1983

BRITANNICA
BOOK OF THE YEAR

1983

BRITANNICA
BOOK OF THE YEAR

ENCYCLOPÆDIA BRITANNICA, INC.

CHICAGO
AUCKLAND, GENEVA, LONDON, MANILA, PARIS, ROME, SEOUL, SYDNEY, TOKYO, TORONTO

THE UNIVERSITY OF CHICAGO

*The Britannica Book of the Year is published with the editorial advice
of the faculties of the University of Chicago.*

CONTENTS

8 *Feature article:* **The Great Disarmament Debate** by *Lawrence Freedman*
A professor of war studies at the University of London who has written extensively on the subject of nuclear strategy, Lawrence Freedman examines the current public pressure for disarmament, particularly in Western Europe and the U.S. He traces the history of arms control and disarmament attempts since World War I and discusses the outlook for arms limitation.

15 *Feature article:* **The Russian Giant: 60 Years After Formation of the Soviet Union**
by *Zhores A. and Roy A. Medvedev*
Two famous Soviet authors, Zhores A. and Roy A. Medvedev, have written an enlightening article that details the flow of events in the U.S.S.R., from the formation of the Soviet Union in 1922 to the death of Leonid Brezhnev and the ascent to power of Yury Andropov.

22 **Calendar of Events of 1983**

26 **Chronology of Events of 1982**
A month-by-month summary of the significant events of 1982.

52 **Unusual but Noteworthy Events**
Peculiar and unusual happenings that were reported around the world in 1982.

56 **Disasters**
A catalog of the most destructive events of 1982, including man-made and natural disasters.

60 *Feature article:* **"You Can't Foreclose a Country"** by *F. John Mathis*
An international economist for one of the largest U.S. commercial banks explains who owes what to whom in the world today and why banks find it necessary to continue lending money to debtor nations that are already behind in their repayments. He discusses the problems plaguing debtor nations and explains the difficulty some nations are having in meeting their obligations in world money markets.

65 *Feature article:* **Stresses in the Western Alliance** by *Edward Heath*
The Western Alliance, which took shape in Europe after World War II, is facing what many believe is its most serious crisis. A former British prime minister, Edward Heath possesses first-hand knowledge of the tensions besetting the alliance, and in a clearly written article he tells what they are and how they came about.

People of the Year
Individuals around the world whose names figured prominently in the news in 1982:

70 Biographies

96 Nobel Prizes

99 Obituaries

129 *Feature article:* **China's Uncertain Future** by *Richard H. Solomon*
The teeming, sprawling nation of China has long been a mystery to Westerners. Richard H. Solomon of the Rand Corporation, a noted sinologist who has traveled extensively in China, brings his understanding of its history and peoples to this article telling why China has remained a largely agrarian society instead of becoming an industrial power like its neighbour Japan and why it is so difficult to predict China's future.

138 **Excerpts from the 1983 Printing of Encyclopædia Britannica**

149–738 **Book of the Year**
An alphabetically organized treatment of the people, places, and developments of significance during 1982, including the following areas:
  Economic Development
  Environment and Natural Resources
  Food and Agriculture
  Health and Disease
  Human Affairs
  Industrial Review
  Literature and the Arts
  National and International Affairs
  Science and Technology
  Social Sciences
  Sports and Games
  Special Reports on many subjects
Frontispiece photo credits (page 149): (top left) Milner—Sygma; (top right) Cindy Karp—Black Star; (centre left) Franceschi—Sygma; (centre right and bottom) Sygma

739 **Contributors**

747 **Index** Cumulative for issues of 1981, 1982, and 1983

SPECIAL REPORTS

181 *Archaeology:* **The Raising of the "Mary Rose"**
In October a 17-year project to raise one of Henry VIII's warships, which sank in 1545, was completed. Margaret Rule, who headed the committee to raise the "Mary Rose," describes the efforts that went into this undertaking to salvage a specimen of British naval history.

202 *Australia:* **Tasmania Debates Progress**
Tasmania lacks jobs because it lacks energy. There is a potential for hydroelectric energy, but developing it would mean damming some of Tasmania's most beautiful rivers and conservationists are vigorously opposed. A. R. G. Griffiths describes the debate.

229 *Canada:* **Strains Along the Border**
The traditionally cordial and cooperative relations between Canada and the U.S. are becoming strained for a number of reasons. Canadian parliamentary observer and newsman Peter Ward lists the causes of dissension between these two North American neighbours.

263 *Crime and Law Enforcement:* **Computers Don't Sin: People Do**
With computers becoming more and more commonplace, the possibilities for computer crimes are increasing. A computer specialist, Donn B. Parker, details the kinds of crime being committed with computers and the efforts to thwart potential wrongdoers.

285 *Defense:* **Lessons from the Falklands**
The Falklands conflict was a curious sort of war, fought in an area 400 miles from one of the combatants and 8,000 miles from the other. Old fashioned in some ways, it also provided the first test in battle of various ultramodern weapons systems. Robin Ranger describes how the conflict was waged and examines its possible lessons for the world's military planners.

335 *Education:* **The Promise of Early Learning**
Every mother knows that her baby is probably the smartest one in the world, and she is probably right, according to James M. Wolf, director of U.S. Department of Defense Dependents Schools, Panama Region. Dr. Wolf discusses the learning potential of very young children and the pioneers who are helping mothers to learn how to utilize that potential.

415 *Health and Disease:* **The New Prohibition**
Richard Whittingham has written an engrossing report in which he draws parallels between the rum runners of the Prohibition era and the drug smugglers of today. Upon investigation, it became clear that they and their methods are amazingly similar.

465 *Japan:* **Japan's Economic Secret**
Those who marvel at the Japanese industrial machine will come to understand why it is so successful when they read Frank Gibney's account. Gibney traces how management–labour–government cooperation transformed a once medieval nation into a modern industrial power.

485 *Libraries:* **The "New" Censors**
When *Huckleberry Finn* was removed from the library of the Mark Twain school in Fairfax, Va., it caused immediate concern in publishing and civil libertarian circles. Self-appointed censors have become more and more active in recent years. John Berry, editor in chief of *Library Journal*, examines their techniques and finds that the situation is not altogether new.

497 *Life Sciences:* **Reevaluating Darwin**
One hundred years after the death of Charles Darwin, controversy still swirls around his theory of evolution. Jeremy Cherfas describes current thinking about Darwin's theory, including some of the knowledge that supports it and some that seems to refute it.

556 *Nigeria:* **Africa's Awakening Giant**
Africa's largest and currently most successful black nation, though still facing many difficulties, is rapidly becoming both example and spokesman for the continent. So says Guy Arnold, a free-lance writer living in London, in a report that analyzes this new power on the world scene.

586 *Race Relations:* **The Latinization of the U.S.**
High immigration (some legal and some illegal) and high birthrates have combined to produce large Hispanic populations that are changing the cultural complexion of many U.S. cities. In a revealing report, John T. Kenna, a writer specializing in cultural affairs, describes the similarities and differences within the Hispanic community and its—as yet unrealized—political potential.

601 *Religion:* **New Roles for Women**
The percentage of people in seminaries who are women has risen each year for the last decade. More and more women are being ordained, and many are rising to positions of power and influence within church bodies. Martin E. Marty, one of the best-known theologians in the U.S., appraises the current position of women in organized religion.

627 *Space Exploration:* **Who Benefits from the Shuttle?**
The successful flights of the U.S. space shuttle "Columbia" demonstrated that this expensive vehicle is not a toy but is capable of performing much useful work. Dave Dooling describes the benefits that can accrue to industry and to the public at large from the space shuttle flights.

656 *Television and Radio:* **Revolution in the Soaps**
When the prime-time soap opera "Dallas" attracted nearly 90 million viewers for its episode revealing "who shot J.R.," it was apparent that the soaps, once confined to the daytime TV ghetto, had come of age. Robert Feder of the *Chicago Sun-Times* has written an account of how the soaps gained respectability and even social significance.

698 *United States:* **PAC's—The New Force in Politics**
Laws sometimes have unintended results, an example being the U.S. electoral reforms that resulted in the growth of Political Action Committees (PAC's). These powerful groups, according to *Time* magazine correspondent David Beckwith, are changing the way parties function, the way elections are conducted, and even the way the government operates.

THE GREAT DISARMAMENT DEBATE

by Lawrence Freedman

> Great armaments lead inevitably to war. The increase of armaments . . . produces a consciousness of the strength of other nations and a sense of fear.

This comment of British foreign secretary Sir Edward Grey on the Anglo-German naval arms race gained immense authority with the subsequent onset of World War I. He appeared to have identified a virtual Law of International Relations. According to this law, those who wished to prevent further war must prevent further arms races. The key to this was disarmament: fixing the armed forces of all countries at the lowest possible level.

Seventy years later voices are warning once again that an arms race must inevitably end in catastrophe. The warnings are given even greater urgency by the fact that the weapons involved are nuclear and the consequences of their use would move beyond mass slaughter to the destruction of whole civilizations. In these circumstances, the cause of disarmament is understandably popular. However, the relationship between arms races and war is not a simple one of cause and effect. Wars are not just the product of the accumulation of armaments but reflect real conflicts over such things as territory and ideology. To address the arms race without considering the political differences between nations is often to address the symptoms rather than the cause. Furthermore, as is evident from a survey of postwar efforts at disarmament and the current debate, unless the underlying political differences can be moderated, the "arms race" symptoms are extremely resistant to treatment.

After Hiroshima. The pro-disarmament sentiment of 1918 was not evident in the international community in 1945. Explanations of the origins of World War II looked more to a failure to react to the German military challenge of the 1930s than to an arms race. There had been no equivalent to the Anglo-German naval competition, nor was it possible to point to military machines impressing their own timetables on a crisis and forcing the hand of the diplomats. Memories of interwar efforts to promote disarmament were of cynical wrangling and deadlocks. Those treaties that had been adopted failed to affect the course of the war, with the possible exception of the 1925 Geneva Protocol outlawing the use of poison gas. No disarmament treaty could have prevented Belsen and Auschwitz.

In plans for a postwar world, centred on the new United Nations, the prevention of further conflicts was seen to lie in the political rather than the military sphere. The victorious powers expected to maintain military capabilities that would enable them to act swiftly and decisively against any renewed outbreaks of aggression. Otherwise, as in 1918, after years of full mobilization and having imposed total disarmament on their defeated enemies, the Allies were only too happy to run down their own armed forces as quickly as possible.

Nevertheless, disarmament was still high on the international agenda. The reason was the impression of awesome power and destructiveness created by the atomic bomb, whose use against the Japanese cities of Hiroshima and Nagasaki had dramatically ended the war. Whatever might be done about the generality of weapons, urgent action was needed in this special case. Even in the United States, with its monopoly of atomic weapons, there was a disposition to nip this dangerous new development in the bud. Accordingly, in 1946 the U.S. put forward a plan to internationalize atomic technology and prevent its full exploitation for military purposes.

Unfortunately, the U.S. plan was framed in such a manner as to excite Soviet suspicions, and it soon got bogged down with the onset of the cold war. The political conditions became unfavourable, and the relevant UN committees devoted themselves to scoring propaganda points rather than serious negotiating. The warning signs were the tendencies toward utopian and all-embracing plans. Argument could not be limited to the area of atomic weapons,

Lawrence Freedman is professor of war studies at King's College, University of London. He is the author of The Evolution of Nuclear Strategy and Britain and Nuclear Weapons.

9

where for much of the 1950s the U.S. had a clear lead, but inevitably began to include all other weapons as well. Why should the West forgo its nuclear superiority if the East would not relinquish its conventional superiority? So the discussion got tangled up in military and political complexities. Agreement depended on an understanding between the superpowers, but their antagonism prevented any agreement. American suspicions of Soviet secrecy meant that the U.S. put an enormous premium on methods to verify compliance with the provisions of any treaty by making the closed Soviet society as transparent as possible. Still, neither side wished to appear responsible for dashing international disarmament hopes, so Washington and Moscow engaged in a sort of competitive bidding, putting forward ever more elaborate and fanciful schemes to ensure General and Complete Disarmament.

Arms Control. Long before this futile process reached its peak at the start of the 1960s, moves had begun on a more fruitful approach to the regulation of armaments. This approach came to be known as arms control. It accepted that nuclear weapons and East-West antagonism would be features of international life for many years. The challenge was to find ways to reduce the consequent dangers. If the nuclear threat could not be eliminated, it could at least be contained. If a military paralysis based on a balance of terror was developing, then perhaps this could be fortified to remove temptations to settle differences once and for all in some decisive battle, or to rush from crisis to war in a preemptive strike through fear of being caught napping.

Superpower political relations had to ease to give even this modest approach an opportunity to show its potential. The opportunity came after the October 1962 Cuban missile crisis when, having gone so close to the brink, the leaders of the U.S. and the U.S.S.R. resolved to develop a less stressful relationship. Additional help was provided by advances in satellite reconnaissance that began to open up Soviet and U.S. territories to each other's penetrating gaze. As there was little that could be done about this, it became recognized as a reliable means of verification. In the ensuing decade, arms control chalked up some impressive achievements: the 1963 Nuclear Test-Ban Treaty, which, while failing to be comprehensive, banned atmospheric explosions and so eased public anxieties over the harmful effects of radioactive fallout; the 1966 Outer Space Treaty, which kept nuclear weapons out of space; the 1968 Non-proliferation Treaty, which constrained the spread of military nuclear technology; the 1970 Seabed Treaty; and, as the first substantive result of the strategic arms limitation talks (SALT) begun by the superpowers in 1969, the 1972 treaty limiting antiballistic missiles. This last pact, combined with a short-term agreement putting a ceiling on the numbers of offensive nuclear weapons, became known as SALT I.

By 1972, with détente in full swing, there seemed every reason to believe that the pattern of regular agreements would continue. The next stage was to be a more comprehensive treaty on offensive nuclear arms, and at Vladivostok, U.S.S.R., in December 1974, Leonid Brezhnev, general secretary of the Communist Party of the Soviet Union, and U.S. Pres. Gerald Ford announced the framework for an agreement. Meanwhile, in 1973, NATO and the Warsaw Pact had begun to discuss ways of reducing the burden of conventional forces in central Europe in the talks held in Vienna on mutual and balanced force reductions.

Loss of Momentum. This promise was not fulfilled. After acrimonious and difficult negotiations, a SALT II treaty was agreed on in June 1979, but it was not ratified by the U.S. Senate. The Vienna talks failed to overcome fundamental disagreements over data. A set of arms control initiatives undertaken in 1977 to breathe life into the enterprise—concerning a variety of issues ranging from a comprehensive test ban to limits on antisatellite and chemical weapons and reform of the arms trade—all faltered. One reason was the loss of momentum in détente, largely as a result of superpower rivalries and interventions in the third world (particularly by the Soviet Union). Under these conditions, negotiations became tougher, with greater domestic suspicion of the motives of the other side.

Another problem was uncertainty over objectives, at least in the West. This was part of a general uncertainty about strategic doctrine, revolving around arguments over whether all that was necessary for

A drawing by a survivor of the Nagasaki atomic bomb blast depicts the blackened body of a five-year-old boy raising his arms to heaven.

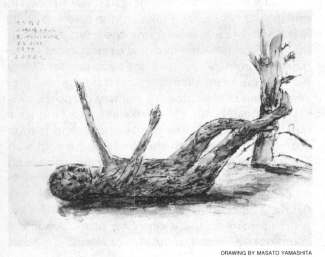

DRAWING BY MASATO YAMASHITA

Former U.S. Pres. Jimmy Carter and Soviet Pres. Leonid Brezhnev exchange copies of the SALT II agreement after the documents were signed in 1979.

deterrence and stability was for both sides to be able to assure destruction of the other. Even if a balance of terror was firmly in place, were there other forms of superiority that might be translated into a decisive political advantage? The promoters of arms control were generally doubtful. In 1974, in a moment of frustration, U.S. Secretary of State Henry Kissinger exclaimed: "We have to ask ourselves . . . what in the name of God is strategic superiority? What is the significance of it, politically, militarily, operationally, at these levels of numbers? What do you do with it?"

There was no agreed answer to this general question, or to the specific question: if "superiority" was believed to be significant, exactly what type and degree of superiority made the difference? For negotiating purposes it seemed sensible to concentrate on simple numbers and rectify any imbalances with common ceilings. East and West could then claim to be "second to none." However, such visible parity seemed artificial to the technically minded, who were more interested in what each side could do in actual warfare than in comparing static inventories. U.S. technicians noted asymmetries in force structure that escaped treaty language, particularly the growing Soviet lead in warheads on intercontinental ballistic missiles (ICBM's). They began to worry that under cover of SALT and an irrelevant numerical parity, the U.S.S.R. was being allowed to attain a potentially decisive strategic advantage.

Even those unimpressed by such fears found the calculation of parity difficult. The negotiations were becoming less manageable as attention moved from the first stage—setting limits to military activity by marking boundaries that few had shown an inclination to cross—to making substantial adjustments to existing capabilities and plans. There was no self-ev-

ident formula for "parity," for the two force structures were quite different in composition. Did one count launchers or warheads? Should an ICBM count the same as a bomber? Should one make allowances for the British, French, and Chinese forces facing the U.S.S.R.? In each country programs with strong political support had to be protected from arms control. To the other country, these were precisely the programs to which a stop had to be put if the exercise was to be worthwhile. Under adverse political conditions, this mix created a barely tractable set of problems.

In retrospect, many of the early successes seemed easy. Underground testing of nuclear weapons was a ready substitute for atmospheric testing; there was no great military interest in putting nuclear weapons in space or in Antarctica or on the seabed; the technology of antiballistic missiles was not showing any particular promise. Once negotiators began to address the more dynamic offensive weapons, they found themselves barely able to cope, bypassed by new developments and outpaced by production programs.

The eventual SALT II treaty of June 1979 was hardly satisfactory. It was enormously complex yet imposed only marginal changes on the nuclear arsenals. If anything, it required most of the U.S.S.R., but that did not prevent a powerful opposition, largely mounted on the right, from developing in the U.S. Critics charged that the treaty threatened valuable U.S. military options, failed to constrain the most dangerous aspects of the Soviet military buildup, and perpetuated an illusion of détente. Although U.S. Pres. Jimmy Carter had answers to all these points, after the Soviet invasion of Afghanistan in December 1979 he no longer felt disposed to make an effort on SALT II's behalf. The treaty languished, unratified, in the Senate.

Pres. Ronald Reagan, entering office in January 1981, described SALT II as "fatally flawed" and argued for a major program of rearmament to regain ground lost in the 1970s. According to his officials, the U.S. had been so preoccupied with arms control that it had neglected to take full note of the Soviet buildup.

The Nuclear Debate. Distrust of all forms of diplomatic contact with the Soviet Union, interest in the possibility of conducting nuclear wars to produce results approximating "victory," and a readiness to increase purchases of all types of military hardware generated some consternation among the U.S.'s allies. The fear in Western Europe was that a breakdown in U.S.-Soviet relations would unravel all the local benefits of détente, from the settlement of the territorial status quo to East-West trade. In addition, a renewed arms race would aggravate the general sense of tension, raise the terrible spectre of nuclear war, and, if the U.S. was deemed responsible, put an added strain on the NATO alliance.

In the early 1980s there was widespread protest in Western Europe against the nuclear policies of NATO. In the latter part of 1981 many of the continent's capitals were filled with demonstrations, sometimes involving up to 250,000 people. The origins of this renewal of the antinuclear movement, which had last peaked in the late 1950s and 1960s, go back to 1977, when the "neutron bomb" gained notoriety. To NATO officials this was an "enhanced-radiation weapon" designed to disable tank crews; to its opponents it would "kill people but leave buildings intact"—the ultimate "capitalist weapon." Revulsion against the neutron bomb led to a massive public outcry. In The Netherlands, with the encouragement of religious leaders, some one million signatures were collected in opposition.

The "Greens," a group of mainly young people campaigning for the environment and against nuclear energy, became a force in West German politics in 1982.

POLY-PRESS/KATHERINE YOUNG

The outcry led President Carter in April 1978 to defer production of the neutron bomb. The protest groups calmed down but then re-formed in 1979 to oppose plans by NATO to base 464 Tomahawk cruise missiles in Belgium, Britain, The Netherlands, Italy, and West Germany, along with 108 Pershing ballistic missiles in West Germany. This deployment was designed to modernize a well-established capability. U.S. nuclear weapons had been based in Europe since the early 1950s, partly to offset Soviet superiority in conventional forces but increasingly to couple the defense of Western Europe with the U.S. nuclear arsenal. The theory was that the Kremlin was deterred from any aggression by the risk that war would "go nuclear" but that the risk would be insufficient if U.S. weapons were stored out of harm's way in North America. In the mid-1970s concern grew in defense circles, at first mainly in Europe, that gradual obsolescence of the long-range aircraft on the NATO side was being exploited by determined improvements in equivalent Soviet capabilities, most notably the Backfire bomber and the SS-20 triple-headed missile. From this perspective, NATO's decision on Dec. 12, 1979, to deploy the cruise and Pershing missiles was seen as merely a prudent measure to fill a gap.

In an attempt to ward off the expected protest, NATO added to the armament program a second track of arms control, offering to limit the number of new NATO missiles in return for severe restrictions on comparable Soviet missiles. Unfortunately, the credibility of this diplomatic alternative was shattered within weeks. The Soviet invasion of Afghanistan undermined all East-West diplomacy and made early ratification of SALT II impossible.

New Fears. The Carter administration then announced, in June 1980, a new doctrine for targeting nuclear weapons that emphasized selectivity, flexibility, and command and control, thus implying an expectation that nuclear exchanges could turn into old-fashioned battles rather than orgies of mutual destruction. No such confidence was actually claimed, only a worry that the U.S.S.R. might try to fight in such a manner, but the critics feared that the U.S. government was now harbouring dangerous notions concerning the utility of nuclear weapons in conventional warfare.

In Europe opponents linked this new doctrine (known officially as Presidential Directive 59) with the highly accurate weapons coming into Europe and the low state of East-West relations. From this, they concluded that the U.S. was shaping up for some confrontation with the Soviet Union which it intended to fight with nuclear weapons all over Europe. This fear grew after the U.S. presidential election in November 1980. Ronald Reagan was known to be distrustful of arms control, a believer in energetic schemes for rearmament, and interested in active nuclear strategies.

Vigorous and determined protest movements gathered strength in Europe. Some, like the "Greens" in West Germany led by Petra Kelly (see BIOGRAPHIES), reflected an environmentalist bias and a history of campaigning against nuclear energy facilities. The British-based campaign for European Nuclear Disarmament, inspired by the social historian E. P. Thompson, linked opposition to cruise missiles with an aspiration to dissolve the two alliances—NATO and the Warsaw Pact—dividing Europe. These movements soon influenced political parties. In Britain the Labour Party resolved to have nothing whatever to do with nuclear weapons. In West Germany immense strains were put on the Social Democratic Party; even the Christian Democrats, whose leader, Helmut Kohl, replaced Helmut Schmidt as federal chancellor in October 1982, were not immune to antinuclear influences. In The Netherlands all but the centre Liberal Party reflected the same trend. The trend, in fact, could be detected throughout northern Europe, though it was much less evident in the south. Pres. François Mitterrand of France, despite his Socialism, upheld the established French faith in nuclear deterrence, while in Italy protest against cruise missiles was rather late in gaining momentum.

It came to be assumed that, whereas opinion in the U.S. was robustly anti-Communist and ready for high levels of defense spending, opinion in Europe was drifting in exactly the opposite direction. This picture was always somewhat misleading. Polls in both the U.S. and Western Europe demonstrated strong support for established policies as well as increasing nervousness over the risk of nuclear war. Toward the end of 1981 the U.S. was beginning to develop its own protest movement, organized around the call for a "nuclear freeze"—that is, cessation of all new work on weapons development, production, and deployment. The idea was to halt the arms race before it was beyond control. The Freeze Resolution was put to both the Senate and the House of Representatives (where it just failed) and to a number of state referenda (where it passed in most cases). Although bipartisan in leadership—Democrat Edward Kennedy and Republican Mark Hatfield sponsored the resolution in the Senate—the movement was animated by opposition to the policies of the Reagan administration.

The Reagan administration's image was not helped by regular Soviet disarmament initiatives. In October 1979 President Brezhnev promised unspecified concessions if NATO would abandon its plans for new missiles in Europe. Then he offered a

DRAWING BY MARTIN © 1982 THE NEW YORKER MAGAZINE, INC.

"I figure the universe was formed with a big bang so it might as well end with a big bang."

moratorium: no new missiles on either side. Later Brezhnev even claimed to have ordered a unilateral freeze on the Soviet side. The impact was not enormous. There was nothing particularly magnanimous about offering to freeze deployments of weapons in an area of substantial Soviet superiority. Nevertheless, the rhetoric and regular initiatives from the Warsaw Pact helped to put the Reagan administration on the defensive.

Reagan's Response. President Reagan insisted that he was not opposed to the principle of arms control negotiations but was only reluctant to sit at the same table with the U.S.S.R. while it was still indulging in unacceptable behaviour in such places as Afghanistan. When, in response to domestic and international pressure, he did eventually put forward initiatives of his own in late 1981, he was anxious to avoid repeating what he saw as the deficiencies of SALT: its failure to deal adequately with the most menacing aspects of the Soviet buildup and its imposition of permissive ceilings, rather than substantial reductions, in armaments.

In the second of these complaints against SALT, President Reagan was quite close to the critique made by the antinuclear movements. They also castigated previous arms control efforts for not achieving disarmament. In fact, Reagan's first major proposal was surprisingly close to an antinuclear slogan. In November 1981 U.S.-Soviet discussions began in

13

Some 30,000 women antinuclear protestors linked arms in a human chain encircling a U.S. Air Force base at Greenham Common, England, a planned site of U.S. cruise missiles.

Geneva on intermediate nuclear forces—a new name for the longer-range nuclear weapons based in and around Europe. At a speech to the National Press Club, President Reagan proposed the "zero option," offering to abandon plans for cruise and Pershing missiles in return for the dismantling of all Soviet SS-20s, along with the older SS-4s and SS-5s.

In the West this was politically effective, but it was certain to be unacceptable to the U.S.S.R. because it required the Soviets to give up something for nothing. Soviet proposals emphasized the need to bring in the British and French nuclear forces and U.S. aircraft in Europe. The asymmetry of the two force structures and the technical problems of deciding on what to count (location or type of weapon; launchers or warheads) make it hard to envision a satisfactory conclusion to the talks. The first anniversary passed without any breakthroughs.

In principle, strategic arms talks appeared to be a better prospect. Many of the technical details and problems of definition had been ironed out in a decade of discussions. The forces were sufficiently comparable to permit some agreement based on parity. However, the political context was less favourable, with every move surrounded by controversy. President Reagan's approach was again calculated to disarm his critics as much as the U.S.S.R. He proposed radical cuts in strategic arms on the eve of the resumption of talks—after a gap of three years—in June 1982. He renamed the negotiations Strategic Arms Reduction Talks (START) and proposed common ceilings of 5,000 missile warheads, half of which could be on ICBM's, and 850 deployed missiles—only 50% of current levels. Skeptics noted that this posed maximum inconvenience to the U.S.S.R., with its heavy dependence on multiple-warhead ICBM's, and minimum disruption to U.S. plans. Nevertheless, the philosophy of cuts was compelling, and the Soviet proposal of ceilings of

1,800 for all missiles and bombers reflected this mood. The two positions were not hopelessly apart, but neither appeared flexible and there were many negotiating pitfalls in the incidental details.

The Future. Arms control was hardly bursting with promise in 1982, but at least serious discussions were beginning once more. Those anxious for more urgent and fundamental action had little cause for comfort. Despite a number of years of sustained pressure by the antinuclear movement, no major NATO country had opted for unilateral disarmament of any sort. Those who dreamed of parallel movements in Eastern and Western Europe, working together to expel nuclear weapons from the continent, saw their hopes dashed with the imposition of martial law in Poland and the crushing of the small independent "peace" groups in East Germany and the Soviet Union. The vision of a "nuclear-free zone"—always unlikely because of France's attachment to its force de frappe and the fact that some 40% of all Soviet nuclear forces are based in the European part of the country—seemed even more impractical. The more modest proposal of a nuclear freeze was critically dependent on a change in U.S. administration, impossible before January 1985.

Meanwhile, there was no progress in attempts to organize old-fashioned disarmament through the UN. In 1978 a special session of the UN achieved a common agenda for disarmament. At a second special session in the summer of 1982, the attempt to move beyond that agenda failed, a victim of the prevailing state of international distrust. A group of senior statesmen and others from all sections of the international community, including the U.S. (former secretary of state Cyrus Vance) and the U.S.S.R. and chaired by Sweden's Olof Palme (the Independent Commission on Disarmament and Security Issues), produced a report for the session that gained credibility only by the moderation of its objectives; these were mainly to urge expeditious completion of all the various negotiations begun in the 1970s.

Thoroughgoing schemes for disarmament require a degree of international accord that is not likely to exist for some time to come. The most optimistic construction on the current situation is that some sort of marriage is taking place between the arms controllers' preoccupation with stability and the disarmers' desire for tangible reductions in armaments. But there is no prospect of reductions to a point where war is anything less than catastrophic—to reduce "overkill" still leaves "kill"—and even progress in this direction is highly dependent on improvements in superpower relations. Ultimately, it is in the political sphere that answers to the problems of war and the peacetime burden of armaments must be found.

THE RUSSIAN GIANT: 60 YEARS AFTER FORMATION OF THE SOVIET UNION

by Zhores A. and Roy A. Medvedev

The Union of Soviet Socialist Republics was declared a multinational federative state at the very end of 1922, the draft of the new constitution having been written by Lenin. There was no unanimous agreement about this draft among Lenin's Bolshevik colleagues. Lenin wanted a federation of "equal" republics, with the right of each to independence. Joseph Stalin and Leon Trotsky wanted more formal Russian domination with strict subordination of the other national republics. Lenin won the constitutional battle, but when he died in January 1924, he left the power over the country and the Communist Party to the newly emerged Communist bureaucracy which had no intention of respecting the constitutional rights either of citizens or of the nations that formed the Soviet Union. The constitution acknowledged the importance of democratic rights, but it included no formula to guarantee them at all levels of social life. Furthermore, it did not solve the problem of leadership succession: the possibility of a power struggle made the choice of leader by democratic process difficult even within the party system.

The year 1982 was declared an official Jubilee year. The Soviet population was reminded of this by countless posters, slogans, and news headlines. While the country had changed enormously in many ways during the intervening 60 years, the lack of consistency and the contradictions between real and constitutional rights were by now even more visible than they were in 1922.

Growth of the U.S.S.R. and World Communism. In 1922 there were only four constituent republics of the U.S.S.R.: the Russian Federal Republic, the

Zhores and Roy Medvedev are co-authors of Khrushchev—The Years in Power and A Question of Madness. Zhores Medvedev, a biologist who until leaving the U.S.S.R. held important posts in Soviet research institutes, has worked at the National Institute for Medical Research, London, since 1973; besides numerous scientific publications, his books include The Rise and Fall of T. D. Lysenko, The Medvedev Papers, and The Nuclear Disaster in the Urals. Zhores's twin brother, Roy, a historian and sociologist still resident in the U.S.S.R., is the author of Let History Judge, The October Revolution, Khrushchev, On Soviet Dissent, Leninism and Western Socialism, and other books.

Ukraine, Belorussia, and the Transcaucasian Republic. Lenin insisted on a federation of independent republics because he believed that the Union would grow in the future, both through internal development and by the voluntary accession of other countries which would become socialist. The Union did indeed grow: the Uzbek and Turkmen republics, formed in 1924, became constituent members in 1925, and the Tadzhik Republic joined in 1929. By 1936, when the new Stalin Constitution was adopted, the number of republics was already 11. A few more were incorporated in 1939 and 1940—the Karelo-Finnish Republic, Moldavia, Estonia, Latvia, and Lithuania; however, they joined not voluntarily but under coercion. The war against Nazi Germany in 1941–45 and against Japan in 1945 brought several Eastern European states and North Korea under Soviet domination, though these did not become republics in the Union.

But it was not only Soviet military power that was responsible for the spread of Communism. The defeat of Fascism in Europe and militarism in Asia increased the worldwide influence of Communist movements. The new Communist regimes in Albania, Yugoslavia, and China emerged essentially as a result of national revolutions and civil wars within those countries. Although the Soviet Union supported their revolutions, it was unable to transform them into satellite states. Greece came very close to Communism in the years from 1944 to 1946. The Communist Party of Italy might also have come to power if the country had not been under Anglo-American occupation during the last stage of World War II. Even France was not immune from the possibility of a Communist takeover during this period because the traditional ruling groups in that nation had collaborated with Germany. When Stalin died in 1953, about one-third of the world's population lived under the banner of Marxism-Leninism. But the structural unity of the world Communist system proved unable to survive nationalistic and ideological disputes. Nevertheless, the Communist movement has continued to attract new adherents, although at a much slower pace. Cuba, Vietnam, Laos, Kampuchea, Angola, Mozambique, South Yemen,

Soviet Pres. Yury Andropov, then KGB chief, addressed Soviet leaders in a Lenin birthday celebration in the Kremlin in April. A portrait of Lenin loomed large in the background.

Ethiopia, Zimbabwe, and several other smaller nations can now be considered to have Marxist-Leninist regimes.

When the capitalist economic system takes the form of Nazism, feudal monarchy, or military dictatorship, and when this is aggravated by poverty and social polarization, the confrontation between right and left often develops into a revolutionary struggle. Thus new Marxist regimes will continue to appear, particularly in Africa, Latin America, and Asia. In the modern world of superpowers the final outcome of a revolutionary struggle often does not depend upon internal factors alone—the examples of Chile, Vietnam, and Angola show this clearly. External aid in the form of arms, training, financial grants, and direct military assistance may be decisive. Who helps whom often (but not always) depends upon ideological considerations.

The survival of the Communist system in the Soviet Union, in China, and even in Eastern Europe is not in serious doubt. It is unrealistic to expect the imminent collapse of the world Communist system, even if some observers see signs of this in Poland. The question of "Whither Communism?" is relevant not to the survival of already well-established Communist states but rather to their ability to generate and support Communist ideology in the rest of the world, to be an attractive model for others. Active assistance to radical Marxist regimes and revolutionary movements in the third world is of huge economic and political cost. Will the Soviet Union be able to continue carrying this burden? This question can only be answered by analyzing the economic and political situation within the Soviet bloc. Since the changes in the Soviet leadership following the death of Leonid Brezhnev (*see* OBITUARIES), the probable priorities of his successor, Yury Andropov (*see* BIOGRAPHIES), and the latter's new team are equally important aspects of the question.

Successes and Failures. The Soviet Union has an impressive list of achievements to show for its 60 years of existence: the rapid industrial reconstruction of agrarian and undeveloped Russia; the difficult victory in World War II against Nazi Germany and its allies; the educational revolution; the building of a modern and powerful army.

But 60 years of Soviet history have also recorded some events that are hardly mentioned in relation to the jubilee. The forced and brutal collectivization of agriculture (1930–33) cost the lives of millions of people; it did not solve the food problem but instead retarded the production of grain, meat, and dairy products for years to come. Stalin's rule of terror and repeated purges from 1928 to 1953 took almost the same toll of human lives—about 20 million—as did the war against Germany. Although the situation began to change during Nikita Khrushchev's era, the image of the Soviet Union as the most repressive postwar regime remained for years. It damaged the structure of the "just society" that the first Communist thinkers had expected would be built upon the foundations of the proletarian revolution.

The plight of the Soviet population under Stalin's regime shows that the current economic and political crisis is certainly not the most serious in Soviet history. The current crisis does not threaten the Communist system, because it has not developed as an isolated problem unique to the Soviet bloc. It appeared simultaneously with the deep postwar recession in Western Europe and the U.S., and the desperate economic plight of many major countries of Latin America and Africa. It can also be seen in relation to China's apparent failure to modernize rapidly and the economic difficulties of the unique Yugoslav model of socialist self-management. However, if the crisis in the West can be explained in economic terms, the problems of the U.S.S.R. are essentially related to an accumulation of errors and the political and economic mismanagement of an inept leadership.

The most serious economic crisis of Lenin's government in 1921 was the result of the arbitrary and repressive system of War Communism. Lenin was the only leader in Soviet history who was bold enough to acknowledge a failure. He replaced War Communism with the successful New Economic Policy, with its mixed socialist and capitalist sectors which competed with and complemented each other. When Stalin became leader, this balanced development quickly became distorted. Stalin's model of rapid industrialization was based mainly upon the forced extraction of human and economic resources from the rural agricultural sector and from the private trade and light industrial sectors. The historical necessity for these methods was far from certain. The losses in light industry, trade, and food production during the 1930s and the horrendous purges did little to help prepare the country for the inevitable war against Germany. The most important factors for the outcome of the war were the enormous size of the country and the significant reserves of the population.

After the war, during the last years of Stalin's life, the economic crisis manifested itself primarily in the form of acute shortages of food and consumer goods and the extreme poverty of the collective farm peasants. Soviet agriculture was now dependent upon a semifeudal system which attached peasants to the collective farms and made them work under the threat of prison camps. During the period 1950–53 the total production of food only reached the level of 1913, and the urban population had significantly increased. Stalin's death in 1953 saved the country from the gloomy prospect of rural starvation and a new series of purges.

After Stalin. Khrushchev's reforms quickly improved the economic and political situation. From 1954 to 1958 the growth of all sectors of the economy was about 11–12% per annum. The most visible growth was in agriculture. The annual production of grain rose from an average of 80 million metric tons (1950–53) to 130 million–140 million metric tons. However, Khrushchev's subsequent reorganizations were carried out hastily. Attempts to produce an artificially accelerated growth rate miscarried and had the reverse effect—the production of food declined again. The bitter quarrel with China split the Communist system into two hostile camps and made it necessary to increase the Soviet defense budget. Khrushchev's errors and blunders continued to mount until they reached a critical level in 1964, when his Politburo colleagues voted him into retirement.

The new leadership of Leonid Brezhnev managed to restore a more balanced economy and began to transform the country into a modern consumer society. However, the leadership was already too old and inflexible to introduce the necessary political and economic reforms when new serious problems started to emerge at the end of the 1970s.

As the history of the U.S.S.R. clearly shows, then, the performance of the system is closely linked to the performance of the men at the top. What is more, their style, their knowledge, their character, and even their tastes are reflected not only in the methods of rule but in almost everything, ranging from literature and the arts to industry, agriculture, and international policy. The dependence of the fate of a country on individual leaders is not, of course, restricted to the Communist system. But in the West this dependence is often temporary, and it is less comprehensive than in the Soviet Union. Western leaders are less involved in day-to-day economic and industrial decision-making processes. The Soviet economy is much more centralized, and it is entirely dependent upon government decisions. Because the Soviet Union is now the centre of a large group of countries linked in the Council for Mutual Economic Assistance (CMEA or Comecon), which is responsible for about 30% of the world industrial output, possible changes of economic policy related to leadership transition attract intense attention.

The Leadership Problem. In no Communist country does the constitution make provision for an orderly succession, nor are the criteria for changing the leader made explicit. In fact, the durability of individual rule has become an integral part of the legitimacy of most such regimes. Aging and ill health are still the main indicators of possible changes at the top, which, when they happen in large powers like the U.S.S.R. or China, can alter the course of world politics.

In the Soviet Union Khrushchev's dismissal prompted the Politburo to set a compulsory retirement age of 70 for its leaders. However, when Brezhnev was approaching 70, the compulsory retirement age was canceled "for outstanding figures of the party and state." The venerable age of the current leaders relates them to the revolutionary period and is a part of their claim to legitimacy. That is why the deaths of Brezhnev, Premier Aleksey Kosygin, and chief party ideologue Mikhail Suslov (see OBITUARIES), together with the retirement of Andrey Kirilenko, mean for the Soviet Union much more than the change of a few leaders—they mean the end of a whole political era. At 68, Andropov is older than any of his predecessors when they assumed power, but for replacements in many important positions he is selecting much younger men who will probably remain in office for at least a decade. They belong to a generation that not only does not remember the Revolution and Civil War but often took only a minor part in World War II. This will make it difficult for them to build up the kind of "personality cult" that proved to be so important for their predecessors. Moreover, they will face difficult decisions. The economy of the U.S.S.R. is in poor shape, and Soviet-style Communism is in a critical condition in such neighbouring countries as Poland and Afghanistan.

Power Base of the Soviet Leadership. Lenin's main power base was the October Revolution itself and all its institutions and reforms. The party had not yet developed a bureaucratic apparatus, and Lenin ruled the country as the chairman of the first revolutionary government, the Council of People's Commissars. When Stalin was appointed general secretary of the Communist Party Central Committee in 1922, he was not a popular figure and was not considered a possible successor to Lenin. But he skillfully began to form an influential party apparatus which he used as his power base in the struggle with the left and right opposition in the 1920s. When he started to become de facto dictator rather than party leader, he made the state security system the powerful instrument of his personal rule, able to carry out comprehensive purges of all ranks of the party, military, and state systems. The party apparatus was not abolished, but its influence declined. From 1934 to 1953 the Soviet Union was, in all practical senses, a police state. Before World War II Stalin abolished the post of general secretary of the Central Committee and assumed the post of chairman of the government, one more convenient for direct rule.

Khrushchev is best remembered in Soviet political history for his elimination in 1953 of Lavrenty Beria and his top security henchmen and for his "secret speech" in 1956, which exposed and condemned many of Stalin's crimes. The exceptional position of the security system was abolished, and the party system and party bureaucracy regained priority. Khrushchev himself was not a typical party bureaucrat—his style of rule was more open, though still far from being democratic. Party power had been restored, but the party only made directives. Final decisions had to be made and implemented by the government. It was, therefore, to Khrushchev's advantage to assume the post of premier in addition to his position as leader of the party in 1958. This step, however, restored the possibilities for personal dictatorship, and Khrushchev was not immune from the misuse of power and the creation of a personality cult. Khrushchev was a de facto dictator, but the party apparatus remained his power base. When he introduced an unpopular reorganization of the party apparatus that reduced the influence of local bosses, his relations with the party bureaucracy were seriously damaged. His seven-year plan for economic development failed, and he had no powerful security system to protect him from his angry colleagues. His removal was a comparatively painless leadership change. Only one man—Khrushchev himself—lost his post. As a precaution against repetition of personal rule, the Central Committee decreed that the positions of party leader and head of government should be separated forever.

The Brezhnev Era. Brezhnev's power was, therefore, much more limited. Leadership was effectively collective, based on Politburo consensus, even after the restoration of the position of general secretary in 1966. Kosygin had independent views about the economy, and both Suslov and Nikolay Podgorny had independent sources of influence. But like previous Soviet leaders, Brezhnev began to consolidate his power. In 1977 he assumed Podgorny's post of chairman of the Presidium of the Supreme Soviet and managed to remove him from the Politburo. This made Brezhnev titular head of state. When Kosygin became ill in 1980, Brezhnev succeeded in replacing him with Nikolay Tikhonov, a rather weak premier but an old friend and protégé. Brezhnev's personality cult grew. But by the time he achieved this concentration of power, he was already too old and too ill to use it or to lead the country efficiently. When his old friends and relatives started to assume important state and party positions, the more technocratic members of the Politburo and Central Committee objected. Brezhnev failed to secure Suslov's position for Konstantin Chernenko, his aide and confidant since the 1950s. Instead, Andropov, then head of the security force (KGB), was appointed to this post, the second most important in the party hierarchy. Until 1967 Andropov was the secretary of the party Central Committee responsible for Soviet relations with other socialist countries. He had his own political objectives, and his rise, supported by the more technocratic group in the Politburo (Dmitry Ustinov, Andrey Gromyko, Mikhail Gorbachev, and Vladimir Shcherbitsky), secured his election as general secretary after Brezhnev's death.

Few new bold initiatives were adopted during Brezhnev's era. Most of the reforms—a limited attempt to introduce market forces into the economy; an increase in the procurement prices paid to farmers; increasing investment in agriculture; the encouragement of more effective use of private plots of land—were Kosygin's ideas. Many of these reforms were half measures, and they generated very modest incentives. But the absence of reorganization and the lack of coercion were welcomed by the managerial groups, and economic growth was persistent, although slower than before. However, the absence of strong leadership also encouraged official corruption.

The policy of détente with the West improved

the international position of the U.S.S.R. The decline of U.S. influence in the world was not directly related to Soviet actions. It was more the result of errors and miscalculations by the administrations of U.S. Presidents Richard Nixon, Gerald Ford, and Jimmy Carter. Just when Soviet international policy was predictable and consistent, U.S. policy was unstable. The peak of Brezhnev's success at home was reached in 1978, when the U.S.S.R. reaped a record harvest of 230 million metric tons of grain. The peak of his détente policy was in June 1979, when the new SALT II (Strategic Arms Limitation Treaty II) was signed in Vienna. However, there were new challenges at home and abroad at the start of the 1980s, and the aging Soviet bureaucracy responded inadequately. The situation was complicated by four poor harvests in a row: 180 million metric tons of grain per annum and a decrease in the production of meat and dairy products created food shortages and the need for massive purchases of food abroad. The popularity of the leadership declined sharply, and the closed, secretive style of Brezhnev's rule increased the gap between the Soviet people and their leaders.

However, discontent did not develop into real opposition, as happened in Poland, where the crisis was much more serious. In the Soviet Union there was a visible slowing down of the growth rate but no actual decline in the gross national product (GNP) or in living standards. The Soviet political system was also much more stable than that of Poland. The alternative extraparty opposition was represented by small and weak groups of dissidents who had no links with workers or peasants. The influence of the Orthodox Church and other religions had been weak ever since religious institutions were repressed under Lenin, Stalin, and Khrushchev. Soviet people tend to wait for change to occur at the top.

From Bureaucracy to Technocracy. The most likely outcome of the Andropov ascendancy is an increase in the influence of the technocratic elements in the Soviet leadership. The emergence of a younger, more pragmatic, and more flexible generation of state and party leaders is inevitable within two to three years, if not sooner. Any significant reduction in the dominant role of the Communist Party is unlikely—it is still the most efficient apparatus of power. But the essence of the Communist doctrine concerning economic and political processes will probably change. Some modest experiments with a mixed economy in agriculture and in the service sectors are likely. The new leadership may also try to reduce the international commitments of the Soviet Union. They may decide that there is no point in giving generous economic assistance to countries that, like Egypt and Somalia, easily

change sides after a change of leadership or for other reasons.

The new generation of Soviet politicians lived through the exposure of Stalin's crimes and of Khrushchev's errors and mismanagement. They will, therefore, realize that public support for party objectives cannot be taken for granted. They will probably be more ready to accept criticism and to introduce the political and economic reforms which are badly needed. The generation born between 1923 and 1935 is much better educated, and its representatives have occupied professional positions for much longer. They should, therefore, know that a Communist economy as such does not guarantee rapid economic progress and that the capitalist system can achieve rapid technological innovation and high productivity, even if it is cyclical. This generation will not be inclined to dogmatism or fanaticism, qualities usually born of revolution. Because they did not occupy high positions before 1980, they often have no basis for claiming past great successes and for building personality cults. They will try much harder to be successful after promotion. In general they will be technocrats rather than bureaucrats. The government may develop more decision-making power, independent of the party, than it has at present. If the new leaders want to be popular, they will have to introduce some liberal reforms. Repression does not win popular support, and probably no one understands this better than Andropov, former head of the KGB.

Economic Problems. This section is purposely headed "economic problems" rather than "the economic crisis." While the economic situation in Poland is critical, and in Romania near critical, it has not reached crisis level in the U.S.S.R. During the last few years the Soviet economy has experienced a decline in the growth rate, but there has been no reduction in total output. Although living standards have not risen, neither have they fallen. The price of food and other essentials has not risen; there has been no budget deficit and no unemployment; and the inflation rate has remained very low. There has been no serious foreign debt problem. Consumers complain about the quality of goods and the lack of diversity, but not about empty shelves. There are shortages of meat and some dairy products, but not of bread and other staple foods. The problems are those of rising expectations and of the disproportion between consumer demands and available stocks. However, the disappointment of consumers and especially their complaints about the quality of their diet indicates that they are disillusioned with the official promises and programs reiterated at party congresses and in official plans. The older generation remembers the deprivation and rationing of food and consumer goods during Stalin's time and is less disturbed about the current problems. But the younger generation, more consumer oriented and westernized, clearly sees the system as being responsible for the country's poor economic performance.

The promises of economic growth made in the 1950s and 1960s and included in the official party program were very inflated. They seemed to ignore the fact that the Soviet Union has natural limits of economic growth. The targets for the 1958–65 seven-year plan and for the subsequent five-year plans were unreasonably high, and the plans were not fulfilled. Nevertheless, the growth of industrial output was substantial, increasing by 270% in the period 1965–80. But agricultural production only grew 35% during those 15 years, and it did not increase at all from 1980 to 1982. Because the urban population grew by 30–32%, there was no improvement in the food situation throughout this period. Nonetheless, the situation in rural areas improved substantially. Rural incomes increased because higher procurement prices were paid for state purchases and because the prices paid for food on the private and collective farm markets in towns were very high. The gap between the incomes of urban workers and peasants was markedly reduced.

The centralized Soviet economy still gives priority to defense and heavy industry. In the production of some military hardware (e.g., tanks) and in the total output of steel, iron, some metals, and some kinds of machine tools and heavy equipment (locomotives, electric trains, tractors, steel pipes), the Soviet Union has already surpassed the U.S. The U.S.S.R. produces more oil and gas than does the U.S. and more gold and diamonds. However, the U.S. has the ascendancy in the production of such high-technology equipment as computers and in the production of consumer goods per capita. The construction of housing in "modernized" Soviet villages and in cities has been impressive. After food, housing is the second most important indicator of living standards. Between 1965 and 1982 about 1.8 million square metres (19 million square feet) of apartment space was built in the Soviet Union, more than for the whole preceding period from the Revolution to 1964. But the annual growth of GNP declined from an average of 10% in the 1960s to 3.5% at the end of the 1970s and 2.8% in 1982.

In the 1970s, however, the Soviet Union improved its internal domestic situation by radically increasing foreign trade. The deficiencies of agricultural production were partly compensated for by large purchases of food abroad. This turn of events became possible because of the dramatic increase in the world prices for oil and gas. The U.S.S.R. is the world's largest producer of these commodities. In Stalin's time the Soviet Union, with even worse food problems, had to export grain to obtain hard currency. In the 1970s oil sales became the main source of export revenue. The world prices for other traditional Soviet exports, such as timber, fur, gold, and diamonds, also increased, and the new revenue was used to import significant quantities of food, machinery, and high-technology equipment. Between 1970 and 1980 Soviet foreign trade rose from 22 billion to 109 billion rubles a year, and there were no signs that this trend would be changed by U.S. attempts to restrict further increases in the export of Soviet energy.

The overall picture of Soviet industrial development reveals some problems, disproportions, and errors of planning but no signs of real crisis. The Soviet bureaucracy has been conservative in using foreign credits. Soviet foreign debts are mostly not related to cash payments but to payments in kind by goods and commodities. Other Eastern European countries were much more liberal in their foreign borrowing, and this has put them in a difficult position. It has also created a great deal of financial difficulty for their Western creditors. (See Feature Article: "You Can't Foreclose a Country": Debtor Nations Worry Bankers.) While a significant number of economic problems certainly accumulated in the final stages of Brezhnev's era, they are of a very different kind from those which occurred at the end of Lenin's, Stalin's, or Khrushchev's tenure. The new leadership will not need to make an economic U-turn, but will no doubt make some adjustments and modifications. If Andropov's attempts to be more pragmatic and more efficient and less tolerant of the widespread official corruption are reflected in reforms that will give more encouragement to local initiative in the industrial and agricultural sectors, that in itself would be enough to stimulate the economy.

The Future: An Optimistic View. The most urgent priority for the future will remain food. The recently introduced ten-year "food program" has been received by Soviet public opinion, with justified skepticism, as yet another empty long-term promise. Something must be done and can be done more quickly. If the new government were to open up a free discussion of the problem, this could help to solve it more quickly; an effective food program should be open for democratic discussion, not simply introduced by the Politburo. Although Brezhnev tried hard to improve agricultural performance, having no wish to leave the political arena as a possible future scapegoat for food shortages, he did not introduce basic changes, such as price reforms. Increases in food prices are certainly not popular. But when food is too cheap, when prices have not changed for decades, much agricultural produce goes to waste. About 20% of cereals are lost in the Soviet Union because of waste, poor storage, and inadequate transport; the proportion of vegetables lost is even higher. Moreover, all the available resources are not being used for food production. Although hydroelectric projects, nuclear power stations, and other industrial projects have absorbed land, there are still large resources available for individual agricultural exploitation, for small, privately cultivated farms. In the early 1960s, when the government gave permission to workers and other urban dwellers to grow fruit and vegetables on small allotments on unused land outside towns, there was no problem in finding land. There are now some four million allotments, and they are extremely popular. This is primitive private agriculture, and it is tax-free. Many thousands of small, productive private farms would cause no harm to the socialist sector of agriculture. Leasing land for private farms and offering credits is a project that can be effective immediately. Gigantic schemes to irrigate the drought-prone south may be valid but would take many years and hundreds of billions of rubles.

The socialist idea that essential services must be free has brought benefits in the form of free health services and free education to many countries. In the U.S.S.R. this idea has led to cheap public transport and cheap rent. These services are state controlled and not easy to misuse. But much public housing is poorly built and inadequately maintained because of lack of funds normally provided by rate (local property tax) or rent payments. Without some such provision a deterioration of living conditions in the near future is inevitable. The provision of free gas for cooking and heating water is not really justified and leads to the misuse of this important energy source. There is nothing wrong with making people pay for some services. The old Communist dream, reiterated by Khrushchev, that "mature Communism" will mean that everything is free, is utopian. The slogan "to each according to his needs" probably seemed reasonable 100 years ago, but it is naive when material needs constantly expand. Moreover, people's needs include not only food and consumer goods but also cultural and intellectual values and freedoms. As soon as food and minimal consumer requirements are met, demands for democratic freedoms are inevitable. What the Soviet public values most about the countries of the West is not the quality of consumer goods but civil liberties and democratic traditions. The propaganda image of an eternally prosperous West is now very tarnished—recession, unemployment, inflation, and other problems are too visible. But trade with the West helps to satisfy consumers and makes it more likely that the Soviet people will demand civil liberties.

Soviet Foreign Policy. Contrary to many Western predictions, the new Soviet international policy will almost certainly be more restrained. There have already been some signs of restraint in the last two years. The Soviet Union has not been actively involved in the major conflicts of 1981–82, the Iraq-Iran war, Poland, the Argentine-British conflict, the Israeli-Palestinian war. Soviet support for radical revolutionary regimes has become a costly economic and political burden and will probably be reduced, although the Soviet Union will continue to exploit the situation in the third world indirectly by capitalizing on economic and political difficulties. But the U.S.S.R. needs partners, not dependents, and the technocrats understand this much better than the bureaucrats and revolutionaries.

The expansion of Comecon will certainly be restricted. Cuba and Vietnam have been admitted but have not become active participants. Experience has shown that real integration is possible only among equally developed countries. The failure of Poland and Romania to westernize their economies through credits and to increase their independent cooperation with the West has helped the long-term Soviet aim of completely integrating the Eastern European economies. Although this project is unpopular in Poland, Hungary, and Romania, these countries have little choice since they are unlikely to receive further economic assistance from the West. They will soon have to redirect their industries and standardize their equipment, technological processes, research and development programs, and distribution of manufactured goods. This will almost certainly mean closer political integration.

For centuries traditional Russian foreign policy was centred on relations with immediate neighbours. The Soviet Union has the longest border in the world, more neighbours than any other country, and an economy relatively independent of overseas resources. Thus the improvement of relations with close neighbours will be the most urgent foreign policy priority for the future. China, Iran, and Turkey will mean more to the U.S.S.R. than Mozambique or Nicaragua. The failure of Soviet-U.S. détente may become less important as the chance of Sino-Soviet détente increases—neither country has anything to gain from the continuing conflict.

A return to a more rational, traditional foreign policy is, certainly, an optimistic prediction for the future. Many chances of better relations with neighbours have been lost by Soviet leaders in the past because of ideological disputes. One can only hope that the new leadership will not repeat the errors and miscalculations of its predecessors.

CALENDAR OF EVENTS OF 1983

JANUARY

1 *New Year's Day; Unicorn Hunters publishes banished words*

6 *Epiphany; Three Kings' Day*

25 *Birthday of Robert Burns (1759)*

26 *Australia Day; Republic Day in India*

27 *Tenth anniversary of Vietnam cease-fire*

31 *25th anniversary of the launching of Explorer 1*

1 Unicorn Hunters publishes banished words. On New Year's Day, a U.S. organization that calls itself the Unicorn Hunters publishes a list of words and phrases that, in its opinion, should be banished from the English language. In past years banned words and phrases have included: revenue enhancement, classic, first time ever, patriate, sit on it, past history, exact same, doable, time frame, no problem, viable alternative, bottom line, meaningful, somewhere down the road, any word used to modify the word unique, preboard as used by the airlines, and any sentence beginning with the words "Surely if we can send a man to the Moon...." The organization also calls attention to neologisms and creative expressions such as "fruitworthy," which was coined by Chicago Mayor Jane Byrne in reference to an investigation. Nominations for words to be banned should be sent between November 15 and December 15 to W. T. Rabe, Lake Superior State College, Sault Ste. Marie, Michigan 49783.

26 Australia Day. In 1786 Arthur Phillip, a retired officer of the British Royal Navy, was selected by Lord Sydney, the secretary of state for the Home Department, to head an expedition to New South Wales. Phillip was commissioned to establish a new settlement on the east coast of Australia and develop the territory as governor. After the 11 ships under Phillip's command reached their destination, a survey of the coast was made to find a suitable location for the new colony. Phillip made his choice on Jan. 26, 1788, and named the spot Sydney Cove. Fifty years later the day was officially proclaimed a public holiday to commemorate the founding of Australia.

31 25th anniversary of the launching of Explorer 1. The launching of this 13.9 kg (30.8 lb) Earth satellite on Jan. 31, 1958, marked the entrance of the United States into the "space race"; it followed by only a few months the successful launch by the U.S.S.R. of Sputnik 1. Explorer 1 was propelled into orbit by a Jupiter-C rocket. A Geiger counter placed on board by James A. Van Allen, a U.S. scientist, detected evidence of an intense belt of particulate radiation surrounding the Earth. In his honour, the doughnut-shaped zone of charged particles was named the Van Allen Belt. The U.S. launched two more satellites in 1958—Van-guard 1 on March 17 and SCORE on December 18. The Soviets' only successful launching in 1958 was Sputnik 3.

FEBRUARY

2 *Candlemas Day; Groundhog Day in the U.S.*

6 *Waitangi Day in New Zealand*

11 *150th anniversary of Melville Fuller's birth; Empire Day in Japan*

12 *Lincoln's Birthday; 250th anniversary of the founding of Georgia*

14 *St. Valentine's Day*

15 *Shrove Tuesday Pancake Race*

16 *Ash Wednesday*

20 *Brotherhood Week begins*

21 *Washington's Birthday official holiday*

22 *Washington's Birthday*

23 *350th anniversary of Samuel Pepys's birth*

27 *Jewish feast of Purim*

28 *450th anniversary of Michel de Montaigne's birth*

2 Groundhog Day in the U.S. According to legend, if the groundhog emerges from his burrow on this date and casts a shadow there will be six more weeks of winter. If, on the other hand, the day is cloudy and no shadow is cast, winter will shortly give way to spring. In most parts of the northern U.S., however, there are almost always at least six more weeks of winter regardless of what the groundhog sees on this date. The legend of the groundhog was brought to the U.S. by immigrants from Great Britain and Germany, and elaborate tongue-in-cheek observances have sprung up in places such as Sun Prairie, Wis., and Punxsutawney and Quarryville, Pa. February 2 is also the Christian feast of Candlemas. On this day certain Christian denominations celebrate the Presentation of the Christ Child in the Temple and the Purification of the Blessed Virgin Mary. The feast carried greater significance before the Reformation than it does today, but the Roman Catholic, Eastern Orthodox, and Anglican churches continue the observance by blessing all the candles that will be used on their altars during the year.

15 Shrove Tuesday Pancake Race. According to legend, the first Shrove Tuesday pancake race was a solitary event that began accidentally in 1445 at Olney in Buckinghamshire, England. It was customary in those days for housewives to fry pancakes on Shrove Tuesday; church law forbade the use of eggs and cooking fat during the Lenten season, which, then, as now, began the following day. Legend has it that a certain Olney housewife was so busy frying her pancakes that she forgot about the shriving service in the church. Hearing the church bells ring, she dashed out of the house and ran to the church—frying pan still in hand. This so amused her neighbours that the following year they gathered with their frying pans to see who would be the first to make it to the church.

MARCH

4 *50th anniversary of the first inauguration of Franklin D. Roosevelt*

13 *250th anniversary of Joseph Priestley's birth*

15 *Ides of March (Julius Caesar assassinated, 44 BC)*

17 *St. Patrick's Day*

20 *Vernal equinox in the Northern Hemisphere; autumnal equinox in the Southern Hemisphere (11:39 PM EST)*

25 *Independence Day in Greece*

29 *First day of Jewish feast of Passover*

4 50th anniversary of the first inauguration of Franklin D. Roosevelt. Having won the election of 1932 over Republican incumbent Herbert Hoover by 22,822,000 to 15,762,000 popular votes, Franklin Delano Roosevelt was inaugurated 32nd president of the United States on this date in 1933. Roosevelt promptly proposed and got Congress to pass a sweeping program of recovery and reform which he called the New Deal. Among its better known components were the Agricultural Adjustment Act, the National Industrial Recovery Act, the Tennessee Valley Authority, legislation regulating the issuance and sale of securities, a broad reform of the nation's banking structure, soil conservation legislation, and the Social Security Act. Reelected three times, Roosevelt served a total of 12 years and 39 days.

13 250th anniversary of Joseph Priestley's birth. Born at Birstall Fieldhead, near Leeds, England, on March 13, 1733, Joseph Priestley attracted attention early in life when he disavowed his strict Calvinist upbringing and at the age of 22 became a freethinking Presbyterian minister. He was later ordained a Dissenting minister and had charge of a congregation for several years, but he is best known for his contributions to the chemistry of gases. Priestley, with the encouragement of Benjamin Franklin, published his first major scientific work, *The History and Present State of Electricity*, in 1767. In 1774, with the aid of a newly acquired burning glass, he obtained a new gas from mercuric oxide. A short time later his experiments were repeated by the French chemist Antoine-Laurent Lavoisier, who named the new gas oxygen. Priestley also discovered several gases besides oxygen, including ammonia, nitrogen, nitrous oxide, hydrogen chloride, and sulfur dioxide. Some of his other experiments resulted in significant contributions in the fields of plant respiration and photosynthesis.

APRIL

1 *April Fools' Day; Good Friday*
3 *Easter Sunday; 200th anniversary of Washington Irving's birth*
4 *Major league baseball season opens in the U.S.*
9 *Bataan Day in the Philippines*
11 *Academy Awards presentations*
14 *Pan American Day*
15 *Income taxes due in United States*
18 *Boston Marathon*
24 *Daylight saving time begins at 2 AM*
29 *Arbor Day in the U.S.; Emperor's birthday in Japan*

3 200th anniversary of Washington Irving's birth. Born on April 3, 1783, in New York City, Washington Irving was the youngest of 11 children reared by a wealthy Presbyterian merchant and his Anglican wife. Though he lived to be 76, Irving spent much of his life in frail health, a condition that may have enhanced his literary attainments. Because of his physical frailties he spent much of his time traveling, rather than suffering the rigours of formal education and family business concerns (although he practiced law for a time and tended briefly to family business affairs in Liverpool). Irving's first venture into literary waters was a series of whimsically satirical essays published in the *Morning Chronicle*, a newspaper owned by his brother Peter. He won his greatest literary acclaim for *The Sketch Book of Geoffrey Crayon, Gent*, a collection of some 30-odd pieces including "The Legend of Sleepy Hollow" and "Rip Van Winkle." After spending 17 years away from New York—most of them in Europe—Irving returned in 1832 and settled down at "Sunnyside," his home on the Hudson River. There he devoted himself chiefly to biography, producing works such as *Oliver Goldsmith* (1849) and five volumes on the life of George Washington (1855–59). Irving died on Nov. 28, 1859.

29 Arbor Day in the U.S. Widely but not universally observed, Arbor Day encourages the planting of trees, an idea that took root largely through the efforts of J. Sterling Morton. A prominent Nebraska newspaper editor and politician during the second half of the 19th century, Morton saw a need for trees on the Nebraska plain and began planting them in earnest sometime after moving there from Michigan in 1854. As a member of the state board of agriculture Morton proposed April 10, 1872, as the first Arbor Day, with prizes to be awarded to both the individual and the county agricultural society that planted the

most trees. Nebraska declared Arbor Day a legal holiday in 1885, setting it on April 22, the anniversary of Morton's birth. By 1888, Nebraskans had planted some 350 million trees. Morton went on to become secretary of agriculture under Pres. Grover Cleveland, as well as president of the American Forestry Association.

MAY

1 *May Day*
5 *Cinco de Mayo*
7 *Kentucky Derby*
8 *Easter in Orthodox churches; Mother's Day in the U.S.; VE Day (1945); World Red Cross Day*
14 *National Windmill Day in The Netherlands*
21 *The Preakness Stakes*
24 *100th anniversary of the dedication of the Brooklyn Bridge*
26 *250th anniversary of John Kay's patent on the flying shuttle*
29 *30th anniversary of Sir Edmund Hillary's ascent of Mt. Everest; Indianapolis 500 auto race*
30 *Memorial Day in the U.S.*

24 100th anniversary of the Brooklyn Bridge. Probably no one will ever know how many times the Brooklyn Bridge has been sold by the unscrupulous to the unwary. But before the pranks and jokes began, the famous bridge had to be built and dedicated, a process beset with considerable adversity. The bridge was designed by John Augustus Roebling. While he was working on the bridge a ferryboat crushed his foot in a piling, and he died of a tetanus infection in 1869. In seeing the project through to completion, Roebling's son, Col. Washington Augustus Roebling, contracted caisson disease (the bends). Suffering from paralysis and partial blindness, he was forced to watch the dedication ceremonies from his house on Columbia Heights. When the 486-m (1,595-ft) span opened on May 24, 1883, 12 people were trampled to death in the excitement. At the time, Brooklyn and New York were the two largest cities in the U.S.

26 250th anniversary of John Kay's patent on the flying shuttle. On this date in 1733 John Kay, an English machinist and engineer, received a patent for a "New Engine or Machine for Opening and Dressing Wool." Weavers were quick to adopt the new invention, but organized a protective club to avoid paying a royalty to Kay. Kay spent most of his money in unsuccessful litigation to protect his patent. His later years are obscure. He is believed to have died in France sometime after 1764.

29 30th anniversary of Sir Edmund Hillary's ascent of Mt. Everest. On this date in 1953 Sir Edmund Hillary and Tenzing Norgay, a Sherpa guide, reached the summit of Mt. Everest in Nepal, the highest

mountain in the world. The two men made their final assault on the mountain from a tent at 8,500 m (27,900 ft) on the southeastern ridge and reached the 8,848-m (29,028-ft) summit at 11:30 AM.

JUNE

5 *200th anniversary of the first balloon flight; 100th anniversary of John Maynard Keynes's birth*
6 *Anniversary of D-Day (1944)*
11 *Kamehameha Day in Hawaii*
12 *Queen's "official" birthday in Great Britain; Philippine Independence Day; First day of Ramadan*
15 *Magna Carta Day (1215)*
19 *Father's Day in the U.S.*
21 *Summer solstice in the Northern Hemisphere; winter solstice in the Southern Hemisphere (7:09 PM EDST)*
25 *Partial eclipse of the Moon*
26 *500th anniversary, Richard III becomes king of England*

5 200th anniversary of the first balloon flight. When three men from Albuquerque, N.M., made the first successful manned balloon flight across the Atlantic Ocean in 1978, they were carrying on a ballooning tradition that had begun in France two centuries earlier. In 1782 the Montgolfier brothers, Joseph-Michel and Jacques-Étienne, discovered that heated air collected inside a large lightweight bag caused the bag to rise into the air. The brothers made their first public demonstration of this discovery on June 5, 1783, from the marketplace of their hometown, Annonay, France. Using heat generated from a fire they had built of wool and straw, they filled a bag with warm air, then watched as it rose to a height of about 1,800 m (6,000 ft). It remained at that altitude for about ten minutes, then settled to the ground about 2.5 km (1.5 mi) away. On September 19 of the same year the Montgolfier brothers launched a larger balloon at Versailles, this time bearing aloft a sheep, a rooster, and a duck. The first manned flight took place over Paris on Nov. 21, 1783. With Pilâtre de Rozier and the Marquis François Laurent d'Arlandes aboard, the balloon traveled almost 9 km (about 5.5 mi) and stayed aloft about 25 minutes.

26 500th anniversary, Richard III becomes king of England. Controversy continues to swirl around Richard III. Was he a hunchbacked monster who ordered the murder of his two nephews in order to protect his claim to the crown, or was he a humane and benevolent ruler? Although Richard has long been viewed as a villain, some recent investigations have cast doubt on that assessment. The Richard III Society, organized in 1924, claims that the jaundiced view of Richard was the product of a vicious Tudor propaganda campaign designed to bolster the claims of Henry VII to the crown. The society claims further that the characterization of Richard as a murderer was unwittingly strengthened by William Shakespeare in his play *Richard III*. Though there is no certain evidence that Richard ordered his nephews killed, neither was he able to produce them after having lodged them in the Tower of London. Richard was born on Oct. 2, 1452, began his rule on June 26, 1483, was formally crowned on July 6, 1483, and died in battle on Aug. 22, 1485.

JULY

1 *Dominion Day in Canada*

3 *100th anniversary of Franz Kafka's birth*

4 *Independence Day in the U.S.*

8 *Calgary Stampede begins*

10 *Tenth anniversary of Bahamian Independence*

12 *Id al-Fitr, Muslim feast day*

14 *Bastille Day in France*

23 *National Day in Egypt*

24 *200th anniversary of Simón Bolívar's birth*

28 *50th anniversary of the first singing telegram*

3 **100th anniversary of Franz Kafka's birth.** Kafka was born on July 3, 1883, in Prague (then the capital of Bohemia), of German-speaking parents. Though he died on June 3, 1924, one month short of his 41st birthday, he is recognized today as one of the great writers of modern times. Few in his own time believed that he would ever attain such stature. Even Kafka himself doubted his talents. Before he died he ordered his literary executor, Max Brod, to destroy all his manuscripts. But Brod disobeyed and published several of Kafka's best-known works after his death. Among these are *Amerika*, *The Trial*, and *The Castle*.

10 **Tenth anniversary of Bahamian Independence.** On July 10, 1973, a new constitution went into force in The Bahamas, and the islands became independent of Great Britain. The government now consists of a two-house parliament, a ministerial Cabinet headed by the prime minister, and an independent judiciary. At the same time the islands belong to the Commonwealth with a governor-general appointed by Queen Elizabeth II. The islands were discovered by Columbus on Oct. 12, 1492. The first English inhabitants came in 1648. Since the early 18th century, apart from brief interruptions caused by foreign invasions, the government has functioned as a parliamentary democracy.

24 **200th anniversary of Simón Bolívar's birth.** The great South American soldier-statesman was born on this date in 1783 to an aristocratic family in Caracas, Venezuela. While in Europe, Bolívar vowed to liberate South America from Spanish control. In 1807 he returned to Venezuela from Europe and quickly rose to prominence in the independence movement. As commander of an expeditionary force, he vanquished the Spanish in six pitched battles and regained control of Caracas. On Aug. 6, 1813, he entered the city, received the title of Liberator, and became dictator. Bolívar eventually succeeded in liberating Colombia, Ecuador, Peru, and Bolivia from Spanish control, despite many setbacks along the way. These arose from internal dissension, nationalistic conflicts, and the grandiose designs and personality of Bolívar himself. He was forced into exile twice and narrowly escaped assassination on another occasion. A few days before his death on Dec. 17, 1830, he wrote, "My last wishes are for the happiness of my country. If my death can contribute anything toward the reconciliation of the parties or the unification of the country, I shall go to my grave in peace."

28 **50th anniversary of the first singing telegram.** In 1933 Western Union, like many other companies in that depression year, faced a dim economic picture. One of those trying to think of a way to revive the company's sagging fortunes was George Osling, a young public relations man who worked for the company at its headquarters in New York. Osling hit upon the idea of a singing telegram and instructed his secretary to find out about any prominent people who were having birthdays. She came up with the name of Rudy Vallee, then appearing at New York's famed Latin Quarter. Osling got Vallee's phone number at the Astor Hotel, called it, then handed the phone to another young Western Union employee named Lucille Lipps. Lipps informed Vallee that she had a message for him and proceeded to sing a lusty rendition of "Happy Birthday to You."

AUGUST

2 *U.S. Declaration of Independence signed*

3 *25th anniversary of the first voyage beneath the North Pole*

5 *400th anniversary of the founding of the first English colony in North America*

6 *Hiroshima Peace Day*

9 *Moment of silence in Nagasaki*

15 *Independence Day in India*

20 *150th anniversary of Benjamin Harrison's birth*

26 *100th anniversary of the eruption of Krakatoa; U.S. women granted suffrage*

29 *Liberation Day in Hong Kong*

3 **25th anniversary of the first voyage beneath the North Pole.** At precisely 11:15 PM Eastern Daylight Saving Time on this date in 1958, the USS "Nautilus," the world's first nuclear-powered submarine, also became the first ship ever to pass beneath the North Pole. The "Nautilus" had submerged two days earlier off the northern coast of Alaska near Point Barrow. It resurfaced August 5 in the Arctic Ocean between Greenland and Spitsbergen, Norway. During the 96 hours that the "Nautilus" was submerged, it covered a distance of 3,390 km (1,830 nautical miles) and passed beneath an ice pack that ranged in thickness from 3 to 24 m (10 to 80 ft). The sub traveled at approximately 120 m (400 ft) beneath the surface. In recognition of their accomplishment, Pres. Dwight D. Eisenhower awarded the Legion of Merit to William R. Anderson, the sub's commander, and the Presidential Unit Citation to the officers and men.

20 **150th anniversary of Benjamin Harrison's birth.** There is no record that Benjamin Harrison ever thought about growing up to be president when he was a boy, but he certainly had a good head start on his contemporaries. His great-grandfather was a governor of Virginia and a signer of the Declaration of Independence; his grandfather was the ninth president of the United States; and his father served two terms in the U.S. House of Representatives. Harrison made two unsuccessful attempts to become governor of Indiana. In 1872 he failed to gain the nomination; in 1876 he was nominated but failed to win the election. His political fortunes took a turn for the better, however, in 1881 when the Indiana legislature elected him to serve in the U.S. Senate. As a U.S. senator, Harrison pushed for expansion into the territories and for the admission of new states. Then in 1888 he won the Republican presidential nomination and went on to beat Grover Cleveland in the general election. (Harrison lost the popular vote but received 233 electoral votes to Cleveland's 168.) As president, Harrison continued to push for the admission of new states, and during his presidency six joined the union: North Dakota, South Dakota, Montana, Washington, Idaho, and Wyoming. Other accomplishments of his administration included the Sherman Anti-Trust Act, the Sherman Silver Purchase Act, the McKinley Tariff Act, a new veterans' pension bill, and legislation strengthening the Army and Navy. In the election of 1892 Harrison ran against Cleveland once again, but this time he lost. He returned to his law practice and died of pneumonia on March 13, 1901.

26 **100th anniversary of the eruption of Krakatoa.** One of the greatest volcanic eruptions ever witnessed by man began on this date in 1883 on the islet of Krakatoa between Java and Sumatra. The eruption took place as a series of explosions. The first occurred at 1 PM on August 26; the climax came at 10 AM on the 27th. The explosions could be heard four hours later as far away as Rodrigues Island, nearly 4,800 km (3,000 mi) to the southwest. The enormous discharge threw nearly 21 cu km (5 cu mi) of rock fragments into the air, and ash blanketed an area of over 800,000 sq km (300,000 sq mi). On several islands nearby, the ash accumulated to a depth of 60 m (200 ft). Eighty kilometres (50 mi) away there was total darkness for two and one-half days. The most disastrous consequence of the eruption, however, was a series of tidal waves. The one that occurred just after the main explosion reached a height of 35 m (120 ft) and took the lives of 36,000 people on the islands of Java and Sumatra.

SEPTEMBER

3 *200th anniversary of the Treaty of Paris*

5 *Labor Day in the U.S.*

8 *Rosh Hashana begins*

17 *Jewish holy day of Yom Kippur*

23 *Autumnal equinox in the Northern Hemisphere; vernal equinox in the Southern Hemisphere (9:42 AM EST)*

28 *Birthday of Confucius*

3 **200th anniversary of the Treaty of Paris.** The long and painful course of the American Revolution formally ended on Sept. 3, 1783, with the signing of the Treaty of Paris. Under its terms Britain recognized the independence of the United States and acknowledged U.S. rights over all the territory from the colonies to the Mississippi River and from Florida to the Great Lakes. The U.S. also was given access to the Newfoundland fisheries. In return, provisions were inserted in the treaty calling for payment of American private debts to British citizens, fair treatment of Loyalists, and British access to the Mississippi River.

8 **Rosh Hashana begins.** This is the Jewish New Year of 5744 and the beginning of a ten-day penitential period that concludes with Yom Kippur, the Day of Atonement. The observation begins at sundown with the blowing of the shofar (ram's-horn trumpet) in the synagogue. During the ten days Jews are expected to pray, meditate, examine their consciences, and repent.

OCTOBER

1 *Founding of the People's Republic of China (1949)*

4 *100th anniversary of the Orient Express*

10 *Thanksgiving Day in Canada; Columbus Day in the U.S.*

20 *Tenth anniversary of the "Saturday night massacre"*

24 *United Nations Day*

30 *Reformation Sunday; Standard time resumes at 2 AM*

31 *Halloween*

4 **100th anniversary of the Orient Express.** There were no transcontinental trains in Europe until this date in 1883 when the Orient Express pulled out of the Gare de l'Est in Paris, bound for the Bulgarian border south of Bucharest. There the passengers were ferried across the Danube. On the other side they took another train to Varna where they boarded a ship to Constantinople.

20 **Tenth anniversary of the "Saturday night massacre."** On Aug. 9, 1974, Richard M. Nixon resigned as president of the United States to avoid facing the possible result of impeachment proceedings stemming from the Watergate investigation. One of the dramatic events that led to Nixon's resignation was the "Saturday night massacre" of Oct. 20, 1973. On that night Nixon ordered the firing of special Watergate prosecutor Archibald Cox because of Cox's insistence that Nixon turn over tapes recording conversations between Nixon and his aides. Attorney General Elliot Richardson submitted his resignation rather than fire Cox, and when Deputy Attorney General William D. Ruckelshouse also refused to dismiss the special prosecutor, Nixon fired him. Cox was finally discharged by the solicitor general. From that time demands for Nixon's impeachment increased in both number and intensity until his resignation. The Watergate investigation sought to discover whether Nixon had known about the plan to break into the national headquarters of the Democratic Party (located in Washington's Watergate complex) and whether he had later taken part in a conspiracy to conceal his role in a cover-up of the break-in plans.

NOVEMBER

7 *Anniversary of the Bolshevik Revolution*

10 *500th anniversary of Martin Luther's birth*

11 *Veterans Day in the U.S.*

13 *150th anniversary of Edwin Booth's birth*

22 *20th anniversary of the assassination of Pres. John F. Kennedy*

24 *Thanksgiving Day in the U.S.*

27 *First Sunday in Advent*

10 **500th anniversary of Martin Luther's birth.** The great German religious reformer was born at Eisleben in Thuringian Saxony (Germany) on this date in 1483. He joined the eremitical order of St. Augustine in 1505 and professed his vows as a monk the following year. In 1507 he was ordained priest. Luther became increasingly distressed with certain practices of the Roman Catholic Church under Pope Leo X. The practice that angered him the most was the selling of indulgences. According to church doctrine, when a priest granted one of the faithful an indulgence, that person's sins were forgiven by God. As an ordained priest and a teacher of philosophy and theology at the University of Wittenberg, Luther objected to the widespread practice of offering indulgences for sale. Luther expressed his objections in the form of the famous Ninety-five Theses, which he nailed to the door of All Saints Church in Wittenberg on Oct. 31, 1517. The rebellious young priest expected the people of Wittenberg to oppose him; instead they gave him their enthusiastic support. It was not long before the Ninety-five Theses were being read all over Germany, helping to incite the Protestant Reformation. Luther was branded a heretic and excommunicated, but with the help of powerful German princes he became the Reformation's acknowledged leader.

13 **150th anniversary of Edwin Booth's birth.** The noted American tragedian was born on a farm near Belair, Md., on Nov. 13, 1833, and died on June 7, 1893. Booth made his acting debut at the Boston Museum on Sept. 10, 1849, playing the role of Tressel to his father's Richard III. Two years later at the National Theatre in New York City Booth's father refused to appear as Richard III, and the 17-year-old Edwin took his place. He went on to become one of the best-known actors of his time, excelling—especially in later life—in roles such as Hamlet, King Lear, Macbeth, Iago, Othello, Brutus, Shylock, and Richard III. Edwin Booth was the older brother of actor John Wilkes Booth, the man who assassinated Pres. Abraham Lincoln.

DECEMBER

1 *First day of Jewish feast of Hanukka*

4 *200th anniversary—Washington took leave of his officers*

10 *Human Rights Day*

17 *Wright brothers' first flight (1903)*

22 *Winter solstice in the Northern Hemisphere; summer solstice in the Southern Hemisphere (5:30 AM EST)*

25 *Christmas Day*

4 **200th anniversary—Washington took leave of his officers.** When the last British troops had set sail from New York Harbor, George Washington, the commander in chief of the Continental Army, gathered his officers together to say goodbye. On Dec. 4, 1783, in Fraunces Tavern in lower Manhattan, Washington spoke briefly: "With a heart full of gratitude, I now take leave of you. I most devoutly wish that your later days may be as prosperous and happy as your former ones have been glorious and honorable." When the men had drunk their wine, Washington continued, "I cannot come to each of you, but shall feel obliged if each of you will come and take me by the hand." According to witnesses Washington and many of his officers were overcome by emotion. When it was over, Washington boarded a barge for Paulus Hook (now in Jersey City), where a small cavalcade waited to escort him to Philadelphia and then to Annapolis, Md., where Congress was in session. He then returned to his beloved Mount Vernon.

22 **Winter solstice in the Northern Hemisphere.** This is the first day of winter, or the exact time that the Sun appears to reach its southernmost point below the celestial equator and begins moving northward again. The apparent movement of the Sun from south to north is a result of the changing declination of the Earth's axis as the Earth orbits the Sun. The winter solstice always occurs on or about December 21. In 1983 it will occur at precisely 5:30 AM, Eastern Standard Time, on December 22. In the Southern Hemisphere it is the first day of summer.

JANUARY

3 *South Korea names new prime minister and lifts curfew*

South Korean Pres. Chun Doo Hwan appointed Yoo Chang Soon, an economics expert, to be prime minister in place of Nam Duck Woo. He also replaced five other members of his Cabinet. The changes, according to a government spokesman, were prompted by a desire to speed up implementation of the nation's five-year economic development plan. Two days later the government declared an end to the four-hour nighttime curfew that had been in effect nationwide for 36 years, since the end of World War II. The curfew, however, remained in effect in areas bordering North Korea.

4 *European Community responds to Polish crisis*

The foreign ministers of the European Community (EC), during a special session in Brussels, denounced the imposition of martial law in Poland but did not endorse the economic sanctions imposed against both Poland and the U.S.S.R. by the U.S. The EC called for an end to martial law and the release of Polish workers who had been arrested.The EC also urged Polish authorities to resume a dialogue with officials of the Roman Catholic Church and Solidarity, the national federation of labour unions.

7 *Reagan backs draft registration*

Presidential counselor Edwin Meese III read a statement by U.S. Pres. Ronald Reagan that reversed his preelection stand on the registration of 18-year-old males for a possible future military draft. Reagan indicated that his continuation of registration did not mean he intended to draft young men into military service. He noted, however, that preregistration would speed up mobilization by as much as six weeks in the event that some future threat to U.S. security required a military response.

11 *Taiwan to get U.S. fighters*

The Reagan administration announced that the Chinese Nationalist government on Taiwan would not be given the advanced fighter aircraft it had requested because "no military need for such aircraft exists." The U.S., however, said the Nationalists could continue to co-produce the U.S. aircraft that currently constituted the mainstay of its air force. The U.S. decision to continue to aid Taiwan was vigorously denounced by the People's Republic of China.

12 *Ghana to be ruled by council*

The West African republic of Ghana, according to an announcement, would be ruled by a seven-man Provisional National Defense Council headed by Jerry J. Rawlings. The former flight lieutenant overthrew Pres. Hilla Limann's government on Dec. 31, 1981.

13 *Stephen named governor-general of Australia*

Sir Ninian Martin Stephen was named to be the next governor-general of Australia. He would replace Sir Zelman Cowen, who was scheduled to retire in July. The announcement ended speculation that Britain's Prince Charles might be given the post.

15 *Spain replaces military chiefs*

The Spanish government identified the four men who would hold the nation's top military posts: the chairman of the joint chiefs of staff and the chiefs of the Army, Navy, and Air Force. Their predecessors had all been summarily retired the previous day. By way of explanation, the Defense Ministry said it seemed appropriate to make the changes before Spain began negotiating its entry into NATO. There was also speculation that the shake-up was related to the upcoming court-martial of officers who were allegedly involved in the abortive attempt to overthrow the government on Feb. 23, 1981.

16 *Vatican and U.K. establish full diplomatic relations*

Great Britain and the Vatican established full diplomatic relations after a period of four and a half centuries of estrangement. Relations between Britain and the Vatican had been severed when King Henry VIII became head of the Church of England. Sir Mark Evelyn Heath, who had headed Britain's Vatican legation, was named U.K. ambassador. His counterpart, Msgr. Bruno Heim, who had been serving as the Vatican's apostolic delegate to Britain, was raised to the rank of apostolic nuncio.

21 *U.K. miners reject call to strike*

About 55% of Britain's nearly 250,000 coal miners, it was announced, had rejected the recommendation of their president-elect by voting to accept a 9.3% wage increase rather than strike. Outgoing president Joe Gormley had defied the union executive by urging the miners to accept management's offer.

24 *Mubarak invites Soviet help*

Egypt announced that it had invited 66 Soviet experts to assist on a number of major industrial projects. The move reversed the policy of the late president Anwar as-Sadat, who in September 1981 ordered the Soviet ambassador and other Soviet diplomats out of the country. Some 1,500 Soviet technicians were also expelled. All were accused of fostering religious turmoil in Egypt. Pres. Hosni Mubarak explained that Egypt was now committed to a policy of nonalignment. This was generally interpreted to mean that Egypt would try to improve relations with other Arab nations and with the Soviet Union.

26 *Reagan proposes "new federalism" in his state of the union message*

In his first state of the union message to the U.S. Congress, President Reagan reaffirmed his support for supply-side economics and proposed a massive but

Pres. Ronald Reagan delivered his first state of the union message to the U.S. Congress on January 26. He urged support for supply-side economics and a transfer of federal social programs to the states.

UPI

gradual shift of federal social programs to the states. In exchange, the federal government would assume responsibility for Medicaid payments and would temporarily distribute revenues to the states from a $28 billion "trust fund." Reagan called the bold concept "new federalism." The cost of the trade-off between the federal government and the states was about equal and was estimated at $47 billion. By 1988, after studying and evaluating local needs, states would be free to decide the fate of individual programs they had taken over.

Haig and Gromyko meet in Geneva

U.S. Secretary of State Alexander Haig and Soviet Foreign Minister Andrey Gromyko met for eight hours in Geneva to review issues affecting relations between their two countries. Despite Gromyko's warning the previous day that he would not discuss the situation in Poland, the two, according to Haig, did in fact pointedly disagree on Poland. Gromyko insisted that the imposition of martial law was an internal matter to be handled by Polish authorities; Haig declared that the military crackdown dealt a serious blow to U.S.–Soviet relations. The U.S. had earlier accused the U.S.S.R. of pressuring Poland's leaders to use force to keep the nation under control.

27 *Salvadoran rebels destroy air force planes at government base*

Salvadoran guerrillas staged a highly successful attack on the government's Ilopango air base outside San Salvador. According to reports, five or six fighter planes were destroyed as were three C-47 transports, a trainer aircraft, and 5 of the 14 helicopters loaned to El Salvador by the U.S. Much of the damage was believed to have been inflicted by saboteurs who went into action as artillery shells were being fired into the base. On February 4 the Reagan administration began replacing helicopters that had been destroyed or severely damaged.

Honduras ends military rule

Honduras ended nine years of military rule with the installation of Roberto Suazo Córdova as president. During his inaugural address, Suazo pledged that officials of his administration would be "servants of the people and not beneficia-

U.S. Brig. Gen. James L. Dozier (right) was rescued by Italian police from Red Brigades terrorists who had held him for 42 days.

ries of the state." The new leader also praised the military for sanctioning elections and recalled that during its 161 years of existence, Honduras had had 126 governments and 385 armed rebellions.

Koivisto chosen Finnish president

Mauno Koivisto was elected president of Finland with 167 of the 301 votes cast by members of the electoral college. Koivisto had vacated the prime ministership on Sept. 11, 1981, to become acting president during the serious illness of Pres. Urho Kekkonen. After 25 years in office, Kekkonen formally resigned on Oct. 27, 1981.

28 *General Dozier rescued in Italy*

U.S. Brig. Gen. James L. Dozier was rescued from his Red Brigades kidnappers when Italian antiterrorist forces carried out a carefully planned raid on an apartment in Padua. Three men and two women were captured. Dozier was described as tired but otherwise in good health after his 42 days of captivity.

29 *U.S. covers Poland's debts with commercial banks*

The U.S. government notified nine of the nation's commercial banks that it would

cover the $71 million in principal and interest that Poland was unable to pay on schedule. The Reagan administration chose to bypass the normal requirement that the banks first declare Poland in default on the loans, which had been guaranteed by the U.S. government. The administration's decision was controversial, but those who defended it noted that, without a formal declaration of default, Poland remained responsible for eventual repayment of the debts.

30 *Hundreds arrested during clashes in Poland*

According to a Warsaw radio report, more than 200 people were arrested in Gdansk after violent clashes with Polish police. The local military council responded by tightening curfew restrictions and suspending all sports activities and public entertainment. In other parts of the country, however, an easing of martial law was still expected to take effect on February 10. No official explanation was given for the trouble in Gdansk, which the Internal Affairs Ministry said was "provoked by propaganda activities of the U.S. administration," but some observers suspected the unrest was related to food prices, which were scheduled to rise by several hundred percent on February 1.

FEBRUARY

2 *Uprising reported in Hamah, Syria*

An antigovernment rebellion erupted in Hamah, Syria, a stronghold of the outlawed fundamentalist Muslim Brotherhood. According to unconfirmed sources, the uprising followed on the heels of a disastrous attempt by government forces

to raid a Muslim Brotherhood hideout. Though the government denied reports of a conflict for about two weeks, it then announced that the main road through Hamah had been reopened. Numerous casualties on both sides and heavy damage in the city's centre were said to have resulted

3 *Mubarak underscores Palestinian issue during U.S. visit*

Egyptian Pres. Hosni Mubarak declared, during welcoming ceremonies in Washington, D.C., that the "Palestinian problem" was the key to peace and stability in the Middle East. He also asserted that

FEBRUARY

"both sides [Israelis and Palestinians] have an inherent right to exist and function as a national unity." Addressing President Reagan directly, Mubarak said, ". . . the Palestinians need your help and understanding." The Egyptian leader also urged the U.S. to begin discussions with the Palestinians, even though they still refused to concede Israel's right to exist. Later in his visit, Mubarak reiterated his continuing commitment to the Camp David accords.

6 Syria discounts rumours of coup

Syrian Foreign Minister Abdul-Halim Khaddam, according to published reports, categorically denied that a military coup against Pres. Hafez al-Assad had been averted when the conspirators tried to recruit a loyal officer. Khaddam further declared that "Syria is the most stable country in the region," having the support of the common people and the backing of the military.

7 Costa Rica chooses president

Luis Alberto Monge Alvarez was chosen president of Costa Rica in an election that also gave his National Liberation Party a substantial majority in the Legislative Assembly. Monge's victory came at a time when Costa Rica was in the midst of an acute economic crisis and its citizens were fearful they might soon experience the same type of violence that extremist groups had instigated in other Central American countries.

9 Marcos's son-in-law rescued

Philippine Pres. Ferdinand Marcos's son-in-law, Tommy Manotoc, was reported to have been rescued from leftist guerrillas the previous day. Manotoc, who had mysteriously disappeared 41 days earlier, was brought back to Manila by a unit of the special forces. The amateur golfer and professional basketball coach had angered the president and his wife by secretly marrying their daughter, Imee, on Dec. 4, 1981, in Virginia. In an interview after his release, Manotoc read a statement expressing regrets that his family had accused the president of involvement in his abduction. Manotoc was reportedly found in a mountainous area east of Manila, where the Maoist New People's Army was known to operate.

New premier named in Kampuchea

The Kampuchean government, under the domination of Vietnam, appointed Chan Sy president of the Council of Ministers, in effect, the nation's premier. Chan Sy had been acting premier since December 1981 when Pen Sovan was removed from office "for reasons of health." According to unverifiable reports, Pen Sovan was in reality under house arrest.

11 African leaders debate Chad and Western Sahara

Eleven African leaders, all members of the Organization of African Unity (OAU), ended a special session in Kenya called to discuss the problems of peace in the Western Sahara and Chad. Morocco continued to refuse to negotiate directly with the Polisario Front, which was contesting Morocco's right to Western Sahara (former Spanish Sahara). Morocco insisted instead that Algeria be party to the peace negotiations because it was the principal supplier of arms to the Polisario Front.

The African leaders also called on Chad to accept a cease-fire with the rebel forces of Hissen Habré, who was seeking to overthrow the government of Pres. Goukouni Oueddei. Chad was also directed to draft a new constitution and hold new presidential and legislative elections. To give teeth to their demands, the leaders threatened to withdraw the OAU peacekeeping force from Chad by June 30 if there were no cease-fire or negotiations.

Egypt releases 1,000 prisoners

An Egyptian court ordered the release of 1,054 political prisoners after suspending former president Anwar as-Sadat's emergency order that resulted in the arrests of 1,500 persons in September 1981. The court also lifted bans on a Muslim Brotherhood monthly magazine and on a weekly newspaper published by the opposition Socialist Labour Party.

13 Five face investigation in El Salvador for murdering churchwomen

A civil court judge in El Salvador ordered five former national guardsmen to be held for further investigation in the murders of three Roman Catholic nuns and a laywoman co-worker in December 1980. The news was gratifying to U.S. officials because it seemed at times that no serious effort was being made to apprehend those responsible. Physical evidence in the case included a fingerprint on the women's burned-out van and a shell casing. On February 11 Pres. José Napoleón Duarte flatly declared "these men are guilty."

Report coup thwarted in Portugal

Portugal's interior minister, speaking on television, implied that a Communist-led union federation had tried to overthrow the government the previous day while the country was paralyzed by a general strike organized by the union. The union, however, denied there was any connection between the organizers of the strike and the men who were arrested that day in a car loaded with guns, explosives, and recordings calling for a popular uprising.

17 Mugabe drops Nkomo from Cabinet

Robert Mugabe, prime minister of Zimbabwe, relieved Joshua Nkomo of his Cabinet post after accusing him of planning to take over the government. Mugabe had claimed that a sizable cache of arms—including rifles, mines, mortars, and antiaircraft weapons—had been located on property owned by the Zimbabwe African People's Union (ZAPU), an organization founded and still headed by Nkomo. Though Mugabe and Nkomo had long been fierce political rivals, their respective groups formed part of the Patriotic Front coalition that contested white rule in Rhodesia before it achieved independence as Zimbabwe. When Mugabe won Zimbabwe's first election in 1980, he sought to placate Nkomo by giving him

Egyptian Pres. Hosni Mubarak (left) was greeted by U.S. Pres. Ronald Reagan when Mubarak visited Washington. Mubarak pleaded with Reagan to aid the cause of the Palestinians.

J. L. ATLAN—SYGMA

and other members of his party a role in government.

18 Council to replace Khomeini

The Iranian government announced that Ayatollah Ruhollah Khomeini would eventually be replaced by a three-, four-, or five-man elected council. Concurrent reports that Khomeini was seriously ill were denied by the government as "imperialist and Zionist lies."

19 Pope ends visit to Africa

Pope John Paul II ended an eight-day pastoral visit to western Africa that included stops in Nigeria, Benin, Gabon, and Equatorial Guinea. During the pontiff's four days in Nigeria, he did not meet as expected with the nation's Muslim leaders, apparently because the various Muslim factions could not resolve their differences.

Belfast auto manufacturer fails

The De Lorean Motor Co. of Belfast, Northern Ireland, went into receivership after the British government announced it could no longer provide money to the ailing manufacturer of deluxe stainless steel sports cars. The receivers, aware of the high rate of unemployment in Northern Ireland, expressed hopes they could raise up to £50 million (about $90 million) to keep the company operating

23 Rebels attack Ugandan capital

According to official reports, 69 members of the Uganda Freedom Movement were killed by government troops during an eight-hour assault on the army barracks in the capital city of Kampala. The next day government troops broke up Ash Wednesday services in a Roman Catholic church, saying it had been the staging area for the guerrilla attack. Emanuel Cardinal Nsubuga subsequently demanded that the government apologize for "the insults and harm" it had inflicted on the Catholic Church.

Japan denies Poland new credits

The Japanese government announced that it would grant no new credits to Poland until it lifted martial law. Japan, however, promised to fulfill its earlier commitments of economic aid. In a related step, Japan notified the Soviet Union that it would not attend a planned meeting on scientific and technological cooperation and that it was suspending consideration of a Soviet request to enlarge its Japanese trade office.

24 Reagan outlines Caribbean plan

President Reagan, in an address to the Organization of American States in Washington, D.C., warned that "new Cubas will arise from the ruins of today's conflicts" in Central America unless

Wayne B. Williams was led from the courtroom after being convicted of murdering two black youths in Atlanta, Ga. He was also believed to be implicated in a number of other murders.

something is done to prevent it from happening. Reagan accused Cuba and the Soviet Union of supplying arms to the rebels in El Salvador and pledged that the U.S. would undertake "whatever is prudent and necessary" to guarantee peace and security in the area. The heart of Reagan's speech was a proposal to help Central American and Caribbean nations through trade, investments, technology, and military assistance. The U.S. commitment to the region for fiscal year 1982 would amount to nearly $1 billion. That figure included an additional $350 million in economic aid and an extra $60 million for military security.

25 UN expands its Lebanese peace force

The UN Security Council voted 13–0 to increase its 6,000-man peacekeeping force in southern Lebanon by an additional 1,000 troops. The vote was prompted by fears that continued Palestinian attacks against Israel might provoke Israel to retaliate by sending troops into Lebanon.

27 Williams convicted in Atlanta

Wayne B. Williams, a 23-year-old black photographer and talent promoter, was convicted of murdering two of the 28

black children and young adults whose bodies were found in the Atlanta, Ga., area over a two-year period. Though Williams was charged with only two murders, the prosecution was allowed to introduce evidence linking these deaths to those of ten other victims. Superior Court Judge Clarence Cooper immediately, in accordance with Georgia law, sentenced Williams to two consecutive life terms in prison. On March 1 Lee Brown, Atlanta's public safety commissioner, announced that the task force formed to investigate the murders would be disbanded.

28 Israel insists Mubarak must visit Jerusalem on state visit

The Israeli Cabinet announced that if Egyptian Pres. Hosni Mubarak "refuses to visit Jerusalem during the course of his visit to Israel, we would have to do without this important visit." The matter was highly explosive because Israel had infuriated the Arab world in July 1980 by declaring that all of Jerusalem, including the eastern sector captured from Jordan in the 1967 war, would henceforth be the capital of Israel. The Israeli demand effectively ended any hope that Mubarak would visit Israel in the foreseeable future.

MARCH

2 *El Salvador halts drive against rebel forces*

El Salvador ended an all-out ten-day offensive against rebel forces holed up on the slopes of the dormant volcano Guazapa. According to Defense Minister José Guillermo García, the stronghold constituted "a very important concentration of subversion." The government abruptly halted the operation when its troops failed to seal off escape routes.

4 *Mitterrand addresses Knesset*

French Pres. François Mitterrand, in an address to Israel's Knesset (parliament), declared that Palestinians of Gaza and the West Bank had as much "right to live" as did citizens of the state of Israel. After indicating his support for a Palestinian state, Mitterrand asserted that the Palestinians must "reconcile their right with respect for the rights of others." The president then wondered how the Palestine Liberation Organization could ever "hope to sit at the negotiating table as long as it denies the main thing for Israel, which is the right to exist, and the means to maintain security." In his follow-up remarks, Israeli Prime Minister Menachem Begin said that Mitterrand's support for a Palestinian state created an obstacle to better relations between their two countries.

6 *OPEC to cut oil production*

Arab members of the Organization of Petroleum Exporting Countries (OPEC), during an informal meeting in Qatar, agreed to cut their aggregate output of oil by more than one million barrels a day to shore up sagging oil prices. The oil ministers were reportedly miffed at Iran be-

cause it had violated an OPEC agreement in February by unilaterally lowering the price of its oil by $4 a barrel to stimulate demand on the glutted market. An official of Shell Austria reported on February 17 that OPEC production had fallen to a ten-year low and in 1981 had been 16% less than in 1980.

7 *Guevara wins plurality in Guatemalan election*

Gen. Angel Aníbal Guevara outpolled three other candidates in Guatemala's presidential election and seemed destined to succeed Pres. Fernando Romeo Lucas García. Because no candidate received an absolute majority of the popular vote, the National Congress would be permitted to name the next president. Guevara was heavily favoured to win because he was the candidate of Guatemala's ruling rightist coalition. A leftist call to boycott the election was largely ignored, but violence was so widespread during the campaign that armed government troops were stationed at polling places. The U.S. had earlier indicated that the character of the election would influence U.S. policy on future aid to Guatemala.

8 *China restructures government*

The Standing Committee of China's National People's Congress adjourned a 15-day session after approving sweeping changes in the structure of the central government. To improve efficiency, the 13 current vice-premierships would be reduced to 2 and the number of ministries would be halved from 12 to 6. In addition, the 98 state council organizations would merge to form only 52. The reorganization would also reduce the roster of employees

in these agencies from 49,000 to 32,000. Though mandatory retirement was set at age 65 for ministers and 60 for vice-ministers and department directors, exceptions would be permitted if warranted in individual cases. When Premier Zhao Ziyang (Chao Tzu-yang) first explained the nature and extent of the planned shake-up on March 2, he reassured the country that the present leadership was "not making revolution against persons."

9 *Ireland chooses prime minister*

Ireland's Dail (parliament) elected Charles J. Haughey prime minister by a vote of 86–79. The outcome was uncertain until Haughey's Fianna Fail party, which had captured 81 seats in the February 18 elections, won the support of five members of the Dail who sat as independents or members of the minor Sinn Fein party. Garret FitzGerald, who had succeeded Haughey as prime minister on June 30, 1981, was forced to resign on January 27 when the budget submitted by his Fine Gael party was rejected.

10 *U.S. boycotts Libyan oil*

The Reagan administration placed an embargo on oil imported from Libya and on exports to Libya of certain high technology products. The decision, which affected only a small percentage of normal U.S. oil imports, meant Libya would have to find another market for some $2 billion worth of oil—about a quarter of the country's total annual oil revenues. The announcement followed a long series of warnings to Libya to cease its support for international terrorism.

11 *Sen. Harrison Williams resigns*

Sen. Harrison Williams, a Democrat from New Jersey, resigned from the U.S. Senate when it appeared certain his colleagues were prepared to vote for his expulsion. Though Sen. Alan Cranston had introduced a censure resolution two days earlier, this milder form of punishment received only scattered support. Williams had been convicted in 1981 of bribery and conspiracy in connection with the Abscam scandal. Secretly filmed videotapes were used during the trial and Senate hearings as evidence that Williams agreed to help an Arab sheikh (actually a disguised FBI agent) with his immigration problems and turn government business his way in exchange for secret shared ownership of a titanium mine. Williams still proclaimed his innocence.

12 *East-West parley ends bitterly*

Representatives of 35 nations adjourned their conference in Madrid as it became

French Pres. François Mitterrand addressed the Israeli Knesset and declared that the Palestinians of the West Bank and Gaza had as much "right to live" as did citizens of Israel.

ALAIN MINGAM—GAMMA/LIAISON

evident that discussion on East-West cooperation had reached an impasse. The U.S. and its allies used the occasion to denounce the Soviet Union for its role in imposing martial law in Poland. The Soviet bloc reacted by bitterly charging that Western nations were unlawfully interfering in Poland's internal affairs.

Nicaraguan repudiates his confession

The U.S. government was publicly embarrassed when a 19-year-old Nicaraguan told reporters at a news conference in Washington, D.C., that he had lied when he confessed to having been trained as a Marxist guerrilla in Cuba and Ethiopia and then sent to fight alongside leftist insurgents in El Salvador. The young man also repudiated earlier statements when he insisted he had never encountered other Nicaraguans or Cubans in El Salvador. The U.S. Department of State had arranged the news conference expecting the youth to confirm U.S. charges that Cuba and Nicaragua were interfering militarily in El Salvador's civil conflict.

15 *Nicaragua suspends constitution*

Daniel Ortega Saavedra, coordinator of Nicaragua's ruling junta, proclaimed a month-long state of siege and suspended the nation's constitution one day after antigovernment rebels destroyed two important bridges near the Honduran border. The minister of interior accused the U.S. Central Intelligence Agency of complicity in the bombings and closed down a Roman Catholic radio station for an indefinite period because it had broadcast news of the attacks before they had been publicly confirmed by the government.

17 *Four Dutch newsmen killed in El Salvador*

Four members of a Dutch television crew, filming a report in an area of El Salvador controlled by leftist guerrillas, were killed by government troops during a 40-minute firefight. Five other journalists had lost their lives since 1980 while covering the civil war.

18 *Indonesian political campaigns generate violence*

More than 60 persons were reported injured and 240 arrested during riots that broke up an election rally organized by Golkar, whose members dominate Indonesia's House of People's Representatives. Admiral Sudomo, the chief of security, blamed the trouble on extreme right-wing Muslims who supported, but did not belong to, the opposition United Development Party. On May 4 voters would decide who would occupy the 364 elected seats in the House, Indonesia's parliament. On April 12 the government canceled for an indefinite period the license to publish *Tempo* because the weekly magazine, which had a circulation of 100,000, had violated an agreement not to report

JOHN HOAGLAND—GAMMA/LIAISON

Voters turned out in surprisingly large numbers in elections in El Salvador. The Christian Democratic Party of José Napoleón Duarte received more than 40% of the votes.

controversial political topics; *i.e.*, the riots of March 18. Violence and threats of violence, according to various reports, caused many residents to remain indoors during the campaign.

21 *French voters moving to right*

French voters reconfirmed a trend set a week earlier in the first round of voting for departmental assemblies by giving the ruling coalition of Socialists and Communists control of only 37 of the country's 95 assemblies. Lionel Jospin, leader of the Socialist Party, read the results as a "warning" to the government; Georges Marchais, head of the Communist Party, said the swing to the right indicated "there is a problem."

22 *Iran launches offensive against Iraqi-held positions*

Iran launched a spring offensive to regain the territory Iraq had taken from it more than a year earlier. After one week of fighting, Iran reported it had captured more than 13,000 Iraqi soldiers while many of their units retreated in disarray. Iraqi Pres. Saddam Hussein downplayed developments, calling the retreat a "reorganization toward the rear" designed to prevent Iran from penetrating into Iraq and threatening its cities. In a radio broadcast, Iranian Pres. Sayyed Ali Khamenei said Iranian troops could easily cross the border into Iraq but would not do so because Ayatollah Ruhollah Khomeini would not permit it.

"Columbia" makes third flight

The U.S. space shuttle "Columbia" was launched into orbit for the third time, with Marine Col. Jack Lousma acting as flight commander and Air Force Col. C. Gordon Fullerton as pilot. An auxiliary power unit overheated in flight, two television cameras malfunctioned, and about 35 heat-shielding tiles were lost or damaged, but most of the planned experi-

ments were successfully completed. After eight days in orbit, the "Columbia" was landed at the White Sands Missile Range in New Mexico. Lousma said the shuttle had "performed magnificently."

23 *Reagan says "enterprise zones" can revitalize cities*

President Reagan sent Congress a plan to revitalize urban areas by offering businesses attractive incentives to invest in designated "enterprise zones." The inducements would include tax breaks and a relaxation of government regulations as well as tax credits for employees who worked in areas that met the criteria of "pervasive poverty, unemployment and general distress."

Guatemalan government toppled

Guatemalan army officers ousted Pres. Fernando Romeo Lucas García from office and named a three-man military junta, headed by retired Gen. Efraín Ríos Montt, to run the government. The rebel officers, who said they acted because the election of March 7 had been a fraud, pledged to restore "authentic democracy." The following day the junta suspended the constitution and placed a temporary ban on all political activities. The deposed president and his brother, who had been chief of staff in the armed forces, were reported to be under house arrest.

24 *Sattar ousted in Bangladesh*

Lieut. Gen. Hossain Mohammad Ershad overthrew the government of Abdus Sattar, president of Bangladesh. The predawn coup, which terminated three years of civilian rule, came as no great surprise because Ershad, the army chief of staff, had been openly striving for greater power. In a radio broadcast after the coup, Ershad said he sought to end corruption in public life and would "reestablish democracy in accordance with the hopes and aspirations of the people." On March

APRIL

27 Ershad told foreign reporters that he expected martial law to last for two years. That same day A. F. M. Ahsanuddin Choudhury, a retired justice of the supreme court, was sworn in as figurehead president. On March 30 smuggling and tax evasion became crimes punishable by death and severe retribution was threatened against those found guilty of hoarding, profiteering, black-marketing, or criticizing the government.

25 SDP wins vital seat in U.K.

Roy Jenkins, one of the founders of Britain's new Social Democratic Party (SDP), won a seat in Parliament in a by-election held in the Hillhead district of Glasgow. Because preelection polls suggested the SDP had lost much of its initial momentum, the election assumed national signif-

icance. Shirley Williams, a member of Parliament and a founder of the SDP, exulted after the victory: "We have now got back into Parliament the man who is certain to lead the [SDP-Liberal] alliance and will be the prime minister in waiting."

Dozier kidnappers sentenced

A court in Verona, Italy, sentenced 17 Red Brigades terrorists for their roles in the kidnapping of U.S. Brig. Gen. James Dozier on Dec. 17, 1981. Antonio Savasta, the reputed leader of the group and the admitted killer of 17 persons, received a reduced sentence of 16½ years in prison because information he supplied to police reportedly led to the arrests of numerous other terrorists. Others received prison sentences ranging from 27 years to two years and two months.

28 El Salvador holds election

Voters who turned out in surprisingly large numbers to elect members to El Salvador's Constituent Assembly gave the Christian Democratic Party of junta president José Napoleón Duarte a plurality of 40.5% of the popular vote and 24 of the 60 seats in the Assembly. It was not certain, however, that Duarte would continue to head the government because of the combined strength of right-wing groups that opposed him. The leftists had cited fear of assassination for not running candidates. Instead, they urged supporters to boycott the election or to cast useless ballots. About 11% of the ballots, according to reports, were either blank or marred with invalidating marks. Sporadic violence was reported, but the guerrilla threat to disrupt the elections did not materialize.

APRIL

2 Argentina seizes Falklands

Several thousand Argentine soldiers seized control of the British-administered Falkland Islands, which lie about 400 km (240 mi) off the southeastern coast of South America. The first challenge to British sovereignty in the region came on March 19 when some 60 Argentine civilians landed on South Georgia, a dependency of the Falklands. On April 3 British Prime Minister Margaret Thatcher informed Parliament, which had convened in emergency session, that a large British naval task force was being dispatched immediately to retake the islands. On April 5 British Foreign Secretary Lord Carrington resigned because of the "humiliating affront" Britain had suffered. The U.K. had long rejected Argentina's claim to the Falklands on the grounds that the 1,800 inhabitants were of British stock and wished to remain part of Britain. Though sheepherding was the main economic activity on the islands, there were indications that valuable oil deposits might lie offshore.

6 Egypt offers Mideast plan

Egypt's UN Ambassador Ahmad Esmat Abdel Meguid outlined a peace plan for the Middle East during a meeting of nonaligned nations in Kuwait. It was the first high-level meeting of Arab states to which Egypt had been invited since it signed a peace treaty with Israel in 1979. Meguid, adhering closely to a plan proposed earlier by Saudi Arabia, affirmed that all countries in the Middle East had the right to security within borders mutually recognized by Israel and its neighbours. He also called for an end to "Israeli occupation of Arab territories" and for the establishment of "an independent Palestinian state in the West Bank and Gaza within the 1967 boundaries." Algeria, Ye-

men (Aden), Syria, and the Palestine Liberation Organization quickly rejected Meguid's proposals.

7 Uganda arrests thousands

Ugandan police, according to reports, rounded up about 10,000 persons suspected of having ties to or information about guerrillas operating in or near Kampala, the capital. Many were soon released but others were kept incommunicado. Three days later an additional 1,000 were taken into custody. The crackdown, which began on March 14 with the questioning of some 2,000 persons, was apparently related to a guerrilla attack on an army barracks in Kampala on February 23.

10 Ghotbzadeh's arrest in Iran confirmed

The Iranian government confirmed reports that Sadegh Ghotbzadeh, who became Iran's foreign minister shortly after the seizure of the U.S. embassy in Novem-

ber 1979, had been arrested on April 7 for plotting to assassinate Ayatollah Ruhollah Khomeini. Ghotbzadeh's brother was reportedly also taken into custody with some 45 others and charged with complicity. Two mullahs implicated 82-year-old Ayatollah Kazem Shariat-madari in the plot, saying he had given Ghotbzadeh a large sum of money to buy a house from which a rocket could be launched into Khomeini's residence. According to a Teheran radio broadcast on April 20, Ghotbzadeh admitted his guilt on Iranian television.

11 Israeli violates Jerusalem mosque

Alan Harry Goodman, a 37-year-old U.S.-born Israeli soldier, ran amok in Jerusalem's Dome of the Rock, one of Islam's most sacred shrines. An unarmed mosque guard and an Arab youth were killed and a number of worshipers wounded before Goodman was subdued by Israeli police and border guards. Israeli troops and police later in the day used tear gas to control

Queen Elizabeth II of Great Britain formally proclaimed a constitution for Canada in a ceremony witnessed by more than 30,000 people.

JONATHAN WENK—BLACK STAR

WIDE WORLD

The Egyptian flag was hoisted above the Sinai after the territory was returned to Egypt by Israel as part of the treaty signed in 1979.

angry Arab crowds on the Temple Mount. The violence spread to other areas of Jerusalem during the following days as Arabs continued to vent their outrage. Israeli Prime Minister Menachem Begin called the attack a "terrible sacrilege" perpetrated by a man who was mentally ill. On April 13 Goodman was arraigned and charged with murder.

15 Sadat assassins executed

The two military men and three civilians convicted by a military court of assassinating former president Anwar as-Sadat were executed with the approval of Egyptian Pres. Hosni Mubarak, who rejected their final pleas for clemency. The military men were shot, the civilians hanged. Mubarak also confirmed the prison sentences of those found guilty of complicity in the plot to kill Sadat.

17 Canada gets own constitution

Canada lost the last vestiges of legal dependence on Great Britain when Queen Elizabeth II proclaimed the first formal Canadian constitution before more than 30,000 people gathered in Ottawa, the nation's capital. Canada, which had been governed for more than a century under the British North America Act of 1867, retained the British monarch as its official chief of state. Quebec Premier René Lévesque and other French-speaking separatists refused to attend the ceremonies

because certain provisions of the constitution were not to their liking.

23 Solution in Western Sahara still difficult to find

The Organization of African Unity ended a special two-day session in Kenya without resolving differences over the earlier admission of the Polisario Front-led Saharan Arab Democratic Republic to the organization. Kenyan Pres. Daniel arap Moi warned that the new status given the Polisario Front, which was fighting Morocco for control of the Western Sahara, presented the "most serious challenge facing the OAU in its 19-year history."

25 Egypt repossesses Sinai

In a simple but significant ceremony, Egypt regained control over the eastern portion of the Sinai as had been stipulated in the peace treaty signed with Israel in 1979. Israel had occupied the territory since seizing it during the 1967 war. The newly recognized line of demarcation separating Egypt from Israel (essentially the same as that in force before 1967) would run from Rafah in the north to a spot on the Gulf of Aqaba west of Elat.

26 U.S. rounds up illegal aliens

The U.S. Immigration and Naturalization Service began a week-long roundup of illegal aliens working in Chicago, Dallas,

Denver, Detroit, Houston, Los Angeles, Newark, New York, and San Francisco. The purpose of the raids, according to officials, was to open up jobs for unemployed legal residents. Of the 5,635 persons taken into custody, 87% were Mexican. A few of those detained were able to produce proper documentation and returned to work, but more than 4,000 agreed to leave the country voluntarily. Various individuals and groups protested the government's action because, they said, it smacked of racism.

27 National Front wins in Malaysia

The Malaysian government announced that the ruling National Front coalition party of Prime Minister Datuk Seri Mahathir bin Mohamad overwhelmed its opposition in elections for the 154-seat parliament. The victory was generally viewed as an endorsement of Mahathir personally and of programs designed to root out corruption and increase the efficiency of government agencies. Before the election Mahathir replaced about 40% of the party's incumbents with candidates of his own choice.

28 Walesa not among those freed by Polish authorities

Poland's Military Council of National Salvation announced that 800 detainees would be released outright and an additional 200 granted "conditional leave" as part of a program to relax martial law. Lech Walesa, the leader of Solidarity, was not among those freed. The government also promised that the seven-hour nighttime curfew would be relaxed provided there were no "excesses" or social unrest.

29 Magaña named to lead El Salvador

El Salvador's 60-member Constituent Assembly elected Alvaro Alfredo Magaña Borjo provisional president of the country, thereby ending a month of partisan political strife that followed in the wake of elections for the assembly on March 28. The selection of Magaña was rendered easier by the appointment of three vice-presidents, one from each of the major political factions. Magaña, a lawyer and mortgage banker, was supported by the Christian Democrats (the party of outgoing president José Napoleón Duarte) and by the right-wing National Conciliation Party. The military reportedly had threatened to take over the government if the stalemate over the presidency continued.

30 Canada's Alsands project dies

Canada's multibillion dollar project to extract crude oil from the tar sands of Alberta was effectively killed when Shell Canada Ltd. and Gulf Canada Ltd., the last two private investors in the undertaking, announced an immediate end to their participation. Either the federal or provincial government could assume Shell Canada's 25% interest in the operation,

MAY

but neither gave any indication of wanting to do so. Hope, however, remained that the project might be revived at some future date because more than Can$125 million had already been committed to it.

Canada's energy program suffers another setback

Corporate sponsors announced that they were delaying for two years construction of the U.S. segment of the 7,689-km (4,800-mi) Alaska Highway natural gas pipeline that would carry gas from Prudhoe Bay in Alaska into Canada and then into the lower 48 U.S. states. When the U.S. and Canada signed an agreement in 1977 to build the pipeline, the estimated cost was $10 billion, less than one-third of current estimates. Canada had already completed part of its work on the pipeline but it would have no access to Alaskan gas unless the U.S. company built the northern section.

Law of Sea treaty completed

After eight years of complicated negotiations, delegates to the United Nations Law of the Sea Conference overwhelmingly adopted a final version of a comprehensive treaty governing the use of the seas and their natural resources. There were 130 affirmative votes, 4 negative, and 17 abstentions. Among its many provisions, the treaty (one year after ratification by 60 nations) would impose international controls on seabed mining and require mining companies to sell their technical expertise to an international group operating for the benefit of third world countries. Though the U.S. voted against the treaty for a variety of reasons, chiefly related to the seabed mining provisions, it could still ratify the accord sometime in the future.

Botha meets with African leader

South African Prime Minister P. W. Botha and Zambian Pres. Kenneth Kaunda met for several hours in a mobile home set up on the border separating South Africa and Botswana. It was Botha's first meeting with a black African leader. The two men, it was presumed, discussed the issue of South West Africa/Namibia and the internal policies of South Africa, but the short joint communiqué merely stated that the talks were frank and useful.

MAY

2 *Falkland war casualties mount*

Casualties in the war over the Falkland Islands dramatically increased when the Argentine cruiser "General Belgrano" was sunk by a British submarine with the loss of 321 lives. Two days later the British destroyer HMS "Sheffield" was hit by a plane-launched missile and later sank; 20 seamen lost their lives. As Argentine Foreign Minister Nicanor Costa Méndez reiterated on April 30 that sovereignty over the islands was "nonnegotiable," the U.S. ended its efforts to mediate the crisis and publicly declared its support for Great Britain.

3 *Israel won't leave West Bank*

Israeli Prime Minister Menachem Begin, speaking during the opening summer session of the Knesset (parliament), declared that Israel would assert sovereignty over the West Bank at the end of the five-year transitional period specified in the Camp David peace accords. He had reportedly intended to introduce legislation barring future governments from dismantling Jewish settlements in the area as part of a Middle East peace agreement, but such a proposal would have met strong opposition from important politicians and many Israeli citizens.

4 *Indonesia holds elections*

Indonesian voters turned out in large numbers to give government-backed Golkar representatives a resounding victory in elections to the nation's House of People's Representatives (DPR), the equivalent of parliament. Golkar captured 246 of the 364 elected seats (4 had been added for East Timor), an increase of 14 over the 232 it won in the 1977 election. The United Development Party (PPP) captured 94 seats (a loss of 5) and the Indonesian Democratic Party (PDI) 24 (a loss of 5). An additional 96 members of the DPR serve as government appointees, bringing to 460 the total membership of the House. Golkar, which represents numerous segments of Indonesian society ("functional groups"), was especially elated over its victory in Jakarta. In 1977 it won 5 seats in the capital, as did also the PPP, but the PPP outpolled Golkar by a significant margin in the popular vote.

The British frigate HMS "Antelope" exploded and sank after being hit by bombs from Argentine aircraft during the Falklands war.

UPI

Hinckley trial begins in Washington, D.C.

The federal trial of 26-year-old John Hinckley, Jr., for shooting President Reagan and three others in 1981 got under way in Washington, D.C. Hinckley had pleaded not guilty by reason of insanity. The prosecution hoped to persuade the jury of Hinckley's guilt by arguing that the assassination attempt was carefully planned and executed.

11 *Huge loan swindle uncovered in South Korea*

The South Korean government announced the arrests of Lee Chul Hi and his wife, Chang Yong Ja, for alleged fraudulent transactions on Seoul's unregulated curb (over-the-counter) market. Lee had served in the National Assembly and as deputy director of the Korean Central Intelligence Agency and Chang, who was related by marriage to the wife of Pres. Chun Doo Hwan, was well known as a socialite and financial speculator. Chang reportedly obtained huge unsecured loans from several banks, then loaned the money at high interest rates to six corporations. As collateral she received promissory notes worth nearly U.S. $1 billion, far in excess of the amounts of the loans. Chang then disposed of the notes, violating a clear but implicit understanding that all curb market IOU's revert to the borrowers as soon as their loans are repaid. The fraud created panic on the stock market, forced one corporation into bankruptcy, and severely damaged the financial structures of others. Two bank presidents were arrested as was also Lee Kyu Kwang, Chang's brother-in-law, a retired one-star general and former president of the Korea Mining Promotion Corp. Other indictments were expected as the investigation into the scandal progressed.

12 Pope attacked in Portugal

During a candlelight procession at the shrine of the Virgin Mary in Fatima, Portugal, a Spanish priest attempted to assault Pope John Paul II with a bayonet. The priest was identified as Juan Fernández Krohn, an ultraconservative living in France. He reportedly opposed the reforms of Vatican Council II and called the pope an "agent of Moscow." John Paul had made the pilgrimage to Fatima to give thanks for his recovery from wounds sustained in an assassination attempt in St. Peter's Square just one year earlier.

13 Braniff airline in bankruptcy

Braniff International Corp. became the first major U.S. airline to file for reorganization under Chapter 11 of the federal Bankruptcy Act. Burdened with debts and mounting losses, the nation's eighth largest carrier canceled all its flights on May 12 and terminated about 8,000 employees. Howard Putnam, chairman and president of Braniff, insisted that the airline would survive in one form or another, but some industry executives doubted this would ever come to pass.

14 Marcos drops two from Supreme Court in wake of scandal

Philippine Pres. Ferdinand E. Marcos swore in the 15 members of a newly constituted Supreme Court just four days after he had demanded and received the resignations of all 14 members of the former court. Although Chief Justice Enrique Fernando admitted on April 19 that he shared responsibility for fixing the bar examination score of Justice Vicente Ericta's son, he was among the 12 previous justices reappointed to the court. On the advice of a panel of former justices, Marcos replaced Ericta and Associate Justice Roman Fernández, judged to be the central figures in the scandal.

16 Dominican Republic elects Jorge Blanco president

Salvador Jorge Blanco, a member of the Dominican Revolutionary Party, was elected president of the Dominican Republic with something less than half of the popular vote. His closest rival was Joaquín Balaguer, candidate of the Reformist Party. Pres. Antonio Guzmár Fernández did not run, but it was largely due to his efforts that the Army had become depoliticized and played no significant role in the electoral process. Jorge Blanco, who favoured strong ties to the U.S., had campaigned on a platform of fiscal austerity to revitalize the nation's severely crippled economy. He also pledged to initiate programs to help the country's poor.

18 EC in dispute over farm prices and veto rights

A crisis developed in the European Community when seven member nations voted to increase farm prices by 10.7% over Great Britain's forceful objections. The vote meant that Britain, a heavy importer of foodstuffs, would be making a greater net contribution to the EC than it deemed equitable. Britain also resented the apparent disregard of a well-established tradition that required unanimous approval of any measure that affected a "vital national interest" of any member nation. Greece and Denmark reportedly favoured the price increase but abstained in the voting because they worried about the implications of overriding Britain's veto. On May 25 a compromise was reached that at least temporarily settled the issue. Gaston Thorn, president of the European Commission, noted that the crisis was not over even though "violent disruption" of the organization had been avoided.

20 Kenya expels Odinga from ruling party

Kenyan Pres. Daniel arap Moi expelled former vice-president Oginga Odinga from the Kenya African National Union (KANU) party for "divisive and destructive propaganda against the government." Odinga was quoted in London as saying that the presidents of countries with one-party systems "set up cohorts of sycophants" with the sole intention of exploiting the masses. On May 26 KANU endorsed Odinga's expulsion and advocated a change in the country's constitution to legalize Kenya's de facto status as a one-party state.

21 British land on East Falklands

British forces launched a major offensive against East Falkland Island and within a few days were in control of about 155 sq km (60 sq mi) along the west coast. Accurate casualty figures were unavailable but material losses on both sides were heavy. The British lost two frigates, two destroyers, a containership, and a number of Harrier jets and helicopters. Argentina admitted the loss of some 20 aircraft but Britain claimed that nearly three times that number had been downed. On May 26 the UN Security Council requested Secretary-General Javier Pérez de Cuéllar to try to negotiate a settlement but hopes were dim because neither Argentina nor Great Britain appeared willing to relinquish claims of sovereignty over the Falkland Islands (called Islas Malvinas by the Argentines) and their dependencies.

22 Bahrain convicts 73 Shi'ah Muslims

Bahrain's highest court convicted 73 Shi'ah Muslims on charges of planning acts of sabotage against the conservative government of Emir Isa ibn Sulman al-Khalifah, whose family and supporters are mostly Sunni Muslims. Three of those convicted received life sentences and 60 others 15-year terms; ten minors were given 7 years each. During the largely secret trial, the prosecution claimed that most of the defendants were trained as guerrillas in Iran, which also supplied the arms that were to be used in the abortive coup of December 1981. Saudi Arabia also made arrests at that time and joined Bahrain in accusing Iran of attempting to export its religious revolution to Arab nations of the Persian Gulf.

24 Iran retakes Khorramshahr

Iran announced that it had retaken its port city of Khorramshahr and captured about 30,000 Iraqi troops. Iraq had won the fierce battle for control of Khorramshahr in late September 1980 but never succeeded in conquering nearby Abadan, especially important because of its huge oil refinery. The two cities are situated on the Shatt-al-Arab waterway which, before the war, was the principal cargo port for tankers that carried most of Iraq's exported oil, and a great deal of Iran's exported oil, to foreign ports.

SHELLY KATZ—BLACK STAR

The jetliners of Braniff International Corp. rested idly on the ground after the company filed for bankruptcy.

JUNE

27 Japan lowers trade barriers

Japan announced the elimination of tariffs on 96 industrial goods, including machine tools and computers, and a reduction of import duties on 121 other items. The decision, which would be fully implemented within a year, was made public one week before the opening of an economic summit in Versailles, France. Japan also pledged to enforce its antitrust laws to ensure fair competition between domestic and foreign firms. Foreign companies would also be guaranteed equal treatment with local enterprises in matters of banking, insurance, and securities.

30 Spain becomes member of NATO

Spain formally became a member of NATO following ratification by each of the other 15 member nations. Spain had stipulated, as had Norway and Denmark before it, that no nuclear weapons would be based on its soil. Spain's contribution to the alliance would consist of 340,000 troops, nearly 200 planes, 29 warships, and 8 submarines.

31 Colombia elects president

Belisario Betancur Cuartas, a member of the Conservative Party, was elected to a four-year term as president of Colombia. On August 7 he would replace Pres. Julio César Turbay Ayala, who was not permitted to run for a second term. Betancur's victory was partly attributable to a split in the Liberal vote, which was divided between former president Alfonso López Michelsen and Sen. Luis Carlos Galán. Betancur won 47% of the vote against 41% for López Michelson.

JUNE

2 Pope visits warring nations

Pope John Paul II completed a historic visit to Great Britain that was highlighted by an ecumenical service in Canterbury Cathedral on May 29. The pope and the archbishop of Canterbury, the Most Rev. Robert Runcie, pledged to strive "in faith and hope towards the unity for which we long." During his visit the pope also spoke frequently of peace. Antipapist demonstrations were less violent than feared. On June 11 Pope John Paul arrived in Argentina, a predominantly Catholic country that was at war with Britain over control of the Falkland Islands and dependencies. The pontiff spoke of "the absurd and always unfair phenomenon of war, on whose stage of death and pain only remain standing the negotiating table that could and should have prevented it." After addressing a crowd of one million people gathered in Palermo Park, Buenos Aires—the largest religious event in Argentina's history—the pope prayed for all those who had died in the war.

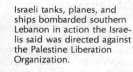

Israeli tanks, planes, and ships bombarded southern Lebanon in action the Israelis said was directed against the Palestine Liberation Organization.

JAMES NACHTWEY-BLACK STAR

3 Spanish rebels sentenced

A panel of 17 military judges meted out 30-year prison sentences to Lieut. Col. Antonio Tejero Molina and Lieut. Gen. Jaime Milans del Bosch for their roles in the abortive antigovernment coup of February 1981. Tejero had directed the seizure of the Cortes (parliament) by civil guards and the holding of the legislators as hostages. Milans del Bosch had ordered his troops into the streets of Valencia and then disregarded orders to have them return to their barracks. Twenty other officers and one civilian were given substantially lighter sentences and ten junior officers were acquitted. The editor of *El Pais*, a large Madrid newspaper, viewed the attempted coup as a rightwing attempt to overthrow Spain's democratic government. Reflecting the anger of like-minded Spaniards at the light sentences given to most of the officers, the editor commented: "The price paid for participating in military rebellion in Spain is incredibly cheap."

U.S. bans identifying agents

The U.S. House of Representatives voted 315–32 for a bill forbidding the identification of current U.S. intelligence agents, informers, or sources of information, even if such information is available in public records. The principal targets of the legislation were those who deliberately sought to expose agents so that U.S. foreign intelligence activities would be impaired or impeded. The most severe penalties were reserved for those with authorized access to government secrets. The Senate was expected to follow the House by voting approval.

6 Israel invades Lebanon

Israel carried out previous threats against the Palestinians by invading Lebanon by land, sea, and air. The immediate objective was to destroy strongholds of the Palestine Liberation Organization (PLO), which was accused of repeated attacks against Israelis and most recently of seriously wounding the Israeli ambassador to

Britain in an assassination attempt in London on June 3. The day after that attack a spokesman for the PLO denied his organization was involved. By June 10 the invading Israeli troops had reached the outskirts of Beirut and had engaged the Syrian peacekeeping force in heavy fighting. When a cease-fire was declared on June 11, Israeli forces controlled most of Lebanon's devastated west coast south of Beirut while Syrian military units continued to hold the Bekaa Valley. On June 19 Israelis moved into the centre of Beirut and took up positions along the "green line" that separated the Christian eastern part of the city from the Muslim western sector.

World leaders confer in France

The leaders of seven major industrialized democracies concluded their eighth annual summit in Versailles, France. The official communiqué, signed by Canada, France, Great Britain, Italy, Japan, the U.S., and West Germany, declared that the participating nations had come closer together on such economic issues as currency exchange rates, aid to less developed countries, and export credits to the U.S.S.R. During the conference French Pres. François Mitterrand called for united efforts to ensure that new technologies would not destroy jobs at a faster rate than they could create them. The war in the Falkland Islands and the fighting in Lebanon were among other topics also discussed.

7 Chad government toppled

After two years of civil war, rebel forces under the command of former premier Hissen Habré captured N'Djamena, the capital of Chad, and toppled the government of Pres. Goukouni Oueddei. Some 3,000 peacekeeping troops of the Organization of African Unity remained passive since they had orders to fight only if attacked.

9 Ríos Montt acquires total power in Guatemala

Brig. Gen. Efraín Ríos Montt dissolved Guatemala's three-man military junta, which had ruled the country since March 23, when Gen. Fernando Romeo Lucas García was ousted from power. The two other members of the junta were reported to have resigned voluntarily. It was then announced that the Army had appointed Ríos Montt president of the country and commander in chief of the armed forces. The new president, who had become a member of the California-based fundamentalist group known as the Christian Church of the Word, reportedly believed that he had been chosen by God to rule Guatemala.

11 Mauritius holds election

The Mauritius Militant Movement (MMM) party and its Socialist allies won

A crowd estimated at more than 600,000 jammed the streets of New York at the start of a special UN session on disarmament.

all 62 elected seats in the 70-member Legislative Assembly. As a result, Aneerood Jugnauth became prime minister. The defeated Labour Party coalition, led by 82-year-old Prime Minister Sir Seewoosagur Ramgoolam, had ruled the island nation and its dependencies since Mauritius gained independence from Great Britain in 1968. One of the major issues during the campaign was sovereignty over the island of Diego Garcia, site of a U.S. military base. In 1965 Ramgoolam had ceded the territory to Great Britain, which subsequently leased it to the U.S. so that country could develop a military presence in the Indian Ocean. The MMM wanted Diego Garcia returned to Mauritius.

12 Peace rally held in New York

A massive parade and peace rally, organized by religious and secular groups, was held in New York City to coincide with the second UN special session on disarmament. The crowd, including those who lined the sidewalks, was estimated to be about 600,000. More than 1,600 demonstrators were arrested two days later for blocking the entrances to the UN missions of five countries that possess atomic weapons. There was no violence because the demonstrators had notified police that peaceful arrests were to be part of their protest.

13 King of Saudi Arabia dies

King Khalid, who had ruled Saudi Arabia since 1975 and held the post of prime minister, died of a heart attack. He was succeeded in both positions by 59-year-old Crown Prince Fahd, the country's foreign minister, who had long been a prominent figure in Saudi government affairs. Fahd designated Prince Abdullah as crown prince and eventual successor to the throne.

15 Argentine troops surrender

The Falklands war formally ended when the Argentine troops, surrounded in Stanley, the capital, surrendered to the British. Britain later reported that 255 of its soldiers and associated civilians had lost their lives in the fighting; Argentina's losses were believed to be three or four times heavier. Many Argentines were reported to be disillusioned and angry over the defeat. On June 17 Lieut. Gen. Leopoldo Galtieri resigned as president of Argentina, as a member of the ruling junta, and as commander in chief of the Army. On June 19 the British repatriated 4,200 Argentine soldiers and hoped to return an estimated 7,000 others within a few days because severe weather and poor food threatened their health.

U.S. rules that illegal aliens must have access to free education

The U.S. Supreme Court in a 5–4 vote struck down a Texas law that permitted local school districts to either bar children of illegal aliens from public schools or charge them tuition. The ruling meant that children of undocumented aliens had

JUNE

to be granted access to free public education. Justice William J. Brennan, writing for the majority, noted that even though public education was not a right granted individuals by the Constitution, the Texas law imposed a "lifetime of hardship" and the "stigma of illiteracy" on such children and did not comport with fundamental concepts of justice.

16 *Cuba announces doubling of military power*

Cuban Vice-Pres. Carlos Rafael Rodríguez told the UN General Assembly, gathered in special session to discuss disarmament, that his country had nearly doubled its military might during the preceding year by acquiring "huge quantities of modern and sophisticated weapons." Cuba, he said, had also increased its military manpower by 500,000 men. Rodríguez explained that the buildup was necessary because the U.S. had adopted a "philosophy of plunder."

18 *U.S. extends voting rights law*

The U.S. Senate overwhelmingly approved renewal of the 1965 Voting Rights Act for an additional 25 years. Five days later the House of Representatives unanimously accepted the Senate version of the bill, which no longer required that challenges to local election laws be supported by evidence that the alleged discrimination was intentional. The act requires 9 states and portions of 13 others, all of which had histories of past racial discrimination or low turnouts of minority voters, to obtain approval of the Department of Justice for changes in their election systems. Any region that could show it had taken steps to encourage the participation of minorities in elections and had been free of discrimination for a period of ten years would no longer fall under the restrictions of the act.

21 *Jury finds Hinckley not guilty*

A federal jury, after four days of deliberation, found John W. Hinckley, Jr., not guilty by reason of insanity of shooting President Reagan and three others on March 30, 1981. The verdict shocked many and brought forth demands for a change in the law that permitted such an acquittal. Federal District Judge Barrington D. Parker, in his instructions to the jury, had stated that an acquittal based on insanity meant that Hinckley could be released from the hospital "only if the court finds by a preponderance of the evidence that he is not likely to injure himself or other persons due to mental disease." After the verdict was handed down, Hinckley was committed to a Washington, D.C., hospital for an indefinite period.

Son born to prince and princess of Wales

Buckingham Palace announced that a son had been born to Prince Charles and Di-

ana, the prince and princess of Wales. The child, named William Arthur Philip Louis, became second in line to the British throne. The child would be known as Prince William of Wales and as King William V when he succeeded his father, Charles, as Britain's monarch.

22 *Japanese accused of conspiring to steal IBM computer secrets*

The U.S. Department of Justice charged 18 Japanese with conspiring to steal industrial secrets from IBM, the world corporate leader in the computer industry. Most of those charged were employees of Hitachi Ltd., which allegedly paid $622,000 for classified information about IBM technology. Mitsubishi Electric Corp., also a leading Japanese computer manufacturer, reportedly paid $26,000. One of those arrested was identified as Thomas Yoshida, the only U.S. citizen among the accused, who was president of NCL Data Inc., located in California's "Silicon Valley" south of San Francisco. The defendants were accused of paying the money to an undercover FBI agent who posed as a "Silicon Valley" businessman willing to steal and sell computer secrets. IBM had informed the FBI in 1981 that certain important technical information and product designs had been stolen. There was consternation in Japan when news broke that six persons had been arrested in California and that arrest warrants had been issued for others in Japan. On June 30 a federal grand jury in San Jose, Calif., indicted Hitachi Ltd., 13 of its employees, and one other person. In a separate indictment, three persons were charged with receiving and transporting stolen IBM documents to Japan. The Mitsubishi company and four of its employees were indicted on July 21.

Kampucheans form government-in-exile

The leaders of three Kampuchean political factions met in Kuala Lumpur, Malaysia, to form a coalition government-in-exile opposed to the Vietnam-controlled regime of Heng Samrin. The three leaders were Prince Norodom Sihanouk, who had formerly headed the government as a neutralist; Khieu Samphan, head of the Khmer Rouge regime that had been overthrown by the Vietnamese; and Son Sann, a rightist. According to the agreement, Sihanouk would be head of state of Democratic Kampuchea (which was still recognized at the UN), Khieu Samphan would be vice-president, and Son Sann premier. Though Sihanouk disliked the Khmer Rouge, he explained that cooperation was the only alternative to continued "Vietnamese colonization" of his country.

Bignone named Argentina's ruler

Retired Army Maj. Gen. Reynaldo Benito Antonio Bignone was named president of Argentina over vigorous objections from the Air Force and Navy, which reported-

ly wanted a return to civilian rule. Despite promises that Argentina would see a return to democracy by early 1984, the commanders in chief of the Air Force and Navy said they would no longer support the junta and would participate in government only in matters affecting national security.

24 *South Korean president names new prime minister*

South Korean Pres. Chun Doo Hwan named Kim Sang Hyup, a jurist and former university president, prime minister in place of Yoo Chang Soon. Three other ministers were also replaced as part of the second Cabinet reshuffle in a month. The government was apparently reacting to the uproar that followed the revelation on May 11 of a gigantic loan swindle.

25 *Alexander Haig resigns*

President Reagan announced "with great regret" the resignation of Alexander M. Haig, Jr., as U.S. secretary of state. In his letter of resignation Haig indicated that an unspecified shift in U.S. foreign policy had played a significant role in his decision to leave government service. George P. Shultz, who had held Cabinet posts in the Nixon administration, was nominated as Haig's successor. The Senate confirmed the appointment 97–0 on July 15. The following day Shultz took the oath of office in a Rose Garden ceremony at the White House.

29 *Haitian refugees to be freed*

A federal judge in Miami, Fla., ruled that "it would not be just or equitable" to continue holding Haitian refugees in detention camps even though they had entered the U.S. illegally. In ordering the parole of most of the 1,900 refugees, the judge stipulated that each Haitian have a written agreement from both a voluntary resettlement agency and an individual sponsor stating that they would abide by the terms of the release. The judge's ruling was based on the government's failure to declare in writing its intention to detain such refugees should they make their way into the U.S. On July 23 the first 17 Haitians were released.

30 *Equal Rights Amendment dies*

Efforts to pass the Equal Rights Amendment (ERA) to the U.S. Constitution ended in failure when legislators in three additional states could not be persuaded in sufficient numbers to vote approval of the measure before the midnight deadline. A total of 38 states was needed for ratification. Eleanor Smeal, president of the National Organization for Women (NOW), said her group would first concentrate on electing women to Congress and to state legislatures before reviving the ERA issue. The amendment, however, was reintroduced in Congress on July 14 by 51 senators and 201 members of the House.

JULY

2 NAACP wins court battle

The U.S. Supreme Court voted 8–0 to overturn a Mississippi Supreme Court decision that held the National Association for the Advancement of Colored People (NAACP) liable for damages that resulted from a business boycott organized in Port Gibson. Justice John Paul Stevens declared that boycotts had constitutional protection and "the use of speeches, marches and threats of social ostracism cannot provide the basis for a damage award." The NAACP, which that same day was concluding a five-day convention in Boston, pledged to use boycotts more frequently to promote equal rights. Benjamin L. Hooks, the executive director, urged his audience to "march by every place that doesn't treat us right and spend our money where they know how to treat us with dignity and respect and compassion."

4 Mexico elects president

Miguel de la Madrid Hurtado was elected president of Mexico with about 75% of the popular vote. The Institutional Revolutionary Party (PRI) that he represented had won every national election since 1929. The conservative National Action Party under the leadership of Pablo Emilio Madero garnered a surprising 14% of the vote, making it the only political party in the country capable of challenging even modestly the near-absolute control exercised by the PRI in Mexico's "one-party democracy."

Dominican president kills self

Antonio Guzmán Fernández, the 71-year-old president of the Dominican Republic, died of a self-inflicted gunshot wound in the head. Guzmán, who was scheduled to be replaced by President-elect Salvador Jorge Blanco on August 16, was reportedly depressed after discovering that some of his most trusted aides had been stealing government funds and depositing them in foreign banks.

5 Penn Square Bank fails

Federal regulators declared the Penn Square Bank of Oklahoma City, Okla., insolvent because of huge losses it had sustained on loans to small oil and gas companies whose collateral only partially covered the amounts they had borrowed. The regulators, who had been aware of Penn Square's precarious situation for some time, had subjected the bank to five examinations during a two-and-one-half-year period but were unable to avert eventual failure. The collapse of Penn Square had far-reaching consequences because other banking institutions had bought about $2 billion worth of Penn Square's loans and now faced losses in excess of $200 million.

7 Poland's unpaid debts to West remain thorny issue

Private Western bankers tried in vain to work out a settlement with Polish officials on that nation's multibillion dollar debts, even though Western governments refused to discuss the problem until Poland lifted martial law. Poland told the bankers it wanted new credits to cover its 1982 interest payments or, as an alternative, a deferment of both interest and principal payments until 1983. Certain European bankers seemed to prefer the latter solution, but others, including U.S. bankers, wanted an entirely new schedule covering several years. Some Polish authorities were reported to favour a formal declaration of bankruptcy. Though such a step would free Poland of its immediate burden of debt, it would have a devastating effect on Poland's future economic relations with the West.

8 Businessmen back Trudeau's program

During a meeting with Canadian Finance Minister Allan MacEachen, representatives of many of the country's major businesses indicated a willingness to support Prime Minister Pierre Elliott Trudeau's efforts to limit wage increases to 6% in 1982 (the hoped-for limit in the rate of inflation) and to 5% the following year. Trudeau had stated earlier that he would not impose full-scale wage and price controls.

Certain businessmen urged MacEachen to take additional measures to combat the recession, such as a reduction in the federal government's projected budget deficit, a freeze on business-crippling regulations, and promotion of foreign investments.

10 The UN conference fails

The UN second special session on disarmament ended with all 157 members of the General Assembly acknowledging their inability to reach agreement on a comprehensive program of disarmament. Neither the U.S. nor the U.S.S.R. supported the progressive approach to disarmament put forth by nonaligned nations. Some delegates took limited satisfaction in the fact that the conference had at least focused attention on the importance of the problem.

OPEC meeting ends bitterly

Ministers of the Organization of Petroleum Exporting Countries (OPEC) ended an emergency two-day meeting in Vienna as divided over prices and production quotas as they had been before coming together. Iran, which along with Libya and Nigeria was accused of exceeding the allotted production quotas agreed to in March, directly challenged Saudi Arabia's domination of the organization and demanded that Saudi Arabia stop "stealing Iran's share" of the market. After the meeting adjourned, the Saudi delegate announced that his country would continue to monitor the state of the market and then decide what steps it would take to protect its interests.

Miguel de la Madrid Hurtado (seen here campaigning) was elected president of Mexico, with 75% of the popular vote, on July 4.

RANDY TAYLOR—SYGMA

JULY

Workers look for bodies beneath the rubble following an Iraqi air raid on Hamadan, Iran. Iranian troops had crossed the border into Iraq in an offensive that began on July 13.

12 India elects president

Zail Singh, a close friend of Prime Minister Indira Gandhi, was elected president of India by members of Parliament and the state assemblies. He would replace N. Sanjiva Reddy, whose five-year term was due to expire on July 25. Gandhi's nomination of a Sikh for the largely ceremonial post of president was seen by some as an attempt to pacify Sikhs in the state of Punjab, who had been clamouring for independence.

Peru faces serious crises

Peruvian Pres. Fernando Belaúnde Terry suspended constitutional rights in three of the country's southern provinces and ordered 100 specially trained policemen into the area to quell violence instigated by a Maoist organization called Sendero Luminoso. In their latest attack in Trujillo Province, the leftists had blown up a police station; one officer was killed and three were wounded. All told, some 40 persons had been killed by the guerrillas since Belaúnde assumed power in 1980. Peru also faced serious problems in its mining industry. In an effort to alleviate the financial stress brought on by falling commodity prices on the world market, the government suspended collective bargaining rights and exempted smaller mining businesses from taxes.

13 Iranian troops push into Iraq

Iranian troops crossed the border into Iraq despite earlier protestations that the purpose of Iran's spring offensive was limited to recapturing the territory it had lost in the early stages of the war. The attack against Basra, Iraq's second largest city, appeared to have been stopped, but Ayatollah Ruhollah Khomeini appeared determined to keep Iranian forces fighting until Iraqi Pres. Saddam Hussein at-Takriti was overthrown.

16 Sun Myung Moon sentenced

A U.S. federal judge in New York City sentenced the Rev. Sun Myung Moon to 18 months in prison for tax fraud and conspiracy to obstruct justice. The Korean founder of the Unification Church was also fined $25,000. His top aide received a six-month prison term and a $5,000 fine. The judge categorically denied that religious persecution was in any way involved in the case, even though Moon's lawyers had used that argument in presenting their defense.

19 Bolivian government resigns

The Bolivian information minister announced that the resignations of Pres. Celso Torrelio Villa and his Cabinet had been accepted. A military junta composed of the chiefs of the Army, Navy, and Air Force took over the government. General Torrelio had resigned July 15, the same day the government announced that general elections would be held on April 24, 1983, to choose a civilian government. It was not immediately clear whether Torrelio's decision was prompted by the news of the 1983 elections or by conflicts with military officers. On July 21 Gen. Guido Vildoso Calderón, the army chief of staff, was installed as president by the ruling junta.

Britain to sell telephone system

Great Britain's secretary of state for industry, Patrick Jenkin, told the House of Commons that the government planned to sell a majority share in British Telecom, the state-owned telephone company. Jenkin noted that the sale would involve the largest number of shares ever to go on the London market and possibly on any market in the world. Telecom's assets were estimated to be worth about $27.7 billion. The decision was in line with Prime Minister Margaret Thatcher's policy of selling off state-controlled operations to the private sector. Jenkin acknowledged the right of the electorate to have a say in the matter by announcing that the shares would not be offered to the public until after the next election.

22 France to honour its pipeline contracts with the U.S.S.R.

The French government announced that French companies had been told to honour previously signed contracts that had been entered into for construction of the Western European–Soviet natural gas pipeline. The statement challenged President Reagan, who had extended a U.S. embargo on such cooperation to include foreign companies operating under licenses from U.S. firms. West German Chancellor Helmut Schmidt's immediate support for France's decision was expected to be echoed by other members of the European Community.

Sindona indicted for fraud

Michele Sindona, already serving a 25-year prison sentence in the U.S. for banking fraud, was indicted in Milan, Italy, on charges of fraudulent bankruptcy, falsification of records, and violations of Italian finance laws. The charges were related to the 1974 bankruptcy of Banca Privata Italiana. According to the indictment, the bank was systematically despoiled by Sindona and his confederates. Luigi Mennini, a lay official who served as managing director of the Institute for Religious Works (the Vatican's autonomous bank), was among 25 others also charged by Italian authorities.

23 Japan to expand its military power

Japan's National Defense Council proposed a five-year military expansion program that would emphasize air and naval power to deter "limited and small-scale aggression." Implementation of the program would depend on annual appropriations voted by the Diet (parliament). The plan, estimated to cost about $18 billion, called for the purchase of antisubmarine and fighter planes, submarines, minesweepers, and antisubmarine warships.

27 Indira Gandhi visits U.S.

Indian Prime Minister Indira Gandhi arrived in the U.S. for her first visit in 11 years. Her "adventure in search of understanding and friendship" was undertaken to clear up misunderstandings and disabuse the U.S. of the notion that India belonged to "the Soviet camp." Gandhi and President Reagan agreed to a compromise solution over nuclear fuel for India's Tarapur power plant. France would be allowed to supply the facility with fuel, but India could not reprocess the spent material without U.S. permission. The agreement would prevent India from producing plutonium that could be used for nuclear weapons. India also agreed to submit its entire operation to international controls. In 1978, four years after India exploded a nuclear device, the U.S. Congress banned nuclear fuel to any nation that rejected international inspection of its nuclear facilities. France and other countries concurred in the ban.

El Salvador to get U.S. aid

The Reagan administration sent a 48-page document to Congress certifying that El Salvador was making tangible progress on human rights and the implementation of economic and political reforms. The document, signed by Secretary of State George P. Shultz, conceded that serious and frequent violations of basic human rights still occurred because fighting continued among various factions within the country. Shultz, however, noted that the March election of a constituent assembly was "widely judged to be fair and honest" and served as an indication that significant progress was being made. Certification every six months was a condition for continued U.S. military aid to El Salvador. Sen. Christopher Dodd of Connecticut described the document as a sham and expressed fears that the Reagan administration was simply encouraging right-wing forces in El Salvador to halt whatever economic and social reforms had been initiated. A number of civil rights organizations also deplored the certification.

29 *South Africa sentences white mercenaries*

A South African judge sentenced 42 white mercenaries found guilty of air piracy for hijacking an airliner to escape from the Seychelles after an unsuccessful coup in November 1981. Michael Hoare, the leader of the group, was given a ten-year prison sentence. Others received sentences ranging from five years to six months. During the trial the government denied Hoare's charge that it had backed the coup attempt. Earlier in the month five other mercenaries who failed to escape from the Seychelles were put on trial in that country. They were found guilty and four of them were sentenced to death.

AUGUST

1 *Israelis continue offensive*

Israeli planes bombed West Beirut for 14 hours in the most devastating attack against Palestinian guerrillas in Lebanon since June 6, when Israel sent its troops across the border. During the air attack Israeli tanks took control of the Beirut airport and moved close to the Bourj al Barajneh refugee camp, Beirut's largest. On August 4 Israel sent its tanks into the outskirts of West Beirut to dislodge some of an estimated 6,000 Palestinian guerrillas. The move was meant to intensify pressure on the Palestine Liberation Organization to agree to proposed conditions for a complete withdrawal from the country. On August 12 Israeli planes again inflicted severe damage on West Beirut in a sustained air attack that lasted 11 hours. Certain members of the Israeli Cabinet accused Defense Minister Ariel Sharon of acting without proper authorization and of attempting to sabotage the negotiations so that the bombings could continue.

Coup fails in Kenya

Army troops loyal to Kenyan Pres. Daniel arap Moi suppressed an antigovernment revolt that had been organized by members of the Air Force. The heaviest fighting occurred in Nairobi, the capital, and at an Air Force base some 200 km (125 mi) away. About 3,000 persons were arrested, including all 2,100 members of the Air Force. On August 21 Moi dismissed the entire Air Force and directed a former army general to form a new unit.

4 *Panama lifts newspaper ban*

Panama's Supreme Court invalidated an order that closed down eight daily newspapers on July 30. Brig. Gen. Rubén Darío Paredes, commander of the National Guard, reportedly ordered the closedown to stifle criticism of government officials. The Supreme Court tempered its ruling by sanctioning a new government policy that permitted a government-appointed "moralizer" to censor each edition. After the shutdown, according to reports, government troops destroyed expensive electronic equipment at *La Prensa*, the most vocal and influential opposition newspaper in the country.

5 *New Zealand cuts personal taxes*

Robert Muldoon, prime minister of New Zealand, unveiled a budget that included substantial cuts in personal income taxes. The prime minister had earlier pledged to grant such tax relief to compensate for the wage and price freeze he imposed in June. The loss of revenues, however, would be made up by increasing taxes on fuel, tobacco, and alcoholic products and by tracking down those who had failed to pay taxes that were due.

6 *PLO accepts pullout terms*

Lebanon announced that the Palestine Liberation Organization had agreed to terms for the peaceful withdrawal of its forces from the country. The negotiations had been mainly handled by U.S. special envoy Philip Habib. One of the few remaining problems was resolved the next day when Syria agreed to accept a large portion of the departing Palestinians. Other Arab nations made similar but lesser commitments, including Egypt, which reiterated its willingness to give asylum to the leaders of the PLO. On August 10 the plan moved closer to fulfillment when the Israeli Cabinet approved the principal elements of the agreement.

Banco Ambrosiano liquidated

Italian authorities ordered the liquidation of Milan's Banco Ambrosiano, Italy's largest privately owned bank. The Nuovo Banco Ambrosiano was then created to carry on the domestic operations of the bank it replaced. This step protected the interests of former customers and employees as well as those of small investors. Roberto Calvi, head of operations at Banco

A column of military vehicles carrying PLO forces left Beirut, Lebanon, after an evacuation plan was accepted by the PLO and Israeli forces.

RANCINAN—SYGMA

AUGUST

Ambrosiano, was found dead in London in June, an apparent suicide. His bank had allegedly made unsecured loans amounting to $1.4 billion. It was said to have had ties to the Vatican bank, which seemed to have been at least indirectly involved in the affair.

8 *Corsica granted own assembly*

Nearly 70% of Corsica's eligible voters cast ballots to select representatives for the region's new 61-seat Assembly. It marked the first time that local residents were allowed to directly elect the members of a French regional council. With 17 party groupings competing for seats, neither the left nor the right succeeded in gaining an absolute majority. That left proponents of autonomy holding the balance of power.

9 *Reagan's new federalism delayed*

A White House spokesman confirmed that the Reagan administration would not submit its "new federalism plan" to Congress until 1983. After six months of debate and negotiations, the governors of the states and federal representatives had been unable to reach agreement on several major issues. The governors, among other things, felt insufficient consideration had been given to the differences that exist among the states and that the proposed transfer of numerous social programs from the federal government to the states would prove disadvantageous to those for whom the programs were designed.

12 *Portugal abolishes Council*

The Portuguese Parliament voted 197–40 to revise the constitution in such a way as to abolish the Council of the Revolution, which had repeatedly used its veto powers to prevent private enterprise from entering such fields as banking and insurance. The Socialists supported the revision but wanted assurances that certain nationalized industries would remain under state control. The most vehement opposition to the change came from the Communists.

EC rejects pipeline ban

The European Community (EC) rejected President Reagan's embargo on the use of U.S. technology for construction of the Soviet-Western Europe natural gas pipeline. The EC protested that the ban violated international law and that failure to participate in the construction would severely injure EC industries. The EC also argued that construction of the pipeline would not jeopardize the security of Western Europe because the completed pipeline would account for less than 4% of the energy consumption of EC's members. France, Italy, and Great Britain had already indicated that they would honour the contracts signed earlier with the Soviet Union.

GAMMA/LIAISON

A line of Polish police was brought up to intimidate crowds of demonstrators who gathered to mark the second anniversary on August 31 of the Solidarity labour movement.

17 *China and U.S. reach agreement on U.S. arms sales to Taiwan*

China and the U.S. announced an agreement whereby the U.S. would gradually decrease its arms sales to Taiwan. No specific date, however, was mentioned for the complete cutoff. The matter had threatened to disrupt amicable relations between the two countries. On August 19 President Reagan gave the required notification to Congress that he intended to sell Taiwan $60 million in spare parts for F-5E fighter jets.

U.S. shaping immigration policy

The U.S. Senate approved a new immigration bill that would grant permanent resident status to illegal aliens who had arrived in the U.S. before 1977. Those who arrived during 1977, 1978, and 1979 would be classified as temporary residents, but after three years they would qualify as permanent residents. All permanent residents could apply for U.S. citizenship after five years. Illegal aliens who had arrived in the U.S. after Dec. 31, 1979, would be subject to deportation. For the first time, employers who knowingly hired illegal aliens could be fined; it they were found guilty of repeated violations of the new law they would face possible imprisonment of six months. Visas issued to legal immigrants, exclusive of refugees, would be limited to 425,000 a year.

U.S. draft resister sentenced

Federal District Court Judge James C. Turk of Roanoke, Va., sentenced 20-year-old Enten Eller to at least 250 hours of public service and placed him on three years' probation for refusing to register for a possible future military draft. In ad-

dition, the judge ordered Eller to comply with the law within 90 days or face a prison term of up to five years. Eller had publicly indicated he would not register because the law conflicted with his religious beliefs. All males who met the age requirement were obliged by law to register, but in the event of an actual military draft many would be excused from serving for a variety of reasons, including religious beliefs and physical disabilities.

19 *U.S. Congress increases taxes*

Both the U.S. House of Representatives and the Senate approved a $98.3 billion increase in tax revenues. President Reagan had urged passage of the bill, saying it was "80% tax reform" and not, as some suggested, the largest tax increase in history. Speaker of the House Thomas ("Tip") O'Neill had also exhorted his fellow Democrats to support the bill. The House vote was 226–207; that in the Senate 52–47. Such bipartisan support for a tax increase was highly unusual in an election year.

21 *Mexico in financial crisis*

Mexican officials ended a three-day emergency meeting in New York with bankers who were deeply worried about Mexico's ability to repay the huge debts it had contracted and the devastating effects a default would have on banks all over the world. After long discussions, Mexico was given a 90-day moratorium on payment of $10 billion in principal but not on payment of interest due. It was also granted new credits that would be supervised by a banking committee representing Canada, France, Great Britain, Italy, Japan, Switzerland, the U.S., and West Germany. In addition, the Bank for International Settlements agreed to give Mexico $1.6 billion in short-term credits to meet its most urgent needs.

PLO pullout gets under way

About 400 members of the Palestine Liberation Organization left Lebanon by ship, the first step in what was planned to be the total evacuation of guerrillas from West Beirut within the next two weeks. Troops from France, Italy, and the U.S. were on hand to monitor the operation. On September 1 the last of an estimated 15,000 Palestinians and Syrians left the city. Yasir Arafat, head of the PLO, had departed for Greece on August 30. The largest number of evacuees went to Syria; Tunisia accepted about 1,000 and other countries the remainder. Several thousand Syrian troops had reportedly left Beirut by truck during the evacuation to join other Syrian troops in Lebanon's Bekaa Valley.

23 *Lebanon elects president*

Bashir Gemayel, a Maronite Christian, was elected president of Lebanon despite efforts by Muslims in the National Assembly to deprive the assembly of the quorum needed for such an election. By tradition, the president of Lebanon was a Christian, the prime minister a Sunni Muslim, and the speaker of the National Assembly a Shi'ah Muslim.

26 Premiers disagree with Trudeau

At the conclusion of their annual meeting in Halifax, Nova Scotia, Canada's ten provincial premiers called for a special conference with Prime Minister Pierre Trudeau to draft a comprehensive plan for the nation's economic recovery. The premiers had rejected Trudeau's call to limit price and wage increases to 6% during 1982 and to 5% in 1983. They also concurred that the federal government paid too little attention to the notable differences among the provinces when it drew up its programs. The premiers also indicated a clear preference for cutting federal spending rather than increasing taxes as a way to control budget deficits.

27 Spanish Parliament dissolved

King Juan Carlos of Spain, acceding to the wishes of Prime Minister Leopoldo Calvo Sotelo, formally dissolved the Cortes (parliament) so that general elections could be held in late October. The prime minister's ruling Union of the Democratic Centre party had gradually lost so much strength that it commanded only 40% of the 350 seats in the lower house. The Socialist Party under the leadership of Felipe González was expected to make a strong bid to take over the government.

28 U.S. soldier defects to North Korea

U.S. Army Pfc. Joseph T. White of St. Louis, Mo., defected to North Korea while on duty at the Demilitarized Zone that separates North and South Korea. All requests by the United Nations Command for a face-to-face interview with White were rejected by North Korean authorities. White was the first U.S. soldier to volun-

tarily flee to North Korea since 1965 and only the fifth to do so since the end of the Korean War in 1953.

31 Poles clash with police on Solidarity anniversary

Polish police used tear gas, water cannons, and noise grenades to control moderate-sized crowds of demonstrators who defied government warnings against holding rallies on the second anniversary of the founding of Solidarity, the suspended federation of free trade unions. The largest reported demonstration was in Wroclaw, where a crowd of 20,000 clashed with police. About 6,000 demonstrated in Warsaw in two different squares, and several thousand in Gdansk, the birthplace of Solidarity. It was later reported that at least five persons were killed during the turmoil and about 4,000 arrested. A government official described the demonstration as Solidarity's "funeral march."

SEPTEMBER

1 Mexico nationalizes banks

Mexican Pres. José López Portillo closed all of the country's private banks so they could be "incorporated directly into the service of the nation." He also announced the imposition of a system of strict currency exchange controls. The president accused private bankers of taking "more money out of the country than all the empires that have exploited us since the beginning of our history." By nationalizing the banks, the government made it much more difficult for Mexicans to invest their money outside the country. Mexicans had spent some $30 billion for U.S. real estate, according to reports, and had an additional $14 billion on deposit in U.S. banks. On August 12 the government had notified those with foreign currency deposits in Mexican banks that their money would be available only in pesos.

Drought hits Australia

Some 60% of all the farms in Australia were being harshly affected by one of the worst droughts in the nation's history. Of the estimated 80,000 farms in critical condition, a large percentage were in the states of Victoria, New South Wales, and Queensland. Government officials acknowledged that substantial government assistance would probably be needed to meet the emergency.

Philippine labour leaders and others arrested

Philippine authorities began a two-day roundup of 23 labour leaders and 6 others said to be members of the outlawed Communist Party. Among those taken into

custody was Bonifacio Tupaz, secretary-general of the Trade Union of the Philippines. Most were accused of plotting against the government. On September 7 an additional 13 persons were charged with plotting to instigate a rebellion during Pres. Ferdinand Marcos's visit to the U.S. later in the month. Similar arrests had been made in August to short-circuit alleged subversive activities.

6 Salvadoran troops accused of killing civilians

During a news conference organized by the Salvadoran Human Rights Commission, three women accused government troops of indiscriminately killing 300 unarmed civilians during a seven-day anti-guerrilla campaign in San Vicente Province. The women insisted that the civilians were unarmed, even though they supported the rebel cause. The government reportedly used planes as well as hand weapons in their sweep through the territory. The government labeled the massacre story "misinformation" but acknowledged that 260 guerrillas had been killed. A civil defense commander, however, confirmed the women's account but estimated that 400 people had been killed.

9 Congress overrides Reagan veto

The House of Representatives voted 301–117 to override President Reagan's veto of a $14.1 billion supplemental appropriations bill that the president had called a "budget buster." The following day 21 Republican senators joined 39 Democrats in voting 60–30 against the president. The 30 votes supporting Reagan included 4 Democrats. A two-thirds majority was

needed in each house of Congress to negate the veto. The override was the first legislative defeat Reagan had suffered on a major issue since he assumed office.

Arab leaders meet in Morocco

Following a four-day conference in Fez, Morocco, the Arab League announced its unanimous approval of a peace plan for

Depositors talk to armed guards stationed in front of a bank after Mexican Pres. José López Portillo ordered all private banks closed on September 1.

UPI

SEPTEMBER

ALAIN NOGUES—SYGMA

Members of the Arab League, meeting in Fez, Morocco, called for a Mideast peace plan which included an independent Palestinian state.

the Middle East. It called for an independent Palestinian state and hinted that such a move would bring about the formal recognition of Israel. The plan, which was generally viewed as a victory for more moderate Arab views, also called for the return of lands occupied by Israel since 1967 and the removal of all Israeli settlements from those areas.

10 Argentine junta reestablished

Argentina's Navy and Air Force chiefs of staff decided to reconstitute the three-man military junta that was in effect dissolved when the two men announced in June that they would cooperate with the head of the Army only in matters of national defense. Their decision had been a protest against the appointment of Gen. Reynaldo Bignone to the presidency. The Navy and Air Force chiefs had argued in vain against the appointment of another army man to head the government. He succeeded Lieut. Gen. Leopoldo Galtieri, who had been forced to step aside after Argentina's troops were defeated by British forces in the war over the Falkland Islands.

11 China concludes party congress

The Chinese Communist Party adjourned its 12th national congress after adopting a new party constitution. The document restructured the party organization in several ways to preclude the type of "personality cult" that had prevailed under former chairman Mao Zedong (Mao Tse-tung). The constitution also asserted that class struggle was no longer a relevant issue in China. In the shakeup, Hua Guofeng (Hua Kuo-feng), Mao's handpicked successor, lost his position on the Politburo in a move designed to remove Maoists still further from positions of power. A number of younger men were elevated to positions of responsibility and

older officials were urged to retire to positions on the newly created Central Advisory Commission. It would offer advice to the Central Committee upon request.

14 Bashir Gemayel assassinated; elder brother chosen as successor

Bashir Gemayel, president-elect of Lebanon since August 23, was assassinated when a bomb demolished the headquarters of the Lebanese Christian Phalangist party in East Beirut. At least 8 other persons were also killed and more than 50 wounded. It was not known immediately who had committed the crime. On September 21 Amin Gemayel, the elder brother of Bashir and a member of Parliament for ten years, was elected president by Parliament, which gave him 77 of 80 votes on the first ballot. Two days later he assumed office.

15 Sadegh Ghotbzadeh executed

Sadegh Ghotbzadeh, who became foreign minister of Iran shortly after U.S. hostages were seized in Teheran in November 1979, was executed by a firing squad. He had been convicted of plotting to assassinate Ayatollah Ruhollah Khomeini and attempting to overthrow the government. During his trial, Ghotbzadeh denied planning to kill Khomeini but admitted he wanted to remove fundamentalist mullahs from their positions of power. According to unconfirmed reports, about 70 other persons were also executed for their involvement in the alleged plot.

Ferdinand Marcos visits U.S.

Philippine Pres. Ferdinand Marcos arrived in the U.S. for an official state visit, his first in 16 years. Two days earlier five Democratic senators had sent a letter to President Reagan protesting the visit,

saying it could be interpreted "as a sign that your administration condones the repression of the Marcos government." Official discussions covered a wide range of topics but reporters several times brought up the question of human rights. On one such occasion, Reagan acknowledged that the Philippines had "had a problem there" but said that progress had been made since the ending of martial law. Appearing before a group of congressmen, Marcos asserted that "there was no such thing as human rights" in the Philippines until he imposed martial law.

16 Palestinians slaughtered in two Lebanese refugee camps

Christian militiamen began a day-long slaughter of Palestinians in the Sabra and Shatila refugee camps in West Beirut. When news of the massacre began to circulate, there was immediate worldwide condemnation of the atrocity. Anger was also directed against Israel, whose troops had entered West Beirut after the death of Bashir Gemayel, for permitting the militiamen to enter the camps, since their hatred of the Palestinians was common knowledge. When reporters entered the camps on September 18 they reported that the scene was more horrible than anyone had imagined. Bodies lay everywhere. Some of the Palestinians had been executed with automatic weapons while others were shot as they tried to run for safety. Still others were buried in the rubble of houses that had been demolished by dynamite or bulldozers. Numerous women and children were among the dead. On September 27 Lebanese officials reported that more than 600 bodies had been removed from the two camps.

17 Thatcher visits Japan and China

British Prime Minister Margaret Thatcher arrived in Japan on the first leg of her first official visit to Asia. In her final press conference in Japan, Thatcher said her principal aim had been to present the problem of Japan's trade imbalance in such a way as to make everyone realize it had to be solved. Earlier she assured Japanese companies that investments in Britain would be warmly welcomed. After her arrival in China, Thatcher and Chinese officials discussed a wide range of topics, but none so pressing as the future of the British crown colony of Hong Kong. Britain's lease was due to expire in 1997 and there was great uneasiness in Hong Kong financial circles about the territory's future prospects. China seemed certain to claim sovereignty over Hong Kong but appeared willing to make certain concessions to ensure its continued prosperity. Thatcher discussed the situation with officials in Hong Kong before returning home.

19 Socialists regain power in Sweden

Sweden's Social Democratic Party (SD) picked up 12 additional seats in elections for the Riksdag (parliament), enough to give it control of the government because it could rely on support from the Communists. Under the leadership of former prime minister Olof Palme, the SD won 46% of the vote and 166 of the 349 seats in the Riksdag. The Communist Party retained its 20 seats. The conservative Moderate Union captured 86 seats, an increase of 13, while the Liberals suffered a substantial loss, winning only 21 seats for an overall loss of 17. The Centre Party also lost strength, its representation dropping from 64 to 56. The SD had promised voters it would restore the cuts that had been made in social programs and would take steps to create 30,000 new jobs. This would be accomplished by increasing the sales tax, which already stood at 22%.

20 Indira Gandhi visits U.S.S.R.

Indian Prime Minister Indira Gandhi began a week-long visit to the Soviet Union. The trip had reportedly been delayed to permit Gandhi to visit the U.S. first. During her visit to Moscow, Gandhi thanked the Soviet Union for "standing by" India but also, according to reports, made it clear that her country counted itself among the nonaligned nations. Gandhi also insisted that substantial trade with Western and other nations was necessary to provide India with badly needed modern technology.

21 Strike halts U.S. pro football

Players belonging to the professional National Football League (NFL) went on strike against all of the league's 28 teams. It was the first in-season strike in the 63-year history of the NFL. The executive committee of the NFL Players Association called the strike on September 20 after failing to reach agreement on a new labour contract with the NFL Management

Council, which represented the owners. The players had originally wanted a share of the teams' gross revenues or a share of the $14 million that each team was on average entitled to receive each year over a five-year period. This was refused by the owners, as was the union's alternative demand for a 50% share of television revenues over the next four years, a sum amounting to $1.6 billion. Both sides appeared to take strong positions on several basic issues so the strike was not expected to be settled without major concessions.

22 Bolivia fails to pay debts

Bolivian Finance Minister Alfonso Revollo revealed that his country had not been able to pay $50 million in foreign debts that had come due earlier in the month. The nonpayment of the first $10 million was attributed to cash flow problems, but overall Bolivia was facing one of the worst financial crises in its history. Three out of four workers were unemployed or working only part time, and inflation stood at 150%. In addition, the price of tin, Bolivia's principal export, was declining. The International Monetary Fund had refused to comply with Bolivia's request for help.

25 Honduran siege ends

Twelve leftist guerrillas ended their nine-day takeover of the Chamber of Commerce building in San Pedro Sula. On September 17, two days after it was learned that the government had captured Salvadoran guerrilla leader Alejandro Montenegro, the terrorists took 107 hostages in the Chamber of Commerce headquarters. The next day they passed out copies of a statement that declared their aim was to combat the "hunger, poor health, illiteracy, lack of housing

and rights to culture, art and science, lack of respect for public and individual rights and the hold of terror and repression of the state." They also demanded the release of political prisoners. The siege ended when the government allowed the guerrillas to take a plane to Panama. From there they went to Cuba.

26 Zenko Suzuki visits China

Japanese Prime Minister Zenko Suzuki arrived in Beijing (Peking) for a six-day series of meetings with top Chinese officials. Development of China's oil and coal reserves and continued aid to revitalize China's factories were among the topics discussed at length. Suzuki also assured Premier Zhao Ziyang (Chao Tzu-yang) that Japan would revise recently published textbooks that has sparked resentment in certain Asian nations by downplaying Japan's aggression before and during World War II. Deng Xiaoping (Teng Hsiao-p'ing) affirmed China's support for a stronger Japanese military and applauded Japanese-U.S. cooperation.

28 Begin accepts investigation of Lebanon massacre

Israeli Prime Minister Menachem Begin reversed his earlier stand and agreed to have an independent three-man board of inquiry investigate the massacre of Palestinian civilians in Beirut on September 16–17. The fact-finding panel would have subpoena powers but lack judicial authority. Two days earlier Israeli troops withdrew from West Beirut and were replaced by a peacekeeping force composed of French, Italian, and U.S. troops. Begin had yielded to intense international pressure and to the unanimous vote of his Cabinet in announcing the full-fledged investigation.

OCTOBER

1 Kohl to lead West Germany

Helmut Kohl, leader of the Christian Democratic Union, replaced Helmut Schmidt as chancellor of West Germany. In a rarely used constructive motion of no confidence, the Bundestag (lower house of Parliament) voted 256–235 in favour of Kohl. Schmidt, head of the Social Democratic Party, knew he was in serious trouble when the liberal Free Democratic Party withdrew from the ruling coalition. The chancellor wanted the question of his continued leadership to be decided in a general election but was overridden. Kohl and his Cabinet were sworn in on October 4.

Sweden sights spy submarine

A submarine was reported sighted in the restricted waters off Muskö Island, the site of a Swedish naval base. Though

Swedish officials declined to speculate on the identity of the submarine, it was widely believed to have been on a spy mission for the Soviet Union or a Soviet-bloc nation. After numerous depth charges failed to force the submarine to the surface, Swedish military officers concluded the submarine had either escaped or lay disabled on the bottom of the bay. Nearly one year earlier a Soviet Whisky-class submarine, possibly carrying nuclear warheads, had run aground in restricted waters off Karlskrona Naval Base. Sweden sent a vigorous protest to the Soviet Union over the intrusion.

2 Teheran bombing kills scores

An estimated 150 kg (330 lb) of explosives that had been placed in a parked truck in the central square of Teheran, Iran, were detonated with devastating effect. At least 60 persons were killed and 700 others in-

jured. Most were aboard passing buses or in nearby establishments. A government spokesman blamed "American mercenaries" for the explosion.

5 Lebanese Army enters Beirut

The Lebanese Army commenced a sweep through West Beirut to begin reestablishing the government's authority over the capital. The goals of the search were to disarm combatants, ferret out caches of arms, and round up illegal aliens and criminals. The action immediately sparked rumours that sooner or later most of the more than one-half million Palestinians in Lebanon would be forced to leave the country. On October 14 the government reported that the sweep had netted tons of arms and ammunition. In addition, 1,441 persons were arrested and some 23,000 forged identification papers confiscated.

GAMMA/LIAISON

Helmut Kohl, leader of the Christian Democratic Union, was sworn in as chancellor of West Germany on October 4, succeeding Helmut Schmidt.

Siles Zuazo elected in Bolivia

The Bolivian Congress voted 113–29 to elect Hernán Siles Zuazo president of the country. Three days later Siles Zuazo returned from exile in Peru and officially assumed office on October 10 as the first civilian president in 17 years. In a clear reference to the military, Siles Zuazo had remarked that those "who do not believe in democracy and have interrupted it many times, depriving people of their liberties, should reflect and understand that their time has come to an end." On October 11 he replaced the commanders of the three branches of the armed forces with officers who supported a civilian government.

7 U.S. stock market goes wild

Trading on the New York Stock Exchange set a one-day record when 147,070,000 shares changed hands. The rally continued through the following week, which registered the highest weekly total on record with 592,460,000 shares traded by Friday, October 15. The Dow Jones industrial average closed at 1012.79 on Monday, October 11, the first time the average had surpassed the 1,000 mark since April 1981. The increase in stock values got under way on August 17 when the Dow rose a record 38.81 points. The unprecedented surge in activity was attributed mainly to declining interest rates.

8 Poland bans Solidarity

The Polish Sejm (parliament) overwhelmingly voted to outlaw Solidarity and all other existing labour unions. The legislation made provisions for new unions, but the limitations placed on their activities and the conditions under which they could operate clearly indicated that the government intended to keep them under rigid restraints. On October 11–12 thou-

sands of workers at the Lenin shipyards in Gdansk went on strike to protest Parliament's action. Police used tear gas and concussion grenades to break up demonstrations. According to government figures, 148 people were arrested. On October 13 all the shipyard workers were drafted into military service, which made them subject to courts-martial for disobedience. That same day violence erupted in Nowa Huta, Krakow, and Wroclaw. One worker was shot and killed.

11 Sikhs storm Indian Parliament

Four persons were killed and scores injured when a group of Sikhs besieged India's House of Parliament in New Delhi. Two hours earlier the members of the Akali Dal, a political entity of the Sikhs, had been told by the security police that only five of their number would be allowed inside to present their demands for a judicial inquiry into a train-bus accident that killed more than 30 Sikh prisoners in the state of Punjab in the previous month. The Sikhs then armed themselves and attacked the building.

12 Zenko Suzuki to retire

Japanese Prime Minister Zenko Suzuki, president of the ruling Liberal Democratic Party (LDP), announced that he would not run for reelection as party head in November because he wanted "to sweep away the bad faith and hard feelings" that had split the LDP. Because of the LDP's majority in the Diet (parliament), the party leader automatically became prime minister. Suzuki's position was undermined when two members of his Cabinet attacked his economic policies, and Nobusuke Kishi, a former prime minister, wavered in his support of the prime minister. If three or more members of the LDP sought the party presidency, the more than one million members of the LDP

would vote their preferences. One of the two receiving the greatest number of votes would be elected president by the LDP members of the Diet. If only two candidates entered the race, rank and file members of the LDP would not vote.

King Hussein and Arafat meet

King Hussein of Jordan and Yasir Arafat, head of the Palestine Liberation Organization, concluded four days of talks on the proposed establishment of a Palestinian state confederated with Jordan. No conclusions were made public, but Arafat later declared there were "positive elements" in the plan suggested by President Reagan. The day after Hussein and Arafat concluded their talks, five hard-line factions within the PLO denounced the idea of a confederation but did not mention Arafat by name. The chairman of the Palestine National Council explained that democratic procedures within the PLO made allowances for disagreements, but he did not foresee anyone successfully challenging Arafat's leadership.

15 Suharto concludes U.S. visit

President Suharto of Indonesia ended a five-day visit to the U.S. after a series of discussions that included U.S. policy in Asia and economic aid for Indonesia. In welcoming Suharto to the White House, President Reagan praised Indonesia for bringing credibility to the concept of nonalignment; he also pledged never to lose sight of the security and economic needs of Indonesia, the world's fifth most populous nation, and of other Asian countries. Reagan later assured Suharto that any request for military aircraft or ships would be sympathetically reviewed. During a banquet given in honour of Suharto, Reagan announced the appointment of John Holdridge as U.S. ambassador to Jakarta. Earlier attempts to fill the vacancy had met opposition.

16 U.S. backs Israel against Arab attacks in UN

U.S. Secretary of State George P. Shultz announced that the U.S. was withholding an $8.5 million payment to the UN International Atomic Energy Agency because it had canceled Israel's credentials. The action had been instigated by Arab nations that wanted to exclude Israel from all UN bodies, including the General Assembly. Shultz warned that the U.S. would refuse to participate in any UN organization that barred Israel.

China fires submarine missile

China announced that it had successfully fired a ballistic missile from a submarine. The event, described as "an embodiment of socialism's excellence," made China the fifth nation to have developed such technology; the other four with this capability were France, Great Britain, the U.S., and the U.S.S.R.

CAMERA PRESS

A crowd of angry Sikhs stormed the House of Parliament in New Delhi, India, after their demands for an inquiry into an accident that killed 30 Sikh prisoners had been rejected.

Chinese pilot defects to Taiwan

A Chinese Air Force pilot landed safely in South Korea in his MiG-19 fighter plane after successfully outrunning other Chinese jet fighters that pursued him. It was the third time since the Korean War that a Chinese pilot had fled to South Korea. The pilot obtained permission from Korean authorities to proceed to Taiwan, where the Nationalist government had a standing offer of $2 million for any pilot defecting from the mainland.

19 De Lorean arrested on drug charge

John De Lorean, whose company had been producing luxury stainless steel sports cars in Northern Ireland, was arrested in Los Angeles and charged with possession of 27 kg (59 lb) of cocaine and conspiracy to distribute it. Two others arrested at the same time faced similar charges. In mid-February the British government had notified De Lorean that it would no longer provide funds for his ailing company, and only hours before the arrest it had announced that the plant would be closed permanently. According to the FBI, De Lorean became involved in drug dealing to salvage his company. Undercover agents from the FBI and the Drug Enforcement Administration were reportedly directly involved in negotiations with De Lorean for several months.

21 Habré becomes Chad president

Hissen Habré was sworn in as president of Chad and quickly appointed a 31-member Cabinet that included former political opponents and the first Chadian woman ever to hold so high a position. The new government replaced the Council of State that had ruled Chad since early June when Habré overthrew Pres. Goukouni Oueddei.

26 Australians invade Parliament

About 50 unemployed Australian workers from Wollongong, New South Wales, fought their way into Parliament House in Canberra demanding to see Prime Minister Malcolm Fraser. The group represented some 800 laid-off miners and steelworkers who insisted that the government take steps to put them back to work. When Fraser sent word that he would meet with union heads to see what could be done, the workers departed.

27 Japanese-U.S. trade talks falter

Trade talks between Japan and the U.S. were cut short in Honolulu when the U.S. delegation, led by Donald Nelson, refused to discuss any other topic except unrestricted Japanese importation of U.S. beef and citrus products. Hiroyo Sano insisted on broadening the talks to include other quotas and tariffs. The Japanese minister of agriculture, forestry, and fisheries later stated that what the U.S. viewed as merely a question of trade involved much more than that from the Japanese point of view, namely, the viability of its domestic agriculture. In early September the minister revealed that Japanese imports of U.S. farm products had totaled about $3.5 billion for the first half of 1982, a drop of 19.2% from the same period in 1981. However, U.S. food entering Japan still accounted for 40% of the country's total agricultural imports during the first half of 1982. Japan's overall food imports during that time had declined by 9.8%.

Poland loses special trade status

President Reagan suspended Poland's most-favoured-nation trading status because it had outlawed Solidarity and other free labour unions. As a consequence, Polish goods entering the U.S. would have to be marketed at higher prices because of increased tariffs. Reagan, justifying his action on technical grounds, pointed out that Poland had not fulfilled its trade obligations under the General Agreement on Tariffs and Trade (GATT) since 1978. GATT obliged Poland to increase its imports from Western nations by 7% a year.

28 Socialists win in Spain

Felipe González led the Spanish Socialist Workers' Party to resounding victories in elections for the lower house of the Cortes (parliament) and the Senate. The Socialists won 201 seats in the lower house, increasing their representation from 121 seats during the government of outgoing Premier Leopoldo Calvo Sotelo. The rightwing Popular Alliance Party made impressive gains, winning 106 seats, an increase of 82. Calvo Sotelo failed to win reelection to the Cortes as his Union of the Democratic Centre (UCD) party suffered a devastating defeat. Its candidates won only 12 seats. Seven minor parties took the remaining 31 vacancies. In the Senate, the Socialists won 134 of the 208 seats, the Popular Alliance 54, and the UCD 4. González would be Spain's first left-wing head of government in half a century.

NOVEMBER

2 U.S. voters go to the polls

U.S. voters went to the polls to elect 33 senators, 433 representatives, 36 governors, and hundreds of local officials. Republicans retained their 54–46 majority in the U.S. Senate but suffered a net loss of 26 seats in the Democrat-controlled House of Representatives. The new total gave the Democrats 267 seats and the Republicans 166; 2 seats remained vacant. Democrats also won 27 of the state races for governor, giving them a net increase of 7. These victories gave the Democrats 34 of the 50 governorships. Many of the Republicans who went down to defeat represented areas that were hard hit by the economic recession.

4 Lubbers replaces Van Agt

Ruud Lubbers was sworn in as prime minister of The Netherlands, replacing Andreas van Agt. The new Parliament, which included 45 Christian Democrats and 36 members of the Liberal Party, was expected to curtail government spending and support NATO's decision to deploy medium-range nuclear weapons in Europe if a reduction of arms could not be worked out with the Soviet Union.

7 Turks back military government

Turkish voters overwhelmingly endorsed the new constitution drawn up by the rul-

NOVEMBER

ing National Security Council. Approval of the document meant, among other things, that Gen. Kenan Evren would begin a seven-year term as president on November 10. The constitution, however, called for general elections no later than the spring of 1984.

9 Gemayel gets special powers

The Lebanese Parliament voted 58–1 with 32 abstentions to give Pres. Amin Gemayel certain emergency powers for a period of six months. The legislature simultaneously gave the government a vote of confidence as it began the arduous task of trying to restore the country to normality after years of civil war and the 1982 Israeli invasion. Gemayel had requested broader powers than those eventually approved by Parliament, but he was authorized to negotiate as he wished for the withdrawal of Israeli and Syrian forces and with members of the Palestine Liberation Organization, who were concentrated in the northern and eastern areas of Lebanon. The new president would also attempt to disarm the Christians in East Beirut so that the central government could establish control over the entire country.

Hundreds die in Afghan tunnel blast

Reports reached New Delhi, India, that hundreds of Afghan civilians and Soviet soldiers had been killed in a mountain tunnel disaster about one week earlier. Though details were sketchy, it appeared that a violent explosion had occurred when the lead truck of a Soviet convoy collided with a fuel truck. Flames then engulfed other vehicles and toxic fumes swept through the 2.7-km (1.7-mi)-long tunnel. According to one report, Soviet soldiers outside the tunnel mistakenly sealed off both entrances because they thought the explosion signaled an attack by Afghan guerrillas.

Pope John Paul visits Spain

Pope John Paul II concluded the first ever papal visit to Spain after making public appearances in 16 cities throughout the country. Arriving as he did just a few days after the Socialists gained power, the pope made it clear that his visit had no political dimensions; his purpose, he said, was to strengthen the faith, hope, and good works of the predominantly Catholic population. On November 6 the pontiff visited the Basque region of Spain, where elements of the population were demanding independence. That same day two men were arrested in a Basque city in France on suspicion of plotting an attack against the pope.

10 Mexico accepts IMF terms

The Mexican government announced that it had reached agreement with representatives of the International Monetary Fund (IMF) on terms for $3,840,000,000 in credits spread over three years. Mexico agreed to cut government spending, increase taxes, and curb imports to prevent badly needed capital from leaving the country. The IMF loan would make it possible for Mexico to service its huge foreign debts. It also improved the government's chances of borrowing additional money from the international banking community so that the nation's economic recovery could be accelerated.

U.K. spy sentenced to 35 years

Geoffrey A. Prime, who had been a translator of Russian at Britain's Government Communications Headquarters in Cheltenham from 1976 to 1977, pleaded guilty to having spied for the Soviet Union and was sentenced to 35 years in prison. Prime said he suffered from psychological problems and was motivated by "a misplaced idealistic view of Soviet socialism." Lord Lane, the lord chief justice, said Prime had caused "incalculable harm" to Great Britain and its allies. Prime had been taken into custody in April on charges of assaulting young girls. His wife then told police she suspected her husband of being a spy. Confronted with the accusation, Prime eventually confessed he had spied for the U.S.S.R. for 14 years. The judge imposed an additional three-year sentence for Prime's sex offenses. The communications centre, which is a joint British-U.S. operation, analyzes data gathered from worldwide sources.

11 Leonid Brezhnev dies; Andropov elected successor

The Soviet people were officially informed that Leonid I. Brezhnev had died

Soviet leader Leonid Brezhnev died on November 10 and was buried in Moscow's Red Square. Yury Andropov was elected his successor.

JOHN BRYSON—SYGMA

the previous day of a heart attack. Brezhnev succeeded Nikita S. Khrushchev as first secretary of the Communist Party in 1964 and became chief of state in 1977. On November 12 the Communist Party Central Committee met in emergency session and elected 68-year-old Yury V. Andropov general secretary of the party, the most powerful position in the Soviet Union. In 1967 Andropov became head of the Committee for State Security (KGB) and in 1973 a full member of the Politburo. He left the KGB in May 1982 after being appointed to the party Secretariat. It appeared that no one would be named chairman of the Presidium of the Supreme Soviet (president) in the near future.

Israeli military headquarters bombed in Lebanon

A shock of unknown origin caused the Tyre headquarters of the Israeli force in Lebanon to collapse. Early reports indicated that at least 26 persons were killed but eventually a total of 89 dead were found. The Israelis initially believed members of the Palestine Liberation Organization were responsible for destroying the seven-story building, which had been the regional headquarters of the PLO before Israel invaded Lebanon in June. But an inquiry later cast doubt on the possibility of sabotage and implied that the building collapsed because it had been poorly constructed.

13 Reagan lifts pipeline ban

President Reagan lifted his controversial ban against the use of U.S. technology for the construction of a natural gas pipeline that would run from Siberia to Western Europe. Reagan asserted that the sanctions had served their purpose and could now be removed because the U.S. had reached "substantial agreement" with its allies on what trade policies it would adopt in dealing with the Soviet Union. Britain and West Germany expressed gratification over Reagan's announcement, but France denied it was a party to any agreement.

14 Lech Walesa rejoins family

Lech Walesa, released by Polish authorities after 11 months of detention, returned home to his family in Gdansk. He told well-wishers awaiting his arrival that in the future he would "talk and act, not on my knees, but with prudence." The official Polish press agency referred to Walesa as "the former head of Solidarity," the national federation of free labour unions that had been outlawed with all other free unions by Parliament on October 8.

16 Chinese and Soviet officials discuss troubled relationship

Chinese Foreign Minister Huang Hua and his Soviet counterpart, Andrey Gromyko, met for an hour and a half in Moscow, following the funeral of Leonid I. Brezhnev. It was the first such high-level meeting between the world's two largest Communist countries since 1969. Gromyko reportedly told Huang that the U.S.S.R. placed great importance on the restoration of normal relations with China. Huang expressed hope that relations between the two countries would "gradually" return to normal.

Football strike may be over

The U.S. National Football League Players Association and the owners of the 28 teams reached a tentative agreement through their bargaining agents that, if ratified by the players, would end the strike that began on September 21. If the season resumed, each team would play only seven more games (two had already been played) before 16 teams commenced play-off eliminations leading to the Super Bowl. The usual six-division structure of the NFL would be abandoned for the current season. Some players immediately indicated dissatisfaction with the proposed contract, but the prospects for ratification by the players seemed good.

17 Ex-CIA agent convicted

Edwin P. Wilson, a member of the U.S. Central Intelligence Agency from 1954 to 1970, was convicted by a federal jury on seven of eight counts of illegally transporting firearms to the Libyan government. Wilson maintained he had merely been a part of a covert CIA operation, but the CIA denied it. The prosecution argued that Wilson had acted on his own and was motivated by greed. Wilson still faced three other trials involving the illegal export of firearms and explosives and conspiracy to assassinate a Libyan dissident.

19 China replaces high officials

Chinese Foreign Minister Huang Hua and Defense Minister Geng Biao (Keng Piao) were replaced, respectively, by Deputy Foreign Minister Wu Xueqian (Wu Hsüeh-ch'ien) and Zhang Aiping (Chang Ai-p'ing). The changes were approved by the Standing Committee of the National People's Congress. Earlier in the month regional military commanders in Nanjing (Nanking), Guangzhou (Canton), and Chengdu (Ch'eng-tu) were also replaced.

24 GATT members meet in Geneva

Representatives of the 38 nations that signed the General Agreement on Tariffs and Trade met in Geneva for the first time since 1979. A major consideration in calling the meeting was President Reagan's concern that protectionist tendencies were increasing around the world. Even though the meeting was extended in the hope of reaching substantive conclusions, no major decisions were announced. The delegates returned home after pledging to promote "liberalization and expansion of world trade."

Yasuhiro Nakasone was sworn in as prime minister of Japan on November 26 following the surprise resignation of Zenko Suzuki on October 12.

Irish choose new Parliament

Irish voters went to the polls to decide, in effect, whether Prime Minister Charles Haughey, representing the Fianna Fail party, would remain in power or be replaced by former prime minister Garret FitzGerald, the leader of the Fine Gael party. A total of 364 candidates had campaigned for the 166 seats in the Dail (lower house of Parliament). It was the third such election in 18 months. Though neither major party gained an absolute majority of the seats, it appeared that FitzGerald would assume the prime ministership in mid-December after forming a coalition with the Irish Labour Party. He had told voters that one of his top priorities if elected would be to settle the "desperate tragedy of Northern Ireland."

Ghana rebellion quelled

Former flight lieutenant Jerry Rawlings, leader of the West African republic of Ghana, announced that troops loyal to the government had suppressed a rebellion led by "misguided individuals" in a military camp outside Accra, the capital. Rawlings had come to power at the end of 1981 by overthrowing Pres. Hilla Limann.

Inquiry board warns Begin

The Israeli commission investigating the slaughter of Palestinians in two Lebanese camps in mid-September fulfilled a legal obligation by officially notifying Prime Minister Menachem Begin and eight other top officials that they "may be harmed" by the findings and conclusions of the commission. Begin and Defense Minister Ariel Sharon might have failed in their duties, the commission said, by ignoring the possibility that the Lebanese Christian militiamen who were allowed to enter the camps might take revenge on

innocent people. Other Israeli officials might be faulted for neglecting to act quickly enough to either stop the killings or report what was happening to higher authorities. Each of the persons cited by the commission had 15 days to reappear before the board to examine the evidence and cross-examine witnesses.

25 Chad affair disrupts OAU

African leaders meeting in Tripoli, Libya, canceled a conference of the Organization of African Unity when it became evident that a dispute over Chad's representation could not be amicably resolved. Libyan leader Muammar al-Qaddafi refused to recognize Hissen Habré as the legitimate president of Chad (he had ousted Goukouni Oueddei from the presidency earlier in the year), and Habré refused to absent himself voluntarily from the meeting in exchange for formal recognition by the OAU.

26 PLO rejects confederation

The 60-member Central Council of the Palestine Liberation Organization issued a statement in Damascus, Syria, rejecting President Reagan's proposal that the Palestinians be given territory in the West Bank and Gaza Strip in association with Jordan. The PLO said the plan, which called for limited autonomy for the Palestinians, failed to "satisfy the inalienable national rights" of the Palestinians because it did not grant them full independence. The rejection, however, was not as absolute as some of the hard-line Palestinian leaders had wanted, so hope remained for a compromise solution.

Nakasone becomes prime minister

Yasuhiro Nakasone was, as expected, elected prime minister of Japan by those

DECEMBER

members of the Diet (Parliament) who belonged to the ruling Liberal Democratic Party (LDP). Following Zenko Suzuki's unexpected October 12 announcement that he had decided to retire as prime minister and party president, four candidates sought the party leadership, which brought with it the prime ministership. In a popular election open only to rank and file members of the LDP, Nakasone won 58% of the vote. The LDP members of the Diet then sanctioned the people's choice by electing Nakasone party president on November 25 and, a day later, head of government.

DECEMBER

2 First permanent artificial heart operation a success

Barney B. Clark, a 61-year-old retired dentist, received the world's first permanent artificial heart during surgery at the University of Utah Medical Center in Salt Lake City. Clark was chosen because he was fast approaching death and had all the psychological attributes doctors desired in a patient undergoing such a critical operation. Soon after the plastic heart began beating, Clark's vital organs showed remarkable improvement. Doctors at the center were cautiously optimistic that Clark could survive for a considerable period of time.

EEC defends farm subsidies

Poul Dalsager, the agricultural commissioner of the European Economic Community (EEC), indicated a willingness to seek solutions to the international problems created by farm subsidies granted to members of the EEC but noted that the subsidies had been legally negotiated during the General Agreement on Tariffs and Trade Conference held in Tokyo in 1979. The U.S. continued to be adamant in its demand that changes be made to ensure fair competition in world markets.

Robert Jarvik holds the artificial heart he invented. The first artificial heart was implanted in Barney B. Clark on December 2. At year's end the patient was still alive.

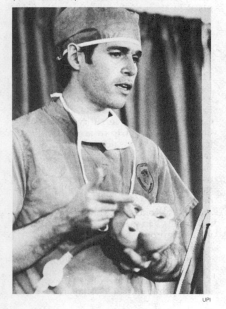

UPI

4 Reagan visits Latin America

President Reagan concluded a visit to four Latin-American nations, undertaken to foster "democratic institutions in the hemisphere." The president was warmly welcomed in Brazil, indicating that relations between the two countries had improved dramatically. During the visit Reagan offered Brazil $1,230,000,000 in short-term credits to cover its emergency needs. Reagan also praised Brazil for holding its first free national elections since 1964. A very different atmosphere awaited Reagan at his next stop in Colombia. He was jeered in the streets and listened politely as Pres. Belisario Betancur Cuartas publicly criticized U.S. policies in Latin America. Betancur also suggested that the U.S. could best stem the flow of illegal Colombian drugs into its cities by suppressing the demand at home. Reagan next visited Costa Rica where he signed an extradition treaty with Pres. Luis Alberto Monge and met briefly with Salvadoran Pres. Alvaro Alfredo Magaña. In Honduras, Reagan conferred with Pres. Roberto Suazo Córdova and Guatemalan Pres. Efraín Ríos Montt.

China adopts new constitution

The National People's Congress of China ratified a new constitution, the fourth since the People's Republic was established in 1949. The document, which "summed up the historical experiences" of the Chinese Communist Party, restored the post of president and in various ways institutionalized China's program of modernization. The role of the People's Liberation Army (PLA) was also redefined, weakening the bonds that tied the PLA to the Communist Party leadership.

Egypt puts 280 on trial

The trial of 280 Egyptians, all accused of conspiring to overthrow the government, got under way in Cairo. Most of the defendants were relatively young members of Al Jihad, an Islamic fundamentalist group bent on turning Egypt into an Islamic state. The accused were, for the most part, linked to crimes connected with the violent uprising that occurred in Asyut shortly after Pres. Anwar as-Sadat was assassinated in October 1981.

6 Zia-ul-Haq visits the U.S.

Pakistani Pres. Mohammad Zia-ul-Haq arrived in the U.S. for his first state visit. His request for economic and military aid was supported by President Reagan but Congress was still debating the details of a proposed $3.2 billion package to be made available over a period of six years. Zia said such aid would lay "the foundation for a credible and enduring relationship" with the U.S. On more than one occasion he tried to allay fears that Pakistan was seeking nuclear technology in order to develop nuclear weapons. Zia insisted that Pakistan intended to use nuclear power for peaceful purposes only.

7 House kills MX missile funds

The U.S. House of Representatives rejected President Reagan's request for $988 million to build and deploy the first five of 100 MX missiles. The 245–176 vote was a major setback for the president, who had said the MX was vital to the nation's security and an essential bargaining chip in disarmament talks with the Soviets. Because the opposition of some congressmen centred on Reagan's choice of the dense pack mode of basing the missiles, the president quickly declared his willingness to discuss alternatives. The House finally appropriated about $2.5 billion for continued research on and development of the MX. On December 17 the Senate agreed to fund the building of the MX missiles but stipulated that Congress must first approve the basing mode. The Senate-House conferees requested the president to present his decision on a new basing mode after March 1, 1983.

10 Peru's prime minister quits

Peruvian Pres. Fernando Belaúnde Terry announced that he had accepted the resignation of Prime Minister Manuel Ulloa Elías, but no mention was made of the 15 members of Ulloa's Cabinet, who also submitted their resignations. The president then announced that Fernando Schwalb López Aldana, who served as first vice-president and ambassador to the U.S., would replace Ulloa in January.

Most nations sign sea law pact

Representatives of 117 sovereign nations signed the United Nations Law of the Sea Treaty during a conference held in Montego Bay, Jamaica. The treaty would take effect one year after it had been ratified by 60 nations. Of the 23 countries that sent representatives to the meeting but did not sign, the U.S. was among the most outspoken in its opposition to that part of the pact calling for a global authority that would determine who could mine metals under the high seas and how much they could remove. Other nonsignatories included Belgium, Ecuador, Great Britain, Italy, the Holy See, Japan, Spain, Venezuela, and West Germany.

12 *Chrysler strike ends*

Canadian auto workers overwhelmingly approved a new 13-month contract, thereby ending a 38-day strike against Chrysler Canada Ltd., a subsidiary of the U.S. company. Because the strike in Canada cut U.S. supplies and resulted in 4,600 layoffs in U.S. plants, U.S. workers decided to reopen their own contract negotiations, which had been postponed until January 1983. Auto workers in the U.S. were also expected to approve their new contract, which differed in some details from that signed in Canada. All the workers received pay increases and other benefits but had to make some concessions on other issues.

15 *Brazil to get large IMF loan*

The International Monetary Fund agreed to give Brazil $4.5 billion in credits so that it could service its huge foreign debt. Brazil's negotiators pledged in return that the government would continue to restrict wage increases, imports, and government spending. The IMF loan was also expected to make it easier for Brazil to get additional credit from foreign banks, which had shown reluctance to continue lending to heavily indebted nations.

Teamsters boss convicted

Roy L. Williams, president of the powerful teamsters' union, was convicted in Chicago along with four co-conspirators on 11 federal charges of plotting to bribe U.S. Sen. Howard W. Cannon and of defrauding the union's pension fund. Each conviction carried a maximum prison sentence of five years. During the trial the prosecution contended that Cannon was offered choice property in Las Vegas, Nev., at bargain prices if he would try to defeat or delay a trucking deregulation bill being considered in the Senate. Cannon, who was not indicted, denied having received a bribe offer and voted in favour of the legislation. Evidence against the defendants consisted mainly of wiretapped conversations recorded over a 14-month period.

16 *Argentines stage demonstration*

An antigovernment rally in Buenos Aires, organized by five of Argentina's largest political parties and sanctioned by the government, turned violent despite the precautions that had been taken to avoid confrontations with the police. After some of the tens of thousands of demonstrators hurled stones through the windows of the presidential palace and began shouting slogans, police tried to

Gen. Wojciech Jaruzelski, premier of Poland, announced on December 19 that martial law would be lifted in that country on December 31.

disperse the crowd with tear gas. The military government had permitted the demonstration in the hope that demands for a speedy return to civilian rule would be muted. The previous week a 24-hour national strike had paralyzed the nation.

19 *Poland to lift martial law*

Poland's Council of State announced that martial law would be suspended on December 31. The previous day the Sejm (parliament) authorized the government to suspend or reimpose martial law as it saw fit. Most political prisoners would be released but certain ones would be charged with serious crimes and made to stand trial. For the indefinite future, many of the country's factories, mines, and transportation facilities would remain under military control. A number of other features of martial law were institutionalized by the Sejm when it amended the civil and criminal laws.

20 *Italy links Bulgaria to attack on Pope John Paul II*

Italian Defense Minister Lelio Lagorio told a special session of the Chamber of Deputies that the attempted assassination of Pope John Paul II in May 1981 by the Turkish terrorist Mehmet Ali Agca was "an act of war" perpetrated by Bulgaria. The Bulgarians, he indicated, acted as puppets of the Soviet Union, which wanted the pope killed because he had supported Solidarity, the Polish labour federation. Lagorio called the attempted assassination "a precautionary and alternative solution to an invasion of Poland." After Agca was convicted and sentenced to life imprisonment, he reportedly told Italian authorities that two Bulgarian accomplices were with him in St. Peter's Square when he shot the pontiff.

Hussein visits U.S. to discuss Middle East peace plans

King Hussein of Jordan began a series of talks in Washington, D.C., with top U.S. officials who were anxious to have Jordan join the peace negotiations that were in progress between Israel and Egypt. The main sticking points were the establishment of a homeland for the Palestinians and Israel's withdrawal from occupied lands. The U.S. hoped that all interested parties would eventually accept the presence of an autonomous Palestinian homeland in the West Bank and Gaza Strip in federation with Jordan. Hussein and President Reagan both expressed satisfaction with the discussions, but Hussein was not prepared to commit himself without laying down certain conditions and consulting with other Arab nations. He noted, however, that the construction of Israeli settlements in occupied lands was a major obstacle to achieving peace in the Middle East.

OPEC drops production quotas

The Organization of Petroleum Exporting Countries (OPEC) ended its meeting in Vienna without reaching agreement on individual production quotas. Iran had reportedly violated OPEC's earlier production quotas and price structures most flagrantly in order to finance its ongoing war with Iraq. The Iranian oil minister made it clear that his country resented Saudi Arabia's attempt to continue dictating what policies OPEC should follow; he also said Iran could not be dissuaded from continuing its current high level of production.

29 *Finnish government shaken*

The Communist-dominated Finnish People's Democratic League (PDL) forced the resignation of Prime Minister Kalevi Sorsa, a Social Democrat, by opposing a parliamentary resolution to increase defense spending. The government's four-party coalition was shattered, Sorsa declared, because the PDL wanted to present itself as a peace party in the March 1983 elections. Pres. Mauno Koivisto, however, refused to accept Sorsa's resignation and appointed three Social Democrats to fill the Cabinet posts previously held by the PDL.

Not all the news events of 1982 made prominent headlines. Among items reported less breathlessly in the worldwide press were the following:

Dorsey Connors of the *Chicago Sun-Times* supplies her readers with a wide variety of practical household hints. During the summer she gave space to Helen Kiska, who said she saved a great deal of sorting time by marking plastic containers and their corresponding lids with identical numbers. She then went on to say, "If you run out of numbers, use the alphabet." No follow-up story appeared on the number of mathematicians who suffered cardiac arrest at the thought of running out of numbers.

In a daring robbery, Melvin Riddell snatched a 4½-carat diamond ring from the finger of Elissa Terry while she was hospitalized in Chicago in early June. A doctor who heard the woman's screams alerted security guards, who nabbed Riddell a few blocks from the hospital. But there was no sign of the missing ring. After Riddell confessed he had swallowed it, doctors located it in the man's esophagus. At first the security guards presumed the fleeing suspect was a member of the hospital staff because he was wearing a green scrub top, but gradually it dawned on them that he was a ringer.

Time and time again, Taiwan's Little League baseball teams have outclassed their U.S. counterparts. The girls at Redwood High in Larkspur, Calif., must have known that and hoped their basketball team would be well prepared when a group of 13 Chinese girls arrived in February. As things turned out they were totally ill-prepared for what took place. The Orientals showed no interest in shooting baskets. But they certainly knew how to sing and dance. Through some misunderstanding, the Chinese had sent a group of entertainers.

A municipal court judge in Bowling Green, Ohio, automatically dropped charges of speeding against Michael Groff when a letter arrived from Hillcrest Hospital in Mayfield Heights certifying that Groff had been admitted on March 6 and died on March 11. The local *Sentinel-Tribune* carried the death notice. Later, in a follow-up story, the newspaper reported that Groff was still attending classes at Bowling Green State University. Faced with a life-or-death situation, Groff showed up at court prepared to pay his fine. The unbemused judge may have thought a death sentence would best satisfy poetic justice, but he settled on a $250 fine for contempt of court by obstructing justice and avoiding prosecution, 80 days of community service, a letter of apology to the public, and $30 plus court costs for the speeding violation.

In early August Lon Haldeman of Harvard, Ill., climbed onto his bike in California and headed in an easterly direction. It took him 9 days, 23 hours, and 15 minutes to reach New York City—exactly one day and 12 minutes faster than anyone else had ever pedaled across the U.S. His female counterpart, Susan Notorangelo of St. Louis, Mo., completed a comparable trip in 11 days, 16 hours, and 20 minutes in July, shortening by nearly three days the record set by Ann Kovich of Texas the previous month.

The Rev. Bob Jones, Jr., was so upset with the U.S. State Department for refusing to issue a visa to the Rev. Ian Paisley, a contentious Protestant leader from Northern Ireland, that he urged the students of Bob Jones University in Greenville, S.C., to pray that the Lord would smite Secretary of State Alexander Haig. In biblical tones, seldom heard in modern times, Jones exhorted the student body: "I hope you'll pray that the Lord will smite him, hip and thigh, bone and marrow, heart and lungs, and all there is to him, that he shall destroy him quickly and utterly." Haig resigned his government post on June 25.

Adrian Pugh, an 18-year-old Londoner, was not much of an art critic, but he knew what he liked in the way of picture frames. In fact, he liked one small frame so much he stole it. When Pugh was brought before an Old Bailey judge in March and charged with theft, he told the court he liked the picture frame but not the etching it enclosed, so he tossed the picture into a Piccadilly Circus sewer. The unrecovered etching was a Rembrandt.

Not all lawyers are willing to fall on their knees before a jury and beg for the acquittal of a client. But the lawyer for Laura E. Clark did just that in August—to no avail. The jury found 82-year-old Clark guilty of possessing nine pounds of marijuana harvested from plants she had cultivated in her vegetable garden. The great-grandmother, who said she got the seeds in Mexico to treat her arthritis, was sentenced to two years of unsupervised probation.

City marathons have become major sports events in recent years, but the annual Bay to Breakers Race in free-spirited San Francisco was in several ways more memorable than the mine run of such happenings. Among the 50,000 people who ran across the city on May 16 were a Roman empress with four loin-clothed slaves, a Mediterranean fruit fly, Pac Man, and a 60-ft-long centipede bearing a 250-lb replica of the Golden Gate Bridge.

Engineers at the Lockheed Missile and Space Co. in Sunnyvale, Calif., had a problem. They were using CAD/CAM techniques in their work and had to get each day's information to the company's test base in Santa Cruz. But the test facility did not have the expensive equipment needed to receive transmissions, and couriers proved to be too slow and too expensive. Finally the perfect solution came to mind: homing pigeons carrying the information on microfilm. The pigeons were found to be swift, cheap, and reliable—as the Allies had proved during World War I.

Mary Ellen Shaver went on strike in February. She posted a notice on the front door of her home in San Ramon, Calif., informing her three children that "this mother, maid, cook, driver, laundress" was on strike until further notice. Mary's husband, a medical

Pierre Leon of Toronto, Ont., wrote the *Globe and Mail* to insist that this hybrid offspring of a female zebra had been improperly called a zebroid because "zebra-like animal" does not reflect its parentage. He suggested either zebkey or donbra because officials at the Tohoku Safari Park near Tokyo think the father was a donkey. Hybrid offspring, of course, don't necessarily bear the names of their parents. A foal of a mare impregnated by a donkey is simply a mule.

UPI

research scientist, had initial doubts that Beth and Meg and John would heed their mother's message, but two weeks later both parents reported that the kids had been doing their own laundry, keeping their rooms neat and clean, setting the dinner table, cleaning the bathroom, and observing the weekday and weekend curfews. Encouraged by such displays of goodwill, Mary Shaver tentatively resumed cooking dinner.

The fish weren't biting in April, at least not in the waters around Baltimore, so a group of 13 fishermen packed up their gear and called it a day. During a final drink together each accepted a dare and swallowed a couple of live minnows they had bought for bait. The next day two were doubled over with severe abdominal cramps and had to be hospitalized. Surgeons later reported that the seemingly harmless minnows contained live worms that had perforated the men's intestines.

Impulse buying can wreak havoc with the family budget, but don't try telling that to newlywed Luann Lingle of Bay City, Mich. The night before she got married, her fiancé asked for a cold beer. Happy to oblige, the 23-year-old bride-to-be rushed to the store. When she returned, she handed her future husband the beer—and a lottery ticket she had purchased on impulse. It was worth $100,000.

A. Donald Fass was the chief designer of security devices for the Rollins Protective Service Co. and the firm's top salesman of burglar alarms in the Hartford area of Connecticut. As a salesman, Fass was not easily discouraged. If he failed to make a sale during his first visit to a potential customer's home, he frequently succeeded on his second try about two weeks later. In August Fass pleaded guilty to nine counts of felony and was sentenced to prison for 13 to 26 years. His impressive sales record, he confessed, had been enhanced by burglarizing customers' homes after his initial unsuccessful visit.

Amelia Salazar was a basketball star at Bledsoe High School in Texas, editor of the yearbook, and top student in her class. Eulogio Guerrero co-captained the varsity basketball team and was president of the student council. He also had the worst academic record among the graduating seniors. None of these things, however, played a role in selecting Amelia as valedictorian of the class of 1982 and Eulogio as salutatorian. Bledsoe's only school, which accepts students from kindergarten through grade 12, had a student body of just 53 and only two high school seniors.

A remarkable eight weeks in the lives of the Hawkins family began in spring when two-year-old Robin bade farewell to her stuffed cat before flushing it down the toilet. A few days later Robin enlisted the help of her newly bathed teddy bear to burn out the dishwasher. Then, after a relatively peaceful weekend trip, the Hawkinses returned home to Michigan to discover that their refrigerator had been put out of commission by magnetic letters Robin had stuffed into the vents. The youngster's next

target was the colour tuner on the television set. This was followed by a joy ride in the family car, which came to an abrupt halt when it hit a tree. The little girl's search and destroy mission then extended to the stereo and tape deck and to the electric garage door, which she bounced off the hood of the car while her parents were unloading the groceries. Robin then turned to theft. While sitting atop a supermarket shopping cart, she surreptitiously removed $620 from the cash register. If the money was meant to cover the cost of her two-month spree, Robin needed a lesson in economics. Her father, a policeman, calculated the cost of her reign of terror at $2,296.37.

Drivers in Homewood, Ill., were under unusual police surveillance during the summer. One by one some of the most law-abiding citizens of the community were pulled over by police and given tickets. Subdued anger quickly gave way to a happy surprise when each was told the ticket was redeemable for $5 at the police station. The village trustees wanted to promote good driving by rewarding those who observed all the rules of the road.

The June issue of *Canada Today* featured the province of Manitoba and some memorable events from its past. Among items of special interest was one on Sir Arthur Conan Doyle, the creator of Sherlock Holmes. In July 1924 Conan Doyle was invited to Winnipeg by Dr. Thomas Hamilton to participate in a séance with members of his family and a few close friends. Conan Doyle was deeply impressed by the experience. He later wrote that a table, invested with mysterious powers by Mrs. Elizabeth Poole, a medium, lunged at him "like an angry dog." According to the story, Conan Doyle visited the Hamiltons twice again after his death.

Moments after a well-dressed San Franciscan boarded a streetcar in March, he was recognized by a woman passenger who blurted out: "You're the father of one of my children!" The woman merely meant he was the father of one of her pupils.

T. S. Schwaner, curator of reptiles at the South Australian Museum in Adelaide, had to hospitalize one of the world's deadliest snakes for nearly half a year. The 4½-ft-long taipan had a severe infection in the cheek that required intensive care and daily antibiotic injections to control. It seems one of the four mice the taipan had been given for dinner decided not to die without putting up a fight.

Most who listened to 66-year-old Yvonne Mary Henderson's ramblings presumed she was merely exhibiting signs of incipient senility. After all, other bag ladies were known to talk in much the same way. For several years Henderson was able to survive on food given to her by a community centre in Miami Beach, Fla., but no one really believed she had been born in China and was the daughter of Sir Herbert Phillips, who once headed the Far East Department of the British Foreign Office. Then an English newspaper published a story about the curious bag lady in Florida who said she had lived in luxury before divorcing her

Jessie Byam graduated from high school in May and publicly pledged to continue her education. Just about everyone in Madison Heights, Mich., cheered the decision because Jessie was still striving to improve herself at the age of 98. She is believed to be the oldest person ever to graduate from a U.S. high school.

fifth husband and moving to the U.S. Anthony Phillips read the account with great attention. In June he flew to the U.S., identified Henderson as his sister, and made preparations to take the bag lady aristocrat home to England.

A teller at Crocker National Bank in San Francisco told a customer in January he would have to produce proper identification before his check could be cashed. The retired policeman immediately pulled out and displayed an unconventional identification that the teller didn't question: a set of dentures bearing the owner's name.

Brazilian police were frustrated in efforts to seize drug smugglers in their jungle hideout until Officer João da Silva Bisteme figured out a solution. He evaded the lookouts posted at all the approaches to the camp by sweeping in on a hang glider. His bursts of gunfire permitted police on foot to rush the camp and arrest eight suspects.

Michigan State University officials announced in September that the school would continue to supply bed linens for resident students but not pillows. The cost of replacing or repairing the 4,000 pillows that had disappeared or were ripped apart during the previous academic year came to $22,000—considerably more than the budget could bear.

In midsummer 85-year-old George Adams had reason to remember his first Fourth of July celebration in the U.S. He was 16 at the time, a teenaged immigrant from Albania living in Philadelphia. During the Independence Day festivities someone randomly fired a gun and Adams collapsed when the bullet lodged near his heart. Doctors were afraid to operate. As the Fourth of July ap-

Parks Bonifay of Pensacola, Fla., became the youngest water skier in history when he was still a toothless six-month-old baby. Though he was obviously flying high at a very tender age, he still hadn't learned to hot dog it through the air.

proached 69 years later, Adams found himself in a Southfield, Mich., rehabilitation centre where he was recovering from an auto accident. During lunch something caught in his throat. After a fit of coughing he brought up the bullet.

Thousands enter newspaper contests even though few believe they will actually win. When the *Chicago Tribune* notified Debra Engle that she had won the "Beat Siskel" contest by correctly predicting the winners of all the major Academy Awards, she was astonished. Engle had not even submitted an entry. Many hours later, after questioning her family and close friends, she learned that Billie Williams, a fellow actress, had sent in several entries—one using Engle's name, address, and phone number—on the mistaken assumption that contestants were permitted only one prediction.

Ronald MacSporran of Saint Catharines, Ont., bought five one-dollar lottery tickets during the Edmonton Klondike Days festival in July. He put his own name on one and those of his wife and two young daughters on others. As luck would have it, five-year-old Rhonda won a $53,000 motor home. As the MacSporrans drove off in their new mobile home, they little suspected the troubles that lay ahead. Lloyd Gardiner, the public trustee of Alberta, warned the parents that the prize had to be sold and a trust fund set up for Rhonda because her name was on the winning ticket. He also warned that the Rotary Club, sponsors of the lottery, could be sued on Rhonda's behalf. James Masson, the attorney for the Rotary Club, also mentioned the possibility that Rhonda might sue her father for the value of the vehicle once she became an adult. He suggested, however, that the father might be able to avoid these problems

if he had himself named legal guardian of the child's property. The public trustee found the whole matter rather frustrating because, he noted, none of these complications would have arisen if the fifth ticket that MacSporran filled out had been drawn rather than Rhonda's. It bore the name of the family dog.

Stanton Powers, an artist in Santa Cruz, Calif., needed the help of a Social Security disability check to make ends meet. Then, according to his attorney, he simply prayed for money in front of an automatic teller installed at the County Bank of Santa Cruz, and his prayers were answered. His balance rose from $1.17 to $26, then up through the hundreds, the thousands, and hundreds of thousands. By the next morning Powers was worth, according to the computer, $4.4 million. Powers was able to withdraw about $2,000 before the machine snatched away his card.

Inmates in Nevada State Prison face virtually insurmountable obstacles if they try to escape. The prison is a maximum-security facility, and the officials are well versed in escape techniques. In May, however, they were taken by surprise when guards reported finding a nearly completed one-man helicopter in the maintenance area. The ingenious contraption had been designed and assembled by a plumber, an electrician, and a welder, all of whom were serving long terms. The trio were charged with misuse of state property, a misdemeanour.

In March six-year-old Scott McKenzie was playing with friends in his backyard in Vinita Park, Mo., when a 100-lb mutt leaped over the fence, attacked the child, and bit off his ear. Scott's father, a policeman, fired six times at the animal, but it escaped. Another policeman later spotted the animal and killed it. When the dog was taken to a veterinarian to be examined for rabies, the boy's ear was found in its stomach. Surgeons succeeded in restoring the ear to the injured child.

U.S. taxpayers often become frustrated trying to figure out the bottom line on their federal returns. But before they reach that point, they sometimes have to make inquiries, only to learn that in some cases the very same query put to different employees of the Internal Revenue Service elicits quite different replies. The General Accounting Office added to taxpayers' grief this year when it reported to Congress in October that the IRS detected about 33 million errors on the 94 million individual tax returns it processed in fiscal 1981. It also noted, on the basis of a sample study of 2,543 returns, that IRS employees made nearly twice as many mistakes in arithmetic as did the taxpayers.

On St. Patrick's Day in 1964 Jack Granger dropped 100 sealed bottles into the sea off Miami Beach, Fla. Each contained a note offering an all-expenses-paid vacation to the lucky finders. In October, nearly 18 years after the event, Barbara Karas happened upon one of the bottles at the mouth of Boston Harbor. She managed to get Granger's phone number and called. Though his hotel no longer existed, he as-

sured Karas that the offer of a 12-day free vacation still stood, compliments of the Miami Beach Visitor and Convention Authority.

Geraldine Gordon's tongue is soft and rubbery even though it is considerably smaller than most. It's a great help, naturally, in eating and talking. And it clamps onto her lower teeth. She lost her own tongue to cancer, but after a five-year interval she received a silicone replacement developed by doctors at the University of California at Davis. It was the first known artificial tongue designed for speech as well as for swallowing.

U.S. narcotics agents frequently use dogs to sniff out illegal drugs, but the animals are not ideal helpers. They obey only one or perhaps two masters, eat a great deal, require considerable space and care, and sometimes frighten innocent people. Canadian law enforcement officials think they can eliminate all those disadvantages by using squads of gerbils—ratlike creatures confined to cages. Gerbils, they think, can be especially useful against drug smuggling in prisons and at airports. Placed behind airport counters, for example, the gerbils could sniff out odours wafted their way as passengers move through checkpoints. But gerbils, too, have their limitations. Each can be trained to react to just one smell. Their trainers, therefore, have no intention of revealing to prisoners or air travelers which gerbils are placed on duty at any given time.

Jeremy Cook was only in kindergarten but he thought it would be great if he could win $500 for his school in Elmira, N.Y. So he sent a helium-filled balloon aloft in March hoping it would travel farther than anyone else's and thereby qualify for first prize. In early May Jeremy received a letter from east Africa. His balloon had drifted one-third the distance around the world before landing in Kenya.

Krysta Roberts became a diabetic when she was four years old and was blind by the time she was a freshman in college. The following year her kidneys failed, and she was put on dialysis. The treatment was so debilitating that doctors concluded her life could be saved only if she received a kidney from a blood relative. Krysta's mother was happy beyond words to be the donor and gave her daughter a new lease on life. Theirs, after all, was an extraordinary story. Krysta had been adopted when she was two days old, and her natural mother had been located only after an often frustrating eight-month search. The courts had made the search possible by providing vital information contained in the sealed adoption records.

Most wives appreciate a little help around the house, but husbands who do everything, and do it perfectly, are about as rare as flying streetcars. A woman in East Germany, however, had a perfect husband. He did more around the house than any wife could hope for: cooking, baking, shopping, laundry, and taking care of the baby. He did everything so perfectly, in fact, that the woman was granted a divorce in October because she couldn't stand the boredom of having nothing to do.

Midyear graduation marked an incredible victory for Adeline Becht, a 48-year-old resident of Oregon. As a young woman she became addicted to drugs while being treated for osteomyelitis and alcoholism. The drugs in turn destroyed her sight and hearing. But Becht took hold of herself and straightened out her life. With the help of an interpreter, who sometimes spent 18 hours a day attending lectures and transcribing them into Braille, Becht completed her studies at the University of Oregon. In June, when she graduated with doctoral degrees in both clinical and counseling psychology, she was confident she would be able to treat patients as effectively as any of her peers.

Sherry Crider, a 28-year-old woman living in Cave Spring, Ga., was rushed to the hospital in August after a serious auto accident. Two months later she gave birth to a healthy six-pound baby boy. The father expressed hope that the normal delivery indicated his still comatose wife would soon return to normal and be able to see and hold her newborn son.

Gertrude Jamison was mighty upset when A. Douglas Thompson notified the Humane Society in Chattanooga, Tenn., that her dog had nipped him while he was delivering mail. She was so angry, in fact, that she phoned Thompson ten times a day to let him know just how she felt. In March a judge threatened to send Jamison to a penal farm if the phone calls persisted. That normally would have satisfied a plaintiff, but Thompson was not convinced his troubles were over. "She'll call again. I guarantee you. As long as she can dial a phone, she'll call." He had good reason to think so. The calls had been going on for 45 years.

Danny Pocock of Wycheproof, Australia, was on his way to work one July morning when he noticed a six-foot kangaroo following close behind. The train engineer reckoned it was someone's pet until it knocked him to the ground. He raced for the safety of the station platform but was floored two more times before he made it. "I did somersaults," he later reported, "that I didn't know I could."

In its May issue, *New Scientist* reported a story that originally appeared in the *Journal of the American Medical Association.* Students at the University of Alabama Medical School were assigned nine human cadavers for dissection. One of the girls looked up from her work and was badly shaken. She informed the director that one of the cadavers appeared to be that of her great aunt. The body had come from out of state, but a check of the records confirmed that the girl was indeed right.

New York City police were preparing to destroy some of the illegal handguns in their collection when they came upon an ornate pair of pistols confiscated in a drug raid nearly ten years earlier. Because the weapons were overlaid with ivory and intricate gold floral patterns, someone decided they should be checked by experts at the Metropolitan Museum of Art. The guns were identified as prized hunting pistols that once belonged to Catherine the Great, empress of Russia, and had an appraised value of $200,000.

A bargain-hunting New Yorker paid $2 in 1981 for a porcelain food stand offered during a tag sale. In January the auction house of Sotheby Parke Bernet found a dealer willing to pay $60,000 for the rare antique. It had been manufactured in the 1770s by Bonin & Morris of Philadelphia, the first porcelain factory in the U.S.

Stephen Thomas complained in January that he had never been paid for the time he served as mayor of Milton, Pa. Some weeks before the election in November 1981 he decided to take another job but at that late date could not legally withdraw his candidacy for mayor. After winning the election, he was duly sworn in as mayor but resigned within half an hour. He figured he was owed eight cents for the time he served as chief executive

Border Patrol Chief Robert Adams contended that a roadblock set up near Florida City, Fla., was so effective it led to the arrests of 25 illegal aliens in five days. Residents of Key West, however, said that its usefulness was inconsequential and that it was destroying the area's vital tourist trade. They supported their allegations by pointing out in April that traffic had been backed up 19 mi the previous weekend. When a federal judge refused to grant a temporary injunction against setting up the checkpoint, the citizens of Key West seceded from the Union. They hoisted the flag of the Conch Republic and declared the pelican the state bird and the hibiscus the national flower. Then, in a facetiously dramatic statement, the mayor declared war on the U.S., but he quickly surrendered in order, he said, to become eligible for $1 billion in foreign aid.

In mid-February Judge Wallace Anktel of Berlin, N.H., gave Rowland Duchasne the option of spending two 12-hour periods at the city dump in freezing weather or facing a $200 fine. Anktel had been found guilty of cruelty to animals for putting four unwanted puppies under a pile of garbage at the dump site.

Mayor Jane Byrne, like most of her predecessors in Chicago, never missed a chance to have her name appear on just about every project associated with the city. The annual ChicagoFest in August was no exception. A brochure was printed showing suburbanites the most convenient routes to the city's lakefront site. Those who tried to follow the map are probably still asking directions at gas stations along the way. The three main highways were all mislabeled.

In late January Judge Alan I. Friess, presiding over a criminal court in New York City, was undecided whether a convicted pickpocket should be imprisoned for 20 or for 30 days on Rikers Island. He thereupon decided to let the defendant participate in the decision saying: "I'm prepared to allow you to decide your own fate and, if you're a gambling man, I'll permit you to flip a coin for that purpose." The defendant correctly called tails and got 20 days. And Judge Friess got ready for another likely censure from the State Commission on Judicial Conduct. In 1981 Friess had been taken to task for releasing a woman on her own recognizance after she had been charged with murder—and then inviting her to spend the night in his Brooklyn home. On that occasion the commission declared that the judge showed "extraordinarily poor judgment and a serious misunderstanding of the role of a judge in our legal system." In the January incident he was, at a minimum, guilty of injudicious flippancy.

Kung Teh-cheng, a university professor in Taiwan, traveled to San Francisco's Chinatown in August to attend the Sacrificial Ceremony to the Sage. His presence was considered so important that officials agreed to hold the ceremony one month early to accommodate Kung's schedule. The honoured guest, after all, represented the 77th generation descended from Confucius, the great Chinese sage born in 551 B.C.

When Larry Walters of North Hollywood, California, was 13 years old, he knew he wanted to take a balloon ride. Twenty years later he strapped on a parachute, fastened the belt that secured him to an aluminum lawn chair, and then told friends to release the tethers. With the aid of 45 1.8-metre (6-feet)-tall weather balloons he shot skyward. Three commercial jet pilots were bug-eyed when they spotted the lawn chair sailing along at 4,880 metres (16,000 feet). But Walters had no interest in passing planes. He was anxiously trying to send off a radio message for help and was feeling for his BB-gun so he could shoot out some of the balloons. After descending safely to Earth, Walters concluded that an improvised balloon ride wasn't much fun after all. He then assured his friends that nothing could ever induce him to take such a ride again.

The loss of life and property from disasters in 1982 included the following:

AVIATION

January 13, Potomac River, Washington, D.C. An Air Florida Boeing 737 jetliner crashed into a crowded bridge, broke into pieces, and sank into the river moments after takeoff from National Airport during a snowstorm; the crash, which was believed to have been caused by ice buildup on the wings of the plane, claimed the lives of 74 of the 79 persons on the plane and 4 others in vehicles on the bridge.

February 5, Cheju, South Korea. A C-123 military transport plane carrying 53 persons crashed into Mt. Halla, the country's highest mountain, when strong winds jerked the aircraft as it approached a landing strip; there were no survivors.

February 7, Jammu and Kashmir State, India. A military transport plane crashed during bad weather; 23 army personnel and crew were killed.

February 9, Tokyo Bay. A DC-8 jetliner dived into Tokyo Bay some 275 m (900 ft) short of the runway at Tokyo International Airport when its captain, who had been experiencing mental difficulties, pushed the control stick forward moments before the crash; 24 persons were killed and some 150 others were injured.

March 19, Wonder Lake, Ill. An Air National Guard KC-135 stratotanker jet exploded into a ball of flames and plunged to the ground; 4 crew members and 23 national guardsmen were killed.

April 2, Crete. A C-1A aircraft carrying 11 navy personnel crashed into a mountain on the island; there were no survivors.

April 13, Near Erzincan, Turkey. A U.S. C-130 cargo plane crashed into a mountain and burst into flames; all 28 military personnel aboard were killed.

April 26, Near Guilin (Kuei-lin), China. A Chinese jetliner carrying 112 persons from Guangzhou (Canton) to the scenic city of Guilin crashed some 45 km (28 mi) short of its destination; all aboard were killed.

June 8, Near Fortaleza, Brazil. A Boeing 727 Brazilian airliner crashed in the Pocatuba Mts. during heavy rains; all 137 persons aboard were killed.

June 22, Bombay, India. A Boeing 707 carrying 111 persons crash-landed during a blinding rainstorm; the Air India jet skidded off the runway, slammed into a wall, and broke into three pieces. Nineteen persons were killed and 24 others were injured.

July 6, Near Moscow, U.S.S.R. An Ilyushin-62 jetliner crashed moments after takeoff in the area of Sheremetyevo Airport; all 90 persons aboard reportedly were killed.

July 9, Kenner, La. A Pan American World Airways Boeing 727 jet carrying 145 persons crashed shortly after taking off from New Orleans, exploded, and plowed through four residential streets; the accident, which killed 153 persons including 8 on the ground, was the second worst air disaster in U.S. history involving a single plane.

September 11, Mannheim, West Germany. A U.S. Army helicopter carrying an international parachuting team crashed minutes after taking off from Neuostheim airfield, the site of an air show; all 44 persons aboard the copter were killed when a propeller blade snapped off and the copter fell to the ground and exploded.

September 13, Malaga, Spain. A DC-10 jetliner en route to New York City crashed during takeoff when one of the engines malfunctioned; at least 46 of the 393 persons aboard were killed, many of them trapped in the tail section of the airplane because the rear exits did not work.

September 29, Luxembourg. A Soviet Ilyushin-62 jetliner skidded off the runway after landing, slammed into a stand of trees, and exploded into flames; 6 of the 77 persons aboard were killed and 26 others were injured.

October 1, Caatiba, Brazil. A helicopter slammed into a mountain peak during severe weather conditions after the pilot had unsuccessfully tried twice to land the craft; all 13 persons aboard were killed, including 3 Brazilian politicians.

October 17, Near Taft, Calif. A C-45H Beechcraft airplane, carrying 12 skydivers, a jumpmaster, and a pilot, crashed and exploded into flames moments after takeoff; all aboard were killed.

November 17, Off the coast of Taiwan. A helicopter carrying workers from an offshore oil drilling rig crashed into the sea; all 15 persons aboard were killed.

November 29, Near Quetame, Colombia. A twin-engine airplane crashed into a mountain during a rainstorm; the craft was completely destroyed and all 22 persons aboard were presumed dead.

December 9, La Serena, Chile. An F-27 Chilean airliner carrying 46 persons from Santiago to La Serena slammed into a hill and exploded in flames; there were no survivors in the crash that occurred when the pilot's vision was obstructed by heavy smoke used by airborne firefighters during a drill.

December 9, Near San Andres de Bocay, Nicaragua. An air force helicopter carrying Indian children crashed and burst into flames; 75 children and 9 women were killed in the crash.

December 24, Guangzhou (Canton), China. A Soviet-built Ilyushin-18 turboprop jetliner was forced to make a crash-landing when the plane filled with smoke; 23 persons were killed and 27 others were injured.

FIRES AND EXPLOSIONS

February 3, Near Porto Velho, Brazil. A box of dynamite exploded in a state police barracks; ten troopers and one civilian were killed in the accidental blast.

February 8, Tokyo, Japan. An early morning fire ripped through the top two floors of a ten-story luxury hotel; 32 persons were killed and more than 60 others were injured.

March 6, Houston, Texas. A fire in one room of a new 165-room high-rise hotel was confined to that room, but 12 persons died of suffocation when thick billowing smoke infiltrated their rooms. The tragedy was complicated by a hotel employee who unwittingly and repeatedly turned off the fire alarm, with the result that many guests never heard the disjointed alarm.

April 25, Todi, Italy. An explosion, followed by a fast-burning fire in a building housing an antique show, claimed the lives of 34 persons; the intense heat prompted patrons to climb to the roof, and many were injured when they jumped onto mattresses piled on a flatbed truck by townspeople.

April 30, Hoboken, N.J. A predawn fire in a four-story hotel claimed the lives of 12 residents; police confirmed that arson was the cause of the blaze.

May 15, Baltimore, Md. A residential home caught fire after a candle affixed to a wall tipped over and ignited a sofa; four persons escaped with minor injuries but ten others were killed.

May 25, Aire, France. A fire in a privately run home for mentally handicapped teenagers resulted in the deaths of 18 persons, including 2 staff members.

July 5, Waterbury, Conn. A fire set by an arsonist ripped through two brick tenement buildings; 11 persons were killed.

August 17, Luanco, Spain. A block of three-story apartment buildings was reduced to rubble after some propane gas containers exploded in a ground-floor restaurant; 10 persons were killed in the blast and 11 others were injured.

September 4, Los Angeles, Calif. A fast-burning fire swept through a four-story tenement house and claimed the lives of 18 persons including 5 children and 4 infants. The fire, which was viewed as "suspicious" by arson investigators, was believed to have started in the rear of the second-floor hallway.

November 8, Biloxi, Miss. A fire believed to have been started by an inmate at the county jail claimed the lives of 27 prisoners, many of whom succumbed after inhaling toxic fumes from burning polyurethane padding in the jail cells.

November 11, Tyre, Lebanon. An explosion rocked an Israeli military headquarters building and claimed the lives of 47 persons; an investigation was being made into the cause of the blast.

A Japan Air Lines jetliner dived into the water of Tokyo Bay just short of the runway at Tokyo International Airport on February 9. Twenty-four persons were killed and 150 others injured.

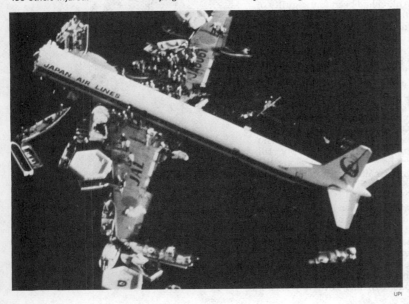

UPI

December 11, Alexandria, Egypt. An early-morning fire gutted a 60-room hotel on the beachfront; 10 persons were killed in the four-hour blaze and 16 others were injured, 2 seriously.

December 19, Near Caracas, Venezuela. A fire erupted at a power plant when a storage tank containing 80,000 bbl of fuel oil ignited while it was being discharged; the tank exploded, ignited two other tanks, and blazed for three days before firemen could control the fire; at least 129 persons were killed and 500 others injured in one of the country's worst disasters.

December 29, Taegu, South Korea. A fire that started in a second-floor room of a six-story tourist hotel swept through the building, killed at least 10 persons, and injured 15 others.

MARINE

January 6, Aleutian Islands. The ship "Akebono Maru" capsized while being boarded by fishermen in the Aleutian Islands; 27 fishermen were missing and presumed dead.

February 13, Atlantic Ocean. The tanker "Victory" broke in two pieces and was drifting in the Atlantic Ocean when a helicopter rescued 16 of the 32 crewmen aboard; the others were missing and presumed dead.

February 16, Off the coast of Canada. A Soviet freighter, the "Mekhanik Tarasov," carrying some 35 to 40 crewmen, sank in heavy North Atlantic seas; 7 men were rescued by a Danish trawler, but all other lives were lost because the remaining men insisted on waiting for a Soviet rescue vessel.

March 28, Boca Raton, Fla. A wooden Haitian freighter called "The Esperancia" broke up and sank in 4.5-m (15-ft) seas; at least 20 persons drowned, many of them believed to be Haitian refugees who were smuggled aboard by crewmen.

March 28, Near Rangoon, Burma. A passenger ferry capsized in a canal and claimed the lives of nearly 130 passengers.

April 11, Near Henzada, Burma. A double-decker ferry carrying more than 300 persons sank after slamming into a sandbar; at least 160 persons were missing and presumed drowned.

April 17, Near Cairo, Egypt. An 11-m (36-ft) ferryboat sank in the Ismailia Canal after overzealous factory workers forced their way onto the small craft in order to attend a soccer match; as many as 100 persons were feared dead.

May 21, South Pacific. A tuna boat sank 2,250 km (1,400 mi) south of Tahiti during a severe typhoon; 18 seamen were feared dead.

June 17, Off the coast of the Philippines. A passenger ferry, the "Queen Helen," exploded and caught fire in shark-infested waters of the Sulu Sea; 36 persons were killed, 12 were missing, and 327 others were rescued.

July 12, Near Cristóbal, Panama. A raging fire on the British tanker "Argol" engulfed the cabin quarters and claimed the lives of ten crewmen.

July 12, Off the coast of Visakhapatnam, India. A fishing boat capsized and 15 persons were feared drowned.

Mid-July, Near Semra, India. A boat traveling on the Ganges River capsized; 20 of the 40 persons aboard drowned.

July 18, Off the coast of Sumatra, Indon. A fire broke out on a motor launch when a gas stove exploded; 25 of the 80 persons aboard drowned when the boat sank.

July 25, Manila Bay. The tourist ship "Coral Island" caught fire at the entrance of Manila Bay when an auxiliary engine exploded; 74 crewmen were rescued but 21 others were missing and presumed drowned.

September 4, Orissa State, India. A ferry capsized crossing a river swollen by heavy flooding; at least 35 persons drowned.

October 17, Java Sea. The "Karya Tambangan" cargo ship sank off the coast of central Indonesia; 89 of the 120 persons aboard were missing and presumed drowned.

November 4, Near Irian Jaya, Indon. A boating accident claimed the lives of scores of people; 30 persons were rescued.

November 8, Off the coast of Alexandria, Egypt. A Greek merchant ship sank off the coast of the country; a week later the bodies of 11 crew members were washed ashore.

MINING

May 12, Zenica, Yugos. Two methane gas explosions in a coal mine claimed the lives of 39 miners; the cause of the blast was unknown.

October 6, Northwestern Liberia. After three days of torrential rain, an avalanche of iron-ore waste descended on sleeping workers at a mining camp on the Mano River; 45 miners were known dead, 150 others were missing and presumed dead, and 29 workers were injured. It was the country's worst mine disaster.

November 29, Bytom, Poland. An explosion of coal gas ripped through an emergency crew that was sent into a mine to battle a fire; 18 miners were killed in the blast.

MISCELLANEOUS

January 17, Near Guaíra, Brazil. A footbridge suspended over a waterfall on the Paraná River collapsed and dropped tourists into the waterfall or the river; at least 30 persons were feared dead at Guaíra Falls, which is on the Brazil–Paraguay border.

February 15, Off the coast of Newfoundland, Canada. The "Ocean Ranger," the largest submersible oil rig in the world, listed and sank in 15-m (50-ft) seas; all 84 men aboard the rig, including those who tried to escape from the structure in lifeboats, were presumed drowned.

February 17, Moscow, U.S.S.R. When the moving surface of an escalator broke during rush hour at the Aviamotornaya subway station, at least 15 persons were killed when they were pitched into the mechanism or thrown down a 46-m (150-ft) shaft beneath the escalator.

April 15, East Chicago, Ind. Two sections of an unfinished bridge known as the Cline Avenue Extension collapsed and hurled 12 construction workers to their death; 17 others were hospitalized with serious crushing injuries. Some experts conjectured that faulty scaffolding failed to support the weight of the concrete being poured and that stress and vibrations caused a ripple effect and the downfall of the second section.

July 10, Mwinilunga, Zambia. A measles epidemic claimed the lives of 51 children.

Early September, Kerala, India. Poisoned homemade liquor that was sold to revelers at a festival killed 54 persons and left more than 600 others hospitalized.

Late September–Early October, Bangladesh. An outbreak of cholera in the northern and eastern parts of the country caused the deaths of at least 75 persons.

Early October, West Bengal, India. An encephalitis epidemic claimed the lives of at least 118 people from the districts of Burdwan, Birbhum, Bankura, and Midnapore.

Late October, Java, Indon. An outbreak of cholera in the area of Banyumas killed 39 persons and affected some 200 others; the lack of clean drinking water was believed to have caused the epidemic.

November 2, Algiers, Algeria. The roof on the August 20 Stadium caved in under the weight of 300 spectators who had illegally climbed on it to watch a soccer match; at least 10 persons were killed and nearly 600 others were injured.

November 29, Igapo, Brazil. A power line fell on a crowd of people who were watching rescuers remove victims from a wrecked van that had crashed into a power post; of the 29 persons killed, some were electrocuted and others died after being hurled into a barbed wire fence.

The collapse of a span of a bridge under construction in East Chicago, Indiana, killed 12 workers and hospitalized 17 others on April 15.

UPI

Early November–December, Irian Jaya, Indon. A severe drought contributed to the deaths of nearly 350 persons who died of starvation during a one-month period.

December 3, Cairo, Egypt. A five-story house collapsed and 55 persons were killed; 15 persons were injured and 32 others escaped unharmed.

NATURAL

January–March, Madagascar. Five tropical cyclones, named Benedict, Frida, Electra, Gabriel, and Justine, ravaged various regions of Madagascar; more than 100 persons were killed, 117,000 others were left homeless, and over 40,000 ha (98,800 ac) of crops were destroyed.

January 3–5, San Francisco Bay area, Calif. A devastating rainstorm that lashed the area with more than 30 cm (12 in) of precipitation triggered flooding and mudslides that killed at least 37 persons in the counties of Santa Cruz, San Mateo, Contra Costa, Marin, and Sonoma, which were declared disaster areas by Pres. Ronald Reagan. The storm caused an estimated $280 million in damage, including the destruction of at least 80 homes that were buried in mudslides; some 150 other homes were also damaged.

January 4, Nariño Province, Colombia. Severe flooding killed 90 persons in southwestern Colombia.

January 5, Rio de Janeiro, Brazil. Heavy rains triggered landslides and floods; 15 persons lost their lives.

January 8, Near Manizales, Colombia. A huge landslide, caused by intense rain, killed nearly 30 persons.

January 9–12, Europe. Frigid cold and wind-whipped snowdrifts battered Europe and claimed the lives of at least 23 persons; hardest hit was Wales, which was cut off from the rest of Britain by 3.7-m (12-ft)-high snowdrifts, making travel impossible.

January 9–17, United States. An onslaught of record-breaking arctic-cold temperatures, combined with fierce, icy winds and, in some cities, heavy snow, was blamed for the deaths of more than 230 persons nationwide.

January 23–24, Western Peru. The swollen Chuntayaco River burst its banks after several days of rain and swept away 17 villages along a 97-km (60-mi) stretch of the river; at least 600 persons were killed and some 2,000 others were missing.

January 26, Australia. Thunderstorms, severe flooding, intense summer heat, and numerous brushfires led to the deaths of at least 13 persons.

January 31, Near Salzburg, Austria. An avalanche on the Elmau-Alm slope in the Tennen Mountain range killed 13 members of a West German student group, including their teacher; rescuers working in blizzard conditions recovered 5 survivors from the snow.

February 2, Kashmir, India. A landslide triggered by heavy rains destroyed six houses and killed at least 23 persons in northern Kashmir.

February 9, Near Mexico City, Mexico. A broken water main in the suburb of Naucalpan prompted a mudslide that killed at least ten women and children.

Mid-March, Santa Cruz, Bolivia. Swirling floodwaters caused by persistent rains destroyed crops and left thousands of persons homeless; some 50 families were missing and presumed drowned.

March 14, Near Tocache Nuevo, Peru. A major landslide claimed the lives of an unspecified number of people.

March 14, France. A spate of avalanches in the French Alps claimed the lives of at least 11 skiers; a late winter thaw triggered the massive slides of snow, rock, and dirt.

Late March, Philippines. Typhoons Mamie and Nelson rampaged across the central and southern islands of the country, leaving some 17,000 people homeless and claiming the lives of at least 90 others.

March 25, Onoluk, Turkey. An avalanche of snow killed 15 persons living in a village in the foothills of Mt. Ararat.

March 29, Near Pichucalco, Mexico. El Chichón, a 2,200-m (7,300-ft) volcano that had been dormant for centuries, erupted, spewed nearly a billion tons of hot ash and rock, and killed as many as 100 persons living in villages on its slopes.

March 31, Squaw Valley, Calif. Avalanches touched off by a four-day, 3.7-m (12-ft) snowfall killed seven persons at the Alpine Meadows ski resort.

Early April, Georgian S.S.R. Record rains created widespread flooding that destroyed some 300 buildings, killed livestock, and claimed the lives of an unspecified number of people.

Early April, Cuzco Province, Peru. Heavy rains inundated the province and precipitated landslides and floods; some 220 persons were believed dead.

Early April, Bangladesh. A week of violent weather conditions that included intense storms and tornadoes killed 24 persons.

April 2–3, Midwestern and southern U.S. A series of deadly tornadoes swirled through Ohio, Texas, Arkansas, Mississippi, and Missouri and left 31 persons dead; hardest hit were Paris, Texas, where 10 persons died, and Arkansas, where 14 others were killed.

April 5, Java, Indon. The Mt. Galunggung volcano erupted and spewed hot rock, mud, and ash on the surrounding area. The

eruption was the first in a series of violent explosions that caused the deaths of at least 20 persons, $25 million in damage to homes and crops, the evacuation of 82,000 persons, and in June and July the near crash of two jetliners whose engines had become clogged with volcanic dust.

April 6, United States. An unseasonable blizzard moving from the Rocky Mountains to the northeastern states inflicted severe damage to crops and property, forced some airports and schools to close, and killed 33 persons.

May 4, Burma. A raging cyclone with 200-km (124-mi) winds damaged homes, public buildings, and rubber plantations; 11 persons were killed in the storm and 7,200 families were left homeless.

May 11–12, Kansas, Oklahoma, Texas. A cavalcade of tornadoes rampaged through Oklahoma, Texas, and Kansas and killed at least seven persons; hardest hit was Altus Air Force Base in southwest Oklahoma, where twisters caused an estimated $200 million in damage.

Mid-May, Guangdong (Kwangtung) Province, China. Torrential rains precipitated the worst flooding in 30 years in the southeastern province of Guangdong; at least 430 persons were killed, 450,000 others were marooned, and some 46,000 homes collapsed.

Late May, Honduras and Nicaragua. The worst flooding in 50 years killed 75 persons in Nicaragua and 125 others in Honduras; the damage to homes, roads, bridges, and crops was estimated at $200 million.

May 29, Hong Kong. Torrential rains caused severe flooding and several landslides that killed at least 20 persons living in hillside shantytowns.

May 29, Marion, Ill. A deadly tornado left a 24-km (15-mi) swath of destruction and killed at least ten persons.

June 3, Sumatra, Indon. Heavy monsoon rains triggered severe flooding that killed at least 225 persons and left some 3,000 others homeless.

June 4, Orissa, India. A severe storm packing winds of up to 221 km/h (137 mph) pummeled coastal villages, claimed 200 lives, and left some 200,000 persons homeless.

June 5–6, Connecticut. A weekend storm lashed the state and dumped between 18 cm (7 in) and 28 cm (11 in) of rain, precipitating severe flooding; at least 12 persons died as a result of the flooding.

June 19–20, Cuba. A weekend storm caused major flooding in Cuba's western provinces; an undisclosed number of people were killed and many factories were damaged or destroyed.

June 26–27, Paraná and São Paulo, Brazil. Swirling 145-km/h (90-mph) winds in the states of Paraná and São Paulo demolished homes and buildings, injured 500 persons, and killed at least 43 others, mostly senior citizens and children who were trapped inside collapsed homes.

Late June, Fujian (Fukien) Province, China. The worst flooding in 30 years left 75 persons dead in the southern province of Fujian.

July 9, Lapilang Village, Nepal. Torrential rains set off a landslide that claimed the lives of 18 persons.

July 12, Semjong, Nepal. A landslide triggered by torrential rains buried alive 15 villagers.

July 17, Sichuan (Szechwan) Province, China. A powerful earthquake measuring 6.0 on the Richter scale killed 10 persons and injured at least 5 others.

July 19, El Salvador. An earthquake measuring 7.0 on the Richter scale wreaked destruction over 25% of the country, claimed the lives of 20 persons, and seriously injured 94 others.

Late July, Southern Japan. Monsoon rains touched off landslides and the worst flooding in 25 years; hardest hit was the Nagasaki area on the island of Kyushu, where 212 persons were known dead and 114 others were missing. The death toll combined with other areas stood at 245 persons; 117 others were missing.

August 12–13, South Korea. A raging typhoon battered the country's southwestern coast; 38 persons were known dead, 26 others were missing, 6,000 were left homeless, and 100 persons were injured in flash floods and landslides.

Mid-August, South Korea. Raging Typhoon Cecil blasted the country, claimed the lives of at least 35 persons, left 28 missing, injured 42 others, and caused more than $30 million in damage; hardest hit was Kyongsang-namdo where at least 42 persons were missing or dead.

Early September, Orissa, India. The worst monsoon flooding in memory displaced nearly 8 million people and swept away more than 2,000 head of cattle; at least 1,000 persons were feared dead in the coastal districts and 5 million others were receiving aid from air force planes dropping food and supplies to those marooned on rooftops and islands.

September 11–12, Japan. Typhoon Judy battered the country with 175 km/h (110 mph) winds and caused hundreds of millions of dollars in damage; 26 persons were killed, 94 were injured, and 8 others were missing.

September 17–21, El Salvador. Five days of relentless torrential rain triggered floods and huge mudslides that buried hundreds of people. The El Salvador government reported that 700 persons were known dead, 18,000 were injured, and 55,000 others were made homeless. The country's crops including corn, beans, and rice were virtually destroyed. Neighbouring Guatemala reported 615 deaths related to the storm and hundreds of others missing.

September 30, Sinaloa, Mexico. Hurricane Paul roared through northern Mexico packing 190 km/h (120 mph) winds; dozens of people were missing and 50,000 others were homeless.

October, Nghe Tinh, Vietnam. A thunderous hurricane pummeled the province of Nghe Tinh and left nearly 200,000 people homeless; hundreds of others were believed dead.

October, Indonesia. A four-month drought, the worst in ten years, dried up rivers and wells and contaminated many others; the clean water shortage led to major outbreaks of cholera and dengue fever which claimed the lives of more than 150 persons.

Mid-October, Spain. Three days of relentless rain in the provinces of Valencia, Alicante, and Murcia led to the deaths of at least 13 persons; 30 others were missing and some 30,000 people were left homeless.

October 14–15, Northern Philippines. A deadly typhoon swept through the provinces of Isabela, Kalinga-Apayao, and Cagayan packing 190 km/h (120 mph) winds; 68 persons were killed, at least 58 were injured, and tens of thousands were left homeless.

November 6–8, Southwestern France. A violent storm producing high winds and rain led to the deaths of at least 11 persons.

November 8, Gujarat, India. A devastating hurricane struck the western coast of the country with gusting winds of 200 km/h (125 mph); the storm leveled 30,000 homes, destroyed crops, cut power and communication lines, and claimed the lives of at least 275 persons.

Early December, Arkansas, Illinois, Missouri. Torrential rains precipitated heavy flooding that caused at least $500 million in damage in three states; 20 persons lost their lives and 4 others were missing.

Early December, Western U.S. Blizzards, rainstorms, and tornadoes swept across the western states; heavy rains and high winds in California burgeoned into a blizzard that dumped 1.8 m (6 ft) of snow in the Sierra Nevada and 1.2 m (4 ft) over the Rocky Mountains. At least 34 persons were killed in the storms.

December 10, Sri Lanka. Heavy monsoon rains triggered landslides that buried several homes and killed at least 22 persons; 12 others were feared dead.

December 13, Dhamar Province, Yemen Arab Republic. A deadly earthquake measuring 6.0 on the Richter scale struck the province, killing more than 2,800 persons and injuring some 1,500 others; nearly 300 villages were either damaged or destroyed.

December 16, Baghlan, Afghanistan. A powerful earthquake measuring 6.0 on the Richter scale killed more than 500 persons, injured 3,000 others, and destroyed thousands of homes.

RAILROADS

January 27, Near Beni Helouane, Alg. A passenger train carrying 450 persons broke free from its locomotive, sped backward down an incline, and struck a stopped cargo train at Beni Helouane station; 130 persons were killed and at least 140 others were injured.

January 27, Near Agra, India. The head-on collision of a passenger express and a freight train resulted in the deaths of at least 70 persons; 20 others were seriously injured.

July 11, Tepic, Mexico. A passenger train carrying 1,560 persons to Guadalajara plunged into a mountain gorge when an eroded roadbed caused the tracks to collapse beneath the coaches; 120 persons were killed.

September 12, Near Zürich, Switz. A locomotive slammed into a tourist bus carrying West German soccer fans after the signalwoman failed to lower the railroad barriers at the crossing; the bus and the first car of the electric train burst into flames and the signal house was gutted. Thirty-nine of the 41 passengers aboard the bus were killed and at least 10 others were injured, including the signalwoman, who was severely burned.

TRAFFIC

January 20, Near Dacca, Bangladesh. An overcrowded bus plunged off a bridge after swerving to avoid a collision with a speeding truck; 28 passengers were killed and some 40 others were injured.

January 26, Near Tuxpan, Mexico. An overcrowded bus fell off a bridge and plunged into a river after one of its tires blew out; 19 persons were killed and 56 others were injured.

January 27, Near Baguio, Phil. A bus carrying a group of Canadian tourists to the resort city of Baguio was struck by a larger tourist bus traveling in the opposite direction; the smaller bus's fuel tank was smashed and the bus exploded, killing 12 persons.

January 30, Near Santiago, Chile. Two buses crashed and toppled into a 18-m (60-ft) gorge; 14 persons were killed and 70 others were injured.

February 6, Near Pasamayo, Peru. A bus ran off a road and plummeted 91 m (300 ft) down a hillside; 11 persons were killed and 17 others were injured.

March 31, Peru. A bus traveling on the Central Highway some 72.5 km (45 mi) east of Lima plunged off the road into a deep canyon; 22 persons were killed and 15 others were injured.

Hearses carry the bodies of some of the 44 children who were killed in the worst road disaster in France's history. The children had been riding in a bus which stopped suddenly, resulting in a ten-vehicle crash near Beaune, France.

April 20, Near al 'Arish, Egypt. A bus accident resulted in the deaths of 14 Greek tourists who were on their way to visit St. Catherine Monastery at the foot of Mt. Sinai; 34 others were injured in the mishap.

May 1, Near Kyongju, Korea. A sightseeing bus veered off the road and plunged down a mountain valley after swerving to avoid an oncoming taxicab; 11 of the 32 persons aboard were killed and several others were seriously injured.

May 19, Pusan, South Korea. An intercity bus carrying 90 passengers veered off the road and plummeted into a water-filled ditch after the driver made a wrong turn; 14 persons were killed and 58 others were injured.

May 25, Near Nkurenkuro, South West Africa/Namibia. A head-on collision between a truck and an army vehicle resulted in the deaths of 15 tribesmen on the truck.

July 14, India. A bus carrying more than 50 passengers careened off a mountain road and plummeted into the Sutlej River.

July 30, Himachal Pradesh, India. An intercity bus plunged down a steep mountain gorge; 33 persons died and 27 others were injured.

July 31, Near Beaune, France. A ten-vehicle pileup resulted in the deaths of 44 children and 9 adults; the worst road disaster in France's history occurred when a bus stopped, two cars smashed into the bus, and then a second bus slammed into the wreckage and exploded in flames. A third bus and five other cars were also involved in the accident.

August 15, Near Tula, Mexico. A speeding bus slammed into a train at a railroad crossing; 23 persons were killed and 11 others were listed in serious condition.

Early November, Northern Afghanistan. A Soviet fuel truck collided with another vehicle in the Salang Tunnel and exploded into flames, sending noxious fumes throughout the 2.7-km (1.7-mi)-long tunnel. Eyewitnesses reported that hundreds of Soviet soldiers and Afghan civilians were asphyxiated by the fumes or burned to death when the Soviets sealed off the tunnel in fear that they were being attacked by Afghans.

November 25, Southwestern India. An overloaded truck carrying passengers and cargo overturned on a winding road; 18 persons were killed and 14 others were injured.

December 3, Near Durban, South Africa. A bus rolled down an embankment and landed upside down in a culvert; of the 60 passengers aboard the vehicle, 12 were drowned and 20 others were injured.

December 26, Brahmanbaria, Bangladesh. An overcrowded passenger bus plunged into a riverbed when the bridge it was traveling over collapsed; of the more than 100 persons aboard, 45 were killed and 30 others were seriously injured.

"YOU CAN'T FORECLOSE A COUNTRY"
DEBTOR NATIONS WORRY BANKERS

by F. John Mathis

During 1982 major commercial banks in the United States, Canada, Europe, and Japan were confronted with a number of very large borrowers who could not make interest and principal payments on their loans. Mexico, Argentina, Venezuela, and a host of other smaller Latin-American and African countries faced a liquidity shortfall and were forced to reschedule their foreign indebtedness to governments and banks.

Mexico and Argentina are among the largest borrowers from commercial banks. During the year they ran out of funds to service their bank debt of $78 billion, almost $40 billion of which matured before the end of 1982. Venezuela, also a major borrower, initiated renegotiation talks with its banks to lengthen the maturity of its debt. Worldwide, 40 countries were in arrears in their foreign debt-service payments, including Poland, which, together with Romania, had rescheduled its debt in 1981. Even countries that were not facing severe economic difficulties or liquidity problems, such as Brazil and South Korea, suffered adverse side effects and found it troublesome to obtain the funds that they needed to maintain their debt payments.

Rescheduling debt is not a new phenomenon for commercial banks—they have done it often for their domestic loans—but the magnitude of the international debt being rescheduled in 1982 was tremendous. For some banks it represented a significant percentage of their capital and reserves. This was particularly true of U.S. banks, which had the largest loans to Latin-American countries. In the case of Mexico, for instance, loans of the ten largest U.S. banks averaged almost 55% of their shareholders' equity, including common and preferred stock. Even so, Mexican exposure accounted for only 3% of total loans for those same banks and, unlike companies that can declare bankruptcy, countries seldom go out of existence.

Since 1975 principal payments have been renegotiated for payback over a longer period for 22 coun-

tries, including Poland. However, most of this rescheduled debt has been owed to governments in industrial countries rather than to banks. Between 1975 and 1981 commercial banks participated in only eight renegotiations—with Peru, Yugoslavia, Zaire, Nicaragua, Sudan, Jamaica, Turkey, and Bolivia—involving about $5.5 billion. Actual bank losses on those loans were negligible in most cases, and in general bank losses on international loans are about half the loss rate on domestic loans.

Beginning in 1982, however, reschedulings with commercial banks began to increase. These financial difficulties have been made more serious because of severe problems in domestic lending by banks as bankruptcies rose sharply after 1979, reflecting persistent worldwide recession. As large corporations in many industrial countries neared collapse and oil prices weakened, the Penn Square became the largest bank to fail in the U.S. In Italy Banco Ambrosiano collapsed, in part because of fraud but also owing in part to depressed economic conditions.

These developments made it more difficult for even the largest banks to raise funds in international financial markets. Therefore, banks were unable to continue to extend their loan portfolios. This, in turn, led to a major slowdown in the amount of net new international lending during 1982, resulting in further strains on the international financial system. During the first half of 1982 net new lending of $50 billion was well below the $65 billion increase recorded in the first half of 1981. It seems likely that because of the external financing difficulties of some major borrowing countries in Latin America, net new lending slowed further in the second half of 1982. Thus, total lending for the year will be well below the $165 billion increase recorded in 1981.

Growth of International Bank Lending. Following the quadrupling of oil prices in 1973, major banks participated aggressively in the recycling of funds from the oil-exporting countries to the oil importers. Between 1974 and 1982 international lending by commercial banks grew by an average annual rate of 26%, significantly higher than before 1974. This growth was concentrated in a relatively small num-

F. John Mathis is vice-president of the Continental Illinois National Bank and Trust Company of Chicago.

ber of large banks, with the world's 50 largest banks accounting for nearly two-thirds of the total and the top 200 banks representing almost 80%.

Total international loans outstanding rose to $1,550,000,000,000 at the end of 1981. If interbank transactions and redepositing among banks are excluded, the net amount is $945 billion, compared with $155 billion in 1973. European banks accounted for almost two-thirds of total international loans; the share of U.S. banks and their offshore branches was almost 30%; while Japanese banks represented 5% and Canadian banks 2%. Almost three-quarters of international loans were to industrial countries and offshore money centres. The remaining 26%, or $415 billion, was loaned to less developed countries, including $61 billion to Eastern Europe, $51 billion to southern Europe, and $72 billion to nations in the Organization of Petroleum Exporting Countries (OPEC). More than 60% of the total amount of loans to the less developed countries was concentrated in 12 countries, as shown in the table.

Offshore loans by U.S. banks and their foreign branches rose to $286 billion at the end of 1981, up from $65 billion in 1973. The table lists the 12 largest less developed country borrowers from U.S. banks. They represent 34% of total offshore borrowing and 70% of all U.S. bank loans to less developed countries. Most international lending by U.S. banks is concentrated in a few of the largest banks. For example, in the case of Mexico the ten largest U.S. banks account for 70% of the loans to that country.

Commercial bank loans are only part of the total debt owed by less developed countries. These nations also receive funds from governments and in-

Major Less Developed Country Borrowers as of the end of 1981

In $000,000,000

Total debt from all sources		Debt from all commercial banks		Debt from U.S. banks	
Mexico	73.0	Mexico	55.4	Mexico	21.5
Brazil	71.4	Brazil	49.5	Brazil	16.8
Argentina	35.6	Argentina	22.9	Venezuela	10.5
South Korea	15.9	Venezuela	22.3	South Korea	8.9
Venezuela	26.0	Spain	21.8	Argentina	8.4
Poland	26.0	South Korea	16.9	Chile	5.8
Spain	25.0	Poland	14.7	Spain	5.8
Yugoslavia	19.3	East Germany	10.1	Philippines	5.4
India	19.0	Yugoslavia	9.7	Taiwan	5.0
Indonesia	18.0	Chile	9.6	Greece	3.1
Algeria	17.0	Greece	9.0	Colombia	2.8
Philippines	16.0	Hungary	7.5	Yugoslavia	2.7

ternational institutions, such as the World Bank, the International Monetary Fund (IMF), and corporations in the form of suppliers' credits. Altogether the total debt of less developed countries rose to $530 billion at the end of 1981 and is estimated to have increased to $630 billion during 1982. About 80% of those funds were received by foreign governments or guaranteed by them. The remainder went to businesses in the private sector and was not guaranteed by the governments. Countries with the largest total foreign debt are ranked in the table.

Debt owed by less developed countries to private creditors rose from 23% of total debt in 1970 to 55% in 1982. In contrast, the share of debt accounted for by official (public-sector) sources dropped from 57% in 1970 to below 40% in 1982. Consequently, the proportion of debt contracted on concessional terms (loans with at least a 25% grant element) declined from 41% to 25% over the past decade. Moreover, almost 70% of the public-sector debt and almost all of the private-sector debt owed to private creditors carries variable interest rates. The trend of rising interest rates over the past decade, combined with heavy reliance on private credit markets, has fundamentally increased the cost of borrowing. This has reduced the amount of funds left to invest in economic development.

Foreign Debt Structure. In evaluating the seriousness of present debt problems, a number of indicators show that there has been a significant change in the structural aspects of foreign debt. For example, during the past five years the ratio of foreign debt to gross national product (GNP) for less developed countries increased little, from 22% in 1977 to 24% in 1981. However, in 1973 foreign debt as a percentage of GNP was below 14%, and in 1982 it was estimated at 28%. Similarly, foreign debt service payments as a percentage of export earnings changed little between 1977 and 1981, remaining about 16%, but in 1973 it was only 11% and it may reach 25% in 1982. These ratios refer primarily to public or publicly guaranteed debt because similar information on private debt is not readily available. The World Bank

In September Mexican Pres. José López Portillo nationalized all of that country's private banks, announcing that the purpose was to prevent more money from fleeing the country.

CINDY KARP—BLACK STAR

estimated that the amount of foreign debt held by the private sector in less developed countries and not guaranteed rose to $94 billion in 1981 from about $25 billion in 1973.

Evaluating the maturity structure of less developed countries' foreign debt indicates that the debt servicing problem may continue for several years because debt service payments will be bunched until the mid-1980s. This bunching of service payments is the result of the sharp increase in lending that began in 1974 immediately after the first oil price increase. Also, lending continued to be strong after the second oil price increase in 1979 and 1980. Commercial bank loans averaging eight years in maturity began to come due in 1982 and will continue to do so until 1984. However, for a less developed country an eight-year loan usually does not allow enough time to finance the establishment of sufficient productive capacity to service the debt.

Deteriorating Economic Conditions. The sharp increase in external borrowing by less developed countries and the resulting debt burden were caused by a number of factors, but particularly important were the two oil price rises of 1973 and 1979. Less developed countries have been especially hard hit by the oil price increases, and their deteriorating economic conditions forced significant policy changes. The less developed nations initially suffered a sharp deterioration in their balances of payments. Subsequent stimulative policies of industrial countries boosted world trade growth temporarily, and commodity export earnings rose sharply with world inflation, causing the less developed countries to stimulate their economies.

The second oil price increase further worsened the current account deficits of the less developed

Poland's massive international debts meant fewer foreign goods on store shelves and a lower standard of living.

countries, but this time there were no stimulative policies by industrial nations. Consequently, real world trade growth stopped, interest rates on foreign borrowings rose to record levels, and the foreign currency reserves of the less developed countries were drawn down to finance their balance of payments deficits. Less developed countries were then forced to almost abandon economic development goals in order to meet the more pressing need for balance of payments adjustment. This process was uneven, and some countries such as Brazil began to adjust sooner than others such as Mexico.

The restrictive economic policies of industrial countries were designed to reduce inflation, but they also caused the growth in the volume of world trade to decline from about a 10% average annual rate of increase prior to 1973 to an average of 3 to 4% since, with almost no growth since 1979. Slower world trade growth will continue to hinder the recovery of export earnings for less developed countries and slow the successful completion of their economic development programs. Also, it will be increasingly difficult for them to earn foreign exchange to meet scheduled debt service payments.

Those less developed countries whose exports are dominated by basic raw material or agricultural products have been hit particularly hard. Not only did the volume of their exports slip but commodity export prices (for both agricultural and industrial materials) also fell, resulting in a deterioration in terms of trade, particularly with respect to oil imports. Thus, the growth in the purchasing power of export earnings was severely eroded, and with oil import costs sharply rising, non-oil imports were reduced adversely, affecting general economic growth. Even the relatively prosperous exporters of manufactured goods experienced only a 1% annual rise in the purchasing power of exports during 1980 and 1981, compared with a 5% yearly increase in 1978 and 1979 and 10% growth in both 1976 and 1977. The less developed countries reacted by depreciating their currencies more often and by larger amounts. However, this aggravated their liquidity problem by raising the cost of imports, which drained scarce foreign exchange reserves.

Another factor adversely affecting the less developed countries is the growing interest rate burden, which since 1973 has led to a hardening of borrowing terms. Increasingly, foreign borrowing by less developed countries has been at variable interest rates based on the London interbank offered rate (LIBOR), adjusted every three or six months, plus a fixed spread. The general trend of rising interest rates over the past ten years was accelerated by the jump in U.S. interest rates beginning in 1979.

Eurodollar rates parallel interest rate movements

Eldon Beller, president of the failed Penn Square Bank in Oklahoma City, testified before a congressional hearing.

in the United States and have risen sharply from an average of 6% in 1977 to 12% in 1979, 14% in 1980, almost 17% in 1981, and 14.5% for 1982. The yearly increase in debt service due solely to the increase in interest rates totaled at least $16 billion between 1978 and 1981. Interest payments by less developed countries now take about 10% of export earnings, up from just 3% in 1973. Consequently, the net inflow of funds (taking into account debt-service outflows) to less developed countries has declined since 1978 and in 1982 was smaller than it was in 1975. This decline was entirely accounted for by private lenders, whose share of the net inflow of new funds to less developed countries fell from 70% in 1978 to about 20% in 1981.

Mixed Prospects for Commercial Banks. Each country will react differently to changes in its external or internal economic environment depending on such factors as social pressures, international reserve levels, and resource endowment. Countries in the newly industrialized category will react differently from oil exporters or the centrally planned economies of Eastern Europe. Consequently, each country's situation and adjustment options must be reviewed independently. In international lending most U.S. and other industrial-country commercial bank loans are concentrated either in the high-income less developed countries or in those that have shown the most potential for strong economic development. Most of those countries are exporters of manufactured goods and should best be able to adjust to economic problems and to service their foreign debt.

Significantly, since World War II only Cuba has defaulted on its foreign debts, and even in that case efforts are under way by the country to reschedule

its loans. Unless a nation is prepared to leave the free world economy—either because it does not need to sell its exports and import products from abroad or is no longer in need of substantial funds from private banks, governments, or international institutions—it must continue to service its foreign borrowings. Not only is it in the country's self-interest to service its foreign debt but it also has little choice, since it needs access to world products and capital markets to raise its standard of living. As illustrated by the reschedulings of debts of Poland and Romania, even members of the Soviet bloc want to maintain access to the free world markets.

Western governments generally have encouraged private banks to take an active part in the transfer of resources to the less developed countries. This is based on the belief that free market forces will yield the most efficient distribution of resources. A conflict in government policy has developed as increased commercial bank lending has prompted attempts to monitor and regulate the growth of this lending. Governments have denied responsibility for bailing individual banks out of any rescheduling problems, but at the same time, they have reacted quickly when the problem was perceived to be a political issue, as in the case of Mexico and Yugoslavia. In the case of Eastern European debt problems, particularly with Poland and Romania, the issue of forced default to embarrass the Soviet Union politically was openly discussed. Such government involvement, as in the case of Eastern Europe, shifts international lending from the realm of economics into that of politics. It undermines the role market forces can play in inducing the required economic adjustment.

Some analysts accuse commercial banks of over-aggressive lending and maintain that this is the source of current debt problems. However, governments and international agencies worry that banks may withdraw from offshore lending, causing major hardship to the vast majority of the world's population. Furthermore, the lender-of-last-resort responsibility of central banks comes into play when a major liquidity shortfall threatens to jeopardize the confidence of the international financial community. In this respect governments and international organizations moved quickly in the cases of Mexico, Brazil, and Argentina to provide substantial amounts of funds. These funds have been made available until the liquidity shortfall can be resolved through domestic policy adjustment under IMF guidelines.

Thus, during December 1982 solutions to the liquidity problems of the large less developed countries began to be worked out. Mexico agreed to implement the necessary economic-adjustment measures to improve its international financial position. In return it received access to $4.5 billion over three years from the IMF, $1 billion in U.S. Commodity Credit Corporation guarantees, $700 million from the U.S. Federal Reserve, and $1,850,000,000 from industrial countries acting through the Bank for International Settlements. Net new funds needed for Mexico from commercial banks were estimated at $1.5 billion in 1982 and $5 billion in 1983. Similarly, Argentina obtained commitments for $1.8 billion from the IMF and in 1982 was attempting to obtain $2.6 billion from commercial banks in short-term loans in order to refinance $4.8 billion of unpaid 1982 debt. Brazil received access to $4.5 billion over three years from the IMF and may obtain an additional $1.5 billion from that agency; Brazil also gained several short-term loans totaling $1,230,000,000 from the U.S. government and a $1.5 billion loan from the United States and three European governments. It also was attempting to arrange a $2.4 billion short-term loan from commercial banks. Finally, Venezuela is in the process of arranging a $3 billion short-term refinancing loan from commercial banks.

Additional Funds Needed. These developments, plus smaller debtor requests, have exhausted a substantial amount of the IMF's loanable resources. If the IMF is to continue to be effective in guiding countries' economic and balance of payments adjustment process, it will require additional funds to lend. The growth in the IMF's resources has lagged far behind the expansion in world trade and inflation and thus diminished its ability to cope with rising imbalances. The U.S. originally objected to a large increase in IMF resources, but more recently it has agreed with other major industrial countries to expand the IMF resources by 50% and to make those funds available as early as 1983 instead of 1985 as originally scheduled.

Despite these additional funds from official sources, there is still a strong need for new funds from commercial banks. These banks will be in-

volved in rescheduling or rolling over outstanding loans, which for Mexico may approximate a $16 billion public-sector debt and as much as $9 billion in the private sector falling due by the end of 1983.

Although the vast majority of offshore lending is done by the 200 largest banks in the world, many of the remaining smaller institutions that comprise the 1,000 to 1,500 banks involved in international lending are likely to reduce their overseas exposure. Since smaller banks tend to emphasize short-term loans, often in the form of trade finance, they are able to reduce their foreign exposure rather quickly. However, both large and small banks have discovered that when a country is experiencing a liquidity shortfall, there may be little difference between short- and long-term debt. The Mexican rescheduling also made clear the distinction between lending to the public versus the private sector as public loans received priority access to available dollars to make service payments. Even so, in some cases the Mexican government has assumed responsibility for private debt and is eventually expected to make dollars available to facilitate the servicing of almost all foreign debt.

The withdrawal of smaller banks from offshore lending may adversely affect creditworthy borrowers and reinforce the slowdown in international lending. The impact of this slowdown, even with increased official lending, will deter world economic growth. The extent of this adverse effect may be softened somewhat by slower world inflation, so that the actual purchasing power of international lending may be maintained.

Rescheduling has certain costs for commercial banks, although it has some benefits. The costs relate to depressed stock prices and management time. So far, actual outright loan losses have remained small. The benefits of a rescheduling are associated with an increase in the average interest rate spread on outstanding debt. In addition, the country concerned may receive special economic management assistance from the IMF. Nevertheless, it may take some time before full confidence is restored in the commercial banking system. In an effort to improve the flow of information on countries' financial situations, commercial banks in major countries are attempting to establish a new institution. This institution, first discussed at Ditchley, England, in early 1982, would attempt to make member banks aware of payment problems in countries and would serve as a forum for banks to communicate their concerns to foreign governments. The objective is to resolve balance of payments difficulties in a more orderly manner so as to avoid repetition of the liquidity problems confronting a number of major countries.

ANDY—RAND DAILY MAIL

STRESSES IN THE WESTERN ALLIANCE

by Edward Heath

Ever since the creation of the Atlantic Alliance more than 30 years ago, there has never been a shortage of those who have concentrated on the strains and tensions to which it has been subjected. Moreover, the issues of policy that have divided it have been a constantly recurring feature of its existence. Differences of opinion over nuclear strategy, over the Arab-Israeli conflict, over the disputes between Greece and Turkey, and, more indirectly, over trading activities between East and West, industrial protectionism, and differing agricultural systems are nothing new.

Ascendancy of Unilateralism. That the Alliance has survived these seemingly endless disagreements and conflicts of national interest should have caused observers, until recently, to regard the prophets of doom with more than a little skepticism. However, there is today a new, and what can only be described as pernicious, tendency within the Alliance that compels one to view its prospects with greater foreboding. This new tendency is the deliberate downgrading, by the present United States administration in particular, of the concept of joint management of the international economy and global security. Inflation is to be solved by each country on its own. Security outside the North Atlantic Treaty Organization (NATO) is to be assured by an unwarranted reliance on the unilateral deployment of military might. Diplomacy is to be downgraded; and partnership with the overwhelming majority of less developed countries is shelved, thus excluding two-thirds of the world's population as far as possible from the governance of the international system.

It is not merely frustration or exhaustion or even plain selfishness that motivates this abdication from international cooperation. Nor is it growing public indifference toward the Alliance that is enabling political leaders increasingly to pursue unilateral policies. It is rather the ascendancy of an ideology in which cooperation is denigrated as a sellout to foreign interests, in which the utility of military power is asserted to be almost absolute, and in which the pursuit of moderation and consensus is dismissed as the negation of strength and fortitude. Under these circumstances consultation between allies, when it is allowed to take place at all, is inevitably in real danger of becoming a ritual, emptied of all substance and direction.

After the disarray among the Allies following the Soviet invasion of Afghanistan and the U.S. unilateral decision to produce the neutron bomb, this alarming conclusion is borne out by at least two further transatlantic disagreements: the first over how to react to the imposition of martial law in Poland and the second over the pipeline to transport natural gas from the Soviet Union to Western Europe.

Concerning Poland, discussions within the Alliance had been going on for one and a half years before the imposition of martial law in that country. Yet it still failed to produce a united reaction or even an agreement on how to gear the extension of credit to Eastern Europe more closely to Western political priorities. As far as the pipeline is concerned, the U.S. administration unilaterally imposed sanctions against European companies that had signed contracts for the export of components made under license to the Soviet Union—a policy that was inconsistent with international law and with all the accepted limitations governing the sovereignty of nations. Subsequently, the U.S. administration unilaterally lifted the sanctions. As a result, the strain imposed on the Alliance has been substantial; and the West has conveyed a signal of disunity and inconsistency to the new Soviet leadership.

Disruptive Forces. The real question that now must be asked, and to which this article is addressed, is whether this new autarchy in political

The Rt. Hon. Edward Heath, MBE, MP, was Conservative prime minister of the United Kingdom from 1970 to 1974, having held office in previous Conservative governments from 1952 onward. A member of the Brandt Commission (Independent Commission on International Development Issues) and a firm supporter of European unity, he has published, among other works, Old World, New Horizons.

and economic affairs is merely a temporary phenomenon, brought about by the strains of a world recession and by the group of political leaders who happen to be in office at the present time, or whether forces are at work that will make this a far longer and deeper crisis in the Alliance—forces that challenge the whole set of assumptions that have governed Western policymaking for more than three decades. It is impossible to disguise the fact that strong forces of this kind do indeed exist.

First, the pursuit of unilateral policies is in danger of becoming a self-sustaining process, not only in the realm of economics but also in matters of security. This is because the inevitable failure of such policies, and the consequent worsening of the problems they are designed to solve, serves to enhance rather than reduce the inclination of governments to be introspective and to pursue national rather than international solutions to their problems. This was seen all too clearly in the 1930s, and with catastrophic results.

The monetary policy of the U.S. provides an example of this process. The unilateral imposition of high interest rates by the U.S. authorities was originally conceived to be a temporary measure to reduce the rate of inflation, after which business confidence, investment, and output would rapidly be revitalized. Nothing of the kind happened. On the contrary, high interest rates increased the cost of borrowing for governments and private investors alike so enormously that investment by both virtually ceased and long-term business planning became all but impossible. At the same time, spiraling public and private debt increased the competition for available funds, which in turn was used by the authorities concerned as a justification for continued upward pressure on interest rates—pressure that resulted not only in thousands of bankruptcies but also in a continuing decline in investment. Yet the deeper the economic quagmire in which the Reagan administration found itself, the more resolutely it seemed to believe in the pursuit of national autarchy in its economic policies.

The second force that is perpetuating the crisis in the Alliance is the continuing shift of the political centre of gravity in the U.S. away from the East Coast. The growing intellectual and political assertiveness of other parts of the U.S., which do not have the tradition of internationalism or the network of contacts in Europe so characteristic of the Eastern Seaboard, appears now to be an irreversible process. As a result, it is increasingly improbable that a president from this old political group will be elected; or, if he is, he will need to be far more closely attuned to the ascendant political views of the rest of the country than was ever necessary in the past.

U.S. sanctions against construction of the Soviet pipeline to Western Europe added to frictions within the Atlantic Alliance.

The third disruptive force stems from the threats to the security of the Alliance and the interests of its members, which have become so much more numerous and complex in recent years that unity has become far more difficult to maintain and far more costly for political leaders to insist upon. This is an inevitable result of the new challenge to Western policy created by the global reach of Soviet power, the growing inhibitions on the full use of Western power—whether military or economic—to deter aggression in the modern world, and the increasing economic strength of countries outside NATO, particularly in East Asia, the Arabian peninsula, and Latin America. Although the Alliance does not formally act as one in economic affairs or in upholding international security outside its own perimeter, it is condemned to seek unity on these matters because the failure to do so would seriously damage both its interests in those areas and its cohesiveness in the face of the Soviet threat to Western Europe.

The crisis precipitated by the Argentine invasion of the Falkland Islands provided a vivid illustration of these realities. It showed how difficult unity is to achieve given the increasingly complex interests of the major countries in the Alliance—for example, in their respective relations with Latin America. At the same time, it demonstrated the overriding and inescapable need for the Alliance to remain united, even on an issue that was clearly outside the scope of its formal purpose—to defend itself from a direct Soviet military threat.

Fourth, there is a danger that the growing cost of defense will heighten tensions between Europe and the U.S. over military strategy. The recession in the West and the rapidly rising cost of conventional forces are exacerbating the old dilemma between placing greater reliance on nuclear weapons for the defense of NATO, so as to minimize costs, and diverting public expenditure from social or economic purposes to conventional defense in order to reduce the need for the use of such weapons. Today, both courses of action are extremely difficult for politicians to undertake, the first because of the unprecedented strength of the antinuclear lobby and the second because the recession is making every additional cut in other spheres of public expenditure to make way for that on conventional arms the object of increasingly strong public opposition.

The absence of any easy solution to this dilemma is undermining the attempt by some European members of NATO to achieve a durable domestic consensus on the priorities for their own defense. This has been reflected in the changes in attitude within some European countries toward the neutron bomb, from being in support of it to opposing it; and it has been seen in the vacillation of some who had previously given full support to the modernization of NATO's long-range theatre nuclear forces, to name but two major issues of defense policy.

These changes in attitude are wrongly interpreted by many in the U.S. administration and Congress as symptomatic of a tendency on the part of governments in Western Europe to appease the Soviet Union rather than to stand up to its growing military strength. One of the dangers of this misconception about European behaviour is that in the minds of many Americans it may justify the current tendency of their administration to pursue unilateral policies. To these people the European allies will no longer seem to be worth the sacrifices and compromises required to maintain unity within the Alliance.

Opportunities for Renewal. What do these various threats to the cohesion of the Alliance portend for the future? Are there any developments within the Alliance that may counterbalance these disruptive forces and thereby give it fresh vigour in the years ahead? There are, in my view, three opportunities for the Alliance to inject itself with renewed vitality and purpose.

The first is the increasingly close cooperation between Spain and the rest of the Western world. Even if Spain decides not to join the integrated military command of NATO, its desire to cooperate with the Alliance reflects the confidence and hopes that the Spanish people have placed in it and the remarkable reintegration of that nation into the family of Western democracies. If Spain does decide to remain in NATO, this will provide an opportunity both to strengthen the Alliance and to rekindle popular support in all its countries for its basic aims of preserving democracy and freedom in the West.

Second, it is a sign of vitality in NATO, and not of decay, that some of its members are now seriously beginning to question doctrines of nuclear warfare that are no longer credible in an age of nuclear parity between the superpowers. In particular, more and more senior generals and politicians on both sides of the Atlantic openly doubt whether a U.S. president would really authorize the first use of nuclear weapons, and thereby the potential destruction of the U.S., in response to a successful conventional assault on Western Europe by the Warsaw Pact forces. The voicing of such doubts has added considerably to the need to find an answer to this question: What happens if deterrence breaks down?

The answer to the question is *not* that more complicated means of fighting "limited" nuclear wars must be elaborated. Nobody has yet shown that a nuclear war could be kept limited, nor that the military has mechanisms for command and control to keep it as such, nor that the Soviets would believe that it would remain so. The attempt to make nuclear "war-fighting" seem more credible will have the effect of making NATO's overall military posture less credible because it will powerfully inflame the anxieties of those in Europe who fear that it will increase the probability of a nuclear exchange between the superpowers confined to the European battlefield. This argument will therefore play directly into the hands of the growing army of "pacifists" who favour the unilateral disarmament of Western Europe.

Strategic logic dictates one overriding answer to the question of how to address the crisis of NATO's nuclear doctrine. It demands an improvement of NATO's conventional forces to such a degree that the Alliance is relieved of the political and psychological burden of appearing to have to rely on the threat to use nuclear weapons in a first strike. This will be expensive, but so great is the fear of nuclear weapons in Europe—and in much of the U.S.—that it would be presumptuous to regard the political obstacles to a major improvement in conventional defense as insurmountable.

Such a strengthening of NATO's conventional defenses would be the single most effective way of diminishing the strength of the pacifist movement. At present, reliance is being placed on arms reduction talks to achieve this objective. Yet the process of arms reduction is likely to be too slow to mollify the fears of Europeans about nuclear war or to prevent fresh calls for unilateral disarmament. And as the technological sophistication of armaments relentlessly increases, so it will become even more difficult to find ways of limiting not only the numbers of weapons but also improvements in their quality.

However, arms reduction talks are, and must remain, a top priority for the Alliance. In particular they can help to make clearer and more visible the capabilities and the military options available to both East and West in conventional as well as nuclear warfare. President Reagan's proposals leading to the strategic arms reduction talks (START), now under way in Geneva, on the limitation of intermediate-range nuclear warfare could make a major contribution to building greater stability into the East-West relationship. Indeed, the growing political consensus in the U.S. on the need for arms control provides a fresh opportunity for a major step forward toward the limitation of nuclear weapons.

What Europe Should Contribute. The third long-term opportunity for the Alliance is the increasing balance in power between the U.S. and Western Europe. Today Western Europe has a gross national product larger than that of the U.S., and it has the potential, through the European Community, to play a major diplomatic role in international affairs. Militarily, the gap between European and U.S. capabilities continues to be reduced. Indeed, if tomorrow NATO had to counter a conventional attack by the Warsaw Pact, 90% of its ground forces and 75% of the sea and air forces available from the outset would be Western European troops.

The existence of a more equal relationship between Western Europe and the U.S. may well make the achievement of consensus more difficult, but it provides a major opportunity to revitalize the Alliance and give added effectiveness to its policies. In particular, it enables Europe to make a far greater contribution to a genuine division of labour in the Alliance. For example, in the diplomatic sphere European governments are sometimes allowed considerably more flexibility by their electorates than is the U.S. administration. This is true of the Cyprus problem, and the lingering dispute in the Aegean, where Europe has uniquely close contacts with all the parties involved. And it is true of the Arab-Israeli dispute, where Europe often has better and more trusted relations with key Arab countries than the U.S. One of the advantages of working through the institutions of the European Community in these tasks is that they are untainted by the legacy of mistrust—justified or unjustified—that the superpowers have acquired for themselves.

In the economic sphere Europe has technological and financial resources with which it can help countries whose security is threatened by their economic weakness—Turkey, Yugoslavia, and Pakistan, particularly after the Soviet invasion of Afghanistan.

In the military sphere Europe can also contribute substantially without deploying large numbers of troops outside the NATO area. It can do this by pro-

ED GAMBLE/THE FLORIDA TIMES-UNION

"Well . . . It looks like I'm going to have to explain the trickle down theory again!"

viding military equipment and training to countries threatened by external aggression. It can also provide logistical and financial support for U.S. military deployments around the world. And it can strengthen the defense of the European theatre itself.

In all these spheres it is essential that Europe should be seen to make an effective and willing contribution to the solution of the problems with which the Alliance is faced. Unless the Europeans do this, the people of the U.S. will inevitably become disillusioned with their allies, and the effectiveness of the Alliance will be further undermined.

At this point, however, a nagging question arises, which refers back to the starting point of this article: What if the U.S. is unwilling to pursue a partnership of equals with Western Europe in the *non*military tasks that currently face the Alliance? What if it refuses to cooperate with Europe in the development of the underprivileged regions of the third world or if it designs its economic policies without regard to the interests of Europe or the stability of the international economy?

It is obviously desirable for Europe to resist as far as it possibly can the temptation to go it alone. Indeed, in the areas of military security and relations with the Soviet Union it remains of overriding importance to maintain compatibility between European and U.S. policies. Moreover, there is still much that can be done to improve mechanisms of consultation within the Alliance. The democracies still have no institutional machinery for addressing economic issues or those relating to the third world. The summit meetings of Western and Japanese leaders are an attempt to fulfill this need, but they are too infrequent and unsystematic in the way they relate to decision-making procedures at lower levels to solve the many substantive problems on the agenda of the Alliance.

Thus, where consultation between Europe and the U.S. can be improved, where the possibility of a convergence of their views and policies remains, and where time permits, every effort must be made to preserve unity of action within the Alliance. However, the new reality of our times is that we must be prepared to face the fact that in some areas of policy this may not be possible, and that Europe will need to take its destiny more into its own hands. It is in the area of economic affairs that this is perhaps most urgent and most immediately feasible.

The Monetary Factor. The constant threat of conflict across the Atlantic over trade and monetary policy can be averted by Europe only if the Community makes a determined effort to insulate its monetary policies and interest rates from those of the U.S. I have proposed that this should be done by devising a "ring fence" of exchange controls around the Community that can be imposed as and when necessary in order to preserve monetary stability in Europe. I have never pretended that this would be easy, either politically or technically. In particular, it would be difficult to attempt without harmonizing taxation on portfolio investments in the member nations. It would also require greater control over the Eurocurrency markets, whose unchecked expansion in any case threatens the attainment by each member state of its own monetary objectives.

Some will say that exchange controls cannot work and that the proposal for a ring fence is therefore doomed to failure. History shows otherwise. For example, the British operations over 50 years, including the experience with the old investment dollar premium, which was often around 20–30% for long periods of time, are evidence that they can work. Others will say that the ring fence is no more than a protectionist device that militates against free trade and all the principles of an open international economy on which the post-World War II prosperity of the West has been based. Such a view is founded on little more than ideological prejudice, for exactly the reverse would occur. Such a ring fence would enable Europe to pursue lower interest rates and therefore higher growth and expanded trade. It would help to reduce the instability of exchange rates, which is a potent cause of protectionist pressures. And, as a result, it would enable the less developed countries to increase their trade with Europe and to reduce their crippling payments of interest. This in turn would help those countries to escape from the appalling quagmire of ever increasing debt in which they now find themselves and that seriously threatens the integrity of the international private banking system. The result would be to underpin the international system of payments and trade rather than to endanger it.

It is the alternative course along which Europe is now being dragged that is more likely to lead to the breakup of the international systems of trade and private lending. It is the relentless multiplication of restrictive trading practices, the futile attempt to defend currencies by constant changes in interest rates, and the irresponsible financing of the internal projects of countries like Poland that most gravely threaten the international economy.

It is now vital to bring into being a system of international monetary affairs of which the U.S. need no longer be the ultimate guarantor. In this system a central role for Europe can be neither escaped nor postponed, even if the U.S. once again becomes more cooperative in international monetary affairs. Indeed, what is needed is the development of a regional approach to the management of global economic and monetary affairs, for no one country is any longer powerful enough to underwrite the system, however benign or altruistic its policies. Under this approach only those responsibilities that cannot be dealt with effectively by cooperation between the major economic zones of the world would be handled by the International Monetary Fund and other global bodies.

The responsibility of Europe in giving renewed strength and purpose to the Alliance is today greater than ever before. This responsibility can be exercised only by a united Europe. This is true whatever the climate of relations with the U.S. happens to be. It will require the European Community to devise a far wider range of policies than those that are currently its mainstay, namely those that exist in the spheres of agriculture, foreign affairs, and the customs union. This would in turn enable the development of a broader constituency with a conscious stake in the growing unity of Europe.

With over nine million people unemployed in the Community, with billions of dollars worth of idle industrial plant, and with Europe's currencies adversely affected by wildly gyrating foreign exchange markets, the ability of the Community to take bold common action to develop the new high-technology industries on which its international competitiveness depends, to create a forward-looking energy policy, to coordinate further monetary and exchange rate policies, and to remove the plethora of nontariff barriers that frustrate millions of businessmen in Europe will be the prime determinant of its ability to rekindle the confidence of the public in its direction and purpose. And the ability of Europe to grow in unity and strength will in turn determine whether the Atlantic Alliance possesses the resilience to withstand the many disruptive forces and conflicting national interests to which it is being increasingly subjected.

PEOPLE OF THE YEAR

Biographies 70

Nobel Prizes 96

Obituaries 99

——— BIOGRAPHIES ———

The following is a selected list of men and women who influenced events significantly in 1982.

Andropov, Yury Vladimirovich

In November 1982, for the first time in the Soviet Union's 60 years of existence, a change at the top of the government was unexpectedly swift and, on the face of it, remarkably harmonious. After Lenin's death Stalin had seized power by ruse and force, doing away with opponents and accomplices alike; when he died, Lavrenty Beria, who had sought to succeed him, was shot, while Georgy Malenkov, who ten days after grasping the rod of power had to pass it to Nikita Khrushchev, was dismissed to oblivion. Khrushchev in turn was pushed aside in a "palace coup" and was succeeded by a group of three until Leonid Brezhnev (*see* OBITUARIES) eclipsed the other two.

Yury Andropov's accession was an altogether smoother affair. During Brezhnev's illness Politburo members began to consider who among them would be the fittest to succeed him. On April 22, 1982, Andropov

NOVOSTI PRESS AGENCY, LONDON

was chosen to make the traditional speech commemorating Lenin's birth, and on May 24 he was reelected to the Secretariat of the party Central Committee. (He then automatically relinquished his previous post as head of the State Security Committee [KGB].) Two days after Brezhnev's death on November 10, the 308-member Central Committee unanimously elected Andropov as the sixth leader of the Soviet Union.

Yury Vladimirovich Andropov was born on June 15, 1914, at the village of Nagutskaya in the Stavropol region, the son of a railway worker. Little was known of his schooling, but at the age of 16 he joined the Young Communist League (Komsomol) while working at Mozdok in the North Ossetian Autonomous Republic. For a time he was a boatman on the Volga River, and in 1936 he graduated from the Inland Waterways Transport College at Rybinsk in the Yaroslavl region, where he became a Komsomol organizer. He joined the Communist Party in 1939, and the following year was appointed first secretary of the Komsomol organization in the Karelo-Finnish Autonomous Republic. In 1944 he was appointed second secretary of the party Central Committee at Petrozavodsk, the chief city of Karelia.

The turning point in Andropov's career was his transfer to Moscow, where he was assigned to the central apparat of the Communist Party. In 1953 Khrushchev appointed him ambassador to Hungary, where he was instrumental in the suppression of the 1956 uprising. Recalled to Moscow in 1957, Andropov became head of the Central Committee's department supervising the Communist parties of the "sister" countries. In May 1967 Brezhnev appointed Andropov head of the KGB. A month later he was made a candidate member and in April 1973 a full member of the Politburo.

(K. M. SMOGORZEWSKI)

Aoki, Rocky

He was nearly killed in a fiery crash while racing an offshore powerboat in San Francisco Bay in 1979; his doctors told him he could never race again. Rocky Aoki, nevertheless, returned to the sport on July 14, 1982, and drove a 11-m (38-ft) speedboat to victory in the Benihana Grand Prix off Point Pleasant, N.J. Then, on September 11, Aoki had another brush with death, breaking both his legs in a crash. But the flamboyant Japanese founder of the Benihana of Tokyo steakhouse chain, which had made Japanese cooking an American household word, had always fancied himself a risk-taker and a champion.

Considered by many to be a Japanese Horatio Alger, the wiry Aoki's meteoric climb to success in both the business and sports worlds overshadowed his uncertain fate in boat racing. Born Hiroaki Aoki in Tokyo in 1938, Aoki spent many of his early years working around his father's coffee shop. He first traveled to the U.S. in 1959 as a member of the Japanese national team to prepare for the 1960 Olympics. He did not make it to Rome but he later became an excellent flyweight wrestler in the Amateur Athletic Union. Lured by the "American life-style," he remained in the U.S., where he attended Springfield College in Massachusetts on a physical education scholarship. But the aspiring wrestling coach quickly realized that big-money opportunities lay elsewhere, so he enrolled in the New York City Community College to study hotel and restaurant management.

While in school Aoki began supporting himself by parking cars and selling ice cream from a truck in Harlem. Working all day and well into the evening, he attracted customers by sticking small red paper parasols into each ice cream. Within months he had saved $10,000. In 1964 he borrowed $20,000 more and opened the first Benihana of Tokyo—a four-table restaurant in New York City. Less than seven years later he ruled a virtual empire of 15 restaurants and 7 franchises around the U.S. By the end of 1982, Benihana of Tokyo was doing $70 million in sales, with 52 restaurants in the U.S. and 24 in Japan.

The highlight—and the selling point—of a meal at one of Aoki's restaurants is the knife-wielding chef who slices up the food with Samurai-like speed and then cooks it on an open steel griddle that is ringed with diners. Aoki, who pioneered the concept, enjoyed being the showman himself and had long counted on his sporting exploits to drum up business for Benihana. He participated in and financially backed the first manned transpacific balloon trip from Japan to California in late 1981. He said he still hoped to undertake a balloon trip from Europe across the Soviet Union to Japan, even though the Soviet government had so far turned down his requests. But there were also times when he doubted whether he should ever take these sorts of risks again. So with his boat racing and ballooning futures in doubt, Aoki was turning his eyes toward business ventures, such as fast food noodle restaurants, to support the expansion of the Benihana empire.

(FRANK B. GIBNEY, JR.)

Arafat, Yasir

Chairman of the Palestine Liberation Organization (PLO) since 1969, Yasir Arafat in 1982 became less secure as leader of the Palestinians' nationalist cause. He was the target of criticism from various factions within the PLO; from the Syrian leadership (Syria having been a mainstay of Arab support for the PLO); and from Palestinian communities in the Israeli-occupied West Bank and Gaza territories, in Kuwait, and in the U.S. The criticism escalated after the Israeli invasion of Lebanon forced Arafat to abandon his Beirut headquarters at the end of August and set up a new base in Tunisia.

Muhammad Abed Ar'ouf Arafat (also known as Abu Ammar—"the builder") was born in 1929 in Jerusalem, one of seven children of a well-to-do merchant whose wife was related to the anti-Zionist grand mufti of Jerusalem, Amin al-Husayni (d. 1974). After schooling in Gaza, Arafat went to Cairo University where he was graduated as a civil engineer. While in Egypt he joined the Muslim Brotherhood and the Union of Palestinian Students, of which he was president during 1952–56. He was also commissioned into the Egyptian Army and in 1956 served in the Suez campaign.

After Suez Arafat went to Kuwait, where he worked as an engineer for the government and set up his own contracting firm. While there, he was a co-founder of al-Fatah, which was to become the leading military component of the PLO. After assuming the PLO chairmanship in 1969, in 1971 he became commander in chief of the Palestinian Revolutionary Forces and two years later head of the PLO's political department. Subsequently, he directed his efforts increasingly toward political persuasion rather than military confrontation and terrorism.

In November 1974 Arafat became the first representative of a nongovernmental organization—the PLO—to address a plenary session of the UN General Assembly. He paid official visits to a number of Eastern bloc countries, but his contacts with Western leaders were generally more informal because of the latters' need not to appear to grant political recognition to the PLO.

After moving to Tunisia, Arafat in September 1982 attended the Arab League summit in Fez, Morocco, where he was received as a head of state. Later that month he visited Rome and had a brief meeting with Pope John Paul II that drew bitter criticism from Israel.   (JOHN WHELAN)

Argüello, Alexis

It might have been a Cinderella story in several respects. Alexis Argüello, born poor in Nicaragua 30 years ago, went to work as a day labourer at the age of 12 to help support his family. While still in his teens he traveled to Canada, where better wages meant more money to send home to his family a continent away. In Canada he also found his way into professional boxing and discovered that prizefighting paid better than construction labour.

In 1974 Argüello won a world boxing title in the 126-lb class. He then moved up twice to win both the World Boxing Council junior lightweight and lightweight championships. Over the years he won 76 professional bouts, 62 by knockouts, and lost only 4. In 1982 he tried to win his fourth title, something that no boxer had ever done. On November 12 he stepped into the ring in the Orange Bowl at Miami, Fla., to face Aaron Pryor, the defending World Boxing Association junior welterweight champion.

However, the Cinderella story was not to be. Argüello, known as a fighter of superb intelligence and savvy intuition, was the bettors' favourite at 12 to 5 odds despite being outweighed. For 13 rounds the boxers fought almost equally, but when round 14 began the challenger's left hand began to drop, and the defender took advantage with his hard right fist. Argüello took six uncontested blows before the fight was called on a technical knockout. Bleeding from a cut below the eye, Argüello also had a severe concussion and was hospitalized. Pryor thus retained his junior welterweight title while Argüello kept his lower division crown.

Argüello's brain concussion prompted new concern about the risks of prizefighting. The death of South Korean boxer Duk Koo Kim from injuries that he suffered in a bout the following day brought further demands for the end of bareheaded boxing as a professional sport.

(PHILIP KOPPER)

Bechtel, Stephen, Jr.

When U.S. Pres. Ronald Reagan needed a new secretary of state in 1982, he turned to a well-tested source and lured George Shultz (q.v.) away from the presidency of the Bechtel Group, Inc. The San Francisco firm had become the "cradle of the Cabinet," almost a proving ground for his administration's top echelon. Caspar Weinberger, the secretary of defense, had been Bechtel's general counsel; W. Kenneth Davis, the deputy secretary of energy, had been an executive; and diplomatic troubleshooter Philip Habib (q.v.) was a consultant. The remarkable engineering company had employed men who had served other administrations as well; former CIA director Richard Helms had helped the firm avoid potential losses in Iran.

The man who acknowledged the company's debt to Helms was Stephen Bechtel, Jr., the family firm's chief executive officer. Bechtel was used to having close contacts in high places throughout the world. When criticized for his connections in foreign cap-

JAMES D. WILSON/NEWSWEEK

itals—sometimes unfriendly ones—he said, "I only feel it is appropriate to see leaders when there is business to conduct and it is worth their time."

A giant among privately owned companies, the Bechtel Group stands like a colossus among the world's engineering and construction firms with recent billings of $11 billion a year and 113 "major" simultaneous projects in 21 countries. Bechtel recruited able men of global experience to build such projects as an industrial city in Saudi Arabia, Canada's largest hydroelectric project, the Alaska pipeline, and the subway for Washington, D.C.

The company began modestly enough in 1898 when Bechtel's grandfather hired himself out with a mule team to help build a railroad through Indian territory. It gained national prominence in the 1930s when it headed the consortium that raised the Hoover Dam across the Colorado River. It spanned San Francisco Bay with the Oakland Bay Bridge, concentrated on launching Liberty ships during World War II, and then turned to oil refineries and pipelines under the leadership of Bechtel's father. When nuclear energy came into fashion, the firm took the lead and built nearly half the reactors that would operate in the U.S.

Born May 10, 1925, in Oakland, Calif., Bechtel gained a B.S. degree in engineering from Purdue University and an M.B.A. from Stanford University. During World War II he served in the U.S. Marine Corps and was awarded the French Legion of Honour.   (PHILIP KOPPER)

Betancur Cuartas, Belisario

Belisario Betancur was elected president of Colombia on May 30, 1982. It was the fourth time that he had been a Conservative candidate in a presidential campaign. The first time was in 1962; the second, when he lost to the official Conservative candidate, Misael Pastrana Borrero, was in 1970; and the third was in 1978, when he was beaten by the Liberal Julio César Turbay Ayala. In 1982 a split in the Liberal Party ensured Betancur's victory, the first Conservative win since 1974, when a 16-year agreement to alternate Liberal and Conservative presidencies had ended. Betancur received 47% of the vote, as against 40% for the official Liberal candidate, former president Alfonso López Michelsen, and 11% for the New Liberal, Luis Carlos Galán.

Betancur was born in the Amagá district of Antioquia in 1923. Brought up in severe poverty, he endured considerable hardship in acquiring an education. At the university in Medellín he studied first architecture, then law. At the same time he worked as a journalist and became increasingly involved in official Conservative politics, moderating his original extreme right-wing opinions. In 1950 Pres. Laureano Gómez appointed him to the constituent assembly, but he was later imprisoned for his opposition to the military rule of Pres. Gustavo Rojas Pinilla. During his career Betancur had been a senator, minister of labour, ambassador to Spain, and professor of law. He was inaugurated in August.

His belief in the Colombian system of power sharing was demonstrated in his first Cabinet, in which six Conservatives and six Liberals were given posts (the Ministry of Defense remained in the hands of the Army). His economic policies pleased the private sector, especially the encouragement of agricultural and industrial exports with increased tax discounts and controls on imports of luxuries and goods that competed unfavourably with domestic products. More important, however, were Betancur's moves to halt guerrilla activity. He restored the Peace Commission (which had resigned under Turbay's administration) and initiated positive steps toward dialogue with the insurgency movements. By the end of September, the two main groups, M-19 and FARC (Colombian Revolutionary Armed Forces), had called cease-fires. One of Betancur's election promises was that guerrilla-dominated areas would receive assistance.   (BEN BOX)

Brown, Charles Lee

You are to reorganize one of the world's largest business enterprises, establishing 22 operating subsidiaries as independent firms and dividing up $100 billion in assets. In addition, you are to do this in a manner that maintains public confidence in your company, protects the investment of your three million shareholders, and satisfies the courts of the United States. You have two years to complete the job.

This was the task presented to Charles Lee Brown, board chairman since 1979 of the American Telephone and Telegraph Co. AT&T operates the Bell Telephone System, which provides telephone service in the U.S. It is also the parent firm to Bell Telephone Laboratories, Inc., where research is performed, and Western Electric Co., a

communications equipment manufacturer. During the 1970s, 37 smaller firms that manufacture telephones and operate telephone systems had filed suit against AT&T, charging it with monopolistic practices and seeking its breakup. Also, the U.S. government had filed an antitrust suit under federal laws that protect the public against business monopolies. After fighting these actions for some time, AT&T negotiated a settlement. In January 1982 the firm agreed to divest itself of 22 state and regional telephone systems, such as Illinois Bell Telephone Co. and New England Telephone & Telegraph Co. In return, AT&T was allowed to expand into new fields, such as data processing.

If anyone could resolve the immense problems associated with AT&T's divestiture, it appeared to be Charles Brown. In 1977–78, as president and chief operating officer, he directed a reorganization of AT&T—one of the largest such corporate actions in history. Prior to that, as AT&T's chief financial officer, he had helped to reduce the firm's debt. Since joining AT&T during the 1940s as a summer employee and maintenance man, Brown had risen through more than 20 positions. Born on Aug. 23, 1921, in Richmond, Va., he earned a degree in electrical engineering at the University of Virginia in 1943 and served as a radioman in the U.S. Navy before joining AT&T.   (VICTOR M. CASSIDY)

Chen Pixian

Chen Pixian (Ch'en P'i-hsien) gained national prominence when he was elected in September 1982 to the Chinese Communist Party's Central Secretariat. The only member selected from the provinces, he brought his vast experience in agricultural and industrial development to the 11-member Secretariat, which replaced the Politburo as the most important party organ to supervise China's transformation into a stable and prosperous modern power during the coming decades.

Born in Shanghang County, Fujian (Fukien) Province, in 1911, Chen joined the Communist Party in 1931. During the 1930s and '40s he was given various party responsibilities in Jiangxi (Kiangsi) Province. After the Communist victory in 1949, Chen worked closely with Chen Yi (Ch'en I), a veteran military commander and mayor of Shanghai, and became the first secretary of the party's Shanghai branch in 1965. Until his purge in 1966, he was a key figure in directing the city's postwar industrial development and economic growth. At the beginning of the Cultural Revolution in 1966, he turned against the leftist movement and was publicly humiliated during televised criticism and self-criticism demonstrations. Returning to power in 1977, he served briefly in Yunnan Province as party secretary and governor. Later that year he was elected to the party's Central Committee and transferred to Hubei Province, where he served as governor and first secretary. During his years there, he received renewed national attention for restoring political calm, increasing agricultural production, and developing industry. Under his leadership the Wuhan steel mills were modernized and Gezhou (Ko-chou) Dam, a key project designed to control floods and produce electricity, was finally completed.

His energetic efforts were also directed at improving transportation, foreign trade, and economic growth in Hubei.

Imaginative, cheerful, and persistent, Chen has stressed the pragmatic approaches to rural development that he outlined in 1982 in the party's official organ Red Flag. Comparatively young and an extremely capable economist, he was expected to play increasingly important roles in carrying out China's modernization program in the coming years.   (WINSTON L. Y. YANG)

Chevènement, Jean-Pierre

At the end of June 1982, Jean-Pierre Chevènement, already minister of state and minister for research and technology, added the office of minister of industry, following a Cabinet reshuffle that made him one of the most prominent figures in France's Socialist government. He thus gained the means to carry out his plans to make France a major power in advanced technology. He believed that national independence depended on technological independence, and his view of nationalization had always been that nationalized industries should be the leaders in development in their fields. In addition, his interest in defense problems should now allow him to approach the long-neglected problem of relations between civil and military research; Chevènement was a supporter of nuclear energy and one of the first in the Socialist Party to defend the French nuclear strike force.

Born on March 9, 1939, in Belfort, Chevènement took a degree in law before studying for the diplomas of the Institut d'Études Politiques and the École Nationale d'Administration from 1963 to 1965. He began his administrative career as a commercial attaché in the Ministry of Economy and Finance. After joining the SFIO (Section Française de l'Internationale Ouvrière) in 1964, he was secretary-general (1965–71) of the Centre d'Études, de Recherches et d'Éducation Socialistes (CERES). In 1971, at the congress on Socialist unity at Épinay-sur-Seine, he became the ally of François Mitterrand. He was appointed national secretary of the Socialist Party that year and was one of the main negotiators of the joint program with the Communists and other left-wing parties. He was first elected a deputy for Belfort in 1973.

In 1975, at the Socialist Party's Pau congress, he was removed from the party leadership and went into a four-year "exile." But at the Metz congress in 1979 he supported Mitterrand, and the Socialist Party Committee extended the National Secretariat to members of the CERES. The main editor of the "Socialist Plan" on which Mitterrand based his presidential manifesto, Chevènement was the author of several books.

          (JEAN KNECHT)

Clark, William P.

As U.S. presidential adviser for national security affairs, William P. Clark had the main qualification for success in Ronald Reagan's Washington—Reagan's trust and confidence. He also has earned the respect of a foreign policy establishment that was highly critical when Clark first came to town to serve as deputy to former Secretary of State Alexander Haig.

The U.S. Senate confirmation hearing for the deputy secretary of state's post was an

embarrassment to Clark. He was unable to answer ever basic questions about foreign affairs, and a number of senators openly expressed doubts about his appointment, which they reluctantly voted to approve. But once on the job, Clark quickly learned what he had to know, and his critics soon were praising him for his intelligence and a calm, judicial manner. Though known as "Reagan's man" in the Department of State, he also gained Haig's confidence and frequently was responsible for smoothing troubled waters between Haig and the rest of the administration.

Clark was chosen to head the National Security Council after the resignation of Richard Allen. In that sensitive and often controversial position Clark's open-mindedness and quiet, methodical approach to problems proved highly effective. Again, his low-profile style was a sharp contrast to Henry Kissinger and Zbigniew Brzezinski, two flamboyant predecessors.

But Clark could be outspoken and blunt when he believed it was necessary. A devout Roman Catholic, he wrote a strong letter to the chairman of the National Conference of Catholic Bishops, which was drafting a pastoral letter that opposed the Reagan policy on nuclear strategy and disarmament. Clark called for the bishops to support U.S. proposals for nuclear arms reduction and charged that their draft letter reflected "fundamental misreadings of American policies."

Like Reagan, Clark is a former Democrat who became a conservative Republican. Born Oct. 23. 1931, in Oxnard, Calif., he gained his law degree at Loyola University in Los Angeles. He was a county chairman in Reagan's first political campaign and became chief of staff when Reagan was elected governor in 1966. As governor, Reagan appointed Clark to be a county judge and, eventually, a justice of the California Supreme Court. (HAL ERUNO)

Compton, John George Melvin

Although the return to power of John Compton and his United Workers' Party (UWP) in St. Lucia's general elections in May 1982 was hailed in the U.S and elsewhere as a victory for Western-oriented democracy, it was probably more a tribute to the quiet but strong leadership exerted by Compton. For while Compton's politics were in Caribbean terms slightly to the right of centre, his party's landslide victory owed more to the planning and organization he had undertaken during his 2½ years in opposition. During that time St. Lucia had experienced weak government as a result of political rivalries, severe economic decline, and constitutional crises.

As an example of his readiness to return to government, the 56-year-old Compton pleased even critics by having ready, on resuming office, a strong team of young and dedicated experts capable of tackling some of the severe economic problems facing the island. Unlike his predecessors he did not pursue a broadening of international relations but instead concentrated on restoring close links with the U.S., the U.K., Canada, Venezuela, and like-minded regional governments.

Head of St. Lucia's government from 1964, first as chief minister and, later, after St. Lucia achieved statehood in association with the U.K. in 1967, as premier, Compton became the nation's first prime minister when full independence was granted in February 1979. He held office for only a little over four months, for in a general election on July 2 the UWP under his leadership was heavily defeated. The St. Lucia Labour Party led by Allan Louisy won 12 of the 17 seats. But two years later the Labour administration was defeated on a budget measure, and Prime Minister Louisy resigned (1981). The governor-general then invited another member of the Labour Party, Winston Cenac, to form a new Labour administration. As with Louisy's government, internal strife continued to plague the new administration. In January 1982 a bill was introduced in Parliament that, in the eyes of the opposition, appeared to condone corrupt practices. Under pressure from both the private and public sectors, the government fell. In the general elections on May 3, 1982, the UWP won 14 of the 17 seats. (DAVID A. JESSOP)

Costa-Gavras

The rare distinction among contemporary filmmakers of having invented a new genre of entertainment film—the political thriller closely based on recent historical events—belongs to Costa-Gavras. The style was imitated, but Costa-Gavras remained its master. Missing, one of the major award-winning films of 1982, was his latest work. Adapted from Thomas Hauser's book The Execution of Charles Horman, its subject—the disappearance of a young U.S. journalist during the Chilean coup of 1973 and the sinister involvement of U.S. agents in Chile—admirably suited Costa-Gavras's style.

Born Konstantin Gavras in Athens in 1933, to a Russian father and a Greek mother, Costa-Gavras settled in France at 18 and adopted French nationality in 1956. As a student he switched from literature at the Sorbonne to cinema studies at the Paris film school, the Institut des Hautes Études Cinématographiques. By 1958 he was writing scripts for U.S. and Canadian television, and during the next seven years he worked as assistant to many French directors, including René Clair, René Clément, Henri Verneuil, and Jacques Demy. His first two films as a director in his own right were tough, American-style thrillers, Compartiment tueurs (1965) and Un Homme de trop (1967). It was with Z (1968) that he discovered his individual forte and established an instant, international celebrity. Z, shot in Algiers and set in an unidentified Mediterranean country, was based on an actual case of political assassination in Greece, just as L'Aveu (1970) was a dramatization of the trial and execution of Rudolf Slansky in Prague in 1952, symbolizing the terrorism of the Stalin years in Eastern Europe.

Costa-Gavras was now wholly dedicated to his cause of exposing political corruption and violence. État de Siège (1973) dealt with a political kidnapping in a South American nation and the infiltration and activities of U.S. agents. Section Spéciale (1975) went further back in history for abuses of justice, dealing with the special court set up by the Vichy government in France to carry out the will of the German occupying forces in World War II. Costa-Gavras's commercial popularity continued, though critically he was increasingly attacked for weakening his moral message for the sake of effective melodrama. (DAVID ROBINSON)

Cresson, Edith

Since her appointment as French minister of agriculture after Pres. François Mitterrand took office in 1981, Edith Cresson had fully justified the new head of state's confidence in her ability. Mitterrand's desire to promote women to responsible positions had been demonstrated in February 1975 at the Pau congress of the Socialist Party (PS), when Cresson took her place in the PS National Secretariat, in charge of youth and students.

At the end of January 1982 Cresson declared "unacceptable" the prices proposed by the European Commission in Brussels for the agricultural year 1982–83. The Commission had offered an average rise of 9%, while the French farmers were demanding 16%, so the agreement reached by the European Economic Community at the end of April for a rise of 13% in the price of French agricultural products—despite the reservations of the U.K.—might be credited to her. A month later, Britain, satisfied with the compensation granted for 1982 by the other European Community countries toward its contribution to the Community budget, stopped blocking the agreement on agricultural prices. European solidarity was maintained—for the time being at least.

Born on Jan. 27, 1934, the daughter of a tax inspector, Edith Cresson was a graduate of the Hautes Études Commerciales—J.F. (the women's section of the business studies school) and joined the Convention des Institutions Républicaines in 1965. She failed in her attempts to be elected a deputy, first in Vienne, then in the canton of Châtellerault-Nord. As mayor of Thuré from 1977, she stood once more in the March 1978 legislative elections but failed again.

From June 1979 Cresson was a member of the European Parliament, where she showed a special interest in agricultural questions. She gained a doctorate in demography on the subject of "the life of farmers' and workers' wives in the rural canton of Guéméné-Penfao (Loire-Atlantique)." In October 1982 she visited the U.S.S.R. with a confidential mission to improve the French balance of payments deficit through exports of cereal crops. She returned with a draft agreement on deliveries of agricultural and food products for 1982–83.

(JEAN KNECHT)

Cuomo, Mario M.

When voters in New York State went to the polls to elect a governor on Nov. 2, 1982, they were faced with a classic choice of the old versus the new. Republican businessman Lewis Lehrman, a strong supporter of Pres. Ronald Reagan's policies, advocated social welfare cuts, tougher anticrime laws, reinstatement of capital punishment, and a 40% tax cut; while Democratic Lieut. Gov. Mario Cuomo harked back to the Great Society of the 1960s and the necessity of aid to the needy, despite budget deficits. Lehrman waged a powerful campaign using effective television ads and was reported to have spent as much as $8 million. But in the end it was Cuomo's old-fashioned coalition of liberals, labour unions, and minorities that prevailed.

Before he could face Lehrman, however, Cuomo had to wage a fierce rematch against Edward Koch, the popular mayor of New York City, who had defeated him in the Democratic primary for that office in 1977. Koch, who was favoured in the polls, blundered early in the campaign, antagonizing upstate New Yorkers. Cuomo, while advocating liberal policies, capitalized on his simple, conservative family life and upset Koch by more than 80,000 votes.

A lifelong resident of the New York City borough of Queens, Cuomo was born there on June 15, 1932. After high school he briefly played baseball for the farm club of the Pittsburgh Pirates before returning to New York City and receiving a B.A. (1953) and a law degree (1956) from St. John's University. He taught law at St. John's from 1963 to 1974 and also practiced law in Brooklyn. In 1966 he gained public attention by arranging an acceptable compromise between New York City and clients whose neighbourhood was to be destroyed for a new school. New York Mayor John Lindsay asked him to mediate a public housing controversy in 1972, and his success in that endeavour led him to seek public office. He was defeated in his 1974 bid for the nomination for lieutenant governor by a ticket headed by an old friend, Hugh Carey. One of Carey's first appointments as governor was Cuomo as his secretary of state. In 1978, having lost his bid to be mayor, Cuomo joined the ticket in Carey's reelection campaign.

Although he had little administrative experience, Governor Cuomo was expected to be an effective negotiator. It was a skill he would need in order to manage the needs of the poor and the business interests while holding a fragile coalition together in the months ahead. (MELINDA SHEPHERD)

D'Aubuisson, Roberto

Maj. Roberto d'Aubuisson, a 38-year-old former army chief of intelligence and currently leader of the extreme right-wing Alianza Republicana Nacionalista (Arena), failed to fulfill his hopes of becoming El Salvador's president following the March 1982 elections but did succeed in securing the powerful position of president of the Constituent Assembly. His ambition for the national presidency remained undeterred, and he frequently stated that he wanted to succeed the more moderate interim president, Alvaro Magaña, who was supported by the U.S. Whether his path to power would be a legitimate one through the national presidential elections scheduled for 1984 or would be by force was a matter of speculation.

D'Aubuisson's record of coup attempts and right-wing terrorist activity was certainly lengthy. It resulted in his being thrown out of the Army in October 1979 when Col. Adolfo Arnaldo Majano Ramos came to power. In May 1980, together with other members of the Broad National Front, he was implicated in an abortive coup to remove Majano Ramos. Later, in March 1981, following allegations that he had been involved in the murder of Archbishop Oscar Romero a year earlier, d'Aubuisson took refuge in Guatemala, returning to El Salvador in late 1981 to form Arena.

His background of some 20 years in the Army, including four (1960–64) at the Gerard Barrios Military School, and several years as a fugitive plotter proved a formidable combination. He gained a reputation for calculating conspiracy and was described by a former U.S. ambassador to El Salvador as a "pathological killer." A fervent nationalist, one of whose slogans was *patria si, comunismo no*, he wished to reverse all reforms carried out by José Napoleon Duarte's regime and succeeded in forcing the government to suspend the third stage of its land reform program. He denounced current peace talks as "treason most vile" and opposed the negotiations with the left, carried on by Defense Minister Gen. José Guillermo García.

Unlike other leaders in El Salvador, d'Aubuisson did not come from the ruling oligarchy of 14 wealthy families but was

WIDE WORLD

born of French immigrant stock. His forebears went to Latin America in the 19th century to work on the building of the Panama Canal with the De Lesseps company and stayed on after the company went into liquidation. (LUCY BLACKBURN)

De Klerk, Fredrik Willem

Member of a South African family with a long tradition of public service, notably in the Afrikaner Nationalist cause, and son of a prominent former Cabinet minister and president of the Senate, Fredrik Willem de Klerk made his own contribution to South Africa's political history in 1982. In March he assumed the Transvaal leadership of the ruling National Party (NP) at a crucial stage in its affairs. A. P. Treuernicht, then Transvaal party leader and minister, had broken away from the NP with a group of supporters representing about 20% of the Transvaal's parliamentary strength. (See SOUTH AFRICA.) De Klerk, a relatively junior minister in P. W. Botha's Cabinet, at first joined in trying to heal the breach. When the attempt failed, he sided with Botha. He was unanimously elected new party leader of the key province over the heads of more senior claimants.

In a rapid organizing tour, de Klerk succeeded in stemming the tide toward Treuernicht's new Conservative Party. The result was seen in the almost undivided support given to Botha and his policies in the subsequent Transvaal NP congress. Observers predicted that de Klerk might well be in line for eventual succession to the national leadership.

Born in Johannesburg on March 18, 1936, de Klerk was educated at Krugersdorp and graduated in law, with distinction, at Potchefstroom University for Christian National Education. He entered Parliament in 1972 as MP for Vereeniging and achieved ministerial rank in B. J. Vorster's last Cabinet in 1976. From then on he held various portfolios, under both Vorster and P. W. Botha. Appointed on July 6, 1982, to replace Chris Heunis as minister of internal affairs, he had to handle such sensitive matters as immigration and passports, censorship, citizenship, and the population register, one of the cornerstones of apartheid. In the opinion of many South Africans, some departmental decisions on such matters might be incompatible with his reputation as a *verligte* ("enlightened") Nationalist.

De Klerk himself saw as his main responsibility the continued task of rallying support for the concept of limited power-sharing across the racial barriers. Therein, he believed, lay the only prospect for stability and peace in South Africa.

(LOUIS HOTZ)

De Lorean, John Zachary

In April 1973 auto executive John Z. De Lorean resigned from his $650,000-per-year job with General Motors Corp. to follow the dream of founding his own auto company. Nine years later the dream became a nightmare as De Lorean was arrested in Los Angeles on charges of drug trafficking on the same day that the British government closed the doors on the bankrupt De Lorean Motor Co. To many people De Lorean's meteoric rise and fall could serve as a symbol for both the benefits and the potential corruption in American business.

De Lorean was born into the automobile industry on Jan. 6, 1925, in Detroit, Mich., the son of a foundry worker at the Ford Motor Co. After graduating from the Lawrence Institute of Technology in 1948, he became a research engineer, first at Chrysler Corp. and then at the Packard Motor Co. He earned master's degees in engineering and business administration, and in 1956 he joined GM as director of advanced engineering at Pontiac. His work showed a flair for marketing as well as design, and he soon gained recognition for his innovative ideas, particularly the popular Pontiac GTO "muscle car." De Lorean rose through the ranks at GM, becoming vice-president of the North American car and truck group in 1972. It was widely believed that he might one day be president of the corporation, but De Lorean was a maverick and combined his innovations with a decidedly uncorporate image. He often disagreed with company policies, and his personal life grew increasingly flamboyant as he divorced his first wife and dated models and actresses before marrying 20-year-old model Kelly Harmon in 1969 and 22-year-old actress-model Cristina Ferrare in 1973.

After his resignation in 1973, De Lorean began to seek financing to develop an "ethical car" that would combine style, fuel efficiency, and a moderate price. In 1978 he announced that the British government would invest at least $110 million in his venture if the new factory were built in Belfast, Northern Ireland. Anticipation was high, but when the first car, the stainless-steel-skinned, gull-winged DMC-12, finally rolled off the assembly line in 1981 it met mixed reviews and carried a $25,000 price tag in the midst of a worldwide recession and falling car sales. By early 1982 the company was in receivership.

Then on October 19 De Lorean was arrested in Los Angeles and charged with bankrolling a drug deal that would have involved 100 kg (220 lb) of cocaine and netted him as much as $24 million. He denied all charges and at the year's end was free on $5 million bond.

(MELINDA SHEPHERD)

Decker Tabb, Mary

Winning race after race in 1982, Mary Decker Tabb literally ran off with the record book for women runners in events ranging from 800 to 10,000 m. In October the U.S. runner, who had set nine world and U.S. track records in 1982, was named amateur sportswoman of the year by the Women's Sports Foundation.

In January 1982 Mary Decker Tabb, who had been sidelined for a year and a half by an injured Achilles tendon, began her comeback by winning the women's 1,500-m race at the U.S. Olympic Invitational meet. In this first effort after her injury she set no world records, though she did establish a new meet record of 4 min 8.32 sec in the event. In February at the Los Angeles Times Games she lowered the world indoor record in the 3,000-m race with a time of 8 min 47.3 sec and achieved a new best time of 5 min 53.4 sec at 2,000 m. A few days later she ran the fastest indoor mile ever at the prestigious Wanamaker Millrose Games at Madison Square Garden, where she was timed at 4 min 21.47 sec, winning the race by a comfortable 65 yd. The following week

she broke her own record by running the mile in 4 min 20.5 sec at the Jack in the Box Invitational indoor track meet in San Diego, Calif. (A 4-min 17.55-sec indoor mile that she ran in 1980 was not recognized because it was run on the Houston [Texas] Astrodome's oversized track.)

Decker Tabb also fared well in outdoor events. In June, in her debut in the 5,000-m race, she set a world record at 15 min 8.3 sec. A month later in Paris she ran a 4-min 18.08-sec mile, the first woman to break 4 min 20 sec outdoors. She set a U.S. record of 8 min 29.8 sec in the 3,000-m in Oslo, just missing the world mark of 8 min 27.12 sec in that event. On her return home to Eugene, Ore., she established a time of 31 min 35.3 sec in the 10,000 m at the University of Oregon, the fastest time ever set on a track (though it had been bettered on a road). With this event Decker Tabb became the fastest U.S. woman at all six distances from 800 to 10,000 m.

Mary Decker was born in Flemington, N.J., on Aug 4, 1958. She discovered track and field in 1970, and by 1974 she held world records in the women's 800 m and the 880-yd and 1,000-yd runs indoors. Severe shin splints kept her from competing in the 1976 Olympics. In 1981 she married marathon runner Ron Tabb.

(JOAN N. BOTHELL)

Defferre, Gaston

Because the two men had been friends for many years, no one was surprised to see Gaston Defferre appointed to the French government after Pres. François Mitterrand took office in May 1981. At the age of 72, Defferre was minister of state, minister of the interior and decentralization, life president of the powerful Socialist Federation of the Bouches du Rhône, and editor of the Socialist newspaper Le Provençal and had been regularly reelected mayor of Marseilles during three decades. His slow southern accent, white hair softening his features, blue eyes, and an engaging smile did not disguise the man of action: Gaston Defferre remained "the boss." During 1982 he was savagely attacked as mayor of Marseilles after various scandals were revealed in the press, but he seemed well able to stand up for himself.

A young Socialist lawyer before World War II, Defferre was already known in Marseilles as a determined fighter. Resistance to the Nazis gave him the opportunity to show his courage. As president of the Socialist group in the National Assembly, he was one of the leading opposition figures under the Fifth Republic, having already been in government under the Fourth, as minister for the merchant navy and, above all, as minister of overseas territories and architect of a bill that made sensible preparations for French decolonization. During the difficult period of restructuring on the Socialist left, which resulted in the creation of the new Socialist Party under Mitterrand, his loyalty to the future head of state never wavered. As minister of the interior he was responsible for the introduction of controversial measures affecting the police and local government, but he denied suggestions that the State Secretariat for Public Security set up in August 1982 would constitute a "political" police force.

Born on Sept. 14, 1910, in Marsillargues

(Hérault), of a Protestant family, Defferre was the son of a lawyer. He also took up the law and studied at Aix-en-Provence. At the age of 23 he joined the Socialist Party. A member of the Executive Committee of the banned party under the German occupation, he was entrusted with missions to London and Algiers. He organized three resistance networks and published a clandestine paper, L'Espoir. After the Liberation, he became mayor of Marseilles (1944–45 and from 1953 onward) and from then on enjoyed a busy political career.

(JEAN KNECHT)

Devine, Grant

In the Saskatchewan provincial election of April 26, 1982, the Progressive Conservative Party won 57 of the 64 seats in the provincial legislature, the largest majority in Saskatchewan history. Party leader Grant Devine, who had never before been elected to public office, thus became the premier of Saskatchewan. His was Saskatchewan's first Conservative government since it became a province in 1905. Once elected, he moved quickly to implement his campaign promises. The legislature abolished the provincial road tax on gasoline and instituted a program giving mortgage relief to homeowners. Saskatchewan was thus provided with the cheapest gasoline and home mortgages in Canada.

Born in Regina, Sask., on July 5, 1944, Devine grew up on his family's farm. He earned three degrees in agricultural economics: a B.S.A. from the University of Saskatchewan (1967), an M.Sc. from the University of Alberta (1969), and a Ph.D. from Ohio State University (1976).

Before making his debut in politics, Devine worked as a marketing specialist and agricultural commodities consultant. From 1970 to 1972 he worked for the Canadian government in Ottawa on agricultural commodities legislation. As an adviser to the Food Prices Review Board, he provided food price comparisons to selected communities across Canada. This endeavour resulted in more competitive retail food prices. In 1970 he obtained a master of business administration degree from the University of Alberta, and in 1976 he opened an economic consulting firm in Saskatoon.

In the late 1970s Devine decided to enter politics. In November 1979 he became the leader of the Progressive Conservative Party of Saskatchewan, winning on the first ballot at the nominating convention. Winning a seat in the Saskatchewan legislature was not as easy. After losing in elections in 1978 and 1980, he was put in the ignominious position of leading his party from a seat in the legislative gallery. In the 1982 provincial election, he finally won a seat as the representative for the riding of Estevan. Thus he could form a government and become premier of the province.

(DIANE LOIS WAY)

Domingo, Placido

Twenty years after his operatic debut, the critics were saying that Placido Domingo had everything: "the heroic sound, the musical intelligence, the actor's instinct, the

APESTEGUY—GAMMA/LIAISON

good looks, the charm, the stamina, and the adoring crowds." He had more even "than Jon Vickers, Carlo Bergonzi, José Carreras, or even Luciano Pavarotti, he of the golden voice and gilded image." In sum, Domingo had perhaps the most sublime combination of assets in a tenor since Enrico Caruso, whom he surpassed in at least one respect: Domingo was busier. By the end of 1982 he had sung 82 roles in more than 1,600 performances, cut 70 records, and worked on a motion picture.

Born Jan. 21, 1941, in Madrid, Domingo was the scion of the first family of *zarzuela*, the Spanish operetta form that includes spoken dialogue and satire. While he was still a small boy, his parents left Spain for Mexico to found a *zarzuela* company there. Domingo began piano lessons at age eight and won his first competition—a song and dance contest—a year later. After brief studies at Mexico's National Conservatory of Music, he dropped out. He played soccer, tried his hand at amateur bullfighting, and supported himself doing musical odd jobs in clubs and other places.

Returning to serious music, the one-time baritone turned tenor and made his operatic debut in Monterrey, Mexico, in 1961. That same year he sang with Joan Sutherland in Dallas, Texas, and with Lily Pons at her farewell performance in Fort Worth, Texas. Moving to Israel, he spent more than two years there singing in multinational productions. He made his New York City debut in 1965 with the New York City Opera and first sang with the Metropolitan Opera in 1968 on 35 minutes' notice. Seven years later he expanded his musical capabilities by working as a conductor.

Domingo attributes his success in part to his early training. Beyond that, he believes the formula for operatic greatness is "a big chest, a big mouth, 90 percent memory and 10 percent intelligence, lots of hard work and something in the heart."

(PHILIP KOPPER)

Douglas-Home, Charles Cospatrick

The Times, traditionally the newspaper of the British establishment, acquired a new editor of impeccable establishment qualifications in Charles Douglas-Home, nephew of the former Conservative prime minister, Lord Home of the Hirsel. In March 1982 he replaced Harold Evans, a journalist with a reputation as an innovator and fervent campaigner; only a year earlier Evans had been appointed editor of *The Times* by a new proprietor, the Australian media tycoon Rupert Murdoch. The Evans style, which included a taste for personal publicity, had been an immense success in his 13 years as editor of *The Sunday Times*, but it failed to fit the traditions of *The Times*, and Evans resigned.

The Times's way of doing things was quietly, firmly, and decisively reaffirmed by Douglas-Home. Nobody was better qualified to do this. He was not only an aristocrat by birth but also a professional journalist of remarkably wide experience, having been military correspondent (1961–62) and political and diplomatic correspondent (1962–64) on the *Daily Express* before joining *The Times* in 1965. Born on Sept. 1, 1937, he attended Eton College, served in the Army in the Royal Scots Greys, and after that was for two years the aide-de-camp of the governor of Kenya. During his 17 years on *The Times* he was defense correspondent (1965–70), features editor (1970–73), home editor (1973–78), foreign editor (1978–81), and deputy editor (1981–82).

Douglas-Home did not build himself up as a media personality. On the contrary, he was self-effacing and not well known outside his own circle of colleagues. Though the editorship of *The Times* was a post of great distinction, Douglas-Home determined to keep out of the limelight. He said that he would refuse to be interviewed by anyone about anything. His views were traditionalist, right of centre. His direct impact on *The Times* had not been easy to detect. If it was seen as a paper that was very much what it used to be only more so, that was no doubt his intention.

(HARFORD THOMAS)

Dozier, James Lee

During the 1960s a group of left-wing Italian university students organized with the purpose of creating anarchy. Over time their speechmaking and pamphleteering evolved into bombings, kidnappings, and murders. In 1978 this group, by then known as the Red Brigades, gained worldwide notoriety when they abducted, held, and then killed Aldo Moro, a former premier of Italy.

On Dec. 17, 1981, the Red Brigades made their first major mistake. Armed members of the group posing as plumbers kidnapped U.S. Brig. Gen. James Lee Dozier from his apartment in Verona, Italy. Dozier was then the North Atlantic Treaty Organization (NATO) deputy chief of staff of logistics and administration for allied land forces in southern Europe. By abducting Dozier, a representative of NATO, the Red Brigades committed a political act with international implications.

Dozier was hardly a model prisoner. Constantly resistant and watchful, he falsified information on his personal history to confuse his captors. During the 42 days of his captivity he spent most of his time in a pup tent pitched in the middle of a Red Brigades apartment in Padua.

On Jan. 28, 1982, the Leatherheads, an antiterrorist unit of the Italian police, rescued Dozier alive and uninjured. This, only the second such police success against the terrorists, was quickly followed by the capture of several Red Brigades leaders and the recovery of numerous documents linking the group to similar organizations in West Germany and Libya, as well as to the Soviet Union.

Dozier's calm courage under constant threat of death did not surprise anyone who knew him. According to a colleague he was "one of the best army officers" to serve in the Vietnam war. Dozier won the Legion of Merit for his leadership there and four additional medals for bravery under fire.

Dozier was born on April 10, 1931, in Arcadia, Fla. After being graduated from the U.S. Military Academy in 1956, he served with the Army in Kentucky, Vietnam, the Pentagon in Washington, D.C., Kansas, Pennsylvania, Texas, and Europe.

(VICTOR M. CASSIDY)

Ershad, Hossain Mohammad

Lieut. Gen. Hossain Mohammad Ershad, who seized power in a bloodless coup and proclaimed himself chief martial law administrator of Bangladesh in March 1982, had fallen out with aging Pres. Abdus Sattar soon after the latter's election in November 1981. The cause of the disagreement was the role of the armed forces in the nation's affairs. Although he was snubbed by Sattar, who insisted that the armed forces had only one role to play—to look after the defense and security of the country—General Ershad did not act hastily. He waited to strike until the Sattar administration showed signs of cracking up, with the president himself openly admitting that the political and economic situation was verging on collapse. The coup turned out to be smooth by the standards of Bangladesh, which had seen two of its former presidents assassinated and had experienced bloodshed and violence throughout most of its 11-year history. General Ershad had built up some popular goodwill when he stood by Sattar and the constitution during the crisis-ridden days that followed the assassination of Pres. Ziaur Rahman in May 1981.

Ershad, made Army chief of staff by his mentor, Maj. Gen. Ziaur Rahman, had risen to power rather quickly. Born in the northern district of Rangpur on Feb. 1, 1930, he was graduated from a local college and commissioned into the Pakistan Army in 1952. He was promoted to the rank of lieutenant colonel in 1969 and given command of the 3rd East Bengal Regiment.

During the Bangladesh war for independence in 1971, Ershad was in Pakistan; he later chose to return to Bangladesh along with other Bengali army officers. In Bangladesh he was taken into the new Army as an adjutant general. As a brigadier in June 1975 he was sent to study at the National Defense College in India. On his return later in the same year he was made a major general and appointed deputy Army chief of staff by Ziaur Rahman, who was then Army chief. Ershad was picked by Rahman to succeed him in his post as chief of the Army staff when the latter became chief martial law administrator and then president in 1977.

(GOVINDAN UNNY)

Fahd ibn 'Abd al-'Aziz al-Saud

On the death of King Khalid (see OBITUAR-IES) of Saudi Arabia on June 13, 1982, his half brother Crown Prince Fahd succeeded him. Fahd came to the throne at a time when Middle Eastern affairs were in greater turmoil than at any time since the Arab-Israeli "October war" of 1973 and when Saudi Arabia's strained relations with the West were also a matter for concern. He was, however, well equipped for the task, having had considerable administrative experience before taking the brunt of government decision-making at the side of the older but less worldly Khalid.

Fahd was born c. 1922 in Riyadh, the son of Ibn Saud. He was the first son of Hassa Sudairi after her remarriage to Ibn Saud, and his full brothers included the minister of defense and aviation, Prince Sultan; the interior minister, Prince Nayif; and the governor of Riyadh, Prince Salman. On being proclaimed crown prince in 1975 after the murder of King Faisal, Fahd made his name as a modernizer, pushing through the ambitious and highly successful second development plan (1975–80). Once thought of as a lazy man, he had from the late 1960s begun an earnest program of self-improvement, making up for his lack of formal schooling. He was minister of education (1953–60) and minister of the interior from 1962 until 1975, when King Khalid, on his accession to the throne, named him crown prince.

The best testaments to Fahd's period as crown prince were the twin industrial cities of Yanbu on the Red Sea and al-Jubayl on the Gulf. Fahd gave them priority and created special agencies to handle projects such as the huge new Jiddah airport, opened in April 1981. His first major political initiative involved his eight principles for a Middle East peace settlement, announced in 1981. These caused considerable interest in Washington because of their implicit recognition of Israel's right to live within secure boundaries. Although the Fahd plan failed to gain Arab endorsement at the Fez, Morocco, Arab summit later in the year, it provided the basis for further progress on a Middle East peace settlement in 1982.   (JOHN WHELAN)

Fedorchuk, Vitaly

The appointment on May 26, 1982, of Col. Gen. Vitaly Fedorchuk as chairman of the Committee for State Security (KGB) of the Soviet Council of Ministers was made by the Presidium of the Supreme Soviet of the U.S.S.R. only two days after Fedorchuk's former chief, Yury Andropov (q.v.), was elected a secretary of the party Central Committee; Fedorchuk was promoted above two deputy heads of the KGB, and it seemed clear that Andropov had picked him as his successor some time earlier. Then, a month after Andropov succeeded Leonid Brezhnev (see OBITUARIES) as general secretary of the Communist Party, came a new promotion for Fedorchuk, when he was appointed minister for internal affairs. He was succeeded as KGB chief by Viktor Chebrikov, one of the deputies he had bypassed.

Fedorchuk was born in 1918 in the Ukraine. After training at a special school for security and intelligence officers, he joined the national security service—then known as NKVD (Narodny Komissariat Vnutrennikh Dyel)—in 1939. A year later he became a member of the Communist Party of the Soviet Union. The secret treaty between Nazi Germany and the Soviet Union that preceded World War II mapped a partition of eastern Europe in general and of Poland in particular. The Polish provinces of Eastern Galicia and Volhynia, which had majority Ukrainian populations, were incorporated with the Ukrainian Soviet Socialist Republic. The Ukrainians, however, dreamed of independence and religious freedom, especially in Eastern Galicia, where they had been Uniate Catholics in communion with Rome.

The liquidation of the Uniate Church and its forcible merger with the Russian Orthodox Church was the task of the KGB, in which Fedorchuk was involved from the outset of his career with the force. When in 1970 he became head of the Ukrainian branch of the KGB he had to lead the incessant campaign against the "nationalist bias" in the Ukraine, the homeland of the second largest nationality of the U.S.S.R. Fedorchuk's latest promotion, besides underlining the way in which Andropov was replacing close associates of Brezhnev with his own former KGB colleagues, suggested that the Ministry for Internal Affairs would initiate more vigorous action to combat the growing Soviet crime rate and widespread corruption among the party elites.
            (K. M. SMOGORZEWSKI)

Gabler, Mel and Norma

Two of the most influential voices in U.S education may belong to a Christian fundamentalist couple—high school graduates who operate the nation's largest textbook-reviewing service from their home in Longview, Texas. Mel and Norma Gabler, through their nonprofit organization, Educational Research Analysts, examine textbooks for material that they consider antifamily, anti-American, and anti-Christian. They distribute their reviews to some 13,000 individuals and organizations and work to have textbooks that do not meet their criteria kept out of the nation's elementary and secondary schools.

The Gablers are against not only books that contain errors or omissions but also books that they believe undermine patriotism, the free enterprise system, religion, and parental authority. They oppose sex education in the schools and favour the teaching of the biblical story of creation along with the theory of evolution. They argue that many textbooks have been written by "secular humanists" who do not believe in God or an absolute value system. Their fund-raising pamphlet states: "Until textbooks are changed, there is no possibility that crime, violence, venereal disease and abortion rates will decrease."

The Gablers' successes, especially in their home state of Texas where a single committee chooses books for the entire state system, have had a national impact. In 1981, of the 15 books against which they testified, 11 were rejected by the Texas textbook committee. Because Texas was expected to spend about $60 million on schoolbooks in 1982, many publishers were believed to consider that state's preferences in planning their books.

The Gablers have been castigated as "self-appointed censors" by such organizations as the National Education Association and the American Library Association. At the 1982 hearings the couple's testimony was opposed by a new group called People for the American Way, which was founded to fight for First Amendment, freedom-of-speech causes.

Mel Gabler, now 67, and Norma Gabler, 59, were married in 1942. He worked as a clerk for the Standard Oil Co. of New Jersey (now Exxon Corp.) for 39 years, though both now devoted full time to their cause, frequently lecturing throughout the U.S. They became concerned with textbooks in 1961, when their 16-year-old son first complained about the view of federal-state relations in his history book.

            (JOAN N. BOTHELL)

Galtieri, Leopoldo Fortunato

As commander of the Argentine Army in December 1981, Lieut. Gen. Leopoldo Galtieri was a member of the three-man junta ruling Argentina under the presidency of Gen. Roberto Viola. Viola had been in office for just nine months, but his own ill health and the armed forces' dissatisfaction with his administration's policies led to his removal. Galtieri, with the support of newly promoted generals, was sworn in as president on Dec. 22, 1981. For the first time since 1978 the posts of president and Army commander were united.

Galtieri's reputation had been that of a moderate, following the policies of the military governments of his predecessors and not associating with civilian political parties. Once installed in the Casa Rosada (the presidential palace), however, he made a number of statements on the need for a gradual return to civilian participation in government. This gained him some popular support, and that support grew enormously when, on April 2, 1982, Galtieri and his fellow junta members decided on the invasion of the Falkland Islands—the Islas Malvinas. It was a national ambition to make the islands, ownership of which had been disputed with Britain for 149 years, a part of Argentina. To some extent, the invasion also diverted attention away from widespread anger over the military's handling of the economy and its refusal to provide information on thousands of desaparecidos, victims of the 1976–79 suppression of opposition.

Born in 1926, the son of an Italian immigrant, Galtieri rose steadily through the ranks of the Army. After his promotion to Army chief, he closed the Argentine–Chilean border in April 1981, thus increasing tension between the two countries. His two visits to Washington in that year were successful in achieving understanding between the U.S. and Argentina on foreign policy and economic planning.

During the war with Britain over the Falklands/Malvinas, Galtieri publicly maintained a rigid attitude toward Argentina's right to the islands, but after the surrender of his forces on June 14, he resigned as Army commander on June 17. He was soon replaced as president by retired general Reynaldo Bignone. In his wake he left much recrimination and further instability within the ruling armed forces.

(BEN BOX)

Garfield

Did two constellations of U.S. culture change their courses in 1982? Traditionally, the dog has been man's best friend, the pet whose picture on a magazine cover assured higher newsstand sales, the very symbol of rectitude and fidelity. Cats of several sorts might be symbols for automobiles and football teams, but they had not worked their way into the nation's heart; even Walt Disney made them villains when he pictured them at all. Horses like Black Beauty and Flicka might enjoy perennial popularity among 13-year-old girls, but it was *Lassie Come Home*—a dog story—that was adapted as a television series. *Pussy Come Home?* Impossible.

Then, nearly a decade ago, a cat named "Heathcliff" was featured in a cartoon strip, followed shortly by Bernard Kliban's popular "Cat." Somewhere along the way a live specimen named Morris hawked cat food on television and gained such a personal following that his death was reported deadpan on obituary pages. In time some 250 books appeared, including *101 Uses for a Dead Cat* and *The Official I Hate Cats Book.* Then came Garfield.

Cartoonist Jim Davis conceived him innocently enough in Muncie, Ind., as straight man in a comic strip that he drew for the local newspaper. But the cat started taking over. When the human character introduced himself to readers and then presented the animal, the latter bubbled "Hello. My name is Garfield. I'm a cat and this is my cartoonist . . ." The beast had no manners, no sense of propriety. It soon tyrannized the strip—and then the strip began to sell; first to United Feature Syndicate in 1978 and then in just four years to 1,200 newspapers. By October 1982, a book of Garfield cartoons had knocked *The Joy of Sex* off the paperback best-seller list—and had become the fifth Garfield book on the list. *New York Times* book review editors called it "an unprecedented triumph, to put it mildly." At that point the Garfield paperbacks accounted for 40% of all sales among the top 15. By Thanksgiving there were seven Garfield books on the list, and there had been a Garfield special feature on television.

In addition, there were stuffed Garfields, Garfield kittybanks, and a line of Garfield

© UNITED FEATURE SYNDICATE, INC.

cat food in Canada, to say nothing of china icons of the orange beast with black stripes and bugeyes. (It could have been worse; Davis, 37, had once vainly tried to make another animal star of a strip called "Gnorm the Gnat.")

(PHILIP KOPPER)

Garvey, Ed

The executive director of the National Football League Players Association (NFLPA), Ed Garvey was called everything from visionary to wild-eyed radical in 1982 as he led the union through the NFL's first regular-season strike in its 63 years. It lasted eight weeks, from September 21 through November 16, shortened the 1982 regular season from 16 games to 9, and confused onlookers because the union did not follow the traditional sports labour path of fighting for less restricted free-agency, which had allowed baseball and basketball salaries to skyrocket in open-market bidding for players.

Garvey approached negotiations more as a conventional union, reasoning that football players had little more individual bargaining power than pipefitters or electricians. NFL teams had a monopoly in the United States, and they had a bottomless reserve of unemployed potential replacements for a game that rewards team coordination more than individual excellence. Garvey maintained that the teams lacked economic incentive to improve because they shared television and play-off revenues equally and played to near-capacity crowds weekly, leaving few tickets to sell on the basis of a newly acquired star player. Therefore, he proposed that the players be paid according to a wage scale based on experience and augmented by bonuses for team and individual achievement and that all salaries come from an independently administered league-wide fund.

But Garvey's demands eventually caved in under the burden of player unrest and an important unfavourable court ruling in an unfair-labour-practice suit. Management's only important new concessions in the settlement were immediate bonuses based on experience, severance pay, and union authority to approve players' agents. In return, the NFLPA backed off from its initial demand of a percentage of gross receipts, and the owners preserved the existing system of paying the bulk of players' salaries through individual contract negotiation.

Garvey was born April 18, 1940, in Burlington, Wis. His athletic career ended after he lettered in freshman golf at the University of Wisconsin, where he later was elected president of the student body. After his graduation in 1961 and service in the Army as an intelligence officer, he returned to Wisconsin for law school and was graduated in 1969. Two years later he became executive director of the NFLPA after serving it almost full-time as an attorney.

(KEVIN M. LAMB)

Gemayel, Amin

The election of Amin Gemayel as president of Lebanon on Sept. 21, 1982, followed the assassination a week earlier of his younger brother, President-elect Bashir Gemayel (*see* OBITUARIES). Bashir had been elected on August 23 to succeed the retiring president, Elias Sarkis.

Amin Gemayel came to power as the can-

didate of the Phalange Party, whose patriarch was his father, Pierre Gemayel. As a politician and businessman Amin was one of the foremost "doves" among Lebanon's Christian leaders. During 12 years as a member of the Lebanese Parliament prior to his election he earned a reputation as a conciliator, maintaining contact with the Palestinian leftist alliance during the 1975–76 civil war and the troubled years that followed. During the Israeli siege of Beirut in 1982 he crossed the front line for meetings with Palestinian leaders at a time of great tension between the two sides of the divided city. Such an act would have been unthinkable for his brother Bashir, who had a reputation as a man of violence. The two brothers differed widely in character and political views. While Bashir took the military road to power, Amin chose politics. He was first elected to Parliament on the death of his uncle in 1970. When the civil war broke out, he fought and was injured when the jeep he was driving came under attack. The command of the militia, nevertheless, went to his warlike brother.

Aged 40, Amin Gemayel, who was deeply interested in Lebanon's history and culture, was trained as a lawyer. Head of a large business empire which he had built up himself, he was co-founder of the rightist French-language daily newspaper *Le Réveil*. His political philosophy was based on the idea of "dynamic coexistence" both for the diverse creeds and communities of Lebanon and for the warring parties in the Middle East. He showed sympathy for the Palestinians, in sharp contrast to his brother who said they should leave. His contacts with the Israelis were distant, and he was better known as a friend of Syria. A month after taking office President Gemayel made his international debut when he addressed the UN General Assembly, which accorded him an unusually warm reception. Afterward he was received by U.S. Pres. Ronald Reagan and had talks with Secretary of State George Shultz. (JOHN WHELAN)

González Márquez, Felipe

The Spanish Socialist Workers' Party (PSOE) won a stunning victory in Spain's October 1982 general election under the cool leadership of Felipe González, who at the age of 40 became Europe's youngest head of government. The victory, though widely predicted, was even more sweeping than expected and was all the more surprising in that the PSOE had only been legalized in 1977. The PSOE election campaign was pitched almost exclusively around González's moderation as a leader, and in his victory speech he soberly promised "dialogue and cooperation to help reach solutions to the problems confronting our motherland." He was also determined to see Spain more prominent internationally; in his inaugural address to Parliament on November 30, he said he expected Spain would become a member of the European Communities by 1986; that a referendum would be held on NATO membership; and that negotiations with Britain on the reintegration of Gibraltar into Spanish territory would be a prime foreign policy objective.

Born in Seville on March 5, 1942, González was the only one of five children to attend the university. There he studied first to be a civil engineer (at his mother's insistence) before transferring to the law faculty. While still a student, he became involved in the Socialist movement, then in 1964 joined the outlawed PSOE. He started a law practice in Seville, specializing in the defense of workers' rights, and in 1965 moved to Madrid. He and his Andalusian comrades gradually gained ascendancy over the exiled PSOE leadership, and at the party congress at Suresnes, France, in 1974 he was elected secretary-general.

González was conscious of the debt he owed to the Socialist International, which had supported him in his fight to win the leadership of the party from its "old guard" of Civil War veterans under Rodolfo Llopis. A vice-president of the International since 1976, he had traveled extensively, especially in Latin America, to promote its aims. He was a close friend of West Germany's Willy Brandt and other leading Western European Socialists. His election campaign stressed social justice and liberty, and his moral stance accorded well with his youthful good looks and openness of manner.

(MICHAEL WOOLLER)

Guare, John

"Theatre is the last refuge for poetry," said John Guare, who wrote plays in prose but with a lyrical quality similar to the poems of Walt Whitman. In 1982 Lydie Breeze and Gardenia, two parts of a projected tetralogy set in 19th-century New England, opened separately for short off-Broadway runs. A year earlier his screenplay Atlantic City won prizes from the National Society of Film Critics, the Los Angeles Film Critics Society, and the New York Film Critics Circle. Also in 1981, the dramatist won an Award of Merit from the American Academy and Institute of Arts and Letters.

Admired for his rich language and satiric vivacity, Guare first gained fame in the 1960s for arranging "shotgun weddings of lunacy and lyricism," according to the Saturday Review. "With a touch of the poet—and the lunatic—Guare conceived contemporary satires that overflowed with lyrical language." Among them were Marco Polo Sings a Solo and the autobiographically tinged House of Blue Leaves, which won a New York Drama Critics Circle award.

The son of a stock exchange clerk, Guare was born Feb. 5, 1938, in New York City. He received an undergraduate degree from Georgetown University and a master's degree from Yale University's celebrated drama school.

After his New York City debut in the mid-1960s, Guare's plays began appearing almost regularly at the Caffe Cino. Muzeeka—about a canned music factory—won him his first Obie (off-Broadway award) in 1968. His adaptation of Shakespeare's The Two Gentlemen of Verona—reset in San Juan, Puerto Rico, and New York City—won several prizes.

Turning to the screen, Guare teamed up with French director Louis Malle (Pretty Baby, My Dinner with Andre) and wrote Atlantic City, a touchingly sleazy murder-romance about an aging second-rate hoodlum and a casino raw bar waitress. (Malle then directed Lydie Breeze on stage.) Their next collaboration was slated to be Moon Over Miami, a farcical film about drug traffic and police entrapment.   (PHILIP KOPPER)

Habib, Philip Charles

For the second time in as many years, Philip Habib was at the eye of the storm in the Middle East in 1982. Once again he performed heroic labours in bringing a tenuous cease-fire to the strife-torn region. U.S. Pres. Ronald Reagan presented him with the Medal of Freedom, and Charles Percy, chairman of the Senate Foreign Relations Committee, nominated him for the Nobel Peace Prize. But true peace in the Middle East proved as elusive as ever.

Heart trouble had forced Habib's retirement in 1978 after a distinguished 29-year career as a U.S. foreign service officer, most of it as a specialist on the Far East. He suffered a series of heart attacks and underwent coronary bypass surgery. But Pres. Jimmy Carter sent him on a fact-finding mission to the Caribbean, and in 1981 President Reagan made him special envoy to the Middle East with the task of damping down the crisis caused by Syria's installation of surface-to-air missiles in Lebanon. While he was there, fighting broke out between Israeli and Palestine Liberation Organization (PLO) forces in southern Lebanon, but he managed to arrange a cease-fire.

In 1982 the situation was even worse. In June Israel invaded Lebanon in force and drove north to Beirut, where it laid siege to the Muslim part of the city. Working 18 hours a day, shuttling from capital to capital and from meeting to meeting for 11 weeks, Habib hammered out an agreement that ended the hostilities, at least temporarily. He was credited with the idea of bringing in U.S. Marines to help oversee the PLO's evacuation of Beirut—an important

point in securing Israeli consent—and with finding other Arab countries where the PLO could go.

With the immediate fire extinguished, it was understood that Habib would leave the working out of a long-range settlement to others, but he was back again in late November, when the Reagan administration became impatient with the lack of progress. In late December he was again shuttling among capitals, but the year ended with Israeli and Syrian troops still firmly ensconced on Lebanese soil.

Habib was born Feb. 25, 1920, the son of a Lebanese-American grocer, and grew up in a Jewish section of Brooklyn. At the time of his retirement he was undersecretary of state for political affairs, the highest career rank in the State Department.

(DAPHNE DAUME)

Habré, Hissen

The 17-year-long civil war in the central African republic of Chad seemed finally to have ended on Oct. 21, 1982, when Hissen Habré was sworn in as president. Five months earlier, on June 7, Habré's Armed Forces of the North (FAN) had entered the capital, N'Djamena; since then he had been in effective control of Chad, although the southern part of the country was not won over until September.

As president, Habré appointed a 31-member Cabinet, broadly representative of the various factions that had been involved in the conflict, to replace the Council of State he had headed since June. He stated that his aim would be to consolidate peace, security, and national unity and to reestablish the authority of the central government.

The long struggle, basically opposing the Muslim north and the Christian and animist south, had involved France, Libya, and Sudan and contributed to the loss of credibility suffered by the Organization of African Unity in 1982. On taking office, Habré accused Libya of planning to destabilize Chad and of supporting the defeated Goukouni Oueddei, whom he had replaced as head of state.

Hissen Habré was born in 1942 and belonged to the Toubou tribe of northern Chad, then part of French Equatorial Africa. After higher political studies in Paris he joined the rebel leader Abba Siddick and his Front de Libération Nationale du Tchad (Frolinat). In 1974 he first attracted international attention when he took hostage the French archaeologist Françoise Claustre, who was subsequently released on payment of a Fr 10 million ransom by the French government. After Oueddei took over as Frolinat leader in 1976, Habré retreated into Sudan. In January 1978 he became commander of the FAN, and in August was appointed premier by Pres. Félix Malloum. He resigned with Malloum in March 1979 after the Kano, Nigeria, agreement that put Oueddei at the head of a Transitional Government of National Union (GUNT). Habré was a minister in the GUNT until disagreement with Oueddei again forced him into exile in Sudan. He returned at the head of the FAN in November 1981, when the final struggle for supremacy began.

Haddad, Saad

At the start of 1982 former major Saad Haddad, one of the most ruthless as well as one of the most enigmatic of Lebanon's many militia leaders, was in control of a narrow strip of territory adjacent to the Israeli border, which extended, snakelike, from the Mediterranean Sea to the foothills of Mt. Hermon and the border with Syria. But within a week of the entrance of Israeli troops into Lebanon on June 6 the Israelis had ceded him authority over the entire south of the country, from the Awali River north of Sidon to Lake Qaraaoun in the Bekaa Valley. Haddad expected a major Israeli attack before it came. On June 2 he called for a quick military strike against the Palestinians. "I have no faith in the cease-fire," he said, referring to the agreement negotiated in July 1981 between Israel and the Palestine Liberation Organization (PLO) that had led to ten months of unparalleled calm in southern Lebanon—a calm broken only by a heavy barrage by Israeli and Haddad artillery, and by Israeli aircraft, on April 23, 1982.

Haddad, a 44-year-old Greek Orthodox who had recruited Shi'ah Muslims as well as Maronite Christians for his 2,500-strong pro-Christian force, had long hated the Palestinian guerrillas in Lebanon. In 1979 he used the presence of Palestinian forces in the south as a pretext for his declaration of independence from Lebanon, when he proclaimed the territory under his control to be "Free Lebanon." All Haddad's military supplies came from Israel. Haddad was cashiered from the Lebanese Army after that incident. He had earlier reached the rank of major and had attended a one-year course at the U.S. Advanced Infantry School at Ft. Benning in Georgia.

Haddad was in Beirut in September when the massacre of Palestinians in the Sabra and Shatila camps took place. He initially told reporters that some 10–20 of his men might have been in the city at the time, but he later told an Israeli judicial commission inquiring into the massacre that none of his men were north of the Awali when it occurred. Israel appeared to be hoping that in 1983 Haddad would achieve a reconciliation with the new authorities in Lebanon and become, de facto if not de jure, the Lebanese government's recognized security arm in the south after an Israeli withdrawal.   (JOHN ROBERTS)

Hamad, Abdel Latif al-

The importance that Arab banking and financial services had assumed within the world banking system during the past decade was underlined at the annual meeting of the World Bank and International Monetary Fund, held in Toronto in September 1982. On this occasion, for the first time, the world's leading financial conference was chaired by an Arab, Abdel Latif al-Hamad of Kuwait.

Hamad, aged 45, first came to international notice as a member of the Brandt Commission on North-South relations. In March 1981 he was appointed Kuwait's finance and planning minister, having served since May 1963 as director general of the Kuwait Fund for Arab Economic Development, which was the oldest of the Arab aid agencies. During his first 18 months as finance minister for one of the world's richest countries, he showed toughness in his desire for economies in state spending and conservatism in his management of reserves. A sharp liquidity crisis on the unofficial Kuwait stock exchange (the curb market) forced him to demonstrate sternness toward Kuwaiti stock dealers who had dishonoured postdated checks. Hamad encouraged the growth of a capital market in the Kuwaiti dinar, and a number of foreign corporate lenders tapped the market in closely regulated operations designed to prevent the dinar from becoming an international currency. In the management of Kuwait's official reserves Hamad was aided by the oil minister, Sheikh Ali Khalifah al-Sabok, and the central bank governor, Hamza Abbas Hussain.

Hamad was born in Kuwait into one of the emirate's most eminent merchant families. After completing schooling in Kuwait, he studied at the American University in Cairo and later obtained degrees at Claremont (Calif.) College and at Harvard University in Cambridge, Mass. In 1962 he was appointed a member of Kuwait's UN delegation. On becoming finance minister he resigned from the chairmanship of two foreign-based banks, the United Bank of Kuwait in London and the Luxembourg-based CAII. From 1965 to 1974 he was chairman of one of Kuwait's leading merchant banks, the Kuwait Investment Company.   (JOHN WHELAN)

Henderson, Rickey

Rickey Henderson of the Oakland A's had thought of major league baseball's base stealing record as more of a distraction than a barrier. Lou Brock's record of 118 bases in 162 games was less than three in every four games, and Henderson wondered why nobody had averaged one a game.

He then nearly accomplished that in 1982, when he broke Brock's eight-year-old record with 130. Henderson stole into the record book despite a .399 on-base percentage, which was the lowest of his four-year career. Although his 116 walks were the most in the major leagues, his .267 batting average was 33 points below his career average and 52 points (or 27 hits) below his 1981 average.

Henderson was not the fastest player in the game, but his acceleration to full speed in two strides enabled him to steal second base in 2.9 seconds. A catcher can rarely receive a pitch and deliver the ball to second base in less than 3.2 seconds. Henderson did set another record by being caught stealing 42 times, but 14 were on pickoff attempts and 3 were on attempted steals of home. He also became the unofficial champion of stealing third base, which accounted for more than a quarter of his total.

Born Dec. 25, 1958, in Chicago, Henderson was raised in Oakland, Calif., where he was not only outstanding at baseball but had a football career at Technical High School that attracted major scholarship offers. In his first full major league season, 1980, Henderson's 100 stolen bases broke Ty Cobb's 65-year-old American League record. In 1981 he was a close second in the league's most valuable player voting, won a Gold Glove for his play in left field, and led the league in hits, runs, and stolen bases.

Henderson's prime years as a base stealer appeared to be ahead of him. Brock set his record at the age of 35, and Maury Wills had set the previous record at 29. As 1982 ended, Henderson talked about winning a batting championship and hitting more home runs, but he still said that stealing a base was as exciting as hitting a game-winning grand slam home run in the bottom of the ninth inning.   (KEVIN M. LAMB)

Hinault, Bernard

During 11 weeks in 1982 French cyclist Bernard Hinault proved beyond all doubt his right to be considered among the sport's all-time greats. Between mid-May and the end of July he won both the Tour of Italy and the Tour de France to join Fausto Coppi, Jacques Anquetil, and Eddy Merckx as the only men to take cycling's two most important stage races during the same season. Although the dominating figure in professional road racing since 1978, Hinault had met with failure when first attempting the double triumph in 1980. As a result he had continued to suffer in comparison with his immediate predecessor Merckx and fellow countryman Anquetil until his victories in 1982 finally ensured the total adulation of an enthusiastic nation.

The Tour of Italy began in Milan on May 13 and finished, after 4,023 km, in Turin on June 6. Winning and then surrendering the jersey of race leader on three occasions, Hinault finally asserted his authority on the mountainous 18th stage between Piamborno and Monte Campione, opening a decisive gap over his nearest challenger when he stretched his advantage to 2 min 35 sec by winning the final time-trial section. In the Tour de France, which began in Basel, Switz., just 26 days later, it was Hinault's ability against the clock on the four individual time-trial stages that gave him the edge; he finished the 3,492-km race by leading the field across the line in Paris on July 25. His total victory margin over Joop Zoetemelk of The Netherlands was 6 min 21 sec and, along with his powerful riding in the Pyrenees and Alps, that last stage confirmed his all-round superiority in the face of unjustified criticism.

Born in Yffiniac, Brittany, on Nov. 14, 1954, Hinault began his reign by winning the Tour de France in 1978 and again the following year. After winning the Tour of Italy in 1980, on the first attempt, Hinault was forced to retire from the Tour de France by tendonitis of the knee. He recovered to win the world championship a few weeks later in front of a jubilant home audience at Sallanches, and the following year he won his national tour for the third time. By the end of 1982 Hinault had planned an additional four years of racing and was poised to break the record total of five Tour de France victories held jointly by Anquetil and Merckx.   (JOHN R. WILKINSON)

Hussein at-Tikriti, Saddam

Regarded by some Western observers as the Middle East's second most skillful politician, after Syria's Pres. Hafez al-Assad, Iraqi Pres. Saddam Hussein took his great-

est political gamble when he launched a war on Iran and its religious leadership headed by Ayatollah Ruhollah Khomeini. The conflict started in September 1980 with initial Iraqi successes, but in 1982 the tide turned in favour of Iran, whose forces retook nearly all the territory lost in the early stages of the fighting. Iraqi casualties were reckoned at 40,000 dead and 70,000 wounded, with 40,000 taken prisoner.

Hussein succeeded Gen. Ahmad Hassan al-Bakr (see OBITUARIES) as chairman of Iraq's Revolutionary Command Council (RCC) and president of the republic on Bakr's retirement in July 1979. At that time Hussein also became secretary-general of the Iraqi Ba'ath Party. He had been an influential figure since the July 1968 coup (in which he played a leading role) that effectively ensured Ba'ath Party control of Iraq. He moved into prominence in November 1969 as vice-chairman of the RCC and deputy to the president. Following the 1972 signing of a treaty of friendship and cooperation with the Soviet Union, in 1973 Hussein visited Moscow. Subsequently, a Soviet-Iraqi intelligence agreement was concluded. In 1975 Hussein negotiated with the shah of Iran a settlement of the Shatt al-Arab border dispute between the two countries, whereby Iran also agreed to withdraw its support from the Kurdish rebels in northern Iraq. After taking over from Bakr in 1979, Hussein, who held the dominant position within the Ba'ath Party as head of its organizational structure, instigated a ruthless purge of "traitors" within the party, 21 of whom were executed.

Born in Takrit, near Baghdad, in 1937, Saddam Hussein attended Cairo and Baghdad universities and graduated in law. In 1959 he was sentenced to death in absentia for the attempted killing of Maj. Gen. Abd al-Karim Kassem, leader of the 1958 revolution. He lived in exile in Egypt, returning after Kassem's execution in 1963 to become a member of the then national Council for Revolutionary Command under the presidency of Field Marshal Abd as-Salam Aref. In October 1964 he was arrested for plotting Aref's overthrow but was subsequently released. (JOHN WHELAN)

Ibuka, Masaru

Masaru Ibuka has long traveled a road different from that taken by most other "early learning" theorists. In his *Kindergarten Is Too Late!* (English trans. 1978) he opted firmly for mother-child bonding—partly on the basis of traditional Japanese experience—and later contributed to the early learning controversy with *Education from Age Zero.*

Superficially, sophisticated electronics have seemingly made it feasible for urban mothers to fulfill themselves without depriving their infants of early learning stimulation. In his latest research studies, however, Ibuka has reemphasized the paramount role of mother-child bonding as an indispensable foundation for ultimate human development. He seeks even further support from nature, which provides the womb as the optimum climate for nurturing one of its frailest offspring. Ibuka holds the view that an infant emerges perhaps ten months too early for its well-being. Such perspectives on early learning would normally attract little public attention, but because they are associated with the man who founded Sony Corp., they are discussed by the general public.

Ibuka was born in Tochigi Prefecture in 1908 and graduated from Waseda University after majoring in science and engineering. By 1933 he had won international recognition for his invention of a modulated-light transmission system. In 1946, with Akio Morita, he founded Tokyo Tsushin Kogyo (the forerunner of the Sony Corp.) and within a few years had developed the world's first practical magnetic-tape-recording systems. The Sony Corp. was already part of modern electronics technology when, in 1967, Ibuka recognized the potential of a patented device developed in California that he marketed as the Trinitron colour television system.

As Sony's honorary chairman in 1982, Ibuka thinks that technological innovation has achieved a plateau that calls for greater attention to application. He believes that the optical fibre cable, for example, might eventually improve human communications through electronic means. But outside the world of business, Ibuka is still developing his theories of early learning and retreating beyond birth to maximize the mother-child bond. He concludes that a loving environment marked by warm and informative communication should surround the mother throughout her pregnancy. This cannot be directed or influenced by "hardware," even of the electronic type. Because a mother-child relationship is instinctive, it cannot be programmed. Nature has intended that the optimum communication between mother and child be effected through a bonding that is total in tactile and all other modes. The mood surrounding a pregnancy is the ultimate programming.

Ibuka's Early Development Association, dating from 1969, has continued to seek out the optimum conditions influencing the mother-child environment. Ibuka, though still a symbol of the sophisticated electronic era, is looking backward beyond even the womb for answers to human questions first posed to him while caring for a mentally retarded child. (ROWLAND GOULD)

Imran, Khan

For Khan Imran 1982 was an *annus mirabilis,* a wonder-year. He was appointed captain for the short Pakistan cricket tour of England, and no man could have made a more thrilling attempt to wrest victory than he in a three-match series in which England won two matches and Pakistan one. Imran's leadership was crucial in Pakistan's victory by ten wickets at Lord's. In the two test matches that Pakistan lost Imran almost played England on his own and was declared Man of the Match each time. At Edgbaston he took 7 wickets for 52 runs and 2 for 84, and scored 22 runs and 65 (top score). At Headingly he took 5 wickets for 49 runs and 3 for 66, and made 67 runs not out and 46. He was rightly acclaimed Man of the Series, unusual for the captain of the losing side.

Imran first came to England as an 18-year-old all-round cricketer with the Pakistan touring team of 1971. His performances on that tour attracted the attention of the Worcestershire Country Cricket Club, for whom he played for the next few years. During this time he had two years at Oxford University, being captain in 1974, making five centuries, and taking 45 wickets. After transferring from Worcestershire to Sussex in 1977, he became a key member of the latter team. His ability as a menacing fast bowler and No. 5 batsman made Sussex formidable opponents in championship and one-day cricket.

Meanwhile, Imran had become an important player for Pakistan in matches against New Zealand, Australia, and West Indies. He took six wickets in each innings against Australia at Sydney in 1976 and was largely responsible for Pakistan's victory by eight wickets. During the English winter of 1980-81, he played in Pakistan against West Indies and in one memorable match scored his first test century and took ten wickets.

Imran was born on Nov. 25, 1952, the only son of five children of a prosperous civil engineer in Lahore, Pakistan. On his mother's side two of Pakistan's foremost cricketers, Javed Burki and Majid Khan, were his first cousins and his early heroes. The name Khan signifies that his family are Pathans from the North-West Frontier and that they belong to the Naizi tribe. Imran studied politics and economics at Keble College, Oxford; he stated that he did not know what career he would choose when he gave up cricket but that it would be work in which he was his own master.

(REX ALSTON)

Jarvik, Robert

Retired dentist Barney Clark was a very special patient when he entered the University of Utah Medical Center in Salt Lake City in November 1982. Possessed of a fierce will to live and a professional interest in advancing science, he suffered a form of heart disease that was amenable to only one form of treatment—a form never before tried. The surgery itself was dangerous and the outcome was unforeseeable. Without the unprecedented operation (which U.S. government authorities approved on an experimental basis) he would have been dead in a matter of days or hours.

When Clark's condition worsened, on December 1 he was wheeled into a specially equipped operating room. Eight hours later he emerged with a new heart—not a transplant from some accident victim's chest but an artificial implant, one made by men out of plastic and aluminum and driven by an electronically controlled air compressor. Because tubes must always connect the new heart to the power source and monitor, Clark would never live a life of normal agility again. But live he did. By Christmas he had taken a few steps around his hospital room, and it appeared that he might soon go home, thanks to the Jarvik-7 beating in his chest.

The device, essentially a pneumatic pump built to exact specifications, was named for its inventor, Robert K. Jarvik, who almost did not make the grade in medicine. Born in Midland, Mich., on May 11, 1946, Jarvik was the son of a surgeon and often observed his father operate. Intrigued with the design of surgical instruments, he invented a surgical stapler to close wounds when he was still a teenager. Going on to Syracuse University, he studied architecture and mechanical drawing while earning a zoology degree in 1968. When his academic record did not open doors to any U.S. medical schools, he studied at the University of Bologna Medical School in Bologna, Italy, for two years. He then dropped out and transferred to New York University, where he earned a master's degree in occupational biomechanics.

Finally receiving an M.D. degree at the University of Utah College of Medicine in 1976, Jarvik went to work at its medical centre's Artificial Organs Division. His assignment was to design a series of mechanical hearts that could be tested on animals. As these hearts improved, one of them kept a calf alive for 268 days. The heart that extended Barney Clark's life is a two-chambered device that receives blood from the patient's right and left atrias and then pumps it to the pulmonary artery and aorta.

(PHILIP KOPPER)

Kadar, Janos

First secretary of the Hungarian Socialist Workers' (Communist) Party, Janos Kadar was one of the most respected leaders within the Soviet bloc. When he assumed power in the sombre November days following the crushing by Soviet tanks of the 1956 Hungarian uprising, most Hungarians believed him to be a puppet of Moscow. Convinced of the Soviet resolve to restore Communism in Hungary, Kadar hoped that if he played a part in this process he would be able to retrieve some of the less contentious goals of the uprising. For a quarter of a century he worked for the welfare of his people and avoided raising hopes impossible to fulfill in the existing world alignment.

Janos Csermanik was born on May 26, 1912, in the then Hungarian Adriatic port of Fiume (now Rijeka, Yugos.). Abandoned by his father, he settled with his mother in Budapest where he worked as a machinist. In 1930 he joined the Union of Young Communist Workers, was twice jailed, and in 1940 went underground, adopting the nom de guerre of Kadar. After the Hungarian Communist Party was restored by Matyas Rakosi in 1945, Kadar became a member of the Politburo. As part of a Stalinist purge he was arrested in April 1951 on charges of

treason and sentenced to four years in prison. However, after Stalin's death and under pressure from Soviet leader Nikita Khrushchev, he was released in July 1954. In February 1956 Khrushchev's denunciation of Stalin and his regime precipitated Rakosi's downfall and also set the scene for the uprising of October 23.

After the Soviet intervention Kadar was installed as head of a new government, having become first secretary of the renamed Hungarian Socialist Workers' Party several days earlier. His first efforts in office were to reconstruct the party and the government, and then he started on the long and difficult uphill road to regain the trust of the Hungarian nation and the sympathy of the free world. On June 9, 1977, Pope Paul VI received him in audience at the Vatican—symbolically marking the end of Hungary's moral isolation.

(K. M. SMOGORZEWSKI)

Kelly, Petra Karin

A delicately built blonde with a degree in political science from American University in Washington, D.C., Petra Kelly in 1982 was the principal leader of West Germany's Green Party. In several state elections during the year the "Greens" outpolled the liberal Free Democrats for third place in the party rankings. Originally dismissed as part of the lunatic fringe, the Greens, a motley collection of ecologists, pacifists, and self-styled "positive dropouts," had won representation in 6 of 11 state assemblies and stood a good chance of entering the Bundestag after a federal election.

Petra Kelly was born in Günzburg, Bavaria, on Nov. 29, 1948, and subsequently took the name of her mother's second husband, a colonel in the U.S. Army. When she was 13 she went with her parents to the U.S., where she completed her education and afterward worked on the political staffs of both Hubert Humphrey and Robert Kennedy. After her return to Europe she became an official at the headquarters of the European Communities in Brussels and a member of the West German Social Democratic Party (SPD). But her political credo was far to the left of the SPD's official policy and made her instead a natural stalwart of

CAMERA PRESS, LONDON

the Greens. She was a tireless campaigner against nuclear weapons, nuclear power, and the "destructive pursuit of economic growth."

Kelly described the Greens as the "anti-party•party" and insisted that they would lose their real function and their appeal should they develop into a political party like any other. Her nightmare, as she once put it, was that the Greens would one day poll so many votes that they would have to play a role in government. This attitude led to accusations that she was irresponsible and naive. Kelly alienated the West German Communists because she insisted that the Greens must fight nuclear rearmament in the Soviet bloc as well as in NATO. The Greens wanted the establishment of a nuclear-free zone in Western Europe and the withdrawal of the two German nations from their respective multinational pacts.

The Green Party adhered strictly to a system of rotating leadership, as a result of which Kelly stepped down from the federal chairmanship of the party in October. However, she remained one of its leading voices.   (NORMAN CROSSLAND)

Kemp, Jack

For U.S. Rep. Jack Kemp, 1982 required a strong will and all of his faith in the "supply side" economic theory. That theory had become "Reaganomics" in 1981, but a year later Pres. Ronald Reagan reluctantly asked for and got an increase in certain taxes in an effort to hold down the federal deficit. Kemp not only opposed the tax hike but continued to preach his tax-cutting gospel as he campaigned for Republican candidates throughout the country.

"A recession is *not* the time to raise taxes," Kemp insisted, blaming the Federal Reserve Board for the nation's tight money supply and high interest rates. He also voted against Reagan's balanced budget amendment to the Constitution and found himself bitterly at odds with the White House that had adopted his economic policy only a year earlier.

But the 47-year-old New York congressman was familiar with adversity and accustomed to hearing boos as well as cheers. His previous career as a professional football star was good preparation for the hard knocks of political life. Kemp was cut or traded by a half-dozen teams before becoming the starting quarterback of the Buffalo Bills. He led them to three division titles and two American Football League championships before retiring as an all-pro in 1969.

Always interested in politics, Kemp had been a volunteer in Richard Nixon's presidential campaigns and a special assistant to Reagan when he was governor of California. In 1970 Kemp capitalized on his football fame to be elected to Congress as a conservative Republican in a Buffalo district where he had to win the support of blue-collar Democratic voters. He held it from then on and in 1982 was easily reelected to a seventh term with 75% of the vote.

Kemp was an early and forceful advocate of "supply side" economics—the theory that lower taxes will stimulate the economy and boost productivity, thereby creating jobs and increasing tax revenue by drawing from a broader base. The Kemp-Roth bill became a cornerstone of the Reagan economic policy. But Kemp believed the president's advisers lacked the courage to stick with it through the recession.

Kemp was born July 13, 1935, in Los Angeles. He was graduated from Occidental College in 1957. (HAL BRUNO)

Kohl, Helmut

Chairman of the West German Christian Democratic Union (CDU) and a former minister president (prime minister) of the Rhineland-Palatinate, Helmut Kohl became his country's sixth federal chancellor on Oct. 1, 1982, succeeding the Social Democrat Helmut Schmidt. He was elected in the Bundestag with the help of the liberal Free Democratic Party, which had decided to change coalition partners in midterm.

Born on April 3, 1930, in Ludwigshafen, of devout Roman Catholic parents, Kohl was brought up amid the hardships of wartime. He had to interrupt his schooling for a period of pre-military training in Bavaria. He financed his studies at Frankfurt and Heidelberg universities, where he read history, philosophy, law, and economics, by working in a chemical plant.

Kohl joined the CDU at the age of 17 and soon proved to be a natural politician. He was elected a member of the Rhineland-Palatinate Parliament in 1959, and four years later he was appointed his party's parliamentary floor leader in the state assembly. He became minister president in 1969 and won a reputation as a sound administrator. Elected chairman of the CDU in 1973, he resigned from the state premiership in 1976 to devote himself to federal politics.

Kohl fought the 1976 federal election as the chancellor candidate of the CDU and its Bavarian sister party, the Christian Social Union (CSU), under the slogan "Freedom Instead of Socialism." The CDU-CSU's poll of 48.6% was its second best result since the formation of the federal republic. But the CSU, led by the conservative Franz-Josef Strauss, had never had a high opinion of Kohl's abilities, considering him dull and provincial. In the 1980 election Strauss again contested the chancellorship and lost decisively.

Kohl was a centrist, and in his first government statement he promised that his coalition would pursue centrist policies at home and abroad. He was considered by his detractors to be too much of a generalist for the top job, although he partly compensated for his lack of specialization by a readiness to delegate authority. He was also handicapped by an inability to speak foreign languages. (NORMAN CROSSLAND)

Koivisto, Mauno Henrik

Elected Finland's chief of state in January 1982, Mauno Koivisto was dubbed the "people's president." The description fitted his background and bearing: born into the family of a ship's carpenter in 1923; a onetime dockworker who wrote a doctorate on conditions in his home port of Turku; a man who did not hide unpalatable truths from his audiences; and an amiable figure with a passion for volleyball and Gary Cooper movies who nevertheless maintained the dignified distance required by high office.

That Koivisto was the first Finnish president to emerge from the left seemed merely incidental. He was always remote from the grinding apparatus of his party, the Social Democrats, and he was obviously bored with simplistic "isms." Pragmatism was his guideline throughout his terms as prime minister (1968–70 and 1979–82) and central bank governor (1968–82), and he was not afraid to impose draconian measures when other politicians dithered.

Koivisto himself had sometimes appeared vacillating, but he could act decisively when necessary—as when his opponents used the services of his predecessor, the ailing Pres. Urho Kekkonen, in an abortive attempt to dislodge him as prime minister in April 1981. Had Koivisto quit then, he might never have become president in the election forced by Kekkonen's premature resignation, but he invoked the constitutional prerogatives bestowed on Parliament. Koivisto was eager to reactivate Parliament's role in the foreign policy debate. This was a departure, since Juho Paasikivi (president during 1946–56) and Kekkonen, whose personalities remained synonymous with Finland's neutral line, had exercised their responsibilities in this field to the fullest.

The freer atmosphere resulting from this attempt to devolve part of the great power constitutionally bestowed on any Finnish president led to some confusion. However, there was no immediate effect on Finland's international position. Koivisto stressed continuity at his meeting with Soviet Pres. Leonid Brezhnev in March. Though primarily an economist, Koivisto was quick to grasp the workings of diplomacy and this, coupled with Finland's innate stability, made the change after the 26 years of Kekkonen's presidency remarkably undramatic. (DONALD FIELDS)

Laurens, André

"The stranger in the house," a name taken from the title of Georges Simenon's novel *Les Inconnus dans la maison*, was given to André Laurens by his colleagues on *Le Monde* when, on July 1, 1982, he took over as the paper's sole manager and editor. It was easy to believe Laurens when he said that he was surprised at his appointment. Before the event it indeed seemed unlikely that, after more than two years of discussion, crises, and internal squabbles, this 48-year-old with his sing-song southern

French accent—until then deputy head of the political service and so not a member of the paper's hierarchy—should overnight become one of the most influential figures in French journalism.

The approximately 200 journalists on the staff of *Le Monde* were jointly owners of 40% of the firm's capital, and since January 1980 they had had the right to choose their editor themselves. From then on the campaign started. After a hard fight Claude Julien, editor of the paper's monthly *Le Monde Diplomatique*, was elected and in April 1981 appointed co-director. But in the fall of that year new disputes arose. Julien wrongly accused a contributor of unprofessional conduct. A majority of the editorial staff moved for a new election, and in November 1981 Julien's appointment was rescinded.

It was then that the "wise men" behind the scenes on the paper noticed Laurens, proposed him, and, to everyone's surprise, had him elected by the editorial staff with 71% of the vote on the first round. Unassuming and easy of manner, with no hint of "star" quality, Laurens had Socialist sympathies and possessed one major trump card in an atmosphere poisoned by interpersonal rivalries. He was the candidate of compromise and unity. As soon as he took office, he had to face the disturbing economic situation of *Le Monde*, which was a reflection of the problems confronting all the leading Parisian papers.

Born on Dec. 7, 1934, in Montpellier (Hérault) and having among his ancestors a grandfather who emigrated from Spain early in the century as an agricultural worker, Laurens started his journalistic career in southern France in 1954 and joined *Le Monde* in 1963. Beginning in 1972 he published several political works. (JEAN KNECHT)

Lubbers, Rudolphus Franciscus Marie

"Ruud" Lubbers became prime minister of The Netherlands in November 1982, the youngest person ever to hold that office.

Like Andreas van Agt, his predecessor, he belonged to the Roman Catholic component of the Christian Democratic Appeal (CDA). His appointment did not surprise anyone. As party leader in the lower house of Parliament since 1978, he had played an important role as mediator between the party and the government. His independence and litheness of mind at times tended to obscure the true nature of his political views and feelings. He had a reputation as a competent negotiator—a person who had at least five solutions for any one problem.

Lubbers was born on May 7, 1939, in Rotterdam. He was educated at Canisius College at Nijmegen and then at Erasmus University, Rotterdam, where he studied economics. After his graduation in 1962 he aspired to a scientific career, but circumstances led him to join the family firm of Lubbers Hollandia Engineering Works, of which he became a director in 1965. During his political career his continuing involvement with this enterprise gave his enemies an opportunity to cast doubts on his integrity. He was reputedly one of the wealthiest of Dutch politicians.

In the 1960s Lubbers belonged to the progressive part of the Catholic People's Party (KVP). He felt emotionally engaged with the Christian Radicals, a movement of progressive politicians within the three great confessional parties, but refused to become a member of the Radical Political Party, founded in 1968, because he felt he owed allegiance to the KVP. During these years he also participated actively in employers' organizations. In 1964 he became chairman of the Christian Young Employers' Organization. Later he was appointed chairman of the Catholic Employers' Organization for the Metal Industry and a member of the board of the influential Dutch Christian Employers' Organization.

From 1973 to 1977 Lubbers served as minister of economic affairs in the government headed by the Socialist Prime Minister Joop den Uyl. During that period he proved his capabilities and succeeded in winning the confidence of the Socialists. In 1977 he became vice-chairman of the CDA in the lower house. After the unexpected and emotional departure of Willem Aantjes in 1978 he was appointed chairman and thereafter was considered to be a key figure in Dutch politics.　　　　　　　　　(DICK BOONSTRA)

Ludlum, Robert

"Robert Ludlum writes spy thrillers the way the rest of us play Scrabble. Ludlum has 25 tiles with words on each, words like World War II, secret documents, Nazi war treasure, CIA.... Each year Ludlum chooses half the tiles, face down and turns them over, arranging them this way and that until some reasonably plausible sequence appears...."

His latest opus "is in fact a lousy book. So I stayed up until 3 AM to finish [reading] it. Storytellers like Ludlum sink their hooks into us, and there is only one way to wriggle free. You have to know how it all comes out...."

Thus did some critics pillory this formula writer. Ludlum's tenth novel, *The Parsifal Mosaic*, spent most of 1982 on everybody's best-seller list. Five years earlier his printings had passed the 10 million mark, and at last count his works were available in 23 languages.

Each book had a certain sameness that began with the title: *The Bourne Identity, The Matarese Circle, The Holcroft Covenant, The Chancellor Manuscript, The Gemini Contenders, The Rhinemann Exchange, The Matlock Paper, The Osterman Weekend, The Scarlatti Inheritance.* Never celebrated for their narrative style or literary complexity, Ludlum's novels are fantasies of international intrigue, vengeance, violence, and final victory for the forces of decency as defended by a spectacularly ruthless hero. Each one mixed similar elements into similar plots, and each coined money.

"I write about things that intrigue me," said the author. "I take a theatrical viewpoint . . . sort of melodramatic," he told an interviewer who described the 55-year-old New York City native as a nondescript short man with gray hair and the look of "an off duty professor." In fact, after graduating from Wesleyan University in 1951, he started out as an actor. In 1960 Ludlum founded the Playhouse on the Mall in Paramus, N.J., and found "if you could set your sights low enough in the theatre you could make a killing." After ten years of that he yearned for a change. "I thought I might get published in a small way and then go into teaching at a university or something. In 1971 his first book, *The Scarlatti Inheritance,* was published. It became an instant hit and a Book-of-the-Month Club selection.　　　　　　　(PHILIP KOPPER)

Ludwig, Daniel K.

In January 1982 U.S. shipping tycoon Daniel K. Ludwig decided to abandon his most ambitious undertaking—perhaps the largest agricultural-industrial effort ever financed by one person—the $1 billion Jari development project in Brazil. The project, named for the Amazon River tributary along which it is situated, began in 1967 with the purchase of 1.6 million ha (3.5 million ac) for a cost of $3 million, with the aim of producing saw timber and pulp. During the course of the project Ludwig created in the jungle four towns, an airport, a hospital, 4,850 km (3,000 mi) of roads, a 60-km (37-mi) freight railway, a deep-water port, and a $250 million paper and pulp mill that was built in Japan and transported by barge the 27,400 km (17,000 mi) to Jari. In addition to 114,000 ha (287,000 ac) of gmelina, pine, and eucalyptus trees for pulp and paper, there were 34,600 ha (86,500 ac) of rice fields, more than 11,000 head of cattle and buffalo, and an enormous mine for kaolin, a clay used in paper production and ceramics.

Although Ludwig's failing health was cited as the reason for abandoning Jari, observers noted many problems in the project, which had recently been losing about $100 million a year. Cost overruns, heavy management turnover (there had been some 30 project directors), disputes with the Brazilian government, and miscalculations about the demand for his products and the adaptability of the fast-growing Southeast Asian gmelina tree to the Amazon soil were all cited. By 1980 financial difficulties had led Ludwig to seek help from the Brazilian government, which was denied. The Jari project was to be taken over by about 20 leading Brazilian companies.

Born on June 24, 1897, in South Haven, Mich., Ludwig left school after the eighth grade. At the age of 19 he went into business for himself, purchasing an excursion boat for $5,000 and converting it into a barge. He later specialized in profitable oil transport. In the 1930s he introduced to the tanker trade the practice of chartering ships before they were built and using the charters as collateral for shipbuilding loans. By the end of World War II Ludwig controlled almost all world oil shipping. He is credited with the development of efficient supertankers, giant ships that can handle cargo more cheaply than several small ships.　　　　　　(JOAN N. BOTHELL)

Madrid Hurtado, Miguel de la

Elected president of Mexico on July 4, 1982, Miguel de la Madrid assumed power on December 1 for a six-year term. At his inauguration he announced a ten-point plan to combat the country's grave financial crisis. The measures he proposed were in line with the economic policies he had outlined in his election campaign as being essential for Mexico's recovery. They included cuts in public spending, selective investment in labour-intensive industries, and a campaign to drive out corruption. His government was expected to adopt a low profile in foreign affairs and to support reasonable free-market policies when the economic situation improved.

Miguel de la Madrid Hurtado was born in Colima (capital of the state of the same name) on Dec. 12, 1934. He received his primary and secondary education in Mexico City and obtained a law degree with honours at the Universidad Nacional Autónoma (UNAM) in 1957, submitting a dissertation on "Economic Thought in the 1857 Constitution." In 1963 he became a member of the Partido Revolucionario Institucional (PRI). He obtained a master's degree in public administration at Harvard in 1964–65.

During 1953–57 de la Madrid worked in the legal department of the National Foreign Trade Bank. In 1960 he became a consultant to management in the Banco de México, the central bank, which he left in 1965 to spend five years as subdirector of credit in the Secretariat of Finance and Public Credit. From 1970 until April 1972 he

operated as subdirector of finance at Petró-leos Mexicanos (PEMEX), the nationalized oil company, but in May he rejoined the Secretariat of Finance as director general of credit. He was appointed undersecretary of finance in October 1975 and from May 1979 occupied the post of secretary for programming and the budget.

On various occasions de la Madrid acted as counselor to bodies concerned with exports and finance, and he was a member of several related technical committees. He attended many economically oriented international meetings on behalf of the government, particularly annual International Monetary Fund, World Bank, and Inter-American Development Bank meetings. He published a book on constitutional law, *Estudios de Derecho Constitucional*, and taught at the UNAM law faculty from 1968.

(BARBARA WIJNGAARD)

Marcinkus, Msgr. Paul Casimir

Archbishop Paul Marcinkus first became known to the general public as the tall, balding bodyguard who was always seen shepherding Pope John Paul II on his many international journeys. But in 1982 he became better known in his other role as president of the "Vatican bank" (strictly, the Institute for Religious Works, IOR). The Italian authorities wished to question him about the involvement of the IOR in the Banco Ambrosiano of Milan, which had failed. Its president, Roberto Calvi, was found hanged under Blackfriars Bridge in London on June 18.

Born Jan. 15, 1922, in Cicero, Ill., to immigrant Lithuanian parents, Marcinkus was ordained a priest in 1947. After serving in a Chicago parish, he entered the Pontifical Ecclesiastical Academy in 1952, served as papal diplomat in Bolivia and Canada, and became one of the inner circle of advisers to Pope Paul VI. The chaos of the first papal journey abroad—to the Holy Land in 1964—persuaded the pope to put Marcinkus in charge of future trips. In this he was highly successful. In Manila in 1970 he helped to subdue a deranged Brazilian painter who had approached the pope, knife in hand.

Marcinkus's brusque style offended some, but Paul VI made him bishop and put him in charge of the IOR in 1969. He had no special training in international finance and had to learn on the job. This brought him into contact with various Italian bankers who were not all above suspicion. He worked first with Michele Sindona (currently serving a 25-year sentence for fraud in New York State) and Roberto Calvi. His most imprudent act was to provide Calvi with "letters of comfort" to reassure Ambrosiano's creditors as late as August 1981, at a time when the bank appeared to be doomed. The fact that Calvi gave him in exchange a secret assurance that the IOR would not be liable for any losses incurred by the Banco Ambrosiano looked like conspiracy.

As of the end of 1982 Marcinkus had escaped questioning by staying inside the Vatican. No one suggested that he gained any personal advantage from his financial deals. His misfortune was to be sucked into the Italian banking world. In December it was announced that the Vatican and the Italian government had agreed to set up a joint six-man committee to investigate the IOR-Banco Ambrosiano connection. Meanwhile, Marcinkus no longer acted as the pope's travel organizer and bodyguard, but he remained governor of Vatican City State.

(PETER HEBBLETHWAITE)

Mercouri, Melina

For Melina Mercouri, the talented Greek actress, the role of culture and science minister of her country's first Socialist government was perhaps the most demanding of her temperamental career. "The first thing this country needs," she said, "is cultural decentralization. The cultural revolution must reach the smallest Greek village." A pet project of hers was to induce the British government to return the Elgin Marbles—"the Parthenon marbles," as she put it emphatically, "which are an integral part of our national heritage." (The marbles, removed from Greece by Lord Elgin during 1803–12, had been housed in the British Museum since 1816.)

Politics might be her second career, but the seed of politics was implanted almost at birth. Her grandfather was mayor of Athens, and her father was a Cabinet minister and later a left-wing politician. Born in Athens on Oct. 18, 1925, Mercouri graduated from the Drama School of the National Theatre of Greece. Her first major role, at the age of 20, was Electra in Eugene O'Neill's *Mourning Becomes Electra*, but perhaps her most memorable parts were Blanche in *A Streetcar Named Desire* and the good-hearted prostitute in the film *Never on Sunday*. It was this film that gained her an international reputation that would serve her well in politics. But what made the seed of politics germinate was her indignation over the military coup that brought a handful of inept army colonels to power in Greece in 1967.

Married to the French-born U.S. film director Jules Dassin (who directed most of her films), she was abroad when the coup occurred. From the first day she dedicated herself to stimulating opposition against the junta in Europe and the U.S., to the extent that she was deprived of her Greek nationality by the colonels' regime. After the collapse of the dictatorship in 1974, she returned to Greece and promptly joined Andreas Papandreou's Panhellenic Socialist Movement (Pasok). She ran unsuccessfully that year for deputy from the same destitute Piraeus district that had made her famous in *Never on Sunday*, but she was luckier the second time round in 1977. Reelected in 1981 when Pasok swept the polls, she was promptly appointed by Papandreou to be his minister for culture. In 1971 Mercouri published an autobiography, *I Was Born Greek*.

(MARIO MODIANO)

Moi, Daniel Torotich arap

Kenya's reputation as one of Africa's stablest countries was severely shaken by an attempted military coup led by elements in its Air Force in August 1982. Although Pres. Daniel arap Moi was able to put down the challenge with relative ease (but at the cost of several hundred lives), it revealed something of the true extent of economic and political discontent in the country, accentuated since the death of the nation's founding father, Jomo Kenyatta, in 1978. Moi was unfortunate in having come to office at a time when Kenya's rapid economic growth had begun to decline, due mainly to the international financial situation. This meant growing unemployment and fewer opportunities for young Kenyans.

Although President Moi was widely respected, he lacked the charisma of Kenyatta and had no strong independent political base of his own, coming as he did from one of the clans of the minority Kalenjin community. An astute politician, he sought to identify his leadership with Kenyatta's by calling for a policy of *nyayo*, that is, following in the "footsteps" of Kenyatta. But while this slogan was popular among many in the dominant Kikuyu community, it found much less appeal among the second strongest community, the Luo, or among the nation's youth. Although himself a former teacher, Moi found it difficult to win the support of the country's intellectuals. Troubles with university students and staff were a continuing feature of his rule.

Moi was born at Sacho in the Baringo district of Rift Valley Province in 1924 and received a traditional Christian missionary education. He first entered politics as a bitter opponent of Kenyatta and an outspoken critic of the Kikuyu-led Mau Mau revolt. Fearing domination by the Kikuyu and Luo, he was prominent in establishing the Kenya African Democratic Union (KADU), which favoured a federal type of constitution for the country. During the colonial period he became minister of education in 1961 and later minister of local government. But after independence in 1963, Moi joined Kenyatta's ruling party and became minister for home affairs in 1964 and vice-president in 1967. He was rewarded by being made Kenyatta's designated successor.

(COLIN LEGUM)

Moseley, Mark

Snow was falling, the wind was swirling, and the Washington Redskins were trailing 14–12 with four seconds to play when Mark Moseley lined up for a 42-yd field-goal attempt on Dec. 19, 1982. An opponent tipped the ball, but Moseley kicked it hard enough to put it between the goalposts, winning the game for Washington and breaking the previous National Football League record of 20 consecutive field goals.

Moseley kicked 23 in a row, including 3 in 1981, before missing his final 1982 attempt from 40 yd. His 20-for-21 kicking in one season set an NFL record for field-goal percentage with .952. He led the league in field goals and made the all-star Pro Bowl team for the second time. Most important, Moseley's kicks were the difference in five Redskin victories, two on the last play, prompting the Associated Press to make him the first kicker ever to win the NFL's most valuable player award. In Washington's 27–17 victory over Miami in the Super Bowl Moseley kicked two field goals.

"We just keep it close and let Mark kick the field goals," Washington coach Joe Gibbs said. But Moseley was nearly released by Gibbs before the season began. His field-goal percentage the previous two seasons had been .587 on 37-for-63, unacceptable even though he had brought the

85

Redskins from behind to win three games with late kicks and even though he had been 22-for-27 from inside 40 yd. For the 1982 season Moseley did not make the team until his rookie challenger missed two field-goal attempts in the final exhibition game.

Moseley, born March 12, 1948, in Lanesville, Texas, was hardly an instant success in the NFL. Philadelphia cut him in 1971 after one season, and Houston cut him in 1973 after one season, one game, and an injury. From there he returned to Stephen F. Austin State University for his degree. But he continued kicking, and Washington signed him in 1974.

Through 1982, Moseley's career field-goal percentage of .641 was not far behind the NFL record of .688, even though more than half his 273 attempts with Washington had been from 40 yd or farther. His percentage from that distance in nine Redskin seasons was a remarkable .493, despite the apparent disadvantage of kicking with his toe instead of using the instep, soccer style, as 26 of 28 NFL kickers did in 1982.

(KEVIN M. LAMB)

Nakasone, Yasuhiro

With the selection of 64-year-old Yasuhiro Nakasone as Japan's prime minister on Nov. 26, 1982, the nation presumed Japanese interests would be more forcefully defended than they had been under the former head of government, Zenko Suzuki. Nakasone, who had been the director general of the Administrative Management Agency, had demonstrated his well-known political talents by first outpolling three other Liberal-Democratic Party (LDP) candidates who challenged him for the party presidency. Only the rank and file members of the LDP were allowed to cast ballots. By garnering 57% of the vote, Nakasone was all but assured of the party presidency when the LDP members of the Diet (parliament) made their choice. The presidency of the LDP brought with it the prime ministership.

Though the LDP had held power in Japan since it was founded in 1955, its rule had been severely hampered by bitter factional divisions. Nakasone's victory, therefore, had to be won with the backing of political kingmakers. Chief among those was former prime minister Kakuei Tanaka, who was driven from office when he was accused of involvement in the Lockheed bribery scandal. Though the still incomplete court proceedings began in 1977, Tanaka had remained a powerful force within the LDP, as was immediately evident when six of his closest associates were named to Cabinet posts in the new government.

Nakasone was born in Takasaki City, Gumma Prefecture, on May 27, 1918, the son of a wealthy lumber dealer. He was graduated from Tokyo University School of Law in 1941 and saw action during World War II with the Imperial Japanese Navy. In 1947 he was elected to the first of 14 successive terms in the Diet and in 1959 received a Cabinet post. Subsequently, he held portfolios in science and technology, defense, and international trade and industry.

Cosmopolitan by choice and capable of carrying on conversations in English and French, Nakasone had earned a reputation among foreign diplomats as a no-nonsense straight talker. Though said to have admired the stubborn independence of the late French president Charles de Gaulle, Nakasone clearly intended to continue Japan's close relationship with the U.S. He nonetheless kept his options open on the role Japan would play in the defense of the free world and what economic and trade policies he would pursue. All of these issues were of paramount importance to the Japanese people.

(ROWLAND GOULD)

Nattrass, Susan

For avid competitor Susan Nattrass winning was always a priority. Gaining the women's world trapshooting championship in 1981 gave her the best-ever record in that sport, six consecutive world championships. In recognition of her achievement the Sports Federation of Canada named her the female athlete of the year (1982). She also received the Lou Marsh Trophy as Canadian overall athlete of the year (1981).

Born on Nov. 5, 1950, in Medicine Hat, Alta., Nattrass was introduced to trapshooting at the age of 12 by her father, Floyd Nattrass, himself a champion in the sport and a member of the 1964 Canadian Olympic trapshooting team. Susan Nattrass's first international win came in Reno, Nev., in 1969, when she triumphed over 1,300 other competitors in a trapshooting meet. After that victory she set her sights on world and Olympic Games competition. She won the North American ladies' trapshooting championship every year, beginning in 1972; and she had been the Canadian women's trapshooting champion since 1968. In 1969 she began competing in women's world championships. She finished fourth in 1969 and 1970, second in 1971, and won the gold medal for the first time in 1975. In the 1976 Olympic Games held in Montreal, Nattrass was a member of the Canadian team, the first woman to participate in trapshooting in Olympic competition. However, she finished a disappointing 25th.

Competing in both American- and international-style trapshooting, Nattrass won all her major victories in international style. In American style the clay pigeon travels 80 km/h (50 mph), and the shooter has the gun at the shoulder when the target is launched. In international style the pigeon travels at 145 km/h (90 mph), and the shooter has the gun below the waist when the target is launched.

During the winter, when training became difficult because of the weather, Nattrass concentrated on volleyball, squash, and skiing to maintain her reflexes. She also worked toward her degree in physical education. She earned a B.A. at the University of Alberta and an M.A. at the University of Waterloo. While working on her Ph.D. in the sociology of sports at the University of Alberta, she taught physical education and was a sports coach there.

(DIANE LOIS WAY)

Palme, (Sven) Olof Joachim

The return to power of Olof Palme in Sweden's general election on Sept. 19, 1982, brought back to centre stage the man who, even in opposition, remained the nation's best-known international politician. He was chairman of the Independent Commission on Disarmament and Security Issues, which presented its report, *Common Security*, in 1982, and a member of the earlier Independent Commission on International Development Issues (the Brandt Commission). He also had the thankless task of being the UN special emissary in peace negotiations between Iran and Iraq.

At 55, Palme remained a contentious figure on the domestic scene, his peppery style somewhat out of keeping with the generally low-key mood of Swedish politics. The 1982 election was a "make or break" one for him. The Social Democrats' fortunes had declined rapidly after he took over the leadership in 1969, a process that culminated in their loss of power in 1976 after 44 years in office. He led the party to a second defeat in 1979, and it was doubtful whether he could have survived a third.

Born on Jan. 30, 1927, into a wealthy Stockholm family, Palme gained a scholarship to the U.S. where he took a B.A. degree at Kenyon College, Gambier, Ohio, in 1948. On his return to Sweden, he graduated in law at Stockholm University and in 1953 was appointed secretary to the then prime minister, Tage Erlander. A Social Democrat member of Parliament from 1957, he held several ministerial positions from 1963 to October 1969, when he was elected party chairman and took over the premiership following Erlander's resignation.

Critics within the Social Democratic Party accused Palme of being "too clever by half." One of the most vociferous, Valter Aman, a 77-year-old veteran of Swedish Socialism and the man responsible for drafting much of Sweden's job security legislation, condemned him for lowering the standard of political debate. Palme's victory in 1982 stemmed the tide of such criticism and secured, at least for the time being, his position at the helm of both party and nation.

(CHRIS MOSEY)

Pawley, Howard

In the Manitoba provincial election of Nov. 17, 1981, the New Democratic Party won a majority of the 57 seats in the Manitoba legislature. Party leader Howard Pawley was sworn in on Nov. 30, 1981, as the 19th premier of the province. Emphasizing economic renewal, Pawley believed that the provincial government should spend money in order to bring Manitoba out of its economic recession. Once in office, he moved to do just that. A mortgage interest rate relief plan was implemented, as was an income stabilization plan for beef producers. Tenants were not neglected; rent increases were limited to 9% on all older buildings.

Pawley's victory surprised many observers. However, with his easygoing demeanour he had shown himself to be an effective grass-roots politician. First elected to the provincial legislature in 1969, he became the most junior minister in the Cabinet of Premier Edward Schreyer. From 1969 to 1976 he was minister of municipal affairs and was so popular in that position that the municipal secretaries in Manitoba complained when in 1973 Schreyer decided to move him to another Cabinet post. As a result, Pawley retained the municipal affairs portfolio when he became Manitoba's attorney general and keeper of the great seal in 1973. Known as a civil libertarian, Pawley had a hand in several pioneering pieces of legislation. Among them were an automobile insurance bill, a bill outlawing wiretapping, and a bill opening credit files to customers.

Pawley was born on Nov. 21, 1934, in Brampton, Ont. He received an undergraduate degree at the University of Winnipeg and a law degree at the University of Manitoba, and before his entrance into politics he was a practicing lawyer in Selkirk. When he first ran for provincial office in 1958, he was defeated. Two attempts to gain political office in federal elections also ended in failure. However, in 1969 the people of the provincial riding of Selkirk elected him to serve as their representative in the Manitoba legislature.

The government of Edward Schreyer was defeated in the provincial election of 1977, but Pawley retained his seat in the legislature. When Schreyer resigned his post as leader of the Manitoba New Democratic Party to accept the position of governor-general of Canada, Pawley succeeded him.

(DIANE LOIS WAY)

Pérez de Cuéllar, Javier

As his second five-year term neared its end late in 1981, Kurt Waldheim, the secretary-general of the United Nations, was seeking reelection. Waldheim, an Austrian, represented an effectively neutral nation in the East-West conflict. He was opposed by Salim A. Salim, foreign minister of Tanzania and a spokesman for the economic interests of the less developed countries.

In order to win election, one of the candidates had to gain the unanimous approval of all five permanent members of the UN Security Council—the United States, the Soviet Union, Great Britain, France, and China. After being chosen by the Security Council, a candidate had to win majority approval from the General Assembly, where every UN member country has a vote.

The U.S. opposed Salim's candidacy and vetoed him in the Security Council. China did the same with Waldheim, and the UN thus appeared to be deadlocked. But on Dec. 11, 1981, in an unexpected move, the Security Council agreed on Javier Pérez de Cuéllar of Peru. Subsequently, he won approval in the General Assembly.

Pérez de Cuéllar's major goal for his term in office was to help achieve independence for Namibia, the territory also known as South West Africa. In 1982 Namibia was controlled by South Africa, a country whose policies of racial separation made it unpopular throughout the world. "I can't forget I come from the third world," Pérez de Cuéllar said. "I have to give priorities. I've committed myself to solve this problem as soon as possible."

Pérez de Cuéllar was born on Jan. 19, 1920, in Lima, Peru. He joined the Foreign Ministry in 1940 after graduating from Catholic University in Lima. Subsequently, he held numerous diplomatic posts in Europe and Latin America. Before his election as secretary-general, Pérez de Cuéllar had been serving as the UN's special representative to negotiate a Soviet withdrawal from Afghanistan.

(VICTOR M. CASSIDY)

Peterson, Roger Tory

More than 30,000 birders hiked through forests and prairies, clambered through thickets, and splashed through swamps in Canada, the U.S., and the Caribbean for the 1982 Audubon Society's Christmas Bird Count. For this important annual wildlife survey, standard equipment included a pair of binoculars and what has become the birdwatcher's bible, Roger Tory Peterson's *A Field Guide to the Birds*. Peterson's *Guide* for the eastern U.S., first published in 1934 and now in its fourth edition (1980), had sold approximately two million copies by 1982. The latest edition made the *New York Times* best-seller list, and the first sold out in one week in the midst of the Depression. A companion volume for the western U.S. had sold more than one million copies.

Peterson's stroke of genius in developing the guides was to realize that what the amateur needed was a mentor in the form of a pocket-sized reference work that grouped similar birds and pointed out the distinctive markings of each, the "field marks" that enabled the birder to identify each species at a distance. The 1980 edition, the first in 33 years, was completely redone to incorporate new observations and add new species, including several escapes into the wild by domesticated species. All birds are pictured in colour, with helpful detail drawings of beaks, feet, and heads. Birds are shown in flight as well as at rest. A description of the behaviour, song, and habitat faces the illustration. The phenomenal success of the two guides to the birds encouraged the issuing of 23 other Peterson *Field Guides*, ranging from mammals through minerals and animal tracks.

In 1982, at age 74, Peterson was at work repainting some of the plates for the western *Guide*. He was born on Aug. 28, 1908, in Jamestown, N.Y., and trained at the Art Students League and National Academy of Design in New York City. He has been engaged in painting birds and illustrating and writing bird books since the 1930s, contributing to more than one hundred titles as author, illustrator, or editor. In 1981 Peterson reached a milestone in his career: he completed his U.S. life list, the ornithologist's tabulation of sightings of all of the bird species that breed in the U.S. On an April day in the sandhills of northern Texas, Peterson sighted his last bird, the lesser prairie chicken. (ANITA WOLFF)

Planinc, Milka

Under the system of rotation of offices within the federal government of Yugoslavia, Milka Planinc took office on May 16, 1982, the country's—and Eastern Europe's—first woman head of government. A Croatian, she was appointed by the Federal Assembly to succeed Veselin Djuranovic, a Montenegrin, as president of the Federal Executive Council for a four-year term.

Because of the active role she played in Croatian politics, Premier Planinc had the reputation of being something of an "iron lady." Once in office, she acted to increase the federal government's effectiveness (previously limited by the national government's decision-making powers) in combating Yugoslavia's mounting economic problems. Among these were an inflation rate of approximately 30%, a per capita for-

CAMERA PRESS, LONDON

eign indebtedness greater than that of Poland, and an unemployment rate exceeding 13% of the work force. Planinc's measures included the introduction of a greater number of technocrats, particularly economists, into the new government; the raising of the price of gasoline, for the third time in a year, to the highest in Europe; a price freeze affecting all goods and services apart from privately grown fruit and vegetables for a minimum six-month period beginning in July; and notice to the effect that a wage freeze might also be imposed.

Milka Planinc was born in November 1924 at Drnis, Croatia. She graduated in 1941 from the Senior Administrative School in Zagreb, the Croatian capital. During the same year she joined the Communist Youth Union of Yugoslavia, and in 1943 she was accepted as a soldier of the Yugoslav Liberation Army. After the war she joined the Yugoslav Communist Party (which in 1952 was renamed the League of Communists). In 1961 Planinc was appointed head of the Secretariat for Education and Culture in Zagreb. Two years later she was promoted to be the secretary for education and science of the republic of Croatia. She established her political reputation as a loyal supporter of Tito, whom she helped to overcome the outbreak of Croatian nationalism in 1971. A member of the Central Committee of the Croatian branch of the League of Communists since 1959, she became its chairman in 1971 and also a member of the federal Executive Committee.

(K. M. SMOGORZEWSKI)

Podborski, Steve

Seven years of disciplined and concentrated training rewarded Steve Podborski when he became the World Cup downhill ski champion for the 1981–82 season. In the ten-race circuit of the World Cup, scoring is based on five races out of the ten. Podborski garnered three first-place, two second-place, and two fourth-place finishes to end the season with 115 points out of a possible 125. He was the first male North American to capture the World Cup downhill title.

Born on July 25, 1957, Podborski grew up in Don Mills, Ont., a section of Toronto. At the age of two he was introduced to skiing by his parents. His mother, Jackie Podborski, Alpine Ski chairman for southern Ontario and a member of the Canadian Ski Association, was the driving force behind his skiing career. He spent his early years training on a 180-m (600-ft) peak in Ontario, a fact many skiers find hard to believe since the minimum fall in a World Cup downhill course is 910 m (3,000 ft). At the age of 9 Podborski started racing in southern Ontario, and at 13 he competed in the Canadian juvenile championships in British Columbia. In 1974 he went to the fall selection competition of the Canadian national ski team. He won all five downhill races there and made the team. Thus began his career as a World Cup racer.

Podborski's first true win on the World Cup circuit took place in 1981 on the Corviglia downhill course in Saint-Moritz, Switz. He won the next two races on the circuit, at Garmisch-Partenkirchen, West Germany, and at Kitzbühel, Austria. He was the first to win three races in a row since world champion Franz Klammer in 1971. At the end of the 1980–81 season Podborski was ranked as the world's premier downhill skier, but he lost the World Cup championship that year by 0.28 sec.

Podborski was a competitor at the 1980 Olympic Games, where he won the bronze medal in downhill skiing. When an accident on the slopes in May 1980 threatened to end his skiing career, he instituted a rigorous training program. Just six months after surgery on his knee he was back on the slopes skiing—and winning. In recognition of his achievements the Sports Federation of Canada named him the Canadian male athlete of the year for 1982.

(DIANE LOIS WAY)

Podhoretz, Norman

Norman Podhoretz, editor in chief since 1960 of *Commentary* magazine, is a neoconservative, a person who relatively recently has been converted to the belief that accommodation with the Soviet Union and other Communist powers is impossible. His views, both past and present, became the subject of controversy in 1982 after he published *Why We Were in Vietnam,* an analysis of U.S. involvement in that war, and "J' Accuse," a defense of Israel and its foreign policy.

In *Why We Were in Vietnam* Podhoretz makes three major points: (1) U.S. entry into the Vietnam war was "an act of imprudent idealism whose moral soundness was overwhelmingly vindicated by the hideous consequences of our defeat"; (2) the effort required to win the war exceeded the "intellectual and moral capabilities" of the U.S. government and its people; and (3) the antiwar movement must accept "a certain measure of responsibility for the horrors that have overtaken the people of Vietnam."

Podhoretz's book provoked a fresh examination of U.S. involvement in Vietnam. Critics accused him of oversimplifying history, confusing the good intentions of American leaders with the evil effects of their deeds, and unreasonably condemning many who opposed the war. (Podhoretz himself had originally been among them).

Podhoretz has become one of the leaders of the neoconservative movement. In the past most Jewish intellectuals in the U.S. were political liberals, and serious Jewish magazines such as *Commentary* reflected a liberal point of view. As U.S. intellectual and political conservatism gained popularity during the 1970s, Podhoretz broke ranks and began to lead *Commentary* rightward.

In "J' Accuse" Podhoretz replied to critics of the Israeli military occupation of Lebanon by arguing that the invasion was a necessity and that Israel was a peace-seeking democracy. He went on to call Israel a tireless enemy of Soviet expansionism, a nation almost uniquely willing among those of the West to make the sacrifices necessary to its survival.

Podhoretz had spent virtually his entire working career at *Commentary*, which is sponsored by the American Jewish Committee. He joined the publication as assistant editor in 1955, left after three years for another publishing job, and then returned to take command in 1960. Born on Jan. 16, 1930, in Brooklyn, N.Y., he obtained bachelor's degrees in 1950 from Columbia University and the Jewish Theological Seminary. He then went to Cambridge University as a Kellett fellow where he obtained a B.A. degree in 1952 and an M.A. five years later. (VICTOR M. CASSIDY)

Pritchard, John Michael

A brisk, thoroughgoing musician of wide sympathies, John Pritchard was confirmed in 1982 as principal conductor of the BBC (British Broadcasting Corporation) Symphony Orchestra in succession to Gennadi Rozhdestvensky. It was a safe choice in a time of considerable economic and artistic uncertainty. He had been chief guest conductor of the BBC Symphony since 1979 and chief conductor of the Cologne (West Germany) Opera from 1978.

The son of a distinguished orchestral violinist, Pritchard was born in London on Feb. 5, 1921. He studied piano, viola, and organ under a number of teachers before, in his teens, visiting Italy to study orchestral and operatic rehearsal methods at first hand. Following a spell as conductor of the largely amateur Derby String Orchestra (to which he was appointed in 1943), Pritchard was invited to the Glyndebourne Festival Opera (Sussex, England) in 1947 as a coach. There Fritz Busch, the doyen of Glyndebourne conductors since the house's foundation in 1934, took a keen interest in Pritchard's abilities, infusing him with his own strict concepts of musical excellence. At the same time, Pritchard served as assistant to other major Glyndebourne conductors, among them Rafael Kubelik, Fritz Stiedry, and the veteran Vittorio Gui.

In 1951 the 30-year-old Pritchard found himself in charge of his first full Glyndebourne production, Mozart's *Don Giovanni.* The previous year he had succeeded Reginald Jacques as conductor of the Jacques Orchestra, and in 1952 he substituted, at short notice, for ailing Swiss maestro Ernest Ansermet at the Edinburgh International Festival. Following a spell at Austria's Vienna State Opera, Pritchard in 1955 was appointed principal conductor of the Royal Liverpool Philharmonic Orchestra, a post he held for a number of years. During that time he promoted an especially enterprising "Musica Viva" series of contemporary music programs, in which (under Pritchard's aegis) other young conductors could gain wide experience. In 1955 he conducted, at London's Royal Opera House, Covent Garden, the premiere of Sir Michael Tippett's *The Midsummer Marriage.* Pritchard was made a CBE in 1962 and was to be knighted in the New Year's honours in January 1983. (MOZELLE A. MOSHANSKY)

Pryor, Richard

In 1980 black comedian Richard Pryor literally caught fire; he accidentally immolated himself while handling a volatile cocaine mixture. In a comic skit concocted after the accident he asks hypothetically what he learned from the experience: "When you're on fire and running down the street, people will get out of your way."

Defusing anxiety with comic common sense is a Pryor trademark: the willingness to look life square in the face and see that it's cross-eyed. As a colleague said, "There is one single reason for his success. Richard tells the truth about the human condition. That's what makes his comedy so wonderful."

Born in Peoria, Ill., on Dec. 1, 1940, Pryor dropped out of school and worked at menial jobs, all the while developing his comic sensibility "on the corner," as he put it. He began working as a comedian in small clubs in Peoria after serving in the Army and first received national exposure in 1966 with appearances on several television variety shows. He acted in his first film role in 1967 and by 1982 had appeared in more than 25 movies.

Successful on the screen and the nightclub stage, Pryor not only drew grist from his own life but wrote all his own material. "Pryor on Fire," his finale at the Hollywood Palladium, was the "reenactment of his incendiary ordeal." The act, according to *Newsweek*'s Jack Kroll, was "a psychodrama at once mirthful and merciless in which he plays everything from himself . . . to the free-base pipe that speaks to Pryor with satanic seductiveness."

Pryor's movies include vehicles shared with black singer Diana Ross (the Billie Holiday biography *The Lady Sings the Blues*) and white comic Gene Wilder (*Silver Streak* and *Stir Crazy*). Other films include *Greased Lightning, The Wiz, Bustin' Loose,* and *California Suite.* While a television series was short-lived, in part because of network censorship, he won an Emmy award for a performance with Lily Tomlin. His most famous works are hybridized: concert performances filmed piecemeal and then edited into one-man movies. Highly unusual in style and content, two have been enormously successful: *Richard Pryor Live in Concert* and *Richard Pryor Live on the Sunset Strip.* (PHILIP KOPPER)

Pym, Francis Leslie

In April 1982, amid the crisis brought by the Argentine invasion of the Falkland Islands, Francis Pym suddenly found himself appointed British foreign secretary. Lord Carrington, seemingly as firm a fixture as anyone in the U.K. Cabinet, had felt obliged to resign as foreign secretary because of the failure of his department to read Argentine intentions correctly. At a moment when international negotiations would be of crucial importance, Prime Minister Margaret Thatcher turned to Pym. He was not a foreign affairs expert, but for the first two years of the Thatcher government he had been secretary of state for defense. Just as important perhaps, he understood the Conservative Party better than anyone in the Cabinet, and the party was in angry disarray.

After becoming an MP in 1961, Pym had spent much of his parliamentary career as a "whip" in the administrative office of the party in the House of Commons. As chief whip in the Edward Heath government of 1970–73 and as leader of the Commons since 1981, he was the recognized professional in the business of keeping the party in line. It might be said to run in the family; his father had been a Conservative MP and a whip before him.

Born on Feb. 13, 1922, Pym had the classic Conservative roots in the landed gentry, the traditional education—at Eton College and the University of Cambridge—and a distinguished war record. This was not necessarily the best qualification for the middle-class, aggressive individualism of the Thatcher wing of the party. In fact, Pym was not in Thatcher's inner ring of confidants and had expressed his doubts about monetarism and the prospects for the economy with some bluntness.

Pym's first mission as foreign secretary, securing a negotiated settlement of the Falklands crisis, failed, but he won the respect and confidence of the diplomatic world by his sharp mind and by a combination of realism and toughness. He had hoped to get the Foreign Office post when the Thatcher government was formed in 1979. After circumstances brought him the appointment, he was soon regarded as a great success. Observers of the Westminster scene even began to talk of Pym as the most likely successor to Thatcher as party leader.

(HARFORD THOMAS)

Reagan, Nancy

If 1981 was a year of criticism for the wife of U.S. Pres. Ronald Reagan because of her social life and expensive tastes, 1982 was a

KATHERINE YOUNG

year of more positive reaction to her work on two social issues—drug abuse among young people, which she believed was related to the breakdown in traditional family life, and the foster grandparents program, which brings together the elderly and handicapped children. In mid-February 1982 Nancy Reagan began her antidrug campaign by traveling to Florida and Texas, where she visited various facilities to draw attention to the problem. In March she participated in the White House Conference on Drug Use and Families. In support of the foster grandparents program she provided an introduction to a book of case studies entitled *To Love a Child*, published in the fall of 1982.

Critics charged that her work on these two issues was intended primarily to draw attention from her public image as a rich man's wife who cared little about the economic problems of ordinary people, an image that arose during her first year in the White House, when she spent some $800,-000 to redecorate the living quarters and $200,000 to buy new china. Although these funds came from private contributions, the expenditures were attacked as insensitive in a time of severe recession and federal budget cuts in social welfare programs. The controversy erupted again in 1982 when it was revealed that Mrs. Reagan had accepted free clothes from high-fashion designers, including a $10,000 gown that she wore to the inaugural ball and that was later donated to the Smithsonian Institution.

Nancy Reagan had always said that her first duty was to her family, particularly to her husband, Ronald Reagan. They were married in 1952, when both were actors in Hollywood. Nancy Reagan soon gave up her acting career to become a homemaker. After her husband was elected governor of California in 1966, she became involved in the foster grandparents program and worked to expand it nationwide.

She was born Anne Frances Robbins in New York City. Her official biography gives her birthday as July 6, 1923, though school records state the year as 1921. After her mother's divorce and remarriage she was adopted by her stepfather, a Chicago surgeon, and became Nancy (a nickname from infancy) Davis. She was graduated from Smith College in 1943 and worked as an actress on Broadway and later in motion pictures.

(JOAN N. BOTHELL)

Reagan, Ronald Wilson

Midway through his term in office, U.S. Pres. Ronald Reagan in 1982 confronted significant tests of his policies. The political momentum that had carried him successfully through 1981 stalled in 1982, primarily because of the nation's deepening recession.

Voter disenchantment with Reagan and his policies was expressed in the congressional elections of November 1982. Although they maintained their six-seat margin in the Senate, the Republicans lost 26 seats in the House of Representatives. Thus it seemed certain that it would be more difficult in the future for administration bills to win the approval of Congress.

The legislative independence of Congress had already stung Reagan when his effort to gain production funding for the MX missile was defeated by the House of Representa-

tives in December. This marked the first time since World War II that either house of Congress had voted to deny a major weapons system to a president. The vote, in which 50 Republicans opposed the president, was an indication that Reagan's policy of increasing military spending while cutting expenditures on other programs would meet increased resistance. Also affecting the outlook for a military buildup were projected annual federal budget deficits of almost $200 billion.

The deficits seemed certain to influence the future of another of Reagan's key policies, the 10% cut in the federal income tax, scheduled to become operative in July 1983. Reagan was expected to be unwilling to compromise on the tax cut, maintaining that it was necessary for the success of his economic program.

The economy presented Reagan with his greatest challenge in 1982. Though he could point with satisfaction to reductions in annual inflation rates from 13.1 to 4.8% and in interest rates from 21 to 11.5% during his first two years in office, he also had to face the slowdown in the growth of the national economy that resulted in an unemployment rate of 10.8% by the end of the year. Congress responded to the problem with Republican- and Democratic-sponsored jobs bills, the latter more far-ranging and expensive.

Reagan was active in foreign affairs in 1982. He traveled to Central and South America and, in his most ambitious initiative, attempted to involve Jordan's King Hussein in talks with Israel and Egypt on Palestinian self-rule.

(DAVID R. CALHOUN)

Ríos Montt, Efraín

According to reliable sources Gen. Efraín Ríos Montt was busy conducting a Bible class when, in a bloodless coup on March 23, 1982, a group of junior army officers asked him to become president of Guatemala. As a born-again Christian (albeit a Protestant in a predominantly Roman Catholic country) and as a man not involved in army infighting, the 55-year-old general was considered a suitable leader to reform his troubled country.

Ríos Montt was remembered by the officers as the commander of the Honour Guard Brigade and chief of staff as well as for teaching at the Military Academy. By others he was respected for his nomination as the Christian Democrat candidate in the 1974 elections. Indeed, had the election votes been counted and adhered to, it was believed he might then have secured the presidency. Instead, he was ousted from the country and given the post of military attaché in Spain. In 1978 he found himself attracted by the evangelical teachings of the California-based Church of the Christian Word. He renounced his Catholic faith, and under Pres. Fernando Romeo Lucas García's new regime was allowed to return home as a lay preacher. The Bible had become his textbook, and even as a military instructor he believed that trust in "God, my master and my King" alone would conquer the iniquities of political parties, which he came to regard as "sick and miserable" species.

The euphoria that greeted his appointment as president was short-lived. Any hopes held for an improvement in Guatemala's human rights situation were soon shattered; the June amnesty for political prisoners was replaced by a state of siege that limited the activities of political parties and labour unions under the threat of death by firing squad, and the campaign known as *frijoles y fusiles* ("beans and guns"), initiated by the president in an attempt to win over the large Indian population to the rule of the army, resulted in a nightmare of chaos and violence. By the end of 1982 Ríos Montt was claiming that the war against the leftist guerrillas had been won and said that the government's program could now become one of *techo, trabajo y tortillas* ("roofs, work, and tortillas"). However, three coups had been attempted since he came to power, the latest on September 25, and a firm date for free and fair elections in 1983 had still to be set.

(LUCY BLACKBURN)

Rossi, Paolo

A major hero of the Italian World Cup soccer triumph in Spain during the summer of 1982, the Juventus (Turin) striker Paolo Rossi was yet another example of the fallen idol returned to his pedestal. Though he strenuously denied any implication, Rossi had been banned for three years by the Italian football authorities in May 1980 for supposed involvement in a football bribery scandal in 1979, a sentence later cut to two years and ending in April 1982. Rossi then so impressed the Italian national team manager, Enzo Bearzot, that he included him in the World Cup team.

Rossi played a crucial part in his country's World Cup triumph by scoring six goals — including three against favoured Brazil and the second of Italy's three goals in the final against West Germany (in which he won his 27th cap). That tally made Rossi top scorer in the finals in Spain and brought him and his family many gifts from a grateful populace, including 1,000 bottles of wine and shoes for his family for life from an Italian shoemaker.

Born in Prato, in the Italian Tirol, on Sept. 23, 1956, Rossi had a far from easy passage to stardom. He was signed by the Turin club as a teenager, but by the time he reached the age of 18 he had had three cartilages removed from his knees. He went on loan to the lakeside club of Como and made his league debut for them in November 1975, against Perugia. The following season he was sold partly to Vicenza, which later had to sell other star players to buy him outright from Juventus, after an auction. That season, 1976–77, he scored 21 times in 36 games to help Vicenza clinch promotion to the First Division.

Rossi took part in the 1978 World Cup in Argentina, where Italy finished fourth, and played in all games. On his return to Italy he recorded another 15 goals in 28 matches for Vicenza but could not stop them going back to the Second Division. A year later he was sent on loan to Perugia

and scored 13 goals, including both in the 2–2 draw with Avellino, over which result the bribery scandal arose. During his two years in the wilderness Rossi was transferred back to Juventus for a fee of about $5 million. He played in the last three games of 1981–82 to help Turin win its 20th championship.

(TREVOR WILLIAMSON)

Rostow, Eugene

When U.S. Pres. Ronald Reagan named Eugene Rostow to head the U.S. Arms Control and Disarmament Agency, it stirred opposition on the right and the left. Conservative Republicans suspected him of being "too liberal," while Democrats objected to his being "too conservative" and a "hawk" on maintaining U.S. military superiority.

Despite these criticisms, the Senate approved Rostow's nomination, and he took over leadership of the new agency charged with managing and conducting arms negotiations. Unlike his predecessor, Ralph Earle II, Rostow did not become the chief arms negotiator for the U.S.; that post went to Paul Nitze, a long-time Rostow friend and colleague. Edward L. Rowny, a retired army general, was appointed to handle the strategic arms limitation talks (SALT) with the Soviet Union. Rostow concentrated on formulating policy and rebuilding an agency that had become somewhat demoralized in previous administrations. He traveled widely, speaking to government leaders, the press, and the public on the need for unity between Western Europe and the U.S. His theme was that U.S. missiles in Europe provided nuclear protection for the NATO nations and strengthened the negotiators' hand in the Geneva talks.

Rostow suggested changing the name of the negotiations from SALT to START — strategic arms reduction talks — a name that more accurately reflected the Reagan administration's view. He encountered a conflict with then Secretary of State Alexander Haig, who insisted on a prominent role and State Department jurisdiction in the arms talks. Rostow lost that bureaucratic battle but quickly adapted by creating an interagency committee to work with the State and Defense departments in support of the Geneva negotiating team. Nevertheless, Rostow was unable to get the deputy he wanted, and his advocacy of a more flexible approach to the arms talks was opposed by some high administration officials.

Born in Brooklyn, N.Y. on Aug. 25, 1913, educated at Yale University, and a former dean of the Yale law school, Rostow had served in the administration of Lyndon Johnson as undersecretary of state. At that time Rostow absorbed much of the anti-Vietnam protest from his own party and was labeled a "hawk." As a conservative Democrat he opposed Pres. Jimmy Carter's approach to disarmament and supported Reagan in the 1980 election.

(HAL BRUNO)

Schell, Jonathan

In February 1982 Jonathan Schell published "Reflections: the Fate of the Earth," three long articles on nuclear war. After their appearance in *The New Yorker* magazine, Schell's articles were republished as a book, *The Fate of the Earth*. Though many books on nuclear war had appeared over the past few years, Schell's had an unusually powerful

impact. A staff writer for *The New Yorker*, Schell had no expert qualifications in military affairs, but he did research the topic for nearly five years. *The Fate of the Earth*, an exceptionally eloquent book, draws upon the ideas of political theorists, military leaders, and scientists.

Schell believes that world leaders have mistakenly approached nuclear warfare as a technical military problem rather than as the moral and political issue that it really is. In *The Fate of the Earth* he begins by describing in detail the presumed effects of an all-out nuclear attack on the United States. He declares that the technology exists for complete destruction of the world's industrial nations and for the extinction of all human beings. In the second part of his book Schell treats the moral and philosophical implications of humankind's disappearance. He moves on to a discussion of the military doctrine of deterrence and concludes that the only hope of avoiding a nuclear apocalypse lies in complete disarmament and the dissolution of all sovereign nations into a world government.

Much of the critical reaction to *The Fate of the Earth* could be characterized as skeptical and hostile. Though everyone appeared to respect Schell's serious-mindedness, some wrote that he vastly exaggerated the devastation that a nuclear war would bring. Others accused him of schoolboy idealism for his belief in the possibilities of world government. We have had the United Nations since 1945, they said, and it has yet to bring peace to the world.

Schell was born on Aug. 21, 1943, in New York City. He began working for *The New Yorker* in 1968. Believing that his work was more important than his personality, Schell refused to provide any details of his background. His mentor was said to be William Shawn, editor of *The New Yorker*.

(VICTOR M. CASSIDY)

Schlüter, Poul Holmskov

Poul Schlüter, chairman of Denmark's Conservative Party, took over as his country's prime minister in September 1982 after Anker Jørgensen and his minority Social Democratic government resigned without forcing an election. Schlüter, who for several months had been advocating a broad national coalition as signs of an approaching economic catastrophe became ever more apparent, formed his government with the participation of the Liberal Democrats (Venstre), the Centre Democrats, and the Christian People's Party.

Schlüter replaced Jørgensen after the latter had held office continuously since October 1972 with only one interruption (Poul Hartling's minority Liberal government of December 1973–January 1975). He inherited formidable problems, including soaring balance of payments and budgetary deficits and growing unemployment. Although his appointment was greeted by left-wing demonstrations outside Christiansborg Castle (the Parliament building) and skepticism on the part of the trade unions, Schlüter enjoyed generally good opinion poll ratings; most Danes undoubtedly wished him well in the tasks that lay ahead.

Schlüter came to office during the half-yearly period for which Denmark assumed the presidency of the Council of Ministers of the European Communities (EC). This in turn coincided with the culmination of intra-Community negotiations over the adoption of a common fisheries policy (CFP). Throughout the negotiations Denmark had been steadfastly opposed to the CFP, and consequently at the EC summit in Copenhagen in December, at which Schlüter was host, he found himself at odds with the other ministers.

Schlüter was born in 1929 in Tønder, southern Jutland, close to the German border. The son of a wholesaler, he attended the universities of Copenhagen and Aarhus, graduating with a master's degree in law, and gained his attorney's license. His interest in politics developed early, and at the age of 16 he chaired the south Jutland Conservative youth organization. He was active in the World Association of Youth and in that connection visited more than 30 countries. He was elected to Parliament in September 1964, became Conservative Party spokesman in 1971, chaired the party parliamentary group in 1974, and in 1980 became party chairman.

(STENER AARSDAL)

Sharon, Ariel

For Ariel Sharon, 1982 was a year of supreme challenge. From his appointment as defense minister in August 1981 until June 6, 1982, when Israel's armed forces swept into Lebanon, he had concentrated every effort toward the destruction of the Palestine Liberation Organization (PLO) in that country. "I wanted them out of Beirut, out of Lebanon," he said afterward in a celebrated interview with Italian journalist Oriana Fallaci. But what should have been the moment of vindication turned sour with the revelation of the September massacre by Christian militiamen of Palestinian refugees at Sabra and Shatila.

Earlier in the year Sharon had won high praise from Prime Minister Menachem Begin, the Cabinet, and the country for the way he had managed the evacuation of Sinai. He had also won the respect of the Pentagon for his firm manner of handling the sometimes abrasive relations between Washington and Jerusalem. In August, when no Arab country appeared ready to accept the Palestinians expelled from Beirut, Sharon proposed that Israel offer a home to those expelled Palestinians who were prepared to live in peace with Israel.

Again, when the Lebanese president-elect, Bashir Gemayel, was killed, Sharon insisted that Israeli forces must go immediately into West Beirut to avert a possible massacre.

All this went for little when scenes at the Sabra and Shatila refugee camps appeared on television screens around the world. The judicial commission of inquiry set up by Israel in response to worldwide condemnation of the massacre, which was still in session at the year's end, did not stem the tide of criticism. Sharon told his critics that he had understood what they failed to see in Lebanon—a dagger that could have destroyed Israel.

Born in 1928, Sharon displayed abilities that were noticed early by Israel's first prime minister, David Ben-Gurion. His army career began before the 1948 war of independence. After law studies at Tel Aviv University, in 1953 he commanded a controversial attack on Jordan and led many cross-border reprisal raids. He resigned in 1973 but was recalled later that year and spearheaded the Israeli counterattack across the Suez Canal in the October Yom Kippur war. A member of the Knesset (parliament) from 1973, he was adviser to Labour Prime Minister Yitzhak Rabin (1975–77) before joining Begin's administration in 1977 as minister of agriculture.

(JON KIMCHE)

Shultz, George

It came as no surprise to government leaders when U.S. Pres. Ronald Reagan named George Shultz to be secretary of state after the forced resignation of Alexander Haig in the summer of 1982. Shultz had wanted the job when the Reagan administration came to power, but he refused to lobby for it and faced strong opposition from some of Reagan's ultraconservative supporters.

In 1982, however, his nomination to be Haig's replacement sailed through the Senate with no opposition. A former dean of the University of Chicago's Graduate School of Business, Shultz previously had served as secretary of labor, director of the Office of Management and Budget, and secretary of the treasury in Richard Nixon's administration. He had been untouched by the Watergate scandal and was one of the most powerful and popular men in Washington when he left government to become president of the Bechtel Corp., an international engineering firm.

Shultz was known as a quiet, soft-spoken team player whose personal style contrasted dramatically with that of the mercurial Haig. Where Haig frequently clashed with the White House and other Cabinet members over questions of policy and jurisdiction, Shultz was willing to compromise for the sake of harmony. He also had the advantage of having worked at Bechtel with Secretary of Defense Caspar Weinberger, who had been involved in a running feud with Haig.

In taking over at the State Department, Shultz made the point that policy would not change, since he served the same president. Because of Bechtel's heavy involvement in Middle Eastern development projects and Shultz's personal contacts in Saudi Arabia, he was careful to appear evenhanded in dealing with Israel and the Arab countries.

Following his visit to Moscow to attend the funeral of Leonid Brezhnev, Shultz warned that there would have to be a "change in behaviour" on the part of the Soviet Union before there could be any change in the Reagan administration's tough policies. At the same time he was instrumental in lifting economic sanctions against the Soviet natural gas pipeline to Western Europe in an effort to ease strains with the European allies.

Shultz was born in New York City on Dec. 13, 1920. He received a bachelor's degree from Princeton University and a Ph.D. from M.I.T.

(HAL BRUNO)

Siles Zuazo, Hernán

Bravery and tenacity were some of the qualities that Bolivia's Pres. Hernán Siles Zuazo had to show in order to return to power against all odds, after having helped destabilize three military regimes that had usurped his election victories in 1978, 1979, and 1980. In September 1982 the military junta, faced with widespread strikes and demonstrations that partially paralyzed the country, agreed to hand over power to a civilian government. The Bolivian Congress elected Siles Zuazo president by 113 votes to 29, and he returned from exile in Lima, Peru, to be sworn in on October 10. The new president had pledged to put the Bolivian economy on its feet through a policy of national government by consensus.

Siles Zuazo was born in 1914, the son of Hernando Siles, who was president from 1926 to 1930. As a young man he took part in the Chaco War against Paraguay, being wounded and decorated for bravery in 1933. After gaining a doctorate in law from the University of San Andrés, he became a practicing lawyer in 1939 but soon entered politics. He was first elected to Parliament in 1942 during the regime of Gen. Enrique Peñaranda (1941–43), having helped form the Movimiento Nacionalista Revolucionario (MNR) together with Víctor Paz Estenssoro, Walter Guevara Arze, and the writer Augusto Céspedes. Members of the MNR, including Siles Zuazo, were forced into exile in July 1946 after the hanging of Maj. Gualberto Villarroel.

Siles Zuazo returned from exile in April 1952 when he joined mining union leader Juan Lechín Oquendo in a successful uprising that resulted in Paz Estenssoro taking power for the first time. Siles Zuazo became vice-president in this government, which was beset by economic chaos and nearly fell owing to uncontrolled labour union demands. Siles Zuazo brought the unions into line by going on a hunger strike, thereby gaining the sympathy of the electorate, and was then able to impose an International Monetary Fund agreement on the country, which helped relaunch the economy. At the end of 1963 Paz Estenssoro and Siles Zuazo came into conflict when the former put himself forward for a third time for president. Siles Zuazo defeated the move and the MNR, but only at the cost of precipitating a coup by Gen. René Barrientos Ortuño, who came to power in November 1964.

(MICHAEL WOOLLER)

Singh, Zail

Sworn in as seventh president of the republic of India on July 25, 1982, Zail Singh was the first Sikh to hold that office; he was also a person with a long record of grass-roots politics. His humble origins recalled the phrase "log cabin to White House." Son of Sardar Kishan Singh, he was born on May 5, 1916, at Sandhwan village in the Faridkot district, in a family of artisans turned small farmers. Originally named Jarnail Singh, when barely 15 he was inspired by the deeds of Bhagat Singh, a revolutionary who was executed by the British in 1931, and became active in the politics of the Akali Dal, a Sikh organization that opposed British rule. Without the benefit of formal education, he pursued traditional studies in Sikh holy books and earned the title of Giani, which means "learned man." In 1938 he established the Praja Mandal (allied to the Indian National Congress) in Faridkot, which was then a princely state. For this act he had to spend four years and ten months in jail. It was about this time that he assumed the name Zail Singh.

In 1946 Zail Singh led a movement to assert the right of people in the state to hoist the national flag. He even set up a "parallel government" and was arrested again. After India became independent, Faridkot was merged in the Patiala and East Punjab States' Union (PEPSU), which itself was integrated with Punjab in 1956. Zail Singh served as a minister in PEPSU and then in Punjab. He was a member of Rajya Sabha (the upper house of Parliament) from 1956 to 1962. Returning to state politics, he was chief minister of Punjab from 1972 to 1977.

When Indira Gandhi was voted out of power in 1977, Zail Singh stood firmly by her. On her return to office he was named Union home minister, having been elected to Lok Sabha (the lower house of Parliament) from Hoshiarpur. He held that position until he was named the Congress candidate for the presidency of India in 1982. In the election he defeated H. R. Khanna.　　(H. Y. SHARADA PRASAD)

Spielberg, Steven

Like the actor who can play Scaramouche and Othello or the musician who can sing plainsong and then conduct Beethoven's Ninth, Steven Spielberg during 1982 proved his virtuosity. The filmmaker responsible for *Jaws, Close Encounters of the Third Kind,* and *Raiders of the Lost Ark* released two impressive box-office smashes back-to-back. They were *Poltergeist,* a horror film in which malevolent spirits haunt a family by coming and going through a television set, and *E.T. The Extra-Terrestrial,* which spun the original space-age fable of a ten-year-old California lad who befriends a creature from a distant planet. *E.T.,* the year's blockbuster, earned $190 million in rentals in the U.S. and Canada, three times as much as runner-up *Rocky III.*

"*E.T.* is my personal resurrection, and *Poltergeist* is my personal nightmare," Spielberg said. *Time* magazine declared that "both succeed beyond anyone's expectations. . . . They re-establish the movie

CAMERA PRESS/PHOTO TRENDS

screen as a magic lantern, where science plays tricks on the eye as an artist enters the heart and nervous system with images that bemuse and beguile. . . . Not since the glory days of the Walt Disney Productions—40 years and more ago . . . has a film [*E.T.*] so acutely evoked the twin senses of everyday wonder and otherworldly awe."

Spielberg was born in Cincinnati, Ohio, on Dec. 18, 1947, a member of the postwar baby boom who was reared in that newly ubiquitous place, suburbia. His father was a computer engineer and his mother a concert pianist, and the family moved frequently from subdivision to subdivision in Ohio, New Jersey, Arizona, and California. "I never mock suburbia," Spielberg said. "My life comes from there," as does the context for both of his latest films, which are peopled by suburbanites who encounter the otherworldly right at home.

After two years at California State University in Long Beach, Spielberg wangled an interview with a film studio executive, showed him a short film that he had made, and by the age of 21 became Hollywood's youngest director with a long-term contract. After directing a number of episodes for television series, he made *The Sugarland Express,* an offbeat tragicomedy with Goldie Hawn. Since then all his features save one (the confused action comedy *1941*) have had remarkable commercial success as well as critical acclaim.

(PHILIP KOPPER)

Stephen, Sir Ninian Martin

Sir Ninian Stephen succeeded Sir Zelman Cowen as governor-general of Australia in July 1982 after a distinguished legal career, climaxed by his appointment as a justice of the High Court of Australia. Australian governors-general had always been in the forefront of political controversy, and Sir Ninian Stephen was no exception. As soon as his appointment was announced, Stephen held a press conference at which he expressed the wish that his term of office be marked by calm. However, most of the reporters wanted to know whether he would follow Sir John Kerr's 1975 example and dismiss an elected government should similar circumstances arise.

Although Stephen could not see this particular piece of history repeating itself, he was prepared to offer a few clues as to his future behaviour. Questioned closely on whether as governor-general he would dis-

solve both houses of Parliament, he replied that the governor-general "must generally follow the advice of his ministers." He added that he would "seek guidance from my own understanding of the past and the vast resources which now exist, including the great amount of written material on the role of the governor-general."

Stephen's hopes that his appointment would be untainted by public controversy were soon dashed. Since Sir John Kerr sacked Gough Whitlam's Australian Labor Party administration, the governor-general had been regarded as fair game for journalists. Stephen was quickly confronted by a press demanding to know why his daughter had been arrested, while working as a journalist for the Communist newspaper *Tribune,* during Aboriginal land rights demonstrations at the time of the 1982 Commonwealth Games in Brisbane.

Ninian Stephen was born on June 15, 1923, near Oxford in England. After schooling in Edinburgh, London, and Melbourne, he studied law at the University of Melbourne. During World War II he served in the Australian Army (1941–46). In 1949 he was admitted as barrister and solicitor in the state of Victoria. A queen's counsel from 1966, he was appointed a judge of the Victoria Supreme Court in 1970 and elevated in 1972 to the Australian High Court bench. He was knighted in 1972.

(A. R. G. GRIFFITHS)

Suazo Córdova, Roberto

The elections held in Honduras on Nov. 29, 1981, resulted in a clear victory for Roberto Suazo Córdova as president and for his Liberal Party, which gained an absolute majority in the 78-seat National Assembly. The election of a civilian after 17 years of almost continuous military rule (the last civilian president was overthrown in 1972 after only 18 months in office) was greeted with relief both within the country and by other nations, especially the U.S. At his inauguration on Jan. 27, 1982, for a four-year term of office, President Suazo reiterated his campaign promise to carry out "a revolution of work and honesty" and pledged to provide a "government of high public morality."

At the age of 54 Suazo had little experience of government office. His career as a medical doctor was successful (after studying medicine at the University of San Carlos he served in the surgical and maternity wards at Guatemala General Hospital in 1953, followed by 25 years of independent practice in La Paz) and was only on three occasions seriously interrupted by politics. The first was in 1979, when on the death of Modesto Rodas Alvorrado he became general coordinator of the Liberal Party. The second occurred in April 1981, when he was selected as candidate for the Liberal Party at their convention and also became president of the Constituent Assembly. Finally, in the November elections he defeated Ricardo Zúñiga Augustinus, leader of the right-wing National Party.

Suazo was strongly anti-Communist and favoured closer relations with the U.S. But his ambitions, to reactivate the sluggish economy and restore peace, were frustrated on two fronts: in the economic sphere by low foreign credit and commodity prices and politically by increased tension on the country's border with El Salvador and, more recently, Nicaragua. Ultimate power appeared to lie not in the hands of the president but with the hard-line commander in chief of the Army, Gustavo Adolfo Alvarez Martínez. Internal security deteriorated after the president came to power, and it appeared that Suazo would find it difficult to consolidate his position within the country. In December his daughter, also a doctor, was kidnapped by Guatemalan guerrillas and released only after an anti-American statement had been published in Mexican and Central American newspapers.

(LUCY BLACKBURN)

Sutter, Bruce

In the game that won the 1982 World Series for the St. Louis Cardinals, Bruce Sutter set down the last six batters with dispassionate ease. He did not glare at opposing Milwaukee Brewer hitters from behind his bushy lumberjack beard. He barely acknowledged them. As was his custom, he concerned himself only with the catcher's glove and the split-fingered fastball he throws for virtually every pitch.

He had learned that pitch in 1974 from Freddie Martin, who was his minor-league pitching instructor in the Chicago Cubs organization. Sutter's ordinary fastball and his uninspiring 4.13 earned run average (ERA) had made him consider quitting baseball until Martin taught him to grip the ball between the inside cuticles of his second and third fingers. Only Sutter has been able to master the split-fingered pitch, which should not spin and should drop dramatically as it reaches home plate, forcing hitters to beat the ball harmlessly into the ground.

The right-handed relief pitcher, 6 ft 2 in and 190 lb, has been most impressive against the strongest competition. He had two victories and two saves in his four All-Star game appearances, 1978–81. In his first postseason championship competition Sutter had one victory and one save as the Cardinals defeated Atlanta three games to none in the National League championship series, and he had one win and two saves as they defeated Milwaukee four games to three in the World Series.

Sutter was born Jan. 8, 1953, in Lancaster, Pa. He barged into hitters' nightmares in 1977, his first full major league season, when he had a career-low 1.35 ERA, 31 saves, and a 7–3 won-lost record for a Chicago Cub team that was 81–81. His best season was 1979, when he won the National League's Cy Young award for the pitcher of the year after tying a league record with 37 saves and winning six more games while the Cubs went 80–82. The Cubs traded him to St. Louis after the 1980 season.

Joining a St. Louis team that had recorded just 27 saves altogether in 1980, Sutter supplied 25 in strike-shortened 1981 and 36 in 1982, when his record was 9–8 for the 92–70 Cardinals. It was the fourth year in a row that Sutter had led the National League in saves.

(KEVIN M. LAMB)

Thatcher, Margaret Hilda

No British prime minister since Winston Churchill in the 1940s enjoyed such massive popular support as Margaret Thatcher did during and after the 1982 Falkland Islands conflict. Her determination to win back the islands by force of arms from the Argentine invaders never faltered. She presented the action as a moral duty and a heroic crusade, and the public for the most part responded to her patriotic appeal. The dominant role she played as war leader was acknowledged by the widely held view that "it was Maggie's war," a judgment that could be taken as critical as well as approving.

The war had come about through miscalculation of Argentina's intentions. An official inquiry was set up to look into the origins of the conflict, including Thatcher's share of responsibility. Apart from that, her leadership improved the reputation of her Conservative government, which was at an exceptionally low ebb at the end of 1981, recording only 25% support in opinion polls. At the time of the Falklands victory the Conservatives' opinion poll rating had risen to 51%, a lead of almost 20 points over the Labour Party. By the end this lead had fallen back to around ten points, but it was still enough to suggest that the Thatcher government could win comfortably at the next general election, which was expected in 1983.

The Falklands dispute was a diversion from Thatcher's primary political objective, to effect a radical shift in the British economy back to private enterprise. She came into office in May 1979 on a program that aimed to cut public sector expenditure, to return state-owned enterprise to private ownership wherever possible, to curb the power of the trade unions, and to squeeze out inflation by monetarist financial policies. She told an exultant party conference in October 1982, "We have done more to roll back the frontiers of Socialism than any other previous government."

Margaret Thatcher, born on Oct. 13, 1925, was the daughter of a successful grocer in the small market town of Grantham. She made her way from the local school to the University of Oxford, where she took a degree in science. Entering Parliament in 1959, she epitomized a new generation of middle-class conservatives who were pushing aside the traditional landed gentry members of the party. She was elected party leader in 1975.

(HARFORD THOMAS)

Trottier, Bryan

On a hockey rink Bryan Trottier rarely comes out of the corner without the puck, and he rarely comes out of the play-offs without the Stanley Cup. His durability and dependability have prompted more than one general manager to call him the best player in the National Hockey League, no matter how many records Wayne Gretzky is breaking.

Trottier's New York Islanders won their third consecutive Stanley Cup championship May 16, 1982, by beating Vancouver in four straight games. Trottier was the leading scorer in the play-offs for the second time in three years. He had 29 points on 23 assists and 6 goals to go with his regular-season totals of 79 assists and 50 goals, the most goals in his seven-year NHL career. In an overtime quarterfinal game against the New York Rangers, Trottier won 11 consecutive face-offs in his own zone and scored the winning goal.

"Every facet of the game is important to me," Trottier said. Beyond being a goal scorer and a passer and a playmaker, he was praised for his defense, his checking, and his face-off skills, ranking in many minds with legendary Gordie Howe as a complete player. Trottier was quiet and businesslike on the rink, moving almost nonchalantly from breakaway spring to body check. Away from the ice his reputation for practical joking made him the first suspect when a teammate found his shirt missing or his skate laces tied together.

Trottier was born July 17, 1956, in Val Marie, Sask. A left-handed shooting centre, he was the NHL's rookie of the year in 1975–76, when he set league rookie records with 63 assists and 95 points. In 1978–79, his second consecutive first-team All-Star season, he was the NHL's most valuable player and scoring leader, with 134 points on 47 goals and 87 assists. The next season he was most valuable player in Stanley Cup play as the Islanders won their first championship. His seven-year regular-season averages after 1981–82 were 40 goals, 69 assists, and 109 points.

(KEVIN M. LAMB)

Tune, Tommy

His real name is Tommy Tune, he was born to dance, and in 1982 he became one of the hottest names on Broadway. But let him tell it as a *Saturday Review* writer reported in May:

"I was born in Wichita Falls, Texas, 43 years ago. My parents met while dancing, if you can believe it. I started dancing in Houston when I was five years old. It was a class of all boys, 30 minutes tumbling and 30 minutes tap. I was good at tumbling but I was a speed at tap." The next year all the other boys dropped out, girls enrolled instead, and ballet was offered. "From then on it was all ballet for me. I loved the sensation of flying. I couldn't get over it. Then I started to grow when I was about 12. Before you know it I was six-foot-six. I just looked ridiculous in tights. Right away I knew I'd never make it as the prince in Swan Lake.... Anyway, one day the star of our dance studio suggested that I major in drama in high school. 'What's drama?' I asked her. You can't imagine how green I was. 'Well, they put on plays,' she told me. So the first day in high school I signed up to major in drama."

Tune went to *The King and I* and there

PETER CUNNINGHAM/TIME MAGAZINE

"for the first time I saw singing and dancing and acting all woven together—colour, movement, laughter, tears—laughter and tears at the same time. I couldn't believe it—and that was the place in the road where I turned. From that moment on it had to be musical comedy. And I never turned back."

After being graduated from the University of Houston in 1962, Tune headed for New York City. Before nightfall on his first day there he landed a job in the *Irma La Douce* road show chorus. More chorus line jobs followed, and then a major role in 1974 dancing in *Seesaw*. "All my life I'd dreamed of dancing on Broadway, and the first time I did I won a Tony." After that Tune turned to directing. In 1977 *The Club*, his presentation of a satirical Victorian revue with women playing all the male roles, won him an off-Broadway Obie award.

In 1982 *Nine* garnered five major Tony awards, including one for Tune as best director. Tune was going into rehearsal with Twiggy, the 1960s model, in an adaptation of the film *Funny Face*. "Twiggy and I dance so well together. We have the same bodies, except that I'm a foot taller."

(PHILIP KOPPER)

Tutu, the Rt. Rev. Desmond Mpilo

The son of a schoolmaster who taught in South African mission schools later taken over by the state under the "Bantu education" policy, Bishop Desmond Tutu abandoned teaching for preaching early in his career in protest against that system. It was a characteristic gesture. Almost prophetically, he was given the second name Mpilo ("life"), for he was destined to become a vital force in South Africa's racial context—a man loved and hated but always to be reckoned with. When, in August 1982, Columbia University awarded him an honorary degree, he was aptly likened by Columbia's president to Martin Luther King, Jr.

Born on Oct. 7, 1931, at Klerksdorp, Transvaal, of mixed Xhosa and Tswana parentage, Tutu was educated at schools headed by his father. Forced by lack of money to give up the idea of a medical career, he turned to teaching and qualified at the Pretoria Bantu Normal College, gaining a B.A. degree at the same time by private study. He taught for a time but resigned in 1957. In 1961 he was ordained as an Anglican parish priest, and in 1967 he became a lecturer in a theological seminary in Johannesburg.

His next move was to London, where he obtained an M.A. degree at King's College and ministered for a time in London and Surrey. Back in South Africa, he worked briefly as student chaplain at Fort Hare and made his first contact with the Black Consciousness movement. Returning to London, he was for three years (1972–75) associate director of theological education funds for the World Council of Churches. His appointment as first black dean of Johannesburg followed; in 1976 he became Anglican bishop of Lesotho and in 1978 assistant bishop of Johannesburg.

The most stormy chapter of his career lay

WIDE WORLD

ahead. Appointed in 1978 as general secretary of the controversial South African Council of Churches, he was brought face to face with the country's basic race and colour problems. As spokesman for an organization radically opposed to apartheid, he was officially cast in the role of "turbulent priest" and agitator. On visits abroad, he did not hesitate to advocate economic pressures on South Africa to hasten change. This led to the withdrawal of his passport in 1981.

While demanding an end to racial discrimination, Tutu repudiated antiwhite feeling and pleaded for moderation.

(LOUIS HOTZ)

Wan Li

Wan Li became one of China's most powerful leaders in September 1982 when he was elected to the Politburo of the Communist Party. Because this promotion followed his election to the Central Secretariat of the party and his appointment as vice-premier in 1980, he became the only figure besides Premier Zhao Ziyang (Chao Tzu-yang) to hold full membership in both the Secretariat and the Politburo as well as a key position in the State Council (Cabinet). After his appointment as first vice-premier, which followed an extensive reorganization of the government in May 1982, Wan played an increasingly important role in streamlining China's inefficient bureaucracy and speeding up its economic modernization.

Wan became a close associate of Deng Xiaoping (Teng Hsiao-p'ing), China's paramount leader, in the early 1950s and one of his chief troubleshooters in the mid-1970s. With Zhao and Communist Party General Secretary Hu Yaobang (Hu Yao-pang), Wan headed a small group of comparatively young but experienced leaders who carried out China's economic readjustment programs and ensured a smooth transition of authority.

Born in Dongping County, Shandong Province, in 1916, Wan studied in France and joined the Communist Party in 1936. As secretary-general of the party's organization in the Hebei-Shandong-Henan Border Region, he organized guerrilla activities against the Japanese during World War II. After the establishment of the People's Republic in 1949, he held several positions in the central government and in Nanjing (Nanking). Appointed vice-mayor of Beijing (Peking) in 1958, he became a key figure in several of the capital's major construction projects, including the Great Hall of the People. Though branded a "bourgeois reactionary" in 1966, he re-

emerged in 1971 and brought a measure of order to China's disrupted communications system as railways minister in 1975–76. He was purged a second time in 1976 but was named the first party secretary and governor of Anhui (Anwei) Province in 1977. It was during his years (1977–80) in that province that he dramatically improved agricultural production.

An experienced and efficient administrator, Wan was known for his organizational ability and for the pragmatic and flexible agricultural policies he outlined in his 1978 article "Conscientiously Implement the Party's Economic Policy in the Rural Areas." These contributions and others related to urban development won him wide support.

(WINSTON L. Y. YANG)

Wilson, Bertha

Bertha Wilson once commented that she decided to study law because she lived across the street from the law school. From the time she finished her studies in 1958, she rose steadily until on March 4, 1982, she reached the pinnacle of her profession in Canada, judge of the Supreme Court of Canada. Thus she became the first woman admitted to the select company of nine judges who hold general appellate jurisdiction in civil and criminal cases in Canada and rule on questions of the constitutionality of laws and the powers of Parliament and the provincial legislatures. In making Wilson's appointment Justice Minister Jean Chrétien asserted that she had been appointed not because of her sex but because she was "a very able judge."

Being the first to hold a position was not a new experience for Wilson. In 1975 she became the first woman in Canada named to a provincial supreme court when she was appointed to the Ontario Court of Appeal.

The former Bertha Wenham was born on Sept. 18, 1923, in Kirkcaldy, Fifeshire, Scotland. She earned a master of arts degree from the University of Aberdeen (1944) and a teaching certificate from Aberdeen Training College for Teachers (1945). In 1949 she emigrated to Canada with her husband, an ordained minister. Bertha Wilson entered Dalhousie University law school of Halifax, Nova Scotia, in 1955 and received her degree in 1958. The next year the Wilsons moved to Toronto, and Bertha Wilson became a partner and research director of a large law firm. In 1973 she was appointed a queen's counsel by the government of Ontario.

In 1975 Wilson became a judge. During her seven years on the bench of the Ontario Court of Appeal she was not afraid to innovate. For her decision in a discrimination case, she was commended by Bora Laskin, chief justice of the Supreme Court of Canada, even though he had to disagree with her decision and overturn it. With her expansive view of the law it was thought that she would be a liberal interpreter of the law in her judgments on legal rights and discrimination cases.

Outside the courtroom Wilson was active in the Canadian Bar Association, becoming in 1970 the first woman elected to the national council of that organization. Always interested in religious affairs, she was a member of the board of trustees of the Toronto School of Theology.

(DIANE LOIS WAY)

Wilson, Edwin

At first the case looked like an espionage thriller bound for best-seller status: a tale of disaffected spies, CIA duplicity, smuggled arms, secret guerrilla training, a fortune stashed in foreign banks, a renegade agent nabbed in a Caribbean trap, an undercover crusader who turned up dead. When it came to trial in Washington, D.C., the agent's defense attorney called it "the Spy Who Was Left Out in the Cold"; he suggested that his client, Edwin Wilson, was just helping foreign powers at the behest of his old employer, the CIA. Refuting that, the prosecutor said Wilson was motivated by simple greed. In the end the jury agreed and found Wilson guilty on seven out of eight counts; he was sentenced to 15 years' imprisonment and fined $200,000. He faced three more trials.

The charges involved accusations that Wilson, after retiring as a U.S. CIA intelligence agent and becoming an international entrepreneur, sold arms, explosives, and training to Libyan dictator Col. Muammar al-Qaddafi's terrorists. Prosecutors said that Wilson had one of his employees buy an M-16 rifle in Washington, D.C., for $10,000 and bring it to Amsterdam. From there Wilson ferried it by chartered jet to Libya as a sample of his stock-in-trade. Some of his employees believed he was working for the CIA at first. One of them, former CIA technician Kevin Mulcahy, blew the whistle that prompted the first official inquiry. Zealously pursuing the matter, he goaded authorities to further action until Wilson was indicted in 1980.

Meanwhile, Wilson took refuge in Libya and only left in the summer of 1982 when offered the chance to discuss a "deal" on a theoretically neutral Caribbean island. Immigration authorities there barred his entry and put him on the next outbound plane—for New York City where he was arrested by U.S. agents. At the November trial, which lasted only two days, Wilson's London office manager testified that Wilson had received more than $20 million from Libya, including an $8 million down payment for 5,000 additional M-16s. Equally telling was the lack of defense testimony to support the claim that Wilson was working for the U.S. government.

The case involved at least two tragedies. A Libyan dissident was assassinated in Bonn, West Germany, with one of the smuggled guns. And the zealous Mulcahy, a second-generation CIA man, seemed to have burned himself out in seeing Wilson brought to justice. Days before the trial he was found dead at a rural motel, apparently of natural causes.   (PHILIP KOPPER)

Woodward, Sir John

The man chosen to command the British task force that recovered the Falkland Islands was a 49-year-old rear admiral who was then unknown to the public and even to the Cabinet ministers who had set the Falklands operation in motion. Rear Adm. "Sandy" Woodward put to sea on April 5 from Gibraltar, without time to return to London for consultations. Less than three months later Woodward's task force had secured the surrender of the Argentine forces on the Falklands in one of the most daring operations ever undertaken by the British

Navy. In Woodward's judgment, adapting a phrase used by Wellington after the Battle of Waterloo, it was a very close run thing. On his return to England he was knighted by Queen Elizabeth.

As it turned out, Woodward was well prepared for the job, with a wide range of experience in different branches of the Navy, though he was too young to have seen action in World War II. Born May 1, 1932, at Marazion, Cornwall, he had fixed his ambitions on the Navy from the time he went, as a small boy, to a preparatory school that had turned out 97 admirals. By the age of 15 he was at Britannia Royal Naval College, Dartmouth, the traditional route to a commission in the Navy. As a young officer he served in submarines, including Britain's first nuclear submarine, and in destroyers. In his 40s he was spotted as a man with a future and was brought into the Ministry of Defence as director of naval plans. He was promoted to rear admiral in July 1981.

Reflecting on the abrupt turn of events that had projected him to the centre of world attention, he said in an interview given as his fleet neared the Falklands, "I am very astonished to find myself in this position. . . . I have been a virtual civil servant for the past three years, commuting into London every day. I do not see myself as a hawk-eyed, sharp-nosed, hard military man leading a battle fleet into the annals of history." In fact he had to make hard decisions, to risk ships and suffer losses in a battle fought almost 13,000 km (8,000 mi) from home bases, without adequate early warning radar systems, with insufficient air cover, and with uncertain supply lines. If the operation was to succeed, it had to succeed quickly. It did.

(HARFORD THOMAS)

Worthy, James

Less than eight minutes into the final game of the 1982 Atlantic Coast Conference basketball tournament, James Worthy had 14 points for the University of North Carolina. He was perfect from the field on seven shots. He had a steal and an assist. He had set a pattern not only for the game, which North Carolina won 47–45 against Virginia, but for the entire tournament season, which culminated March 29 with North Carolina becoming the 1982 national champion of college basketball.

In the championship game Worthy led both teams with 13-for-17 shooting, as North Carolina defeated Georgetown 63–62, but perhaps more significant was his game-saving catch of Georgetown's errant pass in the waning seconds. It was not a spectacular play; he simply was in the right place. Throughout his three college seasons Worthy's value was never so much bellowed by boxcar statistics as it was whispered by the nuances that made him appear to have stepped out of the pages of a basketball textbook. Although his close-cropped hair and beard gave Worthy the look of an intimidator, the 6-ft 8-in, 219-lb forward was more consistent than flamboyant, distinguished by grace, fluidity, and economy of motion.

His numbers were impressive enough. He averaged 15.6 points, 6.3 rebounds, and 2.4 assists per game as a junior in the 1981–82 season, and his sophomore averages

were 14.2, 8.4, and 2.8 despite playing with a six-inch rod in the ankle he had broken midway through his freshman season. But basketball success at North Carolina is measured by won-lost records, and the Tar Heels were 71–13 with Worthy in the lineup, 32–2 in 1981–82.

The national spotlight did not chase Worthy from the cloak of privacy he had worn since his birth in Gastonia, N.C., on Feb. 27, 1961. He remained reserved, forgoing the traditional press conference of the National Basketball Association's first draft choice when the Los Angeles Lakers selected him for that honour on June 29, 1982. In the fall of 1982 he returned to campus to stay on schedule for his graduation in the summer of 1983.   (KEVIN M. LAMB)

Wozniak, Stephen

"I've got enough money to sit back in the pool and watch it all go by," a young "Midas" said; then he added in his generation's idiom, "but I want to be in life." Thus, if Stephen Wozniak got a "black eye" staging a three-day rock concert that lost $3 million, the computer wizard did not blink. What counted in his book, apparently, was the idea of rallying young America around a slogan that echoed John F. Kennedy to older folks' ears: Don't ask "What's in it for me?" Instead Wozniak wanted youth to inquire "What's in it for us?"

Toward that end he founded Unuson (for "Unite Us in Song"), a commercial operation that presented the "Us Festival" and attracted 200,000 people to San Bernardino, Calif. Tickets sold for $37.50 and lemonade for $2, while the pamphlets outlining Wozniakian philosophy were free. When the gate receipts were counted and the books balanced, the event seemed seriously in the red—though sales of records and movie rights were expected to bring additional revenue. If not, Wozniak could still theoretically afford to stage 20 more similar shows before feeling any financial pinch. The reason for this is that computers had already made Wozniak rich.

Six years earlier Wozniak had little more to his public credit than a hand in the "blue box"—a famous or infamous device, depending on one's viewpoint. The contrivance, the size of a cigarette pack, enabled telephonic bootleggers to plug into long-distance systems and chat with friends for free around the world—to the Bell System's anger and despair. Wozniak had made the boxes in concert with Steven Jobs, and underground celebrity followed. Then the partners scraped together $1,300, appropriated the garage of Jobs's parents, and built a prototype computer: the Apple. No bigger than a typewriter, it was packed with surprisingly simple electronics and designed for use by nontechnicians. Apple Computers soon found half a million customers, and the company, still run by the two founders, was doing business amounting to approximately $335 million a year. Wozniak's personal worth amounted to some $60 million.

Wozniak was born in California in 1950. He attended the University of California at Berkeley.   (PHILIP KOPPER)

The 1982 list of Nobel Prize winners contained several surprises, most notably, perhaps, the names of Alva Reimer Myrdal and Alfonso García Robles, two relatively unknown diplomats who were awarded the Prize for Peace for the many years they have spent quietly but effectively lobbying for disarmament. The Prize for Literature, not infrequently conferred on obscure literary figures, was awarded to Gabriel García Márquez, a Latin-American novelist of world renown. The Prize for Physics went to Kenneth G. Wilson of Cornell University for his mathematical studies of the behaviour of matter under the influences of temperature and pressure. Aaron Klug won the Prize for Chemistry for studies into the structures of viruses; he works at the Laboratory of Molecular Biology in Cambridge, England. The Prize for Physiology or Medicine was shared by three men: Swedish chemists Sune Bergström and Bengt Samuelsson and British pharmacologist John Vane. They were selected for their studies of prostaglandins. Though Bergström was chairman of the Nobel Foundation, he was not involved in selecting the Nobel laureates. The economics prize was awarded to George J. Stigler of the United States. The 1982 honorarium accompanying each prize amounted to $157,000.

Prize for Peace

Two senior ambassadors of disarmament, Alva Myrdal of Sweden and Alfonso García Robles of Mexico, shared the 1982 Nobel Prize for Peace. The twin choice seemed to reflect the times because many Western countries had been experiencing antinuclear protests. The official announcement stated: "In today's world the work to promote peace, disarmament and the brotherhood of mankind is carried on in different ways. . . . There is the patient and meticulous work undertaken in international negotiations on mutual disarmament, and there is also the work of the numerous peace movements with their greater emphasis on influencing the climate of public opinion . . ."

Alva Myrdal and Alfonso García Robles have both served at the UN and worked for the UN Disarmament Commission in Geneva; both have criticized the Soviet Union and United States for carrying the world to the brink of thermonuclear disaster.

Alfonso García Robles was born March 20, 1911, in Zamora, Mexico. He joined Mexico's foreign service and was a delegate to the 1945 San Francisco Conference, which founded the United Nations. He then worked in the UN Secretariat for several years.

As Mexico's director general for Europe during the late 1950s, García Robles played a key role at the Law of the Sea conferences. While serving as ambassador to Brazil, he first encountered the proposition of making Latin America a nuclear-free zone. Following the Cuban missile crisis of 1962, García Robles persuaded the Mexican government to pursue the cause of a nonnuclear Latin America. His efforts led to the 1967 Treaty of Tlatelolco, a pact that committed 22 nations to bar nuclear weapons from their territories. A year later he helped write the Nuclear Non-proliferation Treaty.

Alva Reimer Myrdal was born on Jan. 31, 1902. In 1924 she married Gunnar Myrdal, destined to win the Nobel economics prize 50 years later. In 1949 Myrdal became head of the UN Department of Social Welfare, then director of UNESCO's Department of Social Studies. Five years later, to the surprise of the Swedish business establishment, she was named ambassador to India, a job she handled with a competence that even her earlier detractors respected.

When the Swedish foreign minister asked Myrdal to become his special disarmament adviser in 1961, she set out to become an expert on the subject. A year later she was elected to Parliament as a Social Democrat and was named head of the Swedish delegation to the Geneva Disarmament Conference. In 1966 she became minister with portfolio covering disarmament and church affairs and held that post and the one in Geneva until 1973. Since that time she has written and spoken frequently on behalf of disarmament. In her book *The Game of Disarmament: How the United States and Russia Run the Arms Race* (1976) she castigated both superpowers. "The arms race has brought costs that are ruinous to the world economy," she said, and argued that military competition wastes resources better dedicated to education, health, housing, and other social challenges.

Myrdal expressed surprise at her selection though she had received the Albert Einstein Peace Prize in 1980 and the West German Peace Prize (with her husband) ten years earlier. In 1981 she also accepted a People's Peace Prize from a consortium of Norwegian pacifist groups organized after the Nobel Prize was awarded to the UN High Commissioner for Refugees.

Prize for Economics

George J. Stigler, winner of the 1982 Nobel Memorial Prize in Economic Science, wears the "conservative" label and teaches at the University of Chicago, where he has been Charles R. Walgreen Distinguished Professor of American Institutions since 1958. He often collaborates with Milton Friedman, who is also associated with the university and was awarded the Nobel Prize in 1976. Stigler is an advocate of free market economics and a particular proponent of reduced government intervention in markets. In *Roofs or Ceilings?* (1946) Stigler and Friedman wrote: "When rent control is enacted, the original tenants benefit in the short run, but in the long run, property values decline, the tax base is eroded, and the losers wind up losing more than the winners gain. In the end the national income itself is reduced."

Stigler confesses that he is more interested in why things happen than in how to change them. This inclination led him to study the history of economics as well as contemporary phenomena. Along the way he scrutinized numerous regulating agencies, ranging from those overseeing local public utilities to the Securities and Exchange Commission. His conclusion is that government regulators have, at best, no effect.

Given his advocacy of free markets, Stigler's selection for the Nobel Prize delighted the Reagan administration. He was invited to the White House, but things went awry during a news conference. Just hours after Pres. Ronald Reagan had assured small businessmen that there was economic "sunshine on the horizon," Stigler told reporters that the U.S. was "in a depression now". . . comparable in magnitude to the Great Depression of the 1930s. (The White House had sedulously cultivated the use of "recession" rather than "depression" to describe the nation's economic ills.) Stigler also referred to the administration's supply-side economics as a "gimmick." He conceded that the "thesis had a great deal of sense to it. Where it went too far, was claiming too much."

Stigler was born in Renton, Wash., in 1911 and graduated from the University of Washington. He obtained a graduate degree in business from Northwestern University, then studied for a doctorate at the University of Chicago because "it was the middle of the Depression, and it seemed better to go to school than look for work." He subsequently taught at Brown and Columbia universities and at the London School of Economics. He has also served as president of the American Economic Association.

Prize for Literature

When the Swedish Academy announced that Gabriel García Márquez had been awarded the Nobel Prize for Literature, it noted he was not "an unknown writer." Indeed, the choice recognized a literary genius whose works have been translated into at least 32 languages. Ten million copies of *Cien años de soledad* (1967; *One Hundred Years of Solitude*, 1970) alone have been printed.

A decade earlier William McPherson, who in 1977 won a Pulitzer Prize in the field of literary criticism, called the book "a vast jungle of a novel—at once so rich, so dense and so extravagant as to be overwhelming; a fabulous creation of magic and metaphor and myth." Pablo Neruda, the Chilean poet who won a Nobel Prize for Literature in 1971, described the book as "perhaps the greatest revelation in the Spanish language since the *Don Quixote* of Cervantes." García Márquez has frequently been compared with Balzac and sometimes also with William Faulkner because both rooted their stories in fictionalized versions of the places of their origin.

Much of García Márquez's life seems as bizarre as his fictions. Born on March 6, 1928, in Aracataca, a banana port on Colombia's Caribbean coast, he was one of 16 children born to an impecunious telegrapher. When his parents left home to seek a better life elsewhere, he was left in the care of eccentric grandparents. He eventually enrolled in the University of Bogotá law school because the absence of afternoon

Winners of Nobel Prizes in 1982: (left to right, sitting) Gabriel García Márquez and Sune Bergström; (standing) George Stigler, Bengt Samuelsson, Aaron Klug, John Vane, and Kenneth Wilson.

classes made it possible for him to study and still hold a steady job. In 1948 García Márquez, intrigued with the political turmoil that surrounded him, abandoned law for journalism. A naturally gifted reporter, he worked in Bogotá, Geneva, Rome, Paris, and New York. He became an advocate of leftist causes but never joined the Communist Party. Finding conditions in Colombia inimical, he entered into a semi-self-imposed exile in Mexico after severing his relationship with Fidel Castro's propagandists. For the past two decades he has lived mostly in Mexico City, but the Nobel Prize has brought him new esteem at home. When he suggested he might use the money to found a newspaper in Colombia, the Bogotá government seemed to welcome the possibility.

García Márquez's view of Latin autocrats is clearest in his novel *The Autumn of the Patriarch* (1975), a story about a dictator who embodies characteristics of several Latin-American tyrants. The *New York Times* called the book "a most complex and terrible vision of Latin America's ubiquitous, unkillable demon." Other novels include *In Evil Hour* and *Chronicle of a Death Foretold*. In addition, he has published several collections of short stories and reams of reports and commentaries.

At the award ceremonies in Stockholm, García Márquez entitled his acceptance speech "The Solitude of Latin America." A *Washington Post* reporter summed up the speech in these words: "The themes were avowedly political, a catalogue of repression and poverty in his beloved South America, and the risk to the world of annihilation. But it was also a literary event and it ended like this: 'On a day like today, my master William Faulkner said (in his own Nobel speech) "I decline to accept the end of man." I would feel unworthy of standing in this place that was his if I were not fully aware that the colossal tragedy he refused to recognize 32 years ago is now for the first

time since the beginning of humanity nothing more than a simple scientific possibility. Faced with this awesome reality . . . we, the inventors of tales, who will believe anything, feel entitled to believe that it is not yet too late to engage in the creation of the opposite utopia, a new and sweeping utopia of life, where no one will be able to decide for others how they die, where love will prove true and happiness be possible and where the races condemned to 100 years of solitude will have at least and forever a second opportunity on earth.'" (PHILIP KOPPER)

Prize for Physiology or Medicine

An Englishman and two Swedes shared equally in the Nobel Prize for Physiology or Medicine for 1982. The Englishman is John R. Vane, a pharmacologist who is research director of the Wellcome Research Laboratories, a pharmaceutical manufacturing firm in Beckenham, Kent. The Swedish laureates are biochemists at the Karolinska Institute at Stockholm: Sune K. Bergström, who retired as rector in 1977 but continues to do research, and Bengt I. Samuelsson, who succeeded Bergström as dean of the medical faculty in 1967. The three scientists have isolated and identified numerous prostaglandins, a family of natural compounds widely distributed (although in minute amounts) in the bodies of mammals, and they have systematically clarified their biological effects.

During the 1960s the prostaglandins came under intense investigation because of the diversity of their physiological actions and the connections between these actions and many diseases. Prostaglandins have been shown to influence blood pressure, inflammation, body temperature, muscle contraction, blood coagulation, pain, and allergic reactions. The smallness of the quantities present in the body at any time and the rapidity of their breakdown have added to the difficulties of studying

them; a very fast and sensitive bioassay described in 1971 by Vane has been one of his outstanding contributions to prostaglandin research.

In 1933 Ulf von Euler of the Karolinska Institute (a Nobel Prize winner in 1970 for other research) discovered that the blood pressure of experimental animals was reduced by injections of preparations of seminal fluid; he surmised that the effect was due to a substance originating in the prostate gland and named it prostaglandin. At Euler's suggestion Bergström undertook the isolation and identification of prostaglandin in 1947. It became apparent that Euler's proposal of a single compound had been incorrect, and in 1960 Bergström published the elemental compositions of two members of the class. By 1962 he and Samuelsson had determined the molecular structure of a prostaglandin, and in 1964 they announced that the substances are derived from arachidonic acid, a constituent of polyunsaturated oils present in certain meats and vegetables. Samuelsson filled in the details of the process by which arachidonic acid combines with oxygen to form the prostaglandins.

In 1969 Vane found that, in allergic shock, the lungs of rabbits release a substance that causes the aorta to contract; he further observed that this release is inhibited by aspirin and similar drugs. Within two years he had proved that aspirin, acetaminophen, and indomethacin (all used to treat pain, fever, and inflammation) stop the formation of prostaglandins. This finding indicated that prostaglandins are involved in producing the symptoms and probably are connected with the origin of rheumatoid arthritis. It also provided a physiological rationale for the effectiveness of aspirin, which had been introduced in 1899 and has become the world's most widely used drug although no one has been able to show why it works.

Vane demonstrated that the substance that causes the rabbit aorta to contract also causes blood platelets to clump together. Samuelsson found a prostaglandin in this substance, then went on to prove that another component was present. This newcomer proved to be a thromboxane, the first member of a class of compounds similar to the prostaglandins but differing somewhat in molecular structure. The thromboxane was extremely potent in aggregating platelets and constricting blood vessels. In 1976 Vane, in turn, noted that the prostaglandin found by Samuelsson is convertible to a compound of still another class, the prostacyclins; this compound proved to be the most powerful agent yet found to dilate blood vessels and prevent the clumping of platelets. The confusion was finally resolved when it was found that the prostaglandin released by the lung tissue is transformed to a thromboxane by the platelets but to prostacyclin by the walls of the blood vessels.

Vane, who was born in 1927, in Tardebigg, Worcestershire, was graduated from the University of Birmingham, then earned a doctorate at the University of Oxford in 1953. He spent two years on the faculty of

Yale University before returning to England to join the Institute of Basic Medical Sciences of the University of London. He moved to the Wellcome Research Laboratories in 1973.

Bergström was born in Stockholm in 1916 and was educated at the Karolinska Institute, which granted him doctorates in medicine and biochemistry in 1944. He held research fellowships at Columbia University and the University of Basel, then returned to Sweden to accept a professorship of chemistry at the University of Lund. In 1958 he moved to the Karolinska Institute, where he became dean of the medical faculty in 1963 and rector in 1969.

Samuelsson was born in Halmstad, Sweden, in 1934. He was graduated from the University of Lund, where Bergström was one of his professors. He continued his studies at the Karolinska Institute, earning doctorates in biochemistry in 1960 and medicine in 1961. He remained at the institute as a member of the faculty, eventually succeeding Bergström as dean of the medical faculty.

Prize for Chemistry

The Nobel Prize for Chemistry was conferred upon Aaron Klug, a South African expatriate affiliated with the Medical Research Council at Cambridge, England. Klug was cited for his investigations of the three-dimensional structure of the combinations of nucleic acids and proteins; his work on the tobacco mosaic virus has resulted in a detailed understanding of the arrangement of its components and of the selective process by which the molecule of ribonucleic acid and more than 2,000 identical molecules of its protective protein assemble to form the rodlike virus particle. Klug has made his discoveries in biology in conjunction with an outstanding achievement in physics, namely, the development of a versatile technique for studying crystalline materials. In this program, which established the new science of crystallographic electron microscopy, Klug unified the concepts of image formation and the diffraction of beams of X-rays, light, or electrons. Klug has shown how series of electron micrographs, taken from different angles, can be combined to produce three-dimensional images of particles. His method has been widely used to study proteins and viruses.

In 1957 Francis Crick and James Watson (who shared a Nobel Prize in 1962) pointed out that the nucleic acid content of a virus is too small to govern the formation of a single protein molecule large enough to form its own coat. The coat forms from many identical molecules of a small protein that hang together as a stable shell, either a cylinder or a sphere. Klug and D. L. D. Caspar investigated the possibilities of spherelike shells, taking clues from the geodesic domes designed by Buckminster Fuller, and showed that no more than 60 protein units, in 12 groups of five, can be arranged symmetrically on the surface of a sphere. If five- and sixfold clusters could occur, a series of larger numbers of protein units could participate, although the cohesive forces between protein units could not be exactly the same. This scheme, now called the Caspar-Klug quasi-equivalence theory, accurately accounts for the composition of the multi-faceted shells of many small virus particles.

In the presence of certain compounds, the tobacco mosaic virus particle breaks apart into its nucleic acid and the protein molecules that make up its jacket, but if the disruptive ingredient is removed, the virus slowly puts itself back together. Klug found that the slow step in the regeneration is the assembly of 34 protein molecules into a disk like a doughnut with a thin slice cut from it. Klug directed a 12-year study of the arrangement of the proteins in the disks. He showed that the final cylindrical form of the protein coat is not that of a simple stack of individual flat disks but a continuous helical sequence of the protein units.

Klug, who was born in Lithuania in 1926, was taken by his parents to South Africa when he was three years old. He entered the University of the Witwatersrand at Johannesburg intending to study medicine but graduated with a science degree. He then began a doctoral program in crystallography at the University of Cape Town but left with a master's degree upon receiving a fellowship at Trinity College of the University of Cambridge, where he completed his doctorate. He then accepted a research fellowship at Birkbeck College of the University of London, undertaking the study of the structure of tobacco mosaic virus and other viruses. In 1958 Klug became director of the Virus Structure Research Group at Birkbeck. In 1962 (at the invitation of Crick) Klug returned to Cambridge as a staff member of the Medical Research Council; in 1978 he was named joint head of its division of structural studies.

Prize for Physics

The Nobel Prize for Physics was awarded to Kenneth G. Wilson of Cornell University, Ithaca, N.Y., who has developed a general procedure for constructing improved theories concerning transformations of matter called continuous or second-order phase transitions. Exact understanding of these changes had been unattainable, partly because of the mathematical difficulties of dealing with effects that involve neighbouring atoms or molecules as well as those that influence a specimen of material large enough to be experimentally observed.

As the temperature, pressure, or other conditions are varied, most pure substances change from one distinct form or phase to another. At ordinary atmospheric pressure, for example, water exists as the liquid at temperatures between 0° C and 100° C; below 0° the stable phase is ice, a crystalline solid; above 100° the stable phase is steam, a gas. At 0° the liquid and solid forms are equally stable, and as long as no heat is added to or taken from the sample, the amounts of the two will remain unchanged indefinitely—the phases are said to be in equilibrium. When heat is added to water at atmospheric pressure, its temperature rises to the boiling point, then stays the same as it changes into steam at a rate that depends on the intensity of the heat source. Similarly, if heat is taken from liquid water, its temperature falls to the freezing point and stays there as the water solidifies bit by bit. In neither of these so-called first-order transitions does the entire sample change instantaneously from liquid to gas or solid.

Many substances undergo more subtle transitions. These processes, like the first-order transitions already mentioned, take place at characteristic temperatures but, unlike them, occur throughout the entire volume of material as soon as that temperature is reached, in what is called a second-order transition. Examples of such changes are the complete loss of ferromagnetic properties of certain metals when they are heated to their Curie points (about 771° C for iron) and the disappearance of the distinction between a liquid and its vapour at the critical point (about 374° C at a pressure of 217 atmospheres for water). Below 374° in the liquid or the vapour, the density in very small regions may be slightly higher or lower than the average, but the existence of separate phases is not affected by these fluctuations. If the temperature is raised toward the critical point, the bulk density of the liquid falls and that of the vapour rises; as the densities converge upon the same value, larger and larger regions undergo the fluctuations, even though the small ones (involving only a few molecules) persist. Just at the critical point, the density difference vanishes and the largest fluctuations extend throughout the sample; indistinguishable droplets of liquid and bubbles of gas occupy the whole volume.

Generations of physicists have tried to devise theories that could be used to interpret critical points. In the 1930s and 1940s two earlier Nobel laureates, Lev Landau in the Soviet Union and Lars Onsager in the United States, made some progress, but neither of their approaches proved adequate. In 1966 Leo Kadanoff, then at Brown University, sketched a way to deal with the enormous range of the fluctuations; he showed how the interactions of individual molecules form the basis of the properties of successively larger groups. In this way the microscopic fluctuations are smoothed out so that, though the molecular interactions remain responsible for the bulk properties of a substance, it is not necessary to evaluate every single one of them to arrive at the final result. Kadanoff's work validated an earlier suggestion of universality—that the second-order transitions fall into classes, each of which should be described by a single theory—but it did not lead to a specific formulation of any of these theories.

In 1971 Wilson published a demonstration that Kadanoff's concepts could be quantitatively framed by applying the mathematical strategy of the renormalization group. This approach had been developed during the 1950s to unite quantum mechanics and the theory of relativity in explaining the interactions of elementary particles with electromagnetic fields.

Wilson, who was born in 1936, in Waltham, Mass., was graduated from Harvard in 1956. In 1961 he received a Ph.D. from the California Institute of Technology, where he completed a dissertation under Murray Gell-Mann (the winner of the Nobel Prize for Physics in 1969) and Francis Low. After a year at the European Council for Nuclear Research, Wilson was appointed assistant professor at Cornell in 1963; he was named professor of physics in 1971.

(JOHN V. KILLHEFFER)

The following is a selected list of prominent men and women who died during 1982.

Abdullah, Sheikh Muhammad, Kashmiri nationalist (b. Dec. 5, 1905, Srinagar, Kashmir—d. Sept. 8, 1982, Srinagar), fought all his life for the rights of Kashmir and won for it a semiautoromous status within India. Known as "The Lion of Kashmir," he championed the rights of the Muslim majority of the state even before the end of British rule in India and fought against the discrimination exercised by the Hindu ruling house. After Abdullah served the first of many terms of imprisonment in 1931, he founded the Kashmir Muslim (later National) Conference. He supported the concept of a secular state, and when India was granted independence he strongly opposed the idea of joining Muslim Pakistan. In 1948 Abdullah became prime minister of Kashmir. Despite his early support for Indian leader Jawaharlal Nehru, many Indians believed that Abdullah's ultimate aim was succession to the presidency; therefore, in 1953 he was dismissed and imprisoned. During the next 11 years he refused to pledge his loyalty to India and spent most of the time under detention. When he was released by Nehru in 1964, he received an enthusiastic reception from his people. In subsequent talks with the Indian government, he worked out the basis of a possible solution to the Kashmir problem. He was dispatched on a foreign tour to gain the goodwill of Pakistan and Algeria, but India's relations with Pakistan had by then deteriorated and Abdullah's foreign tour was seen as seditious. At the same time his support in Kashmir had been eroded by the apparent lack of progress in negotiations with India. Abdullah was again arrested and not released until 1968. From then until his appointment as chief minister of Jammu and Kashmir in 1975, his Plebiscite Front gained some successes but lost to the Congress Party in the 1972 elections. His relations with Indian Prime Minister Indira Gandhi were sometimes strained, but he persuaded her to allow Kashmir a form of autonomy. Abdullah's government was later accused of corruption but, though his popularity waned, he was still admired for his outstanding contribution to the cause of Kashmiri national rights.

Ace, Goodman, U.S. television and radio comedy writer (b. Jan. 15, 1899, Kansas City, Mo.—d. March 25, 1982, New York, N.Y.), was a theatrical reviewer before starring with his wife, Jane, on the radio show "Easy Aces" from 1928 to 1945 and becoming one of the highest paid comedy writers in television. "Easy Aces" was a 15-minute program flavoured with an array of malapropisms "spontaneously" delivered by Jane, including such beauties as "Home wasn't built in a day," "He's a ragged individualist," and "Familiarity breeds attempt." Ace, who also wrote a regular column on broadcasting for the *Saturday Review,* confessed in 1967 that he had carefully constructed his wife's misused words. Goodman's offbeat humour was well received on television, and he wrote for such stars as Milton Berle, Perry Como, Danny Kaye, Sid Caesar, and Bob Newhart. A perpetual comic, Ace once quipped that he wanted his tombstone inscribed with the message "No flowers, please. I'm allergic."

Adams, Harriet Stratemeyer, U.S. writer (b. 1893?, Newark, N.J.—d. March 27, 1982, Pottersville, N.J.), brought adventure, intrigue, and suspense to generations of young people as the author of some 200 books, including many of the Nancy Drew, Hardy Boys, Bobbsey Twins, and Tom Swift Jr. series. As a member of the Stratemeyer Syndicate founded by her father, Adams was one of many writers to use the pseudonyms Carolyn Keene (for Nancy Drew), Franklin W. Dixon (for the Hardy Boys), Victor W. Appleton II (for Tom Swift Jr.), and Laura Lee Hope (for the Bobbsey Twins). Af-

UPI

ter her father's death in 1930 she became a partner in the syndicate and held firm in her belief that besides providing entertainment the books had to offer an educational element. She traveled widely and interspersed knowledge about Ming pottery and rocket manufacture in her stories. In 1980 when Adams marked her 50th anniversary as an author, the publishers Simon & Schuster honoured her with a celebration featuring costumed characters she had created in her novels.

Aggett, Neil Hutchin, South African union leader (b. 1954?, Kenya—d. Feb. 5, 1982, Johannesburg, South Africa), was found dead in his cell at security police headquarters and was believed to be the first white to have died in detention. The South African authorities reported that Aggett committed suicide by hanging. The announcement caused a storm of controversy both inside and outside the country as opposition politicians called for an inquiry. The inquest, which reported in December, ruled that no one could be held responsible for his death. Aggett moved to South Africa while still a child and later studied medicine at the University of Cape Town. In 1978 he began working for the African Food and Canning Workers' Union (AFCWU), one of a small number of multiracial, though largely black, independent trade unions. He later became a full-time official of that organization. Aggett was put under detention along with several other trade union leaders under the 1967 Terrorism Act on Nov. 27, 1981. At the time of his death Aggett was acting Transvaal regional secretary of the AFCWU.

Alekseyef, Aleksandr, Russian-born film animator (b. April 18, 1901, Kazan, Russia—d. Aug 9, 1982, Paris, France), invented the pinboard technique of film animation which he used in such pioneering works as *A Night on Bald Mountain* (1933) and *En passant* (1943). The technique depends on thousands of sliding pins that, when moved, produce effects of relief, light, and shade. He studied in Paris at the School of Oriental Languages, then turned to stage design and worked as a designer and graphic artist during the 1920s. Alekseyef made other experiments in film and animation techniques and applied his pinboard process to book illustration with *Dr. Zhivago* (1958). He also worked in advertising. By the 1950s his pioneering role was widely recognized at such international

film festivals as the animation festival in Annecy, France.

Allen, (William Ernest) Chesney, British comedian (b. 1894, Brighton, England—d. Nov. 13, 1982, Medhurst, England), together with Bud Flanagan formed the Crazy Gang, one of the best-known British music-hall acts. Allen started as an actor and appeared in farce and melodrama until 1926 when he teamed up with Flanagan at the Keighley Empire as the "straight man" to Flanagan's brash, quick-talking Jewish comedy. "Underneath the Arches," their theme song, took on new meaning during the Depression, and they were successful during the 1930s and in World War II with such numbers as "Run, Rabbit, Run" and "We're Gonna Hang out the Washing on the Siegfried Line." By this time they had joined with Nervo and Knox, Naughton and Gold, and "Monsewer" Eddie Grey in the Crazy Gang. Allen went into virtual retirement after 1945 for medical reasons. He returned later in life, however, as sole survivor of the Gang for Royal Variety Performances (he did 17 in all), a television show, and the musical *Underneath the Arches* produced in 1981 to celebrate the Crazy Gang's contribution to British comedy.

Alvin, Juliette, French-born musician and music therapist (b. 1897, Limoges, France—d. Sept. 30, 1982, London, England), was a pioneer in the use of music for therapeutic purposes. She studied at the Paris Conservatoire and won the Premier Prix d'Excellence and the Medaille d'Or. Alvin later studied cello under Pablo Casals and became a soloist in concert halls and over the radio in the U.S. and many other countries. A specialist in musical education, Alvin experimented in Britain with music therapy on mentally and physically handicapped children, made films and lectured in Europe, the U.S., and Japan, and wrote some of the standard texts in the field, including *Music for the Handicapped Child* (1965) and *Music Therapy* (1966). She was a founder-member of the British Society for Music Therapy and head of the music therapy diploma course at the Guildhall School of Music and Drama in London. The latter was started in 1964 largely due to her success in convincing the medical and educational professions of the value of such work.

Amoroso, Emmanuel Ciprian, British veterinary physiologist (b. Sept. 16, 1901, Trinidad, West Indies—d. Oct. 30, 1982, Cambridge, England), was professor of veterinary physiology at the Royal Veterinary College of the University of London from 1947 to 1968. He studied in Dublin, Berlin, and London before joining the Royal Veterinary College in 1934. Amoroso made outstanding contributions to research in animal physiology, especially to the understanding of the role of the placenta in reproduction. Besides publishing numerous papers on this and a variety of other topics, he was a fellow of the Royal Society and after his retirement was visiting lecturer and special professor at the University of Nottingham. Amoroso was made Commander of the Order of the British Empire in 1969 and was awarded the Trinity Cross by the government of Trinidad and Tobago in 1977.

Aragon, Louis, French poet, novelist, and political activist (b. Oct. 3, 1897, Paris, France—d. Dec. 24, 1982, Paris), was an engaging Renaissance man who became a literary giant with poems, novels, and essays and a committed rebel who embraced Surrealism, Dadaism, and finally Marxism. Though Aragon studied for a medical degree, he was drawn to literary circles and, together with André Breton and Philippe Soupalt, founded the Surrealist review *Littérature* (1919). In 1924 he was a founder of the Surrealist movement. During this period Aragon published such poems as *Feu de joie* (1920), *Le Mouvement perpétuel* (1925), and *La Grande*

Gaite (1929). In 1927 his search for an ideology led him to Communism, and in the following year he met (and in 1939 married) Elsa Triolet (the Russian-born sister-in-law of the poet Vladimir Mayakovsky), who was also a writer and who served as his inspiration for such love poems as *Cantique à Elsa* and *Les Yeux d'Elsa.* In 1930 he visited the Soviet Union, by 1933 had abandoned Surrealism, and in 1935 founded the International Association of Writers for the Defense of Culture. One of his most famous poems during this period was *Le Front Rouge (The Red Front).* In 1934 Aragon acquired an international reputation with the acclaimed *Les Cloches de Bale (The Bells of Basel),* the first of a series of novels collectively called *Le Monde réel* ("The Real World"). The series, which described in some historical detail the class struggle of the proletariat marching toward a social revolution, also included *Les Beaux Quartiers* (*Residential Quarter*), *Les Voyageurs de l'imperiale* (*The Century Was Young*), and *Aurelien.* During World War II, Aragon, who had earlier been decorated for service during World War I, served in Belgium and Dunkirk and received a second Croix de Guerre. When France fell to the Nazis he joined the underground resistance as a patriot and intellectual leader. His resistance poems, including *Le Crève-Coeur* (1941) and *La Diane française* (1945), stirred new patriotism in the French people after the 1940 defeat and made Aragon a national hero. After the war he published the celebrated *Le Semaine sainte* (1958; *Holy Week*), a historical novel about loyalty and treason set during Napoleon's era, and *Henri Matisse: Roman,* a glorification of the painter's works. Aragon was also a member of the Central Committee of the French Communist Party from 1950 to 1960 and editor from 1953 to 1972 of the influential literary and artistic weekly *Les Lettres Françaises,* founded in 1941. Aragon, who produced hundreds of poems, novels, and essays, was France's much-admired *homme de lettres.* An activist to the end, Aragon participated in a peace march through the streets of Paris in 1981.

Arout, Gabriel, Armenian-born playwright (b. Jan. 28, 1909, Armenia—d. Feb. 12, 1982, Paris, France), established his reputation on the French stage soon after World War II with sombre plays, including *Le Bal du Lieutenant Helt* (1950), and adaptations of works by foreign writers, including Dostoyevsky and Vishnevsky. He also wrote screenplays for Claude Autant-Lara's *Marguerite de la nuit* and Luis Buñuel's *La Mort en ce jardin.* He immigrated to France in 1921 and wrote *Orphée,* his first play, which was staged at the Vieux Colombier in 1943. Arout went on to work with many of the leading figures in the French theatre and remained active until the end of his life, winning an award from the Académie Française in 1981.

Askey, Arthur Bowden, British comedian (b. June 6, 1900, Liverpool, England—d. Nov. 16, 1982, London, England), was one of the best-known and best-loved figures in British entertainment. A pioneer of radio comedy, a superbly inventive stage performer, and an irrepressible fount of good humour and fun, Askey worked as a clerk while gaining experience on the amateur stage before his first London engagement in 1924. He became a household name in 1938 with "Band Waggon," the radio variety show in which he starred with Richard Murdoch. After World War II, he continued his successful radio career in such shows as "Arthur's Inn" and "Hello Playmates." He also appeared on television as early as 1953 in "Before Your Very Eyes" and in the film *Charley's Big-Hearted Aunt* (1940), among others. In variety or music hall, he was most successful exploiting his talent for ad-libbing and his feel for an audience. Askey's zest and resilient good humour were genuine and infectious and triumphed even over the illness of his final years. He continued to work despite ill health, appearing in his tenth Royal Command Performance in 1980 and a revival of "Band Waggon" to mark 50 years of radio. Askey published an autobiography, *Before Your Very Eyes* (1975), and was made Officer of the Order of the British Empire in 1969 and Commander of the Order of the British Empire in 1981.

Bader, Sir Douglas Robert Steuart, British World War II flying ace (b. Feb. 21, 1910, London, England—d. Sept. 5, 1982, London), was a legendary figure whose triumph over his physical disability was an inspiration to handicapped people. A rebel against authority and a natural athlete, Bader studied at Oxford and at the RAF College at Cranwell, was picked for the RAF cricket and rugby teams, and graduated second in his class. He joined No. 23 Squadron and in December 1931, while performing an aerobatic stunt, crashed. Bader eventually lost both of his legs and was given a pension in 1933. But he was determined to lead a normal life despite his disability and, moreover, to resume his flying career. His application to rejoin the RAF was refused until 1939, when, with the outbreak of war, his persistence paid off; he passed a flying test and was appointed to No. 19 Spitfire Squadron. Bader was promoted to squadron leader, then wing commander, won the DSO and bar, shot down 22 enemy aircraft, and won a unique reputation as an inspiring leader among "the Few." In August 1941 he was shot down and captured in France, minus one of his artificial legs which was lost in the crash. He escaped from the hospital, was recaptured, and eventually was taken to Colditz after further attempts to escape. He maintained an attitude of unrelenting defiance toward his captors, treating prison camp with the contempt of an unruly schoolboy. After his release in 1945, he organized and led the victory fly-past and in 1946 retired from the RAF with the rank of group captain. Bader then joined the Shell Petroleum Co. and began helping disabled people. His reputation was enhanced by the appearance of his biography by Paul Brickhill, *Reach for the Sky,* and the film based on it. Bader was awarded the Legion of Honour and the Croix de Guerre and in 1976 was knighted for his services to the disabled.

Bagramyan, Ivan Kristoforovich, Soviet army commander (b. Nov. 26, 1897, Gandzha [now Kirovabad], Azerbaijan—d. Sept. 21, 1982, Moscow, U.S.S.R.), commanded the 11th Guard Army which in July 1943 played a decisive role at the Battle of Kursk, the last German offensive on the Russian front. The following year, as army general, Bagramyan commanded the 1st Baltic Front which defeated German forces in Latvia and Lithuania. During World War I Bagramyan served in the Russian Tsarist Army before joining in 1917 the ranks of the independent Army of Armenia and later the Soviet Army, once Armenia was proclaimed a Soviet socialist republic in 1920. He studied at the Frunze Military Academy (1931–34) and at the General Staff Academy of the Soviet Army (1936–40). After World War II he was commander of the Baltic military area until 1954 and later served (1958–68) as deputy minister of defense in the Soviet government.

Bakr, Ahmad Hassan al-, Iraqi army officer and politician (b. 1914, Takrit, Mesopotamia—d. Oct. 4, 1982, Baghdad, Iraq), was president of Iraq from 1968 to 1979. A Sunni Muslim, he trained as a teacher but joined the Army in 1938. Retired after involvement in the Rashid Ali revolt of 1941, he was reinstated in time to participate in Gen. Abdul Karim Kassem's revolution of 1958 which overthrew the monarchy. After falling out with the new regime, he joined the Ba'ath Party, took part in the February 1963 coup, and became vice-president. In November 1963 Field Marshal Abd as-Salam Arif staged a countercoup against the Ba'ath, and Bakr was again retired from office. After Arif's death in a plane crash, his brother took over and in 1968, with other Ba'athist officers, Bakr seized power and proceeded to establish his regime by ferocious purges of his opponents, particularly the Communists, with whom he had negotiated on participation in government. He also negotiated with the Kurdish minority in the North, established an uneasy peace in the region, and finally defeated the Kurdish rebellion with the help of the shah of Iran, who cut off supplies to the Kurdish army. But Bakr's health was failing and by 1976 power was largely in the hands of his nephew Saddam Hussein (*see* BIOGRAPHIES), though Bakr remained as a figurehead president until three years later.

Balmain, Pierre Alexandre, French couturier (b. May 18, 1914, St.-Jean-de-Maurienne, Savoie, France—d. June 29, 1982, Paris, France), founded a fashion house that made his name a byword for elegance during the post-World War II years. His clients included the duchess of Windsor, the queen of Belgium, and many of the leading film stars of the 1950s. But one of the first and most important was the U.S. writer Gertrude Stein, who encouraged him and publicized the House of Balmain when it opened in 1945. Balmain had abandoned his architectural studies because of lack of money and in 1934 joined Edward Molyneux as a designer. In 1939 he went to Lucien Lelong, where he worked with Christian Dior, who was to become his main rival during their heyday in the postwar years. Balmain's was an immediate success, its clothes characterized by superb quality, particularly in his evening gowns, which combined femininity with imposing, slightly unattainable elegance. He rapidly expanded, opening branches in New York and Caracas, Venezuela, and diversifying into perfume and accessories. He designed for films and for film stars, among them Marlene Dietrich, Katharine Hepburn, Sophia Loren, Ingrid Bergman, and Brigitte Bardot. As haute couture gave way to ready-to-wear, he opened boutiques and developed his ancillary interests in handbags, scarves, luggage, and even furniture. He published his memoirs, *My Years and Seasons,* in 1964 and in 1978 was made an officer of the Legion of Honour.

Barr, Stringfellow, U.S. educator (b. Jan. 15, 1897, Suffolk, Va.—d. Feb. 2, 1982, Alexandria, Va.), as president (1937–46) of St. John's College, Annapolis, Md., abolished the elective course system and instituted a curriculum that required study of some 100 Great Books, with a heavy emphasis on science and mathematics. Besides earning degrees from the Universities of Paris and Virginia, Barr was a Rhodes scholar at the University of Oxford. After serving as professor of history at the University of Virginia from 1924 to 1937, he assumed the presidency at St. John's College and astonished the academic community with an innovative program that introduced students to the works of Plato, Copernicus, Darwin, and Marx. Barr later served as president (1948–58) of the Foundation for World Government, professor (1955–64) at the Newark College of Arts and Sciences of Rutgers University, and fellow (1966–69) at the Center for the Study of Democratic Institutions in Santa Barbara, Calif. He was also the author of 11 books including a cookbook, a children's book, history books, and a satiric novel on education entitled *Purely Academic* (1958).

Barsky, Arthur Joseph, U.S. plastic surgeon (b. Dec. 7, 1899, New York, N.Y.—d. Feb. 9, 1982, near Le Beausset, France), as the pioneering chief of plastic surgery at Mount Sinai Hospital in New York City led a team of surgeons that in 1958 performed more than 150 operations on deformed orphans maimed in the 1945 Hiroshima bombing. Besides participating in the " Hiroshima Maidens Project," Barsky and lawyer Thomas R. Miller established (1966) Children's Medical Relief International and, with U.S. federal assistance, a 50-bed hospital in Saigon, which opened in 1969 to treat children in war-torn South Vietnam. From 1969 to 1975 he saw some 7,000 children, whom he treated for severely burned faces and hands as well as other ailments. Barsky, who was educated at the University of Pennsylvania and New York Medical College, founded plastic-surgery services in several New York hospitals and wrote *Principles and Practice of Plastic Surgery* (1950), one of the first textbooks in the field.

Belushi, John, U.S. comic actor (b. Jan. 24, 1949, Chicago, Ill.—d. March 5, 1982, Hollywood, Calif.), was an irreverent entertainer whose humorous and outrageous assaults on society's con-

NBC PHOTO

ventions earned him a cult following. After performing with the Second City improvisational group in Chicago, Belushi vaulted to stardom as one of "The Not Ready for Prime Time Players" on television's "Saturday Night" (later renamed "Saturday Night Live"). As a member of the troupe from 1975 to 1979, he became an audience favourite with his killer bee and Samurai warrior impersonations. In one of his most famous motion pictures, *National Lampoon's Animal House,* Belushi sent audiences into peals of laughter as John ("Bluto") Blutarski, a campus derelict who majored in toga parties and food fights. His other film credits include *Goin' South, 1941, Ole' Boyfriends, Continental Divide, Neighbors,* and *The Blues Brothers,* in which he played a white soul singer. Belushi died of a drug overdose resulting from intravenous injections of heroin and cocaine.

Benelli, Giovanni Cardinal, Italian prelate of the Roman Catholic Church (b. May 12, 1921, Poggiole, near Pistoia, Italy—d. Oct. 26, 1982, Florence, Italy), was archbishop of Florence from 1977 and widely expected to succeed John Paul I as pope in 1978. Ordained in 1943, Benelli studied at the Gregorian University and the Pontifical Academy before becoming secretary to Giovanni Montini, the future Pope Paul VI. Benelli served in diplomatic posts in Europe and South America and was appointed apostolic delegate to West Africa. In 1967 Paul VI made him undersecretary of state in charge of the reform of the Curia. During his ten years in this post, he was the pope's "right-hand man," establishing his reputation as an energetic administrator, a conservative in doctrinal matters, and an opponent of the Christian-Communist dialogue. Benelli left to become archbishop of Florence and cardinal, played a leading role in the election of John Paul I in 1978, and was thought to have failed narrowly to succeed him when the new pope died after only 33 days in office. Instead, Benelli returned to Florence, where he remained in relative obscurity until his death.

Benyahia, Muhammad Seddik, Algerian politician (b. 1934, Djidjolli, Algeria—d. May 3, 1982, on the Iraq–Iran border), Algeria's foreign minister from 1979 to 1982, played a major role in securing the release of the U.S. hostages held after the seizure on Nov. 4, 1979, of the U.S. embassy in Iran. He had previously served as his country's special envoy in Moscow and as minister of information, minister of education, and minister of finance. Benyahia studied law at the University of Algiers, where he became president of the Union of Algerian Muslim Students and was an early member of the Front de Libération Nationale (FLN). He represented the FLN in Indonesia in 1956 and later in London during the struggle for Algerian independence. He played a significant role as a member of the negotiating team that achieved the agreement with France on independence at Evian in 1962 and was a member of the committee that drafted the

FLN's "Tripoli Charter," setting out the political bases of the new socialist state. Benyahia died in a plane crash.

Bergman, Ingrid, Swedish actress (b. Aug. 29, 1915, Stockholm, Sweden—d. Aug. 29, 1982, London, England), would be remembered both as a star in the classic era of Hollywood movies and as an actress whose talent allowed her to rebuild her career when it was threatened by scandal in her private life. Even before moving to Hollywood in 1938, she had achieved success in Sweden with her performance in Gustav Molander's *Intermezzo* (1936). Bergman's first Hollywood role was in the 1939 remake of *Intermezzo,* with Leslie Howard. Her beauty and her naturalness shone through in some otherwise mediocre films, and, with Humphrey Bogart in *Casablanca* (1942), transformed melodrama into magic in a work that has come to symbolize Hollywood's golden age. Bergman won her first Oscar for *Gaslight* (1944) and made three extraordinary films with Alfred Hitchcock, starring as a worried psychiatrist trying to cure Gregory Peck in *Spellbound* (1945), as a despairing secret agent helping Cary Grant in *Notorious* (1946), and as the suffering wife of an ex-convict in *Under Capricorn* (1949). In the late 1940s she fell in love with the Italian director Roberto Rossellini and had his child

UPI

before her divorce from her first husband. Though she eventually married Rossellini, the public was outraged and the films she made with her new husband were artistic and commercial failures. But Bergman triumphed again with *Anastasia* (1956), winning her second Oscar and confirming her place among the Hollywood "greats." Her intelligence and unaffected charm were qualities evident in all her films and in *Indiscreet* (1958), playing opposite Cary Grant, she also displayed a sense of humour. In the same year she made *The Inn of the Sixth Happiness,* one of her greatest popular successes. Once more in demand, she was able to exploit her virtuosity in such films as *The Visit* (1964), *Cactus Flower* (1969), *A Matter of Time* (1976), and *Murder on the Orient Express* (1974), for which she won her third Oscar. By this time she had remarried and in 1974 discovered that she had cancer. *Autumn Sonata* (1978), in which she was directed by Ingmar Bergman, was to be her last film and was the artistic high point in her career, but she returned to play Israeli leader Golda Meir on television. Bergman did not conceal her illness but faced it with courage and optimism, despite a serious operation in 1979. In the following year, with Alan Burgess, she published her autobiography, *Ingrid Bergman: My Story.* Although less widely known as a stage actress, Bergman first appeared on the stage in 1940 and in more recent years enjoyed notable successes in New York and London.

Bernbach, William, U.S. advertising executive (b. Aug. 13, 1911, New York, N.Y.—d. Oct. 2, 1982, New York), as the creative founder (1949) and president (1949–68) of Doyle Dane Bernbach advertising agency, revolutionized advertising by adhering to a soft-sell sales policy with believable sales messages rather than a hard-sell pitch. Bernbach, Ned Doyle, and Maxwell Dane founded the agency with less than $500,000 in billings and built it into the tenth largest agency in the U.S. Their clients included Avis Rent A Car, Polaroid, Levy's Jewish Rye bread, and American Airlines. Bernbach believed in quietly conducting round-table creative discussions to solicit ideas from his personnel rather than holding brainstorming sessions with writers and artists. Earlier Bernbach worked for William H. Weintraub Inc., Coty Inc., and Grey Advertising. After serving as president of Doyle Dane Bernbach for nearly 20 years he was named chairman and chief executive officer in 1968 and in 1976 became chairman of the executive committee, a post he held until his death.

Béthouart, Antoine, French army officer (b. Dec. 17, 1889, Dôle, Jura, France—d. Oct. 17, 1982, Fréjus, France), during World War II held off a 1940 German advance in Norway, took Narvik, but was obliged by the course of events to withdraw. Later, as commander (1940–42) of the French division at Casablanca, he assisted the Allied landings in North Africa, was arrested for treason by the pro-Vichy resident-general, but was released on the arrival of the U.S. forces in November 1942. He then served as head of the French military mission in the U.S. and, at the end of the war, as commander of French forces in Austria (1945–50). After his retirement in 1950, he became a senator and served as vice-president to the French delegation at the NATO parliamentarians' conferences in 1965 and 1968. He was a member of the Legion of Honour and received many decorations from France's wartime allies.

Bettis, Valerie Elizabeth, U.S. choreographer and dancer (b. Dec. 20, 1919, Houston, Texas—d. Sept. 26, 1982, New York, N.Y.), was a vivacious modern dancer who was also heralded as a dramatic actress, a star dancer in musical comedies, and a choreographer for both Broadway plays and Hollywood motion pictures. Acclaimed for her earthy dance routines, she mesmerized audiences with her alluring stage presence. Bettis, who studied under Hanya Holm, danced in Holm's company from 1937 to 1940, but it was not until her showstopping solo performance in *The Desperate Heart* that Bettis became a major figure in modern dance. In 1941 she made her debut as a choreographer, and in 1947 she became the first modern dance choreographer to present a work for a major ballet company when she directed *Virginia Sampler* for the Ballet Russe de Monte Carlo in New York City. Bettis also choreographed such experimental works as *As I Lay Dying, Yerma, The Golden Round,* and *Winesburg, Ohio.* On the Broadway stage Bettis received rave reviews for her portrayal of an enchantress who pushed her lovers off cliffs in *Tiger Lily.* She also triumphed in *Haunted Heart* and *Bless You All* and replaced Lotte Lenya in the role of Jenny in Kurt Weill's *Threepenny Opera.* Bettis also choreographed dances for such television shows as the "Colgate Comedy Hour" and "Your Show of Shows" and directed the dances for Rita Hayworth in the films *Affair in Trinidad* and *Salome.*

Bhave, Acharya Vinoba, Indian ascetic and social reformer (b. Sept. 11, 1895, Gagode, Baroda, India—d. Nov. 15, 1982, Paunar, India), was a spiritual disciple of Mohandas K. Gandhi, a leader in the country's civil disobedience movement, and founder of the Bhoodan Yajna (land gift movement). Bhave, who abandoned his high school studies to join Gandhi's ashram (ascetic community), took a vow of celibacy at ten, often went for months without speaking, and walked more than 40,000 mi to dramatize the needs of the landless In-

dian peasants. After Gandhi was assassinated in 1948 Bhave assumed his position as spiritual leader of the country, and in 1951 he formulated a land reform program that urged wealthy landowners to donate one-sixth of their holdings to the poor. After traversing the country Bhave was successful in securing 600,000 ha (1.5 million ac) of farmland for the poor. During the 1920s and 1930s he was imprisoned several times because of his passive resistance to British rule, and during the 1940s he spent five years in prison as the leader of the civil-disobedience movement against British efforts to mobilize India during World War II. After suffering a heart attack, Bhave refused food and medication and succumbed.

Birley, Sir Robert, British educator (b. July 14, 1903—d. July 22, 1982, Somerset, England), was headmaster at two leading British "public" schools, Charterhouse (1935–47) and Eton College (1949–63). He also played a significant role in the educational life of Germany, where he was educational adviser (1947–49) to the military government in the British zone after World War II. In South Africa Birley was visiting professor of education at the University of Witwatersrand (1964–67). He was educated at Rugby School and at the University of Oxford, where he studied history. He then taught at Eton and at the age of 32 was appointed headmaster of Charterhouse, an unusual choice not only because of his youth but because the post had previously gone almost exclusively to classical scholars. He managed the school during World War II and was granted a sabbatical to assist in reestablishing the German educational system, which had been destroyed by the Nazis and the war. After returning to England he went to Eton, where he maintained the classical and religious traditions of the school while at the same time encouraging the sciences. He was a leading member of the 1944 Fleming Committee, formed to examine the integration of the private sector (the "public" schools) with the state sector of education. When Birley went to South Africa, he faced the immense task of keeping liberal and humanist traditions alive under a notably illiberal and antihumanist regime; his achievement in this field, particularly for black education, was discreet but real. He then returned to Britain and became head of the social sciences and humanities department at the City University, London. He was knighted in 1967.

Bodley Scott, Sir Ronald, British physician (b. Sept. 10, 1906, Bournemouth, England—d. May 12, 1982, Italy), was physician to the household of King George VI from 1949 and from 1952 to 1973 physician to Queen Elizabeth II. He was a world authority on diseases of the blood, a noted writer and editor of medical works, and an outstanding clinician. Bodley Scott studied at the University of Oxford and at St. Bartholomew's Hospital, London, qualifying in 1931 and becoming a member of the Royal College of Physicians in 1933. He obtained a doctorate of medicine at Oxford in 1937. From 1936 to 1971 he was consultant to the Memorial Hospital in Woolwich and during World War II served with the Royal Army Medical Corps in the Middle East. Elected a fellow of the Royal College of Physicians in 1943, he served as a consultant to many hospitals, to the armed services, and to British Railways. Bodley Scott edited *Price's Textbook of the Practice of Medicine* and *The Medical Annual.* He was knighted in 1964 and made Knight of the Grand Cross of the Royal Victorian Order in 1973.

Bohusz-Szyszko, Zygmunt, Polish general (b. Jan. 19, 1893, Chełm Lubelski, Poland—d. June 20, 1982, London, England), joined the Russian Tsarist Army in 1914 and in the following year was taken prisoner of war by the Austrians. In 1916 he volunteered to serve with the Polish Legions fighting Russia under Austrian command. In 1918, however, when his brigade broke through the front into the Ukraine to join the Polish Army as a protest

against the hypocrisy of the Vienna government, Lieutenant Bohusz-Szyszko was captured and, until the fall of the Habsburg Empire, was interned in Hungary.

Having graduated from the Polish Military Academy in 1923, he was in command of an infantry division when Germany attacked Poland in 1939. When the Red Army assaulted the Polish forces from the rear, tens of thousands of Polish soldiers, including Colonel Bohusz-Szyszko, escaped through Hungary and Romania to France. In 1940 General Bohusz-Szyszko was appointed commander of a Polish brigade which, as part of the Allied Expeditionary Corps, reconquered the Norwegian port of Narvik from the Germans. In June, however, the Allied force was withdrawn and returned to France, which capitulated on June 22. Most of the Polish Army in France was evacuated to Britain and Bohusz-Szyszko became an organizer of a Polish army corps in Scotland. In 1941 Bohusz-Szyszko negotiated a military agreement with the Soviet high command stipulating that a Polish army would be organized in the U.S.S.R. In December 1941 Bohusz-Szyszko was appointed commander of one of the two divisions of the Polish army in Russia. But in 1942, 75,000 Polish soldiers were evacuated from the U.S.S.R. to the Middle East. With British help the 2nd Polish Army Corps was formed in Palestine and in 1943 it was transferred to Italy. Fighting alongside the British 8th Army, the Polish Corps captured Monte Cassino in 1944. The following year, under the command of General Bohusz-Szyszko, the Polish Corps captured Bologna. After the war he was deprived of his citizenship by the Warsaw government and lived in London.

Bolton, Sir George Lewis French, British expert in international finance (b. Oct. 16, 1900, London, England—d. Sept. 2, 1982, London), was a director (1948–68) of the Bank of England, which he joined in 1933 after working for a merchant banker in London and Paris. He was British executive director (1946–52) with the International Monetary Fund and a director (1949–57) of the Bank for International Settlements, and he played a major role in the management of sterling and foreign exchange control during that time. As chairman (1957–70) of the Bank of London and South America, he presided over a period of considerable prosperity and expansion and later became a director of Lloyds Bank International. Bolton also served on the boards of several industrial companies. He published *A Banker's World* in 1970.

Brahms, Caryl, British playwright, scriptwriter, novelist, and critic (b. 1901, Surrey, England—d. Dec. 5, 1982, London, England), in a long career that centred on the theatre and show business, was the author, sometimes in collaboration, of an astonishing variety of plays, film and television scripts, novels, adaptations, and theatrical and ballet criticism. Her first book, *The Moon on My Left* (1930), was followed by *Footnotes to the Ballet* (1936, frequently reprinted). The satirical thriller *A Bullet in the Ballet* (1937) began a fruitful collaboration with S. J. Simon. Together they wrote a dozen books, including such comic historical fantasies as *Don't, Mr. Disraeli* (1940), *No Bed for Bacon* (1941), and *Trottie True* (1946), about an Edwardian chorus girl. A second prolific collaboration was with the television producer Ned Sherrin. In 1959 they adapted *No Bed for Bacon* for the stage, worked together on scripts for the innovative satirical television show "That Was The Week That Was," and wrote a number of musicals, including *Cindy Ella* (1962), *Sing a Rude Song* (1970), and *The Mitford Girls* (1981), as well as plays, novels, and radio and television scripts. From 1980 Brahms was a member of the board of the National Theatre.

Brezhnev, Leonid Ilyich, Soviet statesman (b. Dec. 19, 1906, Kamenskoye [now Dneprodzerzhinsk], Ukraine—d. Nov. 10, 1982, Moscow, U.S.S.R.), became head of the Communist Party of the Soviet Union (CPSU) on Oct. 14, 1964, and remained in that post for 18 years, longer than any other Soviet leader apart from Stalin. Brezhnev became a full member of the CPSU in 1931 and, after his military

service in a tank regiment, joined the party apparatus. In 1938 he was appointed deputy chairman of the regional committee in Dnepropetrovsk. Called to military service as a political commissar, by the end of World War II he had attained the rank of major general. After the war he assisted Nikita Khrushchev, at the time first secretary of the party in the Ukraine, and was sent to Moldavia in 1950 to sovietize the Romanian population of that province. Rapid promotion followed in 1952: Brezhnev was elected a member of the Central Committee (CC) of the CPSU, a candidate member of its Politburo, and a member of its Secretariat.

After Stalin's death Brezhnev lost his seat on both the CC inner bodies. But Khrushchev, who had gained full power in Moscow, sent Brezhnev to Kazakhstan to supervise the "Virgin Lands" scheme: its success brought Brezhnev reelection to his posts within the CC. He became a full Politburo member in 1957. From May 1960 to June 1964 Brezhnev was chairman of the Presidium of the Supreme Soviet (titular chief of state). He masterminded the coup that ousted Khrushchev from the posts of party first secretary and head of government, and was elected first secretary (general secretary from 1966) in his place.

After Warsaw Pact forces entered Czechoslovakia in 1968, he was instrumental in establishing the so-called Brezhnev Doctrine that upheld the right of intervention in cases where "the essential common interests of other socialist countries are threatened by developments in one of their number." In his dealings with the West, however, he sought to normalize relations between West Germany and the Warsaw Pact countries and pushed for détente. Soviet–U.S. relations improved when Pres. Richard Nixon journeyed to Moscow in 1972; Brezhnev returned the visit the following year. In May 1977 he became the first person in Soviet history to hold the posts of party leader and chief of state at the same time. Submitting the draft of a new constitution to the CC in May 1977, he spoke of the "repression of the 1930s that must never be repeated."

Though Brezhnev met U.S. Pres. Jimmy Carter in Vienna in 1979 to sign a new bilateral strategic arms limitation treaty (SALT II), the encounter was later viewed as the end of détente, since the U.S. Senate refused to ratify the treaty. Brezhnev's rejoinder was the Soviet Army's intervention in Afghanistan in December 1979. Three days before his death Brezhnev warned any "potential aggressor that a crushing retaliatory strike would be inevitable." Ambitious but circumspect, he clung to office to the end, despite the fact that his increasingly frail health had opened up a pre-succession struggle. (*See* Feature Article: *Signposts to the Future of Communism;* Union of Soviet Socialist Republics.)

Among the many awards made to Brezhnev

during his lifetime was the Lenin Prize for Literature (1979) for his volume of memoirs.

Bushmiller, Ernest Paul, U.S. cartoonist (b. Aug. 23, 1905, New York, N.Y.—d. Aug. 15, 1982, Stamford, Conn.), was the inventive creator of the "Nancy" comic strip, which relied heavily on sight gags and appeared in 700 U.S. dailies and some 100 overseas newspapers. Bushmiller, who dropped out of high school to become a copy boy at the *New York Evening World,* took night classes at the National Academy of Design. In 1925 he began drawing the "Fritzi Ritz" comic strip and in 1931 continued sketching the strip for the United Features Syndicate. During the early 1930s he introduced Nancy as Fritzi's niece, and the cheeky simplicity of the chunky child with the red bow atop her head became an instant sensation. In 1940 the strip was renamed "Nancy," and during the 1950s and 1960s "Nancy" was one of the most widely followed comic strips. In 1978 Bushmiller was named cartoonist of the year for "Nancy" by the National Cartoonists Society.

Butler of Saffron Walden, Richard Austen Butler, BARON, British politician (b. Dec. 9, 1902, Attock Serai, India—d. March 8, 1982, Great Yeldham, Essex, England), was the architect of Britain's 1944 Education Act, served as chancellor of the Exchequer, home secretary, and foreign secretary, and three times failed in his bid for the leadership of the Conservative Party. One of the most respected figures in British politics, he represented the liberal wing of modern Conservatism and remained a much-admired elder statesman after his appointment in 1965 as a life peer and master of Trinity College, University of Cambridge. A brilliant scholar, "Rab" Butler gained double firsts in French and history from Pembroke College, Cambridge. After being elected to Parliament in 1929 he served as member for Saffron Walden, the seat he represented throughout his parliamentary career. Butler served as private secretary to Sir Samuel Hoare and helped draw up the Government of India Act, 1935. In 1938, as undersecretary of state at the Foreign Office, he became one of the main defenders in the House of Commons of the policy of appeasement, and this had an adverse effect later on in his career. In 1941 he was moved to the Board of Education and reorganized the educational system, his first major political achievement. Under the 1944 act the age for leaving school was raised, elementary schooling was replaced by primary and secondary education, and the status of church schools was protected.

In 1951 Butler was appointed chancellor of the Exchequer and between then and 1955 presided over a period of economic expansion that allowed him to make considerable and popular tax concessions in his last budget. These proved, however, to have been overoptimistic, and he suffered a further setback in the following year because of his outspoken and inflexible line during the Suez crisis. In the debacle that followed, it was probably this that explained his failure to be chosen as successor to the prime ministership when Anthony Eden resigned. Butler served as home secretary under Harold Macmillan and remained in this office until 1962. As head of the Central African Office, he played a major role in the 1963 conference that ultimately led to the independence of Zambia and Malawi. In October 1963 Macmillan fell ill, and Butler, as deputy prime minister, became acting head of the government. Once more, however, he failed in his bid for the party leadership. He served as foreign secretary under Sir Alec Douglas-Home until the Conservative defeat in 1964, then retired into academic life. He was president of the Royal Society of Literature from 1951 and remained an active member of the House of Lords until a few years before his death.

Camus, Marcel, French film director (b. April 21, 1912, Chappes, France—d. Jan. 13, 1982, Paris, France), won international acclaim for his film *Orfeu negro* (*Black Orpheus*), which gained first prize at the 1959 Venice Film Festival and an Oscar for best foreign film. Camus had already achieved some notoriety with his first feature, *Mort en fraude* (1956), set in Indochina during the war against France. But his later work, including *Os Bandeirantes* (1959) and *Le Chant du monde* (1965), failed to repeat the success of his modern version of the Orpheus legend. Camus then turned to commercial cinema and to television. His last Brazilian film, *Otalia de Bahia* (1976), attracted little attention. Trained as an artist and taken prisoner during World War II, Camus started his career in films as an assistant to such directors as Henri Decoin and Luis Buñuel before making his first short film in 1950.

Canham, Erwin Dain, U.S. editor (b. Feb. 13, 1904, Auburn, Maine—d. Jan. 3, 1982, Agana, Guam), was a highly respected journalist who spent nearly five decades contributing to the *Christian Science Monitor,* first as a reporter and then as chief of the Washington bureau (1932–39), general news editor (1939–41), managing editor (1941–45), editor (1945–64), and finally editor in chief (1964–74). In the latter capacity Canham strengthened the newspaper's worldwide coverage and inspired its staff specialists to produce thoughtful and analytical pieces. After graduating from Bates College in Maine, Canham worked briefly for the *Monitor* before attending the University of Oxford as a Rhodes scholar. The indefatigable Canham also covered the League of Nations Assembly while there. This energy characterized his entire career; besides his work on the paper, Canham held a variety of governmental posts and also spent part of his one-year term as president (1966) of the Church of Christ, Scientist, on a worldwide lecture tour.

Carr, Edward Hallett, British historian (b. June 28, 1892—d. Nov. 3, 1982, Cambridge, England), spent the last 30 years of his life writing the 15-volume *History of Soviet Russia,* one of the major achievements of British historiography in the 20th century. The monumental work traced the establishment of Soviet power from the Revolution against the background of Russian culture and traditions. Some critics, however, felt that Carr's patient analysis of the documentary evidence in *History of Soviet Russia* took on the colour of the bureaucracy it was describing. Carr studied classics at Trinity College, Cambridge, and joined the Foreign Office, becoming a member of the delegation to the 1919 Paris peace conference. From 1925 to 1929 he was second secretary at the British embassy in Riga, Latvia, and two years after his return from this post published a study of Dostoyevsky. He left the Foreign Office in 1936 to become professor of international relations at the University of Aberystwyth and in 1941 became assistant editor on *The Times,* where he defended controversial views on Anglo-Soviet relations and domestic policies. Resigning his post in Aberystwyth in 1947, he went to Oxford, and in 1955 he was appointed fellow of Trinity College, Cambridge. His works included *The Romantic Exiles* (1933), *The Twenty Years' Crisis 1919–39* (1939), and *What Is History?* (1961).

Carritt, (Hugh) David Graham, British art dealer (b. April 15, 1927—d. Aug. 3, 1982, London, England), had a sensational knack for discovering Old Master paintings, based on his expert knowledge of the Italian Renaissance and the 18th century. In 1977, at the sale of the contents of Mentmore Towers, Buckinghamshire, England, he bought a painting attributed to the minor painter Carle van Loo for around £8,000, having correctly identified it as a lost work by the 18th-century French painter Fragonard. Fragonard's "Toilet of Psyche" now hangs in the National Gallery, London, and is estimated to be worth some £600,000. As a student at Rugby School and later at the University of Oxford, Carritt had already developed a passion for the fine arts. In 1952, in a private collection in England's Lake District, he discovered a painting by Caravaggio, now in the Metropolitan Museum of Art, New York City. Carritt became a director of the London art auctioneers Christie's, leaving them for Artemis in 1970, the same year he founded David Carritt Ltd.

Carter, Harry Graham, British typographer (b. March 27, 1901, Croydon, Surrey, England—d. March 10, 1982, London, England), was responsible for design and layout with Her Majesty's Stationery Office and from 1954 to 1980 was archivist with the Oxford University Press. In both posts he made a major contribution to typography and book design. Carter's own type designs included a Hebrew alphabet that he engraved while working as a postal censor in Palestine during World War II, a Russian type, and the small Bible type for the Oxford University Press. He was also a leading writer on typography whose works included *Printing Explained* (with Herbert Simon; 1931), *A View of Early Typography* (1969), and *A History of the Oxford University Press* (1975). He collaborated with Stanley Morison to produce *John Fell, the University Press, and the 'Fell' Types* (1967). Carter studied law before attending classes in engraving at London's Central School of Art and Design, joined the Monotype Corp. in 1928, and exploited his gifts as a linguist by translating Pierre-Simon Fournier's classic work on typefounding (*Fournier on Typefounding;* 1930). After working for the Kynoch Press, he became production manager at the Nonesuch Press, where he worked with Francis Meynell. He was made an officer of the Order of the British Empire in 1951.

Cavalcanti, Alberto de Almeida, Brazilian-born film director and producer (b. Feb. 6, 1897, Rio de Janeiro, Brazil—d. Aug. 23, 1982, Paris, France), established his reputation as a documentary filmmaker in Britain during the 1930s and went on to produce some notable films for Ealing Studios. In the 1950s he returned to Brazil and was a leading figure in the revival of Brazilian cinema. Cavalcanti studied architecture in Geneva, worked in French cinema as an art director, and in 1926 made the pioneering documentary *Rien que les heures,* which portrayed the lives of Paris workers during a single day. In 1934 he went to Britain and joined John Grierson on the General Post Office (GPO) Film Unit to make *Pett and Pott, Coalface* (with Grierson and W. H. Auden), and *We Live in Two Worlds.* The GPO's productions were important milestones in the development of documentaries. Moving to Ealing Studios in 1941, he produced such wartime propaganda films as *The Foreman Went to France* and, after 1943, directed the features *Champagne Charlie, Nicholas Nickleby,* and *They Made Me a Fugitive.* After returning to Brazil, he made *O Canto do mar* and *Mulher de verdade* with his own company; but he fell under official suspicion because of his left-wing stance and in 1954 returned to Europe. Cavalcanti eventually settled in France, where he continued his work in television.

Chapman, (Anthony) Colin, British car designer and businessman (b. 1928, Richmond, Surrey, England—d. Dec. 16, 1982, Norfolk, England), was the dynamic founder of the Lotus Engineering Co. (later Lotus Cars Ltd.) in 1952 and a master designer who built both Lotus sports and racing cars. Chapman, who specialized in suspension systems and lightweight cars, was a giant in Grand Prix racing. In 1962 he built the Lotus MK25, the first race car with the engine and framework integrated with the body. This innovation replaced the tubular chassis and became known as the monocoque chassis. He also introduced the modern "ground effects" race car, which is held to the ground by aerodynamic pressure. In 1963 his Lotus team began racing in the U.S. and though some felt his cars were too lightweight and fragile, Chapman's Lotus racers captured seven Formula One world championships. Chapman was also credited with launching the careers of such superb race drivers as Jim Clark, Emerson Fittipaldi, and Mario Andretti. Chapman was instrumental in the development of John De Lorean's gull-winged auto, but in 1981 Lotus accounts came under scrutiny when the company shareholders asked probing questions about funds paid to Lotus via a Swiss-based Panamanian company run by a De Lorean distributor. In 1970 Chapman was honoured as Commander of the Order of the British Empire.

Chaudhri, Fazal Elahi, Pakistani politician (b. Jan. 1, 1904, Gujrat, Punjab, India—d. June 1, 1982, Lahore, Pakistan), was president of Pakistan from 1973 to 1978 and a supporter of Zulfikar Ali Bhutto's Pakistan People's Party. When Bhutto was ousted as the country's prime minister by the military regime of Gen. Mohammad Zia-ul-Haq in 1977, Chaudhri remained in office but resigned in the following year, reportedly after differences with the new regime. He trained and practiced as a lawyer until his election to the Punjab Legislative Assembly in 1945 as a member of the All-India Muslim League. He became successively a member of the Punjab provincial government, speaker of the provincial assembly, and, from 1971 to 1973, speaker of the National Assembly. When Bhutto relinquished the position of chief of state in 1973 under the new constitution enacted by the directly elected National Assembly, Chaudhri became president.

Cheever, John, U.S. short-story writer and novelist (b. May 27, 1912, Quincy, Mass.—d. June 18, 1982, Ossining, N.Y.), was a Pulitzer Prize-winning writer who comically and ironically chronicled the daily lives of upper-middle-class people, many of whom were spiritually imprisoned by their suburban estates and swimming pools. Cheever's works began appearing in *The New Yorker* magazine during the 1930s. As the author of such collections of short stories as *The Enormous Radio* (1953), *The House-*

UPI

breaker of Shady Hill (1958), *Some People, Places, and Things that Will Not Appear in My Next Novel* (1961), and *The Brigadier and the Golf Widow* (1964), Cheever was praised for his rich, elegant prose and for a purity of style. His novels *The Wapshot Chronicle* (1957; winner of the National Book Award in 1958) and *The Wapshot Scandal* (1964) focused on the human possibilities and failures of the Wapshot family of St. Botolphs, Mass.; *Bullet Park* (1969) and *Falconer* (1977) revealed a less optimistic vision. In 1978 *The Stories of John Cheever* topped the *New York Times* bestseller list, becoming one of the few collections of short fiction ever to do so, and it was awarded the 1979 Pulitzer Prize for fiction. In 1981 Cheever was the recipient of the National Medal for Literature, and in 1982 he published the novella *Oh What a Paradise It Seems.*

Chenoweth, Dean, U.S. hydroplane driver (b. 1938?, Xenia, Ohio—d. July 31, 1982, Pasco, Wash.), was the four-time winner of both the unlimited hydroplane national championships and the American Power Boat Association's prestigious Gold Cup. Chenoweth, who was the reigning national champion, had three bonecrushing mishaps in hydroplanes; two on Lake Washington in Seattle and one at Pasco. Chenoweth was killed when his "Miss

Budweiser" boat flipped and crashed during a qualifying run for the annual Columbia Cup race.

Chloros, Alexander George, Greek-born British jurist (b. Aug. 15, 1926, Athens, Greece—d. Nov. 15, 1982, Luxembourg), was a leading expert in comparative law and a judge at the Court of Justice of the European Communities (EC). He studied in Athens and at University College, Oxford, before teaching at the University of Wales in Aberystwyth (1954–59) and at King's College, London, where he was professor of comparative law (1966–81) and director of the Centre of European Law (1974–81). Chloros helped establish a degree course in French and English law jointly with the University of Paris and lectured in many countries, including France, Greece, Sweden, and Yugoslavia. He was involved in advising the government of the Seychelles on the creation of a revised legal system during the early 1970s and in negotiating Greece's entry to the EC. Chloros's books included *Yugoslav Civil Law* (1970) and *Codification in a Mixed Jurisdiction* (1977). From 1976 he was general editor of *European Studies in Law.*

Churchill, Sarah (SARAH LADY AUDLEY), British actress (b. Oct. 7, 1914, London, England—d. Sept. 24, 1982, London), was the daughter of Sir Winston Churchill and an actress whose three marriages and unhappy private life at times overshadowed her real achievements. She made her debut in 1936 and went on to play in classical and modern roles on the London and New York stage, notably as Nastasya in *The Idiot.* During World War II she gave up her career to accompany her father to the summit conferences at Teheran and Yalta. After the war Churchill returned to the theatre and developed her talent as a painter. She also published two books of poetry and two volumes of memoirs, *A Thread in the Tapestry* and *Keep on Dancing.*

Chuykov, Vasily Ivanovich, Soviet Army commander (b Jan. 31, 1900, Serebryanye Prudy, Tula Province, Russia—d. March 18, 1982, Moscow, U.S.S.R.), led the 62nd Army to victory at Stalingrad (1942–43), the battle that marked the turning point in the German campaign against the U.S.S.R. during World War II. Chuykov's unit, renamed the 8th Guards Army, went on to take part in a series of offensive operations that led the Soviet forces to Berlin. Chuykov joined the Red Army when it was founded in 1918. After graduating from a military academy in 1925, he spent some time in China as military adviser to Chiang Kai-shek. Returning home in 1937, he commanded an army corps that occupied northeastern Poland in 1939. After World War II Chuykov remained in East Germany and was appointed commander in chief of the Soviet forces there in 1949. During the period 1960–64 he served as deputy minister of defense and commander in chief of the Soviet land forces. In 1961 he was elected a member of the Central Committee of the Communist Party of the Soviet Union and was a member of the Supreme Soviet during the years 1946–66.

Cody, John Patrick Cardinal, U.S. prelate of the Roman Catholic Church (b. Dec. 24, 1907, St. Louis, Mo.—d. April 25, 1982, Chicago, Ill.), was from 1965 to 1982 the stalwart archbishop of Chicago, the largest Roman Catholic archdiocese in the U.S. Cody earned Ph.D.'s in philosophy, theology, and canon law. He was ordained a priest on Dec. 8, 1931. Two years later he was assigned to the staff of the Vatican secretariat of state, headed by Giovanni Battista Montini, who later became Pope Paul VI and Cody's patron and mentor. Cody then returned to the U.S. and served the church in various capacities in St. Louis and Kansas City, Mo. In 1964 he became archbishop of the New Orleans (La.) archdiocese and came to national attention in executing his predecessor's order to integrate archdiocesan schools. The following year Pope Paul VI named Cody archbishop of Chicago, the spiritual leader of 2.3 million Catholics; in 1967 he was named a cardinal. During his tenure in Chicago, Cody became a controversial figure. Although he was given unwavering support by the Vatican and

was applauded for his skills as an administrator, Cody encountered dissension within the clergy. He largely ignored the Second Vatican Council directive to open the church to more broad consultations and decision-making responsibilities. He angered priests who viewed his rule as autocratic, and during Cody's pastorship diocesan clergy resigned at a rate exceeding the national average. In 1981 Cody came under fire when the *Chicago Sun-Times* charged him with diverting church funds. A federal grand jury began investigating allegations that the cardinal misused as much as $1 million in church funds to benefit his stepcousin, Helen Dolan Wilson. In reply to allegations made by his detractors, Cody said, "Any accusations against the shepherd are also against the church." On Dec. 8, 1981, the ailing Cody celebrated 50 years as a priest with a special mass.

Collins, the Rev. Canon (Lewis) John, British Anglican clergyman (b. March 23, 1905, Hawkhurst, Kent, England—d. Dec. 30, 1982, London, England), was a nonconformist who in 1946 founded the interdenominational Christian Action movement, of which he was chairman until 1973. He was also prominent as chairman (1958–64) of the Campaign for Nuclear Disarmament (CND) and of the Martin Luther King Foundation (1969–73). As a residentiary canon of St. Paul's Cathedral, London, from 1948 until 1981, he was an outspoken preacher whose sermons on current topics of national and international concern often struck a controversial note. Collins, who was educated at Cranbrook School and at Sidney Sussex College and Westcott House, Cambridge, was ordained deacon in 1928. After a year as curate at Whitstable he returned to Sidney Sussex as chaplain. In 1931 he was appointed to a minor canonry at St. Paul's and lectured for a time at King's College, University of London, before becoming vice-principal at Westcott House in 1934. In 1937 he moved to Oxford, where he was first lecturer and chaplain and then dean (1938–48) of Oriel College. During World War II he was a chaplain with the Royal Air Force. At that time the seeds of Christian Action were sown, and the year after his return to Oxford the movement was launched with the support of a number of prominent churchmen and others, including the economist Barbara Ward. One of Christian Action's main areas of concern became South Africa, and funds were raised to support passive resistance to apartheid and to help opponents of the system who were arrested. Collins played a leading role in the inauguration of CND in 1958, taking part in the original and subsequent "Aldermaston marches." However, the CND changed its character after the formation in 1960 of Bertrand Russell's Committee of 100 and after the inclusion of anarchist groups; in 1964 Collins resigned his chairmanship. Among his publications were (with Victor Gollancz) *Christianity and the War Crisis* (1951) and the autobiographical *Faith Under Fire* (1966).

Collins, Norman Richard, British writer, publisher, and broadcasting executive (b. Oct. 3, 1907—d. Sept. 6, 1982, London, England), was the author of a best-selling novel, *London Belongs to Me,* and a pioneer in commercial television. After leaving school, he joined the Oxford University Press, wrote a study of publishing, and in 1934 published his first novel. Collins joined the publishing firm of Victor Gollancz Ltd. and established his reputation with *London Belongs to Me* (1945; adapted as a television series, 1977). In 1941 he joined the British Broadcasting Corporation (BBC), was chosen in 1944 to launch the General Overseas Service, and two years later became controller of the Light Programme which he established as the most popular BBC radio station. From 1947, as controller of television, he was responsible for many innovations in the new medium, notably coverage of the 1950 election results. But in that year he resigned. Collins criticized BBC policies and campaigned for the formation of a commercial television service. When the latter was established Collins was named deputy chairman of the Associated Television Corporation, a post he held until his retirement in 1977. He remained active as a director of

Independent Television News. His last novel, *The Husband's Story*, appeared in 1978.

Conried, Hans, U.S. actor (b. April 15, 1917, Baltimore, Md.—c. Jan. 5, 1982, Burbank, Calif.), had a mastery of a vast array of foreign accents and continental mannerisms that led to a successful career

as a character actor on stage, radio, and television. After Conried first gained applause for his role as a wacky Bulgarian sculptor in the Broadway musical *Can-Can*, he played Professor Kropotkin on the radio show "My Friend Irma." On television he portrayed the eccentric Lebanese Uncle Tonoose on "Make Room for Daddy." Conried also appeared in about 100 motion pictures, usually in villainous roles and often donning Nazi uniforms. His films included *Dramatic School* (1938), *Mrs. Parkington* (1944), *Rock-A-Bye Baby* (1958), *The Patsy* (1964), and *Oh God Book II* (1980). During his latter years Conried made guest appearances on such television shows as "Love Boat" and "Fantasy Island."

Coote, Robert, British actor (b. Feb. 4, 1909, London, England—d. Nov. 25, 1982, New York, N.Y.), was a character actor known for his portrayal of engaging buffoons and elderly army officers. Of the latter, his most successful part was as Colonel Pickering in *My Fair Lady*, which he played in the original 1956 Broadway production and later in London. The son of a comedian, Coote acted in repertory in Britain and South Africa, making his London debut in 1931. He served with the Royal Canadian Air Force during World War II and in 1953 appeared in Peter Ustinov's *The Love of Four Colonels* in New York, establishing one of his most successful character types. His other stage parts included Colonel Lukyn in *The Magistrate* and Colonel Richardson in *The Jockey Club Stakes*. He also appeared in many films, including *A Yank at Oxford* (1938), *Forever Amber* (1947), *Rommel* (1951), and *Prudence and the Pill* (1968).

Corbett, Harry H., British actor (b. Feb. 28, 1925, Rangoon, Burma—d. March 21, 1982), was best known for his role as scrap merchant Harold Steptoe in the television situation comedy "Steptoe and Son." The series, first shown in 1962 and revived in 1970, was highly popular and led to his being typecast as the frustrated and ineffectual son constantly struggling to free himself from his domineering father (played by Wilfrid Brambell). The role, successful as it was, tended to overshadow Corbett's other work, especially his appearances on stage in a variety of modern and classical parts. He left school at the age of 14 and worked in various jobs before serving in the Royal Marines during World War II. In 1948 he joined the Chorlton repertory company. Corbett went on to play with Joan Littlewood's Theatre Workshop and made frequent appearances in films as a supporting actor in comedy roles; these included two adaptations of the "Steptoe" series. He also played Hamlet, Macbeth, and Richard II on stage and acted in productions of *Volpone* and *The Way of the World*. He started

the Langham Group for television drama and helped form a film company, Wimpole Productions. Corbett was made Officer of the Order of the British Empire in 1976.

Curzon, Sir Clifford Michael, British pianist (b. May 18, 1907, London, England—d. Sept. 1, 1982, London), was one of the few British pianists to enjoy an international reputation and was a superb technician whose rare concerts and infrequent recordings were much prized. He studied at the Royal Academy of Music and later with Artur Schnabel, who was a major influence on Curzon's work. Though a brilliant exponent of Romantic music, Curzon later concentrated on earlier composers, notably Mozart, though he made few recordings of Mozart's work. Throughout his life Curzon devoted long periods of time to study and

made exceptionally high demands on himself and those who played with him. His interpretations of Schubert, Tchaikovsky, Brahms, and Beethoven were especially admired. Curzon was made Commander of the British Empire in 1958 and was knighted in 1977. In 1980 he was awarded the Royal Philharmonic Society's Gold Medal.

Dannay, Frederic, U.S. author (b. Oct. 20, 1905, Brooklyn, N.Y.—d. Sept. 3, 1982, New York, N.Y.), together with his cousin Manfred B. Lee wrote under the pseudonym Ellery Queen and during their 42-year collaboration turned out some 60 detective novels that intrigued readers worldwide. Their Ellery Queen novels depicted Queen as a highly intelligent author and sleuth whose finely tuned powers of deduction made it possible for him to aid his father, a New York police detective, in solving highly complex crimes. Some of their best-known works included *The Four of Hearts* (1938), *The Devil to Pay* (1938), and *A Fine and Private Place* (1971), their last novel. They also published an anthology of detective stories, *Ellery Queen's Challenge to the Reader* (1938); novels about a detective named Drury Lane, published under the pseudonym Barnaby Ross; and in 1941 the first issue of *Ellery Queen's Mystery Magazine*. There were also an Ellery Queen radio program, a television series, and motion pictures.

Dantine, Helmut, Austrian-born actor (b. Oct. 7, 1917, Vienna, Austria—d. May 2, 1982, Beverly Hills, Calif.), spent three months in a concentration camp before he fled to the U.S. in 1938 and then embarked on a successful film career portraying Nazis in such classic World War II motion pictures as *Mrs. Miniver*, *Casablanca*, *Mission to Moscow*, and *Passage to Marseilles*. Dantine, who played both sympathetic German soldiers and sadistic Nazi SS officers, was given his first starring role in *Hotel Berlin* in 1945. His leading roles in *Edge of Darkness* and *Shadow of a Woman* were followed by a stint on Broadway, but he later returned to Hollywood in the 1950s in supporting roles. His other credits included *Call Me Madam*, *War and Peace*, and *The 5th Musketeer*. In 1959 he curtailed his acting career to

produce such films as *Bring Me the Head of Alfredo Garcia* and *The Killer Elite*, but he usually could not resist the temptation to cast himself in a small role. Dantine's last production was *Tarzan the Apeman* (1981).

de Freitas, Sir Geoffrey Stanley, British politician (b. April 7, 1913—d. Aug. 10, 1982, Cambridge, England), was Britain's high commissioner in Ghana and in Kenya during the early 1960s. A Labour member of Parliament for some 30 years and a strong supporter of British entry into the European Economic Community, he was vice-president of the European Parliament from 1975 to 1979. De Freitas studied law at the University of Cambridge and then in the U.S. at Yale University. He joined the Labour Party before starting his practice as a lawyer. After service with the Royal Air Force during World War II, he was elected to Parliament in 1945 and was successively appointed parliamentary private secretary to the prime minister and undersecretary of state for air. After the Labour defeat in 1951, he became a distinguished member of the opposition, and the Conservative government in 1961 took the exceptional step of appointing him, rather than a Conservative, as high commissioner in Ghana. In 1963, during an abortive attempt to form an East African Federation, he went to Kenya, but he returned to Britain to fight in the 1964 election. He led the British delegation to the Consultative Assembly of the Council of Europe in 1965, was elected president of the Assembly the next year, and chaired the Labour Committee for Europe from 1965 to 1972. De Freitas was knighted in 1961.

Del Monaco, Mario, Italian opera singer (b. July 27, 1915, Florence, Italy—d. Oct. 16, 1982, Mestre, near Venice, Italy), enjoyed an international reputation as one of the outstanding operatic tenors of the post-World War II period. He studied at the Rome Opera School and made his official debut in 1941 in *Madama Butterfly* in Milan. Five years later Del Monaco appeared at Covent Garden, London, and in 1951 he joined the Metropolitan Opera in New York City where he was so successful that in 1957 he was awarded the Golden Orpheus as the world's best tenor by an international jury. In 1962, at Covent Garden, he sang *Otello*, achieving probably the greatest triumph of his career. After his retirement in 1973, Del Monaco taught young singers in Venice.

De Rochemont, Richard Guertis, U.S. filmmaker (b. Dec. 13, 1903, Chelsea, Mass.—d. Aug. 4, 1982, Flemington, N.J.), as executive producer (1943–51) of "The March of Time," a series of film news features that combined newsreel material and specially staged scenes and interviews, received an Academy Award in 1949 for his production of *A Chance to Live*, a riveting story about Boys Town in Italy. After succeeding his brother Louis as executive producer of the series, de Rochemont turned out some of the most acclaimed "March of Time" reels, including *Underground Report*, *What to Do with Germany*, *Sweden Takes the Middle Road*, and *The Story of the Vatican*, the first sanctioned feature-length film of the papal state. Besides working for Time-Life during most of his film career, de Rochemont also served as president of Vavin Inc., a firm he founded in 1955 to produce informational films.

Dubinsky, David (DAVID DOBNIEVSKI), U.S. labour leader (b. Feb. 22, 1892, Brest Litovsk, Russian Poland—d. Sept. 17, 1982, New York, N.Y.), was the dynamic president of the International Ladies Garment Workers Union (ILGWU) from 1932 to 1966, a foe of Communism and racketeering, and an influential labour leader who played a major role in the formation of the Committee for Industrial Organization (later the Congress of Industrial Organizations). As a master baker in Russia, Dubinsky was elected secretary of his local bakers' union at age 15 and the following year was arrested as an agitator and exiled to Siberia, spending 18

WIDE WORLD

months in several prisons en route. He escaped and resumed his work as a baker but eventually immigrated to the U.S. In 1911 he became a cloak cutter in New York, joined Local 10 of the ILGWU, and became a U.S. citizen. A cloakmakers' strike in 1916 sparked Dubinsky's interest in union affairs, and in 1918 he was elected to the executive board of Local 10. He successively served in Local 10 as vice-chairman (1919), chairman (1920), and general manager and secretary-treasurer (1921). In 1922 he was elected vice-president and a member of the executive board of ILGWU. Dubinsky was elected secretary-treasurer of the ILGWU in 1929 and became acting president when Benjamin Schlesinger became ill. After he was elected president of the ILGWU in 1932, Dubinsky reduced the union's debt by $1 million, brought 410,000 new members into the union, helped oust racketeers from union leadership, published financial statements before it was legally required, reduced work hours and increased wages, established research and engineering departments to improve efficiency in the garment trade, and instituted educational and cultural programs for union members. Besides helping John L. Lewis set up the Committee for Industrial Organization in 1935, he served as a vice-president of the American Federation of Labor and helped form the American Labor Party, but when that came under Communist influence, he helped organize the Liberal Party, which became a major force in New York politics. Dubinsky also served on many U.S. government boards and was engaged in helping countries overseas.

Dubos, René Jules, French-born microbiologist (b. Feb. 20, 1901, Saint-Brice, France—d. Feb. 20, 1982, New York, N.Y.), conducted pioneering work in bacteriology and discovered that by isolating antibacterial substances from certain organisms, he could obtain germ-fighting drugs. This 1939 research led to the production of the first commercial antibiotics. After Dubos earned a Ph.D. (1927) from Rutgers University, he spent the bulk of his scientific career at Rockefeller Institute and the Rockefeller University, where he also did research on acquired immunity, soil bacteria, human fungal infections, and the organisms that cause dysentery, pneumonia, and tuberculosis. In the 1960s Dubos became a concerned environmentalist who warned of man's harm to himself through environmental pollution. He was also the author of 20 books including *Bacterial and Mycotic Infections of Man* (1948), *Pasteur and Modern Medicine* (1960), *Only One Earth* (written with Barbara Ward for the 1972 UN Conference on the Human Environment), and *So Human an Animal,* which won the

Pulitzer Prize for nonfiction in 1969. Dubos's last book, *Celebrations of Life,* was published in 1981.

Duncan, Ronald Frederick Henry, British dramatist and poet (b. Aug. 6, 1914, Salisbury, Rhodesia—d. June 3, 1982, Barnstable, England), was a highly individual writer and the author of such plays as *This Way to the Tomb* (1945) and *Stratton* (1949), which expressed in intense, poetic language his sense of the decline in moral values in contemporary society. *This Way to the Tomb,* a "masque and antimasque" with music by Benjamin Britten, was his greatest success, and he collaborated with Britten again in the opera *The Rape of Lucretia* (1946), for which he adapted the libretto. He also helped to found the English Stage Company at the Royal Court Theatre. Educated in Switzerland and at the University of Cambridge, he edited *The Townsman* from 1938 to 1946 and later wrote for the *Evening Standard* from his farm in Devon. His play *Saint Spiv* (1950) was adapted as a novel, and his other works included the plays *Our Lady's Tumbler* (1951), *Don Juan* (1953), and *The Seven Deadly Virtues* (1968). Duncan's volumes of autobiography were *All Men Are Islands* (1964) and *How to Make Enemies* (1968). He also wrote *A Memoir of Benjamin Britten* (1981).

Durant, Henry William, British market researcher (b. 1902, London, England—d. June 8, 1982, London), pioneered the use in Britain of the opinion polling techniques developed in the U.S. by George Gallup. His work, and the high standards he set, did much to establish scientific market research and polling in Britain and to gain public confidence for the idea. A man of humble origins, he left school at 14 and, while working for an insurance company, took his matriculation and eventually was graduated in economics at the London School of Economics and Political Science. He went on to earn a Ph.D. In 1936 he was chosen by the Gallup organization to undertake research in Britain and set up the British Institute of Public Opinion, later renamed Social Surveys (Gallup Poll) Ltd. During World War II the company carried out a range of opinion surveys for the Ministry of Information and other government bodies and after the war gained much credit for correctly forecasting the Labour Party victory in the 1945 elections. Durant helped found the Market Research Society, becoming its first chairman in 1947. He was also president (1952–54) of the European Society for Marketing and Opinion Research.

Eberhard, Fritz, German publicist and politician (b. Oct. 2, 1896, Dresden, Germany—d. March 30, 1982, West Berlin), devoted his life to opposing Fascism and, after World War II, to defending the constitution of the Federal Republic. The son of Baron Adolf von Rauschenplat, he took the name Eberhard under the Nazi regime when, as a member of the German Social Democratic Party (SPD), he was in opposition to Hitler. In 1937 he went to London, where he remained, engaging in psychological warfare as a broadcaster with the BBC, until the end of World War II. He later helped to draft the West German constitution, was an SPD member of the Baden-Württemberg parliament (1946–49) and secretary of state (1947–49) in the provincial government, and became director (1949–58) of Süddeutscher Rundfunk, a leading radio station. He was subsequently a professor at the Institute of Publicistics at Berlin's Free University. Respected as both an academic and a journalist, Eberhard subordinated personal political ambition to the task of defending the democratic ideals in which he believed and remained an independent voice in West German politics.

Eldjarn, Kristjan, Icelandic scholar (b. Dec. 6, 1916, Tjorn, Iceland—d. Sept. 13, 1982, Cleveland, Ohio), was president of Iceland from 1968 to 1980 and an expert in Icelandic literature and history. He studied at the University of Copenhagen, as well as in Iceland, and was director of the National Museum, Reykjavik, from 1947 to 1968. He also wrote several books on history and archaeology. Eldjarn, who was elected by a large majority to the presidency in 1968, was returned unopposed in 1972 and 1976.

Engel, Lehman, U.S. conductor (b. Sept. 14, 1910, Jackson, Miss.—d. Aug. 29, 1982, New York, N.Y.), was the eminent musical director of more than 100 musicals, including such classics as *Show Boat, Annie Get Your Gun, Guys and Dolls,* and *Carousel,* and the accomplished composer of incidental music for such productions as *The Time of Your Life, Anne of the Thousand Days,* and *A Streetcar Named Desire.* Engel also used his expertise to instruct students in musical lyrics at Broadcast Music Inc. in New York, Los Angeles, and Toronto. He compiled his theories on musical theatre in such books as *Words with Music* (1972), *Getting Started in the Theater* (1973), *The American Musical Theater* (1975), and *Their Words Are Music* (1975). Engel, who studied at the Cincinnati Conservatory and the Cincinnati College of Music, both in Ohio, was then awarded a graduate scholarship at the Juilliard School in New York. During the 1930s he composed music for the Martha Graham Dance Company and had the distinction of conducting the first U.S. performance of Kurt Weill's *The Threepenny Opera.* A musician who composed for radio, television, and film, he also recorded more than 60 albums, many featuring selections from popular musicals. Besides earning esteem for his technique in conducting musical comedy, Engel was awarded two Antoinette Perry (Tony) Awards. The first, in 1950, was for conducting Gian Carlo Menotti's opera *The Consul,* and the second, in 1953, paid tribute to his direction of *Wonderful Town* and operettas by Gilbert and Sullivan. Engel published his autobiography, *This Bright Day,* in 1974.

Evans of Hungershall, Benjamin Ifor Evans, BARON, British author and educator (b. Aug. 19, 1899, London, England—d. Aug. 28, 1982, London), was provost of University College, London, from 1951 to 1966 and an English literature scholar whose love of his subject was perhaps best illustrated in his popular compendiums *A Short History of English Literature* (1940) and *A Short History of English Drama* (1950). Evans studied at University College and was professor at the Universities of Southampton, Sheffield, and London before becoming principal of Queen Mary College, London, in 1944. As provost of University College he demonstrated extraordinary gifts as a fund raiser and administrator and made an exceptional contribution to the post-World War II development of higher education in London. His books reflected a liberal and eclectic approach rather than profound scholarship. Evans published studies of William Morris, Ben Jonson, Victorian poetry, and the language of Shakespeare's plays. He also co-edited with W. W. Greg an edition of *Most Virtuous & Godly Susanna,* a previously unknown 16th-century play. His horror of 20th-century materialism was reflected both in *English Literature Between the Wars* (1948) and in his three novels—*In Search of Stephen Vane* (1946), *The Shop on the King's Road* (1947), and *The Church in the Markets* (1949). He was knighted in 1955 and made a life peer in 1967.

Fassbinder, Rainer Werner, West German film director (b. May 31, 1946, Bad Wörishofen, Germany—d. June 10, 1982, Munich, West Germany), was a leading figure in the young German cinema which gained international recognition during the 1970s. As director of 41 films for the cinema and television in a career of less than 14 years, he was a passionate and often bitter critic of German society. His work gave a pessimistic view of a world hostile to individual happiness and self-fulfillment. Fassbinder started his career as an actor and played with the Munich Action Theatre in 1967 before founding his Antitheater, which performed his own plays and his free adaptations of the classics. He made his first full-length feature film, *Liebe ist kälter als der Todt,* in 1969, and he maintained a prodigious output until he completed his last work, *Querelle,* shortly before his death. Influenced aesthetically and ideologically by the radical French film director Jean-Luc Godard, Fassbinder portrayed the sufferings of individuals who were on the fringes of society: immigrant workers, homosexuals, and lonely women. *Die bitteren Tränen der Petra von Kant* (1972; *The Bitter Tears of Petra von Kant*), the story of a fashion designer, was an international success, as was *Die Ehe der Maria Braun* (1978; *The Marriage of Maria Braun*), which won first prize at the Berlin Film Festival. His other notable works included *Der Händler der vier Jahreszeiten* (1971; *The Merchant of Four Seasons*), *Angst essen Seele auf* (1973; *Ali* and *Ali: Fear Eats the Soul*), and *Effi Briest* (1974). His last works, including *Lili Marleen* (1980) and *Lola* (1981), seemed less austere and were intended as part of a series portraying women against the background of German history.

Feldman, Marty, British comic, actor, and motion picture director (b. July 8, 1933, London, England—d. Dec. 2, 1982, Mexico City, Mexico), was a zany comedian whose wide-set bulging eyes became his trademark. Feldman, a star on such British television shows as "Every Home Should Have One" and "Marty," earned a European cult following before he came to the U.S. (1974), where he appeared in such Mel Brooks films as *Young Frankenstein* and *Silent Movie* and in *The Bed-Sitting Room* and *The Adventures of Sherlock Holmes' Smarter Brother*. Feldman later wrote, directed, and starred in his own films, most notably *The Last Remake of Beau Geste* (1977), a satire on French Foreign Legion films. At the time of his death Feldman was working on *Yellowbeard* in Mexico City.

Felici, Pericle Cardinal, Italian prelate of the Roman Catholic Church (b. Aug. 1, 1911, near Rome, Italy—d. March 22, 1982, Foggia, Italy), made his career in the Vatican administration, specializing in legal matters and becoming mainly responsible for the reform of canon law completed in draft form in 1981. Ordained in 1933, he became a doctor of philosophy, theology, and civil and canon law and in 1938 was appointed rector of the pontifical seminary in Rome. At the same time, he was auditor on the tribunal of the Rota and held a number of other Vatican posts. Secretary to Domenico Cardinal Tardini, whom Pope John XXIII had entrusted with the task of preparing for the Second Vatican Council, Felici was ordained bishop in 1960 and became secretary-general of the council, playing a major role in its proceedings. He was a close associate of Pope Paul VI, who appointed him cardinal in 1967 and put him in charge of reforming canon law. In 1977 he was appointed prefect of the Tribunal of the Signatura Apostolica.

Fenton, Clyde Cornwall, Australian "flying doctor" (b. May 16, 1901, Warrnambool, Victoria, Australia—d. Feb. 27, 1982, Melbourne, Australia), was a pioneer of Australia's "flying doctor" service and a folk hero whose exploits were appreciated more by his patients and the general public than by the civil aviation authorities. He graduated as a doctor in 1925 and learned to fly four years later. After conducting research in England, Fenton was appointed medical officer at Katherine, Northern Territory, in 1934 and started to use his own Gipsy Moth biplane to attend patients in the outback, thus initiating the Northern Territory Medical Service. A fearless and even a reckless pilot, he flew in all weather and was forced down several times, surviving, sometimes for days, in a desert or jungle. Fenton also indulged in feats such as landing in the main street of Katherine to buy a drink, which added to his legend but did not endear him to the authorities. In 1940 he was appointed Officer of the Order of the British Empire for his work in the flying doctor service, and he served with the Royal Australian Air Force during World War II as an instructor. His other pioneering exploits included the first solo flight across the Gulf of Siam. Fenton's autobiography, *Flying Doctor*, describes his adventurous career.

Ferras, Christian, French violinist (b. June 17, 1933, Le Touquet, France—d. Sept. 15, 1982, Paris, France), was a virtuoso performer, noted for his interpretations of Romantic music. His performance of Alban Berg's violin concerto was reputed to be among the finest ever heard. A prodigy, Ferras gained the first prize at the Paris Conservatoire at the age of ten. He toured Europe, the U.S., the Soviet Union, and the Far East, played with many outstanding orchestras and conductors, and made recordings that long retained their popularity. Ferras performed all the Bach sonatas for unaccompanied violin in Munich, West Germany, and with Yehudi Menuhin recorded the Bach double violin concerto. Ferras, who taught at the Conservatoire, briefly retired, but in 1981 he performed again in public with his accompanist, the pianist Pierre Barbizet.

First, Ruth, South African writer (b. 1925, Johannesburg, South Africa—d. Aug. 17, 1982, Maputo, Mozambique), was a lifelong activist in the struggle against white supremacy in southern Africa. First studied at the University of the Witwatersrand, joined the Communist Party, and actively supported the African miners' strike of 1946. She became Johannesburg editor of radical newspapers and embarked on a career as a brilliant investigative journalist, exposing the appalling conditions of nonwhite workers and farm labourers in South Africa under apartheid. She and her husband, Joe Slovo, a leading member of the Revolutionary Council of the African National Congress, were among the defendants in the mass 1956 treason trial. They were acquitted, but she was banned from journalism in the early 1960s and during 1963 held in solitary confinement, an experience she recorded in her book *117 Days*. First settled in London, became a lecturer in sociology at the University of Durham, and published studies of African politics, including *The Barrel of a Gun*. She also wrote with Ann Scott a biography of the South African writer Olive Schreiner. She and Joe Slovo continued to play an active role in the political opposition to apartheid, and she went to Mozambique primarily to study the conditions of migrant workers from the South African mines. First was killed by a letter bomb sent to the Centre for African Studies in Maputo, Mozambique, where she had been research director since 1978.

Fitzmaurice, Sir Gerald Gray, British international lawyer (b. Oct. 24, 1901, Storrington, Sussex, England—d. Sept. 7, 1982, London, England), served as a judge of the International Court of Justice and the European Court of Human Rights and was one of the most outstanding international lawyers of his time. He studied at Cambridge, was called to the bar in 1925, and became a legal adviser at the Foreign Office. During the late 1940s Fitzmaurice was involved in the drafting of major international treaties and defended the British position in disputes at the International Court of Justice. After his appointment as principal legal adviser in 1953 he played an important role in preparing the four conventions on the Law of the Sea in Geneva. Fitzmaurice served on the International Court of Justice from 1960 to 1973 and during his tenure became involved in a controversy over the court's competence to examine the case of South West Africa/Namibia. From 1974 to 1980, he was a judge with the European Court of Human Rights and reviewed a number of cases involving the U.K., including the issue of human rights in Northern Ireland. Fitzmaurice was also president of the tribunal for the Beagle Channel arbitration and, even after his retirement, negotiated a dispute involving Kuwait and the Aminoil Company.

Fonda, Henry Jaynes, U.S. actor (b. May 16, 1905, Grand Island, Neb.—d. Aug. 12, 1982, Los Angeles, Calif.), had a sterling acting career that was climaxed by his best actor Academy Award-winning role as a crotchety octogenarian facing death in *On Golden Pond* (1981). Fonda, who represented the noble, honest man of conscience in more than 80 films, made his film debut in *The Farmer Takes a Wife* (1935). Fonda's unaffected manner, Midwestern twang, and long, purposeful strides became a familiar hallmark to moviegoers who embraced him as their homespun hero. A giant in the film industry, he created an array of poignant characters including a backwoods presidential candidate in *Young Mr. Lincoln* (1939), the farmer Tom Joad in *The Grapes of Wrath* (1940), the naive womanizer in *The Lady Eve* (1941), the troubled cowpoke who fails to stop a lynching in *The Ox-Bow Incident* (1943), Wyatt Earp in *My Darling Clementine* (1946), and the idealistic navy officer in *Mister Roberts* (1955), one of his most celebrated roles both on stage and in

film. His list of credits was both lengthy and impressive; Fonda also appeared in *The Wrong Man, Twelve Angry Men, Jesse James* (as brother Frank), *Jezebel, Advise and Consent, Fail Safe, Once upon a Time in the West,* and *The Battle of Midway.* Besides his many extraordinary film roles, Fonda repeatedly returned to the theatre, where he played in *The Caine Mutiny Court-Martial, Clarence Darrow,* and *Mister Roberts.* Fonda, who earlier had received only one Academy Award nomination (for his performance in *Grapes of Wrath*) and an honorary Oscar (1981), realized a lifetime dream a few short months before his death when he received an Academy Award for best actor for his inspired characterization of Norman Thayer in *On Golden Pond.* Earlier, in 1978, Fonda had received the sixth Life Achievement Award of the American Film Institute. He also appeared on such television series as "The Deputy" and "The Smith Family" and received wide acclaim for his portrayals in the 1980 television productions of "The Oldest Living Graduate" and "Gideon's Trumpet." Fonda, who married five times, was the father of Jane (actress and social activist) and Peter (actor and director).

Fortas, Abe, U.S. lawyer (b. June 19, 1910, Memphis, Tenn.—d. April 5, 1982, Washington, D.C.), was a prominent Washington lawyer with the influential

firm of Arnold, Fortas & Porter before being appointed associate justice of the Supreme Court by Pres. Lyndon B. Johnson in 1965. Fortas, who graduated first in his class from Yale Law School, played a significant role in Franklin D. Roosevelt's Brain Trust, which helped shape the programs of the New Deal. As a lawyer he argued the landmark case of *Gideon* v. *Wainwright* before the Supreme Court, which ruled that poor defendants were guaranteed the right to free counsel. After his appointment to the Supreme Court, Fortas wrote numerous majority opinions that expanded individual rights. A 1966 court decision stated that juveniles facing court proceedings were entitled to many of the constitutional protections afforded to adults, and in 1969 a decision upheld the right of high school students to wear black armbands to protest the Vietnam war. In the same year, Fortas was forced to resign under pressure when Attorney General John Mitchell disclosed that in 1966 Fortas had accepted $20,000 from Louis Wolfson, who had been under investigation for violating securities laws. In this way Fortas became the only justice ever to resign under the threat of impeachment.

Foster, Harold R., U.S. comic strip artist (b. Aug. 16, 1892, Halifax, Nova Scotia—d. July 25, 1982, Spring Hill, Fla.), was a foremost illustrator and the creator of the "Prince Valiant" comic strip in 1937 and of its companion strip, "The Medieval Castle," in 1944. In 1921 Foster arrived in Chicago on a bicycle to attend classes at the Art Institute. He then studied at the National Academy of Design and the Chicago Academy of Fine Arts before working as an illustrator and advertising artist. Foster also drew the first "Tarzan" comic strip in 1929, but it was not until 1931 that he began sketching the strip for the Sunday newspaper. Foster, who was widely praised for his precise figure drawings and authentic costuming, turned over the "Prince Valiant" comic strip to his associates in 1979.

Frazier, Brenda (BRENDA DIANA DUFF FRAZIER KELLY CHATFIELD-TAYLOR), U.S. socialite (b. 1920?—d. May 3, 1982, Newton, Mass.), was one of the most photographed debutantes of the pre-World War II era and possibly the most famous society glamour girl of the century. At the age of 12 she became an heiress, and after a lavish debutante ball at age 18 she became a permanent fixture in New York café society. Her escorts, including John F. Kennedy and Howard Hughes, never failed to make front-page news. Frazier's fortune, however, could not compensate for two failed marriages (John Simms Kelly and Robert F. Chatfield-Taylor), years of psychoanalysis, and ill health, which forced her to abandon her exhausting social activities in the early 1960s.

Frei Montalva, Eduardo, Chilean politician (b. Jan. 16, 1911, Santiago, Chile—d. Jan. 22, 1982, Santiago), was a self-styled radical social reformer who became the first Christian Democratic president in the Western Hemisphere when he was convincingly elected president of Chile in 1964. After Frei graduated in law from the Catholic University of Chile in 1933, he was a delegate to the Congress of Catholic Young People held in Rome in 1934. The following year he helped establish a youth department within the Chilean Conservative Party, but in 1938 he became disenchanted with the Conservative Party and joined other youth department leaders to form the National Falange, an anti-Fascist social Christian party. Frei was elected president of the Falange in 1941, 1943, and 1945, served as minister of public works in the governments of José Antonia Ríos in 1945–46 and Gabriel González Videla in 1946–49, and was elected to the Senate in 1949. The Falange merged in 1957 with the Social Christian Conservatives to form the Christian Democratic Party, and in 1958 Frei placed third in the presidential election running as a Christian Democrat. In the 1964 presidential elec-

tion Frei defeated the Marxist candidate, Salvadore Allende, with a program of "chileanization" of U.S.-owned copper mines and land redistribution among peasants. Frei's domestic policies were defeated in the legislature, but he played a significant role in foreign policy by promoting Latin-American economic integration and independence from the U.S. Frei, who was ineligible under the constitution to succeed himself, joined the opposition when Allende was elected president. After a 1973 military coup ousted Allende, Frei's party was outlawed, but he continued to work behind the scenes from his law offices and led a campaign to oust Gen. Augusto Pinochet's military government and to return the country to democracy.

Freud, Anna, Austrian-born psychoanalyst (b. Dec. 3, 1895, Vienna, Austria—d. Oct. 9, 1982, London, England), was a pioneer in the field of child psychoanalysis. The youngest child of Sigmund Freud, and the only one to follow her father in the profession of psychoanalysis, she was his close collaborator during his last years. She studied at the

CAMERA PRESS, LONDON

Cottage Lyceum in Vienna and later taught there. Freud became a member of the Vienna Psychoanalysis Society in 1922 and acted as its chairman from 1925. Her specialized interest in child psychology was evident in her first major work, *The Ego and the Mechanisms of Defence* (1937), and, after the family was obliged by the Nazi occupation to move to London in 1938, she set up a nursery in Hampstead and published *Young Children in War Time* (1942) with her close friend Dorothy Burlingham. The Hampstead Child Therapy Clinic, which Freud set up after World War II, became a leading centre for the study of child development, engaging in research, training, and therapy and attracting students from all parts of the world. Her publications at this time confirmed her as an outstanding authority and her inspiration was felt by her many colleagues and students. Her later publications, including *Beyond the Best Interests of the Child* (1973), reflected her growing concern with social problems in relation to child psychology and the legal rights of young people.

Frisch, Karl von, Austrian zoologist (b. Nov. 20, 1886, Vienna, Austria—d. June 12, 1982, Munich, West Germany), was joint winner (with Nikolaas Tinbergen and Konrad Lorenz) of the 1973 Nobel Prize for Physiology or Medicine and was widely known for his remarkable research into insect behaviour. Dedicated from childhood to the study of biology, he attended the Universities of Munich and Vienna and later served briefly as professor at the Universities of Rostock, Breslau, and Graz. Most of Frisch's career was spent at Munich's Zoological Institute, where he served as director for nearly 30 years. Before World War I he undertook research into sense perception in fish and found them to have exceptionally acute hearing. Frisch

made similar studies of sensory perception in insects. In 1919 he began his most astounding work, which was to prove that bees communicate by means of ritual "dancing" movements to show the location of food. His studies in the late 1940s proved bees can navigate by the sun and duplicate an excursion by remembering patterns of polarized light. The results of Frisch's early research, described in his book *Aus dem Leben der Bienen* (1927; *The Dancing Bees,* 1954), were so unexpected that the scientific community at first doubted their validity.

Gale, Sir Richard Nelson, British army officer (b. July 25, 1896, London, England—d. July 29, 1982, Kingston-on-Thames, England), was an outstanding commander of airborne forces during World War II and later served as commander in chief (1952–57) of the British Army of the Rhine (BAOR) and deputy supreme allied commander in Europe (1958–60). Gale attended the Royal Military College, Sandhurst, before serving in World War I on the Western Front and winning the Military Cross. He then spent some 18 years in India. At the beginning of World War II, he was with the War Office and in 1941 was appointed to command the newly formed 1st Parachute Brigade. Before the D-Day landings, as commander of the 6th Airborne Division, Gale was sent into France with his men and fought many fierce battles behind enemy lines. He was awarded the Companion of Distinguished Service Order and the U.S. Legion of Merit and continued to play an important role in the later stages of the war. In 1946 Gale commanded the 1st Division of British troops in Palestine under the mandate, and two years later he took command of British troops in Egypt. In 1949, as an acknowledged expert on the tactical use of airborne troops, he was made director general of military training at the War Office, where he stayed until his appointment to the BAOR. After his formal retirement in 1957 he succeeded Lord Montgomery of Alamein as deputy to Gen. Lauris Norstad at Supreme Headquarters Allied Powers, Europe, where he remained until 1960. He was also aide-de-camp (general) to Queen Elizabeth II from 1954 to 1957. Gale, who was knighted in 1950, published his autobiography, *Call to Arms,* in 1968.

Gardner, John Champlin, Jr., U.S. novelist and poet (b. July 21, 1933, Batavia, N.Y.—d. Sept. 14, 1982, near Susquehanna, Pa.), was a philosophical novelist whose fiction revealed the inner conflicts of man within a physical world. His novels included *The Wreckage of Agathon* (1970), *Grendel* (1971), *The Sunlight Dialogues* (1972), and *October Light,* which won the National Book Critics Circle Award in 1976. Gardner was also a gifted poet and critic who expressed his views about writing in *On Moral Fiction* (1978), in which he declared war "not between art and science but between the age-old enemies, real and fake." Gardner, who taught at various colleges and universities including Oberlin College in Ohio, California State University, San Francisco State University, the University of Detroit, Northwestern University, and Bennington College in Vermont, was a conspicuous presence on campus with his black leather jacket, blue jeans, and motorcycle. Gardner was killed when his motorcycle ran off the road after making a sharp turn.

Garroway, David Cunningham, U.S. television broadcaster (b. July 13, 1913, Schenectady, N.Y.—d. July 21, 1982, Swarthmore, Pa.), as the offbeat pioneering host (1952–61) of the "Today" show was a familiar fixture to early-morning viewers with his thick horn-rimmed glasses, bow tie, and furry sidekick, a chimpanzee named J. Fred Muggs. Garroway, who had a special knack for communicating with audiences, had a wide spectrum of interests including astronomy, photography, jazz, golf, and sports cars. He often regaled audiences with an eclectic assortment of guests; one notable roster included Eleanor Roosevelt, Yogi Berra, and Miss Concrete Life Preserver. Garroway's low-keyed "Chicago style" of broadcasting was developed and perfected in the late 1940s when he launched his television career with the variety show "Garroway at Large." After he moved to New York as host of "Today," his career skyrock-

UPI

eted, but in 1961 Garroway, who was also host of a nighttime variety series, "The Dave Garroway Show," was both physically and mentally exhausted. Garroway never returned to "Today" from a several-months-long leave of absence he had taken in order to attain the "peace" that he had routinely wished his viewers at the close of each show. In later years he was virtually invisible to television audiences although he produced "Exploring the Universe" for public television and briefly served as host of "Nightlife" and "The CBS Newcomers." Garroway, deeply despondent over a heart condition, took his own life.

Gemayel, Bashir, Lebanese politician (b. Nov. 10, 1947, Beirut, Lebanon—d. Sept. 14, 1982, Beirut), was president-elect of Lebanon from August 23 until his assassination, ten days before he was due to take office. Gemayel, who was the youngest child of Phalangist leader Pierre Gemayel, took control of the party in 1980, having already established himself as its military leader. Gemayel studied in Beirut and briefly in the U.S. before making his mark as a Christian militia leader in the 1975 civil war. Noted for his ruthlessness, he was believed to be responsible for the 1978 killing of Tony Franjieh, son of former president Suleiman Franjieh. Gemayel led his Maronite wing of the Phalangists in bloody battles against the National Liberal Party in 1980 and ultimately gained effective military control of a section of the country. But by the time of his election to the presidency he had made peace with some of his former rivals and had called for a reconciliation between Lebanon's warring communities. He was therefore viewed, in Lebanese terms, as a moderate.

Ghotbzadeh, Sadegh Iranian politician (b. 1936—d. Sept. 15, 1982), was foreign minister of Iran from

SVEN SIMON/KATHERINE YOUNG

November 1979 to August 1980. During his student days in Britain and the U.S., he was a leader of opposition to the shah and a supporter of the National Front of Mohammad Mossaddeq. Ghotbzadeh joined Ayatollah Ruhollah Khomeini during the latter's exile and became one of Khomeini's closest associates; he was appointed head of the National Iranian Radio and Television after the revolution. During the crisis caused by the detention of U.S. hostages following the seizure of the U.S. embassy in Tehran, Ghotbzadeh was appointed foreign minister. Though his efforts to resolve the situation were viewed as sincere, he finally resigned over the deadlock in negotiations. In the same year he was arrested briefly after criticizing the Islamic Republican Party and retired from public life. He was arrested in 1982 and accused of plotting against the regime, but he denied any conspiracy to take Khomeini's life. He apparently admitted complicity with Ayatollah Kazem Shariat-Madari in a plot against the government and was executed by a firing squad.

Giauque, William Francis, U.S. chemist (b. May 12, 1895, Niagara Falls, Ont.—d. March 28, 1982, Oakland, Calif.), won the 1949 Nobel Prize for Chemistry for his studies concerning the behaviour of substances at extremely low temperatures. Giauque invented a magnetic cooling device that allowed him to attain temperatures within one degree of absolute zero $(-273.15°\ C)$. His research confirmed the third law of thermodynamics, which states that the entropy of ordered solids reaches zero at the absolute zero of temperature, and established a firm experimental basis for quantum statistics. His work led to improved gasoline, stronger steel, longer wearing rubber, and better glass. In the course of his low-temperature studies of oxygen, Giauque discovered with Herrick L. Johnston the oxygen isotopes of mass 17 and 18. This revelation upset the periodic table of elements and warranted the creation of a second table with altered weights. After earning his Ph.D. from the University of California in 1922, Giauque served as professor of chemistry there until he retired in 1962. However, he rejoined the university in the same year to direct research in the chemistry department and held that post until 1981.

Goldmann, Nahum, Israeli Zionist leader (b. July 10, 1895, Wisznewo, Lithuania—d. Aug. 29, 1982, Bad Reichenhall, West Germany), was an outspoken critic of Israeli politics. The son of a professor of Hebrew, in 1900 Goldmann moved with his family to Germany, where he later attended the Universities of Heidelberg, Marburg, and Berlin. During World War I he worked in the Information Department of the German Foreign Office before escaping from the country in 1934. He took part in many international gatherings of the Zionist movement during the 1920s, and as one of the leading figures in the World Zionist Organization he was instrumental in setting up the 1936 World Jewish Congress. Goldmann declined to take office in the government of Israel when the state was proclaimed in 1948, but in 1952, acting as plenipotentiary of Prime Minister David Ben-Gurion, he negotiated with West German Chancellor Konrad Adenauer a reparations agreement that resulted in payments of some $822 million to Israel and the Jewish survivors of the Holocaust. Goldmann served as president of both the World Zionist Organization (1956–68) and of the World Jewish Congress (1951–78). Always a realist, he repeatedly advocated peaceful coexistence between Arabs and Israelis, saying: "There can be no future for the Jewish state unless agreement is reached with the Arabs."

Gomulka, Wladyslaw, Polish leader (b. Feb. 6, 1905, Krosno, southern Poland—d. Sept. 1, 1982, Warsaw, Poland), was head of the Polish United Workers' (Communist) Party from 1956 to 1970. He first became a member of the clandestine Communist Party of Poland in 1926. After a skirmish with police in Lodz in 1933, he served two years in prison and after his release fled to the U.S.S.R., where he studied at the International Lenin School near Moscow. Gomulka returned to Poland at the

end of 1935 but was rearrested the following year. He escaped when World War II broke out and remained in hiding in German-occupied Poland, where he resumed his activity as a Communist organizer. On Nov. 23, 1943, Gomulka was elected first secretary of the Polish Workers' Party, reorganized under the auspices of Stalin. Gomulka was appointed deputy head, under Boleslaw Bierut, of the Soviet-supported provisional government in Lublin. Accused by Stalin of "nationalist deviation," he was dismissed from the government, expelled from the party, and finally arrested in July 1951. His rehabilitation began after Stalin's death in 1953 but was not completed until after the Poznan riots in June 1956. Gomulka was readmitted to party membership in August and in October became a member of the Central Committee and the Politburo. Deeply disturbed over the Poznan riots, Soviet leader Nikita Khrushchev unexpectedly visited Warsaw on October 19 and had a stormy confrontation with Gomulka. Two days later Gomulka was elected first secretary of the Central Committee. Though his earlier persecution by Stalin had endeared Gomulka to the people, the Poles became disillusioned with Gomulka's halfhearted reforms. Most of the Stalinist features were eliminated but intellectual freedom remained restricted and no major economic reform was carried out. In 1968 riots against Gomulka's regime greatly weakened his political strength. He tried to adopt some new policies and on Dec. 7, 1970, West German Chancellor Willy Brandt signed a treaty by which West Germany recognized the Oder-Neisse line as Poland's western frontier. But on December 20 Gomulka was thrown out of office after he had ordered security forces to open fire on striking workers, 44 of whom were killed in Gdansk and Gdynia.

Gonella, Guido, Italian politician (b. Sept. 18, 1905, Verona, Italy—d. Aug. 19, 1982, Nettuno, Italy), was for many years an influential figure within Italy's Christian Democratic Party. Gonella, who was educated at the Universities of Milan, Rome, Paris, London, and Berlin, taught the philosophy of law at the Universities of Bari and Pavia. His anti-Fascist concerns led him to take part in the founding of the Christian Democratic Party and also, in 1943, of the underground newspaper *Il Popolo*. Gonella held ministerial posts in the post-World War II governments, including that of minister of education (1946–51) and minister of justice on several occasions, the latest being 1968. He was vice-president of the Chamber of Deputies (1966–72) before moving to the Senate and in 1979 was elected to the European Parliament.

Gosden, Freeman F(isher), U.S. radio comedian (b. May 5, 1899, Richmond, Va.—d. Dec. 10, 1982, Los Angeles, Calif.), delighted radio listeners for 32 years (1929–60) as the straight and solid Amos Jones to Charles Correll's gullible Andy Brown on the "Amos 'n' Andy" show, which chronicled the adventures of two southern blacks who traveled north to make their fortune. The two found themselves the owners of a broken-down topless jalopy and they established the Fresh-Air Taxicab Co. in Harlem. Gosden and Correll created more than 550 characters for the program; Gosden also portrayed the bamboozling George "Kingfish" Stevens and the shuffling Lightnin'. In later years Gosden and Correll's mimicry of Negro dialect became an irritation to the National Association for the Advancement of Colored People, which described the show as "a gross libel on the Negro and a distortion of the truth." The radio production of "Amos 'n' Andy" went off the air in 1960, and the television show derived from it was forced off the air in 1966, to the chagrin of Gosden and Correll, who insisted that they had admiration and respect for blacks.

Gotovac, Jakov, Yugoslav composer (b. Nov. 11, 1895, Split, Croatia—d. Oct. 16, 1982, Zagreb, Yugos.), used the folk traditions of his native Croatia to create music of distinctive character and harmonies. Probably the best-known modern Yugoslav composer, he studied law before attending the Musical Academy in Vienna. After returning to Yugoslavia in 1922, he organized a philharmonic society in Sibenik and became conductor and musical director at the Zagreb opera. Gotovac's compositions include the choral piece *Koleda* and the orchestral works *Symphonic Reel* and *The Ploughmen*, all of which showed the influence of folk music and his preference for strong rhythmical expression. He also achieved international success with his comic opera *Ero the Joker*, which was performed in several countries during the 1950s.

Gould, Glenn Herbert, Canadian pianist (b. Sept. 25, 1932, Toronto, Ont.—d. Oct. 4, 1982, Toronto), was an eccentric musical genius who made daring interpretations of Johann Sebastian Bach's music and aroused controversy with his provocative concert style in which he sat on a low chair slumped over the keyboard with his legs crossed, humming tunelessly. At the age of 3 Gould learned to read music; he was composing at 5 and at age 12 was the youngest graduate of the Toronto Conservatory of Music, where he studied piano with Alberto Guerrero, organ with Frederick C. Silvester, and theory with Leo Smith. On Dec. 12, 1945, he made his debut as an organist in a Casavant Society recital in Toronto and was heralded for his technique and his remarkable interpretive intuition. The following year he made his debut as a pianist playing Beethoven's Concerto No. 4. In 1950 he made his broadcasting debut on "Sunday Morning Recital" and detected that he could manipulate the sound of the piano by taking a recording of the broadcast and suppressing the bass and boosting the treble. This discovery became a dominant factor in his approach to performing and recording. In the early 1950s he made several tours of eastern and western Canada, and in 1955, after performing in Washington, D.C., and New York, where he received critical acclaim, Gould became a concert pianist. In 1955 he began his recording career with Columbia and produced the famous recording of Bach's *Goldberg Variations*. Gould made 65 albums during his career. As a concert pianist from 1955 to 1964 he performed works by Bach, Berg, Beethoven, Gibbons, Sweelinck, and Webern and dazzled audiences with his technique but sometimes enraged critics with his stage mannerisms. Gould felt that audiences should be more concerned with the auditory aspects of a concert than with the visual and for this reason in 1964 he abandoned his career as a concert pianist in favour of recording, broadcasting, and writing. In the recording studio Gould was free to experiment to extremes of tempo and articulation and, probably more than any other classical artist, stretched the technological possibilities of recorded music. In addition Gould constructed a series of radio documentaries for the Canadian Broadcasting Corporation; they combined the spoken word with other sound-track materials and described his life of isolation in "The Solitude Trilogy." He also produced "The Idea of North," which is concerned with the isolation in the Canadian Arctic. During the 1970s Gould created a series of programs for Canadian television on 20th-century music. Gould, who had decided to begin conducting after his 50th birthday, suffered a stroke two days after that milestone and died one week later.

Grace, Princess, of Monaco (GRACE KELLY), U.S. actress and princess of Monaco (b. Nov. 12, 1929, Philadelphia, Pa.—d. Sept. 14, 1982, Monte Carlo, Monaco), was a stunning blond whose intriguing, chilly demeanour cast her as the "ice princess"; she starred in 11 motion pictures before abandoning a Hollywood career to marry Prince Rainier of Monaco in 1956 and becoming the much beloved princess of that country. During her six-year (1951–56) heyday in Hollywood she appeared as Grace Kelly in such films as *Fourteen Hours* (1951), in which she made her screen debut; *High Noon* (1952), as Gary Cooper's Quaker wife; *Mogambo* (1953), opposite

UPI

Clark Gable; and *The Country Girl* (1954), for which she won an Academy Award for best actress as Bing Crosby's dowdy wife. But perhaps her most memorable roles were in such Alfred Hitchcock films as *Dial M for Murder* (1954), *Rear Window* (1954), and *To Catch a Thief* (1955). Kelly was the perfect Hitchcock heroine and had what he described as "sexual elegance." After making *The Swan* (1956) and *High Society* (1956), she married Prince Rainier and became princess of Monaco. The couple had three children—Princess Caroline, Prince Albert, and Princess Stephanie—and remained devoted to each other and their family. Princess Grace died of injuries sustained in an automobile accident. She and her daughter Stephanie were driving on a snaking road at Cap-d'Ail in the Côte d'Azur region of France when Princess Grace suffered a stroke and lost control of the car, which plunged down a 13.7-m (45-ft) embankment.

Greenwood of Rossendale, Arthur William James Greenwood (Anthony Greenwood), BARON, British politician (b. Sept. 14, 1911, Leeds, England—d. April 12, 1982, London, England), held ministerial office in Harold Wilson's government from 1964 to 1969 and was a leading figure of the left wing of the Labour Party. He failed, however, to achieve the success or prominence for which he had seemed destined early in his career. The son of a former Labour Party leader and Cabinet minister, he attended the University of Oxford and served during World War II with the Ministry of Information and the Royal Air Force. Greenwood entered Parliament in 1946 and in 1954, already a member of the shadow Cabinet, was elected to the party's national executive committee. His support for unilateral nuclear disarmament brought him into conflict with Hugh Gaitskell, whose party leadership he challenged in 1961. Greenwood was defeated 59 votes to 171, but in 1963 he was elected chairman of the party and, after the 1964 elections, became secretary of state for colonial affairs. After serving as minister for overseas development, he was appointed (1966) minister of housing and local government, a field with which he had been particularly concerned. Ten years earlier, he had played a leading role in drafting the party's policy document *Homes for the Future*. But despite good results in his first year in office, economic difficulties led to a severe cut in the 1968 building program, and in 1969, after a departmental reorganization, he lost his seat in the Cabinet. Greenwood also failed in the election for the Labour Party general secretaryship. In 1970 he did not stand for reelection to Parliament and was made a life peer. He continued to take an active part in public life both in the House of Lords

and through membership in the Commonwealth Development Corporation, the British Council for the Rehabilitation of the Disabled, and the Housing Corporation.

Gregory, Horace, U.S. poet, critic, and translator (b. April 10, 1898, Milwaukee, Wis.—d. March 11, 1982, Shelburne Falls, Mass.), was a literary scholar who in his poetry and contributions to such left-wing magazines as *New Masses* and the *New Republic* advocated a rebirth of society through revolutionary change. Gregory, who graduated from the University of Wisconsin in 1923, married poet Marya Zaturenska in 1925 and became an important Depression-era poet. He rejected his middle-class background after viewing New York tenements and wrote verse in the idiom of the common man. Gregory also published criticism, translated the poems of Catullus and Ovid, and wrote biographies of such luminaries as James Whistler and Amy Lowell. In 1965 he was awarded the prestigious Bollingen Prize, regarded as the highest honour in poetry in the U.S. Besides writing such books of poetry as *Chelsea Rooming House* (1930), *Selected Poems* (1951), *Collected Poems* (1964), and *Another Look* (1976), Gregory taught at Sarah Lawrence College from 1934 to 1960.

Grosvenor, Melville Bell, U.S. magazine editor (b. Nov. 26, 1901, Washington, D.C.—d. April 22, 1982, Miami, Fla.), as the enterprising editor and president (1957–67) of the National Geographic Society increased membership from 2.1 million to 5.5 million, increased funds for research, exploration, and public service, and launched numerous important expeditions. Grosvenor's great grandfather, Gardiner Greene Hubbard, founded the society in 1888 and served as its first president. Grosvenor's grandfather, the inventor Alexander Graham Bell, was its second president, and his father, Gilbert Hovey Grosvenor, served as the editor of the magazine from 1899 to 1954. When Grosvenor became editor in 1957 he abandoned the traditional gold bordered cover in favour of colour photographs and turned out the massive *Atlas of the World*. Under his leadership members of expeditions scaled the highest peak in Antarctica, planted the first U.S. flag on Mt. Everest, reconstructed ancient ruins of Mayan cities in Yucatán, and conducted underwater exploration of the Red and Mediterranean seas. In 1967 Grosvenor became editor in chief and chairman of the board.

Grumman, Leroy Randle, U.S. industrialist (b. Jan. 4, 1895, Huntington, N.Y.—d. Oct. 4, 1982, Manhasset, N.Y.), was founder of Grumman Aerospace Corp. and the master designer of the fighter planes that reportedly shot down more than 60% of enemy aircraft during World War II. In 1929 Grumman formed an aircraft-repair company that he built into one of the nation's top defense contractors. After graduating from Cornell University, Grumman joined the U.S. Navy and served as a flight instructor and later as a test pilot. After World War I he worked for Loening Aeronautical Engineering Corp. but in 1929 founded his own company. During the 1930s Grumman's inventions earned him countless Navy contracts. He designed a retractable landing gear that converted Navy scout planes into amphibians; the XFF 1, a fighter plane that employed retractable landing gear; and a folding wing used on the Wildcat carrier fighter planes. His other airplanes included the Hellcat, the first plane built to pilot specifications, the first produced in mass before a test flight had been conducted, and an aircraft that set production records because it was built so quickly. Grumman later devised the Avenger torpedo bomber, when it was predicted that fighter planes would become obsolete. Shortly before the end of World War II Grumman contracted pneumonia and was permanently blinded after he was given a shot of penicillin and suffered an allergic reaction. In 1946 he stepped down as president of his company, but remained chairman of the board until 1966.

Guzmán Fernández, Silvestre Antonio, Dominican politician (b. Feb. 12, 1911, La Vega, Dominican Republic—d. July 4, 1982, Santo Domingo, Dominican Republic), was sworn in as president of the country on Aug. 16, 1978, three months after a hotly contested election in which the Army suspended the counting of the votes the day after the May 16 balloting. On July 8, however, following international protests and charges of fraud, Guzmán was proclaimed winner of the presidency over Joaquín Balaguer. It was the first peaceful transfer of power between constitutionally elected governments in 100 years. Before becoming involved in politics, Guzmán was an enterprising agricultural entrepreneur. He joined the Partido Revolucionario Dominicano (PRD) in 1963 and served as minister of agriculture under Pres. Juan Bosch. After Bosch left the PRD in 1973, Guzmán and José Francisco Peña Gomez assumed leadership of the party. In 1974 the PRD joined in a national front called the Santiago Agreement and offered Guzmán as its presidential candidate, but at the last moment the Front abstained from voting. As president (1978–82) Guzmán was criticized for his economic policies but was generally regarded as an honest politician. Shortly before handing over power to Salvador Jorge Blanco, who had been chosen to succeed him in the election of May 16, 1982, Guzmán discovered that some of his closest aides were skimming government funds and sending money abroad into personal bank accounts. This disclosure prompted Guzmán to shoot himself in the head to prove that he was "an honest and serious man." The official government statement ruled the suicide an accident so that Guzmán could be buried in a Catholic cemetery.

Gwynne-Jones, Allan, British painter (b. March 27, 1892—d. Aug. 5, 1982, Northleach, Gloucestershire, England), made still lifes notable for their lyrical refinement and was an esteemed portrait painter whose subjects included Queen Elizabeth II (as Princess Elizabeth) and many well-known figures in British public life. He was professor of painting at the Royal College of Art and senior lecturer at the Slade School of Fine Art. Although Gwynne-Jones showed an early talent for art and design, he qualified as a lawyer before becoming a student at Slade, where he rapidly gained a reputation as a sensitive painter of landscape and still life. His varied talent was best displayed in the retrospective exhibitions that marked his 80th and 90th birthdays, the first in London in 1972 and the second at the Welsh National Eisteddfod in Swansea shortly before he died. His works are represented in the collections of the Tate Gallery, London, and other museums and galleries in Britain, Australia, and South Africa. He was elected a member of the Royal Academy of Arts in London in 1955 and appointed Commander of the Order of the British Empire in 1980. Gwynne-Jones was the author of such books on painting as *Introduction to Still-Life* and *A Way of Looking at Pictures.*

Hall, Joyce Clyde, U.S. greeting card manufacturer (b. Dec. 29, 1891, David City, Neb.—d. Oct. 29, 1982, Leawood, Kan.), was the enterprising founder and president (1910–66) of Hallmark Cards Inc., the largest greeting card concern in the world, and the manufacturer of some eight million cards daily. Hall launched his business in 1910 with two shoeboxes of imported postal cards and then, with his brother Rollie, opened a specialty store named Hall Brothers Inc. When a fire completely destroyed their inventory in 1915, the brothers bought an engraving company and produced their own cards with the Hallmark label. During his 56 years as president of Hallmark, Hall conducted extensive market research and oversaw the artwork and approved the verses for each card, always insisting that "good taste is good business." He introduced eye-catching displays for greeting cards, pioneered the use of radio and television to promote the sale of cards, and was the first to sell unfolding cards that tell a story. Besides introducing Walt Disney characters on his cards, Hall enhanced many cards with the work of such noted artists as Norman Rockwell and Grandma Moses. Hall was even successful at obtaining permission to use the paintings of Winston Churchill on his Christmas cards. Hall, who inspired the slogan that propelled his company to success, "When you care enough to send the very best," stepped down as president in 1966.

Hallstein, Walter, West German jurist and diplomat (b. Nov. 17, 1901, Mainz, Germany—d. March 29, 1982, Stuttgart, West Germany), was one of the founding fathers of the European Communities (EC) and the first president (1958–67) of the executive Commission of the European Economic Community (EEC—the Common Market). His years in office were marked by his conflict with French Pres. Charles de Gaulle over the principle of supranationality in the Community. Hallstein, a firm believer in European unity, eventually witnessed the triumph of the French belief in a Europe of distinct national entities. His name had earlier been associated with the "Hallstein Doctrine," formulated while he served (1951–58) as secretary of state in the West German Foreign Ministry. The doctrine called for the breaking of diplomatic relations with any country other than the U.S.S.R. that recognized East Germany.

Hallstein studied law and received his Ph.D. from the University of Berlin in 1925. He lectured in law there and was appointed professor in 1930 at the University of Rostock, where he remained until taking up the chair of law in Frankfurt am Main in 1941. After serving during World War II, Hallstein became guest lecturer in law and foreign policy at Georgetown University, Washington, D.C., and rector of the University of Frankfurt. In 1948 he met Chancellor Konrad Adenauer, who later appointed him to the Foreign Ministry, where he worked for the improvement of Franco-German relations. He led the West German delegation to the talks that set up the European Coal and Steel Community (ECSC), a forerunner of the Common Market. Hallstein also headed the German delegation at the Messina Conference of 1955, which led directly to the formation of the EEC three years later. As president of the EEC Commission he found himself in confrontation with President de Gaulle, who had come to power only months after the Community was formed. De Gaulle, a nationalist determined to establish French supremacy in the EEC, was firmly opposed to any move toward political unity among its members and despised the Commission's "technocrats." In 1965 Hallstein attempted to persuade France to agree to the strengthening of Community institutions, and in protest the French withdrew from most EEC activities for several months, causing the most serious crisis in the Community since its creation. When the previously separate executive bodies of the EEC, ECSC, and Euratom were merged in a single EC Commission in 1967, Hallstein anticipated French opposition and resigned. He served as a member of the Bundestag (West German parliament; 1969–72) and was president of the European Movement (1968–74). His books included *Wissenschaft und Politik* (1949), *United Europe: Challenge and Opportunity* (1962), and *Europe in the Making* (1972).

Hama, Boubou, Niger politician and writer (b. 1906, Fonéko, French West Africa—d. Jan. 30, 1982, Niamey, Niger), was former president of the Niger National Assembly, one of his country's best-known writers and cultural figures, author of some 50 books, and an influential figure in the development of Niger culture and science. A Songhai Muslim, he trained as a teacher and entered politics in 1947 as a member of the Rassemblement Démocratique Africain. Hama was a noted parliamentarian in the French-controlled institutions of preindependence Niger and French West Africa and became president of the National Assembly after Niger was proclaimed a republic in 1958. In 1974, after a military coup, he was arrested but was liberated in 1977 owing to his age and in response to pressure from friends in Europe and Africa. An instigator of the UNESCO project to produce a history of black Africa, he inspired the systematic recording of Niger's oral culture. His own works included stories, political studies, history, and ethnography. Hama won the Grand Prix Littéraire d'Afrique Noire for *Kotia-Nima,* a chronicle of his childhood and youth published in 1969. He continued to write during his imprisonment and after his release.

Hampton, Hope, U.S. actress and opera singer (b. 1898?, Philadelphia, Pa.—d. Jan. 23, 1982, New York, N.Y.), starred in 28 silent films, sang with the Philadelphia Grand Opera in the 1930s, and for the remainder of her life was a glamorous socialite who, bedecked in jewels, sequined gowns, and furs, became a fixture at New York City opening nights. Hampton, who was dubbed "The Duchess of Park Avenue," was a frequent patron of the Peppermint Lounge nightclub, where she basked in the limelight and helped usher in the Twist dance craze of the 1960s. She confided that "the thing about the Twist is you've got to have the body for it and I have the body for it." By 1978 Hampton had curtailed her demanding social calendar, and after once seeing a young woman in dungarees at the opera she lamented that "glamour is finished" and never went to another opening night. Some of her films included *Star Dust* (1921), *Lawful Larceny* (1923), *The Price of a Party* (1924), and *The Road to Reno* (1938).

Harkness, Rebekah West, U.S. philanthropist and composer (b. April 17, 1915, St. Louis, Mo.—d. June 17, 1982, New York, N.Y.), was the distinguished writer of some 100 popular songs, including such compositions as *Safari* (1955), *Musical Chairs* (1958), and *Letters to Japan* (1961), and as founder and president in 1959 of the Rebekah Harkness Foundation (later the Harkness Ballet Foundation, Inc.) became a leading patron of dance in the U.S. In 1964 Harkness founded and became artistic director of the Harkness Ballet; the following year she established the Harkness Home for Ballet Arts, an opulent school and home for dancers. She then converted an old movie house into the Harkness Theatre (which was demolished in 1976). For two years she sponsored the Joffrey Ballet. As executor of the William Hale Harkness Foundation, she was also a generous donor to medical research. In 1975 the Harkness Ballet disbanded.

Havemann, Robert, East German scientist (b. March 11, 1910, Munich, Germany—d. April 9, 1982, Grüneheide, East Germany), was a leading figure in the East German regime until the mid-1960s and one of its most powerful critics. He had been a member of the Communist Party for 40 years and, as an active opponent of Nazism, was sentenced to death in 1943, but he was spared because of the importance of his scientific work. Havemann survived the war and became a professor at the Humboldt University in East Berlin, a member of Parliament, and president of the Peace Council. Loaded with honours by the Communist regime, he became increasingly disenchanted, called for parliamentary opposition and freedom of speech, and, after heretical lectures at the university and an interview with the West German magazine *Der Spiegel,* was forbidden to teach in 1964 and expelled from the party. His reputation protected him from further trouble, however, and he continued to state his case whenever and wherever possible, taking a stand in later years in favour of nuclear disarmament. After the publication in 1970 of his political biography in West Germany, Havemann was put under house arrest, but he refused to remain silent, calling for a pan-German peace initiative in 1981. His political philosophy was summed up in the ten theses he published in the Spanish Communist paper *Mundo Obrero* in October 1979; he demanded full freedom of expression and the liberation of political prisoners in East Germany.

Heinze, Sir Bernard Thomas, Australian musician, conductor, and teacher (b. July 1, 1894, Shepparton, Victoria, Australia—d. June 9, 1982, Sydney, Australia), was director general for music with the Australian Broadcasting Company from 1929 to 1932 and afterward musical adviser to the Australian Broadcasting Commission. He enthusiastically encouraged musical education through youth concerts, notably the series of radio concerts that he founded in 1947. In 1912 he won a scholarship to attend the Royal College of Music in London and, after service with the Royal Artillery in World War I, also studied in Paris and Berlin. In 1923 he returned to Australia and in 1925 was appointed Ormond professor of music at the University of Melbourne, a post he retained until 1956. From 1957 until 1966 he directed the New South Wales State Conservatorium. In 1938 he toured Europe, conducting at concerts in Britain, Germany, France, Finland, and Hungary. He was a fellow of the Royal College of Music from 1931, knighted in 1949, and made Companion of the Order of Australia in 1976.

Helen, Queen of Romania (b. 1896, Athens, Greece—d. Nov. 28, 1982, Lausanne, Switz.), was married to Crown Prince Carol of Romania from 1921 to 1928 and played a central role in Romanian life as adviser to her son, King Michael. The eldest daughter of King Constantine of the Hellenes, she followed him into three years of exile after the assassination of his father, King George. Her marriage was unhappy and ended in divorce in 1928, three years after her husband had given up his rights to the throne in favour of their son, Michael. But in 1930 Carol returned, seizing the throne until 1940; then King Michael was restored to power and invited his mother to return as his adviser. With her son, she faced the drama of his coup against the pro-Hitler dictator Ion Antonescu in 1944, the negotiations with the Soviets and the Romanian Communists, and King Michael's eventual deposition and exile. Most of her later years were spent in Lausanne and Florence, Italy.

Herring, Sir Edmund Francis, Australian lawyer and soldier (b. Sept. 2, 1892, Maryborough, Victoria, Australia—d. Jan. 5, 1982, Melbourne, Australia), was chief justice of the Supreme Court of Victoria (1944–64) and lieutenant governor of Victoria (1945–72). As a soldier he had a distinguished career in both World Wars, receiving a Distinguished Service Order and Military Cross during World War I. After attending the University of Oxford for two years on a Rhodes scholarship, he volunteered to serve in France and Macedonia. Herring resumed his studies after the war and was called to the bar in 1920. His legal career was interrupted with the outbreak of war in 1939, and he served in North Africa and Greece before becoming commander of the New Guinea Force. Many years later he was embroiled in a controversy over his decision that Papuans who had delivered missionaries to the Japanese should be executed. Herring was knighted in 1943.

Hertzog, Albert, South African politician (b. July 14, 1899, Bloemfontein, South Africa—d. Nov. 4, 1982, Pretoria, South Africa), led the extreme right-wing Herstigte Nasionale Party (HNP) in its break in 1968 with the ruling National Party. But the HNP failed to make its mark at the polls and in 1977 Hertzog was replaced as leader by Jaap Marais. Hertzog was educated at universities in South Africa, Britain, and The Netherlands and practiced as a lawyer before entering national political life in 1948. He served as minister of health and minister of posts and telecommunications, being notable in the latter post for his opposition to the introduction of television. A fanatical Afrikaner nationalist, he never disguised his racial views and finally broke with the National Party over the issue of allowing multiracial sports visits to South Africa. The HNP called for total separation of the races in South Africa and Afrikaner dominance within the white community, but it failed to win any seats after the 1970 election and Hertzog moved increasingly toward the extreme and even fascist right.

Hicks, Granville, U.S. critic, novelist, and teacher (b. Sept. 9, 1901, Exeter, N.H.—d. June 18, 1982, Franklin Park, N.J.), as a leading writer during the 1930s proletarian movement, created a furor in academic circles with his Marxist critiques of American and British literature. Hicks, who graduated with highest honours in English from Harvard University, studied briefly for the ministry before openly joining the Communist Party in 1934. While teaching (1929–35) at Rensselaer Polytechnic Institute in Troy, N.Y., Hicks published *The Great Tradition: An Interpretation of American Literature Since the Civil War* (1933), which established his reputation as a critic. When Hicks was discharged from his post at the institute in 1935, *The Nation* magazine decried his dismissal as "a flagrant violation of academic freedom," although the college said his removal was due to retrenchment. As literary editor (1934–39) of the *New Masses*, Hicks exerted considerable influence and became one of the party's chief cultural spokesmen; he also wrote *John Reed: The Making of a Revolutionary* (1936), the first biography of the radical journalist. In 1939 *Figures of Transition* appeared, a Marxist study of British literature which he wrote on a Guggenheim fellowship. But in the same year, Hicks became disillusioned with Communism and quit the party after the Nazi-Soviet pact. In 1942 *Only One Storm* disclosed the feelings of an American whose way of life was threatened by his intellectual doubts. Hicks, who remained an active writer, also published *Part of the Truth* (1965) and *Literary Horizons* (1970), a 25-year collection of book reviews.

Holloway, Stanley, British actor (b. Oct. 1, 1890, London, England—d. Jan. 30, 1982, Littlehampton, Sussex, England), was an authentic East End Cockney whose name became synonymous with his portrayal of Alfred Doolittle in *My Fair Lady*, the musical adapted from George Bernard Shaw's play *Pygmalion*. He created the part on Broadway, then in London's Drury Lane, and finally in the 1964 film, bringing to it a lifetime's experience in music hall, film, and theatre and an unforgettable stage presence. He started his career before World War I as a singer and, after war service, achieved his first notable success with The Co-Optimists concert party in a variety program that ran for six consecutive years in London and the provinces. From this he derived his series of comic monologues that during the 1930s, owing to the growing popularity of phonograph records, made him a household name. His routines were enthusiastically imitated by many parlour reciters. After World War II he played the First Gravedigger in the film of *Hamlet* and other Shakespearean parts on stage until his international success in *My Fair Lady*. His films included some of the most notable postwar British comedies (*Passport to Pimlico*, *The Lavender Hill Mob*), as well as *This Happy Breed* and *Brief Encounter*. He continued to appear in films and on stage until shortly before his death, touring Australia and Hong Kong at the age of 87 in *The Pleasure of His Company*. He was appointed Officer of the Order of the British Empire in 1960. His autobiography, *Wiv a Little Bit o' Luck*, appeared in 1967.

Hopkins, Sam ("LIGHTNIN'"), U.S. blues singer, composer, and guitarist (b. March 15, 1912, Centerville, Texas—d. Jan. 30, 1982, Houston, Texas), was a legendary country blues singer, composer of some 600 songs, and an improvisational guitarist whose style was a major influence on rock guitarists of the 1960s and '70s. Hopkins, who was ranked with such blues greats as B. B. King and Muddy Waters, was renowned for his spontaneous style. On his guitar he played single-note runs on the high strings and then alternated to a hard-driving bass in irregular rhythms that corresponded to his brooding autobiographical lyrics. During his 50-year career Hopkins recorded more than 200 singles and 10 albums, but for many years Hopkins's talent was unheralded; he performed in tough dives in Houston's ghetto until 1959, when folklorists sparked a blues revival. Though he gave concerts at Carnegie Hall, his music was better suited to clubs, coffeehouses, and juke joints, and between tours he continued to perform in the ghetto. In 1970 he appeared in the documentary *Blues Accordin' to Lightnin' Hopkins*, a tribute to the man and his music.

Horikoshi, Jiro, Japanese aeronautical engineer (b. June 22, 1903, Gumma Prefecture, Japan—d. Jan. 11, 1982, Tokyo, Japan), designed the Zero (Mitsubishi A6M) airplane, a single-engine fighter that was used in the air attack on Pearl Harbor. After Horikoshi graduated from Tokyo Imperial University, he joined (1927) Mitsubishi Heavy Industries, Ltd., which manufactured 10,947 Zeroes. The Japanese Navy used these planes extensively in the early stages of World War II because Zeroes could outfly the heavier U.S. airplanes. The Zeroes, which were equipped with two machine guns and two 20-m cannon, were also often used in kamikaze (suicide) attacks on Allied ships. After the war Horikoshi helped design Mitsubishi's YS-11, a short-haul commercial aircraft. He also taught at Japan's Defense Institute and at Nippon University.

Irish, Edward Simmons ("NED"), U.S. sports promoter (b. May 6, 1905, Lake George, N.Y.—d. Jan. 21, 1982, Venice, Fla.), was an enthusiastic promoter of college basketball, founder and president of the New York Knickerbockers professional basketball team, and one of the founders in 1946 of the 11-team Basketball Association of America, which merged in 1949 with the National Basketball League to become the present National Basketball Association. During the Depression Irish left his job as a sportswriter for the *New York World-Telegram* to gain fan support for college basketball games held at Madison Square Garden. His successful campaign helped to make college basketball into a major arena sport. Irish, who served as president of Madison Square Garden from 1943 to 1974, was also president of the Knicks from 1946 to 1974. He was inducted into the Basketball Hall of Fame in 1964.

Iwama, Kazuo, Japanese business executive (b. Feb. 7, 1919, Aichi Prefecture, Japan—d. Aug. 24, 1982, Tokyo, Japan), together with Akio Morita and Masaru Ibuka built the Sony Corp. into a world-renowned electrical products giant. Iwama served as president of the company from 1976 to 1982. Although he was trained as a geophysics engineer, Iwama was persuaded by Morita to join Tokyo Tsushin Kogyo (the forerunner of Sony). Iwama quickly ascended Sony's executive ladder and became company director at age 31. He was instrumental in the manufacture of Japan's first transistor radio in 1954, and he was credited with premiering the world's first transistorized television receiver in 1960. From 1971 to 1973 Iwama directed the Sony Corp. of America and was responsible for engineering the construction of the first Japanese colour television manufacturing plant in the U.S. In 1979 he was awarded a blue ribbon medal of honour by Emperor Hirohito for his contributions to the electronics industry.

Jakobson, Roman, Russian-born linguist (b. Oct. 11 [Sept. 29, old style], 1896, Moscow, Russia—d. July 18, 1982, Boston, Mass.), was internationally known for his expertise in Slavic languages and for his theory that all languages have a similar fundamental structure. After earning a Ph.D. from Prague University, Jakobson and his colleagues Nikolay S. Trubetskoy and S. I. Karcevskij proposed that their method of studying the function of speech sounds could be applied both synchronically (to a language as it exists) and diachronically (to a language as it changes). Their theory represented a dramatic departure from the tenets of the acclaimed Swiss linguist Ferdinand de Saussure, who held that the principles and methodology of each approach are distinct and mutually exclusive. During the 1930s Jakobson taught at Masaryk University in Brno, Czech., but when the Nazis invaded the country he fled successively to the Universities of Copenhagen, Oslo, and Uppsala (Sweden). In 1941 he immigrated to the U.S. and taught at Columbia (1943–49) and at Harvard (1949–67) universities. He was later named institute professor at the Masssachusetts Institute of Technology, where he was given an office and secretary for his lifetime. Jakobson, who was fluent in 6 languages and could read 25 others, wrote some 600 scholarly papers. His earlier works included *Remarques sur l'évolution phonologique du russe comparée à celle des autres langues slaves* (1929; "Comments on Phonological Change in Russian Compared with

That of Other Slavic Languages") and *Kharakteristichke yevrazi-yskogo yazykovoyo soyuza* (1931, "Characteristics of the Eurasian Language Affinity"). He later produced *Kindersprache, aphasie und allgemeine Lautgesetze* (1941; "Child Language, Aphasia, and Phonological Universals"), *Preliminaries to Speech Analysis* (1952; with G. Fant and M. Halle), and *Fundamentals of Language* (1956). At the time of his death Jakobson had just completed *Dialogues.*

Jaworski, Leon, U.S. lawyer (b. Sept. 19, 1905, Waco, Texas—d. Dec. 9, 1982, Wimberly, Texas), rose to national prominence in 1973 when he was sworn in as Watergate special prosecutor and made constitutional history when he convinced the U.S. Supreme Court that Pres. Richard M. Nixon was bound to obey a subpoena and turn over the 64 White House tapes needed for testimony in the trial of Watergate defendants. The release of the tapes revealed to the U.S. Senate investigators

UPI

Nixon's long-standing involvement in the cover-up of the 1972 burglary at Democratic national headquarters by members of his reelection staff and led to Nixon's resignation. Jaworski, a top Texas lawyer, served the government as a prosecutor in the 1945–46 Nuremberg trials of Nazi war criminals and as a counsel in the 1977–78 House investigation of the "Koreagate" bribery scandal. Jaworski also represented Lyndon B. Johnson and handled the litigation that allowed Johnson to run simultaneously for the Senate and the vice-presidency. In 1912 she was invited to join the Vienna The highlight of Jaworski's career, however, was as the dauntless Watergate special prosecutor, who resolutely pursued Nixon. Jaworski's controversial decision not to prosecute Nixon, however, outraged both the public and some members of the White House staff. Jaworski explained, if the "court asked me if I believed Nixon could receive a prompt, fair trial . . . I would have to answer, as an officer of the court, in the negative." Jaworski resigned as special prosecutor on Oct. 25, 1974, and never argued another court case after the landmark *United States* v. *Nixon.*

Jeritza, Maria (MITZI JEDLICKA), Austrian-born opera singer (b. Oct. 6, 1887, Brünn, Austria [now Brno, Czech.]—d. July 10, 1982, Orange, N.J.), was a magnificent soprano whose striking appearance and flair for the dramatic made her a favourite of opera audiences, who dubbed her the golden girl of opera's "golden age." Jeritza, who divided her career between Vienna and New York, enjoyed mass adulation wherever she performed. The opera diva made her professional debut in 1910 with the Olmütz Opera company in the role of Elsa in *Lohengrin.* In 1912 she was invited to join the Vienna Opera after Emperor Franz Joseph was enchanted by one of her performances at Bad Ischl, a summer

spa. After making her debut with the Vienna Opera singing the title role in *Aphrodite,* she added 50 roles to her repertory before joining the Metropolitan Opera in 1921. There she sang 20 roles including Santuzza, Sieglinde, Elsa, Octavian, and Turandot, but it was her performance in the title role of *Tosca* that brought her thunderous ovations. Her innate theatrical stage presence reached its pinnacle when she sang her second-act aria "Vissi d'arte," prostrate before the diabolical Scarpia. In 1932 Jeritza left the Met but continued to perform in Europe and the U.S.

Johnson, Dame Celia, British actress (b. Dec. 18, 1908, Richmond, Surrey, England—d. April 25, 1982, Nettlebed, Oxfordshire, England), reached the pinnacle of her career in 1945 playing opposite Trevor Howard in the film *Brief Encounter,* a bittersweet love story. Johnson poignantly conveyed the emotions beneath a surface of characteristically English refinement and restraint. She appeared in other films by Noël Coward, including *In Which We Serve* (1942) and *This Happy Breed* (1944). Johnson made her stage debut in *A Hundred Years Old* in 1929 and during the 1930s appeared on London's West End stage in such plays as *The Wind and the Rain* (1933) and *Pride and Prejudice* (1936). After World War II she had a mixed reception for her performance in *Saint Joan* (1947). Though she acted in Shakespeare and produced some outstanding performances in plays by Ibsen and Chekhov, her talents were more often displayed in modern sentimental drama and comedy, such as William Douglas Home's *The Reluctant Debutante* (1955) and *The Dame of Sark* (1974) or Alan Ayckbourn's *Relatively Speaking* (1967). Her faultless technique, charm, and sense of fun endeared her to her audiences and to her fellow actors. She was appointed Commander (1958) and Dame Commander (1981) of the Order of the British Empire.

Joseph, Sir Maxwell, British businessman (b. May 31, 1910, London, England—d. Sept. 22, 1982, London), started to build a property empire during the years immediately following World War II and eventually made Grand Metropolitan Ltd. into a vast international hotel group. Joseph diversified and expanded through his purchase of such companies as Express Dairies, Berni Inns, Mecca, and Watney Mann. Prior to World War II Joseph worked for a real estate agent and in 1948 began to acquire the hotels that were the foundation of his business empire. His career escalated in the late 1960s with a series of takeover deals and later with the acquisition of the Watney Mann brewing organization. During the next decade the group concentrated its position until in 1980 it moved to take over the U.S. Liggett group. This acquisition was achieved despite bitter opposition, though a subsequent bid for Coral Leisure in the U.K. was thwarted by the Monopolies Commission. In 1981, less than a year before his retirement, Joseph acquired Intercontinental Hotels from Pan American World Airways. He was knighted in 1981.

Jurgens, Curt (CURD JÜRGENS), West German actor (b. Dec. 13, 1912, Munich, Germany—d. June 18, 1982, Vienna, Austria), achieved international fame in 1955 as the Nazi officer in the film *The Devil's General* and was later cast in many roles exploiting his brand of virile Teutonic charm. Success had not, however, come easily. His acting career started in 1936 when he abandoned journalism to play in the first of a long series of films, notably operettas, and from 1941 to 1953 he was a member of the Vienna Burgtheater company. In 1944 he was sent to a concentration camp for criticizing Nazi propaganda minister Joseph Goebbels. After the success of *The Devil's General* he moved to France, appearing with Brigitte Bardot in *And God Created Woman* (1956), then to Hollywood, where he made *Me and the Colonel* (with Danny Kaye), *The Inn of the Sixth Happiness* (with Ingrid Bergman), and *Lord Jim.* He continued to work occasionally in the theatre, notably playing Sigmund Freud in the 1963 Paris production of Henry Denker's *Le Fil rouge.* His last international film success was as a villain in the James Bond film *The Spy Who Loved Me* (1977). Jurgens, who married five times and was a millionaire,

cultivated the image of a fast-living playboy. His autobiography was entitled *Sixty and Not Yet Wise.*

Kamanin, Nikolay Petrovich, Soviet aeronautical and space pioneer (b. Oct. 18 [Oct. 5, old style], 1908, Melenki, Vladimir District, Russia—d. March 14, 1982, Moscow, U.S.S.R.), was associated with his nation's military and space programs from 1928. In 1934 he piloted an aircraft that rescued marooned members of an expedition from ice floes. The party had been aboard the ship "Chelyuskin," which sank in the Arctic Ocean. For his heroism Kamanin received the title Hero of the Soviet Union. During World War II he commanded the 5th Assault Aviation Corps, which helped liberate the Ukraine, Poland, Romania, Hungary, and Czechoslovakia from the Germans. Following the war he held posts in civil aviation, commanded an air army, and was deputy chief of staff of the Soviet Air Force. In 1960 Kamanin became an air force representative on the State Selection Commission that in 1961 designated Yury Gagarin as the man to be launched in orbital flight. Kamanin was named colonel general of aviation in 1967 and became increasingly involved in the operations and planning of astronaut training at the space centre in Zvezdny Gorodok, an installation built especially for that purpose some 30 km (19 mi) northeast of Moscow. Kamanin commanded the centre from 1966 until his retirement in 1971.

Karayev, Kara Abulpaz, Soviet composer (b. Feb. 5, 1918, Baku, Azerbaijan, Russia—d. May 1982, Baku, U.S.S.R.), was a leading exponent of Azerbaijani music. His works, opera, ballet, and orchestral music, were often inspired by the folk tradition of his native region but interpreted in a thoroughly modern idiom. Karayev studied in Baku and Moscow and taught at the Azerbaijan Conservatory from 1946, becoming professor there in 1957. A member of the Communist Party, he found inspiration for many of his works in contemporary events, from his first symphony, the *Great Patriotic War Symphony* (1944), to his *Vietnam Suite.* His ballet scores, *The Seven Beauties* (1953) and *The Path of Thunder* (1957), also carried a political message. His other stage works included the verse opera *Aina* (1941) and *Tenderness* (1973), and he wrote scores for *Othello* and for a highly praised production of Vishnevsky's *An Optimistic Tragedy,* which the Leningrad Pushkin Theatre played in Paris in 1959. Karayev's orchestral works included the symphonic poem *Don Quixote* and a violin concerto. He won many prizes, including the Lenin Prize, was a deputy to the Supreme Soviet, and was a member of the Azerbaijan Academy of Sciences.

Keynes, Sir Geoffrey Langdon, British surgeon and scholar (b. March 25, 1887, Cambridge, England—d. July 5, 1982, Brinkley, Suffolk, England), had a distinguished medical career and was at the same time a respected litterateur. Younger brother of the economist John Maynard Keynes, he studied at the University of Cambridge and afterward at St. Bartholomew's Hospital, London, before serving with the Royal Army Medical Corps in World War I. Already recognized as an outstanding surgeon, he became a fellow of the Royal College of Surgeons in 1920, was Hunterian professor from 1923, 1929, and 1945, and served on the staff of St. Bartholomew's. During World War II he was consulting surgeon to the Royal Air Force. He was an authority on blood transfusion, the thyroid gland, and cancer, and he received many honours for his work. In 1969 he was awarded an honorary gold medal by the Royal College of Surgeons. Keynes developed an exceptional private library, specializing notably in the 17th century, and, with his bibliographies of John Donne (1914, 1932, 1958, and 1972) and John Evelyn (1937, 1968), produced standard works that demonstrated his scholarship, his broad culture, and his originality of thought. He was president of the Bibliographical Society in 1953. A friend of writers, including Rupert Brooke and Siegfried Sassoon, he also patronized the visual arts, encouraged the sculptor Eric Gill, was chairman (1958–66) of the National Portrait Gallery, and won the James Tait Black Memorial Prize for his *Life of William Harvey* (1966; 2nd ed., 1978). His autobiography, *The Gates of Memory,* appeared in 1981.

Khalid 'ibn Abd al-'Aziz Al Saud, king of Saudi Arabia (b. 1913, Riyadh, Arabian Peninsula—d. June 13, 1982, Ta'if, Saudi Arabia), succeeded his half brother Faisal as king when Faisal was assassinated in 1975. A moderate influence in Middle East politics and a relatively retiring man, he left much of the administration of the country to his half brother Prince Fahd (*see* BIOGRAPHIES), who was his successor. The fourth son of Ibn Saud, the kingdom's founder, he served as viceroy of the Hejaz

SVEN SIMON/KATHERINE YOUNG

and minister of the interior during the 1930s and as deputy prime minister from 1964. He was nominated crown prince in 1965, but from 1970 illness inhibited his role in public life and cast doubt on his eventual succession to the throne. However, he did take over following Faisal's assassination and was welcomed as a figure who enjoyed much popularity, especially with the Bedouin. He reacted moderately to Egyptian Pres. Anwar as-Sadat's Israeli peace initiative and benefited from the success of the 1979 visit to his country of Queen Elizabeth II. Saudi-British relations were clouded, however, in 1980 by the broadcasting on British television of the dramatized documentary "Death of a Princess" and did not fully recover until Khalid's return visit to the U.K. in 1981. An intensely religious man, he retained many of the habits of a desert prince, spending some time each year among the Bedouin tribesmen in his favourite pursuit of falconry and maintaining the tradition of hearing the petitions of his subjects in public audience.

Khan, Fazlur R(ahman), Bangladesh-born structural engineer (b. April 3, 1929, Dacca, India [now Bangladesh]—d. March 27, 1982, Saudi Arabia), was an innovative skyscraper designer who invented the "bundled tube" system, a structural network consisting of a group of narrow cylinders that are clustered together to form a thicker tower. The system was innovative because it minimized the amount of structural steel needed for high towers and eliminated the need for internal wind bracing since the perimeter columns carry wind loadings. His most spectacular projects included such Chicago landmarks as the 110-story Sears Tower and the 100-story John Hancock Center; he also designed the One Shell Plaza building in Houston, Texas. Khan, who completed his undergraduate studies at the University of Dacca, qualified for a scholarship and entered the University of

Illinois, Champaign-Urbana, where he earned two master's degrees and a Ph.D. in structural engineering. For a short period he served as executive engineer for the Karachi Development Authority in Pakistan, but he returned to the U.S. in 1960 to rejoin the Chicago architectural firm of Skidmore, Owings & Merrill. During his long association with the firm he also devised engineering designs for the solar telescope at Kitt Peak, Arizona, the U.S. Air Force Academy in Colorado Springs, Colo., and the Hubert H. Humphrey Metrodome in Minneapolis, Minn. His long-span structural designs led to the construction of the Haj Terminal of the King Abdul Aziz International Airport in Jidda, Saudi Arabia.

King, Henry, U.S. motion picture director (b. Jan. 24, 1886?, Christiansburg, Va.—d. June 29, 1982, Toluca Lake, Calif.), was an actor in vaudeville, burlesque, and films before he found his niche as the director of such acclaimed silent films as *Tol'able David* (1921), *The White Sister* (1923), and *Stella Dallas* (1925). During the following three decades King specialized in Americana in his films. He helped launch the careers of Tyrone Power, Jennifer Jones, and Ronald Colman (who sported a trademark mustache after King first penciled one on the actor). Besides mastering the art of adapting such novels to the screen as *A Bell for Adano, The Sun Also Rises,* and *Tender Is the Night,* King directed musicals, westerns, and biblical and war films including *Carousel, The Gunfighter, Twelve O'Clock High, David and Bathsheba, The Song of Bernadette,* and *Love Is a Many-Splendored Thing.* He retired from filmmaking in 1961.

Kinmonth, John Bernard, British surgeon (b. May 9, 1916, County Clare, Ireland—d. Sept. 16, 1982, London, England), held the chair of surgery at St. Thomas's Hospital, University of London (1955–81), and made a notable contribution to the study of the lymphatic vascular system. He studied at St. Thomas's Hospital and served with the Royal Air Force (RAF) Medical Service during World War II, later becoming consultant in vascular surgery to the RAF. From 1948 to 1949 he was research fellow at Harvard Medical School and after returning to England he joined the teaching staff at St. Bartholomew's Hospital. Kinmonth then became director of the surgical professional unit at St. Thomas's in 1955. He was a member of the Council of the Royal College of Surgeons and an honorary fellow of the Royal College of Radiologists and the American College of Surgeons. His publications included *Vascular Surgery* (1963), *The Lymphatics: Diseases, Lymphography and Surgery* (1972), and *The Lymphatics, Lymph and Chyle* (1982).

Kipphardt, Heinar, West German playwright (b. March 8, 1922, Heidersdorf, Upper Silesia—d. Nov. 18, 1982, Munich, West Germany), was a committed exponent of political theatre whose greatest international success came in 1964 with *In the Matter of J. Robert Oppenheimer,* a documentary describing the hearings against the U.S. nuclear scientist. Kipphardt served on the Eastern Front during World War II, then trained as a psychiatrist in Düsseldorf. After working in East Berlin, he joined the Deutsches Theater as director and chief dramatist. In 1959, however, his *Die Stühle des Herrn Szmil* brought him into conflict with the East German authorities and he returned to the West. His antiwar play *Der Hund des Generals* (1962) was followed by such works as *Joel Brand, die Geschichte eines Geschäfts* (1965) and the novel *März* (1976). Kipphardt remained a Marxist, despite his experience in East Germany, and the chief influence on his work was the political theatre of Erwin Piscator, who staged *In the Matter of J. Robert Oppenheimer* in Munich in 1964. Kipphardt was the recipient of a number of prizes, including the Bremer Literature Prize and a Prix Italia (both 1976).

Koenigswald, G. H. Ralph von, Dutch paleoanthropologist (b. Nov. 13, 1902, Berlin, Germany—d. July 10, 1982, Bad Homburg, West Germany), was a pioneer in the discovery of hominid fossils. Koenigswald, who made his most important finds in the Far East, believed that it was there, rather

than in Africa, that mankind first emerged. From 1928 to 1930 he was assistant at the Munich Geological Museum; then he joined the Geological Survey for the Dutch East Indies, where, between 1936 and 1941, he made his major discoveries of *Pithecanthropus* and *Meganthropus.* When the Japanese occupied Java during World War II, Koenigswald was imprisoned but managed to conceal his most important materials, which escaped loss or destruction. He specialized in the study of fossil teeth, tracing them by means of their use in Chinese medicine in apothecaries' shops. After World War II he continued his work until his appointment in 1948 as professor at the State University of Utrecht. He was also curator of paleoanthropology at the Senckenberg Museum, Frankfurt am Main. Koenigswald published two books on early man (*Begegnungen mit dem Vormenschen,* 1956; *Geschichte des Menschen,* 1968) and many scientific papers. He was awarded the Royal Anthropological Institute's Huxley medal in 1964.

Kogan, Leonid Borisovich, Soviet violinist (b. Nov. 14, 1924, Dnepropetrovsk, U.S.S.R.—d. Dec. 17, 1982, place not reported), was a famed classical violinist who exhibited technical virtuosity and was acclaimed for the purity of tone he elicited from his 1726 Guarneri del Gesu violin. Kogan was revered for his refined poker-faced performances, although some critics felt he played without passion. After winning the 1951 Queen Elisabeth Competition in Brussels, he made debuts in London and Paris (1955), South America (1956), and the U.S. (1957). In 1952 he became professor at the Moscow State Conservatory and in 1965 was awarded the Lenin Prize. Though Kogan was a Jew, he denied in 1970 that Moscow was guilty of anti-Semitic discrimination; he also supported Soviet foreign policy and publicly criticized dissidents, including Andrey Sakharov.

Koirala, Bisheshwar Prasad, Nepalese politician (b. September 1915, Biratnagar, Nepal—d. July 21, 1982, Kathmandu, Nepal), became prime minister after his country's first democratic election in 1959 but was dismissed in 1960 when King Mahendra seized power and dissolved the government. Much of his life thereafter was spent in imprisonment or exile. Koirala was educated at Banaras and Calcutta universities, joined the Indian Congress Party, and, after India became independent, formed the Nepali National Congress. His party split, leaving him as leader of the Nepali Congress, which he led to victory in 1959. His policy of good relations with China led to accusations of Communist sympathies, but the reason for his dismissal, in December 1960, was that his reforms would have established Nepal as a constitutional monarchy, severely limiting the power of the king. With the help of the Army, the king overthrew the government, and Koirala was imprisoned. Under Mahendra's successor, King Birendra, he suffered further imprisonment, exile, and trial for treason. Amnestied, in 1980 he campaigned for restoration of the multiparty system, which was, however, rejected by a 55% majority in that year's referendum.

Kollsman, Paul, U.S. aeronautical engineer (b. Feb. 22, 1900, Freudenstadt, Germany—d. Sept. 26, 1982, Los Angeles, Calif.), during the 1920s invented the altimeter, an instrument that measures and registers the altitude of an airplane. The Kollsman altimeter revolutionized aviation because it converted barometric pressure into feet and enabled the pilot to "fly blind." Kollsman's altimeter was first tested on Sept. 24, 1929, by Lieut. Gen. James H. Doolittle, who made a historic 24-km (15-mi) flight guided exclusively by instruments. Kollsman's invention was considered an aviation milestone in the advance of piloted aircraft. After immigrating to the U.S. from Germany, Kollsman was unable to sell an automobile engine that he had invented so he joined the Pioneer Instrument Co. in New York. When the latter refused to consider his recommendation for an altimeter, he founded Kollsman Instrument Co. and marketed the invention himself. In 1940 he sold his company to the Square D Co. of Detroit and served as a consultant and vice-president of that company.

Lamas, Fernando, Argentine-born actor (b. Jan. 9, 1915, Buenos Aires, Arg.—d. Oct. 8, 1982, Los Angeles, Calif.), was a charming silver-haired entertainer who starred in numerous "Latin lover" films including *Rich, Young and Pretty, The Merry Widow, Diamond Queen,* and *Jivaro.* The dashing actor, who made his Hollywood debut in 1951 after appearing in more than 20 European and Latin-American films, also directed more than 60 television shows including "The Bold Ones," "Mannix," and "The Rookies." Lamas, who was also a champion swimmer, married Esther Williams in 1963.

Laskov, Haim, Israeli general (b. April 1919, Russia—d. Dec. 8, 1982, Tel Aviv, Israel), was a disciplined professional soldier who in the 1948 war for independence led a tank battalion, helped break the Arab siege of Jerusalem, and captured Nazareth for Israel. Laskov moved to Israel with his family in 1924 and later joined the Haganah, the Jewish self-defense organization that fought Palestinian Arabs opposed to Jewish settlement of Palestine. When World War II broke out he joined the British Army and served with the Palestine Battalion in North Africa. After the 1948 war for independence, Laskov was promoted to colonel. As a tribute to his organizational skills, Laskov was in 1951 appointed officer commanding the Air Force, helping to establish a framework for that branch of the military, even though he never learned how to fly. From 1953 to 1955 Laskov studied at Oxford but was called back to Israel to serve as deputy chief of staff under Moshe Dayan. Laskov then commanded the armoured corps and southern command before he was appointed chief of staff in 1958. He retired from military service in 1961 and served briefly as director general of the Port Authority; he returned to the Army in 1972 as ombudsman, a post he held until his death.

Leek, Sybil, British-born mystic (b. Feb. 22, 1917, Staffordshire, England—d. Oct. 26, 1982, Melbourne, Fla.), was a self-styled witch and Druid (priest) who maintained that witchcraft was a legitimate religion. Leek, who traced her psychic ancestry back to the Crusades, was the author of more than 60 books on numerology, phrenology, and astrology. Her mystical volumes included *Diary of a Witch, Numerology: The Magic of Numbers, Guide to Telepathy,* and *The Story of Faith Healing.* She also published *The Assassination Chain* (1976), which divulged her theories about the assassinations of Pres. J. F. Kennedy, Robert Kennedy, and Martin Luther King, Jr. Leek was Britain's most visible witch, giving lectures on ESP and the occult until she came to the U.S. in 1964 after having a dispute with the Witchcraft Research Association. She was also the president of four companies and the promoter of cosmic cosmetics.

Lloyd, Albert Lancaster, British ethnomusicologist (b. Feb. 29, 1908, London, England—d. Sept. 29, 1982, London), was the author of *Folk Song in England* (1967), the standard work on the subject, and a guiding influence in the folk song movement. A committed Socialist, he saw his work as a contribution to working-class culture although his belief in the importance of economic factors in the shaping of folk music was sometimes challenged. Lloyd seriously began to collect folk songs when, as a young man, he spent nine years in Australia. His Socialist beliefs matured during a long period of unemployment in the 1930s, when he spent his time conducting research in music and politics. Lloyd served as a deckhand on a whaling ship, then traveled widely as South American correspondent for *Picture Post* magazine until he left to become a free-lance folklorist in 1950. Besides speaking several languages, Lloyd translated works by the Spanish poet Federico Garcia Lorca. The diversity of Lloyd's interests was brought to light in the many radio programs he wrote for the BBC and in his documentary films, one of which, on Bela Bartok, won the Golden Harp award in 1981. He was director of Topic Records and a member of the English Folk Dance and Song Society, the European Permanent Commission for the study of industrial folklore, and the International Folk Music Council. His books included *Come all ye Bold Miners: Songs and Ballads of the Coalfields* (1952) and, with Ralph Vaughan Williams, *The Penguin Book of English Folk Song* (1959).

Lockridge, Richard, U.S. mystery writer (b. Sept. 26, 1898, St. Joseph, Mo.—d. June 19, 1982, Tryon, N.C.), was a reporter (1923–29) and a drama critic (1929–42) for the *New York Sun* but was better known as the co-author, with his wife, Frances, of the "Mr. and Mrs. North" mystery series. A prolific author, Lockridge wrote or co-wrote 89 books including the detective series "Inspector Heimrich" and "Captain Heimrich." His stories about Mr. and Mrs. North appeared in *The New Yorker* magazine before Lockridge published their adventures in such novels as *Death Takes a Bow* (1948), *Murder Comes First* (1951), and *Murder Has Its Points* (1961). In 1941 "Mr. and Mrs. North" became a successful stage play, then a film and a popular radio and television program. Lockridge's last book, *The Old Die Young,* appeared in 1981.

Loring, Eugene (LEROY KERPESTEIN), U.S. dancer and choreographer (b. 1914, Milwaukee, Wis.—d. Aug. 30, 1982, Kingston, N.Y.), exerted a dramatic influence on American ballet as the choreographer and dancer in the lead role of the ballet *Billy the Kid,* which premiered Oct. 16, 1938, at the Opera House in Chicago. Loring choreographed and Aaron Copland supplied the music for the one-act ballet that became one of the classic examples of American folk ballet. While studying at the School of American Ballet, Loring made his professional dancing debut with the Fokine Ballet as Pantalon in *Carnaval.* In 1936 and 1937 Loring appeared with the American Ballet before joining the experimental Ballet Caravan, in which he made his debut as a choreographer with *Harlequin for President.* In 1940 Loring became a member of Ballet Theatre and choreographed *The Great American Goof,* with words by William Saroyan. Loring then briefly left dance to appear in 120 performances of Saroyan's *The Beautiful People.* In 1941 Loring founded Dance Players, but the company disbanded in 1942. For the next decade he worked in Hollywood, first as a minor actor in such films as *National Velvet* and *Torch Song,* then as choreographer of *Yolanda and the Thief* (1945), *Ziegfeld Follies* (1946), and *Deep in My Heart* (1954). One of his most notable contributions to dance, however, was the founding of the American School of Dance in 1948. Loring's Freestyle teachings, which combined elements of ballet, modern dance, and jazz, schooled dancers in an entire range of dance techniques. From 1965 to 1981 he served as chairman of the dance department at the University of California at Irvine.

Loughran, Tommy, U.S. boxer (b. Nov. 29, 1902, Philadelphia, Pa.—d. July 7, 1982, Hollidaysburg, Pa.), as reigning world light-heavyweight champion from 1927 to 1929 was dubbed the "Phantom of Philly" because his lightning reflexes enabled him to elude punches. During his career Loughran, who had 172 professional bouts, won 18 by knockout, 77 by decision, and one on a foul. He had eight draws, lost 21 decisions, was knocked out twice, and fought 45 no decisions. On Oct. 7, 1927, Loughran won the light-heavyweight crown by outpointing Mike McTigue in 15 rounds. Loughran then successfully defended his title six times but moved into the heavyweight division after winning his last title defense in a 15-round decision over James Braddock on July 18, 1929. As a heavyweight Loughran fought such champions as Jack Sharkey, Max Baer, and Primo Carnera, who outweighed him by 39 kg (86 lb). Loughran went 15 rounds with Carnera but lost the 1934 title bout on points. Loughran retired in 1937 and was inducted into the Boxing Hall of Fame in 1956.

Lowe, Arthur, British actor (b. Sept. 22, 1915, Hayfield, Derbyshire, England—d. April 15, 1982, Birmingham, England), was best known as the Home Guard captain in the BBC television series "Dad's Army." The irascible and pompous Captain Mainwaring was a part ideally suited to him; he displayed a subtlety and a faultless sense of timing that was so polished it was undetected by most viewers. Lowe started acting during World War II while serving with the Army and made his West End stage debut in 1950. In the following year he secured his first television role and eventually played in "Coronation Street," in the series "Bless Me, Father," and in "Dad's Army." Lowe took supporting parts in many films, including *Kind Hearts and Coronets* (1949), *If* (1968), and *O Lucky Man* (1972). He also appeared on stage, in musicals, and in the original production of John Osborne's *Inadmissible Evidence* (1965). In 1974 his comic gifts and his range were evidenced in his fine performance as Stephano in the Old Vic production of *The Tempest.*

Lynd, Helen Merrell, U.S. sociologist (b. March 17, 1896, La Grange, Ill.—d. Jan. 30, 1982, Warren, Ohio), together with her husband, Robert, compiled the Middletown books, in which they applied the methods of cultural anthropology to the study of a modern Western community. The first, *Middletown: A Study in Contemporary American Culture* (1929), was the first all-encompassing study of the daily lives and values of the people in a small middle-class U.S. city. Based on field observations in Muncie, Ind., it was innovative in the treatment of the middle class as a tribe (in the anthropological sense). The second volume, *Middletown in Transition: A Study in Cultural Conflicts* (1937), examined the social changes precipitated by the Depression of the 1930s. The two books became classics in the field. Lynd, who graduated (1919) from Wellesley (Mass.) College, was also a leading educator. She taught social philosophy at Sarah Lawrence College, Bronxville, N.Y., from 1928 to 1964, helping to construct the school's flexible, interdisciplinary curriculum and grading system. After earning (1944) a Ph.D. in history and philosophy from Columbia University, Lynd wrote such scholarly works as *England in the Eighteen-Eighties* (1945), *On Shame and the Search for Identity* (1958), and *Toward Discovery* (1965).

Lynde, Paul, U.S. performer (b. June 13, 1926, Mount Vernon, Ohio—d. Jan. 9, 1982, Beverly Hills, Calif.), was a sharp-tongued comedian who was best remembered for his one-line wisecracks on the television game show "Hollywood Squares." Lynde, who made his Broadway debut in *New Faces of 1952,* also played in such stage productions as *New Faces of 1956, New Faces of 1962,* and *Bye Bye Birdie* (1960). On television he starred in "The Paul Lynde Show" and portrayed Uncle Arthur on "Bewitched" from 1965 to 1972. Lynde's motion picture credits included *Son of Flubber, Send Me No Flowers,* and *Bye Bye Birdie.*

Macdonald, Dwight, U.S. author and critic (b. March 24, 1906, New York, N.Y.—d. Dec. 19, 1982, New York), as a staff writer for *The New Yorker* magazine from 1951 to 1971 and a film critic for *Esquire* magazine reveled in his position as a gadfly. In his essays Macdonald took keen delight in criticizing middle-brow culture, *Webster's Third New International Dictionary,* and the Revised Standard Version of the Bible. A staunch individualist, Macdonald at various times embraced such ideologies as Trotskyism, anarchism, and pacifism. He also encouraged civil disobedience as part of opposition to U.S. involvement in World War II and in Vietnam. In literary circles Macdonald often aroused controversy, especially with a series of articles in which he defined cultural divisions between those he termed American "mass-cult" and "mid-cult." His essays containing classifications of those belonging to each group appeared in *Against the American Grain* (1963). Macdonald's other books included *Henry Wallace: The Man and the Myth* (1948), *The Ford Foundation: The Men and the Millions* (1956), *The Memoirs of a Revolutionist: Essays in Political Criticism* (1957), and *The Ghost Conspiracy* (1965), in which he took to task the Warren Commission findings in the assassination of Pres. John F. Kennedy. Despite Macdonald's polemics, his literary merits were recognized when he was inducted into the National Institute of Arts and Letters in 1970.

BOOK OF THE YEAR

MacLeish, Archibald, U.S. litterateur and statesman (b. May 7, 1892, Glencoe, Ill.—d. April 20, 1982, Boston, Mass.), won wide renown as the winner of three Pulitzer Prizes and later as his country's unofficial poet laureate. MacLeish, who drew his

UPI

themes from the political and social issues of the day, was especially concerned with the preservation of individual liberty. He also wrote poems of a more personal nature, and these contained probably his most memorable lyrics. After being graduated from Harvard Law School, MacLeish practiced as an attorney for three years (1920–23) before leaving for France to cultivate his poetic craft. During his five expatriate years he published such verse as *The Happy Marriage* (1924), *The Pot of Earth* (1925), *Streets in the Moon* (1926), and *The Hamlet of A. MacLeish* (1928), which received critical acclaim. He returned to the U.S. in 1928, became a writer for *Fortune* magazine, and established his reputation with *Conquistador* (1932), a narrative poem describing the conquest of Mexico by Cortés as seen through the eyes of a Spanish soldier. For this "public" poem he won a Pulitzer Prize. During this period he also composed some of his most famous pieces, including "You, Andrew Marvell," "The End of the World," and "Ars Poetica." As a political activist MacLeish penned such famous radio verse plays as *The Fall of the City* (1937) and *Air Raid* (1938); he also wrote the collections *Public Speech* (1936) and *America Was Promises* (1939), which were less successful. He became a political figure and served as librarian of Congress (1939–44), assistant secretary of state (1944–45), and chairman of the U.S. delegation to the 1945 London conference drafting the UNESCO constitution. In 1953 he was awarded a second Pulitzer, the Bollingen Prize in Poetry, and a National Book Award for his *Collected Poems, 1917–52*. His verse drama *J.B.,* based on the book of Job, was a smash hit on Broadway and earned him a Pulitzer Prize for drama. MacLeish's last book of poems, *The Wild Old Wicked Man,* was published in 1968, and his verse drama *Scratch* appeared in 1971.

Magee, Patrick, Irish actor (b. 1924, Armagh, Northern Ireland—d. Aug. 14, 1982, London, England), interpreted the works of the writer Samuel Beckett on stage and on radio. Beckett wrote the radio play *Embers* for Magee after his performance in *Krapp's Last Tape* at the Royal Court Theatre, London, and he later appeared in the same theatre in *Endgame* and *That Time*. His sinister, croaking voice, beautifully modulated, seemed ideally suited to the mood of Beckett's work. Magee made his London debut in 1958 in Eugene O'Neill's *The Iceman Cometh,* and in 1964 he joined the Royal Shakespeare Company, appearing in *Hamlet* and in Harold Pinter's *The*

Birthday Party. Under Peter Brook's memorable direction, he played the role of the Marquis de Sade in Peter Weiss's (*q.v.*) *Marat/Sade*. This last performance won him a Tony award in New York. He appeared in 1966 with Paul Scofield in the two-man play *Staircase* and in such stage productions as *The White Devil* in 1976 and *Doctor Faustus* in 1980. Magee was also a noted performer on television and in such films as *A Clockwork Orange* and *Barry Lyndon*. His last role, though not broadcast at the time of his death, was in Beckett's radio monologue *Ill Seen, Ill Said.*

Margulies, Lazar, U.S. obstetrician-gynecologist (b. 1895, Galicia, now in Poland—d. March 7, 1982, New York, N.Y.), invented a flexible plastic intra-uterine coil that was used to prevent conception. The device, which was the first made from molded polyethylene, was widely used because it was well tolerated by the body and it did not have to be surgically inserted. Margulies, who earned his M.D. at the University of Vienna, practiced medicine there from 1929 to 1938. In 1940 he immigrated to the U.S. and established a practice in New York. He joined the staff of Mount Sinai Hospital in 1953 and at the time of his death was lecturer in the department of obstetrics and gynecology at the Mount Sinai School of Medicine of the City University of New York and senior clinical assistant in the department of obstetrics and gynecology at Mount Sinai Hospital.

Markey, Lucille Parker, U.S. Thoroughbred horse breeder and owner (b. Dec. 14, 1896, Maysville, Ky.—d. July 24, 1982, Miami, Fla.), for over half a century was the proprietor of Calumet Farm in Lexington, Ky., the famed Thoroughbred racing nursery and stable that boasted eight Kentucky Derby winners and two Triple Crown champions, Whirlaway and Citation. Together with her first husband, Warren Wright, Markey helped transform Calumet from a small trotting-horse farm into the leading money-winning stable in the U.S., with purses in excess of $26 million. During her long association with racing Markey was especially admired for her outstanding organizational skills.

Marsh, Dame (Edith) Ngaio, New Zealand novelist (b. April 23, 1899, Christchurch, New Zealand—d. Feb. 18, 1982, Christchurch), was among those who in the 1930s raised the detective story to the level of a respectable literary genre, combining style, ingenuity, and believable characters. Marsh studied at art school and acted in repertory before going to England in 1928. Her first book, *A Man Lay Dead,* appeared in 1934. The art world and the theatre provided the background for many of her novels, including *Artists in Crime* (1938), *Final Curtain* (1947), and *Opening Night* (1951), all featuring her detective hero, Roderick Alleyn of Scotland Yard. These books, with *A Surfeit of Lampreys* (1941) and *Black as He's Painted* (1974), were classic examples of the traditional detective story, giving their readers the delights of a cleverly contrived puzzle involving well-observed characters against an authentic background. Marsh's interest in the theatre continued; she directed plays and in 1944 helped to found a theatre guild that became an important mainstay of New Zealand cultural life. She was made Officer of the Order of the British Empire in 1948 and Dame Commander of the Order of the British Empire in 1966, as much for her services to the theatre as for her novels. She published an autobiography, *Black Beech and Honeydew,* in 1966.

Mendès-France, Pierre, French politician (b. Jan. 11, 1907, Paris, France—d. Oct. 18, 1982, Paris), as an outstanding statesman during the French Fourth Republic, ended the colonial war in Indochina during his brief premiership (June 1954 to February 1955). He became a symbol of opposition to the Gaullist Fifth Republic, was loyal to parliamentary tradition, and lived to see the Socialist Party triumph in 1981. But Mendès-France was never a dogmatic Socialist and, though he knew the importance of power, was something of a loner. Though his middle-class Jewish background was a detriment in prewar French politics, he had a brilliant

CAMERA PRESS, LONDON

academic career and in 1932 became the youngest deputy in the National Assembly. During World War II Mendès-France joined de Gaulle's Free French Air Force in London, after escaping from prison, and was a member of the National Committee in Algiers. After the Liberation he became minister for economic affairs but resigned in 1945 after a dispute with de Gaulle. In 1954 when Mendès-France came to power he pledged to end the Indochina war within 30 days and did so with the Geneva Agreement, which provided for an honourable French withdrawal. He later continued the process of decolonization by granting autonomy to Tunisia. The latter, and the outbreak of war in Algeria, lost him support and outraged the right; after stormy debate, his government fell. Mendès-France served briefly as minister of state under Guy Mollet in 1956 and was expected to rally to de Gaulle in 1958 but voted against the new regime and lost his seat in the Assembly. He regained his seat in 1967 but never attracted a substantial group of followers who shared his hostility to the Fifth Republic's presidential government.

Merchant, Vivien, British actress (b. July 22, 1929, Manchester, England—d. Oct. 3, 1982, London, England), played the female leading roles in the best-known plays of her husband, Harold Pinter. From the early 1960s she appeared in all his main works, including *The Room, The Lover,* and *The Homecoming;* the last, which she also filmed, was her greatest success. Merchant met Pinter while they were acting in repertory, married him in 1956, and rapidly established her reputation as a sensitive actress of great emotional power. In 1965 she joined the Royal Shakespeare Company and played many parts while touring with the company in the U.S. and other countries. During the 1970s her name was also associated with productions of the Greenwich Theatre. Merchant's film roles included *Alfie* (1966), *Accident* (1967), and *Frenzy* (1972), and she acted in several of Pinter's plays on television. Her marriage to Pinter ended in divorce in 1980.

Merrill, Henry Tindall (DICK MERRILL), U.S. pilot (b. 1894?, Iuka, Miss.—d. Oct. 31, 1982, Lake Elsinore, Calif.), was a crack pilot for Eastern Airlines for 33 years and an aviation daredevil who became the first pilot to have flown the North Atlantic nonstop four times in a heavier-than-air machine. In 1936 Merrill made the first round-trip Atlantic flight, and in the following year he made aviation history by piloting the first commercial transatlantic flight in an airplane. The trip was notable because Merrill delivered photographs of the burning of the zeppelin "Hindenburg" to England, and on his return to the U.S. he carried newsreels and stills of the coronation of King George VI, setting a record for the fastest picture delivery by a photo syndicate in newspaper history. During his 41 years as a pilot, Merrill logged 41,709 hours in the air and was the recipient of the International Federation of Aeronautics School Gold Medal for logging more flying time than any other pilot. After retiring from Eastern in 1961, Merrill, who hobnobbed with celebrities, flew a corporate jet around the world in 1966 with the entertainer Arthur Godfrey and set 21 world speed records.

Micunovic, Veljko, Yugoslav diplomat (b. Jan. 16, 1916, Cetinje, Montenegro—d. Aug. 2, 1982, Belgrade, Yugos.). as ambassador to the Soviet Union (1956–58) witnessed the Soviet leadership's reactions to the 1956 upheavals in Poland and Hungary. After studying law at the University of Belgrade, Micunovic joined the underground Communist Party of Yugoslavia and in 1941 was one of the first to become part of Tito's partisan movement. After World War II he became a member of the federal government, serving as deputy minister of the interior and deputy minister of foreign affairs before being sent to Moscow. Yugoslav-Soviet relations, only recently resumed after the split between Stalin and Tito, were put under severe pressure as a result of the events of 1956. Micunovic's record of these years, published as *Moscow Diary* (Eng. trans., 1980), was recognized as an important work on the period. He later served as ambassador to the U.S. (1962–67) and returned in the same capacity to Moscow (1969–71).

Mills, Harry, U.S. singer (b. Aug. 19, 1913, Piqua, Ohio—d. June 28, 1982, Los Angeles, Calif.), was a baritone with the original Mills Brothers, a quartet known for its mellow sound, four-part harmonies, and vocal instrumental imitations. Together with his brothers Herbert, Donald, and John Jr., Mills formed a group called Four Boys and a Guitar in 1925. The group was later billed as the Mills Brothers, and in the early 1930s they catapulted to stardom with "Tiger Rag," the first of more than 2,000 records. They later popularized such songs as "Paper Doll," "Lazy River," "Glow Worm," "Bye-Bye Blackbird," "You're Nobody till Somebody Loves You," and "Sweet Sue." After the death of John Jr. in 1936 the Mills Brothers' father filled out the foursome. He retired in 1956 but occasionally performed on recording dates; after his death in 1968 the brothers continued as a trio. Mills, who enjoyed a 57-year-career, felt that his songs endured because "Maybe people want to hear plain, simple songs and easy harmony."

Mitchell, Sir Godfrey Way, British building contractor (b. Oct. 31, 1891—d. Dec. 9, 1982, Beaconsfield, England), as chairman (1930–73), executive director (1973–79), and from 1979 life president of George Wimpey & Co. Ltd. was an outstanding figure in the British construction industry. After serving as an officer in the Royal Engineers during World War I, in 1919 he acquired a small mason and stonelaying firm from its founder and owner, George Wimpey, and over the years built it into one of the biggest construction companies in Europe. In 1928 the firm expanded into building houses and became the world's largest in that field. During World War II Mitchell was a member of several committees advising government departments and was controller of building materials at the Ministry of Works. He was knighted in 1948 and the same year was elected chairman of the Federation of Civil Engineering Contractors.

Monk, Thelonious Sphere, U.S. composer and pianist (b. Oct. 10, 1917, Rocky Mount, N.C.—d. Feb. 17, 1982, Englewood, N.J.), was an innovative and eccentric jazz composer and pianist who together with Dizzy Gillespie and Charlie Parker pioneered the 1940s bebop music jazz form. Monk's music was characterized by distinctive harmonic progressions and dissonant melodies that converged logically to form a unified composition. During the late 1930s and early 1940s Gillespie, Parker, Monk, and Kenny Clarke conducted jam sessions at Minton's Play House in Harlem, N.Y., where the four gave birth to bebop music. Because of his angular piano style, Monk was largely ignored until the late 1950s bop movement. He then gained recognition

UPI

with a series of outstanding recordings and performances with saxophonist John Coltrane, and during the 1960s Monk was the leader of small jazz bands that gave concerts worldwide. In the 1970s his public appearances were sparse, and in 1976 he gave his last concert at Carnegie Hall. An eccentric who kept his grand piano in the kitchen, fashioned his own middle name to indicate he wasn't square, and spontaneously danced in sly elflike steps, Monk remained an enigma throughout his life. His jazz compositions, including "Round About Midnight," "Blue Monk," "Epistrophy," "Straight, No Chaser," "Hackensack," and "Ruby My Dear," became jazz standards. Other works in his repertoire included "Little Rootie Tootie," "Criss Cross," and "Well, You Needn't." Monk also exerted a powerful influence on modern jazz musicians.

Moore, Stanford, U.S. biochemist (b. Sept. 4, 1913, Chicago, Ill.—d. Aug. 23, 1982, New York, N.Y.), shared the 1972 Nobel Prize for Chemistry for his fundamental contributions to enzyme chemistry. Specifically, Moore and William H. Stein, his co-researcher for 40 years, were the first to apply chromatographic procedures for the separation of amino acids, which are the basic components of proteins. By separating biological substances in amino acids, the two were able to establish the molecular structure of proteins. In 1959, using these analyses, Moore was able to determine the structure of the enzyme ribonuclease. The discovery paved the way to a clearer understanding of how a biological malfunction might be repaired in the human body. Moore, who earned a Ph.D. from the University of Wisconsin in 1938, joined the staff of the Rockefeller Institute (now Rockefeller University) the following year and remained there throughout his career. At the time of his death he was John D. Rockefeller professor.

More, Kenneth Gilbert, British actor (b. Sept. 20, 1914, Gerrards Cross, Buckinghamshire, England—d. July 12, 1982, London, England), gave screen portrayals of essentially English types, from the happy-go-lucky medical student in *Doctor in the House* (1954) to the unflappable butler who takes charge after a shipwreck in *The Admirable Crichton* (1957). He achieved his greatest success, however, as the legless pilot Douglas Bader (q.v.) in *Reach for the Sky* (1956). In this role he gave life to the caricature of the "British wartime spirit," undemonstrative, decent, courageous, and even cheerful in misfortune. More had worked in various jobs before joining the Windmill Theatre, where he acted in revue in 1936. He took his first important film role in *Scott of the Antarctic* (1948), made a notable stage appearance as a Royal Air Force pilot in Terence Rattigan's *The Deep Blue Sea* (1952; filmed 1955), and became a household name with the de-

lightful film comedy *Genevieve* (1953). Other successes followed, but by the time of *The Comedy Man* (1963), despite his attempts to avoid typecasting and his considerable acting skill, his career had begun to falter. He made a comeback on television as Young Jolyon in the immensely popular adaptation of Galsworthy's *The Forsyte Saga* (1966–67). He later starred in "The White Rabbit" and the "Father Brown" series. In films he made only cameo appearances in *Oh! What a Lovely War* (1968) and *Scrooge* (1970), and on stage he preferred the traditional well-made play, giving accomplished performances in *The Secretary Bird* (1968), *The Winslow Boy* (1970), and *Getting On* (1971). More, who was diagnosed as suffering from Parkinson's disease in 1980, had published two volumes of autobiography, *Happy Go Lucky* (1959) and *More or Less* (1978), and a book of reminiscences, *Kindly Leave the Stage* (1965). He was made Commander of the Order of the British Empire in 1970.

Morrow, Vic, U.S. actor (b. Feb. 14, 1932, Bronx, N.Y.—d. July 23, 1982, Castaic, Calif.), was best known as Sgt. Chip Saunders in the television drama "Combat" (1962–67), a World War II saga that chronicled the landing of the U.S. infantry on D-Day and the Allied victory one year later. Morrow, who made his motion picture debut in *The Blackboard Jungle* (1955), was especially noted for his tough guy roles in such other films as *Tribute to a Badman, Cimarron,* and *Portrait of a Mobster.* Morrow died when a helicopter carrying a camera crew crashed after it was hit by debris from bombs set off during the filming of a movie version of the television series "The Twilight Zone." Morrow, who was on the ground, was decapitated, and two Vietnamese children he was holding were killed.

Morton, Thruston Ballard, U.S. politician (b. Aug. 19, 1907, Louisville, Ky.—d. Aug. 14, 1982, Louisville), was a seventh-generation Kentuckian who became a towering figure in state politics while representing Louisville in the House of Representatives from 1947 to 1953 and serving as U.S. senator from 1957 to 1969. Morton, a graduate of Yale University, was also assistant secretary of state (1953–56) under Pres. Dwight D. Eisenhower and was national chairman (1959–61) of the Republican Party during the 1960 presidential campaign. Morton was opposed to the war in Vietnam and called for bold U.S. leadership in world affairs. At the peak of his career in 1968, Morton surprised his constituents by deciding to not seek reelection. After retiring from politics he served on the board of directors of several leading companies.

Muus, Flemming B., Danish businessman and writer (b. Nov. 21, 1907, Copenhagen, Denmark—d. Sept. 23, 1982, Copenhagen), was a leading member of the Danish resistance movement during World War II. He worked in Liberia from 1931 and was there on business at the outbreak of war. In 1942 he managed to reach England and joined the British Army. During the following year Muus was parachuted into Denmark, undertook sabotage and other resistance work, and helped to persuade the Danish government to end its policy of collaboration with the Nazis. He was a founder-member of the Liberation Council which ultimately took over the reorganization of the country after its liberation. During the postwar years, he lived for some time in South Africa and wrote over 20 books including travel and children's books. Muus was vice-chairman of the board of the Museum of the Danish Resistance Movement in Copenhagen and editor of *Resistance Veterans.*

Namgyal, Palden Thondup, deposed *chogyal* (king) of Sikkim (b. May 22, 1923, Kham Province, India—d. Jan. 29, 1982, New York, N.Y.), was king of Sikkim, a small Himalayan protectorate of India, from 1963 until he lost power in 1973 and was formally deposed in 1975. At the time of Palden Thondup's birth he was proclaimed a living saint and spiritual head of the Phodong and Rumtek monasteries. He was trained as a monk but when his elder brother was killed in an airplane crash, Palden Thondup became heir apparent. After being educated at the administrative college in Dehru Dun, India, he served as an adviser to his father and led the Sikkimese delegation that negotiated the 1950 treaty with India. Six years after the death (1957) of his first wife, Palden Thondup defied Buddhist tradition and made international headlines by marrying New York socialite Hope Cooke. On Dec. 5, 1963, Palden Thondup was formally proclaimed maharaja of Sikkim. During his reign he and his consort sought to modernize the Himalayan kingdom with roads, schools, and hospitals. In 1973 he lost power when he pressed too hard for Sikkimese autonomy. In 1975 he was deposed, the monarchy was abolished, and on April 10 Sikkim became the 22nd state of the Republic of India. After the uprising his wife returned to the U.S. The couple divorced in 1980.

Nesbitt, Cathleen, British actress (b. Nov. 24, 1888, Cheshire, England—d. Aug. 2, 1982, London, England), had a stage career that lasted 70 years and was constantly in demand as one of the great names of the London and New York theatre. After Nesbitt made her debut in 1910, she was asked by the poet W. B. Yeats to join the Irish Players; she toured with them in the U.S. When she returned to London she met and fell in love with the poet Rupert Brooke. Their friendship, which lasted until Brooke's death in 1915, was recalled many years later in her autobiography, *A Little Love and Good Company* (1975). In the U.S. and in England, she played classical and modern roles in such productions as *The Doctor's Dilemma* (1923), *Hassan* (1923), and *Spring Cleaning* (1925), exhibiting the stage presence and versatility that helped her win so many notable parts prior to the outbreak of World War II. In 1949 at the Edinburgh Festival, she was Julia in T. S. Eliot's *The Cocktail Party.* She later toured with the same play in the U.S., where she spent much of the 1950s and performed in *My Fair Lady* (as Mrs. Higgins), *The Chalk Garden,* and *The Sleeping Prince.* Nesbitt also appeared in such films as *Nicholas Nickleby* and *Three Coins in the Fountain,* and she appeared on television in "The Crucible" and "Upstairs, Downstairs." She made her last appearances on stage in 1980–81, touring with *My Fair Lady* in the U.S. and performing in the Chichester Theatre production of *The Aspern Papers* in Britain. Nesbitt was made Commander of the Order of the British Empire in 1978.

Neveux, Georges, French poet and dramatist (b. Aug. 25, 1900, Poltava, Ukraine, Russia—d. Aug. 27, 1982, Paris, France), collaborated with the actor and manager Louis Jouvet at the Comédie des Champs-Elysées and was the author of several successful plays and film scripts. Though he studied to be a lawyer, during the 1920s Neveux came into contact with the French Surrealists whose work inspired his first play, *Juliette; ou, la clé des songes* (*"Juliet, or the Key to Dreams"*). His experimental production was a commercial failure, so he went to work for Jouvet and turned to writing for the cinema. Neveux was also the author of many translations, notably of Shakespeare, Chekhov, and Shaw, and of an adaptation of *The Diary of Anne Frank.* He later worked extensively for television and adapted his own play *Zamore* in 1970. He was awarded the Grand Prix of the Société des Auteurs in 1973.

Nicholson, Ben, British artist (b. April 10, 1894, Denham, Buckinghamshire, England—d. Feb. 6, 1982, London, England), was the leading British abstract painter of his generation. His austere painted reliefs, inspired by the aesthetics of Cubism, Constructivism, and the Dutch De Stijl group, influenced many younger British artists during the post-World War II period. The son of painter Sir William Nicholson, he studied briefly at the Slade School and traveled in France, Italy, and the U.S. before holding his first one-man show in London in 1922. During the 1930s Nicholson was associated with such groups as Unit One and Abstraction-Création, which were concerned with the application of geometric forms to both painting and architecture. His work moved toward greater purity and restraint, typified by his white reliefs of this period. In 1940 he settled in St. Ives, Cornwall, where he remained until 1958; with his second wife, the sculptress Barbara Hepworth, he was a leading figure in the Cornish art colony. It was during this time that he began to receive international recognition, notably in 1954 with a major retrospective exhibition shown in many European countries and with the award of the Ulissi prize at the Venice Biennale. This was followed by numerous other awards, including the Guggenheim Prize and the Grand Prix at Lugano in 1956 and the Rembrandt Prize in 1974. Nicholson's work continued to evolve along the lines he had first mapped out for it, and his 75th birthday was marked by a major retrospective exhibition at the Tate Gallery in London and by the publication of two monographs. He was appointed Member of the Order of Merit in 1968.

Noel-Baker, Philip John Noel-Baker, BARON, British politician (b. Nov. 1, 1889—d. Oct. 8, 1982, London, England), was a Labour member of Parliament from 1929 to 1970, a tireless campaigner for world peace, and the winner of the 1959 Nobel Prize for Peace. He studied at Haverford (Pa.) College and King's College, Cambridge, and at the Universities of Munich and Paris. Noel-Baker was also a gifted athlete who took part in the 1912 Olympic Games and, as captain of the Olympic team at Antwerp in 1920, won the silver medal in the 1,500 m. During World War I he had served courageously in ambulance duties and won the Mons Star and the Italian Silver Star and the Croce di Guerra. Noel-Baker then served as a member of the League of Nations secretariat and professor (1924–29) in international relations at the University of London. He continued to work for disarmament, served as joint parliamentary secretary at the Ministry of War Transport in World War II, as minister of state in the postwar Labour government, and as secretary of state for air and minister of fuel and power. From 1946 to 1947 he was chairman of the Labour Party. In his book, *The Arms Race* (1958), which was awarded the 1960 Albert Schweitzer Book Prize, Noel-Baker supported realistic arms control, but he opposed unilateral disarmament. He was also president of the Socialist Campaign for Multilateral Disarmament.

O'Gorman, Juan, Mexican architect and painter (b. July 6, 1905, Coyoacán, Mexico—found dead Jan. 18, 1982, Mexico City, Mexico), created imaginative mosaic designs that adorned the facades of buildings, the most elaborate example being the exterior walls of the Library of the National Autonomous University of Mexico, which he planned and built in 1950. The windowless library featured a tower containing book stacks and covered with mosaics constructed of natural minerals. After being graduated in 1927 from the school of architecture of the National University of Mexico, Mexico City, O'Gorman began designing houses and buildings in Mexico in the International Style, including the house and studio of muralist Diego Rivera. Some of O'Gorman's major works in Mexico City included murals and frescoes at the National Museum of Anthropology, the airport, and the Museum of National History in Chapultepec Castle. His important mosaics appear on the Secretaría de Comunicaciones y Obras Públicas (1952) and on the facade of the Posada de la Misión Hotel in Taxco. His own house outside Mexico City (1953–56, demolished 1969) was considered his most extraordinary work. It was in part a natural cave in rocks and was designed to accentuate the lava formations of the landscape and was also decorated with mosaic symbols and images from Aztec mythology. O'Gorman, despondent over a heart ailment that prevented him from working, apparently took his own life.

Opie, Peter Mason, British folklorist (b. Nov. 25, 1918, Cairo, Egypt—d. Feb. 5, 1982, West Liss, Hampshire, England), was co-author with his wife, Iona, of the delightful and scholarly *Lore and Language of Schoolchildren* (1959) and *Children's Games in Street and Playground* (1969; Chicago Folklore Prize). These works, which followed their *Oxford Dictionary of Nursery Rhymes* (1951), were the product of a lifetime study of folklore, meticulous collection of oral evidence, and a profound sympathy with the minutiae of childhood lore, pursuits, and customs. Opie was educated at Eton College and served in the Army during World War II until invalided out in 1941. His marriage in 1943 and the birth of his first child led him to specialize in the branch of folklore that the Opies were to make their own. Their other publications included *The Classic Fairy Tales* (1974), anthologies of children's verse, and the article "Children's Sports and Games" in *Encyclopædia Britannica.* Peter Opie was awarded the Silver Medal of the Royal Society of Arts in 1953 and was president of the anthropology section of the British Association (1962–63).

Orff, Carl, German composer and musical educator (b. July 10, 1895, Munich, Germany—d. March 29, 1982, Munich, West Germany), strove for a simplicity in musical form that would give contemporary music greater popular appeal. The work in which he most successfully demonstrated this concern was the cantata *Carmina Burana,* which he composed to a sequence of 13th-century lyrics. The simple melodies and rhythmical vitality of *Carmina Burana* made it an immediate success when first performed in 1937. Orff, who profoundly influenced the principles and practice of elementary school music education, co-founded the Güntherschule in Munich in 1924. The centre coordinated the teaching of music, gymnastics, and dance. Orff's improvisational system of music education was largely based on group performance with percussion instruments. He illustrated these principles in his manual *Orff-Schulwerk.* Orff's many stage works, which reveal his interest in Monteverdi and other early composers, include *Der Mond* (1939), *Die Kluge* (1943), *Die Bernauerin* (1947), and *Trionfo di Afrodite* (1953). He also wrote Easter and Christmas plays, first performed in 1957 and 1960. His work was sometimes criticized as crude and oversimplified, but as an educator his influence was considerable. He gained West Germany's Orden Pour le Mérite in 1956 and awards from the Italian and Swedish academies.

Ovando Candía, Alfredo, Bolivian politician (b. April 6, 1918, Cobija, Bolivia—d. Jan. 24, 1982, La Paz, Bolivia), was commander in chief of the military campaign during which Che Guevara, the Cuban revolutionary, was captured and executed in 1967, and also twice served as president of Bolivia. Ovando, who became a soldier in the Army in 1936, was credited with rebuilding the country's armed forces after their dissolution in 1952. He served as co-president in 1965–66 with Gen. René Barrientos after they overthrew Pres. Víctor Paz Estenssoro. Ovando became president again in 1969 when he ousted the constitutional civilian president, Luis Adolfo Siles Salinas, in a bloodless military coup. In 1970 Ovando resigned under pressure from the military.

Paige, Leroy Robert ("SATCHEL"), U.S. baseball player (b. July 7, 1906?, Mobile, Ala.—d. June 8, 1982, Kansas City, Mo.), was a phenomenal right-handed pitcher whose precision and stamina became a hallmark of his career first in the Negro leagues and then when he entered (1948) the major leagues as a rookie at age 42. Paige, who for 20 years pitched for various teams in the Negro Southern Association and the Negro National League, claimed a minor league record of 2,000 wins, 500 losses, and 100 no-hitters. As a barnstormer he traveled some 30,000 mi a year playing in the Caribbean, Central America, and South America for anyone who would pay his price. In 1935 he pitched 153 games, starting 29 times in one month. After Jackie Robinson broke the major league colour barrier in 1947, Bill Veeck signed Paige in 1948 to play with the Cleveland Indians. Though many were skeptical, Paige stunned batters with his fastball and slow, hesitant delivery and helped spark

his team to an American League pennant and World Series victories. After Veeck bought the St. Louis Browns, Paige served as the team's most effective relief pitcher from 1951 to 1953. Paige played intermittently in the major leagues for some six seasons, and during that time he faced some of baseball's most formidable hitters and opposed legendary pitchers. During an exhibition game he had struck out the power hitter Rogers Hornsby five times, and in 1934 he bested Dizzy Dean by scoring a 1–0 victory in 13 innings over the pitcher who had won 30 games for the St. Louis Cardinals that year. In 1965, during his last professional appearance, Paige pitched three scoreless innings against the Boston Red Sox for the Kansas City A's; he was 59 years old. A homespun philosopher who never admitted his age, Paige was also known for his most famous maxim, "Don't look back. Something might be gaining on you." He was inducted into the Hall of Fame in 1971.

Parry, Clive, British jurist (b. July 13, 1917, Astley, Shropshire, England—d. Sept. 10, 1982, Cambridge, England), was professor of international law at the University of Cambridge from 1969 and the author of many standard works on international legal questions. Parry was the notable editor, from 1965, of the *British Digest of International Law,* five volumes of which were published before his death. After studying at the University of Birmingham, Cambridge University, and the Max Planck Institute and army service during World War II, he spent a year as professor of public law at the University of Ankara, Turkey, then became lecturer at the London School of Economics and Political Science. In 1946 he returned to Cambridge where he spent the rest of his career and became recognized as an exceptional, though uncompromising, teacher. Parry's many publications included *The Sources and Evidences of International Law* (1965) and works on British nationality law; he was the editor of many journals and collections, including the monumental *Consolidated Treaty Series,* 231 volumes of annotated text covering all treaties concluded between 1648 and 1918.

Pepper, Art, U.S. saxophonist (b. Sept. 1, 1925, Gardena, Calif.—d. June 15, 1982, Los Angeles, Calif.), established himself as one of the greatest altoists in post-bebop jazz with tortured yet elegant rhythms that mirrored his own personal anguish. Pepper, who became a star playing (1947–52) with the Stan Kenton Orchestra, was credited with ushering in progressive jazz. Riddled with self-doubt, however, Pepper became a heroin addict in the early 1950s; despite his drug dependency he turned out (1956–60) such masterpieces as "I Surrender Dear," "Pepper Pot," "What Is This Thing Called

Love?," and "Winter Moon." After his release from a three-year prison term in 1966, Pepper performed briefly (1968–69) with Buddy Rich's Big Band but spent most of his time in hospitals or in prisons until he was cured of his addiction in 1972. He returned triumphantly to the music scene with the album "Living Legend," which showcased his distinctive and fiery lyricism. In 1979 Pepper published his autobiography, *Straight Life: The Story of Art Pepper,* a lurid account of his tumultuous career.

Perham, Dame Margery, British historian (b. Sept. 6, 1895, Bury, Lancashire, England—d. Feb. 19, 1982, Burcot, Oxford, England), enjoyed a unique advisory role at the Colonial Office and helped to smooth the path of Britain's African colonies toward independence during the post-World War II period. Perham helped to establish the School of Colonial Studies and the Institute of Colonial (later Commonwealth) Studies at the University of Oxford and was an active member of the Inter-University Council for Higher Education in the Colonies. Perham was a reader in colonial administration and a fellow of Nuffield College at Oxford, and she was a leading historian of British colonial rule in Africa. She had studied history at Oxford and lectured at the University of Sheffield before her first visit to Africa in 1922. This and subsequent visits led in 1937 to the publication of *Native Administration in Nigeria,* a study of the policy of indirect rule developed by Lord Lugard. Her travels in Africa were described in *African Apprenticeship* (1974) and *East African Journey* (1976). She delivered the BBC Reith Lectures in 1961–62 and published a two-volume collection of her articles on African affairs in *Colonial Sequence* (1967 and 1970). She was made Commander of the Order of the British Empire in 1948 and Dame Commander of St. Michael and St. George in 1965 and was elected fellow of the British Academy in 1961.

Petri, Elio, Italian film director (b. 1929—d. Nov. 10, 1982, Rome, Italy), won an Oscar for *Investigation of a Citizen Above Suspicion* (1970), a complex satire on the Italian middle class and the psychology of Fascism. He studied at Rome University and wrote for the Communist daily newspaper *L'Unità* before working as a scriptwriter and making documentaries. Petri's first feature was *The Assassin* (1961), which introduced his theme of analysis of the bourgeois mentality. This, and his taste for the macabre, were evident in his later works, which included *The Tenth Victim, Property Is No Longer Theft,* and *Todo Moro,* a satire on the Christian Democrat leader Aldo Moro who was killed by terrorists in 1979.

Pilyugin, Nikolay Alekseyevich, Soviet scientist (b May 18, 1908, Krasnoye Selo, St. Petersburg [now Leningrad] region, Russia—d. Aug. 2, 1982, Moscow, U.S.S.R.), was a key figure in the early stages of the Soviet space program. His major contribution was to the development of control systems, first for satellite-launching rockets and later for the first Soviet spaceships and space stations, of which he was chief designer. Educated at the Bauman Higher Technical College in Moscow, from which he was graduated in 1935, he later taught at the Moscow Institute of Radiotechnology, Electronics, and Automation, where he was appointed professor in 1969. He became a member of the Communist Party of the Soviet Union in 1940 and among other decorations was awarded the Lenin Prize (1957) and the U.S.S.R. State Prize (1967).

Powell, Eleanor Torrey, U.S. dancer (b. Nov. 21, 1912, Springfield, Mass.—d. Feb. 11, 1982, Beverly Hills, Calif.), was a leggy, agile tap dancer whose extraordinary terpsichorean skills vaulted her to stardom in a series of "Broadway Melody" musical extravaganzas. Powell, who made an impressive film debut in *George White's 1935 Scandals,* became a star in *The Broadway Melody of 1936.* She likewise gave lustrous performances in *Born to Dance* (1936), *Rosalie* (1937), and *Honolulu* (1939), in which she tap danced while skipping rope. In *Broadway Melody of 1940* Powell danced on a glittering mirrored floor, matching Fred Astaire step for step in a fast-paced rendition of Cole Porter's "Begin the Beguine,"

and in *Lady Be Good* (1941) she was the critics' choice as the best woman tap dancer in motion pictures. After marrying actor Glenn Ford in 1943 she retired from show business. In 1961 she made a brief comeback but then returned to private life.

Powell, Sandy, British music hall and radio comedian (b. Jan. 30, 1900, Rotherham, England—d. June 26, 1982, Eastbourne, England), started in variety at the age of seven, became the star of the BBC's first radio variety series, "Sandy's Hour," in 1928, and appeared in his last Royal Variety Performance at the London Palladium when he was 80 years old. A Northern comedian, he owed his first success to music hall and to seaside audiences in Blackpool, but he was equally popular in the South and eventually settled in Eastbourne on the south coast. He made more than 100 phonograph records and starred in eight films, which were enormously successful, during the 1930s. He went on to tour South Africa, New Zealand, Canada, and the U.S. and performed on television and radio. A modest man, much loved by audiences and his fellow artists, he insisted that he had never cracked a dirty joke and that his success had been due mainly to good luck.

Praz, Mario, Italian scholar (b. Sept. 6, 1896, Rome, Italy—d. March 23, 1982, Rome), was professor of English language and literature at the University of Rome from 1934 to 1966 and an outstanding literary historian who contributed to every field of English studies from the Middle Ages to the present day. His *La carne, la morte e il diavolo nella letteratura romantica* (1930), published in English as *The Romantic Agony,* was his best-known work and became a standard text. Praz studied in Rome and Florence before going to England to conduct research. He lectured in Italian at the University of Liverpool (1924–32), then spent two years as professor of Italian studies at Victoria University of Manchester before returning to Rome. He published studies of 17th-century poetry and the Elizabethans, as well as work on the Romantics. Praz exhibited a combination of scholarship and eclecticism that was evidenced in his brilliant *Storia della letteratura inglese* (1937), a one-volume history of English literature. The breadth of his erudition was also demonstrated in *Studi sul concettismo* (1934) and *Gusto neoclassico* (1940). He was designated an honorary Knight Commander of the British Empire by the British government in 1962.

Primrose, William, Scottish-born violist (b. Aug. 23, 1904, Glasgow, Scotland—d. May 1, 1982, Provo, Utah), was a virtuoso who achieved a pure, sweet tone that helped elevate the viola to the rank of a solo instrument. Primrose was a violin prodigy before he was persuaded to switch to the viola by his teacher Eugene Ysaye. After studying at the Guildhall School of Music and Drama in London, Primrose was a violist with the London String Quartet from 1930 to 1935. For the following two years he toured as a recitalist before settling in the U.S. and becoming in 1937 first viola of the NBC Symphony, then under the direction of Arturo Toscanini. As a member of the latter he organized the Primrose Quartet, which gave radio performances of chamber music. He remained with the NBC Symphony until 1942, when he accelerated his solo engagements. Primrose, who also worked closely with composers, commissioned Bela Bartok to write a viola concerto and played the first performance of the completed work. After a heart attack in 1963 impaired his hearing, Primrose turned his expertise more to teaching. He was a faculty member of the University of California at Los Angeles, Indiana University, the Tokyo National University of Fine Arts and Music, and Brigham Young University, Provo, Utah.

Quandt, Herbert, West German industrialist (b. June 22, 1910, Pritzwald, Germany—d. June 2, 1982, Bad Homburg, West Germany), headed one of the last major private business empires in West Germany. The enterprise was launched by his father, Günther Quandt, who started in textiles during the years before World War II, then diversified into batteries and arms, including Mauser pistols. Herbert, who suffered from poor sight, left school at the age of ten and studied at home before joining the business as a worker on the shop floor. During the war the business was nearly destroyed, but Günther started to rebuild it; after his death in 1954 it passed to Herbert and his half brother Harald. Harald died in 1967 in a plane crash, and after a dispute over the inheritance Herbert became principal owner. In 1970 he bought the Bayerische Motoren Werke (BMW) automotive company, then close to bankruptcy, and developed it into one of West Germany's leading car manufacturers. By the time of his death, his combined businesses, including BMW and the Varta battery concern, had a turnover of DM 13 billion (U.S. $5.3 billion).

Rambert, Dame Marie (DAME MARIE DUKES), Polish-born ballet teacher and director (b. Feb. 20, 1888, Warsaw, Poland—d. June 12, 1982, London, England), as a dominant figure in British ballet established Ballet Rambert, which served as a nursery for talent and a creative force from the time of its foundation in 1926. Although she went to Paris to study medicine, Rambert was inspired by Isadora Duncan and took to dance. Rambert became a pupil of Émile Jaques-Dalcroze and, later, Enrico Cecchetti. In 1912 she was asked by Sergey Diaghilev to help Vaslav Nijinsky with his work on *The Rite of Spring*. She also danced with Diaghilev's Ballets Russes and, on the outbreak of war, moved to London, where she taught dance. In 1918 she married the playwright Ashley Dukes and with his encouragement in 1920 opened the Rambert School of Ballet. One of her protégés was the eminent choreographer Frederick Ashton, whose first ballet, *A Tragedy of Fashion*, she produced in 1926. The Ballet Rambert's first season, with Tamara Karsavina, was at the Lyric Theatre, Hammersmith, in 1930. During the next decade her husband's Mercury Theatre (headquarters of their Ballet Club, founded 1930) realized the first successes of many of her pupils, with ballets created by Antony Tudor, Andrée Howard, Walter Gore, and Frank Staff. During World War II she produced lunchtime ballets at the Arts Theatre, and after the war the company was enlarged. Rambert was more interested, however, in encouraging new talent, and after a financial crisis in 1966 the company, renamed the Modern Dance Company, was made smaller and concentrated on experimental work. She was made Commander (1953) and Dame Commander (1962) of the Order of the British Empire. Her autobiography, *Quicksilver*, appeared in 1972.

Rand, Ayn, U.S. writer (b. Feb. 2, 1905, St. Petersburg [now Leningrad], Russia—d. March 6, 1982, New York, N.Y.), was a controversial novelist and philosopher who enraged liberals and inspired conservatives but nonetheless delighted readers with the publication of *The Fountainhead* (1943), which introduced her philosophy of objectivism. Rand defined objectivism as embracing "reason, individualism, and capitalism" and denouncing altruism in favour of "rational selfishness." Her novel, about an architect whose uncompromising integrity prompted him to blow up his own construction project rather than have others interfere in his design, was made into a motion picture in 1949. Two years after Rand graduated from the University of Petrograd (1924), she immigrated to the U.S. and became a screenwriter in Hollywood. Her first novel, *We the Living* (1936), was not well received, but *The Fountainhead* earned her a following. Other works in which she expounded on objectivism were *Atlas Shrugged* (1957), an examination of the role of the individual in industrial society, *The Virtue of Selfishness* (1965), and *Capitalism: The Unknown Ideal* (1966). Her other nonfiction works included *For the New Intellectual, The Romantic Manifesto,* and *The New Left*. Rand also was editor of two journals, *The Objectivist* (1962–71) and *The Ayn Rand Letter* (1971–76).

Randall, Sir Richard John, Australian economist (b. Oct. 13, 1906, Birkdale, Queensland, Australia—d. Nov. 15, 1982, Canberra, Australia), was secretary to the Commonwealth of Australia Treasury from 1966 to 1971. He studied economics at the University of Sydney where he later conducted research. Randall also worked on a sheep farm and was in the premier's office in New South Wales before joining the Commonwealth Treasury in 1940. A conscientious official whose wide knowledge and judgment were highly esteemed, he served as adviser to Australian prime ministers and Treasury ministers for many years. Randall was knighted in 1964.

Reader, (William Henry) Ralph, British theatrical producer (b. May 25, 1903, Crewkerne, Somerset, England—d. May 13, 1982, London, England), created the first of the Boy Scout movement's "Gang Shows" in 1932 and continued to produce what became an annual event until it ended with his retirement in 1974. The "Gang Shows," naive and jolly, reflected qualities of good humour, decency, and camaraderie that were the essence of the Boy Scout movement and of Reader's own outlook on life. At the last show he revealed that they had been used as a cover during the 1930s for the recruitment of British counterintelligence agents. Reader also produced wartime spectaculars at the Albert Hall. Such show business talents as Peter Sellers and Tony Hancock launched their careers performing for him. Reader's first theatrical experience was in the 1920s in New York, where he acted and produced dance numbers before returning to England in 1928. He worked with *The Cochran Revue* in 1930, and he continued to act and direct musicals and pantomimes into the 1950s. However, his greatest talent lay in marshaling large amateur casts and channeling their enthusiasm to create an atmosphere summed up in one of the best-known "Gang Show" songs, "Riding Along on the Crest of a Wave." The title of his autobiography, *It's Been Terrific* (1953), and of his television series, *"It's a Great Life,"* expressed the same hearty optimism. A second autobiographical volume, *Ralph Reader Remembers,* appeared in 1974.

Redcliffe-Maud, John Primatt Redcliffe Redcliffe-Maud, BARON, British university administrator and civil servant (b. Feb. 3, 1906—d. Nov. 20, 1982, Oxford, England), chaired the royal commission set up in 1966 to examine the reform of local government in Britain. After studying at New College, University of Oxford, and at Harvard he served as a city councillor (1930–36) in Oxford. Redcliffe-Maud was dean of University College, Oxford (1932–39), then master of Birkbeck College, University of London (1939–43), before working in the Ministry of Food. He then served at the Ministry of Education (1945–52) and as permanent secretary in the Ministry of Fuel and Power (1952–59). In the latter post, he was responsible for administering fuel supplies during the Suez crisis. In 1959 he became high commissioner in South Africa, a key post at a time when that country was in the throes of leaving the Commonwealth. Redcliffe-Maud worked assiduously to avoid this outcome, though he was entirely sympathetic to Prime Minister Harold Macmillan's 1960 "wind of change" speech delivered in Cape Town. After South Africa left the Commonwealth, Redcliffe-Maud remained there as ambassador (1961–63), then returned to Britain to become master of University College (1963–76). As chairman of the commission designated to review local government, he produced radical proposals for reform in the report published in 1969, but they were only partially implemented in the Local Government Act 1972. Among his publications were *English Local Government Reformed* (1974) and an autobiography, *Experiences of an Optimist* (1981). Redcliffe-Maud was made a life peer in 1967.

Rexroth, Kenneth, U.S. poet and painter (b. Dec. 22, 1905, South Bend, Ind.—d. June 6, 1982, Montecito, Calif.), who as co-founder with Allen Ginsberg and Lawrence Ferlinghetti of the San Francisco Poetry Center helped shape the emergence of the Beat movement, a social and literary trend originating in San Francisco in the 1950s that rejected the accepted mores of conventional society. Rexroth later denounced the movement and became a correspondent (1953) for *The Nation* and a columnist (1960) for the *San Francisco Examiner*. His poetry used eroticism, Marxism, and witticisms to deliberately enrage the bourgeoisie. His volumes of poetry included *The Phoenix and the Tortoise* (1944), *The Art of Worldly Wisdom* (1949), and *The Heart's Garden, the Garden's Heart* (1968). Rexroth also published collections of essays including *Bird in the Bush* (1959), *Assays* (1962), and *With Eye and Ear* (1970), and translated Japanese, Chinese, Greek, and Spanish poetry. He was one of the country's first abstract painters and throughout his life held numerous one-man shows. In 1966 he received critical acclaim with *An Autobiographical Novel,* which described his stints as a pharmacy clerk, soda jerk, insane asylum attendant, and fruit picker. Rexroth was voted into the National Institute of Arts and Letters in 1969.

Richard, Marthe (MARTHE BETENFELD), French war heroine (b. April 15, 1889, France—d. Feb. 9, 1982, Paris, France), was a legendary figure who became a spy during World War I and a resistance organizer during World War II but gained perhaps her greatest notoriety following the liberation as a campaigner against brothels. One of the first women to take her pilot's license, she was recruited by the French secret service to seduce a German naval attaché during World War I and obtain military secrets from him. The truth about her adventures and the significance of the information she obtained were obscured, rather than revealed, in the subsequent series of best-selling books written about her and in a film made in 1937, starring Edwige Feuillère and Erich von Stroheim. During World War II she helped organize an escape line for Allied airmen and in 1945 was elected municipal councillor for Paris. In the following year, as a result of her efforts, a law was passed closing the officially tolerated brothels which became known as the "Loi Marthe Richard."

Ritchie-Calder, Peter Ritchie Ritchie-Calder, BARON, British science writer (b. July 1, 1906, Forfar, Scotland—d. Jan. 31, 1982, Edinburgh, Scotland), trained as a journalist and used his skill as a publicist to interpret developments in science in light of his concern for social justice. He began writing in Dundee, Scotland, in 1922 and later worked for the *Daily News* (1926–30) and the *Daily Herald* (1930–41). As a reporter he experienced the social deprivation of the 1930s firsthand and became an active member of the Labour Party. During World War II he was director of plans at the Foreign Office Political Warfare Executive. Afterward he returned to journalism as science editor of the *News Chronicle* (1945–56) and served on the British delegations to the first UNESCO General Conference and to those in 1947, 1966, and 1968. He also attended the 1955 and 1958 UN conferences on the Peaceful Uses of Atomic Energy. Ritchie-Calder was a prominent member of the Campaign for Nuclear Disarmament and president of the National Peace Council. In 1961 he was appointed professor of international relations at the University of Edinburgh, where he remained until 1967. In 1969 he became chairman of the Metrication Board. Ritchie-Calder was made a life peer in 1966, and from 1972 to 1975 he was senior fellow at the Center for the Study of Democratic Institutions, Santa Barbara, Calif.

Ritola, Ville, Finnish long-distance runner (b. Jan. 18, 1896, Peräseinäjoki, Finland—d. April 24, 1982, Helsinki, Finland), met his rival Paavo Nurmi in memorable duels at the 1924 and 1928 Olympic Games and, with Nurmi, helped to establish Finland's supremacy in long-distance running. Ritola trained in the U.S. and first raced against Nurmi in the 1924 Paris Olympics, when they met in the 5,000 m and Nurmi beat him by less than a second. In the 10,000 m Ritola competed without Nurmi, captured a gold medal, and set a new world record of 30 min 23.2 sec. Ritola gained another gold in the 3,000-m steeplechase and, with Nurmi, shared the Finnish victories in the 3,000-m and the 10,000-m cross-country team races. Four years later, in Amsterdam, the two men met again in one of the classic athletic confrontations of all time, and Ritola took the gold in the 5,000 m, some two seconds ahead of Nurmi, but was beaten by a still narrower margin in the 10,000 m. In all, at the Olympic Games of 1924 and 1928, Ritola gained three gold and three silver medals in individual events and two team gold medals.

Roa García, Raúl, Cuban government official (b. April 18, 1907, Havana, Cuba—d. July 6, 1982, Havana), as Cuba's foreign minister from 1959 to 1976 promoted a Cuban-Soviet alliance and, despite his contempt for U.S. policy, played a major role in negotiating two important agreements between Cuba and the U.S. The first accord in 1965 sanctioned the airlifting of Cuban emigrants to the U.S. In 1973 the countries signed an antihijacking agreement that permitted both countries to prosecute air and sea pirates where they landed for theft, illegal entry, or other crimes. Roa entered the political arena when he was elected a member of the students directorate in 1930; he was jailed in 1931 for antigovernment activities and in 1933 joined the revolt (led by Fulgencio Batista) that overthrew the government of Gerardo Machado. After participating in a failed general strike against the Batista government, Roa fled to the U.S. and organized a Cuban revolutionary association. From 1948 to 1952 Roa served as director of culture for the Cuban government. With the return to power of Batista in 1952, Roa went into exile. After the 1959 revolution Fidel Castro named Roa foreign minister, a post he held until 1976. He served as vice-president of the National Assembly and member of the Council of State until 1981.

Robarts, John Parmenter, Canadian lawyer (b. Jan. 11, 1917, Banff, Alta.—d. Oct. 18, 1982, Toronto, Ont.), was elected leader of the Ontario Conservative Party in 1961 and served as the formidable premier of Ontario from 1961 to 1971. During his administration, Robarts used his common sense to preserve calm and balance. He was particularly dedicated in his approach to English-French relations and in helping to unite French Canada. Robarts became a legendary figure in Canada after serving as the levelheaded co-chairman of the 1977 Task Force on Canadian Unity. In 1971 Robarts retired as premier. Deeply disturbed over the physical disabilities he suffered as a result of a stroke in 1981, Robarts took his life.

Robbins, Marty, U.S. singer (b. Sept. 26, 1925, Glendale, Ariz.—d. Dec. 8, 1982, Nashville, Tenn.), was a versatile performer who became a top country-western star with a string of pop and country ballads that were a mixture of cowboy and Mexican mariachi music. Robbins's music ran the gamut from cry-in-your-beer balladry when he was known as "Mr. Teardrop" to rock, pop, and various styles of country music. He won two Grammy awards for his recordings of "El Paso" and "My Woman, My Woman, My Wife" and produced such smash hits as "A White Sport Coat and a Pink Carnation," "Devil Woman," and "Tonight Carmen." During his career Robbins had 43 songs in the country music top 10, recorded nearly 70 albums, and was a favourite at the Grand Ole Opry in addition to being one of the first country musicians to appear in Las Vegas. After he had reached stardom on stage, Robbins became a stock-car racer on the Grand National circuit and ranked among the top ten drivers. Robbins was also deluged with music awards; he was named Man of the Decade by the Academy of Country Music in 1970, was elected to the Nashville Songwriters' Hall of Fame in 1975, won in 1979 the Golden Trustee Award given by the National Cowboy Hall of Fame, and was inducted into the Country Music Hall of Fame in 1982. Robbins, who appeared regularly on television, also had motion-picture roles, his last in *Honky Tonk Man* (1982).

Rogge, Bernard, German naval officer (b. Nov. 4, 1899, Schleswig, Germany—d. June 29, 1982, West Germany), commanded the "Atlantis," one of the most successful of the German raider ships during World War II. The "Atlantis," which was a converted merchantman, preyed on British merchant ships en route to Australia in the South Atlantic and the Indian Ocean. Between March 1940 and November 1941 the "Atlantis" destroyed 22 vessels totaling 146,000 tons. Rogge relied on the elements of surprise and concealment, disguising the ship as a Soviet or Japanese vessel, frequently repainting it at sea, and sailing the ship close to its victims before opening fire. The "Atlantis" was eventually sunk by the HMS "Devonshire," and Rogge was rescued by a U-boat. A naval officer from the latter part of World War I, he worked in the chemical industry after World War II but returned to the Navy in 1957 as commander of the Schleswig-Holstein and Hamburg area, with the rank of rear admiral. He retired, after a disagreement on territorial defense with Defense Minister Franz-Josef Strauss, in 1962.

Roskill, Stephen Wentworth, British naval historian (b. Aug. 1, 1903, London, England—d. Nov. 4, 1982, Cambridge, England), was the author of the official British account of naval operations in World War II, *The War at Sea 1939–1945.* He served during World War I after training at Dartmouth College and was made a commander in the Royal Navy in 1937. During World War II he served as commander and then as captain in the Far East and after the war was appointed deputy director of naval intelligence. In 1949 he was appointed official naval historian. His four-volume history (1954–61) was an authoritative account, though Roskill was unable to use some intelligence material and was later involved in controversy over his interpretation of events with the U.S. historian Arthur Marder. Roskill became a fellow of Churchill College, Cambridge, in 1961. His other works included *The Strategy of Sea Power* (1962), *Naval Policy Between the Wars* (vol. 1, 1968; vol. 2, 1976), and *Churchill and the Admirals* (1977).

Rotha, Wanda, Austrian-born actress (b. 1910?, Vienna, Austria—d. Aug. 5, 1982, London, England), had a striking stage presence and was at her best in powerful dramatic roles such as the empress in *Elisabeth of Austria,* which she played in London in 1938. Trained at the Vienna Academy of Dramatic Art, she played in Vienna, Germany, and Czechoslovakia before making her debut on the London stage in 1937 in *The Astonished Ostrich.* In 1942 she was Sadie Thompson in *Rain* and in 1944 Anna Christie in Eugene O'Neill's play of that name. During the late 1950s and 1960s she toured in Europe, appearing particularly in *Who's Afraid of Virginia Woolf?* and *The Rose Tatoo.* Rotha also acted on television and in films.

Rothschild, Alain James Gustave Jules de, French banker (b. Jan. 7, 1910, Paris, France—d. Oct. 17, 1982, New York, N.Y.), was vice-president of the Banque Rothschild from 1968 until its nationalization in 1982 and a leading member of the French Jewish community. It was in the latter role that he was best known, as president of the Conseil Représentatif des Institutions Juives de France (CRIF) and other organizations that defended the interests of French Jews in the post-World War II years. Rothschild studied law and joined the family bank until entering military service in 1939. He was taken prisoner and after his liberation devoted himself to working for the Jewish community, showing particular concern for Jewish schools and refugees from North Africa. Rothschild's relations with the government were sometimes clouded by its changing attitude toward Israel, and in 1982 he called for better protection against terrorist attacks. His presidency of CRIF demanded exceptional diplomatic skills in an increasingly delicate situation, and he was highly respected for his fervent defense of Jewish interests and his ability to maintain a moderate stance.

Rubinstein, Arthur, Polish-born pianist (b. Jan. 28, 1887, Lodz, Poland—d. Dec. 20, 1982, Geneva, Switz.), was considered one of the greatest concert pianists of the century and a keyboard virtuoso who produced a golden sound and a distinctive tone that was unequaled by any other. A prodigy, Rubinstein began at age four to issue calling cards that read "Artur the Great Piano Virtuoso" (his name was spelled Artur until he later anglicized it). At the age of eight he studied at the Warsaw Conservatory and the following year became a pupil of Heinrich Barth in Berlin. When Rubinstein was six he made his first public appearance, and he made his European debut in Berlin at 13. In 1906 he made his U.S. debut with the Philadelphia Orchestra at Carnegie Hall but got a cool reception. During World War I Rubinstein, who was fluent in eight languages, served as a military interpreter in London and performed there with the violinist Eugène Ysaye. In 1916 Rubinstein visited Spain and became a sensation by introducing works by Manuel de Falla and Enrique Grandas. Another trip to the U.S. in 1919 proved lacklustre. By his own admission Rubinstein was content to be "an unfinished pianist who played with dash." A contemporary of such international figures as Pablo Picasso and Ernest Hemingway, Rubinstein was an international playboy and a "cynical bad boy," but in 1928 he met his future wife, Aniela Mlynarski, began recording, and analyzed his artistry. He renewed his dedication to music, practiced six to nine hours a day, and brought a new discipline to his already brilliant technique. When he returned once again to the U.S. in 1937 and performed at Carnegie Hall

he was hailed as a genius. Throughout the rest of his career Rubinstein took the world by storm with a huge repertoire that included Beethoven, Mozart, Albéniz, Ravel, Stravinsky, and Chopin. As an interpreter of the latter's work, Rubinstein was considered a master. During World War II he took up residence in California and played in such motion pictures as *Carnegie Hall* (1947) and *Of Men and Music* (1950). Not only was Rubinstein a witty extrovert and irrepressible raconteur, he was a serious musician whose stage presence enhanced his playing. Rubinstein, who made more than 200 recordings, was the largest selling classical pianist in history; 10 million copies of his records were sold. At the age of 76, afflicted with failing eyesight, Rubinstein gave his last concert in London, but in 1977 U.S. music lovers were treated to a 90-minute television special, "Rubinstein at 90," which was part of public television's "Great Performances" series.

Sackler, Howard, U.S. playwright (b. Dec. 19, 1929, Brooklyn, N.Y.—found dead Oct. 14, 1982, Ibiza, Spain), won the 1969 Pulitzer Prize for the Broadway blockbuster *The Great White Hope,* the fictional story of boxer Jack Johnson, who in 1908 became the first black heavyweight boxing champion. Sackler's drama, which opened on Broadway on Oct. 3, 1968, traced Johnson's downfall after he flaunted society's conventions. The play starred James Earl Jones and won the 1969 Tony award for best play. Sackler also wrote the screenplay for the motion picture, which also featured Jones in the lead role. Sackler's other plays included *Goodbye Fidel, Semmelweiss,* and *Klondike.* For the screen Sackler co-wrote *Saint Jack* and *Jaws 2.* Besides directing for the theatre, Sackler served as a director of Caedmon Records, responsible for recording poetry and plays by such men of letters as Shakespeare, Lewis Carroll, and James Joyce.

Sánchez, Salvador, Mexican boxer (b. Feb. 5, 1959, Santiago Tianguistengo, Mexico—d. Aug. 12, 1982, near Querétaro, Mexico), was a disciplined and colourful fighter who captured the World Boxing Council featherweight crown in February 1980 by knocking out Danny López in the 13th round. Sánchez, who prided himself on wearing down his opponents, had a record of 43–1–1 including 31 career knockouts. During a rematch against López four months after Sánchez was crowned champion, Sánchez scored another knockout in the 14th round. He dominated his division for the following two years and defended his title nine times. But probably his most spectacular bout was against the popular contender Wilfredo Gómez on Aug. 22, 1981. Sanchez pummeled Gómez before knocking him out in the eighth round. Sánchez was named Fighter of the Year for 1981 together with Sugar Ray Leonard by *Ring Magazine.* Sánchez, who enjoyed collecting cars, was killed when he collided with a truck while driving his Porsche 928. He had planned to retire in 1983 and study to become a doctor.

Sandham, Andrew, British cricketer (b. July 6, 1890, Streatham, London, England—d. April 20, 1982, London), was an outstanding batsman for Surrey and England and, as Surrey coach from 1946 to 1958, helped develop a side that won seven successive county championships. Sandham joined Surrey in 1911, but it was not until after World War I that, as opening batsman in partnership with Sir Jack Hobbs, he showed his real potential. He was the first batsman to score more than 300 in a test innings (during the West Indies tour of 1929–30), and his partnership score of 428 with Hobbs for Surrey against the University of Oxford in 1926 remained an unbeaten county record. During his career Sandham scored 41,284 runs (the 11th highest total in the history of cricket) and 107 centuries, and he held the record for a score by a county player against the Australians (219, in 1934). He was an honorary life member of Surrey, its vice-president in 1979, and an honorary member of the Marylebone Cricket Club (the game's ruling body).

Santos Costa, Fernando dos, Portuguese army officer (b. Dec. 19, 1899, northern Portugal—d. Oct. 15, 1982, Lisbon, Portugal), was minister of defense under António de Oliveira Salazar from 1944 until 1958 and a leading figure in Salazar's regime. He was commissioned in 1918 and became acquainted with Salazar during the 1920s. In 1936 Santos Costa was appointed deputy minister of war and during World War II, when he was viewed as sympathetic to the Axis, rose to become a key figure in the government. After the discovery of a plot in 1947, Santos Costa, who had been accused by the opposition of complicity in the death in custody of the leading conspirator, established his role as the mainstay of Salazar's power. Santos Costa saved the dictator again in 1958 from the electoral challenge of Gen. Humberto Delgado, but by this time Salazar was wary of Santos Costa's own power and dismissed him. He made a bid to replace Salazar in 1968, when the dictator retired due to ill health, but failed and in the revolution of 1974 stayed in Portugal where, surprisingly, he was allowed to live on unmolested.

Sargeson, Frank, New Zealand writer (b. March 23, 1903, Hamilton, New Zealand—d. March 1, 1982, Auckland, New Zealand), documented contemporary New Zealand life in novels and short stories that established him as the most authentic and internationally the best-known literary portrayer of his country's people. His works included *Conversation with My Uncle* (1936), *Joy of the Worm* (1969), and *The Hangover* (1967), the latter telling in his ironic and highly polished prose the story of a young man growing up. Many of Sargeson's works were autobiographical, describing his struggles against poverty and ill health. Except for a brief visit to Europe, he remained in New Zealand, but he achieved international success with the publication of *That Summer, and Other Stories,* and *I Saw in My Dream.* His collected short stories appeared in 1964.

Saville, (Leonard) Malcolm, British children's writer (b. Feb. 21, 1901, Hastings, Sussex, England—d. June 30, 1982, Hastings), was the author of more than 80 books for children, among them the highly popular "Lone Pine" stories and a series featuring the special agent Marston Baines. Saville was associate editor of *My Garden* magazine from 1947 to 1952, worked with Kemsley Newspapers until 1955, and was editor of *Sunny Stories* magazine and general books editor for George Newnes Ltd. and C. Arthur Pearson Ltd. until 1966. His first children's story and the first of the "Lone Pine" stories was written in 1943, and he continued the series with 19 other adventures set in different parts of the country. Widely translated, they sold over two million copies. Saville's approach was idealistic, and his stories were wholesome and founded on the Christian values in which he believed and which he hoped to inculcate. He had a talent for storytelling and the depiction of believable characters, though his plots were often improbable. Saville wrote a life of Christ, *King of Kings* (1958), and a number of nonfiction works, as well as scripts for the Children's Film Foundation.

Schneider, Romy, Austrian-born film actress (b. Sept. 23, 1938, Vienna, Austria—d. May 29, 1982, Paris, France), made her name portraying the Empress Elizabeth of Austria in the series of *Sissi* films but escaped the threat of typecasting as a "Shirley Templehof" to become one of the best-known and most versatile international stars. She was born Rosemarie Albach-Retty, the daughter of an actor and of Magda Schneider, a popular film star. After her parents' divorce she adopted her mother's name. She made her cinema debut in 1953 and, after the *Sissi* series, acted in the French film *Christine,* which marked the beginning of her association with the French cinema and her friendship with her co-star Alain Delon. Schneider acted for many leading European and U.S. directors: Luchino Visconti (*Ludwig*), Claude Chabrol (*Les Innocents aux mains sales*), Orson Welles (*The Trial*), Otto Preminger (*The Cardinal*), Joseph Losey (*The Assassination of Trotsky*), and Bertrand Tavernier (*La Mort en direct*), making more than 50 films in her career. Though she appeared in many second-rate films, her talent and her screen presence were considerable and, at her best, Schneider showed a mature understanding of her craft. Twice married, she suffered a personal tragedy in 1981 with the accidental death of her 14-year-old son.

Scholem, Gershom, Israeli cabalistic scholar (b. Dec. 5, 1897, Berlin, Germany—d. Feb. 20, 1982, Jerusalem, Israel), was professor of Jewish mysticism at the Hebrew University of Jerusalem from 1933 to 1965 and the unchallenged modern authority on the Kabbala. He studied mathematics at the Universities of Berlin and Jena, then Semitics in Berne, Switz., and Munich, Germany, before immigrating to Palestine in 1923. There Scholem undertook a vast work of scholarship, collecting and publishing some 500 manuscripts relating to the Kabbala and elevating the mystical element in Jewish tradition to a place of honour it had previously been denied. A man of wide culture, he was president (1968–74) of the Academy of Sciences and Humanities in Jerusalem and was awarded the Goethe Prize for his contribution to German literature. The range of his interests was perhaps best illustrated in his correspondence from 1929 to 1946 with Walter Benjamin and Theodor Adorno. His most important works, published in several languages, included *Bibliographica Kabbalistica* (1927), *Major Trends in Jewish Mysticism* (1946), and *The Beginnings of Kabbalism* (1949).

Schuster, Sir George Ernest, British financial expert (b. April 25, 1881—d. June 5, 1982, Middle Barton, Oxfordshire, England), served with the colonial governments in the Sudan and India and, even when he was more than 80 years old, played an important role in managing the financial affairs of Voluntary Service Overseas and the United World College of the Atlantic. He studied at the University of Oxford and was called to the bar in 1905. During World War I Schuster served with the Oxfordshire Yeomanry and in 1918 joined the Murmansk Force, winning the Military Cross. After the war he worked with the League of Nations and in 1922 became financial secretary to the Sudan government. For his work there during a period of unrest, he was knighted in 1926. In 1928 he was appointed finance minister with the viceroy's government in India, and he remained in that post until 1934, serving during a time of civil disturbance and grave financial crisis. He was elected to Parliament as a Liberal National in 1938. During World War II he brought his outstanding gift for financial administration to the problems of war production and planning and to the field of industrial relations, which he discussed in his book *Christianity and Human Relations in Industry* (1951). He also took a major part in setting up the United World College of the Atlantic at St. Donat's Castle, Wales, raising funds, managing finances, and remaining as chairman of the governors until 1973. His other books were *India and Democracy* (1941) and *Private Work and Public Causes* (1979).

Scott, Sir Robert Heatlie, British official (b. Sept. 20, 1905, Peterhead, Scotland—d. Feb. 26, 1982, Lyne, Peebles, Scotland), was in charge of the British Ministry of Information branch in Singapore in 1941. He was taken prisoner by the Japanese and confined in Changi jail, where he became a symbol of resistance to the occupying forces. Accused of complicity in a commando raid, he was tortured, tried, and confined in a cell at the top of the prison tower. After his release he gave evidence at the war crimes trials and surprised even the accused by his lack of animosity. Scott had studied law at Oxford before he joined the consular service, serving in many parts of the Far East and learning Chinese, Japanese, and other languages. Presumed dead during his captivity, he returned to Britain and soon faced a demand for back income tax. After a period of convalescence, Scott served as undersecretary of state at the Foreign Office in London and as minister (1953–55) at the British embassy in Washington, D.C. In 1955 he was appointed U.K. commissioner general for Southeast Asia in Singapore. Then in 1960 he became the first civilian head of the Imperial Defence College and in 1961 permanent undersecretary at the Ministry of Defence. He retired in 1963 and during 1968–80 served as lord lieutenant of Tweeddale. He was knighted in 1954 and made a Knight Grand Cross of the Order of St. Michael and St. George in 1958.

Searle, Humphrey, British composer (b. Aug. 26, 1915, Oxford, England—d. May 12, 1982, London, England), was an early exponent in Britain of serial music. Searle's work, which was once dismissed as excessively avant-garde, had been overtaken by the time of his death by still more radical experiments. What he achieved, however, was to show that 12-note serialism could be the basis of expressive and appealing music and not just an intellectual fad. Searle studied at the University of Oxford and at the Royal College of Music before going to the Vienna Conservatory, where he came under the influence of Anton von Webern. Searle worked for the BBC for a time before and after World War II, serving with the Intelligence Corps during the war, and he was later music adviser to Sadler's Wells Ballet. He wrote three works for the stage, including an opera based on Shakespeare's *Hamlet* (1968). His early chamber works, such as *Night Music* (1943), seemed revolutionary at the time, but tastes changed, and his major orchestral works (First Symphony, 1953; Fifth Symphony, 1964) remained under the influence of Webern and Arnold Schoenberg. Searle was the author of several books, including *The Music of Liszt* (1954; rev. ed. 1966) and *Ballet Music: An Introduction* (1958; rev. ed. 1973).

Selye, Hans Hugo Bruno, Austrian-born endocrinologist (b. Jan. 26, 1907, Vienna, Austria—d. Oct. 16, 1982, Montreal, Canada), in 1936 discovered that the human body's physical response to stress could cause disease and even death. Selye first detected the effects of stress when he injected ovarian hormones into the glandular system of laboratory rats. He found that the hormone stimulated the outer tissue of the adrenal glands of the rats, caused deterioration of the thymus gland, and produced ulcers and eventually death. Selye correlated his findings to man and demonstrated that a breakdown of the body's hormonal mechanism could initiate disease and lead to death. He published his discovery in *Nature* magazine in 1936 and later gained world renown for his expertise on stress. He wrote 33 books, most notably *Stress Without Distress,* which was translated into more than 12 languages. Selye, who by 1931 earned both his M.D. and Ph.D. in chemistry at the German University in Prague, Czech., then came to the U.S. to serve as a research fellow in the department of biochemical hygiene at Johns Hopkins University. In 1932 he continued his fellowship at McGill University in Montreal, where he conducted his pioneering studies. Selye was later director of the International Institute of Stress at the University of Montreal.

Sender, Ramón José, Spanish novelist (b. Feb. 3, 1902, Alcolea de Cinca, Aragon, Spain—d. Jan. 15, 1982, near San Diego, Calif.), was a leading novelist who recounted his experiences in the Spanish Civil War in a number of works, including *Réquiem por un campesino español* (1960; Eng. trans. *Requiem for a Spanish Peasant*). A lifelong Republican, he studied at the University of Madrid, was imprisoned for his political activities, and served with the Spanish Army in Morocco (1923–24). From 1924 to 1931 he edited the Madrid *El Sol;* he then spent some years abroad. Sender established his literary reputation with such novels as *Imán* (1929; Eng. trans. *Pro Patria,* 1935); *Siete domingos rojos* (1932; Eng. trans *Seven Red Sundays,* 1936), and *Mr. Witt en el Cantón* (1935; Eng. trans. *Mr. Witt Among the Rebels,* 1937), for which he was awarded the 1935 National Prize for Literature. He was a staff major in the Spanish Republican Army during the Civil War and after the Nationalist victory he left for exile in Guatemala and Mexico. Sender then settled in the U.S. and became professor of Spanish literature at Amherst (Mass.) College (1943–44), the University of New Mexico (1947–63), and the University of

Southern California (1965–73). From 1965 his work could once more be published in Spain, and two years later he received the City of Barcelona Prize for the definitive version of his series of nine novels, *Crónica del Alba (Chronicle of Dawn);* characteristic of his later work, these novels explored the relationship between individual and social needs. In 1969 he was awarded Spain's major literary prize, the Planeta Prize, for the novel *En la vida de Ignacio Morel.*

Shalamov, Varlam Tikhonovich, Soviet writer (b. June 18, 1907, Vologda, Russia—d. Jan. 17, 1982, Moscow, U.S.S.R.), spent 17 years in a Siberian labour camp and reflected on this experience in *Kolyma Tales;* despite his official rehabilitation, these stories were never published in the Soviet Union, where he was officially recognized only as a poet. As a student Shalamov had already come into conflict with the Soviet authorities and spent five years in jail before being accused in 1937 of "anti-Soviet Trotskyist agitation" because of his defense of the emigré writer Ivan Bunin. He was not released until after the death of Stalin in 1953. His stories, offering a chilling witness to the horrors of the Kolyma camp but written without propagandist motives, first appeared in abridged form in France in 1969, having previously circulated clandestinely in the Soviet Union. Shalamov was forced to deny having authorized their publication. In 1981 the French PEN Club awarded him its Prix de la Liberté.

Shimura, Takashi, Japanese actor (b. 1905, Hyogo Prefecture, Japan—d. Feb. 11, 1982, Tokyo, Japan), was a leading film star whose most memorable performances were made in films directed by Akira Kurosawa. Shimura was noted for such riveting portrayals as a bitter doctor in *Drunken Angel* (1948), a woodcutter in *Rashomon* (1950), the dying civil servant in *Ikiru* (1952), and a masterful samurai leader in *Seven Samurai* (1954). He also appeared in *Godzilla, King of the Monsters* (1954), a popular Japanese horror film. Shimura was honoured for his contributions to the performing arts with Japan's Medal of Honour with Purple Ribbon in 1976 and the Fourth Class Order of the Rising Sun in 1980. His last film was *Kagemusha.*

Simmons, Calvin, U.S. conductor (b. April 27, 1950, San Francisco, Calif.—d. Aug. 21, 1982, near Lake Placid, N.Y.), was the promising music director of the Oakland Symphony in California and at the time of his appointment in 1979 the first black conductor of a major U.S. symphony. Simmons who attended the Cincinnati College-Conservatory of Music in Ohio, studied under Max Rudolf. In 1969 Simmons followed Rudolf to the Curtis Institute in Philadelphia, where he also came under the influence of Rudolf Serkin. At the age of 25, Simmons, who had been an associate conductor of the Los Angeles Philharmonic under Zubin Mehta, made his New York debut conducting the American Symphony. His international reputation blossomed when he conducted at the Glyndebourne Festival in England in 1974. Four years later he served as maestro with the San Francisco Opera, the Metropolitan Opera, the San Francisco Symphony, and the New York Philharmonic. Simmons drowned in a canoeing accident.

Slone, Dennis, South African-born epidemiologist (b. Jan. 9, 1930, Pretoria, South Africa—d. May 10, 1982, Lexington, Mass.), together with his research team examined the link between birth defects and drugs used by pregnant women and concluded that common painkillers, sleeping pills, and tranquilizers posed little risk to fetuses. After Slone published his findings in *Birth Defects and Drugs in Pregnancy* (1977), he conducted other research on the incidence of heart attacks in women who use or had used birth-control pills. Slone found that women who were longtime users of oral contraceptives faced a double or triple risk of heart attack up to nine years after they had discontinued the Pill. He also reported that women who both smoked and used birth-control pills were at much higher risk than those who did not smoke. Slone, who earned his medical degree from the University

of the Witwatersrand Medical School in Johannesburg, South Africa, was trained as a pediatrician there before he continued his studies in pediatrics and endocrinology at Harvard University. He later served (1969–75) as co-director of the Boston Collaborative Drug Surveillance Program and then as research professor of epidemiology and co-director of the drug epidemiology unit at Boston University Medical Center.

Smith, Red (WALTER WELLESLEY SMITH), U.S. sportswriter (b. Sept. 25, 1905, Green Bay, Wis.—d. Jan. 15, 1982, Stamford, Conn.), was a much admired sportswriter whose columns sparkled with a lively imaginative wit that was evocative of some of lit-

erature's finest writers. After graduating (1927) from the University of Notre Dame, Smith, an exceptionally prolific writer, worked for a string of newspapers before joining (1945) the *New York Herald Tribune,* where he turned out five columns a week for 21 years. In 1971 he was hired by the *New York Times* and spent the next ten years polishing his style in four weekly columns. Smith, who centred his attention on his favourite sports, including baseball, boxing, horse racing, and football, composed his first story from the viewpoint of a glowworm overwhelmed by the competitive glare of field lights at a night football game. Though many of his columns were lighthearted, others criticized the owners of professional sports teams in their labour-management relations, and in 1980 a political column encouraged a U.S. boycott of the 1980 Olympic Games in Moscow. His writing was so masterful that a sample of it was sandwiched between an essay by Winston Churchill and a short story by Dylan Thomas in the college textbook *A Quarto of Modern Literature,* and in 1976 he was awarded the Pulitzer Prize for commentary, though many felt it was some three decades overdue. Smith, who was considered the best sportswriter of his time, described himself as "a seedy amateur with watery eyes behind glittering glasses, a receding chin, a hole in his frowzy haircut." In his last column, Jan. 11, 1982, he explained that he would begin writing three columns a week instead of four and humbly added, "We shall have to wait and see whether the quality improves."

Sobhuza II, king of Swaziland (b. July 22, 1899, Mbabane, Swaziland—d. Aug. 21, 1982, Mbabane), was before his death the world's longest reigning monarch. The son of King Ngwane V, who died a few months after he was born, Sobhuza ascended the throne in 1921, his grandmother having ruled as regent in the intervening years. He led his kingdom to independence in 1968 but five years later, soon after the first National Assembly elections had taken place, Sobhuza abandoned the U.K.-designed constitution and reverted to a system of government in which he and his personal advisers exercised power: Swaziland's prime minister and Cabinet were appointed by the king himself. The tribal elders were, in accordance with tradition, entrusted with choosing which of Sobhuza's many male heirs should succeed him. One of his senior wives, Indovukavi, the "Great She Elephant," was appointed regent until the choice was named. Sobhuza's successor faced the task of maintaining the political and economic stability that the late king's pragmatism had promoted.

Soboul, Albert Marius, French historian (b. 1914, Tizi-Ouzou, Algeria—d. Sept. 13, 1982, Nîmes, France), was one of the leading modern historians of the French Revolution and professor of history (from 1967) at the University of Paris-Sorbonne. A disciple of George Lefebvre, Soboul joined the Communist Party as a student in the 1930s and was dismissed from his teaching post during World War II. The author of many studies of the revolutionary period, he also served as director of the Institut d'Histoire de la Révolution Française. Soboul established his reputation with the publication in 1956 of his masterly doctoral thesis on the sansculottes, which was translated into many languages. Soboul was attacked at various times both from within the Communist Party and from outside it, but he managed to reconcile his concern for historical truth with his loyalty to the party. He was also secretary on the *Annales historiques de la Révolution française.*

Spivak, Charlie, U.S. bandleader (b. Feb. 17, 1905, Trilesy, Russia—d. March 1, 1982, Cleveland, S.C.), was a popular orchestra leader during the big-band era of the early 1940s and an accomplished trumpeter who was billed as "the Sweetest Trumpet in the World" in the bands of Tommy and Jimmy Dorsey, Jack Teagarden, and Ray Noble. While performing with his first band Spivak used a mute on his trumpet because he feared that loud music would intimidate audiences and dancers. After Harry James sensationalized swing, Spivak revitalized his second band with open horn solos and with the addition of such sidemen as saxophonist Willie Smith and drummer Dave Tough. Spivak's popularity waned when bebop music came into vogue in the late 1940s.

Stephanopoulos, Stephanos, Greek politician (b. 1898, Pyrgos, Greece—d. Oct. 4, 1982, Athens, Greece), was prime minister of Greece for 15 months from September 1965. He joined Parliament in 1930 as a deputy for the Populist Party, after studying law and political science in Athens and Paris. He served as economics minister in prewar governments and took part in the resistance to German occupation during World War II. After serving as minister of economic coordination until 1950, Stephanopoulos helped set up a right-wing splinter party and, after Alexandros Papagos's Greek Rally had won the 1952 elections, became foreign minister. In 1961 he helped form the Centre Union Party under Georgios Papandreou but defected in 1965 to become prime minister. His government was never stable and eventually fell in a deteriorating political situation that culminated in a 1967 military coup. After the return of democracy Stephanopoulos set up the right-wing National Rally, but he failed to win reelection in 1977 and the party collapsed.

Stitt, Edward ("SONNY"), U.S. saxophonist (b. Feb. 2, 1924, Boston, Mass.—d. July 22, 1982, Washington, D.C.), was a jazz great whose alto saxophone sounds were reminiscent of Charlie Parker, although Stitt developed his style independently. Stitt emerged on the jazz circuit in the 1940s and performed with the big bands of Tiny Bradshaw, Billy Eckstine, and Dizzy Gillespie before forming his own combo. In 1949 Stitt switched to the tenor saxophone in order to avoid comparisons between himself and Parker; he proved to be equally facile on alto, tenor, and baritone. In the mid-1940s Stitt

and Gene Ammons teamed up on the tenor saxophone and produced such swinging albums as *Soul Summit* and *Together Again for the Last Time.* Stitt's other albums included *Sonny Side Up, In Walked Sonny,* and *Night Work.* During the last 30 years of his career Stitt toured mainly as a solo act.

Strasberg, Lee (ISRAEL STRASSBERG), U.S. acting coach, actor, and director (b. Nov. 17, 1901, Budzanow, Austria—d. Feb. 17, 1982, New York, N.Y.), as the artistic director of the Actors Studio, brought new dimensions to acting through his teaching of the method technique, a form of dramatic training based on a system developed by the Russian director Konstantin Stanislavsky. Some of Strasberg's most celebrated pupils, including Jane Fonda, Marlon Brando, John Garfield, Robert De Niro, and Al Pacino, were disciples of the method. Through the use of physical, emotional, and vocal exercises, Strasberg taught his students to internalize their roles by drawing on their own inner impulses and experiences. Strasberg, who began his career as an actor in such plays as *Red Rust* and *Green Grow the Lilacs,* later founded with Harold Clurman and Cheryl Crawford the Group Theatre (1931), an experimental company that exerted a lasting influence on the U.S. theatre. With the Group Theatre, Strasberg directed such outstanding productions as *The House of Connelly* and *Men in White,* which won the Pulitzer Prize for drama in 1934. The Group Theatre disbanded in 1941. In 1948 Strasberg was asked to join the Actors Studio founded by Crawford, Elia Kazan, and Robert Lewis. Strasberg served as artistic director of the studio for 34 years (1948–82). He also directed such Broadway hits as *Clash by Night* (1941) and *The Big Knife* (1949). In 1974 Strasberg made his film debut in *The Godfather, Part II* and was nominated for an Academy Award for his portrayal of an aging underworld boss. He also appeared in *And Justice for All, Going in Style, The Cassandra Crossing,* and *Boardwalk* but would be remembered primarily as the quintessential teacher. The day before he died Strasberg was notified that he had been elected to the Theater Hall of Fame.

Stratton, Monty Franklin Pierce, U.S. baseball player (b. May 21, 1912, Celeste, Texas—d. Sept. 29, 1982, Greenville, Texas), was a right-handed pitcher for the Chicago White Sox professional baseball team from 1934 to 1938 before losing his right leg in a hunting accident, after which he attempted to make a comeback and became the subject of a motion picture that won an Academy Award for best original screenplay. Stratton, who won 36 games and lost 23 while pitching for the White Sox, accidentally discharged his shotgun into his right leg, which was then amputated. He was fitted with an artificial leg and worked the following two years for the White Sox as a coach and batting practice pitcher. But in 1946 he stunned baseball enthusiasts by making a comeback with Sherman in the Class C East Texas League and winning 18 games. In 1947 he had a 7–7 record with Waco in the Class B Big State League but retired from baseball when Hollywood filmed his spectacular comeback attempt in the 1949 motion picture *The Stratton Story,* starring James Stewart and June Allyson.

Strong, Sir Kenneth William Dobson, British army officer (b. Sept. 9, 1900—d. Jan. 11, 1982, Eastbourne, England), was Gen. Dwight D. Eisenhower's chief of intelligence (1943–45) at Allied Force Headquarters (AFHQ) during World War II, director (1948–64) of the Joint Intelligence Bureau of the Ministry of Defence, and director general (1964–66) of the Defence Intelligence Staff. An accomplished linguist, Strong joined the Royal Scots Fusiliers in 1920 and served as assistant military attaché in Berlin before entering the German Section of the War Office intelligence directorate. His work there made an outstanding contribution to Britain's ability to assess German plans at the start of World War II, and as chief of intelligence at AFHQ he played a vital role in helping to shape Allied strategy until the German surrender. His extraordinarily acute judgment was displayed in his prediction of the German offensive in the Ardennes. As first head of the Joint Intelligence Bu-

reau he was responsible for providing information to government departments, coordinating British intelligence, and advising Commonwealth countries in intelligence matters. After his retirement in 1966 with the rank of major general, he published two books: *Intelligence at the Top* (1968) and *Men of Intelligence* (1970). He was knighted in 1952 and made Knight Commander of the Order of the British Empire in 1966.

Sunay, Cevdet, Turkish army officer (b. Feb. 10, 1900, Trabzon, Ottoman Empire—d. May 22, 1982, Istanbul, Turkey), was a leading figure in Turkish politics during the 1960s and served as president from 1966 to 1973. He was, however, a soldier rather than a politician, brought to power not by personal ambition but by the Army's guiding role in Turkish politics. The son of a regimental mufti, he fought in Palestine during World War I and, at the age of 17, was captured by the British. Sunay later fought in the war of independence and served in various posts until his promotion to the rank of general in 1958. Following the army coup of 1960, he was appointed chief of staff and, with the restoration of civilian government in the following year, came to play a major role behind the scenes at a time when the Army remained the dominant force in politics. In 1966, after Suleyman Demirel had taken office as prime minister, Sunay was persuaded to accept nomination to the Senate to facilitate his election as president. When Demirel's government fell in 1971, Sunay headed the interim military regime until civilian rule was restored in 1973. Throughout this period he acted as a moderating and stabilizing influence, mediating between rival political factions but never losing sight of the interests of the armed forces.

Suslov, Mikhail Andreyevich, Soviet politician (b. Nov. 21, 1902, Shakhovskoye, Saratov gubenya (now Ulyanovsk region), Russia—d. Jan. 25, 1982, Moscow, U.S.S.R.), was one of the most powerful influences within the Communist Party of the Soviet Union (CPSU). He joined the Communist Party in 1921, graduated from the Workers' Faculty in 1924, and continued his education at the Plekhanov Institute of National Economy. In 1931 Stalin picked Suslov to chair the CPSU's Central Control Commission, and in this capacity he played an important role in the great purges of the 1930s. As chief of staff of the Stavropol partisan formation during World War II he reportedly played a major role in the deportation of the Chechen, Ingush, and other Caucasian nationalities to Kazakhstan. In 1944 Suslov planned and supervised the reestablishment of Soviet rule in Lithuania and the deportation of some 60,000 Lithuanian patriots. Already a member of the CPSU Central Committee, Suslov worked continuously as a secretary to that body from 1947 and was editor in chief of *Pravda* (1949–50). He was first appointed to the CPSU Politburo in 1952, and though he was dropped from it the following year, he returned to that key body in 1955 and remained there until his death. A long-time deputy of the Supreme Soviet of the U.S.S.R., he chaired its Commission for Foreign Affairs from 1954. Suslov was involved in the moves that led to the expulsion of Yugoslavia from the socialist camp in 1948. He helped Nikita Khrushchev's efforts to consolidate his leadership but showed his antipathy toward him after the reconciliation with Yugoslav leader Tito in May 1955. In October 1964 Suslov, the custodian of Marxism as interpreted by Lenin and applied by Stalin, was instrumental in removing Khrushchev from power and raising Leonid Brezhnev (*q.v.*) to the position of party leader.

Swart, Charles Robberts, South African politician (b. Dec. 5, 1894, Winburg, Orange Free State [now South Africa]—d. July 16, 1982, Bloemfontein, South Africa), was president of the Republic of South Africa from 1961 to 1967 and a leading member of the National Party. From 1948 to 1959 he was minister of justice and was responsible for the legal entrenchment of apartheid and for the series of repressive laws against individual freedom that followed the National Party victory. Swart graduated from Grey University College of the Orange Free State and in 1918 was called to the bar. From 1921 to 1922 Swart was in the U.S. studying journalism at Columbia University, New York City. He then worked as a journalist and also for a time as an actor, playing minor parts in several Hollywood films. When he returned to South Africa, he was elected a member of Parliament in 1923. In 1948 the Nationalists were victorious in the general election, and they began the implementation of their policy of apartheid. Swart revised the Immorality Act, making sexual relations between the races illegal, and put through a series of "security laws," including the Suppression of Communism Act (1950). The right of appeal to the Privy Council was abolished, and the government was given extensive and arbitrary powers to interfere with the rights of individuals. From 1954 to 1959 he was deputy (1958, acting) prime minister, and in 1959 he was appointed governor-general of the Union of South Africa. In 1961 South Africa left the Commonwealth and declared itself a republic, with Swart as its president. He wrote several books in Afrikaans and was chancellor (1950–76) of the University of the Orange Free State.

Swinnerton, Frank Arthur, British author and publisher (b. Aug. 12, 1884, Wood Green, London, England—d. Nov. 6, 1982, Guildford, England), was a key figure in English literary life during the first half of the century and an accomplished novelist whose work reflected the society of the time. From 1907, with the publishers Chatto and Windus, Swinnerton published manuscripts submitted by many leading authors. His autobiography, published in 1937, and his critical works, *A London Bookman* (1928) and *The Georgian Literary Scene* (1935), were valuable testimonies to the cultural life of the period, as was the later *Arnold Bennett: A Last Word* (1978). Swinnerton's novels included the highly successful and accomplished *Nocturne* (1917); longer works of the 1930s, were *The Georgian House* (1932), *The Two Wives* (1939), and *A Woman in Sunshine* (1944). Swinnerton was a careful stylist, less interested in formal experiment than in the accurate depiction of London society and characters in contemporary settings.

Szmuness, Wolf, Polish-born epidemiologist (b. March 12, 1919, Warsaw, Poland—d. June 6, 1982, New York, N.Y.), as head of the laboratory of epidemiology (1973–82) at the New York Blood Center designed studies that determined the effectiveness of the first vaccine against hepatitis B. A group of 1,083 male homosexuals were selected to participate in the trials because homosexuals have a tenfold greater risk of contracting hepatitis B than the general population. After spending ten years in a Siberian labour camp, Szmuness received an M.D. degree in 1950 from the Tomsk (U.S.S.R.) V. V. Kuibyshev State University, and he earned advanced scientific degrees from the Kharkov (U.S.S.R.) A. M. Gorky State University and from the Catholic University of Lubin, Poland. In 1968 he immigrated to New York, where he became a medical technician at the New York Blood Center. However, it soon became evident that Szmuness was a brilliant researcher, and by 1970 he was head of his own laboratory there. By 1975 Szmuness was an internationally renowned epidemiologist, and in 1978 he began classic field studies that led to the production of the new hepatitis vaccine in 1980.

Tati, Jacques (JACQUES TATISCHEFF), French film actor and director (b. Oct. 9, 1908, Le Pecq, Yvelines, France—d. Nov. 4, 1982, Paris, France), was one of the most inventive comic talents in the history of cinema, but because of commercial pressures and his own perfectionism he made only five full-length features. However, his characterizations were masterpieces, from the bumbling country postman of *Jour de fête* to the still more accident-prone character of his best-known film, *Mr. Hulot's Holiday*, and the satire of *Mon Oncle, Playtime,* and *Trafic.* Tati started in music hall and mime before making and starring in his first feature, *Jour de fête,* in 1949. Like all his work, it was essentially a silent picture, relying for its humour on visual gags and acrobatics reminiscent of Chaplin or Buster Keaton

rather than the verbal wit that had previously characterized French cinema comedy. In Monsieur Hulot, he perfected a character that was uniquely his own and the film, made in 1952, was a great international success. *Mon Oncle* (1958) retained the character but introduced a new note of satire, directed against the gadgets and snobbishness of contemporary culture. As France grew more prosperous, Tati turned with increasing bitterness against the alienating world of town planners and the motorcar in *Playtime* (1967) and *Trafic* (1971). Perhaps the satire was too barbed (or too accurate) since the films were not box-office successes and, combined with his painstaking methods of work, this meant that he was unable to find backers. In 1974 he directed, in Sweden, a television variety show, "Parade," built around circus acts in which he appeared as Monsieur Loyal, but his plans for another feature were thwarted by lack of funds.

Terry, Walter, U.S. dance critic (b. May 14, 1913, Brooklyn, N.Y.—d. Oct. 4, 1982, New York, N.Y.), was an internationally acclaimed expert on modern dance and ballet and as an enthusiastic champion of dance for nearly 50 years helped bring recognition to all dance forms through his lectures and books. Terry began his career as a critic with the *Boston Herald* in 1936 and later served as dance critic with the *New York Herald Tribune* (1939–42 and 1945–66), the *World Journal Tribune* (1966–67), and the *Saturday Review* (1967–81). Terry, who felt that dance would take root in the U.S., traveled extensively to introduce American dance in foreign countries. During World War II, while serving in the U.S. Army in Egypt and Africa, he taught modern dance at the American University in Cairo, lectured on American dance to the Allied forces there, and starred as the principal dancer in a British production of *Rose Marie* at the Royal Opera House in Cairo. He also conducted lecture tours for the U.S. State Department in Eastern Europe and regaled audiences with his expertise on modern dance. Terry was instrumental in encouraging members of the Royal Danish Ballet to appear in the U.S. and exhibit the Bournonville style at the 1955 Jacob's Pillow Dance Festival. His numerous books included *Star Performance: The Story of the World's Great Ballerinas* (1945), *Ballet in Action* (1954), *The Ballet Companion* (1968), and a biography of the dancer Richard Cragun. In 1980 Terry was the recipient of the Capezio Dance Award.

Theorell, (Axel) Hugo Teodor, Swedish biochemist (b. July 6, 1903, Linköping, Sweden—d. Aug. 15, 1982, Stockholm, Sweden), won the Nobel Prize for Physiology or Medicine in 1955. His work on enzymes was a major contribution to the understanding of cell metabolism, one of the basic processes in all living organisms. Theorell's studies also had an immediate social effect: the development of a valid blood test for suspected drunken drivers. He studied at the Royal Caroline Institute in Stockholm, becoming a member of the staff there and gaining his M.D. in 1930 for his work on red blood cells. Theorell went on to work at the University of Uppsala (1932–36) and at the Kaiser Wilhelm Institute, Berlin (1933–35), where, with Otto Warburg, he began the enzyme research that led to his Nobel award. He also discovered an antibiotic for the treatment of tuberculosis. In 1937 he joined the Nobel Medical Institute in Stockholm; there he served as professor and head of the department of biochemistry. Theorell was president of the International Union of Biochemistry (1967–73) and of the Royal Swedish Academy of Sciences (1967–69).

Trepper, Leopold, Polish-born intelligence agent (b. Feb. 23, 1904, Nowy Targ, Poland—d. Jan. 19, 1982, Jerusalem, Israel), was spymaster of the espionage network known as the Red Orchestra which operated against Nazi Germany during World War II. Trepper reportedly warned Moscow two months in advance that German forces were preparing to invade the U.S.S.R. According to his memoirs, of the 1,500 messages sent to Moscow by the Red Orchestra during the period May 1940–November 1942 only 200 or so were decoded by the Germans. The son of a Jewish shopkeeper,

Trepper was blacklisted by Polish police in the 1920s for his part in organizing strikes. Later he was expelled from Palestine by the British after fighting for the Jewish underground forces. The years 1932–37 were spent in Moscow where he trained to head the Soviet spy network in Western Europe. After World War II Trepper returned to Moscow to face charges of collaboration. In 1947 he was imprisoned until after Stalin's death, when he was cleared of all charges. The last eight years of his life were spent in Israel, after winning a battle with the Polish authorities to gain permission to emigrate there.

Truman, Bess (ELIZABETH VIRGINIA WALLACE), U.S. first lady (b. Feb. 13, 1885, Independence, Mo.—d. Oct. 18, 1982, Independence), was the devoted wife of Pres. Harry S. Truman and an unassuming

WIDE WORLD

first lady who shunned the limelight afforded her position by holding no news conferences and by granting few interviews. Truman attended both primary school and high school with her future husband, but it was not until ten years after their high school graduation in 1901 that the two began courting. In 1917 they became officially engaged when Truman went to war. The couple were married on June 28, 1919, and in 1924 their daughter, Margaret, was born. After holding several political offices in Jackson County, Harry Truman was elected a U.S. senator and the Trumans moved to Washington, D.C. He was reelected to the Senate in 1940 and against his wife's advice accepted the nomination for vice-president in 1944. On April 12, 1945, Pres. Franklin D. Roosevelt died, and Truman took the oath of office as 33rd U.S. president. Bess was propelled into the White House and faced with the prospect of filling Eleanor Roosevelt's shoes. After unsuccessfully trying to emulate Mrs. Roosevelt, Mrs. Truman adopted a private style. She was sometimes criticized for her lack of accessibility to the public, but by the president's own account she served as a "full partner in all my transactions—politically and otherwise." In 1952 she played a major role in persuading him not to seek reelection. The couple then returned to Independence, where Mrs. Truman lived quietly until she died at the age of 97.

Tsvigun, Semyon Kuzmich, Soviet security officer (b. Sept. 27, 1917—d. Jan. 19, 1982), was the second most powerful person in the Committee for State Security (KGB). He first attained prominence when in 1957 he was appointed head of state security in the Tadzhikistan republic. In 1963 he took up the same post in Azerbaijan before being transferred in 1967 to Moscow as a deputy director within the KGB. His promotion to deputy head followed closely upon the appointment of Yury Andropov (*see* BIOGRAPHIES) to the post of head of that organization. Though Tsvigun was a prominent member of both the government and the Communist Party of the Soviet Union, no official obituary of him appeared in the Soviet press. This fact gave rise to speculation that he had fallen out of favour as a result of a KGB investigation into high-level corruption which, it was rumoured, had assumed political overtones.

Tung, C. Y. (TUNG CHAO-YUNG), Chinese shipowner (b. 1911, Shanghai, China—d. April 15, 1982, Hong Kong), was the owner of the second largest private merchant fleet in the world, surpassing the flamboyant Greek shipowners. Unlike them, however, he exercised his immense power without ostentation, and his name first became widely known in 1970 when he bought the former Cunard liner "Queen Elizabeth"; his ambition to convert it into a floating university ended when the vessel caught fire in 1972. Tung moved to Hong Kong in 1949 and founded the Chinese Merchant Navigation Co. Eventually, his group owned 150 vessels, including the world's largest ship, and was able to take over Furness, Withy & Co., a major British shipping group, for £113 million. He was the creator of the first Chinese international liner service and a pioneer in the field of containerization. He also had interests in oil, banking, insurance, and property. From 1977 he gradually handed over control of his Orient Overseas Containers consortium to his son, C. H. Tung.

Tuve, Merle Antony, U.S. physicist (b. June 27, 1901, Canton, S.D.—d. May 20, 1982, Bethesda, Md.), made the observations of short-pulse radio waves reflected off the ionosphere that became the theoretical foundation for the development of radar. After Tuve received a Ph.D. from Johns Hopkins University in 1926, he joined the staff of the Carnegie Institution, where he used high-voltage accelerators to define the structure of the atom. In 1933 he confirmed the existence of the neutron and measured the bonding forces in atomic nuclei. During World War II Tuve conducted research that led to the development of the proximity fuse, which was highly effective against both German V-1 buzz bombs aimed at Britain and Japanese kamikaze air strikes. Tuve then returned to Carnegie, where as director of the department of terrestrial magnetism he made seismic measurements of the Earth's crust. In recognition of his achievements Tuve was knighted in 1948 and received numerous awards in the U.S., including the Presidential Medal of Merit.

Twining, Nathan Farragut, U.S. Air Force officer (b. Oct. 11, 1897, Monroe, Wis.—d. March 29, 1982, San Antonio, Texas), was a decisive air force general who was instrumental in directing air assaults against Japan during World War II; he later served (1957–60) as chairman of the Joint Chiefs of Staff. After graduating from the U.S. Military Academy, West Point, N.Y., Twining became a U.S. Army pilot in 1926 and quickly rose through the ranks. As commander of the 13th Air Force in the South Pacific in 1943, Twining organized strategic air assaults on Guadalcanal and Bougainville in the Solomon Islands. The crack pilots easily annihilated enemy planes and referred to their missions as "turkey shoots." From 1944 to 1945 he led the 15th Air Force in the strategic bombing campaign against Germany and the Balkans. In the final days of the war Twining commanded the 20th Air Force, which dropped the first atomic bombs on Hiroshima and Nagasaki, Japan. After the war he served as vice-chief of staff of the Air Force (1950–53) and air force chief of staff (1953–57). In the latter post he fostered the development of nuclear air weapons and supersonic missiles and jets. In 1957 Twining was named chairman of the Joint Chiefs of Staff and earned a reputation for his judicious decisions concerning military policy. Twining, who retired in 1960 because of ill health, was inducted into the Aviation Hall of Fame in 1976.

Tworkov, Jack, Polish-born painter (b. 1900, Biala, Poland—d. Sept. 4, 1982, Provincetown, Mass.), was a leading Abstract Expressionist painter whose work was characterized by flamelike brush strokes and controlled rhythms and a distinguished member of the New York School, a term given to those painters who participated in the development of contemporary art in or around New York City during the 1940s. Tworkov immigrated to the U.S. in 1913, and although he earned a degree in creative writing from Columbia University, he began working as an artist. In order to support himself he worked as a puppeteer and as an associate of the U.S. writer John Dos Passos at the Playwrights' Theatre. During the 1920s he studied at the National Academy of Design and the Art Students' League. Tworkov's early paintings reflected the influence of the 19th-century French painter Paul Cézanne, but while working from 1935 to 1941 for the government-sponsored WPA (Works Progress Administration) federal arts project, he met Willem de Kooning and began experimenting with abstract painting. During World War II he worked as a tool designer and after the war joined the Abstract Expressionist movement, an approach that dictates complete freedom from traditional social values in favour of a free, spontaneous personal expression. Though his early painting was more gestural, by 1955 his work was relying heavily on geometry. The progression of Tworkov's style was exhibited in such paintings as "Watergame" and "Height," in which he built up countless diagonal strokes of paint that completely obliterated all references to objects or scenes; "Homage to Stefan Volpe," in which he used broad strokes instead of flickering lines; and "Variable," in which he created a gridlike format. In his series "Crossfield," which he began in 1968, Tworkov's gridwork became literal. Tworkov, who had more than a dozen one-man shows in his career, was also chairman of the art department at the Yale School of Art and Architecture from 1963 to 1969. In 1981 he was elected to the American Academy and Institute of Arts and Letters.

Vernov, Sergey Nikolayevich, Soviet physicist (b. July 11, 1910, Sestroretsk, near St. Petersburg [now Leningrad], Russia—d. Sept. 26, 1982, Moscow, U.S.S.R.), was director of the Nuclear Physics Research Institute at Moscow University and much honoured for his work, which included research into the action of cosmic rays in the stratosphere. During the 1930s he worked at the Radium Institute of the Academy of Sciences and became professor at Moscow University in 1944. Vernov was twice awarded the Order of Lenin and in 1960 gained the Lenin Prize.

Vidor, King Wallis, U.S. motion picture director (b. Feb. 8, 1894, Galveston, Texas—d. Nov. 1, 1982, Paso Robles, Calif.), was the masterful and visionary director of such silent film classics as *The Big Pa-*

UPI

rade (1925) and *The Crowd* (1928) and a maverick who defied Hollywood conventions to make motion pictures marked by social realism. Vidor, who worked in a nickelodeon as a schoolboy, went to Hollywood with his first wife, Florence Vidor, in 1915 and by 1919 directed his first film, *The Turn in the Road.* In 1925 Vidor persuaded MGM to produce *The Big Parade,* a World War I saga that chronicled the realities of war in the trenches for an ordinary soldier. The film was a box-office smash hit, made $15 million, and established John Gilbert as a star. Vidor's other technical successes included *The Crowd,* a quasi-documentary drama about the drab life of a New York City clerk and his wife, and its sequel, *Our Daily Bread* (1934), the story of the same couple leaving the city for a farming community. Vidor also directed *Hallelujah!* (1929), the first Hollywood film with an all-black cast; *The Champ* (1931), the mawkish story of a washed-up boxer and his small son; and *The Citadel* (1938), the screen adaptation of A. J. Cronin's novel about a young Scots doctor who rises from Welsh slums to Harley Street only to resume serving the poor. During his more than 40-year career, Vidor directed more than 50 feature films including *Peg o' My Heart* (1923), *Show People* (1928), *Billy the Kid* (1930), *Street Scene* (1931), *Northwest Passage* (1939), *The Fountainhead* (1949), *War and Peace* (1956), and *Solomon and Sheba* (1959). Vidor was honoured for his directorial accomplishments in 1979 when he received a special Academy Award for his achievements over four decades. In 1982 Vidor appeared in the film *Love and Money.*

Villeneuve, Gilles, Canadian racing driver (b. Jan. 10, 1952, Berthierville, Que.—d. May 8, 1982, Zolder, Belgium), captured six Grand Prix title events in Formula One racing and was touted as one of the fastest and most spirited of the up-and-coming drivers. From 1970 to 1976 Villeneuve, a daredevil speedster, raced snowmobiles. His prize money enabled him to buy his first single-seat race car. Villeneuve, who made his Formula One debut in a McLaren at the 1977 British Grand Prix, was involved in a massive accident in his third race at the 1977 Japanese Grand Prix. His Ferrari somersaulted off the back of Ronnie Peterson's car, and the disintegrating Ferrari killed a marshal and a spectator, though Villeneuve escaped unharmed. He was later involved in several other spectacular accidents, but he never failed to exhibit an almost reckless bravado. In 1979 he was named Canada's male athlete of the year after placing second in the drivers' world championship. Villeneuve was killed in a final practice session at the Belgian Grand Prix when his Formula One Ferrari catapulted off the rear wheel of a slow-moving car driven by Jochen Mass. Villeneuve died of massive head injuries after his car disintegrated, the safety harness snapped, and he was thrown into a steel catchfence.

Villiers, Alan John, Australian mariner (b. Sept. 23, 1903, Melbourne, Australia—d. March 3, 1982, Oxford, England), devoted his life to the sea and to sailing ships and was president (1970–74) of the Society for Nautical Research and a trustee (1948–74) of the National Maritime Museum. His first experience of the vanishing way of life he was to adopt and record was during the early 1920s on a Norwegian whaling expedition. Villiers then worked as a journalist until 1931, when he bought a share in a four-masted barque. In 1934 he acquired his own full-rigged ship, "Joseph Conrad," in which he logged 58,000 nautical miles in the following three years. During World War II he served with the Royal Naval Volunteer Reserve and was awarded the Distinguished Service Cross. He continued to write and lecture after the war and to sail, as master of the training ship "Warspite" and, in 1957, as commander of a replica of the "Mayflower" in a transatlantic crossing. He also handled ships in the films *Moby Dick* and *Billy Budd.* Perhaps his most lasting contribution was as the historian of sail, bringing his practical experience to bear on his biography of Captain Cook and his account of the last race around Cape Horn. His own adventures were recorded in *Give Me a Ship to Sail* (1958).

Walker, Fred ("DIXIE"), U.S. baseball player (b. Sept. 24, 1910, Villa Rica, Ga.—d. May 17, 1982, Birmingham, Ala.), as the crowd-pleasing outfielder for the Brooklyn Dodgers from 1939 to 1947 was dubbed "The People's Cherce" after he helped spark the team to National League pennants in 1941 and 1947. Walker sustained two shoulder injuries and a torn knee during his stints with the New York Yankees, the Chicago White Sox, and the Detroit Tigers, who traded him to the Dodgers when it seemed likely that his career was ebbing. As a Dodger he wowed the fans by hitting .357 to win the 1944 National League batting crown. In 1945 he led the league with 124 RBI's, and during his 18-year career he had a lifetime .306 batting average. His blissful association with the Dodgers ended abruptly in 1947 when Walker voiced his reluctance to accept as his teammate Jackie Robinson, the first black major league player. At his own request Walker was traded to the Pittsburgh Pirates in 1948 and retired from baseball the following year. In later years, however, Walker praised Robinson both as a man and as a player.

Wallenberg, Marcus, Swedish financier (b. Oct. 5, 1899, Stockholm, Sweden—d. Sept. 13, 1982, Stockholm), controlled the Stockholms Enskilda Bank, which his grandfather had founded in 1856, presided over its merger to form the Skandinaviska Enskilda Bank, and, with his brother Jacob who died in 1980, had holdings in some 20 leading Swedish companies, including Saab-Scania, SKF, Ericsson, and Electrolux. Wallenberg also participated in the creation of the airline SAS and in setting up the system of shareholding that protected Swedish industry from foreign takeovers. He joined the Enskilda Bank in 1925, was vice-chairman from 1958 to 1969 and chairman from then until 1971. During World War II Wallenberg was a member of the Swedish trade delegation that negotiated with Britain, Finland, and the U.S. He later served as chairman of the Council of European Industrial Foundations and the OECD Business and Industrial Advisory Committee. Wallenberg's influence in Swedish industry was immense, and as an outspoken defender of the capitalist system, he spoke out against the extent of Swedish welfare programs. He was also a keen tennis player who won the Swedish indoor championships twice during the 1920s and was the first Swede to play on the centre court at Wimbledon.

Warburg, Sir Siegmund George, British banker (b. Sept. 30, 1902, Germany—d. Oct. 13, 1982, London, England), was founder and head of S. G. Warburg and Co., a leading merchant bank, and enjoyed a reputation as an influential and respected British financier. He joined the family bank in Hamburg during the 1920s and established the firm's Berlin branch in 1930. However, the accession to power of the Nazis led him to immigrate to London in 1934, and he founded the New Trading Company Ltd., which in 1946 became S. G. Warburg. He was determined that the firm not expand beyond the manageable limits of a family bank, and he acted more as financial adviser than as a major lender to his clients. During the 1950s, the British financial establishment was critical of Warburg's role in such deals as the bid to take over British Aluminium, but his methods later became accepted practice and Warburg was applauded for his pioneering role in modernizing London banking procedures. A man of considerable culture, he approached his profession almost as an academic discipline and continued to play an influential role as president of Warburg's even after his retirement from the chairmanship of the bank in 1964. He was knighted in 1966.

Webb, Jack, U.S. actor (b. April 2, 1920, Santa Monica, Calif.—d. Dec. 23, 1982, Los Angeles, Calif.), who was better known as the stone-faced Sgt. Joe Friday on the television series "Dragnet" (1951–59 and 1967–70), a detective show based on actual crime files from the Los Angeles Police Department. Webb, who began his career on radio in 1945, created "Dragnet" in 1948. The program ran for seven years on radio, and when it appeared on television, two separate shows were broadcast.

UPI

During the height of the program's popularity "Dragnet" had 38 million viewers, and Sergeant Friday's laconic "Just the facts, ma'am" passed into the language. After reviving "Dragnet" in 1967, Webb also directed and produced the series. He later headed the Mark VII Ltd. production company that made such television shows as "Emergency!," "Adam-12," "Mobile One," and "Hec Ramsey."

Weiner, Joseph Sidney, South African-born environmental physiologist and anthropologist (b. June 29, 1915, Pretoria, South Africa—d. June 13, 1982, Oxford, England), helped to uncover the Piltdown forgery. The Piltdown skull "discovered" by Charles Dawson had long been accepted as that of an early hominid of previously unknown type. Weiner became convinced that it was not genuine and called on Sir Wilfred Le Gros Clark and Kenneth Oakley to help him show that it was a hoax. They did so, implying (though they never openly said so) that Dawson was responsible. Weiner studied at the University of the Witwatersrand, then qualified as a doctor at St. George's Hospital Medical School in London. Reader in physical anthropology at the University of Oxford in 1945, he became director (1962–80) of the Medical Research Council's Environmental Physiology Unit and professor (1965–80) of environmental physiology at the University of London. He helped found the Society for the Study of Human Biology and was its chairman (1968–71). From 1964 to 1974 he was world convener of the Human Adaptability Section of the Human Biological Programme. Weiner's numerous books and papers included *The Piltdown Forgery* (1955) and *The Biology of Human Adaptability* (1966). In 1978 he was awarded the Huxley Medal of the Royal Anthropological Institute.

Weiss, Peter (Ulrich), German-born writer (b. Nov. 8, 1916, Nowawes, near Berlin, Germany—d. May 10, 1982, Stockholm, Sweden), won international recognition with his play *Marat/Sade,* which reflected perhaps better than any other work the concerns of the European theatre in the 1960s. *Marat/Sade* (full English title, *The Persecution and Assassination of Jean-Paul Marat as Performed by the Inmates of the Asylum of Charenton Under the Direction of the Marquis de Sade*), described as an analysis of revolution and individualism, was a powerful mixture of ideological debate, music, and spectacle. Staged in West Berlin in 1964 by Konrad Swinarski and in London (1964) and New York (1965) by Peter Brook (who filmed it in 1967), it was a resounding success with audiences seeking an alternative to bourgeois drawing-room drama. Weiss, the son of an industrialist of Hungarian-Jewish origin with Czechoslovak nationality, fled Nazi Germany in 1934 for Britain (1934–36) and Prague (1936–38), where he studied painting. Weiss continued to

work as an artist and held a one-man exhibition in Stockholm in 1941 and a traveling retrospective in the 1970s. After a brief interval in Switzerland, in 1939 he settled in Sweden, took Swedish nationality (1946), and wrote his first published works in Swedish; he also made documentary films and radio plays. Weiss returned to his native Germany for the setting of his first (semiautobiographical) novels, *The Shadow of the Coachman's Body* (1960), *The Leavetaking* (1961), and *Exile* (1962). After *Marat/Sade* he worked mainly in the theatre, using his plays to attack fascism, imperialism, and colonialism: *The Investigation* (1965), an oratorio based on the Auschwitz trials, was premiered on the same day in 17 theatres in Berlin, East and West Germany, and London; *The Song of the Lusitanian Bogey* (1967), staged in 1968 by the New York Negro Ensemble, denounced Portuguese colonialism; *The New Trial* (1982) attacked multinational companies. His stance in such works as *Trotsky in Exile* (1970) did not always please orthodox Communists, but it was more often the right than was outraged by his overtly Marxist message. He devoted much of his later years to a three-part autobiographical work, *The Aesthetics of Resistance* (1975–81). He received the Charles Veillon (1963), Lessing (1965), Heinrich Mann (1966), and Thomas Dehler (1978) prizes for literature. In 1964 Weiss married the Swedish ceramic artist Gunilla Palmstierna, who designed the costumes for the Berlin and London-New York productions of *Marat/Sade.*

Welter, Erich, West German economist and newspaper publisher (b. June 30, 1900, Strasbourg, Germany [now France]—d. June 10, 1982, Frankfurt am Main, West Germany), played an important role in the creation of the *Frankfurter Allgemeine Zeitung* after World War II and in its establishment as a leading West German independent daily. It was the successor in the postwar period to the *Frankfurter Zeitung,* which Welter joined in 1921 after studying law and political science at the University of Berlin. He left in 1933 to edit the *Vossische Zeitung,* but this paper was closed in the following year by the Nazis. Welter returned to the *Frankfurter Zeitung* as economic correspondent in Paris, then as deputy chief editor and managing editor until it too was closed down in 1943. In 1946 he was co-founder of *Wirtschaftszeitung* and in 1949 negotiated the publication of the *Frankfurter Allgemeine Zeitung,* which he later protected as an independent publication by setting up in 1961 a foundation holding a majority of its shares. Welter was lecturer (1931–48) at the University of Frankfurt and in 1951 founded the Research Institute for Political Economy, which he directed, at the University of Mainz.

Whitelock, Dorothy, British Anglo-Saxon scholar (b. Nov. 11, 1901, Leeds, England—d. Aug. 14, 1982, Huntingdon, Cambridgeshire, England), was vice-principal of St. Hilda's College, Oxford (1951–57), and professor of Anglo-Saxon at the University of Cambridge (1957–69). She had studied at Cambridge, made a standard edition of Anglo-Saxon wills, and established her reputation as a teacher and scholar by the time she published her first major book, *The Audience of Beowulf* (1951). Combining literary, linguistic, and historical scholarship, she wrote with an understanding of the Anglo-Saxon period's many facets and an appreciation of Anglo-Saxon contributions to later British history. Whitelock also published a popular study of *The Beginnings of English Society* (1952), articles for *Encyclopædia Britannica,* and a biography of Alfred the Great, which appeared posthumously. Her other essential contributions to her field were her studies of Wulfstan, archbishop of York, and her *English Historical Documents, c. 500–1042* (1955; 2nd ed., 1979). Whitelock's many honours included fellowships of colleges in Oxford and Cambridge and of the British Academy. She was made Commander of the Order of the British Empire in 1964.

Whitney, John Hay ("JOCK"), U.S. multimillionaire, publisher, and sportsman (b. Aug. 17, 1904, Ells-

UPI

worth, Maine—d. Feb. 8, 1982, Manhasset, N.Y.), at the age of 23 inherited the largest estate that had ever been appraised to that time and thereafter had a multifaceted career as a publisher, financier, philanthropist, and Thoroughbred horse breeder. After graduating from Groton preparatory school and Yale University, Whitney became an internationally ranked polo player and captain of the Greentree team that won national championships. During the 1930s he added to his coffers by astutely backing the motion picture *Gone with the Wind* and the Broadway hit *Life with Father.* He also invested in Minute Maid orange juice, Pan American World Airways, some 25 small newspapers, and six radio stations. His greatest disappointment was his inability to revitalize the *New York Herald Tribune,* which he served (1961–66) as editor in chief and publisher until the newspaper folded. A keen sportsman, Whitney enjoyed polo, golf, tennis, billiards, and swimming and had an enduring enthusiasm for horse breeding. The family stables, Greentree, twice produced the horse of the year. In 1946 he set up the John Hay Whitney Foundation, to which he contributed $1 million annually, and in 1970 he donated $15 million to his alma mater. From 1956 to 1961 he served as ambassador to the Court of St. James's and was effective in subduing tensions stemming from the 1956 Suez crisis. Whitney, whose estate was estimated at some $200 million at the time of his death, never flaunted his wealth and disdained the inclusion of his name in the *Social Register.*

Wiener, Jean, French pianist and composer (b. March 19, 1896, Paris, France—d. June 8, 1982, Paris), was one of the first musicians in France to realize the possibilities of jazz and throughout his life rejected conventional distinctions between "popular" and "serious" music. He started to play the piano at the age of six and became a pupil of Gabriel Fauré. He attended the Conservatoire National Supérieur de Musique, Paris, with Darius Milhaud, a lifelong friend. After military service during World War I, he founded, with Jean Cocteau, the cabaret Le Boeuf sur le Toit, where he played with Clément Doucet. The cabaret was a famous meeting place for leading musicians, writers, and painters, including Pablo Picasso, Tristan Tzara, and the group of composers known as Les Six. Jazz rhythms had inspired Wiener's *Concerto Franco-Américain* of 1924, and he moved effortlessly into writing film music, eventually composing more than 300 scores for such films as *Touchez pas au grisbi, Les Bas-Fonds,* and *Le Crime de Monsieur Lange.* Later he composed 429 impromptu accompaniments for the television series "Histoires sans paroles." He joined the Communist Party during World War II and was an active member of the Société des Auteurs, Compositeurs et Editeurs de Musique, a union of writers, musicians, and artists.

He wrote popular music, was the singer Mireille's first accompanist, and continued to produce works such as his concerti for accordion (1957) and for two guitars (1966). His autobiography was entitled *Allegro Appassionato* (1978).

Williams, Frederick Ronald, Australian painter (b. Jan. 23, 1927, Melbourne, Australia—d. April 22, 1982, Melbourne), was a noted painter of the Australian landscape and an important figure in the Australian art world. He studied at the National Gallery Schools in Melbourne and at the Chelsea Art School in London. Though Williams was best known for his landscapes and seascapes and particularly for the quality of light he brought to his depiction of Australian scenes, he was also an accomplished printmaker and portraitist. He held a one-man exhibition at the Museum of Modern Art, New York City, in 1977 and another in London in 1980. Williams was a member of the council of the Australian National Gallery and a founder and president of the Print Council of Australia. His awards included the Wynne Prizes for 1966 and 1977. Williams was made Officer of the Order of the British Empire in 1976.

Williams, Gluyas, U.S. cartoonist (b. July 23, 1888, San Francisco, Calif.—d. Feb. 13, 1982, Boston, Mass.), as longtime cartoonist for *The New Yorker* magazine produced finely crafted pen-and-ink drawings that featured children and adults over 35 in humorous or ironic situations. Williams, who was especially adept at satirizing suburbanites, showed his characters at family reunions, vacation resorts, commuter stations, and in the workplace. Williams attended Harvard University, where he contributed stories and cartoons to the *Harvard Lampoon* and established a lifelong association with humorist Robert Benchley. Williams supposedly advised Benchley to abandon art and concentrate on writing. After graduating from Harvard in 1911, Williams studied fine art at Colarossi's in Paris. He then returned to the U.S. and successively served as art editor of *Youth's Companion* magazine, cartoonist and caricaturist of the *Boston Transcript,* and writer and cartoonist for *Life* magazine. From 1925 to 1930 he contributed cartoons to both *Life* and *The New Yorker* but after 1930 continued with only the latter. Besides illustrating many Benchley books, Williams produced some volumes of his own including *Fellow Citizens* (1940) and *The Gluyas Williams Gallery* (1957). He retired in 1953.

Wilson, Don, U.S. radio and television announcer (b. Sept. 1, 1900, Lincoln, Neb.—d. April 25, 1982, Cathedral City, Calif.), was the jovial and bombastic radio announcer for "The Jack Benny Program" on both radio and television and served as the perfect foil for Benny's humour. Wilson, who joined the show in 1933 after working as a sports announcer, was best remembered for his attempts to get a commercial on the air while Benny tried to thwart him. Occasionally Wilson would interject a song by the Sportsmen Quartet at the beginning of a commercial, a maneuver that delighted audiences. For more than 30 years Wilson and his wife, Lois Virginia Corbet, both played characters on the show, and after the program went off the air in 1965, they appeared in the theatre.

Winkler, Paul, French journalist (b. July 7, 1898, Budapest, Hung.—d. Sept. 23, 1982, Melun, near Paris, France), was director of *France-Soir* and founder of the press agency Opera Mundi. He came to France as a newspaper correspondent in 1925, was naturalized in 1932, and became a leading figure in popular journalism through his press agency and such periodicals as *Le Journal de Mickey* and *Confidences,* which he created. During World War II he served in the U.S. as foreign commentator for the *Washington Post* until he was able to return to France and resume his activities in popular publishing. But Winkler's ambition was to acquire a leading daily newspaper, and in 1976 he purchased *France-Soir.* In the following year Winkler was obliged to sell 50% of his holding to press baron Robert Hersant, though he remained as managing editor. Winkler was the author of several books including *The Thousand-Year Conspira-*

cy (1943) and *Les Sources mystiques des concepts moraux de l'Occident* (1957).

Woods, George David, U.S. investment banker (b. July 27, 1901, Boston, Mass.—d. Aug. 20, 1982, near Lisbon, Port.), as a founder and chairman of First Boston Corp. became one of the world's most influential and respected investment bankers and, before serving as president (1963–68) of the World Bank, was a frequent consultant on special assignments. In the latter capacity he helped to alleviate the financial chaos that resulted from the nationalization of the Suez Canal by Egypt. As an executive with the First Boston Corp., Woods helped finance the Kaiser Engineering and Aluminum Co. of Canada while other Wall Street firms ignored Kaiser's request for backing. During his tenure as president of the World Bank, Woods promoted innovative policies including giving poor countries freer access to loans and establishing loans for agriculture and education. A modest man and a patron of the arts, Woods was convinced that "you can accomplish an awful lot of good if you don't care who gets the credit."

Wright, Helena (HELENA ROSA LOWENFELD), British gynecologist (b. Sept. 17, 1887, London, England—d. March 21, 1982, London), was a pioneer in birth control and sexual education. She helped found the National Birth Control Council in 1930 and, as a result of her work in Britain and in the less developed countries, established a unique reputation as a publicist of birth control methods. Wright was the daughter of a Polish immigrant whose business enterprises enabled him to advance from poverty to wealth and to have her educated at Cheltenham Ladies College. She rebelled against her father, trained as a doctor, and during World War I worked at Bethnal Green Hospital. In 1922 she left with her husband for China, where she was associate professor of gynecology at the Shantung Christian University. Returning to Britain in 1927, Wright met E. Gräfenberg, inventor of the intra-uterine device, devoted herself to the study and promotion of contraceptive techniques, and was increasingly drawn into the field of sexual education through her counseling of patients with sexual problems. Wright worked actively with both the National Birth Control Council (later Family Planning Association) and the International Planned Parenthood Federation. In 1930 she published *The Sex Factor in Marriage,* remarkable at the time as a clear, popular exposition of the subject. Even after her retirement from the FPA in 1957, Wright continued working in private practice and was especially active as an inspiring teacher and lecturer in the third world. She paid her last visit to India in 1976. In 1968 she published *Sex and Society,* in which she explored the most recent developments in her field.

Zworykin, Vladimir Kosma, Russian-born electronics engineer (b. July 30, 1889, Mourom, Russia—d. July 29, 1982, Princeton, N.J.), was dubbed "the father of modern television" after inventing the iconoscope (1923; the first practical television camera tube) and the kinescope (1924; a television picture tube). The two inventions comprised the first all-electronic television system and paved the way for future technological advancements. After Zworykin immigrated to the U.S. in 1919, he joined the Westinghouse Electric Corp. The company showed little interest, though, in Zworykin's 1924 demonstration of his television or in his subsequent improvements. In 1926 he earned a Ph.D. from the University of Pittsburgh, and three years later he was recruited by RCA, where he obtained his first patent for colour television. Zworykin, who held more than 120 patents, also developed an early form of the electric eye, initiated development of the electron microscope, and constructed an electron image tube, which was sensitive to infrared light. The latter was the basis for the snooperscope and sniperscope used during World War II. He also perfected a secondary-emission multiplier often used for sensitive radiation detection. Zworykin, who retired from RCA in 1954, was honoured for his technical achievements in 1966 when he was awarded the National Medal of Science, the highest scientific award in the U.S.

(1919) era, the decade of the Nationalist government at Nanking after 1928, and the 1949 Communist victory in the civil war now seem notable as false starts or periods in which high hopes for national rebirth were dashed by domestic political turmoil, foreign intervention, and the burdens of bringing a vast, decentralized peasant society into the mainstream of 20th-century industrial civilization. In contrast, the Japanese—despite the destructiveness of World War II—have hardly missed a step on the road to social and economic modernization.

The past three decades of Communist Party rule of China—the era of Mao Zedong's (Mao Tse-tung's) leadership—have been no less a time of shifting experiments and disappointed hopes that a way could be found to modernize China rapidly. During the early 1950s the Chinese Communists adopted the Soviet model of development, only to reject it after 1958 in favour of a Great Leap Forward in economic construction. This experiment in the mass mobilization of peasant labour had failed by 1961, and it was followed by a decade of uncertain economic policies as the country succumbed to leadership feuds and the political chaos of the Cultural Revolution.

The decade of the 1970s was one of continuing leadership conflict and policy alterations as the Communists who established the People's Republic of China (PRC) continued to search for a path to China's modernization. Three developments give special meaning to the past decade:

- Communist Party Chairman Mao Zedong and many of the other senior revolutionary figures who led the People's Liberation Army to victory in the civil war, and who subsequently shaped policy during three decades of national reconstruction, died in the 1970s.
- China's foreign relations, which in the first two decades of Communist rule shifted from alliance with the Soviet Union to self-isolation during the years of Cultural Revolution turmoil, took a major turn toward an opening to the non-Communist world—to Western Europe, the United States, and Japan.

Richard H. Solomon is director of International Security Policy research at the Rand Corporation and head of Rand's Political Science Department. A professor of Political Science at the University of Michigan from 1966 to 1971, he subsequently served on the National Security Council staff with particular responsibility for Chinese affairs (1971–76). His books include Mao's Revolution and the Chinese Political Culture (1971), A Revolution Is Not a Dinner Party (1976), Asian Security in the 1980s (1979), and The China Factor: Sino-American Relations and the Global Scene (1980).

EASTFOTO/SOVFOTO

"... Mao's answer to China's modernization needs: ... to mobilize the peasants for agricultural and industrial production by organizing them into military-style units..."

- Efforts of China's revolutionary leaders to bring about economic development through political mobilization of the country's 800 million peasants gave way to the building of socialism through the training of a technically competent party cadre, material incentives for the workers and peasants, and the bureaucratic management of China's huge agricultural economy.

Mao and the Succession. Mao Zedong—Chairman Mao—emerged as a leading figure in the Chinese Communist movement after the 1935 emergency leadership conference held at Zun-yi (Tsun-yi) during the Long March. From that time he played the primary role in developing the military and political strategies and the organizational forms that led the Communists to victory in the civil war and, after the founding of the People's Republic in 1949, that built a socialist economy. A major issue in China's leadership politics from the early 1960s was Mao's effort to ensure that his policies would survive his death and that leaders whom he believed would sustain his revolutionary legacy would remain in control of the Communist Party. In both respects Mao's final years of rule were a failure.

The Cultural Revolution that began in the spring of 1966 was, in part, an effort by Mao to remove from positions of leadership men such as State Chairman Liu Shaoqi (Liu Shao-ch'i) and Party Gen-

把工作的重点转到四化建设上来

CHINA'S UNCERTAIN FUTURE

by Richard H. Solomon

China and Japan began their struggles to transform agrarian, feudal societies into industrial nation-states at about the same time in the late 19th century. But while Japan, since the Meiji Restoration of 1868, has single-mindedly grown to become the world's third largest industrial power, China, from the time of Li Hung-chang's self-strengthening movement in the 1870s and '80s, has repeatedly floundered in its search for a path to national political and economic restoration.

Sun Yat-sen's 1911 revolution against the Manchu dynasty, the intellectual ferment of the May Fourth

eral Secretary Deng Xiaoping (Teng Hsiao-p'ing), who—according to the chairman and his supporters—wanted to take China down the "capitalist road" of national development. While such leaders were purged in 1967, by the end of the 1960s the chaos and violence of what the Chinese now term the "ten wasted years" of political terror had generated a strong reaction against Mao's more radical policies and serious leadership factionalism.

At the second plenum of the ninth Central Committee in August 1970, Mao's long-time associate Chen Boda (Ch'en Po-ta), the theoretician of the Great Leap Forward and the Cultural Revolution, was purged on grounds of having incited Red Guard violence and factional intrigue within the party. Just over a year later, in September 1971, the man named in the ninth party constitution as Mao's heir to party leadership, Defense Minister Lin Biao (Lin Piao), mysteriously died in a plane crash while fleeing to the Soviet Union. It was later said that Lin had organized an assassination plot against the strong-willed and unpredictable chairman.

During the next three years it appeared that under the pragmatic direction of Premier Zhou Enlai (Chou En-lai), China was finally emerging from its nightmare of political violence. Zhou even succeeded in bringing Deng Xiaoping back to national leadership to assist him in his efforts. But Zhou's attempt to reestablish regularized bureaucratic administration of China's huge state system and economic planning mechanism was criticized by radicals within the party leadership centred on Mao's wife, Jiang Qing (Chiang Ch'ing). As Mao's health deteriorated after 1974 because of a series of debilitating strokes, Zhou and his plan to bring the Four Modernizations to China (the modernization of agriculture, industry, science and technology, and national defense) were attacked as being contrary to the chairman's legacy. The popular Zhou succumbed to cancer in January 1976, and not long thereafter the radicals engineered the second purge of Zhou's choice for the succession, Deng Xiaoping.

Thus, on the eve of Mao's death on Sept. 9, 1976, China's leadership seemed firmly in the hands of his wife and the radicals. Indeed, less than a month after Mao's passing, party leadership was placed in the hands of a provincial official from Mao's home province of Hunan, Hua Guofeng (Hua Kuo-feng). It was said that Mao's deathbed testament was that with Hua in charge of his revolution, he—the chairman since 1935—was "at ease" as he passed on to a Marxist heaven.

However, the deep hatred within China for Mao's wife and the radicals who had led the country into the decade of Cultural Revolution turmoil erupted within only weeks of Mao's death. Jiang Qing and her close supporters were arrested and accused of being a "gang of four" who acted against the will of the party and the chairman. Deng Xiaoping was rehabilitated for the second time nine months later, and by 1978 he had begun restoring to leadership many of the senior figures of China's Communist movement who had been purged by Mao during the Cultural Revolution. Liu Shaoqi was exonerated

"... the deep hatred within China for Mao's wife and the radicals who had led the country into the decade of Cultural Revolution turmoil erupted within only weeks of Mao's death."

HENRI BUREAU—SYGMA

"Invoking the slogan of past periods of intellectual liberalization, 'Let a hundred flowers bloom,' Deng and his colleagues encouraged China's intellectuals to vent their bitterness against the turmoil and persecution suffered during the Cultural Revolution." The "Democracy Wall" in Beijing.

posthumously, and Mao's chosen successor, Hua Guofeng, was demoted from the posts of party chairman and premier in 1981 and replaced by associates of Deng Xiaoping. Hu Yaobang (Hu Yao-pang), a former Communist Youth League official, assumed the post of Communist Party general secretary, and the Sichuan (Szechwan) provincial official Zhao Ziyang (Chao Tzu-yang) became premier.

Pragmatic Bureaucratism. More significant to the ending of Chairman Mao's revolution than the intrigues within the party leadership that followed his death has been the almost complete abandonment of Mao's policies for building China into a socialist state. A party leadership plenum in the summer of 1981 paid lip service to the chairman's role in bringing the Communist Party to power in China, but it also attacked him for his "cult of personality," for serious policy misjudgments dating back to the time of the Great Leap Forward, and for his "gross mistakes" made during the Cultural Revolution. And while Mao's contributions to the revolution were said to outweigh his errors, in fact, China's contemporary leaders have all but eliminated the style of leadership and the policies for economic development that were the distinguishing characteristics of his three decades of rule.

From the mid-1960s until Mao's death the Communist Party had become little more than an instrument for the chairman's personal rule. During those

years the party's propaganda machinery preached "the thought of Mao Zedong" as the only vision of China's future. Mao's successors, at the 12th party congress in September 1982, abolished the post of party chairman and asserted their intention to "break the fetters of dogmatism and the personality cult" by rebuilding a party that would "seek truth from facts" and perfect a socialist legal system to guard against abuses of power. In the Maoist era the party cadre had asserted its authority by means of "redness" or political loyalty. The new party leadership proclaimed its intention to train a younger generation of leaders that instead had both technical competence and organizational ability.

To give force to these intentions party General Secretary Hu Yaobang asserted that all of the Communist Party's membership of 38 million would have to turn in their party cards and be examined for reregistration based on these new criteria for leadership. But future political battles can be expected as Deng Xiaoping and his associates seek to purge the party of the aged and incompetent as well as those members still supportive of "ultraleft" policies.

Under Chairman Mao the Communist Party, or its Cultural Revolution incarnation of "revolutionary committees," had virtually run China—formulating policies, assigning personnel, and administering the economy, the Army, and the state bureaucracy. In the era of Deng Xiaoping the party's role, it is asserted, will be restricted to that of a policy-formulating institution. The power to make laws and administer a society of more than 1,000,000,000 people will be returned to the National People's Congress, the State Council, and its various administrative organizations. Whereas in Mao's time "class struggle" and the promotion of policies through military-style mass campaigns were the hallmarks of economic and political life, the Deng Xiaoping leadership now seeks to stabilize administrative power in the various bureaucracies of the State Council.

Intellectual Liberalization. Deng Xiaoping's modernization program, by its very definition, will transfer power in China from the rural "masses" to the urban intellectuals and bureaucrats. This shift in emphasis became evident in the summer of 1978 as Deng began to assert his alternative to Mao's policies. Invoking the slogan of past periods of intellectual liberalization, "Let a hundred flowers bloom," Deng and his colleagues encouraged China's intellectuals to vent their bitterness against the turmoil and persecution suffered during the Cultural Revolution. "Big character posters" were displayed on what was known as Democracy Wall in Beijing (Peking) and in other cities; on them personal tales of mistreatment during Jiang Qing's reign of terror were recounted for China, and the world, to see. Writers and artists purged during the 1960s by the gang of four were rehabilitated and their works published. Even Western literature, music, and films were widely circulated.

To compensate for the destruction of China's educational system during the Cultural Revolution, Deng ordered in 1978 that more than 10,000 students be sent abroad—largely to the United States—to gain the scientific, technical, and managerial skills that they needed to become leaders in a more pragmatic Communist Party. Also, such institutions as the Chinese Academy of Sciences and the newly created Academy of Social Sciences were given the resources to help formulate policies for China's modernization.

The intellectual ferment unleashed by Deng, however, was not long in generating a political reaction from more conservative elements in the party and the People's Liberation Army. By late 1979 criticism of the Communist Party and socialism by the intellectuals had reached sufficient proportions that fears were raised of a loss of all party authority. Countercriticism of the danger of "bourgeois liberalism" began to appear in official publications. Democracy Wall was closed down. And the party asserted its authority once again by proclaiming that intellectual life had to remain within the bounds of the Four Fundamental Principles: Communist Party leadership, the working class dictatorship, a commitment to Marxism-Leninism, and the building of socialism.

Economic Development. For Mao Zedong and the other Communist revolutionaries who struggled for more than three decades to gain political power in China, the establishment of the People's Republic in 1949 presented a profound personal challenge to their leadership skills. Could they be as successful as economic developers as they had been as political revolutionaries? From the perspective of 1982 it is clear that Mao, in particular, tried to adapt the style of leadership that had succeeded in the years of revolutionary warfare to the tasks of economic construction—but with catastrophic results.

In the early 1950s the Chinese Communists adopted the Stalinist approach to economic construction, with its stress on the development of heavy industry through a centralized bureaucratic planning system that set production targets and allocated key resources. It did not take long for Mao, a man of rural background, to see that such an approach would not work in a technologically backward and undercapitalized country like China, in which more than 80% of the population were unlettered peasants. Some of the first strains in Sino-Soviet relations appeared in the mid-1950s as Mao

In a move to increase the flow of consumer goods, China's first international Auto Salon was held in Guangzhou (Canton) in January 1981.

"But material incentives rather than political appeals were to be used to motivate the labour force . . ."

rejected the Stalinist approach and began to formulate his own solution to China's economic development dilemmas.

The Great Leap Forward of 1958 represented Mao's answer to China's modernization needs: to substitute for capital the country's great surplus resource, its labour power, and to mobilize the peasants for agricultural and industrial production by organizing them into military-style units as had been done during the years of revolutionary warfare—into production "brigades" and agricultural communes. Mao went so far as to encourage population growth because, he said, it would enlarge the country's labour force.

The Great Leap Forward was a drastic failure. Between 1959 and 1962 China's national income dropped by 35%, a greater decline than occurred in the United States during the Great Depression of the 1930s. While some economic recovery was achieved during the years 1962–65, the onset of the Cultural Revolution in 1966 destroyed China's economic management system and central planning bureaucracy as party members were attacked by student Red Guards for practicing "revisionism." Labour productivity similarly dropped as peasants and workers devoted considerable time to studying Mao Zedong's "little red book" of quotations and attending political rallies. In 1978 China's leaders had to face the stark fact that over the 20-year period 1957–77 per capita income in the nation had actually declined somewhat as unabated population growth outpaced the increases in agricultural and industrial output attained during two decades of economic experimentation and political turmoil.

Mao devoted scant attention to economic matters in his last decade of rule, instead concentrating his failing energies on the political succession struggle and on China's growing national security problems with the Soviet Union. It was only in 1975 that the ever pragmatic Zhou Enlai—only a year from death—raised again the need for China to pursue the Four Modernizations, a theme he had first expressed in 1964 just before the country was engulfed in the Cultural Revolution. Zhou's call for a return to economic construction was delayed for several years, however, first by the struggle against the gang of four, and then by two years of renewed Soviet-style planning in 1977–78 under the leadership of Hua Guofeng. In an effort to restart the engine of economic development rapidly, Hua stressed the development of heavy industry through high levels of capital accumulation (at the expense of popular consumption) and unrealistically high production targets. His policy, however, did not survive Deng Xiaoping's reassertion of power in the summer and fall of 1978.

China's current policy lines for pursuing the Four Modernizations were basically set at the third plenum of the 11th Central Committee in December 1978—the leadership convocation at which Deng Xiaoping reaffirmed the Zhou Enlai approach to economic development. Deng stressed that in pursuit of the goal of quadrupling national income by the year 2000, China would abandon Mao's mass campaign style of economic construction and return to a pattern of planned, centralized management of the economy by technically proficient bureaucrats. Deng sustained Mao's legacy to the extent that he stressed the primacy of agricultural output and encouraged a significant decentralization of decision making in the rural economy to the production teams and individual peasant households. But material incentives rather than political appeals were to be used to motivate the labour force, including allowing the peasants to earn extra income by selling the produce of their private plots at free markets.

By the end of 1982 Deng Xiaoping's policies had begun to improve China's economic performance, particularly in the rural areas. Yet even if the Communist Party is able to sustain these policies until the end of the century, it faces major barriers to sustained economic growth. Among these the most significant are the difficulty of increasing agricultural productivity given China's fixed quantity of arable land and the great effort needed to modernize rapidly the nation's agricultural technology, serious bottlenecks in the production of energy and in transportation, and the country's limited number of well-trained scientists, engineers, and managers.

Although the Western world has been prepared to help facilitate China's economic modernization program through sales of advanced production technologies, the Chinese discovered in the late 1970s that they lack the economic and managerial capacity to absorb large quantities of foreign technology, even if they can find ways of financing such imports. And although the Chinese economy, in aggregate terms, is likely to rank among the world's largest by the end of the century, unless the country is able to stabilize its population growth quickly, further gains in agricultural and industrial production will do little to raise per capita income—estimated in 1982 to be less than $320 (compared with $9,780 in Japan and $2,460 in Taiwan).

Foreign Relations. China's foreign relations since 1949 fall into three distinct, decade-long periods of shifting alignments, each of which was influenced in a major way by Mao Zedong. In the summer of 1949 Mao proclaimed that the soon-to-be-established People's Republic of China would "lean to one side"—to an alliance with the Soviet Union and the socialist world. By 1960, however, after a decade of experimenting with the Stalinist model of development, leadership and policy differences in the Sino-Soviet relationship had grown so serious that China's "unbreakable" friendship with the U.S.S.R. had dissipated in public feuding. During the 1960s China withdrew from active involvement with the world—despite Mao's calls for revolution in the third world—as the leadership preoccupied itself with the domestic chaos of the Cultural Revolution. All but one of China's ambassadors were recalled

home during the latter half of the decade. In 1969, however, serious military clashes along the Sino-Soviet frontier forced the Chinese to confront a major and growing Soviet military buildup. This development led Mao to initiate the third major phase in China's foreign relations—an opening to the United States and other non-Communist countries of the Western world.

In early 1970 China and the United States privately informed each other, after 134 unproductive ambassadorial talks at Warsaw, that they wished to normalize relations. This set the stage for what was probably the most dramatic development in international relations since the end of World War II, the journey to Beijing of U.S. Pres. Richard Nixon. Concurrently, Premier Zhou Enlai initiated efforts to establish diplomatic relations between China and the countries of Western Europe and the third world. During the 1970s 70 governments broke ties with the Republic of China on Taiwan and established diplomatic relations with Beijing.

Intrigue and political pageantry marked the opening of the high-level Sino-U.S. dialogue in the summer of 1971 as President Nixon's national security adviser, Henry Kissinger, traveled secretly to Beijing to pave the way for Nixon's visit to the Chinese capital in February of the following year. The Kissinger trip probably accelerated China's long-resisted

Among China's problems are its "limited number of well-trained scientists, engineers, and managers."

"... and most profoundly, China's economic progress and political stability will be hostage to the effectiveness with which population growth can be restrained while the technical modernization of agriculture and industry is promoted."
NOGUES—SYGMA

admission to the United Nations, which finally occurred in October 1971—along with Taiwan's expulsion from the world organization.

The Nixon visit to China in early 1972—projected worldwide by satellite television—concluded with publication of the Shanghai Communiqué, a political document in which China and the United States agreed to seek the full normalization of their bilateral relations while expressing a common opposition to Soviet "hegemony." Trade and cultural exchanges between the two countries were initiated, and the leaderships continued to discuss ways of reconciling their differences over Taiwan—with which the U.S. continued to maintain formal diplomatic relations.

Normalization did not come quickly, however. President Nixon's resignation over the Watergate scandal in August 1974, conservative Republican resistance to breaking U.S. ties with Taiwan, and political uncertainties in China associated with the deaths of Zhou Enlai and Mao in 1976 slowed down the process of Sino-U.S. accommodation until 1978. In December of that year the administration of U.S. Pres. Jimmy Carter and Deng Xiaoping finally reached agreement on establishing diplomatic relations, which was accomplished on Jan. 1, 1979. The U.S. severed formal ties to the government of the Republic of China on Taiwan and agreed to maintain

only unofficial relations with the island even as it asserted its intention to sustain the island's defenses through continuing sales of American arms.

For both China and the United States the process of normalizing relations, from its beginning in 1970, was given political impetus by a common concern with the worldwide growth of Soviet military power. Indeed, the timing of the establishment of diplomatic relations in early 1979 was influenced, in part, by Moscow's support for Vietnam in its invasion of Kampuchea—a development highly threatening to China's security. By the late 1970s, however, China's post-Mao leadership had begun to place its highest priority on economic development, and it was in this context that Deng Xiaoping in the summer of 1978 ordered the training abroad of a new generation of scientists, engineers, and managers. At the same time, China began to import sizable amounts of foreign technology in order to speed up the process of economic development. Nonetheless, Soviet military pressures continued to impart a national security rationale to the Sino-U.S. relationship. After Moscow invaded Afghanistan in December 1979, the U.S. and China exchanged visits of senior defense officials in order to explore ways of cooperating in response to the seemingly implacable military threat from Moscow.

This decade of positive developments in U.S.-

China relations slowed abruptly after 1980, however, as the Chinese began placing greater emphasis on reunification with Taiwan and the administration of U.S. Pres. Ronald Reagan asserted its intention to sustain U.S. arms sales to the island. During the 1980 presidential campaign in the U.S., Reagan had stressed his desire to strengthen ties with Taiwan. In this context the Chinese curtailed defense-oriented contacts between the two countries and threatened to downgrade relations with the U.S. if arms sales to Taiwan were not terminated. This impasse led to more than a year of negotiations, which culminated on Aug. 17, 1982, with the publication of a joint Sino-U.S. communiqué. In this document the U.S. pledged to gradually reduce its sales of defense weaponry to Taiwan in view of Beijing's "fundamental policy of striving for peaceful reunification" with the island.

Not long after publication of this understanding, the Chinese initiated what may turn out to be a major new phase in their foreign relations by opening talks with the U.S.S.R. designed to explore the possibility of normalizing Sino-Soviet relations. In the era of Chairman Mao unremitting hostility to the Soviets had been almost a touchstone of political virtue, but under Deng Xiaoping's more pragmatic leadership diplomatic efforts to defuse the growing Soviet military threat to China are seen as holding the promise of allowing China to concentrate its scarce resources on economic development. However, China's intention is not to reestablish the Sino-Soviet alliance of the 1950s but to create for itself an independent foreign policy of balance between the two "superpowers." Thus, Hu Yaobang, in his political report to the 12th party congress in September 1982, stressed that "China never attaches itself to any big power or groups of powers." At the same time, PRC propaganda began to criticize *both* the United States and the Soviet Union as "hegemonic" states and stressed China's alignment with the third world of less developed countries.

Whether China, in fact, can pursue a more independent foreign policy will be shaped primarily by actions of the Soviet Union. If the new leadership in Moscow significantly reduces the Soviet military threat to China, the latter can conduct a more balanced foreign policy between the U.S. and the Soviet Union. Conversely, unremitting Soviet pressures on China will sustain Beijing's resistance to Moscow's "hegemonic" actions. Also of importance for the evolution of China's foreign relations will be the future China policy of the United States, which in 1982 was still being pulled between a strategic interest in good relations with the PRC and long-standing ties of friendship, cooperation, and trade with Taiwan.

The Uncertain Future. The death of Mao Zedong marked the onset of a new phase in China's struggle for economic and social development. Given Mao's profound influence over the Chinese people for more than a quarter of a century, it is remarkable that his policies dissipated so rapidly after his death. Deng Xiaoping and China's other contemporary leaders have all but abandoned the chairman's legacy in favour of policies of bureaucratic pragmatism, and these must now be tested against several intractable realities.

Four problem areas will have particular influence on this new phase in China's struggle for modernization. First, Deng Xiaoping's efforts to rejuvenate the Communist Party with a technically competent younger generation will face resistance from the aged, the radical, and the reactionary among the party membership. Further leadership feuding could seriously disrupt the country's development efforts, as it has so often in the past.

Second, current attempts to reestablish centralized planning and the bureaucratic management of the Chinese economy will once again expose the country to the stifling weight of the state bureaucracy, something that Mao fought against during much of his life. As is attested to by the sluggishness of the Soviet economy, the bureaucratic control of an economic system of continental size can be as stultifying as political turmoil can be disruptive. Only the future will tell if the Chinese can find the means to establish an effective balance between centralized planning and managerial initiative given to industrial enterprises and farm families.

The third problem area involves the new generation of scientific and managerial talent that has been trained abroad since Mao's death. This is a valuable human resource that compensates only in part for the destruction of China's educational system during the Cultural Revolution. Many times in China's past, however, a xenophobic reaction to foreign ways has led to the rejection of those trained abroad. If the Chinese fail to use effectively their newly trained talent, they are likely to pay a great cost in terms of the pace of modernization.

Finally, and most profoundly, China's economic progress and political stability will be hostage to the effectiveness with which population growth can be restrained while the technical modernization of agriculture and industry is promoted. The Chinese people today seem cynical of ideology and distrustful of Communist Party rule after so many years of political turmoil, and they are likely to measure their contemporary leaders according to how rapidly their living standard improves rather than in terms of the promotion of "class struggle," as characterized the era of Mao Zedong.

ARTICLES FROM THE 1983 PRINTING OF THE BRITANNICA

Once it was possible to transmit information instantly only when the informer and informee were face-to-face or, at least, within sight of one another. Improvements were made with the coming of the telephone and telegraph (and the attendant chore of laying wires) and with the development of wireless communications--radio and telegraph.

Then, nearly half a century after a science-fiction writer wrote about them, man-made satellites were fired into orbit around the Earth to serve as reflectors or retransmitters of electronic information. Today, no spot on the planet is out of sight of one of these communications satellites and, providing that proper receiving equipment is available, no spot is out of reach of another.

The revised article Satellite Communication in the 1983 Britannica traces the history and technology of this modern marvel from the first signals bounced off the Moon in the 1950s and the giant Echo balloon satellites a few years later, through such early Earth-launched "switchboards in the sky" as Telstar, Syncom, and Early Bird, to the placing of a communications satellite directly into orbit from the space shuttle "Columbia" in 1982.

The story of communicating via the heavens is fast-breaking and difficult to keep up with. However, the new Britannica article will help the inquisitive reader keep newly announced wonders concerning this field in perspective with what has gone before.

Satellite Communication

Satellite communication, the use of man-made satellites travelling in Earth orbits to provide communication links between various points on Earth, is the most important nonmilitary exploitation of space technology. Communication satellites permit the exchange of live television programs between nations and continents. International telephone and data services are provided through Earth stations located in more than 100 countries, and a number of other satellite systems provide regional and domestic service, as well as communication with ships. The technique basically involves transmitting signals from an Earth station to an orbiting satellite. The equipment aboard the satellite receives these signals, amplifies them, and transmits them to a region of the Earth. Any station within this region can pick up the signals, thus providing a communication link.

The International Telecommunications Satellite Organization, usually referred to as Intelsat, is responsible for all international nonmilitary satellite communication outside the Soviet bloc. Intelsat also provides domestic service in a number of countries. A government-regulated private corporation known as the Communications Satellite Corporation (Comsat) is the U.S. member of Intelsat. An organization called Intersputnik manages satellite communication within the Soviet bloc.

Satellites provide communication circuits between widely separated locations via microwaves. To transmit television and telephone signals between population centres requires high-capacity circuits. Over land such circuits can be provided in many ways, including pairs of wires, coaxial cables, waveguides, optical fibres, and microwave radio relay systems. Improved submarine cables can carry thousands of telephone signals across oceans, but satellites can provide even greater capacity, in many cases at less cost per channel. Moreover, a satellite system can be put into service quickly, for it does not require the laying of wires or cables from one point to another or, as does a ground microwave system, the construction of intermediate relay or repeater stations. Once a satellite has been launched, communication between two points can be established merely by constructing two Earth stations, and one satellite can serve many stations.

Microwaves are very short radio waves, of wavelengths ranging from 10 centimetres to one centimetre (four inches to $^2/_5$ inch). This corresponds to a frequency range of from three to 30 gigahertz ([GHz]; a gigahertz is 1,000,000,000 [10^9] hertz [Hz], or cycles per second). Microwaves are launched from and received by parabolic (bowl-shaped) antennas. The waves diverge along straight lines in narrow beams; microwave repeaters or amplifiers, therefore, must be located within line of sight of one another. On land this can be achieved by using towers and hilltop locations, but transoceanic microwave systems were impossible until the stationing of satellites in the sky.

The width of a beam of microwaves is proportional to the ratio of the wavelength of the microwaves to the diameter of the antenna. Thus, a small antenna on a satellite will receive from or transmit to the part of the Earth that is visible from the satellite, nearly a complete hemisphere, while a larger antenna will receive from and transmit to a more limited region of the Earth's surface. Similarly, a large antenna at an Earth station will transmit to and receive from only the satellite to which it is pointed and not from other nearby satellites.

HISTORY

Rockets were first seriously considered as a means for sending humans through space by the Russian scientist Konstantin E. Tsiolkovsky and the U.S. scientist Robert H. Goddard early in the 20th century. The use of unmanned space vehicles has been appreciated only since World War II, when German V-2 rockets were used in air assaults on London. Although early proposals envisioned manned satellites, the great success of satellite communication has been achieved by the use of highly reliable unmanned satellites.

The theoretical stage. The idea of radio transmission through space is at least as old as the space novel *Ralph 124C41+* (1911), by the U.S. science fiction pioneer Hugo Gernsback. Yet the idea of a radio repeater located in space was slow to develop. In October 1942 the U.S. science fiction writer George O. Smith published the story "QRM Interplanetary" in the magazine *Astounding Science-Fiction*. Smith's "Venus Equilateral" radio repeater, that was located in a position equidistant from Venus and the Sun, was used to relay signals between Venus and the Earth.

In 1945 the British author-scientist Arthur C. Clarke proposed the use of an Earth satellite for radio communication between, and radio broadcast to, points widely removed on the surface of the Earth. Clarke assumed a manned space station with living quarters for a crew, built of materials flown up by rockets. The station would be positioned at an altitude of about 35,900 kilometres (22,300 miles) so that its period of revolution about the Earth would be the same as the period of the Earth's rotation. This synchronous satellite, which would always appear in the same place in the sky, would be provided with receiving and transmitting equipment and directional antennas to beam signals to all or parts of the visible portion of the Earth. Clarke suggested the use of solar power, either a steam engine operated by solar heat or photoelectric devices. Three such space stations would provide broadcast to or communication among all locations on Earth except for the most remote regions of the Arctic.

Early satellites. The first satellite communication experiment was the U.S. government's Project SCORE (Signal Communication by Orbiting Relay Equipment), which launched a satellite on December 18, 1958. This satellite circled the Earth in an elliptical orbit, with a 180-kilometre perigee, its closest point to Earth, and an apogee, its greatest distance from Earth, of 1,490 kilometres. The satellite operated in a real-time (immediate) and a delayed-repeater mode, in which messages were recorded on magnetic tape and retransmitted. SCORE functioned for 13 days, until its batteries ran down. It reentered the atmosphere and was destroyed on January 21, 1959.

Echo 1, a balloon 30 metres (100 feet) in diameter, made of a plastic called Mylar and coated with a thin layer of aluminum, was launched on August 12, 1960. The satellite was placed in an almost exactly circular orbit at an altitude of 1,600 kilometres and an inclination of 47.3°. The satellite stemmed from two sources: the construction of such a balloon by the U.S. engineer William J. O'Sullivan as a means for measuring the atmospheric density in a 1,600-kilometre orbit and from Pierce's proposal for a passive satellite in his 1955 article.

Communications tests carried out by reflecting radio signals from Echo 1's surface were completely successful. The first transmissions were made between terminals built on the East and West coasts of the United States. Bell Telephone Laboratories built a terminal in New Jersey, the U.S. National Aeronautics and Space Administration (NASA) paying for its use. A terminal on the West Coast was built at Goldstone, California, by NASA's Jet Propulsion Laboratory. Echo 1 was used for experimental telephone, data, and facsimile transmission. Signals from Echo 1 were detected in Europe, but no messages were transmitted across the ocean. Echo 1 remained in orbit for almost eight years and was a conspicuous object in the night sky. Echo 2, launched in 1964, remained in orbit for five years.

Margin notes:
Early plan for a manned space station

Project SCORE

Echo 1

Echo 1 stimulated a great deal of interest in the development of active satellite communication and led American Telephone and Telegraph Company (AT&T) to build Telstar, launched on July 10, 1962. Telstar was an active satellite with a microwave receiver and transmitter. It was the first satellite to transmit live television and telephone conversations across the Atlantic, which it did on an experimental basis. Telstar was turned off on February 21, 1963. A second Telstar satellite was launched on May 7, 1963 and operated for about two years.

Syncom 2, the first synchronous communication satellite, was launched on July 26, 1963. This simple but effective satellite was conceived by Harold A. Rosen of Hughes Aircraft Company. The satellite weighed only 39 kilograms (86 pounds); its light weight made insertion into a synchronous orbit possible with the small boosters available at the time. The satellite performed well.

Syncom 3, launched on August 19, 1964, relayed the first sustained transpacific television picture from the the Olympic Games in Tokyo. The first commercial communication satellite, Intelsat 1 (Early Bird), launched on April 6, 1965, was a modified version of Syncom.

Other early experiments. In the early days of satellite communication it was not clear what techniques would prove to be practical or useful, and many were proposed and tested. The very earliest communication by means of a satellite made use of signals reflected from the Moon. As early as 1954 the U.S. Naval Research Laboratory transmitted voice messages in this way, and a naval communications link was established between Washington, D.C., and Hawaii in 1960. The goal of the West Ford project, which originated in 1958, was communication by reflection from a cloud of wires that had been launched into orbit; 20 kilograms of wires were put into a 3,000-kilometre orbit in May 1963. Measurements were made of microwave signals reflected from them, but there was little further development of the project.

The success of Echo decided the issue in favour of man-made satellites, and the success of Telstar in favour of active satellites. The success of Syncom led to the universal use of active synchronous satellites for communication.

Margin notes:
Telstar

First synchronous satellite

SATELLITE AS A RADIO REPEATER

A typical communication satellite has a number of transponders, or repeaters, each providing a channel of information. Each transponder consists of a receiver tuned to a channel, or range, of frequencies lying in the uplink (receive) band of frequencies; a frequency shifter to lower the received microwaves to a downlink (transmit) range of frequencies; and a power amplifier to produce an adequate microwave output power. The number of transponders, or channels, indicates the communication capacity of a satellite. Typically, one channel (a half-circuit) can carry a colour television signal or 1,200 telephone voice signals in one direction.

Margin note:
Satellite capability

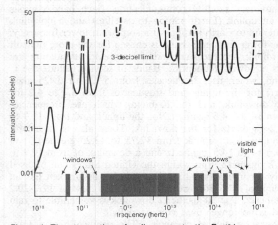

Figure 1: The attenuation of radio waves by the Earth's atmosphere as a function of frequency for an Earth-to-space signal. The chart assumes that the waves originate in clear weather at a high and dry location on the Earth and are directed upward toward space within 45° of vertical (see text).

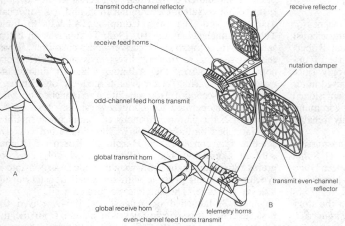

transmit odd-channel reflector

receive reflector

receive feed horns

nutation damper

odd-channel feed horns transmit

global transmit horn

transmit even-channel reflector

A

global receive horn

telemetry horns

B

even-channel feed horns transmit

Figure 2: *Antennas.*
(A) Cassegrain Earth station antenna. The parabolic dish directs received microwaves to the convex secondary reflector, which in turn reflects the microwaves in a beam through a hole in the centre of the dish, where they are collected and sent to the receiver. (B) Antennas of the Intelsat 4A satellite. The large reflectors are illuminated by complex arrays of small horns so that the microwave beam covers only a portion of the Earth's surface.
By courtesy of Hughes Aircraft Co. Space and Communications Group

Propagation. As shown in Figure 1, electromagnetic waves are attenuated (*i.e.*, lose power) in passing through the ionosphere and the lower atmosphere. In general, an atmospheric attenuation greater than three decibels (dB), corresponding to a loss of half of the transmitted power, is considered excessive. Deliberate attenuation, made by using high microwave frequencies for which atmospheric absorption is great, may be used in communication between military satellites in order to avoid interception of such signals on the ground. For satellite communication with Earth stations, however, only low microwave frequencies are suitable.

Rain also attenuates microwaves. In dealing with rain attenuation, it is useful to consider the attenuation in decibels that is exceeded 0.01 percent of the time, or 52.5 minutes a year. In a region that is neither very dry nor very rainy, the attenuation for this period of time exceeds 43 decibels at 28 gigahertz, 22 decibels at 19 gigahertz, nine decibels at 14 gigahertz, and only one decibel at four gigahertz. In regions where rain attenuation is a serious problem, two Earth stations can be used to communicate with one satellite (diversity), since it is less likely that rainfall will be heavy at both stations simultaneously. Diversity may be desirable at 12 gigahertz in some areas of the world. Except in very dry regions, diversity is necessary for reliable commercial service at 20 gigahertz.

Frequency allocations. Through international agreement, three major frequency bands have been assigned for nonmilitary satellite communication. Each band consists of an uplink (Earth station to satellite) and a downlink (satellite to Earth station) at a somewhat lower frequency. The lower frequency band is chosen for the more difficult downlink because rain and atmospheric attenuation are less at lower frequencies. Bands in service include the C band, which uses frequencies from 5.925 to 6.425 gigahertz for the uplink and frequencies from 3.7 to 4.2 for the downlink, and the K band, which uses frequencies from 14 to 14.5 gigahertz for the uplink and from 11.7 to 12.2 gigahertz for the downlink. There also is an assignment, with an uplink from 12.75 to 13.25 gigahertz and from 14 to 14.5 gigahertz and a downlink of from 10.7 to 11.7 gigahertz, that within the United States can be used only for international service. Another assignment has an uplink of 27.5–30 gigahertz and a downlink of 17.7–20.2 gigahertz. The 20-gigahertz downlink is vulnerable to rain and is no longer used commercially.

Characteristics of channels. The bandwidth of a transponder is commonly 36 megahertz (MHz). Such a channel will transmit about 1,200 telephone signals, each with a bandwidth of 4,000 hertz, or one television signal. The total bandwidth of 1,200 telephone signals is only 4.8

megahertz, and the 36-megahertz channel that is used to transmit these signals has seven and a half times this bandwidth. Either wide-deviation frequency modulation is used in satellite communication, or the telephone signals are transmitted as binary pulses by pulse-code modulation. In either case, the use of a broad band of radio frequencies reduces the transmitter power necessary to attain an adequate signal-to-noise ratio in the overall system.

Path loss and power requirements. The power necessary for satisfactory transmission between a satellite and the Earth depends on the total received power necessary at the input of the Earth-based receiver and on the fraction of the power transmitted from the satellite that is picked up by the Earth station antenna. This fraction is the ratio of the area of the receiving antenna on Earth to the area covered by the microwave beam on the Earth. A standard Earth station antenna, for example, has a diameter of about 30 metres. If the antenna beam from the satellite just covers the Earth, the 30-metre antenna receives about $^4/_{1,000,000,000,000}$ (4×10^{-12}) of the transmitted power, and the received signal is 114 decibels weaker than the transmitted signal. If the antenna beam of the satellite just covers the continental United States, the received power is about 103 decibels weaker than the transmitted power, or about 11 decibels (14 times) stronger than the power received from a satellite whose antenna beam covers the entire Earth. Because the path loss for transmitting between a pair of antennas is the same in either direction, it is also advantageous to use a narrow receiving beam on a satellite. Thus, it can be advantageous to use a satellite with narrow transmitting and receiving beams, pointed only toward those regions with which communication is desired. Advanced satellites, such as Intelsat 5, have global coverage beams for communicating with nations that have relatively small amounts of traffic, as well as hemispheric and spot beams for areas of heavy traffic.

In order to get a narrow antenna beam, the antenna on the satellite must have a considerable area. The minimum beam width, measured in radians, that can be attained with an antenna of a given diameter is roughly equal to the wavelength divided by the diameter of the antenna. Thus, for a given beam width the diameter of the antenna must be greater at lower frequencies (longer wavelengths) than at higher frequencies. In order for the antenna beam to cover a limited area on Earth, the antenna on the satellite must be quite large (about 2.5 metres in width in Intelsat 5), and the feed, which directs the transmitted power toward the antenna dish or collects the received power from it, must consist of an array of microwave sources such as feed horns. The relative phases and

Major frequency bands

Types of beams

amplitudes of the signals going to the feed horns determine the area of the Earth covered by the antenna beam. This area can be shifted by changing the phases of the signals to the feed horns, either mechanically or electronically. If the phases are shifted electronically, the beam can be made to scan, or hop, from one point to another. By dividing signals among the feed horns it is possible to produce several simultaneous beams aimed at different spots on the Earth. Figure 2 indicates the general configuration of some microwave antennas used for Earth stations and satellites.

The power that must be received at an Earth station for satisfactory operation of a communication satellite channel is proportional to the required ratio of the carrier (received power) to the noise. In normal operation the carrier-to-noise ratio is about 13 to 20 decibels. Signals can be received with some degradation in quality with a carrier-to-noise ratio as low as six or seven decibels, so the design carrier-to-noise ratio provides some protection against rain attenuation or other loss of signal strength.

Some noise in the receiver can be Johnson, or thermal, noise from rain; thermal noise from space is negligible unless the antenna is pointed at the Sun. Part of the noise comes from the receiver itself. Because Johnson noise is proportional to temperature in kelvins (K; $-273.15°$ C), the noisiness of a receiver is specified by a noise temperature T, such that Johnson noise for temperature T added at the input of the receiver doubles the observed output noise. Thus, in the absence of rain noise, power is proportional to the receiver noise temperature T. It is also proportional to the bandwidth, which for a satellite channel is about 36 megahertz (the noise power is $N = kTB$ watts, where B is the bandwidth in hertz and k is the Boltzmann constant $[k = 1.38062 \times 10^{-23}$ joule per degree]). The received power per channel is typically about 126 decibels less than a watt (2.5×10^{-13} watt).

The power received at an Earth station depends on the power transmitted by the satellite (usually from five to 10 watts per transponder), on the area of the Earth's surface covered by the satellite's transmitting beam, and on the area of the Earth station antenna. The gain G of an antenna is related to its area, being proportional to the area divided by the square of the wavelength. The "figure of merit" of an Earth station receiving system is defined as the ratio G/T, the ratio of antenna gain to receiver noise temperature. This ratio may be expressed in decibels. A typical Earth receiver noise temperature is 50 kelvins, and a typical antenna gain is 60 decibels, giving a figure of merit of 20,000, or 43 decibels.

The transmitter power on a satellite is limited by considerations of weight and life; it is important, therefore, that Earth stations have antennas with large areas and that they have low-noise receivers. It is of little use to provide the receiver on a satellite with low-noise receivers because noise at between 200 and 300 kelvins is received from the Earth. Large Earth station antennas can be used for transmitting to satellites as well as receiving from them, and high powers can be used in transmitting (about three kilowatts [kW] for all channels combined).

Limitations. The maximum amount of communication available from satellites is limited by the number and bandwidth of frequency assignments and by other considerations. For a given bandwidth the amount of communication can be increased several ways. Sending independent signals on two polarizations doubles the communication capacity. The first use of two polarizations was on the domestic satellites Satcom, launched on December 12, 1975, and Comstar, launched on May 13, 1976. In addition, using narrow beams from satellites to various regions of the Earth allows reuse of the same frequencies.

The more satellites that can be used simultaneously in synchronous orbit, the greater the total communication capacity. Larger, and hence more directive, Earth station antennas allow the simultaneous use of more satellites. Some Intelsat satellites are spaced as closely as 3° from other satellites. Satellites spaced as far as 14° apart can interfere, however, if small Earth station antennas and correspondingly high powers are used. The U.S. Federal Communications Commission (FCC) has proposed that

domestic satellites be spaced 2° apart, even though this spacing is considered too close by some experts.

SATELLITE TECHNOLOGY

Communication satellites are put into orbit by means of rocket launch vehicles, or boosters. During insertion into orbit, control is maintained partly by inertial guidance, using gyroscopes and accelerometers, and partly by microwave radar observations, by means of which the position and velocity of the vehicle is determined and commands are given for correcting the orbit.

Launch sequence. Satellites are put into synchronous orbits in the plane of the Equator from sites that do not lie on the Equator. This requires adjusting the plane of the orbit during or after the initial launch phase. The first, or boost, stage lifts the satellite out of the atmosphere and gives it considerable velocity. When this stage burns out, it is separated from the satellite and other stages, falls to Earth, and is destroyed as it passes through the atmosphere. The fairing, which protects the payload (the satellite and associated final stages) as it passes through the atmosphere, is jettisoned. The second stage is then fired, putting the satellite into an intermediate orbit. After the second stage is jettisoned, it remains in orbit for some time. The perigee stage is then fired and ejected; this puts the satellite in an inclined elliptical orbit, an orbit whose apogee is at synchronous altitude (35,900 kilometres above the surface of the Earth). While the satellite is in this transfer orbit, tests are performed, and the satellite is positioned for the firing of the apogee motor, which is commonly built into the body of the satellite. (The Titan IIIC transtage can eject into synchronous orbit, so that no apogee motor is needed.) At the apogee of the transfer orbit, the apogee motor is fired, which puts the satellite in a circular synchronous orbit. Satellite antennas and the solar panels can then be extended and the satellite put into its final physical configuration.

The orbit at this point will not be exactly right, nor will the satellite have the correct attitude (point in the right direction). Throughout the life of the satellite the attitude must be controlled and the station kept (the orbit adjusted), because irregularities in the gravitational fields of the Earth, Sun, and Moon—as well as the pressures of light from the Sun and of the solar wind—tend to change the attitude and station.

Launch vehicles. Advances in satellite communication have been made possible by the development of powerful boosters that can launch heavier satellites. In the early 1960s Syncom was launched by a Delta vehicle, which at that time was just able to insert the 39-kilogram satellite into a synchronous orbit. By the 1980s the Delta vehicle could launch a satellite such as the 550-kilogram SBS (Satellite Business System). Heavier satellites, such as Intelsat 5, which weighs almost 2,000 kilograms, can be launched with the Atlas-Centaur. Military satellites have been launched with these vehicles, and several at a time have been launched with the more powerful Titan IIIC.

Figure 3 shows the relative sizes of various launch vehicles. All of the launch vehicles used through the early 1980s—the Delta, Atlas-Centaur, and Titan—have been refinements and developments of military ballistic missiles—the Thor, Atlas, and Titan, respectively. The Japanese N launch, in some ways similar to the U.S. Delta, is a civilian vehicle. The French Ariane, which has made several successful flights, is a civilian vehicle with capabilities somewhat greater than the Delta or Atlas-Centaur; in its most powerful configuration it should be capable of launching two communication satellites, and a number of commitments have been made to use the Ariane to launch commercial satellites. The U.S. STS (Space Transportation System), or space shuttle, is a manned vehicle; the manned portion is recoverable through a gliding landing on an airfield, and the solid rocket shells through descent into the ocean by parachute. The space shuttle itself can put a payload consisting of several satellites into a low Earth orbit. Propulsion such as the Inertial Upper Stage (IUS), under development in the early 1980s, or propulsion incorporated in the satellite itself is necessary for insertion into synchronous orbit. The first use of the space shuttle

Thermal noise (margin note)

Control of attitude and station (margin note)

The reusable U.S. space shuttle (margin note)

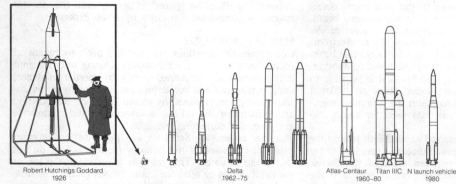

Figure 3: Relative sizes of launch vehicles.
From Harold A. Rosen, *Hughes Aircraft Space Telecommunication;* used with permission from Hughes Aircraft Co. Space and Communications Group

for commercial satellite communication was scheduled for late 1982, with the launching of both an SBS and a Canadian Anik satellite.

The space shuttle is designed to put up to 30,000 kilograms into a low orbit. Manned space shuttle flights might make it possible to assemble or to repair large communication satellites in low Earth orbit. Assembly in orbit would be extremely expensive, however, and does not appear to be necessary. Space shuttle plans provide no means for sending astronauts into synchronous orbit, where they would have to go in order to repair communication satellites. In addition, communication satellites have proved to be very long-lived; they tend to become obsolete before they wear out. Repair costs may greatly exceed the cost of launching a new satellite.

Electronic technology. Solar cells are the universal source of electric power in operational communication satellites, although some experimental satellites have used thermoelectric generators heated by radioisotopes. A synchronous satellite, which is eclipsed by the Earth during two 44-day seasons each year, for times as long as 70 minutes, carries secondary batteries to provide power during the eclipse. The power necessary for the operation of a communication satellite is considerable; the solar cells of Intelsat 4A, for example, provide 600 watts.

The most common source of microwave power for transmitting signals from communication satellites is the traveling-wave tube. Transistors have been used in some transmitters, but by the early 1980s they were not as efficient for microwave frequencies as were traveling-wave tubes. Linearity is another consideration when signals from Earth stations must be transmitted through the same transponder. As improvements are made, the transistor or some other solid-state amplifier may eventually replace the traveling-wave tube, the last vacuum tube used in communication satellites.

As noted, it is important to have a low-noise receiver at an Earth station in order to reduce the signal power that must be transmitted from the satellite. In some early satellite experiments a very low-noise microwave amplifier, called a maser, was used. The maser is expensive, for it must operate at the temperature of liquid helium, only slightly above absolute zero. The signal received from a satellite is weakest during a rainstorm. Unfortunately, during a rainstorm a considerable amount of Johnson noise is received, corresponding to a temperature of more than 200 kelvins. For this reason there is little advantage in using a receiver with a noise temperature below the 50 kelvins that can be attained with a parametric amplifier. Thus, parametric amplifiers rather than masers are used even in large and costly Earth stations.

Almost all electronic functions in satellites are carried out by means of solid-state devices, especially transistors, which are used to generate and amplify signals and to operate various control functions. LSI and VLSI (large-scale integration and very large-scale integration) circuits, in which many complex on–off or digital functions are performed by a silicon chip about 0.4 square centimetre (1/16 square inch) in size, have come to play an increasingly important part in satellite communication.

Although satellites use both wide-deviation frequency modulation (FM) and digital transmission of voice by pulse-code modulation in order to conserve power and reduce interference, the trend is toward digital transmission. In part this is a general trend in all voice communication, in switching as well as in transmission. Digital transmission also is more efficient than FM when more than one Earth station uses the same satellite repeater. If several FM signals are sent through one repeater, the transponder must operate at a reduced power level in order to reduce nonlinearities that cause one signal to interfere with the others. In digital transmissions Earth stations can be assigned different, short repetitive time intervals for their transmissions (time-division multiplex), and the repeater can operate at full power.

SATELLITE SYSTEMS

Several satellites of the same or of different designs used in communicating among a group of Earth stations form a satellite communication system. A system may provide international communication, as does the Intelsat system, or both international and domestic communication; the Soviet Intersputnik organization provides communication within the Soviet Union and among countries of the Soviet bloc. Other satellite systems provide regional or domestic communication. Some systems, such as the Marisat and Marecs and a number of military satellites, provide mobile communication, primarily to ships. Other satellites serve military uses only. Several experimental satellites have been launched, and there are some satellites reserved for use by amateur radio operators.

Intelsat. The first use of communication satellites was to provide international communication. When the U.S. Congress passed the Communications Satellite Act in 1962, creating Comsat and giving it a U.S. monopoly on international satellite communication, no clear provision was made for the supplying of other forms of satellite service.

International satellite communication required the participation of other nations. Intelsat originated as a joint venture in August 1964, when 11 countries signed agreements to form a global communication system. It has become an international legal entity, which by 1980 had an owner's investment of about $672,000,000, and in which more than 100 countries held investment shares. Comsat is the designated U.S. participant in Intelsat, which is responsible for the design, development, and maintenance of the space segment of the global telecommunication system. Earth stations used for international communication are owned and operated by entities in the countries in which they are located.

Nations that are not members of Intelsat, including those that cannot join because they are not recognized by the United Nations, can obtain satellite communication through Comsat General, a domestic subsidiary of Comsat. An example is Taiwan, which has a large international telecommunications traffic.

By the 1980s the Intelsat system included about 400 Earth stations with some 500 antennas, located in about 150 countries. By 1980 Intelsat was providing about

The international communication system

20,000 two-way telephone circuits that were leased full time and a great deal of television and other transmission.

By 1981 Intelsat had successfully launched 24 satellites, of which eight were either primary (serving all countries) or major (serving a few countries with heavy traffic), or were providing leased transponders; three satellites were available for limited use or for contingencies. The advance in satellite communication has been outstanding. Intelsat 1, launched in 1965, has one transponder, which provides 240 two-way telephone circuits or one television channel. Intelsat 5, launched in 1980, provides 12,000 telephone circuits and two television channels. Intelsat 1 operates in the 6/4-gigahertz band only. In Intelsat 5 the 6/4-gigahertz frequencies are used four times, and the 14/11-gigahertz frequencies are used twice. Intelsat 5 also has six communication antennas: two global-coverage beams, two hemispheric beams, and two steerable spot beams. The specifications for additional Intelsat satellites provide for even greater capabilities.

The reduction in rates for satellite communication also has been remarkable. The annual charge for satellite use per telephone circuit dropped from $64,000 in 1965 to $9,360 in 1981.

Soviet satellites. There are two major types of Soviet satellites. The Molniya satellites, first launched in 1965, are placed in elliptical orbits with a 65° inclination. At this angle the perigee moves very slowly, and the apogee remains in the Northern Hemisphere. Under suitable conditions, the angular velocity near apogee roughly matches the angular velocity of the Earth, and the satellite appears almost stationary in the sky. The satellite is positioned over the Soviet Union every other revolution for about eight hours. Due to its inclination, the Molniya satellite is visible in the most northerly regions of the Soviet Union, where a synchronous satellite would be below the horizon. The second type of Soviet communication satellite is the Statsionar. It is a synchronous satellite and was first launched in 1975.

By the end of 1979, 75 Molniya satellites had been launched, of which 28 were known to be out of service. Only one of the 14 synchronous satellites launched was no longer operating. Technical details of Soviet satellites are known only in part. Their communication capacity appears to be less than that of Intelsat satellites.

Domestic systems. Some domestic satellite systems have been established because the communication they provide would be difficult to obtain in any other way. Canada's Telesat system provides communication to the sparsely populated regions of the Northwest Territories as well as to the nation's urban areas. Indonesia's Palapa system provides communication among many islands that would be hard to link otherwise.

Domestic satellite systems in the United States add communication capacity to a range of other communication channels. Such satellite service has several advantages. In the distribution of programs for cable television the same signal must be sent simultaneously to stations in many parts of the country. The transmission of plates from which newspapers and magazines can be printed simultaneously in many locations is a similar application. Satellites can provide many additional long-distance circuits more quickly than laying cables or building ground microwave systems. Once in place, a satellite system can be used to supplement other long-haul facilities when they become overloaded because of regional changes in traffic or because of disasters. The SBS, for example, provides large industries with private networks in which the Earth station is on company premises, thus avoiding the use of cables or ground microwave systems to link the networks to communication facilities.

Canada. Canada's Telesat system uses satellites, called Anik, built by U.S. companies. Three Anik A satellites were in service by the early 1980s; the first was launched in 1972. They have antennas with beams that cover Canada and have 12 transponders. One Anik B satellite, launched in 1978, has 12 transponders in the 6/4-gigahertz band that cover all of Canada and six transponders in the 14/12-gigahertz band that serve a fourth of the nation. Advanced Anik satellites have been designed.

Indonesia. The first two satellites of Palapa A, Indonesia's satellite system, were launched in 1976 and 1977. They are of the Anik A type, and the antenna beams cover some 3,000 islands. The larger and more powerful Palapa B system is designed to use both polarizations and to have 24 transponders.

United States. The United States has the greatest number of domestic satellites. Western Union launched two Westar satellites in 1974 and one in 1979. These operate in the 6/4-gigahertz band and have 12 transponders. The antennas cover the conterminous United States and, with less power, Alaska and Hawaii. Plans have been made for a TDRSS, or Advanced Westar, satellite (TDRSS stands for Tracking and Data Relay Satellite to Satellite) to be used for domestic communication and for picking up signals from various spacecraft and relaying them to Earth. Launch of this satellite is possible only with the space shuttle.

RCA launched Satcom satellites in 1975, 1976, and 1981. These operate in the 6/4-gigahertz band, use both polarizations, and have 24 transponders. Half of the transponders are used in conjunction with separate antennas so that they cover Hawaii as well as the rest of the United States; the other transponders cannot be used for traffic with Hawaii.

Four Comstar satellites were in service by the early 1980s; the first was launched in 1976. They are Comsat General satellites, but their entire communication capacity is leased by AT&T. The satellites operate in the 6/4-gigahertz band and use both polarizations to provide 24 transponders. Communication is provided within all of the United States, including Alaska, Hawaii, and Puerto Rico. In 1981 AT&T ordered three advanced communication satellites, called Telstar 3, which can operate in a higher frequency and have an increased life expectancy of 10 years, instead of the average seven years.

Maritime communication. In general, mobile satellite communication is difficult because of the problem of placing microwave antennas on vehicles. Some narrowband communication can be provided by ultrahigh frequency (UHF) using essentially nondirectional antennas, but the amount is limited. In contrast to automobiles and airplanes, ships are suitable platforms for microwave antennas of moderate size; the first commercial mobile service was to ships.

The Marisat system, developed by Comsat General, began serving both the U.S. Navy and commercial shipping in 1976. Three satellites were launched, operating in three frequency ranges. The UHF capability, in the 300/250-megahertz band, was leased by the U.S. Navy for five years. Commercial maritime traffic is carried in the 1.6/1.5-gigahertz range. The 6/4-gigahertz range is used for commercial communication links between satellites and Earth stations on both coasts of the United States. Each satellite provides 16 voice and 88 telex channels in the high-power mode (60 watts transmitter power), eight voice and 44 telex channels in the medium-power mode (27 watts), and one voice and 44 telex channels in the low-power mode (seven watts). By 1980 ships flying the flags of more than 35 nations were using Marisat, and more than 460 shipboard terminals had been commissioned for operation with the satellites.

Inmarsat (International Maritime Satellite Organization) was established in July 1979; Comsat was designated the U.S. participant. Marecs, the first Inmarsat satellite, was launched in 1981 from French Guiana, using an Ariane vehicle. Marecs are designed to communicate between shore and satellite in the 6/4-gigahertz band and between ship and satellite in the 1.6/1.5-gigahertz band.

Military satellites. In 1960 ARPA (Advanced Research Projects Agency of the U.S. Department of Defense) proposed an elaborate military communication satellite called Advent. The satellite proved far beyond the state of the art and was abandoned in 1962. In June 1965 the Department of Defense directed the U.S. Air Force to launch simple near-synchronous satellites in equatorial orbits. Some 26 of these IDCSP (Initial Defense Communication Satellite Program, later renamed Initial Defense Satellite Communication System [IDSCS]) satellites were launched from 1966 to 1968, usually eight at a time, using the Titan IIIC vehicle. Although these satellites provided useful communication, they were soon outdated.

By the early 1980s the major U.S. military communication satellites were the DSCS 2 and FLTSATCOM satellites. The DSCS 2 satellite, of which 10 had been successfully launched by 1981, is a spinning satellite with both global coverage and spot beam antennas. It has a capacity of 1,300 two-way voice circuits. The uplink frequency band ranges from 7.9 to 8.4 gigahertz; the downlink varies from 7.25 to 7.75 gigahertz. The FLTSATCOM satellite began operation in 1978, and by 1981 five had been launched. Each satellite provides high-frequency communication between military forces through more than 20 channels.

The initial requirement of U.S. military satellites was that they provide adequate and reliable communication. The armed forces have become more and more dependent on satellite communication for both strategic and tactical use, but it had become increasingly apparent by the 1980s that existing military satellites would be vulnerable in a number of ways during a war: to jamming by high-power ground-based jammers; to destruction of ground facilities that are used in connection with satellite station keeping and internal operation; to high-altitude nuclear explosions, whose electromagnetic fields and radiation could destroy or cause errors in the operation of satellite electronic equipment; and, finally, to enemy antisatellite weapons. In the future military communication satellite systems will diverge increasingly from commercial systems in several respects.

New, more survivable military satellites will utilize broad bandwidths to transmit comparatively small amounts of teletypewriter and coded voice communication, which works against jamming and allows operation with relatively small Earth antennas. Multiple steerable satellite antenna transmitting and receiving beams also will be helpful in both respects. Electronic equipment that is carried aboard the satellites will be both shielded against electromagnetic radiation and made to withstand radiation. Satellites will be made more autonomous; that is, their operations will be made to depend less on control from Earth. Some protection will be provided against direct attack. It is believed that such a military satellite system can provide vital communication to small land-, ship-, and aircraft-based terminals even during major hostilities.

IDSCP satellites were used to provide early communication for the North Atlantic Treaty Organization (NATO). Two NATO satellites were launched in 1971 and 1972, and three NATO 3 satellites were launched in 1976, 1977, and 1978. The NATO 2 satellites are spinning satellites, with an antenna coverage optimized for NATO use. The up-band is 7.976–8.005 gigahertz, and the down-band is 7.257–7.286 gigahertz. The NATO 3 satellite has one global beam antenna and one spot beam antenna for Europe; it operates in about the same frequency band as NATO 2. Skynet 1 and 2 are British satellites. They were launched in 1969 and 1974 and are similar to DSCS 2.

The United States has planned two chief military satellites: DSCS 3 and LEASAT. The communication capacity of DSCS 3 is with a 7.9–8.4-gigahertz uplink and a 7.25–7.75-gigahertz downlink. A channel with a 300–400-megahertz uplink and a 225–260-megahertz downlink is designed for communication with UHF equipment. LEASAT, to be built and operated by Hughes Aircraft Company and leased for military use, is designed for launch from the space shuttle to provide UHF communication.

Amateur satellites. From 1961 to 1978 the United States successfully launched eight OSCAR (Orbiting Satellite Carrying Amateur Radio) satellites for the use of amateur radio operators; by 1980 five remained. OSCAR 7 has two channels: a 145.85–145.95-megahertz uplink with a 29.40–29.50-megahertz downlink and a 432.125–432.175-megahertz uplink with a 145.925–145.975-megahertz downlink. In 1978 the Soviet Union launched two RS satellites for amateur use.

Experimental satellites. In addition to early experimental satellites such as Echo, Telstar, and Syncom, a large

number of other experimental satellites have been launched. NASA launched a series of ATS's (Applications Technology Satellite) that were used mainly to explore various technological features and to gather data on microwave propagation. The last satellite in the series, ATS 6, was used in an experiment in India for direct broadcasting of educational programs to receiving equipment in numerous villages.

There were several joint ventures in the mid-1970s. Two French–German Symphonie satellites were launched in 1974 and 1975. These three-axis stabilized satellites have global and spot beams in the 6/4-gigahertz band and four transponders. The CTS (Communications Technology Satellite), or Hermis, a U.S.–Canadian experimental satellite launched in 1976, operates in the 14/11-gigahertz band. It has a high-power (200 watts) transmitter for use with small Earth stations, as well as a transmitter of moderate power. Among other options, it can transmit FM television with up to three simultaneous channels.

Other programs include the Italian Sirio, launched in 1977, with beams that cover Europe. The European Space Agency's OTS (Orbital Test Satellite), a three-axis satellite, was launched in 1978. It operates in the 14/12-gigahertz band, uses dual polarization, two European spot beams, and six repeaters of various bandwidth.

Japan had two major experimental programs by the late 1970s. The CS, or Sakura satellite, launched in 1977, has six repeaters in the 30/20-gigahertz band and two repeaters in the 20/18-gigahertz band. The BSE (Medium-Scale Broadcasting Satellite for Experimental Purposes), or Yuri satellite, was launched in 1978 and operates in the 14/12-gigahertz range. It can transmit two FM high-power (100 watts) colour television signals to Japan for experimental broadcasting to homes.

Disadvantages and prospects. Satellites cannot provide separate circuits to individual homes and offices, as can telephone wires, cables, and optical fibres. Although the SBS can link various corporate locations, wires, cables, or fibres must connect individual users to the Earth station. Thus cables compete successfully with satellites between Europe and the United States, and cables with optical fibres are expected to perform even more successfully. The amount of communication that satellites can provide is limited further by the number of orbital positions and the frequencies available.

Although it was suggested early in the history of satellite communication, the advantages of direct broadcasting of television signals from satellites to individual users has been questioned. The U.S. experimental Intelsat 4 (1974) was used for a time by India to broadcast educational programs to villages. The joint U.S.-Canadian CTS satellite (1976) had a transmitter powerful enough to transmit television signals to small Earth stations. The Japanese Yuri satellite (1978) was capable of transmitting television signals to small rooftop antennas, but part of the motivation for doing this was a law that required television service to all parts of Japan, a country with regions where cable is uneconomical and reception from Earth-based transmitters impractical. In the United States, by the early 1980s, a number of people had erected antennas to pick up cable and network television programs relayed by satellite. One satellite alone relayed 24 channels, but tens of channels were available from other satellites.

The practicality of commercial direct-to-user satellite television service should be settled in the 1980s. Comsat has announced plans to initiate such service early in 1986. It would begin with a satellite providing three television channels to the most densely populated Eastern states. Ultimately, four satellites would cover the U.S. time zones. The satellites would operate in the 12/14-gigahertz band, and the transmitters would be powerful enough to allow reception with a small rooftop antenna.

BIBLIOGRAPHY. J.R. PIERCE, *The Beginnings of Satellite Communications* (1968); MARTIN P. BROWN, JR. (ed.), *Compendium of Communication and Broadcast Satellites 1958 to 1980* (1981); COMMUNICATION SATELLITE CORPORATION, *Report to the President and Congress* (annual), and *COMSAT Guide to the Intelsat, Marisat, and Comstar Satellite Systems* (1981).

(JOHN R. PIERCE)

Direct television broadcasts

The past is unchanged and unchangeable, an axiom brought home at one time or an-other to everyone who wishes a hasty word or an ill-advised action could be called back. However, our perception of the past can easily change as scientists and histori-ans uncover new evidence about a subject or develop new techniques for investigat-ing it.

When this occurs, as in the case of the Australopithecines (a species that existed from about 8,000,000 to 1,500,000 years ago in Africa and which may well constitute an intermediate stage of development between ape and man), encyclopaedists must reconsider their presentation of the subject.

Thus the Britannica article Australopithecus *had to be changed because the latest word on these ape-like men (or man-like apes) was no longer the latest word. New discoveries, dating techniques, and the inferences drawn from them by anthropolo-gists (who are not always in agreement) had to be brought to the attention of Britan-nica subscribers.*

Information and speculation about family organization, living conditions, hunting skill, diet, and tools are discussed as well as a fascinating alternate theory that the skeletal structure of the Australopithecines indicates that he walked upright, or it might mean something entirely different.

In any event, one must remember that this is not the last word on these creatures that might be our ancestors--only the latest.

Australopithecus

Australopithecus (literally "southern ape") was the generic name given to the first discovered member of a series of fossils of creatures closely related, if not ancestral, to modern human beings. Since the first discovery—of a child's skull in a cave at Taung, South Africa, in 1924—similar hominid remains have been found at numerous sites in East and southern Africa. The term australopithe-cine is often used to refer to all the fossil hominid material that dates between the end of the Miocene Epoch (about 8,000,000 years ago) and the beginning of the Pleistocene Epoch (around 1,500,000 years ago). Fossil remains that date from before 8,000,000 years ago are widely regarded as those of fossil apes, while evidence of *Homo erectus* ("upright man") dates to 1,500,000 years ago. There are few hominid fossils from the period between 8,000,000 and about 3,500,000 years ago, and little can be said except that their apelike features are less pronounced than those of earlier fossils.

From 3,500,000 to 1,500,000 years ago, the fossil record is much richer and open to varied interpretations of the fossils themselves and of the course of hominid evolution. The fossil evidence of the australopithecines has been seen by some scholars as merely representing temporal stages within a single evolving lineage leading to *Homo erectus*. Others have stressed the extent of the adaptive differences among the various fossils and have suggested that there may have been two, or even three, lineages evolving in parallel, only one of which led to the later species of *Homo*. Whatever the details of their interpretations, however, most hominid paleontologists are agreed that the australopithecines represent a link between the fossil apes and human beings. Thus, study of the australopithecines is regarded as the study of one of the most important stages in the emergence of our own species, *H. sapiens*.

FOSSIL EVIDENCE

Discovery of the main South African cave sites

The South African australopithecines. More than two decades were to elapse between the recognition of the importance of the Taung child's skull by Raymond Dart in 1924 and the next series of discoveries of australopithe-cines in South Africa. These discoveries were made by Robert Broom in 1936 and 1938 as the direct result of mining operations at the caves of Sterkfontein and Krom-draai, many hundreds of miles south of Taung, in the Transvaal. When research activities resumed in earnest in South Africa after World War II, two additional cave

sites were discovered at Swartkrans and Makapansgat. After the early discoveries the rate of recovery of fossils from these hard, breccia-filled cave deposits diminished. During the 1970s, however, there was renewed activity at these sites, and the total number of hominid remains re-covered from southern African caves was well in excess of 1,000 by the early 1980s.

As each series of discoveries was announced, it was usually marked by a new taxonomic classification, or taxon, for the newly found fossils. Scientists are now agreed, however, that the evidence did not justify the multiplicity of taxa that resulted. It is generally accepted that the australopithecine fossils recovered from the South African cave sites belong to either *Australopithecus africanus*, the species usually referred to as the "gracile" australopithecine, or *A. robustus*, the species called the "robust" australopithecine. (Some workers support the recognition of a second species of robust australopithe-cine, at Swartkrans, called *A. crassidens*, but this is a minority view.) The classification into two main species within one genus won the support of Raymond Dart and Sir Wilfred Le Gros Clark, and, with minor modifications, it is the scheme that has come to be supported by the majority of scholars.

Two main species

Features of the gracile australopithecines. The skull of *Australopithecus africanus* has a braincase that is roughly spherical in shape, with the greatest width across the base of the skull. The cranial capacity of the species depends upon which estimates are used; the average value is probably between 450 and 500 cubic centimetres (cc), a capacity just within the range of that of living apes. Brain size is best judged in relation to body size, however, and on this count the gracile australopithecines have a relative brain size intermediate between that of modern apes and that of modern human beings. The area of attachment on the gracile australopithecine skull for the neck muscles is reduced when compared to that of equivalent-sized apes. Although bony crests mark the attachment of the jaw muscles onto the skull, these are not obvious features and, in particular, do not form large midline, or sagittal, crests. The foramen magnum (the area of the skull through which the spinal cord passes) lies nearer the centre of the skull in these fossil hominids than it does in the apes. The face is projecting, but it does not form the marked "muzzle" that is a feature of most modern and fossil ape skulls.

The teeth of the gracile australopithecines are not arranged in the characteristic U-shaped fashion of the apes, but instead lie in a more rounded arcade. The incisor teeth are set vertically in the jaw, and the canines are small and do not project well above the other teeth, which is always the case in the apes. There is no gap, or diastema, between the canines and the premolars, and the upper canines do not form a shearing unit with the first lower premolars. The milk teeth resemble those of the later hominids, and the order of eruption and the rate of maturation of the teeth follow the human pattern more closely than they do that of apes.

There are fewer limb bone fossils than skull remains. Upper limb bones are particularly poorly represented and provide little or no information about manipulative ability, but there are indications from remains of the shoulder that this region of the gracile australopithecine was well adapted for climbing. The remains of the lower limbs and vertebral column provide good evidence for a more or less upright posture and suggest that these creatures walked bipedally in a way that was much more efficient than the occasional bipedal walking observed in apes. An important aspect of this evidence is the low, posteriorly expanded blade of the ilium with the characteristic sciatic notch. The greatly increased width of the pelvic cavity, when compared to that of the apes, allowed for the birth of infants with larger heads and is additional evidence of the increase in relative brain size (see Figure 1). Estimates of stature and body weight are necessarily imprecise, but they suggest that the height of the gracile australopithecines was about 5 feet (1.5 metres) and that they weighed between 55 and 100 pounds (25 and 45 kilograms).

Evidence of upright posture (margin note)

From W. E. Le Gros Clark, *The Fossil Evidence for Human Evolution* (1964); The University of Chicago Press

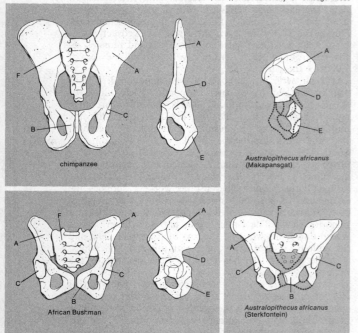

Figure 1: *Front and side views of pelvis.*
(A) Iliac blade. (B) Pubic bone. (C) Acetabulum (hip joint).
(D) Sciatic notch. (E) Ischium. (F) Sacrum.

chimpanzee

Australopithecus africanus
(Makapansgat)

African Bushman

Australopithecus africanus
(Sterkfontein)

Features of the robust australopithecines. The robust australopithecines found at sites in southern Africa share many of the basic features of the gracile group, the main points of difference being in the skull, the teeth and jaws, and, to a lesser extent, the region of the hip joint. The average brain size of the robust australopithecines is a little larger than that of the gracile form. Because estimates of the robust form's body weight are between 10 and 25 percent greater than those of the gracile form's weight, however, the relative brain size of the two species is of the same order. The skulls of the robust australopithecines are more rugged than those of the graciles, the crests that mark the attachment of the jaw and neck mus-

cles are better developed, and the face is flatter and broader.

The dental arcade of the robust sample differs from that of the gracile remains in several ways. The molars of the robust form are larger, and the premolars of the lower jaw tend to develop extra cusps and so to appear more like molar teeth. The anterior teeth of the robust form show no corresponding increase in size; in fact, their average size is smaller than in the graciles. The canines of the robust dentition are conical and more like those of later hominids, while the canines of the graciles are unusually asymmetrical. All of these features, taken with microscopic evidence of tooth wear, suggest that the face of the robust australopithecines had become specialized to increase the tooth area devoted to chewing and to concentrate the power of the jaw muscles on the molar and premolar teeth.

The extent and functional significance of the differences between the pelvic and hip regions of the two types of australopithecines has been vigorously debated. J.T. Robinson has contended that the robust australopithecine pelvis is adapted more for activities that emphasize power, such as climbing, than for length of stride and is thus significantly different from that of the gracile form. He and others have also maintained that the shape of the top end of the femur is distinctive. Many other scholars, however, interpret the fossil evidence as indicating no major differences in the gait of the two types of australopithecines.

The East African australopithecines. *The Olduvai fossils.* The next important series of australopithecine discoveries was made at Olduvai Gorge, Tanzania, by L.S.B. Leakey and Mary Leakey. In 1959 they discovered a well-preserved cranium that showed, in an exaggerated form, many of the features of the robust australopithecines from Swartkrans and Kromdraai. Although the cranium was initially attributed to a new genus and species—*Zinjanthropus boisei*—it was later suggested that the fossil be included as a separate species in *Australopithecus*. The discovery in 1964 of a massive robust australopithecine jaw at Lake Natron in Tanzania confirmed the presence of this species in East Africa.

A series of fossils recovered from Olduvai Gorge during this period clearly did not belong to the same taxon, however. The crania were fragmentary, but they suggested a brain size of around 650 cc. Features of skull shape, including a better developed frontal region, or forehead, and smaller and narrower teeth—together with aspects of the preserved hand and foot bones that were interpreted as indicating considerable manipulative abilities and a more stable platform for standing and walking—prompted L.S.B. Leakey, P.V. Tobias, and J.R. Napier to redefine the genus *Homo* and to include this material within it as a new species, *Homo habilis*. Excavations had also revealed comprehensive evidence that at least one of the species of hominids living in Olduvai Gorge at the same time as the newly discovered fossils was making and using stone artifacts. It was natural, perhaps, for Leakey and his co-workers to associate these with the more human-like of the two hominids, hence the species name *habilis*, meaning "able, handy, and mentally skillful." More than 50 specimens were found at Olduvai Gorge between the years 1964 and 1981, and most of them were included in *H. habilis*. (The evidence assumed particular importance because Olduvai Gorge was the first site where the methods of radiometric and geomagnetic dating were combined to provide the first well-dated sequence of hominid fossils.

The assessment of Leakey and his co-workers did not go unchallenged. Robinson, who had worked with Robert Broom and who was familiar with the australopithecine remains from South Africa, considered that the allegedly *Homo* features of the earliest of the *habilis* remains could be encompassed within the range of variability of the gracile australopithecines.

Evidence from Omo and Koobi Fora. The next major contribution to knowledge of the australopithecines came from research at sites on the Omo River, in Ethiopia, and at Koobi Fora (formerly East Rudolf), on the northeast-

Discovery of Homo habilis (margin note)

Late-surviving gracile Australopithecines (margin note)

ern shore of Lake Turkana (Lake Rudolf). At both sites there is evidence of both gracile and robust hominids. The more robust remains clearly belong to *Australopithecus boisei* (*Zinjanthropus boisei*), the East African variety of the robust australopithecines. There is a good deal of size variation among the skulls, jaws, and teeth belonging to *A. boisei*. This suggests that the males and females of this taxon may have been markedly different in body size, an observation that has implications for any attempts to reconstruct the social organization of these creatures.

The interpretation of the more gracile, smaller-toothed remains is more problematic. Evidence from the earliest fossil-bearing strata at both sites consists mainly of isolated teeth, and they most closely match teeth belonging to the gracile australopithecine, *Australopithecus africanus*. The gracile fossils from slightly younger strata at both sites are more difficult to interpret and resemble in many ways the *habilis* material recovered from Olduvai Gorge.

The 1470 skull

Some of the cranial remains (*e.g.*, KNM-ER 1470 and 3732) suggest that the brains of these creatures were significantly larger than those of *A. africanus*, yet other gracile crania (*e.g.*, KNM-ER 1813) have brain capacities between 500 and 600 cc, clearly within the accepted range for gracile australopithecines. Jaws and teeth show a mixture of australopithecine and later *Homo* features, and some of the limb bones suggest affinities with later *Homo erectus* remains. The result of this mosaic of features is that opinions differ about how this material should be classified. Some scholars regard it as strengthening the case for *H. habilis*, yet others consider it to be a geographical variant of *A. africanus*. A third interpretation, favoured by Richard Leakey, is that the gracile fossils from Olduvai, Koobi Fora, and Omo are a mixed sample composed of the remains of two taxa, *H. habilis* and *A. africanus*. The discovery at Sterkfontein of an apparently more advanced cranium (StW 53) from layers more recent than those yielding the gracile australopithecines has reopened the debate about whether *H. habilis* is present in the Transvaal cave site.

Fossils from Laetoli and Hadar. Fossil evidence of australopithecines from Laetoli, Tanzania, and from Hadar, Ethiopia, represents hominids from the beginning of the crucial period of 3,500,000–1,500,000 years ago. In 1935–39 the site at Laetoli (then called Garusi) yielded fragmentary remains of two upper jaws. The site was reexplored in the mid-1970s by Mary Leakey, resulting in a series of fossil hominid discoveries that included trails of hominid footprints (see below). Fieldwork carried out at Hadar, an extensive fossil site located in the Afar triangle of Ethiopia, in 1972–77 by an international expedition led by Donald Johanson and Maurice Taieb resulted in a remarkable collection of several hundred fossil hominid remains. Two discoveries were particularly notable. One is an individual specimen (AL 288, popularly called "Lucy"), that includes nearly half of the bones of the preserved skeleton; the other is a series of fossils, popularly called the "First Family," from locality AL 333 that includes remains from at least 13 individuals.

The initial assessment of the material from Laetoli suggested that the remains most closely resembled the allegedly early *Homo* fossils from Koobi Fora, and thus the Laetoli evidence was also tentatively referred to the genus *Homo*. Similar inferences were made about part of the Hadar sample, while the remaining material from Hadar was considered to show affinities with the gracile and the robust australopithecines. More detailed examination, however, resulted in a new interpretation that links the remains at the two sites in an entirely new australopithecine

Proposal of *Australopithecus afarensis*

species, *Australopithecus afarensis*. The authors of this proposal, Johanson and Timothy White, listed a series of features that they consider differentiate *A. afarensis* from *A. africanus*, the existing taxon that it most closely resembles. The features they find important include a more projecting face; a long, narrow, straight-sided dental arcade, with relatively and absolutely large anterior teeth (canines and incisors); and the shape of the canine and premolar teeth.

The distinctiveness of these features that, together with aspects of the mandible and cranium, make up the diagnosis of *Australopithecus afarensis* has been challenged by other researchers. In their view the features cited either overlap with the known samples of *A. africanus* or are features that are common to australopithecines as a whole. Such shared features, these researchers argue, are of no value in defining a single species within the same group of fossil taxa. Some researchers have also pointed to the large range in size of mandibles and teeth in the Hadar collection and have questioned whether such variability can be accommodated within a single taxon.

ARCHAEOLOGICAL EVIDENCE

The relative richness of the archaeological record at the principal East African australopithecine sites contrasts with the meagre evidence recovered from the cave sites of southern Africa. The probable explanation for this has come from careful studies of the animal bones found together with the hominid remains in the South African caves. The results of these studies suggest that the australopithecines were not living in the caves but were simply part of the bone refuse accumulated by a predator, most likely a leopard-sized creature. Even if these gracile and robust australopithecines had been making stone artifacts, it is most unlikely that their tools would have found their way into a carnivore's lair.

Bone "tools" from Makapansgat. Perhaps the best-known so-called archaeological evidence from the South African cave sites came from Makapansgat. Two discoveries there were thought to be particularly significant. The first was an unusual abundance of the jaws and forelimb bones of fossil antelopes, and the second was a series of baboon skulls that had been extensively fractured. The evidence of the antelope bones led Dart to propose the existence of the so-called osteodontokeratic culture, in which the jaw and forelimb bones were prized as weapons and used to butcher baboons. Dart's speculations were later to foster the idea that the early australopithecines were "killer-apes." Research on the way predators and scavengers deal with animal skeletons, however, has cast considerable doubt on this interpretation. These findings suggest that the natural breakup of antelope skeletons leads to the differential survival of particular bony parts, and that this, along with the preferences of predators and damage to the bones by stones falling from the cave roof, would be sufficient to account for the bone accumulations and the pattern of breakage found at Makapansgat. These studies do not exclude the use of bone tools at Makapansgat, but they do suggest that the present evidence for it is, at the very least, ambiguous.

Stone artifacts. No stone artifacts have been found at Makapansgat, but small collections of such artifacts have been recovered in the robust australopithecine-bearing layers at Swartkrans and in strata of similar age at Sterkfontein. The Swartkrans artifacts are relatively crude choppers made of quartzite; the artifacts at Sterkfontein, also made of quartzite, are technologically more advanced and include small scrapers and primitive hand axes.

Although artifacts have been recovered from older levels at Hadar, the earliest substantial and comprehensive archaeological evidence from East Africa occurs in strata dating from around 2,000,000 years ago. The earliest of this series of occurrences is at the Omo River in Ethiopia, where collections of small quartz flakes have been found. It is, however, the sites at Olduvai Gorge and Koobi Fora that have provided the richest evidence of early hominid technology and behaviour. At both sites there is evidence that by about 1,750,000 years ago hominids had developed sufficient manipulative skills and cognitive ability to fashion a range of stone tools. The best known of these early industries is the Oldowan, first described from sites in Bed I of Olduvai. The artifacts range from choppers to small flakes, and variants (and, perhaps, developments) of this basic tool kit have since been described in later strata at Olduvai and other East African sites.

Archaeological evidence is not, however, restricted to stone artifacts themselves. At some sites remains of bones associated with artifacts suggest these were places where hominids butchered carcasses. The association of artifacts with the remains of animal carcasses is not necessarily

Evidence of butchery

evidence of organized hunting, however. Modern hunter-gatherers are known to chase scavengers from carnivore kills, and this may have been the type of early hominid behavior from which organized hunting developed.

Early living sites. The pattern of bone and artifact refuse at other localities indicates that hominids returned several times to the same place. It has been suggested that these "living sites" may have functioned as a home base for the activities of small groups of early hominids. At one site in Olduvai Gorge are the remains of a stone circle that may have formed the base of a shelter. Many researchers link the beginning of a rich archaeological record with the appearance in the fossil record of more advanced gracile hominid remains, which have been attributed to *Homo habilis*.

Interpretation of the living sites

Two points must be emphasized in relation to this archaeological evidence. First, the interpretation of assemblies of artifacts and animal bones as living sites has been challenged by some distinguished archaeologists who suggest that other agencies, such as the action of gently flowing streams, can cause such objects to be gathered together. Second, the durability of stone artifacts means that they may serve to bias interpretations of the activities of early hominids and may lead to an overemphasis of the role of hunting and the eating of meat. Studies of modern hunter-gatherer groups have all pointed to the crucial importance of gathering and to the relatively sophisticated technology and social behaviors that are involved in the finding, recovering, and preparing of gathered vegetable foods. Because digging sticks, baskets, and bowls are usually made of organic materials, however, they would seldom, if ever, be preserved in the Plio-Pleistocene archaeological record.

HABITAT

Since the 1960s scientists have paid particular attention to reconstructing the palaeoenvironment of the australopithecines. Information about the strata, fauna, and flora (from pollen analysis) of the period have been combined to provide reliable assessments of the habitat of the early hominids.

The evidence from both East and South Africa suggests a similar pattern of climatic change. Bovids, which include the antelopes and bucks, are especially sensitive to environmental change. Their distribution in the southern cave sites suggests that the deposits in the earlier sites of Makapansgat and Sterkfontein (Member 4) accumulated under more wooded conditions than those of the later sites of Swartkrans and Sterkfontein (Member 5), where the types of bovids found indicate a drier climate with more open grassland. The early sites in East Africa seem to indicate an open land environment, but evidence from Omo, Olduvai, and Koobi Fora suggests that a marked change in climate and vegetation occurred throughout East Africa just after 2,000,000 years ago. The evidence, ranging from oxygen isotope analysis of lake sediments to the detailed examination of microfauna, all points to a shift at that time to a drier climate and a more open, relatively treeless, scrub-type savanna environment.

BEHAVIORAL INFERENCES AND EVOLUTIONARY IMPLICATIONS

Fossil and paleoenvironmental evidence from the Miocene Epoch, the finds at Hadar, and the bipedal footprints and other remains from Laetoli have led paleontologists to revise their theories about the emergence and adaptations of the australopithecines. The paleoenvironment at most of the fossil ape-bearing Miocene sites was open woodland, similar to the habitats reconstructed for the early australopithecine sites. The footprints at Laetoli are unambiguous evidence for bipedal walking, and the pelvic remains from Hadar confirm that modifications for upright posture were well established by 3,000,000 years ago. There is, however, increasing evidence from studies of the limb bones of the australopithecines that the skeletal adaptations for climbing and bipedal walking are similar. That the skeletal changes necessary for climbing may be preadaptive for bipedal running and walking suggests that the early gracile australopithecines from East and South Africa may have used both these modes

Bipedal locomotion

of locomotion and may well have spent more time resting and feeding in trees than has hitherto been believed. The dental remains of the gracile australopithecines do not suggest any particular dietary adaptation, and researchers have suggested that they subsisted mainly on a plant diet of fruits, berries, and tubers. The lack of any archaeological evidence at Laetoli, together with its relative paucity at Hadar, suggests that these early australopithecines were not regularly making and using stone artifacts.

The change to a drier climate at about 2,000,000 years ago coincides with the emergence of the robust australopithecines and the appearance of the more advanced gracile hominids. Studies of the molar teeth belonging to robust australopithecines have suggested that they would have been well adapted to crushing hard objects, such as the casings and husks of fruits. Thus, it may be that the drier climate forced the robust australopithecines to occupy a specialized, and ultimately limited, niche in the open savanna grasslands. During the same period it seems most likely that the more lightly built australopithecines were adapting in a different direction, and it is natural to link them with the quickening pace of cultural advance and the emergence, at 1,500,000 years, of *Homo erectus*. Uncertainty about the classification of these "advanced" australopithecines and their evolutionary relationship with *H. erectus* are reflected in the tentative phylogenetic scheme presented in Figure 2.

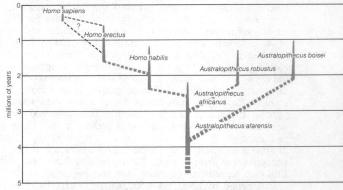

Figure 2: Tentative phylogenetic scheme for early hominid evolution. Adaptive features of the genus *Homo* include brain enlargement, reduction of jaws and teeth, and an increasingly complex stone technology. Features of the australopithecines, who may not have had a stone technology, include jaws and teeth for crushing and grinding.

New evidence about the fossil hominids and their context is needed and will surely come. Equally important, however, is the need for palaeontologists to refine their methods for analyzing and interpreting the evidence. During the 1970s there were important conceptual debates about many important aspects of evolutionary biology and paleontology. The lessons learned from those discussions may well contribute as much to an understanding of this crucial stage in hominid evolution as the discovery of additional fossil evidence.

BIBLIOGRAPHY. JOHN READER, *Missing Links: The Hunt for Earliest Man* (1981), an excellent historical account and perceptive review of the fossil evidence; RICHARD E. LEAKEY, *The Making of Mankind* (1981), a comprehensive popular account of the fossil and archaeological evidence; DONALD C. JOHANSON and MAITLAND A. EDEY, *Lucy: The Beginnings of Humankind* (1981), a popular account of the discovery and interpretation of the Hadar hominids; NANCY MAKEPEACE TANNER, *On Becoming Human* (1981), a comparative review of the relationship between early hominid behaviour and evolution; MICHAEL H. DAY, *Guide to Fossil Man*, 3rd ed. (1977), an authoritative guide that includes many of the most important early hominid fossils; BERNARD A. WOOD, *Human Evolution* (1978), a short introduction that includes details of dating methods; GLYNN LL. ISAAC and ELIZABETH R. MCCOWN (eds.), *Human Origins* (1976), a useful collection of papers giving the background of much of the fossil and archaeological evidence; F.C. HOWELL, "Hominidae," in VINCENT J. MAGLIO and H.B.S. COOKE (eds.), *Evolution of African Mammals* (1978), perhaps the most comprehensive and reliable detailed account of the australopithecine fossil record.

(BERNARD WOOD)

Lebanon

El Salvador

Afghanistan

Falklands

Iran/Iraq

CONFLICT

events
of
1982

Aerial Sports

The stunning flights of the space shuttle "Columbia" produced the greatest aerial sports achievements of 1982, a year unfortunately marred by some tragic accidents. Eclipsing records set by U.S. space shuttle pilots John Young and Robert Crippen in their first orbital flight in April 1981, pilots Jack R. Lousma and C. Gordon Fullerton in March 1982 set the aerospacecraft world record for duration and distance covered with an 8-day, 4-minute 45-second flight of 5,367,009 km (3,332,912 mi) from a launch at Cape Canaveral, Fla., to a landing in New Mexico. Shuttle astronauts Thomas K. Mattingly and Henry W. Hartsfield, Jr., also set a world record of 325.64 km (202.2 mi) for altitude in an elliptical orbit in their June 27–July 4 flight in "Columbia" from Cape Canaveral to Edwards Air Force Base in California. (For further information on the space shuttle see Space Exploration.)

Other high points of the year included confirmation by the Fédération Aéronautique Internationale (FAI) of a record by Erwin Müller and Otto Schäffner. The two West Germans set the multiplace glider speed record over a 100-km triangular course in an Mü II at Bitterwasser, South Africa, with a speed of 158.3 km/h (98.3 mph). Also confirmed was Müller's claim of a 500-km triangular course multiplace glider speed record of 146.69 km/h (91 mph) set at Bitterwasser on Dec. 13, 1981, in an Mü II. The FAI also confirmed the Dec. 29, 1981, claim of Luc de Preter and Dietmar Spohn of Belgium for a multiplace motorglider record for out-and-return distance to a goal with a

617.95-km (383.7-mi) flight from Kenilworth, South Africa, to Britstown, South Africa, and back in a Janus CM.

Former world sailplane champion George Moffat won the prestigious U.S. National open class championship held August 3–12 at Caddo Mills, Texas. He flew a Nimbus 3B.

In the world gas balloon championship held September 25–October 3 at Bern, Switz., the Swiss team took first place with 2,975 points. West German teams finished second and third with 2,970 and 2,892 points. Both the world gas balloon and hot-air balloon championships would be held in 1983 in France in honour of the 200th anniversary of the Montgolfier brothers' first balloon flights.

Coy Foster of the U.S. set a world distance record for category AX-2 free balloons with a 38.46-km (23.88-mi) flight from Stavby to Brunna in Sweden on Jan. 6, 1982, in a Colt 14A. John Petrehn of the U.S. set a category AX-6 duration record, flying for 13 hours and 24 minutes in a Barnes Firefly 6b from Prior Lake, Minn., to Richland Center, Wis., on February 5–6.

The International Balloon Festival at Albuquerque, N.M., was marred by a fire aboard one of the balloons that killed four and injured three.

Maxie Anderson and Don Ida of the U.S. made a third unsuccessful attempt to go around the world in a balloon. The helium-filled balloon, the "Jules Verne," lifted off from Rapid City, S.D., on November 7, but a leak forced it down some 15 hours later at a ski resort about 95 km (60 mi) north of Toronto.

In the world parachuting championships at Lucenec, Czech., August 6–20, Bernard Weisner of East Germany finished first in individual men's

Aden:
see Yemen, People's Democratic Republic of

Advertising:
see Industrial Review

Aerospace Industry:
see Defense; Industrial Review; Space Exploration; Transportation

A host of balloons took to the air in September in the world gas balloon championship, held in Bern, Switzerland. Teams from nine countries participated, with the Swiss taking the championship.

WIDE WORLD

Small light planes called "ultra-lights" became popular during the year. These tiny craft fly at low altitudes and at speeds of about 40 miles per hour.

accuracy with a one-centimetre total. Nicolaj Usmajev of the Soviet Union was second with a four-centimetre score, and Jurgen Roehme of East Germany was third with five centimetres. In men's style competition Maurice Fernandez of the U.S. was first, Jan Sofranek of Czechoslovakia placed second, and Vjacslav Valgunas of the Soviet Union finished third. In individual men's overall performance Weisner was first, Christian Lubbe of France second, and Usmajev third. France, West Germany, and Australia finished first, second, and third in men's team accuracy.

Record-holding Cheryl Stearns of the U.S. was first in women's individual accuracy with an 8-cm showing, Elena Burkova of the Soviet Union took second with 9 cm, and Heike Glau of East Germany finished third with 15 cm. First in women's style went to Irina Walhkoff of East Germany, second to Barbara Harzbecker of East Germany, and third to Larisa Koriceva of the Soviet Union. Koriceva was women's overall champion, with Stearns and Walhkoff tied for second. Bulgaria won the women's team accuracy competition followed by Canada and Czechoslovakia.

On January 25, at Bukhara, U.S.S.R., Soviet parachuting teams set world records for group precision jumps in categories of group of four, two landings on a disk, 0.04 m; group of eight, one landing on a disk, 0.04 m; and women's group of four, one landing on a disk, 0.01 m. A U.S. team set the record for largest canopy formation with a four-person jump executed at Jenkinsberg, Ga., on March 27.

In the world aerobatics championships August 8–22 at Spitzerberg, Austria, Victor Smolin finished first in men's individual competition with 16,404.4 points in a Yak 50. Henry Haigh of the U.S. was second with 16,399.4 points in his Haigh Superstar, and Manfred Stroessenreuther of West Germany was third with 16,310.8 points in a Zlin 50L. First in the women's individual contest was Betty Stewart of the U.S. with 15,482.4 points in a Pitt Special; second was Liubow Nemkova of the Soviet Union with 15,243.9 points in a Yak 50; and Halida Makagonova of the Soviet Union was third with 15,139.3 points in a Yak 50. The Soviet Union

placed first in the men's team competition, with the U.S. second and Czechoslovakia third. The Soviets won the women's team championship with the U.S. women second and France third.

Three people were killed in the aerial collision of two light aircraft in a flyby demonstration during the Experimental Aircraft Association annual meet August 1–7 at Oshkosh, Wis. In another fatal accident four jet planes belonging to the Thunderbirds, a U.S. Air Force precision flying team, crashed near Indian Springs, Nev., on January 18 while practicing a "loop and tail" maneuver. All four pilots were killed.　　(MICHAEL D. KILIAN)

Afghanistan

Afghanistan

A people's republic in central Asia, Afghanistan is bordered by the U.S.S.R., China, Pakistan, and Iran. Area: 652,090 sq km (251,773 sq mi). Pop. (1981 est.): 16.4 million, including (1978 est.) Pashtoon 53%; Tadzhik 20%; Uzbek 9%; Hazara 9%; other 9% (by 1982 the exodus to Pakistan and Iran accounted for more than 3.7 million). Cap. and largest city: Kabul (pop., 1979 prelim., 749,000). Language: Pashto and Persian. Religion: Muslim 99% (including 80% Sunni; 20% Shi'ah); Hindu, Sikh, and Jewish 1%. President of the Revolutionary Council in 1982, Babrak Karmal; prime minister, Sultan Ali Keshtmand.

Fighting in Afghanistan between the *mujaheddin* (Islamic guerrillas) and the Afghan Army backed by Soviet forces was less widespread during 1982 as the government appeared to be in better control of the insurgency problem in general. Pres. Babrak Karmal, whose position had been considered shaky, was also firmly in command as his Parcham faction of the ruling People's Democratic Party managed to eliminate most of the pro-Khalq elements from the government and the party.

Diego Cordovez, UN special representative for Afghanistan, visited the capitals of Afghanistan, Pakistan, and Iran to convince their leaders of the necessity to find a peaceful settlement. Afghan Foreign Minister Shah Mohammad Dost and his Pakistani counterpart, Sahabzada Yaqub Khan,

Afghanistan

Soviet soldiers, captured by rebels in Afghanistan, were held in an Afghan rebel camp. Fighting between the Soviets and Afghan rebels continued throughout the year.

AFGHANISTAN

Education. (1979–80) Primary, pupils 1,006,094, teachers 32,937; secondary, pupils 116,714, teachers 4,903; vocational, pupils 16,784, teachers 1,211; higher, students (1978–79) 21,118, teaching staff (universities only) 817.

Finance. Monetary unit: afghani, with (Sept. 20, 1982) a free rate of 58 afghanis to U.S. $1 (99 afghanis = £1 sterling). Gold and other reserves (May 1982) U.S. $311 million. Budget (1980–81 est.): revenue 23,478,000,000 afghanis; expenditure 19,213,000,000 afghanis. Money supply (March 1982) 48,509,000,000 afghanis.

Foreign Trade. (1980–81) Imports 23,482,000,000 afghanis; exports 32,362,000,000 afghanis. Import sources (1977–78): U.S.S.R. 22%; Japan 20%; Iran 13%; West Germany 6%; India 5%. Export destinations (1977–78): U.S.S.R. 37%; U.K. 12%; Pakistan 12%; India 8%; West Germany 6%; U.S. 5%; Saudi Arabia 5%. Main exports: natural gas 39%; fruits and nuts 32%; carpets 10%.

Transport and Communications. Roads (1978) 18,752 km. Motor vehicles in use (1978): passenger 34,506; commercial 22,100. Air traffic (1980): c. 163 million passenger-km; freight c. 21 million net ton-km. Telephones (Jan. 1979) 31,200. Radio receivers (Dec. 1978) 823,000. Television receivers (Dec. 1979) 11,000.

Agriculture. Production (in 000; metric tons; 1981): wheat c. 3,000; corn c. 800; rice c. 475; barley c. 350; grapes c. 460; cotton, lint 34; wool, clean c. 13. Livestock (in 000; 1981): cattle c. 3,710; karakul sheep c. 4,500; other sheep c. 14,200; goats c. 2,850; horses c. 420; asses c. 1,320; camels c. 265.

Industry. Production (in 000; metric tons; 1980–81): coal 119; natural gas (cu m) 2,790,000; cotton fabrics (m) 43,300; rayon fabrics (m) 14,800; nitrogenous fertilizers (nutrient content) 106; cement 87; electricity (kw-hr) c. 959,000.

met in Geneva in June, while Iran, after agreeing to attend, later backed out. Cordovez said that at the meeting he broadly outlined the principles of an agreement in separate talks with Khan and Dost and that he also kept Iran informed of progress. Both sides, Cordovez maintained, accepted the main agenda items: withdrawal of troops, resettlement of an estimated three million refugees, and international guarantees on noninterference in the internal affairs of Afghanistan. Khan commented that talks were "still at a preliminary stage" and reiterated Pakistan's refusal to hold direct talks with Kabul until Pakistan recognized the Kabul government.

President Karmal repeated in March that Afghanistan was ready to discuss proposals for a "flexible peace policy" with its neighbours but was thwarted by the hostile reaction of the U.S. and its allies. He also stressed his government's agreement with the U.S.S.R. on all policy matters.

The U.S., the U.K., and other Western countries again condemned the Soviet intervention in Afghanistan on March 21, the start of the Afghan new year, which was proclaimed Afghanistan Day by Western nations. On the same day the U.S.S.R. declared its intention of staying in Afghanistan until the Kabul government was secure. The Soviet media criticized the proclamation of Afghanistan Day as part of a "slanderous campaign" against the Soviet presence in Afghanistan.

Clashes between insurgents and security forces were mainly centred on the Panjsher Valley, about 70 km (45 mi) northeast of Kabul. According to Western diplomatic sources, bitter fighting took place in this region during June–August. The Afghan Army and the Soviets committed a large number of ground troops supported by helicopter gunships and MiG jet fighters to dislodge rebels from the valley. Rebel sources in Pakistan admitted that the rebels had to take refuge in nearby mountains but insisted that they were preparing to fight back. As a result of large-scale operations by Soviet and Afghan forces, Kandahar City, in the south, also seemed more secure. Western news agency reports estimated casualties in fighting since the Soviet intervention at 20,000 Afghan and 10,000 Soviet troops. Little was known about rebel losses.

Early in November an explosion in a mountain tunnel north of Kabul was reported to have killed hundreds of Soviet soldiers and Afghan civilians. According to accounts that reached the West, the lead truck of a Soviet military convoy collided with an oncoming fuel truck. The resulting blast and burning gasoline ignited other vehicles, and most of the deaths were believed to have been caused by asphyxiation from the smoke and fumes that filled the tunnel.

In February Karmal signed a trade protocol with the Soviet Union that thrust Afghanistan further into the Soviet economic orbit. Most Afghan exports were going to the U.S.S.R., which allowed a credit of 10 million rubles to Afghanistan for essential imports.

Agricultural production continued to suffer. The farm-labour force remained depleted, as able-bodied men, refusing to be forced into the Army, either fled the country or joined the rebels. In August Karmal chose Abdul Ghaffar Lakanwal as the new agriculture minister, replacing Fazil Mohmand. In September Gen. Abdul Qader was appointed minister of defense in place of Gen. Mohammad Rafi.   (GOVINDAN UNNY)

African Affairs

Africa's three major concerns during 1982 were the steadily worsening economic conditions throughout the continent, a serious crisis within the Organization of African Unity, and the failure to achieve an international settlement in regard to South West Africa/Namibia. These three elements contributed in varying degrees to the creation of political instability and to increasing military and political violence.

The Organization of African Unity. For the first time since its founding in 1963, the 50-nation Organization of African Unity (OAU) failed to muster a quorum for its annual summit meeting, which was scheduled for August in Tripoli, Libya. The two principal reasons for the failure to obtain the requisite attendance of two-thirds of the member nations were, first, a decision to admit to membership in the OAU the Saharan Arab Democratic Republic (SADR), Western Sahara's government-in-exile led by the Popular Front for the Liberation of Saguia el Hamra and Río de Oro (Polisario Front); and, second, objections by a number of African leaders to the choice of Libya's capital as the site for the summit, since this automatically conferred the OAU chairmanship for the ensuing year on Libyan head of state Col. Muammar al-Qaddafi.

Three months of intensive diplomacy produced a compromise formula that was acceptable to all the parties directly involved in the Western Sahara conflict. It required the Polisario Front to absent itself voluntarily from the summit but did not withdraw recognition of the SADR as a member,

pending the holding of an internationally supervised referendum to test the wishes of the Saharans. Acceptance of this compromise appeared to allow the summit to be reconvened in Tripoli on November 23. However, a new dispute broke out concerning two rival delegations from Chad. Qaddafi wanted the one headed by former president Goukouni Oueddei to be seated. Oueddei had seized power with Libyan military backing in November 1981 but had been ousted in 1982 by forces led by Hissen Habré (see BIOGRAPHIES), head of the rival delegation (see below). Several nations favoured Habré and walked out of the meeting. Again a quorum could not be obtained, and the summit was canceled.

Southern Africa. The level of military activity and political violence in southern Africa rose significantly during the year, with the South African Army making repeated military thrusts deep into Angola, and the guerrilla forces of the South West Africa People's Organization (SWAPO) and the African National Congress (ANC) intensifying their incursions into Namibia and South Africa, respectively. In addition to Angola, a number of other neighbours complained that the South African government was engaged in destabilizing their regimes; these included Zimbabwe, Mozambique, Lesotho, Zambia, and Botswana. Nevertheless, Zambia's Pres. Kenneth Kaunda agreed to meet with South Africa's Prime Minister P. W. Botha on neutral ground in Botswana to try to advance a negotiated settlement of the region's most pressing problems.

Substantial progress was made by the contact group of five Western countries (the U.S., the U.K., France, West Germany, and Canada) in persuading both South Africa and SWAPO to agree to

Libyan leader Muammar al-Qaddafi gazed at a number of empty chairs at the Organization of African Unity summit meeting in Tripoli, Libya. Nineteen African nations boycotted the meeting, which failed to register a quorum.

REZA—SIPA PRESS/BLACK STAR

terms for implementing the UN Security Council's resolution 435. The resolution called for an international settlement of the Namibian conflict and the introduction of a peacekeeping force to maintain a cease-fire during an 11-month transition period leading to free elections. By November most of the difficult problems relating to implementation had been resolved, and the only serious obstacle to agreement was the joint insistence by South Africa and the U.S. that Cuban troops should start to withdraw from Angola simultaneously with the confinement to barracks of South Africa's troops.

Although the Angolan government remained publicly committed to the withdrawal of Cuban troops once agreement had been reached over Namibia, it firmly rejected the idea of linking the two issues in this way. The U.S. sought to overcome this obstacle through separate talks with the Angolans. All that still held up final agreement on this thorny issue was essentially a diplomatic impasse over the exact timing of the Cuban withdrawal and the form of its announcement. On December 8 South Africa announced that South African and Angolan delegations had met in Cape Verde, although no particulars were given.

The Horn of Africa. While Ethiopia's relations with Sudan improved considerably during the year, those with Somalia deteriorated. In July Somalian Pres. Muhammad Siyad Barrah claimed that Ethiopian troops had invaded his country. Ethiopia insisted that the transborder fighting was being carried on entirely by Somali opponents of the Barrah regime. However, since those forces were based inside Ethiopia and seemed to rely on Ethiopian arms, it was difficult to dissociate entirely the regime of Lieut. Col. Mengistu Haile Mariam from the attempt to overthrow President Barrah by force of arms.

Coups and Inter-African Affairs. Only one African government was changed by means of a military coup in 1982: in November the military regime of Upper Volta was overthrown by junior officers. An attempt by elements in the Kenya Air Force to oust Pres. Daniel arap Moi (*see* BIOGRAPHIES) in August was quickly suppressed. An unsuccessful attempt by mercenaries to overthrow the government of Seychelles in November 1981 had international repercussions during 1982. The mercenaries who had hijacked a plane to South Africa were, after international pressure, brought to trial by the South African government.

The regime of Pres. Goukouni Oueddei of Chad was defeated in June by the military forces of Col. Hissen Habré, who was believed to have had the support of Sudan and Egypt. Libya, which had earlier withdrawn its army from Chad when an OAU peacekeeping force was introduced, was sharply critical of this new development in Chad. Sudan, which accused Qaddafi of wishing to intervene again in Chad, remained on bad terms with the Libyan leader, as did Egyptian Pres. Hosni Mubarak, Somali President Barrah, and the leaders of Senegal, The Gambia, Cameroon, and Zaire. The Ugandan government accused the Libyans of helping to arm the opponents of Pres. Milton Obote. However, Qaddafi's policies in Africa appeared to be less interventionist than in recent years, partly because of his wish to secure the chair of the OAU for 1982–83 and partly because of his involvement in the events in Lebanon.

The five-year conflict in the Western Sahara between Morocco and the Polisario forces, the latter strongly backed by Algeria, showed no sign of bringing military victory to either side. It continued to contribute to hostile relations between Morocco and Algeria. With 26 OAU members giving diplomatic recognition to the independence of the SADR and 14 giving their strong support to Morocco's claims on the territory, the conflict tended to polarize relations in Africa as few issues had done since the civil wars in Angola and Nigeria.

Political Systems. The decision of Senegal and The Gambia to establish the new Senegambia confederation—a decision prompted by their desire to guarantee The Gambia's fragile security following an almost successful military coup there in 1981—came into effect on Feb. 1, 1982. Sudan and Egypt also agreed in November to go ahead with their long-proposed plan for a union along confederal lines. In December 1980 Léopold Sédar Senghor of Senegal had become the first African president voluntarily to relinquish his presidency while under no immediate political pressure to do so; his example was followed in November 1982 by Pres. Ahmadou Ahidjo of Cameroon, who, though still at the peak of his political career, decided to step down in favour of his prime minister.

The most sensational election held during the year was that in Mauritius when the ruling party of Prime Minister Sir Seewoosagur Ramgoolam failed to win a single seat in the new Parliament. Elections in Sierra Leone were characteristically violent and controversial. In Madagascar a hard-fought contest for the presidency was won by the incumbent, Pres. Didier Ratsiraka, against the veteran nationalist Monja Joana.

External Relations. Although most African countries continued to pursue policies of nonalignment, their closest relations remained largely with the Western community, mainly due to economic links. This relationship was considerably strengthened by the world economic crisis, which compelled African countries, more than ever before, to look for trade and aid from Western Europe, the U.S., and Japan. The two Marxist governments of Angola and Mozambique, which had previously indicated an intention to become associate members of the Soviet-led Council for Mutual Economic Assistance, signed the Lomé convention, a trade agreement between African, Caribbean, and Pacific countries and the European Communities. Both countries were anxious to attract Western, including U.S., investment and trade. Both also reestablished warm relations with Portugal, the former colonial power.

Despite French Pres. François Mitterrand's promise that his Socialist government would not continue to seek to play the role of gendarme in Africa, none of the French-speaking African countries indicated any desire to loosen their military ties with Paris. The long-standing hostility between Guinea and France was finally ended with a visit by Pres. Ahmed Sékou Touré to Paris. The annual summit of the Franco-African community,

Prime Minister P. W. Botha (left) of South Africa and Pres. Kenneth Kaunda (right) of Zambia met in April. President Kaunda reportedly tried to convince Prime Minister Botha to give greater leadership roles to South African blacks.

held in Zaire in October, was the biggest meeting since its inception, attracting 36 delegations. There, Mitterrand promised to increase French overseas aid by 50% in 1983.

If the African countries looked primarily to the West for trade and aid, they were no less eager to turn to the Soviet bloc when it came to buying arms. Overall, the Warsaw Pact powers and the U.S. supplied roughly equal amounts of weapons to the continent. The U.S.'s military aid went largely to Egypt, Sudan, Somalia, Morocco, Tanzania, and Kenya. The Soviet bloc's main arms clients included Libya, Angola, Mozambique, and Ethiopia. The U.K. remained a major arms supplier to Nigeria, Kenya, and Zimbabwe. French military supplies went mainly to French-speaking countries, while Spain and Italy became increasingly important suppliers of weapons, especially to nations in North Africa.

The Soviet Union showed a renewed interest in Africa during the year, highlighted by a speech by Pres. Leonid I. Brezhnev in November in which he accused the U.S. of seeking to "encircle" Africa by acquiring bases and military allies around the continent's periphery. China's interest in the continent remained consistently high, primarily because of its third world interest in strengthening the nonaligned alliance against the major powers, especially the U.S.S.R. But the Beijing (Peking) leadership told African visitors to China that, for the present, they were unable to give as much economic aid as in the past.

Israel's hopes of reestablishing relations with African countries, broken after the 1973 war, received a setback as a consequence of its military intervention in Lebanon. Only Zaire risked the sanctions of Arab League countries by restoring diplomatic ties with Jerusalem.

Social and Economic Conditions. For most of the continent, the only marginal exceptions being the larger oil producers, the state of the economy in 1982 was little short of disastrous. Every recognized indicator of economic and social development was markedly negative. The increase in the continent's real productive output averaged about 3.5%, just slightly above the average rise in its population; this meant that most countries were getting poorer. Export earnings continued to decline; they fell by $1 billion in 1981 to $28 billion and were expected to be still lower in 1982. Africa's aggregate trade deficit increased again, by $2 billion in 1981 to reach $13 billion. By early 1982 the continent's long-term external public debt stood at $38.5 billion, an increase of $4 billion over 1979. A World Bank forecast was that the annual income per head in the poorest of the African countries would fall by 10% during the 1980s to $235 by 1990.

The continuing failure of the continent to feed itself remained a critical factor in its economic development, both in terms of human suffering and because of the need to spend precious foreign exchange earnings on importing essential foodstuffs. Total food production increased by only 1.4% in 1979 and by 2.4% in 1980. Set against the average population growth of about 3%, these figures represented a growing gap between food needs and production. The UN-sponsored World Food Council (WFC) reported that food consumption was 10% per capita less than it had been ten years earlier, although grain imports had doubled in that period and were expected to triple by the mid-1980s. The WFC warned that hunger and malnutrition could be expected to become far more widespread in future years unless successful remedial action was taken. The WFC and the UN Economic Commission for Africa listed five major causes for Africa's serious economic condition: natural causes; the absence of adequate infrastructure; the failures of government policies; the adverse terms of international trade; and the severe impact of higher oil prices.　　　　　　　　　　　(COLIN LEGUM)

See also Dependent States; articles on the various political units.

Agriculture and Food Supplies

Despite the leveling off of world agricultural production in 1982, the amount of output continued to support the buildup of stocks of a wide range of agricultural products, particularly in the major exporting countries. World prices of several agricultural farm commodities were depressed, and the worldwide economic recession helped hold them down because of reduced demand by consumers. Those poor economic conditions also contributed to growing trade tensions throughout the world, particularly between the European Economic Community (EEC) and the United States over agricultural trade. International food security issues were overshadowed by these disputes, and food aid and foreign assistance for agricultural development in the less developed countries felt the effect of budgetary restraints imposed in the developed nations.

Production. INDEXES. World agricultural and food production may have declined somewhat less than 1% in 1982, according to preliminary estimates (in December 1982) of the U.S. Department of Agriculture's Economic Research Service. The heaviest losses in output were in the Soviet Union, where the harvest was small again for the fourth year in a row. Among the other centrally planned economies China registered gains in agricultural production, and Eastern Europe matched its performance in 1981. Agricultural output fell slightly in the developed countries as a group because farm surpluses and low prices led to cutbacks in U.S.

The financial woes of farm equipment manufacturer International Harvester were exemplified by an auction of unsold machinery at one of the firm's warehouses in Marshalltown, Iowa.

SARA KRULWICH/THE NEW YORK TIMES

production, while bad weather hurt grain crops in Australia and South Africa.

Agricultural output was unchanged in the less developed countries, as gains in West Asia and Africa were offset by losses in Latin America and South Asia. The decline in Iranian agricultural output was finally arrested, while Morocco partially recovered from the severe drought in 1981. Mexico was hard hit by drought in 1982, while India experienced a moderate retreat from the previous year's record output.

On a per capita basis world food production may have fallen as much as 2% in 1982. The decline was smallest in the developed countries and greatest in the centrally planned economies, where the effect of Soviet production shortfalls dominated despite modest gains by the Chinese.

Among the less developed regions only West Asia did not record a decline in per capita output, and only a few of the larger agricultural economies grew faster than their populations—Bangladesh perhaps being the most notable. Per capita food production for less developed Africa as a region was 13% lower than in 1970, but some of the severest shortages experienced by several African countries early in the year eased considerably.

Nevertheless, the United Nations Food and Agriculture Organization (FAO) reported that, as of October 1982, 17 African countries were experiencing abnormal food shortages. Of the other nations with considerable shortages, four were in Asia, one was in the Middle East, and one was in Latin America. The FAO noted that of the 45 new or expanded emergency operations conducted by the World Food Program during the first nine months of 1982, more than 75% were to relieve "man-made situations" rather than natural disasters.

GRAINS. Another year of ample grain supplies (wheat, coarse grains, and rice) was in prospect (in December) for 1982–83. The continuing increase in world grain output was the result of an expected rise in grain yields despite cutbacks in planted area. Most of the estimated increases in 1982–83 grain production were in the EEC and in the centrally planned economies, which should make possible a substantial recovery in world grain utilization. The increases in production in major grain importing countries were expected to reduce the overall world demand for grain imports in 1982–83, compounding the demand-dampening effects already being experienced as a result of slow economic growth throughout the world.

World grain production was likely to exceed grain consumption for the second year in a row. Thus, world stocks of grain, which continued to grow in 1981–82, were forecast to become the largest (measured as a percentage of utilization) in a decade by the end of 1982–83. Those stocks had become increasingly heavily concentrated in the developed exporting countries, and the U.S. share had increased dramatically in recent years.

World wheat production was expected to reach a record high in 1982–83 despite an estimated 1.4% decline in harvested area from 238 million ha in 1981–82 (1 ha = 2.47 ac). The largest increases in output were in exporting countries other than the United States—the EEC, Argentina, and Canada,

Family farmers were hard hit by bad times down on the farm. This farm auction in Minnesota in April was one of many across the U.S. as small farmers fell victim to high interest rates and low crop prices.

all of which had larger harvested areas — and in the centrally planned economies. Although Soviet wheat output was estimated to be almost 8% above the 80 million-ton harvest in 1981–82, it was still the fourth poor crop in a row, one-third lower than that of 1978–79. Severe drought cut Australian harvested wheat area and production by nearly one-half, raising the possibility of a need to import wheat in order to maintain that nation's export commitments. U.S. wheat production was little changed from 1981–82; increased yields offset the only partially successful influence of government programs aimed at reducing wheat plantings in the face of large domestic stocks.

Global utilization of wheat fell in 1981–82 largely because of the sharply lower 1981 Soviet wheat harvest that forced a nearly 18 million-ton decline in Soviet wheat use, mainly in that fed to livestock. Nearly all of the forecast increase in wheat consumption in 1982–83 was based on expected larger production in major wheat importing countries, especially the U.S.S.R., China, and India.

The annual rate of increase in the consumption of wheat in the less developed countries slowed to about 2% in the early 1980s after averaging about 4% in the 1970s. Much of the reduction was the result of slower economic progress in those countries, which restrained both the growth in

Table I. Indexes of World Agricultural and Food Production
1969–71 = 100

Region or country	Total agricultural production						Total food production						Per capita food production					
	1977	1978	1979	1980	1981	1982¹	1977	1978	1979	1980	1981	1982¹	1977	1978	1979	1980	1981	1982¹
Developed countries	113	116	119	118	122	121	113	117	120	118	123	122	107	110	111	109	112	111
United States	118	118	124	118	132	130	118	119	125	119	132	132	111	112	114	107	117	117
Canada	116	119	115	118	128	132	119	122	118	121	131	136	109	111	107	107	115	119
Western Europe	109	115	119	124	121	122	109	116	119	124	121	123	105	111	114	119	115	116
EEC	111	114	115	122	119	119	107	114	118	122	120	121	104	110	114	118	115	115
Japan	107	105	105	94	95	98	106	105	105	94	95	98	98	95	94	84	85	87
Oceania	112	120	113	107	116	104	120	130	120	111	122	107	107	115	105	96	104	90
South Africa	129	133	128	135	151	132	133	136	131	139	157	136	111	111	105	108	120	101
Centrally planned economies	118	126	125	123	124	122	118	127	126	123	124	121	106	113	110	106	106	102
U.S.S.R.	114	123	115	112	110	103	114	123	114	111	109	101	107	115	105	101	99	91
Eastern Europe	121	126	124	121	124	123	122	127	125	122	124	124	116	120	117	114	116	115
China²	119	131	143	142	148	151	121	133	146	143	148	151	106	115	125	120	123	124
Less developed countries	122	127	126	123	135	135	123	129	128	131	137	137	104	106	102	102	104	102
East Asia³	135	143	144	143	155	155	138	147	147	151	159	160	117	121	119	119	123	119
Indonesia	125	135	141	152	159	157	129	139	144	157	165	164	109	114	115	123	126	121
South Korea	155	165	161	143	153	151	153	164	161	143	153	152	135	142	137	119	125	118
Malaysia	146	147	159	167	171	176	159	161	182	195	203	212	133	131	144	151	153	157
Philippines	135	137	134	133	149	150	136	138	135	140	150	151	112	111	106	107	111	110
Thailand	132	162	144	163	174	170	141	175	150	179	186	180	118	142	119	139	140	134
South Asia	119	124	118	120	128	127	120	124	118	120	129	127	102	104	96	96	100	97
Bangladesh	110	114	114	120	118	126	112	115	115	124	122	130	93	93	91	95	92	97
India	120	126	118	120	130	127	120	126	117	120	130	127	103	105	96	95	101	97
Pakistan	119	113	128	129	139	141	126	123	132	133	145	145	103	98	102	100	106	103
West Asia	134	140	139	142	142	146	134	142	141	143	143	148	110	113	109	108	104	104
Iran	149	158	147	132	125	126	152	162	152	136	128	129	124	128	116	101	91	89
Turkey	128	132	132	135	138	143	128	132	133	136	140	146	107	108	106	106	107	107
Africa⁴	107	113	113	117	119	121	109	114	115	119	121	123	90	92	90	90	89	87
Egypt	108	113	117	122	123	125	115	120	123	127	129	134	98	100	100	100	99	99
Ethiopia	92	95	93	95	95	93	90	93	91	93	93	90	74	72	73	70	70	66
Morocco	94	121	118	123	100	114	94	120	117	123	99	114	75	94	88	89	70	76
Nigeria	107	110	111	113	120	121	108	110	112	117	120	122	86	85	84	85	85	83
Latin America	126	132	135	139	146	144	129	134	138	143	149	149	108	110	110	111	114	111
Argentina	121	134	139	127	136	138	121	135	141	129	139	140	109	120	122	110	117	116
Brazil	140	136	144	160	168	164	148	143	150	170	171	177	125	118	121	135	133	133
Colombia	126	141	149	153	161	166	127	143	152	161	163	169	112	125	130	137	137	140
Mexico	122	129	128	136	145	131	124	133	131	140	150	136	98	102	97	100	105	93
Venezuela	141	146	154	153	155	165	144	148	159	163	160	170	109	106	108	105	98	99
World	117	123	124	123	127	126	118	124	124	124	127	127	103	107	106	103	104	102

¹ Preliminary. ² Represents about two thirds of all field crops (includes all major field crops), but excludes livestock products. ³ Excludes Japan. ⁴ Excludes South Africa.
Source: USDA, Economic Research Service, International Economic Division, December 1982.

World Production and Trade of Principal Grains (in 000 metric tons)

	Wheat			Barley			Oats			Rye			Corn (Maize)			Rice		
	Production		Imports− Exports+	Production		Imports− Exports+	Production		Imports− Exports+	Production		Imports− Exports+	Production		Imports− Exports+	Production		Imports− Exports+
	1961–65 average	1981	1978–81 average	1961–65 average	1981	1978–81 average	1961–65 average	1981	1978–81 average	1961–65 average	1981	1978–81 average	1961–65 average	1981	1978–81 average	1961–65 average	1981	1978–81 average
World total	254576	459554	−79188[1] / +79483[1]	98474	158372	−15040[1] / +14968[1]	47775	43997	−1377[1] / +1474[1]	33849	24530	−965[1] / +1013[1]	216429	451413	−74431[1] / +74886[1]	254711	414071	−11619[1] / +11418[1]
Algeria	1254	c1400	−c1544	476	c750	−c365	28	c100	−c18[1]	—	—	—	4	c1	−c160	7	c1	−c15[1]
Argentina	7541	7900	+3535	679	c200	+29	676	c500	+152	422	200	+25	4984	c13500	+6112	193	286	−4[1] / +97
Australia	8222	16,400	+11140	978	3430	+1859	1172	1530	+290	11	c16	—	176	118	−3[1] / +16	136	761	−1[1] / +347
Austria	704	1025	−1[1] / +194	563	1220	−12 / +27	322	304	−8	393	320	+22[1]	197	1374	−23 / +1[1]	—	—	−45
Bangladesh	37	1092	−c1269	15	c12	−c11[1]	—	—	—	—	—	—	4	c1	—	15048	20422	−c195
Belgium	826	c910	−1282[2] / +644[2]	485	c760	−1315[2] / −693[2]	389	c130	−62[2] / +6[2]	120	c30	−14[2] / +8[2]	2	c25	−2453[2] / +1211[2]	—	—	−156[2] / +85[2]
Brazil	574	2207	−4276	26	101	−71	20	90	−29	17	20	—	10112	21098	−1321 / +9	6123	8261	−280 / +59
Bulgaria	2213	4429	−c125 / +356	694	1401	−91 / +11	141	61	—	58	35	—	1601	2477	−588 / +43	37	71	−7[1]
Burma	38	c80	—	—	—	—	—	—	—	—	—	—	58	c100	+13[1]	7786	c14636	+573
Canada	15364	24519	+14590	3860	13384	+3758	6075	3570	+112	319	964	+337	1073	6214	−922 / +634	—	—	−90
Chile	1082	686	−925	74	91	−28 / +11	89	131	−c2[1] / +c11[1]	7	9	—	204	518	−301	85	100	−21 / +111
China	22200	58490	−c10560	c5700	c3400	−c485 / +c1[1]	c1600	c600	—	c1500	c1000	—	c22500	c60000	−c4240 / +c60	c86000	143205	−c125 / +c1340
Colombia	118	62	−c490	106	56	−c69	—	c5	−c10	—	—	—	826	880	−c88	576	1799	−14[1] / +23
Czechoslovakia	1779	c4400	−437 / +c1	1556	c3500	−55 / +20	792	c400	−c11[1] / +c11[1]	897	c500	−12	474	c800	−913 / +c11[1]	—	—	−77
Denmark	535	792	−38 / +140	3506	6010	−84 / +792	713	c165	−16 / +2	380	c200	−5[1] / +76	—	—	−236	—	—	−12 / +2
Egypt	1459	1806	−c4071	137	103	−c4[1]	—	—	—	—	—	—	1913	3308	−c705	1845	2236	+c118
Ethiopia	540	c491	−c259	628	c750	−c16[1]	5	c12	—	—	—	—	743	c1100	−c12[1]	—	—	—
Finland	448	235	−235[1] / +2[1]	400	1080	−32 / +54	828	1008	+6[1]	141	64	−46	—	—	—	—	—	−16
France	12495	22782	−609 / +8752	6594	c10180	−157 / +4061	2583	1754	−1[1] / +269	367	342	−4[1] / +78	2760	9100	−679 / +2802	120	c21	−275 / +27
Germany, East	1357	c3000	−687 / +54	1291	c3800	−717 / +c146	850	c500	−113 / +c116	1741	c1800	−49[1] / +c70	3	c2	−c1692 / +c11[1]	—	—	−c42
Germany, West	4607	8314	−1251 / +572	3462	8687	−1159 / +342	2185	2678	−149 / +12	3031	1729	−62 / +216	55	832	−2561 / +c167	—	—	−175 / +42
Greece	1765	2750	+c162	248	790	−56	143	82	−c1[1]	19	5	—	239	1250	−c988	88	74	+14[1]
Hungary	2020	c4800	−1[1] / +803	970	c950	−128 / +13	108	c80	−8	271	c135	−9[1] / +1[1]	3350	c6500	−83 / +148	36	c35	−24
India	11191	36460	−c540 / +c480	2590	2242	+c7[1]	—	—	—	—	—	—	4593	c7000	−c4[1]	52733	c82000	−c73 / +c386
Indonesia	—	—	−1116	—	—	—	—	—	—	—	—	—	2804	4648	−41 / +12	12396	c32776	−1578
Iran	2873	c5800	−c1450	792	c1300	−c420	—	—	—	—	—	—	24	c50	−c540	851	c1400	−c330
Iraq	849	c1100	−c1650	851	c600	−c230	—	—	—	—	—	—	2	c90	−c160	142	c250	−c340
Ireland	343	c250	−c248 / +c29	575	c1425	−c23 / +c191	357	c96	−c11	1	c1	—	—	—	−c196 / +3[1]	—	—	−c3[1]
Italy	8857	8921	−3163 / +26	276	993	−1392 / +19[1]	545	429	−109 / +11[1]	87	31	−2	3633	7250	−3154 / +32	612	931	−202 / +533
Japan	1332	612	−5701	1380	c390	−1498	145	c10	−160	2	c1	−48	96	c3	−12091	16444	12824	−42 / +557
Kenya	122	212	−c80	15	c80	−2[1] / +1[1]	2	c7	—	—	—	—	1110	2250	−c171 / +36	14	40	−c5[1] / +11
Korea, South	170	57	−c1763	1148	771	−c27	—	—	—	18	c5	−1[1]	26	145	−c2334	4809	7032	−922 / +14[1]
Malaysia	—	—	−c465	—	—	—	—	—	—	—	—	−c6[1]	8	8	−c500 / +c1[1]	1140	2147	−c270
Mexico	1672	3189	−876 / +c15	175	559	−100	76	106	−c3[1]	—	—	—	7369	14766	−2196	314	644	−c52 / +16
Morocco	1516	c892	−c1626	1514	c1039	−13[1]	18	c5	—	2	c2	—	405	c90	−c113	20	c17	—
Netherlands, The	606	882	−1479 / +641	390	249	−422 / +160	421	c115	−27 / +41	312	29	−49 / +10	—	c2	−3108 / c660	—	—	−184 / +114
New Zealand	248	368	−41	98	187	+c50	34	52	—	—	c1	—	16	177	+c32	—	—	−71
Nigeria	16	c21	−c1040	—	—	—	—	—	—	—	—	—	997	c1580	−c139	207	c1241	−c510
Norway	19	c61	−353 / +2[1]	440	c650	−31	126	c417	−1[1] / +9[1]	3	c5	−39	—	—	−61	—	—	−8
Pakistan	4153	11340	−1086	118	c131	+32	—	—	—	—	—	—	514	1104	−3[1]	1824	5093	+1060
Peru	150	c117	−c804	185	c160	−26	4	c1	−c5[1]	1	c1	—	490	587	−270 / +c2[1]	324	712	−150
Philippines	—	—	−740	—	—	—	—	—	—	—	—	−c4[1]	1305	3176	−161	3957	7720	+143
Poland	2988	4203	−3038 / +13[1]	1368	3575	−1480 / +3[1]	2641	2731	−100 / +2[1]	7466	6731	−300 / +c17	20	79	−2238	—	—	−93
Portugal	562	310	−c748	61	38	−c47	87	71	−1[1]	177	125	−13	617	417	−c2217	167	112	−c76
Romania	4321	c5800	−c660 / +c698	415	c2500	−c94	154	c60	−c23[1]	95	c35	−c9[1]	5853	c11200	−c1004 / +c820	40	c65	−c62
South Africa	834	2090	−3[1] / +c141	40	97	+c36	107	c80	−5[1] / +c11[1]	10	8	−1[1]	5248	14645	−4[1] / +c3240	2	c3	−c124 / +11
Spain	4365	3356	−c264 / +c16	1959	4709	−c340 / +1[1]	447	454	+3[1]	385	216	—	1101	2151	−c4260 / +1[1]	386	441	−1[1] / +c61
Sweden	909	1034	−39 / +378	1167	2510	−3[1] / +208	1304	1732	+258	142	195	−1[1] / +59	—	—	−46	—	—	−22
Switzerland	355	391	−358	102	220	−417	40	57	−145	52	32	−18	14	c117	−255	—	—	−28
Syria	1093	2086	−c53 / +7[1]	649	1406	−c77 / +c31	2	c2	—	—	—	—	7	89	−c116	1	—	−c95
Thailand	—	—	−c166	—	—	—	—	—	—	—	—	—	816	c4000	+2097	11267	c19000	+2562
Turkey	8585	17040	−c18 / +c836	3447	5900	+c108	495	300	—	734	500	+21	950	1100	+3[1]	222	290	−21
U.S.S.R.	64207	c88000	−c11520 / +c1630	20318	c43000	−c2060 / +c50	6052	c15000	−c150 / +c12	15093	c8500	−c275 / +c7[1]	13122	c8000	−c12900 / +c133	390	c2400	−c615 / +c16
United Kingdom	3520	8409	−c2565 / +c629	6670	10321	−c266 / +c1080	1541	635	−c34 / +c5	21	24	−c20 / +c11[1]	—	c1	−c3030 / +c18	—	—	−185 / +35
United States	33040	76026	−2 / +36237	8676	10414	−133 / +1199	13848	7375	−13 / +92	828	473	−1[1] / +73	95561	208314	−35 / +56131	3084	8408	−1[1] / +2708
Uruguay	465	c400	−c84	28	c100	−19 / +1[1]	66	c28	−10[1]	—	—	—	148	196	−c21 / +c6[1]	67	326	−3[1] / +c150
Venezuela	1	c1	−c783	—	—	—	—	—	—	—	—	−c4	477	c415	−c690 / +11	136	730	+c6
Yugoslavia	3599	4270	−544 / +c36	557	720	−c26 / +c11	343	311	−1[1]	169	75	—	5618	c9800	−300 / c170	23	c40	−14[1]

Note: (—) indicates quantity nil or negligible. (c) indicates provisional or estimated. [1]1978–80 average. [2]Belgium-Luxembourg economic union.

Sources: FAO Monthly Bulletin of Statistics; FAO Production Yearbook 1981; FAO Trade Yearbook 1980.

(M. C. MacDONALD)

DAVID VON REISEN—THE NEW YORK TIMES

Wheat farmers in the U.S. Midwest were troubled by a fungous disease that hit their grain, causing the creation of vomitoxin, a chemical that can cause dizziness and vomiting in animals.

expected to continue to increase its share of world wheat exports to about 16% of the world total with the aid of heavy export subsidies. The Soviet Union remained the single largest importer of wheat, almost 20 million tons in 1981–82, but China has been importing 13 million to 14 million tons annually since 1980–81.

Less developed countries by 1982 accounted for almost 50% of world wheat imports. The region comprising North Africa and the Middle East im-

Table II. World Cereal Supply and Distribution
In 000,000 metric tons

	1979–80	1980–81	1981–82	1982–83[1]
Production	1,418	1,437	1,490	1,523
Wheat	423	440	447	470
Coarse grains	741	730	767	785
Rice, milled	254	266	277	268
Utilization	1,443	1,455	1,450	1,481
Wheat	444	446	440	456
Coarse grains	741	741	733	751
Rice, milled	258	268	277	273
Exports	200	212	216	209
Wheat	86	94	102	100
Coarse grains	101	106	102	98
Rice, milled	13	13	12	12
Ending stocks[2]	195	177	217	259
Wheat	80	74	81	94
Coarse grains	92	80	114	148
Rice, milled	24	22	22	17
Stocks as % of utilization	13.5%	12.1%	15.0%	17.5%
Wheat	18.0%	16.7%	18.5%	20.7%
Coarse grains	12.3%	10.8%	15.6%	19.7%
Rice, milled	9.3%	8.2%	7.9%	3.5%
Stocks held by U.S. in %	40.0%	35.1%	48.9%	53.4%
Wheat	30.7%	36.2%	39.0%	43.5%
Coarse grains	57.6%	43.2%	64.1%	73.2%
Rice, milled	3.3%	2.3%	7.3%	11.8%

[1] Forecast.
[2] Does not include estimates of total Chinese or Soviet stocks but is adjusted for estimated changes in Soviet stocks.
Source: USDA, Foreign Agricultural Service, December 1982.

effective domestic demand for food and the availability of foreign exchange with which to purchase grain imports. Recession in the developed countries, besides reducing the stimulus to growth that results from demand for exports from less developed countries, also reduced the flow of commercial credits and foreign aid to those nations.

The U.S. captured most of the rise in world wheat exports in 1981–82, but it was also expected to face the largest cutback in exports in adjustment to the rise in world wheat output. Canada and Argentina were expected to increase their wheat exports in 1982–83 as an offset to the substantial decline in Australia's shipments because of its drought. The EEC—which only became a consistent net wheat exporter in the early 1970s—was

ported about 20% of the world total, having grown 7% annually during the 1970s. But the countries of South Asia (India, Bangladesh, and Pakistan), which in the mid-1960s took 15% of world wheat imports, accounted for only 3%, thanks in part to strong growth in domestic grain production.

World wheat stocks increased moderately during 1981–82, and a further buildup was forecast for 1982–83. The level was generally considered comfortable in terms of world food security, although for the most part stocks were heavily concentrated

Israel's dairy cows, among the highest milk producers in the world, average about 7,000 litres per year per cow. The herd is bred and fed using computerized techniques.

AUTHENTICATED NEWS INTERNATIONAL

in the exporting countries—especially in the United States. Prices for wheat weakened in 1982, reaching about $182 per ton in December, compared with an average of about $194 in 1981–82 and about $218 in 1980–81.

World rice production, which reached a record high in 1981–82 based upon both expanded area and rising yields, was forecast to decline in 1982–83. A 16% reduction in Indian rice output because of erratic rainfall was mainly responsible, although Thailand also experienced significant losses. The Chinese harvest was estimated to rise about 3% above the 96 million tons of milled rice produced in 1981–82.

The level of rice consumption is usually closely related to production because most of it is consumed in the countries where it is produced. Only about 5% of world rice production enters into international trade, and stocks historically have been maintained at much lower levels than for wheat. Thus, world rice consumption was expected to decline slightly in 1982–83 after a strong rise in 1981–82. India, however, was expected to reduce its consumption of rice much less than its output by drawing down rice stocks to their lowest level in eight years and by sharply cutting its rice exports, 500,000 tons of which might otherwise have moved to the Soviet Union.

The strong expansion of world stocks of coarse grains that reached record levels by the end of 1981–82 was likely to continue unabated in 1982–83. For the second year in a row stocks were expected to decline outside the U.S. while increasing there to about three-fourths of the world total. The price of corn, which averaged about $164 per ton in 1980–81, fell to about $135 in 1981–82 and stood at only $118 per ton in December 1982.

The vigorous expansion of North American

coarse grain production in 1981–82, following the severe drought in 1980, pushed world output of coarse grains to a record high. An even larger crop was forecast for 1982–83 based mainly upon production increases in the centrally planned economies and Western Europe. Among the major exporters only the United States and South Africa were expected to register increases in the output of corn in 1982–83.

Global utilization of coarse grains in 1981–82 did not keep pace with the rise in production and actually declined. The use of those grains fell sharply in the U.S.S.R. and China, where production shortfalls were only partially offset by larger imports. Eastern Europe also recorded large reductions in utilization of coarse grains because a shortage of foreign exchange seriously limited grain imports. The recession and increased use of grain substitutes, which are subject to much less stringent import barriers than are grains, contributed to a reduction in both the use and importation of coarse grains by the EEC in 1981–82.

The predicted recovery in utilization of coarse grains in 1982–83 was based primarily upon the expected recovery of output—and, thus, use—in the centrally planned countries and upon more grain use in the United States. Poor economic growth prospects in the developed grain-exporting countries were expected to dampen further the demand for livestock products and, thus, reduce further the level of coarse grain imports in 1982–83.

CASSAVA. World production of cassava (also called manioc) rose only an estimated (in July) 1% in 1982, according to FAO, to the equivalent of about 50 million tons of grain. Output fell in Thailand because land previously devoted to cassava was being planted in corn, pulses, oilseeds, and rubber. Thailand accounted for about 90% of world cassava trade in 1981 with shipments of 6.3 million tons (processed product weight) and was estimated to export 6 million tons in 1982, almost all to the EEC.

The EEC in 1982 accepted from Thailand about 500,000 tons more cassava products than provided in the quota it had negotiated with that country. The restrictions were designed to protect the EEC's domestic production of feed grains, with which cassava competes. The EEC also proposed quotas on shipments from Brazil, China, India, Indonesia, and Tanzania at about the level of their aggregate

With surplus cheese piling up in U.S. government warehouses and with more than ten million Americans out of work, U.S. federal officials decided to give away tons of the stockpiled cheese.

UPI

Table III. World Cassava Production
In 000,000 metric tons (root equivalent)

Region	1980	1981[1]	1982[2]
Far East	42.8	47.6	48.0
China	3.2	3.3	3.1
India	5.8	5.8	5.9
Indonesia	13.5	13.7	13.9
Thailand	13.6	17.9	16.2
Vietnam	3.3	3.4	3.5
Africa	46.4	47.7	48.4
Mozambique	2.8	2.9	2.9
Nigeria	11.0	11.0	11.2
Tanzania	4.6	4.7	4.7
Zaire	12.2	13.0	13.3
Latin America	29.9	31.6	31.9
Brazil	23.4	25.1	25.4
Total	119.5	127.3	128.6

[1] Preliminary.
[2] Forecast.
Source: FAO, *Food Outlook* (July 1982).

AGIP/PICTORIAL PARADE

In France farmers took their tractors to the streets of Paris to protest their decreasing incomes.

shipments in 1981, which totaled approximately 1 million tons.

PROTEIN MEAL AND VEGETABLE OIL. Global output of oilseeds was forecast (in November) to increase about 8% in 1982–83 above the 161.4 million tons produced during the previous year. The increase reflected the expansion of the 1982 U.S. soybean harvest, the Soviet and Chinese oilseed harvests in 1982, and the predicted large Southern Hemisphere soybean crops in early 1983. World production of protein meal and vegetable oil from oilseeds was expected to increase slightly faster than the output of oilseeds, but the production of fats and oils from other sources was not expected to change much in 1982–83.

Although world stocks of soybeans fell 6% during 1981–82 to about 14.6 million tons, the large expansion in 1982–83 soybean production was expected to push stocks up as much as 40% during 1982–83. This would raise the U.S. share of the total from 50 to 60%. World soybean output (55% of all oilseeds) was forecast to climb about 13% above the 86.2 million tons harvested in 1981–82. Much of the growth in soybean output in the U.S. resulted from weak grain prices there that led to the diversion of land from grains to soybeans because of government grain-acreage reduction programs. The expected recovery in Brazilian soybean production was slowed by more favourable prices there for corn, which competes for land with soybeans, and by rising production costs. Argentine soybean output was rising most rapidly in areas where double cropping with wheat was being expanded.

World demand for soybeans, as measured by the soybean crush, rose about 2.3% in 1981–82 to about 73.5 million tons despite the slow growth in the livestock industry that dampened the demand for feed. Depressed soybean prices created an incentive for the greater use of soybean meal, relative to corn, in livestock feed. This effect was especially strong in the EEC, where soybeans and

Table IV. World Oilseed Products and Selected Crops			
In 000,000 metric tons			
Region and product	1980–81	1981–82[1]	1982–83[2]
Selected Northern Hemisphere crops			
U.S. soybeans	48.8	54.4	62.6
Chinese soybeans	7.9	9.2	9.8
U.S. sunflower seed	1.7	2.1	2.5
U.S.S.R. sunflower seed	4.7	4.7	5.3
U.S. cottonseed	4.1	5.8	4.3
U.S.S.R. cottonseed	5.1	5.0	5.0
Chinese cottonseed	5.4	5.9	6.5
Canadian rapeseed	2.5	1.8	2.1
Chinese rapeseed	2.4	4.1	4.7
Indian rapeseed	2.2	2.5	2.3
U.S. peanuts	1.0	1.8	1.6
Chinese peanuts	3.6	3.8	3.8
Indian peanuts	5.0	6.2	6.5
Selected Southern Hemisphere crops			
Argentine soybeans	3.5	4.0	4.6
Brazilian soybeans	15.2	12.8	14.3
Argentine sunflower seed	1.3	1.8	1.9
Malay palm oil	2.8	3.3	3.5
World production[3]			
Total fats and oils	56.3	59.3	62.9
Edible vegetable oils	39.1	42.0	45.7
High-protein meals[4]	85.3	91.3	99.3

[1] Preliminary.
[2] Forecast.
[3] Processing potential from crops in year indicated.
[4] 44% protein meal equivalent.
Source: USDA, Foreign Agricultural Service, May and November 1982.

soybean meal are imported freely but where import barriers restrict the importation of feed grains that compete with high-priced domestic feed grains. In 1981–82 the EEC drew even with the U.S. in soybean utilization—each using 16.1 million tons out of a world total of 58.2 million—and it was likely to draw ahead in 1982–83.

World trade in soybeans increased about 16% in 1981–82 to 29.2 million tons, with U.S. exports representing about 86% of the total. Soybean meal exports increased 3% to 20.4 million tons; Brazil had 42% of that total and the United States, 31%.

Prices for soybean oil also declined, pulled down by both larger supplies and the continued rapid expansion of palm oil production. The price of soybean oil was $416 per ton in October 1982, compared with an average of $463 for 1981–82 and $540 for 1980–81. High prices for petroleum deriva-

Agriculture and Food Supplies

UPI

Marvin Meek (right), president of the American Agricultural Movement, recommended in January that farmers reduce production to force food shortages and thereby raise prices of their crops. Beside him is Wayne Cryts, a Puxico, Missouri, farmer.

Table V. Livestock Numbers and Meat Production in Major Producing Countries[1]

In 000,000 head and 000,000 metric tons (carcass weight)

Region and country	1981	1982	1981	1982
	Cattle		Beef and veal	
World total	945.4	942.9	40.58	40.63
Canada	12.5	12.5	1.02	1.04
United States	115.7	115.2	10.35	10.42
Mexico	32.3	28.5	1.13	1.25
EEC	78.0	78.7	6.92	6.65
Eastern Europe	37.9	37.4	2.37	2.47
U.S.S.R.	115.8	116.0	6.60	6.60
Argentina	57.8	58.2	2.96	2.60
Uruguay	10.9	10.5	0.41	0.40
Australia	24.5	23.0	1.42	1.62
New Zealand	8.0	8.0	0.50	0.52
	Hogs		Pork	
World total	421.0	412.1	37.69	37.07
Canada	9.3	9.0	0.87	0.84
United States	58.7	52.5	7.20	6.41
Mexico	16.5	16.0	1.09	1.20
EEC	78.4	78.1	9.46	9.49
Eastern Europe	72.3	69.2	6.67	6.68
U.S.S.R.	73.2	73.9	5.20	5.10
Japan	10.0	10.1	1.40	1.44
	Poultry		Poultry meat	
World total	...	...	22.04	22.36
United States	...	...	6.99	7.03
EEC	...	...	4.15	4.33
U.S.S.R.	...	...	2.30	2.50
Brazil	...	...	1.49	1.59
Japan	...	...	1.13	1.21
	Sheep and goats		Sheep, goat meat	
World total	...	...	4.55	4.51
			All meat	
Total	...	...	104.86	104.57

[1] Preliminary. Livestock numbers at year's end. Consists of 48 countries for beef, veal, pork, sheep, and goat meat and 40 for poultry. Includes all but a few countries in the Western Hemisphere, Europe, Turkey, Israel, Morocco, South Africa, Oceania, Japan, India, South Korea, Taiwan, and Philippines.
Source: USDA, Foreign Agricultural Service, November 1982.

tives, relative to edible vegetable oils, led to the increasing substitution of the latter in the manufacture of fatty acids and other organic chemicals used to make such products as soaps and pesticides.

MEAT AND LIVESTOCK. World meat production in 1982 in the major producing countries was estimated (in November) to continue at about the same level as in 1981, with small increases in poultry output offset by declines in pork. Both cattle and hog numbers declined in some countries because of feed or forage shortages. Many producers also reduced herds or were reluctant to increase them because of expectations of continuing low revenues and dampened consumer demand for red meat that was the result of recession in many countries.

Drought in both Australia and Mexico reduced the availability of both forage and feed in 1982, resulting in a larger cattle slaughter and smaller cattle herds. The cattle and calf slaughter was also heavy in Poland because of feed shortages and low government price guarantees.

In Argentina, however, strong domestic retail prices for beef and devaluation of the peso caused producers to hold cattle back from the market. Nevertheless, Argentina—the single largest exporter—continued the level of its shipments to its major markets, the Soviet Union and the EEC. The Soviet Union in 1982 was again able to support a small increase in cattle numbers, although output leveled off because of lower slaughter rates. During September and October 1982 Australia, New Zealand, and Canada agreed to restrict their beef exports to the United States in order to avoid triggering mandatory import quotas by exceeding the 1,300,000,000-lb limit for 1982 of the U.S. Meat Import Law.

The decline in world pork production in 1982 resulted largely from a sharp drop in U.S. output. U.S. producers reduced their hog breeding stocks because of low profits and debt problems, but falling feed prices, lower interest rates, and strength-

ened retail pork prices appeared to be resulting in a turnaround late in the year. Short feed supplies in both Poland and Mexico led to increased hog slaughter and larger pork output there.

The world sheep inventory may have grown more slowly in 1982 because of reduction in flocks in Australia caused by drought and in the U.S.S.R. because of feed shortages. Nevertheless, Australia maintained its level of production of sheep meat, while domestic price supports for wool and continued strong demand for live sheep in the Middle East gave strong encouragement for resumption in

John Deere, a major farm equipment manufacturer, built a vehicle operation simulator to help company engineers design safer and more comfortable equipment.

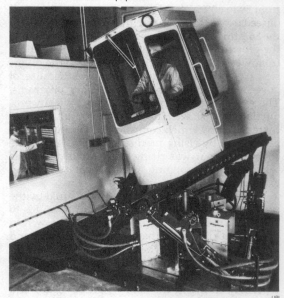

UPI

the buildup of flocks. Minimum price guarantees were also encouraging the creation of larger flocks in New Zealand.

The growth in world poultry production slowed in 1982 primarily because of sharp reductions of output in Poland, resulting from feed shortages, and only small gains in the United States. U.S. producers faced weakened domestic demand and increased competition with its exports—particularly to the Middle East—from subsidized shipments from Brazil and the EEC. Output of poultry meat continued to expand in the Soviet Union despite tight feed supplies.

DAIRY PRODUCTS. The growth in world milk production accelerated in 1982, intensifying the problem of increasingly heavy surpluses of dairy products in several countries. Although the total number of cows throughout the world had increased little since the mid-1970s, the output of milk per cow had risen about 10% because of technological improvements. With the exception of India the largest gains in productivity were in developed countries—particularly France, the United Kingdom, Italy, Ireland, and the United States—where daily output grew much faster than consumption. The world recession contributed to the problem by slowing the growth in demand for such dairy products as cheese and butter.

Because consumption of fresh milk grew little or actually declined in many developed countries in 1982, most of the increased milk output was diverted to the manufacture of processed products, mainly nonfat dry milk (NFDM), butter, and cheese. Production of all those products exceeded their consumption in 1981, and the output of butter and NFDM was increasing more rapidly than consumption. One result was large and expensive additions of those products to government stocks in the U.S., the EEC, and New Zealand. The U.S. Congress attempted to slow the growth in U.S. milk output by freezing dairy price supports, which were scheduled to rise in October, for two years, and by authorizing assessments on commercial sales of milk by producers. Nonetheless, low feed prices were expected to lead to larger U.S. milk output again in 1983. Milk production was also expected to continue to grow in the EEC,

Pres. Ronald Reagan (left), during a farm visit near Des Moines, Iowa, met with farmers Allan and Eric Dee and their father, Donald. Reagan visited the Dees' farm in August after addressing the National Corn Growers Association.

where target prices were increased 10.5% in October.

Production of NFDM in 36 major producing countries was estimated (in December) to have increased 4% in 1982 (double the rise in 1981), and world stocks of NFDM were expected to expand about 32% to a total of 1,429,000 tons (equal to 40% of annual consumption). U.S. stocks of NFDM jumped 56% to 629,000 tons, while the EEC's stocks rose 21% to 465,000 tons. New Zealand also recorded a substantial rise in NFDM stocks. In an attempt to reduce its stocks the EEC subsidized both the feeding of NFDM to hogs and poultry and its exportation, while the U.S. government began to increase sharply its donations of NFDM to needy persons overseas.

Output by major producers of butter (including anhydrous butterfat such as butter oil) rose 2.6% in 1982, while world stocks climbed almost 19% to 751,000 tons (13% of annual consumption). U.S. stocks of butter grew 25% to 243,000 tons, while EEC stocks expanded 22% to 294,000 tons. Total production of cheese rose about 3% in 1982, while stocks of cheese increased 8% to 1,399,000 tons (17% of total consumption). Again the U.S. recorded the largest increase, 17% to 517,000 tons, compared with a 5% rise to 561,000 tons for the EEC. The U.S. attempted to reduce its stocks of butter and cheese through special domestic donations, as did also the EEC for butter.

SUGAR. The world sugar surplus was expected (in November) to continue to expand in 1982–83, despite a likely decline in world sugar production. The sharp jump in world output of centrifugal sugar in 1981–82 led to a large buildup in sugar stocks until they represented nearly 40% of total world sugar production. Market prices of sugar in international trade have tended historically to be depressed whenever the level of stocks has exceeded 25% of consumption. The world price of sugar as measured under the International Sugar Agreement (ISA), which averaged nearly 29 cents a

Table VI. World Milk Production[1]
In 000,000 metric tons

Region	1980	1981	1982
North America	73.2	75.3	76.7
United States	58.3	60.2	61.3
South America	18.6	19.1	19.3
Brazil	10.3	10.5	10.7
Western Europe	131.0	131.4	134.6
EEC	108.1	108.3	111.3
France	28.3	28.4	29.1
West Germany	24.8	24.9	25.4
Italy	11.4	11.2	11.5
Netherlands, The	12.0	12.4	13.2
United Kingdom	16.0	15.9	16.5
Other Western Europe	22.9	23.1	23.3
Eastern Europe and U.S.S.R.	128.5	125.7	126.3
Poland	16.5	15.3	15.3
U.S.S.R.	90.6	88.9	89.5
India	30.0	31.0	32.5
Australia and New Zealand[2]	12.4	12.0	12.0
Japan and South Africa	8.9	8.9	8.9
Total	402.6	403.4	410.4

[1] Based on 36 major producing countries.
[2] Year ending June 30 for Australia and May 31 for New Zealand.
Source: USDA, Foreign Agricultural Service, December 1982.

Table VII. World Production of Centrifugal (Freed from Liquid) Sugar In 000,000 metric tons raw value			
Region	1980–81	1981–82	1982–83[1]
North America and Caribbean	17.2	18.4	17.7
United States	5.4	5.5	5.2
Cuba	7.5	8.2	7.9
Mexico	5.4	5.5	5.2
South America	13.6	13.5	14.6
Argentina	1.7	1.6	1.6
Brazil	8.5	8.3	9.4
Europe	19.7	23.9	22.4
Western Europe	14.9	18.1	16.6
EEC	12.9	15.8	14.3
France	4.2	5.5	4.8
West Germany	3.0	3.7	3.4
Italy	1.9	2.9	1.3
Eastern Europe	4.8	5.8	5.8
U.S.S.R.	7.2	6.4	7.3
Africa and Middle East	7.4	8.8	9.2
South Africa	1.7	2.2	2.3
Asia	17.8	23.3	21.5
China	3.0	3.4	3.7
India	6.5	9.7	8.4
Indonesia	1.3	1.5	1.6
Philippines	2.4	2.5	2.5
Thailand	1.7	2.8	2.1
Oceania	3.8	4.1	4.1
Australia	3.4	3.6	3.6
Total	88.3	100.0	98.5

[1] Preliminary.
Source: USDA, Foreign Agricultural Service, November 1982.

pound in 1980, had fallen to about 6.5 cents per pound in November 1982. Stocks could reach an unprecedented 45% of consumption by the end of 1982–83, even if low prices succeeded in stimulating a more rapid rise in the rate of world sugar consumption than was achieved in 1981–82. Of course, protective trade policies in many countries prevented the effects of low world prices from being fully transmitted to consumers.

Except for February 1982 the ISA price for sugar remained below the ISA minimum of 11 cents per pound. Consequently, ISA members continued to be permitted to export to the free market only 85%

U.S. scientists have developed a moisture-sensing device that can determine the moisture content of the soil beneath the surface. Farmers require such knowledge in order to plan their irrigation schedules.

USDA SCIENCE AND EDUCATION ADMINISTRATION

of their "basic export tonnages" under the ISA. However, the 15.6 million tons of sugar that this represents still exceeded by about 3.6 million tons the estimated needs of ISA members trading in the free market.

In a further attempt to raise sugar prices the ISA members advanced the date by which exporting members were to accumulate 2.5 million tons of special sugar stocks from July 1984 to the end of 1983. The members failed to reach agreement in November 1982 on a proposal to have exporters acquire mandatory additional special stocks, but they authorized applications to the ISA stock financing fund by countries in support of voluntary acquisitions of special stocks.

Negotiations were tentatively scheduled for May 1983 with the aim of replacing the extension of the current ISA with a new agreement by Jan. 1, 1984. The EEC—whose nonmembership in the ISA had been a principal obstacle to its success—planned to participate fully in the renegotiations. ISA members were unwilling to make additional specific proposals to further strengthen the agreement until the EEC indicated a willingness to bind itself to reciprocal actions.

Cocoa. World production of cocoa was forecast (in November) to fall slightly in 1982–83, but stocks were expected to continue growing. Although Ivory Coast's output was expected to decline in 1982–83 because of weather problems and the tightening of the influx of contraband cocoa from Ghana, increases in its production were anticipated thereafter, at least through 1985. One-fourth of the area planted to cocoa in the Ivory Coast had not yet matured. However, the Ivory Coast government reduced the rate of new cocoa plantings and eliminated planting subsidies because of low world cocoa prices.

Although Brazilian cocoa production was expected to recover because of improved weather, the Brazilian government set reduced goals for expanding the area planted to cocoa. The new targets of a 315,000-ha increase by 1985 and a 550,000-ha increase by 1992 represented reductions of 30 and 21%, respectively. Malaysia continued to expand cocoa plantings rapidly in response to high yields and low production costs. Its output could exceed 100,000 tons by 1983–84.

The cocoa-bean grind was estimated at 1.6 million tons in 1982, 1.5% above that in 1981. A nearly 2% increase was forecast for 1983, based upon lower prices for both cocoa and sugar throughout the world. Stocks of cocoa beans increased an estimated 93,000 tons during 1981–82, and the 54,000-ton growth forecast for 1982–83 would be the sixth consecutive annual rise in stocks.

The International Cocoa Organization (ICCO) was attempting—so far unsuccessfully—to push cocoa bean prices up to the minimum price objective of $1.06 per pound. The New York futures price for cocoa beans (average of the nearest three months), which averaged 91.7 cents per pound in December 1981, fell to 66 cents in August 1982 but recovered to about 72 cents in October on reports of a smaller 1982–83 crop.

From the implementation of the International Cocoa Agreement in August 1981 until March 8,

Table VIII. World Cocoa Bean Production
In 000 metric tons

Region	1980–81	1981–82	1982–33[1]
North and Central America	88	103	103
South America	497	466	480
Brazil	351	315	325
Ecuador	84	85	87
Africa	1,002	1,029	990
Cameroon	120	120	122
Ghana	258	222	220
Ivory Coast[2]	412	455	425
Nigeria	155	175	165
Asia and Oceania	97	112	128
Malaysia	50	60	75
Total	1,635	1,710	1,703

[1] Forecast.
[2] Includes some cocoa marketed from Ghana.
Source: USDA, Foreign Agricultural Service, October 1962.

1982, the ICCO's Buffer Stock Fund had expended $235.4 million to purchase 100,345 tons of cocoa beans, mostly from Ivory Coast, Brazil, and Nigeria. In June 1982 the ICCO accepted a $75 million loan from Brazilian banks to continue the fund's operation, but it deferred a decision on the loan's use. The banks had offered an additional $45 million in March 1982 if the ICCO would agree to increase the 2-cents-per-pound export levy that became effective Oct. 1, 1982, to 3 cents. The ICCO could not reach agreement on this proposal at either its July or September 1982 meeting. The impasse revolved around proposals by producing countries to use the loan to purchase up to 150,000 tons of the 1982–83 crop from members and also around proposals by consumer members to reduce the floor price for cocoa beans to 80 or 90 cents per pound. Action on the latter proposal was deferred to the ICCO's meeting in March 1983.

COTTON. World cotton production was forecast (in November) to fall sharply in 1982–83, largely because of a nearly one-third reduction in planted cotton area in the U.S. Large U.S. stocks and sluggish demand favoured the adoption of a voluntary acreage reduction program there. China was expected to move ahead of the U.S.S.R. as the world's leading cotton producer, based on government incentives that had led to larger cotton plantings. Demand for cotton had been depressed as a result of the worldwide economic recession. Estimated world utilization of cotton fell 0.3% in 1981–82 to about 65.5 million bales (480 lb), and forecasts of a modest increase in 1982–83 were scaled down because of delayed economic recovery throughout the world.

Table IX. World Cotton Production
In 000,000 480-lb bales

Region	1980	1981	1982
North and Central America	13.9	18.0	13.6
Mexico	1.6	1.4	0.9
United States	11.1	15.6	11.9
South America	4.8	5.0	4.6
Brazil	2.8	2.9	2.9
Europe	0.9	0.9	0.8
U.S.S.R.	14.3	13.5	13.3
Africa	5.3	5.3	5.4
Egypt	2.4	2.3	2.1
Asia and Oceania	26.5	28.4	29.5
China	12.4	13.6	15.0
India	6.1	6.3	6.2
Pakistan	3.3	3.5	3.7
Turkey	2.3	2.2	2.1
Total	65.6	71.0	67.2

Source: USDA, Foreign Agricultural Service, May and November 1982.

World stocks of cotton at the beginning of 1982–83 amounted to 28.1 million bales, 23% above a year earlier and the largest total since 1974–75. They represented 42% of estimated world use of cotton. The rise in stocks during 1981–82 pushed the average price of cotton (Outlook "A" Index) down to 67.7 cents per pound in December 1981, from which it recovered to 78.5 cents in July 1982; it then slipped back to 70.2 cents by October, reflecting the unlikely prospects for stock reductions in 1982–83.

Trade Tensions. A large number of trade disputes occurred in 1982, many of which had agricultural questions as their central focus. Depressed economic conditions in many countries generated pressures that exacerbated many of these disputes. The U.S. and the EEC were the principal protagonists in the agricultural area.

The agricultural sectors in both the U.S. and the EEC had faced serious difficulties in recent years, which intensified their trade differences. In the U.S. farm income was down because of the price-depressing effects of large agricultural supplies and also because operating costs had been driven up rapidly by inflationary forces. Thus, U.S. net farm income, which amounted to $32.3 billion in 1979, fell to $20.1 billion in 1980, recovered to $25.1 billion in 1981, and slipped again to an estimated $19 billion in 1982. The crop sector was hit the hardest—the livestock sector at least benefited from low feed prices—as prices for wheat and corn fell below the loan rate to the lowest levels since 1978–79. These developments also greatly added to government spending through automatic deficiency payments designed to support farm income and through acquisition of surplus agricultural commodities just at a time when budgetary deficits were becoming a central preoccupation of U.S. economic and political life.

"Does this mean I gotta start pulling the plow myself?"

MAULDIN © 1982 CHICAGO SUN-TIMES

**Agriculture and
Food Supplies**

Japanese farmers protested in April against relaxed import rules that would allow greater imports of U.S. beef, citrus fruits, and other crops.

Under such conditions U.S. agriculture was particularly prone to look abroad to find an outlet for its agricultural surpluses in foreign markets. U.S. farmers had become accustomed to a rapid expansion of sales of their products overseas during the last decade when U.S. agricultural exports rose annually by an average of 13%. During that time U.S. agriculture became much more dependent upon foreign sales for its income. About two acres out of every five on U.S. farms were used to produce for export; 35% of the corn produced in the U.S. in 1980–81, 64% of the wheat, 40% of the soybeans, and 53% of the cotton were exported. But in fiscal 1982, the value of U.S. agricultural exports fell for the first time since 1969, dropping 11% to an estimated $39.1 billion.

One of the immediate factors contributing to the decline was the strengthening of the U.S. dollar during 1981 and 1982 in important markets for U.S. agricultural exports. This made U.S. commodities more expensive in those foreign currencies. Another was the dampening effect of low economic growth upon domestic demand for agricultural products in many of those markets, particularly in the industrialized world. Among agricultural commodities sales of meat and dairy products were the most likely to contract in response to a rise in price or a reduction in consumer income. Feedstuffs destined for use in foreign livestock and dairy industries, together with livestock products, make up a high proportion of U.S. farm exports. In addition, the U.S. is an important export market for many

countries, especially for manufactured products, and the U.S. recession reduced the U.S. demand for their exports.

Another source of difficulties for U.S. farm exports was the aftermath of the U.S. embargo on the sale of its agricultural products to the Soviet Union, imposed in January 1980 by Pres. Jimmy Carter in response to the Soviet invasion of Afghanistan and ended by Pres. Ronald Reagan in April 1981. The resulting loss in grain sales by U.S. farmers contributed substantially to the buildup in U.S. grain stocks that helped depress prices and added to governmental budget outlays.

Total U.S. grain shipments to the U.S.S.R. in 1980–81 (July–June) were cut nearly in half to the minimum guaranteed by the U.S.-Soviet grain agreement. The U.S. export cutback was most severe for corn, the grain in greatest oversupply in the United States. Although U.S. grain shipments to the U.S.S.R. recovered to the pre-embargo level in 1981–82, the U.S. did not capture any of the large expansion in Soviet grain imports that occurred in those two years as the result of successive poor grain harvests. Argentina, which was the only major grain exporter not to agree to join in trade sanctions against the U.S.S.R., made the most gains in the Soviet market, although Canada and the EEC also increased their market shares.

In addition to these apparently short run problems, U.S. farmers were faced with the growing irritant of the expanding, heavily subsidized agricultural exports of the EEC. In terms of overall world agricultural trade the EEC's share of exports increased from 9.5% in 1973 to 11.1% in 1980, while the U.S. share fell from 19.8 to 18.9%. The largest EEC gains since 1970 were in commodities that touched U.S. nerves: wheat (from under 3 to 10% of total exports), wheat flour (34 to almost 50%), dairy products (22 to about 33%), and broiler chickens (from being the world's largest importer to 35% of world exports).

Under the EEC's common agricultural policy (CAP) the EEC stood ready to purchase commodities produced by its farmers at a floor "intervention" price as part of its overall policy to support EEC farm income. That price was considerably higher than either the price of those commodities in world trade or the roughly comparable "loan rate" in the United States. For instance, the intervention price in 1982 for bread wheat was almost the equivalent of $10 per bushel and almost $6 for corn, compared with, in October 1982, a U.S. export price of $3.84 and a loan rate of $3.55 for wheat and $2.38 and $2.55, respectively, for corn. To keep out lower-cost imports the EEC imposed a "variable levy" on imports which raised their cost to the "threshold" price, or desired ceiling. But in order to avoid accumulating ever larger stocks of domestic commodities, the CAP provides for "restitutions" (export subsidies) to exporters equal to the difference between the intervention price and the much lower price needed to be competitive in world markets. The purchase of surplus commodities and payment of export subsidies (estimated at $6.5 billion in 1980) was the reason that the annual operating costs of the CAP rose from $2 billion in 1970 to almost $14 billion in the 1980s. In the long run the internal political pressures generated by these costs might themselves force reform of the CAP.

The U.S., which had been concerned about its restricted access to the EEC's agricultural market, began to press harder for both the elimination of import barriers and the elimination of subsidies on EEC exports that competed with U.S. products in third-country markets. The U.S. was already pursuing a number of complaints against the EEC under the General Agreement on Tariffs and Trade (GATT), including separate cases dealing with wheat flour, sugar, poultry, pasta, canned fruit, and citrus.

U.S. fears were intensified when the EEC asked the U.S. in May 1982 to negotiate under GATT what it called temporary restrictions on importation of corn gluten, an animal feed U.S. sales of which to the EEC totaled about $500 million annually. Many U.S. exporters feared that the action would be a precedent for restrictions on soybean products, the most important U.S. export to the EEC. Their fears were plausible since importation of those products undermined the EEC's grain policies.

Agricultural issues, thus, suddenly emerged as perhaps the most central and contentious topic discussed at the November 1982 GATT ministerial conference, the first meeting of the GATT's governing council since completion of the 1979 Multilateral Trade Negotiations. The meeting was preceded by apparent threats and counterthreats of trade wars, including statements about dumping U.S. wheat and dairy products on world markets in retaliation against the EEC.

The United States entered the meeting advocating a "standstill" on export subsidies for agricultural products together with their phaseout over a specified period. The EEC adamantly refused, and the conference nearly broke apart over the issue. However, differences were papered over at the last minute with a jointly agreed declaration that, among other things, included a loose commitment "to refrain from taking or maintaining any measures inconsistent with GATT and to make determined efforts to avoid measures which distort international trade."

Roger West (right) of the U.S. Department of Agriculture checks a Japanese ship upon its arrival in New York City. The department was waging a battle to make sure that no foreign pests arrived on U.S. shores.

Many veal producers in France were
accused by government officials of
injecting their calves with an illegal
hormone that caused the calves to
grow rapidly but could also be a
health hazard to human consumers.

International Food Security. Food security issues received much less prominence than trade problems in 1982. The earlier efforts to achieve some international system of food security in the form of a new International Wheat Agreement appeared to have lost all momentum. The U.S. opposition to any form of international management or coordination of grain reserves along with preferences for more informal consultative procedures, such as those carried out in the International Wheat Council, was probably decisive, although none of the other grain-exporting nations showed enthusiasm for a new agreement. The secretariats of the World Food Council and FAO encouraged consideration of a coordinated grain reserve for less developed countries, and some interest was expressed in regional reserves for Africa and Asia, but none went beyond the exploratory stage.

Shipments of food aid in the form of cereals rose from about 8.6 million tons in 1980–81 to about 9.4 million tons in 1981–82. Preliminary estimates of allocations for 1982–83 indicated a reduction, based on budgetary allocations for food aid in the U.S. Some of the U.S. dairy surplus was expected to be channeled into increased food aid.

As of October 1982 pledges of contributions for 1981–82 were $170 million short of the $1 billion target. For the 1982–83 biennium pledges equal to

83% of the $1.2 billion target had been made. Budgetary restraints were delaying the U.S. contribution, which totaled $220 million in 1981–82. Contributions to the International Emergency Food Reserve for 1982 amounted to 413,000 tons as of November, short of its 500,000-ton target and below the 610,000 tons contributed in 1981.

Foreign Assistance to Agriculture. Official commitments of external assistance to agriculture in the less developed countries—narrowly defined to include only direct support to agriculture—fell in 1981 according to the Organization for Economic Cooperation and Development (OECD) and FAO. Direct support of agriculture in recent years had averaged about 70% of assistance defined broadly by the OECD to include rural infrastructure, agro-industries, fertilizer production, and regional river basin projects. The component of total assistance that declined the most, and for the second year in a row, was bilateral aid. Its share of total official external assistance fell below 40% for the first time since 1973.

The International Fund for Agricultural Development (IFAD) was the only multilateral source of assistance not to increase its commitments to agriculture in 1981. It was forced to reduce its commitments by 50%. Disagreement between the industrialized IFAD members and the Organization of Petroleum Exporting Countries (OPEC) over the appropriate shares of their respective pledges delayed replenishment of the fund. OPEC continued to object to the United States' stretching out of its commitment over a five-year, rather than a three-year, period, claiming that the U.S. action constituted a reduction in its commitment. The IFAD Governing Council in late 1982 finally agreed to a $1.1 billion replenishment, the same level as the Fund's original endowment.

The continuing effects of world recession and budgetary constraints in donor countries probably also ruled out an increase in official foreign assistance to agricultural development in 1982. As an indication the World Bank's International Development Association (IDA) had to reduce its lending for all purposes (including nonagricultural) from

	Table X. Shipments of Food Aid in Cereals			
	In 000,000 metric ton grain equivalent			
Country	Average 1977–78, 1979–80	1980–81[1]	1981–82[1]	1982–83[2]
Australia	294	394	511	400
Canada	783	600	600	600
EEC				
By members, directly	607	478	775	722
By organization	639	622	914	928
Japan	392	567	683	700
Sweden	102	94	123	120
United States	5,856	5,216	5,341	5,098
Others	524	483	434	384
Total[3]	9,197	8,454	9,381	8,952

[1]Partly estimated.
[2]Allocations, some estimated.
[3]Includes Argentina, Austria, China, Finland, India, Norway, OPEC Special Fund, Saudi Arabia, Spain, Switzerland, Turkey, and World Food Program, but not necessarily for all years.
Source: FAO, *Food Outlook* (November 30, 1982).

Table XI. Official Commitments of External Assistance to Agriculture in Less Developed Countries[1] In $000 000				
Commitments	Average 1976–78	1979	1980	1981[2]
Total				
Multilateral	2,850	3,634	4,732	4,616
Bilateral	2,049	3,323	3,188	2,710
Current prices	4,899	6,957	7,920	7,326
1975 prices[3]	4,388	4,865	5,013	4,884
Concessional				
Multilateral	1,515	2,028	2,638	2,247
Bilateral	1,988	3,220	3,159	2,420
Current prices	3,503	5,248	5,797	4,661
1975 prices[3]	3,104	3,670	3,669	3,111
Nonconcessional				
Multilateral	1,334	1,606	2,094	2,369
Bilateral[4]	61	103	29	290
Current prices	1,395	1,709	2,123	2,659
1975 prices[3]	1,234	1,195	1,344	1,773

[1] "Agriculture" conforms to OECD "narrow" definition. Excludes commitments by centrally planned countries.
[2] Preliminary.
[3] Deflated by the UN unit-value index of exports of manufactured goods.
[4] Partial estimates.
Source: OECD and FAO, November 1982.

$3.5 billion in fiscal year 1981 to $2.7 billion in 1982. However, chances appeared to be good that the IDA would be able to increase its lending to $3.3 billion in both fiscal 1983 and 1984.

A sustained cutback in foreign aid to agriculture in less developed countries could have a serious effect upon nations facing the most persistent food problems. The World Bank pointed out, for example, that foreign aid accounted for an average of 20% of public investment in agriculture in the poorest countries of Africa. Little private foreign investment or lending had flowed to agriculture in the low-income countries in recent years, and foreign aid had become, according to the Bank, the main external source of foreign exchange and technical support. (RICHARD M. KENNEDY)

Illinois Gov. James Thompson (right) announced in September that 170,000 metric tons of Illinois-produced corn and soybeans would be sold to Taiwan.

WIDE WORLD

See also Environment; Fisheries; Food Processing; Gardening; Industrial Review: *Alcoholic Beverages; Textiles; Tobacco.*
[451.B.1.c; 534.E; 731; 10/37.C]

Albania

A people's republic in the western Balkan Peninsula, Albania is on the Adriatic Sea, bordered by Greece and Yugoslavia. Area: 28,748 sq km (11,100 sq mi). Pop. (1982 est.): 2,862,000. Cap. and largest city: Tirana (pop., 1978 est., 198,000). Language: Albanian. Religion: officially atheist; historically Muslim, Orthodox, and Roman Catholic communities. First secretary of the Albanian (Communist) Party of Labour in 1982, Enver Hoxha; chairmen of the Presidium of the People's Assembly (presidents), Haxhi Leshi and, from November 22, Ramiz Alia; chairman of the Council of Ministers (premier) from January 18, Adil Carcani.

On Jan. 14, 1982, the Albanian People's Assembly approved Pres. Enver Hoxha's nomination of Adil Carcani as premier to succeed Mehmet Shehu, who allegedly committed suicide in December 1981. Carcani had become first deputy premier in 1965 and a member of the Albanian Party of Labour's Politburo in 1974.

In his maiden speech, Carcani did not refer to his predecessor; however, Mehmet Shehu's nephew, Fecor Shehu, formerly minister of the interi-

Albania

ALBANIA
Education. (1973–74) Primary, pupils 569,600, teachers 22,686; secondary, pupils 32,900, teachers (1971–72) 1,318; vocational and teacher training, pupils 69,700, teachers (1971–72) 1,712; higher (1971–72), students 28,668, teaching staff 1,153.
Finance. Monetary unit: lek, with (Sept. 20, 1982) a free exchange rate of 5.89 leks to U.S. $1 (10.10 leks = £1 sterling). Budget (1981 est.): revenue 8.2 billion leks; expenditure 8,150,000,000 leks.
Foreign Trade. (1979) Imports c. 900 million leks; exports c. 1 billion leks. Import sources: Czechoslovakia c. 12%; Yugoslavia c. 12%; China c. 10%; Italy c. 8%; Poland 8%; West Germany c. 7%. Export destinations: Czechoslovakia c. 11%; Yugoslavia c. 10%; Italy c. 10%; China c. 9%; Poland c. 7%; West Germany c. 7%. Main exports (1964; latest available): fuels, minerals, and metals (including crude oil, bitumen, chrome ore, iron ore, and copper) 54%; foodstuffs (including vegetables and fruit) 23%; raw materials (including tobacco and wool) 17%.
Transport and Communications. Roads (1971) 5,500 km. Motor vehicles in use (1970): passenger c. 3,500; commercial (including buses) c. 11,200. Railways: 1979 c. 330 km; traffic (1971) 291 million passenger-km, freight 188 million net ton-km. Shipping (1981): merchant vessels 100 gross tons and over 20; gross tonnage 56,127. Shipping traffic (1975): goods loaded c. 2.8 million metric tons, unloaded c. 760,000 metric tons. Telephones (Dec 1965) 13,991. Radio receivers (Dec. 1979) 201,000. Television receivers (Dec. 1979) 5,000.
Agriculture. Production (in 000; metric tons; 1980): corn c. 330; wheat c. 440; oats c. 30; potatoes c. 130; sugar, raw value c. 40; sunflower seed c. 24; olives c. 50; grapes c. 61; tobacco c. 14; cotton, lint c. 9. Livestock (in 000; 1980): sheep c. 1,170; cattle c. 475; pigs c. 125; goats c. 670; poultry c. 2,400.
Industry. Production (in 000; metric tons; 1979): crude oil c. 2,100; lignite c. 1,100; petroleum products c. 2,060; chrome ore (oxide content) c. 465; copper ore (metal content) c. 12; nickel ore (metal content) c. 8; fertilizers (nutrient content) c. 90; cement c. 1,000; electricity (kw-hr) c. 2,400,000.

Aircraft:
see Aerial Sports; Defense; Industrial Review; Transportation

Air Forces:
see Defense

or, was not included in the new government, and the late premier's widow, Ficreta Sandiaktari, was removed from her post of secretary in charge of ideology on the party's 81-member Central Committee. The chief ideologist was now Ramiz Alia, one of the 13 members of the Politburo. A further purge of Shehu's associates was reported in November, when Alia replaced Haxhi Leshi as chairman of the Presidium of the People's Assembly (president). In a speech at the time of the November Assembly elections (won overwhelmingly by the single slate of candidates), Hoxha said Shehu had been an agent for the U.S., the U.S.S.R., and Yugoslavia. Relations with Yugoslavia remained strained following further demonstrations in February by ethnic Albanians in the Yugoslavian province of Kosovo.

According to a communiqué issued by the Ministry of the Interior, an armed gang led by "the bandit Xhevdet Mustafa" landed on the Albanian coast on the night of September 25–26. Five hours later, however, the invaders were "liquidated."

(K. M. SMOGORZEWSKI)

Algeria

Algeria

A republic on the north coast of Africa, Algeria is bounded by Morocco, Western Sahara, Mauritania, Mali, Niger, Libya, and Tunisia. Area: 2,381,741 sq km (919,595 sq mi). Pop. (1982 est.): 19,954,000. Cap. and largest city: Algiers (pop., 1978 est., 1,998,000). Language: Arabic (official); with Berber and French minorities. Religion (1980): Muslim 99.1%; Christian 0.8%; none 0.1%. President in 1982, Col. Chadli Bendjedid; premier, Mohamed Ben Ahmed Abdelghani.

The major issue for Algeria during 1982 was the prolonged struggle to gain a fair price for its major resource, natural gas. This was caused by Algeria's decision to index natural gas prices to crude oil prices. In February 1982 France agreed to buy Algerian gas at slightly more than the world price. Other agreements followed, including one with

ALGERIA

Education. (1981–82) Primary, pupils 4.6 million, (1980–81) teachers 88,481; secondary, pupils 999,937, teachers 38,845; vocational, pupils 12,903, teachers 1,168; teacher training, students 13,315, teachers 1,124; higher, students (1979–80) 57,208, teaching staff (1978–79) 7,401.

Finance. Monetary unit: dinar, with (Sept. 20, 1982) a free rate of 4.64 dinars to U.S. $1 (7.95 dinars = £1 sterling). Gold and other reserves (June 1982) U.S. $2,775,-000,000. Budget (1981 est.): revenue 68,305,000,000 dinars; expenditure 36,195,000,000 dinars (excludes 31,593,000,000 dinars development expenditure). Money supply (Nov. 1981) 95,153,000,000 dinars.

Foreign Trade. (1981) Imports c. 46 billion dinars; exports 50,902,000,000 dinars. Import sources (1979): France 18%; West Germany 18%; Italy 13%; Belgium-Luxembourg 7%; U.S. 6%; Spain 5%; Japan 5%. Export destinations (1979): U.S. 52%; France 14%; West Germany 11%; Italy 6%. Main exports (1979): crude oil 86%; natural gas 6%; petroleum products 5%.

Transport and Communications. Roads (1977) c. 78,000 km. Motor vehicles in use (1978): passenger 396,800; commercial (including buses) 206,500. Railways (1978): 3,908 km; traffic 1,644,000,000 passenger-km, freight 2,177,000,000 net ton-km. Air traffic (1980): c. 2,300,000,000 passenger-km; freight c. 13 million net ton-km. Shipping (1981): merchant vessels 100 gross tons and over 129; gross tonnage 1,287,833. Shipping traffic (1978): goods loaded 49,829,000 metric tons, unloaded 13,498,000 metric tons. Telephones (Jan. 1980) 422,010. Radio receivers (Dec. 1979) 3,220,000. Television receivers (Dec. 1979) 750,000.

Agriculture. Production (in 000; metric tons; 1981): wheat c. 1,400; barley c. 750; oats c. 100; potatoes c. 618; tomatoes c. 197; onions c. 118; dates c. 206; oranges c. 300; mandarin oranges and tangerines c. 140; watermelons c. 178; olives c. 140; wine c. 284. Livestock (in 000; 1980): sheep 12,500; goats c. 2,850; cattle c. 1,433; asses c. 538; horses c. 176; camels c. 150; chickens c. 18,000.

Industry. Production (in 000; metric tons; 1980): iron ore (53–55% metal content) 3,500; phosphate rock 1,025; crude oil (1981) 36,500; natural gas (cu m) 19,347,000; petroleum products (1979) c. 5,600; fertilizers (nutrient content; 1980–81) nitrogenous c. 24, phosphate c. 31; cement (1979) 3,773; crude steel (1979) 462; electricity (kw-hr) 6,200,000.

Italy for gas transported via the new Trans-Mediterranean pipeline, which was completed in 1981 but lay idle until September 1982 because of the dispute. These agreements meant that Algeria was able to counter the fall in crude oil sales, which dropped to 37.5 million metric tons for 1981.

Presidents Chadli Benjedid (left) of Algeria and François Mitterrand of France waved to the crowd from their motorcade during Mitterrand's state visit to Algeria on May 19.

GAMMA/LIAISON

Alcoholic Beverages:
see Industrial Review

A bilateral economic cooperation convention was signed between France and Algeria on June 21. Among other provisions, France was to supply 5,000 trucks, construct a subway system for Algiers, and build two gasification plants. The agreement was worth over $3 billion. This renewed cooperation between Algeria and France was crowned by the visit to Algiers of Pres. François Mitterrand on May 19. However, a return visit to Paris by President Bendjedid on December 17 was marred by disagreement over France's immigration policy and its application to Algerians.

Algeria also looked elsewhere for support. An economic agreement with Libya for cooperation over oil and gas exploration and production was signed in early April. However, despite Libyan requests, Algeria did not increase its support for the Popular Front for the Liberation of Saguia el Hamra and Río de Oro (Polisario Front) in the Western Sahara conflict.

Festivities planned for the 20th anniversary of Algeria's independence on July 5 were canceled because of the Israeli invasion of Lebanon. Internal unrest among industrial workers and young people occurred during the year. National Assembly elections on March 5 underlined the domination of the National Liberation Front (FLN), the sole political party. Marxist tendencies within the FLN were purged in favour of Arabo-Islamic socialism. The government continued to emphasize Algeria's Arabo-Islamic heritage. When Foreign Minister Muhammad Seddik Benyahia (see OBITUARIES) died in May, his replacement was Ahmed Taleb Ibrahimi, a well-known Arabist.

The $16 billion budget for 1982 was directed toward infrastructure and communications. Industrial development continued to slow, and the private sector received modest encouragement. Algeria was considered sound by the international financial community, and this fact, together with its developing role as a mediator in international affairs, added to its growing international stature.

(GEORGE JOFFÉ)

Andorra

An independent co-principality of Europe, Andorra is in the Pyrenees Mountains between Spain and France. Area: 468 sq km (181 sq mi). Pop. (1982): 38,050. Cap.: Andorra la Vella (commune pop., 1982, 14,900). Language: Catalan (official), French, Spanish. Religion: predominantly Roman Catholic. Co-princes: the president of the French Republic and the bishop of Urgel, Spain, represented by their *veguers* (provosts) and *batlles* (prosecutors). An elected Council General of 28 members elects the first syndic; in 1982 Estanislau Sangrà Font and, from January 4, Francesc Cerqueda Pascuet; chief executive from January 8, Oscar Ribas Reig.

On Jan. 4, 1982, the Council General elected Francesc Cerqueda Pascuet as first syndic of Andorra. Four days later, in response to the demand for institutional reform expressed in January 1981 by the two co-princes, the Council General elected Oscar Ribas Reig, the nephew of former first syn-

Andorra

ANDORRA
Education. (1979–80) Primary, pupils 4,711, teachers 305; secondary, pupils 2,134, teachers (1974–75) 120.

Finance and Trade. Monetary units: French franc and Spanish peseta. Budget (1979 est.) balanced at 3,209,-000,000 pesetas. Foreign trade: imports from France (1979) Fr 933,809,000 (U.S. $219.5 million), from Spain (1980) 10,924,000,000 pesetas (U.S. $152.4 million); exports to France (1979) Fr 22,201,000 (U.S. $5.2 million), to Spain (1980) 788,850,000 pesetas (U.S. $11 million). Tourism (1978) 6.4 million visitors.

Communications. Telephones (Jan. 1980) 12,200. Radio receivers (Dec. 1979) 7,000. Television receivers (Dec. 1979) 3,500.

Agriculture. Production: cereals, potatoes, tobacco, wool. Livestock (in 000; 1980): sheep c. 12; cattle c. 4.

dic Juliá Reig-Ribò, as chief executive. On January 15 Ribas Reig announced his Cabinet—the first in Andorran history—of four ministers. Their responsibilities were finance, agriculture, public works, and education.

In April six Basque terrorists, members of the Euzkadi ta Azkatasuna (ETA), carried out armed robberies at two banks in Andorra la Vella, stealing 2 million pesetas from one and 16 million pesetas from the other. The latter sum was recovered by police when the culprits were arrested. Three terrorists were sentenced to imprisonment, and Andorran authorities refused the demands of the Spanish government to extradite the group.

Andorra was virtually isolated by a severe storm on November 7–8 that caused nine deaths and heavy damage.   (K. M. SMOGORZEWSKI)

Angola

Located on the west coast of southern Africa, Angola is bounded by Zaire, Zambia, South West Africa/Namibia, and the Atlantic Ocean. The small exclave of Cabinda, a province of Angola, is bounded by the Congo and Zaire. Area: 1,246,700 sq km (481,353 sq mi). Pop. (1982 est.): 6,943,700. Cap. and largest city: Luanda (pop., 1979 est., 475,300). Language: Bantu languages (predominant), Portuguese (official), and some Khoisan dialects. Religion (1980): Roman Catholic 68.7%; Protestant 19.8; tribal 9.5%; other Christian 1.5%; none 0.5%. President in 1982, José Eduardo dos Santos.

Planning Minister Lopo do Nascimento announced early in January 1982 that Angola could not hope to avoid the food crisis that was affecting the whole of Africa, thus heralding another year of nationwide shortages. As a result of two years of drought and the continuing internal security problems, the amount of home-grown food sold in 1981 had declined by 26% from 1979; this could not be offset by purchasing food overseas because of the shortage of foreign exchange. In December 1982, faced by a worsening economic situation, Pres. José dos Santos assumed emergency powers.

Angola's difficulties were aggravated by the fact that the government had to spend more than half of its revenue and foreign exchange earnings on financing military operations against Jonas Savimbi's National Union for the Total Independence of Angola (UNITA) guerrillas and in responding to

Angola

American Literature: see Literature

Anglican Communion: see Religion

WIDE WORLD

Pres. Fidel Castro of Cuba announced in July that his troops would remain in Angola until South Africa withdrew from Namibia.

South African armed incursions over the southern border. UNITA operations were undiminished along the Benguela Railway in the centre of the country as well as in the south, where there was more direct support from South Africa. Savimbi himself visited the U.S. and several African countries early in the year, raising money for his guerrilla campaign and collecting Soviet-made missiles. In January he claimed that he had been approached by the Angolan government with a view to negotiating a peace settlement. He had replied that UNITA was willing to negotiate but that a condition of any agreement must be the withdrawal of all Cubans from Angola.

This requirement was a clear reflection of the policy of UNITA's South African supporters, and it recurred throughout the year during the negotiations on the future of South West Africa/Namibia. In this way Angola was drawn still more deeply into discussions that involved the U.S. as well as a number of European countries. Pres. Fidel Castro of Cuba also intervened in July to confirm that Cuban troops would not pull out of Angola until South Africa withdrew from Namibia and ended its aggression toward Angolan territory. The Angolan government stressed that the two matters were in no way linked because the presence of Cubans in Angola was the result of a bilateral agreement between those two countries and was outside the jurisdiction of any other power. Nevertheless, it was widely believed that the U.S., in its anxiety to settle the Namibian problem, was bringing pressure on Angola to remove what appeared to be an important obstacle in the way of South African participation in negotiations.

The Angolan government was itself anxious for a Namibian settlement, which, it was hoped, would remove the South African threat from the southern border and thereby weaken the challenge presented by UNITA. Angola could then concentrate on building up its economy with the assistance of the U.S. and Western Europe. Already Angola was trying to borrow $100 million from Western banks to help cover its balance of payments deficit.

Relations with South Africa remained strained. In March Angola joined with five other southern African nations meeting in Maputo, Mozambique,

ANGOLA

Education. (1978) Primary, pupils 1,388,110, teachers (1977) 25,000; secondary and vocational, pupils 153,000, teachers (1972–73) 4,393; teacher training (1972–73), students 2,005, teachers 173; higher, students 4,746, teaching staff (1972–73) 333.

Finance and Trade. Monetary unit: kwanza, with a free rate (Sept. 20, 1982) of 30.21 kwanzas to U.S. $1 (51.80 kwanzas = £1 sterling). Budget (1981 est.) balanced at 108,874,000,000 kwanzas. Foreign trade (1981): imports c. U.S. $1,639,000,000; exports c. U.S. $1,744,000,000. Import sources: Portugal c. 15%; France c. 11%; Soviet Union c. 9%; South Africa c. 9%; Brazil c. 8%; U.K. c. 7%; Japan c. 6%; Sweden c. 6%; West Germany c. 5%; The Netherlands c. 5%. Export destinations: U.S. c. 49%; The Bahamas c. 15%; Spain c. 7%; Brazil c. 7%. Main exports (1979): crude oil 68%; coffee 14%; diamonds 11%; petroleum products 6%.

Transport and Communications. Roads (1974) 72,323 km. Motor vehicles in use (1979): passenger 144,000; commercial (including buses) 43,000. Railways: (1980) c. 3,999 km; traffic (1974) 418 million passenger-km, freight 5,461,000,000 net ton-km. Air traffic (1980): c. 553 million passenger-km; freight c. 21 million net ton-km. Shipping (1981): merchant vessels 100 gross tons and over 44; gross tonnage 79,889. Shipping traffic (1977): goods loaded c. 9.4 million metric tons, unloaded c. 1.9 million metric tons. Telephones (Dec. 1978) 28,000. Radio receivers (Dec. 1979) 125,000. Television receivers (Dec. 1979) 2,000.

Agriculture. Production (in 000; metric tons; 1981): corn c. 250; cassava c. 1,900; sweet potatoes c. 180; dry beans c. 45; bananas c. 309; citrus fruit c. 81; palm kernels c. 12; palm oil c. 40; coffee c. 40; cotton, lint c. 11; sisal c. 20; fish catch (1980) 78; timber (cu m; 1980) c. 8,759. Livestock (in 000; 1980): cattle c. 3,209; sheep c. 225; goats c. 935; pigs c. 400.

Industry. Production (in 000; metric tons; 1979): cement c. 400; diamonds (metric carats; 1980) 1,500; crude oil (1981) c. 7,160; petroleum products c. 1,000; electricity (kw-hr) c. 1.4 million.

to issue a communiqué promising increased support for the African National Congress in its campaign against the South African government. In the meantime, South African troops continued to harass Angola's southern frontier. In March a member of Angola's defense staff stated that South Africa still occupied 129,500 sq km (50,000 sq mi) of Angolan territory. The South African government consistently denied all such claims but almost simultaneously announced that its forces operating in Angola had killed 201 guerrillas belonging to the South West Africa People's Organization (SWAPO) and had captured large quantities of ammunition. Again, in August, after repeatedly denying claims by the Angolan government that it had embarked upon a major incursion into Angolan territory, South African defense headquarters admitted having pursued SWAPO guerrillas over the Angolan border, killing more than 300 of them. In May South African Air Force planes carried out a number of raids over the border, and in September South Africa claimed to have shot down a Soviet-made jet fighter over Angolan territory.

(KENNETH INGHAM)

Antarctica

The Antarctic Treaty nations began to formulate a regime for the exploitation of mineral resources during a consultative meeting in Wellington, N.Z. Major international research efforts occurred in the Weddell Sea, where a U.S.-U.S.S.R. expedition

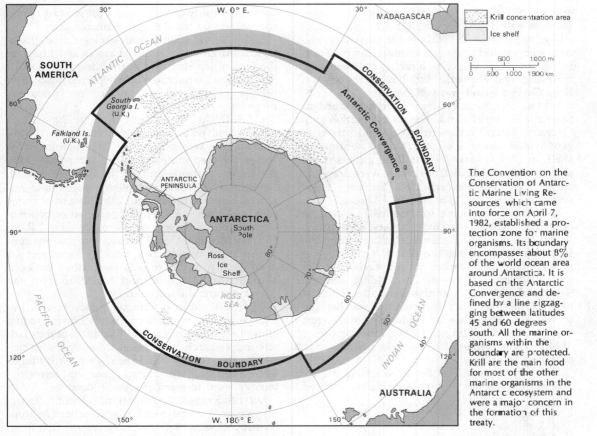

The Convention on the Conservation of Antarctic Marine Living Resources which came into force on April 7, 1982, established a protection zone for marine organisms. Its boundary encompasses about 8% of the world ocean area around Antarctica. It is based on the Antarctic Convergence and defined by a line zigzagging between latitudes 45 and 60 degrees south. All the marine organisms within the boundary are protected. Krill are the main food for most of the other marine organisms in the Antarctic ecosystem and were a major concern in the formation of this treaty.

searched without success for the Weddell Polynya, an area of ice-free water; in North Victoria Land, where major geologic investigations were conducted by 60 scientists; and near the Antarctic Peninsula, where researchers in the BIOMASS (Biological Investigation of Marine Antarctic Systems and Stocks) program discovered a swarm of krill estimated at ten million metric tons. The Convention on the Conservation of Antarctic Marine Living Resources was ratified and went into effect. A permanent secretariat was organized in Hobart, Tasmania.

Disasters struck several expeditions. The West German expedition to North Victoria Land lost its ship "Gotland II" when it sank in heavy ice within 24 hours of being pinched by the pressure of the ice. The passengers and crew were rescued by the five helicopters on board, but all scientific equipment and supplies were lost. Fire destroyed the transportation building at the U.S. McMurdo Station, doing $2 million worth of damage to the building and vehicles. A fire also destroyed the generator facility at Vostok Station (U.S.S.R.), located in the coldest part of Antarctica. The war between Argentina and Britain over the Falkland (Malvinas) Islands had adverse effects on both nations' Antarctic programs, although the specific damage would not be realized until later. The British Antarctic Survey lost its two Twin Otter aircraft in a storm, eliminating much of the planned summer research program.

A new research expedition, Operation Gangotri, was sent by India to the Prince Olav Coast of Enderby Land, not far from Japan's Syowa Station.

Oceanographic research was conducted en route; glaciologic, meteorologic, seismic, and magnetic research was conducted on the continent, and automatic weather stations were left behind. Data were transmitted to India via satellite. China continued to develop plans for a major national expedition, probably scheduled for 1985. Five Chinese scientists worked with the Australian and New Zealand expeditions. Brazil announced plans to field an expedition under the auspices of the Navy during the 1982–83 summer season. The ice-strengthened supply ship "Thala Dan" was purchased for the expedition's use.

National Programs. ARGENTINA Geologic research predominated at the nine bases in and near Antarctica. Some economic investigations were conducted in the South Shetland Islands. At Marambio base on Seymour Island, the National Space Research Commission joined with the U.S. National Aeronautics and Space Administration to launch balloons and rockets to study the ozone, winds, and temperatures in the stratosphere. Biological research was conducted at sea from the "Almirante Irizar."

AUSTRALIA. Glaciologists recovered an ice core to bedrock from fast-moving ice on the Law Dome at Cape Folger. The core was over 300 m (980 ft) in length and was returned to Australia for analysis. Other expedition members established a second automatic weather station some 70 km (40 mi) inland from Mawson Station.

CHILE. Two active volcanoes were discovered by Chilean scientists working on the Weddell Sea side of the Antarctic Peninsula. Both volcanoes had erupted recently and covered parts of the Larsen Ice Shelf with debris. Other biological, glaciologic, and geologic research continued at the two permanent stations and at several summer camps. Tourist flights on Chilean aircraft between the mainland and Teniente Rodolfo Marsh base on King George Island were offered.

JAPAN. Station operations were continued at Syowa in Enderby Land. The oil exploration ship "Hakurei Maru" completed its second season of geophysical surveys of Antarctica's continental shelf. In 1981 it surveyed the Bellingshausen Sea and in 1982 the Weddell Sea. Plans were drawn to survey the Ross Sea in early 1983. "Shirase," a new research icebreaker, was launched.

NEW ZEALAND. Some 160 scientists, including exchange scientists from four nations, participated in the New Zealand Antarctic Research Program. In addition to joining the North Victoria Land project, scientists worked on Mt. Erebus and at several locations between Cape Adare and the South Pole. The 25th anniversary of continuous New Zealand research in Antarctica was marked by a visit to Scott Base by Prime Minister Robert Muldoon and Sir Edmund Hillary, the conqueror of Mt. Everest. Hillary had been the first officer in charge of Scott Base.

POLAND. Scientists continued working at Arctowski Station, but economic restraints reduced

Fossil remains of the first land mammal ever found in Antarctica were discovered by a team of U.S. scientists. The bones were those of a small marsupial about the size of a rat.

manning to only nine persons. Future work would concentrate on smaller-scale krill research.

SOUTH AFRICA. Biological, geologic, and glaciologic research was conducted at SANAE III base on the Fimbul Ice Shelf and in the King Haakon VIII Sea. Expedition members also deployed doppler receivers as part of an international geodetic program.

U.S.S.R. The 27th Soviet Antarctic Expedition, which involved some 800 men and women during the summer, worked at seven permanent stations and established summer stations at the base of the Antarctic Peninsula and on the Ronne Ice Shelf. Glaciologists discovered pollen, spores, and microorganisms at the 200-m (650-ft) depth of an ice core from Vostok Station and reported evidence of the occurrence of a major thaw of some kind about 15,000 years ago. Geophysical investigations continued in the Weddell Sea, possibly for oil and gas deposits. An air route was established between Maputo (Mozambique) and Molodezhnaya, the Soviet Antarctic headquarters.

UNITED KINGDOM. Summer season research at four permanent stations was limited owing to loss of the Twin Otter aircraft. While much of the earth sciences research was canceled, several ship-carried parties were able to do fieldwork. Krill studies were successfully conducted at sea, and terrestrial biology went forward at several locations.

UNITED STATES. An important scientific discovery occurred on Seymour Island, where helicopter-supported geologists discovered the first fossil marsupial in Antarctica. The discovery supports the theory of marsupial migration from the Americas to Australia via Antarctica. Large-scale fieldwork was conducted in North Victoria Land. A 203-m (660-ft) ice core was drilled at the South Pole, and scientists estimated that it represented a 1,600-year climatic record. Laboratory analyses seemed to indicate that several meteorites discovered in Antarctica probably originated from Mars and not from the asteroid belt. A major review of U.S. policy toward Antarctica resulted in a presidential announcement that the government would maintain an active and influential presence in Antarctica. However, Siple Station would be closed at the end of its useful life—about 1985—

.5 cm.

INSTITUTE OF POLAR STUDIES, OHIO STATE UNIVERSITY; ILLUSTRATION, R. W. TOPE

and only three permanent stations would be maintained.

WEST GERMANY. A new icebreaker, "Polarstern," was commissioned in January 1982 and underwent sea trials. Research continued at George von Neumayer Station, which was resupplied by the Norwegian ship "Polar Queen," and on the Filchner Ice Shelf. Only the North Victoria Land geology program was canceled when "Gotland II" sank.

OTHER NATIONS. Norwegian scientists worked with other expeditions, and the Norsk Polarinstitutt leased "Polar Circle" to the Indian expedition. Belgium did not field an expedition but participated in the political meetings. East Germany participated in the Soviet expedition. Italy acceded to the Antarctic Treaty and began to develop plans for an expedition in 1983.   (PETER J. ANDERSON)

Anthropology

Modern humans are characterized by specific physical and behavioural characteristics. The main physical features are a large brain, bipedal or two-footed walking, and certain features of the dentition such as small canine teeth and thick enamel covering the molars. Among the behavioural characteristics are the use of tools and fire, food sharing, and village or home-base sites. Although other species may be characterized by one, or even a few, of these features, humans are unique in possessing the entire complex.

Since the early 1960s, a group of fossils known as Ramapithecus have been considered the first representatives of the human line because they possess relatively small canine teeth and have thick enamel on their molars. Ramapithecus is known from the middle of the Miocene period, approximately 16 million–10 million years ago, and has been found in East Africa, Europe, and Asia. However, over the last ten years the dental features common to humans and Ramapithecus have been recognized in other apelike fossils of the same age as Ramapithecus, known as Sivapithecus.

The major problem in interpreting the evolutionary significance of Ramapithecus and Sivapithecus has been the very fragmentary nature of their fossil remains. However, a relatively complete face of a large species of Sivapithecus (Sivapithecus indicus) was discovered in Pakistan in 1979–80. This skull shows clear affinities not only with the modern orangutan but also with Ramapithecus. The similarity between Ramapithecus and Sivapithecus is so great, in fact, that Ramapithecus was renamed Sivapithecus punjabicus. Because of the similarities between the orangutan and all of the Sivapithecus fossils, it was suggested that all of these fossils, including Ramapithecus, have only a remote relationship to the human line and are actually on that branch of the evolutionary tree leading to the orangutans.

The authors of this analysis point out that this interpretation is in line with the interpretation of the early course of human evolution drawn from the molecular evidence. Through the comparisons of proteins of living apes and humans, molecular biologists have claimed that the line leading to the modern orangutans could not have separated from that leading to humans and the African apes until the Middle Miocene, and the human line itself could not have separated from the line leading to the African apes prior to 6 million ± 3 million years ago. By removing Ramapithecus from the human line, the interpretation of the early course of human evolution based on the fossil material is brought more nearly into line with this alternative reasoning.

There are also no known fossils prior to those from Laetoli, Tanzania (3,750,000–3.6 million years old), and Hadar, Ethiopia (approximately 3.7 million–3.3 million years old), that are definitely on the human line (hominids). This more recent African material clearly shows the development of another hominid feature, bipedal locomotion. At the Laetoli site there is a trail of footprints showing that the gait of these hominids was virtually identical to that of modern humans except that the stride length appears to have been very short. Recent analyses of well-preserved skeletal fossils from Hadar support this conclusion. The muscle patterns on the bones indicate the possibility of a well-controlled bipedal gait, but the length of the hind limbs in relation to the inferred body size is very short compared with modern Homo sapiens. The author of this analysis concludes that bipedalism developed in an ancestral form with short hind limbs, and the legs have lengthened in response to the need for increased stride length and the associated improvement in energetic efficiency.

The bipedal gait of these hominids has one important implication for the development of human culture. Bipedalism frees the forelimbs from their locomotor function. Ever since the time of Darwin, free forelimbs in hominids have been associated with the use and manufacture of tools. However, there is no evidence for the use of stone tools in sites of the same age as the early hominids from Hadar and Laetoli. Tools could have been made from perishable material, but there is no conclusive evidence that tool use was associated in a causal relationship with the evolution of bipedal locomotion.

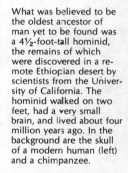

What was believed to be the oldest ancestor of man yet to be found was a 4½-foot-tall hominid, the remains of which were discovered in a remote Ethiopian desert by scientists from the University of California. The hominid walked on two feet, had a very small brain, and lived about four million years ago. In the background are the skull of a modern human (left) and a chimpanzee.

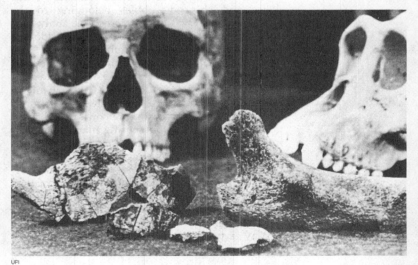

UPI

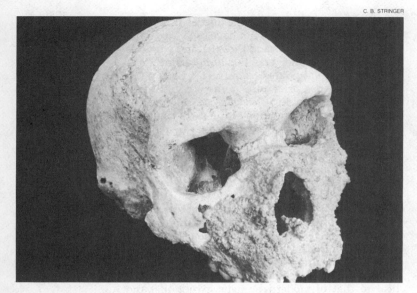

The Petralona skull from Greece belongs to a group of Middle Pleistocene hominid fossils from Europe and Africa that differ sufficiently from *Homo erectus* of Asia to suggest that they represent a different species.

Antigua and Barbuda

It has been suggested that upright posture may have been associated with feeding on food that grew off the ground, at standing height. However, it has also been suggested that bipedalism may have been associated with another basic human feature, food sharing. If hominids collected food and brought it back to their home bases to share and consume, they would have had to carry it. Unfortunately, no convincing argument has been put forward for the development of food sharing at this stage.

Meat eating in the early hominids has been suggested as a possible cause of food sharing and, by extension, bipedal locomotion, but again there is no evidence for hunting or meat eating at the time of the Hadar and Laetoli hominids. It should also be remembered that humans are unique among mammals in sharing not only meat but also vegetable food. Any convincing argument for the development of food-sharing behaviour should include the sharing of plant foods.

Direct evidence for home bases, meat eating, and tool use does not appear in the fossil record until later. The earliest stone tools appear in later levels at Hadar (2.5 million–2 million years old) and at the Omo Valley, Ethiopia, at the same approximate time. These tools are relatively crude flakes and chipped cobbles belonging to the Oldowan industry. Recent microscopic analysis of later tools belonging to a variant of the Oldowan industry (Karari industry from Koobi Fora, Kenya, 1.5 million years) shows that they were used to butcher animals, cut soft plants containing plant silica, and cut wood. In addition, new microscopic analysis of animal bones in early hominid sites suggests that at least some bones as old as 1.8 million years carried butchering marks that may indicate both the removal of meat and the possible removal of skins. This suggests a more complex reliance on animal food than is found in other primates and also the use of tools on vegetable material, the direct collection of vegetable food, and possibly the preparation of wooden tools such as digging sticks.

Why early hominids began to eat meat in larger quantities than other primates is also a question for which there is no immediate answer. It has been suggested that the early hominids went through a stage of scavenging meat before they began to hunt with any great frequency or efficiency. This is an attractive hypothesis, because early hominids did not have large canine teeth or claws and as a result were not physically equipped as hunters and carnivores. In support of the scavenging model, it has been suggested that the proportions and types of animal bones left in some of the hominid sites would be more consistent with scavenging than with hunting behaviour. However, if the hominids went through a stage of scavenging, this would also require explanation. No nonprimate animals are exclusively scavengers, and scavenging is extremely rare in nonhuman primates. Although the remains of nonhominid animal bones found in the early hominid sites, along with the associated stone tools, do not give much information about the origins of hunting, they do provide evidence that some of these sites were home bases and not merely butchering sites or sites at which the hominids spent only short periods of time.

There was also new evidence that fire may have been a relatively early occurrence. Until recently the earliest substantiated use of fire was from sites in northern latitudes dating around 500,000 years old, and it was associated with the spread of the hominids to more temperate environments. However, newly reported baked clay patches from Chesowanja, Kenya, have been interpreted as evidence of controlled hearths or "campfires" dating to 1.4 million years ago.　(LESLIE C. AIELLO)

See also Archaeology.
[411; 10/36.B]

Antigua and Barbuda

An independent state and a member of the Commonwealth, Antigua and Barbuda comprises the islands of Antigua (280 sq km), Barbuda (161 sq km), and Redonda (uninhabited, 1 sq km) and lies in the eastern Caribbean approximately 60 km north of Guadeloupe. Total area: 442 sq km (171 sq mi). Pop. (1982 est.): 77,000. Cap.: Saint John's (pop., 1979 est., 25,000). Language: English. Religion: Church of England (predominant), other Protestant sects, and Roman Catholic. Queen, Elizabeth II; governor-general in 1982, Sir Wilfred E. Jacobs; prime minister, Vere Cornwall Bird.

During its first year of independence Antigua and Barbuda set about forging a major regional role for itself in the eastern Caribbean. It was particularly active in the generation of the Organization of East Caribbean States and at the Caribbean Community summit at Ocho Rios, Jamaica, in November 1982. Despite this high regional profile, Antigua remained economically depressed, although tourism, the economic mainstay, continued buoyant in contrast to the downward regional trend. A dormant oil refinery was refurbished, and this generated additional employment. Aid came from South Korea, Venezuela, and Brazil in addition to that received from traditional sources in the U.S., Canada, and the U.K. The U.S. re-

ANTIGUA AND BARBUDA

Education. (1977–78) Primary, pupils 10,159, teachers 414; secondary (1976–77), pupils 6,685, teachers 333; vocational (1976–77), pupils 153, teachers 18; teacher training (1976–77), students 89, teachers 7.

Finance and Trade. Monetary unit: East Caribbean dollar, with (Sept. 20, 1982) a par value of ECar$2.70 to U.S. $1 (ECar$4.63 = £1 sterling). Budget (1980): revenue ECar$62 million; expenditure ECar$69 million. Foreign trade (1977 est.): imports ECar$110 million; exports ECar$35 million. Import sources (1975): U.K. 19%; U.S. 19%; Trinidad and Tobago 11%; The Bahamas 11%; Venezuela 9%; Iran 7%; Canada 5%. Export destinations (1975): bunkers 57%; U.S. 10%; Guyana 5%. Main export (1975): petroleum products 87%. Tourism (1980) 97,901 visitors.

tained three military bases on the island for which Antigua received substantial rents.

During the year, a left-leaning opposition party made allegations of corruption against the government, which were strenuously denied. Politically, the opposition was weakened by factionalism. In contrast, the ruling Antigua Labour Party, though subject to internal disagreement, maintained its strong national support under the leadership of Prime Minister Vere Bird.   (DAVID A. JESSOP)

Archaeology

Eastern Hemisphere. As often happens, what was probably the single most spectacular find of the year was not made by professional archaeologists. It was a magnificently decorated bronze Celtic helmet, discovered by speleologists in a cave near La Rochefoucauld (Charente), France. Covered with gold leaf, it was also ornamented with inlays of coral.

On October 10, the day before the U.S. national holiday celebrating Christopher Columbus's "discovery" of the New World, the *New York Times* reported that a "hunter of sunken treasure" had recovered specimens of Roman amphorae from a bay near Rio de Janeiro, Brazil. Encountered earlier by fishermen, the jars were said to be scattered over an area on the seabed comparable in size to three tennis courts. Both Plutarch and the elder Pliny remarked that the Romans knew the Atlantic as far as the Canary Islands. It is possible that a Roman vessel, caught in the trade winds, was blown across the ocean. Quite clearly, it never got back home again to announce its discovery.

Public support appeared to be growing in the United States for federal control of the antiquities trade and for adherence to the 1970 UNESCO Convention on the Means of Prohibiting and Preventing the Illicit Import, Export and Transfer of Ownership of Cultural Property. Unfortunately, a measure, pending in various forms for a decade, was blocked in the Senate Finance Committee. A compromise was, however, in prospect.

The year had its usual archaeological whimsies. Mt. Ararat was again climbed in search of Noah's Ark. One of the climbers broke a leg, but no ark was found. Thanks, doubtless, to a current movie, another group sought and was even rumoured to have found a different ark, the "gold-plated Ark of the Covenant," on Mt. Pisgah in Jordan. The responsible authorities, both Jordanian and foreign,

knew nothing of the matter. Melina Mercouri (*see* BIOGRAPHIES), a former actress and now minister of culture in Greece, in a strongly worded demand again reminded the British Museum that it must return the Elgin Marbles.

PLEISTOCENE PREHISTORY. The newly found fossil hominid bones from the Awash River valley, Ethiopia, at four million years old, predated the so-called Lucy fossils by about half a million years, but artifacts (hence, archaeology proper) discovered so far dated back to only about 2.5 million years. In 1982 a British-French-U.S. group, working in Kenya, pushed the use of fire back almost a million years to 1.4 million years ago. The firemakers were believed to have been of the *Homo erectus* taxonomic group. In Ethiopia a *Homo erectus* skull fragment showed jagged cut marks suggesting that the individual was scalped.

A report by A. J. Jelinek of the University of Arizona on recent excavations in the Tabun cave in Israel covers the long sequence of artifacts from about 130,000 to 50,000 years ago. These finds support an earlier suggestion "that a continuous biological evolution from Neanderthal to anatomically modern *Homo sapiens* took place in the southern Levant." In the Nile River valley a Belgian team closed an important gap in Egyptian prehistory between 40,000 and 20,000 years ago. Blade tools of flint, previously believed missing, were found.

Arlette Leroi-Gourhan reported on the 40 years of detailed analyses of the paintings and engravings in the great Lascaux cave in France. A new basis for the study of Old Stone Age art and symbolism is provided by these analyses. Vadim Ranov of the Archaeological Institute at Dushanbe, Tadzhik S.S.R., reported finding approximately 6,000 rock engravings in the Pamirs Mountains.

NEAR EAST. The Royal Ontario Museum's research project at the Dakhileh oasis, 250 km (155 mi) west of the Nile in the Egyptian desert, located several hundred formerly inhabited sites, ranging from about 100,000 years ago to Roman times. There was a thin forest cover and grassland condition adjacent to the oasis until close to 3000 BC; this supported a variety of "neolithic" settlements. Thereafter, settlement clustered within the oasis itself.

In Israel a concentrated program of survey and excavation begun in the Sinai in 1970 was completed before the region was returned to Egypt. Ofar Bar-Yosef of the Hebrew University of Jerusalem reported on a variety of important prepottery Neolithic sites from the period in which agriculture was just beginning. In Jerusalem, despite the continued opposition of ultra-Orthodox zealots, Israeli archaeologists continued their work outside the old walled city. A French-Israeli excavation at Tell Yarmouth recovered new information from the 3rd-millennium BC levels at the base of the mound. In Jordan the American Centre of Oriental Research was active, continuing its excavations on the large mound of Bab edh-Dhra and also mounting several important surveys covering periods from Pleistocene into historic times.

In Turkey, in a region where more new dams were being built on the Euphrates River, U.S.,

Archaeologists uncovered the remains of what was presumed to be Santa Catalina de Guale, the northernmost Spanish mission on the Atlantic coast of North America, in what is now Georgia.

British, Dutch, French, West German, and Turkish salvage teams were at work. Much was being learned of the 4th- to 2nd-millennium BC developments in this previously unexamined region. It was becoming increasingly clear that the stretch of the Euphrates in upper Syria and southern Turkey, with its linkages to southern Mesopotamia, Anatolia, and the Mediterranean coastal cities, is a region of critical importance for the understanding of ancient Near Eastern history. Elsewhere in Turkey a new West German excavation was begun on the northwest coast near the site of Troy, and Mehmet Ozdogan of Istanbul University continued his important survey in European Turkey, an area unknown archaeologically.

For the Islamic period, the Syrians were reconstructing the city of Raqqa on the Euphrates. The Royal Ontario Museum began research in northern Yemen, and the Oriental Institute made clearances on a site with important Islamic and Chinese contact materials in Sri Lanka.

GRECO-ROMAN REGIONS. In northern Greece, at Vergina in Greek Macedonia, Greek archaeologists found the town's ancient theatre. On both Crete and Cyprus, excavations were continued on various pre-Greek sites with good results. The Royal Ontario Museum's team at Kommos in southern Crete cleared a broad Minoan road leading from the town to the seaside.

The year's fresh news from Italy included word of further work at Pompeii and at Herculaneum, where the remains of more than 20 people who died in the fire and lava of Mt. Vesuvius's eruption were found. It now seemed likely, contrary to previous belief, that few of the people of Herculaneum had had time to escape the eruption by sea.

Farther east, in regions affected by Greco-Roman culture, a fine yield of gold jewelry was re-

covered in a tomb in the Tadzhik S.S.R. The Jordanian government's Department of Antiquities organized a multinational team to investigate the great Greco-Roman site of Jerash. The Oriental Institute continued its excavation at the Red Sea port of Quseir in Egypt, an important link in the Roman and early Islamic spice trade.

In Western Europe the remains of nine Roman ships were recovered at Mainz, West Germany, on the Rhine, where foundations for a new hotel were being dug. They appear to have been in a shipyard abandoned by the Romans about AD 400, as the empire's garrison began to retreat. A large and well-planned Roman villa was being exposed at Echternach in Luxembourg. Various Gallo-Roman finds were reported from France, and the fine bronze helmet from La Rochefoucauld, described above, has workmanship suggesting Greek or Italic models. In England there were also various finds of Roman date, the most important being the recovery in London of timbers believed to be from the Roman bridge and riverside wharves on the Thames. In January the old London market at Billingsgate was closed to permit excavations.

ASIA AND AFRICA. In China excavation was being discontinued on the great tomb mound of Qin Shi Huang (Ch'in Shih Huang, the first Chinese ruler to call himself emperor, builder of the Great Wall and codifier of laws). Xia Nai (Hsia Nai), director of the Archaeology Institute of the Chinese Academy of Social Sciences, decided that—given the overwhelming potential yield from the tomb—the large number of artifacts already recovered must be subjected to the best preservation technology possible. Most of the news from Africa was concerned with finds from prehistoric times, as already mentioned above.

(ROBERT J. BRAIDWOOD)

Western Hemisphere. As in most multidisciplinary, labour-intensive, and generally long-term research activities, archaeology in 1982 was not immune from the fiscal and political perturbations that rocked the countries of North and South America. This was true especially in countries important both as centres of pre-Columbian development and as foci of national and international research efforts. Within the U.S. inflation and general fiscal uncertainty left both state and federal preservation programs uncertain about their future and financial solvency. In Mexico and South America high inflation rates, heavy foreign debts, recession, and political upheavals forced the curtailment or cancellation of many planned or even ongoing government-sponsored surveys and excavation projects. Finally, the civil wars in Guatemala and El Salvador all but stopped archaeological research in much of Central America.

TECHNICAL STUDIES. Despite these fiscal and political limitations, 1982 was marked by several significant breakthroughs in applied technology that greatly expanded the ability of archaeologists to identify and define buried and vegetation-obscured archaeological sites. Radar equipment carried aboard the U.S. space shuttle demonstrated the capacity to see features below the surface of sand-covered desert regions in both Africa and the Americas. Scientists were able to identify the presence of ancient rivers and landforms buried as much as 4.5 m (15 ft) below the desert sand. Because prehistoric peoples commonly worked or lived next to rivers, this new space-born radar technology held the promise of helping to locate and identify deeply buried archaeological sites, which previously had been unrecognized and undetectable.

The penetration of sand-covered desert regions with airborne radar followed similar breakthroughs with the long-standing problem of site detection in heavily forested areas, such as the almost impenetrable Maya lowland jungles of southern Mexico and Guatemala. Between 1977 and 1982 airborne radar surveys provided scientists with the first glimpses through this heavy overgrowth and, with them, some major new insights into the extent and economic foundations of ancient Maya culture. Using synthetic aperture radar (SAR), Walter E. Brown of the Jet Propulsion Laboratory, working with archaeologist Richard E. Adams of the University of Texas, identified an extensive system of between 1,250 and 2,500 sq km (500 and 1,000 sq mi) of prehistoric raised fields and canal networks in lowland swamp areas previously thought to have been uninhabited wastelands. The extent and magnitude of these previously unknown canal networks suggested how the Maya could have supported their large populations with an adequate agricultural food base.

Another major development of the past year based on applied technology was the symbiotic use of archaeology to aid other sciences concerned with nonarchaeological issues, such as the study of past environmental change, animal and plant extinctions, and climatic shifts. For example, until recently the Hawaiian Islands had been perceived as an apparently harmonious balance between man and nature, with environmental degradation and animal extinctions taking place only in the last several hundred years as a result of European settlement. However, recent combined research by archaeologists and biologists severely altered this assumption with the discovery that long before the arrival of the Europeans, the native Polynesian settlers had both drastically altered their island environments and caused the extinction of large numbers of animals and plants.

HISTORICAL ARCHAEOLOGY. The realization that the written record often is not as thorough as was once thought and is, in fact, often a biased reflection of past events, combined with recent legislation stressing the need to address both recent and ancient archaeological remains as part of the overall cultural fabric of the past, precipitated a shift in emphasis over the past several years to a more broad-based coverage of relatively recent 16th–20th-century remains. The results often either were at odds with or simply were not reflected by the written record.

With this change in understanding among archaeologists of the potential of the unwritten historical record to refine and even redefine history came the realization that, although the contempo-

The discovery of human skeletons at the ancient site of Herculaneum was announced in February. The people were killed in the eruption of Mt. Vesuvius in AD 79, which also buried the city of Pompeii.

rary landscape has been heavily altered by urban development and industrial growth, even modern cities may contain a wealth of unsuspected data. In 1982 perhaps the most dramatic example of the archaeological value of even heavily developed urban centres was demonstrated by an unexpected discovery in one of the most heavily developed cities in North America, New York. Work initiated by the New York Landmarks Commission to salvage an area of 18th- and 19th-century settlement beneath the modern pavement of a parking lot destined to become the site of a 30-story office complex in lower Manhattan resulted in the discovery of a 25-m (85-ft)-long hull of a buried wooden ship sunk to expand the shoreline in 1747–55. The ship was excavated and removed for preservation.

MESOAMERICA. In Mexico, despite the continuing economic crisis that curtailed or caused the cancellation of numerous programs, work continued on the exposure of the Aztec Great Temple, which had been found by chance in 1978 during the installation of a power transformer by the Mexico City Light and Power Co. From 1978 Mexican archaeologists under the direction of Eduardo Matos Moctezuma continued to clear and stabilize the massive temple complex in what became one of the most energetic examples of New World urban rescue archaeology. The first look at the entire temple layout revealed seven major stages of construction and a total area indicating that the previous hypothetical reconstructions were at least 30% larger than the actual structure.

In the southern Mayan area continuing work in Belize by Norman Hammond of Rutgers University revealed what could be the earliest lowland Maya stela yet discovered. The 80-cm (32-in)-long rectangular and undecorated stela was dated to the 1st century AD, contemporary with the earliest Mexican stone monuments found off the Pacific

coast but several centuries earlier than the next most ancient examples of stela construction in the Maya lowlands.

SOUTH AMERICA. In addition to a number of foreign expeditions to Latin-American countries, 1982 was noteworthy for an upsurge in survey and excavation programs undertaken by professional Latin-American archaeologists. For example, in Peru National Institute of Culture field teams made two significant discoveries in the highland drainages of Cuzco and Ayacucho. In Cuzco, centre of the 15th-century Inca empire, a National Institute team discovered an entire buried and previously unknown sector of the otherwise well-known Inca site Orllantaytambo in the Urubamba Valley to the east of Cuzco. This sector consisted of a matrix of well-preserved buildings and courts with intricate fountains and baths buried below the fields. What appeared to be randomly deposited boulders protruding from the valley-bottom farmlands proved to be carefully engineered elements in a multilevel subterranean nonirrigation canal system for open-air baths and fountains.

Approximately 800 km (500 mi) to the north a second team of Peruvian archaeologists under the direction of González Carre of the Universidad de Huamanga in Ayacucho completed the excavation and stabilization of a large ceremonial complex at the 8th-century pre-Inca Huari capital. This find abruptly altered archaeologists' understanding of the development of pre-Inca architectural and cultural history. The excavation cleared a large segment of a buried temple complex consisting of rows of multistoried rectangular rooms facing a central courtyard having a circular building with cut stone columns in its centre. The walls were decorated with incised three-dimensional Huari-style motifs and painted in at least three colours. The shape and composition of this complex differed markedly from previously known Huari structures and helped link a continuum of development in Andean architecture from the 1000 BC Chavin civilization to the elaborate stone workmanship characteristic of the 15th-century Incas.

NORSE CONTACTS. The old controversy over transatlantic Norse contact with the Americas was shifted to a new perspective with the assertion that not only did a group of weather-stranded Norse explorer-refugees arrive in eastern Greenland about AD 981 but also, while there, they conducted the first New World archaeological excavations. Ralph Rowlett of the University of Missouri cited a recently translated semiofficial medieval account of the settlement of Iceland in which two 10th-century Norse refugees from marital problems passed the winter by conducting excavations at a coastal Dorset mound site that reportedly yielded valuables that were both noted and fought over. Rowlett observed that since the Arctic Eskimo Thule culture postdates the arrival of the Icelandic explorers in Greenland, the "mound" excavation probably took place in a stone-lined Dorset pit house of the type that commonly yields elaborate artifacts such as carved bone animal forms.

(JOEL W. GROSSMAN)

See also Anthropology.
[723.G.8.c; 10/41.B.2.a.ii]

A large number of Roman amphorae were discovered in a bay near Rio de Janeiro. The jars were of the type carried by Roman ships in the 2nd century BC.

THE RAISING OF THE "MARY ROSE"

by Margaret Rule

At 9:03 AM on Oct. 11, 1982, the remains of the Tudor era warship "Mary Rose" were lifted through the surface of the Solent, one mile from the entrance to Portsmouth Harbour on the south coast of England. After being buried in the seabed for 437 years, less than half the hull survived, but the 200 metric tons of waterlogged oak recovered and brought ashore for conservation and display in the Royal Naval Base at Portsmouth will provide ship historians and naval architects with the only surviving example of a north European carrack fitted with a gun deck built for that purpose and equipped with a battery of guns capable of firing a broadside through lidded gun ports cut low in the side of the hull.

The Ship. The "Mary Rose" was built in Portsmouth by command of King Henry VIII in 1509–10, and a document dated July 29, 1511, refers to the payment of £120 by the king to Robert Brygandyne, the clerk of the king's ships, for the "conveyance of our two new ships from Portsmouth to the River Thames, the one being the 'Mary Rose' and the other the 'Peter Gernerde.'" By Christmas 1511 the ship lay in the Thames close to the royal palace at Greenwich, fully equipped, fitted out with banners and streamers and ready for war.

During the following spring the lord high admiral, Sir Edward Howard, chose the "Mary Rose" as his flagship for a short and successful campaign in the English Channel. Later that year the "Mary Rose" again served as his flagship during the English attack on the French fleet at Brest, which resulted in the destruction or capture of 32 French ships.

Undoubtedly the "Mary Rose" was a stable warship, and in 1513, after trials in the Channel, Sir Edward Howard reported to the king, "The 'Mary Rose,' Sir, she is the noblest ship of sail and a great ship at this hour that I trow to be in Christendom. A ship of 100 tons will not be sooner about than she." This ability to "go about" quickly and safely was essential in ships built like the "Mary Rose," with a high protruding summer castle at the bow and an even higher fighting castle at the stern causing it to be sluggish and unwieldy.

Although no drawings or plans survive to show how the "Mary Rose" was constructed in 1509, it seems possible that the hull lines remained unaltered after it was refitted and rebuilt in 1536. If so, it was a stable ship with a length-to-beam ratio of 3:1 and a keel length of 32 m (105 ft) from the skeg at the stern to the keel stem scarf. The only contemporary picture of the ship comes from an inventory of King Henry VIII's royal ships prepared by Anthony Anthony, an officer of the Board of Ordnance at the Tower of London in 1546, and it shows the ship after the rebuilding in 1536. At that time it was uprated from 600 to 700 tons and equipped with 91 guns, including 15 brass guns with iron shot, 76 iron guns with shot of stone or lead, and 50 hand guns.

The Sinking. Why an apparently stable ship should sink in calm weather within 1.6 km (1 mi) of its home port is a mystery, but the occasion was well documented, and both French and English eyewitness accounts of the tragedy survive. A fleet of 235 French ships under the command of Monsieur d'Annebault, admiral of France, lay in St. Helen's Roads off the northeast corner of the Isle of Wight on July 19, 1545. On board, 30,000 French soldiers waited the command to invade and destroy, but first King Henry's fleet of barely 60 ships had to be engaged and defeated. The king had good intelligence reports of the proposed invasion, and on July 15 he had arrived in Portsmouth as commander in chief of his navy and army.

The day was calm with only light winds, and the English carracks moved sluggishly through the water to meet the French fleet. Four French galleys, propelled by oarsmen, moved forward to challenge the English flagship the "Henry Grace à Dieu" and, as the "Mary Rose" moved forward to join its sister ship, it suddenly heeled on its starboard side and sank. English eyewitness accounts suggest that the disaster was caused by indiscipline among the crew, but the French admiral claimed that the "Mary Rose" was sunk by his ships.

The truth may lie somewhere between the two accounts. The ship's normal crew was 514 soldiers and mariners, but when it sank there were nearly 300 extra soldiers on board, many in armour and deployed high in the fighting castle. This extra weight may have made the ship dangerously unstable. The gun ports were open and secured against the sides of the hull, and all the guns on the starboard side of the hull were loaded, primed, and run forward

Margaret Rule, a fellow of the Society of Antiquaries, has worked on the "Mary Rose" salvage project since its inception in 1965 and is archaeological director of the Mary Rose Trust, established in 1979.

181

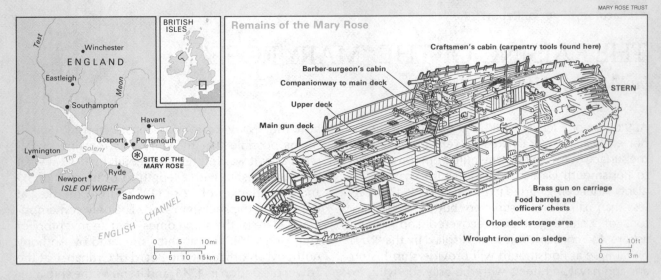

Remains of the Mary Rose

Craftsmen's cabin (carpentry tools found here)

Barber-surgeon's cabin

Companionway to main deck

Upper deck

Main gun deck

STERN

Brass gun on carriage

Food barrels and officers' chests

Orlop deck storage area

Wrought iron gun on sledge

BOW

through the open ports. Under these conditions the normally stable ship would have been vulnerable, and any slow response to orders while hoisting sail would have been disastrous. As the ship heeled to go about, water poured in over the sills of the open gun ports, and some of the guns on the port side in the aftercastle broke loose and swept across the deck, carrying equipment and men with them. This additional weight and the extra weight of water pouring into the ship sealed its fate, and the "Mary Rose" sank rapidly to lie on its starboard side in the soft mud of the seabed 12 m (39 ft) below.

The Rising. There were immediate attempts to pull the ship upright and salvage it by securing it to two empty hulks and using the tide to lift it from the seabed, but eventually these attempts were abandoned. The ship lay forgotten until 1836, when John and Charles Deane, pioneer "hard-helmet" divers, recovered a bronze 32-pounder gun from the ship. During the following four years they recovered other guns, some longbows, pottery, and quantities of wood, but archaeological evidence reveals that they did not enter the surviving starboard section of the hull but simply "harvested" the material that lay among the collapsed timbers from the upper hull on the port side of the ship.

In 1965 a deliberate program of seabed search and documentary research was initiated to find the remains of the ship but, although a buried mass was detected in the general wreck area in 1967, it was not until 1971 that the tops of eroded frames on the port quarter at the stern were seen for the first time. By 1979 enough evidence had been obtained to justify the formation of the Mary Rose Trust and the appointment of a team to excavate and survey the hull and prepare it for recovery in 1982.

The program of underwater work was demanding, and between 1979 and 1982 almost 28,000 dives were made at the site by professional divers, archae-

ologists, and volunteers from aquatic clubs. Approximately 17,000 registered objects were removed from the wreck, and 3,000 timbers were surveyed and removed before the empty hull was strengthened and prepared for recovery. A steel cradle was built to conform with the hull lines deduced from the archaeological survey of the internal sections of the hull, and an underwater lifting frame was constructed of tubular steel to spread the load when the ship was lifted from the seabed and moved underwater to its final position in the cradle.

The underwater transfer was completed on Oct. 9, 1982, using acoustics (sonar) to locate the legs of the underwater lifting frame and fit them into the guides on the sides of the cradle. Eventually, however, only three of the legs could be successfully placed in the cones of the guides. The cradle was lifted with parts of the load that should have been on the fourth leg supported by an auxiliary wire from the shackles on the lifting wires.

The total "package"—cradle, hull of the "Mary Rose," and underwater lifting frame—weighed 560 metric tons in the air. It was lifted and placed on a barge for transport ashore by the crane barge "Tog Mor," on loan from the Howard Doris Co. Two months later, on December 8, the "Mary Rose" was "dry docked" at the Royal Naval Base alongside Lord Nelson's flagship HMS "Victory," only a few hundred yards from where it was built 473 years earlier.

The task now is to restore the hull to the condition in which it was found underwater. The dismantled deck planks will be replaced, and the cabins, companionways, and bulkheads will be reconstructed. The objects of wood, leather, steel, and bronze will be prepared for display, and the public will then have a unique opportunity to study the material remains of a 16th-century community of seafaring men alongside a half section of the ship within which they worked, lived, and died.

Architecture

High interest rates and continuing recession throughout the Western world kept the construction outlook bleak in 1982, yet architects seemed full of ideas for new projects. Classicism was the dominant stylistic trend, much of it deriving from a renewed interest in architectural history and a renewed study of buildings of the past Even where no distinct classical allusions appeared, there was often a discernible reliance on the straight line and the flat plane arranged geometrically, with colour and graphics as important accents. The same influences were apparent in architects' drawings. Renderings reminiscent of the 1920s, with formalistic layouts and pale washes, were common. The Sir Edwin Lutyens (1869–1944) exhibition in London at the end of 1981 reflected an existing neoclassical trend and probably gave it an additional boost.

In Paris the work of Spanish architect Ricardo Bofill and his French contemporaries attempted to promote classicism as a means of providing economical low-cost housing that would be more acceptable to the public than the high-rise towers of a decade earlier; their efforts resulted in concrete Greco-Roman "palaces for the people." The influence of the 19th-century classical revival Beaux-Arts style was unmistakable. For example, the newly established Institute of French Architecture in Paris decorated its exhibition rooms (to show French architecture of the last decade) with classical details. Worldwide, the influence of the U.S. postmodernists such as Michael Graves was felt. There were to be no more flat roofs. Works of the Milton Keynes Development Corp. in England were clearly influenced by this trend. Foster Associates' Hong Kong Bank project showed that firm also moving away from the hard smooth sheen of glass and metal toward a new interest in colour, pattern, and surface decoration.

The June 1982 issue of the *Architectural Review* was devoted to the classical revival. Among the buildings featured were works by Bofill in France. There was also a corrugated classical pavilion in Eugowra, New South Wales, Australia, designed as a farmhouse by John Andrews. The Simon-Bellamy House, Stony Creek, Conn., by Moore Grover Harper, was a renovation of a bungalow in the clapboard tradition by means of a design that exaggerated its regularity of outline and classical antecedents. Kiyoshi Nakagome's house for himself in Tokyo took the formality of the classical revival even further: his structure consisted essentially of a formal pedimented framework within which a rounded volume contained the living accommodation.

The McKay Trading Estate in west London was also strongly in the new classical idiom. Comprising a series of factory units, the estate was designed by architect John Outram. There, in an unprepossessing part of the city, between Kensal Road and the Grand Union Canal, the architect had grouped together the factory elements to achieve a classical effect, complete with pediments, columns, recesses, and details, all somehow abstracted yet clearly derived from the temple model. The factories or workshops, designed in pairs, had pitched roofs, with each pair forming a pedimented gable on the street side. The pediment was in turn supported on a brick column that contained the services. Symmetrically placed offices, delineated by dark glass and red window frames, were slightly recessed under the pediment, one office for each factory. The offices were cantilevered over the entrance area from the industrial sheds behind, the latter being fronted with great doors. Each individual element required by the function of the building was incorporated into a decorative and classical composition in an original and entertaining manner. The units had charm, something rare in industrial architecture, and were of human scale. The materials were simple. There was dark blue brick at the base, yellow London stock brick above, and a band of red brick for emphasis. Colour played an important part. The roofs were like lids, with gable ends and soffits clad in white corrugated sheet steel. This was as far removed from the "high tech" shed as imaginable. The building won a Civic Trust Award.

Colin Amery, the architectural critic for the *Financial Times,* reviewing an exhibition at the Royal Institute of British Architects (RIBA) entitled "British Architecture 1982," criticized some of the architects working in the classical idiom and exhorted architects to consider more than revivalism. In his view many of the architects of postmodernism failed to understand that classicism already had a language of its own with rules and regulations and that picking and choosing bits and reassembling them at random reduced this language to an "absurd slang." He urged architects to look again at the work of Sir John Soane and Lutyens, who used the language properly but still managed to experiment and produce buildings of originality and wit within the rules.

Awards. Twelve projects received American Institute of Architects (AIA) Honor Awards, presented at the 1982 AIA national convention in Honolulu in June. Eight of the awards were for buildings designed and completed within the past seven years; the others were for older structures renovated or adapted to new uses. Included were the Illinois Regional Library for the Blind and Physically Handicapped, Chicago, by Joseph W. Casserly, city architect, and consulting architects Stanley Tigerman and Associates; a residence at East Hampton, N.Y., by Eisenman/Robertson Architects; and an addition to the Schulman House, Princeton, N.J., by Michael Graves.

The AIA Gold Medal for 1982 went to Romaldo Giurgola of Mitchell/Giurgola Architects of New York City and Philadelphia. The firm's most recent competition success was for a new Parliament House for Canberra, Australia. The 1982 medal honouring artists whose work relates to architecture was given to Jean Dubuffet, a French sculptor who had made an important contribution to the harmony of sculpture and architecture. The architectural historian Sir John Summerson was honoured with the 1982 AIA medal for recorders of architectural accomplishments. The Architectural

Archery:
see Target Sports

A Civic Trust Award was won by the McKay Trading Estate erected in west London. The architect was John Outram.

Firm award for the year went to Gwathmey Siegel & Associates of New York City.

Two widely contrasting buildings received RIBA awards for architectural elegance. The Roman Catholic Church of St. John Ogilvie at Irvine in Ayrshire, Scotland, designed by Gerard Connolly and Douglas Niven, was a minutely detailed exercise in postmodernism. On a much larger scale, in high-tech style, was the radioisotope factory designed by the Percy Thomas Partnership for Amersham International Laboratories at Whitchurch, Cardiff, Wales.

The RIBA 1982 Royal Gold Medal was presented to Berthold Lubetkin, best known for his modern buildings of the 1930s, especially the Penguin Pool at London Zoo of 1938 and his High Point I and II apartment blocks in Highgate, London. Lubetkin, born in Russia in 1901, settled in England at the age of 30 in 1931 and in 1932 formed the Tecton partnership, which was one of the leading proponents of the International Style in Britain.

The Pritzker Architecture Prize for 1982 was won by the U.S. architect Kevin Roche of Kevin Roche-John Dinkeloo and Associates. Roche's works included the Oakland (Calif.) Museum (1968), and the General Foods Corp. headquarters at Rye, N.Y. (under construction in 1982). Roche announced his intention of using the prize to establish an Eero Saarinen chair of architecture at Yale University.

Educational and Cultural Buildings. In 1982 museums undoubtedly led in the category of educational and cultural buildings; they seemed to be springing up everywhere and in 1982 were often in the news for their architectural qualities. Indeed, the Whitney Museum of American Art in New York City devoted a summer exhibition to the wave of new U.S. art museums as well as museums that were planning large additions. These included the Dallas (Texas) Museum of Fine Arts, by Edward Larrabee Barnes; the High Museum of Art in Atlanta, Ga., by Richard Meier; the Museum of Contemporary Art, Los Angeles, by Arata Isozaki; the Museum of Modern Art, New York City, by Cesar Pelli; the Joseph Price Collection (site undecided), by Bruce Goff; the Portland (Maine) Museum of Art, by Henry Cobb of I. M. Pei and Partners; and the Virginia Museum of Fine Arts at Richmond, by Hardy, Holzman, Pfeiffer Associates.

Late in January the Los Angeles County Museum of Art approved in principle plans by Hardy, Holzman, Pfeiffer Associates for expansion and reorganization of the museum. The design reversed the original concept of the museum, which was of pavilions in a park, to a scheme with a continuous enclosure of buildings around a courtyard. The new Atlantic Richfield Gallery for Modern Art would front directly onto Wilshire Boulevard and would be a monolithic structure with a stepped profile to the west and a 20-m (65-ft)-high doorway leading to a new courtyard occupying space formerly used as a public plaza and sculpture court.

Architects Belzile Brassard Gallienne Lavoie; Sungur Incesulu; and Moshe Safdie and Desnoyers Mercure, Quebec, won a limited competition for a new National Museum of Civilization for Quebec City. The design was for a waterfront site with terraced steps and gardens integrating the building into the old street plan of the city. The galleries beneath the terraces were skylit, and the design featured copper roofs with dormers punctuated by a tower.

A new west wing for the Boston Museum of Fine Art, opened in July 1981, was designed by I. M. Pei, architect of the East Wing of the National Gallery in Washington, D.C. The new air-conditioned galleries were not easily added to the 1909 Beaux-Arts building. The architect's instructions were to provide additional space for traveling exhibitions and contemporary art and also a new restaurant and other service functions. His design made a 76-m (250-ft)-long skylighted vault the heart of the wing. This "galleria" provided a circulation loop for the whole museum. The new wing was clad in Maine granite to relate it visually to the old building. A new home for the art museum in Akron, Ohio, was a conversion of a historic post office by architects Dalton, van Dijk, Johnson and Partners.

Great public interest was generated in London by the competition for an extension to the National Gallery. The works of the seven finalists were put on public display in late summer and attracted such large crowds that the exhibition was extended. The public was asked to vote for its first and last choices, and the winner of the competition was to be announced in October by the secretary of state for the environment. The addition was re-

A small elementary school, equipped with solar collectors, was fitted onto a steep hillside near Coit Tower in San Francisco. The architects were Esherick, Homsey, Dodge & Davis.

PETER AARON—ESTO

quired to have some 2,800 sq m (30,000 sq ft) of toplit gallery space to house the Renaissance masterpieces of the collection. Underneath, the building had to provide 5,600 sq m (60,000 sq ft) of office space. Each architect teamed with a developer, who would gain an office building on a prime site in exchange for providing the galleries. The site would be leased for 125 years for a nominal rent but would then revert to the crown. Thus the government could gain its gallery space without having to foot the huge bill.

Of the seven plans chosen as finalists, by far the most controversial was that by Richard Rogers & Partners. The Rogers design featured galleries raised on stilts above a metallic-looking office building with a curved face and a high tower at one side. The structure and metallic skeleton showed the technological bravura of the architect's Beaubourg Centre in Paris and was criticized by some as out of place on the sensitive site; others thought it the most exciting, romantic, and "architectural" entry. Buildings by the other six finalists ranged from a severely neoclassical entry by the one U.S. firm represented, Skidmore, Owings & Merrill, to the restrained entries by Arup Associates and Ahrends Burton and Koralek. In the event, although Skidmore, Owings & Merrill's entry was the one that came closest to satisfying the National Gallery's requirements, none of the competing designs was selected; Ahrends Burton and Koralek, however, were to be asked to submit an entirely new design.

The Federal Commission of Fine Arts approved a design by Hartman-Cox for a four-level addition for the John F. Kennedy Center for the Performing Arts in Washington, D.C. The centre was originally designed by Edward Durell Stone. The entire structure would be underground, with terraced gardens and light wells replacing the grassed area on the city side of the building. A recital hall, parking spaces, theatre, and music studios would be provided. The funding of the required $25 million would be from private sources.

An international competition was held to select a design team, including a landscape architect, for a new park at La Villette in northeast Paris. The 30-ha (75-ac) site would be the first Paris park to be created in more than 100 years and would include a museum devoted to science, technology, and industry and also a music centre. Entries would be exhibited to the public early in 1983 at the Beaubourg Centre. Other major architectural projects in Paris in the planning stage included an opera house for the Place de la Bastille, a jazz and rock music centre for the Place de Bagnolet, and an international communications centre in La Défense. All would be the subject of competitions.

In London the Barbican Centre finally opened in the spring, after years of planning and construction. It housed two theatres, a concert hall and opera house, and an art gallery and library.

Public, Commercial, and Industrial Buildings. The limited design competition for the Humana Headquarters for downtown Louisville, Ky., was won by Michael Graves & Associates of Princeton, N.J. The four runners-up were Cesar Pelli & Associates, Murphy/Jahn Associates, Ulrich Franzen/ K. Kroeger & Associates, and Foster Associates of London. The winning design was a formalist conception reminiscent of 19th-century buildings, featuring covered arcades, a tower, a loggia at the base, granite- and marble-clad façades red and bluish in colour, tripartite elevations, and a north-facing cantilevered porch. The mass of the 27-story-high building was broken into a number of disparate elements with classical overtones and

The Akron (Ohio) Art Museum's new home was formerly a deserted post office across the street from the old museum. A benefactor gave $3 million to help renovate and endow the building.

was far removed from the traditional single-volume slab skyscraper. The building was to form the headquarters of an international hospital management committee and provide 41,800 sq m (450,000 sq ft) of space.

Two office buildings by Skidmore, Owings & Merrill were under construction and scheduled for completion in 1983. The Hartford Tower, CityPlace, Hartford, Conn., featured a cutaway corner design in which bay windows allowed a wide view from each office. The 38-story-high tower would be the tallest in Connecticut. In San Antonio, Texas, the First International Plaza, a $50 million project, would at 28 stories be the largest building in the downtown area. The arched façade with pointed detailing again showed the tendency to break up the slab.

The new Barbican Arts Centre in London is equipped with concert theatres, cinemas, libraries, cinemas, and theatre halls.

Helmut Jahn, of the Chicago firm Murphy/Jahn, won a design competition for an 82-story office building in Houston, Texas. The steel, granite, and glass design is reminiscent of the skyscrapers of the 1920s and 1930s. At 373 m (1,222 ft) the tower would be one of the tallest in the U.S.

In Los Angeles the Intercontinental Centre by Pereira Associates would replace the 1930s Streamlined Moderne Broadway Department Store (recently demolished) on Wilshire Boulevard. The project attempted to re-create some of the traditional Wilshire Boulevard motifs in the 30-story tower building with its stepped profile, monumental door, roof terraces, and motor court at the rear. A smaller "sister building," either hotel or residential, was planned for the back of the site. The tower, which would have retail space at ground-floor level and ornate elevator lobbies in the traditional manner, would be the tallest in the immediate area.

Kohn, Pedersen, Fox Associates were architects for a new corporate headquarters for Procter & Gamble Co. in Cincinnati, Ohio. The building, which would provide 74,300 sq m (800,000 sq ft), featured squat twin octagonal towers rising from a piazza in downtown Cincinnati to 17 stories from an L-shaped six-story base. A gray granite colonnade at street level and open atria at fourth- and sixth-floor levels were features. A heat pump system was used to recover energy from lights, equipment, and people. The same architects designed the Tampa (Fla.) Financial Center, a $45 million project with a curved wall of tinted glass facing Tampa City Hall. The 30-story building, with a granite fascia frame and picture windows in the tower walls, was scheduled for completion early in 1984. (SANDRA MILLIKIN)

See also Engineering Projects; Historic Preservation; Industrial Review.
[626.A.1–5; 626.C]

Arctic Regions

Alaska. Two British adventurers became the first to cross both the North and South poles in a single voyage when they planted the Union Jack at the North Pole on April 11, 1982. After covering 56,300 km (35,000 mi) of their planned 84,000-km (52,000-mi) trip, the attainment of the North Pole was the climax of a three-year voyage for Sir Ranulph Fiennes and Charles Burton.

In September the Associated Press reported that charter aircraft business to the North Pole was booming. The short mid-April to mid-May season is terminated when the ice breaks up, making landings dangerous. The visits to the area last no longer than 30 minutes because after that the planes' engines could freeze. After a year-long study by the U.S. National Petroleum Council, it was reported that undeveloped Arctic regions in the United States contain enough oil and gas to make a significant contribution to the nation's energy supply. The report estimated that approximately 44,000,000,000 bbl of undiscovered recoverable oil and gas resources are expected to be found in those regions. In October, 23 companies made high bids totaling $2.1 billion for the right to drill for oil in the Beaufort Sea off Alaska's North Slope.

In addition, as reported in the *Anchorage Times*, the state is believed to contain 50% of the nation's peat resources and more than half of the coal resources. Prudhoe Bay, which holds 29% of the confirmed U.S. reserves of crude oil, already was supplying 9% of the nation's petroleum needs.

After a ruling by the U.S. Supreme Court, an estimated 419,000 Alaskans were due to receive an initial dividend of $1,000 each from the Permanent Fund Dividend, a savings account for Alaska oil revenues. For the year ended June 30, 1982, the state's $2 billion fund earned interest of 16%.

A study by the University of Alaska's Institute of Social and Economic Research showed that, because of high oil revenues, beginning in 1980 the U.S. government collected almost twice as much in taxes as it spent in the state. This important shift in the economy was expected to continue as long as revenues remained high.

As reported in the April issue of *Alaska*, it was expected that the state of Alaska would be requested to invest in the Alaska Highway gas pipeline, perhaps through the building of a $4 billion gas conditioning plant. As a start toward meeting the cost of the project, estimated at $40 billion, pledges of nearly $15 billion were organized by the Northwest Alaskan Pipeline Co. Late in the year a company official informed the Federal Regulatory Commission that the pipeline would be delayed and that 1989 was the earliest expected completion date.

Canada. Planning for the Arctic Pilot Project (APP) continued during 1982 with the submission of a number of applications to the National Energy Board. The joint undertaking by Petro-Canada, Nova Corp., Dome Petroleum Ltd., and Melville Shipping Ltd., if approved by the Canadian gov-

ernment, would eventually move natural gas from Melville Island through the Northwest Passage and Baffin Bay-Davis Strait to markets in eastern North America and Europe.

In July the Canadian government released a report entitled "The Lancaster Sound Region, 1980–2000." It outlined six options for the management of Lancaster Sound, the eastern entrance to the Northwest Passage. They ranged from strict environmental protection to concerted economic development.

The first agreement under the new Canada Oil and Gas Act was signed in May between Esso Resources Canada, Ltd., and the government of Canada. The agreement covered the company's $600 million exploration program in the Mackenzie Delta-Beaufort Sea region.

As reported in the fall issue of the *APOA Review*, the encouraging exploration results in the Beaufort Sea led the petroleum industry to begin designing systems to extract hydrocarbons and deliver them to market. Further drilling was planned during the 1982 season; administrative and technical support bases were being established; and a comprehensive environmental impact statement was submitted for public review in preparation for recommendations to the federal government.

Some progress was made toward settling the many outstanding Indian land claims in Canada. In December 1981 the Department of Indian and Northern Affairs reaffirmed its commitment to negotiate claims by issuing a comprehensive claims policy entitled "In All Fairness." This was followed in May 1982 by a revised policy entitled "Outstanding Business." Land claims negotiations were a major issue in the Yukon general election held June 1982. Some Indian spokesmen alleged that the winning Conservative territorial government was resisting a settlement favourable to native people, and the Council of Yukon Indians threatened to take the issue to court.

In May the Dene Nation and Métis Association of the Northwest Territories announced that agreement had been reached on the definition of "Dene" for the purposes of negotiating a land

Two British adventurers, Charles Burton and Sir Ranulph Fiennes, left England in 1979 determined to circle the globe, pole to pole. They reached the South Pole in December 1980, where a plane met them to replenish their supplies. On April 11, 1982, they arrived at the North Pole.

Areas:
see Demography; see also the individual country articles

claims settlement in the western Canadian Arctic. "Dene" would include descendants of seven native groups including the Métis, who traditionally used and occupied lands that are now in the Northwest Territories, Yukon, and northern British Columbia.

In May the legislative assembly of the Northwest Territories voted in favour of asking the Canadian government to divide the Northwest Territories and to establish a commission to recommend boundaries for a new eastern territory, which would be named Nunavut. This action followed a plebiscite held in April in which 56% of voters signified they were in favour of division.

During the year the Northwest Territories and federal governments signed an agreement to create a 39,500-sq km (15,250 sq mi) national park on northern Ellesmere Island. Under the agreement the land would be withdrawn for two years from development for other purposes while public consultation and planning proceeded.

In July the Dene, Indians, Inuit, and Sami of the circumpolar countries participated in the first World Assembly of indigenous peoples held in Regina, Sask. The chairman of the conference stated that indigenous peoples did not intend to "ask for sovereignty, for they had never given it up" and that they wanted to coexist, as culturally and socially different nations, with those peoples who shared their lands. The Inuit (Eskimo) Circumpolar Conference, an organization representing the Eskimo populations of Alaska, Canada, and Greenland, planned to ask for affiliation with the United Nations. Related to this development was the hope of the Conference to define the differences between commercial and subsistence whaling and to have that definition accepted by the International Whaling Commission.

The Soviet North. In May it was reported that Soviet scientists believed that relics ranging from 15,000 to 20,000 years old found in northeastern Siberia confirmed that the first inhabitants of America migrated from Asia. The relics indicated that the people hunted deer, mammoth, and bison and also tamed dogs.   (KENNETH DE LA BARRE)

See also Environment.

Argentina

The federal republic of Argentina occupies the southeastern section of South America and is bounded by Chile, Bolivia, Paraguay, Brazil, Uruguay, and the Atlantic Ocean. It is the second-largest Latin-American country, after Brazil, with an area of 2,758,829 sq km (1,065,189 sq mi). Pop. (1982 est.): 28,438,000. Cap. and largest city: Buenos Aires (pop., 1980, 2,922,800). Language: Spanish. Religion: Roman Catholic 92%. President until June 18, 1982, Lieut. Gen. Leopoldo Galtieri; interim chief executive from June 18 to July 1, Maj. Gen. Alfredo Oscar Saint Jean; president from July 1, Maj. Gen. Reynaldo Bignone.

Lieut. Gen. Leopoldo Galtieri (*see* BIOGRAPHIES), who assumed the military presidency of Argentina on Dec. 22, 1981, faced increasing civilian opposition to military rule during the first months of

Argentina

1982. The principal reason for this was the worsening economy. Gross domestic product fell by 6% in 1981; the foreign debt was $32 billion; and the annual rate of inflation, estimated at 138.1% at the end of 1981, was reported by the International Monetary Fund (IMF) to be the highest in the world in January 1982. Finance Minister Roberto Alemann introduced a program of austerity: cuts in public sector spending; denationalizations in the banking, energy, and military-industrial sectors; devaluation of the peso; and a wage freeze. Repeated outcries against Alemann's policies, rising unemployment, and falling wages led to a violent protest by the Peronist Confederación General de Trabajo on March 30, during which about 2,000 people were arrested.

Efforts at cutting budgetary expenditure were likened to the policies of U.S. Pres. Ronald Reagan, and a general rapprochement between Argentina and the U.S. was observed, especially in foreign policy. Argentine involvement in Central America, in support of the U.S. position, continued in the form of advisers in El Salvador, but reports of plans to destabilize the Sandinista regime in Nicaragua were denied.

The failure to resolve the dispute over sovereignty of the Falkland Islands/Islas Malvinas during 17 years of talks with the U.K. returned to the headlines in March. After reportedly cordial but unproductive talks in New York City on February 26–27, the Argentine Foreign Ministry stated that an alternative measure to negotiation would be taken if a solution were not found quickly.

Rumours of a possible Argentine invasion of the Falkland Islands met with no response from the U.K. until the arrival on March 19 of a group of Argentine scrap-metal contractors on South Georgia, a Falklands dependency, developed into a confrontation between Argentine warships and the British Antarctic patrol vessel HMS "Endurance." On April 2 Argentine troops landed on the Falkland Islands, easily overcoming the small garrison of U.K. Royal Marines stationed at Port Stanley.

In Argentina Galtieri received much popular support for the invasion. The U.K.'s immediate reaction was to break off diplomatic relations and to dispatch a naval task force to the South Atlantic. On April 3 the UN Security Council supported the U.K.'s call for an Argentine withdrawal. During the three weeks that it took the British fleet to reach the vicinity of the Falklands, negotiations at the UN for a peaceful settlement and mediation attempts by U.S. Secretary of State Alexander Haig and by Pres. Fernando Belaúnde Terry of Peru proved unsuccessful.

Trade sanctions were imposed on Argentina by the European Communities (EC), and the U.K. received further support from many of its Commonwealth allies. Argentina, on the other hand, was backed by the majority of Latin-American countries, although many did not approve of the initial use of force as a means toward settlement. Soviet support for Argentina was cautious and did not extend to voting for Argentina in the first UN debate. The U.S., while not joining its partners within the Organization of American States in condemning the British position, did not openly support the U.K. until April 30, after British forces had retaken South Georgia.

On June 14 the Argentine military governor of the Falklands, Gen. Mario Benjamín Menéndez, surrendered. (For an account of the military campaign see DEFENSE: *Special Report.*) For Argentina, the repercussions of defeat were serious. Public morale had been bolstered by a visit by Pope John Paul II during the conflict, but the Army's capitulation on the islands, the Navy's relative inactivity, and feelings that the U.S. could no longer be counted on as an ally brought a sense of pessimism.

Galtieri resigned as army commander and president on June 17. The former post was taken by Gen. Cristino Nicolaides; the presidency was temporarily given to Interior Minister Maj. Gen. Alfredo Oscar Saint Jean. After much debate within the armed forces, retired army general Reynaldo Bignone was named president until March 29, 1984. Since the plan for a speedy return to democracy seemed unlikely to be adopted, the Air Force, together with the Navy, retired from the ruling junta in protest against Bignone's appointment. Brig. Basilio Lami Dozo, commander of the Air Force, was dismissed in August after his proposal to form an official party to further the process of national reconstruction met with disapproval. He was replaced by Brig. Augusto Jorge Hughes. The navy commander in the conflict, Adm. Jorge Isaac Anaya, announced his retirement in September. His successor was Adm. Rubén Oscar Franco. On September 10 the junta, consisting of the three service commanders, was restored in order to provide a stronger approach to the country's debt crisis. Opposition civilian parties were heartened by moves toward the signing of a statute on the organization and activity of political parties.

The politically sensitive issue of the *desaparecidos* ("disappeared persons") remained prominent in domestic affairs. Human-rights groups continued to press the government for a full investigation of the issue, especially after the claim that nearly 1,000 unidentified bodies found in six cemeteries during October and November were those of victims killed during the 1976–79 suppression of opposition. The government's proposed pact with civilian parties for a transition to democracy included an agreement not to investigate the armed

LAFFAILLE—SIPA PRESS/BLACK STAR

Argentine soldiers dug in to fight off British troops during the brief war on the Falkland Islands.

forces' actions at that time or their handling of the Falklands campaign and the economy. On September 26 censorship was imposed on the reporting of all "subversive" matters.

On the international front the war had forged some unexpected alliances, notably between Argentina and Cuba. Argentina's trading links with Latin America, socialist countries, and the Middle East were reinforced, but the end of hostilities brought a gradual reinstatement of trade ties with the U.S. and the EC. Argentina, however, retained some sanctions against selected EC countries. Although the future of the Falklands seemed to rest firmly in the hands of the British government, a UN General Assembly resolution calling for the resumption of direct negotiations on the islands' future was passed in November. Argentine/British trade embargoes were not lifted, but in September financial sanctions were ended. Agreement on Argentine debts to the U.K. was reached in October.

Since June 16 Argentina had been unable to make repayment on its external debts, which had risen to $37 billion. Economy Minister Jorge Wehbe (who replaced Alemann's successor, José María Dagnino Pastore, when he resigned in August) succeeded in obtaining a delay in debt repay-

ARGENTINA

Education. (1979) Primary, pupils 4,003,670, teachers 224,673; secondary and vocational, pupils 1,295,815, teachers 178,681; higher, students 475,799, teaching staff 45,089.

Finance. Monetary unit: peso, with (Sept. 20, 1982) a free financial rate of 39,000 pesos to U.S. $1 (66,865 pesos = £1 sterling). Gold and other reserves (May 1982) U.S. $3,217,000,000. Budget (1980 actual): revenue 48,939,000,000,000 pesos; expenditure 54,015,000,000,000 pesos. Gross national product (1978) 50,717,000,000,000 pesos. Money supply (Dec. 1980) 36,158,000,000,000 pesos. Cost of living (Buenos Aires; 1975 = 100; June 1982) 91,776.

Foreign Trade. (1980) Imports 19,555,-000,000,000 pesos; exports 14,703,000,000,000 pesos. Import sources: U.S. 23%; Brazil 10%; West Germany 9%; Japan 9%; Italy 6%. Export destinations: U.S.S.R. 20%; Brazil 10%; U.S. 9%; The Netherlands 9%; Italy 6%; West Germany 5%. Main

exports: meat 12%; wheat 10%; corn 6%; machinery c. 5%.

Transport and Communications. Roads (1978) 207,630 km. Motor vehicles in use (1978): passenger 2,866,000; commercial (including buses) 1,244,000. Railways (1980): c. 34,600 km; traffic 12,593,000,000 passenger-km, freight 9,742,000,000 net ton-km. Air traffic (1981): 6,936,000,000 passenger-km; freight 214.8 million net ton-km. Shipping (1981): merchant vessels 100 gross tons and over 521; gross tonnage 2,306,760. Shipping traffic (1980): goods loaded 20,650,000 metric tons, unloaded 10,540,000 metric tons. Telephones (Jan. 1980) 2,759,736. Radio receivers (Dec. 1978) 10.2 million. Television receivers (Dec. 1979) 4,715,000.

Agriculture. Production (in 000; metric tons; 1981): wheat 7,900; corn c. 13,500; sorghum c. 7,550; millet 238; barley c. 200; oats c. 500; rice 286; potatoes 2,247; sugar, raw value 1,624; linseed c.

531; soybeans 3,600; sunflower seed c. 1,260; tomatoes 453; oranges 654; lemons 300; apples c. 905; wine c. 2,075; tobacco 52; cotton, lint 82; cheese c. 240; wool, clean 89; beef and veal c. 3,000; fish catch (1980) 384; quebracho extract (1980) 95. Livestock (in 000; 1981) cattle 54,325; sheep 30,000; pigs 3,900; goats 3,000; horses 3,000; chickens 40,000.

Industry. Fuel and power (in 000; metric tons; 1981): crude oil 25,513; natural gas (cu m) 9,790,000; coal 487; electricity (excluding most industrial production; kw-hr) 35,250,000. Production (in 000; metric tons; 1981): cement 6,912; crude steel 2,199; cotton yarn (1980) 74; man-made fibres (1980) 38; petroleum products (1979) c. 24,300; plastics and resins 136; sulfuric acid 232; newsprint 109; other paper (1980) 504; passenger cars (including assembly; units) 143; commercial vehicles (including assembly; units) 29. Merchant vessels launched (100 gross tons and over; 1981) 95,300 gross tons.

ments to the country's major creditors. An IMF delegation arrived in September to prepare studies for renegotiating the foreign debt, which by then stood at $40 billion.

Debts and high interest rates forced businesses into bankruptcy, and confidence was lost as money left the country to purchase black-market dollars. The black-market peso stood as low as 60,000 to U.S. $1 in September, when, on the reintroduced two-tier exchange system, the commercial peso was 26,850 to U.S. $1 and the financial peso 39,000 to U.S. $1. Wehbe's strategy aimed to close the gap between the commercial and financial peso so as to lead eventually to a unified rate. Despite a virtual halt in exports after reimposition of the two-tier rate, Argentina had a trade surplus of $1,964,000,000 in the first seven months.

Wehbe also initiated attempts to resuscitate industry and provide a real rise in living standards for workers. Unemployment was estimated at 18%. Wage increases were given in August, September, and October, but these did not prevent strikes and demonstrations on September 22 and October 17. Annual retail inflation stood at 175.5% as of September.

The dispute with Chile over the sovereignty of three islands in the Beagle Channel was not resolved. Mediation by the Vatican produced no lasting result, although in September both parties agreed to a ten-year extension of their treaty on frontier disagreements. It was feared that the Yacyretá hydroelectric project on the Río Paraná, planned in cooperation with Paraguay, would be postponed because of Argentina's financial difficulties. However, talks with French and Italian contractors, at the request of the Argentine government, cleared the way for construction to begin in 1983.   (BEN BOX)

Art Exhibitions

There would be no more large loan exhibitions, or so the experts had been saying for some years. Certainly the lending policies of the major institutions, reflecting the increased costs of insurance and transport and the problems of conservation, militated against the major loan retrospectives that had been common 20 years earlier. Loans were approved only for works robust enough to travel and for shows of outstanding importance.

The rare large loan retrospectives were now greeted with more enthusiasm and excitement than ever. Such was the London Royal Academy's winter exhibition, "Painting in Naples from Caravaggio to Giordano," a loan exhibition devoted to Caravaggio and his followers which drew on many Italian private and public collections and churches. Not only were many of the paintings lent for the first time but works often difficult to view properly in churches were displayed under gallery conditions. Of the more than 150 paintings comprising the show, the highlights undoubtedly were Caravaggio's "Seven Works of Mercy" and his "Flagellation." Jusepe de Ribera, Guido Reni, Francesco Solimena, and Giordano were other artists whose work was represented.

The largest exhibit of El Greco's paintings ever mounted opened at the Prado in Madrid in April before traveling to the National Gallery of Art, Washington, D.C., the Toledo (Ohio) Museum of Art, and the Dallas (Texas) Museum of Fine Arts. Titled "El Greco of Toledo," the show originated as part of the celebration of 50 years of "sisterhood" between Toledo, Ohio, and Toledo, Spain, where El Greco spent most of his career. Of the 66 paintings in the exhibit, 32 were from Spain and the remainder were on loan from museums and collections outside the country, several of them in the U.S. Besides the paintings executed in Toledo, the show included works from the painter's early years in Italy.

If loan exhibitions in which works of art were borrowed from various owners were becoming less and less frequent, a new type of show was on the increase: the exhibition of a whole collection made by one man or family. Not only did such exhibitions afford an opportunity to see fine works of art, they also provided an insight into the history of private collecting, taste, and connoisseurship. The goals and achievements of private collectors differ from those of museums. A museum director

"St. Martin and the Beggar" was one of 66 paintings that made up the "El Greco of Toledo" exhibit. The exhibit was shown in galleries in Madrid; Washington, D.C.; Toledo, Ohio; and Dallas, Texas.

NATIONAL GALLERY OF ART, WASHINGTON, D.C.; PHOTOGRAPH, AUTHENTICATED NEWS INTERNATIONAL

Armies:
see Defense

Art:
see Architecture; Art Exhibitions; Art Sales; Dance; Literature; Museums; Theatre

must bear in mind the suitability of a new acquisition for the whole collection. The great private collector can satisfy his own artistic taste. If he has a good eye, his collection will be coherent and unique.

The National Gallery of Art in Washington, D.C., mounted "Lessing J. Rosenwald: Tribute to a Collector" in the winter. Rosenwald was the foremost donor of prints and drawings to the gallery, and the Rosenwald collection contains works dating from medieval times to the present. It was described as the finest collection of its kind ever formed by a single individual in the U.S. Lessing Rosenwald was the son of the chairman of Sears, Roebuck & Co. and succeeded his father in that position, retiring in 1939. Between 1926 and 1979 he collected about 22,000 Old Master and modern prints and drawings.

George Costakis, born in Moscow of Greek parents, formed a unique collection of modern Russian art between 1908 and 1932. A show based on his collection was organized by the Guggenheim Museum, New York City, in the winter of 1981–82 and later toured the U.S., Europe, and Asia, including the Museum of Fine Arts, Houston, Texas, and the Royal Academy, London. Titled "Art of the Avant-Garde in Russia: Selections from the George Costakis Collection," the show consisted of 275 works of art made in the first quarter of the 20th century by 40 artists, some little known in the West. There were important works of Futurism, Suprematism, and Constructivism and examples of works by the major artists of the period, including the sculptors Aleksandr Rodchenko and Vladimir Tatlin. Costakis, through his contacts in Moscow, was able to meet many of the artists personally and collect at a period when the works of this group lacked official recognition.

The families of artists sometimes have an unrivaled opportunity to collect. "Max Ernst—From the Collection of Mr. and Mrs. Jimmy Ernst" was organized by the Glenbow Museum, Calgary, Alta., and shown also at the Art Gallery of Hamilton, Ont. Jimmy Ernst was the son of the Surrealist artist Max Ernst and was himself a leading American painter. The works forming the core of the show were from Max Ernst's personal collection. There were 16 paintings, 23 works of sculpture, 34 prints, and 15 pieces of primitive art from which the artist drew some inspiration. The exhibition included some of the concrete gargoyles made by Max Ernst to decorate his own home in Arizona.

"An American Perspective: Nineteenth Century Art from the Collection of JoAnn and Julian Ganz, Jr." was shown in the summer at the Los Angeles County Museum of Art. The Ganz collection, formed in the last 20 years, was considered one of the finest collections of 19th-century American art and included works by such major artists as Winslow Homer, Thomas Cole, and J. S. Sargent. An exhibition devoted to the works of the New York postwar Abstract Expressionist Adolph Gottlieb was shown in Los Angeles at the same time.

Shows with an American theme remained common, and one of the finest in 1982 was the definitive exhibition organized by the Philadelphia Museum of Art and devoted to the work of Thomas

An exhibit entitled "The Indian Heritage: Court Life and Arts under Mughal Rule" went on display at London's Victoria and Albert Museum. The painting shown dates to 1617.

Eakins (1844–1916). The show was part of Philadelphia's celebrations of the city's 300th anniversary. Both the famous "clinical" scenes—"The Agnew Clinic" and "The Gross Clinic"—were on view. Eakins emerged as possibly the greatest of all American artists. The show would travel to Boston later, but without a number of the paintings seen in Philadelphia.

"American Portraits in the Grand Manner, 1720–1920" was organized for the Los Angeles County Museum of Art and was also on view at the National Portrait Gallery, Washington, D.C. It was the first major loan exhibition to be devoted to formal portraiture in the U.S. as a distinct artistic type. The works shown included notable examples by Frank Duveneck and Robert Henri as well as earlier works. The paintings were mostly full-length and many were life-size. Circus art was the subject of "Center Ring: The Artist," organized by the Milwaukee (Wis.) Art Center and also seen at the Corcoran Gallery of Art, Washington, D.C.

Many exhibitions in 1982 were again devoted to Far Eastern subjects. Indian art was shown at a number of places in London as part of the Festival of India. The British Museum's "From Village to City in Ancient India" focused on works dating from the neolithic period to the 10th century. "In the Image of Man" at the Hayward Gallery was devoted to 2,000 years of Indian painting and sculpture, with many works lent from India. The British Museum lent some examples of 3rd-century sculpture that were not normally on public view. At the Victoria and Albert Museum, "The Indian Heritage: Court Life and Arts Under Mughal Rule" included paintings and objects from private and public collections in Britain, India, France, and the U.S. Among the exhibits were a silver tiger's head from Tippu Sultan's throne, lent by the queen. Another exhibition at the Victoria and Albert, "India Observed," took as its theme British artists and photographers in India. It included 200 paintings, drawings, and prints. A number of commercial galleries also held shows with an Indian theme.

The Kimbell Art Museum, Fort Worth, Texas, celebrated its tenth anniversary with an exhibition of Japanese Buddhist sculpture from the 7th to the 13th centuries, the first show of its kind ever to travel from Japan to the West. Many of the fragile wooden pieces were lent by active Buddhist temples. Included were seven "national treasures" and over 30 "important cultural properties." The show was also seen at the Japan House Gallery in New York City. "Arts of the Islamic Book: The Collection of Prince Sanruddin Aga Khan" at the Asia Society Gallery, New York City, featured some of the finest examples of Islamic painting and calligraphy. It consisted of 90 paintings, drawings, manuscripts, and calligraphies collected by the prince over 30 years, most of which had never before been exhibited and many of which were unpublished. Said to be one of the most important collections of its kind in private hands, the show was slated to travel in 1983 to Fort Worth and Kansas City, Mo.

"Treasures of Asian Art from the Idemitsu Collection" was organized by the Seattle (Wash.) Art Museum and also seen in New York City at the Japan House Gallery and in Colorado at the Denver Art Museum. The Idemitsu Museum of Arts is a private Japanese museum, 15 years old, regarded as one of the finest in Japan. Its collection is particularly strong in Far Eastern ceramics and Japanese painting. Treasures of Chinese and Japanese art from the Kuboso Collection were shown at the Tokyo National Museum and later at the Museum of Art, Osaka, Japan. Among the works on view were paintings and decorative art and a group of

early Chinese bronze mirrors. The collection was formed by Sotaro Kubo and presented to the Imuzi municipality, where a new museum was built to house it.

Exhibitions held at the Israel Museum, Jerusalem, during 1982 included "Ethnic Arts" in March and April, a selection from the museum's own collection of African, Oceanic, and pre-Columbian objects. Also at the Israel Museum were an exhibition of photographs by Bill Brandt and "Royal Hunters and Divine Lovers," a display of 16th- to 19th-century Rajput miniatures.

An important Canaletto exhibition at the Fondazione Giorgio Cini in Venice, Italy, included many rarely seen privately owned paintings. Works from all phases of Canaletto's life were included, distinguishing this from the recent London exhibition devoted to his later works. Some of the paintings predated Canaletto's departure from Venice for England. Many of the later works had never before been exhibited in Italy. Three rooms were devoted to drawings and sketches, with many drawings lent by Queen Elizabeth. Works on show included the "View of the Piazza San Marco" from the Thyssen-Bornemisza Collection, Lugano, of about 1723, Canaletto's first painting of the Piazza and one that shows the influence of the theatre on his early works. There were also a number of works from the artist's final years after he returned to Venice from England.

In the autumn the Museo Correr in Venice held a show called "Venezia: Piante e Vedute," which was made up of a series of plans and views of Venice, some taken from bound volumes. Works by Jacopo de'Barbari and the Combatti brothers and vistas by Dutch mapmakers were among the items shown.

"De Stijl — 1917–1931: Visions of Utopia," organized by the Walker Art Center, Minneapolis, Minn., was also seen at the Hirshhorn Museum, Washington, D.C., and in The Netherlands at the

An exhibition of Dutch avant-garde paintings, "De Stijl—1917–1931: Visions of Utopia," went on display in Minneapolis, Minnesota, in February. At right is Theo van Doesburg's "Card Players."

Stedelijk Museum, Amsterdam, and at Otterlo. It included paintings by Mondrian and Theo van Doesburg and furniture by Gerrit Rietveld, the leading names in this Dutch modern movement.

London continued to attract important art exhibitions. The Arts Council staged the largest exhibition of new Italian art ever seen outside Italy at the Hayward Gallery from October 1981 to January 1982. The exhibition, called "Arte Italiana, 1960–1982," comprised a major roundup of what had happened in Italian art since 1960, from the abstract, the conceptual, and the minimal to the recent return to representation. The exhibition was organized by the city of Milan in exchange for the British exhibition "English Art Today," seen in that city in 1976.

The Mauritshuis in The Hague, Neth., held an exhibition devoted to the work of Jacob van Ruisdael which attracted an average 2,000 people daily. Forty paintings from the museum's permanent collection of Dutch masterpieces would travel to the U.S. and Canada as part of the bicentennial of diplomatic relations between The Netherlands and the U.S. The works, which would be seen in Washington, Boston, Chicago, Los Angeles, and Toronto, included Vermeer's "Head of a Girl."

Two notable exhibitions were devoted to women. The Metropolitan Museum of Art, New York City, showed "The Eighteenth-Century Woman," an exhibition comprising costumes, clothing, furniture, desk sets, toilet articles, and other objects from the museum's collection demonstrating how fashion and femininity influenced the aesthetics of the age. "The Substance or the Shadow: Images of Victorian Womanhood" was the first loan exhibition of Victorian painting to be organized by the Yale Center for British Art, New Haven, Conn. It included works by Millais, Frith, Rossetti, and others.

There were a number of important retrospectives devoted to modern artists. Among them was the first major show devoted to the Surrealist Giorgio de Chirico since his death in 1978. Organized by the Museum of Modern Art, New York City, it was seen in London at the Tate Gallery. The show emphasized the artist's early years, from 1911 to 1915, and included drawings and documents as well as 65 paintings. A large retrospective of the work of Fernand Léger was organized by the Albright-Knox Art Gallery, Buffalo, N.Y., in the winter. Most of the 65 paintings shown dated from 1905 to 1954 and were borrowed from European collections. Many were being shown in the U.S. for the first time. Included were "La Lecture" of 1924, lent by the Beaubourg Centre, Paris, and "Étude pour Adam et Eve" of 1939, from the Musée National Fernand Léger.

Works by the artist and sculptor Jean Tinguely were shown at the Tate Gallery. Many of his strange mobile constructions were made of scrap metal and found objects. The show was an entertaining and witty one devoted to this Swiss-born artist, who had worked in Paris from the mid-1950s and was influenced by the Dadaism of Marcel Duchamp. The Tate also held a comprehensive exhibition devoted to the work of English painter Graham Sutherland (1903–80), designed as a me-

An exhibit of 40 outstanding examples of 17th-century Dutch painting from the Royal Picture Gallery of The Netherlands opened at the National Gallery of Art, Washington, D.C., in April. The Jan Steen (1626–79) painting, "Girl Eating Oysters," was included.

morial to the artist. It included his 1977 self-portrait and a number of his menacing but characteristic thorn heads.

Chaim Soutine (1893–1943) was the subject of an exhibition at the Hayward Gallery, previously shown in West Germany. Soutine, a Russian-born artist who worked in Paris, produced works that are expressive in character, with strong colours, thick paint, and violent brush strokes. The exhibition comprised a number of works executed between 1919 and 1925 when the artist was living at Céret and at Cagnes in southern France. An exhibition at the Museum of Fine Arts, Ghent, Belgium, was devoted to the turn of the century work of Belgian sculptor Georg Minne (1866–1941). All of his works from the period 1886 to 1900 were shown.

As part of the celebrations of the 250th anniversary of the Royal Opera House, Covent Garden, an exhibition titled "The Royal Opera House Retrospective 1732–1982" was shown in London in the private rooms of the Royal Academy in the winter of 1982–83. The works on exhibit included oils, watercolours, sculpture, and engravings showing the artist's view of the development of the theatre. The Georgian period was illustrated by Hogarth and Zoffany and the Neoclassical by fine portraits by Gainsborough, Lawrence, and Reynolds.

An exhibition organized by the Tower of London Armouries, which has one of the finest collections of arms and armour in the world, was shown at the Sainsbury Centre for Visual Arts, University of East Anglia, Norwich, and later traveled to the U.S. and Canada. The arms and armour, displayed as works of art, included such historic and decorative items as the swords of Cromwell and Wellington.   (SANDRA MILLIKIN)

[613.D.1.b]

Art Sales

Market Trends. The worst recession in the art market since 1974–75 took place in 1981–82. High interest rates discouraged dealers from buying for stock and made art significantly less attractive as an investment medium. Sotheby's turnover was down 25% from the previous year, while Christie's was 10% lower. The main problems lay in the middle market. Prices for exceptionally fine items were generally buoyant and sometimes ran beyond expectations. At the bottom of the market, cheap collectors' items or decorative furnishing pieces continued in demand.

Virtually every field was affected in this way, from paintings to furniture, silver to books, glass to antiquities. The explanation appeared to be a virtual disappearance of investment buying, which had been concentrated in the middle market area. Serious collectors and museums continued to compete for rarities whenever they appeared on the market. The recession also discouraged owners from selling, and fewer important works of art came on the market than in previous years. The financial difficulties of Sotheby's, the market leader, had a further depressing effect. The worldwide company reported a loss of £1.5 million before taxes for the year to February 1982. Staff was cut by 25%, the Los Angeles and Belgravia, London, auction rooms were closed, and in New York the Madison Avenue galleries were closed and all business transferred to York Avenue. There was also a major management reshuffle.

The lawsuit brought against Sotheby's and Christie's by the British Antique Dealers Association and the Society of London Art Dealers, alleging collusion over the introduction in 1975 of the buyer's premium, which required a purchaser to pay 10% of the bid price for a work of art, was settled out of court in September 1981. In May 1982 the British Office of Fair Trading ruled that the auctioneers had not acted irregularly. In September a request from the Art Dealers' Association of America that the charging of a buyer's premium be

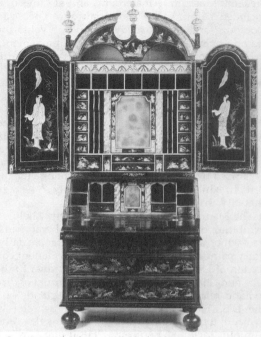

A Queen Anne bookcase sparked a bidding war when it appeared at auction in New York City. It eventually sold for $860,000.

prohibited at auctions in New York City was denied by the commissioner of consumer affairs.

Works of Art. One of the most eccentric high prices of the year was the $860,000 paid at Christie's in New York in October 1981 for a Queen Anne black lacquer bureau bookcase. It had formerly belonged to Queen Mary and when auctioned in Los Angeles in 1973 had reached only $90,000. The price was three times the dealers' valuations and was generated by a bidding battle between Wendell Cherry of Chicago, head of the Hospitals Corp. of America and the eventual winner, and the California financier David Murdoch, proprietor of Stair & Co., furniture dealers. A more calculated high, also underlining the strength of prices at the top of the market, was the SFr 1.5 million paid at a Christie's sale in Geneva in May 1982

Samuel F. B. Morse's famous 1832 painting "The Gallery of the Louvre" was sold for $3,250,000 by Syracuse University, which had owned it since 1884. The purchaser, shown at left, was Daniel J. Terra, founder of the Terra Museum of American Art in Evanston, Illinois.

for a small jeweled snuffbox made for Frederick the Great of Prussia in the late 18th century. The price doubled expectations and quadrupled the previous high for a snuffbox. It was bought for stock by S. J. Phillips, Ltd., London jewelers.

The shortage of top-quality items was also highlighted by two major museum purchases in which gambles were taken on attribution. The Cleveland (Ohio) Museum of Art spent an undisclosed price, probably about $3 million, on a version of Poussin's "Madone à l'escalier" that was previously considered a copy of the painting of the same name in the National Gallery, Washington, D.C., but was recognized as authentic by Cleveland's experts. The Städelsches Kunstinstitut of Frankfurt am Main, West Germany, spent DM 3 million in March 1982 on a version of Watteau's "Ladies and Gentlemen Embarking for the Isle of Cythera," again previously considered a copy of another painting. In July Daniel Terra paid $3,250,000 for "The Gallery of the Louvre," an 1832 painting by Samuel F. B. Morse, inventor of the telegraph. It was the highest price ever paid for a work by a U.S. painter. The painting was displayed at the Terra Museum of American Art in Evanston, Ill.

Auctions of Impressionist and modern paintings, generally the most expensive field, were often 50% or more unsold, but a few outstanding works brought top prices. A Cézanne "Still Life with Apple and Napkin" of around 1890 made $1,980,000 at Sotheby's in New York in November 1981, while Monet's "Pleasure Boats at Argenteuil" brought $1,430,000 in the same sale. In March 1982 Toulouse-Lautrec's "La Toilette: Le Repos du Modèle" made £759,000 at Sotheby's in London. In May in New York, Christie's offered the highest quality sale of contemporary art in many years, setting 14 new auction records for individual artists. Frank Stella's "Reichstag" of 1958 made $462,000; Jackson Pollock's "Night Dancer (Green)" of 1944, $330,000; and Mark Rothko's "No. 1—1962," $297,000. Also in May, Sotheby's sold Henry Moore's carved elmwood sculpture "Reclining Figure" for $1,265,000, an auction record price for a work by a living artist.

Fewer Old Master paintings of distinction came on the market, and prices were weak in the middle range. However, a group of British 18th- and early 19th-century pictures sold by Christie's in July brought outstanding returns. Turner's "Temple of Jupiter Panellius Restored" made £648,000; Constable's "Landscape with Ploughmen near East Bergholt," £324,000; Reynolds's "Countess of Eglington," £259,200; and a Lawrence portrait of Sir Robert Peel's daughter, £216,000.

The market in Chinese ceramics, another expensive field, recorded stronger prices than most other areas. A massively potted 15th-century blue and white jar (with damage) sold for £792,000 at Sotheby's in December 1981 to Hirano, a Japanese dealer, the highest auction price ever recorded for Chinese art.

Prices for the applied arts in general crept into the top bracket when exceptional items were on offer. A suit of armour made at the Greenwich Royal Armoury about 1610 sold for £418,000 at Christie's in November 1981; of outstanding magnifi-

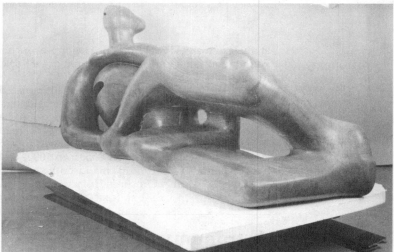

Henry Moore's carved elmwood sculpture "Reclining Figure" went for $1,265,000 in an auction at Sotheby's in New York City. The price was a record for a work by a living artist.

SOTHEBY PARKE-BERNET INC./ EDITORIAL PHOTOCOLOR ARCHIVES

cence, it had been ordered by Henry, prince of Wales, for his kinsman the duke of Brunswick. In December Christie's sold a French library table by J. F. Leleu, a pioneering example of neoclassical design of the 1770s, for £330,000. In March Sotheby's in Monte Carlo sold for Fr 1,155,500 a Vienna Secession bureau of 1903 with rich marquetry inlay, made by Soloman Moser for the Charlottenlund Palace near Stockholm.

In July a superb clock in an ebony and silver case made by Thomas Tompion for King William III of England in the late 17th century was withdrawn from a Christie's auction and sold privately to the British Museum by Lord Mostyn, its owner. The museum paid £500,000, but this was a special price since direct sales to institutions in Britain are not subject to capital taxes. The clock would have to have sold for between £800,000 and £1 million at auction to provide Lord Mostyn with the same sum after payment of tax.

Books. The market for rare books began the season on a sluggish note, book dealers being significantly less prepared to buy for stock than in previous years. In the spring and summer of 1982, however, some remarkable material reached the salesroom and prices picked up. A sprinkling of oddities came on the market in the autumn of 1981: Sotheby's sold a recently discovered manuscript of Edward Lear's *Book of Nonsense*, with 54 pen and ink drawings, for £17,600; a manuscript of *Les Grandes Chroniques de France*, written and illuminated for Jean, duc de Berry, the great medieval art collector and bibliophile, for £220,000; and, in New York, a 15th-century Latin translation of an 11th-century Arabic health manual, *Tacuinum Sanitatis*, with 132 illuminated illustrations, for $225,000.

A two-day sale in London of books and manuscripts concerning Australia in April 1982 demonstrated a new surge of interest among Australians in the documentation of their past. A 1786 pamphlet, *A Narrative of the Death of Captain James Cook*, sold for £15,400, against an expected £400–£700. On April 20–21 Israeli librarians and collectors packed Sotheby's for a sale of Hebrew books from the Valmadonna Trust; a scroll of the book of Esther, written and illustrated in Holland about 1620–40, was sold for £66,000 on behalf of the Liverpool Athenaeum. The following week Islamic collectors set new high price levels for calligraphy at a sale of manuscripts from the Hagop Kevorkian Foundation; a magnificent large Koran of 1488 sold for a record £88,000.

In June Sotheby's sold 20 Western illuminated manuscripts from the library of Prince Fürstenberg at Donaueschingen, a collection begun in the 15th century. H. P. Kraus of New York paid £308,000 for the illuminated *Sacramentary* of Augsburg Cathedral, written about AD 1000, and £220,000 for an 8th-century manuscript, written in France, of Paulus Orosius's *History of the World*.

(GERALDINE NORMAN)

Astronomy

Solar System. In 1979 a comet hit the Sun. But this remarkable event, the first evidence for the collision of an astronomical body with the Sun, only came to light in reports in late 1981 and 1982. Furthermore, the event was not seen from any ground-based observatory, some of which continuously monitor the Sun for unusual activity. It was detected by a U.S. Air Force research satellite, P78-1, launched in February 1979.

The SOLWIND orbiting coronagraph aboard the satellite, a device that effectively blots out the intense optical radiation from the solar disk itself while allowing a view of the much dimmer hot corona surrounding the Sun, revealed the event in a series of photographs taken at ten-minute intervals. The Naval Research Laboratory group that built the coronagraph, headed by Donald J. Michels, reported that late on Aug. 30, 1979, the comet approached the Sun. The path of its head on the photo images was straight, and a typical cometary tail pointed away from the Sun. In succeeding photographs a brightly lit gassy region appeared around the Sun, but the comet did not reappear, suggesting that it either hit the Sun directly or

totally evaporated because of the Sun's intense radiation. The calculated orbit suggested that it was a member of a previously known class of comets called sungrazers, comets whose highly eccentric orbits are opposite the orbital direction of the planets and bring them very close to the Sun.

Astonishingly, after their first announcements the same group reported that two more comets hit the Sun, on Jan. 27 and July 20, 1981, both with orbits similar to that of the first comet. These also did not reappear, suggesting a direct hit or complete evaporation. Probably the most intriguing aspect of this series of discoveries is that either cometary collisions with the Sun are quite common, possibly occurring as often as once a week, or the satellite was launched at a particularly auspicious time.

The year 1982 also marked the first sighting of Halley's Comet since it vanished from view in 1911. Early on October 16 David Jewitt and G. Edward Danielson spotted it using the 200-in Hale telescope on Mt. Palomar. At 24th magnitude it was still 100 million times too dim to be seen by the unaided eye. It was expected to pass the Earth in 1985, at which time a worldwide flurry of satellite- and ground-based observations would be made of the object. At its rediscovery the comet was about 1,600,000,000 km (1,000,000,000 mi) from the Earth, but it appeared within eight arc seconds of its predicted position in the sky.

In another story of belated discovery Edward F. Guinan, his student Craig C. Harris, and Frank P. Maloney of Villanova (Penn.) University announced in June 1982 the discovery of rings around the planet Neptune. In recent years all of the other giant gaseous planets of the solar system had been found to contain ring systems, though those of Uranus and Jupiter were far less easily seen from Earth than that of Saturn. The possible discovery (since it was unconfirmed, though not

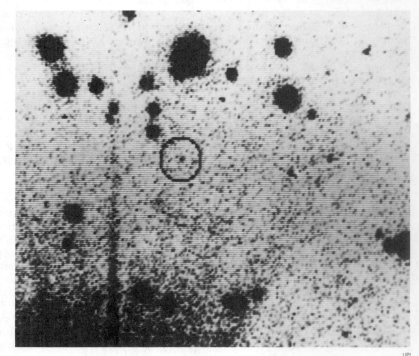

The first photograph of the return of Halley's Comet was taken in October with the Hale telescope on Mt. Palomar near Escondido, Calif. The comet, which becomes visible in the Earth's sky every 76 years, will make its closest approach to the Sun in February 1986.

Association Football:
see Football

Astronautics:
see Space Exploration

UPI

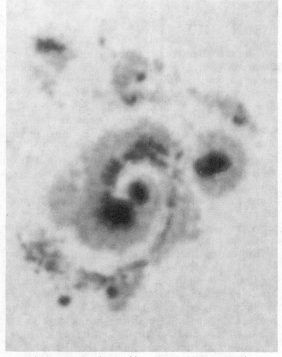

A spiral sunspot was observed by astronomers at Kitt Peak National Observatory in February. It was the first time that a spiral sunspot had been seen.

contradicted, by subsequent observations) was based on measurements made in 1968 to study Neptune's atmosphere. Guinan had been watching the occultation of a distant star by Neptune, looking for the diminution of the light as the star went behind the planet. The data, analyzed 13 years later, showed the partial drop in starlight characteristic of the presence of a ring system lying between 1.2 and 1.4 times the radius of the planet.

Following two years of spectacular observations of Jupiter and Saturn by the U.S. Voyager space probes, no new American planetary spacecraft were launched or were active during 1982. The one major planetary mission was the soft landings by the twin Soviet probes Venera 13 and 14 on Earth's sister planet Venus on March 1 and 5. These two probes provided the sharpest images of the rock-strewn planetary surface to date. Because of the enormous pressure on the surface of Venus, nearly 90 times that on Earth's surface, and intense heat (with measured temperatures of about 460° C, or 860° F) the craft had to make their measurements rapidly before being destroyed by the severe environment. Venera 13 touched down on a plain to the east of the Phoebe region of the Beta area, a rolling upland considered to be young and highly volcanic. It promptly photographed (in both black and white and colour) and sampled the soil and atmosphere for 127 minutes. Venera 14 landed some 900 km (560 mi) to the southeast at a location about a half kilometre lower in elevation than the Venera 13 site; it survived only 57 minutes.

Though short-lived, the two craft managed to provide a wide array of information and insights, among them the findings that there are at least two major volcanic regions on Venus, Beta Regio and the "Scorpion Tail" of Aphrodite Terra; that Venus

apparently has a thicker crust than that of Earth; and that the planet shows no evidence for the sort of plate tectonic activity that dominates Earth's surface features. Because of the thick crust most of the planet's internal heat vents itself through volcanically active regions. Not only are Venus's thick clouds the main absorber of sunlight for the planet, they appeared to be "upside down" with a thick smog layer on top. Finally, the probes found new evidence that the planet once had been covered with an ocean, which it lost early in its history.

Galaxies and Quasars. In recent years observations of spectacular outbursts or prodigious luminosities from quasars and active galaxies have tended to make our own Galaxy appear rather unspectacular. The past year, however, produced at least three independent lines of evidence that pointed to much greater activity within the nucleus of the Milky Way than had been suspected heretofore. Robert L. Brown of the National Radio Astronomy Observatory used the Very Large Array radio telescope in New Mexico to produce a radio "photograph" of the galactic centre. He found radio-emitting regions with an S-shaped symmetry around the galactic centre, suggesting the ejection of radiating material from some type of rapidly rotating central object. Though the galactic nucleus is shrouded in dust, it can be viewed with infrared, radio, X-ray, and gamma-ray telescopes.

A group using the Anglo-Australian Telescope managed to get a photograph of the same region in the near infrared, revealing what appeared to be a pair of objects at the position of the galactic centre. These could be simply two infrared stars, but the group interpreted them as a manifestation of non-thermal activity in the galactic centre. On the other hand, George Rieke of the University of Arizona's Steward Observatory reported on infrared observations of the galactic centre that he interpreted as evidence for a recent burst of star formation in the region.

Though quasars (quasi-stellar sources) usually show single starlike images on an optical photograph, several double or triple quasar images were known. The images of a quasar pair or triplet appear to be at the same distance from the Earth but separated by a few arc seconds in the sky. They were interpreted as being multiple images of a single object produced by the gravitational deflection of its light by an intervening galaxy. The first of these was found in 1979, and a second in 1981. In 1982 Daniel W. Weedman of Pennsylvania State University and a team at the University of Arizona headed by Ray J. Weymann discovered a third gravitationally split quasar image using the 3.6-m telescope on Mauna Kea in Hawaii. This find changed the question from why such quasars were found to be split to why many more of them had not already been discovered.

Although the list of quasars continued to grow each year, the most distant known quasar, called OQ 172, had held that record for a decade—until a group of British and Australian optical and radio astronomers, headed by Bruce A. Peterson of Mount Stromlo and Siding Springs Observatories, bettered it in 1982. They found that the quasar called PKS 2000-330 has a red shift (shift of its

Earth Perihelion and Aphelion, 1983

Jan. 2	Perihelion, 147,096,000 km (91,401,000 mi) from the Sun
July 6	Aphelion, 152,105,000 km (94,513,000 mi) from the Sun

Equinoxes and Solstices, 1983

March 21	Vernal equinox, 04:39[1]
June 21	Summer solstice, 23:09[1]
Sept. 23	Autumnal equinox, 14:42[1]
Dec. 22	Winter solstice, 10:30[1]

Eclipses, 1983

June 11	Sun, total (begins 02:09[1]), visible in Madagascar, extreme SE Asia, Indonesia, Australia, W New Zealand.
June 25	Moon, partial (begins 05:43[1]), visible in S. America except the NE part, N. America except the N and NE part, extreme E Australia, New Zealand, Antarctica, the Pacific O., and W Atlantic O.
Dec. 4	Sun, annular (begins 09:41[1]), visible in extreme NE N. America, NE S. America, British Isles, Iceland, S. Europe, Africa, and SW Asia.
Dec. 19– 20	Moon, penumbral (begins 23:46[1]), visible S. America, N. America, Arctic regions, Greenland, Atlantic O., Africa except the E part, Europe, N Asia, W. Asia, and the eastern part of Pacific O.

[1] Universal time.
Source: *The Astronomical Almanac for the Year 1983* (1982).

spectral lines toward the red end of the spectrum due to its motion away from the Earth) of 3.78, compared with the previous record holder of 3.53. This figure places the quasar at a distance of about 12,000,000,000 light-years.

Cosmology. Though the big-bang model of the universe enjoyed wide support based on its successful prediction of the microwave background radiation and helium abundance left over from the original cosmic fireball as well as its compatibility with observations of the overall expansion of the universe, a number of puzzles came to the forefront in 1982 to lead many astronomers to question the picture. In the usual scenario the universe formed in a vast explosion with all present-day matter and radiation ultimately emanating from an original singularity of space and time. But what caused the explosion? In recent years attempts to apply the so-called grand unified theories (GUTS) of the strong, weak, and electromagnetic interactions to the early universe led to a picture in which the universe forms spontaneously out of an original void. In 1982 A. D. Linde of the Lebedev Physical Institute in Moscow proposed a model in which the entire "universe" is essentially a bubble appearing in an even larger region of space and time in which other such "universes" form continuously, thus avoiding the problem of finding a unique origin of the universe.

GUTS also led to the prediction of the existence of magnetic monopoles, or "charges" of magnetism that consist of either north or south poles. In 1982 Blas Cabrera of Stanford University reported the possible detection of such a particle. Whether the event that he recorded is an example of the type of monopole predicted to be left over from the big bang remained to be seen. (*See* PHYSICS.)

Assuming that the expansion of the universe has continued at a constant rate, the ratio of the distance of a galaxy to its speed of recession from observers on the Earth is a measure of the time since the original explosion, or the age of the universe. T. Matilsky of Rutgers University, New Brunswick, N.J., and collaborators, reporting on X-ray observations of the quasar 1525-227, suggested this age to be about 9,000,000,000 years. Using observations of supernova explosions in distant galaxies, W. D. Arnett of the University of Chicago reported a value of about 13,000,000,000 years. Although these values lay between previously deduced ages for the universe, both were less than the ages determined for the oldest stars of about 15,000,000,000 years.

Probably the most intriguing (if true) cosmological report came from Paul Birch of the University of Manchester's Nuffield Radio Astronomy Laboratories at Jodrell Bank, England. Based on a study of 94 radio galaxies distributed over the sky, Birch concluded that the universe as a whole is rotating at a rate equivalent to one rotation every 6×10^{13} years. Though quite a long time, it was the first suggestion that the universe, like planets, stars, and galaxies, is rotating at all.

(KENNETH BRECHER)

See also Earth Sciences; Space Exploration.
[111.H.2 and 7; 131.A.1.b–c; 131.A.3.c; 131.E.1; 132.B.6.b; 133.A.4.b; 133.C.1.b]

Athletics:
see articles on the various sports

Australia

A federal parliamentary state and a member of the Commonwealth, Australia occupies the smallest continent and, with the island state of Tasmania, is the sixth largest country in the world. Area: 7,682,300 sq km (2,966,200 sq mi). Pop. (1982 est.): 15,054,000. Cap.: Canberra (statistical district pop., 1981, 220,400). Largest city: Sydney (metro. pop., 1980 est., 3,231,700). Language: English. Religion (1981): Roman Catholic 29.6%; Church of England 27.7%; Methodist 7.3%; Presbyterian 6.6%; Lutheran 1.4%; Baptist 1.3%; other Christian 8.6%; Jewish 0.5%. Queen, Elizabeth II; governors-general in 1982, Sir Zelman Cowen and, from July 29, Sir Ninian Martin Stephen; prime minister, Malcolm Fraser.

Domestic Affairs. The usual equilibrium of the Australian nation was disturbed during 1982 by a continual round of political crises. Prime Minister Malcolm Fraser and the leader of the opposition, William Hayden, faced challenges to their respective leaderships, and both the ruling coalition of Liberal Party and National Country Party (LCP) and the opposition Australian Labor Party (ALP) were shaken by unforeseen reverses.

Fraser tried to head off his problems by taking the battle to the enemy within his own Liberal Party. In April he seized the initiative and called a special party meeting to resolve the LCP leadership question "once and for all." He had taken this bold step, he said, because speculation about his leadership, and whether or not it would be contested from within the Liberal Party, had continued for a year. This speculation had come to a head during the Commonwealth heads of government meeting in Melbourne in 1981 and during the state election in Victoria in April 1982. It had, continued Fraser, proved a distraction to the people of Australia and had disturbed the Liberal Party profoundly. When the party meeting was held, former Cabinet minister Andrew Peacock, who had resigned his office in 1981, challenged Fraser for the leadership. He was unsuccessful and later was treated without magnanimity by the prime minister, who excluded him from the fourth Fraser ministry when he announced a major Cabinet reshuffle on May 7. On October 11, however, Peacock rejoined the Cabinet as minister for industry and commerce in an apparent effort to strengthen the government in the face of its economic and other difficulties. The by-election to fill the seat of Sir Phillip Lynch, who had resigned as industry minister for health reasons, was won by the LDP.

The ALP had little time to capitalize on the disarray in the government camp. During the national conference of the ALP in July, tension surfaced between opposition leader Bill Hayden and the ALP's talented and temperamental industrial relations spokesman, Robert J. Hawke. A public opinion poll showed that the ALP would romp home in an election if Hawke were leader but might well lose under Hayden. As Hawke explained, he had decided to challenge Hayden for the leadership of the parliamentary Labor Party in the belief that only

MICHAEL COYNE—CAMERA PRESS/PHOTO TRENDS

Traffic was brought to a standstill in Melbourne when thousands of sympathizers and members of the Movement Against Uranium Mining took to the streets to protest nuclear proliferation.

he could save the ALP from electoral defeat at the next general election and "rid Australia of Fraserism." When the vote was held, the result was 42 to 37 in Hayden's favour. Hayden subsequently embraced Hawke, promoting him to the influential ALP Election Strategy Committee. Even so, neither leader could feel secure. While Hayden and Hawke agreed to "fix things up" and heal the wounds, Hawke refused to disclaim his ultimate leadership ambition.

The leadership challenges had been prompted by the result in Victoria's state election in April. The ALP won in Victoria for the first time in 27 years. Peacock's supporters saw this as a portent for the LCP if Fraser's hard-line approach to economic management continued. The balance was maintained, however, when, in a similar upheaval in Tasmania in May, a long-term Labor administration was swept out by reformist Liberals. (See Special Report.)

The new ALP leader in Victoria was John Cain, a suburban lawyer who had led the state ALP for only seven months. Cain, however, embarrassed his leader, Hayden, with a serious miscalculation involving the sensitive issues of the Australian-U.S. alliance, nuclear weapons, and state rights. Cain announced in June that the Victorian government planned to introduce legislation that would make Victoria a nuclear-free state. Under the proposed new law, nuclear-powered and nuclear-armed vessels from the U.S. were not to be allowed to use the state's ports. Hayden supported Cain and precipitously announced that, if elected, a federal Labor government would follow the Cain approach and grant itself the right to ban visits to Australia by nuclear-armed ships.

Fraser was jubilant over this blunder. He pointed out that the states had no constitutional rights over what amounted to defense questions and that the ANZUS defense treaty, linking Australia, New Zealand, and the U.S., would be threatened by such a policy. Hayden changed his mind, and his vacillation helped draw supporters to the Hawke faction in the leadership conflict. Fraser sent the message home by sending federal police to oversee the visit of a U.S. warship to Melbourne and by

introducing a new bill, the Defence (Visiting Warships) Bill, into Parliament. Under the planned new law the federal government was given explicit supreme authority over the states on the visit to Australian ports of either nuclear-armed or nuclear-powered warships. The new law was to give the defense minister the power to order people to allow vessels to enter or leave port and to be loaded or unloaded; it also provided a A$1,000 fine and up to six months imprisonment for anyone seeking to prevent, hinder, or obstruct visits by warships.

The Victoria branch of the Returned Servicemen's League (RSL) came under fire in 1982 for controversial statements on Aboriginal and immigration policy. The state president of the Victorian RSL, Bruce Ruxton, deplored the prospect that Australia would become a "coffee-coloured society." He declared that the Victorian RSL wanted Australia to retain its original identity, just as countries like Japan wanted to retain theirs, and he called upon the government to restrict Asian immigration. He also reported that there was a strong feeling among RSL members that the Communist Party was behind the Aboriginal land-rights movement.

Other trends worried the minister for immigration and ethnic affairs, Ian Macphee. Macphee announced that Australia's population was growing at a faster rate than almost any other developed country because of a rise in birthrate and immigration. Macphee said that it was essential for Australia to monitor the new demographic trends because substantial fluctuations in the numbers of persons reaching primary, secondary, and tertiary education ages required flexibility in educational planning. Moreover, he warned, although an aging labour force was more experienced, it was less mobile, and the growing number of elderly people would result in changes in patterns of demand for goods and services.

Participants in the Queensland Aboriginal rights movement took the occasion of the Brisbane Commonwealth Games in September–October to demonstrate their disapproval of the plight of Aboriginals. A Black Protest Committee attempted to organize a boycott of the Games by African countries through the Organization of African Unity. The National Aboriginal Conference, on the other hand, opposed militancy and urged its Aboriginal members to stage only peaceful protests at the Commonwealth Games.

On July 29 Sir Ninian Stephen (*see* BIOGRA-PHIES) succeeded Sir Zelman Cowen as governor-general.

The Economy. Tax avoiders and militant trade unions were the whipping boys chosen by the Fraser government to help explain the failure of Australia to live up to its economic promise in 1982. Billions of dollars were said to have escaped the Taxation Department as a result of the promotion of such tax-avoidance measures as the notorious scheme involving "bottom of the harbour" companies—that is, companies that no longer existed.

The extent of the tax-avoidance schemes was revealed by a royal commissioner, Frank Costigan, who uncovered the abuses as an indirect consequence of an inquiry into the Federated Ship Painters and Dockers Union. The crimes of the trade union movement paled into insignificance compared with those of the white-collar tax avoiders. In his fourth interim report, Costigan found that the deputy crown solicitor's office in Perth had "failed grossly" in its duty to stop major frauds on the tax revenues between 1973 and 1980. All deputy crown solicitors in Australia were soon under suspicion, and a Public Service Board official confirmed that members of the Sydney office were interviewed.

Prime Minister Fraser was aghast to find that even prostitution appeared to have been run from the Perth crown solicitor's office and moved quickly to avoid the charge that there was one rule for the trade unions and another for corporate criminals. The prime minister declared that the Costigan report and other royal commissions had shown that traditional law-enforcement methods had failed against white-collar crime. He also agreed that high-priced lawyers and accountants who devised and promoted tax-avoidance schemes did more economic damage than a thousand corrupt or bad trade unions. He warned that if any members of the Liberal Party were avoiding tax, he "would like to see them leave the Liberal Party before they get caught by our special prosecutor."

Fraser's conflict with tax avoiders and such trade unions as the Builders' Labourers Federation had the air of Nero fiddling while Rome burned. By mid-1982 the Australian economy was in poor shape. The unemployment rate reached 6.6%, and by November, with 552,600 out of work, had exceeded the 8% that Macphee, appointed minister for employment and industrial relations in May, predicted would be reached by the end of 1982. Some of the unemployment was blamed on the 50,000 illegal immigrants working in violation of their entry permits, and these illegal workers were threatened with deportation if caught.

High inflation joined unemployment as a major feature of the economy. During 1982 Australia's inflation rate reached its highest level in five years. The Australian Chamber of Commerce-National Bank survey revealed the worst trading situation since the survey was begun 14 years earlier and the worst profitability in 7 years. The Australian dollar also weakened in 1982, reaching its lowest value in history when measured against the U.S. dollar. Federal Treasurer John Howard summed things up by saying that the Australian economy had "come off the top fairly sharply" and that he could not see anything that would produce a kick in the opposite direction. He continued to assert that many Australians had received wage increases that were beyond the capacity of industry to pay and that this had put other Australians out of work.

Symptomatic of the economic crisis was the plight of Australia's biggest company, Broken Hill Proprietary Co. Ltd. BHP was hit hard by steel imports and was forced to lay off thousands of workers at its factories in Port Kembla, New South Wales, and Whyalla, South Australia, when the government refused to grant increased tariff protection. In resisting the BHP appeal Prime Minister Fraser was conscious of his earlier public statements on the need for less protectionism in the world economy. Although Australia was not among the seven major industrialized Western nations attending the economic summit conference at Versailles, France, in June, Fraser himself visited the U.S., Canada, and Japan to lobby for Austra-

---

AUSTRALIA

Education. (1981) Primary, pupils 1,871,617, teachers 91,386; secondary and vocational, pupils 1,115,782, teachers 86,364; higher, students 331,678, teaching staff 33,172.

Finance. Monetary unit: Australian dollar, with (Sept. 20, 1982) a free rate of A$1.04 to U.S. $1 (A$1.79 = £1 sterling). Gold and other reserves (June 1982) U.S. $4,477,000,000. Budget (1981 actual): revenue A$37,435,000,000; expenditure A$38,744,000,000. Gross national product (1981) A$138.7 billion. Money supply (May 1982) A$16,772,000,000. Cost of living (1975 = 100; April–June 1982) 197.8.

Foreign Trade. (1980–81) Imports A$18,965,000,000; exports A$19,189,000,000. Import sources: U.S. 22%; Japan 19%; U.K. 8%; West Germany 6%; Saudi Arabia 5%. Export destinations: Japan 27%; U.S. 11%; New Zealand 5%. Main exports: coal 10%; wool 9%; wheat 9%; beef 6%; sugar 6%; iron ore 6%; nonferrous metals 5%; alumina 5%. Tourism (1980): visitors 903,299; gross receipts U.S. $725 million.

Transport and Communications. Roads (1980) 810,918 km. Motor vehicles in use (1980): passenger 5,898,000; commercial (including buses) 1,462,000. Railways: (government; 1979) 39,888 km; freight traffic (1976–77) 31,995,000,000 net ton-km. Air traffic (1980): 25,506,000,000 passenger-km; freight 515.6 million net ton-km. Shipping (1981): merchant vessels 100 gross tons and over 527; gross tonnage 1,767,930. Shipping traffic (1979–80): goods loaded 187,780,000 metric tons, unloaded 26,220,000 metric tons. Telephones (June 1979) 6,677,000. Radio receivers (Dec. 1978) c. 14.8 million. Television receivers (Dec. 1979) 5,515,000.

Agriculture. Production (in 000; metric tons; 1981): wheat 16,400; barley 3,430; oats 1,530; corn 118; rice 761; sorghum 1,090; potatoes 896; sugar, raw value 3,450; tomatoes c. 220; apples 342; oranges c. 380; pineapples c. 122; wine 350; sunflower seed 147; wool, clean 410; milk 5,324; butter 79; cheese 137; beef and veal 1,481; mutton and lamb 588. Livestock (in 000; March 1981): sheep 133,396;

cattle 25,177; pigs 2,427; horses 489; chickens 52,967.

Industry. Fuel and power (in 000; metric tons; 1981): coal 100,869; lignite 32,903; crude oil 18,624; natural gas (cu m) c. 11,260,000; manufactured gas (including some natural gas; cu m) c. 21,400,000; electricity (kw-hr) 103,194,000. Production (in 000; metric tons; 1981): iron ore (64% metal content) 84,670; bauxite 25,510; pig iron 6,830; crude steel 7,635; aluminum 379; copper 164; lead 208; tin 4.2; zinc 296; nickel concentrates (metal content; 1979–80) 64; uranium (1979) 0.7; gold (troy oz) 521; silver (troy oz) 26,400; sulfuric acid 2,000; fertilizers (nutrient content; 1980–81) nitrogenous c. 223, phosphate c. 800; plastics and resins (1980) 678; cement 6,006; newsprint 243; other paper (1979) 1,149; cotton yarn 22; wool yarn 20; passenger cars (including assembly; units) 359; commercial vehicles (including assembly; units) 40. Dwelling units completed (1981) 139,500.

lian interests, which, he believed, would be served by reductions in protectionism.

Things were scarcely any better on the farms than they were in the factories. The furor over the substitution of kangaroo, goat, and horse meat for beef being exported to the Japanese and U.S. markets had hardly died down when a royal commission reported in June that federal meat inspectors had been paid bribes of A$200 a week to turn a blind eye to the substitution of mutton for export lamb. To make matters worse, the lack of rain in agricultural and pastoral areas led to widespread drought. By September it was so serious that massive government aid had to be granted to farmers. The drought was so severe that the treasurer predicted it could cause Australia's current account deficit for 1982–83 to reach double the predicted A$1,670,000,000.

In the August budget session of Parliament the treasurer outlined government policies for the coming year. He explained that, although relatively abundant energy endowments had created a more favourable investment climate in Australia than in most other countries, by mid-1982 the continued deterioration of economic activity around the world was affecting Australian exports. Australia's rate of wage and price inflation also moved sharply above that of its major trading partners, causing the competitiveness of Australian industry to be severely eroded despite the considerable depreciation of the exchange rate. Over the year ended June 1982, the inflation rate as measured by the consumer price index was 10.4%, almost 2% above the rate of the previous 12 months and 4% above the average of Australia's major trading partners within the Organization for Economic Cooperation and Development. Even so, with the possibility of an early election in prospect, Howard granted tax cuts, home mortgage relief, and increased family allowances and unemployment benefits in the budget.

Foreign Affairs. The Falklands crisis, the Australian-U.S. alliance, and instability resulting from the wars in the Middle East were the preoccupations of Australia's foreign-policy makers in 1982. Australia agreed to participate in the Sinai multinational peacekeeping force, and Prime Minister Fraser criticized what he regarded as Israel's destruction of Lebanon. Fraser called upon the U.S. to use its influence to restrain the Israeli war effort, and the Australian government used its influence with the U.S. to underline the point. Personal high-level diplomatic talks were held between Australia and the U.S.; Fraser visited Pres. Ronald Reagan in Washington, D.C., and U.S. Vice-Pres. George Bush visited Australia in May.

Australia's major diplomatic problem, however, was how to react to the conflict between Great Britain and Argentina in the Falkland Islands. Aware of its significant trading links with South America, Australia nevertheless threw its diplomatic weight behind the U.K. Fraser condemned the Argentine invasion of the Falkland Islands in the strongest terms. He said that the use of armed force against a small and peaceful territory was a grotesque reminder of an era that all hoped had receded into the past. Argentine Foreign Minister

LONDON EXPRESS/PICTORIAL PARADE

Outrage erupted in Britain's Parliament when it was announced that the aircraft carrier HMS "Invincible" was to be sold to Australia for £175 million. The British ultimately backed down and canceled the sale.

Nicanor Costa Méndez was informed that Australians felt the most serious concern and abhorrence over the unprovoked use of force in the Argentine invasion of the Falklands and the dangerous situation which this action had generated The Australian government supported the UN Security Council in its concern for a diplomatic solution.

Australia did not follow New Zealand's lead in giving military assistance to the U.K. On the contrary, in the face of pro-British public opinion, Fraser detached Australian service personnel from British units due to be sent to the Falkland Islands. Fraser also used the Falklands crisis as the opportunity to withdraw from an agreement, widely criticized in Australia, to buy the British aircraft carrier HMS "Invincible." While the war continued, Fraser sent U.K. Prime Minister Margaret Thatcher a telex, giving her the option of canceling the sale. Remarking that it was "the only decent course an Australian government could take in the circumstances," Fraser said that he believed Britain would want to keep the "Invincible" to cover its naval losses in the Falklands conflict. Britain subsequently announced that it would exercise this option and retain the carrier. While the crisis gave the opportunity for a reappraisal of defense priorities, no immediate solutions presented themselves in regard to the problems of how to defend Australia's own huge coastline.

Australia's migration selection system was again changed on April 19. Under the new policy, brothers, sisters, and nondependent children of Australian residents had a better chance of migration than previously. But, in order to be considered under the new plan, a person would have to be sponsored by a close relative in Australia, and the relative was required to provide financial support, accommodation, and employment.

A minor but embarrassing diminution of Australia's sovereignty was revealed when it was found that a Hutt River passport had been used by a television reporter to get through Customs and Immigration in Beirut, Lebanon. The responsible minister responded to this situation by pointing out that the "Hutt River Province" in Western Australia, set up by the self-styled Prince Leonard, was not a state in international law and that any passports issued by the "Hutt River Province" were not valid travel documents.

(A. R. G. GRIFFITHS)

See also Dependent States.

TASMANIA DEBATES PROGRESS

by A. R. G. Griffiths

The island state of Tasmania was the area hardest hit by the Australian economic recession in 1982. Almost 9% of the Tasmanian work force was unemployed; the state treasury was A$40 million in the red; and such leading local firms as Electrolytic Zinc Co. of Australia Ltd. and the Mount Lyell Mining and Railway Co. threatened to put more Tasmanians out of work when their ventures proved unprofitable in the wake of falling world commodity prices. Isolated from the rest of the continent, often cut off from the mainland by maritime strikes, and with a comparatively small industrial base, the Tasmanian economy quickly slumped.

To save Tasmanians from mass unemployment, many political leaders sought to increase energy resources by an ambitious public works scheme involving the creation of a huge hydroelectric project. The Tasmanian Hydro Electric Commission had always shown aptitude and determination in harnessing the abundant water resources of the island, which, with its mountainous topography and snowy peaks, resembles Norway. Enthusiasts for the hydroelectric project predicted that when it was completed, Tasmania could attract industry by providing cheap power to investors and entrepreneurs. It might even become a net exporter of electricity to mainland Australia, piping power through the Victorian grid via an undersea cable in Bass Strait, the 240-km (150-mi) channel separating Tasmania from the state of Victoria.

Mainland Australia was not impressed by these suggestions, nor indeed were a large minority of Tasmanians. Southwest Tasmania, the area where the new hydroelectric scheme would be located, was one of only three remaining temperate wilderness areas left in the world. The Tasmanian Wilderness Society led the environmentalist backlash and mobilized antihydroelectric public opinion. Nationwide publicity campaigns were mounted to show

---

A. R. G. Griffiths is a senior lecturer in history at the Flinders University of South Australia.

the beauty of the wild rivers in the wilderness areas, and Tasmanians were told that they were custodians of natural beauty not merely for their own fellow islanders but also for all Australians who respected their natural heritage.

Prince Philip, the duke of Edinburgh, threw his considerable public weight behind the conservationists. He had concerned himself with Tasmanian environmental issues as early as 1972–73, when the Hydro Electric Commission flooded Lake Pedder. Prince Philip visited Tasmania in 1981 and repeated in 1982 his sadness and concern that the wild rivers and wilderness areas of the state would be destroyed forever.

The Dams Referendum. Worried, threatened, and puzzled by the growing divisions in the community, the Tasmanian Australian Labor Party (ALP) government held a referendum of voters to help decide how to resolve the issue. The referendum paper was badly drawn, however, and many thought it had been drafted by the Hydro Electric Commission. The referendum gave the voters the choice of two dams. The first alternative proposed the construction of a dam on the Gordon River above the junction of the Olga River, which would preserve the Franklin River, and the second proposed the construction of a dam below the Franklin, which would flood that wild river.

The environmentalists responded to a Tasmanian form of Hobson's choice by writing "no dams" on their ballot papers in what the *Sydney Morning Herald* described as "an unprecedented gesture of defiance, resolve, and disgust." This "no dams" write-in was an informal vote that could be counted and exactly measured as a sample of public opinion. The "no dams" vote was also an expression of disapproval for the ALP, which appeared to be trying to confront the electorate with a fait accompli, merely allowing Tasmanians to name their poison. When the votes were counted, 47% were in favour of the Franklin dam, 45% voted informal, and 8% voted for the Olga plan.

The May Elections. The dams referendum and its results revealed deep divisions both in the community and in the ALP state government. Parliament was adjourned and went into recess in December 1981, while the ALP, always sensitive to environmental issues, tried to make up its mind on the dams question. During the parliamentary recess, however, the ramshackle nature of the ALP became more and more obvious. Doug Lowe, the premier who had staged the dams referendum, was challenged for party leadership by Harry Holgate. Holgate was successful, but Lowe caused a new political crisis by leaving the ALP. When he defected, Lowe took with him a former party whip, Mary Willey, and together they joined forces with Australian Democrat member Norm Sanders to pass a no-confidence motion and bring the Labor government down, thus forcing a state election.

By the time the May 15 elections were held the ALP had a new dams policy, but procrastination by the party had driven the pro-hydroelectric voters into the camp of the Liberals. Willey expressed the widespread feeling of disillusionment felt by many former ALP voters, declaring that the Independents represented the only true opposition in Tasmania. Both the Liberals and the ALP had identical platforms, claimed Willey, and the only real argument between them was which could flood the wild rivers first. Labor Premier Harry Holgate went into his first and last election as party leader with an approval rating of only 15%, and after the May poll Tasmania became a national stronghold for the Liberals. The new premier, Robin Gray, was the first Liberal Party leader ever to govern in his party's own right. No National Country Party member was returned in rural Tasmania. The independents, who had fought on the "no dams" platform, all lost.

For the ALP, dithering over the dams proved disastrous. Liberals already held all five Tasmanian House of Representatives seats in the national Parliament, seats that had been in ALP hands during the Gough Whitlam era of 1972–75. The ALP strategy involved the intervention of the federal secretariat in local politics, the replacement of Holgate with an experienced federal senator, and the convening of a series of closed special meetings designed to preselect better candidates and reduce what was seen as excessive trade union influence. While party reorganization was on the whole successful, the dams-versus-environment issue refused to go away.

At the ALP's federal conference it was decided that, if elected at the next federal election, the party ought to oppose dam construction in the wilderness area. Instead, the conference called for the provision of funds to establish alternative means of electricity generation, as well as to expand tourism. Most Tasmanian ALP members of Parliament were unconvinced, if not aghast, in regard to this policy, and some considered that the conference decision made hopeless the task of regaining the five vital seats in the federal House of Representatives at the next general election.

Challenge in the Courts. After the May 15 elections the conservationists abandoned their faith in the ALP and put their trust in the legal system. The Tasmanian Wilderness Society briefed a queen's counsel to seek an injunction in the High Court to prevent the Commonwealth government from granting special funds for the project through the Loan Council, the body set up by agreement between the states and the Commonwealth to divide taxation revenue. The High Court refused to grant the society an injunction; Prime Minister Malcolm Fraser declared that the scheme was a state matter and that he would comment further only in the event of World War III; and Premier Gray pushed the project ahead without delay.

Gray swept aside suggestions that energy could be provided by huge windmills or that nuclear power could be used to save the wilderness area, and argued that the Franklin dam was so much required for the good of the state that even if the Loan Council refused special Commonwealth funds for dam construction Tasmania would go it alone and provide the necessary capital from its own resources. His point of view was that his Liberal Party could not raise world commodity prices or provide enough assistance to help the industries that had gotten into a nonprofitable phase, but it could plan for the future when the recession ended.

Gray squarely blamed the general loss of confidence in Tasmania on the previous ALP government's procrastination over the state's energy needs, claiming that the Labor government's two-year delay in deciding on the state's next major power scheme was largely responsible for record unemployment. Believing that the government's role was to create the right economic environment and to try to do things that, when the economy was performing well, would encourage people to invest in development, he sent the earthmovers and bulldozers to begin work at the site of the dam. While the environmentalists were predominantly nonviolent, they were not exclusively so. Sabotage of the public works program began almost before the first sod was turned. For example, sand and water were put in the fuel and hydraulic systems of earth-moving equipment. The level of physical obstruction to the work was low, but it did indicate that hydroelectric progress in Tasmania and the concomitant destruction of the wilderness would be accompanied by continuing opposition.

Austria

Austria

A republic of central Europe, Austria is bounded by West Germany, Czechoslovakia, Hungary, Yugoslavia, Italy, Switzerland, and Liechtenstein. Area: 83,853 sq km (32,376 sq mi). Pop. (1981): 7,555,300. Cap. and largest city: Vienna (pop., 1981, 1,515,700). Language: German. Religion (1980): Roman Catholic 88.8%. President in 1982, Rudolf Kirchschläger; chancellor, Bruno Kreisky.

Under Austria's proportional representation system, results of the 1981 census necessitated a redistribution of provincial seats in the Nationalrat (National Council; the lower house of Parliament). Vienna's entitlement was reduced to four seats, while Upper Austria, Salzburg, Tirol, and Vorarlberg each gained one. The number of seats in the Bundesrat (Federal Council; the upper house) rose from 58 to 65. An election in Styria in October 1981 had left the Austrian People's Party (övp) with an unchanged 30 seats in the provincial assembly, while the Socialist Party of Austria (spö) increased its seats by one to 24 and the Austrian Freedom Party (fpö) lost one of its previous 3 seats.

After much political debate, construction began in July 1982 on a new conference centre that would greatly extend the facilities already provided by Vienna's "UN City." Following an opinion poll in Vienna that indicated opposition to the new centre, the övp had initiated a national referendum in which 1,360,000 (26% of those entitled to vote) rejected the project. A special parliamentary committee was appointed to consider the issue. The opposition criticized the high cost of a "superfluous project," while the ruling spö invoked undertakings given to the UN and the boost to employment that could be expected to result from construction of the centre.

Chancellor Bruno Kreisky continued to support the rights of the Palestinians and to afford the Palestine Liberation Organization (PLO) diplomatic contact with the West. He was one of the sharpest critics of the Israeli government's intervention in Lebanon. The official visit to Austria in March, at Kreisky's invitation, of Libyan leader Col. Muammar al-Qaddafi brought a wave of protest from the opposition; it was also criticized by the U.S. and Western-oriented Arab states.

The arrest of Bahij Younis, believed to have organized the 1981 attack on a Viennese synagogue and the murder of Heinz Nittel, a Socialist city councillor, and the trial of two of the suspected assassins indicated that these acts of terrorism were instigated not by the PLO but by other Arab groups. Several bombings of Jewish homes and businesses in Vienna during 1982 were attributed to right-wing extremists and neo-Nazis.

Despite the unfavourable economic climate, Austria continued to admit refugees on a liberal scale. Some 35,000 were admitted in 1981, and a further 4,500 were granted, or applied for, asylum in the first eight months of 1982. The majority were Poles, whose care and administration caused considerable problems, since their onward movement to the traditional receiving countries was hindered by worldwide unemployment. An Austrian national committee was set up to administer aid to the Polish people.

In the wake of the previous year's corruption case in connection with Vienna's new general hospital, another financial scandal, involving a building firm, shook the country in January 1982. Among those implicated were members of Parliament and a deputy provincial governor, who were

Austrian Chancellor Bruno Kreisky (right) seems not to share the exuberance of Libyan leader Muammar al-Qaddafi when Qaddafi arrived at Vienna in March for a state visit. It was Qaddafi's first official visit to a Western country.

AUSTRIA

Education. (1980–81) Primary, pupils 401,396, teachers (1979–80) 26,369; secondary, pupils 549,061, teachers (1979–80) 45,213; vocational (1979–80), pupils 144,885, teachers 14,169; teacher training (1979–80), students 5,471, teachers 742; higher (1979–80), students 123,463, teaching staff 11,792.

Finance. Monetary unit: schilling, with (Sept. 20, 1982) a free rate of 17.51 schillings to U.S. $1 (30.02 schillings = £1 sterling). Gold and other reserves (June 1982) U.S. $5,810,000,000. Budget (1980 actual): revenue 204,650,000,000 schillings; expenditure 236,860,000,000 schillings. Gross national product (1981) 1,043,600,000,000 schillings. Money supply (June 1982) 148,890,000,000 schillings. Cost of living (1975 = 100; June 1982) 146.

Foreign Trade. (1981) Imports 334,660,000,000 schillings; exports 251,730,000,000 schillings. Import sources: EEC 59% (West Germany 39%, Italy 8%); U.S.S.R. 6%; Switzerland 5%. Export destinations: EEC 53% (West Germany 29%, Italy 10%); Switzerland 7%. Main exports: machinery 23%; iron and steel 10%; chemicals 9%; textile yarn and fabrics 7%; paper and board 5%, metal manufactures 5%. Tourism (1980): visitors 13,879,024; gross receipts U.S. $6,441,000,000.

Transport and Communications. Roads (1980) 106,303 km (including 938 km expressways). Motor vehicles in use (1980): passenger 2,246,950; commercial 183,700. Railways: (1980) 6,482 km; traffic (1981) 7,735,000,000 passenger-km, freight 10,320,000,000 net ton-km. Air traffic (1981): 1,235,000,000 passenger-km; freight 17.3 million net ton-km. Navigable inland waterways in regular use (1980) 358 km. Shipping (1981): merchant vessels 100 gross tons and over 8; gross tonnage 62,190. Telephones (Jan. 1980) 2,812,700. Radio licenses (Dec. 1979) 2,640,000. Television licenses (Dec. 1979) 2,114,000.

Agriculture. Production (in 000; metric tons; 1981): wheat 1,025; barley 1,220; rye 320; oats 304; corn 1,374; potatoes 1,310; sugar, raw value c. 490; apples 243; wine c. 200; meat c. 614; timber (cu m; 1980) 14,827. Livestock (in 000; Dec. 1980): cattle 2,538; sheep 191; pigs 3,706; chickens 14,160.

Industry. Fuel and power (in 000; metric tons; 1981): lignite 3,062; crude oil 1,338; natural gas (cu m) c. 1,290,000; manufactured gas (cu m) 610,000; electricity (kw-hr) 42,881,000 (69% hydroelectric in 1980). Production (in 000; metric tons; 1981): iron ore (31% metal content) 3,057; pig iron 3,477; crude steel 5,079; magnesite (1980) 1,318; aluminum 141; copper 39; zinc 24; cement 5,282; newsprint 178; other paper (1980) 1,068; petroleum products (1980) 9,486; plastics and resins 504; fertilizers (nutrient content; 1980–81) nitrogenous c. 300, phosphate c. 111; man-made fibres (1979) 140.

suspected of taking bribes to enrich party funds and had to resign.

Austria's economic situation remained relatively favourable, with growth estimated at 1.5–2%, inflation at 5.5%, and unemployment at 3.5% for 1982. Nevertheless, insolvencies cost thousands of jobs; building and construction stagnated; small and medium-sized concerns suffered difficulties; and falling demand and fluctuating raw-material prices necessitated massive financial support, especially for the nationalized industries. The important arms industry suffered a setback when the delivery of tanks to Argentina was suspended because of the Falklands conflict.

(ELFRIEDE DIRNBACHER)

Bahamas, The

A member of the Commonwealth, The Bahamas comprises an archipelago of about 700 islands in the North Atlantic Ocean just southeast of the United States. Area: 13,864 sq km (5,353 sq mi).

BAHAMAS, THE

Education. (1979–80) Primary, pupils 30,974, teachers (state only; 1976–77) 768; secondary, pupils 17,520, teachers (state only; 1976–77) 649; vocational (1975–76), pupils 1,823, teachers 92; teacher training (1975–76), students 731, teachers 21; higher (College of the Bahamas), students 4,396.

Finance and Trade. Monetary unit: Bahamian dollar, with (Sept. 20, 1982) a par value of B$1 to U.S. $1 (free rate of B$1.71 = £1 sterling). Budget (1981 actual): revenue B$278.2 million; expenditure B$284.1 million. Cost of living (1975 = 100; June 1982) 164.4. Foreign trade (1980): imports B$5,481,000,000; exports B$4,834,000,000. Import sources (1977): U.S. 35%; Saudi Arabia 24%; Iran 10%; Nigeria 9%; Libya 7%; Angola 5%. Export destinations (1977): U.S. 81%; Saudi Arabia 10%. Main exports: crude oil and petroleum products 96%. Tourism (1980): visitors (excludes cruise passengers) 1,181,000; gross receipts U.S. $650 million.

Transport and Communications. Shipping (1981): merchant vessels 100 gross tons and over 105; gross tonnage 196,682. Telephones (Jan. 1980) 68,000. Radio receivers (Dec. 1979) 99,000. Television receivers (Dec. 1979) 31,000.

Pop. (1982 est.): 240,000. Cap. and largest city: Nassau (urban area pop., 1979 est., 138,500). Language: English (official). Religion (1970): Baptist 28.8%; Anglican 22.7%; Roman Catholic 22.5%; Methodist 7.3%; Saints of God and Church of God 6%; others and no religion 12.7%. Queen, Elizabeth II; governor-general in 1982, Sir Gerald Cash; prime minister, Lynden O. Pindling.

In a general election on June 10, 1982, Prime Minister Lynden O. Pindling and his Progressive Liberal Party (PLP) were again returned to office. The PLP won 32 of the 43 seats in the House of Assembly, taking 55.18% of the popular vote, while the main opposition Free National Movement won the other 11 seats. The left-wing Vanguard Party gained only a few votes.

During the year divisions between the Bahamian and U.S. governments became public. Pindling criticized the U.S. for not extending the same tax concessions granted to companies holding conventions in Jamaica to such companies wishing to hold such affairs in The Bahamas. Also criticized was the fact that to benefit from certain aspects of the Caribbean Basin Initiative, The Bahamas would have to provide tax information on nationals and nonnationals, thereby breaching its own banking secrecy laws. In May the Getty Oil Co. was awarded licenses to explore for oil at the northeastern end of the Bahama chain. Efforts against the smuggling of narcotics through The Bahamas to the U.S. were stepped up, and joint Bahamian-U.S. operations were mounted. (DAVID A. JESSOP)

The Bahamas

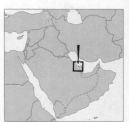

Bahrain

Bahrain

An independent monarchy (emirate), Bahrain consists of a group of islands in the Persian Gulf, lying between the Qatar Peninsula and Saudi Arabia. Total area: 669 sq km (258 sq mi). Pop. (1981): 350,800. Cap. and largest city: Manama (pop., 1981, 115,000). Language: Arabic (official), Persian. Religion (1980): Muslim 95%, of which 50% are Shi'ah Muslim; Christian 4%; others 1%. Emir in 1982, Isa ibn Sulman al-Khalifah; prime minister, Khalifah ibn Sulman al-Khalifah.

Automobile Industry:
see Industrial Review; Transportation

Automobile Racing:
see Motor Sports

Aviation:
see Defense; Transportation

Badminton:
see Racket Games

BAHRAIN
Education. (1979–80) Primary, pupils 48,672, teachers 2,479; secondary, pupils 22,141, teachers 929; vocational, pupils 2,048, teachers 193; teacher training, students 99, teachers 18; higher, students 4,059, teaching staff 125.
Finance and Trade. Monetary unit: Bahrain dinar, with (Sept. 20, 1982) a free rate of 0.377 dinar to U.S. $1 (0.646 dinar = £1 sterling). Gold and other reserves (June 1982) U.S. $1,487,000,000. Budget (1981 actual): revenue 477 million dinars; expenditure 378 million dinars. Foreign trade (1980): imports 1,313,000,000 dinars; exports 1,357,500,000 dinars. Import sources: Saudi Arabia 57%; U.S. 8%; Japan 7%; U.K. 7%. Export destinations: United Arab Emirates 18%; Japan 12%; Singapore 10%; U.S. 6%. Main export: petroleum products 89%.
Industry. Production (in 000; metric tons; 1980): crude oil 2,412; natural gas (cu m) 2,760,000; petroleum products c. 12,000; aluminum (1979) 126; electricity (kw-hr) 1,290,000.

In Bahrain the first half of 1982 was dominated by the aftermath of an attempted coup planned for Dec. 16, 1981. The plot was foiled as a result of information supplied to the security police by Saudi Arabia and the United Arab Emirates. The plotters belonged to an Iranian-backed underground movement, the Islamic Front for the Liberation of Bahrain.

The trial of 73 accused, most of whom were Shi'ah Muslims, ended late in May. All were found guilty, and three people were sentenced to life imprisonment. Prior to the coup attempt, it had been thought that the rift between Sunni and Shi'ah Muslims in Bahrain was healing. Among the plotters were 11 Saudi Arabians, one Kuwaiti, and one Omani. Prime Minister Khalifah ibn Sulman al-Khalifah accused Iran of involvement in the plot and said that training camps existed in that country for revolutionaries bent on creating unrest in all the Arab Gulf states.

The attempted coup had little effect on development plans for the island or on the growth of its banking, insurance, refining, and aluminum industries. Bahraini politicians continued to have faith in the Gulf Cooperation Council as a sign of stronger relations with their Arab neighbours. The start of contracting work on the $600 million causeway link to Saudi Arabia was regarded as proof of close ties with the mainland. An important new project agreed on in 1982 was a $1 billion heavy-oil conversion plant, a joint venture with Saudi Arabia and Kuwait. (JOHN WHELAN)

Bangladesh

An independent republic and member of the Commonwealth, Bangladesh is bordered by India on the west, north, and east, by Burma in the southeast, and by the Bay of Bengal in the south. Area: 143,998 sq km (55,598 sq mi). Pop. (1981): 89,940,000. Cap. and largest city: Dacca (1981 prelim., city pop. 2,244,000; metro. pop. 3,459,000). Language: Bengali. Religion (1980): Muslim 85.9%, Hindu 12.7%, with Christian and Buddhist minorities. Presidents in 1982, Abdus Sattar to March 24 and, from March 27, Abul Fazal Mohammad Ahsanuddin Choudhury; prime minister to March 24, Shah Azizur Rahman; chief martial

Bangladesh

Balance of Payments:
see Economy, World

Ballet:
see Dance

Ballooning:
see Aerial Sports

law administrator from March 24, Hossain Mohammad Ershad.

The seizure of power and the proclamation of martial law on March 24, 1982, by Lieut. Gen. Hossain Mohammad Ershad (*see* BIOGRAPHIES) came as no surprise, since the army chief of staff had often expressed dissatisfaction with the way the affairs of the country were being looked after by aging Pres. Abdus Sattar. Ever since his victory in the presidential election of November 1981, Sattar had steadfastly refused to yield to Ershad's demand that the armed forces be given a formal role in the administration. Appointing himself chief martial law administrator after a bloodless coup, Ershad attempted to justify his takeover, saying, "Bangladesh is facing a crisis on every front: economic, political, social, and law and order."

Ershad moved swiftly to keep control by arresting some government ministers suspected of corruption, banning political and trade union activities, and announcing stiff penalties, including the death sentence, for those found guilty of corruption or political agitation. Within days the military government was said to have arrested at least 200 persons, including six former ministers. Parliament was dissolved, and under a martial law order announced on April 12 Ershad was empowered to make laws that would have the same force

BANGLADESH
Education. (1979) Primary, pupils 8,219,313, teachers 187,504; secondary, pupils 2,737,568, teachers 110,096; vocational, pupils 19,600, teachers 1,059; teacher training, students 6,704, teachers 772; higher (1978), students 154,496, teaching staff 15,784.
Finance. Monetary unit: taka, with (Sept. 20, 1982) a free rate of 22.63 taka to U.S. $1 (38.80 taka = £1 sterling). Gold and other reserves (June 1982) U.S. $107 million. Budget (1981–82 est.): revenue 28,620,000,000 taka; expenditure 16,624,000,000 taka (excludes development budget 30,150,000,000 taka). Gross domestic product (1980–81) 195,960,000,000 taka. Money supply (March 1982) 20,828,000,000 taka. Cost of living (1975 = 100; May 1982) 176.2.
Foreign Trade. (1981–82) Imports 34,545,000,000 taka; exports 11,491,000,000 taka. Import sources (1980): U.S. 14%; Japan 11%; Saudi Arabia 9%; U.K. 6%; United Arab Emirates 5%. Export destinations (1980): U.S. 9%; Singapore 8%; Pakistan 7%; Iran 6%; U.K. 5%; U.S.S.R. 5%. Main exports: jute manufactures 54%; jute 17%; leather 11%; fish 7%; tea 6%.
Transport and Communications. Roads (state maintained; 1980) 5,691 km. Motor vehicles in use (1979): passenger 29,400; commercial 11,900. Railways: (1980) 2,884 km; traffic (1980–81) 5,198,000,000 passenger-km, freight (1976–77) 739 million net ton-km. Navigable waterways (1977) 8,430 km. Air traffic (1980): 1,179,000,000 passenger-km; freight c. 20 million net ton-km. Shipping (1981): merchant vessels 100 gross tons and over 208; gross tonnage 401,054. Shipping traffic (1979–80): goods loaded 988,000 metric tons, unloaded 7,618,000 metric tons. Telephones (Dec. 1980) 116,500. Radio licenses (Dec. 1980) 706,400. Television licenses (Dec. 1980) 78,100.
Agriculture. Production (in 000; metric tons; 1981): rice 20,422; wheat 1,092; potatoes 999; sweet potatoes c. 795; sugar, raw value c. 550; onions c. 140; mangoes c. 210; bananas c. 625; pineapples c. 143; rapeseed 155; tea c. 39; tobacco 47; jute 868; meat c. 326; fish catch (1980) c. 650; timber (cu m; 1980) c. 10,643. Livestock (in 000; 1981): cattle c. 35,000; buffalo c. 1,600; sheep c. 1,070; goats c. 11,800; chickens c. 73,000.
Industry. Production (in 000; metric tons; 1980–81): cement 345; crude steel 139; natural gas (cu m) 1,390,000; petroleum products 1,208; fertilizers (nutrient content) nitrogenous 160, phosphate 33; jute fabrics 590; cotton yarn 46; newsprint 30; other paper 34; electricity (kw-hr; 1980) c. 2,587,000.

Artillery pieces were seen around the airport in Dacca two days after a military takeover of Bangladesh in March.

as acts of Parliament. He also assumed authority to appoint top civilian judges.

To the people of Bangladesh, used to political upheavals, violence, and large-scale poverty, the peaceful changeover appeared to be welcome, at least on the surface. Ershad's choice of a new figurehead president fell on Justice Abul Fazal Mohammad Ahsanuddin Choudhury, a retired Supreme Court judge, who was sworn in on March 27. Soon after taking over, Ershad said that he had no political ambitions and would hand over power to a democratically elected government once stability was restored.

The economic situation in Bangladesh was extremely grave. Before the coup, the Bangladesh Bank reported that the balance of payments deficit had increased by more than 1 billion taka to 4,160,500,000 taka during 1981. The International Monetary Fund continued to maintain that it would not release loans already sanctioned unless Bangladesh rectified the balance of payments position. Prime Minister Shah Azizur Rahman admitted before Parliament on March 2 that the food deficit was on the order of 2,265,000 metric tons; unofficial estimates had put it at approximately 2.8 million metric tons.

On June 1 Ershad denationalized almost all industries, 70% of which had been in the public sector. All public sector units operating at a loss were to be closed, and private participation in all existing industries was to be encouraged. The policy was to affect automobile assembly plants, dry docks, machine-tool factories, and paper mills. Also opened to private investment were the jute, fertilizer, sugar, and newsprint industries and mineral and petroleum exploration. Foreign investment was welcomed in the form of joint ventures. Other economic measures included an immediate ban on the importation of 14 industrial and other items in order to protect indigenous industries. A conditional ban was imposed on several other items.

Ershad tried to improve relations with India by inviting Indian Foreign Minister Narasimha Rao

to visit Dacca in May. Relations had been strained for some time because of disagreement over the sharing of the Ganges River waters and the sovereignty of New Moore Island in the Bay of Bengal. Ershad himself visited India on October 6–7 in an attempt to find political solutions to several bilateral issues. (GOVINDAN UNNY)

Barbados

The parliamentary state of Barbados is a member of the Commonwealth and occupies the most easterly island in the southern Caribbean Sea. Area: 430 sq km (166 sq mi). Pop. (1982 est.): 254,300; 91% black, 4% white, 4% mixed. Cap. and largest city: Bridgetown (pop., 1980 prelim., 7,600). Language: English. Religion: Anglican 53%; Methodist 9%; Roman Catholic 4%; Moravian 2%. Queen, Elizabeth II; governor-general in 1982, Sir Deighton Lisle Ward; prime minister, J. M. G. Adams.

During 1982 Barbados began to experience problems similar to those of other less developed Caribbean nations. A reduction in tourism, a decline in sugar production, and increasing regional trade restrictions all served to depress the economy. In

Barbados

BARBADOS

Education. (1978–79) Primary, pupils 35,555, teachers 1,261; secondary and vocational, pupils 27,770, teachers 1,453; higher (university only), students 1,330, teaching staff 270.

Finance and Trade. Monetary unit: Barbados dollar, with (Sept. 20, 1982) an official rate of Bar$2.01 to U.S. $1 (free rate of Bar$3.45 = £1 sterling). Budget (1980–81 actual): revenue Bar$482 million; expenditure Bar$530.4 million. Cost of living (1975 = 100; May 1982) 210.9. Foreign trade (1981): imports Bar$1,148,100,000; exports Bar$422.6 million. Import sources (1980): U.S. 34%; Trinidad and Tobago 14%; U.K. 14%; Canada 7%; Venezuela 5%. Export destinations (1980): U.S. 38%; Trinidad and Tobago 12%; Ireland 7%; U.K. 6%. Main exports (1980): sugar 23%; electrical equipment c. 20%; clothing c. 16%; petroleum products 12%; chemicals 7%. Tourism (1980): visitors 370,000; gross receipts U.S. $252 million.

Agriculture. Production (in 000; metric tons; 1981): corn c. 2; sweet potatoes c. 4; sugar, raw value c. 96.

Banking:
see Economy, World

Baptist Churches:
see Religion

addition to putting forward a strongly deflationary budget, the government decided to seek special standby credits of $33.8 million over a 20-month period beginning in October 1982. Its deflationary policies brought the government into conflict with the trade unions.

Relations with Grenada remained poor, but the personal acrimony between Prime Minister J. M. G. ("Tom") Adams and Prime Minister Maurice Bishop of Grenada evidenced in 1981 did not reemerge. Substantially closer relations with Trinidad and Jamaica developed in the period preceding the Caribbean Community (Caricom) summit meeting in Jamaica in November. In April U.S. Pres. Ronald Reagan visited Barbados in an effort to draw attention to the U.S. Caribbean Basin Initiative.

Barbados continued efforts toward establishing a joint coast guard and fisheries protection service among eastern Caribbean governments. An agreement on cooperation in security matters was signed in November. (DAVID A. JESSOP)

Baseball

After the seven-week players' strike during the summer of 1981, baseball officials looked to the 1982 season with caution and some fear. Their apprehensions were unwarranted, however. The public reaction was positive, and the major leagues established an attendance record as the American League drew in excess of 23 million paid admissions and the National League topped 21.5 million. Some play-off and World Series telecasts also shattered previous marks for nationwide ratings.

World Series. The St. Louis Cardinals, who had finished fourth and were 14 games below .500 only two years earlier, captured the 1982 World Series by defeating the Milwaukee Brewers, four games to three. The Brewers trounced the Cardinals 10–0 in the opener at St. Louis, Mo., on October 12. Mike Caldwell, a former Cardinal, limited St. Louis to only three hits while Milwaukee pounded Cardinal pitchers for 17.

In the second game the next evening the Brewers mounted an early 3–0 lead, but veteran right-hander Don Sutton was unable to hold it. A two-run double by St. Louis catcher Darrell Porter tied the game 4–4 in the sixth inning. Then, in the eighth inning, Milwaukee relief pitcher Pete Ladd walked pinch hitter Steve Braun with the bases loaded to force home the winning run. The Cardinals prevailed 5–4.

The Series then moved to Milwaukee, Wis., where the Cardinals captured the third game 6–2 on October 15. Willie McGee, a 23-year-old rookie centre fielder, clubbed two homers and batted in four runs for St. Louis. Joaquin Andujar, a hard-throwing right-hander, had the Brewers shut out until the seventh inning, when he was injured by a batted ball and had to depart. In game four on October 16 the Cardinals were leading 5–1 when rookie pitcher Dave LaPoint dropped a throw while covering first base with one out in the seventh inning. The Brewers seized the opportunity;

before they were retired they scored six runs. A single by Cecil Cooper tied the game 5–5, and then Gorman Thomas singled for two more runs. The Brewers triumphed 7–5 to even the best-of-seven Series at two games each.

In the fifth game on October 17 Milwaukee shortstop Robin Yount registered his second four-hit game of the Series to pace the Brewers to a 6–4 conquest. The Brewers, not noted for their defense, made several outstanding plays in the field as Caldwell won his second game despite yielding 14 hits. Yount hit a home run before 56,562, the largest crowd in the history of Milwaukee's County Stadium.

In game six at St. Louis on October 19 the Cardinals averted elimination by routing the Brewers 13–1 in a contest that was twice delayed by rain—once for 2 hours and 13 minutes. The Cardinals capitalized on four Milwaukee errors and amassed 12 hits—including homers by Darrell Porter and Keith Hernandez, who had gone hitless in his first 15 times at bat. John Stuper outlasted the inclement weather and pitched a complete game for the Cardinals.

In the seventh game, at St. Louis on October 20, the Cardinals rallied for a 6–3 victory to win their first World Series championship in 15 years. Making use of their artificial turf surface, the Cardinals garnered 15 hits (13 singles and 2 doubles) and won the game with a three-run outburst in the sixth inning to erase a 3–1 Milwaukee lead. Hernandez stroked a two-run, bases-loaded single to create a 3–3 deadlock. Then George Hendrick singled through the right side for what proved to be the winning run. Bruce Sutter (see BIOGRAPHIES), the premier relief pitcher in the National League, used his split-fingered fastball to work two perfect innings and save the game.

Perhaps the happiest Cardinal was Porter, the bespectacled catcher who was voted most valuable player for the World Series. He batted a modest .286 for seven games but contributed several key hits and was a steadying influence for St. Louis pitchers.

Though the 1982 World Series featured a tactic used exclusively by the American League—the designated hitter—the Cardinals profited. Dane Iorg, their appointed "DH," batted .529, while Milwaukee's Don Money and Roy Howell—who were accustomed to the role—fared poorly, totaling only 3 hits in 24 at bats.

Play-offs. The St. Louis Cardinals advanced to the World Series by sweeping the best-of-five National League championship series from the Atlanta Braves three games to none. Bob Forsch hurled a three-hitter to win the opener in St. Louis 7–0, and Ken Oberkfell's single scored the winning run for the Cardinals' 4–3 victory in game two. In Atlanta on October 10 the Cardinals clinched their first pennant since 1968 with a 6–2 decision behind the pitching of Andujar and Sutter.

The Brewers had a more difficult time achieving the first pennant in their history. They lost the first two games of the American League championship series to the star-studded California Angels by scores of 8–3 and 4–2. But when they returned home, the Brewers came to life and became the first team in play-off history to win despite losing the first two games. They tied the series with 5–3 and 9–5 conquests. Then, on October 10, Cooper singled for two runs in the seventh inning to give Milwaukee a 4–3 triumph. Gene Mauch, the California manager, resigned shortly after the bitter defeat.

Regular Season. Baseball was blessed with four uncommonly close division races during the season—a situation that no doubt contributed to the record attendances. Only one team, the Minnesota Twins, failed to draw one million fans; seven franchises cracked the two-million barrier. The California Angels broke the American League season mark by attracting 2,807,360 customers. The Los Angeles Dodgers bettered their own major league record with 3,608,881 for 80 dates, an average of 45,111 fans per game.

The Brewers were an also-ran until Harvey Kuenn replaced Buck Rodgers as manager on June 2. Under Kuenn, the Brewers finished 72–43 and hit 216 home runs en route. But the Brewers had to win the last game of the season at Baltimore to take the American League East title. The Brewers had appeared to have a comfortable lead in the division, but their excellent relief pitcher, Rollie Fingers, was injured on September 2 and missed the rest of the season.

The Angels, a veteran team with several past and present All-Stars, finished three games in front of the Kansas City Royals in the American League West. The Angels were helped by off-season acquisitions such as Reggie Jackson, who hit 39 home runs, and Doug DeCinces.

The Cardinals, who hit fewer home runs than any team in the major leagues, employed speed and defense to win the National League East by three games over the Philadelphia Phillies. The Cardinals never lost more than three games in a row and finished strongly. Their success was attributed mostly to their cagey manager, Whitey Herzog, who had joined the organization two years earlier and effected several trades in his role as general manager.

The Atlanta Braves probably had the most difficult time of any division champion. They began the season with a record 13 consecutive victories but then were inconsistent for much of the summer, at one point losing 19 of 21 games. With only 10 games left they were 3½ games behind the Los Angeles Dodgers, defending World Series champi-

Frank Robinson (left) and Hank Aaron waved to fans when they arrived in Cooperstown, N.Y., for induction into the Baseball Hall of Fame on August 1. Robinson was the only player in history to win the most valuable player award in both leagues.

LARRY DOWNING—NEWSWEEK

UPI

(Left) Bruce Sutter and Darrell Porter (with glasses) are joyous after Sutter struck out the last man in the last game of the World Series to give the championship to the St. Louis Cardinals. Porter was named the Series' most valuable player. (Right) Robin Yount of the Milwaukee Brewers was named the American League's MVP. He finished the season with a .331 batting average and 29 home runs.

Rickey Henderson of the Oakland A's stole his 119th base of the season on August 27, beating the previous record for the total number of bases stolen during a complete season.

ons. But the Dodgers then faded, losing eight in a row.

Willie Wilson of the Kansas City Royals took the American League batting title with a .332 average, slightly better than the .331 by Yount. Hal McRae, also of the Royals, batted in the most runs (133), while Thomas of Milwaukee and ex-Yankee superstar Jackson of the Angels tied for home run leadership with 39. Rickey Henderson (*see* BIOGRAPHIES) of the Oakland A's broke all base-stealing records with 130.

Lamarr Hoyt of the Chicago White Sox recorded the most victories (19) among American League pitchers. Dan Quisenberry, the relief ace of the Kansas City Royals, earned 35 saves.

At the season's end Billy Martin was fired as manager of the Oakland A's, and Earl Weaver, considered by many to be the best manager in baseball, retired after a brilliant career with the Baltimore Orioles. In November Bowie Kuhn was deposed as commissioner of baseball after 14 years when five National League team owners voted not to renew his contract.

Al Oliver, obtained from the Texas Rangers, batted .331 for the Montreal Expos to win the National League title. Dave Kingman of the New York Mets took the home run crown with 37, while Oliver and Atlanta's Dale Murphy shared the RBI leadership with 109.

Steve Carlton, the brilliant 37-year-old left-hander of the Philadelphia Phillies, was the only pitcher in the major leagues to win 20 or more games, with a record of 23–11. Sutter of the Cardinals was the front-runner in saves for relief pitchers with 36.

If the National League had feelings of superiority after the 1982 season, it was not only because of four consecutive successes in the World Series. Also, in the annual midsummer All-Star Game, the National League beat the American League 4–1 at Montreal. It was the 11th straight victory for the National. Steve Rogers of the Montreal Expos was the starting and winning pitcher. Shortstop Dave Concepcion of the Cincinnati Reds hit a two-run home run in the second inning and was voted most valuable player.

Among the postseason awards Yount was named most valuable player in the American League and Dale Murphy of the Braves won the honour in the National. The Cy Young awards for outstanding pitching went to Pete Vuckovich of the Brewers in the American League and the Phillies' Carlton in the National; it was a record fourth Cy Young for the Phillie veteran. Dodger second

Final Major League Standings, 1982

AMERICAN LEAGUE
East Division

Club	W.	L.	Pct.	G.B.
Milwaukee	95	67	.586	—
Baltimore	94	68	.580	1
Boston	89	73	.549	6
Detroit	83	79	.512	12
New York	79	83	.488	16
Cleveland	78	84	.481	17
Toronto	78	84	.481	17

West Division

Club	W.	L.	Pct.	G.B.
California	93	69	.574	—
Kansas City	90	72	.556	3
Chicago	87	75	.537	6
Seattle	76	86	.469	17
Oakland	68	94	.420	25
Texas	64	98	.395	29
Minnesota	60	102	.370	33

NATIONAL LEAGUE
East Division

Club	W.	L.	Pct.	G.B.
St. Louis	92	70	.568	—
Philadelphia	89	73	.549	3
Montreal	86	76	.531	6
Pittsburgh	84	78	.519	8
Chicago	73	89	.451	19
New York	65	97	.401	27

West Division

Club	W.	L.	Pct.	G.B.
Atlanta	89	73	.549	—
Los Angeles	88	74	.543	1
San Francisco	87	75	.537	2
San Diego	81	81	.500	8
Houston	77	85	.475	12
Cincinnati	61	101	.377	28

baseman Steve Sax was rookie of the year in the National League, and Baltimore shortstop Cal Ripken, Jr., won the award in the American. Managers of the year were Joe Torre of the Braves for the National League and Kuenn for the American.

(ROBERT WILLIAM VERDI)

Latin America. The 1981–82 winter Caribbean baseball season benefited from the 1981 U.S. major league strike. Many major league players felt that they had to continue working through the winter after a shortened summer season.

The Orange Growers of Hermosillo won the championship of the Mexican Pacific League. In Venezuela the Caracas Lions gained the national title for the second year in a row, while the Lions of Escogido achieved the same feat in the Dominican Republic. In Puerto Rico the Ponce Lions became the new champions.

All of these teams met in February in Hermosillo, Sonora, Mexico, for the 24th Caribbean Series, a yearly contest of national winter champions that had been suspended in 1981. The Caracas Lions became for the first time the Caribbean champions. Led by Manager Alfonso ("Chico") Carrasquel, they defeated the Ponce Lions in the last and decisive game of the series.

The Indians of Ciudad Juárez were the surprising champions of the Mexican League, played during the spring and summer. They emerged from the Western Group of the Northern Division, considered by some the weakest group within the league, and were not even favoured to win there. But win they did, and then they went on to defeat the heavily favoured Nuevo Laredo team for the Northern Division title. In the final championship series, they played the Mexico City Tigers, a five-time champion that had staged a remarkable comeback after being at the bottom of their group at midseason. The Indians, managed by José ("Zacatillo") Guerrero, defeated the Tigers four times in a row and left no doubts about their superiority.

(SERGIO SARMIENTO)

Japan. The Seibu Lions of Tokorozawa, winners of the Pacific League pennant, defeated the Chunichi Dragons of Nagoya, the Central League pennant winners, four games to two in the best-of-seven Japan Series. The Lions, a team organized only four years earlier, won the first two games 7–3 and 7–1 but lost the next two 4–3 and 5–3. In the fifth and sixth games the Lions won 3–1 and 9–4 behind explosive batting by former U.S. major leaguers Steve Ontiveros of the Chicago Cubs and Terry Whitfield of the San Francisco Giants and also by Takuji Ota, the most valuable player of the first half of the split season. Among the pitchers worthy of special mention was Osamu Higashio, who pitched 13⅔ innings and had two wins against one loss.

In the Central League the Dragons won the pennant in the last game, their first title in eight years. Their winning percentage was .577, beating by only .008 the second-place Yomiuri Giants of Tokyo.

Keiji Nagasaki, outfielder of the Taiyo Whales of Yokohama, won the Central League batting award with .351. Infielder Masayuki Kakefu of the Hanshin Tigers of Osaka captured both the home run and runs-batted-in crowns with 35 and 95, respectively. The most valuable player award was won by catcher Takayoshi Nakao of the Dragons, who batted .281 and had 18 home runs and 47 runs batted in.

In the Pacific League the Lions, the first-half winner, beat the Nippon Ham Fighters, the second-half winner, three games to one. No Lion players were prominent enough to capture individual titles, and much of the credit for the team's championship went to the manager, Tatsuro Hirooka.

Hiromitsu Ochiai of the Lotte Orions of Kawasaki won the triple crown of the Pacific League, batting .325 with 32 home runs and 99 runs batted in. The fourth triple-crown winner in Japanese professional baseball history, he was also named the league's most valuable player.

(RYUSAKU HASEGAWA)

Basketball

United States. PROFESSIONAL. It was Earvin ("Magic") Johnson's turn to work wonders once more during the 1981–82 National Basketball Association (NBA) season. First, the charismatic superstar made Los Angeles Lakers' Coach Paul Westhead disappear merely by saying "I want to be traded." Then, with new coach Pat Riley permitting Johnson to mix and match his bag of tricks at will, the Magic Man conjured up the formula for another NBA championship.

It was the Lakers' second title in Johnson's third pro season, proving that the 6-ft 8-in guard was much more substance than shadow. Despite uproar about Johnson's 25-year, $25 million contract and the image-tarnishing Westhead incident, he regained the fans' favour.

When Westhead was fired, assistant coach Riley quickly ended grumbles about the Lakers' slow-down offense. Merely by letting Johnson and backcourt running mate Norm Nixon trigger fast breaks at every opportunity, Riley unleashed a juggernaut on the NBA. And, even though he turned 35 on the eve of the play-offs, 7-ft 2-in centre Kareem Abdul-Jabbar was still at the top of his game, adding power to his teammates' speed.

That was fortunate, because the inspired Philadelphia 76ers staved off another collapse in the Eastern Conference finals to enter the championship round feeling like a team of destiny. They were not, despite Julius ("Dr. J.") Erving's valiant effort.

In a typical bitterly fought play-off with the Boston Celtics, the 76ers rolled to a 3–1 edge over the defending NBA champions in the best-of-seven series. Philadelphia had been in the same situation a year earlier and then had stunned their fans by dropping three straight games and the series to the Celtics. This time the 76ers again won three of the first four. They then lost the next two, forcing a showdown in Boston Garden, where the Celtics had humiliated them by 40 and 29 points earlier in the Eastern final. Even more ominous was the fact that in ten previous seventh-game play-off tests on their home court the Celtics had won nine times.

WIDE WORLD

Earvin "Magic" Johnson of the Los Angeles Lakers, being guarded by Julius Erving (6) and Maurice Cheeks of the Philadelphia 76ers, searches for a teammate to pass to. The action came during an NBA championship play-off game in June.

But the magnificent Erving refused to let Celtic tradition prevail once more, sparking the 76ers to a convincing 120–106 triumph.

Meanwhile, Los Angeles had breezed through two Western Conference play-off rounds with 4–0 sweeps and then had to sit for a week while Philadelphia and Boston went the limit. Instead of rusting during that enforced idleness, the rested, relaxed Lakers landed the knockout punch against Philadelphia in the third quarter of the first game. They let the 76ers grab a big lead in Philadelphia and then shocked them with a 40–9 explosion in the third quarter to win going away. That made the outcome predictable, the new champions never losing control before they wrapped up the series with a 114–104 victory in the sixth game. Demonstrating his versatility, Johnson racked up 13 points, 13 rebounds, and 13 assists in the final game to earn the play-off's most valuable player award. Johnson was only the second man in NBA history to earn that award twice, the first being New York Knicks' centre Willis Reed, who did so in 1970 and 1973.

After the season the 76ers offered a $13.2 million, six-year contract to Moses Malone, all-professional centre of the Houston Rockets. The Rockets eventually traded Malone to Philadelphia for centre Caldwell Jones and a first-round draft choice.

The large amount of money for one superstar's services really reflected a league-wide struggle for survival. Caught in the squeeze between soaring salaries and sinking revenue, the NBA had a number of shaky franchises. The hope for salvation lay in the steadily increasing use of cable and home subscription television, but the players threatened to strike if they did not get a slice of that potential bonanza.

COLLEGE. The jinx that had plagued North Carolina Coach Dean Smith finally was shattered in

Beer:
see Industrial Review

1982. Seven proved to be Smith's lucky number when a pass stolen by All-America forward James Worthy (see BIOGRAPHIES) in the closing seconds of the title game preserved North Carolina's first National Collegiate Athletic Association (NCAA) championship. The Tar Heels prevailed 63–62 over Georgetown in a splendid final played before a record crowd of 61,612 in the mammoth New Orleans Superdome.

One of America's most respected collegiate coaches, Smith had reached the final four in the NCAA tournament six times previously, only to be rebuffed. The spell was broken by his poised team's refusal to panic, despite a shaky start against Georgetown's shot-blocking 7-ft centre, Patrick Ewing.

Rallied by Worthy's clutch shooting, North Carolina gradually took control of the thrilling contest, getting the lead on a jump shot by freshman Michael Jordan with 16 seconds left. Coach John Thompson of Georgetown refused to call time out in order to set up a play, and that proved fatal to the Hoyas. Worthy capped a magnificent career at North Carolina with one more defensive gem, anticipating a midcourt pass by Georgetown's Fred Brown and stepping in for the interception.

That, plus a game-high 28 points, earned the tournament's most valuable player award for Worthy, soon to become the top choice in the NBA draft. Los Angeles made the 6-ft 8-in forward its number one pick, signing him to a lucrative contract.

But the exciting climax to another record-break-

Kareem Abdul-Jabbar (left) of the Los Angeles Lakers was a member of the National Basketball Players Association team that journeyed to Beijing for an exhibition game in July. The U.S. team beat the Chinese 100–76.

WIDE WORLD

ing season could not hide the fact that college basketball was in danger of being swallowed by its own success. With his coaching colleagues gathering in New Orleans for the NCAA finals, Notre Dame's Digger Phelps dropped a bombshell by disclosing that he knew of at least three schools illegally paying athletes up to $10,000 a year to play basketball. Phelps asserted that fewer than 10% of the top 100 universities were engaging in such practices, sticking to his guns despite criticism from coaches who felt he was tarring the profession with sweeping charges.

The pressure to make the NCAA tournament field provoked more controversy, even with 48 berths allotted. Coach Dick Versace of Bradley erupted when the Braves from Peoria, Ill., were not invited to the meet despite winning the Missouri Valley Conference title. He blasted the selection committee for alleged favouritism to Boston College and other Eastern schools.

Ironically, Boston College promptly recorded the tournament's most stunning upset by knocking out DePaul of Chicago. It was the third straight year the highly rated Blue Demons had been embarrassed in their NCAA opener. But Bradley had something to prove and did so convincingly, sweeping to its fourth National Invitation Tournament crown. Paced by David Thirdkill's smothering defense, the Braves beat Purdue 67–58 for the title.

In women's basketball, Louisiana Tech took NCAA Division I honours, defeating Cheney (Pa.) 76–62. Rutgers beat Texas 83–77 to capture the Association of Intercollegiate Athletics for Women (AIAW) tournament. After losing a court challenge of the NCAA decision to stage women's championship events, the AIAW's major role in college athletics appeared over. Most nationally ranked teams switched to the NCAA. (ROBERT G. LOGAN)

World Amateur. The ninth World Championship for Men was played in Colombia during August 1982. Thirteen teams competed; Colombia had a bye to the final round, and the other 12 were divided equally into three groups playing in Bogotá, Medellín, and Bucaramanga. In Bogotá there was an early surprise when Spain beat the U.S. 109–99. In Medellín, Australia beat Brazil, which failed to qualify. Qualifiers for the final pool were: Group A, Spain, U.S.; Group B, U.S.S.R., Australia; Group C, Yugoslavia, Canada. The finals were played in the Cali stadium, which seated 25,000 spectators.

The results of the preliminary rounds were carried forward into the finals, the Soviet Union and Yugoslavia being the only two undefeated teams with maximum points. When the two met in the final pool, the Soviet Union struggled home to win 99–94. Yugoslavia was again in trouble when it lost to the U.S. 88–81. The Soviet Union remained undefeated and clearly would be playing in the final, but at this stage it lost to the U.S. 99–93. Yugoslavia had to be content with a narrow win against Spain 119–117, which gave it the bronze medal.

The final match between the Soviet Union and the U.S. was a thrilling exhibition of basketball. At the half the U.S. led 49–47. With just seconds remaining at the end, and the score Soviet Union 95,

One of the reasons North Carolina won the NCAA championship was James Worthy, shown slamming home 2 of his 28 points in the final championship game. Worthy was awarded the MVP title for the series.

U.S. 94, a jump ball was called by the French referee. The U.S. got the ball and shot on the buzzer but missed. Thus, the Soviet Union won the gold medal for the third time and the U.S. the silver. The other placings were: (4) Spain, (5) Australia, (6) Canada, and (7) Colombia.

The 11th Asian Basketball Championship for Men took place in Calcutta during November 1981. China won the championship, being undefeated throughout the tournament. In the final game, against South Korea, the score was 96–64 for China.

The African Championship for Men was held in Mogadishu, Somalia, during December 1981. Eleven teams took part. The competition for the championship took place between the Ivory Coast and Egypt. The first time they met, the Ivory Coast won 66–62, and in the final contest they were convincing winners 81–65.

The ninth Asian Basketball Championship for Women took place in Tokyo during April and May 1982. When South Korea and China met in the final, the former won 65–64, thereby gaining the championship and placing China second.

(K. K. MITCHELL)

Belgium

A constitutional monarchy on the North Sea coast of Europe, the Benelux country of Belgium is bordered by The Netherlands, West Germany, Luxembourg, and France. Area: 30,521 sq km (11,784 sq mi). Pop. (1981 est.): 9,863,400. Cap. and largest urban area: Brussels (pop., 1981 est., metro. area 1,000,200, commune 141,900). Language: Dutch,

Belgium

French, and German. Religion: predominantly Roman Catholic. King, Baudouin I; prime minister in 1982, Wilfried Martens.

The new Social Christian-Liberal government led by Wilfried Martens, which took office in December 1981, immediately sought emergency powers to deal with Belgium's serious economic and financial crisis. Despite Socialist filibustering, the final vote in the Senate took place on Feb. 2, 1982, and the government at once published a first series of special decrees aimed at stimulating employment, in particular by a reduction of value-added tax on the construction of dwellings. The most surprising measure was an 8.5% devaluation of the Belgian franc, on February 21. This was accompanied by a prices and wages freeze to last until May 31, the previously sacrosanct automatic wage indexation system being replaced by a lump sum increase. The Socialist Fédération Générale du Travail de Belgique (FGTB) called several 24-hour general strikes to protest the government's decisions but only roused the workers, to a limited extent, in French-speaking Wallonia.

The government, meanwhile, busied itself with the still pending 1982 budget, which had to be completely revised in order to bring down the expected deficit from BFr 322 billion to BFr 252 billion. This was done in part by reducing child allowances and imposing wage reductions for childless couples and unmarried persons. The economies stirred up considerable discontent, and FGTB Secretary-General Georges Debunne, in an interview in early September, warned that he would initiate action to bring down the government. Martens stood his ground, proposing discussions over delicate questions such as the financial balance of the social security system, redistribution of the available amount of work, industrial policy, and the introduction of new technologies. Unemployment continued to climb but at a slower pace than in 1981. Most worrisome was the high proportion of unemployed under 25. Local elections in October indicated broad support for the government.

The constitutional changes approved in 1980

BELGIUM

Education. (1979–80) Primary, pupils 877,138, teachers 48,423; secondary, pupils 562,610; vocational, pupils 287,848; secondary and vocational, teachers (1976–77) 71,170; higher, pupils 188,232, teaching staff (university level) c. 9,000.

Finance. Monetary unit: Belgian franc, with (Sept. 20, 1982) a free commercial rate of BFr 48.09 to U.S. $1 (BFr 82.45 = £1 sterling) and a free financial rate of BFr 49.84 to U.S. $1 (BFr 85.45 = £1 sterling). Gold and other reserves (June 1982) U.S. $4,697,000,000. Budget (1981 actual): revenue BFr 1,059,300,000,000; expenditure BFr 1,534,-700,000,000. Gross national product (1981) BFr 3,552,-000,000,000. Money supply (March 1982) BFr 820 billion. Cost of living (1975 = 100; June 1982) 158.9.

Foreign Trade. (Belgium-Luxembourg economic union; 1981) Imports BFr 2,296,600,000,000; exports BFr 2,059,-900,000,000. Import sources: EEC 61% (West Germany 19%, The Netherlands 17%, France 14%, U.K. 7%); Saudi Arabia 7%; U.S. 7%. Export destinations: EEC 70% (West Germany 20%, France 19%, The Netherlands 15%, U.K. 9%, Italy 5%). Main exports: chemicals 12%; machinery 11%; motor vehicles 11%; food 9%; iron and steel 9%; petroleum products 8%; precious stones 6%; textile yarn and fabrics 6%. Tourism (1980) gross receipts (Belgium-Luxembourg) U.S. $1,810,000,000.

Transport and Communications. Roads (1980) 126,800 km (including 1,192 km expressways). Motor vehicles in use (1980): passenger 3,158,700; commercial 267,700. Railways: (1980) 3,971 km; traffic (1981) 7,078,000,000 passenger-km, freight 7,514,000,000 net ton-km. Air traffic (1981): 5,202,000,000 passenger-km; freight 454 million net ton-km. Navigable inland waterways in regular use (1980) 1,509 km. Shipping (1981): merchant vessels 100 gross tons and over 312; gross tonnage 1,916,765. Shipping traffic (1979): goods loaded 38,301,000 metric tons, unloaded 65,555,000 metric tons. Telephones (Jan. 1980) 3,447,700. Radio licenses (Dec. 1979) 4,450,900. Television licenses (Dec. 1979) 2,924,800.

Agriculture. Production (in 000; metric tons; 1981): wheat c. 910; barley c. 760; oats c. 130; potatoes c. 1,400; tomatoes c. 90; apples c. 130; sugar, raw value c. 1,000; milk c. 3,760; pork c. 670; beef and veal c. 310; fish catch (1980) 46. Livestock (in 000; Dec. 1980): cattle 2,896; pigs 5,011; sheep 86; horses 33; chickens 27,047.

Industry. Fuel and power (in 000; 1981): coal (metric tons) 6,139; manufactured gas (cu m) 2,030,000; electricity (kw-hr) 50,640,000. Production (in 000; metric tons; 1981): pig iron 9,786; crude steel 12,288; copper 437; lead 110; tin 2.5; zinc 250; sulfuric acid 2,001; plastics and resins 1,943; fertilizers (nutrient content; 1980–81) nitrogenous c. 740, phosphate c. 490; cement 6,698; newsprint 102; other paper (1980) 797; cotton yarn 47; cotton fabrics 48; wool yarn 78; woolen fabrics 32; man-made fibres (1979) 64. Merchant vessels launched (100 gross tons and over; 1981) 222,000 gross tons.

Belgian steelworkers, concerned for their jobs, protested government actions relating to the steel industry. A demonstration on March 16 degenerated into a fierce clash with police.

were implemented with the designation of, on the one hand, a Flemish Executive (nine members) and, on the other, a French Community Executive (three members) and a Walloon Regional Executive (six members). The newly created bodies did not see eye to eye on several matters. The fact that five major industrial sectors were left under the national government—among them steel and textiles—was openly regretted by the Flemish Executive, which was eager to extend its powers. This attitude was inspired by the steadily deteriorating situation of the recently merged Cockerill-Sambre steel company, which failed to get out of the red despite large-scale injections of public money. A demonstration by worried steelworkers on March 16 in Brussels degenerated into a fierce clash with police in which many were injured.

Criticism was leveled repeatedly at the still incomplete state reform. While regional authorities wanted more power, other voices warned against growing separatist trends. Meanwhile, despite opposition by the Socialists, Parliament approved a bill transferring some powers to the German-language community. Early in September, the antagonism between the two major language communities was rekindled when the European Economic Community included practically all of Wallonia in its list of economically distressed areas, while only two small districts in Flanders were recognized as such.

A long-awaited debate on Belgium's future energy policy was concluded with the carrying of nine resolutions, calling, among other things, for a new coal-powered, 600-Mw generating station near the Limburg coal mines that were still in operation, and the treatment by Eurochemic of no more than 90 tons of radioactive waste material annually. (JAN R. ENGELS)

Belize

A constitutional monarchy on the eastern coast of Central America and a member of the Commonwealth, Belize is bounded on the north by Mexico, west and south by Guatemala, and east by the Caribbean Sea. Area: 22,965 sq km (8,867 sq mi). Pop. (1982 est.): 150,000. Cap.: Belmopan (pop., 1980 est., 4,500). Largest city: Belize City (pop., 1980 est., 42,200). Language: English (official); Spanish, Creole, Maya, and Garifuna. Religion (1980 est.): Roman Catholic 66.8%; Anglican 13.6%; Methodist 13.2%; other 6.4%. Queen, Eliz-

abeth II; governor-general in 1982, Minita Gordon; prime minister, George Cadle Price.

During the year Belize celebrated the first anniversary of its independence and began to participate actively in regional and international affairs. Because the new nation is geographically bound to other Central American countries and tied by political and cultural traditions to the English-speaking countries of the Caribbean, Belize's foreign policy was among its most important concerns. In March Belize became a full member of the African, Caribbean, and Pacific Group. The nation also opened its doors to 5,000 refugees from El Salvador, and a feasibility study got under way for the migration of some 600 Haitian families to Belize over a number of years.

Resolving the border dispute with neighbouring Guatemala remained a major priority for Belize. The possibility of violence crippled Belize's tourist industry despite the presence of a British security force. The British troops were to remain in Belize until the agreement was terminated by both governments. (INES T. BAPTIST)

Belize

Benin

A republic of West Africa, Benin is located north of the Gulf of Guinea and is bounded by Togo, Upper Volta, Niger, and Nigeria. Area: 112,600 sq km (43,475 sq mi). Pop. (1982 est.): 3,756,000, mainly Dahomean and allied tribes. Cap.: Porto-Novo (pop., 1980 est., 123,000). Largest city: Cotonou (pop., 1980 est., 215,000). Language: French and local dialects. Religion: mainly animist, with Christian and Muslim minorities. President in 1982, Col. Ahmed Kerekou.

Pope John Paul II visited Benin briefly on Feb. 17, 1982, in the course of his West African tour. Pres. Ahmed Kerekou used the occasion to give his guest a public discourse on the merits of Marxism-Leninism. In April President Kerekou reshuffled his government, 9 of the 22 portfolios changing hands. Most important, Tiamiou Ajibade replaced Simon Ifede Ogouma as foreign minister, and Amidou Baba Moussa took over from Martin Dohou Azonhiho as information minister.

Benin

Benin was among the Organization of African Unity (OAU) members that supported the admission of the Saharan Arab Democratic Republic (Western Sahara) to the OAU. At a meeting of OAU information ministers in Dakar, Senegal, in March, the Benin delegation was one of 13 that walked out to protest the exclusion of the Western Saharan delegation from the meeting. In August President Kerekou went to Tripoli, Libya, for the annual OAU summit meeting, but the summit did not take place because of disagreement over the Western Sahara issue.

During the year Benin received a $14 million credit from the International Development Association toward the improvement of its primary and lower secondary educational system.

(PHILIPPE DECRAENE)

Bhutan

Bhutan

A monarchy situated in the eastern Himalayas, Bhutan is bounded by China and India. Area: 46,100 sq km (17,800 sq mi). Pop. (1981 est.): 1,174,000, including Bhutia 60%, Nepalese 25%, and 15% tribal peoples. Official cap.: Thimphu (pop., 1979 est., 10,000). Administrative cap.: Paro (population unavailable). Language: Dzongkha (official). Religion (1980): 69.3% Buddhist; 24.8% Hindu; 5% Muslim; 0.9% tribal. Druk gyalpo (king) in 1982, Jigme Singye Wangchuk.

King Jigme Singye Wangchuk visited New Delhi on March 16–19, 1982. Expressing his gratitude for India's financial and technical assistance, the king stated that friendship with India would remain the cornerstone of Bhutan's foreign policy. India announced that economic assistance to Bhutan for the fiscal year 1982–83 would be stepped up to Rs 500 million from the previous year's revised estimate of Rs 480 million.

The Beijing (Peking, China) *People's Daily* of April 6 referred to the Indo-Bhutanese treaty of 1949, stating that the relationship mentioned in the treaty stood in the way of Bhutan's exercising its "free and self-determined policy, and control of its sovereignty." The article was considered significant since it closely followed both the king's visit to New Delhi in March and remarks made by the Bhutanese foreign minister, Lyonpo Dawa Tsering, during a visit to Singapore on April 1. Tsering told Singapore leaders that Bhutan would give its continued support to the Khmer Rouge regime in Kampuchea as opposed to the Vietnam-backed

---

BHUTAN

Education. (1981–82) Primary, pupils 22,288, teachers 797; secondary, pupils 14,546, teachers 520; vocational, pupils 401, teachers 49; teacher training, pupils 121, teachers 17; higher, pupils 204, teaching staff 16.

Finance and Trade. Monetary unit: ngultrum, at par with the Indian rupee (which is also in use), with (Sept. 20, 1982) a free rate of 9.62 ngultrums to U.S. $1 (16.50 ngultrums = £1 sterling). Budget (1979–80): revenue 97 million ngultrums; expenditure 90 million ngultrums. Foreign trade (1980): imports c. $2 million; exports c. $1.5 million. Most external trade is with India. Main exports: timber, fruit and vegetables, cardamom. Tourism (1979–80) 1,500 visitors.

Bicycling:
see Cycling

Heng Samrin government, which India had recognized. He also announced his government's intention to appoint an honorary consul in Singapore to promote trade between Bhutan and Singapore.

(GOVINDAN UNNY)

Billiard Games

Billiards. The 37th world three-cushion billiard championship began May 21 in Guayaquil, Ecuador, under unusual circumstances when both 1981 defending champion Ludo Dielis of Belgium and runner-up Nobuaki Kobayashi of Japan decided not to compete. This placed perennial contenders Yoshio Yoshihara of Japan and Rini Van Bracht of The Netherlands, along with Frank Torres and Carlos Hallon of the United States, in contention for the title.

Play during the first two days of the nine-day tournament was desultory as the field of 12 national champions and runners-up became acclimated to the high heat and humidity. On the third day, however, competition became intense. After a loss to Yoshihara in a close match, Hallon put Mexico's Gilberto Avalos away 60–34 in just 33 innings with a 1.818 average. Torres then won two matches, defeating Luis Doyharzabal of Argentina 60–47 and Yoshihara 60–46. On the fourth day Hallon and Van Bracht traded points to 51–51, whereupon the latter added six more points before yielding the table. Hallon took over, running to 59 before narrowly missing the 60th and winning point. Van Bracht won this important match and went on to oppose Yoshihara on the final day for the world title. Both had decided upon a game of safety. Taking no chances, Van Bracht slowly drew away to claim the championship in 51 innings. Placing third and fifth were Hallon and Torres, while José Viteri of Ecuador took fourth place. Despite the absence of the 1981 winners, the tournament grand average was an exceptional 0.931.

Pocket Billiards. The Billiard Congress of America (BCA) held both its All-American League championships and national eight-ball singles championships in Kansas City, Mo. The fourth All-American, June 24–26, brought together 78 league-winning teams from throughout the U.S. and Canada. By the end of the third day the 46 five-man teams of the men's division had been reduced to two contenders, The Wizards of Colorado Springs, Colo., and The Other End from Taylor, Mich.

The Other End had lost once to The Wizards but had survived the losers' bracket to earn a second and final chance at the championship. As one-time losers, however, they had to defeat their opponents twice to win. At the outset The Other End took the lead and won the first match 8–3, largely due to Bill Patee preventing Charlie Shootman, a member of the three previous championship teams from Colorado, from getting a chance at the table. As the final and deciding match began, The Other End again took an early lead with three straight games before The Wizards rallied to win six straight. Trading games in the "race to eight," the teams had scores of seven each as the final game

BILLIARDS DIGEST

Professional Pool Players Association world open men's champion Steve Mizerak and women's champion Jean Balukas pose with their trophies in New York City after the finals on August 21.

began. Ron Howle, The Other End's steadiest player, made the break. Nothing fell. Coming to the table for The Wizards, Brett Smith pocketed one ball, but then missed. Working methodically, Howle proceeded to clear the table except for his last ball. Smith, encouraged by teammates Shootman, Junior Harris, Stian Woods, Scott Smith, and Gene Dover, then cleared the table and took the crown home to Colorado Springs for the fourth consecutive year.

In the women's division the two finalists from the original 32 teams were Richard's Pigeon Inn from Lansing, Mich., and the Bank Shots from Colorado Springs, Colo., who were the 1981 champions under different sponsorship. In an earlier match the Bank Shots had lost to the Pigeons and had been forced to play and win their remaining games through the losers' bracket. As defending champions they came to the final match with great confidence, a large cheering section, and iced champagne. But there had been no mistake in the earlier contest. The Pigeon team, consisting of Chi Zeeb, Vicki Frechen, DeeDee Bailey, Julie Hunter, Carla Johnson, and Kathy Amiranti, again won by a score of 8–5, taking the women's title away from Colorado Springs for the first time in three years.

The BCA national singles eight-ball championships were held over Labor Day weekend with 82 finalists, ranging in age from 13 to 69, in contention for the men's and women's titles. In the men's final the contest was between undefeated Joe Sposit of Pittsburgh, Pa., and once-beaten Greg Fix of Rochester, Minn., who had come through the losers' bracket in the double-elimination play. Both had displayed forceful style throughout the contest. In the "race to eleven" Sposit took charge ear-

ly, winning six consecutive games before Fix was able to post his first. Subsequently, there was no doubt about the outcome as an unrelenting Sposit reached the required 11 wins in just one hour.

The women's championship play-off was another matter. Linda Hoffman from Fort Worth, Texas, who had learned the game in college while earning an automotive engineering degree, was undefeated. Her opponent, Sher Lively of Vallejo, Calif., had lost just once. Playing deliberate games, the two were tied at five games each after two hours of play. At that point, however, Hoffman took charge and won the next six games to take the 1982 title.

Spurred on by the success of the BCA in producing tournaments that attracted thousands of participants, several private sponsors offered similar competitions. The Miller and Busch breweries and Valley pool tables were successfully attracting tavern participation, leading to national play-offs for hundreds of amateurs. Another notable contest, featuring individual nine-ball and possibly the largest cash awards offered in this century, was co-sponsored by promoter Richard Florence, Caesar's Palace resorts, Budweiser beer, and a cable television network. In September more than 100 of the top-rated players in the U.S. paid entry fees of $1,500 each to compete at Lake Tahoe in Nevada for a $169,000 purse. Among them were such former BCA champions as Joe ("The Meatman") Balsis, Dallas West, Luther ("Whimpy") Lassiter, and Nick Varner. Accepting their challenge were the who's who of contemporary pool: Jim Rempe, Allen Hopkins, Mike Massey, Buddy Hall, Mark Wilson, Mike Sigel, Ronnie Allen, and a host of local sports seeking their first fame away from home. In the end Buddy Hall of Paducah, Ky., went undefeated to claim the $33,000 first prize by defeating Allen Hopkins (second place, $15,000) and Louie Roberts (third place, $10,000).

(ROBERT E. GOODWIN)

[452.B.4.h.v.]

Bolivia

A landlocked republic in central South America, Bolivia is bordered by Brazil, Paraguay, Argentina, Chile, and Peru. Area: 1,098,581 sq km (424,165 sq mi). Pop. (1982 est.): 5,915,800, of whom more than 50% are Indian. Judicial cap.: Sucre (pop., 1982 est., 79,900). Administrative cap. and largest city: La Paz (pop., 1982 est., 881,400). Language (1978): Spanish 46%, Quechua 33%, Aymara 21%. Religion (1980): Roman Catholic 92.5%. Presidents in 1982, Gen. Celso Torrelio Villa until July 19, Brig. Gen. Guido Vildoso Calderón from July 21 until October 10, and, from October 10, Hernán Siles Zuazo.

Gen. Celso Torrelio Villa clung to power as Bolivia's president until July 1982 despite dissension among the armed forces, a burgeoning economic crisis, foreign debt difficulties, and the international isolation of his regime because of its alleged links with paramilitary groups and with the drug trade. As the crisis worsened, President Torrelio became desperate to reach agreement with civilian

Bolivia

Biographies:
see People of the Year

Biological Sciences:
see Life Sciences

Birth Statistics:
see Demography

Boating:
see Rowing; Sailing; Water Sports

Bobsledding:
see Winter Sports

Hernán Siles Zuazo was elected president of Bolivia by Congress on October 6. Siles Zuazo returned from two years of exile to lead that nation after a military junta had given up its attempt to run the country.

leaders so the Army could withdraw from the government. He decreed an amnesty to allow exiled political and trade union leaders to return and lifted the ban on the activities of political parties and unions. An army group, Nueva Razón de Patria, warned that it would start a "bloodbath" if the authorities carried through their plan for democracy by April 1983. Critics in the military stated that Nueva Razón's members were all officers linked to the drug trade who feared investigation into their activity by an incoming civilian regime.

On July 19 Torrelio announced his resignation from the presidency. Power was transferred to a junta composed of the commanders of the three armed services, and soon afterward they appointed Brig. Gen. Guido Vildoso Calderón, the army chief of staff, as head of state. The move was aimed at resolving a leadership crisis brought about by Col. Faustino Rico Toro, who had accused Torrelio of failing to halt deterioration in the economy and had named himself as the general's natural successor. On August 12 the new government announced that the forthcoming election would be contested under the electoral law of 1965 instead of that of 1980. Reaction by the political parties and unions was swift. Most of Bolivia was paralyzed by strikes, which hit all the main cities during August and September.

On September 17, after three days of inconclusive discussions, the senior military commanders decided to recall the Congress elected democratically in 1980. Under the plan the Congress was to reconvene at the beginning of October and confirm the results of the 1980 elections. These had been won by Hernán Siles Zuazo (*see* BIOGRAPHIES) of the left-wing Unidad Democrática y Popular, but the Army had not allowed him to take power. The military junta's decision to resign came at a time when chaotic management of the nation's finances led Bolivia to default on interest payments on its renegotiated foreign debt. The generals had failed to reach agreement with the International

Monetary Fund on austerity measures that might have helped to restart the flow of financial assistance to Bolivia.

On October 6 Congress elected Siles Zuazo president for a four-year term. Jaime Paz Zamora, a Socialist, was elected vice-president. The country's new president returned from exile in Peru and took office on October 10. In early November

BOLIVIA

Education. (1980) Primary, pupils 978,250, teachers 48,894; secondary and vocational, pupils 170,710, teachers (1975) 7,143; teacher training, pupils (1976) 17,000, teachers (1970) 344; higher (1978; universities only), students 44,946, teaching staff 2,797.

Finance. Monetary unit: peso boliviano, with (Sept. 20, 1982) an official rate of 44 pesos to U.S. $1 (free rate of 75 pesos = £1 sterling). Gold and other reserves (June 1982) U.S. $161 million. Budget (1980 actual): revenue 11,793,000,000 pesos; expenditure 21,521,000,000 pesos. Gross domestic product (1980) 134,987,000,000 pesos. Money supply (March 1982) 19,668,000,000 pesos. Cost of living (La Paz; 1975 = 100; April 1982) 1,123.2.

Foreign Trade. (1981) Imports U.S. $825.4 million; exports U.S. $908.5 million. Import sources (1979): U.S. 28%; Japan 18%; Argentina 11%; Brazil 9%; West Germany 8%. Export destinations (1979): U.S. 33%; Argentina 15%; U.K. 9%; Brazil 5%; The Netherlands 5%; West Germany 5%. Main exports: tin 38%; natural gas 38%; silver 8%; lead and zinc 6%; tungsten 5%.

Transport and Communications. Roads (1978) 38,866 km. Motor vehicles in use (1979): passenger 35,900; commercial 50,300. Railways: (1980) 3,929 km; traffic (1978) 398 million passenger-km, freight 593 million net ton-km. Air traffic (1981): 962 million passenger-km; freight 44.2 million net ton-km. Telephones (Dec. 1979) 125,800. Radio receivers (Dec. 1979) 500,000. Television receivers (Dec. 1979) 100,000.

Agriculture. Production (in 000; metric tons; 1981): barley c. 55; corn c. 250; rice c. 100; cassava c. 230; potatoes c. 950; sugar, raw value c. 266; bananas c. 220; oranges c. 88; coffee c. 22; cotton, lint c. 5; rubber c. 5. Livestock (in 000; 1981): cattle c. 4,100; sheep c. 8,900; goats c. 3,050; pigs c. 1,500; horses c. 410; asses c. 780.

Industry. Production (in 000; metric tons; 1980): tin 16; lead ore 17; antimony 15; tungsten (oxide content) 3.4; zinc 50; copper 1.6; silver (troy oz) 6,099; gold (troy oz) 52; cement (1979) 258; crude oil (1981) 1,045; natural gas (cu m) 2,320,000; petroleum products (1979) c. 1,320; electricity (kw-hr) 1,510,000.

President Siles announced an austerity program that he called a "necessary first step" toward economic recovery. Among other measures, strict controls were placed on foreign currency, and the exchange rate was fixed at 200 pesos to the U.S. dollar. Salaries of government officials, including President Siles, were lowered.

(MICHAEL WOOLLER)

Botswana

A landlocked republic of southern Africa and a member of the Commonwealth, Botswana is bounded by South Africa, a part of Bophuthatswana, South West Africa/Namibia, Zambia, and Zimbabwe. Area: 581,700 sq km (224,600 sq mi). Pop. (1981 prelim.): 936,600, almost 99% African. Cap. and largest city: Gaborone (pop., 1981 prelim., 59,700). Language: English (official) and Setswana. Religion: Christian 60%; animist. President in 1982, Quett Masire.

Botswana experienced a difficult economic year in 1982. Depressed diamond sales led to stockpiling, and demand for copper declined. As a result, the budget for 1982–83 forecast negative growth. Total exports for 1981, worth 340 million pula, were down from 389 million pula in 1980. In May 1982 the pula was devalued by 10%.

A conventional abattoir for frozen meat, replacing the planned cannery, was to open at Maun in January 1983, and another was to be built in Francistown. Although the Botswana Vaccine Institute, opened in October 1981, represented a vital advance, the cattle industry experienced a poor year as a result of the worst drought conditions since the 1960s. Contracts were awarded for Gaborone's new international airport.

In July Shell Coal Botswana began a feasibility study for a coal mine project in east central Botswana. Its target production figure of five million metric tons a year could earn Botswana 150 million pula annually. The new diamond mine at Jwaneng was opened in August 1982 by Pres. Quett Masire. Production forecasts of 4.5 million carats a year by 1985 represented a doubling of 1981 output.

(GUY ARNOLD)

BOTSWANA

Education. (1981) Primary, pupils 179,564, teachers (1980) 5,316; secondary, pupils 19,129, teachers (1980) 844; vocational (1980), pupils 2,206, teachers 259; teacher training, students 1,032, teachers (1980) 59; higher (1980), students 928, teaching staff 113.

Finance and Trade. Monetary unit: pula, with (Sept. 20, 1982) a free rate of 1.11 pula to U.S. $1 (1.89 pula = £1 sterling). Budget (1981–82 actual): revenue 265 million pula; expenditure 266.9 million pula. Foreign trade (1981): imports 670.3 million pula (88% from South Africa in 1979); exports 335.4 million pula (67% to Europe, 17% to U.S., 7% to South Africa in 1979). Main exports: diamonds 41%; copper-nickel ore 24%; meat 18%.

Agriculture. Production (in 000; metric tons; 1981): corn c. 15; sorghum c. 45; peanuts c. 2; beef and veal c. 47. Livestock (in 000; 1981): cattle c. 2,950; sheep c. 180; goats c. 680; chickens c. 870.

Industry. Production (in 000; metric tons; 1980): copper ore (metal content) 16; nickel ore (metal content) 15; coal 371; diamond (metric carats) 5,146; electricity (kw-hr) 470,000.

Bowling

Tenpin Bowling. WORLD. The fourth European Cup tournament for individuals was in May 1982 in Borås, Sweden. Each country in Europe was allowed to enter its national men's and women's champion of 1981. The cup was played in head-to-head round-robin matches. After the match games the four best women and men advanced to the finals. In the women's division Shelagh Leonard from Great Britain met Irene Groonert from The Netherlands in the final contest. Groonert won the first game 188–182, but in the second game Leonard closed with four strikes to score 242 and win the match and cup 424–381.

In the men's division the two finalists were Arne Svein Strøm of Norway, bowler of the year in 1981, and Olle Svensson of Sweden. Strøm showed again that world bowling writers had made the right selection when they voted him bowler of the year, winning the cup 374–357.

The European Youth Tenpin championships took place in Stuttgart, West Germany, in April. The nation that topped the tournament was Sweden, with five gold and five silver medals and one bronze. The host, West Germany, won the remaining three gold medals and also two bronze. The individual champions were Karin Glennert from Sweden for girls and Walter Meiburg of West Germany for boys.

The international bowling leaders approved membership applications from Bahrain and San Marino. This increased to 67 the number of national member federations in the Fédération Internationale des Quilleurs (FIQ), the world governing body for bowling sport. (YRJÖ SARAHETE)

UNITED STATES. Pete Weber of St. Louis, Mo., the 19-year-old son of Bowling Hall of Fame member Dick Weber, emerged as one of the most formidable competitors in Professional Bowlers Association (PBA) tournaments in 1982. The young Weber, whose opponents on the national tour sometimes included his father, won the PBA meets in Hartford, Conn., and Portland, Ore., and his earnings of $75,935 placed him sixth in that category with several tournaments remaining on the schedule.

The dominant male professional was Earl Anthony of Dublin, Calif., voted bowler of the year in 1974–76 and 1981 and a likely choice for 1982. Anthony captured three PBA titles and was the money leader with $133,895.

Mike Durbin won the Firestone Tournament of Champions, the $200,000 event that concludes the PBA's nationally televised winter tour. Durbin, from Chagrin Falls, Ohio, rolled strikes in six of the first seven frames in the title match to defeat Steve Cook of Roseville, Calif., 233–203. Durbin, who also won the Firestone in 1972, received $40,000 for his victory.

In the Masters Tournament of the American Bowling Congress (ABC), the winner of the $40,600 first prize was Joe Berardi of New York City. He defeated Ted Hannahs of Zanesville, Ohio, 236–216, in the final game.

Botswana

Bonds:
see Stock Exchanges

Books:
see Art Sales; Literature; Publishing

Bophuthatswana:
see South Africa

Botanical Gardens:
see Zoos and Botanical Gardens

Botany:
see Life Sciences

BOWLERS JOURNAL

Pete Weber, son of a famous bowling father, won two PBA tournaments during the year and was sixth among money winners with prizes totaling $75,935. Pete's father, Dick Weber, is a member of the Bowling Hall of Fame.

In the Regular Division team event of the ABC tournament, a club that competed on the final squad of the three-month-long meet, Carl's Bowlers Paddock, of Cincinnati, Ohio, rolled 3,268 to win. Rich Wonders of Racine, Wis., was the individual star of the tournament, as he won the Regular all-events title with a nine-game total of 2,076, shared the doubles honours with Darold Meisel of Milwaukee, Wis., with 1,364, and was a member of the Kendor Corp. unit from Racine that took the team all-events crown with 9,498. Bruce Bohm of Chicago bowled 748 to win the singles championship.

The largest prize in women's bowling again went to Japan's Katsuko Sugimoto, who triumphed in the Avon/Women's International Bowling Congress (WIBC) Queens tournament for the second successive year. Sugimoto won $20,525 by downing Nikki Gianulias of Vallejo, Calif., 160–137, in the final game, as both bowlers encountered numerous splits. A week later in the women's U.S. Open, Shinobu Saitoh of Japan took the $9,000 first prize by outdistancing a field of the best female professionals.

Open Division champions in the WIBC tournament were: team, Zavakos Realtors, Dayton, Ohio, 2,961; singles, Gracie Freeman, Alexandria, Va., 653; doubles, Shirley Hintz, Merritt Island, Fla., and Lisa Rathgeber, Palmetto, Fla., tied Pat Costello, Dublin, Calif., and Donna Adamek, Duarite, Calif., 1,264; all-events, Aleta Rzepecki, Detroit, 1,905. (JOHN J. ARCHIBALD)

Lawn Bowls. Open bowls and its relationship with the Commonwealth Games provided much of the news in 1982. The Games, held in September and October in Brisbane, Australia, greatly at-tracted amateur sports people, and in order to compete some decided not to accept money prizes in open tournaments. John Watson of Scotland won the Indoor Bowls World Championship, an amateur event, in February 1982 and was invited to the Target Bowls Championship, which carried the world's largest first prize, £5,050. He withdrew, however, in order to preserve his amateur status. Peter Bellis, winner of the New Zealand Open, refused the prize money and took the alternative award for an amateur. Outdoor world champion David Bryant had made his decision in 1980 when he accepted the £2,000 first prize at the first-ever open tournament. In 1982 he won the Kodak masters bowls tournament at Worthing, England, for the third time. Chris Ward won the English Bowling Association singles championship.

The biggest surprise came from Australia when John Snell, a silver medalist at both previous world championships and Commonwealth Games, remained an amateur only to be omitted from the Australian team for the 1982 Games.

In the Games, W. Wood won the singles for Scotland, Zimbabwe won the triples, Australia the fours, and Scotland the pairs.

(C. M. JONES)

Brazil

A federal republic in eastern South America, Brazil is bounded by the Atlantic Ocean and all the countries of South America except Ecuador and Chile. Area: 8,512,000 sq km (3,286,500 sq mi). Pop. (1982 est.): 124,342,600. Principal cities (pop., 1980 prelim.): Brasília (cap.; federal district) 411,300; São Paulo 12,719,100; Rio de Janeiro 9,153,200. Language: Portuguese. Religion: Roman Catholic 90.3%. President in 1982, Gen. João Baptista de Oliveira Figueiredo.

Domestic Affairs. Political events in Brazil were dominated by the elections on Nov. 15, 1982, to the 479 seats in the Chamber of Deputies, one-third of the 69 seats in the Senate, the state governorships and assemblies, and the municipalities. These elections were in connection with the *abertura* policy carried out by Pres. João Baptista de Oliveira Figueiredo's administration since it came to office in March 1979; this policy aimed at gradually returning the country to civilian rule and so ending the period of military government that began in March 1964. Five parties nominated 250,000 candidates for 44,000 posts. The parties were the government-sponsored Partido Democrático Social (PDS) and four opposition groupings: the Partido Movimento Democrático Brasileiro (PMDB), which was by far the largest of the four; the Partido Trabalhista Democrático (PTD); the Partido Trabalhista Brasileiro (PTB); and the Partido dos Trabalhadores (PT). Preliminary results published at the end of November established that the PDS gained 234 seats in the Chamber of Deputies as against the four opposition parties' 245, of which 199 were won by the PMDB. (*See* POLITICAL PARTIES.) The PMDB gained the state governorships of São Paulo, Minas Gerais, Paraná, Goiãs, Espírito

The world's largest hydroelectric facility, the Itaipú project on the Paraná River, was dedicated by the presidents of Braz l and Paraguay on November 5.
UPI

Santo, Amazonas, Pará, Acre, and Mato Grosso do Sul. Leonel Brizola won the state gubernatorial elections for Rio de Janeiro for the PTD; Brizola had been exiled because he was one of the leading figures in the regime of João Goulart in the early 1960s

BRAZIL

Education. (1979) Primary, pupils, 22,025,449, teachers 862,282; secondary, vocational, and teacher training, pupils 2,667,359, teachers 183,476; higher (1980), students 1,770,917, teaching staff 109,788.

Finance. Monetary unit: cruzeiro, with a free rate (Sept. 20, 1982) of 200.62 cruzeiros to U.S. $1 (343.96 cruzeiros = £1 sterling). Gold and other reserves (June 1982) U.S. $5,931,000,000. Budget (1981 actual): revenue 2,161,460,000,000 cruzeiros; expenditure 2,151,400,-000,000 cruzeiros. Gross national product (1981) 25,424,100,000,000 cruzeiros Money supply (June 1981) 1,552,900,000,000 cruzeiros. Cost of living (São Paulo; 1975 = 100; Nov. 1981) 3,223.2.

Foreign Trade. (1981) Imports 2,130,000,000,000 cruzeiros; exports 2,093,000,000,000 cruzeiros. Import sources (1980): U.S. 19%; Iraq 16%; Saudi Arabia 9%; West Germany 7%; Japan 5%. Export destinations (1980): U.S. 17%; West Germany 7%; Japan 6%; The Netherlands 6%; Argentina 5%; Italy 5%. Main exports (1980): coffee 14%; soybeans and products 12%; machinery 9%; iron ore 8%; sugar 6%; motor vehicles c. 5%.

Transport and Communications. Roads (1980) 1,394,686 km. Motor vehicles in use (1980): passenger 9,090,300; commercial 947,200. Railways: (1980) 31,127 km; traffic (1979) 11,395,000,000 passenger-km, freight 73,805,000,000 net ton-km. Air traffic (1981): 10,761,-000,000 passenger-km; freight 528.6 million net ton-km. Shipping (1981): merchant vessels 100 gross tons and over 627; gross tonnage 5,133,224. Shipping traffic (1981): goods loaded 123,990,000 metric tons, unloaded 64,066,000 metric tons. Telephones (Jan. 1980) 6,494,000. Radio receivers (Dec. 1979) 35 million. Television receivers (Dec. 1979) 15 million.

Agriculture. Production (in 000; metric tons; 1981): wheat 2,207; corn 21,098; rice 8,261; cassava 25,050; potatoes 1,911; sugar, raw value c. 8,500; tomatoes 1,493; dry beans 2,339; soybeans 15,290; bananas 6,696; oranges 9,315; coffee 1,878; cocoa c. 345; cotton, lint 613 sisal 243; tobacco 362; rubber c. 28; beef and veal c. 2,250 pork c. 980; fish catch (1980) c. 850; timber (cu m; 1980) c. 217,324. Livestock (in 000; 1981): cattle c. 93,000; pigs c. 35,000; sheep c. 18,000; goats c. 8,000; horses c. 6,300; chickens c. 430,000.

Industry. Fuel and power (in 000; metric tons; 1981): crude oil 10,688; coal (1980) 5,240; natural gas (cu m) c. 1,290,000; manufactured gas (cu m; 1979) c. 730,000; electricity (kw-hr; 1980) 137,383,000 (92% hydroelectric). Production (in 000; metric tons; 1981): cement 25,825; pig iron 11,248; crude steel 13,108; iron ore (exports; 68% metal content) 64,911; bauxite (1980) c. 4,150; manganese ore (1979) 2,809; gold (troy oz) c. 1,100; wood pulp (1979) 2,475; paper (1980) 3,469; fertilizers (nutrient content; 1980–81) nitrogenous c. 384, phosphate c. 1,623; passenger cars (including assembly; units) 662; commercial vehicles (units; 1980) 565. Merchant vessels launched (100 gross tons and over; 1981) 453,000 gross tons.

and had returned to Brazil following an amnesty for exiles introduced in 1979. Thus, opposition nominees were in charge of the administration of the country's three most economically significant and populous states: São Paulo, Rio de Janeiro, and Minas Gerais.

Nonetheless, the PDS gained an overall victory in the elections. Control of Congress was retained through its overall majority in the Senate, and it was expected to arrive at an accommodation with smaller opposition parties to ensure a government majority in the Chamber of Deputies. The PDS also won the remaining 13 of the 23 state governorships and controlled most of the state assemblies and local councils.

The government's authority over political events whatever the outcome of the elections was guaranteed by a package of reform measures introduced in July. This package stipulated that a two-thirds majority in the Chamber of Deputies was required for changes in the constitution; that the term of office for local councillors was extended from four to six years; and that the next municipal elections would take place in 1988 separately from congressional and gubernatorial elections. The reforms also increased representation of state assemblies and municipalities in the electoral college, which in late 1984 was to choose a new president to take office for a six-year term in March 1985. Meanwhile, in late November President Figueiredo undertook to cooperate with state governments administered by opposition forces and guaranteed that all development programs funded by federal government departments would continue.

The Economy. The economic performance in 1982 was not good and was affected by the international recession. Growth in gross domestic product (GDP) was expected to be nil or slightly negative; a decline of 1.9% had been recorded in 1981. Overall industrial output fell by 0.6% in the period January–September 1982 and by 5.2% in the year ended in September; only mining output recorded an increase — of 8% — over the same 12 months, largely because of a rise in iron-ore extraction. Agricultural production was expected to decline following an increase of 6.8% in 1981. The main reasons for this were poor coffee and soybean crops and cuts in official price and credit supports. Expansion in the service sector of the economy was patchy because of poor consumer demand resulting in part from unemployment and job insecurity as well as from

Brazil

Brazilian Literature:
see Literature

Bridge:
see Contract Bridge

Bridges:
see Engineering Projects

Brunei:
see Dependent States

high charges for credit. On the other hand, industrial employment improved. The jobless rate in the six main industrial cities—São Paulo, Rio de Janeiro, Pôrto Alegre, Belo Horizonte, Salvador, and Recife—declined from 8% in December 1981 to 5.4% in September 1982. The rate of inflation remained high, at 95.9%, in the 12 months ended in October 1982, and it was expected to be about 95% for the whole year, compared with the 1981 figure of 95.2%.

The external accounts weakened considerably. There was a trade surplus of $617 million in the period January–October, but the overall 1982 surplus was expected to be only $500 million, well short of the $3 billion target set in January. The current account deficit was estimated to have grown from $11 billion in 1981 to $14 billion because of interest payments on the external debt, which stood at $89 billion at the end of November. The government imposed a variety of stabilization measures between August and December, mainly involving restraints on monetary expansion and import controls. In December the International Monetary Fund tentatively agreed to extend $4.9 billion in credit, and additional loans were also sought from foreign banks.

The construction of the Itaipú hydroelectric project on the Paraná River on the border with Paraguay was completed during the year, and the project was inaugurated by President Figueiredo on November 5.

Foreign Affairs. U.S. Pres. Ronald Reagan visited Brazil in late November and early December: during his stay agreement was reached on creating closer economic and military links between the two countries. President Figueiredo visited the U.S. on May 10–14, but his stay was cut short by one day in protest against U.S. support for the U.K. in its conflict with Argentina in the South Atlantic. He visited Canada in late July and signed agreements for transactions in excess of $1 billion.

(ROBIN CHAPMAN)

Bulgaria

A people's republic of Europe, Bulgaria is situated on the eastern Balkan Peninsula along the Black Sea, bordered by Romania, Yugoslavia, Greece, and Turkey. Area: 110,912 sq km (42,823 sq mi). Pop. (1982 est.): 9,108,000, including 87% Bulgarians, 8.5% Turks, 2.5% Macedonians, and 2% Gypsies. Cap. and largest city: Sofia (pop., 1980 est., 1,056,900). Language: chiefly Bulgarian. Religion: official sources classify 35.5% of the population as religious, although this figure is suspect since the regime promotes atheism. Of those who practice religion, it is estimated that 26.7% are Bulgarian Orthodox, 7.5% Muslim, 0.7% Protestant, 0.5% Roman Catholic, and 0.1% Jewish. General secretary of the Bulgarian Communist Party and chairman of the State Council in 1982, Todor Zhivkov; chairman of the Council of Ministers (premier), Grisha Filipov.

After a two-year trial period in selected state enterprises, Bulgaria launched a "new mechanism" to manage its national economy on Jan. 1,

1982. Its main aims were to make central planning less cumbersome and to improve industrial efficiency. One innovation was to link pay with productivity. General Secretary Todor Zhivkov and Premier Grisha Filipov initially positioned themselves between the Politburo members who supported the reform and those wishing to maintain traditional conservative ideology; they finally joined the reformers.

Filipov visited Moscow in June and signed two agreements: on joint production between appropriate industrial enterprises, and on cooperation in prospecting for oil and gas on the Bulgarian continental shelf. Gen. Kenan Evren, the Turkish head of state, and Greek Prime Minister Andreas Papandreou visited Bulgaria in February and June, respectively. Both discussed the idea of a nuclear-free zone in the Balkans, Papandreou supporting it and Evren rejecting it.

In March Peko Takov retired from the Politburo and was replaced by Milko Balev. On his appointment as premier in June 1981, Filipov had ceased to be a member of the Central Committee; he was replaced by Kiril Zarev. Zhivko Popov, a former deputy foreign minister, was deprived of party membership and sentenced to 20 years' imprisonment for offenses involving illegal hard-currency transactions.

Bulgaria

Buddhism:
see Religion

Building and Construction Industry:
see Engineering Projects; Industrial Review

BULGARIA

Education. (1981–82) Primary, pupils 70,125, teachers 4,514; secondary, pupils 1,064,383, teachers 61,154; vocational, pupils 207,011, teachers 17,976; higher, students 72,386, teaching staff 11,579.

Finance. Monetary unit: lev, with (Sept. 20, 1982) a free exchange rate of 0.99 lev to U.S. $1 (1.70 leva = £1 sterling). Budget (1981 est.): revenue 15,385,000,000 leva; expenditure 15,370,000,000 leva.

Foreign Trade. (1981) Imports U.S. $10.8 billion; exports U.S. $10,685,000,000. Main import sources: U.S.S.R. 55%; East Germany 6%; West Germany 5%. Main export destinations: U.S.S.R. 48%; East Germany 6%; Libya 5%. Main exports (1980): machinery 35%; transport equipment 9%; tobacco and cigarettes 8%; chemicals 6%; fruit and vegetables 5%. Tourism (1980): visitors 5,485,800; gross receipts c. U.S. $260 million.

Transport and Communications. Roads (1980) 36,447 km (including 112 km expressways). Motor vehicles in use: passenger (1980) 815,549; commercial (including buses; 1979) c. 130,000. Railways: (1980) 4,341 km; traffic (1981) 6,960,000,000 passenger-km, freight 18,052,000,000 net ton-km. Air traffic (1980): c. 775 million passenger-km; freight c. 10 million net ton-km. Navigable inland waterways (1973) 471 km. Shipping (1981): merchant vessels 100 gross tons and over 188; gross tonnage 1,193,853. Telephones (Dec. 1980) 1,255,800. Radio licenses (Dec. 1980) 2,148,000. Television licenses (Dec. 1980) 1,652,000.

Agriculture. Production (in 000; metric tons; 1981): wheat 4,429; corn 2,477; barley 1,401; potatoes 407; sunflower seed c. 340; tomatoes c. 911; grapes 1,107; apples 393; tobacco 133; meat c. 650. Livestock (in 000; Jan. 1981): sheep 10,433; cattle 1,796; goats 467; pigs 3,808; horses 120; asses 341; chickens 39,877.

Industry. Fuel and power (in 000; metric tons; 1981): lignite 28,980; coal 250; crude oil (1980) c. 280; natural gas (cu m; 1980) 150,000; electricity (kw-hr) 36,964,000. Production (in 000; metric tons; 1981): cement 5,444; iron ore (33% metal content) 1,750; manganese ore (metal content; 1979) 12; copper ore (metal content; 1980) 62; lead ore (metal content; 1980) 110; zinc ore (1980) c. 87; pig iron 1,511; crude steel 2,483; sulfuric acid 919; nitric acid (1979) 878; soda ash (1979) 1,468; fertilizers (nutrient content; 1980) nitrogenous 730, phosphate 217; cotton yarn 85; cotton fabrics (m) 353,000; wool yarn 33; woolen fabrics (m) 38,000. Merchant vessels launched (100 gross tons and over; 1981) 108,000 gross tons.

Joint maneuvers of land, sea, and air forces of the Warsaw Pact members took place in the Varna area from September 25 to October 1.

(K. M. SMOGORZEWSKI)

Burma

A republic of Southeast Asia, Burma is bordered by Bangladesh, India, China, Laos, Thailand, the Bay of Bengal, and the Andaman Sea. Area: 676,577 sq km (261,228 sq mi). Pop. (1982 est.): 37,065,000. Cap. and largest city: Rangoon (pop., 1980 est., 2,186,000). Language: Burmese. Religion (1980): Buddhist 87%. Chairman of the State Council in 1982, U San Yu; prime minister, U Maung Maung Kha.

After a lull lasting nearly two years, there were indications during 1982 that a new round of clashes had begun between Burma's government security forces and the pro-Chinese Burmese Communist Party (BCP) insurgents. First news of resumed fighting came when the government announced on June 15 that 67 Communists had surrendered with their weapons in April and May. Foreign Minister U Chit Hlaing visited Beijing (Peking) in July to persuade the Chinese government to stop giving moral and material support to the BCP. There was no indication that he had succeeded in his effort, but unconfirmed reports circulating in Rangoon said the Chinese had indeed stopped giving aid to the BCP, which was now

entirely dependent on the opium trade for funds.

On the surface, government-level relations between China and Burma appeared good as China continued to extend technical and financial assistance. The Thai and Burmese armies agreed to increase their cooperation in fighting the Communist, Karen, and other insurgents in border regions. In September a group of five Karens unsuccessfully attempted to take over the Burmese radio and television headquarters in Rangoon.

Relaxation of the rigid isolationist policy of former chairman U Ne Win's government was benefiting the economy. Japan promised a $160 million loan for the fiscal year April 1982–March 1983, to develop liquefied petroleum gas and to modernize the railways. The Asian Development Bank sanctioned $18.5 million for upgrading half of the hospitals in the country and another $5 million for a crop intensification program.

(GOVINDAN UNNY)

Burma

Burundi

Burundi

A republic of eastern Africa, Burundi is bordered by Zaire, Rwanda, and Tanzania. Area 27,834 sq km (10,747 sq mi). Pop. (1982 est.): 4,778,000, mainly Hutu, Tutsi, and Twa. Cap. and largest city: Bujumbura (pop., 1979, 141,000). Language: Rundi and French. Religion (1980): Roman Catholic 78%; Protestant 5%; Muslim 1%; most of the remainder are animist. President in 1982, Col. Jean-Baptiste Bagaza.

During 1982 a number of small-scale but important economic developments took place in Burundi. The European Economic Community (EEC) granted a loan for the construction of two coffee treatment factories near Bujumbura. Burundi received considerable assistance from France. Pres. François Mitterrand visited Bujumbura during his African trip in October.

A sugar project, total cost $71 million, was partly funded by the Abu Dhabi Fund for Arab Economic Development with a loan of 20 million dirhams. The development was to include construction of an agricultural and industrial complex, and its target was to produce 16,000 metric

BURMA

Education. (1978–79) Primary, pupils 3,731,160, teachers 84,593; secondary, pupils 924,739, teachers 31,433; vocational, pupils 9,576, teachers 786; teacher training, students 5,163, teachers 370; higher, students 112,671, teaching staff 3,922.

Finance. Monetary unit: kyat, with (Sept. 20, 1982) a free rate of 7.89 kyats to U.S $1 (13.52 kyats = £1 sterling). Gold and other reserves (June 1982) U.S. $164 million. Budget (1980–81 est.): revenue 24,968,000,000 kyats; expenditure 27,104,000,000 kyats.

Foreign Trade. Imports (1980) 2,337,000,000 kyats; exports (1981) 3,305,000,000 kvats. Import sources (1978): Japan 31%; U.S. 12%; U.K. 9%; West Germany 6%; Singapore 6%; China 5%. Export destinations (1978): Switzerland 12%; Singapore 10%; Hong Kong 10%; Sri Lanka 10%; U.S. 9%; Japan 9%; Indonesia 9%. Main exports: rice 50%; teak 21%; pulses 7%; nonferrous metals and ores c. 6%.

Transport and Communications. Roads (1978) 22,471 km. Motor vehicles in use (1978): passenger 39,900; commercial (including buses) 42,300. Railways: (1978) 4,473 km; traffic (1979–80) c. 3,760,000,000 passenger-km, freight c. 600 million net ton-km. Air traffic (1980): c. 218 million passenger-km; freight c. 1.6 million net ton-km. Shipping (1981): merchant vessels 100 gross tons and over 96; gross tonnage 85,439. Telephones (Dec. 1978) 34,000. Radio receivers (Dec. 1979) 700,000.

Agriculture. Production (in 000; metric tons; 1981): rice c. 14,636; dry beans c. 195; onions c. 105; plantains c. 397; sesame seed 162; peanuts 476; cotton, lint c. 22; jute 34; tobacco c. 55; rubber c. 16; fish catch (1980) 585; timber (cu m; 1980) 26,582. Livestock (in 000; 1981): cattle c. 8,600; buffalo c. 1,950; pigs c. 2,200; goats c. 625; sheep c. 230; chickens c. 24,000.

Industry. Production (in 000; metric tons; 1979–80): cement 376; crude oil c. 1,650; natural gas (cu m) 364; electricity (kw-hr; 1980) 1,433,000; lead concentrates (metal content) c. 12; zinc concentrates (metal content) 6.1; tin concentrates (metal content) 1.4; tungsten concentrates (oxide content) 0.6; nitrogenous fertilizers (nutrient content; 1980–81) 60; cotton yarn 13.

BURUNDI

Education. (1979–80) Primary, pupils 159,729, teachers 4,623; secondary, pupils 7,967, teachers 501; vocational, pupils 1,918, teachers (1977–78) 139; teacher training, students 6,525, teachers 370; higher, students 1,763, teaching staff (1978–79) 248.

Finance. Monetary unit: Burundi franc, with (Sept. 20, 1982) a par rate of BurFr 90 to U.S. $1 (free rate of BurFr 154.30 = £1 sterling). Gold and other reserves (June 1982) U.S. $57 million. Budget (1981 actual): revenue BurFr 12,293,000,000; expenditure BurFr 14,427,500,000.

Foreign Trade. (1981) Imports BurFr 14,509,000,000; exports BurFr 6,423,000,000. Import sources: Iran 20%; Belgium-Luxembourg 15%; France 8%; Japan 8%; West Germany 7%; Kenya 7%; U.S. 5%. Export destinations: U.S. 44%; Belgium-Luxembourg c. 15%; West Germany 13%. Main export: coffee 88%.

Agriculture. Production (in 000; metric tons; 1981): sorghum c. 95; corn c. 140; cassava c. 1,200; sweet potatoes c. 928; peanuts c. 40; dry beans c. 175; bananas c. 983; coffee c. 30; tea c. 2; cotton, lint c. 3. Livestock (in 000; 1981): cattle c. 872; sheep c. 332; goats c. 686; pigs c. 37.

PAUL VAN RIEL—GAMMA/LIAISON

Burundi coffee farmers such as these could look forward to the construction of two local coffee treatment factories with funds loaned to their country by the European Economic Community.

tons of sugar a year. A plan to improve high-altitude food crops was launched with the aid of an EEC grant.

At the end of 1981 the Kagera River Basin project, involving the construction of a dam for hydroelectric purposes, was agreed on by Burundi, Rwanda, Tanzania, and Uganda. Burundi was to be compensated for the loss of 1,200 ha (2,970 ac) of land and the rehousing of 535 families. An International Development Association credit of $16 million, approved during 1982, was to be used to assist 150,000 farm families in Ngozi Province.

(GUY ARNOLD)

followed in September by the southern Chad leader Col. Wadal Abdelkadar Kamougue, who continued to Gabon.

In January Pres. Ahmadou Ahidjo undertook a four-day state visit to Nigeria, designed to improve the previous year's strained relations. Guy Penne, Pres. François Mitterrand's adviser on African affairs, visited Yaoundé in August.

There was slow but steady economic expansion. However, construction of a planned gas liquefaction plant at Kribi was postponed in June following a downward revision of Cameroon's estimated gas reserves.

(PHILIPPE DECRAENE)

Cameroon

Cameroon

A republic of west Africa on the Gulf of Guinea, Cameroon borders on Nigeria, Chad, the Central African Republic, the Congo, Gabon, and Equatorial Guinea. Area: 465,054 sq km (179,558 sq mi). Pop. (1982 est.): 8,853,000. Cap.: Yaoundé (pop., 1979, 400,000). Largest city: Douala (pop., 1979, 500,000). Language: English and French (official), Fang, Doula, and other Benue-Congo language groups. Religion (1980): Roman Catholic 35%; animist 25%; Muslim 22%; Protestant 18%. Presidents in 1982, Ahmadou Ahidjo and, from November 6, Paul Biya; prime ministers, Biya and, from November 6, Bello Bouba Maigari.

Ahmadou Ahidjo, who had served as president of Cameroon since it became independent in 1960, resigned on Nov. 6, 1982, and Prime Minister Paul Biya was sworn in to succeed him. Ahidjo was said to be suffering from exhaustion.

Developments in neighbouring Chad's civil war had repercussions in Cameroon during the year. In March the refugee camp at Kousseri was closed; more than 5,000 of its inmates returned to Chad, while several thousand others were moved to Poli, farther from the border. In June Chad's former president Goukouni Oueddei passed through Cameroon on his way to exile in Algeria. He was

Cambodia:
see Kampuchea

CAMEROON

Education. (1979–80) Primary, pupils 1,302,974, teachers (1978–79) 25,248; secondary, pupils 153,618, teachers (1978–79) 5,112; vocational, pupils 51,561, teachers 1,804; teacher training, students 1,677, teachers 168; higher, students 11,901, teaching staff 439.

Finance. Monetary unit: CFA franc, with (Sept. 20, 1982) a parity of CFA Fr 50 to the French franc and a free rate of CFA Fr 353 to U.S. $1 (CFA Fr 605 = £1 sterling). Budget (total; 1981–82 est.) balanced at CFA Fr 310 billion.

Foreign Trade. (1981) Imports CFA Fr 385.8 billion; exports CFA Fr 301.1 billion. Import sources (1980): France 45%; West Germany 8%; Japan 6%; U.S. 5%; Italy 5%. Export destinations (1980): U.S. 30%; France 22%; The Netherlands 19%; Italy 8%; West Germany 6%. Main exports (1980): crude oil 31%; coffee 23%; cocoa and products 21%; timber 11%.

Transport and Communications. Roads (classified; 1978) 30,167 km. Motor vehicles in use (1978): passenger 73,700; commercial (including buses) 61,200. Railways: (1980) c. 1,320 km; traffic (1981) 280 million passenger-km, freight 710 million net ton-km. Air traffic (1980): c. 477 million passenger-km; freight c. 29 million net ton-km. Shipping (1981): merchant vessels 100 gross tons and over 44; gross tonnage 39,597. Telephones (June 1973) 22,000. Radio receivers (Dec. 1979) 750,000.

Agriculture. Production (in 000; metric tons; 1981): corn c. 500; millet c. 400; sweet potatoes c. 135; cassava c. 1,011; bananas c. 97; plantains c. 1,026; peanuts c. 270; coffee c. 105; cocoa c. 110; palm kernels c. 46; palm oil c. 80; rubber c. 18; cotton, lint c. 22; timber (cu m; 1980) c. 9,976. Livestock (in 000; 1981): cattle c. 3,284; pigs c. 1,257; sheep c. 2,174; goats c. 2,434; chickens c. 10,712.

Industry. Production (in 000; metric tons; 1980): crude oil 2,800; cement (1979) 148; aluminum (1979) 53; electricity (kw-hr) c. 1,250,000.

Canada

Canada is a federal parliamentary state and member of the Commonwealth covering North America north of conterminous United States and east of Alaska. Area: 9,976,139 sq km (3,851,809 sq mi). Pop. (1982 est.): 24,625,000, including (1971) British 44.6%; French 28.7%; other European 23%; Indian and Eskimo 1.4%. Cap.: Ottawa (metro pop., 1981, 718,000). Largest cities: Toronto (metro pop., 1981, 2,998,900); Montreal (metro pop., 1981, 2,828,300). Language (mother tongue, 1981): English 61%; French 26%; others 13%. Religion (1971): Roman Catholic 46%; Protestant 42%. Queen, Elizabeth II; governor-general in 1982, Edward R. Schreyer; prime minister, Pierre Elliott Trudeau.

Domestic Affairs. Canada gained a new constitution in 1982. The document represented a striking personal achievement for Prime Minister Pierre Elliott Trudeau, who had made it a prized goal ever since his entrance into federal politics in 1965. Trudeau's popularity among Canadians slipped badly during the year, however, as his government failed to inspire confidence in its handling of the worst economic recession since the 1930s. Public opinion polls suggested that if an election were held, Trudeau's Liberals would be removed from office. But Trudeau, now 63 and enigmatic about his retirement, remained the dominant figure in Canadian political life.

Canada's new constitution was proclaimed by Elizabeth II, in her capacity as queen of Canada, in a dramatic ceremony on Parliament Hill in Ottawa on April 17. The document, called the Constitution Act 1982, contains the original statute that established the Canadian federation in 1867, the amendments made to it by the British Parliament over the years, and new material drawing on Trudeau's 1980 proposals and his later discussions with the provincial premiers. Of the ten premiers, all were present for the ceremony except René Lévesque, leader of the Parti Québécois (PQ) separatist government of Trudeau's own province.

Lévesque's absence was unfortunate, for it had been Quebec's discontent with Canadian federalism during its "Quiet Revolution" in the 1960s that had launched the momentum for change. Quebec's demands for a special status within the federal system had been rejected by Trudeau and the other provinces, as had its claim that it was entitled to an absolute veto over constitutional change.

The new constitution represented a compromise between Trudeau's vision of "one Canada with two official languages" and the particular concerns of the provinces. A novel part of the document was the Charter of Rights and Freedoms. This set down 34 rights to be observed across Canada, ranging from freedom of religion to language and educational rights based on the test of numbers. Many of the rights could be overridden by a "notwithstanding clause," which allowed both the federal Parliament and the provincial legislatures to set aside guarantees in the Charter. Designed to preserve parliamentary supremacy, a basic political principle in Canada, "notwithstanding clauses" would have to be renewed every five years to remain in force. Thus the Charter of Rights was not fully entrenched in the Canadian constitution as the Bill of Rights was in that of the United States.

The Constitution Act also contained a formula for its amendment in Canada, a subject that had defeated attempts to gain agreement on a new constitution as far back as 1927. Under the formula, resolutions of the Canadian Parliament, accompanied by the concurrence of two-thirds of the provinces (7) representing at least 50% of the country's population, would be sufficient to approve a constitutional amendment. Other sections of the act recognized the aboriginal and treaty rights of native peoples, strengthened the provinces' jurisdiction over their natural resources, and committed the central government to provide public services of reasonable quality across Canada by ensuring revenue (equalization) payments to the provinces.

The constitutional changes having been extensively discussed in Canada since their presentation in 1980, and their mode of procedure having secured judicial endorsement in 1981, there was little opposition when they came before the British Par-

Canada

CANADA

Education. (1981–82 prelim.) Primary, pupils 3,313,231; secondary, pupils 1,709,798; primary and secondary, teachers 271,034; higher, students 675,430, teaching staff 54,980.

Finance. Monetary unit: Canadian dollar, with (Sept. 20, 1982) a free rate of Can$1.23 to U.S. $1 (Can$2.11 = £1 sterling). Gold and other reserves (June 1982) U.S. $2,926,000,000. Budget (1981–82 est.): revenue Can$54.3 billion; expenditure Can$68.3 billion. Gross national product (1981) Can$328.5 billion. Money supply (April 1982) Can$33,170,000,000. Cost of living (1975 = 100; June 1982) 190.2.

Foreign Trade. (1981) Imports Can$83,950,-000,000; exports Can$87,027,000,000. Import sources: U.S. 69%; Japan 5%. Export destinations: U.S. 66%; Japan 5%. Main exports: motor vehicles 16%; machinery 11%; cereals 7%; natural gas 6%; chemicals 6%; crude oil and products 5%; metal ores 5%; newsprint 5%; nonferrous metals 5%; wood pulp 5%. Tourism (1980): visitors 12,426,000; gross receipts U.S. $2,284,000,000.

Transport and Communications. Roads (1976) 884,273 km. Motor vehicles in use (1979): passenger 9,985,150; commercial 2,854,200. Railways: (1979) 67,563 km; traffic (state only; 1980) 2,856,000,000 passenger-km, freight 228,117,000,000 net ton-km. Air traffic (1981): 31,401,000,000 passenger-km; freight 776.5 million net ton-km. Shipping (1981): merchant vessels 100 gross tons and over 1,300; gross tonnage 3,158,864. Shipping traffic (includes Great Lakes and St. Lawrence traffic; 1979): goods loaded 134,639,000 metric tons, unloaded 67,414,-000 metric tons. Telephones (Jan. 1980) c. 17.3 million. Radio receivers (Dec. 1979) 26,142,000. Television receivers (Dec. 1979) 11,040,000.

Agriculture. Production (in 000; metric tons; 1981): wheat 24,519; barley 13,384; oats 3,570; rye 964; corn 6,214; potatoes 2,555; tomatoes c. 480; apples 409; rapeseed 1,794; linseed 477; soybeans 631; tobacco c. 116; beef and veal c. 1,020; fish catch (1980) 1,305; timber (cu m; 1980) c. 161,366. Livestock (in 000; Dec. 1980): cattle c. 12,468; sheep 488; pigs 9,585; horses c. 350; chickens 82,493.

Industry. Labour force (March 1981) 11,585,000. Unemployment (Dec. 1981) 8.5%. Index of industri-al production (1975 = 100; 1981) 117. Fuel and power (in 000; metric tons: 1981): coal 32,854; lignite 6,797; crude oil c. 61,600; natural gas (cu m) c. 73,000,000; electricity (kw-hr) 377,624,000 (68% hydroelectric and 10% nuclear in 1980). Metal and mineral production (in 000; metric tons; 1981): iron ore (shipments; 67% metal content) 49,488; crude steel 14,603; copper ore (metal content) 689; nickel ore (metal content 1980) 195; zinc ore (metal content) 1,096; lead ore (metal content) 332; aluminum (exports; 1980) 1,074; uranium ore (metal content; 1980) 7.5; asbestos (1980) 1,335; gold (troy oz) c. 1,590; silver (troy oz) c. 35,000. Other production (in 000; metric tons; 1981): cement 9,598; wood pulp (1979) 19,322; newsprint 8,946; other paper and paperboard (1979) 5,033; sulfuric acid 4,117; plastics and resins (1978) c. 1,300; synthetic rubber 263; fertilizers (nutrient value; 1980–81) nitrogenous c. 1,755, phosphate c. 724, potash c. 7,337; passenger cars (units) c. 810; commercial vehicles (units) c. 450. Dwelling units completed (1981) 175,000. Merchant vessels launched (100 gross tons and over; 1981) 75,000 gross tons.

Canadian Prime Minister Pierre Trudeau displayed his happiness as Britain's Queen Elizabeth II signed a constitutional proclamation on April 17 for Canada on a visit to Ottawa. About 30,000 people turned out in the rain to watch the historic event.

liament early in 1982. All major parties supported them, although some MP's felt that native rights were inadequately protected. The queen gave royal assent to the Constitution Act on March 29, 115 years to the day after Queen Victoria, her great-great-grandmother, had approved the federation act of 1867. Thus the last legal tie with Great Britain was severed, and Canada became a fully sovereign state.

Though the people of Quebec were deeply divided over the merits of the new constitution, Lévesque's government went ahead with its opposition to the changes. The PQ government took its case to the courts, but the Quebec Court of Appeal, on April 7, held that Quebec did not possess a veto over constitutional change, even if it affected provincial jurisdiction. Again, on September 8, the Superior Court of Quebec held that sections of Quebec's controversial language law, Bill 101, were unconstitutional because they conflicted with the new Charter of Rights. Bill 101 required English-speaking Canadian parents educated outside Quebec to send their children to French schools if they moved to Quebec. The Charter, on the other hand, guarantees minority language education in all provinces for children of Canadian citizens where numbers warrant the establishment of schools. Quebec's claim to a constitutional veto was decisively rejected by the Supreme Court of Canada, 9–0, on December 6.

The unpopularity of the Trudeau government derived from its inability to improve the country's weak economic condition. Finance Minister Allan MacEachen's budget of Nov. 12, 1981, had to be sharply modified in the face of widespread criticism. His second budget, proposed on June 28, 1982, was better received. Nevertheless, MacEachen left the Finance Ministry on September 10, moving to External Affairs, a post he had held

from 1974 to 1976. The new minister of finance was Marc Lalonde, who had promoted the Canadian national thrust in developing oil and gas resources while he was minister of energy, mines, and resources.

In August it was announced that public opinion polls showed the Liberal Party with a 28% popularity rating, its lowest in 40 years. Conservative support stood at 47%. Three federal by-elections on October 12 demonstrated the Liberals' unpopularity. The Conservatives won two seats, a gain of one, and the New Democratic Party (NDP) won the other. The results did not affect the Liberals' comfortable majority in the House of Commons, where the party occupied 146 of 282 seats. The Conservatives held 102 seats, the NDP 33, and there was one independent.

Five provinces went to the polls in 1982, and in four instances sitting governments were returned. The exception was Saskatchewan, where an 11-year-old NDP government under Allan Blakeney was soundly defeated on April 26. Led by Grant Devine (*see* BIOGRAPHIES), the Conservatives won 57 of the 64 seats in the legislature, the remainder going to the NDP. The party capitalized on popular discontent with the Blakeney government and offered tax cuts on gasoline and lower mortgage interest rates. Next door, in Alberta, another Conservative administration, under Edgar Peter Lougheed, won triumphant reelection on November 2. Having presided since 1971 over an oil boom that made Alberta the wealthiest province of Canada, Lougheed's Conservatives gained 75 of the 79 seats in the legislature. The once-powerful Social Credit Party, dominant in Alberta for 36 years before 1971, was eliminated in the legislature, as was a separatist member elected earlier in the year.

The other three elections were in Atlantic Canada. In Newfoundland Conservative Premier Brian

Peckford won a resounding vote of confidence in his struggle with Ottawa over the control of off-shore mineral resources. In an April 6 election the Conservatives captured 44 seats to the Liberals' 8 in the 52-seat House of Assembly. In a quiet contest in Prince Edward Island on September 27, Conservative Premier James Lee, sworn into office ten months earlier, led his party to a 22–10 victory over the Liberal opposition. Finally, in New Brunswick, Richard Hatfield, another Conservative who had been premier since 1970, won an unprecedented fourth term in office on October 12 when his party captured 39 seats in the 58-seat legislature. The Liberals won 17 seats, gaining an additional one in a recount. For the first time in New Brunswick's history, an NDP member was elected. The elections left Conservative administrations in all four Atlantic provinces, in Ontario, and in Saskatchewan and Alberta. No Liberal government was in power in any province in 1982.

The Economy. Throughout 1982 Canada endured the longest and most severe economic slump since the great depression of the 1930s. From mid-1981 to mid-1982 economic production slipped 6%. The gross national product, on a seasonally adjusted annual basis, was expected to total $349.9 billion, but this figure masked a real-term decline in output. The world recession, dampening mineral prices, severely affected the mining and energy sectors of the economy. Merchandise exports were surprisingly strong, and the cumulative surplus of exports over imports for the first nine months of the year amounted to a record $12.7 billion.

High interest rates, a serious problem in 1981, moderated as the Bank of Canada lending rate dropped steadily to 11.6% in mid-October. This brought down loan and mortgage rates, which in turn stimulated stock market gains. The Canadian dollar recovered somewhat from the shocks it had taken in 1981, moving from a low of 76 U.S. cents in June to 81–82 cents four months later. The rate of inflation also fell, although not as steeply as in the U.S. In October it stood at 10% over the previous 12 months, the lowest increase since the summer of 1980. The cost of checking inflation, the prime objective of the Trudeau government, was a disturbing increase in unemployment. The unemployment rate in November was 12.7% on a seasonally adjusted basis, a level unsurpassed since the '30s.

The dismal performance of the economy was symbolized by the collapse of several large projects in the energy field. The first to go was the $13.5 billion Alsands project to recover synthetic crude from the vast oil sands deposits of northern Alberta. It collapsed on April 30 when the last three of the eight companies in the consortium turned down an offer of tax and royalty concessions held out by the federal and Alberta governments. The high cost of construction, reduced cash flows for the oil companies, and uncertain world prices for oil killed the project. At the same time, the Alaska Highway gas pipeline suffered a blow when a further two-year delay in financing the project was announced in New York. Since 1977, when Canada and the U.S. agreed to build the line, costs of construction had soared from about $10 billion to

perhaps $35 billion. Completion was now scheduled for 1989, but there were doubts that the major part of the pipeline would ever be built. The southern portion of the line, the "prebuild" section, was completed on time within budget and began moving natural gas to U.S. markets on September 1. However, it represented only 837 km (520 mi) of the 7,700-km (4,800-mi) route.

The largest Canadian oil company, Dome Petroleum Ltd. of Calgary, Alta., required a massive injection of capital from the federal government and four chartered banks at the end of September. A total of $1 billion in new capital was put into Dome to help offset its $7.4 billion debt. Canada's hopes of achieving self-sufficiency in oil by 1990, a goal of the Trudeau government, now rested on the promising oil and gas exploration in the Beaufort Sea, a new oil field and pipeline at Norman Wells in the Northwest Territories, the Hibernia field off the coast of Newfoundland, and gas exploration activities around Sable Island off the Nova Scotia coast.

There was no agreement among the various levels of government in Canada on how to deal with the economy. This was demonstrated at a conference of first ministers in Ottawa, February 2–4, which broke up without reaching any consensus. In introducing his June 28 budget to the House of Commons, MacEachen admitted that the recession had undercut his efforts to reduce the federal government's deficit. The revised shortfall was placed at $19.6 billion, the largest in Canadian history. MacEachen's budget put limits on the indexing factor for personal income tax exemptions: 6% in 1983 and 5% in 1984. (Since 1973 indexing had been tied to the rate of inflation.) Wage controls at 6% for the current year and 5% for 1983 were imposed immediately on 500,000 federal public employees, ranging from civil servants to judges and members of Parliament. Old-age security payments and family allowances were also to be curtailed by being tied to the same 6 and 5% increases. MacEachen also gave a commitment to try to keep

Peter Lougheed's Conservative Party won a large election victory in Alberta on November 2. The Conservatives captured 75 of the 79 seats in the provincial legislature.

price increases down in all federally regulated industries.

Invited to endorse the federal government's restraint program at a special meeting held in Ottawa two days after the budget, the provinces balked. They insisted that they would control their spending in ways suited to their own circumstances and needs. Over the next few months all the provinces except Manitoba announced plans of restraint for public sector employees, and many of them imposed restraints on their municipalities as well. Lelonde, the new finance minister, issued an "economic statement" on October 27, when Parliament reconvened after the summer recess, explaining that the federal deficit had risen to $23.6 billion from MacEachen's June 28 forecast. The minister announced that $150 million would be redirected from government spending into job creation before April 1983.

Foreign Affairs. Trudeau's efforts to build a bridge between the industrialized North and the less developed South met failure in 1982. Global talks on restructuring the world economy did not get under way, despite guarded encouragement provided by the economic summit conference at Versailles, France, which Trudeau attended in June. The annual meeting of the International Monetary Fund in Toronto, September 6–9, largely failed to mention global negotiations for a new international economic order.

Trudeau made an 11-day trip to Europe to attend the Versailles economic summit (June 4–6), the results of which he described as "disappointing."

One Canadian expressed his opinion over the Trudeau government's budget. After much criticism, the government proposed a revised budget on June 28.

CANADIAN PRESS

Later, at the NATO meeting in Bonn, West Germany, on June 10, he was critical of the failure to discuss the deeper problems of the alliance. He said he did not agree with the Reagan administration's policy of linking disarmament talks to Soviet behaviour in other areas. On June 18, speaking before the UN special session on disarmament, he called on the two superpowers to give their undivided attention to arms reductions.

Canada imposed sanctions against Poland and the Soviet Union on February 23 in order to dramatize the government's unhappiness over the establishment of martial law in Poland. The sanctions, symbolic rather than substantial, resembled those laid down by other members of the Western alliance. Canada condemned Argentina's resort to force to settle the Falkland Islands dispute by banning imports and discouraging exports on April 12. Exports to Argentina amounted to only $150 million in 1981, much of it resulting from the sale of a Canadian-made CANDU nuclear reactor.

Canada was touched by international terrorism on August 27 when the military attaché at the Turkish embassy was murdered in Ottawa. The attack appeared to be the action of extremists seeking revenge for the Turkish massacre of Armenians during World War I. Another incident occurred on October 15 when a powerful blast damaged a Toronto plant making guidance systems for the U.S. nuclear cruise missile. Seven persons, including three policemen, were injured. The plant had been a focus of antinuclear demonstrations since March 17, when the Trudeau Cabinet announced that approval in principle had been given to test unarmed cruise missiles in northern Canada. A Canadian economics professor, Hugh Hambleton, was sentenced in London's Old Bailey court on December 7 to ten years in prison after being convicted of passing top secret NATO information to the Soviets while working for the alliance in Paris between 1956 and 1961.

A record grain sale worth $1.3 billion was made to the Soviet Union in October, the first signed with that country in the 1982–83 crop year. On June 10 Mexico announced the cancellation of its huge nuclear program, thus dashing Canada's hopes of selling it a CANDU reactor. This was a severe blow to the Canadian nuclear industry, which faced large layoffs unless new orders were found. Better news came on May 18 with the award of a contract to Bombardier Inc., a Quebec company, to build 825 subway cars for New York City. Valued at $1 billion, this was the largest export contract ever awarded a Canadian manufacturer. After strong representations by the Canadian government, Japan agreed to limit its car exports to Canada to 153,000 vehicles in 1982, down about 25% from the year before.

Canadian climbers conquered the highest mountain on earth twice in 1982. With two Sherpa guides, Laurie Skreslet, 32, of Calgary, reached the top of Mt. Everest on October 4. Three days later Patrick Morrow, 29, of Kimberley, B.C., also reached the summit. The eight-man Canadian team was the 26th expedition to climb the mountain since the summit was first conquered in 1953.

(D. M. L. FARR)

STRAINS ALONG THE BORDER

by Peter Ward

Hard economic times and conflicting political philosophies in 1982 created what some critics called the worst climate of the century between Canada and the U.S. U.S. policy in Central America came under fire from Canada; Canadian policies of economic nationalism annoyed Washington. Beset with rising unemployment, both countries competed for jobs in the staggering North American automotive industry. Neither capital thought its neighbour was taking the right approach to economic recovery.

Neighbourhood Quarrels. Canadian politicians blamed the high-interest-rate policies of the Reagan administration for even higher Canadian interest rates; Americans were critical about the dismal Canadian performance in productivity, coupled with average wage increases greater than those in the U.S. In both nations businessmen went bankrupt by the thousands, while unemployment soared to post-Depression record levels. Paul Robinson, Jr., the U.S. ambassador to Canada, publicly criticized what he termed overly generous Canadian social policies, and Canada fought U.S. plans to cut back environmental protection budgets, even in the pages of U.S. newspapers.

Acid rain—the result of aerial pollution by industry in both countries—became an important political cause in Canada, and Canadians openly lobbied U.S. legislators to take action. As the year progressed, Americans grew angrier over Canada's Foreign Investment Review Agency, which monitors all foreign investment in Canada. Meanwhile, Canadians lashed out at the U.S. for flexing its economic muscle to stop other nations from cooperating with the Soviet plan to build a natural gas pipeline from Siberia to Western Europe.

Prime Minister Pierre Elliott Trudeau even backhanded Pres. Ronald Reagan in public with a verbal shot at the Bonn, West Germany, summer summit. While the leaders were lining up for photographs, a reporter yelled a question at the president. Trudeau loudly advised the reporter to "ask Al"—a clear indi-

cation that, in Trudeau's opinion, then U.S. secretary of state Al Haig was the one who should answer, not the president. Yet on several occasions Trudeau took pains to downplay the differences between Canada and the U.S. In September, during a lengthy radio interview, he said the Reagan administration, like previous U.S. governments, understood Canadian problems and the difficulties of solving them. Trudeau blamed the world economic recession for exaggerating the difficulties and politicians on both sides of the border for trying to protect their constituencies, even at the expense of the other nation.

The Economic Disagreement. No matter what the economic times, it would be difficult not to notice the difference between the right-wing Reagan administration and Trudeau's Liberal government, which had become almost the North American equivalent of what the Europeans call social democratic.

Reagan's policy was to lessen government involvement with the economy. Trudeau believed in a partnership between business, government, and labour, with government exerting considerable influence over business and competing with the private sector through government-owned enterprises. Canada's national energy policy of 1980, for example, was theoretically designed to increase Canadian ownership over the oil and gas industry, but in fact it increased government control over the industry much more rapidly. Canadian control over the private sector of the industry went from 22.3 to 24.9% during 1981, while government involvement rose from 3.8 to 7.9%. In addition, complex government regulations allowed Ottawa to keep a tight rein on privately owned oil and gas companies.

During 1981 the national energy policy was the pet peeve of the Reagan administration because, in the U.S. view, it allowed Canadians to take over U.S. assets in Canada at fire-sale prices. In 1982 the Foreign Investment Review Agency (FIRA) replaced the energy situation as the aspect of Canadian economic policy most disliked by U.S. critics. Trudeau added salt to the wounds when he switched Marc Lalonde, architect of the national energy policy, from the energy portfolio to the key task of finance minister. Both Trudeau and Lalonde defended FIRA as a mechanism that did for Canada what other governments do by more devious means. On the surface, FIRA appeared to be something of a paper tiger. The agency is empowered to allow or disallow takeovers of Canadian enterprises by foreign investors. It could also prevent a foreign firm from selling assets in Canada to another foreign company. In 1979–80 FIRA approved 92% of the cases it decided, and in 1980–81 it approved 88% of takeovers worth Can$5,350,000,000.

Peter Ward operates Ward News Services Canada in the Parliamentary Press Gallery, Ottawa.

A huge 380-metre (1,250-foot) smokestack rises above the nickel smelter at Sudbury, Ontario; 50–70% of the chemical compounds that fell on Canada in the form of acid rain came from industrial operations in the U.S., but the Sudbury smelter remained the single largest pollutant source in Canada.

Thomas d'Aquino, president of Canada's prestigious Business Council on National Interests, said the major areas of foreign investor concern over FIRA centred around the fact that the agency could block sales of assets by one foreign owner to another, thus diminishing the value of holdings. FIRA also sometimes required foreign investors to buy Canadian, and the agency could take months to make some decisions, then rule without offering explanations.

The reluctance of foreign investors to struggle through the FIRA process, coupled with the international recession, cut off much foreign capital that might have come to Canada. The result was downward pressure on the Canadian dollar, requiring higher Canadian interest rates as a counterbalance. The federal deficit, estimated by the government to be in excess of $23.6 billion for fiscal 1982–83, as well as deficits on other levels of government, placed a terrible strain on the nation's capital resources, again pressuring interest rates upward. Further pressure came from the estimated $20 billion that left the country during 1981 and '82 to buy out foreign ownership of various companies. Canadian government leaders blamed high interest rates in the U.S. for high rates in Canada. Americans argued that economic nationalism and the huge government deficit were the real villains.

Acid Rain. As predicted by economists on both sides of the border, the economic disagreements were spilling over into other areas. Acid rain was the issue that took the spotlight in 1982. Thousands of lakes in both Canada and the U.S. were dying and hundreds were dead because of increased acidic content in the rain and snow. Coal-burning electrical generating stations and smelters like the giant Inco mill at Sudbury, Ont., spew out toxic waste, particularly sulfur dioxide. This mixes with the moisture in the upper atmosphere and falls to Earth as a mild acid. The acid kills aquatic life in lakes and was already affecting the growth of timber. The $10 billion-a-year forestry industry of eastern Canada was in danger.

Canada's environment minister, John Roberts, called acid rain the greatest problem between the U.S. and Canada and probably the most serious long-term problem facing Canada. Opinion polls showed that most Canadians were aware of the threat from acid rain and were concerned about it, while a far lower percentage of Americans realized the dangers. Canada was particularly vulnerable because the lakes in the Precambrian Shield, which underlies much of Canada, are granite-based. Lakes with limestone-base rock are better able to withstand the pollution onslaught because the limestone tends to neutralize the acid.

In the late summer a joint study by the C. D. Howe Institute in Montreal and the Washington-based National Planning Association warned that the acid rain situation was rapidly reaching crisis proportions. The study reported that 50% of the acid rain falling in Canada came from the U.S., primarily from utility generating sites in the Tennessee Valley, while only 15% of U.S. acid rain came from Canadian sources. However, the largest acid rain producer on the continent was the Inco smelter.

President Reagan was slashing environmental budgets and had rated industrial efficiency higher than fighting pollution. Environment Minister Roberts pledged to cut Canadian acid-rain-producing emissions 50% by 1990 if the U.S. would do the same, but installation of the necessary equipment to clean stack gases would add 10% or more to utility bills in the U.S.

Like many of the disagreements between the two close neighbours and best friends, acid rain and the economic issue were subtly related to a basic difference in national philosophies. The U.S. was founded on the ideals of life, liberty, and the pursuit of happiness, and the rights of the individual are considered to be paramount. It has been said that Canadians would rather have peace, order, and good government, even if that means more government involvement in society, more restrictions on freedoms of the individual, and a value system that places security for the poor ahead of creating a "good climate" for the business community.

Cape Verde

An independent African republic, Cape Verde is located in the Atlantic Ocean about 620 km (385 mi) off the west coast of Africa. Area: 4,033 sq km (1,557 sq mi). Pop. (1980 prelim.): 296,100. Cap. and largest city: Praia (pop., 1980 prelim., 37,500). Language: Portuguese. Religion (1980): 96% Roman Catholic. President in 1982, Aristide Pereira; premier, Pedro Pires.

Pres. Aristide Pereira of Cape Verde expressed hope during 1982 that the disagreement between his country and Guinea-Bissau could be resolved. The African Party for the Independence of Cape Verde, however, objected to the fact that the ruling party of Guinea-Bissau continued to call itself the African Party for the Independence of Guinea-Bissau and Cape Verde. In September Cape Verde was host to the other Portuguese-speaking African states, including Guinea-Bissau.

As a result of drought, the harvest was the worst since 1977. Nonetheless, Cape Verde donated flour, rice, and beans to The Gambia to assist its relief program. An agrarian reform bill was aimed at abolishing private leasing of land, but since the Roman Catholic Church was the country's largest landowner, the reform became a sensitive issue.

Supreme Court Judge Antonio Caldiera Marques sought political asylum in Portugal on the grounds that all chances of democratization in Cape Verde had been exhausted and that there was systematic abuse of human rights and freedom. Exiles in Lisbon established a Cape Verde Human Rights Association. The trial of 21 Cape Verdians who had attempted a rebellion in August 1981 resulted in all but 3 receiving prison sentences.

(GUY ARNOLD)

CAPE VERDE

Education. (1980–81) Primary, pupils 50,661, teachers 1,436; secondary, pupils 8,716, teachers (1979–80) 293; vocational, pupils (1979–80) 632, teachers 40; teacher training, pupils (1977–78) 198, teachers (1976–77) 32.

Finance and Trade. Monetary unit: Cape Verde escudo, with (Sept. 20, 1982) a free rate of 54.71 escudos to U.S. $1 (93.80 escudos = £1 sterling). Budget (1979 est.) balanced at 1,327,000,000 escudos. Foreign trade (1979): imports 1,986,900,000 escudos; exports 92.1 million escudos. Import sources (1978): Portugal 33%; The Netherlands 8%; West Germany 7%; U.S. 6%; U.K. 5%; France 5%. Export destinations (1978): Portugal 42%; Angola 18%; U.K. 11%; Zaire 7%. Main exports (1978): fish 32%; salt 17%; bananas 10%; machinery 10%.

Transport. Shipping (1981): merchant vessels 100 gross tons and over 20; gross tonnage 10,793. Shipping traffic (1978): goods loaded 22,000 metric tons, unloaded 218,000 metric tons.

Central African Republic

The landlocked Central African Republic is bounded by Chad, the Sudan, the Congo, Zaire, and Cameroon. Area: 622,436 sq km (240,324 sq mi). Pop. (1981 est.): 2,392,700. Cap. and largest city: Bangui (pop., 1981 est., 387,100). Language: French (official), local dialects. Religion (1980):

CENTRAL AFRICAN REPUBLIC

Education. (1977–78) Primary, pupils 238,605, teachers 3,690; secondary, pupils 46,084, teachers 462; vocational, pupils 2,523, teachers 118; teacher training, students 51, teachers 12; higher, students 7,547, teaching staff 405.

Finance. Monetary unit: CFA franc, with (Sept. 20, 1982) a parity of CFA Fr 50 to the French franc and a free rate of CFA Fr 353 to U.S. $1 (CFA Fr 605 = £1 sterling). Budget (total; 1980 est.) balanced at CFA Fr 25,447,000,000.

Foreign Trade. (1980) Imports CFA Fr 17,009,000,000; exports CFA Fr 24,384,000,000. Import sources: France 61%; Japan 7%. Export destinations: France 52%; Belgium-Luxembourg 14%; Israel 8%; U.S. 5%. Main exports: timber 29%; coffee 27%; diamonds 25%; cotton 7%.

Agriculture. Production (in 000; metric tons; 1981): millet c. 50; corn c. 40; cassava c. 1,021; peanuts c. 125; bananas c. 82; plantains c. 62; coffee 17; cotton, lint c. 8. Livestock (in 000; 1981): cattle c. 1,272; pigs c. 135; sheep c. 86; goats c. 951; chickens c. 1,600.

Industry. Production (in 000): electricity (kw-hr; 1980) 64,000; diamonds (metric carats; 1979) c. 300; cotton fabrics (m; 1978) 2,619.

Protestant 50%; Roman Catholic 33.1%; tribal 12%; Muslim 3.2%; Anglican 1.4%; Baha'i 0.3%. Head of state and chairman of the Military Committee of National Recovery in 1982, Gen. André Kolingba.

An unsuccessful coup attempt on the night of March 3–4, 1982, brought renewed repression of the political opponents of the regime and strained relations with France. Former premier Ange Patassé, who had returned to Bangui on February 27 after several months of voluntary exile in France, was accused of complicity in the attempt and took refuge in the French embassy. French Pres. François Mitterrand's adviser on African affairs, Guy Penne, flew to Bangui and, after negotiations rendered delicate by Gen. André Kolingba's suspicion that the French Socialist Party had encouraged Patassé, the latter was flown in a French military aircraft to asylum in Togo on April 13. Abel Goumba, another leading opponent of the regime, who nevertheless had been appointed rector of the University of Bangui in January, was arrested in August. Relations with France improved when Kolingba visited Paris in October.

Diplomatic relations with Libya, suspended since 1980, were renewed in September 1982.

(PHILIPPE DECRAENE)

Chad

A landlocked republic of central Africa, Chad is bounded by Libya, the Sudan, the Central African Republic, Cameroon, Nigeria, and Niger. Area: 1,284,000 sq km (495,755 sq mi). Pop. (1982 est.): 4,752,000, including Africans (Saras, Tebu, Tama, Masalit) and Arabs. Cap. and largest city: N'Djamena (pop., 1979 est., 303,000). Language: French (official). Religion (1980): Muslim 44%; Christian 33%; animist 23%. President to June 7, 1982, Goukouni Oueddei; head of state from June 19 and president from October 21, Hissen Habré.

For Chad, 1982 was marked by the irresistible rise of Hissen Habré (see BIOGRAPHIES), leader of the Armed Forces of the North (FAN), who in June took over the country's destiny from Goukouni Oueddei and his Transitional Government of Na-

Cape Verde

Central African Republic

Chad

Canadian Literature:
see Literature

Canoeing:
see Water Sports

Catholic Church:
see Religion

Cave Exploration:
see Speleology

Census Data:
see Demography; see also the individual country articles

Central America:
see Latin-American Affairs; articles on the various countries

Ceramics:
see Materials Sciences

Ceylon:
see Sri Lanka

PHILIPPE LEDRU—SYGMA

Hissen Habré, leader of the Armed Forces of the North (FAN), took command of Chad in June. Two of his rivals fled into exile and one was accidentally killed when he was hit by an airplane propeller.

tional Union (GUNT). The Organization of African Unity (OAU) peacekeeping force, which had arrived in N'Djamena in November 1981, left the country in July 1982. The decision to withdraw it was taken by Kenya's Pres. Daniel arap Moi (*see* BIOGRAPHIES) in his capacity as incumbent OAU chairman.

Habré, who reoccupied the eastern town of Abéché in November 1981, went on to take Ati and Largeau and by January 1982 was in control of two-thirds of the country. After capturing Massakory in May, FAN forces made their victorious entry into N'Djamena on June 7. On the same day Oueddei, who in May had returned empty-hand-

ed from a visit to Tripoli to enlist Libya's aid, fled to Cameroon and thence, on June 22, to Algeria. Habré's other two principal rivals were also eliminated. On July 19 Ahmat Acyl, former GUNT foreign minister, was accidentally killed at Laï when he was struck by an aircraft propeller. In the south, Col. Wadal Abdelkader Kamougue, leader of the Chadian Armed Forces (FAT), who had been named president of the GUNT Council of State in May, gave way to forces led by Maj. Ganembang Zamtato; after the loss of Moundou in September, he fled to Cameroon and thence to Gabon.

At first severely critical of the roles of France and Algeria in the Chadian conflict, Habré sought French budgetary aid in July. In October he attended the Franco-African summit meeting in Kinshasa, Zaire, where he met French Pres. François Mitterrand. In a July 4 message to Pres. Ronald Reagan, Habré also sought good relations with the U.S. In September his foreign minister, Idriss Miskine, said Chad would demand that Libya return the Aozou strip in the north to "its motherland."

(PHILIPPE DECRAENE)

Chemistry

Organic Chemistry. The ever narrowing gaps between organic chemistry, biochemistry, and molecular biology were emphasized with the announcement in October of the 1982 Nobel Prize for Chemistry. The award went to Aaron Klug of the University of Cambridge in England for his fundamental work on the application of electron microscopy to solving the structure of nucleic acids and protein complexes. This achievement in turn led to a better understanding of the structure and development of viruses and the mechanisms of protein synthesis in animal cells. (*See* NOBEL PRIZES.)

Chemists continued to improve their skill at building bigger and bigger molecules, but because of the growing variety of synthetic methods and reagents available, they had to rely increasingly on computer assistance. New computing systems allowed chemists to draw the structure of the desired compound on a graphics tablet, to which the computer responded with possible routes of synthesis, starting materials, and reaction conditions using its built-in library. Computer graphics could also provide a colour picture of molecular shape in three dimensions.

Among the many compounds of biological importance synthesized during the year were human parathyroid hormone and the antibiotic milbemycin β_3, which also acts as a potent insecticide. Particularly exciting was the successful culminaton of a 20-year research effort involving more than 100 Chinese scientists and led by Wang Debao in Shanghai to make biologically active transfer RNA (tRNA), a replica of a vital molecule found in living cells. Responding to the genetic code, tRNA brings the correct amino acids into alignment alongside the ribosomes for assembly into proteins. Also fascinating was the news of successful clinical trials in the U.S. of a perfluorocarbon emulsion used as a short-term substitute for human blood. Such blood

CHAD

Education. (1976–77) Primary, pupils 210,882, teachers 2,610; secondary, pupils 18,382, teachers 590; vocational, pupils 649, teachers (1965–66) 30; teacher training, students 549, teachers (1973–74) 26; higher, students 758, teaching staff 62.

Finance. Monetary unit: CFA franc, with (Sept. 20, 1982) a parity of CFA Fr 50 to the French franc and a free rate of CFA Fr 353 to U.S. $1 (CFA Fr 605 = £1 sterling). Budget (total; 1978 est.) balanced at CFA Fr 17,084,000,000.

Foreign Trade. (1977) Imports CFA Fr 11,255,000,000; exports CFA Fr 6,862,000,000. Import sources (1976): France 46%; Nigeria c. 22%; Cameroon c. 5%; Netherlands Antilles c. 5%. Export destinations (1976): Nigeria c. 19%; Japan c. 14%; France c. 13%; West Germany c. 13%; Spain c. 11%. Main exports (1975): cotton 66%; petroleum products 8%; beef and veal 7%.

Agriculture. Production (in 000; metric tons; 1981): millet c. 580; sweet potatoes c. 37; cassava c. 188; peanuts c. 110; beans, dry c. 41; dates c. 27; mangoes c. 30; cotton, lint c. 26; meat c. 53; fish catch (1980) c. 115. Livestock (in 000; 1981): horses c. 150; asses c. 255; camels c. 420; cattle c. 3,800; sheep c. 2,300; goats c. 2,300.

Chemical Industry:
see Industrial Review

substitutes bind oxygen reversibly like hemoglobin, last much longer than natural blood cells, and do not need matching for blood type.

Among the more structurally interesting of new compounds was a chemical Möbius strip (1) having left- and right-handed forms that, like their paper prototype, could be split lengthwise into rings of twice the original diameter. Another new structural marvel was a cycloalkane called dodecahedrane (2), a highly symmetrical, 20-carbon spherical molecule that neatly illustrates the dodecahedron, one of Plato's five perfect solids. The molecule is highly stable and possesses very distinctive physical and chemical properties, according to its maker, chemist Leo Paquette of Ohio State University.

Polymers and plastics were much in the news. The year began with an announcement of a range of novel engineering plastics from General Electric, followed in March by a report that researchers at the University of Edinburgh, Scotland, had produced a polymer for removing lead from drinking water. Throughout the year chemists made real progress in understanding polymer structure and properties, which helped in the design of materials with high performance qualities. Research accelerated on electrically conducting polymers, or organic metals, and many industrial firms took an active interest in such materials as polyacetylene. G. Brian Street at IBM's research centre in San Jose, Calif., made good progress in developing β-dimethylpolypyrrole, believed to be the best conducting plastic to date. One potential application for conducting polymer systems was in lightweight rechargeable batteries.

Inorganic Chemistry. Most newsworthy was the report that on August 29 scientists at the Heavy Ion Research Laboratory (GSI) in Darmstadt, West Germany, made element 109. Led by Gottfried Munzenberg and Peter Armbruster, the team bombarded a bismuth-209 target with iron-58 nuclei for a week. Even though only one atom was made by this fusion technique and decay began five-thousandths of a second later, the researchers were confident of their identification. The work gave encouragement to the collaborative project with the Lawrence Berkeley Laboratory in California attempting to make element 116.

Despite resembling carbon in many respects, silicon had resisted all attempts to form compounds with multiple bonds until late 1981. Then, very soon after German chemists had made the ethylene analog silaethene ($H_2Si=CH_2$), which contains a silicon-carbon double bond, researchers at the universities of Wisconsin and Utah announced the first stable compound with a silicon-silicon double bond (3). Chemist Robert West of Wisconsin said that the new material was probably the forerunner of a large class of compounds and that the work could lead to new materials with unexpected properties.

Zeolites held research attention as newly developed systems of this class of materials offered additional possibilities for commercial application. These crystalline aluminosilicates have a sievelike structure that can sift molecules of different sizes; act as an absorbent or dessicant, trapping water

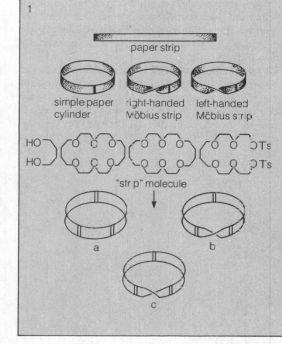

Just as the ends of a paper strip can be joined to form a cylinder or a left- or right-handed Möbius strip, so chemists coupled the ends of a "strip" molecule in an appropriate chemical reaction to create molecular Möbius strips. During the reaction the strip molecules double over and sometimes twist 180° as well, allowing the HO— (hydroxyl) groups at one end to remove and replace the —OTs (tosyl) groups at the other end. The result is a mixture of three products, a cylindrical structure (a) and two Möbius forms (b and c).

from a solution; and offer a high surface area for catalysis. During the year increased volumes of zeolites replaced phosphates in detergents, regarded by environmentalists as major contributors to the biological degradation of lakes and streams. One new application for zeolites was for a simple synthesis of ammonia, an important raw material for fertilizers. Ammonia (NH_3) is normally produced by reacting hydrogen (H_2) and nitrogen (N_2) gases at high temperatures and pressures over an iron oxide catalyst. Researchers led by Po-Lock Yue at the University of Bath in England made their ammonia by shining light on water containing a titanium-based zeolite through which nitrogen was being bubbled.

Metal-cluster compounds, which are molecules containing small groups of metal atoms bonded together, continued to occupy chemists interested in the transition metals. These polynuclear compounds can serve as catalysts, offer possibilities for converting solar energy into a usable form, and include the best superconducting substances yet discovered. During the past year Robert Benfield and

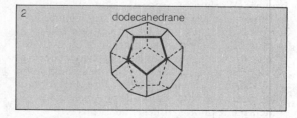

dodecahedrane

Peter Edwards of the University of Cambridge and Angelica Stacey of Cornell University in Ithaca, N.Y., showed that a cluster based on ten osmium atoms behaved as a tiny metal particle, being capable of magnetization in a strong magnetic field; smaller clusters did not show this effect. Clusters involving metals and such nonmetals as sulfur are important in living systems. Metalloproteins, for example, play a vital role in respiration and nitrogen fixation. German chemists made news by synthesizing the first trinuclear iron-sulfur cluster compound, a realistic model for such chemically active centres in biological systems.

Physical Chemistry. Research funding for techniques to separate water photochemically into oxygen and hydrogen remained high during the year, and successive announcements of "breakthroughs" occurred regularly. By midyear the emphasis had turned to developing improved electron relays. In a typical water-splitting system, light energy is trapped by a semiconductor or an

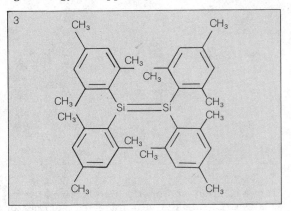

organic molecule called a sensitizer. This process frees an electron, which is passed on through an electron relay and which, with the aid of a platinum-based catalyst, reduces the hydrogen in water to elemental hydrogen. The main research teams were being led by Michael Grätzel of the École Polytechnique in Lausanne, Switz., Melvin Calvin at the University of California at Berkeley, and Sir George Porter at the Royal Institution in London. In October, however, lesser known researchers from Texas A & M University skipped formal publication of their work by excitedly (and exaggeratedly, according to some) disclosing their new process at a press conference. Marek Szklarczyk and A. Q. Contractor used a solar cell with cheap silicon electrodes coated with a very thin layer of platinum to convert solar energy to hydrogen with an efficiency of about 10%.

Running parallel with the photochemical generation of hydrogen was research into the mechanism of photosynthesis in green plants and certain bacteria. Workers at Argonne National Laboratory in Illinois and at Stanford University were providing new insights into what happens only billionths of a second after sunlight shines on the photosynthetic system. In Japan a research team at Kyoto University, led by Toyonari Sugimoto, achieved practical success with a liquid membrane that mimicked the lipid-bilayer membrane on which plant photosynthesis takes place.

Making use of unusual physical phenomena attracted attention during the year as chemists further explored the effect of high-intensity ultrasound on chemical reactions. Ultrasonic waves produce acoustic cavitation (formation of gas cavities) within a solution, causing hot spots with temperatures as high as 1,000° C (1,830° F). Kenneth Suslick at the University of Illinois at Ur-

bana-Champaign found that the isomerization of olefins in the presence of metal carbonyls could be catalyzed using ultrasonics. Sonocatalysis could open a fascinating new area of chemistry.

Of the many advances in spectroscopy recorded during the year, worth noting was the discovery by Canadian researchers of the largest molecule ever detected in space. With 13 atoms and a molecular weight of 147 daltons, the molecule having the formula $HC_{11}N$ was detected in a shell of dust and gas surrounding the star CW Leonis in the constellation Leo.

Analytical Chemistry. The trend toward increased computer control of analytical instruments continued apace, and it became rare to find new instruments without automated control, video displays, or other high-performance features. As computer power has improved it has become possible to synchronize and link instruments together so that, for example, the first device performs the separation of a mixture and the second carries out the identification of the components. In 1982 the best known of these "hyphenated techniques" was gas chromatography-mass spectrometry, or GC-MS, but work progressed well on the development of other linked instrument systems, with a good deal of interest in liquid chromatography-mass spectrometry. The most commercially successful of these new instrument systems, however, was one that combined the separation power of gas chromatography with the powerful identification features of Fourier-transform infrared spectroscopy, GC-FTIR.

A highlight in automated analysis was the unveiling of a laboratory robot at the Pittsburgh Conference on Analytical Chemistry and Applied Spectroscopy held in Atlantic City, N.J., in March. This bench-top robotic arm could weigh, pipette, filter, dilute, and mix samples and should help

Restoration of this ancient Greek bronze to its former glory was aided by modern analytical techniques, which yielded information about its chemical and internal structure.

reduce human exposure to toxic or radioactive materials. It should also offer opportunities for increasing laboratory productivity, permitting unattended sample preparation and analysis around the clock.

Among the newsworthy analytical studies of the year were an elemental analysis of rocks on the surface of Venus by X-ray fluorescence equipment on the Soviet Venera 13 spacecraft and, back home, an investigation using scanning electron microscopy and X-ray microanalysis of the way in which interactions between aluminum wiring and iron screws in residential electrical outlets cause overheating and failure. Analytical chemists helped determine the exact metallic composition and thus prevented the corrosion of two rare 5th-century BC Greek bronze statues found in 1972. Other workers showed that Claudian quadrantes were the purest copper coins of any Roman coins found to date. These studies—and confirmation that the pigment used to colour a beautiful limestone and plaster bust of Queen Nefertiti, who reigned in Egypt in the middle of the 14th century BC, was indeed the blue silicate of copper and calcium known as Egyptian blue—were able to shed light on the remarkable skills of ancient civilizations.　　　　　　(GORDON WILKINSON)

See also Materials Sciences: Nobel Prizes.
[121.B.5.b.ii; 121.C.5; 122.A.6.c; 122.A.7; 122.E.1.c,j,r,u; 123.G,H]

Chess

Anatoly Karpov's easy victory over Viktor Korchnoi in the world championship match at Merano, Italy, in October 1981 obscured the importance of the international tournament at Tilburg in The Netherlands during the same month. In that event, which attracted all the world's strongest players except for Karpov and Korchnoi, the Soviet grand master Aleksandr Beljavsky finished first, half a point ahead of former world champion Tigran Petrosian.

The 49th Soviet championship tournament, held at Frunze in November and December, ended in a tie between Lev Psakhis and the young star

Played in Round 10 of the Lucerne Olympiad 1982

Q. P. King's Indian Defense

White V. Korchnoi	Black G. Kasparov	White V. Korchnoi	Black G. Kasparov
1 P–Q4	N–KB3	19 N(R3)xP (c)	PxP
2 P–QB4	P–KN3	20 BxP (d)	B–Q2
3 P–KN3	B–N2	21 Q–K2 (e)	Q–N3
4 B–N2	P–B4	22 N–R3	QR–K1
5 P–Q5	P–Q3	23 B–Q2 (f)	QxP
6 N–QB3	O–O	24 PxN (g)	BxKP
7 N–B3	P–K3	25 N–B4	NxP
8 O–O	PxP	26 RxR ch	RxR
9 PxP	P–QR3	27 Q–K1	NxB ds ch
10 P–QR4	R–K1	28 K–N2	Q–B7
11 N–Q2	QN–Q2	29 NxB	R–B7 ch (h)
12 P–KR3	R–N1	30 QxR	NxQ
13 N–B4	N–K4	31 R–R2	Q–B4
14 N–R3	N–R4	32 NxB	N–Q6
15 P–K4	R–B1	33 B–R6	QxN
16 K–R2 (a)	P–B4 (b)	34 R–R8 ch	K–B2
17 P–B4	P–QN4	35 R–R8? (i)	K–B3
18 RPxP	RPxP	36 K–B3	QxP ch
		resigns	

(a) Too dangerous is 16. P–KN4 when Black would have the promising sacrifice of 16 . . ., Q–R5. (b) This leads to a sharp interchange good seems 16 . . ., B–Q2 preparing to play P–QN4. (c) Or 19. PxN, BxKP; 20. N–K2, NxP; 21. NxN, P–B5 with an unclear position in which Black has good chances. (d) After 20, NxQP, Kasparov intended playing 20 . . . , Q>N; 21. NxP, Q–N3; 22. PxN, RxR; 23. QxR, BxP with a strong attack. (e) Best after 21. NxP, R–N3; 22. PxN, BxKP; 23. N–B4, BxP ch; 24. K–N1, BxP; Black has an overwhelming attack. (f) Up to this point has chosen the best move every time, but this obvious developing move is a mistake. Correct was 23. Q–N2, and if then 23 . . ., Q–N5; 24. N–B2, Q–N1 when White still has the better game. (g) And not 24. KR–QN1, N–B6 ch! Korchnoi afterward thought 24. R–R2 would have won but to this Kasparov intended replying 24 . . ., Q–N1; 25. PxN RxR; 26. QxR, BxKP; 27. B–K1 BxN; 28. BxB, RxB; etc. (h) A mistake after which White ought to be able to draw. Correct was 29 . . . NxB; 30. NxB, N–B6 ds ch; 31. Q–K2, N–R5 ch; followed by QxN. (i) Now again White is lost; he should have played 35. N–K4, with good drawing chances.

Garry Kasparov. The European junior championship, held early in the year at Groningen in The Netherlands, was won by a 17-year-old Danish player, Curt Hansen. During the same period, a major international tournament took place at Porz, a suburb of Cologne, West Germany. First prize went to the former world champion Mikhail Tal of the U.S.S.R. with 9 points. Second, half a point behind, was the British grand master Tony Miles.

In an official international rating list published on Jan. 1, 1982, Karpov was again ranked first with 2,720 points. He was followed by Jan Timman (The Netherlands) 2,655, Korchnoi (stateless) 2,645, and Kasparov 2,640. The highest placed British player, John Nunn, had a score of 2,590, and the highest placed U.S. competitor was grand master Larry Christiansen with 2,585.

Anatoly Karpov of the U.S.S.R., the world chess champion, took on 15 competitors in a simultaneous game at UNESCO headquarters in Paris in February.

Fourteen computer programmers moved pieces on chessboards as directed by computers at the 13th North American Computer Chess Championships in Dallas. Computers can now play chess at the master level; it is anticipated that within three years computers will be able to beat the world chess champion.

The Soviet women's championship, held at Ivano-Frankovsk, ended in a tie between the former world champion Nona Gaprindashvili and Nana Joseliani. Soviet grand master Viktor Kupreichik-was won the annual Hastings International Tournament, finishing one point ahead of former world champion Vassily Smyslov and the young British grand master Jonathan Speelman. The Wijk aan Zee international tournament that followed immediately after the Hastings event in January ended in a tie for first place between the Soviet grand master Yuri Balashov and Nunn.

The Clarin tournament, which took place in Argentina in February, was one of Karpov's rare failures. The tournament was won by Timman, as Karpov lost two games. The annual Banco di Roma international tournament, held in Rome in February and March, ended in a tie between Korchnoi and the Hungarian master Joseph Pinter.

The Philips and Drew King's tournament, held in London in April, was one of the strongest ever held in Britain. Once again Karpov lost a game, rather badly to the young U.S. grand master Yasser Seirawan, but he managed to recover and ended by sharing first prize with the Swedish grand master Ulf Andersson.

Among the major events of the year were the interzonals, from each of which two players qualified for the candidates matches due to take place in 1983. These, in turn, would decide who should challenge Karpov for the world championship in 1984. The first interzonal was held at Las Palmas (Spain) in July, and the two qualifiers were Zoltan Ribli (Hungary) and the 61-year-old Smyslov. Among those who failed to qualify were Petrosian and Timman. The second interzonal took place in August at Toluca in Mexico, and the qualifiers were Hungarian grand master Lajos Portisch and the Philippine grand master Eugenio Torre. Those who failed included Spassky and Seirawan. In the third interzonal, at Moscow in September, Kasparov won easily and Beljavsky was the second qualifier. Those six would be joined in the candidates matches by the two finalists from previous years, Korchnoi and Robert Hübner of West Germany.

Two women's interzonal tournaments took place during the year. In the first, at Bad Kissingen, West Germany, the three qualifiers were Gaprindashvili, Tatiana Lemachko (Bulg.), and Semyonova (U.S.S.R.). It was later announced that Lemachko had defected from Bulgaria to a Western country. The second interzonal tournament was held in Tbilisi. Two Soviet players, Margareta Muresan and Irina Levitina, finished first and second, respectively.

At the world junior championship held near Copenhagen in August, the Soviet player Andrey Sokolov was the winner. During the same month, the world championship for players under 16 took place at Guayaquil, Ecuador; the winner was Yevgeny Bareyev of the U.S.S.R. The British championship, held at Torquay in August, was won, for the first time, by Miles. Karpov barely won the Tilburg tournament late in the year.

At the Lucerne (Switz.) Olympiad there was a record entry of 91 countries. The Soviet team finished first with 42½ points. Second was Czechoslovakia with 36, and the U.S. was third with 35½. In the women's competition the Soviet team won with 33 points, ahead of Romania with 30 and Hungary with 26.   (HARRY GOLOMBEK)

Chile

A republic extending along the southern Pacific coast of South America, Chile has an area of 756,626 sq km (292,135 sq mi), not including its Antarctic claim. It is bounded by Argentina, Bolivia, and Peru. Pop. (1982 prelim.): 11,275,400. Cap. and largest city: Santiago (metro. pop., 1982 est., 3,992,500). Language: Spanish. Religion: predominantly Roman Catholic. President in 1982, Maj. Gen. Augusto Pinochet Ugarte.

The year 1982 proved to be one of the most difficult and testing of Pres. Augusto Pinochet Ugarte's term in office, as Chile faced a deepening economic crisis. The high level of growth, which averaged 6.8% per year during the period 1976–81, declined markedly. Contributing to this setback were the worldwide recession, low copper prices, and what

CHILE

Education. (1981) Primary, pupils 2,139,319, teachers (1980) 66,354; secondary, pupils 392,940, teachers (1980) 24,387; vocational, pupils 161,809, teachers (1980) 4,176; higher, students 118,978, teaching staff (1975) 11,419.

Finance. Monetary unit: peso, with (Sept. 20, 1982) a free rate of 63 pesos to U.S. $1 (108 pesos = £1 sterling). Gold and other reserves (June 1982) U.S. $2,807,000,000. Budget (1980 actual): revenue 352,406,000,000 pesos; expenditure 299,175,000,000 pesos. Gross domestic product (1980) 1,095,180,000,000 pesos. Money supply (March 1982) 77,085,000,000 pesos. Cost of living (Santiago; 1975 = 100; June 1982) 1,879.

Foreign Trade. (1981) Imports U.S. $6,378,000,000; exports U.S. $3,931,000,000. Import sources: U.S. 21%; Japan 13%; Brazil 9%; West Germany 6%; Venezuela 5%. Export destinations: U.S. 15%; Japan 11%; West Germany 9%; The Netherlands 8%; Brazil 7%; Argentina 5%; Italy 5%. Main exports (1980): copper 46%; chemicals 9%; timber 6%; wood pulp 5%; vanadium and molybdenum ores 5%.

Transport and Communications. Roads (1980) 79,867 km. Motor vehicles in use (1980): passenger 405,000; commercial 188,000. Railways: (1979) c. 10,100 km; traffic (1981) 1,622,000,000 passenger-km, freight 1,727,000,000 net ton-km. Air traffic (1981): 2,220,000,000 passenger-km; freight 104 million net ton-km. Shipping (1981): merchant vessels 100 gross tons and over 182; gross tonnage 563,628. Telephones (Jan. 1980) 553,900. Radio receivers (Dec. 1979) 3,239,000. Television receivers (Dec. 1979) 1,225,000.

Agriculture. Production (in 000; metric tons; 1981): wheat 686; barley 91; oats 131; corn 518; rice 100; potatoes 1,007; rapeseed c. 40; dry beans 138; tomatoes c. 155; sugar, raw value c. 250; apples c. 300; wine c. 585; wool, clean c. 10; beef and veal 172; fish catch (1980) 2,817; timber (cu m; 1980) 11,433. Livestock (in 000; 1981): cattle 3,745; sheep 6,185; goats c. 600; pigs 1,130; horses c. 450; poultry c. 25,000.

Industry. Production (in 000; metric tons; 1981): coal 839; crude oil (1980) 1,590; natural gas (cu m; 1980) 2,820,000; petroleum products (1979) c. 4,600; electricity (kw-hr) 11,724,000; iron ore (61% metal content) 8,355; pig iron 681; crude steel (ingots) 657; copper ore (metal content) 1,079; copper 762; nitrate of soda (1980) 620; manganese ore (metal content; 1980) 9.5; sulfur (1980) 87; iodine (1980) 2.6; molybdenum concentrates (metal content; 1980) 13.7; gold (troy oz) c. 370; silver (troy oz; 1980) 9,598; cement (1980) 1,583; nitrogenous fertilizers (1980–81) 101; newsprint 129; other paper (1979) 171; fish meal (1978) 379.

Chile

in to fill the joint post of minister of finance and economy; Samuel Lira became minister of mines; and Vice-Adm. Patricio Carvajal was named minister of defense, his appointment to take effect on December 15. Lüders, like his predecessor, Sergio de la Cuadra, was a confirmed Chicago-school monetarist, but it was hoped that he would manage to provide greater coherence and flexibility in economic policymaking.

These Cabinet changes and adjustments reaffirmed President Pinochet's resolve to pursue a monetarist course. In a presidential speech made on September 11 to commemorate nine years of military government, he declared: "Neither present economic difficulties nor the permanent aggression of our enemies will make us stray from our goals—all the vigour of the law will be applied to those who foment an artificial atmosphere of political agitation." Under the March 1981 constitution, political parties were allowed to form in time for the congressional elections in 1990, but they were not expected to have full political powers.

In foreign policy the Chilean government continued to strengthen its relations with the West and was one of the few Latin-American supporters of the U.K. during its conflict with Argentina over the Falkland Islands. In March Israel signed a trade and cooperation agreement with Chile, and at the end of September the Federation of Labour in New Zealand lifted its eight-year trade ban. The long-standing dispute with Argentina over the three islands of Picton, Lennox, and Nueva in the Beagle Channel and their territorial waters remained unresolved despite mediation by Pope John Paul II. Finally, in September, after much deliberation and on condition that Chile promise not to take the matter to the International Court of Justice at The Hague, Argentina extended the 1972 agreement, thus allowing for a peaceful settlement.

Repression continued during 1982 with little

Chilean Pres. Augusto Pinochet Ugarte led ceremonies in Santiago marking the ninth anniversary of the military coup that established him in power. He reiterated his ban on political activities.

many considered to be overvaluation of the peso in the first half of the year.

Dissension over economic policy grew, and President Pinochet had to maneuver with increasing care to maintain the political balance. The division between the Chicago-school proponents of the free-market economy (*blandos*, or "wets") and the military nationalists (*duros*, or "hard-liners"), who believed in greater state intervention, widened, fueled by controversy over such measures as mining policy, intervention in the banking system, and exchange-rate policy. The decision on June 14 to devalue the peso from 39 to 46 to the U.S. dollar, followed on August 6 by the floating of the peso, marked a dramatic end to Chile's three-year fixed-exchange-rate policy and represented a victory for those who had proposed that the government should take a more active role in economic management.

No fewer than three Cabinet reshuffles took place in quick succession. The annual change at the end of 1981 was followed by new appointments on April 23 and again on August 30. In the August reshuffle Rolf Lüders, an economist and former executive of the Banco Hipotecario, was brought

UPI

sign of any political liberalization; books could not be published without the government's prior authorization, and the "state of emergency" that gave the president the power to carry out arrests, restrict labour union activity, and expel dissidents from the country was renewed again in 1982. The murder in February of the trade union leader Tucapel Jiménez Alfarao, following a speech made at a press conference in which he called for the formation of a "common front" to oppose the government's economic policy, aroused the suspicions of many; more than 50 people were arrested at the funeral. The International League for Human Rights claimed that a total of 837 political arrests occurred in the first six months of 1982, compared with 614 during the same period in 1981. In September more than 200 law students from the University of Chile and the Catholic University of Santiago demonstrated against the president's powers and demanded the return of Chileans in exile. Jaime Castillo, the president of Chile's human rights commission, who had been exiled in 1981, was again refused entry to the country.

Business confidence deteriorated in 1981 and 1982, and the lack of export growth threatened the closing of many companies. The government found itself increasingly obliged to step in to prevent further bankruptcies. On July 12 the Banco Central offered to take charge of the private banks' overdue loans and high-risk debts by means of nontransferable promissory notes that had a maximum maturity of ten years.

Overall prospects for the Chilean economy were improved by the floating of the peso, but many economists considered that the measure had come too late to have a major effect. Gross domestic product plummeted in 1982 but was expected to pick up in 1983. Exports in the nontraditional sector, such as fruit, forestry, and fish, were likely to improve, but the outlook for copper remained bleak because of low world demand. Imports were restrained by both the current recession and their increased cost. The trade deficit, which widened in 1981 to $2.6 billion, was expected to narrow, but pressure on the current account continued because of the heavy commitment on the $15 billion debt. International reserves, standing at $3.1 billion in July 1982, were depleted. It was predicted that inflation, reduced from an annual rate of 31.2% in 1980 to 9.5% in 1981 and to the remarkably low level of 2.4% during the first seven months of 1982, would rise to reach double digits by the end of 1982. Midyear figures showed that 21% of the work force was unemployed, and as the year progressed the situation showed no sign of improvement.

(LUCY BLACKBURN)

China

China

The most populous country in the world and the third largest in area, China is bounded by the U.S.S.R., Mongolia, North Korea, Vietnam, Laos, Burma, India, Bhutan, Nepal, Pakistan, and Afghanistan and also by the Yellow Sea and the East and South China seas. From 1949 the country has been divided into the People's Republic of China

(Communist) on the mainland and on Hainan and other islands, and the Republic of China (Nationalist) on Taiwan. (*See* TAIWAN.) Area: 9,561,000 sq km (3,691,521 sq mi), including Tibet and excluding Taiwan. Population of the People's Republic (1982): 1,008,175,288. Capital: Beijing (Peking; metro. pop., 1982, 9,230,700). Largest city: Shanghai (metro. pop., 1982, 11,859,700). Language: Chinese (varieties of the Beijing dialect predominate). Chairman of the permanent Standing Committee of the National People's Congress (nominal chief of state) in 1982, Ye Jianying (Yeh Chienying); chairman of the Communist Party to September 12 and general secretary from that date, Hu Yaobang (Hu Yao-pang); premier, Zhao Ziyang (Chao Tzu-yang).

In 1982, the 33rd year of Communist rule under the banner of Marxism-Leninism and Mao Zedong (Mao Tse-tung) Thought, China remained poor and backward in science, technology, and economic development, with a per capita national income of less than $400.

The new pragmatist leadership, effectively headed by Deng Xiaoping (Teng Hsiao-p'ing), car-

CHINA

Education. (1980–81) Primary, pupils 143,330,000, teachers (1964–65) *c.* 2.6 million; secondary, pupils 48,596,000; vocational, pupils 2,220,000; higher, students 1,280,000.

Finance. Monetary unit: yuan, with (Sept. 20, 1982) a market rate of 1.96 yuan to U.S. $1 (3.35 yuan = £1 sterling). Gold and other reserves (May 1982) U.S. $7,056,000,000. Budget (1981 actual): revenue 106.4 billion yuan; expenditure 109 billion yuan. National income (1981) 388 billion yuan. Money supply (March 1982) 102.1 billion yuan. Cost of living (1975 = 100; 1981) 116.5.

Foreign Trade. (1981) Imports 36,770,000,000 yuan; exports 36,760,000,000 yuan. Import sources: Japan 25%; U.S. 18%; Hong Kong 10%; West Germany 5%; Romania 5%. Export destinations: Japan 24%; Hong Kong 24%; U.S. 9%. Main exports: crude oil and products 20%; food 16%; textile yarn and fabrics 15%; clothing 10%; chemicals 6%.

Transport and Communications. Roads (1981) 897,000 km. Motor vehicles in use (1978): passenger *c.* 50,000; commercial *c.* 710,000. Railways (1981): 50,000 km; traffic 147,300,000,000 passenger-km, freight 571,200,000,000 net ton-km. Air traffic (1981): 5,000,-000,000 passenger-km; freight 170 million net ton-km. Inland waterways (1981) 109,000 km. Shipping (1981): merchant vessels 100 gross tons and over 1,051; gross tonnage 7,653,195. Telephones (Dec. 1977) *c.* 5 million. Radio receivers (Dec. 1977) *c.* 45 million. Television receivers (Dec. 1979) 3,248,000.

Agriculture. Production (in 000; metric tons; 1981): rice 143,205; corn *c.* 60,000; wheat 58,490; barley *c.* 3,400; millet *c.* 5,900; sorghum *c.* 7,500; potatoes 15,000; soybeans 9,245; peanuts 3,826; rapeseed 4,065; sugar, raw value *c.* 4,000; tobacco *c.* 850; tea 343; cotton, lint 2,968; jute 1,260; cow's milk 1,291; beef 249; pork 11,884; mutton 476; fish catch (1980) 4,240; timber (cu m; 1980) *c.* 224,600. Livestock (in 000; 1981): horses *c.* 11,100; asses *c.* 7,400; cattle *c.* 53,400; buffalo *c.* 18,850; sheep *c.* 105,200; goats *c.* 82,500; pigs 293,702; chickens *c.* 861,000.

Industry. Fuel and power (in 000; metric tons; 1981): coal (including lignite) 620,000; crude oil 101,220; natural gas (cu m) 12,740,000; electricity (kw-hr) 309,300,000. Production (in 000; metric tons; 1981): iron ore (metal content) *c.* 34,800; pig iron 34,170; crude steel 35,600; bauxite (1980) *c.* 1,500; aluminum (1980) *c.* 360; copper (1980) *c.* 280; lead (1980) *c.* 170; zinc (1980) *c.* 160; magnesite (1980) *c.* 2,000; manganese ore (1980) *c.* 1,600; tungsten concentrates (oxide content; 1980) *c.* 15; cement 84,000; sulfuric acid 7,810; plastics 916; fertilizers (nutrient content) nitrogenous 9,860, phosphate 2,510; soda ash 1,652; caustic soda 1,923; cotton yarn 3,170; cotton fabrics (m) 14,270,000; man-made fibres 527; paper 5,400; motor vehicles (units) 176.

Deng Xiaoping, China's Communist Party vice-chairman and regarded as its strong man, opened his party's first congress in five years in Beijing in September. He stressed modernization, the return of Taiwan, and combating superpower expansionism.

ried out several political and economic reforms during the year, most notably the streamlining of the administrative structure to weed out incompetent and undesirable officials and the punishing of economic criminals to eliminate corruption. Concerning rural economic reform, the revised constitution, adopted by the fifth session of the fifth National People's Congress (the nominal legislature) in December, stipulated reestablishment of the old township and district governments while retaining the people's communes as economic organizations only.

The most important event of the year was the 12th Communist Party congress, which met in

The Chinese government's encouragement of light industry and the production of consumer goods was beginning to bear fruit in 1982, as this couple buying a washing machine could testify.

September to reaffirm the political and economic policies of the pragmatist leadership, adopt a new party constitution, restructure the party organization, and elect a new Central Committee to implement policy for the next five years.

Domestic Affairs. The internal struggle for power between pragmatists and ideologues (or moderates and radicals) continued, with the former in the lead. In January the party newspaper called for a major ideological campaign to broaden and strengthen support for Deng's policies and to win the confidence of the people. A nationwide anticorruption campaign, which had begun in the summer of 1981, became a principal focus of political activity in February. In a detailed directive, the party's ruling Politburo cited 82 senior officials and their children in thefts of state property, bribe taking, and serious abuse of party and government positions. It directed all party organizations to undertake measures to expose corrupt officials and called on the people to rise up against them.

The campaign against corruption was related to the effort to reduce China's huge government and party bureaucracy, which was announced by Premier Zhao Ziyang (Chao Tzu-yang) at the fourth session of the fifth National People's Congress in December 1981. The cooperation of the armed forces, which contained the largest bloc of declared Maoists, was important in this effort. Since he took over as chairman of the party's Military Commission (commander in chief) in 1981, Deng had stressed the need for military obedience to party directives. In February it was reported that the military had agreed not to attack Deng's reforms if he would soften the criticism of Maoists and Maoism, which were considered useful symbols of party legitimacy.

On March 2 Zhao presented to the Standing Committee of the National People's Congress his detailed proposals for reducing the 98 existing government ministries, commissions, and agencies to 52 and cutting their staffs by one-third, or about 200,000 people. The committee approved Zhao's

China

North Korean Pres. Kim Il Sung (right) and his delegation arrived in Beijing on September 16 for a ten-day visit.

plan but decided to carry out the streamlining of the State Council by stages, beginning with the 12 ministries dealing with commerce, trade, power, food, and industries. In April Zhao reported to the Standing Committee on a further trimming, which reduced the number of ministers and vice-ministers from 505 to 167. It was not until May that an official announcement was made on the abolition of 11 posts of vice-premier; only two vice-premiers were retained: Wan Li (*see* BIOGRAPHIES) and Yao Yilin (Yao I-lin), both veteran economic planners and close allies of Deng.

The 12th party congress, with 1,545 delegates and 145 alternates in attendance, opened on September 1 with an address by Deng and a long political report by the party chairman, Hu Yaobang (Hu Yao-pang). Deng reiterated the basic tasks set out for China: to strive for national reunification, including the return of Taiwan; to combat foreign hegemonism or expansionism; and to intensify the Four Modernizations (agriculture, industry, science and technology, and defense). Hu described the party's rule as threatened by bureaucracy, corruption, remoteness from the people, and ideological errors. He asked the congress to undertake a reorganization of the party, including a purge of

U.S. Assistant Secretary of State John Holdridge (left) met with Chinese Deputy Prime Minister Ji Pengfei (Chi P'eng-fei; right) in Beijing in January. Holdridge notified the Chinese that the U.S. would not sell advanced fighter planes to Taiwan.

its ranks. A "rectification campaign" was scheduled to start in late 1983 to purge opponents of the new, liberalized policies, as well as incompetent and corrupt members.

On September 6 the congress approved a new party constitution, superseding the constitution of 1978. It marked a complete break with the radicalism of the late Chairman Mao. The post of chairman was abolished to ensure that no one person would ever dominate the party as Mao had for over three decades. Advisory commissions were created in both Beijing (Peking) and the provinces to take over party posts from veteran leaders, who would retire to advisory roles. Lifelong tenure for leading party officials was eliminated. Discipline inspection commissions were to be established at all levels to police the party.

In the last two days of the session (September 10–11), the congress elected 210 members and 138 alternates to the party's Central Committee and 172 members to the newly created Central Advisory Commission, to which elderly members of the leadership were encouraged to retire. Contrary to expectations, Ye Jianying (Yeh Chien-ying), 85, the nominal chief of state, and Chen Yun (Ch'en Yün) and Li Xiannian (Li Hsien-nien), both 77 and also Politburo members, refused to retreat from the political scene. On the other hand, several prominent aging officials, including Wu De (Wu Te), the former mayor of Beijing, and Chen Xilian (Ch'en Hsi-lien), former commander of the Beijing military region, joined Deng on the Central Advisory Commission. Over 60% of the Central Committee's members were new, and two-thirds were under 60. About a dozen veterans over 70 remained on the new Central Committee, as did Hua Guofeng (Hua Kuo-feng), 61, who had been Mao's designated heir but was forced out as party chairman in 1981.

At the first plenary session of the 12th Central Committee, held on September 12–13, Hua was dropped from the Politburo, now composed of 25 full and 3 alternate members. Only 9 were new, and most of the elderly veterans remained in their posts. With the deletion of Hua, the Politburo's elite Standing Committee consisted of six members in the following order: Hu, Ye, Deng, Zhao, Li Xiannian, and Chen Yun. On the Secretariat, 6 of the 11 members were new, and they were younger and better educated. Hu was named general secretary of the Secretariat, which would handle the party's day-to-day business. It was believed that Deng had the support of at least 15 of the Politburo's full members plus most of the Secretariat.

On November 19 the government announced that Foreign Minister Huang Hua and Defense Minister Geng Biao (Keng Piao) had been replaced, respectively, by Wu Xueqian (Wu Hsüeh-ch'ien) and Zhang Aiping (Chang Ai-p'ing), both supporters of Deng. The changes had been rumoured for some months, but the timing was unexpected; Huang had just returned from the funeral of Soviet Pres. Leonid I. Brezhnev in Moscow. At about the same time there were reports that the commanders of the three military regions had been replaced, apparently signaling a reorganization in the leadership of the armed forces.

The new constitution approved by the fifth session of the fifth National People's Congress, which met November 16–December 10, was the fourth in the history of the People's Republic. Like those of 1954, 1975, and 1978, it reflected the current state of the internal power struggle. Among other provisions it reinstated the post of president/chairman of the republic, established a Central Military Council to replace the party's Military Commission, and stipulated that state leaders should not serve more than two consecutive terms. While it stressed the importance of socialist construction by accelerating the program of Four Modernizations, it retained the Four Fundamental Principles: the leadership of the Communist Party, "the people's democratic dictatorship," the socialist road, and Marxism-Leninism-Mao Zedong Thought.

The Economy. At the opening session of the party congress, Hu reaffirmed that the policy of economic reform included extensive reliance on market forces to spur economic development and growth, as well as expected foreign investment and trade. He stressed that improving conditions for the people would take precedence over new industrial projects. Nevertheless, it was hoped that the combined value of China's industrial and agricultural output would be quadrupled to over $1.7 trillion by the year 2000.

Since 1979 light industry had received priority in a number of fields, and production of major consumer goods had risen substantially. During 1978–81 the output of TV sets increased more than tenfold and that of radios and cameras more than threefold, while production of bicycles, sewing machines, wristwatches, and wine more than doubled. In the agricultural sector, acreage sown to grain crops was reduced while annual grain output rose from 320,520,000 tons in 1980 to 325,020,-000 in 1981. The target for 1982 was 333.5 million tons, but drought in the north, floods in the central and southern areas, and the desire of many farmers to grow industrial crops such as cotton and oil made it unlikely that the grain target would be met. China continued to import 12 million to 16 million tons of grain, including about 8 million tons from the U.S.

Total foreign investment in China over the past three years was estimated at $2.9 billion, including $90 million in joint ventures. In March China invited foreign business to invest $900 million to help develop 30 new industrial projects. The foreign trade deficit for 1981 was $5.8 million, compared with $247 million in 1980. According to official figures, China registered a trade surplus of $2.4 billion in the first six months of 1982, achieved by a surge in exports coupled with severe import cutbacks. In February the newly established China National Offshore Oil Corporation took full charge of cooperation with foreign companies in exploiting oil reserves on China's continental shelf. On September 19 it signed an exploration agreement with the Atlantic Richfield Co., the first U.S. oil concern to win China's permission to start drilling for oil offshore.

The delayed sixth five-year plan (1981–85), which was approved by the National People's Congress, projected modest economic growth of 4% per year. Grain production for 1985 was targeted at 360 million tons and steel output at 39 million tons. Transportation and energy were identified as priority areas.

Foreign Affairs. Since the normalization of Sino-U.S. relations in 1979, China had considered Soviet hegemonism rather than capitalist imperialism to be the major threat to world peace and security. During U.S. Secretary of State Alexander Haig's tenure, Washington's efforts to draw Beijing into strategic cooperation with the U.S. had met with some response. However, China differed sharply with the U.S. over such major issues as the Palestinian question, the Falkland Islands crisis, and the presence of U.S. troops in South Korea. Signaling a chill, Beijing reverted to its characterization of the U.S. as a hegemonistic superpower, like the Soviet Union. It revived Mao's three-world concept in international relations, criticizing both superpowers of the first world, soliciting the cooperation of the industrial nations of Europe and Japan (the second world), and championing the cause of the third world. By equating the two superpowers as hegemonists, China increased its flexibility in moving between them.

The status of Taiwan continued to complicate relations with the U.S. Under the Taiwan Relations Act of 1981, the U.S. was committed to supplying Taiwan with defensive arms, but a request by Taiwan for advanced fighter aircraft to deter Chinese aggression led to a threat by Beijing to downgrade its diplomatic relations with Washington. In January 1982 the Reagan administration rejected Taipei's request for advanced fighters, and it restricted arms sales to Taiwan to $60 million in spare parts. To demonstrate Pres. Ronald Reagan's interest in good relations with China, Vice-Pres. George Bush arrived in Beijing on May 7 to hold wide-ranging talks. Washington and Beijing finally reached a compromise in late summer. In a joint communiqué issued on August 17, the Reagan administration acceded to the Chinese position that the People's Republic is the sole legal government of China. It also agreed that future arms sales to Taiwan would not exceed past sales but would be contingent upon peaceful relations between Taiwan and the mainland.

Japanese troops pictured guarding a Chinese captive during a Japanese invasion of China in the 1930s. Chinese officials were outraged when Japanese history books were revised to downplay Japan's history of aggression in Asia and especially the "rape of Nanking," in which 300,000 Chinese were massacred by Japanese soldiers.

UPI

Early in 1982 both Moscow and Peking appeared to be seeking common ground to improve trade and cultural contacts. Following the exchange of trade missions, Moscow offered to renew the suspended border talks and to revive scientific and technical consultations, and the two countries signed an agreement that allowed China to export goods to Eastern Europe via the Trans-Siberian railway. On March 24, when Sino-U.S. relations were at a low ebb because of the Taiwan issue, President Brezhnev made a conciliatory speech in which he appealed to Beijing to join in a search for ways leading toward normal relations. The immediate response from China's Ministry of Foreign Affairs was cautious and cool, but on May 31 Zhao stated that China consistently stood for maintaining and developing normal relations between the two countries. In a second overture on September 26, Brezhnev said that his country "would deem it very important to achieve a normalization, a gradual improvement of relations" between the two Communist superpowers. The next day Zhao announced that China and the Soviet Union would hold a new series of high-level talks. Soviet Deputy Foreign Minister Leonid F. Ilyichev arrived in Beijing on October 3 to open negotiations with Chinese Vice-Foreign Minister Qian Qichen (Ch'ien Ch'i-ch'en).

To celebrate the tenth anniversary of the normalization of relations with Japan, Zhao paid an official visit to Japan from May 31 to June 5. In talks with Zhao, Prime Minister Zenko Suzuki reaffirmed that Japan would continue to cooperate with China in its economic development and promised to pay a return visit to China in September. Sino-Japanese relations were strained in July, however, when Japan's Education Ministry disclosed a revision of school textbooks that mitigated accounts of Japanese aggression in Asia before and during World War II. (*See* JAPAN.) Beijing was particularly incensed by the textbooks' suggestion that the "rape of Nanking," in which over 300,000 were massacred, was warranted by Chinese resistance to Japan's aggression. After two months of acrimonious dispute, China accepted Japan's pledge that the revision would be changed, and on September 26 Suzuki arrived in Beijing for a six-day official visit.

Bilateral trade between China and Japan exceeded $10 billion in 1981. A new long-term Sino-Japanese trade agreement signed a few days before Suzuki's arrival entitled Japan to 8.6 million tons of Chinese crude oil annually, as well as lesser amounts of Chinese coal. During his visit Suzuki signed an agreement giving China another $250 million in low-interest government loans, bringing total credit from Japan to over $1 billion in the past few years.

British Prime Minister Margaret Thatcher arrived in Beijing on September 22 for a five-day official visit that included talks on Hong Kong's future. Hong Kong Island and the Kowloon Peninsula had been ceded to Britain in perpetuity, but the greater part of Kowloon and the New Territories—90% of the colony's land—were under a 99-year lease, due to expire in 1997. Meanwhile, Hong Kong had become an economic gateway to China, which currently earned about 40% of its foreign exchange through the colony. Thatcher maintained that the treaties permanently ceding parts of Hong Kong to Britain were valid, but on September 30 Beijing issued a statement asserting that China was not bound by the so-called unequal treaties and would recover the colony "when conditions are ripe." On September 24 Thatcher and Deng issued a joint statement in which they agreed to enter negotiations through diplomatic channels "with the common aim of maintaining the stability and prosperity of Hong Kong" in working out a transition for the colony.   (HUNG-TI CHU)

See also Feature Article: *China's Uncertain Future.*

Colombia

A republic in northwestern South America, Colombia is bordered by Panama, Venezuela, Brazil, Peru, and Ecuador and has coasts on both the Caribbean Sea and the Pacific Ocean. Area: 1,141,748 sq km (440,831 sq mi). Pop. (1981 est.): 26,729,200. Cap. and largest city: Bogotá (pop., 1981 est., 4,486,200). Language: Spanish. Religion: Roman Catholic (97%). Presidents in 1982, Julio César Turbay Ayala and, from August 7, Belisario Betancur Cuartas.

Colombia

Chinese Literature:
see Literature

Christian Church (Disciples of Christ):
see Religion

Christianity:
see Religion

Churches of Christ:
see Religion

Cinema:
see Motion Pictures

Ciskei:
see South Africa

Cities:
see Environment

Clothing:
see Fashion and Dress

Coal:
see Energy

Coins:
see Philately and Numismatics

Colleges:
see Education

COLOMBIA

Education. (1979) Primary, pupils 4,337,607, teachers 139,277; secondary, vocational, and teacher training, pupils 1,879,118, teachers 85,938; higher, students 271,302, teaching staff (1978) 25,708.

Finance. Monetary unit: peso, with (Sept. 20, 1982) a free rate of 65.55 pesos to U.S. $1 (112.38 pesos = £1 sterling). Gold and other reserves (June 1982) U.S. $4,438,000,000. Budget (1980 actual): revenue 200,-243,000,000 pesos; expenditure 213,424,000,000 pesos. Gross domestic product (1981) 2,005,010,000,000 pesos. Money supply (Dec. 1981) 257,280,000,000 pesos. Cost of living (Bogotá; 1975 = 100; June 1982) 473.9.

Foreign Trade. Imports (1981): U.S. $5,201,000,000; exports U.S. $2,916,000,000. Import sources: U.S. 34%; Japan 10%; Venezuela 8%; West Germany 6%. Export destinations: U.S. 23%; West Germany 20%; Venezuela 12%; The Netherlands 5%. Main exports (1979): coffee 59%; textiles and clothing 6%. Tourism: visitors (1978) 826,000; gross receipts (1980) U.S. $357 million.

Transport and Communications. Roads (1980) 74,735 km. Motor vehicles in use (1980): passenger 322,000; commercial 33,000. Railways: (1979) 2,912 km; traffic (1980) 310 million passenger-km, freight 860 million net ton-km. Air traffic (1981): 4,212,000,000 passenger-km; freight 209.7 million net ton-km. Shipping (1981): merchant vessels 100 gross tons and over 72; gross tonnage 296,860. Telephones (Jan. 1980) 1,524,000. Radio receivers (Dec. 1979) 3,005,000. Television receivers (Dec. 1979) 2 million.

Agriculture. Production (in 000; metric tons; 1981): corn 880; rice 1,799; sorghum 532; potatoes c. 2,100; cassava 2,150; soybeans 89; cabbages c. 462; onions c. 265; tomatoes c. 243; bananas c. 1,155; plantains 2,400; sugar, raw value 1,185; palm oil c. 88; coffee 808; tobacco 49; cotton, lint c. 87; beef and veal 576; timber (cu m; 1980) 42,783. Livestock (in 000; 1981): cattle 24,251; sheep 2,427; pigs c. 2,245; goats 652; horses c. 1,710; chickens c. 30,650.

Industry. Production (in 000; metric tons; 1981): crude oil 6,926; natural gas (cu m; 1980) 2,790,000; coal (1980) c. 5,260; electricity (kw-hr; 1980) 20,645,000; iron ore (metal content; 1980) 490; crude steel 216; gold (troy oz) 570; emeralds (carats; 1979) 1,228; salt (1979) 634; cement 4,459; caustic soda 18; fertilizers (nutrient content; 1980–81) nitrogenous c. 42, phosphate c. 46; paper (1979) 325.

Belisario Betancur Cuartas and his wife, Helena, waved to crowds after Betancur was sworn in as president of Colombia in August. He gave up the traditional tuxedo and champagne for a business suit and soft drinks.

In the congressional elections of March 14, 1982, the Liberals led by ex-president Alfonso López Michelsen gained 47.4% of the seats in the Senate and 47.7% of the seats in the House of Representatives, respectively 2.7 and 5.5% more than the Conservatives of Belisario Betancur Cuartas (*see* BIOGRAPHIES). Luis Carlos Galán Sarmiento's New Liberals, whose only victory was in the capital district, took 7% of the Senate seats and 9.1% in the lower house. (For tabulated results, *see* POLITICAL PARTIES.)

Despite his disappointing results, Galán withstood pressure from López Michelsen to withdraw his presidential candidacy, thus splitting the Liberal vote in the presidential election on May 30 and preventing that party from repeating its congressional victory. Betancur gained the presidency by obtaining 47% of the vote (3.2 million), while López Michelsen won 41% (2.8 million) and Galán more than 11%; Gerardo Molina of the Socialist-Communist alliance received the remaining 1%. Betancur's first Cabinet maintained the practice of sharing posts between the Conservatives (six ministers) and the Liberals (also six); the Defense Ministry was a military appointment.

One of Betancur's initial tasks was to curb guerrilla activity. In the final months of his predecessor's term of office, military actions against insurgents claimed some success but failed to diminish the operations of the various groups, including those of the right-wing death squad, MAS, formed in late 1981 to attack left-wing activists. An amnesty was proposed in February by the Peace Commission, led by ex-president Carlos Lleras Restrepo and set up to bring the guerrillas back into normal political life. Despite a number of surrenders, the leaders of M-19 (one of the most active movements) insisted that the state of siege, in force since 1976, be lifted before they would lay down arms.

The Peace Commission made direct contact with M-19 in March, but its proposals for negotiation were rejected by the government, causing Lleras and four commissioners to resign. After the commission's collapse, Pres. Julio César Turbay Ayala announced early in June that the state of siege would be lifted on June 20 because the congressional and presidential elections had taken place without the threatened disruptions. M-19 immediately called a cease-fire. On taking office, President Betancur initiated moves to hold direct talks with the guerrillas and recalled the Peace Commission. The guerrilla movements responded positively, and in September M-19 declared that it would cease all armed activity. Twenty-five M-19 members were among the guerrillas freed under an amnesty signed in late November.

Although Betancur proposed that Colombia join the nonaligned movement, he stated that relations with Cuba would not be renewed. However, closer inter-American cooperation would be sought. During U.S. Pres. Ronald Reagan's December visit to Bogotá, Betancur was unusually blunt in his criticism of U.S. policies that "discriminated" among Latin-American nations.

The major economic tasks facing Betancur included reducing the government deficit and arresting the decline experienced by many sectors. Growth in the gross domestic product was not expected to be above the 2.5% rate of 1981 (4% in 1980). The balance of trade was again weakened by falling prices for the country's exports. Colombia's ability to borrow overseas was jeopardized by a series of banking scandals that led to the arrest of several top banking officials and a state governor. (BEN BOX)

Combat Sports

Boxing. World Boxing Council (WBC) champion Larry Holmes (U.S.) retained the heavyweight championship he had won five years earlier, stopping Gerry Cooney (U.S.) in 13 rounds in June in

Colonies:
see Dependent States

Table I. Boxing Champions
as of Dec. 31, 1982

Division	World	Europe	Commonwealth	Britain
Heavyweight	Larry Holmes, U.S.* Michael Dokes†	Lucien Rodriguez, France	Trevor Berbick, Canada	Neville Meade, Wales
Cruiserweight	S. T. Gordon, U.S.* Ossie Ocasio, Puerto Rico†	...	...	...
Light heavyweight	Dwight Muhammad Qawi, U.S.* Mike Spinks, U.S.†	Rudi Koopmans, The Netherlands	Lottie Mwale, Zambia	Tom Collins, England
Middleweight	Marvelous Marvin Hagler, U.S.*†	Louis Acaries, France	vacant	Roy Gumbs, England
Junior middleweight	Thomas Hearns, U.S.* Davey Moore, U.S.†	Luigi Minchillo, Italy	Herol Graham, England	Herol Graham, England
Welterweight	vacant	Colin Jones, Wales	Colin Jones, Wales	Colin Jones, Wales
Junior welterweight	Leroy Haley, U.S.* Aaron Pryor, U.S.†	Roberto Gambini, France	Obisia Nwankpa, Nigeria	Clinton McKenzie, England
Lightweight	Alexis Argüello, Nicaragua* Ray Mancini, U.S.†	Joey Gibilisco, Italy	Claude Noel, Trinidad	George Feeney, England
Junior lightweight	Bobby Chacon, U.S.* Sammy Serrano, Puerto Rico†	Roberto Castañon, Spain	Johnny Aba, Papua New Guinea	...
Featherweight	Juan LaPorte, U.S.* Eusebio Pedroza, Panama†	Pat Cowdell, England	Azumah Nelson, Ghana	Steve Sims, Wales
Junior featherweight	Wilfredo Gómez, Puerto Rico* Leonardo Cruz, Dominican Republic†	...	...	...
Bantamweight	Lupe Pintor, Mexico* Jeff Chandler, U.S.†	Guiseppe Fossati, Italy	Paul Ferreri, Australia	John Feeney, England
Super flyweight	Rafael Orono, Venezuela* Jiro Watanabe, Japan†	...	...	...
Flyweight	Eloncio Mercedes, Dom. Rep.* Santos Laciar, Argentina†	Charlie Magri, England	Steven Muchoki, Kenya	Kelvin Smart, Wales
Junior flyweight	Hilario Zapata, Panama* Katsuo Tokashiki, Japan†	...	...	...

*World Boxing Council champion.   †World Boxing Association champion.

WBC heavyweight champion Larry Holmes retained his crown by defeating Gerry Cooney in a June bout in Las Vegas.

WIDE WORLD

the richest prizefight in history. Both champion and challenger were reported to have grossed about $10 million each. The fight was witnessed by 32,000 in a stadium erected in the parking lot of Caesar's Palace in Las Vegas, Nev., but millions watched it throughout the world on closed-circuit television. Holmes thus remained undefeated in 40 contests, while Cooney was defeated for the first time in 26 bouts. In November Holmes was again successful with a unanimous 15-round victory over Randall "Tex" Cobb in Houston, Texas. Mike Weaver (U.S.), the World Boxing Association (WBA) champion, lost his title to Michael Dokes (U.S.) when he was stopped in the first round of a challenge late in the year.

The cruiserweight division, introduced by the WBC in 1980, raised the weight limit to 195 lb. Carlos de León (Puerto Rico) retained the title, stopping Marvin Camel (U.S.), the former champion, in seven rounds, but then lost his championship to S. T. Gordon (U.S.) when battered to defeat in two rounds. The WBA, which had not previously competed in this division, recognized Ossie Ocasio (Puerto Rico) as champion when he outpointed Robbie Williams (South Africa) in Johannesburg. He retained the title with a points victory over Young Joe Louis (U.S.) in Chicago in December. Dwight Muhammad Qawi (U.S.), formerly Dwight Braxton, retained the WBC light-heavyweight title with wins over Jerry Martin (U.S.) in six rounds and Matthew Saad Muhammad (U.S.), also in six. The WBA championship was retained by Michael "Mike" Spinks (U.S.), who won his four defenses against Mustapha Wasajja (Uganda) in six rounds, Murray Sutherland (U.S.) in eight, Jerry Celestine (U.S.) also in eight, and Johnny Davis (U.S.) in nine.

Marvelous Marvin Hagler (U.S.) continued as undisputed middleweight champion recognized by the WBC and WBA, with knockouts against William "Caveman" Lee (U.S.) in 67 seconds of the first round and Fulgencio Obelmejías (Venezuela) in five rounds. Wilfred Benítez (Puerto Rico) surrendered the WBC junior middleweight crown to Thomas Hearns (U.S.), who beat him on points over 15 rounds in a December bout. Benítez held off a challenge to his junior middleweight title earlier in the year by outpointing Roberto Durán (Panama). Davey Moore (U.S.) became the new WBA champion at that weight by stopping Tadashi Mihara (Japan) in six rounds in Tokyo. Moore then retained his title, stopping Charlie Weir (South Africa) in five rounds in Johannesburg and Ayub Kalue (Denmark) in ten.

Sugar Ray Leonard (U.S.), the undisputed welterweight champion of the WBC and WBA and considered by many the most outstanding boxer since Muhammad Ali, announced his retirement from the ring at the age of 26. This followed months of speculation after his eye operation for a detached retina. Leonard had successfully defended his title by stopping Bruce Finch (U.S.) in three rounds. A former Olympic Games champion, Leonard lost only one decision in 32 professional contests.

Leroy Haley (U.S.) took the WBC junior welterweight crown from Saoul Mamby (U.S.) and successfully defended it against Giovanni Giuseppe Giminez (Italy). Aaron Pryor (U.S.) kept the WBA junior welterweight title by stopping Miguel Montilla (Dominican Republic) in 12 rounds, Akio Kameda (Japan) in 6, and Alexis Argüello (Nicaragua; see BIOGRAPHIES) in 14. Argüello was attempting to win his fourth world title at different weights.

Argüello remained the top man among the lightweights, retaining the WBC title by stopping James Busceme (U.S.) in six rounds and Andy Ganigan (U.S.) in five. This was Argüello's 19th successive championship win in three divisions: featherweight, junior lightweight, and lightweight. The WBA lightweight crown was taken over by Ray Mancini (U.S.) with a one-round win against Arturo Frias (U.S.). Frias earlier had retained the championship with a controversial points decision after nine rounds against Ernesto España (Venezuela). Frias was cut under the left eye, and, because the three judges had Frias ahead on points, he was awarded the decision. España was later matched with Mancini but lost in six rounds. Mancini then knocked out Duk Koo Kim (South Korea) in the 14th round; the 23-year-old Korean never recovered consciousness and later died.

After Rolando Navarrete (Philippines) had retained the WBC junior lightweight championship, knocking out Chung Il-Choi (South Korea) in 11 rounds in Manila, Rafael Limón (Mexico), a former champion, regained the title by knocking out Navarrete in 12 rounds. Limón briefly kept the crown, stopping Chung Il-Choi in seven, but he later lost it on points to Bobby Chacon (U.S.). Sammy Serrano (Puerto Rico) retained the WEA version of this division after a controversial finish against Benedicto Villablanca (Chile). The fight was stopped at the end of the tenth round after Serrano had sustained a badly cut eye, and the decision was given to Villablanca. But later the WBA changed the decision to a technical draw, and, because the referee and two judges had Serrano ahead on points, the referee put the injury down to an accidental butt and Serrano retained the title.

The featherweight division suffered a tragedy when WBC champion Salvador Sánchez (Mexico; see OBITUARIES) was killed in an automobile accident in Mexico City a few weeks after retaining the title with a victory over Azumah Nelson (Ghana) in 15 rounds. Sánchez, who was 23, lost only one of 47 professional contests and won the world title before he was 21. He won ten title bouts. The vacant WBC crown was won by Juan LaPorte (U.S.), who beat Mario Miranda (Colombia) in ten rounds. Eusebio Pedroza (Panama) kept the WBA featherweight crown earlier, outpointing LaPorte and drawing with Bernard Taylor (U.S.) in his 15th defense. Wilfredo Gómez (Puerto Rico) remained WBC junior featherweight king after a total of 17 defenses. His four wins were against Juan Meza (U.S.) in 6 rounds, Juan Antonio López (Mexico) in 10, Roberto Rubaldino (Mexico) in 7, and Lupe Pintor (Mexico) in 14. Sergio Palma (Arg.) won the WBA junior featherweight title from Jorge Luján (Panama) but lost it to Leonardo Cruz (Dominican Republic) on points.

Lupe Pintor (Mexico) continued as WBC bantamweight champion, stopping Seung-Hoon Lee (South Korea) in 11 rounds, and Jeff Chandler (U.S.) retained the WBA version and his unbeaten record by defeating Johnny Carter (U.S.) in six and Miguel Iriarte (Panama) in nine. Chul-Ho Kim (South Korea), the WBC super flyweight champion, won against Koki Ishii (Japan) and Raúl Valdez (Mexico) but in November was stopped in the sixth round by former champion Rafael Orono (Venezuela). The WBA gained a new champion when Jiro Watanabe (Japan) beat Rafael Pedroza (Panama) and retained the title against Gustavo Ballas (Arg.). The WBC flyweight championship changed three times. Prudencio Cardona (Colombia) took the title from Antonio Avelar (Mexico) with a one-round knockout but lost it to Freddie Castillo (Mexico). Later Castillo was outpointed by Eloncio Mercedes (Dominican Republic). The WBA flyweight crown was taken over by Santos Laciar (Arg.), a former champion, who stopped Juan Herrera (Mexico) in 13 rounds and carried on as champion with wins over Betulio Gonzáles (Venezuela) and Steve Muchoki (Kenya), both former champions. The WBC junior flyweight championship changed hands several times. Hilario Zapata

Wrestler Lee Kemp (bandage on leg) seems to be getting the worst of it, but he went on to beat his Iranian opponent, Hossein Mohebbi, 3–2, in World Wrestling Championships in Edmonton, Alberta, in August. The two were competing in the 74-kg (163-lb) class.

Jeno Pap of Hungary (right) won the individual épée class in the World Fencing Championships in Rome by defeating Philippe Riboud of France in July.

Table II. World Wrestling Champions, 1982

Weight class	Freestyle	Greco-Roman
48 kg (105.5 lb)	S. Kornilaev, U.S.S.R.	T. Kazaraszwili, U.S.S.R.
52 kg (114.5 lb)	H. Reich, E. Germany	B. Paszajan, U.S.S.R.
57 kg (125.5 lb)	A. Beloglazov, U.S.S.R.	P. Michalik, Poland
62 kg (136.5 lb)	S. Beloglazov, U.S.S.R.	R. Swierad, Poland
68 kg (149.5 lb)	M. Kharachura, U.S.S.R.	G. Ermilov, U.S.S.R.
74 kg (163 lb)	L. Kemp, U.S.	S. Rusa, Romania
82 kg (180.5 lb)	T. Dzgoev, U.S.S.R.	T. Abhazawa, U.S.S.R.
90 kg (198 lb)	U. Neupert, E. Germany	R. Anderson, Sweden
100 kg (220 lb)	I. Mate, U.S.S.R.	R. Wroclawski, Poland
100+ kg	S. Khasimikov, U.S.S.R.	N. Dinev, Bulgaria

(Panama), the defending champion, was knocked out in two rounds by Amado Ursua (Mexico). Then Tadashi Tomori (Japan) outpointed Ursua, but Zapata earned a split decision against Tomori to become champion again and then defeated Chang Jung-Koo (South Korea). Zapata later defended his title in a rematch with Tomori by stopping the challenger in the eighth round. WBA champion Katsuo Tokashiki (Japan) stopped Masaharu Inami (Japan) in the eighth round.

In December the WBC announced two rules changes for championship fights. All bouts would be limited to a maximum of 12 rather than 15 rounds, and referees must impose a mandatory standing eight count for any fighter who appears to be defenseless.

In Europe Lucien Rodriguez (France) remained heavyweight champion with points victories over Al Syben (Belgium), Dragomir Popovic (Yugos.), and Alfredo Evangelista (Spain). Rudi Koopmans (Neth.) retained the light-heavyweight title, knocking out Cristiano Cavina (Italy) in the first round, stopping Alex Blanchard (Neth.) in the eighth, and beating Domenico Adinolfs (Italy).

Tony Sibson (England) relinquished the middleweight crown, and Louis Acaries (France) earned it in December by stopping Frank Wissenbach (West Germany) in six rounds. Luigi Minchillo (Italy) continued as junior middleweight champion, outpointing Maurice Hope (England) and Jean-André Emmerich (West Germany).

Jørgen Hansen (Den.) retired, relinquishing the welterweight title. Hans Henrik Palm (Den.) eventually met Colin Jones (Wales) in Copenhagen for the vacant crown; Jones knocked out Palm in two rounds. Clinton McKenzie (England) lost the junior welterweight championship to Roberto Gambini (France) on a two-round disqualification. Joey Gibilisco (Italy) retained the lightweight title in a drawn contest against Ray Cattouse (England). (FRANK BUTLER)

Wrestling. The U.S.S.R. continued its domination of amateur wrestling, winning both freestyle and Greco-Roman 1982 world championships. The Soviet victory was most pronounced in the freestyle tournament, which was held August 11–14 in Edmonton, Alta. Soviet wrestlers took seven individual championships, one second place, and two third places. In team scoring the U.S.S.R. had 55 points, followed by the U.S. with 28, Bulgaria with 25, and East Germany with 23.

In the Greco-Roman tournament, held at Katowice, Poland, September 9–11, the Soviets placed all ten of their wrestlers. They finished with four champions, one second place, two thirds, and three fourth places, for a total of 46 points. Poland finished second with 31 points, and Bulgaria and Romania tied for third with 30 points each.

The University of Iowa won its fifth straight U.S. National Collegiate Athletic Association championship and in so doing also set a new NCAA scoring record with 131.75 points. Iowa State University finished second with 111 points.

(MARVIN G. HESS)

Fencing. A pall was cast over the sport of fencing in July when Vladimir Smirnov of the Soviet Union died as a result of a freak accident during the world championships in Rome. The 28-year-old athlete, who had been a 1980 Olympic Games gold medalist with the foil, was mortally wounded when his rival's broken weapon pierced his protective wire-mesh mask. The mishap occurred during a bout with Mattias Behr of West Germany. Behr was attacking, and Smirnov advanced in a counter action. The point of the West German's blade hit the middle of Smirnov's chest with such force that the weapon snapped. The jagged end of the remaining part of the blade then went through Smirnov's mask into his eye.

Robert Berland (left) of Wilmette, Illinois, gave a flip to Brian Germain of Lakeland, Florida, during the 86-kg (189-lb) judo competition in the National Sports Festival. The festival was held in Indianapolis, Indiana, in July.

Despite Smirnov's absence the Soviet Union almost registered a sweep in the four foil events. Aleksandr Romankov captured the individual men's title in an awesome performance in which none of his last four opponents scored more than four touches against him. Led by Romankov, the U.S.S.R. also won the men's team foil tournament; France finished second and Italy third. In women's foil Naila Guliazova gave the Soviets their third straight gold medal by defeating second-place Dorina Vaccaroni of Italy. However, Vaccaroni then led her teammates to victory in women's team foil.

The Soviet Union also showed strength in the individual sabre as Viktor Krouopuskov and Andret Alchan finished first and second in a heated competition. Hungary's Imre Gedovari was third. In team sabre Gedovari succeeded in pacing his countrymen to the first of that nation's two gold medals.

Hungary's other first place was gained in individual épée, as the veteran Jeno Pap turned in one of the tournament's major surprises. The Hungarian outscored Philippe Riboud of France. Hungary's Erno Kolczonay was third. France accounted for its only triumph in team épée, Switzerland finishing second and Hungary third.

In the U.S., Wayne State University captured its third NCAA fencing title in four years by outscoring Clemson 85 to 77. The University of Pennsylvania finished third.   (MICHAEL STRAUSS)

Judo. Japanese *judoka* won the team title as well as six of the seven individual weight classes at stake in 1982's only major world judo tournament, the 33-nation Jigoro Kano International Championships. World champion Yashuhiro Yamashita reinforced his claim to greatness by capturing the All-Japan Judo Championships (the world's only major judo tournament without weight classes) in April for an unprecedented sixth straight year. He also won the over-95-kg event for the fifth consecutive time in the All-Japan Weight Class Judo Championships in Fukuoka. Then, in the Jigoro Kano Cup meet in November, 27-year-old Yamashita took the open-weights title by defeating Hitoshi Saito by *waza-ari* (half-point) in the final. He thus stretched his unbeaten record to 173 matches, including 104 consecutive wins over all foreign opponents since 1974. Other Japanese winners in the Jigoro Kano Cup tourney were heavyweight Takeshi Suwa, middleweight Nobutoshi Hikage, lightweight Hidetoshi Nakanishi, bantamweight Katsuhiko Kashiwazaki, and flyweight Shinji Hosokawa. The only non-Japanese winner was Soviet *judoka* David Bodaveli, a light-heavyweight. In the team competition, Japan and the Soviet Union finished with two wins each and a draw in the finals, but Japan was declared winner "for superior techniques." Altogether, Japan captured seven gold, five silver, and eight bronze medals.

Karate. Karate in 1982 was highlighted by the sixth World Championships held in November under the sponsorship of the World Union of Karate-do Organizations (WUKO) in Taichung, Taiwan. On the eve of the tournament, WUKO directors voted 19–17 to bar South Africa from competing and agreed that the 1984 championships would be held in The Netherlands. Britain defeated Italy 4–0 in the team finals. Japan and Spain tied for third. But Japanese *karateka* won three of the six golds in the *kumite* (free-fighting) competition as well as both golds in the men's and women's *kata* (prescribed forms) contests. *Wado-kai* specialists Hisao Murase and Seiji Nishimura, both of whom had dominated Japanese karate for the past several years, won the open and 65–70-kg classes, respectively, while Yuichi Suzuki took the 60–65-kg category. Other winners were Jukka Vayrynen of Finland in the under-60-kg class, Javier Gomez of Switzerland in the 70–75-kg class, Patrick McKay of Britain in the 75–80-kg class, and Jeffrey Thompson of Britain in the over-80-kg class. Masashi Koyama and Mie Nakayama, both of Japan, took the men's and women's titles, respectively, in the *kata* competition.

Although the major karate styles associated with WUKO did not hold national championships during the year, the main nonaffiliated styles staged their own tournaments. The All-Japan Shotokan Championships was won in September by Masashi Sakata in *kumite* and Yoshiharu Osaka in *kata*. Keiji Sanpei won an unprecedented third karate title in the Kokushin-kai's All-Japan (contact) Championships at the Tokyo Municipal Gymnasium. Kazutoshi Yamamura of Osaka captured the men's open title in the National Athletic Meet in Shimane Prefecture during October, as well as the championship of the Osaka municipal tournament. Murase had previously taken the open title four straight years.

Sumo. After dominating sumo for the past four or five years, *yokozuna* (grand champion) Kitanoumi ("Kita") won only one *yusho* (tournament championship) in 1982. A new *yokozuna*, Chiyonofuji, grabbed the spotlight by winning four of the six *yusho*, including three in a row, and placing second in another. The 27-year-old Chiyonofuji ("Chiyo") also won Rikishi of the Year honours with 74 wins against 16 losses, ending Kitanoumi's seven-year monopoly of that prestigious award. Kita's one victory left him nine *yusho* behind former *yokozuna* Taiho's career record of 32. It now appeared unlikely that 29-year-old Kita would break Taiho's mark. The other *yusho* was won by 30-year-old *ozeki* (champion) Takanosato, who put on a sudden surge in the fifth *basho* (tournament) to finish with a perfect 15–0 record. He missed promotion to sumo's highest rank of *yokozuna* by posting a disappointing 10–5 record in the final tourney. Even so, Takanosato's 1982 total of 68 wins and 22 losses was second only to Chiyo's. Rivaling Chiyo in popularity was Wakashimazu ("Waka"), a new star who racked up the third best annual total with 61 wins and 19 losses. He catapulted from the No. 2 *maegashira* rank to the rank of *ozeki*. Ozeki Kotokaze finished with 58 victories against 32 defeats. Kitanoumi wound up far behind the leaders with an annual mark of 52–38, largely because he was sidelined for 20 bouts. Full-blooded Hawaiian Takamiyama, born Jesse Kuhaulua but now a Japanese citizen named Daigoro Watanabe, completed his 15th year in the top division (of six divisions composed of more than 700 sumo wrestlers) at the age of 38. The heaviest *rikishi* (sumo wrestler) in the history of the 2,000-year-old sport at 204 kg (450 lb), Takamiyama extended his consecutive *basho* record to 90 and moved into third place on the all-time list for most wins with 642.

Kita lost his first two bouts in the Hatsu Basho in January but won the remaining 13 to capture his only *yusho* of the year. Chiyo and Takanosato tied for second with 12–3 marks. Chiyo then won three *yusho* in a row before Takanosato astonished sumo fans with a perfect 15–0 victory in the Aki *basho* in September. Chiyo won his fourth *yusho* in November with a brilliant 14–1 performance.

Kendo. Japan, as expected, completely dominated the World Kendo Championships in São Paulo, Brazil, in midsummer. The Japanese team overwhelmed Brazil 4–1 for the team championships, while the U.S. and South Korea tied for third place. Also competing were Argentina, Canada, China, France, Italy, Mexico, Sweden, Switzerland, and West Germany. In the individual championships, M. Makita of the Osaka University of Physical Education defeated Osaka policeman T. Kosaka. Kosaka was also runner-up in the All-Japan Men's Individual Kendo Championships held in November. Kenichi Ishida took the championship by scoring a *kote* (forearm) strike in overtime. Satomi Fukunojo of Kagoshima won the All-Japan Women's Kendo Championships with a *do* (side) strike against Kanako Omura. In the All-Japan Men's Team Championships, the Saitama Prefecture team scored a 4–1 victory over Osaka. Kiyonori Nishikawa grabbed the individual title in the All-Japan Police Championships with two *men* (helmet) points against Tadayoshi Ito.

(ANDREW M. ADAMS)

Commonwealth of Nations

The member states of the Commonwealth unanimously supported the military action of the United Kingdom in response to the Argentine invasion of the Falkland Islands in April 1982, since many of these nations—among them Belize, Guyana, and Kenya—suffered similar external claims on their land. In June, when the new government of Guatemala stated that it no longer recognized Belize's independence, Britain warned that the Commonwealth Pact (Britain, Canada, Guyana, Jamaica, Trinidad, Barbados, and The Bahamas) would be implemented in the event of military threat. The 1981 Melbourne Declaration specifically supported Commonwealth territorial integrity.

The Maldives became the 47th member state and the fourth with special-member status in July 1982. The establishment of the Senegambian confederation in February combined The Gambia and Senegal, the latter not a Commonwealth nation; each state retained its sovereignty, but finance, foreign policy, and defense were to be shared. In southern Africa, Swaziland was negotiating with South Africa over the transfer of a large area of land in northern Natal and Transvaal. Acquisition of this land would give Swaziland access to the sea and 750,000 more subjects. The move was condemned by both the Organization of African Unity, on the grounds of border inviolability, and by the Zulus, who also claimed the territory. Negotiations were

delayed as a result of the death of King Sobhuza II (*see* OBITUARIES) of Swaziland in August.

There was political unrest in some parts of Commonwealth Africa. Ghana's fourth military coup since independence—and the second to be led by former flight lieutenant Jerry Rawlings—occurred on Dec. 31, 1981. In August 1982 there was a short-lived mutiny by rebel forces in Seychelles. Kenya, long regarded as among the most stable of African nations, suffered an abortive coup in August; this followed the ruling Kenya African National Union's decision in June that it should be the nation's only officially recognized political party. Sierra Leone's first one-party elections in May were marred by violence and corruption. In Mauritius the left-wing alliance of the Mauritius Militant Movement and the Mauritius Socialist Party gained all 62 directly elected seats in the legislature in June elections. Prime Minister Robert Mugabe's open support for a single-party state in Zimbabwe deepened the rift between himself and Joshua Nkomo, who was dismissed from the Cabinet in February.

Echoes of the 1981 Commonwealth heads of government meeting in Melbourne, Australia, sounded during the year. Canada received final patriation of its constitution on April 17 when Queen Elizabeth II signed the Constitution Act, which replaced the British North America Act of 1867. Papua New Guinea joined the Association of Southeast Asian Nations as an observer. The UN Conference on the Law of the Sea was an issue of importance to the Commonwealth, with 23 island nations and 16 coastal states among its members. (*See* LAW.)

Commonwealth finance ministers meeting in London in August agreed to increase aid to the poorest member nations. British aid figures for 1981 were estimated at £1,082 million, the vast majority going to Commonwealth countries. India was the largest single recipient at £86 million; Zimbabwe counted as a special case, as its total of £112 million included some allowances outside aid figures. The Commonwealth Development Corporation made new commitments worth £94.7 million in 1981. These covered 25 projects in 19 countries and brought total commitments to £596 million in 47 countries. (MOLLY MORTIMER)

See also articles on the various political units.
[972.A.1.a]

Comoros

An island state lying in the Indian Ocean off the east coast of Africa between Mozambique and Madagascar, the Comoros administratively comprise three main islands, Grande Comore (Ngazídja), Moheli (Mohali), and Anjouan (Dzouani); the fourth island of the archipelago, Mayotte, continued to be a de facto dependency of France. Area: 1,792 sq km (692 sq mi). Pop. (1982 est., excluding Mayotte): 372,000. Cap. and largest city: Moroni (pop., 1980 prelim., 20,100), on Grande Comore. Language: Comorian (which is allied to Swahili), Arabic, and French. Religion: Islam (official). President in 1982, Ahmed Abdal-

Comecon:
see Economy, World

Commerce:
see Economy, World

Commodity Futures:
see Stock Exchanges

Common Market:
see Economy, World; European Unity

Communications:
see Industrial Review; Television and Radio

Comoros

lah; premiers, Salim Ben Ali and, from February 8, Ali Mroudjae.

During 1982 Pres. Ahmed Abdallah significantly reinforced his personal authority. On January 25 he dissolved the Federal Assembly and the government, and on February 8 he appointed former foreign minister Ali Mroudjae as premier. Legislative elections held on March 7 and 14 resulted in candidates who supported the government winning all seats in the assembly. On October 24 a number of constitutional amendments extended the powers of the head of state at the expense of the island governors. On May 28 President Abdallah pardoned former foreign minister Abdallah Mouzaoir, who had been convicted of subversive activity on May 19. Opposition to the regime was now limited to Comorans resident abroad and to the educational sector; in October 200 teachers were dismissed for taking part in strikes.

Although the status of the island of Mayotte, still a de facto French dependency, remained unresolved, relations with France were good. Pres. François Mitterrand received President Abdallah in Paris in June, and in August French Minister for Cooperation Jean-Pierre Cot visited Moroni. (PHILIPPE DECRAENE)

Computers

The permeation of computers into people's daily lives became increasingly noticeable during 1982. Indications of this trend included the appearance of coin-operated microcomputers at some libraries, the proliferation of automated teller machines at banks, and home banking ventures that allowed a selected number of customers to link their home computers to the bank's computer centre in order to perform transactions.

Evidence of the growing use of computers as standard appliances was seen as increasing numbers of stores began stocking personal computers on their shelves. Personalities such as comedian Bill Cosby touted the utility of these systems on television, and magazines and newspapers carried extensive advertising about them. In fact, the competition among vendors to sell personal computers for home use resulted in a brief price war when Texas Instruments, Inc. offered a $100 rebate on its 99-4A home computer.

"Computer literacy," knowledge about the operation of and language of computers, was at the root

Nearly 200 libraries in the U.S. installed coin-operated computers during the year. Customers pay $2 to $6 for an hour of computer time. It was anticipated that more than 40,000 U.S. libraries would eventually offer this service.

of this growing fascination with the microcomputer. As adults encountered computers more frequently at their places of work and as children used computers as learning tools at school, computer literacy was quickly spreading through society and paving the way for more extensive use of computer-based systems and acceptance of computer technology. Legislation was introduced into Congress that would allow computer vendors to make tax-deductible gifts of computers to educational institutions.

Technology. Although microcomputers had recently begun to capture the interest of the general public, particularly for use at home, the vast majority of computer systems were used for business or scientific purposes and were much larger than personal computers. These larger systems are known as mainframes and minicomputers.

Somewhere between the personal computer and the larger systems was the domain of the desktop computers. Shipments of these powerful, economical devices, priced at below $5,000, were projected to increase annually by about 45% for the next five years. These computers, built around 16-bit or 32-bit processors, allow managers and professionals to access information. Their greatest potential is for distributed processing applications, in which data are downloaded from a company's mainframe to the desktop system, where they are used by

Britannica's New "Quill Pen"

Encyclopædia Britannica, now in its third century, has taken a giant leap into the modern high-tech age with the installation of a specially designed electronic editorial system. For the first time since William Smellie, first editor of the *Encyclopædia Britannica*, took up his quill pen in 1768, Britannica editors can control the final printed results of their work without the intervention of outside typesetters, proofreaders, or printers.

Heretofore, even with the use of electronic typesetting, the editors and other editorial personnel were forced to go through the same steps that Smellie would have found quite familiar—manuscript preparation, typesetting, proofreading, typesetting corrections, proofreading corrections, page design, page layout, page makeup, page correction, etc. Now, however, many of those steps have been eliminated or altered radically. Sitting at a video display tube—not unlike a small television set or arcade game—the editor can edit, correct, or move copy by manipulating a 134-key keyboard. An editor can immediately ascertain how long an article will be when printed and where each line of an article breaks. If there is a need to rearrange paragraphs, scissors and paste-pot are no longer required. The editor simply defines the paragraph to be moved, points to where it should go, strikes the "move" key, and the job is done.

Typographic decisions can also be made instantly. There are keys to change words, sentences, or paragraphs from roman type to *italic* or to **boldface.** If the designer decides that a narrower column is called for, the editor can insert a simple command or code and, without resetting even a single character of the text, the line becomes narrower.

In like manner—by use of codes or keys—the editor can increase the space between lines or, if a special effect is desired, can even cause lines to be centred within the column.

The system that makes possible this new editorial speed and flexibility was designed and installed by Atex, Inc., of Bedford, Mass., a firm well known for its various newspaper editorial computer systems. The Britannica system consists of three Digital Equipment Corp. 11/34 computers that were extensively modified by Atex, six disk drives that can store up to 300 million characters each, 32 video display tubes on which editing functions can be performed, and three soft typesetters—proofing devices that permit electronic review of pages before they are actually turned into type for the press.

One thing, of course, has not changed since 1768. The stern insistence on completeness and accuracy the editors demand of each Britannica publication would make Smellie and his editorial successors proud. But the new electronic "quill pen" makes getting that effort into print faster, easier, and—it may be said—a lot more fun.

(J. THOMAS BEATTY)

managers and professionals for applications specific to their jobs. The communication of data to and among these devices is usually accomplished through a local area network. Many versions of these networks, such as Wangnet from Wang Laboratories, Inc., were introduced during 1982 by the makers of desktop systems.

Although there were no major technological breakthroughs during the year, new technologies such as artificial intelligence and a technique for "growing" computer circuitry in test tubes captured the imaginations of computer watchers. Artificial intelligence (AI) is a technique for programming computers to mimic human thought processes. Computers programmed in such a way are known as "expert" systems. They are designed to aid people in making judgments pertinent to their work specialties.

Expanding their technological horizons, scientists were also experimenting with growing biocircuits. Also called biochips, these were envisioned as a single layer of protein on top of glass and overlaid with metal tracks to form conventional two-dimensional chips. More complex versions consisted of enzymes used to organize a three-dimensional array of molecules that could fit into a human cell and direct pulses of current.

Business. Although the outlook for improved computer technology appeared almost limitless, the continuing recession had a severe effect on the profits of many of the major computer and semiconductor firms. Layoffs and work furloughs were quite common throughout the year.

The year began in noteworthy fashion when the U.S. Department of Justice settled on January 8 its long-standing antitrust suit with AT&T. AT&T agreed to divest itself of its 22 Bell operating companies, thus gaining the approval of the agency to enter the lucrative data-processing market. On the same day the Department of Justice also dropped its 13-year-old antitrust suit against IBM Corp. This action was viewed by many as permission for IBM to compete even more aggressively in all areas of the computer business.

In September IBM introduced the 3084 computer. Almost twice as powerful as the firm's previous top-of-the-line model, it can process 26 million instructions per second. The 3084 consists of four smaller computers acting together as a single unit. A similar machine having almost as high a speed as the 3084 was unveiled earlier in the year by the Univac division of the Sperry Corp.

The threat of Japanese encroachment in the U.S. computer market created considerable uneasiness among U.S. manufacturers. This was heightened dramatically in June, when the U.S. Department of Justice charged two large Japanese firms, Hitachi Ltd. and Mitsubishi Electric Corp., and various persons acting on their behalf, with paying $650,000 for IBM system secrets.

Another major event during the year was the incorporation of the Microelectronics and Comput-

A Computer Showcase Expo, held in Chicago in November, attracted 70 exhibitors and more than 17,000 attendees.

er Technology Corp. Proposed by Control Data Corp. in 1981, this new firm was conceived as a research venture to be funded jointly by major U.S. computer and semiconductor vendors. When in operation, the company expected to perform basic research on computer systems, semiconductor packaging, computer-aided design and manufacturing, and software productivity. The venture marked the first time that leading firms in the industry had pledged wide-scale cooperation in research and was seen as a way of countering the massive government-sponsored research in Japan. Cooperation was also the key to a pledge by Digital Equipment Corp., Tektronix, Inc., Intel Corp., and other vendors to formulate standards for graphics and videotext transmission.

Applications. Computers played a key role behind the scenes in several major events during the year. Systems at the U.S. Food and Drug Administration sorted two million product tests in the wake of seven deaths in the Chicago area associated with cyanide poisoning of Extra-Strength Tylenol capsules. Other systems at Johnson & Johnson were tracing distribution of the contaminated batches of the product. (*See* CRIME AND LAW ENFORCEMENT.)

Computers were also enlisted to search Social Security files in order to trace some 500,000 men who had not registered for the military draft in the U.S. This action raised cries of invasion of privacy among some citizens.

Operation Greenbacks, a project of the U.S. Customs Service's Currency Investigation Division, the Internal Revenue Service, and the U.S. Department of Justice, concentrated on tracing large unexplainable sums of money. This helped lead to a seizure of $25 million in cocaine.

Because computer components were in such demand in the Soviet Union and other Eastern European countries, the Customs Service intensified its Operation Exodus effort in 1982. This led to more than 65 seizures of equipment bound for countries with which U.S. computer vendors were not allowed to trade.

Electronic video games continued their rapid growth. Almost unknown five years earlier, they were plugged into television sets in approximately 15 million homes in the U.S. at the end of 1982. Revenues from these games, which operate with microprocessor chips, were estimated at $1.7 billion in 1982, and many industry observers believed that the figure would rise to $3 billion in 1983. In addition, electronic games in arcades were enjoying great popularity and profitability. At the end of the year, however, two major firms announced fourth-quarter sales that were lower than expected. (*See* GAMES AND TOYS.)

(MARCIA A. BLUMENTHAL)

[735.D.; 10/23.A.6–7]

Congo

A people's republic of equatorial Africa, the Congo is bounded by Gabon, Cameroon, the Central African Republic, Zaire, Angola, and the Atlantic Ocean. Area: 342,000 sq km (132,047 sq mi). Pop. (1982 est.): 1,619,000, including Kongo 52%, Teke 24%, Kota 5%, Mboshi 4%, other 15%. Cap. and largest city: Brazzaville (pop., 1980 est., 422,400). Language: French (official), Kikongo, Lingala, Monokutuba, Sanga, and local Bantu dialects. Religion (1977 est.): Roman Catholic 40.5%; Protestant 9.6%; Muslim 2.9%; animist 47%. President in

Congo

CONGO

Education. (1979–80) Primary, pupils 383,018, teachers 6,852; secondary, pupils 148,857, teachers 3,148; vocational, pupils 8,744, teachers (1978–79) 505; teacher training, students 1,617, teachers (1978–79) 102; higher, students (1977–78) 4,767, teaching staff 254.

Finance. Monetary unit: CFA franc, with (Sept. 20, 1982) a parity of CFA Fr 50 to the French franc and a free rate of CFA Fr 353 to U.S. $1 (CFA Fr 605 = £1 sterling). Budget (1981 est.) balanced at CFA Fr 159.9 billion.

Foreign Trade. (1979) Imports CFA Fr 61,960,000,000; exports CFA Fr 108,460,000,000. Import sources (1978): France 50%; Italy 6%; West Germany 5%; U.S. 5%. Export destinations (1978): Italy 31%; France 24%; Spain 8%; The Netherlands 6%; Chile 6%; Belgium-Luxembourg 5%. Main exports (1978): crude oil 63%; veneers 10%; timber 8%; food 6%; diamonds 6%.

Transport and Communications. Roads (all-weather; 1977) 8,246 km. Motor vehicles in use (1977): passenger 13,250; commercial 3,700. Railways: (1980) c. 800 km; traffic (1979) 286 million passenger-km, freight 470 million net ton-km. Air traffic (including apportionment of Air Afrique; 1980): c. 197 million passenger-km; freight c. 19.3 million net ton-km. Telephones (Dec. 1978) 13,000. Radio receivers (Dec. 1979) 92,000. Television receivers (Dec. 1979) 3,300.

Agriculture. Production (in 000; metric tons; 1981): cassava c. 530; sweet potatoes c. 26; peanuts c. 14; sugar, raw value c. 22; bananas c. 31; plantains c. 34; coffee c. 5; cocoa c. 4; palm oil c. 9; tobacco c. 1. Livestock (in 000; 1981): cattle c. 75; sheep c. 69; goats c. 133; pigs c. 53; chickens c. 1,150.

Industry. Production (in 000; metric tons; 1979): cement 55; crude oil (1981) c. 3,090; lead concentrates (metal content; 1978) c. 2.5; zinc ore (metal content; 1978) 4.8; electricity (kw-hr; 1980) 120,000.

1982, Col. Denis Sassou-Nguesso; premier, Col. Louis Sylvain Ngoma.

Signs of a reconciliation with France, the former colonial power, first became evident in the Congo in 1981 and increased during 1982. In October French Pres. François Mitterrand was received with great enthusiasm in Brazzaville, where he announced plans to increase cooperation between the two countries. Past differences were to be put aside in light of the government's proposed economic development program, which required assistance from France.

Relations with the U.S.S.R. were not in any way adversely affected by the rapprochement with France. On October 23 a delegation from the Communist Party of the Soviet Union paid an official visit to Brazzaville.   (PHILIPPE DECRAENE)

Consumerism

March 15, 1982, marked the 20th anniversary of the "consumer bill of rights." In a speech to the U.S. Congress on that date in 1962, Pres. John F. Kennedy announced four basic rights of consumers: the rights to safety, to be informed, to choose, and to be heard. The rights to redress, to consumer education, and to a healthy environment were subsequently added. The president of the International Organization of Consumers Unions (IOCU) proposed that March 15 be marked as "Consumer Rights Day" throughout the world.

International Cooperation. In 1982 IOCU's membership stood at 118 organizations in 50 countries. In recent years, and especially after the tenth International Consumer Congress in The Hague, Neth., in June 1981, IOCU had played an increasing

role as an "international consumer advocate," particularly through a number of groups that it was instrumental in forming: the International Baby Food Action Network (IBFAN, formed in 1979), Health Action International (HAI, 1981), and the Pesticide Action Network (PAN, 1982). A major IOCU project for the 1980s—Consumer Interpol—was launched in 1982; its aim was to provide a worldwide warning and information exchange system on newly discovered hazardous products, wastes, and technologies.

In 1982 IBFAN released three publications to mark the start of a major new initiative to encourage implementation and monitoring of the World Health Organization's international code for the marketing of breast-milk substitutes. They provided up-to-date information, a practical guide for action, basic resource materials, a summary of industry practices since the code was approved, and a detailed critique of attempts by the baby food industry to rewrite the code.

HAI's first year was spent largely on the question of improving marketing and information for pharmaceuticals in the third world and on policy information from member groups. It produced a critique of the International Federation of Pharmaceutical Manufacturers' Associations' voluntary code of marketing practices that drew attention to inadequacies of the code and the absence of convincing interpretation, monitoring, and enforcement arrangements. An updated version of the critique was included in a HAI briefing pack for delegates to the 35th World Health Assembly, held in May 1982 in Geneva.

A coalition of nongovernmental organizations based in 16 countries, PAN was formed during a meeting in Penang, Malaysia, organized by IOCU and Friends of the Earth in May 1982. With the objective of stopping the indiscriminate sale and widespread misuse of hazardous chemical pesticides, PAN members called for, among other measures, the expansion of traditional, biological, and integrated pest management and an end to the unnecessary sale and use of chemical pesticides. It urged that nine Green Revolution research centres, including the International Rice Research Institute based in the Philippines, reverse their practice of developing and distributing seed varieties that are heavily dependent on chemical pesticides and fertilizers.

Mounting evidence of the dumping of hazardous or potentially hazardous products pointed to the need for an independent worldwide alert system. Consumer Interpol, inaugurated for this purpose during 1982, consisted of a network of correspondents representing consumer groups within the IOCU, as well as IBFAN, HAI, and PAN. The correspondents were to notify the Consumer Interpol coordinator when they received information on any newly discovered or recently regulated hazard. The coordinator, in turn, would inform other correspondents. Local chapters of Consumer Interpol were being organized in Australia and Malaysia. In recognition of the inception of this system, IOCU president Anwar Fazal was awarded the 1982 Alternative Nobel Prize.

In conjunction with World Food Day on October

Congregational Churches:
see Religion

Conservation:
see Environment

Construction Industry:
see Engineering Projects; Industrial Review

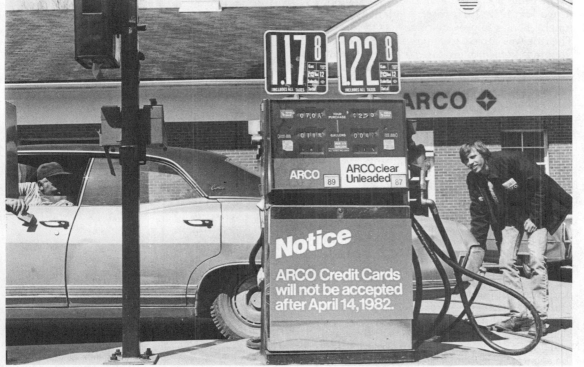

An attendant fills up the tank of a motorist's car at a gas station in New Canaan, Conn., during the final weekend before Arco dropped credit card services for its customers.

16, IOCU launched a food and nutrition resource pack designed to enable third world groups to understand the complex issues surrounding food. The international consumer movement was also breaking into the field of information technology. An IOCU working group decided to cover such subjects as advertising across national boundaries (through satellites), direct marketing through telephone-linked systems, data banks, privacy, and the potential use of satellites and other new technologies as sources of information in the third world.

Regional Developments. The Bureau Éuropéen des Unions de Consommateurs (BEUC), the lobby organization of consumer groups in the European Community (EC) countries, identified two areas related to the current economic recession as cornerstones of its programs for 1982. First, it felt that consumers should be more alert with regard to price-fixing mechanisms, competition problems, and price and quality comparisons. Second, safety and consumer protection should not be foregone because they placed a financial burden on industry. As a direct result of the second consideration, BEUC set up an alert system on hazardous products that would be linked to Consumer Interpol. For the first time, France had a Ministry of Consumer Affairs, established in response to consumer organizations' wishes. In Britain the Consumers' Association celebrated its 25th anniversary. The Arbeitsgemeinschaft der Verbraucher in West Germany named work toward reforming the law on unfair competition as its top priority for 1982.

The Consumers' Association of Penang, probably the best known such group in the third world, published a number of books during the year on topics ranging from the environmental crisis to "traditional" consumer concerns like product safety. The Hong Kong Consumer Council sounded

alerts on a range of products, including ineffective electronic mosquito repellents and face creams containing mercury. Australian consumer groups were giving increasing support to groups in the less developed countries of Asia.

(LIM SIANG JIN)

In the U.S. a study released by the Insurance Institute for Highway Safety in 1982 found that U.S.-made automobiles were safer than Japanese-made automobiles of comparable size. The study used government records on fatal automobile crashes that occurred from 1978 through 1980. The larger models had the best safety records. A rule reinstated by the Civil Aeronautics Board (CAB) on Oct. 1, 1982, allowed passengers of commercial airlines to collect double the face value of a one-way ticket, up to $400, if they were bumped from an airline flight and were unable to arrive at their destinations within two hours of their original scheduled flight. The CAB also changed a rule to allow passengers to obtain $1,000 rather than $750 if their luggage was lost or damaged.

The cyanide-laced Tylenol deaths in Chicago spurred manufacturers to offer a host of tamper-proof sealing devices for food and medicine containers.

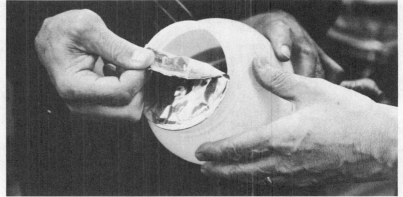

BUCK MILLER/BUSINESS WEEK

The Federal Trade Commission (FTC) completed its work in 1982 on proposed regulations requiring funeral homes to provide price lists to consumers. The rule was subject to congressional veto. In 1982 Congress vetoed a proposed FTC regulation that would have required used-car dealers to tell customers about known mechanical defects.

In September the Food and Drug Administration (FDA) proposed labeling aspirin containers with a warning that aspirin had been linked to Reye's syndrome, a rare and sometimes fatal childhood disease. A House of Representatives subcommittee approved three tough warning labels to be put on cigarette packages. The subcommittee's recommendations would be reviewed by Congress in 1983.

Consumer groups and restaurateurs were opposing revisions of beef grading standards proposed by the U.S. Department of Agriculture that would allow leaner and lower-priced beef to qualify for higher grades and higher prices. USDA officials contended that the current grading system put a price premium on fat content, which may cause health problems. A U.S. district court upheld the FDA's decision to give industry more time to complete safety reviews of 23 colour additives used in foods, drugs, and cosmetics. The colours were on the agency's provisional list, permitting their use until safety tests determined whether they were to be "permanently" approved or withdrawn from the market. In July the FDA issued an ultimatum to 125 marketers and distributors of "starch blocker" diet aids to halt distribution of the products until they were proved safe and effective. Starch blockers were said to assist weight control by impeding the digestion of starch.

Federal restrictions on offering discounts to customers who pay cash were removed, but the ban on surcharges for credit-card purchases was extended to l984. Several oil companies discontinued or discouraged the use of credit cards at their gasoline stations. In some cases consumers were offered discounts if they paid in cash.

(EDWARD MARK MAZZE)

See also Economy, World; Industrial Review: Advertising.
[532.B.3; 534.H.5; 534.K]

Contract Bridge

The sixth World Pairs Olympiad was staged at Biarritz, France, in October 1982. Sixty-one member countries competed and produced fields of 360 for the Open Pairs championship, 140 for the Women's Pairs, 450 for the Mixed Pairs, and 129 teams for the Julius Rosenblum Memorial Trophy. The overall increase in competitors from the 1978 Olympiad in New Orleans, La., was almost 100%. The playing areas were in two casinos in whose corridors and in hotel lounges television screens provided constant tournament information and, in the closing stages of the team championship, board-by-board results as each hand was played. There was also a live screen presentation in a 1,500-seat theatre.

The Mixed Pairs gold medal went to Diana Gor-

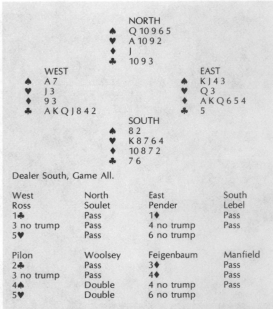

```
                    NORTH
                ♠ Q 10 9 6 5
                ♥ A 10 9 2
                ♦ J
                ♣ 10 9 3
      WEST                        EAST
  ♠ A 7                        ♠ K J 4 3
  ♥ J 3                        ♥ Q 3
  ♦ 9 3                        ♦ A K Q 6 5 4
  ♣ A K Q J 8 4 2              ♣ 5
                    SOUTH
                ♠ 8 2
                ♥ K 8 7 6 4
                ♦ 10 8 7 2
                ♣ 7 6
```

Dealer South, Game All.

West	North	East	South
Ross	Soulet	Pender	Lebel
1♣	Pass	1♦	Pass
3 no trump	Pass	4 no trump	Pass
5♥	Pass	6 no trump	

Pilon	Woolsey	Feigenbaum	Manfield
2♣	Pass	3♦	Pass
3 no trump	Pass	4♦	Pass
4♠	Double	4 no trump	Pass
5♥	Double	6 no trump	

Pilon's opening bid of two clubs showed eight playing tricks based on a long and solid suit (unspecified). Three diamonds showed the ace of diamonds, and four diamonds indicated a diamond suit. At both tables it was reasonable to assume that declarer could take 12 tricks in the two minor suits. At the second table Woolsey had the added information that West held the ace of spades. Woolsey led a diamond, and the declarer took the first 12 tricks. At the first table Soulet led the ace of hearts, and the defense took the first five tricks.

don and George Mittelman (Canada), with Peggy and John Sutherlin (U.S.) second and Jean-Louis and Isabelle Viennois (France) third. In the Open Pairs championship the field of 360 pairs was reduced to 40 pairs, and the U.S. with 14 qualifiers and France with 9 represented more than half of that total. Chip Martel and Lew Stansby of the U.S. were on top when the final results were announced; Max Rebattu and Anton Maas (Neth.) finished second, and Cabriel Chagas and Roberto de Melho (Brazil) placed third.

In the Women's Pairs, the field was also reduced to 40 in the qualifying rounds, and Betty Ann Kennedy and Carol Sanders (U.S.), runners-up in 1978, spent many anxious hours before their 40th place was confirmed. Then, however, they climbed to third place in the first session of the final, moved into the lead in the second, and stayed there to the end. Lynn Deas and Beth Palmer (U.S.) took the silver medals, and Sally Horton and Sandra Landy (Great Britain) the bronze. The team championship was divided into three groups designated as Europe, North America, and the Rest of the World. The Open Pairs champions, Chip Martel and Lew Stansby, associated with Peter Pender and Hugh Ross, Kit Woolsey and Ed Manfield, survived the early rounds and went on to defeat their U.S. compatriots led by Jim Zimmerman in a semifinal. In the other semifinal Luca de Tena of Spain and his team went down to the French team (Pierre Schmeil, nonplaying captain, Michel Lebel, Philippe Soulet, Dominique Pilon, Albert Feigenbaum) by the narrowest of margins. France and the U.S. thus qualified in an 80-board final. France won by 17 international match points to take the Rosenblum Trophy; a choice of opening lead on the hand illustrated cost the U.S. team 18 points. (HAROLD FRANKLIN)

Costa Rica

A Central American republic, Costa Rica lies between Nicaragua and Panama and has coastlines on the Caribbean Sea and the Pacific Ocean. Area: 51,100 sq km (19,730 sq mi). Pop. (1982 est.): 2,339,800, including white and mestizo 98%. Cap. and largest city: San José (metro. pop., 1982 est., 867,000). Language: Spanish. Religion: predominantly Roman Catholic. Presidents in 1982, Rodrigo Carazo Odio and, from May 8, Luis Alberto Monge Alvarez.

General elections held in Costa Rica on Feb. 7, 1982, resulted in a clear victory for Luis Alberto Monge Alvarez and his social democratic Partido de Liberación Nacional, which gained an absolute majority in the Legislative Assembly. The new president took office on May 8.

Costa Rica was allocated $70 million, more than any other country apart from El Salvador, under the U.S. Caribbean Basin Initiative, and further promises to bolster the country against Communism were forthcoming. Israel granted aid, and the International Monetary Fund provided a standby agreement for $105 million scheduled for November. In January Costa Rica established the Central American Democratic Community (CDC) together with El Salvador and Honduras (Guatemala joined later in the year), and in September it organized a forum of nine Caribbean Basin countries to seek peace in the region. U.S. Pres. Ronald Reagan received a warm welcome when he visited San José during his Latin-American trip in December.

The economic chaos inherited from the previous administration was partially resolved by austerity measures. Chief among the remaining problems were a foreign debt of $4.4 billion, an inflation rate

Costa Rica

COSTA RICA

Education. (1980) Primary, pupils 347,708, teachers 10,536; secondary, pupils 103,579, teachers 4,263; vocational, pupils 30,229, teachers 2,056; higher, students (1979) 55,378, teaching staff (1973) 1,967.

Finance. Monetary unit: colón, with (Sept. 20, 1982) a free rate of 69 colones to U.S. $1 (40 colones = £1 sterling). Gold and other reserves (June 1982) U.S. $167 million. Budget (1981 est.) balanced at 11 billion colones. Gross national product (1980) 39,612,000,000 colones. Money supply (Nov. 1981) 10,643,000,000 colones. Cost of living (San José; 1975 = 100; May 1982) 344.6.

Foreign Trade. (1981) Imports 26,360,000,000 colones; exports 22,370,000,000 colones. Import sources (1980): U.S. 33%; Japan 11%; Guatemala 7%; Venezuela 6%; Mexico 5%; West Germany 5%. Export destinations (1980): U.S. 33%; Nicaragua 12%; West Germany 11%; Guatemala 6%; El Salvador 5%. Main exports: bananas 24%; coffee 23%; beef 7%; chemicals c. 6%. Tourism (1980): visitors 345,000; gross receipts U.S. $87 million.

Transport and Communications. Roads (1978) 26,627 km. Motor vehicles in use (1979): passenger c. 79,600; commercial (including buses) c. 58,900. Railways: (1978) c. 1,003 km; traffic (main only; 1976) 99 million passenger-km, freight 16 million net ton-km. Air traffic (1981): c. 530 million passenger-km; freight c. 21 million net ton-km. Telephones (Jan. 1980) 194,500. Radio receivers (Dec. 1979) 180,000. Television receivers (Dec. 1979) 161,000.

Agriculture. Production (in 000; metric tons; 1981): sorghum 42; corn 88; rice 210; potatoes 28; bananas 1,144; oranges c. 76; sugar, raw value 195; coffee 120; cocoa 3; palm oil c. 24. Livestock (in 000; 1981): cattle 2,275; horses 113; pigs c. 240; chickens 5,300.

Industry. Production (in 000; metric tons; 1979): cement 544; petroleum products c. 410; nitrogenous fertilizers (1980–81) c. 40; electricity (kw-hr; 1980) 2,227,000 (96% hydroelectric).

of 100%, and a three-tier exchange rate (official rate 20 colones to the U.S. dollar, commercial 40, and free-market 69). (LUCY BLACKBURN)

Court Games

Handball. Naty Alvarado of Los Angeles won his fourth U.S. National Open handball title in 1982 by defeating defending champion Fred Lewis of Tucson, Ariz., 21–5, 21–9 at the Tucson Athletic

Luis Alberto Monge Alvarez cast his ballot in the general election held in Costa Rica in February. Monge's party gained an absolute majority in the Legislative Assembly; Monge took office as president on May 8.

Cost of Living: see Economy, World

Council for Mutual Economic Assistance: see Economy, World

Club. Alvarado then teamed with Chicago's Vern Roberts to win the national doubles title, becoming the first player since Jim Jacobs in 1965 to win both championships in the same year. Alvarado and Roberts defeated Tom Kopatich of Milwaukee, Wis., and Jack Roberts of Cambridge, Mass., 21–10, 21–8 in the finals.

In women's play Rosemary Bellini of New York City defeated Rosanna Ettinger of Long Beach, Calif., 21–12, 21–12, for her third straight U.S. National Open singles title. Allison Roberts of Cincinnati, Ohio, and Gloria Motal from Austin, Texas, won the doubles title, defeating Bellini and Sue Oakleaf of Austin, Texas, 10–21, 21–20, 11–2.

Seventeen-year-old Alfonso Monreal, Los Angeles, won the U.S. National Junior championship. He defeated Richard Lopez of Los Angeles 21–14, 17–21, 11–9.

Lake Forest (Ill.) College won the national intercollegiate title at Memphis State University. Bob Martin, a Lake Forest senior, won the singles championship, defeating Robert Laarhoven of Memphis State 21–12, 21–14. Charlie Kalil of Lake Forest won the B singles title, defeating Joe Berman of the University of Arizona 21–6, 21–9. Chris Roberts and Steve Kiser of Lake Forest won the doubles title, defeating Laarhoven and Joe Robie of Memphis State 21–5, 18–21, 11–2. Freshman Allison Roberts of Bradley University pulled the upset of the tournament when she defeated two-time defending champion Sue Oakleaf of Texas A&M 21–13, 21–8. (TERRY CHARLES MUCK)

Volleyball. The world championships for men and women were the focal point of volleyball for 1982. Each event qualified a team for the 1984 Olympic Games.

The Soviet Union won the 1982 men's title. Since the U.S.S.R. had already qualified for the 1984 Olympic Games by virtue of being the 1980 Olym-pic champion, the second-place team, Brazil, was awarded a position in the 1984 Games. Third in the men's championship was the host team from Argentina, a great move forward for Argentine volleyball. The two medal positions earned by South American teams were another first. Japan was fourth, and Bulgaria, Poland, China, Korea, Czechoslovakia, and Cuba rounded out the top ten in that order. Although the U.S. men lost only to the Soviet Union and Bulgaria, with whom they were matched in the four-team preliminary group, they officially finished 13th.

China won the 1982 women's world championship and as such qualified for the 1984 Olympic Games. Second place went to the host Peruvians, with the U.S. third.

The victory by the Soviet men was a repeat of their win in the 1978 world championships. For the Chinese women it was their highest finish ever in the world championships, although they were the 1981 World Cup winners.

All other international volleyball activity during 1982 was either dual competition or invitational tournaments. The U.S. women were for all practical purposes undefeated in such competitions during 1982 with significant wins over Japan, the Soviet Union, China, Cuba, South Korea, Bulgaria, and Hungary. The U.S. men were victorious in competitions against Japan, Poland, Italy, South Korea, Yugoslavia, and Canada.

UCLA once again captured the National Collegiate Athletic Association (NCAA) men's championship with Penn State second. In the NCAA women's championship play (in late December 1981) the University of Southern California captured Division I over UCLA; Sacramento State won Division II over Lewis University; and the University of California at San Diego was the NCAA Division III champion over Uniata College.

(ALBERT M. MONACO, JR.)

Jai Alai. The world's jai alai countries converged on Mexico City in October for the 1982 world amateur championships. Teams representing Spain, France, Italy, Mexico, Philippines, and the United States participated in the event.

The defending champion French team of Danial Michelene and Pierre Echeverriay again dominated the play. They won all four of their games, defeating Italy 40–9, Mexico 40–29, and Spain 40–27 in the first three rounds. The final round pitted them against the U.S., which was also undefeated in the first three matches. Billy Schofill and Paul Boornazian of the U.S. took an early lead in the final contest, but the French were eventually victorious by a score of 40–33. Spain captured third place when its team of Marcus Rego and Emilio Rodriguez defeated Mexico's Arturo Lopez and Guillermo Trejo 40–29.

The controversy over professionalism continued during the year. France had been accused of using professional players in world amateur competition for the last three tournaments. The U.S., Mexico, and Spain let it be known that they had played the tournament under protest. Meanwhile, such leading players as Michelene, Echeverriay, Boornazian, and Schofill were planning to become professionals. (ROBERT H. GROSSBERG)

A seemingly unbeatable Naty Alvarado (foreground) of Los Angeles won his fourth U.S. National Open handball title by beating Fred Lewis of Tucson, Arizona. Alvarado then teamed with Vern Roberts of Chicago to win the national doubles title, becoming the first player since 1965 to win both titles in the same year.

TERRY MUCK—UNITED STATES HANDBALL ASSOCIATION

Cricket

England, Australia, India, Pakistan, and New Zealand played test series in 1981–82. They were joined by the new member of the International Cricket Conference, Sri Lanka, which played against England and Pakistan.

England, led by K. W. R. Fletcher, toured India and Sri Lanka. India, under S. M. Gavaskar, won the first test, and the other five were drawn. Much of the cricket was tedious, as India sat on its lead, and neither side achieved an acceptable overrate on the slow pitches. Gavaskar, G. R. Viswanath, K. Dev, and Y. Sharma all made centuries for India, and Dev, fast-medium, and D. R. Doshi, slow left, were the chief wicket-takers. For England, I. T. Botham, G. A. Gooch, G. Boycott, and C. J. Tavare were century-makers, and R. G. D. Willis, D. L. Underwood, and Botham were the leading wicket-takers.

England then moved on to Sri Lanka for the first-ever test match in that country. D. I. Gower (89 and 42 not out) and Tavare (85) shone for England with the bat, and spinners Underwood (5 for 28) and J. E. Emburey (6 for 33) exploited a turning pitch to win the match by seven wickets, despite fine batting by R. L. Dias (77), R. S. Madugalle (65), and A. Ranatunge (54). Sri Lanka proved that it was up to test standard, but the side lacked penetrative fast and seam bowlers.

Meanwhile, Australia, under G. S. Chappell, was at home to Pakistan and West Indies. Australia beat Pakistan 2–1, owing largely to powerful batting by Chappell (201), K. J. Hughes (106), and G. M. Wood (100); the speed of D. K. Lillee (15 wickets); and the off-spin of B. Yardley (18). Pakistan's leading batsmen were Javed Miandad, Wasim Raja, Zaheer Abbas, and Mudassar Nazar, and Imram Khan (see BIOGRAPHIES) took 16 wick-

ets. The West Indies series was tied one all. Australia's chief batsmen were A. R. Border, Hughes, and J. Dyson, each making a century, while Lillee (16 wickets) and Yardley (20 wickets) again excelled with the ball. For the West Indies H. A. Gomes had a fine series (393 runs), supported by the captain C. H. Lloyd (275) and P. J. Dujon (227). Fast bowler M. A. Holding took 24 wickets. Ten one-day matches between the three countries ended in a "best of five" final between West Indies and Australia, which West Indies won easily by three matches to one, owing largely to fine batting by C. G. Greenidge and I. V. A. Richards.

After losing to England, Sri Lanka toured Pakistan and was well beaten 2–0. For Pakistan, Haroon Rashid, Salim Malik, Mohsin Khan, and Zaheer Abbas made centuries; S. Wettimuny became the first Sri Lankan to score a test century, followed by Dias. Imram Khan took 14 wickets in the third test match, and slow left-arm Iqbal Qasim took 15 wickets in the series. Sri Lanka's best bowler was spinner D. S. de Silva (17 wickets).

In March, 15 of England's best cricketers, led by Gooch and Boycott, played three international matches against a full South African team sponsored by South African Breweries. They ignored a warning by the Test and County Cricket Board and were duly banned from all test cricket for three years. They were lavishly paid, and undoubtedly helped South Africa, which treated the matches as "tests." The English team lost one game and drew the other two.

Australia undertook a short tour of New Zealand, and, after rain had washed out the first test, New Zealand won a famous victory in the second by five wickets. B. A. Edgar made a superb 161; fast bowler R. J. Hadlee took 5 for 63; and fierce hitting by L. Cairns (34) ensured victory in a thrilling final day. Wood scored 100 in Australia's second innings. A brilliant 176 by Chappell helped the third test by eight wickets.

Test Series Results, October 1981–September 1982

Test	Host country and its scores		Visiting country and its scores		Result
1st	India	179 and 227	England	166 and 102	India won by 138 runs
2nd	India	428	England	400 and 174 for 3 wkt	Match drawn
3rd	India	487	England	476 for 9 wkt dec	Match drawn
4th	India	208 and 70 for 3 wkt	England	248 and 265 for 5 wkt dec	Match drawn
5th	India	481 for 4 wkt dec and 160 for 3 wkt dec	England	328	Match drawn
6th	India	377 for 7 wkt dec	England	378 for 9 wkt dec	Match drawn
	Sri Lanka	218 and 175	England	223 and 171 for 3 wkt	England won by 7 wkt
1st	Australia	180 and 424 for 8 wkt dec	Pakistan	62 and 256	Australia won by 286 runs
2nd	Australia	512 and 9 wkt dec 3 for 0 wkt	Pakistan	291 and 223	Australia won by 10 wkt
3rd	Australia	293 and 125	Pakistan	500 for 8 wkt dec	Pakistan won by an innings and 82 runs
1st	Australia	198 and 222	West Indies	201 and 161	Australia won by 58 runs
2nd	Australia	267 and 200 for 4 wkt	West Indies	384 and 255	Match drawn
3rd	Australia	238 and 386	West Indies	389 and 239 for 5 wkt	West Indies won by 5 wkt
1st	Pakistan	396 and 301 for 4 wkt dec	Sri Lanka	344 and 149	Pakistan won by 204 runs
2nd	Pakistan	270 and 186 for 7 wkt	Sri Lanka	454 and 154 for 8 wkt dec	Match drawn
3rd	Pakistan	500 for 7 wkt dec	Sri Lanka	240 and 158	Pakistan won by an innings and 102 runs
1st	New Zealand	266 for 7 wkt dec	Australia	85 for 1 wkt	Match drawn
2nd	New Zealand	387 and 109 for 5 wkt	Australia	210 and 280	New Zealand won by 5 wkt
3rd	New Zealand	149 and 272	Australia	353 and 69 for 2 wkt	Australia won by 8 wkt
1st	England	433 and 67 for 3 wkt	India	128 and 369	England won by 7 wkt
2nd	England	425	India	379 for 8 wkt	Match drawn
3rd	England	594 and 191 for 3 wkt dec	India	410 and 111 for 3 wkts	Match drawn
1st	England	272 and 291	Pakistan	251 and 199	England won by 113 runs
2nd	England	227 and 276	Pakistan	428 for 8 wkt dec and 77 for 0 wkt	Pakistan won by 10 wkt
3rd	England	256 and 219 for 7 wkt	Pakistan	275 and 199	England won by 3 wkt

England, under Willis, played two three-match series at home against India and Pakistan. England won the preliminary one-day Prudential games against India by nine wickets and 114 runs. In the tests the English won the first and drew the other two. Botham (403 runs and 9 wickets) predominated with scores of 208, 128 and 67, and 5 for 46 in the Lord's test. D. W. Randall (126), South African-born A. J. Lamb (107), and G. Miller (98) were his chief batting supporters, and Willis celebrated his inaugural test captaincy by taking 15 wickets. Dev was India's answer to Botham. He made the most runs (292) and took ten wickets. S. M. Patil and D. B. Vengsarkar made centuries, and Doshi (13 wickets) was a model of accuracy. Unfortunately, India's two best batsmen, Gavaskar and Viswanath, were out of form. England won both one-day Prudential matches against Pakistan easily by seven wickets and 73 runs, but the tests were a much tougher struggle, England winning 2–1. Imram Khan was the outstanding competitor (212 runs and 21 wickets), rivaling Botham (163 and 18). For England Randall was the only centurian, and Tavare made the most runs (216). Willis took 10 wickets, and 37-year-old R. D. Jackman took eight. For Pakistan Mohsin made 200 at Lord's, where Mudassar took six for 32, and leg-spinner Abdul Qadir (10 wickets) was always a threat.

The English county championship was won easily by Middlesex, with Leicestershire second and Hampshire third. Somerset again won the Benson and Hedges competition, beating Nottinghamshire by nine wickets, and Surrey won the NatWest Trophy, defeating Warwickshire, also by nine wickets. The John Player League was won by Sussex. The first-class batting averages in England were again dominated by overseas players. West Indian A. Kallicharran (Warwickshire) made 2,120 runs, New Zealander G. M. Turner (Worcestershire) played an innings of 311 not out, and West Indian fast bowler M. Marshall (Hampshire) took a record 134 wickets.

South Australia won the Sheffield Shield. In South Africa, Western Province won the Currie Cup and Boland the Castle Bowl. In the West Indies Barbados won the Shell Shield, and in New Zealand Wellington won the Shell Trophy. In India the Irani Trophy was drawn (between Bombay and Rest of India). West Zone won the Duleep Trophy and the Delhi and Ranji Trophy. In Pakistan Habib Bank won the Paco Pentangular and National Bank the Qaid-i-Azam Trophy.

Australia retained the women's World Cup in New Zealand. Others competing for it included England (runner-up), New Zealand, India, and an international team.   (REX ALSTON)

Crime and Law Enforcement

Violent Crime. TERRORISM. The hatred and bitterness flowing from long-festering political conflicts, many of them centred in the Middle East, sparked a rash of terrorist incidents in 1982. Western Europeans, especially the French, bore the brunt of much of this violence. During August and September more than 20 bombings and shootings were reported in Paris alone, including an August 9 machine gun and grenade attack on customers lunching at a famous Jewish restaurant in the French capital. The attack, believed to have been committed by the Black June terrorist group, left 6 people dead and 22 wounded.

Led by Abu Nidal, a renegade Palestinian leader, Black June was known to have waged a six-year campaign of terror against a wide range of targets, including rival Palestine Liberation Organization leaders and Israeli diplomats. It claimed responsibility for the attempted assassination in London on June 3 of Shlomo Argov, Israel's ambassador to Britain, an incident used by Israel as the immediate pretext for its June 6 invasion of Lebanon. Black June was also thought to be responsible for a bloody attack in Rome on October 9, when terrorists wielding machine guns and lobbing grenades cut down worshipers leaving a synagogue. A two-year-old boy was killed, and 34 people, many of them children, were wounded.

In March Italian authorities in Verona put on trial 17 (8 in absentia) Red Brigades terrorists accused of the December 1981 kidnapping of U.S. Brig. Gen. James L. Dozier (see BIOGRAPHIES). After 42 days in captivity, Dozier was rescued on January 28 in a dramatic raid on an apartment in Padua by Italy's elite antiterrorist commando unit, the Leatherheads. The massive manhunt for Dozier resulted in the penetration of the Red Brigades' elaborate underground network as captured terrorists traded information for shorter sentences. In April one of these terrorists, Antonio Savasta, 27, who received a prison term of 16 years for his leading role in the Dozier kidnapping, became a key prosecution witness in the Rome trial of more than 50 Red Brigades members. The defendants faced charges arising out of 19 murders and many gun attacks between 1977 and 1981, including the 1978 kidnapping and murder of former Italian premier Aldo Moro. Italian authorities achieved another success in October with the capture in Bolivia of Pierluigi Pagliai, 28, wanted in connection with the 1980 bombing of the Bologna railway station in which 85 people were killed. In this case, neo-Fascists had committed the outrage.

An international assassination campaign by Armenian nationalists directed against Turkish diplomats claimed several victims during the year, including Kemal Arikan, Turkey's consul general in Los Angeles, and Orhan Gunduz, the honorary Turkish consul general for New England. On August 7 one of the terrorist groups, the Armenian Secret Army for the Liberation of Armenia, made a major assault on Turkish soil for the first time: three men armed with machine guns and bombs killed at least 9 people and wounded 72 at Ankara's Esenboga Airport.

Pope John Paul II, who survived an assassination attempt in St. Peter's Square on May 13, 1981, was attacked again almost exactly one year later while visiting the shrine of Fatima in Portugal to thank the Virgin Mary for sparing his life. Juan Fernandez Krohn, a rebel Spanish priest, was apprehended at the scene after lunging at the pope

France experienced many of the terrorist incidents that occurred throughout the year. An attack on August 9 at a famous Jewish restaurant in Paris left 6 dead and 22 wounded.

Antonio Savasta, one of the ringleaders in the 1981 terrorist kidnapping of U.S. Brig. Gen. James L. Dozier from his apartment in Verona, Italy, was handcuffed after receiving a 16-year prison sentence at his trial in March. He became a key witness against more than 50 other Red Brigades members.

with a bayonet. Controversy continued to surround the earlier assassination attempt by Turkish right-wing terrorist Mehmet Ali Agca. There was speculation that Agca may have had links to the Bulgarian secret service and that the Bulgarians, in turn, acted as agents for the Soviets, who desired the death of the Polish-born pontiff because of his support for the Solidarity movement in Poland. Italian authorities identified three Bulgarians whom they said were implicated in the attack.

In June John W. Hinckley, Jr., who narrowly missed killing U.S. Pres. Ronald Reagan on March 30, 1981, was found not guilty by reason of insanity on each of 13 counts arising from the assassination attempt. The verdict, which followed a highly publicized jury trial in Washington, D.C., provoked a storm of protest across the U.S. and led to a wave of legislative attempts to tighten or abolish the insanity defense. Hinckley was hospitalized for psychiatric treatment.

After holding off police for some ten hours on December 8 by threatening to blow up the Washington Monument in Washington, D.C., a man identified as Norman Mayer, 66, was shot and killed by police when he attempted to leave the Monument grounds. He had demanded a nationwide debate on the use of nuclear weapons.

On July 9 Michael Fagan, 31, an unemployed labourer, was arrested in Buckingham Palace after gaining access to the royal bedchamber and talking to Queen Elizabeth II. Fagan, it was discovered, had also sneaked into the palace on June 7 and drunk some wine belonging to Prince Charles. On July 9 Fagan had merely trespassed on royal property, a civil rather than a criminal offense, so he was charged only in connection with the June 7 incident. In September a jury acquitted him, but

in October, after he had pleaded guilty to a charge of car theft, a judge ordered him detained indefinitely in a mental hospital.

The British public's confidence in its security forces, severely shaken by the Fagan incidents, was further weakened by the explosion on July 20 of two bombs planted by the Irish Republican Army (IRA) in the heart of London. The first blast, in Hyde Park, killed three members of the Queen's

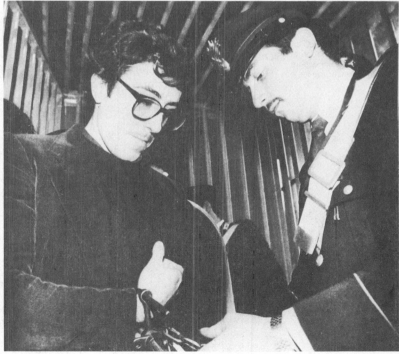

Crime and Law Enforcement

John W. Hinckley, Jr., (centre) accused of attempting to assassinate U.S. Pres. Ronald Reagan in March 1981, was found not guilty by reason of insanity by a Washington, D.C., jury in June. The verdict aroused a storm of protest.

British confidence in its security forces was shattered by two explosions on July 20. The first blast, in Hyde Park (below), killed 3 members of the Queen's Household Cavalry, injured 23 others, and also killed or wounded several horses. Two hours later 6 army musicians were killed and 28 people injured when another bomb exploded at a Regent's Park bandstand during a lunchtime concert.

Household Cavalry as they rode from their barracks to a changing of the guard ceremony at Whitehall. Twenty-three persons were injured in the explosion, which also killed or wounded a number of horses. Two hours later 6 army musicians were blown apart and 28 people were injured when a second bomb exploded under a Regent's Park bandstand during a lunchtime concert by the Royal Greenjackets Band. An offshoot of the IRA, the Irish National Liberation Army, claimed responsibility for an explosion that collapsed the roof of a popular bar in Ballykelly, Northern Ireland, on December 6, killing 11 British soldiers and 5 civilians and injuring an estimated 66 others.

MURDER AND OTHER VIOLENCE. In a sharp departure from the soaring crime rates reported to the police in recent years in the U.S., the FBI's *Uniform Crime Reports* showed that the overall rate of crime in 1981 remained about the same as that of 1980, while violent crimes as a group rose only 1%.

Despite these slightly encouraging trends, there were still almost 25,000 murders committed in the U.S., or roughly 500 per week.

Proponents of gun control pointed out that handguns were used to kill about 10,000 Americans each year and to commit another 500,000 violent crimes. Opinion polls across the country continued to show that a large majority of Americans favoured stricter handgun controls, and a few municipalities adopted local ordinances barring possession or sale of handguns by almost all citizens. In California, however, Proposition 15, which would have mandated strict regulation of handguns, was rejected by the voters in the November election.

Following a retrial that cost taxpayers $4 million, Juan Corona was convicted again for the slayings of 25 farm labourers in California. Corona's original conviction in 1973 had been overturned by the California Court of Appeals in 1978. William Bonin, 34, the so-called freeway killer, was sentenced to death in March for the murders of ten young men and boys whose bodies were found dumped along the freeways crisscrossing Los Angeles. Police said there were similarities between these crimes and more than 40 such murders dating back to 1976. In February an Atlanta, Ga., jury found Wayne Bertram Williams, a 23-year-old free-lance photographer, guilty of two counts of murder. Williams, who was arrested in June 1981, was implicated in at least 12 of 28 apparently related strangulations and knifings of young blacks in Atlanta. He was sentenced to two consecutive terms of life imprisonment.

A nationwide consumer alert was triggered early in October by the sudden deaths of seven Chicago-area residents who had taken capsules of Extra-Strength Tylenol, a popular over-the-counter pain-relieving drug, that were found to contain cyanide. The authorities believed that the capsules had been tampered with after they left the factory and probably after they had been placed on store shelves. The police began a massive hunt for the person or persons responsible for these terrifying acts of random, impersonal mass murder, a task made more difficult by "copycat" incidents of product tampering reported across the country. In December James and LeAnn Lewis, suspected of attempting extortion in connection with the Tylenol slayings, were taken into custody, but it was not known whether they were involved in the murders themselves.

Nonviolent Crime. POLITICAL CRIME. U.S. Sen. Harrison A. Williams, Jr., of New Jersey was sentenced in February to three years in jail and fined $50,000 by a federal court in Uniondale, N.Y. He had been convicted in 1981 on charges of bribery and conspiracy arising from the FBI's Abscam investigation of political corruption. Williams resigned his seat rather than face almost certain expulsion from the Senate, but he appealed both the conviction and sentence. In December Roy L. Williams, president of the teamsters' union, and four others were found guilty of attempting to bribe Sen. Howard J. Cannon (Dem., Neb.) to oppose a bill deregulating the trucking industry. An appeal was expected.

A much publicized investigation by a special federal prosecutor, Leon Silverman, into the conduct of U.S. Secretary of Labor Raymond J. Donovan came to a close in September when the prosecutor said he was unable to find "sufficient credible evidence" to corroborate allegations that Donovan had consorted with known Mafia figures and committed various illegal acts. During the course of the Donovan probe, two government witnesses, both connected with organized crime, were murdered.

The Belgian government ordered a judicial investigation in September into charges that prominent public officials, including two former prime ministers, had been involved in large financial payoffs and transactions with the regime of Zairian Pres. Mobutu Sese Seko. The charges were contained in a "leaked" report by a former official of the International Monetary Fund, Erwin Blumenthal, on the financial status of Zaire. The report also claimed that much of Mobutu's personal wealth, estimated at $4 billion–$5 billion, had come from his corrupt diversion of central bank funds and profiteering in the nation's extensive diamond, copper, cobalt, and other mines.

WHITE COLLAR CRIME AND THEFT. A complex scandal that shook the international banking system and reached into the secret financial apparatus of the Vatican began to take shape after the collapse of the Banco Ambrosiano, Italy's largest private bank, and the apparent suicide of its president, Roberto Calvi. According to investigators, some $1.2 billion in bank funds had been used to provide unsecured loans to "shadowy" Latin-American companies, in association with letters of patronage (financial guarantees) issued by the Institute for Religious Works or Vatican bank. (See RELIGION.) As the inquiries continued, Licic Gelli, an Italo-Argentine financier associated with Calvi and the alleged recruiter of the mysterious Masonic lodge known as P2, was arrested by Swiss police in Geneva. Gelli's arrest came as he sought to withdraw up to $60 million, believed to have come from the Banco Ambrosiano, from numbered accounts in a Swiss bank. Gelli faced possible charges of fraud, political and military espionage, and illegal possession of state secrets in Italy and was thought to be implicated in the Bologna railroad station bombing. The exposure of P2, which allegedly included many prominent Italians, had brought down the Italian government in 1981.

In another case involving a prominent figure, automaker John Z. De Lorean (see BIOGRAPHIES) was arrested by federal agents in California in October on charges of dealing in drugs. After a meteoric career at General Motors, DeLorean, with British government participation, had begun manufacturing expensive sports cars in Northern Ireland. Officials alleged that he became involved in a scheme to sell cocaine in an effort to obtain funds to shore up his failing company.

In the U.S. the FBI reported a 4% decline in car and truck thefts in 1981. Even so, about 1.1 million such thefts occurred during the year, and only 55% of the stolen vehicles were returned to their owners. Police officials stated that the proportion of vehicles recovered had continued to drop over

Famous automaker John Z. De Lorean was arrested in Los Angeles in October and charged with participating in a multimillion dollar cocaine operation. It was alleged that he had hoped to save his floundering automobile enterprise with the proceeds from the drug sale.

the last 25 years, reflecting increased professionalism among car thieves. In many cases vehicles were worth more as parts than as a whole, and "chop shops" had sprung up which could reduce a stolen vehicle to pieces within a very short time.

A new U.S. record for a cash robbery was set on December 12 when an estimated $10.4 million was stolen from an armoured car service depot in the Bronx, New York City. After sawing their way through the roof and overcoming the guard, the robbers backed a truck to a loading dock and filled it with bales of cash.

Law Enforcement. President Reagan announced in October that a major offensive would be launched by federal law enforcement agencies to "cripple the power of the mob in America." The president, who pointed to the enormous profits gained by crime syndicates from illicit drug operations around the nation, said 12 new task forces of federal prosecutors and investigators would be established to focus on drug trafficking.

In a September press interview, FBI Director William Webster said that almost 20% of his agency's resources now went into fighting organized crime. In the first nine months of 1982, the FBI obtained 587 convictions in organized crime cases. Among a further 245 cases in the process of prosecution was one involving a dramatic FBI undercover operation that infiltrated fencing operations in New York City. In August five alleged members of New York's Bonanno crime syndicate went on trial on racketeering charges stemming from the operation, which included three murders, gambling, hijacking, drug conspiracy, and armed robbery. The main witness against the Bonanno group was an FBI agent, Joseph D. Pistone, who was sent undercover in 1976 and posed as a thief named Don Brasco for more than six years.

Crime and Law Enforcement

Technicians tested millions of capsules of Extra-Strength Tylenol after cyanide-contaminated capsules killed seven persons in the Chicago area in October. Sales of Tylenol were barred in many areas.

Italy's top Mafia fighter, Gen. Carlo Alberto Dalla Chiesa, and his wife died in a hail of bullets as they drove through the streets of Palermo, Sicily, on September 3. Following his considerable success in leading the battle against political terrorism, Dalla Chiesa had been sent to Sicily in May by Premier Giovanni Spadolini's government on a special mission to combat the Mafia. In the wake of the assassination, the government created a new and powerful post of high commissioner against organized crime, and a bill was pushed through Parliament giving investigators unprecedented powers to look into Mafia sources of wealth and influence.

The reputation of London's famous police force was tarnished by the Fagan case and by the disclosure that the queen's personal police bodyguard, Commander Michael Trestrail, had been involved in a lengthy homosexual affair with a prostitute. Trestrail resigned, and there were numerous calls for the resignation of London's police chief, Sir David McNee, and Home Secretary William Whitelaw, the minister responsible for the force. Adding to the furor were allegations in Parliament of substantial corruption among members of the London force.

In Montreal a judge dismissed charges in September against three Mounties and a former officer accused of stealing dynamite in 1972. The charges were among more than 50 made by the Quebec Justice Department against 18 current and former RCMP members alleged to have been involved in illegal police operations aimed at terrorist groups in the early 1970s.

The death in February in a Johannesburg police cell of Neil Aggett, 28, a physician and union activist, provoked a storm of protest in South Africa and abroad. Aggett was found hanging in his cell 14 hours after he had signed an affidavit accusing police of torturing him with electric shocks. Arrested in November 1981 as part of a police crackdown on trade unionists, students, and church leaders, Aggett was the first white South African to die while being detained without charge under the country's sweeping security laws.

(DUNCAN CHAPPELL)

Jurors, weighing the fate of Wayne B. Williams of Atlanta, were taken to visit a bridge from which Williams was accused of having thrown two of his victims into the Chattahoochee River. Williams, who was implicated in at least 12 of 28 related strangulations and knifings, was found guilty of two counts of murder and sentenced to life imprisonment.

See also Prisons and Penology.
[522.C.6; 543.A.5; 552.C and F; 737.B; 10/36.C.5.a]

COMPUTERS DON'T SIN: PEOPLE DO

by Donn B. Parker

Because of the speed and efficiency of computerized data processing, business and government have grown dependent on computer and data communication systems to carry on their activities. As the number of computers and the value of data stored and processed by them have increased, so too have reported cases of computers being involved in the commission of such crimes as fraud, theft, larceny, embezzlement, sabotage, espionage, extortion, and conspiracy. Therefore, computer crime and methods to prevent it have become important issues today.

Many definitions of computer crime are used for different purposes. One effective definition is any criminal activity in which a special knowledge of computer technology is essential for its perpetration, investigation, or prosecution. For example, a bank embezzlement accomplished by filling out standard forms for transferring funds among accounts could be a computer crime if the embezzler's knowledge of specific controls in the computer system was essential to avoid detection of the crime. Legal definitions of computer crime are being established in each jurisdiction that has a specific computer crime statute.

In computer crime, computers directly or indirectly play the role of objects, subjects, instruments, or symbols. A computer can be the object of an act when it or its content is attacked, damaged, or destroyed. For example, in five reported cases computers have been shot with guns. A computer can be the subject of a crime when it is the environment in which a criminal act occurs, such as the unauthorized change of personal credit data within a computer by altering a computer program, submitting false data or unauthorized instructions, or withholding authorized data. In addition, a computer can be a tool or an instrument in a computer crime when it is used to process data in an illegal act such as bookmaking, drug smuggling, or forging of investment statements. Finally, as a symbol in a crime, a fictitious computer could be claimed to be used in advertising of a fraudulent service. One or more of

these four roles of computers have been found in all of the more than 1,000 reported cases of computer abuse and crime.

Scope. Although many statistics have been reported on the extent of computer crime and its rate of increase, these statistics are not complete or representative of computer crime. As with other forms of business crime, acceptable mechanisms for collecting comprehensive or valid samples of incidence and loss data, even if a generally accepted definition of computer crime were in use, do not exist. The number and nature of cases that have been reported to criminal justice authorities, or prosecuted by them, has never been determined. Moreover, much suspected computer crime is thought not to be reported to the authorities.

Some analysts believe that the losses to business as a result of crime increase greatly when computers are used. In the Equity Funding insurance fraud in Los Angeles in 1973, for example, a computer was used to create 64,000 fake insurance policies and to disguise their false nature. A loss of $200 million was identified in the criminal trials, but it would be an estimated $2 billion if stockholders' losses were included. The largest recorded bank embezzlement, $21 million, occurred in Los Angeles in 1981. The embezzlers in the latter case had special knowledge about the controls in the targeted computer system. Crimes on this scale would be improbable without the concentration of assets and powerful processing capabilities within computer systems.

The Computer Criminal. For the most part, computer criminals exhibit the same characteristics as the traditional white-collar business criminal, although they more often are young people in the computer technology field. The challenge of winning the game plays a significant role during the perpetration of their crimes, but usually not as the initial motivating factor.

Known computer criminals have been mostly amateurs with no previous criminal history. In fact, they do not perceive of themselves as criminals but only as problem solvers. They differentiate between doing harm to people, which they consider unacceptable and immoral, and doing harm to organizations or computers. These criminals are not necessarily

Donn B. Parker is a Senior Management Systems Consultant at SRI International, Menlo Park, Calif.

exceptionally brilliant or even above average in intelligence, but they often have a capability for intense concentration on a narrow range of detailed activities.

The technical nature of computer crime limits its perpetration to those with sufficiently specialized skills, knowledge, access, and resources. This significantly reduces the number of people who are in a position to engage in business crime involving computers. Therefore, most known and reported computer crimes are perpetrated by trusted employees working in their authorized assignments. However, a growing number of mostly technically competent young people known as system hackers have been gaining access to computers through dial-up telephone connections from their own or their school's computer terminals. These are cases of technological trespassing into computers.

Few career criminals have been found among computer crime perpetrators. This situation is also changing, however, as an increasing number of prison inmates are taught electronic data processing. In addition, organized crime activities are often of such magnitude as to justify or require the use of computer technology for the same reasons that it is used in legitimate business activities.

Methods. The most common technical method in computer crime is false data entry, commonly referred to as data diddling. This technique of changing or withholding data intended for input to computers is least likely to be detected and can be performed by the largest number of people who might engage in business crime. Another basic method is called superzapping. It consists of using a computer program, usually referred to as a utility program, to change, copy, or destroy data and programs in a computer or on computer media. These utility programs do not come under the normal controls of the computer operating system and do not require the use of the more specialized and complex computer application programs that would normally be used to process the targeted data.

A third basic method used in computer crime is the Trojan horse technique of putting secret instructions into computer programs so that programs not only perform their normal functions but also execute the secret instructions so as to perpetrate an additional, unauthorized activity. For example, the program that debits and credits the accounts in a company's accounts payable and receivable system or in a bank's savings or checking system could be modified by inserting several computer instructions. Each time the program is run, these secret instructions would cause unauthorized transfers of credits and debits among the accounts being maintained by the computer program.

Using the Trojan horse method or a separate program, a computer criminal could transfer small amounts of money that might not be missed from each of a large number of accounts into one or more favoured accounts; from these the accumulated money could then be withdrawn by authorized methods. This is known as the salami technique—the taking of large numbers of small slices over a period of time to engage in a fraud not likely to be detected because few if any account holders would complain about small discrepancies. Another technique, known as the logic bomb, involves the use of control transfer and condition testing instructions in a program in order to cause fraudulent acts to be performed at a specific time when conditions are known to be opportune for the fraudulent purposes.

Safeguards. Because of the increasing number of powerful safeguards that can be built into and around computer systems, sophisticated computer crimes have become difficult to commit. Data stored in computer systems and computer media in a well-run computer centre are far safer than such data stored in human-readable form and used in noncomputerized business activities. Hundreds of highly cost-effective controls are routinely being used in computers to reduce the likelihood of business crime to a much greater extent than was ever possible in previous manual systems.

Technical controls are built into computers to create electronic "fences" that prevent or detect the attempts of people using computer programs from gaining access to the storage locations of other programs and data. Technical controls in the computer operating system also can limit the use of sensitive functions in the computer to only authorized persons or their computer programs. In addition, for computer systems accessed by many people from remote terminals, it is common to require knowledge of a secret password in order to gain access to the computer and subsequently to protected computer programs and data files.

At another level, business computer programs can be designed to prevent and detect any deviations from acceptable input data and activity within the computer system. For example, a wide range of controls that examine the reasonableness of data entering or leaving a computer system is available. These controls often trigger a special audit of any transaction that might exceed an acceptable or normal financial value.

One of the most powerful safeguards yet devised to protect data—cryptographic secret coding—is increasingly being used in computer systems and data communications. This technique scrambles or codes data and uses secret keys that must be employed for encoding and decoding the data.

Cuba

The socialist republic of Cuba occupies the largest island in the Greater Antilles of the West Indies. Area: 110,922 sq km (42,827 sq mi), including several thousand small islands and cays. Pop. (1981 prelim.): 9,706,400, including (1953) white 72.8%; mestizo 14.5%; Negro 12.4%. Cap. and largest city: Havana (pop., 1981 prelim., 1,924,900). Language: Spanish. Religion (1980): Roman Catholic 42.1%; atheist 6.4%; other 2.8%; none 48.7%. President of the Councils of State and Ministers in 1982, Fidel Castro Ruz.

Political stability was maintained in Cuba during 1982, but little economic progress was made apart from modest improvements in productivity. The National Assembly of People's Power was inaugurated for its second five-year term in December 1981. Fidel Castro, head of state and first secretary of the Cuban Communist Party, was reelected by the Assembly to the post of president of the Council of State, and Gen. Raúl Castro was reelected as first vice-president.

In January 1982 it was revealed that two months earlier U.S. Secretary of State Alexander Haig had met in secret with Carlos Rafael Rodríguez, a vice-president of the Cuban Council of State, in Mexico. In a bid to begin negotiations that might resolve the differences between the two countries—and perhaps also bring an end to economic sanctions—Cuba had offered to halt military aid to revolution-

ary forces in Central America if the U.S. would make a similar pledge not to intervene militarily in the area. Cuba had also offered to withdraw troops from Angola as soon as South African troops began to leave South West Africa/Namibia.

During the remainder of 1982, however, Cuba's relations with the U.S. wavered. U.S. Pres. Ronald Reagan clearly indicated his administration's attitude to Cuba when he launched the Caribbean Basin Initiative in February. His projected program of economic and development assistance to Caribbean nations was strongly underscored by the political objective of strengthening the region against "the expansion of Soviet-backed Cuban-managed support for violent revolution in Central America." The U.S. planned to set up a Spanish-language radio station—to be named Radio Marti, after Cuban national hero José Marti—to broadcast to Cuba from Florida. In April new limitations were imposed on U.S. citizens traveling to Cuba, further straining relations between the two countries. In August, apparently in response to the Radio Marti proposal, Cuba disrupted U.S. radio programming for one night.

Castro announced that he regarded as a "real threat" the U.S. military maneuvers that took place in the Caribbean in March; these followed major exercises earlier in the month by NATO forces, the aim of which was to practice the protection of merchant shipping in the Florida Strait. Any attempts to normalize relations with Washington were further jeopardized in July when President Castro, during his speech at the annual ceremony to celebrate the start of the Cuban revolution, resorted to a hard-line attitude over Cuban troops in Angola. In August Wayne Smith, who had served the U.S. government's interests section in Havana since 1977, resigned in protest over U.S. policy toward Cuba, particularly what he saw as missed opportunities for serious negotiations.

Cuba's position in Latin America and the Caribbean was strengthened during the year, mainly as a result of its stance during the Falkland Islands conflict between the U.K. and Argentina. In its capacity as chairholder of the nonaligned movement, Cuba called on the members of the group to condemn the "colonialist aggression of Great Brit-

Cuba's Pres. Fidel Castro (left) met with Argentina's foreign minister Micanor Costa Mendez prior to Costa's address to a nonaligned ministerial meeting in Havana in June. Castro called upon the ministers to condemn Britain for its "colonialist aggression" against Argentina in the Falkland Islands conflict.

Cuba

CUBA

Education. (1981–82) Primary, pupils 1 409,765, teachers 83,113; secondary, pupils 918,629, teachers 87,703; vocational, pupils 263,981, teachers 16,154; teacher training, students 92,152, teachers 6,461; higher, students 165,496, teaching staff (1980) 10,736.

Finance. Monetary unit: peso, with (Sept. 20, 1982) a free rate of 0.83 peso to U.S. $1 (1.42 pesos = £1 sterling). Budget (1980 est.): revenue 7,584,000,000 pesos; expenditure 7,581,000,000 pesos. Gross national product (1979 est.) U.S. $13.9 billion.

Foreign Trade. (1980) Imports 4,509,000,000 pesos (58% from U.S.S.R.); exports 3,967,000,000 pesos (64% to U.S.S.R.). Main exports: sugar 84%; nickel, copper, and chromium ores 5%.

Transport and Communications. Roads (1978) c. 31,200 km. Motor vehicles in use (1976): passenger c. 80,000; commercial (including buses) c. 40,000. Railways: (1979) 14,873 km; traffic (1981) 1,835,000,000 passenger-km, freight 2,626,000,000 net ton-km. Air traffic (1980): c. 932 million passenger-km; freight c. 11.1 million net ton-km. Shipping (1981): merchant vessels 100 gross tons and over 408; gross tonnage 920,137. Telephones (Jan. 1978) 321,000. Radio receivers (Dec. 1979) 2,575,000. Television receivers (Dec. 1979) 1,114,000.

Agriculture. Production (in 000; metric tons; 1981): rice c. 578; cassava c. 328; sweet potatoes c. 327; tomatoes c. 211; sugar, raw value c. 7,359; bananas c. 155; oranges c. 360; coffee c. 24; tobacco c. 34; jute c. 10; beef and veal c. 147; fish catch (1980) 186. Livestock (in 000; 1981): cattle c. 5,900; pigs c. 1,950; sheep c. 365; goats c. 100; horses c. 829; chickens c. 25,250.

Industry. Production (in 000; metric tons; 1981): crude oil 362; natural gas (cu m) c. 90,000; petroleum products (1979) c. 6,320; electricity (kw-hr) 10,336,000; copper ore (metal content) 2.9; chrome ore (oxide content; 1979) 9.9; nickel ore (metal content; 1980) 38; salt (1980) 71; paper (1979) 73; sulfuric acid 418; fertilizers (nutrient content; 1980–81) nitrogenous 112, phosphate c. 5; cement 2,290; crude steel (1980) 304; cotton yarn 26; cotton fabrics (sq m) 156,000.

Crops:
see Agriculture and Food Supplies

ain against Argentina." Although the movement did not adopt the resolution in its entirety, in general Cuba gained credibility among the members.

In September the Cuban government sought to reschedule $1.2 billion of its debt to Western banks, delaying repayment of the principal until 1986. Cuba's debts to the West totaled about $3.5 billion, and falling sugar prices, rising interest rates, and the drying up of credit from Western banks had led to severe difficulties with debt repayment. It was estimated that the Soviet Union was subsidizing up to 20% of Cuba's national income, though much aid was in the form of subsidized trading agreements.

Real economic growth in 1981 was abnormally high at 12%, compared with the 1980 growth rate of 3%, chiefly as a result of recovery within the agricultural sector from diseases that affected tobacco and sugar crops in 1980. The forecast for 1982 was much lower, in spite of a good harvest, because world prices for sugar were depressed. Sugarcane still dominated the economy, providing about 80% of export earnings. The 1981–82 sugar crop was officially put at 8.2 million metric tons, just short of the record 1969–70 crop of 8.6 million metric tons. Cuba exported 7.1 million metric tons of sugar during 1981, as against 6.2 million metric tons a year earlier. To achieve improved levels of agricultural output and stem migration to the cities, the government allowed the establishment of limited free markets, where farm produce in excess of state quotas could be sold at freely negotiated prices.

Diversification of the economy away from sugar had been the prime economic policy aim since 1971. There had been some broadening of the manufacturing base, an expansion of fishing, and a development of nonsugar agriculture. The 1982 economic plan aimed at 2.5% growth, offsetting the still low world sugar prices with reduced demand for imports. A new law published in February 1982 encouraged direct foreign investment, particularly in the tourist sector.

In October the Cuban poet Armando Valladares, imprisoned for 22 years after he broke with Castro over Cuba's ties to Moscow, was released following the personal intervention of French Pres. François Mitterrand and left Cuba for Paris.

(FIONA B. MERRY)

Cycling

The 1982 world cycling championships took place in Great Britain, which celebrated an outstanding victory for 20-year-old Amanda Jones in the women's road race at Goodwood, Sussex. Riders from the U.S. dominated the two women's events in the track program. Rebecca Twigg, 19, won the individual pursuit and Connie Paraskevin, 21, the sprint.

Koichi Nakano of Japan won the professional sprint for the sixth successive year, this time by default when his opponent in the final, Gordon Singleton of Canada, crashed twice and was unable to complete the series. The reign of East Germany's Lothar Thoms, winner of an Olympic and

1982 Cycling Champions		
Event	Winner	Country
WORLD AMATEUR CHAMPIONS—TRACK		
Men		
Sprint	S. Kopylov	U.S.S.R.
Tandem sprint	I. Kucirek, P. Martinek	Czechoslovakia
Individual pursuit	D. Macha	East Germany
Team pursuit	K. Khrabtsov, A. Krasnov	U.S.S.R.
	V. Movtchan, S. Nikitenko	
1,000-m time trial	F. Schmidtke	West Germany
50-km points	H.J. Pohl	East Germany
50-km motor-paced	G. Minneboo	The Netherlands
Women		
Sprint	C. Paraskevin	U.S.
Individual pursuit	R. Twigg	U.S.
WORLD PROFESSIONAL CHAMPIONS—TRACK		
Sprint	K. Nakano	Japan
Individual pursuit	A. Bondue	France
50-km points	U. Freuler	Switzerland
One-hour motor-paced	M. Venix	The Netherlands
Keirin	G. Singleton	Canada
WORLD AMATEUR CHAMPIONS—ROAD		
Men		
Individual road race	B. Drogan	East Germany
100-km team time trial	M. Ducrot, G. Schipper	The Netherlands
	G. Solleveld,	
	F. van Bindsbergen	
Women		
Individual road race	A. Jones	Great Britain
WORLD PROFESSIONAL CHAMPION—ROAD		
Individual road race	G. Saronni	Italy
WORLD CHAMPIONS—CYCLO-CROSS		
Amateur	M. Fisera	Czechoslovakia
Professional	R. Liboton	Belgium
MAJOR PROFESSIONAL ROAD-RACE WINNERS		
Milan–San Remo	M. Gomez	France
Het Volk	A. de Wolf	Belgium
Tirenno–Adriatico	G. Saronni	Italy
Paris–Nice	S. Kelly	Ireland
Amstel Gold	J. Raas	The Netherlands
Tour of Flanders	R. Martens	Belgium
Paris–Roubaix	J. Raas	The Netherlands
Ghent-Wevelgem	F. Hoste	Belgium
Flèche Wallonne	M. Beccia	Italy
Liège–Bastogne–Liège	S. Contini	Italy
Grand Prix of Frankfurt	L. Peeters	The Netherlands
Tour of Romandie	J. Wilmann	Norway
Bordeaux–Paris	M. Tinazzi	France
Tour de France	B. Hinault	France
Tour of Italy	B. Hinault	France
Tour of Spain	M. Lejarreta	Spain
Tour of Switzerland	G. Saronni	Italy

The men's and women's winners of the 11-day Coors International Classic cycling events were José Patrocinio Jiminez of Colombia and Connie Carpenter of the U.S. The race ended in Boulder, Colorado.

UPI

four successive world titles, in the 1,000-m time trial was ended by Fredy Schmidtke, a former junior world champion from West Germany.

For the first time in the history of cycling, the winner of a major national tour was subsequently disqualified because of drug abuse. Angel Arroyo, from Spain, was stripped of overall victory in the Tour of Spain when a dope test taken after the end of the 17th stage was found positive, and runner-up Marino Lejarreta was promoted to first place; four other riders were also eliminated. Later in the season in France a number of riders, including Bernard Hinault (see BIOGRAPHIES), were fined by their governing body for refusing to submit to tests after a race in Brittany, and only the intervention of the French minister for sport prevented a boycott of the world championships by the French team. A truce was declared until the end of the season.

Giuseppe Saronni, second in 1981, won the professional world road race championship for Italy from Greg Lemond, who earned the U.S. its first medal ever in that event and then went on to win the Tour de l'Avenir. Phil Anderson of Australia won the award for the best young rider, and Ireland's Sean Kelly finished first in the points competition.

In the Commonwealth Games at Brisbane, Australia, K. Tucker (Australia) won the 1,000-m sprint, C. Adair (N.Z.) the individual time trial, M. Turtur (Australia) the 4,000-m individual pursuit, K. Nichols (Australia) the 10-mi race, and M. Elliott (England) the individual road race.

(JOHN R. WILKINSON)

Cyprus

An island republic and a member of the Commonwealth, Cyprus is in the eastern Mediterranean. Area: 9,251 sq km (3,572 sq mi). Pop. (1982 est.): 645,000, including (1980 est.) Greeks 80.7%; Turks 18.7%; others 0.6%. Cap. and largest city: Nicosia (pop., 1980 est., 161,000). Official population estimates may not take into account the extensive internal migration or the recent and reportedly extensive Turkish immigration and Greek emigration. Language: Greek and Turkish. Religion (1980 est.): Greek Orthodox 76.2%; Muslim 18.7%; other Christian 2.7%; other 0.6%; none 1.8%. President in 1982, Spyros Kyprianou.

The major political development of 1982 in Cyprus was the announcement of an alliance between Pres. Spyros Kyprianou's ruling Democratic Party and the Communist party, AKEL. Its objective was to secure victory for President Kyprianou in the presidential election scheduled for February 1983. Kyprianou announced his candidacy for a second term after reaching agreement on a minimum program of cooperation with AKEL.

The new political alliance brought strong reactions from the main opposition parties, the right-wing Democratic Rally Party of former president Glafcos Clerides and the Socialist EDEK party of Vassos Lyssarides. Both these opposition leaders intended to stand for election but realized that they had little chance of matching the 54% electoral support that President Kyprianou and AKEL proved they could muster in an August by-election.

A more serious result of Kyprianou's alliance with the Communists was a sharp deterioration in relations between Cyprus and Greece after Greek Prime Minister Andreas Papandreou indicated his displeasure with the pact. The Cyprus Communists sharply rebuked Papandreou for "interference," to the great embarrassment of the government, which had accorded the Greek leader a hero's welcome when he visited the island in February–March.

Greek-Cypriot disappointment over the progress of talks with Turkish Cypriots led the govern-

Bernard Hinault of France, leading the way down the Champs-Elysées in Paris, won the Tour de France for the fourth time in five years. A few weeks earlier he had won the Tour of Italy.

Cyprus

Some of the Palestinians evacuated from Beirut were flown to Cyprus for resettlement there and elsewhere. The group pictured was on its way from Cyprus to Jordan.

ment to seek more international action on the Cyprus problem, a move that angered Turkish Cypriots who saw the problem as an internal one.

CYPRUS

Education. Greek schools (1980–81): primary, pupils 48,701, teachers 2,183; secondary, pupils 41,794, teachers 2,408; vocational, pupils 5,805, teachers 502; teacher training, students 117, teachers 16; higher, students 1,823, teaching staff 175. Turkish schools (1978–79): primary, pupils 18,353, teachers 610; secondary, pupils 10,524, teachers 531; vocational, pupils 1,434, teachers 175; teacher training, students 37, teachers 4.

Finance. Monetary unit: Cyprus pound, with (Sept. 20, 1982) a free rate of C£0.49 to U.S. $1 (C£0.84 = £1 sterling). The Turkish lira is also in use in North Cyprus (Turkish Federated State). Gold and other reserves (June 1982) U.S. $415 million. Budget (1981 est.): revenue C£162.8 million; expenditure C£162.5 million. Excludes budget of Turkish Federated State (1981–82 est.) balanced at 6,337,000,000 Turkish liras.

Foreign Trade. (South only; 1981) Imports C£490 million; exports C£235 million. Import sources: U.K. 14%; Italy 10%; Greece 8%; U.S. 7%; West Germany 7%; Japan 7%; Iraq 7%; France 5%. Export destinations: U.K. 19%; Libya 10%; Saudi Arabia 8%; ships' stores 8%; Lebanon 6%; Iraq 6%; Syria 5%. Main exports: clothing 20%; footwear 8%; potatoes 8%; cement 7%; citrus fruit 6%; wine and spirits 6%; paper containers 5%; cigarettes 5%. Tourism (1980): South, visitors 353,000, gross receipts U.S. $199 million; North, visitors 85,000.

Transport and Communications. Roads (1980) 10,257 km. Motor vehicles in use (1980): passenger 92,000; commercial 23,300. Air traffic (1981): 854 million passenger-km; freight 18.1 million net ton-km. Shipping (1981): merchant vessels 100 gross tons and over 588; gross tonnage 1,818,997. Telephones (Jan. 1980) 104,300. Radio receivers (Dec. 1979) 300,000. Television licenses (Dec. 1979) 100,000.

Agriculture. Production (in 000; metric tons; 1981): barley c. 101; wheat c. 21; potatoes c. 216; grapes c. 210; oranges c. 123; grapefruit c. 89; lemons c. 36; olives c. 39. Livestock (in 000; 1981): sheep c. 525; cattle c. 41; pigs c. 183; goats c. 360.

Industry. Production (South only; in 000; metric tons; 1980): asbestos c. 30; iron pyrites (exports) 88; chromium ore (oxide content; 1979) 7.6; petroleum products (1979) c. 510; cement (1981) 1,035; electricity (kw-hr; 1981) 1,061,000.

The Turkish-Cypriot administration in the north showed signs of internal instability and, with both sides having internal divisions, problems between the Greek and Turkish communities tended to be exploited. The result was a number of sharp exchanges between Greek and Turkish leaders, each accusing the other of stockpiling arms. The new tensions reached a dangerous level in September when a Greek-Cypriot national guardsman was shot dead by a Turkish-Cypriot sentry on the Nicosia "green line." Both sides were shocked by the incident and afterward were careful to keep the confrontation at the propaganda level.

All major industries in Cyprus, apart from tourism, appeared to be in decline, a result of the island's reduced competitiveness in traditionally labour-intensive enterprises such as clothing manufacture and citrus farming. Inflation had been cut back from 13.5% in 1980 to 10.8% in 1981 and an estimated 7% in 1982, and the total unemployment rate during 1982 was about 3%. However, Cyprus began during the year to experience its first labour problems ever. Trade unions began to show a previously unknown militancy as fears for the future of jobs grew. The government gave assurances that its pact with AKEL would not in any way affect the island's free-enterprise economy.

(CHRIS DRAKE)

Czechoslovakia

A federal socialist republic of central Europe, Czechoslovakia lies between Poland, the U.S.S.R., Hungary, Austria, and East and West Germany. Area: 127,889 sq km (49,378 sq mi). Pop. (1982 est.): 15,374,800, including (1980) Czech 64.1%, Slovak 30.6%, other 5.3%. Cap. and largest city: Prague (pop., 1981 est., 1,182,400). Language: Czech and Slovak (official). General secretary of

Czechoslovakia

the Communist Party of Czechoslovakia and president in 1982, Gustav Husak; federal premier, Lubomir Strougal.

The problem of the economy, which had dominated Czechoslovakia's affairs for several years, continued to overshadow virtually all other considerations in 1982. If anything, the situation grew more alarming and the leadership's inability to apply remedies more obvious. The figures for 1981 were the second worst since the Communist Party of Czechoslovakia (CPC) took over in 1948. The increase in national income was 0.2% over 1980; the worst year was 1963, when the economy actually declined by 2.2%. In 1981 industrial output went up by 2%, while agricultural output fell by 3.4%. These and other statistics made it clear that Czechoslovakia had exhausted its reserves and was paying for the policies of the 1970s by low output. In effect, the failure to improve investment structure, the continued preponderance of heavy industry, and the reliance on inflexible command planning had resulted in stagnation.

Responsibility lay with the CPC leadership, which had rejected economic reform projects on political grounds and remained wedded to rigid central control. In this respect, the Czechoslovak leadership was the victim of an immobility born of its refusal to countenance any reform, the latter being associated with the "Prague Spring" of January–August 1968. This rigidity manifested itself in the remedies put forward.

In the first place, the leadership stressed austerity. There were to be serious cutbacks in consumption, both individual and social. Affecting the former were the steep increases in meat, drink, and tobacco prices announced in January; energy prices were also raised. Collective consumption, which as a proportion of the budget had risen steadily in the 1970s, would be cut back, with unavoidable deterioration in the provision of health, education, culture, rented accommodation, and transportation. The second goal of the leadership's strategy was autarchy. This had inherent difficulties for a relatively small, industrial country short of many raw materials. Czechoslovakia relied on imports for 40% of its energy needs, 69% of nonferrous and 93% of ferrous metals, and 34.3% of its feed grains.

The raising of productivity, the most pressing requirement according to outside observers, ran into obstacles of inflexibility deriving from politically determined centralization. Yet the scale of inefficiency in Czechoslovak industry was alarming. The rate of consumption of materials was 30–40% higher than in the West. In engineering, waste amounted to one-quarter of the total output of steel, and there were reports of growing inventories of unsold and unsalable goods.

Despite countless official exhortations to the population to improve their working habits and to "face up to the challenge of the economic situation," there was no evidence of any improvement in the figures for the first half of 1982. Although at first the press attempted to present these figures in an optimistic light, by October the newspapers were openly referring to "an emergency situation" in the economy. The January–June increase in industrial output over the same period of 1981 was on the order of 0.4%.

Underlining the extent of the decline, it was clear that, except for cosmetic purposes, the five-year plan was being abandoned. The actual plan targets for the 1981–85 period were not sanctioned until December 1981, and these targets were below the already low figures put forward in the guidelines for the plan. Whereas the guidelines had looked to an annual growth rate of 2.7–3%, the actual target was down to 2%, which meant zero growth in some years. It seemed likely that 1982 would be one of these. The target increase of 0.6% would be effectively wiped out by a population increase of the same order.

In the midst of this economic gloom, political developments were of secondary significance. The Czechoslovak leadership was evidently relieved at the suppression of Poland's reform process before it might spread. Within the leadership there was no evidence of any shift in the relative strengths of hard-liners and conservatives. The former were more than powerful enough to prevent any concessions to genuine reform. The general malaise left

CZECHOSLOVAKIA

Education. (1981–82) Primary, pupils 1,930,634, teachers 90,282; secondary, pupils 149,210, teachers 8,918; vocational, pupils 229,543, teachers 16.391; teacher training, pupils 14,590, teachers 962; higher, students 152,584, teaching staff 18,624.

Finance. Monetary unit: koruna, with (Sept. 20, 1982) a commercial rate of 6.30 koruny to U.S. $1 (10.80 koruny = £1 sterling) and a noncommercial rate of 11 koruny to U.S. $1 (18.90 koruny = £1 sterling). Budget (1979 rev. est.): revenue 294.6 billion koruny; expenditure 292.4 billion koruny. Net material product (1980) $482.5 billion koruny.

Foreign Trade. (1981) Imports 88,107,000,000 koruny; exports 86,634,000,000 koruny. Import sources: U.S.S.R. 40%; East Germany 10%; Poland 6%; Hungary 6%; West Germany 5%. Export destinations: U.S.S.R. 38%; East Germany 10%; Poland 7%; West Germany 6%; Hungary 5%. Main exports (1980): machinery 39%; iron and steel 8%; motor vehicles 8%; chemicals 6%; textiles and clothing 6%.

Transport and Communications. Roads (1974) 145,455 km (including 79 km expressways). Motor vehicles in use (1979): passenger 1,976,700; commercial 324,800. Railways (1980): 13,131 km (including 3,034 km electrified); traffic 18,050,000,000 passenger-km, freight (1981) 73,260,000,000 net ton-km. Air traffic (1981) 1,472,-000,000 passenger-km; freight 14.3 million net ton-km. Navigable inland waterways (1979) c. 480 km. Shipping (1981): merchant vessels 100 gross tons and over 21; gross tonnage 185,225. Telephones (Dec. 1980) 3,150,500. Radio licenses (Dec. 1980) 4,082,000. Television licenses (Dec. 1980) 4,292,000.

Agriculture. Production (in 000; metric tons 1981): wheat c. 4,400; barley c. 3,500; oats c. 400; rye c. 500; corn c. 800; potatoes c. 3,500; sugar, raw value c. 870; grapes c. 234; apples c. 170; beef and veal c. 380; pork c. 840; timber (cu m; 1980) 18,387. Livestock (in 000; Dec. 1980): cattle 5,002; pigs 7,894; sheep 910; chickens 47,283.

Industry. Index of industrial production (1975 = 100; 1981) 128. Fuel and power (in 000; metric tons; 1981): coal 27,204; brown coal 95,223; crude oil 88; petroleum products (1979) c. 17,390; natural gas (cu m) c. 640,000; manufactured gas (cu m) 7,700,000; electricity (kw-hr) 74,065,000. Production (in 000; metric tons; 1981): iron ore (26% metal content) 1,937; pig iron 10,076; crude steel 15,269; cement 10,646; sulfuric acid 1,317; caustic soda 331; plastics and resins 913; fertilizers (nutrient content; 1980) nitrogenous c. 735, phosphate 361; cotton yarn 137; cotton fabrics (m) 636,000; woolen fabrics (m) 60,200; man-made fibres 157; paper (1980) 894; passenger cars (units) 181; commercial vehicles (units) 86. Dwelling units completed (1981) 94,000.

neither the party membership nor the population at large unaffected. The former was repeatedly criticized for "formalism, passivity, and indiscipline," while some party organizations were described as similar to "bourgeois clubs." The mood of disenchantment was widespread, particularly in light of the leadership's insistence that the party membership was primarily responsible for ensuring that its economic strategy was implemented. The popular mood was one of skepticism and apathy. Shortages of consumer goods, services, and foodstuffs were reported, but the response did not go beyond grumbling and deeper involvement in the secondary economy. A rise in the number of prosecutions for economic crimes provided tentative evidence of an increase in semilegal and illegal economic activity.

While the official hard-line attitude to religion was sustained, making Czechoslovakia the most repressive country in Eastern Europe (Albania excepted) in its policy toward the churches, the Charter 77 opposition movement appeared to have found a new lease on life. After the inactivity of 1981, the Charter issued a large number of documents in 1982. They dealt with a variety of subjects, ranging from the situation in Poland to religious freedom, price increases, education, miscarriages of justice, the situation in prisons, and discrimination against certain writers. Nonetheless, the political isolation of the Charter from the population as a whole continued, and apathy characterized the mood of the bulk of the population. (GEORGE SCHÖPFLIN)

Dance

United States. The year 1982 was a disquieting one for dance in the U.S. Major ballet companies were beset with labour disputes, financial crises, and injuries to dancers and choreographers. Large and small troupes struggled to hold ground in a shrinking economy with reduced government support for touring.

American Ballet Theatre (ABT) completed its second season under the artistic helm of Mikhail Baryshnikov, whose contract was renewed through the 1985–86 season. Baryshnikov promoted many young dancers from the ranks but was criticized

for his revisions of 19th-century ballets and unfruitful commissions. ABT staged new ballets by Kenneth MacMillan (*The Wild Boy*, music by Gordon Crosse, sets by Oliver Smith, costumes by Willa Kim), Choo San Goh (*Configurations*), Lynne Taylor-Corbett (*Great Galloping Gottschalk*), and Peter Anastos (*Clair de Lune*). The company also acquired its first Merce Cunningham ballet, *Duets*. Other ABT premieres included George Balanchine's *Bourrée Fantasque*, Eliot Feld's *Variations on 'America,'* and Roland Petit's *Carmen*.

Injuries plagued many ABT dancers, including Baryshnikov, who underwent knee surgery and was out most of the season. In December Natalia Makarova suffered a broken shoulder blade and a head cut when a length of pipe fell on her during a performance of the musical *On Your Toes* in Washington, D.C.'s Kennedy Center. At the expiration of their contracts on August 31 the ABT dancers were locked out by management, and engagements in Paris, Boston, and Washington, D.C., were canceled. A two-month layoff ended in November with a four-year contract (a first for ABT). Dancers won major salary gains, an increased number of performance weeks, and improved fringe benefits. The company resumed rehearsals for a delayed season to begin January 1983 in Washington, D.C. Aleksandr Godunov, who defected from the Soviet Union in 1979, left ABT; a former soloist, Gelsey Kirkland, was rehired for the new season.

New York City Ballet (NYCB) mounted an ambitious Stravinsky Centennial Celebration in June at the New York State Theater, despite the infirmity of the artistic director, George Balanchine, who first underwent cataract surgery and later suffered a fall that necessitated lengthy hospitalization. Compared with the NYCB's landmark 1972 Stravinsky Festival, the 1982 celebration was disappointing. Eleven of the 28 Stravinsky works were newly choreographed. Balanchine mounted new productions of *Persephone* (with Vera Zorina) and *The Flood* (designed by Rouben Ter-Arutunian) and three short works, *Tango, Elegie*, and *Variations*. There were new ballets by Jerome Robbins (*Four Chamber Works*), John Taras (*Concerto for Piano and Wind Instruments*), Jacques d'Amboise (*Serenade en La* and *Pastorale*), and Peter Martins (*Concerto for Two Solo Pianos* and *Piano-Rag-Music*). Lew Christensen's *Norwegian Moods* had its NYCB premiere; Robbins's *Circus Polka* and Balanchine's *Scherzo à la Russe* were revived.

With Balanchine ill there was considerable speculation as to his possible successor, with Martins the most frequently mentioned prospect. The regular season featured Martins's *The Magic Flute* (Riccardo Drigo), staged first in 1981 for the School of American Ballet, Robbins's *The Gershwin Concerto*, and Joseph Duell's *La Création du Monde*. Mel Tomlinson of Dance Theatre of Harlem and David MacNaughton of San Francisco Ballet joined NYCB.

Joffrey Ballet, strapped financially, announced that it would acquire a second home in Los Angeles in 1984 as resident dance company of the Los Angeles Music Center. It thus became the first major company with a home on both coasts of the U.S. The Joffrey celebrated its 25th season with perfor-

The New York City Ballet performed Jerome Robbins's witty *Four Chamber Works*, which used the circus as metaphor, during its Stravinsky Centennial Celebration in June.

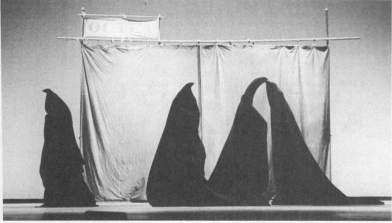

MARTHA SWOPE

mances of a new work by Gerald Arpinc (*Light Rain*), the first U.S. productions of John Cranko's *The Taming of the Shrew* and Jiri Kylian's *Transfigured Night*, revivals of Kurt Jooss's *The Green Table*, Twyla Tharp's *Deuce Coupe II*, the pas de six from Arthur Saint-Léon's *La Vivandière*, Robbins's *Moves*, and Arpino's *Trinity* and *Secret Places*.

Pennsylvania Ballet survived the disclosure of an accumulated debt of close to $2 million; the resignation of founder Barbara Weisberger, a protégé of Balanchine; and Balanchine's withdrawal of his ballets. Under Benjamin Harkarvy's direction the dancers toured nationally before a layoff. Harkarvy, who joined the company in 1972, resigned when he was unable to regain the Balanchine repertory. Robert Weiss, principal dancer with NYCB, replaced him as artistic director on a one-year contract with Martins as artistic adviser.

San Francisco Ballet produced a Stravinsky celebration with in-house choreographers Michael Smuin, Val Caniparoli, John McFall, Robert Gladstein, and Tomm Ruud. The season also included *Vilzak Variations*, staged by ballet master Anatole Vilzak, and a newly designed production of Lew Christensen's *Beauty and the Beast* by José Varona. The company broke ground for a new home.

The Metropolitan Opera's Stravinsky tribute was designed by painter David Hockney. It comprised *Le Sacre du Printemps* (Jean-Pierre Bonnefous), *Le Rossignol* (Frederick Ashton for Makarova and Anthony Dowell), and *Oedipus Rex* (narrated by Dowell).

Dance Theatre of Harlem toured widely during 1982, staging company premieres of Valerie Bettis's *A Streetcar Named Desire*, Geoffrey Holder's *Songs of the Auvergne* and *Banda*, Domy Reiter-Soffer's *Equus*, and Ruth Page and Bentley Stone's *Frankie and Johnny*. There was also a world premiere of Taras's *Firebird*, with sets and costumes by Holder.

Ballet West celebrated founder Willam Christensen's 80th birthday. *Swan Lake* was newly staged by Denise Schultze and Louis Godfrey (formerly of South Africa), and there were premieres by Helen Douglas and company director Bruce Marks. The Feld Ballet, directed by Eliot Feld, inaugurated its home in New York City, the Joyce Theater. a 500-seat converted movie house designed for Feld and other small companies. Feld's new ballets included *Play Bach* and *Over the Pavement*.

The Boston Ballet mounted Rudolf Nureyev's *Don Quixote* and took it on the road with Nureyev. In Miami, Fla., Norbert Vesak's New World Ballet Company made its debut in the New World Festival of the Arts with premieres by Vesak, Vicente Nebrada, Lynn Seymour, and Oscar Araiz. Patricia Wilde, former director of the ABT School, which closed in 1982, replaced Patrick Franz as artistic director of Pittsburgh Ballet. Flemming Flindt and Ted Kivitt completed their first seasons directing the Dallas and Milwaukee ballets, respectively. Indianapolis Ballet Theater staged the first Western production of Marius Petipa's one-act *Cavalry Hall*. Following its production of Bronislava Nijinska's *Les Noces*, the first by a U.S. company, the Oakland Ballet staged Nijinska's *Les Biches*.

Martha Graham, 88 and in ill health, presented two new works in her City Center season, *Dances of the Golden Hall* (Andrzej Panufnik) and *Andromache's Lament* (Samuel Barber), and revived *Dark Meadow*, *Primitive Mysteries*, and *Herodiade*. The José Limón Dance Company celebrated its 35th anniversary and tenth year since Limón's death with a tribute at the Joyce Theater. The Alvin Ailey troupe celebrated its 25th anniversary season with new works by Rodney Griffin (*Sonnets*) and Elisa Monte (*Pigs and Fishes*). In City Center seasons Merce Cunningham presented *Trails* and *Gallopade* and his latest film/dance collaboration with

One of the features of the American Dance Festival in Durham, N.C., in July was *Sea-Dappled Horse* performed by the group Dai Rakuda Kan. The Japanese company, in the words of a critic, "performs living nightmares."

Dams:
see Engineering Projects

Charles Atlas, *Channels/Inserts*; Paul Taylor created *Lost, Found and Lost* and *Mercuric Tidings* and revived *Orbs*. Twyla Tharp presented two new works in Vancouver, B.C. (*Bad Smells* and *Nine Sinatra Songs*). David Gordon's *T.V. Reel* and *Trying Times*, Meredith Monk's *Specimen Days*, and Bill T. Jones's *Social Intercourse* were among notable new works that mixed media, movement, and language.

Foreign companies visiting the U.S. for the first time included Ballet Rambert from Great Britain, the Norwegian National Ballet, and the Cullberg Ballet from Sweden. The Royal Danish Ballet played two-week seasons at the Kennedy Center and New York City's Metropolitan Opera House, with a rich selection of August Bournonville ballets, including the first U.S. showing of *Kermesse in Bruges*. Other major imports included the Grand Kabuki from Japan, Netherlands Dance Theatre, and Dutch National Ballet. Les Grands Ballet Canadiens made its first U.S. appearance in ten years at the New York City Center. There were tributes to dancer Igor Youskevitch in Austin, Texas, and to choreographer Katherine Dunham in Chicago.

The tap dance revival flourished. Among the productions were *Tappin' Uptown* in Brooklyn, a tap festival at New York University, and a tribute to Honi Coles in Washington, D.C.

(SALI ANN KRIEGSMAN)

Europe. During 1982 the frontiers of Europe were crisscrossed by ballet and modern dance. London alone was visited by companies from France (Paris Opéra Ballet and Ballet-Théâtre Français), West Germany (Tanztheater Wuppertal), Italy (Aterballetto), Switzerland (Zürich Opera Ballet), Canada (Les Grands Ballets Canadiens; Royal Winnipeg Ballet; Dancemakers, Toronto), the U.S. (Murray Louis Dance Company), Australia (Australian Dance Theatre), Israel (Kibbutz Dance Company), and Nepal.

In return, several British companies went elsewhere: Ballet Rambert to the U.S.; London Contemporary Dance Theatre to Canada; Northern Ballet Theatre (Manchester) to Hong Kong; the Royal Ballet from Covent Garden to Rome and Venice; and the Sadler's Wells Royal Ballet, which

began the year in Monaco, to New Zealand, Australia, Singapore, and Bangkok, Thailand.

Sadler's Wells Royal Ballet was adventurous in repertory, ranging from a scholarly historical reconstruction of enchanting dances from Saint-Léon's *La Vivandière* (1844) to *The Swan of Tuonela*, a first three-act ballet by company dancer David Bintley. His choice of all-Sibelius music and a tale of fantasy figures from the Kalevala, the national epic of Finland, made him overly reliant on narrative mime at the expense of dance interest.

Younger talent was also featured in the Royal Ballet's Covent Garden premiere of *L'Invitation au voyage* by company dancer Michael Corder, a beguiling suite of mood dances with no specific story, to songs by Henri Duparc. Principal choreographer Kenneth MacMillan created a lacklustre *Orpheus* to mark the Stravinsky centennial (widely celebrated elsewhere in Europe, notably by the Hamburg, Stuttgart, and Netherlands National ballets, as well as by Robert North's diverting *Pribaoutki* for Ballet Rambert).

The Rambert company's first use of a mobile tent theatre in London's Battersea Park was dedicated to the memory of Dame Marie Rambert, who died aged 94 (*see* OBITUARIES). A founding pioneer of the British dance tradition from the 1920s, she was personally responsible for the development of much choreographic talent, from Frederick Ashton to Christopher Bruce. The latter's new *Requiem*, to music by Kurt Weill, was premiered by Ballet Rambert.

London Festival Ballet devoted its major effort to an elaborate new production of *Swan Lake*, in which the received elements of 19th-century classical choreography were supplemented by new details from artistic director John Field. Deemed only partially successful, this gave Britain alone its fourth different version of the ballet classic, alongside those of the two Royal Ballet companies and one by Peter Darrell for Scottish Ballet. The latter staged the first production by a British company of Cranko's *Romeo and Juliet* (1958).

Other British developments included the formation of a new modern dance group, Second Stride, involving a trio of choreographers (Richard Alston, Siobhan Davies, Ian Spink). The group made a successful first tour of the U.K. and the U.S. The independent London City Ballet, with no public funding, became the first classical ballet company to tour the United Arab Emirates. For the London troupe, international ballerina Maina Gielgud created her first professional choreography in *Ghosties and Ghoulies* (music by Debussy).

The Royal Ballet at Covent Garden announced for December a new ballet based on Shakespeare's *The Tempest* by Nureyev (who became an Austrian citizen on January 25, having been stateless since he left the U.S.S.R. in 1961). It was also announced that Nureyev would take his first salaried directorial position, in charge of the Paris Opéra Ballet from September 1983. Among his other activities he continued the so-called Nureyev Festival at the London Coliseum, including a notably successful "Homage to Diaghilev" presentation by the Ballet-Théâtre Français from Nancy.

Paris was host to an outstanding eight-week vis-

Ballerina Olga Chenchikova performed in *Swan Lake* during an eight-week visit to Paris by the Soviet Kirov Ballet directed by Oleg Vinogradov.

DANIEL CANDE/TIME MAGAZINE

it by the Soviet Kirov Ballet from Leningrad, directed by Oleg Vinogradov. His own ballet on Gogol's *The Government Inspector*, to music by Aleksandr Tchaikovsky (no relation to the 19th-century composer), was thought to yield too much to the continuing wish for full-evening story-ballets when it could have been more successful at a shorter length. The repertory also included a *Swan Lake* that brought international acclaim to Olga Chenchikova as a ballerina of extraordinary gifts.

A contingent of the Kirov Ballet went on to Geneva, and Moscow's Bolshoi Ballet also traveled westward, first to the Prague (Czech.) Spring festival, where the repertory included *The Age of Gold*, newly choreographed by artistic director Yury Grigorovich to the 1930 music by Shostakovich that provided one of the early Soviet ballets on the theme of "socialist realism." The Moscow company was again featured in the open-air arena at the Baths of Caracalla, near Rome, and also in Italy at the old-established international ballet festival at Nervi, near Genoa. The Nervi festival also presented, among others, the Ketiak Ballet from Indonesia and the Alvin Ailey and Paul Taylor companies from the U.S.

The Ailey and Taylor troupes were two of several U.S. companies touring Europe. Others included the Washington Ballet, making its European debut at the Festival of Two Worlds in Spoleto, Italy, and return visits there and elsewhere by the Dance Theatre of Harlem and the Houston (Texas) Ballet. The Twyla Tharp modern dance group appeared at Vienna's international dance festival.

One of the year's cancellations was a direct casualty of the Falkland Islands conflict; the announced visit of the Geneva Opera Ballet to the Edinburgh Festival could not be made because musicians necessary to the performance of *Tango*, by Argentine-born Oscar Araiz, the company's director, could not obtain permission to travel from Argentina. The Swiss company was replaced at Edinburgh by the Antonio Gades Spanish Ballet whose production of a ballet on Federico García Lorca's *Blood Wedding* had earlier been the subject of a prizewinning international film.

Scandinavia afforded illuminating contrasts of approach to 19th-century ballets. The Danish-born choreographer Flemming Flindt reproduced Bournonville's *The Wedding at Hardanger* (1853) for the Norwegian National Ballet with his own choreography in the style of Bournonville and a score newly arranged from period folk themes. With *Giselle* for Sweden's Cullberg Ballet, Mats Ek updated the work's 1840s period to 1940; his new choreography had the betrayed heroine enter a mental asylum for the second act, the erstwhile Queen of the Wilis becoming the head nurse.

Other unconventional dance presentations included *Waltz* by Pina Bausch for her Wuppertal Dance Theatre, again reflecting her concern for human relationships, obstacles, and restraints, which premiered at the Holland Festival. Though dependent on trained dancers for its performance, her work had moved conceptually closer to theatre drama and revue. Waltzes were also prominent in Maurice Béjart's *Wien, Wien* for his Brussels-based Ballet of the 20th Century, a ballet about Vienna,

MARTHA SWOPE

For the New York City Ballet's Stravinsky Centennial Celebration, George Balanchine mounted a new production of *Noah and the Flood*, first choreographed for television in 1962. Adam Lüders and Nina Fedorova danced the parts of Adam and Eve.

about death and rebirth, and, in the choreographer's words, "the structural presentation of a mathematical vision of Hell."

The Irish Ballet celebrated the centennial of writer James Joyce with *Pomes Penyeach*, a ballet by the Israeli-born resident choreographer Domy Reiter-Soffer. The title was from a collection of Joyce poems, some of which were spoken in parallel with the dancing as a visualization of them, interspersed with music varying from Bach to Erik Satie. The device was thought to be imaginatively contrived and theatrically effective within the context of the company's classically based and sometimes folk-inspired repertory.

In other European dance centres the pattern of activity continued to be relatively stable in spite of reductions in government funds in some countries as a result of the recession. Major companies in each country, based on classical ballet or other techniques, were supplemented by a variety of smaller modern dance groups.   (NOËL GOODWIN)

See also Music; Theatre.

Defense

Continuing Palestine Liberation Organization (PLO) attacks on Israeli territory from Syrian-occupied Lebanon led Israel to invade Lebanon on June 6, 1982, in an effort to neutralize Palestinian and Syrian troops based there. After several weeks of fighting, the Palestinians evacuated the Lebanese capital of Beirut during August 21–September 1, under the supervision of an international U.S., French, and Italian force; this force then withdrew, only to be reintroduced after the assassination of the newly elected president of Lebanon, Bashir Gemayel (*see* OBITUARIES). The underlying causes of conflict in the Middle East, and the resulting military balance, made it extremely difficult to see how lasting peace could be achieved. (*See* MIDDLE EASTERN AFFAIRS.)

Chief among the basic causes of conflict in the area was the Arab-Israeli dispute. After more than 30 years, the Arab countries (other than Egypt) still refused to accept the existence of Israel. At the same time, their insistence on the creation of a state for the displaced Palestinians was unacceptable to Israel, in large measure because of the dom-

inance within the Palestinian nationalist movement of violent extremists. Fishing in troubled waters, the Soviets encouraged conflict to undercut U.S. influence in the Middle East, as in Syria's 1976 invasion of Lebanon. Adding to unrest in the region were the emergence of Islamic fundamentalism as a major ideological and political force, epitomized by the Ayatollah Ruhollah Khomeini's theocratic regime in Iran; the centuries-old division between the Sunni and Shi'ah branches of Islam; and border disputes such as that leading to the stalemated Iran-Iraq war. Against this background, Israel's reliance on military means to provide for its security was unavoidable. The U.S. had little choice but to support Israel with massive military aid—since Israel could not afford to defend itself—but could influence Israel's military actions only marginally. The U.S. also had to try and protect its interests and those of its allies, including NATO-Europe and Japan's continued access to Persian Gulf oil at stable prices.

Barring the intervention of Soviet forces, the military balance in the Middle East had shifted significantly in favour of Israel. In the Lebanese fighting, the latest U.S. equipment operated by the Israelis proved far superior to older Soviet equipment manned by the Syrians. Syrian losses were

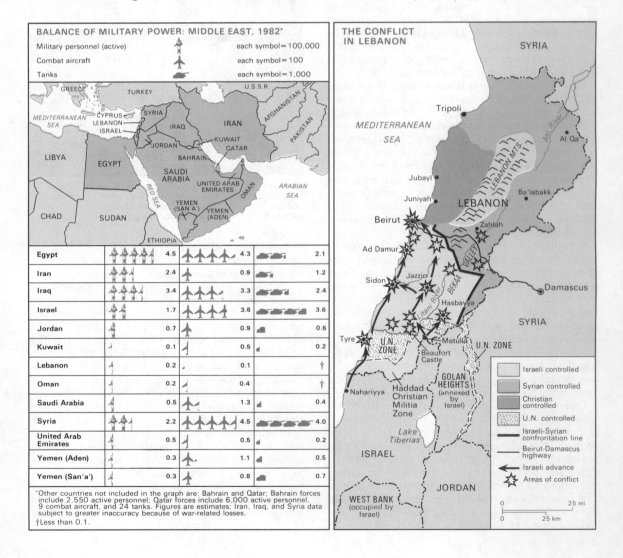

BALANCE OF MILITARY POWER: MIDDLE EAST, 1982*

Military personnel (active)	each symbol = 100,000
Combat aircraft	each symbol = 100
Tanks	each symbol = 1,000

	Military personnel (active)	Combat aircraft	Tanks
Egypt	4.5	4.3	2.1
Iran	2.4	0.9	1.2
Iraq	3.4	3.3	2.4
Israel	1.7	3.6	3.6
Jordan	0.7	0.9	0.6
Kuwait	0.1	0.5	0.2
Lebanon	0.2	0.1	†
Oman	0.2	0.4	†
Saudi Arabia	0.5	1.3	0.4
Syria	2.2	4.5	4.0
United Arab Emirates	0.5	0.5	0.2
Yemen (Aden)	0.3	1.1	0.5
Yemen (San'a')	0.3	0.8	0.7

*Other countries not included in the graph are: Bahrain and Qatar; Bahrain forces include 2,550 active personnel; Qatar forces include 6,000 active personnel, 9 combat aircraft, and 24 tanks. Figures are estimates; Iran, Iraq, and Syria data subject to greater inaccuracy because of war-related losses.
†Less than 0.1.

THE CONFLICT IN LEBANON

Israeli controlled	
Syrian controlled	
Christian controlled	
U.N. controlled	
Israeli-Syrian confrontation line	
Beirut-Damascus highway	
Israeli advance	
Areas of conflict	

0   25 mi
0   25 km

estimated at 70–80 interceptors (out of 244), as against Israeli losses of 2–3 fighter-bombers. The Israeli Air Force (IAF) also destroyed Syria's Soviet-built SA-6 mobile surface-to-air missiles (SAM's) and radar deployed in the Bekaa Valley. Israel's success was attributed to, first, superior electronic countermeasures (ECM/ECCM), including anti-SAM weapons; second, the use of EC-2 Hawkeye airborne warning and control systems (AWACS) aircraft; and, third, superior pilots and equipment.

It is incorrect to conclude, however, that the results proved the overwhelming supremacy of U.S. military technology, although it performed much better than its critics had predicted. The IAF had not had to fight the latest generation of Soviet fighters and air defense systems, manned by Soviet personnel. Similarly, the supremacy of Israeli ground forces, especially armour and artillery, could not be extrapolated to the East-West land balance. Unlike the U.S. and NATO, Israel had enjoyed the overwhelming advantage of escalation dominance. If Syria had escalated the Lebanese fighting to all-out war, it would have lost.

The Middle East military balance is summarized in the accompanying map. However, several additional factors should be kept in mind. Israel's peace treaty with Egypt had neutralized Egypt's armed forces of 320,000 men, 2,100 tanks, and 429 combat aircraft. In addition, Egypt was engaged in the massive task of converting its forces from Soviet to Western equipment while trying to keep Soviet equipment in service without spare parts. Effective Egyptian forces were therefore much less than is shown. Egypt also had to deal with the military threat posed by Libya's unpredictable ruler, Col. Muammar al-Qaddafi. Libya's armed forces were significant, with 55,000 men, 2,600 Soviet tanks, and 555 Soviet and French combat aircraft (some with Soviet pilots). Jordan's 65,000-strong armed forces remained the most professional in the Arab world but were primarily infantry, with only 569 tanks plus an air force of 94 combat aircraft, mainly 82 Tigershark F-5E/F fighter-bombers. The continuing Iran-Iraq war meant that those countries' armed forces could not be used against Israel. Furthermore, equipment estimates for Iran and Iraq in Table II and the map are inflated because serviceability, after three years of war, was low, and equipment losses and casualties had been high.

The resultant isolation of Syria left it militarily vulnerable. Syrian forces totaled 222,500 personnel, with 2,200 T-54/55, 1,000 T-62, and 790 T-72 tanks, plus 448 combat aircraft. Against these Israel, with full mobilization, could deploy some 450,000 personnel, 3,600 tanks (Centurion, M-48, M-60, T-54/55, T-62, and 200 Israeli-built Merkava I/II's), and 634 combat aircraft. Syrian forces had proved no match for the Israelis in the 1967 and 1973 Middle East wars. Thus Syria was unlikely to enter Lebanon in force, and the 30,000-man Syrian occupation force there was essentially on its own, except for its Palestinian supporters. These totaled perhaps 12,000 well-armed but poorly organized guerrilla fighters, who proved unable to offer an effective defense. Indeed, the lack of effective PLO opposition may have led Israel to expand an initially limited operation.

The war in Lebanon fell into two stages. In the first, from June 6 to June 18, the Israeli Defense Force advanced rapidly to Beirut, destroying in the process some 20% of the effective Syrian Air Force and Syrian SAM batteries. The second stage, the siege of Beirut, lasted until September 1, when the PLO completed its evacuation of the city under terms of an agreement negotiated by U.S. special envoy Philip Habib (see BIOGRAPHIES). Two major questions remained unresolved: when, or if, Israeli forces could withdraw from Lebanon; and whether the Lebanese themselves could achieve a viable domestic politico-military settlement. (See LEBANON.)

Politically, the war cost Israel some support in the U.S., at least temporarily. This was the case even though initial media reports of civilian casualties proved to be grossly exaggerated, and the PLO itself used civilian centres as shields. The massacre of Palestinians by Lebanese Christian forces at the Sabra and Shatila refugee camps also had a negative impact, since at the time the camps were under Israeli protection. But this was by no means the only—or the bloodiest—incident in the region during the year. It was estimated that over 100,000 opponents of Iran's theocratic regime had been executed, while Hafez al-Assad's reduction of the rebel city of Hamah killed thousands of Syrians.

UNITED STATES

Contrary to the widespread impression that Pres. Ronald Reagan was undertaking a massive defense buildup, U.S. defense spending as a proportion of gross national product (GNP) increased only slightly, from 5.5 to 6.1%. Because of inflation, the monetary amount seemed large—some $215.9 billion for 1982–83—but U.S. gross domestic product (GDP) had risen to some $3 trillion. The administration's projection for 1984–85 was for a defense budget of about 7% of GNP, compared with average defense spending of 10% of GNP from 1950 to 1965. The impact of this increase was generally overestimated, however. The proportion of GNP spent by the federal government had increased sharply in recent years, and the proportion of government spending allocated to defense had dropped from 41.7% in 1964 to 25.2% in fiscal 1982.

Actual U.S. forces remained too small to meet U.S. alliance commitments in the face of the continuing Soviet buildup, although personnel in the all-volunteer force rose slightly to 2,116,800 (185,680 women). Overdue increases in pay and allowances, plus civilian unemployment, allowed all services to meet their recruitment goals, qualitatively and quantitatively. However, personnel costs amounted to some 30% of the defense budget.

U.S. strategic nuclear forces (SNF) remained inferior to those of the Soviets. (See Table I.) The main changes in U.S. SNF and intermediate nuclear forces (INF) involved the retirement of obsolete systems, including the last of 10 Washington/Allen-class nuclear ballistic missile submarines (SSBN), each carrying 16 Polaris A-3 submarine-launched ballistic missiles (SLBM); 52 Titan II liquid-fueled intercontinental ballistic missiles (ICBM); and 75 B-52D bombers. The only new system deployed was one Ohio-class SSBN with 24

Table I. U.S./NATO–Soviet Strategic and Intermediate Nuclear Force Balance, July 1982

Weapons systems	Range (km)	Payload[1] (000 lb)	Warheads, yield[2]	CEP[3]	Speed (Mach)	Number deployed
UNITED STATES Strategic Forces						
Intercontinental ballistic missiles (ICBM)						1,052
Titan II	15,000	7.5	1 × 9 mt	0.5	...	52–0[4]
Minuteman II	11,300	1–1.5	1 × 1–2 mt	0.4	...	450
Minuteman III	13,000	1.5–2	3 × 350 kt	0.12–0.7	...	550
Submarine-launched ballistic missiles (SLBM; in 36 nuclear submarines)						520
Poseidon C-3	4,600	2–3	10 × 50 kt or 14 × 50 kt	0.15	...	304
Trident C-4	7,400	3+	8 × 100 kt	c. 0.15	...	216
Manned bombers						
B-52G/H	12,000	70	...	...	0.95	241
	16,000				0.95	
FB-111A	4,700	37.5	...	...	2.5	60
U.S./NATO Intermediate Nuclear Forces[5] (Total: 436 weapons, 218 delivery systems)						
Medium/short-range ballistic missiles (M/SRBM)						
U.S. Pershing I	720	...	kt	...	...	108
Manned bombers						
U.S. F-111A/E	4,700	28	2	...	2.5	220[6]
U.K. Vulcan B-2	6,400	21	2	...	0.95	48–0[4]
BRITAIN (Strategic Nuclear Forces only)[7]						
Submarine-launched ballistic missiles (SLBM; in 4 nuclear submarines—SSBN)						
Polaris A-3	4,600	1	3 × 200 kt	0.5	...	64
FRANCE (Strategic and INF)[7]						
Submarine-launched ballistic missiles (SLBM; in 5 nuclear submarines—SSBN)						
MSBS M-20	3,000	...	1 × 1 mt	...	...	80
Intermediate-range ballistic missiles (IRBM)						
SSBS S-3	3,000	...	1 × 1 mt	...	...	18
Manned bombers						
Mirage IVA	3,200	16	2 × mt	...	2.2	34
Mirage IIIE	2,400	19	2 × mt	...	1.8	30
SOVIET UNION Strategic Forces						
Intercontinental ballistic missiles (ICBM)						1,398+
SS-11 Mod 1	10,500	1.5–2	1 × 2 mt	0.3–0.5	...	570
Mod 3			3 × 100–300 kt			
SS-13 Savage	10,000	1	1 × 1 mt	0.7	...	60
SS-16	9,300	2	3 × 150 kt	0.3	...	...
SS-17 Mod 1	10,000	6	4 × 900 kt	(1,500′)	...	150
Mod 2			1 × 5 mt			
SS-18 Mod 1	10,500	16–20	1 × 18–25 mt	0.2–0.34	...	308
Mod 2	9,300	16–20	8 × 2 mt	(600′)		
Mod 3	10,500	16–20	1 × mt	(600′)		
SS-19 Mod 1	11,000	7	6 × 550 kt	(850′)	...	310
Mod 2	10,200	7	1 × 5 mt			
Submarine-launched ballistic missiles (in 69 nuclear plus 15 diesel submarines)						989
SS-N-5 Serb	1,120	1.5	1 × 1–2 mt	1–2	...	57
SS-N-6 Mod 1, 2	2,400	1.5	1 × 1–2 mt	1	...	165
Mod 3	3,000	1.5	2 × 3 kt			288
SS-N-8	8,000	1.5	1 × 1–2 mt	0.5	...	291
SS-NX-17	5,000	3+	1 × 1 mt	0.2–0.3	...	12
SS-N-18	8,000	5+	3 × 1–2 mt	...	...	176
SS-N-20						20
Manned bombers						150
TU-95 Bear	12,800	40	...	...	0.78	105
Mya-4 Bison	11,200	20	...	...	0.87	45
Soviet INF (Total: 1,800 weapons, 990 delivery systems)						
Variable/intermediate/medium-range ballistic missiles (V/I/MRBM)						
SS-4 Sandal	1,900	...	1 × mt	...	...	275
SS-5 Skean	4,100	...	1 × 1 mt	...	...	16
SS-20 Mod 1	5,000	1.2	1 × 1.5 mt	...	...	500–
Mod 2	5,600		3 × 150 kt			756[8]
Mod 3	7,400		1 × 50 kt			(230)
Medium/short-range ballistic missiles and sea-launched cruise missiles[9]						
SS-12/22 SRBM	1,000	...	mt	...	...	c. 500
SS-N-12 SLCM	3,700	...	2 × kt/mt	...	...	c. 100
Manned bombers[10]						880
Tu-16 Badger	6,400	20	2	...	0.8	580
Tu-22 Blinder	2,250	12	2	...	1.5	165
Tu-22M/26 Backfire	8,000	17.5	4	...	2.5	135

[1] Payload refers to a missile's throw weight or a bomber's weapons load.
[2] For MIRV and MRV the figure to the left of the multiplication sign gives the number of warheads and the figure to the right is the yield per warhead. For bombers, weapons per bomber are given.
[3] Circular Error Probable: the radius (in nautical miles) of a circle within which at least half of the missile warheads aimed at a specific target will fall.
[4] To be phased out.
[5] INF systems are missiles with ranges or aircraft with unrefueled combat radii. Combat radii are about one quarter or less of the range.
[6] Total deployed worldwide, including FB-111A; 170 is the inventory normally based in Europe, or within striking range of Europe.
[7] British nuclear forces are under national control, but may be assigned to NATO. French nuclear forces are controlled and targeted independently of NATO.
[8] Total deployed against both NATO and China theatres; two-thirds are thought to be deployed against NATO. Two missiles per launcher.
[9] Although not classified as Soviet INF, Soviet SRBM and SLCM could hit targets in Western Europe and are therefore shown for illustrative purposes.
[10] Total deployed worldwide. Of these, about half are allocated to Soviet Naval Aviation (some 270 Tu-16, 40 Tu-22, and 70 Tu-26). Two-thirds of the remaining strike bombers and ASM carriers are considered deployed against NATO.

Sources: International Institute for Strategic Studies, *The Military Balance 1982–1983*; and *Aviation Week and Space Technology*. Figures for Soviet forces, especially INF, can only be estimates.

Trident C-4 slbm's; one more was on trials and seven were building. The first B-52G/H squadron equipped with long-range air-launched cruise missiles (alcm) became operational. Production of the B-52's replacement, the B-1B, was under way, but the first squadron would not become operational before 1986. The 1,000 aging Minuteman II/III icbm's were being upgraded; some 300 of the 550 Minuteman III's were being retrofitted with the improved Mk 12A multiple independently targetable reentry vehicle (mirv), raising their yield from 3 × 165 kilotons to 3 × 335 kilotons.

Controversy continued to surround the basing mode for Minuteman's successor, the MX icbm, scheduled to become operational in 1986. The latest proposal, advocated by President Reagan in an address in November, was to space MX very close together in a "dense pack" system. Attacking Soviet reentry vehicles would, it was hoped, destroy each other with their own blasts—the fratricide phenomenon—enabling a large proportion of the 100 MX in each dense pack field to survive. Improvements to the basic dense pack system could include the construction of additional silos, so that MX could be shuttled between silos while some were left empty, and its defense by the low-altitude defensive system (loads) antiballistic missile (abm) system being developed by the Army. The lame duck session of Congress refused to fund production of the MX, specifying instead that funding would be contingent on congressional approval of the basing mode within 45 days of a new presidential recommendation, which was to be made on or after March 1, 1983.

Nonetheless, the Reagan administration began to announce a new strategy of prevailing in any major conflict with the Soviets; that is, that the U.S. and its allies would win. This was linked to a strategy of horizontal escalation. A direct, or proxy, Soviet attack on one area of vital U.S. interests (e.g., the Persian Gulf) would be met by U.S. retaliation against one of the Soviets' direct or indirect assets (e.g., Cuba). Hence the administration's emphasis on rebuilding U.S. power-projection forces, notably the Navy, the Air Force, and the Marine Corps.

The 553,000-strong Navy's 600-ship goal was ambitious, given its current force of 201 major surface combat ships and 90 attack submarines (85 nuclear-powered [ssn]). The core of the fleet remained the attack carrier battle group, built around four nuclear carriers and seven conventional carriers. Each normally carried one air wing of 70–95 aircraft. There were also three older carriers, as well as the "Intrepid," used for training. Major surface combatants included 9 nuclear-powered guided weapons (GW) cruisers and 20 conventionally powered GW cruisers, plus the first of the new Aegis-class fleet air-defense cruisers, the uss "Ticonderoga" (8,000 tons). There were also 41 GW and 43 gun/antisubmarine warfare (asw) destroyers and 24 GW and 55 gun frigates. The British experience in the Falkland Islands war with the Invincible-class light carrier meant that the five Tarawa- and seven Iwo Jima-class assault ships represented a significant light carrier capability. Major Navy aircraft included some 400

F-14A/RF-14A Tomcats, 116 A-6E Intruders, 164 A-7E's, 110 S-3A Viking ASW aircraft, and 216 land-based maritime reconnaissance P-3B/C Orions.

The U.S. Marine Corps had 192,000 men and 576 M-60A1 tanks, divided into three heavy divisions, each with its own air wing. Aircraft totaled 440, including the first 28 F-18 Hornet fighters. Deployment afloat was in marine amphibious units, each comprising a composite Marine battalion group (1,800 men). One was deployed with the international force in Lebanon.

The 581,000-strong Air Force had some 3,650 combat aircraft. Major aircraft types, excluding the Strategic Air Command, included 624 F-4 Phantoms, 312 F-16 Falcons, 376 F-15 Eagle interceptors, 252 F-111A/D/E/F medium bombers, 288 A-10A Thunderbolt ground-support fighters, and 126 RF-4C reconnaissance Phantoms. Heavy (strategic) transport included 73 C-5A Galaxys and 254 C-141B's, with additional C-5A's on order. Conversion to modern aircraft types (F-15, F-16, and A-10) was nearly complete; additional aircraft were on order, but numbers remained insufficient. North American air defense was minimal.

The Army, with 790,800 personnel, provided four armoured, six mechanized, four infantry, one airmobile, and one airborne division. These contained more men but fewer tanks than a Soviet division. A U.S. armoured division fielded 18,300 men and 324 tanks, compared with a Soviet division's 11,000 men and 335 tanks, while a U.S. mechanized (motor rifle) division had 18,500 men and 216 tanks, as against 14,000 men and 266 tanks for the U.S.S.R. U.S. tank holdings totaled 12,130, including 300 new Abrams M-1s. Personnel quality, especially among the infantry, remained a problem, despite some improvements.

The central U.S. commitment remained the defense of NATO-Europe, where some 348,600 personnel, including 221,300 troops, were deployed. Other major commitments were in defense of South Korea (28,500 U.S. troops) and Japan (2,500), plus the Persian Gulf. Overall, U.S. military forces had improved, especially in quality, although not enough to counter the Soviets' formidable qualitative and quantitative advantages.

U.S.S.R.

The growth of Soviet military expenditure and power continued. Estimates of Soviet defense expenditure as a percentage of GNP remained at the high end of the 9–15% range, with an annual real growth rate of 4–10%. Soviet S/INF reflected this. Modern Soviet SSBN's included 1 Typhoon class (20 SS-NX-20 SLBM's; larger than the "Ohio") and 13 D-III class (16 SS-N-18 SLBM's; more of both classes building), as well as 4 D-II's, 18 D-1's, 1 Y-II, and 25 Y-I's. Five Y-I's had been converted to attack submarines. ICBM launch silos totaled some 1,398, but this was not an accurate indication of Soviet ICBM numbers since an estimated 2,000–3,000 reserve ICBM's were available. A new strategic bomber, the Ram-K (NATO code name Blackjack), comparable to the B-1, was deployed, while the number of Backfire long-range (8,000 km; c. 5,000 mi) bombers rose to 180.

MX missile dummies are worked on by technicians. In the background is the shroud that covers the missile assembly.

Deployment of modern INF continued rapidly despite Pres. Leonid Brezhnev's claim of a moratorium. By September there were 333 SS-20 intermediate-range ballistic missile (IRBM) launchers deployed in 37 complexes. Each launcher had one or more reload missiles, each with three warheads, for a total of 666 SS-20 IRBM's with 1,998 × 150-kiloton warheads. The Soviets also retained 16 SS-5 and 275 SS-4 intermediate/medium-range ballistic missiles (I/MRBM).

Soviet strategic defenses remained massive. Active defenses included an ABM system around Moscow; 10,000 SAM launchers, with 12,000 SAM's, at 1,400 fixed sites; and the new SA-10 SAM, with ABM capability. Among associated radar systems was a ten-site battle-management ABM radar deployed in violation of the 1972 ABM treaty. The Soviets were also leading in the development of space weapons, including antisatellite weapons. The Air Defense Force (PVO-Strany) and the Ground Forces Air Defense Troops, totaling 630,000 men, were merged.

The U.S. Navy recommissioned its World War II battleship the "New Jersey" to operate as part of an aircraft fleet. The craft was refitted to enable it to launch cruise missiles.

Soviet conventional forces were still the most powerful in the world. Personnel totaled 1,825,000 (1.4 million conscripts), and the quality of their equipment was now comparable to that of the West. This included 50,000 tanks (12,000 new T-72 and older T-62 and 38,000 T-54/55 main battle tanks); 62,000 armoured fighting vehicles (AFV), including the new BTR-70 armoured personnel carrier (APC) and BMP mechanized infantry combat vehicle (MICV); and some 20,000 artillery pieces. These were organized into 46 tank (armoured), 126 motor rifle (mechanized), and 8 airborne divisions, each with more striking power than the Soviet division of a decade earlier.

Deployment remained constant in terms of nominal divisions, with roughly two-thirds deployed against NATO-Europe and one-third against China. The big forward deployment was the Group of Soviet Forces in Eastern Europe, comprising 31 Category 1 (three-quarters to full-strength) divisions plus other deployments for a total of 15 tank and 15 motor rifle divisions. These first-echelon forces were backed up by a second echelon of 69 divisions, half in Category 1 or 2 (half to three-quarters strength) in the European U.S.S.R. military districts. A further 24 divisions (1 tank, 22 motor rifle, 1 airborne), mostly Category 3 (one-quarter strength), were in the southern U.S.S.R., usable against NATO's southern flank or the Persian Gulf. Of the 47 divisions on the Sino-Soviet border, half were in Category 1 or 2. Evidence accumulated concerning Soviet use of illegal chemical and biological weapons (CBW), underlining the threat posed by their massive CBW stockpiles.

Overseas Soviet deployments increased. The largest was in Afghanistan, where Soviet forces had risen to 95,000–120,000 personnel. Casualties since the 1979 invasion amounted to some 20,000–30,000 killed and wounded, but the Soviets still had not gained control of the countryside. Other major deployments included 2,800 personnel in Cuba, 1,800 in Libya, 1,200 in Iraq, 2,500 in Syria, 1,500 in Yemen (Aden), 500 in Yemen (San'a'), and 5,000 in Vietnam. Smaller detachments were deployed to control the operations of Soviet Cuban proxies, often in conjunction with East German security services, in Angola, Ethiopia, Kampuchea, Mali, Mauritania, Mozambique, and Seychelles.

The Soviet Navy had grown to 450,000 personnel, with 290 major surface combat vessels, 273 cruise-missile and attack submarines (105 nuclear, 168 diesel), 755 combat aircraft in the Naval Air Force, and 300 helicopters. Newer Soviet vessels were designed to project Soviet power as well as to defend Soviet SSBN's, attack Western SSBN's, and deny the West use of the sea lines of communication. The Soviet counter to U.S. attack carriers was twofold: first, the 80 Backfire-B, 40 Tu-22 Blinder, and 270 Tu-16 Badger bombers, all land-based and armed with air-to-surface missiles (ASM); and second, the submarine force of 56 nuclear and 148 diesel attack submarines plus 49 nuclear cruise-missile submarines, most of them equipped with eight to ten medium/long-range submarine-launched cruise missiles (SLCM). The new SS-N-12 and SS-N-19 medium/long-range SLCM (1,000-km [620-mi] range, high-explosive 350-kiloton nuclear warhead) was replacing the older SS-N-3 Shaddock. There were also 20 diesel cruise-missile submarines, most with four SS-N-3s.

Construction of a Soviet nuclear-powered attack carrier continued, and a third Kiev-class carrier/cruiser (37,000 tons) was deployed, armed with 14 Yak-36 Forger vertical/short take-off and landing (V/STOL) aircraft, similar to the British Harrier. The two Moskva-class carrier-cruisers had ASW helicopters. Major modern Soviet surface combatants included the unique Kirov-class nuclear-powered, 25,000-ton battle cruisers (1 deployed, 1 fitting out), 18 GW ASW cruisers (7 Kara class, 8,200 tons; 10 Kresta II, 6,000 tons), and 8 GW cruisers (4 Kresta I and 4 Kynda class). The new Sovremenny-type GW destroyers and Udaloy-type ASW GW destroyers were joining the 39 existing GW destroyers and 77 GW frigates. Development of Soviet amphibious warfare/rapid deployment forces continued with the completion of a second Ivan Rogov amphibious assault ship (13,000 tons), surface-effect landing craft, and roll-on/roll-off transports able to unload without port facilities.

The Soviet Tactical Air Force of 475,000 personnel continued to expand its deep-interdiction capability. Older strike aircraft (100 MiG-21s, 150 Su-7s, and 650 Su-17s) were being phased out and replaced by the MiG-27 Flogger D/J and Su-24 Fencer (current deployment 550 each). A new ground-attack aircraft, the Su-25 Frogfoot (formerly Ram-J), comparable to the U.S. A-10 Thunderbolt, was being deployed in Afghanistan. Similarly, 500 MiG-21 Fishbed D/N's were being replaced by 1,250 MiG-23 Flogger B/G's, and 150 MiG-25 Foxbat B/D's supplemented the 130 MiG-21 Fishbed H and 360 Yak-28/Su-17 reconnaissance aircraft. The approximately 2,300 helicopter gunships included 800 Mi-24 Hinds, used against the Afghans. The separate Air Defense Force had some 2,250 interceptors; modern types included 825 MiG-23 Flogger B/G's, 240 MiG-25 Foxbat A's, and 90 new MiG-25 Foxhounds with look-down, shoot-down capability against U.S. cruise missiles. A new fighter, the MiG-29 Fulcrum (Ram-L), was reported. Soviet civil defense, especially of the Communist Party leadership, continued to improve.

NATO

The divisions within NATO, symbolized by the controversy over implementation of the 1979 INF modernization program, remained serious. Adding to the problem was the NATO-European refusal to comply with the U.S. embargo on equipment for the Soviet pipeline being built to carry natural gas to Western Europe. In the view of the U.S. and the U.K., there was a real Soviet politico-military threat that should be contained by rebuilding NATO military capabilities for deterrence and defense. To the NATO-Europeans and Canada, this view exaggerated the threat while understating the importance of détente and arms control. These legitimate differences of interest had been exacerbated by the reemergence of antinuclear, neutralist, nationalistic, and anti-American sentiment in Britain, Belgium, The Netherlands, and West Germany, fanned by a brilliant Soviet propaganda campaign. (*See* Feature Article: *Stresses in the Western Alliance.*)

By late 1982, however, NATO-Europe was moving toward the U.S. and U.K. view, and INF modernization was proceeding. Three factors had contributed to this shift. First was the ongoing Soviet military buildup, coupled with Soviet intransigence in arms control negotiations. Second was the Soviet suppression, via the Polish military government, of the Solidarity trade union movement. Third was the continued Soviet occupation of Afghanistan and the mounting evidence of Soviet use of CBW. Political changes in NATO-Europe, although they occurred mainly for domestic reasons, reinforced this shift. In West Germany, for example, the Free Democratic Party switched its support from Chancellor Helmut Schmidt's Social Democratic Party to the Christian Democratic Union, thereby forcing the resignation of Schmidt's government. He was replaced as chancellor by Helmut Kohl on October 4, and Manfred Wörner was named defense minister. This ensured West German support for INF modernization. Similar shifts were apparent elsewhere, and deployment of 108 Pershing II MRBM's and 464 ground-launched cruise missiles (GLCM) was to start in Britain, Belgium. The Netherlands, Italy, and West Germany in 1983.

This alone would not solve NATO's problems, however. Most NATO-Europe governments were failing to meet the 1978 Long-Term Defense Program goals, especially that of a 3% annual real (corrected for inflation) increase in defense spending. Except for the U.K., they spent, proportionately, much less on defense than the U.S. As a result, pressures were intensifying in the U.S. for

cutbacks in, or elimination of, U.S. troop deployments in NATO-Europe.

NATO's chief military problem remained the weakness of its conventional forces on the crucial Central Front from Norway to southern Germany. NATO could offer an effective conventional defense of only ten days or less before resorting to nuclear weapons. But the Soviets seemed likely to win a theatre nuclear exchange, forcing the U.S. to use its SNF and thus bring on a Soviet strategic counterstrike. Static force comparisons underestimated NATO's weakness because the Soviet forces could mobilize more quickly and concentrate superior forces at chosen points for a breakthrough. But the crude figures themselves pointed up NATO's inferiority on the Central Front, even if the French forces were counted: 10,356 tanks to some 17,000 Soviet tanks, plus reserves; the equivalent of some 66 divisions to 119 for the U.S.S.R./Warsaw Pact.

With the aim of averting escalation to an SNF exchange, four former U.S. government officials, Robert S. McNamara, McGeorge Bundy, George F. Kennan, and Gerard Smith, proposed in the journal *Foreign Affairs* that NATO adopt a doctrine of no-first-use of nuclear weapons while building up its conventional forces, but this was dismissed in most quarters as unrealistic. Equally unrealistic was the argument that NATO could do nothing to offset its conventional weaknesses, advanced by NATO-Europeans who wished to avoid paying more for defense. According to Gen. Bernard Rogers, supreme allied commander for Europe, a credible conventional NATO defense for some 15–20 days could be purchased for a real increase in NATO-Europe defense spending of about 5% annually. Currently, the high contributions to the alliance were made by the U.S. and U.K. (6.1 and 5.4% of GNP, respectively, in 1981). France (4.1%), West Germany (4.3%), Belgium (3.3%), The Netherlands (3.4%), and Norway (3.3%) were in the middle range, while the low contributions were made by Canada (1.7%), Denmark (2.5%), Italy (2.5%), and Spain (1.9%).

WARSAW PACT

The continuing unrest in Poland underlined the dual threat to European security posed by Soviet retention of an Eastern European empire that was unnecessary for defense and an economic liability.

The newest fighter in the U.S. Air Force, the Tigershark, made its first test flight in August.

WIDE WORLD

Table II. Approximate Strengths of Regular Armed Forces of the World

Country	Military personnel in 000s			Warships[1]			Jet aircraft[3]		Tanks[4]	Defense expenditure as % of GNP
	Army	Navy	Air Force	Aircraft carriers/cruisers	Submarines[2]	Detroyers/frigates	Bombers and fighter-bombers	Fighters/reconnaissance		
I. NATO[5]										
Belgium	68.7	4.3	20.5	—		4 FFG	90 FB	36, 18 R	359	3.3
Canada	13.0	5.5	15.3	—	3	23 DDG	—	136	114	1.7
Denmark	18.0	5.8	7.4	—	5 C	5 FFG	56 FB	40, 16 R	208	2.5
France[6]	314.2	68.0	100.4	2 CV, 1 CVH, 1 CG	21, 5 SSBN	19 DDG, 11 FF, 9 FF	34 SB, 291 FB	165, 45 R, 42 MR	1,140	4.1
Germany, West	335.5	36.4	105.9	—	24 C	7 DDG, 1 FFG, 6 FF	457 FB	59, 87 R, 19 MR	3,938	4.3
Greece	163.0	19.5	24.0	—	10	16 DD, 6 FF	232 FB	99, 28 R, 8 MR	1,553	5.7
Italy	257.0	44.0	69.0	1 CVH, 2 CAH	9	4 DDG, 1 DD, 4 FFG, 8 FF	162 FB	72, 24 R, 14 MR	1,810	2.5
Luxembourg	0.7	—	—	—	6	—	—	—	—	1.2
Netherlands, The	67.0	16.9	19.0	—	6	2 DDG, 12 FFG	116 FB	36, 18 R, 11 MR	811	3.4
Norway	24.4	9.4	8.3	—	14 C	5 FFG	69 FB	15, 6 R, 7 MR	116	3.3
Portugal	41.0	13.4	12.0	—	3	17 FFG	71 FB	4 R	85	3.8
Spain	255.0	54.0[7]	38.0	1 CV	8	11 DD, 13 FFG, 7 FF	38 FB	128, 17 R, 6 MR	730	1.9
Turkey	470.0	46.0	53.0	—	16	15 DD, 2 FF	305 FB	36, 43 R	3,650	4.5
United Kingdom	163.1	73.0[7]	91.5	3 CVH	16, 11 SSN, 4 SSBN	12 DDG, 44 FFG	54 SB, 134 B, 44 FB	126, 44 R, 28 MR	900	5.4
United States	790.8	745.0[7]	581.0	4 CVN, 10 CV, 9 CGN, 18 CG, 5 LHA, 7 LPH, 14 LPD, 31 LSD/T	5, 85 SSN, 32 SSBN	41 DDG, 43 DD, 24 FFG, 55 FF	316 SB, 60 B, 2,199 FB	1,020, 191 R, 453 MR	12,130	6.1
II. WARSAW PACT										
Bulgaria	105.0	9.0	34.0	—	2	2 FFG	84 FB	140, 24 R	1,860	4.2
Czechoslovakia	142.5		54.0	—	—	—	164 FB	252, 55 R	3,400	4.0
Germany, East	113.0	15.0	38.0	—	—	2 FFG	47 FB	300, 12 R	1,500	7.7
Hungary	85.0	—	21.0	—	—	—	—	140	1,230	3.0
Poland	207.0	22.0	88.0	—	4	1 DDG	220 FB	430, 55 R, 10 MR	3,060	4.3
Romania	140.0	7.0	34.0	—	—	—	70 FB	240, 18 R	1,800	2.0
U.S.S.R.	1,825.0	450.0[7]	1,498.0[8]	2 CV, 2 CVH, 1 CGN, 26 CG, 7 CA	148, 56 SSN, 69 SSBN, 14 SSB, 49 SSGN, 20 SSG	42 DDG, 27 DD, 77 FFG, 106 FF	150 SB, 925 B, 2,125 FB	4,200, 899 R, 290 MR	50,000	8.4–15
III. OTHER EUROPEAN										
Albania	30.0	3.1	10.0	—	3	—	—	100	100	...
Austria	45.0	—	4.4	—	—	—	32 FB	—	170	1.2
Finland	31.4	2.5	3.0	—	—	—	—	40	—	1.6
Ireland	14.7	0.8	0.9	—	—	—	—	—	—	1.5
Sweden	45.0/700.0[9]	10.0	9.5	—	12	2 DDG	117 FB	216, 54 R	670	3.1
Switzerland	10.5/580.0[9]	—	8.0/45.0	—	—	—	208 FB	101, 25 R	815	1.8
Yugoslavia	190.0	15.5[7]	45.0	—	9	1 FFG	185 FB	150, 35 R	1,300	4.6
IV. MIDDLE EAST AND MEDITERRANEAN; SUB-SAHARAN AFRICA; LATIN AMERICA[10]										
Algeria	150.0	6.0	12.0	—	—	2 FFG	12 B, 140 FB	113, 4 R, 7 MR	630	2.2
Egypt	320.0	20.0	27.0	—	12	5 DD, 3 FF	14 B, 218 FB	152, 38 R	2,100	7.3
Iran[11]	150.0	10.0[7]	35.0	—	—	3 DDG, 4 FFG	140 FB	77, 14 R, 2 MR	1,110	3.6
Iraq[11]	300.0	4.3	38.0	—	—	—	17 B, 167 FB	147	2,300	...
Israel	135.0/450.0[9]	9.0/10.0	30.0/37.0	—	3	—	606 FB	28 R	3,600	28.7
Jordan	65.0	0.3	7.5	—	—	—	29 FB	45	569	11.4
Kuwait	10.0	0.5	1.9	—	—	—	30 FB	20	240	4.3
Lebanon[12]	22.3	0.3	1.3	—	—	—	—	—	—	...
Libya[13]	55.0	5.0	5.0	—	5	1 FFG	7 B, 209 FB	297, 13 R	2,900	...
Morocco	125.0	6.0	10.0	—	—	—	71 FB	—	135	7.0
Oman	15.0	1.0	2.0	—	—	—	20 FB	—	18	...
Qatar	5.0	0.7	0.3	—	—	—	—	8	24	13.6
Saudi Arabia	35.0	2.2	15.0	—	—	—	65 FB	30	450	20.5
Sudan	53.0	2.0	3.0	—	—	—	30 FB	0	190	2.7
Syria	170.0	2.5	50.0	—	—	2 FF	205 FB	244, 2 R	3,990	20.0
Tunisia	24.0	2.6	2.0	—	—	1 FF	—	—	14	...
United Arab Emirates	46.0	1.0	1.5	—	—	—	12 FB	30	118	...
Yemen, North	30.0	0.6	1.5	—	—	—	—	75	714	...
Yemen, South	22.0	1.0	3.0	—	—	—	8 B, 74 FB	36	470	...
Angola[14]	35.0	1.0	1.5	—	—	—	67 FB	1 MR	325	...
Ethiopia[15]	244.5	2.5	3.5	—	—	—	107 FB	—	790	8.9
Kenya	13.0	0.7	3.0	—	—	—	12 FB	—	60	...

The Soviets could retain political control within Eastern Europe only by powerful occupation forces, backed up by reserves in the western U.S.S.R.: 20 divisions in East Germany, 2 in Poland, 4 in Hungary, and 5 in Czechoslovakia. Since in wartime these forces would have to control Eastern Europe while defeating NATO before Eastern Europe revolted, the Soviets would continue to threaten Western Europe militarily. In addition the political oppression and economic failure of Communist Party rule meant that the continued existence of a free and prosperous Western Europe represented a threat to the Soviet empire that had to be countered, either directly by military means or indirectly, using military strength to gain political leverage.

Political unrest and the collapse of the Polish economy — GNP was two-thirds that of 1979 — made it questionable whether Gen. Wojciech Jaruzelski's military government could retain control. If it could not, direct Soviet military intervention might well be fought by the Polish Army. This was the largest non-Soviet force in the Warsaw Pact, with 317,000 personnel (605,000 reserves) plus 85,000 paramilitary forces and 200,000 Citizens Militia. The 207,000-man Army had five armoured, eight mechanized, one airborne, and one amphibious assault division, equipped with 3,000 T-54/55 tanks and 5,500 MICV/APC's. The 88,000-strong Air Force had 705 combat aircraft, mostly second-line (150 MiG-17 and 70 Su-7/20 fighter-bombers, 430 MiG-17 fighters), and there was a small coast defense navy of 22,000. These would be formidable forces for the Soviets to crush, and they were positioned astride the Soviet lines of communication to East Germany.

Country	Military personnel in 000s			Warships[1]			Jet aircraft[3]		Tanks[4]	Defense expenditure as % of GNP
	Army	Navy	Air Force	Aircraft carriers/ cruisers	Submarines[2]	Destroyers/ frigates	Bombers and fighter-bombers	Fighters/ reconnaissance		
Madagascar	20.0	0.4	0.5	—	—	—	12 FB	—	—	...
Mozambique[16]	20.0	0.6	1.0	—	—	—	25 FB	—	200	...
Nigeria	125.0	4.0	9.0	—	—	2 FF	30 FB	—	65	0.9
Somalia	60.0	0.6	2.0	—	—	—	3 B, 9 FB	37	140	...
South Africa	67.4/404.5[9]	5.0[7]	9.0	—	3	1 FF	15 B, 114 FB	30, 11 R, 25 MR	250	3.4
Tanzania	38.5	0.9	1.0	—	—	—	—	29	30	...
Zaire	22.0	1.5	2.5	—	—	—	—	7	—	...
Zimbabwe	60.0	—	3.0	—	—	—	5 B, 14 FB	—	28	...
Argentina	125.0	36.0[7]	19.5	1 CV	3	2 DDG, 6 DD	7 B, 55 FB	20, 20 R, 5 MR	285	8.1
Brazil	182.8	47.3[7]	42.8	1 CV	8	4 DDG, 8 DD, 6 FFG	36 FB	15, 28 MR	75	0.5
Chile	53.0	29.0[7]	15.0	3 CA	3	3 DDG, 4 DD, 2 FFG, 3 FF	38 FB	8, 8 MR	161	4.6
Colombia	57.0	7.0[7]	3.8	—	2	2 DD, 1 FF	—	16, 10 MR	—	...
Cuba	100.0	11.5	16.0	—	3	1 FF	50 FB	169	710	8.5
El Salvador	14.9	0.1	1.0	—	—	—	10	13	—	...
Mexico	95.0	20.0[7]	4.5	—	—	2 DD, 6 FF	7	7, 26 MR	—	0.6
Nicaragua	20.0	0.2	1.5	—	—	—	—	8	—	...
Peru	75.0	20.5[7]	40.0	1 CG, 2 CA	10	2 DDG, 7 DD, 2 FFG	20 B, 66 FB	11 MR	375	2.0
Venezuela	27.0	9.0[7]	4.8	—	3	2 DD, 6 FF	20 B, 16 FB	36, 2 R	75	1.4
V. FAR EAST AND OCEANIA[10]										
Afghanistan[17]	40.0	—	6.0	—	—	—	20 B, 54 FB	25	850	...
Australia	32.9	17.6	22.7	—	6	3 DDG, 8 FFG	24 FB	53, 14 R, 20 MR	103	3.0
Bangladesh	70.0	4.0	3.0	—	—	3 FF	20 FB	6	30	...
Burma	163.0	7.0[7]	9.0	—	—	1 FF	—	—	25	...
China	3,150.0	360.0[7]	490.0	—	101, 2 SSGN	13 DDG, 16 FFG, 5 FF	90 SB, 700 B, 500 FB	4,600, 130 R	10,500	...
India	944.0	47.0	113.0	1 CV< 1 CA	8	2 DD, 21 FF	45 B, 172 FB	400, 8 R, 13 MR	2,128	3.3
Indonesia	200.0	40.0[7]	29.0	—	4	10 FF	15 FB	15, 24 MR	—	3.3
Japan	155.0	45.0	45.0	—	14	18 DDG, 16 DD, 12 FFG, 4 FF	60 FB	240, 16 R, 120 MR	910	0.9
Korea, North	700.0	33.0	51.0	—	19	4 FF	70 B, 382 FB	240	2,675	8.9
Korea, South	520.0	49.0[7]	32.6	—	—	11 DD, 7 FF	320 FB	60, 10 R, 20 MR	1,000	6.3
Laos	46.0	1.7	1.0	—	—	—	—	20	—	...
Malaysia	80.0	8.1	11.0	—	—	2 FF	19 FB	3 MR	—	8.3
Mongolia	31.5	—	3.1	—	—	—	—	12	130	...
New Zealand	5.7	2.8	4.4	—	—	4 FFG	11 FB	5 MR	—	2.2
Pakistan	450.0	11.0	17.6	1 CA	11	9 DD	11 B, 51 FB	144, 13 R, 3 MR	1,285	6.9
Philippines	70.0	26.0[7]	16.8	—	—	8 FF	24 FB	22, 1 MR	—	2.2
Singapore	35.0	3.0	4.0	—	—	—	72 FB	21, 8 R	—	5.7
Taiwan	310.0	38.0	77.0	—	2	15 DDG, 8 DD, 9 FF	422 FB	19, 4 R, 39 MR	310	6.6
Thailand	160.0	30.0[7]	43.1	—	—	6 FF	15 FB	36, 7 R, 22 MR	50	3.5
Vietnam	1,000.0	4.0	25.0	—	—	5 FF	10 B, 295 FB	210	1,900	...

Note: Data exclude paramilitary, security, and irregular forces. Naval data exclude vessels of less than 100 tons standard displacement. Figures are for July 1982.
[1] Aircraft carrier (CV); helicopter carrier (CVH); general purpose amphibious assault ship (LHA); amphibious transport dock (LPD); amphibious assault ship (helicopter) (LPH); dock/tank landing ship (LSD/T); heavy cruiser (CA); guided missile cruiser (CG); helicopter cruiser (CAH); destroyer (DD); guided missile destroyer (DDG); frigate (FF); guided missile frigate (FFG); N denotes nuclearpowered.
[2] Nuclear powered attack submarine (SSN); ballistic missile submarine (SSB); guided (cruise) missile submarine (SSG); coastal (C); N denotes nuclear powered.
[3] Bombers (B), fighter-bombers (FB), strategic bombers (SB), reconnaissance fighters (R); maritime reconnaissance (MR) data include jet combat aircraft from all services including naval and air defense. MR also includes propeller driver ASW and ECM aircraft; data exclude light strike/counter-insurgency (COIN) aircraft.
[4] Main battle tanks (MBT), medium and heavy, 31 tons and over.
[5] Defense expenditure calculated as percentage of gross domestic product (GDP).
[6] French forces were withdrawn from NATO in 1966, but France remains a member of NATO.
[7] Includes marines.
[8] Figure includes the Strategic Rocket Forces (325,000) and the Air Defense Force (630,000), both separate services, plus the Long-Range Air Force (68,000).
[9] Second figure is fully mobilized strength.
[10] Sections IV and V list only those states with significant military forces.
[11] Iranian figures refer to pre-revolutionary situation. Iraqi figures before Iran-Iraq war. War losses uncertain.
[12] Figures approximate, given Lebanon's civil war and division.
[13] Some advanced Libyan aircraft amintained and manned by Soviet/Warsaw Pact crews.
[14] Plus 18,000 Cubans and 450 East Germans serving with Angolan forces.
[15] Ethiopia also has 13,000 Cuban plus other Soviet bloc troops.
[16] Plus Cuban, Warsaw Pact, and Chinese advisers and technicians in Mozambique.
[17] Figures approximate, given civil war in Afghanistan. Exclude 100,000 Soviet occupation troops.

Sources: International Institute for Strategic Studies, 23 Tavistock Street, London, The Military Balance 1982–1983, Strategic Survey 1981–1982.

Any involvement of East Germany could raise questions about the political loyalty of the extremely efficient East German forces. These totaled 166,000 personnel, providing an army of 113,000 (two tank and four motor rifle divisions) with 1,500 T-54/55 and T-72 tanks (plus 1,600 in storage) and 1,700 MICV/APC's. The 38,000-man Air Force had 359 combat aircraft, mainly 300 MiG-21 fighters, while the coast defense Navy of 15,000 had 74 fast attack craft. Overseas deployment included forces in Algeria, Angola, Ethiopia, Libya, Mozambique, Yemen (Aden), and Syria.

Czechoslovakia's armed forces were numerically large — 196,500 personnel — but of doubtful combat value. The Army of 142,500 personnel had 3,400 medium tanks (T-54/55 and T-72) and some 3,000 MICV/APC's, while the 54,000-strong Air Force had 471 combat aircraft, including 250 MiG-21 interceptors. Hungary's armed forces totaled 106,000 personnel, including an army of 85,000 with 1,230 tanks (T-54/55) and 1,400 APC's and an air force of 21,000 with 120 MiG-21 interceptors. Romania, which was semi-independent and not occupied by Soviet forces, had armed forces totaling 181,000, 1,800 T-54/55 tanks, and 240 MiG-21 interceptors.

Warsaw Pact defense spending was relatively higher than NATO-Europe's and had risen sharply, but it varied considerably among countries: 4.3% of GNP for Poland, 7.7% for East Germany, perhaps 4% for Czechoslovakia, but only 3% for Hungary and 2% for Romania.

UNITED KINGDOM

U.K. defense spending rose from the 1981 level of 5.4% of (relatively low) GDP because of the Falklands conflict, but by how much remained uncertain. (*See* Special Report.) The most important costs of the hostilities were human, but the economic costs appeared to have been moderate in relation to the pre-Falklands defense budget of £14,090 million (about $25.4 billion at an exchange rate of $1.70 to £1).

The big issue remained implementation of the 1980 decision to modernize and upgrade Britain's independent nuclear forces by building four or five SSBN's, carrying the U.S. Trident SLBM with British warheads. It was confirmed that these would be the Trident II D-5. The U.S. version had a range of 11,000 km (6,900 mi) and carried 14 × 150 kiloton Mk 500 Evader maneuverable reentry vehicles (MARV). This would represent a major advance over Britain's current force of four Resolution-class SSBN's, each with four U.S. Polaris A-3 missiles with British Chevaline warheads (5,200-km [3,200-mi] range, estimated 6 × 150–200-kiloton reentry vehicles).

The Falklands war had emphasized the extraordinary professionalism of Britain's all-volunteer force and the importance of tradition and of units training and fighting together. Both were typified by the Army's regimental system, but the same principle applied to Navy ships and Air Force squadrons. Despite its losses, the Royal Navy was still the third largest in the world, with 73,000 personnel, 59 major surface combatants, and 27 attack submarines (11 nuclear and 16 diesel). The carrier HMS "Invincible," one of the victors of the Falklands and namesake of the battle cruiser that helped defeat a German squadron under Vice-Adm. Graf von Spee at the Battle of the Falkland Islands, Dec. 8, 1914, was not to be sold to Australia as originally planned. The future composition of the Royal Navy was being reexamined in light of the Falklands war.

So was that of the Royal Air Force, with its 91,500 personnel and 700 combat aircraft. The 54 Vulcan B-2 heavy bombers were obsolete for NATO service and were being retired. More Harrier GR3 v/STOL strike aircraft would be purchased, besides

Polish military forces staged maneuvers, along with other Warsaw Pact troops, in March.

WIDE WORLD

the 44 deployed, since the Harrier had proved surprisingly versatile in the Falklands fighting, especially as a dogfighting interceptor. The first 12 Tornado interceptor/strike fighters entered service. The 7,900-strong Royal Marines and the 163,100-strong Army would have to find manpower for a Falklands garrison of some 6,000–8,000 men, besides 55,000 for the British Army of the Rhine (BAOR). This could include additions to the 9,600-strong Gurkha force, recruited overseas. The BAOR also needed replacements for its 900 Chieftain heavy tanks and 3,000 APC's. Northern Ireland continued to absorb some 9,000 British military personnel.

FRANCE

French defense spending fell slightly in real terms—to some 4.1% of GNP ($19,295,000,000)—despite a nominal increase because of inflation. Socialist Pres. François Mitterrand returned to the Gaullist position of stressing French nuclear forces while reducing conventional forces. The main strategic nuclear force remained France's five SSBN's, with a sixth building. Each carried 16 SLBM's, the M-20 (3,000-km [1,860-mi] range, 1 × 1-megaton reentry vehicle) being replaced by the M-4, with greater range and 3 × 200-kiloton reentry vehicles or MIRV, it was unclear which. Supplementing these were 18 SSBS-3 IRBM's (3,500-km [2,170-mi] range, 1-megaton reentry vehicles) and 34 aging Mirage IVA strategic bombers (3,200-km [1,980-mi] range, 1 AN-22 60-kiloton bomb). French theatre and tactical nuclear forces were being upgraded. The 100,400-strong Air Force had 519 combat aircraft, including 120 Mirage F-1C interceptors and 75 Mirage IIIE, 30 Mirage 5F, and 75 Jaguar strike aircraft.

The French Army of 314,200 comprised eight armoured, two mechanized, two motor rifle, one alpine, one airborne, and one parachute division. Their equipment was lighter than needed to fight Soviet forces but included 1,140 AMX-30/30B2 tanks, 620 AMX-10P MICV's, and 1,050 AMX-13 VTT and 1,100 VAB APC's. Three armoured divisions (48,500 men) were deployed in West Germany, making it almost certain France would fight on NATO's side in the event of a Soviet attack. Some 28,000 men were deployed in support of pro-Western regimes in Africa and the Middle East. The French Navy, the fourth largest in the world, had 68,000 personnel and 46 major surface combat vessels, including 2 Clemenceau-class carriers, 1 GW cruiser, 19 GW destroyers, and 16 GW frigates. The submarine force included France's first SSN and 20 diesel submarines.

WEST GERMANY

The new West German government seemed likely to reverse the steady decline of defense spending, which had fallen to 4.3% of GNP in 1982. Even so, West German defense expenditures, at $18,440,-000,000,000, were still the second largest in NATO, after the U.S. They provided armed forces totaling 495,000 personnel, over half professionals, with a mobilizable strength of 1,250,000. Reorganization stressed the brigade unit (4,500–5,000 men), so the 12 divisions (6 armoured, 4 armoured infantry, 1

U.S. negotiator Edward Rowny (left) greets his Soviet counterpart, Viktor Karpov, at the start of the strategic arms talks in Geneva in June.

mountain, and 1 airborne) comprised 17 armoured, 15 armoured infantry, 1 mountain, and 3 airborne brigades. Equipment included 269 new Leopard 2, 2,437 Leopard 1, and 1,232 older M-48A2/A2G2 tanks; 2,136 Marder MICV's; and 4,016 M-113 APC's.

Tactical nuclear forces, with warheads under U.S. control, included 72 Pershing I surface-to-surface missiles (SSM; 720-km [445-mi] range, kiloton-range warhead), 26 Lance SSM's (110-km [680-mi] range, 50-kiloton warhead), and 216 Nike Hercules SAM's with SSM capability. These were part of the 105,900-strong Air Force, with 548 combat aircraft. Inadequate funding forced the retention of 144 obsolete F-104G Starfighters and 60 F-4F Phantom fighter-bombers. The first 15 Tornado fighter-bombers entered service. The Navy, with 36,400 personnel, had 24 coastal submarines, 4 GW destroyers, 7 frigates, and 39 fast attack craft, and the Naval Air Force had 119 combat aircraft including 54 F-104G fighter-bombers, 27 RF-104G reconnaissance aircraft, and 7 Tornados. Given the high quality of West Germany's armed forces, moderate increases in funding could make a major contribution to improving NATO's defenses.

ARMS CONTROL AND DISARMAMENT

Further evidence emerged, confirmed by an independent Canadian investigation, of massive Soviet violations of the 1925 Geneva Protocol banning the first use of chemical weapons and the 1972 Biological Warfare Convention banning the manufacture, stockpiling, and use of biological weapons. The evidence showed that the Soviets (and their Vietnamese allies) had used CBW in Southeast Asia since 1976–78 and in Afghanistan from the start of the occupation in 1979. This called into question Soviet reliability in observing the terms of any arms control agreement and indicated that U.S. requirements for verification would have to be more rigorous, as would requirements for enforcing compliance by a credible U.S. threat to abrogate any agreement the Soviets violated. The Soviets had also exceeded the limits on strategic

delivery vehicles contained in the 1972 SALT I and 1979 SALT II agreements (although the latter remained unratified). They were in violation of the 1972 ABM treaty, which was undergoing its second five-yearly review in 1982, and of the unratified 1974 Threshold Test Ban Treaty, which banned underground tests of more than 150 kilotons by the U.S. and the U.S.S.R. Ratification of the threshold test ban had been postponed by Pres. Jimmy Carter in favour of a comprehensive test ban, which, however, was rejected by the Soviets.

Despite this pattern, the Reagan administration was still pursuing arms control in the strategic arms reduction talks (START) and the intermediate nuclear force (INF) talks. President Reagan had set out the U.S. START objectives as elimination of the Soviet land-based ICBM first-strike capability and reduction of U.S. and U.S.S.R. strategic forces. He proposed a mutual reduction of warheads to 5,000 on ICBM's and SLBM's (not more than 2,500 on ICBM's), with a ceiling of 850 on ICBM and SLBM launchers. The Soviets replied by proposing a 25% reduction in their ICBM/SLBM launchers in exchange for a 10% reduction in U.S. forces, limiting U.S. SLBM's and banning U.S. cruise missiles. These positions are unreconcilable. So were those at the INF talks. In November 1981 President Reagan had proposed the so-called zero option: elimination of the Soviet SS-20 I/MRBM force (now nearly 700 missiles) in exchange for U.S./NATO cancellation of INF modernization. The Soviets insisted on the cancellation while offering only minor and unverifiable reductions in their SS-20 force west of the Ural Mountains. They claimed to have imposed a moratorium on SS-20 deployment while negotiations proceeded, but deployment continued at the rate of one SS-20 every five days.

It was ironic that a movement supporting a bilateral nuclear freeze should emerge in the U.S. at this juncture, but the movement — however impractical — reflected a growing realization that traditional approaches to arms control had failed. Also ironic was U.S. withdrawal from the International Atomic Energy Agency (IAEA) in October, after IAEA expelled Israel, since the IAEA was important in verifying compliance with the 1968 nuclear nonproliferation treaty. (*See* Feature Article: *The Great Disarmament Debate*.)

SOUTH, EAST, AND SOUTHEAST ASIA

The U.S. visit of Indian Prime Minister Indira Gandhi improved U.S.-Indian relations, lessening the tensions caused by U.S. support for Pakistan as a buffer against further Soviet expansion from Afghanistan. India maintained the third largest armed forces in the area (1,104,000 personnel) at a reasonable cost of $5,260,000,000 (3.3% of GNP). The 944,000-strong Army was organized in 2 armoured, 18 infantry, and 11 mountain divisions and 7 armoured brigades, equipped with some 2,128 tanks (including 78 new T-72s) and 700 APC's. The Air Force of 113,000 had 635 combat aircraft, comprising a wide variety of types. The 47,000-strong Navy included 1 old aircraft carrier (converting to Sea Harriers), 2 GW destroyers, 21 GW frigates, and 8 submarines, with a mix of ex-Soviet and British vessels. Pakistan's armed forces of 478,600 were too small and too poorly equipped to provide security against both India and the Soviet forces in Afghanistan. The Army of 450,000 included 2 armoured and 16 infantry divisions but had only 1,000 T-59 and 250 M-47/48 tanks and 550 APC's. Similarly, the Air Force of 17,600 had 219 combat aircraft, but its only modern types were 17 Mirage IIIEP and 34 Mirage 5PA/DP fighter/ground attack aircraft and some U.S. F-16 fighter-bombers.

China's military weakness relative to the Soviet Union and Vietnam became more pronounced. The People's Liberation Army totaled 4,750,000 (all services), but the Army of 3,150,000 had 119 infantry and only 12 armoured and 27 artillery divisions, with 11,100 tanks. The 490,000-strong Air Force had 5,300 combat aircraft, mostly obsolete ex-Soviet types. Chinese nuclear forces remained minimal; deployment was begun of 4 T-5 ICBM's (13,000-km [8,000-mi] range, 1 × 5–10-megaton reentry vehicle), 10 T-3 IRBM's, 50 T-2 IRBM's, and 50 T-1 MRBM's. Two Han SSGN's with six tubes each carried the CSS-N-4 missile. Otherwise, nuclear weapons were delivered by aircraft. The Navy of 360,000 provided coast defense, mainly with 101 attack submarines and 1,000 fast attack craft plus 800 combat aircraft.

Vietnam retained massive armed forces of 1,029,000, with 40,000 deployed in Laos and 170,000 in Kampuchea. The Army of one million, mainly infantry, had about 2,000 tanks, including Soviet T-34/54/55s and captured U.S. M-48s, and the 25,000-strong Air Force had 470 combat aircraft, many in storage. With 784,000 personnel, North Korea's armed forces remained superior to those of the South. Its Army of 700,000 (43 divisions) had 2,500 tanks, and the Air Force of 51,000 had 700 combat aircraft. By comparison South Korea's armed forces totaled 601,600 personnel, with an army of 520,000 (21 divisions; 1,000 tanks) and an air force of 32,600 (434 combat aircraft). Although Taiwan's 464,000 military personnel and 484 combat aircraft were no threat to the mainland, China objected strongly to its proposed purchase of advanced U.S. FX fighter-bombers, and the Reagan administration substituted the less capable F-5E.

Japan's continued refusal to spend more on its own defense was a source of growing criticism in the U.S. Japan spent less than 1% (0.9%) of GNP on defense ($10,450,000,000). The armed forces had increased slightly to 250,000 personnel, but the Navy had only 33 GW destroyers and 16 GW frigates, plus 14 operational submarines and a naval air arm of 110 combat aircraft. The Air Force of 45,000 had 314 combat aircraft, and the Army of 155,000 had 910 tanks.

AFRICA SOUTH OF THE SAHARA

The conflict between South African forces and the Soviet-controlled Cuban and local forces in Angola escalated, with air battles in which South Africa shot down two Soviet-supplied MiG fighters. (*See* ANGOLA.) South Africa retained control over South West Africa/Namibia. Defense spending was increased to $2,760,000,000 (R 2,465,-000,000), providing armed forces totaling 92,700 personnel (404,500 on mobilization). The 67,400-strong Army had some 250 tanks and 1,450 armoured cars, and modern combat aircraft included 45 Mirage F-1/AZ/CZ and 23 Mirage IIICZ/RZ/R2Z fighter-bomber/reconnaissance aircraft.

These forces were superior to any indigenous sub-Saharan forces but were vulnerable to Soviet intervention, direct or indirect. The U.S.S.R.'s Cuban proxies in Africa now included 19,000 men in Angola (with 2,500 East German troops), 14,000 in Ethiopia (with 1,300 Warsaw Pact troops), 750 in Mozambique, and over 1,000 in the rest of the continent. (*See* AFRICAN AFFAIRS.)

LATIN AMERICA

The destabilizing influence of Cuban interventions combined with local revolutionary movements made the defense of Latin America a major U.S. concern. (*See* LATIN-AMERICAN AFFAIRS.) The opportunities for Soviet/Cuban destabilization were illustrated by the size of El Salvador's armed forces: 9,850 personnel, an all-infantry army, and an air force with 15 elderly jet fighter-bombers in a country of some 5 million. In contrast, Cuba had armed forces of 236,000 and a population of nearly 10 million. A new Soviet base in Latin America was being established, via Cuban proxies, in the tiny but strategic island of Grenada, which was visited by Adm. S. G. Gorshkov, head of the Soviet Navy. Facilities included a major air base and weapons storage facility, with MiG-23 fighter-bombers.

Although the armed forces of the major Latin-American countries were numerically large (*see* Table II), they were essentially infantry forces doubling as internal security troops, mostly with limited training, poor equipment, and little leadership from the politicized officer corps. Argentina's defeat at the hands of Britain in the Falklands war underlined the difference between the armed forces of Latin America and those of developed industrial societies. (ROBIN RANGER)

See also Space Exploration.
[535.B.5.c.ii; 544.B.5–6; 736]

LESSONS FROM THE FALKLANDS

by Robin Ranger

The main lessons learned from the Falkland Islands conflict of April–June 1982 were old lessons relearned. Strategically, the first crucial lesson was the importance of convincing potential aggressors that they will be opposed by force. Argentina's Pres. Leopoldo Galtieri occupied the Falklands because he believed Britain would not fight. The second was that only armed forces can protect a state's vital interests. Force remains the key instrument of foreign policy.

Militarily, the three most important lessons were: first, there is no substitute for large attack carriers in conducting opposed amphibious landings; second, first-class professional troops can defeat much larger numbers of troops who are less well trained, equipped, and led; and third, where forces are roughly equal, as with the Argentine Air Force versus the Royal Navy and Air Force, luck plays a crucial role in deciding the outcome.

The Argentine Forces. The balance of forces involved, together with the geography of the Falklands, determined the basic course of fighting. Argentina's surface fleet was bottled up in port by the Royal Navy's attack submarine force. Its only modern vessels were two Type-42 destroyers and two Type-209 submarines. How many British submarines were deployed was unclear, but the threat they posed was overwhelming and was underlined by the sinking of the obsolete cruiser "General Belgrano" on May 2. The Argentine Navy's contribution was thus limited to its Naval Air Force and its submarines. The latter posed a more serious threat than was realized and may have launched a torpedo attack on the British carriers that narrowly failed.

Argentine aircraft effectively deployed against the Royal Navy task force comprised 51 elderly Skyhawk and 14 Mirage III fighter-bombers, plus 6 Dagger interceptors, the Israeli version of the Mirage III.

Robin Ranger is associate professor, Defense and Strategic Studies Program, School of International Relations, at the University of Southern California.

These were armed only with conventional high-explosive bombs and lacked electronic countermeasures or radars to acquire their targets. Of the 14 French Super Etendards ordered, some 8–10 had been delivered before the war led to an official French arms embargo. In the hands of well-trained pilots, the Super Etendard, a current-generation naval attack aircraft armed with the Exocet air-to-surface missile, proved extremely effective. That Argentina's Skyhawks and Mirages proved as effective as they did was a tribute to their pilots. In comparison, the Argentine land forces, the bulk of them one-year conscripts, performed poorly (with individual exceptions), although they were plentifully supplied with previous-generation equipment. The British soldiers, on the other hand, were professionals, and the qualities required in the Falklands land war were precisely those fostered by the British regimental system.

Geography played a crucial role because the Falklands were at the extreme edge of the Argentine aircraft's combat radius; that is, the distance they could fly with any combat load and return to base. (*See* MAP.) This, plus British defenses, forced them to fly at low levels, using more fuel and leaving only enough for one pass at the task force and little to find it. British forces therefore maneuvered so as to remain out of range except when closing to attack Argentine positions.

The Task Force. For the British, the crucial problem was their dependence on two aircraft carriers, one 30 years old (HMS "Hermes"). Air cover was limited to perhaps 20 short-range Sea Harriers, armed with 30-mm cannon and the latest U.S. AIM-9L Sidewinder air-to-air missile. The loss of even one carrier would almost certainly have forced withdrawal. So would major Argentine successes against the destroyers and frigates screening the carriers or against the main troop carriers, the liners "Queen Elizabeth 2" and "Canberra," and the assault ships HMS "Fearless" and "Intrepid." Although the Royal Navy had a reasonable number of modern guided weapons destroyers and frigates, their primary mission was antisubmarine, not antiaircraft, warfare. Financial constraints had prevented installation of the full antiaircraft systems the British vessels were designed to carry. Only two Type-42 destroyers had the more effective Sea Wolf surface-to-air missile (SAM), while the remainder carried the Sea Dart SAM.

The limited availability of Sea Wolf, coupled with the lack of other close-in weapons systems able to destroy incoming air-to-surface missiles, left the task force vulnerable to any Exocet successfully launched and locked onto its target, unless deflected by British electronic countermeasures. The major British asset was superbly trained and highly motivated naval personnel. The British shore bombardment capability was also excellent, and logistic support was remarkably efficient, given the distances involved.

The Opening Moves. The war fell into four phases. In the first, leading up to the Argentine occupation of the Falklands and South Georgia island, the British made the classic mistake of ignoring unmistakable intelligence indicating an imminent attack. Taking what they called Islas Malvinas had always been a major Argentine objective. (*See* DEPENDENT STATES: *Sidebar.*) Previous Argentine threats had been countered by symbolic British naval movements. This time nothing was done, and some 2,000 Argentine troops landed on the Falklands on April 2, forcing the surrender of the token Royal Marine garrison. Supplies and reinforcements totaling 18,000 to 20,000 men were brought in, but they were lacking in three important respects. First, the Falklands airstrip was too short to accommodate jet fighter-bombers and was not extended. Second, little Argentine armour was landed. Third, although winter was beginning, proper food, clothing, and shelter for the Argentine forces were not supplied.

In the second phase, the British Conservative government under Prime Minister Margaret Thatcher made the difficult decision to retake the Falklands. They assembled, in one week, the Falkland Islands Naval Task Force, built around HMS "Hermes" and the new HMS "Invincible" light carrier (on which the queen's second son, Prince Andrew, served as a helicopter pilot). The RAF built up its small base on Ascension Island, 6,400 km (4,000 mi) from the Falklands. The task force sailed from Plymouth on April 5–6 and was reinforced en route. The Argentine occupation force (perhaps 150 strong) on South Georgia was overcome, and the island reoccupied, on

The Exocet missile, made by the French, proved effective for the Argentine forces in the Falklands conflict.

April 25–26. An elderly Argentine submarine, the "Santa Fe," was also captured after being surprised on the surface in the harbour.

Air-Sea Warfare. The third phase, from May 1 to May 21, was a classic battle between land-based air power and an amphibious assault force, much like the World War II battles in the Pacific. The crucial factor was the cost-exchange ratio between Argentine aircraft and British ships and aircraft. This went in Britain's favour, but by a much narrower margin than appeared from the relative losses. The British would have lost at least four more ships if Argentine bombs had not failed to explode.

Tactically, the battles followed the predicted pattern. The Royal Navy, lacking airborne early-warning aircraft or helicopters, had to station radar picket ships ahead of the main fleet to give warning. These ships were thus exposed to attack, and HMS "Sheffield" was lost on May 4. The crucial carriers were protected by a screen of destroyers and frigates. Argentine losses in this phase were estimated (no official figures were released) at 15 to 20 aircraft, some 20 to 30% of their forces.

Popular attention was caught by the spectacular sinking of HMS "Sheffield," costing some $150 million, by an Exocet missile costing $45,000. The speed with which fire spread in the ship, especially in its aluminum superstructure, also seemed remarkable. But both these apparent lessons were misreadings of the evidence. The real cost of the Exocet was not the missile but its delivery system—aircraft plus pilots and air crews. Viewed in this light, the discrepancy is much smaller. Similarly, the fatal effect of the Exocet's relatively small warhead (136 kg [300 lb] of high explosives on a 590-kg [1,300-lb] missile striking at supersonic speed) on ships of 2,500–4,000 tons displacement is understandable, given that modern warships are eggshells armed with hammers. They carry enormous firepower, a vast quantity of electronic equipment, a small crew (100–200 men), and virtually no armour. Protection is sought in offensive and defensive firepower plus electronic countermeasures to destroy or evade the enemy. Although the number of hits received is reduced, those that are received are likely to be very damaging, especially in the case of missiles, like Exocet, that home in on the vital central portion of the hull.

The Final Phase. The fourth and final phase of the war lasted from the initial British landing near Port San Carlos on May 21 to the surrender of the Argentine garrison at Stanley (Port Stanley) on June 14. The weakened Argentine Air Force kept up its attacks on the task force, while Argentine land forces tried to halt the British advance. The land battle was a traditional infantry engagement, since the terrain was

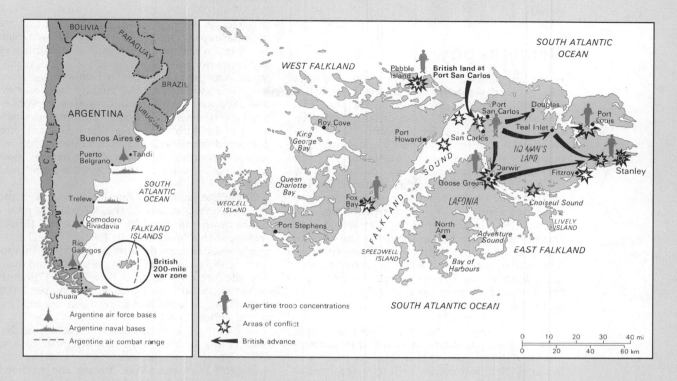

unfavourable for the use of armour, although the British used mechanized infantry combat vehicles to give mobility to their attacks.

The crucial part of the final phase was the initial British landing and consolidation. As in any amphibious operation, the landing force was at its most vulnerable in the first few days, while men and equipment were being brought in. But the bridgehead was consolidated, and the advantage passed to the British. Apparently expecting a direct British assault, the Argentine commander, Gen. Mario Menéndez, had centralized his forces around the capital of Stanley to protect its vital airstrip. Instead, the British force commander, Rear Adm. John Woodward (see BIOGRAPHIES), and the land-force commander, Maj. Gen. Jeremy Moore, decided to make their initial landing at Port San Carlos and then mount an overland attack on Stanley. They calculated that this would avoid casualties to the British civilian population and to the British forces.

Nevertheless, while the initial landing was unopposed, the Argentine defense, about 5,000 strong, quickly organized an effective resistance, and heavy fighting was required to wear it down. Although the Argentine Air Force kept up its attacks on the British fleet, now more vulnerable because it was unloading men and supplies in a conflict area, they were unable to damage either aircraft carrier or to sink enough ships to jeopardize British land operations. They did succeed in sinking the frigates HMS "Antelope" and HMS "Ardent" and the destroyer HMS "Coventry," damaging several other frigates and destroyers, and sinking (with an Exocet) the container-

ship "Atlantic Conveyor," which was carrying important supplies, including 20 Harriers. Two landing ships, "Sir Galahad" and "Sir Tristram," were sunk later at a second bridgehead five miles southwest of Stanley, with considerable casualties to the troops on board.

The British bridgehead was protected by artillery and antiaircraft batteries, including the Rapier Blowpipe SAM, with Harriers providing air support. Some Harriers were flown from Britain, via Ascension Island, with inflight refueling, a major feat for short-range aircraft. During this fighting, Argentina lost a considerable proportion of its remaining jet aircraft, as well as of its Falklands-based helicopters and Pucará light ground attack aircraft, both very effective anti-infantry weapons. British commandos may have succeeded in penetrating the mainland Argentine air base at San Carlos and destroying several aircraft on the ground.

Thereafter, the British advanced rapidly, through forced marches under extremely adverse conditions, capturing the settlements of Darwin and Goose Green and taking the high ground west of Stanley. With British forces surrounding and blockading Stanley, it was clear that the Argentines were cut off and could be starved out. General Menéndez then made the same decision every garrison commander in a similar position has made (including Lord Cornwallis at Yorktown in 1781) and surrendered. At the conclusion of hostilities it was estimated that some 950 servicemen of both sides had been killed during the conflict, British deaths being put at 225.

Demography

World population, increasing at a rate of almost 2% per year, was estimated at 4,600,000,000 at mid-1982. New UN projections to the year 2000 ranged from 5,800,000,000 to 6,300,000,000. An analysis by the Population Reference Bureau emphasized the continuing disparity in the growth of the more developed countries (Europe, North America, Australia, Japan, New Zealand, and the U.S.S.R.) and the less developed countries. The latter contained twice as many persons as the more developed countries in 1940 and three times as many in 1982; by the year 2000, they would have four times as many. The difference in the speed of growth could be illustrated by the number of years it takes to double a population. At current growth rates, doubling time for the more developed countries averaged 116 years (Sweden 999 years), while for the less developed countries the average was 33 years (Kenya 18 years).

In the U.S. immigration added over one million persons to the population in 1980 and 1981, reminiscent of the numbers that entered the country in the early 20th century. According to the Population Reference Bureau, 808,000 persons were legally admitted as immigrants or refugees in 1980, while an estimated 400,000 were illegal migrants.

Birth Statistics. For the sixth consecutive year, the number of births in the U.S. increased; an estimated 3,646,000 live births occurred in 1981, compared with 3,598,000 in 1980. The birthrate was 15.9 live births per 1,000 population, somewhat lower than for 1980. The fertility rate was 67.6 live births per 1,000 women aged 15–44, about the same as in 1980. These trends continued into 1982. For the 12-month period ended in June, there were 3,662,000 births, a 1% increase over the previous 12 months, while the rate continued at the 1981 level.

According to the National Center for Health Statistics, the number of women of childbearing age was stabilizing, and only small annual increases in births could be anticipated for the next several years. An analysis by the Center of the phenomenon of delayed childbearing in the 1970s revealed that not since the 1930s had such large numbers of women postponed marriage and motherhood. The proportion of women aged 25–29 who were still childless in 1979 was almost twice that in 1970.

Reflecting the increased significance of the Hispanic population in the U.S., 19 states now included an item on ethnic or Hispanic origin of the parents on birth certificates. In the nine states where data were available in 1979, the Hispanic birthrate was 25.5 births per 1,000 population, compared with the non-Hispanic rate of 14.7. The Hispanic fertility rate was 100.5 births per 1,000 women aged 15–44, while that for non-Hispanic women was 63.2. (See RACE RELATIONS: *Special Report.*)

As their total fertility rates continued to drop, developed industrialized countries became increasingly aware of the problem of population replacement. A total fertility rate of 2.1 to 2.5 children per woman in her childbearing lifetime indicates replacement level fertility, below which a population will eventually decline. Two-thirds of all European countries, Australia, Cuba, Canada, Japan, and the U.S. had rates below replacement level. In contrast, the total fertility rates of most less developed countries were well over replacement levels; the average was 4.6 children per woman, and in Africa the rate was 6.5. Many less developed countries had policies directed toward reducing population growth. China had the most drastic policy, with a national goal of a one-child family.

Death Statistics. The number of deaths in the U.S. in 1981 was estimated at 1,987,000. The provisional death rate per 100,000 population (866.4) was somewhat lower than in 1980 (874.2). The decrease resulted from declines in deaths for infants under one year of age and for persons 55 and over. The rate continued to fall in 1982; for the 12-month period ended in June it was 8.5 deaths per 1,000 population, as against 8.8 for the corresponding period ended June 1981.

In 1981 there were decreases in deaths from diseases of the heart (2%), cerebrovascular disease (5%), motor vehicle accidents (4%), all other accidents (6%), chronic liver disease and cirrhosis (7%), and leukemia (9%). Increases were noted for malignant neoplasms of respiratory and intrathoracic organs (3%) and of the breast (5%), chronic obstructive pulmonary diseases (7%), and ulcer of the stomach and duodenum (20%). Two-thirds of all deaths were attributed to heart disease (38%), cancer (21%), and stroke (8%). Accidents, suicide, and homicide accounted for 8%.

The leading causes of death in the U.S. in 1981 were:

Cause of death	Estimated rate per 100,000 population
1. Diseases of the heart	330.6
2. Malignant neoplasms	184.3
3. Cerebrovascular diseases	71.7
4. Accidents	44.5
5. Chronic obstructive pulmonary diseases	26.1
6. Pneumonia and influenza	23.7
7. Diabetes mellitus	15.2
8. Chronic liver disease and cirrhosis	12.9
9. Atherosclerosis	12.5
10. Suicide	12.3
11. Homicide and legal intervention	10.7
12. Conditions of the perinatal period	9.2
13. Nephritis, nephrotic syndrome, and nephrosis	7.6
14. Congenital anomalies	5.8
15. Septicemia	4.4

Crude death rates continued to decline in many less developed countries, while death rates in some developed countries were relatively high, reflecting an aging population.

Expectation of Life. The provisional life tables prepared by the National Center for Health Statistics indicated a life expectancy at birth of 74.1 years for the total U.S. population in 1981, a new record. The average length of life for males was 70.3 years and for females, 77.9 years. Nonwhites had made greater gains than whites; since 1970 total white life expectancy had increased by 4% and nonwhite by 8%. White females had the highest life expectancy in 1981, 78.5 years; nonwhite females were

continued on page 292

Table I. World Populations and Areas[1]

	AREA AND POPULATION: MIDYEAR 1981			POPULATION AT MOST RECENT CENSUS					Age distribution (%)[2]					
Country	Area in sq km	Total population	Persons per sq km	Date of census	Total population	% Male	% Female	% Urban	0–14	15–29	30–44	45–59	60–74	75+
AFRICA														
Algeria	2,381,741	19,590,000	8.2	1977	17,422,000	49.7	50.3	40.6	47.9	25.4	12.7	8.2	4.5	1.3
Angola	1,246,700	6,851,000	5.5	1970	5,620,001	52.1	47.9	14.2	41.7	23.2	17.0	7.4	3.8	1.0
Benin	112,600	3,641,000	32.3	1979	3,338,240	47.9	52.1	14.2	49.0	——39.4——			——11.6——	
Botswana	581,700	937,000	1.6	1981	936,600	...	...	...	...	...	...	...	...	...
British Indian Ocean Territory	60	...	...	...	...	...	...	...	...	...	...	...	...	...
Burundi	27,834	4,348,000	156.2	1979	4,111,310	48.4	51.6	...	...	...	...	...	...	...
Cameroon	465,064	8,650,000	18.6	1976	7,661,000	49.9	50.1	28.5	42.2	26.4	16.5	9.7	——5.2——	
Cape Verde	4,033	329,000	81.6	1980	296,093	46.3	53.7	26.2	...	...	...	...	...	...
Central African Republic	622,436	2,393,000	3.8	1975	2,054,610	48.0	52.0	34.6	43.5	23.5	17.1	12.4	2.7	0.8
Chad	1,284,000	4,547,000	3.5	1975	4,029,917	47.7	52.3	16.0	40.6	28.3	17.2	9.5	——4.4——	
Comoros[3]	1,792	369,000	205.9	1980	346,992	50.1	49.9	33.4	...	...	...	...	...	...
Congo	342,000	1,578,000	4.6	1974	1,300,120	48.5	51.5	37.8	...	...	...	...	...	...
Djibouti	23,200	323,000	13.9	1961	81,200	...	...	57.4	...	...	...	...	...	...
Egypt	997,667	43,465,000	43.6	1976	33,626,204	50.9	49.1	43.8	39.9	26.7	16.6	10.6	5.2	1.0
Equatorial Guinea	28,051	372,000	13.3	1965	254,684	50.0	50.0	47.6	...	...	...	...	...	...
Ethiopia	1,223,000	32,158,000	26.3	1970	24,068,800	50.7	49.3	9.7	43.5	27.0	16.3	8.8	3.7	0.7
French Southern and Antarctic Lands	7,366	...	...	...	...	...	...	...	...	...	...	...	...	...
Gabon	267,667	1,409,000	5.3	1970	950,009	47.9	52.1	31.8	35.4	19.1	22.3	16.4	——6.5——	
Gambia, The	10,690	619,000	57.9	1973	493,499	51.0	49.0	15.0	41.3	——44.1——			——14.6——	
Ghana	238,533	12,063,000	50.6	1970	8,559,313	49.6	50.4	28.9	46.9	24.4	15.8	7.5	3.8	1.6
Guinea	245,857	5,147,000	20.9	1972	5,143,284	...	...	...	43.1	——56.9——				
Guinea-Bissau	36,125	810,000	22.4	1979	767,739	48.2	51.8	...	44.3	25.5	15.1	8.2	4.7	2.2
Ivory Coast	322,463	8,298,000	25.7	1975	6,702,866	51.9	48.1	32.4	44.6	27.4	16.8	7.7	2.7	0.7
Kenya	580,367	17,148,000	29.5	1979	15,327,061	49.6	50.4	15.1	43.4	26.9	12.9	7.1	3.5	1.1
Lesotho	30,352	1,374,000	45.3	1976	1,216,815	48.3	51.7	...	33.1	25.5	15.5	10.4	——9.5——	
Liberia	97,790	1,926,000	19.7	1974	1,503,368	50.5	49.5	29.1	40.9	26.7	17.7	8.8	4.6	1.3
Libya	1,749,000	3,096,000	1.8	1973	2,249,237	53.0	47.0	59.8	44.3	22.2	15.4	8.2	4.0	1.6
Madagascar	587,041	8,955,000	15.3	1975	7,603,790	50.0	50.0	16.3	44.4	25.7	14.2	10.0	4.6	1.1
Malawi	118,484	6,370,000	53.8	1977	5,547,460	48.2	51.8	8.3	44.6	25.7	14.2	9.0	——6.5——	
Mali	1,240,192	7,160,000	5.8	1976	6,394,918	49.1	50.9	16.7	47.3	22.2	17.2	8.8	——3.8——	
Mauritania	1,030,700	1,682,000	1.6	1976	1,419,939	...	...	21.9	...	...	...	...	...	...
Mauritius	2,040	971,000	476.0	1972	826,199	50.0	50.0	42.9	40.3	28.6	14.5	11.0	4.9	0.7
Mayotte	378	52,000	137.6	1978	47,246	49.9	50.1	53.3	50.2	23.4	13.9	7.0	3.8	1.7
Morocco	458,730	20,646,000	45.0	1971	15,379,259	50.1	49.9	35.4	46.2	22.4	16.0	8.3	5.3	1.8
Mozambique	799,380	12,458,000	15.6	1980	12,130,000	48.7	51.3	...	...	...	...	...	...	...
Niger	1,189,000	5,479,000	4.6	1977	5,098,427	49.3	50.7	11.8	...	...	...	...	...	...
Nigeria	923,800	79,680,000	86.3	1963[4]	55,670,055	50.5	49.5	16.1	43.0	31.9	16.5	5.1	2.5	1.0
Réunion	2,512	503,000	200.2	1982	515,808	...	...	...	...	...	...	...	...	...
Rwanda	26,338	5,256,000	199.6	1978	4,819,317	48.8	51.2	4.3	——60.0——			——40.0——		
St. Helena & Ascension Islands	412	5,000	12.1	1976	5,866	52.0	48.0	29.4	34.2	27.7	16.3	10.8	8.4	2.6
São Tomé & Príncipe	964	95,000	98.5	1981	95,000	...	...	...	...	...	...	...	...	...
Senegal	196,722	5,811,000	29.5	1976	4,907,507	49.2	50.8	29.6	42.5	27.3	17.2	8.6	3.7	0.1
Seychelles	444	64,000	144.1	1977	61,898	50.4	49.6	37.1	39.7	26.3	14.0	10.8	6.9	2.2
Sierra Leone	71,740	3,571,000	50.0	1974	2,729,479	54.1	45.9	...	36.7	27.2	19.4	9.0	——7.6——	
Somalia	638,000	3,752,000	5.9	1975	3,253,024	...	...	15.0	...	...	...	...	...	...
South Africa	1,133,759	25,085,000	22.1	1980	23,771,970	...	...	...	...	...	...	...	...	...
Bophuthatswana[5]	40,430	1,361,000	33.7	1980	1,328,637	46.8	53.2	15.7	...	...	...	...	...	...
Ciskei[5]	8,300	645,000	77.7	1980	635,631	...	...	...	...	...	...	...	...	...
Transkei[5]	41,002	2,313,000	56.4	1970	1,745,992	41.2	58.8	3.2	46.4	22.8	14.1	——15.3——		1.2
Venda[5]	7,184	335,000	46.6	1970	265,129	38.8	61.2	0.2	48.1	22.7	13.7	6.4	7.6	1.5
South West Africa/Namibia	824,269	1,038,000	1.3	1970	761,562	50.8	49.2	24.9	...	...	...	...	...	...
Sudan	2,503,890	18,395,000	7.5	1973	14,819,000[6]	50.4	49.6	...	46.7	——48.4——			——4.9——	
Swaziland	17,364	566,000	32.6	1976	494,534	45.6	54.4	15.2	47.7	25.2	13.7	7.9	3.7	1.7
Tanzania	945,050	18,511,000	19.6	1978	17,551,925	49.2	50.8	...	46.2	——39.3——			——14.5——	
Togo	56,785	2,784,000	49.0	1970	1,953,778	48.1	51.9	...	49.8	21.5	15.1	8.0	3.6	2.0
Tunisia	154,530	6,554,000	42.4	1975	5,588,209	50.8	49.2	49.0	43.7	25.6	14.7	10.0	4.9	0.9
Uganda	241,139	13,012,000	54.0	1980	12,630,076	49.5	50.5	8.1	...	...	...	...	...	...
Upper Volta	274,200	6,251,000	22.8	1975	5,638,203	50.2	49.8	9.0	47.4	21.1	16.1	9.3	——6.1——	
Western Sahara	266,769	101,000	0.4	1970	76,425	57.5	42.5	45.3	42.9	27.2	16.3	7.4	4.4	1.8
Zaire	2,344,885	29,084,000	12.4	1976	25,568,640	48.5	51.5	...	——52.8——			——47.2——		
Zambia	752,614	5,961,000	7.9	1980	5,679,808	...	...	43.0	...	...	...	...	...	...
Zimbabwe	390,759	7,600,000	19.4	1969	5,099,350	50.3	49.7	16.8	47.2	25.4	15.7	8.4	——3.3——	
Total AFRICA	30,217,894	484,047,000	16.0											
ANTARCTICA total	14,244,900		[7]											
ASIA														
Afghanistan	652,090	16,400,000	25.1	1979	13,051,358[8]	51.4	48.6	15.1	44.5	26.9	15.8	8.6	3.6	0.6
Bahrain	669	351,000	524.7	1981	350,798	58.4	41.6	80.7	32.9	34.5	20.1	8.8	3.0	0.7
Bangladesh	143,998	89,940,000	624.6	1981	87,052,024	51.5	48.5	...	...	...	...	...	...	...
Bhutan	46,100	1,174,000	25.5	1969	931,514	...	...	...	...	...	...	...	...	...
Brunei	5,765	187,000	32.4	1982	191,765	...	...	...	...	...	...	...	...	...
Burma	676,577	36,166,000	53.5	1973	28,885,867	49.7	50.3	...	40.5	——53.4——			——6.0——	
China	9,561,000	982,550,000	102.8	1982	1,008,175,288	51.5	48.5	21.2	...	...	...	...	...	...
Cyprus	9,251	637,000	68.9	1976	612,851	50.0	50.0	...	25.4	29.0	17.9	13.4	10.8	3.5
Hong Kong	1,050	5,154,000	4,908.6	1981	4,986,560	53.2	48.7	...	24.8	32.7	17.7	14.6	——10.2——	
India	3,287,782	683,810,000	208.0	1981	633,810,051	51.7	48.3	23.7	...	...	...	...	...	...
Indonesia	1,919,443	150,520,000	78.4	1980	147,490,298	49.7	50.3	22.3	40.8	27.0	16.4	10.2	4.5	1.1
Iran	1,648,000	39,320,000	23.9	1976	33,708,744	51.5	48.5	47.0	44.5	25.2	14.8	10.1	3.8	1.4
Iraq	437,522	13,542,000	31.0	1977	12,000,497	51.5	48.5	63.7	43.9	24.5	12.3	8.2	4.2	1.9
Israel	20,700	3,954,000	191.0	1972	3,147,683	50.3	49.7	85.3	32.6	26.9	15.6	13.6	9.2	2.0
Japan	377,682	117,645,000	311.5	1980	117,060,396	49.2	50.8	76.2	23.5	21.5	24.2	17.9	9.8	3.1
Jordan	94,946	2,326,000	24.5	1979	2,147,594	52.3	47.7	59.5	51.8	23.3	13.4	7.3	——4.2——	
Kampuchea	181,035	5,746,000	31.7	1962	5,728,771	50.0	50.0	10.3	43.8	24.9	16.8	9.8	4.1	0.6
Korea, North	121,929	18,340,000	84.3											
Korea, South	98,966	38,723,000	391.3	1980	37,448,836	50.1	49.9	57.3	34.0	30.0	18.4	11.5	5.1	1.0
Kuwait	17,818	1,463,000	82.1	1980	1,357,952	57.2	42.8	100.0	40.2	28.2	21.7	7.7	1.9	0.4

Table I. World Populations and Areas[1] (Continued)

	AREA AND POPULATION: MIDYEAR 1981			POPULATION AT MOST RECENT CENSUS					Age distribution (%)[2]					
Country	Area in sq km	Total population	Persons per sq km	Date of census	Total population	% Male	% Female	% Urban	0–14	15–29	30–44	45–59	60–74	75+
Laos	236,800	3,810,000	16.1	—	—	—	—	—	—	—	—	—	—	—
Lebanon	10,230	3,238,000	316.5	1970	2,126,325	50.8	49.2	60.1	42.6	23.8	16.7	9.1	——7.7——	
Macau	16	278,000	17,735.0	1981	276,673	...	...	...	...	...	...	...	...	...
Malaysia	329,747	14,179,000	43.0	1980	13,435,588	50.2	49.8	...	...	...	...	...	...	...
Maldives	298	152,000	510.1	1978	142,832	52.6	47.4	20.7	...	...	...	...	...	...
Mongolia	1,556,500	1,710,000	1.1	1979	1,594,800	50.1	49.9	51.2	...	...	...	...	...	...
Nepal	145,391	15,020,000	103.3	1981	15,020,451	...	...	...	...	...	...	...	...	...
Oman	300,000	919,000	3.1	—	—	—	—	—	—	—	—	—	—	—
Pakistan	796,095	83,782,000	105.2	1981	83,782,000	...	...	...	...	...	...	...	...	...
Philippines	300,000	49,530,000	165.1	1980	48,098,460	50.2	49.8	...	...	...	...	...	...	...
Qatar	11,400	220,000	19.3	—	—	—	—	—	—	—	—	—	—	—
Saudi Arabia	2,240,000	9,319,000	4.2	1974	7,012,642	...	...	...	...	...	...	...	...	...
Singapore	618	2,443,000	3,953.1	1980	2,413,945	51.0	49.0	100.0	27.0	34.7	19.8	11.3	5.9	1.3
Sri Lanka	65,610	14,850,000	226.3	1981	14,850,001	50.8	49.2	21.5	35.3	29.6	17.9	10.6	5.2	1.4
Syria	185,179	9,156,000	49.4	1981	9,172,000	51.1	48.9	47.9	47.9	27.3	12.4	7.9	3.5	1.0
Taiwan	36,002	17,892,000	499.5	1980	18,031,825									
Thailand	542,373	48,125,000	88.7	1980	44,278,000	49.7	50.3	17.3	38.2	29.8	16.3	10.2	——5.5——	
Turkey	779,452	46,248,000	59.3	1980	45,217,556	51.6	48.4	...	38.5	27.7	16.0	11.2	——6.6——	
United Arab Emirates	77,700	1,040,000	13.4	1981	1,043,225	69.0	31.0	80.9	...	...	...	...	...	...
Vietnam	329,465	55,053,000	167.1	1979	52,741,766	48.5	51.5	19.2	...	...	...	...	...	...
Yemen (Aden)	338,100	1,943,000	5.7	1973	1,590,275	49.5	50.4	33.3	47.3	20.8	15.8	8.6	——6.6——	
Yemen (San'a')	200,000	8,557,000	42.8	1981	8,556,974	...	...	...	...	...	...	...	...	...
Total ASIA[9,10]	44,614,399	2,665,412,000	59.7											
EUROPE														
Albania	28,748	2,795,000	97.2	1979	2,591,000	...	...	35.3	37.0	——55.6——			——7.4——	
Andorra	468	36,000	76.9	1982	38,050	53.7	46.3	66.8	...	...	...	...	...	...
Austria	83,853	7,559,000	90.2	1981	7,555,338	...	...	...	...	...	...	...	...	...
Belgium	30,521	9,863,000	323.2	1970	9,650,944	48.9	51.1	...	23.5	21.0	19.4	17.1	14.4	4.6
Bulgaria	110,912	9,059,000	81.7	1975	8,727,771	49.9	50.1	58.0	21.8	22.4	20.6	18.6	13.0	3.4
Channel Islands	194	133,000	685.6	1981	133,000	48.1	51.9	...	...	...	...	...	...	...
Czechoslovakia	127,881	15,314,000	119.8	1980	15,283,095	48.7	51.3	65.5	24.3	22.9	19.8	17.2	11.5	4.3
Denmark	43,080	5,124,000	118.9	1979	5,111,534	49.4	50.6	83.3	21.6	——42.7——		——35.7——		
Faeroe Islands	1,399	44,000	31.4	1977	41,969	52.4	47.6	...	27.6	——58.4——		——14.0——		
Finland	337,032	4,792,000	14.2	1980	4,787,778	48.3	51.7	...	20.2	24.3	22.2	16.9	12.4	4.1
France	544,000	53,963,000	99.2	1982	54,257,000									
Germany, East	108,333	16,736,000	154.5	1971	17,068,318	46.1	53.9	73.8	23.3	19.9	20.1	14.7	16.9	5.1
Germany, West	248,667	61,666,000	247.9	1979	61,439,400	47.7	52.3	...	16.8	23.1	20.1	18.3	13.8	7.9
Gibraltar	6	30,000	5,000.0	1981	29,648	...	...	...	...	...	...	...	...	...
Greece	131,990	9,740,000	73.8	1981	9,740,151	...	...	...	...	...	...	...	...	...
Hungary	93,036	10,711,000	115.1	1980	10,709,536	48.5	51.5	53.2	21.7	——61.4——		——16.9——		
Iceland	103,000	232,000	2.2	1970	204,930	50.6	49.4	...	32.3	25.1	16.4	13.7	9.0	3.5
Ireland	70,285	3,440,000	48.9	1981	3,440,427	50.2	49.8	...	...	...	...	...	...	...
Isle of Man	588	61,000	103.7	1976	61,723	47.5	52.5	51.8	20.5	19.1	15.6	17.3	20.2	7.3
Italy	301,263	56,244,000	186.7	1981	56,243,935	48.7	51.3	...	...	...	...	...	...	...
Jan Mayen	373	—	—	1973	37	...	...	—	...	...	...	...	...	...
Liechtenstein	160	26,000	162.5	1980	25,215	50.0	50.0	...	...	...	...	...	...	...
Luxembourg	2,586	365,000	141.1	1981	364,600	49.0	51.0	...	19.0	23.7	21.0	18.8	——17.6——	
Malta	320	366,000	1,143.7	1967	314,216	47.9	52.1	94.3	29.8	25.9	17.6	13.8	10.2	2.7
Monaco	1.9	26,000	13,684.2	1975	25,029	45.2	54.8	100.0	12.9	17.5	18.4	20.9	21.2	9.1
Netherlands, The	41,160	14,209,000	345.2	1971	13,060,115	49.9	50.1	54.9	27.2	24.6	17.9	15.6	10.9	3.7
Norway	323,895	4,100,000	12.7	1980	4,092,300	49.6	50.4	...	...	...	...	...	...	...
Poland	312,683	35,902,000	114.8	1978	35,061,000	51.3	48.7	57.5	23.8	27.5	——35.6——		——13.2——	
Portugal	91,985	9,931,000	108.0	1981	9,784,201	...	...	...	...	...	...	...	...	...
Romania	237,500	22,457,000	94.6	1977	21,559,400	49.3	50.7	47.8	27.2	24.6	22.7	13.5	9.8	2.2
San Marino	61	22,000	352.5	1976	20,284	50.4	49.6	...	24.4	23.0	19.9	17.4	11.4	3.9
Spain	504,750	37,654,000	74.6	1981	37,746,200	49.1	50.9	...	...	...	...	...	...	...
Svalbard	62,050	—	—	1974	3,472	...	...	...	...	...	...	...	...	...
Sweden	449,964	8,323,000	18.5	1980	8,320,582	49.5	50.5	...	19.4	20.6	21.2	16.7	15.7	6.4
Switzerland	41,293	6,473,000	156.8	1980	6,365,960	48.7	51.3	50.9	19.8	23.2	21.6	17.3	12.8	5.4
United Kingdom	244,035	56,232,000	230.4	1981	55,618,374	48.6	51.4	...	21.1	22.5	19.2	17.3	14.3	5.6
Vatican City	.44	1,000	1,677.3	—	—	—	—	—	—	—	—	—	—	—
Yugoslavia	255,804	22,491,000	87.9	1981	22,418,331	49.4	50.6	...	24.7	25.3	20.0	18.4	8.7	2.9
Total EUROPE[10]	10,504,977	683,820,000	65.1											
NORTH AMERICA														
Anguilla	91	7,000	76.9	1974	6,519	...	...	...	...	...	...	...	...	...
Antigua and Barbuda	442	77,000	175.0	1970	64,794	47.2	52.8	33.7	44.0	24.2	12.0	11.7	——8.0——	
Bahamas,The	13,864	235,000	17.0	1980	209,505	48.6	51.4	...	...	...	...	...	...	...
Barbados	430	253,000	618.6	1980	248,983	47.6	52.4	...	28.9	32.3	14.2	11.2	——13.3——	
Belize	22,965	167,000	7.3	1980	144,857	...	...	...	...	...	...	...	...	...
Bermuda	46	61,000	1,326.1	1980	54,050	48.8	51.2	...	22.7	27.5	22.2	15.7	9.0	2.9
British Virgin Islands	153	12,000	79.7	1980	12,030	...	...	...	...	...	...	...	...	...
Canada	9,976,139	24,343,000	2.4	1981	24,343,181	49.6	50.4	...	22.5	28.1	20.6	——28.8——		
Cayman Islands	264	18,000	68.2	1979	16,677	48.6	51.4	...	29.1	25.8	22.1	13.1	7.3	2.6
Costa Rica	51,100	2,307,000	45.2	1973	1,871,780	50.1	49.9	40.6	43.3	27.0	14.2	8.4	4.4	2.7
Cuba	110,922	9,706,000	87.5	1981	9,706,369	50.6	49.4	...	——57.8——		19.0	12.3	——10.9——	
Dominica	772	84,000	108.8	1970	69,549	47.4	52.6	46.2	49.1	21.2	11.2	10.0	6.3	2.2
Dominican Republic	48,442	5,648,000	116.6	1981	5,647,977	50.1	49.9	52.0	...	...	...	...	...	...
El Salvador	21,041	4,942,000	234.9	1971	3,544,648	49.6	50.4	39.4	46.2	25.1	15.2	8.2	4.3	1.0
Greenland	2,175,600	51,000	.02	1981	41,459	50.9	49.1	...	30.8	34.3	17.2	11.4	——6.4——	

Table I. World Populations and Areas[1] *(Continued)*

Country	AREA AND POPULATION: MIDYEAR 1981 Area in sq km	Total population	Persons per sq km	POPULATION AT MOST RECENT CENSUS Date of census	Total population	% Male	% Female	% Urban	Age distribution (%)[2] 0–14	15–29	30–44	45–59	60–74	75+
Grenada	345	112,000	324.6	1970	92,775	46.2	53.8	25.3	47.1	23.0	11.6	9.4	6.6	2.2
Guadeloupe	1,705	314,000	184.2	1982	328,400	...	...	...	...	...	...	...	...	...
Guatemala	108,889	6,004,000	55.5	1981	6,043,559	49.9	50.1	...	...	...	...	...	...	...
Haiti	27,750	5,104,000	183.9	1981	4,329,991	48.2	51.8	20.4	41.5	25.8	16.5	9.5	5.0	1.7
Honduras	112,088	3,822,000	34.1	1974	2,656,948	49.5	50.5	37.5	43.1	25.8	13.9	7.8	3.6	0.9
Jamaica	10,991	2,220,000	202.0	1980	2,176,762	49.4	50.6	...	33.7	29.8	12.9	10.1	3.0	7.5
Martinique	1,079	308,000	285.4	1982	326,536	...	...	...	...	...	...	...	...	...
Mexico	1,958,201	71,153,000	36.4	1980	67,382,581	49.4	50.6	...	42.9	27.6	14.9	8.5	——5.9——	
Montserrat	102	12,000	117.6	1980	11,606	48.1	51.9	54.1	31.5		——68.5——			
Netherlands Antilles	993	253,000	254.8	1972	223,196	48.8	51.2	...	33.0	26.7	16.7	10.3	6.4	1.8
Nicaragua	128,875	2,465,000	19.1	1971	1,877,972	48.3	51.7	48.0	43.1	25.6	14.1	7.4	3.6	1.1
Panama	77,082	1,940,000	25.2	1980	1,830,175	...	...	...	...	...	...	...	...	...
Puerto Rico	8,897	3,251,000	365.4	1980	3,187,566	...	...	66.8	...	...	...	...	...	...
St. Christopher-Nevis	269	50,000	185.9	1980	44,404	...	...	37.1	...	...	...	...	...	...
St. Lucia	622	122,000	196.1	1970	99,806	47.2	52.8	36.9	43.6	21.3	11.6	9.8	5.5	2.2
St. Pierre & Miquelon	242	6,000	24.8	1982	6,041	...	...	...	...	...	...	...	...	...
St. Vincent & the Grenadines	388	124,000	319.6	1970	86,314	47.3	52.7	...	51.2	21.7	11.0	8.8	——7.2——	
Trinidad and Tobago	5,128	1,185,000	231.1	1980	1,059,825	49.8	50.2	...	...	...	...	...	...	...
Turks and Caicos Islands	500	7,000	14.0	1980	7,436	...	...	...	...	...	...	...	...	...
United States	9,363,123	229,805,000	24.5	1980	226,504,825	48.6	51.4	73.7	22.6	27.4	19.1	15.2	11.3	4.4
Virgin Islands (U.S.)	345	99,000	287.0	1980	95,214	60.5	39.5	18.4						
Total NORTH AMERICA	24,229,885	376,347,000	15.5											
OCEANIA														
American Samoa	199	33,000	165.8	1980	32,395	...	...	...	...	...	...	...	...	...
Australia	7,682,300	15,054,000	1.9	1981	15,053,600	...	...	...	...	...	...	...	...	...
Canton and Enderbury Islands	70	—	—											
Christmas Island	135	3,000	22.2	1981	2,871	66.8	33.2	...	25.9	26.4	35.8	10.8	——1.1——	
Cocos Island	14	600	42.9	1981	569	54.1	45.9	...	27.4	28.3	27.2	11.2	——6.4——	
Cook Islands	241	18,000	73.4	1981	17,753	51.0	49.0	...	42.7	——40.3——			——17.0——	
Fiji	18,273	636,000	34.8	1976	588,068	50.5	49.5	37.2	41.1	29.8	16.2	8.8	3.3	0.8
French Polynesia	4,182	151,000	38.3	1977	137,382	52.5	47.5	39.7	42.0	27.2	17.0	8.9	4.0	0.8
Guam	549	110,000	200.7	1980	105,821	50.0	50.0	...	•	...	...	...	...	...
Johnston Island	3	1,000	333.3	1970	1,007	...	...	0	...	...	...	...	...	...
Kiribati	712	59,000	82.9	1978	57,673	49.5	50.5	...	40.6	28.8	15.3	9.7	4.6	1.0
Midway Islands	5	2,000	400.0	1970	2,220	...	...	0	...	...	...	...	...	...
Nauru	21	8,000	381.0	1981	8,000	...	...	0	...	...	...	...	...	...
New Caledonia	19,079	140,000	7.3	1976	133,233	52.0	47.9	0	33.6	26.3	18.6	10.4	4.9	1.2
New Zealand	269,057	3,176,000	11.6	1981	3,175,737	49.7	50.3	83.6	26.8	25.9	19.0	14.2	10.6	3.5
Niue	259	3,000	11.6	1976	3,843	50.2	49.8	24.8	46.2	23.8	13.6	7.9	5.8	2.6
Norfolk Island	35	2,000	57.1	1981	2,175	...	...	0	...	...	...	...	...	...
Pacific Islands, Trust Territory of the	1,880	140,000	74.5	1980	132,900	...	...	...	...	...	...	...	...	...
Papua New Guinea	462,840	3,061,000	6.6	1980	3,006,799	52.3	47.6	13.1	...	...	...	...	...	...
Pitcairn Island	4	54	13.5	1981	54	...	...	0	...	...	...	...	...	...
Solomon Islands	27,556	235,000	8.5	1981	232,936	52.3	47.7	...	49.0	25.9	——21.6——		——3.5——	
Tokelau	10	2,000	200.0	1981	1,572	49.4	50.6	...	...	...	...	...	...	...
Tonga	747	98,000	131.2	1976	90,085	51.1	48.9	20.3	44.2	26.0	14.7	9.5	4.0	1.6
Tuvalu	26	7,000	269.2	1979	7,349	46.8	53.2	...	31.8	31.7	15.2	13.2	6.3	1.7
Vanuatu	12,190	120,000	9.8	1979	112,300	53.1	46.9	13.3	45.1	27.4	14.9	7.7	5.3	1.6
Wake Island	8	2,000	250.0	1970	1,647	...	...	0	...	...	...	...	...	...
Wallis and Futuna	255	11,000	43.1	1976	9,192	50.0	50.0	...	45.6	23.6	14.0	9.9	5.1	0.8
Western Samoa	2,831	157,000	55.5	1976	151,983	51.7	48.3	21.1	43.2	26.0	12.6	8.7	3.5	1.0
Total OCEANIA	8,503,481	23,229,654	2.7											
SOUTH AMERICA														
Argentina	2,758,829	28,065,000	10.1	1980	27,862,771	49.2	50.8	86.3	...	...	...	...	...	...
Bolivia	1,098,581	5,718,000	5.2	1976	4,613,486	49.1	50.9	41.7	41.5	27.0	15.4	9.8	4.6	1.7
Brazil	8,512,000	121,547,000	14.3	1980	119,098,992	49.7	50.3	67.6	39.1	28.6	16.4	10.0	——5.9——	
Chile	756,626	11,297,000	14.9	1982	11,275,440	49.0	51.0	81.0	32.2	29.1	18.9	11.7	6.3	1.8
Colombia	1,141,748	26,729,000	23.4	1973	22,915,229	48.6	51.4	63.6	44.1	27.3	14.9	8.5	4.1	1.0
Ecuador	281,334	8,644,000	30.7	1974	6,521,710	50.1	49.9	41.3	44.6	26.5	14.7	8.4	4.6	1.3
Falkland Islands	16,265	2,000	0.1	1980	1,855	...	...	...	...	...	...	...	...	...
French Guiana	90,000	67,000	0.7	1982	73,022	...	...	...	...	...	...	...	...	...
Guyana	215,000	903,000	4.2	1970	699,848	49.7	50.3	33.3	47.1	25.1	13.4	9.0	4.4	1.0
Paraguay	406,752	3,158,000	7.8	1972	2,433,399	49.6	50.4	37.4	44.7	25.6	14.4	9.2	4.6	1.5
Peru	1,285,215	18,278,000	14.2	1981	17,031,200	...	...	72.6	...	...	...	...	...	...
Suriname	163,820	387,000	2.4	1980	352,041	49.2	50.8	...	39.1			——60.9——		
Uruguay	176,215	2,927,000	16.6	1975	2,732,000	49.0	51.0	83.0	27.0	22.6	19.2	16.9	10.8	3.5
Venezuela	912,050	14,313,000	15.7	1971	10,721,522	50.1	49.9	73.1	45.0	26.9	14.9	8.5	3.7	1.0
Total SOUTH AMERICA	17,814,435	242,065,000	13.6											
U.S.S.R.[10]	22,402,200	267,700,000	11.9	1979	262,436,200	46.6	53.4	62.0	...	...	...	...	...	...
in Asia[10]	16,831,100	70,000,000	4.2											
in Europe[10]	5,571,100	197,700,000	35.5											
TOTAL WORLD[11]	150,129,971	4,474,920,654	32.9											

[1] Any presentation of population data must include data of varying reliability. This table provides published and unpublished data about the latest census (or comparable demographic survey) and the most recent or reliable midyear 1981 population estimates for the countries of the world. Census figures are only a body of estimates and samples of varying reliability whose quality depends on the completeness of the enumeration. Some countries tabulate only persons actually present, while others include those legally resident, but actually outside the country, on census day. Population estimates are subject to continual correction and revision; their reliability depends on: number of years elapsed since a census control was established, completeness of birth and death registration, international migration data, etc.

[2] Data for persons of unknown age excluded so percentages may not add to 100.0.
[3] Excludes Mayotte, shown separately.

[4] A census was taken in Nigeria in 1973, but the results were officially repudiated.
[5] Transkei received its independence from South Africa on Oct. 26, 1976; Bophuthatswana on Dec. 6, 1977; Venda on Sept. 13, 1979; Ciskei on Dec. 4, 1981. All are Bantu homeland states whose independence is not internationally recognized.
[6] Sudan census excludes three southern autonomous provinces.
[7] May reach a total of 2,000 persons of all nationalities during the summer.
[8] Excludes nomadic population.
[9] Includes 18,130 sq km of Iraq-Saudi Arabia neutral zone.
[10] Asia and Europe continent totals include corresponding portions of U.S.S.R.
[11] Area of Antarctica excluded in calculating world density.

continued from page 288

next at 74.5 years. Life expectancy for white males was 71 years and for nonwhite males, 66.1 years.

The average length of life varied greatly around the world, although there had been considerable improvement in recent years. It was generally highest in northwestern Europe (about 75 years for the Scandinavian countries, The Netherlands, and Switzerland) and North America (Canada 74 years). Japan had computed the highest total life expectancy (76 years), and in many other countries it was now over 70 years (most of Europe, Australia, New Zealand, and Israel).

Infant and Maternal Mortality. There were 42,000 deaths of infants under one year of age in the U.S. in 1981, compared with 45,000 in 1980, and the infant mortality rate fell from 12.5 deaths per 1,000 live births to 11.7, the lowest on record for the U.S. Both neonatal mortality (deaths to infants under 28 days) and postneonatal mortality (deaths to infants aged 28 days to 11 months) decreased by 7%. The declining trend continued into 1982. The rate for January–June 1982 was 11.7, compared with 12.4 for the corresponding period in 1981, and the rate for the 12-month period ended June 1982 was 11.4, a new record low. At the same time, differences in rates continued to exist among various segments of the population. In 1979 the black infant mortality rate was about twice the white (21.8 black infant deaths per 1,000 live births, compared with 11.4 for white infants).

Infant mortality continued to be high in certain African countries, with estimates of about 200 infant deaths per 1,000 live births in The Gambia, Sierra Leone, and Upper Volta. Northern and Western Europe continued to report extremely low rates (Iceland 5.4; Sweden 7; Finland 7.7).

About 280 deaths of women were associated with childbearing in the U.S. in 1981; the maternal mortality rate was 7.7 per 1,000 live births. Although this represented an increase over 1980, the overall trend was downward. In 1951 the rate was 75 deaths per 1,000 live births.

Marriage and Divorce Statistics. Marriages in the U.S. increased for the sixth consecutive year, to an estimated 2,438,000 in 1981. This new national record was 11% higher than the 2,190,481 marriages of 1971. The marriage rate was 10.6 per 1,000 population, about the same as in 1980. The trends continued into 1982. For the 12 months ended in June there were 2,444,000 marriages, 13,000 more than in the previous corresponding period.

People married later in life than they had a decade earlier. The Census Bureau reported that the median age at first marriage in 1981 was 24.8 years for men and 22.3 years for women, about 1.5 years higher than in 1970. The proportion of never married persons in the population rose significantly for young men and women in the age groups from 20–24 through 30–34.

Divorces also reached a record high in 1981, with 1,219,000 being granted, 3% more than in 1980 and 72% more than in 1970. The divorce rate was 5.3 per 1,000 population, compared with 5.2 in 1980. While this rate had not changed significantly for several years, there were some indications that it might decline. During the first six months of 1982 there were 582,000 divorces, with a rate of 5.1 per 1,000 population, 4% below the rate for the corresponding period in 1981.

According to the Census Bureau, the number of families headed by one parent had doubled in a decade, from 3.3 million in 1970 to 6.6 million in 1981. In the same period, the number of one-parent families headed by divorced women rose 182%, from 956,000 to 2.7 million. Reflecting both increased divorces and births to unmarried mothers, 54% more children under 18 lived in a one-parent family in 1981 than in 1970. For the nation as a whole, one of every five children lived in a one-parent family: about one in every seven white children and almost one-half (45%) of all black children.

Table II. Birthrates and Death Rates per 1,000 Population and Infant Mortality per 1,000 Live Births in Selected Countries, 1981*

Country	Registered Birth-rate	Registered Death rate	Registered Infant mortality	Estimated Birth-rate	Estimated Death rate	Estimated Infant mortality
Africa						
Algeria	40.6[1]	7.8[1]	70.8[1]	42.0–47.0	13.0–14.0	127.0[1]
Egypt	37.6	10.1	76.4[1]	41.0–42.0	12.0	92.0[1]
Guinea-Bissau	10.8[2]	1.9[2]	112.7[2]	40.0[3]	23.0[3]	154.3[3]
Madagascar	45.0	18.0	53.2[4]	45.0[3]	19.0[3]	75.7[3]
Mauritius	25.7	7.0	35.0	...	...	...
Nigeria	...	...	...	48.0–51.0	17.0–19.0	140.5[3]
Rwanda	19.5[2]	5.2[2]	50.4[5]	51.0[6]	22.0[6]	127.0[6]
Seychelles[3]	28.9	7.0	24.0	...	...	...
South Africa[2]	...	...	...	37.9	10.3	100.6
Tunisia	34.9[2]	7.6[2]	40.3[7]	...	11.1[3]	106.5[3]
Zaire	...	...	...	43.0–46.0	15.0–19.0	116.6[3]
Asia						
Bangladesh	45.0[1]	17.6[1]	13.2[1]	47.0[3]	17.6[3]	139.6[3]
China[2]	...	...	...	21.3	7.4	48.7
Cyprus	20.6	8.3	16.0	19.6[3]	9.1[3]	19.5[3]
Hong Kong	16.9	4.8	9.8	...	...	...
India	33.5[2]	12.5[2]	...	33.2[7]	14.1[7]	134.0[8]
Israel	23.6	6.6	14.6	...	...	...
Japan	13.0	6.1	7.1	...	...	...
Korea, South	23.4	6.6	37.0[2]	25.3[3]	8.1[3]	36.7[3]
Kuwait	37.2	3.6[2]	31.1[11]	...	...	...
Philippines	30.5[7]	6.5[7]	53.1[7]	36.2[3]	8.6[3]	58.9[3]
Singapore	17.0	5.3	10.8	...	...	...
Turkey	...	...	...	34.9[3]	10.2[3]	131.0[3]
Vietnam	...	...	...	40.1[3]	14.3[3]	106.4[3]
Europe						
Austria	12.5	12.3	12.6	...	...	...
Czechoslovakia	15.5	11.7	16.8	...	...	...
France	14.9	10.3	9.6	...	...	...
Germany, East	14.2	13.9	12.3	...	...	...
Germany, West	10.1	11.7	12.6	...	...	...
Hungary	13.3	13.5	20.6	...	...	...
Ireland	21.0	9.4	11.2[3]	...	...	...
Italy	10.9	9.5	14.1	...	...	...
Poland	18.9	9.2	20.6	...	...	...
Spain	14.1	7.6	10.3	...	...	...
Sweden	11.3	11.1	7.0	...	...	...
Switzerland[2]	11.6	9.3	9.1	...	...	...
United Kingdom	13.1	11.8	12.1[2]	...	...	...
North America						
Canada	15.2	7.0	10.9[1]	...	...	...
Cuba	13.9	5.9	18.5	...	...	...
El Salvador[2]	35.8	8.2	42.0	...	...	...
Greenland	21.2	7.8	32.1[2]	...	...	...
Guatemala[2]	41.8	7.1	65.9	...	...	...
Martinique	17.5	6.6	12.6	...	...	23.0
Mexico	33.5[1]	6.0[7]	44.1[7]	38.3[3]	...	59.8[3]
Panama	26.8[3]	4.0[3]	21.3[3]	...	6.0[2]	36.2[2]
United States	15.9	8.7	11.7	...	...	...
Oceania						
Australia	15.8	7.3	11.0[2]	...	...	...
Guam	28.9	3.9	16.3[2]	...	...	...
New Zealand	16.3	8.0	11.7	...	...	...
Papua New Guinea	...	...	...	42.5[3]	15.7[3]	110.9[3]
Western Samoa	16.0	2.8	15.9	...	...	...
South America						
Argentina	25.2[7]	8.9[7]	40.8[7]	...	...	47.2[3]
Brazil	23.3[2]	6.8[2]	68.1[2]	33.3[3]	9.1[3]	82.4[3]
Chile[2]	22.2	6.7	33.0	...	...	...
French Guiana[2]	29.5	7.8	28.5	...	...	...
Peru	27.5[9]	8.1[7]	70.3[4]	39.6[3]	11.6[3]	93.5[3]
Suriname	28.0	7.9	30.4[10]	...	...	39.2[3]
Uruguay	18.3	9.5	34.1	...	...	...
Venezuela	35.6[2]	5.5[2]	33.1[2]	36.9[3]	6.1[3]	44.8[3]
U.S.S.R.	18.7	10.3	27.7[11]	...	...	...

*Both registered and estimated rates are shown only for countries with incomplete registered rates. [1]1979. [2]1980. [3]1975–80. [4]1972. [5]1975. [6]1970. [7]1978. [8]1973. [9]1976. [10]1966. [11]1974.
Sources: United Nations, *Population and Vital Statistics Report*; various national publications.

Table III. Life Expectancy at Birth in Years, for Selected Countries

Country	Period	Male	Female
Africa[1]			
Burundi	1980–85	45.3	46.6
Egypt	1980–85	55.9	56.4
Ivory Coast	1980–85	46.9	50.2
Kenya	1980–85	56.3	60.0
Nigeria	1980–85	48.3	51.7
Swaziland	1980–85	46.8	50.0
Asia			
China	1980		68.0
Hong Kong	1981	72.0	78.0
India	1981	53.9	52.9
Indonesia	1980–85[1]	51.2	53.9
Israel[2]	1978	71.9	75.6
Japan	1979	73.4	78.9
Kuwait	1980–85[1]	68.1	72.9
Pakistan	1980–85[1]	54.4	54.2
Taiwan	1980	69.6	74.5
Thailand	1980–85[1]	59.5	65.1
Europe			
Albania	1978–79	66.8	71.4
Austria	1976	68.1	75.1
Belgium	1976	68.6	75.1
Bulgaria	1980	69.0	75.0
Czechoslovakia	1979	67.0	75.0
Denmark	1979–80	71.2	77.3
Finland	1980	69.2	77.6
France	1979	70.0	78.0
Germany, East	1979	68.7	74.8
Germany, West	1977–79	69.4	76.1
Greece	1980	71.0	75.0
Hungary	1980	66.0	73.2
Iceland	1979–80	73.7	79.7
Ireland	1980	70.0	75.0
Italy	1978	67.0	73.1
Netherlands, The	1979	72.4	78.9
Norway	1979–80	72.3	79.0
Poland	1980	66.0	74.4
Portugal	1980	66.0	74.0
Romania	1976–78	67.4	72.2
Spain	1975	70.4	76.2
Sweden	1980	72.8	78.8
Switzerland	1980	72.0	78.0
United Kingdom	1977–79	70.0	76.1
Yugoslavia	1978	67.5	72.8
North America			
Canada	1976	70.2	77.5
Costa Rica	1980	63.0	72.0
Cuba	1980	71.0	74.0
Martinique	1980–85[1]	67.8	73.0
Mexico	1975	62.8	66.6
Panama	1980	63.0	72.0
Puerto Rico	1976	70.2	77.1
Trinidad and Tobago	1980	66.0	72.0
United States	1981	70.3	77.9
Oceania			
Australia	1979	71.0	78.0
New Zealand	1975–77	69.4	75.9
South America			
Argentina	1980–85[1]	66.8	73.2
Brazil	1975–80[1]	61.3	65.5
Chile	1980–85[1]	63.8	70.4
Peru	1980–85[1]	56.7	59.7
Suriname	1980–85[1]	66.3	71.5
Uruguay	1980–85[1]	67.1	73.7
Venezuela	1975	65.0	69.7
U.S.S.R.	1980–85[1]	65.5	74.7

[1]Projection.
[2]Jewish population only.
Sources: United Nations, *World Statistics in Brief*, statistical pocketbook, 6th edition (1981), *World Population Trends and Prospects by Country, 1950–2000*, summary report of the 1978 assessment; official country sources.

Censuses and Surveys. By the end of 1982 the World Fertility Survey, established in 1972, had interviewed some 35,000 women in 42 less developed and 20 developed countries. Major findings to date showed that there had been substantial fertility declines in Asia, Latin America, and the Middle East but none in the Saharan African countries.

The field enumeration of the long-awaited census of China began July 1, 1982. About five million enumerators, one million supervisors, and one million or more additional workers, including advisers, took part. Through the UN Fund for Population Activities, the UN provided 21 computers for data processing, as well as consultation. Simple statistical summaries, available on October 1, showed a total population of 1,008,175,288 persons. Plans called for the results of a 10% sample to be released at the end of 1983. Complete results of the census would be available to the government of China at the end of 1985.

(ANDERS S. LUNDE)

[338.F.5.b; 525.A; 10/36.C.5.d]

Denmark

A constitutional monarchy of north central Europe lying between the North and Baltic seas, Denmark includes the Jutland Peninsula and 100 inhabited islands in the Kattegat and Skagerrak straits. Area (excluding Faeroe Islands and Greenland): 43,080 sq km (16,633 sq mi). Pop. (1981 est.): 5,124,000. Cap. and largest city: Copenhagen (pop., 1981 est., 648,700). Language: Danish. Religion: predominantly Lutheran. Queen, Margrethe II; prime ministers in 1982, Anker Jørgensen and, from September 10, Poul Schlüter.

The major economic problems facing Denmark

Denmark

DENMARK

Education. (1979–80) Primary, pupils 448,370; secondary, pupils 61,757; primary and secondary, teachers (1978–79) 64,118; vocational, pupils 223,831, teachers (1974–75) 5,290; teacher training, students 23,626, teachers (1978–79) 502; higher, students 81,352, teaching staff (1978–79) 6,713.

Finance. Monetary unit: Danish krone, with (Sept. 20, 1982) a free rate of 8.73 kroner to U.S. $1 (14.97 kroner = £1 sterling). Gold and other reserves (June 1982) U.S. $2,142,000,000. Budget (1981 est.): revenue 118,049,000,000 kroner; expenditure 139,155,000,000 kroner. Gross national product (1981) 396,590,000,000 kroner. Money supply (Feb. 1982) 83,570,000,000 kroner. Cost of living (1975 = 100; June 1982) 201.

Foreign Trade. (1981) Imports 124,677,000,000 kroner; exports 114,264,000,000 kroner. Import sources: EEC 47% (West Germany 19%, U.K. 12%, The Netherlands 6%); Sweden 12%; U.S. 9%. Export destinations: EEC 47% (West Germany 17%, U.K. 14%, France 5%, Italy 5%); Sweden 11%; Norway 6%; U.S. 5%. Main exports: machinery 19%; meat 14%, chemicals 8%, dairy products 5%; fish 5%. Tourism: visitors (1976) 16,232,000, gross receipts (1980) U.S. $1,337,000,000.

Transport and Communications. Roads (1980) 58,909 km (including 516 km expressways). Motor vehicles in use (1980): passenger 1,389,500; commercial 252,800. Railways (1979): 2,944 km; traffic 3,069,000,000 passenger-km, freight 1,800,000,000 net ton-km. Air traffic (including apportionment of international operations of Scandinavian Airlines System; 1981): 2,967,000,000 passenger-km; freight 132.6 million net ton-km. Shipping (1981): merchant vessels 100 gross tons and over 1,169; gross tonnage 5,047,734. Shipping traffic (1981): goods loaded 7,024,000 metric tons, unloaded 31,636,000 metric tons. Telephones (including Faeroe Islands and Greenland; Jan. 1980) 3,144,558. Radio licenses (Dec. 1979) 1,929,000. Television licenses (Dec. 1979) 1,830,000.

Agriculture. Production (in 000; metric tons; 1981): wheat 792; barley 6,010; oats c. 165; rye c. 200; potatoes 910; rutabagas (swedes; 1980) 801; sugar, raw value c. 522; apples c. 80; rapeseed 310; butter 102; cheese c. 247; pork c. 995; beef and veal c. 240; fish catch (1980) 2,027. Livestock (in 000; July 1981): cattle c. 2,933; pigs 9,856; sheep 56; chickens c. 15,016.

Industry. Production (in 000; metric tons; 1981): crude steel 611; cement 1,602; fertilizers (nutrient content; 1980–81) nitrogenous c. 138, phosphate c. 135; plastics and resins (1976) 145; crude oil 758; petroleum products (1979) c. 8,710; manufactured gas (cu m) c. 300,000; electricity (kw-hr) 18,201,000. Merchant vessels launched (100 gross tons and over; 1981) 306,000 gross tons.

Poul Schlüter (holding flowers) became Denmark's new prime minister in September following the resignation of Anker Jørgensen. Jørgensen resigned during a budgetary dispute.

in 1982 were the rising foreign debt, accumulated over several years, and a growing budget deficit. The balance of payments deficit was estimated at 20 billion kroner, bringing the foreign debt up to a little more than 25% of Denmark's gross national product (GNP).

The Social Democratic minority government on February 21 announced a 3% devaluation of the krone, and in May it set forth plans to raise an extra 6 billion kroner in taxes. About one-third of the total was to be raised from taxing the previously tax-free pension fund and other similar funds. The remainder was to come from increasing the traditional indirect taxes—on wine, beer, liquor, tobacco, gasoline, and heating oil—and from new taxes on coal for heating, videotapes, and bus trips by tourists. Not all the proposals were accepted; the new pension tax in particular was resisted violently. One estimate suggested that this tax package would cost an average family some 3,000 kroner a year in purchasing power. Furthermore, the Federation of Danish Industries calculated that it would add approximately 20,000 to the number of unemployed, which was already a little over 250,000.

In February the people of Greenland voted in favour of leaving the European Communities (EC). (See DEPENDENT STATES.) Greenland—like Denmark itself—was involved in the continuing struggle over fishing rights within the EC.

The grim realities of Denmark's economic situation were spelled out by the finance minister on August 16 when he presented his 1983 budget. It showed national expenditures of 191 billion kroner against income of 117 billion kroner, producing a deficit of 74 billion kroner. This deficit was later revised upward to a little over 80 billion kroner, some 14–16% of the estimated GNP. In 1982 the payment of interest on the money borrowed over the years was estimated at 24 billion kroner. Many economists suggested that these government figures were in fact too optimistic.

Prime Minister Anker Jørgensen tried to find parliamentary support for a way to reduce the deficit by 10 billion kroner. However, there was opposition from right-wing parties to the taxing of pension funds, while the Progress Party claimed that the government should be cutting spending by 60 billion–70 billion kroner. On the left wing, the Socialist People's Party wanted nothing to do with tax increases and was even less in favour of spending cuts.

All this dissent resulted in the resignation of Prime Minister Jørgensen on September 3. Six days later Denmark had its first Conservative prime minister in more than 80 years, Poul Schlüter (see BIOGRAPHIES). Jørgensen withdrew without forcing an election, and Schlüter headed a coalition government comprising the Conservative, Liberal Democratic (Venstre), Centre Democratic, and Christian People's parties. This right-of-centre minority government controlled 66 of the 179 seats in the Folketing (parliament).

On October 5 Prime Minister Schlüter presented his government's program to the Folketing. It was an austerity program similar to (though more severe than) that which Jørgensen had proposed. Among many other features, it planned to cancel automatic wage indexation (cost of living adjustments) for two years, to freeze unemployment benefits (according to analysts this represented a real decrease in purchasing power over two years of 15–20%), to introduce the much-debated tax on pension funds for an interim period of two years, to reduce the state old-age pension for those with earned incomes, and to freeze wages from October 5 until March 1983. This package was approved by 90 votes to 85 on October 17.

The new government planned to set up tripartite negotiations among employers, trade unions, and government to reach settlements in labour contract negotiations. Opinion polls suggested that its policies had the backing of a sympathetic majority in the country.   (STENER AARSDAL)

Dentistry:
see Health and Disease

Dependent States

The conflict between the U.K. and Argentina over the Falkland Islands (Islas Malvinas), which began in April 1982 (*see* SIDEBAR), affected attitudes toward the development of dependent territories and especially toward the principle of self-determination in areas with no permanent or indigenous population, such as St. Helena and the British Antarctic Territory. One result was the request by Brunei, in an oil-rich and strategically important area, that a British Army presence remain on the island after independence in 1983. Another was that British forces continued to be stationed in Belize, a former U.K. colony.

Europe and the Atlantic. With Spain supporting Argentina in the Falklands dispute, the 13-year blockade of its border with Gibraltar, territory that it disputed with the U.K., was not lifted on schedule. An agreement to end the blockade on April 20 was suspended when the Falklands crisis erupted. However, one of the first actions of the new Socialist government that came to power in Spain in December was to open the frontier at midnight on December 14–15.

The response of Commonwealth countries to the invasion of the Falklands was immediate and unequivocal. They condemned the seizure by force and the repudiation of the principle of self-determination which, in their view, the action represented. They cited the possible implications for

continued on page 299

Those Lucky (?) Falklanders

The U.K.'s claim to the Falkland Islands/Islas Malvinas was first contested over two centuries ago. In 1766 the British, deciding that the islands represented the "key to the whole Pacific Ocean," sent Capt. John MacBride to arrange the defense of Port Egmont, a settlement begun the previous year on West Falkland. English Capt. John Strong, who had made the first recorded landing three-quarters of a century earlier, had given the islands their English name, but it was the French who first settled there, in 1764 on East Falkland. They named the islands Les Malouines, after St. Malo, and the Spanish-language name derives from this. MacBride, however, was to find his country's claim contested by the Spanish, to whom the French had sold their rights. Spanish troops expelled the British in 1770, but the disagreement was resolved the following year when the Spanish returned Port Egmont to the British.

Forty-two years before the United Provinces of the Río de la Plata (later Argentina) declared independence from Spain in 1816, the British had abandoned Port Egmont, leaving behind a plaque claiming British sovereignty over the entire Falklands. The Spanish had left in 1811, when news of uprisings in Buenos Aires reached them. A short-lived Argentine presence ended when the U.K. reasserted its claim in 1833. Argentina, therefore, claims sovereignty over the islands in succession to Spain and because of their proximity to the mainland. The U.K.'s argument rests on an unbroken British presence since 1833, coupled with the fact that the islanders themselves expressed the wish to retain association with the U.K.

Attempting to calm the British public's enthusiasm for war against Spain in 1770, Samuel Johnson described the Falklands thus: "An island which not even the southern savages have dignified with habitation." Nevertheless, the settlers who went there a few decades later—mainly Scottish, Irish, and Welsh—stayed on. Reaching a peak of almost 2,400 in 1931, the population had declined by the 1980s to 1,800. The humans were vastly outnumbered by some 650,000 sheep, providing the sole source of income, and an estimated 10 million penguins, part of a unique wildlife.

The position of the Falkland Islands and its dependencies was first discussed at the UN in 1964 by the Special Committee of 24 on colonialism, set up to establish the obligation of UN member states to report regularly to the Security Council on the condition of nonautonomous territories and to work toward decolonization. The following year the emphasis shifted to the question of sovereignty. UN General Assembly Resolution 2065 acknowledged the dispute between the U.K. and Argentina and called on both countries to hold discussions directed at finding a peaceful solution.

Intermittent consultations held over the next 17 years did little to resolve the basic disagreement. The Falkland Islands Economic Survey, carried out by Lord Shackleton in 1976 for the U.K. government, pointed up the dilemma: the development of the islands' economy could take place only as a result of closer cooperation with Argentina, but the sovereignty issue continued to dominate negotiations. In the meantime, the islands suffered. Lord Shackleton recommended the establishment of tourist and fishing industries and offshore oil and gas exploration, but in 1981 the economy was still almost totally dependent on sheep farming.

The effect of the armed conflict that erupted in April 1982 was to push the sovereignty dispute further from the negotiating table. (For the military campaign, see DEFENSE: *Special Report.*) But in the aftermath Lord Shackleton's proposals for development seemed likely to evoke greater response. His 1976 report detected an "underlying tendency to decline" in the economy. Six years later, the proposed measures were of necessity more radical. Shackleton's 1982 report, presented in September, recommended that aid over a five-year (1984–88) period should total £35 million for the development of tourism, agriculture, and small-scale fisheries. A further £75 million would be required to explore the possibility of creating an offshore fishing industry and to build a permanent airfield. This total did not include the cost of defending the islands. Apart from perhaps becoming some of the most heavily aided people in the world, the islanders seemed set to become the most heavily defended. (LOUISE WATSON)

ANTARCTIC

Claims on the continent of Antarctica and all islands south of 60° S remain in status quo according to the Antarctic Treaty, to which 19 nations are signatory. Formal claims within the treaty area include the following: Australian Antarctic Territory, the mainland portion of French Southern and Antarctic Lands (Terre Adélie), Ross Dependency claimed by New Zealand, Queen Maud Land and Peter I Island claimed by Norway, and British Antarctic Territory, some parts of which are claimed by Argentina and Chile. No claims have been recognized as final under international law.

AUSTRALIA

CHRISTMAS ISLAND

Christmas Island, an external territory, is situated in the Indian Ocean 1,410 km NW of Australia. Area: 135 sq km (52 sq mi). Pop. (1981 est.): 3,300. Main settlement: Flying Fish Cove and the Settlement (pop., 1978 est., 1,400).

COCOS (KEELING) ISLANDS

Cocos (Keeling) Islands is an external territory located in the Indian Ocean 3,685 km W of Darwin, Australia. Area: 14 sq km (5.5 sq mi). Pop. (1981 est.): 569.

NORFOLK ISLAND

Norfolk Island, an external territory, is located in the Pacific Ocean 1,720 km NE of Sydney, Australia. Area: 35 sq km (13 sq mi). Pop. (1981): 1,800. Cap. (de facto): Kingston.

DENMARK

FAEROE ISLANDS

The Faeroes, an integral part of the Danish realm, are a self-governing group of islands in the North Atlantic about 580 km W of Norway. Area: 1,399 sq km (540 sq mi). Pop. (1982 est.): 45,000. Cap.: Thorshavn (pop., 1981 est., 12,700).

Education. (1980–81) Primary, pupils 5,879; secondary, pupils 2,837; primary and secondary, teachers 484; vocational, pupils (1979–80) 1,314, teachers (1966–67) 88; teacher training, students 113, teachers (1966–67) 12; higher, students 16.

Finance and Trade. Monetary unit: Faeroese krone, at par with the Danish krone, with (Sept. 20, 1982) a free rate of 8.73 kroner to U.S. $1 (14.97 kroner = £1 sterling). Budget (1979–80 est.): revenue 515,752,000 kroner; expenditure 514,893,000 kroner. Foreign trade (1980): imports 1,235,000,000 kroner; exports 1,058,000,000 kroner. Import sources: Denmark 73%; Norway 14%. Export destinations: Denmark 20%; U.K. 15%; West Germany 12%; U.S. 11 %; Italy 10%; France 8%; Spain 6%. Main exports: fish 81%; ships 8%; fish meal 6%.

Transport. Shipping (1981): merchant vessels 100 gross tons and over 180; gross tonnage 68,564.

Agriculture and Industry. Fish catch (1980) 275,000 metric tons. Livestock (in 000; 1981): sheep c. 71; cattle c. 2. Electricity production (1980) 160 million kw-hr.

GREENLAND (Kalâtdlit-Nunât)

An integral part of the Danish realm, Greenland, the largest island in the world, lies mostly within the Arctic Circle. Area: 2,175,600 sq km (840,000 sq mi), 84% of which is covered by ice cap. Pop. (1982 est.): 51,000. Cap.: Godthaab (Nûk; pop., 1981 est., 9,900).

Education. (1980–81) Primary, pupils 8,104; secondary, pupils 3,432; primary and secondary, teachers 1,076; vocational, pupils 855, teachers (1979–80) 53; teacher training, students 330, teachers (1979–80) 27; higher, students 197.

Finance and Trade. Monetary unit: Danish krone. Budget (1979 est.): revenue 170 million kroner; expenditure 160 million kroner. Foreign trade (1980): imports 1,846,000,000 kroner; exports 1,168,000,000 kroner. Import sources: Denmark 75%; U.K. 6%; The Netherlands 5%. Export destinations: Denmark 51%; France 12%; Finland 10%; West Germany 8%; U.S. 6%. Main exports: fish 66%; zinc ore 17%; lead ore 11%.

Agriculture. Fish catch (1980) 104,000 metric tons. Livestock (in 000; 1981): sheep c. 17; reindeer c. 2.

Industry. Production (in 000; metric tons; 1980): lead ore (metal content) 30; zinc ore (metal content) 92; silver (troy oz) 547; electricity (kw-hr) 160,000.

FRANCE

FRENCH GUIANA

French Guiana is an overseas département situated between Brazil and Suriname on the northeast coast of South America. Area: 83,533 sq km (32,252 sq mi). Pop. (1982 est.): 68,800. Cap.: Cayenne (pop., 1982, 38,200).

Education. (1979–80) Primary, pupils 12,920, teachers 613; secondary, pupils 5,660; vocational, pupils 1,532; secondary and vocational, teachers 483; teacher training, students (1978–79) 39.

Finance and Trade. Monetary unit: French (metropolitan) franc, with (Sept. 20, 1982) a free rate of Fr 7.05 to U.S. $1 (Fr 12.09 = £1 sterling). Budget (total; 1982 est.) balanced at Fr 578 million. Foreign trade (1981): imports Fr 1,355,310,000; exports Fr 192,080,000. Import sources (1980): France 58%; Trinidad and Tobago 15%; U.S. 8%. Export destinations (1980): France 27%; U.S. 26%; Portugal 13%; Japan 12%; Martinique 8%; Venezuela 6%. Main exports (1980): shrimp 36%; timber 29%; instruments 11%; machinery 6%; wood manufactures 6%.

FRENCH POLYNESIA

An overseas territory, French Polynesia consists of islands scattered over a large area of the south central Pacific Ocean. Area of inhabited islands: 4,182 sq km (1,615 sq mi). Pop. (1981 est.): 160,000. Cap.: Papeete, Tahiti (pop., 1981 est., 23,400).

Education. (1981–82) Primary, pupils 28,633; secondary, pupils 11,258; vocational, pupils 3,050; primary, secondary, and vocational, teachers (1980–81) 2,613; teacher training (1979-80), students 225, teachers 20.

Finance and Trade. Monetary unit: CFP franc, with (Sept. 20, 1982) a parity of CFP Fr 18.18 to the French franc and a free rate of CFP Fr 128 to U.S. $1 (CFP Fr 220 = £1 sterling). Budget (1981) balanced at CFP Fr 23.1 billion. Foreign trade (1981): imports CFP Fr 54,843,000,000; exports CFP Fr 2,861,000,000. Import sources (1980): France 48%; U.S. 21%; Singapore 5%; New Zealand 5%. Export destinations (1980): France 61%; Italy 14%; U.S. 9%; New Caledonia 7%. Main exports (1980): firearms 37%; coconut oil 24%; machinery 9%; precision instruments 8%. Tourism (1980): visitors 89,000; gross receipts U.S.$62 million.

GUADELOUPE

The overseas département of Guadeloupe, together with its dependencies, is in the eastern Caribbean between Antigua to the north and Dominica to the south. Area: 1,780 sq km (687 sq mi). Pop. (1982 est.): 314,800. Cap.: Basse-Terre (pop., 1979 est., 15,500).

Education. (1979–80) Primary, pupils 54,703, teachers 2,744; secondary, pupils 38,768; vocational, pupils 10,059; secondary and vocational (1978–79), teachers 2,602; higher (1977–78), students 1,645.

Finance and Trade. Monetary unit: French (metropolitan) franc. Budget (total; 1977 est.) balanced at Fr 1,199,000,000. Cost of living (Basse-Terre; 1975 = 100; April 1982) 201. Foreign trade (1981): imports Fr 3,192,020,000 (71% from France, 6% from U.S. in 1980); exports Fr 509.3 million (73% to France, 18% to Martinique in 1980). Main exports (1980): sugar 41%; bananas 26%; wheat meal and flour 8%; rum c. 7%.

MARTINIQUE

The Caribbean island of Martinique, an overseas département, lies 39 km N of St. Lucia and about 50 km SE of Dominica. Area: 1,100 sq km (425 sq mi). Pop. (1982 est.): 307,700. Cap.: Fort-de-France (pop., 1980, 100,600).

Education. (1979–80) Primary, pupils 50,142, teachers 2,751; secondary, pupils 38,778; vocational, pupils 9,854; secondary and vocational (1978–79), teachers 3,040; higher, students 1,475, teaching staff 77.

Finance and Trade. Monetary unit: French (metropolitan) franc. Budget (1979 est.) balanced at Fr 925 million. Cost of living (Fort-de-France; 1975 = 100;

April 1982) 214. Foreign trade (1981): imports Fr 4,010,000,000; exports Fr 705 million. Import sources (1980): France 63%; Venezuela 6%; U.S. 5%; Saudi Arabia 5%. Export destinations (1980): Guadeloupe 52%; France 39%. Main exports (1980): petroleum products 45%; bananas 21%; rum c. 11%. Tourism (1980) 157,200 visitors.

MAYOTTE

An African island dependency of France that was formerly a part of the Comoros, Mayotte lies in the Indian Ocean off the east coast of Africa. Area: 374 sq km (144 sq mi). Pop. (1981 est.): 53,000. Cap.: Dzaoudzi (pop., 1978, 4,100).

Education. (1980–81) Primary, pupils 9,905, teachers 291; secondary, pupils 662, teachers 39; vocational (1978–79), pupils 62.

Finance and Trade. Monetary unit: French (metropolitan) franc. Budget (1980 est.) balanced at Fr 197 million. Foreign trade (1979): imports Fr 24.7 million; exports Fr 6.6 million. Import sources: Réunion 27%; France 27%; Pakistan 16%; Kenya 14%. Export destination: France 100%. Main exports: ilang-ilang 56%; copra 26%; coffee 10%; vanilla 8%.

NEW CALEDONIA

The overseas territory of New Caledonia, together with its dependencies, is in the South Pacific 1,210 km E of Australia. Area: 19,103 sq km (7,375 sq mi). Pop. (1980 est.): 139,600. Cap.: Nouméa (pop., 1976, 56,100).

Education. (1980–81) Primary, pupils 34,281, teachers 1,516; secondary, pupils 9,366, teachers 545; vocational, pupils 3,961, teachers 315; higher, students 421, teaching staff 60.

Finance and Trade. Monetary unit: CFP franc. Budget (1980 est.): revenue CFP Fr 19,299,000,000; expenditure CFP Fr 18,279,000,000. Foreign trade (1981): imports CFP Fr 40,480,000,000; exports CFP Fr 34,296,000,000. Import sources (1980): France 34%; Bahrain 16%; Australia 11%; U.S. 5%; Japan 5%. Export destinations (1980): France 56%; Japan 31%; U.S. 10%. Main exports: ferroalloys 50%; nickel ores 24%; nickel 20%.

RÉUNION

The overseas département of Réunion is located in the Indian Ocean about 720 km E of Madagascar and 180 km SW of Mauritius. Area: 2,512 sq km (970 sq mi). Pop. (1982 est.): 504,400. Cap.: Saint-Denis (pop., 1981 est., 115,700).

Education. (1981–82) Primary, pupils 125,305, teachers (1980–81) 4,392; secondary and vocational, pupils 63,889, teachers 3,111; higher (university only), students (1980–81) 2,400, teaching staff (1979–80) 63.

Finance and Trade. Monetary unit: French (metropolitan) franc. Budget (1978 est.) balanced at Fr 3,573,000,000. Cost of living (Saint-Denis; 1975 = 100; April 1982) 188.9. Foreign trade (1981): imports Fr 4,281,460,000; exports Fr 571,620,000. Import sources (1980): France 65%; South Africa 6%; Italy 5%. Export destinations (1980): France 85%; U.K. 6%. Main exports: sugar 79%; essential oils 4%.

SAINT PIERRE AND MIQUELON

The self-governing overseas département of Saint Pierre and Miquelon is located about 20 km off the south coast of Newfoundland. Area: 242 sq km (93 sq mi). Pop. (1982 est.): 6,300. Cap.: Saint Pierre, Saint Pierre (pop., 1980 est., 5,600).

Education. (1981–82) Primary, pupils 703, teachers 58; secondary, pupils 530; vocational, pupils 199; secondary and vocational, teachers 61.

Finance and Trade. Monetary unit: French (metropolitan) franc. Budget (1979 est.) balanced at Fr 31.5 million. Foreign trade (1980): imports Fr 177.2 million; exports Fr 24.2 million. Import sources (1976): Canada 64%; France 27%. Export destinations (1976): ship's bunkers and stores 53%; Canada 30%; U.S. 13%. Main exports (1974): petroleum products 53%; cattle 30%; fish 12%.

WALLIS AND FUTUNA

Wallis and Futuna, an overseas territory, lies in the South Pacific west of Western Samoa. Area: 255 sq km (98 sq mi). Pop. (1982 est.): 11,000. Cap.: Mata Utu, Uvea (pop., 1976, 558).

NETHERLANDS, THE

NETHERLANDS ANTILLES

The Netherlands Antilles, a self-governing integral part of the Netherlands realm, consists of an island group near the Venezuelan coast and another group to the north near St. Kitts-Nevis-Anguilla. Area: 993 sq km (383 sq mi). Pop. (1981 est.): 253,300. Cap.: Willemstad, Curaçao (pop., 1970 est., 50,000).

Education. (1973–74) Primary, pupils 33,170, teachers 1,492; secondary and vocational, pupils 12,104, teachers 631; higher (university only), students c. 150, teaching staff c. 15.

Finance. Monetary unit: Netherlands Antilles guilder or florin, with (Sept. 20, 1982) a par value of 1.80 Netherlands Antilles guilders to U.S. $1 (free rate of 3.09 Netherlands Antilles guilders = £1 sterling). Budget (1979 actual): revenue 213 million Netherlands Antilles guilders; expenditure 256 million Netherlands Antilles guilders. Cost of living (Aruba, Bonaire, and Curaçao; July 1975 = 100; July 1981) 172.5.

Foreign Trade. (1977) Imports 5,631,000,000 Netherlands Antilles guilders; exports 4,764,000,000 Netherlands Antilles guilders. Import sources: Venezuela 61%; Nigeria 11%; U.S. 8%. Export destinations: U.S. 49%; Nigeria 11%; Ecuador 5%. Main exports: petroleum products 89%; crude oil 7%. Tourism (1980): visitors c. 500,000; gross receipts U.S. $410 million.

Transport and Communications. Roads (1972) 1,150 km. Motor vehicles in use (1979): passenger c. 51,700; commercial (including buses) c. 8,700. Shipping traffic (1977): goods loaded c. 24.8 million metric tons, unloaded c. 31.1 million metric tons. Telephones (Jan. 1979) 50,000. Radio receivers (Dec. 1979) 175,000. Television receivers (Dec. 1979) 40,000.

Industry. Production (in 000; metric tons; 1979): petroleum products c. 29,100; phosphate rock 45; salt 232; electricity (kw-hr; 1980) c. 1,825,000.

NEW ZEALAND

COOK ISLANDS

The self-governing territory of the Cook Islands consists of several islands in the southern Pacific Ocean scattered over an area of about 2.2 million sq km. Area: 236 sq km (91 sq mi). Pop. (1981 est.): 17,700. Seat of government: Rarotonga Island (pop., 1981 prelim.), 9,500).

Education. (1982–83) Primary, pupils 3,162, teachers 157; secondary, pupils 2,751, teachers 179; teacher training (1977–78), students 48.

Finance and Trade. Monetary unit: Cook Islands dollar, at par with the New Zealand dollar, with (Sept. 20, 1982) a free rate of CI$1.38 to U.S. $1 (CI$2.36 = £1 sterling). Budget (1979–80 est.): revenue CI$15,887,000; expenditure CI$16,414,000. Foreign trade: imports (1980) CI$23,610,000; exports (1981) CI$5,015,000. Import sources (1978): New Zealand 62%; Japan 11%; Australia 6%; U.S. 5%. Export destination (1977): New Zealand 99%. Main exports: clothing 41%; citrus juice 15%; bananas 14%; pawpaws 8%; copra 7%; pearl shell 6%. Tourism (1981): 18,498 visitors.

NIUE

The self-governing territory of Niue is situated in the Pacific Ocean about 2,400 km NE of New Zealand. Area: 259 sq km (100 sq mi). Pop. (1981 est.): 3,400. Capital: Alofi (pop., 1979, 960).

Education. (1981–82) Primary, pupils 564, teachers 38; secondary, pupils 436, teachers 27

Finance and Trade. Monetary unit: New Zealand dollar. Budget (1979–80): revenue NZ$4,078,000 (excluding New Zealand subsidy of NZ$2.8 million); expenditure NZ$4,013,000. Foreign trade (1980): imports NZ$3,384,000 (80% from New Zealand in 1979); exports NZ$308,000 (98% to New Zealand in 1979). Main exports (1978): passion fruit 36%; copra 16%; plaited ware 12%; limes, fresh and juice 9%; honey 9%.

TOKELAU

The territory of Tokelau lies in the South Pacific Ocean about 1,130 km N of Niue and 3,380 km NE of New Zealand. Area: 12 sq km (4.6 sq mi). Pop. (1981): 1,600.

NORWAY

JAN MAYEN

The island of Jan Mayen, a Norwegian dependency, lies within the Arctic Circle between Greenland and northern Norway. Area: 373 sq km (144 sq mi). Pop. (1973 est.): 37.

SVALBARD

A group of islands and a Norwegian dependency, Svalbard is located within the Arctic Circle to the north of Norway. Area: 62,050 sq km (23,957 sq mi). Pop. (1980 est.): 3,600.

PORTUGAL

MACAU

The overseas territory of Macau is situated on the mainland coast of China 60 km W of Hong Kong. Area: 16 sq km (6 sq mi). Pop. (1981 est.): 350,000.

Education. (1979–80) Primary, pupils 33,334, teachers 732; secondary, pupils 13,034, teachers 619; vocational, pupils 2,261, teachers 67.

Finance and Trade. Monetary unit: pataca, with (Sept. 20, 1982) a free rate of 6.33 patacás to U.S. $1 (10.85 patacás = £1 sterling). Budget (1980 est.) balanced at 303 million patacás. Foreign trade (1981): imports 4,132,900,000 patacás; exports 4,018,-900,000 patacás. Import sources (1980): Hong Kong 56%; China 26%; Japan 7%. Export destinations (1980): U.S. 20%; West Germany 19%; France 15%; Hong Kong 13%; U.K. 8%; Italy 6%. Main exports (1980): clothing c. 78%; textile yarns and fabrics c. 9%. Tourism (1980) 641,466 visitors.

Transport. Shipping traffic (1979): goods loaded 781,000 metric tons, unloaded 566,000 metric tons.

SOUTH WEST AFRICA/NAMIBIA

South West Africa has been a UN territory since 1966, when the General Assembly terminated South Africa's mandate over the country, renamed Namibia by the UN. South Africa considers the UN resolution illegal. Area: 824,292 sq km (318,261 sq mi). Pop. (1982 est.): 1,086,000. National cap.: Windhoek (pop., 1978 est., 75,100). Summer cap.: Swakopmund (pop., 1978 est., 16,800).

Education. (1980) Primary, secondary, and vocational, pupils 228,287, teachers 7,741.

Finance and Trade. Monetary unit: South African rand, with (Sept. 20, 1982) a free rate of R 1.15 to U.S. $1 (R 1.97 = £1 sterling). Budget (total; 1982–83 est.): revenue R 660 million; expenditure R 870 million. Foreign trade (included in the South African customs union; 1979 estimate): imports c. R 700 million (c. 80% from South Africa in 1972); exports c. R 1 billion (about 50% to South Africa in 1972). Main exports: diamonds c. 45%; uranium c. 25%; metal ores c. 10%; karakul pelts c. 6%; cattle and meat c. 6%.

Agriculture. Production (in 000; metric tons; 1981): corn c. 30; millet c. 15; beef and veal c. 74; sheep and goat meat c. 27; fish catch (1980) 213. Livestock (in 000; 1981): cattle c. 1,700; sheep c. 4,500; goats c. 2,200; horses c. 45; asses c. 67.

Industry. Production (in 000; metric tons; 1980): copper ore (metal content) 39; lead ore (metal content) 48; zinc ore (metal content) 32; tin concentrates (metal content) c. 1; uranium 4.8; diamonds (metric carats) c. 1,560; salt c. 230; electricity (kw-hr; 1963) 188,000.

UNITED KINGDOM

ANGUILLA

The island of Anguilla is a non-self-governing dependency. It was a part of the associated state of St. Kitts-Nevis-Anguilla until Dec. 19, 1980. It received a constitution separating its government from that of St. Kitts-Nevis-Anguilla in 1976. Area: 91 sq km (35 sq mi). Pop. (1982 est.): 7,000.

Education. (1979) Primary, pupils 1,610, teachers 68; secondary, pupils 450, teachers 20.

Finance and Trade. Monetary unit: East Caribbean dollar, with (Sept. 20, 1982) a par value of ECar$2.70 to U.S. $1 (free rate of ECar$4.63 = £1 sterling). Budget (1981 est.): revenue ECar$6.3 million (excluding U.K. grant of ECar$1.1 million); expenditure ECar$7.5 million. Foreign trade (1979 est.) exports c. ECar$1.6 million. Main export destinations: Trinidad and Tobago c. 40%; Puerto Rico c. 30%; Guadeloupe c. 10%; U.S. Virgin Islands c. 10%. Main exports: salt c. 40%; lobster c. 38%; livestock c. 13%.

BERMUDA

The colony of Bermuda lies in the western Atlantic about 920 km E of Cape Hatteras, North Carolina. Area: 53 sq km (20.5 sq mi). Pop. (1980): 54,000. Cap.: Hamilton, Great Bermuda (pop., 1980, 1,600).

Education. (1981–82) Primary, pupils 5,878, teachers 320; secondary, pupils 4,215, teachers 362; higher (university only), pupils 575, teachers 63.

Finance and Trade. Monetary unit: Bermuda dollar, at par with the U.S. dollar (free rate, at Sept. 20, 1982, of Ber$1.71 = £1 sterling). Budget (1981–82 est.): revenue Ber$132 million; expenditure Ber$129.8 million. Foreign trade (1981): imports Ber$323 million; exports Ber$29.4 million. Import sources: U.S. 53%; Netherlands Antilles 13%; U.K. 11%; Canada 7%. Export destinations: bunkers 38%; U.S. 14%; Australia 9%; South Africa 6%. Main exports: drugs and medicines 40%; petroleum products 37%. Tourism: visitors (1980) 491,600; gross receipts U.S. $258 million.

Transport. Roads (1979) c. 240 km. Motor vehicles in use (1980): passenger 13,600; commercial 1,996. Shipping (1981): merchant vessels 100 gross tons and over 75; gross tonnage 499,029.

BRITISH INDIAN OCEAN TERRITORY

Located in the western Indian Ocean, this colony consists of the islands of the Chagos Archipelago. Area: 60 sq km (23 sq mi). No permanent civilian population remains. Administrative headquarters: Victoria, Seychelles.

BRITISH VIRGIN ISLANDS

The colony of the British Virgin Islands is located in the Caribbean to the east of the U.S. Virgin Islands. Area: 153 sq km (59 sq mi). Pop. (1981 est.): 13,000. Cap.: Road Town, Tortola (pop., 1980, 9,300).

Education. (1979–80) Primary, pupils 2,272, teachers 109; secondary and vocational, pupils 833, teachers 49.

Finance and Trade. Monetary unit: U.S. dollar. Budget (1980 actual): revenue $12,774,000; expenditure $10,853,000. Foreign trade (1980): imports $36 million; exports $1,087,000. Import sources (1976): U.S. 23%; Puerto Rico 24%; U.K. 15%; U.S. Virgin Islands 12%; Trinidad and Tobago 11%. Export destinations (1974): U.S. Virgin Islands 53%; Anguilla 22%; St. Martin (Guadeloupe) 9%; U.K. 5%. Main exports (domestic): fresh fish, sand and gravel, fruit and vegetables. Tourism: visitors (1980) 172,700; gross receipts (1978) U.S. $24 million.

BRUNEI

Brunei, a protected sultanate, is located on the north coast of the island of Borneo, surrounded on its landward side by the Malaysian state of Sarawak. Area: 5,765 sq km (2,226 sq mi). Pop. (1982 est.): 199,600. Cap.: Bandar Seri Begawan (pop., 1982 est., 51,600).

Education. (1980–81) Primary, pupils 31,677, teachers 1,800; secondary, pupils 16,805, teachers 1,326; vocational, pupils 570, teachers 127; teacher training, students 714, teachers 85.

Finance and Trade. Monetary unit: Brunei dollar, with (Sept. 20, 1982) a free rate of Br$2.17 to U.S. $1 (Br$3.71 = £1 sterling). Budget (1980 revised est.): revenue Br$6.3 billion; expenditure Br$1 million. Foreign trade (1981): imports Br$1,264,700,000; exports Br$8,591,730,000. Import sources (1980): Japan 24%; U.S. 20%; Singapore 19%; U.K. 10%. Export destinations (1980): Japan 71%; U.S. 9%; Singapore 7%; South Africa 5%. Main exports (1980): crude oil 62%; natural gas 31%; petroleum products 6%.

Agriculture. Production (in 000; metric tons; 1981): rice c. 10; cassava c. 3; bananas c. 3; pineapples c. 3. Livestock (in 000; 1981): buffalo c. 14; cattle c. 4; pigs c. 14; chickens c. 1,159.

Industry. Production (in 000; 1979): crude oil (metric tons) c. 12,000; natural gas (cu m; 1980) 8,950,000; petroleum products (metric tons) c. 103; electricity (kw-hr; 1980) c. 375,000.

CAYMAN ISLANDS

The colony of the Cayman Islands lies in the Caribbean about 270 km NW of Jamaica. Area: 264 sq km (102 sq mi). Pop. (1981 est.): 18,000. Cap.: George Town, Grand Cayman (pop., 1979, 7,600).

Education. (1980–81) Primary, pupils 2,152, teachers 1,133; secondary, pupils 1,565, teachers 1,097; vocational (1979–80), pupils 12, teachers 1; higher, pupils 119, teachers 8.

Finance and Trade. Monetary unit: Cayman Islands dollar, with (Sept. 20, 1982) a par value of CayI$0.83 to U.S. $1 (free rate of CayI$1.43 = £1 sterling). Budget (1980 est.): revenue CayI$34.9 million; expenditure CayI$25.1 million. Foreign trade (1980): imports CayI$85.8 million; exports CayI$2,227,000. Import sources: U.S. 72%; Trinidad and Tobago 7%. Export destinations: West Germany 34%; U.S. 28%; U.K. 12%; Japan 11%; Jamaica 7%. Main exports: turtle meat 31%; chemicals 25%; turtle fat 12%; pearls and precious stones 11%; turtle shell 5%. Tourism (1980): visitors 120,200; gross receipts U.S. $63 million.

Shipping. (1981) Merchant vessels 100 gross tons and over 241; gross tonnage 279,771.

FALKLAND ISLANDS

The colony of the Falkland Islands and dependencies is situated in the South Atlantic about 800 km NE of Cape Horn. Area: 12,173 sq km (4,700 sq mi). Pop. (1980): 1,800. Cap.: Stanley (pop., 1980, 1,050).

Education. (1979–80) Primary, pupils 215, teachers 15; secondary, pupils 127, teachers 13.

Finance and Trade. Monetary unit: Falkland Island pound, at par with the pound sterling, with (Sept. 20, 1982) a free rate of U.S. $1.71 = FI£1. Budget (excluding dependencies; 1981–82 est.): revenue FI£2,478,000; expenditure FI£2,411,000. Foreign trade (1980): imports FI£2,590,000 (86% from U.K. in 1975); exports c. FI£3.3 million (100% to U.K. in 1975). Main exports: wool c. 81%; postage stamps c. 18%.

GIBRALTAR

Gibraltar, a self-governing colony, is a small peninsula that juts into the Mediterranean from southwestern Spain. Area: 5.80 sq km (2.25 sq mi). Pop. (1982 est.): 30,000.

Education. (1981–82) Primary, pupils 2,844, teachers 168; secondary, pupils 1,794, teachers 125; vocational, pupils 48, teachers 20.

Finance and Trade. Monetary unit: Gibraltar pound, at par with the pound sterling. Budget (1980–81 est.): revenue Gib£41,025,000; expenditure Gib£42,680,000. Foreign trade (1980): imports Gib£63,142,000 (64% from U.K.); reexports Gib£16,994,000 (mainly bunkers and ships' supplies). Main reexports: petroleum products 75%; tobacco and manufactures 20%; wines and spirits 5%. Tourism (1980) 153,800 visitors.

Transport. Shipping traffic (1979): goods loaded 9,000 metric tons, unloaded 307,000 metric tons.

GUERNSEY

Located 50 km W of Normandy, France, Guernsey, together with its small island dependencies, is a crown dependency. Area: 78 sq km (30 sq mi). Pop. (1982 est.): 56,400. Cap.: St. Peter Port (pop., 1976, 17,000).

Education. (1979–80) Primary and secondary, pupils 9,400, teachers 524.

Finance and Trade. Monetary unit: Guernsey pound, at par with the pound sterling. Budget (1980): revenue £44,971,000; expenditure £37,526,000. Foreign trade (1979): imports £150 million; exports £110 million. Main source and destination: U.K. Main exports (1979): manufactures c. 62%; tomatoes c. 21%; flowers and ferns c. 11%. Tourism: visitors (1980) c. 310,000; gross receipts (1979) U.S. $85 million.

HONG KONG

The colony of Hong Kong lies on the southeastern coast of China about 60 km E of Macau and 130 km SE of Canton. Area: 1,060 sq km (409 sq mi). Pop. (1981): 5,021,000. Cap.: Victoria (pop., 1981, 590,800).

Education. (1981–82) Primary, pupils 539,545, teachers 17,972; secondary, pupils 444,718; voca-

tional, pupils 11,485; secondary and vocational, teachers 15,927; teacher training, students 1,632, teachers 215; higher, students 39,695, teaching staff 2,810.

Finance. Monetary unit: Hong Kong dollar, with (Sept. 20, 1982) a free rate of HK$6.10 to U.S. $1 (HK$10.46 = £1 sterling). Budget (1980–81 est.): revenue HK$21,040,000,000; expenditure HK$18,440,000,000.

Foreign Trade. (1981) Imports HK$147,305,-000,000; exports HK$122,381,000,000. Import sources: Japan 22%; China 20%; U.S. 10%; Taiwan 7%; Singapore 7%. Export destinations: U.S. 28%; China 9%; U.K. 7%; West Germany 6%; Japan 5%. Main exports: clothing 25%; machinery (except telecommunications) 12%; textile yarns and fabrics 10%; watches and clocks 8%; telecommunications apparatus 6%; plastic toys and dolls, etc. 6%. Tourism (1980): visitors 2,301,000; gross receipts U.S. $1,320,000,000.

Transport and Communications. Roads (1981) 1,161 km. Motor vehicles in use (1980): passenger 200,000; commercial 58,800. Railways (1981): 51 km; traffic 390 million passenger-km, freight 60 million net ton-km. Shipping (1981): merchant vessels 100 gross tons and over 223; gross tonnage 2,580,492. Shipping traffic (1981): goods loaded 9,172,000 metric tons, unloaded 26,406,000 metric tons. Telephones (Jan. 1980) 1,517,300. Radio receivers (Dec. 1979) 2,530,000. Television receivers (Dec. 1980) c. 1,110,000.

ISLE OF MAN

The Isle of Man, a crown dependency, lies in the Irish Sea approximately 55 km from both Northern Ireland and the coast of northwestern England. Area: 588 sq km (227 sq mi). Pop. (1982 est.): 61,000. Cap.: Douglas (pop., 1976, 20,300).

Education. (1981–82) Primary, pupils 5,731, teachers (state only; 1978–79) 270; secondary, pupils 5,122, teachers (state only; 1978–79) 240; vocational and higher, pupils 3,561.

Finance and Trade. Monetary unit: Isle of Man pound, at par with the pound sterling. Budget (1980–81 est.): revenue £58.3 million; expenditure £50.9 million. Foreign trade included with the United Kingdom. Main exports: herring, beef and lamb, grain, scrap metal. Tourism (1981) 453,000 visitors.

JERSEY

The island of Jersey, a crown dependency, is located about 30 km W of Normandy, France. Area: 116 sq km (45 sq mi). Pop. (1982 est.): 74,000. Cap.: St. Helier (pop., 1981, 24,900).

Education. (1980) Primary, pupils 5,884; secondary, pupils 5,457; primary and secondary (1976–77), teachers 670.

Finance. Monetary unit: Jersey pound, at par with the pound sterling. Budget (1980): revenue £99,625,000; expenditure £81,881,000.

Foreign Trade. (1980) Imports £230,895,000 (85% from U.K.); exports £89,930,000 (67% to U.K.). Main exports: fruit and vegetables 16%; motor vehicles 11%; telecommunications apparatus 10%; works of art 6%; knitted fabrics 6%; jewelry 6%; tea 5%; musical instruments 5%; clothing 5%. Tourism (1980): visitors 1,340,600; gross receipts U.S. $291 million.

MONTSERRAT

The colony of Montserrat is located in the Caribbean between Antigua, 43 km NE, and Guadeloupe, 60 km SE. Area: 102 sq km (40 sq mi). Pop. (1980): 11,600. Cap.: Plymouth (pop., 1980, 1,600).

Education. (1979–80) Primary, pupils 1,740, teachers 87; secondary, pupils 920, teachers 68; vocational, pupils 56, teachers 8.

Finance and Trade. Monetary unit: East Caribbean dollar. Budget (total; 1980 est.): revenue ECar$16,724,000; expenditure ECar$15,092,000. Foreign trade (1981): imports ECar$51 million; exports ECar$6 million. Import sources (1978): U.K. 33%; U.S. 23%; Trinidad and Tobago 9%; Canada 5%. Export destinations (1978): U.S. 54%; Trinidad and Tobago 7%; Antigua 5%. Main exports (domestic only): packaging 50%; clothing 12%; live plants 10%; electrical equipment 10%; fruit and vegetables 8%. Tourism (1980): visitors 15,532; gross receipts U.S. $4.3 million.

PITCAIRN ISLAND

The colony of Pitcairn Island is in the central South Pacific, 5,150 km NE of New Zealand and 2,170 km SE of Tahiti. Area: 4.53 sq km (1.75 sq mi). Pop. (1981): 54, all of whom live in the de facto capital, Adamstown.

ST. HELENA

The colony of St. Helena, including its dependencies of Ascension Island and the Tristan da Cunha island group, is spread over a wide area of the Atlantic off the southwestern coast of Africa. Area: 412 sq km (159 sq mi). Pop. (1981 est.): 5,200. Cap.: Jamestown (pop., 1978 est., 1,500).

Education. (1981–82) Primary, pupils 647, teachers 35; secondary, pupils 604, teachers 32; vocational, pupils 32, teachers 1; teacher training, students 6, teachers 2.

Finance and Trade. Monetary unit: St. Helena pound, at par with the pound sterling which is also used. Budget (1980–81 est.): revenue St.H£4,488,-000; expenditure St.H£4,552,000. Foreign trade (1979–80): imports St.H£1,835,800 (52% from U.K., 36% from South Africa, 5% from Ghana in 1976–77); exports St.H£10,600. Main export: skipjack and tuna 100%.

ST. KITTS-NEVIS

This associated state consists of the islands of St. Kitts and Nevis (Anguilla received a separate constitution in 1976). Area: 269 sq km (104 sq mi). Pop. (1980 prelim.): 44,400. Cap.: Basseterre, St. Kitts (pop., 1980 prelim., 14,700).

Education. (1980–81) Primary, pupils 7,848, teachers 335; secondary, pupils 4,867, teachers 287; vocational, pupils 127, teachers 24; teacher training, students 61, teachers 8.

Finance and Trade. Monetary unit: East Caribbean dollar. Budget (1979 est.): revenue ECar$31.3 million; expenditure ECar$36.4 million. Foreign trade (1979): imports ECar$86.6 million; exports ECar$45.5 million. Import sources (1975): U.S. 29%; U.K. 20%; Trinidad and Tobago 10%; Canada 7%; The Netherlands 5%; Japan 5%. Export destinations (1975): U.S. 51%; U.K. 42%. Main exports (1975): sugar 61%; television sets and parts 34%. Tourism (1980) 38,400 visitors.

TURKS AND CAICOS ISLANDS

The colony of the Turks and Caicos Islands is situated in the Atlantic southeast of The Bahamas. Area: 500 sq km (193 sq mi). Pop. (1980 est.): 7,000. Seat of government: Grand Turk Island (pop., 1980 est., 3,100).

Education. (1980–81) Primary, pupils 1,926, teachers (1978–79) 90; secondary, pupils 691, teachers (1978–79) 38.

Finance and Trade. Monetary unit: U.S. dollar. Budget (1980–81 est.): revenue $7,188,000; expenditure $7,364,000. Foreign trade (1980–81): imports $13,805,000; exports $2,160,000. Main exports: crayfish c. 49%; conch meat c. 48%. Tourism (1980) 11,887 visitors.

UNITED STATES

AMERICAN SAMOA

Located to the east of Western Samoa in the South Pacific, the unincorporated territory of American Samoa is approximately 2,600 km NE of the northern tip of New Zealand. Area: 199 sq km (77 sq mi). Pop. (1981 est.): 33,000. Cap.: Pago Pago (pop., 1980, 2,600).

Education. (1979–80) Primary, pupils 6,680, teachers 355; secondary, pupils 2,911, teachers 175; vocational, pupils 45, teachers 4; teacher training, pupils 256, teachers 6; higher, students 472, teaching staff 54.

Finance and Trade. Monetary unit: U.S. dollar. Budget (1980 est.) balanced at $59 million (including U.S. grants of $34.3 million). Foreign trade (1979–80): imports (excluding fish for canneries) $95.1 million (73% from U.S., 12% from Japan, 6% from New Zealand in 1977–78); exports $127.1 million (99% to U.S. in 1976–77). Main export: canned tuna (1977–78) 93%; pet food 5%. Tourism (1980) 52,721 visitors.

GUAM

Guam, an organized unincorporated territory, is located in the Pacific Ocean about 9,700 km SW of San Francisco and 2,400 km E of Manila. Area: 549 sq km (212 sq mi). Pop. (1981 est.): 109,900. Cap.: Agana (pop., 1974 est., 2,500).

Education. (1981–82) Primary, pupils 17,784, teachers 772; secondary and vocational, pupils 13,183, teachers 587; higher (university), students 2,496, teaching staff 162.

Finance and Trade. Monetary unit: U.S. dollar. Budget (1979–80 est.): revenue $124.3 million; expenditure $130.4 million. Foreign trade (1979–80): imports $544 million (32% from U.S., 7% from Japan in 1978–79); exports $61 million (49% to U.S. Trust Territories, 26% to U.S., 16% to Taiwan in 1978–79). Main exports (1978–79): petroleum products 38%, copra, watches, clothing. Tourism: visitors (1981) 312,900; gross receipts (1979) U.S. $132 million.

Agriculture and Industry. Production (in 000; metric tons; 1979): copra c. 1; eggs 1; fish catch 0.22; petroleum products (1978) c. 1,410; electricity (kw-hr; 1978) c. 1,060,000.

PUERTO RICO

Puerto Rico, a self-governing associated commonwealth, lies about 1,400 km SE of the Florida coast. Area: 8,897 sq km (3,435 sq mi). Pop. (1981 est.): 3,251,000. Cap.: San Juan (pop., 1980 mun., 433,000).

Education. (1980–81) Primary, pupils 470,089, teachers 23,154; secondary, pupils 337,153, teachers 13,297; vocational, pupils 60,045, teachers 1,522; higher, students 130,105, teaching staff 3,300.

Finance. Monetary unit: U.S dollar. Budget (1979–80 actual): revenue $4,148,000,000; expenditure $3,550,000,000. Gross domestic product (1980–81) $14,653,000,000. Cost of living (1975 = 100; May 1982) 149.4.

Foreign Trade. (1980–81) Imports $9,364,000,000 (61% from U.S., 8% from Venezuela); exports $6,799,000,000 (82% to U.S.). Main exports (1974–75): chemicals 25%; petroleum products 14%; clothing 11%; machinery 11%; fish 3%. Tourism (1980): visitors 2,741,800; gross receipts U.S. $596 million.

Transport and Communications. Roads (paved; 1979) 12,366 km. Motor vehicles in use (1979): passenger 838,400; commercial 143,600. Railways (1979) 96 km. Telephones (Jan. 1980) 651,400. Radio receivers (Dec. 1979) 2 million. Television receivers (Dec. 1979) 700,000.

Agriculture. Production (in 000; metric tons; 1981): sugar, raw value 137; pineapples 38; bananas 109; oranges 29; coffee 14; tobacco 1; milk 416; meat 70. Livestock (in 000; Jan. 1981): cattle 489; pigs 241; chickens 7,455.

Industry. Production (in 000; metric tons; 1981): cement 1,151; beer (hl) 727; rum (hl; 1977) c. 600; petroleum products (1979) c. 12,390; electricity (kw-hr) c. 13,060,000.

TRUST TERRITORY OF THE PACIFIC ISLANDS

The Trust Territory islands, numbering more than 2,000, are scattered over 7,750,000 sq km in the Pacific Ocean from 720 km E of the Philippines to just west of the International Date Line. Separate administrative actions within the Trust Territory have, since 1973, created four new administrative entities that are to form the framework for local government upon cessation of the UN trusteeship: the Commonwealth of the Northern Mariana Islands (1978); the Federated States of Micronesia (Yap, Ponape, Kosrae, and Truk; 1979); the Marshall Islands (1979); and the Republic of Palau (early 1981). The government of the Trust Territory will not, however, cease to exist until the UN permits its dissolution, subject to refer-

enda. Area: 1,880 sq km (726 sq mi). Pop. (1981 est.): 135,600 (including the Northern Mariana Islands, 17,300). Seat of government: Saipan municipality (pop., 1930, 14.500).

Education. (1978–79) Primary, pupils 31,250, teachers 1,484; secondary, pupils 7,982, teachers 566; vocational (1976–77), pupils 257, teachers (1973–74) 13; higher, students 1,703, teaching staff 155.

Finance and Trade. Monetary unit: U.S. dollar. Budget (1979–80 est.): revenue $124.6 million (including U.S. grant of $112.7 million); expenditure $109.4 million. Foreign trade (1977–78): imports $39 million (35% from U.S., c. 25% from Japan, 6% from Austral a in 1976–77); exports $19 million (54% to Japan in 1972). Main exports: coconut oil 57%; fish 27%; copra 11%.

VIRGIN ISLANDS

The Virgin Islands of the United States is an organized unincorporated territory located about 60 km E of Puerto Rico. Area: 345 sq km (133 sq mi). Pop. (1981 est.): 99,400. Cap.: Charlotte Amalie, St. Thomas (pop., 1980 prelim., 11,700).

Education. (1980–81) Primary, pupils 20,890, teachers 979; secondary, pupils 12,174, teachers 627; vocational, pupils 2,500, teachers 56; higher, students 593, teaching staff 98.

Finance. Monetary unit: U.S. dollar. Budget (1980–81 est.): revenue $253 million; expenditure $216 million.

Foreign Trade. (1979) Imports $3,766,000,000; exports $3,093,000,000. Import sources (1978): Iran 46%; U.S. c. 12%; Libya 11%; Nigeria 9%; United Arab Emirates 8%; Angola 6%. Export destinations (1978): U.S. 92%. Main exports (1978): petroleum products 91%; chemicals 6%. Tourism (1980): visitors 700,000; gross receipts U.S. $356 million.

continued from page 295

many Commonwealth and other countries. For example, there were some 60 territorial disputes in Asia, Africa, and the Caribbean. More than 30 newly independent states had populations of less than 200,000. Australia and New Zealand supported the U.K. on the issue partly because of their concern over Argentina's actions within the Antarctic region generally. South Georgia, the Falklands dependency where the Argentine flag was raised on March 19—marking the beginning of the crisis—was in fact closer to other islands in the British Antarctic Territory than to the Falklands.

The Argentine forces on the islands surrendered on June 14, and the Falklands returned to U.K. control. The suggestion that a UN trusteeship be set up to administer them seemed unlikely to proceed. The specific aim of such an arrangement would be to move toward independence, a solution that was generally considered to be impractical in this case.

Though events concentrated attention on the Antarctic region during 1982, this did not mean that the Arctic region was free of problems. Greenland, granted a degree of home rule from Denmark in May 1979, indicated a desire to leave the European Communities (EC). The vote in the referendum in February was much closer than might have been expected, since the EC authorities had indicated that if the Greenlanders gave up full membership they could not necessarily expect to retain any special association with the Communities. In a 75% turnout, the decision to leave was carried by 52% for to 46% against. It was reported that Norway became increasingly anxious during

the year about Soviet encroachments in the Svalbard (Spitsbergen) Archipelago, which was regarded as a potential source of offshore oil.

The population of the Isle of Man was rocked by financial scandal when the island's biggest independent bank collapsed in June and small depositors found that they were not protected. The affair severely damaged the island's plans to develop as an international offshore banking centre.

Caribbean. During 1982 the U.K.'s only remaining associated state, St. Kitts-Nevis, began to move toward full independence. Following an announcement to this effect early in the year, a federal constitution was drawn up. The constitution gave substantial power to Nevis, and this became a major source of criticism from the opposition at a constitutional conference held in London in early December. St. Kitts-Nevis experienced many of the same problems as the other less developed countries in the eastern Caribbean. Although it produced some 35,000 metric tons of sugar during the year, the low world price for the commodity was a major factor in keeping the economy depressed.

None of the Caribbean dependencies indicated any interest in proceeding to independence during 1982. The Turks and Caicos Islands were the subject of an inquiry by a U.K. parliamentary select committee looking into the U.K.'s decision to spend some £4 million on providing infrastructure for a resort development, to be created by Club Méditerannée on the island of Provodenciales. The report was highly critical of the expenditure. By year's end it was still unclear whether or not the company would construct the holiday village, and Britain, on behalf of the Turks and Cai-

Dependent States

One (standing, left) of the 30 demonstrators who broke into the territorial assembly of New Caledonia confronts the legislators. The intruder eventually rejoined 4,000 other demonstrators outside who favoured retaining New Caledonia's status as an overseas territory of France.

cos government, was considering legal action. Problems resulting from use of the islands as a transshipment point for narcotics moving to the U.S. were largely brought under control as a result of coordinated action by local police, the U.S. Drug Enforcement Administration and Coast Guard, and The Bahamas coast guard.

In marked contrast to most of the region, the Cayman Islands remained economically buoyant. Contributing to the colony's prosperity were its use as an international offshore banking centre and the continuing growth of tourism. Montserrat's slow but steady development continued throughout the year. The island remained reasonably sound economically, relying heavily on small-scale agriculture, tourism, and income generated by an offshore medical school. The government maintained its right-of-centre position and actively sought investment from sources in the U.K. and the U.S. to finance a large-scale hotel development. Bermuda began to give renewed thought to the issue of independence, but no clear position had emerged by year's end. Premier John Swan began to develop closer links with the eastern Caribbean.

The British Virgin Islands became enmeshed in a row with the U.S. over a proposed new double-taxation treaty. Following lengthy negotiations on the renewal of an existing treaty, the U.S. government sent the document to the Senate for ratification, but it was later recalled by the U.S. Treasury Department. Attempts to renegotiate the treaty during the year failed and, as a result, relations between the U.S. and the British Virgin Islands weakened considerably. Prospecting for oil and minerals proved unsuccessful, and most of the companies involved withdrew from the islands.

Tax advantages for companies — mostly pharmaceutical and electronics firms — earning income in Puerto Rico were limited somewhat in a tax measure passed by the U.S. Congress in August. How-ever, the provision in the final bill was much less stringent than that originally passed by the Senate, and three large companies announced expansion of their Puerto Rican facilities. Puerto Rico's Gov. Carlos Romero Barceló had feared that the Senate version would increase the island's unemployment, already at 24%. In his Caribbean Basin Initiative, announced in February, U.S. Pres. Ronald Reagan promised special measures to ensure that Puerto Rico would benefit from the program.

Africa. Negotiations aimed at resolving the problem of South West Africa/Namibia's independence remained deadlocked. The UN resolution recognizing the South West Africa People's Organization (SWAPO) as the only representative of the Namibian people was reaffirmed in 1982 by the secretary-general to the Council for Namibia, a body not recognized by the U.K. government. The main problem faced by negotiators concerned the timing and nature of the withdrawal of Cuban forces from Angola. The Angolan government insisted that their presence in the country was unrelated to the Namibian issue and therefore their withdrawal, to which they were committed, should not become a precondition of Namibian independence. South Africa set up parliamentary and provincial representation for Walvis Bay during 1982 and extended civil and military port facilities in the exclave.

Indian Ocean. On Jan. 6, 1982, Yves Bonnet was nominated prefect of the island of Mayotte. A general strike took place in August. The leaders of the Mouvement Populaire Mahorais, which supported continuation of the island's status as a dependency of France rather than a return to the independent Comoros group, condemned the political nature of the action.

In March the U.K government concluded a settlement whereby £4 million in compensation was granted to the Ilois, the inhabitants of Diego Garcia who had been removed from the island in 1966 and had since settled on Mauritius. Diego Garcia, an island in the Chagos Archipelago and part of the British Indian Ocean Territory, had been cleared of its population in order to make way for a U.S. military base. The landslide victory of the Mauritius Militant Movement in June elections in Mauritius led to increased pressure on the U.K. for the return to Mauritius of Diego Garcia itself.

Pacific. Elections in French Polynesia on May 23, 1982, in which 398 candidates contested 30 seats, resulted in a change of government. The position of the autonomists had weakened since 1981 when, misreading local as well as French opinion, they abandoned their usual Socialist stance and backed Valéry Giscard d'Estaing in the French presidential election. In 1982 even the Gaullists were demanding greater autonomy than the autonomists. Following the election, the Tahoeraa Huiraatira party led by Gaullist Gaston Flosse, with 13 out of 30 seats in the Assembly, formed a majority coalition with the 3 members of the Aia Api party. France conducted nuclear bomb tests at Mururoa in March and July despite a vote in the Assembly in December 1981 calling for cessation of nuclear testing pending an investigation into radiation leaks and accidents.

In New Caledonia political polarization increased in response to the reforming policies of the French government. A number of bombing incidents in Noumea in November 1981 were followed by riots and damage to urban property by large crowds of demonstrators, spearheaded by unemployed youths. An estimated 25,000 opponents of independence subsequently marched in favour of law and order and the political status quo. In mid-December 1981 the Paris government announced that it was going to rule by decree and gave notice of administrative and land reforms, new mining policies, and new initiatives for the protection and advancement of Melanesian rights and cultures. These new policies led to an easing of pressure for decolonization from the South Pacific Forum, which met in Rotorua, New Zealand, in August 1982. The new government council, formed in June and dominated by centre-left coalitions, was invaded by anti-independence demonstrators on July 22; several members were assaulted, crowds were dispersed with tear gas, and there were serious street riots. In August the vice-president of the government council fixed 1984 as the target date for independence. Despite the alienation of European settler elements, the French government persisted with its reforming policies, although little in the way of tangible results had been achieved.

In negotiations between the U.S. government and the Trust Territory of the Pacific Islands, little progress was made toward solving the constitutional impasse or terminating the UN trusteeship agreement, despite a flurry of constitution-making and compact negotiations. Following the review of the situation by President Reagan's administration, it seemed that the draft compact, signed by the U.S. with three of the four island groups—the Federated States of Micronesia, the Republic of Palau (Belau), and the Marshall Islands—in the last days of the Carter administration, had survived almost intact. When negotiations on the subsidiary agreements were resumed in February, however, a new hard line on the period during which the U.S. could exercise strategic denial over the islands was evident.

During the year the components of the Federated States of Micronesia continued to design their constitutions. They also defined the permissible limits of territorial fragmentation when the people of Faichuk, one region of the Truk Islands, were refused permission to become a separate entity. Palau was the only trust territory to have reached final agreement with the U.S. Under a 50-year compact of free association, the U.S. guaranteed inflation-protected payments which, at the current level, would amount to about $1 billion. Talks between the U.S. and the Marshall Islands were disrupted several times over such issues as compensation for islanders whose lands and lives had been affected by radiation, the military use of Kwajalein Atoll, and the determination among the Marshall Islanders to have independence listed as an option in the plebiscite that was to test feeling on the agreed compact of free association. A UN Trusteeship Council mission visited the Trust Territory in 1982.

Guam, an unincorporated territory of the U.S., rejected statehood in two referenda in 1982 and opted for commonwealth status.

The Cook Islands, a self-governing territory of New Zealand, changed its constitution in 1982, separating the functions of queen's commissioner and New Zealand commissioner. The former position was filled by Sir Gaven Donne, who as chief justice had set a precedent when, in 1978, he dismissed Albert Henry from the office of premier for electoral malpractice. The 1982–85 development plan was to be based on aid funds from New Zealand (about NZ$4.6 million), an Asian Development Bank loan of NZ$1.5 million, and a local contribution of NZ$4.8 million. New Zealand also continued to provide a significant portion of the recurrent budget. Having been blocked by international trade barriers for decades, the Cook Islands finally managed to initiate significant exports to French Polynesia. Even so, exports, earning NZ$5 million, were swamped by imports, which cost NZ$23 million. There were fears that Air New Zealand's withdrawal of DC-10 aircraft in favour of Boeing 737s would affect the NZ$6 million tourist industry, but these apprehensions were partly alleviated by new Air Nauru flights that linked the Cook Islands to American Samoa, Western Samoa, Kiribati, and Nauru.

East Asia. In the wake of the South Atlantic crisis, there was renewed discussion about the future of various states in East Asia, sovereignty over which was disputed by China. In July the Beijing (Peking) government issued a statement to the effect that it foresaw Hong Kong, Macão, and Taiwan all being ruled eventually as "special administrative zones" of China. In response the Hong Kong stock-exchange index fell dramatically, prompting the Chinese to make assurances that measures would be taken to protect the areas's prosperity. In 1981 exports to Hong Kong supplied China with an estimated 40% of its foreign-exchange earnings; thus it was clear that any settlement of the colony's future would have to weigh economic with political objectives.

U.K. Prime Minister Margaret Thatcher visited both China and Hong Kong in September. While in Hong Kong, she insisted that the treaties by which the U.K. governed the colony were valid in international law and that the U.K. would negotiate with China over the future of Hong Kong's New Territories. The 99-year lease on the New Territories, forming the bulk of Hong Kong's land mass, was due to expire in 1997.

(PHILIPPE DECRAENE; DAVID A. JESSOP; BARRIE MACDONALD; MOLLY MORTIMER)

See also African Affairs; Commonwealth of Nations; United Nations.

Djibouti

Dominica

Dominican Republic

Djibouti

An independent republic in northeastern Africa, Djibouti is bordered by Ethiopia, Somalia, and the Gulf of Aden. Area: 23,200 sq km (8,900 sq mi). Pop. (1981 est., excluding refugees): 323,000, including (1978 est.) Cushitic Afar 38%, Somali Issa 28%, Issachar and Gad 20%, European 9%, Arab 5%. Capital: Djibouti (pop., 1980 est., 200,000). Language: Arabic and French (official); Saho-Afar and Somali are spoken in their respective communities. Religion (1980 est.): Muslim 90.6%; Christian 8.7%; other 0.7%. President in 1982, Hassan Gouled Aptidon; premier, Barkat Gourad Hamadou.

On Jan. 5, 1982, former premier Ahmed Dini and six members of his Djibouti People's Party (PPD), formed the previous year in opposition to Pres. Hassan Gouled Aptidon's regime, were released from detention. Six other PPD members had been released shortly after the declaration of a one-party state in October 1981.

Djibouti's first legislative elections since independence from France in 1977 were held on May 21, 1982. Over 90% of the votes were cast for the ruling People's Group for Progress (RPP). Some 7,000 voters abstained—the only way of registering opposition to the RPP. Of the 65 candidates elected, 43 had been members of the previous National Assembly. Premier Barkat Gourad Hamadou, after resigning on May 25 in accordance with the constitution, resumed office on June 1. In October he and Foreign Minister Moumin Bahdon Farah represented Djibouti at the Franco-African summit in Kinshasa, Zaire.

In February a French military aircraft carrying

Disasters:
see page 56

Disciples of Christ:
see Religion

Diseases:
see Health and Disease

Divorce:
see Demography

DJIBOUTI
   Education. (1980–81) Primary, pupils 16,841, teachers 375; secondary, pupils 3,812, teachers 174; vocational, pupils 1,279, teachers 88; teacher training, students 65, teachers 11; higher, students 150.
   Finance. Monetary unit: Djibouti franc, with (Sept. 20,1982) a par value of DjFr 177.72 to U.S. $1 (free rate of DjFr 305 = £1 sterling). Budget (1981 est.) balanced at DjFr 15,730,000,000.
   Foreign Trade. (1979) Imports DjFr 31,477,000,000; exports DjFr 2,023,000,000. Import sources: France 47%; U.K. 8%; Japan 8%; Belgium-Luxembourg 5%. Export destination: France 87%. Main export (most trade is transit; 1977): cattle c. 7%.

31 paratroopers and a crew of 5 crashed in mountains west of Lake Assal; all on board were killed.

(PHILIPPE DECRAENE)

Dominica

A republic within the Commonwealth, Dominica, an island of the Lesser Antilles in the Caribbean Sea, lies between Guadeloupe to the north and Martinique to the south. Area: 772 sq km (300 sq mi). Pop. (1982 est.): 81,000. Cap.: Roseau (pop., 1981 est., 20,000). Language: English (official), French patois. Religion: Roman Catholic. President in 1982, Aurelius Marie; prime minister, Eugenia Charles.

A number of those arrested during the two attempted coups of 1981 were brought to trial in 1982. Among those accused was the former prime minister Patrick John, but in a court judgment, which the government decided to appeal, he and three others were acquitted. Also, in September, Alexander J. McQuirter, former "grand wizard" of the Canadian Ku Klux Klan, was sentenced in Ontario to two years in prison for plotting with others to break the laws of another country, namely Dominica. An aftermath of the coup attempts was that Dominica's complex opposition political scene again became confused, with the leaders of three parties that had split from the Dominica Labour Party again joining together.

Despite these traumas Dominica began to show the first real signs of growth. After it forcefully presented a case for financial assistance to the U.S. government, substantial funding was made available for a number of capital projects, including much-needed road reconstruction. During the year Prime Minister Eugenia Charles was able to announce the creation of some 3,500 additional jobs; 28 new light industries were attracted by the Industrial Development Corporation. Most surprising, considering the political upheavals and previous natural disasters, was a 70% increase in tourism during the first eight months of the year.

(DAVID A. JESSOP)

DOMINICA
   Education. (1978–79) Primary, pupils 15,220, teachers 423; secondary, pupils 9,814, teachers 299; vocational, pupils 400, teachers 21; teacher training, students 49, teachers 6; higher, students 154, teachers 8.
   Finance and Trade. Monetary unit: East Caribbean dollar, with (Sept. 20, 1982) a par value of ECar$2.70 to U.S. $1 (free rate of ECar$4.63 = £1 sterling). Budget (1981–82 est.): revenue ECar$58,354,000; expenditure ECar$63,660,-000. Foreign trade (1980): imports ECar$128.7 million; exports ECar$26.3 million. Import sources (1978): U.K. 27%; U.S. 15%; St. Lucia 7%; Trinidad and Tobago 7%; Canada 5%. Export destinations (1978): U.K. 67%; Barbados 5%. Main exports (1978): bananas 58%; soap 12%; coconut oil 5%; grapefruit 5%.

Dominican Republic

Covering the eastern two-thirds of the Caribbean island of Hispaniola, the Dominican Republic is separated from Haiti, which occupies the western third, by a rugged mountain range. Area: 48,442

Jacobo Majluta Azar (centre) was sworn in as president of the Dominican Republic to finish out the remaining six weeks of the term of Pres. Antonio Guzmán Fernández, who died of a gunshot wound in July. Majluta was succeeded a few weeks later by Salvador Jorge Blanco.

sq km (18,704 sq mi). Pop. (1982 est.): 5,812,900, including mulatto 75%; white 15%; black 10%. Cap. and largest city: Santo Domingo (pop., 1981, 1,313,200). Language: Spanish. Religion: mainly Roman Catholic (98%), with Protestant and Jewish minorities. Presidents in 1982, Antonio Guzmán Fernández until July 4, Jacobo Majluta Azar until August 16, and, from August 16, Salvador Jorge Blanco.

Presidential and congressional elections held on May 16, 1982, showed a shift to the left with 56-year-old lawyer Salvador Jorge Blanco, a moderate leftist within the ruling Partido Revolucionario Dominicano (PRD), being elected president with

DOMINICAN REPUBLIC

Education. (1976–77) Primary, pupils 867,592, teachers (1975–76) 17,932; secondary and vocational, pupils 178,249, teachers (1975–76) 6,702; teacher training (1975–76), students 1,353, teachers c. 49; higher (universities only), students (1978–79) 42,412, teaching staff (1975–76) 1,435.

Finance. Monetary unit: peso, at parity with the U.S. dollar, with a free rate (Sept. 20, 1982) of 1.71 pesos to £1 sterling. Gold and other reserves [June 1982] U.S. $86 million. Budget (1981 est.) balanced at 1,233,000,000 pesos. Gross national product (1980) 6,438,800,000 pesos. Money supply (May 1982) 668.6 million pesos. Cost of living (Santo Domingo; 1975 = 100; March 1982) 183.2.

Foreign Trade. (1981) Imports 1,667,700,000 pesos; exports 1,188,000,000 pesos. Import sources (1980): U.S. 45%; Venezuela 21%; Japan 8%. Export destinations (1980): U.S. 46%; Switzerland 27%; Venezuela 9%; The Netherlands 5%. Main exports: sugar 45%; gold and alloys 17%; ferronickel 9%; coffee 6%; tobacco 6%.

Transport and Communications. Roads (1980) 17,659 km. Motor vehicles in use (1980): passenger 115,300; commercial 77,221. Railways (1980) 588 km. Telephones (Jan. 1980) 155,400. Radio receivers (Dec. 1979) 215,000. Television receivers (Dec. 1979) 300,000.

Agriculture. Production (in 000; metric tons; 1981): rice c. 400; sweet potatoes c. 85; cassava c. 180; sugar, raw value c. 1,032; dry beans c. 42; tomatoes c. 170; peanuts c. 36; oranges c. 72; avocados c. 134; mangoes c. 180; bananas c. 320; plantains c. 625; cocoa c. 35; coffee c. 51; tobacco c. 45. Livestock (in 000; June 1981): cattle c. 2,155; sheep c. 55; goats c. 385; horses c. 204; chickens c. 8,300.

Industry. Production (in 000; metric tons; 1980): cement 1,014; bauxite (1981) 405; nickel ore 16; gold (troy oz) 397; silver (troy oz) 1,623; petroleum products (1979) c. 1,200; electricity (kw-hr) 3,420,000.

48% of the votes cast. Former president Joaquín Balaguer of the Partido Reformista received 35% of the votes. The PRD achieved a majority in both houses of Congress for the first time.

On taking office, President Jorge Blanco stated that he would seek closer links with the U.S. and would hesitate over establishing ties with Cuba. The period leading up to the transfer of power was marred by the suicide of Pres. Antonio Guzmán Fernández (*see* OBITUARIES). Vice-Pres. Jacobo Majluta Azar completed the last six weeks of President Guzmán's term of office.

The country faced an economic crisis in 1982, with the main export crop, sugar, selling at less than half the cost of production, 28% unemployment, and a budget deficit of more than $450 million. President Jorge Blanco announced an austerity program that included a wage freeze, price controls, higher taxes, and an import ban on such farm products as poultry, pork, rice, and beans.   (SARAH CAMERON)

Earth Sciences

GEOLOGY AND GEOCHEMISTRY

The theory of plate tectonics, which revolutionized the earth sciences beginning in the late 1960s, was undergoing its own revolutionary developments 15 years later. The theory gave earth scientists a framework for interpreting geology, geochemistry, and the dynamics of the Earth on a global scale. In 1982 ideas about mountain building were changing as a result of applications of geophysical methods to structural geology. Ideas about the geochemical evolution of continents, viewed as one aspect of the chemical differentiation of the Earth, were being modified by the broader considerations of planetary processes developed during the study of rocks from the Moon.

The Wilson cycle of continental rifting and ocean opening and closing, associated with continental collision, has grown in importance as conti-

Drama:
see Motion Pictures; Theatre

Dress:
see Fashion and Dress

Earthquakes:
see Earth Sciences

nental geology and the geology of mountain-building belts, or orogens, have been fitted into the concept of plate tectonics. The world's mountain systems have been classified into three types, controlled by the mechanisms of (1) continental collision, (2) subduction of oceanic lithospheric plates beneath continental lithosphere, or (3) subduction of oceanic plates beneath oceanic lithosphere. Collision orogens are represented by the Alpine and Himalayan chains, continental-margin orogens by the Andes, and arc-trench orogens by the Aleutian Islands. The historical perspective gained through application of geological investigations to the simple plate tectonic models has revealed complexities and variations through time due to shifting plate patterns. The tectonic evolution of large cordilleran chains is particularly complex.

It recently was reported that more than 70% of the North American Cordillera, the parallel mountain chains that spread from the Rockies to the Pacific coast, is made up of allochthonous terranes, which are large or small geological provinces quite distinct from neighbouring provinces in terms of stratigraphy, structure, metamorphic and magmatic histories, fossilized life, and mineral deposits. These terranes are separated from each other by major faults. The allochthonous terranes have also been called suspect terranes, because their place of origin remains unknown, or accreted terranes, because they have been accreted to continental margins. Paleomagnetic studies of rocks from suspect terranes of the North American Cordillera demonstrated that the terranes have rotated independently and migrated northward along the edge of the continent.

The importance of suspect terranes and accretion recently was recognized for the evolution of the Appalachian orogen. The simple Wilson cycle, with its Andean-type mountain-building mechanism, was found inadequate to account for the observed geology. In 1982 it was anticipated that more detailed geological study of the Andes would reveal suspect terranes as well. The procedure of identifying suspect terranes has led to the formulation of completely new types of tectono-stratigraphic maps. The concept, termed collage tectonics, was bringing new vision to tectonic investigations and to interpretation of the origin of the mineral resources in cordilleras.

Only a few of the suspect terranes of the North American Cordillera are composed of continental rocks; most of them have oceanic character. Modern analogues of many suspect terranes may be represented by the topographic ridges, or plateaus rising above the deep ocean floor, which make up about 10% of the ocean basins. These elevated regions, which may have crustal thicknesses two to five times as great as normal oceanic crust, are fated to collide with continents. Their accretion may be responsible for mountain building comparable to that caused by collision of continents.

Study of the magnetic properties of rocks was contributing significantly to the concepts of collage tectonics and accreted terranes. Another geophysical technique contributing to the revolutionary developments involves seismic reflection profiling of the continental basement, as conducted since the mid-1970s by Cocorp (Consortium for Continental Reflection Profiling). The results demonstrated that thin-skinned thrusting of older rocks onto younger sedimentary rocks of continental margins has occurred on very large scales during mountain building. It appears that thin-skinned thrusting may relate many aspects of continental geology to plate tectonic theory. These conclusions were based on Cocorp studies in eastern North America before collage tectonics was applied to interpretations of the Appalachians. In 1982 seismic reflection profiling was just beginning to be applied to western North America, where the importance of collage tectonics had already been established. Many investigators believed that the earth sciences were about to reach a new level of understanding of the tectonics of the continental crust and the evolution of mountain chains.

The chemical differentiation of the Earth was being deciphered at two levels. Geochemists measuring isotopes and trace elements were developing a new field of chemical geodynamics, evaluating chemical reservoirs of global extent and the rates of transfer of elements from one reservoir to another. Petrologists were studying details of the processes of magma generation, especially in association with the beginning and end of the Wilson cycle: the origin of basalts at divergent plate boundaries and the origin of andesites, basalts, and rhyolites associated with subduction at convergent plate boundaries. Since the early 1960s the

Radar images taken from the space shuttle "Columbia" revealed that the Sahara Desert once was crisscrossed with a lacy network of major waterways. The picture at right shows normal visual imaging; the one at far right shows the same area beneath its layer of sand as revealed by synthetic-aperture radar imaging.

R. TAYLOR—SYGMA

Accumulating dust and ash created both physical obstructions and health hazards in towns and villages surrounding El Chichón volcano.

dominant model has involved the generation of basaltic magma by partial melting of peridotite composing the Earth's mantle and the generation of andesite in a second stage of chemical differentiation by partial fusion of subducted oceanic crust and overlying mantle peridotite, fluxed by aqueous solutions expelled by dehydration of the subducted oceanic crust.

During the decade after plate tectonics was proclaimed (1968–78), geochemists were persuaded that many basalts were little-modified samples derived by various percentages of partial melting of mantle peridotite. The geochemistry of these supposedly primitive basalts therefore was used to survey the major- and trace-element chemistry of the upper-mantle peridotite. Thereafter, however, much evidence from rocks and phase-equilibrium studies indicated that the magma derived from peridotite is not basalt but normally picritic (richer in magnesium oxide, MgO, than basalt) and that basalts have evolved through partial crystallization at shallow levels. The basaltic lavas at mid-ocean ridges erupted from magma chambers within which batches of primitive and evolved lava were mixed.

The study of lunar rocks and their interpretation led to the concept of a magma ocean during the Moon's early existence, a massive layer of molten silicates from which the rocks of the interior and the crust were precipitated. This concept recently was applied to the Earth, with the formulation of models for chemical differentiation differing significantly from the traditional model outlined above. In particular, the solidification of an early magma ocean was thought to have produced a deep layer of eclogite (a dense, high-pressure rock equivalent chemically to basalt or picrite) within mantle peridotite. The hypothesis was evolving, but one important feature was that melting of the eclogite produces the basalts of mid-ocean ridges.

Another recent model for the early Earth involves a subterranean magma ocean composed of komatiite (silicate melt with more MgO and higher temperature than basalt and picrite). The high density of this melt allowed the storage of a global melt layer beneath a buoyant cap of dunite more than 100 km (60 mi) thick. Eruption of komatiite from the melt layer was the Earth's principal means of dissipating excess heat.

While new ideas developed and flourished in geology and geochemistry, old equipment was wearing out. Geochemical and other scientific instruments in universities were deteriorating and becoming obsolete. The urgent need to revitalize the instrumentation base on which future scientific and technological advances would depend was a serious problem in the U.S., one that spawned workshops and survey committees but no solutions to the funding problem.

(PETER JOHN WYLLIE)
[214.B.1.c; 214.B.1.e.ii; 214.D.4; 231.F; 241.A; 241.E–G]

GEOPHYSICS

Seismically 1982 was comparatively quiet, experiencing no great earthquakes (Richter magnitude 8.0 or greater). Among several shocks that reached magnitude 7.0 or greater, the largest occurred on June 19 in El Salvador. At magnitude 7.4 it caused 16 deaths and many injuries. Extensive damage due to seismic vibration and landslides left thousands homeless in El Salvador and southeastern Guatemala. The shock was also felt in Costa Rica, Honduras, and Nicaragua. On December 13 a series of shocks of magnitude 5.4–6.0 struck North Yemen near Dhamar, killing nearly 3,000 and leaving hundreds of thousands of villagers homeless. Two shocks of special interest occurred on January 9 in New Brunswick. Although they were not damaging, they had magnitudes of 5.7 and 5.4 and were the largest in the region since 1855.

Volcanic activity was less destructive than usual. In the state of Washington, Mt. St. Helens, which continued to be studied intensively, exhibited moderate and varied activity until March 19, when it produced the most significant eruption in 17 months. A cloud of tephra (solid particles) rose to an altitude of more than 13.5 km (one kilometre equals 0.62 miles), and a directed blast caused an avalanche down the north slope into Spirit Lake and a mud flow down the North Fork of the Toutle River, where it did minor damage. The volcano remained rather active during succeeding months.

A phenomenon that evoked considerable interest among meteorologists and geophysicists was a stratospheric aerosol cloud first detected by lidar (laser radar) at Fukuoka, Japan, on January 23. On January 28 it was detected at Mauna Loa, Hawaii, and four days later it was reported at Garmisch-Partenkirchen, West Germany. On February 13 a lidar-equipped plane flew from Wallops Island, Va., 3,000 km to Costa Rica, encountering an unbroken cloud along the entire path at altitudes of 16.5 to 19.5 km. Subsequent analysis of cloud samples showed that it contained none of the debris expected from either a nuclear explosion or a meteorite; instead it had a high sulfuric acid content indicative of a volcanic origin. After considering several previous eruptions experts decided that the eruptions of Mt. Nyamulagira in Zaire in late December 1981 were the probable source. Some uncertainty remained because the cloud was detected as far north as West Germany, whereas the volcano is at latitude 1° S.

While these investigations were in progress, El Chichón in Mexico became active for the first time in modern history. Eruptions began on March 26 and continued through mid-May. A particularly violent blast on March 29 killed as many as 100 persons living in nearby villages. On April 4 an explosive eruption produced a cloud that by May 1 had circled the Earth. The cloud reached an altitude of more than 32 km in late June with the densest portions detected at 28 km altitude. On the slopes of El Chichón pyroclastic deposits trapped subsequent rains and formed several lakes. One of these natural dams failed on May 27, releasing the waters of a lake 5 km in length into a nearby river and inundating a hydroelectric plant 35 km downstream.

After a series of four earthquakes ranging in magnitude from 5.5 to 6.1 occurred in Long Valley Caldera in California during May 1980, the U.S. Geological Survey (USGS) began monitoring the area very closely. An earthquake hazard watch was issued in May 1980 and remained in effect at the end of 1982. By May 1982, when seismic activity decreased, 22 earthquake swarms had been recorded in a limited area about 3.5 km from the town of Mammoth Lakes, Calif. The first occurred at a depth of nine kilometres, but as time went on

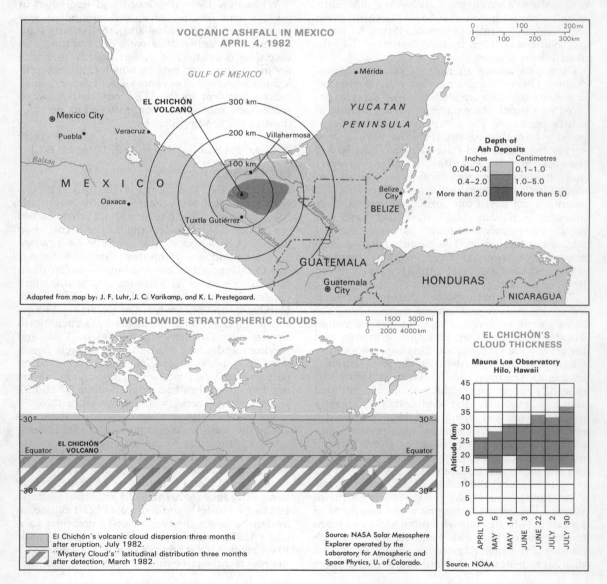

the swarms became progressively shallower until the final hypocentres were only three kilometres deep. In addition to the seismic activity the central dome in the caldera deformed progressively. Because of this combined continuing activity, the USGS issued a volcano notice. A notice is much less definite than a watch and, in this instance, indicated that a volcanic eruption was a possibility but was not nearly as likely as a moderate-size earthquake. The Long Valley Caldera was formed by the Bishop eruption more than 700,000 years ago. That catastrophic event deposited 580 cu km (140 cu mi) of volcanic ash over western North America, more than 500 times the amount produced from Mt. St. Helens. The current deformation of the dome and the upward migration of hypocentres were believed to result from a tongue of lava pushing up from a magma chamber situated eight kilometres below the surface.

Deep-sea drilling by the research ship "Glomar Challenger" continued with improved results due to better techniques for coring and down-hole logging. These included use of a variable-length piston corer, which produced a 90% improvement in obtaining soft cores, and a pressure barrel, which brought back unaltered cores at in situ pressures as high as 3,800 kg/sq cm (54,000 psi). A new heat-flow package was used that allowed temperature measurement every 9.5 m (31 ft) of penetration. The program was concentrating on the study of three environments: active margins, passive margins, and oceanic crusts. Previous analysis had shown the need for corroborative information from some of the earlier drilling sites and that previously competing phases of the exploration—multiple shallow penetrations, single deep-hole penetrations, and down-hole measurements—should be combined more effectively as elements of an integrated experiment. Legs 78 through 84 were reported on during the year. Drilling was performed, sequentially, at the Barbados Ridge, the Mid-Atlantic Ridge, the Mazagan Plateau off Morocco, the Goban Spur in the Bay of Biscay, the Azores Triple Junction, and the Middle America Trench off Guatemala.

Leg 78B marked the first effort to apply the integrated approach mentioned above. A hole drilled five years previously on the Atlantic Ridge was reoccupied. A complete set of geophysical tests was carried out, including packer tests, temperature measurements, water sampling, and standard down-hole logging. In addition to the usual equipment, a bore-hole television system and a Soviet-designed down-hole magnetometer were used. This combination of techniques produced an exceptionally clear picture of the crust.

A long-standing goal of the deep-sea drilling program, deep penetration of the basement, was achieved on Leg 83. A hole drilled during Legs 69 and 70 in the eastern Pacific about 200 km south of the Costa Rica Rift was reoccupied, and a depth of 1,350 m (4,430 ft) below the seafloor was reached. This was the deepest hole ever drilled into the ocean crust. It penetrated 1,075.5 m (3,529 ft) into sub-basement, also a record.

(RUTLAGE J. BRAZEE)

[212.D.4; 213.B; 231.D]

Crew members of a fishing boat struggle to secure it to a dock on the island of Kauai against the force of Hurricane Iwa. The storm, Hawaii's first hurricane in 23 years, blasted Kauai, Niihau, and Oahu in late November with winds clocked at 110 miles per hour.

HYDROLOGY

In contrast to the prolonged droughts and water shortages of 1981, streamflow was at or above the normal range in most of the U.S. during 1982. The combined flow of that nation's "big five" rivers—the Mississippi, St. Lawrence, Ohio, Columbia, and Missouri—was 12% above normal in 1982. Several regions including the Pacific and Gulf coasts, the Midwest, and southern New England experienced severe flooding. More than 150 lives were lost, and monetary damages were in the billions of dollars. The Federal Emergency Management Agency reported that 80% of presidential disaster declarations were related to floods. In the Maumee River basin in Indiana and Ohio, severe flooding occurred during March, and many streams were at or close to the highest discharge of record. As a result 9,000 residents of Fort Wayne, Ind., had to evacuate their homes. Torrential rains in June and July caused flooding on several streams in Connecticut, Iowa, Illinois, Indiana, and Pennsylvania. In early December a week of rainstorms flooded extensive regions of Illinois, Missouri, Arkansas, and other states from the Great Lakes to the Gulf of Mexico, forcing tens of thousands from their homes.

Spirit Lake, a large body of water on the northeast flank of Mt. St. Helens, has presented a potential for catastrophic flooding along the Toutle and Cowlitz rivers since the eruption of the volcano on May 18, 1980. During the summer of 1982 the lake reached a dangerous level because of damming by volcanic debris. On August 19 Pres. Ronald Reagan issued a Declaration of Emergency and ordered remedial action by federal agencies. As a result geologic and hydrologic data were being collected and analyzed to determine the best method to stabilize the debris dam and to prevent additional rises of water levels. The U.S. Army Corps of Engineers was pumping water from the lake to ease pressure on the natural dam.

Acid precipitation, thought to be responsible for deterioration of lakes, crops, and buildings since about 1950 in the northeastern U.S. and the Maritime Provinces of Canada, was the subject of much discussion in the news media in 1982. Many federal and state agencies in the U.S. conducted coordinated, nationwide programs to monitor the chemical composition of streams and lakes that were or could be affected by acid rain or snow. An interagency task force on acid precipitation, consisting of 12 federal agencies, received $18 million in funding in 1982, which would increase to $22 million in 1983. Research also was conducted by state and federal agencies on natural and man-made sources of acidic substances in precipitation. The studies were intended to provide the scientific basis for a national policy on the control of damage due to acid rain. The U.S. Geological Survey reported that the acidity of lakes and rivers in New York State changed little since the late 1960s.

The mining or withdrawal of groundwater in the High Plains area in excess of what was returned received attention during the year. The High Plains Aquifer underlies 451,000 sq km (174,000 sq mi) extending from Texas to South Dakota. The region has abundant sunshine and moderate precipitation (400–460 mm, or 16–18 in, annually). These advantages along with a plentiful supply of groundwater to support irrigation have permitted development of the region into one of the major agricultural areas of the U.S. The increase in groundwater withdrawal since 1949, however, has resulted in extensive declines in water level in the High Plains Aquifer. Since irrigation began, water levels declined more than 3 m (10 ft) in 130,000 sq km (50,000 sq mi) of the aquifer and more than 15 m (50 ft) in 31,000 sq km (12,000 sq mi) of the aquifer. Water-level declines of as much as 61 m (200 ft) have been measured in Texas, where most of the depletion in the aquifer has occurred.

The aquifer underlying Cape Cod, Mass., was

In April and May scientists making deep dives to the Pacific Ocean floor studied giant clams known to flourish in fissures warmed by volcanic hot springs. The water temperature in these fissures was found to be somewhat colder than first assumed, about 4°–10° C (40°–50° F), due to cooling from a subterranean influx of frigid seawater.

designated by the U.S. Environmental Protection Agency (EPA) as a sole-source aquifer. This designation requires that all federally funded projects be evaluated to determine their possible effect on the aquifer. The Cape Cod aquifer supplies drinking water to more than 100 municipal wells and 15,000 private wells. The EPA indicated that localized contamination from chemical spills, leaking fuel tanks, waste-water treatment systems, and individual disposal systems had occurred in the past. (JOHN E. MOORE)

[222.A.2.b; 222.D.4; 232.C.1.d.i; 355.D.5.d.iii]

METEOROLOGY

During 1982 weather events together with world-wide research programs, resulting scientific papers, and the daily efforts of weather bureaus in more than 100 countries reemphasized the complex interrelationships of geology, hydrology, meteorology, and oceanography. The explosive eruptions of El Chichón, Mexico, beginning in late March blew tons of volcanic dust high into the stratosphere, where the normal atmospheric circulation carried it around the globe and slowly northward until it was detected by scientific observatories over practically the entire Northern Hemisphere. It permitted the kind of natural laboratory experiment eagerly sought by atmospheric scientists and astronomers for studying the causes of climatic change and other mysteries of the globe.

The ashy eruption of El Chichón recalled the "year without a summer" of 1816, which was well documented in history and generally was thought to be the result of volcanic dust high aloft that blocked the Sun's rays and thus reduced summer heating of the Earth's surface. There were some predictions in 1982 of a similar effect: below normal temperatures caused by the suspended dust from El Chichón. This forecast, seen in light of an independent long-range prediction of a much colder than normal winter for 1982–83 in the eastern U.S., epitomized the state of the art in long-range weather forecasting. The latter prediction was made by a distinguished specialist on the basis of years of studies of variations and cycles in solar radiation, sunspots, and related phenomena. Nevertheless, as the public knew well, weather forecasting in 1982 was very much an inexact science.

New questions about weather and climate and the significance of man-made changes to them were studied with renewed urgency in 1982. Of particular interest were acid rain, effluents that could increase carbon dioxide (CO_2) in the atmosphere or reduce the protective stratospheric ozone layer, and deliberate cloud-seeding activities. A few authorities in U.S.S.R. and allied countries reported progress in these fields, but in North America reports were mixed with most investigators finding conflicting evidence. Acid rain, once thought to be caused almost exclusively by oxides of sulfur and nitrogen from factory smokestacks, was suspected to come from other sources as well, some of which remained uncertain. Recent measurements of CO_2 and ozone in the atmosphere, although inconclusive, were not as alarming as those done during the 1970s, yet many scientists felt that shifts in the present atmospheric levels of these gases eventually would have negative consequences for life unless solutions to involuntary alterations were found.

Cloud seeding to increase rainfall or to inhibit growth of destructive hailstorms had been heralded widely between 1950 and 1975 as a promising remedy for droughts and other agricultural and water-supply problems, but although these supplements to natural processes were still widely practiced during 1982 with claims of success, truly scientific verifications were less and less positive. An especially pessimistic evaluation gave less than a 5% success rate to attempts at rainmaking since the late 1940s.

Ocean temperatures greatly affect Earth's climate and weather, notably the formation and intensity of hurricanes, typhoons, and tropical cyclones. During 1982 several typhoons struck Japan and eastern Asia causing floods, mud slides, and other heavy damage with loss of life. In late November Hurricane Iwa battered the northern Hawaiian Islands, killing several people and destroying millions of dollars worth of homes and businesses. By contrast, the Caribbean and Gulf of Mexico experienced fewer hurricanes than usual, none very destructive. The reasons included changes in atmospheric wind circulation, ocean temperatures, and possibly other, still unknown causes. Although there was no adequate annual census of storminess worldwide, news reports gave an impression that fewer destructive storms than usual occurred on the whole during 1982.

(F. W. REICHELDERFER)
[212.D.4; 224.A.3.e; 224.B.3.b; 224.C.3; 224 D.2.c.iii]

OCEANOGRAPHY

In more than a century of measuring temperature and salinity in the oceans, oceanographers had never detected any changes of either property in the deep waters of the ocean. Then in recent months it was discovered that water in the North Atlantic many thousands of metres below the surface had cooled by about 0.1° C (0.18° F) and freshened by about 0.02 g of salt per kilogram of seawater between 1972 (when a survey of water properties was made as part of the Geochemical Ocean Sections program) and 1981 (when participants in the Transient Tracers in the Ocean program returned to some of the 1972 stations). These changes occurred in a region of the Atlantic occupied at great depths by water that was once at the surface in the Norwegian and Greenland seas; subsequently this water sank below the surface there and flowed southward into the Atlantic along the Mid-Atlantic Ridge. Examination of still earlier data showed no evidence for similar changes in the decade or so prior to 1972 for which data exist in this region.

The importance of these observations is that they provided the first direct evidence of how much the heat stored in the deep oceans may vary with time, a critical question in understanding global climate fluctuations. It is possible that these changes occurred in response to changes in atmospheric behaviour over the Norwegian and Greenland seas. If this could be demonstrated, these observations would reveal a great deal about the way in which the deep circulation of the ocean is driven.

Success in applying an entirely new observational technique, called acoustic tomography, for mapping ocean currents over many hundreds or even thousands of kilometres was reported in 1982. In preparation for such a study a number of buoys containing acoustic (sound-generating) transmitters and receivers are placed around the perimeter of the region within which currents are to be mapped. As the study progresses, the travel time of sound from each buoy to every other buoy is measured repeatedly with high accuracy. Since the travel time of sound from one buoy to another depends on the velocity of water between the buoys as well as on the sound speed of the intervening water, all of the travel times measured at any instant may be combined to produce maps of water velocity and sound speed in the region enclosed by the buoys.

Sound speed in seawater depends on the temperature and salinity of the water. Because these are closely correlated with the flow, the sound speed map itself furnishes a great deal of flow information. Sound traveling from one buoy to another does so along a number of paths, all centred on a region of minimum sound speed usually about a kilometre or so (about 0.62 mi) beneath the surface but departing vertically from this region by varying amounts. As a result, different paths give information about the flow at different depths throughout the measurement region. Resolution of detail depends on the number of buoys available. With about a dozen buoys, flow features with a size on the order of 100 km may be resolved in a study region many hundreds of kilometres on a side.

Although acoustic tomography was demonstrated by resolving such flow features in a region in the Atlantic, its greatest potential appeared to lie in monitoring flow variations over very large regions such as an entire ocean current gyre. As of 1982 no other technique was able to average small features out of a measurement of the large-scale flow without the need for a prohibitive number of instruments in the water. Since large-scale changes in ocean flow are accompanied by similarly large-scale changes in ocean heat transport and storage, monitoring them is of great importance for climate studies.

In recent years a number of seafloor vents emitting water at temperatures of more than 100° C (212° F) had been discovered along the East Pacific Rise, a mid-ocean ridge running from near Antarctica toward the Pacific coast of Mexico. In 1982 clear evidence of similar vents in an entirely different tectonic setting was found in the form of high methane concentrations in the deep water of the Mariana Trough in the western Pacific (not to be confused with the much deeper Mariana Trench to the east). Such vents are important because they are major sources of metals both in seawater and in ores.

(MYRL C. HENDERSHOTT)
[222.B.3; 223.C; 224.D.1.d; 231.G; 234.D.1.b]

See also Disasters; Energy; Life Sciences; Mining and Quarrying; Space Exploration; Speleology.

Eastern European Literature:
see Literature

Eastern Non-Chalcedonian Churches:
see Religion

Eastern Orthodox Churches:
see Religion

Ecology:
see Environment; Life Sciences

Economy, World

In terms of economic growth 1982 could best be characterized as a year of unfulfilled hopes and disappointment, a year in which the modest improvement seen in 1981 gave way to stagnation and possibly a small decline. During 1981 member countries of the Organization for Economic Cooperation and Development (OECD) recorded a growth of 1.3% and, although the year closed on a fairly sluggish note, it was widely hoped that a similar growth rate would be achieved in the following year. As it happened, however, most governments misread the signs and underestimated the deflationary impact of their policies, with the result that at the year's end there was expected to be no growth or even a decline of about 0.5%.

In the United States Pres. Ronald Reagan's monetarist policy slowed growth dramatically and, despite a modest relaxation halfway through the year, gross national product (GNP) seemed set for a decline of 2%, compared with a rise of a similar magnitude in 1981. In West Germany the authorities eased monetary policy somewhat, but this was not enough to maintain growth, and the economy probably experienced a small decline in output compared with confident early predictions of at least a 1% gain. In Japan the authorities did not seem to know what to do and therefore did not do much, with the result that GNP growth was well below expectations and just about matched the previous year's achievement. Canada's 1981

Table I. Real Gross Domestic Products of Selected OECD Countries
% change, seasonally adjusted at annual rates

Country	Average 1970–80	Change from previous year		
		1980	1981	1982*
United States	3.0	−0.2	2.0	−1.5†
Japan	4.8	4.2	2.9	2.0†
West Germany	2.8	1.8	−0.3	1.0†
France	3.6	1.3	0.3	1.5†
United Kingdom	1.9	−1.8	−2.2	1.2†
Canada	4.0	1.2	3.0	−1.5†
Italy	3.1	0.1	−0.2	1.5†
Total major countries	3.3	1.2	1.2	0.2†
Australia	3.1	2.7	5.0	3.0
Austria	3.7	3.6	0.1	1.5
Belgium	3.2	1.4	−0.6	0.5
Denmark	2.3	−1.0	−0.2	2.2
Finland	3.5	5.3	0.9	1.0
Greece	4.7	0.6	−0.5	1.2
Ireland	4.1	1.0	1.6	1.5
Netherlands, The	2.8	0.8	−1.3	0
New Zealand	2.3	2.7	3.9	0.2
Norway	4.6	3.7	0.8	0.2
Spain	3.8	1.7	0.3	2.2
Sweden	1.9	1.4	−0.9	0.5
Switzerland	1.2	3.2	1.9	−0.5
Total OECD countries	3.3	1.3	1.2	0.5

*Estimate. †GNP.
Sources: Adapted from OECD, *Economic Outlook,* July 1982; National Institute of Economic Review; EIU estimates.

growth turned into a large decline, and most other small countries experienced a deterioration in their relative performance. In fact, the only large countries that did better than in the preceding year were France, Italy, and the United Kingdom. In the case of France the demand-boosting policy of the Socialist government lifted growth from about 0.5% to 1.5% but led to an acceleration in the rate of inflation and acute external instability and had to be revised dramatically in midstream. In the U.K., however, a modest relaxation in fiscal and monetary policy turned a 1.9% fall in gross domestic product (GDP) into a rise of 0.5% without any adverse effect on the trend of prices.

One major casualty of the dismal world economic performance during 1982 was employment. The year started with a total of 26 million people out of work, but by the time 1983 was approaching the total was nearing 31 million, accounting for some 8.5% of the available labour force. Unemployment increased everywhere, but the actual rates varied greatly from country to country. As in 1981 the dubious honour of having the highest unemployment belonged to the U.K. (approximately 13%), followed by Canada (12%) and the U.S., which in October 1982 had an unemployment rate of 10.2%. As in previous years Japan remained the land of full employment by world standards with only about 2.5% of the labour force without a job. Another telling sign of the recession was the trend of industrial production. During 1982 every major OECD country except Japan produced less than in 1981, with the shortfall ranging from around 10% in Canada and 8% in the U.S. to less than 1% in the U.K. Overall, the OECD area probably experienced a fall of about 3.5%, the first time since the 1974–75 oil crisis that industrial output recorded an actual decline.

Another consequence, as well as a cause, of the weakness of the world economy was the sluggishness of world trade. Its underlying volume was largely flat during the first half of the year, and the figures available for the third quarter did not sug-

CHART 1

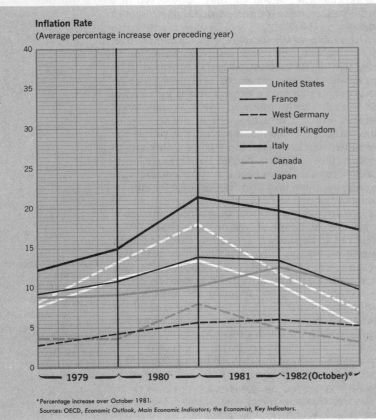

Inflation Rate
(Average percentage increase over preceding year)

Legend:
United States
France
West Germany
United Kingdom
Italy
Canada
Japan

1979 — 1980 — 1981 — 1982 (October)*

*Percentage increase over October 1981.
Sources: OECD, *Economic Outlook, Main Economic Indicators; the Economist, Key Indicators.*

gest any upturn. In early December, therefore, it seemed likely that the result for the full year might have been a volume fall of 1%, compared with a decline of 0.5% in 1981. The year's poor performance was the result of a number of factors. The recession in the developed countries restricted their appetite both for manufactured products and for raw materials. This not only undermined their ability to export to each other but — by adversely affecting the foreign exchange earnings of countries exporting raw materials — had a serious effect on their exports outside the OECD area. This applied to both oil and non-oil producers, whose problems were further aggravated by the weakness of fuel and raw material prices. In fact, the terms of trade (the relationship between import and export prices) moved heavily against those countries partly because of weak demand for their products and partly because of the relative strength of the U.S. dollar. (This meant that they received fewer dollars per unit of export but had to pay more per unit of imports than previously.)

Not unexpectedly, the adverse trade trends played havoc with the external payments position of a number of countries. Overall, the OECD economies were on the winning side largely because of the movement in the terms of trade in their favour; whereas in 1981 those countries incurred a collective current account deficit of $30 billion, the latest available information for 1982 pointed to a surplus of approximately $10 billion. Most OECD countries shared in this improvement, the only major exception being the U.K.; there, partly because of the weakness of oil prices and an acceleration in imports resulting from higher consumer spending, a significant movement in the opposite direction took place. However, oil-exporting countries (a definition that does not include the U.K.) experienced a large reduction in their current surplus from just over £100,000 million to some £60,000 million. The less developed countries without oil saw an already poor situation becoming worse; in 1981 they had incurred a collective deficit of about £80,000 million, but by the time the figures were published for 1982 the total was expected to be nearer the £100,000 million mark.

The one major favourable aspect of the world economy was a further decline in the rate of inflation. In 1981 consumer prices in the OECD countries had risen by an average of 9%, but for 1982 the figure was estimated to be 8% or less. An easing of inflationary pressures was seen in virtually every country; in the U.S. and the U.K. double-digit inflation in 1981 (10.4 and 11.9%) was cut down to single figures (6.5 and 8.5%), while in the case of Italy the reduction was from +19.5 to +16.5%. Even France, which pursued a basically expansionary policy for a substantial part of the year, was believed to have reduced the rise in the retail price index from 13% to about 12%, although this was mainly the result of the four-month wage and price freeze imposed in June 1982. As in previous years Japan managed not only the highest growth in GNP but the lowest rate of inflation as well; the index of retail prices rose by about 3.5–4%, about one-third less than in 1981 and less than half of the OECD average.

In November a broker in Paris posts a record high exchange rate of 7.3040 francs to the U.S. dollar.

As a result of the growing fear of joblessness and the inability of employers to grant large wage increases in order to buy industrial peace, the rise of wages and, therefore, that of unit labour costs slowed down considerably. For example, in the U.S. during the first quarter of 1982 there was a relatively large increase in wages in the manufacturing sector, but the subsequent two quarters exhibited a virtual standstill with the result that the growth for the full year was approximately 7%, as against 9% in 1981. Similarly, in the U.K., where a firm stance by government and industry forced a more realistic approach to wage bargaining by the trade unions, the annual rise in earnings was estimated to have fallen from 14% to below 10%. In Japan the increase appeared to have been largely unchanged at 6%, but in France — where the Socialist government made several early concessions to organized labour — there was a rapid upward trend during the first two quarters. Nevertheless, because of the more realistic economic policy forced on the government halfway through the year, the second half was expected to show less of an increase.

As already mentioned, another significant factor contributing to the fall in the rate of inflation was the weakness of world commodity prices. This was largely the result of excess supply over demand from the recession-hit economies. In the case of crude oil there was persistent oversupply, as the producing countries, themselves in growing need of foreign exchange, could not agree on sufficiently large production cutbacks and as energy conservation measures made further inroads into consumption in many countries. As a result, average oil prices of the Organization of Petroleum Exporting Countries (OPEC) were estimated to have fallen by 3–4% in 1982, as against a rise of 10% in 1981. Poor demand took an even greater toll on the price of non-oil mineral products (−15%), and in the case of primary food products the position was further aggravated by relatively good crops in most producing areas.

Considerable instability in foreign exchange markets was evident during the year. However, one consistent feature was the sustained strength of the U.S. dollar despite the marked fall in U.S. interest rates. During the first ten months of 1982 the effective exchange rate of the dollar was about 12% higher than the average for the previous year, and as 1982 was coming to a close there were no signs of a weakening in the underlying trend. The pound sterling remained relatively stable for the first three quarters, but in November it fell sharply against the dollar, largely as a result of a fall in British interest rates and growing overseas fears that the relative recovery in the nation's private consumption would lead to a significant deterioration in its balance of payments position. France did poorly on the foreign exchange front; its attempt to spend its way out of the recession undermined foreign confidence, and in June 1982 it was forced to devalue the franc against the (West German) Deutsche Mark by 10%. This brought the value of the franc to a figure 18.5% lower than in October 1981. Similarly, against all expectations Japan was confronted with a rapid weakening in the dollar value of the yen up to November; during that period it fell from 220 to 275 per $1, largely because of the wide differential in interest rates between the two nations.

As indicated earlier, 1982 began on the basis of generally restrictive fiscal and monetary policies in most countries except France. This was partly the result of the existence of very large budget deficits, which made it difficult for governments to provide heavy additional fiscal stimulus (in the U.S. and Japan budgeted spending had to be cut back in order to limit the rise in the deficits), and

Table II. Percentage Changes in Consumer Prices in Selected OECD Countries

Country	Average 1961–70	Average 1971–78*	1979	1980	1981	Latest month* 1982
United States	2.8	6.7	11.3	13.5	10.4	4.9
Japan	5.8	9.8	3.6	8.0	4.9	3.2
West Germany	2.7	5.2	4.1	5.5	5.9	4.9
France	4.0	9.0	10.8	13.6	13.4	10.1
United Kingdom	4.1	13.2	13.4	18.0	11.9	7.5
Canada	2.7	7.6	9.1	21.2	12.5	10.4
Italy	3.9	13.0	14.8	10.1	19.5	17.2
Australia	2.5	10.6	9.1	9.9	9.7	12.3
Austria	3.6	6.6	3.7	6.4	6.8	4.9
Belgium	3.0	7.8	4.5	6.6	7.6	9.4
Denmark	5.9	9.6	9.6	12.3	11.7	9.8
Finland	5.0	11.6	7.5	11.6	12.0	8.1
Greece	11.9	28.7	44.1	57.5	51.6	49.2
Iceland	11.9	28.7	13.3	18.2	20.4	17.0
Ireland	4.8	13.2	13.3	18.2	20.4	17.0
Luxembourg	2.6	6.9	4.5	6.3	8.1	17.2
Netherlands, The	4.1	7.8	4.2	6.5	6.7	5.4
New Zealand	3.8	11.8	13.8	17.1	15.4	16.6
Norway	4.5	8.5	4.8	10.9	13.6	10.8
Portugal	3.9	18.2	23.6	16.6	20.0	21.1
Spain	6.0	15.2	15.7	15.5	14.6	14.6
Sweden	4.0	8.7	7.2	13.7	12.1	8.3
Switzerland	3.3	5.3	3.6	4.0	6.5	5.5
Turkey	5.9	24.1	63.5	94.3	37.6	24.4
Total OECD countries	3.4	8.5	9.9	12.9	10.4	7.4

*Twelve-month rate of change (not directly comparable with annual changes). Sources: OECD, *Economic Outlook*, July 1982; OECD, *Main Economic Indicators*; The Economist, *Key Indicators*.

also of a belief that a modest recovery was on the way. It later became clear, however, that the hoped-for recovery could not be counted on. In response most governments relaxed the reins a bit but not enough to prevent a further fall in output. Thus, in the U.S. the discount rate was maintained by the Federal Reserve Board (Fed) at 12% between February and July, but by the end of the year it had been reduced to 8.5%. In the U.K. the banks' base rate started off at 14% but fell later in the year before rising modestly in November; at year's end it stood at 10%. The U.K. also introduced a mildly reflationary budget, made possible by progress in reaching its borrowing targets.

In Japan interest rates were thought to be already too low by international standards and were therefore kept steady, although there were two rather halfhearted attempts to stimulate the economy by larger expenditures on public works and housing. In France the trend was toward higher interest rates as the government sought to support the besieged currency, the position of which was undermined by the nation's policy of spending its way out of the recession.

Another important feature of the year was the heavy strain on the world's banking system. This was the result of the difficult financial position of a number of large debtor countries that were not able to meet their obligations. Poland, which had run up very large debts in the West, fell victim to a disastrous economic policy and the government's inability to come to terms with the national movement in support of independent trade unions. Argentina, which was facing difficulties partly because of the burden of and the lack of confidence created by its ill-fated invasion of the Falkland Islands, was also seeking a rescheduling of its considerable debts. Mexico was in a similar position, and for a time there were widespread fears that a major failure could lead to a chain reaction that would bring about a collapse of several large financial institutions and have a serious effect on the

CHART 2

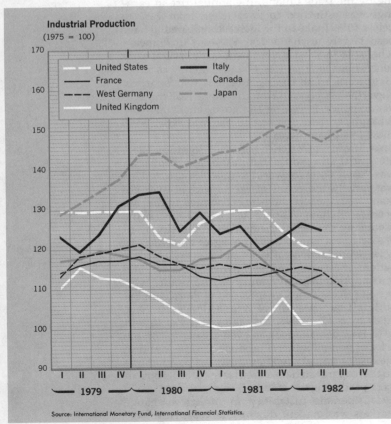

Industrial Production
(1975 = 100)

Legend: United States, France, West Germany, United Kingdom, Italy, Canada, Japan

1979 — 1980 — 1981 — 1982

Source: International Monetary Fund, *International Financial Statistics*.

Table III. Total Employment in Selected Countries
1975=100

Country	1979	1980	1981	1982 First quarter	Second quarter	Third quarter
Australia	104	107	109	109	109	108
Canada	112	115	118	112	115	117
France	96	99	93	92	92	93
West Germany	101	102	101	99	99	98
Italy	103	105	105	104	105	106
Japan	105	106	107	105	109	109
Sweden	103	104	104	102	104	105
United Kingdom	101	99	94	91	91	91
United States	114	115	117	114	116	117

Source: OECD, *Main Economic Indicators.*

world banking system. For the present, however, this danger appeared to have passed, although there was little doubt that serious problems would persist as long as the world recession continued. (*See* Feature Article: *"You Can't Foreclose a Country."*)

NATIONAL ECONOMIC POLICIES

Developed Market Economies. UNITED STATES. The first full year for President Reagan's new economic policies was 1982. Although the celebrated medium-term economic program—the major policy goals of which were a reduction in the inflation rate and faster economic growth—was launched in the spring of 1981, and some of the personal tax cuts became effective that autumn, it did not have much time to influence the economy in that year. The economic results for 1982, however, did not cheer the proponents of the new strategy, for the recession that was much in evidence during the last half of 1981 deepened and lengthened. As a result the GNP was estimated to have declined by nearly 2%, compared with a moderate growth of 2% during the previous year, indicating a downswing almost as sharp as the one in the 1974–75 recession. Industrial production fell by around 8%, canceling the 3% increase registered the year before, and stood at the lowest level in almost seven years. Unemployment rose rapidly, from an average of 7.6% in 1981 to almost 11% by the end of the year. Interest rates followed a fluctuating but generally downward trend. The prime rate started the year at 15.75%, then rose to 16.5% in February and stood at that level until July. The decline to 11.5% after that was highly encouraging. In real terms, however, interest rates remained high, exerting a downward pressure on economic activity.

On the plus side the achievement in reducing the inflation rate was better than expected. The average rate, which stood at more than 10% in 1981, was cut back to 5% on a 12-month basis by November. The dollar remained very firm against other major currencies throughout the year, reflecting the high interest rates and much to the detriment of exports.

As the year opened, the economy was firmly in a downswing, and a decline of 5.1% in the GNP during the first quarter confirmed the severity of the recession. There were tentative signs, however, that the severe destocking which had caused the sharp drop in GNP was at an end, and if the rise in consumer sales could be sustained, the economy

would stabilize and enter into a recovery phase in the second half. Although it had a number of unsatisfactory features, the overall GNP rise of 1.3% during the second quarter encouraged the view that the long climb out of the recession had started in earnest. However, the third quarter's figures were highly disappointing, as they showed that the economy had slowed down significantly. The closing quarter was widely expected to remain flat, dashing the hopes of a sustained recovery in 1982. Apart from the disappointing low overall growth rate in the third quarter, a close analysis of the figures underlined the fragile structure of the recovery since the summer. Most of the improvement in the GNP came from stock movements. Final sales of goods and services actually fell in both the second and the third quarters.

Given the weak final demand, it was not surprising that the industrial production index provided gloomier reading than the overall indicators of economic activity. A cumulative decline of 8.6% as of October masked a much sharper fall in certain sectors, such as business equipment and materials. Surprisingly enough, sales of consumer goods held up reasonably well during the recession and were down by only 2.7%. Capacity utilization rates tumbled generally to around 70%; worst hit sectors, such as steel and automobiles, were operating at 60% capacity or less.

Unemployment moved relentlessly upward in step with the slump in industrial production and the severe squeeze in corporate profitability. From a level of about 9% at the beginning of the year, it rose steadily through the spring and summer, almost equaling the peak of 9.9% last experienced in 1941. At that level 10.8 million persons were out of a job. By October the unemployment rate reached a new post-depression high of 10.4%, or 11.2 million unemployed. Because employment generally tends to lag behind economic recovery, it was expected to inch up in spite of the slight improvement in business conditions during the closing months of the year.

The major success story of the year was the fight against inflation, which was the overriding objective of the economic policymakers. Under the impact of the deepening recession and the flexible stance of the Fed, which allowed interest rates to decline, the inflation rate was effectively halved from the 1981 average of 10.4%. Declining oil prices and depressed raw material prices contributed to the good news, enabling 1982 to be the best year for price stability since 1976, when the consumer price index rose by 4.8% on average. The continuing strength of the dollar also eased the inflationary pressures but at a heavy toll on the trade account. The visible trade deficit in the first ten months was a staggering $35 billion and was heading toward the 1978 record deficit of $42 billion. One worrisome aspect was its suddenness. Nearly $17 billion of the cumulative deficit to October was incurred in the preceding few months, and with an economic recovery forecast for 1983 this would lead to an even higher deficit the following year.

The Fed's policy of monetary restraint was "too successful" in 1981 and went beyond suppressing inflationary pressures. It severely curtailed economic activity by constraining demand because of the high interest rates. Thus in the closing months of 1981 the expansion in monetary aggregates (M1 and M2) was well within the target ranges, prompting the Fed to state that it would permit faster than average growth rates in the final quarter. Similarly, at the beginning of 1982 it adopted a slightly expansionist stance in that while the targets for 1982 set in the previous July were reaffirmed, it was made known that an outcome near the upper end of the range would be more appropriate. The aim of this revision was to enable money supply in 1982 to expand much faster than in 1981 while not straying from the long-range limits. This flexibility was the guiding principle of the Fed throughout 1982.

During the period up to the end of June the money aggregates slightly exceeded the target ranges. M1 (currency plus checkable deposits) rose by 5.6%, as against a 2.5–5.5% target range, while M2 (interest-bearing deposit and savings accounts) rose 9.7%, against a 6–9% target. Since inflation was declining rapidly, the demand for credit weak, and the economy stuck in the doldrums, the Fed agreed to allow money supply to expand faster and exceed the target ranges. Accordingly, the federal discount rate, which remained at 12% throughout February–July, was reduced to 10% in August. The Federal Funds Rate also tumbled, to 10% from 14.5% in the spring. The prime rate, a

more direct indicator of demand/supply relationship for borrowing, dropped by 3 points to 13.5% between July and mid-August.

The fall in interest rates gathered speed in the autumn as it became clear that the Fed was not proposing to offset any excess in money supply in the short term. Indeed, in October it announced a radical change in its short-term monetary policy. The monetary target for M1, which had been the centrepiece of monetary policy since 1979, was to be ignored. Instead, M2, the broader measure of money supply, became the main monetary indicator. Predictably, interest rates continued to fall during November as the Fed demonstrated increased flexibility in interpreting the money supply figures and in its response. At the end of November the discount rate stood at 9%, the Federal Funds Rate at 9.25%, and the prime rate at 11.5%. The flexible stance of the monetary policy, aimed at encouraging economic growth while not abandoning the fight against inflation, pleased the financial markets and touched off a boom in Wall Street and in the other leading stock exchanges throughout the world. (*See* STOCK EXCHANGES.)

The tax cuts provided by the Economic Recovery Act passed in August 1981 and the resulting budget deficits ensured that the stance of fiscal policy would be moderately expansionist. The budget for fiscal year 1982 (beginning October 1981), after all the amendments and revisions, postulated a deficit in the region of $55 billion–$58 billion. As the year unfolded, however, it became clear that the deepening recession was reducing the projected revenues and increasing social payments, causing the deficit to widen. Revised projections available in February, when the fiscal 1983 budget proposals were sent to Congress, estimated a deficit of $101 billion for fiscal 1982. While the tax cuts in July 1983 and the scheduled 7.4% increase in Social Security pensions were seen as positive measures aimed at pulling the economy out of the recession, the size of the proposed deficit in fiscal 1983 and in subsequent years gave rise to concern. It was feared that this level of deficit was too high in relation to the supply of savings coming into the market. Large sums that the Treasury would have to borrow would crowd out the market during a period when the private sector would be borrowing for expansion, leading to higher interest rates.

Not surprisingly, the fiscal 1983 budget, which initially projected a deficit of $91 billion, ran into a storm of opposition in Congress. Revisions of the estimates by bodies outside the government or in the Congressional Budget Office—and subsequently by the Office of Management and Budget itself—indicated that the original deficit would turn out to be too low by at least $80 billion. Therefore, urgent action was required to cut the deficit. The Congressional Budget Measure passed in early June provided for spending cuts (compared with fiscal 1982) of about $275 billion and tax increases of about $95 billion over the fiscal years 1983–85. But the tax provisions were submitted in outline only, and a detailed tax bill was required to put them into effect. In an election year the members of Congress appeared to be reluctant to vote for specific tax measures. Republicans in particular did

CHART 3

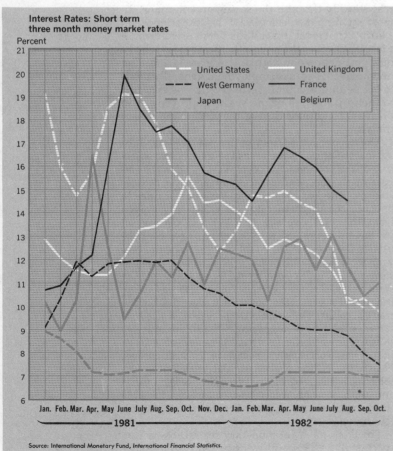

not want to appear to be reneging on the original tax cutting pledges of 1980.

Eventually, after intense lobbying, President Reagan won the day, and in mid-August the bill was passed. The net result was a revised budget deficit for fiscal 1983 more or less as indicated in February. Although greater constraints were placed on fiscal 1984 and 1985, the fact that the July 1983 tax cuts were unaffected was regarded as a victory by the administration.

In conclusion, almost halfway into its term the inherent conflicts within the Reagan administration's economic policies moved away from a collision course. A subsiding inflation rate coupled with sluggish economic recovery had a healing effect. The rigid monetary stance gave way to a more flexible approach and, on the other hand, budget deficits of the order of $100 billion appeared less menacing. The U.S. economy thus ended 1982 with fairly high hopes of a return of non-inflationary and well-balanced economic recovery during the coming year.

JAPAN. During 1982 the Japanese economy laboured under the twin handicaps of the world recession and an irresolute, and at times divided, government. As in other countries, sluggish world conditions and increasing protectionism had an adverse effect on exports and damaged business confidence. At the same time the government, facing a large increase in the budget deficit and a fall in the overseas value of the currency, failed to support domestic demand adequately despite a virtual lack of inflationary pressures. The result was a rather uneven, and uncertain, economic performance, yielding a GNP growth of about 3% for 1982, as against the original official projection of 5.2%. Nevertheless, the expected growth rate of 3% represented no deterioration from the 2.9% chalked up in the previous year, and—as was usually the case—it was likely to be one of the best growth rates among those achieved by the large OECD countries. Furthermore, inflation remained under control with the consumer price index rising by only some 4%, as against a gain of 4.9% in 1981. Although unemployment rose, both the rate of increase (from 2.2% in late 1981 to 2.5% in September 1982) and its absolute level were modest by international standards. Contrary to expectations, however, the overseas value of the yen fell markedly for most of the year, although by November there were signs of a change in trend. There also was an increase in the country's current account surplus; this, despite further moves toward liberalizing Japan's import policy, led to renewed foreign criticism of Japanese trading practices.

During the closing quarter of 1981 there was a marked deceleration in economic growth, with GNP registering a gain of only some 2% over the same period of the previous year. This was not only well below the advance achieved in the third quarter but also represented an actual quarter-to-quarter decline of 0.9%, the first such decline since 1975. It was not surprising, therefore, that 1982 opened on a sluggish note and that most observers regarded the authorities' forecast of a 5.2% growth for the year as unattainable. Nevertheless, the government, arguing that interest rates were already too low by international standards and that a strong fiscal stimulus would be inconsistent with a cut in the budget deficit, did not respond to demands for reflation. In fact, in early March the Diet passed an austere budget that provided for only a modest growth in spending and allowed for no increase at all in public-works-related expenditure. However, in response to growing criticism and the poor figures for the final quarter of 1981, the government announced a halfhearted package of stimulatory measures later in the month; the most important of these concerned the bringing forward of public expenditure projects into the first half of the 1982–83 fiscal year and an extension of the scheme for low-interest public loans for housing construction.

National accounts for the first quarter of 1982 suggested a GNP gain of 2.2%. Although the quarter-to-quarter comparison suggested that growth had been resumed, the results were still far below the government's by-now revised growth forecast of 4.3%. The principal reason for the improvement was a modest increase in the volume of exports in comparison with a poor performance in the previous quarter, as well as a strengthening of private consumption. Another important development in the early months of the year was the slide in the dollar value of the yen. Although the yen gained strength in terms of the dollar during the last few months of 1981 and was widely expected to continue doing so in 1982, by the end of the first quarter it was down to 245, compared with 220 at the end of the previous year. As this was partly attributed to the wide differential between domestic and overseas interest rates, it provided the government with yet another argument against those pressing for a cut in the Bank of Japan's discount rate in order to stimulate economic activity.

The second quarter's figures placed yet another question mark over the government's "do nothing" policy. Although the quarter-to-quarter growth speeded up considerably, on a year-to-year comparison GNP recorded a gain of only 2.3%. Furthermore, as this was largely the result of the

Japanese goods piled up on the docks awaiting shipment overseas. Japan's huge balance of trade surplus was causing concern in many other countries.

bringing forward of public expenditure and a strengthening of private consumption in the wake of the 7% wage award received as part of the usual spring wage offensive, there were widespread fears that the recovery, such as it was, would prove to be temporary. The yen/dollar exchange rate continued to weaken and, as a result of lower than expected tax revenues, the budget deficit grew rapidly. In an attempt to deal with the situation the authorities took the highly unusual step of freezing the recommended pay increase for public employees in September and prepared a supplementary budget providing for a reduction in government spending and greater reliance on bond financing. However, as the economy continued to falter (industrial output fell in August after two consecutive increases), the government was forced to revise its growth forecast for the year to 3.4% and take some reflationary measures. These were unveiled in early October and were worth a total of $7.7 billion; as usual the most important elements were additional appropriations for public works and some measures to boost residential construction. All in all, it was estimated that the net effect of the package would be to increase GNP by 0.6%.

In spite of the recession-induced slowdown in export growth, Japan's current account surplus achieved a higher level during the first ten months of 1982 than in the corresponding period of the previous year. This, together with the country's remaining import restrictions and large exports of certain "sensitive" items such as cars and electronic products, led to renewed overseas criticism—especially by the U.S. and Europe—of its foreign trade policies. The government had announced the removal of 67 of the 99 identified non-tariff trade barriers in January. This was followed by further relaxations and the announcement of a plan to

bring forward some tariff reductions originally scheduled for 1987 to April 1983.

UNITED KINGDOM. During 1982 the British government pursued a somewhat less restrictive fiscal and monetary policy than in previous years. Partly as a result output stopped falling, but the much awaited—and often promised—recovery failed to materialize. Thus, as the year was drawing to a close, the principal economic indicators were suggesting no net gain in GDP, largely static industrial performance, and a further significant rise in unemployment. By the middle of October a total of 3.3 million people were out of work, representing 13.8% of the labour force, compared with 12.3% in December 1981. On the credit side of the balance sheet, however, there was a further decline in inflation, with the rise in the index of retail prices falling back from 12% in December 1981 to 6.3% in November 1982. There was a further moderation in the size of wage settlements, accompanied by a growing reluctance to take strike action. Productivity recorded another modest improvement, but relative export competitiveness appeared to have declined, and export performance was weaker than in the previous year. This resulted in a deterioration in the external payments position, although the current account of the balance of payments remained in surplus.

The year started off on a relatively sombre note as a result of rather poor industrial production figures that suggested continuing weakness rather than the hoped-for recovery. One effect of this was to strengthen pressure, from all sides of industry and commerce, on the authorities to provide some stimulus for the economy. Partly for this reason, and in sharp contrast to the situation during the previous two years, the spring budget was modestly reflationary and provided a £1,300 million injection into the economy in the form of a reduction in personal taxation, a cut in the national insurance surcharge paid by employers, and higher social security benefits partially offset by an increase in excise duties. At the same time the chancellor of the Exchequer announced a less rigid application of monetary targets and a more relaxed approach to monetary policy.

All in all, therefore, the March budget was regarded as a turning point in the previous strategy of regarding a moderation in inflation as the principal objective of economic policy. Together with falling interest rates, this engendered a degree of confidence in the short-term future, with most commentators forecasting a growth of 1–2% in GDP for the year. Optimism, however, gave way to renewed concern after the publication of the second quarter's figures, which showed that, although GDP was somewhat above the level of the corresponding period of 1981, there was no noticeable increase in output between the first and second quarters.

Consumers' expenditure remained relatively weak, and the volume of fixed investment fell back sharply. Government consumption also recorded a decline. Exports, however, increased modestly, although there was growing evidence that, despite a weakening in the sterling exchange rate during the second quarter, sluggish economic conditions

Mexicans, hit hard by their devalued currency and by rising prices, flocked into government pawn shops trying to raise money.

WIDE WORLD

abroad were making foreign orders increasingly difficult to obtain. For a time economic considerations were overshadowed by the Falklands war and the victory over Argentina, but by July the short-term outlook was widely seen to have taken a turn for the worse.

The government was in no position to provide any further stimulus to the economy without endangering its fiscal and monetary targets (the Falklands campaign had already caused a small, unexpected, increase in expenditure). However, taking advantage of the worldwide trend of interest rates, the government encouraged domestic rates to fall in an attempt to reduce industry's costs and encourage investment. This resulted in a marked reduction in interest rates; whereas in June 1982 the base rate was at 12.5% (having fallen from 14% in January), by September it was down to 10.5%, its lowest level in at least four years. Nevertheless, some commentators argued that in real terms (after taking the decline in inflation into account) rates were still too high and acted as a hindrance rather than as a stimulus to growth. In spite of the rapid decline in nominal interest rates, the overseas value of sterling increased during the third quarter. This, together with depressed conditions overseas, had an adverse effect on the volume of exports. Furthermore, although the trend of retail sales—assisted by the abolition of controls on installment buying (hire purchase) in July and a reduction in the mortgage rate—suggested a small recovery in private consumption, a substantial part of this appeared to have been channeled into imports rather than home production. As a result industrial production failed to grow during the third quarter, and manufacturing output was actually below its level in the same period of the previous year.

Nevertheless, the government continued to put its faith into the measures brought in as part of the March budget and a further decline in interest rates. However, during the final quarter of the year falling interest rates caused a sudden collapse in the sterling exchange rate. This, although good for exporters already facing depressed conditions and increasing competition abroad, was regarded as a threat to the objective of achieving a further fall in inflation. Accordingly, the government inspired a rise of 1% in the base rate, which by then had fallen to 9%, and expectations of a further decline gave way to fears of another early increase.

As the year drew to a close, personal consumption appeared to be the most buoyant area of the economy. Investment activities seemed to be depressed, and the underlying trend of exports was weak. Consequently, despite a marked deceleration in the rate of inflation and a decline in interest rates, industrial activity was sluggish and confidence was weakening.

WEST GERMANY. The year was one of major economic disappointments for West Germany. Confident predictions of a significant and sustained export-led upturn failed to materialize. This was all the more disappointing because an export boom came and went without triggering an economic recovery at home. The year drew to a close with both foreign and domestic demand weak and un-

employment at record levels and still rising. Based on the performance of the first three quarters, the GNP would at best show no growth at all. Another small decline was more probable.

Although 1981 had been a bad year for the economy, with the GNP registering a small decline for the first time since World War II, it had closed on a number of hopeful signs. New industrial orders were up by nearly 3%, led by an 18% rise in foreign demand. The strength of external demand fueled the hopes that it would improve the current account, enabling the Deutsche Mark to recover and, in turn, allowing a less restrictive monetary policy.

The strong external demand, however, did not last long. By the first quarter of 1982 it was still 5.7% above the same period of 1981, but by the second quarter it was down by 6.4%. The decline gathered speed in the second half of the year. Industrial production mirrored the trend of orders quite closely. During the first ten months it was down by nearly 2%, accompanied by a larger decline of 4% in retail sales, leading to considerable involuntary stockbuilding. One of the few sectors to show any sign of buoyancy was the automobile industry, which registered a 16% increase during

CHART 4

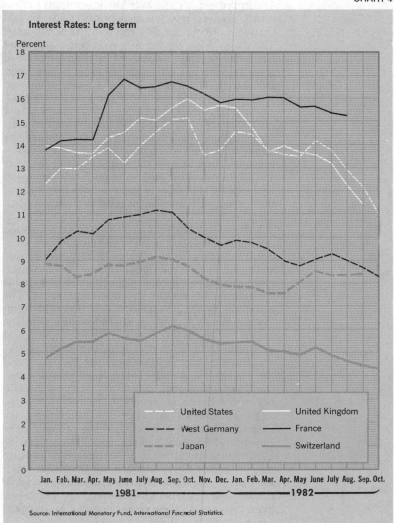

Interest Rates: Long term

Legend: United States, United Kingdom, West Germany, France, Japan, Switzerland

1981 — 1982

Source: International Monetary Fund, International Financial Statistics.

the first half with the promise of more to come later in the year. By contrast, the steel industry was in deep trouble and sought government aid with restructuring and new investment. Bankruptcies rose to new peaks. Hardest hit were construction companies, reflecting the desperate plight of the construction sector.

As in other countries, growing unemployment was the most unsatisfactory feature of the economy. A modest improvement in the spring soon evaporated, and a steady deterioration set in, taking the numbers out of a job to 1,920,000 in October, the highest level in the history of West Germany. This yielded an unemployment rate of 7.9%, compared with 5.9% a year earlier. Although in comparison with other OECD countries the employment situation was relatively good, an increase of over half a million in the number of unemployed during the past 12 months placed West Germany in the lead for the fastest rate of increase in Europe.

Notable success was achieved in the fight against inflation and in correcting the current account imbalance. Inflation stubbornly remained at about 6% throughout 1981, but then it embarked on a gentle downward curve in 1982 and by the end of the year was expected to fall to about 4%. The improvement was aided by low import prices, which allowed raw material prices to rise by less than 2% during the first ten months of the year. Thanks to wage agreements well below the inflation rate, no doubt influenced by the rising tide of unemployment, unit wage costs rose by less than 2% during the first half of the year, compared with 4.8% in 1981 and 7.7% the year before that. The current account balance, which went into a deficit between 1979 and 1981 after years of massive surplus, was once again moving toward the familiar territory of surplus. In spite of a weakening in exports during the second half of the year and higher interest payments on funds borrowed to finance the deficits of the previous three years, the current account was expected to show a modest surplus.

Monetary policy followed the gradual relaxation introduced in October 1981. The moderating inflation rate, improving external trade position, and strengthening of the dollar against other currencies were judged by the authorities to be suitable conditions for easing the monetary reins. The Bundesbank let it be known that it would be allowing money supply to expand in line with the upper end of the 4–7% target range. Although at this time the Lombard rate, which stood at 9%, was 3 percentage points below the 1981 peak and there was a comparable fall in other interest rates, the Bundesbank responded cautiously to the failure of the hoped-for economic recovery. In June, less than nine months after the realignment, the Deutsche Mark was once again revalued in the European Monetary System, to 4.25% against the Central rate and 5.75% against the French franc. In August and again in October and December interest rates were reduced further, and additional liquidity was injected into the system. However, even then real interest rates remained high, exerting a downward pressure on the economy.

Fiscal policy, on the other hand, once again turned out to be slightly more expansionist than intended. Higher-than-expected unemployment and the sluggish rate of economic activity caused public expenditure to rise and reduced the tax yield, thereby widening the budget deficit. The aim of the authorities during 1982 was to reduce the budget deficit to about DM 27 billion (2% of GNP), compared with nearly DM 40 billion in 1981. In June a supplementary budget was presented providing for an additional DM 5 billion expenditure (mainly unemployment pay) and DM 2.1 billion lower tax receipts. The budget deficit was thus revised to more than DM 34 billion. This meant a spending rise of 5.5% in nominal terms rather than the original 3.2%. This was just a technical adjustment, however, and the commitments of the authorities to ride out the recession without a major fiscal package remained intact. The objective remained a steady reduction in the budget deficit so as to free the capital markets from the burdens placed upon them by the financing requirements of the earlier fiscal excesses. The outline of the 1983 budget accepted in the summer provided for an expenditure increase of only 1.8% and aimed to cut the deficit to DM 28.5 billion.

FRANCE. The government's bold attempt to spend its way out of the recession and move on to an economic utopia of full employment, higher living standards, and a 35-hour workweek came badly unstuck—at least in the short term—during 1982. Thus the expansionist Socialist program was replaced by a comparatively restrictive policy aimed at curbing inflation, protecting the franc, and improving the competitiveness of exports. Other policy emphases included restraining wage increases, encouraging industrial investment, and reducing welfare payments.

The government's initial strategy was to break out of the economic stagnation by engineering a consumption-led growth that would be sustained by a rise in exports and new investment. The result, however, was very different. The recovery in economic activity experienced in the second half of 1981 was short-lived, and the GNP fell by 0.2% in the opening quarter of 1982. This was followed by a modest upturn, giving a 1% growth in the second quarter. Throughout the summer and the autumn the economy was sluggish, leading to a downward revision of the full-year growth rate to 1.5% from 2.5%. Although this rate compared well with the 0.5% of 1981 and with the growth rate of OECD as a whole, it was accompanied by large budget and external current account deficits, depreciation of the franc, depletion of external reserves, and an upsurge in inflation.

The overall weakness of the economy was reflected by industrial production, which continued its downward trend during the first half of the year before leveling out in the summer. At this level, however, it was 11% below the mid-1979 peak. Consumer goods appeared to have fared better, reflecting the higher household incomes that had resulted from the expansionary budgets. Business investment, however, took a battering and was expected to be significantly down from 1981.

In spite of the expansionary policies followed

until mid-1982, unemployment continued to deteriorate, reaching a record of just over 2 million, or 9% of the work force, in May. The rise in the summer was fairly modest, and the rate hovered at around 9.6% during the closing months. Unemployment, thus, rose by about 10–11% over the average levels of 1981. Weak industrial output and the slow response of employment to policy measures were the contributory factors behind the higher unemployment levels.

In contrast to the fairly stable situation on the employment front, the inflation rate and the trade deficit gave rise to considerable anxiety among the policymakers. When the measures imposed in October 1981 in the wake of the franc's devaluation were lifted in January, inflation began to accelerate and reached an annual rate of 14% in May. This was largely fueled by a rapid rise in wages, which in the summer stood nearly 20% above the level of a year earlier. To break this wage/price spiral and arrest the large inflation differential between France and its major trading partners, the government imposed a four-month wage-and-price freeze to accompany the devaluation of the franc in June. At the same time the currency was devalued by 10% against the Deutsche Mark, bringing to 18.5% the depreciation since October. This "electric shock," as the finance minister described it, appeared to have had the desired effect in the short term. The inflationary pressures eased during the summer and the autumn, placing the target of 10% within reach.

Fiscal policy during 1982 remained expansionary despite the U-turn halfway through the year. The budget for 1982 originally envisioned a deficit of Fr 95 billion (compared with Fr 78 billion in 1981 and Fr 30 billion in 1980). However, slower-than-expected growth of the economy reduced government revenues and exacerbated the deficit, necessitating a supplementary budget of Fr 11.9 billion in May. The actual deficit was more likely to be about Fr 120 billion, or 3.2% of the GDP. In addition, the separately managed Social Security and Unemployment Benefit funds were in a large deficit position and were expected to reach Fr 70 billion by the end of 1983 in the absence of new measures. In line with the less expansionary approach adopted in the summer, the draft budget for 1983 postulated an increase of 12% in public expenditure, compared with 27% originally budgeted for 1982. It was planned to hold the budget deficit at approximately Fr 100 billion.

Not surprisingly, the monetary policy became progressively more restrictive in the summer following the devaluation of the franc. The authorities moved to check the expansion in money supply, which had been about 15%, to ensure that it remained at the bottom of the originally envisioned 12.5–13.5% range. At the same time the exchange controls were tightened further. Shortly afterward, to reinforce the lower expansion requirement, new and tighter lending quotas were introduced, limiting bank credit expansion to 4.5% by December in comparison with the June level. Although the widening trade deficit meant that the franc remained vulnerable on the foreign exchanges, effectively placing a brake on the interest rates, the sharp fall in U.S. interest rates in the autumn paved the way for a modest downward adjustment in French interest rates. Thus the nationalized banks' base rates, having remained constant at 14% since November, fell to 13.25% in September and stood at around 13% as the year drew to a close.

Less Developed Countries. The less developed countries were adversely affected by a number of unfavourable external features. Chief among them were the persistent recession and high interest rates among the developed nations. Depressed commodity prices and sluggish global trade also exerted a negative influence, sharply lowering export earnings and reducing the capacity of the less developed countries to borrow to sustain existing levels of economic activity. Their already considerable balance of payments deficits and associated external debts took a turn for the worse, exacerbating their economic management problems.

OUTPUT. The rate of real growth in the less developed countries as a whole declined to about 2.2% in 1981 (the latest year available), compared with 5% the year before, according to the World Bank estimates. At the 1981 level it was less than half the long-term average (1960–80) of 5.7%. Coupled with fairly high population growth and existing low income levels, the sharp drop in the tempo of economic activity predictably had a disproportionate effect. Growth in output per head in real terms slumped to 0.2% in 1981, compared with 3% during the previous year and the long-term average of 3.4%. Since there was no letup in the discouraging global environment, no significant

Table IV. Changes in Output in the Less Developed Countries, 1968–81

% changes in real GNP or GDP

Area	Annual average 1968–72	Change from preceding year				
		1977	1978	1979	1980	1981
All less developed countries	5.8*	5.8	5.2	4.8	5.0	2.2
Major oil-exporting countries†	9.0	5.9	1.8	2.9	−2.7	−4.6
Non-oil less developed countries‡	6.0	5.1	5.5	4.7	4.4	2.5
Africa	4.9	3.8	3.5	4.2	3.0	2.0
Asia‡	4.5	6.4	6.2	6.1	5.8	5.0
Europe	6.7	5.3	6.8	7.0	3.0	2.2
Middle East	6.4	3.8	7.2	5.2	6.5	5.4
Western Hemisphere	5.0	5.6	6.0	4.8	3.5	2.0

*1960–70 average.
†Comprises Algeria, Indonesia, Iran, Iraq, Kuwait, Libya, Nigeria, Oman, Qatar, Saudi Arabia, United Arab Emirates, and Venezuela.
‡Weighted average excluding China.
Sources: Adapted from IMF, *Annual Report 1982*; World Bank, *Annual Report 1982*.

Table V. Changes in Consumer Prices in the Less Developed Countries, 1968–81

% changes

Area	Annual average 1968–72	Change from preceding year				
		1977	1978	1979	1980	1981
Major oil-exporting countries*	8.0	15.5	10.2	10.5	12.6	13.1
Non-oil less developed countries†	9.1	27.0	23.6	29.0	36.9	37.2
Africa	4.6	19.2	15.6	19.2	19.4	22.7
Asia‡	6.5	6.8	5.7	9.4	16.0	15.4
Europe	6.1	16.2	21.1	27.5	40.5	25.9
Middle East	4.2	19.5	21.1	25.8	42.7	32.8
Western Hemisphere	15.3	51.4	42.4	49.6	58.3	65.7

*Comprises Algeria, Indonesia, Iran, Iraq, Kuwait, Libya, Nigeria, Oman, Qatar, Saudi Arabia, United Arab Emirates, and Venezuela.
†Weighted average excluding China.
‡Excluding China.
Source: Adapted from IMF, *Annual Report 1982*.

Table VI. Balances of Payments on Current Account, 1976–82
In $000,000,000

Area	1977	1978	1979	1980	1981	1982*
Industrial countries	−4.9	30.5	−10.2	−43.7	−3.7	11.0
Less developed countries						
Oil-exporting countries	30.8	2.9	69.8	116.4	68.6	25.0
Non-oil countries	−28.3	−39.2	−58.9	−86.2	−99.0	−97.0
Africa	−6.6	−9.0	−9.7	−12.7	−13.3	−13.0
Asia†	−0.6	−6.8	−14.2	−24.9	−22.7	−27.0
Europe	−7.6	−5.2	−8.5	−10.9	−7.9	−6.0
Middle East	−5.2	−6.5	−8.5	−7.8	−9.0	−12.0
Western Hemisphere	−8.7	−13.2	−21.3	−33.1	−41.5	−35.5
Total	−2.4	−5.8	0.7	−13.7	−34.1	−61.0

*IMF estimate.   † Excludes China prior to 1977.
Source: Adapted from IMF, *Annual Report 1982.*

improvement was expected in the position of the less developed countries during 1982.

Once again substantial regional variations were in evidence. East Asia and the Pacific turned in an impressive gain of 5.5%, almost as large as the year before thanks to the robustness and vitality of the economies of a number of countries in the region such as South Korea. By contrast, the setback in the economies in Latin America, the Caribbean, North Africa, and the Middle East was so widespread that per capita incomes declined. Africa south of the Sahara did not escape unscathed either; despite a modest increase in the overall economic growth rate, per capita income fell by 0.7%.

The decline in the Middle East was largely attributable to the difficulties experienced by the oil-exporting countries. In 1981 this group as a whole registered a larger decline in the GNP growth rate than it had in 1980, 4.5 and 2.5%, respectively. The weak world demand for oil was the main cause of the decline. Given low oil prices and the continued slump in demand for oil, the fortunes of those countries seemed likely to have worsened significantly during 1982.

CONSUMER PRICES. Progress made by the non-oil less developed countries in reducing very high inflation rates was disappointing during 1981. The weighted average rate in 1981 stood at 31.4%, compared with the record level of 32.1% in 1980. The International Monetary Fund (IMF) sources pointed out that the average was unduly influenced by the extremely high inflation rates in some Latin-American countries. Less expansionary policies adopted by most countries since 1979 appeared to be taking a long time in reducing inflationary pressures. This was partly a reflection of the magnitude of the problem these countries faced. The average annual rate of money expansion, which stood at 35% for the period 1976–78, was slow to respond to progressively restrictive money supply policies. However, the continuation of these less accommodating policies was expected to have had a noticeable effect during 1982.

In the oil-exporting countries, despite the moderate and cautious policy stance of the governments, a slight acceleration in the inflation rate occurred, pushing the average to 13% from the previous year's 12.5%. Downward adjustment from the planned expenditure levels by several governments during 1981 and 1982 in response to lower oil revenues was seen by the IMF as a favourable indicator for easing the inflationary pressures.

TRADE POSITION. Under the impact of weaker commodity prices, the terms of trade of the non-oil less developed countries declined further. During 1981 the current account deficit of this group rose by $13 billion to about $100 billion. Protectionist trade policies of the industrialized countries, the global recession, and sluggish international trade were also significant contributory factors. A modest improvement was in evidence during the early months of 1982, and this was expected to continue during the remainder of the year.

The oil exporters' current account surplus declined to $69 billion in 1981 from the previous year's $116 billion and was expected to continue to slide. IMF projections pointed to a figure of about $25 billion. The external trade position of the oil-exporting countries was weakened in 1981 and 1982 by the lower demand for oil and softer oil prices. With oil exports accounting for nearly 80% of the group's current account receipts, the influence of oil prices and export quantities was clear. By contrast, the imports of the oil exporters showed a volume increase of more than 20% in 1981. The rate of increase was expected to fall back to about 5% in 1982, partly in response to less expansionary policies followed since 1981.

Centrally Planned Economies. The 36th plenary session of the Council for Mutual Economic Assistance (CMEA or Comecon) was held in Budapest, Hung., on June 8–10, 1982. The Council session, in which premiers of the member countries participate, is, at least theoretically, the most important activity of CMEA, though its powers are largely undefined. It makes recommendations and establishes the main directions of the organization's activities, but it is up to the governments of member countries to implement them. As of 1982, the CMEA comprised ten full member countries: the Soviet Union, Bulgaria, Czechoslovakia, East Germany, Hungary, Mongolia, Poland, Romania, Vietnam, and Cuba. Yugoslavia had a "limited participation status," while Afghanistan, Angola, Ethiopia, Laos, Mozambique, and Yemen (Aden) had observer status.

Table VII. Industrial Production in Eastern Europe
1975 = 100

Country	1977	1978	1979	1980	1981
Bulgaria	114	122	128	134	142
Czechoslovakia	112	117	121	125	128
East Germany	111	116	121	127	133
Hungary	112	117	120	118	121
Poland	117	122	126	125	111
Romania	...	...	...	...	...
U.S.S.R.	111	116	120	124	129

Source: UN, *Monthly Bulletin of Statistics.*

Table VIII. Foreign Trade of Eastern Europe
In $000,000

Country	Exports 1979	1980	1981	Imports 1979	1980	1981
Bulgaria	8,869	10,372	...	8,514	9,650	...
Czechoslovakia	13,198	14,891	14,887	14,262	15,148	14,650
East Germany	15,063	17,312	...	16,214	19,082	...
Hungary	7,938	8,677	8,712	8,674	9,235	9,128
Poland	16,233	16,998	13,249	17,488	18,871	15,475
Romania	9,724	12,230	12,610	10,916	13,201	12,458
U.S.S.R.	64,762	76,481	...	57,773	68,523	...

Source: UN, *Monthly Bulletin of Statistics.*

Table IX. Output of Basic Industrial Products in Eastern Europe, 1981

In 000 metric tons except for natural gas and electric power

Country	Anthracite (hard coal)	Lignite (brown coal)	Natural gas (000,000 cu m)	Crude petroleum	Electric power (000,000 kw-hr)	Steel	Sulfuric acid	Cement
Bulgaria	...	28,980	...	...	36,960	2,484	919.2	5,448
Czechoslovakia	27,204	95,220	22,020	84	74,064	15,264	1,317.5	10,644
East Germany	...	...	...	...	...	7,464	...	12,204
Hungary	...	22,872	227,052	2,028	27,204	3,648	573.6	4,632
Poland	163,020	35,544	213,972	...	115,008	15,720	2,775.6	14,232
Romania	...	...	...	...	...	...	...	...
U.S.S.R.	704,100	...	16,214,556	609,000	1,325,004	149,004	24,096.0	126,996

Source: UN, *Monthly Bulletin of Statistics.*

At the end of the session a final communiqué was announced. As far as its economic content was concerned, it was largely devoted to a number of multilateral agreements. Four of these agreements are worth noting: an agreement on joint research and development programs in the production of industrial robots; a specialization and cooperation agreement on the production of the microelectronic base for computers; a multilateral program for cooperation in the field of colour television; and an agreement for the preparation of the "coordinated plan for multilateral integration measures for the 1986–1990 period."

The most important of these was the last agreement, as the problems of integration had already been discussed at several CMEA Council sessions. It is worth noting, therefore, that such a plan for multilateral integration measures was agreed upon as far back as 1971. It was to be carried out mainly through the coordination of national economic plans and was to be implemented during the five years beginning in 1981. The fact that at the 36th session the period mentioned was 1986–90 highlighted the fact that previous agreements had not been implemented. Premier Lubomir Strougal of Czechoslovakia proposed that the coordination plan should be discussed in 1983 and finally concluded in 1984.

There were many reasons for this delay. Most member countries were critical of various aspects of integration, and their leaders found it impossible to agree on concrete measures to be taken. National plans are often not fulfilled, and contractual obligations consequently are not met. This was especially evident during the last few years when the first clear signs of economic crisis began to appear in Poland and in other CMEA countries.

Characteristically, the major problems facing the CMEA countries were not mentioned at the Budapest session. There were only veiled references to the situation in Poland, and nothing was said about the problems of energy, food, and foreign indebtedness, the main stumbling blocks to economic expansion in Eastern Europe. The acute crises in Poland and Romania and significant signs of economic difficulties in other member countries underlined the fact that a reform of the current system was urgently needed. There was, however, an overwhelming reluctance to introduce any change.

The official organ of the Soviet Communist Party, *Pravda,* on Oct. 15, 1982, devoted an editorial to the outlining of the CMEA strategy for the 1980s. *Pravda* quoted Strougal as having said at the 36th Council session that the coordination of plans must be complemented by the harmonizing of overall economic policy. According to *Pravda,* the keystone of this policy was the intensification of production. A new initiative must be taken to solve the problem of international specialization and cooperation in production. Special attention must be paid to multilateral agreements concerning high technology. Also the joint investment in material production, which was the theme in the 1970s, should be supplemented by establishing direct links between enterprises in CMEA countries.

While the principle of integration was virtually endorsed by all European members of CMEA, the practical difficulties of implementing it were enormous. The CMEA countries were unable to work out a united strategy to overcome their major economic problems. No joint program to solve the Polish economic crisis was put forward in spite of the fact that Poland's troubles profoundly affected all CMEA countries. Only the Soviet Union gave limited assistance to Poland, while other member countries, faced with dwindling Polish exports, retaliated by cutting their own exports to Poland.

There was also no agreement on a unified economic policy. East Germany, for example, still advocated dynamic growth, while Hungary maintained that a deliberate slowdown of growth was needed in order to regroup economic forces. All countries except the Soviet Union and Bulgaria were burdened with enormous foreign debts, and all suffered from shortages of either food, as in the case of the Soviet Union, Poland, and Romania, or raw materials and energy.

There were also major differences among CMEA countries concerning economic reforms. Some were trying to introduce or expand certain elements of the market economy. The Hungarians were the main exponents of this strategy while the East Germans and Czechoslovakia were most reluctant to follow it.

All the CMEA countries, including the Soviet

Table X. Soviet Trade with Eastern European Countries

In 000,000 rubles, current prices

Country	Exports			Imports		
	1979	1980	1981	1979	1980	1981
Bulgaria	3,312.7	3,660.2	4,374.5	3,173.7	3,438.9	3,696.9
Czechoslovakia	3,362.9	3,648.1	4,382.3	3,183.4	3,535.9	4,104.8
East Germany	4,216.5	4,873.4	5,526.1	3,917.0	4,326.6	5,154.6
Hungary	2,741.3	2,931.6	3,306.7	2,413.8	2,756.6	3,300.4
Poland	3,837.5	4,405.9	4,931.3	3,717.5	3,596.1	3,220.8
Romania	1,077.8	1,350.3	1,779.1	1,067.8	1,441.2	1,673.1

Source: U.S.S.R. Foreign Trade Statistics/Moscow.

Japan's foreign minister, Yoshio Sakarauchi (centre), headed that nation's delegation to the GATT meeting in Geneva in November. The Japanese came under fire for trade expansionism abroad and protectionism at home.

Union, urgently needed high technology, which could only be obtained from Western industrialized nations. In the 1970s there was a massive inflow of this technology to the Communist bloc. This enabled the CMEA countries to sustain a dynamic growth of their industrial potential. The import of technology was based, however, on Western credits, and as a result the CMEA countries accumulated debts amounting by the end of 1981 to more than $80 billion. First Poland and then Romania found themselves unable to meet financial obligations in repaying these credits. Indeed, they were not even able to keep up the interest payments. Other CMEA countries were also finding it difficult to repay debts or to raise new loans. Deprived of Western technology as well as raw materials, their economies stagnated.

INTERNATIONAL TRADE

The stagnation of world trade continued into 1982 with little immediate prospect of recovery. After world exports had declined in dollar terms in 1981, the first such fall since 1958, it was estimated that the volume of world trade remained constant in 1982 compared with the previous year. OECD countries probably increased their export volumes overall, mainly due to a further expansion of shipments to OPEC. OECD imports from OPEC countries (mainly oil) fell sharply once again. Indeed, demand for OPEC oil by the rest of the world had dropped 50% since the 1979 peak, through a combination of the effects of world recession on demand and increased supplies from such non-OPEC sources as the U.K. and Mexico.

Non-oil less developed countries faced great difficulties. Their export markets were adversely affected by the recession and in some cases were being restricted by protectionist measures. Meanwhile, their imports were increasingly difficult to finance, given the high level of world interest rates and the rising burden of debt service payments coupled with high oil prices. Overall, however, it was likely that the trade balance of the non-oil less developed countries was more or less identical to that in 1981. The improvement in OECD trade balances overall was mirrored by the dramatic tumble of the OPEC nations' trade surplus to approximately

$50 billion, down by over half compared with 1981.

The relatively unrestricted system of world trade that had emerged over the last 20 years came under severe pressure in 1982. This pressure resulted from a combination of three major factors. First was the increased willingness of countries to use trade sanctions as a means of exerting political pressure on other nations. Second, the depth and length of the world recession led to worsening unemployment and increasing trade deficits; with little prospect of a substantial recovery, the imposition of import restrictions seemed an appealing way of improving the situation. Third, the international financial uncertainty that followed the difficulties of Poland, Mexico, and Argentina (among others) spilled over into the provision of suppliers' credit for trade and thus was likely to hold back trade growth for some time.

Protectionist measures (both blatant and covert) became more important during the year as the world recession deepened in many countries. Japanese exporters remained the prime target for most measures because of the large Japanese trade surplus and the tendency for Japanese goods to be concentrated in key sectors (such as automobiles and electronics). Several bills were introduced in the U.S. Congress to force foreign cars sold in the U.S. to have a specified minimum level of domestic content, despite the opposition of the Ford Motor Co. and General Motors Corp. to such legislation. France controlled the level of video tape recorder imports (mainly from Japan) by requiring that these imports pass through a small customs post at Poitiers; this led to considerable delays in processing shipments and thus aided domestic suppliers. Similarly, all import documentation had to be in the French language. But Japan could not complain too loudly; its own system of interlocking industrial groupings and legalized cartels made it difficult for foreign companies to enter the Japanese market, and high tariffs on certain goods also protected local industry.

Probably the most serious manifestation of the trend toward protectionism was the dispute between European and U.S. steel producers. The U.S. producers charged that their competitors in the European Economic Community (principally the U.K., France, Italy, and Belgium) received subsidies of between 15 and 40% of the cost of production, and they wanted tariffs imposed to offset the advantage gained. Eventually an agreement emerged restricting the EEC producers' share of the U.S. market for certain types of steel to 5.75%, together with separate agreements on EEC exports

Table XI. Soviet Crude Petroleum and Products Supplied to Eastern Europe
In 000 rubles

Country	1980	1981
Bulgaria	1,061,006	1,310,920
Czechoslovakia	1,162,706	1,617,945
East Germany	1,420,757	1,744,515
Hungary	755,333	913,503
Poland	1,277,917	1,613,405
Romania	210,540	523,641

Source: U.S.S.R. Foreign Trade Statistics/Moscow.

of alloy steel and of pipes and tubes. There were protectionist features on both sides; the subsidies objected to were designed to help the European countries through a period of intense world competition, while the eventual agreements restricted imports even from those suppliers who remained competitive or unsubsidized (for example, the West Germans).

The buildup of foreign debts by (especially) the less developed countries had been a major concern of the international financial community in recent years. In 1982 the concern became acute as Poland, Mexico, and Argentina plus a number of smaller countries faced difficulties in repaying their international borrowings. This led to a much more cautious approach by banks to their international loans and affected trade in two ways. First, the tightness of credit reduced demand for imports generally. Second, banks (and companies) became more concerned with the solvency of their customers, and supplier credit thus became more difficult to obtain. Even where credit was available, it might be obtained only on onerous terms. A crucial factor as the world economy entered 1983 was how far these international financial difficulties would impinge on normal trade financing; over-cautious lending could cause trade to stagnate or contract, prolonging the world recession and making debtors' problems perhaps even more serious.

Industrialized Nations. After the rapid cutback in trade deficits in 1981 the industrialized nations displayed only slow progress in 1982. Most economies had already slipped into recession in 1981, and there was little leeway for further substantial reductions in imports; exceptions to this were the U.S. and Canada, at least in the first half of the year. The recession left little demand for exports, however, and trade volumes grew very little; exceptions in this regard were West Germany and, among the smaller industrialized nations, Belgium, Ireland, Spain, and Australia. Thus overall import volumes into the OECD area rose by 1–2%, while exports from the OECD to the rest of the world were up by possibly 2%. The combined trade surplus of the seven major economies rose from $6 billion in 1981 to about $11 billion. But a general worsening of invisible account balances resulted in the overall current account deficit of the big seven remaining at around $1 billion–$2 billion. (Invisibles are those transactions not reflected in foreign trade statistics; one example is tourism.) For the other OECD countries trade balances generally improved, with a decline in the combined trade deficit from $30 billion to about $22 billion; the combined current account deficit fell by about $6 billion to reach $21 billion–$22 billion.

The sharp fall in GNP in the U.S. during the last quarter of 1981 and the first quarter of 1982, followed by only moderate increases thereafter, severely curtailed that nation's demand for imports. The cutback in inventories and decline in residential investment spending had a particularly severe effect on import demand. The high level of interest rates also increased the cost of inventories, causing imports of energy to fall dramatically. The strength of the dollar severely hampered the efforts of U.S. exporters. They found it difficult to main-

Table XII. Current Balances of Payments
In $000,000,000

Country	1976	1977	1978	1979	1980	1981	1982
Canada	-3.9	-4.1	-4.3	-4.2	-0.9	-4.5	+3*
France	-5.9	-3.1	+7.0	+5.2	-4.2	-4.9	-9*
West Germany	+3.5	+3.7	+8.6	-7.2	-16.5	-7.4	-1*
Italy	-2.9	+2.4	+6.2	+5.4	-9.8	-8.7	-5*
Japan	+3.7	+10.9	+17.5	-8.8	-10.8	+5.8	+4*
United Kingdom	-1.6	0	+1.8	-1.8	+7.4	+12.3	+2*
United States	+4.4	-14.1	-14.8	-0.5	+1.5	+4.5	0*
OECD total	-17.2	-23.9	+13.6	-29.2	-69.1	-27.4	+10†
Other developed countries	-2.3	-1.4	-0.1	-0.7	+0.6	-6.5	-4†
Centrally planned economies†	-2.7	+2.1	+1.0	+5.2	+7.4	+11.7	+14
Oil exporting countries†	+44.2	+39.3	+14.9	+68.3	+126.4	+102.6	+54
Other less developed countries†	-22.0	-16.1	-29.4	-43.6	-65.3	-80.4	-74
at 1975 prices‡							
OECD total	-17	-22	+11	-21	-44	-18	+7
Other developed countries	-2	-1	0	0	0	-4	-3
Centrally planned economies	-3	+2	+1	+4	+5	+8	+10
Oil exporting economies	+44	+36	+12	+48	+80	+68	+36
Other less developed countries	-22	-15	-24	-31	-41	-54	-50

*First three quarters.   †Estimate.
‡In terms of export prices of manufactured goods.
Sources: International Monetary Fund, *International Financial Statistics;* UN, *Monthly Bulletin of Statistics;* national sources.

tain competitiveness in a world recession when the trade-weighted value of the dollar had risen 30% in two years. Export volumes dropped nearly 10% overall, with the manufacturing sector being particularly hard hit. The U.S. was affected by the difficulties in the Latin-American economies, which took about 15% of U.S. exports in 1981. Coupled with a fall in the traditionally large U.S. surplus on invisibles, the rise in the trade deficit (up $2 billion to $30 billion) led to a decline in the current account surplus to approximately $3 billion.

Japanese exporters also faced difficulties in their major markets. In the U.S. (20% of Japanese exports) demand for imports dropped, while financial problems in some Asian countries held back expansion of export markets there. Restrictions in important markets (for example, on automotive exports to the U.S. and Western Europe) also hindered export growth. Overall export volumes grew by perhaps 1–2% (if at all), despite the undervalued level of the yen and therefore, extremely keen Japanese competitiveness. In spite of a recovery in import volumes in the early part of the year as the inventory rundown that occurred in late 1981 bottomed out, over the year as a whole import volume rose only slightly. Weak oil prices, together with declining commodity prices, helped to keep down the overall value of imports despite the strength of the dollar against the yen. The yen's depreciation aided exporters in keeping export prices in dollar terms almost constant, with the result that the trade balance rose by around $3 billion, to $23 billion. After subtracting the substantial (but slightly reduced) deficit on invisible trade, the current surplus reached $8 billion, nearly double that of 1981.

Improved competitiveness helped West German exporters to register strong gains in world markets during the early part of 1982. But as the world recession continued this increase in market share became more difficult to sustain, especially with economic difficulties in major markets such as France and some of the OPEC countries. Imports held up fairly well, given the generally restrained pace of economic activity, though oil imports fell off in the early part of the year. The trade balance nevertheless improved substantially, up $10 billion to a $28 billion surplus, and this helped to restore the traditional current account surplus.

In France the trade account suffered after the substantial drop in the franc's value against the dollar and most other currencies. The value of imports rose and that of exports fell, in franc terms, reflecting the lower value of the franc and the time lags before such currency changes filter through into volume changes. Thus the trade deficit in franc terms already exceeded that for all of 1981 by July. But with the franc's fall, along with a more restrained growth of the economy likely to follow the government's austerity measures, in the latter part of the year an upturn in export volumes and a slowdown in import growth could be discerned. In dollar terms the trade deficit did not increase much, moving up to $10 billion. With a reduced invisibles surplus, however, the current deficit was of the order of $9 billion.

After the record current account surplus for the U.K. in 1981 there was a substantial fall in 1982. This reflected the $9 billion drop in the trade surplus, down to virtually zero over the year. British exporters were suffering the problems of uncompetitiveness resulting from the delayed effects of the high level of the pound during 1981. Despite the slowdown in inflation, export prices still rose too quickly to offset these currency effects, though some relief appeared to be on the way late in the year. Uncompetitiveness abroad was matched by uncompetitiveness at home, with imports making yet further inroads into the British market. The boost to imports may partly have reflected inventory rebuilding, but nevertheless import penetration appeared undiminished even after such rebuilding had decreased. In the meantime, however, the current surplus totaled a reduced but nevertheless welcome $6 billion, though most of that could be ascribed to the high levels of North Sea oil output and exports, which reached record levels late in the year.

In spite of the lira's rapid decline against the U.S. dollar (down 30% since the beginning of 1981), the volume of imports into Italy rose again in 1982. The effects of the import deposit scheme and the rundown of inventories in 1981 were only temporary and even then only reduced the rate of import advance. After an upsurge in export volumes in the second half of 1981, the rate of growth of exports slowed considerably in 1982 as the high rate of domestic inflation pushed up export prices and wiped out some of the advantage from the lira's depreciation. Thus the trade deficit first rose and then recovered a little in the later months of the year, but overall it still reached an annual total of $9 billion, just $1 billion down from the previous year. After allowing for the invisibles surplus, the current account was in the red to the tune of $7 billion.

Canada's invisibles deficit increased during 1982 to offset an increased trade surplus and keep the current deficit still high at $4 billion. Declining GNP caused a fall in import volumes of substantial proportions. The return of domestic oil production to normal levels led to a major decline in oil imports. The weakness of the U.S. economy (Canada's major export market with over 60% of exports) led to a similar fall in export volumes, though food exports held up well. The net effect was to boost the trade surplus to $9 billion, offset by a large invisibles deficit of around $13 billion.

The other industrialized nations generally managed to improve or stabilize their trade positions, Turkey being the possible exception. The decline in North American imports did not affect the smaller Western European countries. Their prime markets are the big four Western European nations (U.K., France, West Germany, and Italy), where imports held up well. Imports into the smaller nations were subdued, reflecting the general stagnation. An exception was Australia, where the expansion of domestic investment boosted imports. Overall, therefore, the trade deficit of the smaller industrial nations fell from $30 billion to $22.5 billion, though a decreased invisibles surplus meant that the combined current deficit fell only $6 billion, to $21.5 billion.

Less Developed Countries. The less developed countries in general faced a difficult year. Even the OPEC nations found themselves in payments difficulties as the demand for their oil fell off dramatically. High interest rates worldwide made the cost of holding excess oil inventories too expensive and forced a depletion of those stocks. This drop in demand led to an agreement in OPEC on a sharing of production, though not all the oil nations (Iran and Libya, for example) heeded the quotas arranged for them under this agreement. The production cutbacks, since they translated directly into export cutbacks in most cases, severely affected the export receipts of many of the OPEC nations, and late in the year there were signs that the agreement was starting to crumble. For example, Indonesia, facing a turndown in its non-oil commodity export receipts as well, reduced its oil price below the agreed-upon levels to gain a competitive edge in world oil markets. Overall, the OPEC current account crashed into deficit in 1982 for the first time in 20 years, and for some of the so-called "high absorber" nations, with large populations and heavy development expenditures, the current account problems were becoming serious.

As a countermeasure, Indonesia and Malaysia both introduced counterpurchase policies, under which sales of oil were linked to the purchase of an appropriate quantity of non-oil commodities. Portugal had instituted similar measures on its public sector contracts. In a year in which exporters were desperate for business these tactics appeared to be effective. Whether they would be so in more prosperous times remained to be seen.

The non-oil less developed countries faced different problems. They had to fight hard in depressed markets to sell their commodity exports, and not only were export volumes fairly stagnant but prices continued to weaken. At the same time,

CHART 5

the financial problems of several borrowers and the eventual crisis in Mexico made the availability of foreign loans even more difficult. Where loans were available, they were at frighteningly high interest rates, which would only add to the problems of debt repayments in future years. These countries also had to pay the still-high prices for oil, and for many of them the combined bill for debt service payments and oil requirements equaled a substantial percentage of export receipts. Imports were, therefore, held back by financial factors, but even so it appeared that the current account of the non-oil less developed nations remained at about the same level of deficit as in 1981, that is, approximately $75 billion.

Centrally Planned Economies. Although the centrally planned economies faced the same depressed world trading conditions as other nations, other factors were the main influences on their trade positions. The U.S. embargo on exports of technologically useful goods to the Soviet Union and to Poland culminated in the U.S.-EC quarrel about the gas pipeline. Grain trade with the Soviet Union continued, however, though the U.S.S.R. was seeking more reliable sources of imports, notably Canada and Argentina.

Poland's debt problems led to a more stringent review of the ability of the centrally planned economies to repay their debts, and this probably held back imports. China also introduced restrictions on imports of consumer goods, petrochemicals, and textiles. This action was partly political, with Taiwan and South Korea singled out, especially after U.S. sales of arms to Taiwan. But it was also economic, being a continuation of the retrenchment in imports started by the Chinese in 1981. Overall, however, the centrally planned economies stayed in surplus on their trade account, though this was insufficient to offset their deficit in invisibles, and the combined current account remained in the red.

Outlook. The world trade system faced major threats as it entered 1983. The world economy showed no sign of any major upturn, and as unemployment continued to rise in the major industrial markets there was a possibility that protectionist measures would become more widespread and more acceptable. The financial system that had sustained the expansion of world trade after the first oil crisis in 1973 was now showing serious weakness. (EIU)

INTERNATIONAL EXCHANGE AND PAYMENTS

In 1982 the pressures of nine years of recession, with only brief periods of growth, and the growing realization that slow growth was the most optimistic realistic forecast for the next few years led to a series of disruptions in the international economy. The earliest and most obvious effect was the weakening of the price of oil, with its consequences for balances of payments, inflation, and capital flows. Pressures on exchange rates began to increase both because continuing disparities in economic performance reached levels that could no longer be ignored and because policy reactions to the recession diverged. The geographic spread and level of capital movements reacted, both directly

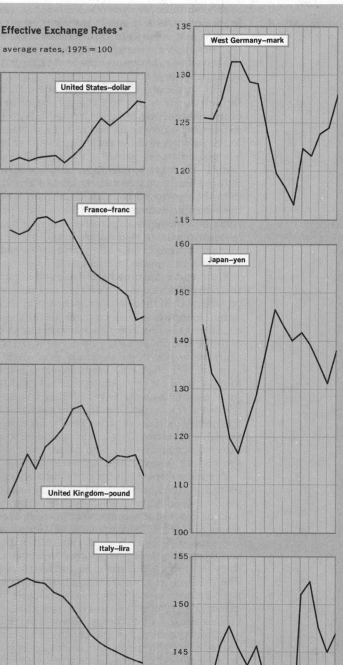

Effective Exchange Rates *

average rates, 1975 = 100

* Measure of a currency's value relative to a weighted average of the values of the currencies of the country's trading partners.
† Fourth quarter figures for 1982 are estimated.

Source: International Monetary Fund, International Financial Statistics.

to those influences and to the related movements in interest rates and also to the changed prospects for different borrowers as pessimism about recovery spread. Protectionist measures continued, and there was no progress on new trading or financing arrangements.

With total trade in oil falling almost 10% for the second year in a row and the volume of OPEC exports consequently falling a further 15%, the OPEC current balance was halved in spite of stagnation in the imports of those nations. The other less developed countries gained only a small improvement in their current balance, partly because they reduced the volume of their oil imports by less than the developed countries but mainly because the recession reduced the prices of their primary commodity exports so that they suffered nearly as severe a decline in terms of trade as did the oil producers. In consequence, they also restrained their imports from the industrial countries.

The centrally planned economies also restrained their imports because of pressure on their external payments, and there was little change in their balance. The result of these changes for the industrial countries was a recovery back into surplus because of the decline in the relative price of oil. In the two years since 1980 they made up all of their move into deficit in the two preceding years. In contrast to most recent years, however, they had no improvement in volume terms in their balance with the rest of the world. The effects of the recession on the nonindustrial countries finally became so severe that they could no longer provide a source of external demand to the OECD countries to help offset the lack of growth in domestic demand.

The improvement in the current balances of the OECD countries was not only weakly based, depending as it did on price movements rather than volume gains, but was also very uneven. Most of it was accounted for by Canada, West Germany, and the smaller European countries, although Italy and Japan might also show some improvement for the year. France and the U.K. suffered large falls. The U.S. was in surplus during the first half of the year because of its very weak economic performance. West Germany achieved a large increase in volume because of its competitiveness at the beginning of 1982, and the smaller countries also improved their volume performance, again possibly because of their greater competitiveness relative to the U.S. The improvement in Italy's balance was

purely the effect of its relatively high inflation on its terms of trade, while Japan gained greatly from the decline in the oil price because oil accounted for almost half its imports.

France failed to participate in the general improvement in terms of trade because of its devaluation in the first part of the year; it also increased its imports relatively rapidly because of its "high" growth rate of 1.3% (against a European average of about zero) and suffered a large drop in exports because of a worsening of competitiveness in 1981. The U.K. also suffered from a falling exchange rate, and its loss of competitiveness on imports and exports in 1977–80 had been much more severe than that of France. The nature of the current balance improvement and its concentration in countries that either had domestic reasons for restraint (Canada and West Germany) or were too small to have independent economic policies suggested that it did not represent a successful permanent adaptation to the new economic conditions.

The effective transfer of part of the OPEC surplus to the developed countries meant that those nations must in the future be the ultimate source of some of the capital flows required to finance the deficit of the non-oil less developed countries. During the 1970s most of the increase in the deficits of the less developed countries was covered by short- and medium-term borrowing on the international capital markets. Between 1974 and 1981, when their combined deficit rose about $50 billion, this type of lending increased by $35 billion, to over $40 billion, while bilateral aid rose only about $10 billion and aid from the international agencies perhaps another $10 billion. This not only offered those borrowers the form of effectively unconditional flexible lending that they preferred but also suited the preferences of the OPEC countries, which were the principal depositors on these markets. Other holders of surplus funds, ultimately the consumers or investors in developed countries whose spending on oil had been reduced, were unlikely to have the same preference for medium-term international bank deposits as did the OPEC governments. Although even at its current level the OPEC surplus still provided a large base for such loans, its decline in 1982 appeared already to have been reflected in a sharp contraction in lending to the non-oil less developed countries. The apparent decline in the current deficit of those non-oil nations, in spite of the reduction in their income from exports, might well reflect a reduction in the availability of funds to finance deficits.

Before the rise in oil prices, foreign direct investment was an important component of capital flows from the developed to the less developed countries. Long-term capital flows from the traditional exporters of capital fluctuated greatly during the 1970s. West Germany, one of the countries currently in surplus, had become an importer of capital while it was in deficit, but it appeared to have moved back into exporting capital in the first half of 1982. Japan and the U.K. also appeared to be increasing their capital outflows. The U.S., however, traditionally the most important source, declined sharply in importance in the second half of the 1970s, and indeed it was in surplus on long-

Table XIII. Foreign Investment by Major Countries
In $000,000,000

Country	1974	1975	1976	1977	1978	1979	1980	1981
Long-term capital flows								
West Germany	−2.4	−7.4	−0.6	−5.6	−1.5	+6.6	+3.5	+4.4
Japan	−3.9	−0.3	−0.9	−3.2	−12.4	−12.6	+2.4	−6.4
United Kingdom	+6.6	+1.5	+2.6	+4.9	−6.2	−6.6	−8.9	−20.6
United States	−7.4	−21.4	−21.2	−17.6	−14.4	−16.9	−11.8	+4.8
Total	−7.1	−27.6	−20.2	−21.5	−34.5	−29.5	−14.8	−17.9
Net interest, dividends, and profits								
West Germany	+0.4	+1.0	+1.3	+0.2	+2.5	+1.7	+1.8	−0.4
Japan	−0.5	−0.3	−0.2	+0.1	+0.9	+2.0	+0.9	−0.8
United Kingdom	+3.3	+1.7	+2.5	+0.2	+1.1	+1.8	−0.1	+2.7
United States	+15.5	+12.8	+16.0	+18.0	+20.6	+31.2	+29.9	+33.0
Total	+18.7	+15.2	+19.6	+18.4	+25.1	+36.7	+32.5	+34.5

Source: National sources.

term capital in 1981. Its increasingly poor performance on current account made any change in this unlikely. The necessary shift to different forms and sources of finance was therefore probably occurring fairly slowly and hesitantly as both investors and borrowers adjusted. This situation probably restrained imports and growth by the less developed countries, even beyond what would be expected from their low export income.

Net exchange rate movements and fluctuations were large in 1982, and they became more important even within the European Monetary System (EMS), the semifixed system that included all EC members except Greece and the U.K. The second half of the year was overshadowed by continuing pressure on the French franc, the level of which within the EMS had to be defended by means of a $4 billion loan on the Euromarkets and other borrowing in addition to the usual intra-EMS arrangements. During the first three quarters of 1982 the Belgian and French francs both fell over 10% against the Deutsche Mark, more than their declines up to that time since the beginning of the EMS in 1979. The Danish krone and Italian lira fell over 5%. The Netherlands guilder and Irish punt showed little change. The EMS currencies together declined by more than 10% against the U.S. dollar, whose effective rate continued its rise; the dollar gained more than 10% during 1982 after a rise of almost 15% in 1981. The U.K. effective rate fell slightly but remained in its now normal position between the EMS and U.S. currencies. The yen's effective rate fell sharply during 1982. These exchange rate movements among currency blocs clearly were not closely related to the current balance performance discussed above, although the movements within the EMS probably reflected the results of the increasing divergence of economic performance and economic policy over the last three years, particularly between France and West Germany.

As in 1981 it was clear that the relative levels of interest rates and expectations about them played a major part. Although they declined somewhat, nominal short-term rates in the U.S. remained extremely high, by historical standards, in absolute terms, and relative to the other industrial countries. Japanese rates, on the other hand, remained extremely low. The West German and U.K. rates moved down to slightly less than that of the U.S. For effects beyond exchange rate movements, however, it is important to note the level of interest rates: in nominal terms, even after the recent declines, all the industrial countries except Japan had rates much higher than they had ever had before 1980. In real terms (that is, with the nominal interest rates deflated by the rise in average output prices for the economies) the comparison was more striking and applied to Japan as well. Not only were the 1981–82 rates unprecedentedly high but they were in sharp contrast to the exceptionally low and negative rates in the mid-1970s.

This coexistence of high real interest rates and recession stemmed in part from 1982's position as a year of transition, with the reduction of inflation and of expectations about growth not yet fully transmitted into interest rates, but it was also the

Table XIV. Nominal and Real Short-Term Interest Rates
In %

Country	1960–66	1967–73	1974–80	1979	1980	1981	1982 First half	1982 Third quarter
			Nominal					
France	...	...	9.8	9.5	12.2	15.3	15.5	14.4
West Germany	4.6	6.8	6.2	6.7	9.5	12.1	9.7	8.9
Japan	5.9	5.4	5.4	4.4	6.3	5.7	5.4	5.4
United Kingdom	5.0	6.9	1.0	13.1	15.0	13.0	13.0	10.6
United States	3.4	5.4	7.5	10.1	11.5	14.0	12.6	9.3
			Real*					
France	...	...	−0.8	−0.5	0.5	3.0	1.1	2.9
West Germany	0.9	2.0	1.4	2.8	4.5	7.5	5.1	4.2
Japan	0.7	−1.0	−1.6	1.9	3.1	2.8	2.7	2.6
United Kingdom	1.2	0.5	−4.7	−1.7	−3.3	1.4	5.5	4.7
United States	1.6	0.7	−0.1	1.5	2.4	4.4	5.3	3.3

*The nominal interest rate divided by the rise in the GDP implicit price deflator.
Sources: OECD, *Historical Statistics, 1966–1980*, *National Institute Economic Review*, November, 1982.

result of the shift in the last few years toward the greater use of monetary restraint in economic policy. This practice had not yet been fully accommodated in international financial arrangements and, combined with the domestic policy priority for controlling inflation, it tended to produce upward pressure on interest rates. This, combined with the heavy use of bank finance during the 1970s recession, helped to produce the crisis in international bank lending, particularly to the non-oil less developed countries, in 1982.

The threat of a serious reduction in lending to all less developed countries, which would inevitably have been followed by large-scale defaulting as borrowers found it impossible to "roll over" existing debt as well as to obtain new finance, was real at the end of the summer, but in the autumn it receded. The nominal level of interest rates was reduced, and the major banks did not withdraw from lending. This may have been at least helped by the intervention of national and international financial authorities. There was a clear and quite sudden shift in pronouncements by the IMF toward emphasizing the need to continue lending and away from stressing the duty of less developed countries to adapt to recession, which had been the theme as late as the summer. There was particular encouragement for banks to lend to the heavy borrowers in Latin America that had turned to the IMF for finance: Mexico, Argentina, and Brazil. There appeared to have been improvements in national arrangements to support banks in temporary liquidity difficulties. There was also a relaxation in U.S. monetary policy.

International action to meet the difficulties created by the recession on a more permanent basis was lacking. The rise in IMF lending in 1981 was not repeated at the same rate in 1982. There was increased discussion of the need for a new set of rules for international exchange rates, interest rates, and monetary management and also for new financing facilities from the IMF, but no action was taken. On the trade side there was retreat; at the General Agreement on Tariffs and Trade (GATT) ministerial conference in November the industrial countries were no longer willing even to pledge themselves to avoid increasing protection.

(SHEILA A. B. PAGE)

Ecuador

Ecuador

A republic on the west coast of South America, Ecuador is bounded by Colombia, Peru, and the Pacific Ocean. Area: 281,334 sq km (108,624 sq mi), including the Galápagos Islands (7,976 sq km), which is an insular province. Pop. (1983 est.): 9,251,000. Cap.: Quito (pop., 1983 est., 918,900). Largest city: Guayaquil (pop., 1983 est., 1,278,-900). Language: Spanish, but Indians speak Quechuan and Jivaroan. Religion: predominantly Roman Catholic. President in 1982, Osvaldo Hurtado Larrea.

The already shaky coalition governing Ecuador came under increasing strain in 1982. Several Cabinet changes were made, reflecting the fluctuations in power within the coalition. In September Energy Minister Eduardo Ortega resigned both that post and the presidency of the Organization of Petroleum Exporting Countries (OPEC) as a result of a congressional vote of censure over his handling of energy policy. Jaime Morillo also resigned as minister of finance rather than face a similar vote. Pres. Osvaldo Hurtado Larrea replaced those ministers with independents so that only four Cabinet posts were affiliated with political parties.

The economy deteriorated rapidly at the beginning of the year as oil revenues declined and international interest rates remained high. In May the official exchange rate for the sucre was devalued, for the first time in over a decade, from 25 to 33 sucres to the U.S. dollar. In spite of this move, the free-market rate continued to depreciate to over 70 sucres to the dollar in July before making a slight recovery later in the year. Foreign borrowing was still necessary to support the balance of payments, and a debt crisis was seen to be imminent as international reserves declined; negotiations were started to reschedule part of the $5.2 billion foreign public debt. It was hoped that new legislation would attract foreign investment and thus increase oil exports, as rising domestic consumption threatened to make Ecuador the first net oil importer within OPEC.

ECUADOR

Education. (1979–80) Primary, pupils 1,427,627, teachers 39,825; secondary, pupils 475,857, teachers (1978–79) 24,120; vocational, pupils 59,588, teachers (1978–79) 5,951; higher, students 274,968, teaching staff 11,998.

Finance. Monetary unit: sucre, with (Sept. 20, 1982) an official rate of 33.15 sucres to U.S. $1 (free official rate of 56.84 sucres = £1 sterling). Gold and other reserves (June 1982) U.S. $587 million. Budget (1982 est.) balanced at 64,770,000,000 sucres. Gross national product (1981) 308,560,000,000 sucres. Money supply (March 1982) 64,802,000,000 sucres. Cost of living (Quito; 1975 = 100; April 1982) 222.7.

Foreign Trade. (1981) Imports U.S. $2,246,100,000; exports U.S. $2,541,600,000. Import sources (1980): U.S. 38%; Japan 14%; West Germany 11%; Italy 5%. Export destinations (1980): U.S. 31%; Chile 9%. Main exports (1980): crude oil 52%; bananas 9%; cocoa and products 8%; coffee 6%.

Transport and Communications. Roads (1980) 37,910 km. Motor vehicles in use (1980): passenger c. 73,700; commercial (including buses) c. 160,700. Railways: (1980) 965 km; traffic (1978) 65 million passenger-km, freight 34 million net ton-km. Air traffic (1980): c. 916 million passenger-km; freight c. 34.6 million net ton-km. Telephones (Jan. 1980) 260,000. Radio receivers (Dec. 1978) 2,540,000. Television receivers (Dec. 1979) c. 400,000.

Agriculture. Production (in 000; metric tons; 1981): rice 402; corn c. 246; potatoes c. 349; cassava c. 236; sugar, raw value c. 359; bananas c. 2,275; pineapples c. 139; oranges c. 530; coffee c. 88; cocoa c. 96; fish catch (1980) c. 671. Livestock (in 000; 1981): cattle 3,032; sheep 3,034; pigs 3,721; horses c. 299; chickens c. 23,479.

Industry. Production (in 000; metric tons; 1979): cement 1,034; crude steel 114; crude oil (1981) 10,732; natural gas (cu m; 1980) 31,642; petroleum products c. 4,440; electricity (kw-hr; 1980) c. 3,155,000; gold (troy oz; 1980) 3.3; silver (troy oz; 1980) 24.

The government faced severe criticism from organized labour. A general strike protesting austerity measures took place on October 21, despite the declaration of a state of emergency. The private sector was also disaffected with the government's economic management, as companies suffered from slack demand coupled with rising costs and falling exports. (SARAH CAMERON)

Education

Judging from UNESCO's statistics, the world illiteracy rate continued its decline in 1982. UNESCO's projections showed that it would fall to 25.7% by 1990 (from a figure of 44.3% in 1950). However, because of the increase in population the actual number of illiterates continued to rise. What caused particular concern in 1982 was evidence of illiteracy in some of the advanced countries. A report drawn up for the European Parliament by Phili Viehoff, on behalf of the Committee on Youth, Culture, Education, Information, and Sport, said that there were some 10 million to 15 million illiterates in the countries of the European Community (not including Greece). Based on an earlier survey, some two million of these were in the United Kingdom. France, West Germany, and Luxembourg denied the existence of illiteracy within their borders, but the evidence suggested that this was untrue. In Greece it was estimated that 14% of the adult population was illiterate and in Portugal, 23%.

At a UNESCO conference of African education ministers in Harare (Salisbury), Zimbabwe, in

A rise in the price of fuel and flour brought rioters into the streets of Quito in October. It took the combined efforts of soldiers and police to quell the demonstrators.

WIDE WORLD

July, Sema Tanguiane, UNESCO's assistant director general for education, said that the overall illiteracy rate in Africa had declined to 60.6%. Nonetheless, as with the world population, the actual number of illiterates on the continent had increased, to approximately 156 million. There were, however, some less gloomy figures to report. Illiteracy in Ethiopia had declined from more than 90% in 1974 to 50%, and Zimbabwe and Tanzania had substantially increased school enrollments.

For most of the advanced industrial countries of the West the problem of illiteracy had a low priority. On the contrary, their principal concern was to contain and, if possible, reduce the cost of public education. There were, however, exceptions. In Europe both Norway and France increased their spending, notably on higher education, at a faster rate than inflation. In Denmark, Sweden, Switzerland, and Austria the rate of increase was somewhat less than that of inflation, and in Belgium, West Germany, The Netherlands, Ireland, and, especially, the United Kingdom it was very considerably below the rate of inflation.

To some extent these differences reflected differing economic and political philosophies. In the U.K. the Conservative Party government stated as one of its main objectives the "privatization" of the economy, and the minister of education declared that he was "intellectually attracted" by ideas of loans for students (unknown in Britain since World War II) and educational vouchers. On the other hand the Socialist government of French Pres. François Mitterrand saw education as a driving force for economic recovery and thus spent considerable public money on it. The new Swedish government espoused a similar policy. But both France and Sweden were affected by the recession and trimmed their spending accordingly.

There was, in any case, some feeling that the expansion of higher education had reached the point where excessive numbers of graduates were being produced. This applied not only to the West but also to the socialist countries of Eastern Europe. In the Soviet Union there were the beginnings of containment of entry to higher education, especially in the universities, and Manfred Loetsch of the

Academy of Social Sciences in East Germany said in June that further expansion of higher education should be ended. In East Germany in 1982 as many as 20% were going on to higher education. Loetsch argued that the figure should be stabilized at no more than 25%.

Expenditure on education continued to rise modestly in the Soviet Union and more rapidly in China, which was still emerging from the depredations of the Cultural Revolution. Most of the oil-rich nations also continued to increase their spending. For example, in Saudi Arabia the share of total government expenditure allocated to education in the third five-year development plan (1980–85) was 18.5%, compared with 16% in the previous five-year plan. In the five years up to 1982, as many as five elementary schools had been opened in Saudi Arabia every week and one secondary school every 11 days.

As the 1982–83 school year opened, some 57,320,000 elementary, secondary, and college students were enrolled in the United States. That was a decrease of 522,000 students from the previous year. Elementary and secondary students numbered 44.8 million, continuing the steady decline since 1970, when there were 51.3 million students in those grades. College students increased by 100,000 to a record enrollment of 12.5 million. The U.S. Census Bureau reported that private school enrollments, especially those of Roman Catholic systems, had declined markedly.

Primary and Secondary Education. Almost all industrialized countries were afflicted by the consequences of falling birthrates, with the result that most governments were almost desperately seeking ways of reducing the number of teachers, both through systems of early retirement and by reducing the number of teacher-training establishments. In Italy particularly generous terms were offered to teachers with 15 years or more of service, namely, to retire at 80% of salary. This led to something of an exodus of teachers from the schools. In the U.K. there were reductions in the number of teachers being trained. In The Netherlands it was expected that there would be a loss of some 12,000 teaching posts in the period up to

Bruce Brombacher, an eighth-grade teacher from Columbus, Ohio, was named 1982 Teacher of the Year. The national event is sponsored by the Encyclopaedia Britannica companies, *Good Housekeeping* magazine, and the Council of Chief State School Officers. Brombacher is the first Ohio educator ever to win the award.

WIDE WORLD

Ecumenical Movement:
see Religion

1985, while in West Germany the reduction was expected to be on the order of 10,000 positions over the same period.

A number of governments attempted to bring about a real reduction in teachers' salaries. In Denmark the principal teachers' union called for a ban on overtime in July in order to protect teachers' jobs; at least 1,000 teachers there were expected to become unemployed because of declining enrollments. In the United Kingdom teachers' unions effectively prevented compulsory layoffs in 1982, although the projections for containing expenditure in 1983 suggested that they would soon be necessary.

In the U.S. a cut of nearly 6% in federal support for elementary and secondary education followed the previous year's 8% reduction. Federal dollars going to education fell from $5,610,000,000 in 1981–82 to $5.3 billion in the 1982–83 school year. In keeping with Pres. Ronald Reagan's "new federalism," there was a shift in federal funding away from categorical grants (for specific, narrowly defined programs) to block grants—distributed to the states on the basis of population—for use in broad, general areas. The result was to give the states considerably more discretion as to how the money was to be spent. However, for the 30 educational programs that were combined into block grants, total federal funding declined from $535 million to $484 million.

Hardest hit by the cutbacks would be districts that had large numbers of students targeted by the federal programs—the economically disadvantaged, the handicapped, and the non-English-speaking. Bilingual education was cut by 15% and vocational education by 4%. It was estimated that by the time President Reagan's proposed education policies were fully implemented, the federal

contribution to education would have been halved and the influence of the federal government in the area of education would have been reduced significantly. Federal officials pointed out, however, that the federal component of local school budgets was relatively small and that, overall, the proportion of local school budgets funded by the federal government only fell from 8.7% in 1981 to 8.2% in 1982.

The Reagan administration concluded that forced busing was ineffective. It explored the idea of assisting school districts that sought to modify busing plans that were not working. At the same time, the administration said that it was not reversing basic policy and was only seeking better, voluntary means of encouraging desegregation. The Department of Justice did not undertake any desegregation action during the first 20 months of the Reagan administration. However, the U.S. Civil Rights Commission strongly endorsed the continuation of mandatory busing to desegregate schools.

The Northeast trailed the rest of the U.S. in promoting school integration, according to a report to the House of Representatives. The Joint Center for Political Studies told a House committee that between 1968 and 1980 the Southern and border states made great progress in achieving integration in the classroom. By 1970 the South was the least segregated region for U.S. blacks. The Northeast had become the most segregated area. The Center reported that segregation of Hispanics had increased in each region.

In its first opinion of the law that provided "free and appropriate" education to handicapped children and youth, the U.S. Supreme Court said that provisions for the handicapped could be limited. In their opinion on the Education for All Handicapped Children Act of 1975, the justices concluded that the Congress intended that education be accessible to the handicapped but did not intend a specific type of education—nor that it necessarily be equal to that provided other children.

A Texas law prohibiting the free education of children of illegal aliens was overturned by the U.S. Supreme Court. State officials estimated that 5% of the Texas population was there illegally. Texas had the only law in the U.S. limiting the free education of the children of illegal aliens. The law required exclusion of the children or the payment of tuition for them. A court majority held that without education the children would suffer a lifetime of hardship. (*See* Law.)

The Reagan administration changed the role of the Internal Revenue Service in denying tax exemptions to private schools that practice racial discrimination. The Department of Justice said that the IRS simply does not have the legal right to deny exemptions. The department denied that its action signaled a retreat on the enforcement of civil rights.

The U.S. Supreme Court decided that when a school district bans certain books and thus deprives students' access to ideas, those students have the right to take their case to federal courts. The Nassau County, N.Y., school board had removed some books from library shelves, an act

The U.S. Supreme Court ruled in June that every handicapped child did not necessarily have to be provided with special assistance to reach full academic potential. The court ruled that a school district in Peekskill, New York, was not required to provide a sign-language interpreter for Amy Rowley, who is deaf.

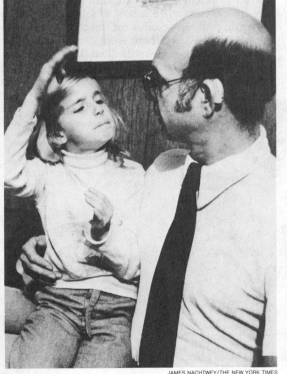

JAMES NACHTWEY/THE NEW YORK TIMES

World Education

Most recent official data

Country	1st level (primary) Students (full-time)	1st level Teachers (full-time)	1st level Total schools	General 2nd level (secondary) Students (full-time)	General 2nd level Teachers (full-time)	General 2nd level Total schools	Vocational 2nd level Students (full-time)	Vocational 2nd level Teachers (full-time)	Vocational 2nd level Total schools	3rd level (higher) Students (full-time)	3rd level Teachers (full-time)	3rd level Total schools	Literacy % of population	Literacy Over age
Afghanistan	1,006,094	32,937	4,146	116,714	4,903	317	16,784	1,211	28	21,118	817	29	28.6	5
Algeria	4,600,000	88,481	9,263[2]	999,937	38,845	1,128[2]	26,218[1]	2,292[1]	71[2]	57,208	7,401	...	26.4	15
Angola	1,388,110	25,000	5,585	153,000[3]	4,393[3]	177	2,005[4]	173[4]	73	4,746	333	1	15.0	15
Argentina	4,003,670	224,679	24,843	1,295,615[3]	178,681[3]	4,952[3]	...	...	...	475,799	45,089	1,001	92.6	15
Australia	1,871,617	91,386	8,180	1,115,782[3]	86,364[3]	1,553	25,219[4]	2,706[4]	...	331,378	33,172	156	98.5	...
Austria	401,396	26,369	3,466	549,061	45,213	2,023	150,356[1]	14,911[1]	1,146[1]	123,463	11,792	37	98.0	15
Bahrain	48,406	2,963	114	23,727	951	21	2,846[1]	233[1]	5[1]	3,650	159	2	63.4	15
Bangladesh	8,219,313	187,504	40,313	2,763,372[1,3]	111,927[1,3]	9,426[1,3]	...	...	...	154,496	15,784	700	25.8	15
Bermuda	5,878	320	22	4,215	362	13	...	...	...	575	63	1	99.9	15
Bolivia	904,874	41,878	7,890	210,385[3]	9,974[3]	2,772[3]	16,206[4]	2,409[4]	39[4]	178,217	6,179	548	40.0	15
Botswana	179,564	5,316	415	19,129	844	38	3,238[1]	318[1]	25[1]	928	113	1	37.5	15
Brazil	22,025,449	862,282	192,723	2,667,359[1,3]	183,476[1,3]	7,133[1,3]	...	...	...	1,770,617	109,788	882	83.0	15
Brunei	31,677	1,800	175	16,805	1,326	27	1,284[1]	212[1]	6[1]	143	57	1	77.8	15
Bulgaria	70,125	4,514	776	1,064,383	61,154	2,774	207,011	17,976	524	72,386	11,579	44	95.0	8
Burma	3,731,160	84,593	23,099	924,739	31,433	1,898	14,739[1]	1,156[1]	68[1]	112,671	3,922	35	69.7	15
Cameroon	1,302,974	25,248	4,721	152,618	5,112	301	53,238[1]	1,972[1]	164[1]	11,901	439	10	47.4	10
Canada	3,313,231	271,034[5]	15,392[5]	1,709,798	...	...	...	...	...	675,430	54,980	66	95.6	14
Chile	2,139,319	66,354	8,220	392,940	24,387	700	161,809	4,176	277	118,978	11,419	15	90.8	15
China	143,330,000	2,600,000	900,000	48,596,000	...	160,000	2,220,000	...	2,000[1]	1,280,000	...	598	95.0	15
Colombia	4,337,607	139,277	32,230	1,879,118[1,3]	85,938[1,3]	3,252	...	...	...	271,302	25,708	70	98.5	15
Congo	383,018	6,852	1,310	148,857	3,148	122	10,361[1]	607[1]	36[1]	4,767	254	1	28.8	...
Costa Rica	347,708	10,536	3,041	103,579	4,263	225	30,229	2,056	74	55,378	1,967	4	84.0	15
Cuba	1,409,765	83,113	11,771	913,629	87,703	827	356,133[1]	22,615[1]	445[1]	165,496	10,736	28	98.0	15
Cyprus	64,274	2,862	604	54,206	13,380	117	7,604[1]	761[1]	22[1]	1,875	186	13	89.0	15
Czechoslovakia	1,930,634	90,282	6,612	149,210	8,918	336	244,133[1]	17,353[1]	554[1]	152,584	18,624	42	99.5	15
Denmark	448,370	40,261	2,263	61,757	44,642	2,516	247,457[1]	5,792[1]	271	104,978	6,713	358	100.0	15
Ecuador	1,427,627	39,825	10,655	475,857	24,120	990	59,588	5,951	221	274,968	11,998	30	79.0	10
Egypt	4,434,557	137,045	10,604	1,994,514	77,095	2,450	598,450[1]	34,782[1]	466[1]	550,171	23,390	12	45.7	10
El Salvador	900,623	16,563	3,103	29,436	2,344[3]	171	48,671[1]	25[4]	9[4]	32,058	2,556	14	49.0	15
Fiji	127,325	4,435	656	35,238	1,766	137	3,186[1]	451[1]	39[1]	2,760	166	1	79.0	15
Finland	583,450	38,311	4,853	341,054	19,530	1,056	143,277[1]	13,547[1]	541[1]	88,244	6,194	21	100.0	15
France	4,609,422	235,415	51,440	5,133,341	349,743	11,147	1,089,439	60,239	231[4]	853,532	41,978	82	100.0	7
Germany, East	2,250,918[6]	168,849[5]	12,233[2]	...	...	5,906	459,485	16,355	1,214	385,600	36,773	290	100.0	15
Germany, West	2,783,867	451,894[5]	23,766[5]	5,950,897	...	...	610,400	35,798	5,350	1,192,755	169,050	3,147	99.0	15
Greece	922,698	35,750	9,593	585,130	26,921	2,162	125,039	...	1,991	99,713	7,077	157	86.0	15
Guatemala	826,613	24,242	7,708	171,903[1,3]	9,613[1,3]	753	...	...	...	34,301	2,845	...	36.7	15
Honduras	582,612	16,612	5,568	125,016[3]	4,417[3]	254	4,250[4]	152[4]	14	24,601	1,507	3	59.5	10
Hong Kong	539,545	17,972	790	444,718	15,927[3]	386	11,485	...	20	41,327	3,025	23	80.9	15
Hungary	1,213,500	78,053	3,800	209,300	15,966	531	157,400	10,700	328[1]	63,400	13,843	57	98.2	15
India	70,949,386	1,311,931	476,249	28,372,339	1,694,651	152,139	421,026[1]	14,024	2,045[1]	4,296,242	235,822	9,805	36.1	15
Indonesia	22,487,053	665,264	105,485	4,364,598	261,864	13,219	802,013[1]	67,312[1]	2,638[1]	397,485	46,668	389	72.0	10
Iran	4,403,106	154,577	40,197	2,370,341	91,960	7,667	314,135[1]	13,029[1]	950[1]	175,675	15,453	244	36.1	15
Iraq	2,609,182	92,603	10,560	897,001	27,987	1,579	72,986[1]	4,700[1]	155[1]	98,327	5,464	62	52.0	15
Ireland	568,364	20,068	3,494	293,809	18,457	822	6,792	202	47	41,928	3,983	58	100.0	15
Israel	574,741	29,940	1,808	181,094	14,434	651	82,173	8,596	376	91,130	...	51	93.4	14
Italy	4,335,911	285,908	29,785	3,482,521	276,987	31,524	1,816,941[1]	149,003[1]	5,334[1]	719,449	48,118	67	94.0	15
Ivory Coast	888,728	21,640	2,697	172,280[1,3]	4,026	...	...	707[1]	...	12,765	580	2	41.2	15
Japan	11,901,526	475,037	25,043	10,224,529[1,3]	517,744[1,3]	16,092[1,3]	...	...	...	2,238,831	128,039	1,043	100.0	15
Jordan	448,411	13,898	1,095	238,763	11,267	1,333	9,360	641	44	27,526	1,178	31	60.0	15
Korea, South	5,586,494	122,727	6,517	3,580,258	87,974	2,955	827,579	25,573	321	734,900	23,750	232	94.3	15
Kuwait	125,114	6,936	180	152,578	13,460	206	7,148[1]	1,220[1]	34[1]	11,621	1,157	1	59.6	15
Laos	441,000	14,416	5,918	67,553	2,996	...	9,060[1]	683[1]	47[1]	1,684	152	3	41.0	15
Lebanon	388,482	33,245[5,6]	2,144	238,773	...	257	29,930[1]	3,161[1]	...	78,628	2,313	15	88.0	15
Lesotho	244,838	4,782	1,081	23,355	940	96	1,952[1]	160[1]	12[1]	1,048	162	9	60.0	15
Liberia	206,876	5,090	1,151	51,231	2,974	275	2,023[1]	80[1]	6[1]	3,789	190	3	25.4	15
Libya	656,541	30,489	2,539	257,479	16,526	1,156	40,145[1]	2,790[1]	129[1]	14,351	1,922	19	52.4	15
Luxembourg	27,927	1,449	541	9,100	1,803[3]	...	16,102[1]	...	...	232	168	2	100.0	15
Malawi	779,676	11,552	2,371	16,431	779	65	2,632[1]	199[1]	13[1]	1,620	203	2	16.5	15
Malaysia	2,033,803	73,881	6,461	1,102,908	48,199	970	17,424	1,430	37	57,139	5,569	34	60.8	10
Mali	293,227	6,877	1,263	64,491	...	15	4,870[1]	666[1]	3	4,789	488	6	2.2	15
Mauritius	123,666	6,177	257	80,881	3,075	148	721[1]	61[1]	3[1]	470	76	1	84.6	15
Mexico	14,282,908	353,538	70,797	3,729,916	212,118	9,138	555,100[1]	38,772[1]	2,888[1]	698,139	57,659	236	78.8	15
Morocco	2,331,000	55,303	2,498	826,500	33,696	644	26,168[1]	847[4]	...	98,515	2,558	19	22.2	...
Mozambique	1,376,865	8,751	5,709	135,956	3,789	138	...	...	...	1,852	224	...	27.5	15
Nepal	1,067,900	27,805	7,275	512,400[1,3]	16,376[1,3]	...	...	...	...	39,900	2,311	55	12.5	15
Netherlands, The	1,425,770	66,026	9,690	823,730	54,369	1,525	571,209[1]	50,100[1]	1,870[1]	280,948	28,500	373	100.0	15
New Zealand	493,856	20,402	2,808	224,926	13,527	396	150,976[1]	2,755[1]	29[1]	31,549	3,043	15	100.0	15
Nicaragua	472,167	13,318	4,421	120,522	3,145[3]	259	19,221[1]	55[4]	81[1]	34,710	1,204	4	87.0	15
Nigeria	12,554,222	309,597	36,287	1,597,877	50,952	...	299,678[1]	19,059[1]	402[1]	115,166	5,748	77	29.9	15
Norway	591,323	30,818	3,518	133,664[3]	14,939[3]	1,419[3]	13,696[4]	1,063[4]	30[4]	40,620	3,652	134	100.0	15
Pakistan	7,090,000	139,300	58,395	1,996,000	115,600	8,989	...	...	...	349,259	19,878	554	26.7	10
Panama	335,239	12,598	2,316	129,787	6,331	186	44,291[1]	2,284[1]	116[1]	43,199	3,035	2	84.6	15
Papua New Guinea	288,267	9,280	2,077	37,068	1,559	99	5,949[1]	419[1]	97[1]	2,637	419	3	30.4	10
Paraguay	504,377	18,038	3,425	110,095[3]	9,830[3]	...	...	...	...	25,232	1,984	2	80.0	10
Peru	3,161,400	77,844	20,775	1,306,400	37,383	2,456	202,100[1]	6,422[4]	682[1]	249,800	13,468	33	76.0	15
Philippines	8,112,536	252,338	33,180	2,917,912[3]	104,657[3]	2,445[2]	...	...	...	1,129,056	38,226	...	89.7	10
Poland	4,341,860	224,300	13,926	392,900	22,500	1,201	1,729,000[1]	82,300	6,310	386,500	55,450	91	98.0	15
Puerto Rico	470,039	23,154	2,287[5]	337,153	13,297	...	60,045	2,600	84	130,105	3,300	27	90.5	14
Romania	3,308,432	156,817	14,361	979,741	46,500	971	182,994[1]	3,611[1]	903[1]	192,769	14,592	44	100.0	8
Rwanda	607,480	10,002	1,573	7,112	903[1,3]	56	5,056[1]	...	62	1,134	213	4	49.5	15
Saudi Arabia	930,436	50,010	4,983	377,681	24,866	1,617	21,967[1]	2,347[1]	68	54,397	5,946	17	25.0	...
Senegal	392,541	8,479	1,493	80,146	2,934	89	9,091	578	124[1]	11,852	571	130	45.6	14
Singapore	289,697	11,108	342	177,238	8,807	144	13,001	889	17	24,156	2,226	4	77.9	10
South Africa	4,480,493	164,149[3,5]	2,511[5]	1,225,153	...	...	29,591	...	153	218,275	16,708	106	89.0	...
Soviet Union	34,400,000	2,636,000[5]	73,700	9,900,000	...	56,200	4,612,000[1]	231,300[1]	4,800	5,235,500	345,000	883	100.0	15
Spain	6,788,877	228,307	216,653	1,091,197	66,160	2,445	558,808	36,556	2,142	649,098	40,321	120	90.1	15
Sri Lanka	1,975,749	138,488[5]	3,588	1,159,967	...	5,501	8,897[1]	1,771[1]	25[4]	17,485	2,498	...	82.0	...
Sudan	1,435,127	41,726	5,729	340,238	15,078	1,701	17,954[1]	1,379[1]	60[1]	26,883	1,934	15	68.6	10
Suriname	75,139	2,803	285	29,790	1,854	96	5,669[1]	397[1]	4[4]	2,353	155	2	65.0	15
Swaziland	119,913	3,586	470	24,826	1,433	86	538	65	1	1,603	267	3	22.0	15
Sweden	565,146	140,600[3,5]	4,923[5]	466,818	...	...	103,485	...	526	158,101	...	...	100.0	15
Syria	1,450,045	49,431	7,594	549,577	29,931	1,285	33,961[1]	4,129[1]	77[1]	95,575	1,332	8	61.5	10
Taiwan	2,202,904	69,143	2,428	1,620,165[3]	70,668[3]	1,023[3]	...	...	...	358,437	17,452	104	85.9	15
Thailand	7,242,123	263,204	32,356	1,489,939	66,965	2,249	287,474[1]	18,720[1,2]	356[1]	288,101	22,261	12	81.8	10
Togo	484,272	8,920	2,000	119,801	2,855	...	8,093[1]	348[1]	21[1]	3,638	291	2	54.9	14
Tunisia	1,045,011	26,989	2,613	210,895	12,629	236	64,238[1]	128[4]	...	31,827	3,869	...	25.0	...
Turkey	5,622,000	199,245	44,098	1,711,000	67,235	5,062	538,988[1]	30,098[1]	1,718[1]	270,000	20,643	331	54.7	6
Uganda	1,223,850	36,442	4,294	66,730	3,108	118	12,185[1]	648[1]	50[1]	6,720	677	4	47.9	15
United Kingdom	5,164,000	225,700	...	4,574,000[5]	274,100[5]	...	...	...	...	330,619	43,017	...	100.0	15
United States	23,733,625[2,6]	1,184,939[2,6]	...	16,417,680[3]	996,077[3]	...	...	...	...	12,300,000	860,000	...	100.0	15
Uruguay	323,235	13,698	2,301	172,969	13,980	259	50,428[1]	4,541[1]	105[1]	39,392	3,263	1	93.9	15
Venezuela	2,453,203	82,226	12,753	758,936[3]	47,496[1,3]	1,447	31,518[4]	...	...	282,074	23,451	68	84.9	15
Western Samoa	33,021	1,913[5]	...	19,299	...	39	264	44	4	388	54	6	98.3	10
Yugoslavia	1,422,871	58,742	13,119	1,880,888	129,176[1,3]	5,905	532,762[1]	...	1,630	447,270	23,969	349	83.5	15
Zaire	5,200,000	80,481	5,924	680,000	14,483[1,3]	2,511	184,899[1]	...	...	35,000	2,782	36	57.9	15
Zambia	960,406	19,868	2,809	91,709	3,539	125	9,690[1]	881[1]	26[1]	9,192	412	1	40.7	15
Zimbabwe	1,934,614	33,516	2,548	224,609	6,107	177	9,701[1]	536[1]	...	2,525	483	...	70.8	15

[1] Includes teacher training. [2] Public schools only. [3] Includes vocational. [4] Teacher training only. [5] Data for primary include secondary. [6] Includes preprimary education.

A Texas state law, which held that the children of illegal aliens were not entitled to public school education unless they paid an annual tuition of $1,000, was overturned in June by the U.S. Supreme Court. The court ruled that Texas could not treat these students differently from others even though they resided illegally in the U.S.

that could be challenged on First Amendment grounds, said the court. The justices did not provide specific guidelines for the trial, which was to be heard in the U.S. 2nd Circuit Court of Appeals.

Few teachers' strikes marked the opening of school in the U.S. Teachers in Detroit staged the largest, with 9,880 teachers out of classes and 200,000 students at home. In Teaneck, N.J., striking teachers were "jailed" in a school for two days for defying a judge's order to return to their jobs. Scattered strikes took place in other Michigan communities and in Illinois, Pennsylvania, Ohio, and Montana. The number of teachers affected in those states was about the same as in Detroit. In some cases teachers worked without contracts. Key issues in negotiations were economic—pay freezes or reductions, layoffs, and job security.

Layoffs of teachers increased. The teachers' unions estimated that 40,000–55,000 teachers were laid off for the 1982–83 school year, more than 20% higher than in 1981–82. The American Federation of Teachers said that it was the worst year ever for firings.

After a long decline and a leveling off in 1981 of Scholastic Aptitude Test scores, there was a 3% improvement in 1982. Approximately one million high-school seniors take the test each year to help colleges determine who will be admitted. The producers of the test claimed that it measures general intellectual aptitude and predicts academic success in college. Educators believed that the rise in SAT scores was an indication that the general quality of the schools had improved.

In regard to the school curriculum, the biggest disturbance of the year was caused by the revised textbooks published by the Japanese Education Ministry for the school year starting April 1983. The changes in the secondary-school history books led to severe condemnation, particularly in China and South Korea. In describing Japanese action in China before and during World War II, the Japanese textbook writers had replaced such words as "aggression" and "invasion" with the more innocuous "advance." The textbooks also were said to have deleted or glossed over atrocities committed by Japanese troops and Japan's oppressive pre-1945 colonial rule of Korea. Both China and South Korea lodged official complaints, demanding correction

of the textbook changes. The president of the Japan Teachers' Union, Motofumi Makieda, was one of the most outspoken critics, not only of those particular amendments but of Japan's textbook authorization methods. Agreement was finally reached with the concerned countries that the "errors" would be corrected. (*See* JAPAN.)

There was also a report in August of differences of opinion between West German and U.S. historians about the postwar images of their respective countries presented in textbooks. The evidence came from the Georg Eckert Institute, which since 1979 had coordinated annual meetings of historians from West Germany and the U.S. The complaint on the West German side was that U.S. schoolchildren were presented with an image of Germany as it was during the era of Adolf Hitler and that little was written about Germany after the Hitler era. U.S. historians complained that German history books concentrated on the Vietnam war and on Watergate and other scandals.

In both Hungary and Romania serious doubts were expressed about secondary-school reforms. In Hungary the school reforms of 1972 reduced failure rates in secondary schools by lowering standards, and there was, in addition, a drive to recruit pupils into vocational schools. Indeed, by 1982 some 80% of the secondary school population was in vocational education. The Central Committee of the Socialist Workers' (Communist) Party called in April for the remedying of the "hasty" reforms of 1972, and a new development program for education was promised for 1983. In Romania a similar trend toward vocational education followed a 1978 reform, and with it a demotion of academic subjects. Again, there was a call to remedy the situation.

There were moves among Muslim populations, in the U.K. and West Germany especially, to introduce an Islamic form of education. Proposals were made in London to introduce an Islamic school, particularly for Pakistani Muslims, and concern was expressed in West Berlin about the growth of private schools teaching the Koran for Turks. As many as 30 had been established in West Berlin with the aim, so it was argued, of re-islamicizing Turks along the lines advocated by Iran's Ayatollah Ruhollah Khomeini. Since there were about 1.5 million Turkish workers in West Germany, there was some alarm. Meanwhile, in Turkey the two-year-old military government proposed to make religious education—that is to say, Islam—a compulsory subject in schools. This, however, was not seen as part of the Islamic revival in the Middle East but rather as an attempt to ensure that religion was taught properly.

Administrative changes were less frequently reported than in past years, although there were underlying moves in the U.K. toward more help for private schools and in Australia to increase the federal government's spending on private schools by 7.7%, as against 2% for government schools. In The Netherlands proposals were made in September to change the three-year basic secondary school after the age of 15, so that there would be a choice, of sorts, between a general (three years) and a vocational course (of two, three, or four years). In Nigeria there was a change from five-year secondary schools to three-year junior secondary schools followed by three-year senior secondary schools. Critics in Nigeria said that this was an ineffective reform, since there were no workshops or technical teachers. The government, however, argued that the reform would work since it would be phased in over three years.

A major preoccupation in many parts of the world was with the plight of those aged 15–18, especially in those countries where they were not provided with full-time education. A report of the European Community on unemployment and vocational training published in October said that of the 11 million jobless in the EC countries, 4 million were under 25. The European Commission proposed that every 16-year-old should be offered at least two years in further education or in vocational training, with work experience.

But it was in the less developed countries that progress in schooling was slowest, although their needs were greatest. There was some criticism of the World Bank's lending policy to less developed countries in regard to basic education, which it was accused of neglecting. World Bank lending on basic education had, however, grown from 5% of the total education loans in 1970–74 to 24% by 1979–83. The familiar argument within the World Bank had been that the Bank was at its best when its lending involved the "transfer of technology." This, it was said, happened least in loans for basic education. Nonetheless, the Bank appeared to have recognized that money spent on basic education could have a powerful role in facilitating locally developed solutions to the chronic difficulties of rural schools.

Higher Education. Federal funds to colleges and universities in the United States were cut by 17%, from $5,540,000,000 to $4,570,000,000. The aid provided for loans to students, construction, and a variety of other kinds of support. Overriding a presidential veto, the U.S. Congress appropriated $169 million more for financial aid for college students. The additional money ensured full funding for student loan programs.

Students in the U.S. found on the average that going to college in 1982–83 cost 11% more than in 1981–82, according to the College Board. The average per-year cost of attending a public four-year college was estimated at $4,388, while expenses for those in private four-year colleges averaged $7,475.

U.S. colleges raised tuition and other direct costs for students. The situation for students worsened as women found it more difficult to find jobs to help pay for their children's educational expenses. A study of the Education Commission of the states found that most education and state officials expected state appropriations to trail inflation. This would require higher tuitions, which were already rising about 15% per year, according to the National Association of Student Financial Aid Administrators. State-supported schools provided education for some 78% of U.S. college students.

College enrollments in the U.S. could drop by 15% by the mid-1990s, according to a study conducted by the Brookings Institution. The decline would result from the fall in births and the subsequent decrease in high-school graduates. For three decades colleges in the U.S. had experienced uninterrupted growth.

The college graduating class in the U.S. in 1983 would be the largest ever. It would also be the most diverse in regard to student backgrounds, would be divided almost equally between men and women, and would have more older students. The number of persons planning to enter graduate schools was expected to decline.

In what two dissenting judges branded "benign neglect" of earlier government pressures to desegregate state education systems, a U.S. Court of Appeals upheld a North Carolina-U.S. Department of Education settlement. The decade-long case was settled when the state agreed to provide new programs at historically black colleges. In a change of policy the state was permitted to leave duplicate programs intact in nearby white institutions.

The traditional open-door admissions policies of U.S. junior and community colleges began to change. The schools began to establish entrance requirements and to drop students who did not maintain acceptable academic standards.

China began 1982 with 704 higher education establishments, 270 more than in 1965, just before the start of the Cultural Revolution. There were then 606,000 students; in 1982 the number had increased to 1,280,000. The demand for graduates remained more than twice the supply. The new Chinese minister of education, He Dongchang (Ho Tung-ch'ang), called for more diversification of higher education, including more two-year practical courses.

In the West it was only in France that there was conspicuous growth. In 1982 the higher education budget was up 15% from the previous year. In March the Claude Jeanette Commission was established by the minister of education, Alain Savary, to draw up a framework for a new higher education law. Savary also spelled out the expectations of the French government for higher education. First was a contribution to combat the recession through teaching and research; the second expectation comprised ways of developing those industrial sectors that would be important in the future, such as biotechnology and computers; the third was collaboration between universities and research bodies; and the fourth was increased effectiveness in spreading new knowledge to the population as a whole.

In West Germany, although student numbers continued to increase, there was growing criticism of the inefficiency of the whole system. In May Ralf Dahrendorf, director of the London School of Economics and formerly a leading liberal politician in West Germany, attacked the German universities at the annual conference of university vice-chancellors at Konstanz, West Germany. He said that in 1978 West Germany had 15 students per 1,000 inhabitants, compared with 12 in France and 7 in Britain. But in West Germany there were only 1.39 graduations per 1,000 inhabitants, compared with 1.76 in Britain and 1.79 in France.

In Italy student numbers continued to decline. The 2 million enrollments in Italian universities in

1978 had been reduced to 1.3 million in 1981–82. The "mass" universities of the 1970s seemed to be disappearing. In August the Italian Parliament passed a reform bill allowing university rectors to close departments or divisions if enrollment in them rose to more than 4,500 students.

Pressure on the higher education system was at its greatest in Greece; during the year 100,000 candidates presented themselves to Greece's higher education institutions. The seven universities and six graduate schools took 15,000 of them; the vocational colleges 25,000; and 10,000 went abroad. Greece had a far higher proportion of students abroad than any other European country, 20% compared with an average of less than 1% for other members of the European Community.

In Canada the number of students in Quebec was allowed to go on rising. Although the Quebec government cut funds to universities, student enrollments continued to increase. The government took the view that the universities must become more productive. In practice this led to a dispute over the allocation of funds between the newer universities, attracting a new class of French-speaking students, and some of the older institutions.

Several governments declared a need to create more productive institutions. There was much argument in the U.K. about the need to reduce the security of tenure held by university teachers. In France, Savary announced something of a crackdown on absentee university teachers. The university academic year was to be lengthened from 25 to 32 weeks, and professors were required to increase the number of lectures they gave per annum from 75 to 96.

There was, unhappily, ample evidence of interference with freedom of inquiry in many parts of the world. In Israel there was serious trouble in the three West Bank universities—Al-Najah, BirZeit, and Bethlehem—over the official demand that teachers refrain from any kind of support for the Palestine Liberation Organization. One hundred foreign teachers in the universities, including 30 from the U.S. and 10 from Great Britain, complained of interference with the right of free expression. The University of Nairobi in Kenya was actually closed down in September because during August students had taken part in an abortive coup against Pres. Daniel arap Moi.

The concept of an open university, pioneered in the U.K., continued to have some influence. The first such university in India was opened in the southern state of Andhra Pradesh in August. It was intended chiefly to help with nonformal education for the rural population. In India, also, the National Adult Education Program, which had been initiated by the Janata Party government in 1978, was given a further lease on life by the government of Indira Gandhi. The original intention was that 100 million illiterates in the 15–35 age group should become literate by 1983–84. Mrs. Gandhi's government took a more realistic approach, and the target date was deferred to 1990.

(JOEL L. BURDIN; TUDOR DAVID)

See also Libraries; Motion Pictures.

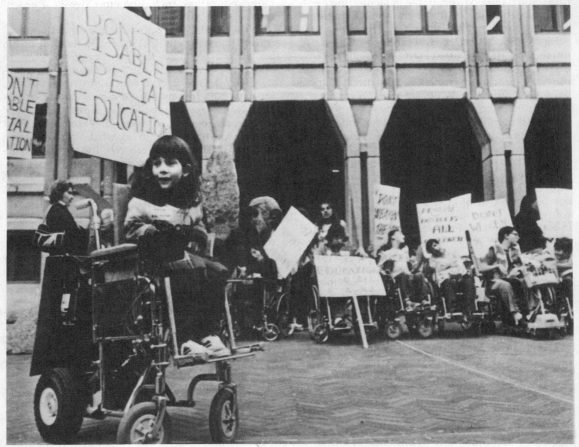

Students protesting a reduction in funds for educating the handicapped demonstrated in front of the federal building in Seattle, Washington, where the U.S. Department of Education was holding hearings on the proposed cutback.

THE PROMISE OF EARLY LEARNING

by James M. Wolf

Interest and support for early learning have been expressed by philosophers and scholars throughout history. Comenius, in the 17th century, espoused the teaching of all knowledge to the child and advocated the "School of the Mother's Knee." John Locke, whose thinking dominated the 18th century, wrote, "I have always had a fancy that learning might be made play and recreation for young children." Lord Henry Brougham in 1828 argued that the child can and does learn more before the age of six than during any other period in his life. However, it was not until the late 1950s and 1960s that evidence and experience were accumulated to support Lord Brougham's notion that children can learn more and more rapidly from birth to age six than at any other period in their lives.

Two books are frequently cited as catalysts for the revolution in early learning that began at that time. Joseph McVicker Hunt's *Intelligence and Experience* (1961) documented the importance of adequate environmental stimulation for a child's optimal development. Benjamin Bloom's classic *Stability and Change in Human Characteristics* (1964) demonstrated that there is a growth curve for each human characteristic. For example, half of a child's future height is reached by age two and a half. By the time a child enters school at age six, he has developed as much as two-thirds of the intelligence he will have at maturity.

As a result of these findings, a wide variety of experimental early childhood programs emerged to challenge the older concepts of child development. The idea of fixed intelligence was no longer a tenable theory. Bloom found that extreme environments—either very favourable or underprivileged—could affect the development of intelligence during the first four years of life. According to Hunt, the

---

James M. Wolf is Director of the U.S. Department of Defense Dependents Schools, Panama Region.

preschool years, especially the first four, appear to be highly important for the achievement of initiative, trust, compassion, curiosity, and intelligence.

The Pathfinders. In 1967 Maya Pines published her epochal book *Revolution in Learning*. It is historically significant because it was written for parents and summarized the work of many of the pathfinders in early learning. Pines discussed such projects as the talking typewriter experiment, in which Omar Moore taught some 60 children as young as three and four to read, write, and compose poetry. The americanization of Montessori methods was also described, particularly the work of Nancy Rambusch at the Whitby School in Connecticut, where she demonstrated the learning potential of three- and four-year-olds from advantaged homes. Bettye Caldwell's work in children's centres where six-month-old babies received cognitive training demonstrated that culturally determined mental retardation in young babies was reversible. Two of the more controversial pathfinders were Carl Bereiter and Siegfried Engelmann, who developed a special preschool program for disadvantaged children that enabled them to start first grade on an equal footing with more privileged children.

Efforts to aid children and adults with deviant conditions frequently provide insights and approaches that can be used for enrichment of the so-called normal child. Glenn Doman and his colleagues, pioneers in the treatment of brain-injured children, have applied their concept and findings about neurological dysorganization in brain-impaired children to the enhancement of neurological organization in the average and superior child. The mastery of reading skills is one of the intervention strategies Doman uses in the treatment of very young brain-injured children. His book *How to Teach Your Baby to Read* has been used successfully by mothers of nonimpaired children throughout the world and is now published in 15 languages. Sylvia Ashton-Warner in New Zealand is another pathfinder in early reading.

Teaching young children to read is a controversial topic among U.S. educators. Some still oppose the practice of having a parent engage in systematized reading instruction with preschool children. Skepticism is also expressed by some teachers, who surmise that learning to read at home interferes with the method used in school and that most children are not ready for reading before the age of six. Too often, it is said, early reading efforts are the result of parental anxieties and pressure and serve primarily to satisfy the parent's ego. In addition, teaching preschoolers to read is an infringement on their precious childhood. However, these statements are more myth than fact.

The Confirmers. Beginning in the mid-1960s, early learning and early childhood enrichment became acceptable to greater numbers of parents and educators. However, there was a need for research to corroborate the pathfinders' results—to confirm the assertion that early learning is beneficial to all children.

Federal programs provided the major source for confirmation of early learning among children from low-income families. In 1965 Pres. Lyndon Johnson hailed Head Start, an early education program, as the principal weapon in his administration's attempt to achieve a Great Society. The results of a national evaluation released by the Westinghouse Learning Corp. and Ohio University in 1969 came close to destroying Head Start and discrediting the concept of early learning and intervention. However, *The Carnegie Quarterly* notes, in an article entitled "New Optimism About Preschool Education," that ". . . recent studies based on new data or reanalysis of the old suggest that the Westinghouse conclusions were premature. . . . Preschool education [early learning] apparently gives youngsters a lasting effect over their peers who get no special help. . . ."

Other research findings have supported this statement. In 1977 Irving Lazar of Cornell University completed his compilation of data from 14 longitudinal studies of children from low-income families who participated in Head Start programs. The findings indicate that, as compared with control groups, children who participated in early childhood and family development programs were placed in remedial special education classes less often, were held back in a grade less often, scored higher on intelligence tests, and were superior in social, emotional, cognitive, and language development after entering school. In a chapter on "Enrichment of Early Childhood Experiences," Caldwell and her associates describe projects that started intervention before age three and that also provide evidence of the effectiveness of these programs in modifying intellectual development.

The Advocates and Resource Materials. Joan Beck was among the first journalists to make a case for early learning. In her book *How to Raise a Brighter Child,* she wrote about the pathfinders in early learning and detailed how all parents can raise their child's useful level of intelligence significantly by the ways in which they care for him or her during the first six years of life. Siegfried Engelmann and his wife, Therese, drawing on their extensive experience with preschool children, developed a programmed step-by-step guide for parents called *Give Your Child a Superior Mind.*

In a 1982 issue of the *Elementary School Journal,* Richard Norton and Doman wrote: "The potential of the young human brain, whether injured or intact, is virtually unlimited and varies inversely with age. Given proper informational, social, nutritional, and emotional nourishment (e.g., speaking, understanding, reading, writing), most children are capable of functioning at the level which is called gifted." The authors propose that an ". . . entire new generation of 'gifted' children is possible." Doman has developed a program on *How to Multiply Your Baby's Intelligence* in which parents are taught how to teach their infants to read, do math, do gymnastics, play the violin, and speak a foreign language.

A group of child development specialists at the Princeton Center for Infancy have condensed the viewpoints of leading experts from over 800 books on child-rearing practices in a complete and easy-to-use guide entitled *The Parenting Advisor.* There are also a number of newsletters that deal with early learning. One of the most interesting, produced monthly by Dennis Dunn and Edwin Hargitt, is called *Growing Child,* with a supplement issue called *Growing Parent.* It should be noted that there is no one method of achieving the goals of early learning, but these materials contain many useful and practical ideas.

The Future. Early learning is an idea whose time has come. Methods now exist to increase the intelligence, creativity, and sociability of all children. However, like most new knowledge, it has the potential for misuse and abuse, and it must be applied with loving care and joyfulness. Early learning, to be successful, must be made "play and recreation" for babies and young children.

Research on early learning during the past two decades has produced exciting findings on how to teach very young children. The next two decades will produce refinements and a new set of challenges. New knowledge gained from brain research will provide more definition for the frequency, duration, and intensity of appropriate early learning activities. This new knowledge will also provide more specific information on the relationship between nutrition and brain chemistry. Although the "School of the Mother's Knee" will never be completely replaced, advancements in technology will affect early learning techniques. The transformation of the ordinary television set into a home-entertainment and educational centre and the proliferation of home computers will offer new opportunities for research and innovative home programs in early learning. Most important, in the decade ahead, early learning will become more accepted and will be demanded by parents and professionals as a common practice to be applied during the first years of life to ensure that all children come closer to reaching and expanding their potential.

Egypt

A republic of northeast Africa, Egypt is bounded by Israel, Sudan, Libya, the Mediterranean Sea, and the Red Sea. Area: 997,667 sq km (385,201 sq mi). Pop. (1982 est.): 45 million. Cap. and largest city: Cairo (pop., 1979 est., 5,399,000). Language: Arabic. Religion (1980 est.): Muslim 81.8%; Christian 17.8%; atheist 0.4%. President in 1982, Hosni Mubarak; prime ministers, Hosni Mubarak and, from January 2, Ahmad Fuad Mohieddin.

During 1982 Pres. Hosni Mubarak's strong personality enabled him to steer Egypt back toward the Arab fold while retaining the confidence of Western leaders, particularly U.S. Pres. Ronald Reagan. At home his grim economic inheritance proved a heavy burden. Although much emphasis had been put on economic reform since the assassination on Oct. 6, 1981, of Pres. Anwar as-Sadat, little had materialized by the end of 1982. The trade gap widened during the year and remittances from Egyptians working in other nations fell. On January 2 President Mubarak appointed Ahmad Fuad Mohieddin to the post of prime minister; Mubarak himself had held the office since he assumed the presidency in October 1981. The day after his appointment the new prime minister announced a reshuffled and enlarged Cabinet, in which the most important reorganizations involved the economic portfolios. Muhammad Abdel Fattah Ibrahim, governor of the central bank and a former minister of finance in the mid-1970s, was named as deputy prime minister responsible for economy and finance and minister for international investment and cooperation. He replaced Abderrazzak Abdel Meguid, who was dropped from the Cabinet. Along with another minister, Abdel Meguid had been named in a corruption case; both were later cleared of suspicion by the attorney general.

The reshuffle was widely interpreted as a temporary measure, since Ibrahim was suffering from poor health. Further changes were announced on August 31: Ibrahim left the Cabinet, together with Fuad Hashim Awad, the economy and foreign trade minister, and five other ministers. Although Ibrahim's position was left vacant, Wagih Shindy, as minister of investment and international cooperation, took over part of his former responsibilities. The new economy and foreign trade minister was Mustafa Kamel Said.

At the congress of the ruling National Democratic Party on January 26, President Mubarak was elected unopposed to the post of chairman of the party. In his speech to the congress, Mubarak reaffirmed the priority that had guided the Cabinet reshuffles; the national economy, he stressed, was Egypt's primary interest. A five-year economic plan was to be drawn up with the advice of a conference of experts.

Relations with Israel remained a thorny question for President Mubarak in his dealings with the other Arab nations. In a low-key ceremony on April 25, Israel handed back to Egypt the last remnants of the occupied Sinai Peninsula as part of the agreement reached at Camp David. Egypt's ambassador to Israel was recalled in September, however, in response to the massacre by Lebanese Christians of Palestinians in Beirut. Nevertheless, Israel remained Egypt's main oil customer, taking 40,000 bbl a day.

In welcoming the unified Arab position on the Middle East reached at the Arab summit meeting in Fez, Morocco, in September, Foreign Affairs Minister Kamal Hassan Ali suggested Egypt's ambivalence. Hailing Fez as "an important landmark and turning point in the Arab countries' position, directed toward achieving peace and recognizing the existence of Israel," Ali added that the proposals that emerged were "goals and principles" that still needed to be discussed further by the Arab countries and the U.S. government. Although the Fez declaration was closer to Egypt's position than the solution proposed by President Reagan, Egypt nevertheless supported the Reagan plan. This was because President Mubarak took the view that the U.S. held the key cards in any comprehensive Middle East peace plan. (See MIDDLE EASTERN AFFAIRS.)

Egypt's drift back toward Arab orthodoxy was emphasized by the president's enthusiastic espousal of a union with Sudan. On October 23 at El Arish, where six months earlier the Sinai had been formally handed back, a ceremony took place at which Mubarak and Pres. Gaafar Nimeiry of Sudan formally declared the "integration" of Egypt and Sudan. It was the third time since the overthrow of King Farouk in 1952 that Egypt had attempted a confederation with another Arab nation. The other two attempts, with Syria and with Libya, both broke down. This time, under President Mubarak, the union was to be more

Egypt

On April 25 the Egyptian flag was raised over the Sinai Peninsula. Israel had agreed to return the Sinai to Egypt as part of the Camp David accord.

BARRY IVERSON—GAMMA/LIAISON

gradual, with a ten-year trial period. At the same time, Foreign Minister Ali was at pains to stress in September that while Egypt welcomed resumed relations with the Arab world, it was in no hurry and would not put pressure on any Arab country over the issue of Egypt's exclusion from the Arab League.

Five men convicted of killing Sadat were executed in Cairo on April 15, two by firing squad and three by hanging. Prison sentences on 17 other conspirators were upheld. A crackdown on Muslim fundamentalists announced on September 16 resulted in 58 arrests. The government was forced to ask the People's Assembly for a renewal of the emergency powers granted for one year after Sadat's death. The Coptic patriarch, Shenuda III, having been stripped of his official status in 1981 for allegedly contributing to tension between Copts and Muslims, remained incommunicado.

In spite of these events, President Mubarak appeared to be taking a comparatively lenient line with political opponents. Many opponents of Sadat, arrested before his assassination, were released during the year. On July 17 the Interior Ministry announced a decision to release 453 detainees. They included Sheikh Shawqi Istanbuli, father of one of Sadat's assassins. The 453 were among a group of more than 1,500 people who had been held since September 1981. But the president also showed his hand against confidants of Sadat. Reports from Cairo on October 26 said that the younger brother of the late president, Esmat as-Sadat, was to stand trial on charges of corruption.

Egypt's economic problems included a trade gap that had deteriorated in 1981 to $4.8 billion; declining remittances, down 19%; lower income from tourism, down 24%; and reduced income from Suez Canal tolls. Tourism, particularly from the U.S., was affected by the aftermath of Sadat's assassination. On September 24 a young Muslim extremist attacked a tourist bus near the pyramids at Giza, slightly injuring two Soviet visitors. In addition, Egypt had become the world's tenth largest debtor nation, with foreign debts estimated at $16 billion.

Although inflation was officially estimated at 9.6%, a more realistic figure was thought to be 20–30%. Maintenance of subsidies—currently at $2.4 billion a year—was becoming more burdensome. Some $975 million, equivalent to more than the entire annual income from the Suez Canal, was being used to subsidize bread sales alone. With a population increasing by 1.2 million a year, Egypt had become partly dependent on imported food. Once an exporter of more than 640,000 metric tons of rice a year, the nation had exported no rice since 1980.

Crude oil production was expected to rise to 740,000 bbl a day in the financial year ending July 1, 1983, compared with 660,000 bbl a day in the financial year 1981–82. Gas output in the same period was expected to rise to 2.8 million metric tons, compared with 2.5 million metric tons in the previous year.

An aid agreement worth $284 million was signed in Brussels on May 25 by Minister of State for Foreign Affairs Boutros Boutros-Ghali and Léo

EGYPT

Education. (1979–80) Primary, pupils 4,434,557, teachers 137,045; secondary, pupils 1,994,514, teachers 77,095; vocational, pupils 552,151, teachers 31,130; teacher training, students 46,299, teachers 3,652; higher (1977–78), students 550,171, teaching staff 23,390.

Finance. Monetary unit: Egyptian pound, with (Sept. 20, 1982) an official rate of E£0.83 to U.S. $1 (free rate of E£1.43 = £1 sterling). Gold and other reserves (April 1982) U.S. $801 million. Budget (1979 actual): revenue E£4,343 million; expenditure E£4,517 million. Gross national product (1979) E£13,260 million. Money supply (April 1982) E£6,737 million. Cost of living (1975 = 100; Feb. 1982) 218.

Foreign Trade. (1981) Imports E£6,147 million; exports E£2,263 million. Import sources: U.S. 20%; West Germany 10%; France 9%; Italy 7%; U.K. 5%. Export destinations: Italy 26%; Israel 17%; Japan 5%; Greece 5%. Main exports (1980): crude oil 58%; cotton 14%; petroleum products 6%; cotton yarn 6%; fruit and vegetables 5%.

Transport and Communications. Roads (1979) 28,910 km. Motor vehicles in use (1980): passenger 325,500; commercial 113,300. Railways: (1980) 4,667 km; traffic (1978) 9,290,000,000 passenger-km, freight 2,302,000,000 net ton-km. Air traffic (1981): 3,264,000,000 passenger-km; freight 40.2 million net ton-km. Shipping (1981): merchant vessels 100 gross tons and over 307; gross tonnage 599,042. Telephones (Dec. 1977) 473,000. Radio receivers (Dec. 1979) 5.4 million. Television receivers (Dec. 1979) 1.3 million.

Agriculture. Production (in 000; metric tons; 1981): wheat 1,806; barley 103; millet 653; corn 3,308; rice 2,236; potatoes c. 1,120; sugar, raw value 679; tomatoes c. 2,632; onions c. 527; dry broad beans c. 262; watermelons c. 1,267; dates c. 428; oranges c. 1,137; grapes c. 294; cotton, lint c. 520; cheese c. 247; beef and buffalo meat c. 245. Livestock (in 000; 1981): cattle 1,912; buffalo 2,347; sheep 1,599; goats 1,451; asses c. 1,746; camels 84; chickens c. 27,903.

Industry. Production (in 000; metric tons; 1981): cement 3,432; iron ore (50% metal content; 1980) 1,780; crude oil 31,795; natural gas (cu m) 2,430,000; petroleum products (1979) 11,480; sulfuric acid 46; fertilizers (nutrient content; 1980–81) nitrogenous 400, phosphate c. 93; salt (1980) 636; cotton yarn 244; cotton fabrics (m) 631,000; electricity (kw-hr; 1980) 18,520,000.

Tindemans, chairman of the Council of Ministers of the European Communities. U.S. aid to Egypt remained the largest single commitment of any Western nation; on May 26 contracts were signed with the U.S. for the enrichment of uranium for four proposed nuclear power plants. On March 26 the World Bank announced a $90 million loan to finance development of the Abu Qir offshore gas field.

Energy remained the brightest element in the economy. Substantial oil finds, particularly one discovered in the Gulf of Suez in November 1981 by the Suez Oil Co., were expected to yield between 50,000 and 100,000 bbl a day. On the basis of the find, British Petroleum, a partner in the Suez Oil Co. along with Royal Dutch Shell, Deminex of West Germany, and the Egyptian General Petroleum Corp., proposed to make Egypt, over the next five- or six-year period, second only to the North Sea in its development budget. The output of the Morgan Field, Egypt's largest in production in 1982, was 150,000 bbl a day. The Suez find was, therefore, a substantial addition to known reserves. Royal Dutch Shell also announced that it had struck oil in the Western Desert.

In the area of defense spending, President Mubarak was anxious to diversify sources of weapons procurement. France seemed likely to be the country to which Egypt would turn; it was reported in

January that Egypt had agreed to purchase 20 Mirage 2000 interceptors as part of an arms agreement worth $1 billion. Nevertheless, the U.S. connection, essential to Mubarak in political terms, remained the strongest Western influence. The presence of U.S. troops in Sinai as part of the peacekeeping force there, as well as the continued joint operations between U.S. and Egyptian troops, demonstrated that the new president intended to stand shoulder to shoulder with his American ally.

(JOHN WHELAN)

El Salvador

A republic on the Pacific coast of Central America and the smallest country on the isthmus, El Salvador is bounded on the west by Guatemala and on the north and east by Honduras. Area: 21,041 sq km (8,124 sq mi). Pop. (1982 est.): 5,087,000. Cap. and largest city: San Salvador (pop., 1980 est., 433,000). Language: Spanish. Religion: Roman Catholic (1980) 96.2%. President of the civilian-military junta to May 2, 1982, José Napoleón Duarte; president from May 2, Alvaro Alfredo Magaña Borjo.

The elections to El Salvador's Constituent Assembly held on March 28, 1982, failed to provide, as the U.S. and many others had hoped, a clear majority for the Partido Demócrata Cristiano (PDC) and Pres. José Napoleón Duarte. Instead, they resulted in an unstable and unruly coalition of five parties: the PDC; Alianza Republicana Nacionalista (Arena); Partido de Conciliación Nacional (PCN); Acción Democrática (AD); and Partido Popular Salvadoreño (PPS). All parties were to the right of the political spectrum because the left-wing umbrella organization, the Frente Democrático Revolucionario (FDR), did not participate in the elections. Duarte was forced to resign from the presidency and was replaced on May 2 by Alvaro Magaña Borjo, a man previously involved not in mainstream politics but in banking and economics. The leader of the far-right party Arena, Maj. Roberto d'Aubuisson (*see* BIOGRAPHIES), was elected president of the assembly and planned to campaign in national presidential elections scheduled to take place in the spring of 1984.

U.S. policymakers regarded the elections, in the words of one official, as a "unique experiment in democracy." In the U.K. they were also seen as a legitimate process, and the two official observers sent to cover the elections were reasonably satisfied with their fairness. However, all other nations of the European Community remained skeptical. In March the European Parliament passed a resolution declaring that the elections "cannot be regarded as free elections as no political liberties have been guaranteed and opposition politicians have to face the possibility of assassination." In February France and Mexico denounced the elections, issuing a peace initiative calling for recognition of the FDR as a representative political force. Within El Salvador itself allegations were made about intimidation and bribery, and a report produced by the Jesuit-run University of Central America suggested that the number of votes had been inflated to

PHILIPPOT—SYGMA

represent an unusually high level of participation.

In July U.S. Pres. Ronald Reagan certified that the Salvadoran government had made a "concerted and significant effort" to comply with international human rights standards. However, the U.S. Congress was not convinced, rejecting a proposed increase in military aid from $66 million to $166 million and securing a reduction in the proportion allocated to El Salvador from the much-publicized U.S.-funded Caribbean Basin Initiative; El Salvador's share was reduced from $128 million to a maximum of $75 million. The International Monetary Fund also laid down conditions to be met before it released the remainder of the 75 million Special Drawing Rights promised for balance of payments assistance in 1983.

Litter bearers carry away one of the wounded from a skirmish in El Salvador. Clashes between government forces and guerrillas resulted in thousands of civilian deaths and injuries.

EL SALVADOR

Education. (1979) Primary, pupils 900,623, teachers (1976) 16,563; secondary, pupils 29,436; vocational, pupils 47,086; secondary and vocational, teachers (1975) 2,844; teacher training, students 1,585, teachers (1975) 25; higher (1978), students 32,058, teaching staff 2,556.

Finance. Monetary unit: colón, with (Sept. 20, 1982) a par value of 2.50 colones to U.S. $1 (free rate of 4.29 colones = £1 sterling). Gold and other reserves (June 1982) U.S. $108 million. Budget (1981 actual): revenue 1,068,200,000 colones; expenditure 1,581,500,000 colones. Gross national product (1981) 8,331,000,000 colones. Money supply (April 1982) 1,484,000,000 colones. Cost of living (1975 = 100; April 1982) 231.1.

Foreign Trade. (1981) Imports 2,464,500,000 colones; exports 1,979,800,000 colones. Import sources (1979): U.S. 29%; Guatemala 18%; Venezuela 8%; Japan 8%; Costa Rica 5%; West Germany 5%. Export destinations (1979): U.S. 27%; West Germany 20%; Guatemala 16%; The Netherlands 9%; Costa Rica 6%; Japan 6%. Main exports: coffee 58%; cotton 7%; textile yarns and fabrics c. 5%.

Transport and Communications. Roads (1977) 11,667 km. Motor vehicles in use (1980): passenger c. 56,600; commercial (including buses) c. 69,000. Railways (1980): c. 763 km; traffic c. 26 million passenger-km, freight 57 million net ton-km. Air traffic (1980): c. 178 million passenger-km; freight c. 13 million net ton-km. Telephones (Dec. 1978) 78,000. Radio receivers (Dec. 1979) 1,508,000. Television receivers (Dec. 1979) 276,000.

Agriculture. Production (in 000; metric tons; 1981): corn c. 487; sorghum c. 138; dry beans c. 37; sugar, raw value 174; bananas c. 53; oranges c. 98; coffee c. 150; cotton, lint 41. Livestock (in 000; 1981): cattle 1,211; pigs 386; horses c. 88; chickens c. 5,050.

Industry. Production (in 000; metric tons; 1979): cement 490; petroleum products c. 730; fertilizers (nutrient content; 1979–80) nitrogenous c. 15, phosphate c. 2; cotton yarn (1977) 6.4; electricity (kw-hr; 1980) 1,589,000.

El Salvador

Eire:
see Ireland

Electrical Industries:
see Energy; Industrial Review

Electronics:
see Computers; Industrial Review

Polarization between the left and right continued, leading to increased guerrilla and counterinsurgency activity. According to the majority of sources, the number of civilian deaths amounted to approximately 13,000 during 1981, with a somewhat lower total for the first eight months of 1982. Violence spread to the western provinces of Santa Ana, Sonsonate, and Ahuachapán.

All attempts at reconciliation, even within the government, failed. The Pact of Apaneca, signed in August by Arena, the PCN, and the PDC, which proposed three commissions to discuss municipal elections, human rights, and peace, was termed a panacea. No agreement was reached on the dates for municipal elections, nor indeed their procedure, since the far-right parties feared that the PDC would win a majority if there was no prior distribution of seats. The Government's Commission on Human Rights was not appointed until December, shortly before President Magaña's meeting with President Reagan in Costa Rica during the latter's Latin-American trip. Relations with neighbouring countries deteriorated despite the formation of the Central American Democratic Community in January by El Salvador, Honduras, and Costa Rica, later joined by Guatemala.

The widespread political unrest resulted in severe disruption of the economy. Some 45 bridges, 20 railway lines, and 650 electricity generators were attacked over the period of 18 months up to mid-1982, and guerrilla kidnappings continued. Gross domestic product fell by 9.6% in 1981 and was expected to decline still further in 1982. The trade deficit for 1981 showed a marked deterioration. Exports fell by 18% to $792 million, while imports increased by 1.5% to $986 million. In September the government introduced a parallel exchange rate of 3.50 colones to the U.S. dollar beside the official rate in an attempt to prevent a further decline in the level of international reserves.   (LUCY BLACKBURN)

Energy

The slack demand for petroleum as a result of the continuing worldwide recession kept oil prices soft throughout the year and created severe strains within the Organization of Petroleum Exporting Countries (OPEC). During the first quarter of 1982 there were many price cuts by both OPEC members and other exporting countries. Iran, desperate for income to support its war with Iraq, cut its price three times within two weeks in February. An emergency OPEC meeting in July broke up in disagreement, as members quarreled over production allocations and the price differentials that reflect the quality of the crude oil. For the remainder of the year official posted prices were maintained, but all countries engaged in discounting. Saudi Arabia, with mounting dissatisfaction, countered other members' above-quota production by cutting its own output. This brought the Saudi production level down to 5.5 million bbl a day, less than one-half capacity. The action was prompted by the fear that, without it, the relatively small discounting would degenerate into an all-out price

Employment:
see Economy, World

war, possibly leading to a collapse of the international market. OPEC's final meeting of the year in December also failed to produce any agreement on price differentials and production levels. This heightened the possibility that continued worldwide recession in 1983, with the consequent lack of any strengthening in the demand for oil, could lead to a collapse of international oil prices.

As it was, the persistent slack oil demand and weak prices had many unpleasant consequences. The unexpected decline in oil revenues brought Mexico to the brink of formal default on its international loans, from which it was rescued by emergency arrangements with international financial institutions and by the advance payment of $1 billion by the United States for additional oil to be delivered to the U.S. Strategic Petroleum Reserve. (A $12 billion loan offer from Saudi Arabia was not accepted, reportedly because it was conditional on either Mexican membership in or formal cooperation with OPEC.) The number of laid-up oil tankers reached a record high. Utilization of U.S. refining capacity declined to 61.5% in February, the lowest level since the 1930s. The permanent closing of some entire refineries and obsolescent facilities at others occurred in the U.S., Canada, and Europe. (U.S. refining capacity dropped by more than 10% in the first nine months of the year.) The slump in oil drilling in the U.S. led to many bankruptcies in the drilling and supply industry and to the failure of one bank that had specialized in oil industry loans.

In the oil industry there were also noteworthy events not associated with markets and prices. After several years of planning and success in obtaining all other government permits and approval, a project to transport Alaskan oil by pipeline from Puget Sound to Minnesota met with rejection from the governor of the state of Washington, who refused on environmental grounds to issue the necessary final permit. In February the world's largest semisubmersible drilling rig sank in a storm off Newfoundland with the loss of all 84 aboard. Also in February China announced that its offshore waters were open for exploration and production by foreigners and sent letters of notification to 46 companies in a dozen countries, inviting bids. In June the first oil production from the Dutch sector of the North Sea was delivered ashore. This sector had previously produced only natural gas.

Oil companies drilling offshore from Point Conception, Calif., revealed the largest discovery in the U.S. since the gigantic Prudhoe Bay field was found on the north coast of Alaska in 1968. The new discovery was estimated to have reserves of 500 million to 1,000,000,000 bbl. In October deliveries through the Trans-Panama Pipeline System began. The pipeline was built to bypass the Panama Canal in delivering crude oil from Prudhoe Bay to refineries on the Gulf and East coasts of the U.S. The pipeline reduced transportation time by four days and enabled the use of larger tankers on the eastern leg of the route.

News of natural gas was dominated by a dispute between the U.S. and its European allies over a project to deliver gas from the Soviet Union to Austria, Belgium, France, Italy, The Nether-

One of the world's largest solar power plants was completed in California's Mojave Desert. The plant has a 90-metre (300-foot) tower surrounded by 1,800 giant movable mirrors. It was expected to generate 10,000 kilowatts.

lands, Switzerland, and West Germany. Delivery was scheduled to begin in 1984 through a 4,500-km (2,800-mi) pipeline from western Siberia at an eventual rate of 39,620,000,000 cu m (1.4 trillion cu ft) per year. The project was to be financed by loans from the buying countries and would involve the purchase of equipment and the use of technology from those countries.

Contracts for the equipment had been signed in 1981, and during 1982 several Western European countries signed gas purchase contracts with the Soviet Union. The U.S. government attempted to discourage the Europeans from proceeding with the project on the grounds that it would make them energy hostages to the Soviets and constitute acquiescence, in trade policy, to Soviet actions in Afghanistan and to the Polish military dictatorship. In June U.S. Pres. Ronald Reagan brought the dispute to a head by prohibiting U.S. firms and their European subsidiaries from supplying the Soviet Union with pipeline equipment that was based on U.S. technology. Viewing this as an unwarranted infringement on their sovereignty, France, Italy, West Germany, and the United Kingdom promptly ordered the local firms to honour their contracts, which they did. The U.S. retaliated by invoking sanctions against the firms involved, prohibiting them from receiving U.S. oil and gas equipment. The end result was that the equipment was delivered to the U.S.S.R., some firms were placed at a competitive disadvantage, and work proceeded on construction of the pipeline.

An equally large pipeline project in North America ran into difficulties of its own. The Alaska Highway gas pipeline would bring gas through Canada from the giant Prudhoe Bay field on the Beaufort Sea to the lower 48 states. After several years of struggle to raise the necessary capital in the face of rising costs, backers of the project decided in May to postpone for two years the construc-

tion of the Alaskan portion of the line. In the meantime a portion from Montana to Iowa was completed. In the absence of Alaskan gas, it was to be used to bring gas from Alberta to the Midwestern states.

In June it was announced that exploration in the Atlantic Ocean off Sable Island, near Nova Scotia, had found sufficient gas to justify commercial development. Construction of the offshore structures and the pipeline facilities necessary to bring the gas to the Canadian Maritime Provinces and New England was scheduled to begin in 1984, with deliveries in 1987 or 1988.

The coal industry, like the oil industry, faced slack demand as a result of the recession. Coal stockpiles mounted in consuming countries, and the anticipated boom in coal exports from the U.S., Australia, Canada, and South Africa failed to materialize. Polish coal miners confounded the expectations of Western observers by responding to government inducements such as extra food ra-

The largest privately financed turbine complex in the U.S. went into operation near Byron, California, in July. Each of the five turbines is higher than a ten-story building; together they produce 1,250,000 kilowatts of energy annually. The wind farm was selling its electricity to a public utility for distribution to customers.

tions, and Polish coal exports in 1982 began to increase from the near total halt that had resulted from the imposition of martial law at the end of 1981. In May the first commercial use of a coal-oil mixture began at a power plant near Tampa, Fla. The mixture of one-half finely ground coal and one-half heavy fuel oil is burned in a conventional boiler designed to burn straight oil. The result is a considerable cost saving.

One of the richest uranium deposits ever found in the U.S. was discovered during the year in Pittsylvania County, Va. If developed, it would provide the first commercial production of uranium east of the Mississippi. In March Brazil's first nuclear power reactor went critical, the first of an eventual eight plants to be operating or under construction by the year 2000. The Canadian National Energy Board in April authorized the first export of nuclear-generated electricity, from a plant at Point Lepreau, N.B., to consumers in Maine and Massachusetts.

The November election in the U.S. included several referenda on nuclear power. In Maine a proposal to force the closing by 1987 of the state's only nuclear power plant was defeated. Nuclear power also received support from Idaho voters, who prohibited the state legislature from blocking, without voter approval, construction of any new nuclear plant. In Massachusetts, on the other hand, voters approved a proposition requiring a referendum on the construction of any nuclear plant or nuclear waste facility.

There were several noteworthy events in unconventional energy. The most dramatic was the sudden and wholly unexpected cancellation, in May, of the most ambitious shale oil project in the United States, an undertaking that would have produced more than 50,000 bbl a day of synthetic crude oil by 1987. Exxon Corp., the project's sponsor, cited the combination of continuing cost increases and lower oil prices as the reason for the cancellation. An almost simultaneous announcement by other oil companies signaled the end of a similarly ambitious project to produce synthetic oil from the huge deposit of tar sands in the Athabasca region of Alberta, Canada, for the same reason.

Progress continued, however, in the harnessing of solar energy for commercial use. In April a solar

thermal power facility began operation in the Mojave Desert near Barstow, Calif. Known as "Solar One," the plant uses an array of mirrors to track the Sun and reflect its light onto a boiler mounted on a central tower. The steam thus generated drives a conventional turbine with a capacity of 10 MW. Two other solar installations to supply utilities with power also began operation during the year. A plant using Sun-tracking photovoltaic cells to produce one megawatt of electricity started up at Phoenix, Ariz., in July, and in December a one-megawatt photovoltaic plant went on line in San Bernardino County, Calif.

Other new projects began supplying energy directly to industrial plants. In May a 400-kw facility began supplying electricity and steam for heating, cooling, and process use to a knitwear plant at Shenandoah, Ga., and in the same month another installation began supplying steam to a chemical plant at Haverhill, Ohio. In February construction began on a "solar breeder" factory at Frederick, Md., for the manufacture of photovoltaic cells with 600 kw of electricity supplied by cells on its roofs.

In still another unconventional energy application, construction began in March on a compressed-air power plant near Springfield, Ill. When completed in 1986, the plant would use electricity generated by conventional power plants during the offpeak period at night to store compressed air in caverns 545 m (1,800 ft) below ground at a pressure of 800 psi. This would provide enough energy to generate 220 MW for 11 hours during daytime periods of peak electricity demand.

In December 1981 President Reagan announced his plan to abolish the Department of Energy and shift about 70% of its functions to the Department of Commerce, with the remainder to be scattered among other departments. (The Department of Energy had been created in 1977.) This proposal fulfilled one of Reagan's pledges made during his 1980 election campaign. Congressional reaction to the proposal was so lukewarm, however, that it was never formally submitted, and the administration contented itself with continuing the reduction in the department's work force and programs that it had begun on taking office. In March the U.S. Senate sustained the presidential veto of a bill that would have given him the power to allocate oil and control its price during a future emergency. Reagan said that he was declining the authority because he believed the free market would work better during a crisis than would any system of government controls. In September the U.S. Congress continued the funding for the controversial Clinch River (Tenn.) demonstration breeder reactor project. Work on the project had been halted while opponents of the project sought to kill it on environmental grounds through court action. Almost simultaneously with the congressional action a federal appeals court overturned a lower court order that had blocked site-clearing work. Bulldozing began the day after the court decision. In another court action, in January, the U.S. Supreme Court upheld the right of Indian tribes to impose severance taxes on mineral resources produced on their lands.   (BRUCE C. NETSCHERT)

Some of the 2,100 workers who lost their jobs at Exxon's Colony Shale Oil Project line up to draw their last paychecks. The workers were stunned when Exxon unexpectedly abandoned development of the plant, which had been expected to produce 50,000 barrels a day of synthetic crude oil by 1987.

COAL

In 1981–82 energy analysts continued to look into the future, even though the more immediate prospect remained confusing. In its review *Coal Prospects and Policies in IEA Countries, 1981*, the International Energy Agency—an autonomous body within the 21-nation Organization for Economic Cooperation and Development (OECD)—summarized the sources of uncertainty. Coal could meet the needs of producers for stable supplies at competitive prices, but the uncertainties arose from: (1) weakening of oil prices, reducing coal's competitive advantage; (2) low economic growth, reducing investment in coal-fired plants; (3) low and uncertain projections of electricity demand; and (4) concern about environmental impact.

Nevertheless, IEA forecast that solid fuels would provide 45% of the incremental energy growth expected by member countries between 1980 and 1990. This additional total was equivalent to 347 million metric tons of crude oil, almost as much as current annual oil output from Saudi Arabia. But the IEA's own Coal Industry Advisory Board (CIAB) commented that this review understated the strategic importance of substituting for oil and the risk that consumers might look only to short-term price comparisons. In a separate document, *The Use of Coal in Industry*, the CIAB broadly confirmed the conclusions of the 1980 World Coal Study that a large expansion of industrial coal use was possible. However, the board added that the opportunities had not been fully developed. In terms of fuel economics, the steam coal potential was estimated at 500 million metric tons for 1990 and 700 million tons for the year 2000 because opportunities for increased use of coal and reduction in oil use had yet to be fully recognized. Industry had a stock of boilers and furnaces designed for oil and gas, and these would change very slowly. The CIAB urged governments to identify priority target sectors for conversion and to determine the constraints. Target sectors suggested were those having the fewest constraints, such as blast furnaces and cement kilns, and those where bulk heat requirements were high (chemical plants, aluminum smelters, textile mills). Governments were also encouraged to pay attention to environmental and any other similar factors that would be constraints on conversion to coal and examine ways of removing them.

There was also some concern about the implications of a study by the International Union of Producers and Distributors of Electrical Energy which found that nuclear power undercut the cost of coal-generated power in five European countries. However, this involved other problems of public acceptability.

ATMOSPHERIC ACIDIFICATION. Combustion of coal and oil was indicted as the main source of "acid rain." For its Environment 82 conference on the tenth anniversary of the first UN Conference on the Human Environment, the Swedish Ministry of Agriculture published a report titled *Acidification Today and Tomorrow*. This stated that almost 100 million metric tons of man-made sulfur emissions were being discharged into the atmosphere, mainly from Europe and North America. This was causing acidification of lakes, watercourses, forests, farmland, and groundwater; it damaged plants, caused corrosion, and might disturb the climate and directly affect human health. The Swedes urged adoption of an international program for gradually reducing sulfur emissions to a common level for all countries, determined by the environmental effects. (*See* ENVIRONMENT.)

In 1979 a European convention was adopted on Long Range Transboundary Air Pollution; techniques considered included coal cleaning and flue gas desulfurization (FGD). Two years later a UN seminar in Salzburg, Austria, concluded that FGD could reduce emissions of sulfur dioxide by 90% or more at a cost of 10 to 20% of the total investment costs of power stations.

COAL PRODUCTION. Reflecting the continuing weakness of economic activity in most of the world, global production of hard coal was reported by the UN as 2,811,000,000 metric tons for 1981, a decline of 0.9% compared with 1980. (All production figures given below are in metric tons.) The U.S., with an output of 685.6 million tons (a fall of 4.9%), was the largest producer, followed by China (620 million tons, no change) and the U.S.S.R. (544.2 million tons, a drop of 1.6%). Other producers of between 1 and 6% of the world's output were, in descending order, Poland, South Africa, the U.K., India, West Germany, Australia, and North Korea. These ten largest producers together yielded 93.3% of the world's hard coal. (For a percentage breakdown by region, *see* TABLE.)

China planned a large expansion and modernization of its industry. For ten specific large projects it invited foreign financing and organized a seminar to promote negotiations with foreign companies. All of those projects were for multimillion-ton annual production. Most striking was a surface mine at Yuanbaoshan, Nei Monggol (Yüanpao Shan, Inner Mongolia), with planned capacity of 80 million tons a year; three others were for 15 million tons a year, and one was for 10 million tons a year.

Poland seemed to have succeeded in starting to fight its way back to recovery. The nation's political troubles were accompanied by a decline of 15.6% in coal output from 1980 to 1981 (to 163 million tons) and a cut of 52% in exports. But in the first half of 1982, daily production rose from 595,000 tons to 630,000 tons, and a struggle to gain or regain export markets around the world was under way.

World production of brown coal at 1,003,000,000 tons in 1981 increased 3.2% over 1980. East Germany was again by far the largest producer, accounting for 26.6%, followed by the U.S.S.R. with 16.6% of world output.

ENERGY STRATEGY AND TRADE. Countries generally aimed at reducing their dependence on petroleum. Between 1979 and 1981 the European Community nations succeeded in raising the share of solid fuel in energy supply from 31 to 34% and reducing that of oil from 42 to 37%. There were similar trends in the U.S., but the share of oil in Eastern Europe remained much the same over this period and actually rose in the U.S.S.R.

Trade patterns in 1981 included a large rise in coal exports from the U.S. and Canada to Western Europe, rises in total exports from Australia, and a gain in Soviet exports to Eastern Europe. These changes coincided with declines in exports from Poland and the U.S.S.R. to Western Europe.

COAL-OIL DISPERSIONS. Interest continued in coal-oil dispersions (sometimes with added water). They were intended to be used with minor adjustments on oil-fuel equipment as a compromise that would reduce oil burn and increase coal burn but did not demand conversion of facilities already installed. In the U.K. British Petroleum had a plant making 100,000 tons a year for practical trials of the mixtures for stability and combustion properties. Shipments of U.S.-produced material to a 125-MW unit in Florida by conventional tank barges were satisfactorily handled by loading and unloading equipment designed for oil. The combustion units had to be fitted with electrostatic precipitators (to clean the flue gas) and an ash-handling system. China embarked on a demonstration program of testing these mixtures in three boilers, currently oil-fired, two of them each burning 100 tons an hour. The Chinese were also testing stability during storage and transport. In all cases the interest arose because the cost of coal was half that of oil per British thermal unit (BTU), and also because of the stability of long-term supplies of coal.

COAL CONVERSION. Developments in connection with the conversion of coal to liquid and gas presented a mixed picture. The West German Technology Ministry commented that coal-to-oil projects were technically satisfactory but made little economic sense; a few months later there were substantial cutbacks in the federal subsidies for coal liquefaction projects. However, the funds allotted still allowed a considerable effort to continue. Meanwhile, the Japanese effort was described as "alive and well"; it included cooperation with the West German Ruhrkohle and formed part of the Japanese government's "Sunshine Project" for commercializing energy sources that could substitute for oil. The Sasol 3 facility in South Africa produced its first synthetic crude oil from coal, and Sasol was considering building Sasol 4. In the U.S.S.R. scientists regretted the smallness of the effort put into coal liquefaction, while in the U.S. there were continuing uncertainties about the scope and scale of such efforts.

(ISRAEL BERKOVITCH)

ELECTRICITY

In 1982 companies and authorities concerned with the bulk generation of electricity continued their retreat from the use of oil as a fuel. The main fuels were seen in-

World Production of Hard Coal by Region
(% of total)

Region	1980	1981
Europe (excluding U.S.S.R.)	17.7	16.8
U.S.S.R.	19.5	19.4
North America	26.4	25.6
South America	0.6	0.6
Asia	28.8	29.5
Africa	4.2	4.8
Oceania	2.8	3.3
Total	100.0	100.0

344

Energy

creasingly as coal and uranium. In the U.S. utilities were converting from oil to coal—six units in Florida alone—and no more oil-fired power stations were planned in the U.K. New stations in almost all countries were based on coal or uranium. The exceptions to this general rule were those countries where the topography is suitable for the use of hydroelectric power, the cheapest source of electricity. For example, Norway generated almost all its electricity in hydroelectric power stations and claimed to have the greatest per capita consumption in Western Europe. Sweden generated about 65% of its capacity in this way, and China announced in 1982 ambitious plans for hydroelectric stations with a total capacity of 11,540 MW; the first stage of its earlier, more modest, projects was completed in 1981. In Brazil the hydroelectric potential was estimated at well over 100,000 MW, of which only 25% was being utilized or built; nevertheless, hydroelectricity constituted approximately 90% of Brazil's production, and the nation had the largest hydroelectric project in the world (12,000 MW) under construction at Itaipú. The U.S.S.R. also had extensive hydroelectric projects, with which it generated almost 20% of its electricity. Canada produced nearly 70% of its electricity from water power.

However, hydroelectricity constituted only a fraction of total production in the industrially developed countries, and the fuels of the foreseeable future were coal and uranium. (There was some use of gas but the effect of the pipeline for natural gas from the U.S.S.R. to Western Europe could not yet be estimated.) The costs of both had been increasing and that of coal was still rising, but nuclear fuel showed signs of declining. In general the result was that electricity had risen in price everywhere and continued to rise. The effect of this was complex, one aspect of inflation and trade recession. Increased costs resulted in less usage, affecting long-term planning and calling for closer attention to improved efficiency and utilization. Use of electricity fell by 1.9% in the U.S. over the past year, and sales in the U.K. to industry fell by 1.7%, although this was an improvement over the previous year's fall of 8.4%. In France Électricité de France lost some Fr 400 million because of the drop in consumption.

These figures were fairly indicative of the trend in all developed nations. (Comparisons do not apply to less developed countries, which have no criteria of past usage. They could make use of every advance made in the industrial countries, and every new generating station was a clear gain.)

The overall result was that there was great emphasis on economy in both production and use. Many new plants were postponed or canceled in the U.S. In the U.K. the Electricity Council was able to report a rise in efficiency of coal-fired generation from 33.77 to 34.12% in one year on average. Some 85% of its research spending was devoted to problems of generation. Some research also went into ways of reducing the amount of expensive metal in a generator. From the U.S.S.R. there was a report that Electrosila, a manufacturer of machin-

ery, was making turbo-generators with 15–20% less copper.

In the usage of electricity there were many developments in economy. Prizes were awarded in the U.K. for energy saving, and many of these went to enterprises that achieved savings in electricity, especially in lighting. During the year one well-known international lamp manufacturer publicized a new fluorescent lamp with an output of over 40 lumens per watt that could be plugged into the usual lamp-holders without any special fittings, thus bringing greater lighting efficiency to the domestic user.

Research was also being done in the U.K., with government backing, into the improvement of induction motors to make them more economical. One company devised a system of house wiring that could be installed by semiskilled personnel. All these developments and many others, however trivial they might seem in a global picture, were signs of the times.

Another development in Western countries meriting discussion was the growth of the environmentalist lobby, especially those opposing nuclear power. The latter became so vocal and effective that they were able to influence Western governments to slow down nuclear-power development. This led to the emergence of the U.S.S.R. as an exporter of nuclear-power stations to less developed countries that did not have coal. The U.S.S.R. made a 440-MW standardized reactor and was successful in selling it. West Germany, Japan, and France followed the Soviet lead. The U.K. and the U.S., pioneers of the nuclear-power industry, were left behind.

In the development of the fast breeder reactor the U.S. was well behind, although

in 1982 licensing rules were waived for preparatory site work on the 375-MW Clinch River, Tenn., reactor station. France's 1,200-MW fast breeder reactor was nearing completion, and the Soviet 600-MW fast breeder was operating. In West Germany the federal government ruled that work should resume on the fast breeder being built at Kalkar; construction had been halted pending a review of the project's financing. In the U.K. the Dounreay Prototype Fast Reactor was successfully operated. An important achievement was that the used fuel was successfully reprocessed at a 99.8% recovery of plutonium; therefore, much less waste had to be disposed of, thus meeting one of the main objections of the antinuclear protesters. No decision was made, however, about a fully commercial fast breeder reactor power station of 1,200 MW.

A second environmental issue claimed much attention during the year. This was the matter of "acid rain" caused by sulfur dioxide and nitrogen oxides in the gas emitted from the chimneys of coal-fired power stations. (See *Coal*, above.)

It was increasingly realized that electronics was no longer entirely separable from the electrical industry. In the U.K. the electrical suppliers ordered 2,000 microprocessor-based radio teleswitch receivers ready for trials in 1983. Along with the employment of radio transmissions for switching—already in use in the U.S.—electronics was also replacing conventional circuit-breaker technology. By incorporating suitable sensors that monitored the state of a circuit breaker—temperature, contact position, etc.—the information could be dealt with in a central processing unit. The most general application of microelectronics was homeostatic control, which involved spot

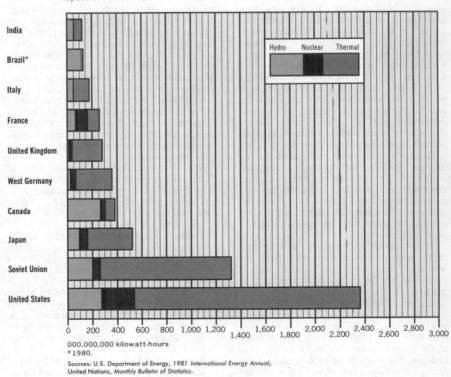

Electrical Power Production of Selected Countries, 1981
By source

000,000,000 kilowatt-hours
*1980.

Sources: U.S. Department of Energy, *1981 International Energy Annual;*
United Nations, *Monthly Bulletin of Statistics.*

pricing of equipment and continuous inter-action between supplier and customer.

Another recent development was the use of fibre optics in connection with the supply and use of electricity. In the U.K. a 21-km (13-mi) link had optical fibres incorporated in a 400-kv transmission line. The U.S., Japan, and the U.K. were all actively involved in this technology. It was developed primarily for telecommunications, and in the making of suitable fibre both the U.S. and the U.K. had been pioneers, with the latter already installing many miles of cable in its trunk telephone lines. Optical fibres were immune to electromagnetic interference, light in weight, and intrinsically safe in hostile surroundings. Furthermore, the light transmitted, being of much shorter wavelength, could carry a much wider waveband of signals. The utilization of optical fibre in the power sector of the electrical industry was likely to be of increasing importance.

Finally, there was the matter of renewable sources of energy for the generation of electricity. These were not likely to be important in size in developed countries, but in the less developed nations the utilization of both solar and wind sources might well increase. The direct conversion of sunlight into electricity appeared attractive for pumps and refrigerators (for medical materials and food) because the costs of photovoltaic cells were falling. Considerable research was under way on the development of still cheaper cells, and it appeared that photovoltaic installations might soon be cheaper than those dependent on diesel fuel. The use of wind appeared very attractive for remote areas, such as offshore islands, even in developed countries. In the U.K. a 200-kw wind turbine of U.S. design was connected to the national grid, and on the Swedish island of Gotland a prototype 2-MW aerogenerator was completed.

(C. L. BOLTZ)

NATURAL GAS

World proven reserves of natural gas on Jan. 1, 1982, were estimated to be 84,959,000,000,000 cubic metres (34,959 billion cu m or bcm). This compared with world reserves of 77,711 bcm a year earlier and 38,099 bcm in 1970. The marked increase in the estimate for reserves between 1981 and 1982 was chiefly due to the revision of figures for the U.S.S.R. and the inclusion of new discoveries in Norway, Abu Dhabi, and Qatar. The U.S.S.R.'s reserves of 34,000 bcm were equivalent to 40% of the world total; Iran had 12.4%, the U.S. 6.6%, Algeria 3.7%, Qatar 3.3%, Abu Dhabi 3.1%, and Canada 3% of total reserves. Between them, the OPEC countries had 32.6% of the world's reserves.

World commercial gas production in 1981, excluding gas flared or reinjected, was 1,558.1 bcm, 1.7% higher than in 1980. The leading gas-producing countries were the U.S. (554.7 bcm), U.S.S.R. (465.2 bcm), The Netherlands (80.8 bcm), Canada (73.9 bcm), and the U.K. (36.8 bcm). The OPEC countries produced 94.1 bcm. The life of the world's proven reserves was estimated to be 55 years at current production rates.

The volume of gas in international trade in 1981 was estimated to be 183 bcm, about 84% of which was transported by pipeline and the remainder as liquefied natural gas (LNG). The leading exporting countries were the U.S.S.R. (57.5 bcm), supplying its Eastern European allies as well as several Western European countries; The Netherlands (42 bcm), supplying much of Western Europe; Norway (26.2 bcm), exporting gas to the U.K. and to Western Europe via Emden; and Canada, providing 21.6 bcm to the U.S. All four of these exporters transported their gas by pipeline. The next three largest exporters were involved in the LNG trade: Indonesia (11.75 bcm), Algeria (7.1 bcm), and Brunei (7 bcm). Most of the LNG traded went to Japan, which took all the exports of Indonesia, Brunei, Abu Dhabi, and Alaska, 22.9 bcm out of the total 30.8 bcm of LNG in international trade. The other LNG importers in 1981, France, Spain, the U.S., and the U.K., were supplied by Algeria and Libya.

During 1981–82 the international gas trade achieved an unaccustomed political prominence. Gas companies in France and Italy had for a long time found themselves unable to agree with Algeria over the terms of new contracts for gas imports, but their respective governments made agreements based on political rather than commercial considerations. A major new pipeline, bringing increased supplies from the U.S.S.R. to Western Europe, raised questions about European dependence on Soviet energy supplies and caused an international controversy linked with events in Poland.

The U.S.S.R. planned to supply Western Europe with an additional 40 bcm a year of gas from western Siberia through the new pipeline, intended to begin deliveries in 1984. Agreements to import this gas, at least in principle, were reached with Italy in October and West Germany in November 1981, followed by France in January and Austria in June 1982. Declining gas demand in The Netherlands made it likely that the Dutch would pull out of the group of importers. Italy was uncertain about its share of the gas, but by the autumn of 1982 it seemed that the U.S.S.R. had firm commitments from West Germany to take 10.5 bcm a year, from France to take 8 bcm a year, and from Austria to take 1.5 bcm a year, with an option for an additional 1 bcm annually. Italy could take up to 6 bcm a year. As was usual in international gas agreements, none of the parties involved

The first nuclear boiling water reactor to be put into service since the Three Mile Island accident began generating in September. The plant is Commonwealth Edison's La Salle station near Seneca, Illinois.

346

disclosed many details of the price or the formula by which it would be increased. Reportedly, the French and West German contracts were similar, fixing a base price equivalent to $4.65 per million BTU for gas delivered at the Czechoslovak-West German border and a minimum price of $5.50 per million BTU for gas delivered all the way to each country. One of the attractions of these deals for Western Europe was the prospect of orders for Western companies to supply equipment for the pipeline. The sanctions on trade with the U.S.S.R. imposed by the U.S. following the crisis in Poland affected the supply of pipeline and compressor technology by U.S. companies, their subsidiaries in Europe, and those European companies which used U.S. technology under license. Although such sanctions might delay completion of the pipeline, their main effect seemed to be to strain relations between the U.S. and its European allies.

In February 1982, after two years of negotiations, France and Algeria agreed on the price to be paid for all France's imports of LNG. The deal was unusual because Gaz de France was unwilling to pay the price required by Algeria, and agreement was only reached when the French government intervened and offered to contribute 60 cents per million BTU in addition to the $4.50 reportedly to be paid by Gaz de France. Apparently, Algeria also undertook to place more orders in France. Similarly, the Italian government took over negotiations with Algeria from the state gas company.

The trans-Mediterranean pipeline was completed in 1981, but no gas was flowing in the absence of an agreed-upon price. An agreement signed in September 1982 was understood to provide for Italy to pay an initial $4.41 per million BTU for gas at the Algerian border and for the Italian government to compensate the gas company for the difference between the contract price and what the company believed to be an economic price. By the terms of the agreement Italy was to take some 12 bcm a year, and Algeria would remove its freeze on commercial contracts with Italy. Algeria also achieved nonpolitical settlements to its differences over pricing with two U.S. companies, Panhandle Eastern and Distrigas.

European gas companies, led by Gaz de France, began discussions about taking gas from the Arctic Pilot Project, intended to demonstrate the feasibility of using ice-breaking LNG carriers to exploit gas from the Canadian Arctic. On the other hand, the Bonny LNG consortium, which planned to export LNG from Nigeria, broke up; the projected LNG terminal at Cojo Bay, Calif., was shelved; and the planned start of exports of LNG from Australia's North-West Shelf to Japan was postponed a year to 1987. The most radical proposal of 1982 was probably the project of General Dynamics Corp. for giant submarines to take LNG from Alaska beneath the ice of the Arctic to Europe.

(RICHARD J. CASSIDY)

PETROLEUM

During 1982 much attention focused on the manner in which OPEC would respond to the downward movement not only of prices but of production. Some prematurely presumed that the disarray of OPEC portended the collapse of the organization; others, forgetting the price rises of previous years, hoped that it would play its part as a price stabilizer. OPEC's 62nd conference in Abu Dhabi in December 1981 did not provide decisive direction, and by the next month, with the spot market prices continuing to slide, some were remarking that the situation had become "a structural oversupply which is incapable of responding to any normal fine tuning of the price mechanism." However, considerably more than fine tuning was required to meet the national budgetary requirements of the OPEC states. For additional information about OPEC, see *Introduction*, above.

The fluctuation of oil prices was not a temporary OPEC phenomenon; behind the political and economic controversies lay a change in the oil marketing structure. Whereas previously the oil companies had balanced the supply and demand situation within their own networks, this role had been replaced by an open marketing system of short-term contracts and increasing use of the spot market. The creation of a new futures exchange in oil products in London in 1982 confirmed this trend toward more opportunistic and less traditional trading conditions. Furthermore, the fall in consumption, like that of production, was not at all uniform. It was most marked in the industrialized nations, whereas consumption in the less developed countries was actually rising. Moreover, while OPEC production fell to 47.5% of the world total in the first half of 1982, non-OPEC production for the same period in the non-Communist world rose from 38 to 48%.

RESERVES. There was a further increase in the total world "published proved" reserves at the end of 1981, to 678,200,000,000 bbl, compared with 654,900,000,000 bbl a year earlier. The share of reserves in the Western Hemisphere again increased, to 19.1% (16.6% in 1980 and 15% in 1979) or 129,400,000,000 bbl, while that of the Middle East, the principal area of concentration, dropped to 53.5 from 55.3% the year before. China's share marginally decreased from 3.1 to 2.9% as did Africa's, 8.4 to 8.3%, whereas that of Western Europe slightly increased to 3.7 from 3.6%. Latin-American reserves increased from 10.6 to 12.5% and U.S. reserves from 4.9 to 5%, but Soviet reserves dropped slightly, from 9.6 to 9.3%. The overall ratio of reserves at the end of the year divided by production in that year, expressed as number of years' supply remaining at that date, continued its improvement since 1979 and was 32 at the end of 1981.

PRODUCTION. World oil production again decreased significantly in 1981, by 6.2%. This followed a 4.7% decline in 1980 and a 0.4% drop during 1976–81. Output averaged 59.1 million bbl a day, as against 62,705,000 bbl a day the previous year. Among the producing countries of the Middle East only Oman (+11.4%) and Dubai (+2.6%) registered increases. Total Middle East production was 152,980,000 bbl a day, down by 15% following a decrease of 14.2% in 1980. Production in Iraq dropped by 66.1% to 900,000 bbl a day; Kuwait 32.4% to 965,000 bbl a day; the Neutral Zone 30.9% to 370,000 bbl a day; Abu Dhabi 15.5% to 1,140,000 bbl a day; Qatar 15.3% to 405,000 bbl a day; and Iran 11.1% to 1,315,000 bbl a day. Saudi Arabia remained almost constant at 9,990,000 bbl a day. Middle East production amounted to 27.3% of the world total.

African production dropped considerably, by 22% to 4,860,000 bbl a day, with

Work on a Soviet natural gas pipeline to Western Europe continued despite U.S. attempts to impose sanctions to prevent its construction.

only Egypt again registering a rise, 7.9% to 690,000 bbl a day. Libya was down by 37.5% to 1,120,000 bbl a day, compared with a five-year annual decrease of 10.4%; Nigeria declined by 30.3% to 1,445,000 bbl a day; Gabon by 14% to 150,000 bbl a day; and Algeria by 10% to 1,010,000 bbl a day. Southeast Asia fell by 5% to 2,020,000 bbl a day, but Indonesia was almost unchanged, being up by 0.8% to 1,605,000 bbl a day. Australasia rose only 2.8% to 415,000 bbl a day. China dropped by 3.5% to 2,035,000 bbl a day, 3.5% of the world total.

Latin-American production showed a slight rise of 1.1% to 18,045,000 bbl a day, though Venezuela was down 3.3% to 2,170,000 bbl a day, 3.9% of world production. Mexico overtook Venezuela, achieving a rise of 19.5% to 2,585,000 bbl a day, 4.4% of the world total. Elsewhere in Latin America there were rises of 13.4% in Trinidad to 240,000 bbl a day; 12.9% in Brazil to 220,000 bbl a day; and 7% in Colombia to 135,000 bbl a day. U.S. production hardly changed, up by just 0.7% to 3,560,000 bbl a day, 14.7% of the world total. Canada dropped by 9.8% to 1,565,000 bbl a day, 2.5% of the world total.

Western European production increased by 6.5% to 2,735,000 bbl a day, 4.6% of the world total. The largest output was by the U.K., up by 11.1% to 1,845,000 bbl a day, 3.1% of the world total; Norway with 505,000 bbl a day was down by 3.7%, compared with a previous five-year average increase of 12.5%. The U.S.S.R. remained the greatest single producer, up by 1% to 12,370,000 bbl a day, 21% of the world total. Between 1979 and 1981 OPEC production fell from 31 million to 23 million bbl a day.

CONSUMPTION. Throughout the world consumption had been dropping since the peak of 64,145,000 bbl a day in 1979; it fell by 3.3% to 59,845,000 bbl a day in 1981 and, exclusive of the U.S.S.R., Eastern Europe, and China, by 4.4% to 47,045,000 bbl a day. Nevertheless, consumption in 1981 was still double that of 1965. Western Europe, down by 7.4% to 12,985,000 bbl a day, showed the greatest decline with only Portugal and Turkey being up, by 5.4% and 180,000 bbl a day and 3.5% and 315,000 bbl a day, respectively. Otherwise all the main European consuming nations fell. Denmark by 13.6% to 240,000 bbl a day; Sweden by 12.6% to 440,000 bbl a day; West Germany by 10.3% to 2,465,000 bbl a day (4.1% of total consumption); Austria by 10.7% to 220,000 bbl a day; France by 9.6% to 2,070,000 bbl a day; The Netherlands by 8.6% to 730,000 bbl a day; and the U.K. by 7.7% to 1,555,000 bbl a day. Over the years 1976–81 the average fall was 2.4% annually.

Other areas where consumption fell included the U.S., down by 6.4% to 15,480,000 bbl a day, with 25.6% of the world total; Canada 6.8% to 1,745,000 bbl a day; Japan by 5.6% to 4.7 million bbl a day (third greatest at 7.7% of the world total); and China by 3.6% to 1,705,000 bbl a day. Eastern Europe at 2,110,000 bbl a day and Australasia at 770,000 bbl a day each registered a slight fall of 0.2%. Consumption increased overall in Latin America by 2.2% to 4,745,000 bbl a day (7.8% of the world total); in South Asia by 7.3% to 890,000 bbl a day; Africa by 5.4% to 1,565,000 bbl a day; the Middle East by 3.3% to 1,685,000 bbl a

day; and the U.S.S.R. by 1.9% to 8,985,000 bbl a day (the second largest consumer, 15.3% of the world total).

REFINING. In 1981 there was a surplus of world refining capacity (82.1 million bbl a day) in comparison with consumption (59,845,000 bbl a day). Nevertheless, overall capacity rose by 1.1% in 1982 with the U.S. up by 0.2% to 18,290,000 bbl a day (the biggest share, 22.3%, of the world total) and Latin America up 1.1% to 9,015,000 bbl a day (11% of the world total). Western European capacity was down by 0.6% to 20,365,000 bbl a day (24.9% of the world total), but Spain increased by 8.6% to 1,550,000 bbl a day. Figures for the Middle East were distorted by the loss of the refinery at Abadan in Iran, which reduced capacity there by 47.8% from 1,225,000 bbl a day to 640,000 bbl a day, still the most in the Middle East. Total capacity in the Middle East fell by 9.5% to 3,230,000 bbl a day. Saudi Arabia's capacity increased by 18.4% to 585,000 bbl a day.

African capacity rose by 3.8% to 2,160,000 bbl a day, less than the previous five-year average annual increase of 9.4%; South Asia by 1.6% to 890,000 bbl a day; Southeast Asia by 1.3% to 3,510,000 bbl a day; and Australasia by 1.2% to 820,000 bbl a day. The U.S.S.R., Eastern Europe, and China together increased by 7.3% to 15,990,000 bbl a day. Once again North America produced the greatest volume of gasolines, 48% of the world total. Western Europe led in middle distillates with 34% of the total, and Japan in fuel oil with 35%. Since 1965 refinery capacity had increased by 15%.

TANKERS. The size of the world tanker fleet continued to drop from its peak of 332.7 million long tons deadweight (dw) in 1977, and at 320.2 million tons dwt in 1981 (9.8% less than in 1980) it was lower than

the 1976 figure. The drop was almost entirely in tankers below 45,000 tons dwt. Tonnage flying the Liberian flag remained the largest single fleet but dropped by 9.1% to 91.6 million tons dwt, 28.6% of the world total. Japan owned 9.2% of the world tanker fleet with 29.7 million tons dwt; Norway 7.6% with 24.4 million tons dwt, a minor increase over the previous year; and the U.K. tanker fleet dropped below that of Norway for the first time, falling 6.6% to 21.3 million tons dwt. The U.S. tanker fleet increased slightly to 16.4 million tons dwt, 5.1% of the total. Tankers between 10,000 and 45,000 tons dwt, at 39.8 million tons dwt, comprised 12.4% of the world total tonnage; between 45,000 and 205,000 tons dwt, 103.2 million tons dwt, 32.2%; and between 205,000 and 285,000 tons dwt, 177.2 million tons dwt, 55.4%.

In interarea total oil movements the main employment of tankers was in voyages from the Middle East, 14,605,000 bbl a day or just over half the total movements of 28,655,000 bbl a day, down by some 20% from 1980. The main movements were to Western Europe, 5,750,000 bbl a day, 39.3%; Japan, 3,020,000 bbl a day, 20.6%; Southeast Asia, 1,775,000 bbl a day, 12%; Latin America, 1,395,000 bbl a day, 9.9%; and the U.S. 1,255,000 bbl a day, 8.6%. The second main employment of tankers was from Latin America, 4,380,000 bbl a day, 15.2% of the total, of which the U.S. took the greatest share, 1,950,000 bbl a day, 44.5%, followed by Western Europe, 880,000 bbl a day, 20%. (R. W. FERRIER)

See also Engineering Projects; Industrial Review; Mining and Quarrying; Transportation.
[214.C.4; 721; 724.B.2; 724.C.1–2; 737.A.5]

The largest oil strike to be discovered in the U.S. since the Prudhoe Bay field was found in 1968 is off the shore of Point Conception, near Santa Barbara, California.

Engineering Projects

Bridges. The frequency of heavy trucks on the roads of Western Europe had increased so much in recent years that the "design load" that engineers use for calculations on long-span bridges was to be increased threefold over the figure used 20 years earlier. Most existing bridges that had a loaded length exceeding 100 m (1 m = 3.3 ft) failed to satisfy the proposed regulations. While that did not mean that such bridges were unsafe for normal daily traffic, there was a risk of occasional excessive loading when bunching of heavy trucks occurred. Engineers and highway administrations were consequently faced with the question of whether to strengthen the bridges or whether to install traffic load-measuring devices linked with traffic controls, so that if the weight of traffic on a bridge approached an unacceptable level the traffic flow could be checked temporarily. The latter method was usually cheaper, and because ensuing traffic delays were minimal it was likely to be widely adopted in preference to costly modifications of existing structures.

In North America the battle of concrete versus steel for long-span bridges followed the pattern already set in Europe, with concrete being used where, a few years earlier, steel would have been the automatic choice. A showdown developed between concrete and steel interests over the replacement for the Sunshine Skyway Bridge across Tampa Bay, Florida, a structure requiring a 370 m cable-stayed main span and 2,300 m of high-level approach spans. The final decision was that concrete would be used throughout. However, the encroachment by the concrete contractors into bridge work formerly the preserve of the U.S. steel firms did not go technically unchallenged. For the 418-m-long four-lane Bonners Ferry Bridge across Idaho's Kootenai River, the contractors all chose a cable-stressed steel bridge rather than the alternative of cast-in-place, post-tensioned concrete design. By using cables to stress the top flange, the designers reduced by 10% the steel required for a conventional plate-girder structure; in so doing they exploited the principles developed by the concrete engineer. Generally, however, the battle between steel and concrete continued to be waged over bridge spans of about 350 m; above that, steel still had an advantage, while concrete was more economical for the shorter spans.

North America also followed Europe with the construction of large concrete cast-in-place cantilevered bridges. Several such projects were under way in the U.S., including the Houston Ship Canal Bridge with a main span of 228 m. Not only was it the longest span of its kind in North America; the largest traveling forms ever made were used for pours of 60 to 84 cu m. This method of bridge construction, described as an "on-site assembly-line factory," reduced the need for costly labour to a minimum.

In West Germany the 1,160-m-long Aichtal Bridge near Stuttgart neared completion. Most of the deck spans were 51 m long and consisted of twin concrete boxes, each 3.5 m deep and 13.5 m wide at the top, to carry two lanes of traffic. Each box was put into place with the aid of a 30-m-long steel-framed nose and by launching off the top of the already erected spans. The first 21-span deck was finished in 15 months; the second deck was scheduled to take 12 months.

Following the ramming of the Sunshine Skyway Bridge by a cargo vessel in 1980, a study showed that, worldwide, a ship hit and damaged a major bridge every year. Not surprisingly, empty ships were found to be more accident-prone than loaded ships because they rode high in the water and were more sensitive to winds. Providing protection for large bridge piers against wayward ships was costly, requiring either massive dolphins (clusters of closely driven piles) or large man-made islands. Wherever possible, therefore, very long span bridges were to be preferred so that the bridge piers could be situated on dry land.

The French and British governments appeared finally to have abandoned the Channel Tunnel project, which could handle only rail traffic, and were moving in favour of a bridge crossing that could cope with the ever increasing demands of road traffic. A principal objection to such a bridge had been the possible damage if it were hit by a ship. To forestall this, engineers proposed an ingenious protection of the piers utilizing a large "hydraulic cushion." Each pier would be built at the centre of a water-filled flexible structure resembling a large inverted umbrella. If struck by a ship, the "umbrella" would distort inward, raising the level of the contained water and generating a hydraulic head that would resist the continued movement of the ship toward the pier. Model tests indicated that this protection would be very effective and relatively cheap.　　(DAVID FISHER)

Buildings. The U.S. engineer Fazlur Khan (*see* OBITUARIES) pioneered the use of the "tube within a tube" principle of resisting lateral loads on tall buildings. Traditionally, lateral forces had been dealt with by either a shear wall core or by frame action. In Khan's concept advantage was taken of the external mullions and spandrel beams to provide an external pierced tube that would share the

The world's largest movable flood barrier, spanning the River Thames at Woolrich, was completed in 1982. Designed to protect London from flooding by freak high tides, the barrier took ten years to build and cost £435 million. The huge revolving floodgates normally rest on the river bed.

load with an internal core, thereby saving construction material. The recently completed 49-story First City Tower in Houston, Texas, used this principle. The building also made extensive use of composite steel and reinforced concrete in the floors, columns, and the elevator and service core. It was believed to be the first time that these two concepts had been used in one high-rise structure.

Another recently constructed building of note in the U.S. was the 84-m-clear-span Moscone Convention Center in San Francisco. A requirement was that the main exhibition hall roof was to be at ground level and designed to support a public park, amusement area, or low-rise shop and theatre buildings. In order to provide maximum headroom without having to excavate deeply into the ground and incur excessive groundwater problems, a shallow arch solution was chosen. Because the arch was shallow, the side thrusts were large, and the ground could not carry the loads without excessive movement. The floor was therefore prestressed to fulfill a threefold function: first, to tie the arch; second, to enable an initial prestress to be put into the arch; and third, by appropriately profiling the tendons, to resist the water pressures in the ground under the floor.

In Europe much use was made of the external structural frame with the roof suspended underneath. Notable examples of this concept were the factory of the Fleetguard International Corp. in northwestern France and the Inmos factory in southern Wales. The object in France was to allow the perceived height of the building to be kept to a minimum and to leave the interior roof zone free for services and unhampered by internal structure. The suspension principle was continued throughout the building with the cooling towers, air handling units, and ducting all being supported in this way. The main steel columns were on an 18-m grid, but the suspension structure above the roof enabled the latter to be supported on a 6-m grid, thereby minimizing its structural depth and weight. The Inmos factory took a different form, having a relatively heavy spine structure housing the main services plant above the roof and using its height to support sloping tendons that provided intermediate support to long-span (36-m) steel trusses. In this way large areas uninterrupted by internal columns were provided.

External framing was also used on a new gymnasium in southern England for IBM. In this case the main load-bearing elements were triangular-section space frame portals. With spans of 18 m and a length of 21 m, the structure was not large, but interesting use was made of large-span industrial door panels for the walls. The joints between the opaque walls and roof were made with rounded, translucent, glass-reinforced plastic, double-skinned panels. Heating and cooling was provided by heat pumps situated above the roof and supported on subframes between the main portal frames. Secondary supporting steelwork was not required.

A recently completed institutional building of note was the European Investment Bank in Luxembourg. The site chosen for the bank was the Kirchberg Plateau, a broad ridge separated from the old city of Luxembourg by a gorge. The architect developed a double-L plan with four fingerlike wings and chose a stratified appearance having a horizontal emphasis. The narrow wings allowed natural light and ventilation, and this showed considerable economy in energy costs over a deep plan building. The structure of the building was in concrete, partly poured at the site and partly precast. The main concrete floor areas were of waffle construction reminiscent of the National Theatre in London and were designed by the same architect. This type of structural form was both visually interesting and suited to relatively large spans where a shallow construction depth was required. In other areas voided precast concrete floor units provided ducts for a supplementary mechanical ventilation system as well as serving their primary structural function.

An example of a successful marrying of new and old was to be seen at the library of the Roman Catholic seminary at Eichstätt, West Germany. There, what was once a yard bounded on three sides by three-story baroque buildings was enclosed on the fourth side by a new five-level library, and the whole was covered with a steel and glass roof. Attention to detail helped the two styles to complement one another; the old buildings were not changed in any way.

(GEOFFREY M. PINFOLD)

Dams. As an outgrowth of the Safety of Dams program of the International Commission on Large Dams, public safety planning was initiated in many countries during the year. The topography in the vicinity of the dam dictates the direction and velocity of flow of water in case of a failure of the dam. Maps were being prepared to show the probable path and extent of damage that could occur. This helped planners designate evacuation routes to safety. Warning procedures were being established so that people living near dams could be alerted rapidly in case of danger.

The Moscone Convention Center in San Francisco incorporated a column-free underground hall 84 metres wide.

Dam building continued throughout the world in 1982, although activity was more pronounced in less developed countries where the demand for water for irrigation and energy was greater. Brazil had the greatest number of large dams actively under way. The main dam of the $14 billion Itaipú project was completed in October 1982, and initial power delivery from the 12,600-MW plant was scheduled to begin in April 1983. During the peak of construction 28,000 workers were employed on the project. When the plant began full operation, Brazil expected to save an equivalent of 300,000 bbl of oil per day. The dam was designed as a hollow gravity type, in which large segments are made to form a hollow chamber with the upstream face supported by two buttress sections and with a downstream face slab. This feature saved about 25% of concrete and about $130 million in cost as compared with other gravity dams. While not the first of this type, Itaipú was the highest and largest.

In Thailand and Laos the proposed Mekong River project would include a dam 100 m high and cost $2 billion to construct. Thailand had under way the 100-m-high Khao Laem dam, scheduled for completion in 1984. China announced plans for ten hydroelectric dams at a cost of $6.7 billion to supply 10,000 Mw of power. During 1982 China constructed more than 1,000 small hydroelectric dams. Even so the nation had developed only 3% of its hydroelectric potential.

In Europe Sweden planned to construct 1,300 mini-hydroelectric plants in the next five years in order to conserve oil use. The U.S.S.R. announced plans for large-scale diversion of several Siberian rivers, the Ob, Irtysh, and Yenesey, which flow

Major World Dams Under Construction in 1982[1]

Name of dam	River	Country	Type[2]	Height (m)	Length of crest (m)	Volume content (000 cu m)	Gross reservoir capacity (000 cu m)
Altinkaya	Kizilirmak	Turkey	E, R	195	604	15,310	5,763,000
Amaluza	Paute	Ecuador	A	170	410	1,157	120,000
Atatürk	Euphrates	Turkey	E, R	179	1,700	84,500	48,700,000
Baishan	Songhuajiang	China	G	150	677	1,663	900,000
Boruca	Terraba	Costa Rica	E, R	267	700	43,000	14,960,000
Canales	Genil	Spain	E, R	156	340	4,733	7,070,000
Chapeton	Paraná	Argentina	E, G	34	6,550	200,000	53,700,000
Dabaklamm	Dorferbach	Austria	A	220	332	1,000	235,000
Dongjiang	Laishui	China	A	157	438	1,389	8,120,000
Dry Creek	Dry Creek	U.S.	E	110	915	23,000	310,000
El Cajon	Humuya	Honduras	A	226	382	1,480	5,650,000
El M'Jara	Ouergha	Morocco	E	87	1,500	25,000	4,000,000
Grand Maison	Eau d'Olle	France	E, R	160	550	18,450	140,000
Guavio	Orinoco	Colombia	E, R	250	461	17,000	10,000,000
Guri (Raúl Leoni)	Caroní	Venezuela	E, R, G	162	11,409	75,700	136,335,000
Ihla Grande	Paraná	Brazil	E, G	29	7,060	11,573	30,000,000
Inguri	Inguri	U.S.S.R.	A	272	680	3,880	1,100,000
Itaipú	Paraná	Brazil/Paraguay	E, R, G	185	7,900	27,000	29,000,000
Itaparica	São Francisco	Brazil	E, R	105	4,700	16,530	11,500,000
Karakaya	Euphrates	Turkey	A, G	180	420	2,000	9,580,000
Kenyir	Trengganu	Malaysia	E, R	150	920	15,900	13,600,000
Kishau	Tons	India	E, R	253	360	N.A.	2,400,000
La Grande No. 2	La Grande	Canada	E, R	160	2,835	23,000	61,720,000
La Grande No. 3	La Grande	Canada	E, R	100	3,855	22,187	60,020,000
La Grande No. 4	La Grande	Canada	E, R	125	7,243	20,000	19,390,000
La Honda	Uribante	Venezuela	E	150	600	10,500	775,000
Lakhwar	Yamuna	India	G	192	440	2,000	580,000
Lungyangxia	Huanghe	China	G	172	342	1,300	24,700,000
Maqarin	Yarmouk	Jordan	E, R	164	700	21,000	486,000
Menzelet	Ceyhan	Turkey	E, R	150	420	7,000	19,500,000
Mihoesti	Aries	Romania	E, R	242	242	180	6,000
Mosul	Tigris	Iraq	E	100	3,600	36,000	11,100,000
Naramata	Naramata	Japan	E, R	158	520	12,000	90,000
Nurek	Vakhsh	U.S.S.R.	E	300	704	58,901	10,500,000
Oosterschelde	Vense Gat Oosterschelde	The Netherlands	E, G	45	8,400	35,000	2,000,000
Oymapinar	Manavgat	Turkey	A	185	360	575	310,000
Özköy	Gediz	Turkey	E, R	180	420	11,251	940,000
Porto Primavera	Paraná	Brazil	E, G	38	11,385	8,441	18,500,000
Revelstoke	Columbia	Canada	E, R, G	162	1,615	8,900	5,310,000
Rogun	Vakhsh	U.S.S.R.	E	325	660	75,500	11,600,000
Roncador	Uruguay	Brazil/Argentina	E, R	78	1,600	6,500	33,580,000
Salvajina	Cauca	Colombia	E, R	154	368	4,000	773,000
São Felix	Tocantis	Brazil	E, R	160	1,950	34,000	55,200,000
Sterkfontein	Nuwejaarspruit	South Africa	E	93	3,060	19,800	2,656,000
Tehri	Bhagirathi	India	E, R	261	570	25,200	3,539,000
Thein	Ravi	India	E, R	47	878	21,920	3,670,000
Thomson	Thomson	Australia	E, R	165	1,275	13,200	1,100,000
Tokuyama	Ibi	Japan	E, R	161	420	10,000	660,000
Tres Irmaos	Tiete	Brazil	E, G	90	3,700	15,000	14,200,000
Tucurui	Tocantis	Brazil	E, G	93	10,677	64,300	43,000,000
Upper Wainganga	Wainganga	India	E	43	181	N.A.	50,700,000
Yacambu	Yacambu	Venezuela	E, R	158	110	3,400	427,000
Yacyreta-Apipe	Paraná	Paraguay/Argentina	E, G	36	65,000	73,000	21,000,000
Zillergründl	Ziller	Austria	A	180	505	980	90,000
Major World Dams Completed in 1981 and 1982[1]							
Caniapiscau	Caniapiscau	Canada	E, R	56	3,493	11,810	53,800,000
Chicoasen	Grijalva	Mexico	E, R	245	584	14,500	1,680,000
Emborcacao	Paranaíba	Brazil	E, R	158	1,607	25,650	17,600,000
Finstertal	Nederbach	Austria	E, R	150	652	4,500	60,000
Foz do Areia	Iguaçu	Brazil	E, G, R	160	850	13,000	6,100,000
Gura Apelor Retezat	Riul Mare	Romania	E, R	168	460	9,000	225,000
Los Leones	Los Leones	Chile	E	179	510	9,200	106,000
Sayano-Shushenskaya	Yenisei	U.S.S.R.	A	242	1068	9117	31,300,000
Wujiangdu	Wujiang	China	G	165	368	1920	2,300,000

[1] Having a height exceeding 150 m (492 ft); or having a volume content exceeding 15 million cu m (19.6 million cu yd); or forming a reservoir exceeding 14,800 x 10⁶ cu m capacity (12 million ac-ft).
[2] Type of dam: E = earth; R = rockfill; A = arch; G = gravity.
NA = not available.

(T. W. MERMEL)

into the Arctic Ocean, to supply water to the arid lands in the Kazakh, Kirghiz, and Uzbek regions in the south. The Soviets also planned to divert the Pechora and Kolva rivers to the Volga. While these projects might take many years to complete, environmentalists were alarmed that they could have a worldwide impact. This scheme paralleled a similar study for North America, which proposed that Canadian rivers be diverted to the southern United States.

In the Philippines a $1 billion municipal water supply project for Manila was to include the construction of a 100-m-high dam. India joined the countries interested in developing tidal power. More than $200 million was made available to study the feasibility of tidal power in the Gulf of Kutch on the nation's northwestern coast.

Canada planned to build an arch dam 270 m high, the second highest in the world. The highest, Inguri, was under construction in the U.S.S.R. and would be 272 m high.

In the U.S. work was under way on the first roller-compacted concrete dam, Willow Creek in Oregon. Its dimensions included a volume content of 300,000 cu m, a height of 52 m, and a crest length of 518 m. It represented a major change in the method of construction of a concrete gravity-type dam. The principal difference was that damp gravel is blended with cement and spread and compacted by large, efficient earth-moving equipment, eliminating the labour-intensive, bucket-by-bucket placing procedures used in the past.

(T. W. MERMEL)

Roads. In 1982 figures revealed that there were almost 20 million km of roads in the world (1 km = 0.62 mi). Of these, 1.1 million km were in Africa, 3 million km in Asia, 4 million km in Europe, 2 million km in Latin America, 7 million km in North America, and 1 million km in Oceania. Vehicle population using the world's roads amounted to 420 million at the end of 1981, with 180 million of those in the United States.

In many of the industrialized nations revenues from vehicle and fuel taxes were no longer sufficient to meet current and projected highway financing needs. Inflation was raising costs at a faster rate than revenues, while the increased fuel efficiency of vehicles was reducing income from gasoline taxes. This situation, coupled with the deterioration of many major highways constructed after World War II, resulted in exploration of new methods of financing highway construction and maintenance.

In the U.S. federal tax receipts fell below outlays by $5.6 billion in 1980 and $5.2 billion in 1981. Legislation to add 5 cents in taxes to the cost of each gallon of gasoline was passed by the U.S. Congress in December, with four cents dedicated to rehabilitation of roads and one cent dedicated to financing of urban transit projects. In the United Kingdom representatives of the Department of Transport proposed a road financing system under which highway contractors would arrange financing and pay for new road projects and then would be repaid by the British government over a period of 15 years.

Despite economic problems major highway pro-

grams were initiated or completed in all continents. Approximately 95% of the 68,260-km Interstate System in the U.S. was in service, while extensive reconstruction and rehabilitation programs were under way on some segments of the system that had been in service for more than a quarter of a century.

The Inter-American Development Bank was helping finance construction of 61,587 km of roads in eight countries in Latin America and the Caribbean, with a combined value of $7,329,000,000. The last link in the section of the Pan-American Highway between Buenos Aires, Arg., and Santiago, Chile, was opened to traffic.

Colombia, with 75,000 km of existing roads, was planning a $2.5 billion road construction program between 1982 and 1986, while Guatemala implemented a seven-year, $1.4 billion program including a four-lane highway connecting Guatemala City with the Pacific port of San José. In Brazil a 1,500-km highway was under construction between Cuiba and Porto Velho. The Brazilian Ministry of Transport developed an important program of feeder highways to benefit the large agricultural population and was rebuilding approximately 1,000 km of highways in the northwest at a cost of $687 million.

China built 10,000 km of new roads and upgraded 4,000 km of existing roads in 1981 (latest figures available), bringing the nation's total road network to 900,000 km. Major new roads included the 965-km Yichuan–Lanzhou (Yi-ch'uan–Lan-chou) highway and the 2,000-km highway from Iqe, Qinghai (Tsinghai) Province, to Hetan (Ho-t'an). A 240-km, six-lane toll highway was under construction from Guangzhou (Canton) to Macao and Hong Kong at a cost of $420 million.

Japan, with 40,000 km of roads, was planning completion of its 7,600-km national expressway system by the end of the century. A total of 5,415 km were already completed or under construction.

Thirty-nine African countries submitted plans for highway projects worth $26 billion as part of the second phase of the UN Transport and Communications Decade in Africa. Included were the 1,200-km highway connecting Annaba, Constantine, Algiers, and Oran in Algeria and the 1,085-km Aaium–Akjoujt road in Morocco.

More than 1,800 km were completed on the Trans-European North-South Motorway, which was to pass through Austria, Bulgaria, Czechoslovakia, Greece, Hungary, Italy, Poland, Romania, Turkey, and Yugoslavia. Italy's government lifted a six-year ban on the building of new expressways and was expected to implement a new $5 billion program that included a bypass around Rome.

(HUGH M. GILLESPIE)

Tunnels. Hard rock tunnel boring machines (TBM's) continued to improve their performance and reliability when used under suitable conditions. Norwegian engineers claimed a world record for an advance of 240.5 m in one week achieved by a Robbins 3.5-m-diameter TBM in a rock tunnel for a hydroelectric project. A TBM achieved an impressive performance at the Hausling pumped storage project in Austria, where in eight months it bored a 950-m-long, 4.2-m-diameter pressure shaft inclined at 42° through a hard grained gneiss. In the U.K. the machine-driven Kielder water tunnel through hard rock between the Rivers Tyne and Tees was finally completed in 1982. The 29-km-long, 3.5-m-diameter tunnel was Britain's longest.

The need to ensure that ground conditions were suitable for the employment of TBM's was demonstrated at the Talave irrigation tunnel in Spain; during construction of the 31.6-km-long rock tunnel, the longest in Spain, a roof fall buried a 4.2-m-diameter TBM, which was eventually recovered two years later.

Despite the increasing use of TBM's they were unlikely to supersede drill and blast methods in the foreseeable future. In Finland the Pajainne 18-sq-m-section tunnel providing water to Helsinki was completed by drill and blast methods. This 120-km-long unlined tunnel was claimed to be the longest in the world. Pipe jacking continued to increase in popularity with engineers. In the range of small diameters of from one to two metres, West German engineers developed a slurry shield for pipe jacking in which the cutting action was performed by oscillating high-pressure water jets. Japanese engineers introduced small-diameter slurry shields equipped with conventional cutting heads but operated completely by remote control from the surface. Also developed by the Japanese were large-diameter slurry shields using high-density slurry and incorporating crushers to deal with boulders up to 50 cm (20 in) in diameter.

At Frankfurt am Main, West Germany, one of Europe's largest tunnel shields began to be used in 1982 on the new extensions to the city's subway. Weighing 450 metric tons, the 10.56-m-diameter shield was equipped with three excavators. The equipment could be rebuilt to excavate the 8.7-m-diameter tunnels in the same project.

A new development in tunnel lining was the completion of over 1,400 m of 3.6-m-diameter lining using fibre-reinforced concrete extruded behind the shield. It was claimed that if a waterproof lining was required the system could prove up to 30% cheaper than conventional segmental lining.

The protection of tunnels and underground structures against damage by earthquake was a subject of continuing interest as more and more cities throughout the world constructed subway systems. After five years of operation, Soviet engineers reviewed the effectiveness of the measures taken to withstand seismic shocks on the subway at Tashkent. Major sections of the tunnel lining and station structures had been built using precast concrete sections to combine flexibility with strength. By 1982 more than 300 tremors had been experienced without any damage to structures in tunnels.

In the U.S. bids were asked for in the construction of the largest soft ground tunnel in the country, at Seattle, Wash.; estimated to cost up to $100 million, it would be 19 m in diameter and 457 m long. The interesting feature of this huge tunnel was the proposed method of construction, using a minimum of 24 drifts located around the circumference.   (DAVID A. HARRIES)

[733; 734.A]

England:
see United Kingdom

English Literature:
see Literature

Entertainment:
see Dance; Motion Pictures; Music; Television and Radio; Theatre

Entomology:
see Life Sciences

Environment

The tenth anniversary year of the 1972 UN Conference on the Human Environment in Stockholm saw some signs of improvement in the management of the global environment. The continuing recession led to further cuts in the budget of the UN Environment Program (UNEP), and the new treaty on the Law of the Sea, though signed by 117 nations in December, failed to gain general acceptance. At the same time, some hard-fought campaigns made substantial progress.

Internationally, the most contentious issue was "acid rain," which was debated at a conference held in Stockholm to mark the anniversary of the 1972 conference. Here, too, there were gains, as the scientific evidence for damage caused by this type of pollution persuaded countries where the pollution originated to accept the reality of the problem.

In part, the recognition was due to the political success of the environmentalist "Green" candidates in the West German elections. Partly as a result of their rising popularity and partly because of the Free Democratic Party's decline, they emerged as the third most important political party in the country, with opinions that had to be respected. (*See* BIOGRAPHIES: *Kelly, Petra.*)

INTERNATIONAL COOPERATION

UN Environment Program. Speaking at a two-day anniversary meeting held in London on June 15–16 to review progress made by UNEP, a spokesman for West German Chancellor Helmut Schmidt revealed that, at Schmidt's insistence, the global environment was to be included on the agenda of the next summit meeting of Western leaders. At UNEP's own conference, which opened in Nairobi, Kenya, on May 10, the emphasis was on funding. Kenya's Pres. Daniel arap Moi and UNEP Executive Director Mustafa Tolba urged the 100 delegates to increase their contributions. Great Britain agreed to do so, from £600,000 to £750,000; Libya pledged $1 million; The Netherlands said it would raise its contribution by 50%; and Japan, Finland, Malaysia, Uganda, and Thailand all promised more. However, these offers were insufficient to offset the reduction in the U.S. contribution. In October 1981 a State Department internal document had proposed that the U.S. cancel its entire contribution to UNEP as an economy measure. It was persuaded not to take so drastic a step, but the $10 million it had been expected to contribute was reduced to $7 million, with the likelihood that in 1983 it might be lowered to $3 million.

UN Conference on the Law of the Sea. During the period leading up to the final session of the third UN Conference on the Law of the Sea (UNCLOS), several industrialized countries expressed deep reservations about the draft treaty. It was felt that the treaty was biased toward third world countries. Also, because the proposed International Seabed Authority would be funded mainly by taxes levied on Western firms, which were required to share the technologies they developed

Mustafa Tolba, executive director of the United Nations Environment Program, urged delegates at a UNEP conference in Kenya in May to increase their financial contributions to the UNEP. At right is Philip Leakey, a Kenyan MP who served as host for the meeting.

with third world countries, seabed mining could be penalized to the point of nonprofitability.

UNCLOS reconvened in New York City from March 9 to April 30. The U.S. attended but sought major changes in the treaty. On April 17 the Supreme Soviet of the U.S.S.R. decreed that it would allow industrial organizations to exploit seabed mineral resources outside its territorial waters, a measure it said had been forced on it by U.S. attempts to alter the draft treaty to its own advantage. When the text of the Soviet decree was released, it appeared to contain much more detail than would have been needed for a mere tactical document to be used in negotiation. It covered safety zones around drilling sites, the notification of hazards to navigation, methods of resolving disputes with other states, and provision for non-Soviet participation in projects.

The treaty, running to 175 pages in 17 parts, with 320 articles and 8 annexes, was signed at the end of the conference by most of the states present. The U.S., Israel, Turkey, and Venezuela voted against it; Great Britain, West Germany, The Netherlands, Belgium, Spain, and the whole Eastern bloc abstained. Although the treaty covered many issues, including the establishment of 12-mi territorial and 200-mi exclusive economic zones, objections centred on its proposals for the mining of seabed minerals.

On July 10 the U.S. announced it would not agree to the treaty. By the end of July it was clear that the U.S. government, with the aim of devising a "mini-treaty," was negotiating with Great Britain, West Germany, France, Belgium, The Netherlands, Italy, and Japan to reach an agreement covered by the U.S. Deep Seabed Hard Mineral Resources Act of 1980. The treaty was opened for formal signature on December 10 at Montego Bay, Jamaica, and signed by 117 nations. A number of industrialized countries besides the U.S. abstained but did not rule out the possibility of adhering at a later date.

European Communities (EC). Environmental ministers of EC member countries, meeting in Brussels on Dec. 3, 1981, adopted a directive de-

signed to regulate the discharge of mercury into water by the chloralkali industry, although no permissible limits were set. Agreement was reached on the "Seveso directive." This obliged industries to notify the authorities, local residents, and workers of stocks of dangerous chemicals they held and stipulated the quantities of particular substances that might be stored within 500 m (1,640 ft) of one another. Where installations were situated close to international frontiers, consultations would take place directly between the governments involved.

The EC took further steps to control the production and use of trichlorophenoxyacetic acid (2,4,5-T). In January 1982 the Commission received a report produced by an independent research team, which showed that the herbicide was safe provided its dioxin content was reduced. The report recommended that the permitted level for dioxin contamination be reduced to 0.005 parts per million, half the level imposed by Britain, Bel-

World's 25 Most Populous Urban Areas[1]					
Rank	City and Country	City proper		Metropolitan area	
		Population	Year	Population	Year
1	Tokyo, Japan	8,334,900	1981 estimate	29,002,000	1981 estimate
2	Osaka, Japan	2,635,200	1981 estimate	16,224,000	1981 estimate
3	New York City, U.S.	7,071,600	1980 census	16,121,300	1980 census
4	Mexico City, Mexico	9,373,400	1980 census[2]	15,032,000	1980 estimate
5	São Paulo, Brazil	7,033,500	1980 census	12,719,100	1980 census[2]
6	Cairo, Egypt	5,399,000	1979 estimate	12,000,000	1980 estimate
7	London, U.K.	6,608,600	1981 census	11,962,100	1981 census
8	Shanghai, China	6,320,872	1982 census	11,859,748	1982 census
9	Rhine-Ruhr, West Germany	[3]	[3]	11,777,800	1980 census
10	Los Angeles, U.S.	2,966,800	1980 census	11,497,600	1980 census
11	Buenos Aires, Argentina	2,922,800	1980 census	9,766,000	1980 census[2]
12	Beijing, China	5,597,972	1982 census	9,230,687	1982 census
13	Calcutta, India	[4]	[4]	9,165,700	1981 census[2]
14	Rio de Janeiro, Brazil	5,093,200	1980 census[2]	9,153,200	1980 census[2]
15	Paris, France	2,168,300	1982 census[2]	8,505,800	1982 census[2]
16	Seoul, South Korea	[4]	[4]	8,367,000	1980 census[2]
17	Bombay, India	[4]	[4]	8,227,300	1981 census[2]
18	Moscow, U.S.S.R.	[4]	[4]	8,015,000	1981 estimate
19	Nagoya, Japan	2,089,200	1981 estimate	7,968,000	1981 estimate
20	Chicago, U.S.	3,005,100	1980 census	7,869,500	1980 census
21	Tianjin, China	5,142,565	1982 census	7,764,141	1982 census
22	Jakarta, Indonesia	[4]	[4]	6,556,000	1981 estimate
23	Chongqing, China	[4]	[4]	6,000,000	1978 estimate
24	Delhi, India	[4]	[4]	5,713,600	1981 census[2]
25	Manila, Philippines	1,630,500	1980 census	5,664,000	1980 estimate

[1]Ranked by population of metropolitan area.
[2]Preliminary figures.
[3]An industrial conurbation within which no single central city is identified.
[4]City proper not identified by reporting countries.

A device weighing 350 tons and measuring 100 by 100 ft (30 by 30 m) at its base was towed into the ocean off Santa Barbara County, California, and lowered to the ocean floor. The device was designed to capture oil and gas seeping from fissures in the sea floor.

gium, and West Germany. In July the Commission recommended reduction to 0.1 parts per million immediately and, as soon as it became technically feasible, to 0.005 parts per million. At the same time, it urged governments to ensure that 2,4,5-T did not contaminate food by banning its use on cereal crops, in woodlands when edible fungi were in season, and as a domestic weed killer.

Acid Rain. The main air pollution issue of the year was "acid rain," which was affecting parts of North America and parts of Europe. The tenor of the debate changed as certain countries that had been skeptical in previous years—and which were regarded as principal sources of this form of pollution—found that they, too, were its victims. On Oct. 5, 1981, the U.S. National Wildlife Federation published a report identifying 15 states east of the Mississippi in which the pH level of rain varied from 4.8 (South Carolina) to 4.1 (Mississippi). Disagreement between the U.S. and Canada over the issue continued, but it was clear that not only Canada was being affected.

The Swedish government announced in February 1982 that it would celebrate the anniversary of the 1972 UN conference by holding a conference in Stockholm during June 16–30, to be called "Environment 82" and devoted to discussion of the acid rain problem. On June 11 the British Department of the Environment was given a report by scientists at the Warren Spring Laboratory showing that, in all but 4 of 37 rural sites monitored between 1978 and 1980, rain was as acid as in Scandinavia for at least one of the years.

As the conference opened, the delegates expected West Germany to support Britain and the U.S. in opposing any action to deal with the problem effectively, but the West German government had received two shocks. The first was the growing popularity of the "Green" environmentalist political candidates. The second was the result of studies by Bernhard Ulrich of the University of Göttingen, who had found that 40% of West German forests were suffering from damage caused by acid rain pollution. The conference ended with agreement among the signatories of the 1979 Geneva convention on transfrontier air pollution that the convention would be ratified in New York in July

(which it was) and would come into force by the end of the year. West Germany promised to halve its sulfur emissions.

Marine Environment. A report published by UNEP in October stated that, while the deep oceans remained clean, coastal waters in certain areas suffered from pollution, although not yet seriously. The report called for stricter control of the discharge of sewage into coastal waters and drew attention to the condition of the southern part of the Bay of Bengal, where 1,000 tons of tar were believed to be floating.

On January 1 the Persian Gulf states assumed responsibility for protecting the Gulf from pollution, taking over a $6 million program from UNEP and forming a Regional Organization for the Protection of the Marine Environment. The organization held its first meeting in January, when plans for research projects on oceanography and oil pollution were approved. It was also agreed to establish a centre at Bahrain to combat oil pollution and to mount an antipollution publicity campaign throughout the region.

The fourth protocol of the Mediterranean Action Plan was signed in April by the 18 countries bordering the sea. The $7 million budget for 1982–84 would be contributed mainly by Italy, France, and Spain, with the EC members subscribing $400,000.

Fresh Water. Tentative agreement among the five countries concerned (France, Switzerland, West Germany, Luxembourg, and The Netherlands) was reached on Nov. 17, 1981, on ways to reduce pollution of the Rhine caused by the discharge of salt from French potash mines in Alsace. Under the agreement, France was to inject nearly one million tons of salt a year below ground in Alsace and open a salt mine with a 500,000-ton annual capacity which would also recycle sulfur waste.

Also in November 1981, the West German government agreed to start discussions with the governments of East Germany and Czechoslovakia on ways to reduce pollution of Germany's second most important river, the Elbe. Most of its industrial pollution occurred in the East, although treated domestic sewage and industrial effluent were added at Hamburg.

UNITED NATIONS

After eight years of difficult negotiations, delegates to the UN Conference on the Law of the Sea finally adopted a Law of the Sea Treaty on April 30. The treaty received 130 favourable votes, 4 against, and 17 abstentions.

NATIONAL DEVELOPMENTS

"Ecopolitics." During the year West Germany's "Greens" (the Grün-Alternative-Liste) increased their support dramatically to become the third most important political grouping in the country. On March 7 they won more than 5% of the votes in the Schleswig-Holstein state elections; on March 21, 6.5% in Lower Saxony; on June 6, 7.7% in Hamburg; and on September 26, 8% in Hesse. By the end of the year they had seats in six state parliaments, and in some they held the balance of power. It seemed likely that federal elections scheduled for 1983 would bring Green representatives into the Bundestag (federal parliament).

Environmentalist candidates were less successful in France. In the first round of the cantonal (local government) elections on March 14 they won only 0.44% of the votes cast, and in the second round, on March 21, 0.006% of the total. These figures were little different from those achieved in the last cantonal elections, in 1979.

U.S. Secretary of the Interior James G. Watt continued to arouse hostility among environmentalists. William Turnage of the Wilderness Society described as "a duplicitous hoax" Watt's promise, made in February, to "prohibit drilling or mining in the wilderness to the end of the century" in his draft bill on the subject. The objectors maintained

that, far from closing the issue of mining in wilderness areas and leaving it closed, this would allow it to be reopened after 18 years. The proposal did not permit the establishment of a buffer zone around protected areas, and it might exclude from protection areas being considered for designation as wilderness.

The federal budget for fiscal 1983 included a 12% reduction in the operating budget of the Environmental Protection Agency (EPA). This would lead to a loss of more than 1,000 jobs through natural attrition and would be reflected in reduced state and local grants made by the EPA to treat wastes, recover resources, and clean lakes. In May the administration introduced proposals to amend the Clean Water Act; they would relax mandatory requirements for industry to treat effluent before discharging it into municipal sewers, but in general they aroused no strong opposition. However, Congress failed to act on them before it adjourned in December.

Seas, Rivers, Lakes. In the U.K. the eighth report of the Royal Commission on Environmental Pollution, dealing with oil pollution of the sea, proposed an immediate extension of territorial waters to 12 mi. This would increase control over the movement of shipping and make it possible to secure compensation from the owners of ships that caused pollution. The commission also called for better charts of British coastal waters, only 20% of which were charted adequately.

In January a study by the engineering department of Istanbul Technical University drew attention to serious pollution in the Bosporus and the Golden Horn, from untreated sewage, oil, market refuse, industrial wastes, and other debris. It warned that unless pollution were curbed it would begin to affect the Sea of Marmara.

Fears were expressed in September over the effects of a scheme to dam the Kara-Bogaz-Gol, a shallow water gulf linked by a narrow inlet to the Caspian Sea. Rising demands for water, combined with dry weather, had caused the water level in the Caspian to fall 2.6 m (8.5 ft) in the last 50 years, with the greatest evaporation loss occurring in shallow water. If the gulf was dammed, water could not enter from the Caspian, and one large shallow-water area would be sealed and allowed to dry. The gulf contains a large brine lake, rich in sodium sulfate that is exploited industrially, and it was feared that the scheme was already leading to contamination of the valuable brine with chlorides; eventually the Caspian might become more saline, while dry salts from the gulf might be blown onto farmlands.

An October 1981 report by the U.S. Public Interest Research Group stated that toxic wastes, including dioxin, were being pumped from the Hyde Park, N.Y., waste dump into the Niagara River. The dump, owned by the Hooker Chemicals and Plastics Corp., was alleged to be discharging 1,655,000,000 litres (440 million gal) of waste a day. The company offered to install a plant to clean the waste, but its opponents demanded that the waste be removed and burned, at an estimated cost of $200 million. Hooker had previously been held responsible for the dumping of wastes that led in 1978 to the evacuation of the Love Canal area of Niagara Falls. (See *Toxic Substances*, below.)

In July 1982 the California state health department reported that many private wells in the state were contaminated with DBCP (dibromochloropropane), a pesticide banned in the state in 1977 after it had been in use for 20 years. Levels in wells were said to be 50 to 60 times higher than the recommended limit, and the affected area extended more than 965 km (600 mi) south from Sacramento and contained 10,000 wells.

The U.K. National Water Council reported in December 1981 that financial constraints made it unlikely that resources could be diverted in the near future from maintaining existing water supplies and sewerage systems. This meant that little could be done to improve the quality of polluted rivers. In July 1982 the first provisions of Part II of the Control of Pollution Act 1974 came into force, modified to prevent members of the public from using the register of discharges into water, which water authorities were required to keep, as the basis for prosecutions. Despite the general lack of progress, in April a painted goby was caught in the River Thames. The Thames Water Board chairman, Geoffrey Edwards, claimed that the river was now the cleanest metropolitan estuary in the world.

Land Conservation. During the Israeli occupation of Sinai, scientists studied the ecology of the region, establishing the El Arish bird migration monitoring station, a field studies school near Santa Caterina, and the Ras Muhammad underwater observatory. Tourists were forbidden to remove seaweed or coral from beaches for fear they might drop them in the desert and cause ecological disturbances. When Sinai was returned to Egypt in 1982, Israeli scientists offered to make all their data available to their Egyptian opposite numbers. Egyptian plans included the development of solar ponds for energy and the creation of an artificial lake in the Quattana depression, southwest of El Alamein, which lies below sea level. Inflowing water would generate power, and the salt lake formed would feed chemical industries.

In February the Malaysian government announced plans to dam the Tembelins River to provide hydroelectric power and to form a large lake in the Taman Negara National Park. The park contains the only protected forest in the country, parts of which are believed to be 130 million years old, as well as valuable archaeological sites. The project had been suggested in 1971, but studies by Australian and Soviet teams advised great caution, and in 1976 the scheme was shelved.

On January 4 it was announced that U.K. Secretary of State for the Environment Michael Heseltine had rejected applications for two schemes to build dams on Lakes Ennerdale and Wastwater, in the Lake District, to supply water to British Nuclear Fuels Ltd. and the North West Water Authority. Late in March Heseltine announced his decision concerning the application of the National Coal Board (NCB) to open three pits in the Vale of Belvoir, a project that had been opposed strenuously by environmental and amenity groups. Hose, the only pit actually inside the vale, was rejected completely, and the NCB was required to submit new applications for the pits at Asfordby and Saltby. Neither of these pits would be permitted to have waste tips nearby.

In Norway the People's Movement to Save the Alta River ceased to oppose the planned construction of a dam and hydroelectric plant on the river, renowned for its salmon fishing. The huge Jari Project for development of the Amazon basin in Brazil, much criticized by ecologists, was abandoned by its originator, U.S. financier Daniel K. Ludwig (*see* BIOGRAPHIES), and taken over by the Brazilian government.

Toxic Substances. In February the U.S. Consumer Product Safety Commission decided to ban foam insulation made from urea formaldehyde. It had been found that after installation the foam may release formaldehyde gas, a suspected carcinogen. There were fears that the downgrading of the EPA would impede the program of the Organization for Economic Cooperation and Development for the control of toxic chemicals. The U.S. government was accused of failing to release data. In the U.S., the Natural Resources Defense Council cited EPA figures indicating that the Toxic Substances Control Act was being implemented loosely.

The report of a two-year study of contamination

Members of Greenpeace, an environmental protest group, tried to prevent dumping of atomic waste by the British in the Atlantic Ocean off the northwest coast of Spain. The protest failed and the dumping continued.

in Michigan was published in May. Scientists from the Mount Sinai School of Medicine, New York City, found that 97% of the population of Michigan was contaminated with polybrominated biphenyls (PBB's), as well as with DDT and polychlorinated biphenyls (PCB's). The PBB's resulted from an accident in 1973, when the Michigan Chemical Corp. mixed flame retardant with a feed for dairy cattle. In August the EPA issued regulations to control PCB's in electrical equipment where they might contaminate food or animal feedstuffs. The regulations would come into force on Oct. 1, 1985.

On the basis of a 1980 study carried out on behalf of the EPA, "Ring 3," the evacuated area farthest from Love Canal at Niagara Falls, N.Y., was declared safe for human habitation in July by the Center for Disease Control. The statement was challenged, especially by Beverly Paigen, one of a group of consultants who reviewed the original EPA study for the centre. Arguing that the chemical and statistical analyses were faulty and the sampling techniques questionable, Paigen expressed the view that the population should not return to the area.

On March 21 an explosion at a waste tip at Graigmillar, Edinburgh, Scotland, made a crater 12 m (40 ft) deep and 27 m (90 ft) across and showered debris over a nearby housing estate. Following an inquiry, the Health and Safety Executive reported on September 16 that the explosion probably had two causes. The burial 12 years earlier of eight tons of chemicals from an abandoned fireworks factory might have caused hydrogen to accumulate as a result of chemical reactions involving aluminum and magnesium with acids, eventually rupturing the concrete chamber in which the materials were housed. There may also have been a spontaneous ignition of escaping, un-

identified, chemicals or escaping gas ignited by surface fires.

The team investigating the Somerset, England, village of Shipham, where lead and cadmium residues from old mine workings had been found to be contaminating soil and garden produce, reported on September 13 that the villagers were in no danger. They advised continued monitoring, however, and warned people not to eat leafy vegetables grown locally, to grass over unused vegetable plots, and to prevent children from eating soil.

In Britain one of the year's leading issues was the campaign to prohibit the addition of lead to petrol (gasoline). On February 8 The Times published a letter written on March 6, 1981, by Sir Henry Yellowlees, chief medical officer at the Department of Health and Social Security, to Sir James Hamilton, permanent secretary at the Department of Education and Science. In it, Sir Henry said that in his view the risk to children from airborne lead was sufficiently well established to warrant action to "reduce markedly the lead content of petrol in use in the U.K." On the same day, the British Medical Association (BMA) released a statement describing environmental lead as a serious health hazard. The Campaign for Lead-Free Air (CLEAR) pressed its advantage by publishing on February 15 a report, commissioned from a firm of management consultants, that called for government action. On February 22 it was announced that Frazer Alexander, a consultant pediatrician at Newcastle General Hospital, had detected a statistical relationship between lead levels in fetal placentas and the incidence of stillbirths and fetal abnormalities.

By March public opinion polls showed that some 90% of those questioned would favour a ban on lead in petrol, and there was growing support for CLEAR in Parliament and among the medical profession. On May 5 the BMA approved a report by its own science and education board that acknowledged the risk of mental impairment to children from lead at levels lower than had been considered safe and called for a reduction in lead in the environment. A week later Michael Rutter chaired a symposium arranged by CLEAR. Rutter was regarded by the government as the most respected member of the Lawther Committee, which in its 1980 report cast doubt on the validity of evidence linking lead in petrol with brain damage. To everyone's surprise, he sided strongly with CLEAR.

In September the government made its decision, in the form of a circular sent to local authorities by the Department of the Environment. The safe level would be reduced from 35 to 25 micrograms of lead per millilitre of blood and the permitted level of lead in petrol would be reduced from 0.4 to 0.15 grams per litre by 1986. However, exposure to lead was to be monitored by teachers, social workers, and others in close contact with children, and no funds were to be provided for remedying defects such as old and flaking paint, or for examining children to identify those with unacceptably high blood lead levels. The circular was attacked at once by several groups, including the Institution of Environmental Health Officers, the National Society for Clean Air, and the National Association of Community Health Councils for England and Wales. The debate continued with support for strict controls on environmental lead growing rapidly.

In the U.S. the EPA announced in August that, despite pressure from the Office of Management and Budget, gasoline would not be allowed to contain more than 1.1 grams of lead per gallon (0.24 grams per litre) as of November 1. It was estimated that the effect of the new regulation would be to reduce airborne lead by 31% after eight years.

At an international symposium on asbestos held in Montreal in May, William Nicholson, professor at the Mount Sinai Medical School, forecast that more than 8,000 workers in Canada and the U.S. would die in 1982 as a result of exposure to asbestos, and the toll might be expected to reach 10,000 a year by 1990. In Britain calls for a total ban on asbestos intensified following the screening in July of a television documentary, "Alice: A Fight for Life." Two leading British manufacturers of asbestos products faced compensation claims running into millions of dollars, mainly from employees of their U.S. subsidiaries. In August the Manville Corp., the largest producer of asbestos in the U.S., filed for protection from creditors under Chapter 11 of the federal bankruptcy laws. Although Manville had suffered some losses, the chief reason for the move was the large number of lawsuits—estimated in the thousands—that had been filed against the firm by persons who claimed they had suffered permanent damage as a result of exposure to asbestos.

Pesticides. It was alleged in April that the U.S. State Department was considering resumption of a program—conducted with the cooperation of the Mexican authorities—to destroy Mexican marijuana crops by spraying them with the herbicide paraquat. An earlier spraying program had been

People complaining about the leakage of radiation paraded in front of the Rochester (New York) Gas and Electric building in January. The Ginna nuclear power plant, owned by the company, had released radiation when a pipe broke.

successful, but growers were said to have moved to new sites. Doubts about the health risks of smoking marijuana contaminated with paraquat had been not so much resolved as evaded by mixing the herbicide with capsules of a foul-smelling substance, dilimonen-dimercaptan, known as "essence of skunk." The capsules adhere to the plant and remain stable until heated to the 800° C achieved when the leaf is smoked; at that point they burst, warning the smoker that the leaf is contaminated.

It was reported in August that Electronorte, the Brazilian state power company, planned to spray defoliants containing 2,4-D and 2,4,5-T over a large area of rain forest that was to be cleared to make way for dams on the Amazon. The area included Indian reserves and a designated biological reserve. A proposal for a research project to test the scheme led to sharp disagreement between the country's environment minister, Paulo Nogueira Neto, who opposed the project, and Enrique Bergamin, director of the National Institute for Amazonian Research, who favoured it.

Atmospheric Pollution. Smog continued to be a serious problem in Athens. High levels of smog continued for several days in November 1981, even after some 65 factories in the Attica area had been ordered to reduce production by 30%. On Jan. 11, 1982, mild weather encouraged smog levels to rise again, and a 30% reduction in output was imposed on all factories in the Athens-Piraeus area for 24 hours. In June the smog returned, and private cars and trucks were banned from the centre of Athens between 8 AM and 4 PM from Mondays to Fridays; outside the prohibited area, vehicles were allowed on alternate days, depending on whether their license numbers ended with an odd or even digit. The scheme was not entirely successful; taxis were permitted to operate, and many moved into Athens from other areas.

All schools were closed in Ankara, Turkey, on January 11, and automobile travel was restricted as air pollution levels rose. Carbon monoxide concentrations reached 141 mg per cu cm of air, more than double the acceptable maximum, and sulfuric acid levels rose to 520 mg per cu cm, compared with an acceptable maximum of 150. Children under 12, persons over 50, and sufferers from respiratory complaints were advised to remain indoors.

In April the U.K. Department of the Environment reduced substantially its funding of research into air pollution. This affected investigations of the effects of atmospheric chlorofluorocarbons (CFC's), photochemical pollution, and the atmospheric chemistry and effects of sulfur and nitrogen oxides. There was a disagreement between the department and the Greater London Council (GLC), which continued through the year. The department claimed that during the winter of 1980–81 sulfur dioxide pollution levels in London were below the acceptable limits and that no further action was needed. The GLC disagreed; in July it published a report claiming that air in London contained more sulfur dioxide than that of any other British city and exceeded the EC limit until the exceptional winter of 1980–81.

Ozone, produced mainly by vehicle exhausts, might be causing crop losses valued at $3.1 million a year, according to figures published in February by the U.S. National Crop Loss Assessment Network. However, fears that CFC compounds might be damaging the atmospheric ozone layer receded. The U.S. National Aeronautics and Space Administration published figures showing estimated depletion by the end of the century to be between 5 and 9%, compared with 15–18% in earlier predictions.

Nuclear Protest. Greenpeace, the environmental protest group, attempted to halt the dumping of radioactive waste on two occasions in 1982. On August 5 the Greenpeace ship "Sirius" sailed from Amsterdam with 27 people on board and intercepted the British cargo ship "Gem" 788 km (490 mi) from the northwest coast of Spain. Protesters occupied all four of the platforms from which waste canisters were to be dumped, but the crew of the "Gem" improvised new platforms and continued dumping. The action ended on August 13, shortly before the U.K. Atomic Energy Authority's application for an injunction was to be heard in an Amsterdam court. On September 8 three Greenpeace members seized cranes used to dump waste on board the Dutch ship "Rijnborg" and occupied the crane cabins for a short time.

On the night of January 18, five shells fired from a 1960s-vintage Soviet bazooka at a range of 600 m (2,000 ft) struck the Super-Phénix fast breeder reactor under construction at Creys-Malville, France. Two shells hit the steam generator, one hit the reactor building, and two entered the reactor building and struck maintenance equipment. Damage was slight and did not delay work on the plant. Two hours after the attack, police were in-

formed by telephone that a "pacifist ecologist" group was responsible.

The only violent antinuclear demonstration of the year took place in France, at the Chooz nuclear site at Viruex-Molhin in the Ardennes, on the weekend of June 26–27. Following a peaceful protest involving about 500 people but watched by more than 1,000 motorized and riot police with three light armoured tanks and a helicopter, about 100 demonstrators hid in a steel factory and fought police by throwing stones, metal bolts, and gasoline bombs. Four demonstrators and 13 police were injured, and a five-year-old girl was struck in the face by a tear gas canister. In an earlier demonstration at the site, on March 27, Belgian protesters released balloons and threw gasoline bombs. They hoped to persuade their own government to withdraw from the joint Franco-Belgian project.

Urban Problems. In an attempt to prevent the building of a third runway, hundreds of demonstrators blockaded the Frankfurt am Main, West Germany, airport on Nov. 15, 1981. They used burning barricades made from tree trunks and branches, parked cars, and their own bodies to block approach roads. Police replied with water cannon when they were pelted with sticks at one of the airport entrances and by sticks, stones, and gasoline bombs near the building site. On Jan. 30, 1982, the demonstrations resumed. Police estimated the crowd at 8,000 and the demonstrators placed it at 20,000; 90 were arrested. The Citizens Action Group said more than 100 people were injured; police said 104 of their own men were hurt, 6 of them seriously. The following day another crowd of several hundred was dispersed by police. The Citizens Action Group, which favoured peaceful protest, believed other organized groups had joined the demonstration and started the violence; they claimed to have photographs that showed the same men attacking uniformed police and arresting demonstrators.

On April 26 squatters were evicted from a house in the Kreuzberg district of West Berlin, and during the following two days some 3,000 people demonstrated in protest. The protest was mainly peaceful, but on both nights about 200 youths rioted. Eight policemen were injured, there was considerable damage to property, and some 24 demonstrators were arrested. Rioting also followed the eviction of squatters from a building in Amsterdam in October. The building, which had been the centre of serious rioting in 1980, was acquired by the municipality earlier in 1982 for the purpose of housing other homeless families.

(MICHAEL ALLABY)

WILDLIFE CONSERVATION

On Jan. 31, 1982, ten Arabian oryx (*Oryx leucoryx*) were released into the open desert in Oman under strict legal protection. Twenty years earlier, when a few of these oryx still existed in the wild, Operation Oryx was launched by the Fauna Preservation Society (now the Fauna and Flora Preservation Society, FFPS) in an attempt to save the species from extermination by captive breeding. This was finally accomplished in the U.S. The Harasis tribe in Oman were to be the guards of the rehabilitated oryx. A calf was born in March, raising the number of animals to 11.

During the Southern Hemisphere spring and summer, the New Zealand Wildlife Service joined forces with the Royal Forest and Bird Society to save the unique black stilt from extermination. Predator-proof fences were built in the Lake Tekapo region, nesting areas were guarded, and eggs in places at risk were transferred to safer places. The result was 13 fully fledged young, the biggest increase in the black stilt population in five years.

For many years the world's chelonians (tortoises and turtles) had been the subject of anxious study by both scientists and conservationists, in the course of which egg-laying turtles were turned on their backs for tagging. In May the *Marine Turtles Newsletter* drew attention to the possibility that such treatment might rupture the eggs within a female turtle and result in breeding failure or even death. In Western Australia improved regulations were issued to protect both sea turtles and the dugong (*Dugong dugong*) in Shark Bay. Stakes for fishnets in the seabed were banned and hourly attention to all nets became compulsory.

On May 4 Spain acceded to the Convention on Wetlands of International Importance (the Ramsar Convention), thereby guaranteeing two habitats vital for migrating waterfowl—the Doñana and the Daimiel. In the U.S., also in May, a decision to open up for development 2.6 million ha (9 million ac) of the California coast posed a threat to the whole Californian habitat of the sea otter. Following the ten-year-old ban on the use of the pesticide DDT in the U.S., some birds such as bald eagles, brown pelicans, and ospreys showed signs of increasing due to an improvement in egg fertility. However, birds migrating from South America, where DDT was still used, remained at risk. The Charles Darwin research station in the Galápagos Islands, Ecuador, reintroduced 37 young land iguanas from captivity into their native habitat on Isabella Island; 115 young giant tortoises were already reestablished there.

In South Africa two extraordinary threats arose to the Cape vulture (*Gyps caprotheres*), a vulnerable species. These vultures used to rely on hyenas to break the larger carcass bones of carrion and so provide bone fragments from which the young vultures obtained calcium for bone building. With the hyenas gone, the larger bones remained unbroken. The other threat to the vultures was electrocution on existing types of electricity towers. Fortunately, the Vulture Study Group persuaded the Electricity Supply Commission to modify its towers and itself established "vulture restaurants" to provide suitable bones in nesting areas.

Following the discovery in September 1981 in Wyoming of a black-footed ferret (*Mustela nigripes*), the first seen since 1979, 24 of these ferrets had been found. Formerly they inhabited the prairie-dog (marmot) "towns" as a predator on the "dogs," but they had vanished with the cultiva-

A man carries a fawn which he captured in the Florida Everglades. Conservationists tried to save as many deer as they could from starvation or from hunters who were authorized to thin out the herds.

UPI

tion of the prairies and the disappearance of the "dogs" on which they preyed. As long ago as 1918, the naturalist E. W. Nelson had foretold the end of the black-footed ferret as a result of the inevitable extinction of the prairie dog. Although the ferret's newly found area was already threatened by development, urgent measures, with adequate financial support, might still save this species.

In June 1982 Eric Endrom, writing in *Oryx* (the journal of the FFPS), reported the extinction of the square-lipped (or white) rhinoceros in Uganda ("white" is a corruption of the Afrikaans word *weit*, meaning wide). The price obtainable for rhinoceros horn in East Africa, nearly $700 per kilo, and lawlessness in Uganda were to blame. The subspecies of the square-lipped rhinoceros in South Africa remained in good numbers, under careful conservation, and all rhinoceros hunting had been forbidden in Zambia since January to protect the black rhinoceros (*Diceros bicornis*). A new threat to the rarest of rhinoceroses, the Javan rhinoceros (*Rhinoceros sondaicus*), arose in the Ujong Kulon reserve, Java, where disease, possibly anthrax, killed 5 of the remaining population of between 40 and 60.

In June the Convention on the Conservation of European Wildlife and Natural Habitats came into force. All countries in the EC undertook to protect endangered species, including birds of prey and owls. No less urgent was the strict protection to be given to tortoises, especially the Mediterranean land tortoise (*Testudo hermanni*) and the Greek tortoise (*Testudo graeca*). Both were threatened by the pet trade, especially to England, where as late as 1960 tons of tortoises were imported annually (about 3,000 tortoises per ton), few of which survived their first winter. Credit for the recent reduction in this traffic was due to the Universities Federation for Animal Welfare, the FFPS, and the Royal Society for the Prevention of Cruelty to Animals.

In July the Vincent Wildlife Trust published its Otter Survey of Ireland. The European otter, known by farmers in the west of Ireland, in Gaelic, as *dobha-chu* ("dark hound") or *madra uisce* ("water dog") and protected under the Republic of Ireland Wildlife Act, was shown to retain a fair population in the wetland areas of Ireland—areas regarded as of international ecological importance. The density of Ireland's otter population surpassed densities in Scotland, Wales, and England (ranking in that order) by a comfortable margin.

In Australia the dispute between conservationists and the growing kangaroo products industry was heightened by the showing of *Goodbye Joey*, a graphic documentary on kangaroo hunting. Conservationists hoped to convince the U.S. to reinstate its ban on the importation of kangaroo products, lifted in 1980 on the grounds that kangaroo numbers were larger than previously thought.

In July the International Whaling Commission (IWC), meeting in Brighton, England, resolved to phase out commercial whaling entirely after three more years. But the resolution, opposed by Brazil, Iceland, Japan, Korea, and Norway, was dearly bought by an increase in quotas for some species during the intervening period. Moreover, the res-

olution could be revoked at either of the IWC's next two meetings.

In August the International Union for Conservation of Nature, in conjunction with the World Wildlife Fund, opened an office in Tokyo under the name Traffic Japan. This followed Japan's acceptance, in 1980, of the Convention on International Trade in Endangered Species of Wild Flora and Fauna (CITES) Traffic Japan would help the Japanese authorities bring the huge trade in wildlife and its products, centred in Japan, within the bounds of CITES regulations. It would also play an educational role.   (C. L. BOYLE)

See also Agriculture and Food Supplies; Energy; Fisheries; Historic Preservation; Life Sciences; Transportation.
[355.D; 525.A.3.g and B.4.f.i; 534.E.2.a; 724.A; 737.C.1]

Equatorial Guinea

Equatorial Guinea

The African republic of Equatorial Guinea consists of Río Muni, which is bordered by Cameroon on the north, Gabon on the east and south, and the Atlantic Ocean on the west; and the offshore islands of Bioko and Annobon. Area: 28,051 sq km (10,831 sq mi). Pop. (1982 est.): 380,000. Cap. and largest city: Malabo, on Bioko (pop., 1974 est., 25,000). Language: Spanish. Religion (1980): Christian 88.8%; tribal 4.6%; atheist 1.4%; Muslim 0.5%; other 0.2%; none 4.5%. President of the Supreme Military Council in 1982, Lieut. Col. Teodoro Obiang Nguema Mbasogo.

Relations with Spain were the most important aspect of Equatorial Guinea's politics during 1982. Spain took charge of security arrangements, sending two Guinean security force companies to Spain for training. At the same time, the Army was to have Spanish instructors, and Spanish advisers, experts, and technicians were in the country. Pres. Teodoro Obiang Nguema Mbasogo said he wanted Spain to become the predominant foreign influence again. In October the first Hispano-African conference was held in Malabo. Exports to Spain exceeded 1 billion pesetas in value for the first time. In contrast, however, a top Guinean official, Severo Moto, fled to Spain, allegedly forced out on the grounds that he was too pro-Spanish.

In April an International Conference of Donors met in Geneva to consider a program of rehabilita-

---

EQUATORIAL GUINEA

Education. (1973–74) Primary, pupils 35,977, teachers 630; secondary (1975–76), pupils 3,984, teachers 115; vocational (1975–76), pupils 370, teachers 29; teacher training (1975–76), students 169, teachers 21.

Finance and Trade. Monetary unit: ekwele (bikwele for more than one), with (Sept. 20, 1982) a par value of EK2 to 1 Spanish peseta (free rate of EK225 = U.S. $1; EK385 = £1 sterling). Budget (1981 est.): revenue EK1,951,-000,000; expenditure EK2,025,000,000. Foreign trade (1981): imports c. U.S. $58 million; exports c. U.S. $26 million. Import sources: Spain c. 54%; China c. 17%; Italy c. 12%; France c. 6%. Export destinations: Spain 40%; The Netherlands c. 28%; West Germany c. 23%. Main exports (1975): cocoa c. 60%; coffee c. 30%.

Agriculture. Production (in 000; metric tons; 1981): sweet potatoes c. 34; cassava c. 54; bananas c. 16; cocoa c. 8; coffee c. 6; palm kernels c. 3; palm oil c. 5. Livestock (in 000; 1981): sheep c. 34; cattle c. 4; pigs c. 4; goats c. 7; chickens c. 134.

Epidemics:
see Health and Disease

Episcopal Church:
see Religion

Pope John Paul II made a stop in Equatorial Guinea when he visited several countries on an African tour in February.

tion for Equatorial Guinea. The UN Development Program, which organized the conference, set a target of $141 million in aid. The chances of securing this appeared reasonable.

A new constitution, approved by 95% of the electorate, gave President Obiang a mandate for a further seven years in office.   (GUY ARNOLD)

Equestrian Sports

Thoroughbred Racing and Steeplechasing.
UNITED STATES AND CANADA. In a year marked by brilliance and tragedy, Conquistador Cielo was voted horse of the year for 1982 in the closest result since the Eclipse Award balloting was inaugurated in 1971. In the voting by the National Turf Writers Association, *Daily Racing Form,* and the Thoroughbred Racing Associations, the three-year-old colt narrowly defeated the four-year-old colt Lemhi Gold and the two-year-old filly Landaluce, both of which were awarded titles in their divisions as was Conquistador Cielo in his.

Conquistador Cielo (Mr. Prospector-K D Princess, by Bold Commander), owned by Henryk de Kwiatkowski and trained by Woodford C. ("Woody") Stevens, defeated older rivals in the Metropolitan Handicap in late May and six days later won the Belmont Stakes by 14½ lengths. In the Metropolitan, his first stakes start, the bay colt established a track record of 1 min 33 sec for one mile and won by more than seven lengths. He increased his victory streak to seven with triumphs in the Dwyer and Jim Dandy, but a recurring leg problem ended his career after he finished third to Runaway Groom and Aloma's Ruler in the Travers Stakes in August. He was syndicated for $36.4 million and retired to stud. Winners of the other Triple Crown events (with the Belmont

Stakes) for three-year-olds were Gato del Sol, owned by Arthur Hancock III and Leone J. Peters, in the Kentucky Derby and Nathan Scherr's Aloma's Ruler in the Preakness.

Misfortune struck many other promising three-year-olds but none as severely as Timely Writer, which suffered a broken left front cannon bone during the running of the Jockey Club Gold Cup and had to be destroyed. Earlier the colt had undergone surgery for an intestinal disorder and was forced to miss the Triple Crown races after having gained the early top ranking in his division with victories in the Flamingo and Florida Derby.

Landaluce's death was less dramatic but just as tragic. The unbeaten two-year-old daughter of Seattle Slew-Strip Poker, by Bold Bidder, succumbed to a bacterial infection after a one-week illness the nature of which baffled attending veterinarians. Racing solely in California for owners L. R. French and Barry Beal, Landaluce made a spectacular debut in early July at Hollywood Park by winning a six-furlong race by seven lengths in 1 min 8.2 sec. Her second start was even more dramatic, a 21-length decision in the Hollywood Lassie in 1 min 8 sec. She won three other stakes: the Debutante, Anoakia, and Oak Leaf.

Aaron U. Jones's Lemhi Gold (Vaguely Noble-Belle Marie, by Candy Spots) accumulated $1,066,375 while winning stakes over both turf and dirt. His most important victories were in the Marlboro Cup and the Jockey Club Gold Cup.

Other Eclipse Award winners included: two-year-old colt, Roving Boy; three-year-old filly, Christmas Past; older filly or mare, Track Robbery; male turf horse, Perrault; female turf horse, April Run; sprinter, Gold Beauty; steeplechase, Zaccio, for the third consecutive year.

Jockey Angel Cordero, Jr., apprentice jockey Alberto Delgado, owner Viola Sommer, breeder Fred

W. Hooper, Jr., and trainer Charles Whittingham also won Eclipse honours, Whittingham for the second time. Cordero's mounts earned more than $9.7 million in purses to establish a one-year record for a jockey. Cordero, however, lost to Pat Day 399–397 in number of winning mounts. Whittingham's horses earned $4,588,897 to break his own record. Sommer's stable was the top money winner with earnings in excess of $2 million.

Robert E. Hibbert's Roving Boy (Olden Times-Black Eyed Lucy, by Prince Royal II), California-based but Kentucky-bred, captured his title in head-to-head competition with Eastern champion Copelan in the Hollywood Futurity. Roving Boy defeated Desert Wine by a neck, while Copelan finished a distant fifth after having been struck in an eye by a clod of dirt. Roving Boy won three other stake races and earned $800,425.

Cynthia Phipps's Christmas Past (Grey Dawn II-Yule Log, by Bold Bidder) won five stakes, including the Coaching Club American Oaks, Monmouth Oaks, and the Ruffian Handicap to defeat several other aspirants to the crown. She finished third in the Jockey Club Gold Cup. Competition for the older filly and mare award was close, but Summa Stable's Track Robbery (No Robbery-Left at Home, by Run for Nurse) gained the honours with triumphs in four stakes, including the Apple Blossom and Spinster. Perrault, a five-year-old English-bred (Djakao-Innocent Air, by Court Martial), earned $1,197,400 for owners Serge Fradkoff and Baron Thierry van Zuylen after winning four stakes, including the Budweiser Million. A versatile campaigner, he triumphed in the Hollywood Gold Cup on dirt in the excellent time of 1 min 59.2 sec. for 1¼ mi.

Runaway Groom took two of the Triple Crown events for Canadian-foaled three-year-olds, the Prince of Wales and the Breeders' Stakes, while Son of Briartic won the third event, the Queen's Plate. Avowal was victorious in the Canadian Oaks, and Majesty's Prince triumphed in the Rothmans International. The four-year-old gelding Frost King was named Canada's horse of the year.　　　　　　　(JOSEPH C. AGRELLA)

EUROPE AND AUSTRALIA. Akiyda, a three-year-old filly, beat the best that Europe could put against her in the Prix de l'Arc de Triomphe at Longchamp, Paris, on Oct. 3, 1982. The performance, which was her last, did not make Akiyda the best horse on the continent, but it was a year in which there was no true champion. Owned by the Aga Khan, trained by François Mathet, and imaginatively ridden by Yves Saint-Martin, she held off the challenges of two British-trained rivals, Ardross and Awaasif, by a head and half a length.

Ardross had won six of his seven races at home, including the Ascot Gold Cup, and also gave Lester Piggott, who was on his way to his 11th riding championship, his 4,000th winner in his career in Britain in the Geoffrey Freer Stakes at Newbury in August. Awaasif had beaten the Irish Oaks winner, Swiftfoot, by a neck in the Yorkshire Oaks. However, the ease with which the fourth-place horse in the Arc, April Run, won her two subsequent races in the U.S., both by 6½ lengths, suggested that she might have been the best horse in the Arc field.

Gato del Sol led the pack to the finish in the 108th Kentucky Derby on May 1. Mounted on the victor was Eddie Delahoussaye.

UPI

Major Thoroughbred Race Winners, 1982

Race	Won by	Jockey	Owner
United States			
Acorn	Cupecoy's Joy	A. Santiago	Ri-Ma-Ro Stable
Alabama	Broom Dance	G. McCarron	Christiana Stable
American Derby	Wolfie's Rascal	R. Hernandez	Wolfie Cohen and Sidney Port
Arkansas Derby	Hostage	J. Fell	Mrs. Paul Hexter
Arlington Classic	Wolfie's Rascal	A. Cordero, Jr.	Wolfie Cohen and Sidney Port
Arlington Handicap	Flying Target	R. Cox	Dixiana Stable
Arlington-Washington Futurity	Total Departure	E. Fires	Jay Templeman and Steve Lyons
Beldame	Weber City Miss	A. Cordero, Jr.	Joseph Allen
Belmont	Conquistador Cielo	L. Pincay, Jr.	Henryk de Kwiatkowski
Blue Grass	Linkage	W. Shoemaker	Christiana Stables
Brooklyn	Silver Supreme	A. Cordero, Jr.	Michael Berry
Budweiser Million	Perrault	L. Pincay, Jr.	Serge Fradkoff and Baron Thierry van Zuylen
Champagne	Copelan	J. Bailey	Fred W. Hooper
Charles H. Strub	It's the One	W. Guerra	Amin Saiden
Coaching Club American Oaks	Christmas Past	J. Vasquez	Cynthia Phipps
Delaware	Jameela	J. Kaenel	Peter M. Brant
Flamingo	Timely Writer	J. Fell	Nitram Stable
Florida Derby	Timely Writer	J. Fell	Nitram Stable
Futurity	Copelan	J. Bailey	Fred W. Hooper
Gulfstream Park	Lord Darnley	M. L. Russ	Mrs. Ivan Phillips
Hialeah Turf Cup	The Bart	E. Delahoussaye	F. N. Groves
Hollywood Derby (2 divisions)	Racing Is Fun	W. Shoemaker	Mrs. Connie Ring
	Victory Zone	E. Delahoussaye	Honeybee Farm, Ben Perkins, and Mr. and Mrs. Martin Ritt
Hollywood Gold Cup	Perrault	L. Pincay, Jr.	Serge Fradkoff and Baron Thierry van Zuylen
Hollywood Invitational	Exploded	L. Pincay, Jr.	Mrs. Mary Jones Bradley
Hopeful	Copelan	J. Bailey	Fred W. Hooper
Jockey Club Gold Cup	Lemhi Gold	C. McCarron	Aaron U. Jones
Kentucky Derby	Gato del Sol	E. Delahoussaye	Arthur B. Hancock and Leone J. Peters
Kentucky Oaks	Blush With Pride	W. Shoemaker	Stonereath Farm
Ladies	Tina Tina Too	D. MacBeth	Albert Fried, Jr.
Laurel Futurity	Cast Party	J. Velasquez	Greentree Stable
Man o' War	Naskra's Breeze	J. Samyn	Broadmoor Stable
Marlboro Cup Invitational	Lemhi Gold	J. Vasquez	Aaron U. Jones
Matron	Wings of Jove	H. McCauley	Helmore Farm
Metropolitan	Conquistador Cielo	E. Maple	Henryk de Kwiatkowski
Monmouth	Mehmet	E. Delahoussaye	A. J. Chlad, Sam Mevorach, and Elizabeth Vallone
Oak Tree Invitational	John Henry	W. Shoemaker	Dotsam Stable
Preakness	Aloma's Ruler	J. Kaenel	Nathan Scherr
Ruffian	Christmas Past	J. Vasquez	Cynthia Phipps
San Juan Capistrano Invitational	Lemhi Gold	W. Guerra	Aaron U. Jones
Santa Anita Derby	Muttering	L. Pincay, Jr.	Tartan Stable
Santa Anita	John Henry	W. Shoemaker	Dotsam Stable
Santa Susana	Blush With Pride	W. Shoemaker	Stonereath Farm
Sapling	O.K. By You	C. Perret	Timber Creek Farm
Selima	Bemissed	F. Lovato, Jr.	Ryehill Farm
Sorority	Singing Susan	W. Passmore	Robert Quinichett
Spinaway	Share the Fantasy	J. Fell	Gerald Robins
Spinster	Track Robbery	P. Valenzuela	Summa Stable
Suburban	Silver Buck	D. MacBeth	C. V. Whitney
Swaps	Journey At Sea	C. McCarron	Fred W. Hooper
Travers	Runaway Groom	J. Fell	Albert P. Coppola
Turf Classic	April Run	C. Asmussen	Mrs. Bert Firestone
United Nations	Naskra's Breeze	J. Samyn	Broadmoor Stable
Vanity	Sangue	W. Shoemaker	Charlene R. Parks
Washington (D.C.) International	April Run	C. Asmussen	Mrs. Bert Firestone
Whitney	Silver Buck	D. MacBeth	C. V. Whitney
Widener	Lord Darnley	M. L. Russ	Mrs. Ivan Phillips
Wood Memorial	Air Forbes Won	A. Cordero, Jr.	Edward Anchel
Woodward	Island Whirl	A. Cordero, Jr.	Elcee-H Stable
England			
One Thousand Guineas	On the House	J. Reid	Sir P. Oppenheimer
Two Thousand Guineas	Zino	F. Head	G. Oldham
Derby	Golden Fleece	P. Eddery	R. Sangster
Oaks	Time Charter	W. Newnes	R. Barnett
St. Leger	Touching Wood	P. Cook	Maktoum al-Maktoum
Coronation Cup	Easter Sun	B. Raymound	Lady Beaverbrook
Ascot Gold Cup	Ardross	L. Piggott	C. St. George
Eclipse Stakes	Kalaglow	G. Starkey	A. Ward
King George VI and Queen Elizabeth Diamond Stakes	Kalaglow	G. Starkey	A. Ward
Sussex Stakes	On the House	J. Reid	Sir P. Oppenheimer
Benson & Hedges Gold Cup	Assert	P. Eddery	R. Sangster
Champion Stakes	Time Charter	W. Newnes	R. Barnett
France			
Poule d'Essai des Poulains	Melyno	Y. Saint-Martin	S. Niarchos
Poule d'Essai des Pouliches	River Lady	L. Piggott	R. Sangster
Prix du Jockey Club	Assert	C. Roche	R. Sangster
Prix de Diane	Harbour	F. Head	Écurie Aland
Prix Royal-Oak	Denel	Y. Saint-Martin	Mme S. Nathan
Prix Ganay	Bikala	S. Gorli	J. Ouaki
Prix Lupin	Persepolis	L. Piggott	S. Niarchos
Grand Prix de Paris	Le Nain Jaune	H. Samani	Baron G. de Rothschild
Grand Prix de Saint-Cloud	Glint of Gold	P. Eddery	P. Mellon
Prix Vermeille	All Along	G. Starkey	D. Wildenstein
Prix de l'Arc de Triomphe	Akiyda	Y. Saint-Martin	Aga Khan
Ireland			
Irish Two Thousand Guineas	Dara Monarch	M. Kinane	Mrs. L. Browne
Irish One Thousand Guineas	Prince's Polly	W. Swinburn	K. Fitzpatrick
Irish Guinness Oaks	Swiftfoot	W. Carson	Lord Rotherwick
Irish Sweeps Derby	Assert	C. Roche	R. Sangster
Irish St. Leger	Touching Wood	P. Cook	Maktoum al-Maktoum
Italy			
Derby Italiano	Old Country	P. Eddery	Mrs. O. Abegg
Gran Premio del Jockey Club	Friendswood	M. Jerome	N. B. Hunt
West Germany			
Deutsches Derby	Aki	E. Schindler	Miss S. Seiler
Grosser Preis von Baden	Glint of Gold	P. Eddery	P. Mellon
Grosser Preis von Berlin	Orono	P. Alafi	Gestüt Zoppenbroich
Preis von Europa	Ataxerxes	A. Tylicki	Gestüt Schlenderhan

Vincent O'Brien won the English Derby at Epsom Downs with Golden Fleece, which beat Touching Wood and Silver Hawk, while his son David took both the French Derby (Prix du Jockey Club) and the Irish with Assert. Assert also won the Benson and Hedges Gold Cup and the Joe McGrath Stakes, but he was second to Golden Fleece on the only two occasions that they met. He was also second to Kalaglow in the King George VI and Queen Elizabeth Diamond Stakes but finished well behind when favoured to win the Arc.

Kalaglow also was disappointing in his final appearance, finishing far behind Time Charter in the Dubai Champion Stakes. Time Charter, which won by seven lengths, also won the Oaks at Epsom and finished second to On the House in the One Thousand Guineas. The Champion Stakes was sponsored by the three al-Maktoum brothers from Dubai, who were building up large stables of top-class horses in Britain and planned to expand to France and the U.S. Awaasif and Touching Wood, which won the English and Irish St. Legers, were their best horses, but one of the brothers bought the William Hill Futurity winner, Dunbeath, at the end of the season.

Dunbeath was one of the best two-year-olds in Britain in company with the Middle Park Stakes and Dewhurst Stakes winner, Diesis. Gorytus was hailed as the champion, after winning his first two, but he failed in mysterious circumstances in the Dewhurst. Saint Cyrien was the best in France, while Danzatore was Ireland's champion. French-trained Ma Biche won the Cheveley Park Stakes at Newmarket, but her reportedly superior stable companion, Maximova, finished behind Goodbye Shelley in the Prix Marcel Boussac.

Sharpo proved himself the best European sprinter by winning the Prix de l'Abbaye de Longchamp, a race in which he had been second in the two previous years. He also won the July Cup and the William Hill Sprint Championship at home in Britain. After his earlier pending disqualification following a dope test, Vayrann was allowed to retain his victory in the 1981 Champion Stakes. A Jockey Club inquiry, held after eight months of investigation, concluded that the horse had produced its own testosterone and that any other male horse was capable of producing this same steroid naturally. In September it was announced that Queen Elizabeth II had bought the West Ilsley stables, where Major Dick Hern already trained some of her horses. Henry Cecil was leading trainer with earnings of £872,704.

Gurner's Lane won Australia's most important race, the Melbourne Cup, catching the nation's most popular horse, Kingston Town, 22½ m (25 yd) from home to beat him by a neck. Gurner's Lane and the top-class Sovereign Red were sons of Sir Tristram, a U.S.-bred horse at stud in New Zealand that also sired the Victoria Derby winner, Grosvenor, and Dalmacia, victorious in the Grade One Epsom Handicap.

In National Hunt racing in Britain Grittar became the first favourite to win the English Grand National in nine years, beating the best of 7 other survivors from 39 starters by 15 lengths. Dick Saunders, the 48-year-old amateur who rode the

UPI

Conquistador Cielo breezed to a 14½-length victory in the Belmont Stakes in New York on June 5. The winner was ridden by Laffit Pincay.

winner, immediately announced his retirement. The race itself appeared to be in danger of dying: a British Jockey Club appeal at first made little progress, but the future of the event seemed more assured by the autumn. Silver Buck beat his stable companion Brewgawn in the Cheltenham Gold Cup, and the Irish-trained For Auction took the Champion Hurdle. John Francome and Peter Scudamore shared the jockeys' championship. Metatero established himself as the best jumper in France when winning the Grand Steeplechase de Paris. (ROBERT W. CARTER)

Harness Racing. World race records were broken frequently in the U.S. in 1982. In races on mile tracks they included: fastest two-year-old pacer, Trim The Tree 1 min 53⅗ sec; fastest three-year-old, Trenton 1 min 51⅗ sec; fastest older horse, Genghis Khan 1 min 51⅘ sec. Among the trotters, more than one-third of the age, gait, and sex records were broken, notably by New Zealand's Arndon, which took the mile race record of 1 min 57⅖ sec on five-eighths-mile tracks and then trotted an incredible 1 min 54 sec at Lexington, Ky., making him the fastest Standardbred trotter ever. Fan

UPI

Tommy Haughton drove Speed Bowl to a close victory over Jazz Cosmos in the final heat of the 57th run of the Hambletonian in East Rutherford, New Jersey, in August.

Hanover paced a one-mile time trial in 1 min 50⅘ sec to become the fastest mare ever.

The final of the International World Cup at the Meadowlands in New Jersey went to Genghis Khan. The Hambletonian for three-year-old trotters was won by Speed Bowl; Idéal du Gazeau of France won the Roosevelt International Trot; Jazz Cosmos took the Kentucky Futurity; Merger won the Little Brown Jug; and Hilarion won the Million Dollar Meadowlands pace.

In Australia Popular Alm twice recorded 1 min 55.9 sec at the Harold Park half-mile track in Sydney, beating other top pacers with ease. The Grand Circuit champion was Gammalite (1 min 56.1 sec and $575,683). High Valley (dam of Gammalite) was brood mare of the year. Thor Hanover for the eighth year was the leading sire, his stock earning $551,093. The Inter-Dominion championship, raced in Perth, Western Australia, was won by Rhetts Law, and Gundary Flyer took the Miracle Mile in Sydney. In New South Wales, Flushing Meadow earned $42,116 in the two-year-old fillies' ranks, Welcome Frost with $40,835 proving best of the colts. In Victoria, Grand Victory earned $44,988, and War Department was the richest filly with $31,884. In Queensland, President's Dancer was the top colt with $33,660, and Luck of the Irish headed the fillies with $31,225. Champion Australian pacer Pure Steel retired with record earnings of $915,102.

In New Zealand, Bonnie Chance won the New Zealand Cup from another mare, Armalight, which took horse of the year honours. Bonnie Chance with a 1-min 56.2-sec win at Timaru equaled the New Zealand mile race record of Lord Module. Gammalite won the $100,000 Auckland Cup.

In Europe the Swedish Criterium for three-year-olds, worth $170,000, was won by Ex Hammering with a 2-min 5.4-sec rate over the 2,640 m, a race record. The Swedish Derby, worth $175,000, was won by Rex Haleryd. Idéal du Gazeau won the Abbey Greater Prix in Sweden. The Norwegian Grand Prix 2,020-m final was taken by Johnson Lobell in a time of 2 min 6 sec, with Pluvier Lee second. In Helsinki, in the Finlandia Grand Circuit Trot, Darster F. won from Idéal du Gazeau, earning 285,000 markkaa. The Finland Derby was won by Viking Faker. The fastest trotter ever bred in Finland, Billy the Kid, won the Suur Hollola, the Finnish-bred trotters' championship. Ejnar Vogt won the Danish Derby (and also Helsinki's Golden Shoe trot). The Copenhagen Cup was won by Idéal du Gazeau, and in the Tuborg Open Scapester F. triumphed over Copperfield.

In France the $285,986 Prix d'Amérique was won by nine-year-old French stallion Hymour, his fourth successive win after returning from stud duties. The French Critérium for three-year-olds went to Mokar. In the West German Greyhound Stake for four-year-olds, the French entry Moscandiddo was the winner with a time of 2 min 4 sec over 2,100 m. In West Berlin the Matadoren Rennen was won by Keystone Patriot in 1 min 59.3 sec, with Pluvier Lee second.   (NOEL SIMPSON)

Show Jumping. Norbert Koof of West Germany rode his Westphalian-bred Fire II to the world championship in show jumping at Dublin in June 1982. Malcolm Pyrah (U.K.) on Towerlands Anglezarke finished second after a jump-off with Michel Robert (France) on Idéal de la Haye. Fourth was Capt. Gerry Mullins (Ireland) on Rockbarton. In the world team competition the young French team of Gilles Bertrand de Ballande (Malesan Galoubet), Patrick Caron (Malesan École IV), Frédéric Cottier (Flambeau C), and Robert (Idéal de la

Golden Fleece, with Pat Eddery, won the English Derby at Epsom Downs in June. His time was the fastest since that of Mahmoud in 1936.

Haye) emerged victorious; West Germany finished second and Great Britain, the defending champion, was third.

At Luhmühlen, West Germany, in September Britain regained the world three-day event championship for the first time since 1970. The U.K. was represented by Green (formerly Lucinda Prior-Palmer) on Regal Realm, Richard Meade on Kilcashel, Virginia Holgate on Priceless, and Rachel Bayliss on Mystic Minstrel. West Germany was second and the U.S. third. The individual world title was won by Green, riding the Australian-bred Regal Realm; Helmut Rethemeier (West Germany) on Santiago was second and Kim Walnes (U.S.) on The Grey Goose finished third.

(PAMELA MACGREGOR-MORRIS)

Polo. An immediate effect of the Falklands conflict between the U.K. and Argentina was the banning of the use of Argentine professional players by British-based polo patrons. Many of the teams had to be reshaped, and players were imported from Australia, New Zealand, and the U.S. to fill the gaps. The ban also extended to ponies. Despite this, the annual international at the Guards Polo Club, Windsor Great Park, sponsored for the first time by Ceresit of West Germany, was a successful affair. New Zealand contested the Coronation Cup and only just failed to match England, losing 6–4. In the second game, for the Silver Jubilee Cup, England II met the U.S. II, which scored the winning goal in overtime to take the trophy 6–5. Stuart Mackenzie of New Zealand was voted the most outstanding player.

Earlier in the year New Zealand defeated South Africa by three matches to none, 10–5, 8–7, and 7–2. Helen Boehm's team won the World Cup in Florida and, with a different lineup, also took the prestigious Queen's Cup and the Cowdray Park Challenge Cup in England. The major English trophy, the British Open championship, was won by Southfield, which also won the Warwickshire Cup. In the European Polo Academy's new-style tournament played on a league basis, the Gold Medal for the Open section was won by the BB's Polo Team and the Silver Medal for the Handicap section by Laurent Perrier.   (COLIN J. CROSS)

[452.B.4.h.xvii; 452.B.4.h.xxi; 452.B.5.e]

Ethiopia

A socialist state in northeastern Africa, Ethiopia is bordered by Somalia, Djibouti, Kenya, the Sudan, and the Red Sea. Area: 1,223,600 sq km (472,400 sq mi). Pop. (1982 est.): 32,580,000. Cap. and largest city: Addis Ababa (pop., 1980 est., 1,277,200). Language: Amharic (official) and other tongues. Religion (1980 est.): Ethiopian Orthodox 57%; Muslim 31%; tribal 11%; other 1%. Head of state and chairman of the Provisional Military Administrative Council in 1982, Lieut. Col. Mengistu Haile Mariam.

The keynotes of Ethiopian domestic policy in 1982 were the fight against corruption, the consolidation of worker-peasant alliances, and the launching in January of the "Red Star Campaign" in the northern region of Eritrea. The campaign combined intensified military activity against the secessionists with the diversion of funds to the region from other parts of the country for the reconstruction and development of basic facilities, industry, and social services. Government sources claimed successes against rebel guerrillas, and there was much evidence of the revitalization of the Eritrean economy. The government's hand was strengthened by the growing accord with Sudan on border control. Since 1979, the government claimed, more than 8,000 Ethiopians had returned from Sudan or voluntarily abandoned their association with rebel groups.

A concerted program for the elimination of corruption began during the year. People's and workers' control committees were established in neighbourhood associations (Kebeles), peasant associations, industry, and government organizations. A special hierarchy of courts was set up to deal with offenders. The objective was to underline the fact that the means of production and the wealth of the country were no longer to be regarded as the monopoly of an elite and that this transfer of real power brought with it new responsibilities, the fulfillment of which depended upon the creation of new attitudes toward national resources. This action was closely linked with the reorganization of the All-Ethiopia Trades Union and the All-Ethiopia Peasants Association, which was carried out in 1982.

In October it was announced that the second national congress of the Commission to Organize the Party of the Working People of Ethiopia

Ethiopia

ETHIOPIA

Education. (1979–80) Primary, pupils 1,811,251, teachers 30,597; secondary and vocational, pupils 371,301, teachers 8,992; higher, students (1978–79) 13,674, teaching staff (1977–78) 476.

Finance. Monetary unit: birr, with (Sept. 20, 1982) a par value of 2.07 birr to U.S. $1 (free rate of 3.55 birr = £1 sterling). Gold and other reserves (June 1982) U.S. $254 million. Budget (total; 1979–80 est.): revenue 1,971,800,000 birr; expenditure 2,365,000,000 birr. Gross national product (1980–81) 8,785,000,000 birr. Money supply (April 1982) 1,789,000,000 birr. Cost of living (Addis Ababa; 1975 = 100; Dec. 1981) 226.2.

Foreign Trade. (1981) Imports 1,528,300,000 birr; exports 774.5 million birr. Import sources (1980): U.S.S.R. 19%; Italy 11%; West Germany 10%; Japan 9%; U.S. 8%; U.K. 7%; Kuwait 5%. Export destinations (1980): U.S. 18%; Djibouti 11%; Italy 10%; U.S.S.R. 9%; Saudi Arabia 8%; West Germany 8%; France 7%; Japan 6%. Main exports: coffee 61%; hides and skins 13%.

Transport and Communications. Roads (1980) 35,937 km. Motor vehicles in use (1980): passenger 38,600; commercial 11,700. Railways: (1980) 988 km; traffic (including Djibouti traffic of Djibouti–Addis Ababa line; excluding Eritrea; 1978–79) 171 million passenger-km, freight 148 million net ton-km. Air traffic (1981): c. 750 million passenger-km; freight c. 22.3 million net ton-km. Telephones (Jan. 1980) 83,800. Radio receivers (Dec. 1979) 220,000. Television receivers (Dec. 1979) c. 25,000.

Agriculture. Production (in 000; metric tons; 1981): barley c. 750; wheat c. 491; corn c. 1,100; millet c. 190; sorghum c. 687; potatoes c. 240; sugar, raw value c. 165; sesame seed c. 35; chick-peas c. 82; dry peas c. 130; dry broad beans c. 277; bananas c. 73; coffee c. 198; cotton c. 20. Livestock (in 000; 1981): cattle c. 26,100; sheep c. 23,300; goats c. 17,200; horses c. 1,535; mules c. 1,450; asses c. 3,895; camels c. 990; poultry c. 53,500.

Industry. Production (in 000; metric tons; 1978–79): cement c. 93; petroleum products c. 530; cotton yarn (1977–78) 7.9; cotton fabrics (sq m; 1977–78) 65,500; electricity (kw-hr; 1980) 675,000.

Ethiopia, suffering from drought and famine, was rated as one of Africa's ten poorest countries.

(COPWE) would be held in the near future, and that it would play a "decisive role in party formation." An accompanying commentary explained: "Although COPWE is not a party, it is a political organization which functions as a party in its day-to-day operations, guided by the decisions of its periodic Central Committee plenums to intensify the class struggle and provide leadership in the political, ideological, organizational, economic, military, and social fields."

In September 716 detainees imprisoned in 1974–75 were released. These included senior officials of the previous regime and a number of former ministers, several of whom were recruited into the government.

The ten-year (1983–93) social and economic development plan was in preparation. There was expected to be a heavy emphasis on the development of agriculture and an underlying general requirement for self-reliance and the mobilization of national resources. However, projected economic growth rates depended upon a continuing high level of external assistance.

Nevertheless, significant progress was made in the economic sector. The road between Mizan Teferri and Tepi was completed. The construction industry was reorganized and supported by measures taken to increase cement production. In general the industrial sector, hampered by lack of capital input over the previous two decades, found it difficult to meet production targets. However, new industry was progressing. A car and truck assembly plant in Addis Ababa produced more than 24,000 vehicles over a six-year period; the printing industry provided over 42 million books

between 1979 and 1982; and the tourist industry expected to benefit from the construction of new hotels.

The government commitment to action against "ignorance, ill health, and want," announced in the early years of the revolution, was producing a noteworthy effect. In the three years since the national literacy campaign was launched in mid-1979, more than six million certificates had been issued to new literates. The health sector also made great strides forward in primary health care and immunization. The national population and housing census, to be implemented with support from the UN Development Program in 1983, was to be the country's first complete census.

A visit by the head of state, Mengistu Haile Mariam, to Moscow in October resulted in an agreement to broaden cooperation between Ethiopia and the U.S.S.R. In January the fifth session of the Ethiopian-East German Cooperation Commission was conducted in Addis Ababa. In October Addis Ababa was the site of a meeting of the Organization of African Unity Contact Committee, established after the failure of the OAU summit meeting in Tripoli, Libya. Its objective was to define the conditions under which a full meeting of the OAU could take place in the near future.

French Foreign Minister Claude Cheysson paid an official visit to Ethiopia in January, and in July an Ethiopian-Italian cooperation agreement was signed in Addis Ababa. The European Economic Community announced a grant to Ethiopia worth 57 million birr for the second phase of the Coffee Improvement Project under the second Lomé Convention.

European Unity

Throughout 1982 the European Communities (EC; the European Economic Community [EEC], the European Coal and Steel Community [ECSC], and Euratom) faced both unresolved internal problems and increasingly difficult relations with the U.S., their major political, defense, and commercial partner. The internal problems had their origins in the stresses induced by the EC's enlargement to include three new member states—above all, Britain—in 1973 and Greece in 1981. The external problems with the U.S. owed much to the failure of the Western economies as a whole to find a way out of the protracted recession that had really begun with the 1973 oil price rise. Another year of recession and high unemployment brought to the surface a potentially serious number of trade conflicts.

Economic Affairs. The danger of a trade war with the U.S. was sparked in January when U.S. steel producers sought to impose higher import duties on the exports of European steel firms, which, they claimed, were unfairly benefiting from governmental financial aid. This was followed during the summer by U.S. Pres. Ronald Reagan's decision, announced just after the Western economic summit that had been held at Versailles, France, to impose sanctions on European firms supplying equipment for the planned Soviet gas pipeline from Siberia to Western Europe. The pipeline issue, unlike the dispute over steel and—later in the year—agricultural trade, was by no means a purely commercial question. It went to the heart of differences that had developed between the Reagan administration and most EC governments in regard to relations with the Soviet Union. The closing months of 1982 were largely preoccupied with urgent diplomatic moves aimed at defusing what had become known as the "transatlantic trade war" and ensuring that it did not undermine the wider Western alliance in NATO. (*See* Feature Article: *Stresses in the Western Alliance.*)

The tensions between the EC and the U S. first attracted wide attention on January 4 when the EC refused to join the wholesale economic sanctions that the U.S. proposed should be established against the Soviet Union for its moral involvement in the Polish government's suppression of the Solidarity free trade union movement. Although subsequently the Community countries—other than Greece—did agree to make some minor adjustments in trade with the Soviet Union, the U.S. administration was clearly disappointed by the reaction of its European allies. There were hopes that the Versailles summit, which was held June 4–6, would find a formula designed to express the West's criticism of Soviet policy toward Poland, and it was agreed there that the Soviet Union should have to pay more for export credits provided by the West and that the seven leading economic powers would exercise more caution in increasing trade with the Soviet Union in the future.

Shortly after the Versailles summit it became clear that the EC countries did not intend to cut back heavily on trade with the Soviet Union, and most European governments made it clear that they would not be parties to a Western campaign of trade sanctions that might threaten détente between Eastern and Western Europe. At this point President Reagan announced the pipeline sanctions and provoked a storm of condemnation in EC capitals—including London, where the Conservative government of Margaret Thatcher, as a firm advocate of "Reaganite" policies, felt betrayed by Washington's action.

Throughout the spring and summer months efforts were made by both the European Commission and the U.S. administration to head off the imposition of higher import duties on U.S. steel producers. At the same time, other trade frictions surfaced, and there were fears that, unless answers were found, the autumn ministerial meeting of the signatory countries of the General Agreement on Tariffs and Trade might be wrecked. In the event, the GATT ministers, after considerable wrangling, agreed to "resist protec-

European Community members refused to go along with U.S. President Reagan's call for economic sanctions against the Soviet Union over its actions in Poland. Shown are four of the EC ministers, at a meeting in Brussels, in January, from left: Max van der Stoel of The Netherlands, Claude Cheysson of France, Hans-Dietrich Genscher of West Germany, and Léo Tindemans of Belgium.

WIDE WORLD

European Economic Community: *see* Economy, World; European Unity

European Unity

Leaders of the European Communities held a meeting in Brussels on March 29 to plan their response to the world economic crisis. Left to right, front: Prime Minister Margaret Thatcher of Britain; Pres. François Mitterrand of France; King Baudouin and Queen Fabiola of Belgium; and Chancellor Helmut Schmidt of West Germany. At back from left: Joseph Luns, secretary-general of NATO; Lord Carrington, foreign minister of Britain; French Foreign Minister Claude Cheysson; and Foreign Minister Emilio Colombo of Italy.

tionist pressures" and to study trade in services and agricultural products and safeguards for industries that have been injured by import surges. There were widespread warnings on both sides of the Atlantic that trade war and spreading protectionism would make a concerted international recovery from the recession even more difficult to achieve. In October agreement was finally reached, less than two hours before U.S. steel import duties were to have been introduced, on the limitation of European steel exports.

Friction between Europe and the U.S. over trade was matched by continuing difficulties between the EC and Japan over Japan's mounting trade surplus with the Community. Visits by Japanese ministers to Brussels and other EC capitals in March and June resulted in some action in Tokyo to liberalize import restrictions, but the yen's declining value tended to exacerbate the trade imbalance.

European Community summit meetings in Brussels in March and June and in Copenhagen in December were largely preoccupied with the continuing recession and the seemingly relentless rise in unemployment within the EC. The numbers out of work rose to more than 11 million during the year, with industries such as steel, textiles, and automobiles particularly hard hit by plant closings and production cutbacks. However, the consensus among EC leaders was that priority should be given to reducing government budget deficits and public spending rather than to expanding output and reducing unemployment. The political swing to the right in Belgium, Denmark, and The Netherlands and financial and currency pressures brought to bear on France, whose Socialist government had until August given priority to growth, ensured that by the end of the year conservative financial orthodoxy prevailed.

The severe budget pressures on member nations ensured that the negotiations about the future of

the EC's own budget and finances would be particularly difficult. This problem involved a wholesale review of the Community's spending policies—above all on agriculture—and the distribution of the burden of financing the budget among member governments. Between January and May, under the chairmanship of Belgium, which currently held the presidency of the Council of Ministers, efforts were made to secure an agreement. The British government insisted on major reforms of the common agricultural policy, curbs on higher farm prices, and a long-term arrangement limiting its own net contributions to the EC budget.

The negotiations eventually overlapped with the annual fixing of farm prices by the EEC. On May 18 a majority within the EEC Council of Agriculture Ministers pushed through a decision increasing prices by an average of more than 10%, despite British protests and an attempt by the U.K. government to use its veto powers. The disregard of the veto triggered a major political row in Britain, where the national veto (known as the Luxembourg compromise) was thought sacrosanct.

At the end of May it was agreed in principle to extend the ceiling on Britain's budget payments for 1982 and to consider a longer term arrangement later in the year. Although this gave Britain a smaller rebate on its budget payments than the nation's ministers had wanted, it was accepted, and Britain withdrew its opposition to the farm price decision. The conclusion of the Community policy reform was widely seen in Britain as a disappointment, and in the closing months of 1982 there were warnings that, with agricultural spending rising once again and with the strains likely to result from the planned admission of Portugal and Spain, the EC could face its most serious ever budgetary crisis in 1983 or 1984. The establishment of a common fisheries policy by the end of 1982 was blocked by Denmark.

Political Relations. Statements by French Pres. François Mitterrand during an official visit to Spain in June appeared to throw doubt on the possibility of completing the negotiations about Spain's accession to the EC in time to permit it to join in January 1984. However, the electoral successes of the Spanish Socialists in the general election, combined with fears about the political consequences of the EC's shutting the door on Spain, put pressure on the negotiators to break the deadlock. It became clear by mid-September that the negotiations with Portugal were proceeding much more rapidly than those with Spain, and there was even speculation that the two nations might join on different dates. Although the joining of NATO by Spain (May 30) was widely welcomed in the EC, the continuing problems with Britain, even after the border with Gibraltar was opened in December, cast a further shadow over Community-Spanish relations.

In a referendum held on February 23, Greenland became the first territory in the EC to vote for withdrawal from the Community. Negotiations were due to begin at the end of 1982 on Greenland's future relations with the EC, a subject in which Denmark took a very close interest, both as Greenland's sovereign power and as holder, for the half year from July 1, of the presidency of the Council of Ministers. In Denmark itself the anniversary of the October 1972 referendum that preceded the country's entry into the EC the following year was marked by widespread demonstrations by anti-EC groups.

Despite the difficulties experienced by the EC in resolving its internal problems, European political cooperation—the coordination of a common Community foreign policy—also assumed great significance in 1982. The ten member states met frequently during the year to draw up their own policies on issues such as the Middle East, Poland, and the war between Britain and Argentina.

The differences between the EC and the U.S. in their approaches to the Arab-Israeli dispute were dramatically reduced when President Reagan produced his ideas for a political settlement of the Palestine problem in the aftermath of the Israeli invasion of Lebanon. The European leaders saw in the new U.S. emphasis on Palestinian rights and self-determination justification of the stand they had taken since the Venice summit of June 1980. On the other hand, relations between EC governments and Israel reached a new low when the former denounced the massacre of Palestinians by Israel's Lebanese Phalangist allies in September.

The European Community at 25

The celebrations to mark the 25th anniversary of the signing of the Treaty of Rome, which gave birth to the European Community on March 25, 1957, were far from being euphoric. Throughout the ten member countries there was general realization of how far the Community still was from achieving the basic objective of the Rome Treaty—"to lay the foundations of an even closer union among the people of Europe." Most European Community leaders were all too aware of the lack of progress toward full economic—let alone political—union, particularly in the past decade. At the same time, as the incumbent president of the European Commission, Gaston Thorn of Luxembourg, pointed out in an anniversary speech, the Community had great achievements to its credit and had been responsible for creating the basis for stability and reconciliation in Europe, on what had been a war-devastated continent.

At a ceremony in Brussels to honour the founding fathers of the Community, King Baudouin of Belgium spoke on March 29 of some of those achievements: the creation of the European Coal and Steel Community; a genuinely common market in internal trade; a common agricultural policy; enlargement from the original six member states to ten (and possibly to 12 before long); and the setting up of Community institutions such as the Commission, the Court of Justice, and the European Parliament.

It was generally agreed that overcoming the preoccupation with national sovereignty and persuading the member states to pool sovereignty at a Community level had proved far more difficult than imagined in 1957. Member nations had been most concerned to retain their powers over economic policy. However, there had been a growing realization in recent years that the most intractable of contemporary economic problems—such as inflation, unemployment, industrial decline, and adjustment to meet wider international change—could not be tackled on a purely national basis. In recent years the creation of the European Monetary System, linking the currencies of all the EC countries except Greece and the U.K., was a potentially important advance toward monetary union. However, there was recognition that in economic policy, as elsewhere, the EC had little option but to proceed cautiously.

A quarter of a century after its inception the European Community faced a number of important challenges, including the prospective accession of Portugal and Spain at a time of growing economic difficulty. There were inevitably some suggestions that the member states should reexamine the original purpose of the Community. But any such reexamination was unlikely, if only because no one had an interest in further weakening any of the bonds that had been subject to so much strain in recent years. On the other hand, given the challenge of further enlargement and the fact that the EC faced very different internal problems and a very different international environment from those anticipated when the Treaty of Rome was signed, the members might have to make some radical changes in the way the Community functions. This would almost certainly involve reforms to existing policies and the development of new forms of cooperation (such as the extension of security and possibly defense to foreign policy coordination), as well as a review of the decision-making institutions. (JOHN PALMER)

France and Italy provided troops for the international peacekeeping force in Beirut, and EC foreign ministers were active in the autumn seeking common ground between the ideas of the U.S., the EC, and the Arab League countries for a political settlement of the Palestine problem.

The same unity that the Community displayed over the Middle East and Poland was not quite so evident in the discussions on the Falkland Islands war. Although the EC countries condemned Argentina's invasion and initially backed Britain with trade sanctions against Argentina, Italy and Ireland subsequently withdrew their support for the sanctions.

The European Parliament (of which a new president, Pieter Dankert of The Netherlands, was elected on January 19 to succeed Simone Veil of France) made it clear during the year that it expected to play a more influential role in the formulation of Community policy. Successive presidencies of the Council of Ministers attempted to improve liaison with the Parliament over the procedures for adopting the annual EC budget. In September the Parliament passed a resolution threatening to take the Council before the European Court of Justice in Luxembourg for failing to adopt a common EC transport policy. The European Court itself was very active throughout the year, particularly in giving judgments affecting interpretations of EC rules. At the end of October the court gave a provisional judgment that obliged the Ford Motor Co. of Britain not to restrict the import of right-hand-drive cars from the continent to Britain—a move seen as threatening the British motor industry's desire to keep out inexpensive automobiles.

During the year there was also a remarkable number of "informal" meetings of EC ministers on a wide variety of issues, ranging from the adjustment of exchange rates involving a number of the currencies linked within the European monetary system to matters involving industry, employment, justice, and cultural affairs. The 25th anniversary year of the EC's existence was marked by low-key celebrations in most member countries. (*See* Sidebar.)   (JOHN PALMER)

See also Defense; Economy, World.
[534.F.3.b.iv; 971.D.7]

Fashion and Dress

During the winter of 1981–82 women's fashion focused on ponchos and knickers. The latter, carried through into spring, culminated in the rhinestone-trimmed black satin pair worn by Nancy Reagan at a reception given on the occasion of the Versailles summit meeting in June 1982. Ponchos, glorifying in their seamless cut, gave a pleasing alertness to the winter street scene. Adding to the whirl and swirl, stunning giant shawls were tossed over one shoulder and left to flow freely. They came in muted plaids or bold florals, fringed, and often with metallic threads running through the soft wool material like streaks of lightning. Shawls were an essential part of dressing during the winter and early spring. Having become a basic, the fur-lined, belted raincoat in neutral shades

of poplin was the only fitted shape. Regarded as rather cumbersome, it was accepted more for its warmth and convenience than for its looks. Unfitted raincoats were pepped up with contrasting colour bands in checkerboard patterns.

Knickers served their purpose in getting the eye accustomed to more leg and were instrumental in the rapid acceptance of the above-knee hemline. The same applied to Bermudas and sturdy, cuffed shorts in the spring, followed by the miniskirt for full summer. The cuffed bubble dress, which hung down straight from the shoulders, came closest to knickers, with one knee-level cuff instead of two. In view of its tightness at the knees, this type of dress was reserved for fancy occasions; quick movement was limited and measured steps were advisable. Pert little hats, feather-trimmed, veiled, and tipped forward, signaled that this manner of dressing was part of a game and not to be taken seriously.

Hemlines were very much in the news. Snappy, knee-level skirts accompanied the new spencer suit jacket as well as the more traditional one over the hipline, fitted at the waist with darts and seaming and squared off at the shoulders. Completed by a silk blouse with a ruffle-trimmed high neckline and topped with a mannish slouch hat, this was the typical hard chic look worn by the young executive. Suit materials were borrowed from men's wardrobes, mainly small or large checks and preferably black and white. But a blue cornflower or a red poppy slipped through the buttonhole, a brooch at the throat, dangling earrings, and high-heeled sandals or the newest bicolour pumps revived from the 1930s in black and white relieved the stark look and reminded one that the young executive was also feminine.

The revival of gloves was another indication of the readiness to reinstate a long-frowned-on word—elegance. In Paris it seemed a silent reaction to the new social climate: "Now that the Left's in power let's drop jeans for minks." This did not mean that jeans were discarded and stored away in mothballs for the curiosity of future generations. Jeans were still there and as skintight as ever, but they were dressed up with very elaborate white cotton blouses. Full-sleeved and high-necked with no end of frills, wavy flounces, hairline-pleated yokes and bibs, embroidery, and fluting, these blouses came straight out of John Galsworthy's *Forsyte Saga* for a portrait of Irene.

Though at first quite a few were taken with the bright red of the Socialist rose that crowded the early displays of spring clothes in Paris shop windows, very soon all that remained of the vivid red was on the plain low-heeled pumps worn with the all-white summer look. All white were the two- or three-flounced petticoat skirts worn with a fitted corselet top with wide straps, dairy-maid style, or with a high-necked frilly blouse in the "square dance" manner, with a wide belt with metal disks adding a Western touch. The above-knee hemline, however, had made its point and shared honours with a low and droopy waistline. In this case there was very little skirt left. Short, soft, and wavy, it was reduced to a high flounce below a high-necked, bloused top with full sleeves and was

Evangelical Churches:
see Religion

Exhibitions:
see Art Exhibitions; Museums; Photography

Faeroe Islands:
see Dependent States

Falkland Islands:
see Dependent States

Farming:
see Agriculture and Food Supplies

christened the "Charleston" dress. Worn with ballet slippers, it became the favourite look of the teenage Valley Girls of California, whose clothes-conscious life-style and vocabulary were parodied with brio by Moon Unit Zappa, daughter of rock musician Frank Zappa, in a hilarious recording in the U.S.

Shorter still, the skirt could be slick and neat, and quite flat—strictly reserved for girls with perfect legs. For dressy occasions, wedding receptions, or garden parties the "Charleston" dress hovered around knee level and the top had a boat neckline edged with wide triple or quadruple ruffles—all very gentle and feminine and emphasized by wide-brimmed floppy capeline hats in fine straw, usually untrimmed. The accompanying high-heeled sandals were made of narrow strips of leather, multicoloured and metal-hued. A "gondolier bag," shoulder-slung and reduced to the needed size for indispensables, was worn hanging in front to discourage purse snatchers.

The seaside version of fashion emphasized the barrel shape off the beach. Above-knee skirts were gathered into a straight band or flounce. Mini-skirts were light and wavy like a tennis player's. Trousers, soft and full, were tightened below calf, Persian fashion. Shorts had high cuffs. High cuffs also appeared on above-ankle boots in bright shades contrasting with the all-white look.

After dark there was a lot of glitter and shimmer, in checked silk gauze for shawls and in shot taffeta for blouses featuring "fin de siècle" shades such as puce, bronze, and ruby. Knits sparkled with metallic threads, a persistence of the Midas touch. In the fall the new short suit jacket was puffed out at the shoulders and fitted at the waist, sometimes trimmed with velvet at the collar, lapels, and cuffs. Great, gyrating skirts in full flare balanced the short jacket. Some skirts were occasionally propped up by a stiff petticoat but most of them were allowed to fall naturally. Pulled-in waists, rigid cummerbunds, and low, deep armholes moved dresses away from the "Charleston" model. Little berets with a bow at the side of the headband competed with the mannish Borsalino felts for town wear.

The black and white of spring pumps was replaced by russet or claret red, with black arrow-shaped insets front and back. Low boots with high cuffs continued the summer trend in all colours. Worn indifferently with trousers or with a slim skirt, the spencer jacket surfaced again in subdued autumn shades such as Burgundy red or black. In some cases the points were omitted, the fit was looser, and black braid trimming was added. In contrast with the fully flared skirt and big-sleeved top for short evening wear, the "smoking" or black dinner jacket with a white blouse frilled at the neck, a narrow ribbon tie, and a slim knee-length skirt also had its supporters.

Autumn colours ranging from black currant and puce to misty mauves, heather, and deep purple were worn in graduated effects, typically a dark heather for the poncho, a light misty mauve for the

The above-knee skirt returned in 1982, as exemplified by this Geoffrey Beene outfit (left) that also featured such feminine touches as embroidery and patterned lace stockings. Squared shoulders and a greater emphasis on fit were the hallmarks of many collections. Calvin Klein designed this jacket and pants ensemble, topped off by that newly popular item of clothing, the hat.

UPI   UPI

full skirt, and both colours combined in the bulky knitted sweater. A bright fuchsia pink was the winner for light wool sweaters trimmed with a little frill at neck and cuff, like the blouses. Ponchos took on a new lease. The finest were in soft, plain cashmere in natural shade, black, or red; the others were in more rustic and weatherproof woollen materials. Shawls, huge and colourful and indispensable as ever, were slung over the left shoulder and allowed to hang to the ground.

Colours for makeup tended to be soft and misty for daytime but bold and theatrical for evening. For a delicate complexion Helena Rubinstein recommended "Fragile Peach" and a cranberry red named "Medicis Wine" for lips and nails. Elizabeth Arden suggested a soft halo on eyelids in twilight shading named "Midnight Shadows," with a "Scandalous Scarlet" on lips and nails. Estée Lauder favoured a "Violet Mist Tender Blusher" and a halo of pinky-mauve on eyelids, with "Raspberry Glaze" on lips and nails. Natural effects were dominant for hairdos, with length best suited to the wearer. Curls were fine, but no more tousled heads with hair covering forehead and eyebrows; everything was light and off the face.

(THELMA SWEETINBURGH)

Men's Fashions. The year 1982 was one of pure nostalgia. What the film version of *The Great Gatsby* did for men's fashions in the mid-1970s, the television series "Brideshead Revisited," shown originally in Great Britain and subsequently in Europe, the U.S., and Australia, achieved even more dramatically in 1982. This adaptation of Evelyn Waugh's novel of the 1920s and 1930s, and to a lesser extent the film *Chariots of Fire*, helped to revive at least some of the fashions of that period, while the British Menswear Guild's promotion of the "Duke of Windsor" look for 1983 also drew its inspiration from the flamboyance of those halcyon days for men's fashions.

Wing- and pin-collar shirts and the cutaway-style collar for accommodating the Windsor knot of the tie were part of this nostalgic fashion image; so too were scarlet cloth braces, metal armbands, and Fair Isle, argyle, and cable-patterned knitwear, the last in white wool and worn with white flannel trousers and a club or regimental striped blazer. Gloves, too, were worn on many more occasions; panamas and boaters, striped scarves, tweed hats, and caps all enjoyed a resurgence; and one did not have to be either a Liberal politician or a family doctor to carry the Gladstone bag. It was hardly surprising, then, that Anthony Andrews, one of the stars of "Brideshead Revisited," was named the "Best Dressed Man of 1982" by the Menswear Association of Britain.

The business suit itself changed little in style. It was still elegant but less formal, and the interest was centred in the cloths, both lighter in weight and colour and with a greater diversity of designs. The country suit was again influenced by the fashions of the '20s and '30s, with full and semi-hacking jackets in colourful tweeds in big and bold designs. Another touch of nostalgia was the attempt to revive the spencer, a truncated and tailless version of the tailcoat worn with a black tie for either day or evening wear.

S. H. Costin, London

Inspired by television and movie dramas set in the 1920s, patterned sweaters returned. Adding to the mood of nostalgia were such '20s touches as wing and pin collars.

There were signs of jeans losing their hitherto universal popularity to the more traditional trouser. Sports shirts in soft pastel shades and with either half sleeves or with the sleeves rolled above the elbow were a popular international summer fashion when worn with Bermuda shorts or slim-fitting full-length slacks, with cotton and linen the favoured materials. (STANLEY H. COSTIN)

See also Industrial Review: *Furs.*
[451.B.2.b and d.i; 629.C.1]

Field Hockey and Lacrosse

Field Hockey. At Bombay in January 1982 Pakistan retained the World Cup that it had won four years earlier in Buenos Aires. The final standings were: Pakistan, West Germany, Australia, The Netherlands, India, the U.S.S.R., New Zealand, Poland, England, Malaysia, Spain, and Argentina. The tournament was played on natural grass. The first Asia Cup was won by Pakistan, which defeated India at Karachi in the final in April. China won the bronze medal for third place. Three months later, on artificial turf at Amstelveen, Neth., the first six nations from the World Cup tournament took part in a round-robin series, The Netherlands retaining the Champions Trophy that it had won from Pakistan in 1981. The final standings were: The Netherlands, Australia, India, Pakistan, West Germany, and the U.S.S.R.

In October the Hockey Association's annual tournament was played on artificial grass at Queen's Park Rangers football ground in London.

There, England defeated both France and Spain, while Wales, after a tie with Spain, lost to France. Earlier, Scotland beat both Switzerland and Italy at Glasgow to qualify for the European championship in 1983; Ireland and Austria also qualified in Vienna. Indoors, England recovered the home countries' title from Scotland.

In women's hockey England gained the triple crown among the home countries for the third year in succession, clinching the title by beating Ireland 2–1 at Cork. Ireland took second place by defeating Scotland at Glasgow. In the annual match at Wembley, England was beaten 4–2 by The Netherlands in March. Three months later an England team visited Zimbabwe, which beat them 1–0 at Harare. In September two women's tournaments were held simultaneously: at Edinburgh Canada finished ahead of West Germany, Scotland, and Spain; and at Durham, between England, Ireland, Belgium, the U.S., and New Zealand, England had the best record. A week later at Cardiff New Zealand won a tournament in which Wales, Canada, and the U.S. also played.

(SYDNEY E. FRISKIN)

Lacrosse. MEN. In the world championship held in Baltimore, Md., in June 1982 between the U.S., Australia, Canada, and England, the U.S. defeated Australia in the final match 22–14 before 11,000 spectators. The U.S. had previously beaten Canada 23–12 and England 26–9. Australia defeated Canada 24–18 and England 25–5. Canada finished third in the series by defeating England 20–19 in overtime. "Best player" awards went to Tom Sears, U.S., goalkeeper; Mark Greenburg, U.S., defenseman; John Butkiewiez, Australia, midfielder; and Brook Sweet, U.S., attackman.

The intercollegiate final match, played at Charlottesville, Va., between Johns Hopkins University and the University of North Carolina was a closely fought game. North Carolina won 7–4. In another contest the North beat the South 14–9. Tom Sears from North Carolina received the awards as the best goalkeeper and the best player in the U.S. In Australia, where the interstate competition was again won by Western Australia, the popularity of the modified box lacrosse, which required fewer players to form a team, increased.

In England Lancashire won the county championship and Sheffield University the Iroquois Cup (the English club championship). Sheffield University also won the North of England Senior Flags by defeating Cheadle 13–11. Cheadle was the North of England league winner, and Sheffield University won the University Cup by beating Oxford University.

(CHARLES DENNIS COPPOCK)

WOMEN. The first women's lacrosse world tournament, sponsored by the U.S. firm W. H. Brine Co., took place in Nottingham, England, in September 1982. The six competing nations, England, Scotland, Wales, Canada, Australia, and the U.S., played each other in a round robin. Joint favourites England and the U.S. both lost their opening matches, England defeated by Scotland and the U.S. losing to the fast, fit Australians. Play-offs on the last day left Canada third, Scotland fourth, England fifth, and Wales sixth. In a sensational final between Australia and the U.S., Australia stormed ahead to a 6–1 lead at half time, but the U.S. pulled back to make the final score in regular time 7–7. During the overtime period the U.S. scored three goals to win the world championship. The defeated finalists, Australia, then toured Britain and won all nine matches played, defeating the North and South Territories 7–4 and 6–4, respectively, in their closest games.

The South Territory swept the board in the British national competitions. Surrey once again emerged as champions, defeating Hertfordshire in the final of the National Counties Tournament.

Janet Colarusso (left) went airborne after she scored a field hockey goal for the North team during a game at the National Sports Festival in July in Indianapolis, Indiana. The North went on to defeat the South 2–1.

WIDE WORLD

The South Reserves won the Territorial Reserves Tournament, which for the first time was held over two days with the Home Scots team invited to participate. The South recovered quickly from a surprising defeat by the West to win the territorial championship.

In the home internationals England suffered its first defeat ever by Scotland in a thrilling, close match, which the Scots won 6–5. England then defeated Wales 9–3.

(MARGARET-LOUISE FRAWLEY)

Fiji

Finland

Fiji

An independent parliamentary state and member of the Commonwealth, Fiji is an island group in the South Pacific Ocean, about 3,200 km E of Australia and 5,200 km S of Hawaii. Area: 18,273 sq km (7,055 sq mi), with two major islands, Viti Levu (10,388 sq km) and Vanua Levu (5,535 sq km), and several hundred smaller islands. Pop. (1981 est.): 636,000, including 49.9% Indian, 46% Fijian. Cap. and largest city: Suva (pop., 1978 est., 64,000). Language: English, Fijian, and Hindi. Religion (1980): Christian 49.7%; Hindu 40.9%; Muslim 7.8%; other 1.6%. Queen, Elizabeth II; governor-general in 1982, Ratu Sir George Cakobau; prime minister, Ratu Sir Kamisese Mara.

In a general election in July 1982, the Alliance Party government of Ratu Sir Kamisese Mara was returned to office with a much reduced majority after a campaign that accentuated Fiji's ethnic division between indigenous Fijians and Indians. (For tabulated results, *see* POLITICAL PARTIES.) During October 14–18 the Commonwealth regional meeting of heads of government was held in Fiji, followed at the end of the month by the visit of Queen Elizabeth II.

Fiji coped with difficult economic conditions better than most of its neighbours. The annual in-

FIJI

Education. (1980) Primary, pupils 127,325, teachers (1978) 4,435; secondary, pupils 35,238, teachers (1978) 1,766; vocational, pupils 2,568, teachers (1978) 390; teacher training, students (1979) 618, teachers (1978) 61; higher, students (1978) 2,760, teaching staff (1975) 166.

Finance and Trade. Monetary unit: Fiji dollar, with (Sept. 20, 1982) a free rate of F$0.96 to U.S. $1 (F$1.64 = £1 sterling). Budget (1980 actual): revenue F$220.4 million; expenditure F$255.3 million. Foreign trade (1981): imports F$540,070,000; exports F$268,-760,000. Import sources: Australia 36%; Japan 16%; New Zealand 14%; U.S. 7%; Singapore 7%; U.K. 5%. Export destinations: U.K. 33%; U.S. 12%; Malaysia 12%; New Zealand 10%; Japan 10%; Australia 9%; Canada 5%; Singapore 5%. Main exports (domestic): sugar 68%; fish 8%; gold 6%. Tourism (1980): visitors 190,000; gross receipts U.S. $134 million.

Transport and Communications. Roads (1979) 2,960 km. Motor vehicles in use (1981): passenger 25,500; commercial 16,400. Railways (1980) 1,062 km. Air traffic (1980): 253 million passenger-km; freight c. 3.3 million net ton-km. Shipping traffic (1981): goods loaded 801,000 metric tons, unloaded 903,000 metric tons. Telephones (Jan. 1980) 37,500. Radio receivers (Dec. 1979) 300,000.

Agriculture. Production (in 000; metric tons; 1981): sugar, raw value c. 450; rice c. 18; cassava c. 95; copra c. 24. Livestock (in 000; 1981): cattle c. 155; pigs c. 28; goats c. 55; horses c. 39; chickens c. 957.

Industry. Production (in 000; 1980): cement (metric tons) 83; gold (troy oz) 25; electricity (kw-hr) 306,000.

flation rate was reduced to 8.5% by the end of the year, and overseas borrowing was decreased. In the 1982 budget, taxes on fuel, alcohol, and tobacco were raised and, in anticipation of lower world prices, the export tax on sugar and income taxes on cane farmers were lowered. The Fiji Sugar corporation took over from the government the now well-established Seaqaqa sugar development on Vanua Levu.

Fiji supplied a battalion to the Sinai peacekeeping force and continued its involvement in the UN force in Lebanon. (BARRIE MACDONALD)

Finland

The republic of Finland is bordered on the north by Norway, on the west by Sweden and the Gulf of Bothnia, on the south by the Gulf of Finland, and on the east by the U.S.S.R. Area: 337,032 sq km (130,129 sq mi). Pop. (1982 est.): 4,818,000. Cap. and largest city: Helsinki (pop., 1981 est., 483,700). Language: Finnish, Swedish. Religion (1980): Lutheran 97.1%; Orthodox 1.2%; other 1.7%. President from Jan. 27, 1982 (acting president to that date), Mauno Koivisto; prime ministers, Eino Uusitalo (acting) and, from February 25, Kalevi Sorsa.

Mauno Koivisto (*see* BIOGRAPHIES) was sworn

FINLAND

Education. (1980–81) Primary, pupils 583,450, teachers 38,311; secondary, pupils 341,054, teachers (1979–80) 19,530; vocational, pupils 140,602, teachers (1979–80) 13,427; teacher training, students 2,675, teachers (1979–80) 120; higher, students 88,244, teaching staff 6,194.

Finance. Monetary unit: markka, with (Sept. 20, 1982) a free rate of 4.78 markkaa to U.S. $1 (8.19 markkaa = £1 sterling). Gold and other reserves (June 1982) U.S. $1,205,000,000. Budget (1981 actual): revenue 51,698,-000,000 markkaa; expenditure 51.4 billion markkaa. Gross national product (1981) 205,710,000,000 markkaa. Money supply (May 1982) 17,615,000,000 markkaa. Cost of living (1975 = 100; June 1982) 204.7.

Foreign Trade. (1981) Imports 61,269,000,000 markkaa; exports 560,308,000,000 markkaa. Import sources: U.S.S.R. 23%; West Germany 12%; Sweden 11%; U.K. 8%; U.S. 8%. Export destinations: U.S.S.R. 25%; Sweden 13%; U.K. 11%; West Germany 9%; Norway 5%. Main exports: paper 22%; machinery 13%; timber 8%; wood pulp 6%; chemicals 6%; clothing 6%; ships 5%.

Transport and Communications. Roads (1980) 74,960 km (including 208 km expressways). Motor vehicles in use (1980): passenger 1,225,900; commercial 149,150. Railways: (1980) 6,096 km; traffic (1981) 3,273,000,000 passenger-km, freight 8,392,000,000 net ton-km. Air traffic (1981): 2,508,000,000 passenger-km; freight 56.2 million net ton-km. Navigable inland waterways (1980) 6,057 km. Shipping (1981): merchant vessels 100 gross tons and over 341; gross tonnage 2,444,504. Telephones (Jan. 1980) 2,244,400. Radio receivers (Dec. 1979) c. 2.5 million. Television licenses (Dec. 1979) 1.5 million.

Agriculture. Production (in 000; metric tons; 1981): wheat 235; barley 1,080; oats 1,008; rye 64; potatoes 478; sugar, raw value 89; rapeseed 69; butter 75; cheese c. 73; eggs 74; meat 328; fish catch (1980) 141; timber (cu m; 1980) 47,961. Livestock (in 000; June 1981): cattle 1,753; sheep 103; pigs 1,467; reindeer (1979) 205; horses 20; poultry 7,807.

Industry. Production (in 000; metric tons; 1981): pig iron 1,964; crude steel 2,429; iron ore (66% metal content) 863; cement 1,787; sulfuric acid 1,095; petroleum products (1979) c. 11,050; plywood (cu m; 1980) 548; cellulose (1980) 4,606; wood pulp (1979) mechanical 2,238, chemical 4,600; newsprint 1,557; other paper and board (1980) 4,374; electricity (kw-hr) 39,262,000; manufactured gas (cu m) 21,000.

Mauno Koivisto was sworn in as Finland's president on January 27. He succeeded Urho Kekkonen, who had resigned because of illness. Kekkonen had served in office since 1956.

in as Finland's ninth president on Jan. 27, 1982, ending almost 26 years of unbroken rule by Urho Kekkonen, who had resigned in October 1981 because of illness. In the popular vote for an electoral college, the Social Democratic and independent candidates backing Koivisto secured 43.4%, against 18.7% for Conservative nominee Harri Holkeri, best placed of the other seven contenders. Koivisto then secured 167 of the 301 votes in the electoral college, thus gaining a decisive majority in the first round of voting.

Koivisto, the first Finnish head of state to emerge from the left, vowed to continue the external policy pursued by his post-World War II predecessors, based on good-neighbourly relations with the U.S.S.R. During a visit to the U.S.S.R. in March he was amiably received by Soviet Pres. Leonid Brezhnev. Koivisto also traveled to Sweden, Norway, Iceland, and Hungary.

As a result of Koivisto's elevation from prime minister to president, his centre-left government resigned. A new coalition drawn from the same four parties—Social Democratic, Centre, Swedish People's, and Communist—took office on February 25. Again, a Social Democrat became prime minister: Kalevi Sorsa, who had occupied the post twice before (1972–75 and 1977–79).

Domestic politics were overshadowed by the approach of a general election due in March 1983. Opinion polls showed the Social Democrats and Conservatives poised to pick up votes, the Centre holding its own, and the Communists clear losers. The most heat was generated at an extraordinary

Communist Party congress in mid-May, when retiring chairman Aarne Saarinen, a reformist, made a sensational attack on Moscow for siding with the Finnish hard-line minority and implicitly charging the party with harbouring "anti-Soviet elements." The minority then absented itself from the sessions until August, when the new chairman, Jouko Kajanoja, engineered an unconvincing truce between the feuding factions. In December the Communists left the government to go into opposition, preparatory to the upcoming election. Sorsa's resignation was refused by Koivisto, and on December 30 the prime minister reconstituted his Cabinet with Social Democrats replacing the three Communist ministers.

Attempts to balance bilateral trade between Finland and the U.S.S.R. over a five-year period posed problems. By the fall the Finns had built up a 5 billion markkaa surplus. To restore equilibrium, they needed to reduce eastward-bound deliveries. This factor, coupled with the continued recession in Western markets and a loss of competitive edge, served to dull economic prospects. Unemployment rose toward 6% as growth rates, forecast at 1% or lower, were insufficient to sustain jobs. Inflation, though waning, was not brought significantly below the average within the Organization for Economic Cooperation and Development. In October the government finally followed the example of the other Nordic countries and devalued the markka—twice in a single week.

In some respects the economy remained well balanced, however, with a reasonably healthy current account, a respectable foreign debt profile, and no need to apply sharp monetary adjustments. In the budget only 12.4% of expenditure had to be financed by borrowing, a low percentage by Scandinavian standards. Soviet Premier Nikolay Tikhonov visited Finland in December, when a trade agreement was signed that set total turnover in the exchange of goods and services in 1983 at 38 billion markkaa.

On December 30 Sorsa submitted his resignation when the Communists in the coalition voted against an increase in defense spending in the 1983 budget. President Koivisto asked him to remain in office until the 1983 election and he then reformed his government as a three-party coalition.

(DONALD FIELDS)

Fisheries

The UN Food and Agriculture Organization announced a 2% rise in the world fish catch during 1982, but this was by no means a sign that the industry's problems were coming to an end. Although investment in underexploited fisheries, both marine and freshwater, was producing results, high operating costs continued to threaten some fisheries with extinction. Fuel economy was still a dominant factor. Engine builders were quick to introduce fuel-saving outboard and diesel motors, while designers were as anxious to improve the efficiency of West Indian canoes as they were the underwater lines of giant tuna boats.

The ubiquitous microchip appeared in every

electronic navigation aid and fish finder, in an automatic winch system used to shoot and haul the trawl net, and in a "black box" that lowered a hand line to a preset depth and hauled it in when fish of a desired weight were caught, doing the work of two men. Most important, the microchip made possible a whole flock of fuel economizers. One Norwegian company fitted 400 in the home fleet alone, claiming an annual fuel saving of $17 million. New propellers, new engines, and even a more fuel-economic fish-meal plant appeared, designed to reverse the steady rise in costs set in motion by the previous years' quadrupled energy prices. Less energy-intensive fishing methods such as gillnetting and longline fishing, previously neglected, were developed anew on both sides of the Atlantic.

During the year there was a record increase in exports of fish and fish products, whether frozen, dried, or canned, but the very scale of these operations led to problems. In Spain the continued repercussions of the 1981 poisoned cooking oil scandal had a disastrous effect on the sale of any product suspected of being canned in oil. One Dutch company selling canned cockles in Spain had to close down. Sales of canned salmon also declined when a perforated can caused a death from botulism in Belgium, requiring the recall of enormous quantities of U.S. salmon in cans produced by a certain type of can-forming machine. Untold damage was done to the salmon-canning industry, leading to a massive lawsuit by the industry against the machinery manufacturers.

The year's most notable casualty was undoubtedly the U.S. Pacific tuna industry, which experienced an unprecedented slump in demand that tumbling prices did little to check. The blame was placed on the recession, which swung consumer buying to cheaper chicken and cheese products. By August half the Inter-American Pacific tuna fleet was idle, and both Bumble Bee and Van Camp Seafoods had closed big canneries in California. It was an additional bitter pill for this two million-ton-a-year fishery to be told of an estimated ten million-ton tuna resource in the western Pacific,

Table II. World Fisheries, 1980[1]
in 000 metric tons

Country	Catch		Trade	
	Total	Freshwater	Imports	Exports
Japan	10,410.4	220.8	940.0	716.6
U.S.S.R.	9,412.1	747.4	181.8	541.1
China	4,240.0	1,240.0	...	93.4
United States	3,634.5	69.6	963.1	466.5
Chile	2,816.7	0.1	1.8	618.9
Peru	2,731.4	11.7	0.3	586.0
India	2,423.5	875.3	...	74.5
Norway	2,398.2	...	83.5	659.3
South Korea	2,091.1	39.1	46.6	412.3
Denmark	2,026.8	16.4	259.8	754.2
Indonesia	1,653.2	439.1	23.1	69.4
Thailand	1,650.0	150.0	48.2	295.8
Philippines	1,536.6	421.4	48.9	63.9
Iceland	1,514.9	0.5	0.2	542.9
North Korea	1,400.0	70.0		
Canada	1,305.3	53.0	104.7	474.5
Mexico	1,240.2	37.8	41.0	60.4
Spain	1,240.0	32.9	288.7	157.2
Vietnam	1,013.5	176.3	...	...
Brazil	850.0	170.0	70.7	37.0
United Kingdom	796.5	...		
France	765.4	...	478.6	136.6
Malaysia	736.7	3.1	139.9	115.2
Ecuador	671.3	...	...	149.0
Bangladesh	650.0	525.0	...	5.5
Poland	640.0	18.7	236.0	82.0
South Africa	639.5	100.0	44.4	125.9
Burma	585.1	155.8	...	1.1
Nigeria	479.6	187.2	...	1.5
Italy	444.5	36.4	383.4	92.4
Turkey	429.6	32.3	[2]	6.4
Argentina	383.9	7.1	9.3	162.2
Senegal	359.2	7.8	16.9	84.0
Netherlands, The	340.4	1.2	347.7	346.7
Morocco	297.7	0.4	...	70.6
West Germany	296.9	15.0	888.3	229.7
Pakistan	279.3	46.3	[3]	35.1
Faeroe Islands	274.6	...	2.1	112.1
Portugal	265.2	...	82.2	57.3
Tanzania	247.3	198.1	3.7	[2]
Sweden	237.1	10.0	195.2	127.7
East Germany	235.3	12.2	38.6	...
Ghana	224.1	40.0	76.6	2.2
Uganda	223.8	223.8	...	[2]
South West Africa/ Namibia	213.0	[2]	...	...
Other	5,666.4	...	...	...
World	72,190.8	7,614.6[3]	9,198.9[3]	10,044.5[3]

[1]Excludes whaling.
[2]Less than 100 metric tons.
[3]Includes unspecified amounts in Other category.
Source: United Nations Food and Agriculture Organization, *Yearbook of Fishery Statistics*, vol. 50 and 51.

which could have boosted the U.S. catch if there had been a market for it. Meanwhile, Japan was building 20 new tuna boats of the superseiner class to replace old-style line boats.

Low tuna prices in the U.S. were causing concern in France, where prices were fixed at the beginning of each year and, if necessary, supported by the government. Even more worrisome was Mexico's ambitious building program, with 66 tuna boats on order to bring its tuna fleet to a massive 113 vessels. With little home market and with U.S. markets closed to Mexico by a long-standing fishing dispute, it was difficult to conceive of an adequate number of customers for such a potentially large catch. To what extent the Mexican financial crisis would affect this building program was yet to be seen. Possibly it would force the sale of much of the fleet to the Far East, with serious effects on the world market. Prior to the crisis, Mexico had had plans for an eventual total fish catch of two million tons, compared with a 1976 total of 628,000 tons.

The U.S. total catch had risen by 27% since the advent of the 200-mi fishing limit, and in 1982 it was nearing four million tons, valued at $2.4 billion at dockside. The potential value was estimated at $8 billion–$10 billion, and it was believed that continued growth would lead to the possible cre-

Table I. Whaling: 1980–81 Season (Antarctic); 1980 Season (Outside the Antarctic)
Number of whales caught

Area and country	Fin whale	Sei/ Bryde's whale	Hump-back whale	Minke whale	Sperm whale	Killer whale	Total	Percentage assigned under quota agreement[1]
Antarctic pelagic (open sea)								
Japan	—	—	—	3,120	—	—	3,120	44.1
U.S.S.R.	—	—	—	3,120	—	—	3,120	44.1
Brazil	—	—	—	—	—	—	—	11.8
Total	—	—	—	6,240	—	—	6,240	100.0
Outside the Antarctic								
Japan	—	307	—	379	1,192	2	1,880	
U.S.S.R.	—	—	—	—	—	—	178[2]	
Brazil	—	—	—	902	30	—	932	
Peru	—	215	—	—	450	—	665	
Iceland	236	100	—	201	101	—	638	
Spain	219	2	—	—	13	—	234	
Norway	—	—	—	2,002	—	52	2,054	
Greenland	13	—	13	141	1	—	168	
Others	4	—	19	926	304	—	1,253	
Total	472	624	32	4,551	2,091	54	8,002	

[1]Minke; Antarctic only.
[2]Represents gray whales.
Source: The Committee for Whaling Statistics, *International Whaling Statistics*.

Ralph Maggioni, president of L. P. Maggioni & Co., the last remaining oyster cannery on the Atlantic coast of the U.S., surveys his empire from atop a mountain of oyster shells. Hard financial times, coastline developments, and pollution gradually had forced the closure of the 50 other canneries along the coast.

ation of 300,000 new jobs. Much of this potential lay in the estimated 20 million tons of Alaskan pollack that were within reach of U.S. vessels.

Canada had been suffering from an oversupply of canned mackerel, and the government had to support the market by buying stocks for distribution to third world countries. Measures were introduced to cut the fleet by 25%; these included a subsidy for scrapping old vessels and restrictions on the introduction of more efficient ones.

During the year two large Canadian companies, Nickerson and National Sea Products, decided to combine their marketing activities. In the field of conservation, long-awaited legislation was introduced to protect fish habitats from logging and construction activities. Canada reacted sharply to pressure by the European Economic Community (EEC) to ban seal-based products and to reduce the harp seal cull. It was pointed out that one harp seal consumed 1.5 tons of fish every year.

Europe was trying desperately to adjust to a situation of overcapacity. While vessels were becoming ever more efficient, their number had not decreased accordingly, and the EEC nations were finding it difficult to divide a 'mutually owned" resource in a way that was satisfactory to all concerned. Quota allocations were bitterly argued, as was the total allowable catch (TAC) for popular species such as herring, mackerel, and haddock. Denmark was accused of taking ten times its permitted share of the herring TAC and of ignoring requests to stop fishing. Faced with falling prices and costs that were 33% higher than in 1981, EEC nations were tempted to save the industry at the expense of the fish stock.

In Britain the long-established White Fish Authority had been largely disbanded and was replaced by a new Sea Fish Industry Authority, the policies of which were oriented toward marketing rather than increased catching efficiency. Demands by the industry for financial aid were loud and desperate, particularly in Scotland, but were frustrated by the economic climate and by the inability of the EEC to agree on a common fisheries policy. This was vital in order to make planned in-

vestment possible and to share EEC fish stocks equitably. Under the Treaty of Rome the rich and carefully husbanded fish stocks around Britain's coasts could be opened to an "up to the beaches" free-for-all in 1983, failing a new agreement. British fishermen prepared themselves for a unilateral battle to keep out an EEC fleet that would soon include Spain and Portugal.

When an acceptable agreement appeared to have been reached in Brussels in June, it was vetoed by Denmark, which maintained its opposition throughout the year despite strong pressure from its EEC partners. The U.K. had the most to lose by an unfavourable common fisheries policy, a loss that would be a gain for France. The Netherlands, and Belgium. Prospects in Ireland were also bleak, and the industry registered a £14 million loss in 1981. With Spain scheduled to join the EEC in 1983, there were fears of a new Spanish Armada in Ireland's previously protected fishing grounds.

Outside the EEC, Iceland was reaping a rich harvest in its protected waters and was joined by Greenland, which in February chose to leave the European Communities. Norway was not doing so well, however, with some fish stocks so depleted that catch restrictions were applied even to the small boat fleet. While aid to the tune of $170 million was announced, there were accusations by Norway of illegal fishing by Spain, Denmark, and the U.S.S.R. The need to export was vital to Norway's fishing gear and equipment industry, and the nation was busy with projects to aid small-boat fisheries of less-developed countries.

Norway announced the successful production of fish protein concentrate, which had gained expanding markets in the fish product industry. Trondheim was again the site of Europe's largest fisheries exhibition, where business was reported to be encouraging.

Changes in the Humboldt Current brought new prosperity to fishing in Chile, where the annual catch now topped three million tons. Peru was still in trouble despite the prospect of an improvement in total fish landings, which in 1981 had reached 2.7 million tons. The giant Pepesca canning plant, built by the government in 1975 as the ultimate in design, was in liquidation, and other state-owned companies were up for sale. Fish-meal production—once the world's highest—amounted to only one million tons in 1982, and the plan to switch to fishing for human consumption and to fit refrigeration into fishing boats was given a further extension. Farther south, off the Falkland Islands, the U.S.S.R. was taking 400,000 tons of krill for processing. These small, shrimplike creatures had proved valuable as fish farm food and showed promise as a human food source.

In the search for better utilization of fish resources, attention in Britain turned to small fish that sometimes failed to find a market, particularly whiting and haddock. Torry Research Station, at Aberdeen, Scotland, developed a method of forming 170–225-g (6–8-oz) frozen fillets from very small fillets on a production basis; they scored high in acceptability trials. A similar development was reported in Norway, using a different process. Another plentiful small fish was capelin, which had traditionally been used for fish-meal production.

With so much uncertainty in the marine fisheries, it was not surprising that greater attention was being given to the more stable aquaculture industry. This was one of Western Europe's fastest growing industries, worth approximately $400 million a year. China's aquaculture production had risen 30% since 1978 to 370,000 tons a year, and Chinese researchers were claiming a breakthrough in the induced spawning of freshwater prawns. Prawn ponds in Central America continued to develop their enormous potential, and Panama received a $13 million loan from the Inter-American Development Bank for prawn farm development.

What was seen by the International Whaling Commission (IWC) as a major step toward a total ban on whaling was regarded by others as a shift of emphasis from one species to another. Whaling nations such as the U.S.S.R., Japan, and Iceland joined in condemning a total ban, claiming that it would cause additional unemployment and a reduction of food supply. In November the U.S.S.R., Japan, Chile, Norway, and Peru served notice that they would not consider themselves bound by the IWC decision. (See ENVIRONMENT.)

(H. S. NOEL)

See also Food Processing.
[731.D.2.a]

Food Processing

The continuing recession, escalating legislative controls, health controversies, and the costly complexities of safety assurance absorbed an undue proportion of manufacturers' resources in 1982. They contributed to the liquidation of many food processors and the absorption of others by multinational corporations. Overproduction of a number of agricultural products confronted many farmers with disaster rather than riches, and in the European Economic Community (EEC) mountains of surplus butter, milk powder, wheat, beef, and sugar compounded the problem.

There was a growing tendency on the part of some scientists to label all physiologically active components of foods as "toxins." Lists of such constituents, running into the hundreds, included substances found in fruits, vegetables, cereals, seafood, and meat. The *FAO Food and Nutrition Series No. 2* contained such a list, although its avowed objective was to demonstrate that "natural" foods may be more "toxic" than processed ones since the so-called toxins can be removed during manufacture.

Fruits, Vegetables, and Cereals. To meet the growing demand for fruit juices, a plant with 20 million litres (5,280,000 gal) of storage capacity was installed in Belgium for the European distribution of concentrates from Latin America. A wild fruit extremely rich in vitamin C, yielding 2.3 to 3.1 grams per 100 grams, was discovered in Northern Australia. The fruit, *Terminalia ferdinandiana*, was eaten by the aboriginal people and especially by children. Spanish technologists made a significant development in paprika processing by replacing the traditional sun-drying with a continuous process involving washing, dicing, seed separation, liquidizing, low-temperature concentration, pasteurization, and, finally, aseptic packaging.

Indian research on an alga (*Spirulina*), consumed for centuries by the peoples of Chad and Mexico, established its nutritional value, and recommendations were made for its wider use as a protein source. New potato strains were developed in The Netherlands for chip manufacture in less developed countries; when dried, they did not require refrigeration or special storage. The discovery that the local potatoes of Taiwan were particularly suitable for french fries led to a fast-food development there.

The U.S. organization Intsoy was providing many African and Asian countries with new soybean genotypes capable of utilizing local nitrogen-fixing bacteria for growth. It also provided specialist assistance on the processing of soybeans and their use in traditional products. Other U.S. scientists investigated an African preparation (*akara*), made from dehulled cowpeas, which proved to be a good source of vegetable protein.

Declining bread consumption led to further bakery closures in Britain, and the survivors were installing improved technology to meet new consumer and legal requirements. This included the extension of microelectronic control of flour-milling operations, installation of small batch mixers and dough sheeting machines, and the synchronization of continuous bakery-oven output with packaging operations. Many nutritionists who had previously condemned bread and potatoes as fattening supported a government campaign to increase their consumption in view of their nutritional value. The proportion of brown to white bread consumed in Britain increased substantially. A gastroenterologist told the Royal Society that consumption of brown bread could eliminate the National Health Service's £20 million-a-year expenditure on laxatives. In the U.S. pasta became a fashionable food, and stores specializing in different varieties of pasta opened in a number of cities. China launched a campaign to

Floods:
see Earth Sciences; Engineering Projects

The U.S. Department of Agriculture was considering relaxing its standards to allow lower quality beef to qualify for higher grades. The move raised a storm of opposition from restaurateurs and consumers.

encourage bread consumption, assisted by a Japanese company that installed a large plant for bread and doughnut manufacture.

Dairy Products. World stocks of dairy products continued to rise. At the International Dairy Federation conference in Moscow there was discussion of how to reconcile overproduction in developed countries with undernutrition in the third world. One proposal was to blend milk fat and protein with vegetable oils and proteins to make cheaper products. However, the growing market for such cheaper products in the U.S., Britain, and other Western countries had already increased the surpluses. Imitation cheese had captured 7% of the U.S. cheese market, and imitation mozzarella was used in 35% of the pizzas sold there. Considerable research in the U.S., Britain, and The Netherlands was devoted to the use of surplus milk protein in bakery and meat products, the development of new beverages, and milk protein fractionation and modification for novel applications.

The concentration of milk by ultrafiltration (UF) on the farm was studied in the U.S. as a means of reducing transportation costs. The concentrate could be stored for four days without deterioration, and it improved the yields of cheese and cultured products. Canadian workers used milk powder made from UF-concentrated milk in cheese manufacture, making it possible for dairies to cope with the summer surge and to keep operating throughout the year.

British scientists demonstrated that the storage of refrigerated milk could be improved by the use of carbon dioxide which prevented the growth of cold-tolerant bacteria. French scientists made the interesting discovery that the adverse effect of refrigerated milk in cheesemaking could be overcome by the use of certain proteolytic enzymes that also improved cheese quality. The use of enzymes to augment flavour and hasten the ripening of cheeses was the subject of research in several countries. Their use halved the ripening time of many cheeses, resulting in substantial savings in labour and storage costs.

Meat and Seafood. Manufacturers of meat products in the U.K. had a difficult year as a result of regulatory problems arising from new technological developments. However, all parties agreed that such developments should not be hindered if they reduced waste and provided cheaper alternative products. Still to be resolved were matters of definition, labeling, and analytical problems relating to "lean meat" content, water content, the use of rind, the proportion of connective tissue in different cuts of meat, and the use of binders and vegetable proteins. Meanwhile, serological tests developed in Austria and West Germany made it possible to differentiate between different kinds of meat in manufactured products. A similar test developed in Britain detected 3% kangaroo meat in beef products. A British company developed a fluorimetric method for determining "lean meat"

Aseptic paper bottles, common in Europe for more than 20 years, were introduced into the U.S. following approval by the Food and Drug Administration in January. The paper packaging eliminates the need for refrigeration during storage.

content, and the Danish Meat Research Institute (DMRI) developed a rapid method for determining the collagen content of meat.

The British Meat Research Institute developed an optic probe, capable of examining 200 carcasses per hour, to detect the effects of preslaughter stress on the quality of uncut pig carcasses. Animals exhausted before slaughter developed an "unattractively dark, translucent and sticky" meat that was vulnerable to spoilage. The probe also detected pig meat susceptible to a "pale, soft, exudative" defect that rendered it unsuitable for processing. DMRI carried out experiments on the canning of cured hot-boned hams without the use of phosphates. The products proved similar to traditional canned hams except that they were slightly darker in colour. Italian scientists studying the utilization of slaughterhouse blood for human nutrition demonstrated that 70% of the total blood protein could be recovered by the use of microbial proteases or papain to digest the cellular elements. The red pigment of the red blood cells was easily extracted.

The conservation of fisheries was discussed at an International Seafood Conference in Munich, West Germany. Strong measures were urged to combat overfishing, pirating of stocks, and exploitation for fish meal. The conference also called for restructuring of the industry to enable it to make a better contribution to protein resources. A British government report recommended that the fishing industry place more emphasis on quality than on quantity, and fish processors were criticized for failing to encourage sales of frozen fish through supermarkets and retail grocers. The canned salmon trade suffered a serious setback as a result of several cases of botulism and one death attributed to produce of Alaskan origin. The trouble arose from damage caused during the in-cannery erection of can bodies that had been flattened for transit. Traders in Britain faced a bill of some £500,000 for the mechanical checking of ten million suspect cans by an officially approved procedure.

New Products. A great many of the new products that appeared during the year were specially formulated preparations with reduced fat and/or energy content, variously combined with nonnutrient fillers and sometimes aerated or with increased water content. Such products satisfied the desire for variety and customary levels of food consumption without exceeding calorie requirements; they also helped to maintain manufacturing and sales turnover. Products of this type appeared in the EEC, the U.S., Australia, New Zealand, Eastern Europe, and the U.S.S.R. Other growth areas included new low-salt and low-cholesterol products and sugarless foods. The growth of new products high in polyunsaturated fats was affected by medical statements that they increased the risk of cancer, although other medical spokesmen expressed the opinion that high intake of saturated fats was actually the culprit.

The transition of Japan toward a Western lifestyle resulted in a spate of new products that were compromises between traditional and Western-style foods. Among them were a soy protein-derived blue cheese resembling Roquefort, soymilk yogurt, snacks made from meat and algae (*Chlorel-*

la), and food preparations made from gelatinized seaweed combined with fruit juices, fish eggs, meat products, or noodles. Kangaroo meat was reported to have become popular in Japan, where it was known as "jumping steak."

Similar new product adaptations were made in many other countries to meet tourist and ethnic demands. A line of cheese spreads made from soy flour was developed in Yugoslavia, and a custard-like product was made in the U.S. from *villia* (a Scandinavian cultured milk), soy milk, and honey. The Chinese developed a cola drink prepared from haws and another soft drink from soy flavoured with hibiscus. Many new Chinese specialties adapted to overseas tastes were developed in Taiwan, among them pigs' knuckles with black mushrooms, roast gluten, winter cabbage with white fungous jelly, and Buddhist vegetarian foods. A line of ethnic Mexican-style products was developed in Britain, including tacos, tostados, and taco casserole. Mexican foods, often adapted to American tastes, were also gaining in popularity in the U.S. A British connoisseur reported on rare Chinese specialties not consumed elsewhere: braised python, bear's paw, braised whole guinea pig, soup prepared from snake, cat, and chicken, water snake cooked with ginger and onions, civet cat, monkey brains, and grainy dog meat with chili sauce. (H. B. HAWLEY)

See also Agriculture and Food Supplies; Fisheries; Health and Disease; Industrial Review: *Alcoholic Beverages.*
[451.B.1.c.ii; 731.E–H]

Football

Association Football (Soccer). WORLD CUP. Italy's captain and goalkeeper Dino Zoff led his men up the steps to the main stand of the Santiago Bernabeu stadium in Madrid on July 11, 1982, to receive the golden World Cup and medals from King Juan Carlos of Spain after Italy's victory in the final of that tournament. Italy decisively defeated West Germany in that match, estimated to have been watched on television by 1,000,000,000 people. Thus the Italians equaled Brazil's record of three victories in the World Cup, the finals of which had been enlarged to accommodate the teams of 24 nations playing in 17 centres in Spain during June and July.

Perhaps the key to the Italians' success was the decision to include Paolo Rossi (see BIOGRAPHIES) of Juventus, who had only played a handful of league games before traveling to Spain. Rossi had been completing a two-year ban for being implicated—a charge he had always strenuously denied—in the Italian football betting scandal of 1980. (A by-product of the Italian triumph was that players and officials banned after the scandal were amnestied.)

The Italians, masterminded by their manager, Enzo Bearzot, showed a rare resilience to adversity in the final match. They started without one of their key midfielders, Giancarlo Antognoni, injured in the semifinals against Poland in Barcelona, and Francesco Graziani limped out of the game

UPI

Jubilant Italian soccer players Antonio Cabrini (left) and Claudio Gentile embrace after Italy defeated West Germany 3–1 in the 1982 Football World Cup final in Madrid.

after ten minutes with further damage to a shoulder also hurt against the Poles. Italy also withstood the disappointment of Antonio Cabrini's driving a penalty kick wide of Harald Schumacher's goal in the first half, the first time a penalty had not been converted in a World Cup final. But Rossi, Marco Tardelli, and Bruno Conti hit peak form and made most of the West Germans' attacks look stereotyped and robotish. The West Germans also showed fallibility near the goal, as Klaus Fischer sent chances off target and Wolfgang Dremmler scooped a shot, following a pass from the far-from-fit Karl-Heinz Rümmenigge, over the bar.

Rossi broke the 0–0 deadlock 11 minutes into the second period after a free kick—there were many more as the game became more robust—by Tardelli. Claudio Gentile crossed the ball, and there was Rossi to tap it home. Tardelli scored the second goal when he cracked Gentile's pass into the net (after 69 minutes), and Allessandro Altobelli prodded in the third (81 minutes) to cap a superb run by Conti almost half the length of the field. Paul Breitner reduced the margin to 3–1, but he did not stamp his authority on the midfield. Frenetic efforts to try and get the ball into the Italian penalty area caused the Germans to lose some of their discipline—and the glittering prize.

But there was no fluke about the triumph of the Italians. They had already eliminated the favoured Brazil and defending champion Argentina. Brazil gave Italy a close run in their contest before bowing out 3–2 as European soccer gained the ascendancy, supplying all four semifinalists. France lost one semifinal (3–3) to West Germany on penalty kicks and then went down 3–2 to a spirited Polish team in Alicante, in the play-off for third place.

West Germany was involved in a boring clash against Austria with the worst aspects of possession play being paraded in an exploitation of the "league" points system to enable both teams to qualify for the second phase amid a chorus of criticism laced with charges of collusion. The tournament did produce some surprises. The unheralded Cameroon team tied its three games against Poland, Italy, and Peru; Kuwait showed remarkable resilience, and Honduras rocked Spain by holding the tournament hosts to a draw.

The standard of refereeing was criticized. Some was weak, some inept, and much inconsistent; blatant fouls were unpunished, a glaring example being West German goalkeeper Schumacher's charge into the French player Patrick Battiston, which left Battiston badly injured.

The forthcoming retirement of England's manager, Ron Greenwood, was announced before the finals in Spain. Managers of some unsuccessful teams were dismissed.

EUROPEAN CHAMPIONS' CUP. England maintained its domination of the cup for national champions with Aston Villa's 1–0 victory over West

German champion Bayern Munich in Rotterdam's Feyenoord stadium on May 26. Striker Peter Withe scored his goal (67 minutes) with clinical efficiency, but much of the credit went to Tony Morley, who turned Wolfgang Dremmler inside out before sending the ball over the centre for Withe to drill past Manfred Muller. Aston Villa's Nigel Spink, replacing Jimmy Rimmer who was injured after nine minutes, proved a stumbling block to the Bayern players. The West Germans launched a tremendous onslaught against the Villa defense early in the second half, but Spink did everything asked of him and stopped a series of shots and headers hurled at him by the likes of Karl-Heinz Rümmenigge, Dieter Hoeness, Paul Breitner, Wolfgang Kraus, Udo Horsmann, and Bernd Durnberger. True, Hoeness had the ball in the net a couple of minutes before the end of the game, but he was patently offside.

EUROPEAN CUP-WINNERS' CUP. With its emphasis on the game's physical rather than skillful aspects, the final of the Cup-Winners' Cup was a poor advertisement for European football. Some tackling was not far removed from thuggery, but only one man was expelled from the game, Standard Liège's defender Walter Meeuws in the last seconds, a surprise and probably an error of judgment. Some of the earlier offenses from the Barcelona players deserved the same treatment, and their policy seemed to be to win at all costs. They achieved their aim by two goals to one in Barcelona on May 12.

New York Cosmos soccer star Giorgio Chinaglia scored his team's only goal as the Cosmos beat the Seattle Sounders 1–0 in the Soccer Bowl in San Diego on September 18. Chinaglia was named the game's most valuable player.

Table I. Association Football Major Tournaments

Event	Winner	Country
World Cup	Italy	
Inter-Continental Cup	Peñarol	Uruguay
European Champions' Cup	Aston Villa	England
European Cup-Winners' Cup	Barcelona	Spain
UEFA Cup	IFK Göteborg	Sweden
Libertadores Cup (South American Champions' Cup	Peñarol	Uruguay

Table II. Association Football National Champions

Nation	League winners	Cup winners
Albania	Nendori Tirana	
Austria	Rapid Vienna	FC Austria
Belgium	Standard Liège	Waterschei
Bulgaria	CSKA Sofia	Lokotmotiv Sofia
Cyprus	Omonia Nicosia	Appollon Limassol
Czechoslovakia	Dukla Prague	Slovan Bratislava
Denmark	Hvidøvre	B 93, Copenhagen
England	Liverpool	Tottenham Hotspur
Finland	HJK Helsinki	HJK Helsinki
France	Monaco	Paris St.-Germain
Germany, East	Dynamo Berlin	Dynamo Dresden
Germany, West	SV Hamburg	Bayern Munich
Greece	Olympiakos	Panathinaikos
Hungary	Rabo Eto	Ujpest Dozsa
Iceland	Vikingur	Vestmannaey
Ireland	Dundalk	Limerick
Italy	Juventus	Inter-Milan
Luxembourg	Avenir Beggen	Red Boys Differdange
Malta	Hibernians	Sliema Wanderers
Netherlands, The	Ajax	AZ '67 Alkmaar
Northern Ireland	Linfield	Coleraine
Norway	Valerengen	Lillestrøm
Poland	Widzew Lodz	Lech Poznan
Portugal	Sporting Lisbon	Sporting Lisbon
Romania	Dinamo Bucharest	Dinamo Bucharest
Scotland	Celtic	Aberdeen
Spain	Real Sociedad	Real Madrid
Sweden	Öster Växjö	IFK Göteborg
Switzerland	Grasshoppers	Sion
Turkey	Besiktas	Galatasaray
U.S.S.R.	Dynamo Kiev	Dynamo Kiev
U.S.	New York Cosmos	
Wales		Swansea
Yugoslavia	Dynamo Zagreb	Red Star Belgrade

Standard gained a 1–0 lead in the seventh minute when Guy Vandermissen flicked home a centre by Benny Wendt following a free kick. That perked up Standard, but they could not add to the goal. Then, seconds before the halftime interval, a blunder by goalkeeper Michel Preud'homme allowed a free kick from the right by Estaban to float through the Danish striker Allan Simonsen and tie the score. During the second half the same mixture prevailed with tackles rough and tough, but after an hour's play Barcelona took the lead, again from a free kick. Simonsen quickly tapped the ball to Quini while the Standard defenders were organizing themselves, and the little striker drove it into the Belgians' net. The play became more skillful after that, and Barcelona showed that it could have won without resorting to clattering tackles.

UEFA CUP. IFK Göteborg surprised the pundits by winning both legs of the UEFA Cup final to bring Sweden its first major European trophy. IFK, a team of part-time professionals, was confronted by SV Hamburg, which in the first leg in the Ullevi stadium, Göteborg, on May 5 played for a goalless draw with the aim of applying the finishing touches back in West Germany a fortnight later. The plan appeared to be working well, and the West Germans were helped when IFK lost key man Torbjörn Nilsson and later Tommy Holmgren. However, the Swedes stuck to their task, in heavy rain, of breaking down a Hamburg defense that included World Cup player Manfred Kaltz, and three minutes before the end of the match Glenn Hysen headed down a long centre and Tord Holmgren drilled the ball into the net.

The return match in Hamburg started with SV frantic in its search for goals and wanting to do all at breakneck speed. IFK contained its efforts, grew in confidence, and exploited the gaps created by the West Germans' excess of zeal to take the lead midway through the opening half, when Tommy Holmgren's centre was topped off by Dan Corneliusson. That goal rattled Hamburg, and the game slipped gradually into the Swedes' hands. Nilsson whipped in the second goal after an hour following a splendid solo run, and Stig Fredriksson converted a penalty after Nilsson had been fouled. Thus, IFK romped home 4–0 on aggregate for a deserved victory.

U.K. HOME INTERNATIONAL CHAMPIONSHIP. In 1982, competition for the U.K. home title was spread over three months because of the requirements of the World Cup finals in Spain, for which England, Northern Ireland, and Scotland had qualified. In the U.K. tournament England won all of its three games, the first 4–0 over Northern Ireland at Wembley on February 23 with goals by Bryan Robson (Manchester United), Kevin Keegan (Southampton), Ray Wilkins (Manchester United), and Glenn Hoddle (Tottenham).

A goal by Trevor Francis (Manchester City) gave England victory over Wales at Cardiff on April 27. On April 28 Scotland drew with Northern Ireland in Belfast when Sammy McIlroy (Stoke) answered a first-half goal by Ipswich's John Wark. Scotland beat Wales with a goal by Asa Hartford (Manchester City) at Hampden Park, Glasgow, on May 24, and so the scene was set for the deciding contest at the same site five days later against England. A single goal by England's Paul Mariner (Ipswich) settled a far from memorable game. Wales beat Northern Ireland 3–0 at Wrexham on May 27.

NORTH AMERICAN SOCCER LEAGUE. The New York Cosmos regained their champions' tag when they beat the Seattle Sounders in the Soccer Bowl in San Diego, Calif., on September 18, with a single goal after 30 minutes by Italian-born striker Giorgio Chinaglia, again the league's leading scorer with 20 goals and 15 assists in 32 games. It was the Cosmos' fourth title in the past six years, and the final game marked the end of the career of their Brazilian defender Carlos Alberto after 21 seasons as a professional.

The small crowd of 22,634—some 14,000 fewer than the previous year—demonstrated the trend of declining attendance in the NASL. Even the Cosmos dropped to below an average of 30,000 for the first time since the arrival of Pelé in 1975; six teams attracted average attendances of less than 10,000, and three put their franchises up for sale at the end of the season. High ticket prices, unexciting playing, and the general economic depression contributed to the decline.   (TREVOR WILLIAMSON)

Rugby. RUGBY UNION. Many overseas tours by various countries took place in 1981–82. Among them were Romania's tour of Scotland, a 23-match tour of the British Isles by the Australians, and a first-ever tour of Canada and the U.S. by the full England squad.

In September 1981 the Romanians won two of their three games in Scotland. In their only international match they were beaten 12–6 by Scotland at Murrayfield. The Australians, touring the British Isles between October 1981 and January 1982, won 16 of their 23 games but lost three of their four internationals. Wales beat them 18–13 at Cardiff; Scotland won 24–15 at Murrayfield, and England beat them 15–11 at Twickenham. In Dublin, however, Australia defeated Ireland 16–12.

In October and November 1981 New Zealand played two games in Romania—their first visit—and eight in France. In their three internationals New Zealand beat Romania 14–6 in Bucharest and France 13–9 at Toulouse and 18–6 in Paris.

In the home international championships Ireland, which had lost all four matches the previous season, came out on top. France, undefeated champions in 1981, tied for last place with Wales; England and Scotland tied for second.

Ireland won the triple crown for the first time in 33 years by beating Wales 21–12 in Dublin, England 16–15 at Twickenham, and Scotland 21–12 in Dublin. In their last match in Paris the French defeated them 22–9. England opened its campaign by drawing 9–9 with Scotland at Murrayfield but then had the misfortune of losing its long-standing and much-respected captain, Bill Beaumont, who was forced to retire from rugby because of an injury.

Under Beaumont's successor, Steve Smith, England lost to Ireland but then won its last two matches convincingly, beating France 27–15 in Paris and Wales 17–7 at Twickenham. Scotland finished impressively by defeating Wales 34–18, its first victory at Cardiff in 20 years and Wales's first championship defeat at Cardiff since 1968. Scotland's 34-point total was the highest ever recorded against Wales in Wales.

England played eight matches in Canada and the U.S. in May and June 1982, winning them all by large margins. In the two internationals England defeated Canada 43–6 at Vancouver and the U.S. 59–0 at Hartford. Scotland played eight games in Australia in June and July 1982, winning the first international 12–7 at Brisbane and losing the second 33–9 in Sydney. The Australians then toured New Zealand in August and September 1982, playing three international matches. New Zealand won the first 23–16 at Christchurch, lost the second 19–16 at Wellington, and won the third 33–18 at Auckland.

Perhaps the most extraordinary result of the year came on April 3, 1982, when the South Americans (all in fact from Argentina) defeated the South African Springboks 21–12 at Bloemfontein, South Africa, Hugo Porta scoring all their points. The previous weekend the Springboks had beaten the South Americans 50–18 in Pretoria.

RUGBY LEAGUE. In two tests Britain beat France 37–0 at Hull, and France beat Britain 19–2 at Marseilles. In the other international England beat Wales 20–15 at Cardiff. Of the new English clubs, Carlisle, in its first season, was runner-up in the second division of the Slalom Lager Championship. Cardiff, also in its first season, finished eighth out of 17 in the same division. Fulham, in its second season, was relegated from the first to the second division.   (DAVID FROST)

U.S. Football. PROFESSIONAL. Led by the record-setting performance of running back John Riggins, the Washington Redskins won their first Super Bowl by defeating the Miami Dolphins 27–17 on Jan. 30, 1983, in Pasadena, Calif. It was the Redskins' first National Football League (NFL) championship since 1942. Riggins ran for 166 yd on 38 carries, both Super Bowl records, and set another mark with a 43-yd touchdown run from scrimmage. Miami's Fulton Walker also set a Super Bowl record by returning a kickoff 98 yd for a touchdown. Although Miami led 17–10 at halftime, the Redskins dominated the second half, holding the Dolphins to two first downs and 34 yd gained.

Washington reached the Super Bowl by defeating Detroit 31–7 and Minnesota 21–7 in the first two rounds of the play-offs. The Redskins then won the National Football Conference championship with a 31–17 victory over Dallas. Miami's road to the Super Bowl included 28–13 and 34–13 triumphs over New England and San Diego in the first two rounds and a 14–0 win over the New York Jets in the American Football Conference title game.

The season was most memorable for its 57-day players' strike, which reduced the schedule from 16 games to 9. The strike ended Nov. 16, 1982, when player unrest coaxed Players Association executive director Ed Garvey (*see* BIOGRAPHIES) to withdraw his demand for a fixed pay scale distributed from a league fund that would have increased with the NFL's television revenue.

After the strike the league temporarily abandoned its six-division structure and expanded its postseason play-offs to include 16 teams instead of 10. The top eight teams in each conference qualified for the play-offs, two with losing records. Even so, four 1981 play-off teams failed to return to the tournament: Buffalo, the New York Giants, Philadelphia, and San Francisco, the defending Super Bowl champion, which fell from a 13–3 record to 3–6. The most improved team was New England, which climbed from 2–14 to 5–4 under new

coach Ron Meyer. The next most improved teams were regular-season champions Washington in the NFC and the Los Angeles Raiders in the AFC, both at 8–1.

The Raiders, who moved from Oakland after years of legal battles that still were being appealed at the year's end, had been 7–9 the previous season. Their star rookie halfback, Marcus Allen, led the league in touchdowns with 14, and their defense led the league with 38 quarterback sacks.

Washington improved its record from 8–8, largely because kicker Mark Moseley (*see* BIOGRAPHIES) set two league records with 23 consecutive field goals (20 of them in 1982) and with a .952 field-goal percentage (20 for 21). The Redskins also allowed the fewest points in the league, and their quarterback, NFC passing leader Joe Theismann, threw to unheralded first-year wide receiver Charlie Brown, the league leader with 21.6 yd per catch.

San Diego's average of 324.7 passing yards per game set an NFL record, and its average of 450.8 total yards per game was the highest since 1951. Quarterback Dan Fouts became the first quarterback to pass for 400 yd in consecutive games and tied Terry Bradshaw of Pittsburgh with a league-high 17 touchdown passes. Wide receiver Wes Chandler led the league with 1,032 yd on pass receptions and nine touchdown catches. San Diego's Kellen Winslow led the AFC with 54 receptions, and the Chargers also led the league in points, first downs, and yards per play.

Cincinnati quarterback Ken Anderson won his fourth NFL passing championship, broke a 37-year-old record by completing 70.6% of his passes, and completed 20 consecutive passes on January 2 to break a record that Denver quarterback Steve DeBerg had set two weeks earlier. When San Diego defeated Cincinnati 50–34 on December 20, the teams combined for 66 completions and 883 passing yards, both NFL records.

San Francisco led the NFC in total yards and passing yards as quarterback Joe Montana passed for at least 300 yd in five consecutive games, another

In an attempt to recoup lost income and to provide some excitement for the fans during the long football strike, players from the American Football Conference and the National Football Conference held an "all-star" game in the Los Angeles Coliseum in October. A sparse crowd of fewer than 5,000 showed what the fans thought of the idea.

UPI

John Riggins of the Washington Redskins got 43 of his record 166 yards rushing in the Super Bowl on this fourth-and-one play that produced the game-winning touchdown against the Miami Dolphins.

record. Also for San Francisco, Dwight Clark led the league with 60 receptions and the conference with 913 yd on receptions. Los Angeles Ram quarterback Vince Ferragamo's 509 yd passing in one game was the most since 1951.

On the ground Tony Dorsett of Dallas set a record with a 99-yd run, but with the shortened season he was unable to extend his own record of five 1,000-yd seasons in five years. Dorsett's 745 yd rushing led the NFC, trailing only Freeman McNeil of the New York Jets, who led the NFL with 786. Walter Payton of Chicago became the fourth NFL player with a career total of 10,000 yd rushing.

Defensively, Miami led the NFL by allowing 256.8 yd and 114.1 passing yards per game. Tampa Bay led the NFC in those categories. Pittsburgh led the league in rushing defense, yielding 84.1 yd per game.

Before the season the NFL signed a five-year contract worth $2.1 billion with three television networks, attesting to its economic stability but also igniting a share-the-wealth uprising that contributed to the lengthy strike and prompted key players for Buffalo, Detroit, and the Giants to hold out for more money before the strike. Rookie linebacker Tom Cousineau of Cleveland signed a five-year contract worth a reported $3.5 million, the most lucrative in NFL history.

Fans voted against both players and management late in the season. Dramatic increases in no-shows and unsold tickets climaxed with a season-ending game at Kansas City, where 56,671 tickets were unsold and the attendance of 11,902 was the second-lowest in modern NFL history.

As the year ended, the NFL's first U.S. competition in nearly eight years was preparing to begin its first season in March 1983 with network television backing. The United States Football League had 12 franchises: in Birmingham, Ala.; Boston; Chicago; Denver, Colo.; Los Angeles; Philadelphia; Tampa, Fla.; Washington, D.C.; Oakland,

Calif.; suburban Phoenix, Ariz.; Detroit; and New York–New Jersey.

COLLEGE. Pennsylvania State University won the national collegiate football championship on Jan. 1, 1983, by defeating the University of Georgia 27–23 in the Sugar Bowl game at New Orleans. Georgia, the Southeastern Conference champion, had been the only major college team with a perfect record before the Bowl games. Its star junior halfback, Herschel Walker, won the Heisman Trophy, honouring the best college player. Walker's 1,752 yd rushing ranked second in the National Collegiate Athletic Association's (NCAA's) Division 1-A, and he finished his third season just 824 yd short of the four-year career rushing record.

Penn State's national championship with a record of 11 victories and one defeat was the first for Joe Paterno, named college football's coach of the year in his 17th season at Penn State. Paterno's teams had finished lower in the polls despite perfect records in three previous seasons, and so he could understand the claim of Southern Methodist University that SMU should be champion because its record was 11 victories, no defeats, and 1 tie. However, Penn State won its 1982 championship on the same basis that it had lost earlier ones—it played the stronger schedule, including six Bowl teams.

Southern Methodist, the Southwest Conference champion and a 7–3 Cotton Bowl winner over Pittsburgh, ranked second. Penn State had beaten both Pittsburgh and third-ranked Nebraska, which finished 12–1 with a 21–20 Orange Bowl victory against Louisiana State. Georgia (11–1) ranked fourth.

The other top ten teams in the Associated Press writers' poll were, in order: UCLA (10–1–1), Arizona State (10–2), Washington (10–2), Clemson (9–1–1), Arkansas (9–2–1), and Pittsburgh (9–3). The coaches voting in the United Press International poll omitted Clemson, the Atlantic Coast Confer-

Table III.
NFL Final Standings and Play-offs, 1982

AMERICAN CONFERENCE

	W	L	T
* Los Angeles Raiders	8	1	0
* Miami	7	2	0
* Cincinnati	7	2	0
* Pittsburgh	6	3	0
* San Diego	6	3	0
* New York Jets	6	3	0
* New England	5	4	0
* Cleveland	4	5	0
Buffalo	4	5	0
Seattle	4	5	0
Kansas City	3	6	0
Denver	2	7	0
Houston	1	8	0
Baltimore	0	8	1

NATIONAL CONFERENCE

	W	L	T
* Washington	8	1	0
* Dallas	6	3	0
* Green Bay	5	3	1
* Atlanta	5	4	0
* Tampa Bay	5	4	0
* St. Louis	5	4	0
* Minnesota	5	4	0
* Detroit	4	5	0
New York Giants	4	5	0
New Orleans	4	5	0
San Francisco	3	6	0
Philadelphia	3	6	0
Chicago	3	6	0
Los Angeles Rams	2	7	0

*Qualified for play-offs.

NFL Play-offs
First round
Los Angeles Raiders 27, Cleveland 10
Miami 28, New England 13
New York Jets 44, Cincinnati 17
Dallas 30, Tampa Bay 17
Washington 31, Detroit 7
Green Bay 41, St. Louis 16
San Diego 31, Pittsburgh 28
Minnesota 30, Atlanta 24
Second round
Miami 34, San Diego 13
New York Jets 17, Los Angeles Raiders 14
Dallas 37, Green Bay 26
Washington 21, Minnesota 7
AFC Championship
Miami 14, New York Jets 0
NFC Championship
Washington 31, Dallas 17
Super Bowl
Washington 27, Miami 17

Penn State was judged national collegiate champion after defeating Georgia 27–23 in the Sugar Bowl at New Orleans. In photo Penn State's Gregg Garrity catches a 47-yard touchdown pass.

ence champion and defending national champion, because the NCAA had put it on probation for more than 100 rules violations, mostly involving recruiting. UPI otherwise ranked its top ten teams the same as did the AP and made Florida State (9–3) number ten.

Alabama coach Paul ("Bear") Bryant retired after 38 seasons and the most victories in college football history. Bryant's record was 323–85–17, including 232–46–9 in 25 years at Alabama. But Alabama, the only team to beat Penn State, lost three games in a row before defeating Illinois 21–15 in the Liberty Bowl, and Bryant, 69, decided that someone younger should coach the team. Ray Perkins, who resigned as coach of the NFL New York Giants, was named Bryant's successor.

Pacific Ten Conference champion UCLA defeated Big Ten champion Michigan 24–14 in the Rose Bowl. Other conference champions were: Montana in the Big Sky; Fresno State in the Pacific Coast Athletic; Brigham Young in the Western Athletic; Tulsa in the Missouri Valley; Bowling Green State in the Mid-American; Furman in the Southern; Louisiana Tech in the Southland; Jackson State in the Southwestern; and Harvard, Dartmouth, and Penn sharing the Ivy League crown.

Nebraska was the national leader in total offense (518 yd per game), rushing offense (394 yd per game), and scoring (41 points per game). Its centre, Dave Rimington, became the first player ever to win a second Outland Trophy, honouring the best collegiate lineman. Long Beach State led the country in passing offense with 327 yd per game, and its quarterback, Todd Dillon, was the individual leader with 3,587 yd of total offense.

Other individual statistical leaders included Ernest Anderson of Oklahoma State with 1,877 yd rushing; Tom Ramsey of UCLA with a passer rating of 153.5; Wayne Peace of Florida with a pass completion percentage of .707; Henry Ellard of Fresno State with 1,510 yd and 15 touchdowns on pass receptions; Greg Allen of Florida State with 21 touchdowns and 126 points; Paul Woodside of West Virginia with 28 field goals; Terry Hoage of Geor-

gia with 12 interceptions; Chuck Nelson of Washington with a record field-goal percentage of .962; Carl Monroe of Utah with a 30.1-yd kickoff return average and 2,036 yd on rushes, pass receptions, and kick returns; Reggie Roby of Iowa with a 48.1-yd punting average; and Lionel James of Auburn with a 15.8-yd punt return average.

Arizona State's defense gave up the fewest yards (229 per game), and its 11.3-point scoring yield was second to the average of 10.5 by Arkansas. Missouri had the leading pass defense, and Virginia Tech the best rushing defense.

Canadian Football. The Edmonton Eskimos extended their record of Canadian Football League (CFL) championships to five when they defeated the Toronto Argonauts 32–16 for the Grey Cup on November 28 at Toronto. The Eskimos won ten consecutive games after lounging in last place of the Western Division with a midseason record of 3–5. The Argonauts improved from 2–14 the previous season to win the Eastern Division with a regular-season record of 9–6–1 behind rookie coach Bob O'Billovich and quarterback Conredge Holloway, named the league's most outstanding player.

Edmonton quarterback Warren Moon set a CFL record with 5,000 yd passing, led the league with 36 touchdown passes, and won his second award in three years as the outstanding offensive player in the Grey Cup game. Also for Edmonton, linebacker James Parker led the league with 17½ quarterback sacks and was named its most outstanding defensive player, and Dave Cutler led the league with 170 points.

Joey Walters of Saskatchewan set a CFL record with 101 pass receptions and led the league with 1,670 yd on receptions. Hamilton running back Rocky DiPietro was named most outstanding Canadian player. Ottawa had three award winners: Rudy Phillips was most outstanding offensive lineman; quarterback Chris Isaacs was rookie of the year; and Alvin Walker led the league with 1,141 yd rushing and 18 touchdowns.

(KEVIN M. LAMB)

Foreign Aid:
see Economy, World

Foreign Exchange:
see Economy, World

France

A republic of Western Europe, France is bounded by the English Channel, Belgium, Luxembourg, West Germany, Switzerland, Italy, the Mediterranean Sea, Monaco, Spain, Andorra, and the Atlantic Ocean. Area: 544,000 sq km (210,040 sq mi), including Corsica. Pop. (1982 prelim.): 54,257,300. Cap. and largest city: Paris (pop., 1982 prelim., 2,168,300). Language: French. Religion: predominantly Roman Catholic. President in 1982, François Mitterrand; premier, Pierre Mauroy.

Domestic Affairs. The "honeymoon" period that marked the start of Pres. François Mitterrand's term of office was followed in 1982 by a deterioration in the political and economic situation. This led to a notable success for the conservative opposition in the spring cantonal elections and a second devaluation of the franc, resulting in the adoption of austerity policies by the Socialist government.

The government's success in carrying its nationalization bill was the major event of the start of Mitterrand's seven-year term. In February the Constitutional Council rejected the opposition's petition and declared that the bill was consistent with the constitution; it was published two days later in the *Journal Officiel*, thus becoming law. Accordingly, the state found itself in control of a public sector the extent of which was unequaled in the West. It managed 75% of credits and deposits in the banking system, held 29% of industrial turnover, exerted its influence in 3,500 firms or industrial concerns, and employed 23% of industrial wage-earners. In mid-February the Cabinet appointed "general administrators" (in effect, managing directors) of the 5 nationalized industrial groups, the 2 financial companies and the 18 banks. Nonetheless, Mitterrand declared that "National enterprises must have complete executive autonomy and autonomy in decision-making."

Also in the economic field, Soyouz Gas Export and Gaz de France signed an agreement in Paris for the annual delivery to France of 8,000,000,000 cu m of gas over a period of 25 years. beginning in 1984. This would make France dependent on the U.S.S.R. for some 35% of its gas. After two years of negotiation, a third Franco-Algerian agreement on gas was signed in early February. From 1983 on, France was to receive 9,150,000,000 cu m of Algerian gas annually at a price slightly above that on the world market. Later in the year, relations between Paris and Algiers received further stimulus with the conclusion of contracts to extend technical and economic cooperation.

Despite the enactment of a statute reducing the workweek from 40 to 39 hours and introducing a standard five weeks' paid vacation, there were tensions in the government's relations with the trade unions, and the number of strikes increased. The government was confronted with discontented white-collar workers, angry farmers, impatient trade unionists, and restless Socialists. Farmers protested over the level of subsidy being offered by the Ministry of Agriculture, headed by Edith Cresson (*see* BIOGRAPHIES). The situation on the industrial front deteriorated, with factory occupations and sometimes violent clashes between strikers and nonstrikers. In addition, the confrontation between the two main trade union confederations, the Confédération Général du Travail (CGT) and the Confédération Française Démocratique du Travail (CFDT), intensified; there was a break in relations between the two unions, which had been drifting apart since 1980.

In this hostile climate, the Socialist government suffered some stunning political defeats. In January four by-elections (one in the Marne, one in Siene-et-Marne, and two in Paris) were all won by the opposition. Moreover, the candidates put up or supported by the Socialist Party (PS) signally failed to collect all the left-wing votes.

In the cantonal elections on March 14 and 21 to fill half the seats on the *conseils généraux*, the final results appeared to be an undeniable defeat for Mitterrand and the government. The first round gave a majority of votes (51.5%) to the major opposition parties, the Rassemblement pour la République (RPR) and the Union pour la Démocratie Française (UDF), while the majority parties, the PS, the Left Radicals (MRG), the Communist Party

France

FRANCE

Education. (1980–81) Primary, pupils 4,609,422, teachers 235,415; secondary, pupils 5,183,341, teachers 349,743; vocational (1979–80), pupils 1,089,439, teachers 60,239; higher (universities only), students 853,532, teaching staff (1978–79) 41,978.

Finance. Monetary unit: franc, with (Sept. 20, 1982) a free rate of Fr 7.05 to U.S. $1 (Fr 12.09 = £1 sterling). Gold and other reserves (June 1982) U.S. $18,307,000,000. Budget (total; 1981 actual): revenue Fr 683.4 billion; expenditure Fr 716.1 billion. Gross domestic product (1981) Fr 3,096,900,000,000. Money supply (April 1982) Fr 762 billion. Cost of living (1975 = 100; June 1982) 208.9.

Foreign Trade. (1981) Imports Fr 654,850,000,000; exports Fr 576,660,000,000. Import sources: EEC 45% (West Germany 16%, Italy 9%, Belgium-Luxembourg 7%, The Netherlands 6%, U.K. 5%); Saudi Arabia 10%; U.S. 8%. Export destinations: EEC 46% (West Germany 14%, Italy 11%, Belgium-Luxembourg 8%, U.K. 7%); U.S 5%. Main exports: machinery 19%; food 14%; chemicals 12%; motor vehicles 11%; iron and steel 6%. Tourism (1980): visitors 30.1 million; gross receipts U.S. $8,235,000,000.

Transport and Communications. Roads (1980) 802,964 km (including 5,264 km expressways; excluding c. 700,000 km rural roads). Motor vehicles in use (1980): passenger 19,130,000; commercial 2,457,000. Railways: (1980) 33,886 km; traffic (1981) 55,670,000,000 passenger-km, freight 64,398,000,000 net ton-km. Air traffic (1981): 36,498,000,000 passenger-km; freight 2,239,400,000 net ton-km. Navigable inland waterways in regular use (1980) 6,568 km; freight traffic 12,151,000,000 ton-km. Shipping (1981): merchant vessels 100 gross tons and over 1,199; gross tonnage 11,455,033. Telephones (Jan. 1980) 22,212,000. Radio licenses (Dec. 1979) 18 million. Television licenses (Dec. 1979) 15,609,000.

Agriculture. Production (in 000; metric tons; 1981): wheat 22,782; barley c. 10,180; oats 1,754; rye 342; corn 9,100; potatoes 6,480; sorghum 320; sugar, raw value c. 5,600; rapeseed 1,023; tomatoes c. 800; cauliflowers 481; carrots 501; green peas c. 419; apples 1,840; peaches 480; wine 5,791; tobacco c. 46; milk 33,700; butter c. 530; cheese c. 1,185; beef and veal 1,984; pork 1,786; fish catch (1980) 765; timber (cu m; 1980) 30,829. Livestock (in 000; Dec. 1980): cattle 23,553; sheep 12,980; pigs 11,629; horses 317; chickens 185,965.

Industry. Index of production (1975 = 100; 1981) 114. Fuel and power (in 000; 1981): coal (metric tons) 18,583; electricity (kw-hr) 260,759,000; natural gas (cu m) 7,080,000; manufactured gas (cu m; 1978) 5,516,000. Production (in 000; metric tons; 1981): iron ore (30% metal content) 21,577; pig iron 17,911; crude steel 21,152; bauxite 1,828; aluminum 595; lead 167; zinc 280; cement 28,229; cotton yarn 214; cotton fabrics 164; wool yarn 137; man-made fibres 294; sulfuric acid 4,352; petroleum products c. 84,000; fertilizers (nutrient content; 1980–81) nitrogenous c. 1,640, phosphate c. 1,351, potash c. 1,933; passenger cars (units) 2,953; commercial vehicles (units) 473. Merchant shipping launched (100 gross tons and over; 1981) 246,000 gross tons.

(PC), and the other left-wing parties, obtained only 47.5%.

This outcome was confirmed by the second round. Final results for the 2,014 seats contested showed that—except for the far left, which took five seats for a gain of one—all the parties in the government coalition lost. The PC took 198 seats, a loss of 44; the PS took 509 seats, a loss of 5; the MRG took 61 seats, a loss of 27; and the remaining left-wing parties took 54 seats, a loss of 24. The opposition parties, on the other hand, all improved their positions. The RPR took 336 seats, a gain of 146; the UDF took 470 seats, a gain of 69; and the various right-wing parties took 380 seats, a gain of 51. The far right retained its one seat. On March 24 the *conseillers généraux* elected the presidents of their councils, and this saw a gain of two presidencies for the government majority while the opposition took ten. Of the *conseils généraux* in metropolitan France, the left now controlled 35 as against the opposition's 58.

This was the last time that the *préfets* would be responsible for summoning the *conseils généraux*. Under the March 2, 1982, law on decentralization, the *conseils généraux* were to meet at least once every three months on the initiative of their presidents. Each *préfet* read a message from Minister of the Interior and Decentralization Gaston Defferre (*see* BIOGRAPHIES) solemnly confirming the transfer of executive powers by the *préfet* to the president of the *conseil général*. The *préfet* was expected to retain his or her role as representative of the state in the *département* or region, but henceforth the presidents of the *conseils régionaux* would play a decisive part in regional affairs.

On the first anniversary of his election to the presidency, Mitterrand launched an appeal for national unity. In early June, in the second press conference of his term, he surveyed his government's achievements and outlined the second phase of his policy: the speeding up of recovery on the home front and moves to ensure the country's technological future, to carry on the work of social justice, to restore savings, and to develop the regions.

However, a few days earlier a devaluation of the franc, the second since the president took office, was announced. At their meeting on June 12 in Brussels, the finance ministers of the European Communities (EC) decided to adjust parity of four out of seven currencies in the European Monetary System. The West German mark and the Dutch guilder were revalued by 4.25% each, while the French franc and the Italian lira were devalued, the first by 5.75% and the second by 2.75%. Thus the franc was effectively devalued by some 10% against the West German currency. This adjustment was accompanied by a number of other measures, including a freeze on all wages and prices until October 31 except for producer agricultural prices, fresh food prices, and fuel prices; and the suspension of contractual clauses on wage increases and the indexing of unearned incomes.

Meanwhile, there was a minor Cabinet reshuffle. Pierre Dreyfus left his post as minister for industry because of ill health, and Nicole Questiaux left the Ministry of National Solidarity when her plan for the reorganization of social security was judged too costly. Jean-Pierre Chevènement (*see* BIOGRAPHIES) took up the portfolio of industry in addition to his post as minister of state for research and technology. Pierre Bérégovoy, until then general secretary at the Elysée, took over the national solidarity portfolio. His place at the Elysée went to Jean-Louis Bianco who, as *maître de requêtes* to the Cabinet, would be responsible for the operation of the machinery of government, while Jacques Attali remained in charge of political questions. Jean Auroux, former minister of labour, was appointed delegate minister to assist Bérégovoy. Jean Le Garrec, former secretary of state in charge of the extension of the public sector (nationalization), became a delegate minister to Premier Pierre Mauroy responsible for employment. In December the minister for cooperation and development, Jean-Pierre Cot, was replaced by Christian Nucci.

A major problem facing the government was the renewed wave of terrorist attacks in various parts of the country, especially Paris. In the Rue Marbeuf, near the Champs-Elysées, a car bomb killed or injured some 60 people and caused extensive damage, and in the Rue des Rosiers a terrorist gang opened fire in a Jewish restaurant, leaving 6 dead and many wounded. In August, after several other outrages in the capital, the government set up an antiterrorist plan involving the dissolution of the *Action directe* group and surveillance of foreign diplomats suspected of illegal activities. Other measures included the establishment of a state secretariat for public security.

Among the measures approved by the National Assembly were the government's economic and financial program; an amended bill on security and freedom; an electoral reform bill; a bill that set out to reorganize transport within France on a national basis; and a bill relating to the status of Paris, Lyon, and Marseilles. Also passed was the social security bill introduced by Bérégovoy, which represented a turning point in social and political policy because it aimed to balance the social security budget. Most French people would have to make sacrifices to achieve this goal.

Among the many acts of terrorism that occurred in France during the summer was the explosion of a car bomb in July that killed the PLO's deputy director, Fadel ad-Dani, in Paris. Hundreds of people attended his funeral.

LAURENT MAOUS—GAMMA/LIAISON

U.S. Pres. Ronald Reagan's visit to Paris was greeted on June 5 by a large crowd of hostile demonstrators carrying red flags and banners.

The debate on the 1983 finance bill in the National Assembly confirmed the government's wish to pursue a policy of austerity. Laurent Fabius's budget was marked by considerable restraint in public expenditure, the curbing of taxes, and limiting of the deficit. It represented a decisive move away from the policies of reflation and reform pursued until then and showed that the battle against inflation had become the government's primary target. To consolidate the foreign currency reserves in the Banque de France and protect the franc, the Treasury opened a credit of $4 billion (Fr 28 billion) in foreign banks. However, the poor trade figures for September—a deficit of Fr 12.2 billion for the month and Fr 73.5 billion for the first nine months of the year—led the government to consider protectionist measures to wipe out the balance of trade deficit.

The government laid down strict guidelines for the relaxation of the freeze on prices and incomes after November 1. The resulting general dissatisfaction was manifested in an unprecedented wave of strikes—especially in the automobile and steel industries and in transport—as well as various protest demonstrations. The rise in retail prices during the third quarter slowed to about 0.4%, but unemployment continued to stand at more than two million, and some price rises caused resentment in the trade unions. In a further policy reorientation, Premier Mauroy announced a lifting of the burden on employers, especially the gradual transfer, over five years, of the cost of financing family allowances from firms to households. President Mitterrand, meanwhile, made an impassioned appeal for increased business investment. Government strategy aimed to end the sliding scale of prices and wages and to consolidate the four-month freeze on both by an 18-month plan to reduce inflation to 10% in 1982 and 8% in 1983.

Foreign Affairs. Unlike domestic policy, French foreign policy under the PS government was not subject to any major change, and in fact it showed remarkable continuity in relation to that of the previous government. The Falkland Islands conflict between the U.K. and Argentina generally strengthened the solidarity of the ten members of the EC behind the U.K. However, the fact that France had supplied the Argentine Air Force with its Super-Étendard fighter planes, equipped with the Exocet missiles that caused so much damage to Royal Navy ships during the hostilities, resulted in strained relations between France and the U.K. Nevertheless, the seventh Franco-British summit took place in Paris early in November in a cordial atmosphere, and relations improved overnight after France decided to abstain in the UN vote on a Latin-American motion calling for a resumption of negotiations on the sovereignty of the Falklands. Delegations from France and the U.K. were to meet every month in an attempt to resolve contentious EC issues, notably budgetary contributions and agricultural prices.

Following several meetings between West German Chancellor Helmut Schmidt and President Mitterrand, the 40th Franco-German summit in October brought together, for the second time, the French president and the new West German chancellor, Helmut Kohl. It confirmed that cooperation remained a constant factor in the diplomacy of both countries, despite any changes in the political complexion of the governments of France and West Germany. President Mitterrand's visits to Rome, Athens, and Madrid gave him the opportunity to develop a theme dear to his heart, namely, that "there cannot be a Europe which does not include a Mediterranean dimension." France was drawing closer to Greece and Spain since those countries had also opted for Socialist regimes.

Mitterrand also went to Washington to meet Pres. Ronald Reagan; to Tokyo on the first official visit of a French president; to Denmark; to Hungary, where no French head of state had been for eight centuries; and to India. In August, when the U.S. announced that it was imposing sanctions on companies supplying hardware to the U.S.S.R. for the Soviet-European gas pipeline, the government ordered French companies to defy the ban. Sanctions were lifted in November as part of a wider agreement between the U.S. and Western Europe on the nature of East-West trade, but France immediately declared that it was not a party to the agreement.

Mitterrand's "historic" visit to Israel, another country that no French head of state had visited officially, led to mixed comments because of France's support for "the principle of a Palestinian state." With Italy and the U.S., France participated in the multinational force that went to Lebanon as part of the cease-fire agreement there. In early June the leaders of the major industrial countries met at Versailles, but with no concrete results. Mitterrand made two extensive visits to Africa during the year. In May he visited Niger, the Ivory Coast, Senegal, and Mauritania, and in October he went to Burundi, Rwanda, Zaire, and the Congo. These visits to francophone Africa left no doubt about the continuing interest of the French government in this part of the world.   (JEAN KNECHT)

See also Dependent States.

February, antigovernment tracts were distributed, supposedly by members of the clandestine Movement for National Renewal (Morena). A number of persons believed to be Morena members were arrested in mid-March but released in April.

Although the French Socialist Party was undoubtedly sympathetic toward Morena, and the French press treated Pres. Omar Bongo with scant respect, Gabon nevertheless enjoyed good relations with France. Early in the year French Premier Pierre Mauroy confirmed the grant of a large loan toward construction of the second phase (Booué to Franceville) of the trans-Gabon railway. The expanding economy was given a further boost in April by the discovery of new petroleum deposits.

Gabon also remained on good terms with its neighbours, with the exception of Cameroon. However, the resignation of Cameroon's president, Ahmadou Ahidjo, in November seemed likely to favour a reconciliation between the two states.   (PHILIPPE DECRAENE)

Gabon

The Gambia

French-Canadian Literature:
see Literature

French Guiana:
see Dependent States

French Literature:
see Literature

Friends, Religious Society of:
see Religion

Fuel and Power:
see Energy

Furniture Industry:
see Industrial Review

Furs:
see Industrial Review

Gabon

A republic of western equatorial Africa, Gabon is bounded by Equatorial Guinea, Cameroon, the Congo, and the Atlantic Ocean. Area: 267,667 sq km (103,347 sq mi). Pop. (1981 est.): 1,409,000. Cap. and largest city: Libreville (pop., 1978 est., 225,200). Language: French and Bantu dialects. Religion: traditional tribal beliefs; Christian minority. President in 1982, Omar Bongo; premier, Léon Mébiame.

Faced by a growing student protest movement, the government closed the University of Libreville from mid-December 1981 until Jan. 11, 1982, and a number of students and faculty members were arrested. During the visit of Pope John Paul II in

Gambia, The

A small republic and member of the Commonwealth, The Gambia extends from the Atlantic Ocean along the lower Gambia River in West Africa and is surrounded by Senegal. Area: 10,690 sq km (4,127 sq mi). Pop. (1982 est.): 635,000, including (1973) Malinke 37.7%; Fulani 16.2%; Wolof 14%; Dyola 8.5%; Soninke 7.8%; others 15.8%. Cap. and largest city: Banjul (pop., 1980 est., 47,700). Language: English (official), Malinke, Fulani, and Wolof. Religion: predominantly Muslim. President in 1982, Sir Dawda Jawara.

In May 1982 Pres. Sir Dawda Jawara and his People's Progressive Party won presidential and parliamentary elections in The Gambia. Sheriff Mustapha Dibba, at the time in prison accused of involvement in the 1981 coup attempt, polled 27.5% of the vote to Jawara's 72.5% in the presidential contest. This victory was seen as an endorsement of the president's policies, including the decision to form a confederation with Senegal. The merger came into effect on February 1, and in November the confederation's Council of Ministers was formed, with Jawara as deputy chairman.

The peanut (groundnut) crop for 1981–82 was almost 83,000 metric tons, nearly double the previous year's disastrous total. Tourism suffered badly

---

GABON

Education. (1981) Primary, pupils 155,081, teachers 3,281; secondary, pupils 22,005, teachers 1,088; vocational, pupils 3,465, teachers 266; teacher training (1978–79), students 2,119, teachers 120; higher (1981), students 3,878, teaching staff 231.

Finance. Monetary unit: CFA franc, with (Sept. 20, 1982) a parity of CFA Fr 50 to the French franc (free rate of CFA Fr 353 = U.S. $1; CFA Fr 605 = £1 sterling). Budget (1982 est.) balanced at CFA Fr 453.5 billion.

Foreign Trade. (1980) Imports CFA Fr 142.3 billion; exports CFA Fr 459.1 billion. Import sources (1978): France 55%; U.S. 6%. Export destinations (1978): France 25%; U.S. 20%; Argentina 11%; Brazil 8%; Gibraltar 8%; West Germany 6%; Chile 5%. Main exports (1978): crude oil 72%; manganese ore 10%; uranium and thorium ores 8%; timber 6%.

Transport and Communications. Roads (1979) 7,082 km. Motor vehicles in use (1976): passenger *c.* 17,400; commercial (including buses) *c.* 12,700. Railways (1979) *c.* 185 km. Air traffic (1980): *c.* 374 million passenger-km; freight *c.* 27.3 million net ton-km. Telephones (Jan. 1980) 11,600. Radio receivers (Dec. 1979) 96,000. Television receivers (Dec. 1979) 9,000.

Agriculture. Production (in 000; metric tons; 1981): cassava *c.* 100; corn *c.* 10; peanuts *c.* 7; bananas *c.* 8; plantains *c.* 63; palm oil *c.* 2; cocoa *c.* 4; timber (cu m; 1980) *c.* 2,312. Livestock (in 000; 1981): cattle *c.* 4; pigs *c.* 7; sheep *c.* 100; goats *c.* 90.

Industry. Production (in 000; metric tons; 1981): crude oil 7,654; natural gas (cu m) 60,000; uranium (metal content) 1.1; manganese ore (metal content) 1,015; petroleum products (1979) *c.* 1,510; electricity (kw-hr; 1980) 450,000.

GAMBIA, THE

Education. (1979–80) Primary, pupils 37,468, teachers 1,377; secondary, pupils 8,314, teachers 457; vocational, pupils 371, teachers 51; teacher training, students 255, teachers 29.

Finance. Monetary unit: dalasi, with (Sept. 20, 1982) a free rate of 2.33 dalasis to U.S. $1 (par value of 4 dalasis = £1 sterling). Budget (1980–81 actual): revenue 85 million dalasis; expenditure 97 million dalasis.

Foreign Trade. (1981) Imports 243,690,000 dalasis; exports 51,460,000 dalasis. Import sources (1979–80): U.K. 25%; China 16%; France 9%; The Netherlands 8%; West Germany 7%. Export destinations (1979–80): The Netherlands 24%; U.K. 18%; Italy 16%; Belgium-Luxembourg 7%; Switzerland 6%; France 5%. Main exports (1979–80): peanuts and byproducts 67%; fish 8%.

during 1982, partly as a result of adverse publicity following the coup attempt. The International Monetary Fund agreed to give a standby credit for 16.9 million SDR's to help pay for imports.

The July budget revealed that real gross domestic product in 1981–82 increased by 8.9% over the previous year, while inflation declined slightly to 7.9%. A major development for the port at Banjul was to be financed by loans from the World Bank, the African Development Bank, and the Islamic Development Bank. (GUY ARNOLD)

Gambling

In the United States casino gambling at Atlantic City, N.J., flourished in 1982 despite the recession. Though the city had only nine casinos and one-fifth the casino floor space of Las Vegas, Nev., gambling during the summer produced $446.5 million in revenues. This was 24% more than in the previous summer and only slightly less than the $455 million generated by the Las Vegas casinos during the same period. During October Atlantic City's revenues were 39% higher than in October 1981. By contrast, growth in the Nevada casinos slowed for the first time in 25 years. Observers attributed Atlantic City's comparative success to the fact that most of its customers were day-trippers and did not have to pay for overnight lodging as was generally the case in Nevada.

In a statewide referendum in September Oklahoma voters approved parimutuel betting on horse races and thus became the 32nd state to allow that form of gambling. The District of Columbia in August inaugurated a lottery, thus joining 15 states that had done so in previous years. Later in 1982 Colorado and Washington followed suit. Officials in Arizona announced in March that sales during the first six months of the state's lottery totaled $71 million, double the amount that had been expected. In general, states were promoting increased sales by replacing their relatively infrequent and high-priced games with daily contests and instant "rub-off" tickets selling for 50 cents to $1.

The gambling boom enjoyed by London bookmakers and casino operators during the late 1970s was finally laid to rest in 1982, many of the most familiar and popular casinos having lost their licenses. During 1982 the recession hit firmly in the betting office business, with static turnovers and rising overhead costs forcing many shops to close. This industry, once so profitable, was struggling for survival, and it seemed inevitable that some rural areas would be without betting facilities in the near future. The four major bookmakers, Ladbrokes, Mecca, William Hill, and Coral, increased their share of betting offices to approximately one-third of the total. The prohibitive level of betting tax charged by the government, coupled with the betting levy, gave rise to a large increase in illegal gambling.

In racing circles 1982 became known as the "Year of the Knockout." This practice evolved when, because of lack of money at the racetracks, the "on-course" betting offices were manipulated. The "knockout," artificially lengthening the odds

on favoured horses that were backed off course to win and place, was conducted by certain unscrupulous on-course bookmakers. The powerful betting office chains were affected to such an extent that changes were made in their rules, and discussions on a new system of starting price returns were held.

During 1982 the sale of lottery tickets showed a marked decline, with local authorities and football clubs turning to other means of obtaining a cash influx. Revenue from football pools, however, seemed to be keeping pace with inflation. Bingo, which in 1981 attracted stakes totaling £472.5 million, suffered a tax increase from 7½ to 10%; duty paid in the year to March 31, 1982, was estimated at £39 million. A new trend was the "free bingo" started by several popular newspapers, offering prize money totaling nearly £1 million.

(DAVID R. CALHOUN; ROBERT M. POOLE)

Games and Toys

The major growth segment of the toy market in 1982 was electronics, and during the year there was a significant trend in the U.S. toward video games. The coin-operated electronic arcade games, which throughout the U.S. had been satisfying youngsters' need for a place to congregate, paved the way for the rapid development of home games of the same kind. But the video games market was very different from the battery-operated, hand-held games market because, unlike the latter, it was not predominantly concerned with products designed to amuse children. As a result, in the U.S. the growth of video games brought the greatest sales benefits not to the specialty toy shops but to the electronic stores, and the same pattern was developing in the U.K. and other European countries. Understandably, there was some reluctance on the part of toy stores to deal in the hardware of electronic games, mainly because of the lower than usual profit margins. Furthermore, since adults

Monopoly, a game that has been around since 1934 and has sold 80 million sets, has finally gone electronic. An electronic accessory rolls the dice and keeps track of property ownership.

COURTESY, PARKER BROTHERS, INC.

were the main purchasers of these items, manufacturers were distributing their products to retail outlets that could provide good demonstration facilities and electronics know-how.

The importance of the growth of video games was emphasized during the year when two major U.S. manufacturers entered the field for the first time. CBS Inc. unveiled plans to market, through its subsidiary Gabriel Industries, Inc., home versions of Bally Manufacturing Corp. arcade games. CBS then followed this by purchasing Ideal Toy Corp., which had outlets for video games in the U.K., France, and West Germany, and merged Ideal with Gabriel Industries. In another development Quaker Oats Co., the parent company of Fisher-Price Toys, acquired the home video games assets of the U.S. Games Corp.

Solar power came to the toy field in 1982 through the enterprise of the Bandai group of Japan. The company evolved a line of hand-held electronic games that operated when exposed to the Sun or to any normal electric light. In the U.K. the Mettoy Company Ltd., the manufacturers of Corgi diecast toys, launched a family computer in midyear. This surprising move by a leading British toy company was further evidence that the toy industry was coming to grips with the needs of the modern market. Traditional toys were ceasing to be of interest to children at a much earlier age. In elementary school they were using computers, and Mettoy decided that a home computer, when added to its traditional toy products, spanned the age spectrum of consumers and would be a family purchase with year-round sales potential.

In June Lesney Products & Co. Ltd., the British-owned Matchbox toys group, went into receivership. The company owed £25 million to the British banks and a further £10 million to trade creditors. In addition, its overseas marketing subsidiaries had £10 million in bank loans. Many companies were involved in the possible purchase of the Matchbox firm, whose brand name was a world leader in the field of diecast toys. Eventually the company was acquired by Universal International (Holdings) Ltd. of Hong Kong. The new owners quickly announced the closing of one of the two Matchbox factories. Universal International also acquired subsidiary companies of the former Lesney group operating in France, West Germany, and Australia.

Much of the financial difficulty experienced in recent years by the toy industry had been due to the uneven pattern of business, which in the majority of countries continued to be heavily concentrated in the Christmas gift-buying season. In an effort to alter this pattern, trade associations representing toy manufacturers, wholesalers, retailers, and importers in the U.K. carried out an experiment in 1982. They launched a pilot scheme in northern England under the title "Give a toy at Easter." The promotion was widely advertised in the chosen area and achieved sufficient success to warrant the holding of a fully national promotion in the U.K. in 1983.

Rubik's Cube, the best-selling toy of 1981, declined in popularity in 1982. Taking its place along with video games were dolls and toys based on the successful motion picture *E.T. The Extra-Terrestrial.*

In September the European Parliament called on European Community governments to ban war toys. The European MP's voted 82 to 45 in favour of a resolution recommending progressive reduction in the manufacture and sale of such toys and their replacement by toys that were "constructive and develop creativity." The governments of the member countries of the Community planned to consider the resolution. The International Committee of Toy Industries (ICTI), meeting in Montreal in April, agreed to set up a committee to examine all current advertising standards in its 11 member countries. Canada had proposed that ICTI members should adopt and then observe a voluntary international standard for advertising directed toward children. The ICTI had already achieved a measure of success in harmonizing safety standards for toys throughout the world.

(THEODORE V. THOMAS)

[452.B.6; 452.C–D]

Gardening

The number of U.S. households engaged in gardening has generally paralleled changes in the Consumer Price Index for food, with a one- to two-year lag. According to surveys by Gardens for All, a national nonprofit gardening association, 47% of the nation's households, or 38 million, grew some or all of their own vegetables. This represented a gain of one million households a year. Of these gardeners, 51% were between the ages of 18 and 29, and more than half lived in the Midwest and South, although the West was the fastest growing area. Tomatoes were the most popular garden vegetable in all regions. About 15 million households indicated that they would like to garden if they had land, and 52% of them would support community gardening programs.

Lack of space did not deter many households from growing plants of some kind; over 76.4% of U.S. households with members in the 25 to 49 age group had indoor plants. The growing trend toward the use of plants in commercial and public areas had spawned a new industry called interior plantscaping. Among the most popular indoor foliage plants were palms, *Schefflera, Dracaena, Ficus,* Chinese evergreens, peace lilies, and Norfolk Island pines, but flowering houseplants were gaining in popularity.

Outdoor bedding plants continued to win favour with home gardeners, who found that these seedlings were good shortcuts to instant garden displays. Geraniums, grown primarily from seed by commercial growers, showed a 14% rise in sales. Tissue culture or test-tube production of perennials increased the availability of these relatively permanent summer flowers. Garden centres and mail-order catalogs had stimulated interest in these plants, as well as renewed interest in home fruit orchards and berry patches. Most mail-order sources reported sales increases of up to 33%. With the housing market depressed, many homeowners were revamping their old houses, a process that often included the redesigning of old landscapes

Community gardening plots such as this one in New York City turned unpromising urban wasteland into sources of produce, pride, and even profit for growing numbers of city dwellers.

with renovation plantings. The most important plants for this purpose were dwarf or low-growing evergreens, longer-lasting lawn-grass mixtures, and the smaller-sized flowering trees.

In the continuing battle against the gypsy moth, which destroyed more than 4.8 million ha (12 million ac) of forest and residential trees and shrubs in 21 states and Canada during the year, progress was reported in the use of biological controls. Several parasitic wasps were proving effective in attacking the moth larvae; one species imported from the Kulu Valley in India had excellent prospects since it multiplies rapidly and is harmless to humans. The synthetic sex attractant or pheromone Disparlure was also being integrated successfully into pest management.

A herbicide for the control of a pernicious perennial weed, couch grass (Agropyron repens), was introduced in the U.K. in small packs for amateur gardeners. The active ingredient, alloxydim-sodium, acts systemically and will control the weed without damaging most ornamental plants. Fire blight, a serious bacterial disease of pears and apples in some parts of the U.K., also attacks ornamental plants in the same botanical family, such as hawthorn and rowan, and these plants in small gardens may form a source of infection for commercial orchards. Suitable control measures had not yet been developed, but it was hoped that a forecasting method would be established.

In the annual all-Europe seed trials (Fleuroselect), the 1983 award and bronze medal went to the F_1 hybrid grandiflora petunia Red Picotee, which was raised in Japan (T. Sakata & Son of Yokohama). The flower is dark red with a white margin and measures about three inches across

when wide open. (It also won a 1983 bronze medal in the All-America seed trials.) At the Royal National Rose Society's trials in the U.K., the President's International Trophy for the best new rose and a gold medal went to a blood red, cluster-flowered seedling (tentatively called Korpeana), raised in West Germany by W. Kordes and Son.

The use of micropropagation techniques (increasing plants vegetatively from very small parts, such as buds) for roses received considerable publicity in 1982. One firm in the U.K. multiplied a miniature rose by micropropagation to produce a large quantity of plants for marketing. Another firm was using the technique for several rose varieties, although it is known that not every variety will grow satisfactorily on its own roots. Some 20 varieties of large flowered and cluster-flowered roses were grown from bud to salable plant in 21 months, and larger-scale trials were in progress with eight varieties. The main advantage for the gardener is that roses propagated by this method produce no unwanted suckers from the roots.

(JOAN LEE FAUST; ELSPETH NAPIER)

See also Agriculture and Food Supplies Environment; Life Sciences.
[355.C.2–3; 731.B.1]

German Democratic Republic

German Democratic Republic

A country of central Europe, Germany was partitioned after World War II into the Federal Republic of Germany (Bundesrepublik Deutschland; West Germany) and the German Democratic Republic (Deutsche Demokratische Republik; East Germany), with a special provisional regime for Berlin. East Germany is bordered by the Baltic Sea, Poland, Czechoslovakia, and West Germany. Area: 108,333 sq km (41,827 sq mi). Pop. (1981 est.): 16,736,000. Cap. and largest city: East Berlin (pop., 1981 est., 1,152,500). Language: German. Religion (1969 est.): Protestant 80%; Roman Catholic 10%. General secretary of the Socialist Unity (Communist) Party and chairman of the Council of State in 1982, Erich Honecker; chairman of the Council of Ministers (premier). Willi Stoph.

The East German people increasingly felt the pinch of the world economic recession during 1982. There were severe shortages of food items, including meat, butter, and cheese. Reports of a drop in morale and falling production came from various parts of the country. Lack of foreign currency caused a sharp cutback in imports of vital components for industry, and in some sectors short-time working had to be introduced. Dissatisfaction was frankly voiced at meetings of works councils and of local branches of the Socialist Unity (Communist) Party.

In March the East German Parliament adopted a law regulating the use of firearms by East German border guards. It did not, however, make them less trigger-happy. The ink was hardly dry on the statute book when an East German farmer, trying to escape across the demarcation line into the West German state of Hesse, was shot and killed. Since

Garment Industry:
see Fashion and Dress

Gas Industry:
see Energy

Gemstones:
see Industrial Review

Genetics:
see Life Sciences

Geochemistry:
see Earth Sciences

Geology:
see Earth Sciences

Geophysics:
see Earth Sciences

Polish Premier Gen. Wojciech Jaruzelski (right) arrived in East Berlin on March 29 for a one-day visit at the invitation of East Germany's leader, Erich Honecker.

approaching shortage of recruits, a consequence of the introduction of the contraceptive pill. Should mobilization be necessary, the law provided for the call-up of women between the ages of 18 and 50. Otherwise, the new legislation was not expected to cause much change in East German life, already firmly militarized. The subject of defense had been introduced into East German schools in 1979, and paramilitary units at factories had existed for three decades. One of the purposes of the legislation was to counter the propaganda of the burgeoning peace movement. The "Swords into Plowshares" badges were declared illegal by the government.

In a leading article headed "No to Nuclear Madness," the Communist Party newspaper, *Neues Deutschland*, expressed sympathy for the hundreds of thousands of people in Western Europe who were standing up for the elementary right to life and peace. A demonstration of 50,000 people in Potsdam in October protested against NATO nuclear rearmament. But the authorities said nothing about the peace movement, centred in the churches, which was campaigning against the nuclear buildup in both East and West. In addition, young Christians were demanding recognition of conscientious objectors and introduction of a period of social service as an alternative to conscription. Western observers believed that the situation in Poland was bound to preclude any liberalization in neighbouring East Germany.

Restrictions were placed on travel to the Warsaw Pact countries for the first time in many years. Journeys to Poland were banned, except for those necessitated by urgent business. At the same time, propaganda against the West was stepped up. In the political sparring match between East and West Germany, the East Germans appeared to be winning with ease. The East German leadership was convinced that the division of Germany would be finally sealed only when the number of East Germans with relatives and friends in West Germany was reduced from several million to a few thousand.

The West German government had no success in persuading East Germany to reduce the compulsory currency-exchange fee imposed on Westerners entering East Germany. This had been tripled in October 1980, with the effect that the East German authorities managed to achieve a 40% drop in

1961 at least 180 East Germans had died attempting to reach West Germany. In spirit and practice the law changed nothing. All that had happened was that the Army's orders concerning the "protection" of the border were now enshrined in a parliamentary act similar, it was claimed, to the border regulations of many other countries. The motive was not clear, but it was assumed that East Germany wished to demonstrate that it was a *Rechtsstaat*, a state based on the rule of law.

The people's Parliament also passed a law obliging schools, universities, factories, and all state organizations to ensure that the "citizen is prepared for defensive service." One of the reasons the law was needed, according to Gen. Heinz Hoffmann, the defense minister, was that in a crisis the strength of U.S. forces in West Germany, at the time numbering 230,000, could be increased to 480,000. In a reference to those young East Germans who wore badges inscribed with the peace slogan "Swords into Plowshares," Hoffmann said, "Much as we would like to scrap our weapons one day, socialism and peace still require plowshares *and* swords."

Contrary to expectations, the East German government decided not to extend the period of conscription beyond 18 months. Instead, reservists were to fill the gaps in the ranks caused by an

GERMAN DEMOCRATIC REPUBLIC

Education. (1980–81) Primary and secondary, pupils 2,250,918, teachers 168,849; vocational, pupils 459,485, teachers 16,355; higher (1978–79), students 385,600, teaching staff 36,773.

Finance. Monetary unit: Mark of Deutsche Demokratische Republik, with (Sept. 20, 1982) a free rate of M 2.50 to U.S. $1 (M 4.28 = £1 sterling). Budget (1980 est.): revenue M 160,652,000,000; expenditure M 160,283,000,000. Net material product (at 1975 prices; 1980) M 173.9 billion.

Foreign Trade. (1980) Imports M 62,970,000,000; exports M 57,131,000,000. Import sources (1979): U.S.S.R. c. 36%; Czechoslovakia c. 7%; Poland c. 7%; West Germany c. 6%; Hungary c. 6%. Export destinations (1979): U.S.S.R. c. 36%; Czechoslovakia c. 9%; Poland c. 8%; West Germany c. 6%; Hungary

c. 6%. Main exports (1975): machinery 37%; transport equipment 12% (ships 5%); chemicals; textiles.

Transport and Communications. Roads (1980) c. 119,000 km (including 1,687 km autobahns). Motor vehicles in use (1980): passenger 2,677,703; commercial 234,148. Railways: (1980) 14,248 km (including 1,695 km electrified); traffic (1981) 23,027,000,000 passenger-km, freight 55,824,000,000 net ton-km. Air traffic (1979): 1,848,000,000 passenger-km; freight 67.3 million net ton-km. Navigable inland waterways in regular use (1980) 2,302 km; goods traffic 2,159,000,000 ton-km. Shipping (1981): merchant vessels 100 gross tons and over 449; gross tonnage 1,570,158. Telephones (Jan. 1980) 3,071,500. Radio licenses (Dec. 1979) 6,288,-000. Television licenses (Dec. 1979) 5,634,000.

Agriculture. Production (in 000; metric tons; 1981): wheat c. 3,000; barley c. 3,800; rye c. 1,800; cabbages c. 337; rapeseed c. 330; apples c. 522; pork c. 1,370; beef and veal c. 417; fish catch (1980) 235. Livestock (in 000; Dec. 1980): cattle 5,722; sheep 2,038; pigs 12,871; goats 24; poultry 51,611.

Industry. Index of production (1975 = 100; 1981) 133. Production (in 000; metric tons; 1981): cement 12,204; lignite (1980) 258,000; electricity (kw-hr; 1980) 98,800,000; iron ore (39% metal content) 51; pig iron 2,440; crude steel 7,466; sulfuric acid (1980) 958; petroleum products (1979) c. 19,600; fertilizers (nutrient content; 1980) nitrogenous 943, phosphate 370, potash 3,422; synthetic rubber (1980) 170; man-made fibres (1979) 292; passenger cars (units) 180; commercial vehicles (units) 41.

the number of Westerners visiting relatives and friends while maintaining the amount of hard currency derived from the border traffic. Far from being moved by West German ultimatums, the East German Communist leader, Erich Honecker, let it be known that he would respond to West German toughness by administering a further dose of *Abgrenzung*, making the demarcation line still less permeable. Clearly, Honecker was worried about the spread of the Polish sickness and about the possible repercussions of the East German peace movement. When Poland's leader, Gen. Wojciech Jaruzelski, went to East Berlin in March, Honecker expressed support for his martial-law policies.

(NORMAN CROSSLAND)

Germany, Federal Republic of

A country of central Europe, Germany was partitioned after World War II into the Federal Republic of Germany (Bundesrepublik Deutschland; West Germany) and the German Democratic Republic (Deutsche Demokratische Republik; East Germany), with a special provisional regime for Berlin. West Germany is bordered by Denmark, The Netherlands, Belgium, Luxembourg, France, Switzerland, Austria, Czechoslovakia, East Germany, and the North Sea. Area: 248,667 sq km (96,011 sq mi). Pop. (1982 est.): 61,713,000. Provisional cap.: Bonn (pop., 1981 est., 288,100). Largest city: Hamburg (pop., 1981 est., 1,645,100). (West Berlin, which is an enclave within East Germany, had a population of 1,896,200 in 1981.) Language: German. Religion (1970): Protestant 49%; Roman Catholic 44.6%; Jewish 0.05%. President in 1982, Karl Carstens; chancellors, Helmut Schmidt and, from October 1, Helmut Kohl.

The year 1982 proved to be one of change in West Germany. A steady deterioration of relations between the government coalition partners, the Social Democratic Party (SPD) and the liberal Free Democratic Party (FDP), reached a dramatic climax on September 17. In a statement to the Bundestag the federal chancellor, Helmut Schmidt, made it clear that he could no longer cooperate with the Free Democrats, whom he accused of plotting to switch support to the Christian Democratic Union (CDU) and its Bavarian wing, the Christian Social Union (CSU). The Free Democrats thereupon resigned from Schmidt's government and joined forces with the CDU–CSU. On October 1 Schmidt was replaced as chancellor by the CDU chairman, Helmut Kohl (*see* BIOGRAPHIES).

Domestic Affairs. The SPD–FDP alliance had endured since 1969, with Schmidt succeeding Willy Brandt as head of the alliance and chancellor in 1974. At the 1980 federal election it was returned with an increased majority of 45 seats, compared with only 10 in the previous Bundestag. All seemed set for another stable four-year term in office. But decay set in rapidly. The Social Democrats, divided over defense policy and bearing the brunt of the blame for the country's economic malaise, suffered an alarming loss of public support.

The Free Democrats, who had always lived in fear of their parliamentary lives, were confronted with the prospect of going down with a sinking ship. Moreover, genuine political differences between the two parties became increasingly evident as the government got down to the task of balancing the federal budget in a period of economic recession.

By mid-1981 the chairman of the FDP, Hans-Dietrich Genscher, had begun to talk of an approaching "turning point" in German politics, and thereafter there was constant speculation as to whether the coalition would stay the course. The SPD failed to retain its absolute majority in elections to Hamburg's state parliament in early June 1982. On June 17 the Free Democrats in the Hesse state assembly took a decision that was bound to have far-reaching consequences: they undertook to join a coalition with the CDU should the state election on September 26 make this feasible. Clearly, this represented an important nail in the coffin of the federal government, although immediately after it was hammered home the Schmidt coalition survived yet another crisis. After long and nervous negotiations, the two parties reached a compromise on the outline of the 1983 federal budget.

Matters came to a head quickly after the summer recess. A memorandum presented in early September by the Free Democrat minister of economics, Count Otto Graf Lambsdorff, was widely interpreted as a statement of grounds for divorce. The minister's strategy for restoring economic growth and combating unemployment contained proposals for severe cuts in social welfare and was obviously unacceptable to the SPD. In background conversations with journalists, Genscher made no secret of his party's intention to leave the coalition;

Federal Republic of Germany

Signs protesting the deployment of U.S. nuclear weapons in West Germany began appearing in that country during the spring.

JEAN GUICHARD—SYGMA

German Literature: *see* Literature

the only question was when. The ideal time for the FDP leadership was after the Hesse election and after the FDP conference in West Berlin in November. Genscher's idea was that a majority of delegates would vote for a change of coalition partners once it was clear that the old coalition could not agree on economic and financial policy.

However, the chancellor decided to launch a preemptive strike, and in his state of the nation speech on September 9 he challenged Kohl to try to topple the government with a constitutional lever known as a constructive vote of no confidence. Under the constitution, which was designed to promote political stability, the federal Parliament could express its lack of confidence in the chancellor only if a majority of its members agreed on a successor. Schmidt could be replaced by Kohl if the FDP switched horses in midstream. But Kohl at this stage was not taking the risk, although he knew that he could already count on the support of a good many Free Democrats. He rejected Schmidt's challenge, suggesting instead that the chancellor resign. Schmidt replied that he had no intention of resigning or of trying to soldier on as head of a minority government. Should the opposition assume power on the strength of a parliamentary vote, he added, the new government would have to pave the way for an early election, since a change of administration by this means would require the sanction of the people.

In his statement to the Bundestag on September 17, Schmidt reported that doubts about the intentions of the Free Democrats had grown daily. The chancellor remained convinced that his party and the FDP still had much in common. However, he added, the Lambsdorff memorandum had indeed marked a turning point—from the concept of a socially caring state to that of an "elbowing society." The period of uncertainty could not continue. "In the interest of our country, of our democratic system of government, and of the Social Democrat coalition partner, I can no longer tolerate any further damage to the effectiveness and the reputation of the federal government." The chancellor repeated his demand for new elections, although he admitted that his party was in poor shape to contest them.

The chancellor's appeal for an immediate decision was again refused. The Free Democrats left the coalition and opened negotiations with the CDU–CSU, while Schmidt carried on as head of a minority government. However, Genscher's eagerness for a change of partner caused a deep rift in his party. In the Hesse election the charge of treachery leveled at the Free Democrats stuck; they polled a derisory 3.1%, below the minimum share needed to win seats, and thus ended with no representation in the state parliament. The Social Democrats were carried to a respectable finish on a wave of public sympathy, and the Christian Democrats, who had been expected by most observers to win an absolute majority, astonished everyone by polling only 45.6%.

To secure election as federal chancellor, Helmut Kohl needed at least 249 votes, 23 more than the total parliamentary strength of the CDU–CSU. In the event, in a secret ballot on October 1, he polled 256, indicating that 30 of the 53 Free Democrat members voted for him. There were 235 votes against and 4 abstentions. Kohl, who was sworn in as chancellor on the evening of the same day, announced his intention to hold a federal election on March 6, 1983.

In the debate on the constructive vote of no confidence, Schmidt made a scathing attack on the FDP leadership. Less than two years earlier, he pointed out, his coalition government had been convincingly confirmed in office by the electorate for a further four-year term. During that election campaign, he went on, Genscher had said, "A vote for us helps to keep Schmidt as chancellor . . . the voter must know where he stands." Schmidt claimed that although the method adopted by the CDU–CSU and the FDP to elect Kohl was legal, it had no moral justification. The case for the no-confidence motion was put by former CDU chairman Rainer Barzel, who in 1972 had tried unsuccessfully to take the chancellorship from Brandt by using the same device. On this occasion he accused Schmidt's government of running up massive

---

GERMANY, FEDERAL REPUBLIC OF

Education. (1980–81) Primary, pupils 2,783,867; secondary, pupils 5,950,897; primary and secondary, teachers 451,894; vocational, pupils 610,400, teachers 35,798; higher, students 1,192,755, teaching staff 169,050.

Finance. Monetary unit: Deutsche Mark, with (Sept. 20, 1982) a free rate of DM 2.50 to U.S. $1 (DM 4.28 = £1 sterling). Gold and other reserves (June 1982) U.S. $45,442,000,000. Budget (federal; 1981 actual): revenue DM 207.8 billion; expenditure DM 247.7 billion. Gross national product (1981) DM 1,551,900,000,000. Money supply (May 1982) DM 236.4 billion. Cost of living (1975 = 100; June 1982) 136.7.

Foreign Trade. (1981) Imports DM 369,120,000,000; exports DM 396,990,000,000. Import sources: EEC 47% (The Netherlands 12%, France 11%, Italy 7%, United Kingdom 7%, Belgium-Luxembourg 7%); U.S. 8%. Export destinations: EEC 47% (France 13%, The Netherlands 9%, Italy 8%, Belgium-Luxembourg 7%, United Kingdom 7%); U.S. 6%; Switzerland 5%; Austria 5%. Main exports: machinery 27%; motor vehicles 15%; chemicals 12%; iron and steel 6%; food 5%; textiles and cloth-

ing 5%. Tourism (1980): visitors 9,710,000; gross receipts U.S. $6,640,000,000.

Transport and Communications. Roads (1979) 482,000 km (including 7,292 km autobahns). Motor vehicles in use (1980): passenger 23,236,100; commercial 1,288,100. Railways: (1980) 31,626 km (including 11,482 km electrified); traffic (1981) 41,559,000,000 passenger-km, freight 62,037,000,000 net ton-km. Air traffic (1981): 21,636,000,000 passenger-km; freight 1,583,700,000 net ton-km. Navigable inland waterways in regular use (1980) 4,395 km; freight traffic 51,435,000,000 ton-km. Shipping (1981): merchant vessels 100 gross tons and over 1,820; gross tonnage 7,708,227. Shipping traffic (1981): goods loaded 40,327,000 metric tons, unloaded 96,573,000 metric tons. Telephones (Jan. 1980) 26,632,300. Radio licenses (1979) 22,664,000. Television licenses (Dec. 1979) 20,672,000.

Agriculture. Production (in 000; metric tons; 1981): wheat 8,314; barley 8,687; oats 2,678; rye 1,729; potatoes 8,045; sugar, raw value c. 3,600; apples 772; wine 750; cow's milk c. 24,817; butter 545;

cheese 818; beef and veal c. 1,490; pork c. 2,614; fish catch (1980) 297. Livestock (in 000; Dec. 1980): cattle 15,069; pigs 22,553; sheep 1,179; horses 382; chickens 85,461.

Industry. Index of production (1975 = 100; 1981) 116. Unemployment (1981) 5.5%. Fuel and power (in 000; metric tons; 1981): coal 88,459; lignite 130,618; crude oil 4,463; coke (1979) 27,438; electricity (kw-hr) 368,772,000; natural gas (cu m) 19,170,000; manufactured gas (cu m) c. 13,460,000. Production (in 000; metric tons; 1981): iron ore (32% metal content) 1,577; pig iron 31,724; crude steel 41,240; aluminum 1,120; copper 387; lead 304; zinc 523; cement 31,543; sulfuric acid 4,828; newsprint 676; cotton yarn 146; woven cotton fabrics 148; wool yarn 52; man-made fibres 914; petroleum products c. 78,800; fertilizers (1980–81) nitrogenous 1,436, phosphate 687, potash 2,701; synthetic rubber 415; plastics and resins (1980) 6,787; passenger cars (units) 3,590; commercial vehicles (units) 312. Merchant vessels launched (100 gross tons and over; 1981) 665,000 gross tons. New dwelling units completed (1981) 365,500.

debts, boosting unemployment, and generally mismanaging the economy.

The new Cabinet included four Free Democrat ministers, one fewer than before. Genscher remained as foreign minister, Lambsdorff as economics minister, and Josef Ertl as minister of agriculture. But the leftish liberal Gerhart Baum of the FDP was replaced as minister of the interior by a right-wing conservative, Friedrich Zimmermann of the CSU.

In the Bavarian state election on October 10, the Free Democrats polled only 3.5% and were thus eliminated from a state assembly for the second time within two weeks. Unlike their colleagues in Hesse a fortnight previously, the environmentalist Green Party did not succeed in winning parliamentary seats in Bavaria. Even so, the Green Party, which opposed nuclear energy and nuclear rearmament and whose leaders included Petra Kelly (see BIOGRAPHIES), was represented in 6 of 11 state assemblies and had reason to be confident of winning Bundestag seats in a federal election. Brandt, the SPD chairman, suggested that his party could collaborate with the Greens on certain issues, without entering into a formal coalition. At their party congress in November the Greens indicated that they would only pledge support to a chancellor who had renounced nuclear arms and nuclear energy.

Four weeks after losing office, Helmut Schmidt announced that he would not stand again for the chancellorship. This robbed the Social Democrats of their biggest electoral asset and opened up the prospect of a move to the left. The leader of the opposition in the West Berlin assembly, Hans-Jochen Vogel, a 56-year-old lawyer with a distinguished career as mayor of Munich and later as federal minister of justice, was nominated to succeed Schmidt as the SPD's candidate for the chancellorship. Meanwhile, about 6,000 members of the FDP quit the party in protest over the alliance with the CDU. In late November some 1,500 of them met in Bochum to form a new left-liberal party, to be known as the Liberal Democrats. The leader of the new grouping was Ulrich Krüger, a former deputy in the state parliament of Hesse.

The policy statement by Chancellor Kohl to the Bundestag on October 13 should have caused no unease, at home or abroad. He described his government as a coalition of the centre, dedicated to giving society a human face, and there was nothing in his rather vaguely phrased program to suggest that the label was false. Nobody could deny his assertion that he had taken office at a time when West Germany was experiencing a major economic crisis or that this crisis had shaken many people's confidence in the state's ability to cope with it.

The year was one of economic disappointments, and 1983 seemed unlikely to prove better. Almost everyone's projections turned out to be too optimistic—those of government, banks, and economic research institutes. An export boom came and went without proving to be the forerunner of an economic upswing at home. Kohl was planning a federal election campaign as the unemployment figures rose to around two million. Soon after tak-

Helmut Kohl (centre left) replaced Helmut Schmidt in October as chancellor of West Germany.

ing office the new administration announced measures to stimulate the crisis-ridden building industry and to encourage those planning to found businesses of their own. The new government was expected to be more receptive than its predecessor to pressure for the development of new communications technology and to resist more strongly pressure against an extension of nuclear power. It also said that it was determined to cut public borrowing.

Foreign Affairs. Kohl's government stressed continuity in foreign and security policies. In his first few weeks of office Kohl visited Paris and London, and soon afterward he received Pres. François Mitterrand of France and U.K. Prime Minister Margaret Thatcher in Bonn. In mid-November Kohl went to Washington for talks with U.S. Pres. Ronald Reagan. In his policy statement on October 13 he declared that West Germany's foreign and security policies were founded on NATO and friendship with the U.S. His government, he said, would dispel the doubts that were troubling West German-U.S. relations by reaffirming and stabilizing that friendship. The federal government, the chancellor went on, was wholly committed to the NATO dual-track decision of 1979, which proposed negotiations on the reduction and limitation of Soviet and U.S. intermediate-range nuclear systems. It would stand by the two parts of the decision, both the part relating to negotiations and, if necessary, the part on arms modernization.

However, Kohl pointed out, every West German government must take into account the special responsibility deriving from the division of the country and its geographic location. This meant that the pursuance of an active policy for peace toward the countries of Central and Eastern Europe remained a fundamental task of West German foreign policy. On the basis of the Eastern treaties, concluded in the early 1970s by an SPD–FDP coalition, and the Final Act of the Helsinki conference, the government would continue to work for genuine détente. Particular attention was

Former flight lieutenant Jerry J. Rawlings returned to power in Ghana following a period of internal strife. His Provisional National Defense Council installed a civilian Cabinet but named Rawlings as chairman. Rawlings then toured the countryside to explain the new order.

Ghana

to be devoted to relations with the Soviet Union. Kohl added that, nevertheless, his government could not overlook the severe obstacles and setbacks caused by the Soviet intervention in Afghanistan, the oppressive situation in Poland, and Soviet arms stockpiling.

The NATO summit meeting in Bonn in June reiterated the Western alliance's determination to seek détente from a position of military balance. The Schmidt government welcomed President Reagan to Bonn as a man of peace, although a good many members of the SPD believed that the U.S. was primarily concerned with achieving military superiority over the Soviet Union. As the NATO leaders met, some 300,000 people gathered on the other side of the Rhine to demonstrate for peace. When the summit meeting was over, President Reagan spent a few hours, closely guarded, in West Berlin. Relations with the U.S. were strained by the Reagan administration's attempts to obstruct the Soviet-European gas pipeline project.

West Germany's initial support for the U.K. in its reaction to Argentina's aggression against the Falkland Islands gave way to strong misgivings once the military campaign began. In the interests of Western solidarity the West German government voted for the indefinite extension of trade sanctions imposed against Argentina by the European Communities, but this action belied Bonn's true feelings.

Schmidt's government believed that the British response to the seizure of the islands was inappropriate and anachronistic. Furthermore, it believed that the conflict in the South Atlantic would cause severe and lasting damage to relations between Western Europe and the whole of Latin America. Argentina's claim to sovereignty over the Falkland Islands was widely regarded in West Germany as justified, and it was notable that the government had always been careful to avoid expressing an opinion on the sovereignty issue. But the Falklands conflict did not seem to impair relations between West Germany and the U.K. When Thatcher visited West Berlin in October, she was widely applauded for her powerful speech in defense of freedom. (NORMAN CROSSLAND)

Ghana

A republic of West Africa and member of the Commonwealth, Ghana is on the Gulf of Guinea and is bordered by Ivory Coast, Upper Volta, and Togo. Area: 238,533 sq km (92,098 sq mi). Pop. (1982 est.): 12,439,000. Cap. and largest city: Accra (pop., 1980 est., 998,800). Language: English (official); local Sudanic dialects (1978 est.): Akan 52.6%, Mole-Dagbani 15.9%, Ewe 11.8%, Ga-

GHANA

Education. (1978–79) Primary, pupils 1,294,872, teachers 48,397; secondary, pupils 588,823, teachers 29,775; vocational, pupils 21,377, teachers 1,101; teacher training, students 3,510, teachers (1977–78) 212; higher, students (1979–80) 9,745, teaching staff (1975–76) 1,103.

Finance. Monetary unit: cedi, with (Sept. 20, 1982) a free rate of 2.75 cedis to U.S. $1 (4.71 cedis = £1 sterling). Gold and other reserves (June 1982) U.S. $183 million. Budget (1979–80 est.): revenue 2,950,000,000 cedis; expenditure 4,179,000,000 cedis. Gross domestic product (1978) 20,986,000,000 cedis. Money supply (Feb. 1982) 9,435,300,000 cedis. Cost of living (Accra; 1975 = 100; Jan. 1982) 3,535.

Foreign Trade. (1978) Imports 1,681,800,000 cedis; exports 1,580,600,000 cedis. Import sources: U.K. 19%; West Germany 13%; U.S. 11%; Nigeria 10%; Japan 5%; Switzerland 5%. Export destinations: The Netherlands 18%; U.S. 16%; U.K. 16%; U.S.S.R. 10%; West Germany 8%; Japan 6%; Switzerland 6%. Main exports (1978): cocoa 69%; aluminum 10%; timber 6%.

Transport and Communications. Roads (1980) c. 32,000 km. Motor vehicles in use (1980): passenger c. 66,000; commercial (including buses) c. 48,000. Railways: (1980) 953 km; traffic (1974) 521 million passenger-km, freight 312 million net ton-km. Air traffic (1980): c. 324 million passenger-km; freight c. 2.8 million net ton-km. Shipping (1981): merchant vessels 100 gross tons and over 123; gross tonnage 254,595. Telephones (Jan. 1980) 68,850. Radio receivers (Dec. 1979) 1.2 million. Television receivers (Dec. 1979) 50,000.

Agriculture. Production (in 000; metric tons; 1981): corn c. 420; cassava c. 1,850; taro c. 1,500; yams c. 1,000; millet c. 73; sorghum c. 142; tomatoes c. 140; peanuts c. 90; oranges c. 30; cocoa c. 230; palm oil c. 21; meat c. 116; fish catch (1980) 224; timber (cu m; 1980) c. 9,577. Livestock (in 000; 1981): cattle c. 950; sheep c. 1,700; pigs c. 415; goats c. 2,100; chickens c. 12,000.

Industry. Production (in 000; metric tons; 1980): bauxite 226; petroleum products (1979) c. 1,200; gold (troy oz) 412; diamonds (metric carats) 1,258; manganese ore (metal content) c. 120; electricity (kw-hr) 4,768,000.

Adange 7.6%, other 12.1%. Religion (1980 est.): Christian 63%; Muslim 16%; animist 21%. Chairman of the Provisional National Defense Council in 1982, Jerry John Rawlings.

The return to power in Ghana of former flight lieutenant Jerry John Rawlings on the eve of 1982 was followed by the establishment of a Provisional National Defense Council (PNDC) with Rawlings as chairman. Former president Hilla Limann was placed under house arrest within days of the coup. The PNDC then appointed a civilian Cabinet, though it retained responsibility for defense.

People's defense committees were set up in villages and workplaces to defend democratic rights and to fight corruption, and a National Economic Review Committee was established to assess the economy. Producer prices for cocoa and peanuts were tripled, and stringent cost cutting was adopted to curb public-sector spending. Road rehabilitation was given major priority. The new economic policy aimed to reduce inflation, increase food production, instill financial discipline in the public sector, and achieve a balanced budget.

In July an unidentified armed group abducted and killed three judges and a retired military officer. On November 24 the government announced that it had put down an attempted coup.

(GUY ARNOLD)

Golf

Although Craig Stadler, winner of the Masters and the World Series of Golf, was the leading money winner in the United States during 1982, Tom Watson's victories in the U.S. and British Open championships made him the outstanding golfer of the year. This feat had only been achieved five times previously, by Bobby Jones (1926, 1930), Gene Sarazen (1932), Ben Hogan (1953), and Lee Trevino (1971). It stamped Watson as one of the great players of the generation.

Prior to his triumph in the U.S. Open at Pebble Beach, Calif., there had been reservations as to Watson's overall quality. He had never won a U.S. Open, and that tournament seemed always to be a stumbling block in his career. In 1982, however, he survived a tremendous contest with Jack Nicklaus and deprived Nicklaus of a record fifth victory. No recent Open had produced a more fitting climax than that between the two foremost competitors of the time, and the way it was contested was magnificent.

Watson began the last round tied for first with Bill Rogers, runner-up in 1981 and reigning British champion, and three strokes ahead of Nicklaus. The latter, however, quickly charged for the lead with five successive birdies beginning with the third hole. Although Bobby Clampett and Dan Pohl bravely sustained their efforts, Rogers slipped a couple of strokes, and battle finally was joined between Watson and Nicklaus, who was playing ahead of him. A long putt on the 14th green put Watson two ahead, but Nicklaus birdied the 15th and when Watson bogeyed the 16th the match was even. The 17th is a menacing short hole, and Watson's no. 2 iron shot drifted into

thick rough just off the green and about 40 ft (12 m) from the pin. Nicklaus, watching on television in the scorer's tent, then felt certain that Watson would need a birdie on the 18th to win, but Watson thought differently. The lie was better than he expected, and he told his caddie that he was going to hole the delicate little chip shot. To everyone's astonishment and Watson's boundless delight he did just that. Had the ball missed the hole, it could have run several feet past and Nicklaus might have been champion. As it was, it would be remembered as one of the great winning shots. That Watson's lay-up putt for a winning par on the last green went in for a birdie and victory by two strokes was purely academic.

All the great champions have known the crushing bitterness of narrow failure, especially when it was of their own making. In years to come Clampett might profit from the fate that befell him a few weeks later in the British Open. His first two rounds of 67 and 66, only one stroke over the record, made light of the links at Troon, Scotland, and gave him a five-stroke lead over the field. But the old course was in no mood for further trifling, and a terrible eight at the par-five sixth hole in the third round began Clampett's plunge from the heights.

Watson was no stranger to harsh disappointment and could sympathize with Nicky Price of South Africa, who had the lead during the last round but could not take the pressure. If Price could have played the last four holes at Troon in one over par, he would have won. By then Watson had finished in 284, four under par, having just missed his putt for a birdie on the 18th hole. The 15th had proved the most difficult hole in relation to par throughout the Open, and on it Price shot a double bogey six; he then underclubbed to the short 17th green, and when his putt of 30 ft missed, Watson won by one stroke his fourth British Open in eight years, all of them taking place in Scotland.

Watson's victory was achieved by superb long driving, particularly in the last round, whereas in other championships this had occasionally been a vulnerable part of his game. It would be unfair to say that he was a lucky champion. Such tournaments are a severe test of nerve, and in the last analysis it was Price and not Watson who failed. An opening 77 proved too great a burden for Nicklaus, but the British made a good showing. Peter Oosterhuis, not for the first time, was runner-up, sharing second place with Price; and Nick Faldo (286) and Sandy Lyle (287) were each a stroke further behind. Watson had now won seven major championships, and by the end of the season only lacked a victory in the Professional Golfers' Association (PGA) championship to share the rare distinction with Sarazen, Hogan, Gary Player, and Nicklaus of having won all four major titles — the U.S. and British Opens, the U.S. Masters, and PGA.

One of the worst experiences that can befall any golfer is to suffer the erosion of a commanding lead. When Stadler was six ahead at the last turn in the final round of the U.S. Masters, many thought that he was assured of the victory. But tragedy and triumph often march together amid the woods and

Gibraltar:
see Dependent States

Glass Manufacture:
see Industrial Review

Gliding:
see Aerial Sports

water on the back nine at Augusta, Ga. While Stadler was bogeying the 12th, 14th, and 16th, Dan Pohl was posting a second successive 67 after starting with a pair of 75s. Jerry Pate and Severiano Ballesteros were also making moves, and eventually Stadler came to the 18th needing a par to win. An awful first putt finished six feet short, and one could imagine the agony he felt when he missed the second one and had to go into a sudden-death play-off with Pohl. That Stadler played the tenth, the first extra hole, in a solid par, while Pohl went one over spoke highly of his composure and proved that he could control the lively temperament that on occasion in the past had betrayed him. For once at Augusta the air was alive with complaint at the pin positions and pace of the greens on the second day. The committee admitted that some of the contours were wrong and said that 12 greens would be reshaped for 1983. The greens for the second round proved so troublesome that the cut score of 154 was the highest ever.

Stadler made almost certain of leading the money list by beating Ray Floyd and winning $100,000 on the fourth sudden-death hole of the World Series of Golf at Akron, Ohio. Had the result been reversed, Floyd would probably have retained the honour. He had won the PGA championship in commanding style with a score of 272, shooting a 63 in the first round at the Southern Hills course in Tulsa, Okla., and leaving everyone else wondering if one of the game's famous front runners could be caught. But except for a light tremor in the last round while Lanny Wadkins, Fred Couples, and Calvin Peete were mounting late counterattacks, Floyd was never in danger and won by three strokes.

Discounting the major championships, the golfer of the year was Calvin Peete. His four victories, two by seven shots, and total winnings of well over $300,000 far surpassed the achievements of any other black golfer in the history of the game. The PGA statistics also proved that he was the most accurate golfer in terms of hitting fairways and greens in regulation figures. In 1981 and 1982 he was first in both categories. Of all the golfers on the U.S. tour, Peete probably had the fewest advantages when young. One of a family of 18, he had to leave school and work to help with family expenses. He became a traveling salesman following migrant farm workers from Florida to Rochester, N.Y. He had no interest in golf until friends persuaded him to try. He was 23 at the time but took to the game quickly and, without any formal teaching, became a good amateur. Eventually he turned professional and at 32 passed the PGA qualifying school on his third attempt. His subsequent success was one of the most remarkable in modern professional golf.

For the second time Greg Norman, the most powerful of Australian golfers, headed the European money list with £66,405, and Lyle, leader in 1979–80, was second. Lyle lost a memorable final to Ballesteros in the Suntory match play championship at Wentworth, England. Otherwise Ballesteros had, for him, a moderate season, and Manuel Pinero was the leading Spanish golfer, winning the European Open at Sunningdale, England,

with a record last round of 63. Bernhard Langer of West Germany declined somewhat after his record year in 1981 but still finished sixth. A pleasing aspect of the European tour was the play of several young men in their first season as professionals. Gordon Brand, Jr., son of a professional, actually won two tournaments—a performance for a first-year professional without precedent in British golf—and over £38,000 in prize money. Paul Way also won a tournament, and Ronan Rafferty and Roger Chapman made steady progress.

The victory of Jay Sigel in the U.S. amateur championship was a triumph for a generation of amateurs who had gradually been thrust aside by the uprush of young golfers from colleges and universities. Sigel, whose attractive style and easy rhythm had impressed everyone when he won the British title in 1979, had every right to be counted the premier amateur (in the true sense of the term) in the world. He led the U.S. to victory in the World Team championships in Lausanne, Switz. In this he was assisted by Jim Holtgrieve, Robert Lewis, and Nathaniel Crosby, whose 68 on the final day steadied the U.S. performance when Japan and Sweden were mounting a serious threat. Considering the attention always upon him as Bing Crosby's son, Nathaniel Crosby, who had won the U.S. amateur championship in 1981 and was leading amateur in the U.S. Open, showed remarkable golfing character.

In women's golf the U.S. professional scene was

Jan Stephenson anxiously watches a putt during the LPGA tournament at Kings Island, Ohio, in June. She went on to win the $200,000 tournament.

dominated by JoAnne Carner with five victories and record winnings of $308,759, a total surpassed by only a few on the men's tour. No woman had ever approached this total before, and one of the greatest natural talents the game had known showed no sign of waning at 43. Sandra Haynie, who turned professional in 1961 but lost some years through injury, returned to peak form and was Carner's closest challenger, together with Sally Little, Patty Sheehan, and Beth Daniel. In view of the supremacy of these women, one of the most remarkable achievements was that of Janet Alex, wife of a professional, who joined the small and distinguished group whose first victory as a professional was in the most important event of all. Her final round of 68 swept her clear of the field, and she won the U.S. Women's Open by six shots.

The outstanding woman amateur of the season was Juli Inkster, who won the U.S. championship for the third successive year, a feat that had not been accomplished since Virginia Van Wie did so in 1932–34. Inkster played a leading part in overwhelming victories in the Curtis Cup match in Denver, Colo., and the World Team championship in Geneva, Switz. Britain and Ireland won only $3^1/_2$ points out of a possible 18 in the Curtis Cup, and New Zealand finished 17 strokes behind the U.S. in Geneva. Britain and Ireland finished third, two strokes further behind.

(P. A. WARD-THOMAS)

Greece

A republic of Europe, Greece occupies the southern part of the Balkan Peninsula. Area: 131,990 sq km (50,962 sq mi), of which the mainland accounts for 107,194 sq km. Pop. (1981): 9,740,200. Cap. and largest city: Athens (pop., 1981 prelim., 885,100). Language: Greek. Religion: Orthodox. President in 1982, Konstantinos Karamanlis; prime minister, Andreas Papandreou.

During 1982, the first full year of Socialist change in Greece, Prime Minister Andreas Papandreou and his government tackled the country's problems with a vigorous realism that spared them untimely confrontations but was not without political cost. In foreign affairs, the Socialist government sought to reassert the independence of its opinions at international meetings on such topics as the Middle East, Poland, and détente. However, on the issues that were truly vital for Greece, it showed a moderation that was, in practice, a renunciation of its election slogans about leaving NATO and the European Communities (EC) and dismissing the U.S. bases. At home, faced with a rapidly deteriorating economy, the government refrained from introducing its more radical reforms. Yet uncertainty lingered, undermining business confidence, prolonging recession, and posing a problem of unemployment.

The effect of these contradictions was reflected in the results of municipal elections held in October. Although the ruling Panhellenic Socialist Movement (Pasok) gained control of three-fifths of Greece's towns and villages, it did so only with the help of the pro-Moscow Greek Communist Party

Greece

GREECE

Education. (1978–79) Primary, pupils 922,698, teachers 35,750; secondary, pupils 585,130, teachers 26,921; vocational, pupils 125,039; higher, students 99,713, teaching staff 7,077.

Finance. Monetary unit: drachma, with (Sept. 20, 1982) a free rate of 70.46 drachmas to U.S. $1 (120.60 drachmas = £1 sterling). Gold and other reserves (May 1982) U.S. $980 million. Budget (1981 actual): revenue 402,770,000,000 drachmas; expenditure 550.1 billion drachmas. Gross national product (1981) 2,091,-000,000,000 drachmas. Money supply (Dec. 1981) 377,-380,000,000 drachmas. Cost of living (1975 = 100; June 1982) 325.

Foreign Trade. (1981) Imports 493,760,000,000 drachmas; exports 233,010,000,000 drachmas. Import sources: EEC 50% (West Germany 20%, Italy 10%, France 7%, The Netherlands 5%, U.K. 5%); Japan 11%; Egypt 6%; Saudi Arabia 6%; U.S. 5%. Export destinations: EEC 43% (West Germany 18%, Italy 7%, France 7%); U.S. 9%; Saudi Arabia 6%; Libya 5%. Main exports: fruit and vegetables 15%; textile yarns and fabrics 11%; petroleum products 9%; clothing 9%; iron and steel 5%; cement 5%; chemicals 5%. Tourism (1980): visitors 4,796,000; gross receipts U.S. $1,733,000,000.

Transport and Communications. Roads (1980) 37,132 km (including 91 km expressways) Motor vehicles in use (1980): passenger 877,900; commercial 401,970. Railways (1980): 2,479 km; traffic 1,464,000,000 passenger-km, freight 814 million net ton-km. Air traffic (1981): 5,196,000,000 passenger-km; freight 75,138,000 net ton-km. Shipping (1981): merchant vessels 100 gross tons and over 3,710; gross tonnage 42,004,990. Telephones (Dec. 1980) 2,781,200. Radio receivers (Dec. 1979) 2.9 million. Television receivers (Dec. 1979) 1.4 million.

Agriculture. Production (in 000; metric tons; 1981): wheat 2,750; barley 790; oats 82; corn 1,250; rice 74; potatoes 953; sugar, raw value 340; tomatoes c. 1,666; onions c. 132; watermelons c. 710; apples 320; oranges c. 611; lemons c. 185; peaches 448; olives c. 1,350; olive oil 280; wine c. 540; raisins 164; tobacco 122; cotton lint 117. Livestock (in 000; Dec. 1980): sheep 7,920; cattle 899; goats 4,650; pigs 1,000; horses 120; asses 250; chickens 30,000.

Industry. Production (in 000; metric tons; 1981): lignite 27,718; electricity (kw-hr) c. 21,800,000; petroleum products (1979) c. 15,010; iron ore (43% metal content) 1,278; bauxite 3,185; aluminum 148; magnesite (1979) 1,376; cement 13 259; sulfuric acid 982; fertilizers (1980–81) nitrogenous c. 311, phosphate c. 170; cotton yarn 110. Merchant vessels launched (100 gross tons and over; 1981) 23,000 gross tons.

(KKE), which had deplored the government's failure to fulfill its campaign promises.

The Socialist government at first tried to ignore its differences with Turkey over the Aegean Sea. It was, however, forced to agree to the resumption of a diplomatic dialogue after Turkish aircraft systematically challenged Greek sovereignty in the Aegean. Preliminary Greek-Turkish talks were resumed at the foreign minister level in October, but only after Turkey had promised to discontinue its sorties. Pasok's plan to alienate Greece from NATO was shelved in the hope of extending the protection guaranteed by the alliance to Greece's frontiers with Turkey.

Negotiations with the U.S. to determine the status of U.S. military bases in Greece were begun in October, in exchange for the supply of sophisticated U.S. weapons that would help Greece preserve the balance of power with Turkey. A plan to get rid of Western nuclear warheads stockpiled in Greece, as a first step toward the creation of a nuclear-free zone in the Balkans, was put on ice, partly because of reservations expressed by Yugoslavia but also because Papandreou had become more sensitive to the exigencies of maintaining the East-West equilibrium.

Great Britain:
see United Kingdom

Greek Orthodox Church:
see Religion

Greenland:
see Dependent States

JEAN-CLAUDE FRANCOLON—GAMMA/LIAISON

Yasir Arafat, chairman of the Palestine Liberation Organization, was welcomed by Greek Prime Minister Andreas Papandreou and a naval guard of honour on his visit to Greece in September.

Cyprus was declared a top priority, and Papandreou made a triumphant visit to the island on February 28. However, his opposition to continuing the intercommunal dialogue between Greek and Turkish Cypriots under UN auspices brought him into direct conflict with Pres. Spyros Kyprianou of Cyprus; to ensure his reelection in February 1983, Kyprianou made an alliance with the island's powerful Communist party, AKEL, which, like Moscow, wanted the dialogue to continue.

The most flamboyant aspect of Papandreou's foreign policy was his unstinted support of the Arabs and his espousal of the Palestine Liberation Organization cause. Greece became the only EC country to grant the PLO diplomatic recognition. This line of policy sprang naturally from Pasok's ideological affinity with several Arab states. It was also designed to distract Pasok's supporters from foreign-policy reversals. But if the government hoped that it would trigger an avalanche of Arab petro-investments, it was disappointed.

With Greece still financially dependent on the West, the government drastically revised its attitude toward the EC. Before coming to power, the Socialists had promised to call a nationwide referendum to decide whether or not Greece should stay in the EC. One year later, faced with a foreign payments deficit of over $2 billion, the government no longer talked about a referendum. Instead it applied to the EC for help in solving its economic problems.

Perhaps the government's most disappointing performance was in its handling of the economy. Pasok let 1982 go by without introducing a program that could have stimulated enough confidence to curb the recession. A change of guard in the economic ministries in July reversed whatever trust the previous ministers had managed to inspire. By the end of the year, the only hope for the economy was the promise of a 1983–87 five-year plan that would allow businesses to plot their course.

The government systematically purged the public administration. All directors general and their deputies were retired, and civil servants loyal to

Pasok were appointed to key positions. Through some legalistic devices, the court deposed several antigovernment trade union executives and appointed temporary councils consisting of Pasok trade-unionists. Most of the militant unions, however, remained under KKE control, and they tended to cause trouble whenever Pasok's relations with KKE soured.

The municipal elections in October allowed the government to go ahead with its plan for drastic administrative decentralization—perhaps the most popular of the government's planned reforms. Other reforms included a new law on universities giving students a say in the advancement of their professors; the abolition of illiberal labour legislation; the lowering of the voting age to 18; the introduction of civil marriage; and the recognition of wartime left-wing resistance organizations as patriotic. Minister of Culture Melina Mercouri (*see* BIOGRAPHIES) campaigned for the return of the Elgin Marbles from the British Museum.

The popularity of Pasok remained undiminished, but cracks appeared in Pasok's monolithic structure that raised questions about whether Papandreou was running his party along democratic lines. Four Pasok deputies who questioned government policy were expelled from the party. At the end of 1982, Pasok was the only party in Parliament that—eight years after its foundation—had not yet staged its first national congress.

(MARIO MODIANO)

Grenada

Grenada

A parliamentary state within the Commonwealth, Grenada, with its dependency, the Southern Grenadines, is the southernmost of the Windward Islands of the Caribbean Sea, 161 km N of Trinidad. Area: 345 sq km (133 sq mi). Pop. (1981 est.): 112,000, including black 84%, mixed 11%, white 1%, and East Indian 3%. Cap.: Saint George's (pop., 1978 est., 30,800). Language: English. Religion: Roman Catholic 64%; Anglican 22%; Methodist 3%; Seventh-day Adventist 3%. Queen,

Education. (1980–81) Primary, pupils 23,065, teachers 704; secondary, pupils 6,120, teachers 284; vocational (1978–79), pupils 497, teachers 10; higher, students 153, teaching staff 23.

Finance and Trade. Monetary unit: East Caribbean dollar, with (Sept. 20, 1982) a par value of ECar$2.70 to U.S. $1 (free rate of ECar$4.63 = £1 sterling). Budget (1980–81 est.) balanced at ECar$103 million. Foreign trade (1980): imports ECar$135.6 million; exports ECar$46.8 million. Import sources (1979): U.K. c. 21%; Trinidad and Tobago c. 20%. Export destinations (1979): U.K. 40%; West Germany 17%; Belgium-Luxembourg 16%; The Netherlands 11%. Main exports: cocoa 39%; bananas 24%; nutmeg 18%. Tourism (excluding cruise passengers; 1980: visitors 29,500; gross receipts U.S. $17 million.

Education. (1980) Primary, pupils 826,613, teachers 24,242; secondary, vocational, and teacher training, pupils 171,903, teachers 9,613; higher (1978), students 34,301, teaching staff 2,845.

Finance. Monetary unit: quetzal, at par with the U.S. dollar (free rate, at Sept. 20, 1982, of 1.71 quetzales to £1 sterling). Gold and other reserves (June 1982) U.S. $162 million. Budget (total; 1980 actual): revenue 754 million quetzales; expenditure 1,116,000,000 quetzales. Gross national product (1980) 7,793,000,000 quetzales. Money supply (May 1982) 897 million quetzales. Cost of living (1975 = 100; May 1982) 188.7.

Foreign Trade. (1981) Imports 1,715,000,000 quetzales; exports 1,271,000,000 quetzales. Import sources (1980): U.S. 35%; Venezuela 10%; Netherlands Antilles 8%; Japan 8%; El Salvador 6%; West Germany 5%. Export destinations (1980): U.S. 27%; El Salvador 13%; West Germany 8%; Nicaragua 6%; Costa Rica 6%; Italy 5%. Main exports (1980): coffee 30%; cotton 11%; chemicals c. 8%; bananas 5%; textile yarns and fabrics c. 5%.

Transport and Communications. Roads (1979) 17,278 km. Motor vehicles in use (1980): passenger 166.900; commercial (including buses) 81,500. Railways: (1980) c. 967 km; freight traffic (1976) 117 million net ton-km. Air traffic (1980): 159 million passenger-km; freight 6.4 million net ton-km. Telephones (Jan. 1980) 81,600. Radio licenses (Dec. 1979) 285,000. Television receivers (Dec. 1978) 150,000.

Agriculture. Production (in 000; metric tons; 1981): corn 1,052; sugar, raw value c. 448; tomatoes 90; dry beans 81; bananas c. 650; coffee 173; cotton, lint 126; tobacco c. 9. Livestock (in 000; 1981): sheep 734; cattle 1,730; pigs 835; chickens 14,237.

Industry. Production (in 000; metric tons; 1980): cement 583; nickel ore (metal content) 6.7; petroleum products (1979) c. 800; electricity (kw-hr) 1,602,000.

Guatemala

Elizabeth II; governor-general in 1982, Sir Paul Scoon; prime minister, Maurice Bishop.

Throughout 1982 Grenada maintained an economic and political course unique in the eastern Caribbean. Utilizing aid from the European Communities, Eastern Europe, and the Middle East, the government concentrated on improving basic infrastructure. Work continued on the construction of an international airport with assistance from Cuba. Prime Minister Maurice Bishop came away from a visit to Moscow with agreements for aid from the U.S.S.R., a new source of assistance. Other new sources were Libya, East Germany, and Bulgaria. Grenada was excluded from the U.S. Caribbean Basin Initiative. During the conflict in the South Atlantic between the U.K. and Argentina, Grenada was the only English-speaking Caribbean government to support the latter.

At the Caribbean Community (Caricom) summit meeting in November, the government came under increased pressure, from Jamaica and Barbados in particular, to hold elections and to free political detainees. It was announced during the summit that 28 political prisoners had been released. (DAVID A. JESSOP)

Guatemala

A republic of Central America, Guatemala is bounded by Mexico, Belize, Honduras, El Salvador, the Caribbean Sea, and the Pacific Ocean. Area: 108,889 sq km (42,042 sq mi). Pop. (1981

prelim.): 6,043,600. Cap. and largest city: Guatemala City (pop., 1981 prelim., 1,307,300). Language: Spanish, with some Indian dialects. Religion: Roman Catholic (1976) 88%. President to March 23, 1982, Fernando Romeo Lucas García; head of a three-man ruling junta from March 23 and president from June 9, Gen. Efraín Ríos Montt.

Presidential elections held in Guatemala on March 7, 1982, were won by Gen. Angel Aníbal Guevara, the candidate chosen by the outgoing regime. On March 23, however, a coup brought Gen. Efraín Ríos Montt (see BIOGRAPHIES) and two other officers to power, and the election results were declared void. General Ríos Montt dissolved the junta and declared himself sole leader and head of the armed forces on June 9.

Initial hopes that the internal security situation

Members of the military junta that seized power in Guatemala on March 23 declared null and void an election that had been held on March 7. Gen. Efraín Ríos Montt (centre) was president of the junta.

UPI

Guinean Pres. Ahmed Sékou Touré (left) journeyed to France in September and was welcomed by France's Pres. François Mitterrand.

might improve under the new president were short-lived. Violence escalated in the countryside, and only a temporary lull was experienced in urban areas. An Amnesty International report estimated that over 2,600 Indians and peasant farmers were killed in the period March–July. Political parties boycotted the Council of State, established on September 15 in an attempt to provide a forum for discussion between politicians and members of the university, judiciary, and private banks.

Relations with the U.S. administration were strengthened following the admission of Guatemala to the Central American Democratic Community on July 7. However, as a result of the deterioration in human rights, full resumption of U.S. military aid was no longer assured, and Guatemala received only a $10 million share of the total $350 million in direct aid granted under the U.S. Caribbean Basin Initiative. Relations with the U.K. remained uneasy, since the president refused to recognize the independence of Belize.

The economy was adversely affected by the decline in Central American trade and a marked fall in investment. The trade deficit widened to $409 million in 1981, compared with $63 million in 1980.   (LUCY BLACKBURN)

Guinea

Guinea

A republic on the west coast of Africa, Guinea is bounded by Guinea-Bissau, Senegal, Mali, Ivory Coast, Liberia, and Sierra Leone. Area: 245,857 sq km (94,926 sq mi). Pop. (1982 UN est.): 5,278,000. Cap. and largest city: Conakry (pop., 1980 est., 763,000). Language: French (official), Basari, Fulani, Kissi, Koniagi, Kpelle, Loma, Malinke, and Susu. Religion (1980 est.): Muslim 69%; tribal 30%; Christian 1%. President in 1982, Ahmed Sékou Touré; premier, Louis Lansana Beavogui.

In May 1982 Pres. Ahmed Sékou Touré, sole candidate of the ruling Democratic Party of Guinea, was reelected, virtually unanimously, for another

Guinea-Bissau

GUINEA

Education. (1978–79) Primary, pupils 272,000, teachers 6,413; secondary and vocational, pupils 106,000, teachers 3,700; higher, students 24,000, teachers 650.

Finance. Monetary unit: syli, with (Sept. 20, 1982) a free rate of 22.86 sylis to U.S. $1 (39.20 sylis = £1 sterling). Budget (total; 1979 est.) balanced at 11,250,000,000 sylis.

Foreign Trade. (1977) Imports 5,664,000,000 sylis; exports 6,629,000,000 sylis. Import sources: France c. 20%; U.S.S.R. c. 11%; U.S. c. 6%; Italy c. 6%. Export destinations: U.S. c. 18%; France c. 13%; West Germany c. 12%; U.S.S.R. c. 12%; Spain c. 12%; Canada c. 7%; Italy c. 7%. Main exports (1975–76): bauxite c. 57%; alumina c. 31%.

seven years. Meanwhile, opposition to his single-party regime continued; in December 1981 Guinea's ambassador to France denounced the activities of a subversive group there, and in February 1982 President Touré himself claimed to have foiled a new plot.

In September, when Touré visited France for the first time since his country's independence in 1958 (when he rejected membership in the then French Community), he encountered demonstrations organized by the Guinean opposition. Among the French Socialist Party leadership there was also opposition to the visit because of Guinea's poor civil rights record. Pres. François Mitterrand justified it on grounds of diplomatic courtesy, former French president Valéry Giscard d'Estaing having paid an official visit to Guinea in 1978. Other considerations included French participation in mineral exploitation in Guinea and the desirability of Guinea's reintegration into the circle of French-speaking African nations. Touré himself was anxious to reinforce links with the West, and in June he visited the U.S.   (PHILIPPE DECRAENE)

Guinea-Bissau

An independent African republic, Guinea-Bissau has an Atlantic coastline on the west and borders Senegal on the north and Guinea on the east and

Guyana

south. Area: 36,125 sq km (13,948 sq mi). Pop. (1982 est.): 811,500, including (1979) Balante 27.2%; Fulani 22.9%; Malinke 12.2%; Mandyako 10.6%; Pepel 10%, other 17.1%. Cap. and largest city: Bissau (pop., 1979 prelim., 105,300). Religion (1980 est.): tribal 52%; Muslim 38%; Christian 10%. President of the Council of the Revolution in 1982, João Bernardo Vieira; prime minister from May 14, Victor Saúde Maria.

Uneasy relations between Guinea-Bissau and Cape Verde continued for much of 1982, although many Cape Verdians retained important positions in Guinea-Bissau. The two countries announced in June that they would begin the process of restoring governmental relations. On January 1 former president Luis de Almeida Cabral, deposed in the 1980 coup, was released from prison and went into exile in Cuba.

A reshuffle in May purged left-wing ministers from the Cabinet and placed greater power in the hands of Pres. João Bernardo Vieira. A plot against Vieira was uncovered in July, and a number of arrests were made. It was claimed that a counter-revolutionary organization had been exposed, and a former health minister was reported to have confessed complicity.

Guinea-Bissau remained heavily dependent upon aid to combat food shortages. President Vieira visited Cuba and Panama in March with a ministerial team, and in April he visited China and North Korea. Pres. António Ramalho Eanes of Portugal visited Guinea-Bissau in November.

(GUY ARNOLD)

Guyana

A republic and member of the Commonwealth, Guyana is situated between Venezuela, Brazil, and Suriname on the Atlantic Ocean. Area: 215,000 sq km (83,000 sq mi). Pop. (1982 est.): 924,000, including (1978) East Indian 50%; African 30%; mixed 10%; Amerindian 5%. Cap. and largest city: Georgetown (pop., 1979 est., 195,000). Language: English (official). Religion (1980 est.): Hindu 34%; Protestant 34%; Muslim 9%; Roman Catholic 8%; other 15%. President in 1982, Forbes Burnham; prime minister, Ptolemy Reid.

For Guyana, 1982 was dominated by two major issues: the renewal of the claim by Venezuela to more than half its territory; and the near collapse of the economy. Politically, the nation remained irreconcilably divided, with opposition parties alleging systematic abuses of human rights by the government and its supporters.

Alleged incursions by Venezuelan troops into Guyana were followed by proposals and counterproposals for a settlement of the border dispute, whether by the International Court of Justice, the UN secretary-general, or direct negotiation, but no agreement was reached. Although Guyana was able to elicit support at the November Caribbean Community meeting in Jamaica, some nations were concerned about their relations with Venezuela and held back. Guyana developed significantly closer ties with Brazil, to which Pres. Forbes Burnham paid an official visit in October.

The effect of the dispute and the consequent military expenditure further weakened the economy. Discussions with the World Bank and the International Monetary Fund (IMF) took place, but by year's end there was no agreement on implementing any IMF proposals. Demand for bauxite and sugar, the nation's two main products, remained depressed.

(DAVID A. JESSOP)

Gymnastics and Weight Lifting

Gymnastics. The World Cup championships that were held in Zagreb, Yugos., from October 22 to 24 featured 20 men and 20 women who had participated in the 1981 world championships in Moscow. Soviet athletes captured both team titles. The U.S.S.R. women gymnasts also took home the lion's share of the individual medals. In the men's team competition, China finished second to the Soviet Union, and East Germany was third. The Soviet women's team finished far ahead of the teams representing East Germany, China, Romania, and the U.S. Li Ning (China), however, was by far the brightest star in the men's individual competitions.

Guiana:
see Dependent States; Guyana; Suriname

UPI

Winner of the men's division in the American Cup gymnastics competition in March was Bart Conner (left) of the U.S. Julianne McNamara of the U.S. (right) and Zoya Grant-charova of Bulgaria (centre) shared the championship in the women's division.

In the men's all-around, Li Ning and Tong Fei (China) outperformed Yury Korolev (U.S.S.R.), the 1981 world champion, who had to be content with third place. In the individual events, Li was superb. He won the floor exercise, the pommel horse, and the long horse vault. In addition, he tied for the gold medal in both the horizontal bar and rings competitions and placed third in parallel bars, the only event Korolev won.

In the women's all-around, Olga Bicherova (U.S.S.R.), the 1981 world champion, shared first place with newcomer Natalia Yurchenko (U.S.S.R.). In the individual events, Bicherova won a gold medal for the floor exercise and shared the vaulting title with Yurchenko; the latter won a second gold medal for her balance beam routine. Maxi Gnauck (East Germany) was crowned champion in the uneven parallel bars competition.

The best U.S. performances were given by Jim Hartung, who placed tenth in the all-around, and by Julianne McNamara, who won a bronze medal in the vault and placed eighth in the all-around.

The most impressive U.S. victories during the year came at the International Invitational held in Fort Worth, Texas. The U.S. won both team titles. Though Li Ning won the all-around title, Hartung was second and Mitch Gaylord (U.S.) fourth. Li again displayed his remarkable talents by winning the floor exercise, the pommel horse, and the rings. None of the U.S. gymnasts won a gold medal in the individual events. Kathy Johnson (U.S.) captured the women's all-around title, finishing just ahead of her teammates Diane Durham and Amy Koopman. Johnson and Michelle Goodwin (U.S.) shared first-place honours on the balance beam, and Durham was tops in the vault.

In the U.S. national championships for men held in early June in Syracuse, N.Y., Peter Vidmar succeeded Hartung as all-around champion. Gaylord was second and Hartung third. Hartung, however, won four of the six individual events: the floor exercise, pommel horse, rings, and long horse vault. Vidmar won the parallel bars and Gaylord the horizontal bar. During the women's U.S. national championships held in Salt Lake City, Utah, in late May, Tracee Talavera retained her crown as national all-around champion by defeating McNa-

Haiti

mara 75.95 to 75.75. Talavera triumphed despite a fifth-place subpar performance in the floor exercise. The next two top places were taken by Koopman and Gina Stallone. First-place honours in the individual events went to Koopman in the floor exercise, McNamara on the balance beam, Marie Roethlisberger on the uneven parallel bars, and Yumi Mordre in the vault.

Weight Lifting. The world championships demonstrated once again that the Soviet Union and Bulgaria are in a class by themselves. Each won four gold medals, but in the final team standings the U.S.S.R. finished in first place because it also captured five silver medals and one bronze.

In the superheavyweight division, world champion Anatoly Pisarenko (U.S.S.R.) again emerged victorious. Sergey Arakelov, competing in the 110-kg category, set a new world record of 241.5 kg in the clean and jerk and captured the gold medal. Victor Sots (U.S.S.R.) successfully defended his 100-kg crown, as did Blagoi Blagoev in the 90-kg class. Another world record was established when Asen Zlatev (Bulg.) snatched 180 kg and became world champion in the 82.5-kg class.

One of the finest performances of the competition was given by Yanko Rusev (Bulg.), the 1980 Olympic champion and the 1981 world champion in the 75-kg class. He retained his world title with ease by setting two world records: 209 kg in the clean and jerk and 365 kg for his total lift. In the 67.5-kg class Piotr Mandra (U.S.S.R.) won the gold medal, and in the 60-kg class Yurik Sarkisian (U.S.S.R.) finished in first place. Anton Kodjabashev (Bulg.) had a total lift of 280 kg and captured a gold medal in the 56-kg category. Stefan Leletko (Poland), competing in the 52-kg weight class, won a second gold medal for Poland by setting a world record of 143.5 kg in the clean and jerk. (CHARLES ROBERT PAUL, JR.)

Haiti

The Republic of Haiti occupies the western one-third of the Caribbean island of Hispaniola, which it shares with the Dominican Republic. Area: 27,750 sq km (10,715 sq mi). Pop. (1982 est.): 5,195,200, of whom 95% are black. Cap. and largest city: Port-au-Prince (pop., 1978 est., 745,800). Language: French (official) and Creole. Religion: Roman Catholic; Voodoo practiced in rural areas. President in 1982, Jean-Claude Duvalier.

Pres. Jean-Claude Duvalier ordered several Cabinet reshuffles during 1982. The most significant changes involved Marc Bazin, a former World Bank official, who was appointed minister of finance following pressure from the U.S. and international financial institutions to carry out a campaign against corruption and financial mismanagement. Bazin took up the post in February but was dismissed in July after losing a power struggle with Duvalier's wife, Michèle Bennett. In the main, the changes brought more power to the political hard-liners.

A retrial was ordered in the case of Sylvio Claude, leader of the suspended opposition Christian Democratic Party, whose 15-year prison sen-

HAITI

Education. (1978–79) Primary, pupils 546,097, teachers 13,209; secondary (1977–78), pupils 72,651, teachers 3,833; vocational (1975–76), pupils 5,356, teachers 747; higher, students 4,186, teaching staff 493.

Finance. Monetary unit: gourde, with (Sept. 20, 1982) a par value of 5 gourdes to U.S. $1 (free rate of 8.57 gourdes = £1 sterling). Gold and other reserves (June 1982) U.S. $11 million. Budget (1979–80 actual): revenue 775 million gourdes; expenditure 1,012,000,000 gourdes. Cost of living (Port-au-Prince; 1975 = 100; Dec. 1981) 176.4.

Foreign Trade. (1980) Imports 1,888,000,000 gourdes; exports 973 million gourdes. Import sources (1978): U.S. 45%; Netherlands Antilles 10%; Japan 9%; Canada 8%; West Germany 5%. Export destinations (1978): U.S. 59%; France 13%; Italy 7%; Belgium-Luxembourg 6%. Main exports (1977–78): coffee 39%; bauxite 11%; toys and sports goods 10%; essential oils 6%; electrical equipment 5%.

Transport and Communications. Roads (1980) c. 4,000 km. Motor vehicles in use (1980): passenger c. 25,500; commercial (including buses) c. 9,500. Railways (1979) c. 250 km. Telephones (Jan. 1980) 34,900. Radio receivers (Dec. 1979) 101,000. Television receivers (Dec. 1979) 15,000.

Agriculture. Production (in 000; metric tons; 1981): rice c. 90; corn c. 180; sorghum c. 110; sweet potatoes c. 270; cassava c. 255; sugar, raw value c. 52; dry beans c. 50; bananas c. 210; plantains c. 300; mangoes c. 330; coffee c. 33; sisal c. 10; timber (cu m; 1980) c. 5,018. Livestock (in 000; 1981): cattle c. 1,200; pigs c. 600; goats c. 1,000; sheep c. 90; horses c. 415.

Industry. Production (in 000; metric tons; 1980): cement 240; bauxite (exports) 470; electricity (kw-hr) 315,000.

tence was thus reduced to six. In September he was released from prison but was rearrested in December. In January and March there were reports of unsuccessful invasion attempts by small bands of Haitian exiles.

Haiti's real gross domestic product fell by 1% in 1982 and by 2.1% in 1981. The decline was attributed to bad weather, which affected agricultural production and greatly reduced bauxite output. The International Monetary Fund approved a standby credit of $37 million in August. Bilateral and multilateral aid in 1982 was estimated at $140 million.   (ROBIN CHAPMAN)

Health and Disease

General Developments. Much of the medical news during 1982 reflected the increasingly complex relationship between the providers of health care and the rest of society and pointed up a growing awareness of the effect of life-style on health and longevity.

The Institute of Medicine, part of the U.S. National Academy of Sciences (NAS), issued a report that claimed that as much as 50% of the mortality from the ten leading causes of death in the U.S. could be traced to life-style, adding that three of four Americans die from heart disease, stroke, cancer, accidents, or violence, in all of which behaviour plays a part. The report quoted the surgeon-general's estimate that 320,000 deaths a year in the U.S. are related to smoking and stated that more than 200,000 deaths a year are due to alcohol-related causes, including accidents and violence.

The World Bank and the UN Food and Agriculture Organization announced their intention to reduce support for tobacco cultivation in the less

developed nations but showed reluctance to condemn the trade altogether because of short-term profitability. Stronger action would have been welcomed by the World Health Organization (WHO), which stated that controlling cigarette smoking in the less developed countries "could do more to improve health and prolong life than any other single action in the whole field of preventive medicine."

In another report from the Institute of Medicine, chronic, heavy marijuana smoking was blamed for inflammation and precancerous changes in the bronchial airways similar to those produced by tobacco smoking. The report stated that although marijuana may be less toxic in the short term than cigarettes, in combination the two are more dangerous than either alone. Total opposition to any attempts to legalize cannabis was pledged by ministers from 12 Council of Europe countries at the end of a two-day conference on drug abuse and illicit trafficking.

During the summer the NAS advised the American public that it could reduce its risk for cancer by following a diet that emphasizes fruit, vegetables, and whole-grain cereals and that is low in fat, alcohol, and cured or smoked foods. The anticancer diet was similar to the prudent diet recommended in 1977 by the American Heart Association to prevent heart disease, although it seemed to partially contradict an NAS report from 1980, which had found no reason for healthy Americans to reduce fat intake.

In 1982 a mysterious disease that killed 40% of its victims came under medical scrutiny. Called acquired immunodeficiency syndrome (AIDS), the disease results in failure of the body's immune system, which normally wards off cancer and infection. AIDS victims are ravaged by disease, including rare cancers and stubborn fungal infections. In some cases doctors were able to control patients' cancers and infections with drugs, but no AIDS victim regained normal health.

At first it was thought that AIDS was a new disease of homosexual men. Continued investigation, however, identified other groups of people with

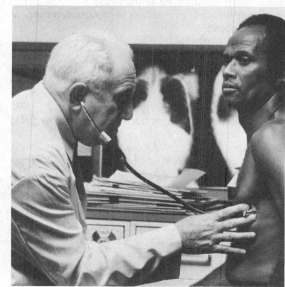

Environmental health specialist examines an asbestos victim suffering from mesothelioma, a type of cancer. Thousands of present and former employees of asbestos maker Manville Corp. filed damage suits against the company claiming work-related illnesses.

JIM POZARIK

Handball:
see Court Games

Harness Racing:
see Equestrian Sports

the disease; of the approximately 500 AIDS victims identified by late 1982, 27 were women and more than 60 were men who said they were not homosexual. Nevertheless, the epidemiological pattern strongly suggested that whatever triggers the disease can be sexually transmitted. Some medical researchers thought the cause to be a virus harboured in blood, semen, and other body fluids. They feared that, like hepatitis, the virus may be spread to the general population through blood transfusions and noted that several nonhomosexual AIDS victims were hemophiliacs who required frequent transfusions. The alarming spread of AIDS was arousing immense concern among public health specialists.

In May the 35th World Health Assembly in Geneva endorsed WHO's recommended list of 240 essential drugs that could serve virtually all the needs of the less developed nations and that would reduce their dependence upon imported and expensive pharmaceuticals, many of which were of doubtful use. The following month Bangladesh became the first country to adopt the WHO guidelines and announced legislation establishing a list of 250 essential medicines, banning 237 as dangerous, and directing that supplies of 1,500 others should not be renewed. The pharmaceutical industry worldwide expressed concern at the WHO policy, which threatened a large and expanding export trade to the third world.

Iatrogenic disease—disease resulting from the effects of treatment—claimed attention, most notably in the case of benoxaprofen, marketed under the trade name Opren in the U.K. and Oraflex in the U.S. Benoxaprofen is one of a group of nonsteroidal, anti-inflammatory agents widely used for the treatment of rheumatoid arthritis and osteoarthritis. It was approved for use in the U.K. in 1980 but was given clearance in the U.S. by the Food and Drug Administration (FDA) only in April 1982. Its manufacturer, Eli Lilly and Co., vigorously promoted benoxaprofen as being different from similar drugs already on the market. It had "different activity," the company said, and "preliminary evidence also suggests the disease process may be retarded in human patients" who take the drug. As a result of this promotion benoxaprofen became a market leader.

Concern over the drug began in May with publication in the *British Medical Journal* of two papers recording an unacceptably high incidence of side effects, notably death from liver poisoning. These papers stimulated a rash of reports from other sources, and by the beginning of August 3,500 reports of adverse reactions, including 61 fatal cases, prompted prohibition of further sales of benoxaprofen in the U.K. with immediate effect and for an initial period of three months. Almost immediately Eli Lilly suspended sales worldwide. In Washington a congressional hearing was told that Eli Lilly had made unsubstantiated claims for benoxaprofen when it was launched in a blaze of publicity, but the manufacturers made it clear that they still thought it to be safe when properly used. Benoxaprofen might yet return to the market, depending on the results of further studies, but not likely as the best-seller it was in 1982.

A major study of heart disease in the U.S. was concluded in 1982 with a surprising result: widely prescribed diuretics used to treat high blood pressure could be dangerous to some patients. The study, called the Multiple Risk Factor Intervention Trial (MRFIT), was conducted by the National Heart, Lung and Blood Institute at a cost of $115 million over ten years. Its aim was to determine whether men who reduced their blood cholesterol, blood pressure, and cigarette smoking—three major risk factors for heart disease—would live longer. The 12,866 MRFIT participants were divided into two groups. One group, the experimental group, was given intensive counseling and assistance in reducing its risk factors, whereas the other group, a control group, was referred to its members' doctors for medical treatment.

Both groups of men reduced their risk factors, but the experimental group reduced them more. So the MRFIT analysts predicted that this group would have a lower mortality rate. But the two groups had the same mortality rate. On the face of it, risk factor reduction was not beneficial. The MRFIT investigators, however, suspected that something unforeseen had influenced the results. They proposed that most of the subjects who reduced their risk factors indeed had been helped but that these positive results were canceled by negative ones in certain men who appeared to have been harmed by reducing their risk factors. In particular, those participants who had high blood pressure, abnormal electrocardiograms, and who were given diuretics to control their blood pressure had a 66% higher death rate than expected. It was felt that most men in the control group who had high blood pressure were given lower doses of diuretics or none at all.

The MRFIT researchers speculated that diuretics, particularly in high doses, may be depleting the body of potassium. For people whose hearts are already damaged, as evidenced by their electrocardiograms, this depletion may encourage rhythm disturbances leading to sudden death. The MRFIT study was the first in which it was ever suspected that diuretics may be toxic to some patients. The implications were far-reaching because diuretics were among the most commonly prescribed medicines.

In August Great Britain's Association of Anaesthetists produced a report suggesting that about 300 people in the U.K. die from surgical anesthesia every year and that in a further 1,800 postoperative deaths the anesthetic was a significant factor. The report stated that doctors were still making the same mistakes with anesthetics that they did 30 years earlier, despite improved knowledge, equipment, and drugs. Too many patients were given anesthetics without having been previously examined by the anesthetist for the presence of heart or lung disease or other relevant disabilities, and too many were anesthetised by insufficiently supervised trainees.

Doctors at the Karolinska Institute in Stockholm transplanted tissue into the living human brain for the first time in May. They injected cells taken from an adrenal gland of a patient with Parkinson's disease into a part of his brain known as the caudate nucleus in the hope that the cells would

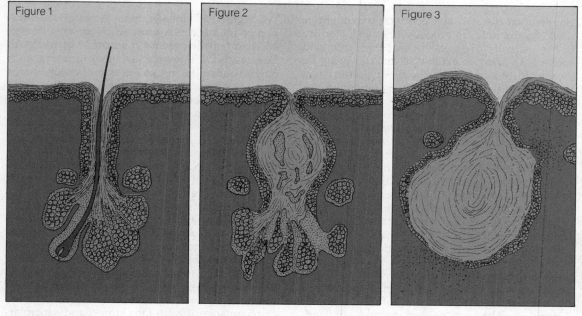

Sufferers from acne were given hope by a new drug, Accutane. Acne develops in hair follicles when surrounding sebaceous glands (Fig. 1) oversecrete oily sebum; pressure builds within the follicle (Fig. 2); and the wall of the follicle then ruptures, forming a deep lesion filled with sebum, bacteria, and pus (Fig. 3).

continue to secrete a key chemical, dopamine, that is deficient in the brains of Parkinson's disease victims. After several months the patient was showing slight improvement, but whether the effect was due to the transplant was not certain.

In early December medical history was made again when a surgical team led by William C. De-Vries of the University of Utah Medical Center implanted a permanent artificial heart into a human for the first time. The aluminum-and-plastic device, called the Jarvik-7 after its inventor, bioengineer Robert Jarvik (*see* BIOGRAPHIES), replaced the two lower chambers (ventricles) of the natural heart; its two rubber diaphragms, designed to mimic the pumping action of the natural heart, were kept beating by an external compressor connected to the implant by hoses. At year's end recipient Barney Clark, a 61-year-old retired dentist, was making remarkable progress despite setbacks that included a bout of brain seizures and further operations to close air leaks in his lungs and to replace one of the artificial ventricles, which had developed a crack.

Regulation and Legal Matters. The Department of Health and Human Services (HHS) announced in June that it would seek a warning label on aspirin sold in the U.S. The popular drug was suspected of being linked to Reye's syndrome, a serious and often fatal disease that strikes children recovering from flu or chicken pox. Reye's syndrome starts with vomiting and progresses to coma and brain swelling; patients who survive often suffer brain damage. But the link between aspirin use and Reye's syndrome was not well established, and some medical researchers felt that a warning label was unwarranted. Nonetheless, HHS Secretary Richard Schweiker announced that the agency would run a public awareness campaign to publicize the putative link between aspirin and Reye's syndrome as well as press for warning labels on the drug.

New FDA regulations to make packages for nonprescription drugs sold in the U.S. more tamper-resistant followed in the wake of a rash of bizarre poisonings that left seven people dead in the Chicago area during late September and early October. All of the victims had taken capsules of Extra-Strength Tylenol, a popular analgesic, that apparently had been individually opened, contaminated with cyanide, and returned to bottles that were then placed on the shelves of several retail stores in the city and nearby suburbs. The deaths resulted in the recall of all Tylenol capsules, both regular- and extra-strength, and brought a halt to their manufacture until appropriate packaging changes were implemented. In November the FDA announced that beginning in January 1983 most nonprescription drugs, many cosmetics, and certain "devices" like contact-lens solutions would be required to be made with tamper-resistant packaging; by the following May these products would need to carry a label warning consumers to avoid breached packages. Drug companies had several techniques at their disposal to discourage tampering, including capsules that indicate if they have been pulled apart, sealing of tablets and capsules in individual cells of plastic or foil, membrane seals over the mouths of bottles, and metal or plastic seals around bottle caps.

In April the British government took the unprecedented step of rejecting the advice of its official Committee on Safety of Medicines (CSM) by refusing to approve the use of the injectable contraceptive Depo-Provera for long-term use. Over the past decade the drug had been given to some ten million women, amassing a safety record better than that of oral contraceptives, with no deaths attributed to its use. A single injection is effective for three months, and the agent had been approved for short-term use in the U.K. under special circumstances; for example, to provide protection against pregnancy for the limited period after a male sexual partner has been vasectomized but is still capable of delivering sperm.

The CSM decided that the drug was safe for long-term use, and the government's refusal to grant a license for such use was based on political rather than scientific considerations. Objectors had claimed that the injectable contraceptive might be used, for example, to produce functional sterility in the mentally disabled without their informed consent, an injection every three months being far more readily administered without protest from the recipient than, say, the fitting of an intrauterine contraceptive. This appeared to be the first time that any drug apart from drugs of addiction had its use limited on social rather than clinical grounds. The decision produced strong protests from doctors and the manufacturer, Upjohn.

The FDA began deliberations in September on whether Depo-Provera should be approved for use in the U.S. More than 80 countries had approved the drug in the 15 years since Upjohn first applied to market it, but the FDA was hesitating because of hints that the drug might cause cancer.

During the year a new prescription drug to help acne sufferers was approved by the FDA. Accutane, a synthetic derivative of vitamin A, had been shown effective in clinical trials against cystic acne, a disfiguring disorder that afflicts 360,000 Americans. Although neither the FDA nor Hoffman-La Roche, the manufacturing company, knew how Accutane works, both believed it to be a major medical breakthrough.

In November 1981 a major medical cause célèbre came to an end when respected British pediatrician Leonard Arthur was acquitted of the attempted murder of a three-day-old victim of Down's syndrome (mongolism). The infant had been rejected by his parents, and the doctor had written on the case notes "Parents do not wish baby to survive" and the instructions "Nursing care only." He was further alleged to have prescribed a morphinelike drug at a dosage that could have favoured the development of the pneumonia from which the child died. The jury decided that Arthur had committed no crime or, in the words of the judge, "strayed beyond the bounds of proper medical ethics." Although the verdict was greeted with relief by the medical profession and made similar prosecutions unlikely for some time to come, it did nothing to clarify the law concerning the legal position of doctors who handle grossly disabled newborns.

The case stimulated intense public interest in the issue, and debate continued into 1982. In February Great Britain's director of public prosecutions, Sir Thomas Hetherington, suggested that a new charge should be devised for doctors accused of procuring the deaths of patients to distinguish these cases from common murder charges. The British Medical Association strongly objected but agreed that "the whole of this area of speeding the death of someone needs a good deal more clarification and lucid thinking." The British anti-abortion group Life placed an advertisement in the *Nursing Times* urging nurses to report doctors who breach abortion regulations as well as instances of late abortions carried out with no resuscitation equipment on standby, instances of children born alive as a result of abortions, and cases of handicapped babies who had been deliberately sedated.

U.S. courts saw an increase in a novel variety of lawsuits during the year. With the legalization of abortion more and more couples were suing doctors for "wrongful birth" or (on behalf of a child)

"wrongful life" following unsuccessful sterilization or the birth of a diseased infant after doctors had assured the parents of a normal birth. South Dakota and Minnesota had laws banning such claims, and at the instance of anti-abortion groups similar legislation was pending in Illinois, Michigan, and Missouri.

In September abortion foes were blocked in the U.S. Senate after 18 months of efforts to pass some sort of federal anti-abortion legislation. The bill that was defeated was sponsored by Sen. Jesse Helms (Rep., N.C.), who had tried to attach it to a debt-ceiling bill that had to be passed by October 1 to keep the government operating. Before its defeat Sen. Orrin G. Hatch (Rep., Utah) withdrew a companion bill he had sponsored for a constitutional amendment that would have permitted Congress and each state to restrict abortion. Hatch later said his bill would be brought to the Senate floor in the spring of 1983 for a full debate.

Starch blockers, one of the hot diet fads of 1982, came under attack by the FDA. Marketed as tablets in pharmacies, health food stores, and supermarkets under many different brand names, the products contain a protein obtained from beans that reportedly prevents the body from digesting starch, thus allowing consumption of starchy foods like breads and pasta without weight gain. The FDA contended that starch blockers are not a food, as their manufacturers claimed, but unapproved drugs that should be removed from the market. The agency was concerned that the drugs may be ineffective in promoting weight loss, may

The U.S. Food and Drug Administration in July prohibited the marketing of starch blockers, which had become enormously popular with dieters in the U.S. The FDA asserted that the pills were a drug and required testing before they could be sold over the counter.

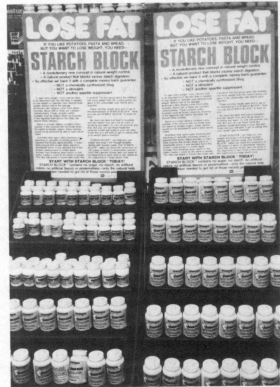

JACQUES M. CHENET/NEWSWEEK

interact with prescription drugs, may harm diabetics and pregnant women, and may have serious long-term effects. In addition, some users reported nausea, flatulence, diarrhea, vomiting, and stomach pains. Following orders in July that manufacturers discontinue marketing starch blockers, the FDA began seizure of the tablets in several states in September. The following month a federal district judge legally classified starch blockers as drugs and issued a ban on further manufacture and sale until experts could evaluate their safety.

Economic Aspects. Britain's National Health Service (NHS) was disrupted by industrial action from the spring onward. Low-paid hospital workers, which included porters, cleaners, cooks, laboratory technicians, clerks, and laundry staff, demanded a 12% pay increase, but the government claimed to be able to afford only 4%. Workers responded with such job actions as preventing delivery of supplies to hospitals, refusing to make clinical records available, refusing to deal with dirty linen, and, perhaps most importantly, refusing to allow hospital admission of nonurgent cases. The ancillary workers' cause earned wide support from the trade union movement, which made it a major political issue, and also attracted the backing of much of the medical profession. Late in the year the dispute remained unresolved, with neither side showing any inclination to give way.

Such troubles in Great Britain reflected a worldwide problem posed by the rapidly escalating costs of health care. Expenditure in the U.K. on the NHS rose from £165 per person in 1979 to £260 in 1982, while more than $1,200 (£650) in medical costs were spent on the average American in 1981, compared with $350 in 1970. According to a report from the HHS issued in July, national health care expenditures reached $287 billion in 1981, which represented a record 9.8% of the gross national product and a 15% increase over 1980. While inflation accounted for 70% of the increase, 10% was attributed to population growth and 20% to the growing proportion of elderly in the population. Medicare costs totaled nearly $45 billion for 1981—up 21.5% over 1980—and averaged $2,400 per beneficiary. The report noted that in 1981 the average person paid only one-third of personal health care expenses directly, compared with slightly more than half in 1965; two-thirds were covered by governments, private insurers, and other "third party" agencies.

(DONALD W. GOULD; GINA KOLATA)

[421.B.2.d; 421.C; 423.C.2.k; 424.B.1.a.i; 424.C.1.b; 425.D.3.a–b; 425.I.2.d–e; 425.J]

MENTAL HEALTH

The use of electroconvulsive therapy (ECT) in the treatment of mental illness remained a matter for dispute. At the end of 1981 Great Britain's Royal College of Psychiatrists published a major report based on more than 3,000 questionnaires that had been sent to every doctor in the U.K. known to be using ECT. The investigators also visited many of the 400 hospitals and clinics where the treatment was employed. More than 80% of the psychiatrists interviewed agreed that the technique was of greatest value in treating severe depression that

Paralyzed from the waist down as a result of a car crash, a patient was able to stand up and even ride a bicycle after being fitted with a prosthesis developed by Jerrold Petrofsky and Roger Lazglar of Wright State University in Dayton, Ohio. The device consists of electrodes connected to a microcomputer and strapped to the hip, knee, and ankle joints.

had proved resistant to drug therapy, but there was great divergence of opinion concerning its value in such other conditions as acute schizophrenia, for which half thought it occasionally appropriate and a quarter said it was "probably not appropriate." Only 1% thought that ECT should never be used, which seemed surprising in view of the controversy that had surrounded this treatment in recent years.

A disturbing aspect of the report revealed that administration of ECT usually was left to junior members of the medical staff who had received little training or guidance in the use of the technique and who had to be told what to do by attendant nurses or anesthetists familiar with the routine. Very few of the clinics displayed diagrams showing the correct positioning of ECT electrodes. ECT machines are so made that the strength and duration of the current pulse can be varied to suit the needs of individual patients, but in 72% of the clinics visited the settings on the machines were never altered. In more than a quarter of the clinics the machines were obsolete and did not conform to hospital safety standards. Many of the older machines had no automatic timer, so that the duration of the delivered shock depended entirely upon the manipulations of the operator, a particularly serious fault because overdoses can lead to prolonged memory impairment. Although research had shown that ECT is beneficial only if a convulsion is induced, many patients do not convulse, but this fact was unrecognized by some doctors, who mistook a tonic jerking of muscles for the desired effect.

As a result of the report the college set up a working party to prepare improved guidelines on the use of ECT for members, and the secretary of state for social services set up another working group to investigate the adequacy of apparatuses available in National Health Service hospitals.

A worrisome tendency among old people toward violence was noted during the year by Bernard

Knight of the University of Wales, Cardiff, and William Petrie of Vanderbilt University, Nashville, Tenn. In a survey of patients in the geriatric unit of a state psychiatric hospital in Nashville, Petrie discovered that 139 had committed or had threatened acts of violence. The weapon of choice was a gun or a knife. He classified 18 of the 139 as "violent." The patients had an average age of 74. Knight told a British Medical Association symposium that he had dealt with three cases of extreme violence among elderly people within as many weeks. He said that in such cases years of pent-up frustrations seemed to be released in one great outpouring and suggested that brain degeneration of the elderly might release inhibitions in much the same way as alcohol.

A panel convened by the National Institutes of Health in the U.S. concluded that there was insufficient evidence to support claims for the efficacy of the Feingold diet first proposed by California allergist Ben Feingold in 1973. He advocated the exclusion of all artificial food additives and natural salicylates as an effective treatment for hyperactivity in children. Children diagnosed as hyperactive had been subjected to various forms of treatment in recent years, particularly in the U.S., including administration of amphetamines and even brain surgery. In the early 1980s the condition was still poorly understood, too loosely defined, and sometimes confused with behaviour resulting from other, better understood disorders such as lead poisoning and perhaps even with the natural ebullience of youth.

Guy Chouinard, director of clinical psychopharmacology at the Royal Victoria Hospital in Montreal, reported that one-third of all patients taking major tranquilizers, or antipsychotic drugs (*e.g.*, Thorazine, Stelazine), are likely to suffer from tardive dyskinesia as a side effect. This condition involves distressing involuntary muscular movements, particularly of the face, lips, and tongue. His findings supported earlier recommendations that these drugs should be used only for the short-term treatment of patients with acute schizophrenia, who can benefit greatly from such medication.　　　　　　　　(DONALD W. GOULD)

[321.C.4.c.iii; 423.C.2.i; 438.D.1.a–b; 438.D.4.a]

DENTISTRY

In a sweeping report on the future of dentistry the American Dental Association (ADA) during 1982 projected that, although new methods of financing and delivering dental care were gaining popularity, the mainstream of services would continue to take place in the offices of the private practitioner. As an example of alternate care the ADA noted the slowly growing number of dental centres in department and drug stores, which increased from one such clinic in California in 1977 to 91 retail-store dentistry centres in 17 states and in the District of Columbia in 1982.

A specific strain of bacterium that inhibits the function of certain white blood cells offered a new clue to researchers at the State University of New York at Buffalo who were studying ways of fighting periodontal, or gum, disease. Gum disease, the major cause of tooth loss in adults, causes the underlying bone to resorb into the jaw, thus allowing the teeth to loosen. T. E. Van Dyke reported that cells of the immune system called neutrophils guard the gum crevices against bacterial attacks. His research suggested that one kind of bacterium specifically inhibits binding of stimulatory molecules to the neutrophil surface. This action at the site of the gum crevices indicated that periodontal disease may be of local rather than of systemic nature.

One successful attempt at a less expensive substitute for increasingly costly silver-based dental alloys came from L. B. Johnson of the University of Virginia. A conventional alloy contains mainly tin, silver, and copper, which generally are melted together and then powdered. This powder is then mixed with mercury at the time of treatment. The outside of each alloy particle reacts with the mercury to form a matrix in which the unreacted portions of each particle set, resembling pebbles in cement. These particles, however, still contain about 60% silver. Johnson replaced the powdered alloy with copper granules to which enough silver and tin had been plated to allow the matrix to form as usual. The difference is that the particles set in the matrix are mostly copper and thus much less expensive than granules of silver alloy.

In recent years one approach to the prevention of cavities has been to replace sucrose with non-sucrose sweeteners. According to Larry Breeding of the University of Kentucky College of Dentistry, two such sweeteners, saccharin and Acesulfame-K, may curb dental caries (decay) by means other than simple substitution. Breeding found that these synthetic sweeteners actively inhibit the growth of the tooth-decay bacterium, *Streptococcus mutans*, and also restrict the ability of this organism to use such dietary carbohydrates as sucrose in the development of caries.　　　　(LOU JOSEPH)

[422.E.1.a.ii; 10/35.C.1]

See also Demography; Life Sciences; Nobel Prizes; Social Security and Welfare Services.

Citizens in Berkeley, Calif., succeeded in getting a referendum on the ballot to ban electric shock therapy. The movement was led by a man who had undergone such therapy in the past.

WILLIAM THOMAS

THE NEW PROHIBITION

by Richard Whittingham

Deep in the night a large fishing boat plows through the ocean under a star-studded sky. A little more than 12 mi off the Florida coast, the engines are cut, and the ship's anchor splashes into the water. A short while later, the silence is broken by the harsh rasp of a speedboat's motor, then another, and another. . . . The sleek boats close on the mother ship like metal shavings drawn to a magnet. As they tie up alongside, the deck above is suddenly awash with activity as men rush to pass the cargo down to those in the speedboats. Satchels of cash are thrown up to eager hands on the fishing boat. Minutes later, the small boats are racing back toward shore, every cubic inch filled with contraband. At a remote docking place, trucks wait to take the illicit cargo on the next leg of its journey, one that will eventually end with the surreptitious sale of the goods to a variety of consumers.

Scenes like this were played out countless times in the 1920s and early '30s, and they are occurring in almost the same fashion in the 1980s; only the commodities have changed. Marijuana, cocaine, heroin, and Quaaludes have replaced the beer and bootleg whiskey of Prohibition. The smugglers, once called "rum runners," are now known as "reefer runners."

The illegal manufacture of the substance, the methods of smuggling, and the channels of distribution are astonishingly similar. For example, raw alcohol was manufactured in one place, distilled in another, watered down in still another; pure cocaine or heroin goes through a similar process of reduction before it hits the street. In both cases, huge profits were—or are—made at each stage. From the astronomical amount of cash involved to the killings and the political and police corruption, the parallels cut deeply into the moral and economic heart of the United States.

The Noble Experiment. The Prohibition era began one minute after midnight on Jan. 16, 1920. The 18th Amendment to the U.S. Constitution had rendered the nation dry, and the Volstead Act was passed to enforce the ban on the manufacture, importation, and sale of alcoholic beverages. But the nation was hardly ready for that kind of reform. On the contrary, the "flappers and philosophers" of the 1920s, as F. Scott Fitzgerald called them, were about to launch what he termed "the greatest gaudiest spree in American history."

To supply the wants of the wets, a vast illicit trade arose, manipulated by organized crime. In the lucrative but bloody business, names like Al Capone, Johnny Torrio, Dion O'Banion, Hymie Weiss, Bugs Moran, Machine Gun Jack McGurn, Legs Diamond, Dutch Schultz, Frank Costello, and Detroit's Purple Gang soon became the stuff of infamous legends.

Throughout the U.S., secret stills and breweries were set in operation. (Some distilleries controlled by crime bosses turned out as much as 2,000 gal of whiskey a day.) Their crude output was bottled and trucked to the speakeasies and roadhouses that catered to a legion of thirsty consumers.

On the coasts, the rum runners (who ran everything from whiskey and beer to raw alcohol) flourished. Whiskey that was "right off the boat" was known to be far superior to that manufactured in the clandestine stills. The smugglers loaded up in the West Indies, the Bahamas, Cuba, and other south-of-the-border ports and moved their cargo into the U.S. through Florida, the Louisiana bayous, and the Virginia capes. Farther north, other boats set out from Canada and delivered their illegal freight along the shores of Long Island, New Jersey, and the Great Lakes. Even the fragile airplanes of the '20s were pressed into service to ferry loads of booze on short hops from Canada to U.S. soil.

Federal officials inspect cardboard boxes filled with packets of illegal narcotics. The huge drug shipment was seized in the Miami area.

MIAMI HERALD/BLACK STAR

Richard Whittingham, a free-lance writer, is the author of Martial Justice, The Rand McNally Almanac of Adventure, *and many other books on contemporary affairs.*

415

Competition was fierce. There were "rum wars" waged between rival importers on the high seas and in the ports, and there were "beer wars" in the cities between factions of the crime syndicate that sold and distributed the "hootch." Blood flowed freely. The "St. Valentine's Day Massacre" of 1929, when seven men were machine-gunned to death in a Chicago garage, was a notorious but relatively minor incident, measured against the 300 to 400 bootleg-booze-related murders that took place in Chicago each year during those times.

The government tried to combat the rampant disregard for the new law, but it was a hopeless task. The Coast Guard captured thousands of boats used to smuggle alcohol into the U.S., but they were only a drop in the proverbial bucket. In the cities, practically everyone was on the take. In New York City alone, there were an estimated 32,000 speakeasies in existence by 1929 (and 219,000 nationwide). As Mayor Fiorello La Guardia said: "To enforce the Volstead Act in New York you would need 250,000 policemen and another 200,000 to keep the police within the law."

A Case of Déja Vu. It all ended when Prohibition was repealed in 1933 by the 21st Amendment. The stills disappeared; the smugglers went back to fishing; and the gangsters channeled their energies into prostitution, gambling, extortion, and other sordid endeavours.

Some 50 years after repeal of the 18th Amendment, however, there has been a reprise of Prohibition-type activities. Instead of stills and breweries turning out illicit beverages, there are fields and gardens sown with marijuana, and clandestine chemical laboratories for refining and cutting narcotics and manufacturing other drugs. As in the '20s, the best quality goods are imported (now from places like Colombia and Bolivia). And the smugglers use the same methods, although today's reefer runners may have $250,000 speedboats capable of reaching 70 mph (113 km/h) and equipped with radar scanners, infrared night-vision scopes, even satellite navigational gear.

There is the same intramural warfare, though leisure suits and gold chains have replaced the shoulder-padded suitcoats and flip-brim hats of the hoodlums who once killed each other over territories and profits, and today's feuding parties often speak Spanish. (One thing remains the same as in the Prohibition days: among the preferred weapons for drug-related executions is the machine gun.) Like Chicago in the '20s, Miami, as the capital city of the illicit drug business, has the worst crime rate in the nation. Of the 250 to 300 murders committed in Miami each year in the 1980s, approximately one-third are believed to be drug-related.

Big Business. In an inflationary era, the drug trade involves sums of money that dwarf the crime syndicate operations of the '20s. Whereas Al Capone allegedly grossed between $100 million and $200 million a year from his Chicago bootlegging operation, the drug industry's figures are calculated in the multibillions. One federal bust alone (a government operation called "Grouper") resulted in the confiscation of $1 billion worth of drugs and the indictment of 155 people. It is estimated that cocaine with a street value of $28 billion is smuggled into the U.S. each year. The drug smuggling traffic in south Florida is estimated at between $7 billion and $12 billion annually. In California, the largest agricultural cash crop in that fertile land of fruits and vegetables is thought to be marijuana.

Offenders commonly come up with $1 million in bail—in cash—within hours of being arrested. Smugglers abandon $200,000 yachts and $500,000 airplanes after a single run; when the cargo is worth perhaps $10 million, such losses are a small proportion of sales.

Putting the financial aspect of today's drug trade in startling perspective, *Time* magazine reported the story of a young drug dealer in Florida, one Donald Steinberg. At the age of 28, he owned an estate in Fort Lauderdale, a townhouse in Manhattan worth $2 million, a fleet of cars that included a Rolls-Royce and a Ferrari. At his peak earnings (1978), Steinberg, according to estimates by the U.S. Drug Enforcement Administration, had an annual revenue of $100 million from the sale of 500,000 lb (2,270 kg) of marijuana. In the course of one 90-day period, he reaped a $12 million profit.

Steinberg was caught, convicted, and sent to prison, but others have taken up where he left off. The Coast Guard and Customs Service are continually fighting the smuggling of narcotics and marijuana, and federal agents and local authorities are combating the dissemination and use of the drugs inside the country. Their job is no less difficult than it was in the 1920s.

Drugs constitute a criminal and economic problem of international proportions. The United Nations Commission on Narcotic Drugs has established a major five-year program (1982–86) aimed at developing a strategy to mobilize international efforts to check both drug abuse and the proliferating international traffic in drugs. Among its stated objectives are the improvement of drug-control systems, eradication of illicit sources of supply, prevention of the inappropriate use of narcotic drugs, and reduction of the demand for them.

It will not be as easy to achieve these aims as it was to curb the abuses of the old Prohibition era. There is no simple solution like Repeal.

Historic Preservation

As of August 1982, 67 states had deposited an instrument of ratification or acceptance of the International Convention Concerning the Protection of the World Cultural and Natural Heritage; the "World Heritage Convention," as it was usually called, was adopted by the General Conference of UNESCO in 1972 and came into effect in 1975 after 20 UNESCO member states had adhered to it. States which adhered after late 1981 were Benin, Burundi, Malawi, Peru, Spain, and Zimbabwe.

By the end of 1981, 112 sites had been inscribed on the World Heritage List. Among the most recent were the Roman and romanesque monuments of Arles, the Roman theatre and triumphal arch of Orange, and the Chateau of Chambord (all in France); the archaeological park and Maya ruins of Quirigua (Guatemala); and the Olympic National Park (Washington State). *A Legacy for All: The World's Major Natural, Cultural and Historic Sites*, published by UNESCO, presented 57 sites on the World Heritage List that were inscribed in 1978 and 1979. Essentially a photographic essay with descriptive text, this publication was the first in a series that would be updated approximately every two years.

Monumentum, the international architectural conservation journal of the International Council of Monuments and Sites (ICOMOS), had a new format and now appeared as a quarterly. Edited by Derek Linstrum of the University of York's Institute of Advanced Architectural Studies, *Monumentum* continued to have a leading role in the international dissemination of general and technical knowledge in the field of historic preservation. A third exchange of East-West specialists in the "Field of Preservation and Rehabilitation of Historic Quarters in the European Region," co-sponsored by ICOMOS and UNESCO, took place in October–November 1982. Pursuant to the recommendations of the Conference on Security and Cooperation in Europe held in Helsinki, Fin., in 1975, these exchanges were to take place biennially after their inauguration in 1978. There was a growing recognition of the importance of this program among those concerned with European and North American cooperation for the safeguarding, restoration, and preservation of historic monuments and sites.

Two of UNESCO's 27 campaigns to preserve monuments and sites of international significance had ended successfully. The Nubian campaign had been completed in 1980, and work on the 9th-century Buddhist monument of Borobudur on the island of Java was finished in 1981. A grand ceremony at Borobudur paid tribute to this immense undertaking and to the remarkable demonstration of international support it elicited. The government of Indonesia contributed approximately $14 million, and over $6 million was donated by 25 member states of UNESCO.

Another of UNESCO's international campaigns, launched in 1974, was to save the archaeological site of Mohenjo-daro in Pakistan, one of the main

urban centres of a civilization that flourished in the Indus Valley about 5,000 years ago. Since the initial excavations over 50 years ago, Mohenjo-daro had been threatened by rising groundwater caused by the development of irrigation in this arid area of Sind and by the wanderings of the Indus River. A system of pumping stations, drainage canals, and protective embankments was almost complete, but work had yet to begin on the essential deflector spurs at the river's edge. In 1981 the U.S. government contributed almost $1 million to support the project.

At the invitation of the Mexican government, the World Conference on Cultural Policies (Mondiacult) took place in Mexico City during July 26–Aug. 6, 1982. Convened by UNESCO, the conference was attended by 970 participants. Its purpose was to review the experience acquired since the Intergovernmental Conference on Institutional, Administrative and Financial Aspects of Cultural Policies in 1970; to consider fundamental problems regarding culture in the contemporary world; and to formulate new guidelines. Over 200 resolutions were adopted, the significance of which—particularly in relation to historic preservation—had yet to be assessed. Nevertheless, in Mondiacult's

A massive campaign launched by UNESCO restored the 9th-century Buddhist temple of Borobudur on the island of Java. Workers dealt with 750,000 pieces of the deteriorating monument during the restoration process.

Hebrew Literature:
see Literature

Highways:
see Engineering Projects; Transportation

Hinduism:
see Religion

Hockey:
see Field Hockey and Lacrosse; Ice Hockey

Holland:
see Netherlands, The

Workers erected a scaffold around the Erechtheum temple on the Acropolis in Athens in an effort to save the eroding building. Iron clamps were removed and were replaced with noncorrosive metals.

WIDE WORLD

"Mexico Declaration," the international community affirmed its belief in the importance of culture (defined as the identity of a people) as an essential element for "development." This came at a time when the preservation and, indeed, the very existence of such monuments as Angkor Wat (Kampuchea) and Tyre (Lebanon) were in question, and when the survival of many national preservation programs was being threatened by budget cuts.

The return or restitution of cultural property also figured prominently in the Mondiacult discussions. Support had grown for the principle that art treasures whose absence "causes the greatest anguish" should be returned to their countries of origin. The process was not seen in isolation but as accompanied by the strengthening of museums and the training of personnel.

In the U.K. an important addition to the official list of ancient monuments was the Tudor warship "Mary Rose," which sank off Portsmouth in 1545 and was raised in 1982 after a salvage operation initiated in 1965. (*See* ARCHAEOLOGY: *Special Report*.)　　　　　　　　(JOHN POPPELIERS)

　　See also Architecture; Environment; Museums.

Honduras

Honduras

A republic of Central America, Honduras is bounded by Nicaragua, El Salvador, Guatemala, the Caribbean Sea, and the Pacific Ocean. Area: 112,088 sq km (43,277 sq mi). Pop. (1981 est.): 3,822,000, including 90% mestizo. Cap. and largest city: Tegucigalpa (pop., 1980 est., 444,700). Language: Spanish; some Indian dialects. Religion: Roman Catholic. Presidents in 1982, Brig. Gen. Policarpo Paz García (provisional) and, from January 27, Roberto Suazo Córdova.

The election of a civilian president, Roberto Suazo Córdova (*see* BIOGRAPHIES), in November 1981 ended nearly nine years of military rule in Honduras and raised hopes for peace, but these were shattered in 1982. On the one hand, Gen. Gustavo Alvarez Martínez, commander in chief of the Army, consolidated his position and strengthened the Army to 20,000; on the other, leftist guerrilla activity increased, culminating in the eight-day siege of the chamber of commerce at San Pedro Sula in September when about 80 people, in-

Roberto Suazo Córdova (right) was inaugurated as president of Honduras on January 27. His accession to power ended more than ten years of military rule in that country.

SUSAN GREENWOOD—GAMMA/LIAISON

HONDURAS

Education. (1980) Primary, pupils 582,612, teachers 16,612; secondary and vocational, pupils 125,018, teachers 4,417; teacher training, students 4,250, teachers 152; higher (university only), students 24,601, teaching staff 1,507.

Finance. Monetary unit: lempira, with (Sept. 20, 1982) a par value of 2 lempiras to U.S. $1 (free rate of 3.43 lempiras = £1 sterling). Gold and other reserves (April 1982) U.S. $105 million. Budget (1981 actual): revenue 738.7 million lempiras; expenditure 883.2 million lempiras. Gross national product (1981) 4,943,000,000 lempiras. Money supply (March 1982) 614.2 million lempiras. Cost of living (Tegucigalpa; 1975 = 100; June 1982) 189.5.

Foreign Trade. (1980) Imports 2,017,400,000 lempiras; exports 1,658,800,000 lempiras. Import sources: U.S. 42%; Venezuela 11%; Japan 10%; Guatemala 6%. Export destinations: U.S. 52%; West Germany 12%; The Netherlands 5%; Guatemala 5%. Main exports: bananas 27%; coffee 25%; beef 8%; metal ores c. 6%.

Transport and Communications. Roads (1980) 13,448 km. Motor vehicles in use (1980): passenger 21,600; commercial (including buses) 45,000. Railways (1980) c. 1,928 km. Air traffic (1980): c. 394 million passenger-km; freight c. 3.5 million net ton-km. Shipping (1981): merchant vessels 100 gross tons and over 143; gross tonnage 207,280. Telephones (Jan. 1980) 27,400. Radio receivers (Dec. 1979) 176,000. Television receivers (Dec. 1979) 49,000.

Agriculture. Production (in 000; metric tons; 1981): corn c. 338; sorghum c. 45; sugar, raw value 220; dry beans c. 42; bananas c. 1,330; plantains c. 167; oranges c. 28; pineapples c. 34; palm oil c. 12; coffee c. 90; cotton, lint c. 7; tobacco c. 8; beef and veal c. 50; timber (cu m; 1980) c. 5,283. Livestock (in 000; 1981): cattle 2,336; pigs c. 580; horses c. 151; chickens c. 4,900.

Industry. Production (in 000; metric tons; 1980): lead ore (metal content) 15; zinc ore (metal content) 22; cement (1979) 288; petroleum products (1979) c. 410; electricity (kw-hr) 800,000.

HUNGARY

Education. (1981) Primary, pupils 1,213,500, teachers 78,053; secondary, pupils 209,300, teachers 15,966; vocational, students 157,400, teachers 10,700; higher, students 63,400, teaching staff 13,843.

Finance. Monetary unit: forint, with (Sept. 20, 1982) a free rate of 38.54 forints to U.S. $1 (66.08 forints = £1 sterling). Gold and other reserves (Dec. 1981) U.S. $1,568,000,000. Budget (1981 actual): revenue 472.6 billion forints; expenditure 482.1 billion forints. Gross domestic product (1981) 774.2 billion forints. Money supply (Dec. 1981) 167.6 billion forints. Consumer prices (1975 = 100; June 1982) 152.6.

Foreign Trade. (1981) Imports 314,284,000,000 forints; exports 299,405,000,000 forints. Import sources: U.S.S.R. 29%; West Germany 12%; East Germany 7%; Austria 6%; Czechoslovakia 5%. Export destinations: U.S.S.R. 33%; West Germany 9%; East Germany 7%; Czechoslovakia 6%. Main exports (1980): machinery 21%; food 19%; motor vehicles 10%; chemicals 9%.

Transport and Communications. Roads (1980) 87,689 km (including 209 km expressways). Motor vehicles in use (1980): passenger 1,021,330; commercial 124,540. Railways: (1980) 7,826 km; traffic (1981) 12,372,000,000 passenger-km, freight 23,850,000,000 net ton-km. Air traffic (1980): c. 998 million passenger-km; freight c. 79 million net ton-km. Inland waterways in regular use (1980) 1,302 km. Telephones (Jan. 1980) 1,186,500. Radio licenses (Dec. 1979) 2,608,000. Television licenses (Dec. 1980) 2,766,000.

Agriculture. Production (in 000; metric tons; 1981): corn c. 6,500; wheat c. 4,800; barley c. 950; rye c. 135; potatoes c. 1,600; sugar, raw value c. 587; cabbages c. 170; tomatoes c. 372; onions c. 150; sunflower seed 625; rapeseed 105; green peas c. 197; plums c. 170; apples c. 1,100; wine c. 550; tobacco c. 15; milk c. 2,680; beef and veal c. 178; pork c. 950. Livestock (in 000; Dec. 1980): cattle 1,918; pigs 8,330; sheep 3,090; horses 120; chickens 61,347.

Industry. Index of production (1975 = 100; 1981) 121. Production (in 000; metric tons; 1981): coal 3,065; lignite 22,878; crude oil 2,024; natural gas (cu m) 6,010,000; electricity (kw-hr) 24,206,000; iron ore (24% metal content) 422; pig iron 2,204; crude steel 3,646; bauxite 2,950; aluminum 74; cement 4,636; petroleum products c. 10,200; sulfuric acid 573, fertilizers (1980) nitrogenous 651, phosphate c. 216; cotton yarn 58; man-made fibres 29; commercial vehicles (units) 12.

Hungary

cluding the finance minister, the economy minister, and the president of the central bank, were held hostage. In December President Suazo's daughter was held captive for several days by leftists in Guatemala.

Turmoil in neighbouring countries spread into Honduras. Refugees from El Salvador entered the country, and supporters of the late president Anastasio Somoza of Nicaragua continued to use Honduras as a base from which to conduct raids. In an attempt to maintain Honduras as a buffer state, the U.S. sent additional military advisers. U.S. Pres. Ronald Reagan visited Honduras in December.

Because of its vulnerability to fluctuating commodity prices and severe lack of working capital, Honduras seemed likely to remain one of the poorest countries in the region. On September 1 trade was resumed between Honduras and El Salvador, following a 13-year break after the 1969 war.

(LUCY BLACKBURN)

Hungary

A people's republic of central Europe. Hungary is bordered by Czechoslovakia, the U.S.S.R., Romania, Yugoslavia, and Austria. Area: 93,036 sq km (35,921 sq mi). Pop. (1982 est.): 10,702,000, including (1978 est.) Magyar 98.6%; Gypsy 0.3%; German 0.3%; other 0.8%. Cap. and largest city: Budapest (pop., 1982 est., 2,062,000). Language: Hungarian 95.8%. Religion (1980 est.): Roman Catholic 54%; Protestant 21.6%; atheist 7.2%; other 8.5%; none 8.7%. First secretary of the Hungarian Socialist Workers' (Communist) Party in 1982,

Janos Kadar; chairman of the Presidential Council (chief of state), Pal Losonczi; president of the Council of Ministers (premier), György Lazar.

The two major events of 1982 were Hungary's admission to the International Monetary Fund (IMF) and the official visit of Pres. François Mitterrand of France. On May 5 the executive board of the IMF approved Hungary's application for membership, and the following day it became the 146th member of that institution. Hungary's quota was set at $415 million, giving it access to up to $2 billion of credit. Automatically, Hungary also became a member of the World Bank. A $580 million IMF credit was agreed to on November 11.

Seven months earlier, on Oct. 1, 1981, the National Bank of Hungary had taken the unprecedented step—for a member country of the Soviet-dominated Council for Mutual Economic Assistance (Comecon)—of introducing a single official rate for the Hungarian forint in relation to each of the convertible Western currencies. This decision, however, did not mean a change in the rates of the forint against the "transferable" ruble and other Comecon currencies. It seemed certain that Hungary had not taken such an initiative without clearing it in advance with the U.S.S.R.

A $260 million loan to the National Bank of Hungary was signed on August 9 in London. At the

Hong Kong:
see Dependent States

Horse Racing:
see Equestrian Sports; Gambling

Horticulture:
see Gardening

Hospitals:
see Health and Disease

end of 1982 the total Hungarian debt in hard currencies was estimated at $7.2 billion, representing about $770 per head of population. This was not an enormous burden for a country with a gross national product estimated at $2,000 per head by IMF officials and as high as $3,850 per head according to the World Bank.

In order to reduce state subsidies and ensure economic equilibrium, the government introduced a series of considerable price increases. They included 100% on the price of rail travel, 14–25% on fuel, and 20–25% on bread, flour, and rice.

President Mitterrand's visit on July 7–9 was formally a reciprocation of the official visit to France undertaken by First Secretary Janos Kadar (see BIOGRAPHIES) in November 1978, but in reality it became something more. In his public statements the president described his trip to Budapest as "the shortest road toward the East-West dialogue," and he duly acknowledged Hungary's unique position within the Socialist camp. He brought with him five ministers and promised to expand Franco-Hungarian economic and cultural relations.

Kadar replied that though Hungary and France belonged to different political regimes and were members of opposite alliances, President Mitterrand's visit was of particular importance because it went beyond the normal framework of bilateral relations. Kadar also alluded to the fact that the part played by France in Hungary's foreign exchanges was too modest and expressed a hope that it would increase as a result of talks between the French ministers and their Hungarian counterparts. At the time France was occupying 59th place in the list of countries supplying goods to Hungary.

In 1981 Hungarian foreign trade amounted to $9.2 billion in imports and $8.7 billion in exports. Although in 1975 about two-thirds of Hungary's total trade was with other Comecon countries, that share was reduced in 1982 to slightly more than one-half of the total.

In June some important changes of personnel took place in the ruling Hungarian Socialist Workers' (Communist) Party. Gyorgy Aczel, a reformer, a deputy premier, and a Politburo member, returned to the Central Committee as a secretary, an important position that he had occupied during 1967–74. He was replaced as deputy premier by Istvan Sarlos, another Politburo member. Andras Gyenyes retired not only from his post as secretary but also from membership in the Central Committee. (K. M. SMOGORZEWSKI)

Ice Hockey

North American. The New York Islanders capped a brilliant season-long effort by winning their third consecutive Stanley Cup, defeating the Vancouver Canucks in four straight games. The greatest peril to their success came in the five-game opening round of the play-offs when the Pittsburgh Penguins led by two goals late in the last game before the Islanders rallied to win that series in overtime.

The Islanders went on to a rousing series against

Hydroelectric Power: see Energy; Engineering Projects
Hydrology: see Earth Sciences

The New York Islanders won their third consecutive Stanley Cup on May 16 by defeating the Vancouver Canucks in four straight games. Mike Bossy (left) of the Islanders was awarded the Conn Smythe Trophy.

the New York Rangers, rejuvenated by U.S. Olympic coach Herb Brooks, and then eliminated the Quebec Nordiques in the Wales Conference championship before defeating the Canucks. It was the first year of the divisional play-off format in which most of the National Hockey League's strongest teams were in the Islanders' conference.

During the season the Islanders set a league record for consecutive wins of 15. The ascendancy of their dynasty was paralleled by the decline of another: the Montreal Canadiens were ousted in the opening round of the play-offs by the Quebec Nordiques.

The 1981–82 season also was notable for the greatest individual performance by a player in NHL history. Twenty-one-year-old Wayne Gretzky in his third season with Edmonton swept through the record book again, setting marks for most goals in one season (92), most assists (120), and most points (212). His point total broke his own record of the previous year and gained him the Art Ross Trophy. For the third year in a row Gretzky was also awarded the Hart Trophy as the most valuable player during the regular season.

Gretzky's performance overshadowed another great year for the New York Islanders' 25-year-old right wing, Mike Bossy, who scored 147 points, the fourth highest in league history. Bossy also won the Conn Smythe Trophy for most valuable competitor in the play-offs.

During the summer there were some ownership changes, including the transfer of the Colorado

Rockies to the New Jersey Meadowlands Arena, where the team was to be known as the New Jersey Devils. The Devils would take their place in the heated Patrick Division with the nearby New York Rangers, New York Islanders, and Philadelphia Flyers, creating a tight geographic rivalry. The new arena seated 19,000 people for hockey and could make ice in about eight hours, half the usual time.

Another ownership change was the sale of the Detroit Red Wings by Bruce Norris, whose family had owned the team for 50 years. The new owner was Mike Ilitch, who promptly induced the first management defection from the championship Islanders, hiring their assistant general manager and chief scout, Jimmy Devellano, to be Detroit's general manager. Herb Brooks, who sharpened the Rangers considerably in his first year as coach, signed a new contract with the team for $200,000 annually. This made him the highest paid coach ever in the league.

In contrast to the strife caused by the disputes in the National Football League, the NHL and its Players Association quietly and smoothly struck a deal for a new four-year collective bargaining agreement. Its main provision provided for easier movement of free-agent players.

The league, still unable to woo national television revenues because of ice hockey's regionalism, turned to the new technology of cable television and signed a contract with the USA network for exclusive national cable TV rights over the next two years. Individual teams increasingly were turning to this medium in their local areas. For example, the New York Islanders signed a groundbreaking 30-year agreement with the SportsChannel network.

The year was not without the usual controversy over violence on the ice, but this time there was a new twist. A federal jury in Detroit awarded $850,000 in damages to Dennis Polonich, who had brought a personal injury suit against Wilf Paiement, then with the Colorado Rockies. Polonich had sued Paiement for hitting him with a stick during a game, breaking his nose and giving him a concussion and numerous cuts. It was the first suit of its kind in NHL history. Previously, players had only been brought to court for violent actions during games by local criminal prosecutors, and therefore the award was said to constitute a landmark.

Among end-of-year honours, the Vezina Trophy for the single top goalkeeper was awarded to the Islanders' Bill Smith. The Jennings Trophy for goalies with the best goals-against average went to Denis Herron and Rick Wamsley of Montreal, who posted a 2.79 average. The rookie-of-the-year award was won by Dale Hawerchuk, a forward with Winnipeg. Rick Middleton of Boston received the Lady Byng Trophy for sportsmanship and standard of play. The Masterton Trophy for perseverance went to the Colorado Rockies' embattled goalie, Glenn ("Chico") Resch. The Norris Trophy for best defenseman was won by Doug Wilson of Chicago. The best defensive forward was Steve Kasper of Boston, who wrested the Selke Trophy from Montreal's Bob Gainey, the recipient for each of the four previous years it had been awarded.

The Adams Trophy for coach of the year was won by Tom Watt of Winnipeg. His team showed the greatest one-year improvement, 48 points, in NHL history.

The American Hockey League champions were the New Brunswick Hawks. In the Central Hockey League the winners were the Indianapolis Racers, a team affiliated with the New York Islanders.

(ROBIN CATHY HERMAN)

European and International. The 1981–82 season provided a fairer opportunity than in previous years to assess the relative merits of top Canadian and Soviet talent, the latter this time achieving enough to suggest that the pendulum of suprema-

Twenty-one-year-old Wayne Gretzky (99) of the Edmonton Oilers maneuvered the puck past Don Edwards to score his record-breaking 77th goal on February 24. Gretzky broke NHL records by getting the most goals in one season (92), most assists (120), and most points (212).

cy had tilted from west to east. Games between national teams were more numerous, but any development of a transatlantic interclub contest remained a pipe dream, largely because of financial problems and the ties of domestic competitions.

The 48th world championships retained the now customary format, with the 24 participating nations divided into three sections. The eight in Group A contested the title on April 15–29 in Tampere and Helsinki, Finland. As usual, preliminary round-robin matches decided which four teams would play on for the medals; unexpectedly, the U.S. was relegated to Group B for the following season.

A fifth straight win for the Soviet Union brought its total number of victories to 18, only one short of Canada, whose last championship had been secured in 1961. But, whereas it could be argued that the Canadians in recent years had not fielded their best players, this time a fairly representative team of leading NHL competitors could offer scant excuse. Undefeated in their ten games,

the Soviets dropped just one point when held to a rare goalless tie by Czechoslovakia. This final contest enabled the Czechoslovaks to win the silver medal from Canada by superior goal difference; Sweden finished fourth.

Wayne Gretzky, Canada's remarkable centre from Edmonton, topped the points scorers with 14 from 6 goals and 8 assists. Victor Skalimov and Sergey Makarov of the Soviet Union each had 13, while Skalimov and the Canadian left wing Bill Barber shared the highest number of goals with eight apiece.

Jiri Kralik of Czechoslovakia was voted the best goalkeeper; Aleksey Kasatanov and Vyalcheslav Fetisov, both from the U.S.S.R., were elected the most successful defenders; and the "all-star" choice was completed by Gretzky, flanked by Makarov and Barber.

The East Germans gained promotion to Group A by convincingly heading the eight nations in Group B at Klagenfurt, Austria. They too were undefeated, conceding one point in a tied game. The Austrian runners-up in this section were the season's most improved team, having won promotion from Group C the previous winter. Austria owed its success largely to the inclusion of six Austro-Canadians, notably Brian Stankiewicz, the outstanding goalie of Group B. The biggest upset was the disappointing showing of The Netherlands, which finished last and thus was relegated to Group C only a year after competing in Group A. China, next to last, was also demoted.

Japan decisively won Group C at Jaca, Spain, scoring 70 goals in seven games. Yugoslavia earned second place behind Japan, and thus the two nations regained the Group B status that each had lost the previous season.

The sixth world junior (under 21) championship, in January at Rochester, Minn., was won by Canada for the first time, with Czechoslovakia second and Finland third. The U.S.S.R., which had won in each of the first four years of the championship, could finish only fourth, while Sweden, the defending champion, was fifth of the eight competing nations. Undefeated in their seven games, the Canadians routed the Soviets 7–0 with a four-goal third period and conceded a point to Czechoslovakia in a tense 3–3 draw that decided the title. The Canadians were helped when Sweden stunned the Czechoslovaks with a five-goal second period to win 6–4, the only defeat for the Czechoslovaks.

(HOWARD BASS)

Iceland

Iceland is an island republic in the North Atlantic Ocean, near the Arctic Circle. Area: 103,000 sq km (39,769 sq mi). Pop. (1982 est.): 232,000. Cap. and largest city: Reykjavik (pop., 1981 est., 84,600). Language: Icelandic. Religion: 97% Lutheran. President in 1982, Vigdís Finnbogadóttir; prime minister, Gunnar Thoroddsen.

The Icelandic economy gradually entered into recession in the course of 1982. Real gross national product (GNP) was estimated to have declined by some 3.5%, and the current account deficit for the

Table I. NHL Final Standings, 1982

	Won	Lost	Tied	Goals	Goals against	Pts.
NORRIS DIVISION						
Minnesota	37	23	20	346	288	94
Winnipeg	33	33	14	319	332	80
St. Louis	32	40	8	315	349	72
Chicago	30	38	12	332	363	72
Toronto	20	44	16	298	380	56
Detroit	21	47	12	271	351	54
SMYTHE DIVISION						
Edmonton	48	17	15	417	295	111
Vancouver	30	33	17	290	286	77
Calgary	29	34	17	334	345	75
Los Angeles	24	41	15	314	369	63
Colorado	18	49	13	241	362	49
ADAMS DIVISION						
Montreal	46	17	17	360	223	109
Boston	43	27	10	323	285	96
Buffalo	39	26	15	307	273	93
Quebec	33	31	16	356	345	82
Hartford	21	41	18	264	351	60
PATRICK DIVISION						
Islanders (N.Y.)	54	16	10	385	250	118
Rangers (N.Y.)	39	27	14	316	306	92
Philadelphia	31	36	13	310	337	87
Pittsburgh	31	36	13	310	337	75
Washington	26	41	13	319	338	65

Table II. World Ice Hockey Championships, 1982

	Won	Lost	Tied	Goals	Goals against	Pts.
GROUP A Championship Section						
U.S.S.R.	9	0	1	58	20	19
Czechoslovakia	5	3	2	38	20	12
Canada	5	3	2	36	30	12
Sweden	3	4	3	26	35	9
GROUP A Relegation Section						
Finland	3	3	1	21	31	7
West Germany	2	4	1	19	30	5
Italy	1	5	1	20	44	3
United States	0	6	1	21	39	1
GROUP B						
East Germany	6	0	1	48	25	13
Austria	4	2	1	33	26	9
Poland	4	2	1	42	23	9
Norway	3	4	0	24	43	6
Romania	2	4	1	27	30	5
Switzerland	1	3	3	20	27	5
China	2	4	1	32	47	5
Netherlands, The	2	5	0	22	27	4
GROUP C						
Japan	7	0	0	70	14	14
Yugoslavia	5	2	0	59	22	10
Denmark	4	2	1	35	20	9
France	4	3	0	46	30	8
Hungary	4	3	0	43	29	8
Bulgaria	2	4	1	29	30	5
Spain	1	6	0	26	49	2
South Korea	0	7	0	13	127	0

Iceland

year as a whole was expected to amount to 10–11% of GNP. This followed several years during which production had grown slowly but steadily and the balance of payments had been close to achieving equilibrium. Inflation rose from a 40–45% annual rate at the beginning of the year to some 55–60% at the end. The main cause was the fall in the fish catch, the result of declining fish resources off Iceland's coast. Sales of fish were also suffering because of difficulties in certain export markets, especially Nigeria where there was an important market for Icelandic stockfish.

The economic downturn led to considerable strain within the three-party government coalition, composed of members of the left-wing People's Alliance, the Progressive Party, and a splinter group from the Independence (Conservative) Party. With some difficulty, the government agreed in August to economic measures that consisted mainly of an attempt to break the inflationary spiral by cutting wage increases that were due in compensation for price rises. It was agreed to cut the September 1 increase by 2.7% and the December 1 increase by 8–9%. At the same time, the currency was devalued by 13%, in addition to a 12% devaluation at the beginning of 1982 and gradual devaluation during the course of the year.

During the summer, when Parliament was not in session, one member who had previously supported the government in the upper house switched his allegiance to the opposition, with the result that the government lost its majority in that house. However, it still commanded a majority of one vote in the lower house and a similar majority in a joint legislative session, and was thus protected from a motion of no confidence. This situation created a stalemate in Parliament, since the government was unable to pass any legislation other than the fiscal budget, which was dealt with in joint session.

The government offered to guarantee that it would step down from office early in 1983 provided the opposition agreed to the passage of several important pieces of legislation in the autumn term. The opposition did not refuse this deal out of hand.

It was the intention of all the political parties to pass a constitutional amendment redrawing electoral districts to reflect population movements in the previous two decades. Since the last such amendment was passed in 1959, large population shifts had taken place toward urban areas.

On May 22 local elections were held throughout most of the country. The results showed considerable gains for the Independence Party, the main opposition party, while the chief losers were the People's Alliance and the Social Democrats. The election outcome indicated a substantial swing to the right, reflecting dissatisfaction with the government.

Iceland's Pres. Vigdís Finnbogadóttir paid state visits to the U.K. in February and to the U.S. in September. In the U.S. she also represented all the heads of state of the Nordic countries at the opening of the exhibition "Scandinavia Today." The recently elected president of Finland, Mauno Koivisto, paid a state visit to Iceland in October.

Iceland's former president Kristján Eldjárn (*see* OBITUARIES) died in September.

(BJÖRN MATTHÍASSON)

India

A federal republic of southern Asia and a member of the Commonwealth, India is situated on a peninsula extending into the Indian Ocean with the Arabian Sea to the west and the Bay of Bengal to the east. It is bounded (east to west) by Burma, Bangladesh, China, Bhutan, Nepal, and Pakistan; Sri Lanka lies just off its southern tip in the Indian Ocean. Area: 3,287,782 sq km (1,269,420 sq mi), including the Pakistani-controlled section of Jammu and Kashmir. Pop. (1981 prelim.): 683,810,100; Indo-Aryans and Dravidians are dominant, with Mongoloid, Negroid, and Australoid admixtures. Cap.: New Delhi (pop., 1981 prelim., 272,000). Largest cities: Calcutta (metro pop., 1981 prelim., 9,165,700) and Greater Bombay (metro pop., 1981 prelim., 8,227,300). Language: Hindi and English (official). Religion (1971): Hindu 83%; Muslim 11%; Christian 3%; Sikh 2%; Buddhist 0.7%. Presidents in 1982, N. Sanjiva Reddy and, from July 25, Zail Singh; prime minister, Indira Gandhi.

During 1982 India made several moves to improve its relations with other countries. On the domestic scene, the agitation for an autonomous state for Sikhs by the Akali Dal in Punjab caused anxiety, and the three-year-old Assam issue remained unresolved. The republic acquired its seventh elected president in Zail Singh (*see* BIOGRAPHIES), who succeeded N. Sanjiva Reddy on July 25.

Domestic Affairs. The year started with the rejection by the Akali Dal of Prime Minister Indira Gandhi's award on the sharing of the waters of the

India

Ice Skating:
see Winter Sports

ICELAND
   Education. (1979–80) Primary, pupils 25,600, teachers (including preprimary) 3,074; secondary and vocational, pupils 26,500, teachers 1,340; teacher training, pupils (1976–77) 266, teachers (1975–76) 30; higher, students 4,200, teaching staff 779.
   Finance. Monetary unit: króna, with (Sept. 20, 1982) a free rate of 14.51 krónur to U.S. $1 (24.87 krónur = £1 sterling). Gold and other reserves (June 1982) U.S. $220 million. Budget (1980 actual): revenue 4,088,000,000 (new) krónur; expenditure 3,388,000,000 (new) krónur. Gross national product (1981) 20,196,000,000 krónur. Money supply (June 1982) 1,781,000,000 krónur. Cost of living (Reykjavik; 1975 = 100; May 1982) 1,192.1.
   Foreign Trade. (1981) Imports 7,484,800,000 krónur; exports 6,542,600,000 krónur. Import sources: West Germany 11%; Denmark 10%; Norway 10%; Sweden 8%; U.S.S.R. 8%; U.K. 8%; U.S. 8%; The Netherlands 8%; Japan 5%. Export destinations: U.S. 21%; U.K. 14%; Nigeria 13%; Portugal 11%; West Germany 6%; U.S.S.R. 6%. Main exports: fish and products 78%; aluminum 10%.
   Transport and Communications. Roads (1980) 11,707 km. Motor vehicles in use (1980): passenger 85,924; commercial 8,531. There are no railways. Air traffic (1981): 1,140 million passenger-km; freight 21.4 million net ton-km. Shipping (1981): merchant vessels 100 gross tons and over 384; gross tonnage 183,088. Telephones (Dec. 1980) 108,800. Radio licenses (Dec. 1980) 68,900. Television receivers (Dec. 1980) 60,500.
   Agriculture. Production (in 000; metric tons; 1980): potatoes 15; hay c. 388; turnips 0.9; milk 119; mutton and lamb 14; fish catch 1,515. Livestock (in 000; Dec. 1980): cattle 60; sheep 828; horses 52; poultry 311.
   Industry. Production (in 000; 1981): electricity (kw-hr) c. 3,230,000; aluminum (exports; metric tons) 63.

BALDEV—SYGMA

Zail Singh was the first Sikh to be elected president of India. He succeeded N. Sanjiva Reddy as India's seventh president on July 25.

Ravi and Beas rivers among Punjab, Haryana, and Rajasthan. The demands of the party included the declaration of Amritsar as a holy city, an all-India act for *gurudwaras* (Sikh temples), the right to carry *kirpans* (daggers) on aircraft, the transfer of the union territory of Chandigarh to Punjab, and the acceptance of the party's Anandpur Sahib resolution. This resolution, adopted in 1973, declared Sikhs to be a separate nation and demanded greater powers for Punjab, including a separate constitution. Having failed to obtain satisfaction during talks with the union (central) government in April, the Akali Dal asked its members to defy laws and court arrest. Some 25,000 were taken into custody but were released in October. The Dal organized a march on Delhi on November 19 to coincide with the opening of the Asian Games but, partly because of tight policing, they caused only very minor disruption. Sikh-Hindu clashes occurred in Amritsar in April, and two extremist Sikh groups, Dal Khalsa and the National Council of Khalistan, were banned in May.

Several rounds of talks were held during the year regarding the demand of Assam students that "foreigners" who had come to that state from Bangladesh be detected, deleted from the electoral rolls, and deported. Some opposition parties joined the discussions, but no breakthrough was achieved. In January K. C. Gogoi of the Congress (I) formed a government in Assam, but he resigned in March, and president's rule was reimposed. Under the Indian constitution, president's rule had to end within 12 months and elections had to be held. With the Assam agitators refusing to permit polling until the electoral rolls had been purged of "foreigners," a proposal was considered in November for amending the constitution to allow an extension of president's rule.

Elections were held in May to legislative assemblies in West Bengal, Haryana, and Himachal Pradesh, where the five-year legislative terms had

been completed, and in Kerala because the government led by K. Karunakaran of Congress (I) fell in March after being in office for less than three months. In West Bengal the Left Front, led by the Communist Party of India (Marxist) or CPI(M), retained power, capturing 238 out of 294 seats; the Congress (I) and its allies won 54, and 2 went to a smaller party. Jyoti Basu continued as chief minister. In Kerala an alliance led by Congress (I) won 77 seats as against the Left Front's 63 in a house of 140. Karunakaran was sworn in as chief minister. In Himachal Pradesh, Ram Lal of Congress (I) formed a government again with the support of independents. In Haryana no party secured a majority. The governor called Bhajan Lal of Congress (I) to form the government, and several members elected on other tickets crossed over. There was bitter resentment among the Lok Dal and the Bharatiya Janata Party (BJP), and the governor's action was challenged, but the Supreme Court held that he had acted within his constitutional discretion. Elections were held in Nagaland in November, resulting in a Congress (I) ministry under S. C. Jamir.

There were governmental changes in four other states—Maharashtra, Andhra Pradesh, Uttar Pradesh, and Jammu and Kashmir. In January A. R. Antulay, chief minister of Maharashtra, was adjudged by the Bombay High Court to be guilty of misuse of office in collecting funds for trusts started by him. Following his resignation, Congress (I) chose Babasaheb Bhosale to succeed him. T. Anjiah resigned as chief minister of Andhra Pradesh in February and was succeeded by B. V. Reddy, who made way for Vijaya Bhaskar Reddy in September. In Uttar Pradesh, Vishwanath Pratap Singh resigned in June after a massacre of 21 villagers by dacoits (bandits), and Sripat Mishra was sworn in as chief minister. The chief minister of Jammu and Kashmir, Sheikh Muhammad Abdullah (*see* OBITUARIES), died in September, and his son, Farooq Abdullah, was appointed in his place.

The Bihar chief minister, Jagannath Mishra, came under attack by the press and opposition parties after the Bihar legislature adopted a bill amending the penal code to deal with writings that were "grossly indecent or scurrilous or intended for blackmail." The operation of similar legislation in Tamil Nadu was stayed by the Supreme Court. The president sought the court's opinion on the constitutionality of a bill passed in Jammu and Kashmir to permit the return and resettlement of persons who had migrated.

The presidential election held in July evoked considerable excitement, although the victory of the Congress (I) nominee, Home Minister Zail Singh, was a foregone conclusion. He secured 754,113 electoral votes against 282,685 for the candidate of the combined opposition, H. R. Khanna, a former Supreme Court judge. In elections for one-quarter of the seats in the Rajya Sabha (upper house of Parliament) in March, the Congress (I) improved its strength to 125 seats out of 244. Of the eight by-elections to the Lok Sabha (lower house) during the year, the Congress (I) won three, BJP two, and the Democratic Socialist Party, the CPI(M), and the All-India Anna Dravida Munnetra Kazhagam one each. The Lok Dal split into two groups, led respectively by Charan Singh and Karpoori Thakur. The opposition, although unable to unite, was heartened by the decision of Maneka Gandhi, widow of Sanjay Gandhi, to defy Prime Minister Gandhi. After being ordered from her mother-in-law's residence in March, Maneka Gandhi formed a group to promote the ideas of her late husband and, in November, announced that it would contest two state elections in January 1983.

There were several changes in the union Cabinet. In January the prime minister made over the defense portfolio to R. Venkataraman and appointed Pranab Mukherjee as finance minister. On Zail Singh's election as president, Venkataraman also took charge of home affairs, but in September P. C. Sethi was named home minister.

Hindu-Muslim riots occurred in Meerut, Uttar Pradesh, and in Baroda, Gujarat. The report of the second Press Commission was submitted to Parliament in November. It recommended the appointment of an organization to assist newspaper development, the reintroduction of a page-price

On August 2 in New Delhi thousands of Indian women, sponsored by an opposition political party, marched toward the Parliament to protest against traditional marriage practices involving dowries.

schedule, and restriction of advertisement space. It also suggested the appointment of boards of trustees on large newspapers as buffers between editors and owners.

The failure of the India National Satellite System's INSAT-1A, a Rs 700 million satellite for communications and weather watching, caused disappointment. It was launched in April from Cape Canaveral, Florida, in the U.S., but its solar sails failed to open, and the fuel ran out in September.

The Economy. Grain production in the agricultural year ended June 1982 was placed at 133,060,000 metric tons, compared with 129,590,000 metric tons the previous year. But the June–September monsoon was erratic, subjecting vast areas to drought and others to floods. Orissa, Andhra Pradesh, Maharashtra, and Gujarat were hit by cyclones. Sugar production reached a record 8,430,000 metric tons. The wholesale price index on Oct. 9, 1982, was 0.6% above the level of Oct. 10, 1981. In January Prime Minister Gandhi announced a revised 20-point program to expedite production in key areas and help weaker sectors.

In February railway fares and freight rates were increased to bring in additional income of Rs 2,614,000,000. The union government's budget for 1982–83 provided some relief in direct taxes, but overall revenue was increased by Rs 5,330,000,000. With revenue and capital receipts of Rs 278,540,000,000 and disbursements of Rs 292,190,000,000, the uncovered deficit amounted to Rs 13,650,000,000.

In June the Aid-India Consortium undertook to give development assistance of $3,660,000,000 for 1982–83. Among the major projects completed during the year were the thermal powerhouses of Korba, Ramagundam, and Singrauli, a hydroelectric station at Srisailam, and a bridge across the Ganges River in Bihar. A strike by 160,000 textile workers in Bombay that began in January remained unresolved throughout the year.

INDIA

Education. (1979–80) Primary, pupils 70,940,386, teachers 1,311,931; secondary, pupils 28,372,339, teachers 1,694,651; vocational, pupils (1978–79) 318,956, teachers (1970–71) 14,024; teacher training, pupils 102,072; higher, students (1978–79) 4,296,242, teaching staff (1975–76) 235,822.

Finance. Monetary unit: rupee, with (Sept. 20, 1982) a free rate of Rs 9.62 to U.S. $1 (Rs 16.50 = £1 sterling). Gold and other reserves (April 1982) U.S. $5,105,000,000. Budget (1981–82 est.): revenue Rs 143,272,000,000; expenditure Rs 152,995,000,000. Gross national product (1980–81) Rs 1,257,400,000,000. Money supply (March 1982) Rs 235.5 billion. Cost of living (1975 = 100; May 1982) 143.9.

Foreign Trade. (1981) Imports Rs 179.8 billion; exports Rs 62,840,000,000. Import sources (1979–80): U.S. 10%; Iraq 10%; U.S.S.R. 9%; U.K. 8%; West Germany 7%; Iran 7%; Japan 7%. Export destinations (1979–80): U.S. 13%; Japan 10%; U.S.S.R. 10%; U.K. 8%; West Germany 6%. Main exports (1979–80): food 26%; textile yarns and fabrics 15%; clothing 8%; leather 8%; diamonds 7%.

Transport and Communications. Roads (1979) 1,282,042 km. Motor vehicles in use (1979): passenger 1,035,300; commercial 440,200. Railways: (1980) 60,933 km; traffic (1979–80) 198,642,000,000 passenger-km, freight 155,955,000,000 net ton-km. Air traffic (1981): 12,090,000,000 passenger-km; freight 448.4 million net ton-km. Shipping (1981): merchant vessels 100 gross tons and over 620; gross tonnage 6,019,902. Telephones (March 1980) 2,615,100. Radio licenses (Dec. 1978) 21.7 million. Television licenses (Dec. 1979) 680,000.

Agriculture. Production (in 000; metric tons; 1981): wheat 36,460; rice c. 82,000; barley 2,242; corn c. 7,000; millet c. 10,500; sorghum c. 11,500; potatoes 9,599; cassava 5,817; sugar, raw value 5,587 sugar, noncentrifugal c. 7,851; chick-peas 4,652; mangoes 8,516; bananas c. 4,500; cottonseed c. 2,720; rapeseed 2,247; sesame seed c. 500; linseed 428; peanuts c. 6,000; tea c. 565; tobacco 456; cotton, lint c. 1,360; jute (including substitutes) c. 1,450; meat c. 916; fish catch (1980) 2,423. Livestock (in 000; 1981): cattle c. 182,000; sheep c. 41,500; pigs c. 10,200; buffalo c. 61,500; goats c. 72,144; poultry c. 147,000.

Industry. Production (in 000; metric tons; 1981): coal 122,453; lignite 5,964; crude oil 14,918; natural gas (cu m) 1,970,000; iron ore (63% metal content; 1980) 40,920; pig iron 9,755; crude steel 10,630; bauxite (1980) 1,776; aluminum 213; gold (troy oz) 84; manganese ore (metal content; 1980) 619; cement 20,771; cotton yarn c. 1,010; woven cotton fabrics (m) c. 8,070,000; man-made fibres (1980) 170; petroleum products (1980) 23,601; sulfuric acid (1980) 1,937; caustic soda 512; electricity (kw-hr; 1980) 116,332,000; passenger cars (units; 1980) 48; commercial vehicles (units; 1980) 70.

Foreign Affairs. Prime Minister Gandhi visited the U.S. and the Soviet Union in quick succession. After her talks with U.S. Pres. Ronald Reagan in Washington, D.C., it was announced that the two countries would work more closely in scientific research and that the U.S. obligation to supply nuclear fuel to the Tarapur power station would be taken over by France. In Moscow arrangements for increased trade and economic cooperation were agreed on. Gandhi returned to Moscow in November to attend the funeral of Soviet Pres. Leonid Brezhnev (*see* OBITUARIES) and to have talks with his successor, Yury Andropov (*see* BIOGRAPHIES). There were major developments in relations with Pakistan, culminating in a brief visit to New Delhi by Pres. Mohammad Zia-ul-Haq on November 1, when a decision to establish a joint commission was announced. Senior officials of the two countries were to meet to examine proposals for a no-war pact put forward by Pakistan and a treaty of peace, friendship, and cooperation suggested by India. In December it was announced that agreement had been reached on a prisoner exchange.

In March Prime Minister Gandhi went to the U.K. to launch a six-month-long "Festival of India." While there, she had discussions with Prime Minister Margaret Thatcher, which were continued when Thatcher made a stopover in New Delhi in September. The prime minister also traveled to Japan, Saudi Arabia, Mauritius, and Mozambique, and Pres. Sanjiva Reddy went to Ireland and Yugoslavia.

India undertook to play host in March 1983 in New Delhi to the seventh summit conference of the nonaligned movement. The conference, scheduled for Baghdad in September 1982, had been postponed because of the Iran-Iraq war.

(H. Y. SHARADA PRASAD)

Indonesia

A republic of Southeast Asia, Indonesia consists of the major islands of Sumatra, Java, Kalimantan (Indonesian Borneo), Celebes, and Irian Jaya (West New Guinea) and approximately 3,000 smaller islands and islets. Area: 1,919,443 sq km (741,101 sq mi). Pop. (1982 est.): 154,274,900. Area and population figures include former Portuguese Timor. Cap. and largest city: Jakarta (pop., 1981 est., 6,556,000). Language: Bahasa Indonesia (official); Javanese; Sundanese; Madurese. Religion: mainly Muslim; some Christian, Buddhist, and Hindu. President in 1982, Suharto.

On May 4, 1982, Indonesia's 82 million registered voters went to the polls to elect a new (lower) House of People's Representatives (DPR) to a five-year term, amid sporadic acts of violence that claimed 81 lives. Two thousand candidates contested for 364 seats. (The remaining 100 seats were appointed by the president, largely from the military, who were barred from the general election.) The outcome was no surprise. The government-sponsored Golkar (Functional Groups) won 246 seats, 14 more than in 1977, to retain control of the DPR. The Islamic-oriented United Development Party (PPP) garnered 94 seats for a loss of 5, and the

Indonesia

largely secularist Indonesian Democratic Party (PDI) won 24 seats, also for a loss of 5. The parties were essentially strained coalitions of the many traditional parties, which President Suharto had compelled to merge in an effort to simplify the country's fractious party system. The opposition charged irregularities at the polls.

The election was only a step toward the selection of a president in 1983 by the People's Consultative Assembly (MPR). The MPR consisted of 924 members, including the DPR, 140 regional delegates, 113 additional party representatives, and 207 appointed members. Suharto was expected to win a fourth five-year term. In 1981 he announced that his fourth term would be his last. In another internal development, the DPR adopted a defense act in September that bolstered the concept of *Hankam Rata* ("people's defense") and the "dual function" of the Army in Indonesia's sociopolitical as well as its military life.

Indonesia denounced the continuing Soviet occupation of Afghanistan and the Vietnamese occupation of Kampuchea. Many Indonesians considered Vietnam a Soviet client state. Relations with Moscow worsened in February when the Indonesians broke up a major Soviet spy ring in Jakarta. Radio Moscow was assailed on the floor of the DPR for broadcasts defending the abortive Partei Kommunist Indonesia (PKI) coup of 1965.

INDONESIA

Education. (1980–81) Primary, pupils 22,487,053, teachers 665,264; secondary, pupils 4,364,598, teachers 261,864; vocational and teacher training, pupils 802,013, teachers 67,312; higher, students 397,485, teaching staff (1976–77) 46,668.

Finance. Monetary unit: rupiah, with (Sept. 20, 1982) a free rate of 668 rupiah to U.S. $1 (1,146 rupiah = £1 sterling). Gold and other reserves (March 1982) U.S. $5,356,000,000. Budget (1981–82 est.): revenue 12,274,-000,000,000 rupiah (excluding foreign aid of 1,626,-000,000,000 rupiah); expenditure (total) 13,900,-000,000,000 rupiah. Gross national product (1980) 41,596,-000,000,000 rupiah. Money supply (March 1982) 6,776,-800,000,000 rupiah. Cost of living (1975 = 100; April 1982) 252.1.

Foreign Trade. (1981) Imports U.S. $13,272,000,000; exports U.S. $22,260,000,000. Import sources (1980): Japan 32%; U.S. 13%; Saudi Arabia 9%; Singapore 9%; West Germany 6%. Export destinations (1980): Japan 49%; U.S. 20%; Singapore 11%. Main exports (1980): crude oil 53%; natural gas 13%; timber 8%; food 6%; petroleum products 5%; rubber 5%.

Transport and Communications. Roads (1979) 128,899 km. Motor vehicles in use (1979): passenger 577,300; commercial 383,600. Railways (1980): 6,877 km; traffic 6,229,000,000 passenger-km, freight 980 million net ton-km. Air traffic (1980): 5,907,000,000 passenger-km; freight 127.4 million net ton-km. Shipping (1981): merchant vessels 100 gross tons and over 1,260; gross tonnage 1,744,958. Telephones (Dec. 1979) 460,100. Radio receivers (Dec. 1979) 6 million. Television receivers (Dec. 1979) 1,539,000.

Agriculture. Production (in 000; metric tons; 1981): rice 32,776; corn 4,648; cassava 13,726; sweet potatoes 2,079; sugar, raw value c. 1,449; bananas c. 1,622; tea 95; copra c. 1,254; soybeans 687; palm oil 716; peanuts 842; coffee c. 265; tobacco 85; rubber c. 937; fish catch (1980) 1,853. Livestock (in 000; 1981): cattle c. 6,435; buffalo c. 2,506; pigs c. 3,296; sheep c. 4,196; goats c. 7,925; horses c. 617; chickens c. 111,969.

Industry. Production (in 000; metric tons; 1981): crude oil 78,849; natural gas (cu m) 19,650,000; petroleum products (1980) c. 20,400; coal 354; bauxite 1,203; tin concentrates (metal content) 31; cement (1980) 5,260; electricity (kw-hr; 1980) 7,140,000.

While relations with Moscow cooled, Jakarta was dismayed by Washington's policy of weapons sales to China and its promotion of Japanese rearmament. Indonesia viewed both China and Japan as potential threats to Southeast Asia. In July Defense Minister Mohammed Jusuf flew to Washington to confer with Pres. Ronald Reagan. Suharto followed this up in October with a state visit to the U.S., during which he elicited a pledge from President Reagan that the U.S. would not let its China and Japan policies undermine Indonesian security. During Suharto's visit, 102 members of Congress called on the U.S. to investigate allegations of starvation and violations of human rights in East Timor, which had been integrated into Indonesia. In 1975, after the end of Portuguese colonial rule, the Indonesians had moved into East Timor to prevent a takeover by Fretilin, a left-wing independence faction supported by Moscow and the Portuguese Communists. The U.S. State Department strongly refuted the allegations. During the year independent visitors to East Timor reported a relatively quiet situation with about 100 to 200 armed Fretilin guerrillas holed up in the mountains.

Despite the world recession, Indonesia's economy maintained one of the world's highest growth rates at 7.6% annually. During the year Indonesia entered the ranks of the middle-income nations when its per capita gross national product rose to $520. (The World Bank defined a middle-income nation as one with a per capita GNP of at least $410.) Inflation eased to 7%, compared with 16% the year before, and rice output, a barometer of political stability, rose by 10% to 22.2 million tons. However, a rash of strikes marred the favourable economic outlook. (ARNOLD C. BRACKMAN)

Industrial Relations

Economic adversity was the main force shaping industrial relations in 1982. In many countries unemployment reached record levels and, although inflationary pressures abated somewhat, economic growth was generally low. There were few signs of early improvement. The main concerns of workers and their unions in this climate were to preserve jobs and living standards. They were not always successful. Closings of plants and reductions of the work force increased in many countries, and in many cases workers had to accept wage increases that did not fully compensate for the rise in the cost of living.

In most of the countries where wage increases had customarily been linked with the price index, such as Belgium, Denmark, Italy, and Luxembourg, that process was halted or limited. Wage freezes or restrictions on increases were imposed in some countries, including Denmark, France, and New Zealand. In the public service, as governments found it necessary to cut back on public expenditure, salary increases were often limited, and in some cases, as in France and Ireland, intended increases were postponed. In Canada the federal government required that public servants should receive no more than a 6% increase in 1982 and 5% in 1983, and Canadian provincial govern-

Ten thousand Canadian workers at the Chrysler Corp. plant in Windsor, Ontario, went on strike in November. The employees had taken wage cuts to help Chrysler and were now demanding some of the money back in wage increases.

ments commonly made comparable arrangements. In September in Japan the then prime minister announced that the government would not implement the increase proposed by the National Personnel Authority for government employees.

United Kingdom. With record postwar unemployment and generally low levels of business activity, there was little likelihood that most people would receive high wage increases. The challenge came inevitably in the public sector, where ability to pay has a different dimension from private business. The first major dispute of the year, however, related more to productivity and working conditions than to pay, though pay was a factor. It centred on the determination of the British Railways Board to achieve flexibility in the daily work scheduling of train drivers. In July, after protracted negotiations and after a series of work stoppages had caused considerable disruption to rail services, the Associated Society of Locomotive Engineers and Firemen had to call off its campaign of industrial action. Meanwhile, at the end of June the executive committee of the main railway union, the National Union of Railwaymen, had called a strike on pay and productivity; this decision, however, was overturned by the union's annual delegate meeting the following day, and the dispute was referred to arbitration, which recommended wage increases of 6% along with measures to accelerate progress on productivity.

In April unions representing the great majority of health service workers started a campaign of industrial action on their pay claim; this continued for eight months and was supported nationally by a "day of action" called by the Trades Union Con-

Nurses supported a national "day of action" in London by joining in a mass demonstration called by the Trades Union Congress on September 22. The strike was called in support of health workers' demands for pay raises.

gress (TUC) on September 22. The year's major challenge to the government's policy of restraint seemed likely to come from the coal miners, led by their new and militant president, Arthur Scargill. However, after balloting its members the union accepted the employers' offer.

The report of the Megaw inquiry into civil service pay appeared in July. It proposed annual wage adjustments based on current pay rates in the private sector with a pay information board established to provide data. Weight should also be given to financial constraints and market factors, such as recruitment and retention of staff, and to the job security and pension rights enjoyed by civil services. The right of unilateral reference of claims to binding arbitration should be reviewed or withdrawn. The Employment Act 1982 contained provisions concerning the closed shop; trade union immunities in industrial disputes and the legality of disputes; and the strengthening of workers' involvement in enterprises. The TUC in September agreed upon an important change in the structure of its General Council, providing for automatic representation by all unions with more than 100,000 members.

United States. In the U.S. 1982 also was a year of retrenchment, with unions frequently accepting modification of cost-of-living adjustments and making other concessions, usually in the interest of job security. In a heavy year for collective bargaining, with a large number of contracts up for renewal, the negotiations in the automobile industry were particularly interesting. The bargaining between the United Automobile Workers and the Ford Motor Co.—which had been particularly seriously hit by bad economic conditions—came first, in February, though the existing agreement was not due to end until September. The Ford workers gave up expected pay increases, and cost-of-living adjustments were deferred; certain holidays and

other benefits were also yielded. New employees would start at 85% of the hourly rate for a given job and would receive 5% pay increases every six months until they reached union scale. On the other hand, the company agreed to a range of measures, including a two-year moratorium on plant closings, supplemental unemployment benefits, and a profit-sharing plan. In April General Motors Corp. made a similar comprehensive deal. At the Chrysler Corp., which had obtained earlier concessions, a tentative one-year contract that restored cost-of-living adjustments but tied pay increases to company profits was rejected by the workers and work continued under the old contract. Many were subsequently laid off, however, when workers at Chrysler Canada staged a 38-day strike that won them an immediate pay raise. Employees of the U.S. company approved a similar contract in late December.

The most publicized strike in the U.S. was a lengthy work stoppage by players of the National Football League. (*See* FOOTBALL.) Rich Trumka, a 33-year-old lawyer, defeated Sam Church as president of the troubled United Mine Workers. Roy Williams, president of the powerful teamsters' union, was convicted of conspiring to bribe a U.S. senator and defrauding the union pension fund, but he would continue as president while appealing the verdict.

Continental Western Europe. French industrial relations were particularly eventful as the government sought to give effect to its substantial program of reforms. A decree of January 13 reduced normal weekly working hours to 39 and introduced a fifth week of paid vacation. Overtime arrangements were also revised. Other decrees gave workers the right to take their pension at age 60 (as of April 1983) if they had paid 37½ years of contributions and introduced new arrangements for part-time and temporary workers. Four major acts were passed dealing with such matters as work place discipline and the rights of workers and their representatives in the enterprise; the strengthening of collective bargaining; the strengthening of works committees and establishment of new committees in enterprises concerned with health, safety, and working conditions; and the "democratization of the public sector."

In West Germany the main trade union organization, the Deutscher Gewerkschaftsbund (DGB), held its congress in May and elected a new president, Ernst Breit, formerly president of the postal workers' union. For the first time a woman, 40-year-old Monika Wulf Mathies, was elected, in September, to lead the public service and transport workers' union, the second largest within the DGB. As usual, West German wage settlements were relatively modest. A new conciliation agreement was introduced in the chemical industry.

In Italy discussions between the government and the principal trade unions and employers went on intermittently throughout the year, centring on the country's economic problems and on labour costs. The main problem was the *scala mobile*, the sliding scale arrangement keying wage increases to price increases, which the employers and government viewed as highly inflationary

The United Auto Workers union and the Ford Motor Company signed a concessionary contract calling for a freeze on wages and benefits in return for job security and profit sharing. Signing the agreement are (from left to right): Donald Ephlin, UAW vice-president; Douglas Fraser, UAW president; Philip Caldwell, Ford chairman; and Donald Petersen, Ford president.

and workers as a vital means of protecting their living standards. On June 1 the central employers' organization in the private sector, Confindustria, gave notice of termination of its agreement of 1975 with the unions on indexation. This action precipitated a number of strikes and demonstrations, and a one-day general protest strike called for June 25 attracted considerable support. In the public sector the employers' organization Intersind on June 30 also announced its desire to end the existing indexation system. Employers were not, however, adamant about refusing any form of indexation, and discussions continued with a view to finding some acceptable arrangement. Indexation of severance payments caused a stir in the spring and at one time a referendum seemed likely, but a basis was found for settling the problem by a new law.

Ireland and Norway followed Denmark in moving from normally centralized to decentralized collective bargaining in the private sector. Ireland also passed the Trade Disputes (Amendment) Act, extending the protection of the 1906 act to all workers except the police and the defense forces. Norwegian unions and employers negotiated a revised Basic Agreement, which provided the ground rules of industrial relations; the main innovations concerned the rights of workers and their representatives in the enterprise.

Belgian industrial relations experienced another difficult year as the government sought, with unions and employers, to put together a package that would help to reduce the high level of unemployment without increasing costs and as far as possible would maintain the existing social services. In Greece a 43-day strike of bank workers, about the implementation of a new salary structure, attracted considerable attention, as did a bakery strike in September. The normal work week was reduced from 42 to 41 hours on January 1 (and would be reduced to 40 hours in January 1983), and holidays were extended to a minimum of four weeks a year. The new Greek government enacted a law on union rights and labour disputes. In Spain the National Employment Pact took effect at the beginning of 1982. It set pay limits for the year, with some qualifications, and made provision for negotiations below central levels on early-retirement and productivity schemes.

In Sweden an agreement by employers and unions in April concerned the method of application of the Co-determination Act 1976 in the private sector; subjects covered included work organization, technological development, and the economic operation and resources of enterprises. The agreement laid stress on efficient working and on consultation and participation. One of the most prominent and controversial planks of the electoral program of the Social Democratic government that took office in October was the proposal for wage-earners' funds which would give workers' representatives a gradually increasing share in the ownership of industry. On taking office, Prime Minister Olof Palme stressed that the funds would be the subject of lengthy consultation and that it might take until after the next election to work out complete details.

Eastern Europe. Industrial relations in Poland were dominated by the martial law regulations imposed in December 1981 (suspended in December 1982). There were sporadic strikes and demonstrations, sometimes put down violently, but the authorities kept control of the situation. In October 1982, despite continued public disquiet, the Sejm (parliament) passed legislation formally dissolving the free (but suspended) trade union Solidarity and providing for nonpolitical and factory-based unions that would recognize the leading role of the Polish United Workers' (Communist) Party. New labour courts would be established. The proposed unions seemed unlikely to be able to pursue what the Western world regarded as normal union functions.

South Africa. Employers and unions in South Africa were still getting used to recent reforms affecting industrial relations, which were somewhat troubled during the year. Strikes and riots by black gold miners resulted in hundreds of arrests and deportations. There were strikes too, largely centred on wages, in Eastern Cape automobile plants—with 10,000 workers on strike at times—and a go-slow about union recognition at Port Elizabeth harbour. Meanwhile, the government pressed on with its reforms, and new disputes arrangements were proposed to speed conciliation and to give unregistered unions access to official conciliation machinery. There was a considerable growth of the 30 or so black and nonracial unions, which by the end of 1982 probably had more than 200,000 members as well as an increasing readiness on the part of employers to recognize them.

Industrial Review

Manufacturing activity was only very slightly higher in 1981 than in 1980; a fractional increase in output followed the similarly small decline a year earlier in the free market economies. There was a marginal advance in the industrialized countries, while the level of production did not change in the less developed areas. The rate of growth in the centrally planned economies was markedly reduced.

Table III. Annual Average Rates of Growth of Manufacturing Output, 1968–81
Percent

Area	1968–73	1973–78	1978–81
World[1]	6.0	2.1	1.6
Industrial countries	5.7	1.5	1.5
Less industrialized countries	8.7	5.9	2.6
Centrally planned economies	8.8	7.5	4.2

[1] Excluding centrally planned economies; for definitions see Table I.

The outlook for 1982, as judged by the results of the first half of the year (when output in the advanced countries was more than 2% lower than in the same period a year earlier), was for another decline. Recent developments clearly pointed to an unfavourable medium-term trend. The rapid advance in the five-year period to 1973 (and earlier) was followed by strongly reduced growth, influenced by the deep recession in 1975, in the subsequent five-year period to 1978 and a further decline into quasi-stagnation afterward. The trend was most marked in the advanced countries; the less industrialized nations and those with centrally planned economies followed with some lag.

Economic policies in most advanced countries remained deflationary in 1982 with the main objective of checking inflation. A monetary squeeze, high interest rates, and cuts in public expenditure were the most frequently applied instruments. These and the resulting high unemployment weakened domestic demand for both consumption and investment, acting also as an incentive to reduce inventories at all levels. Another effect was the decline in prices of world commodities to low levels, limiting the earnings of the primary producing less industrialized countries. Thus, the rate of expansion of world trade in manufactures also fell significantly, from $6^1/_2$% per year in 1970–80 to 2% in 1981. The combination of depressed domestic and weak export demand was reflected in the unsatisfactory state of the manufacturing industries, which in many advanced countries also had to face the difficult problem of adapting to structural changes in the wake of technological advance

Table I. Index Numbers of Production, Employment, and Productivity in Manufacturing Industries
1975 = 100

Area	Relative importance[1] 1975	Relative importance[1] 1981	Production 1980	Production 1981	Employment 1980	Employment 1981	Productivity[2] 1980	Productivity[2] 1981
World[3]	1,000	1,000	123	124	…	…	…	…
Industrial countries	868	859	122	123	…	…	…	…
Less industrialized countries	132	141	133	133	…	…	…	…
North America[4]	315	325	125	128	…	…	…	…
Canada	27	25	115	117	102	103	113	114
United States	288	300	126	129	111	111	114	116
Latin America[5]	74	77	133	127	…	…	…	…
Brazil	27	25	143	115	…	…	…	…
Argentina	15	10	96	81	…	…	…	…
Mexico	12	14	134	142	136	143	99	99
Asia[6]	159	184	138	142	…	…	…	…
India	11	12	126	136	115	…	110	…
Japan	109	129	143	147	100	101	143	146
South Korea	…	…	216	239	137	163	158	147
Europe[7]	416	381	116	113	…	…	…	…
Austria	8	8	125	123	98	96	128	128
Belgium	14	13	117	113	…	…	…	…
Denmark	6	6	120	119	99	94	121	126
Finland	6	7	125	128	101	103	124	124
France	80	72	117	110	97	93	121	118
West Germany	115	96	118	116	101	99	117	117
Greece	3	3	129	128	119	120	108	107
Ireland	1	1	137	141	114	110	120	128
Italy	43	44	131	128	105	…	125	…
Netherlands, The	16	15	116	115	89	85	130	135
Norway	6	5	100	99	95	…	105	…
Portugal	4	6	143	144	109	…	131	…
Spain	24	22	115	111	78	…	147	…
Sweden	17	14	98	94	89	86	110	109
Switzerland	13	13	114	115	93	94	123	122
United Kingdom	50	38	95	89	91	81	104	110
Yugoslavia	11	13	140	146	125	128	112	114
Rest of the world[8]	36	33	…	…	…	…	…	…
Oceania	18	16	107	110	…	…	…	…
South Africa	7	8	127	133	106	110	120	121
Centrally planned economies[9]	…	…	133	137	…	…	…	…

[1] The 1975 weights are those applied by the UN Statistical Office; those for 1981 were estimated on the basis of the changes in manufacturing output since 1975 in the various countries.
[2] This is 100 times the production index divided by the employment index, giving a rough indication of changes in output per person employed.
[3] Excluding Albania, Bulgaria, China, Czechoslovakia, East Germany, Hungary, Mongolia, North Korea, Poland, Romania, the U.S.S.R., and Vietnam.
[4] Canada and the United States.
[5] South and Central America (including Mexico) and the Caribbean islands.
[6] Asian Middle East and East and Southeast Asia, including Japan.
[7] Excluding Albania, Bulgaria, Czechoslovakia, East Germany, Hungary, Poland, Romania, and the U.S.S.R.
[8] Africa and Oceania.
[9] These are not included in the above world total and consist of the European countries listed in note 7 above.

Table II. Pattern of Output, 1978–81
Percent change from previous year

	World[1] 1978	World[1] 1979	World[1] 1980	World[1] 1981	Developed countries 1978	Developed countries 1979	Developed countries 1980	Developed countries 1981	Less developed countries 1978	Less developed countries 1979	Less developed countries 1980	Less developed countries 1981	Centrally planned economies 1978	Centrally planned economies 1979	Centrally planned economies 1980	Centrally planned economies 1981
All manufacturing	4	5	−0.3	0.4	4	5	−1	0.5	6	4	4	0	6	4	5	3
Heavy industries	5	5	−0.3	0.7	5	6	−1	1	7	5	4	−2	7	5	5	3
Base metals	5	6	−5	−0.5	5	5	−6	−1	9	11	4	0	4	1	3	−1
Metal products	5	5	1	1	5	5	1	2	7	7	4	−6	8	7	6	5
Building materials, etc.	4	5	−0.5	−3	5	5	−1	−3	7	4	3	0	4	.2	3	2
Chemicals	5	6	−2	0.5	5	7	−3	0.5	5	1	3	1	6	3	4	−1
Light industries	3	4	−0.2	−0.3	2	4	−1	−1	5	3	4	2	4	3	4	4
Food, drink, tobacco	4	3	3	2	4	3	1	2	6	5	7	5	2	3	2	3
Textiles	0.5	4	−2	−3	0	5	−2	−3	3	2	0	−2	4	2	2	0
Clothing, footwear	0	1	−3	−2	−1	1	−5	−4	3	3	1	4	4	5	3	3
Wood products	1	4	−3	−4	0	3	−4	−4	4	4	6	0	4	0	2	2
Paper, printing	4	5	1	1	5	5	1	0	6	6	5	4	4	−2	3	2

[1] Excluding centrally planned economies.   [2] Excluding China.
Source: UN, Monthly Bulletin of Statistics.

Table IV. Output per Hour Worked in Manufacturing
1975=100

Country	1976	1977	1978	1979	1980	1981
France	111	115	121	129	131	132
West Germany	107	110	113	118	116	119
Italy	109	108	111	122	127	130
Japan	110	115	124	134	142	146
U.K.	105	106	107	109	107	113
U.S.	106	108	110	112	115	119

Source: National Institute, Economic Review.

Table V. Manufacturing Production in the U.S.S.R. and Eastern Europe[1]
1975=100

Country	1978	1979	1980	1981
Bulgaria[2]	122	128	134	142
Czechoslovakia	117	122	126	129
East Germany[2]	116	121	127	133
Hungary	117	121	118	121
Poland	123	126	126	111
U.S.S.R.	117	121	124	127

[1] Romania not available.
[2] All industries.
Source: UN, Monthly Bulletin of Statistics.

A Michigan real estate broker decided to aid two of that state's depressed industries by giving purchasers of condominiums a free automobile.

and sharp competition from newly industrializing nations, chiefly in Latin America and the Far East.

In 1981 the heavy industries fared somewhat better than did the light ones in the advanced countries, but in all other areas the opposite was true. Among the heavy industries the output of building materials fell most because of depressed construction activity, followed by the production of base metals, greatly influenced by the weak demand for steel and automobiles. The advance in the light industries was mainly due to the continued growth of the food and allied industries; output in most other light industries fell, and their development, especially that of clothing and wood products, indicated clearly the shift of production from the advanced to the less (or newly) industrialized countries.

In the three established centres of industrial activity—North America, Japan, and Western Europe—output developed differently. In contrast to the growth in 1981 in the other two areas, production in Europe fell. In the first half of 1982, however, output in North America suffered a sharp decline, while a further fall in Europe was avoided and a moderate advance took place in Japan. Among the Western European countries only Italy, Finland, Switzerland, and Portugal could raise production somewhat in 1981; output fell in all the other countries, most markedly in the United Kingdom and France. Changes in manufacturing output varied in the less developed countries: considerable growth in India, South Korea, and Mexico was in sharp contrast to declines in Brazil and Argentina.

The difficult conditions in domestic markets and the strong competition in exports—as well as rising wages—compelled manufacturers to make their production processes as efficient as possible. The result was a rise in labour productivity, despite stagnating output.

In the Soviet Union manufacturing output grew slowly, at just over 2%, for the second year in succession. Because of domestic political troubles production fell by 12% in Poland. Output rose rapidly in Bulgaria and more moderately in East Germany and Czechoslovakia; after the decline in 1980, expansion was resumed at a slow rate in Hungary. (G. F. RAY)

Japan is one of the world's leaders in the use of robots for boring and tiresome mechanical chores. In photo employees who take neither coffee breaks nor vacations apply a coat of paint to an automobile.

Industrial Review

ADVERTISING

Advertisers on college football telecasts were affected by a federal district court ruling in September 1982 allowing individual schools, not the National Collegiate Athletic Association, to sell broadcasting rights for their games. The ruling, if upheld, would create an open market in which each school would negotiate with networks and cable TV for the best deal. More immediately unsettling to advertisers' plans was the strike of National Football League players in the fall that resulted in the cancellation of 112 games. Professional football telecasts had proved to be an unparalleled vehicle for advertising men's products. The networks substituted action movies and other sports events, principally boxing, but these did not have the same appeal.

The recession led many companies to offer more giveaways, sweepstakes, come-ons, and rebates to promote sales. Airlines, for example, offered free tickets and lower rates to frequent flyers. Manufacturers stressed quality, value, price reductions, and new uses of products in their advertising. General Electric, among others, used a technique called "flighting"—running a large number of high-visibility advertisements for fast-selling products over a short period.

Ted Bates Worldwide Inc. and William Esty Co. merged during the year, the largest merger in U.S. advertising agency history. Together, the agencies billed $2.4 billion in 1982. Bates paid $50 million for the Esty agency. The U.S. Supreme Court in 1982 rejected a Missouri state rule that barred lawyers from using direct-mail advertising and limited their advertising claims to specific, state-approved phrases. The decision could affect similar rules in 38 other states. As of March 1982, over 50% of U.S. households were "passed" by cable systems, and approximately half of them, 23 million, were subscribers. Fifty percent of cable households also subscribed to pay television. Advertisers were beginning to exploit this new medium, which allowed them to target particular consumer groups more selectively than with over-the-air television.

The $35 billion beef industry spent $7 million in advertising in 1982 in an effort to reverse declining beef sales. Beef thus joined such products as avocados, eggs, oranges, raisins, and potatoes in advertising directly to the public. In 1976 the Florida Department of Citrus, an early advertiser, began an effort to convince the public that orange juice "isn't just for breakfast anymore." The California Avocado Commission's campaign to change the perception that avocados are fattening had raised the percentage of U.S. households buying the fruit from 5 to 50.

In an effort to force Burger King, the U.S.'s second-largest fast-food chain, to withdraw a comparison advertising campaign, McDonald's (no. 1) and Wendy's (no. 3) filed suit in federal court, charging that the ads were false and misleading. The hard-hitting commercials, devised by the J. Walter Thompson agency, claimed that Burger King's hamburgers were broiled rather than fried, that they had been preferred in nationwide taste tests, and that Burger King's Whopper sandwich contained more meat before cooking than McDonald's Big Mac. An out-of-court settlement was reached in October under which Burger King agreed to phase out the ads. The episode pointed up the growing use of comparison ads in which competing products are mentioned by name.

Procter & Gamble also took to the courts, filing libel suits against individuals who allegedly had spread the rumour that the firm's man-in-the-moon trademark was a Satanist symbol. A publicity campaign had been launched to counter the persistent rumour, but an *Advertising Age* survey indicated that it had not reached the people most likely to believe the story and may actually have spread it. All advertising for Tylenol was withdrawn when seven people died after taking Extra-Strength Tylenol capsules contaminated with cyanide. (*See* CRIME AND LAW ENFORCEMENT.) In late fall Johnson & Johnson, parent company of McNeil Consumer Products Co. which produced the popular painkiller, began a carefully calibrated campaign to restore confidence in the product.

Doylestown Township, Pa., lost a fight in the U.S. Supreme Court to curb unsolicited door-to-door distribution of "shoppers,"

free papers devoted to advertising. The controversy involved a conflict between advertising's First Amendment rights and the township's police power. The trial court upheld the township, which contended that the accumulation of unsolicited circulars at vacant homes identified targets for housebreakers. In doing so, the court noted that the ordinance barring door-to-door distribution left open the opportunity for advertising through the mails or through distribution in response to residents' requests. The appeals court upheld the shopper, however, and the Pennsylvania Supreme Court allowed the appeals court decision to stand.

Each year *Advertising Age* profiles the 100 top national advertisers in the previous year. In 1981 these advertisers spent an estimated $14.8 billion, a 14% increase over 1980. Procter & Gamble remained in the number one position, followed by Sears, General Foods, Philip Morris, and General Motors. Procter & Gamble had been the largest advertising spender in the U.S. since 1963, when it replaced General Motors. In 1981 it spent $671 million on advertising and promotion, 3.4% more than in 1980.

The five leading newspaper advertisers were R. J. Reynolds Industries, Philip Morris, General Motors, Loews Corp., and B.A.T. Industries, PLC. Procter & Gamble led in television advertising with an expenditure of almost $522 million. Next were General Foods, General Motors, American Home Products Corp., and the Ford Motor Co. The 100 leading national advertisers accounted for 36.5% of all newspaper advertising, 50% of all magazine advertising, 76% of network television advertising, and 61% of network radio advertising.

(EDWARD MARK MAZZE)

AEROSPACE

The sorry financial plight of the world's airlines took the edge off a major milestone in the aerospace industry—the entry into service of the Boeing 767 airliner, the intended replacement for a host of mid-1950s, first- and second-generation transports such as the Boeing 707 and 737, Douglas DC-8, and Vickers VC-10. This all-new airplane first flew in September 1981, was certified in the extraordinarily short space of 11 months, and went into commercial operation on

One of the year's most aggressive advertising campaigns was launched by Burger King, which took on rival fast-food chains McDonald's and Wendy's by name.

Early in the year Boeing introduced its new 757, a twin-engine jet designed for short/medium-range flights.

Sept. 8, 1982. It embodied the technical refinements developed since the days of the early jetliners: highly refined aerodynamic shape; new high-bypass, quiet, economical engines; computer-optimized structure; and digital, automatic, self-checking instruments and electronics.

A few months after the 767 came the same company's 757, for shorter ranges, and also Europe's Airbus Industrie A310, both of which made their first flights in 1982 and embodied the technology introduced by the 767. The A310 and 767 were virtually identical to one another in performance, economics, and capacity. The European transport consolidated the reputation built by its predecessor, the A300 short-range airliner, the two designs putting Europe for the first time on equal footing with the U.S. in this class of aircraft.

Unfortunately, the airlines now lacked the capital to buy the new aircraft that were specifically designed to give them the profitability they so badly needed. At the same time the new transports had to battle

against a huge secondhand market. A U.S. credit company in August estimated that 550 transport aircraft, representing 9.5% of the world's fleet of 5,900 transports and many of them new models, had been put up for sale.

Throughout the year airlines sought to delay, cancel, or transfer orders for the 767 and 757. United Airlines was discussing the possibility of canceling orders for 25 of the 767s, while American Airlines converted its order for 757s into 727s of similar capacity with a saving of about $3 million on each aircraft. The latter airline was putting into practice the widely held conviction that expenditure on the new transports could be justified only at a time of steeply rising fuel prices, when the differences in operating costs between old and new aircraft would be greatest. With the slump in orders Lockheed in December 1981 announced the phasing out of TriStar production. This trijet medium-range widebody airliner was perhaps the most advanced commercial transport in operation, and the news was

greeted with sadness by the aeronautical community. Rumours that the almost identical rival, the McDonnell Douglas DC-10, might go the same way could have materialized had not the U.S. Air Force come to the rescue with orders for more of the KC-tankers, a military version of the DC-10. For the first time in its 50-year career Lockheed was out of the commercial aircraft business and seemed likely to remain so for the foreseeable future.

With business so flat little was heard of the 150-seat projects that in 1981 had looked so promising. Boeing still claimed that a viable aircraft could not be available before 1988 because the engine manufacturers would not be able to provide sufficiently advanced power plants to justify the outlay before then. However, the Airbus A320 design might go ahead under the terms of the "order" announced by Air France at the 1981 Paris air show, thus getting the jump on Boeing (which was likely to be in cash flow difficulties with the 767 and 757 for some time), Lockheed, and Douglas. The technically magnificent but economically disastrous supersonic Concorde, in the hands of its only two operators, British Airways and Air France, was gradually dying, with routes being closed down and aircraft being cannibalized for spare parts.

The year was also disastrous for the less-publicized but mammoth general aviation industry, covering everything from two-seater "fly-for-fun" aircraft to multimillion-dollar business and corporate jets. Sales in that sector were down by no less than 50%, with a mere 4,500 U.S. aircraft sold, as compared with the previous figure of some 9,000 annually.

Recession and high prices affected air shows as well, and big-name manufacturers continued to withdraw their support. They objected to paying $1 million for disrupting the life of busy executives for two weeks, hiring expensive chalets, entertaining, and operating demonstration aircraft. Thus, McDonnell Douglas pulled out of the Farnborough Air Show in 1982, and Lock-

Europe's entry into the short/medium-range jet fleet was the Airbus Industrie A310, which could carry 195 to 225 passengers. Airlines had ordered 180 of the airbuses by mid-1982.

Industrial Review

heed announced that it would not be appearing at any more major shows.

The principal military events were the air wars in the Falkland Islands and over Lebanon. The Falklands war was notable for being the first conflict to involve fixed-wing v/STOL (vertical/short take-off and landing) aircraft. The superiority of the British Aerospace Sea Harriers and their U.S.-supplied AIM-9L Sidewinder missiles was such that 31 Argentine aircraft—including 19 Mirages and 5 Skyhawks—were shot down in air combat with no losses to the British fighters. By a fluke of timing the Royal Air Force's Vulcan heavy bombers were used (to bomb the runway at Port Stanley airfield) within days of being retired after 25 years of service. It was their combat debut. Five Vulcan missions were accomplished from Ascension Island, involving a round trip of more than 12,800 km (8,000 mi) and ten air refuelings for each. These were almost certainly the longest bombing raids ever carried out.

By contrast the Israeli invasion of Lebanon was supported by aircraft operating near their bases. Israel's success in the air war made one thing clear: the era of electronic battle management and automated combat was at hand. The Israeli Air Force in air combat and ground attack demonstrated a technical sophistication and integration of forces previously unequaled. Its E-2C Hawkeyes provided early warning of Syrian Air Force fighters taking off to intercept Israeli attackers, and its Boeing 707s then jammed the Syrians' radio communications so that they could not receive steering instructions. Meanwhile, Israeli fighter-bombers knocked out Palestine Liberation Organization and Syrian positions with great accuracy with laser-guided bombs, using ECM (electronic countermeasures) to protect themselves from antiaircraft missiles. To check on damage, Israel then sent in model-aircraft-sized RPV's (remote piloted vehicles) to monitor Syrian positions and radio and televise results. (*See* DEFENSE.)   (MICHAEL WILSON)

ALCOHOLIC BEVERAGES

Beer. Estimated world beer production in 1981 was 948 million hectolitres (hl), with the top ten brewing nations producing some 65% of the total. The U.S. remained the world's biggest brewer, producing almost 214 million hl, about 13 million hl less than in 1980. All other countries in the top ten increased output except the U.K., where the total fell by almost 5% to 61.7 million hl. West Germany increased production by 1.5% to 93,716,000 hl, and the U.S.S.R. became the world's third biggest brewer with 65 million hl.

In the early part of 1982 high prices were being paid in Europe for top quality malting barley. By the end of the year, however, harvest returns were suggesting a record crop in European Community (EC) countries of over 41 million metric tons, more than 1½ million tons higher than in 1981. The 1982 hop crop was also up from 1981, with a hop-growing area of 68,080 ha (168,160 ac) in Europe, Australia, and the U.S. producing 2,263,000 centners (1 cent-

Anheuser-Busch, the largest brewer in the U.S., increased its market share to 29.5% with a record of 54.5 million barrels sold in 1982.

ner = 50 kg). In Europe there were developments in packaged beers to comply with EC labeling directives. From Jan. 1, 1983, packaged beers would display a "Best Before" date if the beer was of an alcoholic strength of under 10% by volume. For bottled beers Best Before dates tended to be indicated by edge-notched labels. For canned beers both non-contact ink-jet systems and laser marking were used.

In May 1982 the Biochemistry Group of the European Brewery Convention (EBC) met in Oporto, Portugal. Topics discussed included malting processes, fermentation, and haze particles in beer. Papers were presented by brewers from the U.K., Ireland, France, West Germany, The Netherlands, Switzerland, Sweden, Norway, and Denmark.   (MICHAEL D. RIPLEY)

Spirits. The spirits industry experienced a depressing year in 1982. In the U.K. the market slumped by 14%, continuing a downward spiral from its drop of 5% in 1981. Heaviest declines were in the home-produced sectors with gin down 44% and vodka down 53% in the first four months of 1982. Scotch whisky retained its 50% share of the U.K. market despite a decline in volume sales of about 12%. Production had dropped by 40% in the last four years. The U.S. market for Scotch whisky fell 22% to 12.8 million U.S. proof gallons in the first five months of the year. In Japan, U.K. brands continued to lead the Scotch market, but bulk exports of malt were allowing home-produced blends to develop a strong base for the future.

Cream liqueurs, a product sector created only five years earlier, continued to flourish at the expense of such after-dinner drinks as port and traditional liqueurs. A renewed interest in cocktails prompted the recent launch of many new liqueurs. There were signs that the domination of the U.S. and European spirits market by white spirits was beginning to wane with a revival by such darker spirits as Canadian whiskey and cognac. Imported liqueurs advanced by

9% in the U.S. to 6 million U.S. proof gallons in 1981, chief suppliers being Mexico, with its tequila and brandy, followed by Italy and France. Ireland's share, thanks to cream liqueurs, jumped above that of the U.K. with a 47% increase to 653,000 gal, while rum imports to the U.S. fell 32%, further suggesting that the white spirits boom had reached its peak.

Future prospects for spirits remained bleak with consumers being forced to moderate their drinking habits during the recession. In the U.K. the government agreed to a credit period for payment of duty on spirits. This concession, which the industry had requested for many years, would free capital and allow for increased promotional investment.

(ANTONY C. WARNER)

Wine. World production of wine in 1982 was expected to be well above the revised 1981 total of 312 million hl. Throughout Western Europe harvests generally were abundant and of high quality. EC countries together produced an estimated 175 million hl, as compared with an average of 150 million hl over the past decade. In France overall production was estimated at 79 million hl, the second highest since World War II; production of quality wines, at 18.6 million hl, was higher than ever before. In Alsace, Bordeaux, Bourgogne, Beaujolais, Côtes-du-Rhône, and Val de Loire the vintage was expected to be of exceptionally high quality. In Champagne a harvest of 2.2 million hl, or well over 250 million bottles, would enable depleted stocks to be replenished after the bad harvests of the three preceding years. The Cognac harvest produced 11.2 million hl of white wines suitable for distillation.

The Italian harvest totaled some 80 million hl, or about 14% higher than in 1981; only in Sicily and Sardinia was production lower than in 1981. In all regions producing quality wines the 1982 vintage was expected to be well above average, with alcoholic content 1–1½ degrees above that of the pre-

Table VI. Estimated Consumption of Beer in Selected Countries
In litres[1] per capita

Country	1979	1980	1981
West Germany	145.1	145.7	147.0
Czechoslovakia	137.0	137.8	140.1
East Germany	135.0	138.7	137.5
Australia[2]	134.2	134.3	134.1
Belgium[3]	125.8	131.3	124.2
Luxembourg	111.0	121.0	123.0
Denmark	120.38	121.63	122.18
New Zealand	118.5	120.9	121.8
Ireland	122.7	121.76	116.4
United Kingdom	122.1	117.1	111.5
Austria	103.9	101.9	104.8
United States	90.1	92.0	93.3
Netherlands, The	84.95	86.39	89.47
Hungary	86.1	87.0	87.0
Canada[4]	84.2	87.0	85.0
Switzerland	68.2	69.0	70.5
Venezuela	79.9	62.5	...
Bulgaria	57.7	60.9	...
Finland	56.18	57.39	57.24
Spain	53.7	53.4	56.0
Sweden	48.2	47.2	45.0
Colombia	40.5	43.9	45.0
Romania	43.4	43.8	45.0
Norway	45.88	48.28	44.81
Yugoslavia	39.7	44.2	44.2

[1] One litre = 1.0567 U.S. quart = 0.8799 imperial quart.
[2] Years ending June 30.
[3] Excluding so-called household beer.
[4] Years ending March 31.

Table VII: Estimated Consumption of Potable Distilled Spirits in Selected Countries
In litres[1] of 100% pure spirit per capita

Country	1979	1980	1981
Luxembourg	5.8	9.0	9.5
East Germany	4.3	4.7	4.7
Hungary	4.15	4.75	4.5
Poland	5.6	6.0	4.3
Czechoslovakia	3.24	3.52	3.6
Canada[2]	3.51	3.38	3.5
U.S.S.R.	3.3	3.3	3.3
United States	3.1	3.07	3.04
Peru	1.4	3.0	3.0
Spain	4.0	2.0	3.0
West Germany	3.37	3.09	2.9
Finland	2.75	2.79	2.76
Netherlands, The	3.41	2.72	2.52
Sweden	3.03	2.75	2.48
Iceland	2.35	2.25	2.23
Belgium	2.26	2.37	2.13
Switzerland	2.04	2.05	2.11
Cyprus	1.9	2.0	2.1
New Zealand	2.11	1.94	2.0
France[3]	2.53	2.53	2.0
Yugoslavia	1.8	2.0	...
Romania	2.3	2.3	2.0
Italy	2.0	1.9	1.9
Japan	1.73	1.83	1.9

[1] One litre = 1.0567 U.S. quart = 0.8799 imperial quart.
[2] Years ending March 31.
[3] Including aperitifs.

Table VIII. Estimated Consumption of Wine in Selected Countries
In litres[1] per capita

Country	1979	1980	1981
France[2]	92.8	91.0	90.0
Portugal	62.6	72.9	77.0
Italy	90.0	80.0	74.0
Argentina	77.0	75.0	73.0
Spain	53.7	53.4	60.0
Switzerland[3]	45.8	47.4	48.4
Greece	40.5	44.9	44.9
Chile	48.0	46.9	43.7
Luxembourg	39.4	48.2	40.2
Austria[4]	35.8	35.8	35.1
Hungary	34.0	35.0	35.0
Romania	35.5	28.9	28.9
Yugoslavia	27.3	28.2	...
Uruguay	25.0	25.0	...
West Germany	24.3	25.5	24.7
Bulgaria	22.0	22.0	...
Belgium	20.4	20.6	20.97
Australia[4]	16.5	17.4	18.3
Denmark	13.88	14.0	16.09
Czechoslovakia	15.5	15.5	16.0
New Zealand	11.2	13.3	14.5
U.S.S.R.	14.0	14.4	14.5
Netherlands, The	11.96	12.85	12.95
Cyprus	9.0	9.8	10.8
Sweden	9.43	9.54	9.72
East Germany	9.3	9.6	9.5

[1] One litre = 1.0567 U.S. quart = 0.8799 imperial quart.
[2] Excluding cider (c. 20 litres per capita annually).
[3] Excluding cider (c. 4.9 litres per capita 1980–81).
[4] Years ending June 30.

Source: Produktschap voor Gedistilleerde Dranken, *Hoeveel alcoholhoudende dranken worden er in de wereld gedronken?*

---

vious year. Estimates of the Spanish harvest varied from about 39 million to 45 million hl, the lower figure being well above that for 1981. In general, quality and alcoholic content were expected to be good, in some cases exceptional. In North Africa harvests in Algeria, Morocco, and Tunisia were considerably lower than in 1981 as a result of lack of rain throughout the summer.

In California the 1982 vintage, which early in September had promised to be abundant and of high quality, was ruined by exceptionally bad weather at the end of the month. Rot appeared and spread rapidly, and despite every effort at prevention about 25% of the harvest was lost. Australia's production for the third consecutive year was high in both quantity and quality.

A new development in English viticulture was the purchase of an East Sussex vineyard by a large-scale West German producer; current annual production of 12,000–15,000 bottles was expected to increase to 50,000 bottles within three years.

(MARIE-JOSE DESHAYES-CREUILLY)

AUTOMOBILES

Chrysler Corp. seemed to be on the road to recovery in 1982, even though the automobile industry was still mired in a sales depression. But De Lorean Motor Co. was on the road to ruin after John Z. De Lorean (see BIOGRAPHIES), former General Motors vice-president and founder of the company bearing his name, was arrested for allegedly conspiring to sell cocaine in hopes of making enough money to bail out his ailing firm.

After losing more than $1 billion in 1980, Chrysler trimmed its losses to $476 million in 1981 and expected to break even or perhaps earn slightly more than $100 million in 1982. Chrysler was able to retire all outstanding bank debt in 1982 and still have $1 billion in cash reserves.

In contrast, De Lorean Motor Co. was placed in receivership by the British government, and production was halted after an estimated 7,000 to 10,000 of the $25,000 gull-wing sports cars had been built at the plant in Belfast, Northern Ireland. Ironically, the British government closed the plant only hours before De Lorean was arrested in Los Angeles.

Though Chrysler was showing signs of recovery, the U.S. automobile industry was still struggling. In the 1982 model year, ended Sept. 30, 1982, sales totaled only 5.5 million units, down from the 6.5 million sold in the 1981 model year and the lowest total since 5.4 million domestic cars were sold in 1961.

General Motors sold 3,387,607 new cars, down from 4,032,727 in the '81 model year. Ford sold 1,289,987, down from 1,487,961; Chrysler sold 658,720, down from 764,535. Volkswagen sold 107,396 versus 159,588; and American Motors sold 99,300, down from 145,206. GM's share of the market totaled 61.1%, compared with 60.7% a year earlier; Ford rose from 23.2 to 23.3%; Chrysler increased to 11.9 from 11.5%; AMC declined to 1.8 from 2.2%; and VW fell to 1.9 from 2.4%.

Imports, which report sales on a calendar and not model-year basis, continued to hold around the 2.3 million-unit mark. Japanese automobiles were limited to sales of 1,680,000 units under voluntary agreements with the U.S. government to give U.S. manufacturers time to develop more fuel-efficient cars. The final Japanese import total fell short of the maximum ceiling by one vehicle. Since the Japanese were limited in the number of cars they could sell in the U.S., there was a marketing shift toward the luxury and sports models and away from the low-price, high-mileage economy cars. Toyota began to promote its $10,000 and up Celica Supra sports model and Cressida luxury sedan, Datsun its 280ZX sports car and Maxima luxury sedan, Honda its Accord LX sedan and Prelude sports car, and Mazda its RX7 sports model and 626 sedan. By midyear Detroit was complaining that the Japanese were selling fewer cars but making more money than ever before.

In an effort to spur car sales in 1982, U.S. automakers resorted to a variety of incentives. They used cash rebates, offers of free air travel, 24-month/24,000-mi or 36-month/36,000-mi free service warranties that included oil and filter changes, and new car loans with interest rates below the national average of 15–16%. GM started the interest program by introducing a 12.8% ceiling on loans financed through its General Motors Acceptance Corp. financing subsidiary. Ford and Chrysler responded. Late in the year GM went down to 10.9%, but Ford improved on this by going to 10.75% while including $200–$1,000 cash rebates and a choice of an added rebate or 24-month/24,000-mi free service.

As a rule sales picked up when the low interest rates were offered and then slid back when they were halted. Despite concern over reduced sales when the interest programs were off, GM and Ford gained a side benefit; both reported record earnings for their financing subsidiaries as a result of the increased loan business.

One other effort was made to bring buyers back into the showrooms. At the outset of the 1983 model year in the fall of 1982, the U.S. automakers limited price increases to less than 2% while either freezing the 1982 price or reducing it on selected small cars. In many cases, however, the price reductions were achieved by making previously standard equipment optional.

Small-car demand cooled during the year. One reason was that gas prices stabilized or declined, but also the industry's downsizing effort had resulted in mid- and full-size cars that could achieve 20 mi per gal (mpg). U.S. manufacturers also stalled demand for small cars in the 1982 model year by raising prices so that many subcompact models with typical options carried stickers of $10,000 and up and in some cases were priced at the same level or higher than full-size models. For 1983 mid- and full-size cars were raised in price. An example of the industry's new pricing policy revealed a subcompact four-door Ford Escort reduced by $109 to $6,154 for 1983, while the full-size Ford LTD Crown Victoria rose by $1,425 to $10,574.

For the outset of the 1983 model year GM raised the base price of its cars an average of $57 to $9,679; Ford by $515 to $8,819; Chrysler by $380 to $8,580; and AMC by $55 to $7,474. Industry-wide, the base price average was $9,157 for 1983.

There were only a few new models added for 1983. At GM the subcompact J-body Buick Skyhawk and Oldsmobile Firenza were added in the spring. Other midyear entries included the Buick Riviera convertible and a more powerful 1.8-l, Brazilian-built four-cylinder engine for use in the subcompact J-cars (Skyhawk, Firenza, Chevrolet Cavalier, Pontiac J2000, and Cadillac Cimarron). For 1983 an even more powerful 2-l, four-cylinder engine was added for use in all but the Pontiac car, which was waiting instead for a turbocharged 1.8-l engine in 1984.

GM's S-10 and GMC's S-15 new U.S.-built compact pickup trucks introduced late in '81 served as the basis for new small four-wheel-drive utility vehicles for 1983. These included the new "baby" Chevrolet Blazer and GMC Jimmy.

Changes at Ford were more numerous. The subcompact Escort and Lynx added larger engines for increased performance; the subcompact Mustang and Capri were restyled with Mustang adding convertible models and Capri glass-bubble hatchbacks; and the compact Granada and Cougar were discontinued but their platform feature was retained to serve as the basis for new smaller LTD and Marquis models with standard four-cylinder engines under the hood. The full-size LTD and Marquis remained but under the Crown Victoria and Grand Marquis names. The Thunderbird and Cougar XR7 were dramatically restyled, with the for-

One of the major attractions at the Automotive News World Expo was Ford Motor Co.'s high-styled car called the "Flare." More than 150 exhibitors showed their wares at the exposition, held in Detroit in September.

mer sporting rounded lines and a laid-back aerodynamic grille while Cougar had a look similar to a Buick Riviera with a long hood, short deck, and notchback roofline. Thunderbird planned to add a five-speed transmission late in the model year.

The compact Fairmont and Zephyr were continued but only for a brief time, as the next line of front-wheel-drive models, a compact Ford Tempo and Mercury Topaz, were scheduled to replace them later in the 1983 model year. Tempo-Topaz were to be stretched versions of the Escort and Lynx with wheelbases expanded to 99 in from 94 in. Ford, like GM, also planned a "baby" Bronco four-wheel-drive utility vehicle based on its new compact Ranger pickup truck.

At Chrysler a new series of front-wheel-drive offshoots for the compact K-body platform appeared, the Chrysler E-Class and Dodge 600. Both were offered in four-

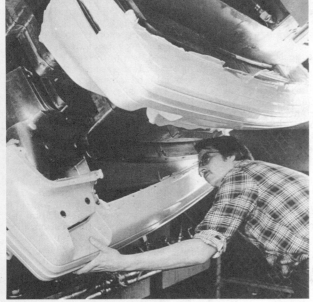

Polyurethane bumpers that are reputed to be lighter and more shock resistant than steel bumpers were being installed on Renault Alliance automobiles for fall delivery.

door models only and were built on stretched 103-in wheelbases versus 99 in on a compact Aries or 100 in on a mid-size Le-Baron. Chrysler's own 2.2-l and the Mitsubishi-built 2.6-l were the only four-cylinder engines that were offered.

Tagged for later midyear entry were a new front-wheel-drive New Yorker based on the E-body and a luxury limousine based on the same but with the wheelbase stretched at least a foot. Early in 1982 Chrysler brought out the LeBaron and Dodge 400 convertibles. The firm also announced that it was devoting attention and money to bringing out in 1984 a new high-performance sports car called the G-24 and a mini (actually compact based on the Reliant) front-wheel-drive van.

At American Motors a subcompact, front-wheel-drive Fuego sports car from Renault was introduced in the spring of 1982, and later in the year came the new subcompact Alliance, the first joint venture car from the partnership between AMC and Renault. In the first month that it was offered it accounted for 60% of AMC's sales and helped the firm report its highest one-month sales (12,722 in October 1982) in more than 14 months. To make room for the car the subcompact Spirit sedan (at one time called the Gremlin) was discontinued.

Among the imports changes were few. Toyota restyled the subcompact front-wheel-drive Tercel and added a four-wheel-drive Tercel wagon. Datsun replaced the 210 rear-wheel-drive subcompact with a new front-wheel-drive Nissan Sentra and the 310 rear-drive model with the front-drive Nissan Pulsar. Mazda restyled its 626 and converted it to front-wheel drive.

Volkswagen, considered an import by the U.S. government and a U.S. producer by VW, added a sports GTI version of the Rabbit and a new engine for a limited-edition Rabbit (only 3,000 were to be built) that automatically shuts off when the driver's foot is removed from the accelerator for more than 1.5 seconds. That engine, in a diesel-powered Rabbit, helped VW capture the top spot in the annual Environmental

Protection Agency fuel economy rankings of 1983 cars. It was the sixth consecutive year in which a diesel Rabbit took the honours and the first year that any car reached the 50-mpg city mileage level. A diesel-engine Nissan Stanza and a Rabbit with non-shutdown engine tied for second with 48 mpg in the city. The lowest rated car was the Maserati Quattroporte at 8 mpg. In 1983 the government-mandated Corporate Average Fuel Economy law, which required each automaker to obtain a prescribed average from its fleet of cars, was set at 26 mpg. It had been 24 mpg in 1982.

In another ranking of some importance, the top ten sales leaders in the auto industry as the 1982 model year closed on September 30 were the Ford Escort, Oldsmobile 88-98 duo, Chevrolet Chevette, Chevrolet Citation, Chevrolet Impala-Caprice duo, Honda Accord, Nissan Sentra, Toyota Corolla, Oldsmobile Cutlass Supreme, and the Buick LeSabre-Electra duo. Though the Toyota Corolla had previously finished in the top ten (highest was fifth in 1980), 1982 was the first year in which three imports (Corolla, Accord, and Sentra) were among the sales leaders.

In other developments Checker Motors Corp. stopped producing taxicabs and cars after 60 years in the business, and Avanti Motor Corp. of South Bend, Ind., was sold to S. Harvard Blake, a Washington, D.C., businessman. The Japanese industrial giant Mitsubishi began sales operations in the U.S. by marketing the Starion, Tredia, and Cordia cars on an exclusive basis without its normal ties with Chrysler dealers. Honda, on October 31, built the first Accord four-door model at its new Marysville, Ohio, assembly plant. The Japanese firm thus joined Volkswagen (Rabbits in Pennsylvania) as the only foreign automakers with manufacturing plants in the U.S. Nissan was planning to build trucks in Tennessee. (JAMES L. MATEJA)

BUILDING AND CONSTRUCTION

The depressed U.S. construction industry experienced its fourth year of declining activity in 1982. While total dollar outlays for new construction put in place reached an all-time high of $238 billion in 1981, inflation concealed the real downtrend that had been occurring since 1978. On a constant dollar basis (1977 = 100), outlays for new construction had fallen steadily from approximately $182 billion in 1978 to $156 billion in 1981. The outlook for 1982 was that total outlays would not exceed $147 billion in constant dollars.

A major contributor to the decline was the downturn in the number of new housing units being built. In the peak year of 1978, over two million housing units had been started, while in 1981 the number was just over one million. On a seasonally adjusted basis, the rate of private housing starts was below one million units per year in each of the months from August 1981 through April 1982. There was some evidence that activity would improve in the last half of 1982 and in 1983 In May, July, and August 1982, the seasonally adjusted annual rate for private housing starts was one million or more units.

In addition, figures released by the U.S. Department of Commerce showed that gross private investment in residential property had stabilized during the first six months of 1982. While the department predicted that the number of private housing starts would be lower in 1982 than in 1981, its forecast for 1983 was for 1.2 million to 1.3 million units. This anticipated slow recovery was based in part on the fact that the number of persons in the prime home-buying category had increased in the late 1970s and early 1980s. Mortgage interest rates were declining somewhat, and it was expected that employment and disposable personal income would rise as the economy recovered.

Private nonresidential construction was the only component of the industry that was not depressed in 1982. The value of new private nonresidential buildings put in place reached $65.4 billion in May 1982 (seasonally adjusted annual rate basis), and it appeared that outlays for the year would exceed the record of $60.8 billion set in 1981. At the same time, dollar outlays for public construction fell from $55 billion in 1980 to $52.9 billion in 1981, and the forecast for 1982 was even lower. Much of the downturn was due to curtailments by state and local governments.

The softening of inflation was a favourable development for the construction industry. The Department of Commerce composite construction cost index stood at 157.6 (1977 = 100) in June 1982, 5% above June 1981. This increase was lower than the comparable 12-month increases during each of the preceding five years, and the index changed less than 1% over the first half of 1982. In late 1982 preliminary figures released by the Department of Commerce showed that the average sale price of a new home was $84,700 and the median sale price was $69,200, up 2% and less than 1%, respectively, over 1981. By late 1982 prices had declined slightly.

In Canada, which was experiencing severe recession, housing starts turned down sharply toward the end of 1981, and the outlook for 1982 was not good. Much the same situation pertained in Western Europe. Construction activity in Great Britain continued at low levels in 1982, and the outlook for 1983 was for very little if any recovery. France planned to increase public investment in housing, but it was expected that this would be more than offset by a decline in private investment. Bad weather conditions in West Germany in 1981 made matters worse for an already depressed construction industry; however, the 1982 forecast was for gradual recovery. Little or no growth was predicted in the smaller countries of Western Europe.

In Japan all types of construction were expected to show some improvement in 1982. The gross national product rose about 4.7% in 1981, and continued expansion of the economy in 1982 was expected to come mainly from domestic-induced growth. It was also forecast that higher industrial profits would lead to increased investment in plant and equipment. (CARTER C. OSTERBIND)

CHEMICALS

The performance of the chemical industry during the last quarter of 1981 and the first three quarters of 1982 reflected the depressed condition of the world economy. Demand for chemicals dropped, and profitability plummeted.

In the U.S. shipments of chemical and allied products, which had risen 8% in 1981, declined during the first half of 1982 from the corresponding period in 1981, according to the U.S. Department of Commerce. Shipments for the full year 1981 reached $175,131,000,000; for the first half of 1982 they were $87,043,000,000, 4.6% lower than they had been in the first half of 1981.

Production activity followed the same general trend. In 1981 the Federal Reserve Board's index of chemical production averaged 215.6 (1967 = 100), 8.5% higher than the average for 1980. But the index started to fall during the third quarter of 1981, and by June 1982 it had dropped to 192.2.

Even the trade picture for chemicals in the U.S. dimmed somewhat. In 1981 chemical exports, as reported by the Department of Commerce, rose 2.2% from 1980 to $21,167,000,000. Imports for the year rose 10.1% to $9,446,000,000. The favourable balance of chemical trade, as a result, declined from $12,157,000,000 in 1980 to $11,741,000,000 in 1981. During the first half of 1982 chemical imports were $4,709,000,000, while exports amounted to $10,388,000,000. Net chemical exports for the period of $5,679,000,000 were 6.8% below the first-half figures for 1981.

Chemical prices in the U.S. continued to rise, although at a slower pace and at a rate below that of overall inflation. The U.S. Department of Labor's index of producer prices for chemicals averaged 287.8 (1967 = 100) in 1981, 10.6% higher than in 1980. The index moved erratically in the first half of 1982, reaching a high of 296.2 in May before falling to 291.6 in July.

Figures available late in 1982 indicated that earnings for the third quarter were sharply below those of the same quarter in 1981. The notable exception to the trend was the pharmaceutical industry, in which companies were generally reporting higher profits.

Lower interest rates and reduced inflation during the fourth quarter of 1982 were encouraging many to hope that the demand for housing and automobiles in the U.S. would increase. Because those markets are big users of chemicals, such a rise would benefit the chemical industry. The industry, however, was not expecting any significant improvement until the economy in general rebounded.

In Japan chemical makers were struggling with a recession that first affected their industry in mid-1980. Early estimates were that Japanese chemical sales in 1981 reached $90 billion, and there was optimism early in the year that they would increase to $100 billion in 1982. The feeling was predicated, however, on a strong economy in the U.S. and on an increase in Japan's domestic spending program. But chemical production in Japan declined across the board during the first half of 1982 despite a 1.3% increase in the nation's gross national product during the second quarter. Production of ethylene, the important petrochemical building block, was down more than 4%, and the output of large-volume plastics was off by 4 to 6%. Japan's Ministry of International Trade and Industry forecast that chemical exports for the fiscal year 1982, which would end on March 31, 1983, would drop 1.3% to $7.6 billion.

The chemical industries in Western Europe were also feeling the effect of the recession. In West Germany chemical sales in 1981 according to preliminary figures increased 8.5% to $51 billion. Exports continued to play an important role in the nation's chemical program. They were estimated to be $24 billion in 1981, 47% of the total chemical sales. Imports during the year of $14.5 billion gave the country a $9.5 billion favourable balance of trade in chemicals.

Like their Japanese counterparts, West German chemical companies in early 1982 were anticipating a healthier year. And, indeed, sales in the first quarter increased 4% to $13.5 billion. But the increase was caused by higher prices as physical output actually declined 1.4%. By the end of the third quarter hopes for 1982 had effectively been dashed. Rudolf Sammet, chairman of West Germany's second biggest chemical concern, predicted that overall chemical production in 1982 would be at least 1% lower than in 1981.

Though chemical sales in France surpassed $40 billion in 1981, the large firms lost money. On Dec. 18, 1981, the National Assembly passed a bill nationalizing a large part of the chemical operations in the private sector. The goal of the nationalization was to spur investment, reduce unemployment, and slow the rate of inflation. However, the government was also determined to hold its budget deficit to approximately $15 billion, and for this reason the chemical industry was not receiving the funding that it desired. The nationalized chemical companies had sought $1.2 billion in new financing, but the government decided to grant only $666 million.

The lower value of the franc did help chemical exports in France during 1981, when they rose 14%. Imports for the year increased only 8%.

In the United Kingdom the chemical industry increased its sales in 1981 by 6% to reach $31 billion. An export drive during the year succeeded in increasing chemical exports by 9% to $10.8 billion. The goal for 1982 was to achieve chemical exports of $12.3 billion. However, the reduced demand for chemicals throughout the world in 1982 seemed to make that objective unattainable. In fact, the U.K.'s Chemical Industry Association reported that exports declined during the first quarter of 1982, although imports increased marginally. Production of chemicals in the U.K. declined 1% during the first four months of 1982. That represented a 10% decline from 1979 levels for the period.

The Italian chemical industry was also beset with troubles. Sales in 1981 increased to $24.6 billion, but during that year the country had a trade deficit in chemicals that amounted to $2.2 billion. The largest chemical company, Montedison Spa, lost $544 million in 1981, following a $523 million loss in 1980. Two of the country's major

chemical companies, SIR and Liquichimica, went bankrupt.

To revitalize the industry, some important structural changes were being made. A notable one was the formation early in 1982 of Enoxy, a joint venture between ENI, the state-owned oil company, and Occidental Petroleum Corp. of the U.S. Enoxy took over much of the plant of the bankrupt SIR and some plant of the state-owned Anic. The new organization also signed a letter of intent with Montedison that would permit it to acquire much of Montedison's primary production capacity.   (DONALD P. BURKE)

ELECTRICAL

Talks in June between Lord Weinstock of Britain's General Electric Co. Ltd. (GEC) and Heinz Duerr of West Germany's AEG-Telefunken raised expectations that the long-anticipated reorganization of the electrical equipment manufacturing sector in the European Economic Community (EEC) would soon begin. The talks began as AEG (150,000 employees and a DM 15 billion turnover in 1981) headed for bankruptcy after years of financial problems.

Reorganization of the AEG group in 1980 had come too late, and Duerr was forced to produce a new plan, Konzept 83, which proposed a carving up of the group into profitable and unprofitable parts. Weinstock was reported to have proposed that GEC take a 40% stake, totaling about DM 300 million, in the profitable part and extend an interest-free loan of DM 450 million.

In July the West German government stepped into the situation with a DM 600 million loan guarantee, and a consortium of 24 German banks agreed to lend DM 200 million to save the group from immediate collapse. While the bankers, who had already provided DM 930 million in 1980, were hesitating over further support, Duerr applied in August for *Vergleich*, a form of partial bankruptcy that would allow 60% of AEG's unsecured debt to be written off. During this period Weinstock withdrew the GEC offer because of determined opposition by the AEG workers to what was said to be a "takeover."

In late August the consortium of German banks grudgingly gave AEG a DM 1.1 billion credit, some bankers openly saying that even more support would be needed in a year or two. A week later the West German government completed the rescue with another DM 1.1 billion, but there was still doubt as to whether this would merely provide a breathing space or enable AEG to survive and prosper. The price of the rescue was the sale or closing of AEG's unprofitable operations. Grundig (West Germany), Electrolux (Sweden), Zanussi (Italy), and United Technologies (U.S.) were buying, or thinking of buying, some of AEG's subsidiaries in that sector. Thus, although there was no dramatic takeover of AEG by GEC, much the same reorganization would occur but possibly at a somewhat slower pace.

Apart from reorganization, the European electrical manufacturing industry was revitalizing itself in other ways. They included buying into new geographic markets, especially in the less developed countries, gaining access to the new advanced technologies through acquisitions, and main-

taining large research and development efforts.

In the U.S., where the electrical equipment manufacturing sector was dominated by only two companies, General Electric Co. (GE) and Westinghouse Electric Corp., future profitability was firmly based on massive in-house research and development. GE said that "a combination of innovation and cost leadership is the essence of the General Electric worldwide thrust," and again, "Among future-oriented expenditures, those for research and development are paramount." In 1981 GE spent about $1.7 billion on research and development (about 50% in-house and the remainder customer-funded). GE's turnover in 1981 was some 9% above that of 1980 at $27,240,000,000, with a similar increase in net earnings to $7,260,000,000 in 1981.

Westinghouse in-house research and development expenditure in 1981 was $230 million and customer-funded, $462 million. Together with government-funded programs, total research and development expenditure was $1.2 billion. Turnover in 1981 was $9,367,500,000 (up 10% over 1980) and net income, $438 million (up 8.7%). Westinghouse also bought into new technology with the $646 million acquisition of Teleprompter, a leader in the fast-growing cable television market.

Probably the best performance during the year was that of Britain's GEC, which announced, for the year ended March 31, 1982, a 23% rise in pre-tax profits on turnover that was up by 20%. Turnover was £4,949 million.

Siemens, the major West German group, saw its profits plunge 20% in 1981 to DM 509.4 million on turnover of DM 34,561,-000,000 (up 8%). However, this trend seemed to have been stemmed with the announcement of DM 464 million profits for the first nine months of 1982.

One of the first moves of the Socialist government in France was to nationalize the largest French electrical manufacturing company, Compagnie Générale d'Électricité. However, the firm continued to enjoy complete autonomy of decision and action.
                                    (T. C. J. COGLE)

FURNITURE

Negative growth characterized the U.S. household furniture industry during 1982. High interest rates that discouraged consumer spending, the lowest level of housing starts in 30 years, and a sizable inventory of unsold homes contributed to the poorest furniture sales since 1975. The National Association of Furniture Manufacturers' "Econometric Forecast" projected that the value of wholesale furniture shipments would recede from a 1981 total of $10,720,000,000 to $9,350,000,000, a drop of 12.8%. Adjusted for inflation, and more accurately reflecting the number of units shipped, the decline for 1982 was estimated at 17.8%. Wood furniture (down 9.5%) fared better than upholstery (down 14.5%), while metal household furniture suffered the most (down 18.1%). Furniture store sales fell from $18,250,000,000 in 1981 to $16,990,000,000. Retail prices for furniture rose less than those of other consumer durable goods.

Business failures at both the manufacturing and retail levels increased dramatically.

Between 1979, when the household furniture industry decline began, and 1982, retail store bankruptcies doubled to an estimated 800. The dollar loss approached $200 million. Furniture factory employment fell by 51,000, from 329,200 workers in April 1979 to 278,200 in April 1982, according to the U.S. Bureau of Labor Statistics. Many furniture plants operated on short time.

U.S. dining room and dinette furniture and wall system manufacturers were especially hard hit by low-priced imports from the Far East and central Europe. Though furniture imports represented only about 4¹/₂% of domestic wholesale volume, they were concentrated in certain low-priced categories. Total imports were estimated by the International Tariff Commission at about $480 million. U.S. furniture exports amounted to an estimated $280 million.

The depressed economy kept design innovation at a low level. Many manufacturers introduced promotional occasional pieces in designs compatible with their most successful sellers. Eighteenth century led traditional styles, and "Country," a casual mixture of many design influences, continued to be strong. Early American strengthened its position as the most stable style in the marketplace. Lacquer, one of the oldest furniture-finishing processes, gained popularity as a result of new technology that made it possible to fashion furniture in an assortment of multicoloured finishes. Oak remained the most popular furniture wood. The style leader in upholstered fabrics continued to be velvet.

The flotation sleep industry continued its amazing growth. The Waterbed Manufacturers Association reported 25% growth for 1981, with industry volume at $1.9 billion and 1982 sales increasing to $2.2 billion. Another fast-rising segment was unfinished furniture. The almost entirely separate office furniture industry enjoyed relative prosperity, with growth in 1982 projected at 7% for a total volume of $4.3 billion.　　　(ROBERT A. SEELMAN)

FURS

Sales of furs at retail were largely flat in 1982, reflecting ailing economies throughout most of the world. The inflation rate subsided in many of the developed countries, but unemployment increased and consumer spending generally turned conservative. Bolstered by the residual financial strength of middle- and higher-income customers, U.S. furriers fared relatively better than their retail colleagues in most other countries. At year's end it appeared that U.S. retail sales would equal or surpass the 1981 total of $1,030,000,000. Even fur consumers were more price-conscious, however. More of them bypassed conventional retailers and went directly to wholesale suppliers. From the consumer's standpoint, this reflected a lack of selection in the stores—a result of high interest rates that caused retailers to defer purchases. At the same time, manufacturers, in need of cash flow, increasingly opened their showrooms to the retail trade.

The important European markets—principally West Germany and Italy—which normally are major consumers of North American furs, were adversely affected by the strong dollar in relation to their own currencies. In addition, heavy carry-overs of inventories and relatively high interest rates curbed buying by many European operators. Retail sales were about even with 1981, which was down from the previous year. The booming Japanese market apparently slowed a bit, reflecting a hesitation in that nation's economy and the approximately 20% decline in the value of the yen against the dollar.

Fur skin production was generally up in 1982, in both the ranched and wild sectors. The worldwide mink crop was estimated at about 24 million pelts, slightly above the previous year. Blue fox and fitch production also rose a bit, but karakul continued to decline, a direct result of consumer apathy. Ideal weather conditions contributed to generally good wild fur crops in North America.

The U.S. Congress approved in 1982 a three-year continuation of the 1973 Endangered Species Act with some revisions, which contained many provisions backed by the fur industry. One of them vacated an earlier ban on exports of bobcats.

　　　(SANDY PARKER)

GEMSTONES

Decline in all commercial activity was reflected in the gemstone industry during 1982. Although prices of almost all but the finest rubies and emeralds fell, diamond was probably the worst sufferer. Diamond investment companies largely held their own, but the newly emerging coloured stone investment firms had to move toward the establishment of "normal" trading channels or diversify into training gemmologists.

The new and extensive emerald deposits of Zambia produced fine stones, some in large sizes. Plausible fakes also emanated from Zambia and could be expected from other countries. In the case of Zambia it was the rough material that was being simulated, largely by green glass ground to the hexagonal shape characteristic of emerald crystals. Following the example of Burma and Sri Lanka, Pakistan had established a State Gem Corporation to channel goods from mine to buyer, but it had not yet become operational. East Africa continued to supply garnets of interesting colour and some fine green tourmaline. Tanzanite supplies were sporadic, and ruby from Kenya appeared to have vanished from the market.

There was no outstanding change in the amount or quality of stones offered by the Sri Lanka Gem Corporation, but there was a slight improvement in the sale position with respect to Burma. Some fine rubies and red spinels reached the market, and while the source might not be official, this seemed to indicate a burst of mining activity. The discovery of extensive diamond deposits in Australia would pose both technical and distribution problems when mining began in earnest in a year or so.

There was still some difficulty in the identification of diamonds that had been treated in atomic piles to alter or enhance colour. It seemed that in some cases diagnosis of yellow diamond could be difficult. It was now the practice for important stones to be certified by an independent gem testing laboratory, and some of the firms that had been established to market stones for investment turned part of their attention to certification.

The salerooms were not too badly affected by recession. While jewelry departments did considerable business, the falloff in other areas meant that firms as a whole showed a downturn in profits. At retail, there was still strong demand for the finest jewelry, but cheap lines were hard hit.

　　　(MICHAEL O'DONOGHUE)

GLASS

The glass industry continued to suffer from recession during 1982. There were several closings in the U.K. container industry, in-

A method for branding diamonds was developed by scientists at General Electric. The distinguishing mark is invisible (left) in normal light but becomes visible when given an electrostatic charge and dusted with a special powder (right).

GENERAL ELECTRIC RESEARCH & DEVELOPMENT CENTER

cluding the New Cross and Kinghorn factories of United Glass Containers and the St. Helens plant of Rockware Group Ltd. Also in St. Helens, Pilkington Brothers Ltd. shut one of its fibreglass plants. In West Germany Gerresheimer Glas announced its intention to shut its Minden works, and Nippon Glass of Japan filed for rehabilitation under the country's bankruptcy procedures.

In the face of competition from other forms of packaging, efforts were made to maintain glass container sales through computer-aided design, milk bottle advertising, and emphasis on lighter weight. The Glass Packaging Institute in the U.S. launched an advertising campaign with the theme that "products taste great in glass." In the U.K., 1982 was designated Glass Recycling Year by the Glass Manufacturers' Federation.

There was a struggle for market share in the flat-glass industry in Europe. The start of manufacture in Luxembourg by Luxguard, a subsidiary of Guardian Industries of the U.S., added another 3% to European capacity—a large amount, considering that most other flat-glass producing plants were running at less than 80% of capacity. Guardian Industries withdrew from an agreement made in 1981 with the Spanish firm Vidrierase de Llodio whereby Guardian was to have financed an $88 million float-glass plant at the Spanish firm's factory in return for a controlling share in the company. Pilkington Brothers entered the U.S. flat-glass market by agreeing to buy a 30% stake in Libbey-Owens-Ford, subject to review under U.S. antitrust laws. A technological achievement in the flat-glass industry was the development of Kappafloat by Pilkington Brothers; this had a coating on one surface that prevented heat from escaping and yet allowed the sun's warmth to penetrate the glass.

In the domestic glassware industry, Galway Crystal of Ireland, previously part of Josiah Wedgwood & Sons Ltd., was sold to a group of Irish investors and Towle Mfg. Co. Corning Glass Works of the U.S. launched Vision, a new line of transparent glass cookware, in the U.K.; made from an amber-coloured glass called Calexium, it could withstand very high direct heat and extreme thermal shocks. In the field of laboratory glassware, J. Bibby and Sons Ltd., a Liverpool-based industrial and agricultural group, announced an agreement to buy Corning's European laboratory glassware business.

Philip's, the Dutch electrical group, announced plans that would make it one of the first companies to undertake large-scale production of optical fibres. The company's new $7.5 million factory at Eindhoven, Neth., would initially produce 300,000 km (186,000 mi) of optical fibre cable annually. British Telecom (BT), the state-owned telecommunications corporation, set a world record when it achieved the transmission of light pulses along 100 km (62 mi) of optical glass fibre without intermediate amplification. BT also inaugurated a 204-km (127-mi) optical fibre link between London and Birmingham which it claimed was the longest

of its kind in the world. Schott Kem Ltd. and the civil engineering firm Sir Robert McAlpine and Sons developed a joint system for conveying potentially active substances in nuclear power stations which utilized Schott's borosilicate glass pipeline for the primary containment. TSL Thermal Syndicate of the U.K. won a Queen's Award for Technological Achievement for an innovation in the manufacture of infrared radiant heaters. (JOANNA TUDOR)

INSURANCE

Sales volume of private insurance worldwide rose above the $500 billion mark for the first time in 1982. About 45% of the premiums were written by the U.S. and 35% by the next four leading markets combined: Japan, West Germany, the U.K., and France. Premiums averaged 7% of GNP in North America, about 4–6% in Europe, and less than 2% in the rest of the world. The world insurance supply was provided by approximately 2,700 life, 6,800 nonlife, and 900 mixed companies.

In the U.K. the Insurance Companies Act came into force in 1982, adding consumer protection to comply with EEC standards. Progress toward an EEC insurance common market made little progress, however. Insurers could establish branches in other member countries, but negotiations were deadlocked on "freedom of services" to transact insurance across frontiers. Premium income of U.K. insurers grew about 20% to £9,600 million in general insurance, with profits dependent on investment income counterbalancing losses on underwriting. Adverse weather in the U.K. early in 1982 cost the companies £250 million. Life insurance sales increased to £8,330 million. Some British companies joined together in appointing an ombudsman bureau to adjudicate policyholder complaints.

Parliament passed Lloyd's Act 1982, which created a new governing body, the Council of Lloyd's, with 8 elected representatives of the 20,000 underwriting members who provide capital, 16 active members, and 3 nonmembers. The council had disciplinary powers that formerly rested with all the members. Insurance brokers would be required to divest themselves of controls over underwriting syndicates within the next five years. Investigations of malpractice by underwriters were in progress, and several suspensions were made. Contrary to expectations, the latest Lloyd's accounts (which under a three-year rule were for 1979) showed satisfactory profits of £173 million on a premium volume of £2,860 million.

As reported by the Institute of Life Insurance in 1982, U.S. life insurers reached an all-time high of $4 trillion of life insurance in force, with an average $53,000 of protection for each insured family. Premium receipts were about $120 billion (44% life, 31% health, and 25% annuities), and benefit payments were nearly $50 billion. Assets exceeded $575 billion, and policy reserves were $475 billion. About one-third of the purchased policies insured women, up from one-fourth ten years earlier. The shift to term insurance continued; approximately 60% of the total amounts bought were for temporary protection, although permanent (cash-value) insurance was included in

three-fourths of the policies. Group life insurance purchases expanded by about 20%.

The Tax Equity and Fiscal Responsibility Act of 1982 brought some major changes to life insurance and pensions, effective in 1983. Federal taxation of life insurers was overhauled for the first time in 20 years. For individuals, medical expenses and health insurance premiums were deductible only when they exceeded 5% of adjusted gross income. The market for "universal life" insurance contracts could expand rapidly, since their taxation was clarified if they were substantially comparable to traditional whole life insurance. The maximum annual limit for payments was lowered from defined-benefit pension plans, to $90,000 at age 62 and to lesser amounts for earlier retirements. Income taxes would be withheld on pension and annuity payments unless the recipient elected not to have withholding apply.

Broader financial services were being provided by more large insurance groups that owned stock brokerage firms, mutual or money market funds, and other investment affiliates. The first major federal legislation prohibiting bank holding companies from insurance activities, with some exceptions, was passed in 1982. Insurers, however, faced increased competition from other businesses expanding to become "financial supermarkets," such as American Express, Transamerica, and Sears.

Property and liability insurance in the U.S. during the first half of 1982 rose to $50 billion in premiums, with underwriting losses of $5.5 billion—only $500 million less than for all of the previous year. Operating earnings, including investment income, were down in the same period by more than $1 billion, and catastrophic losses topped $1.5 billion, the highest ever recorded. Four storms caused insured property losses of more than $100 million each, and one airliner crash near New Orleans, La., killed 153 persons. Product liability claims continued to mount; asbestos-related claims caused the Manville Corp. to file for reorganization under the bankruptcy laws. Increasing workers' compensation costs caused four more states to enact open competition rating laws.

(DAVID L. BICKELHAUPT)

IRON AND STEEL

The long steel recession continued and worsened. World production in 1981 fell by 10 million metric tons from the 1980 level to 707 million metric tons. This was close to the production level in 1974, the last precrisis year, and so represented seven years of stagnation. Production in 1982 was likely to be appreciably lower. The most dramatic change occurred in the U.S. The industry was working at a high rate of capacity in early 1981 but encountered a severe decline in demand around midyear and remained depressed throughout 1982. Production during the first nine months of the year was 38% below the corresponding period of 1981.

Most of the traditional producers were working at even lower levels in 1982 than in 1981. These included several Eastern European countries, most notably Poland, which continued to experience unrest and disruption of output. Some of the smaller producers whose markets had previously

What to do with worn-out blast furnaces? U.S. Steel solved the problem by setting demolition charges to outmoded blast furnaces at its Youngstown, Ohio, plant.

wide range of steel products from several countries, including those of the EC.

The legal and administrative procedures relative to these cases progressed through their appointed course during the year against a background of discussions between the U.S. administration and the European Commission, acting on behalf of EC member governments, with the objective of achieving a negotiated settlement of the steel trade problem. An agreement was signed on October 21, the last practical date before the duties leviable under the countervailing cases would have become definitive. The arrangement provided essentially for restraint of EC exports to the U.S. on the basis of export licensing, to be operated by EC member states, such that imports into the U.S. would not exceed defined percentages of U.S. consumption, as estimated quarterly by independent forecasters. The arrangement was in terms of ten product categories covering most of the steel industry (but not stainless, on which agreement had so far proved impossible).

The condition of acceptance of this restraint by the EC was that the current cases against the products covered by the arrangement would be withdrawn, and that no new cases would be brought by the petitioning companies under any of the enumerated clauses of the U.S. trade legislation for the duration of the agreement: Nov. 1, 1982, to Dec. 31, 1985. If cases were to be brought by new petitioners, the EC would be entitled to terminate the arrangement if a defined consultation process produced no solution.

held up quite well also felt the full weight of the recession in 1982, including South Africa and, to a high degree, Australia. On the other hand, several of the newer producers continued to advance, some spectacularly, such as North Korea, Taiwan, Venezuela, Argentina, and Turkey.

The continuation and deepening of the steel recession predictably evoked an increase in intervention by the public authorities. In the U.S. the severe decline in demand in mid-1981 coincided with an increase in imports, especially from the EC countries. This created pressures that the trigger price system, which had been reconstituted in the fall of 1980, proved unable to contain. In early 1982 the trigger price system was suspended, and major U.S. producers brought antidumping and countervailing (subsidy) cases against a

Table IX. World Production of Crude Steel
In 000 metric tons

Country	1977	1978	1979	1980	1981*	1982 Year to date	No. of months	Percent change 1982/81
World	675,430	717,230	747,520	717,380	707,600			
U.S.S.R.*	146,660	151,440	149,000	147,930	149,000	62,200	5	−2.4
U.S.	113,700	124,310	123,280	101,700	108,790	53,400	9	−38.3
Japan	102,410	102,110	*111,750	111,400	101,680	75,800	9	+0.4
West Germany	38,980	41,250	40,040	43,840	41,610	28,740	9	−8.1
China*	23,700	31,780	34,436	37,040	35,600	†	9	
Italy	23,340	24,280	24,250	26,520	24,780	18,530	9	+1.3
France	22,090	22,840	23,360	23,180	21,260	14,310	9	−11.0
United Kingdom	20,470	20,370	21,550	11,340	15,570	10,970	9	−2.5
Poland‡	17,840	19,250	19,200	19,490	15,600	4,400	4	−25.8
Czechoslovakia‡	15,050	15,290	14,800	14,930	15,200	5,010	4	−3.2
Canada	13,630	14,900	16,080	15,900	14,810	9,680	9	−17.7
Romania‡	11,460	11,780	12,910	13,180	13,500	†		
Belgium	11,260	12,600	13,440	12,320	12,280	7,770	9	−14.0
Brazil	11,250	12,210	13,890	15,310	13,210	9,810	9	−3.4
Spain	11,170	11,340	12,250	12,670	12,920	9,640	8	+0.4
India	10,010	10,100	10,130	9,510	10,780	7,800	9	−1.7
Australia	7,340	7,600	8,120	7,590	7,640	5,170	9	−13.7
South Africa	7,300	7,900	8,880	9,070	8,940	6,550	9	−3.8
East Germany‡	6,850	6,980	6,950	7,310	7,500	2,940	5	−5.4
Mexico	5,600	6,710	7,010	7,100	7,610	5,440	9	−4.8
Netherlands, The	4,920	5,560	5,810	5,260	5,460	3,420	9	−20.3
South Korea	4,350	4,970	7,610	8,560	10,750	8,700	9	+9.5
Luxembourg	4,330	4,730	4,950	4,620	3,790	2,510	9	−0.8
North Korea*	4,000	5,080	5,400	5,600	5,500	†		
Austria	4,090	4,540	4,920	4,620	4,660	3,340	9	−3.4
Sweden	3,970	4,330	4,730	4,240	3,770	2,920	9	+8.6
Hungary‡	3,720	3,380	3,900	3,770	3,600	1,250	4	−0.6
Yugoslavia	3,180	3,460	3,540	3,630	3,980	2,870	9	−2.3
Argentina	2,680	2,780	3,200	2,680	2,540	2,150	9	+14.7
Bulgaria‡	2,590	2,470	2,390	2,570	2,600	1,110	5	−3.1
Finland	2,200	2,330	2,460	2,510	2,410	1,800	9	+2.2
Turkey	1,900	2,170	2,340	2,540	2,430	2,050	8	+14.3
Iran‡	1,830	1,300	1,430	1,200	1,200	†		
Taiwan	1,770	3,430	4,250	4,230	3,140	3,000	9	+27.5
Venezuela	800	860	1,510	1,820	2,030	1,730	9	+15.7
Greece‡	760	940	1,000	1,200	910	†		

* Estimated series.   †1982 figures not yet available.   ‡1980 and 1981 figures estimated.
Sources: International Iron and Steel Institute; British Steel Corporation.

Table X. World Production of Pig Iron and Blast Furnace Ferroalloys
In 000 metric tons

Country	1977	1978	1979	1980	1981*
World	480,760	498,150	519,770	498,940	492,520
U.S.S.R.	107,370	110,700	109,000	108,000	109,000
Japan	85,890	78,590	83,830	87,040	80,050
U.S†	73,780	79,540	78,900	62,350	66,560
West Germany††	28,980	30,160	35,180	33,670	31,660
China‡	20,000	26,000	28,000	30,000	30,000
France†	18,260	18,500	19,410	18,690	16,960
United Kingdom	12,270	11,470	12,930	6,280	9,340
Italy	11,410	11,340	11,330	12,150	12,260
India	9,800	9,270	8,770	8,510	9,470
Czechoslovakia	9,720	9,940	9,530	9,530	10,000
Canada	9,660	10,340	11,080	10,890	9,710
Poland†	9,650	11,240	11,100	11,600	9,200
Brazil	9,380	10,040	11,590	12,680	10,310
Belgium	8,910	10,130	10,780	9,850	9,770
Romania	7,780	8,160	8,880	8,900	9,300
Australia	6,730	7,280	7,760	6,960	6,830
Spain	6,640	6,250	6,510	6,380	6,560
South Africa	5,810	5,900	7,020	7,200	7,130
North Korea†	4,000	5,000	5,000	5,400	5,000
Netherlands, The	3,920	4,610	4,810	4,330	4,600
Luxembourg	3,570	3,720	3,800	3,570	2,890
Mexico	3,000	3,510	3,490	3,630	3,770
Austria	2,970	3,080	3,700	3,490	3,480
Germany, East	2,630	2,560	2,390	2,400	2,500
South Korea	2,430	2,740	5,050	5,580	7,930
Sweden	2,330	2,360	2,910	2,440	1,780
Hungary	2,320	2,330	2,370	2,370	2,200
Yugoslavia	1,930	2,080	2,370	2,440	2,770
Finland	1,760	1,860	2,040	2,050	1,980
Turkey	1,620	1,710	2,300	2,230	2,000
Bulgaria	1,610	1,490	1,450	1,600	1,500
Argentina	1,100	1,440	1,110	1,040	920
Norway	500	550	650	600	570

*Provisional.
†Including ferroalloys.
‡Estimated.
Source: International Iron and Steel Institute.

In the EC the system of compulsory production quotas under the "manifest crisis" provision of the European Coal and Steel Community (ECSC) treaty had been renewed for a year in mid-1981 in regard to a range of major steel products. Comparable voluntary producer commitments to the European Commission were operating for most other steel products. In mid-1982 these arrangements were extended for a further year; compulsory quotas were reintroduced for wire rod.

Late in 1981 and during the early part of 1982 it appeared that these crisis market support measures were permitting attainment of more remunerative price levels in the ECSC, in accordance with the European Commission's objective. However, destocking and a sharp decline in demand, together with an appreciable rise in imports, progressively undermined the market. Consequently, for the October–December quarter the Commission judged it necessary, with the support of the steel industry, to issue a yet more restrictive quota program. Meanwhile, the Commission and member governments were considering the framework for import restraint in 1983 to be negotiated with the principal supplying countries. The Council of Ministers had authorized a measure of relaxation in 1982 compared with 1981. For 1983 some tightening appeared likely, though by no means as great as desired by the ECSC steel producers.

In the longer-term perspective, member governments and the Commission continued to examine steel companies' restructuring plans within the framework of the ECSC Decision on State Aids to the Steel Industry, promulgated in August 1981. The objectives of the plans were the phasing out of public subsidies by the end of 1985 and the achievement of a slimmer and more competitive industrial structure.

(TREVOR J. MACDONALD)

MACHINERY AND MACHINE TOOLS

In 1981 the United States was the largest producer of machine tools. Total production was $5.1 billion, with roughly $4.1 billion accounted for by metal-cutting machine tools and $1 billion by metal-forming machine tools. About 86% of total U.S. machine-tool production went to domestic customers, while 14% was sold to customers in other countries.

Japan, with total production of $4.8 billion, was the second largest manufacturer of machine tools in 1981. West Germany, which had been in second place in 1980, was third with production equal to $4 billion. The Soviet Union was again the fourth largest producer with production estimated at $3.2 billion, and Italy was again the fifth largest at $1.5 billion. Total worldwide production of machine tools in 1981 was estimated at $26.4 billion.

For the U.S. both exports and imports of machine tools grew at faster rates than did domestic shipments. During the ten years since 1971 exports had increased about 300% and by 1981 exceeded $1 billion. On the other hand, imports also rose and in

1981 totaled nearly $1.5 billion. The year 1981 was the fourth in a row during which imports of machine tools to the U.S. exceeded exports. In 1981 imports accounted for one out of every four machine tools installed in the U.S., including 55% of the lathes and 31% of the boring machines. The largest supplier of machine tools to the U.S. was Japan, which in 1981 shipped tools worth $690 million. The second major supplier was West Germany with shipments worth $190 million. Taiwan continued its steady increase in shipments to the U.S., from an insignificant amount in the early 1970s to more than $100 million in 1981.

Export markets for U.S.-built machine tools most notably included Mexico and Canada. In 1981 each of these countries received shipments valued at just under $260 million. Other principal markets included the United Kingdom, West Germany, France, and Brazil.

The U.S. was the leading consumer of machine tools and in 1981 installed equipment worth $5.6 billion. The Soviet Union was the second leading consumer with machine tools worth an estimated $3.9 billion having been installed. Japan placed third with a total of $3.3 billion, and West Germany and Italy followed with $2.1 billion and $1 billion, respectively.

In September 1982, as is the case in the fall of each even-numbered year, the International Machine Tool Show was held in Chicago. More than 96,000 people attended this exposition, which included over 1,200 exhibitors from all parts of the globe. It was estimated that machine tools and related equipment worth more than $250 million were on display during the nine-day show. A similar major machine tool exhibition is held in Europe during odd-numbered years.

(JOHN B. DEAM)

MICROELECTRONICS

Progress in microelectronics continued at a fast pace in 1982. Microprocessors were becoming highly visible because of their effect on the home. They had been used during the past few years in automobiles for fuel and emission control, but they were now also being incorporated into video games. By the end of 1982 approximately four million homes in the U.S. had video games, with an average of eight cartridges per game. Most of the games used an eight-bit microprocessor and 32 kb of ROM (read-only memory) in the cartridge. (1 kb, or kilobit, = 1,024 bits.) The next-generation games would continue to use the eight-bit microprocessor but would employ 64 kb and 128 kb ROM's for improved graphic capability and for more complex games. These home games, along with similar games in arcades, were exposing many young people to computer technology.

In addition to the video games, microprocessors were being increasingly used in the home in personal computers. As of 1982 fewer than one million homes in the U.S. had personal computers, but the number was growing at 50% per year. With the lowering of the prices of the Intel 8086/8088 and Motorola 68000 microprocessors, home computers with performance equivalent to that of minicomputers would be available with base prices of less than $2,000. Though high-quality printers, large-capacity disk drive memories, and software packages could increase this cost substantially, microelectronics was well on the way to making the computer a household staple.

The performance of microelectronic products would continue to improve with reduced lithography. The speed of logic gates would more than double with a decrease in line width from three micrometres to two micrometres. (One micrometre equals one-millionth of a metre.) There would be another doubling in speed with a reduction to 1½ microns. Products with 1½-micron gates were expected to be in production by 1985. This increase in speed would be accompanied by a decrease in the sizes of the microelectronic chips with a consequent reduction in cost per function.

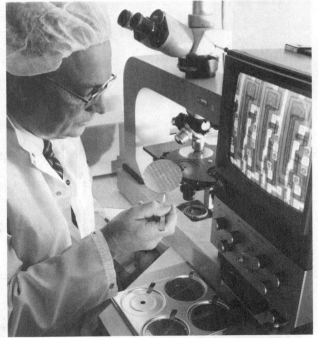

Scientists at General Electric developed a wafer containing nearly 200 tiny circuits to improve radio communication under conditions hampered by extreme electromagnetic interference. The device was developed to produce jam-resistant radio communications systems for military use.

This would continue the reduction in memory costs.

The cost of 64,000 bits of dynamic memory was $5 in 1982, giving a price per bit of 7.8 millicents. It was projected that by 1985 this would be reduced to 2 to 3 millicents per bit and by 1990 to about 1 millicent. Even though inflation had increased the costs of microelectronics production, technological progress was continuing to dramatically reduce the cost per function.

For very-high-speed uses, as in very fast computers and in signal processing, gallium arsenide products were expected to replace silicon. Gallium arsenide was potentially a hundred times faster than silicon with comparable design rules. It was not expected to be used extensively in the home in the near future, but its performance capabilities would be required for the direct broadcasting satellite system that was soon to be inaugurated.   (HANDEL H. JONES)

NUCLEAR INDUSTRY

Prospects remained poor for the nuclear power industry in 1982 as far as new orders for plants were concerned. The most important new project, the 2,000-MW plant for Laguna Verde in Mexico, was suspended due to the Mexican economic crisis.

Statistics released for 1981 and published in 1982 for nuclear reactors of over 150 MW (excluding Soviet-bloc countries) showed that 17 new reactors were commissioned in 1981. The total number of units in service as of Jan. 1, 1982, was 207, with a total generating capacity of 145,408 MW. They included 102 pressurized water reactors (PWR's), 57 boiling water reactors (BWR's), 13 pressurized heavy-water reactors (PHWR's), and 26 Magnox. Analysis of 1981 reactor performance placed two Canadian PHWR's (Candu) in the top two places, followed by a PWR and a BWR, both in Switzerland.

The nuclear power industry in the United States, suffering still from the effects of the regulatory problems that had arisen since the accident at the Three Mile Island nuclear plant in Pennsylvania in 1979 and also from the continuing recession, experienced further cuts by a number of utilities. Of the 13 projects canceled, several were well into the construction phase. Utilities in the U.S. were forced to reappraise the economic advantages of nuclear-generated electricity, advantages that had been eroded by regulatory problems leading to construction delays and, the industry claimed, by the overengineering of nuclear plants. As part of the U.S. government's effort to overcome these problems, the Nuclear Regulatory Commission drew up proposals for new licensing procedures for submission to Congress.

A "quick look" inside the damaged Three Mile Island reactor with a television camera showed that the top portion of the core had collapsed into a bed of rubble and had not fused together. The main area above the core appeared substantially undamaged.

In other countries the costs of nuclear power remained competitive with the main alternative, coal-fired power generation. A European study indicated that, on average, coal-generated electricity cost about 60% more than nuclear power. In 1981 the average cost of nuclear power in France was 14.84 cents per kilowatt-hour, while that of coal was 28.23 cents per kilowatt-hour.

Eight nuclear units began producing power in France in 1982, and although the new Socialist government was expected to cut the program drastically, six new projects were started. By the end of 1981 nuclear power represented 11.8% of France's primary energy consumption.

Four Candu PHWR reactors went into operation: three in Canada, at Point Lepreau (630 MW), Gentilly (600 MW), and Pickering B (515 MW); and one at Wolsung in South Korea (600 MW). A fourth unit of the 600-MW series was scheduled to start up soon in Argentina. Despite the consistently top-rated performance of the Candu type of reactor, the nuclear industry in Canada faced cutbacks due to the lack of new orders. Canadian utilities were active during the year negotiating possible sales of electricity to the northeastern United States.

In Britain test drilling in various hard rock formations, part of the nuclear waste disposal research and development program, was halted by the government. It was generally believed that this was due to the political unpopularity of the program. The electricity-producing and nuclear industries completed preparations for the public inquiry, to be held in January 1983, into the proposed Sizewell-B power station, the first British PWR project.

In West Germany the government under Chancellor Helmut Schmidt affirmed plans to speed up the licensing process for the end of the fuel cycle (waste treatment, etc.). Increasing concern had been expressed over the rate at which the French program was overtaking the West German one. The opposition to the controversial Brokdorf plant (1,300 MW) was dropped by the city of Hamburg, and in the fall the Parliamentary Commission of Inquiry into Future Energy Policy recommended that the government withdraw its veto on the commissioning of the Kalkar SNR-300 fast breeder reactor. A risk assessment study of the design concluded that it would be as safe or even safer than a PWR.

The Japanese government also approved the construction of a prototype fast breeder reactor, Monju, a project that had been facing economic problems. The heavy water Advanced Thermal Reactor was also given the green light during the year. A joint study announced between the U.S. PWR vendor, Westinghouse Electric Corp., its Japanese licensee, Mitsubishi Heavy Industries, and five Japanese utilities sought to improve the performance of the PWR. This five-year project would cost $150 million.

Progress in the Soviet Union also suffered from delays on a number of projects. These included the first of the four 1,000-MW PWR reactors for the combined hydroelectric and nuclear plant on the Bug River in the southern Ukraine. The State Planning Committee warned about the escalating costs occasioned by these delays. Romania and Cuba both announced new agreements with the Soviet Union for the purchase of PWR's.

The new director general of the International Atomic Energy Agency, Hans Blix, found his agency facing one of the most important crises of its recent history. The U.S. delegation walked out of the annual general meeting and was followed by other Western countries in protest against the conference decision to reject the credentials of the Israeli delegation. The U.S., which had hinted at withdrawal from the IAEA, said that the agency had become too "politicized." The expulsion of Israel was proposed in retaliation for the 1981 Israeli raid on the Osirak reactor in Iraq.

(RICHARD A. KNOX)

PAINTS AND VARNISHES

Paint manufacturers in most countries had to work hard in 1982 merely to stand still. Few countries achieved substantial gains in volume over the depressed levels of 1981, and some, such as France, suffered further contraction. In the U.K. sales by volume ran some 3% ahead of the previous year—with sterling value about 6% ahead—thanks mainly to a strong performance by the do-it-yourself sector. In West Germany the economic slowdown was reflected in a 2.7% drop in paint volume, although value rose by 8.7%. The U.S. paint industry estimated a volume gain of approximately 2%, with dollar income about 9% ahead of the previous year.

A digest of results for the period 1971–81, compiled by the European paint makers' federation, placed Italy on top with a 62% gain in output. Finland, with 57%, ran a close second, reflecting large sales to Eastern Europe. U.K. sales fell by 23% and that of Sweden by 12%. For Europe as a whole, total production varied by only a narrow margin over the decade. Looking ahead, a study of the U.S. industry predicted negligible growth before 1986, with volume stagnant at 3,955,315,000 l (1,045,000,000 gal).

The European paint industry continued to be plagued by differing regulations in the various countries. Despite efforts at harmonization by the EEC, adoption of the appropriate labeling directives into national legislation proceeded fitfully. Some major British companies lost patience with the U.K. authorities and adopted their own interpretations of the EEC rules.

The antilead lobby gained ground in some countries. Although not widely used since World War II for pigmentation, lead compounds continued in use as efficient driers in gloss paints. Research into this and other possible health hazards was slowed by the economic climate. The Paint Research Institute in the U.S. came under scrutiny and was reorganized. The U.K. Paint Research Association came near to closing and had to lay off a substantial number of employees.

The most interesting merger of the year was that in the U.K. between the giant Imperial Chemical Industries Ltd. (ICI) and the far smaller Holden Surface Coatings Ltd. It was the subject of a six-month investigation by the official Monopolies Commission but was eventually allowed to proceed.   (LIONEL BILEFIELD)

PHARMACEUTICALS

Two disasters struck the pharmaceutical industry in 1982. The first involved Eli Lilly & Co., which had to withdraw the promising new arthritis drug Oraflex from the market. The second stemmed from the deaths of seven persons in the Chicago area after taking capsules of Extra-Strength Tylenol, a popular over-the-counter (OTC) analgesic, that had been laced with cyanide. (*See* CRIME AND LAW ENFORCEMENT.)

The Oraflex incident, which peaked in August after more than 60 older patients in Britain died as a result of taking the drug, involved a seemingly well-researched drug that had cost the company some $70 million to develop, promote, and manufacture. Besides losing a potential market of possibly $120 million a year, Lilly underwent temporary buffeting in the stock market, faced strong criticism from the Food and Drug Administration (FDA) for mishandling the reports on fatal reactions in Britain, and witnessed a surge in sales of arthritis drugs marketed by its competitors.

The Tylenol poisonings were followed by less serious incidents of tampering with OTC drugs elsewhere in the country, regarded by law officials as the products of a "copycat" mentality. Working through a joint task force with the FDA, the Proprietary Association, the trade association of the OTC drug industry, recommended that the FDA issue a new closure regulation requiring antitampering devices or seals for ingestible drugs, and the FDA did so early in November. The industry hoped to forestall the adoption of different closure regulations in different jurisdictions. By mid-October OTC drug marketers were rushing to install machinery and devices to tamper-proof most of their products.

Standing to lose the most was Johnson & Johnson Inc., whose McNeil Consumer Products Co. division marketed Tylenol. The company had to mobilize its entire sales force to aid in the quick recall of Extra-Strength Tylenol capsules and to handle panic calls from consumers and the press, while some of its competitors took up the slack in sales with their own products. Tylenol had been the unquestioned leader in the analgesics market and contributed almost $500 million in annual sales to the company. In November the firm began an extensive advertising campaign to reintroduce the product, but its future remained in doubt.

The pharmaceutical industry suffered other setbacks during the year. Tax reform legislation sharply reduced the special tax benefits accorded to pharmaceutical manufacturers with plants in Puerto Rico. Although the final version of the bill came short of what was threatened in the initial proposal, some observers suggested that the cost to the industry might be more than $300 million in 1982 and twice that in 1983. A second legislative defeat was the failure of the House of Representatives to pass the so-called Patent Extension Bill, which would have added to the life of patents to make up for the delays sustained in meeting the requirements of regulatory agencies. (DONALD A. DAVIS)

PLASTICS

In the three major manufacturing areas of the world, total production of the five major commodity thermoplastics fell by just over 2%, from 29 million metric tons in 1980 to 28 million tons in 1981. (*See* TABLE

Table XI. Production of Commodity Thermoplastics Materials in the U.S., Western Europe, and Japan
In 000 metric tons

	1980	1981	Percent change
U.S.			
Low density polyethylene	3,307	3,490	+5.5
High-density polyethylene	1,998	2,129	+6.6
Polypropylene	1,655	1,794	+8.4
Polyvinyl chloride	2,481	2,586	+4.2
Polystyrene	1,597	1,643	+2.9
Total	11,038	11,642	+5.5
Western Europe			
Low-density polyethylene	4,231	3,764	−11.0
High-density polyethylene	1,699	1,557	−8.4
Polypropylene	1,421	1,655	+16.5
Polyvinyl chloride	3,619	3,215	−11.2
Polystyrene	1,292	1,220	−5.6
Total	12,262	11,411	−6.9
Japan			
Low-density polyethylene	1,179	1,033	−12.4
High-density polyethylene	680	637	−6.3
Polypropylene	927	959	+3.5
Polyvinyl chloride	1,429	1,129	−21.0
Polystyrene	1,129	1,183	+4.8
Total	5,344	4,941	−7.5
Total	28,644	27,994	−2.3

Source: Association of Plastics Manufacturers in Europe.

XI.) The 5.5% growth in the U.S. from 1980 to 1981 was more than offset by a 7% decline in both Western Europe and Japan. This uneven pattern was likely to be repeated in 1982. The primary reason was not that the recession was any less sharp in the U.S. but that its plastics industry was more disciplined. Western Europe in particular continued to be plagued by massive overcapacity for commodity plastics manufacture, leading to reckless competition and an increasing number of shut-down plants. The major European petrochemical groups all reported serious reductions in profitability during 1982—and laid the main blame for these reductions on their commodity plastics operations.

Adding to this troubled scene was the realization that the overcapacity situation would, at best, take at least the rest of the decade to correct and that the advantage for economical production of ethylene, the basic feedstock for plastics production, was rapidly swinging toward areas with abundant supplies of natural gas such as Canada and the Middle East. In plastics terms the implications were that in the future European (and Japanese) material suppliers must concentrate on products with a high amount of added value and also on the supply of know-how to less developed nations.

In this light it was not surprising that there was a beginning—in 1982—of more than cosmetic action to streamline the industry. Most spectacular was the decision of Imperial Chemical Industries (ICI) to abandon (in the U.K.) the manufacture and sale of low-density polyethylene (LDPE)—the material discovered in its own laboratories in 1933. In an exchange deal with ICI, BP Chemicals at the same time agreed to move out of the field of polyvinyl chloride (PVC). Among the largest West German manufacturers, who in 1982 fared no better than others in Europe, Badische Anilin und Soda Fabrik was a notable leader in its promptness in closing plants operating at losses. In The Netherlands Shell Chemicals and Akzo Chemie agreed to pool their resources in the production of vinyl chloride monomer,

A sterile filter (shown highly magnified), designed to trap bacteria that could find their way into hospital drug solutions, was developed by a Chicago-based company. The plastic membrane can trap up to 10,000,000,000 microorganisms in an area less than a half-inch square.

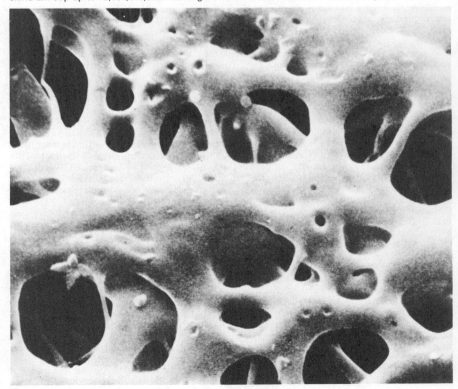

UPI

while in France it was the government that imposed efficiency measures on its plastics materials manufacturers.

The situation continued to be further complicated insofar as LDPE was concerned by the continuing penetration of the market, especially that for packaging film, by the new linear variant (LLDPE), which was stronger than LDPE and thus allowed material of thinner gauge to be used for a given application. LLDPE was reported to have accounted for 15% of the U.S. LDPE market in 1981 (over 500,000 metric tons), and this proportion was expected to grow rapidly over the next few years, possibly to as high as 85%. The same story was being repeated in Europe. The implications for the established manufacturers of traditional LDPE were serious and were receiving the deepest attention.

Apart from gains by those suppliers able to offer LLDPE without harm to their existing business, another success story in the packaging field continued to be registered by polyethylene terephthalate (PET) in its rapidly growing use for clear, blow-molded bottles as a replacement for glass. In the U.K. alone about 275 million PET bottles were used in 1982, compared with only 25 million in 1978, when they first appeared. They were now moving from the carbonated drink bottle market, in which they had done well already, to other packaging uses, notably for beer.

There were few other such areas of encouragement in the bread-and-butter conversion of plastics into end products in 1982. Particular activity was, however, noticeable in the provision of molded thermoplastics housings for the vast array of microelectronics-based communications equipment.   (ROBIN C. PENFOLD)

PRINTING

Despite a worldwide slowdown in investment, impressive sales were reported at the world's largest printing equipment show, in Düsseldorf, West Germany. High-technology companies in pre-press electronics did especially well. Scitex of Israel stood out with its new Vista system, which promised eventually to enable the designer, advertiser, and publisher to plan complete picture and text products electronically. Vista and the U.S. Triple-I system linked text, pagination, picture graphics, and colour reproduction. Triple-I was working with Crosfield Electronics to merge text and colour. The world's largest Hell scanner was installed at Scanart DS Colour in London, complete with two Chromaskop automatic makeup and Kugelmann layout coordinators. In Japan, which had the largest number of Crosfield and Hell scanners anywhere in the world, large scanner users developed their own subsystems for colour analysis and makeup.

Japan was also making a major impact on the general printing materials and equipment market. Fuji developed new plate coatings to handle laser exposure in offset, and Process Shizai introduced the Algraf nonsilver water-development line of daylight films and black-and-white laser scanners. Dainippon Printing introduced the remarkable Video Printing System, which allowed editors to obtain still pictures from video recordings. A viewing screen held the picture, while a second manipulating screen enabled the editor to crop, change size, or even change colour nuances. The picture was then reproduced instantly by exposure onto 70-mm transparency or Polaroid film.

Japan remained the third most important market for West German-built sheet-fed offset machines, after the U.S. and West Germany itself. However, Japanese-built web-offset presses were finding good markets in the U.S. Komori's new plate scanner allowed automatic setting-up of inking according to the plate image. Intergrafica, a trading house active in Latin America and Southeast Asia, introduced a simple-system 16-page web-offset press for less sophisticated and less affluent markets. Some 14 eight-page web-offset press models were available worldwide from almost as many manufacturers.

Web-offset continued to dominate the industry's thinking. Time Inc. decided to switch to that process, taking perhaps $25 million in orders away from the printers R. R. Donnelley. Ease in printing editions tailored to different regions and demographic groups seemed to have influenced the move. China decided to have West German-designed Albert web-offset presses built there under license. This was seen by some observers as the long-awaited breakthrough into one of the largest markets in the world. However, manufacturers tended to be at least equally excited about India's decision to free imports of printing equipment. Huge opportunities for new investment existed, once manufacturers came up with equipment geared to a market with an abundance of low-paid labour.

(W. PINCUS JASPERT)

RUBBER

All segments of the rubber industry were feeling the effects of recession in 1982. This included growers of natural rubber, producers of synthetic rubber, and suppliers of various chemicals and pigments, as well as manufacturers. With the automobile industry suffering its worst slump in years, demand for original equipment tires was down from 1981. The replacement tire business was good, however, as motorists tended to keep their car in service longer.

Productivity of tire firms reportedly increased 13.3% per man-hour in 1981 over 1980, due to the closing of old, inefficient plants. All rubber manufacturers reported some reduction in the number of workers. Production of both natural and synthetic rubber fell in 1981, and a further reduction was predicted for 1982. In the first seven months of 1982, consumption of synthetic rubber declined by 16.1% and of natural rubber by 7.7%, compared with the corresponding period of 1981. Only 50 to 60% of synthetic rubber production capacity could be sold, and the plants could not be operated profitably at this low rate.

The use of rubber as a single-ply roofing material for large, flat-roofed buildings appeared to be gaining wide acceptance. The Rubber Manufacturers Association formed a committee to study one-ply elastomeric roofing, since manufacture and sale of the material were increasing rapidly. Firestone was building a multimillion-dollar plant for its manufacture in Prescott, Ariz., capable of producing 37.2 million sq m (400 million sq ft) of ethylene propylene diene monomer roofing annually.

The closing of tire production by General Tire in Akron, Ohio, in 1982 marked the end of an era. Only a few experimental and aircraft tires were being produced in Akron, once the tire capital of the U.S. The Akron-based rubber companies had kept

Reels of high-pressure hose, combining synthetic rubber braided with wire reinforcement, are checked by a worker at a Goodyear plant. The hose was developed for automotive and industrial use.

UPI

Table XII. Natural Rubber Production
In 000 metric tons

Country	1979	1980	1981
Malaysia	1,570	1,552	1,529
Indonesia*	905	1,020	868
Thailand	531	501	504
India	147	155	151
China*	98	113	128
Sri Lanka	153	133	124
Liberia	73	70	66
Philippines*	60	65	65
Vietnam	50	50	40
Nigeria*	56	44	40
Others	217	127	150
Total*	3,860	3,830	3,665

*Estimate, or includes estimate.
Source: The Secretariat of The International Rubber Study Group, *Rubber Statistical Bulletin.*

Table XIII. Synthetic Rubber Production
In 000 metric tons

Country	1979	1980	1981
United States	2,720	2,241	2,248
U.S.S.R.*	2,025	2,040	2,000
Japan	1,107	1,094	1,010
France	541	511	487
West Germany	418	390	397
Canada	283	253	263
Italy*	270	250	235
Brazil	224	249	223
Netherlands, The	238	212	211
United Kingdom	278	212	190
Romania	149	150	160
East Germany*	150	150	155
Poland	130	118	111
Belgium*	125	115	108
Mexico	84	91	105
China*	80	90	85
Korea	60	75	82
Spain	87	81	75
Taiwan	85	73	71
Czechoslovakia	59	60	63
Australia	43	46	43
South Africa	31	39	36
Argentina	37	33	28
Others	106	97	104
Total*	9,330	8,670	8,490

*Estimate, or includes estimate.
Source: The Secretariat of The International Rubber Study Group, *Rubber Statistical Bulletin.*

their headquarters, general offices, and laboratories there, but the tires were being made in newer, more efficient plants in the South and West.

Foreign tire makers were attempting to tap the U.S. market. Yokohama of Japan entered the performance-tire market with low-profile tires designed to compete with those of Pirelli, Goodyear, Goodrich, and Firestone. Bridgestone of Japan was buying a modern Firestone plant at Nashville, Tenn., while Continental of West Germany contracted with General Tire for production of 500,000 tires per year.

The Gila River Indian community of Sacaton, Ariz., was awarded a $400,000 contract by the Naval Air Systems Command for work on the cultivation and processing of guayule. Guayule rubber, derived from a bush native to some sections of the southwestern U.S. and northern Mexico, showed considerable promise as a replacement for natural rubber. The Indians' job would be to improve the yield and quality of the rubber by seed selection and cultivation, as well as the processing of the bush to remove the rubber.

The U.S. National Highway Traffic Safety Administration (NHTSA) was still examining the merits of the Uniform Tire Quality Grading standard. One major tire manufacturer, Goodrich, had demonstrated that the basic concepts involved in the testing were in error, and, of the other tire makers, only Uniroyal had agreed that the testing was valid. A decision by the NHTSA on the next step with regard to Uniform Tire Quality Grading and its usefulness was due early in 1983.

As a result of competitive forces stemming from the supply-demand situation, materials prices during the year did not necessarily reflect costs or inflation. The New York spot price of natural rubber fell from 46¾ cents per pound on Oct. 1, 1981, to 43½ cents on Oct. 1, 1982, a 7% decrease. The list price of the most widely used synthetic rubber, SBR (styrene butadiene rubber), showed no change from the 70 cents per pound quoted on Oct. 1, 1981; widespread discounting existed, with actual selling prices falling as low as 46 to 48 cents per pound.

World production of natural rubber in 1981 was estimated at 3,665,000 metric tons, a decrease of 165,000 tons compared with 1980. Production for 1982 was estimated at 3,625,000 tons, representing a further decline of 40,000 tons. World production of synthetic rubber was estimated at 8,490,000 metric tons in 1981, down by 180,000 tons from the preceding year. Estimates by country are given in TABLES XII and XIII.

The U.S. continued to be the largest single user of natural rubber, consuming 635,000 metric tons in 1981, 50,000 tons more than in 1980. World consumption of natural rubber latex (dry basis) was estimated at 296,000 tons in 1980; statistics for 1981 were incomplete, but they suggest a decline. Statistics on world consumption of synthetic latices were also incomplete, but U.S. consumption was 101,856 metric tons (dry basis) of the styrene butadiene type. Consumption of both natural and synthetic rubber worldwide was estimated at 12,135,000 metric tons for 1981.

(JAMES R. BEATTY)

SHIPBUILDING

Despite predictions to the contrary, world shipbuilding did not continue the slow recovery that had appeared to be under way in 1981, and by the end of 1982 the amount of tonnage on order showed a reduction from 1981 of more than 13 million tons deadweight (dw) to 61 million tons dw. There were no hopeful signs that the situation would improve, the level of ship orders being related to the world freight markets, which, in turn, depended upon an overall upturn in the world economy for their recovery.

New construction of bulk carriers and oil–bulk-ore carriers declined sharply as owners finally acknowledged that an overtonnage situation existed. The situation was worse in the tanker sector as a result of reduced oil production, and even a fairly high scrapping rate did little to help. The ship category having the largest drop in orders during the past year was tankers, where orders fell from over 20 million tons dw to just under 15 million tons. Orders for bulk carriers decreased from 41.5 million tons dw to 33.3 million tons. Dry cargo ship orders recorded only a modest fall from 9.3 million tons dw to just under 9 million tons. The only sectors to show increased orders were cruise ships and certain types of specialized tonnage such as a new generation of containerships and ships serving the offshore oil and gas fields.

Japan stayed at the top of the world shipbuilding table with 27.2 million tons dw on order, followed at some distance by South Korea with 6 million tons, Spain with 3.8 million tons, and Brazil with 3.2 million tons. A newcomer to the upper part of the table was Taiwan with 3,140,000 tons, just ahead of Poland with 2,830,000 tons.

For most of the shipyards in Europe and the U.S., the situation remained very bad in terms of new orders. The worst hit yards were those in the U.S., where no orders were placed for new merchant ships above

A $46.7 million shipyard expansion proved to be an economic boon to the Bath (Maine) Iron Works, near Portland.

5,000 tons dw. It was significant, however, that even the Japanese shipbuilding industry, which had been drastically streamlined, was facing an acute shortage of new orders and had turned its attention to more specialized ships, such as the 100,000-ton-dw coal carrier with an ultrashallow draft, a very wide beam, and a "split" stern with a propeller at the after end of each skeg. This remarkable vessel, which was offered as a standard design, had the same draft as the popular Panamax-class bulk carrier of 60,000 tons dw; the large beam of 60 m (197 ft) provided the greatly increased cargo capacity.

It became generally accepted that without some form of state financial aid many European shipyards could not survive the current crisis. In Belgium the important Cockerill shipyard virtually shut down with four bulk carriers still to be completed, and in France negotiations started for the merging of the three shipyards at Dunkirk, La Seyne, and La Ciotat as well as of the shipyard of Dubigeon Normandie with the St.-Nazaire yard of Alsthom Atlantique. The major reason for the desperate plight of the U.S. shipbuilding industry was the virtual ending of the construction differential subsidy, which had been a valuable cushion for the yards against the realities of the commercial market. There were signs, however, that some of the yards were prepared to invest capital in new facilities.

After several good years serving foreign customers, the major Brazilian shipyards became mainly concerned with domestic orders, which accounted for all of the 1 million tons dw ordered in 1982. South Korea kept up the pressure on Japanese shipbuilders, but it too booked orders for less tonnage than in 1981 and began to feel the recession. In the U.K., British Shipbuilders was able to secure a better intake of orders than in 1981, and at mid-1982 the group's order book was valued at £1,047 million, half of which was accounted for by merchant ship orders.   (W. D. EWART)

TELECOMMUNICATIONS

Compared with the previous year, technological advances in the telecommunications industry slowed in 1982. But it was just as well that they did so, as legislative and regulatory agencies spent the year scrambling to come up with new rules that could cope with the flood of modern communications technology. The need for new regulations was equally evident in the home, office, and factory.

In the home and office there was great potential competition for the television viewer's eye from two new sources of information. The first of these, the direct broadcasting services, send their signals from an orbiting Earth satellite to an antenna at the viewer's site. The second comprises the suppliers of data base information for interactive television services such as teletex and videotext. These allow users to gain access to computer data bases at a place and time of their own choosing.

For direct broadcasting from an Earth satellite to the home to be successful, the home system must be small in size and low in cost. The most important component of the system for accomplishing this is the semiconductor gallium arsenide. Ideal for use at

the microwave frequencies that a satellite uses to beam television signals down to the Earth, gallium arsenide also allows the making of inexpensive, mass-produced receivers of such great sensitivity that an acceptably small antenna—about 1 m (3 ft) in diameter—can provide high-quality reception.

France, West Germany, and the U.S. were all active in the development of direct broadcasting. But major regulatory questions remained to be answered. For example, it would have to be decided which microwave frequencies would be used and where in space the orbiting satellites would be placed.

While work on direct broadcasting was under way, the proponents of teletex and videotext made progress toward their goal of placing suitably modified television sets in living rooms and offices throughout the world. With teletex a viewer can watch a screen that provides him, by means of text and graphics, with various kinds of information, such as the times and places of airline flights to Chicago.

Mere transmission of the contents of a data base requires nothing from a viewer except a desire to watch. In contrast, videotext, while also transmitting data base contents, calls for interactivity. The viewer is expected to stop the transmission if he or she is not interested. Moreover, viewers can request different kinds of information or focus on those specific aspects of the data base in which they are interested. This interactivity is accomplished by using a hand-held key pad or a full keyboard to send requests—usually over telephone

lines—back to the information provider.

As of 1982 teletex and videotext services were more popular in Europe than in the U.S. and, indeed, originated there. There were problems in marketing the services at both locations since they often duplicated what was otherwise available.

Another problem for the new technology to overcome involved the two conflicting standards for the technical details necessary for providing the service. Thus, several European nations had their own approach, while the U.S. and the Canadians had another. Fortunately, while the standards were different, in practice advanced versions of both teletex and videotext could be made to conform to either or both of them.

During the year the U.S. government dropped two long-standing lawsuits, against AT&T and IBM. One expected result of this action was increased competition between the two firms in areas where computer and communications technology overlap.

As part of settling its business with the U.S. Department of Justice, AT&T agreed to divest itself of its operating companies and make other adjustments in the way it does business. But, most important for AT&T, a new unregulated subsidiary, American Bell, Inc., was allowed to be established. This new firm was expected to compete directly with IBM and other computer firms. Its first offering was a computer-communications package known as the Advanced In-

A collapsible earth station that folds up like an umbrella and can pick up any of 105 U.S. television channels relayed by an orbiting satellite was unveiled in California in September.

UPI

Table XIV. Countries Having More than 100,000 Telephones

Telephones in service, 1981

Country	Number of telephones	Percentage increase over 1970	Telephones per 100 population	Country	Number of telephones	Percentage increase over 1970	Telephones per 100 population
Algeria	484,973	163.5	2.5	Kuwait	214,763	222.7	15.3
Argentina	2,880,754	65.0	10.4	Lebanon[2]	321,500	67.4	11.2
Australia	7,684,336	96.4	52.5	Luxembourg[1]	198,905	17.3	54.8
Austria	3,010,110	110.9	39.8	Malaysia	596,972	234.0	4.4
Belgium	3,636,074	80.1	36.7	Mexico	5,082,718	237.2	7.6
Bolivia	135,100	260.0	2.6	Morocco[1]	227,000	115.1	1.1
Brazil	7,496,000	274.7	6.3	Netherlands, The	7,230,000	112.0	50.8
Bulgaria	1,255,792	165.5	14.1	New Zealand	1,798,802	42.5	56.7
Canada	16,178,158	65.9	67.2	Nigeria[1]	154,236	93.2	0.2
Chile	569,969	54.4	5.0	Norway	1,851,683	61.7	45.3
Colombia	1,623,105	66.6	5.9	Pakistan	367,080	77.1	0.4
Costa Rica	236,132	285.4	10.4	Panama	191,913	163.3	9.9
Cyprus	113,437	178.4	17.9	Peru	487,123	118.7	2.8
Czechoslovakia	3,150,477	57.3	20.6	Philippines	537,795	73.5	1.1
Denmark	3,316,709	95.5	63.7	Poland	3,387,396	81.4	9.4
Dominican Republic	165,253	248.6	2.9	Portugal	1,371,731	82.9	13.7
Ecuador[1]	260,000	175.0	3.3	Puerto Rico	696,805	108.8	20.3
Egypt	534,021	...	1.2	Romania[1]	1,479,627	236.0	6.7
Finland	2,374,461	101.1	49.6	Saudi Arabia	442,514	...	5.3
France	24,686,319	181.3	45.8	Singapore	702,219	335.3	29.1
East Germany	3,156,661	51.1	18.9	South Africa	2,932,983	88.8	12.2
West Germany	28,553,622	106.4	46.4	Spain	11,844,623	157.2	31.0
Greece	2,796,435	167.7	28.9	Sweden	6,621,000	46.9	79.5
Hong Kong	1,676,298	187.4	32.7	Switzerland	4,612,382	52.4	72.4
Hungary	1,261,295	53.1	11.7	Syria[1]	236,020	127.6	2.7
Iceland	108,767	53.3	47.5	Taiwan	3,166,169	685.0	17.8
India	2,785,096	123.6	0.4	Thailand	496,558	224.6	1.1
Indonesia[1]	392,563	95.8	0.2	Tunisia	188,476	146.8	0.3
Iran	1,227,293	299.1	3.1	Turkey	1,902,081	229.7	4.3
Ireland	650,017	111.4	18.7	U.S.S.R.	23,707,000	115.5	8.8
Israel	1,230,000	140.9	31.2	United Kingdom	27,784,447	85.6	49.6
Italy	19,269,340	105.7	33.7	United States	191,595,000	59.4	83.7
Jamaica	119,402	66.2	6.0	Uruguay	287,140	33.4	9.9
Japan	58,007,409	121.1	49.5	Venezuela[1]	1,165,016	208.5	8.5
Kenya	198,294	155.9	1.2	Yugoslavia	2,133,225	189.8	9.5
Korea, South	3,386,800	434.3	9.1	Zimbabwe	224,452	70.6	3.0

[1] 1980.
[2] 1979.
Sources: American Telephone and Telegraph Company; The World's Telephones, 1971; 1981.

formation System. It was designed for customers with a need for extensive, nationwide, computer-based communication and data-processing services.

(HARVEY J. HINDIN)

TEXTILES

Continuing problems of excess capacity and overproduction confronted the textile industries of both developed and less developed countries in 1982. With capital for investment unavailable, manufacturers had to content themselves with existing plant, making yarns and fabrics at uncommercial prices. This was reflected in the failure of a number of major Western European textile-machine builders.

There was growing polarization between the textile industries of the developed countries (mainly Western Europe, North America, and Japan) and those of the less developed countries. In the future the labour-intensive industries of the latter would have to fight against the products of highly automated manufacturing in those countries that could afford new technology.

An example was the almost completely automatic, open-end spinning machine. This produced yarn that, though about 10% weaker than conventionally made yarns, was of much greater regularity and thus highly suitable for weaving on air-jet looms (in which a jet of air—or water, if man-made fibres are being processed—replaces the shuttle). Also reliant on very regular yarn was the multiphase loom currently being developed, which would be able to produce cloths at more than double the speed of conventional weaving. However, there would probably always be a place for manufacturers who could make specialities and novelty cloths that had fashion appeal and could command high prices.

(PETER LENNOX-KERR)

Wool. World production of wool in the 1981–82 season (ended June 1982) was 1,644,000 metric tons clean, 1½% higher than in the 1980–81 season and the highest recorded since the mid-1960s. Only a nominal increase was expected in the 1982–83 season as drought in Australia, the largest producer, reduced sheep numbers. Preliminary estimates of virgin wool consumption showed a slightly declining trend overall in 1981, amounting to 4% in 11 leading reporting countries. The fall was most substantial in the EC; there was a rise of 11% in the U.S., but manufacturing activity there declined toward the close of the year. Early statistics suggested that the overall downtrend in consumption was not halted in 1982.

Price fluctuations were narrow in the 1981–82 season, and there was no indication of alteration during the first half of the 1982–83 season. In both periods seasonally larger supplies tended to depress the price basis during the earlier months. The Australian Wool Corporation increased its floor price by 2.9% for the 1982–83 season. Its stockpile rose from 509,312 bales (50,390 metric tons clean) to nearly 1 million bales toward the end of 1982. South Africa's reserve price purchases were heavy in the early stages of the 1982–83 season, and some support was needed again in New Zealand.

Deep or deepening recession, especially in developed countries, continued to affect usage. Manufacturing activity was low compared with capacity, retail sales were discouraging, and the level of commercial stocks was down as a result of general uncertainty and high financing costs.

(H. M. F. MALLETT)

Cotton. After hovering around the 22 million-bale mark for some time, world stocks of raw cotton suddenly advanced sharply in the 1981–82 season. At more than 27 million bales, carry-over supplies were the highest in seven years, covering requirements for almost five months. The basic reason was a major gain in production. Global output was a record 17.4 million bales, an improvement of 5.8 million bales over the previous season. Better yields accounted for about 75% of the increase, while the acreage planted was around 2.4% higher. The gain centred on the U.S., China, India, and Sudan. There was a fallback in the Soviet Union, Mexico, Egypt, and Zimbabwe, largely caused by bad weather.

Consumption of the raw material, though 700,000 bales below the record 1980–81 season, was still the third highest on record at 65.7 million bales. Demand in the industrialized areas was depressed by the economic recession, but this was offset by gains in the socialist countries, notably China and the Soviet Union.

Average prices for cotton in Liverpool began the 1981–82 season at 86.60 cents per pound but declined to a low of 67.20 cents by December 1981. In April–May 1982 values reached 77.30 cents, with 79.13 cents quoted just before the season ended. There was a sharp decline to 70 cents in the first quarter of the 1982–83 season. For the first time in several years, world production and consumption of raw cotton appeared to be roughly in balance.

(ARTHUR TATTERSALL)

Silk. Developments in 1982 confirmed that China, now the world's premier producer of silk, was fostering the export of finished goods with the aim of increasing the industry's capacity as a foreign currency earner. For some years China had been providing funds for the promotion of silk in Europe. Other Asian silk-producing countries—such as India, Thailand, and to some extent the U.S.S.R.—had traditionally confined their exports of fabric to silk that was surplus to domestic requirements. However, China, since the demise of Japan as an exporter in 1967, had set itself up as a consistent supplier of raw silk to the West, fulfilling that role with much discretion. The price of 51.70 yuan fixed for 3A 20/22 denier in January 1980 held firmly until June 1982 (and then the adjustment was little more than 1½%). This was in striking contrast to the wild fluctuations of the past.

Japan, meanwhile, faced the problem of unwieldy stocks. Even with stricter import controls, a lighter crop of cocoons, and domestic promotion, the volume of stocks was reduced by no more than 10%. Worldwide demand for silk was healthy throughout the year, but Japan's contrived price plateau debarred exports except at a considerable loss. Hopes of restoring the kimono to its ancient status did not seem promising.

(PETER W. GADDUM)

Man-Made Fibres. The continuing decline of the textile industries in the richer countries resulted in the closing of a number of man-made fibre production facilities. This affected not only polyester and polyamide (nylon) but also the cellulosics such as viscose rayon. Since they are based on natural raw materials rather than petroleum, the cellulosics had seemed to have a secure future.

One bright spot was polypropylene, previously considered a somewhat inferior substitute for nylon or polyester. The latest developments opened the way for the production of polypropylene fibres of incredibly brilliant colours. In the past pigments were used, and these tended to produce a somewhat muddy colour. With new technology, it was now possible to incorporate the colour into the raw material before it was converted into fibre. Another development that could bring wider acceptance of polypropylene in clothing manufacture was the feasibility of extruding it as a very fine fibre.

Similarly, nylon appeared to be undergoing something of a transformation. An Italian company launched a version that could be dyed rapidly at only 40° C (104° F), compared with the usual 100° C (212° F) or more. This not only simplified dyeing but also saved energy. Another development, especially useful for carpeting, was the incorporation of soil-release or repellent compounds, such as fluorocarbons, into the nylon. Such finishes were permanent for the life of the product. Carbon-fibre production continued to rise, and considerable research was devoted to developing new types with improved properties.

(PETER LENNOX-KERR)

TOBACCO

Despite tax disincentives and antismoking campaigns, world tobacco consumption rose again in 1982, by about 2%. The main gains were in less developed areas; growth was slight in North America and Japan, and consumption fell in Western Europe. With sales of some 4,650,000,000, cigarettes remained the most favoured mode of tobacco consumption. Cigar smoking declined almost everywhere, though a modest swing to chewing tobacco and snuff persisted.

The world's tobacco farmers sold some 5,650,000,000 kg (12,440,000,000 lb) of tobacco—more than in 1981—but for the third successive year that did not match the rise in manufacturers' needs, and stocks shrank again. Raw tobacco prices in the main markets lost some of their pre-1982 buoyancy. The slide in interest rates started too late in the year to affect buying of a commodity that had to mature for at least 15 months before manufacture.

Signals from the market were encouraging farmers to grow more flue-cured and Burley tobacco, used in the American-blend and English-type cigarettes that, despite their higher cost, were displacing black-tobacco blends in all but the most deeply depressed economies. However, the fuel-cost implications of producing more flue-cured tobacco in the third world, instead of sun-cured or air-cured black tobaccos, became more controversial. The cigarette industry was accused of denuding poor countries' forests, and it also faced health-oriented criticism and restraints on its publicity in third world countries.

In the U.S. a hotly debated reform of the tobacco price-support program left farmers' profits down slightly, but the industry felt

less vulnerable politically, since under the new program price supports were paid to farmers at no net cost to the taxpayer. In Western Europe, which since World War II had been using more and more third world tobacco, interest revived in tobacco self-sufficiency. The strategy assumed continued subsidies to farm and factory in the EC.

Steep increases in tobacco taxes raised the cost of smoking in several developed countries, stimulating contraband trade wherever geography favoured it. The federal tax on cigarettes was doubled in the U.S., to the dismay of the individual states, which for decades had had a near-monopoly of this revenue. Soaring tobacco taxes depressed retail sales in West Germany and Britain and led to an increase in hand-rolling of cigarettes.

The international cigarette export trade, which had long been growing faster than the exporting countries' home sales, turned its attention to Japan as the last big market ripe for exploitation. (China and the U.S.S.R. were not considered penetrable on a large scale for years.) There was intense pressure on Japan, which had a tobacco monopoly, to open its almost closed doors to foreign cigarettes. Japan, meanwhile, had international cigarette-trade ambitions of its own.   (MICHAEL F. BARFORD)

TOURISM

International tourism continued to weather the recession in 1982, though a slight decrease in overall arrivals marked a year in which stagnation of arrivals was frequent and declines were not uncommon. World Tourism Organization (WTO) preliminary estimates revealed a 1.3% drop in international arrivals to 279.9 million, while dollar receipts edged forward by 4% to about $110 billion. However, total tourist movements, including domestic travel within national frontiers, were calculated at almost 3,000,000,000 in 1982.

In the industrialized countries, which were the main generators of tourism, there were moves to reduce working hours and grant longer annual holidays, both of which promoted leisure travel. However, the increasing number of unemployed persons contributed to a fall in disposable income per capita, while growth in real terms slowed significantly, offering an inadequate basis for an increase in tourism.

As demand for energy continued to decline in the face of the world recession, concern for supplies ceased to be a problem, though the relatively high cost of energy, especially for transport, consolidated the trend toward holidays spent closer to home. While the stronger U.S. dollar stimulated outbound U.S. travel, it made North American destinations relatively expensive, leading to a sharp decline in travel to the U.S. Likewise, recovery of Caribbean tourism was delayed because of the high prices of these destinations, most of them with currencies linked to the U.S. dollar.

Countries faring well in 1982 included Spain, where 37.7 million visitors were received in the first ten months of the year, a 5% increase over 1981. Receipts for the first nine months of 1982 reached $5.6 billion, almost 10% more than in 1981. Despite the considerable publicity that attended the World Cup football (soccer) championships held in Spain in June and July 1982, the

449

Industrial Review

Table XV. International Tourist Arrivals and Receipts, 1970–82

Year	Arrivals In 000,000	Arrivals % change	Receipts In $000,000,000	Receipts % change
1971	172.2	7.8	20.8	16.2
1972	182.3	5.9	24.7	18.8
1973	191.3	4.9	31.3	26.7
1974	197.8	3.4	34.1	8.9
1975	215.1	8.7	41.1	20.5
1976	221.6	3.0	44.9	9.2
1977	239.9	8.3	54.4	21.2
1978	253.1	7.6	68.7	26.3
1979	270.0	4.6	82.2	19.7
1980	279.0	3.3	95.3	15.9
1981	283.6	1.6	106.1	11.3
1982	279.9*	−1.3	110.0*	4.0

*Preliminary estimates. International receipts exclude international fares.
Source: World Tourism Organization, *World Tourism Statistics*, 1982.

Table XVI. Major Tourism Earners and Spenders in 1981
In $000,000

Major spenders	Expenditure
West Germany	$17.8
United States	11.5
United Kingdom	6.5
France	5.7
Japan	4.6
Netherlands, The	3.6
Canada	3.2
Austria	2.8
Belgium/Luxembourg	2.6
Sweden	2.2
Switzerland	2.1
Australia	1.9
Italy	1.7
Norway	1.4
Denmark	1.3
Spain	1.0

Major earners	Receipts
United States	$12.2
Italy	7.6
France	7.2
Spain	6.7
West Germany	6.3
United Kingdom	5.9
Austria	5.7
Switzerland	3.0
Canada	2.5
Greece	1.9
Belgium/Luxembourg	1.6
Netherlands, The	1.6
Australia	1.2
Denmark	1.2
Portugal	1.0
Mexico	...
Hong Kong	...

Source: World Tourism Organization, 1982.

success of the season seemed to have been attributable mainly to poor summer weather in northern Europe and a weak peseta. In the United Kingdom, where arrivals rose by 4% to 9.5 million during the first nine months of the year, the North American segment of the market was the most buoyant, with a 7% increase attributable to the use of marketing skills to halt an incipient decline in the "stately home" industry. In comparison, arrivals from EC countries rose less than 1%, those from all of Western Europe by 3%, and the small "rest of the world" segment by 9%. Receipts expressed in pounds sterling grew by 13% in 1982 over the first nine months and, though expenditures grew by only 9% over the same period, the travel account deficit that had marred 1981 persisted as U.K. tourists spent £265 million ($425 million) more on foreign travel than international tourists spent

"Journey into Imagination," part of the Epcot Center, a large tourist attraction in central Florida built by Walt Disney Productions, was presented by the Eastman Kodak Co.

in the U.K.

Other countries reporting favourable trends in 1982 included Japan with a 20% increase, while Finland, Yugoslavia, Austria, Portugal, France, and Greece all showed positive growth rates of up to 10% in the early months of the year. The tiny Indian Ocean nation of the Maldives reported a half-year increase of 28%, bringing arrivals to 38,000. Among countries reporting stagnation or modest declines in international tourist arrivals were Turkey, West Germany, Sweden, and Switzerland.

In North America there was a decline of 11% in arrivals in Canada, though hopes were that the weakness of the Canadian dollar in comparison with the U.S. dollar would shift the balance in Canada's favour as the year progressed. Arrivals in the U.S. were reported down by more than 7%, and a midsummer survey of U.S. travel intentions foreshadowed a 14% decline in person-trips (covering both domestic and international travel). However, the number of tourists intending to travel by air continued above 1981 levels, while business and convention travel intentions were strong, implying that the U.S. economy was beginning to climb out of its recession.

In the Caribbean, tourism demand continued to be mixed. Jamaica showed a 26% increase at midyear with 271,000 visitors. This success was attributed to a return of customer confidence and a strong marketing effort. Antigua registered a 5.5% increase over eight months, aided by a considerable increase in hotel capacity. But Barbados declined 12% over the first eight months, possibly owing to dependence on Canadian visitors and the collapse of some leading Canadian tour operators. Aruba, the Cayman Islands, and The Bahamas also declined from their 1981 visitor levels. Currency movements were seen as undermining the competitive position of some Caribbean destinations, notable exceptions being the French overseas territories of Guadeloupe and Martinique, where the

weakness of the French franc led to higher visitor levels. Mexico's successive peso devaluations made that country an especially good value for money, leading to strong off-season demand from U.S. travelers from June through August.

(PETER SHACKLEFORD)

WOOD PRODUCTS

A radical change in estimates of how much wood Americans would use in future decades marked 1982 as a watershed year for the U.S. forest products industry. Studies by the U.S. Forest Service, based on data collected in the mid-1970s, had projected a doubling of demand for wood by the year 2030. However, research conducted in 1982 by forest industry economists pointed to a surplus of available raw material by the turn of the century, making the prospect of "timber famine" in the U.S. highly unlikely. Such long-range forecasts are important to forest products companies because trees planted in commercial forests take between 25 and 50 years to reach the point where they can be harvested.

The new findings indicated a sharp course change for wood and paper companies, long concerned with maintaining an adequate supply of timber and fibre. It now appeared that concern would shift to the demand side of the equation: finding new domestic markets as well as developing much-needed foreign ones.

The year was a dismal one for the housing market, which traditionally consumes about 80% of the softwood timber harvested in the U.S. Nationwide, the number of housing starts in 1982 was around 1.1 million, about the same as in 1981. However, a major share of this was accounted for by small attached houses that consume less raw material than the traditional suburban detached house. This change in building styles contributed to declines in U.S. lumber shipments of about 25% from 1979 levels and 5% from 1981. Continued high interest rates and consumer anxieties about

other economic factors helped keep home sales sluggish for most of 1982. Interest rates began to fall in the autumn, however, and this accounted for much of the 24% increase in new home sales in September over the previous month. Residential construction in 1983 was expected to rise 31%.

A similar pattern was evident in another important wood market: furniture. Furniture production fell some 15% in 1982, following drops of around 2% in each of the two previous years. However, sales picked up in the autumn of 1982 and shipments were projected to rise 16% in 1983.

Despite these optimistic signs, wood product shipments and company profits were among the indicators off sharply in 1982. Of 22 leading forest products companies studied, only 6 reflected profitability gains over 1981, and most of those gains were in single digits. The total value of lumber shipped in 1982 fell to $5 billion from $5.5 billion in 1981.

Consumer demand for paper remained the strongest side of the forest products picture. Overall production continued at a level about 24% above 1980, and mills functioned at better than 90% of capacity. U.S. paper and paperboard production in 1982 totaled 67 million tons, 5 million tons more than in 1980.

With domestic demand soft, wood and paper companies placed greater emphasis on building foreign markets. The U.S. exported wood to more than 150 countries, with Japan, Australia, and Saudi Arabia the major markets, but it was still a net importer of wood, mostly from Canada for use as newsprint. All imports made up perhaps a quarter of total U.S. lumber consumption. In 1982 this amounted to 35,000,000,000 bd-ft, down from 1981 by almost 2,000,000,000 bd-ft. (JAMES BEEK)

See also Agriculture and Food Supplies; Computers; Consumerism; Economy, World; Energy; Food Processing; Games and Toys; Industrial Relations; Materials Sciences; Mining and Quarrying; Photography; Television and Radio; Transportation.

Iran

An Islamic republic of western Asia, Iran is bounded by the U.S.S.R., Afghanistan, Pakistan, Iraq, and Turkey and the Caspian Sea, the Arabian Sea, and the Persian Gulf. Area: 1,648,000 sq km (636,000 sq mi). Pop. (1982 est.): 40,476,000. Cap. and largest city: Teheran (pop., 1980 est., 6 million). Language: Persian. Religion (1976): Muslim 99%; Christian, Jewish, and Zoroastrian minorities. President in 1982, Sayyed Ali Khamenei; prime minister, Mir Hossein Moussavi.

The tide of the Gulf war turned strongly in Iran's favour during 1982. The main breakthrough began on March 22, when Iraqi forces in Khuzestan were driven back across a broad front. In a further offensive launched at the end of April, an Iranian bridgehead was established west of the Karun River. At the end of May the final withdrawal from Khuzestan was effected when Iraqi troops left Khorramshahr. The Iranian leadership could claim with some truth that the Islamic Republican Army had swept all before it in the liberation of Iranian territory. Iraq announced that it would unilaterally withdraw from all remaining Iranian lands captured earlier and seek a peace agreement through the Islamic Conference.

Encouraged by its military successes, the Iranian regime hardened its stance on peace conditions. It demanded that Iraqi Pres. Saddam Hussein at-Takriti (see BIOGRAPHIES) be removed from office, that an independent commission be established to allocate blame for the war, and that reparations be paid to Iran. In addition to these publicly stated aims, there appeared to be consensus in Teheran that the war should continue until the regime in Baghdad was changed, that the Shi'ah Muslims of Iraq should be liberated by force if necessary, and that all Iranian territorial claims should be met.

A first step toward implementing these expanded goals came with the invasion of Iraq that began on July 14. The offensive was directed toward Basra in southern Iraq. Although some early gains were made, Iranian troops were ultimately expelled with heavy losses. On October 1 a major Iranian assault on the border town of Mandali was followed by a drive westward from Dezful on November 1, when a number of roads and oil installations were captured. A thrust into Iraqi territory in the region of Amarah opened up the road to Baghdad, but Iraq claimed the offensive was contained.

The war had an appreciable effect on Iran's foreign relations. Both the U.S. and the U.S.S.R. remained officially neutral and refused arms supplies to both sides, though materials slipped through these embargoes with comparative ease. Iranian relations with the Arab world deteriorated sharply when Iranian troops invaded Arab soil; only Syria and Libya remained aligned with Iran.

Domestic political events were largely controlled by the ruling Islamic Republican Party, which became increasingly associated with policies of an Islamic and conservative nature. Left-wing influences were attacked and removed wherever possible. The threat from the Mujaheddin-i Khalq opposition was largely negated during the year, though occasional violence erupted. The Tudeh (Communist) Party was no longer tolerated. While the aging Ayatollah Ruhollah Khomeini showed increasing signs of frailty, he remained the final point of reference for all political forces. On December 10 an election was held to select an 83-member assembly that would choose a successor to Khomeini after he died. In September Sadegh Ghotbzadeh (see OBITUARIES) was executed for plotting to overthrow the government. As foreign minister during the crisis that followed the capture of U.S. hostages in 1979, he had been highly visible in the West.

Iran's economic plight worsened in 1982. Poor demand for Iranian oil, Iraqi air attacks on the Kharg Island oil terminal, and prohibitive insurance rates for vessels visiting Iranian ports exacer-

Iran

ALFRED ZADEH—GAMMA/L'AISON

Former Iranian minister Sadegh Ghotbzadeh (second from right) was found guilty at his trial of plotting to overthrow the Iranian government. He was executed on September 15.

Information Science and Technology: see Computers; Industrial Review

Insurance: see Industrial Review

International Bank for Reconstruction and Development: see Economy, World

International Law: see Law

International Monetary Fund: see Economy, World

Investment: see Economy, World; Stock Exchanges

Iraq

IRAN
Education. (1978–79) Primary, pupils 4,403,106, teachers (1977–78) 154,577; secondary, pupils 2,370,341, teachers (1977–78) 91,960; vocational, pupils 256,303, teachers (1976–77) 10,041; teacher training, students 57,832, teachers (1977–78) 2,988; higher, students 175,675, teaching staff (1977–78) 15,453.

Finance. Monetary unit: rial, with (Sept. 20, 1982) a free rate of 85 rials to U.S. $1 (145.70 rials = £1 sterling). Budget (1981–82 est.) balanced at 3,166,000,000,000 rials. Gross national product (1979–80) 6,010,000,000,000 rials. Money supply (Feb. 1981) 2,322,870,000,000 rials. Cost of living (1975 = 100; May 1982) 310.1

Foreign Trade. (1981) Imports (f.o.b.) c. 830.3 billion rials; exports c. 818.7 billion rials. Import sources: West Germany c. 14%; Japan c. 13%; Italy c. 7%; U.K. c. 6%; France c. 6%. Export destinations: Japan c. 17%; The Bahamas c. 14%; Spain c. 12%; Italy c. 6%; West Germany c. 6%; India c. 6%; Romania c. 5%; Turkey c. 5%. Main export: crude oil c. 92%.

Transport and Communications. Roads (1980) 63,100 km. Motor vehicles in use (1980): passenger 1,079,100; commercial (including buses) 406,000. Railways: (1980) 4,567 km; traffic (1978) 2,981,000,000 passenger-km, freight 4,083,000,000 net ton-km. Air traffic (1981): 1,600,000,000 passenger-km; freight 40.9 million net ton-km. Shipping (1981): merchant vessels 100 gross tons and over 234; gross tonnage 1,201,667. Telephones (Jan. 1980) c. 730,000. Radio receivers (Dec. 1978) 2,288,000. Television receivers (Dec. 1979) 2 million.

Agriculture. Production (in 000; metric tons; 1981): wheat c. 5,800; barley c. 1,300; rice c. 1,400; potatoes c. 705; sugar, raw value c. 400; onions c. 265; tomatoes c. 338; watermelons c. 946; melons c. 494; dates c. 301; grapes c. 999; apples c. 467; soybeans c. 120; tea c. 22; tobacco c. 24; cotton, lint c. 87. Livestock (in 000; 1981): cattle c. 8,139; sheep c. 34,377; goats c. 13,709; horses c. 350; asses c. 1,800; chickens c. 72,176.

Industry. Production (in 000; metric tons; 1978–79): cement 6,228; coal 900; crude oil (1981) 65,991; natural gas (cu m; 1981) 7,200,000; petroleum products (1979) c. 33,600; lead concentrates (metal content; 1979–80) 28; chromium ore (oxide content; 1979–80) 67; electricity (kw-hr; 1980) 17,150,000.

of electricity and raw materials, while agriculture, an officially favoured area, showed a further decline in output. Imports of agricultural products rose dramatically to an estimated $4.5 billion. By November Iranian holdings of foreign exchange were thought to be worth $3 billion, compared with $500 million four months earlier.

(KEITH S. MCLACHLAN)

Iraq

A republic of southwestern Asia, Iraq is bounded by Turkey, Iran, Kuwait, Saudi Arabia, Jordan, Syria, and the Persian Gulf. Area: 437,522 sq km (168,928 sq mi). Pop. (1982 est.): 14,014,000, including (1978 est.) Arabs 76.9%; Kurds 18.6%; Turkmens 1.5%; Iranians 1.3%; other 1.7%. Cap. and largest city: Baghdad (pop., 1977, 3,205,600). Language: Arabic (official), Kurdish. Religion (1980 est.): Muslim 95.8%; Christian 3.5%; other 0.7%. President in 1982, Saddam Hussein at-Takriti.

Iraq suffered severe military setbacks in the war with Iran during 1982, and this, coupled with lower oil production and the need for austerity at home, gave Pres. Saddam Hussein at-Takriti (*see* BIOGRAPHIES) a difficult year. The military pressure began in September 1981 when the Iraqi Army was pushed back across the Karun River. This phase culminated on May 24, 1982, with a humiliating capitulation at the Iranian port of Khorramshahr. The Iraqis appeared to hold the line with a successful defensive action in the Basra sector in July, and an Iranian offensive at Mandali in October was also contained. Iraqi casualty esti-

bated existing problems. Oil output, averaging 1,519,000 bbl a day in the first half of 1982, rose to 1.7 million bbl a day in November. However, the recovery was bought with large discounts on oil prices; revenue flows, though improving, were barely adequate to buy imports.

Economic development activity came to a virtual halt. Changes were effected in the organization of foreign trade, much of which was nationalized. Otherwise, unemployment persisted and economic activity diminished. Industry suffered shortages

About 4,000 Iraqis were taken prisoner and several thousand were reported to be dead during violent fighting between the soldiers of the Ayatollah Ruhollah Khomeini of Iran and those of Saddam Hussein of Iraq.

IRAQ
Education. (1979–80) Primary, pupils 2,609,182, teachers 92,603; secondary, pupils 897,001, teachers 27,987; vocational, pupils 54,026, teachers 3,928; teacher training, students 18,960, teachers 772; higher (1978–79), students 98,327, teaching staff 5,464.

Finance. Monetary unit: Iraqi dinar, with (Sept. 20, 1982) a par value of 0.295 dinar to U.S. $1 (free rate of 0.506 dinar = £1 sterling). Budget (total; 1981 est.): revenue 19,435,000,000 dinars; expenditure 19,750,000,000 dinars. Gross domestic product (1977) 5,692,000,000 dinars.

Foreign Trade. (1981) Imports (f.o.b.) c. 4,932,000,000 dinars; exports 3,130,000,000 dinars. Import sources: Japan c. 18%; West Germany c. 17%; France c. 8%; Italy c. 8%; U.K. c. 7%; U.S. c. 5%. Export destinations: Italy c.18%; Turkey c. 13%; Brazil c. 9%; Japan c. 8%; France c. 6%. Main export: crude oil 98%.

Transport and Communications. Roads (1977) 15,123 km. Motor vehicles in use (1980): passenger c. 164,400; commercial (including buses) c.192,700. Railways: (main; 1978) 1,589 km; traffic (1977–78) 821 million passenger-km, freight 2,497,000,000 net ton-km. Air traffic (1981): c. 1,280,000,000 passenger-km; freight c. 50 million net ton-km. Shipping (1981): merchant vessels 100 gross tons and over 148; gross tonnage 1,491,489. Telephones (Jan. 1978) 319,600. Radio receivers (Dec. 1979) 2 million. Television receivers (Dec. 1979) 600,000.

Agriculture. Production (in 000; metric tons; 1981): wheat c. 1,100; barley c. 600; rice c. 250; cucumbers c. 170; watermelons c. 683; onions c. 82; tomatoes c. 485; dates c. 405; grapes c. 447; tobacco c. 12; cotton, lint c. 5. Livestock (in 000; 1981): cattle c. 2,624; sheep c. 11,650; goats c. 3,675; camels c. 242; asses c. 462.

Industry. Production (in 000; metric tons; 1980): cement 5,300; crude oil (1981) 44,894; natural gas (cu m; 1981) 650,000; petroleum products (1979) c. 6,400; electricity (kw-hr) c. 8,000,000.

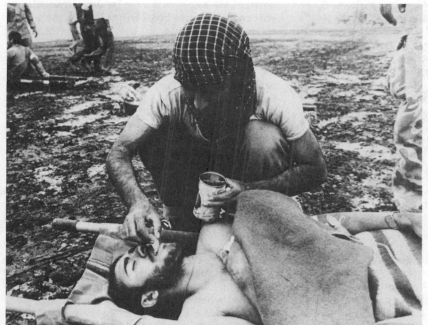

During a cease-fire, Iranian soldiers attend their wounded and clear the battlefront of dead soldiers. The Iranians had invaded southern Iraq in July.

mates stood at 40,000 dead, 70,000 wounded, and some 40,000 captured.

President Hussein survived a difficult political period in May and June but emerged with a stronger hand. On June 27 a shake-up in the ruling Revolutionary Command Council was announced. The purge was less stringent than that carried out in July 1979, when a number of council members and a deputy premier were executed. The average age of the new ministers was 46; most had university degrees; and two had military backgrounds. Ten new ministers were appointed, and a new Ministry for Light Industries was created. Prominent among the new appointees was Oil Minister Qassem Ahmad Taki.

Hussein's position was secure enough for him to ride out the cancellation of the nonaligned movement summit, scheduled to take place in Baghdad in September 1982. The president suggested that the eighth summit be held in Baghdad in 1985. There was some evidence that Iranian-inspired terrorism in Iraq was responsible for the cancellation.

Arab aid to Iraq, estimates of which varied from $16 billion to $30 billion since the start of the war with Iran, were vital to Iraq's survival. By October 1982 oil exports had fallen to 600,000 bbl a day, and only the pipeline to Turkey was in use. Annual revenue from the sale of this oil in depressed world market conditions was estimated at some $6 billion–$10 billion. Foreign currency reserves held by Iraq were down to about $8 billion. The war effort was estimated to be costing Iraq $1 billion a month, while development spending for 1982 was put at about $12 billion.

Against this background of austerity, it seemed likely that the ambitious $130 billion five-year (1981–85) development plan would be shelved. Instead, new projects would be amended annually within the guidelines of the plan and annual budget allocations. A further worry was that Iraq

might have to pay war reparations to Iran for a guarantee of peace. It was thought likely, however, that in such an event Arab Gulf neighbours would step into the breach. Hussein made it clear that the war would take priority as long as he governed. He was quoted as saying, "If we are required to stop any of our development projects to meet battlefield requirements, we will do so."

Within the nonaligned movement, Iraq had a powerful friend in Yugoslavia, with which it had strong business relations. There were similar ties with India and certain other third world countries, which had been helped in the past by the Iraqi Fund for External Development. The president retained a pragmatic view of relations with the Soviet Union and the U.S. but had no diplomatic relations with the latter. Within the Gulf, Hussein was still regarded with suspicion as a past supporter of elements hostile to the sheikhly system. Iraq was pointedly not invited to join the Gulf Cooperation Council grouping of conservative Arab Gulf states formed in 1981.

In October former president Ahmad Hassan al-Bakr (see OBITUARIES), who handed over the presidency to Hussein in July 1979, died. During Hussein's unstable period in the summer, he had been named as a possible caretaker president in the event of Hussein's overthrow or fall from power.　　　　　　　　　　　　(JOHN WHELAN)

Ireland

Separated from Great Britain by the North Channel, the Irish Sea, and St. George's Channel, the Republic of Ireland shares its island with Northern Ireland to the northeast. Area: 70,285 sq km (27,137 sq mi), or 83% of the island. Pop. (1981 prelim.): 3,440,400. Cap. and largest city: Dublin (pop., 1981 prelim., 525,400). Language (1971): mostly English; 28% speak English and Irish or

Ireland

Charles J. Haughey (left) and Garret FitzGerald continued to succeed one another as prime minister in Ireland.

Irish only. Religion: 94% Roman Catholic. President in 1982, Patrick J. Hillery; prime ministers, Garret FitzGerald, Charles J. Haughey from March 9, and FitzGerald from December 14.

Political instability cast a shadow over events in Ireland again in 1982 but was resolved in November by the year's second general election. The recession deepened, and unemployment rose. John Bruton, minister for finance in the Fine Gael-Irish Labour Party coalition government, brought in a

IRELAND

Education. (1980–81) Primary, pupils 568,364, teachers 20,068; secondary, pupils 293,809, teachers 18,457; vocational, pupils 6,792, teachers 202; higher, students 41,928, teaching staff 3,983.

Finance. Monetary unit: Irish pound (punt), with (Sept. 20, 1982) a free rate of I£0.73 to U.S. $1 (I£1.25 = £1 sterling). Gold and other reserves (June 1982) U.S. $2,438,000,000. Budget (1981 actual): revenue £4,064 million; expenditure £5,853 million. Gross national product (1980) £8,557 million. Money supply (June 1982) £1,757 million. Cost of living (1975 = 100; May 1982) 272.2

Foreign Trade. (1981) Imports £6,575.5 million; exports £4,845.9 million. Import sources: EEC 71% (U.K. 50%, West Germany 8%, France 5%); U.S. 12%. Export destinations: EEC 70% (U.K. 40%, West Germany 9%, France 7%, The Netherlands 6%); U.S. 6%. Main exports: machinery 20%; chemicals 13%; textiles and clothing 8%; dairy products 8%; beef and veal 7%; livestock 5%. Tourism: visitors (1979) 1,676,000; gross receipts (1980) U.S. $612 million.

Transport and Communications. Roads (1978) 92,294 km. Motor vehicles in use (1980): passenger 734,400; commercial 65,100. Railways (1980): 1,987 km; traffic 1,032,000,000 passenger-km, freight (1981) 620 million net ton-km. Air traffic (1981): 2,270,000,000 passenger-km; freight 86.4 million net ton-km. Shipping (1981): merchant vessels 100 gross tons and over 156; gross tonnage 267,524. Telephones (Dec. 1980) 642,000. Radio receivers (Dec. 1979) 1,250,000. Television licenses (Dec. 1980) 667,300.

Agriculture. Production (in 000; metric tons; 1981): barley c. 1,425; wheat c. 250; oats c. 96; potatoes c. 1,100; sugar, raw value c. 196; cabbages c. 172; cow's milk c. 4,770; butter c. 107; cheese c. 53; beef and veal c. 410; pork c. 120; fish catch (1980) 149. Livestock (in 000; June 1981): cattle 6,696; sheep 3,363; pigs 1,082; horses c. 77; chickens 8,102.

Industry. Production (in 000; metric tons; 1981): coal 69; cement (1980) 1,812; petroleum products c. 2,040; electricity (kw-hr) 10,910,000; manufactured gas (cu m) c. 610,000; wool fabrics (sq m; 1979) 3,300; rayon, etc., fabrics (sq m; 1979) 67,500; fertilizers (nutrient content; 1980–81) nitrogenous c. 190, phosphate c. 44.

particularly harsh budget in January in an effort to reduce the massive borrowings abroad. As a result of the vote on this budget, the government of Prime Minister Garret FitzGerald was defeated, and a general election, the second within nine months, was called for February 18. In the balloting, neither of the two main parties, Fine Gael and Fianna Fail, gained a majority in the Dail (parliament).

Until the Dail reconvened on March 9, there was uncertainty about who would form a government. In the event, the 81 Fianna Fail deputies, supported by 3 left-wing Sinn Fein Workers' Party deputies and 2 independents, elected Charles J. Haughey as *taoiseach* (prime minister). The opposition parties, Fine Gael and Labour, held 63 seats and 15 seats, respectively, and were consistently supported by one independent.

The apparent stability of these figures was undermined by several factors. An attempt by Prime Minister Haughey to strengthen his position by provoking a by-election in Dublin West in May rebounded when the seat was retained by Fine Gael. The death of a Fianna Fail deputy further weakened the government during crucial debates on finance measures. A July by-election restored the original strength of Fianna Fail, but the death of another deputy and the serious illness of yet another member of the government party placed the administration in an almost untenable position when the Dail resumed after the summer recess.

Haughey faced further embarrassment in August when a murder suspect was found in the apartment of the attorney general, Patrick Connolly. As details emerged, it became clear that Haughey, a close friend of Connolly, had permitted the attorney general to leave the country for a holiday in the U.S. the day after the suspect was arrested. This decision was widely condemned as a grave error of judgment on Haughey's part. Recalled to Dublin, Connolly returned the day after leaving, and the following day he resigned.

In spite of the unstable situation, the government adopted stringent measures to deal with the economy. Nevertheless, the current budget deficit soared to more than I£1,000 million, and unemployment rose to a record 160,000. There was some reduction in inflation from 20 to 14%, but it was still the second highest among the country's main trading partners. A national economic plan based on optimistic forecasts about world recovery, published in the autumn, was widely regarded as an election document rather than a government program. The popularity of the Haughey administration sank to an all-time low.

This grave economic situation was seriously aggravated by discord within the Fianna Fail party. A motion of no confidence in Haughey's leadership was moved in October, and in an open roll-call vote an unprecedented 22 deputies supported it. Two Cabinet ministers—Martin O'Donoghue, minister of education, and Desmond O'Malley, minister of trade, commerce, and tourism—resigned, and the open wrangle did major damage to the credibility of the administration. Finally, a motion of no confidence moved on November 4 was passed, resulting in the downfall of

Haughey's government. Elections were called for November 24. The three-week campaign resulted in no party gaining an overall majority. After discussions between the Labour Party and Fine Gael, which together commanded 86 seats in a 166-seat Dail, a coalition was formed under FitzGerald's leadership which promised the possibility of stable government for a full term. Alan Dukes was the new finance minister while John Bruton, who had held the post in FitzGerald's previous Cabinet, became minister for industry and energy.

Ironically, much of the year's political wrangling took place against a background of centenary celebrations for Eamon de Valera (1882–1975), founder of Fianna Fail and Ireland's greatest 20th-century statesman.

Ireland's relations with the U.K. deteriorated considerably during the year. Ireland withdrew from the economic sanctions imposed by the European Communities against Argentina during the Falklands hostilities, thus estranging U.K. Prime Minister Margaret Thatcher's government. The rift was widened in the autumn when Haughey withheld approval from the October 20 elections to set up a consultative assembly in Northern Ireland. Haughey claimed that this initiative toward devolution had been carried out by the U.K. government without consulting the republic. He therefore interpreted the move as a termination of the joint Anglo-Irish process aimed at resolving the Northern Ireland impasse.

Abortion continued to be a widely debated issue. This was the result of efforts by a pro-life group to have a referendum on the proposal that the country's antiabortion laws be incorporated into the constitution. Although abortion was already illegal (it was estimated that 7,000 Irishwomen annually traveled to the U.K. to attend abortion clinics), the pro-life group feared that a test case might be taken to the Supreme Court and that abortion might be made legal as a result. The Irish Council of Churches came out strongly against the sectarian aspect of the proposed referendum, and opposition to it was growing. However, political leaders had agreed to the referendum without considering the implications, and it seemed likely that they might be faced with a dilemma as the issue gained momentum.

(MAVIS ARNOLD)

See also United Kingdom.

Israel

A republic of the Middle East, Israel is bounded by Lebanon, Syria, Jordan, Egypt, and the Mediterranean Sea. Area (not including territory occupied in the June 1967 war): 20,700 sq km (7,992 sq mi). Pop. (1982 est.): 4,032,500. Cap. and largest city: Jerusalem (pop., 1982 est., 415,000). Language: Hebrew and Arabic. Religion: predominantly Jewish (1979 est., 84%) with Muslim, Christian, and other minorities. President in 1982, Yitzhak Navon; prime minister, Menachem Begin.

For the first four months of 1982, Israel's attention was focused on one date, April 25, when Israel was to complete its withdrawal from the Sinai

Israel

ISRAEL

Education. (1980–81) Primary, pupils 574,741, teachers 29,940; secondary, pupils 181,094, teachers 14,434; vocational, pupils 82,173, teachers 8,596; higher, students 91,180, teaching staff (1974–75) 13.981.

Finance. Monetary unit: shekel, with (Sept. 20, 1982) a free rate of 29.10 shekels to U.S. $1 (49.70 shekels = £1 sterling). Gold and other reserves (June 1982) U.S. $3,592,000,000. Budget (1980–81 actual): revenue 57,139,000,000 shekels; expenditure 81,229,000,000 shekels. Gross national product (1980) 101,604,000,000 shekels. Money supply (Feb. 1982) 15,976,000,000 shekels. Cost of living (1975 = 100; May 1982) 4,550.

Foreign Trade. (1981) Imports 91,079,000,000 shekels (excluding military goods); exports 64,745,000,000 shekels. Import sources: U.S. 20%; West Germany 11%; U.K. 8%; Switzerland 6%; Italy 5%. Export destinations: U.S. 22%; U.K. 8%; West Germany 7%; France 6%. Main exports: diamonds 25%; chemicals 15%; machinery 12%; fruit and vegetables 10%; metal manufactures 7%; aircraft 6%. Tourism (1980): visitors 1,065,800; gross receipts U.S. $866 million.

Transport and Communications. Roads (1979) 12,160 km. Motor vehicles in use (1980): passenger 409,900; commercial 87,600. Railways (1980): 830 km; traffic 264 million passenger-km, freight 828 million net ton-km. Air traffic (1981): 4,815,000,000 passenger-km; freight 302.6 million net ton-km. Shipping (1981): merchant vessels 100 gross tons and over 62; gross tonnage 580,996. Telephones (Dec. 1980) 1,230,000. Radio receivers (Dec. 1979) 802,000. Television licenses (Dec. 1979) 530,000.

Agriculture. Production (in 000; metric tons; 1981): wheat 215; potatoes 195; watermelons c. 32; tomatoes c. 268; onions 36; oranges c. 920; grapefruit c. 536; grapes 84; apples c. 107; olives 17; bananas 64; cotton, lint 92; cheese c. 57; poultry meat c. 195; fish catch (1980) 26. Livestock (in 000; 1981): cattle 265; sheep c. 270; goats c. 119; pigs c. 99; camels c. 11; chickens c. 24,645.

Industry. Production (in 000; metric tons; 1981): cement 2,298; crude oil 16; natural gas (cu m) 380,000; phosphate rock (1980) 2,610; petroleum products (1979) c. 6,970; sulfuric acid 255; fertilizers (nutrient content; 1980–81) nitrogenous 77, phosphate 35, potash 787; paper (1979) 117; electricity (kw-hr; 1980) 12,528,000.

Peninsula as agreed under the Camp David accords. While it waited for this military process to be completed, Egypt, in its relations with Israel, had been correct and friendly if not fulsome. Pres. Hosni Mubarak of Egypt had assured the Israeli government that there would be no change, and that Egypt would stand by its peace treaty with Israel. Nevertheless, in Israeli eyes, the move was the one big gamble in the Camp David agreement. There was no lack of voices abroad suggesting that, once Israel had withdrawn, Egypt would proceed to mend its fences with the rest of the Arab world.

In the event, the military withdrawal from Sinai presented the least difficulty, despite the costly dismantling of the two largest and most sophisticated military airfields in the Middle East and other sensitive Israel Defense Forces (IDF) installations. Far more serious for the government of Prime Minister Menachem Begin was the opposition of the civilian settlers—religious and nationalist—who refused to abandon and dismantle their homes. They had built up a flourishing community—in places literally making the desert bloom—and they resented the government's agreeing to Egypt's demand that no Israeli be permitted to remain in Sinai once it was returned to Egyptian sovereignty. The Begin government called in troops that had been specially selected for the difficult and unpopular task of forcing the settlers to leave. Harrowing scenes were witnessed on Israeli

Ireland, Northern:
see United Kingdom

Iron and Steel Industry:
see Industrial Review

Islam:
see Religion

Antiwar Israelis held a massive demonstration to protest Israel's invasion of Lebanon against Palestinian guerrillas. The demonstrators carried signs asking for "Peace Now" and chanted: "No more war."

Israel's Defense Minister Ariel Sharon (centre foreground) testified before a commission of inquiry in Jerusalem investigating the circumstances surrounding the Beirut massacre of September 16–18.

television as the settlers were moved out and their homes and plantations were bulldozed.

A small multinational peacekeeping force supervised the demilitarization of the Sinai region, with only nominal Egyptian forces on the Sinai banks of the Suez Canal. Egypt belied the many Western and Arab forecasters who had predicted the abandonment of the Camp David undertakings once Egypt regained possession of Sinai. President Mubarak and his government maintained their strict adherence to the treaty with Israel, and neither then nor later in the year, when other crises intervened, did Egypt take any action that might undermine the peace with Israel.

Possibly the most important consequence of the withdrawal went largely unnoticed, even in Israel. In a remarkable interview on Israeli television on April 27, Israel's chief of staff, Lieut. Gen. Raphael Eitan, spoke frankly about the new character of the IDF in the post-Sinai era. He emphasized that Israel's armed forces needed virtually no more quantitative growth. Their efforts would be concentrated on improving the quality of their equipment and the training of their troops.

But even while attention was centred on Sinai, there were ominous rumblings on Israel's northern border with Lebanon and Syria. The Palestine Liberation Organization (PLO) in Lebanon had not been quiescent during Israel's preoccupation with the south. Both Israeli and U.S. intelligence sought to establish an accurate profile of the PLO presence and strength in southern Lebanon. The Israelis concluded that a formidable PLO arms buildup was under way and that this presented a real threat to Israel's security. The U.S. did not agree. However, when U.S. Secretary of State Alexander Haig, Jr., appeared before the U.S. House Foreign Affairs Committee on March 2, he appeared to share the Israeli rather than the U.S. assessment. This discussion about the status of the PLO was refueled by media reports and claims by PLO leadership that Israel was about to launch a major attack on the PLO in Lebanon.

Meanwhile, Israel was receiving decisive support from the U.S. in blocking punitive proposals in the UN directed at Israel because of the application in December 1981 of Israeli law to the Golan Heights, occupied by Israel in 1967. The UN described the move as tantamount to annexation. There was clear recognition in Israel that U.S. support was all that stood between Israel and much greater condemnation by the UN, including the possible suspension of Israel's membership as proposed by Syria on January 29.

On January 19 Prime Minister Begin assured U.S. Pres. Ronald Reagan that Israel would not attack Lebanon without unquestionable provocation from either the Palestinian or the Syrian forces there. Thereafter the Israeli government repeatedly assured President Reagan that no action against Lebanon had been ordered, especially after terrorist attacks inside Israel and attacks on Jewish or Israeli targets elsewhere.

In March a third element was added to Israel's preoccupations in the form of widespread unrest among elements of the Arab population of the West Bank, stemming from the dismissal by the Israeli authorities of elected Palestinian councils and mayors in several West Bank districts. A number of people died when Palestinian demonstrators clashed with Israeli troops. Menachem Milson, civil administrator of the West Bank, accused some Arab mayors of being PLO agents and questioned the fairness of the elections that had brought them to power in 1976. Further Arab protests in the Gaza Strip and Jerusalem followed the shooting of two Muslims by a deranged Jewish immigrant in Jerusalem on April 11.

Despite the repeated limited assurances given to the U.S., and also to France's Pres. François Mitterrand during his state visit to Israel on March 3–5, it was evident in Jerusalem that an Israeli strike against the PLO would not be delayed much longer. Negotiations between the Israeli authorities and the leaders of Lebanon's Maronite Christian community—especially with the commanders of its military forces, led by Bashir Gemayel (see OBITUARIES)—had been under way for years rather than months. The Lebanese Christian leaders were becoming impatient for action against the PLO. According to the information relayed to the Israelis by Gemayel and his associates, the PLO was preparing to block Gemayel's intended candidacy in the Lebanese presidential election due in September. But the PLO could do this effectively only if it first neutralized Israeli assistance to the Maronites. In order to do this, PLO forces began to deploy guns and rockets directed at northern Israel. Convinced by Gemayel's arguments, the Israelis agreed that the operation against the PLO, if it was to be of lasting effect, would have to aim at Beirut and the PLO heartland position.

On June 3 Israel's ambassador to the U.K., Shlomo Argov, was shot and gravely wounded in London. Two days later Israeli jets bombed PLO targets in Beirut. By the early hours of June 6, the operation against Lebanon was under way: Tyre was occupied on June 7; Sidon on June 8; Damur on June 9. The encirclement of Beirut was complete by June 14. At this point the Israeli government came under heavy pressure from the U.S. not to let its troops enter Beirut. Prime Minister Begin and a majority of Cabinet ministers agreed, and Defense Minister Ariel Sharon (see BIOGRAPHIES) had to accept the majority opinion. The advance was halted and replaced by indirect negotiations with the PLO through the U.S. special envoy to the Middle East, Philip Habib (see BIOGRAPHIES), and the Lebanese government. These proceeded inconclusively while the military situation remained suspended.

By July 4 Habib informed the Israeli negotiators that the PLO was ready to sign an undertaking to evacuate Beirut. This was followed by a long process of equivocation and delay while the PLO leaders sought political reassurances from the U.S. In the event, it was only after massive Israeli bombardments of West Beirut, which resumed toward the end of July and reached their fiercest pitch on August 12, that the PLO accepted the evacuation terms.

The PLO evacuation on August 21, supervised by a multinational force of U.S., French, and Italian troops, was followed by the election of Bashir Gemayel as president of Lebanon. On September 14, however, Gemayel was assassinated, and Israeli plans were hastily revised. Reversing previous policies and undertakings, Defense Minister Sharon ordered the IDF into West Beirut in order, he claimed, to make certain that there would be no large-scale massacre of Palestinians and Muslims in the wake of Gemayel's death. Nevertheless, Lebanese Christian forces entered the Sabra and Shatila refugee camps in West Beirut on September 16, and hundreds of Palestinian men, women, and children were massacred. Israel received widespread condemnation for its alleged complicity in the tragedy. Yielding to internal and external pressure, the Cabinet finally voted on September 28 to set up a state commission inquiry under Chief Justice Yitzhak Kahan to investigate Israel's possible involvement. The inquiry was still under way at year's end.

While virtually all the Israeli media were hostile to the government's position and particularly toward Sharon, the government's popularity among the voters remained high. It far surpassed that of the opposition Labour Alignment parties who, in varying degrees, had criticized the inception and conduct of the war in Lebanon.

The validity of the government's justification for launching the attack on the PLO would depend on the extent to which it could uphold its indictment of the PLO as a "form of gangster state within the state of Lebanon." The display of equipment captured in southern Lebanon lent credence to the claim that the PLO was preparing a major assault on northern Israel. The IDF took intact some 500 pieces of artillery from PLO positions in southern Lebanon. On the other hand, the IDF was singularly unwilling to produce its estimates of civilian casualties. President Reagan had hoped that the evacuation of all foreign troops from Lebanon could be completed by year's end, but it was not until the end of December that Israeli and Lebanese delegations, with a U.S. delegation headed by special envoy Morris Draper in attendance, began talks. The initial meetings, held at Khaldah in Lebanon and Qiryat Shemona in Israel, produced no substantive results.

Other events during the year were no less traumatic for Israelis. They included the dismantling of much of the Israel built by the founding fathers and dramatic changes in the economic basis of the state. A number of enterprises were returned to the private sector, not least among them the national airline, El Al, which went into liquidation after a long series of punishing labour conflicts. The Begin regime was replacing Labour stalwarts with its own people in the administrative and diplomatic fields. It also intensified the process of rewriting the history of the state to meet the ideological requirements of the Likud majority and appointed a state commission to reinvestigate the death of the best-known Labour leader of the 1930s, Chaim Arlosoroff.   (JON KIMCHE)

See also Middle Eastern Affairs.

Italy

Italy

A republic of southern Europe, Italy occupies the Apennine Peninsula, Sicily, Sardinia, and a number of smaller islands. On the north it borders France, Switzerland, Austria, and Yugoslavia. Area: 301,263 sq km (116,318 sq mi). Pop. (1982 est.): 56,223,700. Cap. and largest city: Rome (pop., 1981 prelim., 2,830,600). Language: Italian. Religion: predominantly Roman Catholic. President in 1982, Alessandro Pertini; premiers, Giovanni Spadolini and, from November 30, Amintore Fanfani.

As the Italian authorities battled to bring political terrorism under control, with considerably more success during 1982 than had been the case in recent years, there was a significant increase in Mafia (organized) crime in Sicily and in the Naples area. Two coalition governments fell, in August and in November, a sign of continuing political instability and a worsening economic crisis. The Italian lira declined 20% against the U.S. dollar. Details came to light of an alleged international plot behind the attempted assassination of Pope John Paul II in St. Peter's Square in Rome in May 1981. The official allegations led to a freezing of diplomatic relations with Bulgaria, and one Bul-

garian citizen was arrested by Rome police in connection with the plot.

Domestic Affairs. The release on Jan. 28, 1982, in Padua by a special police commando unit of Brig. Gen. James Dozier (*see* BIOGRAPHIES), a senior U.S. NATO officer taken hostage by Red Brigades terrorists from his Verona home in December 1981, marked a turning point in the Italian authorities' fight against terrorist crime. Dozier's five captors, including two women, were arrested inside the apartment where they had held Dozier prisoner. They were sentenced to long terms in prison.

Information gathered by police from the Padua operation and from captured terrorists who decided to turn state's evidence in exchange for promises of leniency in sentencing led to the arrest and prosecution of hundreds of terrorist suspects during the year. Five police officers were arrested in June on charges of having tortured terrorist suspects. They were later released after the case created a furor among Italy's police forces.

The most important and longest terrorist trial ever held in Italy began in Rome on April 14, when 63 alleged members of the Red Brigades appeared in a heavily guarded courtroom set up in a former gymnasium to face charges of kidnapping and murdering former premier Aldo Moro in 1978. The accused were also charged with a total of 16 murders and 11 attempted murders during a four-year period from 1976. Evidence was given in the judge's chamber in September by Giulio Andreotti, premier at the time of the Moro kidnapping, that the government had decided not to negotiate with the kidnappers. He denied rumours of secret negotiations. A verdict was expected in the spring of 1983.

Another terrorist trial, of members of the Front

A bullet-riddled car, over 30 people injured, and one child dead were the results of an attack on the main synagogue of Rome on October 9.

FABIAN—SYGMA

Education. (1981–82) Primary, pupils 4,335,911, teachers 285,908; secondary, pupils 3,482,521, teachers 276,987; vocational, pupils 1,575,791, teachers 135,614; teacher training, students 241,150, teachers 13,389; higher, students 719,449, teaching staff 48,118.

Finance. Monetary unit: lira, with (Sept. 20, 1982) a free rate of 1,406 lire to U.S. $1 (2,410 lire = £1 sterling). Gold and other reserves (June 1982) U.S $16,873,000,000. Budget (1981 actual): revenue 110,290,000,000,000 lire; expenditure 154,352,-000,000,000 lire. Gross national product (1981) 395,682,000,000,000 lire. Money supply (Dec. 1981) 188,085,000,000,000 lire. Cost of living (1975 = 100; June 1982) 287.8.

Foreign Trade. (1981) Imports 103,676,-000,000,000 lire; exports 86,071,000,000,000 lire. Import sources: EEC 41% (West Germany 16%, France 12%); Saudi Arabia 9%; U.S. 7%. Export destinations: EEC 43% (West Germany 16%, France 14%, U.K. 6%); U.S. 7%; Libya 6%. Main exports: machinery 23%; motor vehicles 7%; chemicals 7%; petro-

leum products 6%; food 6%; clothing 6%; iron and steel 5%; textile yarns and fabrics 5%; metal manufactures 5%. Tourism: visitors (1979) 21,954,000; gross receipts (1980) U.S. $8,914,000,000.

Transport and Communications. Roads (1980) 293,799 km (including 5,901 km expressways). Motor vehicles in use (1980): passenger c. 17.6 million; commercial c. 1.3 million. Railways: (1979) 19,855 km; traffic (1981) 39,480,000,000 passenger-km, freight 16,630,000,000 net ton-km. Air traffic (1980): 14,096,000,000 passenger-km; freight 542.1 million net ton-km. Shipping (1981): merchant vessels 100 gross tons and over 1,677; gross tonnage 10,641,242. Telephones (Jan. 1980) 18,085,000. Radio receivers (Dec. 1980) 13,781,000. Television licenses (Dec. 1980) 13,361,000.

Agriculture. Production (in 000; metric tons; 1981): wheat 8,921; corn 7,250; barley 993; oats 429; rice 931; potatoes 2,863; sugar, raw value c. 2,170; cabbages 523; cauliflowers 508; onions 530; tomatoes 4,457; grapes 12,400; wine 7,650; olives 2,800; oranges 1,600; mandarin oranges and tangerines 340;

lemons 750; apples 1,750; pears 1,160; peaches 1,550; tobacco 123; cheese c. 600; beef and veal 895; pork 1,060; fish catch (1980) 445. Livestock (in 000; Dec. 1980): cattle 8,734; sheep 9,277; pigs 8,928; goats 1,009; poultry c. 110,000.

Industry. Index of production (1975 = 100; 1981) 127. Unemployment (1981) 8.4%. Fuel and power (in 000; metric tons; 1981): lignite 1,958; crude oil 1,466 natural gas (cu m) 13,950,000; manufactured gas (cu m) 3,560,000; electricity (kw-hr; 1980) 186,305,000. Production (in 000; metric tons; 1981): iron ore (44% metal content) 121; pig iron 12,477; crude steel 24,773; aluminum 274; zinc 182; cement 42,094; cotton yarn 160; man-made fibres c. 540; fertilizers (nutrient content; 1980–81) nitrogenous 1,388, phosphate 581, potash 95; sulfuric acid 2,412; plastics and resins 2,159; petroleum products c. 83,500; passenger cars (units) 1,256; commercial vehicles (units) 175. Merchant vessels launched (100 gross tons and over; 1981) 236,000 gross tons. New dwelling units completed (1979) 136,700.

Line Urban Guerrilla Organization, ended in Bergamo in August after eight months of hearings. The jury took a record 16 days to reach its verdict. Sentences totaling more than 450 years in prison were handed down to 87 of the accused.

Middle East violence spilled over into Italy in two incidents in Rome. In June Kamal Hussein, second in command of the Palestine Liberation Organization's office in Italy, was murdered by a bomb placed under his car. In October unidentified gunmen opened fire on a group of worshipers coming out of Rome's main synagogue, killing a two-year-old boy and injuring 35 Jews in Italy's worst anti-Semitic incident in years.

Italy's most serious single act of terrorism in 1982 was, however, carried out not for political ends but as a warning by the Sicilian Mafia. Gen. Carlo Alberto Dalla Chiesa and his wife were assassinated in Palermo, Sicily, on September 3. General Dalla Chiesa, the antiterrorist chief credited with a major role in the authorities' previous battles against the Red Brigades, had been sent to Sicily in May as the civilian prefect of Palermo with a mandate to challenge and beat the power of the Mafia, which was based on the lucrative heroin trade with the U.S. In attacking the Mafia bosses he had decided to concentrate on fiscal weapons, investigating tax and currency offenses committed in the channeling of millions of dollars of illegal profits back into Italy.

The Rome government responded to the assassination by pushing through Parliament a new anti-Mafia law that gave the police wider powers to tackle Mafia crime. Pope John Paul II visited Palermo in November to add his voice to the general denunciation of the Mafia and to confirm the decision of his bishops in Sicily to excommunicate those committing Mafia crimes of violence. But at the year's end the toll of dead in Palermo's gang war waged by local Mafia clans battling for the profits of the heroin trade had risen to more than 150, and the Italian state's conflict with the Mafia appeared far from concluded. The biggest Mafia trial in many years got under way in Palermo in November with more than 100 suspects charged with heroin smuggling; observers from the U.S. Drug

Enforcement Agency were present in court for the first time at a Mafia trial.

The arrest of a Bulgarian airline official, Sergey Antonov, in Rome on November 25 was the first official confirmation of the Italian government's allegations that there had been an international plot hatched in Eastern Europe to kill Pope John Paul II in May 1981. An Italian investigating magistrate, Ilario Martella, acting mainly on evidence given from the jail cell of Mehmet Ali Agca, the Turkish terrorist who actually shot the pope and was sentenced to life imprisonment for his crime, also accused two Bulgarian diplomats formerly accredited to Rome of complicity in the shooting. In Parliament Defense Minister Lelio Lagorio described the shooting of the pope as "an act of war in time of peace" and implicitly pointed an accusing finger at the Soviet Union.

Bekir Celenk, a Turkish businessman living in Sofia, Bulg., was accused by Italian police of complicity in what was described as the biggest arms- and drug-smuggling ring ever discovered in Italy. According to Italian newspaper reports Agca claimed that Celenk offered him over $1 million to kill the pope. But the prospects of the Italian judiciary's finding out the truth about a Bulgarian connection with the plot to kill the pope appeared dim, notwithstanding an offer by Bulgaria to allow the Italian investigating magistrate to visit Sofia to question Celenk.

In May Italy's ruling Christian Democrat Party elected a new party secretary, Ciriaco De Mita. The Christian Democrats, despite a series of government crises during the year, showed no signs of loosening their hold on power. They regained the premiership after a hiatus of almost 18 months when in November the veteran Christian Democrat politician Amintore Fanfani, 74, took over from Giovanni Spadolini, leader of the small Republican Party, who had headed the two previous coalitions. Spadolini had failed to settle constant squabbling between his two main coalition partners, the Christian Democrats and the Socialists, over how to distribute the ever growing burden of public expenditure among taxpayers. The Republicans refused to join Fanfani's coalition.

Italian Literature:
see Literature

Ivory Coast

It was the hottest June in 36 years, with temperatures rising to over 45° C (113° F) in Sicily. More than a dozen people died from the heat, and 70% of Italy's grain crop was lost. There were two natural disasters, neither of which led to loss of life. In Umbria in October a series of earth tremors shook a large area around Perugia, making over one thousand families homeless. Damage was reported to the historic basilica of San Francesco in Assisi. In December a massive landslide cut road and rail communications and destroyed hundreds of homes in the Adriatic port city of Ancona. Geologists said that it was probably a seismologic movement and began an investigation into the phenomenon.

Foreign Affairs. Italy and the Vatican exchanged diplomatic notes over the involvement of the Vatican bank, the Institute for Religious Works, in a major Italian banking scandal. The Banco Ambrosiano of Milan, formerly Italy's biggest private banking group, in which the Vatican bank was a shareholder, went into forced liquidation after the death in London in mysterious circumstances of its chairman, Roberto Calvi. A joint commission was set up by Italy and the Vatican to sort out the losses involved in a series of complex financial deals concluded between Calvi and Archbishop Paul C. Marcinkus (*see* BIOGRAPHIES), president of the Vatican bank.

The Italian government rejected U.S. Pres. Ronald Reagan's ban on U.S. technology for turbines manufactured in Italy for the Siberian gas pipeline, due to bring Soviet natural gas to Western Europe by the mid-1980s. The government signed a long-term agreement with Algeria for the supply of natural gas through a newly completed undersea pipeline between North Africa and Sicily. There was criticism, however, of the excessive cost to the Italian taxpayer of future supplies of gas under the Algerian agreement.

Vadim Zagladin, a top Soviet Communist Party official in charge of relations with foreign Communist parties, spent a week in Italy in October, during which time he had talks with Italian Communist leaders. Relations between the Soviet and Italian parties had been deteriorating for some time. Earlier in the year Italian Communist Party Secretary Enrico Berlinguer had described the Soviet political system as bankrupt. An internal split developed over the extent to which the Soviet party should still be regarded as a model for the future.

The Economy. In June Italy's employers' federation, Confindustria, announced that it was pulling out of a wage-indexing agreement because of its inflationary effect. Protracted negotiations between labour unions and employers to find a substitute basis for wage indexing failed to produce any agreement. The economy stagnated, while inflation stood at 16% at year's end, one of the highest rates in Western Europe.

A $1 billion joint venture between the Italian state oil company, ENI, and Occidental Petroleum Corp. of the U.S. aimed at helping Italy's ailing chemical industry was abandoned shortly after it came into force when the U.S. parent company objected to plans to take over an unprofitable fac-

tory. A modest offshore oil find took place off the southern coast of Sicily, but Italy's future energy prospects were gloomy, with slow progress recorded in a nuclear-energy program and a heavy trade deficit incurred because of oil imports.

(DAVID DOUGLAS WILLEY)

Ivory Coast

A republic on the Gulf of Guinea, the Ivory Coast is bounded by Liberia, Guinea, Mali, Upper Volta, and Ghana. Area: 322,463 sq km (124,504 sq mi). Pop. (1982 est.): 8,937,600, including (1978 est.) Bete 20%; Senufo 14.4%; Baule 12%; Anyi 10.5%; Malinke 7%; other 36.1%. Cap. and largest city: Abidjan (metro pop., 1981 est., 1,686,100). Language: French (official), Akan, Mossi, Dyola, Malinke, and other local dialects. Religion (1980 est.): animist 44%; Christian 32%; Muslim 24%. President in 1982, Félix Houphouët-Boigny.

A series of demonstrations by students of the University of Abidjan in February 1982 resulted in the arrest of some 100 students and the closing of the university from February 10 until March 4. The demonstrations were rooted in dissatisfaction with the consequences of the economic downturn, caused by the slump in world coffee and cocoa prices, and in the uneasy political situation arising from Pres. Félix Houphouët-Boigny's continued failure to nominate a successor.

In May the U.S. assistant secretary of state for African affairs, Chester A. Crocker, visited Abi-

---

IVORY COAST

Education. (1978–79) Primary, pupils 888,728, teachers 21,640; secondary, pupils 172,280, teachers 4,026; vocational, pupils 22,437, teachers (1974–75) 620; teacher training, teachers (1970–71) 87; higher, students (university only) 12,765, teaching staff 580.

Finance. Monetary unit: CFA franc, with (Sept. 20, 1982) a parity of CFA Fr 50 to the French franc (free rate of CFA Fr 353 = U.S. $1; CFA Fr 605 = £1 sterling). Gold and other reserves (May 1982) U.S. $7 million. Budget (1980 actual): revenue CFA Fr 495 billion; expenditure CFA Fr 410 billion. Money supply (March 1982) CFA Fr 472,250,000,000. Cost of living (Abidjan; 1975 = 100; Feb. 1982) 246.9.

Foreign Trade. (1981) Imports CFA Fr 653,320,-000,000; exports CFA Fr 689.8 billion. Import sources: France 31%; Venezuela 8%; U.S. 5%; Japan 5%. Export destinations: France 19%; The Netherlands 13%; U.S. 11%; Italy 8%; West Germany 7%. Main exports: cocoa and products 34%; coffee 18%; timber 14%; petroleum products 8%; cotton 5%.

Transport and Communications: Roads (1980) 45,350 km. Motor vehicles in use (1978): passenger 112,000; commercial (including buses) 67,200. Railways (1980): 655 km; traffic 1,210,000,000 passenger-km, freight 600 million net ton-km. Air traffic (including apportionment of traffic of Air Afrique; 1980): c. 215 million passenger-km; freight c. 18.6 million net ton-km. Telephones (Jan. 1980) 78,400. Radio receivers (Dec. 1978) 900,000. Television receivers (Dec. 1980) c. 300,000.

Agriculture. Production (in 000; metric tons; 1981): rice c. 550; corn c. 300; millet c. 48; yams c. 1,800; cassava c. 780; peanuts c. 54; bananas c. 160; plantains c. 830; pineapples c. 350; palm kernels c. 30; palm oil c. 190; coffee c. 350; cocoa c. 430; cotton, lint c. 55; rubber c. 23; fish catch (1980) 77; timber (cu m; 1980) c. 11,942. Livestock (in 000; 1981): cattle c. 720; sheep c. 1,250; goats c. 1,300; pigs c. 360; poultry c. 13,000.

Industry. Production (in 000; metric tons; 1979): petroleum products c. 1,570; cement 1,000; cotton yarn 3; diamonds (metric carats) 25; electricity (kw-hr; 1980) 1,800,000.

djan. Relations with France remained close. There were visits in March by French Minister for Cooperation Jean-Pierre Cot; in April by Defense Minister Charles Hernu, who announced increased military aid in addition to the permanent 500-strong French military contingent in Ivory Coast; in May by Pres. François Mitterrand; and in October by former president Valéry Giscard d'Estaing. Also in October, President Houphouët-Boigny attended the Franco-African summit in Kinshasa, Zaire.

Ivory Coast was among those members of the Organization of African Unity (OAU) that opposed the admission to membership of the self-proclaimed (Western) Saharan Arab Democratic Republic. Because of this stance, President Houphouët-Boigny absented himself from the August OAU summit at Tripoli, Libya.

(PHILIPPE DECRAENE)

Jamaica

A parliamentary state within the Commonwealth, Jamaica is an island in the Caribbean Sea about 145 km S of Cuba. Area: 10,991 sq km (4,244 sq mi). Pop. (1982 est.): 2,222,000, predominantly African and Afro-European but including European, Chinese, Afro-Chinese, East Indian, Afro-East Indian, and others. Cap. and largest city: Kingston (metro pop., 1980 est., 671,000). Language: English. Religion: Christian, with Anglicans and Baptists in the majority. Queen, Elizabeth II; governor-general in 1982, Florizel Glasspole; prime minister, Edward Seaga.

Though the Jamaican economy under Prime Minister Edward Seaga had shown positive growth during 1981, it was clear toward the end of 1982 that some of the government's forecasts had been too optimistic. Low world prices for bauxite, sugar, and bananas meant that the planned growth rate of 4% had to be scaled down.

There was some concern among government supporters about the introduction of a structural

---

JAMAICA

Education. (1978–79) Primary, pupils 381,293, teachers 11,247; secondary, pupils 240,664 teachers 6,583; vocational, pupils 6,663, teachers (1976–77) 340; higher, students 13,556, teaching staff 367.

Finance. Monetary unit: Jamaican dollar, with (Sept. 20, 1982) a par value of Jam$1.78 to U.S. $1 (free rate of Jam$3.05 = £1 sterling). Gold and other reserves (June 1982) U.S. $118 million. Budget (1979–80): revenue Jam$1,102,000,000; expenditure Jam$1,266,000,000.

Foreign Trade. (1981) Imports Jam$2,669,200,000; exports Jam$1,746,500,000. Import sources (1980): U.S. 32%; Venezuela 22%; Netherlands Antilles 14%; U.K. 7%; Canada 6%. Export destinations (1980): U.S. 37%; U.K. 20%; Norway 11%; U.S.S.R. 5%; Spain 5%; Ghana 5%. Main exports: alumina 60%; bauxite 18%; sugar 5%. Tourism (1980): visitors 395,300; gross receipts U.S. $242 million.

Agriculture. Production (in 000; metric tons; 1981): sugar, raw value c. 203; bananas c. 100; oranges c. 27; grapefruit c. 29; sweet potatoes c. 25; yams c. 130; cassava c. 26; corn c. 7; copra c. 7. Livestock (in 000; 1981): cattle c. 305; goats c. 390; pigs c. 260; poultry c. 4,300.

Industry. Production (in 000; metric tons; 1980): bauxite 12,052; alumina 2,478; cement 140; gypsum 95; petroleum products c. 1,040; electricity (kw-hr) 2,330,000.

---

adjustment program aimed at generating export industries and the government's decision to take over the Exxon petroleum refinery and a local port operation. The opposition People's National Party remained divided, though it became clear that former prime minister Michael Manley was determined to see the party chart a more moderate course.

The special relationship between Prime Minister Seaga and U.S. Pres. Ronald Reagan continued to develop; the president paid a brief visit to Jamaica in April. Jamaica was the main Caribbean beneficiary of the U.S. Caribbean Basin Initiative, receiving a $50 million share. In November the island was host to the Caribbean Community (Caricom) summit meeting.   (DAVID A. JESSOP)

Jamaica

Japan

A constitutional monarchy in the northwestern Pacific Ocean, Japan is an archipelago composed of four major islands (Hokkaido, Honshu, Kyushu, and Shikoku), the Ryukyus (including Okinawa), and minor adjacent islands. Area: 377,682 sq km (145,824 sq mi). Pop. (1982 est.): 118,460,000. Cap. and largest city: Tokyo (pop., 1982 est., 8,138,000). Language: Japanese. Religion (1930): primarily Shinto and Buddhist; Christian 3%. Emperor, Hirohito; prime ministers in 1982, Zenko Suzuki and, from November 26, Yasuhiro Nakasone.

Japan

Domestic Affairs. In November 1981 Prime Minister Zenko Suzuki had reshuffled his Cabinet with an eye on factional strength within the ruling Liberal-Democratic Party (LDP) and a view toward the next election for LDP president, scheduled for late fall of 1982. He named Susumu Nikaido to be secretary-general of the party. Nikaido had been nominal head of the powerful 105-member faction actually led by former prime minister Kakuei Tanaka. A veteran politician, Yoshio Sakarauchi, was selected as foreign minister, and Kiichi Miyazawa was retained as chief Cabinet secretary. Among established faction leaders, Yasuhiro Nakasone (see BIOGRAPHIES) remained director general of the Administrative Management Agency, charged with the sensitive issue of administrative reform, and Toshio Komoto was retained as head of the Economic Planning Agency (EPA). Suzuki also recognized so-called new leaders of the LDP: Michio Watanabe, who became finance minister, and Shintaro Abe, minister of international trade and industry.

On Jan. 18, 1982, the 96th regular session of the Diet (parliament) was reconvened in the presence of the emperor. In his policy speech, Prime Minister Suzuki promised to restructure the government in order to rehabilitate the national finances, burdened with a cumulative debt of 82 trillion yen. He vowed to work out prompt solutions to the frictions with other nations over external trade and predicted a steady defense buildup so that Japan could assume appropriate responsibilities as a major power. Again, on February 3, Suzuki declared that he would assume "political responsibility" if his fiscal program failed to achieve the goal of eliminating deficit bond issues by the end of fiscal year

Jai Alai: see Court Games

Members of the ruling Liberal-Democratic Party elected Yasuhiro Nakasone to succeed Zenko Suzuki as prime minister of Japan. Nakasone had previously held five cabinet posts over the past 23 years.

UPI

former transport minister, was also found guilty of "accepting bribes upon entreaties." LDP leaders freely admitted that, within the year, Tanaka would probably be found guilty in the case.

Meanwhile, the LDP maintained its solid majority in both houses of the Diet. Party strength in the (lower) House of Representatives as of July 1982 was as follows: LDP 287; Japan Socialist Party (JSP) 104; Clean Government Party (Komeito) 34; Democratic Socialist Party (DSP) 32; Japan Communist Party (JCP) 29; New Liberal Club (NLC) 10; Social Democratic Federation (Shaminren) 3; independents 7; vacancies 5 (total 511). In the (upper) House of Councillors the lineup was: LDP 136; JSP 47; Komeito 27; DSP 11; JCP 12; independents 16; vacancies 3 (total 252).

On October 12 Suzuki suddenly announced that he would not stand in the forthcoming party primary and, therefore, would also relinquish the prime ministership. Although LDP leaders tried desperately to settle the succession issue behind the scenes, four faction leaders announced their candidacies for the preliminary party primary held November 23. In the poll Nakasone received 560,000 (58%) of the nearly one million votes cast by eligible members of the LDP. His chief competitors, Komoto and Abe, withdrew, and Ichiro Nakagawa, also a member of the Suzuki Cabinet, was eliminated. On November 25 the LDP members of the Diet selected Nakasone to be president of the party, and a day later, on November 26, he was elected by the Diet to become Japan's 17th postwar prime minister.

The first test of the new LDP government was expected in upper house elections scheduled for 1983. On August 18 the Diet had adopted rules to alter election procedures for the House of Councillors under a proportional representation system in the national constituency (50 seats).

Final figures for the fiscal year April 1980–March 1981 showed Japan's gross national product (GNP) at 239,155,000,000,000 yen (nominal terms). In December 1981 the EPA estimated nominal GNP at 250,658,300,000,000 yen ($1.2 trillion) and the adjusted annual growth rate at 4–5% for fiscal 1981.

Late in December 1981 the Cabinet had approved a 1982 budget with expenditures of

1984. The press interpreted the statement as a de facto declaration that he intended to remain in office at least two more years. Nevertheless, according to a *Yomiuri* newspaper opinion poll taken February 20–21, support for the Suzuki administration had dropped by 6.2 points in the space of a month, to 31.7% of those polled. It was the lowest level since the regime was inaugurated in 1980.

Yet another factor affecting the fate of the Suzuki government—and, indeed, of the LDP majority leadership—was the long-awaited outcome of the Lockheed affair, which had first surfaced in February 1976. The scandal, which directly involved former prime minister Tanaka, had to do with procurement of aircraft for All Nippon Airways (ANA). On January 25 Tokuji Wakasa, board chairman of ANA, was given a suspended three-year prison term, and in June Tomisaburo Hashimoto,

---

JAPAN

Education. (1982) Primary, pupils 11,901,526, teachers 475,037; secondary, vocational, and teacher training, pupils 10,224,529, teachers 517,744; higher, students 2,238,831, teaching staff 128,039.

Finance. Monetary unit: yen, with (Sept. 20, 1982) a free rate of 264 yen to U.S. $1 (452 yen = £1 sterling). Gold and other reserves (June 1982) U.S. $26.4 billion. Budget (1981–82 est.) balanced at 46,788,000,000,000 yen. Gross national product (1981) 248,689,000,000,000 yen. Money supply (May 1982) 74,417,000,000,000 yen. Cost of living (1975 = 100; June 1982) 147.6.

Foreign Trade. (1981) Imports 31,464,-000,000,000 yen; exports 33,469,000,000,000 yen. Import sources: U.S. 18%; Saudi Arabia 15%; Indonesia 9%; United Arab Emirates 6%; Australia 5%. Export destinations: U.S. 26%. Main exports: machinery 35%; motor vehicles 22%; iron and steel 11%; instruments 5%; ships 5%.

Transport and Communications. Roads (1980) 1,113,387 km (including 2,579 km expressways). Motor vehicles in use (1980): passenger 23,659,500; commercial 13,948,500. Railways: (1979) 27,493 km; traffic (1981) 316,200,000,000 passenger-km, freight (1980) 39,585,000,000 net ton-km. Air traffic (1980): c. 51,217,000,000 passenger-km; freight c. 2,002,000,000 net ton-km. Shipping (1981): merchant vessels 100 gross tons and over, 10,422; gross tonnage 40,835,681. Telephones (March 1980) 55,421,500. Radio receivers (Dec. 1979) 90 million. Television licenses (Dec. 1979) 28,439,000.

Agriculture. Production (in 000; metric tons; 1981): rice 12,824; wheat 612; barley c. 390; potatoes c. 3,250; sweet potatoes c. 1,317; sugar, raw value c. 770; onions c. 1,067; tomatoes c. 1,000; cabbages c. 3,667; cucumbers c. 1,030; aubergines (eggplants) c. 620; watermelons 999; apples 847; pears 522; oranges 395; mandarin oranges and tangerines 2,841; grapes 339; tea c. 103; tobacco 143; milk 6,620; eggs 1,999; pork 1,396; fish catch (1980) 10,410; timber (cu m; 1980) c. 34,034. Livestock (in 000; Feb. 1981): cattle 4,385; sheep 16; pigs 10,065; goats 62; chickens 286,284.

Industry. Index of production (1975 = 100; 1981) 147. Fuel and power (in 000; metric tons; 1981): coal 17,687; crude oil 392; natural gas (cu m) 2,390,000; manufactured gas (cu m) 8,740,000; electricity (kw-hr) 521,873,000. Production (in 000; metric tons; 1981): iron ore (54% metal content) 441; pig iron 81,686; crude steel 101,675; aluminum 1,616; copper 1,050; petroleum products c. 199,000; cement 84,827; cotton yarn 456; woven cotton fabrics (sq m) 2,067,000; man-made fibres 1,798; newsprint 2,575; sulfuric acid 6,572; caustic soda 2,865; plastics and resins 5,910; fertilizers (nutrient content; 1980–81) nitrogenous 1,202, phosphate 648; cameras (35 mm; units) 13,158; wrist and pocket watches (units) 103,389; electronic desk calculators (units) 52,435; radio receivers (units) 15,196; television receivers (units; 1979) 14,236; passenger cars (units) 6,978; commercial vehicles (units) 4,206. Merchant vessels launched (100 gross tons and over; 1981) 9,140,000 gross tons. New dwelling units started (1981) 1,359,000.

49,680,800,000,000 yen. Defense appropriations were increased by 7.8% (to a total representing 0.9% of GNP). It was the first time that such expenditures had outpaced the increase in general accounts. On July 9 the Cabinet approved a policy of reducing budgetary requests for fiscal 1983 by 5% across the board.

During the year the Japanese staggered under a series of blows dealt by man-made and natural disasters. On February 8, in the worst hotel fire since World War II, 32 guests were killed and 30 injured in a predawn blaze that swept through the Hotel New Japan in Tokyo. The next day a Japan Air Lines DC-8 crashed in shallow waters off Tokyo's Haneda Airport, killing 24 and injuring 150. On March 14 a violent earthquake (force 6 on the Japanese scale of 7) shook Hokkaido and northern Honshu, injuring 99 persons and causing extensive damage. In August in Nagasaki a public funeral service was held for 275 victims who died in the July 23–25 flood that wreaked havoc throughout Kyushu. On August 1 Typhoon No. 10 cut a swath of destruction across central Honshu, leaving 59 persons dead and 24 missing.

Foreign Affairs. During June Japan, represented abroad by Prime Minister Suzuki, played out the role of an advanced industrial power. At the eighth summit meeting of industrialized Western democracies, held at Versailles, France, June 4–6, Suzuki emphasized the importance of "assurance of employment through promotion of science and technology" in order to overcome world economic problems. Specific issues of Japan's merchandise trade balance were put off until the General Agreement on Tariffs and Trade (GATT) ministerial conference, to begin at the end of November. Japanese business leaders—specifically, Yoshihiro Inayama of Keidanren, Bumpei Otsuki of Nikkeiren, and Tadashi Sasaki of Keizai Doyukai—hailed the summit agreement on the need for free trade and for technological cooperation.

After the summit, on June 9, Suzuki flew to New York to attend the UN special session on disarmament. As the first speaker, he spelled out a three-point proposal calling for disarmament, the transfer of resources to promote economic development, and reinforcement of UN peacekeeping functions. From New York, Suzuki went on to South America, for official visits to Peru and Brazil.

At Versailles Suzuki found himself under considerable pressure because of trade surpluses with the U.S. and with the European Community (EC). Customs clearance statistics for 1981 revealed that Japan had chalked up its biggest ever surplus with the U.S., a total of $13.4 billion. With the EC, a record surplus of $10.3 billion was recorded. In late February and early March, delegations led by a former minister, Masumi Esaki, visited the U.S. and the EC nations to help ease the intensifying trade frictions. Esaki was chairman of a special LDP Committee on International Economics Measures.

With the U.S., Japan's closest ally, Tokyo faced a number of critical issues, including the trade surplus, the sanctions proposed against the Soviet Union for its actions in Poland, and the question of the level of Japan's defense effort. In March, in Washington, U.S. Secretary of State Alexander Haig, in talks with Foreign Minister Sakarauchi, openly criticized congressional moves toward protectionist legislation directed at Japan. The two failed, however, to agree on the U.S. request that Tokyo delay fulfillment of a contract between Komatsu, the nation's largest earth-moving-equipment firm, and the Soviet Union. On April 1 in Tokyo, U.S. Vice-Pres. George Bush urged Japan to support U.S. proposals to tighten all credit offerings from the U.S., Japan, and the EC nations to

Chinese Premier Zhao Ziyang (left) and Japan's Prime Minister Zenko Suzuki proposed a toast during a state dinner in May honouring Zhao. The Chinese leader was on a six-day visit to Tokyo celebrating the tenth anniversary of the normalization of relations between the two nations.

UPI

the U.S.S.R. On June 4 in Paris, however, Suzuki asked U.S. Pres. Ronald Reagan to exempt the Japan-Soviet Sakhalin oil-development project, agreed upon before sanctions were suggested.

In the area of trade, Washington was calling on Tokyo to abolish some 22 import quotas on fishery and agricultural products, specifically on beef and on citrus fruits. On April 16 in Tokyo, the president of a national federation of agricultural cooperatives, Shizuma Iwamochi, told about 8,000 demonstrating farmers that his organization would defend the nation's agriculture "to the death." Gov. Heidayu Nakagawa of Fukui, president of the governors' association, was applauded when he stated, "Liberalization for cheap American agricultural products may lead Japan to become an American colony."

Although Japan, responding to U.S. pressure, had built an increase in defense expenditures into its current budget, Washington was not satisfied. U.S. Defense Secretary Caspar Weinberger, visiting Tokyo in March, proposed that expansion of Japan's defense capability be designed to protect sea lanes up to 1,000 nautical miles from its coasts.

In what was called in Tokyo a "sting" operation, the FBI on June 22 arrested five employees of the Hitachi and Mitsubishi electronics firms in the San Francisco area on charges that they had paid $648,000 to an undercover agent to steal computer data from IBM. Warrants were also issued for 12 employees in Japan. By July 21 the men had been indicted by a federal grand jury in San Jose, Calif. Hitachi claimed that its employees had "bought" computer technology from "a consulting firm," while Mitsubishi flatly denied the FBI allegations. Meanwhile, on July 20 in San Francisco, a federal grand jury indicted Mitsui & Co. (U.S.A.) for allegedly conspiring to sell steel in the U.S. below market prices. Mitsui, claiming that the case involved a misunderstanding of import procedures, agreed to seek an out-of-court settlement.

Japanese-Soviet relations during the year were dominated by developments in Poland. In December 1981, Zdzislaw Rurarz, Poland's ambassador to Japan, was protected until he left Tokyo for the U.S., after Washington had granted him political asylum. He was the first ambassador in Japan ever to defect. On February 23 Japan joined the U.S., Britain, and West Germany in imposing limited sanctions on Poland's military regime and its Soviet supporters. The government announced that it would honour pledges for "humanitarian aid" to the Polish people. In April Timofei Guzhenko, a Soviet marine official, made a week-long visit to Tokyo as head of a delegation to a U.S.S.R.-Japan roundtable conference. Guzhenko did not enter on a diplomatic passport.

Japan's relations with its nearer neighbours were mixed. In July Foreign Minister Lee Bum-suk of South Korea, in consultation with Foreign Minister Sakarauchi in Tokyo, agreed to accept Japan's offer of $4 billion in aid to help Seoul's five-year plan (1982–86). At a joint ministerial meeting in Tokyo in December 1981, Japan pledged to provide $1.4 billion in aid to China in an attempt to revive China's stalled industrial projects.

Ties with both China and Korea were severely strained, however, by the so-called Japanese textbook issue. Late in July it was revealed that Japan's Education Ministry had approved alterations in schoolbooks so that, for example, the nation's aggression in China prior to 1945 was described as an "advance." Similarly, pre-World War II opposition to Japanese colonial rule in Korea was called a "riot" against authority. The Chinese reacted angrily, and in Seoul sentiment built steadily as the August 15 anniversary of Korea's national liberation from 35 years of Japanese rule approached. On August 4 Prime Minister Suzuki stated that there was no change in his government's policy, first articulated in the 1972 Sino-Japanese joint communiqué, that Japan "repents its faults in the past." On August 20 Tokyo offered reassurances to Seoul that the issue would be settled in good faith.

Chinese Premier Zhao Ziyang (Chao Tzu-yang) had visited Tokyo in May to commemorate a decade of normalized Sino-Japanese relations, and a return visit by Suzuki was scheduled. Despite expectations that the visit would be postponed, the prime minister arrived in Beijing (Peking) on September 26 and, in his first public move, promised to take "swift steps" to resolve the tensions arising from the disputed textbook problem. On August 26, Tokyo announced that Japan intended "to do its best to make textbook descriptions in question more appropriate." The scheduled revision of textbooks would be advanced one year and, meanwhile, corrections of approach would be made through the Education Ministry's "administrative guidance" system.　　(ARDATH W. BURKS)

Yasukichi Hatano, head of the computer division of Hitachi, explained to reporters that Hitachi had "bought" computer technology from members of "a consulting firm" who turned out to be FBI agents. Hitachi and Mitsubishi electronics firms were charged with stealing computer data from IBM.

JAPAN'S ECONOMIC SECRET

by Frank Gibney

The rest of the world's business leaders—not to mention the economists and the politicians—continue to be alternately impressed, puzzled, or angered by the extraordinary success of Japan's "economic miracle" and the alert, toughly competitive business society that made it. During the past two decades Japan's economy has weathered oil shortages, foreign export restrictions, and domestic recessions; and its statistics are business history. In 1960 Japan's $39.1 billion gross national product (GNP) was not quite 8% of that of the U.S. Japan's $1 trillion GNP in 1980 was almost 40% of the U.S. total. In per capita GNP Japan will probably pass the U.S. before 1990. Exports worth $12 billion in 1968 had become $140 billion by 1980.

Nowhere has the rate of productivity risen so fast or so steadily. If the 1960 level of Japanese productivity in manufacturing is set at 100, the 1980 level is more than 450. Japanese steel, Japanese cars, Japanese television sets, ships, cameras, and chemicals—and now Japan's semiconductor chips, computers, and overseas factories—have made consumers throughout the world satisfied and dependent. No other nation's private entrepreneurs have carried off such brilliant marketing strategies.

Although the Japanese over the past two years have experienced something of a recession in the domestic economy, their productivity and GNP figures continue to rise—if at a reduced rate—and the flood of high-quality exports continues to pose problems for home-grown industry in the U.S., Europe, and some of the other East Asian countries. Despite their economic successes the Japanese have not been good international politicians. Their attitude remains determinedly insular. Continuing trade restrictions on some imports into Japan—especially on such highly visible products as tobacco and citrus fruits—have brought angry threats of retaliation from U.S. producers. Suffering unemploy-

---

Frank Gibney is vice-chairman of the Board of Editors of Encyclopædia Britannica. This article is based on his recent book: Miracle by Design: The Real Reasons Behind Japan's Economic Success.

ment and the worst business depression of recent history, U.S. automakers and labour union officials alike are demanding protectionist legislation; and Congress is listening to them.

People-Centred Capitalism. There is some truth to their charges of "unfair" competition in certain areas. But instead of simply dismissing Japan's success as "unfair competition," it would be more useful to see how this success was achieved—and what lessons can be learned from it.

One can neither understand the nature of Japan's economic success nor learn from it unless it is seen in its social as well as economic context. Much of Japan's business society is strange to those in the West. Everyday words such as law, contract, board of directors, labour union, manager, and stockholder—even such basic terms as company and employee—hold different meanings for the Japanese than they do for those in the Western world. Whereas business society in the West is based on the Christian ethic of individuals, that in Japan grew from the Confucian ethic of relationships. The Japanese have different priorities—different views of wealth, of sufficiency, and of satisfaction. Yet the philosophy of their business as well as its techniques—indeed their modern version of free enterprise democracy—resembles that of the U.S. more than it does anyone else's, and owes much to it.

To begin with, the Japanese are for our time the original practitioners of supply-side economics. They accumulated capital and used it in the classic way—for plant modernization and technology development. They saved prodigiously to provide ever more investment funds. But then they took the standard idea of capital one step further. Western economists tended to think of capital in terms of money, plant, material, and technology. To this, however, the Japanese capitalist adds people. The most conspicuous characteristic of Japanese capitalism is its belief that long-term investment in people—which includes training them, partly educating them, and developing them within a company—is fully as important as long-term investment in plant.

Those in the West have worried about the individual worker's self-fulfillment or alienation. They have shaken their heads at "soulless" corporations that treat workers as virtually interchangeable parts—by definition separated from the management and ownership of their companies. The Japanese, partly from old tradition and partly from modern necessity, simply infused human values into the corporation. They made the company a village. And in so doing they have not only given the worker a sense of belonging, they have also given the company a constituency that speaks up for it: its own workers. The system of lifetime employment used by

Employees of Japan's Matsushita Electric Co. take a break for a wedding ceremony in the company's club.

Japan's major corporations, the seniority system, the companywide bonuses or "base-ups" founded on profits and paid out to blue-collar and white-collar workers alike—all add up to a unique kind of "people-centred" capitalism.

Once he has been put in charge of a corporation, the average U.S. businessman will want to make the major decisions himself and lead his people after him. By contrast, the Japanese leader's ideal is to encourage those under him to formulate decisions. Although there are "dynamic leader" types in Japan and "consensus" types in the U.S., the ideals of the two capitalisms differ. A Japanese economist contrasted them this way: "Our system is rather like an electric train, with each car having its own motor, whereas your system is more like a long train drawn by two or three strong locomotives, with no motors in the other cars. You tell your workers to follow. We like people to have their own motivation—and move together."

Japan's top executives continue to be distinguished also by their relatively low rates of compensation, at least compared with the galloping expansion of corporate salaries in the U.S. The gap between the president's salary and stock option package and the wages of the average worker is nowhere so vast in Japan as it is in the U.S. Prestige and power the Japanese president seeks. But money does not seem to be a primary motivation.

Role of the U.S. Yet despite their strong work ethic—and the advantages of a well-educated, homogeneous society—the Japanese could not have got where they are today without U.S. aid and example. In the first years after World War II the U.S. occupation first fed the Japanese and then supplied enough technical skill, money, and direction to start the wheels of Japan's industry slowly turning again.

And without the sweeping "rationalization" of Japanese business and industry under the 1949 Dodge Plan, the economy could not have gone ahead. The Korean War also provided Japan with an unexpected windfall, in the form of $3 billion worth of arms, military equipment, and supplies purchased there for the U.S. and UN war effort.

Through the 1950s and 1960s there was a rush to acquire U.S. technology. This the Japanese imported wholesale, through a variety of licensing arrangements used and adapted to great advantage. Although the Japanese have had since 1973 a favourable trade balance in technology licensing revenues, the opposite was once true. The Japanese drive to a greater productivity was inspired by the U.S. as part of the effort during the postwar occupation to make Japan more self-sufficient. The Japan Productivity Center, a pioneer in this work, was originally set up with U.S. government funds. In the 1960s, as postwar Japanese business came of age, a procession of pilgrims crossed the Pacific to worship at the shrines of U.S. management efficiency techniques, as taught by various U.S. business schools. These lessons were duly brought back to Japan, digested—and modified.

Besides these tangible contributions there has been the effect, less measurable but immense, of U.S. democracy, innovation, and optimism on the thinking of the Japanese. The attempted U.S. "democratization" of Japan served to ventilate the closed world of Japanese capitalism and semidemocratic practice. It imposed on the Japanese—some would say restored—a feeling for wider freedoms and broader horizons.

Nihachiro Hanamura, vice-chairman of the powerful Keidanren (Federation of Economic Organizations), has labeled this U.S. influence, along with Japan's political stability, one of the major factors underlying Japan's high-growth economy. He said: First, there was a thorough democratization by the occupation forces in the early postwar years of all old systems—political, economic, social, cultural, and educational. The breaking up of the zaibatsu—giant financial, industrial, and business groups—and agricultural land reform were at the core of the policy of economic democratization. As a result every Japanese stood at the same starting point, and an environment was provided in which everyone was rewarded according to his efforts. This generated in every Japanese a willingness to study and work hard, just as in the frontier days of the U.S.

One should not underrate the importance of this U.S. inspiration, however much it may have been modified. The so-called 21st-century capitalists of Japan owe much to the 20th-century capitalism of the United States.

Jordan

A constitutional monarchy in southwest Asia, Jordan is bounded by Syria, Iraq, Saudi Arabia, and Israel. Area (including about 5,440 sq km [2,100 sq mi] occupied by Israel in the June 1967 war): 94,946 sq km (36,659 sq mi). Pop. (excluding Israeli-occupied West Bank, 1982 est.): 2,415,700. Cap. and largest city: Amman (pop., 1979 prelim., 648,600). Language: Arabic. Religion (1980 est.): Muslim 93%; Christian 5%; atheist 0.4%; none 1.6%. King, Hussein I; prime minister in 1982, Mudar Badran.

Jordan was assured a central role in talks on a Middle East peace settlement when, on Sept. 1, 1982, U.S. Pres. Ronald Reagan revived what had come to be termed the "Jordanian option." This option ruled out the Palestinians' principal demand for total independence, substituting instead proposals for "self-government by the Palestinians of the West Bank and Gaza in association with Jordan." The proposal implicitly revived U.S. plans for the Middle East that originally had circulated in 1978 at the time of the Camp David agreement.

There was no immediate reaction from Jordan, but only days earlier, after greeting a contingent of Palestine Liberation Organization (PLO) guerrillas who had been evacuated from Lebanon, King Hussein reiterated his support for the efforts of the PLO to recover the West Bank and Gaza and declared that the PLO was not finished as a force in the Middle East. In mid-September Hussein described the U.S. peace plan as "a very constructive

Jordan

and a very positive move." Following two days of talks in mid-December, the Jordanian government and the PLO agreed that Jordan should have a "special and distinctive relationship" with any future Palestinian entity. During a visit to Washington later in the month, however, Hussein indicated that conditions were not yet ripe for Jordan to enter the negotiations on Palestinian autonomy.

Israel's outraged reaction to a visit by U.S. Secretary of Defense Caspar Weinberger to Jordan in February elicited a denial by President Reagan that his administration was planning to sell advanced military hardware to Jordan. Nevertheless, reports in the *New York Times* in September suggested that the U.S. was indeed prepared to sell Jordan a package that was thought to include mobile Hawk antiaircraft missiles, F-5 interceptors, and possibly F-16 fighter-bombers.

Jordan's support for Iraq in the latter's war against Iran continued. In January King Hussein announced that a contingent of Jordanian volunteers, to be named the "Yarmouk Brigade," was to be formed to fight alongside Iraqi forces. He called for an "arabization" of the war against Iran.

Another type of assistance granted to Iraq put considerable pressure on the southern Jordanian port of Aqaba, where in 1981 some 62% of incoming shipments were in transit and in the main destined for Iraq. Jordan offered to help in the building of a terminal for Iraq's proposed trans-Arabian oil pipeline, while, if Iraq's finances im-

U.S. Secretary of Defense Caspar Weinberger (left) toured an army base when he visited Jordan in February. King Hussein and Secretary Weinberger were reportedly negotiating the sale of antiaircraft missiles and fighter-bombers by the U.S. to Jordan.

DAVID HUME KENNERLY—GAMMA/LIAISON

JORDAN

Education. (1979–80) Primary, pupils 443,411, teachers 13,898; secondary, pupils 238,763, teachers 11 267; vocational, pupils 9,880, teachers 641; higher, students 27,526, teaching staff 1,178.

Finance. Monetary unit: Jordanian dinar, with (Sept. 20, 1982) a free rate of 0.35 dinar to U.S. $1 (0.61 dinar = £1 sterling). Gold and other reserves (June 1982) U.S. $1,047,000,000. Budget (total; 1982 est.): revenue 729 million dinars; expenditure 765 million dinars. Gross national product (1980) 1,073,800,000 dinars. Money supply (Dec. 1981) 701,660,000 dinars. Cost of living (1975 = 100; April 1982) 203.9.

Foreign Trade. (1981) Imports 1,047,480,000 dinars; exports 269,740,000 dinars. Import sources (1980): Saudi Arabia 16%; West Germany 10%; U.S. 9%; U.K. 8%; France 7%; Japan 7%; Italy 6%. Export destinations (1980): Iraq 24%; Saudi Arabia 16%; Syria 11%; India 7%; Turkey 5%. Main exports (1980): phosphates 28%; vegetables 10%; fruit 7%; chemicals 9%; beverages 5%. Tourism (1980): visitors 1,635,600; gross receipts U.S. $512 million.

Transport and Communications. Roads (excluding West Bank; 1980) 4,950 km. Motor vehicles in use (1980): passenger 90,400; commercial 27,400. Railways (1980) c. 618 km. Air traffic (1981): 3,173,000,000 passenger-km; freight 112.4 million net ton-km. Telephones (Dec. 1980) 60,500. Radio receivers (Dec. 1979) 536,000. Television receivers (Dec. 1979) 165,000.

Agriculture. Production (in 000; metric tons; 1981): wheat c. 60; barley c. 30; tomatoes c. 163; aubergines (eggplants) c. 52; watermelons c. 33; olives c. 10; oranges c. 26; lemons c. 9; grapes c. 18. Livestock (in 000; 1981): cattle c. 37; goats c. 490; sheep c. 1,000; camels c. 13; asses c. 27; chickens c. 26,000.

Industry. Production (in 000; metric tons; 1980): phosphate rock 3,911; petroleum products 1,522; cement 913; electricity (kw-hr) 1,070,000.

proved, it was to pay for three new berths south of Aqaba's container terminal. Even if the Iran-Iraq war were to end quickly, salvage experts predicted that it would take several years to clear the Shatt al-Arab waterway of bombs and wreckage.

The Arab Potash Co.'s ambitious Dead Sea extraction plant was opened on March 18 by the king. Commercial production started late in 1982, with a planned rate of 240,000 metric tons a year to be achieved by 1986. Overall, the economy was guided by the five-year (1981–85) social and economic development plan. Revisions to the plan in 1982 raised projected spending to $9,970,000,000. As in the previous plan, a heavy commitment from the private sector was envisioned as well as a continuing reliance on foreign aid. Remittances from Jordanians in other countries were also forecast to grow, despite a decline in the number of Jordanians going to work in the Persian Gulf nations. Income from this source had grown from the equivalent of $100 million in 1974 to more than $2 billion in 1980. In an interview in June, Crown Prince Hassan said that Jordan's manpower pyramid was "upside down"; technical skills acquired by Jordanians working abroad had not been exploited at home because of the failure to build a technical base there.   (JOHN WHELAN)

See also Middle Eastern Affairs.

Kampuchea

Kampuchea

A republic of Southeast Asia, Kampuchea (formerly Cambodia) is the southwest part of the Indochinese Peninsula, on the Gulf of Thailand, bordered by Vietnam, Laos, and Thailand. Area: 181,035 sq km (69,898 sq mi). Pop. (1982 est.): 5,882,000. It is estimated to comprise: Khmer 93%; Vietnamese 4%; Chinese 3%. Cap.: Phnom Penh (urban area pop., 1981 est., 500,000). Language: Khmer (official) and French. Religion: Buddhist. Secretary-general of the People's Revolutionary (Communist) Party of Kampuchea and president of the Council of State in 1982, Heng Samrin; president of the Council of Ministers (premier) from February 9, Chan Sy.

Kampuchea reemerged into the international limelight in 1982, as the three principal anti-Vietnamese Khmer forces formed a coalition to combat

Japanese Literature:
see Literature

Jazz:
see Music

Jehovah's Witnesses:
see Religion

Jewish Literature:
see Literature

Journalism:
see Publishing

Judaism:
see Religion

Judo:
see Combat Sports

KAMPUCHEA

Education. Primary, pupils (1980–81) 1,328,033, teachers (1979–80) 12,000.

Finance. Monetary unit: riel, with (end 1981) a reported official rate of 4 new riels to U.S. $1 (7.70 riels = £1 sterling). Budget (1974 est.): revenue 23 billion old riels; expenditure 71 billion old riels.

Foreign Trade. (1979) Imports c. U.S. $150 million; exports c. U.S. $2 million. Import sources (1973): U.S. c. 69%; Thailand c. 11%; Singapore c. 5%; Japan c. 5%. Export destinations (1973): Hong Kong c. 23%; Japan c. 22%; Malaysia c. 18%; France c. 12%; Spain c. 10%. Main export (1973): rubber 93%.

Transport and Communications. Roads (1976) c. 11,000 km. Motor vehicles in use: passenger (1972) 27,200; commercial (including buses; 1973) 11,000. Railways: (1980) c. 600 km; traffic (1973) 54,070,000 passenger-km, freight 9,780,000 net ton-km. Air traffic (1977): 42 million passenger-km; freight 400,000 net ton-km. Inland waterways (including Mekong River; 1980) c. 1,400 km. Telephones (Dec. 1975) 71,000. Radio receivers (Dec. 1978) 171,000. Television receivers (Dec. 1977) c. 35,000.

Agriculture. Production (in 000; metric tons; 1981): rice c. 1,160; corn c. 98; bananas c. 67; oranges c. 23; dry beans c. 12; rubber c. 10; tobacco c. 5; jute c. 4. Livestock (in 000; 1981): cattle 956; buffalo 404; pigs 223.

Vietnam's continued military occupation of their homeland. At the same time, there were continued efforts by the Vietnam-backed government of Pres. Heng Samrin to consolidate its position and restore normal life to the war- and famine-ravaged country. In February Chan Sy was confirmed as premier in succession to Pen Sovan, who had been removed from office in December 1981.

Not long after agreeing in principle in September 1981 to form a "loose coalition," the Communist Khmer Rouge, former premier Son Sann of the anti-Communist Khmer People's National Liberation Front, and Prince Norodom Sihanouk of the neutralist National Liberation Movement of Kampuchea (Moulinaka) were publicly at odds over power distribution and administrative arrangements. In February 1982 the trio's principal backer, the Association of Southeast Asian Nations (ASEAN), voiced impatience over the lack of progress. Apparently fearful that ASEAN might drop its support for the Chinese-aided Khmer Rouge as the legitimate occupant of the Democratic Kampuchea seat at the UN, China agreed to act as host to a meeting of the Khmer resistance leaders. In late February Sihanouk parleyed with the Khmer Rouge's Khieu Samphan in the Chinese capital

Prince Norodom Sihanouk (left), former Cambodian head of state, and former premier Son Sann formed a coalition government-in-exile of Democratic Kampuchea on June 22. Sihanouk became president and Son Sann was made premier.

UPI

and, after making certain compromises, announced he had reached "initial agreement" with his former enemies.

It took a few more months before the firm-principled Son Sann was brought around to joining forces with the Khmer Rouge, under whose regime in 1975–79 more than a million Kampucheans were reportedly killed. Prodded by ASEAN and China, however, Sihanouk, Son Sann, and Khieu Samphan met in Kuala Lumpur, Malaysia, and on June 22 signed a declaration that they would form a coalition government of Democratic Kampuchea. Sihanouk, once his country's head of state, became president, while the post of premier went to Son Sann. Khieu Samphan was made vice-president.

Most observers saw the alliance as one of convenience. It was to be guided by four principles: tripartitism, equality among members, consensus in decision-making, and adherence to the "legitimacy and framework of Democratic Kampuchea." Each faction, however, would retain its own "organization, political identity, and freedom of action, including the right to receive and dispose of international aids specifically granted it."

Though Vietnam publicly scorned the coalition, privately it was clearly worried, particularly about the political respectability Sihanouk and Son Sann lent Democratic Kampuchea. It tried to gain ASEAN's goodwill by withdrawing some 10,000 of its estimated 180,000 troops in Kampuchea, but the move was widely decried as a "meaningless" rotation of soldiers. Vietnam's fears became reality when the UN General Assembly voted that Democratic Kampuchea should retain its seat.

The Heng Samrin administration launched an intensive propaganda campaign to discredit Sihanouk and Son Sann as well as the Khmer Rouge. The tactics included radio broadcasts, seminars for Khmers of all ages, and harsh measures against people suspected of having contacts with elements of the coalition. Even so, Sihanouk remained generally popular, while Son Sann retained strong sympathy among the country's educated class.

Kampuchea's once-critical food situation improved. Increased agricultural yields, together with international assistance, made starvation largely a thing of the past. The Phnom Penh government began to move from emergency relief to reconstruction and development. Further increases in food production, however, were slowed by increased collectivization of agriculture. Attempts to raise a national army met with limited success; problems included desertion, draft evasion, low-quality training, and lack of enthusiasm in fighting resistance forces. Though most Kampucheans continued to fear the return of the Khmer Rouge, there was also growing resentment of the Vietnamese presence.

(THOMAS HON WING POLIN)

Kenya

An African republic and a member of the Commonwealth, Kenya is bordered on the north by Sudan and Ethiopia, east by Somalia, south by Tanzania, and west by Uganda. Area: 580,367 sq

km (224,081 sq mi), including 11,230 sq km of inland water. Pop. (1982 est.): 17,142,000, including African 98%; Asian and European 2%. Cap. and largest city: Nairobi (pop., 1981 est., 919,000). Language: Swahili (official) and English. Religion (1980): Protestant 26.5%; Roman Catholic 26.4%; tribal 18.9%; African indigenous 17.6%; Muslim 6%; Orthodox 2.5%; other 2.1%. President in 1982, Daniel arap Moi.

A bitter and unexpected attack on Asian businessmen by Kenya's president, Daniel arap Moi (see BIOGRAPHIES), was made during a speech in February 1982. Asians, the president said, were guilty of hoarding essential goods and selling them on the black market and were ruining the economy by smuggling currency out of the country; any Asians, even citizens of Kenya, found guilty of these charges would be deported.

Kenya certainly suffered from serious shortages throughout 1982, and the economy faced considerable problems. This may have been one reason for the radical reshuffling of the Cabinet in February; although no minister was dropped, only 9 out of the 25 retained their original portfolios. Most surprising was the transfer of Vice-Pres. Mwai Kibaki from the Ministry of Finance to the Home Affairs Ministry and his replacement by Arthur Magugu, who was not known to have had any experience with financial issues.

On August 1 some members of the Kenya Air Force and several hundred students tried to overthrow the government in Nairobi. Army troops raise their guns in victory after successfully crushing the attempted coup.

Kenya

Kiribati

Kiribati

Vigorous criticism of the government's economic policies was voiced by former vice-president Oginga Odinga in February. He claimed that Kenya's resources had been subjected to systematic plunder, leading to mass unemployment, and that this situation could not be explained away by reference to high oil prices and international inflation. Odinga was not the only critic of the government; a play by the novelist and playwright Ngugi wa Thiong'o was banned without explanation in May. It was known that the play pursued the theme of some of Ngugi's novels, which had drawn parallels between the condition of Kenyan Africans under the colonial regime and that of peasants under the independent government.

The government reacted severely to Odinga's speech. In May he was expelled from the ruling Kenya African National Union (KANU) by the president, who accused him of having engaged in violent and divisive propaganda against the government; in July his passport was withdrawn, and in November he was placed under house arrest. Meanwhile, in June three other persons were detained under the Preservation of Public Security Act. One, Mwangi Stephen Muriithi, had been deputy director of intelligence until relieved of his post in 1981. The second, George Anyona, had been expelled from KANU along with Odinga after advocating the formation of another political party. (Kenya became officially a one-party state in June 1982 when Parliament amended the constitution.) The third, John Khaminwa, was a lawyer who had acted on behalf of the other two. In July George Githii, editor of Kenya's *The Standard*

newspaper, was dismissed after writing an article critical of the detentions.

Whether the government's fear of its critics was justified or whether its severe action against alleged subversives actually provoked resistance was difficult to determine, but on August 1 a number of air force personnel, enlisting the support of several hundred university students, tried to overthrow the government. The government reacted swiftly, and the uprising was soon put down by the Army and police. There was a brief wave of opportunist looting, mainly of Asian shops and houses because of the feeling that had been generated against the Asian community, but there was little overt support for the attempted coup.

The organizers of the uprising were difficult to locate. Although an air force private and sergeant who had fled to Tanzania claimed to have been its leaders, there was some doubt about their ability to plan such an operation. In any case the Tanzanian government refused to repatriate the two refugees as requested by Kenya. As a precaution the president disbanded the Air Force, and heavy sentences were passed by courts-martial on a number of persons accused of some responsibility for the coup attempt. Some civilians, members of the Luo tribe, were also arrested, including the son of Oginga Odinga. (KENNETH INGHAM)

Kiribati

An independent republic in the western Pacific Ocean and member of the Commonwealth, Kiribati comprises the former Gilbert Islands, Banaba (Ocean Island), the Line Islands, and the Phoenix Islands. Area: 712 sq km (275 sq mi). Pop. (1982 est.): 60,000, including (1978) Micronesian 98%; Polynesian 1.4%; non-Pacific islanders 0.6%. Cap.: Bairiki (pop., 1979 est., 1,800) on Tarawa atoll (pop., 1980 est., 22,100). Language: English (official). Religion (1973): Roman Catholic 48%; Protestant 45%. President (*beriti-tenti*) in 1982, Ieremia Tabai.

In a series of elections held from late March to early May 1982, Pres. Ieremia Tabai was returned to office in Kiribati. The nation had no political parties, but members of factions tended to act in accord. In the first round of voting only 13 candidates for the House of Assembly received the required absolute majority; 23 were elected in a second round, which was confined to the leaders

Karate:
see Combat Sports

Kashmir:
see India; Pakistan

Kendo:
see Combat Sports

Korea

among the candidates from the first round. Although most established politicians were returned, two former Cabinet ministers, Abete Merang and Otiuea Tamentoa, lost their seats. Four candidates were selected by and from the members of the House to contest the presidency; in that election Ieremia Tabai won 49% of the votes.

During 1982 Kiribati signed a $3 million aid agreement with Japan but continued to rely on British subsidies to meet its budget requirements. In August President Tabai attended the South Pacific Forum meeting in New Zealand, at which a resolution was passed regretting the failure of the U.S. to sign the UN Law of the Sea Treaty. In October Queen Elizabeth II made the first visit to the country by a ruling monarch.

(BARRIE MACDONALD)

Korea

A country of eastern Asia, Korea is bounded by China, the Sea of Japan, the Korea Strait, and the Yellow Sea. It is divided into two parts roughly at the 38th parallel.

The efforts of the rival governments in South Korea and North Korea to win friends and influence people, both at home and abroad, dominated events in Korea in 1982. Just over a year after North Korean leader Kim Il Sung announced his plan for reunification of the country, South Korean Pres. Chun Doo Hwan responded with the most detailed blueprint ever to emerge from Seoul. The proposal, which Chun unveiled before Parliament in January, called for the convening of a bilateral, Cabinet-level conference to set up a summit meeting between the two heads of state; they would then negotiate a provisional agreement that would ultimately lead to a new and mutually acceptable constitution and also to free elections for a unified government on the peninsula. The proposal would leave intact South Korea's mutual defense treaty with the U.S. as well as the North's alliances with China and the U.S.S.R.

Chun's plan was quickly rejected by North Korean Vice-Pres. Kim Il, who merely repeated Kim Il Sung's proposal for a Korean confederation and such demands as the withdrawal of the 40,000 U.S. troops in the South, President Chun's resignation, abrogation of internal security laws, and the release of political prisoners. Analysts believed that, in the absence of drastic changes, neither side was likely to alter its position on reunification.

Indeed, there was no sign of a thaw in relations between the two regimes. After the arrest in Seoul of two Canadians in February, the South accused the North of financing a plot to kill President Chun in 1981. North Korea, for its part, continued its fierce attacks on the U.S. armed presence in the South. Amid growing fears that the military balance on the peninsula was tilting heavily in the North's favour, U.S. Secretary of Defense Caspar Weinberger promised to shore up South Korea's security by strengthening the U.S. forces there.

Republic of Korea (South Korea). Area: 98,966 sq km (38,211 sq mi). Pop. (1981 est.): 38,723,000. Cap. and largest city: Seoul (pop., 1980, 8,366,800). Language: Korean. Religion (1979): Buddhist 38.7%; Christian 19%; Confucian 13.1%; Tonghak (Chondokyo) 3%; other 26.2%. President in 1982, Chun Doo Hwan; prime ministers, Nam Duck Woo, Yoo Chang Soon (acting) from January 3, and Kim Sang Hyup from June 24 (acting to September 21).

Pres. Chun Doo Hwan announced in January 1982 that the country's 36-year-old midnight-to-4 AM curfew was to be scrapped and that Prime Minister Nam Duck Woo was to be replaced by Yoo Chang Soon, an economics expert. The lifting of the curfew, widely welcomed, was seen as a sign of confidence in increased social stability since Chun's seizure of power during the turbulent peri-

---

KOREA: Republic

Education. (1981–82) Primary, pupils 5,586,494, teachers 122,727; secondary, pupils 3,580,258, teachers 87,974; vocational, students 827,579, teachers 25,573; higher, students 734,900, teaching staff 23,750.

Finance. Monetary unit: won, with (Sept. 20, 1982) a free rate of 741 won to U.S. $1 (1,271 won = £1 sterling). Gold and other reserves (June 1982) U.S. $2,567,000,000. Budget (total; 1980 actual): revenue 6,833,200,000,000 won; expenditure 6,562,000,000,000 won. Gross national product (1981) 43,155,000,000,000 won. Money supply (May 1982) 4,091,000,000,000 won. Cost of living (1975 = 100; June 1982) 290.5.

Foreign Trade. (1981) Imports 17,796,-000,000,000 won; exports 14,484,000,000,000 won. Import sources: Japan 24%; U.S. 23%; Saudi Arabia 14%; Kuwait 6%. Export destinations: U.S. 27%; Japan 16%; Hong Kong 5%; Saudi Arabia 5%. Main exports (1980): clothing 17%; textile yarns and fabrics 13%; electrical machinery and equipment 11%; iron and steel 9%; transport equipment 7%; footwear 5%. Tourism (1980): visitors 819,000; gross receipts U.S. $369 million.

Transport and Communications. Roads (1980) 46,951 km (including 1,225 km expressways). Motor vehicles in use (1980): passenger 249,100; commercial 226,900. Railways (1981): c. 6,070 km; traffic 21,235,000,000 passenger-km, freight 10,637,-000,000 net ton-km. Air traffic (1981): 11,240,-000,000 passenger-km; freight 933.6 million net ton-km. Shipping (1981): merchant vessels 100 gross tons and over 1,634; gross tonnage 5,141,505. Telephones (Jan. 1980) 2,898,700. Radio receivers (Dec. 1978) 14,882,000. Television licenses (Dec. 1979) 5,661,000.

Agriculture. Production (in 000; metric tons; 1981): rice 7,032; barley 771; potatoes 554; sweet potatoes 1,108; soybeans 249; cabbages 3,457; watermelons 291; onions 407; apples 523; oranges 209; tobacco 87; fish catch (1980) 2,091. Livestock (in 000; Dec. 1980): cattle 1,531; pigs 2,140; goats 201 chickens 51,300.

Industry. Production (in 000; metric tons; 1981): coal 19,985; iron ore (56% metal content) 495; pig iron 8,058; crude steel 5,892; cement 15,617; tungsten concentrates (oxide content; 1980) 3.2; zinc concentrates 57; gold (troy oz; 1980) 38; silver (troy oz; 1980) 2,339; sulfuric acid 1,294; fertilizers (nutrient content; 1980–81) nitrogenous c. 688, phosphate c. 494; petroleum products c. 24,600; man-made fibres (1980) 681; electricity (excluding most industrial production; kw-hr) 40,206,000; radio receivers (units; 1980) 4,143; television receivers (units; 1980) 6,819. Merchant vessels launched (100 gross tons and over; 1981) 1,207,000 gross tons.

KOREA: Democratic People's Republic

Education. (1976–77) Primary, pupils 2,561,674; secondary and vocational, pupils c. 2 million; primary, secondary, and vocational, teachers c. 100,000; higher, students c. 100,000.

Finance and Trade. Monetary unit: won, with (Sept. 20, 1982) a nominal exchange rate of 0.99 won to U.S. $1 (1.69 won = £1 sterling). Budget (1981 est.) balanced at 20,480,000,000 won. Foreign trade (approximate; 1981): imports c. 1.6 billion won; exports c. 1.4 billion won. Import sources: China c. 25%; U.S.S.R. c. 24%; Japan c. 20%; France c. 5%. Export destinations: China c. 30%; U.S.S.R. c. 25%; Japan c. 9%; Saudi Arabia c. 8%; India c. 5%. Main exports (1975): lead and ore c. 30%; zinc and ore c. 20%; magnesite c. 15%; rice c. 6%; cement c. 5%; coal c. 5%; fish c. 5%.

Agriculture. Production (in 000; metric tons; 1981): rice c. 4,900; corn c. 2,200; barley c. 400; millet c. 450; potatoes c. 1,600; sweet potatoes c. 382; soybeans c. 350; fish catch (1980) c. 1,400. Livestock (in 000; 1981): cattle c. 960; pigs c. 2,200; sheep c. 300; goats c. 245; chickens c. 18,050.

Industry. Production (in 000; metric tons; 1980): coal c. 45,000; iron ore (metal content) c. 3,200; pig iron c. 4,000; steel c. 4,000; lead ore c. 70; zinc ore c. 120; magnesite c. 2,620; silver (troy oz) c. 1,550; tungsten concentrates (oxide content) c. 2.2; cement c. 8,000; petroleum products (1979) c. 1,450; electricity (kw-hr) c. 35,000,000.

WIDE WORLD

Chang Yong Ja, wife of Lee Chul Hi, former deputy director of the Korean Central Intelligence Agency, was taken to court in July in Seoul. She and her husband were defendants in what prosecutors called the biggest financial scandal in Korean history.

od following the assassination of former president Park Chung Hee in 1979. The replacement of Nam, chief architect of South Korea's high-growth, high-inflation economic policies, was interpreted as a sign of Chun's determination to break with the legacy of his predecessor. Yoo's mandate was to curb inflation while speeding up the economy's recovery from the negative growth of 1980.

Chun moved to broaden support for his Democratic Justice Party by attempting a dialogue with North Korea. He proclaimed a general amnesty on March 3, the first anniversary of his inauguration as president under the country's new constitution. Religious groups and human-rights activists complained, however, that only one-tenth of the 2,863 people pardoned were, in fact, political offenders. The country's best-known opposition leader, Kim Dae Jung, whose life sentence had been reduced to 20 years by President Chun earlier in the year, was allowed to leave South Korea for the U.S. in late December.

Then, suddenly, things seemed to spin out of Chun's control. On April 26 a young policeman shocked the nation by going on a murderous rampage in rural Uiryong, killing 56 innocent people before blowing himself up. Questions were raised as to why security personnel had been unable to stop the killer and whether there had been a serious neglect of duty on the part of those who, among other things, were supposed to protect the country from North Korean infiltration and sabotage. Home Affairs Minister Suh Chung Hwa resigned after the tragedy.

A much bigger scandal erupted in May. Socialite Chang Yong Ja and her husband, Lee Chul Hi, were charged with defrauding six companies of $250 million by manipulating South Korea's vast underground "curb" money market, in which private loans were transacted. Chang, whose brother-in-law was an uncle of President Chun's wife, and Lee were also accused of using connections in high places to extract large sums of money from government-controlled banks. The affair quickly developed into South Korea's most serious financial crisis in memory.

The political repercussions were no less drastic. Chun, whose presidency had been marked by a strong stress on integrity and moral purity, found himself obliged to replace half of his 22-member Cabinet. Tempers flared anew in June, when the government put on trial a group of students and a priest for alleged involvement in a serious case of arson at the U.S. cultural centre in Pusan three months earlier. A leading group in the country's Christian community urged Chun to "speedily . . . step down for the sake of national security." The arson, explained a group spokesman, was the result of "U.S. support of a dictatorial regime." Chun again revamped his Cabinet in June. Yoo Chang Soon was replaced as prime minister by educationist Kim Sang Hyup, while Kang Kyong Shik took over the important finance portfolio.

After two decades of remarkably rapid growth, the economy since 1980 had been buffeted by rising oil prices, the global recession, soaring interest rates, and increasing foreign restrictions on Korean exports. The government announced a series of dramatic steps to lift the country's debt-ridden big business out of recession. Bank interest rates were immediately cut by four percentage points, while corporate taxes were to be trimmed by up to 18 percentage points by 1983. In a determined attack on the abuse-prone curb market, the government decreed that by January 1983 all new depositors with $40,000 or more would have to identify themselves by showing passports.

The most notable feature of the proposed budget for 1983 was exceptionally tight government spending. The 9.8% rise in the main component ($13 billion) of the budget's public sector contrasted sharply with the 20% average increase over the last two decades. South Korea's gross national product grew an estimated 6% in 1982, while inflation was likely to be held below 10%.

Meeting in Seoul with Australian Prime Minister Malcolm Fraser in May, President Chun proposed a summit of heads of government of major Asian and Pacific countries. In August the president embarked on a tour that took him to Kenya, Nigeria, Gabon, and Senegal. One motive for the trip was to counter the considerable influence North Korea had built up in black Africa through its membership in the nonaligned movement, of which Seoul was not a member. The journey was also intended to promote trade.

South Korea's efforts to negotiate a massive development loan from Japan were suddenly disrupted in July by a fierce controversy over the latter's attempt to revise its history textbooks in order to downplay Japanese atrocities during the occupation of Korea in World War II. (See JAPAN.) The storm abated in September, however, and the two governments settled on a Japanese aid package worth $4 billion.

Democratic People's Republic of Korea (North Korea).

Democratic People's Republic of Korea (North Korea). Area: 121,929 sq km (47,077 sq mi). Pop. (1982 est.): 18,789,000. Cap.: Pyongyang (pop., 1981 est., 1,283,000). Language: Korean. Religion (1980 est.): atheist 68%; animist 16%; Buddhist, Confucian, Tonghak (Chondokyo), and other 16%. General secretary of the Central Committee of the Workers' (Communist) Party of Korea and president in 1982, Marshal Kim Il Sung; chairman of the Council of Ministers (premier), Li Jong Ok.

Events in North Korea centred on the continuing efforts of Pres. Kim Il Sung to pass power on to his son, Kim Chong Il. Over the past few years Kim Chong Il had been in charge of most day-to-day affairs of the Workers' Party of Korea, and he was expected to be named a vice-president in 1982. But he failed to gain any top government post when a new Cabinet was selected in April, after general elections in February. Analysts attributed this to resistance to the younger Kim by veteran military officers, who believed that he was too young and inexperienced to inherit his father's mantle.

Even so, the apparent setback was likely to be only temporary, for Kim Chong Il continued to appear by his father's side. The prospect of Kim Chong Il's eventual rise to supreme power worried the government in South Korea, which viewed him as being even more dogmatic and martial-minded than his father.

With North Korea currently spending a quarter of its $16.2 billion gross national product on defense (against South Korea's 6% of $58 billion), South Korean and U.S. intelligence analysts feared that the North might be tempted to strike at the South while it enjoyed a distinct military advantage. (Pyongyang had about 780,000 men under arms to Seoul's 600,000, some 700 combat aircraft to 400, and 3,000 tanks to 1,200.)

Reliable economic indicators for North Korea were difficult to obtain, but economists believed that the country's performance had been generally indifferent. It continued to have problems repaying its $2 billion foreign debt. It was largely to boost North Korea's limited overseas trade that Premier Li Jong Ok undertook a 12-day tour of non-Communist Southeast Asia in February. Although concrete achievements were few, Li met top leaders in Indonesia, Malaysia, and Thailand. A more important journey was that of Kim Il Sung to China in September. China was North Korea's premier trading partner and political ally, and it was reported that the Chinese, anxious to ensure that Kim was friendlier to them than to the Soviets, gave their Korean guest 20 MiG-21 jet fighters.

(THOMAS HON WING POLIN)

Kuwait

An independent constitutional monarchy (emirate), Kuwait is on the northwestern coast of the Persian Gulf between Iraq and Saudi Arabia. Area: 17,818 sq km (6,879 sq mi). Pop. (1982 est.): 1,562,200. Cap.: Kuwait City (pop., 1980 prelim., 60,400). Largest city: Hawalli (pop., 1980 prelim.,

152,300). Language: Arabic. Religion (1980): Muslim 91.5% (of which Sunni 85%; Shi'ah 15%); Christian 6.4%; other 2.1%. Emir, Sheikh Jabir al-Ahmad al-Jabir as-Sabah; prime minister in 1982, Crown Prince Sheikh Saad al-Abdullah as-Salim as-Sabah.

In 1982 Kuwait experienced a year of introspection brought about by the continuing Iran-Iraq war, lower prices for crude oil, and a liquidity crisis on the unofficial Kuwaiti stock exchange or curb market. A U.S. survey ranked Kuwait as the 17th most prosperous country in the world. Yet Finance Minister Abdel Latif al-Hamad (see BIOGRAPHIES) warned in April that Kuwait faced bankruptcy within four years if the increase in government spending was not checked.

Early in 1982 oil production dropped as low as 600,000 bbl a day, about half the ceiling introduced in 1981. Part of the fall was cushioned by government investment income, estimated at $9 billion a year, but as a consequence of lower revenue the actual growth in government spending between 1981 and 1982 was expected to be in single figures. Foreign currency reserves were reported to be in excess of $60 billion.

The greatest challenge to Kuwait's free economy and system of government was posed by the Gulf war. An Iraqi defeat or change of government would be deeply embarrassing to Kuwait, which had supported Iraq with grant aid of more than $6 billion. About 3.5 million metric tons of cargo bound for Iraq passed through Kuwait in 1981.

The stock market crisis, brought about by uncontrolled forward trading using postdated checks, some of which were not honoured, brought the government into direct conflict with elements of the merchant community. Some estimates put the value of the outstanding checks at more than $60 billion. In late December the government began paying off some of the investors.

(JOHN WHELAN)

KUWAIT

Education. (1980–81) Primary, pupils 125,114, teachers 6,936; secondary, pupils 152,578, teachers 13,460; vocational, pupils 5,564, teachers 931; teacher training, pupils 1,584, teachers 289; higher (1978–79), students 11,621, teaching staff 1,157.

Finance. Monetary unit: Kuwaiti dinar, with Sept. 20, 1982) a free rate of 0.29 dinar to U.S. $1 (0.50 dinar = £1 sterling). Gold and other reserves (May 1982) U.S. $4,270,000,000. Budget (total; 1980–81 actual): revenue 6,351,000,000 dinars; expenditure 2,577,000,000 dinars. Gross domestic product (1981–82) 6,764,000,000 dinars. Money supply (June 1982) 1,695,700,000 dinars. Cost of living (1975 = 100; Dec. 1981) 157.4.

Foreign Trade. (1981) Imports (f.o.b.) c. 2,030,000,000 dinars; exports 4,886,000,000 dinars. Import sources (1980): Japan 21%; U.S. 14%; U.K. 9%; West Germany 9%; Italy 6%. Export destinations (1980): Japan 20%; The Netherlands 12%; South Korea 8%; U.K. 7%; Singapore 7%. Main exports: crude oil 62%; petroleum products 24%.

Transport. Roads (1978) 2,400 km. Motor vehicles in use (1980): passenger 398,900; commercial (including buses) 144,000. Air traffic (1981): 2,882,000,000 passenger-km; freight 112.1 million net ton-km. Shipping (1981): merchant vessels 100 gross tons and over 237; gross tonnage 2,317,275.

Industry. Production (in 000; metric tons; 1981): crude oil 56,715; natural gas (cu m) 5,920,000; petroleum products (1979) c. 17,770; electricity (kw-hr; 1980) 9,270,000.

Kuwait

Laos

Laos

A landlocked people's republic of Southeast Asia, Laos is bounded by China, Vietnam, Kampuchea, Thailand, and Burma. Area: 236,800 sq km (91,400 sq mi). Pop. (1982 est.): 3,901,000. Cap. and largest city: Vientiane (pop., 1978 est., 200,000). Language: Lao (official), French, and English. Religion (1980 est.): Buddhist 58%; tribal 34%; Christian 2%; other 2%; none 4%. President in 1982, Prince Souphanouvong; premier, Kaysone Phomvihan.

The highlight of 1982 for Laos was the convening in late April of the third national congress of the ruling Lao People's Revolutionary (Communist) Party (LPRP). It had been a decade since the last congress was held, and the 1982 meeting took up the tasks of assessing and defining the country's leadership structure, economic and political development, and foreign policy.

The third congress unequivocally confirmed the leading position of Kaysone Phomvihan, secretary-general of the LPRP and premier. There had been rumours that Kaysone, who had headed the party since its founding in 1955, would relinquish the premiership, but he emerged apparently all the stronger as several of his closest allies, as well as his wife, were elevated to the important LPRP central secretariat. Though he shed his finance portfolio in September, Deputy Premier Nouhak Phoumsavan seemed secure in his standing as the regime's second most powerful figure. The composition of the seven-member Politburo remained unchanged, but 30 new faces, including representatives of ethnic minorities and women, graced the 49-member LPRP Central Committee.

The congress struck a decidedly reformist note as it drafted the country's first five-year (1981–85) development plan. Of the rigidly Marxist line pursued by the LPRP since its accession to power in 1975, Kaysone said candidly: "We . . . indulged in subjectivism, failed to grasp economic laws and strongly promote the people's mastery as a motive force." Remedies prescribed included a slowdown in the drive toward full-scale socialism, the lifting of restrictions on private trade, wage increases, and the training of technocrats and efficient economic managers.

The third congress also scrapped the earlier target of eliminating Laos's huge trade deficit by 1985, and it halved the projected increase in internal revenue to about 90%. A bright spot was rice production, which had risen from 700,000 metric tons in 1976 to over 1 million metric tons in 1981, when the country became self-sufficient in the food grain for the first time. Laos was also increasingly able to obtain finance for its projects from non-Communist countries and international institutions.

Vientiane remained a loyal ally of Vietnam in Vietnamese-dominated Indochina. At the third party congress, Kaysone hailed his country's "special relationship" with Vietnam and identified Hanoi's archfoe China as "the most dangerous enemy" of Laos. Vientiane's ties with neighbour-

Labour Unions:
see Industrial Relations

Lacrosse:
see Field Hockey and Lacrosse

ing Thailand continued to be strained by what the Laotians saw as Bangkok's sanction of Lao rebel activity on Thai soil. Late in the year, former Lao deputy premier Phoumi Nosavan, who had lived in exile in Thailand since 1965, announced his intention to form an anti-Communist "United Front of Lao People for the Liberation of Laos." He claimed to have some 40,000 supporters inside the country. (THOMAS HON WING POLIN)

Latin-American Affairs

During 1982 Latin-American affairs were dominated by the crisis that resulted in armed conflict between Argentina and the U.K. in the South Atlantic. On March 19 a group of scrap merchants who had been contracted to dismantle a disused whaling station raised the Argentine flag on South Georgia, a dependency of the British colony of the Falkland Islands/Islas Malvinas. The crisis escalated quickly. On April 2 Argentine forces occupied the Falkland Islands, and the U.K. broke off diplomatic relations with Argentina. The U.K. called an emergency session of the UN Security Council, which on April 3 passed Resolution 502 condemning the Argentine actions; on the same day, the British government announced the dispatch of a naval task force to the South Atlantic area and imposed sanctions on Argentina.

On April 17 the European Communities (EC) imposed trade sanctions on Argentina for 30 days, and in May some member countries renewed their support for the U.K. in this way. On April 7 Britain imposed a 200-nautical mile (370-km) exclusion zone in waters around the islands. U.S. Secretary of State Alexander Haig shuttled between London, Washington, D.C., and Buenos Aires from April 8 to 19 in an endeavour to find a peaceful solution to the dispute. British forces retook South Georgia on April 25, and soon afterward the U.S. formally declared its support for the U.K. Extended negotiations on peace formulas sponsored by Peru and the UN broke down on May 6 and May 20, respectively. The main military action between Argentina and the U.K. took place between May 1 and June 14, the date on which the Argentine commander on the Falklands surrendered to the British. (*See* DEPENDENT STATES: *Sidebar*; for an account of the military campaign, *see* DEFENSE: *Special Report*.)

Latin-American countries supported Argentina throughout the crisis in varying degrees. Their attitude was expressed in the resolution passed by the Organization of American States meeting in Washington, D.C., in late April. The resolution supported Argentina's claim to the Falklands but called for a truce; it was passed by 17 votes to 0 with 5 abstentions. Peru and Bolivia offered limited military assistance to Argentina, which was not taken up. Chile followed a policy of strict neutrality, as it was already in dispute with Argentina over the islands of Picton, Lennox, and Nueva in the Beagle Channel at the southern tip of South America. Brazil adopted an evenhanded stance and made available reexport facilities for Argentine goods from its southern ports and some aircraft for submarine-tracking purposes.

Early in November the UN voted for a Latin-American draft resolution calling for renewed negotiations between Argentina and the U.K. over the sovereignty of the islands. The fact that the U.S. voted in favour of the resolution was interpreted as a gesture toward repairing relations with Latin America, which had been damaged when the U.S. declared its formal support for the U.K. during the hostilities. U.S. Pres. Ronald Reagan visited Brazil, Costa Rica, Honduras, and Colombia in late November and early December as part of the process of restoring links. British efforts to ameliorate relations with the region in the wake of the crisis centred on a visit by Peter Rees, British trade minister, to Chile, Paraguay, and Ecuador in September. The Irish commissioner to the EC, Richard Burke, visited La Paz, Bolivia, in October as part of an effort to remove Latin-American suspicions of the Communities. Negotiations proceeded slowly on an agreement between the European Economic Community (EEC) and the Andean Group countries (Bolivia, Colombia, Ecuador, Peru, and Venezuela), and at the same time the European Coal and Steel Community was arranging a $700 million investment for Brazil to develop minerals needed by the European steel industry.

At a meeting of the board of governors of the Inter-American Development Bank (IDB), held in Rio de Janeiro, Brazil, in late October, the U.S. was in dispute with Brazil, Mexico, Venezuela, and Argentina over access to multilateral finance. The U.S. delegation insisted that those four countries were to limit credits from the IDB in the period 1982–86 to a maximum of $3 billion; Latin-American countries requested an 18% annual growth in bank lending, as opposed to a U.S. proposal of 12%, and a large volume of concessionary lending, totaling at least $2,750,000,000.

The Latin American Integration Association (LAIA), set up by the August 1980 Montevideo Treaty to replace the 20-year-old Latin American Free Trade Association (LAFTA), was fully ratified in March by the signatories (Argentina, Bolivia, Brazil, Chile, Colombia, Ecuador, Mexico, Paraguay, Peru, Uruguay, and Venezuela). The Montevideo Treaty provided for regional preferential tariff arrangements, to be applied by all members on their internal trade within the grouping; regional agreements on trade, industrial and agricultural cooperation, science and technology, tourism, financial flows, and environmental protection, which also extended to member countries; and partial agreements between individual members, which in the long term were to be extended to other members through negotiation.

At a meeting in Jamaica in August, central bank representatives of LAIA member countries and the Dominican Republic agreed to bring under the aegis of LAIA a multilateral reciprocal payments and credits system that had been operated by central banks in the region since 1965. The system provided for clearing bank services for payments of intraregional trade transactions. About 85% of all intraregional trade, valued at $9.3 billion, was channeled through the system in 1981. Under the arrangement the Peruvian central bank settled balances stemming from 63 credit lines every four months, eliminating the need for member countries to make available foreign exchange for individual transactions. A further strengthening of LAIA took place when private-sector representatives from Argentina, Brazil, Mexico, and Uruguay met in Montevideo, Uruguay, in July to discuss mutual tariff reductions for imports of office machinery under its auspices.

Argentine Foreign Minister Nicanor Costa Méndez addressed a meeting of the Organization of American States in April in Washington, D.C., regarding the Falkland Islands dispute. He urged Britain to withdraw its fleet from the South Atlantic.

CONSOLIDATED NEWS PICTURES/KEYSTONE

In August a ministerial meeting of the Latin American Economic System (SELA) was held in Caracas, Venezuela, to outline a new strategy for Latin-American economic relations. This body, established in October 1975 by 25 Latin-American and Caribbean nations, including Cuba, was designed to complement rather than rival or replace the existing regional organizations.

The Andean Group was in the doldrums during the year. The one event of significance was an agreement on new rules for multinational Andean corporations. By Group Decision 169 of March, these corporations were required to have at least 80% Andean ownership, with foreign, non-Pact, holdings being limited to 20% at most. In the case of concerns to be established in Bolivia and Ecuador, the decision allowed for a gradual transition from 40% to 20% maximum foreign capital.

In Central America events were dominated by political violence and social disturbances, especially in El Salvador and Guatemala, and by economic difficulties, in Costa Rica in particular. The Central American Common Market was largely in a state of suspension, but there were some encouraging developments. At a meeting of the Central American Monetary Union in April, the central bank presidents of the five member countries (Costa Rica, El Salvador, Guatemala, Honduras, and Nicaragua) authorized credits of $80.4 million to finance intraregional trade. In February Honduras and El Salvador ratified a bilateral free-trade treaty, which ended an 11-year gap in trade between the two countries. The European Parliament in October discussed the granting of an aid package worth approximately $30 million to Central America and the Caribbean. The Central American Democratic Community, a regional body established to promote cooperation in political and security matters, was formed in January by El Salvador, Costa Rica, and Honduras, which were joined in July by Guatemala.

On February 24 President Reagan announced a program of aid and of trade and investment incentives designed to develop the economies of countries of the Caribbean Basin, excluding Mexico, Cuba, Grenada, and Nicaragua; it was known as the Caribbean Basin Initiative (CBI). The CBI sought to achieve economic benefits through a reduction in state controls, liberalization of trade, and encouragement of foreign investment. Its centrepiece was the proposed free entry of Caribbean products into the U.S. market for 12 years. (Exceptions included textiles, clothing, and sugar, which were subject to quotas.) The U.S. Congress passed the aid component of the program, and a total of $350 million was made available in 1982 for short-term balance of payments support, including $75 million for El Salvador, $50 million for Jamaica, $70 million for Costa Rica, and $40 million for the Dominican Republic. Also envisioned was longer-term development aid, which would total $675 million by 1984. The trade and investment sections of the CBI proposal failed to gain congressional approval during the year. Concomitantly with the program, the U.S. was negotiating bilateral treaties for investment, and the first of these was signed with Panama in October. On November 30

Latin-American Literature:
see Literature

Latter-day Saints:
see Religion

President Reagan began a five-day tour of Latin America.

Latin America's economic performance in 1981 was its worst in 35 years. Overall growth in the region was only 1.2%, a large drop from the 5.8% of 1980 and well below the population increase. The average rate of inflation during the year was 60%, the worst figure ever recorded except for 1976. The overall balance of payments registered a deficit for the second successive year. Although the volume of exports rose by 11%, there was a record current account deficit of $33.7 billion in 1981; this was an increase of nearly $6 billion over 1980. The region's disbursed foreign debt was estimated to have grown by 15% to $240 billion by the end of 1981, four times the figure registered in 1977. During 1982 Mexico, Bolivia, Brazil, Costa Rica, Honduras, Ecuador, and Argentina were at various stages of discussion with their creditors about debt renegotiation and with the International Monetary Fund about stabilization programs. Cuba also sought the rescheduling of some of its $3 billion debt to non-Communist countries.

(ROBIN CHAPMAN)

See also articles on the various political units. [971.D.8; 974]

Law

Court Decisions. In 1982, as in past years, the most important judicial decisions handed down by the many courts of the world emanated from the U.S. Supreme Court. This reflected the fact that the common law system prevalent in the English-speaking world attaches more significance to judicial decisions than does the civil law applicable in most other countries, as well as the fact that the U.S. Constitution vests extraordinary powers in the Supreme Court. Nevertheless, a number of remarkable decisions also were rendered in the civil law countries and in England.

EXECUTIVE PRIVILEGE. According to most U.S. constitutional lawyers, the most important decision handed down by the U.S. Supreme Court in 1982 involved the question of whether the president and his staff are immune from civil actions arising out of their official decisions on behalf of the government. In an apparent reversal of earlier-held views, the court in *Nixon* v. *Fitzgerald* decided that U.S. presidents are absolutely immune from civil liability for acts performed during their tenure in office, but that such blanket immunity does not necessarily attach to the president's chief aides.

The case involved a suit by A. Ernest Fitzgerald, a management analyst allegedly fired from his government job by Pres. Richard Nixon and his chief aides in retaliation for his testifying, before a Senate subcommittee, that the cost overruns on the C-5A transport plane could amount to $2 billion over original estimates. Justice Lewis Powell, writing for the majority, stated that the president was absolutely immune from civil liability because of the special nature of the office. He opined that the particular nature of the responsibilities of certain other officials, such as judges and prosecutors, also require absolute exemption from civil liability, but that no blanket recognition of absolute exemption for all federal executive officials from such liability was warranted.

In a related case, *Harlow* v. *Fitzgerald*, Justice Powell drew the line: a presidential aide is entitled to absolute immunity from civil liability only upon a showing by him or her that the official responsibility in question was so sensitive as to require such a shield from liability; for example, certain areas of national security or foreign policy. In other cases where executive officials are performing discretionary functions, they are entitled to a qualified immunity that protects them from liability for civil suit insofar as their conduct does not violate "clearly established statutory or constitutional rights of which a reasonable person would have known."

The case surprised some constitutional law experts, because recent Supreme Court decisions had increasingly shown a rejection of blanket claims by governmental officials of absolute immunity from civil suit. Some of these experts had erroneously predicted that the court, in *Nixon* v. *Fitzgerald*, would hand down a decision strongly recognizing the rights of injured parties to recover damages from government officials, including the president, who knowingly had deprived them of their rights, thus fortifying the maxim that "no man, not even the President, is above the law."

WOMEN'S RIGHTS. In *Mississippi University for Women* v. *Joe Hogan*, the court faced the question of whether a publicly supported college that admitted only women as regular degree students was guilty of sex discrimination, thus violating the Equal Protection Clause of the 14th Amendment. Hogan, a licensed practical nurse, had been de-

nied admittance to the MUW nursing program because he was male. The court held that the college's single-sex admissions policy could not be justified as "affirmative action" to compensate for discrimination against women. Justice Sandra Day O'Connor opined that a state can invoke affirmative action in favour of women only where they have suffered a disadvantage related to the classification. Here, she said, the opposite was true, since the discrimination tended to perpetuate the stereotyped view that nursing is a job to be done exclusively by females.

In recent years the European Court of Justice had handed down a number of decisions under Art. 169 of the treaty establishing the European Economic Community (EEC), which requires member nations to treat men and women equally. In 1982 it held in *O'Brien* v. *Sim* that Britain's Equal Pay Act violated the EEC treaty because it did not provide for recognition of the principle of "work for equal value."

In related legislative developments, the Convention on the Elimination of all Forms of Discrimination Against Women, passed by the UN in 1979, came into force, and East Germany enacted a law allowing women to be called into active military service at times of general mobilization. Liechtenstein ratified the European Convention on Human Rights, but with a reservation on the article dealing with the equality of men and women. Women have no political rights in Liechtenstein.

ALIENS. One of the most publicized cases coming before the U.S. Supreme Court in 1982 concerned the rights of illegal alien schoolchildren. The case, *Plyer* v. *Doe*, involved the constitutionality of a Texas statute that withheld from local

American Telephone and Telegraph Company and the U.S. government were involved in one of the biggest antitrust cases in U.S. history. After a seven-year court battle, a complex settlement was reached. From left to right are Assistant Attorney General William Baker, AT&T Chairman Charles Brown, and Vice-President and general counsel Howard Trienes.

WIDE WORLD

school districts any state money to be used for the education of students not legally admitted into the U.S. The statute also authorized the various schools to deny enrollment to such students. By a vote of 5–4, the court held that the statute violated the Equal Protection Clause of the 14th Amendment. The majority held that illegal aliens are "persons" within the meaning of the Constitution and thus entitled to the same equal protection of laws and due process as individuals legally present in the country.

DEATH PENALTY. Questions regarding the validity and efficacy of the death penalty for serious crimes continued to be debated throughout the world. In one significant case, *Enmund* v. *Florida*, the U.S. Supreme Court held that the death sentence may not be imposed on a "felony murderer." A person may be guilty of "felony murder," even though he did not kill anyone or even intend the death of the victim, if he took part in the crime during which the murder occurred. Earl Enmund had driven the getaway car as a member of a gang that had robbed an elderly couple and shot them to death. He was not physically present when the murder occurred, and there was no evidence that he intended it. Nevertheless, he was found guilty of felony murder under Florida law and sentenced to death. The court held that the sentence constituted "cruel and unusual" punishment in violation of the Eighth Amendment.

Justice O'Connor, in a dissenting opinion, indicated the implications of the decision by pointing to the fact that roughly two-thirds of the states have laws similar to Florida's. Justice Byron White, writing for the majority, countered Justice O'Connor's contention that the widespread enactment of felony murder statutes militates against a finding that such statutes involve cruel and unusual punishment by asserting that such statutes are rarely used: "We are not aware of a single person convicted of felony murder over the past quarter century who did not kill or attempt to kill, and did not intend the death of the victim, who has been executed."

France abolished the death penalty in 1981, replacing all references to the death penalty in its Criminal Code with references to perpetual imprisonment or detention.

PRIVACY AND PERSONAL LIBERTY. In *Dudgeon* v. *United Kingdom*, the European Court of Human Rights held that a law of Northern Ireland making a criminal act of homosexual relations in private between consenting adults violates Art. 8 of the European Convention on Human Rights, which guarantees the right to respect for private life.

New scientific devices to discover "truth" or to expedite trials met different fates with regard to their use in criminal cases. In an important decision, the Federal Constitutional Court of West Germany held that the use of a lie detector in a criminal trial interfered with the personal rights of the accused and thus violated Art. 2 of the country's Basic Law. The court said this right could not be waived, so it made no difference whether the lie detector was used with the consent of the defendant.

Similarly, the Supreme Court of New Jersey held in *State* v. *Hurd* that evidence obtained through hypnosis is generally not admissible in a criminal trial. A New York court, however, determined that a criminal court may hear the evidence of a murder charge on videotape. This method of presenting the case, it said, aimed at the efficient use of a court's time and could be permitted where the two sides had settled the matter in advance. Videotape had been used in New York in civil cases, but this was the first time it had been approved for criminal cases.

Following the normal common law approach, Ireland for many years had held that one accused of crime may be tried only by the courts of the jurisdiction in which the crime was committed. In 1982 it made a sharp departure. Gerard Tuite, charged in Ireland with having committed an explosives offense in England, objected to the jurisdiction of the Irish court. The court held that it could try him, and he was subsequently convicted. The court found its authority in the new Criminal Law Jurisdiction Act.

The European Court of Human Rights handed down an important decision on the question of corporal punishment in schools, but some scholars found it somewhat confusing. In *Campbell and Cosans* v. *United Kingdom*, the court held that corporal punishment is not prohibited as "torture or inhuman or degrading treatment" within the meaning of Art. 3 of the European Convention on Human Rights. Apparently, however, a school may not impose corporal punishment if the parents of the child are philosophically opposed to it, nor may a school make parental acceptance of corporal punishment a condition of access to the school because Art. 2 of the Convention guarantees the right to education.

While some Europeans continued to complain that the European Court of Human Rights had gone too far in interfering with domestic matters, the court continued to deny jurisdiction where applicants had not exhausted local remedies. For example, in the case of *Helmers* v. *Sweden*, the court refused to hear the complaint of a Swedish civil servant, who alleged that certain misrepresentations had caused him to lose a lectureship, because he had not first brought actions in Sweden for defamation or tort.

The U.S Supreme Court announced that it would reconsider the "exclusionary rule," which requires U.S. courts, state and federal, to set aside evidence obtained in searches that are not conducted in accordance with the Fourth Amendment. The court's decision made many U.S. legal scholars unhappy. Liberals had been staunch supporters of the rule and opposed any reconsideration of it. Conservatives, however, would have preferred that the court confront the basic absurdity, pointed out long ago by Justice Benjamin Cardozo, that "the criminal is to go free because the constable has blundered." Their solution would be to punish the constable for overstepping his authority while admitting the fruits of the wrongful search into evidence.
(WILLIAM D. HAWKLAND)

International Law. International lawlessness took a more serious turn in 1982. There were the usual border violations by South Africa into Angola, by Indonesia into Papua New Guinea, and by Afghanistan into Iran. The war in the Horn of Africa between Somalia and Ethiopia continued. Iran expelled Iraqi troops from most of its territory and made unsuccessful attempts to carry the war into Iraq itself. In addition there were two new acts of armed aggression.

In April Argentina landed troops on the Falkland Islands and South Georgia, territories to which it had laid claim for many years and expelled the British garrisons. The U.K. responded by assembling a task force and recapturing both groups of islands, thus restoring the status quo ante. (See DEFENSE: *Special Report*; DEPENDENT STATES: *Sidebar*.) The hostilities were localized, and no general state of war was declared between the two countries, although economic sanctions were imposed on Argentina by the U.K , its European Community (EC) partners, other European and Commonwealth states, and by the U.S. France and Sweden sought the extradition of one Argentine officer who was captured, Lieut. Cmdr. Alfredo Astiz, in connection with the alleged torture of French and Swedish nationals in Argentina; however, he was repatriated in accordance with the third Geneva Convention on prisoners of war.

The second aggression was Israel's invasion of Lebanon in July, in order to expel the Palestine Liberation Organization from Lebanese territory. It culminated in a classic siege of the capital city of Beirut, which did not end until the city surrendered under international pressure and the Palestinians were evacuated under the protection of an international force. After the latter's departure, Lebanese military units, with the permission of the Israeli occupying authorities, entered certain Palestinian ghettoes, where they massacred many of the inhabitants. The siege itself raised questions of compatibility with the laws of war, involving indiscriminate shelling of civilian targets, including hospitals, and the use of phosphorus shells against civilians. During the siege and subsequent occupation, the U.S. embassy was fired upon, the Soviet embassy compound was forcibly entered, and Arab embassies were entered and ransacked. (See MIDDLE EASTERN AFFAIRS.)

REGIONAL AGREEMENTS. In May 1982 a summit meeting of the Economic Community of West African States agreed on the harmonization of internal taxation, citizenship, and interstate road transport. Saudi Arabia, Kuwait, the United Arab Emirates, Bahrain, Qatar, and Oman, which in 1981 had combined to form a Gulf Cooperation Council, reached agreement in June 1982 on the lifting of customs duties on interstate trade and on free movement of residents; a working group was appointed to formulate a common customs tariff on imports into member states. The Association of Southeast Asian Nations (Indonesia, Malaysia, Philippines, Singapore, Thailand) set up a working party to consider harmonization of member states' tax systems and tax incentives connected with foreign multinational corporations.

Australia, Japan, Canada, and the U.S. created the Pacific Association of Tax Administrators, designed to combat tax evasion by enterprises in the Pacific area, particularly through transfer pricing

UPI

Mayor Dianne Feinstein of San Francisco handed in her .38 calibre handgun to police chief Cornelius Murphy in July. Although licensed to carry a gun, Mayor Feinstein turned it in to call attention to the city's ban on handguns.

in low-tax countries. Australia and New Zealand went so far as to agree in principle on the formation of an economic community between them. The monetary union between Belgium and Luxembourg, which had been experiencing strain in recent years, established a new framework of ministerial meetings to be held three times a year. Senegambia, the confederation of The Gambia and Senegal, came into existence on Feb. 1, 1982.

SOVEREIGNTY. An aspect of sovereignty that caused much discussion during the year was the extraterritorial application of laws by the U.S. In particular, in order to bring political pressure on the U.S.S.R., it required all foreign subsidiaries of U.S. companies and all foreign companies licensing U.S. technology not to carry out contracts connected with the construction of the Soviet gas pipeline from Siberia to Western Europe. This led many European governments to protect their sovereignty by ordering companies within their territorial jurisdiction to fulfill their contractual obligations, even though they would suffer reprisals from the U.S. government as a consequence.

In other fields, the U.S. toned down the full rigour of its extraterritorial law enforcement. Thus a draft agreement was drawn up to resolve disputes between the U.S. and Australia arising out of conflicting extraterritorial exercise of antitrust powers; and U.S. attempts to apply the Sherman Act to foreign shipping lines organized in the "conference" system were replaced by a more tolerant approach. The long-standing attempts by the U.S. to penetrate Swiss banking secrecy culminated in publication of a Swiss bill to reduce such secrecy; and the Swiss Supreme Court upheld an application by the U.S. Department of Justice to require Swiss banks to assist the U.S. Securities and Exchange Commission in its investigation into the diversion of a company's funds into a private numbered account.

In April Panama assumed jurisdiction over the

Law Enforcement:
see Crime and Law Enforcement

Lawn Bowls:
see Bowling

Lawn Tennis:
see Tennis

Canal Zone (courts and police) after the expiration of a 30-month transitional period under the 1977 treaty with the U.S. The Canadian constitution was repatriated from the U.K. (*See* CANADA.) The conference of Australian state premiers approved a number of constitutional changes that would abolish all remaining links to the U.K. Parliament and state appeals to the Privy Council.

INTERNATIONAL ADJUDICATION. The Iran Claims Tribunal began work. It was agreed that the UN Commission on International Trade Law conciliation rules would apply to its procedure, but a number of procedural difficulties emerged, especially with regard to out-of-court settlements and access to the escrow account held by the Bank of England and the security account held by The Netherlands Central Bank.

The International Court of Justice (ICJ) delivered an important judgment in the Libya-Tunisia continental shelf case in which it again refrained from using the equidistance principle and instead repeated its reliance on general equitable principles, taking all circumstances into account. Libya and Malta agreed to submit their continental shelf dispute to the ICJ; and the U.S. and Canada submitted their dispute over fishing in the Gulf of Maine to a chamber of the court, the first time a chamber had been used in this way. In July the ICJ delivered an advisory opinion upholding a judgment of the UN Administrative Tribunal concerning a repatriation grant to a UN official.

MARITIME AFFAIRS. The most important event was the agreement on the final text of a treaty at the spring meeting of the UN Conference on the Law of the Sea, despite U.S. disapproval. Presented for signature in December and signed by 117 nations, it would go into effect when 60 had ratified it. Among those who did not sign were several major industrialized nations, including the U.S., the U.K., West Germany, and Japan. The most controversial section was devoted to an international regime for deep-sea mining. Legislation on that topic had been passed unilaterally by the U.S., the U.K., France, West Germany, and the U.S.S.R. over the past two years, and the U.S. was urging the U.K., France, and West Germany to coordinate

their rules on a go-it-alone basis. An agreement for research on seabed resources in the South Pacific was signed in July by Australia, New Zealand, and the U.S. under the auspices of the UN Committee for the Coordination of Joint Prospecting for Mineral Resources in the Offshore Areas of the South Pacific.

The U.K. and Irish governments continued work on the procedure for submission to arbitration of their dispute over the continental shelf around the island of Rockall and in the Irish Sea. Norway and Iceland concluded a treaty on the shelf between Iceland and Jan Mayen Island. Discussions also took place between Norway and the U.S.S.R. on oil exploration in the Barents Sea, notwithstanding the disputed zone between them. The boundary between Canada's 200-mi zone and the newly proclaimed 200-mi zone around the French overseas département of Saint Pierre and Miquelon continued to be discussed. The U.K. reached agreement with France on the boundary in the eastern part of the English Channel and reached agreement in principle with Belgium on the boundary in the North Sea.

In January Argentina denounced its 1972 treaty with Chile on settlement of the Beagle Channel dispute, but a new agreement was signed in September accepting the continued mediation of the pope. Australia and France signed a boundary agreement covering the overlap between their respective 200-mi zones in the southwest Pacific.

Sweden's difficulties with trespassing foreign submarines in its territorial waters flared into a major problem. More than eight such incidents were officially admitted during the year, and legislation was passed to permit the Swedish Navy to use force to cripple such intruders if they could not be forced to surface. (*See* SWEDEN.) Similar intrusions by unidentified, probably Soviet, submarines were reported by Norway in Narvik Fjord, Finland, Italy in the Gulf of Taranto, and Scotland in the Firth of Clyde.

The Intergovernmental Maritime Consultative Organization changed its name to the International Maritime Organization and agreed to revisions to the Conventions on Safety of Life at Sea. The UN Conference on Trade and Development held a session on flags of convenience; it reached agreement in principle on some points but was boycotted by the U.S., Liberia, and Panama. In the same month The Bahamas amended its Merchant Shipping Act to allow it to operate an open registry system. A nonbinding intergovernmental agreement was signed by the EC, Norway, Finland, Spain, and Portugal to introduce port controls on shipping for the prevention of marine pollution. The International Whaling Commission agreed to the phasing out of all commercial whaling by 1985. A conference of European countries and six international organizations agreed on a plan to set common European safety standards for oil drilling rigs. The International Law Commission, which increased its membership from 25 to 34, devoted part of its 34th session to the law on the nonnavigational uses of international watercourses.

(NEVILLE MARCH HUNNINGS)

See also Crime and Law Enforcement; United Nations.

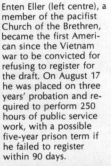

Enten Eller (left centre), a member of the pacifist Church of the Brethren, became the first American since the Vietnam war to be convicted for refusing to register for the draft. On August 17 he was placed on three years' probation and required to perform 250 hours of public service work, with a possible five-year prison term if he failed to register within 90 days.

Lebanon

A republic of the Middle East, Lebanon is bounded by Syria, Israel, and the Mediterranean Sea. Area: 10,230 sq km (3,950 sq mi). Pop. (1982 est.): 3,316,000. Cap. and largest city: Beirut (metro. pop., 1975 est., 1,172,000). The populations of both Lebanon and its capital city, Beirut, are thought to have declined since the outbreak of civil war in 1974, but reliable figures are not available. Language: Arabic (official), French, Armenian, and Kurdish. Religion: available estimates show Christians comprising variously from 40 to 55% of the population and Muslims from 45 to 60%; there is a Druze minority. Presidents in 1982, Elias Sarkis and, from September 23, Amin Gemayel; prime minister, Shafiq al-Wazzan.

The Israeli invasion, which began on June 6, 1982, and the assassination of President-elect Bashir Gemayel (*see* OBITUARIES) on September 14 were the key events in a year that saw Lebanon occupied by foreign troops. The Israeli invasion rapidly escalated into a full-scale pursuit of the Palestine Liberation Organization (PLO) guerrillas by the Israeli Army. By mid-June Beirut was effectively surrounded, and a long siege began. Thousands were reported to have died during the bombardment of the city. The Israelis' second objective—to drive the Syrians from their military positions in Lebanon—was also being achieved. Israeli military successes against Syria were largely attributable to superior military hardware supplied by the U.S. (*See* DEFENSE.)

The PLO fighters and their leader, Yasir Arafat

The bodies of victims of the Sabra and Shatila massacres in Beirut in September were lined up to await identification by relatives. Unidentified bodies were buried in mass graves.

LEBANON

Education. (1979–80) Primary, pupils 388,482; secondary, pupils 238,773; preprimary, primary, and secondary (1972–73), teachers 33,245; vocational, pupils 28,298, teachers 2,956; teacher training, students 1,662, teachers 205; higher, students (1978–79) 78,628, teaching staff (1972–73) 2,313.

Finance. Monetary unit: Lebanese pound, with (Sept. 20, 1982) a free rate of L£4.69 to U.S. $1 (L£8.03 = £1 sterling). Gold and foreign exchange (April 1982) U.S. $1,663,000,000. Budget (1980 est.): revenue L£3,026 million; expenditure L£3,868 million.

Foreign Trade. (1981) Imports (f.o.b.) c. L£13,977 million; exports c. L£3,824 million. Import sources: Italy c. 12%; Saudi Arabia c. 11%; France c. 10%; U.S. c. 8%; West Germany c. 6%; Romania c. 6%; Switzerland c. 5%. Export destinations: Saudi Arabia c. 31%; Syria c. 8%; Kuwait c. 6%; Jordan c. 5%. Main exports (1977): financial papers and stamps 21%; food, drink, and tobacco 17%; chemicals 11%; machinery 9%; metals 8%; textiles and clothing 7%.

Transport and Communications. Roads (1980) c. 7,100 km. Motor vehicles in use (1978): passenger 282,400; commercial 28,600. Railways: (1980) 417 km; traffic (1974) 2 million passenger-km, freight 42 million net ton-km. Air traffic (1981): 1,438,000,000 passenger-km; freight 470.8 million net ton-km. Shipping (1981): vessels 100 gross tons and over 230; gross tonnage 320,077. Telephones (Dec. 1978) 231,000. Radio receivers (Dec. 1979) 2 million. Television receivers (Dec. 1979) 600,000.

Agriculture. Production (in 000; metric tons; 1981): potatoes c. 147; wheat 28; tomatoes c. 76; grapes c. 125; olives c. 15; bananas c. 20; oranges c. 238; lemons c. 65; apples c. 115; tobacco c. 5. Livestock (in 000; 1981): cattle c. 60; goats c. 445; sheep c. 148; chickens c. 7,113.

Industry. Production (in 000; metric tons; 1980): cement c. 2,200; petroleum products (1979) c. 1,850; electricity (kw-hr) c. 1,800,000.

(*see* BIOGRAPHIES), finally agreed to leave Beirut, and on August 21 the evacuation began under French, U.S., and Italian military supervision. The plans for their departure to other Arab countries were negotiated by U.S. special envoy to the Middle East Philip Habib (*see* BIOGRAPHIES).

Worse was to come for Lebanon, however. An election brought about by the retirement of Pres. Elias Sarkis was won by Christian (Phalangist) militia leader Bashir Gemayel on August 23. His election was not popular with some Lebanese leaders because of his association with sectarian violence, but he himself was to die violently, when a bomb planted in the Phalangist headquarters in East Beirut exploded on September 14. The assassination triggered an immediate advance by the Israeli forces into Beirut on September 15.

On September 16 a massacre of hundreds of Palestinian men, women, and children began at the Sabra and Shatila refugee camps in West Beirut. The final casualty toll was placed at 328 dead and 991 missing. Reports suggested that those responsible for the killings were Christian militia forces loyal either to the late Bashir Gemayel or to Maj. Saad Haddad (*see* BIOGRAPHIES). Allegations were subsequently made about Israeli complicity in the killings. The Israeli government claimed it was not aware of the massacre until September 18, but an Israeli inquiry later in the year cast some doubt on this assertion.

The election of Pres. Amin Gemayel (*see* BIOGRAPHIES) at the end of September brought hopes of a new start. Bashir Gemayel had been hailed as a

Rounds of symbolic gunfire and patriotic cheers and gestures saluted PLO fighters as they left Beirut to take refuge in other Arab countries.

LESOTHO

Education. (1980) Primary, pupils 244,838, teachers (1979) 4,782; secondary, pupils 23,355, teachers (1979) 940; vocational, pupils (1979) 1,140, teachers (1978) 121; teacher training, students (1979) 822, teachers (1976) 39; higher (university), students (1979) 1,048, teaching staff (1977) 162.

Finance and Trade. Monetary unit: loti (plural maloti), at par with the South African rand, with (Sept. 20, 1982) a free rate of 1.15 maloti to U.S. $1 (1.97 maloti = £1 sterling). Budget (1978–79 est.): revenue 77,443,000 maloti; expenditure 50,532,000 maloti (excludes development expenditure of 87.7 million maloti). Foreign trade (1979): imports 304 million maloti; exports 37.9 million maloti. Main exports (1979): diamonds 56%; mohair 11%; wool 9%. Most trade is with South Africa.

Agriculture. Production (in 000; metric tons; 1981): corn *c.* 130; wheat *c.* 25; sorghum *c.* 75; dry peas *c.* 7; wool *c.* 1.3. Livestock (in 000; 1981): cattle *c.* 600; sheep *c.* 1,180; goats *c.* 780.

"messiah" by some Christian groups in Lebanon, and it was feared that his presidency would be divisive. Amin Gemayel, on the other hand, was a more moderate figure than his brother. It was thought that the new government would take a strong line with Israel and refuse to agree to a peace treaty except within the context of an overall Arab-Israeli settlement.

Amin Gemayel immediately sought to achieve three objectives: the withdrawal of all foreign troops from Lebanon, the restoration of security, and the reconstruction of a country devastated by war and sectarian strife. In October he visited the U.S., France, and Italy. In an address to the UN, Gemayel pleaded for the withdrawal of Israeli, Syrian, and Palestinian forces from Lebanon. He also requested that the 7,000-strong UN Interim Force in Lebanon remain for a further three-month period until Jan. 19, 1983; this request was granted.

Prime Minister Shafiq al-Wazzan named an entirely new Cabinet on Oct. 8, 1982. The Lebanese press heralded the administration as a technocratic rather than a political group. Beirut airport was reopened on September 30 after the last Israeli soldiers had left it, an event that appeared to mark the return of normality to the city. Late in the year, however, factional fighting was reported between Christian and Druze militiamen in the mountains east and southeast of Beirut and between pro- and anti-Syrian Muslims in Tripoli. On December 28, largely as the result of intense U.S. pressure, negotiations began between Lebanese and Israeli delegations. (JOHN WHELAN)

See also Israel; Middle Eastern Affairs.

Lesotho

Lesotho

A constitutional monarchy of southern Africa and a member of the Commonwealth, Lesotho forms an enclave within the republic of South Africa, bordering the Republic of Transkei to the southeast. Area: 30,355 sq km (11,720 sq mi). Pop. (1982 est.): 1,407,000. Cap. and largest city: Maseru (pop., 1976 prelim., 14,700). Language: English and Southern Sotho (official). Religion (1980): Roman Catholic 43.5%; Lesotho Evangelical Church

29.8%; Anglican 11.5%; other Christian 8%; tribal 6.2%; other 1%. Chief of state in 1982, King Moshoeshoe II; prime minister, Chief Leabua Jonathan.

Political assassination returned to Lesotho during 1982 with the killing in July of Koenyame Chakela, secretary-general of the underground Basotho Congress Party, and the shooting of Minister of Works Jobo Rampeta in August.

On December 9 South African commandos attacked several residences in a predawn raid in Masuru and killed some 30 persons, most of them exiled South African members of the banned African National Congress. The South African claim that they were "trained terrorists" was vigorously denied by spokesmen for the exiled community and by the Lesotho government.

The largest item in Lesotho's 1982–83 budget was a 36 million maloti public debt, starkly illustrating the country's dependence upon outside finances. The budget included a new sales tax and higher charges for liquor, vehicle registration, and trading licenses. New aid granted during the year included loans from the Commonwealth Development Corporation and the World Bank.

More than 100,000 Basotho were working in South African mines; total deferred pay and remittances from this source for 1981, at 47,220,000 maloti, were 50% higher than in 1980. The future of Lesotho's Letseng-la-Terai diamond mine was in doubt. At 2.8 carats per 100 metric tons of ore, it had the lowest recovery rate in the De Beers diamond group, and the world market remained depressed. (GUY ARNOLD)

Liberia

A republic on the west coast of Africa, Liberia is bordered by Sierra Leone, Guinea, and Ivory Coast. Area: 99,067 sq km (38,250 sq mi). Pop. (1982 est.): 1,990,000. Cap. and largest city: Monrovia (pop., 1980 est., 243,200). Language: English (official) and tribal dialects. Religion (1980): tribal 43.5%; Christian 35%; Muslim 21.2%; Baha'i 0.3%. Head of state and chairman of the People's Redemption Council in 1982, Gen. Samuel K. Doe.

The year 1982 was one of consolidation for the regime of Gen. Samuel K. Doe, Liberia's head of

LIBERIA

Education. (1979) Primary, pupils 206,876, teachers 5,090; secondary, pupils 51,231, teachers 2,974; vocational, pupils 1,717, teachers (1976) 63; teacher training, students 306, teachers 17; higher, students (1980) 3,789, teaching staff (1978) c. 190.

Finance. Monetary unit: Liberian dollar, at par with the U.S. dollar, with a free rate (Sept. 20, 1982) of L$1.71 = £1 sterling. Budget (1980–81 actual): revenue L$219 million; expenditure L$228 million.

Foreign Trade. (1981) imports L$477,420,000; exports L$531,420,000. Import sources (1980): Saudi Arabia 27%; U.S. 23%; West Germany 10%; The Netherlands 7%; Japan 7%; U.K. 6%. Export destinations (1980): West Germany 24%; U.S. 21%; France 13%; Italy 10%; The Netherlands 9%; Belgium-Luxembourg 6%. Main exports (1979): iron ore 54%; rubber 16%; timber 11%; diamonds 7%; coffee 5%.

Transport and Communications. Roads (1980) 10,823 km. Motor vehicles in use (1979): passenger 13,070; commercial 8,999. Railways (1980) 490 km. Shipping (1981): merchant vessels 100 gross tons and over 2,281 (mostly owned by U.S. and other foreign interests); gross tonnage 74,906,390. Telephones (Jan. 1980) 7,740. Radio receivers (Dec. 1979) 319,000. Television receivers (Dec. 1979) 21,000.

Agriculture. Production (in 000; metric tons; 1981): rice c. 216; cassava c. 315; bananas c. 75; palm kernels c. 7; palm oil c. 20; rubber c. 76; cocoa c. 4; coffee c. 13; timber (cu m; 1980) 4,939. Livestock (in 000; 1981): cattle c. 40; sheep c. 210; goats c. 210; pigs c. 107.

Industry. Production (in 000; metric tons; 1980): iron ore (68% metal content) 18,350; petroleum products (1979) c. 470; cement 140; diamonds (metric carats) 300; electricity (kw-hr) c. 900,000.

state, following his announcement in December 1981 in which he set April 1985 as the target date for a return to civilian rule. In April 1982 Doe lifted the curfew that had been in force since the 1980 coup. In June it was reported that preliminary work on the draft of a new constitution had been completed. Also during that month Doe revealed plans to build a new capital city to replace Monrovia.

Liberia's head of state, Samuel K. Doe (left), was greeted on a visit to Washington in August by U.S. Pres. Ronald Reagan. The visit was seen as granting legitimacy to Doe's government.

WIDE WORLD

The economic situation continued to deteriorate. The rubber industry faced a decline in world demand and increased taxes. Aid agreements were completed with Italy, the U.S., China, and France, and in late 1981 a $100 million foreign debt was rescheduled. The World Bank and other institutions financed a $57 million package to rehabilitate the iron-ore industry, while agriculture benefited from an International Development Association credit worth $15.5 million.

Doe visited a number of countries during the year, including China, North Korea, France, and Morocco. In August his reception in Washington, D.C., was seen as conferring legitimacy on his regime. At that time the U.S. agreed to help develop Liberia's Air Force. (GUY ARNOLD)

Liberia

Libraries

The worldwide drift into recession created problems for library and information services in 1982. Budgets for the purchase of books and periodicals were reduced while prices continued to rise. Reactions varied from country to country. In West Germany, for instance, there were pressures to introduce charges for the loan of books from public libraries. This was strongly opposed by the majority of professional librarians and information scientists as being in conflict with UNESCO's precept that "access to [information] is one of the basic human rights."

In the U.K. economies in the operation of public library services that had begun in 1973–74 reached a stage where further reductions would make it difficult to provide the comprehensive library ser-

A new stamp to honour libraries in the U.S. was issued on July 13 by the U.S. Postal Service.

U.S. POSTAL SERVICE

vice required by statute. During the past five years, staff in England and Wales had been reduced by over 5% and 472 libraries (11% of the total) had been closed. It was not just the public libraries that were under pressure. In 1981–82, 21% of university libraries received less funds than in the previous year, compared with 2% in 1980–81. Many university libraries reported cuts in book purchasing of up to 40%, and reductions in hours and staff continued to have serious effects. In the school library sector, standards of provision, already poor, worsened.

France was one of the few bright spots in Europe. The advent to power of a Socialist government had injected not only money but also new life into the system. Responsibility for libraries, particularly public libraries, was decentralized to the provinces, and almost unprecedented opportunities were provided for expansion. But if most other countries in Europe suffered badly, the less developed countries faced greater threats. Not only was the purchase of books and periodicals made difficult by increased costs and transport charges; problems were exacerbated by the inability to purchase new technology and to provide the necessary skilled manpower to use it.

Indeed, the increasing confluence of computers and telecommunications, the development of cable networks for television and radio, the evolution of videotext systems and of relatively inexpensive microcomputers, and the introduction of microcomputers into educational institutions were changing the environment in which library and information services were provided. The effect of the new technology on libraries and information services was examined and the consequences for the profession in the U.K. were made clear in a Library Association report.

The coincidence of technological developments and reductions in expenditure forced the library and information science professions to consider ways to best exploit the resources already allocated to them. Many countries in Europe continued to examine the machinery—and in some cases the legislation—required to improve resource allocation to library and information services. Reductions in library budgets affected employment opportunities in all types of library and information work. This situation, along with the advent of the new technology, indicated a need to reexamine library and information science education programs.

At the international level two important meetings took place, sponsored by UNESCO. An international World Congress on Books, held in London in June, produced the "London Declaration." This document encouraged progress toward a reading society and made 12 recommendations to UNESCO, urging it in turn to persuade member states to protect and encourage the use of books in education and library and information services. In Paris, in May, UNESCO held a conference on the Universal Availability of Publications, seen as complementary to the program encouraging universal bibliographic control. The latter recommended that each country be responsible for the production of the bibliographic record books published

The new logo approved by the American Library Association was a stylized figure of a person reading a book. The logo is white against a blue background and was being put on T-shirts, tote bags, and other items.

within its boundaries and for making that information freely available to other countries. The object was to ensure that a book is cataloged only once to an adequate and recognized international standard. (RUSSELL BOWDEN)

The Index of American Public Library Circulation, released in July 1982 by the University of Illinois, showed that U.S. circulation figures for 1981 had passed the 1,000,000,000 mark for an all-time high. U.S. public libraries spent some $2 billion in 1981, but with barely a one-point increase in purchasing power. Although state aid to libraries was up 9% overall, federal funding was flat, and many urban communities cut library services severely. Dramatic gains, however, were made by the libraries of Houston, Texas, Hennepin County, Minn., and Oklahoma County, among others. A California law authorized up to $23 million in matching funds for the state's public libraries beginning in July 1983. In December the National Endowment for the Humanities announced $5.3 million in matching grants to 13 libraries, including $2 million to the New York Public Library.

District-level allocation of federal funds for schools, along with school-based management trends, resulted in increased spending for microcomputers and software, and school media centres were eager to ride the wave. In October the second national conference of the American Association of School Librarians in Houston devoted some 20 sessions to microcomputers. An American Library Association (ALA) survey showed that most libraries were charging fees to help support on-line reference searching, one of the proliferating nonbasic library services.

In April, Dallas, Texas, opened its new state-of-the-art Central Library, with on-line computer catalogs for patrons, a cable television studio, and a full range of community services. The Newberry Library of Chicago completed a ten-story, free-standing facility with 7,150 sq m (77,000 sq ft) for storage of rare materials. The Library of Congress began a deacidification program to prolong the life of some 50,000 items that were self-destructing because of chemicals used in the paper.

The ALA and other library groups waged a year-long battle against qualification standards for federal library posts proposed by the U.S. Office of Personnel Management. Librarians charged the standards would diminish the importance of the master of library science degree and raise the status of managerial posts above that of service posts. (ARTHUR PLOTNIK)

[441.C.2.d; 613.D.1.a; 735.H]

THE "NEW" CENSORS

by John N. Berry III

When officials of the Mark Twain Intermediate School in Fairfax, Va., decided to restrict the use of the novel *The Adventures of Huckleberry Finn* in that school, the incident became the most widely reported censorship story of 1982. No reporter could resist the delicious irony of a case where school officials banned a book by the namesake of the school in which they served. In the eyes of U.S. intellectual freedom fighters, the incident proved what they had been anxiously asserting for nearly two years: Censorship is on the rise, and the freedoms guaranteed in the First Amendment to the U.S. Constitution, particularly those of speech and the press, are in danger.

In June Judith F. Krug, director of the American Library Association's Office for Intellectual Freedom, which monitors censorship activity in the U.S., told reporters that the number of censorship complaints reported to her office had tripled in the last three years. According to Krug, at the beginning of the 1970s the ALA received about 100 complaints of attempted library censorship a year, but this number grew to 300 in the later years of the decade, "and since mid-1980 we get nearly 1,000 a year."

Recent Attempts at Censorship. A sampling of the censorship challenges of 1982 provides some insight into the motivation and beliefs of those who would "protect" others from words and pictures on paper, on the screen, or in live public utterances. Commissioners in Coral Gables, Fla., voted to ask the Miami-Dade Public Library System to ban the showing of several "racy" films (*Airplane, The Wiz, Ordinary People, Urban Cowboy, The Shining, Stripes, The Blue Lagoon*) in branch libraries. The complaint was brought by two Protestant ministers on the grounds that the films presented premarital sex, foul language, and the occult in a favourable light. In Orlando, Fla., a group called the Movement for Moral Decency objected to having works by author Judy Blume (*Deenie; Forever; Are You There God? It's Me, Margaret;* and *Then Again, Maybe I Won't*) in Orange County schools.

John N. Berry III is editor in chief of the Library Journal.

In Coleman, Wis., the school board voted to restrict access to *A Handbook for Conscientious Objectors* and *Words of Conscience: Religious Statements of Conscientious Objectors.* The books were requested by a mother who wanted her two teenage sons to have access to their point of view, as well as to the views of military recruiters who were allowed to work in the schools. In Renton, Wash., a group of parents formally complained against the use of Peter Stillman's *Introduction to Myth* in the schools on the grounds that, by including Christianity in the book, Stillman had implied that it was a myth.

During the past year Chicago author Studs Terkel traveled to Girard, Pa., to defend his book *Working.* Students and parents in Girard objected to the use of profanity in the interviews of workers describing their work that make up the book. As well as being attacked by the Virginia school officials, *Huckleberry Finn* was also the target of complaints by parents in Houston, Texas; Warrington, Pa.; and a host of other cities.

Challenged books came from nearly every era (*Huckleberry Finn,* 1884; *Gone with the Wind,* 1936; *The Grapes of Wrath,* 1939; *The Stupids Die,* 1981) and ranged across subjects from science fiction to psychology. Under fire since its publication in 1951, J. D. Salinger's *The Catcher in the Rye* returned to the fray in 1982, along with two Kurt Vonnegut novels of the 1960s, *Slaughterhouse-Five* and *Cat's Cradle.*

Magazines caught in the attack included *Ms., National Lampoon, Penthouse, Playboy, The Humanist,* and even such apparently "safe" titles as *McCall's, Ladies' Home Journal,* and *Newsweek.* The censors' lists also included games (Dungeons and Dragons), television programs ("Lou Grant"), and a number of newspapers.

New Sources of Censorship. Censorship challenges have always been a part of life in the U.S. They have come from every place on the political, social, racial, and religious spectra of American society. In 1982, however, observers claimed that attempts at censorship had increased dramatically, and most agreed that conservative political and religious individuals and groups were responsible for the increase over what used to be a "normal" amount of censorship. The "new" censors, then, are apt to be politically conservative and believers in "fundamentalist" Christian religious principles.

It was an organization called the Christian Research Center that wanted to ban Isaac Asimov's *In the Beginning* from high-school libraries in San Diego, Calif. The campaign to remove several psychology and sociology textbooks from schools in Escambia County, Fla., was led by members of the

Crossroads Baptist Church. In Shreveport, La., the charges against two Guidance Associates films were brought by a group called the Pro-Family Forum. Other censors have called themselves "creationists" (opposed to scientific theories of evolution) or "pro-life" (opposed to abortion).

The objections that arise from such would-be censors centre on three areas: sex, religion, and politics. The use of dialogue that is perceived to be obscene or profane is the fastest way to get a book challenged by the new censors. Books or movies that appear to condone activities that are threatening to what are called "traditional" values are always in danger of being challenged. Materials that portray premarital sex or any of a number of other varieties of sexual activity are regularly challenged, even in works recommended as purely educational. Any public or published views that oppose defense spending, draft registration, or favour sex education in public schools will draw opposition. The broadest brush with which the new censor paints his or her target, however, is the label "secular humanism." By that the censor means any work or works that either convey doubts about or disbelief in a more or less literal interpretation of the King James Version of the Christian Bible.

Not all censorship efforts originate from these "new" censors, however. There are still substantial attempts at censorship emanating from other segments of the political and religious spectra. It was black parents who objected to Twain's use of the word "nigger" in *Huckleberry Finn,* and it was feminists who campaigned under the banner of Women Against Pornography. Still, it is apparent that the increase in current attempts to censor is coming from the political and religious right.

First Amendment Rights. It is also important to note that, of the "nearly 1,000" complaints that ALA's Judith Krug reports, most (about 750) are aimed at books and other materials in institutions serving children. One of the most perplexing questions that this raises, and that the courts have been unable to resolve, concerns the nature of the First Amendment rights of children and of the librarians and teachers who serve them. One side takes the view that only parents can decide what these rights are and that tax money should not be spent on the purchase of books or other materials for use in schools and libraries serving children if taxpayers and parents disapprove of those materials. The other side asserts that such materials are protected by the First Amendment, as are the teachers, librarians, and children. Court decisions in such cases have been less than definitive.

To complicate the situation, many observers seriously doubt that the incidence of censorship is as

The American Library Association reports that attempts at library censorship more than tripled in the early 1980s. Above, a conservative religious group in Kansas burns books they consider offensive.

great as the reports would suggest. Even if the reported increase in censorship activity is real, there is evidence that the censors are defeated more often than they succeed. Lillian Gerhardt, the editor of *School Library Journal,* points out that the "universe" of libraries in the U.S. numbers more than 83,000, "So, we have a less than 0.01% of the libraries serving the young encountering some parent or patron disapproval." Gerhardt goes on to assert, "In a citizen-run democracy, a rate of one percent or less . . . of complaints, or even demands of any public institution probably represents democratic good health."

This society has never experienced a time with fewer constraints on freedom of expression. It is inevitable that attempts at censorship will increase as freedom of expression is enhanced. As Ervin Gaines, director of the Cleveland Public Library, pointed out in the *Cleveland Press,* would-be censors are "more of a nuisance than a threat." He cited the series of censorship decisions of the U.S. Supreme Court in the 1960s as dramatically reducing constraints on freedom of expression.

The censors are seldom victorious. In August a school board that removed nine books (including *Slaughterhouse-Five, The Fixer, Black Boy,* and *Soul on Ice*) from the school library ordered them returned to the shelves. *The Adventures of Huckleberry Finn* is back in use in the Mark Twain Intermediate School. A federal court ordered *365 Days* returned to the school library in Baileyville, Maine. Studs Terkel convinced the authorities and students in Girard, Pa., to keep and read his book *Working.* Throughout the U.S. school boards, library trustees, judges, and librarians have turned away the censors, both "new" and old. Thus, in 1982 the freedoms guaranteed by the First Amendment held their own.

Libya

A socialist country on the north coast of Africa, Libya is bounded by the Mediterranean Sea, Egypt, the Sudan, Tunisia, Algeria, Niger, and Chad. Area: 1,749,000 sq km (675,000 sq mi). Pop. (1982 est.): 3,425,000. Cap. and largest city: Tripoli (pop., 1981 est., 858,500). Language: Arabic. Religion: predominantly Muslim. Chief of state in 1982, Col. Muammar al-Qaddafi; secretary-general of the General People's Committee (premier), Jadallah Azzuz at-Talhi.

For the first time in more than two decades, Libya in 1982 entered a protracted period of reduced oil revenues, with important consequences for both consumption and economic development. The scale of the reduction in revenues could not be determined exactly because a significant proportion of oil was moved through barter arrangements with Eastern-bloc trading partners, and oil was also offered under a barter agreement to Ireland and Cyprus, among many others. Revenues fell from over $20 billion in 1980 to only $10 billion in 1982.

The shortages reported in Libyan shops could be attributed only partly to a shortage of the means to pay suppliers. The Libyan marketing system continued to adjust to the nationalization of all wholesaling and retailing initiated in 1980. State supermarkets dominated the urban retail trade, and smaller versions were set up throughout the country. These adjustments were more significant than any dislocations in imports, and Libya re-

mained financially competent to provide for the needs of its small population.

Development spending, however, was severely affected. Existing schemes were sustained, but there was a marked slowing in new ventures. One major exception was the initiation of the pipeline to bring water from Tazerbo and Wadi as-Sarir in the south to the coastal tracts behind the Gulf of Sidra for agricultural, industrial, and urban use. The pre-construction phases of the work were not expected to demand much capital. It remained to be seen, however, whether the huge $10 billion bill for construction would be contracted, especially as a similar and less costly venture in the west of the country was being investigated. Industrial investment overtook agricultural investment.

At a special emergency session of the General People's Congress on March 3, a number of changes were made in the composition of the General People's Committee (GPC). Jadallah Azzuz at-Talhi retained the post of secretary-general of the GPC (premier), but two outgoing secretaries, for internal affairs and foreign affairs, were not replaced, though a secretary for foreign liaison remained on the GPC. A new post, that of secretary for economy and light industries, was created. In April the premier was appointed to the post of secretary-general of the General People's Congress. At a regular session of the Congress in January, it was decided to draft a bill that would bring into force the plan to replace the Army with a national militia composed of all Libyan citizens. The necessary measures for the merger with Syria which were proposed in September 1980 were to be undertaken immediately.

During Col. Muammar al-Qaddafi's visit to Algeria in January, a merger between Libya, Algeria, and Syria was discussed. Relations with Egypt were resumed, and some border movements took place for the first time since 1977. Colonel Qaddafi maintained a statesman-like approach throughout the first part of the year, prior to the August summit meeting of the Organization of African Unity in Tripoli. Nevertheless, 19 countries boycotted the meeting, with the result that the necessary two-thirds quorum was not attained, and no formal sessions could take place. A second effort to convene the summit in November failed because of a dispute over the seating of Chad.

Libya blamed the U.S. for influencing members to stay away, and relations with the U.S. remained poor; no oil was exported there, and U.S. nationals were impeded by their own government from going to Libya. In late summer, when the U.S. fleet once again exercised in the southern Mediterranean Sea, the anniversary of the 1981 clash between U.S. and Libyan forces passed without incident.

Qaddafi continued to cultivate relations with Eastern-bloc countries and visited Poland on September 8–10. In his first official visit to a Western state, Qaddafi spent four days in Austria in March. Later in the year when he visited China and North Korea, a coup planned to coincide with his return was uncovered, and on November 3 some 100 officers of the armed forces reportedly were arrested.

(J. A. ALLAN)

Libya

LIBYA

Education. (1979–80) Primary, pupils 656,541, teachers 30,489; secondary, pupils 257,479, teachers 16,526; vocational, pupils 8,918, teachers 637; teacher training, students 31,227, teachers 2,153; higher (1973–79), students 14,351, teaching staff (1977–78) 1,922.

Finance. Monetary unit: Libyan dinar, with (Sept. 20, 1982) a par value of 0.296 dinar to U.S. $1 (free rate of 0.508 dinar = £1 sterling). Gold and other reserves (May 1982) U.S. $7,281,000,000. Budget (administrative; 1982 est.) balanced at 1,255,000,000 dinars. Gross national product (1978) 5,407,000,000 dinars. Money supply (Nov. 1981) 3,290,700,000 dinars.

Foreign Trade. (1981) Imports (f.o.b.) c. 4,162,000,000 dinars; exports 4,635,700,000 dinars. Import sources (1980): Italy 30%; West Germany 13%; Japan 8%; U.K. 7%; France 7%; U.S. 6%. Export destinations (1980): U.S. 35%; Italy 19%; West Germany 13%; The Bahamas 5%; Spain 5%. Main export: crude oil 99.9%.

Transport and Communications. Roads (including tracks; 1976) c. 20,000 km (including 8,700 km surfaced). Motor vehicles in use (1980): passenger c. 367,400; commercial (including buses) c. 278,900. Air traffic (1980): c. 1,101,000,000 passenger-km; freight c. 17 million net ton-km. Shipping (1981): vessels 100 gross tons and over 103; gross tonnage 888,643. Shipping traffic (1979): goods loaded 91,531,000 metric tons, unloaded 7,360,000 metric tons. Telephones (Dec. 1977) 141,700. Radio licenses (Dec. 1979) 131,000. Television receivers (Dec. 1979) 160,000.

Agriculture. Production (in 000; metric tons; 1981): barley c. 79; wheat c. 141; potatoes c. 103; watermelons c. 171; tomatoes c. 238; onions c. 69; oranges c. 35; olives c. 162; dates c. 85. Livestock (in 000; 1981): sheep c. 6,258; goats c. 1,500; cattle c. 185; camels c. 134; asses c. 60.

Industry. Production (in 000; metric tons; 1981): crude oil 53,858; petroleum products (1979) c. 6,070; natural gas (cu m) c. 3,980,000; electricity (kw-hr; 1980) c. 3,100,000.

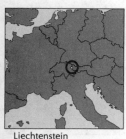

Liechtenstein

Liechtenstein

A constitutional monarchy between Switzerland and Austria, Liechtenstein is united with Switzerland by a customs and monetary union. Area: 160 sq km (62 sq mi). Pop. (1982 est.): 26,200. Cap. and largest city: Vaduz (pop., 1982 est., 5,000). Language: German. Religion (1980): Roman Catholic 88%; Protestant 10.7%; Jewish 0.3%; none 1%. Sovereign prince, Francis Joseph II; chief of government in 1982, Hans Brunhart.

Liechtenstein had been admitted to the Council of Europe in 1978 on the understanding that it would grant voting rights to women, but once again only men voted in the February 1982 general election. Among the excuses given to justify such discrimination was the argument that, if women were given the right to vote, the elections might be influenced by foreigners, since about one-half of the men in the principality were married to women from Switzerland, Austria, or Germany.

The election was contested by the two traditional parties: the Patriotic Union, led by Prime Minister Hans Brunhart, and the Progressive Citizens' Party, led by Hilmar Ospelt. The Patriots obtained a 53.5% share of the vote, retaining eight seats, while the Progressives, with 46.5%, retained their seven seats. Since the elections did not alter the balance of power within the Landtag (parliament) and no important issues divided the two parties, they renewed the coalition government formed in 1978. (K. M. SMOGORZEWSKI)

LIECHTENSTEIN

Education. (1981–82) Primary, pupils 1,899, teachers 95; secondary, pupils 1,831, teachers 92.
Finance and Trade. Monetary unit: Swiss franc, with (Sept. 20, 1982) a free rate of SFr 2.14 to U.S. $1 (SFr 3.66 = £1 sterling). Budget (1981 est.): revenue SFr 217,293,000; expenditure SFr 211,315,000. Exports (1980) SFr 887 million. Export destinations: EEC 41%; Switzerland 22%; EFTA (other than Switzerland) 8%. Main exports: postage stamps, metal manufactures, chemicals, instruments, furniture, pottery. Tourism (1980) 85,033 visitors.

Life Sciences

The efforts of creationists notwithstanding, the theory of biological evolution remained alive and healthy and a powerful intellectual stimulus in 1982, a hundred years after the death of Charles Darwin. As emphasized in the accompanying report on Darwin's centenary (*see* Special Report) the ongoing debates among evolutionary biologists did not at all question the fact that evolution took place but concerned the exact details of how it operated. The primary raw materials for resolving those details, *i.e.*, the fossilized remains of earlier life, continued to be unearthed and analyzed and the results added to the emerging picture of life's pageant on Earth.

For example, new evidence documenting man's presumed transition from a tree-dwelling creature to an upright-walking, tool-using one was de-

COURTESY, E. M. FRIIS, BEDFORD COLLEGE, LONDON

Fossils of ancient flowers were found in clay beds in Sweden. The flowers bloomed about 80 million years ago, making them the oldest flowers presently known to scientists.

scribed during the year, and researchers in Antarctica offered their discovery of the first mammalian fossil ever found on that continent as support for a theory of early animal migration from South America to Australia (see *Zoology*, below). E. M. Friis of the University of London and A. Skarby of the Geological Institute in Stockholm reported their find of whole, structurally preserved flowers in Sweden in clay beds dating from the Upper Cretaceous, about 80 million years ago. Only 2 mm (0.08 in) long, the rare fossils represented the oldest flowers known and came from an age in which it is believed that the flowering plants were diversifying and coming into dominance. Also reported in recent months was the discovery of the earliest known seeds, by William H. Gillespie of the U.S. Geological Survey and colleagues. About 5 to 6 mm (0.2 in) long and enclosed in seed-bearing cupules, the fossils lay in clays and shales associated with coal beds in West Virginia that were formed in the Late Devonian, about 350 million years ago.

A nearly complete skeleton of *Diacodexis*, the earliest known member of the order of mammals (Artiodactyla) that includes cattle, pigs, sheep, giraffes, hippos, camels, deer, and antelope, was described by Kenneth D. Rose of Johns Hopkins University, Baltimore, Md. Previous knowledge of this rabbit-sized species had been limited to a few bone fragments, from which it had been concluded that the animal had a short-limbed, generally unspecialized body and thus might well be the common ancestor of all present-day artiodactyls. The new skeleton, however, showed *Diacodexis* to have long, slender limb bones and other advanced features, suggesting a swift, graceful running and jumping animal much like today's mouse deer, or chevrotain, and not the shrewlike creature first pictured.

George O. Poinar, Jr., and Roberta Hess of the University of California at Berkeley described one of the more spectacular paleontological events of the year: the discovery and microscopic examination of a fly whose abdominal soft tissues had undergone remarkable preservation in Baltic amber believed to be 40 million years old. Calling the find "an extreme case of mummification, involving the preservation of insect tissue by drying and natural embalming [with] plant sap," the researchers were able to observe cells, cell organelles such as mitochondria and ribosomes, nuclei, and clumps of genetic material called chromatin, and to compare them with the structure of present-day insects. The level of preservation appeared to rival that previously seen in 3,000-year-old Egyptian mummies and mammoths exhumed from Siberian ice. Late in the year Poinar and colleagues were exploring the possibility that some of the fly's DNA had remained intact and might be cloned for further study. (CHARLES M. CEGIELSKI)

[312.A.5.C.iii; 312.B–E; 313.J.7.c.xii]

ZOOLOGY

Charles Darwin died in 1882, and hence the centenary year became a focal point for numerous conferences and symposia on evolutionary theory. The past year's discussions and reviews could spawn new approaches, insights, and challenges to evolutionary theory, which states that natural selection operates at the level of the individual organism and has been the primary force modifying species over time. Stephen Jay Gould of Harvard University concluded that the strictest interpretation of Darwin's basic premises eventually may be refuted. He based his opinion on recent scientific challenges to and extensions of Darwinism, such as the concept of punctuated evolution and hierarchical models in which natural selection operates on individual units at various levels of biological organization. Despite modern research tools, innovative interpretations, and new fields of science such as biochemical genetics, most evolutionary biologists still consider Darwin's basic concepts to be solid. (*See* Special Report.)

WIDE WORLD

The well-preserved remains of a fly were found embedded in tree sap believed to be 40 million years old. Scientists were able to study structures within individual cells of the insect.

Certain strides were reported in the field of biochemical genetics by Leonard DiMichele and Dennis A. Powers of Johns Hopkins University, Baltimore, Md., in studies with a small coastal fish known as the mummichog. Their research focused on allelic difference (gene alternatives) at the lactate dehydrogenase (LDH-B) locus since mummichogs in colder parts of their range are known to be genetically different at this particular genetic locus from those in warmer regions. They found that fish having the cold-region genotype (genetic makeup) hatched several days later than those having the warm-region genotype. They also discovered that fish with the cold-region genotype swam significantly faster at 10° C (50° F) than did the other genetic group. Both hatching time and swimming rate are affected by respiration, which in turn is influenced by temperature. Furthermore, differences in respiratory qualities of red blood cells have been related directly to genetic variation at the LDH-B locus. Importantly, this research revealed the physiological function of previously identified allelic patterns at a single genetic locus and could provide insight into the

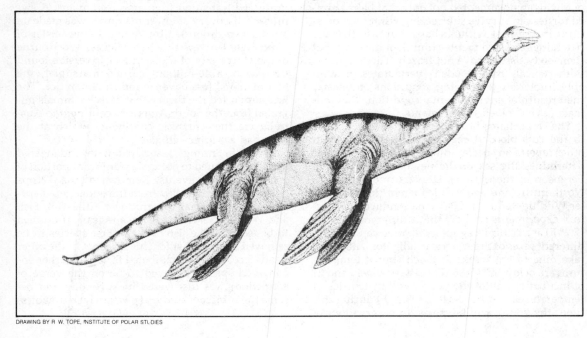

DRAWING BY R. W. TOPE, INSTITUTE OF POLAR STUDIES

The fossilized remains of at least ten large marine reptiles called plesiosaurs, believed to have lived 75 million years ago, were found in early 1982 on Seymour Island off Antarctica. The expedition, led by William Zimsmeister of the Institute of Polar Studies, also uncovered 40-million-year-old fossils of giant penguins as tall as seven feet.

evolutionary significance of such biochemical variations. In addition, few other vertebrate studies have quantified and confirmed that allelic variation at a single genetic locus can affect the whole organism.

An example of how natural selection might operate to shift the frequency of appearance of one gene alternative over another at a critical genetic locus in an entire population was identified by Michael H. Smith and associates at the Savannah River Ecology Laboratory in South Carolina. They documented that the frequency of the most common allele at the beta-hemoglobin (BHB) locus changed significantly over a five-year period in a population of white-tailed deer subjected to hunting pressure. Alleles at the BHB locus affect oxygen transport and other respiratory characteristics that may be important to an animal whose survival is influenced by an ability to run rapidly under certain circumstances. Based on this set of investigations and other examples of how deer herds respond genetically to particular hunting regimes, Smith and his colleagues proposed that wildlife agencies should consider the genetic makeup of wildlife populations in formulating management programs.

Representatives of two groups of vertebrates, frogs and turtles, were found to have unsuspected adaptations to below-freezing temperatures. William Schmid of the University of Minnesota investigated cold-tolerance mechanisms in three species of frogs that are exposed to freezing temperatures in winter. He found that each species produced measurable levels of glycerol, a liquid fat product that during winter functions as an antifreeze. Individual frogs could tolerate temperatures as low as −9° C (16° F) without damage, although as much as one-third of their body liquids actually froze. Many turtles are known to remain in their nest for several months after hatching but usually have been suspected of being in situations where freezing temperatures are not encountered. Justin D. Congdon and Gary Breitenbach of the University of Michigan documented not only that baby painted turtles can survive subfreezing winter temperatures in the nest without harm but also that the hatchlings react to tactile stimuli, indicating that their body tissues have not frozen. These findings with typical "cold-blooded" vertebrates presumably intolerant to freezing conditions emphasize the breadth of environmental conditions that animals have evolved to withstand.

The importance of environmental temperature to the cold-blooded reptiles was emphasized in other reports on species in which nest temperature determines the sex of the newborn. Mark W. J. Ferguson of the Queen's University of Belfast in Northern Ireland and Ted Joanen of the Rockefeller Wildlife Refuge in Louisiana conducted laboratory experiments to show that a difference of 4° C (7.2° F) at a critical stage of incubation can result in different sexes of the American alligator. Alligators take nine to ten weeks to hatch, but if temperatures are below 30° C (86° F) between days 7 and 21 of incubation, all of the young will be females. If temperatures are above 34° C (93.2° F) during this time, the young will be males. In observations of natural alligator nests in Louisiana they found that nests in warm sites produced males, whereas those in cooler, shaded sites produced all females. In those nests with intermediate temperatures males hatched from eggs deposited in the warm, upper portion; eggs on the bottom of the nest, which stayed at cooler temperatures, produced females. They extended the significance of their findings to a possible explanation for extinction of many dinosaurs at the end of the Cretaceous geologic period in that widespread climatic shifts could have resulted in persistent temperature changes that resulted in the virtual elimination of one sex or the other of a species.

In contrast to alligators, green sea turtles produce female hatchlings at warm incubation temperatures and males at cooler temperatures, according to studies by Stephen J. Morreale and colleagues of State University College at Buffalo, N.Y. Based on experiments conducted on nesting beaches in Costa Rica, they found that shaded nests with temperatures below 28° C (82.4° F) resulted in male hatchlings, whereas on the open beach, where temperatures were above 30° C (86° F), the young were females. Morreale and his associates cautioned that these findings are pertinent to sea turtle hatcheries, in which eggs are raised at relatively constant temperatures. Thus, well-meaning conservationists who release hatchlings into the sea as a means of replenishing declining sea turtle populations may be unwittingly producing only one sex.

Fossil finds resulted in advancements in understanding evolutionary relationships among vertebrates. In a development associated with human lineage, R. L. Susman and J. T. Stern of the State University of New York at Stony Brook reported on the earliest known human species (*Homo habilis*, 1,760,000 years ago from Tanzania). They presented evidence of a fossil specimen that shared both the primitive feature of being arboreal and the more advanced humanlike characteristics of walking upright and making tools, documenting the presumed transition from apes to humans. A significant discovery of lower mammals was made on a polar expedition led by William Zinsmeister of Ohio State University when Michael Woodburne of the University of California at Riverside found the jaw of a 40-million-year-old marsupial, the first mammal fossil ever found in Antarctica. The find supported the theory that early mammals migrated from the South American continent to Australia via the Antarctic continent, which at the time had a warmer climate.

Research findings associated with endangered species continued to occupy a significant portion of zoological news events. Removal of the Tecopa pupfish of Death Valley from the endangered species list was official recognition by the U.S. Fish and Wildlife Service that the species is presumed to be extinct. The fish was the first species to be removed from the list for this reason. On the other hand, a colony of black-footed ferrets, another endangered species believed to be on the verge of extinction, was discovered in Wyoming and became the subject of study. (J. WHITFIELD GIBBONS) [312.C.3.c; 312.D.; 354.C.; 413.B; 10/34.B.6.d–e]

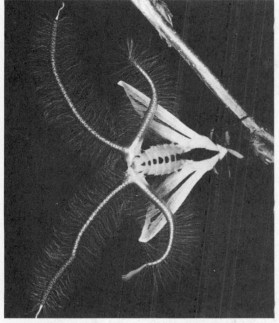

DR. MICHAEL BOPPRÉ, UNIVERSITÄT REGENSBURG INSTITUT FÜR ZOOLOGIE

Scientists in West Germany discovered that the larvae of certain moths ingest plant substances that are poisonous to other insects. In male moths these poisons regulate the development of their prominent scent organs, which function in adult courtship.

Entomology. Hopes that the previous year's widespread outbreak of Mediterranean fruit flies in California had been eradicated were dashed when in mid-1982 a fly turned up in the San Joaquin Valley, near the heart of California's immensely valuable horticultural industry. The minimal indication, however, and the state administration's prompt response, including aerial spraying with the insecticide malathion and a ban on movement of produce in a large surrounding area, gave promise that eventually the threat would indeed be eliminated.

Nevertheless, international and interstate repercussions continued. Fumigation with ethylene dibromide (EDB), required of fruit from California's medfly quarantine areas, is the most effective and economical way of ensuring disinfestation of commercial fruit, but the chemical has been shown to be carcinogenic. California's Occupational Safety and Health Administration proposed stricter permissible concentrations of EDB in work places and required signs to be posted where vapours could be present. Dock workers, alerted to the danger, refused to load fumigated citrus for Japan, while California supermarkets refused to market fruit from Texas and Florida—which had their own fumigation programs—because signs were thought likely to deter customers. Japan eventually agreed to an alternative treatment of fruit en route and, subject to later review, to allow entry of unfumigated lemons from beyond the "regulated areas." Clearly, however, this $100 million annual trade would remain jeopardized while the medfly risk persisted.

Entomologists throughout the world worked to better understand the way insects select and are selected according to the plants on which they feed. Insects adapted to feed on plants that contain chemicals toxic to other species may use such compounds for their own protection and as starting materials for elaboration of sex pheromones. Dietrich Schneider of the Max Planck Institute at Seewiesen, West Germany, and co-workers found that larvae of arctiid moths of the genus *Creatonotos* take up highly toxic pyrrolizidine alkaloids, which not only accumulate in the males but also regulate the development of their "hair pencils"—scent organs that function in courtship Thomas Eisner of Cornell University, Ithaca, N.Y., reported to a meeting of the American Association for the Advancement of Science that the Spanish fly beetle and another species of arctiid, *Utetheisa ornatrix*, are subject to sexual selection for their content of repellent substances, which are transferred from male to female during mating. With William Conner and other associates, Eisner had found that *Utetheisa* possessing a full complement of alkaloid are so distasteful to spiders that the latter free the moths from their webs; but if larvae are reared on bland food, resultant males are less attractive to the females and are eaten by spiders if caught. Eisner quoted evidence that alkaloids passed from the males during mating were subsequently incorporated into the eggs, helping to provide them with protection and supplying a further rationale for sexual selection.

Donald Roberts and others from the University of Brazil and the U.S. Army Environmental Hygiene Agency, working on malaria control in the Amazon basin, investigated local stories of "DDT-eating bees" and found them to be males of a native bee, *Eufriesia purpurata*, that collect inside sprayed houses, noisily scraping DDT off walls and roofing with no apparent ill effects. The researchers postulated that DDT resembles some naturally occurring plant substance and is rapidly detoxified by the bees and used as a pheromone.

An insect's picture of the world is strongly influenced by angles between objects and the rate at which they pass across its visual field. The housefly decelerates and initiates landing as the rate of image expansion of the landing site reaches a critical value, according to Hermann Wagner of the Max Planck Institute at Tübingen, West Germany. L. P. S. Kuenen and T. C. Baker of the University of California, Riverside, found that moths fly at speeds that achieve an optimum rate of movement of retinal images of ground objects; thus the higher the moth, the faster it attempts to fly. Meanwhile, in ingenious experiments in which bees were trained to visit food in a room empty except for a few large reference objects, B. A. Cartwright and T. S. Collett of the University of Sussex in the U.K. found that the bee retained a "snapshot" of the scene. Thus, if the reference objects had been moved farther apart, the bee searched at a spot predictably farther away from them.

(PETER W. MILES)

[321.B.9.c.ii; 321.E.2.a; 731.A.5]

Ornithology. The 18th International Ornithological Congress was held in Moscow in August 1982. For the first time in recent decades ornithologists from the Soviet Union and other Eastern bloc countries were fully represented, to the mutual benefit of themselves and Western visitors.

A study of the urban bird life of Moscow by K. N. Blagosklonov showed that the 110 species that nest within the city's 900 sq km (350 sq mi) fall into two groups: a larger group of species whose natural habitats have been retained despite urbanization and a smaller number that have adapted to the essentially man-made habitats. In many cities one member of the crow family comes to predominate. In Moscow it is the hooded crow; in Riga, the raven; in Lublin, the rook; in Kharkov, the jay; in Tartu, the jackdaw; and in Gorky and Berlin, the magpie. Urban selective pressures on birds allow the evolution of populations clearly tamer than their country cousins. The timing and frequency of breeding have changed, as has diet. In three remarkable cases the more hospitable conditions in Moscow have allowed rooks, starlings, and mallards, formerly as absent as swallows in winter, to occupy the city all year.

Another Soviet study of urban birds concerned the new town of Puschino-on-Oka, a "science town" built from 1965 onward in a "virgin" agricultural area. The status of 127 bird species was examined and related to the building program, to the pollution effects of pesticides, motor vehicles, and river transport, and even to populations of domestic pets.

The ecological counterpart in northern Asia of the very rare North American Eskimo curlew is the little curlew. Some scientists regard the two populations merely as different races of the same species. The little curlew is familiar to ornithologists in northern Australia where it spends the winter, but it was almost totally unstudied in its breeding grounds in northeastern Siberia. There Boris Veprintsev studied, photographed, filmed, and tape-recorded the species. Among several discoveries was the fact that, as part of its sexual and territorial song-flight, the bird has not only a vocal element but also an element of instrumental sound production; as it dives, a "jet plane" effect is achieved by the passage of air through the bird's feathers.

Recordings of the little whimbrel's sound production and of 62 other Euro-Asiatic birds were made available on three long-playing records, the first three of a projected set of 25 under the title *The Birds of the Soviet Union: A Sound Guide*. This monumental work would take ten years to complete and would cover 750 species of the U.S.S.R.

In 1940 it was estimated by the noted biologist Ernst Mayr that, of the total number of bird species in the world, 3% were yet to be discovered. This would add 260 to his figure of 8,600 known species in 1940. It was difficult to evaluate the accuracy of Mayr's estimate because, although only 140 new species had been discovered by 1982, the rate of discovery showed little sign of dropping off. Between 1941 and 1955 it was 2.5 yearly, increasing to 3.6 yearly for 1962–82. Recent discoveries included *Tijuca condita*, a cotinga from Brazil; the Neblina metaltail (*Metallura odomae*), a hummingbird from Peru; the enigmatic shortwing (*Brachypteryx cryptica*), a thrush from India; the Okinawa rail (*Rallus okinawae*) from the Pacific; and the white-headed flightless steamer duck (*Tachyeres leucocephala*) from Argentina.

A new technique growing swiftly in popularity among those who trap birds to put identifying bands on their legs was the use of sound recordings to lure birds toward the net. A startling example was that of three ornithologists who, in five three-month seasons, summoned from the sea by broadcasting their calls at night from rocky headlands no less than 16,500 storm petrels. The retrapping of previously banded birds threw much light on the movements and longevity of the species. A fulmar, a seabird of the petrel family, was banded in Scotland on June 8, 1982, and had crossed the Atlantic to Newfoundland three weeks later.

A new human use of birds was introduced in The Netherlands. To control flies in livestock houses, a Dutch company first fitted the structures with special bird-proof doors and then let loose purple glossy starlings imported from Africa. Two birds were allocated to either eight sows with piglets or to 60 calves.   (JEFFERY BOSWALL)
[313.J.6]

MARINE BIOLOGY

During recent dives by the submersible "Alvin" to 3,650 m (12,000 ft) in the North Atlantic and to 1,300 m (4,270 ft) off southern California, studies were made of the respiration and feeding behaviour of lysianassid amphipod crustaceans. These animals form an important component of deep-sea animal communities, and they aggregate much more rapidly than other scavengers at baited cameras and traps. Their metabolic strategy appeared to involve very rapid responses to food odour, rapid rate of food consumption, and an ability to withstand long periods of starvation. Other studies from "Alvin" were made on the crab *Bythogrea thermydon* from the vicinity of hydrothermal vents at 2,500 m (8,200 ft) depth off the Galápagos Islands. Experiments were aimed at understanding the effects of high pressure on the crabs' neuromuscular system. During decompression of the animals from 238 atmospheres to 1 atmosphere their electrocardiogram pattern was disrupted and heart rate was reduced, both effects being retarded at low temperatures. Observations by scuba diving in the open ocean revealed new associations between zooplankton organisms; for example, a highly specific association between the stromateoid fish *Tetragonurus* and pelagic salps and pyrosomes, which are free-swimming tunicates.

The first new duck species to be reported since 1917 was discovered in the Atlantic off the coast of Argentina. Named the white-headed flightless steamer duck, it escapes from predators by rapid surface swimming.

COURTESY, PHILLIP S. HUMPHREY, UNIVERSITY OF KANSAS ENDOWMENT ASSOCIATION. PHOTO, BRADLEY C. LIVESEY

Studies at Discovery Bay, Jamaica, showed that the symbiotic zooxanthella algae contained in shallow-living colonies of the reef coral *Montastrea annularis* were adapted to function at high intensities of light and did poorly when coral was transplanted to low light intensities at greater depths. Conversely, deeper forms that had become adapted to low light did poorly when transplanted to high light intensities nearer the surface. Growth of the commercially important large brown alga *Macrocystis* was studied in New Zealand and California; localized parts of the alga doubled their fresh weight in just over two days. The growth rate is fast for a macroalga but not as fast as that in some land plants. In the past the nutritional importance of macroalgae to marine fishes that eat them had been questioned.

For the first time for a temperate-zone marine fish (*Cebidichthys violaceus*) assimilation of macroalgal constituents was demonstrated; protein, carbohydrate, and total organic material were absorbed more efficiently from red algae than from green. Conversely, lipid was absorbed more efficiently from green than red. Fecal pellets of midwater fish, like those of euphausiid and copepod crustaceans studied earlier, were shown to exhibit slow rates of sinking and release of dissolved organic compounds; fecal matter represents a major source of organic transfer from the pelagic (open-ocean) community to the benthos (sea bottom). Experiments in Hawaii on respiratory activities of *Alpheus mackayi* showed this burrowing shrimp to be important in transporting water and materials from the sediment into the water above; it enhanced the physical release of silica from sediment pore water by a factor of five. Estimates of chemical fluxes across the water-sediment interface would be unrealistic if they were based solely on physical considerations and excluded the macrofauna as "biological pumps."

The omnivorous copepod crustacean *Calanus pacificus* was found to feed disproportionately on the prey in greatest abundance when given mixtures of diatoms (*Thalassiosira*) and copepod nauplii (newborn larvae). Switching from herbivory to carnivory may be significant in nature during the decline of phytoplankton blooms in summer. The polychaete worm *Nereis virens* is a predator that, on intertidal mudflats in Maine, was shown to "crop" the abundant amphipod crustacean *Corophium volutator*. Removal of the polychaetes in field experiments enhanced *Corophium* abundance, and introduction of *Nereis* led to a decrease.

The sea hare *Aplysia*, unusually for a gastropod mollusk, is capable of sustained directional swimming, which in *A. brasiliana* was shown to be around 0.4 kilometres per hour (0.25 mph) for more than 30 minutes. Orientation in offshore swimming was by rhinophore-mediated detection of wave surge, with visual cues predominating once the animals were in open water. A harbour seal trained to swim at six kilometres per hour (3.7 mph) subsequently remembered how to swim at that rate from day to day; removal of the vibrissae (whiskers) from the snout did not impair this unusual speed sense. The intertidal barnacle *Balanus glandula* of western North America responded with prolonged cirral (arm) withdrawal and tight closure of the shell valves on exposure to the predatory gastropod mollusk *Thais*, but not to the herbivorous gastropod *Tegula*.

Luminescence was shown to be very widespread in amphipod crustaceans, notably in two oceanic genera, *Scina* (Gammaridea) and *Cyphocaris* (Hyperiidea). Sychronous flashing of the peripheral luminescent organs probably serves to deter predatory fish by enhancing the amphipods' apparent size. Tests on Atlantic herring, American pollack, winter flounder, Atlantic salmon, and cod showed that toxins produced by the "red tide" dinoflagellate *Gonyaulax excavata* were fatal when administered orally in low doses. (ERNEST NAYLOR)

[313.H.3; 354.B.2]

BOTANY

Since the element nitrogen (N) is a constituent of nucleic acids and proteins, it is essential for the growth and maintenance of all plants. Although copious amounts of nitrogen are present in the atmosphere, where nitrogen exists in gaseous form (N_2), atmospheric nitrogen is not available to plants. The nitrogen in N_2 can only be used by plants following fixation, a process during which N_2 is converted into ammonia (NH_3).

Nitrogen fixation can be accomplished industrially and biologically. Because production of nitrogen fertilizer by means of industrial fixation consumes large quantities of energy, in recent years efforts have been made to understand and exploit biological fixation.

The capacity to fix nitrogen in biological systems is restricted to certain procaryotic (essentially bacterial) organisms, some of which can accomplish fixation only after forming symbiotic associations with the roots of legumes such as soybean. Invasion of legume roots by the nitrogen fixing bacterium *Rhizobium* results in a proliferation of root tissues leading to the formation of bulbous structures called root nodules. The latter consist of greatly enlarged plant cells infected with *Rhizobium* together with smaller uninfected cells. A recent ultrastructural study showed that the infected and uninfected cells of soybean (*Glycine max*) nodules are markedly different from one another. Uninfected cells possess numerous enlarged microbodies and an extensive network of smooth endoplasmic reticulum (ER), whereas infected cells are almost devoid of these cell organelles.

In soybean root nodules, newly fixed nitrogen becomes incorporated into allantoin and allantoic acid, two of a class of compounds called ureides, which are subsequently exported to the shoot. Ureide synthesis within the nodule cells involves the conversion of the nitrogenous base xanthine into uric acid. The latter interacts with the enzyme uricase to form allantoin, from which allantoic acid is produced by the enzyme allantoinase. Since soybean root-nodule homogeneates yielded a microbody fraction with uricase activity and an ER-containing microsome fraction with allantoinase activity, it was suggested that the uninfected cells in soybean root nodules may play an essential role in the nitrogen metabolism of the nodule. It was conjectured that allantoin synthesis occurs in the microbodies, whereas allantoic acid synthesis takes place in the smooth ER.

When fossil fuels containing sulfur are burned and ores containing sulfur are smelted, the pollutant sulfur dioxide (SO_2) is released into the atmosphere. Automobile exhausts contain nitrogen dioxide (NO_2), which in the presence of light is split into nitrous oxide (NO) and atomic oxygen (O). The latter is extremely reactive and combines with molecular oxygen (O_2) to form the pollutant ozone (O_3). Since human activities result in the release of SO_2 and O_3 into the atmosphere, plant biologists have become concerned with plant responses to these pollutants.

In a study conducted recently in central England the effect of mixtures of SO_2 and O_3 on the net photosynthetic rate of the broad bean (*Vicia faba*) was investigated. The concentrations of SO_2 and O_3 used were typical of the concentrations of the two pollutants in the atmosphere of central England. It was found that in plants exposed to an atmosphere containing 40 ppb (parts per billion) SO_2 photosynthesis was significantly depressed. Similar results were obtained with plants maintained in atmospheres containing 60–150 ppb O_3. However, when plants were maintained in atmospheres containing 40 ppb SO_2 plus O_3 in a concentration range of 60–150 ppb, decreases in the net photosynthetic rates greater than those in either gas alone were observed.

In another investigation ambient air from Washington, D.C., which contains ozone, was supplemented with SO_2. The effects of 0.06, 0.12, and 0.30 ppm (parts per million) of SO_2 on yields of snap bean (*Phaseolus vulgaris*) were studied. Greater decreases in snap bean yields occurred in air containing SO_2 and ambient O_3 than in SO_2-supplemented air from which ozone had been removed. A threefold greater reduction in yields occurred with 0.30 ppm of SO_2 and ambient O_3 than with 0.30 ppm of SO_2 alone.

Although the two highest concentrations of SO_2 used in this study were probably greater than the atmospheric SO_2 concentrations of most industrial areas, the observed linear relationship between increasing concentrations of SO_2 and yield loss prompted the suggestion that SO_2 concentrations even lower than 0.06 ppm, when in the presence of ambient O_3, could bring about a significant reduction in yields of susceptible crop plants.

(LIVIJA KENT)

[313.C.2; 352.B.2.c.ii]

MOLECULAR BIOLOGY

Bacterial Chemotaxis. A bacterium such as the common intestinal inhabitant *Escherichia coli* is exceedingly small, but it is by no means simple. Although it would take 4,000 *E. coli*, end to end, to span one centimetre, each of them is made up of thousands of different kinds of molecules in specific arrangments. Furthermore, an *E. coli* can make more *E. coli* when provided only with a single source of carbon, such as glucose, plus a few inorganic salts. The chemistry involved in this metabolism, as of the early 1980s, was far beyond the best efforts of any group of human chemists, however large the group and however well equipped.

E. coli can also swim. It achieves this ability by the rotation of long spiral appendages, called flagella, which operate much like a propeller on a ship. The swimming of *E. coli* has a purpose. The cell will swim up a concentration gradient (*i.e.*, in the direction of an increasing concentration) of usable nutrients such as sugars, amino acids, and oxygen and away from or down a concentration gradient of toxins such as phenols. This behaviour allows each *E. coli* to seek out an environment optimal for survival and reproduction. Although first noted a century earlier, the details of this bacterial chemotaxis were only recently being unraveled by clever and painstaking observation, experimentation, and analysis. Foremost in this effort has been Daniel E. Koshland, Jr., at the University of California at Berkeley.

The smallness of *E. coli* makes the instantaneous sensing of a chemical gradient infeasible for the bacterium. Separated by only 0.00025 cm (0.0001 in), at any instant the two ends of the cell would experience only trivial differences in concentration, even in a steep gradient. Thus, *E. coli* must contrive to sense the chemical gradient over a distance much greater than its own body length. In fact, it must measure changes in concentration with time as it swims along the gradient. This temporal sensing of gradients implies memory, because the cell somehow must compare the concentration currently experienced with that encountered tens of seconds earlier. How is this managed in a cell that weighs only 10^{-12} gm, or 3.5×10^{-14} oz?

E. coli swims for a few tens of seconds in a straight line and then tumbles briefly before beginning another straight run. The tumbling, which is caused by a reversal of direction of rotation of the flagella, changes the direction in which the cell is pointing, so that the next straight run will be in a new direction. When there is no chemical gradient, runs interspersed with tumbles make for a random motion. Suppose, however, that movement up a concentration gradient of an attractant somehow inhibited tumbling. The cell would then tend to continue moving in the favourable direction. In contrast, if movement down a gradient of attractant increased tumbling, the cell would more quickly and repeatedly reorient itself until it was swimming in the right direction. Gradients of repellents could be handled profitably by the same strategy, except that for repellents up-gradient movement would increase tumbling and down-gradient movement would inhibit tumbling. This is exactly what *E. coli* does.

If *E. coli* responds to a gradient of glucose, it must have receptors for glucose. Indeed, it needs receptors for each of the compounds to which it responds. *E. coli* contains about two dozen kinds of receptors for attractants and half that number for repellents. A cell with a genetic inability to make one of these receptors will be blind to one aspect of its chemical environment. Thus, a cell unable to make functional glucose receptors will not respond to gradients of glucose. *E. coli*, like other gram-negative bacteria, has two membranes in its cell envelope. The outer of these is quite permeable to small molecules, while the inner membrane exhibits a very limited and selective permeability. The receptors that function in chemotaxis are located either in the space between the two envelope membranes or on the inner membrane.

Also on the inner membrane are a few proteins that control the direction of flagellar rotation. These might be called trigger proteins. Each of them communicates with a group of receptors, and for the approximately three dozen types of receptors in *E. coli* there are only four or five kinds of trigger proteins. Combination of an attractant or repellent with its specific receptor changes the receptor in a way that fosters its binding to the appropriate trigger protein. In turn, binding of the receptor to the trigger protein makes the trigger protein more susceptible to both methylation and demethylation (addition and removal of methyl groups), and it is the degree of methylation that controls the direction of flagellar rotation. However, the rate of the methylation reaction is affected rapidly, while the rate of demethylation is affected more slowly. A sudden increase in some attractant therefore would lead to only a transient change in methylation of the trigger protein. Rapid activation of methylation would lead to increased methylation of the trigger, but this state would then be reversed when the more slowly activated demethylation process caught up.

This arrangement of rapid activation of methylation with a slower activation of demethylation guarantees that only changes in concentration will be sensed. Here is the heart of the bacterial memory. At any constant concentration both methylation and demethylation occur at equal rates. However, the difference in the rate of responsiveness of methylation and demethylation to changes in concentration of attractant or repellent means that methylation of the trigger protein will increase when attractant concentration is increasing and will decrease when attractant is decreasing. For repellents the opposite statements apply. The fact that there are numerous receptors funneling their signals through a few trigger proteins means that the cell could integrate its response to simultaneous gradients of several attractants and repellents. The cell thus can make the best compromise response in the face of multiple chemical signals.

The flagella ordinarily rotate at 1,000 rpm, and the flagellar motor somehow is driven by the gradient of protons across the cell envelope of the bacterium. Part of the energy, made available by cell metabolism, is always devoted to maintaining this transmembrane proton gradient. The flow of protons through the flagellar motor drives it, just as a flow of electrons drives a man-made electric motor. Although this facile analogy should not be allowed to mask scientists' complete ignorance of the mechanism of the flagellar motor, there is no doubt that it is driven by the proton gradient, since its rate of rotation is proportional to that gradient.

Also unknown is the exact means by which the degree of methylation of the trigger proteins controls the direction of rotation of the flagellar motor. Yet scientists have gone a long way in dissecting and analyzing this mechanism and in the process have learned something about the way bacteria perceive their chemical environment, remember that environment for short times, adapt to constant factors in that environment so as to allow detection of small changes, and finally respond to their environment in a way that benefits themselves. It seems likely that this analysis will lead ultimately to a better understanding of the behaviour of more complex organisms which achieve the same ends by means that are not yet understood.

(IRWIN FRIDOVICH)

Antibody Diversity. One of the most remarkable aspects of human beings and other vertebrates is their immune system, which serves to protect the body against invasion by microorganisms and other foreign substances and possibly against the growth of cancer cells. When a foreign substance such as a microorganism or a large molecule enters the body it is detected by the immune system and usually inactivated. The components of the immune system responsible for this recognition are called antibodies, and the foreign substances recognized by the antibodies are called antigens.

Antibodies are members of a group of proteins called immunoglobulins (Ig's), of which there are several distinct but closely related classes. Immunoglobulin molecules are composed of two basic types of subunit, called light (L) chains and heavy (H) chains. A complete Ig molecule consists of two identical light chains (molecular weight about 23,000 daltons each) and two identical heavy chains (molecular weight about 60,000 daltons each) held together in a very specific arrangement, forming a Y-shaped antibody molecule (*see* Figure 1). The two sites on an antibody that bind antigen,

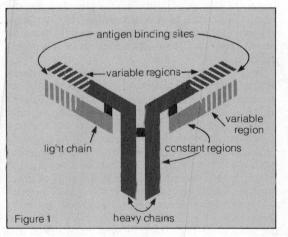

Figure 1

the antigen binding sites, are at the tips of the arms of the Y and are molecule-sized pockets formed by the apposition of the end of one L chain and the end of one H chain.

Every different Ig has a unique antigen binding site that binds tightly to some structural feature (the antigenic determinant) of the antigen. The L chains of all antibodies are similar in structure but display important differences in a region at one end, the so-called variable (V) region. The other end, being much less variable, is called the constant (C) region. The H chains also have a variable region similar in size to that of the L chains and a constant region about three times as long as that of the L chains. It is in fact the variable regions of the H and L chains that form the antigen binding site.

It is known that the body can respond to many different antigenic determinants. For example, if a person is injected with an inactivated polio virus— *i.e.*, immunized—his immune system responds by producing antibodies specifically against this virus. Injection of a different antigen, *e.g.*, a flu virus or ragweed pollen, induces the production of antibodies specifically reactive toward that substance. The body in fact can respond to an enormous number of different antigens. It has been estimated that the immune system can produce well over a million different kinds of antibodies. How the information for such a vast assortment of protein molecules is stored and used by the immune system has been one of the major puzzles of modern biology. The recent technical breakthroughs of recombinant DNA technology, molecular cloning of genes, and rapid sequencing of the genetic material have allowed molecular biologists to solve much of this puzzle.

The protein chains of the Ig's, like other proteins, are linear polymers of building blocks called amino acids. The linear order or sequence of the amino acids in each H or L chain is determined by the gene for that chain. Each gene consists of a stretch of DNA (deoxyribonucleic acid), also a linear polymer, containing a specific sequence of four kinds of DNA building blocks called deoxyribonucleotide bases. The information in the DNA comprising a gene is decoded by being transcribed into a messenger molecule with the same base sequence as the DNA but composed of ribonucleotides. This messenger molecule is called messenger RNA (mRNA). The mRNA serves as a template for the synthesis of the L or H chain protein; the sequence of bases in the mRNA determines—and its information is translated into—the sequence of amino acids in the protein chain.

To encode the millions of different antibody molecules that the immune system is capable of producing, the vertebrate genome (the organism's total genetic complement) should contain a similar number of different antibody genes. Yet, if every different antibody were encoded by a separate gene, the amount of required DNA would represent too large a fraction of the genome, and not enough would be left to code for the thousands of other necessary proteins. This apparent paradox recently was solved by experiments in which antibody genes themselves were isolated by molecular cloning and their organization was analyzed at the DNA sequence level. Much of the progress in this field was due to pioneering work from the laboratories of Philip Leder, currently at Harvard Medical School, and Susumu Tonegawa at the Basel (Switz.) Institute for Immunology.

The key to generating enormous antibody diversity with a limited amount of genetic information lies in organization of the genes encoding the different regions (variable and constant) of the heavy and light chains. There are in fact multiple coding sequences for the variable and constant regions of the Ig chains, but these are dispersed on the DNA. In other words, antibody genes exist in pieces. When a cell develops into an antibody-producing cell (an immunocyte), only then are the pieces of the genes combined in one of many possible ways

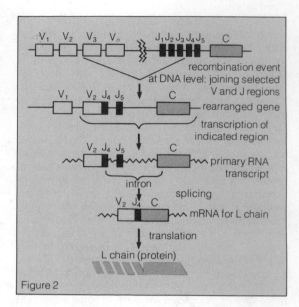

Figure 2

to form a complete gene, which is then used to make a unique antibody chain.

The details of the arrangement (and rearrangement) of the L chain genes are represented schematically in Figure 2. In the DNA of cells not yet making an antibody there is an array of 300 to 500 different variable-region coding sequences (V_1, V_2, V_3, etc.). Elsewhere along the DNA there is a constant-region coding sequence, with five small joining (J) elements flanking it (J_1 through J_5). To form a functional L chain gene, a remarkable recombination event occurs such that one of the V regions becomes fused with one of the J regions, the intervening DNA sequences being deleted. After recombination there exists a VJ region, which codes for the variable half of the L chain.

Transcription (mRNA synthesis) can now occur to form the primary transcript, as illustrated. This transcript contains all the coding information for the L chain, but it still has excess RNA between J and C. This excess RNA (called an intron) is "spliced" out, by mechanisms not yet well understood, to form the actual mRNA. The V, J, and C coding information is now arranged in a contiguous linear fashion and can be translated into protein to form an L chain. Since any V region can be joined to any J region, this device of recombination of genes in pieces can generate 1,500 to 2,500 ($5 \times$ 300 to 500) kinds of L chains.

It is also known that H-chain genes are arranged similarly to L-chain genes and that at least as many different H chains can be formed by analogous recombination mechanisms. Since two of any H chain can associate with two of any L chain to form a functional antibody molecule, combinations of the possible H and L chains can create well over a million kinds of antibodies, each with a different antigen binding site. Using this elegantly efficient mechanism for generating antibody diversity, the immune system can thus recognize and protect the body from a bewildering array of foreign substances without carrying an unacceptably large burden of DNA.   (ARNO GREENLEAF)

[321.B.3; 321.B.5; 339.C; 421.B.2.d]

See also Earth Sciences; Environment.

REEVALUATING DARWIN

by Jeremy Cherfas

Charles Robert Darwin, who died quietly on April 19, 1882, at the age of 73, may safely be said to have changed the way we perceive the natural world of which we are a part. Although Darwin did not discover evolution, he documented the evidence that living things had undergone change and provided a mechanism to explain that change. Natural selection is the force that has shaped living things, and with it we can make sense of both the enormous variety of life and the seemingly exquisite perfection of design.

Darwin is believed to have become an evolutionist at some point on the voyage of the HMS "Beagle" around the world. In the Galápagos Islands he saw that each island had its own distinct giant tortoise. And the birds that he collected there turned out, despite their dissimilar appearance, to be closely related finches. Darwin could hardly suppose that a Creator had made each of the varieties independently. But then how had the varieties arisen?

When he returned to England he threw himself into the work of describing and cataloging the prodigious number of specimens—animal, vegetable, and mineral—that he had collected, giving the collections to the experts of the day. He began a notebook devoted specifically to "the species question" and filled it with observations, thoughts, and untried theories that might illuminate the transmutation of one type of living organism into another. The great insight came in 1838, when Darwin read again Malthus's *Essay on the Principle of Population*.

Theory of Natural Selection. Malthus explained how living things reproduce much more quickly than the resources they need and will very quickly outstrip those resources. This gave Darwin the selection he needed: potential growth coupled with constant resources means that there is an inevitable struggle for survival. This is the first part of Darwin's

Jeremy Cherfas, demonstrator in animal behaviour at the University of Oxford, is life sciences consultant to New Scientist *magazine, whose volume* Darwin Up to Date *he edited. He is the author of* Man Made Life *and co-author of* The Monkey Puzzle.

argument. He then documented the variability of living things. If any such variation gave its owner an advantage in the struggle for survival so that it left more offspring, the variation would be favoured. The struggle for survival selects certain variants, and those variations come to dominate the population. That is the essence of natural selection, a phrase Darwin chose specifically to point up the analogy with artificial selection, in which man breeds specific varieties for his own purposes and in the process changes the plant or animal.

Natural selection, Darwin suggested, could account for all the diversity of life and for design. Anything that gave its possessor an advantage in the reproductive race would be favoured, and so organisms would come to exploit whatever niches they could. And because natural selection worked by accumulating modifications to a basic ground plan, it would produce the obvious similarities as well as the differences.

Darwin had worked out the theory by 1842, when he wrote the so-called "Sketch," later elaborated into the "Essay" of 1844, but only his closest colleagues were aware of his discovery. He knew that his ideas would create uproar, for the powerful doctrine of biblical creation still held sway, and so he settled down to gather the evidence and marshal the arguments that would make his case irrefutable. He was two-thirds of the way through this major work on natural selection when on June 18, 1858, a letter arrived from Alfred Russel Wallace, a young collector and naturalist in the Malay Archipelago. In a malarial fever Wallace had come up with exactly the same notion of natural selection to explain evolution. The timing of this coincidence was remarkable. Like Darwin, Wallace had even been influenced by Malthus, but ever after Wallace regarded the theory as Darwin's and was unstinting in sharing the credit.

Darwin could delay no longer. His friends J. D. Hooker the botanist and Sir Charles Lyell the geologist arranged for a joint contribution from Darwin and Wallace to be presented to the members of the Linnean Society, of which Darwin was a member. This took place on July 1, and evolution by natural selection was made public. Darwin immediately set to and completed what he described as an "abstract" of the larger book. *On the Origin of Species by Means of Natural Selection* was published in November 1859 and sold out before noon on the day of publication. There was furious public debate of the subject, but most scientists of the day accepted the force of Darwin's argument and saw that natural selection could indeed operate like an intelligent designer. From the chaos of minute random variations, survival selected those best designed to do a particular job. The outcome looked as though

THE TIMES, LONDON

A statue of Charles Darwin presides over an exhibit on the theory of evolution at the Natural History Museum in London. The exhibit reflects the controversies that continue to surround his theories on the 100th anniversary of his death.

an artificer had been at work, but in fact none was needed.

Creation Science. A century after his death it may look as if Darwin's theory too is dead. Increasingly vociferous attacks, particularly by right-wing fundamentalist Christians, culminated in the passage of legislation in several U.S. states demanding equal time within the educational system for an alternative doctrine, that of creation science. One such law in Arkansas was challenged by a group of religious leaders and teachers, coordinated by the American Civil Liberties Union, on the grounds that it infringed upon the constitutional separation between church and state. Judge William R. Overton, in his decision delivered on Jan. 5, 1982, agreed, saying that creation science "is not a science because it depends upon a supernatural intervention which is not guided by natural law." The Arkansas law was dismissed as was another in Louisiana ten months later, but at the end of 1982 suits against similar legislation were still pending in other states, and anti-evolutionists continued to exercise considerable influence. In a counterblow the Board of Regents of New York State's Department of Education decided not to approve certain science textbooks because their treatment of evolution was not sufficiently thorough.

The fundamentalist attack on Darwin and evolution makes use of the considerable debate among biologists over the nature of the processes that underlie evolution, pointing to disagreements within biology as evidence that evolution is false. This is not the case. None of the biologists' disagreements involves doubts that evolution has taken place; they are arguing over the details of the mechanism.

Continuing Debate. One of the most prominent arguments is over the tempo of evolution and in particular the very question of the origin of species, which Darwin's great work does not really address. Darwin believed that evolution is slow and gradual, one species shading more or less imperceptibly into another with the passage of geological time. His friend and defender, Thomas Henry Huxley, found this the weakest part of his argument and warned Darwin that he had saddled himself with too great a burden in stating so forcibly that "*natura non facit saltum*" ("nature does not make jumps").

The fossil record does contain evidence of intermediate forms, like the famous *Archaeopteryx*, which is neither wholly bird nor wholly reptile, but there is little evidence of gradual change in the form of a given fossil species through the geological record. Rather, a species exists unchanged for some length of time and then is replaced by another species that is different and yet clearly related to the earlier form. Bearing this in mind, Stephen Jay Gould and Niles Eldredge, two U.S. paleontologists, put forward the theory of punctuated equilibrium in 1972. This stated that most change was concentrated into the event of speciation, and that speciation took place in a relatively brief period among a small subgroup of the original species. For these reasons, and the vagaries of fossilization, one would not expect to see intermediates or gradual change in the fossil record.

The theory received support in 1982 with the publication by Peter Williamson of Harvard University of his findings from the thick fossil beds around Lake Turkana in northern Kenya. Williamson was able to track certain fossil snails through the deposits, which are remarkably complete, and show that all change is indeed concentrated into the transition between species. The change could take place in as short a period as 5,000 years, with a million years or more of stasis thereafter. Other fossil series, however, are neither as detailed nor as complete as Williamson's, and arguments often can be made for either punctuated equilibrium or gradualism. Nevertheless, this example shows that evolutionary change is not always gradual.

Other arguments in evolution concern such things as the level at which selection occurs and the role of nonselective forces in shaping evolution. Is it possible, for example, to account for certain trends seen in the fossil record, like the increasing size of ancestors of the horse, by saying that larger species were more successful and hence more likely to give rise to descendant species? And what part do random processes play in evolution? These are some of the questions that cannot yet be answered, but they reveal that, even a century after his death, the legacy of Charles Darwin continues to provide considerable intellectual income.

Literature

The 1982 Nobel Prize for Literature was awarded to Gabriel García Márquez (*see* NOBEL PRIZES). A Colombian exiled in Mexico, he was one of the Spanish-American writers who had contributed to what was known as "el boom" in Western publishing circles. His most celebrated novel, *One Hundred Years of Solitude*, was often described as a classic. In 1975 he declared that he would not publish any fiction until the president of Chile was deposed; nevertheless, his new novel, *Chronicle of a Death Foretold*, appeared in English in 1982. British awareness of Latin America was stimulated by the Argentine invasion of the Falkland Islands. The political condition of the continent attracted more attention and, with it, an increased respect for the writers who struggled to speak up for their peoples.

The literature of Latin America was also promoted by the Iraqi government during the planning for the seventh conference of nonaligned nations in Baghdad. In the Iraqi journal *Ur: The International Magazine of Arab Culture*, there was much discussion of the literary traditions of Ecuador, Bolivia, Mexico, and Guatemala—the last represented by an earlier Nobel Prize winner, Miguel Angel Asturias. In this tradition writers "offer a spirited defense of the native populations, oppressed since the Spanish conquest," affirmed Nissa Torrents of the University of London. Torrents suggested, however, that "the so-called boom of the Latin American novel" was in part "a commercial phenomenon, the brainchild of a Catalan literary agent," built on the prizewinning success of the Peruvian Mario Vargas Llosa in Spain in 1962.

Sa'ad al-Bazzaz, the editor of *Ur*, eager to count the Latin Americans among the denizens of the third world, urged his Arab readers to recognize

Gabriel García Márquez

UPI

that "the East" need not be merely a label for the right-hand side of the world map; in another sense it was "co-extensive with the 'south,' the *lower* world as distinct from the upper world." Apart from the Latin Americans, *Ur* promoted the writings of several candidates for international fame from other continents. Among them were two left-wingers who had suffered at the hands of their respective governments: Ngugi wa Thiong'o from Kenya, whose *Devil on the Cross* was a strong, populist assault on the new ruling classes of Africa, and Pramoedya Ananta Toer from Java, author of *This Earth of Mankind*, a rich historical novel about the old Dutch East Indies.

Religious books were the theme of the influential Frankfurt (West Germany) Book Fair—according to an Italian publisher, because "Only God can save the publishing business!" The choice of religion in 1982 was appropriate at a time when (as remarked by James Bentley in the London *New Statesman*) Islamic clergy were leading a revolution in Iran and Polish workers were carrying a portrait of the Black Madonna.

ENGLISH

United Kingdom. Readers of fiction looked back a century to 1882, the year when Anthony Trollope died and James Joyce was born. It was noted that the Victorian conservative was still popular and the experimental Irishman was still obscure, needing interpreters. Trollope's novels were dramatized and entertainingly broadcast on radio and television. Joyce was discussed and read aloud on BBC's Radio Three, for a smaller audience. Shirley Robin Letwin published *The Gentleman in Trollope*, a provocative account of Trollope's conservative values. There were also several new books about Joyce—*The Joycean Way*, *A Starchamber Quiry*, and *James Joyce's Odyssey: A Guide to the Dublin of Ulysses* among them—but none of the large scholarly enterprises engaged in Joyce research were ready for the centenary. However, Oxford University Press brought out a new edition of Richard Ellmann's celebrated biography of Joyce.

Anthony Burgess continued to celebrate and, to some degree, emulate Joyce. A composer as well as a novelist, Burgess brought Joyce to the fore in his set of essays about the relationship of music to literature, *This Man and Music*, and in his charming disquisition *On Going to Bed*. Burgess's third book of 1982 was a playfully experimental novel, *The End of the World News*, in which he mingled the lives of Freud and Trotsky with a science-fiction yarn in a variety of styles, with Joycean musicality and wordplay.

The censors of Joyce's time often found his work offensive, charging it with blasphemy and obscenity. Since then a spirit of "permissiveness" had become conventional, and a new sort of censoriousness had emerged; it was represented by the scandal sheet *Private Eye*, a journal that had had an extraordinary influence on British literary values during the past 21 years. Patrick Marnham's anniversary history of *Private Eye* was reviewed with great solemnity by most of its contributors, especially by the deeply religious Christopher Booker. Under the influence of the veteran journalist Malcolm Muggeridge (who was received into the Roman Catholic Church in 1982), *Private Eye* had assailed almost everyone in "the public eye," sometimes truthfully, eager to pull down the mighty. At the same time, it thundered against all modern or progressive trends in religious life, sexual practices, or artistic experiment. All such were labeled "trendy" or "pseud."

The word pseud appeared in the valuable new *Supplement to the Oxford English Dictionary: O–Scz* — itself a permissive work, accepting new and deviant forms in a nonprescriptive spirit. (Anthony Burgess called it "Brilliant lexicography and admirable librifacture in the great tradition of British workmanship.") The *Private Eye* hostility to "trendiness" was expressed in an assault by its editor, Richard Ingrams (a church organist), upon *Hymns for Today's Church*, an attempt to "modernize" the songs of the Church of England on the lines of the modernized Bible and liturgy. Ingrams's colleague Christopher Booker denounced the permissiveness toward pornography that had been apparent in the last 20 years when he reviewed John Sutherland's book *Offensive Literature: Decensorship in Britain 1960–82*.

There were a number of valuable new books by professional philosophers, accessible to the general reader. Richard Hare, professor of moral philosophy at the University of Oxford, surprised his readers by finding moral justification for utilitarianism in his book *Moral Thinking: Its Levels, Methods, and Point*. His Oxford colleague Hugh Lloyd-Jones, professor of Greek, was another scholar with a good command of English; he published two books of essays on scholarship. These were but two of several volumes from the house of Duckworth, a publisher maintaining classical studies almost single-handedly in a threatening

climate. The most influential book on their list was a stimulating Marxist study, *The Class Struggle in the Ancient Greek World*, by another Oxford scholar, G. E. M. de Ste. Croix.

Books about Jews always command an interested readership, and the shifting of political positions during this period of argument about Zionism helped to inspire a special interest in four scholarly books. Stephen Wilson wrote *Ideology and Experience: Anti-Semitism in France at the Time of the Dreyfus Affair*, and Hyam Maccoby offered an anthropological explanation of the anti-Semitic tradition in *The Sacred Executioner*. More cheeringly, David Katz discussed a fascinating episode of Christian history in *Philo-Semitism and the Readmission of the Jews to England 1603–1655*. From Dan Jacobson, a distinguished novelist, Jewish by birth but not by religion, came a poetic inquiry into the mystery of his people's faith and fate, *The Story of the Stories: The Chosen People and Its God*.

FICTION. The year began with literary critics congratulating the general public on its good taste; ambitious, high-quality novels such as Anthony Burgess's *Earthly Powers* and William Golding's *Rites of Passage* had proved to be best-sellers in paperback. But it was also noticed that both Burgess and Golding had followed the traditional narrative pattern of popular fiction and that their work was spiced with the excitements of cruelty and sexual deviation.

The prestigious Booker Prize attracted strong interest in the mass media, and the prizewinning ceremony was televised. The winner was an Australian, Thomas Keneally, with *Schindler's Ark*. This choice caused argument. Keneally's book seemed more like a factual report than an example of fiction. Apparently a true story about a German who protected Jews during World War II while pretending to collaborate with the Nazis, *Schindler's Ark* offered encouragement to well-meaning, unheroic spirits.

It was contrasted with Lawrence Durrell's fictional treatment of wartime life, *Constance: Or Solitary Practices*, fanciful, gamy, and surrealistic. Another unsuccessful competitor was Alice Thomas Ellis with *The 27th Kingdom*, a Roman Catholic fantasy about a flying nun. Also on the list for the Booker were two more down-to-earth novels. William Boyd's *An Ice-Cream War*, a historical novel about the clash between British and German troops in East Africa during World War I, was a worthy successor to his *A Good Man in Africa* of the previous year (which received a 1982 Somerset Maugham Award). *Sour Sweet* by Timothy Mo was an intriguing novel about a Chinese family in the catering trade. The sixth competitor was John Arden, the left-wing historical playwright; his first novel, *Silence Among the Weapons*, was a historical romance, set in the world of the theatre in ancient Rome and imaginatively expressing his concern for subject races and classes. John Wain and Alan Sillitoe, who made their names in the 1950s—that decade of youthful, antisnobbish radicalism—both returned with the quieter work of their maturity. Wain's novel (which won the Whitbread Prize) was called *Young Shoulders* and movingly described the bereavement of a young boy after the

Thomas Keneally

death of his sister. Sillitoe's *Her Victory* came to terms with modern feminism, persuasively representing the struggle of a downtrodden middle-aged housewife while retaining a gruff masculine courtesy.

Graham Greene, the senior British novelist, offered a light, humorous variation on his old theme—dialogue between Catholics and Communists. *Monsignor Quixote* was set in Spain and told of the travels of an innocent priest (a descendant of Cervantes's hero) in the company of his friend, a Communist ex-mayor, who acts as his Sancho Panza. This pleasing morality, with its odd thoughts about faith, dogma, and permissiveness, won immediate popularity. Doris Lessing, who continued her science-fiction series *Canopus in Argos—Archives* with *The Making of the Representative for Planet 8*, received the Shakespeare Prize awarded annually by the West German FVS Foundation.

LIVES AND LETTERS. The most admired biography of the year was George Spater's new account of William Cobbett, the great 19th-century journalist and political reformer, appraising his soldierly combination of conservatism and radicalism. His support for his friend Thomas Cochrane was noted in the year of the Falklands crisis; with José de San Martín, the national hero of Argentina, Cochrane had helped to liberate that nation from the Spanish empire, only to pave the way for a succession of military juntas. The Falklands crisis stimulated many books but, so far, little "literature"—apart from one collection of letters, *A Message from the Falklands*, written by a young naval officer, David Tinker, who was killed during the fighting; Tinker was deeply angry about this "pointless" campaign and critical of his government's policy.

Several British prime ministers were commemorated in biographies and collections of letters, with interesting new material about Benjamin Disraeli, William Gladstone, H. H. Asquith, and Clement Attlee. The cuckoo in this nest of politicians was the British Fascist Sir Oswald Mosley (1896–1980), whose talents were wasted by his selfish arrogance and inconsideration. His son, Nicholas Mosley, attempted the difficult task of appraisal in *Rules of the Game: Sir Oswald and Lady Cynthia Mosley 1896–1933*.

Admirable biographies of poets, including Roy Campbell and Robert Graves, were appreciated. Among the theatrical lives, Sir Laurence Olivier's *Confessions of an Actor* attracted particular attention; usually unwilling to be interviewed, Olivier appeared in two television programs that offered a physical, visual illustration of his contentious, well-written book. The thoughtful novelist C. P. Snow was currently out of fashion and favour; a biographical essay by his brother, Philip Snow, *Stranger and Brother*, offered his detractors an opportunity of which they took advantage. Nevertheless, *Stranger and Brother* was an interesting piece of history, especially valuable for C. P. Snow's letters of the 1930s and '40s.

POETRY. The most severe critic of English verse, Geoffrey Grigson, now 77, brought out his own *Collected Poems, 1963–1980*. No one dared to flatter him. At the same time, he published *The Private Eye: A Poetry Notebook*, with valuable reflections on good poets of the past, and a collection of his reviews, *Blessings, Kicks and Curses*, offering an opportunity for readers to complain of his severity.

Grigson responded by writing fairly gently about his juniors' new anthology, *The Penguin Book of Contemporary Verse*, though not approving of their attempt at a manifesto for a "movement." He highly praised James Fenton, whose collection, *The Memory of War*, was the most acclaimed of 1982, and he was not unsympathetic to Fenton's 32-year-old contemporary, Christopher Reid, whose new book, *Pea Soup*, was described elsewhere as "the acceptable face of Martianism." The Scottish poet Douglas Dunn won the 1982 Hawthornden Prize.   (D. A. N. JONES)

United States. FICTION. The threat of nuclear war was the subject of a large number of the year's books, both fiction and nonfiction. Bernard Malamud's *God's Grace* was an odd, muddled fable, both sardonic and silly, that began with a nuclear holocaust and a second Flood and ended with the destruction of an Eden peopled by the last man and his primate companions, including a gifted chimpanzee with an artificial larynx that allows him to speak. Another version of (among other things) *Robinson Crusoe* was Paul Theroux's *The Mosquito Coast*, a brilliantly executed story of the rise and fall of Allie Fox, self-taught polymath and free-thinking dropout, who decides to abandon a corrupt, doomed America with his wife and children and create a utopia in a backcountry village in Honduras. Kurt Vonnegut's *Deadeye Dick*, the usual catalog of grotesque disasters climaxing this time in the depopulation of a Midwestern town in the explosion of a neutron bomb, was a mechanical, uncertain work.

Although it did provide some of the pleasures for which his work has been celebrated, *The Dean's December*, Saul Bellow's first novel since winning the Nobel Prize in 1976, was a disappointment. Chicago journalist-turned-academic Albert Corde, Bellow's thinnest and most complacent fictional disguise to date, is stranded in Bucharest one Christmas. While his Romanian wife, a distinguished emigré scientist, is baffled by malicious bureaucrats in her attempts to visit her dying mother, he kills the time thinking chiefly about a

Bernard Malamud

IRA WYMAN/NEWSWEEK

murder trial back in Chicago, contrasting the "hard nihilism" of the Communist countries and the "soft nihilism" of the West. Another disappointing work was John Barth's *Sabbatical: A Romance.* Like Bellow, Barth seemed unjustifiably enamoured of his central characters, a pair of married academics who confront a number of "life-choices" as well as nautical perils while on a cruise in their sailboat, and the book founders in self-satisfied liberal priggishness and Barthian scholarly apparatus.

John Cheever, who died in June at the age of 70 (*see* OBITUARIES), published his last novel, the elegiac *Oh What a Paradise It Seems,* a brief, beautiful story that included a wealth of narrative invention within its small, elegant compass. At its centre is elderly, affluent Lemuel Sears, a typical Cheever suburbanite, made melancholy by the fragile fading beauty around him. He asserts his hold over life by taking a mistress and battling an attempt to turn a pond he had loved as a child into a garbage dump. A less satisfactory last novel was *Mickelsson's Ghosts* by John Gardner, who was killed in a motorcycle accident in September at the age of 49 (*see* OBITUARIES). It was a vast, loosely organized, and ponderously speculative work about a philosophy professor who attempts to flee from a variety of personal and professional problems by holing up in an old farmhouse on the edge of a decaying town in eastern Pennsylvania.

Louis Auchincloss's *Watchfires,* based on an incident from the diary of George Templeton Strong, "the Pepys of nineteenth-century New York," was another of his accomplished studies of manners, full of the "enthusiasm for personalities" with which he credits Strong in a note to the book. Less conventional in their approach to historical subject matter were Stanley Elkin's *George Mills* and Joyce Carol Oates's *A Bloodsmoor Romance.* Elkin's book was a rambling, thousand-year chronicle of the ancestral line of his working-class hero. Moving

back and forth from the life of the present George Mills to those who drudged in the past, the novel is enlivened by Elkin's colloquial, blackly comic lyricism. *A Bloodsmoor Romance* was a massive, mock-gothic tale of five independently minded sisters in the late-19th-century U.S., an irreverent blending of fact and fiction in the manner of Oates's recent novel *Bellefleur.*

The pseudonymous William Wharton published a powerful antiwar novel, *A Midnight Clear,* about a small group of bright, teenaged GI's trying to survive Christmas 1944 in a snowbound no-man's-land. Like Wharton's highly original earlier novels, *Birdy* and *Dad, A Midnight Clear* powerfully integrated fantasy into a realistic narrative. Another strongly didactic work was Marge Piercy's typically blunt and energetic seventh novel, *Braided Lives.* Largely autobiographical, it was a middle-aged writer's frequently powerful account of the painful process of growing up female in the 1950s. Gail Godwin's quietly affirmative and carefully detailed *A Mother and Two Daughters* told of three women coping with change today and triumphing in an idyllic epilogue set in 1984.

Poppa John by Larry Woiwode was largely the events of a single day in the life of an elderly actor who had been idled several months previously by the television "death" of the famous soap-opera character he had long played. An untypically brief and spare narrative for Woiwode, *Poppa John* was also unlike his earlier work in being somewhat implausible and unrewardingly awkward in style. Anne Tyler's ninth novel, *Dinner at the Homesick Restaurant,* a witty and compassionate study of an unhappy family, demonstrated a new mastery of both character and form. Glimpsed through the eyes of their dying mother and at their brief, calamitous family reunions, two brothers and a sister reveal their bondage to a childhood diminished by a father's truancy. Alice Walker's *The Color Purple* was a brilliant and affecting novel covering 30 years in the lives of two Southern black women, sisters separated as adolescents.

A number of impressive first novels were published during the year. Ivan Doig's *The Sea Runners,* an account of four men's flight from indentured labour in Russian Alaska in the 1850s, had the convincing matter-of-factness and understated violence of an Icelandic saga. Another powerfully realistic novel was John M. Del Vecchio's *The 13th Valley,* a massive, vivid documentation of the day-to-day horrors of the Vietnam war that is only occasionally flawed by improbable philosophizing by his characters. Two interesting debuts were comic novels about publishing. Alice McDermott's *A Bigamist's Daughter* was a lively, cynical story about a young woman working for a sleazy vanity press who drifts into a love affair with one of her hapless authors. *A Novel Called Heritage* by Margaret Mitchell Dukore consists of the correspondence between an 18-year-old precociously determined to write the Great American Novel and her somewhat bewildered editor, alternating with chapters of her odd, incipient masterpiece. *Sassafrass, Cypress & Indigo* by black playwright Ntozake Shange was a strange, poetic story of three sisters that was realistic and fantastic by

Marge Piercy

THOMAS VICTOR © 1982

Carolyn Forché

turns. Playwright and screenwriter Steve Tesich also published his first novel, *Summer Crossing*, about an adolescent's coming of age in East Chicago, Ind., in the summer of 1961.

Among the year's popular fiction were books by publishing phenomena Robert Ludlum and Stephen King. Ludlum's new thriller, *The Parsifal Mosaic*, longer than any of his previous books and at least as opaquely byzantine, led the *New York Times* best-seller list a week before publication. King's latest book, *Different Seasons*, was a quartet of short novels. Although the stories were uneven in execution (and only the last contained any element of supernatural horror), *Different Seasons* had a sufficiently Grand Guignol character to recommend it to King's legions of fans. In his latest research project, *Space*, James Michener presented the entire history of the space program (along with a half dozen major plots). Along the way he unhesitatingly addressed such weighty issues as the value of space exploration, the existence of extraterrestrial life, and even the debate between evolutionists and creationists. The first novel in ten years by Isaac Asimov, *Foundation's Edge*, was the well-executed sequel to his 30-year-old science-fiction classic, the Foundation trilogy.

Among the year's notable short fiction was a new, expanded edition of *Progress of Stories*, by poet, critic, and controversialist Laura (Riding) Jackson. Praised by critics when it first appeared in 1935, *Progress of Stories* was challenging, rewarding reading from a major, if neglected, 20th-century writer. In the seven stories of *Bech Is Back*, John Updike brilliantly reintroduced Henry Bech, Jewish academic and reluctant novelist, who first ap-

peared a dozen years earlier in *Bech: A Book*. Ursula LeGuin, one of the few writers of science fiction and fantasy who had become known to a wider audience, gave further evidence of her depth, versatility, and growing virtuosity in *The Compass Rose*. Other fine collections of short fiction included Alice Adams's *To See You Again*, Cynthia Ozick's *Levitation: Five Fictions*, Ann Beattie's *The Burning House*, and poet Maxine Kumin's *Why Can't We Live Together like Civilized Human Beings?*

HISTORY, BIOGRAPHY, AND BELLES LETTRES. The year's nonfiction also showed the effects of a rapidly worsening arms race. Among the dozens of books on the subject of nuclear war, the most discussed was *The Fate of the Earth* by Jonathan Schell (*see* BIOGRAPHIES), first published in installments in *The New Yorker* magazine. In the first of the book's three essays, Schell presented technical information about nuclear weapons and the possible effects of their use; in the second he offered moral reflections about human extinction; and in the third he discussed political responses to the problem of the arms race.

A number of the year's books dealt with the U.S. presidency. In *The Kennedy Imprisonment: A Meditation on Power*, columnist and academic Garry Wills produced a vigorous if somewhat simplistic piece of debunking in which he traced an almost unremittingly hostile history of the family, leading to an Edward Kennedy both created and crippled by a self-serving, self-defeating dynastic myth. Robert Caro's *The Years of Lyndon Johnson: The Path to Power* was an illuminating account of Johnson's youth and his political apprenticeship in Franklin Roosevelt's New Deal. *Tumultuous Years: The Presidency of Harry Truman, 1949–1953*, by Robert J. Donovan, was an ably done reappraisal of Truman's second term. For all its 1,300-page bulk, Henry Kissinger's second volume of memoirs, *Years of Upheaval*, dealt only with the 19 months from his first visit to Hanoi in February 1973 to

Richard Reeves

Richard Nixon's resignation as president in August 1974. A third volume, describing the period of Gerald Ford's presidency, was still to come.

Clare Boothe Luce, by novelist and critic Wilfred Sheed, was an overly enthusiastic treatment of its subject. Although beginning admirably with a memoir of a youthful, halcyon summer spent visiting Mrs. Luce in 1949 that vividly evoked the period, Sheed was much less effective in dealing with her career before and after that episode. Another portrait of a controversial woman, Elisabeth Young-Bruehl's *Hannah Arendt: For Love of the World*, was the first full-length biography of the political scientist. Once a student of Arendt's, Young-Bruehl was an informative if, like Sheed, an insufficiently objective biographer.

Louise Brooks, ex-Ziegfeld showgirl and impassively beautiful femme fatale in a number of silent films, recalled her brief movie career in *Lulu in Hollywood*, an elegant, perceptive memoir. Another book on Hollywood was David McClintick's *Indecent Exposure*. Journalism given a novelistic treatment, McClintick's book was an account of the scandal and corporate power struggle that resulted when, early in 1977, it was accidently discovered that David Begelman, then president of Columbia Pictures, was guilty of forgery and theft.

Among the year's best literary biographies was Eileen Simpson's *Poets in Their Youth*, a straightforward, compassionate, and fascinating account of the tangled lives of a group of poets who knew each other in New York City, Cambridge, Mass., and Princeton, N.J., in the 1940s and '50s—chiefly Robert Lowell, Randall Jarrell, Delmore Schwartz, and Simpson's husband of 14 years, John Berryman. The latter was also the subject of a capably done life by John Haffenden, and a well-researched and well-balanced critical biography of Lowell was written by the British poet Ian Hamilton.

The Journals of Sylvia Plath, edited by her former husband Ted Hughes and her former editor Frances McCullough, begin in the summer before Plath entered Smith College and end just before her separation from Hughes. Regrettably, two notebooks containing a record of the last three years of her life have been lost, but Plath's journals still present a moving account of her development as a poet. The *American Diaries 1902–1926* of Theodore Dreiser were published by the University of Pennsylvania Press, which in 1981 issued a "restored" edition of Dreiser's *Sister Carrie*.

Pursuing an intriguing journalistic experiment, columnist Richard Reeves retraced the route traveled in 1831 by the young French aristocrat Alexis de Tocqueville, whose nine-month tour of the U.S. produced the classic *Democracy in America*. The *Second American Revolution* was a collection of recent journalism by novelist and pamphleteer Gore Vidal. About evenly divided between review and polemic, his writing was typically glittering and hyperbolical. In the columns collected in *The Pursuit of Virtue and Other Tory Notions*, Pulitzer Prize-winning journalist and New Right pundit George F. Will elegantly and often irritatingly detailed his own conservatism in considering a great variety of subjects.

Despite some weak spots, *The Tugman's Passage*, Edward Hoagland's fourth book of essays, still possessed the acute, offbeat observation and fine literary style of his earlier work. Paul Fussell, who won a National Book Award in 1976 for *The Great War and Modern Memory* and more recently published the widely praised *Abroad: British Literary Traveling Between the Wars*, put together an interesting if uneven collection of his literary journalism, *The Boy Scout Handbook and Other Observations*. Annie Dillard's *Living by Fiction* was a brief, enthusiastic study of the writers whom she describes as "contemporary modernists," figures such as Jorge Luis Borges and Italo Calvino, whose works are typically fantastic or abstract. She also published *Teaching a Stone to Talk: Expeditions and Encounters*, a wide-ranging collection of essays in the manner of her Pulitzer Prize-winning *Pilgrim at Tinker Creek*.

POETRY. *This Journey* was a ninth, posthumous collection of the work of James Wright, who died in 1980 at the age of 52. *Our Ground Time Here Will Be Brief* by Maxine Kumin included selections from her six earlier books as well as a number of new poems, some of her best work to date. Mona Van Duyn published the elegiac *Letters from a Father and Other Poems*, her first substantial collection since *To See, to Take*, which won the National Book Award in 1971. Among the other new volumes were Denise Levertov's *Candles in Babylon*, Adrienne Rich's *A Wild Patience Has Taken Me This Far*, A. R. Ammons's *Worldly Hopes*, Robert Bly's *The Man in the Black Coat Turns*, and Carolyn Forché's *The Country Between Us*, winner of the 1982 Academy of American Poets Lamont Award.

(FITZGERALD HIGGINS)

Canada. The exuberance of Canadian poetry continued unabated during 1982. Among the more experimental offerings were *Sa N His Crystal Ball* by bill bissett, in which Sa enters the occult and encounters weird beings—an ogopogolist, a littul king—described in a language of cracked, distracted, haunting beauty. Another enchanter from the West Coast with her first major collection in more than 20 years of writing was Maxine Gadd with *Lost Language*, while b. p. Nichol was up to tricks new and old in *Zygal*.

Among other notable volumes of selected poems were *Earthlight: Selected Poetry of Gwendolyn MacEwan* with poems as early as 1963 and as late as 1982 marking the development of this magical voice; *Into a Blue Morning: Poems Selected and New* by C. H. Gervais, edited by Al Purdy; *The Land They Gave Away: Selected and New Poems* by Andrew Suknaski, edited by Stephen Scobie; *The Beauty of the Weapons: Selected Poems 1972–1982* by Robert Bringhurst; and a definitive selection of 150 of Irving Layton's best and best-known works, *A Wild Peculiar Joy, 1945–1982*.

The long poem was also well represented, including a sonnet sequence by Milton Acorn, *Captain MacDougal and the Naked Goddess*, written from the captain's point of view, and *Kissing the Body of My Lord: The Marie Poems*, in which Douglas Beardsley uses the life and times of Marie de l' Incarnation to explore the conflicts between the Old World and the New. A double publication was *The Foetus Dreams and Dedications for a Book Entitled*

Robertson Davies

'Century of Man' by Lorna Uher and Anne Szumigalski.

Other collections of new works by well-known authors included Patrick Lane's *Old Mother*, in which the poet quarries the dark places for images old as coal and brilliant as diamonds; *The Presence of Fire* by George Amabile, dealing with such themes as love and friendship, the family and the self; *The Phases of Love*, in which Dorothy Livesay explores her theme over a span of 60 years; and *I Might Not Tell Everyone This* by Alden Nowlan.

The fiction lists were fat and sassy. They included Katherine Govier's *Going Through the Motions*, the story of a stripper's struggle for justice and survival; Elizabeth Brewster's *Junction*, a time-travel novel in which a woman finds the fantastic and romantic inextricably entangled in the realistic; Graeme Gibson's *Perpetual Motion*, in which an obsession for the impossible culminates in a lunatic but moving tragedy; *The Ruined Season* by M. T. Kelly, a bleak and brawling story in an imaginary northern Ontario setting; the fourth in David Helwig's Kingston tetralogy, *It Is Always Summer*; *Cutting Through*, Keith Maillard's sequel to *The Knife in My Hands*; and *A Fairly Conventional Woman*, the other side of the coin from Carol Shields's previous work, *Happenstance*.

First novels included *The Ivory Swing* by Janette Turner Hospital, the $50,000 Seal First Novel Award winner of 1981, in which a Canadian couple in India find themselves caught between traditional ways and new freedoms; Aviva Layton's *Nobody's Daughter*, in which a poet's ex-wife finally finds her own voice; and Gail Scott's *Spare Parts*, a comic-tragic treatment of a woman's confrontations with crisis from puberty to womanhood.

The short story also continued to flourish, as exemplified by Guy Vanderhaghe's *Man Descending*—proud but weak protagonists who are prisoners of their own minds as much as their bodies are prisoners of circumstance; Robertson Davies's *High Spirits*, which having once enlivened the annual Gaudy Nights at Massey College are now free to entertain us all; and Alice Munro's *The Moons of Jupiter*, stories in which what has always been known is learned in new forms.

(ELIZABETH WOODS)

FRENCH

France. An opinion poll taken during the year showed that readers still claimed to prefer the novel to other literary forms. They might have been excused for answering with a puzzled "don't know," since the borderline between fiction and fact was not easy to draw. Romanticized history and biography, adopting fictional techniques, had long been popular, while the novel increasingly turned to real events and characters for its material. In choosing to describe the life and death of an Italian homosexual film director called Pier Paolo, murdered outside Rome in 1975, Dominique Fernandez seemed on the face of it to have disqualified himself from a chance for France's major prize for fiction. Nonetheless, *Dans la main de l'ange* did win the Prix Goncourt; its first-person narrative, its individual view of Italian society and homosexual psychology, and its subjective interpretation of what may or may not have been the personality of the real Pier Paolo Pasolini were enough to justify calling it a "novel."

The traditional preserve of fiction was attacked from the opposite direction by Zoé Oldenbourg in what seemed at first to be a conventional memoir of childhood, especially of her debt to her father whose passion for literature found an outlet in the invention of stories to which his daughters were asked to contribute. Oldenbourg was to find her conflicts with him being played out on the battleground of these fictions, and *Le Procès du rêve* was gradually invaded by characters from this imaginary world, ending as a pitiless indictment of the novelist's flight from reality and perversion of relationships to suit his imaginative ends.

Dominique Fernandez

This mistrust of the usual creative domain of the novelist was perhaps reflected in the number of journalists writing novels about their own profession. One could believe in the growing cynicism of Olivier Todd's central character in *Un Cannibale très convenable*, in Gilbert Toulouse's "mercenary" who joins the Saharan Polisario guerrillas (*Le Mercenaire*), and even in Pierre Joffroy's small-time reporter in search of a scoop (*Le Cheval chauve*). It was less easy to accept Vladimir Volkoff's premise of wholesale Soviet "disinformation" in the French press (*Le Montage*), which at times verged on paranoia.

The historical novel succeeded better in blending fact and fiction. Serge Bramly described an elaborate exercise in Renaissance "disinformation" in *La Danse du loup*, but it hardly mattered whether the reader believed his tale of Byzantine forgery; he was concerned with more oblique themes, such as the love of learning and the survival of the human spirit. This was one of many works in a genre that retained its popularity; others included Irène Frain's *Le Nabab*, Bruno Racine's *Le Gouverneur de Morée*, and Frédérick Tristan's *La Cendre et la Foudre*.

Robert Pinget, a veteran of the "new novel," ironically explored the relationship of literature to life in *Monsieur Songe*. But the conventional approach to fiction survived, its strengths shown in Henri Troyat's *Le Pain de l'étranger*, the story of a doctor's exploitation of his Portuguese servant. Women writers often proved most competent on the terrain of the psychological novel, notably Anne Philipe (*Les Résonances de l'amour*), Hélène Parmelin (*Le Diable et les jouets*), Michèle Perrein (*Ave César*), and Brigitte Lozerec'h, whose first novel, *L'Intérimaire*, promised to be one of the year's successes.

The Prix Renaudot went to Georges-Olivier Chateaureynaud for *La Faculté des songes*, and there were new novels from Patrick Modiano, Pierre-Jean Rémy, Marc Cholodenko, and René Belleto. Two novelists who had never quite fulfilled their early promise in the 1960s had a mixed critical reception: J. M. G. Le Clézio for his collection of stories, *La Ronde et autres fait divers*, and Christiane Rochefort for the provocative *Quand tu vas chez les femmes*.

The Breton writer Pierre Jakez Hélias drew on the fund of regional custom for his first novel, *L'Herbe d'or*. The Belgian-born Marguerite Yourcenar, first woman member of the French Academy, gave a digest of her life's work in the three stories of *Comme l'eau qui coule*. The problems of Algerian women in France were the subject of Leila Sebbar's *Sherazade*, the recent history of Algeria was evoked in Rachid Mimouni's *Le Fleuve détourné*, and there were new works from the Moroccans Driss Chraïbi and Abdellatif Laâbi.

The death of the poet and novelist Georges Perec, in March, deprived France of an original and exacting talent. Though there was a good deal of minimalist poetry, represented by Marc Guyon's *Les Purifications* and Bernard Mazo's *Dilapidation du Silence*, it lacked the disciplined submission to formal constraints that had made Perec's work so impressive. A more accessible tradition was illustrated in Louis Aragon's *Les Adieux* and Yves Martin's *De la Rue elle crie*, while poetry criticism also ranged from Gérard Genette's demanding study of intertextuality, *Palimpsestes*, to Robert Sabatier's history of French poetry, now brought into the 20th century.

New volumes in the correspondence of Chateaubriand, the collected works of Joe Bousquet, and an unpublished work by Proust, *Matinée chez la princesse de Guermantes*, were published during the year. Philippe Lavergne's translation of Joyce's *Finnegan's Wake* was a staggering achievement. Jean Kelay, in the third volume of his family history, *Avant Mémoire*, gave a fascinating insight into 18th-century society. The Revolutionary period, losing one of its best-known historians with the death of Albert Soboul (*see* OBITUARIES), was the subject of books by Serge Bianchi, Françoise de Kermina, and Claude Nicolet.   (ROBIN BUSS)

Canada. Anne Hébert, the recipient of the Prix Fémina for 1982 for *Les fous de Bassan*, continued to explore the enigmatic world of the characters she first created in *Le Torrent*. Her latest novel tells the story of Nicolas Jones, the pastor of Griffin Creek, who, after a lifetime spent in his village, reconstructs his past and that of the members of his "family." The story would be banal were it not for the narration, which picks up and propels the tale continuously, each time from a new perspective— that is to say, from the point of view of several characters (the pastor, Stevens, Nora, Olivia, and others), who, one by one, take charge of the story. The dynamics of the writing place the book in company with *Les Chambres de bois*, *Kamouraska*, and *Les Enfants du sabbat*.

Another award winner (Prix David for 1982 for the body of her works) was Marie-Claire Blais, who during the year published *Visions d'Ana*. With this novel the author penetrates a turbulent world, charged with revolt and disorder. Facing the decadence of modern society, Ana seeks in the motions of daily life a solution that can satisfy her. Violence, anguish, drugs, tenderness, all are present, but everything is obliterated in and by powerlessness.

Even before its publication, *Le Meurtre d'Ovide Plouffe* by Roger Lemelin was a best-seller. The return of one of the most colourful of the Plouffe family was made in the most dramatic of settings: an airplane crash. Inspired by an actual event that took place in Quebec some 30 years earlier, this work could not fail to please the many readers who had remained loyal to Lemelin. Indeed, they found once again not only his verve but also the attention to detail that characterizes him so well.

(ROBERT SAINT-AMOUR)

GERMAN

In a year dominated by the 150th anniversary of the death of Goethe, Germany's greatest writer, the more recent German past continued to figure prominently in literature. Walter Kempowski completed his Kempowski saga; *Schöne Aussicht* described in his familiar graphic style the interwar years from the viewpoint of a bourgeois family whose members preferred not to think about the wider significance of events around them. Horst

Bienek continued his chronicle of Silesia; *Erde und Feuer* brought the story up to the closing months of World War II. A more optimistic account of history was furnished by Rudolf Hagelstrange, whose *Das Haus* traced the fortunes of a liberal doctor and his family through the Wilhelminian era to the victory of social democracy in 1918. Numerous semiautobiographical works appeared on the subject of growing up in the immediate post-1945 years: Paul Kersten's *Die toten Schwestern*, George Hozwarth's peasant novel *Das Butterfass*, and, most vividly, Birgitta Arens's imaginative *Katzengold*.

Wolfdietrich Schnurre's impressive if sombre *Ein Unglücksfall* had a more specific topic: relations between Germans and Jews. The rebuilding of a synagogue in West Berlin leads to the confrontation of a rabbi with a German who believes he recognizes in him a Jew he had tried to conceal from the Nazis. The most absorbing work on the subject of the Jews in history, however, was by Stefan Heym. *Ahasver* treated the story of the Wandering Jew as a myth of revolution. Ahasver refuses to help Jesus because Jesus' message is passive acceptance; for similar reasons he becomes the antagonist of Luther and his disciples in the 16th century and of the East German establishment in the 20th. This was Heym's masterpiece, witty, intelligent, imaginative, and showing great linguistic virtuosity.

Comparable to *Ahasver* in both quality and its use of myth was Tankred Dorst's much more pessimistic *Merlin*, the retelling of the Arthurian legends through a remarkable set of visions reaching into the future; just as Camelot is subject to death and decay, so humanity itself will one day become extinct. Further examples of literature that used the fantastic were Gerd Jonke's Hoffmannesque *Erwachen zum grossen Schlafkrieg* and Hermann Kinder's *Der helle Wahn*.

Literary reminiscences were found in a number of works centred on woman and her search for identity. In Ria Endres's *Milena erwacht*, the recipient of Kafka's love letters had the opportunity to reply. Andrea Wolfmayr's prizewinning *Spielräume* and Karin Lindemann's *Sie verschwanden im erleuchteten Torbogen* both betrayed their authors' professionally wide reading in European literature. The last mentioned was the most ambitious: the heroine, an émigré from East Germany at the beginning of the 1960s, finds her difficulties compounded by East-West misunderstandings. On a comparable topic, Joseph Zoderer's *Die Walsche*, set in the South Tirol, was less pretentious and more satisfying. Olga has left her German-speaking peasant origins to live with an Italian in the city. When she returns for her father's funeral she finds that she belongs nowhere, neither among the coarse German peasants nor among the urbane Italians.

The year was remarkable for the impressive debuts of a number of young Swiss writers: Thomas Hürlimann (*Die Tessinerin*), Matthias Zschokke (*Max*), Hansjörg Schertenleib (*Grip*), and Rahel Hutmacher (*Dona*). Of their longer established compatriots, Max Frisch published *Blaubart*, a version of the Bluebeard story using his old themes of the question of identity and the problem of guilt;

Adolf Muschg some Kleistian parable stories on wasted lives (*Leib und Leben*); and Hugo Loetscher a satirical portrayal of life in Los Angeles (*Herbst in der grossen Orange*).

In lyric poetry the most exciting nova was Ulla Hahn, whose *Herz über Kopf* successfully rehabilitated emotionalism by the matter-of-fact tone in which it was conveyed. Among numerous others, Sarah Kirsh (*Erdreich*), Wolfgang Bächler (*Nachtleben*), and Erich Fried (*Das Nahe suchen*) produced new collections that were well received.

The two most notable novels to appear in East Germany were both set in the 18th century. Martin Stade's *Der närrische Krieg*, on a brief and trivial war of 1747, culminated in an impressive appeal to reason and independence of mind. Joachim Walther's *Bewerburn bei Hofe* concerned the role of the poet in society. Other novels of interest included Karl Hermann Roehricht's *Waldsommerjahre*, the final part of his trilogy on the artist Waldemar, and Benito Wogatzki's *Das Narrenfell*, a socialist pendant to West German nostalgia for the immediate postwar years. Manfred Jendryschik's *Der feurige Gaukler* was an entertaining, often provocative series of snapshots, while Franz Fuhmann entered the sphere of science fiction with seven stories jokingly entitled *Saiäns-Fiktschen* but implying much more than the genre usually does. Lyric poetry was well represented with volumes from Walter Werner (*Der Baum wächst durchs Gebirge*) and Elke Erb (*Trost*). Karl Mundstock produced an exciting account of his early life (*Meine tausend Jahre Jugend*), which afforded an interesting contrast to Sibylle Muthesius's touching documentation of a teenager's suicide in contemporary East Germany (*Flucht in die Wolken*).   (J. H. REID)

SCANDINAVIAN

Denmark. It was a good year for Danish literature. Henrik Stangerup's *Vejen til Lagoa Santa* was a documentary novel about the philosopher Søren Kierkegaard's relative Peter Lund. Tage Voss's *Kanonerne*, about the Dreyfus affair, had overtones of espionage and counterespionage. The poet Benny Andersen's partly autobiographical *På broen*

Henrik Nordbrandt

was outstanding for its understanding portrayal of boyhood. Vagn Lundbye's *Den store by* completed the trilogy begun in 1978. Klaus Rifbjerg again criticized modern society in *De hellige aber* (1981), in which two boys enter a cave in 1940 and emerge into an alien world in 1981. In *Programmeret til kærlighed* (1981), Dorit Willumsen (Danish Academy prize) created a female robot to fulfill man's dreams and sexual needs.

Rifbjerg's stories, *Mænd og Kvinder*, illustrated the contrast between a rational exterior and the more chaotic being beneath the surface. Soya, on the other hand, tried in *Usynlige tråde* to find a pattern in apparently chance events. Peter Seeberg's *Om fjorten dage* was a sombre and unromantic picture of a southern Jutland village in a past age. *Blixeniana* (1981) contained some hitherto unpublished stories written by Karen Blixen (Isak Dinesen) in her 20s.

Henrik Nordbrandt, recently called one of today's most important European poets, reflected in *Armenia* on man's inhumanity to man and on individual responsibility. Rifbjerg's *Spansk motiv* (1981) scarcely aspired to the same profundity, while Jørgen Gustava Brandt's *Hop* was also written with a certain lightness of touch, though indicating presentiments of approaching catastrophe. By contrast, his *Serie* was a complex attempt to plumb the depths of human personality. Another attempt to interpret life was Ole Wivel's *Skabelsen. Et digt om Guds-elskværdighed*. Suzanne Brøgger (Danish Academy prize) in *Tone* (1981), about one of Copenhagen's now dead eccentrics, gave symbolic significance to a specific personality. Bo Green Jensen's *Det absolutte spil* maintained the promise of his first volume of poems.

Memoirs included Hans Jørgen Lembourn's *Op lille Hans* (1981); former prime minister Poul Hartling's *Politisk udspil*; and *Sådan set*, in which P. G. Lindhardt, one of Denmark's most respected, though at times most controversial, theologians, wrote of himself and his views.

(W. GLYN JONES)

Norway. Outstanding novels were provided by Johannes Heggland in *Brød frå havet. Born av støv*, continuing the story of Anna Gyria in a fishing community in western Norway in the mid-19th century, and by Tor Edvin Dahl in *Abrahams barn*, where lesbianism and incest were central issues in a riveting discussion of moral values, projected against a backdrop of stern Old Testament attitudes. The painful way back from mental and marital breakdown was dealt with convincingly by Carl Frederik Prytz in *Mannen som hadde rett*. Jan Kjærstad's novel *Speil* traced the personal development of an artist shaped by 20th-century world history. Concern over developments pointing toward fascism was at the centre of Øyvind Mhyre's novel *1989*, and similar pessimism concerning political and ecological developments was expressed by Finn Alnæs in *Dynamis*.

The Nazi Holocaust formed the sombre background to the life story of a sexually frustrated middle-aged woman in Åge Rønning's *Kolbes reise*. Jon Michelet's novel *Terra roxa* described the experiences of a young woman doctor and missionary in Brazil. Much discussion was caused by Sverre

Lars Gustafsson

Asmervik's semidocumentary novel *Men tankene mine får du aldri*, which painted an almost unbearably grim picture of the life of prostitutes in the Norwegian capital. In Ragnhild Magerøy's well-written historical novel *Jorsal*, 13th-century Norwegian pilgrims finally reach the Holy Land, only to find that dream and reality can be very different.

Several poems were printed in revised form in Stein Mehren's *Samlede dikt 1960–1967*. Personal war experiences formed the background to Harald Sverdrup's collection of poems *Vårt trygge liv. Krigsnotater*. Outstanding among publications marking the 150th anniversary of the birth of Bjørnstjerne Bjørnson were a study of Bjørnson's early peasant novels by Olaf Øyslebø, *Bjørnsons "bondefortellinger." Kulturhistorie eller allmennmenneskelig diktning?*, and a fascinating biography of Bjørnson's wife by Øyvind Anker, *Boken om Karoline*. A charming close-up of Sigrid Undset was provided by her niece, Charlotte Blindheim, in *Moster Sigrid. Et familie portrett av Sigrid Undset*. The undisputed master of Norwegian documentaries in the postwar period, Per Hansson, died in June 1982. (TORBJØRN STØVERUD)

Sweden. The sensation of the year was Lars Ahlin's return, after an 11-year silence, with the novel *Hannibal segraren*, written with his wife, Gunnel Ahlin. The text, which taxes the reader's hermeneutic skills, conveys the thoughts of the poet Yadamilk as he accompanies Hannibal marching on Rome in 218 BC. By contrast, P. C. Jersild provided lucid but highly uncomfortable reading in *Efter floden*, a "scenario" depicting a sprinkling of survivors after a nuclear war.

Much interest centred on human relationships and individuals. The autobiographical angle was represented by *Realism*, the third volume of octogenarian Ivar Lo-Johansson's memoirs, and by *Barndom*, which described the lonely childhood of Jan Myrdal (son of famous parents Alva [awarded the 1982 Nobel Prize for Peace] and Gunnar). Fiction included Rita Tornborg's *Systrarna*, a middle-aged narrator's memories of three repressed sisters. Women's problems were also at the heart of *Samuels döttrar* by Sven Delblanc, who in *Samuels bok* (1981; awarded the 1982 Nordic literature prize) had written of his grandfather's struggles; this sequel presented the grandfather's daughters with the dice of heredity and environment loaded against them.

Johan Bargum's lively novel *Pappas flicka* featured a married woman helped by psychotherapy to overcome her crippling illusions after her adored father dies. Per Gunnar Evander also wrote of a child-parent relationship in *Hundarnas himmel*, in which the narrator returns home to sell his deceased father's boat and instead gives it to his father's worst enemy, thereby making symbolic atonement for the guilt he has inherited. Guilt and atonement were central as well in Torgny Lindgren's powerful historical novel *Ormens väg på hälleberget*. Love, in varied guise, was the theme of the distinguished short-story writer Margareta Ekström's collection *Kärlekens utland*.

Konny Isgren's second collection of poems, *Simmaren*, confirmed his promise as a metaphysical poet. In the imagistic poems of *Tecken till Europa*, Kjell Espmark moved down the centuries of a Europe of violence and oppression. Lars Gustafsson, in *Världens tystnad före Bach*, wrote of the boundaries between the personal and the infinite and the riddles of existence. Finally, a gem. Barbro Lindgren's *En liten cyklist*, poems about the last days of her aunt's life expressed with rare and luminous simplicity.

(KARIN PETHERICK)

ITALIAN

There was little sense of common purpose in the Italian literature of the year. Few novelists attempted to analyze imaginatively the country's endemic problems of violence and terrorism. Most compelling was Luce D'Eramo's *Deviazione*, which, in the form of a thriller, represented the degradation of terrorism both from within the social personalities of its followers and as a collective phenomenon.

Veteran authors were noticeably in the forefront. Romano Bilenchi published *Il gelo*, in which an adolescent's gradual recognition of the myths of his childhood and the evils of adult life was narrated with rare firmness and sensitivity. Alberto Moravia's *1934*, despite historical references—beginning with the title itself—to the full nazification of Germany, was concerned mainly with a private case of metaphysical despair. Ferdinando Camon, using the device of a psychoanalysis, expressed in *La malattia chiamata uomo* the sense of loneliness and loss experienced by a generation deprived of church and political party, defeated by emerging feminism, and even forced, by the obliteration of its mother tongue dialect, to think in the terms of national language. Equally gloomy, but without the humour that occasionally leavens Camon's novel, was Goffredo Parise's *Sillabario n.2*, a series of short narratives—following *Sillabario n.1* of 1972—written in a desolate and lucid style.

Halfway between novel and autobiography were books by Mario Tobino and Ugo Pirro. *Gli ul-*

GUILIO EINAUDI EDITORE

Primo Levi

timi giorni di Magliano was Tobino's touching farewell to his patients and the clinic in which he spent most of his working life as a psychiatrist; as the institution is closed down by a new law, he pours out his bitterness at the demagogic decree that negates insanity and, in the name of freedom and progress, condemns the sick to loneliness and self-destruction. Pirro's *Mio figlio non sa leggere* was the story of the author's impassioned efforts, against the background of a crumbling family, an uncomprehending environment, and inadequate social structures, to cure his dyslexic son, only to see him leave, once cured.

Primo Levi returned to print with a volume of short stories, *Lilit*, and, overshadowing this, the masterful novel *Se non ora, quando?* Poised between fantasy and historical documentation, between epic and irony, biblical yearning and stark immediacy, it recounts the struggles and sufferings of a motley group of Jewish partisans as they move southward from White Russia to Italy in 1943–45. On a different note, Sebastiano Vassalli's *Mareblu* was a rambling monologue by a deceptively eccentric character who plots revolution; its effervescent language concealed a bitter allegory of the nonexistence of a genuine revolutionary movement in contemporary Italy.

Among young writers, Andrea De Carlo, after the 1981 success of his *Treno di panna*, confirmed his remarkable narrative talent with *Uccelli da gabbia e da voliera*. Set in contemporary Milan, it tells of a young man who finds a sense of purpose only in the pursuit of an elusive woman, herself involved with terrorism. What impressed most was De Carlo's objective, almost cinematic style. Finally, Ignazio Silone's last novel, *Severina*, left uncompleted when he died in 1978, was published by his wife.

Two eminent poets produced collections of enduring quality. Vittorio Sereni's *Stella variabile* dwells on the passing of time and the enigma of life; at the heart of the book mysterious apparitions seem to hold the ever elusive answers he seeks, but life escapes the poet's disquieting and ceaseless quest. Equally suggestive was Giorgio Caproni's *Il franco cacciatore*, which distilled the relationship of man to God into an essential language, brilliantly suited to the theme of the hunter discovering his prey only in its absence.

Turning to nonfictional prose, Leonardo Sciascia's *Il teatro della memoria* was a Pirandellesque reconstruction of a true case of double identity that divided public opinion in Italy in the late 1920s; the same author's *Kermesse* was a melancholy collection of Sicilian idioms explained with an eye to their social implications. A spate of books on Fascism anticipated the centenary of Benito Mussolini's birth (1883). Two were particularly successful: Roberto Gervaso's *Claretta*, a biography of Mussolini's mistress, Claretta Petacci, and Denis Mack Smith's *Mussolini*, a political biography of the dictator during the period 1920–45.

(LINO PERTILE)

SPANISH

Spain. Late in 1981 the Ministry of Culture awarded the Miguel de Cervantes Prize, for the second consecutive year to a Latin-American writer, to the prolific Mexican poet and essayist Octavio Paz. In 1982 the prestigious award went to the Andalusian lyric poet and literary scholar Luis Rosales. In the 38th annual competition for the Premio Nadal, awarded each January by the publisher Destino for outstanding new fiction, the winner was Carmen Gómez Ojea for her semihistorical, semifantastic novel *Cantiga de agüero*.

The deaths of Ramón Sender, considered by many the most important novelist of his generation, and the Basque novelist Juan Antonio de Zunzunegui stimulated fresh critical assessments of their respective contributions. Important new works by well-established writers included Gonzalo Torrente Ballester's novel *La isla de los jacintos cortados*, awarded the National Literature Prize at the end of 1981; *Antagonía*, the last novel of Luis Goytisolo's quartet *Teoría del conocimiento*; Juan Benet's *Trece fábulas y media*; the best-seller by Miguel Delibes, *Los santos inocentes*; *Buscando un tesoro*, a dark satire by Catalan novelist Juan Gomis; and *Octubre, octubre* by José Luis Sampedro. Stylistic and thematic influences of García Márquez and Valle-Inclán were strongly suggested in a promising first novel by Juan Pedro Aparicio; in *Lo que es del César* a dictator's brain, preserved after his death, continues to lust for power.

Poet and playwright Rafael Alberti and essayist José Bergamín shared the Pedro Salinas Humanities Award, instituted by the Menéndez Pelayo International University to commemorate the 50th anniversary of its foundation. Two noteworthy events were the posthumous award, late in 1981, of the National Poetry Prize to Vicente Gaos, coincident with the formal presentation of Gaos's *Obras completas* by the president of the Royal Spanish Academy, Dámaso Alonso; and the publication of Rafael Morales's *Obra poética, 1943–1981* in the popular Selecciones Austral series.

The publishing house Planeta judged Luis Romero's *Por qué y cómo mataron a Calvo Sotelo* the winner of the Espejo de España Prize for outstanding nonfiction. Published under the pseudonym "Graciano Hervás," Romero's analysis of the assassination, in 1936, of the rightist leader José Calvo Sotelo both reflected and perpetuated the seemingly insatiable appetite of Spanish readers for serious, if not always scholarly, inquiries into the country's political and social crises. Intimate memoirs of important writers are a rarity in Spanish letters, so the appearance of Francisco Ayala's *Recuerdos y olvidos* was perhaps the most unusual literary event of the year. (ROGER L. UTT)

Latin America. Latin-American literature's reputation for excellence was reaffirmed with the awarding of the 1982 Nobel Prize for Literature to the Colombian novelist Gabriel García Márquez. Other major writers who published during 1982 were Manuel Puig, Jorge Luis Borges, Mario Benedetti, Julio Cortázar, and Antonio Skármeta.

García Márquez received the Nobel Prize at the age of 54 after having published six novels, numerous short stories, and a considerable amount of journalism. His most successful novel was *Cien años de soledad* (1967), which gained him instant fame in the Hispanic world and appeared in English in 1970 as *One Hundred Years of Solitude*. His book of conversations with Plinio Apuleyo Mendoza, *El olor de la guayaba*, was a best-seller in much of the Hispanic world during the second half of 1982. The other dominant figure during 1982 was the Peruvian novelist Mario Vargas Llosa. His monumental *La guerra del fin del mundo* (1981), a relatively straightforward account of political conflicts in 19th-century Brazil, was one of the best-selling novels in the Hispanic world during most of the year, while his play *La señorita de Tacna* was performed successfully in Spain, Argentina, and other countries.

Several important books were published by

Octavio Paz

writers from Argentina, although many were written in exile. Jorge Luis Borges's *La cifra*, a volume of poems written from 1978 to 1981, appeared in late 1981, as did Julio Cortázar's *Territorios*, a book of stories, photographs, paintings, and poems. Their compatriot Osvaldo Soriano won the prize for the best foreign novel of the year in Italy with *Cuarteles de invierno*. Mempo Giardinelli living in Mexico, published his second novel, *El ciclo con las manos*.

Chile's Antonio Skármeta also continued to live in exile. His novel *La insurrección* (published by Ediciones del Norte in New Hampshire) dealt with the political struggle in Nicaragua. Enrique Lihn, living in Chile, published the unique *Derechos de autor*, a collage of poems, narrative, and other writings. A complementary book, *Conversaciones con Enrique Lihn*, was produced by Pedro Lastra late in 1981. Mauricio Wacquez, writing in virtual anonymity in Europe, completed a novel about the structures and forms of power, *Frente a un hombre amado*. Other notable Chilean novels were Antonio Ostornol's *Los recodos del silencio* and Eugenio Rodríguez's *El cercopies*. The distinguished Chilean poet Gonzalo Rojas published *Cincuenta poemas*.

Younger writers were the most productive in Mexico. Ignacio Solares wrote a nostalgic novel, *La fórmula de la inmortalidad*. A writer of the same generation, René Avilés Fabila, published a novel that was primarily a character sketch, *La canción de Odette*. Josefina Vicens, of an older generation, used sexual roles as her theme in *Los años falsos*. *Cuadernos de Gofa* by Hugo Hiriart, a spoof on academic research, appeared late in 1981. Other noteworthy Mexican novels published in late 1981 were Jorge Ibargüengoitia's *Los pasos de López* and Jesús Gardea's *La canción de las mulas muertas*. Two significant volumes of poetry were Homero Aridjis's *Espectáculo del año dos mil* and Carlos Montemayor's *Finisterra*.

Literary activity in Colombia was overshadowed by the presence of García Márquez. Albalucía Angel published her fourth novel, *Misiá señora*, and Oscar Collazos his third, *Todo o nada*. Newcomers included Alvaro Pineda Botero with *El diálogo imposible* (1981), Ramón Molinares Sarmiento with *Exiliados en Lille*, and Fernando Ayala Poveda with *La década sombría*. A new prize, the Premio de Novela Jorge Isaacs, was awarded to Carlos Castro Saavedra for his first novel, *Adán ceniza*.

Elsewhere in Latin America, the Uruguayan Mario Benedetti's fifth novel, *Primavera con una esquina rota*, appeared after a volume of stories, *Con y sin nostalgia*. The Peruvian Alfredo Bryce Echenique completed another humorous novel dealing with the crisis of his protagonist, *La vida exagerada de Martín Romaña*. His compatriot Isaac Goldemberg published poems in *Hombre de paso / Just Passing Through* (bilingual edition). The Cuban poet in exile Heberto Padilla brought out a novel, *En mi jardín pastan los héroes*.

Mexicans received two major literary prizes. The Rómulo Gallegos Prize went to the novelist Fernando del Paso for *Palinuro de México*. In Spain the 1981 Miguel de Cervantes Prize was given to the Mexican Octavio Paz. One of the highlights for Latin-American literature in the U.S. was Borges's tour of the country, culminating with an international symposium on his work at the University of Chicago in April. A major symposium on Latin-American theatre took place at the University of Kansas the same month. Hispanicists in the U.S. published two major critical studies: Angel Rama's *La novela latinoamericana 1920–1980* and John S. Brushwood's *Genteel Barbarism: New Readings of Nineteenth-Century Spanish-American Novels* (1981).　　　(RAYMOND L. WILLIAMS)

PORTUGUESE

Portugal. The search continued for a new style and a new narrative mode suited to describing the changes that had occurred in Portuguese life since the military coup of April 1974. Among the new novelists who had distinguished themselves in the following years, Olga Gonçalves, winner of the prestigious Ricardo Malheiro prize in 1975, published in 1982 *Ora esguardae*, a sensitive and dramatic account of experiences lived through by Portuguese men and women from all walks of life since the "carnation revolution" that put an end to a 400-year-old colonial empire. The book's structure is fragmentary, and the narrative has an effective cinematic quality; by making the past and present overlap in swift sequences, Gonçalves succeeds in showing the depth of the social changes and the resilience of the old regime. The book closes on a note of deferred hope, signaling the emergence of a dubious individualism totally unconcerned with the warnings of the past.

Unlike Gonçalves, Américo Guerreiro de Sousa maintained the traditional structure of the novel in *Os Cornos de Cronos*. The action also takes place in the post-revolutionary era and is described in the first-person singular. Yet the devices of the traditional narrative are only used so they can be more effectively discredited by the narrator, who shows his inability, and that of those he knows, to live up to the events in which they are involved.

The most ambitious novel of the year, however, was *O Cais das Merendas* by Lídia Jorge. The narrative spins around a small group of people who gather through many summers in a seaside hotel. The philanderer of the group satisfies his egotism in casual encounters with foreign tourists and polarizes the emotions and reminiscences of all the other characters. Built on a web of complex musical patterns, the novel enacts the drama of a loss of individual and national identity, an alienation that is enhanced by a succession of tangible and unreal events. By breaking through the time-space veil, the story changes into an allegory of the state of contemporary Portugal.　　　(L. S. REBELO)

Brazil. A remodeled censorship council was decreed in 1982 to supervise the moral as well as the artistic content of cultural productions. Many critical studies were concerned with the effect of censorship over the last few years. Sônia Khede's *Censores de pincenê e gravata* provocatively compared 19th-century theatrical censorship with that of the post-1964 period. In her *Impressões de viagem* and other critical analyses, Heloísa Buarque de Holanda studied the strained relationship between culture and creativity during the severest periods of repression. Adélia Bezerra de Meneses's *Desenho* *mágico* was a structural study of the language of Chico Buarque's songs; she judged them to have been one of the major popular escape valves during recent Brazilian history.

The 1982 Brazilian Goethe Institute prizes for the best prose works of the last four years were awarded to Autran Dourado for *Imaginações Pecaminosas* and to Antônio Callado for *Sempreviva*. Callado also published *A expedição Montaigne*, in which a quixotic photographer conspires to return Brazil to its Indian roots. Darcy Ribeiro's *Utopia selvagem* focused on Indian culture and anthropology in a handsomely produced volume. A fantasy about a medieval castle in the tropics was the theme of J. J. Veiga's *Aquele mundo de Vasabarros*, while another view of a hypothetical future for Brazil that was shockingly similar to the present was given by Ignácio de Loyola Brandão in his *Não verás país nenhum*. Dias Gomes's fiction *Sucupira, ame-a ou deixe-a* took a comic look at life in contemporary Rio, and Dalton Trevisan published yet another fine series of tepid short stories, *Chorinho brejeiro*. A serious fictional diary of Graciliano Ramos, *Em liberdade*, was prepared by Silviano Santiago in order to question the role of the intellectual within a politically and socially repressed society.

The major theatrical success was Millôr Fernandes's adaptation of the 19th-century classic *Memórias dum sargento de milícias* into the colourful production *Vidigal*. Posthumous poetry by Lúcio Cardoso and Joaquim Cardozo was published. Lêdo Ivo's new collection of poems, *A noite misteriosa*, included a critical study by the Mexican poet Carlos de Montemayor. Spanish American writers dealing with Brazilian themes were notable bestsellers in Brazil; *e.g.,* Vargas Llosa's *A guerra do fim do mundo* and Manuel Puig's *Sangue do amor correspondido*. Finally, Alberto Dines's biography of Stefan Zweig, *Morte no paraíso*, reflected the newly revived interest in this writer, who died in Brazil.

(IRWIN STERN)

RUSSIAN

Soviet Literature. The links between contemporary Soviet writers and the traditions of Russian classical literature were much discussed during the year. Books such as *Voices* by Vladimir Makanin, *Traveling via Moscow* by Anatoly Kurchatkin, *Preliminary Acquaintance* by Anatoly Afanasiev, and *Rough Notes* by Ruslan Kireyev testified to an increasing element of analysis in their authors' work and to their attempts to raise important social and philosophical, moral, and psychological questions by using the destinies of their contemporaries as material. This led one critic to suggest that these writers had a penchant for the creative principles of Chekhov.

Many authors took the history of the development of Soviet society as their background. Vladimir Lichutin (*Winged Serafima*) and Vladimir Krupin (*The Fortieth Day*) continued the traditions of "rustic prose," with its in-depth attention to the eternal moral values of the people and to events and processes that are changing the appearance of the countryside. Sergey Zalygin's novel *After the Storm* spoke of Siberia in the 1920s; Mikhail Alekseyev's *The Pugilists* was devoted to the era of the

collectivization of agriculture; the second part of Oles Adamovich and Daniil Granin's *Blockade Book*, based on documentary material, re-created the days of the heroic defense of Leningrad during the Great Patriotic War (World War II); and Oleg Smirnov's novel *Inevitability* showed the role of Soviet troops in the defeat of militarist Japan. The posthumous novel of Yury Trifonov (d. 1981), *The Time and the Place*, and the first notable prose work of the well-known poet Yevgeny Yevtushenko, *Berry Patches*, were both distinguished for their penetrating analyses of social and ethical problems. Valentin Rasputin, in his preface to *Berry Patches*, described it as "an agitational novel in the best sense."

The anthology *Young Voices* demonstrated that many promising poets had appeared. But while books of poems by Tatiana Rebrova, Andrey Chernov, Aleksandr Korolev, and Tatiana Bek enjoyed well-deserved popularity, critics noted that the creative potential of the beginner-poets had not yet been fully realized. It was the older generation of poets who made the greatest contribution. Among these were David Samoilov (*The Bay*), Yury Levitansky (*The Letters of Katerina or a Walk with Faust*), Andrey Voznesensky (*The Subconscious*), and Aleksandr Kushner (*Canvas*).

The celebration of the jubilees of prose writers Aleksandr Fadeyev and Konstantin Paustovsky and of the children's writer and literary historian Korney Chukovsky once again drew attention to the traditions and legacy of the Soviet classical writers. Publication of the writings of Vissarion Belinsky, the 19th-century critic and revolutionary democrat, neared completion. An edition of the works of the poet and dramatist Aleksandr Blok (1880–1921) was in preparation.

(SERGEY CHUPRININ)

Expatriate Russian Literature. The large number of books by exiled Russian authors (or by those still in the U.S.S.R. whose work did not get past the censor) included Joz Aleshkovsky's new novel, *Kenguru* ("Kangaroo"), which followed the example of Aleksandr Solzhenitsyn and Georgy Vladimov in presenting a picture of Soviet society seen through the prism of life in jails and labour camps. A satirist often thought of as a contemporary Gogol or Swift, Aleshkovsky set his latest book predominantly in the future while clearly holding up a mirror to the present.

Ardis of Ann Arbor in Michigan, publishers of *Kenguru*, brought out a volume of stories by the Caucasian writer Fazil Iskander, *Sandro iz Chegema: Novye glavy*, including five that did not appear in the Soviet edition of 1977. Ardis also published a collection of 35 short stories by Yevgeny Popov, the young Siberian writer whose work had been banned in the U.S.S.R. since he took part in the production of the *Metropol* literary almanac in 1979. Lev Kopelev continued the publication of his memoirs with the third volume in the series, *Utoli moya pechali* ("Calm My Sorrows"). *Volja* ("Freedom"), a collection of verse by Semyon Lipkin, was the first book by this 70-year-old writer to be published outside the U.S.S.R. It was edited by the exiled poet Joseph Brodsky.

Another leading writer living in the U.S., Vasily

Yevgeny Yevtushenko

Aksyonov, published an entertaining new novel, *Ostrov Krym* ("Crimea Island"). Writing in the July–August issue of the London *Index on Censorship*, Aksyonov compared the censorship that existed in tsarist Russia with the more 'powerful, comprehensive, total' censorship of the Soviet Union today. He also drew a fascinating picture of his generation of Russian writers, who had been born in the '30s "in the very storm centre of the world's unfreedom" and who, in the '60s, came to be called "the new voices" by the Soviet literary establishment. "We were supposed to turn out to be the ideal slaves," wrote Aksyonov. "Somehow we turned out to be the opposite. . . . In the days of our literary youth it went without saying that the calling of Soviet author implied some sort of warped conscience. . . . but as the years passed, compromise began to shrink and a feeling of freedom to grow."

Two anthologies, one in English and the other in German, were noteworthy. *Contemporary Russian Prose*, edited by Carl and Ellendea Proffer in Ann Arbor, brought together the work of seven Russian authors, including Aksyonov and Iskander. (The others were Valentin Rasputin, Vasily Shukshin, Andrey Bitov, Yury Trifonov, and Sasha Sokolov.) *Russische Lyrik: Gedichte aus drei Jahrhunderten*, compiled by Efim Etkind and published in Munich, West Germany, contained a selection of the finest Russian poetry from the 18th century to the present.

In the U.S.S.R. persecution of nonconformist writers continued. In February the KGB searched the home of novelist Georgy Vladimov, confiscating all foreign editions of his works. Another search was carried out at the end of December, and the author was ordered to report, with his wife, Natasha, for questioning at Lefortovo prison in Moscow.   (GEORGE THEINER)

Poland continued to dominate the world's headlines in 1982. The offices of the Polish PEN Club were closed down by the martial law authorities, and ten of its leading members were detained, together with a number of other Polish writers. Most had been released from custody by the time martial law was suspended at the end of December. The poet Anka Kowalska was released for health reasons in May and allowed to go to Paris for treatment. Also in Paris was the poet Jacek Bierezin, freed from detention at the same time. The secretary of the Polish PEN, Wladyslaw Bartoszewski, was released and allowed to travel to West Germany, where he was to spend a year before returning to Poland. Another author, Jan Jozef Lipski, was arrested on his return from London, where he had gone for a medical checkup; seriously ill with a heart condition, he faced trial on charges of subversion.

Under these difficult conditions, Tadeusz Konwicki managed to complete his novel *Wschody i zachody ksiezyca* ("Moonrises, Moonsets"). The manuscript found its way to London, where the book was published as the 21st issue of the six-year-old *samizdat* literary quarterly *Zapis*. The rights to Konwicki's earlier novel *Mala apokalipsa* ("A Small Apocalypse"), which came out in Polish as *Zapis* 10 in 1979, had been sold to publishers in almost every Western European country, as well as the U.S. (Farrar Straus Giroux) and Yugoslavia. A Czech émigré edition was published in West Germany, and a dramatized version, put on in London by a Polish theatre company, was broadcast in an English translation by the BBC.

The Czech playwright Vaclav Havel, still serving the sentence of 4½ years' imprisonment meted out to him in October 1979, wrote an interesting personal account of his attitude to the theatre. It appeared in the new *samizdat* journal *Kriticky sbornik* ("Critical Review"), launched toward the end of 1981 as a successor to the earlier *Spektrum*, which discontinued publication with its third issue. By the end of 1982, six issues of *Kriticky sbornik*, consisting of literary criticism and articles on various aspects of Czech literature—official and unofficial—had been produced and distributed in typescript. Havel sent his article from prison piecemeal, each section contained in a letter to his wife, Olga.

One of the most popular of all contemporary Czech authors, the novelist and short-story writer Bohumil Hrabal, made his peace with the authorities and was allowed to publish. Nevertheless, his novel *Obsluhoval jsem anglickeho krale* ("I Served the King of England") was still obtainable only in the Edice Petlice ("Padlock") *samizdat* edition.

Some 70 *samizdat* publications were confiscated in police raids as part of a widespread drive against Czech unofficial religious publishing. Josef Barta, a Franciscan priest, was sentenced to 18 months' imprisonment in April for these activities. The writers Eva Kanturkova and Milan Simecka, who had spent almost a year in custody in connection with the smuggling of literary material in and out of Czechoslovakia, were released without trial. The poet and novelist Jiri Grusa, who had been allowed to visit West Germany, was stripped of his Czechoslovak nationality while still abroad and thus prevented from returning home.

In Hungary the end of 1982 brought a sudden worsening of the position of dissident writers, with repeated police raids on their homes. Unofficial publications continued to appear, however, including the literary journal *Beszelo* ("Spokesman"). William Lomax, a sociology lecturer from the University of Nottingham in England and author of a book on the 1956 Hungarian uprising, was ordered off a train by Hungarian officials at the frontier in December while en route to Budapest.

The Romanian writer Ion Caraion asked for political asylum in Switzerland in January, stating that he did not wish to return to Romania because of the censorship there, which had prevented publication of his book containing the testimony of former political prisoners. Of the books that did get published in Bucharest, Florenta Albu's *Umbra arsa* ("Singed Shadow") was praised as "a landmark" and "undoubtedly among the most important new books of verse" by a reviewer in *World Literature Today* (winter 1982). Another Romanian writer whose work was commended by this U.S. journal was Fanus Neagu. His latest book, a collection of essays entitled *Insomnii de matase* ("Insomnias of Silk"), "reveals a strong concern for political themes . . . raps the iron knuckles of totalitarianism." His "every sentence, every phrase shows verbal mastery, poetic creativity."

(GEORGE THEINER)

JEWISH

Hebrew. In observance of the 100th anniversary of modern Jewish settlement in the Land of Israel, Hebrew writers in symposia and essays discussed the relationship between Jewish nationalism and modern Hebrew literature. A continuing trend was the nurtured mutuality between Hebrew writers and authors in Israel who write in other languages. Especially significant were Arab authors, writing in Hebrew or Arabic, whose works were increasingly available. Overshadowing these literary developments was the war in Lebanon, and many writers were active in both protest and support groups. Two plays heightened the social and political tension: *Nefesh Yehudi* by Yehoshua Sobol and *haPatriot* by Hanoch Levin.

Celebrating his 80th birthday was the eminent man of letters Dov Sadan, whose reminiscences had appeared in three volumes to date. Yisrael Gur, long-time editor of the theatre journal *Bama*, died during the year. A new journal, *Mar'ot*, was established in Jerusalem.

Collections of poetry were published by D. Barak, Yosef Bar-Yosef, Mosheh Ben-Sha'ul, O. Bernstein, S. Davidovitch, Yair Hurwitz, Dan Pagis, and A. Sivan. Noteworthy were *Ulai* by Simon Halkin, *haShoni haMarhiv* by Zelda, a 1940–80 collection of verse by Nathan Yonatan, and a book of "oral essays" by Abba Kovner. Works of fiction included *Menuha Nekhona* by Amos Oz and *Gerushim Me'uharim* by Abraham B. Yehoshua. The Bialik Prize for poetry was awarded to Natan Zach. Israel's highest honour, the Israel Prize for Litera-

Yehuda Amichai

ture, was given to two prominent poets, Amir Gilboa and Yehuda Amichai.

Significant critical works included N. Sadan-Lowenstein's monograph on Yehoshua; Y. Bahat's study of Shlonsky; N. Govrin's *Shorashim Vetsamarot*, on early Hebrew writing in Palestine; and Hillel Barzel's *Shira Tse'ira: Mavo*, on recent Israeli poetry. Barzel also edited a volume of critical essays on Samuel Joseph Agnon. A momentous literary event was publication of vol. i of the *Collected Works* of Uri Nissan Gnessin, edited by Dan Miron and Y. Zemora. (WARREN BARGAD)

Yiddish. Yiddish poets continued to produce works in a surprising variety of styles. Both Asia's refined *No Albatross: Poems* and Hannah Shalit's *In Constant Trembling* were disciplined volumes, expressing a feminine eloquence. Freed Weininger's *Letters, Words, and Stanzas* reflected on beauty and tragedy, while Moyshe Yungman's *The Way My Father Made His Living* cultivated a folk idiom with care and delicacy. Martin Birnbaum's *Poems About the Poem* were meditative and keenly contemporary.

But of all the genres it was the Yiddish novel that flourished most. The resolution of life choices in interwar Poland was the theme of Josef Okrutny's *Between Borders. Unfinished Pages*, a novelistic biography of Esther Frumkin by Lily Berger, constituted a milestone in the history of Yiddishism and Jewish socialism. Tevye Gen's family chronicle, *In the Extra Telegram*, sketched the panorama of Jewish life in the U.S.S.R. Imre Druker's eponymous novel, focusing on the struggle of *Mikhl Yoysef Guzikov* to become a musician in the early 1800s, described shtetl life with its mores, music, and profound philosophical conflicts. Shimshn Apter took the reader to Brazil and Portugal a century earlier in his *The Marrano Family Da Silva*, a powerful novel about the religious and social life of secret Jews. Shlomo Worzoger's collection of stories, *Here*, portrayed Germany and Poland during World War II and Israel in the postwar period. Polish Jewry found its bard in Heshl Klepfish, whose essays were published in *Echoes from a Time that Is Gone: 1929–1939.*

Among noteworthy volumes of criticism were Itche Goldberg's *Essays*; Dan Miron's formalist analysis, *The Shtetl Image*; Arye Shamri's impressionistic collection of essays about writing and writers, *Ingathering*; and Itzhak Korn's provocative *The Struggle for Yiddish*. Three significant contributions to Yiddish reference works were published: Joshua Fishman's monumental anthology about the present and future of Yiddish, *Never Say Die!*; *Dictionnaire Yiddish-Français*, edited by Noyekh Gris and Shmuel Kerner; and Mordkhe Tsanin's *Yiddish-Hebrew Dictionary*.

The death on June 26, 1982, of Chaim Grade, arguably the finest contemporary Yiddish prose writer, was an irreplaceable loss.

(THOMAS E. BIRD; ELIAS SCHULMAN)

CHINESE

China. In 1982 an intense debate was waged between the more moderate critics and writers of the *Literary Gazette*, which advocated that "art and literature serve the people," and the hard-liners and Army-connected leftists of *Report of the Times*, which launched attacks on Bai Hua's (Pai Hua's) *Bitter Love* and advocated the Maoist policy that "art and literature serve politics." Though China continued its crackdown on "bourgeois liberalism" and Western "decadent values and influences," the authorities came out in support of the more moderate line that artistic and literary works should support socialism, socialist modernization, and the people's interests. Hu Qiaomu (Hu Ch'iaomu), a member of the ruling Politburo, stressed that "all works that reflect the feelings of the people should be welcome so long as they do not split or insult the people." After the 12th Communist Party congress in September, a new director of the Army's Political Department was named, and the editors of *Report of the Times* were transferred.

Meanwhile, Chinese writers made significant contributions. Dai Houying's (Tai Hou-ying's) novel *Oh Man!* became an instant best-seller because of its intense emphasis on human nature and its powerful revelations of the sufferings of intellectuals during past decades. Chang Jie's (Ch'ang Chieh's) *Heavy Wings* revealed the dark side of Communist society and some of the serious problems in post-Mao China. Liu Ke's (Liu K'e's) *Fei Tian*, a novel on the tragic life of a village girl, was widely read. Chinese playwrights also turned personal tragedies experienced during the Cultural Revolution into popular plays and films, such as Yang Yuanjin's (Yang Yüan-chin's) *The Small Street*. Mao Zedong (Mao Tse-tung) and other Chinese leaders were summoned back to life on the stage in Ding Yisan's (Ting Yi-san's) *The September 13 Affair*, which attacked Mao's personality cult and the radical faction known as the gang of four.

Taiwan. In contrast to debates on the mainland, Taiwan's literary scene was unusually peaceful. While a few writers were criticized for their political views, most continued to work with little political interference. Chang Yi-ning's *She Has not yet Reached Maturity*, which realistically portrayed the tragic life of a young girl who turned into a drug-addicted prostitute, attracted great attention for its believable poignancy.

Attracting even more attention were many native Taiwanese writers. In contrast to the earlier interest in the lives of intellectuals and professionals, shown mostly by writers from the mainland, many native writers, such as Ch'en Ying-chen and Hung Hsing-fu, dealt with life among the lower-class native Taiwanese living in small towns and remote villages.

(WINSTON L. Y. YANG; NATHAN MAO)

JAPANESE

The year 1982 was an unusually productive one for fiction. Some critics even spoke of the regeneration of the dying novel. Whether this diagnosis was accurate or not, there were certainly several brilliant achievements in the genre. One of the most impressive was Nobuo Kojima's voluminous *Reasons for Separation*, which was 13 years in the making. It grew out of the short story of the same title and went on and on without much dramatic progress, but somehow the reader could not put it down. The main story was commonplace enough—the daily routine of a middle-aged professor-novelist and his wife and their relationships with mutual friends—but Kojima's narrative technique was not tame at all; free from conventional boundaries, it jumped from one episode to another and back and forth in time, introducing mythological parallels without any trace of artificiality. It was an amazing literary tour de force.

Shotaro Yasuoka's *Story of the Wanderers* could be called a historical novel of the Meiji Restoration period, but it was based on careful investigation of family documents, and most of the important characters were the author's own ancestors or close relatives. It was a Japanese version of *Roots*—though with a more solid factual basis—since what engrossed Yasuoka was the search for his familial identity as well as for the origins of modern Japan. Saiichi Maruya claimed that his *Sing Kimigayo* [the Japanese national anthem] *Falsetto* was "a political novel by a nonpolitical, or even antipolitical, writer." The main story concerned Nationalist Chinese activists working for an independent Taiwan, but the action was described from the detached point of view of a middle-aged, hedonistic, Japanese art dealer. The novel was highly entertaining and became a best-seller.

Minako Ohba's *Lonesome*, a Tanizaki Prize winner, was a fantastic love story rich in poetic evocation. The plot was rather arbitrary, but Ohba's style was both frank and subtle in a characteristically feminine way. Tetsuro Miura's *Hymn to the Boys' Mission*, an elaborate historical novel, dealt with the heroic but futile travels of young samurai emissaries sent to Rome at the close of the 16th century. Haruki Murakami's *Adventures in Search of Sheep* was a clever, fantastic fable by a promising young novelist.

Yasuo Irisawa's *New Poems* was an impressive achievement rich in mythological overtone. Readable and stimulating literary criticism was provided by Koichi Isoda's *Inscapes in Post-war Japan* and Hideaki Oketani's biographical essays.

(SHOICHI SAEKI)

See also Art Sales; Libraries; Nobel Prizes; Publishing.

[621]

Luxembourg

Madagascar

Luxembourg

A constitutional monarchy, the Benelux country of Luxembourg is bounded on the east by West Germany, on the south by France, and on the west and north by Belgium. Area: 2,586 sq km (999 sq mi). Pop. (1981): 364,600. Cap. and largest city: Luxembourg (pop., 1981, 78,900). Language: French, German, Luxembourgian. Religion (1980): Roman Catholic 94.3%; Protestant 1.2%; atheist 1%; none 3.5%. Grand duke, Jean; prime minister in 1982, Pierre Werner.

The 8.5% devaluation of the Belgian franc on Feb. 21, 1982, put the 1922 economic union between Belgium and Luxembourg under strain. Under the terms of the union there were no customs barriers between the two countries, and Belgian and Luxembourg coins and bank notes circulated interchangeably. On international markets the National Bank of Belgium had largely assumed responsibility for managing the monetary affairs of both nations.

Stung in both the pocketbook and national prestige by Belgium's unilateral decision to devalue, made known to the Grand Duchy only hours in advance, Luxembourg expressed its displeasure. Pierre Werner, Luxembourg's prime minister, invited Wilfried Martens, his Belgian counterpart, to Luxembourg for an urgent discussion.

Although few in the Grand Duchy seriously proposed ending the economic union with Belgium, the terms of that relationship were a matter for renegotiation as the 60-year agreement ran out in 1982. Luxembourg delayed ratification of an extension. It was perhaps true that, as a senior Belgian official said, the Luxembourg franc on its own would last "about three weeks"; on the other hand, it was suggested that either the Bank for International Settlements in Switzerland or the West German Bundesbank could eventually prove a staunch supporter of an independent Luxembourg currency.   (K. M. SMOGORZEWSKI)

Livestock:
see Agriculture and Food Supplies

Lumber:
see Industrial Review

Lutheran Churches:
see Religion

Macau:
see Dependent States

Machinery and Machine Tools:
see Industrial Review

LUXEMBOURG

Education. (1981–82) Primary, pupils 27,927, teachers (1978–79) 1,449; secondary, pupils 9,100; vocational, pupils 15,950; secondary and vocational, teachers (1975–76) 1,801; teacher training, students 152; higher, students 232, teaching staff (1980–81) 168.

Finance. Monetary unit: Luxembourg franc, at par with the Belgian franc, with (Sept. 20, 1982) a free rate of LFr 48.09 to U.S. $1 (LFr 82.45 = £1 sterling). Budget (1982 est.): revenue LFr 54,616,300,000; expenditure LFr 55,953,700,000. Gross national product (1980) LFr 169.8 million. Cost of living (1975 = 100; June 1982) 158.1.

Foreign Trade: see BELGIUM.

Transport and Communications. Roads (1980) 5,094 km (including 44 km expressways). Motor vehicles in use (1980): passenger 173,100; commercial 11,400. Railways: (1980) 270 km; traffic (1981) 300 million passenger-km, freight 584 million net ton-km. Air traffic (1980): c. 55 million passenger-km; freight c. 200,000 net ton-km. Telephones (Jan. 1980) 198,900. Radio receivers (Dec. 1979) 186,000. Television receivers (Dec. 1979) 89,000.

Agriculture. Production (in 000; metric tons; 1980): barley 59; wheat 27; oats 27; potatoes 34; wine c. 5. Livestock (in 000; May 1980): cattle 225; pigs 79; poultry 131.

Industry. Production (in 000; metric tons; 1981): iron ore (29% metal content) 429; pig iron 2,888; crude steel 3,791; electricity (kw-hr) 1,208,000.

Madagascar

Madagascar occupies the island of the same name and minor adjacent islands in the Indian Ocean off the southeast coast of Africa. Area: 587,041 sq km (226,658 sq mi). Pop. (1982 est.): 9.4 million. Cap. and largest city: Antananarivo (pop., 1982 est., 600,000). Language: Malagasy and French (official). Religion: animist 50%; Roman Catholic 25%; Protestant 20%; Muslim 5%. President in 1982, Didier Ratsiraka; prime minister, Lieut. Col. Désiré Rakotoarijaona.

On Nov. 7, 1982, Pres. Didier Ratsiraka was reelected for a second seven-year term, winning 80% of the votes cast. The only other candidate, Monja Jaona, whose left-wing Madagascar National Independence Movement (Monima) stood in the forefront of peasant opposition to the government, gained 20%. However, a narrow advantage for Ratsiraka in the capital detracted significantly from his victory.

The year had begun with a ministerial reshuffle. The most important of the changes announced by President Ratsiraka on January 15 were the appointment of Pascal Rakotomavo as minister of finance, replacing the former minister of finance and planning (responsibility for planning now reverting to the presidency), and of Georges Solofoson as minister of industry and trade (economy and trade under his predecessor). Both these changes appeared to be politically motivated. Neither of the ministers who were replaced was thought to be an ardent socialist. Then on January 24 the government claimed to have uncovered a subversive plot.

Madagascar's ailing economy and its social consequences, aggravated by severe flooding in Feb-

MADAGASCAR

Education. (1978) Primary, pupils 1,311,000, teachers 23,937; secondary, pupils (1976) 114,468, teachers (1975) 5,088; vocational, pupils (1976) 7,000, teachers (1973) 879; teacher training (1973), students 993, teachers 63; higher, students (1979) 22,857, teaching staff 557.

Finance. Monetary unit: Malagasy franc, with (Sept. 21, 1981) a free rate of MalFr 373 to U.S. $1 (MalFr 640 = £1 sterling). Budget (1982 est.) balanced at MalFr 257 billion.

Foreign Trade. (1980) Imports MalFr 126,780,000,000; exports MalFr 84,780,000,000. Import sources: France 41%; West Germany 10%; Japan 5%; Iraq 5%. Export destinations: France 20%; U.S. 19%; Japan 10%; West Germany 9%; Spain 8%. Main exports: coffee 53%; cloves 8%; vanilla 5%.

Transport and Communications. Roads (1979) 27,556 km. Motor vehicles in use (1980): passenger c. 56,000; commercial (including buses) c. 49,000. Railways: (1979) 1,036 km; traffic (1980) 274 million passenger-km, freight 201 million net ton-km. Air traffic (1980): 310 million passenger-km; freight 21.3 million net ton-km. Shipping (1981): merchant vessels 100 gross tons and over 55; gross tonnage 74,050. Telephones (Dec. 1978) 29,000. Radio receivers (Dec. 1979) 1,150,000. Television receivers (Dec. 1980) c. 9,000.

Agriculture. Production (in 000; metric tons; 1981): rice c. 1,999; corn c. 126; cassava c. 1,745; sweet potatoes c. 410; potatoes c. 258; mangoes c. 174; dry beans c. 51; bananas c. 280; oranges c. 86; pineapples c. 58; peanuts 38; sugar, raw value c. 112; coffee c. 95; cotton 10; tobacco c. 5; sisal c. 20; beef and veal c. 128; fish catch (1980) c. 54. Livestock (in 000; Dec. 1980): cattle c.10,150; sheep c. 620; pigs c. 700; goats c. 1,400; chickens c. 15,000.

ruary, gave rise to civil disturbances in the north in March and in the southwest in May, when more than 100 deaths were reported. Under pressure from the International Monetary Fund, President Ratsiraka announced a 15% devaluation of the Malagasy franc on May 17.

Madagascar's foreign relations remained closest with France. President Ratsiraka received Pres. François Mitterrand's adviser on African affairs, Guy Penne, in February and the French minister for cooperation, Jean-Pierre Cot, in August.

(PHILIPPE DECRAENE)

Malawi

A republic and member of the Commonwealth in east central Africa, Malawi is bounded by Tanzania, Mozambique, and Zambia. Area: 118,484 sq km (45,747 sq mi). Pop. (1982 est.): 6,587,000. Cap.: Lilongwe (pop., 1977, 98,700). Largest city: Blantyre (pop., 1977, 219,000). Language: English (official) and Chichewa (national). Religion (1980): Christian 64.5%; tribal 19%; Muslim 16.2%; other 0.3%. President in 1982, Hastings Kamuzu Banda.

In yet another attempt to strengthen Malawi's economy, Pres. Hastings Kamuzu Banda again reorganized his Cabinet on Jan. 5, 1982. Several ministerial posts were left vacant, including housing, created the previous year. Probably the most significant change was the appointment of Dick Tennyson Matenje as minister without portfolio and secretary-general of the ruling Malawi Congress Party in succession to Bakili Muluzi, previously regarded as a possible successor to President Banda. Muluzi became minister of transport and communications and then retired from the Cabinet in May for personal reasons. On April 24 the kwacha was devalued by 15% against the Special Drawing Right of the International Monetary Fund.

On January 6 it was announced that Orton Chirwa, together with his wife and son, had been

---

MALAWI

Education. (1979–80) Primary, pupils 779,676, teachers 11,552; secondary, pupils 16,431, teachers 779; vocational, pupils 1,077, teachers 91; teacher training, students 1,855. teachers 108; higher, students 1,620, teaching staff 203.
Finance. Monetary unit: kwacha, with (Sept. 20, 1982) a free rate of 1.12 kwacha to U.S. $1 (1.91 kwacha = £1 sterling). Gold and other reserves (June 1982) U.S. $46 million. Budget (1980–81 actual): revenue 199 million kwacha; expenditure 181 million kwacha.
Foreign Trade. (1981) Imports 319.7 million kwacha; exports 254.7 million kwacha. Import sources (1980): South Africa 37%; U.K. 18%; Japan 7%; West Germany 5%. Export destinations (1980): U.K. 28%; U.S. 16%; The Netherlands 8%; West Germany 7%; Zimbabwe 5%. Main exports: tobacco 40%; sugar 26%; tea 12%.
Transport and Communications. Roads (main; 1980) 10,772 km. Motor vehicles in use (1980): passenger 11,800; commercial 13,300. Railways (1981): 789 km; traffic 77 million passenger-km, freight 229 million net ton-km. Air traffic (1981): 83 million passenger-km; freight 1.2 million net ton-km. Telephones (Jan. 1980) 28,800. Radio receivers (Dec. 1979) 250,000.
Agriculture. Production (in 000; metric tons; 1981): corn c. 1,600; cassava c. 90; sorghum c. 140; sugar, raw value c. 175; peanuts c. 180; tea c. 32; tobacco c. 52; cotton, lint c. 9. Livestock (in 000; 1981): cattle c. 850; sheep c. 78; goats c. 650; pigs c. 182; poultry c. 8,100.

---

arrested a fortnight earlier after entering Malawi illegally. Chirwa, a former attorney general and minister of justice, had been living in Tanzania since clashing with President Banda in 1964. Later in the year Chirwa was charged with treason as an alleged leader of the Malawi Freedom Movement, which was said to be plotting the overthrow of the government. His supporters claimed the police had illegally arrested him on Zambian soil.

(KENNETH INGHAM)

Malaysia

A federation within the Commonwealth comprising the 11 states of the former Federation of Malaya, Sabah, Sarawak, and the federal territory of Kuala Lumpur, Malaysia is a federal constitutional monarchy situated in Southeast Asia at the southern end of the Malay Peninsula (excluding Singapore) and on the northern part of the island of Borneo. Area: 329,747 sq km (127,316 sq mi). Pop. (1982 est.): 14,344,000, including (1980 est.) Malays 47.1%, Chinese 32.7%; Indians 9.6%; and Dayaks 3.7%. Cap. and largest city Kuala Lumpur (pop., 1980, 937,900). Language: Malay (official). Religion: Malays are Muslim; Indians mainly Hindu; Chinese mainly Buddhist, Confucian, and Taoist; indigenous population of Sabah and Sarawak (1980 est.) 47% animist, 38% Muslim, and 15% Christian. Supreme head of state in 1982, with the title of *yang di-pertuan agong*, Tuanku Sultan Haji Ahmad Shah al-Musta'in Billah ibni al-Marhum Sultan Abu Bakar Ri'ayatuddin al-Mu'adzam Shah; prime minister, Datuk Seri Mahathir bin Mohamad.

Elections to the federal Parliament and all 11 state assemblies in peninsular Malaysia were held on April 22, 1982, while the two east Malaysian states voted for federal seats only on April 22–26. Employing the campaign slogan of "clean, effective, and trustworthy government," the ruling National Front (Barisan Nasional) coalition achieved an electoral triumph. It secured 132 parliamentary seats out of 154 and also retained control of all the peninsular state assemblies.

A notable feature of the parliamentary results was the loss of seven seats by the Chinese-based opposition Democratic Action Party, which won only nine seats. The dominant Malay party, the United Malays National Organization (UMNO), consolidated its strong position within the ruling coalition through the efforts of Prime Minister Datuk Seri Mahathir bin Mohamad and also by attracting as a parliamentary candidate the charismatic figure of Anwar Ibrahim, who resigned as head of the Malaysian Islamic Youth Movement in order to run for office. There were no major changes in the Cabinet, but new chief ministers were appointed in the states of Selangor, Pahang, Johore, Malacca, and Negri Sembilan.

An election for one state seat in Negri Sembilan was postponed until May because of the murder on April 14 of UMNO candidate Datuk Mohamad Taha Abdul Talib, speaker of the outgoing state assembly. In July federal minister for Culture, Youth, and Sports Datuk Mokhtar bin Haji Hashim and

Malawi

Malaysia

Magazines:
see Publishing

Maldives

four associates were arrested and charged with the murder. One of the associates died in prison before the beginning of the trial in October.

The government reaffirmed its policy, first stated in October 1981 by Prime Minister Mahathir, of not buying British products if similar goods were available from other countries. *The Times* of London estimated that between October 1981 and mid-1982 contracts worth £30 million–£40 million had been lost to U.K. firms as a result of the Malaysian government's stance.

Malaysia's economic circumstances declined during the year. In March Deputy Prime Minister Datuk Musa bin Hitam announced an early review of the country's fourth economic plan. During the same month, the prime minister assured senior executives of 45 multinational firms from the U.S., Europe, Japan, and Australia that Malaysia would continue to offer stability and a good investment climate. Malaysia was also afflicted by a serious drought that adversely affected its rice harvest. In April the National Padi and Rice Board announced its intention to import approximately 400,000 metric tons of rice.

In August, alongside an independence-day amnesty for 47 people detained under the Internal Security Act, Datuk Harun Idris, the former chief minister of Selangor imprisoned for six years in 1978 on charges of fraud and corruption, was granted a full pardon. He had already been released from prison by remission of sentence in August 1981, but the pardon permitted him to hold political office.

In June Kuala Lumpur served as the site for a meeting between leaders of Khmer Communist and non-Communist Kampuchean factions, who agreed to form a coalition government to challenge the Vietnamese-backed administration in their country. Australian Prime Minister Malcolm Fraser visited Malaysia in August in an attempt to improve relations, which had deteriorated since Mahathir came to office in 1981. A more fruitful visit was made by Singapore's prime minister, Lee Kuan Yew, also in August; agreements were reached on the purchase by Singapore of Malaysian liquefied natural gas and also on the operation of an air shuttle service between Kuala Lumpur and Singapore. (MICHAEL LEIFER)

Maldives

Maldives, a republic in the Indian Ocean consisting of about two thousand small islands, lies southwest of the southern tip of India. Area: 298 sq km (115 sq mi). Pop. (1982 est.): 155,000. Cap.: Male (pop., 1978, 29,600). Language: Divehi (official), Arabic, Hindu, and English. Religion: Muslim. President in 1982, Maumoon Abdul Gayoom.

On July 9, 1982, members of the Commonwealth welcomed the association's 47th member, the Republic of Maldives. In a letter seeking membership, Pres. Maumoon Abdul Gayoom said that his government in so doing had the support of the Majlis (parliament). Following consultations with heads of government by the Commonwealth secretary-general, the republic was admitted as the fourth special member, the other three being Nauru, St. Vincent and the Grenadines, and Tuvalu. Special members of the Commonwealth were free to take part in all its technical cooperation programs and they could attend all meetings except the full heads of government conferences. They did not have to contribute to the Secretariat budget, although they could make voluntary contributions.

Practical benefits of membership for the Maldives were mainly to be gained from the Commonwealth Fund for Technical Cooperation (CFTC), which organized training programs in food production and fisheries development. In October the Maldives attended the third summit of Commonwealth leaders from the Asia-Pacific region, held in Fiji.

MALAYSIA
Education. (1981) Primary, pupils 2,033,803, teachers 73,881; secondary, pupils 1,102,908, teachers 48,199; vocational, pupils 17,424, teachers 1,430; higher (including teacher training colleges), students 57,139, teaching staff 5,569.

Finance. Monetary unit: ringgit, with (Sept. 20, 1982) a free rate of 2.36 ringgits to U.S. $1 (4.05 ringgits = £1 sterling). Gold and other reserves (May 1982) U.S. $3,404,000,000. Budget (1981 est.): revenue 14,972,-000,000 ringgits; expenditure 14.6 million ringgits. Gross national product (1981) 54,402,000,000 ringgits. Money supply (May 1982) 11,223,000,000 ringgits. Cost of living (Peninsular Malaysia; 1975 = 100; June 1982) 144.9.

Foreign Trade. (1981) Imports 26,674,000,000 ringgits; exports 25,782,000,000 ringgits. Import sources: Japan 24%; U.S. 15%; Singapore 13%; Australia 6%; Saudi Arabia 5%; U.K. 5%. Export destinations: Singapore 24%; Japan 22%; U.S. 10%; The Netherlands 6%. Main exports: crude oil 27%; rubber 14%; timber 14%; palm oil 11%; tin 8%; thermionic valves and tubes c. 8%.

Transport and Communications. Roads (1979) 28,971 km. Motor vehicles in use (1979): passenger 696,500; commercial c. 158,700. Railways (1981): 2,681 km; traffic (Peninsular Malaysia only; including Singapore) 1,640,000,000 passenger-km, freight 1,130,000,000 net ton-km. Air traffic (1981): c. 4,540,000,000 passenger-km; freight c. 136 million net ton-km. Shipping (1981): merchant vessels 100 gross tons and over 258; gross tonnage 879,468. Telephones (Jan. 1979) 434,000. Radio receivers (Dec. 1979) 2 million. Television receivers (Dec. 1979) 850,000.

Agriculture. Production (in 000; metric tons; 1981): rice 2,147; rubber c. 1,590; copra c. 210; palm oil c. 2,800; tea c. 4; bananas c. 460; pineapples 207; pepper (Sarawak only; 1980) 31; tobacco c. 10; meat c. 235; fish catch (1980) 737; timber (cu m; 1980) c. 43,486. Livestock (in 000; Dec. 1980): cattle c. 540; buffalo c. 293; pigs c. 1,750; goats c. 365; sheep c. 65; chickens c. 52,000.

Industry. Production (in 000; metric tons; 1981): cement 2,833; tin concentrates (metal content) 60; bauxite 701; iron ore (56% metal content) 531; crude oil 12,310; petroleum products (1979) c. 4,960; electricity (kw-hr) 9,541,000.

MALDIVES
Education. (1980) Primary, pupils 33,741, teachers 669; secondary, pupils 1,760, teachers 94; vocational, students 23, teachers 9; teacher training, students 86, teachers 8.

Finance and Trade. Monetary unit: rufiyaa (Maldivian rupee), with (Sept. 20, 1982) a free rate of 7.55 rufiyaa to U.S. $1 (12.94 rufiyaa = £1 sterling). Budget (1980 est.): revenue 44 million rufiyaa; expenditure 44.1 million rufiyaa. Foreign trade (1979): imports 86.6 million rufiyaa; exports 23 million rufiyaa. Main import sources: India c. 25%; West Germany c. 15%; Japan c. 14%; Sri Lanka c. 11%; Burma c. 7%; Pakistan c. 7%. Main export destinations: Japan c. 44%; Sri Lanka c. 14%; Switzerland c. 14%; Mauritius c. 12%; Pakistan c. 9%. Main exports: fresh fish 56%; dried salt fish 36%. Tourism (1979): 33,100 visitors.

Most of the population of the Maldives continued to live by fishing or collecting coconuts. Food and manufactured goods were the main imports, followed by fuel and machinery. The modern sector of the economy depended upon shipping and tourism, both especially vulnerable to recession. The islands remained heavily dependent upon international aid. (GUY ARNOLD)

Mali

A republic of West Africa, Mali is bordered by Algeria, Niger, Upper Volta, Ivory Coast, Guinea, Senegal, and Mauritania. Area: 1,240,192 sq km (478,841 sq mi). Pop. (1981 est.): 7,160,000. Cap. and largest city: Bamako (pop., 1980 est., 440,000). Language: French (official), Bambara, Malinke, Fulani, Soninke, Dogon, Senufo, Berber, and Arabic. Religion: Muslim 65%; Christian 5%; animist 30%. President in 1982, Gen. Moussa Traoré.

Pres. Moussa Traoré received French Minister for Cooperation Jean-Pierre Cot at Bamako in March 1982 and was himself received by Pres. François Mitterrand in Paris in October. However, despite discrete efforts at mediation by France, Mali's hoped-for reintegration into the West African Monetary Union was blocked by Upper Volta because of the continuing frontier dispute between the two countries. Mali's relations with Niger were also strained following apprehension there of a group of Tuaregs using Malian territory as a base for an intended sabotage operation.

The proposal that Mali's foreign minister, Blondin N'Gueye, succeed Edom Kodjo of Togo as secretary-general of the Organization of African Unity (OAU) met with interest in view of President Traoré's active mediatory role in the intra-OAU dispute over Western Sahara.

Elections to Mali's National Assembly on June 13 were a formality. All the candidates on the single list represented the ruling Democratic Union of the Malian People—the only permitted party. (PHILIPPE DECRAENE)

Malta

Mali

Malta

The Republic of Malta, a member of the Commonwealth, comprises the islands of Malta, Gozo, and Comino in the Mediterranean Sea between Sicily and Tunisia. Area: 320 sq km (124 sq mi), including Malta, Gozo, and Comino. Pop. (1981 est.): 366,000. Cap.: Valletta (pop., 1981 est., 14,000). Largest city: Sliema (pop., 1979 est., 20,100). Language: Maltese and English. Religion: mainly Roman Catholic. Presidents in 1982, Anton Buttigieg and, from February 16, Agatha Barbara; prime minister, Dom Mintoff.

Following elections in December 1981, Malta's new Parliament was inaugurated on Feb. 15, 1982, but 31 of its 65 elected members boycotted its sittings. The boycott, which continued throughout the year, was undertaken by members of the Nationalist Party, the only opposition party. They claimed that Prime Minister Dom Mintoff's Malta Labour Party kept a three-seat majority in the house, despite obtaining only 49% of the vote, through deliberate gerrymandering (manipulating the boundaries of electoral districts).

Malta and Libya finally implemented their 1976 agreement to refer their continental shelf dispute to the International Court of Justice at The Hague. On July 26 Maltese and Libyan delegations jointly notified the registrar of the court of their agreement. The two sides were then expected to present their case to the International Court in writing.

On September 1 the highly controversial Foreign Interference Act came into force. This law was specifically designed to curb Nationalist Party broadcasts from neighbouring Sicily and disrupt aid to the party from the West German Konrad Adenauer Foundation.

On October 20 Malta was elected a member of the UN Security Council for the first time.

(ALBERT GANADO)

Manufacturing:
see Economy, World;
Industrial Review

Marine Biology:
see Life Sciences

Materials Sciences

Ceramics. Although in 1982 low-loss optical fibres were under study primarily for telecommunications purposes, advances in their use as sensors also made news. In pursuing advanced sonar systems the U.S. Navy and the Defense Advanced Research Projects Agency developed fibre-optic acoustic sensors that were more sensitive than the best conventional underwater microphones. Acoustic (sound) waves moving through water in which the sensor is immersed elongate the fibre and change its refractive index through pressure-induced strains. Because the change is small, often less than one wavelength of the light used, sensitive interferometers must be used to detect and measure the effect. Nearer term, less-sensitive approaches using fibre bending and vibration effects also were developed.

In addition to sound, fibre optics can be used to sense rotation. Light beams traveling in opposite directions in a rotating glass-fibre ring travel different distances to return to their starting point. This effect can be employed, for example, in small, low-cost navigation devices. Work also was progressing rapidly toward the use of fibre optics as sensors of temperature, pressure, magnetic fields, current, and voltage based on various effects of the environment on their transmission.

Ceramics were appearing in integrated optical circuits, in which the objective is not to convey large volumes of information over long distances, as in fibre optics, but to condense a large number of optical devices into a single tiny chip. Light waves in these optical, or photonic, circuits would perform important functions in the way that electrons do in electronic circuits. In current hybrid photonic devices, discrete light sources, modulators, filters, switches, detectors, and waveguides are built into or mounted on a suitable substrate such as gallium arsenide. Although hybrid devices are comparatively bulky and inefficient, their construction is fairly straightforward. For example, a small lithium niobate crystal can be used to modulate or deflect a light beam at any desired point in a circuit. Work was already under way, however, to produce monolithic integrated circuits in which very large numbers of electronic and photonic functions are performed in one device. Such military applications as radar signal processing were being pursued, and wider commercial applications were expected to follow.

Flat-panel displays have long been sought as less bulky, more efficient, distortion-free replacements for cathode ray tubes. The technology for small active flat-panel devices based on gas-plasma effects was quite mature, and Japan was already experimenting with television displays. Work also progressed on small passive devices, based on liquid-crystal, electrophoretic, and electrochromic effects, that can operate at extremely low power levels. Thin-film electroluminescent panels, however, appeared the most promising for full-colour capability and would soon appear commercially as oscilloscope and computer display screens.

Almost all of these devices are highly dependent on ceramic components and processing. Gas-plasma displays use ceramic dielectric layers to form capacitors in series with each pixel (picture element) to provide a sustaining voltage for image storage. In electrochromic displays, normally colourless tungsten oxide becomes dark blue when a voltage is applied. In thin-film electroluminescent displays, which are entirely solid-state and have no gas or liquid sealing problems, vapour-deposited zinc sulfide is normally the luminescent material itself, which emits light under an applied electric field. Almost all of these devices use tin and indium oxides deposited on glass substrates as their transparent electrodes.

Ceramics also played a major role in continuing efforts to make solar energy conversion a more cost-effective, reliable, and durable source of energy. Texas Instruments, Inc., announced development of a closed-loop system combining a novel photovoltaic solar energy converter with an attractive approach to energy storage. Unlike most photovoltaic systems that use relatively expensive silicon wafers or films, the TI system uses tiny, cheaply produced silicon spheres that are appropriately doped and embedded in a glass matrix. When placed in a hydrogen bromide electrolyte and illuminated, the spheres generate electrical potentials that separate the hydrogen bromide into gaseous hydrogen and liquid bromine. These elements are stored separately and later are recombined in a fuel cell to produce electricity on demand. The electrolyte regenerated in the fuel cell is returned to the solar collector for reuse. (NORMAN M. TALLAN)

[127.B.5.b; 724.C.5; 735.K.2.c]

Metallurgy. Advances in metallurgy during 1982 were almost entirely moderate changes in established technology. Implementation was restrained by economic conditions. The newest technology reaching practical application was that related to amorphous, or glassy, metals and very rapidly solidified crystalline metals.

In the production of metals, energy requirements continued to be a major consideration not only in terms of overall efficiency but also in the choice of energy source. In the iron blast furnace, injection of oil with the air to reduce coke consumption was almost entirely stopped due to cost.

Full realization of the energy efficiency potential of the direct reduction of iron ore to metal remained elusive. Direct reduction plants were being built in countries with abundant, cheap natural gas. The use of coal for direct reduction, which was almost the only option in the developed countries, still had problems, largely due to the ash. Modifications of the shaft furnaces were being tried, but efficiency probably would be only moderate. Coal gasification was not cost-effective. A direct smelting process that partially reduces iron-ore concentrate in a fluidized bed with coal and then finishes the reduction to iron in a melting furnace seemed promising. The molten iron could be charged directly to a steel-making converter.

Production of aluminum from fly ash, which accumulates in quantity at coal-fired power plants, was shown to be practical. The value of the metal should cover the cost of processing and waste disposal; the residue is a chemically inert solid that could be used, for example, as road fill.

Commercially available high-power lasers were finding expanding use in metallurgy in addition to their use in precision cutting and in welding, with a capability similar to electron beams but without the need to operate in a vacuum. Almost unique for metal-surface treatment, they can rapidly melt a surface layer only a few thousandths of a centimetre thick with little heating of the underlying metal. A second metal, perhaps in the form of a powder, can be fused to the surface of a part or allowed to alloy with the substrate. Insoluble particles can be incorporated in the surface for wear resistance or dispersion strengthening while the zone of heat-degraded properties near the surface is held to a minimum. Cooling of the very thin molten layer on the cold underlying metal can be as fast as a billion degrees per second, ample to produce glassy metals or rapid-solidification structures in the surface layer. These structures have exceptional properties, such as resistance to corrosion and wear, that are difficult to achieve with the thin ribbons or powders of glassy metals that were previously available.

Very efficient transformer cores were being made of glassy metal powder by dynamic compaction that welds the particles together without heating the bulk of the material enough to destroy the glassy structure.

Another high-energy-input process is induction heating with a small induction coil powered by millisecond pulses of several kilowatts. Close control of the area hardened is achieved by accurate scanning with the coil. The depth of hardening can be controlled by coil design, frequency of the heating current, and length of pulse. Very rapid quenching of the heated volume results from the adjacent mass of unheated metal.

(DONALD F. CLIFTON)

[125.F; 722.C.6.b; 724.C.3.g; 725.A.5.a.ii; 725.B]
See also Industrial Review: *Glass; Iron and Steel; Machinery and Machine Tools; Mining and Quarrying.*

Mathematics

Fields medals, the equivalent in mathematics of the Nobel prizes, are awarded every four years at the quadrennial meetings of the International Congress of Mathematicians. In 1982 three prizes were announced for research in diverse areas of geometry and analysis that all bear on fundamental issues in physics and relativity theory.

The 1982 recipients, all in their 30s, were Alain Connes of the Centre Nationale de la Recherche Scientifique in Paris, Shing Tung Yau of Princeton University's Institute of Advanced Studies, and William Thurston of Princeton. Their awards had been scheduled to be presented at the August 1982 meeting of the congress in Warsaw, but owing to the political situation in Poland both the congress and the awards ceremony were postponed.

Connes, a 35-year-old analyst, was cited for two major works. He extended a major theorem linking analysis and topology, the Atiyah-Singer theorem, to certain infinite surfaces. This result, a vast generalization of the fundamental theorem of calculus, helped move mathematics toward a grand unification of its fundamental theories. He also solved many of the major open questions in operator theory that pertain to the mathematical foundations of quantum theory. Connes's work relies heavily on the theory of C* algebras, which are abstractions from ordinary algebra that encompass the special properties of operators.

Yau, 33, became famous five years earlier when he contributed to the solution of the Calabi conjecture concerning the relation between the ways volume and distance can be measured in abstract, high-dimensional spaces. Yau proved that the natural measure of volume on certain complex manifolds—curved spaces whose coordinates are complex numbers—determines a unique metric, or measure of length, that is intrinsically related to the geometry of the manifold. Recently he applied these ideas to an important problem in relativity theory; he showed that the mass of an isolated system, like its energy, must always be positive.

Thurston, 35, was a topologist working with three-dimensional surfaces and manifolds. Surprisingly, the mathematical classification of surfaces has been carried out with greater success in higher dimensions than in low dimensions. Thurston's intensive study of three-dimensional surfaces revealed links to eight possible three-dimensional geometries, raising hopes that finally the complete classification of three-dimensional manifolds was close at hand.

The work for which Thurston was cited in his Fields medal award was closely related to work of Michael Freedman of the University of California at San Diego, who startled the mathematical community in 1982 with two major results involving four-dimensional manifolds. Freedman completed in four dimensions what Thurston was working on in three dimensions—a complete classification of all surfaces and manifolds. (The classification for higher dimensional spaces had already been done more than a decade earlier.)

As a result of his classification Freedman verified the four-dimensional case of one of mathematics' most famous unsolved problems, the Poincaré conjecture. A sphere, the most basic object of elementary geometry, has the property that any circle drawn on its surface can be shrunk continuously to a point. (A doughnut-shaped surface, in contrast, does not have this property; for example, a circle that wraps around the hole cannot be shrunk to a point.) Henri Poincaré, France's preeminent mathematician of the late 19th century, conjectured that this fundamental property must be true of spheres in any dimension. Previously Poincaré's conjecture had been proved in all dimensions except 3 and 4. Freedman's work completed the verification in dimension 4, leaving only dimension 3 unresolved.

No one was surprised that Poincaré's conjecture in dimension 4 turned out to be correct. Another consequence of Freedman's work, however, did surprise many people; together with Simon Donaldson, a graduate student at the University of Oxford, Freedman discovered that there is more

Mauritania

Mauritius

than one manifestation of the standard four-dimensional space-time geometry employed in Einstein's relativity theory. Freedman's classification of four-dimensional manifolds provided the key link in a chain of results obtained earlier by several mathematicians and theoretical physicists who were trying to understand the theory of "connections," mathematical abstractions of the forces between subatomic particles. It was still too early to tell whether the new models for space-time would yield physically significant results or whether they were just a theoretical possibility that is not implemented in nature.   (LYNN ARTHUR STEEN)

Mauritania

The Islamic Republic of Mauritania is on the Atlantic coast of West Africa, adjoining Western Sahara, Algeria, Mali, and Senegal. Area: 1,030,700 sq km (398,000 sq mi). Pop. (1982 est.): 1,731,000. Cap.: Nouakchott (pop., 1977, 135,000). (Data above refer to Mauritania as constituted prior to the purported division of Spanish Sahara between Mauritania and Morocco.) Language: Arabic, French. Religion: Muslim. President of the Military Committee for National Salvation in 1982, Lieut. Col. Mohamed Khouna Ould Haidalla; premier, Lieut. Col. Maaouya Ould Sidi Ahmed Taya.

During the night of Feb. 6–7, 1982, a new attempt to overthrow the military regime headed by Lieut. Col. Mohamed Khouna Ould Haidalla was foiled. Among those implicated were Lieut. Col. Mustafa Ould Salek, who had ousted Pres. Moktar Ould Daddah in July 1978 and headed the Military Committee for National Salvation until June 1979, and Sid Ahmed Ould Bneijara, premier from December 1980 until April 1981. They and two others were sentenced to ten years' imprisonment by a special tribunal on March 5, 1982. In an extensive reshuffle of ministerial portfolios in July, Lieut.

MAURITANIA
   Education. (1978–79) Primary, pupils 82,408, teachers 1,857; secondary, pupils 11,957, teachers 511; vocational, pupils (1974–75) 1,591, teachers (1973–74) c. 117; teacher training, students (1977) 430; higher (1977–78), pupils 477, teaching staff 110.
   Finance. Monetary unit: ouguiya, with (Sept. 20, 1982) a free rate of 51.30 ouguiya = U.S. $1 (87.95 ouguiya = £1 sterling). Gold and other reserves (June 1982) U.S. $141 million. Budget (1981 est.) balanced at 10.3 million ouguiya.
   Foreign Trade. (1981) Imports 12,793,000,000 ouguiya; exports 12,505,000,000 ouguiya. Import sources: France c. 17%; Spain c.12%; The Netherlands c. 6%; Senegal c. 5%; U.S. c. 5%. Export destinations: Spain 25%; France c. 19%; Japan c. 14%. Main exports: iron ore 65%; fish 35%.

Col. Maaouya Ould Sidi Ahmed Taya retained the post of premier.

French Minister for Cooperation Jean-Pierre Cot visited Mauritania in January, and Lieutenant Colonel Haidalla was received in Paris by Pres. François Mitterrand in March. In May President Mitterrand spent a few hours in Nouakchott at the end of his first official visit to black Africa. The sixth summit meeting of Saharan states was held in Nouakchott in March.

Faced by the threat of famine, in November Mauritania urgently appealed for relief food supplies.   (PHILIPPE DECRAENE)

Mauritius

The parliamentary state of Mauritius, a member of the Commonwealth, lies about 800 km east of Madagascar in the Indian Ocean; it includes the island dependencies of Rodrigues, Agalega, and Cargados Carajos. Area: 2,040 sq km (787.5 sq mi). Pop. (1982 est.): 963,900, including (1980 est.) Indian 69.5%; Creole (mixed French and African) 28%; Chinese 2.4%; other 0.1%. Cap. and largest city: Port Louis (pop., 1980 est., 147,400). Lan-

At the end of an eight-day state visit to African countries in May, French Pres. François Mitterrand (left) drinks camel milk at an official dinner with Mauritania's head of state, Lieut. Col. Mohamed Khouna Ould Haidalla.

WIDE WORLD

MAURITIUS

Education. (1980) Primary, pupils 123,666, teachers 6,177; secondary, pupils 80,881, teachers 3,075; vocational, pupils 295, teachers 38; teacher training, students 426, teachers 23; higher (university only), students 470, teaching staff 76.

Finance and Trade. Monetary unit: Mauritian rupee, with (Sept. 20, 1982) a free rate of MauRs 11.11 to U.S. $1 (MauRs 19.04 = £1 sterling). Gold and other reserves (June 1982) U.S. $42 million. Budget (1980–81 actual): revenue MauRs 2,070,000,000; expenditure MauRs 2,950,000,000. Foreign trade (1981): imports MauRs 4,976,700,000; exports MauRs 2,997,800,000. Import sources (1980): South Africa 13%; U.K. 12%; Bahrain 11%; France 11%; Australia 6%; Japan 5%; India 5%; U.S. 5%. Export destinations (1980): U.K. 68%; France 13%; U.S. 5%. Main exports (1980): sugar 65%; clothing 17%. Tourism (1980): visitors 115,100; gross receipts U.S. $45 million.

Agriculture. Production (in 000; metric tons; 1981): sugar, raw value 610; bananas c. 7; tea c. 5; tobacco c. 1; milk c. 25. Livestock (in 000; 1981): cattle c. 57; pigs c. 6; sheep c. 4; goats c. 70; chickens c. 1,600.

guage: English (official); French has official standing for certain legislative and judicial purposes, and Creole is the lingua franca. Religion (1980 est.): Hindu 46%; Christian 35%; Muslim 16%; Buddhist 3%. Queen, Elizabeth II; governor-general in 1982, Sir Dayendranath Burrenchobay; prime ministers, Sir Seewoosagur Ramgoolam and, from June 16, Aneerood Jugnauth.

In general elections held on June 11, 1982, the coalition government of Prime Minister Sir Seewoosagur Ramgoolam, which had governed the islands since before independence in 1968, was defeated. World recession, the effects of three cyclones, and record unemployment all contributed to his defeat. The alliance of the socialist Mauritius Militant Movement (MMM) and the smaller Mauritius Socialist Party (PSM) won all 60 elective seats on Mauritius. Two seats on Rodrigues were won by a local party that supported the alliance. Four seats went to other parties under the "best loser" system.

The new prime minister was Aneerood Jugnauth, president of the MMM. Harisun Boodhoo, leader of the PSM, became deputy prime minister and minister of information and cooperatives, while MMM Secretary-General Paul Berenger was appointed minister of finance. In October the PSM left the alliance because it disagreed with austerity measures introduced by Berenger at the behest of the International Monetary Fund.

The government began negotiations with the U.K. over the sovereignty of the Chagos Archipelago, including Diego Garcia. (*See* DEPENDENT STATES.) In August Indian Prime Minister Indira Gandhi, while visiting Mauritius, backed the country's claim to the archipelago.

(GUY ARNOLD)

Mexico

Mexico

A federal republic of Middle America, Mexico is bounded by the Pacific Ocean, the Gulf of Mexico, the U.S., Belize, and Guatemala. Area: 1,958,201 sq km (756,198 sq mi). Pop. (1981 est.) 71,193,000, including about 55% mestizo and 29% Indian. Cap. and largest city: Mexico City (pop., federal district, 1980 prelim., 9,373,400; metro. area, 1980 prelim., 15 million). Language: Spanish. Religion (1980): Roman Catholic 89.4%; Protestant (including Evangelical) 3.6%; Jewish 0.1%; others 6.9%. Presidents in 1982, José López Portillo and, from December 1, Miguel de la Madrid Hurtado.

The year 1982 in Mexico was dominated by a financial crisis engendered by the lack of early adjustments in economic policy as oil prices continued to decline. In February Minister of Finance David Ibarra Muñoz introduced a stabilization program under which the peso was devalued by 40%, but the crisis was not averted. Ibarra and Gustavo Romero Kolbeck, director of the central bank, resigned in March. They were replaced by Jesús Silva Herzog and Miguel Mancera, respectively, both close associates of the presidential candidate of the ruling Partido Revolucionario

"The peso must be down again...it's another batch of Mexican bankers."

PETERS/©1982 DAYTON DAILY NEWS

Medicine:
see Health and Disease

Mental Health:
see Health and Disease

Merchant Marine:
see Transportation

Metallurgy:
see Materials Sciences

Metals:
see Industrial Review; Materials Sciences; Mining and Quarrying

Meteorology:
see Earth Sciences

Methodist Churches:
see Religion

On July 4 Miguel de la Madrid was elected president of Mexico. The Partido Revolucionario Institucional that he represented had won every national election since 1929.

Institucional (PRI), Miguel de la Madrid Hurtado (*see* BIOGRAPHIES), and both known for their economic caution.

Miguel de la Madrid was elected president on July 4 with 74.4% of the vote. Pablo Emilio Madero of the Partido de Acción Nacional (PAN), the main opposition party, polled 16.4%, while Arnaldo Martínez Verdugo, leader of the Partido Socialista Unido de México (PSUM), obtained 3.7%. In concurrent congressional elections, the PRI won all 64 seats in the Senate and 299 in the Chamber of Deputies, with the remaining one going to the PAN. Of the 100 seats allocated by proportional representation to parties outside the PRI, 54 went to the PAN and 17 to the PSUM; three centre and left-wing parties shared the remaining 29.

The new president, who assumed office on December 1, inherited the economic problems caused by the sudden drop in international oil prices in 1981 at a time of rapid domestic expansion. Massive outflows of capital drained the country's foreign exchange reserves between January and August 1982, particularly as inflation began to gain momentum after the first devaluation. Wage increases of 10–30% were granted to compensate for the rise in prices. In spite of strong denials prior

to a further devaluation, partial exchange controls were introduced in August, and the International Monetary Fund (IMF) was called in to discuss a $4.5 billion standby credit. At the beginning of September a stringent two-tier exchange rate was finally established, involving a preferential rate of 50 pesos to the U.S. dollar for foreign-debt interest payments and essential imports and an ordinary rate of 70 pesos to the dollar for all other purposes, including conversion of dollar deposits. On December 19 the preferential rate was changed to 95 pesos to the dollar, and a free rate for other transactions was introduced.

Outgoing president José López Portillo announced that all Mexican private banks were being nationalized in order to reestablish financial stability. Following this move, Mancera resigned as head of the central bank and was replaced by Carlos Tello Macias, a former planning minister who advocated greater public-sector involvement in the economy. The government later said that compensation to shareholders in the banks of at least 144 billion pesos would be paid over ten years. At the end of September, however, bank owners and major shareholders filed a lawsuit against the government, stating that the takeover

MEXICO

Education. (1979–80) Primary, pupils 14,282,908, teachers 353,538; secondary, pupils 3,729,916, teachers 212,118; vocational, pupils 374,900, teachers 27,246; teacher training, students 180,200, teachers 11,526; higher (1978–79), students 698,139, teaching staff 57,659.

Finance. Monetary unit: peso, with (Sept. 20, 1982) an ordinary rate of 70 pesos to U.S. $1 (free rate of 120 pesos = £1 sterling) and a preferential rate of 50 pesos to U.S. $1 (86 pesos = £1 sterling). Gold and other reserves (Dec. 1981) U.S. $4,166,000,000. Budget (total; 1981 est.) balanced at 2,333,-000,000,000 pesos. Gross domestic product (1980) 4,159,300,000,000 pesos. Money supply (April 1982) 647.8 billion pesos. Cost of living (1975 = 100; May 1982) 470.9.

Foreign Trade. (1981) Imports 590,140,000,000 pesos; exports 474,340,000,000 pesos. Import sources (1980): U.S. 62%; Japan 5%; West Germany 5%. Export destinations (1980): U.S. 63%; Spain 7%.

Main exports (1980): crude oil 62%; food 11%. Tourism (1980): visitors 4,144,600; gross receipts U.S. $1,670,000,000.

Transport and Communications. Roads (1980) 213,192 km (including 978 km expressways). Motor vehicles in use (1980): passenger 4,031,970; commercial 1,534,100. Railways: (1980) 25,047 km; traffic (1981) 5,306,000,000 passenger-km, freight c. 42,800,000,000 net ton-km. Air traffic (1980): 13,870,000,000 passenger-km; freight 138.1 million net ton-km. Shipping (1981): merchant vessels 100 gross tons and over 456; gross tonnage 1,134,625. Telephones (Jan. 1980) 4,532,600. Radio receivers (Dec. 1979) 20,000,000. Television receivers (Dec. 1979) 7.5 million.

Agriculture. Production (in 000; metric tons; 1981): corn 14,766; wheat 3,189; barley 559; sorghum 6,296; rice 644; potatoes 868; sugar, raw value c. 2,518; dry beans 1,469; soybeans 712; tomatoes c. 1,370; bananas c. 1,562; oranges c. 1,600; lemons c.

530; cottonseed 530; coffee 217; tobacco 66; cotton, lint 344; beef and veal c. 634; pork c. 490; fish catch (1980) 1,240. Livestock (in 000; Dec. 1980): cattle c. 31,784; sheep c. 7,990; pigs c. 12,900; goats 7,185; horses c. 6,502; mules c. 3,260; asses c. 3,233; chickens c. 153,500.

Industry. Production (in 000; metric tons; 1981): crude oil 105,944; coal (1980) 7,010; natural gas (cu m) 30,840,000; electricity (kw-hr) 73,071,000; cement 17,842; iron ore (metal content) 5,182; pig iron 5,512; crude steel 7,449; sulfur (1980) 2,102; petroleum products (1979) c. 43,000; sulfuric acid 2,177; fertilizers (nutrient content; 1980–81) nitrogenous c. 753, phosphate c. 196; aluminum 43; copper (1980) 84; lead 138; zinc 125; manganese ore (metal content; 1980) 161; gold (troy oz) 160; silver (troy oz) 45,300; woven cotton fabrics c. 70; man-made fibres (1979) 224; radio receivers (units; 1979) 1,291; television receivers (units; 1979) 847; passenger cars (units) 357; commercial vehicles (units) 171.

was unconstitutional. In mid-November the government announced that it would close 106 of its 743 state companies and agencies to help reduce the public-sector deficit. (*See* Feature Article: *"You Can't Foreclose a Country."*)

At the end of October there were demonstrations in Mexico City calling for an emergency wage increase of at least 50%. The minimum wage was subsequently raised by 30%, and the average increase in private-sector salaries was 12%. Also in October, 17 officials of the Communications and Transport Ministry were charged with misappropriating funds to the value of some $1 million. Two senior officials of Petróleos Mexicanos (Pemex), the state oil company, were charged in November with receiving almost $12 million in bribes from a U.S. oil equipment company.

Two natural disasters affected Mexico in 1982. In March the El Chichón volcano near Pichucalco, southeastern Mexico, became active and showered ash, killing over 100 people. At least 200 people were injured and thousands made homeless in October by a hurricane that battered the coast of Baja California, northwestern Mexico.

Relations with the U.S. were mixed in 1982. The two countries failed to agree on a bilateral trade arrangement under which proof of damage to U.S. economic interests would be required before countervailing duties could be imposed on heavily subsidized Mexican exports. Following the August devaluation, Mexico banned exports of foodstuffs across the U.S. border in order to safeguard supplies to it own residents. In mid-1982 Mexican politicians were angered by a U.S. television program in which the U.S. ambassador to Mexico, John Gavin, stated that Central American turmoil could spread into Mexico. Relations worsened in August when it was alleged that two U.S. State Department documents predicted that Mexico would adopt a lower profile in international affairs and become a more willing partner of the U.S. at the economic level. In October U.S. Pres. Ronald Reagan met president-elect de la Madrid at Tijuana. Both men pledged to cooperate while respecting each other's independence.

Within Central America, relations were affected by incursions from Guatemala into Mexican territory. At the end of September Mexico publicly protested against counterinsurgency troops operating inside its borders. Guillermo Ungo, leader of the Frente Democrático Revolucionario in El Salvador, met Mexican political leaders in October in an attempt to gain support for ending the civil war in his country. (BARBARA WIJNGAARD)

Middle Eastern Affairs

The Arab-Israeli dispute entered a new dimension in 1982 when the Israeli Army invaded Lebanon on June 6. Israel had two objectives: the first was to destroy Palestine Liberation Organization (PLO) bases in Lebanon, and the second was to drive the Syrians out of the Chouf Mountains of central and southern Lebanon back toward the Bekaa Valley. While these aims could in no sense be described as a "sixth Middle East war," their consequence was

Iranian families bury those who were killed in continued fighting between Iran and Iraq in July.

to harden Arab resolve and to rally international opinion behind the anti-Zionist cause.

Elsewhere in the Middle East Iran made considerable gains in the conflict with Iraq that had erupted in September 1980. With the incursion into Arab territory represented by Iran's invasion of Iraq in July 1982, there followed a hardening of attitudes among other Arab nations, though most maintained their officially neutral stance.

Arab-Israeli Relations. Two important political initiatives toward a settlement of the Middle East's problems were launched during 1982. On September 1 U.S. Pres. Ronald Reagan revived the so-called Jordanian option for the future of the Palestinians and their occupied territories in the West Bank and Gaza Strip. Reagan recommended the establishment of an autonomous entity for the Palestinians that was to be linked with Jordan, thus reviving the 1978 proposals originally circulated at the time of the Camp David accords. Arab nations considered this the most evenhanded approach yet by a U.S. president. On September 2 the Israeli Cabinet rejected the proposals.

The Reagan declaration mentioned the PLO only in passing and gave little indication as to how the U.S. believed the question of the 2.5 million Palestinian refugees should be settled. Nor did it mention the issue of the Golan Heights, which Israel effectively annexed in December 1981 after having captured the area from Syria in 1967. It was believed that the hand of U.S. Secretary of State George Shultz (*see* BIOGRAPHIES), who replaced Alexander Haig on June 25, could be seen in the

Microbiology:
see Life Sciences

Microelectronics:
see Computers; Industrial Review

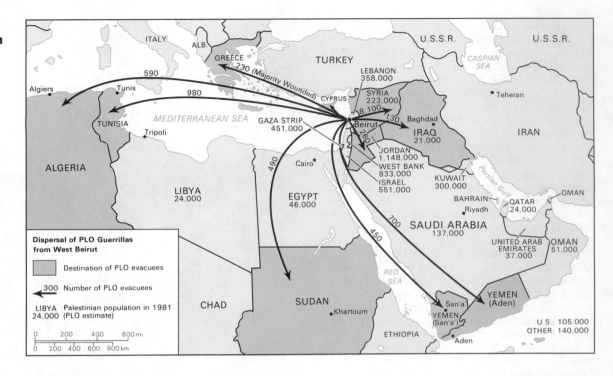

Dispersal of PLO Guerrillas from West Beirut

Destination of PLO evacuees

300 Number of PLO evacuees

LIBYA Palestinian population in 1981
24,000 (PLO estimate)

proposals; Shultz was considered to be an Arab sympathizer, close to the Saudi Arabians in particular.

The Arab League Summit. At a resumed Arab League summit in Fez, Morocco, in September, an eight-point peace plan was adopted as a response to the Reagan proposals. Under this plan: (1) Israel would withdraw from all Arab territories occupied in 1967, including Al Qods (Arab East Jerusalem); (2) Israeli settlements established in Arab land after 1967 would be dismantled; (3) all religions would be guaranteed freedom of worship in holy places; (4) the rights of the Palestinian people to self-determination, the exercise of their rights under the leadership of the PLO (their sole and legitimate representative), and the compensation of those Palestinians who did not wish to return would be reaffirmed; (5) the West Bank and the Gaza Strip would be placed under UN supervision for a transitional period not exceeding a few months; (6) an independent Palestinian state would be set up with East Jerusalem as its capital; (7) the UN Security Council would guarantee peace among all nations of the region, including the independent Palestinian state; and (8) the UN Security Council would guarantee the respect of these principles.

Thus, for the first time, the Arab nations made positive and collective proposals for peace. With the exception of Libya, all the members of the hardline Arab Steadfastness Front agreed to the plan. It had been the absence of those—Syria, Algeria, and Yemen (Aden), together with Libya and the PLO—that effectively wrecked the first meeting of the Fez summit in November 1981. It floundered over a peace plan put forward by King Fahd (*see* BIOGRAPHIES) of Saudi Arabia, at the time crown prince. In particular the radical states could not bring themselves to recognize implicitly the right of Israel to live within secure boundaries.

The new plan was virtually identical to the Fahd scheme with two important exceptions. First, it explicitly recognized the PLO as the sole legitimate representative of the Palestinian people in their progress toward achieving statehood within the Arab nation. Second, the plan specifically called upon the UN Security Council to guarantee the security of all nations in the region. This latter alteration was seen as a means of bringing the Soviet Union back into the Middle East peace process and thereby helping to quell Syrian objections. In early December a committee of seven Arab League members visited the U.S.S.R. in an attempt to rally support for the plan.

Israel reacted by rejecting the summit proposals out of hand. A Cabinet representative in Jerusalem described the plan as "a declaration of war." The U.S. welcomed the implicit recognition of Israel that was retained from the August 1981 Fahd proposals but reiterated objections to the establishment of a Palestinian state. Shultz told Congress that the U.S. opposed the dismantling of existing Israeli settlements in occupied Arab territories, a condition that formed a linchpin of the Arab plan. PLO chairman Yasir Arafat (*see* BIOGRAPHIES) accepted all eight clauses of the peace plan, although it was thought likely that Palestinian fringe groups would reject the terms because their attitude to Israel was not sufficiently hard-line.

The Fez summit was considered a triumph for King Hassan II of Morocco, although beyond the main issue of agreement on a peace plan diplomatic progress was slow. Pres. Gaafar Nimeiry of Sudan was voted down when he proposed the readmission of Egypt, expelled in 1979 for signing an agreement with Israel. Egypt seemed likely to remain out in the cold at least until the 1983 summit in Saudi Arabia. Hassan failed to bring about a reconciliation between Syria and Iraq. A clear diplomatic winner from the summit was Arafat, who was received as a head of state by the other Arab leaders. Later in September Arafat continued his diplomatic rehabilitation in Italy, where he had a 20-minute audience with Pope John Paul II, met with Italy's Pres. Alessandro Pertini, and gave a speech to the Inter-Parliamentary Union in Rome.

Following the summit, President Reagan gave Arab leaders the option of allowing King Hussein of Jordan to represent the Palestinians in new talks with Israel and the U.S. over the future of the occupied territories. He warned an Arab delegation to Washington led by King Hassan that unless talks got under way the Israeli government of Prime Minister Menachem Begin was likely to proceed with a mass escalation of its policy of settling the occupied territories. The Reagan suggestion put King Hussein in a quandary. Accepting that the king should act as a spokesman for the Palestinians would imply rejection of a principle adopted in 1974 and reaffirmed in 1982, that the PLO was the sole and legitimate representative of the Palestinian people.

The Crisis in Lebanon. The Israeli invasion of Lebanon was triggered by the shooting in London on June 3 of the Israeli ambassador to the U.K., although a full week earlier Israeli Foreign Minister Itzhak Shamir had publicly stated that Israel perceived the need to destroy the PLO as a fighting force. At first Israel stated that its aims were the same as those pursued in March 1978: to push the Palestinians back from the border with Israel in order to create a buffer zone. It became clear within 24 hours of the start of the invasion, however, that the Israelis aimed to clear the PLO from the whole of southern Lebanon, cutting off the 4,000 Syrian troops in Beirut from reinforcements in the Bekaa Valley. Later this objective led to a siege of the PLO strongholds in Beirut itself.

On June 9 Israeli jets attacked Syrian missile positions in the Bekaa. Syrian Pres. Hafez al-Assad's government was quick to agree to a cease-fire on June 12. Skirmishing continued to take place after that, but on June 22 the Israelis declared a unilateral truce with the Syrians. With Beirut under siege from mid-June onward, law and order in the city

broke down. Israeli forces kept a stranglehold on the city to starve out the PLO. On June 28 Israeli planes dropped leaflets making it clear that their bombardment of Beirut would not cease until the PLO pulled out its 6,000 fighters from the city. Following intensive negotiations by U.S. special envoy Philip Habib (*see* BIOGRAPHIES), this was accomplished with the signing of a document providing for the withdrawal of the Palestinians under French, Italian, and U.S. military supervision; the evacuation began on August 21.

On September 20 President Reagan announced that U.S. troops, which had left Lebanon, would go back as part of a peacekeeping force to supervise the withdrawal of Israeli troops from the country. The decision was prompted by the fact that the Israelis had pushed back into West Beirut in the aftermath of the assassination on September 14 of Lebanese President-elect Bashir Gemayel (*see* OBITUARIES). It was on September 18 that the world learned the first details of massacres at the Palestinian refugee camps of Sabra and Shatila. Israeli soldiers were alleged to have stood by while Lebanese right-wing militiamen killed hundreds of men, women, and children in scenes of savagery unprecedented even for Lebanon. In the aftermath of the tragedy the Israeli government set up a commission of inquiry at which Defense Minister Ariel Sharon (*see* BIOGRAPHIES) and Prime Minister Begin, among others, testified.

U.S. Marines returned to Lebanon on September 25 to join a reconstituted peacekeeping force. Disagreements arose almost immediately about how long the foreign troops should remain. Israel maintained that its conditions for withdrawal were the expulsion of the remaining PLO fighters, mainly in the north and the Bekaa plain; a simultaneous withdrawal of Syrian troops and Israeli forces; and a special status for the Israeli-backed Christian militia followers of Lebanese Army rebel Maj. Saad Haddad (*see* BIOGRAPHIES). Arafat said that the PLO would not leave before the Israelis. Syria agreed to withdraw its forces if the Lebanese government requested their departure and if Israeli troops also left. The U.S. expressed the hope that

Reminiscent of the D-Day invasion of Normandy during World War II, U.S. Marines of the international peacekeeping force unloaded matériel on the beaches of Beirut in October, in this case without opposition.

CHIP HIRES—GAMMA/LIAISON

the evacuations could be achieved by the end of 1982, but Israeli-Lebanese talks did not begin until December 28.

Gulf Cooperation Council. The GCC, which grouped Saudi Arabia, Kuwait, Qatar, Bahrain, Oman, and the United Arab Emirates (U.A.E.), held its third heads of state meeting on November 9–10 in Bahrain. The summit concentrated on the objectives of strengthening regional security and improving economic integration. The main topics for discussion were reported to be agreement on a security pact; closer military cooperation; and the establishment of a $2 billion Gulf investment fund. The latter was to include private-sector participation. In addition, the leaders of the Arab world's wealthiest nations reviewed the results of numerous ministerial and technical committees that had met earlier. The proposed abolition of customs tariffs and trade and travel restrictions among member countries—the first major implementation of the June 1981 economic agreement—was to be delayed until March 1983.

Kuwait gave notice of its reluctance to sign a mutual security pact at a meeting of interior ministers held before the summit. Kuwait was the only GCC member state to have refused to sign a bilateral security agreement with Saudi Arabia. The provisions that the agreement contained concerning the cross-border pursuit of criminals aroused fears in Kuwait that its democratic traditions were being threatened.

Shortly before the GCC summit Kuwait's foreign minister called for the GCC to work for a negotiated settlement between Iran and Iraq. This continued to be official policy. With the war costing Iraq about $1 billion a month, the GCC had already lent Baghdad some $30 billion. The GCC states apparently believed that it was in their interests to fund the Iraqi war effort rather than to meet claims for reparations from a victorious Iran.

(JOHN WHELAN)

See also Defense; Energy; articles on the various political units.
[978.B]

Migration, International

The patterns of international migration from the poor countries to the richer continued during 1982. At the same time, rising levels of unemployment in the latter—over 11 million in the European Community countries and 10 million in the U.S.—reinforced the tendencies toward greater restrictions on immigration, rising levels of racism and violence directed against migrants, and increasing pressures—both official and unofficial—to "encourage" migrants to return home.

The political controversies surrounding immigration to the U.S., particularly from Latin America and the Caribbean, continued. In mid-1981 Pres. Ronald Reagan had proposed new legislation that would create a category of "temporary residents," admitted on renewable (subject to acceptability) three-year visas, who would pay full taxes but would be ineligible for welfare, food stamps, and other benefits. This category would be subject to an initial limit of 50,000, revisable by the Department of Labor. "Permanent resident alien" status would be granted only after ten years' continuous residence, and only those with such status would be allowed to bring in families. "Amnesty" would be offered to undocumented workers who could show five years' continuous residence—a requirement that limited its applicability. Fines would be levied on firms employing four or more undocumented workers.

In March and July 1982, federal courts ruled that the 1,800 Haitians being held in camps throughout the U.S. must be released subject to later court appearances to determine their status. In 1981 only five Haitians were granted political asylum, and the administration continued its policy of restricting political refugee status to those coming from Communist countries.

The Population Reference Bureau projected immigration into the U.S. of up to one million people a year during the 1980s. The bureau estimated that half would enter illegally and would come primarily from Latin America. Changes in agriculture throughout the hemisphere and the shortage of permanent urban employment, combined with demand for migrant labour—particularly in low-paid, undesirable jobs in the U.S.—ensured that such migration would continue. (*See* RACE RELATIONS: *Special Report.*)

In 1981 Canada admitted 128,000 immigrants, down from 142,439 in 1980. The two largest sources were Asia, 48,000, and Europe, 46,000 (21,000 from Britain). The effect of rising levels of

Abel Dorvilier (foreground), a Haitian refugee held in Miami, was congratulated by Justin Manuel, a resettlement official, after Dorvilier's release from the Krome Detention Center in October.

WIDE WORLD

unemployment on immigration policy could be seen in new regulations laid down in May 1982. All future potential independent immigrants would have to have a prearranged job, cleared through a government employment centre on the basis that there were no qualified Canadian residents available to fill it. In September Australia introduced measures to reduce the number of illegal immigrants, which was estimated at 50,000. Responding to trade union demands, the federal government also agreed to restrict legal immigration in 1983.

Immigration into Britain in 1981 (58,000 accepted for settlement) was at its lowest level since 1973, and people accepted for settlement on arrival were the fewest since records began in 1962. Deportations, at 2,195, were only slightly below the 1980 figure of 2,472. The British Nationality Act 1981, which would come into force on Jan. 1, 1983, replaced almost all previous nationality laws. It created three categories of citizenship with varying levels of rights: (1) British citizenship; (2) British dependent territories citizenship; and (3) British overseas citizenship. One consequence of the new law was that birth in the U.K. in itself would no longer be enough to confer citizenship

The argument continued over the British government's refusal, in the face of condemnation by the European Court and Commission on Human Rights, to allow women settled and living in Britain the right to bring in husbands and fiancés. In a White Paper issued on Oct. 25, 1982, the government proposed giving the right to bring in husbands to women with British citizenship but not to those settled in Britain. This was unlikely to satisfy either the European Commission and Court or Britain's black and Asian communities.

In West Germany, with a foreign population of 4.6 million (including one million under 16 who were born there), the state premiers called on Chancellor Helmut Schmidt to provide financial incentives for people to return to their home countries. This was on top of federal restrictions, announced in December 1981, that banned children over 16 from joining their parents.

The application of current French immigration controls to Algerian visitors strained relations between the two countries at the time of Algerian Pres. Chadli Bendjedid's visit to France in December 1982. In Switzerland new legislation allowed the government to stabilize the proportion of seasonal workers in accordance with the state of the economy. (LOUIS KUSHNICK)

See also Refugees.
[525.A.1.c]

Mining and Quarrying

Production cutbacks and mine closings dominated the news about mining in 1982. Adversely affected by a recession in heavy industry among the industrialized nations, demand for most metals and minerals declined and prices fell. Mining companies reported financial losses and furloughed thousands of employees. For example, in the iron mines of Minnesota and Michigan 70% of the workers

Immigration and Naturalization in the United States
Year ended Sept. 30, 1979

Country or region	Total immigrants admitted	Quota immigrants	Nonquota immigrants Total	Nonquota immigrants Family— U.S. citizens	Aliens naturalized
Africa	12,838	8,553	4,285	4,013	2,667
Asia	189,293	110,544	78,749	54,088	63,650
China[1]	24,264	17,344	6,920	6,589	11,446
Hong Kong	4,119	3,056	1,063	904	...
India	19,708	17,264	2,444	2,130	6,001
Iran	8,476	4,379	4,097	3,774	1,217
Iraq	2,871	2,464	407	382	754
Israel	3,093	1,923	1,170	1,071	1,280
Japan	4,048	2,032	2,016	1,781	1,298
Jordan	3,360	2,493	867	836	1,383
Korea, South	29,248	13,169	11,079	10,024	13,406
Lebanon	4,634	3,719	915	872	1,223
Philippines	41,300	19,069	22,231	21,057	17,749
Thailand	3,194	1,602	1,592	1,363	1,284
Vietnam	22,546	6,436	16,110	359	720
Europe	60,845	37,285	23,560	21,757	41,760
Germany, West	6,314	1,498	4,816	4,480	3,437
Greece	5,090	3,223	1,867	1,782	4,866
Italy	6,174	4,091	2,083	1,930	7,296
Poland	4,413	3,270	1,143	1,106	2,385
Portugal	7,085	5,877	1,208	1,113	4,073
Spain	1,933	801	1,132	971	911
U.S.S.R.	2,543	2,249	294	268	762
United Kingdom	13,907	8,254	5,653	5,157	8,065
Yugoslavia	2,171	1,516	655	627	2,438
North America	157,579	95,013	62,566	47,291	44,161
Canada	13,772	8,076	5,696	5,038	3,085
Cuba	15,585	3,320	12,265	1,048	13,317
Dominican Republic	17,519	14,835	2,684	2,450	3,350
El Salvador	4,479	3,154	1,325	1,293	770
Haiti	6,433	5,213	1,220	1,185	2,567
Jamaica	19,714	16,673	3,041	2,874	7,632
Mexico	52,096	24,207	27,889	25,249	8,046
Trinidad and Tobago	5,255	4,350	875	831	1,351
Oceania	4,449	2,797	1,652	1,512	668
South America	35,344	25,286	10,058	9,517	10,825
Argentina	2,856	2,004	852	784	1,350
Colombia	10,637	7,435	3,202	3,035	2,923
Ecuador	4,383	3,169	1,214	1,170	1,187
Guyana	7,001	6,262	739	691	1,779
Peru	4,135	2,567	1,568	1,517	1,533
Total[2]	460,348	279,478	180,870	138,178	164,150

Note: Immigrants listed by country of birth; aliens naturalized by country of former allegiance.
[1]Taiwan and People's Republic. [2]Includes other countries not listed separately.
Source: U.S. Department of Justice, Immigration and Naturalization Service, *1979 Annual Report*.

were idle during the summer of 1982, and in the fall in Arizona, after some call-backs, over 40% of the copper workers employed a year earlier were still idle. In the less developed countries the mines continued producing, but those nations' foreign exchange earnings suffered because the mine products brought low prices.

Industry Developments. In 1981 there were six oil shale projects in the U.S., but by mid-1982 that number had dwindled. The shutdown by Exxon Corp. of the Colony oil shale project in Colorado came as a surprise because in the spring Exxon and its partner Tosco had reaffirmed that they were proceeding with the 50,000-bbl-per-day facility. Exxon cited escalated costs as the reason for the closing. In the aftermath Exxon purchased Tosco's 40% interest, which was in accord with their agreement. Surviving the debacle was Union Oil Co. of California, moving ahead at Parachute, Colo., with its 10,000-bbl-per-day facility. When the plant became operational in 1983, it would be the first commercial shale oil producer; the cost was estimated at $600 million.

Existing overcapacity in minerals was discouraging new developments. The oil companies that had diversified into minerals were taking a second look. Phillips Petroleum Co. and Conoco Inc. wiped out their minerals departments. Occidental Petroleum Corp. and Cities Service Co. were attempting to sell their mineral units.

Whereas minerals acquisitions had been fre-

Mining and Quarrying

The most northerly metal mine in the world was put into operation on Little Cornwallis Island at 77° north latitude in Canada in March by Cominco Ltd. of Canada. The facility produced lead and zinc concentrates and employed about 240 persons.

quent in 1981, that scene was comparatively quiet in 1982. Even so, mining men noted actions by big corporations in which Occidental acquired Cities Service and U.S. Steel Corp. took over Marathon Oil Co. Molybdenum miners watched with interest as U.S. Borax, a division of Rio Tinto Zinc of the U.K., continued to press ahead with the large Quartz Hill molybdenum project in Alaska. This development continued in the face of a depressed molybdenum market, existing mines operating at reduced capacity, and rich undeveloped deposits in Colorado and Nevada.

Quartz Hill was typical of the mining conundrum: whether to build during the market troughs and hope to come into production during the market highs, or build when cash flow and courage are better. Anaconda Minerals Co. did the latter when it announced its Nevada molybdenum project in December 1979 and reached design capacity of 12 million to 15 million lb of molybdenum annually early in 1982.

Indexes of Production, Mining, and Mineral Commodities

(1975=100)

	1977	1978	1979	1980	1981	1982 I	1982 II
Mining (total)							
World[1]	112.4	112.7	118.3	115.4	114.0	113.3	...
Centrally planned economies[2]	108.4	112.0	115.1	116.3	115.5	120.3	119.3
Developed market economies[3]	108.3	112.4	119.5	124.2	127.7	130.2	124.0
Less developed market economies[4]	116.1	113.1	118.8	110.2	106.0	101.5	...
Coal							
World[1]	101.7	101.1	106.2	109.4	108.5	112.8	...
Centrally planned economies[2]	104.2	105.8	107.6	106.9	102.0	103.9	104.6
Developed market economies[3]	99.6	97.4	105.0	110.5	111.2	117.1	115.8
Less developed market economies[4]	106.4	107.3	109.8	119.9	138.7	145.7	...
Petroleum							
World[1]	115.5	116.3	122.0	117.2	115.6	113.9	...
Centrally planned economies[2]	112.2	118.2	122.3	125.4	128.1	135.1	131.3
Developed market economies[3]	115.5	126.4	134.8	142.6	151.8	157.5	142.6
Less developed market economies[4]	116.1	113.4	118.7	109.1	104.1	99.0	...
Metals							
World[1]	103.8	101.4	103.8	105.6	103.7	103.7	...
Centrally planned economies[2]	102.9	103.6	104.9	111.0	98.3	99.7	100.8
Developed market economies[3]	102.1	97.2	100.5	99.1	99.9	99.6	96.9
Less developed market economies[4]	107.4	106.9	108.7	112.6	114.1	113.5	...
Manufacturing (total)	113.4	118.9	124.5	125.9	126.7	125.0	...

[1] Excluding Albania, China, North Korea, Vietnam.
[2] Bulgaria, Czechoslovakia, East Germany, Hungary, Poland, Romania, U.S.S.R.
[3] North America, Europe (except centrally planned), Australia, Israel, Japan, New Zealand, South Africa.
[4] Caribbean, Central and South America, Africa (except South Africa), Asian Middle East, East and Southeast Asia (except Israel and Japan).
Source: UN, Monthly Bulletin of Statistics (November 1982).

Kennecott Minerals Co., a subsidiary of Sohio, announced plans with Mitsubishi Corp. to modernize the Hurley, N.M., smelter. When completed in 1985, the facility would comply with environmental regulations and have 66% greater capacity, at 450,000 tons per year of copper metal. In December 1981, Asarco Inc. started up a new mine and concentrator at Troy, Mont. The facility was designed to produce 130 tons of silver and 18,000 tons of copper annually and would employ 300 people. A one million-ton-per-year soda ash mining and milling facility was started up by Tenneco Minerals Co. near Green River, Wyo. The plant began operating at a time when the market was depressed and plans for the expansion of other soda ash mines had been set back.

The most northerly metal mine in the world, on Little Cornwallis Island at latitude 77° N in Canada, was put into operation by Cominco Ltd. of Canada. The facility produced lead and zinc concentrates and employed about 240 persons. Construction methods were noteworthy because of the high degree of prefabrication, the centrepiece being a barge-mounted concentrator that was towed to the site where the barge was settled on a pad as the foundation for the mill.

In New Brunswick, Canada, the Mt. Pleasant tungsten mine was scheduled to come into production at a cost of Can$120 million. In June the Real de Angeles silver mine in the state of Zacatecas, Mexico, started production. When it reached full capacity, producing 220 tons of silver annually, it would be the world's largest silver mine.

The first production of aluminum was achieved by Valesul Aluminio early in 1982 at its new smelter southwest of Rio de Janeiro, Brazil. For the state-owned company Cia Vale do Rio Doce, Valesul was one unit of a much larger enterprise, including the Alunorte 800,000-ton-per-year alumina refinery and the Albras 320,000-ton-per-year aluminum smelter at Bacarena southwest of Belem. The last two projects, costing an estimated $2.5 billion, were to be commissioned in 1985.

Brazil set its sights on even higher goals in its projected development of the Carajás mineral province in the Amazon River area. Since the discovery of iron ore in 1967, a remarkable assemblage of mineral deposits containing 18,000,-000,000 tons of iron ore, 60 million tons of manganese ore, 1,200,000,000 tons of copper ore, 50 million tons of nickel ore, 4,600,000,000 tons of bauxite, 37 million tons of cassiterite, and significant deposits of gold had all been located in a 58-km (36-mi) radius centred in the Carajás Range. Development of iron ore for export was launched by 1982 with construction of a mine, railroad, and port well advanced. These plans would change a sparsely inhabited area into a network of communities and industrial establishments.

Twenty-six years after its discovery, the Cerro Matoso lateritic nickel mine and smelter in Colombia came into production. Although starting up during a period when the nickel market was depressed, it had the advantages of high-grade ore and low energy costs.

Morocco restored production at the huge Bou Craa phosphate mine in the Western Sahara; it had been stopped because of military action in the area. From Iran it was learned that the Sar Chesmeh copper complex in Kerman Province had been brought back into production. It had been delayed for several years because of the revolution in Iran and its aftermath.

A new diamond mine, owned jointly by the Botswana government and De Beers Consolidated Mines, Ltd., was inaugurated in August. With an anticipated capacity of 4.5 million carats per year, it would eventually be one of the largest mines in the world.

The Olympic Dam project, near Roxby Downs, South Australia, with a metal content worth $140 billion, held the potential of being one of the largest mining operations in Australia. Owned 51% by Western Mining Corp. and 49% by BP Australia, the deposit was expected to yield an annual 150,000 tons of copper, 3,000 tons of uranium, and 120,000 oz of gold. Another new diamond project was the Ashton Joint Venture in Western Australia; the partners, the CRA, Ashton Mining Group, and Northern Mining, signed a development agreement.

Technological Developments. The world's first frequency-controlled, three-phase mine-hoisting motors were introduced at the Neu Monopul coal mine in West Germany. The motors, each 4,220 kw, were designed to hoist 9,000 tons per day from a depth of 1,350 m (4,455 ft). Operating experience verified the performance prediction of low maintenance and energy conservation.

A complete mining system for the new phosphate mine of the Agrico/Williams group in North Carolina was purchased from PHB Weserhutte AG of West Germany. The system utilized four bucket-wheel excavators and materials-handling equipment to remove overburden and phosphate from the pit area in a continuous mining system. The first packaged mining system operated in a mine of this type in the U.S., it marked a transition from the conventional dragline and slurry pumping common in the Florida phosphate fields.

Continuous mining, first introduced for coal in the early 1950s and later spreading to such bedded minerals as potash and trona, continued to grow. The *Mining Journal* in 1982 estimated that more than 2,000 fixed-head continuous miners were in operation throughout the world. The machines cut the coal away from the face, load it, and deliver it to a transportation system in a virtually continuous system. In June and July the world record was broken three times by a 120-H2 Heliminer manufactured by Jeffrey Mining Machinery Division of Dresser Industries. The records were for eight-hour shifts producing 3,148 tons, 3,513 tons, and 3,668 tons. The records were set at the Sigma coal mine in South Africa.

The heaviest steel ropes ever constructed, weighing 130 tons each, were fabricated in South Africa by Haggie Rand, Ltd., for use at Western Deep Levels, a South African gold mine. Each of the four ropes had 5,300 km (3,300 mi) of wire and was 14.7 km (9.1 mi) long. The longest wire rope was 15 km (9.3 mi) long, also fabricated by Haggie. The ropes were used for hoisting ore and men from the deep mines.　　　　　　　(JOHN V. BEALL)

Production. The United Nations overall indexes of mining production for 1981 and the first two quarters of 1982 (*see* TABLE) indicated stagnation or decline in most sectors of the industry. Results at the end of 1981 were narrowly mixed, and the only segment showing strong growth was the coal sector of the less developed countries, those generally least able to afford the excess costs of imported petroleum. Metals were not strong, but their broad base of intermediate and end-use consumers insulated them from the sharp drop-offs in consumption visible in the energy-related commodities outside the centrally planned economies.

According to data compiled by the U.S. Bureau of Mines, of a group of 85 mineral commodities for which reasonably complete international data were available output in 1981 rose for 42, declined for 31, and remained about the same (or had to be withheld for proprietary or other reasons) for 12. Among metals the losers outnumbered the gainers 18 to 16; most of the gainers were minor metals, with only copper, zinc, tin, and the precious metals showing increases among those considered major. Among the nonmetals gainers outnumbered losers almost two to one (25 and 13, respectively).

The United States mining sector, with an aggregate value of some $25,451,000.000 in 1981, gained about 1.3% in absolute terms but declined substantially when inflation was taken into account. The raw mineral commodities aggregating this total were estimated to have increased in value to about $246 billion when processed for end use by other industries. The value of metals alone in 1981 was about $8,763,000,000; this represented a decline of 1.5% from $8,897,000,000 in 1980, although in quantitative terms 13 of 22 metals increased their absolute output during the year. The value of nonmetals rose by some 2.8% in 1981 to a total of $16,688,000,000.

Among metals in the U.S. the strongest growth was shown by the platinum-group metals (up 83%), gold (up 42%), and copper (refined and recovered; up 29%); almost all of their growth, however, was attributable to recovery of those industries from 1980 lows rather than to any expansion of the user base in 1981. Losses were mostly of small magnitude, although lead and mercury (−19% and −9%, respectively) suffered much reduction in demand because of environmental considerations and also, in the case of lead, because of reduced consumption by the battery industry, both as a consequence of the poor state of the automobile industry and as a consequence of the introduction of new technologies in battery manufacture.

Among nonmetals the gainers included fluorspar (up 24%) and bromine (up 2%). Although short-term growth in steel production raised fluorspar output, fluorspar and bromine faced longer-term difficulties because of the substitution of alternative materials in their principal applications and, in the case of bromine, because of environmental concerns about some bromine compounds. The losers included perlite, used in applications such as aggregate in concrete (−13%), down because of the weakness of the U.S. construction industry.

Aluminum. World production of bauxite, the primary ore of aluminum, was estimated to have fallen by about 4% during 1981, totaling about 86,360,000 metric tons. The major producer continued to be Australia, at 25,541,000 tons, off about 6% from 1980. Other major producers included Jamaica, with about 11.6 million tons, followed by Guinea with an estimated 12.1 million tons (although other estimates ranged as high as 14 million). Output of alumina (aluminum oxide, the concentrated intermediate stage in the production of aluminum metal) was estimated to have fallen by about 2%, to approximately 32,640,000 tons, about 22% of which was produced by Australia, followed closely by the U.S. with 18.4%. Production of aluminum metal was estimated to be nearly identical in 1981 to that of the preceding year, at about 17 million tons. The United States continued as the leading producer, at about 4,490,000 tons, representing a decline of about 3.5% from 1980. The U.S.S.R. ranked second with an estimated 1.9 million tons, followed by Canada at 1,115,000 tons, Japan 900,000 (a decline of about 25%), and West Germany 728,900 tons. Demand worldwide continued weak in 1981 and 1982, leading to delays in completion and start-up of mine operations, financial problems for governments and power authorities, and both shutdowns and underutilization of refining capacity (at least 15% worldwide).

Antimony. Mine output of antimony was estimated to have declined by about 10% during 1981, falling from 65,056 metric tons in 1980 to about 59,178 tons. The major producer continued to be Bolivia, at 15,292 tons rebounding 17% from its 1979 low. South Africa was second, at 9,810 tons, followed by China and the U.S.S.R. (figures for both were unavailable). In October 1981 the first meeting of the Organización Internacional del Antimonio (OIA) was held at La Paz, Bolivia; it was attended by representatives from Bolivia, Peru, Thailand, and Turkey. The second OIA meeting, in October 1982, included consumers and end-users as well.

Cement. World production of cement was estimated to have risen slightly during 1981, reflecting cutbacks in construction work in the developed countries and expansion in less developed countries. The total was some 888 million metric tons, of which the leading producers were the U.S.S.R. with approximately 127 million tons, about 14% of the world total; Japan and China virtually tied for second at approximately 85 million tons; and the United States, slumping to its lowest levels since 1975, with about 65,050,000 tons.

Chromium. World mine production of chromite, the principal ore of chromium, was estimated by the U.S. Bureau of Mines to have fallen by almost 14% during 1981 to a total of about 8,412,000 metric tons. Most of the decline originated in the two leading producing countries: South Africa, where output fell almost 16% to some 2,869,000 tons, and the U.S.S.R., with about 2,403,000 tons in 1981. Recent estimates reconfirmed Albania's probable third place at about 1.1 million tons. Reflecting generally high stocks in South Africa, the Winterveld mine, the world's largest, was operating at only half capacity by the end of 1982.

Copper. According to figures of the Intergovernmental Council of Copper Exporting Countries, worldwide output of copper rose to an estimated 8,278,000 metric tons in 1981, an increase of about 5.8% over the preceding year. The United States was the leading producer with some 1,529,000 tons, registering a strong 29% gain over a strike-reduced 1980 production level and rising above 1.5 million tons for the first time in eight years. Changes were more modest among other leading countries, chief among which were: Chile 1,080,000 tons, the U.S.S.R. an estimated 1,173,000 tons, Canada 718,000 tons, Zambia 587,000 tons, and Zaire 505,000 tons. Production of blister (unrefined) copper metal was thought to have risen equally strongly, by about 5.7% to a total of about 8,360,000 tons; the major producer was the U.S. with 1,378,000 tons, a strong 30% gain on 1980. Output in the U.S.S.R. was estimated to have risen slightly to about 1,194,000 tons, although the actual figure was unknown. Japan's third-place smelter production rose to some 980,000 tons, nearly regaining the 1,000,000-ton record set in 1973 and not approached since; Chile produced about 954,000 tons, registering no change. World production of refined metal showed smaller increases, output rising by only about 2.1%, to a total of 9,184,000 tons. The principal producing country continued to be the U.S., with 2,037,600 tons, recovering pre-1980 production levels and showing an 18% annual gain. Second and third were the U.S.S.R. with about 1,060,000 tons and Japan with 1,050,000 tons. The next three main producers were unchanged, although each showed slight declines from the previous year: Chile 774,000 tons, Zambia 573,000 tons, and Canada 477,000 tons. The most visible trend in the U.S. industry was the acquisition of five major copper-mining companies by oil interests, the largest domestic producer, Kennecott Corp., being acquired by Standard Oil Co. of Ohio.

Gold. Mine production of gold rose slightly in 1981, gaining about 4.2% and reaching an estimated total of about 1,268 metric tons. This increase occurred despite a 2.5% decline in South Africa's output—representing a 51.8% share of world production—amounting to 657 tons in 1981. Though official figures were unavailable, the U.S.S.R. was probably second at 262 tons, and China third at 52.8 tons, according to the U.S. Bureau of Mines. Canadian production, at 47 tons, was in fourth place but lost ground to a strong 42.7% gain by the U.S., in fifth place with about 42.8 tons and exceeding 40 tons for the first time since 1972. It appeared, however, that a significant portion of the U.S. gain was attributable to figures being supplied for the first time by a number of mines not previously reporting (as well as to the recovery of the copper industry, since 40% of U.S. gold production originates in recovery from base-metal refining). South African companies and governmental planners, probably most sensitive to world market conditions, anticipated further production declines throughout the 1980s and curtailed expansion plans accordingly.

Iron. Production of iron ore worldwide was estimated to have fallen by about 3.6% in 1981, with total output amounting to about 860 million metric tons. The U.S.S.R. was the world leader, with production of 242 million tons, a slight decline from 1980 and amounting to more than 28% of the world total. Brazil was the second leading producer with 100 million tons, despite a 12.8% decline. Australia fell slightly to about 86 million tons. The U.S. remained in fourth place with about 75 million tons of production, followed by China at about 70 million tons. The continued weakness of industrial users of iron and steel in the U.S. led to mine closings, layoffs, and the suspension of operations throughout 1981 and 1982. World production of pig iron fell slightly to an estimated 501.5 million metric tons. The leading producers were the U.S.S.R. at 98 million tons, followed by Japan with 80,048,000 tons, an 8% drop from the preceding year that reflected the export problems of Japan's automobile industry.

Lead. World mine output of lead totaled about 3.4 million metric tons in 1981, down about 0.8% from 1980. The U.S. continued as the main producer at 445,535 metric tons, off about 19% from 1980 principally as a result of strikes at seven of the major Missouri mines (settled in July). Other major producers included Australia with 393,000 tons, Canada 332,000 tons, Peru 187,000 tons, and Mexico 157,000 tons. Output of refined metal totaled some 5,308,000 tons, of which the main producer was the U.S. with 495,000 tons, down almost 10% from 1980. Including 641,000 tons of production from secondary recovery, U.S. output amounted to about 1,136,000 tons.

Magnesium. Production of magnesium in 1981 was estimated to have declined slightly worldwide (about 2.6%), reaching approximately 310,000 metric tons. About half of this, 150,000 tons, was produced (mostly from brines) in the U.S., although no official figures were available. The U.S.S.R. was thought to be the second leading producer at about 75,000 tons (principally from magnesite ore); it was followed by Norway with approximately 40,000 tons.

Manganese. World mine production of manganese ore, at about 23,568,600 metric tons, was down 10.6% from 1980. About two-fifths of the output originated in the U.S.S.R., the leading producer with an estimated 9.4 million tons. Following the Soviet Union were South Africa (5,040,000 tons) and Brazil (about 1.9 million tons). In September 1982 the Brazilian government decided to expand manganese mining at its Carajás site, principally at the Igarapé Azul deposit, although expansion was in part dependent upon the success of the much larger iron development at Carajás.

Mercury. Estimated world mine production of mercury in 1981 was 206,600 34.5-kg (76-lb) flasks, virtually the same as in 1980. The leading producer was the U.S.S.R. at about 62,000 flasks, although authoritative figures were not available. It was followed by Spain at about 50,000 flasks, the U.S. with 27,904 flasks, and Algeria with about 25,000 flasks. The U.S. production represented a 9% decline from 1980, primarily from closings of small mines; by the end of 1981 almost all U.S. production originated at only one facility in Nevada.

Molybdenum. Late estimates of world output by the U.S. Bureau of Mines indicated a 0.56% decline during 1981 because of a 7.2% fall in U.S. production, which accounted for about 63% of the world total in most years. The final U.S. production figure, 63,458 metric tons, was higher than originally expected (though still down 7.2%), and most other major producers showed increases. Thus the revised world production estimate of 240,385 tons was only about 0.5% down from the previous year. The other main producers included Chile with 15,102 tons, Canada 14,134, and the U.S.S.R. with about 10,900 tons. Mine closings and production cutbacks characterized North American operations in 1981 and continued into 1982, although even there new production facilities were being opened; development continued on new operations planned to come on line in Peru, Mexico, and elsewhere during 1981–85.

Nickel. World production of nickel was estimated to have fallen by some 5.9% during 1981, reaching a level of about 700,300 metric tons. Several factors were responsible for the decline, ranging from a strike at Inco, Ltd.'s Thompson, Man., facility in Canada (settled Dec. 1981) to the worldwide decline in the steel industry, reducing demand for a principal alloying metal. The Canadian strike reduced production (155,175 tons, off more than 13% from 1980) to the extent that Canada probably yielded its status as the main producing country to the U.S.S.R., where output was estimated at about 157,850 tons. The next most important producers were New Caledonia with 74,500 tons and Australia with 74,000; among lesser producers only Norway exceeded 40,000 tons. Output of refined metal fell by a somewhat smaller 4.3% to 698,450 tons in 1981. The major producer continued to be the U.S.S.R. with an estimated 178,000 tons; Canada was second with 115,200 tons, and Japan was third with 93,600 tons, based almost entirely on imported stocks. The Canadian output represented a 24% decline, but no other significant changes occurred among major producers.

Phosphate Rock. World production of phosphate rock and guano grew slightly during 1981, with most of the major producers showing some growth. The U.S., the leader with about 53.6 million metric tons, showed about a 1% decline; other top producers included the U.S.S.R. at about 30.9 million tons and Morocco at 19.6 million. A paper prepared by the U.S. Bureau of Mines for the International Fertilizer Industry Association released in mid-1982 painted a gloomy picture of both short- and long-term prospects for the industry, a result of such factors as the shortage of cash in potential consuming countries as a result of energy costs, political conflicts among both producing and consuming countries, and the recent strength of the dollar against other currencies.

Platinum-Group Metals. World production of the platinum-group metals (platinum, iridium, palladium, osmium, rhodium, and ruthenium) was estimated to have fallen by less than 0.2% during 1981. Virtually all of the production was divided between the U.S.S.R., thought to be the leader at about 3,350,000 troy ounces, and South Africa with about 3 million troy ounces. Since those two accounted for about 94% of a world total of about 6.8 million troy ounces and since neither published any detailed figures, estimates of output and change rested largely upon the Canadian output figure of 400,000 troy ounces, which was an increase of nearly 50% from 1979.

Silver. Silver production was estimated to have risen by about 7.3% during 1981 with the world total amounting to about 364.9 million troy ounces. The chief producers were Mexico with 53,204,000 troy ounces, up about 12% from 1980, and Peru, estimated at about 46.9 million troy ounces. They were followed by the U.S.S.R. with 46.5 million troy ounces, up about 9%; the U.S. 40,685,000, almost a 30% gain; and Canada 37,418,000, a 12.2% gain.

Tin. World mine production of tin in 1981 was about 252,509 metric tons, a gain of about 2.4%. The major producing countries included Malaysia with some 59,900 tons, down a little from the previous year, the U.S.S.R. with approximately 36,000 tons, Indonesia 34,870, Thailand 32,000, and Bolivia 29,800. Smelter production of tin metal fell slightly in 1981, about 3.2% to about 242,097 tons. The leading producer was Malaysia with 70,320 tons, about one-third of the world total; it was followed by Indonesia and Thailand, each at about 32,500 tons. During most of 1981 negotiations leading to the sixth International Tin Agreement (ITA) were conducted by the chief producing and consuming countries; the principal issues were the size of ITA buffer stocks and the nature of export controls among producing countries. The new five-year ITA entered into force on July 1, 1982, but it was less successful than the fifth ITA in that fewer consuming and producing countries (16 and 4, respectively) participated.

Titanium. World production of titanium sponge metal grew strongly during 1981, reaching approximately 70,400 metric tons. This was about 13% above 1980, itself a year of strong growth. Most of this increase was in Japanese output, which rose from 19,284 tons to about 25,400 tons. Production of ilmenite concentrates was estimated to have declined slightly to 3,608,600 tons, mostly on the basis of a 0.08% decline in the output of Australia, which accounted for about a quarter of the world total. Rutile was estimated to have behaved more drastically, falling about 13% to approximately 361,000 tons. This was mainly accounted for by a 13% fall in Australian production, about 64% of the world total.

Tungsten. World mine production of tungsten (wolfram) declined by about 5% during 1981 to a total of 49,138 metric tons; China was probably the chief producer at about 13,600 tons, followed by the U.S.S.R. at 8,850 tons. Nonsocialist producing countries included a half-dozen between 3,600 and 1,400 tons (by rank: U.S., Australia, Bolivia, South Korea, Canada, and Portugal).

Zinc. According to data from the U.S. Bureau of Mines, mine output of zinc grew by about 1.13% during 1981, reaching a total of about 5,844,200 metric tons. Canadian output of 1,097,200 tons showed a strong gain of more than 22% in 1981, regaining some of the ground lost in 1980 and approaching the production levels of the late 1970s. Another chief producer was the U.S.S.R.; estimates of its level of output were raised to about 1,030,000 tons. Other important producers included Australia, at 508,400 tons showing a small gain; Peru 496,700 tons, up 1.8%; U.S. 312,400 tons, off about 1.5%; Japan 242,000 tons with little change; and Mexico 211,600 tons, down 11%. Despite the catastrophic year in the U.S. domestic market for zinc's two chief consumers, automobiles and housing, consumption rose about 3% during 1981.

(WILLIAM A. CLEVELAND)

See also Earth Sciences; Energy; Industrial Review: *Iron and Steel;* Materials Sciences.
[724.B.1; 724.C.3]

UPI

Prince Rainier (centre) and two of his three children, Prince Albert and Princess Caroline, leave the cathedral after a funeral mass for Princess Grace, who died on September 14.

Monaco

Monaco

A sovereign principality on the northern Mediterranean coast, Monaco is bounded on land by the French département of Alpes-Maritimes. Area: 1.90 sq km (0.73 sq mi). Pop. (1982 est.): 26,000. Language: French. Religion: predominantly Roman Catholic. Chief of state, Prince Rainier III; minister of state in 1982, Jean Herly.

The sudden and tragic death of Princess Grace (*see* OBITUARIES), announced on the evening of Sept. 14, 1982, plunged into profound grief not only her family but also the whole Monegasque population. According to Jean Duplay, chief neurological surgeon of Nice, Princess Grace suffered a cerebral stroke while driving with her younger daughter, Stephanie, from a holiday villa at La Turbie, France, to Monaco on September 13. The car ran off the narrow road, plunging 36.5 m (120 ft) and overturning several times. Princess Stephanie was seriously injured.

The death of Princess Grace was a shattering blow for Prince Rainier III. By his marriage 25 years earlier to Grace Kelly, he had gained not only her cool and restraining influence but also the business acumen of her American connections. That had helped him to win his struggle with Greek shipping magnate Aristotle Onassis and aided his effort to prevent Saudi Arabian arms dealer Adnan Khashoggi from establishing his European headquarters at Monte Carlo.

The funeral service on September 18 in the cathedral of Monaco was attended by royalty, film stars, and representatives of heads of state from around the world. (K. M. SMOGORZEWSKI)

MONACO

Education. (1979–80) Primary, pupils 1,033; secondary, pupils 1,312; vocational, pupils 719; primary, secondary, and vocational, teachers c 400.

Finance and Trade. Monetary unit: French franc, with (Sept. 20, 1982) a free rate of Fr 7.05 to U.S. $1 (Fr 12.09 = £1 sterling). Budget (1980 est.): revenue Fr 987 million; expenditure Fr 629 million. Foreign trade included with France. Tourism (1980) 220,700 visitors.

Missiles:
see Defense

Molecular Biology:
see Life Sciences

Mongolia

Morocco

Mongolia

A people's republic of Asia lying between the U.S.S.R. and China, Mongolia occupies the geographic area known as Outer Mongolia. Area: 1,566,500 sq km (604,800 sq mi). Pop. (1982 est.): 1,732,400. Cap. and largest city: Ulan Bator (pop., 1981 est., 435,400). Language: Khalkha Mongolian. Religion: Lamaistic Buddhism. First secretary of the Mongolian People's Revolutionary (Communist) Party in 1982 and chairman of the Presidium of the Great People's Hural, Yumzhagiyen Tsedenbal; chairman of the Council of Ministers (premier), Zhambyn Batmunkh.

On the occasion of the Mongolian People's Republic's national day, July 11, 1982, commemorative articles appeared in the press of the Soviet Union and other countries within the Council for Mutual Economic Assistance (Comecon) emphasizing the material and cultural progress of this vast but sparsely populated country. In six decades its population had more than doubled.

Novosti Mongolii, an Ulan Bator daily newspaper published in Russian, reported that the Mongolian Academy of Sciences was wasting state money by sponsoring insignificant and valueless research. Pazarin Sherindib, president of the Academy, was dismissed because he was interested in the study of archaeological and historical connections between Mongolia and China.

In April Chinese and Mongolian officials completed six weeks of border discussions, the first to be held since an agreement signed in 1964 provided for such meetings.   (K. M. SMOGORZEWSKI)

Morocco

Monetary Policy:
see Economy, World

Money and Banking:
see Economy, World

A constitutional monarchy of northwestern Africa, on the Atlantic Ocean and the Mediterranean Sea, Morocco is bordered by Algeria and Western Sahara. Area: 458,730 sq km (177,117 sq mi). Pop. (1982 est.): 21,666,000. Cap.: Rabat (pop., 1979 est., 768,500). Largest city: Casablanca (pop., 1979 est., 2,220,600). (Data above refer to Morocco as constituted prior to the purported division of Western Sahara between Morocco and Mauritania and the subsequent Moroccan occupation of the Mauritanian zone in 1979.) Language: Arabic (official), with Berber, French, and Spanish minorities. Religion: Muslim. King, Hassan II; prime minister in 1982, Maati Bouabid.

During 1982 the continuing war in the Western Sahara against the Popular Front for the Liberation of Saguia el Hamra and Río de Oro (Polisario Front) again dominated events in Morocco. The Moroccan Army completed a defensive wall from southern Morocco through the Western Sahara down to Cape Bujdur, thus preventing Polisario attacks and allowing the Bou Craa phosphate mines to reopen in July. However, Morocco suffered diplomatic reverses. In February Polisario representatives were admitted to the Organization of African Unity (OAU) meeting at Addis Ababa, Eth. In protest, Morocco and 18 other nations walked out, thus halting OAU activities.

Morocco reaffirmed its pro-U.S. stance when

King Hassan II visited the United States in May. Although the U.S. Congress refused Pres. Ronald Reagan's request for a $70 million increase in military aid to Morocco, raising it instead by $50 million, Morocco nevertheless granted the U.S. Air Force landing and refueling facilities.

Morocco also reinforced its position in the Middle East when King Hassan in September was host to the Arab heads of state summit at Fez. There the position of the Palestine Liberation Organization was reaffirmed despite the Israeli occupation of Beirut, Lebanon, and a new plan to resolve the Arab-Israeli dispute was adopted. France moved away from traditionally close relations with Morocco, mainly over the Saharan issue, but a visit to Rabat by Pres. François Mitterrand in October helped to improve the situation.

Political wounds after the Casablanca riots in June 1981 were partly healed when the major opposition party, the Socialist Union of Popular Forces, and its associated trade union were allowed to operate again in April, 1982. A new loyalist party, the National Democratic Party, replaced the old Independents Group. Nonetheless, social and political tensions persisted, marked by violent Muslim fundamentalist demonstrations in several cities. There were widespread student protests over the arrests of student union officials in February.

Morocco continued to suffer from the adverse effects of the 1980–81 drought. The trade balance by mid-1982 had worsened by 18%; the inflation rate had risen to 15%; and phosphate sales were down. Foreign debt had increased to $7 billion. Discriminatory trade practices by European nations forced Morocco to seek markets in the third world, Eastern Europe, and the U.S.S.R. Attempts were made to attract foreign investment; a new law no longer demanded majority Moroccan shareholding in any foreign company based in Morocco. Nevertheless, in April the International Monetary Fund had to grant Morocco a $579 million loan, with a special facility to pay for cereal imports necessitated by the drought.   (GEORGE JOFFÉ)

Motion Pictures

By 1982 in almost all of the technologically developed countries of the West, the videocassette recorder firmly established its place alongside the television set and record player in the standard equipment of the average home. For film industries everywhere this presented a whole new series of problems. With the possibility of renting the cassette of a recent box-office success for less than the cost of a single theatre ticket, the decline in audience numbers could only accelerate. Also, the potentially profitable market for the distribution of feature films in cassette form could be critically eroded by massive, easy piracy—a problem that increasingly exercised the wisest heads of the film industry in many countries.

English-Speaking Cinema. UNITED STATES. In a search for certainties in an essentially unpredictable industry, Hollywood increasingly tended toward a policy of making sequels to past successes.

As *Variety* explained, "With the general decline of the traditional star vehicle, [exhibitors] have latched onto series films as an easily definable, steady source of product." Thus the year saw a *Rocky III*, a *Friday the 13th Part III*, a *Grease 2*, an *Amityville II: The Possession*, a *Star Trek II: The Wrath of Khan*, and other successors, whether signified in Roman or Arabic numerals.

Clearly responding to the tastes of an audience largely made up of late adolescents, two themes predominated in the year's studio production: horror and visions of future worlds. With titles like *Madman, The Beast Within, Bloodsucking Freaks,* and *Basket Case,* the horrors were mostly cheap and very deliberately nasty; but some (John Carpenter's *The Thing,* Paul Schrader's *Cat People*—both new versions of classic horror subjects) were more ambitious, and others (Tobe Hooper's *Poltergeist,* Amy Jones's *The Slumber Party Massacre*) more imaginative than the general run.

The films that speculated on future worlds and technology were generally costly productions, at the opposite end of the economic scale. Among them Steven Spielberg's (*see* BIOGRAPHIES) *E.T. The Extra-Terrestrial* was the major box-office success of the year and one of the most profitable films in motion-picture history. Much of its success seemed due to the innocent charm of its story about a stranded creature from outer space befriended by Earth children. Ridley Scott's *Blade Runner* projected a detective story into a gloomy future of urban decay and general pollution. Steven Lisberger's *Tron* was a more cheerful fantasy, a kind of electronic *Alice in Wonderland* whose characters enter into a video game to become luminous participants in combat.

Other favoured popular entertainment formulas were the high-school film, in which the excitement of adolescent sexual discovery was an important element (Robert Freedman's *Goin' All the Way;* Amy Heckering's *Fast Times at Ridgemont High*), martial-arts fantasies (*The Bushido Blade*), and the

Steven Spielberg's *E.T. The Extra-Terrestrial* was the major box-office success of the year and one of the most profitable films in cinema history. In the photo, E.T. tries to communicate with his home planet with help from Elliott, played by Henry Thomas.

SYLVIA NORRIS—PHOTO TRENDS

Mormons: *see* Religion

"sword and sorcery" picture. The principal representatives of this last genre, John Milius's *Conan the Barbarian* and Albert Puyn's *The Sword and the Sorcerer*, both sacrificed great cost and effort to scripts whose tedium and childishness could not entirely be attributed to the intention of parody. The year's leading animated features included Don Bluth's *The Secret of N.I.M.H.*, made by former employees of Walt Disney Productions, and Jim Henson's $25 million fantasy *The Dark Crystal*.

Among Hollywood's old traditional genres the Western remained in eclipse, the only notable representative during the year being the Australian Fred Schepisi's *Barbarosa*. Two costly though lively and successful musicals were adaptations from Broadway successes—John Huston's *Annie* and Colin Higgins's *The Best Little Whorehouse in Texas*. In contrast, an original musical by Francis Ford Coppola, *One from the Heart*, set in the gambling city of Las Vegas, Nev., achieved no distribution success. Critics charged the director—one of the main innovators of the contemporary U.S. cinema—with allowing technical experiment for its own sake to obscure his narrative sense.

The year's most successful love story was Taylor Hackford's *An Officer and a Gentleman*, about a young man's coming of age during naval officer training, while George Roy Hill made a successful film from John Irving's picaresque novel *The World According to Garp*. In *Sophie's Choice* Alan Pakula effectively dramatized William Styron's powerful post-Auschwitz novel. Sidney Lumet's *The Verdict* dealt with the struggle of a down-and-out lawyer to regain his earlier idealism, and Walter Hill's *48 Hours* was a thriller teaming a white policeman with a hip young black convict.

The year brought several notable comedies. The most outstanding was Sydney Pollack's *Tootsie*, in which an unemployed New York actor dresses as a woman and becomes an overnight star of a daytime television soap opera. Dustin Hoffman created a memorable performance as the actor/actress.

Other comedies had a darker hue: Paul Bartel's low-budget *Eating Raoul* showed a suburban couple finding fun and profit in murder and cannibalism; Ron Howard's *Night Shift* was set in a morgue that employees were using it as a call-girl centre; Carl Reiner's *Dead Men Don't Wear Plaid* was a witty spoof of the 1940s private-eye film, using extracts of period films as direct quotation. Richard Pryor (*see* BIOGRAPHIES) made a second solo concert film, *Richard Pryor Live on the Sunset Strip*.

Another highly successful comedy, *My Favorite Year*, which starred Peter O'Toole as an aging, alcoholic, swashbuckling movie star in the Errol Flynn mold, marked the directorial debut of the actor Richard Benjamin. Other distinguished debuts in the course of 1982 were Barry Levinson, with *Diner*, a study of a group of disenchanted young people, habitués of a Baltimore, Md., eating place in the late 1950s, and Wayne Wang, with *Chan Is Missing*, a low-budget independent production that used the device of two Chinatown taxi drivers in pursuit of a defaulting debtor to illuminate much about the situation of the U.S. Chinese community. Two distinguished European directors made their Hollywood debuts. Costa-Gavras's (*see* BIOGRAPHIES) political thriller *Missing* re-created the true story of the disappearance of a young American during the 1973 Chilean military coup and the disillusion of his WASP-ish father (Jack Lemmon) when he discovered the degree of U.S. complicity in the events. Wim Wenders's *Hammett* was a romantic tribute to the famous private-eye author and his creation.

At the annual awards ceremony of the Academy of Motion Picture Arts and Sciences in Hollywood, a British production, Hugh Hudson's *Chariots of Fire*, took Oscars for best film of 1981, best original screenplay (Colin Welland), best musical score (Vangelis), and best costume design (Milena Canonero). The best foreign-language film was the Hungarian *Mephisto*, directed by Istvan Szabo. The winning director was Warren Beatty, whose film biography of John Reed, *Reds*, also received awards for the best supporting actress (Maureen Stapleton) and best cinematography (Vittorio Storaro). Henry Fonda (*see* OBITUARIES), who died shortly afterward, and Katharine Hepburn were adjudged best actor and actress for their work in *On Golden Pond*, which also took the Oscar for best screenplay adaptation (Ernest Thompson). The film *Raiders of the Lost Ark* was recognized for the best film editing (Michael Kahn), best art direction, best sound, and best visual effects. The best supporting actor was Sir John Gielgud, for his role as the butler in *Arthur*.

GREAT BRITAIN. With the world's highest per capita average of videocassette recorders in use in the U.K., British distributors and exhibitors felt their position more insecure than ever. This was, however, something of a wonder-year for British film production. The success of *Chariots of Fire* in the Oscar awards had given the industry new confidence; and the launching of the fourth television channel provided new stimulus and finance for production. Channel 4 commissioned or financed a considerable group of films, on modest but sufficient budgets, providing overdue opportunities

In Steven Lisberger's *Tron*, Bruce Boxleitner ruled an electronic universe. He approaches a tower where he communicates with his User (programmer).

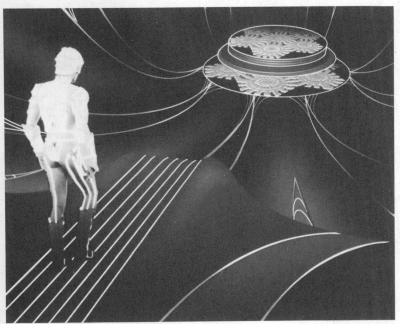

SYLVIA NORRIS—PHOTO TRENDS

for new directors. For Channel 4, Barney Platts-Mills made his first film in more than a decade: *Hero* was a bold if unsuccessful experiment, a dramatization of old Gaelic legends, played by young nonprofessionals, in Gaelic. Karl Francis's *Giro City* was a kind of thriller, with the theme of the political pressures to which television current affairs reporters might be subject. Neil Jordan's *Angel*, entirely Irish-made (and with the new Irish Film Board as Channel 4's partner) was also a thriller, of striking style and metaphysical pretensions in its reflections on the contagious nature of violence.

Co-produced by Channel 4 and the British Film Institute, Peter Greenaway's *The Draughtsman's Contract* was one of the most individual and inventive films made in England for many years: an ironic little anecdote set in the end of the 17th century and treated in a highly formalistic manner. Greenaway's style, already illustrated in his earlier short films, was a game with words, images, and music, enlivened by a rich and quirky sense of humour. Another distinguished Channel 4 production, Colin Gregg's *Remembrance*, was a sad, sympathetic portrayal of young peacetime sailors in port.

Moonlighting, Jerzy Skolimowski's fine comedy and a metaphorical reflection on the tragic events of December 1981 in his native Poland, was jointly financed by Channel 4, the producer, Michael White, and the National Film Finance Corporation. Opening late in the year was Richard Attenborough's $22 million success, *Gandhi*, a more than three-hour biography of the Indian leader. Lindsay Anderson's *Britannia Hospital*, though arguably the most important film of its era, was greeted with hostility from the British critics and indifference from the public; the foreign press (it was shown at the Cannes Film Festival) was more ready to acknowledge the Swiftian energy of this comic metaphor for a society in which institutions had become the masters of the people for whose service they were created. Among more conventional commercial productions, *Victor/Victoria*, a reworking of a German musical of the early 1930s, directed by the American Blake Edwards and starring his wife, Julie Andrews, as a woman who poses as a male transvestite artiste, enjoyed considerable international box-office success.

AUSTRALIA. While government investment in films dropped during the year, a generous tax-shelter scheme encouraged sizable new private investment. The results were more than a score of films, the majority with the combination of technical assurance and indigenous character that could assure international acceptance. Among these the outstanding box-office success of the year was George Miller's *The Man from Snowy River*, adapted from a favourite Australian novel by "Banjo" Peterson. Another early-century book, *We of the Never Never*, Mrs. Aeneas Gunn's memories of the dramatic change in her life when she left a comfortable existence as a Melbourne teacher to join her husband on a remote cattle station, was sensitively and spectacularly brought to the screen by Igor Auzins. Other notable productions of the year were David Atkins's *Squizzy Taylor*, a stylish re-

creation of the career of a small-time gangster of the 1920s; Paul Cox's *Lonely Hearts*, the story of an unlikely romance between two quirky, middle-aged people; and Michael Caulfield's *Fighting Back*, about a young teacher's efforts to reclaim a persistently delinquent child.

Of Australia's internationally reputed directors, Philip Noyce made a disappointing, overly self-conscious thriller about civic corruption, *Heatwave*; Gillian Armstrong a rough-and-tumble musical, *Starstruck*; and Henri Safran an amiable Jewish comedy, *Norman Loves Rose*, about a frustrated wife who finds sexual gratification with her early teenage brother-in-law.

CANADA. Tax-shelter schemes and other government measures to help promote quality film production had as yet had little time to show results. The outstanding French-speaking production of the year was Jean-Pierre Lefebvre's *Les Fleurs Sauvages*, a gentle and humorous account of family relationships, focused on the annual ritual of a mother's visit to her children. The most notable English-speaking films of the year were Rex Bromfield's *Melanie*, a touching story of a backwoods woman who comes to the city to reclaim her child, abducted by its father on his return from the Army; and Phillip Borsos's *The Gray Fox*, a period piece about a turn-of-the century bank robber with Robin Hood instincts.

Western Europe. FRANCE. In a year of generally undistinguished production, two major box-office successes were scored by Francis Veber's detective comedy *Le Chèvre* and Alexandre Arcady's *Le Grand Pardon*, a kind of French *Godfather*, in which Algerian Jews fill the role in organized crime played in the U.S. by Italian immigrants. More distinguished was Eric Rohmer's *Le Beau Mariage*. A fine comedy of manners, it was the intimate observation of a young girl determined on marriage but with not much success in choosing a quarry among the men of her acquaintance. José Pinheiro's *Family Rock*, a road film about a get-away-from-it-all family, and Pierre Granier Deferre's *Une Étrange Affaire*, about the destructive dependence of a boss and an employee, were both attractive films by newer directors. Argentina's Edgardo Cozarinsky made, in *One Man's War*, an outstanding example of the compilation documentary. Rare film of Paris under German occupiers was commentated upon by fragments from the diary of a sensitive and observant officer of the occupation troops.

ITALY. Commercial production in 1982 seemed largely concentrated on comedy, with popular comedians from revue and television starring in vehicles more or less worthy of their talents. Typical were Beppo Grillo in Luigi Comencini's *Looking for Jesus* and Diego Abetantueno in Carlo Vanzina's *Eccezzzionale . . . Veramente*. Somewhat apart was Mario Monicelli's period comedy *Il Marchese di Grillo*, a costly costume vehicle for Alberto Sordi. The year's outstanding box-office attraction was also comedy, Castellano and Pipolo's *Innamorato Pazzo*, a modern fairy tale about a princess and a taxi driver. The most notable prestige productions of the year were the Taviani brothers' *La Notte di San Lorenzo*, a visionary and operatic recollection of

Annual Cinema Attendance[1]

Country	Total in 000	Per capita
Algeria	41,500	2.3
Argentina	66,600	2.5
Australia	36,000	3.0
Austria	17,600	2.3
Bahrain	1,600	4.7
Barbados	1,300	5.2
Belgium	21,700	2.2
Benin	1,100	0.3
Bolivia	36,000	6.8
Brazil	164,800	1.4
Brunei	2,800	14.7
Bulgaria	95,900	10.7
Burma	222,500	8.1
Cameroon	6,500	1.0
Canada	93,200	4.1
Chad	25,400	6.0
Chile	13,300	1.2
Colombia	78,000	2.8
Cuba	31,200	3.2
Czechoslovakia	82,300	5.4
Denmark	16,000	3.1
Dominican Republic	7,700	1.4
Ecuador	38,700	5.6
Egypt	65,200	1.8
El Salvador	15,400	3.4
Finland	10,100	2.1
France	176,400	3.4
Gabon	1,100	2.1
Germany, East	79,500	4.7
Germany, West	135,500	2.2
Ghana	1,000	0.1
Greece	38,900	4.1
Grenada	1,100	12.5
Guatemala	11,200	1.7
Guyana	10,200	12.9
Haiti	2,100	0.4
Hong Kong	65,000	12.6
Hungary	61,000	5.7
Iceland	2,600	11.4
India	2,920,000	4.5
Indonesia	123,600	0.9
Iran	55,000	1.6
Ireland	18,000	5.8
Israel	24,200	6.5
Italy	276,300	4.8
Ivory Coast	6,800	0.9
Japan	164,000	1.4
Jamaica	6,400	3.0
Jordan	12,000	4.0
Kenya	9,200	0.6
Korea, South	53,800	1.4
Kuwait	4,300	3.1
Liberia	1,200	0.7
Libya	11,400	3.8
Luxembourg	1,100	3.2
Macau	2,300	9.3
Madagascar	2,900	0.4
Malaysia	34,000	2.7
Malawi	1,300	0.3
Malta	2,700	8.5
Mauritania	1,500	0.3
Mauritius	8,000	8.7
Mexico	269,800	4.0
Mongolia	15,300	9.3
Morocco	42,500	5.0
Mozambique	3,200	0.4
Netherlands, The	27,900	2.0
New Zealand	15,000	5.1
Nigeria	68,700	1.0
Norway	17,000	4.3
Pakistan	187,400	2.5
Panama	7,100	4.8
Philippines	318,000	7.5
Poland	98,900	2.8
Portugal	34,000	3.5
Puerto Rico	6,800	2.3
Romania	193,600	8.7
Senegal	3,800	0.7
Singapore	40,600	16.8
Somalia	8,000	2.3
South Africa	58,800	2.4
Spain	200,500	5.4
Sri Lanka	68,700	4.2
Sudan	3,000	0.2
Sweden	23,000	2.8
Switzerland	20,000	3.2
Syria	10,000	1.2
Taiwan	229,000	13.0
Tanzania	3,400	0.2
Thailand	71,000	1.7
Tunisia	8,800	1.5
Turkey	81,400	1.9
Uganda	1,900	0.2
U.S.S.R.	4,200,000	15.9
United Arab Emirates	6,900	9.8
United Kingdom	98,800	1.8
United States	1,022,000	4.5
Upper Volta	3,200	0.5
Venezuela	46,200	3.4
Vietnam	253,000	5.1
Western Samoa	1,100	7.4
Yemen (Aden)	5,600	3.1
Yugoslavia	79,400	3.6
Zaire	1,700	0.1
Zambia	1,600	0.3

[1] Countries having over one million annual attendance.

wartime incidents from the filmmakers' boyhood, when an entire Tuscan village set out on a trek to illusory safety; and Ettore Scola's elegant *La Notte di Varennes*, a conversation piece (between Tom Paine, Casanova, Restif de Bretonne, and others) that takes place in a coach following Louis XVI on his ill-fated attempt to escape from Paris in 1791. Michelangelo Antonioni's *Identification of a Woman* and Marco Bellocchio's *The Eyes, the Mouth* both seemed to suffer from being too ingrown in their preoccupation with the spiritual problems of actors and filmmakers and their anchorage in the directors' past.

WEST GERMANY. The death of Rainer Werner Fassbinder (*see* OBITUARIES) confirmed that for most of the past decade he had been the dominant figure in West German filmmaking. He left two new films behind him. *Die Sehnsucht der Veronika Voss*, a scenario based on the life and death of a well-loved star, Sibylla Schmidt, which won the main prize at the Berlin Festival in February, was a worthier memorial than a vulgar and misinterpreted adaptation of Jean Genet's romantic homosexual novel *Querelle de Brest*, titled by Fassbinder simply *Querelle*. Of Fassbinder's contemporaries, Werner Herzog completed a much-fraught epic shot in the Amazonian jungles, *Fitzcarraldo*, recalling the crazy undertaking of a turn-of-the century Irish adventurer who set out to build an opera house in the jungle and to carry a steamship over a mountain range. Hans-Jürgen Syberberg directed a mammoth, five-hour screen version of *Parsifal*; Hans Geissendörffer a faithful adaptation of Thomas Mann's *The Magic Mountain*; and Werner Schröter an indulgent, masochistic account of the sufferings of a young schizophrenic in a bedlam-style madhouse, *Der Tag der Idioten*.

Several promising directors made their feature debuts during the year. Rebecca Horn's *La Ferdinanda* was a precious, stylish, witty parade of bizarre guests in a beautiful Medici villa. Detlev F. Neufert, who had worked as assistant to Krzysztof Zannussi on his German productions, made a sensitive study of the plight of teenagers without families, *Take Away the Night*. Some new, young directors identified themselves as the "Off Kino" (cf. "Off-Broadway") group: Rainer Klaholz's

John Huston's *Annie*, an adaptation of the Broadway success, was a hit on the screen as a family musical.

JOHN BRYSON—SYGMA

Herbskatzen and Manfred Stelzer's *Die Perle des Karibik* were witty and lighthearted comedies; Helmer von Lutzelburg's *Die Nacht der Schicksals,* a diploma work completed in the Munich Film Academy, cleverly parodied the conventions of the horror movie.

SCANDINAVIA. Sweden's most ambitious production—the most costly in its film history—was Jan Troell's *The Flight of the Eagle,* a conscientious account of the ill-fated attempt of the Swedish scientist S. A. Andrée to reach the North Pole by balloon in 1897. With a fine central performance by Max von Sydow, the film was made in both long and short versions, for television and theatrical showing, respectively. In Denmark the distinguished director Henning Carlsen transformed his own experiences of heart illness and financial failure into drama, in *Your Money or Your Life.* Erik Clausen's *Felix* was a wistful comedy about the loneliness of old age, telling how an old lady advertises the loss of a cat that never existed, simply in order to meet people. Iceland enjoyed exceptional success with Agust Gudmundsson's *The Saga of Gisli,* a 10th-century saga vividly re-created as a parable of the conflicts of free will and fate.

Eastern Europe. U.S.S.R. There were few signs of any revitalization of the Soviet cinema. The best that could be said for the films entered in the year's international festivals was that they were concerned with genuine human relationships. *Private Life,* directed by the octogenarian Yuly Raisman, was about the self-examination of a high-ranking bureaucrat, unwillingly retired. Pyotr Todorovsky's *The Woman in Love with Mechanic Gavrilov* was a romantic comedy with the dual attractions of the popular comedienne Ludmilla Gurshenko and its setting in the charming city of Odessa. Iskra Babitsch's *Muzhiki* was a comic and touching story about a soldier who returns from the war to find that his faithless wife has abandoned him, leaving behind three children of uncertain fathering. The good man nevertheless adopts them, despite all advice to the contrary.

HUNGARY. Always the most progressive of Eastern European cinemas—politically as well as artistically—the Hungarian film industry was clearly heartened by the Oscar awarded to *Mephisto*. Characteristic of the resulting liberalism in the choice of themes was Karoly Makk's *Another Way,* whose treatment of a homosexual love affair broke entirely new ground for the socialist cinema. Based on a recent best-seller, the story related how the frustrated love of two women was bound up with the hypocrisies demanded of them as journalists in the late 1950s. The recent past continued to preoccupy filmmakers. Peter Bacso's *The Day Before Yesterday* was a tragic story of the disillusions of the post-World War II era; Pal Gabor's *Wasted Lives* was about the personal effects of the Stalin years. *Time Stands Still,* which confirmed Peter Gothar as the most outstanding new talent of recent years, spoke of the problems of growing up in the years after the 1956 revolution.

Other directors were concerned with the problems of contemporary youth. Zsolt Kezdi-Kovacs's *The Right to Hope* and Janos Rozsa's *Kabala* dealt with the emotional perils of children of broken marriages. In *The Protégé* Pal Schiffer rediscovered a child of an uprooted peasant home whom he had interviewed for a film a decade earlier and found that at 18 he was still finding grave difficulties in fitting into society.

POLAND. Shortages of materials, the constrictions of martial law, and the official disfavour of the filmmakers who had been outspoken in the Solidarity era virtually brought Polish film production to a halt. When possible, directors worked abroad—Andrezej Wajda in Paris, where he was making *Danton*, and Krzysztof Zanussi in West Germany (*The Imperative, The Unapproachable*). A newer director, Filip Bajon, was also working in West Germany, where he completed a West German-Polish co-production, *The Consul*, set in 1939.

Middle East. TURKEY. Turkey's outstanding filmmaker, Yilmaz Guney, escaped from prison, where he had been held for years on an apparently fabricated conviction for murder, to accompany to the Cannes Film Festival a film he had largely directed by proxy, *Yol*. Even though diplomatic pressures forced Guney to go into hiding, the film—exposing social abuses through the story of a group of paroled prisoners—won the Cannes Film Festival's top prize, the Palme d'Or.

EGYPT. A director of ebullient talent and invention, Youssef Chahine made the second part of the impressionist autobiography he had begun with *Alexandria—Why?* The film, *An Egyptian Story*, showed the events of two decades of postwar Egyptian history in the memory flashes of a man undergoing open-heart surgery—a dramatization of the director's own recent personal experience.

LEBANON. Two intelligent and exploratory first features, Borhane Alaouie's *The Beirut Encounter* and Maroun Baghdadi's *Petites Guerres*, attempted to analyze life and events in Beirut just before the Israeli invasion.

ISRAEL. The two most notable productions of the year dealt with themes out of key with the country's aggressive political stance. Shimon Dolan's *Repeat Dive* made no secret of its antimilitarist sentiments, in a story about a group of navy frogmen. Daniel Wachsman's *Hamsun* looked critically at the relations between Jewish agriculturalists and hired Arab labourers.

Latin America. Argentina's biggest box-office success of the year was a sharp satire on current socioeconomic problems, Fernando Ayala's *Easy Money*. The director Maria Luisa Bemberg dealt feelingly with the fate of a betrayed wife in *Señora de Nadie*. One of the better Brazilian films of the year, Roberto Farias's *Ora Frente Brasil*, which dealt with the torture of political prisoners in the 1970s, was officially banned by the censors. Fabio Donato's *India, A Filho deo Sol* focused attention on the position of Indians in Brazilian society, through the story of a police corporal who falls in love with an Indian girl. In Colombia, Luis Ospina made a stylish and propitious debut with *Pura Sangre*, a bizarre horror story about a sick millionaire tycoon who requires a constant supply of the blood of young males to keep him alive.

Asia. JAPAN. Few Japanese films reached Western film festivals during the year. Two above-average pictures dealt with recent history. Sadao

One of the most stunning movie versions of an opera ever made was Hans-Jürgen Syberberg's *Parsifal*, shown at the Cannes Film Festival.

Seitoh's *There Was a War When I Was a Child* was about the troubled wartime friendship of two infants, one of whom is the offspring of a U.S. soldier. *Willful Murder*, directed by Ken Kumai, re-created a labyrinthine scandal of the late 1940s when the president of the Japanese railroads was found killed, apparently the victim of a political plot. Other unusual films were *The Love Suicides at Sonesaki*, an adaptation of a Chikkamatsu play, performed by Bunraku doll puppets and directed by Midori Kurisaki; and Yoichi Takabayashi's *Irezumi—Spirit of Tattoo*, a bizarre, poetic, and erotic tale of an old master tattocist's last doomed assignment to decorate the back of a beautiful young woman with the image of a goddess.

INDIA. The actress Aparna Sen made a noteworthy debut as director with *36 Chowringhee Lane*, a finely observed study of an elderly Anglo-Indian schoolteacher, notably played by Jennifer Kendall. Other Indian directors dealt with contemporary social abuses. A medium-length film intended for television by Satyajit Ray showed the tragedies that could ensue from the caste system. Goutam Ghose's *The Occupation* described the resistance of a Gypsy woman to the oppressions of a rapacious landowner. More remarkable than these for its immediacy and factual content was Tapan K. Bose's horrifying documentary about police brutality to tribal people in Bihar. Another outstanding Indian film released during the year was Adoor Gopalakrishnan's *Mouse Trap*, an unsparing study of a decaying family in South India.

(DAVID ROBINSON)

Nontheatrical Motion Pictures. A documentary film tracing the successful and heroic efforts of medical teams to save the life of Pres. Ronald Reagan was one of the year's best motion pictures in the United States. *The Saving of the President* by Frank Cavenaugh (George Washington University Medical Center) in collaboration with Paul and Holly Fine (WJLA-TV in Washington, D.C.) was selected for showing at the venerable Edinburgh

ALBERT MAGNOLI—HOPE REPORTS

Jazz, a student motion picture made at the University of Southern California, was widely acclaimed as an outstanding amateur film, winning several prizes at the Velden (Austria) Film Festival.

(Scotland) Film Festival, and at the Banff (Canada) Television Festival it was awarded the Jury Prize.

Another television film, *Java Surfing,* by ABC Sports also took international honours at two events. It was awarded the grand prize of the Kracy (Yugos.) Sports Film Festival and the Italia Sul Mare Trophy at the Milan (Italy) Maritime Film Festival. An educational subject, *Continental Drift: The Theory of Plate Tectonics,* by Encyclopædia Britannica Educational Corp., was judged the best science film at the Salerno (Italy) Film Festival.

Certainly the outstanding amateur film of the past two years was a student motion picture, *Jazz,* made at the University of Southern California. It won the grand prize at the Velden (Austria) Film Festival of the Nations and also at the Christchurch (N.Z.) Amateur event.

(THOMAS W. HOPE)

See also Photography; Television and Radio.
[623; 735.G.2]

Motor Sports

Grand Prix Racing. The rules governing the 1982 season of international Formula One racing were in general unchanged from the preceding season, with engine capacity limited to 3 litres for non-supercharged power units and 1½ litres for turbocharged engines, although the increasing power of the latter was thought by some to impose an unfair handicap on the normally aspirated cars. Major aerodynamic changes designed to decrease speed and increase safety, including mandating of flat undersides and elimination of "skirts," were adopted for 1983.

In 1982 the coveted drivers' world championship remained open until the last race, at Las Vegas, Nev., at which a young Finnish driver, Keke Rosberg, took the honours. The deaths of Gilles Villeneuve (*see* OBITUARIES), the Ferrari driver from Canada, during practice at Zolder, Belgium,

and of Riccardo Paletti of Italy at the starting line in Montreal cast gloom over what was otherwise an interesting and stimulating year. Didier Pironi (France), a Ferrari driver, was also involved in an accident during practice that kept him sidelined for the latter part of the season.

The first race, at Kyalami, South Africa, was delayed by a drivers' strike. It proved a runaway win for Renault, with Alain Prost (France) leading the Williams car of Carlos Reutemann (Arg.) home and René Arnoux (France) placing third in another turbocharged Renault. Prost set the fastest lap, at 216.386 km/h. At the Brazilian race in Rio de Janeiro Nelson Piquet (Brazil) won in a Brabham, after he had made the fastest lap at 187.525 km/h. In the U.S. Grand Prix West at Long Beach, Calif., Niki Lauda (Austria) won in a McLaren ahead of Rosberg. Lauda set the fastest lap at 135.861 km/h. Then it was to Imola, Italy, for the San Marino Grand Prix. This resulted in a fierce battle between Renault and Ferrari, with victory for Pironi followed by Villeneuve; the two Ferraris crossed the finish line almost together. Third place went to Michele Alboreto of Italy in a Tyrrell. The Belgian Grand Prix at Zolder was won by John Watson (U.K.) in a McLaren from Rosberg (Williams) and Eddie Cheever of the U.S. (Talbot). Watson confirmed his expertise with quickest lap, at 191.278 km/h.

Riccardo Patrese (Italy) won the Monaco race in a Brabham, followed by Pironi and Andrea de Cesaris (Italy) in an Alfa Romeo. Fastest lap was 138.073 km/h by Patrese. The drivers then returned to North America for the inaugural Detroit Grand Prix, on the new Downland circuit, run counterclockwise. Delayed by an accident, the race finished a lap short owing to a time-limit rule, with Watson first, Cheever second, and Pironi, now Ferrari's top hope, third. Prost (Renault) made best lap at 130.798 km/h. A week later came the tragic Canadian Grand Prix at Montreal, won by Piquet for Brabham with teammate Patrese second and Watson third; the winner recorded the fastest lap at 179.749 km/h.

In the Dutch Grand Prix Pironi's Ferrari won from Piquet and Rosberg, with best lap (191.867 km/h) by Britain's Derek Warwick (Toleman). The British Grand Prix at Brand's Hatch went to Lauda, with Pironi second and Patrick Tambay (France) third in the other Ferrari. In the French race at Le Castellet Renault took first and second places, Arnoux refusing to let Prost past to win. Pironi finished third, and Patrese had the fastest lap at 209.003 km/h. Tambay brought his Ferrari home first in the German Grand Prix, ahead of Arnoux and Rosberg; Piquet had the fastest lap at 214.576 km/h. In the Austrian Grand Prix Italy's Elio de Angelis (Lotus) won from Rosberg; Jacques Laffite (France) in a Talbot was third, and Piquet again lapped fastest at 228.315 km/h.

Rosberg won the Swiss Grand Prix (held at Dijon, France), ahead of Prost and Lauda, although Prost had the fastest lap (202.735 km/h). In the Italian race, at Monza, Arnoux's Renault finished before the Ferraris of Tambay and Mario Andretti (U.S.), the latter making a fine comeback. Arnoux's triumph was endorsed by fastest lap, at

Motorboating:
see Water Sports

Motor Industry:
see Industrial Review

223.031 km/h. The drivers' world championship remained in doubt until the Las Vegas Grand Prix, but Ferrari, in a sad season for them, had already clinched the manufacturers' championship. The year ended with Alboreto winning for Tyrrell, in front of Watson and Cheever, and making best lap at 164.993 km/h, but fifth place was sufficient to give Rosberg the championship.

Rallies and Other Races. The Le Mans 24-hour sports car race was dominated by the Porsche 956s, led by Derek Bell (U.K.) and Jacky Ickx (Belgium). The Spa 24-hour was won by a BMW 528i. In rallying the four-wheel-drive Audi Quattro proved a sensation. Opel won the Monte Carlo Rally, but a Quattro scored in the Swedish event and repeated in Portugal. A Datsun Violet won the tough Marlboro Safari Rally, followed by an Opel Ascona. A Renault 5 scored in the Tour of Corsica, and the Welsh Rally went to a Quattro driven by Björn Waldegard, who also won the New Zealand Rally in a Toyota Celica. In Greece an Audi Quattro won the Acropolis Rally ahead of two Opel Asconas. In Brazil an Audi Quattro defeated an Opel Ascona and a Ford Escort, and in Finland's Thousand Lakes Rally Quattros were first and second, ahead of a Mitsubishi Lancer. Opel held on in Cyprus, from a Sunbeam-Lotus and a Lancer, but in the San Remo Rally in Italy Quattros finished first and second, ahead of an Opel Ascona. The Ivory Coast rally was won by Walter Röhrl in an Opel Ascona 400, which gave him the 1982 world rally drivers' championship. The manufacturers' championship remained a fight between Opel and Audi until the final contest of the year, the Lombard RAC Rally around Britain in November. It was again won by Finnish expert Hannu Mikkola driving for the Audi Sport team; his teammate, the Frenchwoman Michèle Mouton, was second. Audi thus clinched the manufacturers' title.

(WILLIAM C. BODDY)

U.S. Racing. Indianapolis Motor Speedway paid out a record $2,067,475 in prize money in 1982, and that may be more important than the fact that veteran Gordon Johncock defeated Rick Mears to win the Indianapolis 500. Mears, driving a Penske PC-10, had blistered the course for a new pole record speed of 207.004 mph, and he nearly erased an 11-second deficit to pull even with one lap to go (1 mph = 1.61 km/h). But the veteran Johncock in a

René Arnoux of France crossed the finish line in his Renault Formula One car to win the Grand Prix of Italy on September 12.

UPI

Wildcat-Cosworth held him off for his second 500 victory. Pancho Carter, a lap behind, was third, while Tom Sneva and Al Unser, Sr., were two laps farther to the rear in fourth and fifth.

Johncock earned $271,851 and Mears earned $205,151. This astonishing amount of money for averaging 162.029 mph for 500 mi (805 km) emphasized the continued importance of the United States Auto Club as a prime factor in single-seater racing.

Johncock and most of the Indianapolis drivers competed during the year for the rival CART (Championship Auto Racing Team) organization, which clearly established Champ Car (Indianapolis type) primacy in the rest of the U.S. That group ran 11 races, including a new street race on the Cleveland (Ohio) lakefront, and also reclaimed the Pocono International Raceway in Pennsylvania.

However, two conditions remained constant. The Cosworth engine, now called a Ford engine in the U.S., was almost totally dominant, and so was defending champion Rick Mears. Three of the top five cars were Ford-powered while the others were U.S.-made Wildcats. Following Mears in the drivers' standings were rookie of the year Bobby Rahal driving a March Ford, Mario Andretti in a Wildcat, Johncock, and Sneva in a March.

NASCAR (the National Association for Stock Car Auto Racing) enjoyed a successful season financially, but the highlight of the year was a points contest which was not settled until the final race at Riverside, Calif. There Darrell Waltrip, by virtue of taking third place, finally won the Winston Cup title over Alabama's Bobby Allison, who failed to finish. Allison had won the classic Daytona 500 at an average speed of 153.991 mph in a Pontiac, only to switch brands to Chevrolet. Waltrip, the defending champion, stuck to a Junior Johnson-prepared Buick. The NASCAR season was notable for the fact that the teams learned to make the smaller midsize cars run as fast as their 400-plus cu in predecessors and also for the reemergence of Ford as a competitive factor.

The most successful father-son combination in auto racing in 1982 was probably the Paul family. John Paul, Jr., won nine of the 18 International Motor Sports Association's (IMSA's) Camel GT Series en route to the drivers' championship. John

Race	Driver	Car	Average speed	
South African	A. Prost	Renault RE3€B	205.7	km/h
Brazilian	N. Piquet	Brabham BT49	183.000	km/h
U.S. West	N. Lauda	McLaren MP4	131.000	km/h
San Marino	D. Pironi	Ferrari 126C2	187.7	km/h
Belgian	J. Watson	McLaren MP4	187.000	km/h
Monaco	R. Patrese	Brabham BT49	132.2	km/h
Detroit	J. Watson	McLaren MP4	125.850	km/h
Canadian	N. Piquet	Brabham BT50	173.7	km/h
Dutch	D. Pironi	Ferrari 126C2	187.300	km/h
British	N. Lauda	McLaren MP4	200.685	km/h
French	R. Arnoux	Renault RE38B	201.2	km/h
German	P. Tambay	Ferrari 126C2	209.9	km/h
Austrian	E. de Angelis	Lotus 91	222.2	km/h
Swiss	K. Rosberg	Williams FW08	196.8	km/h
Italian	R. Arnoux	Renault RE35B	219.500	km/h
Las Vegas	M. Alboreto	Tyrrell C11	161.094	km/h

Formula One Grand Prix Race Results, 1982

WORLD DRIVERS' CHAMPIONSHIP: Rosberg, 44 pt; Pironi, 39 pt; Watson, 39 pt.
CONSTRUCTORS' WORLD CHAMPIONSHIP: Ferrari, 74 pt; McLaren, 69 pt; Renault, 62 pt.

Paul, Sr., won a separate endurance race championship within the series. The Pauls won the two premier events of U.S. road racing, teaming with West Germany's Rolf Stommelin to take the 24 Hours of Daytona in Florida. Their Porsche Twin Turbo set a record average speed of 114.794 mph. At the 12 Hours of Sebring in Florida the Pauls won with an average of 105.401 mph. Mazda won the manufacturers' title for the third consecutive year. Jim Downing beat fellow Mazda RX-7 driver Roger Mandevelle in the IMSA finale for the drivers' crown in the Champion Spark Plug Challenge Series.

In the Can-Am series of the Sports Car Club of America (SCCA), Al Unser, Jr., won the season crown driving a Chevrolet-powered GR-2 Frissbee and, after midseason, a GR-3. Unser, who won four races, edged Al Holbert in a VDS. In the other professional SCCA series, the Trans-Am, Elliott Forbes-Robinson won the top honours in a Pontiac Firebird. (ROBERT J. FENDELL)

Motorcycles. In world championship road racing the major prize for 1982 went to an Italian when Franco Uncini won the 500-cc class, riding a Suzuki. The 350-cc champion was Anton Mang (West Germany), riding a Kawasaki. Jean-Louis Tournadre (France; Yamaha) won the 250-cc class from Mang by a point. The 125-cc winner was Garelli-mounted Angel Nieto of Spain, and Werner Schwarzel with Andreas Huber (West Germany; Yamaha) won the sidecar category.

At the 75th Isle of Man Tourist Trophy in June, winners included Dennis Ireland (classic), Con Law (junior), Tony Rutter (F2 and 350 cc), Ron Haslam (F1), and Norman Brown (senior). Jock Taylor (sidecar) later crashed at the Finnish Grand Prix and died, as did John Newbold (U.K.) in the North-West 200 race.

At Silverstone the British 500-cc Grand Prix was won by Uncini, from Freddie Spencer (U.S.; Honda). The crash of Barry Sheene (U.K.) in practice ended his season abruptly. In the U.S. the Daytona 200 was won by Graeme Crosby (N.Z.; Suzuki). With Kenny Roberts (U.S.) and Randy Mamola (U.S.) unable to take part, the annual Transatlantic Trophy (U.S. v. U.K.) was won by Britain, with Sheene the top scorer. The world endurance championship was won by Jean-Claude Chemarin, Jacques Cornu, and Sergio Pellandini (Kawasaki).

World champions in motocross included Brad Lackey (U.S.; Suzuki) in the 500-cc class and Danny LaPorte (U.S.; Yamaha), 250 cc; Eric Geboers (Belgium; Suzuki), won the 125 cc. U.S. teams won the Motocross des Nations and the Trophée des Nations, Danny Chandler taking all four races. The speedway world individual title went to Bruce Penhall of the U.S. The world team winner was the U.S. entry of Kelly and Shaun Moran, Penhall, and Bob Schwartz. (CYRIL J. AYTON)

See also Water Sports.
[452.B.4.c]

Mountaineering

Climbers in 1981–82 continued to scale difficult routes on the highest mountains of the world, but there was an alarming increase in the number of fatalities on both the successful expeditions and the unsuccessful attempts. In the last six months of 1981, for example, there were the following deaths: seven Japanese on Nanda Kot, three Japanese on White Sail, two Japanese on Annapurna IV, two Japanese on Gangapurna, two French and two Nepalese on Annapurna I, one French climber on Kanchenjunga, one Northern Irish climber on Bhagirathi II, and two Swiss on Lhotse Shar. In the Karakorum in 1981 there were 33 expeditions, of which only 12 were successful.

On the positive side, Pakistan greatly eased its restrictions on mountaineering. Required application forms were reduced from ten copies to two; helicopter rescue arrangements were to be streamlined; maps and other information were made more readily available; and travel on the KK Highway was freed from permit as far as the Batura Bridge. Pakistan recognized its native mountaineers when Pres. Mohammad Zia-ul-Haq presented medals to the two greatest Hunza mountaineers, Ashraf Aman and Nazir Sahib.

On Mt. Everest a U.S. medical party climbed the Polish Pillar route to the south ridge and the summit in late 1981, but another U.S. expedition failed on the east face, as did a New Zealand party on the west ridge. In the premonsoon season of 1982 a Soviet expedition put 11 members on the summit via a line on the southwest face left of the British route, a creditable achievement for the first visit to the highest mountains of the world by an expedition from the U.S.S.R. A Canadian expedition made the ascent by the South Col route. (See CANADA.) A British attempt on the east-northeast ridge was abandoned after two of the party, Peter Boardman and Joe Tasker, disappeared, and a U.S. attempt on the north face by the Great Couloir was likewise abandoned when a member of the party fell to her death. Yasuo Kato of Japan, who became the first man to scale Mt. Everest in winter and the second to climb it three times, was reported lost on Dec. 28, 1982, together with his partner, Toshiaki Kobayashi.

Pierre Étienne Samin (on bike) and his teammate, Dominique Pernet, both of France, won the 24-hour Le Mans for motorcycles in April.

WIDE WORLD

In central Nepal a new route was established on the south face of Annapurna I by a Japanese party in late 1981, one member being killed. In 1982 an Austrian-German-Swiss expedition climbed the Dutch route on the same mountain. A British expedition failed on a new route on the south face, one member being killed.

In late 1981 a Yugoslav party established a new route on the south face of Dhaulagiri I. A Japanese expedition made the first ascent of the northwest ridge of that mountain in 1982.　(JOHN NEILL)

Mozambique

An independent African state, the People's Republic of Mozambique is located on the southeast coast of Africa, bounded by the Indian Ocean, Tanzania, Malawi, Zambia, Zimbabwe, South Africa, and Swaziland. Area: 799,380 sq km (308,642 sq mi). Pop. (1981 est.): 12,458,000. Cap. and largest city: Maputo (pop., 1980 prelim., 755,300). Language: Portuguese (official); Bantu languages predominate. Religion: traditional beliefs 65%; Christian about 21%; Muslim 10%; with Hindu, Buddhist, and Jewish minorities. President in 1982, Samora Machel.

On Dec. 29, 1981, it was announced that Pres. Samora Machel had reorganized Mozambique's Council of Ministers. The Ministry of Labour was replaced by a state secretariat for labour responsible to the Council of Ministers. Perhaps the most important change was the appointment of Lieut. Gen. Armando Emilio Guebuza, armed forces political commissar, as resident minister in Sofala Province, one of the areas where guerrillas of the Mozambican National Resistance (MNR) had been particularly active.

Instead of reducing their activities in 1982, the guerrillas began to operate on a much broader front. In May the Army launched a strong attack in an attempt to clear the road and rail links with Zimbabwe, which had been sabotaged. The following month the president announced that arms would be distributed to civilians, but guerrilla activities increased, supported by arms supplies from South Africa and sometimes, it was believed, by South African troops.

Apart from severing communications with the inland countries of Zimbabwe and Zambia with the aim of making them more dependent on South Africa for supplies, the guerrillas seemed intent on discouraging foreign technicians from working in Mozambique. In May 40 Swedish workers sought refuge in Zimbabwe after two men had been killed. A Portuguese technician working at a sawmill was shot by guerrillas. Six Bulgarian engineers were held hostage in the north of the country, and in October, in Manica Province, three Portuguese working on the oil pipeline to Zimbabwe were seized, together with their families. This latter action was accompanied by sabotage of the pipeline itself. Particular horror was felt in August when Ruth First (see OBITUARIES), an exile from South Africa, was killed by a letter-bomb explosion in Maputo. First, a member of the South African-banned African National Congress,

was at the time of her death a lecturer at Eduardo Mondlane University. In May a British zoologist, kidnapped by the MNR in December 1981, was released.

These guerrilla activities placed a heavy strain on an economy that showed only limited signs of recovery, and the failure to restore Mozambique's role as a transit state for goods traveling to countries in the interior seriously weakened an important source of income. Agricultural production, the country's main source of wealth, was threatened by the drift of people from rural areas to the towns. In June it was decided to issue identity cards to all city dwellers in an effort to stop this movement.

The need for foreign aid presented a challenge to the government's socialist ideology. In June a Portuguese delegation headed by the premier visited Maputo for discussions that led to the signing of economic cooperation agreements between the two countries. Four months later the government asked to take part in negotiations for the next Lomé Convention, whereby African countries shared in the European Economic Community's common market. This move did not go unnoticed by Mozambique's ally, the U.S.S.R.; Pres. Leonid Brezhnev accused the U.S. and Western Europe of trying to draw African countries into the bondage of debt.

In spite of this warning, the minister of defense visited the U.K. in November to discuss the purchase of communications systems that would facilitate joint action with Zimbabwe against the MNR. President Machel visited Zimbabwe in November with a further appeal for assistance. This followed a secret meeting between Machel and Pres. Julius Nyerere of Tanzania in October, when it was believed that Machel had asked that the 2,000 Tanzanian troops already assisting his forces against the guerrillas be reinforced.

(KENNETH INGHAM)

Mozambique

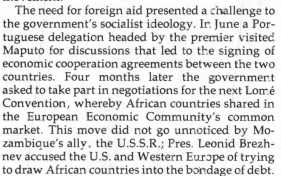

MOZAMBIQUE

Education. (1981) Primary, pupils 1,376,865, teachers 18,751; secondary, pupils 135,956, teachers 3,789; higher, students 1,852, teaching staff, 224.

Finance and Trade. Monetary unit: metical, with (Sept. 20, 1982) a free rate of 30.33 meticals to U.S. $1 (52 meticals = £1 sterling). Budget (1982 est.): revenue 18.5 billion meticals; expenditure 21.4 billion meticals. Foreign trade (1979): imports 23 billion meticals; exports 12.7 billion meticals. Import sources (1977) South Africa 20%; West Germany 15%; Portugal 10%; Iraq 9%; U.K. 7%; Japan 5%. Export destinations (1977): U.S. 27%; Portugal 16%; U.K. 7%; South Africa 7%; The Netherlands 6%; Japan 5%. Main exports (1977): cashew nuts 30%; textiles 9%; tea 8%; cotton 6%; sugar 5%.

Transport and Communications. Roads (1974) 39,173 km. Motor vehicles in use (1980): passenger c. 99,400; commercial (including buses) c. 24,700. Railways (1980): 3,933 km; traffic 556 million passenger-km, freight 970 million net ton-km. Air traffic (1980): 467 million passenger-km; freight c. 9 million net ton-km. Telephones (Jan. 1980) 51,600. Radio licenses (Dec. 1979) 255,000. Television receivers (Dec. 1979) 1,500.

Agriculture. Production (in 000; metric tons; 1981): corn c. 200; sorghum c. 130; cassava c. 2,850; peanuts c. 80; sugar, raw value c. 185; copra c. 70; bananas c. 65; cashew nuts c. 75; tea c. 18; cotton, lint c. 20; sisal c. 12. Livestock (in 000; 1981): cattle c. 1,420; sheep c. 108; goats c. 340; pigs c. 125; chickens c. 17,500.

Industry. Production (in 000; metric tons; 1980): coal c. 408; petroleum products (1979) c. 390; cement c. 275; electricity (kw-hr) 14,000,000.

Museums

The museum boom of recent years showed no signs of abating in 1982. Problems considered by the UNESCO publication *Museum* included financing, training, museum development, facilities for the disabled, and conservation. The magazine also discussed specialist museums in various parts of the world. Some museums experienced economic problems as demonstrated by their reduced numbers of exhibitions and the initiation or raising of admittance fees.

Facilities and Administration. An exhibition at the Whitney Museum of American Art in New York City, "New American Art Museums," with its focus on eight diverse building projects across the U.S., pinpointed the peculiar simultaneity of economic recession and the continuing construction of visual art institutions. Some included in that exhibition, such as the $11.8 million Hood Museum of Art at Dartmouth College in Hanover, N.H., and the Dallas (Texas) Museum of Fine Arts, were already under construction; others, including the Museum of Contemporary Art in Los Angeles and the Virginia Museum of Fine Arts in Richmond, were in advanced planning stages. Among other major museums that announced the construction of large additions were the Cleveland (Ohio) Museum of Art, the Whitney Museum of American Art, and the Des Moines (Iowa) Art Center.

In Baltimore, Md., the Museum of Art completed its three-year renovation with the opening of a new wing, while in St. Petersburg, Fla., the world's largest Dali collection, the Morse from Cleveland, was placed in the permanent Salvadore Dali Museum, a $2 million renovated structure. The Asiatic wing of the Boston Museum of Fine Arts reopened in November following a four-year, $6 million renovation.

Elaborately carved memorial poles from the Pacific line one wall of the Michael C. Rockefeller Wing of the Metropolitan Museum of Art in New York. The wing, opened in February, has one room devoted to Lester Wundermal's collection of Dogon art.

The J. Paul Getty Museum of Art, in Malibu, Calif., became the richest museum in the world when it received $1 billion from the estate of its founder, with another $100 million expected. The National Gallery of Art, Washington, D.C., inaugurated a $50 million endowment fund and was granted $5 million by Paul Mellon. In Pittsburgh, Pa., the Museum of Art at the Carnegie Institute received a grant of $2 million from the Mellon Trust that enabled the museum to resume its international survey of art begun in 1896 and discontinued in 1970.

A new gallery at the Victoria and Albert Museum, London, known as the Boilerhouse Project, opened in January. Established by Terence Conran, founder of Habitat Designs Ltd., it was to provide underground exhibition space dedicated to "encouraging professional and popular interest in the practice, history, and theory of design." The Conran Foundation would own and run the gallery independently of the museum for five years, after which it would move to permanent premises of its own, but the Boilerhouse space would remain a part of the museum as a gift. The first exhibition was "Art and Industry, a Century of Design in the Products We Use." The second was entirely dedicated to the products of Sony, the Japanese electronics firm.

The British government decided in August that plans to establish a Theatre Museum should proceed and that the Museum of Childhood at Bethnal Green should be retained, despite the contrary findings of a report on "wasteful" public expenditure. It was hoped that the Theatre Museum would open in the old flower market premises of Covent Garden in as little as two years.

The City Museum and Art Gallery, Stoke-on-Trent, home of one of the finest collections of ceramics in the world, was chosen as Britain's

The Salvadore Dali Museum, which houses the world's largest Dali collection, opened to the public in St. Petersburg, Florida, in March.

The Australian National Gallery was officially opened by Queen Elizabeth II in November. The building has 11 main galleries on three levels and was described by one critic as combining the "munificence of a cathedral with the austerity of Fort Knox."

Museum of the Year for 1982 in the annual contest sponsored by the *Illustrated London News* and National Heritage. The museum received a prize of £2,000 together with a porcelain sculpture by Henry Moore.

In March a new art museum opened in Silkeborg, Den., as a permanent exhibition centre for the large collection of contemporary art formed by the Danish painter Asger Jorn, amassed from 1953 until his death in 1973. The Museo Civico of Pistoia, Italy, which had been closed for many years for restoration, reopened to the public in February. The Mauritshuis in The Hague, Neth., was closed temporarily for restoration in March. Many of its treasures were on view elsewhere in The Hague; some were part of an important traveling exhibition. (*See* ART EXHIBITIONS.)

The new Australian National Gallery in Canberra was opened by Queen Elizabeth II. It housed the Australian national collection of art and provided more than 7,000 sq m (75,600 sq ft) of exhibition space in 11 main galleries on three levels. The building was designed by Australian architect Colin Madigan and was described by one critic as combining the "munificence of a cathedral with the austerity of Fort Knox."

A new private museum devoted to the cat opened at Reihen, Switz. The "Katzen Museum," with some 10,000 items collected over 20 years, would hold small exhibitions on various subjects, for example, "The Cat in Antiquity" and "Famous Cat-lovers."

New Acquisitions. "Gimcrack, with John Pratt up on Newmarket Heath" by George Stubbs was acquired after a successful appeal by the Fitzwilliam Museum, Cambridge, England. The picture had been "sold" to a U.S. buyer, though prior to the sale it had been on loan to the museum for a long period. In order to prevent the picture's export the museum required over £600,000, nearly half of which it had to raise itself in only 12 weeks.

New acquisitions at the Tate Gallery included Max Beckmann's "Carnival," painted in 1920 in Frankfurt am Main and the first treatment of his later favourite theme, the costume procession. It was the last in a series of important modern German pictures acquired in recent years. Stanley Spencer's last "Self-Portrait," painted in 1959, was presented to the gallery by the Friends of the Tate. The Friends had given Spencer's first "Self-Portrait" of 1914 to the Tate nearly 30 years earlier.

The Scottish National Portrait Gallery acquired the first portrait from life of Mary, Queen of Scots, a small bronze bust modeled in 1559–60 when she was in her teens in France. Four Hogarth drawings related to the series of engravings "Industry and Idleness" of 1747 were acquired by the British Museum. The drawings represent different stages in the development of the series.

Museums continued their recent practice of sharing works of art. Rather than compete with one another, the Minneapolis (Minn.) Institute of Arts and the Des Moines (Iowa) Art Center jointly acquired the Grant Wood painting "The Birthplace of Herbert Hoover." Each museum would display the work in alternate years. The Guggenheim Museum in New York City began a collection decentralization program. Ten museums in other parts of the U.S. would be allowed to borrow art works on a long-term basis from the Guggenheim's permanent collections.

The Metropolitan Museum of Art in New York received two extraordinary gifts from private collections: the Linsky Collection of small-scale three-dimensional works from the Renaissance and Baroque periods included 500 objects valued at $60 million; and 60 examples of Chinese painting and calligraphy, from the John M. Crawford, Jr., collection, were appraised at $18 million. The Art Institute of Chicago incorporated the extensive collections of the long-closed Chicago Harding Museum to give it a comprehensive medieval and Renaissance arms and armour collection. Also in Chicago the Museum of Science and Industry showed the Morse Foundation collection of glass by Louis Tiffany.

(JOSHUA B. KIND; SANDRA MILLIKIN)

See also Art Exhibitions; Art Sales.
[613.D.1.b]

Music

Classical. One thing that became clear during 1982 was that, despite an occasional flash of good news, the classical music business was no longer in the doldrums—it was in trouble. To quote the orchestra manager of one of the U.S.'s most prestigious and highly thought-of symphonic teams, "People here are tying themselves in knots trying to figure out where next season's funding is coming from." In the U.K. the government-sponsored Arts Council issued its most sombre warning ever: without further urgent injections of grant aid some of Britain's best and brightest arts institutions would fold; the Royal Shakespeare Company (its stagecraft enhanced for many seasons by Guy Woolfenden's stylish and inventive music), the Leeds-based English National Opera North (arguably the U.K.'s premier provincial touring company), and at least one of London's leading symphony orchestras were all considered under threat. As 1982 moved into 1983, it no longer appeared to be a question of who was going to be cut back or otherwise "recessed" but who (like the ill-fated English Music Theatre) was going to be eliminated for good.

SYMPHONIC MUSIC. "Safe box office is best" was clearly the watchword among the world's leading orchestras in 1982. Except for a few sparsely scattered, generally undistinguished, and, as always, poorly attended premieres, the symphonic scene in the U.S. reflected the economic climate in its slimmed-down productions and blandly safe programming. The fact that, on the basis of just one album, the Minnesota Orchestra under conductor in chief Neville Marriner failed to achieve the expected long-term recording contract with the giant Phonogram empire (a decision that caused Marriner much bitterness and subsequently led to his London-based Academy of St. Martin in the Fields chamber orchestra withdrawing from a long-time relationship with Phonogram) probably had as much to do with economics as with any short-term

The oldest symphony in the U.S., the New York Philharmonic, conducted by Zubin Mehta, gave its 10,000th performance at Avery Fisher Hall in New York City on March 7.

UPI

weaknesses in the orchestra. The news was a blow nonetheless to the orchestra's managers, despite subsequent rumoured feelers from Angel EMI, Columbia CBS, and Teledec.

Elsewhere, the Pittsburgh Symphony continued to improve steadily under principal conductor André Previn (himself a steadily improving practitioner: in the words of *The Guardian* critic, Edward Greenfield, "strikingly individual . . . beautiful blending rather than brilliance"). Italian-born Riccardo Muti, now fully in charge of the "fabulous Philadelphians" (as their brochure not unreasonably had it), at last got around to promoting at least one piece by a U.S. composer: the late Samuel Barber's second orchestral *Essay*. Under the circumstances it was a shame that the orchestra's previously rich, well-oiled style of playing (qualities well to the fore during a widely applauded European tour) sometimes seemed to be taking on a more hectoring, rasping edge; a Muti/Philadelphia *Petrushka* (Stravinsky) proved an especially ear-lacerating experience. In the same way, a Sir George Solti/Chicago Symphony Haydn *Creation* (subsequently recorded at Orchestra Hall for London-Decca as part of Solti's 70th birthday celebrations) showed plenty of fire but little humour or stylistic adroitness.

Cleveland Orchestra music director Lorin Maazel (still saddled with a fearsome reputation as a martinet) renewed and strengthened an uncommonly rewarding relationship with the Vienna Philharmonic, which lent a particularly bright sparkle to the annual Strauss family jamboree held each New Year's morning in the Austrian capital's historic *Musikverein*. True, Maazel's predecessor at this much-loved annual fête, Willi Boskovsky, might have brought a slightly gentler lilt to certain numbers, but there was no denying either the split-second timing that the younger man gave to the orchestra's playing or the crisp finesse revealed by much-hackneyed favourites such as the "Tritsch-Tratsch" and "Explosions" polkas.

Despite sundry financial problems it was, however, London that once again provided the richest pickings during the year under review. If quantity decreased, quality was undoubtedly on the advance. Simon Rattle's tenure as artistic director at London's South Bank Summer Music Festival yielded numerous gems (the festival's program planning being particularly imaginative), and Bernard Haitink's increasing work load with a healthy-sounding Philharmonia Orchestra pointed to some vintage seasons to come. Already, Haitink's Royal Festival Hall (London) performance with the Philharmonia of Sir William Walton's firebrand First Symphony (subsequently recorded for Angel EMI) had caused a considerable stir. News that additional classics by British masters (among them the two symphonies by Sir Edward Elgar and Gustav Holst's *The Planets* suite) were scheduled for performance and recording by so winning a combination was welcome indeed. British music also appeared to be in for heightened exposure with confirmation of the appointment of John Pritchard (*see* BIOGRAPHIES) as conductor in chief of the British Broadcasting Corporation (BBC) Symphony Orchestra.

Losses to music during the year included composers Carl Orff, Humphrey Searle, and Kara Karayev; pianists Sir Clifford Curzon, Glenn Gould, and Jean Wiener; violinist Christian Ferras; tenor Mario del Monaco; and ethnomusicologist Albert Lloyd. (*See* OBITUARIES.)

OPERA. So far as the world's opera houses were concerned, old standards with established stars were the most frequent offerings in 1982. New York City's Metropolitan Opera enjoyed a particularly jaded season; the fiasco during an October staging of Ponchielli's tuneful but glutinous *La Gioconda* (when an indisposed Placido Domingo's understudy was half-booed, half-tittered off the stage and the conductor, Giuseppe Patane, suffered something approaching a nervous breakdown during the third act) provided light relief to audiences increasingly restless at having to pay $50 and more to hear sometimes inferior productions of box-office regulars. In two of its most successful productions the Metropolitan featured Luciano Pavarotti in Mozart's *Idomeneo* and Joan Sutherland in Donizetti's *Lucia di Lammermoor*.

If opera blossomed anywhere during 1982, it was undoubtedly in France, where (however recklessly) the ruling Socialist regime, headed by Pres. François Mitterrand, poured money into the arts in an attempt to ginger up French interest in something other than food, drink, and sports and to improve the nation's standards of music making and music teaching. Whether as a broader policy this was likely to succeed remained to be seen (the respected music monthly *Diapason* was not alone in asking, in its September 1982 edition, whether the government's appeal to Frenchmen to "learn music" was proving especially productive), but so far as opera was concerned the first fruits were distinctly promising. Apart from English-born Baroque specialist John Eliot Gardiner's unearthing, as part of the 1982 Aix-en-Provence Festival, of yet another lost opera by the 18th-century French master Jean-Philippe Rameau, *Les Boréades*, Paris (courtesy the Opéra) witnessed a new production of Tchaikovsky's *Eugene Onegin*, directed by Gian-Carlo Menotti and conducted by Mstislav Rostropovich, and an enjoyable revival of Gounod's faded but tuneful and ever engaging *Roméo et Juliette*; l'Opéra de Lyon (a centre for excellence for some seasons now) announced a Mozart *Le Nozze di Figaro* starring France's leading dramatic soprano, Colette Alliot-Lugaz, that hailed initially from Italy's Teatro Comunale, Bologna; and the Théâtre de la Ville de Rennes staged a wide range of events from Bizet's *Carmen* (Antoine Bourseiller producing) and Pergolesi's *La Serva Padrona* to a visit by the Pansori "traditional opera" from Korea. As if this were not enough, a fall festival at Tourcoing in northeastern France attracted a considerable variety of performing arts from across the Channel that included a composer-conducted staging of Peter Maxwell-Davies's exciting ballet-cum-music-drama *Vesalii icones*.

Sir Peter Hall (artistic director at the U.K.'s still unsteady-at-the-knees National Theatre) displaced Patrice Chéreau as producer in chief at West Germany's Wagner shrine, the Bayreuth Festspielhaus; the prime attention there focused on a new

MARTY KATZ/THE NEW YORK TIMES

Eugene, Oregon (population about 100,000), boasts one of the newest and finest concert halls in the U.S. The Silva Concert Hall of the Hult Performing Arts Center, built at a cost of $26 million, was inaugurated in September.

Ring cycle under the musical supervision of Sir George Solti, at three score years and ten still the most dynamic Wagnerite around. In London mezzo-soprano Dame Janet Baker announced her retirement from the operatic stage, giving a farewell performance at a Henry Wood Promenade concert at the capital's Royal Albert Hall singing Gluck's *Orfeo ed Euryaice*.

La Scala in Milan went through a difficult period in 1982, with the resignation reported in April of artistic consultant Giorgio Strehler because of his "profound suspicion" of the principles governing the theatre's management. The impending departure of La Scala's artistic director, Claudio Abbado, was also announced.

The year marked the demise of the D'Oyly Carte Opera Company, formed in 1876 to perform the operas of Gilbert and Sullivan. But it also brought to London Joseph Papp's highly successful Broadway production of *The Pirates of Penzance*.

ALBUMS AND CASSETTES. If 1981 had been a difficult year for the recording and hi-fi industries, 1982 was even more so. News that the European launch of the revolutionary Polydor/Sony-developed compact laser disc system had been postponed (though not in Japan) until spring 1983 was hardly surprising; with the death knell of the 30-year-old long-playing disc now officially sounded (most authorities gave it at most a further decade's life), consumer resistance in certain markets was running high.

On the whole, the small companies with the lowest overheads generally fared best. Numerous interesting (and often trailblazing) releases hailed from such apparently homespun but in truth highly professional operations as Abbey Gamut, Hyperion, Lyrita, Meridian, Mobile Fidelity, Pearl, Oriel, and Sheffield Lab. These included an album coupling veteran U.S. composer Roger Sessions's Pulitzer Prize-winning *Concerto for Orchestra* with Polish-born, U.K.-domiciled Andrzej Panufnik's Eighth Symphony, the *Sinfonia Votiva* (Hyperion); Elizabeth Maconchy's Symphony for double string orchestra and *Serenata Concertante* (Lyrita); Alexander Goehr's *Metamorphosis/Dance* and cello *Romanza* (Unicorn Kanchana); William Wordsworth's fifth and sixth string quartets (CRD); and Robin Holloway's *Sea-Surface Full of Clouds* (Chandos). Each of the foregoing was a world first.

Best news from the big names tended to centre less on star-filled new releases (a Herbert von Karajan Wagner *Lohengrin* on Angel EMI and Puccini *Turandot* on DGG notwithstanding) than on an active reissues policy. From the collector's point of view this was all to the good, giving, as it did, a fresh lease on life to a number of vintage readings long out of print. These included the late Italian maestro Tulio Serafin's masterly late-1950s Verdi *Missa de Requiem* (Angel EMI), pianist Julius Katchen's long-absent issue of George Gershwin's Concerto in F Major and *Rhapsody in Blue* (French Decca), Poulenc's *Les Mamelles de Tirésias* and *Dialogue des Carmélites* (both French EMI), and a considerable quantity of material conducted by Sir Thomas Beecham (Columbia CBS). Columbia CBS also scored with a lavish "Stravinsky conducts Stravinsky" reissue, in which 31 of the master's albums (many of them long unobtainable) were sumptuously repackaged as a de luxe limited edition.

Top choice among new issues (in a year in which pressing quality, even in The Netherlands, slipped generally) included *The Cunning Little Vixen*, a further installment in Sir Charles Mackerras's outstanding peregrination around the operas of Leos Janacek (London Decca); Eliot Carter's Symphony for Three Orchestras and *A Mirror on Which to Dwell* (Columbia CBS); Alexander von Zemlinsky's *Lyric Symphony* (DGG); a sequence of middle-period Beethoven piano sonatas played by Charles Rosen (Nonesuch); and a four-disc album of Mozart's complete sacred music conducted by Herbert Kegel (Philips).

(MOZELLE A. MOSHANSKY)

Jazz. In the welter of activity that characterized the jazz world in 1982, no event was more packed with symbolism than a concert that took place in the autumn in honour of the pianist Eubie Blake. As a jazz soloist Blake would probably be content to describe himself as no more than a promising also-ran. In any case, after a boisterous youth

One of the new bands that utilized electronic technology was the Human League of Britain. The "electro-pop" band scored a big hit in the United States.

SIMON FOWLER—RETNA

spent working with such pioneers as Jim Europe, whose infantry band thrived in the aftermath of World War I, and Noble Sissle, who later became his partner, Blake won much greater fame as a writer of such standard songs as "I'm Just Wild About Harry" and, of more relevance in the jazz context, "Memories of You." Even so, it might seem a slender body of achievement on which to build a concert tribute were it not for the most interesting thing of all about Blake, which is that by the time the concert took place, he was less than six months away from his own centenary. His extraordinary longevity, rendered even more extraordinary by the fact that he had remained active as a working musician, was a reminder that convoluted though the evolution of jazz may have been, it was still young enough for its entire history to be encompassed by the life of one musician.

Little of lasting significance took place during the year. Miles Davis, the one-time enfant terrible of modernism, made yet another comeback, but as with his other returns it was characterized by a lamentable lack of creative cohesion and hardly inspired audiences. Connoisseurs of the best in jazz saxophone playing were saddened during 1982 by the deaths of two of the most accomplished apostles of that art. Arthur Edward ("Art") Pepper (*see* OBITUARIES), a Californian born in 1925, was among the earliest white players to understand and echo effectively the ideas of Charlie Parker, and after some years of ill health he had returned in recent years to give further evidence of the incisiveness of his technique. An even more gifted player was Edward ("Sonny") Stitt (*see* OBITUARIES), a contemporary of Parker's who remained true to the teachings of the master through the decades. A player of brilliant facility, ferocious passion, and a truly wonderful melodiousness, Stitt was also one of the few considerable soloists in the history of the saxophone to show equal mastery of the alto, tenor, and baritone instruments. As an alto player he was the wittiest of all of Charlie Parker's shadows, while as a tenor saxophonist he showed some allegiance to the works of Lester Young.

Another modern lion who died in 1982 was that most enigmatic of pianists and composers, Thelonious Monk (*see* OBITUARIES). In conventional terms Monk's piano playing was hamstrung by severe limitations of technique, but a quirky harmonic originality allied to a sly sense of musical humour enabled him to overcome the handicaps of his own style to become a sort of syncopated primitive who occasionally produced startling effects. Were his reputation to stand merely on his playing, then his chances with posterity might look shaky. But in addition Monk achieved much as a composer of jazz themes and, whatever the fate of his idiosyncratic and occasionally willfully eccentric solos, there was no question that such themes as "Round Midnight," "Blue Monk," "Straight No Chaser," "Off Minor," and "Epistrophy" would continue to engage the attentions of sophisticated instrumentalists.

There was one other notable death in 1982, connected with an earlier era of jazz and with a far greater orchestra than any with which Blake, Davis, Pepper, Stitt, or even Monk were associated. Inevitably as the years went by mortality chipped away at the old Duke Ellington orchestra. In 1982 the latest casualty was William Alexander ("Sonny") Greer. Greer spent most of his life under the gaily coloured umbrella of Ellington's art, meeting him as early as 1919, joining his first five-piece band soon afterward, and remaining with him in an unbroken association until 1951. As a big-band drummer Greer stands as one of the great pioneers of the art, a man who was among the first to introduce elaborate kits and who became well known for such special effects as the chimes that may be heard on recordings of "Ring Dem Bells."

(BENNY GREEN)

Popular. There was no orderly development of pop music in 1982. It was a year of rapid change, of styles coming and going, when for economic reasons there was a greater emphasis on single records than on albums and on the happenings in small clubs rather than in big stadiums. The major concert events seemed like relics from the past and exercises in nostalgia rather than pointers to the future, and the most successful bands of the year—in purely economic terms—were the two most famous survivors from the British pop golden years of the 1960s, the Rolling Stones and The Who.

The Rolling Stones followed their 1981 U.S. tour, which had earned them an estimated £60 million, with their first European and British tours in six years. Through the summer of 1982 they gave 40 shows in ten countries, playing to audiences numbering over two million people, who had each paid about £10 for a ticket. The ever athletic Mick Jagger, now 39, gave an exhausting performance as he sprinted around an enormous stage singing such pop classics as "Let's Spend the Night Together," which were once considered outrageous or decadent but were now seen as high-quality, good-time family entertainment. Later in the year The Who gave a lengthy tour of North America, announcing that it would be their last on that continent. Thus once again an economically depressed record industry was able to thank a bunch of veteran rock stars in their late 30s for bringing young audiences swarming back to the vast sports stadiums that rock bands had found so easy to fill in the 1970s.

In both Britain and the U.S. the reaction against big-stadium rock led to a flourishing of new styles. In Britain, whereas the punk bands of the late 1970s had aimed for a return to raw and basic styles, dealing with such everyday realities as unemployment and often snarling at the society around them, the new bands of 1982 emerged more from the escapist world of club-land and the dance floor. As in the 1930s, a period of austerity led to flamboyance in the dress of those with any money to spend, and this apparently escapist trend was reflected in pop music. Much of the new music was based on electronic technology, utilizing synthesizers and computers that could allow one or two performers to sound like a full band, drums and all. The Human League were the most successful exponents of this new "electro-pop" dance music, and they exported the style to the U.S., where they had a massive hit with "Don't You Want Me." Like several other bands they made use of female singers to add glamour to the electronics. Two- or three-piece synthesizer-based bands such as Dépêche Mode, Soft Cell, Yazoo, and Blancmange also made an impact. In keeping with the high-tech mood of the times, some of these bands preferred to make video discs rather than appear live.

The emphasis on the single-record market and good-time dance music also led to a flurry of non-electronic styles, and—as so often in the development of pop music—black American styles were used as inspiration by white bands. The jangling styles of funk music appeared in various guises throughout the year, and the most successful of the new exponents was a young London band, Haircut 100, whose singer, Nick Heyward, mixed light funk guitar rhythms and horns with a bouncy gift for melody that made it seem he could become a possible 1980s equivalent of Paul McCartney. Other new dance bands looked to Africa and South America.

There was a deliberate campaign by several record companies to promote African music in Britain and to show that it did not consist only of the pounding, Burundi drum style that had been copied by bands like Adam and the Ants; the big bands from Nigeria and Tanzania such as King Sunny Ade and Orchestra Makassay played a complex, stirring, and subtle blend of traditional and Western styles using ranks of singers, horn players, percussionists, and distinctive-sounding guitarists. Interest in foreign styles—African, Eastern, and Far Eastern—was shown through the ambitious WOMAD (World of Music and Dance) Festival in July, when hundreds of performers from four continents played alongside British bands. The event was an artistic success, but inevitably it lost money. WOMAD's debts were paid off when one of the organizers, Peter Gabriel, joined his former band Genesis for one massive outdoor reunion in aid of the event.

The new British fascination with dance music, style, and exotic foreign sounds was best summed up by the massive success in Britain of a New York artist, August Darnell, with his band Kid Creole and the Coconuts. Using a big band with a horn section, a comic percussionist (Coati Mundi), and three deadpan, slick dancing girls and singers, Darnell mixed black rhythm-and-blues and disco styles from the U.S. with a variety of Latin influences. His own theatrical personality and black comic hit songs like "Annie I'm Not Your Daddy" ensured that his concerts provided the best party in town.

The U.S., with its enormous size, differences in regional tastes, and musically conservative radio stations, was slower to change to the whims of pop fashion. Many of the most successful artists of the year continued in the tradition of the big-stadium rock styles of the 1970s. The very popular John Cougar was a beat balladeer in the tradition of Bob Seger, while such best-selling bands as REO Speedwagon were in the slick, easy-listening tradition. Even the energetic all-girl group the Go-Gos presented a spirited rerun of old styles.

Changes and innovation were taking place, however, and black American styles were leading the way. "Rap" was the skill of snappily, wittily, and rhythmically talking over a piece of music, and the rap artists of New York, such as Grandmaster Flash and the Furious Five, developed the style to a fine art. Their rap was fast, exhilarating, and funny, but it could also express the hopes and fears of the black community in a poignant and even startling way. "The Message," a rap single that was also a big hit in Britain, was a brilliant description of the sights, smells, and fears of the New York City ghettos, as expressed by a nervous, battered figure who admitted he was "close to the edge."

Elsewhere in the U.S. there was a surprising growth in the new wave or punk scene. Such bands as the blues-based Gun Club or X showed that not everyone in California was "laid-back," while Don Henley, once the prime exponent of California easy-listening with The Eagles, released an intriguing solo album, *I Can't Stand Still,* that showed his concern for youth literacy and the arms race. Once again the greatest U.S. performer of the year was the balladeer Bruce Springsteen, and again he surprised his followers by going against all the trends. *Nebraska,* recorded at home with his own guitar and harmonica backing, was his most bleak, chilling vision yet of the U.S. and blue-collar working life.   (ROBIN DENSELOW)

See also Dance; Motion Pictures; Television and Radio; Theatre.
[624.D-J]

Nauru

Nauru

An island republic within the Commonwealth, Nauru lies in the Pacific Ocean about 1,900 km east of New Guinea. Area: 21 sq km (8 sq mi). Pop. (1981): 8,000, including Nauruan 57%; Pacific Islanders 26%; Chinese 9%; European 8%. Capital: Yaren. Language: Nauruan and English. Religion (1980): Protestant 57.6%; Roman Catholic 24%; Confucian and Taoist 8.4%; Buddhist 1.7%; Baha'i 1.7%; none 6.6%. President in 1982, Hammer DeRoburt.

In February 1982 Nauru was host to a meeting of North and South Pacific island states that aimed to set up an inter-Pacific-island fishing agreement. It was hoped that this would strengthen the islands' bargaining position when negotiations were held with the major fishing nations.

Nepal

Namibia:
see Dependent States; South Africa

NATO:
see Defense

Navies:
see Defense

NAURU

Education. (1978) Primary, pupils 1,500; secondary, pupils 600; primary and secondary, teachers 129; vocational, pupils 61, teachers 4; teacher training (1977), students 6, teacher 1.

Finance and Trade. Monetary unit: Australian dollar, with (Sept. 20, 1982) a free rate of A$1.04 to U.S. $1 (A$1.79 = £1 sterling). Budget (1981–82 est.): revenue A$109.5 million; expenditure A$85.6 million. Foreign trade (1975–76): imports A$14.3 million (c. 58% from Australia, c. 30% from The Netherlands in 1974); exports A$37.3 million (c. 51% to Australia, c. 41% to New Zealand, c. 5% to Japan). Main export: phosphate c. 100%.

Industry. Production (in 000; 1980): phosphate rock (metric tons) 2,087; electricity (kw-hr) 26,000.

Earlier, Nauru had commissioned a land-based ocean thermal energy plant. The pilot plant cost A$4 million and had an output of 100 kw. The Tokyo Electric Power Service Corp. funded the project, which was expected to culminate with the erection of a 1,500-kw generator. If successful, the Nauru project would provide a boost for the construction of other similar plants within the region.

In June Pres. Hammer DeRoburt visited Fiji, where he had talks with Fijian Prime Minister Ratu Sir Kamisese Mara on the question of a Fijian training scheme to help with the education of Nauruan citizens.

On October 21 Queen Elizabeth II and Prince Philip visited the island.   (A. R. G. GRIFFITHS)

Nepal

A constitutional monarchy of Asia, Nepal is in the Himalayas between India and the Tibetan Autonomous Region of China. Area: 145,391 sq km (56,136 sq mi). Pop. (1981 est.): 14,746,000. Cap. and largest city: Kathmandu (pop., 1979 est., 390,000). Language: Nepali (official) 52.5%; also Bihari (including Maithili and Bhojpuri) 18.5%, Tamang 4.8%, Tharu 4.3%, and Newari 3.9%. Religion (1980): Hindu 89.6%; Buddhist 6.1%; Muslim 3%; other 1.3%. King, Birendra Bir Bikram Shah Deva; prime minister in 1982, Surya Bahadur Thapa.

The death of former prime minister B. P. Koirala (*see* OBITUARIES), leader of the banned Nepali Congress, in July 1982 came as a serious blow to the democratic forces in the country. Despite failing health, Koirala had managed to build up a substantial popular following for political and democratic reforms. This was reflected in King Birendra's appointment in November 1981 of a committee with powers to check corruption in the partyless panchayat system and in August 1982 of a royal commission to report on secondary education. The king also decided to allow press coverage of National Assembly proceedings.

In his speech from the throne on June 25, the king stressed the need for economic development,

---

NEPAL

Education. (1980–81) Primary, pupils 1,067,900, teachers 27,805; secondary, vocational, and teacher training, pupils 512,400, teachers 16,376; higher, students (1979–80) 39,900, teaching staff (1978–79) 2,311.

Finance. Monetary unit: Nepalese rupee, with (Sept. 20, 1982) a par value of NRs 13.20 to U.S. $1 (free rate of NRs 22.63 = £1 sterling). Gold and other reserves (May 1982) U.S. $223 million. Budget (total; 1980–81 actual): revenue NRs 2,407,000,000 (excludes foreign aid of NRs 856 million); expenditure NRs 4,186,000,000.

Foreign Trade. (1980–81) Imports NRs 3,796,000,000; exports NRs 988 million. Import sources: India 49%; South Korea c. 8%; Singapore c. 5%; U.S. c. 5%. Export destinations: India 62%; West Germany c. 10%; U.K. c. 8%. Main exports: food 35%; raw materials (excluding food) 31%; manufactures 28%. Tourism (1980): visitors 162,100; gross receipts U.S. $45 million.

Agriculture. Production (in 000; metric tons; 1981): rice c. 2,407; corn c. 720; wheat 477; millet c. 135; potatoes c. 275; jute 43; tobacco 5; buffalo milk c. 489; cow's milk c. 220. Livestock (in 000; 1981): cattle c. 6,973; buffalo c. 4,267; pigs c. 355; sheep c. 2,397; goats c. 2,525; poultry c. 22,412.

harnessing of water resources, enlarging of regional cooperation, and close relations with India and China. A UN report stated that Nepal neither produced nor imported enough food for the needs of its rapidly growing population. In August the government banned rice exports following a series of steep price increases.

The Falklands conflict had repercussions in Nepal; opposition leaders saw the participation of Gurkha troops in the British task force as a threat to Nepalese nonalignment.

(GOVINDAN UNNY)

Netherlands, The

A kingdom of northwest Europe on the North Sea, The Netherlands, a Benelux country, is bounded by Belgium on the south and West Germany on the east. Area: 41,160 sq km (15,892 sq mi). Pop. (1982 est.): 14,285,800. Cap. and largest city: Amsterdam (pop., 1981 est., 712,300). Seat of government: The Hague (pop., 1982 est., 700,800). Language: Dutch. Religion (1971): Roman Catholic 40.4%; Dutch Reformed 23.5%; no religion 23.6%; Reformed Churches 9.4%. Queen, Beatrix; prime ministers in 1982, Andreas van Agt and, from November 4, Ruud Lubbers.

On April 27, 1982, Willem Duisenberg, president of The Netherlands Bank, presented his 1981 annual report. While pointing out the possibility of recovery in the world economy and the opportunities this would present for Dutch industry, he was more concerned about the immediate situation. The number of unemployed had doubled in two years; in real terms the income of the average worker had declined by 4%; and the profits of trade and industry had been seriously undermined.

On May 12 the Socialist Party (PVDA) Cabinet ministers submitted their resignations to Queen Beatrix. The differences of opinion among the coalition partners—the Christian Democratic Appeal (CDA), the Democratic Party (D'66), and the PVDA—had become too great. The immediate cause of the split was the social-economic and financial policy of the government. The CDA and D'66 wanted to give highest priority to measures

The Netherlands

WIDE WORLD

Crosses bearing the names of four Dutch journalists killed in El Salvador were planted in front of the U.S. consulate in Amsterdam in March. Those who placed the crosses were protesting U.S. support for the regime in El Salvador.

intended to reduce the government's financial deficit and thus stimulate economic activity. The PVDA, while acknowledging the desirability of such measures, wanted a policy directed toward the creation of employment. Personal animosity among the leading politicians added to the tensions.

On May 29 Prime Minister Andreas van Agt presented a new Cabinet that excluded the PVDA. The main task of this Cabinet was to prepare for elections to the lower house of Parliament on September 6. One thing was evident from the election results: D'66 had lost its political influence. As a result, Jan Terlouw, the D'66 leader, quit the national political arena. The Liberal Party (VVD) under its new leader, Ed Nijpels, greatly increased its representation, but the PVDA became the largest single party. The CDA lost three seats, and van Agt declared that he was no longer available for the position of candidate-prime minister. (For details of the election results, *see* POLITICAL PARTIES.)

By convention, the biggest single party, in this case the PVDA, was given first chance to form a Cabinet. From the beginning the attempt was doomed to fail. Both the CDA and the VVD let it be known that their differences with the PVDA could not be bridged. After renewed consultations, Queen Beatrix appointed Willem Scholten, vice-president of the State Council and member of the CDA, to form a Cabinet. On November 4 the new Cabinet, headed by Ruud Lubbers (*see* BIOGRAPHIES) as prime minister and supported by the CDA and the VVD, was sworn in. The Cabinet was at once confronted with a five-day strike by teachers. On November 22 the government announced tough austerity measures, including a public-sector wage freeze. Unions representing government workers threatened "massive and lengthy" strikes.

On March 18 the Ministry of Foreign Affairs announced that four members of a Dutch television team had been killed in a gun battle between guerrillas and the Army in El Salvador. Some days before the shooting, Koos Koster, one of the four journalists, had been interrogated by the El Salvador police because a message with his name on it had been found on the body of a guerrilla. The results of an inquiry did not exclude the possibility that the attack was intentional but provided no conclusive evidence.

On March 1 Queen Beatrix and Prince Claus were welcomed to West Germany by Pres. Karl Carstens. During April 19–25 the royal couple visited the U.S., where Queen Beatrix addressed both houses of Congress, and during November 16–19 they visited the U.K.   (DICK BOONSTRA)

See also Dependent States.

New Zealand

New Zealand, a parliamentary state and member of the Commonwealth, is in the South Pacific Ocean, separated from southeastern Australia by the Tasman Sea. The country consists of North and South islands and Stewart, Chatham, and other minor islands. Area: 269,057 sq km (103,883 sq mi). Pop. (1982 est.): 3,190,100. Cap.: Wellington (pop., 1981, city proper 135,700; urban area 321,000). Largest city: Christchurch (pop., 1981, city proper 164,700; urban area 289,900). Largest urban area: Auckland (pop., 1981, city proper 145,000; urban area 769,500). Language: English (official), Maori. Religion (1976): Church of England 35%; Presbyterian 22%; Roman Catholic 16%. Queen, Elizabeth II; governor-general in 1982, Sir David Stuart Beattie; prime minister, Robert David Muldoon.

After providing a speaker in the New Zealand Parliament, which reconvened in April 1982, the National Party (Conservative) administration of Prime Minister Robert Muldoon had a margin of one over the combined opposition of Labour and Social Credit. But Social Credit had agreed not to block government funding measures if it held the

Netherlands Overseas Territories:
see Dependent States

New Guinea:
see Indonesia; Papua New Guinea

Newspapers:
see Publishing

NEW ZEALAND

   Education. (1981) Primary, pupils 493,856, teachers (1980) 20,402; secondary, pupils 224,926, teachers (1980) 13,527; vocational, pupils 145,075, teachers (1980) 2,216; teacher training, pupils 5,901, teachers 539; higher (universities only), students 31,549, teaching staff 3,043.
   Finance. Monetary unit: New Zealand dollar, with (Sept. 20, 1982) a free rate of NZ$1.38 to U.S. $1 (NZ$2.36 = £1 sterling). Gold and other reserves (June 1982) U.S. $401 million. Budget (1980–81 est.): revenue NZ$7,609,-000,000; expenditure NZ$9,133,000,000. Gross national product (1980–81) NZ$23,615,000,000. Money supply (March 1982) NZ$2,977,000,000. Cost of living (1975 = 100; 1st quarter 1982) 251.2.
   Foreign Trade. (1980–81) Imports NZ$5,587,300,000; exports NZ$5,915,100,000. Import sources: Australia 19%; U.S. 18%; Japan 15%; U.K. 10%; Singapore 6%; Saudi Arabia 5%. Export destinations: Australia 14%; U.S. 13%; Japan 13%; U.K. 13%. Main exports: wool 15%; dairy products 14%; lamb and mutton 12%; beef and veal 10%. Tourism (1980): visitors 463,300; gross receipts U.S. $213 million.
   Transport and Communications. Roads (1980) 95,899 km. Motor vehicles in use (1981): passenger 1,346,100; commercial 269,800. Railways: (1980) 4,478 km; traffic (1981) 404 million passenger-km, freight 3,181,000,000 net ton-km. Air traffic (1981): 5,676,000,000 passenger-km; freight 203.9 million net ton-km. Shipping (1981): merchant vessels 100 gross tons and over 114; gross tonnage 243,518. Telephones (March 1981) 1,799,500. Radio receivers (Dec. 1979) 2,750,000. Television licenses (Dec. 1981) 919,100.
   Agriculture. Production (in 000; metric tons; 1981): wheat 368; barley 187; oats 52; corn *c.* 177; potatoes *c.* 278; dry peas *c.* 70; tomatoes *c.* 60; wine *c.* 50; apples 222; milk *c.* 6,550; butter *c.* 247; cheese *c.* 84; wool *c.* 252; sheepskins *c.* 103; mutton and lamb *c.* 606; beef and veal *c.* 500; fish catch (1980) 98; timber (cu m; 1980) *c.* 9,003. Livestock (in 000; June 1981): cattle *c.* 8,581; sheep *c.* 71,200; pigs *c.* 540; chickens *c.* 6,332.
   Industry. Production (in 000; metric tons; 1981): coal 1,949; lignite 218; crude oil 411; natural gas (cu m) 1,770,000; manufactured gas (cu m) 47,000; electricity (excluding most industrial production; kw-hr) 22,707,000; cement 759; aluminum 154; petroleum products 2,502; phosphate fertilizers (1980–81) *c.* 380; wood pulp 1,160; paper 711.

balance of power, and in the key political crisis it voted with the government to overturn a planning tribunal's denial of water rights for a major hydroelectric project. The government was committed to a number of major projects to make the country less dependent on imported fuels and to developing large-scale industry to provide jobs. These policies had a rocky first year in North Auckland, where continuing disagreement with boilermakers threatened a refinery extension.

Tight voting lines did not deter the prime minister from introducing a 12-month wage and price freeze in June, after labour unions had declined an income tax trade-off in place of a wage increase. (The Institute of Economic Research in early October forecast that the 15% inflation would fall to single figures by mid-1983.) The budget, presented in August, increased diesel-oil prices, and inevitably higher transportation costs would be reflected in retail prices. Thaws in the price freeze increased pressure on the government to make exceptions with wages. The budget eased the tax burden on middle-income earners, with less relief for lower earners. It also increased duties on fuels, liquor, and cigarettes; abolished allowances on regional investments, export investment, and fishing investment; and increased an international departure tax from NZ$35 to NZ$40.

In June the prime minister called for the resignation of one of his most outspoken colleagues, Derek Quigley, from his post as minister of housing, works, and development. Quigley had publicly questioned the direction of free-enterprise policies and the extent of government intervention. Muldoon's elderly and most trusted lieutenant, Deputy Prime Minister Duncan MacIntyre, underwent heart surgery during the year, and the National Party elected its first woman president, Sue Wood. In a February reshuffle, Associate Minister of Finance John Falloon relinquished his post office portfolio to Minister of Tourism Rob Talbot. There was some pressure on Labour opposition leader Wallace ("Bill") Rowling, a three-time general election loser, to step down, but he appeared determined to retain his position.

Muldoon moved to the forefront of the Commonwealth finance ministers' conference when he called for the convening of a conference to reform the collapsing international monetary system. He carried the campaign to the International Monetary Fund and World Bank meetings in Toronto. For once he had third world powers behind him.

Parliamentarians were surprisingly in accord in their response to a Privy Council (U.K.) ruling on an appeal by a Western Samoan woman who had allegedly overstayed a visitor permit. The council ruled that she—along with thousands of other Western Samoans—could regard herself as a New Zealand citizen because of a succession of acts in connection with a trusteeship phase of Western Samoa's development. Western Samoans protested when the New Zealand government offered a deal by which 40,000 Samoans in New Zealand, some of them "overstayers," could regard themselves as legally resident there in return for the cancellation of automatic New Zealand citizenship rights for the Samoans at home. One count estimated that 60,000 people in Western Samoa might be penalized by the decision.

Air New Zealand went through a year of re-equipment and reorganization. The nation took a lead in supporting the U.K. in the Falkland Islands conflict. The state railway was reorganized, but continued to lose money, and the east coast of South Island suffered a record drought.

(JOHN A. KELLEHER)

See also Dependent States.

Nicaragua

The largest country of Central America, Nicaragua is a republic bounded by Honduras, Costa Rica, the Caribbean Sea, and the Pacific Ocean. Area: 128,875 sq km (49,759 sq mi). Pop. (1982 est.): 2,643,000. Cap. and largest city: Managua (pop., 1979 est., 552,900). Language: Spanish. Religion: Roman Catholic. Coordinator of the three-member Junta of the Government of National Reconstruction in 1982, Daniel Ortega Saavedra.

The Sandinista National Liberation Front government faced serious political problems in 1982. On the international front, Thomas Enders, U.S. assistant secretary of state for inter-American affairs, promised that the U.S. administration would

UPI

not help the opponents of the Sandinistas if Nicaragua stopped sending arms from Cuba to El Salvador. The Sandinistas replied that negotiations must be linked to a change in the U.S. policy of aiding the military buildup in Honduras. A new military base was established in that country only 19 km (12 mi) from the Nicaraguan border.

Daniel Ortega Saavedra, coordinator of the Sandinista junta, expressed the opinion that a war between Nicaragua and Honduras appeared to be inevitable if the U.S. continued to help the former Nicaraguan national guardsmen, followers of the late president Anastasio Somoza (Somocistas),

During the Falkland Islands conflict, New Zealand offered its most modern frigate, the HMNZS "Canterbury," to the British Navy to replace ships that the U.K. had committed to the Falkland effort.

NICARAGUA

Education. (1980–81) Primary, pupils 472,167, teachers 13,318; secondary, pupils 120,522; vocational, pupils 16,661; secondary and vocational, teachers (1977) c. 3,145; teacher training, students 2,560, teachers (1974) 55; higher, students 34,710, teaching staff (1977) 1,204.

Finance. Monetary unit: córdoba, with (Sept. 20, 1982) a par value of 10.05 córdobas to U.S. $1 (free rate of 17.14 córdobas = £1 sterling). Budget (1980 actual): revenue 4,632,000,000 córdobas; expenditure 6,123,000,000 córdobas. Gross domestic product (1979) 13,409,000,000 córdobas. Money supply (Sept. 1981) 5,783,700,000 córdobas. Cost of living (Managua; 1975 = 100; July 1981) 338.4.

Foreign Trade. (1980) Imports 8,916,500,000 córdobas; exports 4,526,800,000 córdobas. Import sources: U.S. 27%; Venezuela 18%; Costa Rica 13%; Guatemala 12%; El Salvador 6%. Export destinations: U.S. 39%; West Germany 14%; Costa Rica 8%; France 6%; The Netherlands 5%. Main exports: coffee 42%; beef 14%; cotton 8%; chemicals 7%; fish 7%; sugar 6%.

Transport and Communications. Roads (1978) 18,197 km. Motor vehicles in use: passenger c. 36,600; commercial (including buses) c. 30,700. Railways (1980): 373 km; traffic 18.7 million passenger-km, freight 11.8 million net ton-km. Air traffic (1980): c. 76 million passenger-km; freight c. 1.4 million net ton-km. Telephones (Jan. 1980) 57,900. Radio receivers (Dec. 1979) 650,000. Television receivers (Dec. 1979) c. 170,000.

Agriculture. Production (in 000; metric tons; 1981): corn c. 250; rice c. 65; sorghum c. 70; dry beans c. 60; sugar, raw value c. 193; bananas c. 170; oranges c. 53; cottonseed c. 115; coffee c. 63; cotton, lint c. 75; fish catch (1980) c. 20. Livestock (in 000; 1981): cattle c. 2,301; pigs c. 510; horses c. 270; chickens c. 4,800.

Industry. Production (in 000; metric tons; 1980): cement 154; petroleum products (1979) c. 600; gold (troy oz) c. 60; electricity (kw-hr) 988,000.

Nicaragua

RANDY TAYLOR—SYGMA

More than 9,000 Miskito Indians who had fled Nicaragua were housed in refugee camps in Honduras. The Miskitos opposed the Sandinista government in Nicaragua.

who still operated from bases within Honduras. An incident between a Honduran naval ship and a Nicaraguan coast guard vessel was reported on September 18.

In October the Sandinista government received assurances of international backing when Nicaragua was chosen to fill the UN Security Council's Latin-American seat beginning in January 1983.

A serious confrontation was developing between the government and a sector of the Miskito Indian communities on the Atlantic coast. Following heavy fighting in northern Zelaya Province, about 10,000 Indians living along the Coco River were transferred early in 1982 to a new settlement farther from the Honduran border. The Sandinistas justified the transfer on the grounds that it was necessary in order to defend the border more effectively against incursions from Honduras. The Miskito communities opposed to the government were divided; some formed a guerrilla force that supported the Somocistas, while others joined former Sandinista leader Edén Pastora and opposition leader Alfonso Robelo in a new, non-Somocista united front of opposition, the Alianza Revolucionaria Democrática.

Nicaragua's gross domestic product grew by 7% in 1981, as compared with 10.7% in 1980. A similar performance was expected for 1982.

(MARTA BEKERMAN DE FAINBOIM)

Niger

Niger

A republic of north central Africa, Niger is bounded by Algeria, Libya, Chad, Nigeria, Benin, Upper Volta, and Mali. Area: 1,189,000 sq km (459,100 sq mi). Pop. (1982 est.): 5,634,000, including (1978 est.) Hausa 52%; Zerma and Songhai 22.6%; Fulani 10%; Kanuri and Manga 9.1%; Tuareg 3%; other 3.3%. Cap. and largest city: Niamey (pop., 1977, 225,300). Language: French (official), Mausa, Kanuri, Fulani, and other dialects. Religion: Muslim 85%; animist 14.5%; Christian 0.5%. Chief of state and president of the Supreme Military Council in 1982, Col. Seyni Kountché.

In May 1982, on the eve of French Pres. François Mitterrand's official visit to Niger, Pres. Seyni Kountché had to contend with a wave of student agitation. Opposition to the government received support from Libya despite the fact that diplomatic

NIGER
Education. (1978–79) Primary, pupils 187,151, teachers 4,762; secondary, pupils 25,491, teachers 866; vocational, pupils 354, teachers 31; teacher training, students 1,259, teachers 64; higher, students 939, teaching staff 185.
Finance. Monetary unit: CFA franc, with (Sept. 20, 1982) a par value of CFA Fr 50 to the French franc (free rate of CFA Fr 353 = U.S. $1; CFA Fr 605 = £1 sterling). Gold and other reserves (June 1982) U.S. $68 million. Budget (1981–82 est.) balanced at CFA Fr 93.9 billion.
Foreign Trade. (1980) Imports CFA Fr 125 billion; exports CFA Fr 120 billion. Import sources: France c. 45%; West Germany c. 8%; Libya c. 7%; Ivory Coast c. 7%. Export destinations: France c. 74%; West Germany c. 16%; Sweden c. 5%. Main exports: uranium 76%; fruit and vegetables (1977) 10%; livestock (1977) 9%.
Transport and Communications. Roads (1980) 8,219 km. Motor vehicles in use (1980): passenger 25,800; commercial 4,400. There are no railways, but they are planned. Inland waterway (Niger River; 1980) c. 300 km. Telephones (Dec. 1978) 8,000. Radio receivers (Dec. 1979) 200,000. Television receivers (Dec. 1979) 500.
Agriculture. Production (in 000; metric tons; 1981): millet c. 1,117; sorghum c. 273; rice c. 38; cassava c. 225; onions c. 101; peanuts c. 100; goat's milk c. 140. Livestock (in 000; 1981): cattle c. 3,300; sheep c. 2,850; goats c. 7,200; camels c. 365.
Industry. Production (in 000; metric tons; 1980): uranium 4.9; tin concentrates (metal content) 0.1; cement 36; electricity (kw-hr; 1980) 52,000.

relations between the two countries, broken off in January 1981, had been renewed on March 1, 1982. In April a group of Tuaregs, believed to have entered Niger from Mali, were arrested in the uranium mining town of Arlit on suspicion of planning to sabotage installations there. Niger's precarious internal situation was aggravated by severe fluctuations in the price of uranium, reduced sales of which adversely affected economic development.

Relations with France were strengthened during the year, and a visit by French Minister for Cooperation Jean-Pierre Cot in April preceded that of President Mitterrand. The internationally known writer, historian, and former president of the National Assembly, Boubou Hama, died in January (see OBITUARIES). (PHILIPPE DECRAENE)

Nigeria

A republic and a member of the Commonwealth, Nigeria is located in Africa north of the Gulf of Guinea, bounded by Benin, Niger, Chad, and Cameroon. Area: 923,768 sq km (356,669 sq mi). Pop. (1982 est.): 89,117,500, including (1978 est.) Hausa 21.5%; Yoruba 21%; Ibo 18.4%; Fulani 11.1%; other 28%. Cap: Lagos (pop., 1982 est., 1,404,000). Largest city: Ibadan (pop., 1982 est., 1,009,000). Language: English (official), Hausa, Yoruba, and Ibo. Religion (1963): Muslim 47%; Christian 34%. President in 1982, Alhaji Shehu Shagari.

During 1982 Nigeria suffered from its almost total dependence on income from petroleum in the face of world recession, falling demand, and price restrictions imposed by the Organization of Petroleum Exporting Countries (OPEC). Crude-oil exports fell by 41% in 1981, while the cost of living rose by 21%.

In June the National Party of Nigeria (NPN) chose Pres. Alhaji Shehu Shagari as its candidate in the 1983 presidential election. Meanwhile, four opposition parties combined to form the Progressive Parties' Alliance, and a new party, the Nigerian Advance Party, was registered in May. Odumegwu Ojukwu, who had led Biafra during the civil war in the late 1960s, was granted a presidential pardon and returned to Nigeria in June, ending a 12-year exile in the Ivory Coast. later in the year he joined the NPN.

The 1983 elections would be the first test of democracy since the 1979 return to civilian rule. The constitution required that the successful candidate win at least 35% of the vote in two-thirds of the states. New legislation during the year defined the procedure to be adopted when a request for the creation of a new state was made. In September the registration of electors was officially completed amid complaints of inefficiency and corruption. Nigeria, which had not had a reliable census for 30 years, was estimated to have 66 million voters. However, there were fears that the new method of establishing voters' lists—registration was carried out at booths rather than by door-to-door calls—could result in fewer Muslim women registering.

Nigeria mended fences with its neighbours in West Africa. A visit from a Ghanaian delegation in March was designed to quash rumours that Nigeria supported the deposed Ghanaian president, Hilla Limann, while a state visit by Pres. Ahmadou Ahidjo of Cameroon wrote finis to the May 1981 border incident in which five Nigerian soldiers were killed. Pope John Paul II's successful

Nigeria

visit in February pointed up the tolerance of Shagari, himself a Muslim in a country with a sizable Muslim population. Nigeria played a neutral role at the abortive summit meeting of the Organization of African Unity (OAU) in Tripoli, Libya, in August. A Nigerian delegation, excluding the head of state, attended some of the sessions and stated that. while it supported the cause of the Saharan Arab Democratic Republic, the SADR could not yet be defined as a state and therefore was not eligible for OAU membership.

Attempts to increase agricultural production and to stem the population drift away from the countryside continued to fail in the face of corruption and lack of technical skills. Once the leading African exporter of peanuts (groundnuts) and palm oil, Nigeria was paying more than 1 billion naira a year for food imports by the 1980s. Shagari's 1982 budget, announced in December 1981, showed a 1981 balance of payments deficit of more than 1 billion naira. Estimates for 1982 stood at 7.4 billion naira for capital expenditure, 3.5 billion naira for recurrent expenditure, and revenues of 11.6 billion naira. Despite austerity measures in the budget, President Shagari was obliged to pass an Economic Stabilization Act in April to meet an increasing economic crisis, indicating that the budget had been based on overoptimistic estimates of oil production. New measures included import cuts, closing of private jetties, salary cuts for government workers, strict control over external borrowing, and a clampdown on smuggling.

Nigeria's 22nd independence celebrations, held for the first time at the future capital, Abuja, took place on October 1. President Shagari's speech, covering economic planning, education, and the new "ethical revolution," struck a note of cautious optimism.

In late October there were violent clashes between Muslim fundamentalists and police in Kano, Kaduna, and Maiduguri. It was reported that more than 450 people died during the riots. An extremist Muslim sect blamed for the violence was banned in November. (MOLLY MORTIMER)

Pope John Paul II ordained a large group of priests in an outdoor mass in Caduna, his first stop on an African tour.

NIGERIA

Education. (1979–80) Primary, pupils 12,554,222, teachers 309,597; secondary, pupils 1,597,877, teachers 50,952; vocational, pupils 57,492, teachers 2,619; teacher training, students 242,186, teachers 16,440; higher, students 115,166, teaching staff (universities only) 5,748.

Finance. Monetary unit: naira, with (Sept. 20, 1982) a free rate of 0.68 naira to U.S. $1 (1.17 naira = £1 sterling). Gold and other reserves (June 1982) U.S. $1,348,000,000. Federal budget (1981): revenue 14,745,000,000 naira; expenditure 12,002,000,000 naira (including 7,154,000,000 naira capital expenditure). Gross domestic product (1978–79) 28,737,000,000 naira. Money supply (April 1982) 9,344,000,000 naira. Cost of living (1975 = 100; Dec. 1981) 272.1.

Foreign Trade. (1981) Imports (f.o.b.) c. 10,239,000,000 naira; exports 11,935,000,000 naira. Import sources: U.K. c. 18%; West Germany c. 13%; Japan c. 13%; France c. 10%; U.S. c. 9%; Italy c. 5%. Export destinations: U.S. c. 46%; France c. 8%; West Germany c. 8%; The Netherlands c. 7%. Main export: crude oil 94%.

Transport and Communications. Roads (1980) 107,990 km. Motor vehicles in use (1980): passenger 215,400; commercial 33,100. Railways: (1980) 3,523 km; traffic (1974–75) 785 million passenger-km, freight 972 million net ton-km. Air traffic (1981): 2,308,000,000 passenger-km; freight 16.9 million net ton-km. Shipping (1981): merchant vessels 100 gross tons and over 127; gross tonnage 475,786. Telephones (June 1980) 154,200. Radio receivers (Dec. 1979) 5.5 million. Television receivers (Dec. 1979) 450,000.

Agriculture. Production (in 000; metric tons; 1981): millet c. 3,230; sorghum c. 3,750; corn c. 1,580; rice c. 1,241; sweet potatoes c. 240; yams c. 15,000; cassava c. 11,000; tomatoes c. 450; peanuts c. 530; palm oil c. 675; cocoa 160; cotton, lint c. 28; rubber c. 43; fish catch (1980) 480. Livestock (in 000; 1981): cattle c. 12,500; sheep c. 12,000; goats c. 25,000; pigs c. 1,150; poultry c. 130,000.

Industry. Production (in 000; metric tons; 1981): crude oil 71,192; natural gas (cu m) c. 1,100,000; cement (1980) c. 2,000; tin concentrates (metal content; 1980) 3; petroleum products (1980) c. 4,040; electricity (kw-hr; 1980) c. 5,000,000.

FRANCOIS LOCHON—GAMMA/LIAISON

AFRICA'S AWAKENING GIANT

by Guy Arnold

Nothing illustrated more clearly the growing importance of Nigeria than the nervous European reactions to the government's economy measures of March and April 1982. No other African country could have achieved such an effect. The West Germans, who had just been hosts to Pres. Alhaji Shehu Shagari, were especially upset at cutbacks affecting what had become a highly lucrative and important market for their goods. The U.K. Department of Trade nervously commented, "It would be a mistake for British firms to turn their faces from Nigeria."

In 1981 Nigeria's gross domestic product (GDP) reached 43.4 billion naira; approximately 28% of this was accounted for by oil and 13.7% by agricultural production. At the end of the 1970s Nigeria passed South Africa to become the leading country on the continent when measured by the size of its GDP. The estimated 89 million Nigerians represented almost one-fifth of the total population of Africa, while the average Nigerian state, of which there were 19, was equal in terms of resources and finances to the average independent country elsewhere on the continent.

The Oil Legacy. Oil has financed Nigeria's huge development plans; it has also led to large increases in consumer and luxury spending that present their own problems. Overdependence on one product is a major handicap: more than 90% of foreign exchange and over 80% of government revenue are derived from the sale of oil. One estimate suggests that by the year 2000 Nigeria could be consuming as much as 950,000 bbl a day of oil, well over one-half of the present rate of production. If energy consumption is taken as a prime indicator of economic development, this would represent a major advance for the Nigerian economy, but such an advance would need to be balanced. It would make economic sense only if in the meantime oil wealth was used effectively to create other industrial and agricultural

Guy Arnold, a free-lance writer, is the author of Modern Nigeria, Kenyatta and the Politics of Kenya, The Last Bunker, and Aid in Africa.

production that would replace the oil income upon which the country now relies.

Although some of the targets of the fourth development plan (1981–85) have been temporarily set aside in response to the 1982 recession crisis, it remains a huge program. The importance of the Nigerian market is testified to by the determination of the major trading nations to penetrate it. Nigeria is the U.K.'s tenth largest overseas market, and the largest outside Europe and North America. West Germany, France, Japan, and Italy are also pushing to increase their exports to Nigeria.

The most important development task facing the country is to convert its oil wealth into other productive enterprises in preparation for the time when the oil becomes depleted. Other mineral resources are limited, although it is estimated that iron ore reserves will last for 150 years. During 1982 Nigeria at last began to produce its own steel after a gestation saga that lasted over 20 years. Critics of the huge investment in this industry suggest that the final product will be among the most costly steel in the world; however, its supporters justify it on the grounds that it is an essential prerequisite for an industrial society. Apart from steel, oil, and the rapidly developing petrochemical and motor-vehicle assembly industries, other industrialization remained small in scale.

The Green Revolution. One of the most interesting political developments in black Africa over the last few years has been the growing recognition of the need to reverse the disastrous deterioration of agriculture and to attempt to make the continent self-sufficient in food once again. A number of countries have embarked upon "green revolutions" with the aim of creating a resurgence of agriculture. Nigeria has launched its own green revolution, and President Shagari has personally identified his political fortunes with it. In 1982 Nigeria imported food valued at more than 1 billion naira.

The green revolution is of crucial importance to Nigeria's reputation in Africa. If the country succeeds in returning to food self-sufficiency and then achieves its secondary target of becoming a net food exporter, this example will be of immense value to Africa as a whole. On the other hand, if the green revolution fails, it could then be argued that if Nigeria with its oil wealth and human resources cannot successfully conduct a green revolution, what chance has any other African country? Increasingly, Africa tends to look to Nigeria for a lead in such matters.

Nigeria's Role in Africa. On the international scene President Shagari has a high reputation, and Nigeria is expected to speak for Africa over a growing range of issues. At the 1981 North-South development summit in Cancún, Mexico, it seemed natural for Shagari to represent black Africa; he drew special attention to the issue of agriculture.

Nigeria's growing role as spokesman for black Africa began in the early 1970s, when, for example, it became the de facto chief negotiator for African countries in discussions that led to the signing of the first Lomé Convention with the European Economic Community. In 1975 Nigeria set out to persuade a majority of the Organization of African Unity (OAU) nations to recognize the Popular Movement for the Liberation of Angola (MPLA) regime of Agostinho Neto; in the teeth of U.S. pressure against such recognition, Nigeria's diplomacy prevailed. Under Lieut. Gen. Olusegun Obasanjo, the country's last military leader, Nigeria mounted a campaign to persuade Western companies that the time must come when they would be faced with a choice: trade with and invest in Nigeria or South Africa, but not both. The implication of possible action by Nigeria in support of this aim remains in the background; it is not something that trading nations such as the U.K. should ignore.

It was no accident that on the opening day of the 1979 Commonwealth summit conference in Lusaka, Zambia, which led to the Lancaster House agreement that produced independence for Zimbabwe, Nigeria announced the nationalization of its assets in British Petroleum. Nigeria's argument with BP had been under way for some time and was unrelated to the conference; the timing, however, was a deliberate reminder, a warning shot to Britain that should it attempt to make a deal with former (white) Rhodesian prime minister Ian Smith rather than work toward full independence for Zimbabwe, then other major British assets in Nigeria would be at risk. The point was not lost on the U.K. delegation. It was, therefore, appropriate that at the 1981 Commonwealth conference in Melbourne, Australia, Nigeria should be invited to lead the discussions about South Africa and South West Africa/Namibia. Such events demonstrate that as of 1982 Nigeria was the only black nation whose wealth, oil, and size of market enabled it to speak on something like equal terms with major countries outside Africa.

Internal Politics. Growing sureness in international affairs has been matched by an equal confidence at home since the return to civilian rule in 1979. Thus, in two gestures of generally acclaimed magnanimity, President Shagari in 1981 pardoned Gen. Yakubu Gowon and then the following year Odumegwu Ojukwu, thereby finally closing the chapter on the 1967–70 civil war. Under the new constitution the Supreme Court demonstrated toughness and independence from the government, refreshing qualities on a continent where too often

the organs of justice are seen only to represent the interests of the ruling party. Indeed, the development of government, parties, states, and press since 1979 has proceeded in a democratic manner that bodes well for Africa's largest nation. The first moves to the proposed new capital of Abuja are important for their symbolic quality: Abuja represents a new sense of nationhood.

But there are problems. Possibly the most noticeable and insistent of these concerns the "get-rich-quick" mentality that has been commented upon by many observers of the Nigerian scene. President Shagari has condemned the "inordinate craze for wealth in Nigeria" and has called for a revival of moral values. This search for wealth, sparked by the prosperity brought by oil, needs to be tempered and channeled; and this is arguably the most difficult of all tasks facing Nigeria's leaders.

Economic Influence. A touchstone of Nigerian power is its relationship with its immediate neighbours and in particular the other members of the Economic Community of West African States. The ECOWAS is now approaching its eighth year, and Nigeria, whose population is equivalent to three-fifths of the Community total, must, above all, use restraint in order to ensure that it does not dominate its smaller partners and cause them to fear that it will swamp their economies.

Nigeria has at last withdrawn its opposition to opening the African Development Bank (ADB) to outside stockholders, a move that will more than double the capital available for development. Nigeria's vote was essential to enable such a change. When the ADB met in Lusaka in May 1982, Minister of Finance Victor Masi, announcing the Nigerian decision, said: "The views of these 47 more needy African countries, whose economic and consequent political stability forms the centrepiece of Nigeria's foreign policy, cannot be overlooked. Nigeria respects this issue and is sensitive to the wishes of African member states." There was a touch of arrogance about the Masi statement, the conscious unbending of Africa's major black power.

Nigeria's potential is hardly in dispute. As a country its interests are overwhelmingly with the Western world, but this inclination is coupled with a determination to resist any Western interference or neocolonialist activity. Nigeria's emergence during the 1970s as a middle-rank power and third-world leader was a fact of considerable political significance. During the 1980s the African continent as a whole faces formidable development problems. Africa urgently needs to speak effectively to and with the outside world, and Nigeria bids fair to be the black African nations' spokesman for the rest of the decade.

Norway

Norway

Oman

A constitutional monarchy of northern Europe, Norway is bordered by Sweden, Finland, and the U.S.S.R.; its coastlines are on the Skagerrak, the North Sea, the Norwegian Sea, and the Arctic Ocean. Area: 323,895 sq km (125,057 sq mi), excluding the Svalbard Archipelago, 62,048 sq km, and Jan Mayen Island, 373 sq km. Pop. (1982 est.): 4,113,000. Cap. and largest city: Oslo (pop., 1981 est., 451,000). Language: Norwegian. Religion (1980 est.): Lutheran 97.6%. King, Olav V; prime minister in 1982, Kåre Isaachsen Willoch.

Norway entered 1982 with a recently elected Conservative government at the helm. Prime Minister Kåre Willoch's minority administration had pledged to cut corporate and personal taxes, reduce public spending, curb inflation, abolish unnecessary bureaucratic controls, and scale down selective subsidies to industries.

Several factors hampered the achievement of these goals. One was the government's dependence on support from the small Christian People's and Centre parties in order to achieve an overall majority in the Storting (parliament). The two parties were only lukewarm about some of the Conservative proposals, particularly spending cuts that threatened welfare or regional development. The main problem, however, was the continuing world recession. World demand and prices slumped for traditional exports such as paper and pulp, ferroalloys, aluminum, and shipping services. The only important industrial sector still working at capacity, and earning good profits, was offshore oil and gas production.

Industrial employment, on the decline since 1974 when it had stood at around 400,000 man-years, had dropped to 360,000 by 1982 and was expected to fall still further in 1983. Although total employment was stable, at about 1,720,000 man-years, the number of registered unemployed climbed steadily throughout the first half of 1982. In August, when the year's school leavers entered

A 23-metre (76-foot) replica of an ancient Viking ship left Duluth, Minnesota, on May 6 and arrived in Bergen on July 19 after a 34-day Atlantic crossing. The voyage was a symbolic return trip of the Viking ships that many believed reached the new world before Columbus.

WIDE WORLD

NORWAY

Education. (1980–81) Primary, pupils 591,323, teachers 30,818; secondary and vocational, pupils 183,664, teachers 14,939; teacher training, students 13,696, teachers 1,063; higher (universities only), students 40,620, teaching staff 3,652.

Finance. Monetary unit: Norwegian krone, with (Sept. 20, 1982) a free rate of 6.92 kroner to U.S. $1 (11.87 kroner = £1 sterling). Gold and other reserves (June 1982) U.S. $6,738,000,000. Budget (1981 est.): revenue 100,520,000,000 kroner; expenditure 104,742,000,000 kroner. Gross national product (1981) 318.2 billion kroner. Money supply (May 1982) 53,490,000,000 kroner. Cost of living (1975 = 100; June 1982) 188.4.

Foreign Trade. (1981) Imports 89,654,000,000 kroner; exports 102,896,000,000 kroner. Import sources: Sweden 16%; West Germany 15%; U.K. 14%; U.S. 9%; Japan 7%; Denmark 6%. Export destinations: U.K. 40%; West Germany 17%; Sweden 9%. Main exports: crude oil 30%; natural gas 16%; machinery 7%; chemicals 6%; fish 5%.

Transport and Communications. Roads (1980) 81,718 km (including 56 km expressways). Motor vehicles in use (1980): passenger 1,233,600; commercial 152,500. Railways: (1980) 4,242 km (including 2,443 km electrified); traffic (1981) 2,420,000,000 passenger-km, freight 2,880,000,000 net ton-km. Air traffic (including Norwegian apportionment of international operations of Scandinavian Airlines System; 1980): 4,070,000,000 passenger-km; freight 137.8 million net ton-km. Shipping (1981): merchant vessels 100 gross tons and over 2,409; gross tonnage 21,674,886. Shipping traffic (1981): goods loaded 34,341,000 metric tons, unloaded 18,321,000 metric tons. Telephones (Dec. 1980) 1,851,700. Radio licenses (Dec. 1979) 1,332,000. Television licenses (Dec. 1980) 1,204,800.

Agriculture. Production (in 000; metric tons; 1981): barley c. 650; oats c. 417; potatoes c. 530; apples 47; milk c. 1,960; cheese 71; beef and veal c. 76; pork c. 87; fish catch (1980) 2,398; timber (cu m; 1980) 8,810. Livestock (in 000; June 1981): cattle c. 988; sheep c. 2,155; pigs c. 690; goats c. 75; chickens c. 3,775.

Industry. Fuel and power (in 000; metric tons; 1981): crude oil 23,579; coal (Svalbard mines; Norwegian operated only) 312; natural gas (cu m) 27,060,000; manufactured gas (cu m) 12,000; electricity (kw-hr) 92,304,000. Production (in 000; metric tons; 1981): iron ore (65% metal content) 4,063; pig iron 1,292; crude steel 848; aluminum 633; copper 26; zinc 80; cement 1,780; petroleum products c. 7,300; sulfuric acid (1980) 354; fertilizers (nutrient content; 1980–81) nitrogenous c. 428, phosphate c. 143; fish meal (1978) 331; wood pulp (1979) mechanical c. 920, chemical c. 680; newsprint 696; other paper (1979) c. 760. Merchant vessels launched (100 gross tons and over; 1981) 278,000 gross tons. New dwelling units completed (1981) 34,700.

the labour market, it hit a postwar record of 43,900, representing 2.7% of the labour force.

The first test of the new government's policies came in the spring, when the unions traditionally bargain with employers over pay and conditions for the coming year. The Conservative government promised to leave bargaining entirely to the unions and employers, although it pointed out that a moderate settlement of around 6.5% would help hold down inflation and stop the decline in Norwegian industry's competitiveness. In the event, settlements averaged 10–11%, slightly less than the rate of inflation, and there were few strikes.

Offshore production workers, however, failed to reach agreement with their employers during the spring wage bargaining. The union was reluctant to order a strike because it feared the government would enforce a settlement, as the previous Labour government had done in 1980 and 1981. Only in mid-October, when members had voted to reject a final compromise proposal, did the union send out strike notices. The government immediately announced that it would ask the Storting to approve a compulsory settlement order. The dispute cost the state an estimated 145 million kroner a day in lost revenues. Because of the strike, moreover, 1982 oil and gas output was expected to be only slightly higher than in 1981. A new field, Valhall A, came on stream in October.

The government's budget for 1983, introduced in October, proposed real reductions in direct company and personal taxation, partly offset by increased indirect taxes and charges for public services. At the same time, spending was to be curbed, in real terms, in virtually every sector except defense and law and order. The result would have been a tightening of fiscal policy. The very week that the draft budget was published, however, the new Swedish government of Prime Minister Olof Palme announced a 16% devaluation of the Swedish krona. This immediately undermined many of the assumptions on which the government's economic strategy had been based.

Despite the Conservatives' opposition, in principle, to selective industrial subsidies, the government announced a package of measures to assist the Norwegian industries hardest hit by the move. Sweden's sudden, steep devaluation was condemned by Norwegian government ministers, who accused the Swedes of "exporting their problems" and undermining "Nordic solidarity." This overlooked the fact that Norway itself had already devalued its currency twice in 1982, in August and September, by 3% each time.   (FAY GJESTER)

See also Dependent States.

Oman

An independent sultanate, Oman occupies the southeastern part of the Arabian Peninsula and is bounded by the United Arab Emirates, Saudi Arabia, Yemen (Aden), the Gulf of Oman, and the Arabian Sea. A small part of the country lies to the north and is separated from the rest of Oman by the United Arab Emirates. Area 300,000 sq km (120,000 sq mi). Pop. (1982 est.): 948,000; for planning purposes the government of Oman uses an estimate of 1.5 million. No census has ever been taken. Cap. and largest city: Muscat (pop., 1981 est., 50,000). Language: Arabic. Religion: Muslim (of which Ibadi 75%; Sunni 25%). Sultan and prime minister in 1982, Qabus ibn Sa'id.

During 1982 Oman was affected by reduced oil revenue resulting from weak world demand. The five-year plan launched in early 1981 depended on a crude-oil production ceiling of 320,000 bbl a day, but by late 1982 the Cabinet was considering raising production to 350,000 bbl a day to make up for the revenue shortfall. Sultan Qabus ibn Sa'id continued to pursue a policy of friendship with Western countries and hostility toward the U.S.S.R. His official visit to the U.K. in March 1982 was to be followed by a visit to the U.S., tentatively scheduled for April 1983.

Security remained a high priority in view of the support given by neighbouring Yemen (Aden; South Yemen) to guerrillas hostile to Qabus. About 30 guerrillas were believed to be at large in

A British officer (left) directs troops on the Oman side of the border between Oman and South Yemen. The Omanis feared incursions from South Yemen.

OMAN

Education. (1980–81) Primary, pupils 91,652, teachers (1979–80) 3,462; secondary, pupils 15,280, teachers (1979–80) 1,075; vocational (1979–80), pupils 817, teachers (1979–80) 157; teacher training (1979–80), students 251, teachers (1979–80) 41.

Finance and Trade. Monetary unit: rial Omani, with (Sept. 20, 1982) a par value of 0.345 rial to U.S. $1 (free rate of 0.592 rial = £1 sterling). Gold and other reserves (April 1982) U.S. $1,091,000,000. Budget (1981 est.): revenue 1,399,000,000 rials; expenditure 1,410,000,000 rials.

Foreign Trade. (1981) Imports (f.o.b.) c 573 million rials; exports 1,525,000,000 rials. Import sources (1980): Japan 20%; United Arab Emirates 17%; U.K. 16%; U.S. 6%; The Netherlands 6%; West Germany 6%. Export destinations: Japan 50%; The Netherlands 11%; West Germany 11%; Singapore 9%; U.S. 8%. Main export: crude oil 99.7%.

Industry. Production (in 000): crude oil (metric tons; 1981) 15,967; electricity (kw-hr; 1980) 792,000.

the mountains above the southern city of Salalah. Oman professed its readiness to cooperate with mediation efforts by Kuwait and the Arab League. On October 27 it was announced that Oman and South Yemen had reached agreement on the cessation of hostilities.

The death of Sayyid Tariq, uncle of Qabus, left no obvious successor to the sultan, who was childless. An increasingly able cadre of commoners was being built up in the government, with Qais al-Zawawi, appointed deputy prime minister for financial and economic affairs in February, one of the leaders. Informed opinion suggested, however, that the sultan's successor would be chosen from within the ruling family.

(JOHN WHELAN)

Pakistan

A federal republic, Pakistan is bordered on the south by the Arabian Sea, on the west by Afghanistan and Iran, on the north by China, and on the east by India. Area: 796,095 sq km (307,374 sq mi), excluding the Pakistani-controlled section of Jammu and Kashmir. Pop. (1981 prelim.): 83,782,000. Cap.: Islamabad (pop., 1981 prelim., 201,000). Largest city: Karachi (metro. area pop., 1981 prelim., 5,103,000). Language: Urdu (official), En-

Nobel Prizes:
see People of the Year

Norwegian Literature:
see Literature

Nuclear Energy:
see Defense; Energy; Industrial Review

Numismatics:
see Philately and Numismatics

Obituaries:
see People of the Year

Oceanography:
see Earth Sciences

Oil:
see Energy

Organization of African Unity:
see African Affairs

Organization of American States:
see Latin-American Affairs

Ornithology:
see Life Sciences

Orthodox Churches:
see Religion

Painting:
see Art Exhibitions; Art Sales; Museums

Paints and Varnishes:
see Industrial Review

Pakistan

Pakistan's Pres. Mohammad Zia-ul-Haq journeyed to New Delhi in November to meet with India's Prime Minister Indira Gandhi.

glish (lingua franca), Punjabi, Sindhi, and Pashto. Religion: Muslim 97% (of which Sunni 70%; Shi'ah 30%); Hindu 1.6%; Christian 1.4%. President in 1982, Gen. Mohammad Zia-ul-Haq.

To consolidate his martial law regime, Pres. Mohammad Zia-ul-Haq in December 1981 set up a handpicked 350-member Federal Advisory Council, which, he said, would act as a bridge between the martial law administration and a future Islamic democratic government. The council, of which all federal ministers and ministers of state were ex-officio members, had no decision-making powers. After the general elections for a National Assembly of Pakistan, the council would cease to exist. President Zia told the council when it began its first session in Islamabad on Jan. 11, 1982, that general elections could not be held under current circumstances without endangering the country's security and integrity.

On Pakistan's national day, March 23, President Zia described Pakistan's armed forces as the only sector in the country that was organized, disciplined, and united. In May President Zia suggested the formation of a Higher Command Council, which would assign a permanent role to the armed forces in decisions of national and international policy. This was to consist of the president, the prime minister, the defense minister, and the chiefs of the Army, Navy, and Air Force.

After a secret meeting in Karachi on Dec. 30, 1981, leaders of the Movement for the Restoration of Democracy, an alliance of various banned political parties, described the formation of the Federal Advisory Council as an attempt to "hoodwink the nation and the outside world." They later suggested that the idea of a Higher Command Council was a blatant deviation from Islamic principles and the unanimously adopted 1973 constitution. The government denied allegations by Amnesty International in January 1982 that an estimated 6,000 political prisoners had been under arrest at one time in the past and that 193 of them had undergone torture.

Universities in Karachi, Lahore, and other cities were closed from March to June when teachers went on strike demanding higher salaries and stu-

Palestine:
see Israel; Jordan

dents demonstrated against right-wing political elements in academic life. Lawyers and barristers in Karachi and elsewhere boycotted courts in July to protest President Zia's order banning legal practitioners from political activity. From mid-1981 to mid-1982 a number of violent incidents between Shi'ah and Sunni Muslims rocked Pakistan. Terrorists linked to Al Zulfikar, an organization headed by Murtaza Ali Bhutto, son of executed former prime minister Zulfikar Ali Bhutto, also carried out several hit-and-run attacks against police guards and pro-Zia politicians in June and September.

The Islamic Shari'ah law reforms and their application in public life came under criticism. After the Women's Action Forum publicly demonstrated against them in Karachi in April, President Zia gave an assurance that the policy of islamization would not involve women being "shunted back into the home." However, Pakistan's women's field hockey teams were banned from playing overseas or in front of men; their national championships were canceled; and the women's athletic events in the national games were also scrapped.

After his successful state visit to China in October, President Zia met Indian Prime Minister Indira Gandhi in New Delhi on November 1 en route to Singapore, Malaysia, and Indonesia. Despite continuing suspicions about each other's motives,

PAKISTAN

Education. (1979–80) Primary, pupils 7,090,000, teachers 139,300; secondary, pupils 1,996,000, teachers 115,600; higher, students 349,259, teaching staff 19,878.

Finance. Monetary unit: Pakistan rupee, with (Sept. 20, 1982) a free rate of PakRs 12.20 to U.S. $1 (PakRs 20.90 = £1 sterling). Gold and other reserves (June 1982) U.S. $879 million. Budget (1981–82 est.) balanced at PakRs 42,470,000,000. Gross national product (1980–81) PakRs 286,690,000,000. Money supply (June 1982) PakRs 79,653,000,000. Cost of living (1975 = 100; June 1982) 186.7.

Foreign Trade. (1980–81) Imports PakRs 53,544,-000,000; exports PakRs 29,565,000,000. Import sources: Saudi Arabia 13%; Japan 12%; U.S. 11%; Kuwait 8%; U.K. 6%; West Germany 5%. Export destinations: China 12%; Japan 6%; U.S. 6%; Saudi Arabia 6%. Main exports: rice 19%; cotton 18%; cotton fabrics 8%; carpet 8%; cotton yarn 7%; petroleum and products 6%.

Transport and Communications. Roads (1981) 96,436 km. Motor vehicles in use (1979): passenger 303,700; commercial 66,500. Railways: (1981) 8,823 km; traffic (1980–81) 17,315,000,000 passenger-km, freight 8,516,-000,000 net ton-km. Air traffic (1981): 6,059,000,000 passenger-km; freight 254.7 million net ton-km. Shipping (1981): merchant vessels 100 gross tons and over 86; gross tonnage 507,389. Telephones (June 1980) 330,000. Radio receivers (Dec. 1979) 5,250,000. Television receivers (June 1980) 664,000.

Agriculture. Production (in 000; metric tons; 1981): wheat 11,340; corn 1,004; rice 5,093; millet c. 315; sorghum c. 230; potatoes 396; sugar, raw value 928; sugar, noncentrifugal 1,810; chick-peas 532; onions c. 435; rapeseed 252; cottonseed c. 1,500; mangoes c. 550; dates c. 205; oranges c. 515; tobacco 67; cotton, lint c. 750; beef and buffalo meat c. 351; mutton and goat meat c. 340; fish catch (1980) 279. Livestock (in 000; 1981): cattle 15,084; buffalo 11,794; sheep 28,468; goats 32,808; camels 867; chickens 65,718.

Industry. Production (in 000; metric tons; 1981): cement 3,587; crude oil 463; coal and lignite 1,563; natural gas (cu m) 8,966,000; petroleum products (1980) c. 4,200; electricity (excluding most industrial production; kw-hr) 17,150,000; sulfuric acid 59; caustic soda 39; soda ash (1980–81) 96; nitrogenous fertilizers (nutrient content; 1980–81) 581; cotton yarn 389; woven cotton fabrics (sq m) 314,000.

India and Pakistan continued attempts to narrow their differences. A U.S. economic aid and military assistance package for Pakistan, spread over a six-year period and estimated to be worth approximately $3 billion, was made final at the end of 1981. Agreements were signed for the delivery to Pakistan of the first part of a consignment of 40 U.S.-built F-16 fighter aircraft. In December 1982 President Zia visited Washington where he had talks with Pres. Ronald Reagan.

Pakistan's budget for the 1982–83 fiscal year envisioned an overall economic growth rate of 6.2%. There was to be a 16% increase in development spending and a 12% increase in defense spending. (GOVINDAN UNNY)

Panama

A republic of Central America, Panama is bounded by the Caribbean Sea, Colombia, the Pacific Ocean, and Costa Rica. Area: 77,082 sq km (29,762 sq mi). Pop. (1982 est.): 1,921,700. Cap. and largest city: Panama City (pop., 1980 prelim., 383,600). Language: Spanish. Religion (1980 est.): Roman Catholic 92%; Muslim 4.5%; other 3.5%. Presidents in 1982, Aristides Royo and, from July 31, Ricardo de la Espriella.

The arrangement dividing governmental authority between the National Guard and the president worked badly in 1982. Col. Florencio Flórez (the successor of military strong man Brig. Gen. Omar Torrijos) found the friction so uncomfortable early in the year that he retired. Late in July Pres. Aristides Royo yielded to pressure and re-

Pres. Aristides Royo of Panama (left) resigned in late July and was succeeded by Vice-Pres. Ricardo de la Espriella. Royo cited health reasons for his resignation.

signed. Their successors, Col. Rubén Darío Paredes del Río and Ricardo de la Espriella, were no more successful. Royo, charged with corruption and blamed for economic troubles, was swept out with hundreds of his government officials. Paredes displayed his dominance by suspending operation of the nation's press.

Many Panamanians had been disturbed by leftist indications in Royo's foreign policy. In the press and at the United Nations he frequently denounced Great Britain during the Falkland Islands conflict. The Panamanian Air Force rescued a number of guerrillas from Honduras. A Soviet trade delegation, interested in a west coast port as a fishing base, was welcomed.

Much attention centred on the economy. The annual rate of inflation reached 15%, and unemployment rose to an estimated 130,000 persons. Panama's financial obligations raised its foreign debt to more than $3 billion. Compared with this figure, the new source of revenue from the canal treaties, $70 million annually, seemed small and of no benefit. Depression and disenchantment prompted marches, demonstrations, and strikes.

On the other hand, the transition from U.S. to Panamanian operation of the canal on April 1 went smoothly. Passage of ships and cargo reached record levels. In October the Morrison Knudsen Co. completed a 130-km (80-mi) oil pipeline not far from the Costa Rican border. It was expected to carry some 800 bbl a day.

(ALMON R. WRIGHT)

Panama

PANAMA

Education. (1981) Primary, pupils 335,239, teachers 12,598; secondary, pupils 129,787, teachers 6,331; vocational, pupils 43,197, teachers 2,236; teacher training, students 1,094, teachers 48; higher (universities only), students 43,199, teaching staff 3,035.

Finance. Monetary unit: balboa, at par with the U.S. dollar, with a free rate (Sept. 20, 1982) of 1.71 balboas to £1 sterling. Gold and other reserves (June 1982) U.S. $157 million. Budget (1981 actual): revenue 826 million balboas; expenditure 1,073,000,000 balboas. Gross national product (1980) 3,247,000,000 balboas. Cost of living (Panama City; 1975 = 100; June 1982) 155.8.

Foreign Trade. (1981) Imports 1,540,100,000 balboas; exports 316.6 million balboas. Import sources (1980): U.S. 34%; Saudi Arabia 18%; Venezuela 8%; Japan 6%. Export destinations (1980): U.S. 49%; Costa Rica 6%; The Netherlands 6%; West Germany 5%. Main exports: bananas 22%; petroleum products 18%; sugar 16%; shrimps 13%.

Transport and Communications. Roads (1980) 8,612 km. Motor vehicles in use (1979): passenger 97,300; commercial 25,800. Railways (1979) 678 km. Air traffic (1980): c. 414 million passenger-km; freight c. 3.7 million net ton-km. Shipping (1981): merchant vessels 100 gross tons and over 4,461 (mostly owned by U.S. and other foreign interests); gross tonnage 27,656,573. Panama Canal traffic (1979–80): vessels 13,507; cargo carried 169.9 million metric tons. Telephones (Jan. 1980) 176,500. Radio receivers (Dec. 1979) 322,000. Television receivers (Dec. 1979) 240,000.

Agriculture. Production (in 000; metric tons; 1981): rice c. 192; corn c. 68; sugar, raw value c. 187; mangoes c. 26; bananas c. 1,082; oranges c. 69; coffee c. 6; fish catch (1980) 195. Livestock (in 000; 1981): cattle c. 1,604; pigs c. 202; horses c. 166; chickens c. 5,195.

Industry. Production (in 000; metric tons; 1980): cement c. 500; petroleum products (1979) c. 2,380; manufactured gas (cu m) 634; electricity (kw-hr) 1,947,000.

Papua New Guinea

Paraguay

Papua New Guinea

Papua New Guinea is an independent parliamentary state and a member of the Commonwealth. It is situated in the southwest Pacific and comprises the eastern part of the island of New Guinea, the islands of the Bismarck, Trobriand, Woodlark, Louisiade, and D'Entrecasteaux groups, and parts of the Solomon Islands, including Bougainville. It is separated from Australia by the Torres Strait. Area: 462,840 sq km (178,704 sq mi). Pop. (1982 est.): 3,126,000. Cap. and largest city: Port Moresby (pop., 1980 prelim., 116,900). Language: English, Hiri or Police Motu (a Melanesian pidgin), and Pisin (also called Pidgin English or Neo-Melanesian) are official, although the latter is the most widely spoken. Religion (1980): Protestant 63.8%; Roman Catholic 32.8%; tribal 2.5%; other 0.9%. Queen, Elizabeth II; governor-general in 1982, Sir Tore Lokoloko; prime ministers, Sir Julius Chan and, from August 2, Michael Somare.

There was a change of government in Papua New Guinea following a general election in June 1982. Prime Minister Julius Chan was defeated by Michael Somare (prime minister during 1975–80), whose Pangu Party candidates won 41 of the 109 seats in the Parliament. The election was marked by an outbreak of rioting in parts of the highlands. Alcohol restrictions were lifted during the campaign, which was contested by 1,122 candidates.

Somare was named prime minister on August 2, when the new Parliament, meeting for the first time, voted 66 to 43 in his favour. Four days later he announced a 27-member government in coalition with the United Party and independents. Somare's new policy was summed up by his aphorism, "We are interested in development, not envelopment." Economies proposed in the November budget included the sacking of 3,300 civil servants.

Papua New Guinea's relations with Indonesia were again strained in 1982. Papua New Guinea's minister for foreign affairs and trade, Noel Levi, protested to the Indonesian foreign ministry after an armed Indonesian patrol crossed the border on June 26. Levi said that the Indonesians had taken 19 Irian Jaya (West New Guinea) refugees back with them.

Queen Elizabeth II began her tour of Pacific islands in Papua New Guinea on October 13.

(A. R. G. GRIFFITHS)

Paraguay

A landlocked republic of South America, Paraguay is bounded by Brazil, Argentina, and Bolivia. Area: 406,752 sq km (157,048 sq mi). Pop. (1982 est.): 3,251,000. Cap. and largest city: Asunción (metro. pop., 1979 est., 673,200). Language: Spanish (official), though Guaraní is understood by more than 90% of the population. Religion: Roman Catholic (official). President in 1982, Gen. Alfredo Stroessner.

Uncertainty as to whether Gen. Alfredo Stroessner would run in the presidential elections, scheduled for February 1983, strengthened rumours circulating in 1982 that the president was suffering from ill health. Stroessner had remained in power for 28 years by balancing his two main power

PAPUA NEW GUINEA
Education. (1980) Primary, pupils 288,287, teachers 9,280; secondary, pupils 37,068, teachers 1,559; vocational, pupils 3,992, teachers 261; teacher training, students 1,957, teachers 158; higher, students 2,637, teaching staff 419.
Finance. Monetary unit: kina, with (Sept. 20, 1982) a free rate of 0.77 kina to U.S. $1 (1.31 kinas = £1 sterling). Gold and other reserves (June 1982) U.S. $259 million. Budget (central government; 1980 actual): revenue 339.2 million kinas (excludes grants of 174.6 million kinas); expenditure 496.6 million kinas.
Foreign Trade. Imports (1980) 787 million kinas; exports (1981) 573 million kinas. Import sources: Australia 41%; Japan 18%; Singapore 15%; U.S. 6%. Export destinations (1980): Japan 35%; West Germany 25%; Australia 15%. Main exports: copper concentrates 49%; coffee 13%; cocoa 6%; coconut products 6%; timber c. 5%.
Transport. Roads (1976) 19,538 km. Motor vehicles in use (1980): passenger 18,480; commercial 27,140. There are no railways. Air traffic (1980): 520 million passenger-km; freight c. 10.2 million net ton-km. Shipping (1981): merchant vessels 100 gross tons and over 81; gross tonnage 27,723.
Agriculture. Production (in 000; metric tons; 1981): bananas c. 932; cassava c. 96; taro c. 250; yams c. 200; palm oil c. 44; cocoa 31; coffee c. 53; copra 144; tea c. 8; rubber c. 4; timber (cu m; 1980) c. 6,611. Livestock (in 000; 1981): cattle c. 132; pigs c. 1,410; goats c. 16; chickens c. 1,400.
Industry. Production (in 000; 1980): copper ore (metal content; metric tons) 147; silver (troy oz) 1,180; gold (troy oz) 452; electricity (kw-hr) 1,290,000.

PARAGUAY
Education. (1980) Primary, pupils 504,377, teachers 18,038; secondary and vocational, pupils 110,095, teachers 9,830; higher (universities only), students 25,232, teaching staff 1,984.
Finance. Monetary unit: guaraní, with (Sept. 20, 1982) an official rate of 126 guaranis to U.S. $1 (free rate of 216 guaranis = £1 sterling) and a noncommercial rate of 160 guaranis to U.S. $1 (free rate of 274 guaranis = £1 sterling). Gold and other reserves (June 1982) U.S. $795 million. Budget (1981 est.): revenue 63,778,000,000 guaranis; expenditure 65,843,000,000 guaranis. Gross national product (1981) 681.1 billion guaranis. Money supply (Feb. 1982) 58,623,000,000 guaranis. Cost of living (Asunción; 1975 = 100; Feb. 1982) 238.7.
Foreign Trade. (1981) Imports 75,567,000,000 guaranis; exports 37,238,000,000 guaranis. Import sources: Brazil 26%; Argentina 20%; U.S. 10%; Japan 8%; West Germany 8%; Algeria 5%; U.K. 5%. Export destinations: Argentina 23%; Brazil 18%; West Germany 11%; Japan 8%; Switzerland 5%; The Netherlands 5%. Main exports: cotton 44%; soybeans 16%; timber 12%; vegetable oils 8%.
Transport and Communications. Roads (1980) c. 15,000 km. Motor vehicles in use (1980): passenger 25,200; commercial 33,500. Railways: (main; 1980) 441 km; traffic (1977) 23 million passenger-km, freight 17 million net ton-km. Air traffic (1980): c. 262 million passenger-km; freight c. 2.8 million net ton-km. Navigable inland waterways (including Paraguay-Paraná River system; 1980) c. 3,000 km. Telephones (Dec. 1978) 48,000. Radio receivers (Dec. 1979) 186,000. Television receivers (Dec. 1979) 57,000.
Agriculture. Production (in 000; metric tons; 1981): corn c. 600; cassava c. 2,000; sweet potatoes c. 115; soybeans c. 600; dry beans c. 68; sugar, raw value c. 80; tomatoes c. 66; oranges c. 220; bananas c. 305; palm kernels c. 16; tobacco 9; cottonseed c. 208; cotton, lint c. 103; beef and veal c. 98. Livestock (in 000; 1981): cattle c. 5,400; sheep c. 430; pigs c. 1,310; horses c. 330; chickens c. 13,300.
Industry. Production (in 000; metric tons; 1980): cement 177; petroleum products (1979) c. 230; cotton yarn (1979) 73; electricity (kw-hr) 930,000.

Paper and Pulp:
see Industrial Review

Parachuting:
see Aerial Sports

bases, the military and the Partido Colorado, and no one had emerged who appeared able to continue the act. In general, the opposition remained divided. The four permitted extraparliamentary parties, which together formed a loose grouping known as the Acuerdo Nacional, seemed likely to run independently in the election. Despite the lack of an organized opposition, the government was anxious to prevent any focus of dissent from appearing in Paraguay. The authorities kept human rights advocate Adolfo Pérez Esquivel of Argentina, as well as a group of exiled Paraguayan politicians, from entering the country.

The economic slowdown continued throughout 1982. International reserves and exports fell, capital inflows slowed, and the balance of payments surplus evaporated. The start of the Yacyreta hydroelectric project, to be built jointly with Argentina, was delayed by that country's financial crisis, and expected revenues from the Itaipú reservoir were postponed by the lack of a high-tension line linking the project to São Paulo, Brazil.

(MICHAEL WOOLLER)

Peru

A republic on the west coast of South America, Peru is bounded by Ecuador, Colombia, Brazil, Bolivia, Chile, and the Pacific Ocean. Area: 1,285,215 sq km (496,224 sq mi). Pop. (1981 prelim.): 17,031,200, including (1978) approximately 50% whites and mestizos and 49% Indians. Cap. and largest city: Lima (metro. area pop., 1981 prelim., 4,600,900). Language: Spanish and Quechua are official; Indians also speak Aymara. Religion: Roman Catholic. President in 1982, Fernando Belaúnde Terry; prime ministers, Manuel Ulloa Elías until December 9 and Fernando Schwalb.

Terrorist activity in Peru, which began in 1980 when democracy was restored under Pres. Fernando Belaúnde Terry, reached new heights in 1982. Most of the attacks were attributed to the Maoist group Sendero Luminoso. In March an attack by 150 guerrillas on a prison in Ayacucho led to the breakout of some 250 prisoners. Subsequent guerrilla violence included dynamite and firebomb attacks in many parts of the country. In several provinces a state of emergency was imposed, lifted, and then reimposed in accordance with the fluctuating levels of violence. There was a lull in June, although bands of escaped prisoners carried out sporadic attacks on isolated villages. An intensification of terrorism followed in July and August. There was a spate of assassinations of local politicians and community leaders in the Ayacucho region, and in a night of violence in Lima and its port of Callao, electricity pylons were sabotaged, shops vandalized, and public buildings attacked. The guerrilla organization, which favoured small groups operating independently, proved difficult for the police to infiltrate. It had close links with the peasant community, but claims of foreign involvement remained unproved.

The economy remained depressed. Low prices for exports coupled with high international interest rates were detrimental to the balance of pay-

ALAIN KELER—SYGMA

ments. A trade deficit of up to $700 million and a current account deficit of at least $1.7 billion were anticipated. In July, after months of negotiations, the government signed a loan agreement with the International Monetary Fund (IMF) for $960 million over three years on condition that immediate steps be taken to introduce stringent austerity in public finance. Initially it was believed that the public sector deficit could be reduced to 4% of

Peruvian troops dressed in battle gear searched for guerrilla forces in the Ayacucho region of that country. Peru was plagued throughout the year with terrorist attacks.

PERU
Education. (1980) Primary, pupils 3,161,400, teachers (1978) 77,844; secondary, pupils 1,306,400, teachers (1978) 37,383; vocational, pupils 56,200; teacher training, pupils 145,900, teachers (1977) 6,422; higher, students 249,800, teaching staff (1978) 13,468.

Finance. Monetary unit: sol, with (Sept. 20, 1982) a free rate of 777 soles to U.S. $1 (1 333 soles = £1 sterling). Gold and other reserves (June 1982) U.S. $1,497,000,000. Budget (total; 1981 actual): revenue 1,522,500,000,000 soles; expenditure 1,938,600,000,000 soles. Gross national product (1981) 8,347,800,000,000 soles. Money supply (June 1982) 1,074,000,000,000 soles. Cost of living (Lima; 1975 = 100; June 1982) 2,136.

Foreign Trade. Imports (1980) 732,430,000,000 soles; exports (1981) 1,353,890,000,000 soles. Import sources: U.S. 37%; Japan 10%; West Germany 9%. Export destinations (1980): U.S. 34%; Japan 8%; West Germany 5%; Italy 5%. Main exports: petroleum and products 21%; copper 18%; silver 16%; lead 10%; fish 7%; zinc 6%; fish meal 5%.

Transport and Communications. Roads (1979) 58,516 km. Motor vehicles in use (1980): passenger c. 318,700; commercial (including buses) c. 169,900. Railways: (1979) 2,508 km; traffic (1977) 651 million passenger-km, freight 612 million net ton-km. Air traffic (1980): 1,974,000,000 passenger-km; freight c. 40.7 million net ton-km. Shipping (1981): merchant vessels 100 gross tons and over 694; gross tonnage 826,493. Telephones (Dec. 1979) 440,000. Radio receivers (Dec. 1979) 2.5 million. Television receivers (Dec. 1979) 850,000.

Agriculture. Production (in 000; metric tons; 1981): rice 712; corn 587; wheat c. 117; barley c. 160; potatoes c. 1,627; sweet potatoes c. 151; cassava c. 410; sugar, raw value c. 493; onions c. 152; oranges c. 152; lemons c. 91; coffee c. 95; cotton, lint c. 87; fish catch (1980) 2,731. Livestock (in 000; 1981) cattle 3,895; sheep c. 14,671; pigs 2,245; goats c. 1,950; horses c. 653; poultry c. 38,000.

Industry. Production (in 000; metric tons; 1980): cement c. 3,000; crude oil (1981) 9,527; natural gas (cu m; 1981) c. 950,000; iron ore (60% metal content) 5,730; pig iron 261; crude steel 471; copper 232; lead 88; zinc 62; tungsten concentrates (metal content) 0.6; gold (troy oz; 1981) c. 230; silver (troy oz; 1981) c. 43,400; fish meal 450; petroleum products (1979) c. 6,150; electricity (kw-hr) 9,805,000.

Peru

Penology:
see Prisons and Penology

Pentecostal Churches:
see Religion

gross domestic product (GDP), compared with 8.3% in 1981, but by August Prime Minister Manuel Ulloa Elías was admitting that it was likely to be around 9%.

Steps were taken to meet the conditions of the IMF loan. Cuts in spending on investment projects were difficult to implement, as many had been contracted one or two years previously, but the government aimed to save 270 billion soles by this means. Plans to reduce subsidies were also difficult because fuel and food price rises had already exacerbated social tensions and led to many strikes and wage claims. Nevertheless, the Cabinet announced further monthly increases of 10–12% in gasoline prices from August, saving 30 billion soles. The wheat subsidy was cut by lifting the control on the price of bread, and other food subsidies were reduced to save 40 billion soles. The government hoped to bring the deficit down to a more acceptable 6% of GDP. However, the spending cuts were expected to provoke a downturn in economic activity. An inflation rate of 65% was predicted, only marginally lower than the 1981 rate of 73%.

The government maintained its policy of opening the economy to more private investment and reducing the role of the state. Congress began debating legislation that proposed the sale of many state-owned companies, or the state's shareholding in mixed companies, to local or foreign investors. Faced by increasing economic difficulties, Prime Minister Ulloa resigned on December 9 and was replaced by Fernando Schwalb, formerly ambassador to Washington.

One of Peru's leading diplomats, Javier Pérez de Cuéllar (see BIOGRAPHIES), was appointed secretary-general of the UN in December 1981. President Belaúnde gained a reputation as an international mediator during the Falkland Islands dispute, but his peace plan was later rejected by the U.K. and Argentina.   (SARAH CAMERON)

Philately and Numismatics

Stamps. During an unsettled year, an important development concerned arrangements for the future of Stanley Gibbons International. The Swedish conglomerate Esselte disposed of the purely philatelic stock to a consortium of Gibbons directors headed by David Stokes, the managing director, who remained when Letraset (the owners since 1978) sold out to Esselte in 1981.

Values continued to slump for stamps in general but held up well for really rare stamps and exceptional pieces of postal history. The collapse was most marked in the 1977 and 1978 "omnibus" issues for the British Silver Jubilee and 25th anniversary of the coronation of Queen Elizabeth II. Auction prices for general collections and run-of-the-mill material reflected the downward trend.

A three-day Robson Lowe-Christies sale in Zürich, Switz., in May realized SFr 1,500,665 (£435,000); Swiss stamps accounted for SFr 119,278, with an 1849 Vaud 4-centime cantonal on cover selling at SFr 40,500. In London, Sotheby's philatelic department enjoyed outstanding progress handling, among other specialized properties,

the remarkable collection of Cape of Good Hope stamps formed by Sir Maxwell Joseph (see OBITUARIES). Sotheby's also sold a copy of the rare *Official History of Postage Stamps of Japan* (published by the Japanese Post Office in 1896) for a remarkable £1,700, a new record for a philatelic publication. A world record for a Chinese stamp, $44,000, was realized in May for the 1897 one-dollar (Chinese) postal surcharge on a three-cent revenue stamp at a George Alevizos sale held in Santa Monica, Calif. At Malmö, Sweden, in March, a record 9,680 kronor was paid at a Postiljonen AB auction for a Sperati forgery of the Swedish three skilling-banco error of colour.

The first International Philatelic Federation-sponsored international exhibitions to be held in India and Japan took place in New Delhi and Tokyo, respectively, at the end of 1981. The main awards at Tokyo were: Grand Prix d'Honneur, E. M. Bustamente (Spain) for Peru; Grand Prix International, G. Barcella (Italy) for Papal States; and Grand Prix National, Y. Watanabe (Japan) for Japan 1871–79. The major international exhibition, PHILEXFRANCE, was held in Paris in June 1982. The main awards were: Grand Prix d'Honneur, E. Antonini (Switz.) for specialized Egypt; Grand Prix International, "Vreneli" (Switz.) for Switzerland 1843–82; and Grand Prix National, F. Pineau (France) for French postal reform of 1848. At the British Philatelic Federation congress held in July at Southampton, two new signatories to the Roll of Distinguished Philatelists were Herman Branz (West Germany) and Bernard A. Henning (U.S.). The Philatelic Congress medal was awarded to Bernard Lucas of Leeds, England, and the Lichtenstein Medal of the Collectors Club of New York to Robert G. Stone of Blue Ridge Summit, Pa.

The newly formed Vincent Graves Greene Philatelic Research Foundation of Ottawa, Ont., published its first two books, one dealing with postal affairs of the Canadian contingents in the Boer War by Kenneth Rowe, the other on the stamps of Newfoundland 1857–66 by Robert H. Pratt. The conflict in the South Atlantic focused attention on Falkland Islands philately.

(KENNETH F. CHAPMAN)

Coins. The U.S. was one of several countries making major coinage changes in 1982 to reduce the cost of manufacturing money. In January U.S. Federal Reserve banks released into circulation the first Lincoln cents minted out of zinc plated with copper. By year's end government bureaucrats had discontinued production of the "traditional Lincolns," comprised mostly of copper, despite warnings of some experts that the new zinc coins would not wear well. Except for the wartime "steel pennies" of 1943, copper had been the primary metal used in all U.S. one-cent pieces since the federal government began issuing coins in 1793. The zinc cents looked almost identical to the traditional copper coins, but Treasury Department executives estimated that the new metal composition would save taxpayers at least $25 million annually.

The government also abandoned production of the Susan B. Anthony dollar coin following a three-year experiment that failed. The coins— made of copper and nickel—were supposed to re-

WIDE WORLD

A Roman gold coin, minted around the year 300, brought a record $120,000 at auction at Sotheby Parke Bernet in Zürich in July. It was the highest price ever paid at auction for an ancient coin.

Petroleum:
see Energy

Pharmaceutical Industry:
see Industrial Review

duce the demand for $1 bills, thus lowering government printing costs. However, most merchants and consumers refused to use the metal dollars, complaining that people mistook Anthonys for Washington quarters.

In another cost-cutting move, Canada introduced a 12-sided one-cent coin dated 1982 that contained about 10% less copper than the country's traditional round cent. Officials also replaced much of the nickel in Canada's five-cent piece with copper, making the 1982-dated coins cheaper to produce than the pure-nickel specimens minted from 1955 until 1981.

Artists in Great Britain prepared designs for a one-pound coin scheduled for introduction in April 1983. Undaunted by the failure of the Anthony dollar in the U.S., the British believed the coin would lessen demand for one-pound notes. Other countries also altered metal mixtures or issued new coins to soften the effect of inflation on money production.

Besides cutting costs with zinc cents, the U.S. Mint generated more than $45 million in revenue during 1982 by selling millions of commemorative half-dollars to collectors. The 1982-dated coins, the country's first commemorative halves since 1954, marked George Washington's 250th birthday by depicting a middle-aged Washington astride a horse. They were identical in size and metal composition to half-dollars made for circulation before 1965, the so-called 90% silver specimens. Each contained more than a third of an ounce of silver mixed with a much smaller amount of copper.

After months of debate, the U.S. Congress passed a bill authorizing three new coins to mark the 1984 Summer Olympics in Los Angeles. During 1983 and 1984 the Mint would produce and sell two types of silver dollars and a $10 gold piece, in part to raise money for the Olympics. The country had last struck a gold coin in 1933.

For persons owning rare coins as an investment, 1982 was a disappointment as prices plummeted. Almost no type of old coin—whether made with gold, silver, or base metal—escaped the downward price spiral. By year's end several numismatic collectibles were worth only half their value at the peak of the market boom in 1979 and early 1980. Still, over the past ten years, the annual return on the typical rare coin collection had been a robust 22.5%, according to a midsummer survey by a Wall street securities firm.   (ROGER BOYE)

[452.D.2.b; 725.B.4.g]

Philippines

Situated in the western Pacific Ocean off the southeast coast of Asia, the Republic of the Philippines consists of an archipelago of about 7,100 islands. Area: 300,000 sq km (115,800 sq mi). Pop. (1981 est.): 49,530,000. Cap. and largest city: Manila (pop., metro. area, 1980, 5,925,900). Language: Pilipino and English are the official languages. Pilipino, the national language, is based on a local language called Tagalog and is spoken by 55.2% of the population but only by 23.8% as a mother tongue. English is spoken by 44.7% of the popula-

Philippines

PHILIPPINES

Education. (1979–80) Primary, pupils 8,112,536, teachers 252,338; secondary and vocational, pupils 2,917,912; teachers (1978–79) 104,657; higher (1978–79), students 1,129,056, teaching staff 38,226.

Finance. Monetary unit: peso, with (Sept. 20, 1982) a free rate of 8.49 pesos to U.S. $1 (14.55 pesos = £1 sterling). Gold and other reserves (June 1982) U.S. $2,075,000,000. Budget (1981 actual): revenue 35,479,000,000 pesos; expenditure 38,880,000,000 pesos. Gross national product (1981) 305.5 billion pesos. Money supply (June 1982) 22,470,000,000 pesos. Cost of living (1975 = 100; June 1982) 214.8.

Foreign Trade. (1981) Imports 66,990,000,000 pesos; exports 44,621,000,000 pesos. Import sources (1980): U.S. 24%; Japan 20%; Saudi Arabia 10%; Kuwait 5%. Export destinations (1980): U.S. 28%; Japan 26%; The Netherlands 6%. Main exports (1979): coconut oil 16%; metal ores 16%; fruit and vegetables 9%; clothing 9%; electrical equipment 9%; timber 8%; sugar 5%. Tourism (1980): visitors 1,008,200; gross receipts U.S. $320 million.

Transport and Communications. Roads (1979) 127,150 km. Motor vehicles in use (1979): passenger 470,800; commercial (including buses) 419,800. Railways: (main; 1980) 1,177 km; traffic (1981) 254 million passenger-km, freight 33 million net ton-km. Air traffic (1981): c. 6,680,000,000 passenger-km; freight c. 197 million net ton-km. Shipping (1981): merchant vessels 100 gross tons and over 827; gross tonnage 2,539,817. Telephones (Jan. 1980) 519,600. Radio receivers (Dec. 1979) 2,100,000. Television receivers (Dec. 1979) 1,000,000.

Agriculture. Production (in 000; metric tons; 1981): rice 7,720; corn 3,176; sweet potatoes c. 1,100; cassava c. 2,300; sugar, raw value 2,394; bananas c. 4,000; pineapples c. 1,200; copra c. 2,275; coffee c. 140; tobacco c. 50; rubber c. 65; pork c. 432; fish catch (1980) 1,557; timber (cu m; 1980) 35,213. Livestock (in 000; March 1981): cattle c. 1,900; buffalo c. 2,850; pigs c. 8,000; goats c. 1,500; horses c. 320; chickens c. 55,000.

Industry. Production (in 000; metric tons; 1981): coal 364; cement 4,007; chrome ore (oxide content; 1980) c. 200; copper ore (metal content) 564; gold (troy oz) c. 800; silver (troy oz; 1980) 2,114; petroleum products (1980) c. 9,400; sulfuric acid (1979) 210; cotton yarn (1980) 38; electricity (kw-hr) c. 19,100,000.

tion but only by 0.04% as a mother tongue. Other important languages spoken as mother tongues include Cebuano 24.4%, Ilocano 11.1%, Hiligaynon 8%, Bicol 7%. Religion (1970): Roman Catholic 85%; Muslim 4.3%; Aglipayan 3.9%; Protestant 3.1%. President in 1982, Ferdinand E. Marcos; prime minister, Cesar Virata.

The National Assembly passed, and Pres. Ferdinand E. Marcos signed into law on Sept. 11, 1982, a bill providing for the succession in case of the president's "permanent disability, death, removal from office or resignation." It gave succession pow-

Imelda Marcos was sworn in by her husband, Philippine Pres. Ferdinand E. Marcos, to a post on that nation's new Executive Committee.

SHOOTERS

ers to a 15-member Executive Committee, headed by Prime Minister Cesar Virata.

Marcos named his wife, Imelda, and his eldest daughter, Imee, to the committee. Mrs. Marcos was already minister for human development and the governor of greater Manila, where a fifth of the nation's people lived. Imee headed the National Youth Movement. The appointments strengthened speculation that Marcos intended his wife to succeed him. He said, however, that "she is not going to be my successor" but that she would be needed to help a successor.

Marcos, president since 1966, said that he intended to ask the New Society Movement, the nation's dominant political party, to find another candidate for president when his term ended in 1987. He added that an emergency or party pressure could make him decide to seek reelection.

Nationwide elections were held May 17 for 280,000 members of 40,000 barangay (village council) units. After more than eight years of martial law, this was a step back toward elective government, to be followed by National Assembly elections in 1984 and the 1987 presidential election. Legislative assemblies were elected June 7 for autonomous regions created for Muslims in the south. Voter turnout was poor, and the government party candidates prevailed.

Political opponents of Marcos united in February as the United Nationalist Democratic Organization. It called for restoring political freedom, which it accused Marcos of suppressing; justice for the oppressed; and economic development. Marcos said on August 8 that his opponents were conspiring to stage nationwide bombings, assassinations, and strikes in September while he visited the U.S. Labour leaders were particular targets of a crackdown. By early September, 39 had been arrested and 42 others accused of plots. From September 15 to 27 Marcos made his first state visit to the U.S. since 1966. He was accorded a cordial reception by Pres. Ronald Reagan, but some Filipinos in the U.S. demonstrated against him.

The government searched for ways to get the country out of its worst economic situation in more than a decade. The 1983 budget was austere, offering little hope of breaking out of deficits or improving living standards unless worldwide demand for the Philippines' primary products (coconut oil, metal ores, fruit and vegetables) increased significantly.

Economic problems contributed to continued growth of the New People's Army, a Communist guerrilla force. The president of the National Defense College estimated that 20% of the nation's villages were under NPA control or soon would be. One government tactic for combating guerrillas, a program of village relocation under which some 100,000 persons had been gathered into 35 strategic settlements on Mindanao Island, was abandoned because of human rights complaints.

Sporadic insurgency operations by Muslim separatists in the southern islands continued to cause bloodshed. The separatists' Moro National Liberation Front intensified efforts to win political backing from Muslim countries but had little success.   (HENRY S. BRADSHER)

Photography

The introduction of Eastman Kodak's new Disc camera-and-film system highlighted 1982 for the world photographic industry, which severely felt the pinch of a continuing recession in Japan and Europe as well as in the United States. Also adversely affected were the collector's market of photography as fine art and the galleries and dealers who depended on it. Despite these problems the number and quality of photographic exhibitions and books were unusually high, although they more often drew upon the past than upon contemporary achievements.

Photo Equipment. By far the most outstanding event in photography for mass consumers was Kodak's introduction in February of its ultraminiature-format Disc system, the result of a long and intense research-and-development effort.

Heart of the system was a wafer-thin disk containing 15 tiny (8×10-mm; 0.3×0.4-in) radially arranged frames of a new high-resolution ISO (ASA) 200 Kodacolor HR Disc film. Three models of Disc cameras, the 4000, 6000, and 8000, were all small and flat enough to slip into a shirt pocket and incorporated a sophisticated 12.5-mm $f/2.8$ four-element glass lens, a built-in flash with a recycling time of about one second, lithium batteries with a claimed life expectancy under normal amateur use of five years, and automatic film advance. As a further attempt to supply what Kodak termed "decision-free" photography, the Disc cameras provided a bright-light exposure of 1/200 sec at $f/6$ but automatically switched to the flash mode, with an exposure of 1/100 sec at $f/2.8$, when the light level dropped sufficiently. In addition, the 6000 and 8000 models included a built-in close-up lens that provided a minimum shooting distance of 46 cm (18 in). The top-of-the-line 8000 also had a self-timer, rapid-sequence film advance, and digital alarm clock.

By year's end other models of the Disc camera had been introduced by manufacturers in Europe and the Far East under Kodak license arrangements, many of which omitted some of the high-technology convenience features of the Kodak models. Kodak hoped that the Disc system would reinvigorate the mass market of snapshooters as the introduction of its 126 and 110 cameras had done before. The initial response was hopeful: late in the year Kodak announced that it had sold more than eight million Disc cameras and that sales were exceeding those of the 110 for the same period following the latter's introduction.

Sales of 35-mm single-lens-reflex cameras (SLR's) declined as a result of overproduction, saturated markets, recession, and shifts in the international monetary exchange rates, but important developments continued. Nikon introduced its FM2 SLR with a titanium focal-plane shutter providing speeds to 1/4,000 sec and electronic flash synchronization at an unusually fast 1/200 sec.

Continued attempts were made to provide sensitive, fast-responding autofocusing and autofocus aids for interchangeable-lens 35-mm cameras.

Canon incorporated its own CCD (charge-coupled device) technology in the Canon AL-1, an aperture-priority 35-mm SLR that provided three focus indicators visible in the viewfinder: a green dot that lit when the focus was correct and two red arrows to indicate which way to turn the lens if the subject was out of focus. Nikon introduced a modified Nikon F3 autofocusing camera and two specially designed lenses, an 80-mm *f*/2.8 and a 200-mm *f*/3.5. When the new lenses were used with the F3 AF, full autofocusing was provided. With conventional Nikon lenses, autofocus aid was supplied.

Olympus was the last of the major Japanese 35-mm SLR makers to bring forth an autofocus model, the OM-30 (OM-F in the U.S.). This camera used the Honeywell TCL (through-camera-lens) focus-detecting module to provide full autofocus with a new 35–70-mm *f*/4 autofocusing zoom lens and autofocus aid with conventional Olympus lenses.

Anxious to keep their highly automated factories busy, major Japanese camera manufacturers introduced dozens of compact, fixed-lens, leaf-shutter 35-mm cameras with numerous convenience features including built-in flash, power film advance and rewind, automatic exposure, and autofocus. Canon dramatically led the way with its line of Snappy compacts available in several colours and set to challenge Kodak's Disc system by offering nearly equivalent decision-free photography plus the advantage of 35-mm film format at a competitive price.

The year's unusually large number of innovations and technical developments in silver-image sensitized materials was led by Kodak's remarkable ISO 1000 Kodacolor negative film, which provided unprecedented speed with moderate grain. The key to this accomplishment was a new type of light-sensitive silver halide grain that was wafer-flat rather than chunky. Called T-grain (T for "tablet"), the new emulsion was expected to lead to other high-speed films and printing papers.

Polaroid demonstrated a unique rapid-process 35-mm colour transparency film, Polachrome, plus high-contrast and continuous-tone black-and-white instant emulsions. The materials were used like conventional film in any 35-mm camera, but they could be fully developed and ready for mounting and projection about 1½ minutes after exposure with provided chemicals and a crank-operated processing unit.

Kodak augmented its Ektaflex colour printing system with a new material, Ektaflex PCT Reversal Film, designed for the rapid production of colour prints from positive transparencies. Agfa announced a rival, even simpler system based on Agfaspeed, a positive-to-positive printing material that developed within 1½ minutes in any tray or processing tube and required only a single-bath activator solution plus a water rinse.

During the year Sony gave public demonstrations of a Mavigraph system for producing colour prints from its prototype all-electronic Mavica camera. Innovative as the Sony concept was, the Mavica was still far from being a practical, available item. Concentrating first on perfecting a black-and-white model for professional use by journalists, Sony maintained a low public profile in this respect during the year. At the trade fair Photokina held in Cologne, West Germany, in October, Kodak demonstrated its potential for creating interfaces between conventional and electronic photography with a device that converted Kodak Disc photographs into images on a colour television screen. Using a 350,000-pixel image-sensing chip developed in Kodak's own laboratories, the unit allowed one to zoom in on the image and reframe it by shifting to the left or right. The data could then be encoded on the film disk's magnetic core to automatically guide a photofinishing machine in making a print according to the customer's directions.

Cultural Trends. The market for photographic prints, which had begun to soften in the previous year, was severely affected in 1982. A number of galleries found themselves in serious financial difficulties, while others, including New York City's Light Gallery and Photograph Gallery, were forced to close their doors. Print prices at major auctions were erratic. Although the work of 19th-century masters and some contemporary photographers continued to fetch high prices, other work dropped. The volume generally was down, and a number of photographs were withdrawn because they did not meet the minimum bid.

Despite this clear farewell to art photography's great boom of the 1970s, an unusually large number of high-quality, well-reproduced photograph-

JACK MANNING/THE NEW YORK TIMES

One of the hottest new photographic items of the year was Eastman Kodak's pocket-sized Disc camera, which incorporates a wide-angle lens system and a wafer-thin disk containing 15 tiny film frames.

ic books were published. Many were retrospective collections of photographers, including Berenice Abbott, Dorothea Lange, Philippe Halsman, Jerry N. Uelsmann, and Wright Morris. *Hungarian Memories* included delightful early photographs, many never before published, by André Kertész. The second in a four-part series on *The Work of Atget*, titled *The Art of Old Paris*, carried that major project a step further. *Extraordinary Landscape* reproduced stunning aerial colour photographs of America by William Garnett, and Beaumont Newhall's classic *The History of Photography* appeared in a revised and enlarged edition.

Among the year's more ambitious photographic exhibitions was "Color as Form," a major attempt to trace the medium's evolution and define its function, mounted by the International Museum of Photography at George Eastman House in Rochester, N.Y. "The Frozen Image," which opened at the Walker Art Center in Minneapolis, Minn., was the first comprehensive overview of Scandinavian photography from its beginnings to be shown in the U.S. The work of contemporary Chinese photographers, also seen in the U.S. for the first time, included "China from Within," which opened at the National Academy of Sciences in Washington, D.C., and "The Face of China," the latter in connection with the first U.S. visit by a cultural delegation from the Chinese Photographers Association. "Subway," a powerful new documentary work by Bruce Davidson, opened at the International Center of Photography in New York City. An unusual photojournalistic project, organized by American Rick Smolan and Australian Andy Park, brought 100 photographers from all over the world to photograph "A Day in the Life of Australia" and resulted in an impressive picture book and a major exhibition at the International Center of Photography.

The 1982 Pulitzer Prize for spot news photography went to Ron Edmonds of the Associated Press for his coverage of the assassination attempt against U.S. Pres. Ronald Reagan and for feature photography to John H. White of the *Chicago Sun-Times*. Among top winners of the 1982 Pictures of the Year awards, co-sponsored by the University of Missouri School of Journalism and the National Press Photographers Association, were Dan Dry of the *Louisville* (Ky.) *Courier-Journal* and *Louisville Times* as Newspaper Photographer of the Year and Harry Benson of *Life* magazine as Magazine Photographer of the Year; winner of the World Understanding Award was Cincinnati free-lancer Gordon Baer for his photographic report on "Vietnam: The Battle Comes Home." The Hasselblad Foundation Award for photography went to Frenchman Henri Cartier-Bresson.

(ARTHUR GOLDSMITH)

See also Motion Pictures.
[628.D; 735.G.1]

Physics

Laser Physics. Three major physical characteristics differentiate the laser from other light sources. First, laser light is emitted in a narrow beam that diverges only very slowly. Second, the radiation is monochromatic; that is, for all practical purposes, of a single frequency. This quality accounts for the characteristic colour of lasers that emit in the visible region of the electromagnetic spectrum: red for the helium-neon laser, blue or green for the argon laser, and so on. Third, laser light is coherent; in other words, all the peaks and troughs of its component wave trains are aligned in phase with each other.

In addition to these major advantages, the appropriate laser design allows the production of laser light in the form of pulses rather than as a continuous wave. These pulses are normally much shorter than a second in duration and can have considerably higher peak power than continuous-wave emission. A typical approach would be to "pump" a solid laser rod with intense bursts of light from a flash tube to stimulate the output of the laser pulse. Yttrium-aluminum-garnet (YAG) crystal doped with the rare earth neodymium (Nd) is a suitable material for a laser rod, and a typical pulse from a Nd-YAG laser is of the order of ten nanoseconds (one-hundredth of a millionth of a second). In the early 1980s standard techniques were available to decrease this time to a few picoseconds (a millionth of a millionth of a second).

These very intense, very short pulses of light have many possible applications, ranging from the cutting and welding of metals to the study of the kinetics of chemical reactions. For some studies in chemical kinetics the shorter the light pulse, the more precisely controlled is the experiment and the less ambiguous are the results. In 1982 brevity achieved a new meaning at Bell Laboratories in the U.S., where C. V. Shank and co-workers generated the shortest ever flash of laser light and therefore the "fastest act of man." Their laser pulse lasted for 30 femtoseconds, or 0.03 picoseconds. The experimenters put such a small period of time into perspective in the following way: in one second a light beam can travel from the Earth to the Moon and back; in 30 femtoseconds light travels about ten micrometres, or one-tenth the thickness of a human hair.

With light pulses this short it might be possible to study in far more detail not only the result of a chemical reaction but also the reaction itself while it is in progress. Applications for picosecond-pulse lasers had grown rapidly in recent years, and it was expected that the femtosecond laser soon would become yet another useful tool for the spectroscopist, the reaction chemist, the medical physicist, the metallurgist, and many other specialists.

Magnetic Monopole. Magnetism has intrigued scientists since the discovery many centuries ago that a naturally occurring form of iron oxide, lodestone, was magnetic. Today schoolchildren study the permanent magnet with its one north pole and one south pole and are taught that like poles repel whereas unlike poles attract.

The origin of these magnetic effects, in the electric charge of the electron, is also well understood. The orbiting electron carries its charge around the nucleus of the atom and, as such, is equivalent to a current loop. It therefore develops a magnetic moment normal to the plane of the loop. The orbiting electron will appear as a very weak, permanent magnet and will, for example, swing like a compass needle under the influence of an external magnetic field. Since an orbiting electron is the fundamental origin of magnetism and since an orbiting electron produces a small magnet with north and south poles, the two poles seem to be only parts of an indivisible whole. This picture of inseparability was firmly supported for many years.

In 1931 the picture changed. British physicist P. A. M. Dirac was studying the theoretical aspects of electromagnetism, and in explaining why the electron had the minimum allowable charge, a single quantum, he found it necessary to propose a particle with a single quantum of magnetic charge, which became known as the magnetic monopole. Subsequent theoretical work considerably resolved scientists' idea of what the monopole must be like. Dirac was able to deduce its strength, and much more recently its mass was estimated to be about 10^{16} times the mass of the proton. Nevertheless, despite considerable experimental effort direct observation of this particle remained elusive. Because of its heavy mass, searches for the magnetic monopole had been carried out, for example, in the depths of the deepest underwater gorges and in the middle of some of the oldest and densest rocks on Earth—all unsuccessfully until a report in April 1982 by Blas Cabrera of Stanford University that a single monopole appeared to have been detected in his laboratory.

The experiment performed by Cabrera was centred around a monopole detector consisting of a superconducting ring of four turns of niobium wire. When cooled to a few degrees above absolute zero by liquid helium the wire loses all electrical resistance, allowing a current to flow indefinitely in the coil. This current will not decay even though no external power is supplied.

Quantum theory shows that the current in the ring can only have "allowed" quantized values that are separated by a forbidden gap. Another way of stating this is that the magnetic flux produced by the current in the ring is quantized and increases in quantum jumps of $hc/2e$. In this expression h is Planck's fundamental constant, c is the velocity of light, and e is the charge on the electron. This value is exactly one-half the magnetic flux produced by Dirac's monopole: hc/e. Therefore, if a monopole were to pass through just a one-turn coil, the current in the coil would be changed immediately by two flux quanta. If the monopole passed through the detector's four-turn coil, it should produce a change equivalent to eight flux quanta. Cabrera monitored his detector for more than 200 days and during that time observed one change in current that corresponded to the passage of a single monopole to an accuracy of ±5%.

There are many other possible causes of such jumps in current, and Cabrera took great care to eliminate all of them. He argued that effects due to voltage fluctuations, radio-frequency interference, external magnetic fields, ferromagnetic contamination, mechanical effects, earthquakes, and cosmic rays could all be discounted. Nevertheless, he pointed out that a possible effect due to the

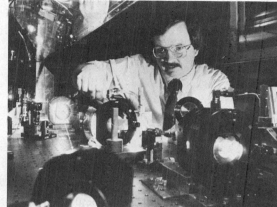

The smallest slice of measurable time ever created was developed by C. V. Shank and co-workers at Bell Laboratories in Phoenix. The laser device creates a burst of light just 30 femtoseconds long—30 millionths of a billionth of a second. The incredible "stop watch" is used to study fundamental changes in nature.

release of internal stresses in the coils could not be ruled out. As an indication of the experimental sophistication required, the measurements had to be made in very low and stable background magnetic fields, and a field of 5×10^{-8} gauss was achieved. This is 10,000,000 times weaker than the Earth's field.

Given the diameter of the detector loop (five centimetres) and making certain assumptions, one can calculate the maximum expected number of monopoles passing through the loop in a particular period of time. First one must calculate how many monopoles there could possibly be in the Galaxy. The total mass of the Galaxy can be estimated from a study of the motion of its various parts, while the visible mass—the stars, gas, and dust that astronomers actually see—can be estimated from direct observation. The visible mass turns out to be less than the total galactic mass, and therefore the difference between the two estimates gives an upper limit to the total mass of monopoles in the Galaxy (assuming that all of the invisible mass is due to monopoles). Estimates of the mass of one monopole then allows one to calculate the maximum number.

Carrying through this analysis yields a maximum of three monopoles passing through a five-centimetre coil every two years. One would surmise that Cabrera was rather fortunate to have made an observation in only 200 days. The statistics would soon be put to the test since the experiment was to be repeated with a ring having a much larger detection area, which should be penetrated by a monopole every 15 days. The great assumption of course is that all the unseen mass of the Galaxy rests in monopoles, an unlikely possibility. Hence one should expect the average interval between observations to be more than 15 days.

Physicists working in magnetism, however, remained unruffled by all of this excitement. Confirmation of the existence of the monopole would hardly solve their problems. In 1982 details of the origins of magnetism in two of the most fundamental magnetic materials, the elements iron and nickel, were still not understood. Indeed they were the basis of an enthralling controversy. Is the magnetism produced by electrons that are mainly localized around their parent atom? Or, on the other hand, is it the electrons that are free to wander through the metal, the conduction electrons, that are responsible? What actually happens to iron and nickel when they are heated to a temperature at which the overall magnetism is destroyed? Do the atoms still have magnetic moments that interact with their neighbours or not? These and other questions would continue to be studied in years to come. (S. B. PALMER)

See also Nobel Prizes.
[111.H.7; 127.C.2; 127.C.5; 128.B.4]

Poland

Poland

A people's republic of Eastern Europe, Poland is bordered by the Baltic Sea, the U.S.S.R., Czechoslovakia, and East Germany. Area: 312,683 sq km (120,727 sq mi). Pop. (1982 est.): 36,062,000. Cap. and largest city: Warsaw (pop., 1982 est., 1,611,600). Language: Polish. Religion: predominantly Roman Catholic. First secretary of the Polish United Workers' (Communist) Party and chairman of the Council of Ministers (premier) in 1982, Gen. Wojciech Jaruzelski; chairman of the Council of State, Henryk Jablonski.

At the end of another eventful year for Poland, on Dec. 12, 1982, Gen. Wojciech Jaruzelski announced the "suspension" of martial law, which had been in force since Dec. 13, 1981, promising to remove all its restrictions as soon as he was able to judge that the "enemy" was totally crushed. A month before, Lech Walesa, leader of the independent trade union Solidarnosc (Solidarity), had been released from his almost year-long detention; at the same time, there were indications that the Polish Roman Catholic hierarchy, in the interest of public order, might be prepared to modify its support for Solidarity in favour of some 2,000 new labour unions that the government intended should become operational on Jan. 1, 1983, and to which Solidarity's assets were to be transferred.

According to Jaruzelski, who besides being first secretary of the Polish United Workers' (Communist) Party (PUWP) was also head of the Military Council of National Salvation and premier, the "enemy" included the people who had organized a "counterrevolution" directed against the Polish "socialist statehood" and the Polish-Soviet alliance. In his speeches and press interviews during 1982 General Jaruzelski constantly reiterated the importance of the Polish-Soviet alliance, describing it as "the cornerstone of Poland's security."

Not only Polish Communists—a minority of the Polish nation—recognized the soundness of this statement. Poles dwelling in the basins of the Vistula and Oder rivers understood that the existing resolution of Poland's long-standing conflict with Germany was a matter of common interest to both Poland and the U.S.S.R. That major consideration explained why Soviet rulers of the post-Stalin era, starting with Nikita Khrushchev, reconciled themselves with the existence of two anomalies differentiating Poland from other members of the Soviet bloc: first, that 70% of Poland's agricultural land was still privately owned by 2.9 million farmers who were responsible for 80% of the nation's total agricultural production; second, that the spiritual influence of the Roman Catholic Church remained strong. Instead of drawing the present Soviet rulers' attention to the importance of accepting a third anomaly—making "socialist statehood" popular among the ten million Polish workers who had joined Solidarity—Jaruzelski had accepted Leonid Brezhnev's advice that the movement must be crushed.

Despite the proclamation of martial law, strikes and violent confrontations continued during 1982. During clashes in Gdansk at the end of January, 205 demonstrators were arrested; two weeks later 194 were arrested in Poznan, including many students, after the reopening of the universities on February 8. By mid-February some 4,000 faced charges for breaches of martial law. Meanwhile, social and economic conditions worsened; there were severe food shortages and price increases of up to 400%.

During March–June Jaruzelski visited all the Warsaw Pact capitals in turn, starting in Moscow on March 1. Brezhnev praised Jaruzelski for "pulling his country out of a protracted and excruciating crisis," adding: "Had the Communists given way to counterrevolution, then the destiny of Poland and stability in Europe and in the world at large would have been jeopardized." In reply Jaruzelski, thanking the U.S.S.R. for its support, said that "the Soviet armed forces, together with the armies of the Warsaw Treaty member states, are the principal guarantee of the security and territorial

Polish riot police used tear gas to disperse demonstrators in Gdansk who gathered in August to mark the second anniversary of the Solidarity trade union. (Right) Lech Walesa, leader of the outlawed union, was released from detention in November.

C.A.F./WIDE WORLD

UPI

Education. (1981–82) Primary, pupils 4,341,800, teachers 224,500; secondary, pupils 392,900, teachers 22,500; vocational, pupils 1,692,000, teachers 82,300; teacher training, students 37,000; higher, students 386,500; teacher training and higher, teaching staff 55,450.

Finance. Monetary unit: zloty, with (Sept. 20, 1982) a commercial and tourist rate of 87.16 zlotys to U.S. $1 (149.43 zlotys = £1 sterling). Budget (1980 est.): revenue 1,215,200,000,000 zlotys; expenditure 1,141,700,000,000 zlotys. Net material product (1980) 1,936,200,000,000 zlotys.

Foreign Trade. (1981) Imports 52,013,000,000 exchange zlotys; exports 44,530,000,000 exchange zlotys. Import sources: U.S.S.R. 34%; West Germany 7%; U.S. 6%; East Germany 6%; Czechoslovakia 5%; France 5%. Export destinations: U.S.S.R. 26%; West Germany 10%; East Germany 6%; Czechoslovakia 6%. Main exports: machinery 38%; transport equipment 10%; chemicals 9%; coal 6%.

Transport and Communications. Roads (1980) 298,512 km (including 139 km expressways). Motor vehicles in use (1980): passenger 2,383,000; commercial 617,800. Railways: (1980) 24,356 km (including 6,868 km electrified); traffic (1981) 48,239,-000,000 passenger-km, freight 109,861,000,000 net ton-km. Air traffic (1981): 2,142,000,000 passenger-km; freight (1980) 18,793,000 net ton-km. Navigable inland waterways in regular use (1980) 2,878 km. Shipping (1981): merchant vessels 100 gross tons and over 827; gross tonnage 3,579,081. Telephones (Dec. 1980) 3,387,400. Radio licenses (Dec. 1980) 8,666,000. Television licenses (Dec. 1980) 7,954,000.

Agriculture. Production (in 000; metric tons; 1981): wheat 4,203; rye 6,731; barley 3,575; oats 2,731; potatoes 42,600; sugar, raw value 1,872; rapeseed 488; cabbages c. 1,600; onions c. 400; tomatoes c. 350; carrots c. 549; cucumbers c. 400; apples c. 800; tobacco c. 81; butter c. 280; cheese c. 386; hen's eggs 494; beef and veal c. 539; pork c. 1,350; fish catch (1980) 640; timber (cu m; 1980) 21,406. Livestock (in 000; June 1981): cattle c. 11,801; pigs c. 18,487; sheep c. 4,100; horses c. 1,780; chickens (adult birds) c. 80,959.

Industry. Index of industrial production (1975 = 100; 1981) 111. Fuel and power (in 000; metric tons; 1981): coal 162,960; brown coal 35,538; coke (1980) 19,800; crude oil c. 300; natural gas (cu m) 6,270,000; manufactured gas (cu m; 1980) 7,602,000; electricity (kw-hr) 115,006,000. Production (in 000; metric tons; 1981): cement 14,225; pig iron 9,351; crude steel 15,718; aluminum (1980) 95; copper (1980) 358; lead (1980) 82; zinc (1980) 217; petroleum products (1980) c. 14,800; sulfuric acid 2,775; plastics and resins 590; fertilizers (nutrient content; 1980) nitrogenous 1,290, phosphate 843; cotton yarn 195; wool yarn 88; man-made fibres 182; cotton fabrics (m) 783,000; woolen fabrics (m) 106,000; passenger cars (units) 240; commercial vehicles (units) 48. Merchant vessels launched (100 gross tons and over; 1981) 350,000 gross tons. New dwelling units completed (1980) 217,100.

integrity of Poland, based on the Yalta and Potsdam agreements." Speeches in the other five Communist capitals reflected similar sentiments.

In the meantime, Solidarity leaders who had escaped the December 1981 roundup formed an underground Coordination Commission, which started organizing demonstrations against martial law. These continued throughout the summer and included a mass gathering in Poznan to mark the anniversary of the 1956 riots that had preceded the advent to power as PUWP secretary-general of Wladyslaw Gomulka (see OBITUARIES). The demonstrations culminated in a series of violent confrontations with security forces in Warsaw and other towns at the end of August, marking the second anniversary of Solidarity's birth as a union. During the summer four workers were killed. On October 5 the authorities announced the arrest of Wladyslaw Frasyniuk, one of the leading Solidarity underground organizers. Then on October 8 the Sejm (parliament) passed an act dissolving all registered trade unions including Solidarity; out of 460 deputies, 10 voted against and 9 abstained.

Underground Solidarity's response to the ban was to call for an eight-hour general strike and public protest meetings on November 10. However, on November 8 Archbishop Jozef Glemp, Roman Catholic primate of Poland, had talks with Jaruzelski, after which it was announced that Pope John Paul II was to be invited to pay a second official visit to Poland in June 1983. The talks were said to have centred on the "common concern" of the church and the government over the trend of events. Before the talks Archbishop Glemp had made it clear that the church would not support street demonstrations. Hedged by massive security measures, the November 10 protest strike was a failure. The following day it was announced that Walesa was being released from his internment as a "private person."

In an interview that Polish state television had taped just before his release, Walesa stated that he wanted a "fair, proper agreement" with the government. On December 18 the Sejm voted unanimously for the suspension of martial law already announced by Jaruzelski six days earlier. But there were nine abstentions when it approved measures

maintaining a tight grip on vital sectors of the economy. Archbishop Glemp sent to the Council of State a letter complaining, in the name of the Roman Catholic hierarchy, of the "repressive" nature of the measures. On December 23 all the remaining 250 or so of those detained when martial law was promulgated were released, with the exception of seven Solidarity leaders who remained under formal arrest.

On November 4 the representatives of 500 Western banks and heads of the Polish state bank signed in Vienna an agreement on the new spread of Poland's financial commitments for 1982, amounting to $3.4 billion.

(K. M. SMOGORZEWSKI)

Political Parties

The following table is a general world guide to political parties. All countries that were independent on Dec. 31, 1982, are included; there are a number for which no analysis of political activities can be given. Parties are included in most instances only if represented in parliaments (in the lower house in bicameral legislatures); the figures in the last column indicate the number of seats obtained in the last general election (figures in parentheses are those of the penultimate one). The date of the most recent election follows the name of the country.

The code letters in the affiliation column show the relative political positions of the parties within each country; there is, therefore, no entry in this column for single-party states. There are obvious difficulties involved in labeling parties within the political spectrum of a given country. The key chosen is as follows: F-fascist; ER-extreme right; R-right; CR-centre right; C-centre; L-non-Marxist left; SD-social democratic; S-socialist; EL-extreme left; and K-Communist.

The percentages in the column "Voting strength" indicate proportions of the valid votes cast for the respective parties, or the number of registered voters who went to the polls in single-party states.

[541.D.2]

Pipelines:
see Energy; Transportation

Plastics Industry:
see Industrial Review

Poetry:
see Literature

Police:
see Crime and Law Enforcement

Country and Name of Party	Affiliation	Voting strength (%)	Parliamentary representation
Afghanistan			
Pro-Soviet government since April 27, 1978	—	—	—
Albania (November 1982)			
Albanian Labour (Communist)	—	99.9	250 (250)
Algeria (March 1982)			
National Liberation Front	—	99.9	281 (261)
Angola (August 1980)			
Movimento Popular de Libertaçao de Angola (MPLA)	—	—	203
Antigua and Barbuda (April 1980)			
Antigua Labour Party	C	59.0	13 (11)
Progressive Labour Movement	L	...	3 (5)
Independents		...	1 (1)
Argentina			
Military junta since March 24, 1976	—	—	—
Australia (November 1980)			
National Country	R	8.7	20 (19)
Liberal	C	37.5	54 (67)
Australian Labor	L	45.4	51 (38)
Other		1.9	0 (0)
Austria (May 1979)			
Freiheitliche Partei Österreichs	R	6.06	11 (10)
Österreichische Volkspartei	C	41.90	77 (80)
Sozialistische Partei Österreichs	SD	51.03	95 (93)
Bahamas, The (June 1982)			
Progressive Liberal Party	CR	53	32 (30)
Free National Movement	L	43	8 (2)
Others	—	...	3 ...
Bahrain			
Emirate, no parties	—	—	—
Bangladesh			
On March 24 Gen. Hossain Ershad seized power from the civilian government			
Barbados (June 1981)			
Democratic Labour	C	47.1	10 (7)
Barbados Labour	L	52.2	17 (17)
Belgium (November 1981)			
Vlaams Blok	ER	...	1 (1)
Volksunie	R	...	20 (14)
Front Démocratique Francophone/ Rassemblement Wallon	R	...	8 (15)
Parti Libéral { Flemish	CR	...	28 (22)
{ Wallon	CR	...	24 (15)
Parti Social-Chrétien { Flemish	C	...	43 (57)
{ Wallon	C	...	18 (25)
Parti Socialiste Belge { Flemish	SD	...	26 (26)
{ Wallon	SD	...	35 (32)
Parti Communiste	K	...	2 (4)
Others	—	...	7 (1)
Belize (November 1979)			
United Democratic Party	R	46.8	5 (6)
People's United Party	C	51.8	13 (12)
Benin (November 1979)			
People's Revolutionary Party	—	—	336
Bhutan			
A monarchy without parties	—	—	—
Bolivia (June 1980)			
Movimiento Nacionalista Revolucionario	R	20.1	44 (43)
Unidad Democrática y Popular	C	38.7	57 (37)
Acción Democrática Nacionalista	L	15.0	...
Five other parties	—	...	...
Botswana (October 1979)			
Botswana Democratic Party	C	...	29 (27)
Botswana People's Party	L	...	1 (2)
Botswana National Front	EL	...	2 (2)
Brazil (November 1982)			
Movimento Democrático Brasileiro	CR	44.1	208
Partido Democrático Social	C	39.4	229
Democratic Labour Party	S	6.7	24
Brazilien Labour Party	S	5.5	13
Workers' Party	EL	4.3	7
Bulgaria (June 1981)			
Fatherland Front { Bulgarian Communist Party	} 99.9	271	400 (400)
{ Bulgarian Agrarian Union		99	
{ No party affiliation		30	
Burma (October 1981)			
Burma Socialist Program Party	—	99.0	464 (464)
Burundi (October 1974)			
Tutsi ethnic minority government	—	—	—
Cameroon (May 1978)			
Cameroonian National Union	—	99.98	120 (120)
Canada (February 1980)			
Social Credit	R	1.9	0 (6)
Progressive Conservative	CR	33.0	103 (136)
Liberal	C	43.9	147 (114)
New Democratic	L	19.8	32 (26)
Cape Verde (December 1980)			
African Party for the Independence of Guinea-Bissau and Cape Verde	—	93.0	—
Central African Republic			
Military Committee of National Recovery took power on Sept. 1, 1981		...	—
Chad			
Military government since 1975	—	—	—
Chile			
Military junta since Sept. 11, 1973	—	—	—
China, People's Republic of (February 1978)			
Communist (Kungchantang) National People's Congress	—	...	3,500
Colombia (March 1982)			
Partido Conservador	R	...	84 (86)
Partido Liberal	C	...	114 (109)
Unión Nacional de Oposisión	L	...	1 (4)
Comoros (March 1982)			
Federal Assembly	—	...	38
Congo (July 1979)			
Parti Congolais du Travail	—	—	115
Costa Rica (February 1982)			
Partido de Liberación Nacional	R	55	33 (25)
Partido Cristiano Democrático	C	30	18 (27)
Three left-wing parties	L	15	6 (5)
Cuba (December 1981)			
Partido Comunista Cubano	—	99.0	499 (481)
Cyprus			
Greek Zone: (May 1981):			
Democratic Rally	R	31.89	12
Democratic Party	CR	19.50	8
Socialist Party (EDEK)	S	8.17	3
Communist Party (AKEL)	K	32.79	12
Turkish Zone (June 1981):			
National Unity Party	—	42.6	18 (30)
Socialist Salvation Party	—	28.6	13 (6)
Republican Turkish Party	—	15.1	6 (2)
Democratic People's Party	—	8.1	2 (0)
Turkish Union Party	—	5.5	1 (0)
Czechoslovakia (June 1981)			
National Front	—	99.5	200 (200)
Denmark (December 1981)			
Conservative	R	14.4	26 (22)
Liberal Democratic (Venstre)	CR	11.3	21 (23)
Christian People's	CR	2.3	4 (5)
Progress	C	8.9	16 (20)
Radical Liberal (Radikale Venstre)	C	5.1	9 (10)
Centre Democrats	C	8.3	15 (6)
Social Democrats	SD	32.9	59 (69)
Socialist People's	EL	11.3	20 (11)
Left Socialists	EL	2.6	5 (6)
Others	—	...	4 (2)
Djibouti (May 1982)			
One-party state: National Assembly	—	...	65
Dominica (July 1980)			
Freedom Party	C	...	17 (3)
Labour Party	L	...	2 (16)
Independents	—	...	2 (2)
Dominican Republic (May 1982)			
Partido Reformista	R	37.0	... (42)
Partido Revolucionario	L	48.4	... (49)
Others	—	...	...
Ecuador (April 1979, figures incomplete)			
Partido Conservador	R	...	10
Concentración de Fuerzas Populares	C	...	30
Izquierda Democrática	L	...	14
Unión Democrática Popular	EL	...	3
Egypt (November 1976)			
Arab Socialist Union	—	...	350
El Salvador (March 1982)			
Alianza Republicana Nacionalista	R	29	19
Partido de Conciliación Nacional	CR	13	14
Partido Acción Democrática	C	18	3
Partido Cristiano Democrático	C	40	24
Equatorial Guinea			
Provisional military government since Aug. 3, 1979		...	—
Ethiopia			
Military government since 1974	—	—	—
Fiji (July 1982)			
Alliance Party (mainly Fijian)	—	...	28 (36)
National Federation (mainly Indian)	—	...	22 (15)
Others	—	...	2 (1)
Finland (March 1979)			
National Coalition Party (Conservative)	R	21.7	47 (35)
Swedish People's	R	4.3	10 (10)
Centre Party (ex-Agrarian)	C	17.4	36 (39)
Liberal	C	3.7	4 (9)
Christian League	C	4.8	9 (9)
Rural	L	4.6	7 (2)
Social Democratic	SD	24.0	52 (54)
People's Democratic League (Communist)	K	17.9	35 (40)
Others	—	1.75	0 (2)
France (June 1981)			
Centre-Right:			
Gaullists (Rassemblement pour la République)	R	...	83 (148)
Giscardians (Union pour la Démocratie Française)	CR	...	64 (137)
Other	—	...	11 (6)
Union of Left:			
Parti Radical	L	...	14 (10)
Parti Socialiste	SD	...	269 (103)
Parti Communiste	K	...	44 (86)
Others	—	...	6 (1)
Gabon (February 1973)			
Parti Démocratique Gabonais	—	...	70
Gambia, The (April 1982)			
People's Progressive Party	C	61.7	27 (28)
Three other parties	—	...	8 (7)
German Democratic Republic (June 1981)			
National Front (Sozialistische Einheitspartei and others)	—	99.2	500 (500)
Germany, Federal Republic of (October 1980)			
Christlich-Demokratische Union	R	34.2	174 (190)
Christlich-Soziale Union	R	10.3	52 (53)
Freie Demokratische Partei	C	10.6	53 (39)
Sozialdemokratische Partei Deutschlands	SD	42.9	218 (214)
The Green (Ecology) Party		1.5	0
Ghana			
Military dictatorship since Dec. 31, 1981	—	—	—
Greece (October 1981)			
Progressive Party	R	1.7	0 (5)
New Democracy Party	CR	35.9	115 (172)
Panhellenic Socialist Movement (Pasok)	SD	48.1	172 (93)
Greek Communist Party	K	10.9	13 (11)
Others	—	2.3	0 (19)
Grenada			
People's Revolutionary Government since March 13, 1979		...	—
Guatemala			
Military government since March 23, 1982	—	—	—
Guinea (December 1974)			
Parti Démocratique de Guinée	—	100.0	150

COUNTRY AND NAME OF PARTY	Affili- ation	Voting strength (%)	Parlia- mentary represen- tation
Guinea-Bissau			
Governed by the Council of the Revolution since Nov. 14, 1980	—	—	—
Guyana (December 1980)			
People's National Congress	—	...	(37)
People's Progressive Party	—	...	(14)
Others	—	...	(2)
Haiti			
Presidential dictatorship since 1957	—	—	—
Honduras (November 1981)			
Partido Nacional	R	42.0	34 (33)
Partido Liberal	CR	54.0	44 (35)
Partido de Innovación y Unidad	C	2.5	3 (3)
Partido Demócrata Cristiano	C	1.5	1 (0)
Hungary (June 1975)			
Patriotic People's Front	—	97.6	352
Iceland (December 1979)			
Independence (Conservative)	R	35.4	21 (20)
Progressive (Farmers' Party)	C	24.9	17 (12)
Social Democratic	SD	17.4	10 (14)
People's Alliance	K	19.7	11 (14)
Independent		...	1 (0)
India (January 1980)			
Congress (I) and allied parties:			
Congress (I)	C	...	351
Dravida Munnetra Kazhagam	R	...	16
Lok Dal (Janata secular)	—	...	41
Three smaller parties	—	...	7
Opposition:			
Janata (People's) Party	C	...	32 (295)
Congress (Urs)	C	...	13 (150)
Communist Party of India (Marxist)	K	...	35 (22)
Communist Party of India (pro-Soviet)	K	...	10 (7)
Anna Dravida Munnetra Kazhagam	R	...	2 (19)
Akali Dal (Sikh Party)	C	...	1 (9)
Six small parties	—	...	11
Independents	—	...	6
Indonesia (May 1982)			
Golkar (Functional Groups)	—	64.3	342
United Development Party	—	27.8	94
Indonesian Democratic Party (merger of five nationalist and Christian parties)	—	7.9	24
Iran (May 1980)			
Islamic Republican Party	R	...	150
Islamic National Party	CR	...	80
Independents	—	...	40
Iraq			
Military and Ba'ath Party governments since 1958	—	...	
Ireland (November 1982)			
Fianna Fail (Sons of Destiny)	C	...	75 (81)
Fine Gael (United Ireland)	C	...	70 (63)
Irish Labour Party	L	...	16 (15)
Others	—	...	5 (7)
Israel (June 1981)			
Likud	R	37.1	48 (43)
National Religious	CR	4.9	6 (12)
Agudat Israel	C	3.7	4 (4)
Labour Alignment	SD	36.6	47 (32)
Democratic Front (Communist)	K	3.4	4 (5)
Others	—	...	11 (24)
Italy (June 1979)			
Movimento Sociale Italiano	F	5.3	30 (35)
Partito Liberale Italiano	CR	1.9	9 (5)
Democrazia Cristiana	C	38.3	262 (262)
Partito Repubblicano Italiano	C	3.0	16 (14)
Partito Social-Democratico Italiano	L	3.8	20 (15)
Partito Socialista Italiano	SD	9.8	62 (57)
Partito d'Unità Proletaria	EL	1.4	6 (6)
Partito Radicale	EL	3.4	18 (4)
Partito Comunista Italiano	K	30.4	201 (228)
Südtiroler Volkspartei	—	0.6	4 (3)
Others	—	2.1	2 (1)
Ivory Coast (October 1980)			
Parti Démocratique de la Côte d'Ivoire	—	99.9	100
Jamaica (October 1980)			
Jamaica Labour Party	L	57.0	51 (12)
People's National Party	SD	43.0	9 (48)
Japan (June 1980)			
Liberal-Democratic	R	...	284 (258)
Komeito (Clean Government)	CR	...	33 (57)
Democratic-Socialist	SD	...	32 (35)
Socialist	S	...	107 (107)
Communist	K	...	29 (39)
Independents and others	—	...	26 (25)
Jordan			
Royal government, no parties	—	—	60
Kampuchea (May 1981)			
Kampuchean United Front for National Salvation (Vietnamese-backed)	—	99.0	117
Kenya (November 1979)			
Kenya African National Union (158 elected, 12 nominated, 2 ex-officio)	—	...	172 (158)
Kiribati (ex. Gilbert Islands, July 1979)			
House of Assembly	—	...	35
Korea, North (February 1982)			
Korean Workers' (Communist) Party	—	100.0	615 (579)
Korea, South (March 1981)			
Korean National	CR	...	25
Democratic Justice	C	...	151
Democratic Korea	L	...	81
Democratic Socialist	S	...	2
Others	—	...	17
Kuwait (February 1981)			
Princely government with elected Parliament, no parties	—	—	30
Laos, People's Democratic Republic of			
Lao People's Revolutionary Party	—	...	...

COUNTRY AND NAME OF PARTY	Affili- ation	Voting strength (%)	Parlia- mentary represen- tation
Lebanon (April 1972)			
Maronites (Roman Catholics)	—	...	30
Sunni Muslims	—	...	20
Shi'ite Muslims	—	...	19
Greek Orthodox	—	...	11
Druzes (Muslim sect)	—	...	6
Melchites (Greek Catholics)	—	...	6
Armenian Orthodox	—	...	4
Other Christian	—	...	2
Armenian Catholics	—	...	1
Lesotho			
Constitution suspended Jan. 30, 1970	—	—	—
Liberia			
People's Redemption Council since April 1980	—	—	—
Libya			
Military government since Sept. 1, 1969	—	—	—
Liechtenstein (February 1982)			
Vaterländische Union	CR	53.5	8 (8)
Fortschrittliche Bürgerpartei	C	46.5	7 (7)
Luxembourg (June 1979)			
Parti Chrétien Social	CR	34.5	24 (18)
Parti Libéral	C	21.3	15 (14)
Parti Ouvrier Socialiste	SD	24.3	14 (17)
Parti Social Démocratique	S	6.0	2 (5)
Parti Communiste Luxembourgeois	K	5.8	2 (5)
Independents	—	...	2 (0)
Madagascar (June 1977)			
Avant-garde de la Révolution Malgache	C	...	112
Parti du Congrès de l'Indépendance	L	...	16
Others	—	...	9
Malawi (June 1978)			
Malawi Congress Party	—	...	87
Malaysia (April 1982)			
National Front (Barisan Nasional)			
United Malays National Organization	70		
Malaysian Chinese Association	24		
Malaysian Indian Congress	4		133 (131)
Gerakan	5		
Sabah and Sarawak	30		
Opposition Parties			
Democratic Action Party	9		
Partai Islam Malaysia	5		21 (23)
Independents	7		
Maldives (February 1975)			
Presidential rule since 1975	—	—	—
Mali			
Military government since Nov. 19, 1968	—	—	—
Malta (December 1981)			
Nationalist Party	R	...	31 (31)
Labour Party	SD	...	34 (34)
Mauritania			
Military government since April 25, 1981	—	—	—
Mauritius (June 1982)			
Independence Party (Indian-dominated)	C	...	2 (28)
Parti Mauricien Social-Démocrate	L	...	2 (8)
Parti Socialiste Mauricien	L	...	18 } 60 (34)
Mouvement Militant Mauricien	EL	...	42
Organization du Peuple Rodriguais	—	...	2
Mexico (July 1982)			
Partido Revolucionario Institucional	CR	...	296 (296)
Partido Demócrata Mexicano	CR	...	
Partido Acción Nacional	C	...	
Partido Auténtico de la Revolución	L	...	104 (104)
Partido Socialista de los Trabajadores	L	...	
Partido Popular Socialista	S	...	
Partido Comunista Mexicano	K	...	
Monaco (January 1978)			
Union Nationale et Démocratique	—	...	18 (17)
Mongolia (June 1981)			
Mongolian People's Revolutionary Party	—	99.9	354 (354)
Morocco (June 1977)			
Independents (pro-government)	CR	44.7	141 (159)
Popular Movement (rural)	CR	12.4	44 (60)
Istiqlal (Independence)	C	21.6	49 (8)
National Union of Popular Forces	L	14.6	16 (1)
Others	—	...	14 (12)
Mozambique (December 1977)			
Frente da Libertação do Moçambique (Frelimo)	—	...	210
Nauru (November 1977)			
Nauru Party (Dowiyogo)	—	...	9
Opposition Party (DeRoburt)	—	...	8
Independent	—	...	1
Nepal (May 1981)			
140-member Parliament, 112 elected and 28 appointed by the King; no parties			
Netherlands, The (September 1982)			
Christian Democratic Appeal	CR	29.3	45 (48)
Liberals (VVD)	C	23.0	36 (26)
Democrats 1966	C	4.3	6 (17)
Labour (Pvd A)	SD	30.4	47 (44)
Others	—	13.0	16 (15)
New Zealand (November 1981)			
National (Conservative)	CR	...	47 (51)
Labour Party	L	...	43 (40)
Social Credit	C	...	2 (1)
Nicaragua			
Provisional government since July 20, 1979	—	...	—
Niger			
Military government since April 17, 1974	—	—	—
Nigeria (July–August 1979)			
National Party of Nigeria	—	...	168
Unity Party of Nigeria	—	...	111
Nigerian People's Party	—	...	79
Great Nigeria People's Party	—	...	48
People's Redemption Party	—	...	49

COUNTRY AND NAME OF PARTY	Affili-ation	Voting strength (%)	Parlia-mentary represen-tation
Norway (September 1981)			
Høyre (Conservative)	R	...	54 (41)
Kristelig Folkeparti	CR	...	15 (22)
Senterpartiet (Agrarian)	C	...	10 (12)
Venstre (Liberal)	C	...	2 (2)
Party of Progress		...	4 (0)
Arbeiderpartiet (Labour)	SD	...	66 (76)
Sosialistisk Venstreparti (Socialist Left)	S	...	4 (2)
Oman			
Independent sultanate, no parties	—	—	—
Pakistan			
Military government since July 5, 1977	—	—	—
Panama			
Since July 1982 a civilian president under "indirect" military supervision.			
Papua New Guinea (June 1982)			
Pangu Party	—	34	50 (39)
United Party	—	7.2	9 (38)
People's Progress Party	—	10	14 (18)
National Party	—	10	13 (3)
Independents	—	20.9	4
Others	—	...	18
Paraguay (February 1977)			
Partido Colorado (A. Stroessner)	R	69.0	...
Opposition parties	—	31.0	...
Peru (May 1980)			
Acción Popular		...	98
Alianza Popular Revolucionaria Americana	—	...	58
Popular Christian Party	—	...	10
Others	—	...	14
Philippines			
Martial law lifted Jan. 17, 1981	—	—	—
Poland (March 1980)			
Front of National Unity { Communists / Peasants / Democrats / Non-party }	—	99.0	{ 261 / 113 / 37 / 49 } 460 (460)
Portugal (October 1980)			
Democratic Alliance	R	47.1	136 (128)
Republican and Socialist Front	SD	28.0	75 (74)
United People's Alliance	K	16.9	41 (47)
Popular Democratic Union	K	...	1 (1)
Qatar			
Independent emirate, no parties	—	—	—
Romania (March 1980)			
Social Democracy and Unity Front	—	98.5	369 (349)
Rwanda (July 1975)			
National Revolutionary Development Movement	—	—	—
Saint Lucia (May 1982)			
United Workers' Party	C	...	14 (5)
St. Lucia Labour Party	S	...	2 (12)
Progressive Labour Party	EL	...	1 (0)
Saint Vincent and the Grenadines (December 1979)			
St. Vincent Labour Party	—	...	11
New Democratic Party	—	...	2
San Marino (May 1980)			
Communist coalition { Partito Communista / Partito Social Democratico / Partito Socialista Unitario }		56.0	{ 16 / 9 / 8 }
Christian Democrats		40.0	26
Independent		...	1
São Tomé and Príncipe (1975)			
Movimento Libertaçao	—	—	—
Saudi Arabia			
Royal government, no parties	—	—	—
Senegal (February 1978)			
Parti Socialiste	CR	82.5	83
Parti Démocratique Sénégalais	L	17.1	17
Seychelles			
People's Progressive Front (alone in power after the June 5, 1977, coup)	—	—	—
Sierra Leone (June 1978)			
All People's Congress	CR	...	85 (70)
Singapore (December 1980)			
People's Action Party	CR	75.5	75 (69)
Solomon Islands			
Independent Group	C	...	...
National Democratic Party	L	...	...
Somalia (December 1979)			
Somalian Revolutionary Socialist Party	—	...	171
South Africa (April 1981)			
Herstigte Nasionale Partij	ER	13.8	0 (0)
National Conservative Party	R	—	0 —
National Party	R	56.1	131 (134)
South Africa Party	CR	—	— (3)
New Republic Party	C	7.7	8 (10)
Progressive Federal Party	L	19.1	26 (17)
Others	—	—	0 (0)
Spain (October 1982)			
Alianza Popular	R	25.35	105 (9)
Unión Centro-Democrático	C	7.26	11 (168)
Partido Socialista Obrero Español	SD	46.07	201 (121)
Partido Comunista Español	K	3.87	5 (23)
Catalan nationalists	—	3.73	12 (8)
Basque nationalists	—	1.91	8 (7)
Herri Batasuna (Basque radicals)	—	0.97	2 (3)
Others	—	—	6 (14)
Sri Lanka (October 1982)			
United National Party	R	53	145 (139)
Freedom Party	C	...	... (8)
People's Liberation Front (Tamil)	—	...	... (17)
Communists and others	—	...	... (2)
Sudan (December 1981)			
Sudanese Social Union	—	...	151
Suriname			
National Military Council since Feb. 25, 1980	—	—	—
Swaziland			
Royal government, no parties	—	—	—
Sweden (September 1982)			
Conservative	R	23.6	86 (73)
Centre	CR	15.6	56 (64)
Liberal	C	5.9	21 (38)
Social Democrats	SD	45.9	166 (154)
Communists	K	5.5	20 (20)
Switzerland (October 1979)			
Christian Democrats (Conservative)	R	...	44 (46)
Republican Movement / National Action (V. Ochen)	R	...	3 (6)
Evangelical People's	R	...	3 (3)
Swiss People's (ex-Middle Class)	CR	...	23 (21)
Radical Democrats (Freisinnig)	C	...	51 (47)
League of Independents	C	...	8 (11)
Liberal Democrats	L	...	8 (6)
Social Democrats	SD	...	51 (55)
Socialist Autonomous	EL	...	3 (1)
Communist (Partei der Arbeit)	K	...	3 (4)
Others	—	...	3 (0)
Syria (November 1981)			
National Progressive Front	—	...	195 (159)
Others	—	...	0 (36)
Taiwan (Republic of China)			
Nationalist (Kuomintang)	—	...	773
Tanzania (October 1980)			
Tanganyika African National Union	C	...	111 (218)
Zanzibar Afro-Shirazi (nominated)	L	...	40 (52)
Thailand (April 1979)			
Social Action Party	—	...	82
Thai Nationalist Party	—	...	38
Democratic Party	—	...	32
Thai People's Party	—	...	32
Serithan (Socialist) Party	—	...	21
Others	—	...	96
Togo (December 1979)			
Rassemblement du Peuple Togolais	—	96.0	67
Tonga (May 1981)			
Legislative Assembly (partially elected)	—	—	21
Trinidad and Tobago (November 1981)			
People's National Movement	C	...	26 (24)
Organization for National Reconstruction	—	...	0 —
National Alliance:			
United Labour Front	L	...	8 (10)
Democratic Action Congress	EL	...	2 (2)
Tunisia (November 1981)			
National Front (led by the Parti Socialiste Destourien)	—	94.6	136 (121)
Turkey			
National Security Council since Sept. 12, 1980; 160-member Consultative Assembly appointed and political parties abolished on Oct. 15, 1981	—	—	—
Tuvalu (September 1981)			
No political parties	—	...	...
Uganda (December 1980)			
Uganda People's Congress Party	—	...	68
Democratic Party	—	...	48
Union of Soviet Socialist Republics (March 1979)			
Communist Party of the Soviet Union	—	99.99	1,500 (767)
United Arab Emirates			
Federal government of seven emirates	—	—	—
United Kingdom (May 1979)			
Conservative	R	43.9	339 (276)
Liberal	C	13.8	11 (13)
Labour	L	36.9	268 (319)
Communist	K	...	0 (0)
Scottish National Party	—	...	2 (11)
Plaid Cymru (Welsh Nationalists)	—	...	2 (3)
Ulster Unionists (four groups)	—	...	10 (10)
Others	—	...	3 (3)
United States (November 1982)			
Republican	CR	...	166 (192)
Democratic	C	...	267 (242)
Independent		...	0 (1)
Upper Volta			
On Nov. 6, 1982, Col. Saye Zerbo's military government was toppled by the Council of Popular Salvation.	—	—	—
Uruguay			
Rule by Council of State from 1973	—	—	—
Vanuatu (New Hebrides) (November 1979)			
Vanuaaku Pati	C	...	26
Others	—	...	13
Venezuela (December 1978)			
COPEI (Social Christians)	CR	...	88 (64)
Acción Democrática	L	...	88 (102)
Movimiento al Socialismo	SD	...	11 (9)
Movimiento Electoral del Pueblo	S	...	3 (8)
Movimiento Institucional Revolucionario	EL	...	4 (2)
Partido Comunista Venezolano	K	...	1 (2)
Vietnam, Socialist Republic of (April 1981)			
Communist Party	—	...	...
Yemen, People's Democratic Republic of			
National Liberation Front	—	—	—
Yemen Arab Republic			
Military government since 1974	—	—	—
Yugoslavia (May 1982)			
Communist-controlled Federal Chamber	—	...	220 (220)
Zaire (October 1977)			
Legislative Council of the Mouvement Populaire de la Révolution	—	...	268
Zambia (December 1973)			
United National Independence Party	—	80.0	125
Zimbabwe (February–March 1980)			
Zimbabwe African National Union	—	63.0	57
Zimbabwe African People's Union	—	24.0	20
United African National Council	—	8.0	3
Rhodesian Front (Europeans)	—		20

(K. M. SMOGORZEWSKI)

Portugal

A republic of southwestern Europe, Portugal shares the Iberian Peninsula with Spain. Area: 91,985 sq km (35,516 sq mi), including the Azores (2,247 sq km) and Madeira (794 sq km). Pop. (1981 prelim.): 9,784,200. Cap. and largest city: Lisbon (pop., 1981 prelim., 812,400). Language: Portuguese. Religion: Roman Catholic. President in 1982, Gen. António dos Santos Ramalho Eanes; premier, Francisco Pinto Balsemão.

The governing Democratic Alliance (AD) coalition's plan to revise Portugal's 1976 constitution, purging it of its references to the achievement of socialism, the People and the Armed Forces Movement, and the irreversibility of nationalizations, led the Communist Party into overt extraparliamentary opposition. As a result, the Communists fully backed the country's first general strike in 40 years on Feb. 12, 1982. Public transport was the principal service disrupted. Without the official support of the Socialist Party-led General Union of Workers (UGT), the striking CGTP-Intersindical trade-union federation represented just slightly more than one-third of the work force.

After the strike was over, the government alleged that a violent coup had been planned to take place at the same time as the union action The Socialist Party (PSP) introduced a motion of no confidence in the government in March, but it was defeated by 130 votes to 116. Shortly afterward the Communist Party introduced its own motion, which was withdrawn after Premier Francisco Pinto Balsemão declined to appear for the debate. On May 1 two men were shot dead and 80 people injured in Oporto when riot police opened fire to quell violence between rival UGT and CGTP May Day demonstrations. The Communist union then called a second general strike, but again support was patchy.

Amid accusations of drift in economic policymaking and rumours of renewed disagreements within the premier's own Social Democratic Party (PSD) over his capacity for leadership, four ministers and six secretaries of state were affected in an unexpected Cabinet reshuffle in June. The education, foreign affairs, and labour ministers were dropped, and a new minister for parliamentary relations was drafted into the government to speed up the constitutional revision, which had stalled in the Assembly. Amid general surprise from the politicians, Pres. António Ramalho Eanes expressed strong disapproval of the reshuffle since he had not been informed of the changes in advance, as required by the constitution. Meanwhile, however, moves were taking place to reduce the president's powers substantially as part of the constitutional amendments. After a week of haggling in early June, the Assembly agreed to devote 100 hours to debate of the new constitution, and the legislature's summer recess was postponed.

Debate over the role of the president was not confined to the AD. The PSP deputies were divided over the matter, though the party demanded that all supporters of the 1980 campaign to reelect the

president would have to recant. On June 23 the PSP suspended Francisco Salgado Zenha, the Socialist leader in the Assembly, for his support of the president.

In July the Assembly, as part of the constitutional revision process, voted to abolish the military Council of the Revolution—the body, headed by President Eanes, that was charged with vetting legislation for conformity with the requirements of the constitution. The outgoing military council reacted loudly, and the left-wing majority pushed through a resolution calling the vote "unjust and disgraceful." The Council of the Revolution was to be replaced by a civilian Council of the Republic with representatives from the political parties, a supreme military defense board, and a constitutional tribunal.

A month later, on August 12, the Assembly completed its debate and approved the revised text of the constitution by 197 votes to 40. The Communist Party and its sympathizers were opposed. The president was deprived of the right to nominate the military chiefs of staff, though he remained supreme commander. Although shorn of their left-wing wording, clauses in the old 1976 constitution governing nationalization and agrarian reform were largely unamended; this was insisted upon by the PSP, which agreed to vote in favour of the new constitution. Zenha, however, introduced a point of order in which he made it clear that he and 34 other Socialist deputies had voted in favour only because of party discipline.

At a press conference after the vote, Premier Balsemão announced legislation designed to free foreign investment from past restraints, place nationalized firms under new management and accounting procedures, and introduce new and more liberal rules for the stock exchange. One of the most controversial decisions was to wind up the state news agency (ANOP) and replace it with a new official organ, Noticias de Portugal (Porpress). While the new constitution did not permit the government to privatize nationalized firms openly, there was nothing to stop it from liquidating them and opening alternative agencies. Balsemão also outlined more general plans along these lines, but without naming the unprofitable state companies concerned.

FRANCOLON/FORNACIARI—GAMMA/LIAISON

A Spanish fundamentalist priest, Juan Fernández Krohn, who attempted to stab Pope John Paul II in Fatima, Portugal, on May 12, was grabbed by security guards.

Portugal

Polo:
see Equestrian Sports; Water Sports

Populations:
see Demography; see also the individual country articles

President Eanes's dissatisfaction with the drift of political events was manifest in the fact that his promulgation of the new constitution, which was required by law, was delayed until the end of September. He also threatened to veto the law governing local government elections and did in fact veto the decree ordering the closure of ANOP.

In a long-awaited television address on November 5, President Eanes criticized many aspects of the process leading up to the constitutional revision. He would not dissolve the Assembly, as the Communists and Socialists had demanded, because of his respect for the electorate and its freely expressed wishes. However, he reaffirmed his vision of the duties of president. In general, these were to act as a moderator of the democratic process, but they included the duty to examine specific laws and new measures to ensure that they complied with the requirements of the new constitution. To aid him in his role, the president demanded, the elected politicians must begin to show the skills needed to attack the deteriorating economic situation, which was threatening to cast Portugal into a gulf of misery and mediocrity. Eanes's challenge to the politicians drew a sharp rebuff from the parties, who tried to represent him as a spent force, bitter as a result of the constitu-

tional revision process. On November 20 President Eanes vetoed a law which put the military under direct government control. Since the law had passed with the two-thirds majority needed to override a veto, the action was mainly a gesture of protest.

In the local elections, held on December 12, the PSD lost 5% of its electoral majority, and on December 18 Premier Balsemão resigned. By year's end the ensuing governmental crisis had not been resolved. (MICHAEL WOOLLER)

See also Dependent States.

Prisons and Penology

How the courts and the penal system should deal with mentally abnormal offenders was a question that came to the fore during 1982. It arose in the U.S. as a result of the trial of John Hinckley, Jr., who, the year before, had attempted to assassinate Pres. Ronald Reagan. After eight weeks Hinckley was found not guilty by reason of insanity. The verdict aroused much controversy. In many other countries such a decision could not have been made by the courts. In the U.K. a verdict of guilty but insane would have been possible. The courts of most European countries could also have passed verdicts involving the concept of diminished responsibility. This might have permitted a reduction in the charge but would still have been likely to lead to long confinement in a secure psychiatric hospital for the criminally insane or one for those with major mental or behavioural abnormalities. Sentences for such offenders were indeterminate because it was difficult to predict dangerous behaviour in future years, but there were regular careful reviews concerning eventual release.

Ordinary prisons nevertheless had to house a great many mentally abnormal prisoners. This occurred despite efforts by official committees to establish more secure psychiatric units, and it placed additional burdens on already overstrained penal facilities. Prison nursing staffs were usually briefly and poorly trained. It was this situation that led to a major scandal in the U.K. Barry Prosser, a prisoner, had died a year earlier in the hospital wing of Birmingham prison of injuries that could not have been self-inflicted. An inquest jury decided that Prosser was "unlawfully killed." But at two different trials it proved impossible to obtain a conviction against the accused prison staff members.

An official report on this same prison later recommended that there should be more training for prison hospital officers, more assignments to outside psychiatric hospitals, and more exact record-keeping of incidents and action taken. The acceptance of these recommendations by Home Secretary William Whitelaw coincidentally came within a few days of the Hinckley verdict in June. Ordinary psychiatric hospitals, used to ordinary mental patients, were generally unsuitable for the containment of mentally disturbed criminals. Nor did nurses and physicians not specialized in forensic psychiatry necessarily have sufficient experience in the management of these often extremely difficult patients to deal with them appropriately.

Portuguese Literature:
see Literature

Power:
see Energy; Engineering Projects; Industrial Review

Presbyterian Churches:
see Religion

Prices:
see Economy, World

Printing:
see Industrial Review

PORTUGAL

Education. (1978–79) Primary, pupils 1,177,868, teachers 58,652; secondary (1977–78), pupils 409,045, teachers 12,363; vocational (1977–78), pupils 82,656, teachers 8,829; teacher training (1977–78), students 8,128, teachers 761; higher, students (1979–80) 84,276, teaching staff 9,441.

Finance. Monetary unit: escudo, with (Sept. 20, 1982) a free rate of 87.05 escudos to U.S. $1 (149.25 escudos = £1 sterling). Gold and other reserves (June 1982) U.S. $1,333,000,000. Budget (1981 est.) balanced at 440 billion escudos. Gross national product (1980) 1,174,900,000,000 escudos. Money supply (Feb. 1982) 534,260,000,000 escudos. Cost of living (1975 = 100; May 1982) 396.7.

Foreign Trade. (1981) Imports 599,710,000,000 escudos; exports 254,920,000,000 escudos. Import sources: EEC 38% (West Germany 11%, U.K. 8%, France 8%, Italy 5%); U.S. 12%; Spain 7%; Saudi Arabia 5%. Export destinations: EEC 54% (U.K. 14%, France 13%, West Germany 12%); Angola 5%; U.S. 5%; The Netherlands 5%. Main exports: clothing 14%; textile yarns and fabrics 13%; machinery 9%; petroleum products 7%; chemicals 6%; cork and manufactures 6%; food 5%; wine 5%. Tourism (1980): visitors 2,708,000; gross receipts U.S. $1,146,000,000.

Transport and Communications. Roads (1979) 51,749 km (including 66 km expressways). Motor vehicles in use (1980): passenger 1,268,970; commercial 186,100. Railways: (1980) 3,588 km; traffic (1981) 5,854,000,000 passenger-km, freight 1,004,000,000 net ton-km. Air traffic (1981): 4,007,000,000 passenger-km; freight 108.6 million net ton-km. Shipping (1981): merchant vessels 100 gross tons and over 351; gross tonnage 1,376,529. Telephones (Jan. 1980) 1,305,600. Radio receivers (Dec. 1979) 1,575,000. Television licenses (Dec. 1979) 1,203,000.

Agriculture. Production (in 000; metric tons; 1981): wheat 310; oats 71; rye 125; corn 417; rice 112; potatoes 936; tomatoes c. 670; apples 97; oranges 92; wine 640; olives c. 220; olive oil c. 33; cow's milk c. 697; meat 461; fish catch (1980) 265; timber (cu m; 1980) 8,152. Livestock (in 000; 1981): sheep c. 5,150; cattle c. 1,000; goats c. 750; pigs c. 3,430; poultry c. 17,500.

Industry. Production (in 000; metric tons; 1981): coal 185; petroleum products c. 7,200; manufactured gas (cu m) c. 136,000; electricity (kw-hr) c. 12,960,000; kaolin (1979) 80; iron ore (50% metal content) 37; crude steel 350; sulfuric acid c. 590; fertilizers (nutrient content; 1980–81) nitrogenous c. 180, phosphate c. 106; plastics and resins (1980) 136; cement 6,040; wood pulp (1979) 753; cork products (1979) 220; cotton yarn 87; woven cotton fabrics 65.

With not enough secure hospitals they had somehow to be coped with in jails.

There was no easing in 1982 of the buildup of pressure on penal institutions. However, the number of people held in custody in proportion to the total population and the known crime rate continued to vary from country to country. For example, in The Netherlands the daily average prison population remained one of the lowest in Europe. France, too, with 30,000 inmates, had almost one-third fewer prisoners than England and Wales, which had 44,000. However, in England tougher measures had been introduced for some young detainees, while French prisons closed their top security wings by government decree in February; this was opposed by some prison staff members, who feared that, without such secure units, they might not be able to control some of the most dangerous convicted murderers. (France had abolished capital punishment the previous year.)

Despite an increase in the number of policemen killed in recent years and a general rise in the level of violence—points strongly stressed in a widespread publicity campaign by the British police federation—the House of Commons in May rejected another attempt to reintroduce capital punishment in England and Wales. In Richmond, Va., in an important test case involving his own wish to die, former policeman Frank J. Coppola was executed on August 10 after four years on death row.

Overcrowding was a serious problem in many countries. So many prisoners, cooped up in inadequate and out-of-date buildings in so many countries, could not fail to produce riots and disturbances. At the Archambault Institute, a jail near Montreal, three guards were killed and seven injured and two prisoners committed suicide in July, and at Brushy Mountain State Penitentiary in Tennessee in February seven white prisoners took four guards hostage and shot four black inmates, killing two of them. Perhaps not surprisingly, uniformed staff sometimes began to take matters into their own hands. An official report on a particularly bad incident of staff overreaction that had occurred the previous year at London's Wormwood Scrubs prison criticized prison management for letting the staff run the place according to their own rules instead of those laid down by the Prison Department. Everywhere fresh means were being sought to devise alternatives to imprisonment. These were not always probation or community service but sometimes imaginative projects run by voluntary agencies. Some of the best schemes were those of the U.S. Vision Quest organization. Vision Quest had pioneered some programs for apparently hopeless young offenders, who were often from chaotic homes and usually had prolonged experience of detention in a penal or mental institution. The programs were action-oriented, posing a physical and mental challenge to these alienated boys and girls, who found that they could overcome considerable hardship and dangers and learn to trust others and themselves. The effort required gave them pride, resourcefulness, self-respect, and a new sense of responsibility. They were confronted instantly with the consequences of their own actions and, whenever

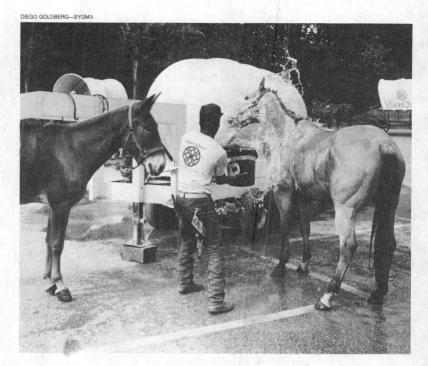

DIEGO GOLDBERG—SYGMA

Prison officials in Arizona tried an experiment of having young offenders made responsible for the care of animals. It was part of an attempt to improve the rehabilitation process.

possible, were helped to rebuild relationships with their parents. So far these schemes had had an approximately 80% success rate. Although not cheap, they were less expensive than juvenile detention.

However, it was early prevention that continued to get the attention of most researchers. Even in Japan, with much the lowest crime rate of any industrialized society, juvenile crime and vandalism continued to rise. The massive work by the Center for Urban Affairs and Policy Research at Northwestern University in Evanston, Ill., suggested broad general factors associated with crime, such as increased affluence; the availability of more and sometimes unguarded goods; and the existence of a large pool of potential offenders, for reasons that were not well understood. Narrower but more specific studies suggested possible practical action. For example, there was proof of a link between television violence and aggressive behaviour in susceptible youngsters, obtained from careful research in the U.S., the U.K., and other countries. Truancy was also connected with juvenile crime. In 1982 in London alone, every day about 20,000 children missed school and roamed the streets, often committing offenses while doing so. Unemployment, too, was a factor—a sense of purposelessness, of not being a part of productive society.

Above all, it was the role of the family that was shown to play a major part in juvenile crime prevention. But lax parenting could be the result of chronic stress, including physical and mental disabilities and long spells of unemployment. In such cases neither the teaching of parent-craft nor the imposition of fines on the parents for their children's offenses would be likely to result in an improvement in the care and control of the children.

(HUGH J. KLARE)

See also Crime and Law Enforcement; Law.
[521.C.3.a; 543.A.5.a; 10/36.C.5.b]

Publishing

During 1982 all branches of publishing continued to suffer from the effects of deep recession, with little expectation of any early improvement. Newspaper publishers, faced with mounting costs and—more often than not—falling circulations, fought to keep mastheads afloat. There were some successes: The *New York Daily News*, in dire straits at the end of 1981, faced a brighter future a year later after reaching agreement with unions on manning reductions and an innovative profit-sharing scheme. Across the Atlantic, *The Times* of London, Rupert Murdoch's prestigious but unprofitable flagship, drifted close to crisis yet again at the end of 1982 when a union dispute over new technology halted production.

At the international level, the UNESCO project for an International Program for the Development of Communications, launched in December 1981, went ahead despite funding problems. A 35-nation conference at Acapulco, Mexico, in January 1982 agreed on the creation of news agencies in Africa, Asia, and Latin America as a step toward the establishment of a "new world information order." A compromise reconciling third world and Western views on what form the "new order" should take was reached at a UNESCO special session in Paris in November–December.

The International Press Institute, at its 31st assembly in Madrid in May, passed resolutions criticizing the increasing concentration of newspaper ownership and subtle forms of censorship practiced by some governments, India and South Africa being named. In Britain the report of a House of Commons select committee's inquiry into "the handling of press and public information during the Falklands conflict," published on December 16, found that misinformation and censorship in wartime were justifiable.

Newspapers. A year that brought the launching of a new national weekly in Britain ended with a symptom of gathering crisis: during the last 11 days of 1982, *The Times* failed to appear because of a dispute with electricians over new technology, which was finally settled on December 31. The recession was beginning to bite hard on the newspaper industry. Circulation in general was down, and the effects of an advertising market that was flat at best were sharpened by desperate competition that threw rates into a downward spiral. The chairman of the Newspaper Publishers' Association predicted a loss approaching £30 million in 1982–83 for all U.K. national newspapers together.

In the year to March 1982, set against the year to March 1981, Britain's four quality national dailies together had lost 2.6% of sales, with slight gains by *The Guardian*, *The Times*, and *Financial Times* wiped out by a 6% loss at *The Daily Telegraph*, by far the largest of the quartet. The five tabloids showed a minimal gain of 1.5%, but all of it was scored by the brash *Sun* (+6.6%) and the smaller and newer *Daily Star* (+35.2%), and most of it was attributable to the "bingo war" in which they fought for circulation with cash prizes through the winter of 1981–82. By the autumn of 1982 it was clear that this had only staved off harsh truths. Official sales figures for April–September showed declines for both sectors. *The Daily Telegraph* again lost enough to offset the gains of the other quality dailies, while the *Sun*, with a 6.8% gain putting its average circulation back over the 4 million mark, was the only tabloid to show an increase. Even the *Daily Star*, whose sales had reached 1.5 million, had slipped back by almost 10%. The *Daily Express* had fallen below 2 million for the first time in its history, from a peak above 4 million in Lord Beaverbrook's heyday.

The Sunday sector was complicated by the newcomer. The *Mail On Sunday* (*MoS*) was launched in May by Associated Newspapers Ltd. as a sister to the *Daily Mail*, the middle-market paper that, in its tabloid format, had proved one of the relative successes of the 1970s. Its Sunday sibling proved an instant flop, and the traditional remedy quickly followed: the editor was removed, and the man behind the *Daily Mail*'s success, Sir David English, was appointed editor of both. The *MoS* was relaunched in October and looked as though it would achieve the plateau above the 1,250,000 level which was said to provide a sustainable base. However, the key to the relaunching was the addition of a colour magazine. This brought to six the number of colour magazines published with Sunday newspapers, and there seemed little likelihood that any of them would get enough of the profitable consumer advertising that was the main reason for their existence.

At Times Newspapers Ltd., the proprietor, Rupert Murdoch, forecast group losses for his News International Ltd. on the order of £20 million and called on his employees to seek no wage increases when current agreements ended. *The Sunday Times*

One of the oldest U.S. dailies, the *Philadelphia Bulletin*, folded in January. The paper was founded in 1847.

Profits:
see Economy, World

Protestant Churches:
see Religion

Psychiatry:
see Health and Disease

UPI

was the market leader of the quality Sundays, and its colour magazine a particular money-maker, but even this was proving to be no help. As for *The Times*, the call for new stringencies came after a quiet summer, during which circulation was gradually pulled back over the 300,000 level of three years earlier, before its 11-month suspension.

At *The Times* the year had begun with a double crisis. It took Murdoch's threat of closure to enforce a major reduction in staffing. Then an unseemly public slanging match ended with the resignation of Harold Evans, whom Murdoch had appointed editor only the previous year. The affair raised doubts about the efficacy of the national directors appointed when Murdoch took over the papers, supposedly to protect editorial independence. The proprietor was evidently in command, and he appointed Charles Douglas-Home (*see* BIOGRAPHIES) to replace Evans.

Murdoch's one consolation in Britain was that his *Sun* was one of only two daily newspapers continuing to make significant gains. The other, at the opposite end of the scale, was *The Guardian*, which, despite a cover-price increase, continued to build on the gains made during *The Times*'s absence. It registered an 8.6% increase in sales for the April–September period, reaching an all-time record for the paper of 421,698.

Another editorial upset occurred in Paris at *Le Monde*, whose journalists elected André Laurens (*see* BIOGRAPHIES) to succeed Jacques Fauvet as editor rather than the previous front runner, Claude Julien. *Le Monde*'s sales (439,124 in 1981) remained the highest of any French daily. Robert Hersant, France's biggest press baron (*Le Figaro*, *France-Soir*, and many others), who early in the year acquired the New York weekly *France-Amérique*, sought (unsuccessfully) to extend his French provincial empire with the Grenoble *Le Dauphiné Libéré*, allegedly in contravention of the law limiting concentration of newspaper ownership.

(PETER FIDDICK)

The recession also took its toll in the U.S. Total daily circulation declined 1.2% to 61,430,745 from the previous year's 62,201,840, according to the 1982 *Editor & Publisher International Year Book*. The total number of daily newspapers published in the U.S. dropped by 15, from 1,745 to 1,730. However, these figures did not tell the entire story. The U.S. was becoming a nation of two newspaper industries: a dwindling core of ailing afternoon papers, most of them published in big cities; and a prosperous group of morning papers in cities large and small. Total afternoon circulation declined 5.8% to 30,878,429, the lowest point in more than two decades, and the number of afternoon papers dropped to 1,352, 36 fewer than the year before. At the same time, morning circulation hit an all-time high of 30,552,316, up 3.9% from the previous year, and the number of morning papers rose to 408, a gain of 21. (The number of dailies publishing editions throughout the day remained constant at 30, and their circulation is divided evenly between the morning and evening categories in the above figures.) It appeared certain that in 1983, for the first time, more Americans would read morning than evening papers.

World Daily Newspapers and Circulation, 1980–81[1]

Location	Daily news-papers	Circulation per 1,000 population	Location	Daily news-papers	Circulation per 1,000 population
AFRICA			**ASIA**		
Algeria	5	31	Afghanistan	13	5[2]
Angola	4	16	Bangladesh	30	6
Benin	1	...	Burma	7	7
Botswana	1	15	China	382	74
Cameroon	1	6	Cyprus	13	137
Central African Republic	1	...	Hong Kong	69	...
Chad	4	...	India	1,087	21
Congo	5	12	Indonesia	172	...
Egypt	9	66	Iran	28	25
Equatorial Guinea	2	...	Iraq	5	20
Ethiopia	3	2	Israel	25	213
Gabon	2	24	Japan	180	500
Ghana	4	48	Jordan	4	63
Guinea	1	3	Kampuchea	15	...
Guinea-Bissau	1	8	Korea, North	11	...
Ivory Coast	1	...	Korea, South	30	193[2]
Kenya	3	13	Kuwait	8	232
Lesotho	3	34	Laos	3	...
Liberia	3	6	Lebanon	14	85
Libya	3	...	Macau	6	28
Madagascar	3	2[2]	Malaysia	38	138[2]
Malawi	1	3	Mongolia	2	106
Mali	1	...	Nepal	28	8[2]
Mauritius	8	72[2]	Pakistan	119	14
Morocco	10	13	Philippines	22	42[2]
Mozambique	2	4	Saudi Arabia	9	29[2]
Niger	2	2	Singapore	11	43
Nigeria	15	5	Sri Lanka	15	62
Réunion	2	91	Syria	7	8[2]
Senegal	1	7	Taiwan	32	215
Seychelles	2	79	Thailand	32	50
Sierra Leone	1	3	Turkey	255	...
Somalia	2	...	Vietnam	4	...
South Africa	25	60	Yemen (Aden)	3	...
Sudan	4	7	Yemen (San'a')	2	...
Tanzania	2	3	Total	2,681	
Togo	2	6			
Tunisia	5	43			
Uganda	1	2			
Upper Volta	2	2[2]	**EUROPE**		
Zaire	6	2[2]	Albania	2	53
Zambia	2	20	Austria	29	423[2]
Zimbabwe	2	16	Belgium	43	314[2]
Total	158		Bulgaria	13	251
			Czechoslovakia	23	824
			Denmark	49	367
			Finland	62	480
			France	84	211
NORTH AMERICA			Germany, East	39	517
Antigua	2	...	Germany, West	626	584
Bahamas, The	3	141	Gibraltar	1	82
Barbados	2	131	Greece	110	88[2]
Belize	2	60	Hungary	29	275
Bermuda	1	245	Iceland	6	569
Canada	122	219	Ireland	10	307
Costa Rica	4	119	Italy	90	132[2]
Cuba	17	132	Liechtenstein	2	538
Dominican Republic	10	...	Luxembourg	5	354
El Salvador	11	71[2]	Malta	5	189[2]
Guadeloupe	1	10	Netherlands, The	80	325
Guatemala	9	25[2]	Norway	89	472
Haiti	4	...	Poland	46	239
Honduras	6	61	Portugal	31	65
Jamaica	3	84	Romania	35	181
Martinique	1	104	Spain	116	...
Mexico	327	130[2]	Sweden	97	528
Netherlands Antilles	7	219[2]	Switzerland	98	475
Nicaragua	3	50	U.S.S.R.	700	312
Panama	7	90[2]	United Kingdom	118	441
Puerto Rico	5	192	Vatican City	1	70
Trinidad and Tobago	4	145	Yugoslavia	27	103
United States	1,731	271	Total	2,666	
Virgin Islands (U.S.)	3	174			
Total	2,285				
			OCEANIA		
			American Samoa	1	180
SOUTH AMERICA			Australia	87	426
Argentina	167	848[2]	Cook Islands	1	250
Bolivia	13	45	Fiji	3	105
Brazil	328	42	French Polynesia	4	98
Chile	37	87	Guam	1	151
Colombia	35	49[2]	New Caledonia	2	146
Ecuador	33	49[2]	New Zealand	43	392
French Guiana	1	...	Niue	1	60
Guyana	1	67	Papua New Guinea	1	9
Paraguay	5	55[2]	Total	144	
Peru	59	...			
Suriname	5	107[2]			
Uruguay	24	220[2]			
Venezuela	51	120[2]			
Total	764				

[1] Only newspapers issued four or more times weekly are included.
[2] Partial circulation only.
Sources: UNESCO, *Statistical Yearbook 1981*; *Editor and Publisher International Year Book* (1982); *Europa Year Book 1982, A World Survey*; various country publications.

A reader outside the offices of Times Newspapers Ltd. in London peruses what might have been the last edition of *The Times*. Proprietor Rupert Murdoch settled with union leaders to end a dispute that halted publication during the last days of 1982.

One of the nation's oldest afternoon dailies, the *Philadelphia Bulletin*, founded in 1847, folded after years of slow decline. A new owner had managed to raise circulation to 405,000 in 1982 from a 64-year low of 397,000, but the paper's share of the city's advertising market had dropped to 24%. The next major afternoon paper to die was the *Minneapolis Star*, which was folded into the city's morning *Tribune* by the firm that owned them both, Cowles Media Co. Though the *Star* was turning a profit at the end, circulation had slipped from 300,000 to 170,000 since the 1950s. The *Star* had attracted attention in recent years for its attempts to introduce a measure of democracy into the newsroom, in the manner of some European newspapers. Shortly after the *Star*'s fall, the afternoon *Cleveland Press* also folded. Circulation had risen from 304,000 to 316,000 under a new owner, Joseph E. Cole, but with stiff competition from the morning *Plain Dealer*, the *Press* continued to lose $500,000 a month.

A few big-city morning papers were in trouble as well. The morning *Seattle Post-Intelligencer* was saved from extinction when the U.S. Justice Department approved a joint operating agreement with a more prosperous all-day rival, the *Times*. The *Boston Herald American* got a last-minute reprieve when Murdoch bought it from Hearst Corp. The nation's largest general-interest daily newspaper, the morning *New York Daily News* (circulation 1.5 million), came close to folding. Circulation had fallen by nearly 500,000 over the past decade, and the paper lost $12 million in 1981. The parent Tribune Co. of Chicago offered it for sale, but there were no buyers. As Tribune Co. executives were deciding whether to close it, 11 of its key production unions agreed to the elimination of the equivalent of 1,340 jobs, saving the company $50 million per year. The company then promised to invest $44 million in new equipment and declared that the paper was saved.

Another major U.S. journalistic institution was rescued from the edge of oblivion. United Press International, which had lost $32 million since 1975, was sold by the E. W. Scripps Co. to a group of young entrepreneurs. Despite UPI's reputation for quality and its heavy investment in new technology, the news service had been unable to gain ground on the Associated Press, and the problem became acute as newspapers that subscribed to both services were forced by rising costs to choose one. The new owners pledged to spend enough money to make UPI profitable again.

Unlike many countries, the U.S. for years had had no general-interest national newspaper, but that picture began to change in 1982. The *New York Times* started printing a version of the paper, minus local news, on a limited basis in Florida and the western U.S. The *Washington Post* announced plans for a tabloid-size national weekly that would be basically a compilation of the daily *Post*'s major nonlocal articles. In the most important development of all, the Gannett Co., which published 88 dailies around the country, launched a true national daily. *USA Today*, with a start-up press run of 200,000, was initially available in four U.S. metropolitan areas and was scheduled to appear in ten more in 1983.

Five of the 12 major Pulitzer Prizes went to Western papers. The *Kansas City Star* and *Times* were both cited for reporting construction flaws in a walkway that collapsed at a local hotel, killing 113 people. *Seattle Times* reporter Paul Henderson received an award for proving that a man had been wrongly convicted of rape, and the *Detroit News* won a prize for its investigations into the deaths of two U.S. Navy personnel. *Los Angeles Times* music critic Martin Bernheimer received the award for criticism, and syndicated humorist Art Buchwald received the award for commentary. The only two prizes won by papers in the northeast went to the *New York Times*, for editorials by Jack Rosenthal and dispatches from Poland by John Darnton.　　(DONALD MORRISON)

Magazines. Just as the effects of recession really began to affect the mainstream of magazine publishing, the titles actually doing well were those like *Vogue*, whose cover price and ethos were increasingly beyond the reach of the vast majority. In fashionable London, it seemed at times that everyone's enterprising son or daughter was involved in planning a new title to be laden with high-gloss photography and aimed at café society, the traditionally rich, or Arabs.

In the mainstream, things were different. International Publishing Corp., the giant of the British magazine business, could announce sales increases for only 10 of its 50-odd titles in the first half of the year, and 4 of these were in the highly volatile juvenile market. All four of the big-circulation women's weeklies lost ground, and a major autumn promotion included the relaunch of one, *Woman's Realm*, which had lost 45,000 sales. Spotlight revamped its younger women's monthly, *Over 21*, reflecting the pressure in another highly competitive sector. Londoners had found themselves with four weekly guides to the theatres and other activities that fewer and fewer of them could afford, but matters were partly resolved by the folding of the oldest title, *What's On In London*, while another, *Event*, tried to realign itself to a younger audience.

New Society celebrated its 20th anniversary in October. Founded by Timothy Raison, currently a junior minister in Prime Minister Margaret Thatcher's government, it tapped the growing interest in sociological matters but combined that with some good writing and enterprising investigation. It was now selling nearly 30,000 a week, not greatly below its peak of ten years earlier and well above the comparable serious weeklies. Of these, the *Spectator* launched an autumn bid to double its sales, which would still not reach *New Society's* levels. The left-wing *New Statesman* was forced to move its headquarters, at the same time precipitating a boardroom row that pushed the editor, Bruce Page, aside and replaced him with Hugh Stephenson, formerly an economics writer for *The Times*.

The journalism of the left hit another murky patch at year's end when *Tribune*, the organ of the Labour Party left wing since the time of Aneurin Bevan, was the scene of a boardroom coup more appropriate for the City of London. The recently appointed editor had aligned the paper with the ideas of Tony Benn, and less leftward-leaning Labour politicians made the move with the intention of reclaiming its voice before a general election campaign. Some noted the irony of this, set against Labour criticisms of the capitalist press.

The main new activity continued to be in areas associated with other consumer activities, notably magazines for home computer or video enthusiasts. Titles multiplied, but prospects of profit—or even survival—seemed doubtful.

(PETER FIDDICK)

The conventional wisdom that controversy is a sure method of building magazine circulation

Interest in cable TV led to the launching of a magazine devoted to the new medium. Time Inc.'s *TV-Cable Week* was scheduled to appear in early 1983.

TIME, INC.

proved correct in 1982 for *The Atlantic*. After running a controversial interview with U.S. Pres. Ronald Reagan's budget director, David Stockman (December 1981), the monthly magazine experienced a threefold increase in readership, as well as gaining wide publicity in other media. Perhaps illustrating Stockman's doubts about the economy, the 58-year-old *Saturday Review* suspended publication after losing $3 million in a two-year effort to remake itself into a monthly cultural journal.

According to a 1982 study, the number of successful commercial periodicals had increased from 500 in 1964 to 1,200 in 1982. The primary reasons were a high literacy rate, higher incomes, and interest in specialized fields. The most popular growth areas were art and antiques; business and finance; crafts, hobbies, and models; dressmaking; cooking; and fishing and hunting. In decline were magazines about babies, campers, and youth.

The usual 100 to 200 new magazines appeared in 1982. Most of the titles were self-explanatory. *Better Times* offered articles on stretching the dollar; *Fit* aimed to help women design their own physical fitness programs; *New Body* offered hope for both men and women; *Performance Horseman* was in step with renewed interest in horse care; *Collectibles Illustrated* came from the publishers of *Yankee*; and *Popular Computing* was directed to microcomputer fans. The most promising new title, to be published early in 1983, was Time Inc.'s challenge to *TV Guide*. Called *TV-Cable Week*, the *Time*-sized magazine would offer news and comprehensive program listings. The record start-up expense, expected to last five years before profit, was an estimated $100 million.

Women's magazines continued to be among the most popular, with the "seven sisters"—*Better Homes and Gardens, Family Circle, Woman's Day, McCalls, The Ladies' Home Journal, Good Housekeeping,* and *Redbook*—reporting a combined circulation of over 44 million. On the other hand, the four leading feminist magazines (*Savvy, Working Woman, Ms,* and *Working Mother*) had a combined circulation of only 2 million. Harvard's *National Lampoon*, the nation's oldest college humour magazine, selected *Newsweek* for its annual parody in 1982 and expected to sell nearly a million copies. For its part, *Newsweek* planned to buy 50,000 copies to use as premiums for subscribers to the campus edition of the real newsmagazine.

Still another way of viewing magazines was offered in 1982 when BRS (Bibliographic Retrieval Service) put the prestigious *Harvard Business Review* on line. Readers could sit at a computer terminal and call up articles or parts of articles on a display screen. Full text computer availability of numerous other periodicals seemed inevitable in the years to come. The problem with on-line computer searching of magazines, however, was cost. The *Review* royalty was $40 per connect hour, contrasted with an annual subscription for the printed version of $24. At the same time, magazine readers were faced with ever increasing prices. The cost of periodicals rose 14.5% in 1982, bringing the average annual subscription price of a periodical to $44.80. Labour and printing costs continued to rise, while advertising revenues in the first half of 1982 were only even with the same period in 1981.

(WILLIAM A. KATZ)

Books. Despite the hopes for an upturn in publishing fortunes, 1982 was an intensely difficult year for publishers all over the world. Continuing recession kept institutional book budgets and general sales at very low levels, and increasing numbers of third world countries experienced severe foreign exchange shortages, restricting imports of books, paper, and printing raw materials. A general improvement in profit performance by U.K. publishers typically resulted from cutbacks in overhead and staffing and from increased international competitiveness (caused by a more realistically valued pound sterling) rather than from any real growth. Book prices remained stable, and average annual increases were well within inflation rates. The growth of "remaindering," heavy competition in all markets, and the pressure of strengthening paperback and book club sales provided very little room for maneuver in pricing, even though average print runs continued to fall. There was a consequent general concern over low gross margin levels and their eventual effect on profitability.

The main event on the international book calendar was UNESCO's World Congress on Books, organized by the British Publishers Association on behalf of UNESCO and held in London on June 7–11. Over 400 delegates from 92 countries attended to debate the full range of international book problems. The 1982 Frankfurt (West Germany) Book Fair was again a quiet and businesslike affair, although background political excitement was provided by a confrontation between the U.S. and British publishers' associations over market infringements. U.K. publishers were once again the largest national group, with over 573 individual exhibitors. The London Book Fair was moved to the recently opened Barbican Centre and held at a new date, April 6–8. It was hoped that, once separated from the immediate pre-Frankfurt period, the London event would take on a distinct and more significant identity.

In the copyright field, Indonesia, Barbados, and Colombia introduced new legislation, and new acts or substantial amendments were expected from India and Jamaica. Long-awaited developments to provide international copyright protection in Korea and China were frustrated once again. Piracy was probably the most serious problem facing international publishing, but there were indications that the campaign against it was growing in strength and effectiveness. In Pakistan a pirate version of Henry Kissinger's memoires resulted in proceedings against two leading booksellers. A legal ruling in Jordan required the establishment of a copyright register, and the Federation of Indian Publishers established its own antipiracy group. In the U.S., despite strong representations from foreign printers and publishers, Congress overrode a presidential veto and voted to retain the "manufacturing clause," which denies copyright protection to books by U.S. authors that are printed outside the country, until 1986.

As a response to the challenge of rapid techno-logical change in the communications industry, 14 major British publishers established Publishers Databases Ltd. A commercial vehicle, open to all publishers, it would undertake to produce common "open access" systems, with compatible standards and an international distribution system. This would probably require the establishment, under the control of publishers, of a system of electronic distribution equivalent to the physical systems built up over the centuries for printed materials. The project attracted interest among member countries of the European Communities.

(ANTHONY A. READ)

In keeping with the rest of the sagging economy, the U.S. publishing industry suffered through a period that ranged from disappointment to disaster. Although net sales of books reached $7,368,000,000 in 1981, an increase of 9.7% over 1980, the growth reflected increased cover prices, and unit sales rose only modestly. The news did not improve in the first half of 1982. According to the Book Industry Study Group, sales in the first six months of 1982 grew only 1.3% in dollars and dropped almost 3% in units. The only bright note was that book sales, while anemic, were outpacing U.S. retailing as a whole. Among those categories hardest hit were adult hardcovers, mail order sales, mass-market paperbacks, and those industry segments dependent on institutional buying.

The perilous state of publishing was reflected on the merger and acquisition scene as large corporations that scrambled to acquire publishing properties in the late 1960s and early 1970s began to cut their losses. The most dramatic example was the departure of CBS from the field of paperback publishing. Although it retained a book-publishing division, CBS sold the assets of Fawcett Books to Random House, itself owned by Newhouse Publications. CBS also sold over 2,000 Popular Library titles to Warner Books. Grosset & Dunlap, once a power in the children's book field, and its paperback division, Ace Books, were sold by Filmways to the Putnam Publishing Group. Putnam also bought Playboy Press, after the troubled Playboy empire decided to withdraw from book publishing, and Quick Fox, a small publisher of trade paperbacks. The Minneapolis Star & Tribune Co. sold its stock in Harper & Row back to the company, and Thomas Nelson, the nation's largest Bible publisher, bought Dodd, Mead and Co. and Everest House. Economics prompted Harcourt Brace Jovanovich to abandon its New York offices for San Diego, Calif., and Orlando, Fla., where the firm's profitable Sea World amusement park subsidiaries were located. Tower Books, a small paperback house, was sold to its creditors.

The news was not much better for bookstores. The American Booksellers Association surveyed its members and found that profitability had fallen sharply during the past four years; by reasonable standards, half of the stores surveyed were operating at a loss. Meanwhile, the war between independent booksellers and the powerful bookstore chains—specifically, Waldenbooks and B. Dalton—grew more heated. The independents charged that publishers regularly offered discounts to the chains, and in August the American

Booksellers Association appealed to the Federal Trade Commission to investigate these discount schedules. In California a regional booksellers' association brought suit against Avon Books charging discriminatory practices.

There was bad news from Washington as well. The Reagan administration's budget proposals called for new cuts in aid to libraries and education. Another budget target was the Postal Service, which threatened to increase postal rates for books by as much as 50%. Toward year's end, however, the president rolled back postal rates and Congress promised more money for the Postal Service.

The American Writers Congress, held in October 1981, had brought together thousands of writers from across the country in the first such meeting since the 1930s. The Congress, which convened to discuss such issues as libel, conglomerate ownership of the media, intellectual freedom, and relationships with publishers, led to a proposal for a U.S. writers union. By the end of 1982 several locals had been formed, but the effectiveness of such a union was widely debated. Publishers also faced the union issue from within the ranks of their own employees, and at one major house, Viking Penguin, the employees voted to organize. Another writer-publisher issue moved toward solution when Viking Penguin became the first major publisher to offer libel insurance to all of its writers. Several other large publishing houses followed suit.

Aside from its practical problems, the book industry faced mounting criticism of the kinds of books being published. Critics decried the proliferation of so-called nonbooks, best represented by such titles as *Real Men Don't Eat Quiche* and the six best-selling books by cartoonist Jim Davis featuring an arrogant cat named Garfield (*see* Biographies). The craze for the Rubik's Cube puzzle and the growing video industry inspired such best-sellers as *The Simple Solution to Rubik's Cube, How to Win at Pac-Man,* and *How to Master Video Games,* while a novelization of the film *E.T. The Extraterrestrial* sold millions of copies. America's passion for diet, fitness fads, and sexual fulfillment produced such winners as *The I Love New York Diet, Jane Fonda's Workout Book,* and Dr. Joyce Brothers's *What Every Woman Should Know About Men.*

Yet seriousness found a place on the country's reading lists. A complex novel, *The White Hotel* by D. M. Thomas, won a million-copy paperback printing and the kind of promotion usually reserved for books of a more popular nature. Another success was James Clavell's *Noble House.* Other familiar names that returned to the best-seller lists included John Irving (*The Hotel New Hampshire*), Stephen King (*Cujo* and *Different Seasons*), and Robert Ludlum (*The Parsifal Mosaic*). Leaving little doubt that publishers were still producing books of substance, *The Fate of the Earth* by Jonathan Schell (*see* Biographies), a disturbing appraisal of the scientific and metaphysical effects of a nuclear war, was a best-seller in hardcover and was sold to Avon for paperback publication for the amount of $275,000. (KENNETH C. DAVIS)

See also Literature.
[441.D; 543.A.4.e]

Qatar

Qatar

An independent monarchy (emirate) on the west coast of the Persian Gulf, Qatar occupies a desert peninsula east of Bahrain, with Saudi Arabia and the United Arab Emirates bordering it on the south. Area: 11,400 sq km (4,400 sq mi). Pop. (1981 est.): 220,000. Capital: Doha (pop., 1981 est., 190,000). Language: Arabic. Religion: Muslim. Emir and prime minister in 1982, Sheikh Khalifah ibn Hamad ath-Thani.

Falling oil revenue and setbacks over a major planned gas field development provided a gloomy outlook for the Arab world's smallest state in 1982. Oil revenue for the year, from production levels of 300,000 bbl a day, was expected to gross $3 billion, significantly less than the $5 billion a year earned in 1980 and 1981. Oil production was reduced by 25% in April 1982 as part of the Organization of Petroleum Exporting Countries (OPEC) strategy aimed at eliminating the world oil glut. Government spending was also cut, adversely affecting the business community.

Qatar's biggest projects, for the recovery of gas at the offshore North Field, advanced more slowly than anticipated. Potential joint venture partners were reluctant to commit new funds for investment in the Gulf because of the Iran-Iraq war, and slackness in the world markets for liquefied gas was another inhibiting factor. The government decided, nevertheless, to go ahead with an interim scheme to harness gas for power generation and desalination. At the North Field a minimum investment of $6 billion would be required to bring the field of nonassociated gas on stream.

A number of development projects were completed in 1982 for Emir Sheikh Khalifah ibn Hamad ath-Thani's tenth anniversary as ruler. They included the Hamad Hospital, designed to service the health needs of Qatar well into the 21st century, and the Sheraton West Bay government hotel and conference centre—big enough to hold a full meeting of OPEC.

In October 1983 the first 3,000 students were expected to move into a new university campus. (JOHN WHELAN)

QATAR

Education. (1982) Primary, pupils 42,392, teachers 3,000; secondary, pupils (1979–80) 14,360, teachers 1,475; vocational, pupils 550, teachers (1979–80) 78; teacher training (1979–80), students 65, teachers 26; higher (1976–77), students 910, teaching staff 300.

Finance. Monetary unit: Qatar riyal, with (Sept. 20, 1982) a free rate of 3.64 riyals to U.S. $1 (6.24 riyals = £1 sterling). Gold and other reserves (Sept. 1981) U.S. $374 million. Budget (total; 1980–81 est.) balanced at 19,243,000,000 riyals.

Foreign Trade. (1981) Imports 5,554,000,000 riyals; exports 20,716,000,000 riyals. Import sources (1980): Japan 18%; U.K. 18%; U.S. 11%; West Germany 6%; France 5%; Italy 5%. Export destinations (1980): Japan 28%; The Netherlands 16%; France 11%; Thailand 8%; Italy 6%; Spain 6%. Main export: crude oil 93%.

Industry. Production (in 000; metric tons; 1981): crude oil 19,612; natural gas (cu m) 4,590,000; petroleum products (1979) c 302; nitrogenous fertilizers (1980–81) 286; electricity (kw-hr; 1980) c. 1,450,000.

Puerto Rico:
see Dependent States

Race Relations

The disabilities and hardships suffered by ethnic minorities in many parts of the world were accentuated in 1982 by the economic recession. Racial prejudice increasingly found expression in demands for the repatriation of foreign workers in countries such as West Germany, France, and Switzerland, and incidents of racially motivated violence proliferated in those and other countries. In South Africa moves toward a liberalization of apartheid—institutionalized racism—were merely cosmetic in effect and met with a backlash from entrenched white supremacists. In the U.S. black civil rights leaders said that under Pres. Ronald Reagan the distance between the White House and black America was greater than at any time in the past 50 years.

Great Britain. The Committee of Enquiry into the Education of Children of Ethnic Minorities in its interim report of June 1981 concluded that "racism, both intentional and unintentional, has a direct and important bearing on the performance of West Indian children in our schools." The committee also said that evidence of racism was found in teacher attitudes and expectations, in the curriculum and teaching materials, and in public examinations. In October 1982 additional support for these findings was provided in a study of a number of London schools by Michael Rutter. His study also related to the operation of institutional racism in the labour market. He found that, although black parents had comparable education, they were twice as likely to be in unskilled jobs as white parents. He also found that among school dropouts more than twice as many blacks were out of work as whites. These findings paralleled Department of Employment figures, which showed that black unemployment had been rising at a rate double that for whites. In Liverpool, the site of the Toxteth uprisings of July 1981, it was estimated that as many as 75% of black youngsters were on the dole.

There was continuing controversy over the government's refusal to establish an effective system for monitoring the employment patterns of government contractors—or indeed its own employment practices. In addition, there was mounting evidence during the year that Department of Health and Social Security officials—on the basis of new regulations and on their own discretion— were refusing benefits to black people, demanding the production of passports by blacks, and passing on information to immigration officials at the Home Office. New procedures determining eligibility for National Health Service treatment brought into force in October 1982 were seen as contributing to what was called a "pass law society" for black people.

Although a number of police liaison committees were established in the wake of the 1981 uprisings, there was still great controversy surrounding police-black relations. The publication by the Metropolitan Police of London on March 10, 1982, of race-coded crime statistics based on the perception of victims of one particular category of crime— "robbery and other violent thefts"—particularly angered the black community as being a distortion of reality and likely to increase racial tensions. Equally disturbing was the view of Jamaicans of the new commissioner of the Metropolitan Police, Sir Kenneth Newman. In an interview for the U.S. *Police Magazine* in January 1982 he declared, "In the Jamaicans you have a people who are constitutionally disorderly. It's simply in their make-up."

The other major aspect of police-black relations, protection—or lack of it—of the black community against racial attacks, continued to be a subject of controversy during the year following the publication of the Home Office *Report on Racial Attacks* on Nov. 17, 1981. The level of racist violence continued to increase, as did charges of lack of interest on the part of the police. Following a series of racist arson attacks that killed black men, women, and children, the Fire Brigades Union began a unique monitoring project of arson attacks in the London area. In this atmosphere 12 young Asians in Bradford made gasoline bombs to protect their community from attack by white "skinheads." They were arrested and charged with conspiracy to cause explosions—a major felony charge—although their assailants, arrested with gasoline bombs at the same time, were charged only with theft of the milk bottles. On June 15, 1982, the jury at Leeds Crown Court acquitted all 12 defendants after accepting their self-defense plea.

The increasing level of deportations that affected black communities throughout Britain did not satisfy the growing body of racists and fascists, including those with links to the right wing of the Conservative Party. Enoch Powell, addressing a fringe meeting at the Conservative Party conference in October 1982, continued his campaign for the repatriation/deportation of Britain's black population. He called for them to be "deliberately and systematically trained in jobs related to the needs and prospects of their home countries in readiness for repatriation."

Starting in October, Vietnam began permitting "Amerasians" to leave that country for resettlement in the U.S. The children were offspring of U.S. servicemen and Vietnamese women. Frederick Eilerman of Manchester, Connecticut, greeted his 10-year-old son and 12-year-old adopted daughter when they arrived in New York on October 15.

Quakers:
see Religion

Quarrying:
see Mining and Quarrying

Continental Western Europe. In France demands for an end to immigration and for the deportation of foreign workers (mainly North Africans) were accompanied by a rising tide of violence. This included a gasoline bomb attack on Feb. 9, 1982, in Avignon on hunger strikers in a church by a group calling itself the "OAS Returns." Violence was also directed against Jews and an attack on a Jewish restaurant in Paris left six dead and a number of wounded. In West Germany violent crimes against foreigners doubled during the year, and racist slogans accompanied by swastikas and SS symbols adorned the walls of German cities.

This crude and ugly racism was paralleled by the "Heidelberg Manifesto" issued in 1981 by a group of university professors. They warned that the West German people were in danger of being swamped by mass immigration of the dependents of foreign workers and the higher birthrate of the foreigners. They opposed integration of foreigners into German society and called for measures to protect the German "Volk," including dismissal of foreign workers and measures to deport immigrants. Such measures received support from politicians in all the main political parties.

South Africa. The central dynamic of apartheid continued to dominate South African society throughout the year. The changes that took place were in those areas characterized as "petty apartheid." Even these limited changes caused a split in the National Party with the *verkramptes*—the hard-liners—led by Andries Treurnicht leaving to form the Conservative Party.

The major pillars of apartheid were the homelands policy, designed to denationalize the black population; the resettlement program, designed to pack as many blacks as possible into the homelands; and the pass laws and influx control regulations, designed to allow out of the homelands only those needed by the white economy. More than three million people had been forcibly relocated over 20 years, and it was estimated that a further one million were scheduled for removal in the near future. The ultimate goal was to make the entire black population statutory foreigners. The homelands were largely overcrowded rural slums.

Blacks in South Africa were resisting these plans in a variety of ways. For example, Bophuthatswana's first general election since "independence" five years earlier brought out the votes of 135 Tswanas in Soweto and Johannesburg—out of 300,000 Tswanas in those areas. Nthato Motlana, chairman of the Soweto Civic Association, declared, "It means no racial planners in Pretoria are going to foreignize us by drawing lines on a map. It means Tswanas in Soweto remain firm in their view of themselves as South Africans—in spite of five years of propaganda."

United States. Race relations in the U.S. were characterized by a worsening in the economic position of blacks and other racial minorities, a shift away from affirmative action by the federal government, and an increasing level of racist violence by resurgent racist and fascist groups. Black unemployment continued to rise during the year and was more than double the white rate. More than

half of young blacks were officially unemployed, with the real figure in ghetto areas substantially higher.

This situation was exacerbated during the year by the collapse of large parts of the unionized basic industries and by the differential effect of cuts in federal government employment—particularly in social service agencies—upon black male and female professionals. Another instance of differential impacts concerned budget cuts; blacks made up one-third of those receiving food stamps, Medicaid, and public housing accommodations and almost half of those receiving Aid to Families with Dependent Children—the programs being cut most severely.

In a clear shift away from the commitment to affirmative action that had characterized the federal government since the mid-1960s, the Reagan administration made it clear that it would no longer support class-action lawsuits and called for the U.S. Supreme Court to overturn its 1978 decision in the Weber case, which authorized voluntary preference schemes for minorities and women in hiring and promotion. Under new regulations announced in August 1981 by Secretary of Labor Raymond J. Donovan, only 4,000 of the total 17,000 government contractors would have to submit affirmative action plans as a condition of being eligible for government contracts. On Nov. 20, 1981, the head of the Civil Rights Division of the U.S. Department of Justice articulated the administration's underlying philosophy when he declared that "school children will no longer be compelled to have an integrated education if they choose against it." The chairman of the U.S. Commission on Civil Rights was fired for supporting affirmative action in a report entitled "Affirmative Action in the 1980s" in which the commission declared that "discrimination experienced by minorities and women is far more pervasive, entrenched, and varied than many critics of affirmative action maintain."   (LOUIS KUSHNICK)

[522.B]

Marchers, hoping to influence Congress to extend the 1965 Voting Rights Act, left Carrollton, Alabama, in February for a long hike that ended in Washington, D.C., in June.

THE LATINIZATION OF THE U.S.

by John T. Kenna

They are known as Hispanics, Latinos, Spanish-surname, Spanish-speaking, or Hispanos. They themselves usually prefer to be identified according to their national heritage. Thus, they are Mexican-Americans (or Chicanos), Puerto Ricans, Cuban-Americans, or people from any of the 16 Spanish-speaking Central American or South American countries.

Unlike European Spaniards, Hispanics in the United States are not sociologically classified as whites. In popular terminology, they are often referred to as "browns." When the Spaniards colonized areas with indigenous populations of Native Americans, they intermarried and produced a mixed race (mestizos). These groups also mixed with Africans brought to the Americas as slaves, and the result was a new breed of people that mingles three races.

Similarities and Differences. The Spanish language is the unifying factor among the Hispanics in the U.S., as it is for the more than 250 million persons who make up Hispanidad throughout the world. Another source of common identity is religion. At least 85% of Hispanics are Roman Catholic.

There are also certain social, economic, and cultural characteristics that most Hispanics share. Eighty-four percent are congregated in large metropolitan areas, compared with 66% of the general population. They are, with some exceptions, poor, having lower incomes per family and higher levels of unemployment than the average American family. Hispanics also have a high degree of family stability and a larger than average number of children per family. With increasing acculturation, however, there is a consistent decline in these factors.

Politically, Hispanics are the most underrepresented ethnic group in the nation. They have only nine members in the U.S. House of Representatives, no U.S. senators, one state governor, mayors of only two major cities (San Antonio, Texas, and Miami), and, except for one state (New Mexico), disproportionately low representation in state legislatures.

Descriptions of common characteristics should

John T. Kenna is a Chicago writer specializing in religious and cultural affairs.

not obscure the vast differences that exist. Within the Hispanic community, there is a rich variety of histories and traditions. Even the way Spanish is spoken differs among the various groups. Some observers believe these differences impede the unity that is necessary for the political success of the Hispanic community as a whole.

A Growing Population. The 1980 U.S. census recorded 14.6 million Hispanics in a total national population of 226.5 million. This made the Hispanics the nation's second largest minority, after the blacks, who numbered 26.5 million. It also gave the U.S. the distinction of having the sixth largest Hispanic population in the world.

During the 1970s, the national growth rate was a low 11.4%, reflecting the decline that began after the baby boom of the 1950s. In sharp contrast, the growth rate for Hispanics during the 1970s was 61%, and even faster growth was likely in the 1980s and 1990s. As of 1980 the median age for Hispanics was 23 years, compared with 30 for non-Hispanics. If the Cubans, who have a surprisingly high median age of 38, were excluded, the median age for Hispanics would be 19 or 20. Hispanic women have a higher fertility rate than that of any other group in the country. Based on these data, together with projected immigration figures, many population authorities believe that by the early 1990s Hispanics could be the largest single ethnic group in the U.S.

Minorities Within a Minority. Mexicans account for 60.6% of the U.S. Hispanic population. They are heavily concentrated in the Southwest and West, areas that were claimed by Spanish explorers and evangelized by Spanish missionaries. Almost all the Hispanics in the Southwest chose to become U.S. citizens in 1848, when Mexico ceded that vast area to the U.S. following the Mexican War.

Until the 1930s, it was common for people to come and go at will across the relatively unguarded 3,060-km (1,900-mi) Mexican-U.S. border. The Mexican Revolution that began in 1910 caused thousands of political refugees to seek asylum in the U.S. Thousands more came later in search of better economic opportunities. Beginning in the early 1940s, temporary seasonal farm workers (braceros) were allowed to come into the U.S. from Mexico in large numbers. A decade later, "illegal alien" or undocumented workers began to pour into the U.S., driven by population pressures and severe economic deprivation and attracted by the need of U.S. industry for low-paid, unskilled labour.

Puerto Ricans, who constitute 14.5% of the country's Hispanic population, are U.S. citizens because Spain ceded the island to the U.S. in 1898 after the Spanish-American War. Internal migration by air between the island and the mainland became heavy in

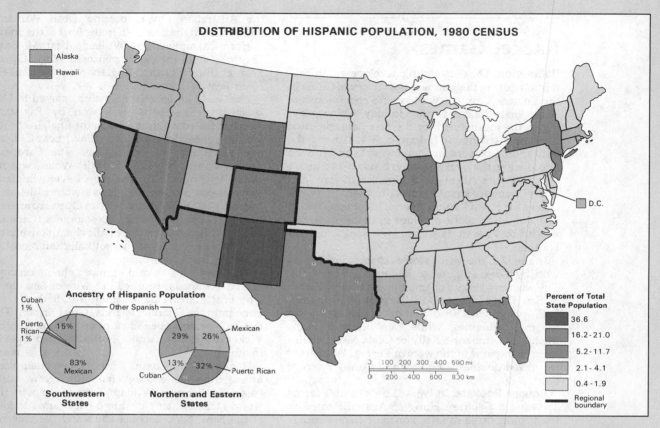

DISTRIBUTION OF HISPANIC POPULATION, 1980 CENSUS

Alaska
Hawaii

Ancestry of Hispanic Population

Cuban 1%
Puerto Rican 1%
Other Spanish
15%
83% Mexican
Southwestern States

Mexican
26%
29%
Puerto Rican 32%
Cuban 13%
Northern and Eastern States

D.C.

Percent of Total State Population

36.6
16.2 - 21.0
5.2 - 11.7
2.1 - 4.1
0.4 - 1.9
Regional boundary

0 100 200 300 400 500 mi
0 200 400 600 800 km

---

the 1950s and 1960s. Most of the Puerto Ricans settled in the Northeastern states, especially in New York City, but there are also fairly large clusters in the big cities of western Pennsylvania and some Midwestern states. Among Hispanics, Puerto Ricans are at the low end of the economic scale.

The most successful economically are the Cubans, who make up 6.6% of U.S. Hispanics. They did not migrate to the U.S. in substantial numbers until 1959, when Fidel Castro came to power. Since then, successive waves of political refugees have flocked to Miami from Communist Cuba, led by the skilled, entrepreneurial classes, then followed by lower middle class workers. Their number exceeds 500,000. Most have remained in the Miami area, where they have become a major success story.

About 125,000 more arrived in 1980, when Castro first eased restrictions on emigration, then emptied Cuban jails and mental institutions and forced the inmates into small boats waiting in Mariel harbour to take the refugees to the U.S. These less desirable newcomers, many of whom were incarcerated upon arrival, caused serious disruptions among the Cuban-Americans already established in Miami.

Immigrants from Central and South American countries, who account for 7% of the U.S. Hispanic population, have come to the U.S. both as political refugees (the most recent being Guatemalans and Salvadorans) and as seekers after economic opportunity. They are a diverse group, ranging from uneducated and unskilled labourers to highly trained professionals. Many of them, especially the affluent and well educated, tend to remain aloof from the other groups of Hispanics. Their aim is to be assimilated into the larger U.S. society.

Issues for the Future. Several broad issues face not only Hispanics but the rest of the nation in the years ahead. Should the U.S. try to reduce immigration across the Mexican-U.S. border—at a huge cost—because, as some claim, the immigrants take jobs Americans need? Or should the U.S. relax border surveillance and/or grant amnesty to undocumented workers and their families who have established themselves in the U.S.?

Should Spanish truly become a second language in the U.S., especially in public schools? Can Hispanics, who have tended to be inactive politically, secure proper representation in federal, state, and city governments? To what degree will Hispanics compete or cooperate with other organized groups, such as blacks and women? Finally, are Hispanics going through the same phase of balancing cultural integrity and acculturation that other ethnic groups have experienced?

Their numbers, their youth, and the stated goal of their leaders to attain full entry into the mainstream of U.S. life could make the 1980s the decade of the Hispanics. Their significant numbers in the relatively prosperous Sun Belt states could provide a golden opportunity.

Racket Games

Badminton. The outstanding development in badminton during the year was the victory of China in the Thomas Cup, the world men's championship. In the finals, held in London in May, China, playing in the tournament for the first time, defeated defending champion Indonesia 5–4. Among the outstanding players for China were Luan Jin, who also during the year placed second in the men's singles in the All-England Open; Han Jian; and Chen Changjie, singles winner in the 1981 World Games for Non-Olympic Sports. Indonesia, which had won seven of the previous eight tournaments, was led by veteran stars Liem Swie King and Rudy Hartono.

In the U.S. the men's singles championship was won by Gary Higgins of Redondo Beach, Calif. The women's singles champion was Cheryl Carton of San Diego, Calif. Don Paup of Washington, D.C., paired with Bruce Pontow of Chicago to win the men's doubles, while Pam Brady of Flint, Mich., and Judianne Kelly of Costa Mesa, Calif., were champions in the women's event. Winners of the mixed doubles were Pam and Danny Brady of Flint. (C. R. ELI)

Squash Rackets. In 1981–82 back trouble forced 35-year-old Geoffrey Hung of Australia to retire from competitive squash. For more than a decade he had been the worldwide supreme artist of the British (softball) version of the game. His successor as British Open champion was an 18-year-old Pakistani, Jahangir Khan, who in the final beat fellow Pakistani Hidayat Jahan by 3–0. A four-glass-walled court was used for the final of the British Open. The Open Veterans championship (age 45 and over) was won for the second year by J. G. A. Lyon (England), who defeated P. G. Kirton (England) in the final. Hashim Khan (Pak.) won his fifth Open Vintage championship (age 55 and over) at the age of 69.

The International Squash Professional Association championship was won by Jahangir Khan, who in the final defeated Maqsood Ahmad (Pak.) without conceding a single point. Khan also won the Australian Open, beating Dean Williams (Australia) in the final 3–0. In the final of the South African championships Williams beat M. Saad (Egypt) 3–0. In the Audi-sponsored World Open, held at Birmingham, England, in November, Khan beat Williams 9–2, 6–9, 9–1, 9–1.

The world junior championship, played in Malaysia and Singapore, was won by Pakistan, which defeated Australia 2–1 in the final. In the individual event Sohail Quiser (Pak.) beat C. Dittmar (Australia) in four games. The European championship, played in Cardiff, Wales, was retained by England. In the men's event England beat Sweden 5–0, and England's women defeated Ireland 3–0. The North American Open championship was won by Michael Desaulniers (Canada) and the U.S. Amateur (hardball) championship by John Limiler. The Canadian softball championship was won by D. Whittaker.

The women's world junior championship, played in Canada, resulted in a win for Lisa Opie, who beat Martine Le Moignan 3–0. Both players came from the Channel Islands, Great Britain. The British women's open championship was won by Vicki Cardwell (Australia), who defeated Opie in the final. (JOHN H. HORRY)

Rackets. John Prenn, British Open champion, unseated the defending champion, New York-based Englishman William Surtees, to win the world rackets championship by six games to four at the New York Racquet Club and the Queen's Club, London, in December 1981. Later Prenn beat Surtees in the final of the U.S. Open in Boston, though he lost when they met in the amateur championship final in Chicago. At home Prenn beat William Boone in the amateur championship and Randall Crawley in the Open. In Montreal Prenn won the Canadian title, beating David McLernon in the final. In doubles Prenn was less successful. Boone and Crawley defeated Prenn and Charles Hue Williams to retain the amateur title and later repeated that victory in the final of the Open. They also retained their British amateur doubles championship title, beating Prenn and Williams in the final at Queen's Club in November. With successes also in the U.S., Boone and Crawley were the outstanding pair of the year.

Dave Peck outplayed Mike Yellen in the finals to win the Ektelon/PONY Racquetball Championships in Anaheim, Calif., in May. Peck won 11–3, 11–2, and 11–10.

MILO MUSLIN

Paul Nicholls won the Under-24 championship (Swallow Trophy). In the final he beat Shannon Hazell, professional at Wellington College, who later won the professional title.

Real Tennis. World champion Chris Ronaldson (Hampton Court) retained the British Open and also the professional championships. In the former he beat Wayne Davies of Australia in the final at Queen's Club, London, in November 1981. In the latter he defeated another Australian, Lachlan Deuchar, in the final at Hatfield House in London. Ronaldson and Michael Dean later won the doubles title at the expense of the two Australians.

Howard Angus, former world, British Open, and amateur champion, having lost all his titles the previous year owing to an eye injury, recovered the amateur championship, beating the defending champion, Alan Lovell, in the final. Davies won the U.S. Open title, thus qualifying to challenge Ronaldson for the world title. Gene Scott won the U.S. amateur championship.

(ROY MCKELVIE)

Racquetball. During 1982 the seven-year domination of Marty Hogan in professional racquetball was seriously challenged. Hogan, whose emergence as a 17-year-old boy wonder in 1975 changed the face of competitive racquetball, finally found life at the top of the ladder too tough to survive. David Peck, a 25-year-old former college linebacker from El Paso, Texas, was the player who ended Hogan's domination, capturing the coveted number one rank in racquetball.

Despite Peck's top position, however, Hogan still managed to lead the sport in prize money earnings, primarily owing to his victory in the season's last event, the $100,000 DP/Leach national championships. Peck had earlier captured the Ektelon/PONY and Catalina Series finals. The two men split their four head-to-head battles.

Lynn Adams of Costa Mesa, Calif., became the dominant player in women's professional competition. She wrested the top-ranked position from former champion Heather McKay with a series of victories over McKay in the finals of various tournaments.   (CHARLES S. LEVE)

[452.B.5.h.xxii; 452.B.4.h.xxvii]

Refugees

Although the status of refugees in 1982 improved in some areas, the worldwide situation was a cause for deep concern by the office of the UN High Commissioner for Refugees (UNHCR). In November there was a sudden influx of some 40,000 refugees from Uganda into Rwanda, a small country ill-equipped to care for an additional population. The massive relief operation continued in Pakistan, where the number of Afghan refugees passed the 2.5 million mark. More than 200,000 Indochinese refugees still awaited resettlement in camps throughout Southeast Asia, while many resettlement countries began to show signs of reluctance toward maintaining high resettlement quotas. There were dramatic increases in the number of refugees from El Salvador in Honduras and of Guatemalans seeking asylum in Mexico.

Refugees from El Salvador fled into Honduras where they established makeshift camps.

In Africa, home of about one-half of the world's refugees, it became possible to shift the emphasis of several major UNHCR programs—notably in the Horn of Africa and the Sudan—from care and maintenance exclusively to self-reliance projects and income-generating activities, which, it was hoped, would reduce the long-term burden on host countries. A major voluntary repatriation program was successfully concluded in Chad, where UNHCR assisted a total of 200,000 people by repatriating them and/or providing emergency food, tools, and other items needed to repair their damaged homes. The special program for returnees in Ethiopia was expanded in an effort to encourage continued voluntary repatriation. Rural settlements for Angolan refugees in Zaire made progress toward self-sufficiency, but the Ugandan refugees continued to need large infusions of relief aid. In southern Africa students and other refugees, both in rural settlements and in urban areas, continued to receive UNHCR support.

In cooperation with the Organization of African Unity (OAU), UNHCR continued to follow up on the recommendations of the 1979 conference on the situation of refugees in Africa held in Arusha, Tanzania, and to monitor the results of the 1981 International Conference on Assistance to Refugees in Africa (ICARA). In December the UN General Assembly adopted a resolution calling for a second ICARA to be held in 1984.

A major development in Pakistan was the agreement by the World Bank to assist UNHCR in setting up pilot projects in the sectors of infrastructure construction and reforestation. These enterprises would depend on the refugee population for 50% of their manpower.

During the year UNHCR participated in the overall UN relief effort to aid victims of the conflict in Lebanon. The high commissioner authorized allocations of $5.5 million from the UNHCR emergency fund to assist Lebanese displaced persons in Lebanon as well as Lebanese citizens in a refugee-like situation in Syria.

The number of arrivals of Indochinese refugees

Radio:
see Television and Radio

Railroads:
see Transportation

Real Tennis:
see Racket Games

Recordings:
see Music

Reformed Churches:
see Religion

ALI NUN—SYGMA

It was reported during the year that Afghan refugees who fled into neighbouring Pakistan were costing that nation more than $500 million per year in emergency aid.

continued to decrease throughout the world, and the number of refugees resettled also declined. A total of 47,115 Indochinese refugees arrived by boat or overland in countries of temporary asylum in the region between January 1 and November 30, 1982, while 71,641 were selected for resettlement. This compared with over 99,600 arrivals and 168,500 departures in 1981. Following 393,500 arrivals in the peak year of 1979, 261,800 people had been resettled in 1980, the highest yearly number of departures. By the end of 1982 more than 800,000 Indochinese had been resettled with the assistance of UNHCR. The agency also continued to promote long-term solutions within the region for small groups of refugees. About 1,000 Laotians had repatriated voluntarily, and a program for Kampuchean returnees was helping about 400,000 people to readapt and become self-sufficient.

The work of UNHCR in Central America had to focus on emergency relief for Salvadoran, Nicaraguan, and Guatemalan refugees. Camps had to be enlarged and facilities improved to accommodate continuous arrivals throughout the year. Several hundred refugees were able to be integrated into small agricultural developments in Belize, Costa Rica, Nicaragua, and Panama.

During 1982 three more nations became parties to the 1951 Convention or the 1967 Protocol relating to the status of refugees, bringing the total number of countries acceding to these major international instruments to 93. Despite these accessions, however, there were an alarming number of incidents in violation of internationally accepted principles.

In December 1982 the UN General Assembly adopted a resolution extending the mandate of the UNHCR for five more years beginning on Jan. 1, 1984. The Assembly also elected the incumbent high commissioner, Poul Hartling of Denmark, to a second term of office to last three years. Hartling became high commissioner in 1978.   (UNHCR)

See also Migration, International.

Religion

"Religion and Power" was the theme when the Society for the Scientific Study of Religion gathered for its annual October convention in Providence, R.I. Conference organizers noted the "unusually large number" of scholarly papers submitted that dealt with "religion and politics" in all parts of the world. It was a timely theme. News of religion in 1982 was dominated by stories about the relationship between religion and power. Next in importance were stories about major developments in the ecumenical movement.

Worldwide, religious leaders increased the momentum of their efforts to ward off the threat of nuclear war. The religious peace movement crossed the dividing lines among denominations and normal differences between "conservatives" and "liberals." At a Boston rally in April, evangelist Billy Graham began what aides described as the most ambitious crusade of his career—to alert the nations to the peril of nuclear war. Keynoting his crusade, Graham said: "We are living at this moment on the very edge of the annihilation of the human race."

A month later, Graham and 587 other religious leaders of all "living faiths" met in Moscow at the World Conference of Religious Workers for Saving the Sacred Gift of Life from Nuclear Catastrophe. Called by the Russian Orthodox Church, the session prompted the U.S. State Department to warn 28 American participants about the dangers of being used as pawns of Soviet propaganda. Although some acrimonious statements were made, the conference ended with the delegates in basic accord on the need for an end to "hostile rhetoric" and for a freeze on the development, deployment, and testing of nuclear weapons. (See *Baptist Churches,* below.)

In May the World Council of Churches (WCC),

representing 300 churches in more than 100 nations, contributed to the peace debate by issuing a document, "Before It's Too Late." The declaration stated that "the time has come when the churches must unequivocally declare that the production and deployment, as well as the use, of nuclear weapons are a crime against humanity." Especially noteworthy was the participation in the antinuclear movement by the American hierarchy of the Roman Catholic Church. Bishop Leroy T. Mattheison of Amarillo, Texas, went so far as to urge Catholics working at a nuclear assembly plant to consider switching jobs. However, it was easier for individual bishops to speak and act than it was for the whole hierarchy to speak with one voice. For 18 months the Bishops Committee on War and Peace of the National Conference of Catholic Bishops laboured to prepare a "pastoral letter" on the subject, but the document hit snags when the next-to-last draft was mailed to all the bishops in early summer. Some bishops believed it did not go far enough in calling for the abandonment of nuclear deterrents, while others felt it did not take U.S. security needs seriously enough. All told, the bishops sent in 700 pages of recommended changes, and a final vote on the document was deferred from November to 1983.

The religious peace movement was not without its backlash, however. Typical of the critics was "neoconservative" Catholic commentator Michael Novak, who charged that the peace bishops were guilty of promoting a "Catholicism of very simple judgments that are deeply felt. The liberal Catholic has become mush-headed."

Caught in the clash between religion and power—or, more accurately, between the power of religion and the power of secular states—was Pope John Paul II, whose planned visit to his troubled Polish homeland was postponed until 1983. (See *Roman Catholic Church,* below.) The pope also faced problems at home when the Vatican was rocked by a scandal centring around its Institute for Religious Works, popularly called the Vatican bank. The Vatican bank and its president, U.S.-born Archbishop Paul C. Marcinkus (*see* BIOGRAPHIES), gained unwanted world publicity after auditors

uncovered $1.4 billion in questionable loans made by Italy's largest private bank, the Banco Ambrosiano. Convicted the year before on charges of violating Italian laws by exporting $26.4 million to Switzerland, Roberto Calvi, Ambrosiano's president, fled to England. A short time later, his body was found hanging from the Blackfriars Bridge in London. The day before, his secretary had fallen to her death from a fourth-floor window in Milan.

In news accounts, Calvi was described as an adviser to Marcinkus who, in 1974, came into the world spotlight as a result of his dealings with another adviser, Michele Sindona, now serving a prison sentence in the U.S. for bank fraud and related charges. Reportedly, the Vatican lost millions in the Sindona and Calvi affairs. Faced with these losses and damage to the church's credibility, John Paul took the unprecedented step of appointing four international financiers to examine the relationship between the Vatican Bank and the Banco Ambrosiano. At a special meeting of the College of Cardinals, the pope pledged that the Vatican would cooperate with Italian authorities to see that the whole truth came to light.

In the U.S. piety and politics were interwoven throughout 1982. Elected in 1980 with help from the well-organized "New Christian Right," Pres. Ronald Reagan disappointed his most conservative backers at the beginning of his term by putting on the "back burner" some of the issues most important to his right-wing constituents. As the 1982 congressional elections neared, however, Reagan began to push for legislation that would solidify his support in many large conservative constituencies. In particular, he urged adoption of tuition tax credits for parents of children attending nonpublic schools and passage of two constitutional amendments, one sanctioning prayers in public schools, the other aimed at circumventing the Supreme Court decision legalizing abortion. The amendments were defeated by liberal filibusters just before Congress's pre-election recess, but their supporters vowed to continue the fight.

All these issues sharply divided the nation's religious communities. Civil libertarians joined numerous mainline church leaders in opposing the

The religious peace movement spurred efforts—such as this demonstration in front of the White House—to halt the arms race and to ward off the threat of nuclear war.

WALLY MCNAMEE/NEWSWEEK

"prayer amendment." Reflecting this viewpoint, Dean M. Kelley of the National Council of Churches charged that the amendment "makes the rights of members of the religious minorities dependent upon the self-restraint of religious majorities." Countering this point of view, E. E. McAteer of the Religious Roundtable called upon Congress to undo court decisions that declare "God unwelcome in our classrooms." The other two measures elicited equally strong statements from both supporters and critics. After the votes were counted in the November election, it became obvious that the power of the New Christian Right had waned significantly since 1980.

The power of religion and the power of secular "principalities and powers" also met head-on in the nation's courts. In Little Rock, Ark., a federal judge struck down a state law passed in 1981 that required the teaching of "scientific creationism" in the public schools. Judge William R. Overton ruled that the legislation violated constitutional separation of church and state by introducing "the biblical version of creation into the public school curricula." In November a federal judge handed down a similar ruling in Louisiana, arguing that the state legislature had exceeded the limits of its power by enacting legislation that dictated to public schools "not only that a subject must be taught, but also how it should be taught."

In New York City the Rev. Sun Myung Moon, Korean-born evangelist and founder of the controversial Unification Church, was sentenced to an 18-month prison term after being found guilty of tax fraud and conspiracy to obstruct justice. The prosecution accused him of using his organization to avoid personal income taxes, but his followers contended that the verdict was an act of "religious persecution." Moon had incurred widespread hostility from parents of his youthful followers, who believed their children had been brainwashed by cultic indoctrination techniques. Nevertheless, his work expanded. After the *Washington* (D.C.) *Star* was shut down, Moon began the *Washington Times* as a "new national daily."

In another notable development, the ecumenical movement began to move again after more than a decade of near stagnation. In January the Faith and Order Commission of the wcc unanimously approved a resolution that, in the words of one ecumenist, provided a "framework for church union" by reaching general consensus on such once controversial issues as baptism, the Eucharist, and the nature of ministry.

The Anglican-Roman Catholic study commission completed 12 years of work on an ecumenical document stating that there was no reason in principle why Anglicans could not unite with Catholics under the primacy of the bishop of Rome. Old wounds were healed within Presbyterianism and Lutheranism as well. The general assemblies of the United Presbyterian Church and the Presbyterian Church in the United States approved resolutions that soon could rejoin those two bodies, separated since the Civil War. (See *Reformed, Presbyterian, and Congregational Churches*, below.) Three branches of Lutheranism in the U.S. approved steps leading to a merger that would bring a 5.4 million-member denomination into being by Jan. 1, 1988. (See *Lutheran Churches*, below.) Meanwhile, these same three branches of Lutheranism and the Episcopal Church reached a historic accord allowing "common joint celebrations" of communion led by clergy of both traditions.

Although ecumenical relations flowered, interfaith relations withered under the pressures of war. Jewish-Christian relationships deteriorated sharply after the Israeli invasion of Lebanon. Numerous mainline church leaders denounced Israel for attacking civilian populations in and around Beirut and for failing to prevent the massacre of Palestinians by Lebanese Christians in two West Beirut refugee camps. (See *Judaism*, below.) Tensions were further exacerbated in September when Pope John Paul agreed to meet in Rome with Yasir Arafat, the leader of the Palestine Liberation Organization (PLO). A senior Israeli official charged: "The same church that did not say a word about the massacre of Jews for six years in Europe [during World War II] and did not say much about the killing of Christians in Lebanon for seven years is ready to meet the man who perpetrated the crime in Lebanon and is bent on the destruction of Israel, which is the completion of the work done by the Nazis in Germany." In an unusually angry response, the Vatican described that statement as an "outrage to the truth."

Although the ecumenical outlook was much brighter than it had been, it was not completely rosy. Some Anglicans and Roman Catholics were both mystified and angry when a former Episcopal priest, married and the father of two daughters, was accepted into the priesthood of the Roman Catholic Church. At a rite on June 29 in Springfield, Mo., the Rev. James Parker was reordained and two days later celebrated his first mass, serving communion to his wife. The angriest outcries came from Roman Catholics who for years had called for an end to mandatory clerical celibacy and recognition of priests who were ordained in the Catholic Church and later married.

Also deserving mention in an account of the world of religion in 1982:

A federal grand jury investigation into charges that John Cardinal Cody (*see* OBITUARIES), Roman Catholic archbishop of Chicago, had diverted tax-exempt church funds to a lifelong friend ended when Cody, the chief target of the probe, died in April. He was succeeded by Archbishop Joseph L. Bernardin of Cincinnati, Ohio, a major figure in world Catholicism, who was received with joy by Chicago Catholics.

Although moderates made a strong showing, biblical literalists continued to dominate the Southern Baptist Convention, the largest Protestant denomination in the U.S. with 13.6 million members. Conservative dominance was reaffirmed when James T. Draper was elected president, defeating his more moderate rival, theologian Duke McCall. (See *Baptist Churches*, below.)

Leaders of the Baha'i faith continued to report that their co-religionists in Iran were being systematically persecuted and put to death by the radical Shi'ah Muslim regime of Ayatollah Ruhollah Khomeini.   (ROY LARSON)

Archbishop of Canterbury Robert Runcie (left) and Pope John Paul II prayed together in Canterbury on May 29. The meeting was regarded as a historic one by both Anglicans and Roman Catholics.

PROTESTANT CHURCHES

Anglican Communion. For Anglicans, the high point of the year was undoubtedly the history-making visit on May 29 of Pope John Paul II to Canterbury, cradle of English Christianity and founding city of Anglicanism. Pope and archbishop knelt together in prayer in the ancient cathedral and later issued a common declaration spelling out "the next stage of our common pilgrimage in faith and hope toward the unity for which we long."

Among other things, the declaration revealed that a second body would carry on the work of the Anglican-Roman Catholic International Commission (ARCIC), whose final report had been published two months earlier. Having managed to agree on a great deal, including the idea of the pope as "universal primate" in any future unity scheme, the ARCIC members felt their 12 years of discussions should now be followed by a new and closer relationship between their two churches. The Vatican's Sacred Congregation for the Doctrine of the Faith was less enthusiastic, although it did call for the dialogue to continue and to be extended to new themes.

Ecumenical hopes suffered a major blow in another quarter when the General Synod of the Church of England, in July, rejected the proposed scheme for a covenant with three Free churches. In the U.S. the General Convention of the Episcopal Church, meeting in New Orleans, La., in September, approved closer ties with Lutherans. (See *Lutheran Churches*, below.)

Several times during the year the Church of England had the unusual experience of being at odds with the Conservative government. The lack of patriotic fervour in the service at St. Paul's Cathedral marking the end of the Falklands conflict drew angry reaction, as did a revision of the national anthem in a new hymnbook. In October a report drawn up for the General Synod, advocating unilateral nuclear disarmament

by Britain, was considered unrealistic by Prime Minister Margaret Thatcher.

In South Africa the bishop of Kimberley and Kuruman resigned, having been, in effect, forced out of office by the South African government. It was thought that the authorities were reacting to the bishop's championship of black detainees. However, there was one pleasant surprise out of South Africa in 1982: Bishop Desmond Tutu (*see* BIOGRAPHIES), who had earlier had his passport withdrawn, was suddenly allowed to leave the country for a short period in order to address the General Convention of the Episcopal Church.

(SUSAN YOUNG)

Baptist Churches. Baptists in Eastern Europe continued to give and receive mixed signals. While faith was tolerated in many places, in Estonia Dmitry Vasilevich Minyakov, a member of the Council of Evangelical Christian Baptist Churches in the U.S.S.R., was sentenced to five years in a forced labour camp. In Romania one of the few highly trained pastors, Josif Ton, was granted a visa to leave the country with the proviso that he not return.

The Baptist evangelist Billy Graham attended an antinuclear conference in the U.S.S.R., where he made remarks about religious freedom in the Soviet Union that were interpreted in the U.S. as "soft" on Communism. Graham's defenders insisted that his natural good will and optimism led him to believe it was possible to talk, privately if not publicly, to the Soviets about religious freedom. His critics accused him of naiveté.

U.S. evangelist Billy Graham (foreground) and other religious leaders attended an antinuclear conference in Moscow. The conference received wide publicity in the Soviet Union.

Religion

At the annual meeting of the Southern Baptist Convention, held in June in New Orleans, Jimmy Draper, pastor of a large church in Texas, was elected president. He succeeded the controversial Bailey Smith, who stated in one speech during his incumbency that he did not believe God heard the prayers of Jews. Draper was considered somewhat more moderate than Smith, but the battle between the conservative champions of biblical inerrancy and the moderates went to the conservatives. In a possibly more significant though less publicized move, the SBC went on record supporting the passage of a school prayer amendment. This was inconsistent with the traditional Baptist stance on the separation of church and state and reversed an anti-school-prayer statement passed by the Southern Baptists in 1980.

At the annual meeting of the largely black Progressive National Baptist Convention, 8,000 delegates from the 1.5 million-member denomination condemned Israel for invading Lebanon. After serving as president of the National Baptist Convention, U.S.A., for 29 years, Joseph H. Jackson was defeated for reelection by T. J. Jemison at the annual meeting of the nation's largest black Baptist group.

The American Baptist Churches in the U.S.A. filed an amicus curiae brief with the Supreme Court in opposition to the government's position in a case involving Bob Jones University, a fundamentalist school in Greenville, S.C. In a letter to Bob Jones, president of the school, Robert Campbell, general secretary of the ABC, USA, stated, "... even though we repudiate any form of racism for any reason and believe that yours is a racist institution, [we oppose] the government's position with respect to the revocation of the [tax] exempt status of your institution, ... solely because of our commitment to religious and constitutional principles of separation of church and state."　(NORMAN R. DE PUY)

Christian Church (Disciples of Christ). Completing five years of bilateral talks, a joint international commission of the Disciples of Christ and the Roman Catholic Church agreed that baptism is the source of Christian unity and the Lord's Supper its nourishment. Representatives of the two bodies called for further dialogue, noting that while the churches are quite different in size, origins, tradition, and style, both celebrate the Eucharist weekly and have a common concern for the wholeness of the church.

The Disciples and their United Church of Christ counterparts on a union steering committee acknowledged their advocacy of union but delayed making a recommendation until studies of mission, ministry, and sacraments begun by more than 700 congregations were completed. The small body of Canadian Disciples voted to continue union conversations with the United Church of Canada.

Disciples experienced a major leadership turnover, losing nearly half of their division heads to retirement in a 13-month period. Most had helped forge the restructure in the late 1960s that brought the church into being from a convention of congregations, individuals, and agencies.

"Peace with Justice" was the church's program priority, and Disciples took part in a demonstration at the UN. Regional and general leaders implored members to involve themselves in peace efforts, an Advent Peace Sunday was established, and a peace consultation was set up at the church's Eureka (Ill.) College.
　　　　　　　　　(ROBERT LOUIS FRIEDLY)

Churches of Christ. Churches in the U.S. and Europe contributed over $2 million for 392 tons of food and other supplies for Christians in Poland in 1982. Churches of Christ in Poland were officially recognized on April 14, ending 20 years during which they had been forced to meet secretly.

World Christian Broadcasting received a permit from the U.S. Federal Communications Commission to begin construction of a shortwave radio station at Anchor Point, Alaska. At least one-third of the world's population would be within broadcast range of the station, scheduled for completion in July 1983. Initial broadcasts would be in Mandarin Chinese and Russian. Missionary Stephen Ma baptized 1,295 people during six months spent in two campaigns into China. The Garden Oaks Church in Houston, Texas, was recognized by the governments of Guatemala and Honduras as a Friend of the Nation for its efforts to aid disaster victims there.

In its 150 years of existence, the church in the U.S. had grown from a small group in West Virginia and two in Kentucky to two million members in 13,250 congregations. In 1981, 58,702 baptisms were reported by 1,328 congregations and the World Bible School.　　　　(M. NORVEL YOUNG)

Church of Christ, Scientist. A new nondenominational Bible exhibit at the church's Boston headquarters was visited by more than 20,000 persons during its first nine months. Focusing on the theme "A Light Unto My Path," the exhibit featured a 13.5-m (44-ft) carved Plexiglas map of the Bible lands, on which important biblical journeys were traced by means of fibre optics; a multimedia film on the Holy Lands and the Scriptures' message today; and a Bible study-reference centre. Scholars from nearby Harvard and Boston universities had lent their expertise to the exhibit, which was 14 years in the making.

At the church's annual meeting in June, Michael Thorneloe, chairman of the denomination's Board of Directors, spoke of "a great yearning throughout the world for the elimination of nuclear dangers. The only answer to this yearning," he continued, "comes from an understanding of God and divine power."

The endowment fund for the *Christian Science Monitor* continued to grow; *Monitor* stories were being syndicated in 206 newspapers. An international youth meeting in August attracted some 2,000 young Christian Scientists from around the world.
　　　　　　　　　(ALLISON W. PHINNEY)

Church of Jesus Christ of Latter-day Saints. The discovery of an 1829 letter, the earliest known dated document concerning the Latter-day Saint movement, was announced in August. Written by Lucy Mack Smith, mother of church founder Joseph Smith, the letter provided information about Smith's translation of materials related to the Book of Mormon and about his early revelatory experiences.

Early in 1982 church membership surpassed five million. The first stake (diocese) in Spain was organized in March.

Policy changes announced in April sought to encourage energy conservation and tithing and to facilitate construction of meetinghouses in areas of rapid church growth. Nearly the entire burden of meetinghouse construction and maintenance was shifted to general church funds, while local congregations would pay utility costs. Meanwhile, in view of greatly increased expenses, individual missionaries' terms of service were limited to 18 months.

President Reagan and several members of Congress called attention to the church's welfare services as a successful example of voluntarism and private initiative. Three Latter-day Saints had been appointed in December 1981 to a White House task force assigned to encourage private welfare help.

In a New Year's message for 1982, the church's First Presidency condemned "organizations and individuals that foster racial prejudice, feed upon religious intolerance, and resort to terrorism." The Ku Klux Klan, which had been seeking adherents in Utah, was seen as a primary target of the statement.
　　　　　　　　　(LEONARD J. ARRINGTON)

Jehovah's Witnesses. *You Can Live Forever in Paradise on Earth*, the title of a new book released by Jehovah's Witnesses during 1982, expressed a fundamental hope held by the vast majority of the 2.4 million Witnesses worldwide. The doctrine of an eternal, earthly paradise, inhabited by peaceful, meek humans, is unique to Jehovah's Witnesses. They do not believe God will permit a nuclear holocaust but that he will, as promised, "bring to ruin those ruining the earth."

Jehovah's Witnesses believe that an elect and chosen "little flock" who are "redeemed from among men" will assist Christ Jesus in administering God's kingdom government from heaven. The selection of these co-rulers, beginning with the 12 apostles, has spanned 1,900 years. A small remnant remains and today directs the worldwide preaching of the Jehovah's Witnesses.

Reminiscent of the festivals of God's people in ancient times, Jehovah's Witnesses hold annual conventions. During 1982 there were 104 "Kingdom Truth" conventions attended by 1,110,000 persons in the U.S. alone. The same program continued in conventions throughout the world.
　　　　　　　　　(FREDERICK W. FRANZ)

Lutheran Churches. Ecumenical relations, church union, southern Africa, and peace issues were major items on Lutheranism's 1982 agenda. In September the Lutheran Church in America (LCA), the American Lutheran Church (ALC), and the Association of Evangelical Lutheran Churches (AELC), accounting for about two-thirds of Lutheran membership in the U.S., committed themselves to formation of a united church body by 1988. A parallel united denomination was expected in Canada by 1985.

In East Germany efforts continued to integrate the eight regional (including three Lutheran) churches more fully into that country's Federation of Evangelical

Churches. The president of the small Lutheran denomination in The Netherlands suggested it might be best to merge it with the numerically dominant Reformed Christians. Relations with Anglicans were especially noteworthy. In the U.S. the LCA, ALC, and AELC and the Episcopal Church formally recognized each other as churches where the gospel is preached and taught and authorized "interim sharing of the eucharist" as a major step toward full communion. The official theological dialogue between representatives of the two traditions in Europe recommended similar steps.

The World Alliance of Reformed Churches proposed steps toward greater cooperation with the Lutheran World Federation (LWF), building on the full communion that exists between most European Lutheran, Reformed, and United denominations. The Baptist World Alliance accepted an invitation to begin theological dialogue with Lutheranism. The English text of a Lutheran-Roman Catholic joint theological statement on ministry was released.

Church-state relationships were a major concern. Additional steps were taken in Norway and Sweden toward the slow loosening of church-state ties. In East Germany Lutheran and other church authorities were at odds with the Communist government over church support for a youth peace movement, which included some questioning of the government's military policies. Lutheran concern for peace issues was also reflected in the proposal by Tanzanian Bishop Josiah Kibira, president of the LWF, for an international ecumenical peace commission. Swedish Lutheran Archbishop Olof Sundby announced plans for a world church peace conference to be held in April 1983.

The situation in southern Africa, especially regarding independence for South West Africa/Namibia, continued to be a Lutheran priority. The LWF executive committee urged Lutherans around the world to pray and work for that goal. (Most Namibians are Lutherans.)

(THOMAS HARTLEY DORRIS)

Methodist Churches. Implementation of the first stages of the "Mission to the Eighties" program of world evangelism, adopted by the World Methodist Council meeting in Honolulu in July 1981, united Methodist churches around the world in mission. Pentecost 1982 was chosen as "Making Disciples Sunday," the climax of a program of challenge and teaching between Easter and Pentecost. It was proposed to repeat the program in 1983. Sunday, Sept. 19, 1982, was observed by Methodists as "Prayer for the World Day." Special prayer events were held in Berlin; Belfast, Northern Ireland; Washington, D.C.; South Africa; and India.

The first Methodist Institute for World Evangelism was formally inaugurated at Candler School of Theology, Emory University, Atlanta, Ga. With the aim of training men and women from all nations as evangelists in their own cultures, the institute planned to hold seminars in every region of the world, the first in Seoul, South Korea, in December 1982.

The first meeting of the executive committee of the World Methodist Council appointed in Honolulu the previous year took place in Brussels in September. At the same time, the Social and International Affairs Committee began planning for an international consultation, and the Youth Committee went ahead with proposals for the second International Youth Conference, to be held in Nassau, The Bahamas, in August 1983.

In South Africa a nationwide candle-lighting ceremony on October 31 launched celebrations of 150 years of Methodist witness in the country and 100 years since the formation of the independent Methodist Church in southern Africa. The church, now with 828,500 members, continued its active opposition to apartheid.

The Oxford Institute of Methodist Theological Studies, normally held every fourth year for intensive theological discussion, met at Keble College, Oxford, in July. It dealt with the "future of the Methodist theological traditions" and attracted more than 140 professional theologians, pastors, and laypersons from 26 countries.

The annual conference of British Methodists, meeting in Plymouth during June–July, voted by an 80% majority to implement proposals toward unity with the Anglican, United Reformed, and Moravian churches. However, the vote of the Church of England General Synod was not sufficient to implement the proposals and the scheme was abandoned. The controversial report on human sexuality, first put forward in 1979, which included proposals regarding the place of homosexuals in the church, was not adopted.

(PETER H. BOLT)

Pentecostal Churches. Pentecostals, with 51 million members worldwide, now constituted the largest family of Protestants, according to David Barratt, editor of the *World Christian Encyclopedia*, which appeared in May 1982. This did not include the 11 million charismatic pentecostals in the traditional churches. The scope of world Pentecostalism was demonstrated by the presence of 12,000 delegates at the 13th World Pentecostal Conference, which convened in Nairobi, Kenya, in September. Although delegates attended from 56 nations, over 90% of those present were Africans.

In the U.S. the International Church of the Foursquare Gospel appointed Roy H. Hicks as general supervisor to succeed M. E. Nichols, who died in office. In July the Open Bible Standard Churches celebrated its 50th year at a "Golden Anniversary Convention" in Des Moines, Iowa.

The Church of God (Cleveland, Tenn.) also chose new leadership at its General Assembly, held in August in Kansas City, Mo. C. E. Thomas was chosen to lead the denomination, which numbered some 1.4 million worldwide. The assembly adopted resolutions reaffirming the right of voluntary prayer in public schools and the importance of lay ministries and deploring the continuing growth of pornography in the U.S.

Also in August, the Assemblies of God conducted its first transdenominational "Conference on the Holy Spirit" in Springfield, Mo. Almost 10,000 persons attended the three-day event, which featured charismatic speakers from mainline denominational churches, among them Dennis J. Bennett (Episcopalian) and Harold Carter (Baptist). (VINSON SYNAN)

Reformed, Presbyterian, and Congregational Churches. At the General Council of the World Alliance of Reformed Churches (WARC), held in Ottawa August 17–27, 1982, the issue that drew most public attention was apartheid in South Africa. The General Council suspended two white South African churches (the Nederduitse Gereformeerde Kerk and the Nederduitse Hervormde Kerk) because of their position upholding separate development of the races. The WARC held practice of racial discrimination to be sin and theological support for it as heresy. This stand was reinforced by the election as new president of the WARC of Alan A. Boesak, a 36-year-old biblical scholar and member of the Dutch Reformed Mission Church in South Africa; closely identified with the Coloured community to which he belonged, Boesak was a well-known campaigner for human rights.

On a different level, the General Council decided to create a Women's Section and a Civil and Religious Liberties Section within the existing Department of Cooperation and Witness. At the same time, a higher proportion of women and of representatives of the third world (7 and 16, respectively) were included in the new 32-member executive committee.

In the ecumenical field, the General Council decided not only to continue the various theological dialogues in progress with other Christian communions but also to revive that with the Lutherans, to develop a second phase with the Roman Catholics, and to open up an entirely new field of contacts with the Jewish people and Islam. A 20-page document summarizing the General Council findings on "Reformed Witness Today" was to be circulated among the WARC member churches.

Total membership of the WARC reached 157 with the admission of eight new churches (one each from Brazil, Botswana, and Zaire and five from Indonesia).

The two main branches of Presbyterianism in the U.S., separated since the Civil War, moved a step closer to reunion when the general assemblies of the United Presbyterian Church (Northern) and the Presbyterian Church in the United States (Southern) voted for merger. The proposal would now go to the presbyteries of the two bodies, which were expected to vote in February 1983. If the merger was consummated, the resulting 3.1 million-member body would be the fourth largest Christian denomination in the U.S. (ALDO COMBA)

Religious Society of Friends. The attention of Quakers worldwide was focused in August 1982 on Kenya, where the largest international gathering of Friends since 1967 was held at Kaimosi. With some 40,000 members, the Quaker community in Kenya was the second largest national group in the world, after the U.S. The choice of a third world country for the gathering was intended to stress to Friends that their Society was outgrowing its Anglo-Saxon origins. While the main theme was devotional, peace, racial prejudice, and the role of women were also discussed.

Peace was the common thread running

Religion

through Quaker concerns during the year. In the U.S. the third "New Call to Peacemaking" conference brought together the three "historic peace churches"—the Brethren, Mennonites, and Friends—and coincided with the UN second special session on disarmament in New York.

In general, Quakers took heart from the growing strength of peace movements in the U.S., Europe, and Australia. British Friends, however, found their pacifist convictions challenged by the Falkland Islands episode and the militant public reaction to it.   (DAVID FIRTH)

Salvation Army. The Salvation Army celebrated its centenary in four countries during 1982: Canada, India, Sweden, and Switzerland. Special congress gatherings were held in each of those countries, conducted by the Army's 12th international leader, Gen. Jarl Wahlström. Many individual centres in Great Britain celebrated similar anniversaries during the year, among them the internationally known Regent Hall Corps in London's West End. As part of the celebrations, and by royal command of Queen Elizabeth II, the Regent Hall Band played music in the forecourt of Buckingham Palace during May.

On April 1 Commissioner Caughey Gauntlett succeeded Commissioner W. Stanley Cottrill, following the latter's retirement, as the Army's chief of staff and the general's second-in-command.

The work of Sundar Egbert, manager of the Salvation Army's Catherine Booth Hospital Vocational Training Centre in southeastern India, was acknowledged at the International Conference on Social Welfare, held in Brighton, England, in September. Egbert received the René Sand Award, the highest that can be bestowed by the International Council on Social Welfare.
                                  (ROB GARRAD)

Seventh-day Adventist Church. The most ambitious church growth program in the history of the denomination was launched Sept. 18, 1982. Entitled "One Thousand Days of Reaping," the program would extend to 1985 and was designed to bring an average of 1,000 people a day into the church for 1,000 days. To launch the program, Neal C. Wilson, president of the General Conference, conducted an evangelistic crusade in Manila early in September. During the year church work was established in Mali, making a total of 185 countries in which the church was operating. Membership was about 3,750,000.

In April representatives from the ten world divisions met in Washington, D.C., for an International Prophetic Guidance Workshop, the first of its kind. Delegates reaffirmed the historic view of the church that, in communicating truth to the human race, God inspires persons who, under the guidance of the Holy Spirit, draw upon many sources to communicate that truth accurately. The conference reaffirmed its confidence in Ellen G. White, one of the founders of the church, as a true prophet. Current criticism directed against Mrs. White and her writings was rooted largely in a defective understanding of the revelation inspiration process.

Upon receiving the report of an investigation into church involvement with a bankrupt California physician–real-estate developer who obtained loans of about $20 million from church entities, the church president set up a review commission to determine whether incompetence, poor judgment, or other factors on the part of church administrators had contributed to the loss and to suggest procedures that would prevent similar problems in the future. In spite of its apparent losses, the church had met its obligations to all members who placed their funds with it in trust.
                                  (KENNETH H. WOOD)

Unitarian (Universalist) Churches. Despite the worldwide economic depression, the North American body of this international movement experienced increased giving to its programs, new congregations added for the third consecutive year, and a modest net growth in the number of adult members. The 21st anniversary of the merger of the Unitarian and Universalist denominations was celebrated by 1,800 delegates and friends from Canada and the U.S. who assembled June 21–26 on the campus of Bowdoin College, Brunswick, Maine. Resolutions were passed supporting a bilateral nuclear freeze, the Law of the Sea treaty, and a comprehensive peace in the Middle East based on respect by all parties for the sovereignty and territorial integrity of the others.

Lay chaplains recommended by the Canadian Unitarian Council were empowered and registered legally by provincial governments in most areas of the country to perform weddings and funerals. This solved a problem caused by a shortage of ordained clergy.

The General Assembly of Unitarian and Free Christian Churches in Britain, meeting April 3–5 in Lampeter, Wales, elected Kathleen Woodhouse of Sheffield, England, as its new president. At a time when many religious bodies were questioning the value of passing resolutions, the British body devoted the first two of its three sessions almost entirely to this purpose. An overwhelming majority voted for unilateral nuclear disarmament, and the government was called on to provide safeguards against the amassing of secret, computerized information, often inaccurate, about its citizens.

Unitarianism in Transylvania, a part of Romania, once a cradle of the movement, was being served by over 100 churches under the leadership of Bishop Lajos Kovacs. Bishop Joseph Ferencz led a small but healthy Unitarian presence in a dozen or more centres in Hungary. The International Association for Religious Freedom was currently headed by its first Asian president, Nikkyo Niwano of Tokyo.
                                  (JOHN NICHOLLS BOOTH)

The United Church of Canada. At the church's 29th biennial General Council meeting in Montreal, Aug. 9–15, 1982, the 453 commissioners (lay and clergy delegates) elected W. Clarke MacDonald as moderator of Canada's largest Protestant denomination. The theme of the 29th Council was "Jesus Christ—the Life of the World," originated by the WCC for its sixth Assembly, to be held in Vancouver, B.C., in August 1983.

The United Church made history—some delegates said rewrote it—when it offered

an apology to a minister it had censured 36 years earlier for supporting the Chinese revolution. James G. Endicott, 83, a missionary in China for 21 years, had resigned from the church in 1946 in the face of extreme criticism by some church leaders. A resolution approved by Council acknowledged the "personal hurt and anxiety" caused to Endicott and recognized that "events in the past 30 years have borne out many of his predictions and prophetic actions. . . ."

Council accepted the recommendation of the Committee on International Affairs that the church endorse the "Canada as a Nuclear Weapon Free Zone" campaign of the interdenominational peace group Project Ploughshare. The committee also won Council's approval for its suggestion of a peace advocate for the church and a recommendation that the federal government take the following actions: (1) conduct a full review of current mechanisms for controlling the export of military goods; (2) do an intensive study of the relationship between nuclear power/weapons and between the arms race and third world development and oppression; and (3) establish a policy of not using food as a weapon to secure changes in policies of governments whose people need famine relief.

Support for Quebec's English minority in their efforts to gain control over their own educational system was endorsed by Council, as was the equivalent right of French-speaking Canadians in other provinces.
                                  (NORMAN K VALE)

United Church of Christ. The United Church of Christ celebrated its 25th birthday in 1982, having come into being as a result of a merger between the Evangelical and Reformed Church and the Congregational Christian Churches on June 25, 1957. Affirming themselves as "A People Alive," UCC members met in hundreds of celebrations throughout the U.S., culminating in a gathering of more than 5,000 people at St. Louis, Mo., on June 27.

Along with other religious bodies in the U.S., the UCC poured time and energy into peace advocacy during 1982. Church leaders, through the media and by their presence in the nation's capital, pressed Congress and the administration to take unilateral initiatives toward disarmament and to move toward negotiation of a nuclear peace. In the spring UCC members participated in the planning of the Interfaith Service of Worship and March for Peace with Justice, held in New York City on June 11 and 12. In May, in Moscow, the UCC was represented by its president at the World Conference of Religious Workers for Saving the Sacred Gift of Life from Nuclear Catastrophe.

At a February 1982 meeting of UCC executives held in Nashville, Tenn., the conference ministers and instrumentality executives present gave a strong signal that the ecumenical agenda was becoming increasingly central in the life of the church. One of the busiest ecumenical calendars in recent years included the 15th plenary of the Consultation on Church Union; widespread local church participation in studies related to the covenant between the UCC and the Christian Church (Disciples of Christ); 30th anniversary celebrations of the National Council of Churches; preparations for the 1983 General Assembly of the wcc; delegated participation in the General Council of the WARC in Ottawa (see *Presbyterian, Reformed, and Congregational Churches,* above); and policy clarifications of UCC relationships with partner churches around the world, voted by the United Church Board for World Ministries.

(AVERY D. POST)

[827.D; 827.G.H; 827.J.3]

ROMAN CATHOLIC CHURCH

The life of the Roman Catholic Church in 1982 was marked by an increasing involvement in international affairs. The traditional Vatican policy of neutrality was abandoned as Pope John Paul II plunged into one controversy after another. His recovery from the bullets of Mehmet Ali Agca was remarkable and almost complete. On May 12 he went to Fatima, Portugal, on the eve of the first anniversary of the assassination attempt, to thank Mary for having saved his life. His visit to Nigeria, Benin, Gabon, and Equatorial Guinea in February was largely unreported outside Africa.

The same could not be said of the long-planned visit to Britain at the end of May, put in jeopardy by the—undeclared—war in the Falkland Islands. It was saved at the 11th hour by making it purely "pastoral" (no meetings with politicians) and promising a visit to Argentina immediately afterward. As it turned out, the pope's role was to declare the unacceptability of war in Britain, while in Argentina he had to console the defeated and collapsing regime of Lieut. Gen. Leopoldo Galtieri (see BIOGRAPHIES).

Two other visits never happened. After the Israeli action in Lebanon, the pope expressed his readiness to go to Beirut if it would help. In the event he dispatched Mother Teresa of Calcutta instead. Much closer to realization was the visit to Czestochowa, Poland, shrine of the Black Madonna, planned for August 26, the 600th anniversary of the arrival of this mysterious icon. The visit was regretfully canceled because military rule was still in force in Poland. In November, however, the Polish government and the primate, Archbishop Jozef Glemp, announced that a papal visit had been set for June 1983.

Throughout the year, the new primate of Poland preached moderation and counseled patience—which some Solidarity members found rather supine. But he continued to press for release of the remaining internees and recognition of Solidarity as a nonpolitical union. After Solidarity was outlawed in October, he urged workers to ask for it "in another form."

Other trouble spots were offered the prospect of a papal visit in 1983. Notable was Central America, which throughout the year was the object of a media battle. Nicaragua, where four priests were Cabinet ministers, was presented either as the vindication of "liberation theology" or as a Soviet-inspired bridgehead in "America's backyard." In El Salvador the elections were interpreted either as a modest triumph for democracy or as an irrelevant farce. John Paul wrote letters to these countries, declaring, in effect, a plague on both ideological houses. Violence, from whatever side, was denounced.

Many Catholics had come to feel that reliance on nuclear weapons was an unacceptable form of violence. The widespread and growing commitment to the "peace movement" was the most striking feature of the year. In January Archbishop Raymond Hunthausen of Seattle, Wash., announced that he would withhold half his taxes as a protest against nuclear weapons. In April so establishment a figure as John Cardinal Krol of Philadelphia said that the arms race was "an irrational and suicidal way" to try to maintain peace. Then came a disappointment. In July the first draft of a pastoral letter from the U.S. bishops was leaked. Though it said that "continued reliance on nuclear weapons is fundamentally abhorrent," it did not absolutely rule out their usefulness as a deterrent. Archbishop Joseph Bernardin, who had just been named to Chicago as successor to John Cardinal Cody, explained that the text was merely a draft that would need much revision before its hoped-for publication in November. A final vote on the document was delayed until 1983, but by then peace activists had been discouraged by the pope's message to the UN special session on disarmament in June. It said: "Deterrence based on balance may be recognized as morally acceptable only as a step toward progressive disarmament." It was carefully stated, it was casuistic, and it dashed the hopes of many.

On humbler levels, financial scandal drew dangerously near to the Vatican with the Banco Ambrosiano affair. (See *Introduction,* above.) Traditionalist Archbishop Marcel Lefebvre, 77, announced his resignation but had not abandoned his sense of the heretical nature of the new liturgy.

The Jesuits emerged without too much damage from the imposition on them of an unprecedented "personal delegate of the Holy Father," while Opus Dei, founded in Spain in 1928, was given greater autonomy in August. The Spanish bishops had opposed this move, judging Opus Dei to be secretive and sinister, but Pope John Paul found them reliable and so presented the bishops with a fait accompli before his scheduled October visit to Spain. Timed to mark the 400th anniversary of the death of St. Teresa of Ávila, the visit chanced to fall just before a general election. With the right-wing parties claiming that the pope was on their side in such matters as divorce and the left-wing parties complaining of papal interference, the visit was moved forward to November, after the election.

On October 10 Maximilian Kolbe, a Polish Franciscan who perished in the Auschwitz concentration camp, was canonized. The requirement of a miracle was waived.

The most important ecumenical event was the delayed publication of the final report of the Anglican-Roman Catholic International Commission on March 22. It reached a great measure of agreement on the Eucharist, ministry, and authority in the church, including papal authority. Despite sniping from Roman bureaucrats, the report was warmly received. More important still, Pope John Paul's visit to Canterbury on May 29 revealed a new and more "collegial" way of exercising the papal office that put some flesh on the bare bones of the final report. All in all, 1982 was a somewhat ragged year, with no clear pattern emerging. (See VATICAN CITY STATE.)

(PETER HEBBLETHWAITE)

[827.C; 827.G.2; 827.J.2]

Archbishop Raymond Hunthausen (right) was one of a number of Roman Catholic clergymen in the U.S. who came out strongly in favour of nuclear disarmament. He is pictured here at an antinuclear demonstration in Seattle, Washington.

ZE OR BURN!

SHERRY BOCKWINKEL/TIME MAGAZINE

THE ORTHODOX CHURCH

A second meeting of the commission for the preparation of a pan-Orthodox "Great Council" was held in Chambésy, Switz., on Sept. 4–8, 1982. It discusssed several items of the approved agenda, including the problem of the computation of Easter. According to the present Orthodox computation, Easter often falls after the western Easter. The possibility of adjusting the computations was generally admitted but awaited a pan-Orthodox consensus.

In Greece the Papandreou administration pushed through Parliament several measures leading toward total separation of church and state. The measures included obligatory civil marriage (making ecclesiastical marriage optional) and abolition of laws making adultery a crime. Texts legalizing abortion on demand and automatic divorce after seven years of separation were also introduced. The hierarchy of the church violently protested the measures. However, some churchmen, including professors of theology, welcomed the trend toward separation of state and church as an opportunity for a more conscious, voluntary witness to Christianity.

In the Middle East, and particularly during the fighting in Lebanon, Orthodox communities tended to adopt an attitude of neutrality. The Orthodox bishop of Beirut, Elias, traveled regularly into West Beirut during the siege and condemned Israeli violence in the city.

In Romania the former bishop of Buzau, Antonie Plamadeala, was elevated to the post of metropolitan of Sibiu. The new metropolitan, who now occupied the third position in the Romanian hierarchy and was in charge of external affairs, had had wide international experience and was recognized as a theologian. At the same time, information coming from Romania, particularly from Bucharest and Banat, indicated that younger priests committed to mission and more lively preaching were being harassed by the police and often deprived of their posts.

In the U.S.S.R. wide publicity was given to the World Conference of Religious Workers for Saving the Sacred Gift of Life from Nuclear Catastrophe. The conference, visibly approved by the state and sponsored by the patriarchate, was attended by foreign "religious personalities," including evangelist Billy Graham. Following the conference, Patriarch Pimen of Moscow came to New York to address the UN special session on disarmament. It was learned that new Orthodox churches had been erected—a very rare event—in remote places in Siberia (Yakutsk, Komsomolsk-on-the-Amur), indicating some relaxation in antireligious pressures.

Metropolitan Theodosius, head of the autocephalous Orthodox Church in America, made an unprecedented visit to the Orthodox Church in Poland (June 24–July 2). The declared purpose of the visit was to show that Orthodox Poles (a religious minority of 500,000), as well as Roman Catholics, had friends in the West.

For the first time in history, a convert from Anglicanism, Kallistos Ware, a professor at Oxford University, was consecrated Orthodox bishop in England by Greek archbishop Methodios.

(JOHN MEYENDORFF)

EASTERN NON-CHALCEDONIAN CHURCHES

In Egypt the situation of the Coptic Church remained abnormal. Patriarch Shenuda, head of the Coptic Church, was still in the monastic retreat assigned to him by the late president Anwar as-Sadat. Bishop Samuel, president of the bishops' commission that held an interim authority, had been killed along with Sadat on Oct 6, 1981, as he stood near the president. His position was taken by Bishop Athanasius, who represented the church at national and international meetings.

There was contradictory and practically unverifiable information concerning the fate of the church in Ethiopia. On the one hand, the government-approved patriarch, Tekle Haimanot, visited West Germany and the Vatican (November 1981) and denied any persecution of religion. On the other, Abba Mathia, formerly in charge of Ethiopian monasteries in Jerusalem and now in exile, formally accused the Marxist government of closing churches and selling church properties. (JOHN MEYENDORFF)
[827.B; 827.G.1; 827.J.1]

JUDAISM

Judaism in the U.S. showed signs of continuing change in 1982, as a long-established order gave way to new patterns of religious and social life. The politics of American Jews remained moderate and centrist, which meant, in effect, a move to the right. The religious life of the community showed a decline in the established institutions and a revival in new forms.

As to politics, Murray Friedman wrote (*Commentary*, December 1981), "The various social crises of the 80's pose a serious challenge to the organized Jewish community. Large numbers of Americans have come to question liberal ideology and programs in favor of a moderate conservatism. . . . The Jewish agencies can take pride in having helped to shape the American conscience on issues of civil liberties and civil rights over the years. What they have not done is to confront some of the implications and consequences of their activities, their policies, and their ideas. . . ." During the year the challenge framed by Friedman dominated public discourse, as such issues as tax exemption for private and parochial education, prayer in the public schools, and other shibboleths of times past came to the fore once again.

In the religious life of the community, two contradictory patterns continued to play themselves out. On the one side, numbers and commitment within moderately Orthodox, Conservative, and Reform synagogues continued to decline, with the aging of the population. On the other, among younger elements in all three movements—but particularly among the Orthodox—an increasing emphasis on stronger individual and collective commitment emerged. While moderated religiosity was on the wane, extreme piety and commitment flourished. The larger part of the community, however, still found itself at home within the conventional synagogues and other organizations.

Alongside the continuing nurture of Jewish culture and learning in America, the year witnessed what appeared to be a continuing decline in the American Jews' focus of their inner life upon events in the State of Israel. Sol Roth, then president of the Rabbinical Council of America, the Orthodox rabbis' association, observed that "the center of gravity of American Jewish interests is moving away from Israel and towards the American Jewish community." He pointed out that allocations of funds in Jewish philanthropy have tended to favour American Jewish needs at the expense of Israel, a development he found deplorable.

Rabbi Zvi Yehuda Kuk, the principal figure in the Israeli movement Gush Emunim, responsible for setting up Jewish settlements in Judea and Samaria (the "West Bank"), died in 1981 at the age of 91. Kuk was the prophet of the Land of Israel united and under Jewish rule, rejected the Egyptian peace treaty, and fostered the view that the resettlement of Jews throughout the Land of Israel marked a step in the coming of the Messiah. It was a considerable distance from the Messianic politics he represented to the slow but steady, step-by-step rebuilding of a viable Judaism in the U.S. and Canada.

Certainly the single most dramatic and telling event in Judaism during the year was the response in both the State of Israel and the U.S. Jewish community to the tragic slaughter of Palestinian Arabs in Beirut refugee camps subject to the protection of the Israeli Army. (*See* LEBANON.) While the murders were committed by Lebanese Christians and were part of a centuries-old blood feud, the fact that Israeli troops stood by shook the moral conscience of world Jewry to its foundations. American Jews were described by *Newsweek* (Oct. 4, 1982) as deeply stunned and anguished. Israelis, for their part, held a mass rally in Tel Aviv that involved an estimated 400,000 persons, more than 10% of the country's entire population. They demanded, and got, a judicial inquiry into the role and responsibility, if any, of Israeli forces in the pogrom.

On one hand, the trend Rabbi Roth discerned was vastly accelerated, but on the other, the events made many American Jews rethink the character and depth of their feeling for and commitment to a Jewish state. On balance, the importance of the Jewish state to Judaism throughout the world proved to be enhanced. Partly this was because, for the first time, people faced the alternative of having no state and rejected it. Partly, it was because they were forced to examine their own deepest moral convictions and discovered that their co-religionists in the State of Israel both shared and embodied them. The tragedy left a sense of shame, but also pride in the moral outrage of the Israeli population. But the Messianic politics of an important sector of Israeli Judaism bore ever less relevance to the religious life of American and other diaspora Jewries. (JACOB NEUSNER)
[826]

BUDDHISM

Events in Southeast Asia during 1981–82 lent little support to Asian Buddhists' conviction of and fervent hope for unity, soli-

The Dalai Lama (right), exiled Tibetan leader, met with followers in Rome in September on a European trip.

darity, and brotherhood among their co-religionists in that region. Religious activities had been severely curtailed by the hostilities and uncertainties in Indochina. This was the case despite Vietnam's announcement that it intended to withdraw a significant portion of its forces from Kampuchea and despite the formation of a shaky three-way coalition of rebel groups headed by Prince Norodom Sihanouk, the country's former chief of state and an ardent advocate of a Buddhist social welfare state.

In 1982 Thailand celebrated the 200th anniversary of the birth of its royal dynasty, the religious and political symbol of the nation. Burmese Buddhists pondered their future as U Ne Win, who in recent years had been conciliatory toward Buddhism, relinquished his power. In Sri Lanka the establishment of development councils, designed to decentralize governmental power, increased the tension between Sinhalese Buddhists and Hindu Tamils.

Under the pragmatic policy of the current Beijing (Peking) regime, Chinese Buddhists began to resume more public activities, including publication of their quarterly magazine, *Po-on*. It was reported that more temples had been reopened. Japanese Buddhists celebrated with fanfare the 700th anniversary of the death of Nichiren in June 1981 and the 850th anniversary of the birth of Honen in April 1982. Both were seminal figures in Japanese Buddhism. The 14th Conference of the World Fellowship of Buddhists, scheduled to be held in Jakarta in the fall of 1982, was postponed until 1983 because of the Indonesian election.

Buddhist delegates were prominently represented at the second meeting of the Asian Conference on Religion and Peace, held in New Delhi, India, in the fall of 1981. Buddhists also took an active part in the UN General Assembly's special session on disarmament in June 1982. The exhibit "Along the Ancient Silk Routes," shown at the Metropolitan Museum of Art in New York City, gave Americans a rare view of 152 precious works of art that had adorned Buddhist caves and temples during the 5th–10th centuries. Buddhist groups, especially those of the Tibetan, Zen, and Pure Land

traditions, were steadily—though not dramatically—growing in various Western nations. The fifth conference of the International Association of Buddhist Studies was held in August 1982 at Oxford, with the Ven. Walpola Rahula as president.

(JOSEPH M. KITAGAWA)

[824]

HINDUISM

In January the state of Uttar Pradesh was the scene of bloody violence between upper-caste Hindus and Harijans (former untouchables). Thirty-four Harijans, including women and children, were gunned down by upper-caste Hindus in the village of Sarhupur, located in the same district where, in the preceding November, 24 Harijans had been murdered. Although local police at first attributed the killings to bandits, it was believed that local landlords instigated the attacks in response to efforts by Harijans to claim land transferred to them by legislation. Also in January, 13 Harijans were murdered by caste Hindus in the state of Madhya Pradesh.

Elsewhere in India, violence between caste Hindus and Harijans occurred throughout the year, usually as a result of the refusal of the untouchables to accept without complaint their traditional subordination to caste Hindus. The resistance of the Harijans had been stimulated not only by legislation according them a range of rights but also by social activists representing a variety of political and religious positions. In an effort to aid the Harijan cause, the central government commissioned for national television a film called *Sadgati* ("Deliverance"), directed by Satyajit Ray and based on a short story by the Hindi writer Prem Chand that depicted the anguish of Harijans.

Communal violence broke out in March between Hindus and Christians in Kanyakumari, on the southern tip of India, over alleged anti-Christian activities by Hindu leaders. A much more serious clash occurred in April in the Punjab. In the Sikh holy city of Amritsar, members of an extremist Sikh group, the Dal Khalsa ("Association of the Pure"), dedicated to the

establishment of a separate Sikh state, desecrated two Hindu temples with the severed heads of cows in retaliation for the Hindus' refusal to support a ban on tobacco, forbidden to Sikhs. Riots followed, and the state government imposed a strict curfew. Prime Minister Indira Gandhi appealed to both communities for calm, and the Dal Khalsa was banned. However, violence continued sporadically throughout the summer.

During the year, followers of Vinoba Bhave, who died on Nov. 15, 1982 (*see* OBITUARIES), agitated for stricter enforcement nationwide of laws forbidding cow slaughter. In response, the prime minister requested state governments (except in West Bengal and Kerala, where large Muslim and Christian populations, respectively, eat beef) to work for enforcement.

The religious leader Shri Abhinav Sachidanand Tirth Maharaj, the *shankaracarya*, or abbot, of the Dwarka monastery, died on April 7.   (H. PATRICK SULLIVAN)

[823]

ISLAM

Israel's June invasion of Lebanon and the tragic massacre of refugees in Beirut in September overwhelmed news of Muslim religious developments elsewhere in the world. (*See* MIDDLE EASTERN AFFAIRS.) However, violence was prominent also in other areas of the Middle East. In Syria in February the Army destroyed much of the city of Hamah, killing many persons, in the government's attempt finally to end resistance there. The government claimed that the Muslim Brotherhood, a fundamentalist group that had continued active even when forced underground in various Arab countries, had encouraged resistance and threatened the ruling Ba'thist government. Behind the claims and counterclaims were political and cultural differences between the 'Alawite Syrian leaders and more traditional, fundamentalist Sunnis.

The ongoing border war between Iran and Iraq became considerably more active with Iran's spring counteroffensive, which for a time appeared to threaten the Iraqi port of Basra. Executions and assassinations of prominent Muslim leaders in Iran and elsewhere added to the climate of violence, as did incidents such as that in February when a group of Shi'ah gunmen held a Kuwaiti airliner at the Beirut airport to protest the 1978 disappearance of their leader, Imam Moussa Sadr. In April an Israeli soldier born and raised in the U.S. shot his way into the Dome of the Rock, the Muslim sacred precinct in Jerusalem, killing and wounding a number of persons; riots and demonstrations were the immediate reaction.

Other occurrences, though not marked by violence, were shaped by current political situations. In February the Turkish government proposed legislation legalizing abortion and voluntary sterilization, which had been defeated by Parliament in 1978. The rising tide of fundamentalism in Pakistan placed increasing pressure on the Ahmedi sect, a strong missionary movement considered to be heterodox. The Izala movement in Nigeria called for a purge of what it

Religion

saw as corruption in Islamic religious practices there.

In the U.S. the former Black Muslim movement had been steadily undergoing changes since the death of its leader, Elijah Muhammad, in 1975. Led by one of Elijah Muhammad's sons, Wallace, now called Warith Muhammad, the principal group had taken the name American Muslim Mission. Claiming some 60,000 to 100,000 followers, it preached mainstream Islam, rejected a number of the tenets held by Elijah Muhammad, upheld the U.S. political system, and welcomed all Muslims and other interested persons, white or black, to join. A number of high-cost businesses formerly operated by the movement had been disposed of, and the personal bodyguard, called the Fruit of Islam, had been disbanded.

A smaller group now known as the Nation of Islam, led by Louis Farrakhan, claimed an increase in numbers. It continued to espouse the principles and practices of Elijah Muhammad, whose follower Farrakhan was. Some 5,000 people attended a Nation of Islam rally in Los Angeles during the summer. (REUBEN W. SMITH)
[828]

WORLD CHURCH MEMBERSHIP

Reckoning religious adherence is a precarious exercise. Different religions and even different Christian churches vary widely in their theories and methods of counting and reporting. Some simply depend upon government population figures. For others, "numbering the people" is blocked by religious law. Where religious liberty obtains, some count contributors; others estimate communicants or constituents.

Differing procedures are followed even within the same religion. Quite reliable statistics are available on the mission fields, for Buddhism, Islam, and Hinduism as well as Christianity. In areas where a reli-

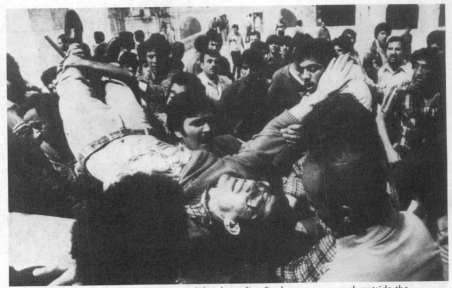

Palestinians help a wounded Arab after Israeli border police fired on an angry mob outside the Dome of the Rock in Jerusalem. The crowd had gathered after a Jewish man shot his way into the holy site, killing and wounding several worshipers there before he was subdued.

gion has been dominant for centuries (*i.e.,* Christianity in Europe, Hinduism in India), official figures usually report whole populations as adherents, although the decline of religious observance and the rise of antireligious ideologies calls this casual procedure into question. Although Albania is the only officially atheist state, the 20th century has produced a number of governments hostile to all traditional religions. It is difficult if not impossible to get reliable religious estimates for the populations such governments control.

The traditional listing of religions, used by scholars since the comparative study of religions became an academic discipline, makes no provision for several religions or faiths now numerous and/or influential; *e.g.,* Baha'i, Ch'ondokyo, the Unification Church. Nor does it make a place for Marxism, which functions in some ways like a state church. Within the traditional classifications, special problems arise. Reports on "Hinduism" sometimes include Sikhs and Jains. Under "Chinese ethnic religions," Taoism and Confucianism are frequently lumped together. For scholarly purposes, combining Hindus, Sikhs, and Jains as a single religious category is seriously misleading, and in the adjoining table, where possible, neither Sikhs nor Jains have been included in the statistics on Hinduism. On the other hand, over the centuries Taoist and Confucian motifs have become interwoven in Chinese culture, and Taoism is subsumed under reports of Confucian adherents outside China.

The reader is advised to reflect carefully upon the statistics reported and to refer to articles discussing the different countries and religions when pursuing the subject in depth. (FRANKLIN H. LITTELL)

Estimated Membership of the Principal Religions of the World

Religions	North America[1]	South America	Europe[2]	Asia[3]	Africa	Oceania[4]	World
Total Christian	240,745,200	191,046,100	336,868,700	100,975,700	140,013,900	18,520,700	1,028,170,300
Roman Catholic	134,411,300	180,251,200	176,039,500	55,979,100	54,921,400	5,191,300	606,793,800
Eastern Orthodox	5,185,500	408,000	49,946,900	2,784,500	9,131,800[5]	406,600	67,863,300
Protestant[6]	101,148,400	10,386,900	110,882,300	42,212,100	75,960,700[7]	12,922,800	353,513,200
Jewish	7,266,900	699,950	4,470,800	4,096,870	213,530	72,800	16,820,850
Muslim[8]	1,326,200	405,400	20,959,600	375,105,400	150,192,200	86,700	548,075,500
Zoroastrian	2,750	2,600	14,000	236,200	900	1,000	257,450
Shinto[9]	60,000	75,000	—	38,000,000	—	—	38,135,000
Taoist	—	—	—	25,000,000	—	—	25,000,000
Confucian	107,600	69,700	507,000	167,907,800	3,500	19,400	168,615,000
Buddhist[10]	214,100	290,100	188,600	248,833,900	16,600	26,100	249,569,400
Hindu[11]	254,600	673,700	392,500	454,955,800	1,263,800	340,700	457,881,100
Totals	249,977,350	193,262,550	363,401,200	1,415,111,670	291,704,430	19,067,400	2,532,524,600
Population[12]	381,818,000	257,798,000	758,889,000	2,760,514,000	498,080,000	23,427,000	4,680,526,000

[1]Includes Central America and the West Indies.
[2]Includes the U.S.S.R. and other countries with established Marxist ideology where continuing religious adherence is difficult to estimate.
[3]Includes areas in which persons have traditionally enrolled in several religions, as well as mainland China with a Marxist establishment.
[4]Includes Australia and New Zealand as well as islands of the South Pacific.
[5]Includes Coptic Christians, of restricted status in Egypt and precariously situated under the military junta in Ethiopia.
[6]Protestant statistics vary widely in style of reckoning affiliation. See *World Church Membership.*
[7]Including a great proliferation of new churches, sects, and cults among African Christians.
[8]The chief base of Islam is still ethnic, although missionary work is now carried on in Europe and America. In countries where Islam is established, minority religions are frequently persecuted and accurate statistics are rare.
[9]A Japanese ethnic religion, Shinto declined rapidly after the Japanese emperor surrendered his claim to divinity (1947); a revival of cultic participation in the homeland had chiefly literary significance. Shinto does not survive well outside the homeland.
[10]Buddhism has produced several renewal movements in the last century which have gained adherents in Europe and America. Although persecuted in Tibet and sometimes elsewhere in Asia, it has shown greater staying power than other religions of the East. It also transplants better.
[11]Hinduism's strength in India has been enhanced by its connection with the national movement, a phenomenon also observable in the world of Islam. Modern Hinduism has developed several renewal movements that have won adherents in Europe and America.
[12]United Nations, Department of International Economic and Social Affairs; data refer to midyear 1982.

(FRANKLIN H. LITTELL)

NEW ROLES FOR WOMEN

by Martin E. Marty

The defeat of the Equal Rights Amendment to the U.S. Constitution in 1982 led to much stocktaking on the part of American women. Behind the political activities that brought about the defeat were cultural attitudes. Those who make profound studies of culture are agreed that religious symbols, fears, and hopes animate troubling issues such as those having to do with feminism. Proponents of the ERA had long recognized that opponents like Phyllis Schlafly appealed to conservative religious forces. The New Christian Right also spoke of the biblical commands for women to be "submissive," to know that their place was in the home and not in the arena where they had to be guaranteed full rights.

The Ordination Issue. The stocktaking has uncovered many positive changes in the way women and religion meet. Some of these can be chronicled with hard data. An important symbolic issue is the ordination of women to the Jewish and Christian clergy. Some may argue that too much focus on the theme is a mark of clericalism and professionalism. People should concentrate on the great masses of "ordinary" women in their life calling, not on the minorities who make up elites. The elites in religion, however, have enormous power in determining what is taught, who has authority to bring about change, and even how God is to be thought of and addressed. Whether or not women are admitted to the ordained and professional ministry tells much about the deepest religious beliefs of a faith-system.

The hard data on progress come from the Association of Theological Schools in the United States and Canada. The authors of its annual *Fact Book* recognize that far more than half of practicing religionists in America are women and that far fewer than half of the seminarians and even fewer of the active clergy are women. In the decade since the ATS started keeping track, the percent increase of women in theological schools was 241.4%, while the number of men rose only 35.3%. Even so, these 12,473 fu-

---

Martin E. Marty is Fairfax M. Cone distinguished service professor of history of modern Christianity at the University of Chicago, and associate editor of The Christian Century.

ture religious professionals still make up only 23.7% of the seminary population.

What is more, many of the women are in two-year programs that prepare them for traditional roles in nonordained religious education positions. What counts for symbolic change is the number in pre-ministerial courses. There they make up only 16% of the total. The figure varies greatly by denomination. The United Church of Christ and the United Church of Canada are highest, with 49.5 and 41.1%, respectively. About one-third of the United Presbyterian, United Methodist, and Lutheran Church in America seminarians are women.

Roman Catholicism forbids the ordination of women, so only 6.5% of the Catholic theological students are women—yet they make up much higher percentages in select schools. The Southern Baptist Convention, the largest Protestant body, allows for women's ordination but discourages it, and only 9.7% of the students in its huge seminaries are women. More and more women are completing doctorates and going on into teaching in colleges and universities, a fact that portends more change in the future.

The bad news for women accompanying the good news of high enrollments is the existence of a low ceiling in their profession. Few Conservative or Reform Jewish women ordained to the rabbinates have congregations of their own. After a decade of women's ordination in the Episcopal Church, some bishops still refuse to do the ordaining and few par-

Sandra Antoinette Wilson (right) became the first black female priest in the Episcopal Diocese of New York when she was ordained in January in New York's Cathedral of St. John the Divine. The Rev. James Parks Morton, dean of the cathedral, is at left.

SARA KRULWICH/THE NEW YORK TIMES

ishes have a woman as head rector. Even in the mainline Protestant and Lutheran churches, where the ministry of women is very widely accepted, most women remain assistant pastors, educators, or in other posts outside the highest congregational ministry.

Many denominations have had women as presidents, moderators, and high executives and have seen to it that they are in important policymaking roles. Thus when three Lutheran bodies voted in September 1982 to form a single Lutheran church, they stipulated that a large percentage of the 70-member commission that would effect the new church policies would be women.

A Matter of Language. Controversies have raged in recent years over the language denominations use in their constitutions, liturgies, and sacred texts. Even the more conservative church bodies have had no difficulty removing sexist language from their constitutional vocabularies and procedural documents. Only the moderate-to-liberal groups, however, have changed the language of their hymns and orders of public worship. Some opposition to the changes has come from people of aesthetic sensitivity who believe that words about "men" should not be changed to language about "persons," since this is taking license with others' art. Others have opposed it because they see feminist ideology as subverting the religious message.

The most heated debate has come about in the aftermath of efforts by some to produce what the public press seized upon as a "Non-Sexist Bible" translation. In this case, the translators would take liberties with the text. God would no longer be God the Father, a male patriarchal figure. While the work in progress was more tempered and moderate than some of the rumours and releases first suggested, there is no question but that such Bible translations will continue to meet opposition, not only from those who oppose feminism, but also from language purists and those who fear violation of the integrity of sacred texts.

Jewish and Christian feminist thinkers recognize that while women may have had honoured and dignified roles in biblical literature, the texts of these ancient scriptures reflected and reinforced a culture in which women were secondary kinds of human beings, subject to men. These theologians, therefore, lift out and accent the biblical passages that *do* point to female roles for the deity: God is pictured in the prophets as giving birth to Israel and nurturing it. The word for the divine presence, the *shekinah*, is feminine. There were women prophets, judges, and visionaries in Israel and women deacons and preachers in early Christianity. Over against the biblical texts that preach female submission there are

others that envision the breaking down of barriers as a result of Jesus' work: in Christ there is to be "neither male nor female," for "all are one in Christ" (Gal. 3:28).

Old and New Roles. Battles of this sort are most intense in evangelicalism, the moderately conservative Protestant form of church life that is less rigid than fundamentalism. Many of the best-selling books in this camp have appealed to what Marabel Morgan called *The Total Woman*. The writers are expressive, fulfilled women in the bounds of marriage, devoted chiefly to pleasing their husbands and bringing up their children.

In the opposite camp is the Evangelical Women's Caucus, led by theologians like Virginia Ramey Mollenkott of William Paterson College. She argues that the biblical message of liberation shatters even the cultural limits of women in the biblical world. The Evangelical Women's Caucus takes pains not to be seen as a mere religious branch of secular feminism. Instead, it argues that women have always had a higher potential in the context of biblical faith than the church has permitted until now.

A small but articulate group of women have not only given up on the Judeo-Christian tradition but have openly rejected it. Charlene Spretnak, in her introduction to the essays in *The Politics of Women's Spirituality* (1982), blasted "patriarchal religion" of biblical descent. At the same time, she and her co-authors do advocate a "spirituality" that draws on other sources. Violently rejecting "God the Father," they appeal to goddesses, mythic Heras and Amazons, and witchcraft lore. Some of this spirituality is both lesbian and antimale. Others simply argue that male imagery has reinforced men's hold on power.

As important as radical feminist spirituality may be in the culture at large, the decisive battles in cultures influenced by Jewish and Christian faith and institutions will take more moderate and persistent forms. Pope John Paul II will not authorize the ordination of women, but Catholic women will still prepare and press for extensions of their ministry. The evangelical patriarchs and their female allies will still preach submission, but every year more women become ministers, more people see their consciousness changed, more women find new roles, more men "see the light."

Only the most sanguine Jewish and Christian women would say that all this amounts to "the end of patriarchy," but it does contribute greatly to the spiritual realization of women's being and power. The issue of "women and religion" is not yet settled in the synagogues, churches, or culture at large. It promises drama long after Equal Rights Amendment battles have been quieted.

COURTESY, PROFESSIONAL RODEO COWBOYS ASSOCIATION

Chris Lybbert became the all-around world champion when he won the National Finals Rodeo steer wrestling average on December 12.

Rodeo

The 1982 rodeo season began on a dismal note, but it turned into another record-breaking year for competitors in the Professional Rodeo Cowboys Association (PRCA). Cowboys and cowgirls from the U.S. and Canada traveled to Sydney, Australia, in January to compete in a World Cup Rodeo that promised to pay winners $1 million. However, the rodeo, which was not sanctioned by the PRCA, was a financial failure, and the total prize money never materialized.

By the end of the year, though, PRCA cowboys had won $13.2 million—a new high—at 645 sanctioned rodeos in North America, and Chris Lybbert of Coyote, Calif., became the first man to win more than $100,000 in a single season prior to competing in the National Finals Rodeo in Oklahoma City, held in December. The Finals was once again the most lucrative rodeo of them all, with $700,860 in prize money. Lybbert gained his first world all-around championship with total winnings of $123,704. All-around titles in the PRCA and other rodeo associations are awarded on the basis of most money won in two or more events.

Individual event champions in the PRCA included Roy Cooper of Durant, Okla., $95,694 in calf roping; Stan Williamson of Kellyville, Okla., $50,798 in steer wrestling; Tee Woolman of Fredonia, Texas, $56,739 in team roping; Bruce Ford of Kersey, Colo., $113,644 in bareback riding; Monty Henson of Mesquite, Texas, $97,716 in saddle bronc riding; and Charles Sampson of Los Angeles, $91,402 in bull riding. Sampson was the first black world champion in PRCA history.

Jan Hansen of Tucson, Ariz., won the Women's Professional Rodeo Association barrel racing championship with $40,966 in earnings. And in September, Guy Allen of Lovington, N.M., won the PRCA single steer roping title with $25,524.

The PRCA reached an important milestone in 1982 through PRCA Properties, Inc., which formed its own television network. Seven major rodeos, including the Finals, were televised and aired on stations throughout North America. Another milestone of sorts came at the end of the year when Don Gay, the seven times world champion bull rider from Mesquite, announced his retirement. The popular 29-year-old cowboy, who in 1981 tied legendary Jim Shoulders's record by winning the most bull riding championships, finally called it quits after earning $501,573 in the arena over the past 12 years. The rigours of riding had taken a toll on Gay physically; he was suffering from torn groin and stomach muscles. He intended to become a rodeo producer.

The International Rodeo Association's versatile Dan Dailey of Franklin, Tenn., was headed for his sixth all-around title with more than $50,000 in earnings going into the International Finals, held each January in Tulsa, Okla. Mel Coleman, a rancher from Lloydminster, Sask., and the top-ranked saddle bronc rider in the U.S. and Canada, reigned as all-around champion in the Canadian Professional Rodeo Association. Jerry Small, a Northern Cheyenne from Busby, Mont., won his third all-around crown at the Indian National Finals in Albuquerque, N.M., in November.

The National Intercollegiate Rodeo Association's all-around champions were Sabrina Pike of Southeastern Oklahoma State University at Durant and Cody Lambert of Sul Ross University at Alpine, Texas. All-around champions in the National High School Rodeo Association were Janis Akins of Phenix City, Ala., and Mark Eldridge of Elko, Nev.

A new rodeo, the Youth National Finals, was held in November at the old Northside Coliseum in Fort Worth, Texas. The contest was open to the top two competitors in each event—from each of six youth rodeo associations—and more than $50,000 in scholarships and prizes was awarded to the winners.   (RANDALL E. WITTE)

Romania

A socialist republic on the Balkan Peninsula in southeastern Europe, Romania is bordered by the U.S.S.R., the Black Sea, Bulgaria, Yugoslavia, and Hungary. Area: 237,500 sq km (91,700 sq mi). Pop.

Rhodesia:
see Zimbabwe

Roads:
see Engineering Projects; Transportation

Rockets:
see Defense; Space Exploration

Roman Catholic Church:
see Religion

(1982 est.): 22,510,000, including (1977) Romanian 88.1%; Hungarian 7.9%; German 1.6%. Cap. and largest city: Bucharest (pop., 1981 est., 1,960,000). Religion (1980 est.): Romanian Orthodox 70%; Greek Orthodox 10%; Muslim 1%; atheist 7%; other 3%; none 9%. General secretary of the Romanian Communist Party, president of the republic, and president of the State Council in 1982, Nicolae Ceausescu; chairmen of the Council of Ministers (premiers), Ilie Verdet and, from May 21, Constantin Dascalescu.

The year 1982 was critical for Romania both economically and politically. The standard of living, always among the lowest in Europe, had deteriorated markedly during the previous five years. In February food prices were increased by an average of 35%, while salaries went up 16%. There were shortages of meat, while quality wines and *tsuica* (the national plum brandy) were added to the list of goods for export only. The Romanian Communist Party (RCP) newspaper *Scinteia* on July 14 published a "program of scientific nourishment" that reduced the daily intake of 3,300 calories by 300–

500. The *Lumea*, a political weekly, announced on October 15 that the 1982 harvest of grain, including corn (maize), was expected to reach 22 million metric tons—almost one ton per person.

Speaking on October 7 at a session of the RCP Central Committee, Pres. Nicolae Ceausescu proclaimed that Romania had modern, competitive industry and that by 1985 the country would be self-sufficient in energy. That goal was to be reached by building new hydroelectric and nuclear power stations and by increasing the output of coal. The U.S.S.R. was to supply to Romania three 1,000-MW-capacity nuclear power plants but there was doubt about its readiness to make up Romania's crude petroleum deficit. In 1981 Romania extracted 11.6 million metric tons of crude, as compared with the planned 12.5 million tons, and imported 13.1 million tons; for the first time the quantity imported was higher than that produced at home.

In September 1977 Ceausescu and Bulgarian Communist Party First Secretary Todor Zhivkov had agreed to begin construction of the Turnu Magurele-Nikopol Romanian-Bulgarian hydroelectric power project in 1978. However, the work had not started by 1982. Work did continue at the Romanian-Yugoslav Iron Gates II project. The major Romanian industrial enterprise, the construction of the Danube-Black Sea canal, was making progress.

Ceausescu's reaction to policy setbacks was to conclude that members of the Council of Ministers (Cabinet) were to blame. A few were replaced in 1981, but the announcement of May 21, 1982, was more like a mass purge as about one-third of the 50-odd portfolios changed hands. Ilie Verdet was replaced as premier by Constantin Dascalescu, but the former was compensated by appointment as a vice-president of the Council of State. Addressing the Central Committee on June 2, Ceausescu stressed that the reshuffles were not merely routine; instead, some ministers had revealed themselves to be incompetent or had "embezzled . . . money from the state." In November Chairman of the State Planning Committee Emilian Dobrescu was replaced by Stefan Birlea.

On July 29 Pres. François Mitterrand of France canceled his planned visit to Romania, apparently because Virgil Tanase, a Romanian dissident writer, had reportedly been killed on the order of the Romanian security services. A few days later, however, the French newspaper *Le Monde* revealed that the kidnapping of Tanase from the Place de la Bastille, Paris, on May 20 was a fake staged by the French counterespionage service to foil an assassination attempt, and that Tanase was alive and well. It was also claimed that Mitterrand had known all along of the subterfuge. The affair soured relations between France and Romania.

On December 7 an agreement signed with 14 of Romania's biggest Western bank creditors rescheduled over 6½ years 80% of the country's 1981–82 outstanding debt of almost $2 billion. Speaking at the RCP national congress later in December, Ceausescu said that Romania's total foreign debt, estimated at $10 billion–$14 billion, would be liquidated by 1990.

(K. M. SMOGORZEWSKI)

Romania

ROMANIA

Education. (1980–81) Primary, pupils 3,308,462, teachers 156,817; secondary, pupils 979,741, teachers 46,500; vocational, pupils 168,138, teachers 2,211; teacher training (1979–80), students 14,856, teachers 1,400; higher, students 192,769, teaching staff 14,592.

Finance. Monetary unit: leu, with (Sept. 20, 1982) an official rate of 4.47 lei to U.S. $1 (free rate of 7.66 lei = £1 sterling), a noncommercial rate of 11 lei to U.S. $1 (free rate of 18.86 lei = £1 sterling), and a commercial rate of 15 lei to U.S. $1 (free rate of 25.72 lei = £1 sterling). Gold and other reserves (June 1982) U.S. $611 million. Budget (1981 actual): revenue 280.3 billion lei; expenditure 271.8 billion lei. Gross national product 641.6 billion lei. Money supply (June 1982) 150,030,000,000 lei.

Foreign Trade. (1980) Imports 59 billion lei; exports 53.9 billion lei. Import sources: U.S.S.R. 16%; U.S. 7%; Iraq 7%; West Germany 6%; Iran 5%; China 5%. Export destinations: U.S.S.R. 18%; West Germany 8%; East Germany 6%; Italy 5%; China 5%. Main exports: machinery and transport equipment 26%; petroleum products c. 19%; food 12%; chemicals 10%.

Transport and Communications. Roads (1975) c. 95,000 km (including 96 km expressways). Motor vehicles in use (1980): passenger c. 250,000; commercial c. 130,000. Railways: (1979) 11,113 km; traffic (1980) 23,220,000,000 passenger-km, freight 75,535,000,000 net ton-km. Air traffic (1981): 1,252,000,000 passenger-km; freight 11.3 million net ton-km. Inland waterways in regular use (1975) 1,628 km. Shipping (1981): merchant vessels 100 gross tons and over 335; gross tonnage 2,031,524. Telephones (Dec. 1980) 1,617,700. Radio licenses (Dec. 1980) 3,205,000. Television receivers (Dec. 1980) 3,714,000.

Agriculture. Production (in 000; metric tons; 1981): wheat c. 5,800; barley c. 2,500; corn c. 11,200; potatoes c. 4,500; cabbages c. 1,000; onions c. 340; tomatoes c. 1,600; sugar, raw value c. 640; sunflower seed c. 824; soybeans c. 268; linseed c. 40; plums c. 590; apples c. 395; grapes c. 1,755; tobacco c. 39; cheese c. 134; beef and veal c. 329; pork c. 980; timber (cu m; 1980) 21,284. Livestock (in 000; Jan. 1981): cattle c. 6,258; sheep 15,865; pigs 11,542; horses c. 566; poultry c. 89,200.

Industry. Fuel and power (in 000; metric tons; 1980): coal 8,100; lignite 27,100; coke 3,033; crude oil 11,500; natural gas (cu m) 33,450,000; electricity (kw-hr) 67,486,000. Production (in 000; metric tons; 1980): cement 14,607; bauxite 700; iron ore (26% metal content) 2,333; pig iron 9,012; crude steel 13,175; petroleum products c. 24,700; sulfuric acid 1,756; caustic soda 723; fertilizers (nutrient content) nitrogenous 1,707, phosphate 687; cotton yarn (1979) 175; cotton fabrics (sq m) 748,000; wool yarn (1979) 71; woolen fabrics (sq m) 128,000; man-made fibres (1979) 205; paper 633. New dwelling units completed (1978) 166,700.

The U.S. team, the Charles River Rowing Association, breezed to a three-length victory over the Thames Rowing Club team to win the Thames Challenge Cup in the Henley Royal Regatta in England.

Rowing

East Germany and Norway were the most successful nations in the men's events at the world rowing championship in Lucerne, Switz., in 1982. The Soviet Union dominated the women's events and Italy the lightweight events, while East Germany collected most of the titles in the world junior rowing championships. Overall, Eastern European countries won 52 of the 96 world rowing medals, including 22 of the 32 titles.

East Germany won three of the men's events and Norway won two; the other gold medalists were New Zealand, Italy, and Switzerland The Soviet Union won five of the women's titles and East Germany took the sixth. Italians were medalists in all four lightweight events, winning three while Austria took the fourth. The East Germans retained the men's coxed fours and quadruple sculls, won the single sculls, but surrendered the double sculls title to Norway, which also defeated them in coxless pairs.

Italy successfully defended its coxed pairs title by beating East Germany, but the surprise of the championships was New Zealand's emphatic victory over East Germany and the Soviet Union, the defending champion, in eights. Switzerland beat the Soviet Union in coxless fours. Czechoslovakia won bronze medals in double sculls and coxed pairs and the silver medal in coxed fours. The U.S. took the bronze medals in coxed fours and single sculls.

The Soviet Union missed only one gold medal in the women's events. The Soviets won the coxed fours, double sculls, single sculls, quadruple sculls, and eights, leaving East Germany to win the coxless pairs. East Germany also won silver medals in double sculls and quadruple sculls, as well as the bronze medal in eights. The Romanians were the silver medalists in single sculls and took the bronze medals in coxed fours and quadruple sculls. The U.S. did well, with silver medals in coxed fours and eights, as did Canada with bronze medals in double sculls and coxless pairs. The only other medalist was Poland with the silver in coxless pairs.

In lightweight events, Italy won the coxless fours, double sculls, and eights and finished third behind Austria in single sculls. The U.S. won two more silver medals in the single and double sculls, Spain and Denmark won a silver and a bronze each, and Switzerland completed the lightweight medal table with a bronze.

Ten of the 14 titles in the world junior championships, held in Piediluco, Italy, were won by East Germany, and another three were taken by the Soviet Union. However, neither country was a medalist in men's eights, in which West Germany beat the U.S. with France finishing third. East Germany finished second in two events; the Soviet Union, West Germany, and Italy collected three silver medals each; and the other two went to France. West Germany and the Soviet Union both won three bronze medals, Bulgaria won two, and the remainder went to Belgium, Czechoslovakia, France, Italy, The Netherlands, and Sweden.

In England the Amateur Rowing Association, the governing body of the sport, celebrated its centenary. Three open trophies at the Henley Royal Regatta were won by overseas crews: Charles River Rowing Association took the Thames Cup (eights) to the U.S.; Neptune R.C. won the Britannia Cup (coxed fours) for Ireland; and the Silver Goblets (coxless pairs) went to M. Ivancic and Z.

Celent of the Veslacki Klub "Gusar" of Yugoslavia. Oxford won the 128th University Boat Race by 3¼ lengths, reducing Cambridge's lead in the series to 68–59.　　　　　　　　　　　　(KEITH OSBORNE)

Rwanda

Rwanda

A republic in eastern Africa and former traditional kingdom whose origins may be traced back to the 15th century, Rwanda is bordered by Zaire, Uganda, Tanzania, and Burundi. Area: 26,338 sq km (10,169 sq mi). Pop. (1981 est.): 5,256,000, including (1978) Hutu 90%; Tutsi 9%; and Twa 1%. Cap. and largest city: Kigali (pop., 1981 est., 156,650). Language (official): French and Kinyarwanda. Religion (1980): Roman Catholic 56%; Protestant 12%; Muslim 9%; most of the remainder are animist. President in 1982, Maj. Gen. Juvénal Habyarimana.

On Dec. 28, 1981, Rwanda held elections, setting up the first elected Parliament since the military takeover in 1973. All candidates belonged to the National Revolutionary Development Movement, the only permitted political party, which had been formed by Pres. Juvénal Habyarimana in 1975. Candidates were required to have four years of secondary schooling and to speak French. The voting, which was mandatory, proceeded calmly. Of the 64 deputies elected to Parliament, five were women.

Problems of transport for landlocked Rwanda remained acute in 1982; tea and coffee exports had to be flown to Mombasa, Kenya. West Germany and China between them undertook the construction of a road from Kigali to Ruhengeri in the north. The country received training aid, mainly in the form of scholarships, from both the U.S.S.R. and the U.S.; most assistance, however, came from the European Economic Community (EEC) and Belgium.

Revenue from tin output for 1981 was adversely affected by the rise in the value of the pound sterling against the U.S. dollar, since the Rwanda franc was tied to the dollar and tin sales were conducted in pounds sterling.　　　(GUY ARNOLD)

RWANDA

Education. (1979–80) Primary, pupils 607,480, teachers 10,002; secondary, pupils 7,112; vocational, pupils 2,177; teacher training, pupils 2,879; secondary, vocational, and teacher training, teachers 903; higher (1977–78), students 1,134, teaching staff 213.

Finance. Monetary unit: Rwanda franc, with (Sept. 20, 1982) a par value of RwFr 92.84 to U.S. $1 (free rate of RwFr 159.17 = £1 sterling). Gold and other reserves (June 1982) U.S. $138 million. Budget (1981 est.) balanced at RwFr 14,406,000,000.

Foreign Trade. (1980) Imports RwFr 22,568,000,000; exports RwFr 7,025,000,000. Import sources: Belgium-Luxembourg 16%; Japan 12%; Kenya 11%; France 10%; China 9%; Iran 9%; West Germany 9%; U.S. 5%. Export destinations: Tanzania 63%; Kenya 13%; Belgium-Luxembourg 9%. Main exports: coffee 55%; tea 18%; tin 8%.

Agriculture. Production (in 000; metric tons; 1981): sorghum c. 175; corn c. 85; potatoes c. 228; sweet potatoes c. 938; cassava c. 494; dry beans c. 178; dry peas c. 48; pumpkins c. 70; plantains c. 2,100; coffee c. 24; tea c. 7. Livestock (in 000; 1981): cattle c. 650; sheep c. 300; goats c. 920; pigs c. 140.

Rubber:
see Industrial Review

Rugby Football:
see Football

Russia:
see Union of Soviet
Socialist Republics

Sabah:
see Malaysia

Sailing

At the end of 1981 the Whitbread Round the World race had reached the halfway stage in New Zealand. Cornelis van Rietschoten's "Flyer" was leading with the shortest elapsed time, but with the handicap taken into consideration Andrew Viant's smaller Foers-design "Kriter III" was in first. During the first two legs incidents and breakages were rampant, but the main interest in the race from the start of the second leg in Cape Town, South Africa, was whether or not the New Zealand entry "Ceramco" could catch "Flyer." "Ceramco" kept "Flyer" close company on that leg, and on the next legs from New Zealand to Australia, Australia to Argentina, and Argentina back to the U.K. This struggle continued until in the last 1,600 km (1,000 mi) to Portsmouth "Flyer" not only got away from "Ceramco" but also won first place on handicap as a huge high-pressure area left the smaller yachts struggling in light fickle winds.

At the end of 1981 the Southern Cross series ended with the Sydney–Hobart race. Eleven teams, each consisting of three yachts, had entered the series, which was won by New South Wales. The Southern Cross series allows a wide rating range, and with the Sydney–Hobart race a protracted affair with light winds, the leading places were taken by small yachts. Because this race counted triple points, the New South Wales team of three small boats gained a great advantage.

During 1982 several syndicates were preparing for the 1983 America's Cup Challenge. From Britain Peter de Savery was challenging with his "Victory" syndicate. Having gained the services of both Phil Crebbin and Harold Cudmore, he had two of the world's best yachtsmen around which to build his team. A group of more than 50 spent the summer training in Newport, R.I., and annoyed the defending U.S. "Freedom" syndicate, led by Dennis Connor, by conducting a surveillance of their sailing activities and obtaining information therefrom. The Australians had three separate challenges with some five or six new 12-m yachts. The Canadians, while training hard, were awaiting completion of their new Bruce Kirby-designed boat.

For the U.S. Connor and Tom Blackaller were the two best-known helmsmen involved. Connor's "Freedom" syndicate had two new boats, "Spirit" and "Magic," but neither seemed to be a match for "Freedom," the cup's successful defender in 1980.

The ton cup events suffered in the world recession. In the smaller-size classes—Micro, Mini, and ¼ ton—a few countries still mustered reasonable fleets. However, rising costs and rule changes took their toll, and the 1982 one-ton series scheduled for British waters had to be canceled because of the lack of entries.

In the Round Britain race the first leg of the course from Plymouth to Crosshaven was won by Robert and Naomi James in "Colt Cars GB," with Chay Blyth and Peter Bateman second in "Brittany Ferries GB." "Exmouth Challenge" won the second leg to Barra and appeared to like the heavy head

Bill Dunlop, from Mechanic Falls, Maine, brought his tiny yacht to dock in Falmouth, England, on August 29, 78 days after leaving Portland, Maine.

WIDE WORLD

winds. The third leg to Lerwick gave way to fresh reaching conditions, which suited the larger trimarans. Blyth was first to arrive in the record-breaking time of 1 day 14 hours and 7 minutes, taking 16 hours off the old record. In fact, the first 14 boats all broke the old record.

In the fourth leg, to Lowestoft, "Brittany Ferries" arrived first, but "Colt Cars" gained nearly 1¾ hours when it finished only 19 minutes later. "Exmouth Challenge" finished four hours after that. On the fifth and final leg to Plymouth the two large trimarans virtually match-raced all the way with "Exmouth Challenge" close behind. Robert and Naomi James were first home, closely followed by Blyth and Bateman and not long afterward by Mark Gatehouse and Peter Rowsell in "Exmouth Challenge." "Colt Cars" set a new Round Britain record of 8 days 15 hours and 3 minutes, and "Voortrekker II" took 1 day and 2 hours off the old monohull record when it finished with a time of 10 days 16 hours and 10 minutes.

Bill Dunlop of Mechanic Falls, Maine, set a new record for crossing the Atlantic Ocean from west to east in the smallest boat. His 9-ft 1-in "Wind's Will" crossed the ocean in 78 days and was only eight inches shorter than the craft in which Tom McClean of the U.K. had sailed the Atlantic earlier in the summer.   (ADRIAN JARDINE)

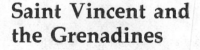

World Class Boat Champions

Class	Winner
Cadet	Raul Saubicet (Argentina)
Enterprise	Stuart Teasdale (U.K.)
Europe	Marc Pirinoli (France)
420	William Sanchez (France)
470	Bjorn Borowski (East Germany)
505	Gary Knapp (U.S.)
Finn	Lasje Hjortnæs (Denmark)
Fireball	Chris Tillett (Australia)
Flying Fifteen	Peter Gale (Australia)
Hornet	Malcolm Goodwin (U.K.)
J24	Mark Bethwaite (Australia)
Optimist	Njaal Sletten (Norway)
Solo	Rob van Ooyen (Neth.)
Taser	David Jones (Australia)
Topper	Ian Fryett (U.K.)
Tornado	Randy Smyth (U.S.)

Saint Lucia

Saint Lucia

A parliamentary democracy and a member of the Commonwealth, St. Lucia, the second largest of the Windward Islands in the eastern Caribbean, is situated 32 km NE of St. Vincent and 40 km S of Martinique. Area: 622 sq km (240 sq mi). Pop. (1981 est.): 122,000, predominantly of African descent. Cap. and largest city: Castries (pop., 1979 est., 45,000). Language: English (official) and a local French dialect. Religion (1970): Roman Catholic 91%, Anglican 3%, Seventh-day Adventist 2%, others 4%. Queen, Elizabeth II; governor-general in 1982, Boswell Williams; prime ministers, Winston Francis Cenac to January 16, Michael Pilgrim from January 17 (interim), and John Compton from May 3.

After the resignation of the St. Lucia Labour Party government in January 1982, an interim government was appointed until elections took place on May 3. The opposition United Workers' Party led by former prime minister John Compton (see BIOGRAPHIES) was returned to power.

The political unrest of the 12 months preceding the election had resulted in a decline in tourism and a general lessening of economic activity, so that 1981 figures showed a negative growth rate. Compton's right-of-centre approach to the problem placed heavy emphasis on construction, tourism, and agriculture. But in spite of generous assistance from the U.S., the U.K., Canada, and others, by late 1982 the prime minister was warning that economic recovery would be slow. He turned to local commercial banks for an ECar$8 million loan and to regional institutions for soft loans. In a speech at the UN he indicated that St. Lucia would follow a truly nonaligned path but would continue to look for help from traditional Western friends.   (DAVID A. JESSOP)

Saint Vincent and the Grenadines

ST. LUCIA

Education. (1979–80) Primary, pupils 30,610, teachers 942; secondary, pupils 4,879, teachers 220; vocational, pupils 198, teachers (1978–79) 24; teacher training, students (1978–79) 152, teachers 13.

Finance and Trade. Monetary unit: East Caribbean dollar, with (Sept. 20, 1982) a par value of ECar$2.70 to U.S. $1 (free rate of ECar$4.63 = £1 sterling). Budget (1980–81 est.): revenue ECar$98,870,000; expenditure ECar$101,310,000. Foreign trade (1979): imports ECar$273.2 million; exports ECar$75.6 million. Import sources (1978): U.S. 36%; U.K. 19%; Trinidad and Tobago 10%; Japan 5%. Export destinations (1978): U.K. 49%; Barbados 9%; Trinidad and Tobago 8%; Dominica 6%; St. Vincent 6%; Jamaica 6%. Main exports (1978): bananas 45%; cardboard cartons 11%; beverages 8%; coconut oil 7%. Tourism (1979): visitors 87,900; gross receipts U.S. $34 million.

Saint Vincent and the Grenadines

A constitutional monarchy within the Commonwealth, St. Vincent and the Grenadines (islands of the Lesser Antilles in the Caribbean Sea) lies southwest of St. Lucia and west of Barbados. Area (including Grenadines): 388 sq km (150 sq mi).

ST. VINCENT

Education. (1979–80) Primary, pupils 24,222, teachers 1,211; secondary, pupils 6,384, teachers (1977–78) 284; vocational, pupils 1,252; teacher training, students 107; vocational and teacher training, teachers (1977–78) 35.

Finance and Trade. Monetary unit: East Caribbean dollar, with (Sept. 20, 1982) a par value of ECar$2.70 to U.S. $1 (free rate of ECar$4.63 = £1 sterling). Budget (1981–82 est.): revenue ECar$70.8 million; expenditure ECar$68.4 million. Foreign trade (1980): imports ECar$154.6 million; exports ECar$42.9 million. Import sources (1976): U.K. 30%; Trinidad and Tobago 20%; U.S. 9%; Canada 9%; St. Lucia 5%; Guyana 5%. Export destinations (1976): U.K. 75%; Trinidad and Tobago 13%. Main exports (1976): bananas 62%; vegetables c. 20%; arrowroot starch 5%.

Pop. (1981 est.): 124,000, predominantly of African descent. Cap. and largest city: Kingstown (pop., 1979 est., 23,200). Language: English (official). Religion (1970): Anglican 47%; Methodist 28%; Roman Catholic 13%. Queen, Elizabeth II; governor-general in 1982, Sir Sydney Gun-Munro; prime minister, Milton Cato.

St. Vincent continued its slow if unspectacular development during 1982. In common with other eastern Caribbean islands, the country suffered a decline in tourism caused by recession in North America. The economic problems this created were compounded by the low value of the pound sterling against the U.S. dollar, to which the currency was tied. Export earnings from bananas fell substantially, and the problem was compounded by disease and concern over the future of the protected U.K. market for Caribbean bananas.

The government introduced a 3% tax on the gross profits of businesses, and in response the business community organized a strike. However, support for the tax measure on the part of most Vincentians meant that the trades had little local sympathy. Former premier James Mitchell emerged as leader of the opposition in Parliament.

St. Vincent received most of its aid from the U.S., Canada, and the U.K. Prime Minister Milton Cato met with U.S. Pres. Ronald Reagan in Barbados in April. (DAVID A. JESSOP)

San Marino

São Tomé and Príncipe

Salvador, El:
see El Salvador

Salvation Army:
see Religion

Samoa:
see Dependent States; Western Samoa

San Marino

A small republic, San Marino is an enclave in northeastern Italy, 8 km SW of Rimini. Area: 61 sq km (24 sq mi). Pop. (1982 est.): 21,800. Cap. and largest city: San Marino (metro. pop., 1981 est., 8,600). Language: Italian. Religion: Roman Catholic. The country is governed by two *capitani reggenti*, or co-regents, appointed every six months by a Grand and General Council. Executive power rests with three secretaries of state: foreign and political affairs, internal affairs, and economic af-

SAN MARINO

Education. (1980–81) Primary, pupils 1,509, teachers 145; secondary, pupils 1,219, teachers 112; vocational, pupils 695; teacher training, pupils 76.

Finance. Monetary unit: Italian lira, with (Sept. 20, 1982) a free rate of 1,406 lire to U.S. $1 (2,410 lire = £1 sterling); local coins are issued. Budget (1981 est.) balanced at 144,103,000,000 lire. Tourism (1979) 3.5 million visitors.

fairs. In 1982 the positions were filled, respectively, by Giordano Bruno Refi, Alvaro Selva, and Emilio della Balda.

On Aug. 29, 1982, Pope John Paul II paid an official visit to the republic of San Marino. It was the first such visit by the head of the Roman Catholic Church since the Vatican recognized San Marino's independence in 1631. The pope was greeted at the government palace by Giuseppe Maianni, the elder of the two co-regents, and was presented to the members of the Grand and General Council. The sovereign pontiff went on to meet representatives of San Marino's clergy. The visit ended with a papal mass.

Reversing existing law, the republic's judiciary gave women born in San Marino the right to keep their nationality if they married outside the republic, a right until then granted only to men. (However, a man in such a situation could pass his nationality on to his children, whereas a woman still could not.) The change was the result of moves initiated by Maria Lea Pedini-Angelini, who, when elected co-regent for a six-month term in March 1981, became the first woman head of state in San Marino's history.

In August San Marino took part in a conference of nine neutral and nonaligned European states.

(K. M. SMOGORZEWSKI)

São Tomé and Príncipe

An independent African state, the Democratic Republic of São Tomé and Príncipe comprises two main islands and several smaller islets that straddle the Equator in the Gulf of Guinea, off the west coast of Africa. Area: 964 sq km (372 sq mi), of which São Tomé, the larger island, comprises 854 sq km. Pop. (1981 est.): 95,000. Cap. and largest city: São Tomé (pop., 1978 est., 25,000). Language: Portuguese. Religion: mainly Roman Catholic. President in 1982, Manuel Pinto da Costa.

Early in 1982 São Tomé and Príncipe experienced the aftermath of violent disturbances that took place at the end of 1981 as a result of food shortages. Separatists on the island of Príncipe accused the authorities in São Tomé, the capital, of deliberately withholding supplies. Some people were injured in clashes with police. According to the government, the shortages were the result of a delay in the arrival of a food-supply vessel, an indication of the narrow margin on which the island worked. The government blamed the riots on "internal reactionary forces." Pres. Manuel Pinto

SÃO TOMÉ AND PRÍNCIPE

Education. (1977) Primary, pupils 14,162, teachers 527; secondary, pupils 3,145, teachers 81; vocational, pupils 155, teachers 30.

Finance and Trade. Monetary unit: dobra, with (Sept. 20, 1982) a free rate of 41.91 dobras to U.S. $1 (71.85 dobras = £1 sterling). Budget (1977 est.): revenue 180 million dobras; expenditure 454 million dobras. Foreign trade (1975): imports 288,469,000 dobras; exports 180,432,000 dobras. Import sources: Portugal 61%; Angola 13%. Export destinations: The Netherlands 52%; Portugal 33%; West Germany 8%. Main exports: cocoa c. 82%; copra c. 6%; palm kernels and nuts c. 5%.

da Costa reshuffled his Cabinet in the wake of the disturbances, taking on the portfolios of defense and national security himself.

During the year talks were held with Cape Verde about the return there of an estimated 10,000 Cape Verdians in the islands. A target of resentment, Cape Verdians were traditionally identified with the former colonial administration. Foreign Minister Maria de Amorim visited Algeria and Libya, and cooperation agreements were completed with both countries. Agreement was reached on a European Development Fund project to improve oil palm cultivation.   (GUY ARNOLD)

Saudi Arabia

A monarchy occupying four-fifths of the Arabian Peninsula, Saudi Arabia has an area of 2,240,000 sq km (865,000 sq mi). Pop. (1982 est.): 8,905,000. Cap. and largest city: Riyadh (pop. 1980 est., 1,044,000). Language: Arabic. Religion: Muslim, predominantly Sunni; Shi'ah minority in Eastern Province. Kings and prime ministers in 1982, Khalid and, from June 13, Fahd.

Khalid ibn 'Abdal-'Aziz (see OBITUARIES), king and prime minister of Saudi Arabia, died of a heart attack on June 13, 1982. He was immediately succeeded in both these capacities by his half brother Fahd (see BIOGRAPHIES), who had been crown prince and first deputy prime minister. Fahd's half brother Prince Abdullah, previously second deputy prime minister and commander of the National Guard, was promoted to the government post vacated by Fahd and named crown prince. Prince Sultan, a full brother of Fahd, was appointed second deputy prime minister and retained the defense portfolio.

The succession of King Fahd to the throne took place smoothly, although in his first six months the new monarch served notice of a change of style. While pledging himself to continue the work of the late King Khalid, Fahd showed every sign of continuing the modernizing stand that he had espoused as crown prince. Crown Prince Abdullah represented the more traditional side of the Saudi regime. Prince Sultan, who could be considered third in line to the throne, was also a modernizer and was thought to be more pro-Western than Fahd.

The smoothness of the transition was not surprising to most observers because of the perceived need of the royal house of Saud to stand together. King Fahd, who was born in 1922, had been groomed for power. As crown prince he took the brunt of responsibility for government from his saintly brother Khalid, who had been regarded as a caretaker monarch when he became king after King Faisal's assassination in 1975. Even the most important foreign-policy effort during Khalid's reign was associated with Fahd: the Fahd plan, an eight-point plan proposed by Saudi Arabia in August 1981, that aimed to bring about a Middle East peace settlement based on recognition of Israel's right to exist within secure boundaries as well as the establishment of an independent state for the Palestinians. Khalid's rule was nevertheless remarkable because of his ability to infuse it with the values derived from his background as an Arab of the Nejd and as a Muslim devoted to the Tarikh — the path followed by the Muslim true believer.

On July 23 Fahd renewed Khalid's promises to introduce the country's first democratic institution—the *majlis al-shura*, a consultative assembly of commoners—into the political administration. He pledged himself to continue Khalid's work and said that the next five-year (1985–90) development plan would ensure a "wide distribution of the national income." Fahd could be expected to fulfill this pledge, since he himself had largely inspired the last two Saudi Arabian development plans. These had impressed foreign observers with their effectiveness in bringing about the transformation of the kingdom into a society served by modern hospitals, ports, airports, roads, universities, and telecommunications.

In his address to mark the Hajj (pilgrimage to Mecca) on September 27, Fahd attacked Israel for

Saudi Arabia

Mourners carried the coffin of King Khalid of Saudi Arabia through the streets of Riyadh. The monarch, who died on June 13 at age 69, had reigned since 1975.

GAMMA/LIAISON

SAUDI ARABIA

Education. (1980–81) Primary, pupils 930,436, teachers 50,010; secondary, pupils 377,681, teachers 24,866; vocational (1979–80), pupils 4,557, teachers 748; teacher training (1979–80), students 17,410, teachers 1,599; higher, students 54,397, teaching staff 5,946.

Finance. Monetary unit: riyal, with (Sept. 20, 1982) a free rate of 3.44 riyals to U.S. $1 (5.90 riyals = £1 sterling). Gold and other reserves (June 1982) U.S. $31,528,000,000. Budget (total; 1982–83 est.) balanced at 313 billion riyals. Gross national product (1979–80) 391.2 billion riyals. Money supply (Sept. 1981) 68,670,000,000 riyals. Cost of living (1975 = 100; March 1982) 154.

Foreign Trade. (1981) Imports 119.3 billion riyals; exports 383.3 billion riyals. Import sources : U.S. 21%; Japan 18%; West Germany 10%; Italy 7%; U.K. 6%; France 6%. Export destinations: Japan 17%; U.S. 13%; France 10%; Italy 7%; The Netherlands 6%; Singapore 5%. Main export: crude oil 95%. Tourism (1980): gross receipts U.S. $1,343,000,000.

Transport and Communications. Roads (1980) 47,700 km. Motor vehicles in use (1980): passenger 630,800; commercial 522,200. Railways: (1979) c. 680 km; traffic (1980) 82 million passenger-km, freight 261 million net ton-km. Air traffic (1980): 9,938,000,000 passenger-km; freight c. 174.6 million net ton-km. Shipping (1981): merchant vessels 100 gross tons and over 286; gross tonnage 3,121,821. Telephones (Jan. 1980) 280,500. Radio receivers (Dec. 1979) 300,000. Television receivers (Dec. 1979) 310,000.

Agriculture. Production (in 000; metric tons; 1981): sorghum c. 100; wheat c. 150; barley c. 16; tomatoes c. 170; onions c. 95; grapes c. 60; dates c. 429. Livestock (in 000; 1981): cattle c. 410; sheep c. 4,201; goats c. 2,043; camels c. 162; asses c. 118; poultry c. 5,598.

Industry. Production (in 000; metric tons; 1981): crude oil 490,796; petroleum products (1979) c. 34,000; natural gas (cu m) 10,150,000; electricity (excluding most industrial production; kw-hr; 1980) 9,000,000; gypsum (1980) 80; cement (1980) 3,500.

its intervention in Lebanon. He also condemned the Soviet Union for its actions in Afghanistan. In calling for an end to the Gulf war between Iran and Iraq, King Fahd was identifying strongly with his partners in the Gulf Cooperation Council (GCC), which grouped the kingdom with Kuwait, the United Arab Emirates, Qatar, Bahrain, and Oman. In a wider context, Fahd also criticized what he termed "big-power influence" in the Muslim world. The Hajj was disrupted by demonstrations mounted in the holy cities of Mecca and Medina by Iranian pilgrims. In a statement in October, Interior Minister Prince Nayef laid the blame on Ayatollah Ruhollah Khomeini of Iran. Among a group of 69 Iranians expelled on October 7 was an Iranian religious leader, Hojatoleslam Khoeina. With the memory of the 1979 siege of Mecca fresh in the minds of Fahd and his associates, subversion and incitement in the holy cities by foreign pilgrims was clearly a matter of intense concern.

Although the official attitude of the GCC toward the Gulf war was one of neutrality, these internal disruptions and other, earlier incidents served to bring Saudi Arabia, as well as other members of the council, into closer alignment with Iraq. It was suggested that Iran was cooperating with Israel by diverting Iraq's energies away from the Arab-Israeli conflict. Iran was also accused of involvement in an alleged coup attempt in Bahrain in December 1981, seen as part of a plan to destabilize the Gulf region. Saudi Arabia signed a frontier treaty with Iraq at the end of 1981, after which Prince Nayef called on all Arab countries to abandon their neu-

trality in favour of Arab solidarity with Iraq in its fight to defend the entire Arab nation.

In January 1982 Saudi Arabia played a prominent part in a meeting of defense ministers from GCC member countries. It was agreed that the six should work toward creating a regional defense plan, in response to the instability in the Gulf area brought about by the Gulf war and the Soviet intervention in Afghanistan.

Saudi Arabia and Libya restored diplomatic relations on Dec. 31, 1981, after a break of 14 months. However, this move did not result in a significant improvement in relations between the two countries during 1982. In March Libya's Col. Muammar al-Qaddafi accused Saudi Arabia of acting in league with the U.S. by "drowning the world market with crude oil at the cheapest price." Saudi Arabia, in turn, called for the expulsion of Libya from the Arab League and the Organization of African Unity, in condemnation of Qaddafi's foreign policies.

At the Arab summit meeting in Fez, Morocco, in September, consensus on a Middle East peace plan was achieved among the Arab nations. The set of proposals was a slightly modified version of the Fahd plan, which the same summit had rejected a year earlier. The revised version put greater emphasis on the role of the UN Security Council in guaranteeing "peace among all states of the region including the independent Palestinian state." (*See* MIDDLE EASTERN AFFAIRS.)

Within the Organization of Petroleum Exporting Countries (OPEC), Saudi Arabia absorbed much of the slump in demand for crude oil in 1982. Output in late 1982 was running at less than 6 million bbl a day, compared with the all-time high of 10.5 million bbl a day achieved at one point in 1981. In the same period, combined OPEC production fell by not more than 3 million bbl a day. The loss of about one-half of the kingdom's export revenue appeared to have little immediate effect on the development plan. The 1982–83 budget called for spending the equivalent of $91 billion, but most analysts agreed that the kingdom needed no more than 7 million bbl a day to finance that sum. Unofficial reports in early November suggested that the Saudi Arabian government might consider drawing down its official reserves, possibly by as much as $25 billion, in order to avoid incurring a budget deficit. Previous reports had ruled out such a step. In oil policy, Saudi Arabia was committed to maintaining the $34 a barrel price for Arabian light crude oil with no discounts.

With imports estimated at $9.8 billion in the first quarter of 1982, Saudi Arabia maintained its attraction for Western business as a buoyant market for capital goods and consumer products. Contractors' payments were nevertheless being squeezed, and advance payments on contracts were kept to 10% of the contract value on the express orders of King Fahd. (Previously they had been 20%.) Saudi Arabia's pro-Western stand was maintained, although a reply was made to Soviet Pres. Leonid I. Brezhnev's message to mark Saudi Arabia's national day on September 23. The king said he was glad to observe that Moscow wanted to see a lasting peace settlement between Israel and the Arabs.

The Saudi Arabian economy had grown used to massive injections of public funds in the 1979–82 period. The squeeze on oil revenue in 1982 dictated that the private sector and the commercial banks would have to play a bigger role in financing projects. Medium-term lending by the banks for productive industries and agriculture still provided only a small percentage of the total finance. The main government agencies, such as the Public Investment Fund, the Saudi Industrial Development Fund, and the Real Estate Development Fund, had borne the main burden of investment under the previous two five-year plans.

It was understood that the government had pledged that oil production would not fall below 5 million bbl a day. This was intended to prevent any catastrophic curtailment of public spending while still allowing a considerable margin for funding by the emerging private sector.

(JOHN WHELAN)

Senegal

A republic of West Africa, Senegal is bounded by Mauritania, Mali, Guinea, and Guinea-Bissau and by the Atlantic Ocean. The independent nation of The Gambia forms an enclave within the country. Area: 196,722 sq km (75,955 sq mi). Pop. (1982 est.): 5,991,000, including Wolof 37%; Serer 17%; Peulh 17%; Dyola 9%; Mandingo 9%; Tukulor 6%; other 5%. Cap. and largest city: Dakar (pop., 1978 est., 914,500). Language: French (official); Wolof, Serer, Fulani, Dyola, Malinke, and other tribal dialects. Religion (1980 est.): Muslim 91%; Christian 6%; animist 3%. President in 1982, Abdou Diouf; premier, Habib Thiam.

Senegal's economy improved slowly but steadily during 1982. Democratic institutions continued to thrive, and under the extended multi-party system inaugurated the previous year, the number of parties rose to 14 with the formation of the Communist League of Workers and the African Party for the Independence of the People. Communal violence at Casamance in July resulted in more than a dozen deaths, and in December there were demonstrations for the province's independence.

Presidents Abdou Diouf of Senegal and Sir Dawda Jawara of The Gambia became, respectively, president and vice-president of the Senegambia confederation, which formally came into existence on February 1. The two countries would retain their individual sovereignty but would adopt joint defense, foreign, and monetary policies. On November 4 a confederal council of ministers was formed.

Faithful to its policy of support for the Organization of African Unity (OAU), Senegal contributed a contingent to the OAU peacekeeping force in Chad during November 1981–July 1982. However, President Diouf opposed the (Western) Saharan Arab Democratic Republic's admission to OAU membership, and he stayed away from the abortive Tripoli, Libya, OAU summit in August. In February diplomatic relations were established with Angola for the first time since 1975. French Pres. François Mitterrand visited Senegal in May. Throughout the Falkland Islands conflict, Senegal's Yoff Airport served as a refueling stop for British military aircraft. (PHILIPPE DECRAENE)

Senegal

Seychelles

A republic and a member of the Commonwealth in the Indian Ocean consisting of 100 islands, Seychelles lies 1,450 km from the coast of East Africa. Area: 444 sq km (171 sq mi), 166 sq km of which includes the islands of Farquhar, Desroches, and Aldabra. Pop. (1982 est.): 67,800, including Creole 94%, French 5%, English 1%. Cap.: Victoria, on Mahé (pop., 1980, 23,900). Language: English and French are official; creole patois is also spoken. Religion: Roman Catholic 90%; Anglican 8%. President in 1982, France-Albert René.

The year 1982 was an exceptionally troubled one for Seychelles. A deeply embarrassed South Africa denied complicity in the failed coup attempt of November 1981, although one of the accused mercenaries was a South African intelligence officer. Seychelles exiles in London claimed responsibility, while Pres. France-Albert René accused former president James Mancham of involvement.

Seven mercenaries captured in Seychelles faced trial in Victoria; they included four South Africans, two white Zimbabweans, and a Briton. Six pleaded guilty, and four of them were later sentenced to death. Meanwhile, the 45 mercenaries who had escaped to South Africa were brought to trial there in March, and their leader, Col. Michael ("Mad Mike") Hoare, was sentenced to ten years in prison for hijacking.

In August 1982 a group of soldiers in Victoria

Seychelles

Scandinavian Literature:
see Literature

Schools:
see Education

Scotland:
see United Kingdom

Sculpture:
see Art Exhibitions; Art Sales; Museums

Securities:
see Stock Exchanges

Seismology:
see Earth Sciences

Seventh-day Adventist Church:
see Religion

SENEGAL

Education. (1979–80) Primary, pupils 392,541, teachers 8,479; secondary, pupils 80,146, teachers (1978–79) 2,934; vocational, pupils 9,091, teachers (1978–79) 578; higher, students 11,852, teaching staff (1978–79) 571.

Finance and Trade. Monetary unit: CFA franc, with (Sept. 20, 1982) a par value of CFA Fr 50 to the French franc (free rate of CFA Fr 353 = U.S. $1; CFA Fr 605 = £1 sterling). Budget (total; 1981–82 est.) balanced at CFA Fr 220.2 billion. Foreign trade (1980): imports CFA Fr 222.3 billion; exports CFA Fr 100.8 billion. Import sources: France 37%; Iraq 8%; Thailand 7%; Niger a 6%; U.S. 5%. Export destinations: France 34%; Ivory Coast 8%; Mauritania 7%; U.K. 6%; Mali 6%. Main exports: fish and products 24%; petroleum products 18%; phosphates 16%; peanut oil 12%; animal fodder 6%; chemicals 5%.

SEYCHELLES

Education. (1980) Primary, pupils 14,516, teachers 685; secondary, pupils 1,261, teachers 80; vocational, pupils 466, teachers 70; teacher training, students 194, teachers 24.

Finance and Trade. Monetary unit: Seychelles rupee, with (Sept. 20, 1982) a free rate of SRs 6.60 to U.S. $1 (SRs 11.32 = £1 sterling). Budget (1980 est.): revenue SRs 374 million; expenditure SRs 370 million. Foreign trade (1981): imports SRs 589 million; exports SRs 89 million. Import sources (1979): U.K. 21%; France 11%; South Africa 10%; Yemen (San'a') 9%; Kenya 9%; Bahrain 7%; Japan 6%; Singapore 5%. Export destinations (1979): ship and aircraft bunkers and stores 68%; Pakistan 17%; Reunion 5%. Main exports (1980): petroleum products 65%; copra 15%. Tourism (1980): visitors 71,800; gross receipts U.S. $41 million.

mutinied. While President René was on a tour of outlying islands, the rebels seized the radio station. Initially they claimed to be loyal to René, but their leader then called for his removal from office. The mutiny was crushed by loyal troops, five rebels being killed. In October the British Foreign Office apprised the Seychelles government of a plot uncovered in London for a new coup attempt, again allegedly with South African support.

(GUY ARNOLD)

Sierra Leone

Sierra Leone

A republic within the Commonwealth, Sierra Leone is a West African state on the Atlantic coast between Guinea and Liberia. Area: 71,740 sq km (27,699 sq mi). Pop. (1982 est.): 3,672,000, including (1979) Mende and Temne tribes 60%; other tribes 39.5%; non-African 0.5%. Cap. and largest city: Freetown (pop., 1974, 314,340). Language: English (official); tribal dialects. Religion: animist 51.5%; Muslim 39.5%; Christian 9%. President in 1982, Siaka Stevens.

General elections were held in Sierra Leone on May 1, 1982. There was some violence, and the results in 13 constituencies (out of a total of 85) were canceled because of serious electoral irregularities.

SIERRA LEONE
   Education. (1980–81) Primary, pupils 238,100, teachers (1978–79) 7,260; secondary, pupils 57,800, teachers (1977–78) 2,507; vocational (1977–78), pupils 2,060, teachers (1978–80) 154; teacher training (1978–79), students 2,510, teachers (1977–78) 121; higher, students 1,780, teaching staff (1976–77) 327.
   Finance and Trade. Monetary unit: leone, with (Sept. 20, 1982) a free value of 1.26 leones to U.S. $1 (2.16 leones = £1 sterling). Budget (1981–82 est.): revenue 266.3 million leones; expenditure 316.6 million leones. Foreign trade (1980): imports 447,480,000 leones; exports 225,350,000 leones. Import sources: U.K. c. 22%; Japan c. 9%; West Germany c. 7%; France c. 6%; U.S. c. 5%. Export destinations: U.K. 41%; U.S. 11%; The Netherlands 8%; Switzerland 7%. Main exports: diamonds 55%; coffee 14%; cocoa 11%.
   Agriculture. Production (in 000; metric tons; 1981): rice c. 400; cassava c. 95; palm kernels c. 30; palm oil c. 50; coffee c. 6; cocoa c. 9; fish catch (1980) 49. Livestock (in 000; 1981): cattle c. 348; sheep c. 268; goats c. 150; pigs c. 38; chickens c. 3,850.
   Industry. Production (in 000; metric tons; 1980): bauxite 746; diamonds (metric carats; 1979) 855; petroleum products (1979) c. 350; electricity (kw-hr) 235,000.

New elections for these seats were conducted peacefully in June, except that further irregularities in Koinaduga North led to the cancellation of its results.

Pres. Siaka Stevens completed his list of government appointments after the by-elections. Stevens retained the presidency, despite his promise to stand down after general elections. The most important new appointment was that of Salia Jusu-Sheriff, former opposition leader, as minister of finance. In presenting his budget on June 30, the new finance minister pointed out that the economy faced severe problems, including a chronic shortage of foreign exchange. The budget deficit for 1981–82 was 141 million leones, as opposed to an estimated 91 million leones.

(GUY ARNOLD)

Ships and Shipping:
see Industrial Review;
Transportation

Singapore

Singapore, a republic within the Commonwealth, occupies a group of islands, the largest of which is Singapore, at the southern extremity of the Malay Peninsula. Area: 618 sq km (239 sq mi). Pop. (1982 est.): 2,472,000, including (1981 est.) 76.8% Chinese, 14.6% Malays, 6.4% Indians, and 2.2% other. Language: official languages are English, Malay, Mandarin Chinese, and Tamil. Religion: Malays are Muslim; Chinese, mainly Buddhist; Indians, mainly Hindu. President in 1982, Chengara Veetil Devan Nair; prime minister, Lee Kuan Yew.

In a speech on the eve of Singapore's national day in August 1982, Prime Minister Lee Kuan Yew provided official confirmation of a pessimistic economic outlook. He stated that after a decade of 10% average annual growth, Singapore would experience a sharp decline in its economy. An acute sense of foreboding was expressed when Prime Minister Lee suggested that Singapore could become another Lebanon or Kampuchea unless properly defended against external and internal threats.

In January the authorities arrested ten members of an alleged clandestine group, the People's Liberation Organization of Singapore. Those arrested included members of the opposition Workers' Party. They had distributed pamphlets during a Muslim rally. In February the government expelled two Soviets accused of spying. In September the government released the political detainees it had held the longest, Poh Soo-Kai and Lim Hock Siew, both originally arrested in 1963. In November the ruling People's Action Party approved proposals for a new constitution.

SINGAPORE
   Education. (1981) Primary, pupils 289,697, teachers 11,108; secondary, pupils 177,238, teachers 8,807; vocational, pupils 13,001, teachers 889; higher, students 24,156, teaching staff 2,226.
   Finance. Monetary unit: Singapore dollar, with (Sept. 20, 1982) a free rate of Sing$2.17 to U.S. $1 (Sing$3.71 = £1 sterling). Gold and other reserves (May 1982) U.S. $7,589,000,000. Budget (total; 1981–82 est.) balanced at Sing$6,335,000,000. Gross national product (1981) Sing$26,390,000,000. Money supply (May 1982) Sing$7,547,000,000. Cost of living (1975 = 100; June 1982) 134.1.
   Foreign Trade. (1981) Imports Sing$58,248,000,000; exports Sing$44,291,000,000. Import sources: Japan 19%; Saudi Arabia 18%; U.S. 13%; Malaysia 12%. Export destinations: Malaysia 16%; U.S. 13%; Japan 10%; Hong Kong 9%. Main exports: petroleum products 32%; machinery 22%; ship and aircraft fuel 7%; rubber 6%; food 5%. Tourism (1980): visitors 2,562,100; gross receipts U.S. $845 million.
   Transport and Communications. Roads (1981) 2,478 km. Motor vehicles in use (1981): passenger 175,100; commercial 87,800. Railways (1981): 38 km (for traffic see Malaysia). Air traffic (1981): 17,280,000,000 passenger-km; freight 667.4 million net ton-km. Shipping (1981): merchant vessels 100 gross tons and over 828; gross tonnage 6,888,452. Shipping traffic (1981): goods loaded 34,239,000 metric tons, unloaded 54,383,000 metric tons. Telephones (Dec. 1981) 775,000. Radio licenses (Dec. 1981) 592,200. Television licenses (Dec. 1981) 414,500.
   Industry. Production (in 000; 1981): electricity (kw-hr) 7,442,000; manufactured gas (cu m) 121,000; petroleum products (metric tons; 1979) c. 32,240. Merchant vessels launched (100 gross tons and over; 1981) 46,000 gross tons.

In April a significant change occurred in the structure of the nation's press. A plan to begin a second English-language morning paper was set aside. The *Straits Times*, following the appointment of the former permanent head of the Foreign Ministry as executive chairman, gave the title of its evening English-language paper, the *New Nation*, to the company that was to have published the other morning paper. There would be a Chinese-language morning newspaper.

The annual ministerial meeting of the Association of Southeast Asian Nations (ASEAN) was held in Singapore in June. The following month Singapore's director of education, Chan Kui-Yao, was appointed secretary-general of ASEAN. In June Prince Norodom Sihanouk, former head of state of Kampuchea, visited the republic after signing an agreement to form a coalition government of Kampuchean anti-Vietnamese resistance leaders. Singapore's support for that coalition prompted a cool reception for Vietnam's foreign minister, Nguyen Co Thach, when he visited in July.

(MICHAEL LEIFER)

Social Security and Welfare Services

During 1982 rising unemployment continued to cast a dark shadow over social security programs in many countries, not only because increasing numbers of workers were receiving unemployment benefits but also because large amounts of social security contributions and tax revenue were being lost as a result of the recession. The problems were compounded by the fact that many governments were becoming more and more reluctant to subsidize social security schemes or to impose higher contributions on employers. As a result, there was pressure to cut expenditure on benefits and to raise more money from the insured persons, both workers and benefit recipients. Nevertheless, several countries instituted improvements in social security coverage, affecting mainly rural workers and the self-employed; in the scope of protection (for example, regarding unemployment and disability); and, to a small extent, in the level of benefits.

International Developments in Social Security. France was virtually the only major industrialized country in 1982 to make large-scale improvements in its social security provisions. These measures were seen as a way of relating the economy and stemming the rise in unemployment. In particular, the electoral commitment to reduce the standard pension age to 60 was duly honoured, although not without considerable debate on certain points. During the year, however, unemployment continued to rise and the franc came under increasing pressure, leading to a tightening of economic policy.

Following the June replacement of the minister responsible for social affairs, two sets of austerity measures were announced, the first in July, the second in September. Planned increases in benefits were postponed or reduced, and pensions were to be adjusted in 1983 in line with prices rather than earnings. Workers who retired early on a "prepension" were to pay much higher social insurance contributions. Farmers' social insurance contributions were increased by 16% and those of other self-employed persons by about 17%. Special taxes were to be levied on alcohol, tobacco, and drug advertising, and hospital patients would be charged Fr 20 a day. Finally, there was to be a major reform of hospital financing so that, starting in 1984, hospitals would have a fixed annual budget rather than being paid a daily rate for each patient.

Financing health care for the elderly was an issue in Japan. Under an act passed in August, a new system was introduced, designed to share the cost more equally among the various sickness insurance plans. Some plans covered far more old people than others, and the National Health Insurance Plan, which covered the vast majority of the elderly, had to be very heavily subsidized by the government. The new arrangement would shift a large part of the burden from public funds to employee health insurance programs. The act also imposed charges on elderly patients for visits to the doctor and for hospitalization. However, free preventive health services financed out of public funds were to be introduced for all persons over the age of 40.

In West Germany financial problems underlay a series of changes in unemployment insurance introduced at the beginning of the year. Unemployment insurance contributions were increased; the minimum period of employment required to establish eligibility was raised from 6 to 12 months; overtime and special holiday pay were excluded from the earnings figure used in the calculation of benefits; and all forms of unemployment benefit were made taxable. Belgium was to change its early retirement arrangements at the end of 1982; 60 would be the earliest age at which benefit would be payable (previously women were eligible from age 55), and the benefit would be markedly less than before. In The Netherlands the employee contribution for unemployment insurance was raised in July from 2.55 to 3.55%, while the employer contribution remained at 1.85%. In 1982 Sweden started to adjust benefits only once a year, whereas previously they rose whenever the price index increased by 3%. From the beginning of 1982 the social insurance contributions payable by enterprises in the U.S.S.R. were raised on average by around 2.5 percentage points.

In the U.K. earnings-related unemployment benefit was abolished in January, and the flat-rate benefits paid to the unemployed became taxable in July. From October unemployed persons no longer had to register for work in order to receive benefits. In September, before registration became voluntary, registered unemployment stood at a record 3,343,075, or 14% of the working population. Legislation was passed in June transferring responsibility for sick pay during the first eight weeks of sickness from social security to employers. This was a low, flat-rate payment that, unlike the social insurance sickness benefit it replaced, was taxable and had no supplements for dependents. The new scheme would take effect in April 1983, at which time industrial injury benefit (paid

Skating:
see Ice Hockey; Winter Sports

Skeet Shooting:
see Target Sports

Skiing:
see Water Sports; Winter Sports

Soccer:
see Football

at a higher rate than standard sickness benefit) would be abolished. Overseas visitors not covered by European Community or other reciprocal agreements now had to pay the full costs of any hospital treatment they received.

On the brighter side, rural workers stood to benefit from changes in Ecuador, Finland, and Nicaragua. In Ecuador the Rural Social Insurance Scheme was to be extended gradually to cover all members of families belonging to communes, cooperatives, or other rural organizations, as well as other families who wished to join. Heads of families contributed 1% of the minimum wage, and the remainder of the funding consisted of 1% of the revenue of the social insurance scheme for employees. In Finland accident insurance was introduced in July for farmers, fishers, and reindeer farmers. Regulations governing the award and amount of benefits were the same as those applying to employees. A major social security reform was enacted in Nicaragua in March. It greatly extended compulsory social security coverage, particularly as regards the rural population, and improved benefits, especially for the lower paid.

New programs or benefits were introduced in Barbados, Czechoslovakia, and Switzerland. Unemployment benefits were introduced in Barbados in July, payable at the rate of 40% of earnings for up to 13 weeks in any one year. Czechoslovakia introduced pensions for young disabled persons aged 18 and over. Switzerland finally passed legislation making occupational pensions mandatory, almost ten years after the principle had been inscribed in the Swiss constitution. The legislation, to take effect in 1984, did little to help the present generation of workers, but special minimum benefits, yet to be defined, would be payable during a nine-year transitional period.

A number of major improvements were introduced in Greece. Complementary schemes that previously covered about 40% of employees were extended to cover almost 100%; the minimum pension was raised in two stages from 8,000 to 18,000 drachmas; and pension rights of farmers' wives doubled with the introduction of equal treatment for men and women.

(ROGER A. BEATTIE)

U.S. Developments. The revolution in social welfare policy, promised and begun by Ronald Reagan in the first year of his presidency, expanded in the U.S. in 1982. Programs to assist the poor were reduced even as the ranks of the poor increased. The number of persons receiving welfare and food stamps stopped growing, and spending was cut for subsidized housing, public services, employment and job training, and other programs for the needy. One notable exception to this trend was Social Security, the largest social program of all. It continued to grow, as did concerns about its future, but no action was taken on this politically explosive issue.

The new direction for social welfare programs had been set by the budget passed in 1981, which cut family support spending by $25 billion. However, the effect was not fully felt until the cuts took effect in the fiscal year running from Oct. 1, 1981, to Sept. 30, 1982. Another $8.5 billion was trimmed from these programs in the fiscal 1983 budget, bringing the human resources share of the federal budget to about 50.8%, compared with 53.8% in the peak year of 1976.

The number of people receiving Aid to Families with Dependent Children (AFDC) fell from 11.1 million in 1981 to 10.4 million in 1982, and the federal outlay dropped from $7.9 billion to $7.6 billion. The estimated AFDC expenditure for 1983 was $6.8 billion. A major change in the structure of the AFDC program took effect in 1982, as benefits to the working poor were eliminated or cut back sharply. In addition, inflation continued to take its toll. The Department of Health and Human Services reported that welfare benefits had fallen by an average of 29% in real terms over the past decade.

Although food costs rose, the federal outlay for food stamps declined from $11.4 billion in 1981 to

STEVE STACK/THE MINNEAPOLIS TRIBUNE

$11.3 billion in 1982, and the number of recipients dropped from 22.4 million to 22.2 million. That figure was slated to fall to 20.1 million in 1983. Food stamp recipients received their first cost-of-living increase in almost two years on Oct. 1, 1982—an 8% boost that raised the maximum allotment for a family of four from $233 a month to $253. The number of children participating in the school lunch program fell from 26.8 million in the 1980–81 school year to 23.6 million in 1981–82, and more than 2,700 schools dropped out of the program. The reductions occurred after Congress lowered federal subsidies for school meals in 1981, leading to increased prices at schools.

State Medicaid officials used new authority to restrict eligibility and reduce benefits. Medicaid provided $32.4 billion in 1982 to help pay the medical bills for 22.9 million poor Americans, about one in every ten. The Comprehensive Employment and Training Act (CETA) expired on Sept. 30, 1982, but Congress approved new legislation that could provide job training for as many as one million disadvantaged workers and youths. Unlike CETA, it would not subsidize public service jobs but would concentrate on skills instruction and other employment-related assistance for low-income workers with severe problems in the job market.

In his state of the union address in January, President Reagan suggested another basic change in social policy. As part of his "new federalism," he proposed to transfer at least 30 federal programs to state and local control, including AFDC, energy assistance, legal services for the poor, and child nutrition. In return, the federal government would assume full responsibility for Medicaid. No action was taken on this plan during the year. Meanwhile, the states continued their efforts to cope with the change in federal funding of many social programs from categorical grants (i.e., for specific, narrowly defined programs) to block grants covering large program areas.

The Urban Institute, a nonprofit, nonpartisan research organization, reported that President Reagan's domestic policies had brought about the most dramatic shift in economic and social policy since Franklin D. Roosevelt's New Deal. It noted that cuts in benefit payments and other programs hit the poor and jobless hardest. The report said the full impact of the Reagan "revolution" was yet to come and would continue long after Reagan left office. The cutbacks came as the Census Bureau reported that 2.2 million additional Americans had joined the ranks of the poor in 1981, for a total of 31.8 million or 14% of the population. The poverty line was defined as $9,287 for a family of four in 1981.

With unemployment at its highest level since the depression of the 1930s, unemployment insurance became one of the most important benefit programs. The Reagan administration estimated that 10.9 million people received a total of $21.1 billion in unemployment benefits during the year. The average payment was $115 a week (in July). Even so, a study by the Center on Budget and Policy Priorities found that 59%, or 6.2 million, of those out of work in September received no unemployment benefits. One reason was that the "ex-

JOHN SOTOMAYOR/THE NEW YORK TIMES

tended" benefits program, which had increased the basic 26 weeks of insurance to 39 weeks in hard-hit states, had been cut back by a 1981 law. Another factor was the length of the recession, which resulted in workers using up their benefits before they could find new jobs. Congress passed a temporary $2.1 billion supplemental benefits program in 1982, providing six to ten additional weeks of coverage.

Meanwhile, there was only debate over Social Security, which paid about $156 billion to 36.2 million persons in 1982. After decades of unchecked expansion, Social Security was running out of cash. The largest of the system's three trust funds, Old-Age and Survivors Insurance, was borrowing from the others (Medicare and disability payments), but these, too, would be without money in 1984. In the long term, the system faced a major crisis when the huge baby-boom generation reached retirement age in about 30 years. A 15-member National Commission on Social Security Reform, appointed by President Reagan and headed by economist Alan Greenspan, was to have reported at the end of the year, but the members failed to agree and it was given an extension. Some of the possibilities included increased payroll taxes; expansion of coverage to government employees; a delay or reduction in cost-of-living increases; taxes on all or part of retirement benefits; and borrowing money from general revenues.

(DAVID M. MAZIE)

See also Education; Health and Disease; Industrial Review: Insurance.
[522.D; 535.B.3.e; 552.D.1]

With cuts being made in various U.S. social welfare programs, needy families were forced to rely more and more on voluntary agencies. Above, a Roman Catholic nun distributes food to a family in the East Harlem section of New York City.

Solomon Islands

Solomon Islands

The Solomon Islands is an independent parliamentary state and member of the Commonwealth. The nation comprises a 1,450-km (900-mi) chain of islands and atolls in the western Pacific Ocean. Area: 27,556 sq km (10,640 sq mi). Pop. (1981 est.): 235,400 (Melanesian 93.3%; Polynesian 4%; Micronesian 1.4%; others 1.3%). Cap. and largest city: Honiara (pop., 1981 prelim., 21,300). Language: English (official), Pidgin (lingua franca), and some 90 local languages and dialects. Religion (1980): Anglican 33.6%; Roman Catholic 19.1%; South Sea Evangelical 24.6%; other Protestant 15.2%; traditional 7.3%. Queen, Elizabeth II; governor-general in 1982, Baddeley Devesi; prime minister, Solomon Mamaloni.

SOLOMON ISLANDS

Education. (1980–81) Primary, pupils 28,870, teachers 1,148; secondary, pupils 3,547, teachers 196; vocational, pupils 367, teachers 37; teacher training, students 116, teachers 24.

Finance and Trade. Monetary unit: Solomon Islands dollar, with (Sept. 20, 1982) a free value of SI$1.05 to U.S. $1 (SI$1.81 = £1 sterling). Budget (total; 1981 est.): revenue SI$34.8 million (excluding SI$23.5 million U.K. aid); expenditure SI$61.3 million. Foreign trade (1980): imports (f.o.b.) SI$61.5 million; exports SI$60.8 million. Import sources: Australia 31%; Japan 20%; Singapore 15%; U.K. 9%; New Zealand 7%; Papua New Guinea 5%. Export destinations: Japan 26%; U.S. 20%; The Netherlands 14%; U.K. 11%; Mexico 6%; American Samoa 6%. Main exports: fish 38%; timber 26%; copra 17%; palm oil 11%.

During 1982 the Solomon Islands continued to weather the economic recession better than most of its neighbours, but a sharp decline in export prices left a significant trading deficit for the first time since independence. Aid continued from the U.K. and other traditional sources, while assistance from the Asian Development Bank and Japan increased. Speaking at the conclusion of the parliamentary session in February, Prime Minister Solomon Mamaloni criticized foreign governments that sought to interfere in the Solomons' affairs.

Mamaloni reaffirmed his government's support for the Kanak independence movement in New Caledonia and again suggested the formation of a "Melanesian Alliance" to include Papua New Guinea, the Solomon Islands, Vanuatu, and New Caledonia. He called for a democratically elected South Pacific regional parliament to supersede a number of regional organizations, including the South Pacific Forum. At a meeting of the latter, in New Zealand in August, he joined other leaders in calling for a clarification of French policy in New Caledonia.

On October 18 Queen Elizabeth II visited the islands. (BARRIE MACDONALD)

Somalia

A republic of northeast Africa, the Somali Democratic Republic, or Somalia, is bounded by the Gulf of Aden, the Indian Ocean, Kenya, Ethiopia, and Djibouti. Area: 638,000 sq km (246,300 sq mi). Pop. (1982 est.): 3,863,000, mainly Hamitic, with Arabic and other admixtures. Cap. and largest city: Mogadishu (pop., 1981 est., 400,000). Language: Somali spoken by a great majority (Arabic also official). Religion: predominantly Muslim. President in 1982, Maj. Gen. Muhammad Siyad Barrah.

In 1982 Pres. Muhammad Siyad Barrah of Somalia continued to demonstrate his staying power in spite of considerable pressures. In February and again in April disturbances in the northern city of Hargeisa resulted in several deaths. This apparently reflected feelings among the population of the north of the country that they were being neglected by the Mogadishu government, which drew most of its strength from the south.

Despite the troubles in Hargeisa, President Barrah felt sufficiently secure in March to end the national state of emergency that he had declared more than 16 months earlier. He disbanded the Supreme Revolutionary Council, through which he had ruled during this period, and reinstated the People's National Assembly and also the state party, the Somali Revolutionary Socialist Party (SRSP). He went on to make a tour of Western countries, including the U.S., which had become Somalia's principal ally since its break with the U.S.S.R. after the latter supported Ethiopia in the 1978 Ogaden war.

Further indications of divisions within the country were seen in June, when seven high-ranking politicians were arrested for treason. They included the third vice-president of the SRSP, Brig. Gen. Ismail Ali Abokor, who was one of the few men of northern origin in the government.

In July fighting began near the Ethiopian border, where Somali Army units were attacked. Responsibility was claimed by the Somali Democratic

---

SOMALIA

Education. (1981–82) Primary, pupils 418,935, teachers 12,007; secondary (1979–80), pupils 17,020, teachers 925; vocational, pupils 23,810, teachers 2,380; teacher training (1979–80), students 2,156, teachers 540; higher (1977–78), students 2,801, teaching staff (1975–76) 324.

Finance. Monetary unit: Somali shilling, with (Sept. 20, 1982) a free rate for essential imports of 6.35 Somali shillings to U.S. $1 (10.88 Somali shillings = £1 sterling), and a free rate for other transactions of 12.46 Somali shillings to U.S. $1 (21.36 Somali shillings = £1 sterling). Gold and other reserves (June 1982) U.S. $5 million. Budget (1981 est.): revenue 2,520,000,000 Somali shillings; expenditure 2,750,000,000 Somali shillings. Cost of living (Mogadishu; 1975 = 100; Feb. 1982) 455.6.

Foreign Trade. (1981) Imports 1,253,100,000 Somali shillings; exports 1,257,800,000 Somali shillings. Import sources (1978): Italy 30%; West Germany 11%; U.K 10%; The Netherlands 5%; Iraq 5%; Kenya 5%. Export destinations (1978): Saudi Arabia 86%; Italy 8%. Main export: livestock 91%.

Transport and Communications. Roads (1979) 19,780 km. Motor vehicles in use (1979): passenger 4,291; commercial (including buses) 5,665. There are no railways. Air traffic (1980): c. 140 million passenger-km; freight c. 500,000 net ton-km. Shipping (1981): merchant vessels 100 gross tons and over 21; gross tonnage 35,095. Telephones (Dec. 1979) c. 7,000. Radio receivers (Dec. 1979) 80,000.

Agriculture. Production (in 000; metric tons; 1981): sorghum c. 150; corn c. 120; cassava c. 33; sesame seed c. 11; sugar, raw value 38; bananas c. 65; goat's milk c. 286. Livestock (in 000; 1981): cattle c. 3,950; sheep c. 10,200; goats c. 16,500; camels c. 5,550.

Somalia

Salvation Front (SDSF), a Somali group opposed to Barrah's regime. However, there were also reports, strongly denied by the Ethiopian government, that most of the invaders were Soviet-armed Ethiopian troops backing an SDSF initiative. In response to this allegation the U.S. finally delivered the $40 million package of defensive armaments that had been promised to Somalia since 1980 in exchange for the use of the port of Berbera as a naval and air base; an additional $40 million worth was promised by the U.S. for future delivery.

After August, however, the fighting appeared to die down. The antigovernment forces held territory about 32 km (20 mi) inside Somalia. In October the SDSF announced that it had formed a joint military committee with the northern-based Somali National Movement, another major opposition group.

The situation of the refugees who had fled from the war in the Ethiopian-ruled province of Ogaden had apparently become stabilized, in that the people still living in camps—who according to the official estimate of the UN High Commissioner for Refugees numbered 700,000—were said to be receiving adequate food and health care. There remained the problem of what was to become of them and also of the unknown but perhaps equally large number scattered among the general population of Somalia.

In the middle of the year the government ordered several measures aimed at financial stabilization, including devaluation of the Somali shilling, easing of import restrictions, and firmer control of government expenditure. This was the second phase of a program begun in 1981 and backed by the International Monetary Fund.

(VIRGINIA R. LULING)

South Africa

The Republic. Occupying the southern tip of Africa, South Africa is bounded by South West Africa/ Namibia, Botswana, Zimbabwe, Mozambique, and Swaziland and by the Atlantic and Indian oceans on the west and east. South Africa entirely surrounds Lesotho and partially surrounds the four former Bantu homelands of Transkei (independent Oct. 26, 1976), Bophuthatswana (independent Dec. 6, 1977), Venda (independent Sept. 13, 1979), and Ciskei (independent Dec. 4, 1981), although the independence of the latter four is not recognized by the international community. Walvis Bay, part of Cape Province since 1910 but administered as part of South West Africa since 1922, was returned to the direct control of Cape Province on Sept. 1, 1977. Area (including Walvis Bay but excluding the four former homelands): 1,125,459 sq km (435,868 sq mi). Pop. (1982 est.): 25,687,000 (excluding the four homelands), including black (Bantu) 67%, white 19%, Coloured 11%, Asian 3%. Executive cap.: Pretoria (pop., 1980, 528,400); judicial cap.: Bloemfontein (pop, 1980, 230,700); legislative cap.: Cape Town (pop., 1980, 1.5 million). Largest city: Johannesburg (pop., 1980, 1,536,400). Language: Afrikaans and English (official); Bantu languages predominate. Religion:

mainly Christian. State president in 1982, Marais Viljoen; prime minister, P. W. Botha.

DOMESTIC AFFAIRS. The year 1982 was marked by significant political developments. An open split in the ruling National Party (NP) was the culmination of a period of internal strife that was primarily focused on the issue of nonwhite participation in government. The central figure in the rift was Andries Treurnicht, minister of state administration and of statistics and Transvaal leader of the NP. He and his supporters, including Minister of (Black) Education and Training Ferdinand Hartzenberg, accused Prime Minister P. W. Botha of seeking to deviate from the traditional race and colour policies of the NP by proposing to extend political rights to the Coloured and Asian populations.

In March Treurnicht and Hartzenberg, with a group of some 20 members of Parliament and provincial councillors, chiefly in Transvaal, seceded from the NP. They formed the Conservative Party of South Africa (CP), with a parliamentary representation of 18, and were joined by other dissidents outside Parliament. While opposing any form of political sharing in decision making in South Africa, they were prepared to concede limited rights of self-determination and some participation, with advisory powers, to Coloureds and Asians in their own areas. But they were not willing to extend these rights to urban blacks who, they contended, could exercise political rights in their respective homelands.

The right-wing opposition Herstigte Nasionale Party (HNP) under Jaap Marais turned down Treurnicht's offer of an alliance but later agreed to a future election pact. In the first test of strength for the new arrangement, a provincial by-election in the Germiston district, the two groups fought the NP separately. The NP retained the seat with a slender majority over the CP and a substantial minority against the combined opposition. In a later series of by-elections in the Cape and the Orange Free State, the NP retained all its seats, in the latter province against a considerable vote for the combined right-wing opposition. The new Transvaal NP leader, F. W. de Klerk (see BIOGRAPHIES), did much to rally support for the government.

In May the President's Council submitted a draft constitution designed, it was declared, to break with the "Westminster" system of parliamentary democracy. The draft embodied a far-reaching range of proposals. Among them were the appointment by an electoral college, for a seven-year term, of an executive president who would have a white, Coloured (mixed black and white), and Asian Cabinet not chosen on party lines and with authority to choose a prime minister; the setting up of separate parliaments for each group; representation for blacks not at the government level but in their own local authorities; multiracial representation on metropolitan councils and on Group Areas Act committees; replacement of provincial councils by eight regional councils with white, Coloured, and Asian representation; and residential separation on ethnic lines but with no enforced segregation or integration. The principle of "one man: one vote" was ruled out. The Council later

South Africa

Soil Conservation:
see Environment

JORDAN—GAMMA/LIAISON

South African tanks return to their bases after a raid against SWAPO guerrillas in southern Angola. South Africa feared that the continued presence of Cuban troops in Angola could lead to a Communist takeover of Namibia.

supplemented and to some extent modified the proposals in a second report.

The government, on the whole, accepted the Council's original draft. The main alteration it proposed was to replace the suggested three parliaments by three chambers in one parliament, each to manage its own affairs but with an elaborate system of consultation and consensus subject to a final decision by the President's Council. There would also be an overall Cabinet to deal with matters of common interest. The general effect was to give the executive president and the President's Council, with its white majority, the dominant voice.

The draft had a mixed reception, largely critical, from other quarters. The official opposition, the Progressive Federal Party, while prepared to discuss the plan, objected to the omission of blacks from virtually all participation and argued that in fact it entrenched apartheid (racial separation) and white supremacy. Coloured and Asian opinion was strongly critical of the exclusion of blacks. Black leaders, with KwaZulu's Chief Gatsha Buthelezi in the forefront, rejected proposals that left their people in the cold. Right-wing Nationalists were firmly opposed.

In the short term the general trend of government race relations policy was to endeavour to improve the quality of life for urban blacks in particular. But words were not always matched with deeds, and such problems as the squatters' camps, a by-product of unemployment in the black homelands, remained unsolved. Industrial unrest among black workers reflected not only more intensive trade union activity and the pressures of inflation and recession but also a spirit of rising economic and political expectations. One result was an increase in police security action, to the accompaniment of detentions without trial. By midyear some 200 persons were reported to be in detention, many of whom had been active in the trade union movement. A case that attracted widespread attention was that of Neil Aggett (*see* OBITUARIES), who was found hanging in his cell in February.

Security legislation as a whole had come under review by a judicial commission. Its recommendations, broadly accepted by the government, included provisions for tighter safeguards against terrorism and subversion, the protection of secret information, and the power to intercept mail and telephone calls. It endorsed the principle of detention without trial but proposed some changes in prison procedure affecting detainees and special ministerial approval for detentions exceeding 30 days. An official code on the treatment of detainees, though welcomed, was regarded as not going far enough.

FOREIGN RELATIONS. The search for a peaceful independence settlement in South West Africa/Namibia remained a central factor in South Africa's foreign relations. Headed by the U.S. representatives on the five-nation Western contact group (the U.S., the U.K., France, West Germany, and Canada) that was acting on behalf of the UN, discussions with the southern African frontline states, South Africa, and the South West Africa People's Organization (SWAPO) produced a broad agreement in principle on a cease-fire and the holding of a free and fair UN-supervised election as required by UN Resolution 435.

However, fresh issues were raised even before the first phase of actual implementation was reached. Above all, the problem of the presence of Cuban forces in Angola emerged as the most formidable stumbling block. South Africa called for the withdrawal of the Cubans as a precondition to Namibian independence. The argument was that, in the event that SWAPO achieved victory in the envisioned election, it would have Cuban backing for the establishment of a pro-Communist regime that might become a threat to South Africa itself. The U.S., for other reasons, also pressed for a Cuban withdrawal, while the Angolan government maintained that the presence of the Cubans was its own affair and had nothing to do with Namibia.

In the meantime, sporadic military activity continued on the Namibian border. South Africa launched periodic raids into Angola with the declared object of preempting a buildup of SWAPO forces or countering the less and less frequent SWAPO incursions into Namibia. A ministerial-level meeting between Angola and South Africa in early December discussed terms for a cease-fire.

South Africa's relations with Zimbabwe were eased by an extension of South Africa's preferential trade agreement before it was due to expire at the end of March. A meeting between Botha and Pres. Kenneth Kaunda of Zambia was aimed at improving occasionally strained relations and exchanging views on the problems of southern Africa. Proposals to cede to Swaziland the homeland territory of KaNgwane and the Ingwavuma region on Kwa-Zulu's border with Swaziland met with determined resistance from the inhabitants of those areas, many of them Swazi-speaking, and resulted in legal battles in which South Africa's competence to transfer the land was challenged. In December the Appeal Court ruled that a proclamation providing for the transfer of Ingwavuma was invalid. Also in December South African troops carried out a raid on African National Congress (ANC) bases in Maseru, Lesotho; 42 people were reported to have been killed. The ANC claimed responsibility for the bombing of the Koeberg nuclear power plant, still under construction, on the day some of the dead were being buried.

Efforts at the UN to secure international approval for mandatory economic and general sanctions against South Africa failed in the face of U.S. and other mainly Western opposition. UN investigators found no conclusive evidence of alleged official South African complicity in an unsuccessful bid by a group of mercenaries to overthrow the Seychelles government in November 1981. The allegations were denied by South Africa. After the abortive coup most of the men returned to Durban in a plane that they had seized. Following a trial in a South African court on a hijacking charge, they were sentenced to terms in prison. Testimony given at the trial claimed that some had past links with the South African security services.

The murder, by a letter bomb, in Maputo, Mozambique, in August of South African antiapartheid activist Ruth First (see OBITUARIES) was attributed by the Mozambique government to South Africa's security services, a charge denied by South Africa.

THE ECONOMY. Introducing his budget in March, Minister of Finance Owen Horwood stressed that it was being presented against a background of serious and long-term world recession. He pointed out that while South Africa had in real economic terms outperformed most other countries up to then, it had become more and more evident that the decline in the gold price and the worldwide recessionary situation were adversely affecting the balance of payments in particular.

The economy appeared to have entered a gradual downward trend, with the rate of real economic growth almost certain to be lower and with no immediate prospect of reflation or stimulation.

As the year proceeded, a series of measures to that end were taken in conjunction with the Reserve Bank. They took the form of fluctuating interest rates and bank credit adjustments. An imports surcharge and a de facto depreciation of the rand in dollar terms cut down a balance of payments shortfall of approximately R 3 billion. Further relief for the balance of payments situation came in the form of a loan of R 1,240,000,000 granted by the International Monetary Fund against strong UN and third world opposition. State expenditure, allowing for inflation, showed little increase in real terms over the previous year. The biggest single item, in a budget of R 18.2 billion, was defense expenditure amounting to R 2,696,000,000, an increase of R 203 million.

Amid growing concern, shared by the government and the general public, over the continued depopulation and underdevelopment of rural areas and small towns, first steps were taken to implement a policy of economic decentralization. The scheme was a comprehensive attempt to arrest the drift of both black and white people to a few highly developed metropolitan areas by creating favourable conditions for the development of the economically backward regions. The country was divided into eight regions, each with a central growth point and each incorporating one or more of the existing and former homelands. Industrialization was to be the main target of the plan, but the development of mineral, agricultural, and commercial potentials was also an essential part of the program. As part of the decentralization scheme the leaders of South Africa, Bophuthatswana, Transkei, Ciskei, and Venda met in November and announced the setting up in 1983 of the Southern African Development Bank.

Bophuthatswana. The republic of Bophuthatswana consists of six discontinuous, landlocked geographic units, one of which borders Botswana on the northwest; it is otherwise entirely surrounded by South Africa. Area: 40,430 sq km (15,610 sq mi). Pop. (1982 est.): 1,347,000, including 99.6% Bantu, of whom Tswana 69.8%, Northern

BOPHUTHATSWANA

Education. (1979–80) Primary, pupils 343,482, teachers 6,015; secondary, pupils 91,372, teachers 2,501; vocational, students 1,557, teachers 71; teacher training, students 3,298, teachers 151; higher, students 114, teachers 36.

Finance and Trade. Monetary unit: South African rand. Budget (1981–82) balanced at R 421 million. Foreign trade included in South Africa.

CISKEI

Education. (1981) Primary, pupils 180,214, teachers 4,058; secondary, pupils 45,661; vocational, pupils 304; teacher training, students 1,252; secondary, vocational, and teacher training, teachers 1,495.

Finance and Trade. Monetary unit: South African rand. Budget (1975–76) balanced at R 64.2 million. Most trade is with South Africa.

TRANSKEI

Education. (1978) Primary, pupils 647,985, teachers 12,627; secondary, pupils 33,636, teachers 1,179; vocational, pupils 908, teachers 59; teacher training, students 3,034; higher, students 503, teaching staff 96.

Finance and Trade. Monetary unit: South African rand. Budget (total; 1981–82 est.) balanced at R 374.6 million. Most trade is with South Africa.

VENDA

Education. (1981) Primary, pupils 121,601, teachers 2,630; secondary, pupils 30,094, teachers 870; vocational, pupils c. 300; teacher training, students 826.

Finance and Trade. Monetary unit: South African rand. Budget (1981–82) balanced at R106.5 million. Most trade is with South Africa.

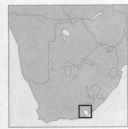

Bophuthatswana

Ciskei

Transkei

Venda

Sotho 7.5%. Cap.: Mmabatho. Largest city: Ga-Rankuwa (pop., 1980 prelim., 48,300). Language (official): Central Tswana, English, Afrikaans. Religion: predominantly Christian (Methodist, Lutheran, Anglican, and Bantu Christian churches). President in 1982, Lucas Mangope.

In the first elections for the National Assembly since the area was declared independent in 1977, the ruling Bophuthatswana Democratic Party of Pres. Lucas Mangope made a clean sweep of all contested seats; voter turnout was light. On the eve of the poll President Mangope announced that he would abolish the 24 seats reserved for nominated chiefs in the 102-member assembly and would replace them by elected members. This meant that it would become an almost wholly elected chamber, with only six nominated members.

Economic development was encouraged by a relatively modest tax policy. There was a steady increase in the number of factories built or planned. The Bophuthatswana Development Corporation received many inquiries from industrialists in South Africa, Israel, and Western Europe. The question of the final consolidation of the fragmented territory remained an outstanding issue in relations with South Africa.

Ciskei. Bordering the Indian Ocean in the south and surrounded on land by South Africa, Ciskei is separated by a narrow corridor of land from Transkei to the east. Area: 8,300 sq km (3,200 sq mi). Pop. (1981 est.): 645,000, including Bantu 99.4%, of whom 97% are Xhosa. Cap.: Bisho (pop., 1970 est., 4,800). Largest city: Mdantsane (pop., 1980, 150,000). Language: Xhosa (official); English may be used for official purposes. Religion: predominantly Christian (Methodist, Lutheran, Anglican, and Bantu Christian churches). President in 1982, Lennox Sebe.

In its regional decentralization program the South African government rated Ciskei as one of the areas most in need of special economic aid. During the first year of independence the Ciskei government showed that it was fully aware of the problems it faced. Pres. Lennox Sebe went abroad in an effort to interest foreign investors in his country; he claimed to have received high-level encouragement despite the fact that Ciskei was not internationally recognized as independent.

The Ciskei Development Corporation reported that since independence the number of new investments was double that of the past five years. Loans were made to Ciskeians for the opening of small business firms. Though some 3,100 new jobs were created, an acute unemployment problem remained, and Ciskei experienced a good deal of labour unrest.

Transkei. Bordering the Indian Ocean and surrounded on land by South Africa, Transkei comprises three discontinuous geographic units, two of which are landlocked. Area: 41,002 sq km (15,831 sq mi). Pop. (1982 est.): 2.4 million, including (1970) Bantu 99%, of whom 95% were Xhosa. Cap. and largest city: Umtata (pop., 1978 est., 30,000). Language: Xhosa (official); English and Sesotho may be used for official purposes. Religion: Christian 65.8%, of which Methodist 25.2%; non-Christian 13.8%; 20.4% unspecified. President in 1982, Kaiser Daliwonga Matanzima; prime minister, George Matanzima.

Pres. Kaiser Matanzima, reacting to the exclusion of blacks from South Africa's constitutional plans, reiterated his previously expressed objections to the concept of a constellation of southern African states, as envisioned by Prime Minister Botha. Instead, he supported a proposal for a federation of all independent black nations in the subcontinent. He urged Cedric Phatudi, chief minister of the Lebowa homeland, who had suggested the idea, to convene a conference of leaders to frame a draft constitution along those lines.

Transkei, like Ciskei, was considered by South Africa to be one of the areas most in need of economic aid under the projected decentralization plan. The Transkei Development Corporation offered entrepreneurs the right to own land in the Transkei on a freehold basis in contrast with the South African policy of granting ownership on leasehold only in black areas under its control. An area of land in the Queenstown district of the eastern Cape was ceded to Transkei.

Venda. The independent republic of Venda comprises two geographic units in extreme northeastern South Africa separated by a narrow corridor belonging to its eastern neighbour, the Gazankulu homeland. Area: 7,184 sq km (2,448 sq mi). Pop. (1982 est.): 374,000, including (1970) 90% Venda, 6% Shangaan, and 3% Northern Sotho. Cap.: Thohoyandou. Largest town: Makearela (pop., 1976 est., 1,972). Language (official): Venda, English, and Afrikaans. Religion: traditional religions predominate; Christian minority. President in 1982, Patrick Mphephu.

In a second report by the commission appointed in 1981 to investigate the question of land ownership, earlier recommendations were elaborated for the protection of the traditional rights of chiefs, headmen, and Venda citizens generally to tribal lands while also providing for private property rights. Sales of land, the commission recommended, should take place only with the permission of the tribal authorities. In the event of a resale of such land the government would have the first option. The principle remained that Venda citizens alone would be entitled to own land; companies registered in Venda would be regarded as citizens and thus eligible for the acquisition of land. Under an agreement with South Africa, Venda was to lose an area of land on the border with Zimbabwe and was to receive in exchange some land on the northwestern border with Transvaal.

Following the attack in October 1981 on a police station at Sibasa in which two Venda policemen were killed, a number of persons were held in detention without trial. Among them were several Lutheran ministers, one of whom allegedly died in detention. The ANC claimed responsibility for the attack.   (LOUIS HOTZ)

See also Dependent States.

Southeast Asian Affairs

In 1982, for the fourth consecutive year, Kampuchea (Cambodia) was the issue upon which the political and strategic interests of both Southeast Asian countries and global powers converged. Though the divergences of those interests continued to produce much tension, the Kampuchean imbroglio seemed to be edging more distinctly toward a resolution than at any time since Vietnamese troops toppled the Khmer Rouge regime of Pol Pot in 1979 and replaced it with one headed by their ally, Heng Samrin. At the same time, the five members (Indonesia, Singapore, Malaysia, Thailand, the Philippines) of the Association of Southeast Asian Nations (ASEAN) felt sufficient pressure from big-power rivalry in the region to address again the controversial subject of closer military cooperation.

Kampuchea was undoubtedly the question that consumed the most energy among diplomats of both ASEAN and the Communist Indochinese nations in the opposite camp. Through patient, deft, behind-the-scenes maneuvering, ASEAN was able to pull off a major political coup by persuading the leaders of the three principal anti-Vietnamese Khmer groups to form a coalition to combat Hanoi's occupation of their troubled homeland. (*See* KAMPUCHEA.) Reconstituted with former head of state Prince Norodom Sihanouk as president, former Cambodian premier Son Sann as prime minister, and Khieu Samphan of the Khmer Rouge as vice-president, the tripartite alliance of Democratic Kampuchea and its backers, ASEAN and China, scored a major diplomatic victory against the Phnom Penh regime and its Vietnamese and Soviet supporters when the UN General Assembly voted in October 90–29 to recognize the alliance as the sole legitimate government of Kampuchea.

The ASEAN countries played a pivotal role in holding together the tenuous coalition. Shortly after they agreed in principle in September 1981 to form an alliance, the neutralist Sihanouk, anti-Communist Son Sann, and Khmer Rouge leaders began to argue bitterly, seriously jeopardizing the chances of forming a coalition. China, eager to see the Khmer Rouge retain a dominant role, also took an inflexible line. It was only when ASEAN discreetly threatened to drop support for Democratic Kampuchea at the UN and consider accommodating Heng Samrin that all parties concerned agreed to compromise and to form the coalition.

Vietnam spared little effort trying to prevent formation of the alliance and to weaken the unity and resolve of the ASEAN members. In chorus with its clients in Phnom Penh, Hanoi continued to remind the world of the atrocities that took place under Khmer Rouge rule and to paint a picture of a Kampuchea gradually returning to normal under Heng Samrin's administration. In July, shortly after the tripartite coalition was born, Vietnam offered ASEAN an ostensible olive branch by withdrawing some 8,000 of its 180,000 troops from Kampuchea. ASEAN, however, spurned the overture, judging it a mere rotation of soldiers. The association made it plain to visiting Vietnamese Foreign Minister Nguyen Co Thach that it would not be satisfied with anything less than full compliance with a UN resolution calling for a complete withdrawal of foreign forces from Kampuchea, followed by free elections. After a stiff confrontation in Singapore, Thach dropped hints that if ASEAN continued to maintain its tough stance, Vietnam might consider supporting long-festering Communist insurgencies within the association's member countries and also might grant the Soviet Union freer access to military facilities in Vietnam.

Yet toward the year's end it seemed that developments were becoming increasingly unfavourable to continued Vietnamese occupation of Kampuchea. With an accelerating thaw in Sino-Soviet relations, many analysts thought it increasingly likely that the Soviets might, in great-power terms, concede that Kampuchea was within the Chinese "sphere of influence" in return for improved ties with China. In such circumstances Moscow would scale down its support for Vietnam, China's archenemy. Indeed, Vietnam since mid-1982 had given subtle hints that it might be prepared to compromise.

The continued interest of the great powers in the Kampuchean question and the resulting competition was unsettling for the smaller countries of Southeast Asia. At a meeting of ASEAN foreign ministers in June, conference host and Singapore Prime Minister Lee Kuan Yew noted that "over Indochina, China and the Soviet Union are engaged in a sustained contest of will and power for preeminent influence. Until one side finds it burdensome and not worth the cost, there is little hope for peace [in the region]." Lee, one of Southeast Asia's most astute strategic thinkers, added that "we were premature in assuming that the congruence of American and Chinese interests in containing Soviet expansionism will make them de facto allies."

It was amid such uncertainty that Lee raised in September the delicate issue of a possible military role for ASEAN, which since its formation in 1967 had concerned itself largely with economic and social matters. While on a visit to Indonesia, Lee suggested multilateral military exercises involving all five ASEAN members. Though observers noted that this was the closest thing ASEAN had heard to a call to arms, the extremely cautious response seemed to indicate that the association was not quite ready to put Lee's suggestion into practice.

In the absence of a fully developed defense capability of its own, ASEAN was generally reassured by renewed U.S. pledges to protect non-Communist Southeast Asia. U.S. Defense Secretary Caspar Weinberger made two separate visits to the region, during which he reaffirmed his country's "unshakable" commitment to its Southeast Asian allies. In his first trip to the White House in 16 years, Philippine Pres. Ferdinand Marcos was pleased to hear U.S. Pres. Ronald Reagan declare that the security relationship between the two countries, founded on the U.S.'s giant Clark and Subic military bases in the Philippines, "is an essential element in maintaining peace in the region and is so recognized." Reagan's assertion also cheered other Southeast Asian leaders, who had good cause to doubt the resolve of the U.S. to stand up to Communist expansionism after the trauma of the war in Vietnam. Specific acts by the U.S. included an agreement to renegotiate the lease on its Philippine bases a year early in 1983 and its provision to Thailand of additional military assistance.

Australia, under the conservative government of Prime Minister Malcolm Fraser, also decided to contribute more actively to the security of the Asian and Pacific region. Over several months Fraser traveled to Malaysia, the Philippines, China, New Zealand, and Fiji, offering aid packages to some countries and discussing defense strategies with others to keep "enemy" (*i.e.*, Soviet) influence at bay. Australia planned to double its assistance (to $1.8 million) to Thailand in 1982–83 and was considering prolonging its small but significant military presence in Malaysia, Singapore, and Thailand. Practical defense cooperation was discussed when Australian Defense Minister Ian Sinclair toured Southeast Asia in the fall.

One capitalist power that ASEAN was reluctant to see assume a higher military profile was Japan. Though the U.S. had been consistently urging Japan to assume a share of responsibility for regional security more in keeping with its economic strength, memories of Japanese aggression in World War II continued to haunt Southeast Asia. Such unpleasant recollections were sharpened when a region-wide furor erupted at midyear over Japan's efforts to tone down descriptions in secondary-school history textbooks of Japanese Imperial Army atrocities during the war. Despite

Tokyo's protests that it would continue to adhere to its no-war constitution, Ferdinand Marcos proclaimed himself "wary, very wary" of Japan's U.S.-encouraged defense buildup.

The Soviet Union also did not contribute to ASEAN's sense of security. The region's misgivings about Moscow's sustained military expansion in the Pacific were exacerbated by two of the most sensational spy scandals to come to light in Southeast Asia for some time, both involving Soviet agents. In early February Indonesia expelled two Soviet officials for illegal espionage activities and closed the Jakarta office of Aeroflot, the Soviet airline. Barely two weeks later the Singapore government announced that it had caught two Soviet spies trying to gain access to sensitive military information.

China, however, another traditional bugbear of Southeast Asia, offered some reassurance. After finding some common ground with ASEAN on the Kampuchean issue, Chinese leaders publicly hinted that Beijing (Peking) would restrict its support for "fraternal" Communist parties in Southeast Asia to purely the moral kind.

In trade the main challenges that faced the open economies of Southeast Asia in 1982 were the global recession and one of its most insidious by-products, protectionism. When ASEAN's economic ministers met in Manila in May, the battle against mounting international trade barriers was at the top of the agenda. The commodity-rich association concluded that a key weapon would be for member nations to increase trade with one another.

(THOMAS HON WING POLIN)

See also articles on the various political units.
[976.B]

Space Exploration

As 1981 ended and throughout 1982, the U.S. space shuttle continued to record progressively greater achievements, justifying the nation's faith in it as the space transportation system of the future. Meanwhile, the Soviet Salyut 7 space station was launched and visited by two crews, including a French man and a Soviet woman.

On June 17, 1982, an important meeting took place in Paris between James M. Beggs, administrator of the U.S. National Aeronautics and Space Administration (NASA), and Erik Quistgaard, director general of the European Space Agency (ESA). The two discussed a variety of subjects of mutual concern for future planning of the two space agencies. ESA expressed interest in NASA's plans for a manned space station, and NASA showed particular interest in ESA's European Remote Sensing satellite.

During 1982 the Soviet Union lost two of its most prominent space pioneers, Nikolay P. Kamanin and Nikolay A. Pilyugin (*see* OBITUARIES). The latter had been involved in rocket and space vehicle design and development since 1946. In October NASA's Jet Propulsion Laboratory (JPL) gained a new director, Lieut. Gen. Lew Allen, Jr. His appointment was viewed as an effort to enhance JPL's intention to search for business in the U.S. Depart-

South West Africa:
see Dependent States; South Africa

Soviet Literature:
see Literature

Soviet Union:
see Union of Soviet Socialist Republics

NASA

Anik 2, a Canadian-built communications satellite, was launched into space from the U.S. space shuttle "Columbia" in November during the shuttle's fifth mission.

ment of Defense as the civilian space budget continued to decline.

In August representatives of some 90 nations met in Vienna to attend Unispace 82. While the stated purpose of the meeting was to prepare a report to the UN on a program for international space cooperation, the delegates showed more concern about the gradual militarization of space by the superpowers.

Manned Spaceflight. The U.S. space shuttle orbiter "Columbia" lifted off again from Kennedy Space Center at Cape Canaveral, Fla., on March 22 with astronauts Jack R. Lousma and C. Gordon Fullerton. The mission lasted more than eight days, and the "Columbia" landed at White Sands Missile Range in New Mexico on March 30. There were few problems, and the crew performed a variety of experiments, including further operation of the manipulator arm to include lifting an experiment package from the cargo bay, extending it into space, and returning it to the bay. Other experiments included materials processing in near-zero gravity, the separation of kidney and blood cells, and an insect study developed by Todd E. Nelson, a student at Southland High School in Adams, Minn. The astronauts also checked out a payload canister for future "getaway specials," experiments to be flown by industry, schools, individuals, and other organizations as space aboard the orbiter permitted.

"Columbia's" fourth launch from Kennedy Space Center was on June 27, with astronauts Thomas K. Mattingly and Henry W. Hartsfield, Jr. Fittingly enough, it landed on July 4 at Edwards Air Force Base (AFB) in California, greeted by Pres.

Ronald Reagan and an estimated 500,000 fellow citizens. A major problem occurred when the two booster rockets plunged into the Atlantic, apparently because of parachute failures. There was no danger to the "Columbia," however. Experiments included the first one to be developed by a private company. It was designed to produce certain pharmaceuticals continuously with high purity. The astronauts also helped save the first "getaway special" when a defective circuit prevented power from reaching the canister.

On November 11 the "Columbia" again went into orbit, manned on its fifth mission by a four-man crew consisting of Vance Brand, the commander; Col. Robert Overmyer, the pilot; Joseph Allen, a physicist; and William Lenoir, an electrical engineer. During its first two days in orbit the shuttle for the first time delivered two satellites into orbit, the Satellite Business Systems 3 and Canada's Anik 2. The only failure of the mission occurred when the planned walk in space by Allen and Lenoir had to be canceled because of malfunctions in the space suits. After 79 orbits the "Columbia" landed at Edwards AFB on November 16. The shuttle missions in 1983 were to be performed by "Columbia's" more powerful sister ship, the "Challenger."

On July 29 the Soviet Salyut 6 space station reentered the atmosphere and burned after four years and ten months in orbit. But the Salyut 7 had been successfully launched on April 19 and its primary crew on May 13. Cosmonauts Anatoly N. Berezovoy and Valentin V. Lebedev, in Soyuz T-5, docked with Salyut 7 on May 14. Their mission was generally an extension of that of Salyut 6: a

WIDE WORLD

The Conestoga I, a spacecraft launched by a private U.S. corporation, roared into the sky on September 9 from an island in the Gulf of Mexico off the coast of Texas. The company that launched the craft hoped to sell "low cost, market-oriented" space services to customers needing satellite communications and tracking.

woman in space, Svetlana Y. Savitskaya. (Valentina Tereshkova, also of the U.S.S.R., orbited the Earth in 1963.) Savitskaya and her colleagues continued the experiments of previous visitors with special attention to the effects of weightlessness upon female physiology. The T-7 crew returned to the Earth on August 27, using the T-5 satellite.

Launch Vehicles. As 1982 progressed, so did development of a lightweight external propellant tank for the space shuttle. By September the manufacturers of the huge tank had succeeded in reducing its weight by more than 4,525 kg (10,000 lb). Approximately 270 kg (600 lb) were saved simply by not painting the tank. Thus, almost 4,550 kg of additional cargo could be orbited.

ESA's Ariane launch vehicle literally had its ups and downs during the year. On Dec. 20, 1981, the Ariane made its final developmental flight, orbiting two satellites. However, on its first operational mission, on Sept. 10, 1982, from Kourou, French Guiana, a failure in its third-stage propulsion system sent the launch vehicle crashing into the Atlantic Ocean. Two satellites were lost. Despite the failure ESA made the decision to develop the Ariane L4, a much more powerful model of the vehicle, capable of payloads up to 4,300 kg (9,480 lb). It was scheduled to become operational in 1986.

The Soviet Union during 1982 continued development of its heavy booster vehicle, which had a larger payload capability than NASA's former Saturn V. Western experts believed that the booster, variously known as the Lenin and G-1 vehicle, had a payload capability of 220,000 kg (485,000 lb). First launch was expected in 1984. It was expected that the new booster would be used primarily for the orbiting of large space stations with crews of 12 and, later, 20.

Looking forward to the need for a vehicle to ferry such crews to such space stations and back to Earth, the Soviet Union for several years had been developing a mini-shuttle. An unmanned version of it, weighing approximately 900 kg (2,000 lb), was launched on June 3 and designated Cosmos 1374. It traveled for a little more than one orbit and was recovered after impact in the Indian Ocean.

Ventures concerning privately developed launch vehicles during the year experienced both bad and good fortune. The bad news came from West Germany's Otrag Corp., which had to close down its launching site in Libya to avoid political problems with several North African nations. The good news was from Space Services, Inc., of Houston, Texas. On September 9 its Conestoga 1 lifted off from a small island off the coast of Texas and successfully performed a suborbital flight.

Unmanned Satellites. As 1981 ended, the Solar Maximum Mission Satellite, launched on Feb. 14, 1980, detected several important new kinds of emissions from solar flares. It also observed gamma rays with energies never observed before. On Nov. 11, 1981, the Orbital Test Satellite, launched in 1978 by ESA, was successfully pressed into service as a telephone and telegraph exchange when a terrestrial exchange at Lyons, France, was destroyed by fire.

Designed for a lifetime of only three years, Applications Technology Satellite (ATS) 1 marked its

mixture of scientific experiments and military observations. After a record 211 days in space, they returned to the Earth on December 10.

On May 24 the unmanned supply satellite Progress 13 docked with Salyut 7. It brought mail, fuel, water, oxygen, and other supplies. It was detached on June 7 and reentered the atmosphere over the Pacific. Having been resupplied, the space station was in shape to receive its first visiting cosmonauts. Soyuz T-6 was launched on June 24. Its crew consisted of Vladimir Dzhanibekov, Aleksandr Ivanchenkov, and Jean-Loup Chrétien of France, the first astronaut from the West to be orbited by the U.S.S.R. This mixed crew worked for eight days with the primary crew of the Salyut 7 on experiments that included space radiation studies, space processing of materials, and biomedical observations. The international crew returned to the Earth on July 2.

The next visitors to Salyut 7 arrived aboard Soyuz T-7 on August 20. They consisted of Leonid I. Popov, Aleksandr A. Serebrov, and the second

Major Satellites and Space Probes Launched Oct. 1, 1981–Sept. 30, 1982

Name/country/ launch vehicle/ scientific designation	Launch date, lifetime*	Physical characteristics					Orbital elements			
		Weight in kg†	Shape	Diameter in m†	Length or height in m†	Experiments	Perigee in km†	Apogee in km†	Period (min)	Inclination to Equator (degrees)
Venera 13/U.S.S.R./D le/ 1981-106A	10/30/81	5,000 (11,023)	cylinder with two solar panels	2.3 (7.55)	2.7 (8.86)	Venus probe	Trajectory to Venus			
Venera 14/U.S.S.R./D le/ 1981-110A	11/4/81	5,000 (11,023)	cylinder with two solar panels	2.3 (7.55)	2.5 (8.2)	Venus probe	Trajectory to Venus			
STS 2 ("Columbia")/U.S./ Space Shuttle/1981-111A	11/12/81 11/14/81	2,029,494 (4,474,269)	delta with two solid boosters and cylindrical tank	24 (78.7)	37 (121.4)	Scientific payload and second flight of "Columbia"	255 (158)	265 (165)	89.57	38.0
Molniya-1 (51)/U.S.S.R./ A lle/1981-113A	11/17/81	1,800 (3,968)	cylinder with cone and six solar panels	1.6 (5.25)	5 (16.4)	Communications satellite	716 (445)	38,704 (24,050)	717.6	62.8
Satcom 3R/U.S./Delta/ 1981-114A	11/20/81	454 (1,000)	cube with two solar panels	1.17 (3.8)	1.63 (5.3)	Communications satellite	35,679 (22,170)	35,893 (22,303)	1,436.1	0.1
Bhaskara 2/India/C I/ 1981-115A	11/20/81	445 (980)	26-sided polygon	2.4 (8)	1.8 (6)	Television and microwave radiometer experiments	514 (319)	557 (346)	95.2	50.7
Intelsat 5 (F-3)/U.S./Atlas Centaur/1981-119A	12/15/81	1,928 (4,251)	cube with two antennas	‡	‡	Communications satellite	35,777 (22,231)	35,799 (22,244)	1,436.2	0.1
Radio 3–8/U.S.S.R./C I/ 1981-120A–F	12/17/81	40 (88)	‡	‡	‡	Six communications satellites for amateur radio operators	1,685 (1,046)	1,794 (1,115)	120.9	83
Marecs 1/ESA/Ariane/ 1981-122A	12/20/81	563 (1,241)	hexagonal prism with two solar panels	2 (6.6)	2.5 (8.2)	Marine communications satellite	35,703 (22,185)	35,872 (22,290)	1,436.2	1.9
Molniya-1 (52)/U.S.S.R./ A lle/1981-123A	12/23/81	1,800 (3,968)	cylinder with cone and six solar panels	1.6 (5.25)	5 (16.4)	Communications satellite	485 (301)	38,990 (24,227)	699	63
Satcom 4/U.S./Delta/ 1982-004A	1/16/82	454 (1,000)	cube with two solar panels	1.17 (3.8)	1.63 (5.3)	Communications satellite	35,782 (22,234)	35,794 (22,241)	1,436.2	0.1
Statsionar T/U.S.S.R./D le/ 1982-009A	2/5/82	2,000 (4,409)	cylinder with two solar panels	2 (6.6)	5 (16.4)	Communications satellite	35,592 (22,116)	35,997 (22,367)	1,436.5	0.2
Westar 4/U.S./Delta/ 1982-014A	2/26/82	1,100 (2,425)	cylinder	2.16 (7.1)	6.8 (22.4)	Facsimile and television relay communications satellite	35,785 (22,236)	35,789 (22,238)	1,436.1	0.0
Molniya-1 (53)/U.S.S.R./ A lle/1982-015A	2/26/82	1,800 (3,968)	cylinder with cone and six solar panels	1.6 (5.25)	5 (16.4)	Communications satellite	457 (284)	39,889 (24,786)	717.6	63.1
Intelsat 5 (F-4)/U.S./Atlas Centaur/1982-017A	3/5/82	1,928 (4,251)	cube with two antennas	‡	‡	Communications satellite	35,776 (22,230)	35,800 (22,245)	1,436.2	0.1
Horizout 5/U.S.S.R./D le/ 1982-020A	3/15/82	2,000 (4,409)	cylinder with two solar panels	2 (6.6)	5 (16.4)	Communications satellite	35,698 (22,182)	35,872 (22,290)	1,436.1	0.6
STS 3 ("Columbia")/U.S./ Space Shuttle/1982-022A	3/22/82 3/30/82	2,031,619 (4,478,953)	delta with two solid boosters and cylindrical tank	24 (78.7)	37 (121.4)	Scientific payload and third flight of "Columbia"	244 (152)	255 (158)	89.36	38.0
Molniya-3 (18)/U.S.S.R./ A lle/1982-023A	3/24/82	2,000 (4,409)	cylinder with cone and six panels	1.6 (5.25)	4.2 (13.78)	Communications satellite	616 (383)	39,733 (24,689)	717.7	63.0
Meteor-2/U.S.S.R./A I/ 1982-025A	3/25/82	2,750 (6,063)	cylinder with two panels	1.5 (4.92)	5 (16.4)	Weather and Earth resources satellite	935 (581)	960 (597)	104.0	82.5
Insat 1A/India/Delta/ 1982-031A	4/8/82	1,152 (2,540)	box with solar panel	1.5 (4.92)	2.2 (7.22)	Communications satellite	35,395 (21,993)	36,178 (22,480)	1,436.1	0.4
Salyut 7/U.S.S.R./D I/ 1982-033A	4/19/82	19,500 (42,990)	cylinder with three solar panels	4 (13.1)	15 (49.2)	Manned space station	280 (174)	299 (186)	90.3	51.6
Soyuz T-5/U.S.S.R./A II/ 1982-042A	5/13/82 8/26/82	6,850 (15,102)	sphere and cone	2.7 (8.86)	7 (23.0)	Ferried crews to Salyut 7 space station	281 (175)	302 (188)	90.4	51.6
Iskra 2/U.S.S.R./Salyut 7/ 1982-033C	5/17/82	28 (62)	sphere with solar cells	0.5 (1.6)		Amateur radio satellite	249 (155)	255 (158)	89.6	51.6
Progress 13/U.S.S.R./A II/ 1982-047A	5/23/82 6/7/82	7,020 (15,476)	sphere and cone	2.2 (7.22)	7.9 (25.92)	Ferried supplies to Salyut 7 space station	191 (119)	278 (173)	88.9	51.6
Molniya-1 (54)/U.S.S.R./ A lle/1982-050A	5/29/82	1,800 (3,968)	cylinder with cone and six solar panels	1.6 (5.25)	5 (16.4)	Communications satellite	653 (406)	40,633 (25,248)	717.7	62.9
Westar 5/U.S./Delta/ 1982-058A	6/9/82	1,100 (2,425)	cylinder	2.16 (7.1)	6.83 (22.4)	Communications satellite	35,723 (22,197)	35,852 (22,277)	1,436.2	0.1
Soyuz T-6/U.S.S.R./A II/ 1982-063A	6/24/82 7/2/82	6,850 (15,102)	sphere and cone	2.7 (8.86)	7 (23.0)	Ferried crew to Salyut 7 space station	279 (173)	301 (187)	90.3	51.6
STS 4 ("Columbia")/U.S./ Space Shuttle/1982-065A	6/27/82 7/4/82	2,034,173 (4,484,585)	delta with two solid boosters and cylindrical tank	24 (78.7)	37 (121.4)	Military payload and final checkout of "Columbia"	300 (186)	310 (193)	90.6	28.5
Progress 14/U.S.S.R./A IV/ 1982-070A	7/10/82 8/13/82	7,020 (15,476)	sphere and cone	2.2 (7.22)	7.9 (25.92)	Ferried supplies to Salyut 7 space station	192 (119)	258 (160)	88.7	51.6
Landsat 4/U.S./Delta/ 1982-072A	7/16/82	2,037 (4,600)	cube with one solar panel	2 (6.6)	6 (19.7)	Advanced Earth resources satellite	689 (428)	696 (432)	98.5	98.3
Molniya-1 (55)/U.S.S.R./ A lle/1982-074A	7/21/82	1,800 (3,968)	cylinder with cone and six solar panels	1.6 (5.25)	5 (16.4)	Communications satellite	650 (404)	38,900 (24,171)	701.0	63.0
Soyuz T-7/U.S.S.R./A II/ 1982-080A	8/19/82 8/27/82	6,850 (15,102)	cone and cylinder	2.7 (8.86)	7 (23.0)	Ferried three-person crew to Salyut 7 space station	228 (142)	280 (174)	89.5	51.6
Anik D/Canada/Delta/ 1982-082A	8/26/82	922 (2,033)	cylinder	2.2 (7.22)	6.4 (21.0)	Communications satellite	185 (115)	36,474 (22,664)	644.2	24.5
China 12/China/ FB-1 (CSL-2)/1982-090A	9/9/82	‡	‡	‡	‡	Military reconnaissance satellite	172 (107)	392 (244)	‡	63.0

* All dates are in universal time (UT).   † English units in parentheses: weight in pounds, dimensions in feet, apogee and perigee in statute miles.   ‡ Not available.

(MITCHELL R. SHARPE)

15th year of continuous operation in space on Dec. 6, 1981. Shortly after its birthday, the satellite helped save the eyesight of a crewman on a research vessel in the Pacific. Radio communications with his ship were interrupted while a doctor was giving instructions on treatment of the man's infected eye. The ship's radio operator switched to ATS 1, and the instructions continued.

On April 4 the GOES 5 environmental satellite spotted the eruption of the Mexican volcano El Cinchon and tracked its dust cloud. Similar observations were made by the NOAA 7 weather satellite. Measurements made by both satellites assisted scientists in evaluating the effects of the dust on the Earth's weather.

An unusual satellite launching took place on May 17 when the crew of Salyut 7 placed Iskara 2, an amateur radio satellite, into orbit from an air lock in the space station. On September 10 a Soviet satellite, Cosmos 1383, was instrumental in saving the lives of three men whose plane had crashed in northern British Columbia. The satellite had on board a developmental search-and-rescue transponder that detected signals from the plane and provided positional data to Canadian rescue aircraft.

Probes. The news of the year concerning space probes was furnished by the Soviet Union. Its two Venus probes landed successfully on that planet and returned a wealth of scientific data as well as photographs.

Venera 13, launched on Oct. 30, 1981, landed March 1, 1982, on a plain to the east of the Phoebe region of the Beta area. The lander took 62 minutes to traverse the thick atmosphere, and it transmit-

ted data from the surface for 127 minutes. In addition to chemical analyses of the Venusian soil, it took panoramic colour photographs of the surface. The lander reported that the ground temperature was 457° C (854.6° F) and the atmospheric pressure was 89 times that of Earth at its surface. Elements found in the soil included magnesium, silicon, aluminum, sodium, potassium, titanium, manganese, and iron. Photographs showed rust-coloured rocks and an orange or reddish-brown sky.

Venera 14, launched Nov. 4, 1981, landed on March 5, 1982, some 965 km (600 mi) to the southeast of Venera 13 after a 63-minute descent. However, it transmitted data for only 57 minutes. The lander reported a temperature of 465° C (869° F) and an atmospheric pressure 94 times that of Earth.

Information on Saturn continued to accumulate as data from the U.S. Voyager probes were analyzed. For example, there was evidence that at least two of Saturn's rings might be composed of ice rather than the remains of a shattered moon of the planet. Early in 1982 Voyager 2, on its way to an encounter with Uranus in 1986, began to experience failures after a 3,200,000,000-km (2,000,-000,000-mi) flight that began in 1977.

In March Pioneer 10, the first successful probe to Jupiter, completed ten years in space and was continuing to function. It was halfway between the orbits of Uranus and Neptune, 4,000,000,000 km (2,500,000,000 mi) from the Sun.

(MITCHELL R. SHARPE)

See also Astronomy; Defense; Earth Sciences; Industrial Review: *Aerospace; Telecommunications;* Television and Radio.
[738.C]

A mixed team of two Soviet cosmonauts and a French astronaut was launched into space on June 24 to join the crew of the Soviet space station Salyut 7. Astronaut Jean-Loup Chrétien of France was the first Western astronaut to orbit in a Soviet space vehicle. From left to right are: Aleksandr Ivanchenkov (U.S.S.R.), Chrétien, and Vladimir Dzhanibekov (U.S.S.R).

UPI

WHO BENEFITS FROM THE SHUTTLE?

by Dave Dooling

Among the more tangible benefits of the U.S. space program has been the transfer of its technology to larger segments of U.S. industry and the commercial world. This process is called spin-off by the public and technology transfer by the National Aeronautics and Space Administration (NASA). Spin-off cannot be a major justification for the space program because the financial return does not match the huge investment. Nevertheless, the gains from spin-off have proved to be an excellent secondary justification for space exploration, as well as for maintaining the spin-off program itself.

Impetus for Spin-off. When NASA was formed in 1958, one of the charges in its charter was that the agency "shall provide for the widest practicable and appropriate dissemination of information concerning its activities and the results thereof." In 1962 NASA set up a Technology Utilization (TU) Program "to accelerate and broaden the transfer of technology to other sectors of the economy." As a result of such encouragement the various manned and unmanned space programs to date have yielded a wide variety of practical benefits, ranging from pocket calculators to better meal service for the elderly and from insulation for liquefied natural gas (LNG) tankers to smoke detectors for the home.

The fiscal year 1983 budget for NASA included $9 million for technology transfer. This allocation represents a reduction compared with past years, but increased interest by U.S. industry in spin-offs, as productivity becomes ever more crucial to the economy, has heightened business interest in borrowing technology from the space program rather than reinventing it.

The Technology Transfer Network that NASA uses to assist this borrowing consists of several major segments: (1) A TU office at each of ten field centres and headquarters manages centre participation in company-owned regional technology utilization offices. (2) Eight industrial applications centres provide information retrieval services and assistance in applying relevant technical information to user needs. These centres have access to 1.8 million NASA technical reports and ten times that many in 200 other computerized data bases. One is the Computer Software Management and Information Center (Cosmic), which offers government-developed computer programs adaptable to secondary use. (3) Two state technology applications centres provide state governments and small businesses with technology transfer services similar to those of the industrial applications centres. (4) Two applications teams work with public agencies and private institutions in applying aerospace technology to problems in the public sector. In addition, NASA publishes *Tech Briefs* four times a year, *Spinoff* annually, *Patent Abstracts Bibliography* and *Computer Programs Abstracts* semiannually, and technical support packages to back up each item published in *Tech Briefs*.

Harvest from the Shuttle. Although the development of the space shuttle was not intended to do so, it did stimulate advances in technology in many areas. Three major aspects of the shuttle are notable: the thermal protection system—*i.e.*, the spacecraft's heatshield—made of more than 30,000 ceramic tiles that can withstand high temperatures and aerodynamic forces; the main engine, embodying the most advanced blend of turbomachinery and combustion; and the computer system, which can operate the shuttle almost without human intervention. New technologies were required to develop and manufacture these and other parts of the shuttle, including the mass-produced external tank, space suits, life-support system, and parts control and inventory system, even though the successful Apollo lunar landing program was used as the foundation of the shuttle program.

Because most of these technologies are new to the space program, their development as spin-offs is lagging. By the early 1980s spin-offs were still emerging from the Apollo and Skylab programs of the 1960s and mid-1970s. In 1982, for example, the U.S. Army just began looking into adapting an early model of the Apollo manned lunar rover, or Moon buggy, for use as a remote-control vehicle for the battlefield. Yet, even though space shuttle spin-offs are just materializing, a number already have shown a potential for the future.

The manned maneuvering unit, a small rocket backpack, is being developed to let astronauts travel short distances through space between the shuttle and nearby objects in orbit. A training model has been built by Essex Corp. for underwater use in special pools where astronauts practice zero-gravity work on Earth. The underwater model has control features nearly identical to those of the flight model.

Dave Dooling is science editor for the Huntsville (Alabama) Times *and editor of* Space World *magazine.*

Offshore oil companies have expressed interest in this device as well as in a possible robot version to increase the endurance and working abilities of divers.

The remote manipulator system was developed as a giant mechanical arm to let astronauts perform extravehicular tasks without leaving the shuttle cabin. SPAR Aerospace of Canada, the developer of the arm, is investigating applications for the handicapped and for reactor operations. In the former, a prototype model mounted on a wheelchair would provide quadriplegics with an arm for grasping objects. In the latter, the arm would be used for refueling nuclear reactors; for this task a heavy-duty version of the arm is required, but the basic form and control system are unchanged.

Because the shuttle crew must rely on limited resources, care is taken in what they consume. A water filter for the shuttle that acts as a bactericide and deodorizer was adopted by Ray Ward of Mesa, Ariz., for home use because he did not like the taste of the water there. It became popular with friends, and eventually Bon Del Manufacturing Co. had 20,000 distributors selling the filters for use in recreational vehicles and kitchens.

Flying the shuttle into orbit requires precise knowledge of the amount of fuel and oxidizer left so that the flight computers can compute burn time remaining and vehicle weight. Simmonds Precision Products, Inc., Tarrytown, N.Y., adapted its propellant management system for the shuttle to the "custody transfer system" used in offloading LNG tankers and for onshore storage facilities.

With cabin volume in a spacecraft limited, waste paper and food containers quickly can become a problem. Nelson & Johnson Engineering Inc., Boulder, Colo., developed a hand-powered, ratchet-driven trash compactor for the shuttle that can flatten cans. A model was produced for the home and camping.

The shuttle's external tank is insulated with spray-on foam insulation that must have the same thickness all around so that the heat resistance and aerodynamic characteristics are even over the whole structure. To overcome uneven application of the insulation NASA and Martin Marietta Corp., Bethesda, Md., modified spray nozzles such that they looked like rocket exhaust nozzles. This design proved to provide a uniform spray pattern and can be used in any industry where materials are applied by spraying.

Large volumes of data in electronic form are handled in and transmitted to and from the shuttle. For speed and efficiency this information is multiplexed: messages from many sources are interleaved like a precisely shuffled deck of cards, sent over a single transmission path such as a wire or radio signal, and then separated at the other end. SCI Systems, Inc., Huntsville, Ala., adapted the shuttle's multiplexing system to remote computer terminals that have become common at bank tellers' positions.

Efforts are under way to replace the shuttle's ceramic tiles with an improved heatshield. In investigating alternatives Rockwell International Corp. has developed a multilayer, titanium-wall sandwich that would withstand in-use temperatures to 1,930° C (3,500° F). Such a shield could be used on aircraft or in furnaces on the ground.

A variety of other spin-offs, some only published in NASA *Tech Briefs* and awaiting application by industry, are (primary use on the shuttle is in parentheses): a lock for hydraulic actuators (main-engine swivel control); advances in the densification, bonding, manufacture, and repair of ceramics (shuttle heatshield); lightweight thermal blankets using "goldized" film interleaved with fibrous filler (internal thermal protection); high-temperature titanium-niobium rivets (fasteners for parts of shuttle thrusters); three-dimensional air curtains that divide rooms into smoking and nonsmoking sections without walls (barrier to prevent cold residual propellants from freezing on heatshield); high-temperature and high-pressure door seals (payload bay vent doors); a special tool that precisely loads a locknut onto a screw without access to the screwhead (heatshield tile assembly); a tool that eliminates the sharp ends of spread cotter pins (space suit protection); a two-speed valve to allow gas pressure to build up slowly in a system (spacecraft oxygen control); protection from the spatter of electron-beam welding (main-engine powerhead assembly); microwave-scanning-beam landing system (hands-off, precision landings); and myriad computer programs (design and operation of the shuttle).

Often technology is borrowed by the space program from other fields. Tools for extravehicular activity have been taken literally from store shelves. A block-and-tackle system for winching shut the shuttle's cargo doors uses mountain-climbing gear. A helmet-mounted television camera for shuttle astronauts came from the gun camera for the F-16 jet fighter aircraft. It is not uncommon for such borrowings to be returned to industry with space-related improvements. The helmet camera, for example, one day may allow a classroom of medical students to look over the shoulder of a surgeon in the operating room.

As long as industry continues to take an intense interest in the shuttle and in space exploration in general, the spin-off program should remain a healthy part of commercial innovation.

Spain

A constitutional monarchy of southwestern Europe, Spain is bounded by Portugal, with which it shares the Iberian Peninsula, and by France. Area: 504,750 sq km (194,885 sq mi), including the Balearic and Canary islands. Pop. (1981): 37,682,300, including the Balearics and Canaries. Cap. and largest city: Madrid (pop., 1981, 3,158,800). Language: Spanish. Religion: Roman Catholic. King, Juan Carlos I; premiers in 1982, Leopoldo Calvo Sotelo y Bustelo and, from December 2, Felipe González Márquez.

Defections from the ruling Unión Centro Democrático (UCD), which had begun in November 1981, intensified in 1982 when Francisco Fernández Ordóñez formally established the Democratic Action Party (PAD) in March and when the right-wing Popular Democratic Party and the Liberal Democratic Party were both set up in July. During the following month former premier Adolfo Suárez González registered the Democratic and Social Centre. To halt the disintegration of the UCD in the face of these defections and to attain some degree of unity in preparation for general elections, Premier Leopoldo Calvo Sotelo y Bustelo held several meetings in early July with the president of the Congress of Deputies, Landelino Lavilla Alsina.

After a meeting on July 6 Calvo Sotelo told the press that Suárez represented the main obstacle to resolving the crisis in the UCD and accused him of trying to regain his powers through control of the party apparatus. Accordingly, Sotelo offered his resignation as UCD president and proposed Lavilla Alsina as his successor; the latter was elected on July 13. Before consenting to run for the UCD presidency, Lavilla Alsina obtained broad new powers

from the national political council. These included the rights to nominate the party secretary-general, to reorganize the national executive, and to nominate the majority of the electoral committee. A number of Cabinet changes were announced on July 27, with the three outgoing ministers being given key positions in the reorganized party secretariat.

The controversial Organic Law on the Harmonization of the Autonomy Process (LOAPA) was approved in the Congress of Deputies on June 30. Supporting it were the UCD and the Partido Socialista Obrero Español (PSOE), while the regional parties, the Partido Communista Español (PCE), and independents opposed it. An amendment sponsored by the PSOE stated that the autonomy law should not enter into force until five months after its publication in the Official Gazette in order to give the Constitutional Court time to consider it fully. Opponents of the LOAPA, most notably the Basques and Catalans, maintained that the law represented a disfigurement of the spirit of the constitution and of the autonomy statutes since it reinforced central government controls; its proponents argued that the law filled the gap between the more general demands of the constitution and the specific requirements of differing autonomous regions.

The statutes for the uniprovincial regions of Cantabria (Santander) and that of the principality of Asturias entered into force on February 1. Autonomy statutes for Valencia, Murcia, and La Rioja came into effect on July 10, and those for Aragón, Castilla-La Mancha, the Canary Islands, and Navarra on August 16. In elections held on May 23 for a regional parliament in Andalusia the PSOE won 66 seats in the 109-member assembly, while the right-wing Alianza Popular (AP) with 17 and the UCD with 15 placed second and third.

Defections from the UCD from March onward

Spain

JACQUES PAVLOVSKY—SYGMA

Spain's Socialist Workers Party, headed by Felipe González Márquez (arms raised), won a decisive victory in national elections in Spain in October.

SPAIN

Education. (1980–81) Primary, pupils 6,778,877, teachers 228,307; secondary, pupils 1,091,197, teachers 66,160; vocational, pupils 558,808, teachers 36,556; higher, students 649,098, teachers 40,321.

Finance. Monetary unit: peseta, with (Sept. 20, 1982) a free rate of 112.40 pesetas to U.S. $1 (192.70 pesetas = £1 sterling). Gold and other reserves (June 1982) U.S. $9,298,000,000. Budget (1981 actual): revenue 2,592,000,000,000 pesetas; expenditure 2,899,000,000,000 pesetas. Gross national product (1980) 15,239,000,000,000 pesetas. Money supply (June 1982) 4,674,000,000,000 pesetas. Cost of living (1975 = 100; June 1982) 300.5.

Foreign Trade. (1981) Imports 2,970,400,000,000 pesetas; exports 1,888,400,000,000 pesetas. Import sources: EEC 29% (West Germany 8%, France 8%); U.S. 14%; Saudi Arabia 11%; Mexico 6%. Export destinations: EEC 43% (France 14%, West Germany 9%, U.K. 7%, Italy 6%); U.S. 7%. Main exports: machinery 13%; motor vehicles 9%; fruit and vegetables 9%; iron and steel 9%; chemicals 7%; petroleum products 5%; textiles and clothing 5%. Tourism

(1980): visitors 38,027,000; receipts U.S. $6,968,000,000.

Transport and Communications. Roads (including rural paths; 1980) 237,904 km (including 2,008 km expressways). Motor vehicles in use (1980): passenger 7,556,500; commercial 1,338,300. Railways: (1980) 15,345 km (including 5,685 km electrified); traffic (1981) 14,135,000,000 passenger-km, freight 10,450,000,000 net ton-km. Air traffic (1981): 15,938,000,000 passenger-km; freight 454.5 million net ton-km. Shipping (1981): merchant vessels 100 gross tons and over 2,678; gross tonnage 8,133,658. Telephones (Dec. 1980) 11,844,600. Radio receivers (Dec. 1979) 9.6 million. Television receivers (1979) 9,424,000.

Agriculture. Production (in 000; metric tons; 1981): wheat 3,356; barley 4,709; oats 454; rye 216; corn 2,151; rice 441; potatoes 5,571; sugar, raw value 1,054; tomatoes 2,074; onions 1,045; cabbages 462; melons 770; watermelons 550; apples 1,064; pears 520; peaches 441; oranges c. 1,500; mandarin oranges and tangerines 725; lemons c. 431; sunflower

seed 298; bananas 445; olives 1,451; olive oil 305; wine 3,331; tobacco c. 38; cotton, lint c. 65; cow's milk 6,103; hen's eggs c. 690; meat 2,538; fish catch (1980) c. 1,240. Livestock (in 000; 1981): cattle 4,531; pigs 10,692; sheep 14,887; goats 2,170; horses 242; mules 190; asses 184; chickens c. 52,500.

Industry. Index of industrial production (1975 = 100; 1981) 114. Fuel and power (in 000; metric tons; 1981): coal 14,266; lignite 20,674; crude oil 1,378; manufactured gas (cu m) c. 1,650,000; electricity (kw-hr) 110,701,000. Production (in 000; metric tons; 1981): cement 28,751; iron ore (50% metal content) 8,411; pig iron 6,524; crude steel 13,170; aluminum (1980) 386; copper (1980) 172; zinc 180; petroleum products (1979) c. 46,900; sulfuric acid (1979) 2,950; fertilizers (nutrient content; 1980–81) nitrogenous 960, phosphate 497, potash 691; cotton yarn (1978) 94; wool yarn (1978) 32; man-made fibres (1979) c. 245; passenger cars (units) 861; commercial vehicles (units) 127. Merchant vessels launched (100 gross tons and over; 1981) 605,000 gross tons.

---

meant that the government lost its majority in the Cortes, and by late August its strength was reduced to 149 deputies. The PSOE had 117, the Communists 23, and the Coalición Democrática 9. Final blows to UCD hopes for reelection were their poor showing in the Andalusian elections and the tensions that were generated in June when light sentences were passed on 32 members of the armed forces and one civilian accused of trying to overthrow the Spanish government in February 1981.

King Juan Carlos I signed a decree on August 27 dissolving the Cortes in preparation for an early election on October 28. During preparation for the election the national executive of the UCD rejected a proposal to form an electoral alliance with the AP. Lavilla Alsina had threatened to resign as UCD president if the proposal were accepted. His principal complaint concerned the AP's plans to reform the constitution should it gain power in the elections. The PSOE, meanwhile, made a preelectoral alliance with the PAD and proposed in a manifesto

that a referendum be held on Spanish membership in NATO, which had become effective on May 30, and that no postelectoral alliance would be formed with the Communists.

The Vatican announced on September 7 that Pope John Paul II had decided on the advice of the Spanish bishops to postpone until early November a visit to Spain that had been planned for mid-October. The major left-wing opposition parties had expressed the view that the pope's visit would bolster conservative voting in the elections.

The PSOE swept to a landslide victory in the general elections. (For details, *see* POLITICAL PARTIES.) On November 18 the Cortes convened and took the oath to the constitution. Gregorio Peces Barba and José Federico de Caravajal, both Socialists, were elected speakers of the Congress and the Senate, respectively. Following the election the UCD executive committee resigned; Santiago Carrillo stepped down as PCE secretary-general and was replaced by Gerardo Iglesias. Blás Piñar's Fuerza Nueva, the extreme right-wing Fascist organization, decided to cease operating as a political party because it had failed to return a single member to the new Cortes.

King Juan Carlos formally opened the new session of the Cortes on November 25. During his discourse the king lent crucial support to the normalization process of Spain's young democracy by condemning terrorism and any future attempt to overthrow the system by military or civilian elements. The following day Premier-elect Felipe González Márquez (*see* BIOGRAPHIES) announced a 14-member Cabinet. Among the first measures taken by the new government were the devaluation of the peseta by 8% and the opening of Spain's frontier with Gibraltar. (*See* DEPENDENT STATES.)   (MICHAEL WOOLLER)

Speleology

The most spectacular explorations of 1982 were in the very deep caves rather than the very long ones. In France the Groupe Spéléo Vulcain set a new world depth record at 1,494 m (4,900 ft) in the

Alonso Alvarez de Toledo (left), Spain's chargé d'affaires, and U.S. Deputy Secretary of State Walter J. Stoessel, Jr., shook hands after depositing Spain's instrument of ratification of the North Atlantic Treaty at the State Department on May 30. Spain thus formally became the 16th member of NATO.

UPI

Gouffre Jean Bernard. They achieved this during a five-day expedition in February by passing the former terminal sump at 1,455 m (4,774 ft) after a bivouac 1,200 m (3,937 ft) down. The Snezhnaya Cave (U.S.S.R.) was explored to a new depth of 1,340 m (4,397 ft), making it the second deepest in the world. The explorers noted a current of air blowing through the rubble at the bottom and so future extensions were hoped for. If the possible link with the Mtchishta Cave were to be established, that would give a record combined depth of 1,800 m (5,906 ft).

The eighth place in the table of deep caves was taken by the Mammuthöhle, Dachstein, Austria, after a linkup with the Däumelkogelschacht gave a combined depth of 1,174 m (3,852 ft). In ninth place was the Spanish cave Pozo del Zitu, where the Oxford University Caving Club reached 1,139 m (3,737 ft) in the summer of 1981. Back in Austria again, in the Tennengebirge mountains, Batmanhöhle (also known as C2) was explored to a depth of 1,105 m (3,626 ft), making it the world's 12th deepest. The U.S., despite possessing the world's longest cave (the Mammoth Cave-Flint Ridge System of 361.6 km [224.7 mi]), still did not approach other areas for depth. The U.S. depth record was, however, increased to 453 m (1,486 ft) in the Columbine Crawl cave in Wyoming.

A West German expedition worked in the rather sparse caves of India. They discovered the longest there (Belum Guhalu, 2,114 m [6,936 ft]) and the deepest (Borra Guhalu, 86 m [282 ft]), and they also extended the Harpan River Cave of Nepal—the longest in the Indian subcontinent—to 2,929 m (9,610 ft).

Lucayan Caverns in the Bahamas, with the longest underwater cave in the world at 8.534 km (5.3 mi), was made a national park to protect it from vandalism. On Sept. 21, 1981, the cave diver Jochen Hasenmayer reached a depth of 145 m (476 ft) beneath the water surface in the French karst spring Fontaine de Vaucluse—the greatest under water depth ever reached in a cave. A few months later Claude Touloumdjian dived there to a new record depth of 153 m (502 ft). A helium-oxygen breathing mixture was used for the dive.

Important archaeological excavations in the Tabun Cave on Mt. Carmel (Israel) suggested that continuous evolution of man, from Neanderthal to anatomically modern *Homo sapiens,* took place in that region from about 130,000 to 50,000 years ago. In northern Spain unusual Magdalenian remains were found by a joint U.S.-Spanish excavation in the El Juyo cave near Santander. A sculptured stone head had the right side of its face representing a bearded man, while the other half face was of a catlike animal. Judging by its position on a stone altar it evidently represented a deity.

(T. R. SHAW)

[232.A.5.e]

Anthropologist Charles Faulkner of the University of Tennessee studies ritual mud drawings in a cave in the eastern part of that state. Faulkner estimates that the ancient graphics were drawn in the 12th century.

WIDE WORLD

Sri Lanka

Sri Lanka

An Asian republic and member of the Commonwealth, Sri Lanka (Ceylon) occupies an island in the Indian Ocean off the southeast coast of peninsular India. Area: 65,610 sq km (25,332 sq mi). Pop. (1981 prelim.): 14,850,000, including Sinhalese 74%; Tamil 17.5%; Moors 7.1%; other 1.4%. Cap. and largest city: Colombo (pop. 1981 prelim., 585,800). Language: Sinhalese (official), Tamil, English. Religion (1981): Buddhist 69.4%; Hindu 15.5%; Muslim 7.6%; Christian 7.5%. President in 1982, Junius Richard Jayawardene; prime minister, Ranasinghe Premadasa.

The government of Pres. Junius Jayawardene announced in August 1982 that Sri Lanka's presi-

SRI LANKA

Education. (1979) Primary, pupils 1,975,749; secondary, pupils 1,159,967; primary and secondary, teachers 138,488; vocational (1976), pupils 4,778, teachers 1,239; teacher training, students 4,119, teachers 532; higher, students (1978) 17,485, teaching staff (1976) 2,498.

Finance. Monetary unit: Sri Lanka rupee, with (Sept. 20, 1982) a free rate of SLRs 20.82 to U.S. $1 (SLRs 35.70 = £1 sterling). Gold and other reserves (June 1982) U.S. $237 million. Budget (1981 actual) revenue SLRs 16,228,000,000; expenditure SLRs 29,493,000,000. Gross national product (1981) SLRs 83,671,000,000. Money supply (May 1982) SLRs 11,050,000,000. Cost of living (Colombo; 1975 = 100; June 1982) 209.9.

Foreign Trade. (1981) Imports SLRs 35,251,000,000; exports SLRs 20,585,000,000. Import sources (1980): Japan 13%; Saudi Arabia 10%; U.K. 9%; Iraq 6%; Iran 6%; India 5%. Export destinations (1980): U.S. 11%; U.K. 7%; West Germany 5%; China 5%. Main exports (1980): tea 36%; petroleum products 15%; rubber 15%; clothing 10%.

Transport and Communications. Roads (1978) 24,911 km. Motor vehicles in use (1980): passenger 120,900; commercial 61,200. Railways (1980) c. 1,453 km; traffic 3,822,000,000 passenger-km, freight 166 million net ton-km. Air traffic (1981): 1,438,000,000 passenger-km; freight 28.4 million net ton-km. Telephones (Dec. 1978) 78,700. Radio licenses (Dec. 1979) 700,000.

Agriculture. Production (in 000; metric tons; 1981): rice 2,229; cassava c. 537; sweet potatoes c. 136; onions c. 67; mangoes c. 73; lemons c. 50; pineapples c. 46; copra 123; tea 210; coffee c. 12; rubber c. 133; fish catch (1980) 186. Livestock (in 000; June 1981): cattle c. 1,644; buffalo c. 843; sheep c. 29; goats c. 493; pigs c. 71; chickens c. 6,405.

Industry. Production (in 000; metric tons; 1981): cement 707; salt (1980) 114; graphite (1980) 7.8; petroleum products (1980) c. 1,670; cotton yarn (1979) 8.5; electricity (kw-hr) 1,870,000.

Squash Rackets:
see Racket Games

dential election would be held on October 20, more than a year ahead of schedule, giving a splintered opposition little time to select a common candidate. The main opposition to President Jayawardene, candidate of the ruling United National Party (UNP), was provided by Hector Kobbekaduwa, nominee of former prime minister Sirimavo Bandaranaike's Sri Lanka Freedom Party (SLFP). The SLFP had earlier split into two camps, but it hastily patched up its internal differences soon after the Election Commission gave recognition to the faction led by Bandaranaike. Bandaranaike herself was barred from contesting the election because of the 1980 court order stripping her of civil rights for seven years for alleged abuses of power. Four other candidates, representing the Trotskyist groups and the Tamil Congress, commanded only limited support. In the election Jayawardene was returned with almost 53% of the vote.

The year was another turbulent one for Sri Lanka. President Jayawardene declared a state of emergency on July 30 after Sinhalese and Muslims clashed in the southern part of the island, leaving three dead and more than 100 injured. There was another state of emergency on election night, as UNP and SLFP supporters clashed after polling had taken place peacefully.

After the election Jayawardene claimed that a faction of the SLFP had planned to assassinate him if their candidate had been elected. He announced that, rather than wait for elections due in 1983, a referendum would be held to decide whether the life of the current Parliament—in which the UNP held 143 of the 168 seats—should be extended by six years until August 1989. The referendum was held on December 22, and a 55% majority approved the measure.   (GOVINDAN UNNY)

Stock Exchanges

The world's major stock markets posted mixed performances in 1982. As usual, stock price movements were influenced by a mixture of economic and psychological factors. Of 17 major stock price indexes, 9 were higher at the end of 1982 than at the end of 1981 (TABLE I).

During 1982 the world economy continued to suffer from a steep recession, which had initially surfaced in several major industrial countries in 1979. The pace of economic activity in the Western industrial world was the slowest in the postwar period. The length and depth of the global recession · produced widespread unemployment, mounting debt burdens, and a sharp reduction in world trade. The fragility of the international financial system as well as poor domestic economies forced many governments throughout the Western world to ease monetary policy. At the same time, the worldwide slump threatened the political stability of several industrial nations and created worries about creeping protectionism as governments imposed trade restrictions in the hope of reviving economically depressed industries. While the dismal economic environment had the salutary effect of lowering interest rates, they still remained very high by postwar standards and

tended to retard consumer spending, discourage capital investment, and increase the volatility of foreign exchange rates in world financial markets.

Consequently, the increases in equity values in most countries in 1982 were often in the opposite direction from economic conditions. This reflected the tendency of stock price movements to anticipate future changes in business conditions, especially the prospects for improved corporate earnings. Severe cuts in business costs promised lower break-even points and good productivity gains once the economic recovery began. Moreover, the decline in interest rates was also a bullish factor, as lower rates both reduce business costs and increase the capitalized value of corporate earnings.

As 1982 drew to a close, the road to sustained worldwide prosperity was paved with obstacles. Steady economic growth was hindered by structural imbalances, such as the worldwide fundamental shift away from old-line heavy industries and toward the service and high-technology sectors. This shift was expected to act as a strong impediment to reducing unemployment even after economic activity picked up. The long and painful process of moving from inflation to disinflation raised fears of global banking failures and a worldwide depression. On the other hand, the beginning stages of worldwide economic recovery were clearly evident at the year's end, and the foundation was in place for a sustainable and less inflationary economic recovery in the years ahead.

(ROBERT H. TRIGG)

United States. The stock market turned in one of its best postwar performances in 1982 with record highs achieved by the leading indexes and very heavy turnover as a result of major institutional participation. On August 18 volume on the New York Stock Exchange (NYSE) reached 132.7 million shares, the first time in the history of the exchange that trading during one day had exceeded 100 million shares. Volume exceeded 100 million shares per day on 25 days during the last few months of 1982. The one-day record was set Nov. 4, 1982, when 149.4 million shares changed hands.

On August 17 Henry Kaufman, a leading stock market economist, predicted that interest rates would decline in 1983. This set off a major rally that lasted from mid-August until November 3. The Dow Jones Industrial Average advanced 37% from 777 to 1,065 in the period. It ended the year at 1,046.54, a 19.6% gain for the year. The Standard & Poor's 500 at 140.64 was up 14.8% for the year, and the Nasdaq composite index of over-the-counter issues gained 18.7% to 232.41. The American Stock Exchange (Amex) market value index, however, gained only 6.2% for the year to end at 340.60.

The stock market's advance came in the midst of the worst economic slump since the Great Depression of the 1930s. The unemployment rate, at 10.8% in December, was the highest in three decades; car sales were the lowest since 1961; housing and construction were badly depressed; and the federal budget deficit for fiscal 1982 was a record $110,660,000,000. Interest rates fell sharply in 1982, with the prime rate dropping from 17% in

Stamp Collecting:
see Philately and Numismatics

Steel Industry:
see Industrial Review

February to 11.5% at the year's end. Dividend payouts were off by 24%, and the number of corporations cutting or omitting dividends was the largest since record-keeping by Standard & Poor's began in 1961. Financial intermediaries prospered in 1982 as many major mergers, acquisitions, and financings occurred.

The fundamental explanation for the market's sharp advance and its volatility lay in the sharp decline in interest rates, expectations of a lower rate of inflation, and optimistic projections for economic recovery. The markets were increasingly dominated by institutional investors making trades of large blocks of shares. Erosion in the size of stock commissions, as discount brokers absorbed a larger share of the small investors' trades and block traders negotiated lower commission rates, improved communications, and the development of options and stock futures were all factors that contributed to the boom in the last half of 1982.

The Dow Jones Industrial Average rose by 171.54 points over the year as a whole, ending at 1,046.54. From its starting point at 875, the average trailed irregularly through March, when the lowest level in 23 months was achieved at 795.47. In June increases in most short-term interest rates were blamed for a dip to 791.48, the lowest finish since April 1980. By August a further retreat occurred, and the average fell to 776.92, a decline of 11.21% from January and the low for the year. Then in mid-August the bull market took off, and records began to be established on a daily basis as volume and price levels climbed. All of the averages participated. On December 27 the Dow Jones reached 1,070.55, an all-time high.

Interest rates remained at 1981 levels during the first half of 1982, with the prime rate beginning the year at 15.75%, rising to 17% in February, and remaining in the 16.5% range until July. At that time interest rates began one of their sharpest plunges in postwar history. The prime rate slid to 13.5% in September and ended the year at 11.5%. Thirty-year U.S. Treasury bonds, which started 1982 at 14% and peaked at 14.1% in June, dropped to 10.4% by the year's end. The discount rate, which is the rate charged by the Federal Reserve on loans to banks and savings institutions, was 12% in mid-July but only 8.5% at the end of the year.

Volume on the NYSE established many records in 1982. Stock sales were 16,458,036,768, up 39% from the 1981 figure of 11,853,740,659. The largest daily volume was set on November 4, when 149,385,480 shares were traded; the largest number of blocks (10,000 shares or more) traded was 2,530, set on October 7; and the largest single block, 6,290,700 shares of Federal National Mortgage Corp., was traded on September 10. Average daily turnover was 65 million shares, well above the 1981 level of 46.8 million per day.

Spurred by institutional investors, the well-known stocks led the turnover race. The most active stocks on the NYSE were IBM Corp. with 216,642,200 shares traded, Exxon Corp. 213,104,000, AT&T 181,655,700, Sony Corp. 137,316,600, and Sears, Roebuck and Co. 129,202,300. The lead-

ing gainers in 1982 were the automobile companies, the average prices of which rose 31.62%; they were led by Chrysler Corp., which increased 419% for the year. Airlines and mobile home firms also performed well. The worst performing groups were offshore drilling, coal, and oil-well equipment. Bond sales on the NYSE were $7,155,443,000 (at par value), up 41% from the 1981 level of $5,059,309,000.

While all of the major exchanges topped their 1981 volume totals, the gains were less impressive than those posted by the NYSE. On the Amex turnover was 1,337,820,000 shares, a slight decline from the corresponding 1981 figure of 1,343,525,000. Bond sales on the Amex rose $325,240,000 in 1982, up only 8% from the 1981 level of $301,385,000 and below the level achieved in 1980. The regional markets enjoyed a banner year in regard to their turnover in NYSE-listed issues. The Midwest Stock Exchange recorded a volume of 983,988,000 shares for the first 11 months, a gain of 283,158,000 shares over the 1981 total. The Pacific Stock Exchange traded 593,559,000 during the first 11 months, 141,968,000 above all of 1981. The Na-

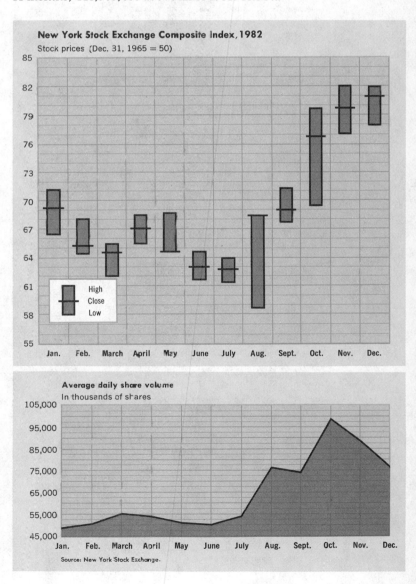

New York Stock Exchange Composite Index, 1982
Stock prices (Dec. 31, 1965 = 50)

High / Close / Low

Average daily share volume
In thousands of shares

Source: New York Stock Exchange.

tional Association of Securities dealers reported 484,651,000 NYSE stocks traded over-the-counter through November 1982, 165,570,000 above the full year of 1981. Over-the-counter activity expanded by 7.7% as volume on Nasdaq reached 8,432,274,885 shares, compared with the 1981 level of 7,832,315,841.

Mutual funds of all types enjoyed record sales growth in 1982, with total industry assets of $300 billion and 21 million shareholder accounts by the year's end. Mutual funds other than short-term

funds registered sales of $14.9 billion in 1982, a 50% gain over the previous sales record set in 1980. Short-term funds set sales records of their own. Assets of short maturity tax-exempt bond funds rose to $14 billion in 1982, three times their size in 1981. Money market funds, which fell sharply in the last half of December, had assets of about $215 billion, up nearly 20% in 1982. Common stock funds also posted record sales. Equity mutual funds gained an average of 25.03%, better than the 21.57% return of the Standard & Poor's 500. Money market fund assets began dropping in December as new deposit accounts offered by banks and thrift institutions drained off funds.

The Standard & Poor's Composite Index of 500 stocks, which had drifted downward listlessly in 1981 and early 1982, made a turnaround in August and moved past the 1981 corresponding month level at 122.43 in September (TABLE II). The 400 stocks represented in the Industrial Average paralleled the composite, surpassing the monthly figure for 1981 in September. Public utilities also moved to higher ground in September. While the railroad index lagged, it too was moving ahead by August 1982.

Yields on U.S. government long-term bonds (TABLE III) began 1982 at 13.73, well above the corresponding January 1981 figure of 11.65, but they then dipped progressively through May, at that time falling below the corresponding month in 1981. After a short pickup in June to 13.32, the average dropped steadily through the remainder of the year. Although the rally cooled off in the final two months of 1982, prices of long-term Treasury issues at the year's end were up more than 30% from June levels and about 25% from the end of 1981. High-grade U.S. corporate bond prices were well below 1981 levels in the early months of 1982 (TABLE IV) but rose from 30.9 in January to 34 in May. After an interruption in June and July, prices rose in August and continued to increase throughout the last half of the year. Average yields were 15.18 in January 1982 but were down to 12.94 in September and fell through the balance of the year. Salomon Brothers Inc. said that for the 12 months ended in October 1982, its index measuring the total return to investors on 850 high-grade corporate bonds had its largest gain since the series began in 1970—49.92%. Total return measures interest income as well as price appreciation of the investment.

Options trading rose sharply in 1982 as the bull market took hold and new products, new markets, and the internationalization of financial futures became more widespread. Volume on the Chicago Board of Trade Options Exchange (CBOE) rose nearly one-third in 1982. The CBOE traded 75.7 million contracts, up 31% from the 57.6 million in 1981. Options trading on the Amex increased 11% to 38.7 million contracts from 34.9 million in 1981. (An options contract is a right to buy or sell 100 shares of stock at a certain price before a specified date.)

Financial futures were becoming a major factor in the money and capital markets. During 1982 U.S. Treasury bond futures became the most widely traded futures in the world, ahead of wheat,

Table I. Selected Major World Stock Prices Indexes*

Country	1982 range† High	1982 range† Low	Year-end close 1981	Year-end close 1982	Percent change
Australia	596	443	596	486	−18
Austria	57	47	57	52	− 9
Belgium	104	86	87	103	+18
Denmark	128	108	119	128	+ 8
France	112	94	100	101	+ 1
West Germany	763	650	675	763	+13
Hong Kong	1,445	676	1,406	784	−44
Italy	213	147	195	166	−15
Japan	8,021	6,850	8,019	8,017	—
Netherlands, The	86	63	63	84	+33
Norway	130	106	126	111	−12
Singapore	811	557	781	732	−6
South Africa	738	508	701	737	+ 5
Spain	107	79	124	82	−34
Sweden	903	563	613	903	+47
Switzerland	288	237	259	288	+11
United Kingdom	637	518	530	597	+13

*Index numbers are rounded and limited to countries for which at least 12 months' data were available on a weekly basis.
†Based on the daily closing price.
Sources: *The Economist, Financial Times,* and the *New York Times.*

Table II. U.S. Stock Market Prices

Month	Railroads (10 stocks) 1982	Railroads (10 stocks) 1981	Industrials (400 stocks) 1982	Industrials (400 stocks) 1981	Public utilities (40 stocks) 1982	Public utilities (40 stocks) 1981	Composite (500 stocks) 1982	Composite (500 stocks) 1981
January	80.86	102.31	131.08	151.06	51.81	52.01	117.28	132.97
February	75.99	97.69	127.56	145.70	51.39	49.81	114.50	128.40
March	67.73	101.32	122.85	151.03	52.33	50.36	110.84	133.19
April	71.20	103.25	129.19	152.29	54.25	50.96	116.31	134.43
May	71.16	94.77	129.68	149.06	54.88	50.37	116.35	131.73
June	65.49	90.91	122.61	148.70	52.13	52.15	109.70	132.28
July	63.15	92.55	122.49	145.30	51.87	52.28	109.38	129.13
August	64.71	91.12	122.29	145.95	53.34	54.06	109.65	129.63
September	77.20	78.81	137.09	132.67	56.48	51.01	122.43	118.27
October	...	83.83	...	133.98	...	51.41	...	119.80
November	...	89.68	...	136.76	...	54.52	...	122.92
December	...	90.84	...	138.35	...	53.53	...	123.79

Sources: U.S. Department of Commerce, *Survey of Current Business;* Board of Governors of the Federal Reserve System, *Federal Reserve Bulletin.* Prices are Standard & Poor's monthly averages of daily closing prices, with 1941–43 = 10.

Table III. U.S. Government Long-Term Bond Yields

Month	Yield (%) 1982	Yield (%) 1981	Month	Yield (%) 1982	Yield (%) 1981
January	13.73	11.65	July	12.97	13.05
February	13.63	12.23	August	12.15	13.61
March	12.98	12.15	September	11.48	14.14
April	12.84	12.62	October	...	14.13
May	12.67	12.96	November	...	12.68
June	13.32	12.39	December	...	12.88

Source: U.S. Department of Commerce, *Survey of Current Business.* Yields are for U.S. Treasury bonds that are taxable and due or callable in ten years or more.

Table IV. U.S. Corporate Bond Prices and Yields
Average price in dollars per $100 bond

Month	Average 1982	Average 1981	Yield (%) 1982	Yield (%) 1981	Month	Average 1982	Average 1981	Yield (%) 1982	Yield (%) 1981
January	30.9	38.0	15.18	12.81	July	32.8	33.0	14.61	14.38
February	31.1	36.1	15.27	13.35	August	35.7	31.8	13.71	14.89
March	32.9	36.5	14.58	13.33	September	38.0	29.9	12.94	15.49
April	33.3	34.5	14.46	13.88	October	...	30.0	...	15.40
May	34.0	32.9	14.26	14.32	November	...	33.7	...	14.22
June	32.1	35.1	14.81	13.75	December	...	33.2	...	14.23

Source: U.S. Department of Commerce, *Survey of Current Business.* Average prices are based on Standard & Poor's composite index of A1 + issues. Yields are based on Moody's Aaa domestic corporate bond index.

soybeans, and pork bellies. Market participants used financial futures to reduce interest-rate risk. Daily dollar volume of trading in Treasury bill futures ranged between $25 billion and $30 billion. While Treasury bonds and bills were the most actively traded contracts, certificates of deposit, Eurodollars, Treasury notes, and stock indexes were also listed for trading.

Canada. The Canadian stock markets in 1982 failed to reflect significant gains on a year-to-year basis. The averages of stock prices followed a V-shaped pattern, declining during the first half of the year and rising in the second. Share prices on the Toronto Stock Exchange ended 1982 almost where they started. The broadly based 300-stock composite index stood at 1,958.08, up 0.2% for the year. It sank steadily to its low of 1,332.2 in July and then recovered in the second half. Volume was 1,580,000,000 shares, up 4% from 1981. Dome Petroleum was the most active issue, its price plummeting from $15 at the beginning of the year to a low of $3.30 at the end. The best performing groups on the Toronto Stock Exchange were finance and leasing, up 59.4%; tobacco stocks, up 46.4%; electrical and electronic, up 45.6%; autos and parts, up 42.2%; and breweries, up 40%. Worst performers were developers and contractors, down 60.7%; real estate and construction companies, down 45%; asbestos, down 41.3%; gas producers, down 39%; and steels, down 34.2%. Renewed interest in gold stocks, a copper price increase, and price rises in U.S. steel products gave the market a lift in the last half of December. On the Montreal Stock Exchange, the indexes of prices showed little change from 1981 levels.

The stock markets in Canada reflected the poor economic performance of the country as the recession deepened. Gross national product on a price-adjusted basis was down from $134.5 billion to $128.1 billion for the year. The unemployment rate rose from 7.6% in 1981 to 11% in 1982, and after-tax corporate profits were very sharply down in the third quarter at $11.6 billion, off 41% from the prior year and down 56% from the fourth quarter of 1979. Interest rates were lower, and the prime rate dipped to 12.5%, the lowest in several years. Canadian 91-day treasury bill yields were above 16% in June 1982 but fell to 12.5% in September and to 10% by the year's end. Similarly, long-term Canada bonds averaged 15% in January, peaked at 16.5% in June, and then fell irregularly to end the year at 11.8%. (IRVING PFEFFER)

Western Europe. Stock markets throughout Western Europe generally experienced a rising trend in 1982. Of the four largest European economies, Great Britain, West Germany, and France posted higher stock prices, while in Italy prices declined sharply. Among the smaller countries bullish markets prevailed in Sweden, The Netherlands, Belgium, Switzerland, and Denmark. On the bearish side were Austria, Norway, and Spain.

The stock market in Great Britain rose for the third year in a row. The *Financial Times* index of 30 industrial issues traded on the London Stock Exchange increased 13% from the end of 1981 to the end of 1982. The index reached an all-time high on

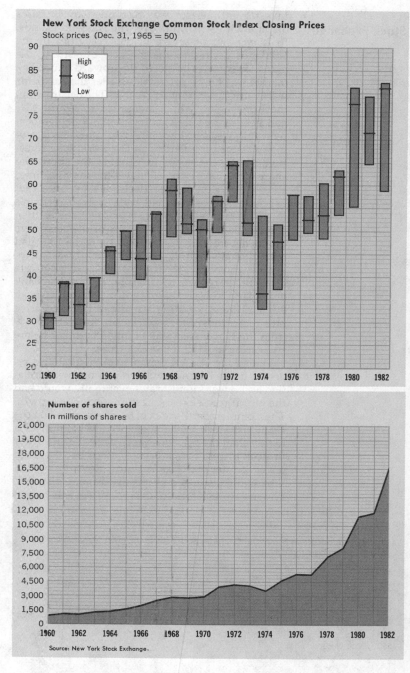

New York Stock Exchange Common Stock Index Closing Prices
Stock prices (Dec. 31, 1965 = 50)

Number of shares sold
In millions of shares

Source: New York Stock Exchange.

November 12, while the low for 1982 was recorded on January 5. The strength in British stock prices occurred despite a low rate of economic growth, a record number of unemployed, a relatively high level of inflation, and persistent labour unrest. However, equity investors chose to focus on the declines in the inflation and interest rates, both substantially below peak levels.

Following advances of 15% in 1980 and 12% in 1981, stock prices entered 1982 on a strong uptrend. January's rise amounted to 9%, but the index had given back 6% of that gain by the end of February. In March Prime Minister Margaret Thatcher announced that the government would continue its monetarist strategy in the hope that tight money would further reduce the rate of inflation. Stock prices turned higher in April, although investor enthusiasm was restrained by Britain's dispute with Argentina over the Falkland Islands. In May news of severe British casualties in the Falklands depressed the market, but strong demand for equities bolstered the upward trend. The market was hit by profit taking after the Falklands were recaptured from Argentina. The decline from the June highs, which amounted to almost 9%, had been erased by the first week of September, reflecting steadily lower interest rates and growing investor confidence that the worldwide recession would end soon. In October the industrial share index broke the 600 level for the first time, and stock prices moved decisively up once that psychological barrier had been pierced. Britain's inflation rate fell to a ten-year low, and British commercial bank lending rates to prime borrowers dropped below 10%, the first time the rate had been a single-digit figure since April 1978. In November, however, the international exchange rate of the British pound fell sharply, causing the Bank of England to lift its base lending rate to 10% from 9% and thereby ending a string of 14 consecutive rate reductions. Stock prices dropped about 8% from the November peak to mid-December before recovering as 1982 drew to a close.

The strong West German stock market also reflected hopes that a slowdown in worldwide inflation and lower interest rates eventually would end the global recession and restore economic growth. The Commerzbank index of 60 issues traded on the Frankfurt Stock Exchange ended 1982 almost 13% higher than the previous year's close. The recovery in stock prices, which began in October 1981, did not encounter profit taking until late April. By that time equity values had increased more than 7%. The strong performance in stock prices was helped

by news that the Bundesbank's restrictive monetary policy had slowed the annual inflation rate to 5.1% in March from 6.3% in December and also by the lowering of the Bundesbank's interest rate to commercial banks to 9.5%. The market's subsequent retreat, which wiped out the earlier gain, was fueled by the threatened bankruptcy of a major West German electrical company. Equity prices rallied during November and set the year's high on the final trading day of the year.

In France the stock market finished 1982 with a gain of 1%. Prices on the Paris Bourse reached their highest point on May 12. The rally was stimulated by news that payments to stockholders of 5 major nationalized industrial companies and of 36 banks would be raised by nearly $2 billion and also by Pres. François Mitterrand's plan to lower corporate taxes and stimulate private investment. However, stock prices retreated as investor concern over an inflation rate double that of West Germany, declining industrial production, and rising unemployment outweighed the government's economic policy shift. The market remained in a downtrend until mid-August, when the government announced measures to encourage savings and investment in financial assets. Share savings accounts were created, which allowed participating equity investors to earn a maximum tax credit of $1,500, or the equivalent of 20% of their net annual purchases of French stocks. In addition, the double taxation of corporate dividends and the withholding tax on bond interest income were eliminated, and the tax exemption on income derived from bonds was increased. The ensuing rebound in stock prices gathered strength in November after the wage/price freeze was lifted, and sweeping cuts in unemployment benefits were announced to reduce the deficit in the country's unemployment insurance program. At the year's close, stock prices were 7% above the August 12 low and 11% below the May highs.

Economic, social, and political turmoil had a disruptive influence on stock price movements in Italy. After rising 13% in 1981, prices on the Milan Stock Exchange reversed the bullish trend and lost 15% in 1982. Stock prices experienced a modest decline in January, largely a continuation of the downtrend that began in August of the previous year following the imposition of new regulations to curb speculation in equity securities. The upswing initiated in early February, which topped out on March 19, added 13% to equity values. The threatened collapse of Premier Giovanni Spadolini's ten-month-old government and the decision by Confindustria, the Italian employers' association, to revoke its 1975 agreement with the country's major labour union on wage-inflation indexation sent shock waves through the investment community. By mid-July equity values had plunged nearly 31% from the March peak. As worldwide interest rates eased, stock prices staged a strong rally over the next five weeks, adding 20% to equity values. However, Spadolini's government resigned after it was unable to obtain parliamentary approval of an economic plan to cut the public deficit and lower the country's 17% inflation rate. The plan was considered crucial to la-

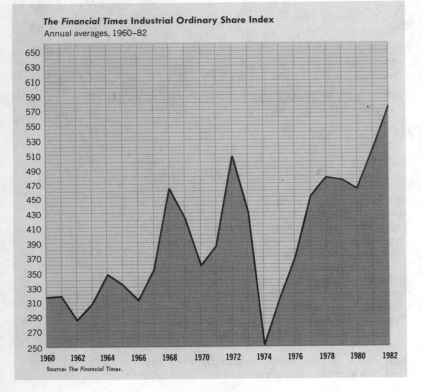

The Financial Times Industrial Ordinary Share Index
Annual averages, 1960–82

Source: The Financial Times.

bour-management peace, since wage adjustments would be linked to the government's projected inflation rate. Subsequently, Spadolini formed a new coalition, but he was forced to resign in November when his Cabinet was unable to agree on an economic program. From August 20 to mid-November stock prices fell 10%. After Amintore Fanfani became premier, the market trimmed its losses, but the rally was without strong conviction.

For the third year in a row the broad trend of stock prices in Sweden was bullish. The index of shares traded on the Stockholm Stock Exchange was up 47%, the largest increase among the world's major stock price indexes. In September Olof Palme was elected prime minister and announced a 12-point economic program to bolster the economy, including a 16% devaluation of the krona, an increase in corporate taxes, a temporary price freeze, and a 20% tax on corporate dividends. The news led to the heaviest volume of trading in the history of the Stockholm Exchange. Equity prices rose 47% from mid-August to the end of December, ending 1982 at a new all-time high.

In Austria the price index of shares listed on the Vienna Stock Exchange fell 9% from the end of 1981 to the end of 1982. After a relatively modest rise during the early part of January, average share prices moved steadily lower until the end of March, when they began to drop much faster. In late June prices were almost 15% lower than at the end of December 1981. The stock market was relatively trendless in July and August, but in September the decline resumed. The low point in equity values was reached on October 28. The subsequent rebound left share prices at the end of 1982 halfway between the January highs and the October lows. The primary forces behind the market's bearishness were the failure of the economy to respond to the softening in interest rates and the highest level of joblessness in 29 years.

The stock market in Norway also took a beating in 1982, reflecting a drop in industrial output to 1973 levels, the highest number of bankruptcies since World War II, a sharply higher government deficit due to a steep decline in tax and royalty payments from oil and gas companies, and a steady decline in international competitiveness owing to one of the highest tax burdens in the Western world. To address these problems Prime Minister Kåre Willoch, who took office in September 1981 as the head of the first Conservative government in Norway since 1928, devalued the Norwegian krone and cut taxes for individuals and businesses to stimulate the economy and reduce unemployment. For the year as a whole prices on the Oslo Stock Exchange plunged 12%.

Other Countries. Among stock markets in countries outside Europe, lower prices were generally the rule. In the Pacific Basin region Japan's stock market ended the year about where it began, while lower stock markets prevailed in Australia, Hong Kong, and Singapore. Stock prices in South Africa posted a small gain over the year.

The stock market in Japan was virtually unchanged from the end of 1981 to the end of 1982. Nevertheless, the index of 225 issues traded on the Tokyo Stock Exchange managed a new all-time

high on December 7, surpassing the previous high of Aug. 17, 1981.

In Australia the economy suffered from the slowdown in world demand for raw materials. To alleviate unemployment, which reached 8.2% in October to register the highest monthly increase in joblessness ever recorded, the Australian government called for a 12-month freeze on all wages in both the private and public sectors. The proposal was aimed at reducing wage costs to enable Australian industry to regain competitiveness in international markets. After dropping 17% in 1981, average share prices on the Sydney Stock Exchange finished 1982 with a loss of 18%.

Stock markets in Hong Kong and Singapore followed a similar bearish pattern. The index of 33 issues traded on the Hong Kong Stock Exchange recorded its high on January 12, while the year's high in Singapore was reached on January 6. The year's decline in equity values in Singapore amounted to 6%, while prices in Hong Kong sank 44% — the largest average loss among the major world stock indexes, largely due to the collapse of speculative momentum in the real estate market and uncertainty over the crown colony's future.

In South Africa the increase in prices of industrial shares traded on the Johannesburg Stock Ex-

Traders on the floor of the New York Stock Exchange were jubilant after the stock market surged ahead 38.81 points on August 17, a record advance.

CAMERA PRESS/PHOTO TRENDS

Trading was lively when the London International Financial Futures Exchange opened in September. The market was devoted to trading in money and money futures.

Strikes:
see Industrial Relations

change was 5%. Average industrial share prices dropped 19% in the first quarter and slipped another 10% during the April–June period. But the stock market then staged a strong rally over the next 16 weeks, adding 38% to equity values. After sinking 7% from mid-October to mid-November, the market resumed its uptrend and closed the year slightly below its all-time high.

Commodity Markets. World commodity markets experienced generally lower prices in 1982. Reuters United Kingdom commodity index, which measures spot or futures prices for 17 primary commodities weighted by their relative importance in international trade, fell from 1,614 at the end of 1981 to 1,580 at the end of 1982. The 2% decline continued the downward trend that began in September 1980, when record highs were established, and left the index 11% below its all-time peak. Price weakness in copper, lead, zinc, aluminum, and other industrial metals was largely attributable to the worldwide recession that sharply reduced operations in industries such as automobiles, construction, and electrical equipment, which are heavy users of those commodities. Abundant harvests in many parts of the world placed downward pressure on the prices of grains, sugar, cocoa, and coffee.

Metals and agricultural commodities also heavily influenced the four major components of *The Economist*'s index of commodity prices. In terms of the U.S. dollar the average price level of metals from mid-December 1981 to mid-December 1982 plunged 18%, while industrial materials prices dropped 15%, foodstuffs slid 11%, and fibres dipped 4%. The price indexes of metals, industrial materials, and foodstuffs reached their 1982 highs in the first two months of 1982 and finished the year not far above their September lows. In contrast, fibre prices were strong until May but also ended the year only slightly above September levels. Weak demand for commodities stemmed from sluggish conditions worldwide and from relatively high short-term interest rates. High interest rates discouraged manufacturers from tying up cash in inventories and aggravated international debt problems. The financial woes of many less developed countries tended to depress commodity prices, as those nations were forced to produce and export commodities regardless of price in order to earn sufficient foreign exchange income to meet debt burdens.

The price of gold changed direction several times during 1982. At the end of 1981 gold closed in the London market at $400 an ounce. By mid-March a steady slide had dropped the price to below $316 before a rally pushed it to $363 on April 15. After the price threatened to break the $300 level in late June, it rebounded and by the end of August had soared above $400. Rising international tensions in the Middle East and the threatened collapse of several European and Canadian banks triggered the rally. Gold prices reached $481 on September 7, but profit taking drove the price under $400 during the first week of October. From that time until the end of the year, the price of gold bullion traded between $398 and $460.

The demand for bullion was buoyed by worries about an international banking crisis due to the inability of such countries as Poland, Brazil, Mexico, and Argentina to service their foreign debt and by fears that governments of the industrial nations might abandon counterinflationary policies in order to fight unemployment. The price of gold finished 1982 at $448 an ounce for a net gain of 12% for the year as a whole but 24% below the all-time high set in January 1980.   (ROBERT H. TRIGG)

See also Economy, World.
[534.D.3.g.i]

Sudan

A republic of northeastern Africa, the Sudan is bounded by Egypt, the Red Sea, Ethiopia, Kenya, Uganda, Zaire, the Central African Republic, Chad, and Libya. Area: 2,503,890 sq km (966,757 sq mi). Pop. (1982 est.): 19,435,000, including (1978 est.) Arab 49% and black 51%. Cap. and largest city: Khartoum (pop., 1980 est., 1,621,000). Language: Arabic (official), various tribal languages in the south. Religion (1980 est.): Muslim (73%) mainly in the north; animist (18%) and Christian (9%) in the south. President and prime minister in 1982, Gen. Gaafar Nimeiry.

Formal approval was given by the International Monetary Fund (IMF) on Feb. 24, 1982, for a stand-by credit of $220 million in support of the Sudanese government's new economic stabilization program. A prolonged decline in exports and neglect of agriculture meant that by the end of 1981 the Sudan was unable to service its foreign debt. The new program, first announced in November 1981, had been prepared in consultation with the IMF and had been followed later that month by the restructuring of the Cabinet to exclude its opponents. Nevertheless, in June 1982 the government defaulted on interest payments, and the IMF suspended the credit arrangement until further spending cuts were implemented.

On January 25 Lieut. Gen. Abdul Magid Hamid Khalil was dismissed as first vice-president and minister of defense and also as secretary of the Sudanese Socialist Union (SSU), the sole legal party. Pres. Gaafar Nimeiry dissolved the party organizations and appointed a 41-member committee with himself at its head to reorganize the SSU.

These changes took place soon after demonstrations in various parts of the country. The first involved students in Khartoum, who marched to protest sharp increases in the price of sugar introduced on the advice of the IMF. Several people died in clashes with police. In the south there was concern that the region might be weakened by administrative subdivision, as the government pursued its policy of decentralization. This fear was intensified by the arrest on January 4 of 21 leading politicians, who had formed a council to protect southern interests. (KENNETH INGHAM)

Sudan

Suriname

A republic of northern South America, Suriname is bounded by Guyana, Brazil, French Guiana, and the Atlantic Ocean. Area: 181,455 sq km (70,060 sq mi). Pop. (1982 est.): 356,000, including (1971) Hindustanis 37%; Creoles 30.8%; Indonesians 15.3%; Bush Negroes 10.3%; Amerindians 2.6%. Cap. and largest city: Paramaribo (pop., 1980 prelim., 67,700). Language: Dutch (official); English and Sranan (a creole) are lingua francas; Hindi, Javanese, Chinese, and various Amerindian languages are used within individual ethnic communities. Religion: predominantly Hindu, Christian, and Muslim. Presidents in 1982, Hendrick R. Chin A Sen until February 4 and, from March 31 to December 9, Lachmipersad F. Ramdut-Misier; prime ministers, Chin A Sen until February 4 and, from March 31 to December 9, Henry Neyhorst; chairman of the National Mili-

Suriname

Sumo:
see Combat Sports

Surfing:
see Water Sports

tary Council and head of state from December 9, Daysi Bouterse.

During 1982 Suriname faced a worsening economic situation resulting from low world prices for bauxite and rice. On February 4 Hendrick R. Chin A Sen and his government resigned, and the National Military Council (NMC) announced that a new administration would be sworn in on March 15. On March 11, however, right-wing elements mounted a rebellion. Sgt. Maj. Willem Hawker, imprisoned after leading an attempted coup in 1981, was released by the rebels.

By March 12 the NMC had regained control and Hawker was executed. The Netherlands suspended aid until a civilian government was appointed, and NMC leader Daysi Bouterse, bowing to this pressure announced a new Cabinet headed by Henry Neyhorst. In December, however, the NMC once again took control. An attempted coup was put down with considerable bloodshed, and aid was suspended by The Netherlands and the U.S.

(DICK BOONSTRA)

Swaziland

Swaziland

A landlocked monarchy of southern Africa and a member of the Commonwealth, Swaziland is bounded by South Africa and Mozambique. Area: 17,364 sq km (6,704 sq mi). Pop. (1982 est.): 589,000. Cap. and largest city: Mbabane (pop., 1982 est., 33,000). Language: English and siSwati (official). Religion (1980): Christian 77%; animist 23%. King until Aug. 21, 1982, Sobhuza II; prime minister, Prince Mandabala Fred Dlamini.

Swaziland experienced a sluggish economic year in 1982. The government conceded that it was unlikely to meet the targets of its third development plan.

The year was dominated by the contentious issue of South Africa's offer to cede the territory of KaNgwane and part of KwaZulu to Swaziland.

Some 20,000 mourners followed the body of King Sobhuza II of Swaziland as it was carried to a secret mountain cave near the royal palace.

The Swazis claimed that the areas, both of which adjoined Swaziland, were part of their ancestral lands, but tribal leaders living there maintained that their people had long accepted the Zulu king. Should the transaction go through, 750,000 black South Africans who would otherwise claim South African citizenship would become Swazis, which was suggested as one attraction of the proposal for South Africa. Furthermore, South Africa would obtain recognition of its Bantustan policies from a respected African country. The proposal was opposed by the Organization of African Unity and by black Africa generally. In December Swaziland authorities arrested some 90 members of the African National Congress, banned in South Africa.

In August 1982 King Sobhuza II (*see* OBITUARIES) died. A traditional burial took place in a secret mountain cave near the Lombamba royal palace. The passing of the king, a conservative but greatly respected figure, was expected to presage change.

(GUY ARNOLD)

Sweden

A constitutional monarchy of northern Europe lying on the eastern side of the Scandinavian Peninsula, Sweden has common borders with Finland and Norway. Area: 449,964 sq km (173,732 sq mi). Pop. (1982 est.): 8,327,500. Cap. and largest city: Stockholm (pop., 1982 est., 647,100). Language: Swedish, with some Finnish and Lapp in the north. Religion: predominantly Lutheran. King, Carl XVI Gustaf; prime ministers in 1982, Thorbjörn Fälldin and, from October 7, Olof Palme.

Sweden ended a six-year flirtation with non-Socialist rule when, in a general election on Sept. 19, 1982, the Social Democratic Party led by Olof Palme (*see* BIOGRAPHIES) swept back to power, gaining 166 seats in the 349-seat Riksdag (parliament). With the Communists retaining 20 seats, the left-wing parties had an overall majority of 23 over the non-Socialist parties. The latter had governed since 1976, when the Social Democrats were defeated after an unprecedented 44 years in office. (For election results, *see* POLITICAL PARTIES.) The result reflected dissatisfaction with a succession of weak coalition governments and one minority Liberal government. The prime minister for most of this time had been Thorbjörn Fälldin, the leader of the agrarian-based Centre Party.

The Social Democratic election manifesto contained a pledge to introduce so-called wage-earner funds, under which elected committees of trade unionists would buy shares in private industry. This proposal became the central issue in the election, opposed by the three non-Socialist parties and the subject of a massive advertising campaign by Swedish industry. The Social Democrats' leading economist, Assar Lindbeck, resigned from the party because he said it would lead to "the collectivization of society."

After his return to power, however, Palme offered "an outstretched hand" to industry in future negotiations on the funds issue, choosing instead to devalue the krona by a massive 16% and to impose an indefinite price freeze. Palme said the devaluation was intended to restore confidence in the krona and improve conditions for Swedish industry on the international and home markets. He

maintained that increased production and fuller employment should result.

Another of Palme's first actions on assuming office was to announce that in the future foreign submarines caught inside Swedish waters ran the risk of being sunk on direct orders from the government. His tough statement came after the Swedish Navy claimed to have trapped a foreign submarine off its top-secret naval base on the Baltic island of Musko, 32 km (20 mi) south of Stockholm. Journalists from all over the world had flocked to the site, expecting a rerun of the 1981 incident in which a Soviet Whisky-class submarine ran aground on rocks near the southern naval base of Karlskrona, but they were disappointed. The submarine was generally thought to have smashed its way through an underwater barrier six days after the hunt started on October 1 and to have escaped back into international waters.

The incident raised grave questions concerning Sweden's traditional policy of armed neutrality and the Navy's ability to defend its coastline, and the government announced a commission of inquiry into the affair. This followed a summer during which more than 50 sightings of unidentified submarines in Swedish waters were reported. A further reminder of Sweden's proximity to the Eastern bloc was the steady stream of refugees from Poland following the imposition of martial law on Dec. 13, 1981. More than 3,000 Poles were

Former prime minister Olof Palme, leader of Sweden's Social Democratic Party, returned to power after six years when his party was victorious in the general election on September 19.

Sweden

granted political asylum in Sweden. The most spectacular escape was the flight of 20 refugees in an old-fashioned crop-spraying biplane across the Baltic Sea to Malmö in October.

There was also a reminder of Sweden's vulnerability to the phenomenon known as acid rain when a four-day ecological symposium took place in Stockholm in June to mark the tenth anniversary of the Stockholm UN Conference on the Human Environment. (*See* ENVIRONMENT.) The symposium called for urgent action to cut sulfur emissions from heavy industry. Scientists claimed that the acid was responsible for killing plant and animal life in about 20,000 Swedish lakes. Sweden was particularly sensitive because its topsoil lacked significant quantities of chalk, which might have had a neutralizing effect on the acid.

(CHRIS MOSEY)

Swimming

The IV World Aquatics Championships, from July 30 to Aug. 7, 1982, at Guayaquil, Ecuador, were expected to produce the best swimming since the 1976 Olympic Games. Fifty-six nations entered the competition, which consisted of swimming, diving, water polo, and synchronized swimming (synchro). It was the first meeting of all world swimming powers since the 1978 world championships at Berlin.

In the Berlin championships the U.S. women had regained their number one position from East Germany, winning nine gold medals to the latter's one. The U.S. men had continued their dominance, though not as impressively as in the 1976 Olympics. At Guayaquil it was a different story. The medal count proved the U.S. was the top nation overall with 13 gold, 10 silver, and 11 bronze in swimming, diving, and synchro. For the first time points were scored, and the combined total from swimming, diving, water polo, and synchro

determined the overall champion. The U.S. scored 840, followed by the Soviet Union with 587.5 and East Germany with 583.5. But in swimming, at the new multimillion-dollar Alberto Vallarino pool, the U.S. team won 8 of 29 events, as compared with 20 of 29 in Berlin. The East Germans won 12 gold medals, 8 silver, and 5 bronze. Ten of the gold were won by women. The U.S. won 8 gold, 8 silver, and 9 bronze. Six of the gold were won by men. The Soviet Union was third, with 4 gold, 7 silver, and 3 bronze.

The ten-day tournament produced seven world swimming records. The outstanding swimmer of the meet was East Germany's Petra Schneider, who set a world record of 4 min 36.10 sec in the 400-m individual medley. Her old mark was 4 min 36.29 sec. Schneider also won the 200-m individual medley, placed second in the 400-m freestyle, and fourth in the 800-m freestyle. Another outstanding East German was Cornelia Sirch, who swam the 200-m backstroke in 2 min 9.91 sec, lowering the previous world mark by almost two seconds. An East German team of Kristin Otto, Ute Geweniger, Ines Geissler, and Birgit Meineke set a new 4 x 100-m medley relay world record of 4 min 5.88 sec. Annemarie Verstappen of The Netherlands became the first Dutch woman to win a major swimming title since the 1968 Olympic 200-m butterfly victory of Ada Kok, taking the gold in the 200-m freestyle and a silver in the 100-m freestyle. The U.S. women gold medalists were Kim Linehan in the 800-m freestyle and Mary T. Meagher in the 100-m butterfly.

In men's competition Canada's Victor Davis was timed in 2 min 14.77 sec in the 200-m breaststroke to erase the six-year-old mark of 2 min 15.11 sec by David Wilkie of the U.K. at the 1976 Olympics. Steve Lundquist, the U.S. world record holder in the 100-m breaststroke, held off Davis by 0.07 sec to win his specialty. On July 19 at the U.S. team trials Lundquist had lowered his world record with a 1 min 2.62 clocking, and then on August 21 at the U.S. championships in Indianapolis, Indiana, he set another new record of 1 min 2.53 sec. Ricardo Prado of Brazil set a world record and won the first world title by a South American by taking the 400-m individual medley in 4 min 19.78 sec, faster by 0.27 sec than the old mark established by Jesse Vassallo of the U.S. in 1978. Vassallo did not compete due to illness. U.S. relay teams set two world records; the 4 x 100-m freestyle mark was lowered to 3 min 19.26 sec and that of the 4 x 100-m medley relay to 3 min 40.84 sec.

Rowdy Gaines, the U.S. world record holder in the 100-m and 200-m freestyle, could do no better than second in those events, losing to East Germany's Jorg Woithe in the 100 m and West Germany's Michael Gross in the 200 m. Gaines did win three gold medals, but he did so as a member of three winning relays. In July Gaines had set a world mark of 1 min 48.93 sec for the 200-m freestyle at the U.S. team trials.

Earlier in the year Soviet Olympic champion Vladimir Salnikov set new world records in the 400-m, 800-m, and 1,500-m freestyle events with times of 3 min 49.57 sec, 7 min 52.83 sec, and 14 min 56.35 sec, respectively. Salnikov and team-

Brazil's Ricardo Prado flashed a smile and a victory salute after winning the men's 400-metre individual medley world swimming championship in Guayaquil, Ecuador. Prado set a new world record time for the distance of 4:19.78.

UPI

A 19-year-old college student managed to better Johnny Weissmuller's record for winning swimming titles. Tracy Caulkins won her 37th U.S. swimming title on April 8 at the University of Florida.

World Swimming Records Set in 1982

Event	Name	Country	Time
MEN			
200-m freestyle	Rowdy Gaines	U.S.	1 min 48.93 sec
400-m freestyle	Vladimir Salnikov	U.S.S.R.	3 min 49.57 sec
800-m freestyle	Vladimir Salnikov	U.S.S.R.	7 min 52.83 sec
1,500-m freestyle	Vladimir Salnikov	U.S.S.R.	14 min 56.35 sec
100-m breaststroke	Steve Lundquist	U.S.	1 min 2.62 sec
100-m breaststroke	Steve Lundquist	U.S.	1 min 2.53 sec
200-m breaststroke	Victor Davis	Canada	2 min 14.77 sec
200-m individual medley	Alex Baumann	Canada	2 min 2.25 sec
400-m individual medley	Ricardo Prado	Brazil	4 min 19.78 sec
4 × 100-m freestyle relay	U.S. national team (Chris Cavanaugh, Robin Leamy, David McCagg, Rowdy Gaines)	U.S.	3 min 19.26 sec
4 × 100-m medley relay	U.S. national team (Rick Carey, Steve Lundquist, Matt Gribble, Rowdy Gaines)	U.S.	3 min 40.84 sec
WOMEN			
200-m backstroke	Cornelia Sirch	E. Ger.	2 min 9.91 sec
400-m individual medley	Petra Schneider	E. Ger.	4 min 36.10 sec
4 × 100-m medley relay	East German national team (Kristin Otto, Ute Geweniger, Ines Geissler, Birgit Meineke)	E. Ger.	4 min 5.88 sec

mate Sviatoslav Semenov finished one-two in both the 400-m and 1,500-m freestyle in the world championships.

The second major international event in 1982 was the XII Commonwealth Games, September 30–October 9 at Brisbane, Australia. The outstanding swimmer was Alex Baumann of Canada, who on October 4 lowered his world record in the 200-m individual medley from 2 min 2.78 sec to 2 min 2.25 sec. He also won the 400-m individual medley crown. Illness prevented him from competing at Guayaquil. Lisa Curry of Australia was the outstanding woman swimmer, winning titles in the 100-m butterfly and 200-m and 400-m individual medley. Commonwealth records were set in five men's events and five women's. Canada won six gold medals in men's races, followed by Australia with five and the U.K. with four. In women's competition Australia won eight gold medals with Canada and the U.K. winning three each.

On August 26–28 at Knoxville, Tenn., a U.S. national team defeated the Soviet Union, the women winning 113 to 77 and the men 111 to 79. Gaines won three freestyle events at distances from 50 to 200 m and swam on three winning relays. On August 26–28 at Kishinev, U.S.S.R., a U.S. junior team lost to the Soviets, the women losing 83 to 81 and the men 91 to 89.

Diving. At the world championships in Guayaquil the U.S., led by Greg Louganis, made diving history. Louganis completed an almost faultless dive by scoring four 10s out of a possible seven for a forward 3½ somersault. His winning springboard aggregate of 752.67 was an amazing 116.52 points over silver medalist Sergey Kuzmin of the Soviet Union. In the platform competition, for the first time in modern international diving, Louganis obtained a clean sweep of seven 10s for his inward 1½ somersault. This perfect dive enabled him to outpoint Vladimir Aleinik of the Soviet Union 634.26 to 629.85. In the women's springboard U.S. divers finished first and second, the first time a nation had ever achieved this in world championship diving. Megan Neyer outpointed teammate Chris Seufert by 11.01 points, 501.03 to 490.02. In the platform event Wendy Wyland moved up on the leaders from China, and after her seventh dive clinched the gold medal with a score of 438.78. Ramona Wenzel of East Germany slipped by the favoured Chinese for second place. At the Commonwealth Games Chris Snode of the U.K. repeated his 1978 performances, winning both the springboard and platform titles. In women's competition Australia's Jenny Donnet and Valerie Beddoe won the springboard and platform, respectively.

Synchronized Swimming. For the first time since the event was included in the world championships the U.S. failed to win the team title. Nor did it win the duet crown. The Canadians won two gold medals and one silver, led by Kelly Kryczka and Sharon Hambrook, victors in the duet. Tracie Ruiz won the solo for the only U.S. gold medal. (For the results of the water polo competition, *see* WATER SPORTS.) (ALBERT SCHOENFIELD)

[452.B.4.a.i]

Switzerland

A federal republic in west central Europe consisting of a confederation of 26 cantons (six of which are demi-cantons). Switzerland is bounded by West Germany, Austria, Liechtenstein, Italy, and France. Area: 41,293 sq km (15,943 sq mi). Pop. (1982 est.): 6,384,300. Cap.: Bern (pop., 1982 est.,

Switzerland

SWITZERLAND

Education. (1981–82) Primary, pupils 469,700, teachers (1970) 14,672; secondary, pupils 420,900, teachers (1970) 1,758; vocational, pupils 231,100; teacher training, students 9,700; higher, students 80,900, teaching staff (1978–79) 5,665.

Finance. Monetary unit: Swiss franc, with (Sept. 20, 1982) a free rate of SFr 2.14 to U.S. $1 (SFr 3.66 = £1 sterling). Gold and other reserves (June 1982) U.S. $16,876,000,000. Budget (1981 actual): revenue SFr 15,939,000,000; expenditure SFr 17,140,000,000. Gross national product (1981) SFr 191.5 billion. Money supply (May 1982) SFr 81,120,000,000. Cost of living (1975 = 100; June 1982) 126.5.

Foreign Trade. (1981) Imports SFr 60,090,000,000; exports SFr 52,860,000,000. Import sources: EEC 66% (West Germany 28%, France 12%, Italy 10%, U.K. 6%); U.S. 7%. Export destinations: EEC 49% (West Germany 18%, France 9%, Italy 8%, U.K. 6%); U.S. 8%. Main exports: machinery 30%; chemicals 22%; precious metals and stones 10%; watches and clocks 7%; instruments, etc. (excluding watches and clocks) 5%; textile yarns and fabrics 5%. Tourism (1980): visitors 8,872,000; gross receipts U.S. $3,149,000,000.

Transport and Communications. Roads (1980) 64,029 km (including 876 km expressways). Motor vehicles in use (1980): passenger 2,246,800; commercial 169,400. Railways: (1980) 5,041 km (including 5,015 km electrified); traffic (1981) 9,094,000,000 passenger-km, freight 7,152,000,000 net ton-km. Air traffic (1981): 11,628,000,000 passenger-km; freight 489.9 million net ton-km. Shipping (1981): merchant vessels 100 gross tons and over 33; gross tonnage 315,297. Telephones (Dec. 1979) 4,446,200. Radio licenses (Dec. 1980) 2,252,900. Television licenses (Dec. 1980) 1,979,518.

Agriculture. Production (in 000; metric tons; 1981): wheat 391; barley 220; oats 57; corn c. 117; potatoes 1,048; rapeseed c. 34; apples c. 240; pears c. 130; sugar, raw value c. 136; wine c. 82; milk c. 3,700; butter c. 35; cheese c. 125; beef and veal c. 160; pork c. 280. Livestock (in 000; April 1981): cattle c. 1,954; sheep c. 336; pigs c. 2,071; chickens c. 6,146.

Industry. Index of industrial production (1975 = 100; 1981) 115. Production (in 000; metric tons; 1979): aluminum 83; cement 3,934; petroleum products (1981) c. 3,800; man-made fibres 82; cigarettes (units) 29,282,000; watches (exports; units) c. 33,700; manufactured gas (cu m) 53,000; electricity (kw-hr; 1981) 49,088,000.

145,300). Largest city: Zürich (pop., 1982 est., 366,200). Language (1980): German 65%; French 18.4%; Italian 9.8%; Romansh 1%; other 5.8%. Religion (1980): Roman Catholic 48%; Protestant 44%; other 8%. President in 1982, Fritz Honegger.

The year's most dramatic event was the federal plebiscite of Nov. 28, 1982, in which a majority of voters unexpectedly approved introduction of a constitutional amendment calling for a system of permanent price control. That this was the case

Hostages held by a group of Polish dissidents in the Polish embassy in Bern in September were quickly rescued and released by Swiss police.

UPI

demonstrated that the rest of Switzerland's economic and political life remained as stable as it had been for years. The new constitutional article, which was to be implemented by federal legislation, was proposed in a popular initiative launched by consumer organizations. In a rather normal 32% turnout, 57.9% voted in favour and 42.1% against. As in the case of other popular initiatives, the federal government submitted its own counterproposal, which called for control of prices only in emergencies and for a limited period. This counterproject was defeated by a vote of 75% against. The simultaneous submission of a popular initiative and a government counterproposal, with the proviso that the citizens could vote "no" for both but "yes" for only one, was in itself a topic of controversy, involving as it did the increasingly complex procedures of "direct" democracy.

Toward the end of the year two members of the federal government, representing the Radical Democratic and Christian Democratic parties, respectively, handed in their resignations for the coming year. Apart from the election of their successors by Parliament, there were no important federal elections in 1982. However, the parliamentary elections scheduled for 1983 motivated a review of party ranks and programs. The first to enter into such discussions at a general congress were the Socialists, who in the event proved to be somewhat divided.

Against a general background of prosperity, apprehension about the future of the economy spread toward year's end in the wake of successive statistical reports on the "partial" unemployment introduced in the machine and watchmaking industries, in particular. While the proportions involved were modest compared with those experienced in other industrialized nations, one high official noted that "we are approaching dimensions to which our country is unaccustomed." It was feared that outright dismissals might follow the partial layoffs and reductions in working hours. At a meeting in Bern with the federal government, representatives of the four leading parties discussed ways of dealing with what by then was being called a recession.

The inflationary trend continued, though the rate of increase remained much lower than in other industrialized countries. In October the cost of living was reported to have risen by 6.2% within a year. The rise of public indebtedness was a cause for concern; the deficit of the federal budget was expected to approach the SFr 3 billion mark. Even at that figure, however, the government budget remained—in the words of a high official—"one of the least unbalanced."

Social security and national defense continued to be the two main priorities of the budget, receiving SFr 4,227,000 and SFr 3,995,000, respectively. While the federal government pleaded for a reduction in military expenditure, the head of the military department called for spending SFr 6 billion on new armaments and installations during 1984–87. At the same time, he appealed for a vote in favour of final and total adhesion to the UN. (The referendum on the issue was unlikely to take place before 1984.) Meanwhile, a committee of centre and right-wing parliamentarians was founded to combat adherence to the UN.

Assistance to less developed countries followed the "Swiss pattern," giving preference to selected bilateral arrangements. Total governmental aid still failed to reach the level stipulated by international authorities. During the year Swiss delegations took an active part in European and international bodies. The occupation of the Polish embassy in Bern by a group of Polish dissidents in September was quickly and efficiently ended by the Swiss police, the federal government having declined an offer of assistance from Warsaw.

(MELANIE STAERK)

Syria

A republic in southwestern Asia on the Mediterranean Sea, Syria is bordered by Turkey, Iraq, Jordan, Israel, and Lebanon. Area: 185,180 sq km (71,498 sq mi). Pop. (1981 prelim.): 9,172,000. Cap. and largest city: Damascus (pop., 1981 prelim., 1,251,000). Language: Arabic (official); also Kurdish, Armenian, Turkish, Kabardian, and Syriac. Religion: predominantly (over 80%) Muslim. President in 1982, Gen. Hafez al-Assad; premier, Abdul Rauf al-Kasm.

Pres. Hafez al-Assad of Syria survived a difficult year in 1982, with military setbacks in Lebanon and an uprising by the banned Muslim Brotherhood in the city of Hamah. The balance of payments deficit reached crisis proportions. The Soviet Union was approached for aid on a number of development projects. Crude-oil supplies were

SYRIA
Education. (1979–80) Primary, pupils 1,450,045, teachers 49,431; secondary, pupils 549,577, teachers 29,931; vocational, pupils 23,349, teachers 2,988; teacher training, students 10,612, teachers 1,141; higher, students 95,575, teaching staff (universities only; 1975–76) 1,332.
Finance. Monetary unit: Syrian pound, with (Sept. 20, 1982) a par value of S£3.925 to U.S. $1 (free rate of S£6.73 = £1 sterling). Gold and other reserves (Dec. 1981) U.S. $326 million. Budget (total; 1981 est.) balanced at S£30,480 million. Gross domestic product (1980) S£50,651 million. Money supply (Dec. 1981) S£24,832 million. Cost of living (Damascus; 1975 = 100; March 1982) 222.
Foreign Trade. (1981) Imports S£20,302 million; exports S£8,254 million. Import sources (1980): Iraq 18%; West Germany 11%; Italy 9%; France 6%; U.S. 5%. Export destinations (1980): Italy 55%; Romania 11%; U.S.S.R. 6%. Main exports: crude oil 61%; cotton 7%.
Transport and Communications. Roads (1979) 17,724 km. Motor vehicles in use (1979): passenger 66,200; commercial 86,000. Railways: (1979) 1,871 km; traffic (1980) 382 million passenger-km, freight 580 million net ton-km. Air traffic (1980): 948 million passenger-km; freight 16.2 million net ton-km. Telephones (Jan. 1980) 236,000. Radio receivers (Dec. 1978) 2,022,000. Television receivers (Dec. 1979) 377,000.
Agriculture. Production (in 000 metric tons; 1981): wheat 2,086; barley 1,406; potatoes 272; pumpkins c. 192; cucumbers c. 285; tomatoes 527; onions 169; watermelons c. 923; melons c. 210; grapes 359; olives 297; cottonseed c. 213; cotton, lint c. 119. Livestock (in 000; 1981): sheep 11,738; goats 1,200; cattle 817; horses c. 53; asses c. 244; chickens c. 14,183.
Industry. Production (in 000; metric tons; 1980): cement 1,810; crude oil 8,282; natural gas (cu m) c. 250,000; petroleum products (1979) 9,040; cotton yarn 20; phosphate rock 1,319; salt 90; electricity (kw-hr) 4,082,000.

SPENGLER—SYGMA

being purchased from Iran, underlining a radical alliance between Assad's government and the regime of Ayatollah Ruhollah Khomeini.

The Israeli invasion of Lebanon, which began on June 6, met no significant resistance from the 26,000 troops of the all-Syrian Arab Deterrent Force in Lebanon. They had been deployed in a wide arc curving from Tripoli in the north through the town of Shtawrah in the centre to Sidon in the south. The Syrian Air Force challenged the Israelis as they fired on Syrian missile sites in the Bekaa Valley, but to no avail. Israel claimed to have shot down 86 Syrian aircraft and reported no losses, although in October Syria claimed that it had shot down 26 Israeli aircraft. The Bekaa sites were destroyed. A further blow to Syrian prestige was its agreement to withdraw its forces from Beirut after August 20. On November 20 President Assad said that Syria would impose no conditions for the withdrawal of all its troops from Lebanon "after a total evacuation of Israeli troops."

The Hamah uprising dramatized the continuing internal opposition to Assad. On February 11 government forces started a drive against antigovernment Muslim Brotherhood militants in the city. Heavy fighting ensued, resulting in the destruction of the city centre and a death toll estimated by Western sources at 3,000–10,000. On February 24 Assad claimed the fighting was over. Government spokesmen alleged that Iraq had supplied weapons to the dissidents.

Syria's antagonism toward Iraq was evident in a decision in April to close its border with Iraq and also the trans-Syrian pipeline. This corresponded with a move to buy 8.7 million metric tons of crude oil a year from Iran starting on April 1. Teheran subsequently announced its willingness to supply Syria with phosphate. This was a far cry from the mood of 1979, when Syria had ambitions for a political union with Iraq. The plans had foundered after the discovery of a coup attempt in which Iraqis were said to be implicated.

The economic picture was bleak. Although oil exports brought in more than $1 billion in 1981, the economic trends were far removed from the forecasts contained in the five-year (1980–85) plan. The plan targeted an average annual increase in imports of 3.4%, but in 1981 — the first full year of the plan — imports rose by 22%. Exports, scheduled to grow by 6.5%, remained almost static. Several European countries complained that they had

Members of the Muslim Brotherhood (shown plotting strategy above) staged a fierce three-week-long rebellion in Hamah in February.

Syria

not been paid for goods or services supplied, while letters of credit were experiencing delays of six to eight months. The only bright spot was the announcement in August by Marathon Petroleum of a significant gas find at the western edge of its Homs block concession.

In January it was reported that the Soviet Union had agreed to supply additional arms to Syria, while Soviet technical help was expected to increase significantly as the result of an economic cooperation agreement signed on October 31. A specific agreement was initialed on a Soviet study for converting the Damascus-Dara railway to standard gauge. Land improvement, dam building, oil drilling, and expansion at Latakia port were covered in the protocol. It was reported on October 27 that agreement had been reached on the supply of nuclear expertise by the Soviets in exchange for power generation.

At home a rigorous crackdown against corruption was mounted by the government. On September 4 in Hamah, security forces arrested 29 government employees accused of offenses against the state. The manager of a bank in Dara was hanged on August 23 after being convicted of embezzling public funds.   (JOHN WHELAN)

Table Tennis

The third World Cup competition was held in Hong Kong in early October and featured 16 of the top ranked players from five continents. Guo Yuehua (China) defeated Mikael Appelgren (Sweden) in three sets to take the singles title. Appelgren had earlier in the year established himself as one of the world's best players by winning the singles crown during the 13th European Championships held in Budapest, Hung. His victory came at the expense of Jan-Ove Waldner (Sweden). Bettine Vriesekoop (Neth.) took the women's singles title with a five-set victory over Jill Hammersley (England). The men's doubles title went to Dragutin Surbek and Zoran Kalinic (Yugos.); the women's doubles crown to Flura Bulatova and Inna Kovalenko (U.S.S.R.); and the mixed doubles to Andrzej Grubba (Poland) and Vriesekoop. Hungary won both the men's and women's team championships. During the tournament the presidents of the International Olympic Committee and the International Table Tennis Federation discussed procedures for including table tennis in the 1988 Olympics.

The sixth Asian championships, held during the summer in Indonesia, were totally dominated by the Chinese. They won both team titles and all the individual titles after monopolizing the finals in every event. Japan and North Korea finished second and third, respectively, in both the men's and women's team standings. Cai Zhenhua captured the men's singles crown and Cao Yanhua the women's.

The sixth Commonwealth Championships were held in India in February. England won both team titles, with Nigeria's men and Canada's women runners-up. Atanda Musa (Nigeria) captured the men's singles title and Carole Knight (England) the women's. The men's doubles championship

Taiwan

1982 World Rankings	
MEN	**WOMEN**
1. Guo Yuehua (China)	1. Tong Ling (China)
2. Cai Zhenhua (China)	2. Cao Yanhua (China)
3. Xie Saike (China)	3. Zhang Deying (China)
4. Mikael Appelgren (Sweden)	4. Qi Baoxiang (China)
5. Tibor Klampar (Hungary)	5. Chen Lili (China)
6. Ziang Zialiang (China)	6. Dai Lili (China)
7. Dragutin Surbek (Yugoslavia)	7. Lee Soo Ja (South Korea)
8. Zhi Zhihao (China)	8. Huang Junqun (China)
9. Teng Yi (China)	9. Pak Yong Sun (North Korea)
10. Seiji Ono (Japan)	10. Bettine Vriesekoop (Netherlands)

was won by Nigeria, but both the women's and mixed doubles crowns were taken by England. Meanwhile, in February in France Europe's top 12 men and women tested their skills. Appelgren again emerged in first place, followed by Milan Orlowski (Czech.) and Desmond Douglas (England). Vriesekoop took the women's title with a victory over Hammersley. That same month Latin America's "Best 16" convened for a tournament in the Dominican Republic. Juan Vila (Dominican Republic) finished first, while Ricardo Tetuo Inokuchi (Brazil) was second and D. Marchallek (Jamaica) third.

The European League winners for 1981–82 were: Yugoslavia in the superdivision, Denmark in Division 1, Norway in Division 2, and Turkey in Division 3.

The U.S. Open was held during the summer in Michigan. Zoran Kosanovic (Canada) won the men's singles championship and Kayoko Kawahigashi (Japan) the women's title. Dan and Rick Seemiller (U.S.) won the men's doubles, Kawahigashi and Rie Wada (Japan) the women's. The mixed doubles title went to Koichi Kawamura and Tomoko Tamura (Japan). The men's and women's team titles were won, respectively, by Japan and South Korea.

During May the first unofficial world championships for veterans were held in Sweden. The four categories for players were spaced at ten-year intervals, beginning at age 40.

(ARTHUR KINGSLEY VINT)

Taiwan

Taiwan, which consists of the islands of Taiwan (Western conventional Formosa) and Quemoy and other surrounding islands, is the seat of the Republic of China (Nationalist China). It is north of the Philippines, southwest of Japan, and east of Hong Kong. The island of Taiwan has an area of 35,779 sq km (13,814 sq mi); including its 77 outlying islands (14 in the Taiwan group and 63 in the Pescadores group), the area of Taiwan totals 36,002 sq km (13,900 sq mi). Pop. (1982 est.): 18,271,000. Area and pop. exclude the Quemoy and Matsu groups, which are administered as an occupied part of Fukien Province. Their combined area is about 160 sq km; their population at the end of 1980 was 61,000. Cap. and largest city: Taipei (pop., 1982 est., 2,298,000). Language: Mandarin Chinese (official). Religion (1980 est.): Confucian and Taoist 48.5%; Buddhist 43%; Christian 7.4%; other 1.1%. President in 1982, Chiang Ching-kuo;

president of the Executive Yuan (premier), Sun Yun-suan.

The future security and status of Taiwan continued in 1982 to cause serious concern to the government and the people of the islands. In 1981 the Chinese Communists laid down a nine-point "peace proposal" for reunification with the mainland. The Communists also pressured the United States to discontinue arms sales to the Nationalists and demanded that countries that had recognized mainland China not have representative agencies on Taiwan. In the midst of those actions and in spite of the strong protests and boycott by China, the fifth World Women's Softball Championship was held in Taipei July 2–12, 1982, with two dozen countries participating.

Because of the development of new weapons by the Communists in recent years, the Nationalists sought to maintain air superiority over the Taiwan Straits by purchasing FX aircraft from the U.S. The administration of U.S. Pres. Ronald Reagan rejected Taiwan's request for the purchase of such advanced aircraft because of China's threat to curtail diplomatic relations with the U.S. if it did so. Instead, the U.S. decided to limit arms sales to Taiwan to spare parts while extending the F-5E co-production line in Taiwan to strengthen its defensive capability.

The four-day visit to China in May by U.S. Vice-Pres. George Bush demonstrated the interest of the U.S. in maintaining good relations with the Communist regime. From his arrival to his departure Bush reaffirmed that the Reagan administration unequivocally accepted that the Communist regime was the sole legal government of China and that Taiwan was a part of China. While Bush was in Beijing (Peking), President Reagan's letters to the three top Chinese leaders were released; in them Reagan restated the "one China policy" of the U.S. and linked the reduction and termination of U.S. arms sales to Taiwan with the peaceful resolution of the Taiwan question. The Nationalist government and the general public on Taiwan viewed the pronouncements of Reagan and Bush as a setback in relations between the U.S. and Taiwan.

On August 17 the U.S. and China issued a new communiqué on arms sales to Taiwan. In it the U.S. government "recognized the government of the PRC [Communist China] as the sole legal government of China" and stated that it had no intention of "infringing on Chinese sovereignty and territorial integrity . . . or pursuing a policy of 'two Chinas' or 'one China, one Taiwan.'" Acceding partly to China's demand to end arms sales to Taiwan, the U.S. pledged, for the first time, to reduce, limit, and eventually end such sales. President Reagan stated that the pledge was made on the basis of the Chinese promise to seek reunification with Taiwan by peaceful means only. On August 21 the New China News Agency on the mainland denied any commitment by China to the U.S. to pursue only a peaceful solution of the Taiwan question. In Taipei the Nationalist government expressed profound regret over the U.S. statement that "it does not seek to carry out a long-term policy of arms sales to Taiwan."

The official Nationalist response to Communist overtures and pressure for unification negotiations, as stated repeatedly by Pres. Chiang Ching-kuo, remained "no contacts, no talks, no compromise" with the Communists. It was feared that under the present circumstances negotiations would only lead to Taiwan's surrender.

The economy of Taiwan, primarily under the system of free enterprise, was approaching the status of a developed country; per capita income rose from $2,378 in 1980 to $2,570 in 1981, ten times that of the Chinese mainland.

The economic growth rate declined from 6.7% in 1980 to 5.5% in 1981. The slowdown was caused by a number of factors, including stagnation in the international economy and a wall of protectionism in world markets.   (HUNG-TI CHU)

TAIWAN

Education. (1981–82) Primary, pupils 2,202,904, teachers 69,143; secondary and vocational, pupils 1,620,165, teachers 70,668; higher, students 358,437, teaching staff 17,452.

Finance. Monetary unit: new Taiwan dollar, with (Sept. 20, 1982) a free rate of NT$37.42 to U.S. $1 (NT$64.15 = £1 sterling). Budget (1980–81 est.): revenue NT$275,054,000,000; expenditure NT$241,705,000,000. Gross national product (1981) NT$1,703,700,000,000. Money supply (April 1982) NT$314,556,000,000. Cost of living (1975 = 100; April 1982) 180.

Foreign Trade. (1981) Imports NT$778.6 billion; exports NT$829.8 billion. Import sources: Japan 28%; U.S. 22%; Kuwait 11%; Saudi Arabia 8%. Export destinations: U.S. 36%; Japan 11%; Hong Kong 8%. Main exports: machinery 22% (including telecommunications apparatus 10%); clothing 13%; textile yarns and fabrics 9%; food 7%; footwear 6%; toys and sports goods 6%. Tourism (1980): visitors 1,111,100; gross receipts U.S. $988 million.

Transport and Communications. Roads (1981) 17,522 km. Motor vehicles in use (1981): passenger 506,300; commercial 277,900. Railways (1981): 3,700 km; traffic 7,982,000,000 passenger-km, freight 2,527,000,000 net ton-km. Air traffic (1981): 7,271,000,000 passenger-km; freight 924.4 million net ton-km. Shipping (1981): merchant vessels 100 gross tons and over 498; gross tonnage 1,887,836. Telephones (Dec. 1981) 2,818,000. Radio licenses (Dec. 1976) 1,493,100. Television receivers (Dec. 1980) 3,993,000.

Agriculture. Production (in 000; metric tons; 1981): rice 2,375; sweet potatoes 834; cassava (1980) 185; sugar, raw value 728; citrus fruit 389; bananas 185; pineapples 181; tea 25; tobacco (1980) 20; pork c. 630; fish catch 912. Livestock (in 000; Dec. 1981): cattle 128; pigs 4,826; goats and sheep 177; chickens 43,899.

Industry. Production (in 000; metric tons; 1981): coal 2,466; crude oil (1980) c. 180; natural gas (cu m) 1,502,000; electricity (kw-hr; 1980) 42,013,000; cement 14,341; crude steel 1,601; sulfuric acid 818; plastics and resins 489; petroleum products (1980) 15,253; cotton yarn 156; man-made fibres 687; paper and board (1980) 1,470; radio receivers (units; 1980) 9,490; television receivers (units) 6,239.

Tanzania

Tanzania

An East African member of the Commonwealth, the republic of Tanzania consists of two parts: Tanganyika, on the Indian Ocean, bordered by Kenya, Uganda, Rwanda, Burundi, Zaire, Zambia, Malawi, and Mozambique; and Zanzibar, just off the coast, including Zanzibar Island, Pemba Island, and small islets. Total area of the united republic: 945,050 sq km (364,886 sq mi). Total pop. (1982 est.): 19,112,000, including 98.9% African and 0.7% Indo-Pakistani. Cap. and largest city:

TANZANIA

Education. (1980–81) Primary, pupils 3,359,966, teachers 81,153; secondary (1979–80), pupils 68,301, teachers 3,357; vocational (1979–80), pupils 1,097, teachers 126; teacher training (1979–80), pupils 9,567, teachers 685; higher (1977–78), students 2,534, teaching staff 553.

Finance. Monetary unit: Tanzanian shilling, with (Sept. 20, 1982) a free rate of TShs 9.42 to U.S. $1 (TShs 16.15 = £1 sterling). Gold and other reserves (April 1982) U.S. $15 million. Budget (1981–82 est.): revenue TShs 12,445,000,000; expenditure TShs 12,205,000,000 (excludes development expenditure of TShs 6,622,000,000). Gross national product (1980) TShs 40,315,000,000. Money supply (March 1981) TShs 13,226,000,000. Cost of living (1975 = 100; 4th quarter 1981) 270.

Foreign Trade. (1980) Imports TShs 10,211,000,000; exports TShs 4,776,000,000. Import sources: U.K. 17%; West Germany 10%; Japan 9%; Iraq 6%; The Netherlands 6%; U.S. 6%; Italy 5%. Export destinations: U.K. 18%; West Germany 13%; Indonesia 10%; Italy 5%; The Netherlands 5%. Main exports (1979): coffee 27%; cotton 11%; fruit and vegetables c. 9%; cloves 6%; diamonds 6%; sisal 6%.

Transport and Communications. Roads (1980) 45,631 km. Motor vehicles in use (1980): passenger c. 42,900; commercial (including buses) c. 52,100. Railways (1980) 3,550 km. Air traffic (1980): 284 million passenger-km; freight c. 2.4 million net ton-km. Telephones (Dec. 1978) 82,000. Radio receivers (Dec. 1979) 500,000. Television receivers (Dec. 1979) 6,000.

Agriculture. Production (in 000; metric tons; 1981): corn c. 750; millet c. 140; sorghum c. 220; rice c. 200; sweet potatoes c. 330; cassava c. 4,650; sugar, raw value c. 124; dry beans c. 150; mangoes c. 178; bananas c. 790; cashew nuts c. 72; coffee c. 68; tea c. 16; tobacco c. 21; cotton, lint c. 57; sisal c. 81; meat 189; fish catch (1980) 247; timber (cu m; 1980) 34,887. Livestock (in 000; 1981): sheep c. 3,586; goats c. 5,784; cattle 12,701; chickens c. 24,000.

Industry. Production (in 000; metric tons; 1980): cement c. 340; salt 17; diamonds (metric carats) 274; petroleum products (1979) c. 420; electricity (kw-hr) c. 710,000.

Dar es Salaam (pop., 1978 prelim., 757,300) in Tanganyika. Language: Kiswahili (official) and English. Religion (1980 est.): traditional beliefs 23%; Christian 44%; Muslim 33%. President in 1982, Julius Nyerere; prime minister, Cleopa David Msuya.

To mark the 20th anniversary of Tanzania's independence on Dec. 9, 1981, Pres. Julius Nyerere released 2,749 prisoners and commuted 48 death sentences. The released prisoners did not include persons charged with economic sabotage, and the government's campaign against those believed to have damaged the country's economy continued into 1982. In a Cabinet reorganization carried out on February 4, Minister of Agriculture Joseph Mungai was dismissed following accusations of nepotism and embezzlement. Another Cabinet minister to lose his post was Abel Mwanga, minister of state in the prime minister's office, who had lost his seat in Parliament in December 1981 when the High Court ruled that his 1980 election victory had been influenced by gifts of food to voters.

The prospect of the country's starting the year with a desperate food shortage because of severe drought in 1981 was averted when a number of nations volunteered assistance. Nevertheless, Tanzania's economic position continued to be grave, and President Nyerere announced on March 25 that in its next budget the government would be concentrating upon improving existing industries and services. No funds would be provided for new projects. Thanks to the cooperation and assistance of Bulgaria, however, it was possible to contemplate the establishment of a new factory in Mwanza to produce agricultural equipment.

The annual congress of the ruling Revolutionary Party (Chama Cha Mapinduzi, or CCM) in October put into effect some of the constitutional changes recommended by an extraordinary session in January. The proposals were aimed at increasing the power of the party and reducing the power of the state, which, in the president's view, had grown disproportionately. Thus the national chairman and vice-chairman of the CCM would no longer be elected by popular acclaim in the meeting of the whole conference in case this should inhibit anyone wishing to propose a rival candidate. Instead, the National Executive Committee of the party would nominate a candidate for each post and would then vote on the nominations by secret ballot before submitting the names of the successful candidates to the whole conference for approval.

In the 1982 election President Nyerere, chairman of the CCM for 20 years, and Vice-Pres. Aboud Jumbe, vice-chairman since 1972, were elected for additional terms of five years. The president took the opportunity offered by his reelection to reaffirm his commitment to a policy of socialism whatever the difficulties ahead.

At a meeting between President Nyerere and Zambian Pres. Kenneth Kaunda in Lusaka, Zambia, in March an agreement was signed establishing a joint commission of cooperation between their two countries. The presidents also agreed on measures to improve the operation of the Tanzam Railway, which had been working at only a fraction of its capacity because of frequent breakdowns and congestion in the port of Dar es Salaam. Relations with Kenya were further strained when, in October, Tanzania granted political asylum to two men believed to have led the attempted coup against the Kenyan government in August.

(KENNETH INGHAM)

Target Sports

Archery. At the 1982 National Sports Festival, held in Indianapolis, Ind., in July and August, Rick McKinney of Glendale, Ariz., won the men's gold medal with a new Festival record score of 2,586 points. Second place went to Darrell Pace of Hamilton, Ohio, with 2,557; Pace had won the

A British soldier lurks by a Tanzanian airliner that was hijacked while en route to Dar Es Salaam and flown to Britain. The hijackers, who were political opponents of Tanzanian president Julius Nyerere, eventually surrendered to antiterrorist police.

archery gold medal in the 1976 Olympic Games, the last Summer Games in which the U.S. competed. Ed Eliason of Seattle, Wash., took third place with a score of 2,523. In women's competition the winner, who also set a new Festival record with a score of 2,510, was Luann Ryon of Parker Dam, Calif.; Ryon had also won the gold medal in the 1976 Olympics. Ruth Rowe of Gaithersburg, Md., finished second at the Festival with 2,489, and Eileen Pylypchuk of Brooklyn, N.Y., was third with 2,436.

At the first Asian-Oceanian archery championships, held at Obihiro, Hokkaido, Japan, in July, three South Korean women broke the world record of 601 points in the 70-m doubles division, a mark that had stood since 1977. Kim Chin-ho won the event with a score of 629, while Park Young-suk finished second with 615 and Kim Mi-young was third with 610. The South Korean team triumphed in the tournament, in which competitors from ten nations participated. (DAVID R. CALHOUN) [452.B.4.h.i]

Shooting. More than 1,200 marksmen representing 54 nations participated in the 43rd world shooting championships at Caracas, Venezuela in 1982. Ten new world records were set there. Twenty-two nations competed at the 44th European championships held at Montecatini Terme, Italy. The 1982 U.S. Internationals took place at Phoenix, Ariz., while the U.S. rifle and pistol championships were held at Camp Perry, Ohio.

TRAP AND SKEET. At the world shooting championships the Italian men's trap team won the gold medal with a new world record score of 587 out of a possible 600. The silver medal was won by France with 582, while the Soviet Union took the bronze with 581. In women's competition the U.S. won the gold medal with a new world record of 396 of a possible 450. Spain took the silver medal with 395, and China gained the bronze with 389. Three individual scores of 197 of a possible 200 were posted in men's trap. The tie-breaking rules awarded Luciano Giovannetti of Italy the gold medal, Eladio Valduvi of Spain the silver, and Daniele Cioni of Italy the bronze. Cioni won the 1982 European trap championship with a 199.

In skeet the U.S. men's team won the world shooting championships gold medal with a 594. France took the silver medal with 587, while Italy won the bronze with 583. For the women China won the gold medal with a new world record score of 136. Svetlana Yakimova of the Soviet Union scored 194 to set a new world record for individual woman's skeet. Bruno Rossetti of France won the 1982 European skeet championship by bettering in the shoot-off two others who had also scored 197.

RIFLES. Two new world records were set at the world championships for mixed runs on the 50-m running game target. Nikolay Dedov of the U.S.S.R. set a new individual record of 392, while the Soviet team's record score was 1,556. The 300-m English Match world record was broken by Malcolm Cooper of the U.K. and by Viktor Danilchenko of the U.S.S.R. (who later won the gold) with 593-27X. The Soviet team's world record score for the 50-m small-bore free rifle standing event was 1,514. The East German women's air rifle team

UPI

set a new 10-m world record score of 1,160 of a possible 1,200. Sigrid Lang of West Germany won the individual gold medal for women's air rifle competition with a 389. The Norwegian team won the men's air rifle gold medal with 2,309 of a possible 2,400, while Frank Rettkowski of East Germany won the individual gold with 587.

Middleton Tompkins won the U.S. national high-power rifle championship with a score of 2,370-87X of a possible 2,400. Patrick McCann placed second with 2,370-86X, while Carl R. Bernosky finished third with 2,366-109X. A new national record for the President's Match was set by Kenneth Erdman, who won over 1,020 competitors with a 298-10X. Presley Kendall won the U.S. national small-bore prone championship with a score of 6,395-528X and the prone metallic sight championship with a 3,198-256X. Mary Stidworthy won the prone any-sight championship with a 3,198-295X. Lones Wigger, Jr., swept the three-position events, taking the small-bore metallic-sight championship with a 1,136, the small-bore any-sight championship with a 1,180, and the three-position national small-bore championship with a 2,316.

HANDGUNS. In the world championships the gold medal for standard pistol went to the Soviet Union with a score of 2,299 of a possible 2,400. Vladas Tourla of the U.S.S.R. won the individual gold medal for his score of 582, which equaled the world record. Tourla also won individual gold medals for his centre-fire pistol score of 592 and air-pistol score of 590. The U.S.S.R. team won the centre-fire event with a 2,356 and the air pistol competition with a 2,327. The women's air pistol championship went to the Soviet team, which scored 1,146, and Marlia Dobrantcheva of the U.S.S.R. took individual top honours with a 386. Ragnar Skanaker of Sweden scored 568 to win the individual gold medal in the 50-m free pistol event. The U.S.S.R. took the team gold medal with a score of 2,248 and also won the 25-m rapid-fire event with a 2,376.

The 1982 U.S. pistol championship was won by

A paraplegic archer, Neroli Fairhall of New Zealand, won the gold medal for archery in the Commonwealth Games at Brisbane, Australia, in October.

Bonnie Harmon, who scored 2,652-159X of a possible 2,700. Ricardo Rodriguez placed second with a 2,634-119X, while James Lenardson was third with a 2,634-115X.   (ROBERT N. SEARS)

[452.B.4.c]

Television and Radio

In some form television and radio service was available in all major countries in 1982. Approximately 850 million radio sets were in use, of which about 470 million, or 55%, were in the United States. Television sets numbered about 430 million, of which 171 million, or 40%, were in the U.S.

The Soviet Union ranked next to the U.S. in number of television sets; its total was about 65 million, and Japan was third with 28.8 million, according to estimates prepared for the 1982 *Broadcasting and Cable Yearbook*. Other *Broadcasting* estimates for television sets included West Germany, 21 million; United Kingdom, 18.3 million; France, 17.6 million; Brazil, 15 million; Italy, 13.2 million; Canada, 11.3 million; Spain, 9.4 million; Mexico, 7.5 million; Poland, 7.2 million; Australia, 5.5 million; East Germany, 5.2 million; Argentina, 5.1 million; and The Netherlands, 4 million.

Approximately 7,850 television stations were in operation or under construction throughout the world. Some 2,200 were in the Far East, 2,110 in Western Europe, 1,240 in the U.S., 920 in Eastern Europe, 180 in South America, 105 in Mexico, 100 in Canada, and 45 in Africa. There were about 16,400 radio stations, most of which were amplitude modulation (AM) stations, though the proportion of frequency modulation (FM) outlets was growing. In the U.S. there were 9,698 radio stations, of which 4,892 were FM.

Organization of Services. Broadcasting organizations throughout the world used communications satellites almost routinely to exchange coverage of important news events. Among the most widely distributed in 1982 were the U.S. elections, events surrounding the death of Soviet president Leonid Brezhnev, the war between Great Britain and Argentina over the Falkland Islands, the visit of Pope John Paul II to Spain, the fifth launch and landing of the U.S. space shuttle "Columbia," and such sports events as the baseball World Series and the Wimbledon tennis matches.

In the United States Pres. Ronald Reagan's policy of deregulation continued to free both broadcasters and cable television operators from some of the restrictions that had limited them. The Federal Communications Commission (FCC) formally opened a proceeding aimed at allowing TV networks to again own cable TV systems, a move it had signaled in 1981 when it granted CBS an exception to its network/cable cross-ownership ban. In another, more controversial, proceeding the FCC was considering whether to repeal its prohibition against the ownership by networks of financial interests in programs produced by others and against their engaging in domestic syndication of any programs. This proposal, much favoured by the networks, was strongly opposed by independent program producers and syndicators on the grounds that, if it were adopted, networks would soon dominate the market.

Along with deregulation there was during the year official authorization of several new services, including FCC grants for low-power television stations capable of serving relatively small communities; for direct broadcast satellite distribution of TV programming, which had the potential of rendering local television stations obsolete except for purely local news and programming; and for experiments in teletext, which offered a virtually limitless variety of information on home screens. In radio the FCC authorized the start of AM stereo broadcasting on a free-market basis, allowing stations—and listeners—to decide which of several FCC-approved systems they preferred.

The U.S. Corporation for Public Broadcasting (CPB), dependent on both federal and private financing, found itself in difficulties under the administration's reductions in federal spending. CPB officials told a congressional hearing in February that cuts contemplated for fiscal year 1984 should be restored and that reductions planned for 1985 could threaten public television's existence, requiring curtailment of program production, hampering stations' ability to attract funds from private sources, and forcing some stations to close. Over a presidential veto Congress restored the 1984 budget to $130 million from the $105.6 million recommended by the administration, but it deferred action on 1985.

The Public Broadcasting Service (PBS), the CPB's programming arm, adopted a reorganization plan to consolidate services and reduce costs and also intensified its efforts to find alternative revenues. These included an experiment, under way at several PBS stations in 1982, in carrying commercial advertising.

In the U.K. 1982 began with major changes to the Independent Television (ITV) network and ended with the start of Channel 4, a new national network. The changes in ITV followed the allocation of new regional contracts by the Independent Broadcasting Authority (IBA). The old ATV (Midlands) was reorganized to form Central TV; Television South (TVS) replaced Southern TV; and Television South West (TSW) replaced Westward. The changes went smoothly except in the Midlands, where the transition from ATV to Central, involving complicated financial and managerial changes, was not completed until well after extended deadlines.

Channel 4, the first new national television network in 18 years, began on November 2, making Britain the only country in the world to have a fourth terrestrial broadcasting network (excepting the U.S. satellite networks). The channel operated as a subsidiary of the IBA, in contrast to the ITV companies also regulated by the IBA, which were given a franchise for a fixed term. Its purpose was to provide a "distinctive" service, with the aim of achieving 10% of the audience (although only 6% was achieved in the first week). Exceptional among European television channels in buying the bulk of its programs from outside producers, it was financed by "subscriptions" paid by the ITV

Tariffs:
see Economy, World

Taxation:
see Economy, World

Telecommunications:
see Industrial Review

companies to the IBA (totaling £120 million in the first year); in return, the companies had the exclusive right to sell advertising.

In France the Socialist government completed its promised reform of the broadcasting system. A draft bill passed by the National Assembly in May incorporated most of the recommendations of the previous year's Moinot report. The seven separate organizations set up by Pres. Valéry Giscard d'Estaing in 1974 remained basically unchanged, but in the future they would operate more independently of the government. The Socialists' objective was a public service rather similar to the British Broadcasting Corporation (BBC). The chief innovation was the establishment of an independent "high authority" to regulate the system and to act as a "buffer" between the government and the operating companies.

Private television in Spain came much closer to existence when the Constitutional Court, responding to an appeal lodged by Antena 3, decided that the constitution, in protecting the right to express and publish, should be understood to support (or, at least, not to forbid) a multiplicity of radio and TV stations. The court said in fact that the question of the television monopoly was not really a constitutional issue but a political matter. The government responded by preparing legislation laying down the principles involved and providing a detailed set of regulations. In Norway the Conservative government elected in 1981 decided to instigate far-reaching reforms of TV and radio broadcasting. Its main priority was the abolition of the monopoly of Norsk Rikskringkasting (NRK), the public broadcasting organization, and the licensing of private companies to provide competitive television services.

On March 4 the British government announced a "modest but early" start of a British direct broadcasting satellite (DBS) system, which would be powerful enough for its signals to be receivable on small household antennae. Both DBS channels were allocated to the BBC, which planned to provide a subscription service of feature films and special programs and a "free" service, called "Window on the World," consisting of new and repeat programs from the U.K. and other countries. Meanwhile, France and West Germany continued with their projects to develop similar national DBS systems.

The possibilities of multichannel cable TV caught the imagination of many governments and media organizations. In the U.K. two government reports (*Cable Systems*, by the Information Technology Advisory Panel, and a report by a committee on "cable expansion and broadcasting policy," chaired by Lord Hunt) recommended that the government give the go-ahead for the rapid expansion of cable TV. The Hunt inquiry recommended a permissive regime in which cablecasters would be licensed by a new supervisory authority but would be free of the constraints of balance and impartiality that governed the broadcasters.

In West Germany, after many postponements, the federal authorities and the states finally agreed to implement four pilot projects of cable TV, in Ludwigshafen, Dortmund, Munich, and Berlin. Each project involved a multichannel, interactive

Comedian Bob Newhart returned to television in the show "Newhart," playing the owner of an ancient inn in Vermont.

system that supplied both television channels and text and data services. The first service, at Ludwigshafen, was scheduled to start on Jan. 1, 1984. Both the West German and French governments announced plans for massive programs of construction of multichannel cable systems.

In Australia the government gave its approval for a national satellite system, to be launched in 1985. A new organization, Aussat, 49% owned by the public, would take over the system's operation when legislation was passed. The services to be distributed by satellite remained undecided. The Australian Broadcasting Tribunal recommended that the government begin subscription TV services both by cable and by broadcasting as soon as possible.

Programming. For the first time in three years the opening of the new prime-time season in the U.S. was not delayed by a strike of actors or writers. The season opened "officially" the week of September 27, although for tactical reasons the networks introduced a few series intermittently before that date and held a few others until later. To make room for the new entries some 18 shows were dropped, including such hits of earlier seasons as "Mork & Mindy," "Barney Miller," and "Taxi" on ABC; "Lou Grant" and "WKRP in Cincinnati" on CBS; and "Harper Valley PTA" on NBC.

For the most part, the shows that were dropped were abandoned by the networks as a result of falling audience ratings. The new shows replacing them continued, as a group, to reflect a diminishing emphasis on sex and a somewhat more cautious approach to violence. The law-and-order theme evident in 1981–82 lost some of its foremost vehicles with the cancellation of "Today's FBI," "Code Red," and "Strike Force," but adventure shows, often containing violent action, remained numerous.

CBS, first in the prime-time ratings again in the 1981–82 season, prepared a new schedule aimed especially at young adults. Its new series included four half-hour situation comedies and three one-hour dramas. Among the comedies were "Square Pegs," about two high-school girls; "Newhart," starring Bob Newhart as the owner of a Vermont inn; and "Gloria," a spin-off from the original "All in the Family" hit series. The new dramas were "Bring 'em Back Alive," based on the exploits of Frank Buck, the big-game hunter; "Seven Brides for Seven Brothers," based loosely on an earlier hit movie of the same name; and "Tucker's Witch," about a private detective whose wife and partner possesses psychic powers.

ABC, second in the 1981–82 prime-time ratings, brought in three new half-hour comedies and four new one-hour shows. The comedies were "Star of the Family," about a fireman whose daughter is a pop singer; "For Better or Worse," about the conflicting goals of a couple in which the husband is a physician and the wife an attorney; and "The New Odd Couple," a black-cast version of the former hit. ABC's new one-hour entries were "Tales of the Brass Monkey," an adventure set in the South Pacific; "The Quest," a madcap adventure set in a mythical Mediterranean kingdom; "Matt Houston," a detective story; and a drama based on "Ripley's Believe It or Not."

NBC offered 11 new series. These included the comedies "Family Ties," about liberal parents bringing up conservative children; "Cheers," set in a Boston bar; and "Silver Spoons," about a young boy adapting to a rich father. The dramas were "Gavilan," the adventures of a former CIA agent; "St. Elsewhere," set in a hospital; "The Devlin Connection," an adventure story with Rock Hudson as star; "Knight Rider," about a former policeman and an "indestructible" car; "Remington Steele," about a female detective; and "Voyagers," a time-travel adventure drama.

The early weeks of the new season produced a somewhat mystifying decline in network prime-time audience ratings. Together, the three networks normally achieved a national Nielsen rating of about 54 at that time of year (each rating point representing 1% of all U.S. TV homes, which in late 1982 numbered about 83.3 million). In October and November 1982, however, their combined ratings were ranging between 49 and 52 each week, and their combined shares of audience—the percentage of sets actually in use that were tuned to one of the networks—had slipped from about 86 to 82. Researchers were unable to agree on where the missing viewers—from 1.5 million to as many

NBC offered a number of new series in the fall season, among them "Cheers," which featured Ted Danson and Shelley Long.

NBC PHOTO

as 4 million in some weeks—had gone. There were strong suspicions that many had switched to independent stations, cable TV, or public television.

Program executives at the networks were concerned about the ratings trends but were nevertheless slower than usual to make major changes in their schedules. In part, this was attributable to the state of the national economy, since canceling series already in production could cost millions of dollars. The executives also speculated that perhaps in past years they had been too quick to cancel low-rated programs; some series, they noted, had become big hits only after enduring months of low ratings—"All in the Family," which in a different format was still a hit as "Archie Bunker's Place," was one of the earliest and most notable examples, and "Hill Street Blues," initially low rated but retained because of the critical acclaim it received, was one of the most recent.

There was nothing to indicate that the old program-mortality rule—that two out of three new series fail to survive into a second season—would not prove true again, but in the opening months the programmers did more tinkering than canceling. CBS withdrew "Alice," "Filthy Rich," and "Tucker's Witch," replacing them with a weekly movie, but said that the programs would return to the schedule, probably in midseason. Similarly, ABC announced that it would put "The Greatest American Hero" and "The Quest" on the shelf for an indefinite period and fill their time period with a movie, effective December 3. At both networks the shows replaced had been running near the bottom of the ratings.

For the period from September 27 through November 21 only three of the season's new series were in the top 20: "Newhart" was tied (with "Three's Company") for 6th place; "9 to 5," a comedy that had been given a test run before the season opened, was 9th; and "Gloria" was 17th. The top of the list was dominated by established programs, led by the "60 Minutes" newsmagazine, the comedy "M*A*S*H," and the nighttime soap opera "Dallas."

News was in the forefront of television programming in 1982. Unable to convince their affiliated stations that the early-evening network newscasts should be expanded from the current half hour to an hour, ABC, CBS, and NBC expanded the number of newscasts they offered. ABC, which had introduced a late-night half-hour newscast during the hostage crisis in Iran, added a one-hour weeknight report and also launched a new early-morning half-hour newscast. CBS added an early-morning half hour of news and also a four-hour report running from 2 AM to 6 AM (Eastern time). NBC added both a late-night hour and an early-morning half hour to its news schedule.

One of the most successful syndicated (non-network) original productions was "A Woman Called Golda," based on the life of the late Israeli Prime Minister Golda Meir and starring Ingrid Bergman (see OBITUARIES). Presented in two two-hour installments by Operation Prime Time, a consortium of independent stations and network affiliates, it was almost invariably the highest rated in its time period in major U.S. cities. "P.M. Magazine," a news and features program, was among the leading weekly series in syndication.

Networks and stations continued to tone down

In October CBS initiated a four-hour news show, "Nightwatch," running from 2 to 6 AM. The show was anchored by Harold Dow, Christopher Glenn, Felicia Jeter, and Karen Stone.

programming for children, reducing elements of violence and of racial and sexual stereotypes and increasing the informational and pro-social content of their Saturday- and Sunday-morning schedules. Game shows and soap operas continued to dominate weekday programming.

In the 34th annual Emmy awards the Academy of Television Arts and Sciences named "A Woman Called Golda" as the year's outstanding drama special. Ingrid Bergman, who starred in it, was named outstanding lead actress in a limited series or special. "Hill Street Blues," a police drama whose audience ratings were beginning to live up to its critical acclaim, was chosen as the outstanding drama series for the second straight year, and "Barney Miller" was voted the outstanding comedy series. "Night of 100 Stars," a one-night extravaganza that featured more than 100 television, motion-picture, and Broadway stars, was named the outstanding variety, music, or comedy program, and "Marco Polo," a ten-hour, $25 million production shown on four nights in May, was chosen the outstanding limited series.

Emmys for lead actor and actress in a dramatic series went to Daniel J. Travanti of "Hill Street Blues" and Michael Learned of "Nurse," and for lead actor and actress in a comedy series to Alan Alda of "M*A*S*H" and Carol Kane of "Taxi." Mickey Rooney, for his work in "Bill," was voted outstanding lead actor in a limited series or special. Supporting actor and actress Emmys were presented to Michael Conrad of "Hill Street Blues" and

Nancy Marchand of "Lou Grant" in the drama category; Lawrence Olivier of "Brideshead Revisited" and Penny Fuller of "The Elephant Man" for limited series or specials; and Christopher Lloyd of "Taxi" and Loretta Swit of "M*A*S*H" for comedy, variety, or music series.

Sports continued to be one of the most popular—and most expensive—forms of programming, with professional and college football and major league baseball the most consistent drawing cards. The popularity of professional football was demonstrated, to the dismay of the networks, during the eight-week early-season strike by National Football League players. The networks substituted other sports on Sunday afternoons and movies on Monday nights, but the audience ratings plunged, in some cases to less than half of what they were when NFL games were shown. The appeal of sports was also reflected in ratings for the 1982 NFL Super Bowl football game; it was seen in 49.1% of all U.S. television homes, commanded a 73% share of audience, and became the highest rated live television program of all time.

With audiences so large, the cost of broadcast rights to major sports continued to rise. *Broadcasting* estimated that television and radio networks and stations paid $493,737,000 for broadcast rights to professional and college football games, an increase of 135% from the 1981 total, and $118,350,000 for major league baseball games, an increase of about 32%. The football total included an estimated $414 million for NFL games, a figure

"Marco Polo," a ten-hour, $25-million production, won an Emmy award for an outstanding limited series. The production was aired in May.

NBC PHOTO

that was later scaled down to take the eight game-less weeks into account. The totals did not, however, include such expenditures as $88 million paid by CBS for college basketball, almost $19 million spent by cable networks for U.S. college and Canadian professional football, about $15 million spent by cable TV and close to $20 million by ABC for games to be played in the spring of 1983 by the new U.S. Football League, or network and station commitments for a variety of other sports including tennis, golf, boxing, ice hockey, and soccer.

Music and news remained the basic format in radio, and station specializations varied widely, from all-news to all-concert music. Broadcasting's annual analysis of the ten highest rated stations in each of the top 50 U.S. markets found that 36% of the stations specialized in contemporary, or currently popular, music, up from 30.9% the year before; 14% featured album-oriented rock music; 12%, "beautiful music"; 11%, country and western music; and 8%, so-called middle-of-the-road music. About 12% offered all-news or news-and-talk formats. Other research indicated that FM stations' share of the listening audience exceeded that of AM stations by a ratio of about 3 to 2.

Public television's audiences continued to grow, though its producers, faced with budget cutbacks, had to watch their dollars more closely. In January a special ratings study showed that the Public Broadcasting Service's audiences—which in 1981 reached an average of some 75 million persons a week—had increased 17% in prime time, compared with the previous January, while its full-day audiences had grown by 9.6%. PBS's presentation of "The Sharks," also in January, was hailed as "the all-time most-watched public television program," and its "Life on Earth" as the highest rated weekly series in PBS history.

The 1982 association football (soccer) World Cup championship was the most important international broadcasting event of the year. More than 1,000,000,000 people watched the finals, which began in Barcelona, Spain, on June 13, through live or recorded broadcasts. The achievement of Spanish Television in providing coverage and facilities for foreign broadcasters was impressive.

Spanish Television also developed an improved drama output. "Los Gozos y las Sombras" ("Joys and Shadows") was notable; a four-part series called "La Plaza del Diamante" ("Diamond Square"), set in Barcelona during and after the Civil War, might not have been made so well, or at all, in the earlier post-Franco era.

Among European countries generally, British television maintained its preeminence for high production values, and among British programs the dramas were best once again. No production achieved quite the status that "Brideshead Revisited" had in 1981, but there was an abundance of excellent programs. The BBC showed "Barchester Chronicles," adaptations of Victorian novels of Anthony Trollope, among its period costume pieces. "Smiley's People" also appeared on the BBC as a sequel to "Tinker, Tailor, Soldier, Spy," drawn from John le Carré's thrillers, and gave an all-too-rare display of the considerable acting skills of Alec Guinness. The best comedy series on BBC

was "Yes Minister" (which had enjoyed a previous incarnation on radio); this political comedy about civil servants and government was at once intellectual, incisive, and funny.

Britain's nearest neighbour, Ireland, produced a small number of excellent programs in 1982. "The Year of the French," a six-part period drama, gave an account of a forgotten period of Anglo-French hostilities on Irish soil. To coincide with the centenary of the birth of James Joyce, Irish Television produced "Is There Anyone Who Understands Me?," a careful and affectionate documentary about his life.

French television remained in the doldrums in 1982 as a result of the considerable uncertainty about the restructuring of French broadcasting. Consequently, nearly all programs needing lengthy forward planning and substantial budgets were left on the shelf.

In West Germany documentary production was the strongest program form. West German documentary makers created much well-researched, incisive, and topical work, and their colleagues in drama departments were beginning to break new ground. One of the interesting new dramas was (in translation) "Six Feet in the Country," set in South Africa, from Bayerischer Rundfunk. A prominent independent production company, Taurus Film, based in Munich, became active in lavish drama production with such offerings as "Confessions of Felix Krull," based on the novel by Thomas Mann, and "Blood and Honour," a portrayal of the Nazi youth movement in the 1930s.

Of the Eastern European countries, Czechoslovakia, Hungary, and Yugoslavia maintained the most impressive production record. Czechoslovakia's "Hospital at the Edge of the City" and "The Golden Eels," two widely differing dramas, were among the most remarkable.

(PAUL A. BARRETT; RUFUS W. CRATER; JOHN HOWKINS; LAWRENCE B. TAISHOFF)

Amateur Radio. The number of amateur, or "ham," radio operators continued to grow in 1982. The American Radio Relay League, the leading organization of ham operators, estimated that there were 410,000 licensed operators in the U.S. at the end of 1982, compared with 403,680 15 months earlier. The number of licensed amateur radio operators throughout the world was estimated at about 1.3 million, with Japan's 530,000 forming the largest national concentration.

Ham operators often provided vital services when normal communications were interrupted. Members of a local Amateur Radio Emergency Service unit, for example, followed the path of a disastrous hurricane in Texas in April, summoning aid to the stricken communities and providing their only links with the outside world until their regular services could be restored. Similarly, amateur radio operators provided emergency communications among rescue units, hospitals, and officials when an airliner struck a bridge and fell into the Potomac River in Washington, D.C., in January.

(RUFUS W. CRATER; LAWRENCE B. TAISHOFF)

See also Industrial Review: Advertising; Telecommunications; Motion Pictures; Music.
[613.D.4.b; 735.I.4-5]

REVOLUTION IN THE SOAPS

by Robert Feder

On a Friday night in November 1980, an estimated 89.9 million people in the United States gathered in front of television sets to watch the climactic "Who Shot J.R.?" episode of the top-rated CBS prime-time soap opera "Dallas." Besides registering the highest Nielsen audience rating ever achieved for a TV series, that program represented a turning point in television history. After 30 years as the most durable and most maligned staple on TV, the soap opera finally had come of age.

Now in full cry, the soap opera revolution has taken television—and mass culture—by storm. Twelve daytime serials air five days a week on the three commercial networks; four soaps air weekly during the evening hours; and several more have been created specifically for the burgeoning cable and pay-television markets. Major motion picture stars who used to regard the soap operas with disdain now make cameo appearances on them with increasing frequency.

A multimillion-dollar industry has sprung up to merchandise soap-related paraphernalia and exploit the public's fascination with the phenomenon. And, largely based on the success of their nighttime off-spring, the daytime soap operas are attracting more men and more young viewers among their 30 million daily devotees than ever before. In short, Americans' attitudes toward the soaps have changed dramatically in the 1980s, prompting more serious attention from the press, greater consideration by scholars and academics as a legitimate social force, and staggering financial returns to the networks and companies that produce them.

Radio to Television. Soap operas made the transition smoothly from radio to television in the 1950s. So named because the first radio serials were sponsored largely by soap companies, they changed little through the 1970s. Housewives comprised the bulk of the audience, and the soaps spoke to them mainly about matters that the networks and sponsors believed would appeal to them most: old-fashioned

morality, small-town family virtues, and contrived romantic entanglements. By and large, the dialogue was unrealistic; the acting and technical quality were uninspired; and the story lines were conceived so as to advance almost imperceptibly from day to day, save for the obligatory cliff-hanger at the end of each episode.

Although some shows tried to break from the hopelessly corny mold of their radio ancestors, few people bothered to notice the exceptions. Agnes Nixon, the most gifted and prolific creator and writer of soap operas (and a housewife herself), summed up the prevailing belief that "soap opera is a Never-Never Land where hack writers and inferior producers, directors, and actors serve melodramatic pap to a lunatic fringe of female children who grow older but never grow up."

True or not, that unfortunate stereotype persisted for decades, and eventually the term soap opera itself became, in Nixon's words, "the classic cliché of derogation." Anyone who had anything to do with soaps, including the millions who watched them faithfully each day, was looked upon with shame or pity by society, the media, and even the networks that profited from them.

New Viewers, New Respectability. Several factors have combined in recent years to change that perception dramatically, most notably the emergence and popularity of evening soap operas, including "Dallas," "Dynasty," "Falcon Crest," and "Knots Landing." Thanks to their acceptance, viewers could follow the week-to-week tribulations of the characters in these high-budget, lavishly produced programs (and discuss them in public) without feeling guilty or fearing the stigma attached to fanatics of the drearier daytime dramas. And, as a result of these converts' becoming "hooked" on nighttime serials, the whole soap opera genre suddenly gained new respectability.

A few years earlier another trend had begun to sweep the daytime soaps, fueled by the fact that more and more housewives—the shows' traditional audience—were getting jobs and leaving the home during the day. In an effort to expand their audiences, programmers at ABC deliberately decided to tap into the youth market by centring much of their action on younger characters, thereby attacting more young women and drawing in high-school and college viewers for the first time. Once the mainstay of the soaps, stories about older, long-established characters were shunted aside to make room for sexier, faster-paced plots about younger people. The strategy worked for ABC, and soon shows on all three networks were courting youth with a vengeance.

The fierce competition for ratings reflected the

Robert Feder is a television reporter for the Chicago Sun-Times.

With top-rated daytime soap operas generating nearly $150 million a year in net profits, networks began spending more money to increase ratings. This scene from NBC's "Search for Tomorrow," showing Rod Arrants and Sherry Mathis, was filmed on a remote Caribbean island.

networks' realization that soap operas make money. While the cost of producing one episode of a weekly one-hour series on prime-time television often exceeds $600,000, daytime soaps cost far less than that for a full week of five hour-long installments. Altogether, in 1981 daytime television accounted for $1.4 billion of the three networks' $5.6 billion in advertising revenue; a few top-rated soap operas each generated as much as $150 million per year in net profits. With stakes that high, the networks frequently resorted to various new devices to improve their ratings, including the use of celebrities for brief appearances and the export of cast and crew to exotic places around the world for taping on location.

New Story Lines. Although none of the soap operas strays far from its mandate to provide entertainment and try to draw the largest share of viewers, several have been noted for their efforts at educating and enlightening their audiences as well. Because they air 260 original episodes a year with no reruns, the daytime soaps have the opportunity to infuse their story lines with thinly disguised messages of public service and social conscience.

Over the years the best of the soaps have explored everything from drug abuse and wife beating to the war in Vietnam and unemployment. Viewers see these issues from various characters' standpoints, and in this way some may come to understand the problems and how to deal with them. For this reason, psychologists and other professionals have begun to pay increased attention to the soap operas as therapeutic devices and as mirrors of society. One university dean observed: "With their realistic characters, daytime serials provide a more accurate representation of the real world than prime-time shows. Prime time is a world of action, power and danger. Daytime is a world of interior turbulence that hits much closer to home."

On ABC's "All My Children," creator and head writer Agnes Nixon, who pioneered the injection of serious social issues on soap operas, conceived two story lines about rape that ran concurrently in 1982. One concerned the effect of rape on the families of both the victim and the rapist, while the other explored the consequences of a situation in which a young white woman falsely accuses a young black man of raping her.

Just before NBC announced the cancellation of "The Doctors" in late 1982, the show launched a major story line involving the dangers of cigarette smoking. Viewers who followed the plight of a physician who tried to kick the habit were invited to send for a free brochure prepared by NBC and the American Cancer Society on how to stop smoking. More than 100,000 of the pamphlets were distributed as a result.

Spin-offs. The television networks are not alone in profiting from the viewers' increased appetite for soap operas. A sizable industry has been spawned to capitalize on the popularity of the genre. Soaps now can be seen on cable and pay-TV systems across the country, and since they are not bound by rigid network censorship, they tend to be more sexually explicit and enjoy greater freedom to employ graphic language. Other new shows to cash in on the soap craze include several nonnetwork programs devoted to following developments on the soaps and the private lives of the shows' stars.

Soap-opera fan magazines, once relegated to lowly places on supermarket checkout racks, have become more critical and incisive while attracting significantly wealthier and better educated readers. They also are making more money than ever before, with the three largest periodicals in the field boasting a combined monthly circulation of almost two million. Add to that the money made by promoters of soap opera "festivals" held throughout the year; the merchandisers of various books, games, calendars, clothing, mugs, tote bags, and other soap-inspired items; and the syndicators of "Dallas" throughout the world, and the total value of the new soap craze is beyond estimate.

But the soap opera revolution relies most, not on audience ratings or money, but on the insatiable curiosity of the public to find out what will happen next to their favourite characters. For that, the only answer is: Tune in tomorrow.

Tennis

The organization of the leading events in men's tennis lost its cohesion in 1982. World Championship Tennis (WCT), controlled by Lamar Hunt of Dallas, Texas, withdrew from the Grand Prix series and revived its independent circuit with a sequence of 22 tournaments in the U.S. and Europe. The Grand Prix series, controlled by the Men's International Tennis Professional Council (MITPC), comprised 85 tournaments played on five continents.

The relationship between the Women's Tennis Association and the Women's Professional Council functioned more smoothly. The women's game was organized in two distinct circuits, the Avon Series played early in the year in the U.S. and a wider ranging International Series under the sponsorship of Toyota. For 1983 one circuit, comprising fewer tournaments in all, was arranged under a revised sponsorship by Virginia Slims cigarettes.

There was controversy early in the year about the decision of Björn Borg (Sweden) not to fulfill the requirements of the Grand Prix rules by undertaking to compete in at least ten tournaments. It meant automatic relegation to the qualifying rounds of all Grand Prix events. Borg did in fact

Jimmy Connors of the U.S. defeated fellow American John McEnroe to win the men's final at Wimbledon in July. It took Connors five sets to achieve the victory.

UPI

challenge in the Monte Carlo tournament in April after qualifying, but without notable success. He competed in no major event during 1982.

Men's Competition. The Australian championship, the last event of the 1981 Grand Prix, was won in Melbourne by Johan Kriek (South Africa). The Volvo Masters' Tournament, the climax event of the series, was again staged in Madison Square Garden, New York City, in January 1982. It was won by Ivan Lendl (born Ostrava, Czech., March 7, 1960), who dominated the early part of the season. Lendl, named as world junior champion for 1978 by the International Tennis Federation, beat John McEnroe (U.S.) in the Masters' semifinal 6–4, 6–2. In the final he beat Vitas Gerulaitis (U.S.) 6–7, 2–6, 7–6, 6–2, 6–4, saving a match point in the tie breaker of the third set. Lendl also won the most important of the WCT tournaments, the Dallas Finals in April. In the final of that tournament he beat McEnroe 6–2, 3–6, 6–3, 6–3.

The Italian championship was won in Rome by Andres Gomez (Ecuador). He beat Eliot Teltscher (U.S.) 6–2, 6–3, 6–2 in the final. Gomez's success reflected the rising standard of the game in many South American countries. The French championship had a precocious singles winner, Mats Wilander (born Aug. 22, 1964, in Växjö, Sweden), victor in the junior event the year before. Wilander, unseeded, beat Lendl 4–6, 7–5, 3–6, 6–4, 6–2 in the fourth round; subsequently he beat three more seeded players, Gerulaitis, José-Luis Clerc (Arg.), and, in the final, Guillermo Vilas (Arg.) by 1–6, 7–6, 6–0, 6–4. Wilander's age when he won was 17 years 288 days, making him the youngest man ever to win a major singles title. Double-fisted on the backhand and with top spin from both sides, he inspired comparisons with his compatriot Borg, who was just over 18 when he first won the same title in 1974. Jimmy Connors (U.S.) was top-seeded for the French title but lost in the quarterfinals to José Higueras (Spain), who subsequently lost to Vilas.

The Wimbledon championships, extended for the first time to 13 playing days, suffered from wet weather, with only one day free from rain. McEnroe, seeded first, was successful in defense of his 1981 title only as far as the final. Connors, seeded second, also reached the last match without danger. In the final Connors rose to the occasion and won 3–6, 6–3, 6–7, 7–6, 6–4 after a contest more notable for its tension than for the quality of play. It was the fifth final and second championship for Connors in nine years, his first victory occurring in 1974.

Connors established himself as the outstanding player of the year when he won the U.S. Open championship at Flushing Meadow in New York City. Lendl beat Wilander 6–2, 6–2, 6–2 in the fourth round and in the semifinal defeated McEnroe, the defending champion, 6–4, 6–4, 7–6. Connors won a semifinal against Vilas 6–1, 3–6, 6–2, 6–3 and then triumphed in the final against Lendl 6–3, 6–2, 4–6, 6–4. It was the fourth U.S. singles championship for Connors since 1974.

In men's doubles Peter Fleming and McEnroe won the Master's title in New York City. The runners-up there, Kevin Curren (South Africa) and

Steve Denton (U.S.), took the U.S. Open title later in the year. Peter McNamara and Paul McNamee (both Australia) won the Wimbledon title, where the bad weather caused a reduction to the best of three sets for the first time. The World Team Cup, formerly the Nations Cup, was again staged in Düsseldorf, West Germany, on clay courts in May. The U.S. (Gene Mayer, Teltscher, and Sherwood Stewart) beat Australia (Kim Warwick, McNamara, and Mark Edmondson) 2–1 in the final.

The Davis Cup was played for the second year under commercial sponsorship and its format of a 16-nation nonzonal championship group above four zonal sections. Ireland, Denmark, Paraguay, and Indonesia were zone winners and qualified for the main competition of 1983. Mexico, India, Spain, and West Germany dropped out of the championship group for 1983 when they lost in both the first round and play-off matches. The U.S. beat India 4–1, Sweden 3–2, and Australia 5–0 to reach the final. The contest with Sweden, held in St. Louis, Mo., was narrowly won in the fifth match when McEnroe beat Wilander 9–7, 6–2, 15–17, 3–6, 8–6 after 6 hours 32 minutes. France beat Argentina 3–2, Czechoslovakia 3–1 (one match unplayed), and New Zealand 3–2 to reach the final. Yannick Noah, a black player from Cameroon, was France's successful number one competitor in that nation's most distinguished progress since its tenure as champion from 1927 to 1932.

The final round, U.S. versus France in Grenoble, was the first between those nations since France won 3–2 in the old challenge round in Paris in 1932. Led by McEnroe, who won two singles matches and teamed with Fleming to win the doubles, the U.S. triumphed 4–1 and thus won the cup for the 28th time. McEnroe defeated Noah 12–10, 1–6, 3–6, 6–3, 6–2 and Henri Leconte 6–2, 6–3 and then, with Fleming, beat Noah and Leconte 6–3, 6–4, 9–7. Gene Mayer triumphed over Leconte 6–2, 6–2, 7–9, 6–4, and Noah gained France's only victory by defeating Mayer 6–1, 6–0.

Women's Competition. The Australian championship, staged in Melbourne in December 1981, was won by Martina Navratilova (U.S.). From a strong field she won the final against Chris Evert Lloyd (U.S.) 6–7, 6–4, 7–5. Later in the month the Toyota championships, the climax tournament of the International Series, was held at the Meadowlands Arena in New Jersey. Tracy Austin (U.S.) beat Evert Lloyd 6–1, 6–2 in the semifinal and Navratilova 2–6, 6–4, 6–2 in the final. On the Avon circuit Navratilova won 5 of the 11 tournaments. In the Avon championship, the climax event at Madison Square Garden in March, Sylvia Hanika (West Germany) surprisingly beat Navratilova 1–6, 6–3, 6–4 in the final.

Evert Lloyd won the Italian championship, played in Perugia, beating Hana Mandlikova (Czech.) 6–0, 6–3 in the final. In Paris Navratilova won the French championship for the first time. Andrea Jaeger (U.S.) beat Evert Lloyd 6–3, 6–1 in the semifinals. Mandlikova, the defending champion, beat Austin 7–6, 6–7, 6–2 in the quarterfinals, but Navratilova defeated her 6–0, 6–2 in the other semifinal. In the final Navratilova triumphed over Jaeger 7–6, 6–1.

The Wimbledon championship brought notable success to Billie Jean King (U.S.), 38 and competing there for the 21st time since 1961. She defeated Austin 3–6, 6–4, 6–2 in the quarterfinals to record her 90th singles victory at the tournament, an unequaled number. Evert Lloyd then beat King 7–6, 2–6, 6–3 in the semifinals. This was King's 104th Wimbledon singles match, and her overall Wimbledon tally was a unique 252 matches played, 214 won. Navratilova reached the final without losing a set and beat Evert Lloyd 6–1, 3–6, 6–2. It was the loser's fifth final in as many years.

Navratilova's victory gave her three legs on the "Grand Slam," holding the Australian, French, Wimbledon, and U.S. titles at the same time, achieved by only two women, Maureen Connolly (U.S.) in 1953 and Margaret Court (Australia) in 1970. However, Navratilova was disappointed in the U.S. championship at Flushing Meadow. Pam Shriver (U.S.), her doubles partner, beat her 1–6, 7–6, 6–2 in the quarterfinals. Also in a quarterfinal match Mandlikova defeated the defending champion, Austin, 4–6, 6–4, 6–4, and then reached the final by beating Shriver 6–4, 2–6, 6–2. Evert Lloyd, competing for the 12th time, beat Jaeger 6–1, 6–2 in the other semifinal and in the final defeated Mandlikova 6–3, 6–1 to win the championship for the sixth time.

Martina Navratilova won the women's title at Wimbledon by defeating former champion Chris Evert Lloyd.

In women's doubles Navratilova rivaled her singles achievements. With Shriver she won both the Toyota and Avon championships. She paired with Anne Smith (U.S.) to win the French title and with Shriver again to triumph at Wimbledon. The U.S. title went to Rosemary Casals (U.S.) and Wendy Turnbull (Australia). The Federation Cup tournament was staged in July at Santa Clara, Calif., and won by the U.S. (Evert Lloyd, Navratilova, and Andrea Leand) for the seventh consecutive year and the 11th time in all. During the competition the U.S. lost no match and only two sets. Navratilova played number one for the U.S. She had also been number one for Czechoslovakia when that country won the trophy in 1975. Navratilova's status as the outstanding player of 1982 was clear-cut.

The Wightman Cup was won for the 44th time by the U.S. (Evert Lloyd, Barbara Potter, Anne Smith, Casals, and Sharon Walsh). At the Royal Albert Hall, London, they beat Great Britain (Sue Barker, Jo Durie, Virginia Wade, and Anne Hobbs) by six matches to one. For the British, Wade, though without success, played for the 18th successive year and extended her total of matches to a record 52. On the U.S. side Evert Lloyd increased her total to 32, a record for a U.S. player, and, unique for either side, won her 22nd singles match out of 22 played.

(LANCE TINGAY)

Thailand

Thailand

A constitutional monarchy of Southeast Asia, Thailand is bordered by Burma, Laos, Kampuchea, Malaysia, the Andaman Sea, and the Gulf of Thailand. Area: 542,373 sq km (209,411 sq mi). Pop. (1981 est.): 48,126,000. Cap. and largest city: Bangkok (pop., 1980 prelim., 4,711,000). Language: Thai. Religion (1970): Buddhist 95.3%; Muslim 3.8%. King, Bhumibol Adulyadej; prime minister in 1982, Gen. Prem Tinsulanond.

For the people of Thailand, 1982 above all marked the 200th anniversary of the establishment of the kingdom's ruling Chakri dynasty. Three months after the nationwide celebrations, King Bhumibol Adulyadej fell ill, but he recovered some six weeks later.

Thailand's King Bhumibol Adulyadej, with Queen Sirikit at his side, celebrated the bicentennial of Bangkok and the 200th anniversary of the dynasty.

UPI

THAILAND

Education. (1979–80) Primary, pupils 7,242,123, teachers (1978–79) 283,204; secondary, pupils 1,489,939, teachers (1978–79) 66,965; vocational, pupils 264,608, teachers 12,680; teacher training (1978–79), students 22,866, teachers 6,040; higher, students (universities only) 288,101, teaching staff 22,261.

Finance. Monetary unit: baht, with (Sept. 20, 1982) a free rate of 23 baht to U.S. $1 (39.40 baht = £1 sterling). Gold and other reserves (June 1982) U.S. $1,609,000,000. Budget (1981 actual): revenue 111,965,000,000 baht; expenditure 133,287,000,000 baht. Gross national product (1981) 785,880,000,000 baht. Money supply (Dec. 1981) 70,970,000,000 baht. Cost of living (1975 = 100; June 1982) 189.2.

Foreign Trade. (1981) Imports 216,746,000,000 baht; exports 153,001,000,000 baht. Import sources (1980): Japan 21%; U.S. 17%; Saudi Arabia 10%; Singapore 6%; Qatar 5%. Export destinations (1980): Japan 15%; The Netherlands 13%; U.S. 13%; Singapore 8%; Hong Kong 5%. Main exports (1980): rice 15%; tapioca 11%; rubber 9%; tin 9%; corn 5%; electrical equipment 5%; precious stones 5%. Tourism (1980): visitors 1,858,800; gross receipts U.S. $867 million.

Transport and Communications. Roads (1980) 67,660 km. Motor vehicles in use (1980): passenger c. 397,900; commercial c. 451,900. Railways: (1981) 3,855 km; traffic (1980) 8,861,000,000 passenger-km, freight 2,805,000,000 net ton-km. Air traffic (1980): c. 6,276,000,000 passenger-km; freight 248.4 million net ton-km. Shipping (1981): merchant vessels 100 gross tons and over 184; gross tonnage 402,705. Telephones (Sept. 1979) 451,400. Radio receivers (Dec. 1979) 5.9 million. Television receivers (Dec. 1979) 800,000.

Agriculture. Production (in 000; metric tons; 1981): rice c. 19,000; corn c. 4,000; sweet potatoes c. 348; sorghum 274; cassava c. 17,900; dry beans c. 275; soybeans 135; peanuts 157; sugar, raw value 1,641; pineapples c. 1,800; bananas c. 2,021; tobacco c. 87; rubber c. 510; cotton, lint 77; jute and kenaf 219; meat c. 639; fish catch (1980) 1,650; timber (cu m; 1980) 38,015. Livestock (in 000; 1981): cattle c. 5,062; buffalo c. 6,299; pigs c. 5,386; chickens c. 71,015.

Industry. Production (in 000; metric tons; 1981): cement 6,286; lignite 1,685; petroleum products (1979) c. 8,460; tin concentrates (metal content) 41; lead concentrates 40; manganese ore (metal content; 1980) 19; fluorspar 306; gypsum 412; sulfuric acid (1980) 35; electricity (kw-hr; 1980) 14,985,000.

The administration of Prime Minister Prem Tinsulanond faced numerous challenges as the nation geared up for general elections in 1983. The tone was set in December 1981, when Prem brought back into his Cabinet members of the country's largest political grouping, the Social Action Party (SAP), which had left the coalition government nine months earlier. Though it promised a measure of political stability, the move nonetheless brought to the surface the SAP's own severe internal divisions. The factionalism came to a head in March when the long-time SAP leader, former prime minister Kukrit Pramoj, announced that, at 71, he would not run in the 1983 election. Frontrunner in the party succession stakes was economics expert Boonchu Rojanastien, former deputy prime minister and head of the Bangkok Bank.

Pressure on the prime minister mounted in June when the parliamentary opposition introduced a no-confidence motion against the government, alleging ineptitude in the conduct of economic and foreign affairs. The motion was defeated.

In an unconfirmed incident on July 16, one or more assailants ostensibly fired an antitank rocket at the prime minister's motorcade as it was traveling in one of Thailand's northern provinces. The attack was unsuccessful. Despite tightened security, a grenade was lobbed into Prem's residential compound on August 15. Prem again escaped unscathed, but so did his assailant. Some insiders said the attacks were the work of elements within the Army disgruntled by the swift rise of Gen. Arthit Kamlang-ek, a Prem protégé who had played a leading role in crushing a coup attempt in April 1981. The controversial Arthit was named commander in chief of the Thai Army in the annual military reshuffles in September, making him effectively the second most powerful man in Thailand.

Prem, himself a former commander in chief, displayed the Thai military's traditional reluctance to participate in democratic politics when he announced in October that he would not join a political party and stand in the upcoming election. However, analysts said that Prem's support within the armed forces virtually guaranteed him another term as prime minister, since no party was expected to win an outright parliamentary majority.

The Thai Army launched three major assaults against the 5,000-strong Shan United Army of the notorious "Golden Triangle" narcotics leader, Khun Sa. An offensive in January succeeded in driving the drug runner's troops from their base in northernmost Thailand into Burma. Follow-up operations in May and October were deemed necessary when it became clear that Khun Sa was determined to reestablish a foothold on Thai soil. Bangkok also reaped results from its judicious carrot-and-stick policy against the Communist Party of Thailand. Promised lenient treatment, thousands of Communists came out of the jungle to surrender to the authorities.

Though affected by the worldwide recession, Thailand's economy performed creditably in 1982. Gross national product was expected to grow at about 5%, and improvements were recorded in several key areas. The current-account deficit was estimated at $1,220,000,000, just half the 1981 figure. After two devaluations the previous year, the baht recovered in 1982 and gained ground against the Japanese yen and most major Western European currencies. However, the government was obliged to introduce sweeping tax changes toward the year's end to raise an additional $440 million in revenue.   (THOMAS HON WING POLIN)

Theatre

The world recession, rising ticket prices, lower attendances, and soaring production costs placed the theatre in Great Britain in increasing jeopardy. Sir Claus Moser, head of the Royal Opera House board, warned of the dangers facing all the arts if appeals for increased grants were ignored. Paul Channon, the minister with responsibility for the arts, had on Britain's first National Arts Day (June 24) expressed optimistic views about the future of the arts in Britain. At the end of the year he allayed the fears of Sir William Rees-Mogg, chairman of the Arts Council, and of the Council's many clients that the Treasury would fail to raise the next grant-in-aid to a sufficient level above that of 1982–83 (£86 million) to prevent the closing of one or

REG WILSON

more leading theatrical companies and to reduce the hardships of those employed in the arts. The Arts Council had applied for a minimum grant of £98.5 million. In a parliamentary statement before the end of the year, Channon announced that the Treasury grant for 1983–84 would be £92 million for the 12 months to March 1984 and a £5 million supplementary grant for the preceding three months. The Arts Council chairman congratulated the minister on having virtually met his full demands and welcomed the decision to investigate the finances of one or more of the major repertory companies. The Council allocations would be made known in early 1983, but the threat to close one of the four major national companies was averted

Several theatres remained "dark" or closed permanently, though the Old Vic was saved by Ed Mirvish of Canada, who paid £550,000 for it and was spending £1 million on refurbishment. The National Youth Theatre was rescued by a grant from Texaco Inc. and the takeover of its home (the Shaw Theatre) by Camden Council. The misguided prosecution of the National Theatre (NT) director, Michael Bogdanov, for allegedly staging an obscene act in Howard Brenton's *The Romans in Britain* in 1981 was stopped, thus vindicating the NT's stand. The Edinburgh Festival conference on the state and the arts raised such problems as the inadequacy of "business sponsorship" (a mere £6 million) to replace the government shortfall.

Everywhere in the West, except France, the crisis bit deep. Cuts in West German budgets imperiled state and city theatres; Stuttgart, for instance, had to drop its theatre festival. The French arts grant, twice that in Britain, was due to rise 12% in the coming year, that for the City of Paris by 13%. Increased grants to new playwrights and a special subsidy to private Paris theatres were also announced. Arts Minister Jack Lang appointed Jean-Pierre Vincent, of the Strasbourg NT, to succeed Jacques Toja as administrator of the Comédie Française and Giorgio Strehler, of the Milan Piccolo, to run an international festival at its 200-year-old subsidiary, the Odéon, due to be renamed the Théâtre de l'Europe. Though theatre attendance in

Geoffrey Hutchings (left) won the SWET award for best comedy actor for his performance as Dodo, the pantomime-dame, in *Poppy*, a musical about Britain's opium trade in China during the Victorian era.

France had dropped 2% in the last five years, the prestigious Avignon Festival welcomed a record 125,000 visitors in 1982.

Great Britain and Ireland. Among the annual Arts Council prizes were six playwrights' bursaries, the John Whiting Prize (David Pownall), and the George Devine Prize (shared by Louise Paget and Andrea Dunbar). A record number of Plays and Players (PP) and Society of West End Theatre (SWET) awards went to the NT, whose spectacular production of the U.S. musical *Guys and Dolls* rated seven: two each to Richard Eyre, director, and John Gunter, designer, the SWET award for best actress in a musical to Julia Mackenzie, for best actor in a supporting role to David Healy, and the outstanding achievement in musicals award to the play. Bill Paterson won the PP best actor award for the title role in *Schweik in the Second World War*, in which Julia Mackenzie also was impressive as Anna Kopecka. In the NT's *The Importance of Being Earnest* the SWET supporting actress award went to Anna Massey and the PP best actress to Judi Dench (as Lady Bracknell and as the lead in Harold Pinter's one-act *A Kind of Alaska*, about a sleeping-sickness patient). This play also shared the PP best new play award with Tom Stoppard's *The Real Thing*, a brilliant Pirandellian comedy of love and marriage among theatricals, which Peter Wood directed in the West End.

Other fine productions at the NT were Edward Bond's *Summer* with Anna Massey, *The Beggar's Opera* with the exciting Imelda Staunton as Lucy, *The Prince of Homburg* with Patrick Drury, a Victorian *A Midsummer Night's Dream* with Paul Scofield as Oberon (also memorable as Don Quixote in Keith Dewhurst's adaptation at the Olivier), and Samuel Beckett's *Rockabye* directed by Alan Schneider, all at the Cottesloe; *Major Barbara* with Penelope Wilton, Alan Ayckbourn's cynical *Way*

Upstream, and Chekhov's *Uncle Vanya*, newly translated by Pam Gems, at the Lyttelton; and, at the Olivier, *Danton's Death* (adapted by Howard Brenton) and a revival of the Peter Hall *Oresteia*, later to be taken to the Athens Festival.

Following the move of the Royal Shakespeare Company (RSC) to the Barbican Centre in the City of London, the company earned four SWET awards: the best musical for Peter Nichols's *Poppy*, a Christmas pantomime type of show with Monty Norman's music, about Britain's opium trade in China in Victorian times; the best comedy actor for Geoffrey Hutchings's pantomime-dame in *Poppy*; and two for best performances in a revival, for Cheryl Campbell's Nora and Stephen Moore's Helmer in *A Doll's House* on the RSC's small stage, The Pit. Before the move to the Barbican the RSC was seen in Schnitzler's *La Ronde* and Ostrovsky's *The Forest* at the Aldwych. Thereafter came charming productions, at the Barbican, of the two parts of *Henry IV* (with Gerard Murphy as a plebeian Prince Hal), *A Midsummer Night's Dream* and *All's Well That Ends Well* (with Peggy Ashcroft), *A Winter's Tale*, and a new version of *Peter Pan*, staged by Trevor Nunn and John Caird, using a male actor for the first time in the title role. At The Pit the RSC staged classics (Bulwer-Lytton's *Money*, *The Twin Rivals*, and *The Witch of Edmonton*) and first-rate plays by Peter Flannery (*Our Friends in the North*, about corruption in modern society) and Peter Whelan (*Clay*, about growing old in a nuclear society).

SWET awards in the private sector went to Rosemary Leach in *84 Charing Cross Road* (best actress in a new play), Roy Hudd in *Underneath the Arches* (best actor in a musical), and Julian Mitchell's *Another Country* (transferred from Greenwich, where it was seen in 1981) as the year's best play; in it Kenneth Branagh won the most promising new-

The biggest show on New York's Broadway during the year was *Cats*, a British import. Production costs were so high for the musical that theatre seats cost $50 each.

MARTHA SWOPE

comer awards, given by PP and by SWET and Benson and Hedges jointly. *Andy Capp*, transferred from the Manchester Royal Exchange Theatre, won the PP best musical, and the philosophical comedy *Insignificance*, by Terry Johnson gained the most promising new play award. Ian McDiarmid won the SWET best actor in a new play award in *Insignificance*, while the comedy of the year award went to Michael Frayn's backstage *Noises Off*, earlier seen at the Lyric Theatre in Hammersmith. Of interest at the Royal Court were Louise Page's drama of old age, *Salonika; Top Girls* by Caryl Churchill; G. F. Newman's drama of police corruption, *Operation Bad Apple*; and the John Byrne working-class trilogy *The Slab Boys*, from Glasgow. The Lyric Theatre, Hammersmith, presented Claire Luckham's *Trafford Tanzi* en route from Liverpool to London's Mermaid, William Gaskill's production of *She Stoops to Conquer*, and Shared Experience's stage version of Evelyn Waugh's *A Handful of Dust*. New at the Mermaid was George Steiner's playwriting debut, *The Portage of A.H.*, in which Alex MacOwen impersonated an 80-year-old Adolf Hitler on the run.

Other novelties in the subsidized sector included a new version of Ayckbourn's *Season's Greetings* and Noel Coward's *Design for Living*, at the Greenwich, both later seen in the West End; *Skirmishes* by Catherine Hayes and *Dreyfus* (Tom Kempinski's version of a J. C. Grumberg play), at Hampstead; *The Lucky Ones* by Tony Marchant and *A Star Is Torn*, starring Robyn Archer, who took it to the West End, at the Theatre Royal, Stratford East; Foco Novo's *Edward II* by Brecht at the Round House and *Woza Albert!* from South Africa at the Riverside Studios (both threatened with closing); Edward Fox's *Hamlet* at the Young Vic, and Anton Lesser's at the Warehouse, under Ian Albery's management; and Robert Walker's rock musical *Yakety Yak*, at the New Half Moon.

The Theatre Royal, Haymarket, launched a repertory season that included Ronald Millar's version of C. P. Snow's *A Coat of Varnish*, starring Peter Barkworth. Among other highlights were Penelope Keith and Trevor Peacock in *Hobson's Choice*, Donald Sinden in *Uncle Vanya*, Peter O'Toole in *Man and Superman*, and Leonard Rossiter in *The Rules of the Game*. Musicals included *Song and Dance* with Wayne Sleep and Marti Webb and a score by Andrew Lloyd-Webber; *Windy City*, based on *The Front Page* (with Carl Toms's eye-catching set); *Destry Rides Again*; and *Camelot. The Mikado* and Joseph Papp's production of *The Pirates of Penzance* appeared in a year when the cradle of Gilbert and Sullivan operetta, the 106-year-old D'Oyly Carte Opera Company, was forced to close. Comedies ranged from the farcical *Key for Two* starring Moira Lister to Eric Idle's absurdist *Pass the Butler*, while more serious fare included *The Little Foxes* with Elizabeth Taylor, Susannah York in *Hedda Gabler*, Glenda Jackson (as Hitler's mistress) in *Summit Conference, Nuts* by Tom Topor, and, more renowned for its authorship than its dramatic skill, *The Jeweller's Shop* by Karol Wojtyla, alias Pope John Paul II.

Helped by the Irish Arts Council grant of £1.9 million, the Abbey Theatre, Dublin, though fac-

ing future cuts, staged Fr. Desmond Forrestal's *Kolbe*, a tribute to the canonized anti-Nazi wartime martyr, at the Dublin Festival. Other new works there included Hugh Leonard's *Kill*, Mary Halpin's *Irish Times*, the prizewinning *Semi-Private*, Jim Sheridan's *The Immigrant* (first seen in Canada), and Fergus and Rosaleen Linehan's *Mary Make-Believe*, a musical based on James Stephens's *The Charwoman's Daughter*. Harveys' of Bristol Theatre Awards went to Frank Conway (*She Stoops to Conquer* at the Abbey, shifted to an Irish setting), Neil Donnelly's *The Silver Dollar Boys* at the Peacock, Alan Standford (for the role of Antonio Salieri in *Amadeus*), Maureen Toal (in *All My Sons*), and Patrick Mason's production of *The Pirates of Penzance*.

France, Belgium, Italy. The French Critics' prizes went to Ariane Mnouchkine's *Richard II*, Peter Brook's *The Tragedy of Carmen* (winner of the Prix Dominique), and the Strasbourg NT's new play, *The Palace of Justice*; to Catherine Sellers (best actress in *Virginia*); and to Patrick Chesnais (best actor in Carlos Semprun's *Le Bleu de l'eau de vie*). The Society of Composers and Dramatists presented its award to Anouilh's *The Navel*, while that of the Plaisir du Théâtre went to Jacques Mauclair, and the French Academy award was given to Georges Neveux (*see* OBITUARIES). The best productions at the Comédie Française were *Mary Tudor*, with Christine Fersen; Henry-François Becque's *The Vultures*, staged by Jean-Pierre Vincent; *Don Juan* by Jean-Luc Boutte; and *Life Is a Dream* by Jorge Lavelli. At its second house, the Odéon, the Comédie Française presented *Hedda Gabler; The Prince of Homburg; Yvonne, Princess of Burgundy*; and new plays by the late Geneviève Serreau, Jean-Luc Lagarce, Bernard da Costa, and J. C. Grumberg.

At the Théâtre de l'Est Parisien the highlight was Denis Llorca's production of Dostoyevsky's *The Possessed*; at the Théâtre de la Ville, *Make and Break*, just in time before fire wrecked the stage; at the Palais de Chaillot, the Grenoble production of the prizewinning *The Giants of the Mountains*; at Jean-Louis Barrault's theatre, *Virginia* and Slawomir Mrozek's *The Ambassador* with Laurent Terzieff; and at the Cartoucherie, *Richard II* and *Twelfth Night*, both staged by Mnouchkine. In the private sector the hits included Chekhov's *Platonov*, staged by Daniel Mesguich, *A Doll's House* with Isabel Dehaas, *Le Charimari* by Pierette Bruno, and revivals of *Moi* by Labiche, *Chéri* by Colette, Montherlant's *Exile, Point H* by Yves Jamiaque, and Giraudoux's *Sodom and Gomorrha*. There were new works by Robert Lamoureux, Marcel Mithois, Rémo Forlani, Gérard Lamballe, Philippe Bruneau, Claude Confortès, and Georges Berreby and foreign plays by, among others, Michael Frayn (*Noises Off*), Charles Dyer, Peter Shaffer (*Amadeus* with François Perier and Roman Polanski, who also directed), and John Murrell (*Memoir* with Delphine Seyrig).

Greece was the country represented at the Belgian Europalia Festival, with the Athens NT, Karolos Koun's Arts Theatre, the Saloniki NT, and the Piraeus Theatre among those taking part. The Belgian NT staged *The Trojan Women*, and the Rideau put on *Zorba the Greek* for the occasion. Also

The first U.S. production of *The Life and Adventures of Nicholas Nickleby* opened at the Great Lakes Shakespeare Festival in Cleveland, Ohio, and went on to tour the U.S. in 1982.

in Belgium Otomar Krejca directed *The Devils* and *The Greek Cockatoo* at the Louvain Atelier. Highlights of the year in Italy were Vittorio Gassman in *Othello*, Anna Maria Guarnieri in *Antony and Cleopatra*, Clauco Mauri in both Oedipus plays, Anna Proclemer in *The Little Foxes*, Rossella Falk in *Duet for One*, Valeria Moriconi in her one-woman show, Lilla Brignone in *Right You Are, if You Think So*, Umberto Orsini in *Nobody Knows Why* (both by Pirandello), and *My Lovers' Lovers Are My Lovers*, by Giuseppe Patroni Griffi with Adriana Asti.

Switzerland, West and East Germany, Austria.
Major Swiss productions included the world premiere of Ionesco's autobiographical *Journey to the Dead* in Basel, Thomas Brasch's adaptation of *Ivanov*, staged by Arie Zinger, and Carlos Trafic's production of Hesse's *Steppenwolf* in Zürich. At his own Geneva Comedy Theatre, Benno Besson staged *A Gozzi Fantasy*.

The West Berlin Spring Meeting was notable for the Free People's Theatre's *Faust*, with Bernard Minetti, later seen in Paris; two new Beckett playlets; and George Tabori's *The Voyeur*. The West Berlin Festival staged Robert Musil's *The Dreamers*, which earned Elisabeth Trissenar the best actress award; also presented in Berlin was Karl Michael Grüber's six-hour-long *Hamlet*, with Bruno Ganz. Elsewhere in West Germany there were new plays by the East Germans Jochen Berg, Heiner Müller, Volker Braun, Peter Hacks, and Stefan Schütz; by Western writers Tankred Dorst, Heinar Kipphardt (*see* OBITUARIES), Botho Strauss (*Kalldewey*, which won the 1982 Mülheim Prize), Gerlind Reinshagen, Thomas Bernhardt, and Karl Otto Mühl; and the world premiere of *Morast* by the Czechoslovak exile Pavel Kohout.

The East Berlin Festival presented Strehler's Milan company with Andrea Jonasson as Shen-Te in *The Good Person of Sezuan* (speaking her monologues in German) and new plays by Volker Braun, Rainer Kerndl, and Hanns Eisler (*Johann Faustus*, staged by Wekwerth and Tenschert at the Berliner Ensemble). The Deutsches NT put on Alexander Lang's production of *Danton's Death*, firstprize winner at the Belgrade bitef festival, and a play by Heinrich Mann about Frederick the Great. *Danton's Death*, staged by Achim Benning, was the Burg Theatre's entry for the Vienna Festival. Other Austrian delights were a new play by Martin Walser; J. M. R. Lenz's forgotten *The New Menoza*, which Benno Besson staged at the Burg; and Christopher Fry's *The Lady's Not for Burning*, directed by Karl Guttmann at the Josefstadt.

Eastern Europe, Scandinavia, Israel. New at the Moscow Taganka were Yury Liubimov's production of a Gogol work and Yevgeny Kucher's of *Five Tales by Isaak Babel*; at the Moscow Arts Oleg Yefremov put on Alexandre Gelman's *Facing Everyone* and Mikhail Shatrov's new Lenin drama *This Way We Shall Win*. East Germany's Hanns Anselm Perten staged Rolf Hochhuth's *The Lady Doctors* at the Malaya Bronnaya; Galina Volchyok presented *Three Sisters* at the Contemporary; Igor Ilinsky put on *The Cherry Orchard* at the Maly; and Valentin Pluchek Erdman's *The Suicide* was produced at the Satire. Despite the state of emergency Polish theatres soon reopened with Jerzy Jarocki staging *Murder in the Cathedral* in the Warsaw Cathedral and Kazimierz Dejmek directing or presenting several novelties headed by Ireneusz Iredynski's *The Terrorists*, set in Central America, at the Polski. Thirty ensembles from four continents took part in the Theatre of the Nations Festival in Sofia, Bulg., where two native plays commemorating the 100th birthday of Georgi Dimitrov (by Ivan Radoev and Georgi Danilov) were also seen. The Csiksomlyo Passion Play at the Castle and Istvan Orkeny's posthumous *The Scenario* (inspired by the 1940s show trials) earned much acclaim in Budapest.

Two contentious productions at Stockholm's Royal Dramatic Theatre were the world premiere of Peter Weiss's (see OBITUARIES) *The New Trial*, directed by a team headed by the author, and *The Tempest*, Göran Järvefelt's directing debut at that theatre. The Danish Royal Theatre put on Klaus Rifbjerg's marital comedy *The Song of the Bed*. Oslo's New Theatre premiered Nell Dunn's *Steaming*, a version of an old Kabuki drama staged by Icelandic guest director Hauken Gunnarsson. Artistic peaks at the Tampere (Finland) Festival included the Turku production of Pam Gems's *Piaf* with Kristiina Elstelä and a visit of the Estonian Drama Theatre from Tartu. Two historic events in Israel were the First Jewish Theatre Festival, with several foreign troupes taking part, and Hanoch Levin's controversial *The Patriot* at the Neve Zedeck theatre, performed twice after being banned for obliquely criticizing the invasion of Lebanon.

(OSSIA TRILLING)

United States and Canada. Although professional theatres throughout the U.S. and Canada continued to be active in 1982, most attention during the year was focused on Broadway. A drab and depressing economy was surely the reason. Audiences seem to have an interest in serious drama when they can enjoy leisure time, but if it becomes escapist time they prefer glamour and tinsel. For that reason primarily the Broadway commercial theatre dominated the U.S. drama in 1982.

During the year the cost of producing a Broadway show hit a new high of $5 million, and the cost of seeing one set a new record at $50 a ticket. The show was *Cats*, a musical extravaganza based on T. S. Eliot's collection *Old Possum's Book of Practical Cats*, set to music by Andrew Lloyd Webber, who also wrote the music for *Evita* and *Jesus Christ Superstar*. This import was a rare example of the British succeeding in an area that Americans had long considered their exclusive domain: the musical theatre. The show became so popular that the $50 price tag did not deter audiences.

Cats became the biggest hit to arrive on Broadway during the year, although *Nine* ran it a close second. The latter was also a musical, this time based on a film—Federico Fellini's *8½*. For legal reasons that source could not be credited in the program. *Nine* won Broadway's Tony award for best musical, *Cats* not being eligible at the time.

Both of these productions were disquieting to serious observers of the theatre because their popularity seemed less related to merit than to successful marketing strategies. They dominated an otherwise thin season during which most of Broadway's theatres were empty and two were even demolished. The biggest noise along Broadway was in fact not the cheering for *Cats* or *Nine* but the explosion of dynamite and the crash of the wrecker's ball as the Helen Hayes and Morosco theatres were razed.

Zakes Mokae won a Tony award for best featured actor in *Master Harold . . . and the Boys*, by the South African Athol Fugard. Originally produced by the Yale Repertory Theatre, it was a well-conceived drama but small in scale and without the muscle usually found in prizewinning plays.

Other Broadway dramas produced during the year included *Hothouse*, an early play that Harold Pinter had relegated to his trunk. It proved historically interesting but worthy of its original fate. William Alfred, a Harvard University English professor, achieved his second New York production in 20 years, but *The Curse of an Aching Heart* was not the success that his earlier *Hogan's Goat* had been. Another futile follow-up was *The Wake of Jamey Foster*, written by Beth Henley, whose *Crimes of the Heart* had won a Pulitzer Prize. This play lasted only a single week.

The only play to originate on Broadway and succeed at all was an uncertainly written religious mystery called *Agnes of God*. Its popularity stemmed from fine performances by Geraldine Page, Elizabeth Ashley, and Amanda Plummer. Audiences evidently still appreciated bravura acting.

This was even more apparent in several productions of classics. Broadway audiences do not usually seek out Shakespeare or Euripides, but a star can attract them. In 1982 the stars were Christopher Plummer and James Earl Jones in *Othello* and Zoe Caldwell and Dame Judith Anderson in *Medea*. Both productions enjoyed successful engagements.

Nonprofit and regional theatres had emerged precisely to do such plays. However, New York's institutional theatres had been floundering in recent years, and in 1982 they continued to do so. They were the first victims of the economic crisis. The theatre at Lincoln Center remained shut for still another season, presumably for renovations. Hopes for its eventual reopening grew dimmer with every work delay and cutback of funds. New York's other major theatrical institution, the New York Shakespeare Festival, continued to operate at a reduced pace. This theatre of Joseph Papp's remained the city's boldest, but it had lost some of its early drive. The Circle in the Square produced a popular revival of Noel Coward's *Present Laughter* with George C. Scott and then dropped the rest of its schedule to capitalize on the hit.

Stars do not always attract audiences. Television's Donny Osmond notwithstanding, a revival of the George M. Cohan musical *Little Johnny Jones* lasted only a single performance. Movie director Robert Altman turned to the stage with a play called *Come Back to the Five and Dime Jimmy Dean, Jimmy Dean* featuring another television star, Cher. The play closed after running little more than a month.

Yet all was not gloomy. Off-Broadway theatre continued to flourish. Despite ticket prices as high as $20, it attracted audiences who were still faithful to serious drama. The year's best plays in fact came from off-Broadway. They were Lanford Wilson's *Angels Fall*, a study of the crisis of faith in a nuclear age, and Harvey Fierstein's *Torch Song Trilogy*, three related one-act plays about a middle-class transvestite. While these plays could not seem more disparate, both were naturalistic works dealing with personal problems.

Throughout the rest of the U.S., theatres pre-

KEN HOWARD

Geraldine Page (left) and Amanda Plummer starred in *Agnes of God*, one of New York's hit Broadway productions.

sented many costume classics, whether Greek, Elizabethan, Restoration, or Chekhovian. It seemed as if the concert-hall mentality of familiar programming had overtaken these theatres. Audiences, however, were hungering for something more recognizable and sympathetic than costume drama. The Actors Theatre of Louisville, Ky., met this need during its popular annual festival of new plays. The Mark Taper Forum in Los Angeles also seemed conscious in its programming of a thirst for relevance, staging Charles Fuller's prizewinning *A Soldier's Play* and Jules Feiffer's *Grown Ups*. Too many of the other regional theatres unfortunately chose their schedules from a short list of standard classics—Shakespeare, Wycherley, Sheridan, Ibsen, Chekhov, and the modern standbys of O'Neill, Miller, Williams, and occasionally Brecht.

One of New York's off-Broadway productions was Harvey Fierstein's *Torch Song Trilogy*, starring Fierstein.

Togo

KEN HOWARD

Although there is a commercial theatre in Canada, that nation's stage life has always centred on the established and prestigious Stratford Festival. With John Hirsch finishing his second year as artistic director, this theatre's days of uncertain leadership seemed over. Playing a 22-week season to an audience that averaged 75% of capacity, the Festival presented *Julius Caesar, The Merry Wives of Windsor, The Tempest,* and Shaw's *Arms and the Man* in the main theatre and *Blithe Spirit* and *The Mikado* in the smaller house.

Arms and the Man was a surprising discourtesy to the nearby Shaw Festival, which is much smaller than Stratford and poses no great competitive threat. The Shaw Theatre in its own summer season presented popular favourites, obviously seeking broad appeal: Shaw's *Too True to Be Good* and *Pygmalion* and Edmond Rostand's *Cyrano de Bergerac.* These were not daring choices but rather the selections of a theatre trying to survive difficult economic times. In that respect it was representative of many U.S. and Canadian theatres in 1982.

(MARTIN GOTTFRIED)

See also Dance; Music.

[622]

Togo

A West African republic on the Bight of Benin, Togo is bordered by Ghana, Upper Volta, and Benin. Area: 56,785 sq km (21,925 sq mi). Pop. (1982 est.): 2,872,000, including (1978 est.) Ewe 46.5%; Kabre 22.4%; Gurma 14.2%; Tem 4.2%. Cap. and largest city: Lomé (pop., 1980 est., 283,000). Language: French (official). Religion (1980 est.): animist 46%; Muslim 17%; and Christian 37%. President in 1982, Gen. Gnassingbe Eyadema.

Togo experienced serious economic and financial difficulties in 1982. These were primarily caused by a slump in the market for phosphates, the country's principal export, and were exacerbated by Ghana's closing in September of the common frontier in order to combat the thriving contraband trade. In November a "national solidarity" surtax of 5% on all wages and salaries was imposed.

Poor relations with Ghana were partly due to tribal antagonisms between Pres. Gnassingbe Eyadema and Ghana's head of state, Jerry Rawlings. With France, which President Eyadema visited in

TOGO

Education. (1979–80) Primary, pupils 484,272, teachers 8,920; secondary, pupils 119,801, teachers 2,855; vocational, pupils 7,793, teachers (1977–78) 326; teacher training, students 300, teachers 22; higher, students 3,638, teaching staff 291.

Finance. Monetary unit: CFA franc, with (Sept. 20, 1982) a par value of CFA Fr 50 to the French franc (free rate of CFA Fr 353 to U.S. $1; CFA Fr 605 = £1 sterling). Budget (1982 est.) balanced at CFA Fr 72.3 billion.

Foreign Trade. (1980) Imports CFA Fr 116,357,000,000; exports CFA Fr 71,285,000,000. Import sources: France 25%; Nigeria 16%; The Netherlands 9%; U.K. 8%; West Germany 6%. Export destinations: The Netherlands 20%; France 15%; Nigeria 10%; West Germany 7%; Cameroon 6%; Yugoslavia 5%; Belgium-Luxembourg 5%. Main exports: phosphates 40%; cocoa 12%; coffee 8%.

September, relations remained good. In November Jean-Christophe Mitterrand, son of French Pres. François Mitterrand and assistant to the latter's adviser on African affairs, Guy Penne, arrived in Lomé to prepare for his father's forthcoming visit; this was scheduled for Jan. 13, 1983, the 16th anniversary of the military takeover in Togo. In April Eyadema granted political asylum to Ange Patasse, leader of the opposition in the Central African Republic, who for some weeks had been a refugee in the French embassy in Bangui.

(PHILIPPE DECRAENE)

Tonga

An independent monarchy and member of the Commonwealth, Tonga is an island group in the Pacific Ocean east of Fiji. Area: 747 sq km (288 sq mi). Pop. (1982 est.): 99,000, 98% of whom are Tongan. Cap. and largest city: Nukualofa (pop., 1980 est., 19,900). Language: English and Tongan. Religion (1976): Free Wesleyan 47%; Roman Catholic 16%; Free Church of Tonga 14%; Mormon 9%; Church of Tonga 9%; other 5%. King, Taufa'ahau Tupou IV; prime minister in 1982, Prince Fatafehi Tu'ipelehake.

Tonga's generally fragile economy, in which exports amounted to only one-quarter of imports with the balance covered by aid and remittances, was shattered by Cyclone Isaac, which killed four people and devastated crops and buildings in March 1982. Another cyclone in June ensured that recovery would be slow. Aid was needed not only to feed and house the victims but to sustain an economy that was heavily based on coconut products. Plantations were expected to take at least two years to recover where trees survived and seven years where replanting was needed. The cyclones came at a time when some progress had been made in establishing small export industries for desiccated coconut and coconut-oil-based soap. An additional fishing vessel arrived from Japan.

In March King Taufa'ahau Tupou provoked a major political row when he sacked Minister of Finance Mahe Tupounuia. Tupounuia was asked to resign after he had twice refused the king's request for additional funds for overseas travel. Tupounuia subsequently returned to his former position as director of the South Pacific Bureau of Economic Cooperation, the economic agency established by the South Pacific Forum.

(BARRIE MACDONALD)

TONGA

Education. (1979) Primary, pupils 19,744 teachers 818; secondary, pupils 12,563, teachers 666; vocational, pupils 280, teachers 19; teacher training, students 134, teachers 9.
Finance and Trade. Monetary unit: pa'anga, with (Sept. 20, 1982) a free rate of 1.04 pa'anga to U.S. $1 (1.79 pa'anga = £1 sterling). Budget (1981–82 est.): revenue 14,744,000 pa'anga; expenditure 14,736,000 pa'anga. Foreign trade (1980): imports 30,134,000 pa'anga; exports 6,630,000 pa'anga. Import sources: New Zealand 38%; Australia 31%; U.S. 6%; Japan 6%; Fiji 5%. Export destinations: Australia 36%; New Zealand 34%; U.S. 14%. Main exports: coconut oil 46%; desiccated coconut 10%; bananas 6%.

Track and Field Sports

Competition was keen throughout the year, but 1982 failed to produce the excitement of either the Olympic Games year of 1980 or of 1981, the "year of the mile." This was especially true of the men's competition, in which world records were set in only four events. The women did somewhat better, setting records in 11 events, but both sexes seemed to be holding something back for the sport's first world championships, scheduled for Helsinki, Finland, Aug. 7–14, 1983.

Men's International Competition. Four of the world's top performers of 1981 missed all or most of the year. Their absence was felt most severely in the mile and 1,500-m runs. Sebastian Coe and Steve Ovett of the U.K., each of whom set three new world standards at those distances in the two previous years, were injured for most of the season and did not approach their form of 1980–81.

The two had been scheduled to compete in a series of three match races, in different cities and in different events, before a worldwide television audience. All three races were canceled, and both runners were unavailable for the Commonwealth Games in Brisbane, Australia, in October. Coe was on hand for the year's most important meet, the quadrennial European Championships in Athens from September 6 to 12. But he was not in peak form and was upset in the 800 m and withdrew from the 1,500 m.

Steve Scott of the United States nearly made up for the loss of Coe. He twice broke the U.S. mile record, running 3 min 48.53 sec at Oslo on June 26 and coming back to record 3 min 47.69 sec on July 7. The latter was the second fastest mile ever run, only 0.36 sec off Coe's mark.

Completely missing from the year's activities were two others from among the five leading athletes of 1981. Renaldo Nehemiah and Edwin Moses, the fastest hurdlers in history, did not continue their well-established assault on the record book. Nehemiah retired from hurdling to play professional football in the U.S., and Moses was injured. In the European Championships Harald Schmid of West Germany ran the 400-m hurdles in 47.48 sec, just 0.35 sec slower than the world record set by Moses.

Of the six new world marks in 1982, three were made in the decathlon. Two of them went to Daley Thompson of the United Kingdom. It was not a new experience for him, as he had established a record of 8,622 points in May 1980. He lost the record the following month, then won the Olympic Games with a nonrecord score and stayed away from major competition in 1981. Rested and eager in 1982, Thompson returned in May to Gotzis, Austria, the scene of his non-Olympic 1980 record. There he again set a new decathlon mark with a total of 8,704 points.

But Thompson's record did not stand for long, falling on August 15 at Ulm, West Germany, to Jurgen Hingsen. The 24-year-old West German had been second to Thompson at Gotzis, where he had established a personal best of 8,535 points.

Tonga

Theology:
see Religion

Timber:
see Industrial Review

Tobacco:
see Industrial Review

Tobogganing:
see Winter Sports

Tourism:
see Industrial Review

Toys:
see Games and Toys

Competing in his national championships, Hingsen narrowly bettered Thompson's record with a score of 8,723. The two met again in the European Championships and Thompson won, this time with a best ever 8,743 points. Hingsen finished second with 8,517. But confronting both of them was Torsten Voss of East Germany, who set a new world junior mark of 8,387 points, 263 more than precocious Thompson had produced as a junior.

First of the other three records set in 1982 was made by Sergey Litvinov of the U.S.S.R. He threw the hammer 83.98 m (275 ft 6 in) at Moscow on June 4. It was an unusually large improvement (2.18 m, 7 ft 2 in) on the record of his countryman Yury Sedykh. The deposed record holder later added a second European title to the two Olympic championships he owned.

The biggest surprise among the record breakers was Dave Moorcroft of the U.K., who lowered the 5,000-m mark by 5.8 sec to 13 min 0.42 sec at Oslo on July 7. The sixth fastest miler ever, Moorcroft at age 29 was not looked upon as a potential world's best at 5,000 m. His best going into 1982 was 13 min 20.6 sec. Moorcroft finished third in the European title meet but won the Commonwealth race.

Sixth of the records to fall was in the 4 x 800-m relay, a non-Olympic event. In this race the U.K. accounted for the fourth of the year's six records when its team of Peter Elliott, Garry Cook, Steve Cram, and Sebastian Coe ran the event in 7 min 3.89 sec at London on August 30.

Carl Lewis, the young sprinter-long jumper from the United States, narrowly missed two world records but did receive unofficial recognition for his significant achievement. He long jumped 8.76 m (28 ft 9 in), just short of the 8.90-m (29-ft 2½-in) mark of Bob Beamon, which many consider the finest performance in track and field. Beamon's effort was made with the maximum allowable wind and at 2,250 m above sea level, gaining added inches from the rarefied air of Mexico City. Lewis's jump was the best ever at low altitude. In 1981 he ran the 100 m in 10.00 sec, a low-altitude record for that event, and he duplicated the feat in 1982.

Indoors, U.S. athletes were by far the most prominent participants. They accounted for nine world bests — indoor records are not approved officially — with Billy Olson responsible for four of them. The Abilene Christian University pole vaulter raised the vault record a centimetre at a time, beginning with 5.71 m (18 ft 8¾ in) at Toronto. In quick succession he vaulted 5.72 m (18 ft 9¼ in) at Louisville, Ky., and 5.73 m (18 ft 9½ in) at San Diego, Calif., concluding his spectacular series at Kansas City, Mo., on February 27. There, just four weeks after his first record, he cleared 5.74 m (18 ft 10 in).

Two other jumping records were set, Lewis long jumping 8.56 m (28 ft 1 in) at East Rutherford, N.J., and Willie Banks triple jumping 17.41 m (57 ft 1½ in) at San Diego. On the track Nehemiah ran the 60-yd hurdles in 6.82 sec at Dallas, Texas, and Don Paige lowered his own world indoor best at 1,000 yd with a 2 min 4.7 sec clocking at Inglewood, Calif.

Women's International Competition. In 1982 the women rebounded from a poor year in 1981, when only two new world marks had been produced. They established 15 records in 11 events, with East Germany leading the way.

The East Germans accounted for four of the records, and Marita Koch, already holder of the international best at both 200 m and 400 m, had a hand in two of them. She dashed 400 m in a rapid 48.16 sec at the European Championships and followed by anchoring the record-breaking 4 x 400-m relay team. Koch's 47.9-sec leg was the second fastest ever, as Kirsten Siemon, Sabine Busch, Dagmar Rubsam, and Koch ran the distance in 3 min 19.04 sec. Veteran Marlies Gohr equaled her world record 10.88 sec for 100 m at Karl-Marx-Stadt in East Germany, while Ramona Neubert bettered her own heptathlon figure with 6,772 points at Halle.

A third record was set at the European Championships when Ulrike Meyfarth of West Germany leaped 2.02 m (6 ft 7½ in) in the high jump. Two other field event records were broken twice. Finland's Tiina Lillak hurled the javelin 72.40 m (237 ft 6 in) at Helsinki, and Sofia Sakorafa of Greece later produced a throw of 74.20 m (243 ft 5 in) at Canea, Greece. Two Romanians bettered the long jump standard on the same day in Bucharest. Anisoara Cusmir leaped 7.15 m (23 ft 5½ in) but soon had her mark eclipsed by Vali Ionescu, who reached 7.20 m (23 ft 7½ in).

Most of the action on the track came in the longer runs, and Mary Decker Tabb (see BIOGRAPHIES) of the United States was the leading lady. She established new records for the 5,000-m and 10,000-m events, which are not on the Olympic program, and for the mile, which never will be an Olympic event because all Olympic distances are metric.

Anne Audain of New Zealand ran a record 15 min 13.3 sec for 5,000 m before it was Tabb's turn. The latter reduced the mark to 15 min 8.3 sec at Eugene, Ore. Her home city also was the site of the 10,000-m record six weeks later, when she ran that distance in 31 min 35.3 sec. In between the Eugene performances she cut the mile best to 4 min 18.08 sec at Paris. But the season ended with the mile mark in the possession of Maricica Puica of Roma-

Table I. World 1982 Outdoor Records—Men

Event	Competitor, country, date	Performance
5,000 m	Dave Moorcroft, U.K., July 7	13 min 0.42 sec
4 × 800 m relay	U.K., August 30	7 min 3.89 sec
Hammer	Sergey Litvinov, U.S.S.R., June 4	83.98 m (275 ft 6 in)
Decathlon	Daley Thompson, U.K., May 23	8,704 points
	Jurgen Hingsen, West Germany, August 15	8,723 points
	Daley Thompson, U.K., September 8	8,743 points

Table II. World 1982 Outdoor Records—Women

Event	Competitor, country, date	Performance
100 m	Marlies Gohr, East Germany, July 9	10.88 sec
400 m	Marita Koch, East Germany, September 8	48.16 sec
One mile	Mary Decker Tabb, U.S., July 9	4 min 18.08 sec
	Maricica Puica, Romania, September 16	4 min 17.44 sec
3,000 m	Svyetlana Ulmasova, U.S.S.R., July 25	8 min 26.78 sec
5,000 m	Anne Audain, New Zealand, March 17	15 min 13.3 sec
	Mary Decker Tabb, U.S., June 5	15 min 8.3 sec
10,000 m	Mary Decker Tabb, U.S., July 16	31 min 35.3 sec
4 × 400 m relay	East Germany, September 11	3 min 19.04 sec
High jump	Ulrike Meyfarth, West Germany, September 8	2.02 m (6 ft 7 ½ in)
Long jump	Anisoara Cusmir, Romania, August 1	7.15 m (23 ft 5 ½ in)
	Vali Ionescu, Romania, August 1	7.20 m (23 ft 7 ½ in)
Javelin	Tiina Lillak, Finland, July 29	72.40 m (237 ft 6 in)
	Sofia Sakorafa, Greece, September 26	74.20 m (243 ft 5 in)
Heptathlon	Ramona Neubert, East Germany, June 20	6,772 points

nia, who ran a race in 4 min 17.44 sec at Rieti, Italy. The final record went to Svyetlana Ulmasova of the U.S.S.R., who covered 3,000 m in 8 min 26.78 sec at Kiev.

Indoors, U.S. women were as prominent as the U.S. men, but athletes from other nations also got into the act. Tabb started her big year with three new mile marks, running 4 min 24.6 sec, 4 min 21.5 sec, and, finally, 4 min 20.5 sec. At 60 yd, a distance not run in Europe, first Jeanette Bolden (6.60 sec) and then Evelyn Ashford (6.54 sec) lowered the world record. At the same distance, but over hurdles, there was unusual action. Stephanie Hightower and Candy Young had the unique experience of tying with a best ever 7.47 sec and then repeated two weeks later when they were each timed in 7.37 sec.

The high jump record was raised twice, Debbie Brill of Canada clearing 1.98 m (6 ft 6¼ in) before Coleen Sommer of the U.S. jumped 2.00 m (6 ft 6¾ in). In the long jump two Soviet Union women matched or increased the standard three times. Margarita Butkiene equaled the record of 6.77 m (22 ft 2½ in) before Svyetlana Vanyushina first jumped 6.82 m (22 ft 4½ in) and then 6.83 m (22 ft 5 in). The only European track record was a 49.59-sec 400-m run by Jarmila Kratochvilova of Czechoslovakia.

U.S. Competition. U.S. men failed to produce a world record for the third year in a row. And for the first time since 1946 no men's world record was established in the United States. But 18 national records were produced.

Scott, who set two U.S. mile marks in Europe, also broke the U.S. 2,000-m figure twice, clocking 4 min 58.8 sec and 4 min 54.8 sec. Multiple records also were established by Alberto Salazar, the marathon record holder. After Matt Centrowitz ran a record 13 min 13.0 sec for 5,000 m, Salazar lowered the U.S. mark to 13 min 12.0 sec. Two weeks earlier Salazar had run 10,000 m in 27 min 25.7 sec, a U.S. best. His times of 27 min 29.1 sec and 27 min 30 sec were the second and fourth fastest ever by an American.

National standards were established in five of the eight field events with the vaulters most active. Olson opened with 5.71 m (18 ft 8¾ in) and in the national championships tied with Dan Ripley at 5.72 m (18 ft 9¼ in). Dave Volz soon moved the record to 5.73 m (18 ft 9½ in) and then to 5.75 m (18 ft 10¼ in), best in the world for 1982. The high jump best of 2.32 m (7 ft 7¼ in) was equaled by Del Davis.

In the throwing events Dave Laut set a shot put record, Dave McKenzie improved the hammer throw mark twice, and Bob Roggy broke the javelin standard three times. Laut's 22.02-m (72-ft 3-in) heave equaled Brian Oldfield's 1981 mark, while McKenzie improved on his own record. He threw 73.56 m (241 ft 4 in) and 74.34 m (243 ft 11 in). Close to the world best was Roggy, who made 93.72 m (307 ft 6 in), 94.46 m (309 ft 11 in), and then became the second best thrower ever with 95.80 m (314 ft 4 in).

In addition to her world marks, Tabb earned a U.S. record when she ran the 3,000 m in 8 min 29.8 sec. Hightower and Sommer, who also had world

indoor bests, set U.S. marks too. The former equaled the 100-m hurdle standard of 12.86 sec and then lowered it to 12.79 sec, while Sommer again high jumped 1.98 m (6 ft 6 in). Veteran Jane Frederick was a two-time record breaker, scoring 6,423 and 6,458 in the heptathlon. And the U.S. national 4 x 100-m relay team ran 42.47 sec with Alice Brown, Florence Griffith, Randy Givens, and Diane Williams carrying the baton.

In team competition the United States men beat East Germany 120½–102½, lost to the Soviet Union 118–100, and defeated West Germany 123–99 and Africa 136–69. U.S. women lost to the East Germans 105–52 and to the Soviets 89–67 but defeated the West Germans 90–56. In team competition within the U.S. the University of Texas at El Paso won the National Collegiate Athletic Association (NCAA) title for the third consecutive time indoors and the fourth straight time outdoors. Ne-

Carl Lewis of the U.S. came close to setting a new world record in the long jump by leaping for 8.76 metres (28 feet 9 inches) at the International Track and Field meet in Zürich, Switzerland.

Tiina Lillak of Finland threw the javelin for a new world record during the World Games in Helsinki in July.

braska won the Association of Intercollegiate Athletics for Women indoor tournament while in outdoor competition UCLA captured the first women's NCAA tournament, held in conjunction with the men. The Athletic Congress national championships went to Athletic Attic for the men both indoors and outdoors and for the women to Tennessee State and Wilt's Athletic Club indoors and Los Angeles Naturite outdoors.

Marathon Running and Cross Country. Alberto Salazar continued his domination of the marathon, but his margins of victory were thin. He won at Boston on April 19 with a race record time of 2 hr 8 min 51 sec, just two seconds ahead of Dick

A series of new U.S. records for indoor pole vaulting was set during the year by Billy Olson of Abilene (Texas) Christian University.

Beardsley. Six months later Salazar won his third consecutive New York City Marathon, running just four seconds faster than Rodolfo Gomez of Mexico, with a winning mark of 2 hr 9 min 29 sec. Salazar was unbeaten in four marathons and was the only man to have broken 2 hr 9 min twice. Charlotte Teske of West Germany led the women at Boston in 2 hr 29 min 33 sec, while Grete Waitz of Norway returned to her winning ways in New York, timed in 2 hr 27 min 14 sec. It was her fourth win in five starts there, after being forced out in 1981.

Salazar was on the other side of a close finish in the International Cross Country Championships at Rome on March 21. He finished three seconds behind Mohamed Kedir of Ethiopia, who clocked 33 min 41 sec for the 11.9-km run. Maricica Puica of Romania won the women's 4.7-km run. Ethiopia won the men's competition, and the Soviet Union the women's.

In NCAA competition Mark Scrutton of the University of Colorado was the individual winner and Wisconsin the team champion. Among the women the leaders were Lesley Welch and her University of Virginia teammates. The Athletic Congress championships were won by Pat Porter and Welch.

Off the Track. While the athletes were competing, the International Amateur Athletic Federation, worldwide governing body of the sport, was busy revamping the rules of amateur competition. They adopted a concept that allows athletes to earn money by running and through business arrangements, with the funds going into a trust. Athletes may draw on the trust account for training and living expenses without losing their amateur status. The IAAF also established strict rules for a limited number of international invitational events, known as permit meetings. Testing for drugs would be mandatory at all such contests as it already was for such events as the Olympic Games and world championships.   (BERT NELSON)

[452.B.3.b]

Transportation

The "Columbia" space shuttle completed its first ten million miles in 1982 but still had some way to go to catch up with the pre-World War II DC-3s. With over 90,000 flying hours, some components of these aircraft must have covered twice the distance of "Columbia."

The worst transportation accident of the year occurred early in November, when several hundred people died 11,000 ft up in the Salang Pass tunnel in the Hindu Kush mountains. Apparently a gasoline tanker collided with the lead vehicle of a troop convoy, causing a holocaust in the 2.7-km (1.7-mi)-long tunnel.

The problems of the aviation industry were reflected in the collapse of Laker Airways, which pioneered low-cost fares across the Atlantic, and of Braniff, the eighth largest airline in the U.S., which filed for reorganization under Chapter 11 of the U.S. Bankruptcy Act in May. The recession also served to highlight the significance of transportation in the poorest nations. It was estimated that three-quarters of such countries had their economies seriously impaired because of inadequate transport. (DAVID BAYLISS)

AVIATION

The air transport industry's problems continued unabated in 1982. The director general of the International Air Transport Association (IATA), the organization representing most international scheduled carriers, described the problems in his annual report as "staggering." He added that the industry was on a financial tightrope with "the abyss of bankruptcy on the one hand and the slippery slope of subsidization or permanent bondage to the loan market on the other." The IATA airlines were expected to suffer a collective operating loss on scheduled services of $260 million in 1982, a figure slightly worse than that for 1981. The association anticipated further deterioration to a $370 million operating loss in 1983 but after that expected a return to profitability.

The full picture, however, was worse. After allowing for interest payments of $1,610,000,000 in 1982, the IATA members' net result for the year was put at a loss of $1,870,000,000. A loss of more than $2 billion was anticipated in 1983, and only a modest improvement was expected in the following year. In his report the IATA director general pointed to the airlines' need to find approximately $50 billion during the current decade just to replace obsolete aircraft and equipment. He noted that, with a drastic worsening of the lines' debt-equity ratios, there could be difficulty in raising capital.

The bleak situation was blamed on such factors as stagnant markets, uneconomic fares combined with illegal discounting, rising costs, overcapacity on many routes, and, in the case of 30–40 airlines, the blocking of some $600 million of their earnings in about 30 countries, mostly in Africa. The effect of illegal discounting—by up to 70% of official fares in some cases—on revenues was a main topic of IATA's November annual general meeting. After considerable argument the meeting approved a resolution obliging the chief executive of each member airline to take steps to deal with the problem and to show positive results by March 1, 1983. Some observers considered the final resolution, which lacked specific disciplinary provisions, to be somewhat weaker than the one initially proposed to the meeting.

In a major effort to control members' operating costs, the IATA launched a campaign to secure stabilization of user charges for navigation and airport services and to persuade governments to make the often circuitous air routes more efficient, particularly in Europe. Measures to be taken by the airlines themselves were likely to include staff cuts, wage freezes, cancellation or postponement of aircraft orders, and the sale of assets.

In the U.S. the 11 major airlines reported an operating loss of $118.1 million for the first nine months of 1982, compared with a loss of $18 million for the comparable period of 1981. Although 9 of the 11 airlines improved their operating results in the third quarter of 1982 from those of a year earlier, and the group as a whole managed a net profit in that quarter, it was considered too early to discern an improving trend.

A review by the U.S. Civil Aeronautics Board considered the effects of deregulation on the U.S. transport industry. It showed that, with the freeing of competition over the years 1978–82, the trunk carriers consistently lost market share to local service carriers and new entrants. In that period the trunks' share fell from 87.2 to 78.9%. The study detected a shift in service patterns, with the trunks pulling out of smaller markets and the locals expanding into longer-haul markets. Fuel and labour costs more than doubled in the period, yet average fares increased by 65%. Certificated airline service to 74 communities was discontinued,

LONDON EXPRESS/PICTORIAL PARADE

Laker Airways, a British concern that pioneered low-cost transatlantic fares, was forced to cease operations in February. Its fleet of planes was impounded so that they could be sold to pay creditors.

Trade, International: see Economy, World

Trade Unions: see Industrial Relations

Transkei: see South Africa

but in general the public's travel convenience improved in large markets and declined only slightly in small ones.

Final figures for world scheduled air traffic in 1981, issued by the International Civil Aviation Organization, showed that the number of passengers, 743 million, represented a decline of 0.8% from 1980. The volume of freight rose 2.8% to 11 million metric tons. Thanks to an increase in the average distance flow, total traffic increased 2.5% to 133,940,000,000,000 metric ton-km, but this was the lowest percentage increase recorded in ten years. The international operations of IATA members, representing about 60% of the world total, rose 5.3% (in ton-kilometre) in 1981; a further rise of 2.4% was expected for 1982, and the association's forecast showed likely gains of 5.7% in 1983 and 6.5% in 1984. (DAVID WOOLLEY)

SHIPPING AND PORTS

Owing to the low level of the world freight markets, particularly those involving bulk cargoes, the international shipping industry was faced with the worst shipping recession since the early 1930s, and as a result the level of idle tonnage reached a new all-time high. Slightly over 10% of world merchant ship tonnage, representing 1,098 ships of nearly 69 million tons deadweight (dw), was laid up for lack of cargo by the end of the summer, compared with about 17 million tons dw in August 1981. By far the largest portion (57 million tons dw) of the laid-up total was tankers, representing 16% of the world's tanker tonnage. Dry-cargo ships that were idle totaled 12 million tons dw or 4% of the world fleet.

The merchant fleets of many of the traditional maritime nations suffered severe reductions because of idled vessels. Denmark was in the lead with 33% of Danish-flag vessels laid up; it was followed by Norway with 32%, Greece 20%, The Netherlands 12%, Liberia 11%, and Panama 8%. The volume of tonnage being sent to scrapyards increased as many owners gave up all hope of finding employment for their older vessels; this fact, coupled with only a modest influx of new tonnage, kept the tonnage total of world shipping almost the same as a year earlier. At the end of 1982 the world total was 75,151 ships of 424.7 million gross registered tons (grt) or 702 million tons dw.

For the first time since such tables were kept, Greece with 42 million grt moved into second place in the overall table of national tonnages, well behind Liberia with 74 million grt (down from 80 million grt in 1981) and just ahead of Japan with 40 million grt.

The war between the U.K. and Argentina over possession of the Falkland Islands had little effect on world freight markets with the exception of grain, which suffered from a reduction in movements from Argentina to the U.S.S.R. A world surplus of steel resulted in cutbacks in production by all the major steel-producing countries, and this in turn led to less demand for ore. Part of the loss in ore cargoes was recovered by an increase in the movement of steaming coal for use in power stations that were converted from oil to coal-firing and in certain industrial processes. It was expected that the long-term future for coal would be good enough to justify the expansion of coal-handling facilities at the major coal ports. At Los Angeles work neared completion on a new $40 million coal terminal, and facilities were improved at New York City and Mobile, Ala. The Sri Lanka government approved a £70 million plan to develop the Port of Colombo, and in Taiwan a $35 million coal-discharging terminal was to be built offshore from Hsinta to serve the Taiwan Power Corporation's electricity generating station. (W. D. EWART)

FREIGHT AND PIPELINES

Continuing pressure on the freight transport sector helped spur the development and application of more flexible and less costly means of transportation. This was reflected in the U.S.S.R., where by 1982 rail container traffic exceeded 50 million tons per year. In the U.S. and West Germany major growth took place in piggyback (truck/trailer and rail flatcar) transport, with the West German annual tonnage having increased from nothing to 6 million in the previous ten years and 20 million expected by the end of the century. A parallel recent development was that of large train ferries, for which there were applications in the Baltic, the Black Sea, and the English Channel.

While pipelines had occasionally led to some regional controversy, they rarely formed a focus of international dispute. A major exception to this general rule was the Siberian–Western European gas pipeline. The scheme involved pumping between 21 billion and 30 billion cu ft per annum of natural gas 3,550 km (2,200 mi) from the Urengoi field in the U.S.S.R. (the largest in the world) to the Czechoslovak border and then on into Western Europe. The contracts, signed in October 1981, would bring relatively cheap gas to energy-poor Western Europe and also would result in substantial orders for pipes, generators, and other engineering equipment. Meanwhile, in response to the continuation of martial law in Poland, the administration of U.S. Pres. Ronald Reagan embargoed the use of equipment made by U.S. manufacturers and their European subsidiaries. Understandably, this led to tension between the U.S. and Western Europe, while the U.S.S.R. maintained that the pipeline could be built without U.S. technology (notably 25-MW compressors). Spiced with ru-

A giant Japanese iron ore carrier, operated with a computerized voice-control system, took to the water in May. The 179,000-ton vessel was built in a shipyard near Tokyo.

UPI

World Transportation

Country	Railways Route length in 000 km	Traffic Passenger in 000,000 pass.-km	Traffic Freight in 000,000 net ton-km	Road length in 000 km	Vehicles in use Passenger in 000	Vehicles in use Commercial in 000	Merchant shipping Number of vessels	Gross reg. tons in 000	Total km flown in 000,000	Air traffic Passenger in 000,000 pass.-km	Freight in 000,000 net ton-km
EUROPE											
Austria	6.5	7,735	10,220	106.3	2,246.9	183.7	8	62	22.0	1,235	17.3
Belgium	4.0	7,078	7,514	126.8	3,153.7	267.7	312	1,917	54.8	5,202	454.0
Bulgaria	4.3	6,960	18,052	36.4	815.5	130.0[1]	188	1,194	c. 12.7	c. 775	c. 10.0
Cyprus	—	—	—	10.3	92.0	23.3	588	.819	9.5	854	18.1
Czechoslovakia	13.1	18,050	73,260	145.5[1]	1,975.7[1]	324.8[1]	21	185	24.7	1,472	14.3
Denmark	2.9[1]	3,069[1]	1,800[1]	68.9	1,339.5	252.8	1,169	5,048	c. 33.0[2]	2,967[2]	132.6[2]
Finland	6.1	3,273	8,392	75.0	1,225.9	49.1	341	2,445	35.5	2,508	56.2
France	33.9	55,670	64,398	803.0	19,130.0	2,457.0	1,199	11,455	276.3	36,498	2,239.4
Germany, East	14.2	23,027	55,824	119.0	2,677.7	234.1	449	1,570	34.5[1]	1,848[1]	67.3[1]
Germany, West	31.6	41,559	62,037	482.0	23,236.1	1,288.1	1,820	7,708	196.2	21,636	1,583.7
Greece	2.5	1,464	814	37.1	377.9	402.0	3,710	42,005	40.1	5,196	75.1
Hungary	7.8	12,372	23,850	87.7	1,021.3	124.5	22	83	c. 15.5	c. 998	c. 19.0
Ireland	2.0	1,032	620	92.3[1]	734.4	65.1	156	268	21.9	2,270	86.4
Italy	19.9[1]	39,480	16,630	293.6	c. 17,500.0	c. 1,300.0	1,677	10,641	139.5	14,096	542.1
Netherlands, The	2.9	9,235	3,321	108.5[1]	4,515.0	344.0	1,271	5,467	108.8	15,317	1,100.1
Norway	4.2	2,420	2,380	81.7	1,233.6	152.5	2,409	21,675	c. 58.1[2]	4,070[2]	137.8[2]
Poland	24.4	48,239	109,861	298.5	2,383.0	617.8	827	3,579	35.1	2,142	18.8
Portugal	3.6	5,854	1,004	51.7[1]	1,269.0	186.1	351	1,377	39.2	4,007	108.6
Romania	11.1[1]	23,220	75,535	95.0[1]	c. 250.0	c. 130.0	335	2,032	19.7	1,252	11.3
Spain	15.3	14,135	10,450	237.9	7,556.5	1,338.3	2,678	8,134	164.3	15,938	454.5
Sweden	12.0	6,934	14,594	129.0	2,883.0	181.6	706	4,034	66.2[2]	5,342[2]	190.9[2]
Switzerland	5.0	9,094	7,152	64.0	2,246.8	169.4	33	315	97.8	11,628	489.9
U.S.S.R.	237.5	331,200	3,507,000	1,346.5	c. 9,250.0	c. 7,910.0	7,867	23,493	...	160,299	c. 3,083.0
United Kingdom	18.0	31,700[3]	17,510[3]	376.0	c. 15,640.0	c. 1,780.0	2,975	25,419	359.1	52,078	1,447.3
Yugoslavia	9.5	10,240	25,444	133.9	2,430.8	190.0	483	2,541	c. 34.8	c. 2,984	c. 41.7
ASIA											
Bangladesh	2.9	5,198	739[1]	5.7	29.4[1]	11.9[1]	208	401	11.8	1,179	c. 20.0
Burma	4.5[1]	2,760	c. 600	22.5[1]	39.9[1]	42.3[1]	96	85	c. 6.1	c. 218	c. 1.6
China	50.0	147,300	571,200	897.0	c. 50.0[1]	c. 710.0[1]	1,051	7,663	c. 46.5	5,000	170.0
India	60.9	198,642	155,955	1,282.0[1]	1,035.3[1]	440.2[1]	620	6,020	84.8	12,090	448.4
Indonesia	6.9	3,229	980	128.9[1]	577.3[1]	383.6[1]	1,260	1,745	88.4	5,907	127.4
Iran	4.6	2,981	4,063	63.1	1,079.1	406.0	234	1,202	15.6	1,600	40.9
Iraq	1.6[1]	821[1]	2,497[1]	15.1[1]	c. 164.4	c. 192.7	148	1,491	12.6	c. 1,280	c. 50.0
Israel	0.8	264	828	12.2[1]	409.9	87.6	62	581	c. 30.2	4,815	302.6
Japan	27.5[1]	316,200	39,585	1,113.4	23,659.5	13,948.5	10,422	40,836	c. 364.8	c. 51,217	c. 2,002.0
Kampuchea	0.6	54[1]	10[1]	c. 11.0[1]	27.2[1]	11.0[1]	3	4	0.8[1]	42[1]	0.4[1]
Korea, South	c. 6.1	21,235	10,637	47.0	249.1	226.9	1,634	5,142	60.7	11,240	933.6
Malaysia	2.7	1,640[4]	1,130[4]	29.0	696.5[1]	158.7[1]	258	879	40.9	c. 4,540	c. 136.0
Pakistan	8.8	17,315	8,516	96.4	303.7[1]	66.5[1]	86	507	49.7	6,059	254.7
Philippines	1.2	254	33	127.1[1]	470.8[1]	419.8[1]	827	2,540	42.4	c. 6,680	c. 197.0
Saudi Arabia	c. 0.7	82	261	47.7	630.8	522.2	286	3,122	91.3	9,938	c. 174.6
Syria	1.9[1]	582	580	17.7[1]	66.2[1]	86.0[1]	45	42	10.5	948	16.2
Taiwan	3.7	7,982	2,527	17.5	506.3	277.9	498	1,888	34.1[1]	7,271	924.4
Thailand	3.9	8,361	2,805	67.7	c. 397.9	c. 451.9	184	403	c. 41.8	c. 6,276	248.4
Turkey	8.2	6,014	5,030	232.2[1]	679.9	327.2	532	1,664	c. 14.5	c. 1,103	c. 13.7
Vietnam	c. 2.5	4,609[1]	995[1]	347.2	c. 100.0[1]	c. 200.0[1]	94	250	c. 0.1	c. 3	c. 0.1
AFRICA											
Algeria	3.9[1]	1,644[1]	2,177[1]	c. 78.0[1]	396.8[1]	206.5[1]	129	1,283	c. 27.9	c. 2,300	c. 13.0
Congo	0.8	286[1]	470[1]	8.2[1]	13.2[1]	3.7[1]	16	8	c. 2.9[5]	c. 197[5]	c. 19.3[5]
Egypt	4.7	9,230[1]	2,302[1]	28.9[1]	325.5	113.3	307	599	30.5	3,264	40.2
Ethiopia	1.0	1711.6	1481.6	35.9	38.3	11.7	19	25	10.5	c. 760	c. 22.3
Gabon	c. 0.2[1]	...	...	7.1[1]	c. 17.4[1]	c. 12.7[1]	17	78	c. 6.4	c. 374	c. 27.3
Ghana	1.0	521[1]	312[1]	c. 32.0	c. 66.0	c. 48.0	123	255	c. 4.3	c. 324	c. 2.8
Ivory Coast	0.7	1,210[7]	600[7]	45.3	112.0[1]	67.2[1]	63	152	c. 2.8[5]	c. 215[5]	c. 18.6[5]
Kenya	4.5	...	1,998	53.6	118.0[1]	111.0[1]	18	5	11.6	863	c. 20.3
Liberia	0.5	—	4,396[1]	10.8	13.1[1]	9.0[1]	2,281	74,906	c. 1.5	c. 17	c. 0.1
Libya	0.8	77	229	c. 20.0[1]	c. 367.4	278.9	103	389	c. 11.7	c. 1,101	c. 17.0
Malawi	0.8	80	247	10.8	11.8	13.3	1	1	2.0	83	1.2
Morocco	1.8	920	3,890	57.6	413.7[1]	157.5[1]	168	374	20.5	1,865	31.3
Nigeria	3.5	785	972	108.0	215.4	33.1	127	476	c. 24.2	2,308	16.9
Senegal	1.2[1]	180[1]	164[1]	13.9	72.9[1]	20.2[1]	12	38	c. 3.2[5]	c. 196[5]	c. 18.4[5]
Somalia	—	—	—	19.8[1]	4.3[1]	5.7[1]	21	35	c. 3.5	c. 140	c. 0.5
South Africa	20.7	...	96,770[8]	183.5	c. 2,456.0	c. 911.0	285	731	c. 67.3	9,286	333.1
Sudan	4.8	1,167	2,620	c. 48.0	c. 34.6	c. 38.0	13	93	c. 10.5	c. 710	c. 12.5
Tanzania	3.6	...	...	45.6	c. 42.9	c. 52.1	35	58	7.5	284	c. 2.4
Tunisia	2.0	1,012	1,720	17.8[1]	120.6[1]	97.7[1]	44	136	c. 13.6	1,441	14.4
Uganda	1.3	...	...	27.9[1]	26.0[1]	5.4[1]	—	—	c. 3.7	c. 120	c. 3.2
Zaire	5.3	467[1]	2,203[1]	c. 145.0[1]	c. 93.9	c. 84.9	34	92	c. 10.0	c. 830	c. 38.0
Zambia	2.2	320[1]	897[1]	36.4[1]	c. 103.0	c. 66.3	—	—	10.5	547	18.2
Zimbabwe	3.4	...	6,610	85.8	167.4	68.7	—	—	7.9	506	9.1
NORTH AND CENTRAL AMERICA											
Canada	67.6[1]	2,856[10]	228,117[10]	884.3[1]	9,985.1[1]	2,854.2[1]	1,300	3,159	c. 337.8	31,401	776.5
Costa Rica	c. 1.0[1]	991	16[1]	26.6[1]	c. 79.6[1]	c. 58.9[1]	27	20	c. 8.4	c. 530	c. 21.0
Cuba	13.9[1]	1,835	2,626	c. 31.2[1]	c. 80.0[1]	c. 40.0[1]	403	920	c. 14.7	c. 932	c. 11.1
El Salvador	c. 0.8	c. 26	57	11.7[1]	c. 56.6	c. 69.0	7	3	c. 3.9	c. 178	c. 13.0
Guatemala	c. 1.0	...	117[1]	17.3[1]	166.9	81.5	9	28	3.7	159	6.4
Honduras	c. 1.9	174[1]	3[1]	13.4	21.6	45.0	143	201	c. 6.8	c. 394	c. 3.5
Mexico	25.0	5,306	c. 42,800	213.2	4,032.0	1,534.1	456	1,135	c. 157.4	13,870	138.1
Nicaragua	0.4	19	12	18.2[1]	c. 36.6	c. 30.7	19	18	c. 1.6	c. 76	c. 1.4
Panama	0.7[1]	...	...	8.6	97.3[1]	25.8[1]	4,461	27,657	c. 6.7	c. 414	c. 3.7
United States	296.9[1]	18,020[9]	1,476,515[9]	6,303.8[1]	120,248.0	33,349.7	5,869	18,908	4,413.4	375,582	10,168.7
SOUTH AMERICA											
Argentina	c. 34.6	12,593	9,742	207.6[1]	2,866.0[1]	1,244.0[1]	521	2,307	c. 93.5	6,936	214.8
Bolivia	3.9	398[1]	593[1]	38.9[1]	35.9[1]	50.3[1]	2	15	c. 13.5	962	44.2
Brazil	31.1	11,395[1]	73,805[1]	1,394.7	9,090.3	947.2	627	5,133	203.4	10,761	528.6
Chile	c. 10.1[1]	1,622	1,727	79.9	405.0	188.0	182	564	24.7	2,220	104.0
Colombia	2.3[1]	310	860	74.7	522.0	33.0	72	297	c. 44.7	4,212	209.7
Ecuador	1.0	65	34	37.9	c. 73.7	c. 160.7	100	299	c. 20.4	c. 916	c. 34.6
Paraguay	0.4	23[1]	17[1]	c. 15.0	25.2	33.5	31	31	c. 4.3	c. 262	c. 2.8
Peru	2.5[1]	651[1]	612[1]	58.5[1]	c. 318.7	c. 169.9	694	826	24.6	1,974	c. 40.7
Uruguay	3.0	418	249	25.0[1]	c. 173.0	c. 91.0	76	200	c. 4.3	c. 178	c. 1.0
Venezuela	c. 0.4	40	20	61.8[1]	1,390.0[1]	639.5[1]	227	742	c. 64.6	c. 4,318	150.8
OCEANIA											
Australia	39.4[1,10]	...	31,995[1]	810.9	5,898.0	1,462.0	527	1,768	198.9	25,506	515.6
New Zealand	4.5	404	3,181	95.9	1,346.1	269.8	114	244	c. 52.1	5,676	203.9

Note: Data are for 1980 or 1981 unless otherwise indicated. (—) indicates nil or negligible; (...) indicates not known. (c.) indicates provisional or estimated.
[1] Data given are the most recent available. [2] Including apportionment of traffic of Scandinavian Airlines System. [3] Excluding Northern Ireland. [4] Peninsular Malaysia only; including Singapore. [5] Including apportionment of traffic of Air Afrique. [6] Including Djibouti traffic. [7] Including Upper Volta traffic. [8] Including Namibia traffic. [9] Class 1 railways only. [10] State system only.

Sources: UN, Statistical Yearbook 1979/80, Monthly Bulletin of Statistics, Annual Bulletin of Transport Statistics for Europe 1980; Lloyd's Register of Shipping, Statistical Tables 1981; International Road Federation, World Road Statistics 1976–80; International Civil Aviation Organization, Civil Aviation Statistics of the World 1980.   (M. C. MacDONALD)

mours of the use of forced labour on the pipeline, the controversy ended when Reagan lifted the embargo in the fall of 1982.

In the U.K., despite considerable opposition, the government announced plans to increase the maximum permitted weight of long trucks from 32.5 to 38 metric tons. Overall in Western Europe road freight still finished second to that on waterways, which carried 185 million metric tons of international freight in 1982 (44% of the total, with the roads taking 40% and rail 16%).

ROADS AND TRAFFIC

The number of automobiles on the world's highways rose to 330 million in 1982. The maintenance of existing roads was a major issue in both developed and less developed countries. In order to keep down construction and maintenance costs, greater emphasis was placed on the use of local materials. In the U.K. the first stage of the widening of one of the world's most densely traveled interurban expressways (the M1) was opened; apart from the problems of designing, constructing, and managing the remodeling of a busy operational motorway, the project provided lessons for long-term highway planning.

The problems of rural road maintenance in less developed countries were different but no less acute. Inadequate maintenance could lead not merely to the deterioration but to the actual disintegration of structures; this appeared to have been the fate of a large portion of the Trans-African Highway in Chad.

New highways were opened between Nicosia and Limassol in Cyprus, Abu Ghraib and Baghdad (Iraq), Hong Kong and Guangzhou (Canton), and

Gudow and West Berlin. This last 200-km (125-mi) highway was the only good standard road link between West Germany and West Berlin and was expected to transform communications between the two areas. The Hong Kong-to-Guangzhou route was a six-lane toll road. As of 1982 Japan's toll roads totaled 2,500 km (1,350 mi) in length. While user toll roads made sense only in certain circumstances, they encouraged private financing—which could be very important during times of restricted public spending. In the U.K. private financing of public highways, whereby the developer received "tolls" from the highway authority rather than the user, was being explored.

Transcontinental road projects continued to attract a good deal of attention, but achievement was slow. Only 1,800 km (1,110 mi) of the planned 10,400-km (6,450-mi) Trans-European Motorway stretching from Gdansk, Poland, to southern Europe was open, and progress was similarly limited on the Trans-African Highway.

Whereas in the past the most spectacular highway projects were to be found in the Western world, the balance was changing. The $460 million Aberdeen Tunnel and East Kowloon Way in Hong Kong and the $175 million Olympic Expressway between Taegu and Kwangju in South Korea were examples of this. The latter project was initiated to mark the holding of the 1988 Summer Olympic Games in Seoul. Traffic congestion was becoming a major problem in some Asian cities, and Hong Kong introduced stiff vehicle taxes to help moderate the growth of car ownership there. On the other hand, Bangkok (Thailand), with much lower traffic density than Hong Kong's, had recently opened its first urban expressway.

INTERCITY RAIL

The most remarkable event of the year was the near completion of the fourth Shinkansen line between Tokyo and Niigata, Japan. This 270-km (170-mi) line had taken 11 years to build through some of Honshu's most difficult terrain. The link through to the Tokyo suburbs was made by the opening of the Di-Shimiyu tunnel, which, at 22.3 km (13.8 mi), was the longest mainline rail tunnel in the world. The opening of this line, which was to extend to central Tokyo in 1986, brought the length of the "bullet train" network to 1,800 km. In California a "bullet-type" railway service between San Diego and San Francisco was being planned.

Expansion of national railway networks continued in other countries, especially those earning oil revenues. In Iraq, despite the war with Iran, work was under way on rail links between Baghdad and Basra (910 km, 565 mi) and Baghdad and Husaiba (404 km, 250 mi). In Venezuela the capital, Caracas, was to be connected to La Guaira on the coast, and in Libya work began on the 194-km (120-mi) Tripoli–Misratah line.

In the U.K. the high-technology Advanced Passenger Train had to be withdrawn from passenger service because of difficulties with its braking system. In West Germany the national airline Lufthansa introduced express rail service between Düsseldorf, Cologne, and Bonn and the Frankfurt airport.

Sentimentalists placed coins on the track as the last of San Francisco's famed cable cars headed into the barn in September. The system was being closed for 20 months while equipment and tracks were rebuilt.

WIDE WORLD

A high-speed express train to link Cologne, Bonn, and Düsseldorf directly with the Frankfurt airport went into service in March in West Germany.

URBAN MASS TRANSIT

During the year the most advanced urban mass transit system came into revenue service in Lille, France, and one of the oldest mechanized systems, the San Francisco, Calif., cable cars, shut down temporarily for rehabilitation. In the U.S. progress was made on rapid transit rail projects in Portland, Ore., and Buffalo, N.Y., and the line from Cleveland, Ohio, to the suburb of Shaker Heights was renovated. In Canada Light Rail Transit (LRT) projects were under way in Vancouver, B.C., and Pickering, Ont. A light rail scheme was approved for London's Docklands, and in The Netherlands the Coalhaven-to-Copelsburg line in Rotterdam was to be extended as a streetcar line to Binnerhof. This form of technology, able to operate as both railway and streetcar, appeared to be increasingly popular where full subways were not merited.

Work on subways proceeded in Paris; in West Germany at Bochum, Dortmund, Duisburg, and Essen; and in Berlin, Rome, Stockholm, Hong Kong, Seoul, Tokyo, Boston, New York, and Mexico City. Openings during the year included Helsinki and the Tsuen Wan line in Hong Kong. By the end of 1982 the system in Mexico City was 85 km (53 mi) long, and the planners were aiming at a 438-km (272-mi) system by the year 2000. Authority to proceed was given to new subways in Singapore and Riga (U.S.S.R.) as well as to extensions of several existing systems, including the connection to the new terminal at Heathrow Airport (London).

Noteworthy developments in urban buses included the successful guided bus in Stuttgart, West Germany, which was to be introduced in Adelaide, Australia. Work also continued on new drive systems including battery diesel hybrids. The number of exclusive urban busways was growing steadily, and there were now at least ten such systems. One of the highest bus flows in any city was in São Paulo, Brazil, where platooning of buses in convoys of up to six vehicles was used to increase busway capacity by 100%.

In London transit fares were first cut by one-third and then doubled. In 1981 transit fares had been more than doubled on some lines in Chicago. This reflected pressures to keep down revenue support for transit on the part of public agencies. In the U.K. new legislation was proposed that sought to restrict external support from either local or central sources. In the U.S. reduction of federal funding led to the crisis in Chicago. In southern California a decision to "go it alone" led to a reduction in transit fares, and in New York and other cities freedom from federal "buy American" policies allowed a wide choice of equipment procurement. This especially benefited Japanese and Canadian train builders and West German bus builders.

(DAVID BAYLISS)

Trinidad and Tobago

Trinidad and Tobago

A republic and a member of the Commonwealth, Trinidad and Tobago consists of two islands off the coast of Venezuela, north of the Orinoco River delta. Area: 5,128 sq km (1,980 sq mi). Pop. (1982 est.): 1,185,000, including (1979 est.) Negro 43%; East Indian 40%; mixed 14%; other 3%. Cap. and largest city: Port-of-Spain (pop., 1979 est., 120,000). Language: English (official), Hindi, French, Spanish. Religion (1980 est.): Christian 64%; Hindu 25%; Muslim 6%; other 5%. President in 1982, Sir Ellis Clarke; prime minister, George Chambers.

Though Trinidad and Tobago continued during 1982 to have the most buoyant economy in the Caribbean, doubts were beginning to be expressed toward the end of the year about the decline in revenue from taxes on the oil industry. Reduced local oil production, the decrease in the world market

TRINIDAD AND TOBAGO

Education. (1978–79) Primary, pupils 181,863, teachers (1975–76) 6,471; secondary, pupils 87,301, teachers (1975–76) 1,631; vocational, pupils 4,200, teachers (1975–76) 114; higher (1975–76), students 4,940, teaching staff c. 500.

Finance and Trade. Monetary unit: Trinidad and Tobago dollar, with (Sept. 20, 1982) a par value of TT$2.409 to U.S. $1 (free rate of TT$4.13 = £1 sterling). Gold and other reserves (June 1982) U.S. $3,153,000,000. Budget (total; 1980 est.) balanced at TT$5,059,600,000. Foreign trade (1981): imports TT$7,469,800,000; exports TT$8,932,200,-000. Import sources (1980) Saudi Arabia 31%; U.S. 26%; U.K. 10%; Japan 7%. Export destinations (1980): U.S. 57%; The Netherlands 6%. Main exports (1980): petroleum products 52%; crude oil 40%.

Transport and Communications. Roads (1980) c. 6,400 km. Motor vehicles in use (1979): passenger 108,000; commercial 20,300. There are no railways in operation. Air traffic (1980): 1,505,000,000 passenger-km; freight 18.3 million net ton-km. Telephones (Dec. 1979) 77,800. Radio receivers (Dec. 1979) 296,000. Television receivers (Dec. 1979) 150,000.

Agriculture. Production (in 000; metric tons; 1981): sugar, raw value c. 90; rice c. 26; tomatoes c. 10; grapefruit c. 4; copra c. 5; coffee c. 2; cocoa c. 2. Livestock (in 000; 1981): cattle c. 78; pigs c. 60; goats c. 47; poultry c. 7,500.

Industry. Production (in 000 metric tons; 1981): crude oil 9,850; natural gas (cu m) c. 2,410,000; petroleum products (1980) c. 11,050; cement (1980) 200; nitrogenous fertilizers (nutrient content; 1980–81) c. 41; electricity (kw-hr; 1980) 1,840,000.

Trapshooting:
see Target Sports

price for crude oil, and new tax concessions to stimulate exploration were all expected to reduce government revenue by up to TT$500 million. Concern grew despite a current account surplus forecast of TT$1,478,000,000 for 1982 and foreign exchange reserves of TT$7.8 billion. State corporations were instructed to reduce losses, and new credit restrictions were introduced.

At home the prime minister adopted the reserved and somewhat remote day-to-day approach of his predecessor, Eric Williams. However, Chambers sought a leading role within the Caribbean Community (Caricom). Aid funds, concessionary loans, and joint ventures were agreed upon with most Caricom nations.

At the Caricom summit conference in Jamaica in November, Chambers emerged as the single most influential figure, taking a strong line on maintaining relations with Grenada. Unlike most other nations in the region, Trinidad maintained relations with the U.S. that were formal rather than close, with the government expressing reservations about the U.S.-inspired Caribbean Basin Initiative. (DAVID A. JESSOP)

Tunisia

Tunisia

A republic of North Africa lying on the Mediterranean Sea, Tunisia is bounded by Algeria and Libya. Area: 154,530 sq km (52,664 sq mi). Pop. (1982 est.): 6,629,600. Cap. and largest city: Tunis (pop., 1975 census, city proper 550,404; 1981 est., governorate 1,133,400). Language: Arabic (official). Religion: Muslim; Jewish and Christian minorities. President in 1982, Habib Bourguiba; prime minister, Mohammed Mzali.

On the domestic scene the main events of 1982 in Tunisia were a series of strikes in February that led to a general increase in wages and violent confrontations between university students and police in March. There also were a number of anti-Jewish incidents at Zarzis, Ben Gardane, and Djerba in October.

The main thrust of Tunisian foreign policy was toward a rapprochement with Libya. At Pres. Habib Bourguiba's invitation, Libyan chief of state Col. Muammar al-Qaddafi paid a five-day official visit to Tunisia in February; this followed a brief unofficial visit by Qaddafi on January 24, when he met Tunisia's Prime Minister Mohammed Mzali. A cooperation agreement was signed during the February visit, but although Qaddafi reportedly again brought up the question of a union between Libya and Tunisia (first proposed by him in 1974), no mention was made of this in the joint communiqué.

Despite the improved relations with Libya, Tunisia was among those member nations that boycotted the August summit in Tripoli of the Organization of African Unity, being opposed to the admission of the self-proclaimed (West) Saharan Arab Democratic Republic. Meanwhile, the dispute between Tunisia and Libya over their respective rights to the oil-rich continental shelf in the Gulf of Gabès was before the International Court of Justice in The Hague.

Trucking Industry:
see Transportation

Trust Territories:
see Dependent States

TUNISIA
Education. (1980–81) Primary, pupils 1,045,011, teachers 26,989; secondary, pupils 210,895; vocational, pupils 60,137; secondary and vocational, teachers 12,946; teacher training, students 4,101, teachers (1979–80) 135; higher, students 31,887, teaching staff (1979–80) 3,591.
Finance. Monetary unit: Tunisian dinar, with (Sept. 20, 1982) a free rate of 0.60 dinar to U.S. $1 (1.03 dinars = £1 sterling). Gold and other reserves (June 1982) U.S. $529 million. Budget (1980 actual): revenue 1,121,000,000 dinars; expenditure 802 million dinars (excludes 333 million dinars capital expenditure). Gross domestic product (1981) 3,992,000,000 dinars. Money supply (May 1982) 1,150,-000,000 dinars. Cost of living (Tunis; 1975 = 100; May 1982) 168.7.
Foreign Trade. (1981) Imports 1,970,180,000 dinars; exports 1,224,760,000 dinars. Import sources (1980): France 25%; Italy 16%; West Germany 9%; Saudi Arabia 9%; U.S. 6%; Greece 5%. Export destinations (1980): Greece 18%; Italy 16%; France 15%; U.S. 15%; West Germany 13%. Main exports (1980): crude oil 50%; clothing 12%; phosphates and products 11%; food *c.* 6%. Tourism (1980): visitors 1,602,100; gross receipts U.S. $605 million.
Transport and Communications. Roads (main; 1979) 17,762 km. Motor vehicles in use (1979): passenger 120,600; commercial 97,700. Railways: (1980) 2,013 km; traffic (1981) 1,012,000,000 passenger-km, freight 1,720,000,000 net ton-km. Air traffic (1981): 1,441,000,000 passenger-km; freight 14.4 million net ton-km. Telephones (Jan. 1980) 173,500. Radio licenses (Dec. 1979) 587,000. Television receivers (Dec. 1979) 300,000.
Agriculture. Production (in 000; metric tons; 1981): wheat *c.* 963; barley *c.* 270; potatoes *c.* 124; tomatoes *c.* 295; watermelons *c.* 206; grapes *c.* 141; dates *c.* 53; olives *c.* 725; oranges 141. Livestock (in 000; 1981): sheep *c.* 4,967; cattle *c.* 950; goats *c.* 987; camels *c.* 170; poultry *c.* 19,000.
Industry. Production (in 000; metric tons; 1981): crude oil 5,406; natural gas (cu m) 380,000; cement 2,024; iron ore (53% metal content) 400; pig iron 157; crude steel 174; phosphate rock (1980) 4,502; phosphate fertilizers (1980–81) *c.* 415; petroleum products *c.* 1,530; sulfuric acid (1980) 1,337; electricity (excluding most industrial production; kw-hr) 2,676,000.

Following a private visit to the U.S. in January by President Bourguiba, Mzali in April went to Washington, D.C., for talks with Secretary of Defense Caspar Weinberger. An agreement was signed for the sale to Tunisia of military equipment that included 12 F-5 fighter aircraft and 54 M-60 tanks; to help pay for this, U.S. aid for 1983 was to be almost doubled from the 1982 figure of $82 million to $140 million.

Following Israel's intervention in Lebanon and the escalation of the civil war there, Tunisia's ruling Parti Socialiste Destourien and the Union Générale des Travailleurs de Tunisie proclaimed their solidarity with the Arab people in Lebanon and Palestine. In August, at President Bourguiba's invitation, Palestine Liberation Organization (PLO) leader Yasir Arafat set up his new headquarters in Tunis, and more than 1,000 Palestinian guerrillas evacuated from Lebanon were housed in the Beja region west of Tunis.

Franco-Tunisian relations were reinforced. Bourguiba visited France for medical treatment in January and September, and members of the French government visited Tunis on several occasions during the year.

In March Tunisia became a member of the Organization of Petroleum Exporting Countries, Libya having withdrawn its opposition. In November serious flooding caused a number of deaths and much damage. (PHILIPPE DECRAENE)

Turkey

A republic of southeastern Europe and Asia Minor, Turkey is bounded by the Aegean Sea, the Black Sea, the U.S.S.R., Iran, Iraq, Syria, the Mediterranean Sea, Greece, and Bulgaria. Area: 779,452 sq km (300,948 sq mi), including 23,698 sq km in Europe. Pop. (1982 est.): 46,312,000. Cap.: Ankara (pop., 1980, 1,887,700). Largest city: Istanbul (pop., 1980, 2,772,700). Language: Turkish (official); Kurdish and Arabic minorities. Religion: predominantly Muslim. Head of state in 1982, Gen. Kenan Evren (president from November 12); prime minister, Bulent Ulusu.

The armed forces commanders who formed the National Security Council (NSC) and took over the government of Turkey in the bloodless coup of Sept. 12, 1980, continued during 1982 to follow their plan for the reform of institutions with a view to the reestablishment of parliamentary rule. A new constitution, drafted by a nominated Consultative Assembly and amended by the NSC, was submitted to a referendum on November 7 and approved by 91% of the votes in a voter turnout also of 91%. Criticism of individual constitutional provisions was allowed before the final text was established. Thereafter the campaign was one-sided, as no one was allowed to urge its rejection.

Under provisional articles, acceptance of the constitution carried with it the election of Gen. Kenan Evren, chairman of the NSC, to the presidency of the republic for a seven-year term and a ban varying from five to ten years on leading members of the old political parties. The constitution provided for a single-chamber Parliament, elected every five years; for an executive headed by a president who was to be elected by Parliament (after the end of General Evren's term) and given enhanced powers; for a Cabinet responsible to Parliament; and for an independent judiciary. Political activity by trade unions and professional associations was banned, as were totalitarian, Marxist, and religious fundamentalist politics. After the constitution was approved, the Consultative Assembly began drafting a law on political parties and an electoral law in preparation for elections scheduled for late 1983.

Bulent Ecevit, leader of the dissolved left-of-centre Republican People's Party, was the only politician to challenge the ruling generals. He served two short prison sentences for giving interviews to foreign publications. On September 1 there were some 18,000 persons under arrest and facing charges for politically motivated offenses, while another 6,500 had received sentences of imprisonment. The military authorities examined 540 complaints of torture and maltreatment and concluded that in four cases death had been caused by torture.

While Turkish political terrorism was largely suppressed, attacks by Armenian terrorists continued. The number of Turkish diplomats and their dependents killed outside the country by Ar-

Turkey

Leon Ekmekjian, an Armenian terrorist, was captured after he and another Armenian engaged in a shoot-out with police at Ankara's airport. The melee left nine dead and scores wounded.

WIDE WORLD

TURKEY

Education. (1979–80) Primary, pupils 5,622,000, teachers 199,245; secondary, pupils 1,711,000, teachers 67,235; vocational, pupils 514,923, teachers 28,644; teacher training (1978–79), students 24,065, teachers 1,454; higher, students 270,000, teaching staff 20,643.

Finance. Monetary unit: Turkish lira, with (Sept. 20, 1982) a free rate of 173.76 liras to U.S. $1 (297.92 liras = £1 sterling). Gold and other reserves (June 1982) U.S. $1,228,000,000. Budget (1981–82 est.): revenue 1,503,944,000,000 liras; expenditure 1,540,965,000,000 liras. Gross national product (1981) 6,576,100,000,000 liras. Money supply (Dec. 1981) 969.3 billion liras. Cost of living (1975 = 100; June 1982) 1,391.

Foreign Trade. (1981) Imports 1,005,300,000,000 liras; exports 530,720,000,000 liras. Import sources: Iraq 18%; West Germany 10%; Libya 9%; U.S. 7%; Switzerland 6%; U.K. 5%; Saudi Arabia 5%. Export destinations: West Germany 14%; Iraq 12%; Libya 10%; U.S. 6%; Switzerland 5%; Italy 5%; Iran 5%. Main exports (1980): fruit and vegetables 32%; textile yarns and fabrics 12%; cotton 11%; tobacco 8%; clothing 5%. Tourism (1980): visitors 1,288,100; gross receipts U.S. $327 million.

Transport and Communications. Roads (1979) 232,162 km (including 189 km expressways). Motor vehicles in use (1980): passenger 579,900; commercial 327,200. Railways (1980): 8,193 km; traffic 6,014,000,000 passenger-km, freight 5,030,000,000 net ton-km. Air traffic (1980): c. 1,103,000,000 passenger-km; freight c. 13.7 million net ton-km. Shipping (1981): merchant vessels 100 gross tons and over 532; gross tonnage 1,663,679. Telephones (Dec. 1980) 1,147,300. Radio licenses (Dec. 1980) 4,281,000. Television licenses (Dec. 1980) 3,343,000.

Agriculture. Production (in 000; metric tons; 1981): wheat 17,040; barley 5,900; corn 1,100; rye 500; oats 300; rice 290; potatoes c. 2,900; tomatoes 3,900; onions c. 1,000; sugar, raw value c. 1,300; sunflower seed 575; cottonseed c. 785; chick-peas c. 280; dry beans c. 170; cabbages c. 588; pumpkins c. 367; watermelons c. 4,457; cucumbers c. 511; oranges c. 723; lemons c. 300; apples c. 1,479; grapes 3,600; raisins c. 365; olives c. 650; tea 52; tobacco 200; cotton, lint c. 490. Livestock (in 000; Dec. 1980): cattle 15,894; sheep 48,630; buffalo 1,031; goats 19,043; horses 794; asses 1,345; chickens 58,584.

Industry. Fuel and power (in 000; metric tons; 1980): coal 3,597; lignite 13,650; crude oil (1981) 2,392; electricity (kw-hr) 23,275,000. Production (in 000; metric tons; 1981): cement 15,041; iron ore (55–60% metal content) 2,882; pig iron 226; crude steel 1,618; petroleum products (1979) c. 13,200; sulfuric acid c. 270; fertilizers (nutrient content; 1980–81) nitrogenous c. 462, phosphate c. 355; bauxite 473; chrome ore (oxide content; 1980) 197; cotton yarn (1979) 184; man-made fibres (1979) 113.

Tunnels:
see Engineering Projects

menian terrorists rose to 24, and on August 7 nine people were killed and 72 injured in an Armenian attack on the Ankara airport.

General Evren in 1982 visited Kuwait, Pakistan, Romania, and Bulgaria, while Prime Minister Bulent Ulusu took part in the Islamic mediation mission in the Iran-Iraq war. Relations with Greece were strained by repeated Greek accusations of Turkish violations of Greek territorial waters and airspace in the Aegean Sea, by Turkish accusations of Greek maltreatment of the Turkish minority in western Thrace, and by the Greek campaign against the presence of Turkish troops in Cyprus, where Turkey continued to support intercommunal talks as the only means to a solution. The situation was temporarily eased, however, when the two governments decided on June 22 to refrain from further polemics.

Relations with Europe were soured by frequent European criticism of the military regime; the European Communities continued to block aid to Turkey. Close relations with the U.S. were promoted by the visit to Ankara in May of U.S. Secretary of State Alexander Haig. The killing of two Turkish soldiers by Soviet border guards on August 10 emphasized the basically antagonistic nature of the outwardly correct relationship between Turkey and the U.S.S.R.

Inflation fell below 30%, and exports increased significantly. However, the tightly controlled monetary policies caused difficulties. The largest private finance house in Turkey, Banker Kastelli, was unable to meet payments and had to be taken over by the government on June 22. This was followed by the resignations of Turgut Ozal, deputy prime minister in charge of the economy, and of the ministers of finance and of housing.

(ANDREW MANGO)

Tuvalu

Uganda

Tuvalu

A constitutional monarchy within the Commonwealth comprising nine main islands and their associated islets and reefs, Tuvalu is located in the western Pacific Ocean just south of the Equator and west of the International Date Line. Area: 26 sq km (10 sq.mi). Pop. (1982 est.): 9,000, mostly Polynesians. Cap.: Funafuti (pop., 1979, 2,200). Queen, Elizabeth II; governor-general in 1982, Penitala Fiatau Teo; prime minister, Tomasi Puapua.

In 1982 the government of Prime Minister Tomasi Puapua, elected in September 1981, had mixed fortunes. It approved a budget of A$3.2 million but began the year in debt for almost one-

third of that amount. This debt was subsequently cleared by special grants from the U.K., Australia, and New Zealand. Exports for the year showed no significant improvement over 1981, when they realized only A$30,000, mainly from copra. Imports during 1981 totaled A$2.6 million. A large portion of the difference was offset by sales of stamps, which were expected to earn A$1.5 million in 1982; A$44,000 of this was given to a Tongan cyclone relief fund.

Tuvalu signed a new fishing-rights agreement with Taiwan worth U.S. $84,000 a year, but a similar agreement with South Korea that would have been worth U.S. $92,000 fell through. An attempt to improve returns from copra by selling husked coconuts proved a failure when the vessel carrying the trial shipment was diverted to Singapore before going to the buyer in Sydney, Australia, and the crop was spoiled. Tuvalu obtained improved shipping from Australia after services by the South Pacific Forum Line were reduced.

Tuvalu was represented at the August meeting of the South Pacific Forum in Rotorua, New Zealand, by the prime minister. On October 26–27 Queen Elizabeth II and Prince Philip visited the islands.

(BARRIE MACDONALD)

> **TUVALU**
> **Education.** (1981) Primary, pupils 1,226, teachers (1979) 44; secondary, pupils 250, teachers (1979) 10.
> **Finance and Trade.** Monetary unit: Australian dollar, with (Sept. 20, 1982) a free rate of A$1.04 to U.S. $1 (A$1.79 = £1 sterling). Budget (1981 est.) balanced at A$2,820,000 (including U.K. aid of A$810,000). Foreign trade (1979): imports A$1,850,800 (48% from Australia, 20% from Fiji, 11% from U.K., 10% from New Zealand); exports c. A$560,000. Main exports: postage stamps c. 54%; copra c. 42%.

Uganda

A republic and a member of the Commonwealth, Uganda is bounded by Sudan, Zaire, Rwanda, Tanzania, and Kenya. Area: 241,139 sq km (93,104 sq mi), including 44,081 sq km of inland water. Pop. (1982 est.): 13,651,000, virtually all of whom are African. Cap. and largest city: Kampala (pop., 1980 prelim., 458,000). Language: English (official), Swahili, and Luganda. Religion: Christian 63%; Muslim 6%; traditional beliefs. President in 1982, Milton Obote; prime minister, Erifasi Otema Allimadi.

Early in 1982 Pres. Milton Obote of Uganda released nearly 200 detainees, including four opposition members of Parliament. His action was dismissed as an empty gesture by a group of his critics meeting in London on January 7 to form a popular front to overthrow the government. The prime mover of the group was former president Godfrey Binaisa; another former president, Yusufu Lule, chairman of the National Resistance Movement, was also present, together with the chairman of the Uganda Freedom Movement. Both Binaisa and Lule insisted, however, that they had had no contact with former president Idi Amin, whom they grouped with Obote as an oppressor of Uganda and its people.

In February Obote appealed to Ugandan exiles to return to their homes, assuring them that they need not fear attack from other tribes. However, acts of violence by guerrillas, particularly in the neighbourhood of Kampala, continued throughout the year, followed by vigorous reprisals from the Army. In February a large group of guerrillas carried out a heavy but ultimately unsuccessful attack on the Malire barracks in Kampala. Both sides claimed to have inflicted serious casualties, and it was reported that 2,000 civilians were sub-

UGANDA

Education. (State aided; 1979) Primary, pupils 1,223,850, teachers 36,442; secondary, pupils 56,730, teachers 3,108; vocational, pupils 4,251, teachers 334; teacher training, students 7,934, teachers 394; higher, students 6,720, teaching staff 677.

Finance and Trade. Monetary unit: Uganda shilling, with (Sept. 20, 1982) a free rate for nonessential imports and private sector of UShs 299 to U.S. $1 (UShs 512.50 = £1 sterling) and a free rate for other transactions of UShs 99.68 to U.S. $1 (UShs 170.90 = £1 sterling). Budget (1981–82 est.): revenue UShs 25.3 billion; expenditure UShs 21.4 billion. Foreign trade (1980): imports UShs 2,175,000,000; exports UShs 2,558,000,000 Import sources (1979): Kenya c. 30%; U.K. 23%; India 13%; West Germany 11%; Italy 8%. Export destinations (1979): U.K. 17%; U.S. 15%; France c. 14%; Spain c. 14%; The Netherlands 14%; Japan 10%. Main export: coffee 99%.

Transport and Communications. Roads (1979) 27,901 km. Motor vehicles in use (1979): passenger 26,000; commercial 5,400. Railways (1980) 1,286 km. Air traffic (1980): c. 120 million passenger-km; freight c. 3.2 million net ton-km. Telephones (Jan. 1980) c. 46,400. Radio receivers (Dec. 1979) 250,000. Television receivers (Dec. 1979) 72,000.

Agriculture. Production (in 000; metric tons; 1981): millet 480; sorghum c. 500; corn 342; sweet potatoes c. 680; cassava c. 1,420; peanuts c. 150; dry beans 240; bananas c. 365; plantains c. 3,550; coffee c. 130; cotton, lint c. 5; meat c. 142; fish catch (1980) c. 224; timber (cu m; 1980) c. 5,788. Livestock (in 000; 1981): cattle c. 5,000; sheep c. 1,075; goats c. 2,160; pigs c. 250; chickens c. 13,300.

Industry. Production (in 000; metric tons; 1979): cement 50; tungsten concentrates (oxide content) c. 0.14; electricity (kw-hr) c. 650,000.

sequently arrested and interrogated. The rough handling meted out by the Army on such occasions aroused further resentment against the government. A small force of Commonwealth soldiers arrived during the year to train and discipline the Ugandan troops.

In areas at a distance from Kampala, security and stability were more in evidence, and a recovery program, backed by the World Bank and the International Monetary Fund, was beginning to take effect. In the drought-threatened northeastern district of Karamoja, however, there were fears that food shortages would again be acute. In February the West German government offered $6 million for development studies.

A further measure aimed at restoring confidence in Uganda's economy was taken in September; a law was enacted by Parliament guaranteeing the return of their property to Asians who had been forced to surrender it by the order of Idi Amin in 1972. It was a condition of the bill that Asians must return to Uganda to register their claim within three months of its becoming law and that they could not resell their property for a period of five years. The law was criticized by many Ugandans who thought it unfair that Africans who had acquired property in good faith and made good use of it should now have to surrender it.

In August a further 1,160 detainees were released, many of them former soldiers under Amin. Almost immediately it was announced that a plot engineered by Binaisa to overthrow the government with the aid of white mercenaries had been postponed owing to lack of money to fund the enterprise. The government was soon challenged from another quarter, however, when Amnesty International published a report charging Obote

and his ministers with responsibility for the torture and group killings of civilians by the Army. The government replied in September that ever since taking office it had been subjected to a hostile campaign of criticism from inside and outside the country and had been given no opportunity to comment on charges before they were published.

In the southwest a new problem arose in October. In the absence of the president, who was receiving medical attention in Europe, officials in Ankole ordered thousands of Rwandan refugees who had been given asylum in Uganda during Obote's first presidency to leave their settlements and enter refugee camps. Finally, the government decided to permit the refugees to live in certain fixed zones. It was announced shortly afterward that thousands of Ugandans living in Kenya who had previously been exempt from the normal immigration laws would have to leave the country because the exemption no longer applied to them.   (KENNETH INGHAM)

Union of Soviet Socialist Republics

The Union of Soviet Socialist Republics is a federal state covering parts of eastern Europe and northern and central Asia. Area: 22,402,200 sq km (8,649,500 sq mi). Pop. (1982 est.): 270 million, including (1979) Russians 52%; Ukrainians 16%; Uzbeks 5%; Belorussians 4%; Kazakhs 3%. Cap. and largest city: Moscow (pop., 1982 est., 8.4 million). Language: officially Russian, but many others are spoken. Religion: about 40 religions are represented in the U.S.S.R., the major ones being Christianity and Islam. General secretaries of the Communist Party of the Soviet Union in 1982, Leonid Ilich Brezhnev to November 10 and, from November 12, Yury Vladimirovich Andropov; chairman of the Presidium of the Supreme Soviet (president) to November 10, Brezhnev; acting president from November 10, Vasily V. Kuznetsov; chairman of the Council of Ministers (premier), Nikolay A. Tikhonov.

Domestic Affairs. An era came to an end on Nov. 10, 1982, with the death of Leonid Ilich Brezhnev (see OBITUARIES; see also Feature Article: *The Russian Giant: 60 Years After Formation of the Soviet Union*). The news of his demise was kept from the Soviet and international public until the following day. Then it was announced that Yury Vladimirovich Andropov (see BIOGRAPHIES) had been made chairman of the funeral commission, clear evidence that he was the front-runner in the struggle to become the new general secretary of the Communist Party of the Soviet Union (CPSU). An extraordinary plenum of the Central Committee duly elected him party leader on November 12. Shortly afterward, the Supreme Soviet convened and elected Andropov to its Presidium but did not make him president. Vasily Kuznetsov, the deputy president, was to continue to act as president.

Andropov's hopes of succeeding Brezhnev had improved in January when Mikhail Suslov (see OBITUARIES) died. Rumoured to have turned

Union of Soviet Socialist Republics

Unemployment:
see Economy, World; Social Security and Welfare Services

Leaders of the Soviet Union flanked the route as the body of Leonid Brezhnev was carried through the streets of Moscow for burial on November 15.

down the post of party leader in 1964, he was the keeper of the CPSU's ideological conscience. Had he lived he would have played a key role in deciding the next party leader. Andropov, head of the KGB security force since 1967, moved back into the Central Committee Secretariat in May, a position he had to hold in order to make an effective bid for the succession. At the same time, Vladimir Dolgikh, Central Committee secretary for heavy industry, was made a candidate (nonvoting) member of the Politburo.

Andropov's main competitors were Konstantin Chernenko and Andrey Kirilenko, but it soon became apparent that the latter was slipping from prominence. Andropov struck a tactical alliance with Defense Minister Dmitry Ustinov and the military. Chernenko seemed to be ambivalent about increased defense spending. Andropov could also rely for support on the KGB under Col. Gen. Vitaly Fedorchuk (*see* BIOGRAPHIES). The security policy-military complex, Andropov's tactical alliance, proved too powerful for Chernenko and his supporters. At 68, Andropov, a Russian, was the oldest man ever to become party leader and a good ten years older than Brezhnev when he took over in 1964.

The Soviet Union needed incisive leadership after the drift of the late Brezhnev era, and Andropov appeared capable of providing it. Since his power base was the party apparatus, he would need to ease out all those closely associated with Brezhnev. His task might be easier given the fact that the average age of the Politburo when Brezh-

nev died was 69. The first demotion was that of Kirilenko, who was dropped from both the Politburo and the Secretariat.

Geidar Aliev, first secretary of the Communist Party of Azerbaijan, was the first man to advance under Andropov. He was promoted from candidate to full member of the Politburo and was also made first deputy premier in preparation, it seemed likely, for the post of premier. His background was revealing. Before becoming party leader in Azerbaijan in 1969, he was a professional KGB officer and headed the organization in that republic in the years 1967–69. His main tasks were to root out corruption, cut through red tape, and get the economy going. The new administration's KGB connection was further emphasized on December 17 when Andropov made Fedorchuk minister of the interior, replacing Nikolay Shchelokov, a close Brezhnev associate. The new KGB head was Viktor Chebrikov. Andropov soon set in motion other changes, promoting younger, more capable officials; for example, a new minister of the railways, a new head of the Communist youth organization, the Komsomol, and a new head of the State Committee on Publishing were appointed. This contrasted with the remarkable stability of cadres under Brezhnev, which had led to complacency and inefficiency.

The military lobby strongly argued its case for higher defense spending and eventually won the day. Chief of Staff Marshal Nikolay Ogarkov, however, was unhappy about the attitude of many Soviet citizens toward the West. Some thought that any peace was good, any war was bad. He advocated an increase in political and educational work in order to inculcate a "class point of view" in foreign affairs. On October 27 Brezhnev told top military leaders in the Kremlin that the time was opportune to raise the combat readiness of the armed forces even further. At the parade in Red Square on November 7 — Brezhnev's last public appearance — Ustinov stated that the armed forces were ready to do their "patriotic and internationalist duty" if called upon. The tone of military self-confidence continued after Andropov became party leader.

A tougher line toward dissent, opposition, corruption, and other social misdemeanours was taken throughout the year. The Helsinki monitoring group, formed six years earlier to check Soviet observance of the 1975 Helsinki accords, was dissolved. Direct dialing between Western Europe and the Soviet Union ceased in July, clearly a move to restrict unofficial contacts, but it was partially restored in September. Soviet citizens were warned against unofficial contacts with Westerners in the Soviet Union. The dissident scientist Andrey Sakharov accused the KGB in October of drugging him and stealing several hundred pages of personal manuscripts and documents.

An unofficial peace committee was set up on June 4 with the aim of establishing trust between the U.S.S.R. and the U.S. It put forward a list of "confidence-building measures," including the suggestion that the Moscow region be twinned with the District of Columbia as a nuclear-free zone. It also wanted war games banned in both states and the introduction of a course on the "propagation of peace" in the schools. It was claimed that some 170 people signed the proposals. The authorities quickly made arrests and threatened signatories with loss of career prospects. Sergey Batovrin, a founding member, was confined in a psychiatric hospital in August but was released after strong protests by Western scientists and nuclear disarmers.

The battle against corruption was given prominence in the press. The most senior official executed was Vladimir Rytov, a former deputy minister of fisheries, for his part in a caviar-smuggling scandal. Parnaoz Ananiashvili, former minister of finance in Georgia, was sentenced for embezzlement, and it was said that his ministry had been riddled with bribery over the last ten years. Thousands of officials, managers, and sales personnel were dismissed, fined, or sentenced for corruption during the year. The arrest of circus officials in February was rumoured to be connected with the succession struggle in the Kremlin. It involved a man known as Boris the Gypsy, a friend of Brezhnev's daughter, Galina. Boris then disappeared from the scene.

Alcoholism continued to be the main social problem. According to a survey, 62% of women filing for divorce cited the "husband's drinking or alcoholism" as the main reason for the breakup of the marriage.

A new Muslim leader was elected in June. After a conference in Tashkent, Shamsutdinkhan Babakhan, aged 45, became mufti and president of the Muslim Board of Central Asia and Kazakhstan, one of the four bodies that govern Islamic practice in the Soviet Union. The Soviet authorities were particularly concerned to counter the potential effect of Islamic fundamentalism.

Among those granted exit visas were Igor, son of chess grand master Viktor Korchnoi, his mother, and his stepmother. Korchnoi, who defected in 1976, had campaigned ceaselessly on their behalf. New defectors included the violinist Nelli Zhkolnikova. It became much more difficult for Jews to emigrate. In 1982 only about 3,000 received exit visas, compared with over 51,000 in 1979. Most of those allowed to leave in 1982 were elderly people with relatives in the U.S. or other Western countries. Soviet officials told Western politicians that all those wanting to leave were being allowed to do so but that the number of requests was decreasing. However, Jewish sources put the number wishing to leave at 380,000.

The Economy. Industry and agriculture failed to achieve their planned targets. Instead of 3.4% industrial growth, only 2.8% was claimed. The harvest was disappointing for the fourth successive year and was unlikely to exceed 185 million metric tons, far short of the planned 239 million metric tons. Labour productivity again failed to meet planned targets, and a whole range of industries turned in disappointing performances. It had been expected that proposals for administrative reform would be presented at the 26th party congress in February–March 1981, but they did not materialize then or during the last period of Brezhnev's rule. Personnel changes had been made, but this did not attack the root cause of the problem, which was that prices did not reflect relative scarcity.

In the opinion of Western experts, the level of investment scheduled for the five-year (1981–85) plan was not sufficient to achieve the planned industrial targets. Investment in the fuel and energy complex had increased sharply, while investment in the industries that provided the support base (e.g., the machine-building industry) had slowed.

New Soviet leader Yury V. Andropov (left) greeted U.S. Secretary of State George Shultz at a reception following Leonid Brezhnev's funeral. Between the two is U.S. Vice-Pres. George Bush, who headed the U.S. delegation to the funeral.

TASS/SOVFOTO

TASS/SOVFOTO

In an attempt to ease tensions between the Soviet Union and China, Chinese Foreign Minister Huang Hua (left), while in Moscow for the funeral of Leonid Brezhnev, met with Soviet Foreign Minister Andrey Gromyko.

The goal of the plan was to raise the share of consumption in total national income, and social goals were accorded priority, but at the same time investment in housing, health, and services had dropped. The performance of the economy in 1982 was the poorest since World War II, with growth of gross domestic product, in real terms, probably zero.

The food situation was serious. Reports circulated that even bread was rationed in certain areas—a psychological blow, since the regime had always been capable of ensuring that enough bread was produced. One of the reasons for the shortage was excessive demand. Prices of all staple foods, including meat, had been frozen for 20 years, while incomes had doubled over the same period. During the agricultural year July 1981–June 1982, the Soviet Union imported an estimated 45 million metric tons of grain at a cost of about $8 billion. In 1982 the state subsidy to agriculture—the difference between what the state paid the farms for their produce and what it got back from retail sales—topped 27 billion rubles.

The dismal performance of agriculture galvanized the Brezhnev leadership into action, and a massive agricultural program, covering the years 1982–90, was announced in May. One of the reasons was the grain embargo imposed by the U.S. Moscow did not wish to find itself in a position where the U.S. could offer grain for Soviet concessions. Because of the high cost of Soviet food production, it might be cheaper to import grain, meat, and other products. However, the leadership rejected this solution because it would make the Soviet Union dangerously dependent.

The agricultural program introduced a new hierarchy of coordinators headed by a deputy premier in Moscow. All the agencies serving agriculture, especially those involved in processing, packing, and transporting produce to the consumer, were to be brought together. Another large increase—totaling 16 billion rubles—in the prices paid by the state for farm produce was to take effect from January 1983, and many farm debts to the state bank were to be written off. Over the next eight years, 160 billion rubles were to be spent on improving rural roads and homes, building new farms, and providing amenities in the villages so as to stem the flow of young people from the countryside. An effort was to be made to improve the quality of machinery and fertilizer delivered to the farms; currently, about 20% of all fertilizer was lost in transit. Private agriculture was also being encouraged, but the performance of the private sector in 1982 was disappointing.

Foreign trade turnover rose by only 5% in 1982, despite considerable sales of gold, diamonds, and precious metals on the world market. One of the reasons for the modest growth was the drop in oil sales on the spot market. However, U.K. trade with the Soviet Union showed a healthy increase, one of the reasons being the purchase of Soviet oil offered at very advantageous prices. The Soviet Union was obliged to run down its hard-currency holdings in Western banks in order to cover its imports of grain and industrial goods. Moscow was slow in reacting to the U.S. offer of an additional 15 million metric tons of grain after the grain embargo was lifted. Increased tension between the superpowers and U.S. reluctance to sell high-technology products to the Soviet Union restricted trade.

Foreign Affairs. Relations with the outside world were unsatisfactory throughout the year. The U.S. administration took a noticeably harder line toward the Soviet Union and set in train heavy increases in defense spending. Although the grain embargo and sanctions against firms participating in the construction of the Urengoi natural-gas pipeline to Western Europe were lifted by Washington, Soviet-U.S. relations deteriorated during the last period of Brezhnev's rule. On November 7 Brezhnev warned "potential aggressors" that the Soviet Union would deal them a crushing retaliatory blow. On the other hand, he stated that the U.S.S.R. would fight consistently for détente. In late October he accused the U.S. government of launching a political, ideological, and economic offensive against Moscow. Only two new weapons were on display during the military parade in Red Square marking the 65th anniversary of the Revolution. Most of the artillery, missiles, and armoured vehicles shown were obsolete, according to Western military observers.

In December Ustinov warned the U.S. that it

should not "hypnotize itself" into believing that it could overtake the Soviet Union in nuclear strength by the end of the decade. "If the present White House leadership . . . challenges us by starting MX missile deployment, then the Soviet Union will deploy in response a new intercontinental ballistic missile of the same class and its characteristics will not be in any way inferior to those of the MX," he claimed. This reflected the new Soviet leadership's tough line toward the West. Andropov needed time to take stock of the situation before he could launch any policy initiatives.

Considerable prominence was accorded Sino-Soviet relations throughout the year. Leonid Ilichev, a deputy foreign minister, journeyed to Beijing (Peking) in October for talks. On the day that Brezhnev died, however, the party newspaper *Pravda* attacked China for "linking up with imperialist reaction" on the Kampuchean question. Evidently there had been little progress on the three main Chinese demands: that the Soviet Union stop aiding Vietnam in Indochina; that Soviet forces withdraw from Afghanistan; and that Soviet troops along the Sino-Soviet border be thinned out. *Pravda* attacked Chinese support for the Khmer Rouge regime, which occupied the Kampuchean seat at the UN, and accused Beijing of distorting both the situation inside Kampuchea and the Soviet Union's support of Vietnam. The Chinese leader Deng Xiaoping (Teng Hsiao-p'ing) suggested that negotiations could resume in Moscow provided the Soviet Union produced actions, not words, on one of the three main questions.

At Brezhnev's funeral, Huang Hua, the Chinese foreign minister, was warmly welcomed by Andropov. He reciprocated by referring to Brezhnev as an "outstanding statesman" and proposing a "genuine improvement" in relations between the two countries. He also wished the Soviet Union well under its new leadership. This was in sharp contrast to his views on the Soviet Union during the 1970s, when he accused the country of conducting an expansionist and hegemonistic foreign policy. After Huang returned to Beijing, he was replaced as foreign minister by Wu Xuegian (Wu Hsüeh-ch'ien). This was thought to reflect a change in policy toward the Soviet Union.

In Afghanistan the war against the Islamic guerrillas continued, with no end in sight. Over 100,000 Soviet soldiers dominated the towns, but the countryside remained in rebel hands. Soviet losses continued to mount, as did those of the guerrillas and the civilian population. The latter were particularly hard hit by the bombing raids carried out by Soviet helicopter gunships. Capture usually meant death for Soviet troops, but two soldiers were handed over to the International Red Cross for internment for two years in Switzerland. Several hundred Soviet personnel were reportedly asphyxiated in the Salang tunnel en route to Kabul in November. According to some reports, the Soviet commander, fearing a guerrilla attack, had closed both ends of the tunnel after a vehicle pileup and explosion. At the UN the Soviet Union failed for the third successive year to convince the third world majority that its troops were in Afghanistan at the request of the Afghan government. In November a resolution calling for the immediate withdrawal of Soviet troops was carried by 114 votes to 21 (13 abstentions).

The situation in Poland stabilized, thus allowing martial law to be suspended after a year. (*See* POLAND.) Nevertheless, Poland became a greater burden to the Soviet Union, especially economically. When Andropov took over he found a demoralized Polish United Workers' Party that would have to be rebuilt. Elsewhere in Eastern Europe, most leaders were in their 70s and well entrenched. Their room for maneuver in relations with the Soviet Union had expanded during the late Brezhnev era, and Andropov was expected to meet resistance if he tried to impose stricter Soviet control. The whole region was in need of economic reform to head off stagnation and decline.

In Western Europe the Soviet Union was encouraged by the strength of the peace movement, which was especially strong in the U.K., The Netherlands, and West Germany. However, Moscow did not welcome the change of government in Bonn when Helmut Kohl (*see* BIOGRAPHIES) re-

---

U.S.S.R.

Education. (1980–81) Primary, pupils 34.4 million; secondary, pupils 9.9 million; primary and secondary, teachers 2,638,000; vocational and teacher training, students 4,612,000, teachers (1979–80) 231,300; higher, students 5,235,500, teaching staff (1978–79) 345,000.

Finance. Monetary unit: ruble, with (Sept. 20, 1982) a free rate of 0.74 ruble to U.S. $1 (1.26 rubles = £1 sterling). Budget (1981 est.) balanced at 271.4 billion rubles.

Foreign Trade. (1981) Imports 52,631,000,000 rubles; exports 57,106,000,000 rubles. Import sources: Eastern Europe 40% (East Germany 10%, Czechoslovakia 8%, Bulgaria 7%, Hungary 6%, Poland 6%); Yugoslavia 5%; Finland 5%; West Germany 5%. Export destinations: Eastern Europe 43% (East Germany 10%, Poland 9%, Czechoslovakia 8%, Bulgaria 8%, Hungary 6%); West Germany 6%; Cuba 5%. Main exports: crude oil and products 38%; machinery 10%; natural gas 10%.

Transport and Communications. Roads (1980) 1,346,500 km. Motor vehicles in use (1980): passenger c. 9,250,000; commercial (including buses) c. 7,910,000. Railways (1980): 237,500 km (including 95,700 km industrial); traffic 331,200,000,000 pas-senger-km, freight (1981) 3,507,000,000,000 net ton-km. Air traffic (1980): 160,299,000,000 passenger-km; freight c. 3,083,000,000 net ton-km. Navigable inland waterways (1980) 142,000 km; freight traffic 244,900,000,000 ton-km. Shipping (1981): merchant vessels 100 gross tons and over 7,867; gross tonnage 23,492,898. Telephones (Dec. 1980) 23,707,000. Radio receivers (Dec. 1979) 125 million. Television receivers (Dec. 1979) 80 million.

Agriculture. Production (in 000; metric tons; 1981): wheat c. 88,000; barley c. 43,000; oats c. 15,000; rye c. 8,500; corn c. 8,000; rice c. 2,400; millet c. 1,500; potatoes 72,000; sugar, raw value c. 6,100; tomatoes c. 6,150; watermelons c. 2,800; apples c. 6,000; sunflower seed c. 4,600; cottonseed c. 5,879; linseed c. 200; soybeans c. 500; dry peas c. 4,000; wine c. 3,200; tea c. 135; tobacco c. 300; cotton, lint c. 2,750; flax fibres c. 300; wool 272; hen's eggs 3,893; milk c. 88,000; butter c. 1,277; cheese c. 1,511; meat c. 15,367; fish catch (1980) 9,412; timber (cu m; 1980) c. 356,000. Livestock (in 000; Jan. 1981): cattle 115,057; pigs 73,382; sheep 141,573; goats 5,914; horses 5,700; chickens c. 988,128.

Industry. Index of production (1975 = 100; 1981) c. 125. Fuel and power (in 000; metric tons; 1981): coal and lignite 704,000; crude oil 609,000; natural gas (cu m) 465,000,000; manufactured gas (cu m; 1980) 36,600,000; electricity (kw-hr) 1,325,000,000. Production (in 000; metric tons; 1981): cement 127,000; iron ore (60% metal content) 242,000; pig iron (1980) 107,000; steel 149,000; aluminum (1980) c. 1,940; copper (1980) c. 1,010; lead (1980) c. 620; zinc (1980) c. 860; magnesite (1980) c. 2,000; manganese ore (metal content; 1980) c. 3,160; tungsten concentrates (metal content; 1980) c. 8.7; gold (troy oz; 1980) c. 8,300; silver (troy oz) c. 46,000; petroleum products (main only; 1979) c. 412,450; sulfuric acid 24,100; caustic soda 2,800; plastics and resins 4,100; fertilizers (nutrient content; 1980) nitrogenous 10,155, phosphate 6,023, potash 8,064; paper (excluding paperboard) 5,400; man-made fibres (1979) 1,100; cotton fabrics (sq m; 1980) 7,068,000; woolen fabrics (sq m; 1980) 762,000; rayon and acetate fabrics (sq m; 1980) 1,769,000; passenger cars (units) 1,324; commercial vehicles (units) 874. New dwelling units completed (1980) 2,055,000.

placed Helmut Schmidt as federal chancellor. Moscow continued its polemics against the Eurocommunists, hitting out especially against the Italians. The latter called into question the historical value of the Soviet experience and the contribution of Lenin to Marxism, as well as criticizing Soviet behaviour in Poland and Afghanistan. The French Communists remained loyal to Moscow, but this made them unpopular with French voters and added to their difficulties in the left-wing coalition led by Socialist Pres. François Mitterrand. Franco-Soviet relations were given a boost when the first Frenchman entered space on board a Soviet spacecraft in July. The Soviet naval attaché, Capt. Anatoly Zotov, was expelled from the U.K. in December for allegedly trying to set up a spy ring.

Soviet commitments around the world became more onerous. The subsidy extended to Eastern Europe amounted to about $20 billion. The Afghan conflict was costing an estimated $7 million a day and Cuba $10 million a day, while Vietnam was also receiving considerable financial support. In total, the burden of empire may have cost the Soviet exchequer about $30 billion in 1982.

(MARTIN McCAULEY)

United Arab Emirates

Consisting of Abu Dhabi, Ajman, Dubai, Fujairah, Ras al-Khaimah, Sharjah, and Umm al-Qaiwain, the United Arab Emirates is located on the eastern Arabian Peninsula. Area: 77,700 sq km (30,000 sq mi). Pop. (1982 est.): 1,121,800, including Arab 42%; South Asian 50% (predominantly Iranian, Indian, and Pakistani); others 8% (mostly Europeans and East Asians). Cap.: Abu Dhabi (pop., 1981 prelim., 243,000). Language: Arabic. Religion: Muslim. President in 1982, Sheikh Zaid ibn Sultan an-Nahayan; prime minister, Sheikh Rashid ibn Said al-Maktum.

The resignation of Brig. Sheikh Sultan ibn-Zaid as commander of the defense forces of the United Arab Emirates (U.A.E.) on February 22 was the major political event of 1982. The appointment of Sheikh Sultan, second son of Sheikh Zaid of Abu

United Arab Emirates

Dhabi, had caused strained relations with the Dubai ruling family; his resignation followed an incident in which soldiers under Sheikh Sultan's command assaulted a group of Bahraini women.

Sheikh Rashid of Dubai was reported to be in better health, but it was expected that a regency council made up of his three sons would act more and more on his behalf. Sheikh Sultan of Sharjah, considered the most radical of the rulers of the seven emirates, opened the Sajaa oil and gas field on June 20. This was expected to boost the emirate's revenues, although by mid-1982 Sharjah was in default on a $200 million loan.

Among the important economic developments were a tightening of laws requiring foreign companies to use local agents, a recommendation for a U.A.E. stock exchange in Sharjah, and the opening on March 10 of Abu Dhabi's Ruwais industrial zone. Cuts in crude oil production to about 1 million bbl a day had little effect on government spending, which continued to be high. A federal budget deficit forecast for 1982 was largely a technical matter, since spending by individual emirates was unaffected.

(JOHN WHELAN)

United Kingdom

A constitutional monarchy in northwestern Europe and member of the Commonwealth, the United Kingdom comprises the island of Great Britain (England, Scotland, and Wales) and Northern Ireland, together with many small islands. Area: 244,035 sq km (94,222 sq mi), including 3,084 sq km of inland water but excluding the crown dependencies of the Channel Islands and Isle of Man. Pop. (1981): 55,618,400. Cap. and largest city: London (Greater London pop., 1981, 6,608,600). Language: English; some Welsh and Gaelic also are used. Religion: mainly Protestant, with Roman Catholic, Muslim, and Jewish minorities, in that order. Queen, Elizabeth II; prime minister in 1982, Margaret Thatcher.

Nobody could have dreamed that 1982 would be a year in which Britain went to war. But that was what happened on April 2, when Argentine forces invaded and quickly captured the Falkland Islands (Islas Malvinas), a tiny British possession 12,800 km (8,000 mi) distant from the U.K. in the South Atlantic. The war for the recovery of the Falklands lasted until June 15, when the British flag flew once again over Government House in Port Stanley. This wholly unexpected incident totally commanded the nation's attention while it lasted—theatre and motion picture attendances fell sharply—and continued to colour its political life for the remainder of the year.

The U.K. had been engaged for some years in desultory talks with Argentina concerning the future of the Falkland Islands. The economic prospects of the islands depended in large part upon the cooperation of neighbouring Argentina. Their effective defense, at such a remove from Britain, was scarcely within the U.K.'s reduced capacity for global operations. In December 1980 the Conservative Party government, led by Prime Minister Margaret Thatcher (*see* BIOGRAPHIES), had gone so

Unions:
see Industrial Relations

Unitarian (Universalist) Churches:
see Religion

United Church of Canada:
see Religion

United Church of Christ:
see Religion

UNITED ARAB EMIRATES

Education. (1979–80) Primary, pupils 88,617, teachers 5,136; secondary, pupils 31,138, teachers 2,736; vocational, pupils 422, teachers 83; higher, students 2,516, teaching staff 344.

Finance. Monetary unit: dirham, with (Sept. 20, 1982) a free rate of 3.67 dirhams to U.S. $1 (6.30 dirhams = £1 sterling). Gold and other reserves (June 1982) U.S. $2,772,000,000. Budget (central total; 1981 actual): revenue 22,460,100,000 dirhams; expenditure 18,666,000,000 dirhams. Gross domestic product (1980) 110.4 billion dirhams.

Foreign Trade. (1981) Imports (f.o.b.) c. 32,782,000,000 dirhams; exports 74,210,000,000 dirhams. Import sources (1980): Japan 17%; U.K. 14%; U.S. 13%; Bahrain 6%; France 6%; West Germany 6%; Italy 5%. Export destinations (1980): Japan c. 36%; U.S. c. 14%; France c. 8%; Netherlands Antilles c. 7%; West Germany c. 7%; U.K. c. 5%. Main export: crude oil 93%.

Industry. Production (in 000; metric tons; 1981): crude oil 73,194; petroleum products (1979) c. 1,140; natural gas (cu m) 11,300,000; cement (1980) c. 1,500; aluminum (1980) 25; electricity (kw-hr; 1980) c. 4,500,000.

far as to suggest a leaseback arrangement whereby sovereignty would pass to Argentina in exchange for continuing British administration over the islands for a substantial period of time. This arrangement was not acceptable to the islanders. A proposal that the sovereignty question be "frozen" for 25 years was unacceptable to the Argentines. (See DEPENDENT STATES.)

Not much attention was paid when on March 19 a group of Argentine scrap-metal merchants dismantling a disused whaling station raised the Argentine flag on South Georgia, a dependency of the Falkland Islands. The incident had too much of low comedy about it. Even in the hours preceding the invasion there was no sense in London of impending crisis. It was true that Foreign Secretary Lord Carrington left early from a meeting of the European Council in Brussels in order to make a statement to the House of Lords on the afternoon of March 30. He decided, nevertheless, to continue with a visit to Israel and left London again that evening. On the next evening Thatcher was informed for the first time that an invasion was imminent or in progress. What miscalculations about Argentine intentions may have been made in the previous weeks, and who had been party to them, was one of the questions being studied by the committee of inquiry under Lord Franks, a former British ambassador to the U.S., which had not reported by the end of the year.

The prime minister's political judgment, on hearing the news on March 31, was that unless the Falklands could be recovered, her government would probably fall. True or false, she was determined from the outset to recapture the islands. The news of what was happening did not break until the night of April 1–2, and throughout the following day the Foreign Office, fueling the accusations of incompetence that were to follow, was unable to confirm to Parliament that an invasion had taken place. The magnitude of the crisis did not begin to become apparent to the public until the morning of Saturday, April 3, when for the first time since the Suez crisis of 1956 Parliament met in an emergency session that was broadcast live to the public. At the close of the debate it was announced that a naval task force would be dispatched to the South Atlantic.

The first contingent sailed out of Portsmouth on April 5 to the playing of bands and the waving of flags. In command of the task force was Rear Adm. John Woodward (see BIOGRAPHIES). Lord Carrington resigned as foreign secretary, stung by the venom of the criticism leveled at him from some sections of his party and in some right-wing newspapers. Secretary of State for Defense John Nott had also offered to resign following what was generally regarded as a disastrously poor showing during the emergency debate. However, the prime minister persuaded him to remain at his post.

The excited, patriotic tone of the Saturday debate had encouraged the public to regard the loss of the Falklands as some kind of major national disaster. Comparisons were made with Suez and with Munich; lessons were drawn from the past about the appeasement of dictators and the consequences of condoning their acts of aggression. Thatcher

quickly made plain her own war aims, which were, first, to show to the world that aggression did not pay and, second, to secure for the Falkland islanders the right to self-determination. These statements of principle, impinging closely as they did upon national pride, struck louder chords with the public than did the questioning of those who, apart from trying to leave room for a diplomatic solution if one could still be found, wondered whether the scale of the British response was commensurate with the interests involved, especially given the tiny population of the islands (some 1,800). This, certainly, was the first reaction of the U.S. and of Britain's partners in the European Communities (EC).

The collapse of the peace initiative by U.S. Secretary of State Alexander Haig led to a declaration of unequivocal support for the U.K. from the U.S. on April 30. Had the Argentine junta been willing or able to respond positively to the Haig proposals, the British Cabinet might have found itself in an embarrassing position, for what Haig was suggesting as an interim solution fell short of Thatcher's declared objectives and might have run into serious trouble with the patriotically aroused Conservative backbenchers. As it was, the intransigence of the junta convinced senior ministers around the prime minister that further dealings with Gen. Leopoldo Galtieri (see BIOGRAPHIES), the president of Argentina, were likely to be useless. So although diplomacy continued, there was from that time little political expectation of its succeeding.

There was a moment in the week of May 10 when it seemed as if diplomacy, then being conducted through UN Secretary-General Javier Pérez de Cuéllar (see BIOGRAPHIES), might make prog-

United Kingdom

A Briton reads the news that British forces have triumphed in the Falklands war.

SUTTON—GAMMA/LIAISON

ress after all. The new British foreign secretary, Francis Pym (*see* BIOGRAPHIES), encountered some criticism from his own party, when he was suspected of being ready to go too far in meeting the Argentines in a compromise. By now also military considerations were paramount in London: ships and troops were in acute danger; the South Atlantic winter was closing in; and the countdown to re-invasion was in progress. The landing of Britain's main force on the Falklands took place on May 21, and the recapture of the islands was completed when, on June 14, the 5,000-strong garrison at Port Stanley surrendered. (For an account of the military campaign, *see* DEFENSE: *Special Report.*)

Domestic Affairs. When the war broke out, the state of British politics was that the three parties were running approximately neck and neck in voter popularity. This indicated that some recovery had already taken place in the fortunes of the Conservative Party during the winter and some decline—in fact about 10%—in the standing of the Social Democratic Party (SDP)-Liberal Party Alliance, which had peaked in November 1981 at an astounding 50% according to a Gallup Poll. The local elections on May 6 produced a result that showed the Conservatives with 40% support against the Labour Party's 32% and the Alliance's 26%. By June the government had notched up a remarkable 20-percentage-point lead. Most of this Conservative gain—the so-called Falklands factor—was at the expense of the Alliance.

When the political season resumed in late September with the annual party conferences, Gallup put the government still at 44%, with Labour at 30.5% and the Alliance at 23%. It began now to look as if factors other than the Falklands might be responsible for the high standing of the government in spite of the fact that unemployment was well in excess of three million. With the most probable date for a general election being the autumn of 1983, party politics began to revolve around the distinct possibility that Thatcher might win a second majority.

During the Falklands crisis the reputation of Labour Party leader Michael Foot reached an unprecedented low in the opinion polls. In by-elections in the Glasgow Hillhead constituency in March and in the Merton, Mitcham, and Morden constituency in June, Labour finished in third place amid the by now familiar canvass reports that the activities of Tony Benn and the left wing were causing disaffection and desertion among the party's traditional supporters. At the party conference in Blackpool at the end of September, Foot scored a victory of a sort when the conference voted to move to oust the Trotskyite Militant Tendency; an inquiry had reported in June that Militant was in effect a party within a party and was thus in breach of Labour's constitution. However, legal difficulties were encountered, and an effective purge appeared increasingly unlikely. In September and again in November, Foot was obliged to deal with speculation that his leadership of the party was under threat. By the end of the year there were signs of a modest Labour revival, but few of the party's own leaders could find much hope or confidence of victory at a general election.

Meanwhile, the Alliance was having troubles of its own. The war in the South Atlantic had deprived it of the limelight in which it had thrived since the launching of the SDP in March 1981 and the formation of an alliance with the Liberal Party in September of that year. Roy Jenkins, the former Labour Party chancellor of the Exchequer and home secretary, was returned triumphantly to Parliament at the Glasgow Hillhead by-election and later was elected leader of the SDP in a contest with David Owen, the former Labour Party foreign secretary. However, Jenkins made little immediate impact in Parliament or the country, and by the autumn the momentum of the new third force in British politics seemed lost, at least temporarily. One cause of its reduced standing may have been the time spent by the SDP in putting into place its own constitutional arrangements and in the painful and troublesome allocation of seats between the two parties. When their deal was finally clinched in September, it was generally concluded that the Liberal Party would do better out of it and overwhelmingly so if the Alliance were to win no more than 50 or so seats in the next Parliament.

The state of the economy was overshadowed by

the Falklands war. By the autumn, with interest rates having fallen sharply and the rate of inflation down into single figures, it had become popular to suppose that the government might be able to win the coming election even with some 3,250,000 unemployed, a total scarcely thinkable a few years earlier. One explanation could be what had happened to actual living standards. In the years 1977–80 real disposable income had risen on average by 5% a year, and during that time there had been a sharp increase in savings. In 1981 and again in 1982 real living standards fell on average (by about 2% each year), but consumption held up for the most part as people drew upon their savings or borrowed. Moreover, falling interest rates, relieving some of the pressure on mortgage payers, combined with a faster decline in the rate of inflation than had been expected — to around an annual 6% by the end of the year from 12% at the beginning — gave the government some claims to success for its economic policies. Nevertheless, unemployment continued to rise during 1982, and the number unemployed for 12 months or more grew to one-third of the total, or about one million people.

The fall in production flattened out, but none of the forecasters, official or unofficial, saw better than a sluggish growth prospect for the economy. Competitiveness improved somewhat, owing to a depreciation of the pound sterling and a slower increase in labour costs than in the past. However, the U.K. was approximately 35–40% less competitive in world markets than it had been in 1978–80, according to a calculation made by the Bank of England. Britain's share in international trade continued to decline during the international trade recession and, in spite of hopes that improvements in productivity might prove lasting, there was little sign in 1982 that the fundamental weaknesses of the British economy were responding to the government's disciplinary treatment.

In three showdowns with trade unions the government came out on top. The most important and the most politically charged of these involved the coal miners. As the agents of the destruction of former prime minister Edward Heath's Conservative government in February 1974, the miners had a special place in British political mythology. Their newly elected national president, the ultraleftist and militant Yorkshireman Arthur Scargill, invited his members in the autumn to authorize a national strike on the twin issues of pay and pit closings. The National Coal Board stood firm with the government behind it, and the miners roundly rejected Scargill's strike call. Earlier in the year the British Railways Board had succeeded in facing down the railway unions, although not until board chairman Peter Parker threatened to close down the entire system.

The third dispute of the year was a more protracted and a murkier affair, involving nurses and ancillary workers employed by the National Health Service. There was a good deal more public sympathy for their cause than there was for the well-paid miners or the railwaymen with their restrictive practices; nevertheless, after a day of action in sympathy for the poorly paid health workers, which was organized by the Trades

THE TIMES, LONDON

Roy Jenkins, a former Labour Party Cabinet minister, was surrounded by well-wishers as he took to the election stump in March. A leader of the new Social Democratic Party, Jenkins was successful in winning a seat in Parliament from Glasgow.

Union Congress in September, the dispute slowly petered out in the face of the government's firmness. By the end of the year such fears as there had been that Prime Minister Thatcher might be plagued by a "winter of discontent," of the kind that had destroyed the Labour Party government of former prime minister James Callaghan in 1978–79, had disappeared.

During the year there was new trade-union legislation, the chief consequence of which was to make union funds liable in civil suits for damages. Unions would be liable when engaging in secondary action (for example, striking against an employer with whom they were not in dispute), including strikes for political ends.

A happier event was the birth of a son, and eventual heir to the throne, to the prince and princess of Wales on June 21. The child was named William Arthur Philip Louis. The princess was soon back in action, and scarcely a day passed in which the popular newspapers did not carry gossip, malicious rumour, or fetching photographs of her. What with an intruder at Buckingham Palace who sat on Queen Elizabeth II's bed and chatted to her, and spies galore, Britain was not without diversion in 1982.

Foreign Affairs. As with everything else, foreign affairs were overshadowed by the preoccupation with the Falkland Islands. The war broke out just as Britain's annual wrangle with the European Economic Community over the costs of the common agricultural policy and the scale of Britain's contributions to the EC budget was coming to its climax. Needing EC support for economic sanctions against Argentina, the government was obliged to abandon hope of achieving any lasting solution and to settle, once more, for a temporary rebate. The continental members of the EC took the opportunity of Britain's distraction to, in effect, override a British veto (in breach of the previous convention about majority voting) and

PACEMAKER

Gerry Adams (third from the right), a candidate of Sinn Fein, the political wing of the Irish Republican Army, greeted a voter before his victory in elections held in Northern Ireland in October. Sinn Fein picked up 5 out of 78 assembly seats in its first appearance on the Northern Ireland ballot.

increase farm prices by more than the British had been willing to agree to.

There was some outrage at first when U.S. Pres. Ronald Reagan appeared to be taking an even-handed approach to the Falklands conflict. Gratitude for the material and political support that the U.S. provided once the Haig mission had failed (U.S. intelligence cooperation was indispensable to the British victory) was later dissipated when in November the U.S. voted at the UN for a resolution sponsored by Latin-American countries that called for a negotiated settlement to the dispute over the sovereignty of the islands. Meanwhile, Britain had sided firmly with its European partners in the transatlantic dispute over the building of the Soviet-Western European gas pipeline. Thatcher, although ideologically sympathetic to Reagan's economic policies and personally sympathetic to Reagan, became increasingly irked by the high U.S. interest rates, which were inhibiting the recovery of the British economy.

Its preoccupation in the South Atlantic prevented Britain from playing any major role in the redefinition of the Atlantic relationship and in responding to the changing (and, in November, changed) leadership in the U.S.S.R., which were the chief items on the international agenda.

Northern Ireland. In the face of considerable opposition from his own Conservative Party, James Prior, the new secretary of state for Northern Ireland, persisted in his plan to revive somewhat the politics of the province by the restoration of an elected, although only consultative, assembly. In spite of the declaration by the Roman Catholic parties that they would boycott the assembly by refusing to take their seats, the elections took place in late October. The Protestant parties, predictably, won a substantial majority, but the chief significance of the event was the success of Sinn Fein, the political wing of the Provisional Irish Republican Army (IRA). Competing for the first time across a broad electoral front, it won 10% of the vote and five seats, puncturing the British claim that the IRA terrorists lacked political support. The more moderate, pro-Irish Social Democratic and Labour Party was outflanked in the process, and politics in Northern Ireland became more polarized than ever before along sectarian and nationalist lines.

Accompanying this endeavour to restore civilized political life to the province was a rash of incidents of sectarian violence, culminating on December 6 in a bombing in Ballykelly that added 16 to the death toll. (PETER JENKINS)

See also Commonwealth of Nations; Dependent States; Ireland.

United Nations

On September 7 UN Secretary-General Javier Pérez de Cuéllar (see BIOGRAPHIES) warned the world that it was "perilously near to a new international anarchy." He asked nations to reverse their "exceedingly dangerous course" and urged them "to render the UN more capable of carrying out its primary function" of preserving international peace and security.

Secretary-General's Report. Instead of surveying UN activities broadly, as secretaries-general have usually done, Pérez de Cuéllar focused, in his first report on the work of the organization since he assumed office on January 1, on the "central problem" of the UN: its "capacity to keep the peace and to serve as a forum for negotiations." Often during 1982, he said, the UN had been set aside or rebuffed. Frequently, the Security Council could not act decisively to remove international conflicts, but even its unanimous resolutions were "increasingly defied or ignored by those . . . strong enough to do so."

In the long run, the secretary-general was sure, disputants would gain from making the UN more effective, and he emphasized that "something must be done, and urgently, to strengthen our international institutions and to adopt new and imaginative approaches" for preventing and resolving conflicts. "More systematic, less last-minute use of the Security Council" was necessary to defuse dangerous situations early before they became full-fledged crises.

The secretary-general appealed to the permanent members of the Council (China, France, the United Kingdom, the Soviet Union, and the United States) not to allow difficulties among them to overshadow their "sacred trust" under the Charter. They and other UN members ought to follow up Council resolutions, especially unanimous ones, and bring their collective influence to bear on nations that ignore Council appeals.

Middle East. The secretary-general's report described the Middle East as "perhaps our most formidable international problem" and called the Security Council "the only place in the world where all of the parties concerned can sit at the same table." It could become "a most useful forum for this absolutely essential effort" of bringing peace and security to the Middle East.

By contrast, during the year, the efforts of the Council, and, indeed, those of the General Assembly, seemed exercises in futility. The Council began a series of meetings on January 6 to consider Israel's decision to impose its laws in the Golan Heights, Syrian territory that Israel had occupied since the 1967 Arab-Israeli war. Israel refused to rescind the measures, as the Council had asked it

UPI

Senji Yamaguchi, a survivor of the Nagasaki atom bombing of 1945, held up a photo of himself taken after the blast as he addressed the UN special session on disarmament in June.

to do in December 1981, insisting that its policy had taken the Golan Heights and its inhabitants out of a legal "limbo." It argued for bilateral negotiations with Syria.

The Council instead considered a draft resolution that would have called on UN members to "consider applying concrete and effective measures in order to nullify the Israeli annexation." In a bid to gain U.S. support, the resolution did not ask for mandatory sanctions, but the U.S. vetoed it anyway, arguing that the resolution itself would aggravate the problem and "sow suspicions and feed hostilities." Moreover, the U.S. insisted it was not at all clear that, in applying its own laws in the territory, Israel had actually annexed it. Then, on January 28, the Council unanimously, with the U.S. and U.K. abstaining, called for an emergency special session of the Assembly to deal with the problem.

In response, the Assembly on February 5 voted 86 to 21, with 34 abstaining, to condemn Israel "strongly" for its Golan Heights decisions and asked UN members "to cease forthwith, individually and collectively, all dealings with Israel in order totally to isolate it in all fields."

During the rest of the year, charges and countercharges by disputants in the Middle East came before the Council and the Assembly, with similar results. On March 24 Arab nations asked the Council to consider "deliberate provocations, assaults, abductions and murder, perpetrated by heavily armed Israeli troops and intruding settlers" in occupied Arab territories. Israel replied that Jordan and the Palestine Liberation Organization (PLO) were conspiring "to eliminate any emerging and promising alternative to the PLO method of violence and terror," were intimidating Arab leaders who favoured peace, and were stirring up violence against Israeli troops.

The Assembly met on April 28 in a resumed emergency session and condemned Israel (86–20–36) for not being a peace-loving state, for not carrying out its Charter obligations, for not complying with resolutions on Jerusalem and not dismantling settlements in occupied territories, for not applying the Geneva conventions that protect civilians in wartime, and for frustrating the exercise of Palestinian rights. It called on the Security Council to recognize the Palestinians' rights to independent statehood and urged the secretary-general to consult with all parties, including the PLO, to find ways to achieve a comprehensive, just, and lasting peace.

Israeli delegate Yehuda Blum denounced the resolution as a "miserable concoction" which "regurgitates" the main components of other anti-Israeli resolutions "steamrollered" through the Assembly by parties seeking to destroy Israel. The U.S., cited in the resolution for misusing its veto to enable Israel to continue its "aggression" and "occupation," said that the resolution was pushing the UN closer to a "political and moral abyss" by questioning Israel's legitimacy and by condemning the U.S. for exercising its constitutional prerogatives. Egypt, to whom Israel had three days earlier returned the final portions of the Sinai, also questioned the resolution's usefulness.

The resolution certainly did not alleviate tensions in Lebanon. The Council had on April 22, after three Israeli air strikes against Lebanon, authorized its president to demand an end to all armed attacks and cease-fire violations. On May 9 Israel launched "retaliatory" raids against Lebanon to put an end to the "terrorist PLO operating from Lebanese territory." It charged the PLO with committing an "ongoing series of atrocities" that caused a steadily mounting toll of dead and wounded Israeli civilians. Once more the secretary-general expressed his anxiety over breaches of the cease-fire.

After Israel's ambassador to Great Britain was critically wounded by Arab assailants in London on June 3, Israel bombed PLO sites in Lebanon again for two days. Then, on June 6, calling Lebanon "the centre of world terrorism," Israel launched an attack that overran positions of the UN Interim Force in Lebanon (UNIFIL) and did not end until nearly all of Beirut was under Israeli control. UN reactions included calls on June 4 by the secretary-general for both sides to "desist from hostile acts" and from the Security Council to "adhere strictly" to the cease-fire. On June 5 and 6 other Council resolutions followed calling for an end to military action, but the Israeli representative asked, "How many Israelis have to be killed by terrorists for this Council to be persuaded that the limits of our endurance have been reached?" On June 26 the U.S. vetoed a resolution calling for all forces to pull back from Beirut because of its "fatal flaw" in not requiring "the elimination from Beirut and elsewhere of the presence of armed Palestinian elements, who neither submit to nor respect" Lebanese sovereignty.

On September 17 the world learned that a massacre of Palestinian and other civilians had occurred in Beirut refugee camps. The Council on September 18–19 unanimously condemned the slaughter and authorized the secretary-general to increase the number of UN observers in the area from 10 to 50. He had also been prepared to deploy additional UNIFIL forces from southern Lebanon to Beirut, but Lebanon requested instead that France, Italy, and the U.S. reconstitute the multinational force that had in the summer overseen the withdrawal from Beirut of PLO forces.

On September 24 the Assembly also condemned (147–2) the Beirut massacre. The U.S. and Israel, which voted no, argued that the resolution would only prolong and embitter conflict. Israel objected that the Assembly was again ignoring the root causes of the agony in Lebanon and stated that its leaders had all expressed their horror at the massacres, which they laid at the door of the Christian Phalangists.

UN officials continued their efforts to end the fighting between Iran and Iraq, which had begun in 1980, but neither the secretary-general himself nor his special representative, Olof Palme of Sweden, succeeded in bridging the gaps between the parties. Security Council resolutions (July 12 and October 4) were likewise unavailing. On October 22 the Assembly affirmed (119–1–15) the Council's calls for a cease-fire, but Iran, which cast the sole negative vote, objected that the Assembly had taken no account of the fact that Iraq started the war and occupied a portion of Iranian territory for more than two years.

Falkland Islands. On April 1 the U.K. warned the Security Council that Argentina was preparing to move militarily against British dependencies in the South Atlantic; at the same time, Argentina complained of "continuous acts of aggression" by Britain over 150 years. The Council and the secretary-general both urged restraint, but on April 2 Argentina invaded and seized the Falklands (which it calls the Malvinas). The Council demanded (10–1–4) that Argentina withdraw and that hostilities cease immediately, but Argentina went on to take South Georgia Island on April 3. Later in April Britain sent a naval task force to the area, and on April 12 Argentina announced that it would comply with the Council resolution if the British would. The U.K. pointed out that Argentina had already violated the resolution by invading South Georgia and increasing its forces on the Falklands and asserted that Britain would do whatever was necessary "in exercise of its inherent right of self-defense" under the Charter.

British military action proceeded while the secretary-general and Council tried without success to resolve the dispute peacefully, and on June 14, Argentina surrendered. It reported its surrender to the Council on June 18, announced a "de facto" end to hostilities, and asked for negotiations within a UN framework to settle the dispute finally. Britain responded on June 23 by saying that its forces would remain to defend the islands against further Argentine attacks.

On November 4 the Assembly called (90–12–52) for Britain and Argentina to settle their "sovereignty dispute." Britain opposed the resolution as

coming too soon after military conflict and insisted that the islanders themselves must choose who should govern them. It called the resolution an "Argentine-inspired charade" because the formula calling for the parties to "take due account of the interests of the population" was not real self-determination. Argentina insisted, however, that the issue was not self-determination but the right of states to maintain their territorial integrity.

Other Political Questions. In Afghanistan the secretary-general and his personal representative, Undersecretary-General Diego Cordovez, could report only "tentative progress" in continuing efforts to arrange for 100,000 Soviet troops to withdraw, to allow the voluntary return of an estimated 3.5 million refugees, and to establish in the dispute the principle of noninterference in the internal affairs of nations. On November 29 the General Assembly renewed its demand (114–21) that the U.S.S.R. withdraw from Afghanistan.

The Assembly on October 28 reiterated (105–23–20) its call for all foreign troops to withdraw from Kampuchea in order to give back the independence and territorial integrity that the people of that nation need to determine their own destiny and that was lost when 150,000 Vietnamese troops invaded in 1978. The Assembly continued to seat the Pol Pot government, deposed at that time.

In regard to Central America the Security Council heard Nicaragua charge that the U.S. was "destabilizing" its government. On April 2 the U.S. vetoed a resolution that would have called on all nations to refrain from "the direct, indirect, overt or covert use of force against any country of Central America and the Caribbean." The U.S. insisted that Nicaragua was intervening on a large scale in the affairs of neighbouring countries and that the issue belonged in the hands of the Organization of American States.

On December 15 the Security Council unanimously voted to condemn "strongly" a raid on Lesotho on December 9 that resulted in some 30 deaths. South Africa described the dead as guerrillas belonging to the outlawed African National Congress, but Lesotho, an independent kingdom entirely surrounded by South Africa, called them refugees from South Africa. On December 20 the secretary-general announced that a UN team would go to Lesotho to ensure the safety of refugees there.

Disarmament. The General Assembly held its second special session on disarmament from June 7 to July 9 and reported progress on some issues but "persistent differences of opinion" on others. Socialist nations wanted to concentrate on practical measures for preventing nuclear war and urged all states to pledge that they would not use nuclear weapons first. The U.S. and some Western European countries reaffirmed that they would not use any weapons, nuclear or otherwise, except to respond to an armed attack.

On December 13 the General Assembly called (112–12–6) on the five nations (China, France, U.S.S.R., U.K., U.S.) that acknowledge they possess nuclear arms to stop producing them and, in a second resolution (adopted 119–17–5), asked states—namely the U.S. and U.S.S.R.—not only to stop making nuclear weapons and fissionable materials but also not to deploy or to test them. The U.S.S.R. voted in favour; the others against. In response to an earlier resolution, adopted 111–1–35, that urged states to outlaw nuclear tests, the U.S. explained that it regarded such a step as appropriate only in the distant future.

International Law. The concluding session of the third UN Conference on the Law of the Sea met in Jamaica from December 6 to 10 to sign the treaty and open it for ratification by governments. Nine years in the making, the treaty was completed during two final sessions at UN headquarters (March 8–April 30; September 22–24) despite strong U.S. pressure to change it substantially. Called by the secretary-general "possibly . . . the most significant international legal instrument [formulated] in this century," the treaty was signed by 117 nations on December 10. The U.S. and 45 others refused to sign, and 24 of the nonsigners actually did not attend. In December the United States announced that it would not pay the UN its share of the costs of a commission set up under the treaty to formulate rules on deep-sea mining.

Organizational Matters. The Assembly's 37th regular session opened on September 21 and elected Imre Hollai (Hungary) as president. On September 24 the Assembly adopted its 138-item agenda but rejected by a vote of 70–30–43 a Cuban proposal to debate the relationship between Puerto Rico and the U.S. Hernan Padilla, mayor of San Juan and alternate U.S. delegate, stated that "Puerto Rico is not an international problem, nor does it want to be" and warned that "there can be no talk of self-determination if Puerto Rico is obliged to pursue the road . . . rejected by 95 percent of the Puerto Rican electorate."

The terms of Ireland, Japan, Panama, Spain, and Uganda on the Security Council ended December 31; they were to be succeeded by Malta, The Netherlands, Nicaragua, Pakistan, and Zimbabwe. The U.S. opposed Nicaragua's election and supported the Dominican Republic but found itself in the minority when Nicaragua won 104–50.

(RICHARD N. SWIFT)

[552.B.2]

United States

The United States of America is a federal republic composed of 50 states, 49 of which are in North America and one of which consists of the Hawaiian Islands. Area: 9,363,123 sq km (3,615,122 sq mi), including 202,711 sq km of inland water but excluding the 156,192 sq km of the Great Lakes that lie within U.S boundaries. Pop. (1982 est.): 231,990,000, including 83.2% white and 11.7% black. Language: English. Religion (1981 est.): Protestant 73.5 million; Roman Catholic 50.4 million; Jewish 5.9 million; Orthodox 3.8 million. Cap.: Washington, D.C. (pop., 1981 est., 636,000). Largest city: New York (pop., 1981 est., 7,070,400). President in 1982, Ronald Reagan.

In national elections held in November 1982 the Democratic Party scored a gain of 26 seats in the U.S. House of Representatives as voters expressed their dissatisfaction with the economic program of Pres. Ronald Reagan (see BIOGRAPHIES) but stopped short of repudiating it altogether. The outcome indicated a considerable amount of voter frustration with a party only two years into national power. The Republican loss in the House was the worst suffered by any governing party at the two-year point in 16 years—since the Democrats under Lyndon Johnson lost 47 seats in 1966.

The Democrats won 269 seats to 166 seats for the Republicans, giving the Democrats a 103-seat advantage in the House. The total included two districts in Georgia where redistricting problems forced postponement of the general election until November 30.

In sharp contrast to the House, the only remarkable thing about the 1982 Senate results was the lack of change. Not only did the party ratio remain the same—54 Republicans and 46 Democrats—but 95 of the 100 senators in the 97th Congress were assured of seats in the 98th. The class of five newcomers was the smallest such group in the history of popular Senate elections.

The outcome was different at the state level, where the Republicans suffered a net loss of seven governorships, leaving them with a total of 16. Of the Republican governors' seats that switched to the Democrats, five were in the Midwest, where the recession was most acute. Michigan, Minnesota, Nebraska, Ohio, and Wisconsin elected Democratic governors. Republican incumbents had decided to retire in all those states except Nebraska, where Gov. Charles Thone was turned out by a margin of about 10,000 votes for Bob Kerrey.

In a surprise announcement on December 1, Sen. Edward Kennedy of Massachusetts said that he would not run for the Democratic presidential nomination in 1984 because he did not want to expose his children to the rigours of another national campaign. Kennedy also said that he would not accept a draft for his party's nomination in 1984, but he did not rule out a presidential candidacy in 1988 or later. The senator's withdrawal appeared to leave Walter Mondale, vice-president in the administration of Pres. Jimmy Carter, as the early favourite to become the Democrats' 1984 presidential candidate.

Domestic Affairs. Economic developments dominated national news in 1982 as the U.S. continued to suffer through its deepest recession since World War II. Unemployment climbed steadily during the year, reaching a rate of 10.8% of the work force in December. This was the highest level of joblessness since 1940. The rising number of unemployed workers severely strained the ability of state and local governments to provide benefits to the jobless.

Also of concern were the more than 30 bank failures, the largest number since 1940. Two events in particular shook the financial community's confidence. The first came in May, when Drysdale Government Securities Inc., a small New York City firm that had been in business only four months, defaulted on $160 million owed to other dealers. Chase Manhattan Bank and Manufacturers Hanover Trust Co., which had acted as Drys-

United States

Sen. Howard Baker, Jr. (left) shakes hands with newly elected Democratic Sen. Frank R. Lautenberg of New Jersey as freshmen congressmen arrive on Capitol Hill on November 29.

dale's intermediaries in the government securities market, were obliged to absorb the firm's losses, at an after-tax cost of $117 million and $8.8 million, respectively.

Then, in July, federal regulators forced the closing of Penn Square Bank, of Oklahoma City, which had managed to make more than $2 billion in loans although it had only about $500 million in deposits. The Continental Illinois National Bank, the nation's sixth largest, was left holding $1 billion in Penn Square credits. Chase Manhattan and Seattle First National Bank also were major partners in Penn Square loan syndications.

Of the many business bankruptcies in 1982, that of Braniff International Corp., the nation's eighth largest airline, was among the most notable. The carrier filed for reorganization under Chapter 11 of the federal Bankruptcy Act on May 13, becoming the first major U.S. airline to do so.

Struggling under heavy losses and laden with debt, Braniff the day before had suspended all its flights. The announcement of the suspension came as a surprise to the company's 9,500 employees, most of whom were told not to come to work the next day. Passengers, travel agents, and many of the airline's creditors were also taken by surprise.

Manville Corp. filed a bankruptcy petition in August in an effort to gain relief from thousands of asbestos-related health lawsuits filed against the company. The company was "completely overwhelmed" by the cost of the lawsuits, according to John McKinney, Manville's chief executive officer and president. The firm faced approximately 16,500 lawsuits at the time, and more were being added at the rate of 500 a month.

Not all the economic news was bad. Inflation eased during the year, triggering a gradual decline in interest rates. The interest rate on government-insured home mortgages issued by the Veterans Administration and the Federal Housing Administration, which had risen as high as 17.5% in 1981, declined in stages to 12%. Conventional mortgage rates fell also, and housing industry spokesmen expressed cautious optimism that the long-awaited revival of the residential construction industry might be at hand. In November home building starts rose 27% above October and were 64% higher than in November 1981.

There was no question about the stock market's revival. Several New York Stock Exchange records were set in frenzied trading during the last two weeks of August. In the week ended August 20,

(Left) Mario Cuomo, Democrat, triumphed over Lew Lehrman, a conservative Republican, in the race for the governor's mansion in Albany, New York. (Right) Republican George Deukmejian edged out Los Angeles Mayor Tom Bradley to win the governorship of California.

the closely watched Dow Jones industrial average climbed 81.24 points to finish at 869.29 and surpass the record of 73.61 points gained in the week ended Oct. 11, 1974. Volume for the week ended August 27 was 549,830,000 shares, also a record. The Dow Jones eventually reached a record closing high of 1070.55 in trading on December 27.

While some businesses were failing, others were merging. Marathon Oil Co. shareholders on March 11 approved a $6 billion merger with U.S. Steel Corp., the second-largest merger in history. The Interstate Commerce Commission on March 25 approved the merger of the Norfolk and Western Railway and the Southern Railway. Directors of Cities Service Co. in August accepted a merger proposal by Occidental Petroleum Co. valued at $4 billion. And on October 26 the California Federal Savings & Loan Association and the American Savings and Loan Association, respectively the third- and fourth-largest savings and loans in the nation, announced an agreement in principle for a merger. The combination would result in the country's biggest savings and loan institution.

But the merger that attracted the most attention in 1982 was the four-way battle involving the Bendix, Martin Marietta, United Technologies, and Allied corporations. Bendix initiated the takeover fight in August by announcing an unsolicited tender offer for 45% of Martin Marietta stock; it already controlled 4.5% of Martin Marietta. In retaliation Martin Marietta made a tender offer for 50.3% of Bendix's outstanding stock. United Technologies entered the fray on September 7, allying itself with Martin Marietta by making a similar bid for Bendix.

For a time it appeared that Bendix and Martin Marietta were headed for a bizarre situation in which each company would own a controlling interest in the other. Then, on September 22, Allied and Bendix reached a tentative agreement calling for Allied to purchase 55% of Bendix's outstanding shares. In a separate deal with Martin Marietta, Allied agreed to allow that company to remain an independent concern.

Perhaps the most significant business story of the year was the settlement of the U.S. Department of Justice's eight-year-old antitrust suit against American Telephone & Telegraph Co. Among other things AT&T agreed to divest itself of its 22 Bell System companies in return for the department's promise to drop the case.

U.S. District Court Judge Harold H. Greene, who had jurisdiction of the case, withheld his approval of the agreement until major modifications were made in it. The changes ordered by Greene would (1) prohibit AT&T from entering the field of electronic information services for a minimum of seven years; (2) allow the divested Bell System companies to publish their own Yellow Pages advertising directories; (3) allow the divested companies to market, but not manufacture, telephones and switchboards. Greene gave his final consent to the amended pact on August 24.

In another antitrust case the Department of Justice dropped its suit against IBM Corp., an action that it had begun in 1969. The suit had charged IBM with monopolizing the general-purpose computer market, but the government finally decided that it was "without merit."

President Reagan scored a major victory in Congress on August 19, when the House and the Senate approved a $98.3 billion tax-increase bill. Reagan, who had committed the prestige of his presidency to passage of the legislation, praised Congress's action as an important part of "our crusade to get this country's economy moving again." Also pressing for the bill's approval was Democratic House Speaker Thomas ("Tip") O'Neill, normally an opponent of the president.

Growing concern about the size of the federal budget deficits was a key factor in winning passage of the tax measure. "This bill is specifically designed to improve the economy by closing the deficit gap and to bring interest rates down," said Rep. Barber B. Conable (Rep., N.Y.). Rep. Leon E. Panetta (Dem., Calif.) put it in more dramatic terms, saying, "Economic survival depends on the passage of this program."

Reagan's biggest legislative setback of the year occurred on December 7, when the House voted to delete initial production funds for the controversial $26 billion MX missile program. It was the first time since World War II that either house of Congress had voted to deny a major weapons system to a president. Reagan reacted angrily, saying: "I had hoped that most of the members in the House had awakened to the threat facing the United States. That hope was apparently unfounded."

One day later the House voted to keep the MX missile alive but only in the development stage, and in a compromise hammered out with the Senate in conference committee, it was agreed that the matter would be reviewed in 1983. Part of the opposition to the MX had concerned the so-called dense pack basing mode—basing the missiles in closely packed clusters—which Reagan had recommended. However, the controversy over the weapon was also viewed as a sign that some members of Congress believed that the administration's military buildup had gone too far. Many also interpreted the initial House vote as a victory for the nuclear freeze movement.

A tent city was erected on Boston Common and labeled a "Reagan Ranch." The encampment was built by demonstrators who wanted to call attention to the needs of the poor and jobless.

JPI

Supporters of the Equal Rights Amendment chained themselves to the brass rails outside the Illinois state senate as that body was debating passage of the amendment. Despite their demonstration, the amendment was defeated.

The proposed Equal Rights Amendment to the U.S. Constitution, banning discrimination on the basis of sex, failed to gain ratification by three-fourths of the state legislatures before the deadline of June 30. Supporters of the amendment vowed to continue their efforts to gain equality for women.

Alarm swept the nation in early October when it was disclosed that seven persons in Chicago and its suburbs had died after taking Extra-Strength Tylenol pain-killing capsules that had been tainted with cyanide. Investigators theorized that the capsules had been removed from their bottles, laced with the poison, and then returned to store shelves. The manufacturer of Extra-Strength Tylenol, the McNeil Consumer Products Co., a subsidiary of Johnson & Johnson, ordered the recall of 264,000 bottles of the pain reliever.

During the following days a number of "copycat" tamperings with various consumer products were reported in other parts of the country. A Colorado man suffered eye damage after using eye drops tainted with acid, and a tourist in Clearwater, Fla., suffered minor throat burns after using mouthwash with hydrochloric acid in it. The person or persons responsible for the Tylenol poisonings was still unknown at the year's end.

John De Lorean (see BIOGRAPHIES), the flamboy-

ant automobile executive who had founded a company that produced expensive sports cars bearing his name, was arrested in Los Angeles in October by federal law enforcement officials and charged with possession of 59 lb (27 kg) of cocaine and with conspiracy to distribute it. De Lorean's arrest was made public only hours after the British government announced that the Northern Ireland plant that manufactured De Lorean cars would be closed permanently.

Wayne Williams, a black free-lance photographer and aspiring talent agent, was convicted in February of murdering 2 of 28 young blacks slain over a two-year period in Atlanta, Ga. Immediately after the verdict, Judge Clarence Cooper sentenced Williams to two consecutive life terms in prison.

In another widely publicized criminal trial, a U.S. District Court jury in Washington, D.C., on June 21 found John W. Hinckley, Jr., not guilty by reason of insanity on all charges of shooting President Reagan and three others in the nation's capital in March 1981. The verdict, reached after four days of deliberation, surprised and shocked many observers, in and out of government. There were calls, including one from Attorney General William French Smith, for a change in the law permitting acquittal in such cases.

Hinckley was committed to a hospital in the District of Columbia. Under the District's law he was entitled to a hearing within 50 days on whether he was capable of being released from custody. After that hearing, in August, U.S. District Court Judge Barrington D. Parker ordered Hinckley confined to a mental hospital for an indefinite period.

After a strike lasting 57 days, negotiators for National Football League players and owners agreed on November 16 to a five-year, $1.6 billion settlement. Two regular-season games had been played before the players struck, and eight were lost during the walkout. It was agreed to play out the remainder of the regular season as originally scheduled and to play one additional game, for a total of nine, prior to the play-offs. A new, one-time play-off format was instituted with a total of 16 teams, 8 from each conference, qualifying for the postseason tournament. (See FOOTBALL: *U.S. Football*.)

Foreign Affairs. As usual, U.S. foreign policymakers were preoccupied in 1982 with relations

U.S. House of Representative Speaker Thomas P. O'Neill (Dem., Mass.) and Majority Leader Jim Wright (Dem., Texas) appeared jubilant after helping to override Pres. Reagan's veto of a $14.2 billion supplemental funding bill for government operations and social programs.

with the Soviet Union and the continuing search for a lasting peace in the Middle East. Their task was complicated somewhat by a midyear change of secretaries of state. Alexander Haig, Jr., who had held the post from the beginning of the Reagan administration, resigned in June and was replaced by George Shultz (*see* BIOGRAPHIES), who had served previous presidents as secretary of labour, director of the Office of Management and Budget, and secretary of the treasury. The nomination of Shultz was unanimously approved by the Senate on July 15. (In the only other Cabinet change of the year, Donald Hodel replaced James Edwards as secretary of energy.)

Another complicating factor was the death on November 10 of Leonid I. Brezhnev, head of the Soviet Communist Party since 1964 and president of the U.S.S.R. President Reagan sent a letter to the Soviet leadership the following day expressing regret for Brezhnev's death and willingness to work for improved relations with his successor. Brezhnev was "one of the world's most important figures for nearly two decades," Reagan wrote to Vasily V. Kuznetsov, first vice-president of the Presidium of the Supreme Soviet. "I look forward to conducting relations with the new leadership in the Soviet Union with the aim of expanding the areas where our two nations can cooperate to mutual advantage."

At a White House news conference the same day, the president called for bilateral arms reductions to ensure world peace. "Our two nations bear a tremendous responsibility for peace in a dangerous time," he said, "a responsibility we don't take lightly." The United States intended to continue negotiations to reduce nuclear arsenals, Reagan said. "I want to reconfirm that we will pursue every avenue for progress in this area."

In what may have been meant as a conciliatory gesture to the new Soviet leadership, Reagan announced on November 13 the lifting of sanctions against U.S. and foreign companies selling U.S.-developed technology for use in the Soviet-Western European natural gas pipeline. "We've

achieved an agreement with our allies that provides for stronger and more effective measures," Reagan declared in a nationwide radio broadcast. "There is no further need for these sanctions, and I am lifting them today."

According to Reagan, the U.S. and its allies had agreed to the following provisions: (1) "not to engage in trade arrangements which contribute to the military or strategic advantage of the U.S.S.R.," with particular attention to trade in high technology, including that used in gas and oil production; (2) not to sign any new natural gas contracts with the Soviet Union, pending the results of "an urgent study of Western energy alternatives"; (3) a strengthening of "existing controls on the transfer of strategic items to the Soviet Union"; (4) establishment of "procedures for monitoring financial relations with the Soviet Union," with the goal of developing a coordinated policy on export credits.

By lifting the sanctions Reagan removed a persistent irritant in relations with Western European allies. Most of them had announced that they would defy the sanctions because they constituted an unacceptable intrusion on their national sovereignty. Reagan may also have been influenced by Shultz. During his confirmation hearings in July, Shultz had said that he supported the gas pipeline sanctions but added that "as a general proposition, I think the use of trade sanctions as an instrument of policy is a bad idea."

Reagan decided in July to authorize U.S. officials to seek a one-year extension of the U.S.-Soviet grain agreement. He called for preserving the terms of the current accord, due to expire on October 1. By the provisions of the agreement the Soviet Union had to purchase a minimum of six million metric tons of grain and was entitled to buy up to eight million metric tons, with larger amounts subject to negotiation.

Early in August Reagan told U.S. farmers that they would be able to sell a "record volume" of grain to the Soviet Union in 1982. "The granary door is open and the exchange will be cash on the

UNITED STATES

Education. (1981–82; public schools only) Primary and preprimary, pupils 23,736,625, teachers 1,189,939; secondary and vocational, pupils 16,417,680, teachers 996,077; higher (including teacher-training colleges), students 12.3 million, teaching staff 860,000.

Finance. Monetary unit: U.S. dollar, with (Sept. 20, 1982) a free rate of U.S. $1.71 to £1 sterling. Gold and other reserves (June 1982) $29.6 billion. Federal budget (1982–83 est.): revenue $666.1 billion; expenditure $757.6 billion. Gross national product (1981) $2,937,700,000,000. Money supply (March 1982) $418.4 billion. Cost of living: (1975 = 100; June 1982) 180.3.

Foreign Trade. (1981) Imports $273.3 billion; exports (excluding military aid exports of $160 million) $233.7 billion. Import sources: Canada 17%; Japan 15%; Saudi Arabia 6%; Mexico 5%; U.K. 5%. Export destinations: Canada 17%; Japan 9%; Mexico 8%; U.K. 5%. Main exports: machinery 27%; chemicals 9%; cereals 8%; motor vehicles 7%; aircraft 6%. Tourism (1980): visitors 22.5 million; gross receipts U.S. $10 billion.

Transport and Communications. Roads (1979) 6,303,771 km (including 88,641 km expressways). Motor vehicles in use (1979): passenger 120,248,000;

commercial 33,349,700. Railways (1979): 296,860 km; traffic (class I railways only) 18,020,000,000 passenger-km, freight 1,476,515,000,000 net ton-km. Air traffic (1981): 375,582,000,000 passenger-km (including domestic services 290,637,000,000 passenger-km); freight 10,168,700,000 net ton-km (including domestic services 6,262,700,000 net ton-km). Inland waterways (1980) 41,099 km; freight traffic (1979) 1,499,341,000,000 ton-km. Shipping (1981): merchant vessels 100 gross tons and over 5,869; gross tonnage 18,908,281. Shipping traffic (1981): goods loaded 369,135,000 metric tons, unloaded 422,706,000 metric tons. Telephones (Jan. 1980) 182,558,000. Radio receivers (Dec. 1979) 450 million. Television receivers (Dec. 1979) 140 million.

Agriculture. Production (in 000; metric tons; 1981): corn 208,314; wheat 76,026; barley 10,414; oats 7,375; rye 473; rice 8,408; sorghum 22,360; sugar, raw value 5,771; potatoes 15,135; soybeans 55,260; dry beans 1,443; cabbages 1,494; onions 1,599; tomatoes 6,339; apples 3,468; oranges 9,547; grapefruit 2,503; peaches 1,430; grapes 4,018; peanuts 1,791; sunflower seed 2,098; linseed 198; cottonseed 5,673; cotton, lint 3,425; tobacco 929; butter 561; cheese 2,212; hen's eggs 4,122; beef and veal c.

10,264; pork c. 7,211; fish catch (1980) 3,635; timber (cu m; 1980) c. 322,265. Livestock (in 000; Jan. 1981): cattle 114,321; sheep 12,936; pigs 64,520; horses c. 9,928; chickens 392,110.

Industry. Index of production (1975 = 100; 1981) 128; mining 126; manufacturing 129; electricity, gas, and water 116; construction 104. Unemployment (1981) 7.6%. Fuel and power (in 000; metric tons; 1981): coal 686,340; lignite 46,430; crude oil 421,317; natural gas (cu m) 554,700,000; manufactured gas (cu m) 18,030,000; electricity (kw-hr) 2,368,000,000. Production (in 000; metric tons; 1981): iron ore (62% metal content) 75,450; pig iron 66,560; crude steel 108,874; cement (shipments) 62,182; newsprint 4,783; other paper (1980) 56,800; petroleum products c. 640,000; sulfuric acid 36,595; caustic soda 9,648; plastics and resins (1980) 12,418; man-made fibres (1980) 3,912; synthetic rubber 2,021; fertilizers (including Puerto Rico; nutrient content; 1980–81) nitrogenous 11,788, phosphate 9,405, potash 2,052; passenger cars (units) 6,238; commercial vehicles (units) 1,690. Merchant vessels launched (100 gross tons and over; 1981) 298,000 gross tons. New dwelling units started (1981) 1.1 million.

barrelhead," the president promised in a speech to the National Corn Growers Association in Des Moines, Iowa. He linked the resumption of U.S.-Soviet talks on a long-term grain accord to the lifting of martial law in Poland.

In a radio talk broadcast to U.S. farm states in October, Reagan said that the United States would soon offer to sell 23 million metric tons of grain to the Soviet Union. He conceded that the Soviets might not buy the full amount offered. "But we know they are shopping," he said, "and they still have large needs." Reagan's announcement followed reports of a large Canadian grain sale to the Soviet Union.

The United States and the Soviet Union continued to discuss nuclear arms limitation, although no formal agreements were reached. In a commencement address May 9 at his alma mater, Eureka College in Illinois, Reagan called for "significant reductions" in U.S. and Soviet nuclear arsenals. He proposed a one-third reduction by both countries of ballistic missile nuclear warheads. In a second stage of his plan an "equal ceiling" would be set on other components of each country's strategic nuclear forces, including "throw weight," or the total payload of destructive power. The president said he had proposed to the Soviet Union that strategic arms reduction talks, known by the acronym START, get under way by the end of June.

Soviet leaders responded favourably to Reagan's initiative, with the result that the START talks opened June 29 in Geneva. The chief Soviet negotiator was Viktor P. Karpov, and his U.S. counterpart was Edward L. Rowny, a retired army lieutenant general. The talks recessed on August 12 and reopened October 6. Rowny expressed optimism early in October: "With good will on both sides, we can make progress toward an equitable and verifiable agreement." But Karpov urged the U.S. to abandon its "one-sided" proposal and "open up the road toward a mutually acceptable agreement." The United States, Karpov claimed, was trying to achieve nuclear superiority over the Soviet Union, while the latter was seeking "radical reductions" in nuclear arsenals.

In the meantime, also in Geneva, negotiations continued between the U.S. and the Soviet Union on limiting intermediate-range missiles stationed in Europe. Negotiators for both sides publicly differed in September on ways to resolve the differences that had emerged during the talks, begun in November 1981.

The U.S. offer to cancel its scheduled deployment of 572 new missiles in Europe, starting in 1983, if the Soviet Union dismantled its nuclear arsenal aimed at Western Europe was still "the best prospect for an enduring and verifiable agreement," said Paul H. Nitze, head of the U.S. delegation. Some progress had been made in the talks, Nitze maintained. Asked whether he agreed that the two sides had made progress, Soviet delegate Yuly A. Kvitsinsky said, "So-so."

The U.S. response to Israel's invasion of southern Lebanon on June 6 was restrained at first. In a formal statement issued on June 7 the Department of State did not directly condemn the Israeli assault. "A divided Lebanon must not be the outcome of this violence," the statement said. "Israel will have to withdraw its forces from Lebanon, and the Palestinians will have to stop using Lebanon as a launching pad for attacks on Israel." President Reagan, who was attending economic and military summit meetings in Europe, dispatched special envoy Philip C. Habib (*see* BIOGRAPHIES) to the Middle East to try to arrange a new cease-fire in Lebanon, as he had done in 1981.

Two weeks later, on June 21, Reagan met for three hours at the White House with Israeli Prime Minister Menachem Begin. In remarks that emphasized their general accord on long-term objectives, the leaders agreed that all foreign troops should be withdrawn from Lebanon as soon as Israeli territory could be made permanently secure from Palestinian attacks.

U.S. involvement in the Lebanon crisis deepened in July, when Reagan confirmed that he had agreed to the use of U.S. Marines in the country to guard a withdrawal of Palestinian forces from West Beirut. The plan called for 800–1,000 U.S. Marines to form the core of an international evacuation and peacekeeping force in Lebanon. Secre-

"The public has got the idea that Dense Pack is a Rube Goldberg"—Senator Jackson

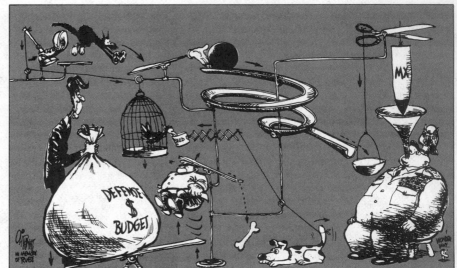

ALLAN TANNENBAUM—SYGMA

A massive crowd, estimated by police at more than 600,000 and said to be the biggest protest rally in U.S. history, filled New York's Central Park in June to plead for nuclear disarmament.

tary of Defense Caspar Weinberger said that the U.S. troops would be used as a "screen" to help Palestinians leave the country and to keep Israeli and Palestinian forces apart.

But the Israeli siege of Beirut continued, culminating in an 11-hour bombardment of the city on August 12 by Israeli aircraft. The bombardment was finally ordered halted by the Israeli Cabinet after an angry confrontation involving Defense Minister Ariel Sharon (*see* BIOGRAPHIES), who had ordered the raid on his own authority.

While the Israeli Cabinet was in session, U.S. Ambassador Samuel Lewis delivered a message from President Reagan sharply condemning the bombardments. Reagan followed the message with a personal call to Begin in which, as the White House described it, the president "expressed his outrage over this latest round of massive military action."

Taking a broader view of the Middle East situation, Reagan on September 1 called for a "fresh start" in the effort to achieve peace in the region. The president advanced new proposals urging "self-government by the Palestinians of the West Bank and Gaza in association with Jordan." To this end he called for the "immediate adoption of a settlement freeze by Israel"; that is, an end to the establishment of additional Jewish settlements in the occupied territories.

The U.S. also became embroiled in the short war that broke out unexpectedly in April between Great Britain and Argentina over ownership of the Falkland Islands, an archipelago in the South Atlantic that was a dependency of Britain but had long been claimed by both countries. The conflict was precipitated by Argentina's military occupation of the Falklands and South Georgia island and Britain's decision to send a naval task force to the South Atlantic to retake them.

The U.S., which counted both combatant countries as allies, at first tried to act as mediator, with Secretary of State Haig conducting shuttle diplomacy. Starting April 8, Haig flew back and forth between London and Buenos Aires in an unsuccessful effort to reach a diplomatic solution to the crisis. The U.S. abandoned this role on April 30, declaring that Argentina was not willing to negotiate. At the same time, the U.S. offered to provide military supplies to Britain and invoked limited sanctions against Argentina, including a suspension of all military exports and certain types of aid. (For a further discussion of the conflict, *see* DEFENSE: *Special Report*.)

The U.S. decision to side with Britain in the Falklands conflict caused deep bitterness in Argentina and indeed in much of Latin America. Some Latin-American officials asserted that it would take years to undo the diplomatic damage. As a first step in that direction, Reagan flew to Brazil on November 30 on the first leg of a five-day trip to Latin America that also took him to Colombia, Costa Rica, and Honduras. On December 1 he announced in Brasília that the U.S. had agreed to extend to Brazil $1,230,000,000 in short-term credit until the government of Pres. João Baptista Figueiredo had finished negotiating with the International Monetary Fund for a possible long-term credit.

Reagan's other major initiative in hemispheric affairs was his program for improving economic conditions and ensuring military security in the Caribbean basin and Central America. Outlined on February 24 in an address to the Organization of American States, the president's plan included $350 million in additional economic aid for the region in fiscal year 1982 and $60 million more in military assistance. The program's other points included special duty-free status for imported products from the Caribbean, tax incentives to encourage U.S. business investment in the region, technical assistance, efforts to increase international aid programs, and protection of the special status already held by Puerto Rico and the U.S.-controlled Virgin Islands.

(RICHARD L. WORSNOP)

See also Dependent States.

PAC'S—THE NEW FORCE IN POLITICS

by David C. Beckwith

Early in 1982, the U.S. Congress overwhelmingly vetoed a Federal Trade Commission (FTC) regulation that would have required used car dealers to inform buyers of any hidden defects they knew about in the autos they were selling. "There was no public interest reason on earth to oppose that rule," Sen. William Proxmire (Dem., Wis.) complained. "The vote can be explained only by campaign contributions." Proxmire's analysis was illuminated later in the year, when campaign finance reports were made public. The National Automobile Dealers Association had donated $950,680 to congressional candidates, the vast bulk of it to incumbents who helped defeat the defect-disclosure rule. The money was channeled through NADA's political action committee, one of the most generous association donors of campaign contributions and clearly one of the most successful.

A Matter of Money. The history of the used car rule illustrates a phenomenon in recent U.S. politics: the rapidly growing influence of the political action committee. PAC's were authorized to gather and spend money freely only ten years ago, and the 113 in existence then accounted for less than $10 million in congressional campaign contributions in 1974. By 1982, however, 3,479 PAC's raised over $200 million, fed about $90 million into congressional campaign coffers, and threatened to overwhelm both individuals and political parties as the dominant source of "the mother's milk of politics." In other words, lobbyists for special interests were fast becoming the dominant financiers of the U.S. electoral process.

The rise of PAC influence paralleled—and encouraged—a dramatic increase in the cost of running for office. The average U.S. House campaign, for example, cost a mere $50,000 in 1974, but that had grown to $150,000 by 1980 and $200,000 in 1982. In some

David C. Beckwith is national economic correspondent for Time *magazine.*

hotly contested races, expenditures of $500,000 or more were not uncommon. The costs of other major campaigns soared proportionately. More than $18 million was spent in the 1982 Texas gubernatorial and Senate races alone, and $2 million was raised and expended on a single race for a seat in the California state legislature (won by former radical Tom Hayden).

Part of the reason was inflation and the expense of reaching a larger population, but most of the increase reflected an indulgence made possible by ever more efficient fund raising. Instead of volunteers, campaign workers now were often paid staffers who were provided with meals and expenses out of campaign funds. Most important, expensive image-building television advertisements were soaking up more and more campaign cash.

Birth of a "Reform." PAC's began taking on major importance in 1974 when, in the wake of the Watergate scandal, Congress approved an election law reform designed to end under-the-table payments by corporations and unions and to put a lid on the influence of wealthy individual contributors. At that time, PAC's were viewed as part of the solution, a well-regulated way for individuals to pool their resources in support of candidates. That much worked. Reports of secretive, bribe-like payments to candidates almost vanished, and the identity of most contributors became a matter of public record. Many small donors to PAC's thought they could have a significant effect on elections, and the power of the smoke-filled room diminished.

But like many other well-intentioned laws, the "reform" bred new problems. The law attempted to curb spending by limiting the amount any single entity could donate. An individual could give only $1,000 to both a congressional candidate's primary and general election campaigns, for example, while a PAC was restricted to $5,000 gifts in both races. But the U.S. Supreme Court subsequently threw out a provision limiting the amount a wealthy person could donate to his own campaign, giving an inordinate advantage to millionaire politicians. Also, the law failed to control the proliferation of separate PAC's. As Rep. Thomas Downey (Dem., N.Y.) noted, "PAC's go with PAC's. If you got one, you got five. It's not $5,000, it's $25,000." The result: more money was pouring into elections every year; the price of running a competitive race was escalating steadily; and the value of an individual citizen's contribution was dwindling apace.

More ominously, the role of major political parties, the great broadening influence in U.S. public life, was being diminished as well. Even with abnormally heavy spending by the Republican Party in 1982, the average congressional candidate got three times as much money from PAC's as from his party. That alarmed PAC critics such as former House legislative counsel Jerome Ziefman. "A whole raft of bills to weaken the antitrust laws is now in danger of passage," he noted. "The principles of both parties support vigorous antitrust enforcement, so you have to conclude that PAC's are driving the process." Added former presidential counsel Stuart Eizenstat: "The PAC's are balkanizing the process, shifting attention away from broad national concerns and towards single-issue, special interest topics." That, in turn, often led to costly special-interest legislation. According to PAC critic James Leach (Rep., Iowa), one of only a dozen congressmen who refused to take PAC money in 1982: "It's not surprising there are no balanced budgets."

Paying the Piper. Four categories of PAC's dominated in national and state elections. In 1982, 613 trade associations such as the National Association of Realtors and the American Medical Association contributed $22 million to congressional campaign war chests. Some 1,500 individual corporation committees, technically funded by employee contributions, gave $30 million more; 350 labour union PAC's, also aggregating individual contributions, added $20 million; and 644 ideological or nonconnected PAC's, of which the National Conservative Political Action Committee (NCPAC) was the most publicized, provided candidates with $6 million and spent at least $25 million on their own advertising and administration.

Whether this money promotes good government and participation in the political process or whether it amounts to an organized payoff system was at the heart of the debate over PAC growth. PAC defenders, such as Rep. Bill Frenzel (Rep., Minn.), asserted that the PAC vehicle allows like-minded individuals to aggregate their contributions and have a legal, wholesome effect on an election. He noted that while $5,000 is a significant contribution, it is not sufficiently overwhelming to cause the abandonment of principles. Other backers of the system suggested that PAC contributions do not buy votes but merely reward those who voted correctly in the past. Another contention was that a PAC contribution merely ensures access to a congressman and exposure for one's point of view. "Talking to congressmen is fine," said California businessman Justin Dart, "but with a little money, they hear you better."

Critics emphatically rejected that argument as disingenuous. "There's no reason to give money except in the expectation of votes," said Rep. William Brodhead (Dem., Mich.) who retired in 1982, partly because he tired of constant fund raising and subsequent pressures for voting allegiance. "Money doesn't always win—just 95 to 98 percent of the time." The relative ease of securing big four-figure checks from lobbyists rather than laboriously scraping up individual $25 contributions also distorts the democratic process. Concluded Common Cause president Fred Wertheimer: "Dependency on PAC's has grown so much that PAC's, not constituents, are now the focus of a congressman's attention."

Certainly, virtually every PAC contribution had some legislative interest behind it. The American Medical and American Dental associations, which had given $2.3 million to House members since 1979, were struggling to exempt doctors and dentists from FTC price-fixing regulation. The beer lobby's PAC, appropriately named SixPAC, was similarly rewarding House members who supported its bill to allow monopoly territory for beer distributors. A half-dozen PAC's led by the American Bankers Association passed out $704,297 to 255 congressmen who were co-sponsoring a bill that would require individuals to repay debts after they declared bankruptcy.

Looming over the fray was the dark spectre of the independent, ideological PAC's, groups that enjoyed constitutional free speech protection. They would doubtless benefit if other PAC activities were somehow curbed. These committees were unaffiliated with any candidate and thus uncontrolled, and they often produced their own advertising—much of it scathing personal assaults on candidates with whom they disagreed. NCPAC, for example, claimed credit for the defeat of four liberal U.S. senators in 1980 via expensive negative television advertising. Two years later, however, the targets were better prepared. Seventeen of 18 NCPAC targets won their races in 1982, but the independent PAC's remained a potent, unguided political force.

There were plenty of ideas for new and improved reforms. One congressman proposed a constitutional amendment to place a ceiling on campaign spending. Another bill would limit a candidate's total PAC take to $75,000 per election. Others would attempt to reduce PAC influence by increasing the limits on an individual citizen's contributions to candidates and political parties. Among academic thinkers, a growing consensus called for public financing of all elections, similar to the system used for presidential campaigns. The prospects for immediate action by Congress were dim, however. "There are too many people [incumbents] doing very well under the present system," observed Sen. Paul Tsongas (Dem., Mass.). Critics thought a national embarrassment would have to precede a serious reform effort. Concluded Rep. James Shannon (Dem., Mass.): "Eventually this scandal—and it is a scandal—will attract so much attention that public financing of elections will be seriously considered."

UNITED STATES STATISTICAL SUPPLEMENT
DEVELOPMENTS IN THE STATES IN 1982

Economic recession and turmoil in federal-state relations made 1982 a stormy year for state governments across the United States. As the national economy completed a fourth consecutive year without significant growth, state legislatures were forced by declining revenues and increased outlay obligations to undo many of the dramatic tax reductions enacted during the relatively good times of the late 1970s.

Pres. Ronald Reagan's call for transferring responsibilities from the federal to state governments continued to lose its allure for state officials during the year as it became clear that the transfers contemplated would severely strain hard-pressed state treasuries. Reagan's "new federalism" idea appeared stalled at the end of 1982, with presidential advisers talking in terms of transferring only minor programs to the states. A nationwide crackdown against drunken drivers, started in 1981, accelerated rapidly, with a majority of states moving to increase penalties and step up traffic enforcement. The drive to require deposits on beverage containers made some progress but was decisively defeated in four western states. Prison overcrowding continued to bedevil penal administrators, and a trend toward mandating physical restraining devices for children in automobiles gained national support.

Forty-three states held regular legislative sessions during 1982. Nineteen staged special sessions, usually to cope with budget problems.

Party Strengths. Democrats made major gains in 1982 state elections, adding a net seven governorships and extending their domination of state legislatures. After picking up 200 seats in the November balloting, Democrats controlled both chambers in 34 state legislatures, while Republicans had a two-house majority in only 11. All states were solidly Democratic except Alaska, Arizona, Colorado, Idaho, Indiana, Kansas, New Hampshire, South Dakota, Utah, Vermont, and Wyoming (where Republicans had control in both houses); Montana, New York, North Dakota, and Pennsylvania (where Republicans controlled the upper house and Democrats the lower chamber); and Nebraska (a nonpartisan, one-house legislature).

Republicans captured the governorship from Democratic control in California and New Hampshire, but Democrats regained the gubernatorial office from the GOP in Alaska, Arkansas, Michigan, Minnesota, Nebraska, Nevada, Ohio, Texas, and Wisconsin. Two races were particularly close. In California Democrat Thomas Bradley narrowly missed becoming the first elected black governor in U.S. history. In a contested election still under legal challenge at the year's end, Illinois GOP Gov. James Thompson apparently defeated Democratic challenger Sen. Adlai Stevenson III by a scant 5,000 votes out of 3.6 million cast. That left the prospective gubernatorial lineup for 1983 at 34 Democrats and 16 Republicans.

Government Structures and Powers. Economic hard times and single-issue enthusiasm led to a 50-year high in voter ballot initiatives during 1982. The National Conference of State Legislatures counted nearly 300 measures on the ballot in 42 states, the highest total since the depression of the 1930s. Some observers feared that the development represented a lack of confidence in elected officials and a weakening of representative democracy.

It was not a boom year for state government. Financial pressures, including declining federal aid, caused employment in state and local public jobs to fall for the first time since World War II. Numerous bond issues were defeated. Georgia voters approved a new state constitution, but proposals to liberalize gubernatorial term length or succession restrictions in Georgia, New Hampshire, North Dakota, and Rhode Island were rejected. New Hampshire voters called for a state constitutional convention. Alaska voters refused to fund, and thus apparently killed, a $2.8 billion project to move the state capital from Juneau to the village of Willow. Voters in the District of Columbia narrowly approved a constitution for a new state of New Columbia. The controversial document guarantees a job or adequate income for all, but observers doubted that even a model draft would prompt Congress to establish a 51st state in the foreseeable future.

Government Relations. For the second consecutive year President Reagan's "new federalism" program bogged down in controversy over funding. Reagan made an attempt to revitalize the concept in his January 1982 state of the union address, calling for "a single bold stroke" that would have the states take over responsibility for basic welfare and food stamp programs while the federal government assumed all costs of Medicaid. He also offered to turn back to the states up to 40 federal programs, from child nutrition to sewerage aid, along with some revenue to fund them.

But critics charged that the presidential initiative was merely a thinly disguised effort to divert attention from shortcomings in the administration's federal budgetary proposals. A Congressional Budget Office study faulted early administration estimates that the Reagan program would be a no-cost "wash," calculating instead that the swap would cost hard-pressed states about $15 billion in the first year and more after that. Negotiations between the White House and state governors later bogged down in a stalemate. As the year wore on and the national economic recession worsened, the spectre of additional future federal budget cuts in state assistance programs caused governors to withdraw early indications of support. Utah Gov. Scott Matheson, chairman of the National Governors Association, said, "The situation in the states is devastating," and suggested that economic recovery would have to precede any further progress in the new federalism proposals.

States were not reluctant to offer the federal government advice in other areas, however. Alaska became the 31st state to demand a constitutional convention that would consider a balanced federal budget; 34 states are required in order to convene such a body. Under that pressure the U.S. Congress hastened to consider a balanced budget amendment, but the House of Representatives defeated it in September. Amendment advocates promised a renewed drive in state legislatures during 1983.

Alaska joined the "Sagebrush Rebellion" as voters laid formal claim to most federal lands within the state. Backers of a worldwide nuclear weapons freeze were successful in persuading 11 states to register advisory opinions on the question during 1982. Legislators in Connecticut and Vermont and voters in California, Massachusetts, Michigan, Montana, New Jersey, North Dakota, Oregon, and Rhode Island approved the freeze recommendation, while Arizona voters rejected it.

States engaged in a significant number of squabbles among themselves, some of them serious. A "Great New England trucking fee war" escalated after Vermont began charging entering truckers a toll of $15, but the warfare wound down after six states agreed to a compact banning all such fees. Another short-lived flare-up started late in the year when New York City authorities discovered that 17-cent Connecticut highway tokens fit into 75-cent city subway turnstiles. South Dakota officials indulged in long-distance name-calling after California temporarily refused to extradite an Indian activist wanted on rioting charges; South Dakota's attorney general was forced to deny formally that some accused criminals in his state were being given a choice of prosecution or moving to California.

Finances. Buffeted by a prolonged recession, cuts in federal aid, high unemployment, and reduced tax revenue, state treasury officials faced unprecedented problems in attempting to balance their budgets during 1982. By midyear 17 states had taken the unpopular election-year step of raising taxes, but many of those same states were forced to cut budgets and boost tax rates again later in the year. The Minnesota legislature, for example, had to trim services and raise taxes three times during the year in an effort to eliminate a yawning revenue shortfall. Even so, seven states ended their fiscal years with an illegal deficit, and a record six states had their bond ratings lowered by a major market service.

A survey by the Tax Foundation reported that 22 states enacted well over $3 billion in tax increases during the year, with four-fifths of the additional revenue being derived from broadly based general sales and personal income taxes that are especially unpopular with voters. Michigan, Minnesota, New Jersey, Ohio, and Oregon raised their personal income taxes, usually by adding a surcharge to existing rates. Florida, Minnesota, Missouri, Nebraska, New Jersey, Washington, and Wisconsin boosted sales taxes, Missouri doing so in exchange for property tax reductions. Nebraska, Rhode Island, and Vermont increased their personal income tax rates to offset decreases in federal taxes to which the state levies are tied.

Ohio, Minnesota, and Wisconsin raised corporate income taxes. Michigan, Missouri, Nebraska, New Jersey, Oregon, Rhode Island, Utah, Washington, and Wisconsin boosted cigarette taxes. Arizona, Idaho, and Maryland lifted motor fuel levies, and Vermont increased diesel taxes. Alabama, Kentucky, Utah, Virginia, and Washington increased excises on alcoholic beverages.

The adverse fiscal situation forced many states into dramatic belt-tightening measures. The U.S. Bureau of the Census reported that the number of state and local government workers declined in fiscal 1982 from 13.3 million to 13.1 million as 43 states reported laying off workers during the year. Indiana, Kentucky, Missouri, New York, Nebraska, and Michigan admitted that they were slowing down payment of income tax refunds in order to harbour cash. Indiana and Mississippi, following the lead of Michigan, established a "rainy day fund" to cushion the state treasury against future recessionary deficits.

Figures accumulated in 1982 showed that state revenue from all sources totaled $310.8 billion during the 1981 fiscal year, an increase of 12.2% over the preceding 12 months. General revenue (excluding state liquor and state insurance trust revenue) was $258.2 billion, up 10.5%. Total state expenditures rose 13.1% to $291.5 billion, creating a surplus of $19.3 billion for the year. General expenditures, not including outlays of the liquor stores and insurance trust systems, amounted to $253.7 billion, up 11.1% for the year. Of general revenue, 58% came from state taxes and licenses; 13.5% from charges and miscellaneous revenue, including educational tuition; and 28.5% from intergovernmental revenue (mostly from the federal government).

The largest state outlay was $96.9 billion for education, of which $31.5 billion went to state colleges and universities and $57.3 billion to local public schools. Other major outlays included $51.5 billion for public welfare, $25.4 billion for highways, and $20.5 billion for health and hospitals.

Ethics. For the first time in a decade present and past state governors avoided involvement in major misconduct charges, a development partially attributable to a national shift in FBI priorities away from white-collar crime and toward combating drug trafficking and organized crime. Charles Roemer, former Louisiana administration commissioner, was sentenced to three years in prison in January after his conviction for conspiring to receive kickbacks from state insurance contracts. New Jersey state senator William V. Musto was convicted in March and sentenced to seven years for arranging kickbacks on school renovation projects. Rep. Tommy Burnett, majority leader of the Tennessee House of Representatives, pleaded guilty in June to three misdemeanour charges; he was accused of failing to report $768,088 in income over three years. Richard Wertz pleaded guilty in October to theft of $18,685 from the Arizona Justice Planning Agency, which he formerly had headed; Wertz was fined $21,800 and sentenced to five years in prison. Nevada state senator Eugene Echols was indicted on bribery charges in December after allegedly accepting $6,000 from an FBI undercover agent.

Oklahoma legislators revamped county commissioner financial laws in the aftermath of a statewide bid-rigging scandal over paving contracts. Alaska also tightened state contracting safeguards. Louisiana mandated financial disclosure for state political candidates. Virginia strengthened legislative ethics rules but weakened its

freedom of information act by allowing more meetings and records to be closed. Arizona opened additional meetings to the public while reducing some penalties for violation of disclosure laws. Ohio and Michigan voters decisively rejected proposals for public financing of utility commissioner election campaigns.

Education. Southern states were stunned by a U.S. Supreme Court decision requiring that a free public education be provided for children of illegal aliens. In dissent, Chief Justice Warren Burger previewed fears of financially strapped state officials by suggesting that court-ordered food stamps, Medicaid, and welfare payments for illegal entrants might be a logical next step.

Federal courts struck down Louisiana and Arkansas laws requiring the teaching of "scientific creationism," the biblical version of creation, alongside scientific evolutionism in public schools. Joining ten other states with existing programs, California, New Mexico, Oklahoma, South Carolina, and Texas provided for mandatory testing of public-school teachers.

West Virginia and Vermont moved to equalize spending between wealthy and poor school districts, but a Colorado appellate court overturned a 1979 lower court decision requiring similar action. Iowa and Massachusetts joined Illinois in selling tax-exempt bonds to replace dwindling federal student loan funds. Numerous states moved to crack down on student loan and other overdue debtors.

Drugs. A nationwide lobbying effort by traffic victim groups such as Mothers Against Drunk Driving (MADD) and Remove Intoxicated Drivers (RID) resulted in a marked stiffening by 27 states of their driving-while-intoxicated laws during 1982. In addition to possible license suspension and fines, some states mandated minimum jail terms even for first offenders under aggravated circumstances: one day in Arizona, Washington, and West Virginia; two days in California, Florida, Iowa, Louisiana, Kansas, Maine, Tennessee, and Virginia; and five days in Idaho. Iowa provided for automatic revocation of license for some first offenders. Maryland, Minnesota, Utah, and Idaho slashed the blood alcohol content level required for a drunk-driving conviction, and Arizona, Kansas, and Wyoming eliminated plea bargaining to ensure integrity of records for repeat offenders.

Attacking the problem in a different way, Connecticut, Maryland, New Jersey, New York, and Ohio raised the minimum drinking age during the year. Of the 29 states that lowered the drinking age during the mid-1970s, 20 had reversed themselves by the end of 1982; only 5 still allowed 18-year-olds to drink liquor. Many states claimed markedly improved traffic death figures following the law changes.

Another trend of the 1970s, decriminalization of possession of small amounts of marijuana, stalled completely, with Georgia and Kentucky among states raising penalties for possession. Another drug liberalization campaign similarly encountered heavy fire. A National Cancer Institute study revealed that laetrile—legalized by 27 states over the past six years—is "a toxic drug that is not effective as a cancer treatment" and, in fact, imparts dangerous amounts of cyanide at the levels recommended by its proponents.

Health and Welfare. Under increasing pressure to slow down spiraling social spending, many states tried methods of re-

ducing health and welfare expenditures. California, Massachusetts, and New York were among states initiating major programs to cut Medicaid outlays, the fastest growing item in state budgets nationwide. Arizona experimented with a prepaid health system, touted by advocates as a possible national alternative to Medicaid.

Arkansas, Connecticut, and Massachusetts cracked down on welfare fraud. Idaho, Iowa, Kentucky, Oklahoma, Pennsylvania, and West Virginia established "workfare" rules designed to force able-bodied welfare recipients to earn their benefits in public service jobs.

Vermont and the District of Columbia joined 11 other jurisdictions having right-to-die legislation; the measures set forth procedures for withdrawing extraordinary care from the terminally ill. Minnesota and South Dakota prohibited so-called wrongful-life and wrongful-birth lawsuits against physicians; the former are based on a failed abortion or sterilization, the latter on alleged failure to prevent the birth of a handicapped child. California, however, specifically authorized suit when medical negligence leads to a genetically disordered birth.

Law and Justice. Reacting to perceived abuses, several states moved to curtail the use of the insanity defense in criminal trials. The acquittal of would-be presidential assassin John W. Hinckley, Jr., by reason of insanity added momentum to a growing protest over alleged misuse of the plea. The most radical reform was taken by Idaho and Montana, which abolished the defense altogether; a similar bill was vetoed by the governor of Louisiana. Alaska, Delaware, Georgia, and Kentucky joined four other states in establishing a new verdict—guilty but mentally ill—that provides mental treatment for a convict but requires a set period of incarceration in the event he or she is cured.

New laws protecting children were enacted by several states. California, Colorado, and Washington toughened laws against child molesting, with California voters abolishing a special diversion program for disordered offenders. Iowa, Vermont, and Washington strengthened laws against child abuse. The U.S. Supreme Court approved a New York law banning the depiction of children in sexually suggestive poses even if the scene is not legally obscene.

Massachusetts joined nine states that had recently expanded the right to use deadly force against intruders in one's home. California, Maryland, and Virginia toughened legal penalties for the use of firearms in commission of a crime, but California voters rejected a major handgun-control initiative. Alabama and Alaska prohibited localities from regulating gun possession, and New Hampshire and Nevada voters expressly reaffirmed their right "to keep and bear arms."

A trend toward limiting the rights of criminal defendants continued nationwide. Voters in Arizona, Colorado, Florida, and Illinois approved the denial of bail under certain circumstances. Arizona, California, and Florida expanded police search powers. Iowa and Louisiana provided compensation for crime victims, and California citizens approved a "victims' bill of rights" initiative that limits plea bargains, lengthens some sentences, and provides for victim restitution.

New Jersey and Massachusetts during 701

the year became the 36th and 37th states to enact capital punishment provisions for first-degree murderers. The number of inmates on death row nationwide continued to mount, passing 1,100, as only two convicts were executed during the year. One of those—Charlie Brooks of Texas—became the first to die by injection of lethal drugs, a technique advocated as less painful and more humane than traditional means of capital punishment. Washington joined four other states that allow use of lethal injections in executions.

In other law revisions Florida banned paramilitary training, and Tennessee prohibited strip searches for minor offenders. Massachusetts, following a national trend to eliminate professional exemptions for jury service, became the first jurisdiction to end all excuses and mandate a one-day or one-trial minimum service for all jury calls. And Kentucky became the 50th state to adopt a uniform automobile registration system, presumably canceling its reputation as a haven for car thieves.

Abortion. Legislatures continued efforts to modify the effect of the 1973 U.S. Supreme Court decision that declared state antiabortion laws unconstitutional. Arizona and Rhode Island required parental notification before a minor can terminate a pregnancy prematurely. Indiana and Pennsylvania went a step further, requiring parental consent. West Virginia's governor, however, vetoed a bill that would have made failure to notify parents a felony, and Alaska voters turned down a proposed ban on state abortion funding.

Gambling. Responding to serious fiscal pressures, additional states moved to expand state revenues via legalized gambling. The District of Columbia, Colorado, and Washington established new lotteries, bringing to 18 the number of jurisdictions with government-run games of chance. Even with the recession, revenues from such sources were up; states grossed $2.8 billion on lotteries in the 1982 fiscal year, compared with $1.5 billion in 1978.

Other gambling measures also won legislative and voter approval. Minnesota authorized pari-mutuel racetrack betting, and West Virginia relaxed bingo restrictions. Although Montana and South Dakota voters turned down expanded casino-style wagering proposals, a measure endorsing North Dakota's $2-limit gaming law won ballot approval.

The vagaries of chance produced several human-interest stories. After a 49-year-old grandmother won $919,559.85 from an Atlantic City slot machine, New Jersey officials promptly suspended her welfare payments. The woman got the final public relations word, however, by repaying $9,500 in past state assistance from her winnings.

Environment. An environmentalist-backed drive to require deposits on beverage containers enjoyed mixed success during the year. New York became the ninth state to require a five-cent deposit on plastic, glass, and aluminum containers of beer and soft drinks, and Massachusetts voters rejected a move to repeal that state's similar law. But well-publicized initiatives to extend the idea of container deposits were rejected by voters in Arizona, California, Colorado, and Washington, dampening hopes for a national deposit law.

State arguments over environmental concerns frequently spilled into federal court. Massachusetts, New Hampshire, New York, and Rhode Island, suspecting adverse impacts on their citizens, sued over plans to build extra-tall smokestacks at several Midwestern pollution centres. And three downstream states, Iowa, Missouri, and Nebraska, filed a legal challenge against South Dakota's 50-year, $1.4 billion contract to provide Missouri River water for a coal slurry pipeline. Under the contested plan up to 50,000 ac-ft of water would be shipped to Wyoming each year, mixed with coal, and then piped to power plants in Oklahoma, Arkansas, and Louisiana.

Indiana, Louisiana, and Mississippi were among states that tightened their hazardous waste disposal laws during 1982. Nebraska voters approved a "Save the Family Farm" initiative that bans new purchases of land by companies that are not owned by families. Oregon voters turned back an assault on the state's strong central planning law, and California rejected a new water conservation initiative.

Energy. With worldwide oil and gasoline prices stabilized during the year, states continued to chafe under a federally imposed 55-mph speed limit. The Montana Supreme Court technically voided the speed restriction as "a blatant handover of the sovereign power of this state." A dozen states approved measures to raise the limit in the event that federal strictures were eased, and Alabama, Arizona, Montana, and Wyoming joined Nevada in drastically reducing fines for minor infractions of the 55-mph limit. South Dakota also forbade insurance companies from considering 10-mph violations of the speed standard.

Controversy over nuclear energy continued to bubble. Idaho and Massachusetts voters ordered a statewide referendum before any new nuclear plant construction could begin, but a federal judge voided a similar Washington law as an undue impairment of existing contracts. For the second time in three years, Maine voters rejected a move to shut down the state's mammoth Maine Yankee nuclear plant. At the year's end the U.S. Congress approved a bill purporting to authorize disposal of used reactor fuel in 10,000-year underground repositories. The action was a response to laws in seven states forbidding any new nuclear plant construction until the waste disposal problem was solved.

While most states grappled with drastic funding problems, oil-rich Alaska arranged to give $1,000 in excess tax receipts to each person residing in the state for at least six months. An earlier plan to give citizens $50 for each year of state residence was struck down by the U.S. Supreme Court as discriminatory. The giveaway quickly hit a snag, however; although latest census data listed Alaska's population at 400,418, more than 475,000 "residents" signed up for the $1,000 payment.

Rhode Island joined New York and Connecticut in imposing a gross receipts tax on oil company revenue. Hawaii started a pilot project to generate electricity through differences in ocean thermal temperature. The U.S. Supreme Court knocked down a New Hampshire law prohibiting the sale of energy to out-of-state customers.

Equal Rights. A proposed U.S. constitutional amendment to ban sex discrimination finally died during 1982. The measure received 35 of 38 necessary state ratifications in four years following its approval by Congress, but no state ratified it after 1977 despite congressional extension of the deadline to June 1982. Demise of the Equal Rights Amendment left only one federal constitutional amendment pending, and it, too, was in trouble. No new state in 1982 joined ten that had previously endorsed full voting rights (including two senators and one representative) for residents of the District of Columbia.

The U.S. Supreme Court threw out a Washington State initiative to curb school busing because it was "effectively drawn for racial purposes." The high court let stand a similar 1979 California initiative, however, noting the absence of civil rights violations in the state's history.

Prisons. Overcrowding in state prisons nationwide continued to intensify during 1982 as officials struggled to house the nation's rapidly growing convict population. A survey at midyear showed 394,380 inmates housed in state and federal prisons, a record 14.3% increase over 1981. Although more than $2.5 billion was spent on new prison construction during the year, officials estimated that the number of prisoners continued to climb at twice the rate of new facility capacity. At the year's end 34 states were under some type of court order to correct overcrowding in penal institutions.

Georgia joined three other states in providing mandatory release of some inmates during overcrowding emergencies. Illinois and New York began converting underutilized mental health centres into prisons. The prisoner explosion was attributed largely to tougher sentencing laws. During the past five years 37 states had passed mandatory prison term requirements for certain crimes, 11 had approved determinate sentences without chance of parole, and 4 had abolished their parole boards altogether.

Consumer Protection. Connecticut, California, and Kentucky became the first states to approve automobile "lemon laws" that require manufacturers to replace chronically defective cars. Georgia and Nebraska became the ninth and tenth states to repeal annual auto inspection laws, leaving only 21 states mandating regular safety checks. Inspection opponents claimed that the accident-reducing effectiveness of the measures was uncertain and that mechanics regularly abused the laws by making unnecessary repairs. The Illinois attorney general sued publishers of the "Red Book," used in 18 states to evaluate car prices for loans and insurance claims, alleging that the book undervalued automobiles and violated consumer laws.

Twelve more states mandated the use of passenger restraints for children under four or five. The National Highway Transportation Safety Administration urged the 31 states without such laws to enact them, noting that auto accidents were the top-ranking cause of death for young children.

Arizona, Maine, and Wisconsin joined Florida in deregulating intrastate trucking. Maine, New Mexico, and Rhode Island regulated condominium sales, while Arizona established rules for condominium time-sharing. South Dakota allowed its banks to pay market-rate interest on checking accounts but reversed itself after the Federal Reserve Bank threatened fines or withdrawal of deposit insurance. Ohio approved a law designed to protect corporate stockholders from being stampeded into selling their shares during a takeover attempt, but the U.S. Supreme Court voided an Illinois antitakeover statute as an unconstitutional burden on interstate commerce.

(DAVID C. BECKWITH)

AREA AND POPULATION

Area and Population of the States

State	AREA in sq mi Total	AREA in sq mi Inland water[1]	POPULATION (000) 1980 census	POPULATION (000) 1981 estimate	Percent change 1980–81
Alabama	51,705	938	3,890	3,917	0.7
Alaska	591,004	20,171	400	412	2.8
Arizona	114,000	492	2,718	2,794	2.8
Arkansas	53,187	1,109	2,286	2,296	0.4
California	158,706	2,407	23,669	24,196	2.2
Colorado	104,091	496	2,889	2,955	2.6
Connecticut	5,018	147	3,108	3,134	0.8
Delaware	2,044	112	595	598	0.5
Dist. of Columbia	69	6	638	631	−1.1
Florida	58,664	4,511	9,740	10,183	4.5
Georgia	58,910	854	5,464	5,574	2.0
Hawaii	6,471	46	965	981	1.6
Idaho	83,564	1,153	944	959	1.6
Illinois	56,345	700	11,418	11,462	0.4
Indiana	36,185	253	5,490	5,468	−0.4
Iowa	56,275	310	2,913	2,899	−0.5
Kansas	82,277	499	2,363	2,383	0.8
Kentucky	40,409	740	3,661	3,662	[2]
Louisiana	47,752	3,230	4,204	4,308	2.5
Maine	33,265	2,270	1,125	1,133	0.7
Maryland	10,460	623	4,216	4,263	1.1
Massachusetts	8,284	460	5,737	5,773	0.6
Michigan	58,527	1,573	9,258	9,204	−0.6
Minnesota	84,402	4,854	4,077	4,094	0.4
Mississippi	47,689	457	2,521	2,531	0.4
Missouri	69,697	752	4,917	4,941	0.5
Montana	147,046	1,657	787	793	0.7
Nebraska	77,355	711	1,570	1,577	0.4
Nevada	110,561	667	799	845	5.7
New Hampshire	9,279	286	921	936	1.6
New Jersey	7,787	319	7,364	7,404	0.5
New Mexico	121,593	258	1,300	1,328	2.1
New York	49,108	1,731	17,557	17,602	0.3
North Carolina	52,669	3,826	5,874	5,953	1.3
North Dakota	70,702	1,403	653	658	0.9
Ohio	41,330	325	10,797	10,781	−0.2
Oklahoma	69,956	1,301	3,025	3,100	2.5
Oregon	97,073	889	2,633	2,651	0.7
Pennsylvania	45,308	420	11,867	11,871	[2]
Rhode Island	1,212	158	947	953	0.6
South Carolina	31,113	909	3,119	3,167	1.5
South Dakota	77,116	1,164	690	686	−0.7
Tennessee	42,144	924	4,591	4,612	0.5
Texas	266,807	4,790	14,228	14,766	3.8
Utah	84,899	2,826	1,461	1,518	3.9
Vermont	9,614	341	511	516	0.8
Virginia	40,767	1,063	5,346	5,430	1.6
Washington	68,139	1,627	4,130	4,217	2.1
West Virginia	24,231	112	1,950	1,952	0.1
Wisconsin	56,153	1,727	4,705	4,742	0.8
Wyoming	97,809	820	471	492	4.5
TOTAL U.S.	3,618,770	79,481	226,505[3]	229,307[3]	1.2

[1] Excludes the Great Lakes and coastal waters.
[2] Less than 0.05 percent.
[3] State figures do not add to total given because of rounding.
Source: U.S. Department of Commerce, Bureau of the Census, *Current Population Reports.*

Largest Metropolitan Areas[1]

Name	Population 1970 census[2]	Population 1980 census	Percent change 1970–80	Land area in sq mi	Density per sq mi 1980
New York-Newark-Jersey City SCSA	17,035,270	16,121,297	−5.4	4,846	3,327
New York City	9,973,716	9,120,346	−8.6	1,384	6,590
Nassau-Suffolk	2,555,868	2,605,813	2.0	1,218	2,139
Newark	2,057,463	1,965,969	−4.4	1,008	1,950
New Brunswick-Perth Amboy-Sayreville	583,813	595,893	2.1	312	1,910
Jersey City	607,839	556,972	−8.4	47	11,850
Long Branch-Asbury Park	461,849	503,173	8.9	476	1,057
Paterson-Clifton-Passaic	460,782	447,585	−2.9	192	2,331
Stamford	206,340	198,854	−3.6	121	1,643
Norwalk	127,595	126,692	−0.7	88	1,440
Los Angeles-Long Beach-Anaheim SCSA	9,980,859	11,497,568	15.2	34,007	338
Los Angeles-Long Beach	7,041,980	7,477,503	6.2	4,069	1,838
Anaheim-Santa Ana-Garden Grove	1,421,233	1,932,709	36.0	782	2,472
Riverside-San Bernardino-Ontario	1,139,149	1,558,182	36.8	27,293	57
Oxnard-Simi Valley-Ventura	378,497	529,174	39.8	1,863	284
Chicago-Gary-Kenosha SCSA	7,726,039	7,869,542	1.9	4,929	1,597
Chicago	6,974,755	7,103,624	1.8	3,719	1,910
Gary-Hammond-East Chicago	633,367	642,781	1.5	938	685
Kenosha	117,917	123,137	4.4	272	453
Philadelphia-Wilmington-Trenton SCSA	5,627,719	5,547,902	−1.4	4,946	1,122
Philadelphia	4,824,110	4,716,818	−2.2	3,553	1,328
Wilmington	499,493	523,221	4.8	1,165	449
Trenton	304,116	307,863	1.2	228	1,350
San Francisco-Oakland-San Jose SCSA	4,630,576	5,179,784	11.9	6,994	741
San Francisco-Oakland	3,109,249	3,250,630	4.5	2,480	1,311
San Jose	1,065,313	1,295,071	21.6	1,300	996
Vallejo-Fairfield-Napa	251,129	334,402	33.2	1,610	208
Santa Rosa	204,885	299,681	46.3	1,604	187
Detroit-Ann Arbor SCSA	4,669,154	4,618,161	−1.1	4,627	998
Detroit	4,435,051	4,353,413	−1.8	3,916	1,112
Ann Arbor	234,103	264,748	13.1	711	372
Boston-Lawrence-Lowell SCSA	3,526,349	3,448,122	−2.2	1,855	1,859
Boston	2,899,101	2,763,357	−4.7	1,232	2,243
Lawrence-Haverhill	258,564	281,981	9.1	307	919
Lowell	218,268	233,410	6.9	179	1,304
Brockton	150,416	169,374	12.6	137	1,236
Houston-Galveston SCSA	2,169,128	3,101,293	43.0	7,193	431
Houston	1,999,316	2,905,353	45.3	6,794	428
Galveston-Texas City	169,812	195,940	15.4	399	491
Washington, D.C.	2,910,111	3,060,922	5.2	2,815	1,087
Dallas-Fort Worth	2,377,623	2,974,805	25.1	8,360	356
Cleveland-Akron-Lorain SCSA	2,999,811	2,834,062	−5.5	2,917	972
Cleveland	2,063,729	1,898,525	−8.0	1,519	1,250
Akron	679,239	660,328	−2.8	903	731
Lorain-Elyria	256,843	274,909	7.0	495	555
Miami-Fort Lauderdale SCSA	1,887,892	2,643,981	40.0	3,261	811
Miami	1,267,792	1,625,781	28.2	2,042	796
Fort Lauderdale-Hollywood	620,100	1,018,200	64.2	1,219	835
St. Louis	2,410,884	2,356,460	−2.3	4,935	477
Pittsburgh	2,401,362	2,263,894	−5.7	3,049	743
Baltimore	2,071,016	2,174,023	5.0	2,259	962
Minneapolis-St. Paul	1,965,391	2,113,533	7.5	4,647	455
Seattle-Tacoma SCSA	1,836,949	2,093,112	13.9	5,902	355
Seattle-Everett	1,424,605	1,607,469	12.8	4,226	380
Tacoma	412,344	485,643	17.8	1,676	290
Atlanta	1,595,517	2,029,710	27.2	4,326	469
San Diego	1,357,854	1,861,846	37.1	4,261	437
Cincinnati-Hamilton SCSA	1,613,414	1,660,278	2.9	2,620	634
Cincinnati	1,387,207	1,401,491	1.0	2,149	652
Hamilton-Middletown	226,207	258,787	14.4	471	549

[1] Standard Metropolitan Statistical Area, SMSA, unless otherwise indicated; SCSA is a Standard Consolidated Statistical Area and combines two or more contiguous SMSA's.
[2] Revised.
Sources: U.S. Dept. of Commerce, Bureau of the Census, *1980 Census of Population, Characteristics of the Population, Number of Inhabitants.*

Population Change

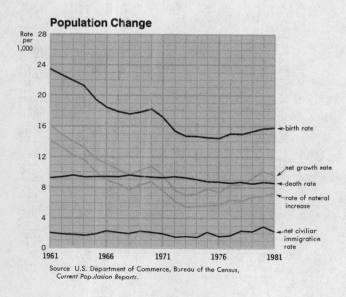

Source: U.S. Department of Commerce, Bureau of the Census, *Current Population Reports.*

Marriage and Divorce Rates

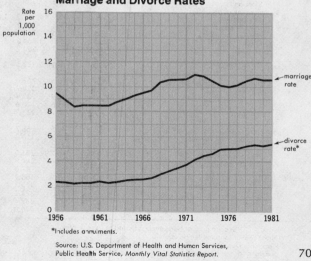

*Includes annulments.

Source: U.S. Department of Health and Human Services, Public Health Service, *Monthly Vital Statistics Report.*

Religious body	Total clergy	Inclusive membership
Baptist bodies		
American Baptist Association	...	225,000
American Baptist Churches in the U.S.A.	6,843	1,607,541
Baptist General Conference	1,227	127,662
Baptist Missionary Association of America	2,000	228,381
Conservative Baptist Association of America	...	225,000
Free Will Baptists	2,864	216,848
General Baptists (General Association of)	1,373	75,028
National Baptist Convention of America	28,574	2,668,799
National Baptist Convention, U.S.A., Inc.	27,500	5,500,000
National Primitive Baptist Convention	636	250,000
Primitive Baptists	...	72,000
Progressive National Baptist Convention	863	521,692
Regular Baptist Churches, General Assn. of	2,045	300,839
Southern Baptist Convention	61,400	13,782,644
United Free Will Baptist Church	915	100,000
Buddhist Churches of America	108	60,000
Christian and Missionary Alliance	1,737	195,042
Christian Congregation	1,435	100,245
Church of God (Anderson, Ind.)	3,072	178,581
Church of the Brethren	1,912	170,267
Church of the Nazarene	7,945	492,203
Churches of Christ—Christian Churches		
Christian Church (Disciples of Christ)	6,608	1,173,135
Christian Churches and Churches of Christ	8,074	1,063,254
Churches of Christ	...	1,600,222
Community Churches, National Council of	...	190,000
Congregational Christian Churches, Natl. Assn. of	720	107,300
Eastern churches		
American Carpatho-Russian Orth. Greek Catholic Ch.	68	100,000
Antiochian Orthodox Christian Archdiocese of N. Am.	132	152,000
Armenian Apostolic Church of America	34	125,000
Armenian Church of America, Diocese of the (including Diocese of California)	61	450,000
Bulgarian Eastern Orthodox Church	11	86,000
Coptic Orthodox Church	25	100,000
Greek Orthodox Archdiocese of N. and S. America	655	1,950,000
Orthodox Church in America	531	1,000,000
Russian Orth. Ch. in the U.S.A., Patriarchal Parishes of	60	51,500
Russian Orthodox Church Outside Russia	168	55,000
Serbian Eastern Orth. Ch. for the U.S.A. and Canada	74	95,000
Ukrainian Orthodox Church in the U.S.A.	131	87,745
Episcopal Church	12,908	2,767,440
Evangelical Covenant Church of America	818	79,523
Evangelical Free Church of America	1,042	103,900
Friends United Meeting	583	60,084
Independent Fundamental Churches of America	1,366	120,446
Jehovah's Witnesses	none	588,503
Jews	5,300	5,921,205

Religious body	Total clergy	Inclusive membership
Latter Day Saints (Mormons)		
Church of Jesus Christ of Latter-day Saints	26,140	3,490,000
Reorganized Church of Jesus Christ of L.D.S.	16,574	190,087
Lutherans		
American Lutheran Church	7,113	2,346,207
Evangelical Lutheran Churches, Association of	676	109,434
Lutheran Church in America	8,145	2,921,829
Lutheran Church—Missouri Synod	7,376	2,636,715
Wisconsin Evangelical Lutheran Synod	1,308	410,288
Mennonite Church	2,523	99,651
Methodists		
African Methodist Episcopal Church	6,550	2,210,000
African Methodist Episcopal Zion Church	6,766	1,134,176
Christian Methodist Episcopal Church	2,877	785,707
Free Methodist Church of North America	1,703	69,949
United Methodist Church	36,502	9,519,907
Wesleyan Church	2,369	103,712
Moravian Church in America	235	56,555
North American Old Roman Catholic Church	139	61,570
Old Order Amish Church	2,368	82,460
Pentecostals		
Apostolic Overcoming Holy Church of God	350	75,000
Assemblies of God	23,898	1,788,394
Church of God	2,737	75,890
Church of God (Cleveland, Tenn.)	10,160	456,797
Church of God in Christ	10,425	3,709,561
Church of God in Christ, International	1,600	200,000
Church of God of Prophecy	...	72,977
Full Gospel Fellowship of Ch. and Min., Intl.	904	65,000
International Church of the Foursquare Gospel	2,690	89,215
Pentecostal Church of God	1,564	83,860
Pentecostal Holiness Church	2,889	86,103
United Pentecostal Church, International	6,063	465,000
Plymouth Brethren	500	98,000
Polish National Catholic Church of America	141	282,411
Presbyterians		
Cumberland Presbyterian Church	711	97,559
Presbyterian Church in America	1,264	136,582
Presbyterian Church in the U.S.	5,744	823,143
United Presbyterian Church in the U.S.A.	14,727	2,379,247
Reformed bodies		
Christian Reformed Church	996	215,411
Reformed Church in America	1,500	345,762
Roman Catholic Church	58,534	51,207,579
Salvation Army	5,153	414,999
Seventh-day Adventist Church	4,480	588,536
Triumph the Church and Kingdom of God in Christ	1,375	54,307
Unitarian Universalist Association	949	131,844
United Church of Christ	10,008	1,726,244

Table includes churches reporting a membership of 50,000 or more and represents the latest information available.
Source: National Council of Churches, *Yearbook of American and Canadian Churches*, 1983.

(CONSTANT H. JACQUET)

THE ECONOMY

Gross National Product and National Income

in billions of dollars

Item	1970[1]	1980[1]	1981[1]	1982[2]
GROSS NATIONAL PRODUCT	982.4	2,633.1	2,937.7	3,041.2
By type of expenditure				
Personal consumption expenditures	618.8	1,667.2	1,843.2	1,945.8
Durable goods	84.9	214.3	234.6	240.2
Nondurable goods	264.7	670.4	734.5	755.0
Services	269.1	782.5	874.1	950.6
Gross private domestic investment	140.8	402.3	471.5	429.7
Fixed investment	137.0	412.4	451.1	447.0
Changes in business inventories	3.8	−10.0	20.5	−17.4
Net exports of goods and services	3.9	25.2	26.1	35.1
Exports	62.5	339.2	367.3	365.3
Imports	58.5	314.0	341.3	330.2
Government purchases of goods and services	218.9	538.4	596.9	630.6
Federal	95.6	197.2	228.9	244.5
State and local	123.2	341.2	368.0	386.0
By major type of product				
Goods output	456.2	1,141.9	1,289.2	1,284.9
Durable goods	170.8	477.3	528.1	505.4
Nondurable goods	285.4	664.6	761.1	779.5
Services	424.6	1,225.5	1,364.3	1,470.7
Structures	101.6	265.7	284.2	285.6
NATIONAL INCOME	798.4	2,117.1	2,352.5	2,425.1
By type of income				
Compensation of employees	609.2	1,598.6	1,767.6	1,850.6
Proprietors' income	65.1	116.3	124.7	118.1
Rental income of persons	18.6	32.9	33.9	34.2
Corporate profits	67.9	181.6	190.6	154.9
Net interest	37.5	187.7	235.7	267.4
By industry division [3]				
Agriculture, forestry, and fisheries	24.5	58.5	68.7	66.6
Mining and construction	51.6	145.9	158.3	158.3
Manufacturing	215.4	525.6	580.8	556.0
Nondurable goods	88.1	216.2	236.0	229.1
Durable goods	127.3	309.4	344.8	326.8
Transportation	30.3	81.2	87.0	87.1
Communications and public utilities	32.5	89.9	103.9	113.1
Wholesale and retail trade	122.2	315.7	353.3	360.3
Finance, insurance, and real estate	92.6	295.5	324.2	345.0
Services	103.3	309.9	349.4	376.1
Government and government enterprises	127.4	306.2	336.0	358.0

[1] Revised.   [2] Second quarter, seasonally adjusted at annual rates.
[3] Without capital consumption adjustment.
Source: U.S. Department of Commerce, Bureau of Economic Analysis, *Survey of Current Business*.

Personal Income Per Capita

State	1960[1]	1970[1]	1980[1]	1981
Alabama	$1,515	$2,903	$ 7,467	$ 8,219
Alaska	2,755	4,726	12,635	13,763
Arizona	2,012	3,688	8,823	9,754
Arkansas	1,370	2,773	7,119	8,044
California	2,729	4,510	10,896	11,923
Colorado	2,272	3,887	10,035	11,215
Connecticut	2,868	4,913	11,536	12,816
Delaware	2,756	4,505	10,079	11,095
District of Columbia	2,830	4,775	12,210	13,539
Florida	1,974	3,779	9,153	10,165
Georgia	1,658	3,323	8,049	8,934
Hawaii	2,305	4,674	10,196	11,036
Idaho	1,842	3,315	8,110	8,937
Illinois	2,639	4,515	10,437	11,576
Indiana	2,169	3,735	8,863	9,720
Iowa	2,010	3,792	9,260	10,474
Kansas	2,125	3,777	9,881	10,813
Kentucky	1,593	3,096	7,552	8,420
Louisiana	1,653	3,041	8,487	9,518
Maine	1,867	3,303	7,671	8,535
Maryland	2,339	4,322	10,399	11,477
Massachusetts	2,464	4,349	10,039	11,128
Michigan	2,339	4,044	9,876	10,790
Minnesota	2,093	3,893	9,687	10,768
Mississippi	1,208	2,556	6,650	7,408
Missouri	2,103	3,706	8,693	9,651
Montana	2,016	3,428	8,417	9,410
Nebraska	2,078	3,748	8,941	10,366
Nevada	2,784	4,691	10,746	11,576
New Hampshire	2,151	3,781	9,034	9,994
New Jersey	2,704	4,737	10,906	12,127
New Mexico	1,821	3,072	7,889	8,529
New York	2,718	4,695	10,256	11,466
North Carolina	1,592	3,220	7,780	8,649
North Dakota	1,780	3,216	8,277	10,213
Ohio	2,332	3,971	9,436	10,313
Oklahoma	1,859	3,337	9,112	10,247
Oregon	2,218	3,711	9,270	10,008
Pennsylvania	2,242	3,928	9,384	10,370
Rhode Island	2,187	3,924	9,188	10,153
South Carolina	1,404	2,975	7,268	8,039
South Dakota	1,824	3,140	7,712	8,833
Tennessee	1,575	3,097	7,613	8,447
Texas	1,904	3,536	9,554	10,729
Utah	1,972	3,220	7,663	8,313
Vermont	1,879	3,530	7,779	8,723
Virginia	1,889	3,712	9,380	10,349
Washington	2,372	4,046	10,282	11,277
West Virginia	1,597	3,043	7,693	8,377
Wisconsin	2,192	3,774	9,313	10,035
Wyoming	2,248	3,686	10,862	11,665
United States	2,216	3,945	9,480	10,491

[1] Revised.
Source: U.S. Department of Commerce, Bureau of Economic Analysis, *Survey of Current Business*.

Average Employee Earnings

September figures

Industry	HOURLY 1981	HOURLY 1982[1]	WEEKLY 1981	WEEKLY 1982[1]
MANUFACTURING				
Durable goods				
Lumber and wood products	$7.16	$7.66	$271.36	$295.68
Furniture and fixtures	6.01	6.40	226.58	241.92
Stone, clay, and glass products	8.53	9.01	346.32	354.00
Primary metal industries	11.22	11.55	457.78	440.06
Fabricated metal products	8.33	8.90	330.70	346.21
Nonelectrical machinery	8.96	9.39	361.98	356.21
Electrical equipment and supplies	7.75	8.32	307.68	322.82
Transportation equipment	10.49	11.24	418.55	443.98
Instruments and related products	7.59	8.44	306.64	307.04
Nondurable goods				
Food and kindred products	7.56	7.90	300.89	315.21
Tobacco manufactures	8.76	9.57	352.15	379.93
Textile mill products	5.69	5.86	221.34	223.85
Apparel and related products	5.04	5.20	177.41	182.52
Paper and allied products	8.95	9.63	386.64	401.57
Printing and publishing	8.37	8.89	313.04	329.82
Chemicals and allied products	9.38	10.21	395.84	420.65
Petroleum and coal products	11.55	12.62	512.82	565.38
Rubber and plastics products	7.29	7.76	289.41	307.30
Leather and leather products	5.09	5.40	183.24	191.70
NONMANUFACTURING				
Metal mining	12.10	12.39	488.84	449.76
Coal mining	12.35	13.05	519.94	502.43
Oil and gas extraction	9.52	10.63	432.21	459.22
Contract construction	11.07	11.70	396.31	431.73
Local and suburban transportation	7.37	7.80	292.59	308.10
Electric, gas, and sanitary services	10.10	10.90	417.13	450.17
Wholesale trade	7.70	8.15	296.45	312.96
Retail trade	5.37	5.52	162.17	166.70
Hotels, tourist courts, and motels[2]	4.90	5.05	148.96	154.03
Banking	5.45	5.91	197.29	215.12

[1] Preliminary.   [2] Excludes tips.   Source: U.S. Dept. of Labor, Bureau of Labor Statistics, *Employment and Earnings.*

Unemployment Trends

quarterly averages, seasonally adjusted

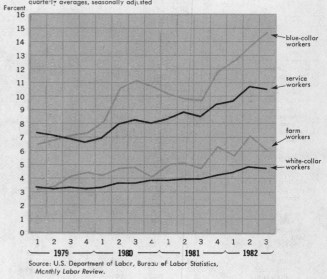

Source: U.S. Department of Labor, Bureau of Labor Statistics, *Monthly Labor Review.*

Value of Agricultural Products, with Fisheries, 1981

in thousands of dollars

State	Corn (grain)	Hay	Soybeans	Wheat	Tobacco	Cotton (lint)	Potatoes	Cattle, calves	Hogs, pigs	Sheep, lambs	Milk	Eggs[1]	Chickens[1]	FISHERIES[2]
Alabama	95,480	69,120	294,688	83,281	[3]	113,562	22,859	322,915	121,224	...	87,358	188,537	7,747	44,148
Alaska	...	...	...	...	...	...	...	1,107	378	25	2,601	670	124	639,797
Arizona	14,105	89,984	...	93,415	...	453,096	10,993	343,115	27,425	8,865	160,093	4,548	56	...
Arkansas	9,077	88,494	643,500	233,393	...	164,573	...	317,971	93,200	...	114,985	213,120	13,992	6,306
California	121,550	584,900	...	439,568	...	1,105,440	216,353	1,013,033	29,192	32,947	1,954,277	398,300	9,656	275,196
Colorado	270,575	217,998	...	309,545	...	...	59,329	917,598	49,007	27,102	141,798	28,060	998	...
Connecticut	...	13,738	...	...	29,978	...	3,038	13,671	2,064	248	91,512	74,580	1,301	2,128
Delaware	48,074	3,758	42,471	5,590	...	...	11,232	3,769	6,432	...	17,732	12,031	467	1,662
Florida	51,257	33,569	68,448	...	38,361	5,054	73,001	315,152	52,554	...	349,776	122,821	3,738	172,726
Georgia	189,750	65,365	265,088	151,833	196,560	43,639	...	248,792	248,546	...	205,212	345,372	14,444	13,158
Hawaii	...	...	...	...	...	...	...	32,567	8,915	...	30,750	15,159	245	18,338
Idaho	22,165	228,008	...	329,855	...	...	364,182	440,837	20,492	22,250	279,504	10,831	170	28
Illinois	3,631,350	201,308	2,304,510	319,125	...	...	2,546	533,731	1,126,252	5,948	359,352	63,100	1,436	994
Indiana	1,536,900	136,488	963,930	220,455	29,304	...	5,699	320,018	673,739	3,537	314,916	197,828	5,057	129
Iowa	4,088,765	505,776	2,095,976	16,146	...	...	1,512	1,668,126	2,456,043	12,873	571,634	85,280	2,112	945
Kansas	404,838	345,990	276,330	1,159,000	...	...	...	1,622,505	307,484	6,670	195,139	18,235	778	41
Kentucky	372,500	209,804	336,005	93,532	911,002	...	1,498	427,717	162,951	940	310,216	24,941	688	...
Louisiana	7,468	41,055	430,532	42,735	106	198,626	127,296	166,850	16,528	176	149,347	31,067	1,257	193,549
Maine	...	25,063	...	...	...	...	127,296	16,078	2,891	563	104,151	108,606	3,521	103,945
Maryland	239,085	46,009	66,600	18,225	50,441	...	2,746	60,126	41,450	537	222,508	37,606	1,033	56,640
Massachusetts	...	22,379	...	...	13,843	...	4,644	12,101	5,705	341	87,336	23,005	822	196,854
Michigan	642,960	192,753	184,785	147,325	...	...	56,432	213,308	125,441	3,693	706,255	69,345	1,993	5,647
Minnesota	1,675,575	590,832	914,760	538,821	...	...	78,853	762,374	743,865	10,801	1,315,979	102,050	1,882	1,960
Mississippi	20,608	58,695	491,400	78,000	...	432,566	...	247,510	47,047	...	122,610	104,308	4,915	30,159
Missouri	512,160	448,875	1,002,173	386,925	11,712	42,504	...	1,013,550	607,242	4,147	385,518	64,395	3,906	231
Montana	2,805	264,440	...	634,740	...	...	13,912	590,731	33,974	13,365	44,652	8,990	204	...
Nebraska	2,006,750	433,483	508,482	329,940	...	...	14,123	1,803,725	606,899	6,684	187,600	31,479	569	29
Nevada	...	74,266	...	6,383	...	363	18,096	106,209	1,303	4,638	29,748	83	2	...
New Hampshire	...	15,075	...	...	...	...	...	8,500	1,516	333	50,671	11,003	456	4,162
New Jersey	32,175	27,324	29,719	7,644	...	...	14,462	15,616	4,820	198	70,938	16,005	385	48,283
New Mexico	25,200	104,248	...	33,300	...	34,560	6,143	265,611	8,468	10,888	104,252	19,663	341	...
New York	186,000	358,564	...	22,176	...	...	77,263	195,115	19,506	1,908	1,538,599	87,791	2,424	45,555
North Carolina	373,412	41,340	298,450	51,968	1,324,916	26,170	18,455	135,307	344,568	159	250,746	174,164	13,021	57,520
North Dakota	95,572	290,421	38,640	1,173,625	...	...	90,563	455,898	37,679	6,755	121,338	2,600	360	117
Ohio	882,000	265,685	648,375	264,990	36,731	...	14,347	314,613	295,792	9,521	606,884	117,498	3,326	2,198
Oklahoma	17,550	219,916	37,584	665,280	...	102,336	...	1,252,432	47,579	3,093	168,015	50,690	1,552	...
Oregon	8,250	170,274	...	297,913	...	...	95,057	307,430	17,342	14,784	173,240	32,585	609	52,461
Pennsylvania	349,440	367,335	17,825	32,562	21,889	...	34,125	310,418	121,342	3,669	1,299,029	213,400	15,413	189
Rhode Island	...	1,558	...	...	...	...	4,800	947	830	...	6,891	6,197	150	48,761
South Carolina	80,997	30,429	209,948	46,638	247,340	44,748	...	83,693	77,663	...	88,430	83,607	2,649	14,161
South Dakota	397,320	413,699	143,220	318,740	...	...	2,527	1,064,121	277,737	33,658	227,180	14,791	328	357
Tennessee	143,608	101,822	381,875	130,900	280,353	81,194	2,734	295,707	158,058	301	319,603	51,479	1,848	...
Texas	369,837	452,335	63,360	669,410	...	1,497,792	22,886	3,354,132	110,418	51,398	547,918	192,365	4,755	174,787
Utah	5,775	134,439	...	32,257	...	...	6,380	173,149	6,364	17,957	146,964	20,655	224	...
Vermont	...	63,245	...	...	...	...	897	34,689	3,052	405	329,503	6,426	135	...
Virginia	151,875	127,100	107,156	58,344	258,841	111	22,388	257,163	103,328	5,904	283,269	63,213	2,472	69,124
Washington	39,269	180,482	...	564,983	...	...	199,044	322,978	12,087	2,716	416,648	64,603	1,229	95,995
West Virginia	16,578	48,203	...	1,314	4,001	...	...	71,144	12,808	3,405	49,280	9,623	387	16
Wisconsin	850,500	652,245	77,344	19,313	32,589	...	80,036	689,435	252,670	4,689	3,037,929	39,625	1,325	5,502
Wyoming	2,650	142,643	...	28,662	...	...	5,830	324,321	4,830	19,263	18,088	403	10	...
TOTAL U.S.	**20,000,805**	**9,211,532**	**12,943,174**	**10,225,881**	**3,487,971**	**4,346,334**	**1,786,281**	**23,472,653**	**9,536,700**	**357,915**	**18,398,974**	**3,662,733**	**136,512**	**2,383,798**

PRINCIPAL CROPS — Corn (grain), Hay, Soybeans, Wheat, Tobacco, Cotton (lint), Potatoes.   **LIVESTOCK AND PRODUCTS** — Cattle, calves, Hogs, pigs, Sheep, lambs, Milk, Eggs, Chickens, FISHERIES.

[1] Gross income, Dec. 1, 1980–Nov. 30, 1981.   [2] Preliminary.   [3] Estimates discontinued.

Sources: U.S. Department of Agriculture, Statistical Reporting Service, Crop Reporting Board, *Crop Values, Meat Animals, Milk, Poultry;* U.S. Department of Commerce, National Oceanic and Atmospheric Administration, National Marine Fisheries Service, *Fisheries of the United States, 1981.*

Income by Industrial Source, 1980

State and region	SOURCES OF PERSONAL INCOME: Total personal income	Farm income	Govt. income disbursements: Federal	Govt. income disbursements: State, local	Private nonfarm income	SOURCES OF LABOUR AND PROPRIETORS' INCOME % OF TOTAL: Total	Farms	Mining	Construction	Mfg.	Wholesale, retail trade	Finance, insurance, real estate	Transportation, communications, public util.	Service	Govt.	Other
United States	$2,162,936	$31,980	$84,400	$177,147	$1,320,475	$1,614,002	%2.0	%1.8	%5.8	%25.8	%16.6	%6.1	%7.7	%17.7	%16.2	%0.3
New England	125,100	457	3,190	9,420	77,756	90,825	0.5	0.1	4.4	32.1	15.8	6.6	5.9	20.1	13.9	0.6
Maine	8,940	109	488	704	5,013	6,315	1.7	[1]	6.0	28.8	15.9	4.1	6.0	17.0	18.9	1.6
New Hampshire	8,429	16	210	574	5,030	5,829	0.3	0.1	6.8	34.0	16.8	5.2	5.5	17.4	13.4	0.5
Vermont	4,013	123	95	343	2,388	2,950	4.2	[1]	5.8	30.7	14.9	4.3	6.2	18.1	14.9	0.9
Massachusetts	58,232	102	1,435	4,883	43,029	43,131	0.2	[1]	3.8	29.5	16.1	6.6	6.5	22.2	14.6	0.5
Rhode Island	8,975	10	293	710	5,205	6,217	0.2	[1]	4.2	32.8	15.8	5.8	4.6	20.0	16.1	0.5
Connecticut	36,510	97	670	2,206	23,409	26,383	0.4	0.3	4.5	36.7	15.4	8.0	5.2	18.3	10.9	0.3
Mideast	431,671	1,920	18,351	35,842	264,472	320,586	0.6	0.6	4.3	25.7	15.6	7.4	8.1	20.5	16.9	0.3
New York	180,646	624	3,818	16,746	113,221	134,410	0.5	0.2	3.4	22.9	16.0	10.4	8.7	22.3	15.3	0.3
New Jersey	80,724	151	1,952	6,170	47,221	55,493	0.3	0.1	4.6	29.6	17.4	5.3	8.9	18.8	14.6	0.4
Pennsylvania	112,220	838	2,914	7,717	71,378	82,847	1.0	1.8	5.1	33.6	15.0	5.2	7.6	17.6	12.8	0.3
Delaware	6,172	92	190	521	4,062	4,866	1.9	[1]	5.9	39.9	13.0	4.3	5.5	14.5	14.6	0.4
Maryland	44,210	216	3,722	3,678	21,823	29,439	0.7	0.2	6.6	16.8	17.1	5.7	6.6	20.7	25.1	0.5
District of Columbia	7,699	—	5,753	1,009	6,768	13,530	—	[1]	2.0	2.9	6.3	5.1	5.3	27.7	50.0	0.7
Great Lakes	408,455	5,077	7,926	31,073	263,017	307,093	1.6	0.8	5.2	35.6	15.9	5.3	6.9	15.7	12.7	0.3
Michigan	92,339	650	1,357	7,954	59,423	69,385	0.9	0.5	4.4	40.2	14.4	4.3	5.8	15.8	13.4	0.3
Ohio	102,410	811	2,238	7,135	67,566	77,750	1.0	1.1	5.3	37.4	15.6	4.6	7.1	15.6	12.1	0.4
Indiana	49,177	878	939	3,336	32,463	37,716	2.3	0.8	5.9	39.2	15.2	4.6	6.9	13.2	11.6	0.3
Illinois	120,434	1,409	2,667	9,003	76,542	89,622	1.6	1.0	5.5	29.0	17.6	7.1	7.9	16.9	13.0	0.4
Wisconsin	44,095	1,329	625	3,645	27,022	32,620	4.1	0.2	5.1	35.5	15.4	5.0	6.4	15.0	13.1	0.2
Plains	160,862	6,014	4,753	12,796	111,867	117,881	5.1	1.2	6.1	23.5	18.2	5.8	9.0	15.9	14.9	0.3
Minnesota	39,744	1,289	719	3,458	24,844	30,309	4.2	1.5	6.1	25.2	18.4	6.0	8.0	16.4	13.8	0.4
Iowa	27,328	1,192	419	2,211	15,297	19,118	6.2	0.3	6.2	27.6	18.0	5.8	7.1	14.6	13.8	0.4
Missouri	44,273	1,179	1,585	3,112	27,553	33,428	3.5	0.6	5.5	25.6	17.7	5.7	10.3	16.7	14.0	0.4
North Dakota	5,723	334	321	461	2,919	4,035	8.3	4.9	8.8	6.5	20.7	5.3	10.0	15.6	19.4	0.5
South Dakota	5,408	287	291	453	2,618	3,649	7.9	1.8	6.5	11.7	20.6	5.5	8.1	17.0	20.4	0.5
Nebraska	14,738	726	566	1,316	8,064	10,672	6.8	0.4	6.0	16.4	19.2	7.1	10.8	15.5	17.6	0.2
Kansas	23,648	1,007	855	1,785	13,023	16,670	6.0	2.5	6.2	22.8	17.0	5.3	9.0	14.9	15.8	0.5
Southeast	428,822	7,369	22,831	35,614	250,116	315,929	2.3	2.6	6.5	23.6	16.8	5.2	8.1	15.8	18.5	0.6
Virginia	50,333	279	5,926	3,870	25,809	35,884	0.8	1.8	6.1	19.7	14.9	4.9	7.2	17.0	27.3	0.3
West Virginia	15,243	45	336	1,293	9,545	11,218	0.4	16.8	6.6	23.3	13.7	3.2	8.8	12.4	14.5	0.3
Kentucky	27,939	624	1,217	2,162	16,800	20,803	3.0	7.9	5.9	25.9	14.9	4.2	7.9	13.7	16.2	0.4
Tennessee	35,525	373	1,734	2,977	22,259	27,342	1.4	0.8	5.2	29.8	17.0	5.1	7.2	15.9	17.2	0.4
North Carolina	46,043	1,277	2,047	4,165	28,783	36,273	3.5	0.3	5.2	33.1	15.6	4.4	6.9	13.5	17.1	0.4
South Carolina	22,726	264	1,528	2,144	3,658	17,594	1.5	0.2	6.9	34.0	14.2	4.2	6.4	11.8	20.8	0.0
Georgia	44,217	649	2,570	3,932	27,736	34,887	1.9	0.4	5.2	23.5	19.4	5.8	9.9	14.8	18.6	0.5
Florida	88,675	1,539	3,186	6,487	47,011	58,223	2.6	0.4	7.8	13.6	20.0	7.4	8.8	21.7	16.6	1.1
Alabama	29,199	517	1,812	2,584	16,875	21,787	2.4	2.3	5.8	28.5	15.2	4.5	7.4	13.3	20.1	0.5
Mississippi	16,626	573	873	1,560	9,378	12,384	4.6	2.0	6.1	26.0	15.9	4.5	7.1	13.5	19.6	0.7
Louisiana	35,645	416	1,049	3,182	23,080	27,726	1.5	8.4	10.3	17.0	16.9	4.6	10.1	15.5	15.3	0.4
Arkansas	16,651	813	554	1,259	9,182	11,808	6.9	1.1	6.1	26.9	16.2	4.6	8.1	14.1	15.3	0.7
Southwest	197,961	3,380	8,555	15,477	124,799	152,211	2.2	6.6	8.0	19.1	18.2	5.7	7.9	16.0	15.8	0.5
Oklahoma	27,645	615	1,360	2,162	16,189	20,328	3.0	9.4	6.2	18.2	16.8	5.0	8.4	15.0	17.3	0.7
Texas	136,146	2,133	5,308	9,998	89,216	106,654	2.0	6.3	8.1	20.2	18.9	5.8	7.9	15.8	14.3	0.7
New Mexico	10,219	207	797	1,217	5,464	7,685	2.7	10.1	7.4	7.2	15.5	4.3	8.5	17.6	26.2	0.5
Arizona	23,951	425	1,090	2,099	13,930	17,543	2.4	3.3	9.0	18.0	16.8	6.2	7.0	18.1	18.2	1.0
Rocky Mountain	59,742	1,297	3,188	5,337	36,090	45,912	2.8	5.0	7.8	15.3	17.1	5.7	9.0	16.6	18.6	2.[illegible]
Montana	6,732	146	326	618	3,613	4,702	3.1	5.2	8.0	10.5	19.0	5.2	11.6	16.9	20.0	0.5
Idaho	7,626	521	327	639	4,119	5,607	9.3	2.0	7.3	17.8	16.8	4.8	7.8	16.0	17.2	1.0
Wyoming	5,152	107	197	490	3,289	4,084	2.6	24.9	11.4	4.8	14.1	3.4	10.2	11.3	16.8	0.5
Colorado	29,029	453	1,555	2,555	18,067	22,630	2.0	4.9	7.3	16.6	17.3	6.7	8.6	17.9	18.1	0.6
Utah	11,203	70	783	1,034	7,002	8,890	0.7	5.6	7.7	18.0	17.0	5.2	8.9	16.0	20.4	0.5
Far West	335,412	6,229	13,429	29,809	201,725	251,193	2.5	0.6	6.1	22.1	16.8	6.7	7.2	20.0	17.2	0.8
Washington	42,677	803	2,044	3,859	25,076	31,783	2.5	0.3	7.6	23.5	17.0	5.7	7.2	16.6	18.6	1.0
Oregon	24,587	430	659	2,299	15,272	18,660	2.3	0.3	6.9	24.7	18.8	6.2	7.9	16.2	15.8	0.9
Nevada	8,597	55	352	721	5,661	6,789	0.8	1.9	9.5	5.4	15.0	4.9	8.0	38.3	15.8	0.4
California	259,551	4,940	10,375	22,930	155,716	193,962	2.5	0.7	5.7	22.2	16.7	6.8	7.2	20.3	17.2	0.7
Alaska	5,136	6	711	896	3,192	4,804	0.1	6.3	9.9	7.7	11.5	3.7	12.5	13.9	33.4	1.0
Hawaii	9,775	231	1,465	883	4,990	7,568	3.0	[1]	7.3	5.4	15.9	7.2	9.3	20.4	31.0	0.5

Dollar figures in millions. Percentages may not add to 100.0 because of rounding.
[1] Less than 0.05%.
Source: U.S. Department of Commerce, Bureau of Economic Analysis, *Survey of Current Business.*

Farms and Farm Income

State	Number of farms 1982[1,2]	Land in farms 1982 in 000 acres[1,2]	CASH RECEIPTS, 1981, IN $000 — Farm marketings: Total[3]	Crops[3]	Livestock and products
Alabama	57,000	12,200	2,194,366	930,478	1,263,888
Alaska	410	1,530[4]	13,050	8,122	4,928
Arizona	7,700	39,600	1,710,693	983,339	727,354
Arkansas	58,000	16,200	3,387,815	1,776,318	1,611,497
California	84,000	34,200	14,044,624	9,823,816	4,220,808
Colorado	27,200	37,200	3,022,391	1,010,056	2,012,335
Connecticut	4,500	510	328,011	141,974	186,037
Delaware	3,400	650	390,746	119,207	271,539
Florida	41,000	13,000	4,044,046	3,014,662	1,029,384
Georgia	60,000	15,500	3,334,160	1,594,342	1,739,818
Hawaii	4,300	1,960	471,557	383,386	88,171
Idaho	23,900	15,100	2,246,540	1,290,338	956,202
Illinois	108,000	29,000	7,484,147	5,259,254	2,224,893
Indiana	89,000	17,000	4,263,883	2,562,028	1,701,855
Iowa	117,000	33,800	10,548,362	4,822,898	5,725,464
Kansas	76,000	48,500	5,246,685	2,069,271	3,177,414
Kentucky	103,000	14,500	2,760,237	1,401,554	1,358,683
Louisiana	38,000	10,100	1,673,513	1,221,048	452,465
Maine	8,100	1,600	463,849	183,913	279,936
Maryland	18,500	2,850	1,055,324	358,182	697,142
Massachusetts	5,400	640	293,501	156,648	136,853
Michigan	67,000	11,600	2,774,086	1,663,029	1,111,057
Minnesota	105,000	30,600	6,738,327	3,347,914	3,390,413
Mississippi	57,000	14,600	2,151,187	1,287,510	863,677
Missouri	121,000	32,400	4,125,714	1,811,794	2,313,920
Montana	24,400	63,200	1,420,677	791,619	629,058
Nebraska	65,000	47,700	6,397,405	2,876,606	3,520,799
Nevada	3,100	8,900	215,214	80,243	134,971
New Hampshire	3,400	545	97,216	26,706	70,510
New Jersey	9,500	1,030	457,492	351,263	106,229
New Mexico	14,000	47,700	829,317	286,929	542,388
New York	49,000	9,900	2,714,236	838,165	1,876,071
North Carolina	90,000	11,100	4,213,314	2,627,879	1,585,435
North Dakota	38,000	41,700	2,607,808	2,013,777	594,031
Ohio	93,000	16,200	3,434,456	2,005,821	1,428,635
Oklahoma	71,000	34,100	2,767,049	935,250	1,831,799
Oregon	38,000	18,300	1,687,409	1,116,691	570,718
Pennsylvania	61,000	8,900	2,897,700	750,088	2,147,612
Rhode Island	820	80	33,710	19,556	14,154
South Carolina	33,000	6,100	1,106,038	707,462	398,576
South Dakota	37,000	45,000	2,727,242	861,812	1,865,430
Tennessee	94,000	13,400	1,805,448	966,715	838,733
Texas	186,000	138,400	9,829,903	4,406,461	5,423,442
Utah	12,900	12,300	552,500	139,679	412,821
Vermont	8,300	1,810	395,925	30,280	365,645
Virginia	59,000	9,800	1,635,076	724,050	911,026
Washington	40,000	16,500	2,807,706	1,911,702	896,004
West Virginia	20,800	4,300	216,935	53,486	163,449
Wisconsin	92,000	18,500	5,222,320	1,075,845	4,146,475
Wyoming	9,400	35,500	611,442	148,674	462,768
TOTAL U.S.	2,437,030	1,045,805	141,450,352	72,967,840	68,482,512

[1] Preliminary. [2] Places with annual sales of agricultural products of $1,000 or more. [3] Excludes Commodity Credit Corporation loans.
[4] Exclusive of grazing land leased from the U.S. Government. Alaska farmland totals about 70,000 acres.
Source: U.S. Department of Agriculture, Statistical Reporting Service and Economic Research Service.

Principal Minerals, Production and Value

State	Principal nonfuel minerals, in order of value, 1980	Value ($000)	% of U.S. total prod.	Crude Petroleum, 1981: Production (000 bbl)	Crude Petroleum, 1981: Value[1] ($000)	Natural Gas, 1981: Production (000,000 cu ft)[2]	Natural Gas, 1981: Value ($000)	Coal, 1981: Production (000 ST)	Coal, 1981: Value ($000)[3]
Alabama	Cement, stone, lime, clays	$328,633	1.31	20,680	$732,486	119,961	$378,000	24,887	921,068
Alaska	Sand and gravel, stone, gold, tin	113,445	.45	587,337	20,803,477	242,503	150,390	800	[4]
Arizona	Copper, molybdenum, cement, silver	2,425,714	9.66	357	12,645	...	...	11,614	[4]
Arkansas	Bromine, stone, cement, sand and gravel	286,631	1.14	18,352	650,028	94,743	163,305	280	11,712
California	Cement, sand and gravel, boron minerals, stone	1,885,695	7.51	384,958	13,635,212	368,295	978,476	...	[4]
Colorado	Molybdenum, cement, sand and gravel, silver	1,264,515	5.04	30,303	1,073,332	192,502	385,541	19,531	388,472
Connecticut	Stone, sand and gravel, feldspar, lime	65,763	.26	...	...	...	...	...	...
Delaware	Magnesium compounds, sand and gravel	2,398	.01	...	...	...	...	...	...
Florida	Phosphate rock, stone, cement, sand and gravel	1,508,754	6.01	34,773	1,231,660	38,653	87,994	...	...
Georgia	Clays, stone, cement, sand and gravel	770,688	3.07	...	...	...	...	5	[4]
Hawaii	Stone, cement, sand and gravel, pumice	59,676	.24	...	...	...	...	...	...
Idaho	Silver, phosphate rock, lead, zinc	522,095	2.08	...	...	...	...	...	...
Illinois	Stone, sand and gravel, cement, lime	443,281	1.77	24,090	853,268	[4]	3,200	51,720	1,261,451
Indiana	Stone, cement, sand and gravel, lime	288,470	1.15	4,721	167,218	[4]	688	29,364	608,422
Iowa	Cement, stone, sand and gravel, gypsum	251,876	1.00	...	...	...	...	655	13,971
Kansas	Cement, salt, stone, sand and gravel	261,593	1.04	65,810	2,330,990	640,111	588,905	785	20,834
Kentucky	Stone, lime, cement, sand and gravel	204,300	.81	6,548	231,930	[4]	61,837	149,068	4,117,258
Louisiana	Sulfur, salt, sand and gravel, cement	583,766	2.33	449,315	15,914,737	6,773,248	14,034,981	...	...
Maine	Cement, sand and gravel, stone, gem stones	36,967	.15	...	...	...	...	...	...
Maryland	Stone, cement, sand and gravel, clays	186,135	.74	...	...	[4]	27	4,453	126,777
Massachusetts	Stone, sand and gravel, lime, clays	91,211	.36	...	...	...	...	...	...
Michigan	Iron ore, cement, magnesium compounds, salt	1,485,450	5.92	32,665	1,156,994	156,921	436,937	...	...
Minnesota	Iron ore, sand and gravel, stone, lime	1,782,310	7.10	...	...	...	...	...	...
Mississippi	Cement, sand and gravel, stone, lime	103,940	.41	34,204	1,211,506	208,189	581,774	...	...
Missouri	Lead, cement, stone, lime	1,056,756	4.21	226	8,005	...	...	4,715	96,658
Montana	Copper, silver, cement, gold	279,550	1.11	30,813	1,091,396	51,191	108,039	33,380	350,490
Nebraska	Cement, sand and gravel, stone, lime	80,474	.32	6,671	236,287	[4]	3,654	...	...
Nevada	Gold, barite, diatomite, sand and gravel	386,149	1.54	700	24,794	...	...	...	...
New Hampshire	Sand and gravel, stone, clays, gem stones	25,406	.10	...	...	...	...	...	...
New Jersey	Stone, sand and gravel, zinc, titanium concentrate	149,448	.60	...	...	...	...	...	...
New Mexico	Copper, potassium salts, molybdenum, silver	765,211	3.05	71,568	2,534,939	1,123,487	2,415,033	18,916	265,013
New York	Stone, cement, salt, sand and gravel	497,891	1.98	841	29,788	[4]	42,869	...	...
North Carolina	Phosphate rock, stone, sand and gravel, cement	379,366	1.51	...	...	...	...	...	...
North Dakota	Sand and gravel, salt, lime, clays	22,376	.09	45,424	1,608,918	53,590	82,677	17,995[5]	134,603
Ohio	Stone, lime, sand and gravel, salt	562,340	2.24	13,551	479,976	[4]	306,261	37,358	1,039,300
Oklahoma	Stone, cement, sand and gravel, gypsum	224,133	.89	154,056	5,456,663	2,018,643	3,805,410	5,250	145,845
Oregon	Stone, sand and gravel, cement, nickel	149,722	.60	...	...	...	13	...	...
Pennsylvania	Cement, stone, lime, sand and gravel	667,606	2.66	3,729	132,081	[4]	285,318	86,223[6]	2,683,260
Rhode Island	Sand and gravel, stone, gem stones	6,170	.02	...	...	...	...	...	...
South Carolina	Cement, stone, clays, sand and gravel	194,779	.78	...	...	...	...	...	...
South Dakota	Gold, stone, cement, sand and gravel	227,701	.91	973	34,464	[4]	3,182	...	...
Tennessee	Stone, zinc, cement, sand and gravel	407,837	1.62	918	32,516	[4]	4,383	10,600	291,924
Texas	Cement, sulfur, stone, sand and gravel	1,734,651	6.91	945,132	33,476,575	7,009,849	12,907,735	32,892[5]	252,282
Utah	Copper, gold, molybdenum, silver	758,918	3.02	25,860	915,961	82,900	100,310	13,809	353,925
Vermont	Stone, asbestos, sand and gravel, talc	42,637	.17	...	...	...	...	...	...
Virginia	Stone, cement, lime, sand and gravel	305,306	1.22	13	460	[4]	19,100	45,500	1,573,390
Washington	Cement, sand and gravel, stone, lime	207,362	.83	...	...	...	...	4,810	[4]
West Virginia	Stone, sand and gravel, cement, salt	106,286	.42	3,473	123,014	160,531	483,753	112,814	3,934,952
Wisconsin	Stone, sand and gravel, iron ore, lime	152,284	.61	...	...	...	...	...	...
Wyoming	Sodium carbonate, clays, iron ore, stone	760,546	3.03	130,563	4,624,541	548,600	1,137,082	102,715	1,082,616
TOTAL U.S.		$25,104,211	100.00	3,128,624	$110,815,862	20,193,817	$39,561,874	820,139	20,216,426

[1] Based on the 1981 average price per barrel of U.S. crude. [2] Preliminary figures. [3] Based on 1980 average mine prices. [4] Figures not available. [5] Lignite only. [6] Includes anthracite.
Sources: U.S. Department of the Interior, *Minerals Yearbook*; Department of Energy, various petroleum, gas, and coal reports.

Services

Kind of service	Number of services 1979	Number of services 1980	Number of employees[1] 1979	Number of employees[1] 1980
Hotels and other lodging places	42,315	41,418	1,064,218	1,085,973
Hotels, tourist courts, and motels	32,685	32,102	1,010,250	1,034,352
Rooming and boarding houses	2,029	1,914	13,799	13,425
Camps and trailering parks	3,679	3,575	17,457	16,620
Sporting and recreational camps	2,012	1,949	10,475	10,147
Personal services	154,914	152,322	965,099	953,081
Laundry, cleaning, garment services	41,399	40,237	371,198	358,812
Photographic studios, portrait	5,636	6,171	35,576	41,376
Beauty shops	67,824	65,669	300,099	285,439
Barber shops	9,612	8,864	27,420	25,353
Shoe repair and hat cleaning shops	2,599	2,515	7,001	6,937
Funeral service and crematories	14,145	13,974	71,864	70,652
Miscellaneous personal services	12,393	14,028	148,466	161,214
Business services	154,313	161,446	2,903,605	2,995,907
Advertising	10,450	10,645	135,110	139,726
Credit reporting and collection	5,714	5,579	68,516	64,826
Mailing, reproduction, stenographic	14,241	14,554	128,635	135,509
Building services	23,368	23,376	501,378	495,916
Employment agencies	7,665	7,991	97,021	109,085
Temporary help supply services	4,923	5,178	436,445	416,071
Computer and data processing services	12,149	13,610	276,554	303,317
Research and development laboratories	2,071	2,300	89,986	99,317
Management and public relations	24,907	27,225	298,133	324,582
Detective and protective services	6,502	6,752	310,333	337,619
Equipment rental and leasing	11,613	12,149	110,556	114,534
Photofinishing laboratories	2,579	2,672	73,527	75,353
Auto repair, services, and garages	101,605	99,514	585,992	559,891
Automobile rentals, without drivers	9,147	8,694	101,051	100,832
Automobile parking	6,957	7,013	36,925	35,309
Automotive repair shops	76,610	75,082	379,009	358,779
Automotive services, except repair	8,149	7,914	66,078	62,323
Car washes	5,130	4,960	44,085	42,498
Miscellaneous repair services	49,140	48,021	313,929	318,982
Radio and television repair	7,689	7,156	38,084	36,759
Motion pictures	15,041	14,941	213,011	207,755
Motion picture production	3,875	4,139	84,028	82,867
Motion picture distribution	1,167	1,157	16,901	15,172
Motion picture theatres	9,732	9,467	110,985	109,192

Kind of service	Number of services 1979	Number of services 1980	Number of employees[1] 1979	Number of employees[1] 1980
Amusement and recreation services	45,317	45,499	692,766	706,288
Producers, orchestras, entertainers	6,067	5,893	97,219	96,031
Bowling and billiard establishments	7,255	7,180	116,355	114,486
Racing, including track operation	1,577	1,529	40,242	40,981
Public golf courses	2,479	2,436	17,759	17,881
Amusement parks	493	502	44,526	44,527
Membership sports, recreation clubs	9,534	9,517	168,068	172,041
Health services	299,378	310,843	5,063,900	5,258,027
Physicians' offices	140,130	147,247	716,739	741,855
Dentists' offices	83,981	85,691	341,771	350,827
Osteopathic physicians' offices	5,293	5,527	23,510	24,011
Chiropractors' offices	8,197	8,861	20,021	22,131
Optometrists' offices	12,304	12,498	37,530	37,836
Nursing and personal care facilities	12,707	12,801	979,844	1,002,037
Hospitals	5,230	5,261	2,557,743	2,672,700
Medical and dental laboratories	10,720	10,849	98,589	98,148
Outpatient care facilities	7,859	8,611	153,300	164,734
Legal services	94,897	97,335	477,744	503,474
Educational services	23,578	23,323	1,219,221	1,245,564
Elementary and secondary schools	11,487	11,332	301,906	302,747
Colleges and universities	2,459	2,433	794,468	819,625
Libraries and information centres	1,332	1,315	13,242	12,893
Correspondence and vocational schools	2,820	2,753	46,171	46,656
Social services	59,867	60,561	1,005,182	1,023,841
Residential care	9,806	9,948	206,533	214,443
Museums, botanical, zoological gardens	1,530	1,496	28,785	28,231
Membership organizations	131,875	130,668	1,225,500	1,214,158
Business associations	11,130	11,097	78,271	78,575
Professional organizations	4,584	4,524	39,656	39,778
Labour organizations	21,141	20,753	175,054	171,815
Civic and social organizations	31,116	30,541	282,785	279,466
Political organizations	933	1,147	3,852	6,287
Religious organizations	56,350	55,998	580,171	573,087
Miscellaneous services	83,042	85,540	858,428	925,470
Engineering, architectural services	36,180	37,456	474,467	523,539
Noncommercial research organizations	2,026	2,023	70,664	73,576
Accounting, auditing and bookkeeping	39,982	40,774	290,508	301,940
TOTAL[2]	1,261,995	1,278,185	16,774,161	17,195,327

[1] Mid-March pay period. [2] Includes other services not shown separately.
Source: U.S. Department of Commerce, Bureau of the Census, *County Business Patterns 1979* and *1980*.

Principal Manufactures, 1977

monetary figures in millions of dollars

Industry	Employees (000)	Cost of labour[1]	Cost of materials	Value of shipments	Value added by mfg.
Food and kindred products	1,520	$18,544	$136,964	$192,912	$56,062
Meat products	309	3,702	...	46,276	7,478
Dairy products	154	1,939	...	26,010	5,648
Preserved fruits and vegetables	235	2,336	...	20,333	7,685
Grain mill products	113	1,576	...	22,344	6,626
Beverages	195	2,849	...	23,329	9,901
Tobacco products	61	751	4,730	9,051	4,334
Textile mill products	876	7,881	24,753	40,551	16,105
Apparel and other textile products	1,334	9,659	20,866	40,245	19,671
Lumber and wood products	692	7,425	23,919	39,919	16,223
Furniture and fixtures	464	4,448	8,187	16,978	8,922
Paper and allied products	629	8,943	30,148	52,086	22,171
Printing and publishing	1,092	14,025	17,795	49,716	31,980
Chemicals and allied products	880	13,839	62,294	118,154	56,721
Industrial chemicals	110	1,847	...	12,845	6,487
Plastics materials and synthetics	157	2,471	...	20,064	7,843
Drugs	156	2,460	...	14,248	9,940
Soap, cleaners, and toilet goods	112	1,526	...	16,331	9,407
Paints, allied products	61	883	...	6,630	2,821
Agricultural chemicals	54	784	...	9,932	3,808
Petroleum and coal products	147	2,696	81,655	97,453	16,378
Rubber, misc. plastics products	721	8,536	20,218	39,553	19,740
Leather and leather products	243	1,860	3,933	7,607	3,719
Stone, clay, and glass products	614	7,943	16,445	35,477	19,130
Primary metal industries	1,114	18,745	66,171	103,179	37,568
Blast furnace, basic steel products	530	10,086	...	50,582	18,318
Iron, steel foundries	222	3,329	...	10,830	6,237
Primary nonferrous metals	57	1,032	...	10,660	3,619
Nonferrous drawing and rolling	177	2,640	...	22,227	5,902
Nonferrous foundries	82	1,044	...	3,826	1,960
Fabricated metal products	1,556	21,036	45,385	90,024	45,512
Ordnance and accessories	70	992	...	2,641	1,737
Machinery, except electrical	2,083	$30,558	$56,532	$122,188	$67,223
Engines and turbines	130	2,238	...	10,426	4,960
Farm and garden machinery	151	2,197	...	11,857	5,490
Construction and related mach.	333	5,097	...	23,682	11,836
Metalworking machinery	298	4,514	...	13,283	8,747
Special industry machinery	185	2,616	...	9,128	5,271
General industrial machinery	314	4,451	...	16,542	9,673
Service industry machines	192	2,516	...	12,416	5,963
Office, computing machines	259	3,949	...	16,842	9,921
Electric and electronic equipment	1,723	22,544	39,370	88,433	50,366
Electric distributing equip.	115	1,431	...	5,772	3,336
Electrical industrial apparatus	198	2,543	...	9,591	5,614
Household appliances	162	1,898	...	10,737	5,276
Electric lighting, wiring equip.	165	1,925	...	8,357	4,741
Radio, TV receiving equipment	98	1,097	...	6,913	3,078
Communication equipment	459	6,995	...	22,744	14,130
Electronic components, access.	374	4,557	...	15,390	9,260
Transportation equipment	1,768	30,674	103,490	166,954	64,291
Motor vehicles and equipment	876	16,038	...	117,747	37,023
Aircraft and parts	431	7,621	...	25,867	14,732
Ship, boat building, repairing	220	2,940	...	8,318	4,681
Railroad equipment	56	889	...	4,278	1,883
Guided missiles, space vehicles	120	2,427	...	6,599	4,422
Instruments and related products	559	7,520	10,504	28,898	18,762
Measuring, controlling devices	200	2,666	...	7,910	5,242
Medical instruments and supplies	114	1,319	...	5,217	3,262
Photographic equipment and supplies	112	1,900	...	9,947	6,732
Miscellaneous manufacturing industries	441	4,406	9,061	19,151	10,291
All establishments, including administrative and auxiliary	19,590	264,013	782,418	1,358,526	585,166

[1] Payroll only.   Source: U.S. Department of Commerce, *Census of Manufactures, 1977*.

Business Activity

Category of activity	WHOLESALING				RETAILING				SERVICES			
	1960	1965	1970	1977	1960	1965	1970	1977	1960	1965	1970	1977
Number of businesses (in 000)												
Sole proprietorships	306	265	274	307	1,548	1,554	1,689	1,862	1,966	2,208	2,507	3,303
Active partnerships	41	32	30	29	238	202	170	164	159	169	176	227
Active corporations	117	147	166	228[1]	217	288	351	417[1]	121	188	281	473[1]
Business receipts (in $000,000)												
Sole proprietorships	17,061	17,934	21,556	33,499	65,439	77,760	89,315	123,595	23,256	29,789	40,869	67,791
Active partnerships	12,712	10,879	11,325	16,624	24,787	23,244	23,546	31,983	9,281	12,442	18,791	37,788
Active corporations	130,637	171,414	234,885	572,364[1]	125,787	183,925	274,808	527,571[1]	22,106	36,547	66,460	146,817[1]
Net profit (less loss; in $000,000)												
Sole proprietorships	1,305	1,483	1,806	2,548	3,869	5,019	5,767	6,880	8,060	11,008	15,063	22,516
Active partnerships	587	548	557	755	1,612	1,654	1,603	1,870	3,056	4,402	6,189	9,245
Active corporations	2,130	3,288	4,441	15,769[1]	2,225	4,052	5,217	10,367[1]	849	1,505	1,199	4,185[1]

Data refer to accounting periods ending between July 1 of year shown and June 30 of following year.   [1] 1976.
Source: U.S. Department of the Treasury, Internal Revenue Service, *Statistics of Income: Business Income Tax Returns* and *Corporation Income Tax Returns*.

Retail Sales

in millions of dollars

Kind of business	1960	1965	1970	1981
Durable goods stores[1]	70,560	94,186	114,288	326,596
Automotive group	39,579	56,884	64,966	180,722
Passenger car, other automotive dealers	37,038	53,484	59,388	160,577
Tire, battery, accessory dealers	2,541	3,400	5,578	20,145
Furniture and appliance group	10,591	13,352	17,778	45,701
Furniture, home furnishings stores	...	...	10,483	27,947
Household appliance, TV, radio stores	...	...	6,073	14,313
Building materials, hardware, farm equipment group	11,222	12,388	20,494	44,491
Lumberyards, building materials dealers	8,567	9,731	11,995	35,059
Hardware stores	2,655	2,657	3,351	9,432
Nondurable goods stores[1]	148,969	189,942	261,239	712,194
Apparel group	13,631	15,765	19,810	47,755
Men's, boys' wear stores	2,644	...	4,630	7,786
Women's apparel, accessory stores	5,295	...	7,582	17,827
Family clothing stores	...	...	3,360	10,441
Shoe stores	2,437	...	3,501	8,613
Drug and proprietary stores	7,538	9,186	13,352	32,999
Eating and drinking places	16,146	20,201	29,689	94,070
Food group	54,023	64,016	86,114	237,586
Grocery stores	48,610	...	79,756	219,324
Meat and fish markets	...	...	2,244	...
Bakeries	...	...	1,303	3,367
Gasoline service stations	17,588	20,611	27,994	101,665
General merchandise group	...	42,299	61,320	127,494
Department stores and dry goods general merchandise stores	...	...	45,000	118,534
Variety stores	...	...	6,959	8,960
Liquor stores	4,893	5,674	7,980	17,461
TOTAL	219,529	284,128	375,527	1,038,790

[1] Includes some kinds of business not shown separately.
Source: U.S. Department of Commerce, Bureau of the Census, *Monthly Retail Trade*; Bureau of Economic Analysis, *1975 Business Statistics*.

Sales of Merchant Wholesalers

in millions of dollars

Kind of business	1960	1965	1970	1981
Durable goods[1]	56,803	82,861	111,970	499,792
Motor vehicles, automotive equipment	7,883	12,140	19,482	94,269
Electrical goods	8,660	12,681	16,667	54,171
Furniture, home furnishings	2,910	3,777	5,199	16,663
Hardware, plumbing, heating equipment	6,422	8,413	10,858	30,286
Lumber, construction supplies	6,680	9,765	10,863	...
Machinery, equipment, supplies	14,287	20,561	27,638	148,130
Metals, metalwork (except scrap)	5,708	9,162	13,647	...
Scrap, waste materials	3,296	4,789	6,040	...
Nondurable goods[1]	80,477	104,470	135,029	674,344
Groceries and related products	27,661	38,068	53,411	167,667
Beer, wine, distilled alcoholic beverages	7,424	9,464	13,332	35,727
Drugs, chemicals, allied products	5,370	7,180	9,135	...
Tobacco, tobacco products	4,164	5,014	6,232	...
Dry goods, apparel	6,675	8,804	10,557	...
Paper, paper products	4,153	5,612	7,679	24,387
Farm products	11,683	13,711	13,987	...
Other nondurable goods	13,346	16,966	22,632	70,575
TOTAL	137,281	187,331	246,999	1,174,136

[1] Includes some kinds of business not shown separately.
Source: U.S. Dept. of Commerce, Bureau of the Census, Current Business Reports, *Monthly Wholesale Trade*.

Commercial Banks[1]

December 31, 1981

State	Number of banks	Total assets or liabilities $000,000	Selected assets ($000,000): Loans	Investments[2]	Reserves, cash, and bank balances	Selected liabilities ($000,000): Deposits: Total[3]	Demand	Time, savings	Capital accounts
Ala.	308	18,719	8,546	5,590	2,585	15,637	4,322	11,199	1,586
Alaska	12	2,460	1,085	726	328	1,924	830	1,094	227
Ariz.	26	14,703	9,090	2,536	1,909	12,153	3,702	8,427	2,354
Ark.	262	12,313	6,246	3,591	1,069	10,318	2,665	7,653	1,038
Calif.	312	262,383	160,126	21,149	43,465	208,882	160,126	109,632	11,828
Colo.	340	18,281	10,266	3,051	2,343	14,659	5,676	8,971	1,396
Conn.	57	14,743	8,478	2,679	2,440	11,949	4,692	6,935	926
Del.	19	4,402	1,964	1,192	625	3,031	790	2,241	576
D.C.	17	9,852	4,959	1,582	2,221	7,966	2,447	3,603	596
Fla.	496	51,838	24,285	13,805	7,600	43,175	14,512	28,083	3,669
Ga.	426	25,598	12,711	5,781	3,449	20,377	7,631	12,265	2,008
Hawaii	9	6,178	3,688	1,168	709	5,433	1,311	3,732	373
Idaho	27	5,477	2,980	1,199	745	4,394	1,035	3,359	373
Ill.	1,252	156,571	88,126	26,466	26,037	119,764	23,946	64,870	8,727
Ind.	405	34,513	17,130	9,537	4,018	28,293	6,498	21,518	2,559
Iowa	649	23,789	11,385	7,210	2,119	19,819	4,023	7,977	1,918
Kan.	617	18,162	8,570	5,452	1,571	15,124	3,943	11,181	1,506
Ky.	343	22,060	10,441	5,771	2,349	17,761	5,073	12,598	1,742
La.	273	28,402	14,061	7,622	3,581	23,829	7,775	15,964	2,206
Maine	36	3,676	1,937	965	461	3,000	785	2,215	266
Md.	94	18,056	9,853	3,524	2,604	14,738	4,426	9,393	1,278
Mass.	138	39,908	19,255	6,758	8,784	29,918	8,945	13,922	2,118
Mich.	375	56,504	29,571	11,644	9,962	46,096	9,674	34,191	3,726
Minn.	759	34,572	18,479	7,669	4,833	27,415	6,723	18,538	2,451
Miss.	170	12,771	6,118	3,937	1,253	10,806	2,830	7,946	966
Mo.	728	38,548	17,995	9,557	5,034	29,738	9,055	20,163	2,738
Mont.	164	5,732	3,040	1,492	633	4,923	1,174	3,749	464
Neb.	457	12,899	6,389	3,059	1,385	2,948	2,871	7,616	1,054
Nev.	12	4,055	2,316	803	539	3,439	1,224	2,215	327
N.H.	71	3,616	2,170	743	431	3,113	710	2,403	270
N.J.	161	38,233	19,502	9,431	5,627	31,769	10,106	21,256	2,555
N.M.	88	6,800	3,419	1,645	792	5,764	1,554	4,210	506
N.Y.	212	482,709	279,738	46,215	94,409	353,264	65,398	97,429	23,327
N.C.	71	29,132	14,011	6,391	4,703	22,051	5,918	13,408	1,886
N.D.	175	5,225	2,612	1,598	503	4,576	971	3,605	443
Ohio	379	59,558	28,501	14,988	9,118	45,704	11,469	32,822	4,670
Okla.	501	27,768	14,176	6,706	3,605	23,580	7,648	15,818	2,012
Ore.	84	13,961	8,083	2,398	1,540	11,013	2,854	8,092	961
Pa.	350	97,613	50,423	23,014	14,903	75,343	17,056	50,674	6,868
R.I.	14	8,003	4,380	1,147	1,310	5,819	1,139	4,398	446
S.C.	83	8,695	3,916	2,522	1,019	7,002	2,737	4,264	704
S.D.	153	7,993	5,281	1,666	527	6,540	879	5,661	694
Tenn.	351	26,103	12,951	6,293	3,745	21,251	5,666	15,489	1,904
Texas	1,523	143,225	74,425	28,087	24,436	114,819	35,912	69,450	9,654
Utah	66	7,553	4,107	1,251	1,334	6,239	1,875	4,233	548
Vt.	27	2,523	1,647	485	212	2,235	464	1,771	186
Va.	223	26,738	15,134	5,831	3,151	21,859	5,623	16,081	1,949
Wash.	98	25,711	15,517	3,109	3,949	20,322	5,249	13,807	1,631
W.Va.	243	11,253	5,203	3,749	926	9,284	2,031	7,252	962
Wis.	636	28,415	15,472	7,161	2,690	23,195	5,553	17,079	2,166
Wyo.	108	3,789	1,970	5,993	377	3,278	928	2,350	333
TOTAL	14,400	2,021,781	1,101,728	350,993	324,508	1,575,529	500,544	872,803	125,671

[1] Excludes noninsured banks.
[2] Excludes federal funds sold and securities purchased.
[3] Includes deposits in foreign offices not shown separately.
Source: Federal Deposit Insurance Corporation, *1981 Bank Operating Statistics.*

Life Insurance, 1981

Number of policies in 000s; value in $000,000

State	Total: Number of policies	Total: Value	Ordinary: Number of policies	Ordinary: Value	Group: Number of certificates	Group: Value	Industrial: Number of policies	Industrial: Value	Credit[1]: Number of policies	Credit[1]: Value
Ala.	11,859	$64,033	2,310	$31,904	1,797	$26,162	6,267	$2,530	1,485	$3,437
Alaska	643	8,986	145	3,507	313	5,126	10	3	175	250
Ariz.	4,216	44,339	1,570	25,261	1,469	16,844	169	124	1,008	2,110
Ark.	2,736	27,931	1,055	14,701	780	11,652	360	198	541	1,380
Calif.	30,337	410,076	10,836	205 061	12,372	192,402	1,681	1,222	5,448	11,391
Colo.	4,868	62,066	1,827	32,142	1,812	27,262	234	158	995	2,504
Conn.	5,840	69,674	2,329	31,936	2,304	35,558	225	201	982	1,979
Del.	1,408	14,644	503	5,702	409	8,102	196	137	300	703
D.C.	2,782	31,034	421	5,539	1,394	24,612	611	373	356	510
Fla.	16,551	151,068	6,118	82,508	3,999	59,282	3,062	2,100	3,372	7,178
Ga.	13,149	102,413	4,064	50,764	2,850	44,344	3,550	2,300	2 685	5,005
Hawaii	1 880	21,801	623	11,473	850	9,359	4	2	403	967
Idaho	1,475	14,834	524	7,931	563	6,074	22	14	366	815
Ill.	21,667	228,607	9,154	111,849	6,983	107,870	2,626	1,886	2,904	7,002
Ind.	9,935	96,807	4,158	47,966	2,813	43,895	1,362	922	1,602	4,024
Iowa	5,076	55,747	2,604	31,064	1,501	22,234	194	124	777	2,325
Kan.	4,234	44,144	1,953	25,902	1,259	16,296	276	174	746	1,772
Ky.	6,222	50,453	2,399	24,853	1,455	22,327	1,209	681	1,159	2,582
La.	9,779	75,782	2,556	40,634	2,060	29,332	3,556	2,066	1,607	3,750
Maine	1,778	15,464	711	7,589	599	7,057	61	49	407	769
Md.	7,824	79,142	3,000	38,516	2,028	37.001	1,530	947	1,216	2,678
Mass.	8,971	101,403	3,852	46,011	2,961	51,981	592	446	1,566	2,965
Mich.	17,139	176,873	5,458	65,020	6,472	103,999	1,641	1,110	3,568	6,744
Minn.	6,719	80,657	2,582	37,419	2,980	40,647	203	143	954	2,448
Miss.	4,060	32,550	1,055	16 521	1,036	13,312	655	386	1,313	2,331
Mo.	8,957	88,277	3,796	42,186	2,717	42,232	1,091	709	1,353	3,150
Mont.	1,195	12,402	448	6,824	466	4,892	22	12	259	674
Neb.	2,835	31,931	1,450	19,181	794	11,431	103	66	488	1,253
Nev.	1,556	16,315	313	6,142	545	7,463	9	6	698	2,704
N.H.	1,594	16,342	694	8,364	506	7,164	76	63	318	751
N.J.	12,089	150,003	5,345	69,867	3,890	74,937	1,216	1,073	1,638	4,126
N.M.	1,849	20,325	654	9,686	585	9,486	77	50	533	1,103
N.Y.	26,306	312,752	10,731	139,334	8,579	160,839	1,535	1,210	5,461	11,369
N.C.	12,558	94,327	4,443	47,416	2,704	40,568	2,847	1,533	2,564	4,805
N.D.	1,075	12,956	479	7,351	352	4,858	3	3	241	744
Ohio	19,833	196,260	8,134	95,537	5,787	91,114	2,689	1,866	3,228	7,743
Okla.	4,944	53,826	1,896	28,548	1,453	22,319	334	206	1,261	2,753
Ore.	3,337	44,208	1,202	19,871	1,369	22,629	70	46	696	1,662
Pa.	23,573	206,828	9,853	99,538	6,259	95,693	3,816	2,626	3,645	8,971
R.I.	1,979	17,961	770	9,043	740	8,233	131	95	338	590
S.C.	7,810	48,921	2,661	24,615	1,640	20,390	2,252	1,365	1,257	2,551
S.D.	1,090	11,670	560	7,212	322	3,856	4	3	204	599
Tenn.	9,421	77,230	2,873	36,064	2,746	36,047	2,063	1,180	1,739	3,939
Texas	25,225	275,549	9,114	144,297	7,525	116,312	3,048	1,936	5,538	13,004
Utah	2,242	23,492	726	12,835	973	9,362	76	41	467	1,254
Vt.	316	7,816	361	4,160	250	3,270	27	23	178	363
Va.	10,629	99,170	3,581	46,155	2,773	47,836	2,302	1,403	1,973	3,776
Wash.	5,525	69,749	1,938	33,771	2,339	33,642	137	83	1,061	2,253
W.Va.	3,297	25,989	1,082	11,425	911	12,641	534	346	770	1,577
Wis.	7,940	80,570	3,405	42,485	3,078	35,191	396	299	1,061	2,595
Wyo.	676	8,198	273	4,290	248	3,477	4	3	151	428
TOTAL U.S.	399,514	$4,063,595	148,539	$1,978,080	122,611	1,888,612	55,209	$34,547	73,055	$162,356

[1] Life insurance on loans of ten years' or less duration.
Source: Institute of Life Insurance, *Life Insurance Fact Book '82.*

Savings and Loan Associations

Dec. 31, 1981[1]

State	Number of assns.	Total assets ($000,000)	Per capita assets
Alabama	52	$5,119	$1,305
Alaska	4	490	1,194
Arizona	12	7,178	2,558
Arkansas	70	4,678	2,024
California	188	130,457	5,440
Colorado	46	10,942	3,722
Connecticut	39	4,695	1,510
Delaware	18	270	451
District of Columbia	10	5,137	8,179
Florida	127	56,853	5,671
Georgia	89	11,544	2,085
Guam	2	73	605
Hawaii	9	4,538	4,636
Idaho	9	1,084	1,125
Illinois	342	47,575	4,154
Indiana	138	10,557	1,915
Iowa	71	7,383	2,525
Kansas	77	7,738	3,258
Kentucky	90	6,195	1,675
Louisiana	128	9,140	2,150
Maine	19	692	611
Maryland	167	11,531	2,722
Massachusetts	149	8,597	1,498
Michigan	59	18,706	2,014
Minnesota	53	10,733	2,615
Mississippi	58	3,003	1,182
Missouri	104	16,360	3,306
Montana	13	1,173	1,475
Nebraska	33	5,629	3,563
Nevada	8	2,577	3,135
New Hampshire	16	1,216	1,299
New Jersey	193	27,754	3,761
New Mexico	33	2,776	2,099
New York	105	26,887	1,534
North Carolina	167	11,888	2,004
North Dakota	11	2,527	3,846
Ohio	362	41,963	3,881
Oklahoma	61	6,428	2,101
Oregon	28	7,519	2,808
Pennsylvania	323	26,087	2,197
Puerto Rico	12	2,809	759
Rhode Island	5	793	834
South Carolina	70	6,720	2,128
South Dakota	18	1,149	1,655
Tennessee	93	7,684	1,656
Texas	311	38,344	2,649
Utah	15	5,267	3,519
Vermont	5	259	501
Virginia	86	10,580	1,960
Washington	47	10,176	2,428
West Virginia	28	1,756	893
Wisconsin	104	12,925	2,730
Wyoming	12	1,058	2,195
TOTAL U.S.	4,347	$663,844	$2,880

[1] Preliminary. Components do not add to totals because of differences in reporting dates and accounting systems.
Source: U.S. League of Savings Associations, *'82 Savings and Loan Sourcebook.*

GOVERNMENT AND POLITICS

The National Executive

December 21, 1982

Department, bureau, or office	Executive official and official title
PRESIDENT OF THE UNITED STATES	Ronald Reagan
Vice-President	George Bush
EXECUTIVE OFFICE OF THE PRESIDENT	
Assistant to the President	James A. Baker III, chief of staff
	William P. Clark
	Richard G. Darman
	Elizabeth Hanford Dole
	Kenneth M. Duberstein
	Craig L. Fuller
	David R. Gergen
	Edwin L. Harper
	Edward V. Hickey, Jr.
	E. Pendleton James
	James E. Jenkins
	Edward J. Rollins
	Richard S. Williamson
Press Secretary to the President	James Scott Brady
Counsel to the President	Fred F. Fielding
Counselor to the President	Edwin Meese III
Special Assistant to the President	Richard Smith Beal
Office of Management and Budget	David A. Stockman, director
Council of Economic Advisers	Martin S. Feldstein, chairman
National Security Council	1
Central Intelligence Agency	William J. Casey, director
Office of Policy Development	Roger B. Porter, director
Office of the United States Trade Representative	William E. Brock, trade representative
Council on Environmental Quality	A. Alan Hill, chairman
Office of Science and Technology Policy	George A. Keyworth II, director
Office of Administration	John F. W. Rogers, director
DEPARTMENT OF STATE	George P. Shultz, secretary
	Walter J. Stoessel, Jr., deputy secretary
Permanent Mission to the Organization of American States	J. William Middendorf II, permanent representative
Mission to the United Nations	Jeane J. Kirkpatrick, representative
African Affairs	Chester A. Crocker, asst. secretary
East Asian and Pacific Affairs	John H. Holdridge, asst. secretary
European Affairs	Richard Burt, asst. secretary
Inter-American Affairs	Thomas O. Enders, asst. secretary
Near Eastern and South Asian Affairs	Nicholas A. Veliotes, asst. secretary
Oceans and International Environmental and Scientific Affairs	James L. Malone, asst. secretary (acting)
Consular Affairs	Diego C. Asencio, asst. secretary
International Narcotics Matters	Dominick L. DiCarlo, asst. secretary (acting)
DEPARTMENT OF THE TREASURY	Donald T. Regan, secretary
	R. T. McNamar, deputy secretary
Office of the Comptroller of the Currency	C. T. Conover, comptroller
Internal Revenue Service	Roscoe L. Egger, Jr., commissioner
Bureau of Government Financial Operations	W. E. Douglas, commissioner
Bureau of the Public Debt	W. M. Gregg, commissioner (acting)
Bureau of Alcohol, Tobacco and Firearms	Stephen E. Higgins, director (acting)
U.S. Customs Service	William von Raab, commissioner
U.S. Secret Service	John R. Simpson, director
U.S. Savings Bonds Division	Angela Buchanan, national director
Bureau of the Mint	Donna Pope, director
Bureau of Engraving and Printing	Harry R. Clements, director
DEPARTMENT OF DEFENSE	Caspar W. Weinberger, secretary
	Frank C. Carlucci III, deputy secretary
Joint Chiefs of Staff	Gen. John W. Vessey, USA, chairman
Chief of Staff, Air Force	Gen. Charles A. Gabriel, USAF
Chief of Staff, Army	Gen. Edward C. Meyer, USA
Chief of Naval Operations	Adm. James D. Watkins, USN
Commandant of the Marine Corps	Gen. Robert H. Barrow, USMC
Department of the Air Force	Verne Orr, secretary
Department of the Army	John O. Marsh, Jr., secretary
Department of the Navy	John F. Lehman, Jr., secretary
DEPARTMENT OF JUSTICE	
Attorney General	William French Smith
Solicitor General	Rex E. Lee
Antitrust Division	William F. Baxter, asst. attorney general
Civil Rights Division	William Bradford Reynolds, asst. attorney general
Criminal Division	D. Lowell Jensen, asst. attorney general
Federal Bureau of Investigation	William H. Webster, director
Bureau of Prisons	Norman A. Carlson, director
Immigration and Naturalization Service	Alan C. Nelson, commissioner
Drug Enforcement Administration	Francis M. Mullen, Jr., administrator (acting)
U.S. Marshals Service	William E. Hall, director
DEPARTMENT OF THE INTERIOR	James G. Watt, secretary
	vacancy (undersecretary)
Minerals Management Service	Harold Doley, director
Territorial and International Affairs	Pedro A. Sanjuan, asst. secretary
Fish and Wildlife and Parks	G. Ray Arnett, asst. secretary
National Park Service	Russell E. Dickenson, director
U.S. Fish and Wildlife Service	Robert A. Jantzen, director
Energy and Minerals	Daniel N. Miller, Jr., asst. secretary
Geological Survey	Dallas L. Peck, director
Bureau of Mines	Robert C. Horton, director
Office of Surface Mining Reclamation and Enforcement	James R. Harris, director
Land and Water Resources	Garrey E. Carruthers, asst. secretary
Bureau of Reclamation	Robert N. Broadbent, commissioner

Department, bureau, or office	Executive official and official title
Bureau of Land Management	Robert F. Burford, director
Office of Water Policy	Thomas Bahr, director
Indian Affairs	Kenneth L. Smith, asst. secretary
DEPARTMENT OF AGRICULTURE	John R. Block, secretary
	Richard E. Lyng, deputy secretary
International Affairs and Commodity Programs	Seeley G. Lodwick, undersecretary
Small Community and Rural Development	Frank W. Naylor, Jr., undersecretary
Farmers Home Administration	Charles W. Shuman, administrator
Rural Electrification Administration	Harold V. Hunter, administrator
Federal Crop Insurance Corporation	Merritt Sprague, manager
Marketing and Inspection Services	C. W. McMillan, asst. secretary
Food and Consumer Services	Mary C. Jarratt, asst. secretary
Natural Resources and Environment	John B. Crowell, Jr., asst. secretary
Forest Service	R. Max Peterson, chief
Soil Conservation Service	Peter C. Myers, chief
Economics	William G. Lesher, asst. secretary
Office of Energy	Earle E. Gavett, director (acting)
World Agricultural Outlook Board	Terry N. Barr, chairperson (acting)
Science and Education	Orville G. Bentley, asst. secretary (designate)
DEPARTMENT OF COMMERCE	Malcolm Baldrige, secretary
	Guy W. Fiske, deputy secretary
International Trade Administration	Lionel Olmer, undersecretary
Economic Development Administration	Mary A. Nimmo, director (Public Affairs)
Minority Business Development Agency	Victor M. Rivera, director
National Bureau of Standards	Ernest Ambler, director
National Oceanic and Atmospheric Administration	John V. Byrne, administrator
National Technical Information Service	Joseph F. Caponio, director (acting)
Patent and Trademark Office	Gerald J. Mossinghoff, commissioner
Bureau of the Census	Bruce Chapman, director
Bureau of Economic Analysis	George Jaszi, director
Bureau of Industrial Economics	Beatrice N. Vaccara, director
National Telecommunications and Information Administration	Bernard J. Wunder, Jr., asst. secretary
United States Travel and Tourism Administration	Peter McCoy, undersecretary
DEPARTMENT OF LABOR	Raymond J. Donovan, secretary
	Malcolm R. Lovell, Jr., undersecretary
Women's Bureau	Lenora Cole-Alexander, director
Occupational Safety and Health	Thorne G. Auchter, asst. secretary
Veteran's Employment	William C. Plowden, Jr., asst. secretary
Employment and Training	Albert Angrisani, asst. secretary
Mine Safety and Health	Ford B. Ford, asst. secretary
DEPARTMENT OF HEALTH AND HUMAN SERVICES	Richard S. Schweiker, secretary
	David B. Swoap, undersecretary
Office of Human Development Services	Dorcas R. Hardy, asst. secretary
Public Health Service	Edward N. Brandt, Jr., asst. secretary
Alcohol, Drug Abuse, and Mental Health Administration	William E. Mayer, administrator
Centers for Disease Control	William H. Foege, director
Food and Drug Administration	Arthur Hull Hayes, Jr., commissioner
Health Resources Administration	Robert Graham, administrator (acting)
Health Services Administration	John H. Kelso, administrator (acting)
National Institutes of Health	James B. Wyngaarden, director
Health Care Financing Administration	Carolyne K. Davis, administrator
Social Security Administration	John A. Svahn, commissioner
Office of Child Support Enforcement	John A. Svahn, director
Office of Community Services	Robert L. Trachtenberg, director (acting)
DEPARTMENT OF HOUSING AND URBAN DEVELOPMENT	Samuel R. Pierce, Jr., secretary
	Donald I. Hovde, undersecretary
Community Planning and Development	Stephen J. Bollinger, asst. secretary
Federal Housing Commissioner	Phillip Abrams, asst. secretary (designate)
Fair Housing and Equal Opportunity	Antonio Monroig, asst. secretary
Policy Development and Research	E. S. Savas, asst. secretary
DEPARTMENT OF TRANSPORTATION	Andrew L. Lewis, Jr., secretary
	Darrell M. Trent, deputy secretary
United States Coast Guard	Adm. James S. Gracey, USCG, commandant
Federal Aviation Administration	J. Lynn Helms, administrator
Federal Highway Administration	R. A. Barnhart, administrator
Federal Railroad Administration	Robert W. Blanchette, administrator
National Highway Traffic Safety Administration	Raymond A. Peck, Jr., administrator
Urban Mass Transportation Administration	Arthur E. Teele, Jr., administrator
Maritime Administration	Harold E. Shear, administrator
Saint Lawrence Seaway Development Corp.	David W. Oberlin, administrator
Research and Special Programs Administration	Howard Dugoff, administrator
DEPARTMENT OF ENERGY	Donald P. Hodel, secretary (acting)
	Guy W. Fiske, undersecretary
Federal Energy Regulatory Commission	Charles M. Butler III, chairman
General Counsel	R. Tenney Johnson
Nuclear Energy	Shelby T. Brewer, asst. secretary
DEPARTMENT OF EDUCATION	Terrell H. Bell, secretary
	Gary L. Jones, undersecretary (designate)
Office of Bilingual Education	Jesse M. Soriano, director
Educational Research and Improvement	Donald J. Senese, asst. secretary
Special Education and Rehabilitative Services	Jean S. Tufts, asst. secretary

1 Council comprised of the President of the United States and certain other members.

Senate January 1983

State, name, and party	Term expires
Ala.—Heflin, Howell (D)	1985
Denton, Jeremiah (R)	1987
Alaska—Stevens, Ted (R)	1985
Murkowski, Frank H. (R)	1987
Ariz.—Goldwater, Barry M. (R)	1987
DeConcini, Dennis (D)	1989
Ark.—Bumpers, Dale (D)	1987
Pryor, David (D)	1985
Calif.—Cranston, Alan (D)	1987
Wilson, Pete (R)	1989
Colo.—Hart, Gary W. (D)	1987
Armstrong, William L. (R)	1985
Conn.—Weicker, Lowell P., Jr. (R)	1989
Dodd, Christopher J. (D)	1987
Del.—Roth, William V., Jr. (R)	1989
Biden, Joseph R., Jr. (D)	1985
Fla.—Chiles, Lawton M. (D)	1989
Hawkins, Paula (R)	1987
Ga.—Nunn, Samuel A. (D)	1985
Mattingly, Mack (R)	1987
Hawaii—Inouye, Daniel K. (D)	1987
Matsunaga, Spark M. (D)	1989
Idaho—McClure, James A. (R)	1985
Symms, Steven D. (R)	1987
Ill.—Percy, Charles H. (R)	1985
Dixon, Alan J. (D)	1987
Ind.—Lugar, Richard G. (R)	1989
Quayle, Dan (R)	1987
Iowa—Jepsen, Roger W. (R)	1985
Grassley, Charles E. (R)	1987
Kan.—Dole, Robert J. (R)	1987
Kassebaum, Nancy Landon (R)	1985
Ky.—Huddleston, Walter (D)	1985
Ford, Wendell H. (D)	1987
La.—Long, Russell B. (D)	1987
Johnston, J. Bennett, Jr. (D)	1985
Maine—Cohen, William S. (R)	1985
Mitchell, George J. (D)	1989
Md.—Mathias, Charles, Jr. (R)	1987
Sarbanes, Paul S. (D)	1989
Mass.—Kennedy, Edward M. (D)	1989
Tsongas, Paul E. (D)	1985
Mich.—Riegle, Donald W., Jr. (D)	1989
Levin, Carl (D)	1985
Minn.—Durenberger, David (R)	1989
Boschwitz, Rudy (R)	1985
Miss.—Stennis, John C. (D)	1989
Cochran, Thad (R)	1985
Mo.—Eagleton, Thomas F. (D)	1987
Danforth, John C. (R)	1989
Mont.—Melcher, John (D)	1989
Baucus, Max (D)	1985
Neb.—Zorinsky, Edward (D)	1989
Exon, J. James (D)	1985
Nev.—Laxalt, Paul (R)	1987
Hecht, Chic (R)	1989
N.H.—Humphrey, Gordon J. (R)	1985
Rudman, Warren (R)	1987
N.J.—Bradley, Bill (D)	1985
Lautenberg, Frank R. (D)	1989
N.M.—Domenici, Pete V. (R)	1985
Bingaman, Jeff (D)	1989
N.Y.—Moynihan, Daniel P. (D)	1989
D'Amato, Alfonse M. (R)	1987
N.C.—Helms, Jesse A. (R)	1985
East, John P. (R)	1987
N.D.—Burdick, Quentin N. (D)	1989
Andrews, Mark (R)	1987
Ohio—Glenn, John H., Jr. (D)	1987
Metzenbaum, Howard M. (D)	1989
Okla.—Boren, David L. (D)	1985
Nickles, Don (R)	1987
Ore.—Hatfield, Mark O. (R)	1985
Packwood, Robert W. (R)	1987
Pa.—Heinz, H. John, III (R)	1989
Specter, Arlen (R)	1987
R.I.—Pell, Claiborne (D)	1985
Chafee, John H. (R)	1989
S.C.—Thurmond, Strom (R)	1985
Hollings, Ernest F. (D)	1987
S.D.—Pressler, Larry (R)	1985
Abdnor, James (R)	1987
Tenn.—Baker, Howard H., Jr. (R)	1985
Sasser, James R. (D)	1989
Texas—Tower, John G. (R)	1985
Bentsen, Lloyd M. (D)	1989
Utah—Garn, Jake (R)	1987
Hatch, Orrin G. (R)	1989
Vt.—Stafford, Robert T. (R)	1989
Leahy, Patrick J. (D)	1987
Va.—Warner, John W. (R)	1985
Trible, Paul S., Jr. (R)	1989
Wash.—Jackson, Henry M. (D)	1989
Gorton, Slade (R)	1987
W.Va.—Randolph, Jennings (D)	1985
Byrd, Robert C. (D)	1989
Wis.—Proxmire, William (D)	1989
Kasten, Robert W., Jr. (R)	1987
Wyo.—Wallop, Malcolm (R)	1989
Simpson, Alan K. (R)	1985

House of Representatives

membership at the opening of the first session of the 98th Congress in January 1983

State, district, name, party

Ala.—1. Edwards, Jack (R)
2. Dickinson, William L. (R)
3. Nichols, William (D)
4. Bevill, Tom (D)
5. Flippo, Ronnie G. (D)
6. Erdreich, Ben (D)
7. Shelby, Richard C. (D)
Alaska—Young, Don (R)
Ariz.—1. McCain, John (R)
2. Udall, Morris K. (D)
3. Stump, Bob (R)
4. Rudd, Eldon D. (R)
5. McNulty, Jim (D)
Ark.—1. Alexander, Bill (D)
2. Bethune, Ed (R)
3. Hammerschmidt, J. P. (R)
4. Anthony, Beryl F. (D)
Calif.—1. Bosco, Douglas H. (D)
2. Chappie, Eugene A. (R)
3. Matsui, Robert T. (D)
4. Fazio, Vic (D)
5. Burton, Phillip (D)
6. Boxer, Barbara (D)
7. Miller, George, III (D)
8. Dellums, Ronald V. (D)
9. Stark, Fortney H. (D)
10. Edwards, Don (D)
11. Lantos, Tom (D)
12. Zschau, Ed (R)
13. Mineta, Norman Y. (D)
14. Shumway, Norman D. (R)
15. Coelho, Tony (D)
16. Panetta, Leon E. (D)
17. Pashayan, Charles, Jr. (R)
18. Lehman, Richard (D)
19. Lagomarsino, Robert J. (R)
20. Thomas, William M. (R)
21. Fiedler, Bobbi (R)
22. Moorhead, Carlos J. (R)
23. Beilenson, Anthony C. (D)
24. Waxman, Henry A. (D)
25. Roybal, Edward R. (D)
26. Berman, Howard L. (D)
27. Levine, Mel (D)
28. Dixon, Julian C. (D)
29. Hawkins, Augustus F. (D)
30. Martinez, Matthew G. (D)
31. Dymally, Mervyn M. (D)
32. Anderson, Glenn M. (D)
33. Dreier, David (R)
34. Torres, Esteban (D)
35. Lewis, Jerry (R)
36. Brown, George E., Jr. (D)
37. McCandless, Al (R)
38. Patterson, Jerry M. (D)
39. Dannemeyer, W. E. (R)
40. Badham, Robert E. (R)
41. Lowery, Bill (R)
42. Lungren, Daniel E. (R)
43. Packard, Ron (R)
44. Bates, Jim (D)
45. Hunter, Duncan L. (R)
Colo.—1. Schroeder, Patricia (D)
2. Wirth, Timothy E. (D)
3. Kogovsek, Ray (D)
4. Brown, Hank (R)
5. Kramer, Ken (R)
6. (vacancy)[1]
Conn.—1. Kennelly, Barbara B. (D)
2. Gejdenson, Samuel (D)
3. Morrison, Bruce A. (D)
4. McKinney, Stewart B. (R)
5. Ratchford, William R. (D)
6. Johnson, Nancy L. (R)
Del.—Carper, Thomas R. (D)
Fla.—1. Hutto, Earl D. (D)
2. Fuqua, Don (D)
3. Bennett, Charles E. (D)
4. Chappell, William, Jr. (D)
5. McCollum, Bill (R)
6. MacKay, Kenneth H. (D)
7. Gibbons, Sam (D)
8. Young, C. William (R)
9. Bilirakis, Michael (R)
10. Ireland, Andrew P. (D)
11. Nelson, Bill (D)
12. Lewis, Tom (R)
13. Mack, Connie, III (R)
14. Mica, Daniel A. (D)
15. Shaw, E. Clay, Jr. (R)
16. Smith, Larry (D)
17. Lehman, William (D)
18. Pepper, Claude (D)
19. Fascell, Dante B. (D)
Ga.—1. Thomas, Lindsay (D)
2. Hatcher, Charles F. (D)
3. Ray, Richard (D)
4. Levitas, Elliott H. (D)
5. Fowler, Wyche, Jr. (D)
6. Gingrich, Newt (R)
7. McDonald, Lawrence P. (D)
8. Rowland, J. Roy (D)
9. Jenkins, Edgar L. (D)
10. Barnard, Doug (D)
Hawaii—1. Heftel, Cecil (D)
2. Akaka, Daniel (D)
Idaho—1. Craig, Larry (R)
2. Hansen, George V. (R)
Ill.—1. Washington, Harold (D)
2. Savage, Gus (D)
3. Russo, Martin A. (D)
4. O'Brien, George M. (R)
5. Lipinski, William O. (D)
6. Hyde, Henry J. (R)
7. Collins, Cardiss (D)
8. Rostenkowski, Dan (D)
9. Yates, Sidney R. (D)
10. Porter, John E. (R)
11. Annunzio, Frank (D)
12. Crane, Philip M. (R)
13. Erlenborn, John N. (R)
14. Corcoran, Tom (R)
15. Madigan, Edward R. (R)
16. Martin, Lynn M. (R)
17. Evans, Lane (D)
18. Michel, Robert H. (R)
19. Crane, Daniel B. (R)
20. Durbin, Richard J. (D)
21. Price, Melvin (D)
22. Simon, Paul (D)
Ind.—1. Hall Katie (D)
2. Sharp, Philip R. (D)
3. Hiler, John P. (R)
4. Coats, Daniel R. (R)
5. Hillis, Elwood H. (R)
6. Burton, Dan (R)
7. Myers, John (R)
8. McCloskey, Francis X. (D)
9. Hamilton, L. H. (D)
10. Jacobs, Andrew, Jr. (D)
Iowa—1. Leach, James (R)
2. Tauke, Tom (R)
3. Evans, Cooper (R)
4. Smith, Neal (D)
5. Harkin, Tom (D)
6. Bedell, Berkley (D)
Kan.—1. Roberts, Pat (R)
2. Slattery, Jim (D)
3. Winn, Larry, Jr. (R)
4. Glickman, Dan (D)
5. Whittaker, Robert (R)
Ky.—1. Hubbard, Carroll, Jr. (D)
2. Natcher, William H. (D)
3. Mazzoli, Romano L. (D)
4. Snyder, Gene (R)
5. Rogers, Harold (R)
6. Hopkins, Larry J. (R)
7. Perkins, Carl D. (D)
La.—1. Livingston, Bob (R)
2. Boggs, Lindy (D)
3. Tauzin, William J. (D)
4. Roemer, Buddy (D)
5. Huckaby, Jerry (D)
6. Moore, W. Henson, III (R)
7. Breaux, John B. (D)
8. Long, Gillis W. (D)
Maine—1. McKernan, John R., Jr. (R)
2. Snowe, Olympia J. (R)
Md.—1. Dyson, Roy (D)
2. Long, Clarence D. (D)
3. Mikulski, Barbara A. (D)
4. Holt, Marjorie S. (R)
5. Hoyer, Steny H. (D)
6. Byron, Beverly (D)
7. Mitchell, Parren J. (D)
8. Barnes, Michael D. (D)
Mass.—1. Conte, Silvio O. (R)
2. Boland, Edward P. (D)
3. Early, Joseph D. (D)
4. Frank, Barney (D)
5. Shannon, James M. (D)
6. Mavroules, Nicholas (D)
7. Markey, Edward J. (D)
8. O'Neill, Thomas P., Jr. (D)
9. Moakley, Joe (D)
10. Studds, Gerry E. (D)
11. Donnelly, Brian J. (D)
Mich.—1. Conyers, John, Jr. (D)
2. Pursell, Carl D. (R)
3. Wolpe, Howard (D)
4. Siljander, Mark D. (R)
5. Sawyer, Harold S. (R)
6. Carr, Bob (D)
7. Kildee, Dale E. (D)
8. Traxler, Bob (D)
9. Vander Jagt, Guy (R)
10. Albosta, Donald J. (D)
11. Davis, Robert W. (R)
12. Bonior, David E. (D)
13. Crockett, George W. (D)
14. Hertel, Dennis M. (D)
15. Ford, William D. (D)
16. Dingell, John D. (D)
17. Levin, Sander (D)
18. Broomfield, William S. (R)
Minn.—1. Penny, Timothy J. (D)
2. Weber, Vin (R)
3. Frenzel, William (R)
4. Vento, Bruce F. (D)
5. Sabo, Martin Olav (D)
6. Sikorski, Gerry (D)
7. Stangeland, Arlan (R)
8. Oberstar, James L. (D)
Miss.—1. Whitten, Jamie L. (D)
2. Franklin, Webb (R)
3. Montgomery, G. V. (D)
4. Dowdy, Wayne (D)
5. Lott, Trent (R)
Mo.—1. Clay, William (D)
2. Young, Robert A. (D)
3. Gephardt, Richard A. (D)
4. Skelton, Ike (D)
5. Wheat, Alan (D)
6. Coleman, E. Thomas (R)
7. Taylor, Gene (R)
8. Emerson, William (R)
9. Volkmer, Harold L. (D)
Mont.—1. Williams, Pat (D)
2. Marlenee, Ron (R)
Neb.—1. Bereuter, D. K. (R)
2. Daub, Harold (R)
3. Smith, Virginia (R)
Nev.—1. Reid, Harry (D)
2. Vucanovich, Barbara (R)
N.H.—1. D'Amours, Norman (D)
2. Gregg, Judd (R)
N.J.—1. Florio, James J. (D)
2. Hughes, William J. (D)
3. Howard, James J. (D)
4. Smith, Christopher (R)
5. Roukema, Marge (R)
6. Dwyer, Bernard J. (D)
7. Rinaldo, Matthew J. (R)
8. Roe, Robert A. (D)
9. Torricelli, Robert G. (D)
10. Rodino, Peter W., Jr. (D)
11. Minish, Joseph G. (D)
12. Courter, James A. (R)
13. Forsythe, Edwin B. (R)
14. Guarini, Frank J. (D)
N.M.—1. Lujan, Manuel, Jr. (R)
2. Skeen, Joseph (R)
3. Richardson, Bill (D)
N.Y.—1. Carney, William (C-R)
2. Downey, Thomas J. (D)
3. Mrazek, Robert J. (D)
4. Lent, Norman F. (R)
5. McGrath, Raymond J. (R)
6. Addabbo, Joseph P. (D)
7. (vacancy)[2]
8. Scheuer, James H. (D)
9. Ferraro, Geraldine (D)
10. Schumer, Charles E. (D)
11. Towns, Edolphus (D)
12. Owens, Major R. (D)
13. Solarz, Stephen J. (D)
14. Molinari, Guy V. (R)
15. Green, S. William (R)
16. Rangel, Charles B. (D)
17. Weiss, Theodore S. (D)
18. Garcia, Robert (D)
19. Biaggi, Mario (D)
20. Ottinger, Richard L. (D)
21. Fish, Hamilton, Jr. (R)
22. Gilman, B. A. (R)
23. Stratton, Samuel S. (D)
24. Solomon, Gerald (R)
25. Boehlert, Sherwood L. (R)
26. Martin, David O'B.(R)
27. Wortley, George (R)
28. McHugh, Matthew F. (D)
29. Horton, Frank J. (R)
30. Conable, B. B., Jr. (R)
31. Kemp, Jack F. (R)
32. LaFalce, John J. (D)
33 Nowak, Henry J. (D)
34. Lundine, Stanley N. (D)
N.C.—1. Jones, Walter B. (D)
2. Valentine, Tim, Jr. (D)
3. Whitley, Charles (D)
4. Andrews, Ike F. (D)
5. Neal, Stephen L. (D)
6. Britt, C. Robin (D)
7. Rose, C. G., III (D)
8. Hefner, Bill (D)
9. Martin, James G. (R)
10. Broyhill, James T. (R)
11. Clarke, James McC. (D)
N.D.—Dorgan, Byron L. (D)
Ohio—1. Luken, Thomas A. (D)
2. Gradison, Bill (R)
3. Hall, Tony P. (D)
4. Oxley, Michael G. (R)
5. Latta, Delbert L. (R)
6. McEwen, Robert (R)
7. DeWine, Michael (R)
8. Kindness, Thomas N. (R)
9. Kaptur, Marcy (D)
10. Miller, Clarence E. (R)
11. Eckart, Dennis E. (D)
12. Kasich, John R. (R)
13. Pease, Donald J. (D)
14. Seiberling, John F., Jr. (D)
15. Wylie, Chalmers P. (R)
16. Regula, Ralph S. (R)
17. Williams, Lyle (R)
18. Applegate, Douglas (D)
19. Feighan, Edward F. (D)
20. Oakar, Mary Rose (D)
21. Stokes, Louis (D)
Okla.—1. Jones, James R. (D)
2. Synar, Mike (D)
3. Watkins, Wes (D)
4. McCurdy, Dave (D)
5. Edwards, Mickey (R)
6. English, Glenn (D)
Ore.—1. AuCoin, Les (D)
2. Smith, Bob (R)
3. Wyden, Ron (D)
4. Weaver, James (D)
5. Smith, Denny (R)
Pa.—1. Foglietta, Thomas (D)
2. Gray, William H., III (D)
3. Borski, Robert A. (D)
4. Kolter, Joseph P. (D)
5. Schulze, Richard T. (R)
6. Yatron, Gus (D)
7. Edgar, Robert W. (D)
8. Kostmayer, Peter H. (D)
9. Shuster, E. G. (R)
10. McDade, Joseph M. (R)
11. Harrison, Frank (D)
12. Murtha, John P. (D)
13. Coughlin, R. L. (R)
14. Coyne, William J. (D)
15. Ritter, Donald L. (R)
16. Walker, Robert S. (R)
17. Gekas, George W. (R)
18. Walgren, Doug (D)
19. Goodling, William F. (R)
20. Gaydos, Joseph (D)
21. Ridge, Thomas J. (R)
22. Murphy, Austin J. (D)
23. Clinger, William F., Jr. (R)
R.I.—1. St. Germain, Fernand (D)
2. Schneider, Claudine (R)
S.C.—1. Hartnett, Thomas F. (R)
2. Spence, Floyd D. (R)
3. Derrick, Butler C., Jr. (D)
4. Campbell, Carroll A., Jr. (R)
5. Spratt, John (D)
6. Tallon, Robert M., Jr. (D)
S.D. Daschle, Thomas A. (D)
Tenn.—1. Quillen, James H. (R)
2. Duncan, John J. (R)
3. Lloyd Bouquard, Marilyn (D)
4. Cooper, Jim (D)
5. Boner, Bill (D)
6. Gore, Albert, Jr. (D)
7. Sundquist, Don (R)
8. Jones, Edward (D)
9. Ford, Harold E. (D)
Texas—1. Hall, Sam B. (D)
2. Wilson, Charles (D)
3. Bartlett, Steve (R)
4. Hall, Ralph M. (D)
5. Bryant, John (D)
6. (vacancy)[3]
7. Archer, William R. (R)
8. Fields, Jack (R)
9. Brooks, Jack (D)
10. Pickle, J. J. (D)
11. Leath, J. Marvin (D)
12. Wright, James C., Jr. (D)
13. Hightower, Jack (D)
14. Patman, William N. (D)
15. de la Garza, E. (D)
16. Coleman, Ronald (D)
17. Stenholm, Charles W. (D)
18. Leland, Mickey (D)
19. Hance, Kent (D)
20. Gonzalez, Henry B. (D)
21. Loeffler, Tom (R)
22. Paul, Ron (R)
23. Kazen, Abraham, Jr. (D)
24. Frost, Martin (D)
25. Andrews, Mike (D)
26. Vandergriff, Tom (D)
27. Ortiz, Solomon P. (D)
Utah—1. Hansen, James V. (R)
2. Marriott, Dan (R)
3. Nielson, Howard C. (R)
Vt.—Jeffords, James M. (R)
Va.—1. Bateman, Herbert H. (R)
2. Whitehurst, G. W. (R)
3. Bliley, Thomas J. (R)
4. Sisisky, Norman (D)
5. Daniel, Dan (D)
6. Olin, James R. (D)
7. Robinson, J. Kenneth (R)
8. Parris, Stanford E. (R)
9. Boucher, Frederick C. (D)
10. Wolf, Frank R. (R)
Wash.—1. Pritchard, Joel (R)
2. Swift, Al (D)
3. Bonker, Don (D)
4. Morrison, Sid (R)
5. Foley, Thomas S. (D)
6. Dicks, Norman D. (D)
7. Lowry, Mike (D)
8. Chandler, Rodney (R)
W.Va.—1. Mollohan, Alan B. (D)
2. Staggers, Harley O., Jr. (D)
3. Wise, Bob (D)
4. Rahall, Nick J. (D)
Wis.—1. Aspin, Leslie (D)
2. Kastenmeier, Robert W. (D)
3. Gunderson, Steven (R)
4. Zablocki, Clement J. (D)
5. Moody, Jim (D)
6. Petri, Thomas E. (R)
7. Obey, David R. (D)
8. Roth, Tobias A. (R)
9. Sensenbrenner, F. J. (R)
Wyo.—Cheney, Richard (R)

Supreme Court

Chief Justice Warren Earl Burger (appointed 1969)

Associate Justices (year appointed)

William J. Brennan, Jr.	(1956)
Byron R. White	(1962)
Thurgood Marshall	(1967)
Harry A. Blackmun	(1970)
Lewis F. Powell, Jr.	(1972)
William H. Rehnquist	(1972)
John Paul Stevens	(1975)
Sandra Day O'Connor	(1981)

[1]Representative-elect John L. Swigert, Jr., died Dec. 27, 1982. [2]Rep. Benjamin S. Rosenthal died Jan. 4, 1983. [3]Rep. Phil Gramm resigned Jan. 5, 1983.

The Federal Administrative Budget

in millions of dollars; fiscal years ending Sept. 30

Source and function	1981 actual	1982 estimate	1983 estimate
BUDGET RECEIPTS	$599,300	$626,800	$666,100
Individual income taxes	285,900	298,600	304,500
Corporation income taxes	61,100	46,800	65,300
Excise taxes	40,800	43,000	41,700
Social insurance taxes and contributions	182,700	206,500	222,500
Estate and gift taxes	6,800	7,200	5,900
Customs duties	8,100	8,900	9,400
Miscellaneous receipts	13,800	15,900	16,800
BUDGET EXPENDITURES	657,200	725,300	757,600
National defense	159,800	187,500	221,100
Department of Defense military functions	156,100	182,800	215,900
Atomic energy defense activities	3,400	4,500	5,200
Defense-related activities	300	200	[1]
International affairs	11,100	11,100	12,000
Conduct of foreign affairs	1,300	1,500	1,800
Foreign economic and financial assistance	4,200	4,300	4,300
Foreign information and exchange activities	500	600	700
International financial programs	2,000	1,300	1,500
International security assistance	3,100	3,500	3,800
General science, space, and technology	6,400	6,900	7,600
Agriculture	5,600	8,600	4,500
Farm income stabilization	4,000	7,000	2,900
Agricultural research and services	1,500	1,600	1,600
Natural resources and environment	13,500	12,600	9,900
Water resources	4,200	4,100	3,400
Conservation and land management	2,600	2,200	1,500
Recreational resources	1,600	1,600	1,400
Pollution control and abatement	5,200	5,400	4,600
Other natural resources	1,500	1,600	1,500
Energy	10,300	6,400	4,200
Commerce and housing credit	3,900	3,300	1,600
Mortgage credit and thrift insurance	700	900	−200
Payment to the Postal Service	1,300	600	500
Other advancement and regulation	2,000	1,700	1,300
Transportation	23,400	21,200	19,600
Air transportation	3,800	3,700	4,000
Water transportation	2,400	2,800	2,600
Ground transportation	17,100	14,700	13,000
Other transportation	100	100	100
Community and regional development	9,400	8,400	7,300
Community development	5,100	5,100	4,300
Area and regional development	2,700	2,800	2,700
Disaster relief and insurance	1,600	500	200
Education, training, employment, and social services	$31,400	$27,800	$21,600
Elementary, secondary, and vocational education	7,000	7,100	5,500
Higher education	6,800	7,000	6,300
Research and general education aids	1,200	1,300	1,300
Training and employment	9,200	5,400	2,800
Social services	6,500	6,400	5,100
Other labour services	600	600	600
Health	66,000	73,400	78,100
Health care services	60,400	68,000	72,700
Health research	3,800	3,800	3,900
Education and training of health care work force	800	600	500
Consumer and occupational health and safety	1,000	1,000	1,100
Income security	225,100	250,900	261,700
General retirement and disability insurance	145,000	162,300	175,700
Federal employee retirement and disability	17,500	19,400	21,100
Unemployment compensation	19,700	25,200	22,600
Public assistance and other income supplements	42,800	44,000	42,500
Veterans benefits and services	23,000	24,200	24,400
Income security for veterans	12,900	14,100	14,800
Veterans education, training, and rehabilitation	2,300	1,900	1,600
Hospital and medical care for veterans	7,000	7,600	8,100
Other veterans benefits and services	900	600	−200
Administration of justice	4,700	4,500	4,600
Federal law enforcement activities	2,400	2,500	2,600
Federal litigative and judicial activities	1,500	1,400	1,400
Federal correctional activities	400	400	400
Criminal justice assistance	500	300	200
General government	4,600	5,100	5,000
Legislative functions	1,000	1,200	1,200
Central fiscal operations	2,600	2,800	3,100
General property and records management	200	400	200
Other general government	1,000	900	900
General purpose fiscal assistance	6,900	6,400	6,700
Interest	82,500	99,100	112,500
Allowances for contingencies, civilian agency pay raises, and management reforms and savings	—	−600	−1,300
Undistributed offsetting receipts	−30,300	−31,500	−43,500
Employer share, employee retirement	−6,400	−7,600	−8,400
Interest received by trust funds	−13,800	−16,100	−16,100
Rents and royalties on the Outer Continental Shelf	−10,100	−7,900	−18,000
Federal surplus property disposition	—	—	−1,000

[1]$50 million or less. Source: Executive Office of the President, Office of Management and Budget, *The United States Budget in Brief: Fiscal Year 1983.*

State Government Revenue, Expenditure, and Debt

1981 in thousands of dollars

State	GENERAL REVENUE: Total	State taxes: Total	State taxes: General sales	State taxes: Income[2]	Intergovernmental	Charges & misc.	GENERAL EXPENDITURE[1]: Total	Education	Highways	Public welfare	Hospitals	DEBT: Total	Issued 1981[3]	Retired 1981[3]
Ala.	4,550,927	2,148,415	595,173	515,870	1,360,892	1,041,620	2,790,584	935,486	413,331	519,423	262,318	1,319,911	284,697	72,823
Alaska	4,867,003	2,316,823	—	7,172	395,198	2,154,982	1,807,631	378,293	199,640	152,075	13,549	2,399,506	934,038	90,676
Ariz.	2,775,904	1,785,775	805,745	364,131	579,698	410,431	1,662,722	591,995	290,442	177,377	94,768	139,843	50,000	4,164
Ark.	2,227,779	1,188,861	398,950	311,929	787,571	251,347	1,496,149	399,401	303,960	358,172	86,621	471,763	112,716	9,481
Calif.	32,623,137	20,504,787	7,262,497	6,589,203	8,621,332	3,497,018	16,946,071	4,278,231	1,152,782	4,494,342	1,112,878	8,982,610	810,322	412,420
Colo.	2,903,689	1,445,777	529,881	437,649	854,497	603,415	1,840,889	680,037	261,236	253,331	151,081	712,930	268,828	29,283
Conn.	3,449,461	2,071,885	916,668	117,786	830,911	546,665	2,511,388	441,784	236,462	671,145	236,314	4,411,442	739,333	222,214
Del.	997,952	550,943	—	261,916	236,880	210,129	727,569	198,466	93,814	104,644	35,485	1,063,786	74,247	68,482
Fla.	8,063,292	5,314,376	2,542,895	—	1,971,345	777,571	4,554,564	958,364	774,757	891,430	309,786	2,815,714	290,175	101,387
Ga.	5,118,285	3,019,847	1,009,237	1,035,899	1,614,260	484,178	3,313,901	802,147	509,564	880,696	250,464	1,378,211	68,805	94,235
Hawaii	1,831,113	1,088,330	548,914	334,750	390,622	352,161	1,672,392	602,089	97,763	271,163	67,930	1,853,594	81,289	99,057
Idaho	988,798	536,681	144,993	185,507	305,763	146,354	672,111	177,567	107,469	115,253	18,820	378,879	64,548	13,003
Ill.	11,891,487	7,322,572	2,333,028	2,037,453	3,283,392	1,285,523	8,028,882	1,569,729	1,183,054	2,707,773	450,483	6,919,662	877,625	355,379
Ind.	4,880,168	2,808,811	1,361,250	642,911	1,241,640	829,717	2,978,930	1,116,047	413,363	511,322	221,066	1,023,933	458,730	38,768
Iowa	3,127,691	1,835,807	514,727	673,470	835,483	456,401	2,000,329	580,490	312,127	526,679	209,663	438,780	64,330	6,549
Kan.	2,374,160	1,392,277	449,213	415,015	643,176	338,707	1,715,068	464,642	342,034	426,461	149,378	420,119	1,000	21,064
Ky.	4,031,314	2,276,170	630,472	573,091	1,205,115	550,029	3,202,267	748,108	709,684	720,649	160,829	3,028,157	318,834	327,489
La.	5,352,227	2,804,570	858,604	185,663	1,369,276	1,178,381	3,672,187	867,211	635,757	771,737	384,176	3,488,824	690,853	105,160
Maine	1,303,116	674,316	235,678	176,600	461,056	167,744	911,233	159,856	126,594	301,608	31,934	833,545	187,278	72,422
Md.	5,259,460	2,956,088	753,674	1,205,507	1,368,734	934,638	3,405,581	764,868	269,413	896,263	319,850	3,981,579	510,192	193,193
Mass.	7,251,518	4,335,648	859,716	2,057,945	2,100,476	815,394	5,105,463	609,269	399,917	1,951,083	333,171	6,282,801	652,689	330,368
Mich.	11,069,444	6,176,957	1,792,675	2,028,437	3,161,246	1,731,241	7,178,214	1,852,187	457,296	2,649,788	518,185	3,471,039	672,675	132,357
Minn.	5,671,909	3,373,726	686,668	1,396,432	1,500,466	797,717	3,157,837	868,768	385,724	695,495	272,182	2,396,438	400,063	95,072
Miss.	2,637,515	1,396,745	723,568	191,138	909,330	331,440	1,750,520	466,044	279,918	413,949	132,239	793,958	39,678	60,768
Mo.	3,793,961	2,142,913	787,185	669,728	1,188,104	462,944	2,823,304	625,434	411,333	794,724	254,768	1,335,337	329,952	12,479
Mont.	1,053,479	465,010	—	146,036	381,512	206,957	702,480	129,867	185,962	114,639	25,099	303,184	—	6,349
Neb.	1,488,481	803,960	281,212	201,161	420,273	264,248	1,017,854	305,163	180,332	191,452	87,543	246,340	50,000	3,001
Nev.	889,033	515,303	203,109	—	261,716	112,014	634,567	130,119	148,838	92,988	21,703	554,571	35,479	8,879
N.H.	710,591	268,752	—	12,618	268,604	173,235	638,463	138,806	114,739	148,112	37,145	1,038,830	173,261	33,461
N.J.	8,163,405	5,029,356	1,263,650	1,147,834	1,916,485	1,217,564	4,866,879	996,197	369,881	1,013,077	539,978	7,620,017	1,224,299	200,069
N.M.	2,476,915	1,179,280	515,692	70,937	480,158	817,477	1,275,303	392,733	215,016	192,086	88,310	762,158	107,765	55,148
N.Y.	23,538,972	13,918,245	2,965,313	6,612,289	7,511,673	2,109,054	12,221,482	2,329,094	1,215,423	1,883,662	1,584,803	24,656,848	2,635,162	1,347,129
N.C.	5,791,771	3,431,002	738,879	1,303,517	1,694,290	666,479	3,654,077	1,070,866	531,178	689,519	320,572	1,351,328	128,119	64,789
N.D.	1,080,093	450,755	129,509	62,419	261,138	368,200	693,656	185,968	109,866	101,523	38,313	212,024	839	15,826
Ohio	9,296,773	5,240,844	1,636,100	1,134,381	2,568,053	1,487,876	6,342,393	1,666,185	584,982	1,748,286	557,209	4,714,807	886,971	267,326
Okla.	3,736,951	2,232,276	382,649	494,023	840,452	664,223	2,373,077	717,131	313,061	619,898	182,001	1,733,102	291,982	95,799
Ore.	3,338,763	1,608,423	—	1,005,104	943,391	786,949	2,293,722	471,651	290,075	476,015	144,752	5,899,900	1,159,080	125,366
Pa.	12,002,736	7,597,010	2,086,165	1,884,756	3,141,418	1,264,308	7,583,357	1,348,276	941,924	2,696,836	686,644	6,329,635	242,150	314,004
R.I.	1,301,649	607,951	177,542	192,976	390,906	302,792	1,087,416	224,762	64,095	308,143	94,140	1,725,068	289,111	90,395
S.C.	3,236,039	1,825,935	616,081	571,001	947,411	462,693	2,306,662	770,873	227,513	437,296	203,124	2,467,093	423,207	71,844
S.D.	733,795	297,813	158,022	—	272,185	163,797	647,319	133,088	143,380	111,026	24,257	693,284	59,151	17,109
Tenn.	3,787,269	1,958,427	1,044,155	35,678	1,354,734	474,108	2,765,012	801,843	431,924	648,718	197,819	1,473,090	138,836	74,973
Texas	13,799,147	8,173,759	2,994,496	—	3,177,736	2,447,652	8,150,161	2,408,457	1,710,588	1,688,237	696,719	2,652,136	291,457	99,441
Utah	1,679,844	849,148	349,502	294,947	540,419	290,277	1,199,573	385,103	204,683	226,154	76,573	578,311	48,000	6,622
Vt.	687,581	294,243	44,761	98,574	262,321	131,017	535,751	143,394	53,388	112,759	22,067	673,446	69,035	38,629
Va.	5,610,949	3,027,348	645,203	1,288,796	1,580,640	1,002,961	3,989,038	1,108,043	738,815	639,527	423,558	2,141,631	260,765	66,017
Wash.	5,347,649	3,125,815	1,716,251	—	1,638,128	583,706	4,027,018	1,258,699	560,749	927,955	286,928	1,793,275	239,221	67,538
W.Va.	2,319,390	1,269,671	623,793	268,124	764,154	285,565	1,741,939	322,963	507,749	264,639	80,741	1,842,833	96,705	75,366
Wis.	6,036,485	3,629,459	901,496	1,654,862	1,656,401	750,625	3,267,227	988,244	308,419	943,106	178,357	2,590,765	263,880	109,492
Wyo.	1,010,127	469,058	197,135	—	295,049	246,020	534,116	99,477	167,732	48,027	20,364	450,500	125,000	37,395
TOTAL	258,159,197	149,737,943	46,412,126	40,895,235	70,785,710	37,635,544	160,474,328	39,663,515	20,687,746	38,580,262	12,696,657	134,846,537	18,222,372	6,260,260

Fiscal year ending June 30, 1981, except Alabama, September 30; New York, March 31; and Texas, August 31. [1]Direct only, intergovernmental excluded. [2]Includes individual and corporation. [3]Long term only. Source: U.S. Department of Commerce, Bureau of the Census, *Governmental Finances in 1981*.

EDUCATION

Public Elementary and Secondary Schools

Fall 1981 estimates

State	ENROLLMENT[1] Elementary	ENROLLMENT[1] Secondary	INSTRUCTIONAL STAFF Total[2]	INSTRUCTIONAL STAFF Principals and supervisors	INSTRUCTIONAL STAFF Teachers, elementary	INSTRUCTIONAL STAFF Teachers, secondary	TEACHERS' AVERAGE ANNUAL SALARIES Elementary	TEACHERS' AVERAGE ANNUAL SALARIES Secondary	STUDENT-TEACHER RATIO Elementary	STUDENT-TEACHER RATIO Secondary	Expenditure per pupil
Alabama	401,000	347,000	41,500	1,800	20,300	19,400	$15,000	$16,010	19.8	17.9	$1,432
Alaska	48,700	39,000	6,291	271	2,926	2,448	31,810	32,060	15.6	15.9	6,015
Arizona	358,032	156,413	30,353	1,235	18,630	8,350	17,821	18,446	19.2	18.7	2,684
Arkansas	238,643	204,849	25,897	1,403	11,803	12,308	13,591	14,361	20.2	16.6	1,711
California	2,623,039	1,335,982	193,700	9,745	104,006	70,438	22,076	22,823	25.2	19.0	2,337
Colorado	309,000	235,000	33,239	1,713	14,777	15,123	19,142	20,102	20.9	15.5	2,691
Connecticut	343,585	181,889	37,347	2,141	19,674	12,929	18,156	18,563	17.4	14.1	3,280
Delaware	46,866	43,206	6,341	395	2,456	3,043	18,715	19,665	19.1	15.8	3,455
District of Columbia	52,744	42,231	6,019	352	3,021	2,111	24,304	24,210	17.4	20.0	3,538
Florida	330,500	721,000	90,690	4,500	43,068	36,553	17,157	16,613	19.3	19.7	2,560
Georgia	660,400	406,300	62,470	2,580	35,330	24,560	16,080	16,770	18.7	16.5	2,001
Hawaii	87,034	75,530	9,277	354	4,778	3,245	23,767	22,537	18.2	23.3	2,904
Idaho	115,850	88,800	11,223	600	5,406	4,691	16,041	16,778	21.4	16.6	1,915
Illinois	1,308,218	619,415	120,924	6,759	71,015	37,340	20,181	22,596	18.4	16.6	2,958
Indiana	542,935	483,754	59,773	4,165	26,305	26,285	18,500	19,433	20.6	18.4	2,358
Iowa	260,000	234,000	34,066	1,341	14,657	16,479	17,312	18,591	17.7	14.2	2,825
Kansas	240,373	166,612	29,538	1,610	14,400	11,928	16,476	16,631	16.7	14.0	2,888
Kentucky	434,940	225,060	37,400	2,150	21,912	11,288	16,740	18,100	19.9	19.9	2,049
Louisiana	540,000	235,000	46,896	2,069	23,994	18,892	17,000	17,600	22.5	12.4	2,128
Maine	150,500	69,357	13,545	1,200	7,600	4,630	14,400	15,650	19.8	15.0	2,359
Maryland	353,128	366,268	44,117	3,303	18,654	20,990	20,206	21,450	18.9	17.5	3,200
Massachusetts	761,709	209,744	100,960	5,574	27,670	38,476	19,631	20,051	27.5	5.5	3,645
Michigan	940,802	874,328	90,790	6,777	40,593	37,590	22,113	22,609	23.2	23.3	3,282
Minnesota	364,270	368,767	44,590	2,220	21,090	22,870	19,152	20,596	17.3	16.1	3,304
Mississippi	259,710	206,779	23,577	1,640	14,030	11,420	13,930	14,400	18.5	18.1	1,965
Missouri	553,014	265,693	55,267	3,150	23,883	23,884	16,098	16,900	23.2	11.1	2,392
Montana	102,438	49,322	10,161	400	5,085	4,040	16,970	18,450	20.1	12.2	2,761
Nebraska	143,883	128,602	18,799	972	8,536	8,255	14,844	16,252	16.9	15.6	2,601
Nevada	80,900	70,900	8,200	400	3,650	3,550	18,100	18,400	22.2	20.0	2,246
New Hampshire	97,623	69,074	11,510	680	5,200	4,700	14,544	14,875	18.8	14.7	2,225
New Jersey	756,500	443,500	90,530	6,000	44,445	30,885	19,336	20,238	17.0	14.4	3,837
New Mexico	147,145	121,249	16,325	903	6,756	7,384	18,621	19,185	21.8	16.4	2,645
New York	1,354,580	1,419,360	184,800	12,600	71,200	92,500	22,600	23,000	19.0	15.3	3,741
North Carolina	781,469	346,703	63,393	3,973	33,618	21,576	16,342	16,563	23.3	16.1	2,256
North Dakota	80,724	31,265	8,190	434	4,767	2,991	14,626	14,992	19.4	10.5	2,180
Ohio	1,130,700	775,700	117,450	5,980	54,910	44,570	17,610	18,740	20.1	17.4	2,496
Oklahoma	323,000	246,000	38,453	2,100	18,150	16,603	16,380	17,220	18.1	14.8	2,432
Oregon	286,385	176,665	30,446	2,192	15,237	10,108	19,561	20,755	18.8	17.5	3,381
Pennsylvania	911,600	933,600	119,960	5,400	48,500	57,300	18,820	19,720	18.8	16.3	2,865
Rhode Island	73,096	69,727	10,703	654	4,632	4,504	21,559	21,428	15.8	15.5	3,329
South Carolina	420,320	188,840	36,880	2,040	19,330	12,110	15,220	16,320	21.2	15.6	1,916
South Dakota	35,757	39,770	9,118	494	5,249	2,820	14,257	14,829	15.3	14.1	1,968
Tennessee	507,950	337,225	47,353	2,612	24,987	15,639	16,123	16,259	20.3	21.6	1,997
Texas	1,626,000	1,288,000	182,000	6,500	92,800	73,200	17,000	18,100	17.5	17.6	2,176
Utah	211,482	143,058	16,689	895	8,368	6,326	17,258	18,693	25.3	22.6	1,968
Vermont	46,831	46,870	8,535	871	3,461	3,312	13,133	14,021	13.5	14.2	2,111
Virginia	509,586	379,962	66,250	3,721	34,256	23,706	16,519	17,914	17.8	16.0	2,525
Washington	391,379	357,823	41,352	3,040	20,011	15,502	21,844	22,961	19.6	23.1	3,037
West Virginia	226,415	151,581	25,103	1,670	12,532	9,654	17,023	17,450	18.1	15.7	2,274
Wisconsin	454,000	352,000	54,900	2,100	28,500	24,300	18,900	19,870	15.9	14.5	2,951
Wyoming	56,900	43,900	8,001	467	3,870	3,271	20,411	21,954	14.1	13.4	2,570
TOTAL U.S.	23,736,625	16,417,680	2,493,891	136,145	1,189,939	996,077	$18,543	$19,494	19.4	16.4	$2,671

[1] Kindergartens included in elementary schools; junior high schools in secondary schools.   [2] Includes librarians, guidance, health and psychological personnel, and related educational workers.

Source: National Education Association Research, *Estimates of School Statistics, 1981–82* (Copyright 1982. All rights reserved. Used by permission).

Universities and Colleges

state statistics

State	NUMBER OF INSTITUTIONS 1981–1982 Total	NUMBER OF INSTITUTIONS 1981–1982 Public	Enrollment[1] fall, 1980	EARNED DEGREES CONFERRED 1979–1980 Bachelor's and first professional	EARNED DEGREES CONFERRED 1979–1980 Master's except first professional	EARNED DEGREES CONFERRED 1979–1980 Doctor's
Alabama	59	37	164,306	17,199	5,527	249
Alaska	15	12	21,296	419	184	0
Arizona	28	19	202,715	10,535	3,890	417
Arkansas	35	19	77,607	7,336	1,782	110
California	272	136	1,790,953	91,613	31,133	3,781
Colorado	45	27	162,976	14,928	4,953	618
Connecticut	47	24	159,632	13,957	5,639	499
Delaware	8	5	32,939	3,276	468	70
District of Columbia	19	1	86,675	8,907	5,488	487
Florida	81	37	411,891	30,428	8,299	536
Georgia	78	34	184,759	18,182	6,820	549
Hawaii	12	9	47,181	3,339	1,009	103
Idaho	9	6	43,018	2,987	660	55
Illinois	158	63	644,245	48,719	16,298	1,872
Indiana	74	28	247,253	25,737	8,313	1,036
Iowa	60	21	140,449	15,186	2,584	532
Kansas	52	29	136,605	12,349	3,126	388
Kentucky	57	21	143,066	12,821	5,210	271
Louisiana	32	20	160,058	16,170	4,190	314
Maine	29	12	43,264	4,958	599	21
Maryland	56	32	225,526	16,655	5,126	529
Massachusetts	118	32	413,415	41,765	14,653	1,839
Michigan	91	44	520,131	40,294	15,056	1,334
Minnesota	70	30	206,691	20,135	3,222	503
Mississippi	41	25	102,364	9,180	2,845	226
Missouri	89	28	234,421	24,137	7,555	637
Montana	16	9	35,177	3,954	638	56
Nebraska	31	16	89,488	8,329	1,689	221
Nevada	7	6	40,455	1,459	425	21
New Hampshire	26	11	46,794	5,926	880	58
New Jersey	61	31	321,610	25,928	7,965	645
New Mexico	19	16	58,283	4,882	1,713	166
New York	294	86	992,237	91,388	32,845	3,375
North Carolina	127	74	287,537	25,157	5,252	757
North Dakota	17	11	34,069	3,813	474	83
Ohio	136	59	489,145	44,263	13,007	1,488
Oklahoma	44	29	160,295	13,701	3,485	377
Oregon	45	21	157,458	11,481	3,268	346
Pennsylvania	202	61	507,716	58,694	13,060	1,669
Rhode Island	13	3	66,869	7,119	1,472	203
South Carolina	60	33	132,476	12,329	3,268	191
South Dakota	20	8	32,761	4,072	604	37
Tennessee	79	24	204,581	19,217	4,848	543
Texas	156	98	701,391	57,464	16,750	1,660
Utah	14	9	93,987	9,678	2,333	453
Vermont	21	6	30,628	4,145	1,164	32
Virginia	69	39	280,504	23,088	5,282	550
Washington	50	33	303,603	17,150	4,281	512
West Virginia	26	16	81,973	7,774	2,167	145
Wisconsin	64	30	269,086	22,741	5,323	760
Wyoming	9	8	21,147	1,392	295	76
TOTAL U.S.	3,243	1,488	12,047,087	996,357	297,052	32,600

Excludes service academies.   [1] Excludes non-degree-credit students.
Source: U.S. Department of Health, Education and Welfare, National Center for Education Statistics, *Digest of Education Statistics* and *Education Directory*.

Universities and Colleges, 1982–83[1]

Selected four-year schools

Institution	Location	Year founded	Total students[2]	Total faculty[3]	Bound library volumes
ALABAMA					
Alabama A. & M. U.	Normal	1875	4,126	321	223,800
Alabama State U.	Montgomery	1874	4,066	179	195,100
Auburn U.	Auburn	1856	18,677	1,091	1,166,000
Birmingham-Southern	Birmingham	1856	1,452	96	126,000
Jacksonville State U.	Jacksonville	1883	7,222	305	415,300
Troy State U.	Troy	1887	8,610	429	253,600
Tuskegee Institute	Tuskegee Institute	1881	3,682	325	230,000
U. of Alabama	University	1831	15,433	919	1,397,800
U. of South Alabama	Mobile	1963	9,411	465	259,900
ALASKA					
U. of Alaska	Fairbanks	1917	5,413	355	500,000
ARIZONA					
Arizona State U.	Tempe	1885	39,919	1,477	2,000,000
Northern Arizona U.	Flagstaff	1899	12,090	650	1,597,800
U. of Arizona	Tucson	1885	33,914	1,446	1,526,800
ARKANSAS					
Arkansas State U.	State University	1909	7,776	339	377,400
U. of Arkansas	Fayetteville	1871	15,108	728	1,004,400
U. of A. at Little Rock	Little Rock	1927	10,065	569	310,000
U. of Central Arkansas	Conway	1907	5,739	299	294,000
CALIFORNIA					
California Inst. of Tech.	Pasadena	1891	1,748	348	380,000
Cal. Polytech. State U.	San Luis Obispo	1901	16,000	1,250	555,000
Cal. State Polytech. U.	Pomona	1938	14,800	800	340,000
Cal. State U., Chico	Chico	1887	13,631	897	471,700
Cal. State U., Dominguez Hills	Dominguez Hills	1960	8,000	300	247,000
Cal. State U., Fresno	Fresno	1911	16,855	1,160	870,000
Cal. State U., Fullerton	Fullerton	1957	23,399	1,301	500,000
Cal. State U., Hayward	Hayward	1957	11,483	610	637,700
Cal. State U., Long Beach	Long Beach	1949	32,034	1,686	815,900
Cal. State U., Los Angeles	Los Angeles	1947	22,500	1,400	895,000
Cal. State U., Northridge	Northridge	1958	28,111	1,502	750,000
Cal. State U., Sacramento	Sacramento	1947	22,660	1,295	75,000
Golden Gate U.	San Francisco	1901	6,132	853	370,000
Humboldt State U.	Arcata	1913	7,500	402	244,000
Loyola Marymount U.	Los Angeles	1911	5,122	351	248,000
Occidental	Los Angeles	1887	1,650	149	350,000
San Francisco State U.	San Francisco	1899	23,227	1,654	530,900
San Jose State U.	San Jose	1857	24,945	1,554	700,000
Sonoma State U.	Rohnert Park	1960	5,508	421	287,000
Stanford U.	Stanford	1885	12,618	1,737	4,487,500
U. of C., Berkeley	Berkeley	1868	28,500	3,100	5,750,000
U. of C., Davis	Davis	1905	18,887	902	1,600,000
U. of C., Irvine	Irvine	1960	10,200	580	930,000
U. of C., Los Angeles	Los Angeles	1919	30,180	3,100	4,230,000
U. of C., Riverside	Riverside	1868	4,600	389	980,000
U. of C., San Diego	La Jolla	1912	11,360	820	1,370,000
U. of C., Santa Barbara	Santa Barbara	1944	14,430	1,100	1,370,000
U. of C., Santa Cruz	Santa Cruz	1965	6,364	350	610,000
U. of the Pacific	Stockton	1851	6,004	371	560,000
U. of San Francisco	San Francisco	1855	6,500	250	366,000
U. of Santa Clara	Santa Clara	1851	6,764	406	396,000
U. of Southern California	Los Angeles	1880	28,129	2,700	1,650,000
COLORADO					
Colorado	Colorado Springs	1874	1,964	153	305,000
Colorado School of Mines	Golden	1874	3,070	200	225,000
Colorado State U.	Fort Collins	1870	18,000	1,200	1,287,300
Metropolitan State	Denver	1963	16,596	821	690,000
U. S. Air Force Academy	USAF Academy	1954	4,544	530	500,000
U. of Colorado	Boulder	1876	21,727	1,162	1,750,000
U. of Denver	Denver	1864	8,099	577	1,005,900
U. of Northern Colorado	Greeley	1889	10,870	620	500,000
U. of Southern Colorado	Pueblo	1933	5,637	293	300,000
CONNECTICUT					
Central Connecticut State	New Britain	1849	12,487	617	350,800
Southern Connecticut State	New Haven	1893	10,481	518	396,400
Trinity	Hartford	1823	1,804	154	650,000
U. S. Coast Guard Acad.	New London	1876	930	113	127,000
U. of Bridgeport	Bridgeport	1927	7,000	539	400,000
U. of Connecticut	Storrs	1881	21,874	1,562	1,476,700
U. of Hartford	West Hartford	1877	6,400	630	280,000
Wesleyan U.	Middletown	1831	2,564	275	830,000
Western Connecticut State	Danbury	1903	5,979	230	142,800
Yale U.	New Haven	1701	10,332	1,353	7,725,400
DELAWARE					
Delaware State	Dover	1891	2,124	146	128,400
U. of Delaware	Newark	1833	18,997	798	1,700,000
DISTRICT OF COLUMBIA					
American U.	Washington	1893	12,500	430	511,000
Catholic U. of America	Washington	1887	7,400	533	900,000
George Washington U.	Washington	1821	21,475	3,104	1,264,000
Georgetown U.	Washington	1789	12,020	682	1,344,000
Howard U.	Washington	1867	11,748	1,922	1,012,500
FLORIDA					
Florida A. & M. U.	Tallahassee	1887	6,011	398	294,200
Florida State U.	Tallahassee	1857	22,424	1,379	1,509,100
Rollins	Winter Park	1885	4,227	112	174,700
U. of Central Florida	Orlando	1963	14,081	546	370,200
U. of Florida	Gainesville	1853	33,772	3,150	2,700,000
U. of Miami	Coral Gables	1925	17,105	1,789	1,343,400
U. of South Florida	Tampa	1960	21,072	1,391	598,800
GEORGIA					
Atlanta U.	Atlanta	1865	1,082	121	533,200
Augusta	Augusta	1925	3,713	174	267,900
Emory U.	Atlanta	1836	7,977	1,173	1,636,300
Georgia	Milledgeville	1889	3,422	170	135,000
Georgia Inst. of Tech.	Atlanta	1885	11,159	572	1,300,000
Georgia Southern	Statesboro	1906	6,800	360	600,000
Georgia State U.	Atlanta	1913	16,657	1,019	698,300
Mercer U.	Macon	1833	5,000	150	240,000
Morehouse[5]	Atlanta	1867	1,950	112[4]	298,500
Oglethorpe U.	Atlanta	1835	1,357	77	200,000
Spelman[6]	Atlanta	1881	1,366	117	60,000
U. of Georgia	Athens	1785	25,886	1,424	2,141,600
HAWAII					
Brigham Young U.-Hawaii	Laie	1955	1,862	96	109,300
U. of Hawaii	Honolulu	1907	20,446	1,615	1,947,500
IDAHO					
Boise State U.	Boise	1932	9,401	378	265,000
Idaho State U.	Pocatello	1901	11,119	421	350,000
U. of Idaho	Moscow	1889	8,998	591	1,015,000
ILLINOIS					
Augustana	Rock Island	1860	2,352	160	245,000
Bradley U.	Peoria	1897	5,637	640	340,000
Chicago State U.	Chicago	1869	7,441	378	31,200
Concordia Teachers	River Forest	1864	1,194	84	127,000
De Paul U.	Chicago	1898	13,300	789	453,500
Eastern Illinois U.	Charleston	1895	10,354	456	489,600
Illinois Inst. of Tech.	Chicago	1892	7,056	741	1,444,800
Illinois State U.	Normal	1857	19,817	930	1,136,000
Knox	Galesburg	1837	963	81[4]	206,200
Lake Forest	Lake Forest	1857	1,138	95	191,800
Loyola U. of Chicago	Chicago	1870	15,857	1,157	821,800
Northeastern Ill. U.	Chicago	1867	11,506	398	355,100
Northern Illinois U.	De Kalb	1895	25,676	1,250	1,070,100
Northwestern U.	Evanston	1851	10,471	1,011	2,838,200
Southern Illinois U.	Carbondale	1869	23,733	1,545	1,792,300
SIU at Edwardsville	Edwardsville	1965	11,342	687	705,000
U. of Chicago	Chicago	1891	9,096	1,021	4,310,000
U. of Illinois	Urbana	1867	34,914	2,646[4]	6,242,600
U. of I. at Chicago Circle	Chicago	1965	21,003	1,008[4]	1,182,700
Western Illinois U.	Macomb	1899	12,411	689	516,000
Wheaton	Wheaton	1860	2,490	194	255,000
INDIANA					
Ball State U.	Muncie	1918	18,244	1,138	1,075,000
Butler U.	Indianapolis	1855	3,800	250	300,000
De Pauw U.	Greencastle	1837	2,425	198	393,400
Indiana State U.	Terre Haute	1865	11,933	717	903,800
Indiana U.	Bloomington	1820	31,877	3,306	1,400,900
Purdue U.	West Lafayette	1869	32,455	5,872	1,502,600
U. of Evansville	Evansville	1854	4,619	234	193,000
U. of Notre Dame du Lac	Notre Dame	1842	9,294	735	1,499,300
Valparaiso U.	Valparaiso	1859	4,254	317	240,000
IOWA					
Coe	Cedar Rapids	1851	1,448	97	190,000
Drake U.	Des Moines	1881	6,592	302	415,000
Grinnell	Grinnell	1846	1,189	119	253,700
Iowa State U.	Ames	1858	24,906	2,116	1,450,000
U. of Iowa	Iowa City	1847	28,140	1,577	2,356,100
U. of Northern Iowa	Cedar Falls	1876	10,988	683	560,900
KANSAS					
Emporia State U.	Emporia	1863	5,768	253	646,800
Kansas State U.	Manhattan	1863	19,497	2,540	900,000
U. of Kansas	Lawrence	1866	24,466	1,296[4]	1,855,100
Wichita State U.	Wichita	1895	17,187	548	685,000
KENTUCKY					
Berea	Berea	1855	1,563	117	271,000
Eastern Kentucky U.	Richmond	1906	13,668	725	500,000
Kentucky State U.	Frankfort	1886	2,342	101	234,200
Murray State U.	Murray	1922	7,722	373	350,000
U. of Kentucky	Lexington	1865	22,258	1,694	1,854,100
U. of Louisville	Louisville	1798	20,057	1,332	906,300
Western Kentucky U.	Bowling Green	1907	12,800	635	515,200
LOUISIANA					
Grambling State U.	Grambling	1901	3,928	234	30,000
Louisiana State U.	Baton Rouge	1860	24,658	1,301	1,965,300
Louisiana Tech. U.	Ruston	1894	11,172	435	855,700
Northeast Louisiana U.	Monroe	1931	9,175	356	649,100
Northwestern State U.	Natchitoches	1884	6,481	367	262,800
Southern U.	Baton Rouge	1880	9,512	430	325,400
Tulane U.	New Orleans	1834	10,040	799	1,818,000
U. of Southwestern La.	Lafayette	1898	15,729	588	499,800
MAINE					
Bates	Lewiston	1864	1,438	238	375,000
Bowdoin	Brunswick	1794	1,395	104	620,000
Colby	Waterville	1813	1,682	140	365,000
U. of Maine, Farmington	Farmington	1864	1,986	76	91,500
U. of Maine, Orono	Orono	1865	11,315	471	562,700
U. of Southern Maine	Portland	1878	8,172	339[4]	433,600
MARYLAND					
Goucher[6]	Towson	1885	1,086	128	197,100
Johns Hopkins U.	Baltimore	1876	8,061	722	1,886,100
Morgan State U.	Baltimore	1867	4,660	256	350,000
Towson State U.	Baltimore	1866	15,528	965	372,000
U.S. Naval Academy	Annapolis	1845	4,607	600	500,000
U. of Maryland	College Park	1807	37,864	1,942	2,000,000
MASSACHUSETTS					
Amherst	Amherst	1821	1,563	171	584,700
Boston	Chestnut Hill	1863	14,069	677	871,500
Boston U.	Boston	1869	28,707	2,513	1,000,000
Brandeis U.	Waltham	1948	3,070	450	850,000
Clark U.	Worcester	1887	2,505	214	406,500
Harvard U.	Cambridge	1636	16,053	3,060	10,261,000
Holy Cross	Worcester	1843	2,519	196	380,000
Mass. Inst. of Tech.	Cambridge	1861	9,510	1,320	1,800,000
Mt. Holyoke[6]	South Hadley	1837	1,903	204	471,700
Northeastern U.	Boston	1898	43,184	3,049	1,123,600
Radcliffe[6]	Cambridge	1879	2,474	...	...
Salem State	Salem	1854	8,320	278	195,900
Simmons[6]	Boston	1899	2,742	167	200,000

Selected four-year schools

Institution	Location	Year founded	Total students[2]	Total faculty[3]	Bound library volumes
Smith	Northampton	1871	2,761	260	866,200
Tufts U.	Medford	1852	4,350	990	530,000
U. of Lowell	Lowell	1894	9,529	552	308,000
U. of Massachusetts	Amherst	1863	24,903	1,201	1,878,000
Wellesley[6]	Wellesley	1870	2,096	292	600,000
Wheaton[6]	Norton	1834	1,328	134	220,000
Williams	Williamstown	1793	1,980	183	532,600
MICHIGAN					
Albion	Albion	1835	1,725	117	235,000
Central Michigan U.	Mt. Pleasant	1892	16,900	770	673,600
Eastern Michigan U.	Ypsilanti	1849	18,274	780	580,300
Ferris State	Big Rapids	1884	11,008	585	184,000
Hope	Holland	1866	2,530	170	190,000
Michigan State U.	East Lansing	1855	40,627	2,515	2,650,000
Michigan Tech. U.	Houghton	1885	7,640	416	543,600
Northern Michigan U.	Marquette	1899	9,576	347	361,300
U. of Detroit	Detroit	1877	6,270	430	467,000
U. of Michigan	Ann Arbor	1817	35,824	4,462	5,400,000
Wayne State U.	Detroit	1868	33,524	2,310	1,839,400
Western Michigan U.	Kalamazoo	1903	20,689	1,013	438,100
MINNESOTA					
Carleton	Northfield	1866	1,877	186	343,800
Concordia	Moorhead	1891	2,553	194	258,000
Gustavus Adolphus	St. Peter	1862	2,314	210	191,900
Hamline U.	St. Paul	1854	1,360	112	175,000
Macalester	St. Paul	1874	1,695	171	280,000
Mankato State U.	Mankato	1867	10,500	590	540,000
Moorhead State U.	Moorhead	1885	8,273	359	271,600
St. Catherine[6]	St. Paul	1905	2,400	160	215,000
St. Cloud State U.	St. Cloud	1869	12,511	500[4]	477,300
St. John's U.[5]	Collegeville	1857	1,936	159	400,000
St. Olaf	Northfield	1874	3,070	275	290,000
St. Thomas	St. Paul	1885	4,236	194	205,200
U. of Minnesota	Minneapolis	1851	58,705	6,481	3,250,000
Winona State U.	Winona	1858	5,130	253	177,900
MISSISSIPPI					
Alcorn State U.	Lorman	1871	2,341	152	131,700
Jackson State U.	Jackson	1877	7,086	406	362,600
Mississippi	Clinton	1826	4,489	177	260,000
Mississippi U. for Women	Columbus	1884	2,307	160	304,100
Mississippi State U.	Mississippi State	1878	12,049	689	653,500
U. of Mississippi	University	1848	9,539	517	661,900
U. of Southern Mississippi	Hattiesburg	1910	10,414	644	633,400
MISSOURI					
Central Missouri State U.	Warrensburg	1871	9,490	455	298,000
Northeast Missouri State U.	Kirksville	1867	6,960	284	248,000
St. Louis U.	St. Louis	1818	9,324	2,185	789,000
Southeast Missouri State U.	Cape Girardeau	1873	9,017	430	250,000
Southwest Missouri State U.	Springfield	1906	15,137	718	373,600
U. of Missouri-Columbia	Columbia	1839	24,304	1,064	2,100,000
U. of Missouri-Kansas City	Kansas City	1929	11,419	665	562,800
U. of Missouri-Rolla	Rolla	1870	7,275	732	330,000
U. of Missouri-St. Louis	St. Louis	1963	11,400	426	383,100
Washington U.	St. Louis	1853	10,804	2,309	1,500,000
MONTANA					
Montana State U.	Bozeman	1893	10,100	743	600,000
U. of Montana	Missoula	1893	8,869	487	650,100
NEBRASKA					
Creighton U.	Omaha	1878	5,682	1,000	457,900
U. of Nebraska	Lincoln	1869	22,477	1,250	2,000,000
U. of Nebraska at Omaha	Omaha	1908	15,000	425	363,000
NEVADA					
U. of Nevada-Las Vegas	Las Vegas	1951	9,064	315[4]	420,100
U. of Nevada-Reno	Reno	1864	8,963	404	705,500
NEW HAMPSHIRE					
Dartmouth	Hanover	1769	4,700	430	1,000,000
U. of New Hampshire	Durham	1866	12,105	643	818,900
NEW JERSEY					
Glassboro State	Glassboro	1923	9,558	500	376,800
Jersey City State	Jersey City	1927	7,700	542	209,000
Kean Col. of N. J.	Union	1855	13,748	775	251,800
Montclair State	Upper Montclair	1908	15,000	500	600,000
Princeton U.	Princeton	1746	5,939	695	3,000,000
Rider	Lawrenceville	1865	5,463	292	323,600
Rutgers State U.	New Brunswick	1766	50,003	2,500	2,000,000
Seton Hall U.	South Orange	1856	9,902	568	300,000
Stevens Inst. of Tech.	Hoboken	1870	2,800	130	103,500
Trenton State	Trenton	1855	11,000	395	400,000
Upsala	East Orange	1893	1,383	71	175,400
William Patterson	Wayne	1855	11,997	393	270,726
NEW MEXICO					
New Mexico State U.	Las Cruces	1888	12,512	549[4]	702,000
U. of New Mexico	Albuquerque	1889	23,701	1,366	1,086,500
NEW YORK					
Adelphi U.	Garden City	1896	11,500	4,000	333,200
Alfred U.	Alfred	1836	2,372	183	239,000
Canisius	Buffalo	1870	4,272	251	211,600
City U. of New York					
Bernard M. Baruch	New York	1919	12,787	865	290,000
Brooklyn	Brooklyn	1930	15,563	1,239	615,400
City	New York	1847	13,161	708	1,000,000
Herbert H. Lehman	Bronx	1931	9,341	438	430,000
Hunter	New York	1870	17,989	637	450,000
Queens	Flushing	1937	17,400	1,250	550,000
Staten Island	Staten Island	1955	3,027	344	165,000
York	Jamaica	1966	4,116	166[4]	156,000
Colgate U.	Hamilton	1819	2,600	240	360,000
Columbia U.	New York	1754	16,812	1,410	5,100,000
Barnard[6]	New York	1889	2,550	200	150,000
Teachers	New York	1887	4,058	135	450,000
Cornell U.	Ithaca	1865	17,329	1,527	4,401,700

Institution	Location	Year founded	Total students[2]	Total faculty[3]	Bound library volumes
Elmira	Elmira	1855	2,709	187	137,955
Fordham U.	Bronx	1841	14,990	986	2,160,000
Hamilton	Clinton	1812	1,660	135	353,800
Hofstra U.	Hempstead	1935	11,110	620	900,000
Ithaca	Ithaca	1892	4,925	407	274,600
Long Island U.	Greenvale	1926	23,300	1,400	600,000
Manhattan	Bronx	1853	4,900	355	226,700
Marymount[6]	Tarrytown	1907	1,112	83	104,500
New School for Soc. Res.	New York	1919	27,000	1,500	175,000
New York U.	New York	1831	32,285	3,792	2,938,400
Niagara U.	Niagara University	1856	3,477	243	166,500
Polytechnic Inst. of N.Y.	Brooklyn	1854	4,700	217	251,500
Pratt Inst.	Brooklyn	1887	3,947	494	186,000
Rensselaer Polytech. Inst.	Troy	1824	5,700	344	500,000
Rochester Inst. of Tech.	Rochester	1829	13,265	993	180,900
St. Bonaventure U.	St. Bonaventure	1856	2,590	160	207,800
St. John's U.	Jamaica	1870	16,412	754	739,600
St. Lawrence U.	Canton	1856	2,432	174	303,000
State U. of N.Y. at Albany	Albany	1844	16,128	830	970,000
SUNY at Buffalo	Buffalo	1846	26,839	1,880	2,137,900
SUNY at Stony Brook	Stony Brook	1957	14,742	866	1,137,100
State U. Colleges					
Brockport	Brockport	1836	7,300	400	387,200
Buffalo	Buffalo	1867	21,759	556	408,400
Cortland	Cortland	1868	6,103	372	235,000
Fredonia	Fredonia	1867	5,262	284	313,600
Geneseo	Geneseo	1867	5,231	290	364,400
New Paltz	New Paltz	1828	6,902	399	345,800
Oneonta	Oneonta	1889	5,855	350	500,000
Oswego	Oswego	1861	7,615	722	400,000
Plattsburgh	Plattsburgh	1889	6,155	375	230,800
Potsdam	Potsdam	1816	5,695	291	250,000
Syracuse U.	Syracuse	1870	16,416	1,204	2,000,000
U.S. Merchant Marine Acad.	Kings Point	1943	1,100	80	100,000
U.S. Military Academy	West Point	1802	4,492	550	400,000
U. of Rochester	Rochester	1850	8,320	1,024	1,900,000
Vassar	Poughkeepsie	1861	2,250	228	500,000
Wagner	Staten Island	1883	2,451	150	260,000
Yeshiva U.	New York	1886	4,452	2,486	850,000
NORTH CAROLINA					
Appalachian State U.	Boone	1899	9,034	550	360,000
Catawba	Salisbury	1851	988	57	180,000
Davidson	Davidson	1837	1,402	203	280,000
Duke U.	Durham	1838	9,794	1,451	3,218,000
East Carolina U.	Greenville	1907	13,304	677	676,900
Lenoir-Rhyne	Hickory	1891	1,325	92	100,000
N. Carolina A. & T. St. U.	Greensboro	1891	5,467	342	294,500
N. Carolina State U.	Raleigh	1887	21,225	1,064	1,000,000
U. of N.C. at Chapel Hill	Chapel Hill	1789	21,465	1,887	2,487,100
U. of N.C. at Greensboro	Greensboro	1891	10,126	628	1,400,000
Wake Forest U.	Winston-Salem	1834	4,773	631	649,100
Western Carolina U.	Cullowhee	1889	6,459	322	310,300
NORTH DAKOTA					
North Dakota State U.	Fargo	1890	6,700	573	344,700
U. of North Dakota	Grand Forks	1883	10,217	501	425,000
OHIO					
Antioch	Yellow Springs	1852	1,000	75	240,000
Bowling Green State U.	Bowling Green	1910	16,335	791	679,800
Case Western Reserve U.	Cleveland	1826	7,869	1,700	1,576,000
Cleveland State U.	Cleveland	1964	18,944	692	515,000
Denison U.	Granville	1831	2,172	192	253,400
John Carroll U.	Cleveland	1886	4,000	250	360,000
Kent State U.	Kent	1910	25,000	800	1,500,000
Kenyon	Gambier	1824	1,450	116	275,800
Marietta	Marietta	1835	1,330	93	257,500
Miami U.	Oxford	1809	17,865	762	988,000
Oberlin	Oberlin	1833	2,799	226	789,400
Ohio State U.	Columbus	1870	57,938	3,681	3,497,900
Ohio U.	Athens	1804	14,149	863	1,200,000
U. of Akron	Akron	1870	26,365	1,366	728,200
U. of Cincinnati	Cincinnati	1819	30,453	2,214	1,500,000
U. of Dayton	Dayton	1850	10,785	575	693,000
U. of Toledo	Toledo	1872	21,117	946	690,000
Wooster	Wooster	1866	1,796	145	300,000
Xavier U.	Cincinnati	1831	6,985	202	325,000
Youngstown State U.	Youngstown	1908	15,584	834	473,000
OKLAHOMA					
Central State U.	Edmond	1890	12,763	415	604,700
Oklahoma State U.	Stillwater	1890	23,053	1,580	1,300,000
U. of Oklahoma	Norman	1890	21,532	908	2,045,500
U. of Tulsa	Tulsa	1894	6,127	416	835,500
OREGON					
Lewis and Clark	Portland	1867	2,320	147	172,100
Oregon State U.	Corvallis	1868	16,743	1,336	949,100
Portland State U.	Portland	1955	15,471	675	646,200
Reed	Portland	1909	1,155	116	280,000
U. of Oregon	Eugene	1872	16,645	1,595	1,540,300
PENNSYLVANIA					
Allegheny	Meadville	1815	1,979	159	310,000
Bryn Mawr	Bryn Mawr	1885	1,722	175	561,900
Bucknell U.	Lewisburg	1846	3,325	251	41,000
Carnegie-Mellon U.	Pittsburgh	1900	5,735	100	618,800
Dickinson	Carlisle	1773	1,685	120	312,000
Drexel U.	Philadelphia	1891	13,714	353	425,000
Duquesne U.	Pittsburgh	1878	6,319	503	450,700
Edinboro State	Edinboro	1857	5,600	396	337,000
Franklin and Marshall	Lancaster	1787	2,018	151	190,000
Gettysburg	Gettysburg	1832	1,916	170	269,200
Indiana U. of Pa.	Indiana	1875	12,503	676	530,000
Juniata	Huntingdon	1876	1,307	94	200,000
Lafayette	Easton	1826	2,398	200	375,000
La Salle	Philadelphia	1863	7,164	363	272,900
Lehigh U.	Bethlehem	1865	6,354	538	770,000
Moravian	Bethlehem	1742	1,494	85	141,000
Muhlenberg	Allentown	1848	2,362	129	177,900
Pennsylvania State U.	University Park	1855	36,693	1,565	1,638,000

Universities and Colleges (continued)

Selected four-year schools

Institution	Location	Year founded	Total students[2]	Total faculty[3]	Bound library volumes
St. Joseph's	Philadelphia	1851	6,235	350	195,700
Slippery Rock State	Slippery Rock	1889	5,600	343	406,700
Susquehanna U.	Selinsgrove	1858	1,417	107	125,000
Swarthmore	Swarthmore	1864	1,316	133	579,900
Temple U.	Philadelphia	1884	31,474	2,686	1,600,000
U. of Pennsylvania	Philadelphia	1740	22,317	3,682	3,054,200
U. of Pittsburgh	Pittsburgh	1787	29,206	2,630	2,386,500
Ursinus	Collegeville	1869	2,085	163	161,000
Villanova U.	Villanova	1842	7,636	666	450,000
West Chester State	West Chester	1812	8,600	512	385,000
PUERTO RICO					
Inter American U.	San Juan	1912	15,401	758	104,000
U. of Puerto Rico	Río Piedras	1903	50,492	2,722	2,156,000
RHODE ISLAND					
Brown U.	Providence	1764	6,784	493	1,709,300
Rhode Island	Providence	1854	7,582	376	275,000
U. of Rhode Island	Kingston	1892	10,133	885	731,000
SOUTH CAROLINA					
The Citadel[5]	Charleston	1842	3,435	197	367,000
Clemson U.	Clemson	1889	11,579	1,789	944,600
Furman U.	Greenville	1826	3,105	166	272,000
U. of South Carolina	Columbia	1801	24,498	1,173[4]	1,904,000
SOUTH DAKOTA					
South Dakota State U.	Brookings	1881	7,289	325	325,000
U. of South Dakota	Vermillion	1882	6,175	487	329,400
TENNESSEE					
Fisk U.	Nashville	1867	1,100	91	189,200
Memphis State U.	Memphis	1909	20,624	852	1,051,000
Middle Tennessee State U.	Murfreesboro	1911	10,933	505	453,000
Tennessee State U.	Nashville	1912	5,698	302	445,000
Tennessee Tech. U.	Cookeville	1915	7,851	530	409,800
U. of Tennessee	Knoxville	1794	45,402	3,392	1,436,000
Vanderbilt U.	Nashville	1873	8,911	2,182	1,439,300
TEXAS					
Austin	Sherman	1849	1,190	114	179,000
Baylor U.	Waco	1845	10,320	983	948,600
East Texas State U.	Commerce	1889	8,752	365	527,700
Hardin-Simmons U.	Abilene	1891	1,948	129	167,200
Lamar U.	Beaumont	1923	14,700	627	650,000
North Texas State U.	Denton	1890	18,928	815	1,350,000
Prairie View A. & M.	Prairie View	1876	4,800	292	195,000
Rice U.	Houston	1891	3,600	410	1,000,000
Sam Houston State U.	Huntsville	1879	10,470	330[4]	659,000
Southern Methodist U.	Dallas	1911	9,112	589	1,700,000
Southwest Texas State U.	San Marcos	1899	16,414	1,257	603,100
Stephen F. Austin State U.	Nacogdoches	1923	10,300	435	254,000
Texas A. & I. U.	Kingsville	1925	5,357	217	633,500
Texas A. & M. U.	College Station	1876	35,000	1,700	1,150,000
Texas Christian U.	Fort Worth	1873	6,881	361[4]	1,044,300
Texas Southern U.	Houston	1947	8,102	390	573,000
Texas Tech. U.	Lubbock	1923	23,100	1,386	2,500,000
U. of Houston	Houston	1927	29,000	1,800	1,100,000
U. of Texas at Arlington	Arlington	1895	22,171	930	750,000
U. of Texas at Austin	Austin	1881	48,039	1,989[4]	4,846,800
U. of Texas at El Paso	El Paso	1913	15,750	663	482,800
West Texas State U.	Canyon	1909	6,803	498	270,100
UTAH					
Brigham Young U.	Provo	1875	27,646	1,286	1,521,000
U. of Utah	Salt Lake City	1850	21,880	1,350	1,500,000
Utah State U.	Logan	1888	10,290	487[4]	638,100
Weber State	Ogden	1889	10,000	425	382,300
VERMONT					
Bennington	Bennington	1925	600	65	80,000
Middlebury	Middlebury	1800	1,900	179	457,000
U. of Vermont	Burlington	1791	11,103	1,355	1,035,000
VIRGINIA					
James Madison U.	Harrisonburg	1908	9,048	521	300,000
Old Dominion U.	Norfolk	1930	15,139	646	638,100
U. of Richmond	Richmond	1830	4,411	295	289,100
U. of Virginia	Charlottesville	1819	16,420	1,637	2,466,800
Virginia Commonwealth U.	Richmond	1838	19,000	2,269	550,000
Virginia Military Inst.[5]	Lexington	1839	1,321	138	268,300
Va. Polytech. Inst. & State U.	Blacksburg	1872	18,214	2,026	1,515,200
Washington & Lee U.[5]	Lexington	1749	1,714	174	290,600
William & Mary	Williamsburg	1693	5,633	557	717,400
WASHINGTON					
Central Washington U.	Ellensburg	1891	7,134	379	300,000
Eastern Washington U.	Cheney	1890	7,469	373	354,000
Gonzaga U.	Spokane	1887	3,532	196	298,800
U. of Washington	Seattle	1861	35,000	2,593	4,025,400
Washington State U.	Pullman	1890	16,746	1,108	1,304,500
Western Washington U.	Bellingham	1893	9,352	425[4]	400,000
Whitman	Walla Walla	1859	1,140	85	272,700
WEST VIRGINIA					
Bethany	Bethany	1840	778	79	144,000
Marshall U.	Huntington	1837	11,741	524	345,500
West Virginia U.	Morgantown	1867	21,337	2,237	1,013,000
WISCONSIN					
Beloit	Beloit	1846	1,081	87	268,600
Lawrence U.	Appleton	1847	1,158	103	236,000
Marquette U.	Milwaukee	1881	13,932	850	700,000
Ripon	Ripon	1851	930	81	114,000
St. Norbert	De Pere	1898	1,706	147	87,000
U. of W.-Eau Claire	Eau Claire	1916	11,054	670	643,600
U. of W.-Green Bay	Green Bay	1965	4,000	242	350,900
U. of W.-La Crosse	La Crosse	1909	8,659	423	333,100
U. of W.-Madison	Madison	1848	42,230	2,175	4,044,100
U. of W.-Milwaukee	Milwaukee	1956	26,122	1,222	1,350,000
U. of W.-Oshkosh	Oshkosh	1871	10,800	544	624,900
U. of W.-Platteville	Platteville	1866	4,713	354	195,000
U. of W.-River Falls	River Falls	1874	5,334	255	201,000
U. of W.-Stevens Point	Stevens Point	1894	9,045	419	522,000
U. of W.-Stout	Menomonie	1893	7,596	333[4]	175,000
U. of W.-Superior	Superior	1896	2,170	136[4]	219,000
U. of W.-Whitewater	Whitewater	1868	10,006	527	287,000
WYOMING					
U. of Wyoming	Laramie	1886	10,210	982	960,000

[1] Latest data available; coeducational unless otherwise indicated. [2] Total includes part-time students. [3] Total includes part-time or full-time equivalent faculty.
[4] Total includes full-time equivalent only. [5] Men's school. [6] Women's school.

LIVING CONDITIONS

Health Personnel and Facilities

State	Physicians Dec. 31, 1980[1]	Dentists 1979	Registered Nurses 1977–78	Hospital facilities 1981 Hospitals	Hospital facilities 1981 Beds	Nursing homes 1980 Facilities	Nursing homes 1980 Beds
Alabama	5,039	1,314	13,372	146	25,838	210	20,651
Alaska	509	232	2,474	26	1,729	9	1,029
Arizona	5,535	1,173	19,139	78	11,636	120	19,209
Arkansas	2,939	714	8,253	96	13,379	211	19,238
California	58,368	14,052	125,308	594	111,774	1,121	101,070
Colorado	5,999	1,701	20,801	98	14,956	161	17,310
Connecticut	8,177	2,194	27,857	65	18,129	320	21,244
Delaware	1,001	265	4,993	15	4,160	32	2,530
District of Columbia	3,626	587	6,613	17	8,730	49	3,180
Florida	20,374	4,323	55,368	252	58,870	355	36,122
Georgia	8,060	2,167	23,628	192	32,353	326	30,041
Hawaii	2,020	599	5,174	27	4,121	243	2,805
Idaho	1,089	459	4,962	52	3,977	57	4,355
Illinois	21,740	5,999	74,262	281	71,498	761	88,383
Indiana	7,415	2,234	28,069	134	32,160	459	44,551
Iowa	3,847	1,396	20,171	139	20,673	489	34,641
Kansas	3,893	1,080	16,143	166	18,283	357	25,208
Kentucky	5,059	1,490	15,583	118	18,948	310	26,265
Louisiana	6,752	1,586	14,298	156	26,546	201	21,672
Maine	1,865	489	8,966	49	6,818	424	11,317
Maryland	11,745	2,591	28,117	85	24,969	187	20,726
Massachusetts	16,342	3,983	61,664	179	42,252	803	55,251
Michigan	15,347	4,772	56,888	236	48,963	514	61,258
Minnesota	8,150	2,429	31,299	184	30,015	409	41,931
Mississippi	2,797	763	8,243	118	17,703	156	12,253
Missouri	8,331	2,303	26,662	166	34,599	867	46,691
Montana	1,100	442	5,326	67	5,204	86	5,652
Nebraska	2,442	931	12,002	110	11,928	262	18,990
Nevada	1,171	340	3,586	25	3,447	31	2,022
New Hampshire	1,655	465	9,457	34	4,742	87	6,672
New Jersey	14,799	4,706	49,969	132	42,193	471	37,825
New Mexico	2,143	511	6,281	56	6,011	72	3,075
New York	49,105	12,611	132,209	345	126,029	828	103,952
North Carolina	9,354	2,175	30,125	160	32,465	940	32,173
North Dakota	919	312	4,735	59	5,959	86	6,450
Ohio	18,342	5,064	69,620	239	64,019	960	76,280
Oklahoma	4,031	1,192	11,949	140	16,995	348	27,101
Oregon	5,119	1,685	15,199	83	11,946	196	17,382
Pennsylvania	23,347	6,272	107,153	312	83,600	550	75,907
Rhode Island	2,102	509	7,991	21	5,999	110	8,653
South Carolina	4,362	1,130	12,982	91	17,274	194	11,990
South Dakota	809	286	4,617	69	5,874	138	8,647
Tennessee	7,480	2,034	18,569	167	31,513	249	21,692
Texas	22,571	5,757	54,549	563	83,147	997	101,328
Utah	2,492	853	6,164	42	5,390	74	5,052
Vermont	1,185	270	4,750	19	2,918	172	4,706
Virginia	9,682	2,599	30,204	136	31,357	436	27,377
Washington	7,921	2,611	29,165	123	16,023	543	39,153
West Virginia	2,745	703	9,440	76	12,887	120	6,423
Wisconsin	7,859	2,654	28,359	164	28,773	427	49,847
Wyoming	567	216	2,506	31	2,741	19	1,759
TOTAL U.S.	**439,249**	**117,223**	**1,375,208**	**6,933**	**1,361,513**	**17,547**	**1,469,039**

[1] Non-federal only. Sources: Bidese, C. and Danais, D., *Physician Characteristics and Distribution in the U.S.*, 1981 Edition, Division of Survey and Data Resources, American Medical Association, Chicago, 1981; American Dental Association, *Distribution of Dentists in the United States by State, Region, District, and County, 1979*; American Nurses' Association; American Hospital Association, *Hospital Statistics, 1981 Edition*; U.S. Dept. of Health, Education, and Welfare, Public Health Service.

Crime Rates per 100,000 Population

State or metropolitan area	VIOLENT CRIME										PROPERTY CRIME								
	Total		Murder		Rape		Robbery		Assault		Total		Burglary		Larceny		Auto theft	
	1976	1981	1976	1981	1976	1981	1976	1981	1976	1981	1976	1981	1976	1981	1976	1981	1976	1981
Alabama	388.8	470.5	**15.1**	11.9	21.7	26.1	96.0	126.5	256.0	306.1	3,419.5	4,428.3	1,170.0	1,450.7	1,987.2	2,693.3	262.3	284.2
Alaska	540.1	615.8	11.3	14.6	46.9	**102.2**	124.9	114.6	357.1	384.5	5,680.5	5,979.1	1,218.1	1,329.9	3,656.8	3,958.7	805.8	690.5
Arizona	455.3	575.8	7.8	8.1	29.7	38.1	129.9	177.6	287.9	352.0	7,431.1	7,038.1	2,366.6	2,064.3	4,642.7	**4,563.9**	421.8	410.0
Arkansas	303.9	310.3	10.1	9.1	24.2	25.2	76.7	77.4	192.9	198.6	3,102.8	3,486.1	937.5	1,078.1	2,013.9	2,221.4	151.4	186.6
California	669.3	863.0	10.3	13.0	44.7	56.2	275.6	388.2	338.7	405.6	6,564.7	6,727.5	2,174.6	2,238.5	3,745.8	3,816.1	644.3	672.9
Colorado	417.0	531.7	6.8	8.1	33.8	45.6	139.7	159.5	236.7	318.5	6,365.4	6,821.4	1,879.9	2,031.6	4,043.5	4,375.9	442.0	413.9
Connecticut	273.2	448.1	3.1	5.4	14.4	21.9	122.9	246.1	132.8	174.6	4,731.4	5,389.2	1,383.9	1,691.9	2,785.8	3,094.1	561.8	602.6
Delaware	321.6	509.0	6.2	6.7	17.7	28.4	128.7	141.1	169.1	332.8	5,942.8	6,180.3	1,542.6	1,609.9	3,915.8	4,140.3	484.4	430.1
Florida	648.3	965.1	10.7	15.0	36.3	56.1	186.4	348.9	415.0	**545.0**	6,368.4	7,067.4	1,954.7	2,375.9	4,074.0	4,241.8	339.7	449.7
Georgia	423.1	548.2	13.9	17.2	24.9	42.4	142.4	196.4	241.9	292.1	4,386.4	5,080.4	1,448.4	1,672.1	2,618.3	3,073.6	319.7	334.6
Hawaii	229.3	247.6	6.2	4.8	23.5	34.7	133.0	148.4	66.5	59.7	6,092.7	6,295.8	1,881.6	1,708.5	3,669.0	4,157.2	542.1	430.1
Idaho	226.7	283.3	5.3	4.5	18.7	20.6	40.0	37.7	162.8	220.4	4,043.8	4,247.4	1,036.7	1,173.6	2,776.9	2,859.5	230.2	214.3
Illinois	468.8	444.1	10.3	10.5	21.5	24.1	219.5	209.3	217.5	200.2	4,586.3	4,506.1	1,089.7	1,163.3	2,991.8	2,852.9	504.8	489.9
Indiana	315.4	341.6	7.1	7.1	23.2	29.6	128.8	129.0	156.3	176.0	4,357.9	4,198.2	1,215.6	1,168.8	2,769.9	2,690.0	372.4	339.3
Iowa	132.9	204.2	2.3	2.6	10.7	13.4	41.1	53.6	78.7	134.5	3,918.6	4,512.4	827.1	1,067.5	2,884.6	3,221.7	206.9	223.2
Kansas	282.6	369.4	4.5	6.3	21.9	30.8	85.8	109.7	170.4	222.6	4,495.8	5,034.9	1,325.5	1,544.2	2,938.1	3,235.6	232.3	255.1
Kentucky	262.2	289.5	10.6	8.4	17.8	20.9	98.7	100.7	135.1	159.5	3,034.7	3,242.0	930.2	1,062.4	1,857.7	1,944.7	246.8	235.0
Louisiana	472.8	638.3	13.2	15.6	26.8	41.4	124.3	202.0	308.5	379.2	3,838.2	4,629.4	1,140.6	1,434.5	2,447.0	2,832.9	300.6	362.0
Maine	220.0	195.6	2.7	3.2	9.9	12.8	37.9	32.5	169.4	147.1	3,864.4	4,047.7	1,313.2	1,243.9	2,337.5	2,610.0	213.7	193.8
Maryland	633.4	887.1	8.5	9.9	32.0	38.8	295.5	424.4	297.4	414.0	5,031.0	5,670.6	1,359.9	1,560.2	3,242.2	3,576.7	428.9	433.7
Massachusetts	399.2	628.6	3.3	3.6	17.7	27.4	180.2	270.9	198.3	326.7	5,421.7	5,206.7	1,662.1	1,647.8	2,446.8	2,559.6	**1,312.7**	**999.3**
Michigan	646.0	641.9	11.1	9.4	36.1	47.5	332.6	257.5	266.1	327.6	5,332.2	6,212.2	1,668.5	1,862.1	3,550.6	3,714.9	613.1	635.2
Minnesota	189.0	228.5	2.3	2.1	18.3	25.8	80.4	104.3	87.9	96.3	4,142.1	4,508.2	1,122.1	1,277.6	2,672.8	2,978.8	347.1	251.8
Mississippi	295.4	304.6	12.5	12.6	16.3	26.0	64.1	81.4	202.5	184.6	2,172.9	3,232.8	811.3	1,170.5	1,239.4	1,880.9	122.2	181.3
Missouri	449.4	540.2	9.3	10.4	27.1	29.7	204.1	215.2	208.9	284.8	4,584.7	4,811.2	1,403.2	1,583.1	2,794.9	2,846.6	386.6	381.4
Montana	180.3	253.0	5.0	3.4	13.5	22.1	35.6	38.1	126.2	189.4	4,081.5	4,765.9	841	966.0	2,932.7	3,519.4	307.8	280.4
Nebraska	210.5	181.5	2.9	3.1	20.5	20.5	63.0	70.7	124.1	87.2	3,351.4	3,996.0	684.2	912.6	2,433.7	2,875.9	233.5	207.5
Nevada	691.0	896.4	11.5	**17.5**	**47.2**	54.9	294.9	458.0	337.4	356.1	**7,615.1**	**7,695.5**	**2,392.5**	**2,727.3**	**4,717.4**	4,373.4	505.2	594.8
New Hampshire	86.3	147.1	3.3	2.9	9.7	16.5	24.8	35.8	48.4	91.9	3,525.1	4,174.8	937.5	1,186.1	2,335.3	2,747.8	252.3	240.9
New Jersey	396.8	630.6	5.2	7.3	19.9	32.1	200.3	334.6	171.4	256.7	5,003.7	5,549.2	1,504.2	1,733.2	2,988.9	3,132.6	510.7	683.3
New Mexico	554.4	671.7	9.7	11.4	41.0	47.3	124.7	140.8	378.9	472.2	5,660.6	5,528.9	1,679.5	1,513.0	3,651.5	3,560.8	329.5	355.1
New York	**858.1**	**1,069.6**	10.9	12.3	25.8	31.1	**529.3**	**684.0**	302.1	342.1	5,357.0	5,835.8	1,763.5	1,991.7	2,855.2	3,066.3	738.2	777.8
North Carolina	403.4	436.6	11.1	9.1	15.3	22.7	70.6	80.8	306.4	324.1	3,477.8	4,083.5	1,175.5	1,336.7	2,124.0	2,548.8	178.3	198.1
North Dakota	71.9	67.5	1.4	2.3	5.6	8.7	16.2	12.9	48.7	43.6	2,442.5	2,923.6	478.5	500.6	1,804.5	2,258.2	159.4	164.7
Ohio	388.7	496.6	7.4	7.4	25.3	31.0	183.8	236.9	171.7	221.3	4,559.5	4,950.8	1,203.2	1,493.6	2,978.2	3,032.4	378.1	424.8
Oklahoma	286.6	426.8	6.4	9.0	27.0	35.2	70.3	115.4	182.8	267.2	4,194.3	4,410.5	1,317.5	1,588.8	2,570.4	2,403.5	306.4	418.2
Oregon	457.4	478.7	4.2	4.4	35.6	41.7	132.7	180.6	285.0	251.9	5,901.4	6,558.2	1,699.7	1,967.0	3,806.8	4,250.8	394.8	340.4
Pennsylvania	294.9	371.7	6.1	6.1	18.1	22.4	138.0	186.6	132.8	156.6	3,045.0	3,311.5	906.0	1,031.5	1,790.8	1,910.8	348.2	369.2
Rhode Island	299.8	441.7	2.4	4.2	8.5	17.9	91.0	132.0	197.8	287.6	5,350.4	5,410.1	1,414.2	1,654.9	3,050.6	2,891.3	885.5	863.9
South Carolina	599.2	640.4	11.6	10.4	31.9	36.3	105.7	120.2	**450.0**	473.5	4,307.7	4,678.7	1,553.5	1,595.7	2,503.2	2,807.5	250.9	275.4
South Dakota	186.2	104.8	1.7	1.8	15.3	11.5	23.2	17.8	145.9	73.7	2,454.2	2,908.3	620.4	634.7	1,684.3	2,129.5	149.6	144.1
Tennessee	393.3	412.6	11.0	9.7	25.4	37.6	147.5	171.7	209.4	193.5	3,865.1	3,898.9	1,320.5	1,384.2	2,218.6	2,180.6	325.9	334.1
Texas	355.7	532.4	12.2	16.6	29.4	46.2	139.0	193.3	175.3	276.3	5,108.7	5,517.9	1,547.8	1,870.4	3,209.5	3,082.9	351.3	564.6
Utah	220.6	298.6	4.5	3.3	20.9	28.4	69.4	84.8	125.8	182.1	4,757.2	5,451.4	1,137.9	1,274.8	3,302.0	3,882.3	317.3	294.3
Vermont	118.3	128.0	5.5	4.3	14.9	33.0	17.9	27.6	80.0	63.1	3,073.9	4,932.8	1,022.7	1,559.8	1,853.2	3,079.6	198.1	293.4
Virginia	307.7	321.7	9.5	8.6	22.2	27.2	108.2	133.2	167.9	152.7	3,895.4	4,349.1	1,019.1	1,167.5	2,650.2	2,979.7	226.1	201.9
Washington	388.6	447.3	4.3	5.1	34.3	50.2	119.5	130.0	230.5	262.0	5,405.4	6,294.8	1,642.4	1,892.1	3,414.3	4,083.4	348.7	319.2
West Virginia	151.6	174.8	6.7	6.0	10.3	14.8	38.0	50.2	96.6	103.7	2,168.0	2,443.9	573.1	775.1	1,459.0	1,480.5	135.9	188.4
Wisconsin	137.7	187.9	3.0	3.4	11.8	15.5	59.3	68.5	63.5	100.2	3,763.0	4,579.0	843.8	1,072.2	2,696.4	3,289.6	222.8	217.2
Wyoming	218.2	430.1	6.9	5.5	24.9	35.4	29.2	41.9	157.2	347.4	3,756.9	4,701.8	754.6	961.0	2,750.3	3,449.6	242.1	291.3
Baltimore	846.6	1,209.9	11.0	13.5	35.3	41.8	416.9	585.8	382.4	**568.9**	5,453.5	6,169.1	1,453.7	1,814.9	3,492.2	3,873.8	507.6	480.4
Boston	484.0	768.1	3.8	4.5	20.1	28.9	246.3	398.3	213.7	336.3	5,617.8	5,555.2	1,562.0	1,628.0	2,407.1	2,605.9	**1,648.7**	**1,321.4**
Chicago	581.1	528.9	13.4	14.2	24.1	26.4	299.4	289.9	244.2	198.4	5,174.9	4,824.1	1,151.7	1,160.1	3,331.9	2,974.9	691.3	689.1
Cleveland	584.6	839.3	15.1	13.9	33.4	42.1	336.2	478.5	199.9	304.7	4,576.3	4,984.4	1,154.2	1,551.4	2,505.9	2,267.2	916.2	1,165.8
Dallas	454.1	730.0	14.5	16.4	39.2	65.1	185.1	294.4	215.3	354.1	6,826.3	**7,465.4**	1,861.5	2,388.9	**4,563.8**	4,514.0	401.4	562.5
Detroit	960.4	848.2	**18.1**	14.7	44.0	50.7	593.8	439.1	304.6	343.7	6,711.9	7,085.1	1,906.4	2,193.0	3,765.5	3,789.1	1,040.1	1,103.0
Los Angeles	951.8	1,300.5	13.8	19.6	**57.9**	**70.3**	400.9	652.3	**479.2**	558.3	6,264.6	6,997.8	**2,271.3**	2,507.0	3,113.3	3,443.2	880.0	1,047.7
Minneapolis	301.1	369.5	2.9	2.7	27.6	37.6	139.3	188.3	131.3	140.8	5,364.5	5,808.8	1,479.2	1,728.4	3,382.9	3,735.2	502.4	345.2
Newark	568.2	1,059.8	7.7	11.9	27.7	52.1	306.1	617.5	226.8	378.3	5,042.0	5,633.8	1,571.0	1,803.5	2,856.2	2,967.8	614.7	862.5
New York	**1,437.2**	**1,785.5**	17.5	**20.7**	37.2	44.8	**915.0**	**1,212.5**	467.5	507.5	6,415.4	7,248.1	2,263.1	**2,555.6**	3,057.3	3,440.2	1,095.0	1,252.3
Philadelphia	446.2	628.9	10.0	10.3	25.6	35.5	226.6	325.6	183.9	257.1	3,781.1	4,677.8	1,132.3	1,486.3	2,131.8	2,550.5	517.1	640.9
Pittsburgh	331.6	425.6	4.3	4.3	21.1	22.5	158.9	249.5	146.7	149.4	3,190.2	2,945.0	896.5	950.6	1,820.8	1,536.7	473.0	457.7
St. Louis	647.4	693.9	13.1	15.7	38.1	35.2	321.5	297.9	274.6	345.1	5,813.5	5,603.0	1,772.4	1,853.7	3,432.7	3,208.9	608.4	540.4
San Francisco	802.3	931.9	12.2	12.4	50.4	58.0	420.5	484.1	319.3	377.3	**7,691.5**	7,443.6	2,458.4	2,243.4	4,487.1	**4,600.3**	745.9	599.9
Washington, D.C.	620.9	870.2	10.1	11.3	38.3	43.1	367.8	557.8	204.8	257.9	5,067.5	6,105.1	1,324.4	1,687.1	3,340.9	3,968.1	402.2	449.9

Boldface: highest rate among states or listed metropolitan areas. Source: U.S. Department of Justice, Federal Bureau of Investigation, *Uniform Crime Reports*.

TRANSPORTATION AND TRADE

Transportation

State	Road and street mi[1] 1982	Motor vehicles in 000s, 1981[2]			Railroad mileage 1980[3]	Airports 1982[4]	Pipeline mileage 1981[5]
		Total	Automobiles	Trucks and buses			
Ala.	87,420	3,026	2,140	886	4,455	137	19,664
Alaska	9,085	259	158	101	550	509	1,212
Ariz.	78,286	2,047	1,458	589	1,865	174	16,817
Ark.	76,764	1,630	1,072	558	2,763	153	18,387
Calif.	176,665	17,744	14,019	3,725	6,862	566	80,837
Colo.	75,708	2,370	1,765	605	3,463	218	23,488
Conn.	19,442	2,189	2,022	167	637	54	6,798
Del.	5,249	402	324	78	280	23	1,339
D.C.	1,102	279	257	22	55	2	1,162
Fla.	97,186	7,882	6,398	1,484	3,681	369	12,651
Ga.	104,253	3,850	2,938	912	5,468	245	25,147
Hawaii	4,107	582	525	57	. . .	37	587
Idaho	57,442	861	531	330	2,413	178	4,435
Ill.	133,672	7,640	6,390	1,250	10,672	763	53,501
Ind.	91,676	3,859	2,900	959	5,948	320	28,762
Iowa	112,487	2,331	1,670	661	5,375	244	18,042
Kan.	132,209	2,038	1,404	634	7,266	355	37,318
Ky.	68,429	2,604	1,813	791	3,515	103	20,110
La.	56,676	2,863	2,016	847	3,373	175	42,256
Maine	21,902	744	525	219	1,487	112	389
Md.	27,005	2,857	2,393	464	1,243	105	8,764
Mass.	33,772	3,809	3,320	489	1,457	78	16,915
Mich.	117,396	6,582	5,326	1,256	4,185	381	44,486
Minn.	130,834	3,142	2,345	797	6,529	408	17,232
Miss.	70,442	1,635	1,269	366	3,063	165	18,101
Mo.	118,403	3,293	2,447	846	6,109	344	21,404
Mont.	71,703	723	455	268	3,815	179	8,538
Neb.	91,828	1,280	849	431	4,857	323	14,149
Nev.	43,442	687	492	195	1,564	102	3,658
N.H.	14,412	724	604	120	599	41	1,162
N.J.	33,490	4,871	4,360	511	1,607	120	23,106
N.M.	53,715	1,097	702	395	2,075	143	25,373
N.Y.	109,639	7,988	6,978	1,010	4,605	362	41,681
N.C.	92,587	4,617	3,421	1,196	3,577	244	12,090
N.D.	85,904	638	370	268	4,966	362	2,950
Ohio	110,645	7,990	6,536	1,454	7,224	518	52,981
Okla.	109,946	2,729	1,844	885	3,930	275	38,578
Ore.	121,408	2,127	1,579	548	2,944	252	10,070
Pa.	117,103	7,131	5,897	1,234	7,197	496	52,527
R.I.	6,275	640	557	83	146	12	2,425
S.C.	62,731	2,020	1,541	479	2,736	127	9,973
S.D.	73,018	608	371	237	1,759	157	2,622
Tenn.	83,497	3,335	2,597	738	3,136	127	16,502
Texas	258,253	10,787	7,606	3,181	13,313	1,184	120,880
Utah	43,735	1,000	682	318	1,656	85	8,504
Vt.	13,942	360	280	80	385	48	404
Va.	64,683	3,704	3,137	567	3,503	207	11,345
Wash.	83,291	3,306	2,344	962	4,378	279	11,883
W.Va.	34,999	1,384	978	406	3,565	60	22,331
Wis.	108,110	3,017	2,449	568	4,838	378	22,197
Wyo.	36,709	479	282	197	1,988	93	8,457
TOTAL	3,852,677	159,760	124,336	35,424	183,077	12,393	1,064,190

[1] Includes federally controlled roads. [2] Estimated registration, excluding military. [3] Class I and II line-haul only.
[4] Public and private. [5] Gas utility industry miles only. Sources: Assn. of American Railroads; Dept. of Transportation, FAA, FHWA; Dept. of Energy; Motor Vehicles Manufacturers Assn.

Communications Facilities

State	Post Offices Oct. 15, 1982	TELEPHONES Jan. 1, 1981 Total	TELEPHONES Jan. 1, 1981 Residential	COMMERCIAL BROADCAST STATIONS, 1980 Radio AM	FM	TV	Public TV stations 1981	NEWSPAPERS Sept. 30, 1981 Daily Number	Circulation	Weekly[1] Number	Circulation	Sunday Number	Circulation
Alabama	611	2,607,952	1,989,175	143	77	17	9	28	739,827	114	494,943	21	692,233
Alaska	186	304,541	185,537	22	12	7	4	8	116,310	12	25,556	2	90,267
Arizona	210	2,109,488	1,563,704	62	32	13	2	18	619,916	52	263,868	10	606,793
Arkansas	618	1,476,741	1,117,994	93	54	9	5	32	487,634	114	340,595	17	486,602
California	1,109	20,880,656	14,822,886	235	208	55	13	124	5,967,900	436	5,520,104	51	5,523,532
Colorado	406	2,451,231	1,744,961	72	53	12	3	27	920,997	123	437,912	10	950,059
Connecticut	242	2,705,133	2,005,660	39	25	5	4	25	896,209	55	655,916	10	755,306
Delaware	55	534,188	388,228	10	7	—	1	3	152,261	14	107,125	2	145,280
District of Columbia	1	1,106,368	522,063	8	9	5	2	1	662,978	. . .	. . .	1	890,079
Florida	459	8,277,482	6,186,830	200	118	32	10	52	2,645,076	140	1,037,646	33	2,781,201
Georgia	628	4,245,999	3,143,861	187	93	19	10	37	1,014,259	196	1,152,509	15	991,305
Hawaii	76	712,095	461,532	26	8	10	2	6	247,349	3	107,581	3	410,215
Idaho	256	707,315	524,239	44	23	8	3	14	212,765	57	134,355	7	191,804
Illinois	1,258	10,314,906	7,740,444	128	132	24	5	76	2,755,023	707	4,148,588	24	2,698,946
Indiana	749	4,166,434	3,183,064	86	95	20	7	76	1,629,089	179	672,130	18	1,442,038
Iowa	949	2,312,255	1,746,776	77	75	13	8	41	868,464	339	765,368	9	797,525
Kansas	686	1,992,067	1,504,871	60	47	12	2	47	580,125	223	440,902	18	493,911
Kentucky	1,200	2,347,628	1,784,088	123	88	11	16	26	745,576	141	631,637	11	932,352
Louisiana	526	2,998,226	2,273,191	95	65	16	6	25	794,077	99	572,529	16	1,100,412
Maine	490	811,841	626,780	38	33	7	5	9	291,793	35	176,727	1	211,758
Maryland	425	3,606,320	2,696,628	50	38	6	4	16	766,862	67	791,188	4	1,122,294
Massachusetts	422	4,629,265	3,371,923	67	39	12	3	46	2,024,932	141	1,059,526	10	2,107,278
Michigan	853	7,305,008	5,567,635	131	122	24	8	52	2,462,535	266	1,927,732	15	2,528,640
Minnesota	852	3,219,112	2,379,016	94	73	12	6	30	1,007,337	326	1,022,046	11	1,631,907
Mississippi	454	1,579,001	1,218,584	107	75	11	8	25	399,855	97	317,598	13	325,573
Missouri	957	3,876,602	2,905,020	112	80	24	4	49	1,511,144	270	1,558,021	18	2,214,847
Montana	359	623,211	455,912	46	25	12	—	11	200,720	72	156,949	8	201,946
Nebraska	541	1,324,919	989,941	49	37	14	9	19	484,891	193	465,156	6	413,074
Nevada	88	761,823	522,082	22	13	8	1	8	230,327	16	43,245	5	234,610
New Hampshire	239	723,589	545,198	28	15	2	5	9	199,186	25	189,703	2	81,092
New Jersey	519	6,724,802	4,999,405	39	36	5	4	26	1,687,084	191	2,118,339	17	1,679,718
New Mexico	326	878,317	616,374	57	29	9	3	20	281,035	25	198,853	14	259,298
New York	1,623	12,972,938	9,492,742	161	120	31	12	78	8,036,466	403	2,333,699	35	5,912,101
North Carolina	772	4,260,509	3,212,481	215	89	19	9	55	1,365,662	119	559,566	25	1,150,900
North Dakota	435	582,152	427,610	28	10	13	4	10	193,685	90	185,084	4	116,408
Ohio	1,069	8,134,567	6,180,998	124	130	25	12	95	3,280,090	262	2,003,802	29	2,841,254
Oklahoma	614	2,446,239	1,799,883	67	53	14	4	53	842,538	190	371,529	43	872,500
Oregon	345	2,046,122	1,462,266	80	37	12	5	21	685,545	92	403,429	7	628,829
Pennsylvania	1,773	9,877,461	7,519,932	179	125	28	8	98	3,298,111	220	1,619,603	19	2,610,707
Rhode Island	55	730,830	549,827	15	7	2	1	7	314,366	15	90,109	2	239,231
South Carolina	387	2,130,377	1,595,719	108	56	12	10	19	607,021	70	290,973	8	505,665
South Dakota	402	526,422	388,923	33	19	11	8	12	169,743	144	212,433	4	122,901
Tennessee	563	3,255,755	2,476,923	164	81	19	6	30	1,063,332	129	584,043	16	1,010,782
Texas	1,484	11,344,044	8,123,163	290	199	59	10	116	3,450,837	497	1,577,999	97	3,974,982
Utah	207	1,077,763	804,001	35	22	4	2	6	283,384	51	220,294	5	282,053
Vermont	282	375,577	276,925	19	12	2	4	8	118,392	20	60,210	3	78,792
Virginia	884	3,947,123	2,932,113	138	74	16	8	38	1,155,339	96	602,645	15	873,097
Washington	460	3,326,258	2,379,959	96	49	15	5	27	1,172,485	138	1,188,292	17	1,145,949
West Virginia	1,005	1,140,361	874,524	63	34	9	3	25	466,259	75	299,197	10	400,219
Wisconsin	774	3,570,248	2,662,194	102	94	20	8	36	1,222,209	230	746,679	10	922,480
Wyoming	165	405,398	281,699	31	10	6	—	10	101,745	33	86,957	4	74,755
TOTAL U.S.	30,049	180,383,387	133,225,484	4,498	3,057	751	291	1,731	61,430,745	7,602	40,970,890	755	55,180,004

[1] Excluding District of Columbia; data for Dec. 31, 1981.   Sources: U.S. Postal Service; Federal Communications Commission; American Telephone and Telegraph Co.; The Editor & Publisher Co., Inc., *International Year Book, 1982* (Copyright 1982. All rights reserved. Used by permission.); National Newspaper Association; Corporation for Public Broadcasting.

Major Trading Partners, by Value

in millions of dollars

Country	EXPORTS 1975	EXPORTS 1980	IMPORTS 1975	IMPORTS 1980
North America	30,100	56,738	30,771	64,281
Canada	21,785	35,395	21,913	41,459
Mexico	5,160	15,145	3,060	12,580
South America	8,808	17,380	7,340	14,389
Argentina	628	2,625	218	741
Brazil	3,062	4,344	1,465	3,715
Chile	533	1,354	138	515
Colombia	643	1,736	593	1,241
Peru	896	1,172	402	1,386
Venezuela	2,243	4,573	3,730	5,307
Europe	33,117	71,376	21,727	48,039
Belgium and Luxembourg	2,442	6,661	1,191	1,914
France	3,031	7,485	2,190	5,265
Germany, West	5,267	10,960	5,394	11,693
Italy	2,867	5,511	2,401	4,325
Netherlands, The	4,194	8,669	1,087	1,913
Spain	2,164	3,179	833	1,220
Sweden	925	1,767	877	1,617
Switzerland	1,180	3,781	968	2,803
United Kingdom	4,787	12,694	3,855	9,842
U.S.S.R.	1,835	1,513	255	454
Asia	28,913	62,041	28,434	80,851
Hong Kong	809	2,686	1,576	4,739
India	1,290	1,689	548	1,098
Indonesia	810	1,545	2,296	5,217
Iran	3,244	23	2,207	472
Israel	1,551	2,045	313	950
Japan	9,570	20,790	11,282	30,714
Korea, South	1,762	4,685	1,416	4,147
Malaysia	393	1,337	766	2,577
Philippines	832	1,999	760	1,730
Saudi Arabia	1,502	5,769	2,732	12,648
Singapore	994	3,033	539	1,921
Taiwan	1,659	4,337	1,940	6,854
Oceania	2,340	4,876	1,513	3,392
Australia	1,815	4,093	1,152	2,509
Africa	4,266	7,187	8,684	33,871
Algeria	632	542	1,359	6,577
Nigeria	536	1,150	3,396	11,105
South Africa	1,302	2,464	847	3,321
TOTAL	108,113	220,786	98,503	244,871

Source: U.S. Department of Commerce, International Trade Administration, *Overseas Business Reports.*

Major Commodities Traded

in millions of dollars

Item	1977	1978	1979	1980
TOTAL EXPORTS [1]	121,293	143,766	182,025	220,786
Agricultural commodities				
Grains and preparations	8,755	11,634	14,450	18,079
Soybeans	4,393	5,210	5,708	5,883
Cotton, including				
linters, wastes	1,899	2,302	3,047	3,929
Nonagricultural commodities				
Ores and scrap metals	1,290	1,839	3,325	4,518
Coal, coke, and briquettes	2,655	2,046	3,394	4,621
Chemicals	10,812	12,623	17,306	20,740
Machinery	32,630	38,105	45,914	57,263
Agricultural machines,				
tractors, parts	1,584	1,337	1,685	3,442
Electrical apparatus	3,264	4,359	5,671	7,763
Transport equipment	730	1,188	1,391	1,756
Civilian aircraft and parts	17,619	21,163	24,577	27,366
Paper manufactures	2,747	3,616	6,177	8,256
Metal manufactures	1,517	1,597	1,967	2,831
Iron and steel mill products	2,608	1,646	2,227	2,998
Yarn, fabrics, and clothing	1,970	2,225	3,189	3,632
Other exports	26,820	32,876	41,997	47,709
TOTAL IMPORTS [1]	150,390	174,762	209,458	244,871
Agricultural commodities				
Meat and preparations	1,276	1,856	2,539	2,346
Fish	2,056	2,212	2,639	2,612
Coffee	3,910	3,728	3,820	3,872
Sugar	1,076	723	974	1,988
Nonagricultural commodities				
Ores and scrap metal	2,732	2,813	3,249	3,696
Petroleum, crude	36,526	34,885	49,361	62,112
Petroleum products	7,846	6,886	9,753	15,525
Chemicals	4,970	6,430	7,479	8,583
Machinery	18,836	24,752	28,530	32,286
Transport equipment	17,571	22,838	25,148	28,260
Automobiles, new	10,623	13,646	14,812	16,775
Iron and steel mill products	5,302	6,681	6,764	6,686
Nonferrous metals	3,380	4,367	4,678	5,183
Textiles other than clothing	1,736	2,200	2,216	2,493
Other imports	32,550	40,745	47,496	52,454

[1] Includes Virgin Islands.
Source: U.S. Department of Commerce, International Trade Administration, *Overseas Business Reports.*

Upper Volta

A republic of West Africa, Upper Volta is bordered by Mali, Niger, Benin, Togo, Ghana, and Ivory Coast. Area: 274,200 sq km (105,900 sq mi). Pop. (1981 est.): 6,251,000. Cap. and largest city: Ouagadougou (pop., 1980 est., 235,000). Language: French (official). Religion: animist 49.8%; Muslim 16.6%; Roman Catholic 8.3%. President of the Military Committee of Recovery for National Progress and premier to Nov. 7, 1982, Col. Saye Zerbo; chairman of the Provisional Committee of Popular Salvation from that date, Maj. Jean-Baptiste Ouedraogo.

On Nov. 7, 1982, some days before he was to have left on an official visit to France, Col. Saye Zerbo was removed from power by a group of subalterns and noncommissioned officers. The organizer of the coup was thought to have been Capt. Thomas Sankara, who in November 1980 had planned to oust Pres. Sangoulé Lamizana but had been forestalled by Zerbo's seizure of power. However, Zerbo's military government was replaced by a Provisional Committee of Popular Salvation representing nationalist and progressive elements and headed by Maj. Jean-Baptiste Ouedraogo of the Army Medical Corps.

Before the coup the year had been marked by a continuing trial of strength between the Zerbo regime and the trade unions. The ban on strikes imposed in November 1981 was lifted in February 1982. In September the secretary-general of the banned trade union confederation, Soumane Touré, was arrested.

Relations with neighbouring Mali remained bad, and early in the year Upper Volta opposed Mali's reintegration into the West African Monetary Union. (PHILIPPE DECRAENE)

UPPER VOLTA

Education. (1979–80) Primary, pupils 185,658, teachers 2,997; secondary, pupils 20,529, teachers 580; vocational, pupils 3,000, teachers 580; teacher training, students 257, teachers 28; higher, students 3,173, teaching staff 166.

Finance. Monetary unit: CFA franc, with (Sept. 20, 1982) a par value of CFA Fr 50 to the French franc (free rate of CFA Fr 353 = U.S. $1; CFA Fr 605 = £1 sterling). Budget (1982 est.) balanced at CFA Fr 47.6 billion.

Foreign Trade. (1981) Imports CFA Fr 91,440,000,000; exports CFA Fr 19,920,000,000. Import sources (1979): France 35%; Ivory Coast 10%; U.S. 8%; West Germany 6%. Export destinations (1979) Ivory Coast 41%; France 18%; China 8%; West Germany 5%; Japan 5%. Main exports (1979): cotton 33%; livestock 26%; oilseeds and nuts 12%; hides and skins 5%; sugar 5%.

Uruguay

A republic of South America, Uruguay is on the Atlantic Ocean and is bounded by Brazil and Argentina. Area: 176,215 sq km (68,037 sq mi). Pop. (1982 est.): 2,967,000, including white 90%; mestizo 10%. Cap. and largest city: Montevideo (pop., 1980 est., 1,260,600). Language: Spanish. Religion (1980): Roman Catholic 59.5%; atheist 3.4%; Protestant 2%; Jewish 1.7%; other Christian 1.7%;

none 31.7%. President in 1982, Gen. Gregorio Conrado Alvarez Armelino.

The Council of State approved a law on political parties on June 3, 1982. Although the legislation introduced a limited form of democracy in preparation for presidential elections due in November 1984, the final text was much more restrictive than had been predicted. Only the Partido Colorado, the Blancos (Nationalists), and the tiny Unión Cívica (a splinter group from the Christian Democrats) were allowed to organize. The Christian Democrats and the left remained excluded. On No-

URUGUAY

Education. (1979) Primary, pupils 326,235, teachers 13,698; secondary, pupils 172,969, teachers (1976) c. 13,980; vocational, pupils (1978) 45,663, teachers (1976) c. 4,200; teacher training, students 4,765, teachers (1973) 341; higher (1977), students 39,392, teaching staff 3,263.

Finance. Monetary unit: new peso, with (Sept. 20, 1982) a free rate of 13.07 new pesos to U.S. $1 (22.40 new pesos = £1 sterling). Gold and other reserves (June 1981) U.S. $537 million. Budget (1980 actual): revenue 20,517,000,000 new pesos; expenditure 18,208,000,000 new pesos. Gross national product (1980) 89,493,000,000 new pesos. Cost of living (Montevideo; 1975 = 100; Feb. 1982) 1,418.

Foreign Trade. (1981) Imports U.S. $1,599,700,000; exports U.S. $1,215,400,000. Import sources (1980): Brazil 17%; Iraq 12%; Argentina 11%; U.S. 10%; Nigeria 8%; West Germany 7%; Venezuela 6%. Export destinations (1980): Brazil 18%; Argentina 13%; West Germany 13%; U.S. 8%; U.S.S.R. 5%. Main exports (1979): clothing 15%; wool 14%; meat 14%; fish 9%; rice 8%; leather 6%.

Transport and Communications. Roads (1977) 24,954 km. Motor vehicles in use (1980): passenger c. 173,000; commercial (including buses) c. 91,000. Railways: (1981) 3,004 km; traffic (1980) 418 million passenger-km, freight 249 million net ton-km. Air traffic (1980): c. 178 million passenger-km; freight c. 1 million net ton-km. Shipping (1981): merchant vessels 100 gross tons and over 76; gross tonnage 200,184. Telephones (Jan. 1978) 268,000. Radio receivers (Dec. 1979) 1,630,000. Television receivers (Dec. 1979) 362,000.

Agriculture. Production (in 000; metric tons; 1981): wheat c. 400; corn 196; rice 326; sorghum 192; potatoes c. 130; sweet potatoes c. 60; sugar, raw value c. 79; linseed 21; sunflower seed 41; apples c. 25; oranges c. 58; grapes 130; wool c. 50; beef and veal c. 404; fish catch (1980) 120. Livestock (in 000; 1981): cattle c. 10,971; sheep c. 20,429; pigs c. 450; horses c. 530; chickens c. 8,000.

Industry. Production (in 000; metric tons; 1980): crude steel 14; cement (1979) 687; petroleum products c. 1,810; electricity (kw-hr) 3,331,000.

A group of Argentine soldiers who were captured by the British during the Falklands war were sent to Montevideo for later transshipment to their homeland.

Upper Volta

Uruguay

Universities:
see Education

Urban Mass Transit:
see Transportation

vember 28 the approved parties held internal elections, which also acted as presidential primaries.

There was an increase in the repression of dissent. Magazines opposed to the junta's policy were closed down, and the military threatened that continued criticism of its actions could lead to a slowdown in the program of political liberalization. Discussion of the bleak economic situation was forbidden. The already faltering economy was adversely affected by the Falkland Islands conflict since Uruguay's economy was heavily influenced by that of Argentina. The country obtained a standby loan from the International Monetary Fund to compensate for a fall in export earnings and held talks with the IMF on wider-ranging support in November. (MICHAEL WOOLLER)

Vanuatu

Vatican City State

Vanuatu

The republic of Vanuatu, a member of the Commonwealth, comprises 12 main islands, the largest of which are Espíritu Santo, Malekula, Efate, Ambrym, Aoba, and Tanna, and some 60 smaller ones in the southwest Pacific Ocean, forming a chain some 800 km in length. Area: 12,190 sq km (4,707 sq mi). Pop. (1982 est.): 125,600, predominantly Melanesian. Cap. and largest city: Vila, on Efate Island (pop., 1979, 14,600). Language: Bislama, a Melanesian pidgin (national); French and English (official). Religion (1979): Presbyterian 36.7%; Roman Catholic 15%; Anglican 15%; other Christian 10%; other 23.3%. President in 1982, George Sokomanu; prime minister, the Rev. Walter Lini.

Despite two attempts to remove him by motions of no confidence, Vanuatu's Prime Minister Walter Lini remained firmly in power throughout 1982. The government produced its first five-year development plan. The plan was aimed at helping the country achieve economic self-reliance, and it advocated the full utilization of natural and manpower resources and the fostering of local businesses while preserving the Melanesian cultural heritage.

VANUATU

Education. (1982) Primary, pupils 23,595, teachers 1,063; secondary, pupils 2,067, teachers 126; vocational, pupils 293, teachers 31; teacher training, students 58, teachers 9.

Finance. Monetary unit: vatu, with (Sept. 20, 1982) a free rate of 98.30 vatu = U.S. $1 (168.50 vatu = £1 sterling). Budget (1980 rev. est.) balanced at 1,964,000,000 vatu (including grants from France and U. K.).

Foreign Trade. (1981) Imports 5,123,000,000 vatu; exports 2,833,000,000 vatu. Import sources: Australia c. 39%; Fiji c. 17%; Japan c. 13%; France c. 10%; New Zealand c. 8%; Spain c. 6%. Export destinations (domestic exports only): Belgium-Luxembourg 34%; France 27%; The Netherlands 25%; New Caledonia 6%. Main exports: copra 38%; frozen fish 29%; beef and veal 6%.

Agriculture. Production (in 000; metric tons; 1981): bananas c. 1; copra c. 34; cocoa c. 1; fish catch (1980) 2.8. Livestock (in 000; 1981): cattle c. 95; pigs c. 68; chickens c. 154.

At the end of 1981 Vanuatu claimed A$5 million from the U.K. and France, holding the former colonial powers responsible for the damage caused during the rebellion on Espíritu Santo that preceded independence in July 1980. The prime minister maintained pressure on France for an end to nuclear testing in the Pacific and for the decolonization of New Caledonia. On the latter issue he disagreed with his colleagues in the South Pacific Forum; in the light of reforms initiated by the French government the other nations in the group were more inclined to await developments.

(BARRIE MACDONALD)

Vatican City State

This independent sovereignty is surrounded by but is not part of Rome. As a state with territorial limits, it is properly distinguished from the Holy See, which constitutes the worldwide administrative and legislative body for the Roman Catholic Church. The area of Vatican City is 44 ha (108.8 ac). Pop. (1981 est.): 738. As sovereign pontiff, John Paul II is the chief of state. Vatican City is administered by a pontifical commission of five

Archbishop Paul Marcinkus, president of the Vatican's Institute for Religious Works, popularly called the Vatican bank, came under scrutiny during an investigation into the relationship between the Vatican bank and the Banco Ambrosiano, Italy's largest private banking group. That bank failed, leaving behind huge debts.

ANSA/TIME MAGAZINE

U.S.S.R.:
see Union of Soviet Socialist Republics

cardinals headed by the secretary of state, in 1982 Agostino Cardinal Casaroli.

In March 1982 a commission of 15 cardinals appointed by Pope John Paul II the previous May to examine the Vatican economy reported that the 1982 budgetary deficit would be some 17% higher than in 1981. Three months later Vatican finances attracted international attention as a result of widely publicized allegations of the involvement of the Institute for Religious Works—the Vatican bank—and its head, Archbishop Paul Marcinkus (*see* BIOGRAPHIES), in the dubious transactions of the collapsed Italian Banco Ambrosiano. A joint commission of experts representing the Vatican and the Italian state was to start its investigations into the affair early in 1983.

Following the example of Great Britain in March, Denmark, Norway, and Sweden established full diplomatic relations with the Vatican (formally, the Holy See) in August. During the year the pope received the presidents of Egypt, France, Greece, Somalia, the U.S., and Zaire. Most controversial was the visit on September 15 of Palestine Liberation Organization chairman Yasir Arafat; bitter Israeli condemnation provoked an unusually sharp response from the Vatican.

In November the pope declared 1983 a Holy Year. (MAX BERGERRE)

See also Religion: *Roman Catholic Church.*

Venezuela

A republic of northern South America, Venezuela is bounded by Colombia, Brazil, Guyana, and the Caribbean Sea. Area: 912,050 sq km (352,144 sq mi). Pop. (1982 est.): 14,714,400, including mestizo 69%; white 20%; Negro 9%; Indian 2%. Cap. and largest city: Caracas (metro area pop., 1981 est., 3,041,000). Language: Spanish. Religion: predominantly Roman Catholic. President in 1982, Luis Herrera Campins.

The economy of Venezuela suffered from a severe cash crisis in 1982, resulting from falling oil revenues, a sharp decline in international reserves, and a lack of confidence by investors. Devaluation of the bolívar and exchange controls were not considered necessary, but by September the government was forced to take action to stem the capital flight, which was reaching alarming proportions, similar to the peak recorded in March when fears about oil income were rife. Dollar sales by commercial banks reached the level of $80 million a day, and private capital flight caused a $3.5 billion drop in international reserves to $5 billion by mid-September. Oil revenues were expected to be 20% below the $16.5 billion earned from this source in 1981, and the money supply was falling despite an increase in oil output to over 2 million bbl a day in September, more than 500,000 bbl a day above the production limit agreed on by the Organization of Petroleum Exporting Countries (OPEC) in March.

In order to improve the country's financial image abroad, the government then resorted to certain accounting methods to boost reserves. These included revaluing its 326 million g (11.5 million

Venezuela

oz) of gold holdings from the official price of $42.22 per ounce to nearer the market value at $300 an ounce, recalling about $1.5 billion deposited in Venezuelan banks in which the state had a shareholding and $850 million from the central bank's stock-market support fund, and placing the foreign reserves of all state agencies (most importantly the state oil company, PDVSA, with reserves worth $5 billion) under central bank jurisdiction. This last step was important because it ended PDVSA's financial independence, maintained since the oil industry was nationalized in 1976.

By these means the government was able to raise international reserves to $15 billion, against a total public foreign debt of $18.5 billion. Attempts were also made to reorganize the debt profile and obtain loans on a longer term; the government negotiated with international banks to convert some $2.5 billion–$3 billion of the total $8.8 billion short-term debt into medium-term obligations.

The domestic political scene was dominated by the launching by the political parties of their campaigns for the December 1983 presidential elections. The ruling Social Christian party, COPEI, chose former president Rafael Caldera as its candidate, while the main opposition party, the social democratic Acción Democrática, nominated Jaime Lusinchi to stand for election.

Guerrilla activity reemerged in 1982 in the eastern part of the country, causing a series of confron-

Venda:
see South Africa

UPI

A policeman rescues an infant from a raging fire in an electric power plant in Caracas. The blaze left at least 129 people dead and 500 others injured.

tations between police patrols and bands of armed left-wing terrorists. One of the worst incidents, a shoot-out between army and guerrilla forces in October, left at least 25 people dead.

The dispute with Guyana over the border region of Essequibo reached a critical stage when the treaty granting a 12-year moratorium on the issue expired on June 18 and was not renewed. Tension had been heightened by news of the discovery of oil by a Canadian firm in the disputed region, and there were frequent Guyanese protests about alleged military incursions across the border by Venezuela. Under the 1966 Geneva agreement signed by Venezuela, Guyana, and the U.K., the two countries in dispute had three months after the expiration of the 1970 treaty to agree to a means of settlement. Venezuela rejected Guyana's proposal to submit the dispute to the International Court of Justice, and in September Pres. Luis Herrera Campins asked the UN to intervene after direct negotiations had failed. If the UN was unable to bring about a satisfactory conclusion, UN Secretary-General Javier Pérez de Cuéllar was to decide the issue. (SARAH CAMERON)

Veterinary Science

Artificial insemination of cattle with semen from proven sires is widely used to improve herd quality. If offspring of predetermined sex could be produced, important economic benefits would be gained. A development that could lead to accurate selection of sex before fertilization was announced in 1982 by International Resource Development Inc. of Norwalk, Conn. By using specific antibodies to identify proteins in the male sperm, scientists can separate female- and male-producing sperm. If this technique could be incorporated into artificial insemination programs, considerable improvement in the productivity of the dairy and beef cattle industries could result.

Other advances in the field of biotechnology led to the production of new vaccines against scours (diarrhea) in pigs and calves. The bacterium *Escherichia coli* is a major cause of infectious diarrhea, which occurs when bacterial components called adhesion factors are present. These factors were isolated and purified; then, by means of cloning techniques, the genes responsible for producing them were transferred to a special laboratory strain of *E. coli* that generated large quantities of antigen, the substance that stimulates the production of antibodies. This, in turn, was used to prepare vaccines that were given to the sow or cow. The vaccinated animal produced protective antibodies that were passed on to the offspring in the colostrum (the mother's first milk).

Increases in the output of beef, milk, and pork were promised by yet another use of such recombinant DNA technology. The production of species-specific bovine and porcine growth hormones was achieved on an experimental basis by researchers at Cornell University, Ithaca, N.Y. Such hormones have the potential to increase daily weight gain by 10–15%, improve the animals' capacity to utilize feed by up to 10%, and raise the milk yield of cows by as much as 40%. Even more important, those increases are made without the risk of side effects or of possibly harmful residues remaining in meat. However, specific growth hormones cannot be marketed until a suitable long-acting dose form can be devised.

One of the hazards that beset fish farms is the disease called white spot or "ich." It is difficult to treat by drugs, and so a vaccine had been sought for some time. Success was achieved by scientists at the University of Georgia School of Veterinary Medicine. The Georgia researchers overcame the difficulty of growing the protozoan parasite responsible for the disease, *Ichthyophthirius multifiliis*, under laboratory conditions. They then grew a similar protozoan that proved suitable for the production of a vaccine. Although the vaccine had to be injected, researchers hoped to develop tech-

A school of veterinary medicine opened at Tufts University, Grafton, Massachusetts, in June. In the photo first-year students check out a patient.

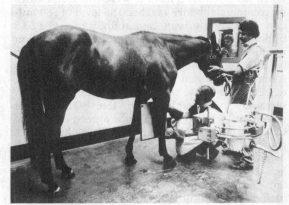

IRA WYMAN/THE NEW YORK TIMES

niques for administration by feed, spray, or immersion in order to facilitate large-scale treatment.

Piglets tend to suffer from anemia unless they are injected with an iron compound early in life. This is relatively costly and can cause such side effects as abscesses. At the Institute for Research on Animal Diseases, Compton, England, it was discovered that anemia could be prevented by simply feeding nursing sows a diet containing added iron in the form of ferrous sulfate. The extra iron was not passed on to the piglets through the sows' milk, but it was obtained by the piglets when they ingested the sows' feces, which they do normally. (EDWARD BODEN)

[353.C]

Vietnam

The Socialist Republic of Vietnam is a southeast Asian state bounded on the north by China, on the west by Laos and Kampuchea, and on the south and east by the South China Sea. Area: 329,465 sq km (127,207 sq mi). Pop. (1982 est.): 55,503,000. Capital: Hanoi (pop., 1979, 2,570,900). Largest city: Ho Chi Minh City (pop., 1979, 3,420,000). Language: Vietnamese, French, English. Religion: Buddhist, animist, Confucian, Christian (Roman Catholic), Hoa Hao and Cao Dai religious sects. Secretary-general of the Communist Party in 1982, Le Duan; chairman of the National Assembly, Nguyen Huu Tho; chairman of the State Council (president), Truong Chinh; chairman of the Council of Ministers (premier), Pham Van Dong.

For Vietnam, 1982 brought important develop-

VIETNAM

    Education. (1979–80) Primary, pupils 7,923,495, teachers 217,493; secondary, pupils 3,703,199, teachers 156,164; vocational (1980–81), pupils 131,000, teachers 12,160; teacher training, pupils (1977–78) 42,583, teachers (1976–77) 2,336; higher (1980–81), students 148,600, teaching staff 16,400.
    Finance. Monetary unit: dong, with (Sept. 20, 1982) a free rate of 9.60 dong to U.S. $1 (16.46 dong = £1 sterling). Budget (1979 est.) balanced at 10.5 billion dong.
    Foreign Trade. (1981) Imports c. U.S. $2 billion; exports c. U.S. $600 million. Import sources: U.S.S.R. c. 50%; India c. 6%; Japan c. 6%. Export destinations: U.S.S.R. c. 39%; Japan c. 6%; Hong Kong c. 5%. Main exports (1974): clothing c. 10%; fish c. 10%; rubber c. 10%; coal c. 5%; beverages c. 5%.
    Transport and Communications. Roads (1980) 347,243 km. Motor vehicles in use (1976): passenger c. 100,000; commercial (including buses) c. 200,000. Railways: (1980) c. 2,510 km; traffic (1978) 4,609,000,000 passenger-km, freight 995 million net ton-km. Navigable waterways (1980) c. 6,000 km. Shipping (1981): merchant vessels 100 gross tons and over 94; gross tonnage 249,848. Telephones (South only; Dec. 1973) 47,000. Radio receivers (Dec. 1978) c. 5 million. Television receivers (Dec. 1978) c. 2 million.
    Agriculture. Production (in 000; metric tons; 1981): rice c. 12,570; sweet potatoes c. 2,400; cassava c. 3,400; bananas c. 900; tea c. 23; coffee c. 7; tobacco c. 28; jute c. 35; rubber c. 48; pork c. 420; fish catch (1980) c. 1,013; timber (cu m; 1980) c. 64,566. Livestock (in 000; 1981): cattle 1,765; buffalo 2,378; pigs 10,500; chickens c. 52,000; ducks c. 30,000.
    Industry. Production (in 000; metric tons; 1980): coal c. 5,800; cement c. 850; salt c. 520; phosphate rock c. 500; fertilizers (nutrient content; 1980–81) nitrogenous c. 40, phosphate c. 40; chromite 15, zinc 6.5; crude steel c. 120; cotton fabrics (m; 1979) 287,000; electricity (kw-hr) c. 3,900,000.

ments on both the domestic and international fronts. The convening in March of the fifth congress of the Vietnamese Communist Party (the last congress had been held in 1976) signified a determined attempt by Hanoi to come to grips with the country's two most pressing problems—putting the tottering economy back on track and infusing the leadership with younger and more capable cadres. Internationally, the formation in late June of a coalition by three leading anti-Vietnamese Khmer resistance forces provided Vietnam with its toughest political challenge over Kampuchea since its troops rolled into Phnom Penh in January 1979 and toppled Pol Pot's Khmer Rouge regime.

Despite widespread rumours that he might resign, 75-year-old Le Duan retained the party secretary-generalship that he had held since 1959. Duan struck a keynote of the fifth party congress when he told delegates frankly that "the party's Central Committee wishes sternly to criticize itself." "Objective conditions," he said, had contributed to the country's manifold difficulties, but so had the "shortcomings and errors committed by our party and state organs."

The dismissal of inefficient and elderly cadres announced at the party congress continued throughout the year, most notably during the major reshuffles of the Council of Ministers (Cabinet) and National Assembly in April and July, respectively. The most notable promotions were those of Politburo member Vo Van Kiet, 59, to vice-premier and head of the State Planning Commission (Vietnam's top economic post) and Foreign Minister Nguyen Co Thach, 62, to alternate membership in the Politburo. The most surprising demotion was the dropping of Dien Bien Phu war hero Vo Nguyen Giap from the Politburo. However, the refusal—or inability—of the most senior men in the hierarchy to step aside triggered doubts about the rejuvenation campaign. Despite their obviously failing health—all three visited the U.S.S.R. for medical treatment during 1982—veterans Le Duan, Pres. Truong Chinh, 75, and Premier Pham Van Dong, 76, retained their positions.

The economy was Vietnam's prime concern throughout the year. Among the nation's "acute problems," Premier Dong told the fifth party congress, were shortages of clothing, medicines, pa-

Vietnam

Deputy Assistant Secretary of Defense Richard Armitage (left) headed a U.S. delegation to Hanoi to inquire into the fate of 2,553 U.S. soldiers still missing since the Vietnam war.

UPI

per, housing, and materials and transport for production; a yawning trade deficit; and fluctuating markets and prices. Although Vietnam had apparently made some headway in the critical area of food-grain production, some analysts believed the country might still be headed for a food crisis of major proportions.

The unmitigated failure of the 1976–80 five-year development plan led Hanoi's leaders to approve one for 1981–85 that displayed marked departures. While the earlier scheme was rigidly Marxist, the new one incorporated such "capitalistic" features as individual enterprise, incentives for workers and peasants, unrestricted movement of goods, and special attention to the production of consumer items. Nonetheless, a flourishing black market remained, and the underground exchange rate for the dong passed 60 to the U.S. dollar (more than six times the official rate of 9.60) despite a 400% devaluation.

Vietnam continued to depend heavily on subsidies and aid from the Soviet Union—the reason good relations with Moscow remained the cornerstone of Vietnamese foreign policy. Yet strains in the alliance became conspicuous. Insiders reported that the Soviets encountered stiff resistance from Hanoi on such sensitive issues as greater Soviet control of Vietnamese economic management and increased access to military facilities. For its part, Moscow came under growing pressure from its Eastern European allies to reduce its massive aid to Vietnam, estimated at some U.S. $3 million a day.

More important to Moscow—and thus disquieting to Hanoi—were the moves, largely on the U.S.S.R.'s initiative, toward improving ties with China, Vietnam's archenemy. Shortly after Soviet Pres. Leonid Brezhnev made his country's most serious "peace overture" in years to China in March, observers wondered how the Kremlin's apparently sincere desire to normalize relations with China would affect Soviet-Vietnamese ties. Hanoi's announcement in July of a withdrawal of some of its occupation troops from Kampuchea was seen in many quarters as the result of Soviet pressure aimed at conciliating China.

The pullout offer came on the heels of the formal announcement of a coalition government-in-exile formed by the three major Khmer groups resisting Vietnamese occupation of their country. (See KAMPUCHEA.) Proclamation of the coalition, after almost a year of difficult negotiations among its mutually suspicious partners, posed the biggest obstacle yet to Vietnam's campaign to gain diplomatic recognition for its client regime in Phnom Penh under Heng Samrin.

In the event, Vietnam's offer of a partial troop withdrawal met widespread skepticism in non-Communist Southeast Asia, as Foreign Minister Thach discovered when he toured key capitals of the Association of Southeast Asian Nations (ASEAN) in July. He was bluntly told that ASEAN still abided by the UN resolution calling for a complete withdrawal of foreign armed forces from Kampuchea. Although Hanoi pulled back thousands of its estimated 170,000 troops in Kampuchea, intelligence sources confirmed that at least as many fresh replacements were being sent in. By

early October a conspicuous military buildup by Hanoi near Kampuchea's border with Thailand had led to new fears of a major Vietnamese offensive against Khmer resistance forces based in the vicinity.

Following the previous year's visit by U.S. Vietnam war veterans, another group visited Vietnam during May 29–June 3, 1982; discussions with Vietnamese officials again centred on missing U.S. servicemen and the effects of chemical defoliants used by the U.S. In what some interpreted as another gesture of goodwill, the Vietnamese government permitted the largest number of Amerasian children in some years to be reunited with their American fathers.   (THOMAS HON WING POLIN)

See also Southeast Asian Affairs.

Water Sports

Motorboating. Lee ("Chip") Hanauer of Seattle, Wash., completed a storybook season in 1982 as he swept to his first American Power Boat Association (APBA) Gold Cup, APBA unlimited hydroplane national championship, and Union of International Motorboating (UIM) world championship aboard the new "Atlas Van Lines." Hanauer had been named in February to succeed Bill Muncey, who died in 1981, as driver for the Atlas Van Lines team.

The 1982 hydroplane season opened with a victory in the Champion Spark Plug Regatta, held on June 6 in Miami, Fla., for defending champion Dean Chenoweth (see OBITUARIES) and "Miss Budweiser." Two weeks later John Walters made history, piloting the turbine-powered "Pay 'n Pack" to its first victory in the inaugural Seneca, N.Y., event.

The turning point of the season came two weeks later when the determined Hanauer staged a dramatic come-from-behind rally to pass Chenoweth and claim the Stroh's APBA Gold Cup in Detroit. Veteran driver Tom D'Eath, of Fair Haven, Mich., returning to unlimited competition after a six-year absence, claimed the Madison, Ind., event in "The Squire Shop" on July 4, but Hanauer returned to the winner's circle in Evansville, Ind., on July 11.

Tragedy struck in Pasco, Wash., on July 31, when Chenoweth was killed in a solo testing run. The four-time national champion (1970, 1971, 1980, 1981) and four-time APBA Gold Cup winner (1970, 1973, 1980, 1981) was the second most successful driver in the history of the sport.

The 1982 offshore racing season featured unprecedented competition, with different winners in each of the first six races. Defending national champion Betty Cook opened the season with a victory in the New Orleans/Michelob Light 200 but lost her APBA national title to 1981 world champion Jerry Jacoby of Old Westbury, N.Y. Jacoby piloted his "Cigarette Hawk" to victory in the Bacardi Trophy Race on May 8 in Miami, the only Class I win of the year for the traditional deep vee designs. Al Copeland of New Orleans, La., won the Stroh Light Challenge on June 22 in Detroit. Copeland's victory in his triple outboard-powered "Popeye's" was the first outboard Class I triumph

Virgin Islands:
see Dependent States

Vital Statistics:
see Demography

Volleyball:
see Court Games

Wages and Hours:
see Economy, World;
Industrial Relations

Wales:
see United Kingdom

Warsaw Treaty Organization:
see Defense

Water Resources:
see Earth Sciences;
Environment

Duke Waldrop of Palestine, Texas, proudly waved his victory flag after winning the Formula II powerboat race at the world championship Grand Prix on August 15 in Fenton, Missouri.

in more than a decade. Copeland also claimed the Harmsworth Trophy.

Restaurateur Rocky Aoki (*see* Biographies) teamed with Howard Quam of Chicago to win the Benihana Grand Prix on July 14 at Point Pleasant, N.J. The boat was destroyed and Aoki injured two months later at St. Augustine, Fla., in the only serious accident of the offshore season.

Ted Toleman of the U.K. posted a new world speed record for offshore boats with a 109.98-mph clocking at Lake Windermere in England. Toleman had set the previous record of 97 mph in 1981.   (JOHN H. LOVE)

River Sports. At the U.S. national flat-water championships, held in late August at Jasonville, Ind., Greg Barton won the 500-m, 1,000-m, and 10,000-m men's single kayak events. Robby Plankenhorn won the 500-m and 10,000-m men's single canoe races, and Blaise Stanek won the 1,000-m event. Cathy Gregory won the women's single kayak event.

The world championships took place in Belgrade, Yugos., in early August. Flat-water competition has traditionally been dominated by Eastern Europe and the Soviet Union, but in 1982 the medals were given to a much larger number of countries. Canada, Sweden, and New Zealand all had unprecedented success. In the overall team standings, the Soviet Union was still in first place, led by Vladimir Parfenovich. East Germany finished second, and Sweden was third.

In white-water racing the U.S. national slalom championships were held in mid-August on the Ocoee River in Tennessee. Sue Norman won the women's kayaking, while Chris McCormick won the men's. The national wild-water championships were held in July on the Arkansas River in Colorado. John Fishburn was the men's champion, and Carol Fisher was the women's.

The top international white-water event during 1982 was the pre-world championships, in Merano, Italy, during June. The best U.S. showings were by Michael and Steven Garvis, who won the double canoe event, and Jon Lugbill, who won the single canoe race.   (ERIC LEAPER)

Water Skiing. A three-member United States water ski team won the 1982 Peter Stuyvesant World Cup Championships at Thorpe Water Park, near London, on September 4–5, but the second and third places were disputed long after the tournament ended following the discovery of a scoring error. The official results showed the U.S. defeating Canada in the finals of the three-round elimination tournament, but after the Australians, listed as finishing third, had returned home, they discovered a 50-point miscalculation in the second-round scoring. If it had not been for that miscalculation, Australia would have met the U.S. in the finals. Australia filed a protest with the sponsoring British Water Ski Federation and the World Water Ski Union, an action that was unprecedented in the 33-year history of international water ski competition.

Members of the U.S. team were Sammy Duvall and Karin Roberge, who had won the overall titles in the biennial world championships at the same site in 1981, and Carl Roberge, Karin's brother, who won the U.S. national open overall title in August for the second year in a row.

The 1982 U.S. national women's overall crown was retained by Cyndi Benzel. Individual event open winners in the U.S. Nationals included: slalom, Kris LaPoint and Deena Brush; tricks, Cory Pickos and Benzel; and jumping, Duvall and Cindy Todd. Overall honours in the prestigious U.S. Masters international invitational at Callaway Gardens, Ga., were won by Duvall and Todd.

(THOMAS C. HARDMAN)

WILLIAM E. SAURO/THE NEW YORK TIMES

Rocky Aoki powered his catamaran to victory in the Benihana Grand Prix off the coast of Point Pleasant, New Jersey, in July. Aoki, who had been nearly killed in a power-boat accident in 1980, was seriously injured in September 1982.

Surfing. The closing rounds of the International Professional Surfers world tour were held in Hawaii with the waves and the weather somewhat less than perfect. Mark Richards and Cheyne Horan, both of Australia, were neck-and-neck at the stretch, with Richards trying for an unprecedented third world championship and Horan the youngest contender for the title in the six-year history of the IPS. When it was all over, Richards won again with a 1981 total of 6,211.52 points to Horan's 5,861.99. Dane Kealoha of Hawaii finished third with 5,212.99. Margo Oberg of Hawaii again won the IPS world championship for women with 3,850 points to second-place Liz Benavidez's 2,283.36. Richards and Oberg were voted Surfers of the Year in the 11th Annual Surfer Poll Awards.

Australia contributed approximately $200,000 in prize money for the four contests in the 1982 IPS circuit. In the Surfabout Wayne "Rabbit" Bartholomew of Australia nosed out Kealoha to claim the first prize of $30,000.

(JACK C. FLANAGAN)

Water Polo. In July the water polo world migrated to Ecuador for the world championships where the top 16 teams competed in a nine-day tournament. When it was completed the Soviet Union, as it had done in the 1980 Olympic Games, again proved its superiority. The Soviets won their first six matches and then were challenged by a strong team from Hungary in the final game. Needing only a tie to take home the gold medal, the Soviets fell behind early but rallied to deadlock the game 7–7 with 25 seconds remaining. Then the Hungarians scored what appeared to be the winning goal, but it was disallowed because the buzzer to end the game had sounded. West Germany, the winner of the 1981 European Championships, was able to finish third, while The Netherlands placed fourth. In the bracket to determine fifth through eighth places, Cuba came out on top followed by the United States, Yugoslavia, and Spain. Italy finished ninth, and a surprisingly strong team from China placed tenth.

In the other major international tournament of 1982, The Netherlands surprised everyone by winning the Tungsram Cup. The Soviet Union placed second and the United States third. Finishing out the eight-team tournament were, in order,

Western Samoa

Weather:
see Earth Sciences

Weight Lifting:
see Gymnastics and Weight Lifting

Welfare:
see Social Security and Welfare Services

Wine:
see Industrial Review

Spain, Italy, Hungary, West Germany, and Yugoslavia.

Industry Hills Aquatic Club, as it had done in 1981, went undefeated to win the 1982 U.S. water polo championships held in August at Stanford (Calif.) University. Newport captured the silver medal, while North Coast finished third.

(WILLIAM ENSIGN FRADY)

Western Samoa

A constitutional monarchy and member of the Commonwealth, Western Samoa is an island group in the South Pacific Ocean, about 2,600 km E of New Zealand and 3,500 km S of Hawaii. Area: 2,831 sq km (1,093 sq mi), with two major islands, Savai'i (1,708 sq km) and Upolu (including several islets, 1,123 sq km). Pop. (1982 est.): 158,000. Cap. and largest city: Apia (pop., 1980, 33,400). Language: Samoan and English. Religion (1976): Congregational 50%; Roman Catholic 22%; Methodist 16%; others 12%. Head of state (O le Ao o le Malo) in 1982, Malietoa Tanumafili II; prime ministers, Tupuola Efi to April 13, Va'ai Kolone to September 18, and Tupuola from that date.

Western Samoa faced serious economic problems in 1982. Furthermore, it emerged that a large development program had been rendered ineffectual by mismanagement; prosecutions followed the uncovering of a major fraud in the Health Department and the World Bank threatened to cut off aid because of the misuse of funds.

Following a general election on February 27, Va'ai Kolone, leader of the Human Rights Protection Party, ousted Prime Minister Tupuola Efi by a single vote in the Legislative Assembly. In September, however, Va'ai was unseated for treating, bribery, and personation, and Tupuola was again sworn in. In October Tupuola lost his majority in a by-election but retained office because Parliament was not in session.

The chief justice held that the Electoral Act, which restricted the franchise for Samoans to *matai* (titled heads of families), conflicted with constitutional requirements for equal rights and was thus void. This decision was later overruled by a specially convened Court of Appeal.

The Privy Council in London ruled that under New Zealand law all Western Samoans born between 1928 and 1949, and their children, were entitled to New Zealand citizenship. Despite pro-

---

WESTERN SAMOA

Education. (1980) Primary, pupils 33,012; secondary, pupils 19,299; primary and secondary, teachers 1,913; vocational, pupils 264, teachers 44; higher (including teacher training), students 388, teaching staff 54.

Finance and Trade. Monetary unit: tala, with (Sept. 20, 1982) a free rate of 1.25 tala to U.S. $1 (2.14 tala = £1 sterling). Budget (1980 est.): revenue 31.4 million tala; expenditure 22.7 million tala. Foreign trade: imports (1981) 69.5 million tala; exports (1980) 15,830,000 tala. Import sources (1980): New Zealand 32%; Australia 20%; Singapore 11%; Japan 9%; U.S. 9%; U.K. 6%. Export destinations: The Netherlands 31%; New Zealand 26%; West Germany 11%; Sweden 8%; American Samoa 7%; U.S. 6%; Japan 5%. Main exports: copra 53%; cocoa 19%; taro and taamu 7%.

tests, New Zealand negotiated a protocol with Western Samoa that granted New Zealand citizenship only to those who were eligible under the decision and were resident in New Zealand when the decision was made.   (BARRIE MACDONALD).

Winter Sports

At both championship and recreational levels, in 1982 all the major sports on snow and ice enjoyed continued expansion in numbers of participants and public following, the latter encouraged by increased television coverage.

Skiing. Extensive additions in various methods of mechanical ascent, ranging from spectacular aerial cabin-car cableways to chair lifts and T-bar tows, generally lengthened the season particularly for holiday skiers, by opening up more high-altitude terrain. Thus, skiing became a more familiar activity in countries associated with warm climates. Areas in the Sierra Nevada, Spain, were a typical example. Countries with little or no appreciable snow, notably the United Kingdom and South Africa, effectively reduced the precious snow time needed for basic instruction by increasing facilities for (roller) skiing on grass and on plastic. The International Ski Federation (FIS) comprised 52 member nations.

ALPINE RACING. The 16th annual Alpine World Cup series covered 28 men's and 27 women's events spanning four months at 24 sites in nine countries. Retaining the men's trophy, Phil Mahre of the U.S. headed both the slalom and giant slalom standings. Ingemar Stenmark of Sweden, the overall runner-up, was deposed in the slalom for the first time since 1975. Steve Mahre, Phil's twin brother, finished third. The best downhill skier was Steve Podborski (see BIOGRAPHIES) of Canada. Stenmark achieved the largest winning margin of 3.16 sec in a World Cup slalom, at Kitzbühel, Austria, on January 17.

Erika Hess of Switzerland, the previous season's runner-up, won the women's trophy from Irene Epple of West Germany and Christin Cooper of the U.S., who finished second and third, respectively. Like Mahre, Hess topped the slalom and giant slalom ratings; the leading downhiller was Marie-Cecile Gros-Gaudenier of France. Austria regained the concurrently decided Nations Cup. Switzerland, the defending champion, was runner-up, and the U.S., whose women racers proved best, finished third.

The 27th biennial world Alpine championships were held at Schladming, Austria, during January 17–February 7; 290 racers from 35 countries contested the four men's and four women's events. New downhill/slalom combination events, although disregarded by some of the top competitors, were an attempt to counteract the trends toward extreme specialization.

Stenmark predictably won the slalom, the first man to do so in three successive world championships. Bojan Krizaj of Yugoslavia proved his closest rival, and another Swede, Bengt Fjällberg, took the bronze medal. Steve Mahre gained the first American giant slalom win in international competition, with Stenmark second and Boris Strel third for Yugoslavia. Harti Weirather of Austria won the downhill, watched by a record attendance of 55,000. His fellow Austrian Erwin Resch finished third behind Conradin Cathomen of Switzerland. The combination event went to Michel Vion of France in front of Peter Lüscher of Switzerland and Anton Steiner from Austria.

Justly dubbed the new Alpine snow queen, Hess dominated the women's events, taking three of the four gold medals with convincing style. Cooper was her runner-up in both the slalom and giant slalom, the respective bronze medals going to Daniela Zini of Italy and Ursula Konzett of Liechtenstein. Cooper finished third in the combination, behind Perrine Pelen of France. In the downhill Gerry Sorensen and Laurie Graham won gold and bronze medals for Canada, split by Cindy Nelson of the U.S. in second place for a North American grand slam—the first world championship race with no European among the top three.

The season's most successful male skier on the professional circuit was Edwin Halsnes of Norway. His compatriot, Toril Forland, decisively retained the women's crown, winning 9 of 21 races.

NORDIC EVENTS. King Olav V of Norway, a former ski jumper, and Crown Prince Harald watched the 34th biennial world Nordic championships at Holmenkollen, Oslo, February 15–28, when 330 competitors from 29 nations contested nine men's and four women's titles. North Europeans took all the cross-country medals except one. In the 15 km Oddvar Braa of Norway outpaced Aleksandr Zaviolov of the U.S.S.R. and Harri Kirvesniemi from Finland. The 30 km went to Thomas Eriksson of Sweden, with Norway's Lars Erik Eriksen runner-up and Bill Koch of the U.S. third—the first American to win a Nordic world championship medal. Thomas Wassberg of Sweden won the demanding 50 km from Yury Burla-

Steve Mahre of the U.S. (right) beamed in victory after winning the world championship giant slalom race at Schladming, Austria. He defeated Ingemar Stenmark of Sweden (left).

UPI

West German skier Maria Epple captured the women's title in World Cup giant slalom in Aspen, Colorado, in February.

kov of the U.S.S.R., with Eriksen third. Braa and Zaviolov, anchoring their Norwegian and Soviet 4 x 10-km relay teams, crossed the finish line in a remarkable dead heat, with Finland third.

The Nordic combination (jumping and cross-country) was won by Tom Sandberg of Norway with two East Germans, Konrad Winkler and Uwe Dotzauer, second and third. A team competition (jumping and relay race) was won by the Soviet Union. The silver medal in that event was shared by Finland and Norway, equal on points. An Austrian, Armin Kogler, outjumped all the Scandinavians in the 70-m event, with Jari Puikkonen of Finland and Ole Bremseth of Norway placing second and third. Approximately 75,000 tried to watch the 90-m jumping finals at Holmenkollen's 90-year-old reconstructed hill, but fog made it difficult to see Finland's Matti Nykaenen outleap Olav Hansson of Norway; Kogler finished third. The team jumping was won by Norway followed by Austria and Finland.

Berit Aunli became the first Norwegian woman to win a gold medal at any world skiing championships when she took the 10 km. Three days later she won the 5 km and two days after that achieved a third gold medal as a member of the winning Norwegian 4 x 5-km relay team, which finished ahead of the U.S.S.R. and East Germany. Aunli placed second in the 20 km, defeated by the Soviet veteran Raisa Smetanina, with Hilkka Riihivuori of Finland third. Riihivuori was runner-up in both the 5 km and 10 km, the bronze medals for those distances going, respectively, to Brit Pettersen of Norway and Kvetoslava Jeriova of Czechoslovakia.

The third Nordic World Cup series resulted in the first U.S. victory, as Koch won the men's cross-country events, and a women's triumph for Aunli. The men's silver and bronze medals were gained by Wassberg and Kirvesniemi. The women's runner-up was Pettersen, followed by Jeriova.

The Nordic World Cup jump title was retained by Kogler, followed by his compatriot Hubert Neuper. Horst Bulau of Canada finished third for the second year. The Nordic Nations Cup was retained by Austria, with Norway second and Finland third, the same order as in the previous season.

East German and Norwegian ski-shooters dominated the world biathlon championships, at Raubichi, U.S.S.R., February 12–17. Frank Ulrich won the 20-km title for East Germany, ahead of two Norwegians, Erik Kvalfoff and Terje Krokstad. Kvalfoff reversed the order to win the 10 km, with Ulrich, the defending champion, second and Vladimir Alikin of the U.S.S.R. third. East Germany retained the 4 x 10-km relay title, with Norway second and the U.S.S.R. third.

OTHER EVENTS. In international speed-skiing championships, held at Silverton, Colo., on April 19–25, a world record men's time of 126.24 mph (203.16 km/h) was set by Frans Weber of Austria. A new women's record of 111.29 mph (179.10 km/h) was achieved by Marty Martin-Kuntz of the U.S.

The men's world cup for freestyle skiing, with emphasis on acrobatic and ballet movements, was won by Frank Beddor of the U.S., calculated from results obtained at selected North American and European locations. The women's overall title went to Marie-Claude Asselin of Canada.

Ice Skating. Keener interest in nonchampionship figure-skating competitions and increased participation in indoor short-track racing were notable trends during 1982. The International Skating Union had 32 member nations.

FIGURE SKATING. The first world figure championships to be held in Denmark drew 132 skaters from 25 countries to Copenhagen on March 9–13. The four events produced two victories for the U.S., one each for Great Britain and East Germany, and, for the first time in 18 years, none for the Soviet Union.

Scott Hamilton, 23 and 5 ft 3 in tall, retained the men's title for the U.S. with apparent ease. His almost flawless long free skating included six triple jumps in a widely varied program entertainingly presented. Norbert Schramm, the season's new European champion from West Germany, finished second ahead of a Canadian, Brian Pockar, whose third place was commendably achieved after he missed much training because of appendicitis complications. Another Canadian, fourth-place Brian Orser, completed a perfect triple axel—3½ midair rotations—which only he and his compatriot Vern Taylor had previously accomplished in a world championship. After leading in the compulsory figures, Jean-Christophe Simond of France could only finish fifth.

Elaine Zayak, 16, became the sixth U.S. skater to gain the women's crown, remarkably pulling up from seventh place in the long free skating after an otherwise undistinguished season. Katarina Witt from East Germany was runner-up despite three faulty landings, and Claudia Kristofics-Binder, the outstanding woman figure tracer from Austria, took the bronze medal in a contest marred by erratic judging. Rosalynn Sumners and Vikki de

Vries, sixth and seventh for the U.S., each demonstrated considerable potential.

Tassilo Thierbach and Sabine Baess became the first East Germans to take the pairs title, with a sound display of powerful overhead lifts, deft throws, and well-controlled death spirals. Neither the winners nor the Soviet runners-up, Stanislav Leonovich and Marina Pestova, appeared to be in the same league as other champions of recent years. An upsurge of North American strength was evident in this division when a U S. brother and sister team, Peter and Caitlin Carruthers, narrowly defeated Canadians Paul Martini and Barbara Underhill in a close duel for third place. Igor Lisovsky and Irina Vorobieva, the Soviet defending champions, were humbled in fifth position, Vorobieva skating with suspected injured cartilage and looking clearly under stress.

Christopher Dean and Jayne Torvill, widely considered to be the best performers ever in their branch of skating, retained the ice dance title for Britain with bewildering technical brilliance. They secured the highest marks ever for a compulsory dance, five of the seven judges awarding 5.9; no one had yet received a six in this section of the event. For their free dance five judges gave them maximum sixes for presentation. Andrey Bukin and Natalia Bestemianova gained a hard-fought silver medal from their Soviet compatriots Andrey Minenkov and Irina Moiseyeva.

During the European championships a month earlier in Lyons, France, Dean and Torvill had received the highest score from a single set of marks in any figure-skating competition when they were awarded sixes for presentation from eight of the nine judges. They received three additional sixes for technical merit, making 11 sixes, a record for any ice dance event.

SPEED SKATING. Hilbert van der Duim won the men's world championship for the host country at Assen, Neth., on February 20–21. Dmitry Bochkarev of the U.S.S.R. was runner-up, and a Norwegian, Rolf Falk-Larssen, came in third. In the individual events Gaetan Boucher of Canada won the 500 m, van der Duim the 1,500 m, and Bochkarev the 5,000 m and 10,000 m.

An East German, Karin Busch, became the new women's world champion at Inzell, West Germany, on February 13–14. Second place went to Andrea Schöne, also of East Germany, and third to the Soviet title defender, Natalia Petruseva. Busch finished first in the 500 m, 1,000 m, and 1,500 m, while Schöne won the 3,000 m.

In the separate world sprint championships, decided at Alkmaar, Neth., on February 6–7, Sergey Khlebnikov of the U.S.S.R. gained the men's title, ahead of Boucher and Frode Rønning of Norway. The women's championship was won by Petruseva, followed by Busch and a West German, Monika Holzner.

Two new men's world records were set. Aleksandr Baranov of the U.S.S.R. skated the 5,000 m in 6 min 54.66 sec at Medeo, U.S.S.R., and a Swede, Tomas Gustafson, covered the 10,000 m in 14 min 23.59 sec in Oslo. In the second world short-track (indoor) championships, at Moncton, N.B., on April 2–4, the men's and women's titles were gained, respectively, by Guy Daigneault and Maryse Perneault of Canada.

Bobsledding. Swiss crews scored a double triumph in the 49th world championships in February at St.-Moritz, Switz. Erich Schaerer, braked by Max Ruegg, won his fourth two-man title for the host country. They hurtled down the 1,550-m course with an aggregate time for the four runs that was over half a second better than their second-place compatriots, driver Hans Hiltebrand and brakeman Ulrich Baechli. Third were Horst Schönau and Andreas Kirchner of East Germany.

Silvio Giobellina steered his Swiss four-man bob to victory, crewed by Heinz Stettler, Urs Salzmann, and Rico Freiermuth; all four were newcomers to the championship. Fastest in three of the four runs, they won by a full second over the East German runners-up, driven by Bernhard Lehman and backed by Roland Wetzig, Bogdan Musiol, and Eberhard Weiss. Schaerer this time took the bronze medal, with Franz Isenegger, Tony Ruegg, and Max Ruegg.

Tobogganing. Uwe Handrich from East Germany gained the men's singles title in the 28th world luge championships at Winterberg, West Germany, on February 13–14. Sergey Danilin was runner-up for the U.S.S.R., with Ernst Haspinger of Italy third. The doubles went to Günther Lemmerer and Reinhold Sulzbacher of Austria. East Germans swept the board in the women's individual event. Bettina Schmidt, the previous year's runner-up, turned the tables on the title defender, Melitta Sollmann, who finished third. Swiss riders again monopolized the medals in both the classic races for skeleton tobogganists on the Cresta Run at St.-Moritz. Nico Baracchi won both the 73rd Grand National, along the full course, and the 59th Curzon Cup, over the shorter distance. Christian Nater placed second and Marcel Melcher third in the Grand National. The Curzon Cup runner-up

In the world championship curling competition in Geneva, the Danish team of (left to right) Marianne Jørgensen, Helena Blach, Astrid Birnbaum, and Jette Olsen emerged as winners.

was Reto Gansser, with Patrick Latscha third.

Curling. Canada increased its record number of wins to 14 in the 24th men's world championship for the Air Canada Silver Broom, during March 28–April 4 at Garmisch-Partenkirchen, West Germany. The winning rink, from Thunder Bay, Ont., was skipped by Al Hackner and included Bruce Kennedy, Bob Nichol, and Rick Lang. One shot decided their 9–7 victory in the final against the Swiss title defenders, the same four from Lausanne who had won the previous year—Jurg Tanner (skip), Patrick Loertscher, Jurg Hornisberger, and Tanner's 54-year-old father, Franz. In the semifinals Canada beat Sweden 5–3 and Switzerland put out West Germany 6–3. The other nations competing were Italy, Norway, the U.S., Scotland, France, and Denmark.

In the fourth women's world championship, in March at Geneva, Denmark gained its first success with an 8–7 victory over Sweden in the final; previous winners had been Switzerland, Canada, and Sweden. The eighth men's world junior championship, sponsored by Uniroyal on March 14–20 at Fredericton, N.B., resulted in a win for Sweden, skipped by Sören Grahn, with Canada runner-up.

(HOWARD BASS)

See also Ice Hockey.
[452.B.4.g–h]

Yemen, People's Democratic Republic of

A people's republic in the southern coastal region of the Arabian Peninsula, Yemen (Aden; South Yemen) is bordered by Yemen (San'a'), Saudi Arabia, and Oman. Area: 338,100 sq km (130,541 sq mi). Pop. (1982 est.): 1,998,000. Cap. and largest city: Aden (pop., 1981 est., 365,000). Language: Arabic. Religion: predominantly Muslim. Chairman of the Presidium of the Supreme People's Council and prime minister in 1982, Ali Nasir Muhammad Husani.

Chief of state Ali Nasir Muhammad Husani of South Yemen was under some pressure in 1982, although reports of an abortive coup against him during the Arab summit in Fez, Morocco, in September were officially denied. It was alleged that former state security minister Muhammad Said Abdullah Muhsin favoured a return to power of the hard-line former president Abd-al Fattah Ismail, who was living in Moscow.

Talks with Oman, with which South Yemen had territorial and ideological disputes, made little progress until, in October, the two countries announced that they had agreed on a formal reconciliation. In November a meeting took place to discuss further the draft joint constitution, set up with Yemen (San'a'; North Yemen) in December 1981. Nevertheless, Aden continued to support the National Democratic Front (NDF) rebels opposed to Pres. Ali Abdullah Saleh of North Yemen. It was understood that Muhammad's stand on unity of the Yemens was opposed by Defense Minister Saleh Musleh Qassam, who advocated a stronger NDF.

(JOHN WHELAN)

People's Democratic Republic of Yemen

Yemen Arab Republic

YEMEN, PEOPLE'S DEMOCRATIC REPUBLIC OF

Education. (1977–78) Primary, pupils 212,795; secondary, pupils 64,388; primary and secondary, teachers 10,078; vocational, pupils 1,223, teachers (1976–77) 68; teacher training, students 1,070, teachers 57; higher, students 2,517, teaching staff 246.

Finance and Trade. Monetary unit: Yemen dinar, with (Sept. 20, 1982) a par value of 0.345 dinar to U.S. $1 (free rate of 0.59 dinar = £1 sterling). Budget (1980–81 actual): revenue 86,020,000 dinars; expenditure 96,020,000 dinars. Foreign trade (1980): imports 527.4 million dinars; exports 269 million dinars. Import sources: Kuwait c. 11%; Qatar c. 11%; United Arab Emirates c. 8%; Japan c. 6%; U.S.S.R. c. 6%; Saudi Arabia c. 5%. Export destinations: United Arab Emirates c. 22%; Italy c. 11%; India c. 5%. Main export: petroleum products 95%.

Transport. Roads (1979) 10,495 km (including 1,356 km with improved surface). Motor vehicles in use (1980): passenger c. 12,200; commercial (including buses) c. 15,300. There are no railways. Shipping traffic (1977): goods loaded c. 1,565,000 metric tons, unloaded c. 3,089,000 metric tons.

Agriculture. Production (in 000; metric tons; 1981): millet and sorghum c. 70; wheat c. 15; watermelons c. 59; dates c. 43; cotton, lint c. 4; fish catch (1980) 75. Livestock (in 000; 1981): cattle c. 120; sheep c. 987; goats c. 1,350; asses c. 171; camels c. 100; chickens c. 1,549.

Industry. Production (in 000; metric tons; 1979): petroleum products c. 1,890; salt c. 75; electricity (kw-hr) c. 245,000.

Yemen Arab Republic

A republic situated in the southwestern coastal region of the Arabian Peninsula, Yemen (San'a'; North Yemen) is bounded by Yemen (Aden), Saudi Arabia, and the Red Sea. Area: 200,000 sq km (77,200 sq mi). Pop. (1981): 7,161,800. Cap. and largest city: San'a' (pop., 1981, 277,800). Language: Arabic (official) and English. Religion: Muslim. President in 1982, Col. Ali Abdullah Saleh; premier, Abdel Karim al-Iriani.

The joint constitution between the Yemen Arab Republic and Yemen (Aden; South Yemen), first drafted in December 1981, was the subject of further talks in November 1982, amid hopes that Aden would halt its backing for the rebel National Democratic Front (NDF) opposed to Pres. Ali Abdullah Saleh. Border skirmishes continued early in 1982 between government and rebel troops. Ac-

YEMEN ARAB REPUBLIC

Education. (1976–77) Primary, pupils 221,482, teachers (1975–76) 6,604; secondary, pupils 24,873, teachers (1975–76) c. 1,172; vocational, pupils 503, teachers (1975–76) 60; teacher training, students 1,650, teachers (1975–76) 113; higher, students (1977–78) 4,058, teaching staff (1973–74) 58.

Finance and Trade. Monetary unit: rial, with (Sept. 20, 1982) a par value of 4.56 rials to U.S. $1 (free rate of 7.82 rials = £1 sterling). Budget (1981 actual): revenue 3,282,600,000 rials; expenditure 6,219,900,000 rials. Foreign trade (1979–80): imports 7,705,000,000 rials; exports 92.8 million rials. Import sources (1978–79): Saudi Arabia 19%; Japan 10%; France 10%; U.K. 8%; West Germany 7%; Italy 6%; Singapore 5%; China 5%. Export destinations (1978–79): Yemen (Aden) 49%; Saudi Arabia 23%; Italy 7%. Main exports (1978–79): biscuits 25%; machinery 15%; sugar 11%; hides and skins 11%; coffee 9%; cement 8%; textile yarn and fabrics 8%.

Agriculture. Production (in 000; metric tons; 1981): barley c. 54; corn c. 49; wheat c. 70; sorghum c. 635; potatoes c. 138; grapes c. 64; dates c. 84; coffee c. 4; tobacco c. 6; cotton, lint c. 2. Livestock (in 000; 1981): cattle c. 950; sheep c. 3,159; goats c. 7,500; asses c. 745; camels c. 115.

More than 2,800 people were killed and 400,000 left homeless when a devastating earthquake struck North Yemen in December.

cording to Western intelligence reports, in early April the NDF captured the border town of Juban. The victory was not considered significant by the government, as the settlement had been surrounded for some time by the rebels.

The government denied reports in July that the powerful Bakil tribal federation was in revolt against the authorities in San'a'. The government nevertheless handed out a stiff prison sentence of ten years to one of its critics, Abdullah al-Asnag, who was convicted on charges of high treason in May. Asnag was regarded as pro-Saudi Arabian and allegedly gave information to that nation about the president's 1981 visit to Moscow.

A major earthquake struck Yemen on December 13. Centred in Dhamar Province, a densely populated mountainous region some 60 mi southwest of San'a', it caused the deaths of more than 2,800 persons and injured some 1,500 others. Approximately 400,000 people were left homeless, and some 300 villages and hamlets were in ruins.

(JOHN WHELAN)

Yugoslavia

A federal socialist republic, Yugoslavia is bordered by Italy, Austria, Hungary, Romania, Bulgaria, Greece, Albania, and the Adriatic Sea. Area: 255,804 sq km (98,766 sq mi). Pop. (1981): 22,418,300, including Serbs 36.3%; Croats 19.7%; Bosnian Muslim 8.9%; Slovenes 7.8%; Albanians 7.7%; Macedonians 6%; Montenegrins 2.6%; others 11%. Cap. and largest city: Belgrade (pop., 1980 UN est., 976,000). Language: Serbo-Croatian, Slovenian, Macedonian, and Albanian. Religion (1953): Orthodox 41%; Roman Catholic 32%; Muslim 12%. Presidents of the Presidium of the League of Communists in 1982, Dušan Dragosavac and, from June 29, Mitja Ribicic; presidents of the Collective Presidency, Sergej Kraigher and, from May 16, Petar Stambolic; presidents of the Federal Exec-

utive Council (premiers), Veselin Djuranovic and, from May 16, Milka Planinc.

Elections were held in Yugoslavia for local, republican, and federal assemblies in March and April 1982. In May the Federal Assembly in Belgrade appointed a new Federal Executive Council with Milka Planinc (*see* BIOGRAPHIES) as premier. Lazar Mojsov became foreign minister, and Stane Dolanc was appointed interior minister. Gen. Nikola Ljubicic, defense minister during the years 1967–82, was replaced by Adm. Branko Mamula. In May the Collective Presidency elected Petar Stambolic president for one year, with Vladimir Bakaric as vice-president.

The congress of the League of Communists in June reaffirmed the main principles of Titoism: self-management, economic decentralization, and nonalignment. It elected a 163-member Central Committee, which in turn elected a 23-member Presidium with Mitja Ribicic as president and Nikola Stojanovic as executive secretary.

Political tension in Kosovo, the scene of nationalist riots in 1981, continued throughout 1982. In November it was officially stated that in the period March–September 1982 some 700 Kosovo Albanians had been arrested for political offenses and that more than 300 had been sent to trial. Three bombs exploded in Pristina, the province's capital, in November. A large-scale purge of Kosovo's state and party administrations, police, and university was carried out. The continuing emigration of Serbs and Montenegrins from Kosovo caused tension in Serbia. Yugoslavia reacted sharply to a speech in November by Albanian leader Enver Hoxha expressing support for the struggle of the Kosovo Albanians. Nevertheless, work was resumed on the joint project for a railway linking Albania with Yugoslavia.

Throughout 1982 Yugoslavia continued to be active in the nonaligned movement, seeking to counter attempts by Cuba and other pro-Soviet members to steer the group toward the Soviet bloc.

Yugoslavia

Wood Products:
see Industrial Review

World Bank:
see Economy, World

Wrestling:
see Combat Sports

Yachting:
see Sailing

Yiddish Literature:
see Literature

YUGOSLAVIA

Education. (1979–80) Primary, pupils 1,422,871, teachers 58,742; secondary, pupils 1,880,888; vocational, pupils 528,628; teacher training, pupils 4,134; secondary, vocational, and teacher training, teachers 129,176; higher, students 447,270, teaching staff 23,969.

Finance. Monetary unit: dinar, with (Sept. 20, 1982) a free rate of 51.14 dinars to U.S. $1 (87.68 dinars = £1 sterling). Gold and other reserves (June 1982) U.S. $923 million. Budget (federal; 1982 est.) balanced at 203.8 billion dinars. Gross material product (1980) 1,553,000,000,000 dinars. Money supply (April 1982) 628.1 billion dinars. Cost of living (1975 = 100; June 1982) 419.8.

Foreign Trade. (1981) Imports 556.6 billion dinars; exports 394.8 billion dinars. Import sources: U.S.S.R. 19%; West Germany 15%; Italy 8%; U.S. 6%; France 5%. Export destinations: U.S.S.R. 33%; Italy 9%; West Germany 8%; Iraq 5%; Czechoslovakia 5%. Main exports: machinery 19%; chemicals 12%; transport equipment 9%; food 8%; clothing 6%; footwear 6%; textile yarn and fabrics 5%. Tourism (1980): visitors 6,410,000; gross receipts U.S. $1,115,000,000.

Transport and Communications. Roads (1980) 133,895 km (including 417 km expressways). Motor vehicles in use (1980): passenger 2,430,800; commercial 190,040. Railways: (1980) 9,465 km; traffic (1981) 10,240,000,000 passenger-km, freight 25,444,000,000 net ton-km. Air traffic (1980): c. 2,984,000,000 passenger-km; freight c. 41.7 million net ton-km. Shipping (1981): merchant vessels 100 gross tons and over 483; gross tonnage 2,540,592. Telephones (Dec. 1979) 1,913,000. Radio licenses (Dec. 1979) 4,634,000. Television licenses (Dec. 1979) 4,189,000.

Agriculture. Production (in 000; metric tons; 1981): wheat 4,270; barley 720; oats 311; corn c. 9,800; potatoes c. 2,500; sunflower seed 320; sugar, raw value c. 850; onions c. 310; tomatoes c. 449; cabbages c. 767; chillies and peppers c. 381; watermelons c. 661; plums 809; apples 380; wine c. 670; tobacco c. 70; beef and veal 348; pork c. 730; timber (cu m; 1980) 16,743. Livestock (in 000; Jan. 1981): cattle 5,484; sheep 7,388; pigs 7,869; horses 580; chickens 65,187.

Industry. Fuel and power (in 000; metric tons; 1981): coal 383; lignite 51,859; crude oil 4,376; natural gas (cu m) 2,240,000; manufactured gas (cu m; 1979) 652,000; electricity (kw-hr) 60,076,000. Production (in 000; metric tons; 1981): cement 10,080; iron ore (35% metal content) 4,793; pig iron 3,078; crude steel 2,358; magnesite (1980) 262; bauxite 3,252; aluminum 197; copper 132; lead 86; zinc 96; petroleum products c. 13,300; sulfuric acid 1,248; plastics and resins 483; cotton yarn 117; wool yarn 56; man-made fibres (1979) 121; wood pulp (1979) 574; newsprint 52; other paper (1979) 898; television receivers (units; 1979) 599; passenger cars (units) 175; commercial vehicles (units) 73. Merchant vessels launched (100 gross tons and over; 1981) 284,000 gross tons.

During the year Yugoslavia was visited by senior representatives of the Sudan, Malaysia, and Cuba as well as Egypt's Pres. Hosni Mubarak, Malta's Prime Minister Dom Mintoff, and Libya's leader Col. Muammar al-Qaddafi. Mojsov traveled to Tunisia and Cyprus in September and to Iran in November. Radovan Vlajkovic, a member of the Collective Presidency, visited India. Stambolic visited Ethiopia in October.

Yugoslav leaders criticized the military takeover in Poland in December 1981, one party official describing it as "a trampling on democracy." Although Soviet Foreign Minister Andrey Gromyko visited Yugoslavia in April, relations between the two countries remained cool.

In order to pay its hard-currency debt, the government in May ordered businesses to sell to the state a percentage of the foreign currency they had previously been allowed to hold for their own purposes and also to repatriate foreign-currency earnings from abroad within 60 rather than 90 days as before. This measure caused much opposition and controversy, particularly in Croatia and Slovenia, which had large tourist earnings and close trade connections with nearby Western countries. In October the dinar was devalued by 20%, and an austerity package was introduced that included gasoline rationing, restrictions on heating and lighting, a prohibitive tax on private journeys abroad, and incentives for exporters to hard-currency areas.

Yugoslavia's request for credit from the Bank for International Settlements in Basel, Switz., in September was turned down. However, in November a consortium of banks granted a $200 million, 18-month credit. Industrial output increased by only 0.6% during January-August 1982. Inflation remained at about 30%; exports to non-Communist countries fell by 3% during January-September.

(K. F. CVIIC)

Milka Planinc became the first woman premier of Yugoslavia after her election by the Federal Assembly in May.

UPI

Zaire

A republic of equatorial Africa, Zaire is bounded by the Central African Republic, Sudan, Uganda, Rwanda, Burundi, Tanzania, Zambia, Angola, Congo, and the Atlantic Ocean. Area: 2,344,885 sq km (905,365 sq mi). Pop. (1982 est.): 29,897,000, including Luba 18%; Kongo 16%; Mongo 13%; Bantu tribes 10%; other 43%. Cap. and largest city: Kinshasa (pop., 1980 est., 3 million). Language: French, Swahili, Lingala, Kikongo, Tshiluba. Religion: animist approximately 50%; Christian 43%. President in 1982, Mobutu Sese Seko; prime minister, N'singa Udjuu.

With receipts from Zaire's main exports — cobalt, coffee, copper, and industrial diamonds — falling well below their anticipated levels and inflation soaring, any prospect of adequately servicing the foreign debt was shattered. The International Monetary Fund (IMF) consequently withdrew permission for Zaire to make use of the loan in the form of Special Drawing Rights agreed upon in 1981. A delegation from the IMF paid a 15-

Zaire

day visit in June 1982, and the government agreed to proposals for reorganizing the mining industry.

This serious economic situation was further undermined by a dispute with the U.S. in May. Following allegations by members of the U.S. Congress that aid given to Zaire had been embezzled, it was proposed that the grant for 1983 should be severely cut. Pres. Mobutu Sese Seko, however, preempted Congress's decision by renouncing all aid from the U.S. because of the "insulting" statements directed against his government. This was particularly disappointing in light of the promise of substantially increased aid made to Mobutu during his visit to the U.S. in December 1981.

Internal opposition to the government was taking an increasingly political form. Thirteen people's commissioners (members of the Legislative Council) who in December 1980 had accused the government of irregular financial dealings were sentenced along with 25 others on July 1, 1982, to 15 years in prison on the charge of having founded a new political party, the Union pour la Démocratie et le Progrès Social (UDPS). They had held political rallies calling for an end to Mobutu's government and, according to the president, had stirred unrest among the supporters of the ruling Mouvement Populaire de la Révolution. Their actions, he said, were in direct conflict with the 1978 constitution, which stated that Zaire should be a one-party nation.

The most immediate result of the sentences was an increase in tension in the government's relations with Belgium, which had already been under strain because of the activities of Zairian exiles in that country. Mobutu planned a visit to Brussels in July, expecting that this would be treated as a state occasion. However, criticism of his action by some of his opponents in exile was so vigorous that the Belgian authorities, fearing demonstrations, preferred to regard the proposed trip as merely a working visit. Such an interpretation would, in Mobutu's view, have constituted a rebuff. He therefore canceled the visit, ostensibly on account of the declaration of state mourning after the death of Gen. Bobozo Adurama, a former army chief of staff. Zairian exiles nevertheless continued their campaign against the government, and in October a number of them formed a popular front aimed at restoring democracy in Zaire.

In May the president himself reformed his government. By reducing the membership of the National Executive Council from 27 to 19 he hoped to "relieve the state's budget and to strengthen regional decentralization." Ten state commissioners lost their ministries. While the president took the opportunity to introduce two new members into the council, his economies were achieved in the main by assigning the portfolios of those who had been dismissed to those who had been retained. Simultaneously he dissolved the general secretariat of the National Security Council.

It was alleged by Zambia that in February Zairian troops had seized a bus and a truck carrying cornmeal inside Zambian territory. This had led to an exchange of shots between Zairian and Zambian soldiers, and thousands of Zambian villagers had fled the area. On March 2 Zaire closed its border with Zambia, and tension continued in the border region in spite of a meeting between President Mobutu and Zambian Pres. Kenneth Kaunda in August. Two meetings of a joint commission were held in September, and both sides agreed to seek a solution to their border problems.

The government restored diplomatic relations with Israel on May 16. The president had earlier announced his intention to take this step because Egypt had already restored diplomatic relations with Israel and the last of the occupied Egyptian territory would be vacated by the Israelis in April. In response, Saudi Arabia, Qatar, Libya, Kuwait, Bangladesh, and the United Arab Emirates broke off diplomatic relations with Zaire, while Algeria and Tunisia recalled their ambassadors. A visit by Israeli Prime Minister Menachem Begin to Zaire was postponed—at first because of Israel's invasion of Lebanon and then, ostensibly, because of the illness of President Mobutu.

Zaire did not send a representative to the abortive Organization of African Unity summit meeting in Tripoli, Libya, in August. President Mobutu had been inclined to respond to the appeal by the Libyan foreign minister who had urged him to rally to the support of the meeting. However, it was thought that he changed his mind as a result of pressure brought to bear by Israel. In December

ZAIRE

Education. (1978–79) Primary, pupils 5.2 million, teachers (1972–73) 30,481; secondary, pupils c. 680,000; vocational, pupils (1977–78) c. 84,995; teacher training, students c. 99,904; secondary, vocational, and teacher training, teachers (1973–74) 14,483; higher, students (1979–80) 35,000, teaching staff (1978–79) 2,782.

Finance. Monetary unit: zaire, with (Sept. 20, 1982) a free rate of 5.86 zaires to U.S. $1 (10.05 zaires = £1 sterling). Gold and other reserves (June 1982) U.S. $133 million. Budget (1982 est.): revenue 7.8 billion zaires; expenditure 8.8 billion zaires. Gross national product (1980) 15,985,000,000 zaires. Money supply (May 1982) 5,599,400,000 zaires. Cost of living (Kinshasa; 1975 = 100; June 1982) 2,375.

Foreign Trade. (1981) Imports 2,950,700,000 zaires; exports 2,836,100,000 zaires. Import sources: Belgium-Luxembourg c. 15%; U.S. c. 11%; France c. 8%; Brazil c. 8%; West Germany c. 8%; Japan c. 6%; Iran c. 5%. Export destinations: Belgium-Luxembourg c. 32%; Angola c. 18%; U.S. c. 14%; Mozambique c. 8%. Main exports: copper 47%; cobalt 16%; coffee 15%; diamonds 7%.

Transport and Communications. Roads (1979) c. 145,000 km. Motor vehicles in use (1980): passenger c. 93,900; commercial (including buses) c. 84,900. Railways: (1980) 5,254 km; traffic (1976) 467 million passenger-km, freight 2,203,000,000 net ton-km. Air traffic (1981): c. 830 million passenger-km; freight c. 38 million net ton-km. Shipping (1981): merchant vessels 100 gross tons and over 34; gross tonnage 92,044. Inland waterways (including Zaire River; 1981) c. 14,000 km. Telephones (Jan. 1980) 30,300. Radio receivers (Dec. 1978) 130,000. Television receivers (Dec. 1979) 8,000.

Agriculture. Production (in 000; metric tons; 1981): rice c. 250; corn c. 520; sweet potatoes c. 309; cassava c. 13,000; peanuts c. 320; palm kernels c. 55; palm oil c. 155; mangoes c. 140; pineapples c. 165; bananas c. 317; oranges c. 143; coffee c. 75; rubber c. 28; cotton, lint c. 10; meat c. 182; fish catch (1980) 115; timber (cu m; 1980) c. 10,280. Livestock (in 000; 1981): cattle c. 1,230; sheep c. 753; goats c. 2,833; pigs c. 737; poultry c. 15,500.

Industry. Production (in 000; metric tons; 1980): copper ore (metal content) 459; zinc ore (metal content) 67; manganese ore (metal content) c. 10; cobalt ore (metal content) 15; gold (troy oz) 40; silver (troy oz) 2,733; diamonds (metric carats) 10,235; crude oil (1981) 993; coal 138; petroleum products (1979) c. 290; sulfuric acid (1979) 135; cement c. 400; electricity (kw-hr) 4,360,000.

it was reported that Israel was to sell arms worth $18 million to Zaire.

In June President Mobutu visited China. Before he did so, an accord was signed between the two countries that granted Zaire military sales credits worth $3.5 million. But on his arrival in Beijing (Peking) the president found that his reception was less splendid than he had anticipated; his visit brought no significant improvement in relations between the two countries. (KENNETH INGHAM)

Zambia

Zambia

A republic and a member of the Commonwealth, Zambia is bounded by Tanzania, Malawi, Mozambique, Zimbabwe, South West Africa/Namibia, Angola, and Zaire. Area: 752,614 sq km (290,586 sq mi). Pop. (1982 est.): 6,330,000, about 99% of whom are Africans. Cap. and largest city: Lusaka (pop., 1980 prelim., 538,500). Language: English and Bantu. Religion: predominantly animist, with Roman Catholic (21%), Protestant, Hindu, and Muslim minorities. President in 1982, Kenneth Kaunda; prime minister, Nalumino Mundia.

Economic problems continued to loom large in Zambia during 1982. In presenting his budget the minister of finance stated that foreign exchange earnings from the mining industry, the country's main source of wealth, were more than 20% below forecast. Subsidies were reduced by one-third, and taxes on fuel, sugar, cigarettes, alcohol, and soft drinks were increased. Subsequently the mining industry was declared exempt from taxes for the current year. The International Monetary Fund refused to allow the government to draw further on

ZAMBIA

Education. (1979) Primary, pupils 980,406, teachers (1978) 19,868; secondary, pupils 91,709, teachers (1977) 3,539; vocational, pupils 5,284, teachers (1977) 510; teacher training, students 4,406, teachers 371; higher, students (1977) 9,192, teaching staff (1976) 412.

Finance. Monetary unit: kwacha, with (Sept. 20, 1982) a free rate of 0.95 kwacha to U.S. $1 (1.62 kwacha = £1 sterling). Gold and other reserves (June 1982) U.S. $80 million. Budget (1980 actual): revenue 765.1 million kwacha; expenditure 1,012,100,000 kwacha. Gross national product (1980) 2,860,000,000 kwacha. Cost of living (1975 = 100; 1st quarter 1982) 249.3.

Foreign Trade. (1981) Imports 1,093,600,000 kwacha; exports 921.5 million kwacha. Import sources (1979): U.K. 26%; Saudi Arabia c. 18%; South Africa 11%; U.S. 9%; West Germany 8%. Export destinations (1979): Japan 19%; France c. 15%; U.K. 13%; U.S. 10%; West Germany 9%; Italy c. 8%. Main export: copper 95%.

Transport and Communications. Roads (1979) 36,415 km. Motor vehicles in use (1980): passenger c. 103,000; commercial (including buses) c. 66,300. Railways (1980) 2,189 km. Air traffic (1981): 54.7 million passenger-km; freight 18.2 million net ton-km. Telephones (Jan. 1980) 60,500. Radio receivers (Dec. 1979) 125,000. Television receivers (Dec. 1979) 60,000.

Agriculture. Production (in 000; metric tons; 1981): corn c. 1,000; cassava c. 178; millet c. 60; sorghum c. 40; peanuts c. 30; sugar, raw value c. 102; tobacco 4. Livestock (in 000; 1981): cattle 2,225; sheep c. 50; goats c. 320; pigs 235; poultry c. 12,500.

Industry. Production (in 000; metric tons; 1980): copper ore (metal content) 736; lead ore (metal content) 13; zinc ore (metal content) 35; coal (1981) 506; petroleum products (1979) c. 890; cement (1981) 143; electricity (kw-hr; 1981) 9,794,000.

the loan negotiated in May 1981. Aid from Japan, the U.S., West and East Germany, and the Arab Bank for Economic Development partly ameliorated the situation; however, the corn (maize) crop produced only one-half of the 1981 yield, thus necessitating large-scale imports.

A Zambian farmer near Lusaka gazes mournfully at his ruined crop after a prolonged drought had scorched his fields. Zambia suffered not only from poor harvests but also from an outbreak of disease among cattle.

ALAN COWELL/THE NEW YORK TIMES

A meeting between Pres. Kenneth Kaunda and Prime Minister P. W. Botha of South Africa in April was strongly criticized by other southern African nations, but the president maintained that the discussions had been of value. Border incidents strained relations with Zaire, but links with both Tanzania and Zimbabwe were strengthened.

(KENNETH INGHAM)

Zimbabwe

A republic in eastern Africa and member of the Commonwealth, Zimbabwe is bounded by Zambia, Mozambique, South Africa, and Botswana. Area: 390,759 sq km (150,873 sq mi). Pop. (1982 est.): 7,730,000, of whom 96% are African and 4% white. Cap. and largest city: Harare (formerly Salisbury; urban area pop., 1981 est., 686,000). Language: English (official) and various Bantu languages (1969 census, Shona 71%, Ndebele 15%). Religion: predominantly traditional tribal beliefs; Christian minority. President in 1982, the Rev. Canaan Banana; prime minister, Robert Mugabe.

The relative tranquillity that had followed the independence struggle in Zimbabwe was disturbed in 1982 by conflicts between the ruling Patriotic Front party, the Zimbabwe African National Union (ZANU [PF]), and Joshua Nkomo's Patriotic Front party, known as the Zimbabwe African People's Union (ZAPU [PF]). In a New Year's message Prime Minister Robert Mugabe forecast an increasingly Socialist program with the state playing an important role in farming, mining, and all other aspects of the economy. He also stated that in the future only policies approved by ZANU (PF) would be adopted by the government. This was denounced by Nkomo, who claimed that it ran counter to the idea of the supremacy of Parliament

contained in the 1979 Lancaster House agreement signed by Mugabe and himself. Ignoring this remark, Mugabe insisted that he was seeking support for a one-party state and that it was only a matter of time before this objective would be achieved.

In February Nkomo rejected a plan to merge the two Patriotic Front parties. Relations between the two leaders then took a turn for the worse with the discovery of large quantities of armaments on farms belonging to Nkomo's supporters. This led on February 17 to the dismissal of Nkomo from the government, along with three others belonging to his party, on the grounds that they allegedly plotted to overthrow the ruling party. Fears that these events would result in an outbreak of violence among Nkomo's angry supporters were not immediately realized, and U.K. Foreign Secretary Lord Carrington, who visited Zimbabwe in February, congratulated the government on the country's stability. Moreover, at a meeting of their party the three remaining ZAPU (PF) members of the government decided that they would not resign in protest against their leader's dismissal. The decision was taken in order to avoid possible victimization of party supporters.

Links between Nkomo's supporters and the Republican Front (RF; previously the Rhodesia Front) were given an ominous twist after four white men were found guilty of plotting to overthrow the government and force the secession of Matabeleland, Nkomo's home province. Nine RF members of Parliament resigned from their party after disagreement over some of its policies. One of the defectors stated that senior members of the RF had known and approved of a proposed armed coup in which Nkomo's supporters would be involved. In April it was claimed that a number of camps had been found where guerrilla fighters

Zimbabwe

Joshua Nkomo, head of the Zimbabwe African People's Union, was removed from the Cabinet of Prime Minister Robert Mugabe, who feared that Nkomo was planning a coup.

JORDAN—GAMMA/LIAISON

loyal to Nkomo were being trained to fight for the overthrow of the government.

Later in the month Nkomo, who was still under investigation for his alleged involvement in the secretion of arms, firmly condemned dissidents thought to be members of his former guerrilla army. But in May, as acts of violence began to spread across the country and to affect Matabeleland in particular, he blamed the government for the unrest, claiming that it stemmed from the prime minister's desire for a one-party state. This, he claimed, was the real cause of his dismissal and subsequent attempts to discredit him.

In June the government was forced to launch a large-scale campaign against the dissidents in Matabeleland, and again Nkomo denounced those who were resorting to violence and called for an all-party inquiry into their activities. "Nobody wants to support these people who are destroying Zimbabwe," he said at a gathering in Bulawayo. Only days later armed men attacked the home of the prime minister and another of his ministers, Enos Nkala, in Harare (the name given in April to Salisbury). Nkomo unreservedly condemned the attacks and called for peace and stability. Meanwhile, government forces arrested hundreds of people in Bulawayo in an attempt to hunt down dissidents, and in no friendly spirit Mugabe accused Nkala of being linked with the Harare attacks.

Worse was to follow. Toward the end of July a night raid on the air base near Gweru resulted in the destruction of 12 fighter planes. A number of both white and black members and former members of the Air Force were arrested by security police. On August 2 Mugabe and Nkomo met, on

Nkomo's initiative, and there appeared to be some prospect of discussions between their two parties. On September 14 Nkomo again called for a political solution to the violence in the west of the country, but at the same time he accused security forces of mistreating civilians. These forces belonged to the 5th Army Brigade, recruited from Mugabe's supporters and trained by North Korean instructors.

It was not reassuring for Nkomo and his supporters when it was admitted that a 6th Army Brigade was being recruited from supporters of ZANU (PF) as a result of the government's concern about the loyalty of the rest of the armed forces. This followed numerous defections of former guerrillas who remained loyal to Nkomo. The new brigade was to be trained by North Koreans, although in October two additional groups of military instructors arrived from the U.K.

On September 30 two condemned murderers became the first people to be executed since independence. They were not political dissidents, but observers believed that their execution was meant to be a warning to dissidents engaged in similar violence for professed political ends. Nevertheless, violence continued, and on December 24 three people were killed and 21 wounded when a band of supposed ZAPU (PF) supporters attacked cars, buses, and a train in western Matabeleland.

In early December it was reported that Ian Smith, former Rhodesian prime minister and leader of the RF, had had his home searched and several papers removed by security forces. The search was believed to be in response to controversial statements made by Smith during an earlier trip to the U.S. and the U.K.

These political activities overshadowed serious economic problems. In March the preferential trade agreement with South Africa, which was due to expire in the same month, was renewed. Not to have done so, an advisory report maintained, would have cost Zimbabwe $50 million in exports and would have put 6,500 jobs at risk. Such a result could not be contemplated after the nation had experienced in 1981 its first visible balance of trade deficit since 1968. One of the main problems was the lack of foreign investment, which the prime minister was inclined to blame on adverse foreign press reports. In fact, world recession and government policy were more important factors. The announcement in March that the constitution was to be rewritten caused consternation among potential investors in spite of an assurance that any change would be introduced by constitutional means and that the property rights of foreign investors would be secure.

In May the economy suffered a further setback when the oil pipeline from Mozambique was sabotaged. The prime minister himself paid a visit to seven European countries in late May and early June in an attempt to reassure would-be investors that Zimbabwe offered secure opportunities for their activities. More important was the government's announcement in October, after prolonged external pressure, of a code to protect foreign investment. The government also reduced subsidies on some basic foods, and the minister of finance cut the allocation of foreign currency to industry

---

ZIMBABWE

Education. (1982) Primary, pupils 1,934,614, teachers (1980) 33,516; secondary, pupils 224,609, teachers (1981) 6,107; vocational (including part-time), pupils 6,217, teachers (1979) 278; teacher training, students (1981) 3,484, teachers (1979) 258; higher (university only), students (1981) 2,525, teaching staff (1979) 483.

Finance. Monetary unit: Zimbabwe dollar, with (Sept. 20, 1982) a free rate of Z$0.77 to U.S. $1 (Z$1.32 = £1 sterling). Budget (1981–82 est.): revenue Z$1,482,000,000; expenditure Z$2,006,000,000. Gross national product (1981) Z$4,418,000,000.

Foreign Trade. (1981) Imports Z$1,,027,400,000; exports Z$942.5 million. Import sources (Aug.–Dec. 1980): South Africa 27%; U.K. 8%; U.S. 7%; West Germany 7%. Export destinations (Aug.–Dec. 1980): South Africa 17%; West Germany 11%; U.K. 5%; Italy 5%. Main exports (1980): tobacco 13%; gold 13%; food 11%; asbestos 9%; ferrochrome 9%; cotton 6%; steel 6%; nickel 6%.

Transport and Communications. Roads (1981) 85,789 km. Motor vehicles in use (1981): passenger 167,400; commercial (including buses) 68,700. Railways: (1980) 3,394 km; freight traffic (1980–81) 6,610,000,000 net ton-km. Air traffic (1981): 506.3 million passenger-km; freight 9,063,000 net ton-km. Telephones (Dec. 1981) 224,500. Radio licenses (June 1981) 224,960. Television licenses (June 1981) 75,200.

Agriculture. Production (in 000; metric tons; 1981): corn 2,814; millet 196; wheat c. 190; sugar, raw value c. 390; peanuts 239; tobacco 70; cotton, lint 60; beef and veal c. 109. Livestock (in 000; 1980): cattle 5,279; sheep 387; goats 982; pigs 132.

Industry. Production (in 000; metric tons; 1981): coal 2,867; cement 583; asbestos 248; chrome ore 536; iron ore (metal content) 1,096; copper ore (metal content) 25; tin concentrates (metal content) 1.2; nickel ore (metal content) 13; gold (troy oz) 371; silver (troy oz) 857; electricity (kw-hr) 4,518,000.

Zoology:
see Life Sciences

and for travel. These changes took effect against a background of concern as the country prepared to negotiate a loan with the International Monetary Fund (IMF) to offset the balance of payments deficit. The government announced a 20% devaluation of its currency on December 8, a move that was interpreted as necessary in order to secure IMF credits. Meanwhile, the long-awaited three-year national economic development program was published in late November.

(KENNETH INGHAM)

Zoos and Botanical Gardens

Zoos. Worldwide recession, with rapidly rising costs, particularly of food and fuel; increasing wages; and declining numbers of visitors caused financial problems for many zoos, especially those in Europe and North America. For totally self-supporting zoos the position in some cases became critical. In Britain, where admissions to the London Zoo had fallen by more than 20% in 1981, a symposium was held in October 1982 at which the reasons for the situation were discussed and a number of possible remedies put forward. It was agreed that to increase attendance it might be necessary to emphasize the entertainment aspect of zoos, although this should not detract from or diminish their essential functions in the areas of conservation, education, and science. It was ironic that some of the zoos that over the last few years had adopted as a top priority the breeding of animals endangered in the wild were now fighting for their own survival.

During 1981–82 the American Association of Zoological Parks and Aquariums committed itself to developing a species survival plan to coordinate the captive breeding of endangered animal species. Thirty species were designated, and detailed plans were drawn up for nearly half that number. Pragmatically, as well as altruistically, a coordinated scientific and practical breeding program was a necessary step forward. There were now fewer sources of wild animals, and high purchasing and shipping costs further reduced the supply. In addition, international and national laws on endangered species, and stricter quarantine regulations, limited animal import and export. The zoos' own preservation thus partly depended on their ability to breed their own animals.

The desire to preserve species for future generations and to maintain a rich genetic pool that might some day be returned to the wild had radically changed the policies of many zoos, replacing competition with cooperation. Zoos now exchanged animals as they would library books, though usually on extended or indefinite loans. Modern technology, particularly the use of computer records, was being used more and more. On an international scale, the Captive Breeding Specialist Group, an important committee of the Species Survival Commission of the International Union for Conservation of Nature, advised and helped to coordinate management and breeding programs. At its meeting in August in London, the committee made a number of important decisions,

particularly in relation to the international management of the Asian wild horse (Przewalski horse) in captivity and its release into reserves in the wild. This meeting followed a well-attended symposium on the status and management of African and Asian rhinoceroses in the wild and in captivity. Organized by the International Union of Directors of Zoological Gardens, the symposium brought together workers from zoos, universities, and the field.

In September pandas again stole the headlines when the female Shao Shao in Madrid gave birth to twins after artificial insemination with semen from the London Zoo's male, Chia Chia. This was the second successful artificial insemination but the first outside China. The tiny mouse-sized cubs, their bodies only sparsely hairy, weighed 88.9 and 59.4 grams (3.14 and 2.1 oz). There were no birth complications, but the mother rejected the smaller offspring and, although it was placed in an incubator, it died after a few days. The other cub was being looked after by the mother and was progressing well.

More refined techniques of artificial insemination led to successful births or hatchings in other species. Two particularly important examples in 1982 were the first whooping crane (*Grus americana*) at the International Crane Foundation in Wisconsin and the first parrot, a cockatiel (*Nymphicus hollandicus*), in Florida.

Successful first-time breedings of special note in

The newest of only 138 Malayan tapirs known to exist was guarded by its mother after the youngster was born on August 2 at the St. Louis (Missouri) Zoo.

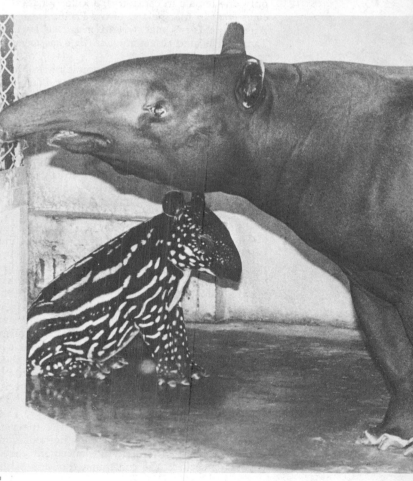

UPI

What was believed to be the first albino wallaby born in captivity in the U.S. arrived at the Jackson, Mississippi, Zoo in the spring.

1982 included Mexican wolves (*Canis lupus baileyi*) in St. Louis, Mo. (only about 30 left in the world; only one female in captivity); a killer whale (*Orcinus orea*) in Marineland of the Pacific, near Los Angeles; a Lear's macaw (*Andorhynchus leari*) in Tampa, Fla.; and Houston toads (*Bufo houstonensis*) in Houston, Texas.   (P. J. OLNEY)

Botanical Gardens. The economic recession seriously affected botanical gardens as well as zoos, and plans for new establishments and the extension and modernization of existing ones were severely curtailed in many cases. Cuts in personnel had a particularly bad effect on the care and maintenance of large collections. There were even some closings, as, for example, at Kassel, West Germany. In the U.S. the national parks, invaluable reservoirs of naturally occurring species, were threatened by proposed changes in their status.

This state of affairs, combined with the current trend of environmentalist thought, focused interest on "wilderness gardens." The theory was that areas given over to natural growth (as, for example, disused railroad station sites in West Berlin) would be richly colonized by flora and fauna, providing valuable material for study without the need for attention. Experience suggested, however, that it was fallacious to assume that no human intervention would be required. Some establishments, such as the National Botanical Gardens at Kirstenbosch in South Africa, continued their valuable service of supplying seeds and plants to public and private gardens so that rare species could be distributed more widely and their survival more effectively ensured.

An outstanding development during the year was the provision of extensive new hothouses for the 50-year-old Zürich, Switz., succulent collection. This secured the continuance of one of the most comprehensive protective collections of cacti and other succulents, greatly increasing its capacity for development and scientific research. (Ironically enough, wild cacti were currently under considerable threat through the depredations of collectors.)

At the Royal Botanic Gardens, Kew, England, the extensively restored temperate house was opened by Queen Elizabeth II in May 1982. The queen planted a young Chilean wine palm (*Jubaea chilensis*) that would eventually replace the one grown from seed in 1846 and transplanted to the temperate house at the original opening in 1860, which now reached the roof. The firm of architects responsible for the restoration, Manning, Clamp & Partners, also won a competition for the design of a new building to be constructed at Kew that would house the reference collection and associated library and offices and also provide space for public exhibitions.

Increasingly, botanical gardens were holding exhibitions devoted to a wide variety of themes within their own grounds or contributing to national and international shows such as the Chelsea Flower Show in London and the European Orchid Congress in Hamburg, West Germany.

Among the year's negative aspects, certain environmental factors predominated. "Acid rain," the precipitation of emissions in the form of various acids, increasingly threatened forests and hothouse cultivation as well as lakes with their plant and animal life. In Hamburg substantial deposits of zinc, lead, and cadmium were recorded in the leaves, roots, and stamens of orchids and bromeliads; protective measures against this would be difficult and costly.   (JOHANNES APEL)

See also Environment; Gardening.
[355.C.6]

CONTRIBUTORS

Names of contributors to the Britannica Book of the Year with the articles written by them.
The arrangement is alphabetical by last name.

AARSDAL, STENER. Economic and Political Journalist, *Borsen*, Copenhagen.
Biographies (*in part*); **Denmark**

ADAMS, ANDREW M. Free-lance Foreign Correspondent; Editor and Publisher, *Sumo World* magazine. Author of *Ninja: The Invisible Assassins; Born to Die: The Cherry Blossom Squadrons.* Co-author of *Sumo History and Yokozuna Profiles; Japan Sports Guide.*
Combat Sports: *Judo; Karate; Kendo; Sumo*

AGRELLA, JOSEPH C. Correspondent, *Blood-Horse* magazine; former Turf Editor, *Chicago Sun-Times.* Co-author of *Ten Commandments for Professional Handicapping; American Race Horses.*
Equestrian Sports: *Thoroughbred Racing and Steeplechasing* (*in part*)

AIELLO, LESLIE C. Lecturer, Department of Anthropology, University College, London.
Anthropology

ALLABY, MICHAEL. Free-lance Writer and Lecturer. Author of *Who Will Eat?; Inventing Tomorrow; World Food Resources; A Year in the Life of a Field.* Co-author of *A Blueprint for Survival; Home Farm.* Editor of *The Survival Handbook; Dictionary of the Environment.*
Environment (*in part*)

ALLAN, J. A. Senior Lecturer in Geography, School of Oriental and African Studies, University of London.
Libya

ALSTON, REX. Broadcaster and Journalist; retired BBC Commentator. Author of *Taking the Air; Over to Rex Alston; Test Commentary; Watching Cricket.*
Biographies (*in part*); **Cricket**

ANDERSON, PETER J. Assistant Director, Institute of Polar Studies, Ohio State University, Columbus.
Antarctic

APEL, JOHANNES. Formerly Curator, Botanic Garden, University of Hamburg. Author of *Gärtnerisch-Botanische Briefe.*
Zoos and Botanical Gardens: *Botanical Gardens*

ARCHIBALD, JOHN J. Feature Writer, *St. Louis Post-Dispatch.* Author of *Bowling for Boys and Girls.*
Bowling: *Tenpin Bowling* (*in part*)

ARNOLD, GUY. Free-lance Writer. Author of *Modern Nigeria; Kenyatta and the Politics of Kenya; Aid in Africa; The Unions; Modern Kenya.*
Botswana; Burundi; Cape Verde; Equatorial Guinea; Gambia, The; Ghana; Guinea-Bissau; Lesotho; Liberia; Maldives; Mauritius; Nigeria: *Special Report*; **Rwanda; São Tomé and Príncipe; Seychelles; Sierra Leone; Swaziland**

ARNOLD, MAVIS. Free-lance Journalist, Dublin.
Ireland

ARRINGTON, LEONARD J. Formerly Church Historian, Church of Jesus Christ of Latter-day Saints. Author of *Great Basin Kingdom; An Economic History of the Latter-day Saints; Building the City of God: Community and Cooperation Among the Mormons; The Mormon Experience: A History of the Latter-day Saints.*
Religion: *Church of Jesus Christ of Latter-day Saints*

AYTON, CYRIL J. Editor, *Motorcycle Sport*, London.
Motor Sports: *Motorcycles*

BAPTIST, INES T. Administrative Assistant, Encyclopaedia Britannica, Yearbooks.
Belize

BARFORD, MICHAEL F. Editor and Director, *World Tobacco*, London.
Industrial Review: *Tobacco*

BARGAD, WARREN. Milton D. Ratner Professor of Hebrew Literature and Dean, Spertus College of Judaica, Chicago. Author of *Hayim Hazaz: Novelist of Ideas; Anthology of Israeli Poetry.*
Literature: *Hebrew*

BARRETT, PAUL A. Managing Editor, *TV World* magazine, London.
Television and Radio (*in part*)

BASS, HOWARD. Journalist and Broadcaster. Editor, *Winter Sports*, 1948–69. Winter Sports Correspondent, *Daily Telegraph* and *Sunday Telegraph*, London; *The Standard*, London; *Toronto Star*, Toronto; *Canadian Skater*, Ottawa; *Skating*, Boston; *Ski Racing*, Denver; *Ski*, London. Author of *The Magic of Skiing; International Encyclopaedia of Winter Sports; Let's Go Skating; Glorious Wembley.*
Ice Hockey: *European and International*; **Winter Sports**

BAYLISS, DAVID. Chief Transport Planner, Greater London Council. Co-author of *Developing Patterns of Urbanization; Uses of Economics.* Advisory Editor of *Models in Urban and Regional Planning.*
Transportation (*in part*)

BEALL, JOHN V. Sales Manager, Davy McKee Corp. Author of sections 1 and 34, *Mining Engineering Handbook.* Frequent Contributor to *Mining Engineering.*
Mining and Quarrying (*in part*)

BEATTIE, ROGER A. Member of Secretariat, International Social Security Association, Geneva.
Social Security and Welfare Services (*in part*)

BEATTY, J. THOMAS. Director of Editorial Production, Encyclopædia Britannica, Inc.
Computers (*Sidebar*)

BEATTY, JAMES R. Retired Research Fellow, B. F. Goodrich Research and Development Center, Brecksville, Ohio. Co-author of *Concepts in Compounding;*

Physical Testing of Elastomers and Polymers in Applied Polymer Science; Physical Properties of Rubber Compounds in the Mechanics of Pneumatic Tires.
Industrial Review: *Rubber*

BECKWITH, DAVID C. National Economic Correspondent, *Time* magazine, Washington, D.C.
United States: *Special Report*; **United States Statistical Supplement:** *Developments in the States in 1982.*

BEEK, JAMES. Editorial Director, American Forest Institute.
Industrial Review: *Wood Products*

BERGERRE, MAX. Vatican Affairs Correspondent. *La Vie Catholique*, Paris.
Vatican City State

BERKOVITCH, ISRAEL. Free-lance Writer and Consultant. Author of *Coal on the Switchback; Coal: Energy and Chemical Storehouse.* Editor of *World Energy: Looking Ahead to 2020.*
Energy: *Coal*

BERRY, JOHN N., III. Editor-in-Chief, *Library Journal*, New York City.
Libraries: *Special Report*

BICKELHAUPT, DAVID L. Professor of Insurance and Finance, College of Administrative Science, Ohio State University, Columbus. Author of *Transition to Multiple-Line Insurance Companies; General Insurance* (10th ed.).
Industrial Review: *Insurance*

BILEFIELD, LIONEL. Technical Journalist.
Industrial Review: *Paints and Varnishes*

BIRD, THOMAS E. Assistant Director, Yiddish Program, Queens College, City University of New York. Contributor to *Lexicon of Modern Yiddish Literature.*
Literature: *Yiddish* (*in part*)

BLACKBURN, LUCY. Economist, Group Economics Department, Lloyds Bank Ltd., London. Contributor to *EEC and the Third World: A Survey.*
Biographies (*in part*); **Chile; Costa Rica; El Salvador; Guatemala; Honduras**

BLUMENTHAL, MARCIA A. Senior Editor, Computer Industry, *Computerworld.*
Computers

BODDY, WILLIAM C. Editor, *Motor Sport.* Full Member, Guild of Motoring Writers. Author of *The History of Brooklands Motor Course; The World's Land Speed Record; Continental Sports Cars; The Bugatti Story; History of Montlhéry; The VW Beetle.*
Motor Sports: *Grand Prix Racing; Rallies and Other Races*

BODEN, EDWARD. Editor, *The Veterinary Record*; Executive Editor, *Research in Veterinary Science.*
Veterinary Science

BOLT, PETER H. Secretary, British Committee, World Methodist Council. Author of *A Way of Loving.*
Religion: *Methodist Churches*

BOLTZ, C. L. Free-lance Industrial Writer, London.
Energy: *Electricity*

BOONSTRA, DICK. Assistant Professor, Department of Political Science, Free University, Amsterdam.
Biographies (*in part*); **Netherlands, The; Suriname**

BOOTH, JOHN NICHOLLS. Lecturer and Writer; Co-founder, Japan Free Religious Association; Senior Pastor of a number of U.S. churches. Author of *The Quest for Preaching Power; Introducing Unitarian Universalism.*
Religion: *Unitarian (Universalist) Churches*

BOSWALL, JEFFERY. Producer of Sound and Television Programs, BBC Natural History Unit, Bristol, England.
Life Sciences: *Ornithology*

BOTHELL, JOAN N. Free-lance Writer and Editor; former Staff Writer, Encyclopaedia Britannica.
Biographies (*in part*)

BOWDEN, RUSSELL. Deputy Secretary-General, Library Association, U.K.
Libraries (*in part*)

BOX, BEN. Free-lance Writer and Researcher on Latin America and Iberia.
Argentina; Biographies (*in part*); **Colombia**

BOYE, ROGER. Coin Columnist, *Chicago Tribune.*
Philately and Numismatics: *Coins*

BOYLE, C. L. Lieutenant Colonel, R.A. (retired). Chairman, Survival Service Commission, International Union for Conservation of Nature and Natural Resources, 1958–63; Secretary, Fauna Preservation Society, London, 1950–63.
Environment (*in part*)

BRACKMAN, ARNOLD C. Asian Affairs Specialist. Author of *Indonesian Communism: A History; Southeast Asia's Second Front: The Power Struggle in the Malay Archipelago; The Communist Collapse in Indonesia; The Last Emperor.*
Indonesia

BRADSHER, HENRY S. Foreign Affairs Writer.
Philippines

BRAIDWOOD, ROBERT J. Professor Emeritus of Old World Prehistory, the Oriental Institute and the Department of Anthropology, University of Chicago. Author of *Prehistoric Men; Archeologists and What They Do.*
Archaeology: *Eastern Hemisphere*

BRAZEE, RUTLAGE J. Geophysical Consultant.
Earth Sciences: *Geophysics*

BRECHER, KENNETH. Professor of Astronomy and Physics, Boston University. Co-author and co-editor of *Astronomy of the Ancients; High Energy Astrophysics and Its Relation to Elementary Particle Physics.*
Astronomy

BRUNO, HAL. Director of Political Coverage, ABC News, Washington, D.C.
Biographies (*in part*)

BURDIN, JOEL L. Professor of Educational Administration, Ohio University, Athens, Ohio. Co-author of *A Reader's Guide to the Comprehensive Models for Pre-* paring Elementary Teachers; Elementary School Curriculum and Instruction.
Education (*in part*)

BURKE, DONALD P. Executive Editor, *Chemical Week*, New York City.
Industrial Review: *Chemicals*

BURKS, ARDATH W. Emeritus Professor of Asian Studies, Rutgers University, New Brunswick, N.J. Author of *The Government of Japan; East Asia: China, Korea, Japan; Japan: Portrait of a Postindustrial Power.*
Japan

BUSS, ROBIN. Lecturer in French, Woolwich College of Further Education, London.
Literature: *French* (*in part*)

BUTLER, FRANK. Former Sports Editor, *News of the World*, London. Author of *A History of Boxing in Britain.*
Combat Sports: *Boxing*

CALHOUN, DAVID R. Editor, Encyclopædia Britannica, Yearbooks.
Biographies (*in part*); **Gambling** (*in part*); **Target Sports:** *Archery*

CAMERON, SARAH. Economist, Group Economics Department, Lloyds Bank Ltd., London.
Dominican Republic; Ecuador; Peru; Venezuela

CARTER, ROBERT W. Free-lance Journalist, London. Author of numerous newspaper and magazine articles.
Equestrian Sports: *Thoroughbred Racing and Steeplechasing* (*in part*)

CASSIDY, RICHARD J. Senior Public Relations Officer, British Gas Corporation. Author of *Gas: Natural Energy.*
Energy: *Natural Gas*

CASSIDY, VICTOR M. Senior Editor, *Specifying Engineer* magazine, Des Plaines, Ill.
Biographies (*in part*)

CEGIELSKI, CHARLES M. Associate Editor, Encyclopædia Britannica, Yearbooks.
Life Sciences: *Introduction*

CHAPMAN, KENNETH F. Former Editor, *Stamp Collecting* and *Philatelic Magazine*; Philatelic Correspondent, *The Times*, London. Author of *Good Stamp Collecting; Commonwealth Stamp Collecting.*
Philately and Numismatics: *Stamps*

CHAPMAN, ROBIN. Senior Economist, Group Economics Department, Lloyds Bank Ltd., London.
Brazil; Haiti; Latin-American Affairs

CHAPPELL, DUNCAN. Professor, Department of Criminology, Simon Fraser University, Vancouver, B.C. Co-author of *The Police and the Public in Australia and New Zealand.* Co-editor of *The Australian Criminal Justice System* (1st and 2nd ed.); *Violence and Criminal Justice; Forcible Rape: the Crime, the Victim and the Offender.*
Crime and Law Enforcement

CHERFAS, JEREMY. Demonstrator in Animal Behaviour, University of Oxford; Life Sciences Consultant, *New Scientist* magazine, London. Author of *Man Made Life*; co-author of *The Monkey Puzzle.* Editor of *Darwin up to Date.*
Life Sciences: *Special Report*

CHU, HUNG-TI. Expert in Far Eastern Affairs; Former International Civil Servant and University Professor.
China; Taiwan

CHUPRININ, SERGEY. Journalist, Novosti Press Agency, Moscow.
Literature: *Russian* (*in part*)

CLARKE, R. O. Writer on Social Affairs and Industrial Relations, Paris.
Industrial Relations

CLEVELAND, WILLIAM A. Geography Editor, *Encyclopædia Britannica* and Britannica Yearbooks.
Mining and Quarrying (*in part*)

CLIFTON, DONALD F. Professor Emeritus of Metallurgy, University of Idaho.
Materials Sciences: *Metallurgy*

COGLE, T. C. J. Editor, *Electrical Review*, London.
Industrial Review: *Electrical*

COMBA, ALDO. Executive Secretary, Department of Cooperation and Witness, World Alliance of Reformed Churches; former President, Federation of Protestant Churches in Italy. Author of *Le Parabole di Gesú.*
Religion: *Reformed, Presbyterian, and Congregational Churches*

COPPOCK, CHARLES DENNIS. Vice-President, English Lacrosse Union. Author of "Men's Lacrosse" in *The Oxford Companion to Sports and Games.*
Field Hockey and Lacrosse: *Lacrosse* (*in part*)

COSTIN, STANLEY H. British Correspondent, *Herrenjournal International* and *Men's Wear, Australasia.* Council of Management Member, British Men's Fashion Association Ltd. Former President, Men's Fashion Writers International.
Fashion and Dress (*in part*)

CRATER, RUFUS W. Senior Editorial Consultant, *Broadcasting*, New York City.
Television and Radio (*in part*)

CROSS, COLIN J. Editor, *The Polo Times*; U.K. Chairman, European Polo Academy.
Equestrian Sports: *Polo*

CROSSLAND, NORMAN. Bonn Correspondent, *The Economist*, London.
Biographies (*in part*); **German Democratic Republic; Germany, Federal Republic of**

CVIIC, K. F. Leader Writer and East European Specialist, *The Economist*, London.
Yugoslavia

DAUME, DAPHNE. Editor, Encyclopædia Britannica, Yearbooks.
Biographies (*in part*)

DAVID, TUDOR. Managing Editor, *Education*, London.
Education (*in part*)

DAVIS, DONALD A. Editor, *Drug & Cosmetic Industry* and *Cosmetic Insider's Report*, New York City. Contributor to *The Science and Technology of Aerosol Packaging; Advances in Cosmetic Technology.*
Industrial Review: *Pharmaceuticals*

DAVIS, KENNETH C. Free-lance Writer, currently at work on a history of the paperback in America.
Publishing: *Books* (*in part*)

DEAM, JOHN B. Technical Director, National Machine Tool Builders Association, McLean, Va. Author of *The Synthesis of Common Digital Subsystems.*
Industrial Review: *Machinery and Machine Tools*

DECRAENE, PHILIPPE. Member of editorial staff, *Le Monde*, Paris. Professor, Institute of Political Studies, Paris. Author of *Tableau des Partis Politiques Africains; Lettres de l'Afrique Atlantique; L'expérience socialiste Somalienne; Le Mali; Vieux Afrique, Jeunes Nations.*
Benin; Cameroon; Central African Republic; Chad; Comoros; Congo; Dependent States (in part); Djibouti; Gabon; Guinea; Ivory Coast; Madagascar; Mali; Mauritania; Niger; Senegal; Togo; Tunisia; Upper Volta

de FAINBOIM, MARTA BEKERMAN. Research Officer, Institute of Development Studies, University of Sussex, England.
Nicaragua

de la BARRE, KENNETH. Director, Katimavik, Montreal.
Arctic Regions

DENSELOW, ROBIN. Rock Music Critic, *The Guardian*, London; Current Affairs Producer, BBC Television. Co-author of *The Electric Muse.*
Music: *Popular*

DE PUY, NORMAN R. Minister, First Baptist Church, Newton Centre, Mass.; Columnist, *American Baptist* magazine. Author of *The Bible Alive; Help in Understanding Theology.*
Religion: *Baptist Churches*

DESHAYES-CREUILLY, MARIE-JOSE. Head of Documentation Services, International Vine and Wine Office, Paris.
Industrial Review: *Alcoholic Beverages (in part)*

DIRNBACHER, ELFRIEDE. Austrian Civil Servant.
Austria

DOOLING, DAVE. Science Editor, *Huntsville* (Ala.) *Times*; Editor-in-Chief, *Space World* magazine.
Space Exploration: *Special Report*

DORRIS, THOMAS HARTLEY. Editor, Ecumenical Press Service, Geneva. Author of several periodical articles on religion, education, and medicine.
Religion: *Lutheran Churches*

DRAKE, CHRIS. Managing Director, MEMO: Middle East Media Operations, Nicosia, Cyprus.
Cyprus

EIU. The Economist Intelligence Unit, London.
Economy, World (in part)

ELI, C. R. Executive Director, U.S. Badminton Association.
Racket Games: *Badminton*

ENGELS, JAN R. Editor, *Vooruitgang* (Bimonthly of the Centre Paul Hymans, liberal study and documentation centre), Brussels.
Belgium

EWART, W. D. Editor and Director, *Fairplay International Shipping Weekly*, London. Author of *Marine Engines; Atomic Submarines; Hydrofoils and Hovercraft; Building a Ship.* Editor of *World Atlas of Shipping.*
Industrial Review: *Shipbuilding;* Transportation (in part)

FARR, D. M. L. Professor of History and Director, Paterson Centre for International Programs, Carleton University, Ottawa. Co-author of *The Canadian Experience.*
Canada

FAUST, JOAN LEE. Garden Editor, *New York Times.*
Gardening (in part)

FEDER, ROBERT. Television Reporter, *Chicago Sun-Times.*
Television and Radio: *Special Report*

FENDELL, ROBERT J. Auto Editor, *Science &Mechanics*; Auto Contributor, *Gentlemen's Quarterly.* Author of *The New Era Car Book and Auto Survival Guide; How to Make Your Car Last Forever.* Co-author of *Encyclopedia of Motor Racing Greats.*
Motor Sports: *U.S. Racing*

FERRIER, R. W. Group Historian, British Petroleum Company Ltd., London.
Energy: *Petroleum*

FIDDICK, PETER. Specialist Writer, *The Guardian*, London.
Publishing: *Newspapers (in part); Magazines (in part)*

FIELDS, DONALD. Helsinki Correspondent, BBC, *The Guardian*, and *The Sunday Times*, London.
Biographies (in part); Finland

FIRTH, DAVID. Editor, *The Friend*, London; formerly Editor, *Quaker Monthly*, London.
Religion: *Religious Society of Friends*

FISHER, DAVID. Civil Engineer, Freeman Fox & Partners, London; formerly Executive Editor, *Engineering*, London.
Engineering Projects: *Bridges*

FLANAGAN, JACK C. Travel Counselor.
Water Sports: *Surfing*

FRADY, WILLIAM ENSIGN, III. Editor, *Water Polo Scoreboard*, Newport Beach, Calif.
Water Sports: *Water Polo*

FRANKLIN, HAROLD. Editor, *English Bridge Quarterly.* Bridge Correspondent, *Yorkshire Post; Yorkshire Evening Post.* Broadcaster. Author of *Best of Bridge on the Air.*
Contract Bridge

FRANZ, FREDERICK W. President, Watch Tower Bible and Tract Society of Pennsylvania.
Religion: *Jehovah's Witnesses*

FRAWLEY, MARGARET-LOUISE. Retired Press Officer, All England Women's Lacrosse Association.
Field Hockey and Lacrosse: *Lacrosse (in part)*

FREEDMAN, LAWRENCE. Professor of War Studies, King's College, University of London. Author of *The Evolution of Nuclear Strategy; Britain and Nuclear Weapons.*
Feature Article: *The Great Disarmament Debate*

FRIDOVICH, IRWIN. James B. Duke Professor of Biochemistry, Duke University Medical Center, Durham, N.C. Contributor to *Oxidase and Redox Systems; Molecular Mechanisms of Oxygen Activation.*
Life Sciences: *Molecular Biology (in part)*

FRIEDLY, ROBERT LOUIS. Executive Director, Office of Communication, Christian Church (Disciples of Christ), Indianapolis, Ind.
Religion: *Christian Church (Disciples of Christ)*

FRISKIN, SYDNEY E. Hockey Correspondent, *The Times*, London.
Field Hockey and Lacrosse: *Field Hockey*

FROST, DAVID. Rugby Union Correspondent, *The Guardian*, London.
Football: *Rugby*

GADDUM, PETER W. Chairman, H. T. Gaddum and Company Ltd., Silk Merchants, Macclesfield, Cheshire, England. Honorary President, International Silk Association, Lyons. Author of *Silk—How and Where It Is Produced.*
Industrial Review: *Textiles (in part)*

GANADO, ALBERT. Lawyer, Malta.
Malta

GARRAD, ROB. Director of Information Services, International Headquarters, Salvation Army.
Religion: *Salvation Army*

GIBBONS, J. WHITFIELD. Research Ecologist, Savannah River Ecology Laboratory, Aiken, South Carolina.
Life Sciences: *Zoology*

GIBNEY, FRANK. Vice-Chairman, Board of Editors, Encyclopædia Britannica, Inc. Author of *Miracle by Design: The Real Reasons Behind Japan's Economic Success.*
Japan: *Special Report*

GIBNEY, FRANK B., JR. Researcher, *Newsweek* magazine, New York City.
Biographies (in part)

GILLESPIE, HUGH M. Director of Communications, International Road Federation, Washington, D.C.
Engineering Projects: *Roads*

GJESTER, FAY. Oslo Correspondent, *Financial Times*, London.
Norway

GOLDSMITH, ARTHUR. Editorial Director, *Popular Photography* and *Camera Arts*, New York City. Author of *The Photography Game; The Nude in Photography; The Camera and Its Images.* Co-author of *The Eye of Eisenstaedt.*
Photography

GOLOMBEK, HARRY. British Chess Champion, 1947, 1949, and 1955. Chess Correspondent, *The Times*, London. Author of *Penguin Handbook of the Game of Chess; A History of Chess; The Encyclopedia of Chess.*
Chess

GOODWIN, NOËL. Associate Editor, *Dance & Dancers*; U.K. Dance Correspondent, *International Herald Tribune*, Paris, and *Ballet News*, New York City. Author of *A Ballet for Scotland*; editor of Royal Ballet and Royal Opera yearbooks for 1978, 1979, 1980. Contributor to the *Encyclopædia Britannica* (15th ed.).
Dance (in part)

GOODWIN, ROBERT E. Formerly Executive Director, Billiard Congress of America: Managing Director, Billiard and Bowling Institute of America.
Billiard Games

GOTTFRIED, MARTIN. Drama Critic, New York City. Author of *A Theater Divided; Opening Nights; Broadway Musicals; Jed Harris Presents Broadway.*
Theatre (in part)

GOULD, DONALD W. Medical Writer and Broadcaster, U.K.
Health and Disease: *Overview (in part); Mental Health*

GOULD, ROWLAND. Free-lance Writer, Tokyo. Author of *The Matsushita Phenomenon; The Concrete Reality of the Japanese Way of Thinking.*
Biographies *(in part)*

GREEN, BENNY. Record Reviewer, BBC. Author of *Blame It on My Youth; 58 Minutes to London; Jazz Decade; Drums in My Ears; Shaw's Champions.* Contributor to *Encyclopedia of Jazz.*
Music: *Jazz*

GREENLEAF, ARNO. Assistant Professor, Department of Biochemistry, Duke University Medical Center, Durham, N.C.
Life Sciences: *Molecular Biology (in part)*

GRIFFITHS, A. R. G. Senior Lecturer in History, Flinders University of South Australia. Author of *Contemporary Australia.*
Australia; Australia: *Special Report;* **Biographies** *(in part);* **Nauru; Papua New Guinea**

GROSSBERG, ROBERT H. Executive Director, U.S. Amateur Jai Alai Players Association, Miami, Fla.
Court Games: *Jai Alai*

GROSSMAN, JOEL W. Archaeologist.
Archaeology: *Western Hemisphere*

HARDMAN, THOMAS C. Publisher, *The Water Skier,* American Water Ski Association. Co-author of *Let's Go Water Skiing.*
Water Sports: *Water Skiing*

HARRIES, DAVID A. Director, Tarmac International Ltd., London.
Engineering Projects: *Tunnels*

HASEGAWA, RYUSAKU. Editor, TBS-Britannica Co., Ltd., Tokyo.
Baseball *(in part)*

HAWKLAND, WILLIAM D. Chancellor and Professor of Law, Louisiana State University, Baton Rouge. Author of *Sales and Bulk Sales Under the Uniform Commercial Code; Cases on Bills and Notes; Transactional Guide of the Uniform Commercial Code; Cases on Sales and Security.*
Law: *Court Decisions*

HAWLEY, H. B. Specialist, Human Nutrition and Food Science, Switzerland.
Food Processing

HEATH, EDWARD. Prime Minister of the United Kingdom (1970–74); Member of Parliament. Author of *New World, New Horizons.*
Feature Article: *Stresses in the Western Alliance*

HEBBLETHWAITE, PETER. Vatican Affairs Writer, *National Catholic Reporter,* Kansas City, Mo. Author of *The Council Fathers and Atheism; Christian-Marxist Dialogue and Beyond; The Year of Three Popes; The New Inquisition?; Introducing John Paul II.*
Biographies *(in part);* **Religion:** *Roman Catholic Church*

HENDERSHOTT, MYRL C. Professor of Oceanography, Scripps Institution of Oceanography, La Jolla, Calif.
Earth Sciences: *Oceanography*

HERMAN, ROBIN CATHY. Reporter, *New York Times.*
Ice Hockey: *North American*

HESS, MARVIN G. Executive Vice-President, National Wrestling Coaches Association, Salt Lake City, Utah.
Combat Sports: *Wrestling*

HIGGINS, FITZGERALD. Editor and Reviewer.
Literature: *United States*

HINDIN, HARVEY J. Senior Systems Editor, *Systems and Software* magazine, Rochelle Park, N.J. Author of numerous articles on electronics and mathematics.
Industrial Review: *Telecommunications*

HOPE, THOMAS W. President, Hope Reports, Inc. Rochester, N.Y. Author of *Hope Reports AV-USA; Hope Reports Education and Media; Hope Reports Quarterly.*
Motion Pictures *(in part)*

HORRY, JOHN H. Former Secretary, International Squash Rackets Federation. Contributor to *The Oxford Companion to Sports and Games.*
Racket Games: *Squash Rackets*

HOTZ, LOUIS. Former Editorial Writer, *Johannesburg (S.Af.) Star.* Co-author and contributor to *The Jews in South Africa.*
Biographies *(in part);* **South Africa**

HOWKINS, JOHN. Editor, *InterMedia,* International Institute of Communications, London. Author of *Understanding Television; Mass Communications in China.*
Television and Radio *(in part)*

HUNNINGS, NEVILLE MARCH. Editorial Director, European Law Centre Ltd., London. Editor, *Common Market Law Reports; European Commercial Cases.* Author of *Film Censors and the Law.* Co-editor of *Legal Problems of an Enlarged European Community.*
Law: *International Law*

INGHAM, KENNETH. Professor of History, University of Bristol, England. Author of *Reformers in India; A History of East Africa.*
Angola; Kenya; Malawi; Mozambique; Sudan; Tanzania; Uganda; Zaire; Zambia; Zimbabwe

JACQUET, CONSTANT H. Staff Associate for Information Services, Office of Research, Evaluation and Planning, National Council of Churches. Editor of *Yearbook of American and Canadian Churches.*
United States Statistical Supplement: *Church Membership table*

JARDINE, ADRIAN. Company Director. Member, Guild of Yachting Writers.
Sailing

JASPERT, W. PINCUS. Technical and Editorial Consultant. European Editor, North American Publishing Company, Philadelphia. Member, Inter-Comprint Planning Committee; Member, Society of Photographic Engineers and Scientists; Life Member, *Eurographic Press.* Author of *State of the Art.* Editor of *Encyclopaedia of Type Faces.*
Industrial Review: *Printing*

JENKINS, PETER. Policy Editor and Political Columnist, *The Guardian,* London.
United Kingdom

JESSOP, DAVID A. Editor, *Caribbean Chronicle* and *Caribbean Insight.* Consultant on Caribbean affairs.
Antigua and Barbuda; Bahamas, The; Barbados; Biographies *(in part);* Dependent States *(in part);* Dominica; Grenada; Guyana; Jamaica; Saint Lucia; Saint Vincent and the Grenadines; Trinidad and Tobago

JOFFÉ, GEORGE. Journalist and Writer on North African Affairs.
Algeria; Morocco

JONES, C. M. Consultant, *World Bowls* and *Tennis.* Member, British Society of Sports Psychology; Associate Member, British Association of National Coaches. Player-Captain, Great Britain's Britannia Cup tennis team (1979–81). Author of *Winning Bowls; How to Become a Champion;* numerous books on tennis. Co-author of *Tackle Bowls My Way; Bryant on Bowls.*
Bowling: *Lawn Bowls*

JONES, D. A. N. Assistant Editor, *The Listener,* London; Novelist and Critic. Author of *Parade in Paris; Never Had It so Good.*
Literature: *Introduction; United Kingdom*

JONES, HANDEL H. Vice-President for Strategic and International Management, Commerical Electronics Operations, Dallas, Texas.
Industrial Review: *Microelectronics*

JONES, W. GLYN. Professor of Scandinavian Studies, University of Newcastle upon Tyne, England. Author of *Johannes Jørgensens modnear; Johannes Jørgensen; William Heinesen; Færo og kosmos; Danish: A Grammar and Exercises.*
Literature: *Danish*

JOSEPH, LOU. Senior Science Writer, Hill and Knowlton, Chicago. Author of *A Doctor Discusses Allergy: Facts and Fiction; Natural Childbirth; Diabetes; Childrens' Colds.*
Health and Disease: *Dentistry*

KATZ, WILLIAM A. Professor, School of Library Science, State University of New York, Albany. Author of *Magazines for Libraries* (4th ed.); *Magazine Selection.*
Publishing: *Magazines (in part)*

KELLEHER, JOHN A. Group Relations Editor, INL (newspapers), Wellington, N.Z.
New Zealand

KENNA, JOHN T. Writer specializing in religious and cultural affairs, Chicago.
Race Relations: *Special Report*

KENNEDY, RICHARD M. Agricultural Economist, International Economics Division of the Economic Research Service, U.S. Department of Agriculture.
Agriculture and Food Supplies

KENT, LIVIJA. Associate Professor, Botany Department, University of Massachusetts.
Life Sciences: *Botany*

KILIAN, MICHAEL D. Columnist, *Chicago Tribune;* News Commentator, WBBM Radio, Chicago. Captain, U.S. Air Force Civil Air Patrol. Author of *Who Runs Chicago?; The Valkyrie Project; Who Runs Washington?*
Aerial Sports

KILLHEFFER, JOHN V. Associate Editor, *Encyclopædia Britannica.*
Nobel Prizes *(in part)*

KIMCHE, JON. Editor. *Afro-Asian Affairs*, London. Author of *There Could Have Been Peace: The Untold Story of Why We Failed With Palestine and Again with Israel; Seven Fallen Pillars; Second Arab Awakening.*
Biographies (*in part*); **Israel**

KIND, JOSHUA B. Associate Professor of Art History, Northern Illinois University, De Kalb. Author of *Rouault; Naive Art in Illinois 1830–1976; Geometry as Abstract Art: The Third Generation.*
Museums (*in part*)

KITAGAWA, JOSEPH M. Professor of History of Religions, Divinity School, University of Chicago. Author of *Religions of the East; Religion in Japanese History.*
Religion: *Buddhism*

KLARE, HUGH J. Chairman, Gloucestershire Probation Training Committee, England. Secretary, Howard League for Penal Reform 1950–71. Author of *People in Prison.* Regular Contributor to *Justice of the Peace.*
Prisons and Penology

KNECHT, JEAN. Formerly Assistant Foreign Editor, *Le Monde*, Paris; formerly Permanent Correspondent in Washington and Vice-President of the Association de la Presse Diplomatique Française.
Biographies (*in part*); **France**

KNOX, RICHARD A. Senior Public Affairs Officer, Atomic Energy of Canada Limited Engineering Company; formerly Editor, *Nuclear Engineering International*, London. Author of *Experiments in Astronomy for Amateurs; Foundations of Astronomy.*
Industrial Review: *Nuclear Industry*

KOLATA, GINA. Writer, *Science* magazine, Washington, D.C. Co-author of *The High Blood Pressure Book; Combatting the Number One Killer.*
Health and Disease: *Overview* (*in part*)

KOPPER, PHILIP. Author and Free-lance Journalist, Washington, D.C.
Biographies (*in part*); **Nobel Prizes** (*in part*)

KRIEGSMAN, SALI ANN. Consultant in Dance, Smithsonian Institution, Washington, D.C. Author of *Modern Dance in America: The Bennington Years.*
Dance (*in part*)

KUSHNICK, LOUIS. Lecturer, Department of American Studies, University of Manchester, England. Editor, *Sage Race Relations Abstracts.*
Migration, International; Race Relations

LAMB, KEVIN M. Sports Writer, *Chicago Sun-Times.*
Biographies (*in part*); **Football:** *U.S. Football; Canadian Football*

LARSON, ROY. Religion Editor, *Chicago Sun-Times.*
Religion: *Introduction*

LEAPER, ERIC. Executive Director, National Organization for River Sports, Colorado Springs, Colo.
Water Sports: *River Sports*

LEGUM, COLIN. Associate Editor (1947–81), *The Observer*; Editor, *Middle East Contemporary Survey* and *Africa Contemporary Record*, London. Author of *Must We Lose Africa?; Congo Disaster; Pan-Africanism: A Political Guide; South Africa: Crisis for the West.*
African Affairs; Biographies (*in part*)

LEIFER, MICHAEL. Reader in International Relations, London School of Economics and Political Science. Author of *Dilemmas of Statehood in Southeast Asia.*
Malaysia; Singapore

LENNOX-KERR, PETER. Editor, *High Performance Textiles*; European Editor, *Textile World.* Author of *The World Fibres Book.* Editor of *Nonwovens '71;* Publisher of *OE-Report*, New Mills, England.
Industrial Review: *Textiles* (*in part*)

LEVE, CHARLES S. Executive Director, National Court Clubs Association. Author of *Inside Racquetball*; co-author of *Winning Racquetball.*
Racket Games: *Racquetball*

LIM SIANG JIN. Research Officer, International Organization of Consumer Unions, Regional Office for Asia and the Pacific, Penang, Malaysia.
Consumerism (*in part*)

LITTELL, FRANKLIN H. Professor of Religion, Temple University, Philadelphia, Pa. Co-editor of *Weltkirchenlexikon*; Author of *Macmillan Atlas History of Christianity.*
Religion: *World Church Membership*

LOGAN, ROBERT G. Sportswriter, *Chicago Tribune.* Author of *The Bulls and Chicago—A Stormy Affair.*
Basketball (*in part*)

LOVE, JOHN H. Executive Director, American Power Boat Association, East Detroit, Mich. Editor, *Propeller*, a publication of the APBA.
Water Sports: *Motorboating*

LULING, VIRGINIA R. Social Anthropologist.
Somalia

LUNDE, ANDERS S. Consultant; Adjunct Professor, Department of Biostatistics, University of North Carolina. Author of *The Person-Number Systems of Sweden, Norway, Denmark and Israel.*
Demography

McCAULEY, MARTIN. Lecturer in Russian and Soviet Institutions, School of Slavonic and East European Studies, University of London. Author of *Khrushchev and the Development of Soviet Agriculture: The Virgin Land Programme 1953–1964; Marxism-Leninism in the German Democratic Republic; The Stalin File; The Soviet Union Since 1917.* Editor of *The Russian Revolution and the Soviet State 1917–1921; Communist Power in Europe 1944–1949.*
Union of Soviet Socialist Republics

MACDONALD, BARRIE. Senior Lecturer in History, Massey University, Palmerston North, N.Z. Author of several articles on the history and politics of Pacific islands.
Dependent States (*in part*); **Fiji; Kiribati; Solomon Islands; Tonga; Tuvalu; Vanuatu; Western Samoa**

MacDONALD, M. C. Director, World Economics Ltd., London.
Agriculture and Food Supplies: *grain table;* **Transportation:** *table;* statistical sections of articles on the various countries

MACDONALD, TREVOR J. Manager, International Affairs, British Steel Corporation.
Industrial Review: *Iron and Steel*

MACGREGOR-MORRIS, PAMELA. Equestrian Correspondent, *The Times* and *Horse and Hound*, London. Author of books on equestrian topics.
Equestrian Sports: *Show Jumping*

McKELVIE, ROY. Sports writer; Rackets and Real Tennis Correspondent, *The Times*, London.
Racket Games: *Rackets; Real Tennis*

McLACHLAN, KEITH S. Senior Lecturer, School of Oriental and African Studies, University of London.
Iran

MALLETT, H. M. F. Editor, *Wool Record Weekly Market Report*, Bradford, England.
Industrial Review: *Textiles* (*in part*)

MANGO, ANDREW. Orientalist and Broadcaster.
Turkey

MAO, NATHAN. Professor of Chinese Studies, Seton Hall University, South Orange, N.J. Author of *Modern Chinese Fiction; Pa Chin.*
Literature: *Chinese* (*in part*)

MARTY, MARTIN E. Fairfax M. Cone Distinguished Service Professor of the History of Modern Christianity, University of Chicago; Associate Editor, *The Christian Century.* Author of *Righteous Empire; A Nation of Behavers.*
Religion: *Special Report*

MATEJA, JAMES L. Auto Editor and Financial Reporter, *Chicago Tribune.*
Industrial Review: *Automobiles*

MATHIS, F. JOHN. Vice-President, Continental Illinois National Bank and Trust Co., Chicago.
Feature Article: *"You Can't Foreclose a Country"*

MATTHÍASSON, BJÖRN. Economist, European Free Trade Association, Geneva.
Iceland

MAZIE, DAVID M. Associate of Carl T. Rowan, syndicated columnist. Free-lance Writer.
Social Security and Welfare Services (*in part*)

MAZZE, EDWARD MARK. Dean and Professor of Marketing, School of Business Administration, Temple University, Philadelphia. Author of *Personal Selling: Choice Against Chance; Introduction to Marketing: Readings in the Discipline.*
Consumerism (*in part*); **Industrial Review:** *Advertising*

MEDVEDEV, ROY A. Historian and Sociologist, U.S.S.R. Author of *The October Revolution; On Soviet Dissent; Leninism and Western Socialism.* Co-author of *Khrushchev—The Years in Power; A Question of Madness.*
Feature Article: *The Russian Giant: 60 Years After Formation of the Soviet Union* (*in part*)

MEDVEDEV, ZHORES A. Biologist, National Institute for Medical Research, London. Author of *The Rise and Fall of T. D. Lysenko; Nuclear Disaster in the Urals.* Co-author of *Khrushchev—The Years in Power; A Question of Madness.*
Feature Article: *The Russian Giant: 60 Years After Formation of the Soviet Union* (*in part*)

MERMEL, T. W. Consultant; formerly Chairman, Committee on World Register

of Dams, International Commission on Large Dams. Author of *Register of Dams in the United States.*
Engineering Projects: *Dams; Dams table*

MERRY, FIONA B. Economist, Group Economics Department, Lloyds Bank Ltd., London. Contributor to *EEC and the Third World: A Survey.*
Cuba

MEYENDORFF, JOHN. Professor of Church History and Patristics, St. Vladimir's Orthodox Theological Seminary; Professor of History, Fordham University, New York City. Author of *Christ in Eastern Christian Thought; Byzantine Theology; Byzantium and the Rise of Russia.*
Religion: *The Orthodox Church; Eastern Non-Chalcedonian Churches*

MILES, PETER W. Dean of Agricultural Science, University of Adelaide, Australia.
Life Sciences: *Entomology*

MILLIKIN, SANDRA. Architectural Historian.
Architecture; Art Exhibitions; Museums (*in part*)

MITCHELL, K. K. Lecturer, Department of Physical Education, University of Leeds, England. Director, English Basket Ball Association.
Basketball (*in part*)

MODIANO, MARIO. Athens Correspondent, *The Times,* London.
Biographies (*in part*); **Greece**

MONACO, ALBERT M., JR. Executive Director, United States Volleyball Association, Colorado Springs, Colo.
Court Games: *Volleyball*

MOORE, JOHN E. Hydrologist, Reston, Va.
Earth Sciences: *Hydrology*

MORRISON, DONALD. Senior Editor, *Time* magazine.
Publishing: *Newspapers* (*in part*)

MORTIMER, MOLLY. Commonwealth Correspondent, *The Spectator,* London. Author of *Trusteeship in Practice; Kenya.*
Commonwealth of Nations; Dependent States (*in part*); **Nigeria.**

MOSEY, CHRIS. Associate Editor, *Sweden Now,* Stockholm; Swedish Correspondent, *The Observer, Daily Mail,* and *The Times.* Contributor to *The Boat People.*
Biographies (*in part*); **Sweden**

MOSHANSKY, MOZELLE A. Music Journalist and Writer, *International Music Guide.*
Biographies (*in part*); **Music:** *Classical*

MUCK, TERRY CHARLES. Editor, *Leadership* magazine, Carol Stream, Ill.
Court Games: *Handball*

NAPIER, ELSPETH. Editor of publications of the Royal Horticultural Society, England.
Gardening (*in part*)

NAYLOR, ERNEST. Professor of Marine Biology, University of Liverpool; Director, Marine Biological Laboratory, Port Erin, Isle of Man. Author of *British Marine Isopods.* Co-editor, *Estuarine, Coastal and Shelf Science.*
Life Sciences: *Marine Biology*

NEILL, JOHN. Consultant, Submerged Combustion Ltd. Author of Climbers'

Club Guides; *Cwm Silyn and Tremadoc, Snowdon South;* Alpine Club Guide: *Selected Climbs in the Pennine Alps.*
Mountaineering

NELSON, BERT. Editor, *Track and Field News.* Author of *Little Red Book; The Decathlon Book; Olympic Track and Field; Of People and Things.*
Track and Field Sports

NETSCHERT, BRUCE C. Vice-President, National Economic Research Associates, Inc., Washington, D.C. Author of *The Future Supply of Oil and Gas.* Co-author of *Energy in the American Economy: 1850–1975.*
Energy: *World Summary*

NEUSNER, JACOB. University Professor, Brown University, Providence, R.I. Author of *Judaism, The Evidence of the Mishnah.*
Religion: *Judaism*

NOEL, H. S. Free-lance Journalist; formerly Managing Editor, *World Fishing,* London.
Fisheries

NORMAN, GERALDINE. Saleroom Correspondent, *The Times,* London. Author of *The Sale of Works of Art; Nineteenth Century Painters and Painting: A Dictionary;* Co-author of *The Fake's Progress.*
Art Sales

O'DONOGHUE, MICHAEL. Curator, Science Reference Library, London. Editor, *Gems, Gemmological Newsletter,* and *Synthetic Crystals Newsletter.* Author of *Encyclopedia of Minerals and Gemstones; Synthetic Gem Materials; Beginner's Guide to Minerals.*
Industrial Review: *Gemstones*

OLNEY, P. J. Curator of Birds and Reptiles, Zoological Society of London. Editor, *International Zoo Yearbook.* Co-editor of *Birds of the Western Palearctic.*
Zoos and Botanical Gardens: *Zoos*

OSBORNE, KEITH. Editor, *Rowing, 1961–63;* Honorary Editor, *British Rowing Almanack, 1961– .* Author of *Boat Racing in Britain, 1715–1975.*
Rowing

OSTERBIND, CARTER C. Associate, Gerontology Center, and Professor Emeritus of Economics, University of Florida. Editor of *Income in Retirement; Migration, Mobility, and Aging;* and others.
Industrial Review: *Building and Construction*

PAGE, SHEILA A. B. Research Officer, National Institute of Economic and Social Research, London.
Economy, World (*in part*)

PALMER, JOHN. European Editor, *The Guardian,* London.
European Unity

PALMER, S. B. Senior Lecturer, Department of Applied Physics, University of Hull, England.
Physics

PARKER, DONN B. Senior Management Systems Consultant, SRI International, Menlo Park, Calif.
Crime and Law Enforcement: *Special Report*

PARKER, SANDY. Publisher of weekly international newsletter on fur industry.
Industrial Review: *Furs*

PAUL, CHARLES ROBERT, JR. Director of Communications, U.S. Olympic Committee, Colorado Springs, Colo. Author of *The Olympic Games.*
Gymnastics and Weight Lifting

PENFOLD, ROBIN C. Free-lance Writer specializing in industrial topics. Editor, *Shell Polymers.* Author of *A Journalist's Guide to Plastics.*
Industrial Review: *Plastics*

PERTILE, LINO. Lecturer in Italian, University of Sussex, England.
Literature: *Italian*

PETHERICK, KARIN. Reader in Swedish, University of London.
Literature: *Swedish*

PFEFFER, IRVING. Attorney. Chairman, Pacific American Group, Inc. Author of *The Financing of Small Business; Perspectives on Insurance.*
Stock Exchanges (*in part*)

PHINNEY, ALLISON W. Manager, Committees on Publication, The First Church of Christ, Scientist, Boston.
Religion: *Church of Christ, Scientist*

PIERCE, JOHN R. Professor of Engineering, California Institute of Technology. Author of *The Beginnings of Satellite Communications.*
Special Preprint: *Satellite Communication*

PINFOLD, GEOFFREY M. Director, NCL Consulting Engineers, London. Author of *Reinforced Concrete Chimneys and Towers.*
Engineering Projects: *Buildings*

PLOTNIK, ARTHUR. Editor, *American Libraries* magazine, American Library Association. Author of *The Elements of Editing; Library Life—American Style.*
Libraries (*in part*)

POLIN, THOMAS HON WING. Assistant Managing Editor, *Asiaweek* magazine, Hong Kong.
Kampuchea; Korea; Laos; Southeast Asian Affairs; Thailand; Vietnam

POOLE, ROBERT M. Director, R & A Racing, Bookmakers, London.
Gambling (*in part*)

POPPELIERS, JOHN. Chief, Section for Operations and Training, Cultural Heritage Division, UNESCO, Paris.
Historic Preservation

POST, AVERY D. President, United Church of Christ, New York City.
Religion: *United Church of Christ*

PRASAD, H. Y. SHARADA. Information Adviser to the Prime Minister, New Delhi, India.
Biographies (*in part*); **India**

RANGER, ROBIN. Associate Professor, Defense and Strategic Studies Program, School of International Relations, University of Southern California; Department of National Defence Fellow in Strategic Studies, 1978–79; NATO Fellow, 1980–81. Author of *Arms and Politics, 1958–1978; Arms Control in a Changing Political Context.*
Defense; Defense: *Special Report*

RAY, G. F. Senior Research Fellow, National Institute of Economic and Social Research, London; Visiting Professor, University of Surrey, Guildford, England.
Industrial Review: *Introduction*

READ, ANTHONY A. Director, Book Development Council, London.
Publishing: *Books (in part)*

REBELO, L. S. Lecturer, Department of Portuguese Studies, King's College, University of London.
Literature: *Portuguese (in part)*

REICHELDERFER, F. W. Consultant on Atmospheric Sciences. Formerly Director, Weather Bureau, U.S. Department of Commerce, Washington, D.C.; formerly President, World Meteorological Organization, Geneva.
Earth Sciences: *Meteorology*

REID, J. H. Senior Lecturer in German, University of Nottingham, England. Co-editor of *Renaissance and Modern Studies*. Author of *Heinrich Böll: Withdrawal and Re-emergence*; Co-author of *Critical Strategies: German Fiction in the Twentieth Century*.
Literature: *German*

RIPLEY, MICHAEL D. Public Relations Officer, Brewers' Society, U.K.; formerly Editor, *Brewing Review*.
Industrial Review: *Alcoholic Beverages (in part)*

ROBERTS, JOHN. Senior Staff Writer, *Middle East Economic Digest*, London.
Biographies *(in part)*

ROBINSON, DAVID. Film Critic, *The Times*, London. Author of *Buster Keaton; The Great Funnies—A History of Screen Comedy; A History of World Cinema*.
Biographies *(in part)*; **Motion Pictures** *(in part)*

RULE, MARGARET. Archaeological Director, The Mary Rose Trust; Fellow of the Society of Antiquaries.
Archaeology: *Special Report*

SAEKI, SHOICHI. Professor of Literature, University of Tokyo. Author of *In Search of Japanese Ego*.
Literature: *Japanese*

SAINT-AMOUR, ROBERT. Professor, Department of Literary Studies, University of Quebec at Montreal.
Literature: *French (in part)*

SARAHETE, YRJÖ. General Secretary, Fédération Internationale des Quilleurs, Helsinki.
Bowling: *Tenpin Bowling (in part)*

SARMIENTO, SERGIO. Editor-in-Chief, Spanish-language publications, Encyclopædia Britannica Publishers, Inc.
Baseball *(in part)*

SCHOENFIELD, ALBERT. Formerly Publisher, *Swimming World*; Vice-Chairman, U.S. Olympic Swimming Committee. U.S. Representative to FINA Technical Committee. Member of 1984 Los Angeles Olympic Organizing Swimming Commission. Contributor to *The Technique of Water Polo; The History of Swimming; Competitive Swimming as I See It; International Swimming and Water Polo* magazine
Swimming

SCHÖPFLIN, GEORGE. Lecturer in East European Political Institutions, London School of Economics and School of Slavonic and East European Studies, University of London.
Czechoslovakia

SCHULMAN, ELIAS. Adjunct Professor, Queens College, City University of New York. Author of *Israel Tsinberg, His Life and Works; A History of Yiddish Literature in America; Soviet-Yiddish Literature; Portraits and Studies*.
Literature: *Yiddish (in part)*

SEARS, ROBERT N. Editor, National Rifle Association, Washington, D.C.
Target Sports: *Shooting*

SHACKLEFORD, PETER. Chief of Studies, World Tourism Organization, Madrid.
Industrial Review: *Tourism*

SHARPE, MITCHELL R. Science Writer; Historian, Alabama Space and Rocket Center, Huntsville. Author of *The Rocket Team; Living in Space: The Environment of the Astronaut; "It Is I, Seagull": Valentina Tereshkova, First Woman in Space; Satellites and Probes, the Development of Unmanned Spaceflight*.
Space Exploration

SHAW, T. R. Associate Editor, *International Journal of Speleology*. Author of *History of Cave Science*.
Speleology

SHEPHERD, MELINDA. Copy Editor, *Encyclopædia Britannica*.
Biographies *(in part)*

SIMPSON, NOEL. Managing Director, Sydney Bloodstock Proprietary Ltd., Sydney, Australia.
Equestrian Sports: *Harness Racing*

SMITH, REUBEN W. Dean, Graduate School, and Professor of History, University of the Pacific, Stockton, Calif. Editor of *Venture of Islam* by M. G. S. Hodgson.
Religion: *Islam*

SMOGORZEWSKI, K. M. Writer on contemporary history. Founder and Editor, *Free Europe*, London. Author of *The United States and Great Britain; Poland's Access to the Sea*.
Albania; Andorra; Biographies *(in part)*; **Bulgaria; Hungary; Liechtenstein; Luxembourg; Monaco; Mongolia; Poland; Political Parties; Romania; San Marino**

SOLOMON, RICHARD H. Director International Security Policy Research, and Head, Political Science Department, The Rand Corporation. Author of *Mao's Revolution and the Chinese Political Culture; A Revolution Is Not a Dinner Party; Asian Security in the 1980s*.
Feature Article: *China's Uncertain Future*

SPELMAN, ROBERT A. President, Home Furnishings Services, Washington, D.C.
Industrial Review: *Furniture*

STAERK, MELANIE. Member, Swiss Press Association. Former Member, Swiss National Commission for UNESCO.
Switzerland

STEEN, LYNN ARTHUR. Professor of Mathematics, St. Olaf College, Northfield, Minn. Author of *Mathematics Tomorrow; Mathematics Today; Counterexamples in Topology; Annotated Bibliography of Expository Writing in the Mathematical Sciences*.
Mathematics

STERN, IRWIN. Assistant Professor of Portuguese, Columbia University, New York City. Author of *Júlio Dinis e o romance português (1860–1870)*; Co-editor of *Modern Iberian Literature: A Library of Literary Criticism*.
Literature: *Portuguese (in part)*

STØVERUD, TORBJØRN. W. P. Ker Senior Lecturer in Norwegian, University College, London.
Literature: *Norwegian*

STRAUSS, MICHAEL. Ski, Sports and Feature Writer, *New York Times*. Author of *Ski Areas, U.S.A.*
Combat Sports: *Fencing*

SULLIVAN, H. PATRICK. Dean of the College and Professor of Religion, Vassar College, Poughkeepsie, N.Y.
Religion: *Hinduism*

SWEETINBURGH, THELMA. Fashion Writer, Paris.
Fashion and Dress *(in part)*

SWIFT, RICHARD N. Professor of Politics, New York University, New York City. Author of *International Law: Current and Classic; World Affairs and the College Curriculum*.
United Nations

SYNAN, VINSON. Assistant General Superintendent, Pentecostal Holiness Church. Author of *The Holiness-Pentecostal Movement; The Old Time Power*.
Religion: *Pentecostal Churches*

TAISHOFF, LAWRENCE B. President, Broadcasting Publications, Inc., and Publisher, *Broadcasting* magazine and other publications.
Television and Radio *(in part)*

TALLAN, NORMAN M. Chief Scientist, Materials Laboratory, Wright-Patterson Air Force Base, Dayton, Ohio. Editor of *Electrical Conductivity in Ceramics and Glass*.
Materials Sciences: *Ceramics*

TATTERSALL, ARTHUR. Textile Trade Statistician, Manchester, England.
Industrial Review: *Textiles (in part)*

THEINER, GEORGE. Assistant Editor, *Index on Censorship*, London. Co-author of *The Kill Dog*; editor of *New Writing in Czechoslovakia*; translator of *Poetry of Miroslav Holub*.
Literature: *Eastern European; Russian (in part)*

THOMAS, HARFORD. Retired City and Financial Editor, *The Guardian*, London.
Biographies *(in part)*

THOMAS, THEODORE V. Free-lance Journalist and Press Consultant. Editor (1961–79), *British Toys and Hobbies*.
Games and Toys

TINGAY, LANCE. Formerly Lawn Tennis Correspondent, *Daily Telegraph*, London. Author of *100 Years of Wimbledon; Tennis, A Pictorial History*.
Tennis

TRIGG, ROBERT H. Assistant Vice-President, Economic Research, New York Stock Exchange.
Stock Exchanges *(in part)*

TRILLING, OSSIA. Vice-President, International Association of Theatre Critics (1956–77). Co-editor and Contributor, *International Theatre*. Contributor, BBC, the *Financial Times*, London.
Theatre *(in part)*

TUDOR, JOANNA. Information Officer.
Industrial Review: *Glass*

UNHCR. The Office of the United Nations High Commissioner for Refugees.
Refugees

UNNY, GOVINDAN. Agence France-Presse Special Correspondent for India, Nepal, Sri Lanka, and Bangladesh.
Afghanistan; Bangladesh; Bhutan; Biographies (*in part*); **Burma; Nepal; Pakistan; Sri Lanka**

UTT, ROGER L. Assistant Professor of Spanish, Department of Romance Languages and Literature, University of Chicago.
Literature: *Spanish (in part)*

VALE, NORMAN K. Retired Director of News Services, The United Church of Canada.
Religion: *United Church of Canada*

VERDI, ROBERT WILLIAM. Sportswriter, *Chicago Tribune*.
Baseball (*in part*)

VINT, ARTHUR KINGSLEY. Counselor, International Table Tennis Federation, Hastings, East Sussex, England.
Table Tennis

WARD, PETER. Owner and Operator, Ward News Service, Ottawa; Parliamentary Reporter and Commentator.
Canada: *Special Report*

WARD-THOMAS, P. A. Golf Correspondent, *Country Life*, London.
Golf

WARNER, ANTONY C. Editor, *Drinks Marketing*, London.
Industrial Review: *Alcoholic Beverages (in part)*

WATSON, LOUISE. Assistant Editor, Encyclopædia Britannica, London.
Dependent States (*sidebar*)

WAY, DIANE LOIS. Historical Researcher, Ontario Historical Studies Series.
Biographies (*in part*)

WHELAN, JOHN. Deputy Editor and Chief News Editor, *Middle East Economic Digest*, London, Managing Editor, *Arab Banking and Finance*.
Bahrain; Biographies (*in part*); **Egypt; Iraq; Jordan; Kuwait; Lebanon; Middle Eastern Affairs; Oman; Qatar; Saudi Arabia; Syria; United Arab Emirates; Yemen, People's Democratic Republic of; Yemen Arab Republic**

WHITTINGHAM, RICHARD. Free-lance Writer and Editor. Author of *Martial Justice* and many other books on contemporary affairs.
Health and Disease: *Special Report*

WIJNGAARD, BARBARA. Economist, Group Economics Department, Lloyds Bank Ltd., London.
Biographies (*in part*); **Mexico**

WILKINSON, GORDON. Information Consultant and Free-lance Science Writer; formerly Chemistry Consultant, *New Scientist*, London. Author of *Industrial Timber Preservation*.
Chemistry

WILKINSON, JOHN R. Sports Writer, East Midland Provincial Newspapers Ltd., U.K.
Biographies (*in part*); **Cycling**

WILLEY, DAVID DOUGLAS. Rome Correspondent, BBC.
Italy

WILLIAMS, RAYMOND L. Assistant Professor of Spanish, Washington University, St. Louis, Mo. Author of *La novela colombiana contemporánea; Aproximaciones a Gustavo Álvarez Gardeazabal; Una década de la novela colombiana.*
Literature: *Spanish (in part)*

WILLIAMSON, TREVOR. Chief Sports Subeditor, *Daily Telegraph*, London.
Biographies (*in part*); **Football:** *Association Football*

WILSON, MICHAEL. Consultant Editor, Jane's Publishing Co. Ltd.
Industrial Review: *Aerospace*

WITTE, RANDALL E. Associate Editor, *The Western Horseman* magazine, Colorado Springs, Colo.
Rodeo

WOLF, JAMES M. Director, Department of Defense Dependents Schools, Panama Region, Miami, Fla.
Education: *Special Report*

WOLFF, ANITA. Manager, Copy Department, Encyclopædia Britannica, Inc.
Biographies (*in part*)

WOOD, BERNARD. Reader in Anatomy, Middlesex Hospital Medical School, University of London. Author of *Human Evolution; Evolution of Early Man.*
Special Preprint: *Australopithecus*

WOOD, KENNETH H. Editor, *Adventist Review*. Author of *Meditations for Moderns; Relevant Religion;* co-author of *His Initials Were F.D.N.*
Religion: *Seventh-day Adventist Church*

WOODS, ELIZABETH. Writer. Author of *The Yellow Volkswagen; Gone; Men; The Amateur.*
Literature: *English (in part)*

WOOLLER, MICHAEL. Economist, Group Economics Department, Lloyds Bank Ltd., London.
Biographies (*in part*); **Bolivia; Paraguay; Portugal; Spain; Uruguay**

WOOLLEY, DAVID. Editor, *Airports International*, London.
Transportation (*in part*)

WORSNOP, RICHARD L. Associate Editor, Editorial Research Reports, Washington, D.C.
United States

WRIGHT, ALMON R. Retired Senior Historian, U.S. Department of State.
Panama

WYLLIE, PETER JOHN. Homer J. Livingston Professor and Chairman, Department of Geophysical Sciences, University of Chicago. Author of *The Dynamic Earth; The Way the Earth Works.*
Earth Sciences: *Geology and Geochemistry*

YANG, WINSTON L. Y. Professor of Chinese Studies, Department of Asian Studies, Seton Hall University, South Orange, N.J. Author of *Modern Chinese Fiction; Teng Hsiao-p'ing: A Political Biography* (forthcoming).
Biographies (*in part*); **Literature:** *Chinese (in part)*

YOUNG, M. NORVEL. Chancellor, Pepperdine University, Malibu, California; Chairman of the Board, 20th Century Christian Publishing Company. Author of *Preachers of Today; History of Colleges Connected with Churches of Christ; The Church Is Building.*
Religion: *Churches of Christ*

YOUNG, SUSAN. News Editor, *Church Times*, London.
Religion: *Anglican Communion*

Index

The black type entries are article headings in the *Book of the Year*. These black type entries do not show page notations because they are to be found in their alphabetical position in the body of the book They show the dates of the issues of the *Book of the Year* in which the articles appear. For example "Archaeology 83, 82, 81" indicates that the article "Archaeology" is to be found in the 1983, 1982, and 1981 *Book of the Year*.

The light type headings that are indented under black type article headings refer to material elsewhere in the text related to the subject under which they are listed. The light type headings that are not indented refer to information in the text not given a special article. Biographies and obituaries are listed as cross references to the sections "Biographies" and "Obituaries" within the article *"People of the Year."* References to illustrations are preceded by the abbreviation "il."

All headings, whether consisting of a single word or more, are created for the purpose of alphabetization as single complete headings. Names beginning with "Mc" and "Mac" are alphabetized as "Mac"; "St." is treated as "Saint."

A

Aaron, Hank il. 209
Abadan, Iran
  energy reduction 347
Abboud, A(lbert) Robert: see **Biographies 81**
ABC (American Bowling Congress) 219
ABC (American Broadcasting Company) 652
Abdallah, Ahmed 249
Abdullah, Prince
  Saudi Arabia 609
Abdullah, Shaikh Muhammad: see **Obituaries 83**
  India 424
Abokor, Ismail Ali 616
Aborigines (people) 199
Abortion
  health regulation and ethics 412
  Ireland's position 455
  United States statistics 702
"Abrahams barn" (Dahl) 508
ABT (American Ballet Theatre) 270
Abu Dhabi 684
  energy production 345
Abu Nidal 258
Accidents and safety
  demography 288
  engineering projects 349
  social insurance 614
Accreted terranes (allochthonous terranes, suspect terranes) 304
Accutane (drug) 412, il. 411
Ace, Goodman: see **Obituaries 83**
Acesulfame-K (sweetener)
  dentistry 414
"Acidification Today and Tomorrow" (Swedish report) 343
Acid rain 352
  botanical gardens 738
  Canada (special report) 230
  earth sciences 308
  energy hazards 343
  Sweden vulnerability 642
Acland, Sir (Hugh) John (Dyke): see **Obituaries 81**
Acne
  drug development 412, il. 411
Acoustic tomography
  oceanography 309
Acquired immunodeficiency syndrome (AIDS) 409
Acuerdo Nacional (pol. party, Paraguay) 563
Aczel, Gyorgy 420
AD (Democratic Alliance, Port.) 575
ADA: see American Dental Association
Adams, Harriet Stratemeyer: see **Obituaries 83**
Adams, J.M.G. 208
Adams, Lynn 589
Adams, Richard E. 179
Adamson, Joy: see **Obituaries 81**
Aden: see Yemen, People's Democratic Republic of
Advanced Information System 447
"Adventures of Huckleberry Finn, The" (Twain) 485
Advertising 432, 699
"Advertising Age" (periodical) 432
Aegean Sea
  Greek-Turkish talks 403
AEG-Telefunken (Company), Federal Republic of Germany) 438
Aerial Sports 83, 82, 81
Aerospace 432
  transportation 671
  see also Space exploration
AFDC (Aid to Families with Dependent Children) 614

Affirmative action
  race relations 585
Afghanistan 83, 82, 81
  "China's Uncertain Future" 136
  defense 278
  demography 289 (table)
  education 331 (table)
  Soviet foreign affairs 683
  United Nations report 690
African Affairs 83, 82, 81
  agriculture and food supplies 156
  Commonwealth of Nations 248
  Cuba-U.S. negotiations 265
  defense 284
  education 329
  energy production 346
  engineering projects 351
  infant mortality 292
  international refugee status 589
  Korean relations 472
  see also African countries
African Development Bank
  Nigeria (special report) 557
African National Congress (ANC)
  African affairs 153, 482, 619
"Africa's Awakening Giant" (Special Report) 556
Agca, Mehmet Ali
  crime and law enforcement 259
  papal assassination attempt 459
Agfa (camera company) 567
Aggett, Neil Hutchin: see **Obituaries 83**
  crime and law enforcement 262
  South African domestic affairs 618
Aging
  mental health 413
  social security 613
"Agnes of God" (play) 665, il. 666
Agriculture, U.S. Department of 156
  consumerism 254
Agriculture and Food Supplies 83, 82, 81
  African economy 155
  European farm prices 370
  fisheries 377
  see Biographies 82
  "Russian Giant: 60 Years after Formation of the Soviet Union, The" 16
  see also various countries
Agropyron repens (couch grass) 395
"Ahasver" (Heym) 507
Ahidjo, Ahmadou 224
  African political developments 154
  Nigerian visit 555
Ahlers, Conrad: see **Obituaries 81**
Ahlin, Gunnel 503
Ahmed Dini 302
AI (artificial intelligence) 250
AIA (American Institute of Architects) 183
AIDS (acquired immunodeficiency syndrome) 409
Aid to Families with Dependent Children (AFDC) 614
Airbus A320 (airplane) 433
Airbus Industrie 433
Aircraft (military) 285
Aircraft carrier 285
Air Force, U.S. 277
Air-launched cruise missiles (ALCM) 276
Airlines 671
  consumer refunds 253
  industrial review 432
Air-Sea warfare 286
Ajman
  United Arab Emirate member 684
Akali Dal (pol. party, India) 423
Akara (food preparation) 380
Akiyda (race horse) 363
Akron, Ohio 184, il. 186

rubber industry production 445
ALA (American Library Association) 484
Alabama, University of 388
Alaska 187, 700
  energy production 345
Alaska Highway gas pipeline
  Canada 227
  energy projects 341
Albania 83, 82, 81
  demography 290 (table)
Alberta, province, Canada 226
Albertson, Jack: see **Obituaries 82**
Albright-Knox Art Gallery, Buffalo, N.Y. 193
Albu, Florenta 514
ALCM (air-launched cruise missiles) 276
Alcoholic beverages 434
Alcoholism
  Soviet domestic affairs 681
Alekseyef, Aleksandr: see **Obituaries 83**
Alemann, Roberto 188
Aleshkovsky, Joz 512
Alex, Janet 403
Alexander, Frazer 357
Alexandrovitch, Prince Andrew: see **Obituaries 82**
Alga
  food processing 380
  life sciences 493
Algeria 83, 82, 81
  demography 289 (table)
  education 331 (table)
  energy production 345
  foreign affairs 460
  French immigration 529
  transportation 673 (table)
  Western Sahara conflict 154
Algiers, Algeria
  France 389
Ali, Kamal Hassan 337
Alia, Ramiz 170
Alianza Popular (AP, Spain) 629
Alianza Revolucionaria Democrática (Nicaragua) 475
Alice, Princess (Alice Mary Victoria Augusta Pauline): see **Obituaries 82**
Aliev, Geidar 680
Allantoic acid 493
Allantoin (chem. compound) 493
Allelic difference
  zoology 489
Allen, (William Ernest) Chesney: see **Obituaries 83**
Allen, Lew
  JPL directorship 622
Allen, Woody
  motion pictures 536
Allergic shock
  Nobel Prizes 97
Allied Corp.
  United States merger 693
Alligator 490
Allison, Bobby 541
All-Japan Judo Championships 247
All Nippon Airways (ANA) 462
Allochthonous terranes (suspect terranes, accreted terranes) 304
Allon, Yigal *see* **Obituaries 81**
Alloy
  dentistry 414
Aloma's Ruler (race horse) 362
ALP (Australian Labor Party) 202
Alpheus mackayi (burrowing shrimp) 493
Alpine ski racing 727
Aluminum 520
  mining and quarrying 532
Alvarado, Naty 255, il. 256
Álvarez Armelino, Gregorio Conrado: *see Biographies 82*
Álvarez Martínez, Gustavo 418
Alvin, Juliette: see **Obituaries 83**
Alvin Ailey American Dance Theatre 271
Amalrik, Andrey Alekseyevich: see **Obituaries 81**
Amarasians
  race relations il. 584
Amateur radio 655
Amendola, Giorgio: see **Obituaries 81**
American Ballet Theatre (ABT) 270
American Bankers Association 699
American Baptist Churches 594
American Bell, Inc. 447
American Bowling Congress (ABC) 219
American Broadcasting Company (ABC) 652
American Centre of Oriental Research 177
American Dental Association (ADA) 414
  U.S. (special report) 699
American Federation of Labor-Congress of Industrial Organizations: *see* AFL-CIO
American Institute of Architects (AIA) 183
American League
  baseball 210
American Library Association (ALA) 484
American Medical Association 699
American Motors 436
American Muslim Mission 600
"American Perspective: Nineteenth Century Art from the Collection

of JoAnn and Julian Ganz, Jr., An" (art exhibition) 191
"American Portraits in the Grand Manner, 1720-1920" (art exhibition) 191
American Power Boat Association (APBA) 724
American Radio Relay League 655
American Samoa 298
  demography 291 (table)
American Savings and Loan Association 693
American Stock Exchange (Amex) 633
American Telephone and Telegraph Co. (AT&T) 447
  computers 250
  United States 693
American Writers Congress 583
America's Cup Challenge
  sailing 606
Amersham International Laboratories (U.K. firm) 184
Amery, Colin 183
Amex (American Stock Exchange) 633
Amichai, Yehuda il. 514
Amino acids 496
Ammonia 233
Amnesty International
  Guatemala report 406
  Pakistan charges 560
  Uganda report 679
Amoroso, Emmanuel Ciprian: see **Obituaries 83**
Amory, Derick Heathcoat Amory, 1st Viscount: see **Obituaries 82**
Amphibious warfare
  defense (special report) 287
Amphora
  archaeology 177, il. 180
Amritsar, India 599
AM stereo broadcast 650
ANA (All Nippon Airways) 462
Anaconda Minerals Co. (U.S.) 530
Ananiashvili, Parnaoz 681
Anaya, Jorge Isaac 189
ANC: see African National Congress
Andean Group (trade org.) 475
Andersch, Alfred: see **Obituaries 81**
Anderson, John Bayard: see **Biographies 81**
Anderson, Ken: see **Biographies 82**
  football 386
Anderson, Lindsay 537
Anderson, Maxie 150
Andorra 83, 82, 81
  demography 290 (table)
Andreotti, Giulio 458
Andretti, Mario 540
Andrews, John 183
Andrews, Julie 537
Andropov, Yury Vladimirovich: see **Biographies 83**
  "Russian Giant: 60 Years after Formation of the Soviet Union, The" 18
  Soviet domestic affairs 679
Anemia
  veterinary science 723
Anesthetics 410
"Angel" (film) 537
Anglican Communion 593
Anglican-Roman Catholic International Commission (ARCIC) 593, 597
Anglo-Australian Telescope 197
Angola 83, 82, 81
  African affairs 153
  Nigeria (special report) 557
  South African relations 618
  defense 284
  demography 289 (table)
  dependent states 300
  education 331 (table)
Anguilla 297
  demography 290 (table)
Anik 2 (Canadian satellite) 623
Ankara, Tur. 359
Annapurna, mt., Himalayas 543
"Annie" (film) 536, il. 538
"Another Way" (film) 538
Ansett, Sir Reginald Myles: see **Obituaries 82**
Antarctica 83, 82, 81
  dependent states 299
  zoology 490
Anthony, Earl 219
Anthropology 83, 82, 81
Antibodies 495
Antigens 495
Antigua and Barbuda
  demography 290 (table)
Antigua Labour Party 177
Antimony (chemistry) 532
Anti-Semitism 204, 459
Antonio Gades Spanish Ballet 273
Antonov, Sergey 459
ANZUS Treaty 199
Aoki, Rocky: see **Biographies 83**
  water sports 725, il. 726
AP (Alianza Popular, Spain) 629
Apeneca, Pact of
  El Salvadoran civil war 340
Apartheid 618
APBA (American Power Boat Association) 724
Aplysia (sea hare) 493
APP (Arctic Pilot Project) 187
Appelgren, Mikael 646
Applications Technology Satellite (ATS) 624
Arab-Israeli conflict: see Middle Eastern Affairs

Arab League Summit 526
Arab Potash Company 468
Arachidonic acid
  Nobel Prizes 97
Arafat, Yasir: see **Biographies 83**
  Lebanon 481
  Middle Eastern affairs 526
  religion 592
Aragon, Louis: see **Obituaries 81**
Arcade games 393
Archaeology 83, 82, 81
Archambault Institute, prison, Canada 577
Archery 648
"Architectural Review" (periodical) 183
Architecture 83, 82, 81
ARCIC: see Anglican-Roman Catholic International Commission
Arctic Pilot Project (APP) 187
Arctic Regions 83, 82, 81
Arctiid moth (*Utetheisa ornatrix*) il. 491
Ardis (U.S. publisher) 512
Ardrey, Robert: see **Obituaries 81**
Ardross (race horse) 363
Argentina 83, 82, 81
  agriculture and food supplies 162
  Antarctica 173
  defense 284, 285
    Falkland Islands conflict 400
  demography 291 (table)
  dependent states 295
  education 331 (table)
  foreign relations
    Canada 228
    Chile 237
    U.K. 684
    United States 697
  international law 479
  literature 511
  motion pictures 539
  transportation 673 (table)
  United Nations report 690
  world economy 312
  "You Can't Foreclose a Country" 60
Argov, Shlomo 457, 258
Argüello, Alexis: see **Biographies 83**
  boxing 245
Ariane (ESA launch vehicle) 624
Arizona 701
Arkansas 701
  life sciences (special report) 498
Arkell, the Rev. A(nthony) J(ohn): see **Obituaries 81**
Armed Forces of the North (FAN)
  Chad civil war 231
Armenians
  Turkish attacks 677
Armenian Secret Army for the Liberation of Armenia 258
Armitage, John: see **Obituaries 81**
Armitage, Richard il. 723
Armour
  art exhibition 193
Arms control: see Disarmament
Arms sales (military) 155
Armstrong of Sanderstead, William Armstrong, Baron: see **Obituaries 81**
Army, U.S. 277
Arndon (race horse) 366
Arnett, W.D. 198
Arnoux, René 540
Aronson, Boris: see **Obituaries 81**
Arout, Gabriel: see **Obituaries 83**
Arroyo, Angel 267
Art: see Architecture; Art Exhibitions; Art Sales; Dance; Literature; Museums; Photography; Theatre
"Arte Italiana, 1960-1982" (art exhibition) 193
Art Exhibitions 83, 82, 81
Arthit Kamlang-ek 661
Arthur, Leonard 412
Artificial insemination
  veterinary science 722
  zoos 737
Artificial intelligence (AI) 250
"Art of the Avant-Garde in Russia; Selections from the George Costakis Collection" (art exhibition) 191
Art Sales 83, 82, 81
Arts Council (U.K.) 661
"Arts of the Islamic Book: the Collection of Prince Sanruddin Aga Khan" (art exhibition) 192
Asarco Inc. (U.S.) 530
Asbestos 358
ASEAN: see Association of Southeast Asian Nations
Ashford, Evelyn 669
Asian Development Bank 223
Asians (people)
  Kenyan accusations 469
Asia Society Gallery, N.Y., N.Y. 192
Asimov, Isaac 503
Askey, Arthur Bowden: see **Obituaries 83**
Askyonov, Vasily 513
Asnag, Abdullah al- 731
Aspirin
  consumer warning table 254

health and disease warning 411
  Nobel Prizes 97
Assad, Hafez al- 275
  Syrian 645
Assam, state, India 424
Assassinations
  Thai attempt 660
Asselin, Marie-Claude 728
Assert (race horse) 364
Association Football 382
Association of Southeast Asian Nations (ASEAN)
  international law 479
  Singapore meeting 613
  Southeast Asian affairs 621
    Kampuchea 468
    Vietnam 724
Association of Theological Schools (ATS) 601
Astaire, Adele Marie (Adele Marie Austerlitz): see **Obituaries 82**
Asther, Nils: see **Obituaries 82**
Astiz, Alfredo 479
Astronomy 83, 82, 81
AT&T: see American Telephone and Telegraph Co.
Athens, Greece 358
Atkins, David 537
Atlanta Braves (baseball team) 209
"Atlantic, The" (magazine) 581
Atlantic City, New Jersey 393
Atlantic Ocean
  energy exploration 341
Atlantic Richfield Co. 241
Atmosphere 343
ATS (Applications Technology Satellite) 624
ATS (Association of Theological Schools) 601
Attenborough, Richard 537
ATV (Midlands)
  television 650
Auchincloss, Louis 502
Auchinleck, Sir Claude (John Eyre): see **Obituaries 82**
Audain, Anne 668
Audi (automobile) 541
Aunli, Berit 728
Aussat (Austr. TV organization) 651
Austerity program
  Somali economic problems 617
Austin, Tracy 659
Australia 83, 82, 81
  Antarctica 173
  consumerism 253
  demography 291 (table)
  dependent states 296
  education 331 (table)
  environment 360
  international law 480
  mining and quarrying 531
  motion pictures 537
  Southeast Asian affairs 622
  sports
    cricket 257
    equestrian sports 366
    lacrosse 375
    water sports 643, 725
  stock exchanges 637
  television and radio 651
  transportation 673 (table)
  wool industry production 448
Australian Labor Party (ALP) 202
Australian National Gallery, Canberra, Austr. 545
Australian Wool Corporation 448
Australopithecus 145
Austria 83, 82, 81
  demography 290 (table)
  education 331 (table)
  energy production 345
  ice hockey 422
  stock exchanges 637
  transportation 673 (table)
Autarchy (pol. sci.)
  "Stresses in the Western Alliance" 65
Automobiles: see Motor vehicles
"Autumn of the Patriarch, The" (García Márquez)
  Nobel Prizes 97
Aviation: see Aerospace
Avocados 432
Avon championship 659
Awaasif (race horse) 363
Ayacucho, department, Peru
  archaeology 180, 563
Aztec Great Temple, Mexico City, Mex. 180

B

B-1B (U.S. bomber) 276
Babakhan, Shamsutdinkhan 681
Bab edh-Dhra, Jordan 177
Bacterium
  dental health 414
Bader, Sir Douglas Robert Steuart: see **Obituaries 83**
Badminton 588
Baess, Sabine 729
Bagaza, Jean-Baptiste il. 224
Bagnold, Enid: see **Obituaries 82**
Bagramyan, Ivan Kristoforovich: see **Obituaries 83**

Baha'i faith 592
Bahamas 83, 82, 81
  demography 290 (table)
  international law 480
Bahrain 83, 82, 81
  demography 289 (table)
  education 331 (table)
Bahonar, Mohammad Javad: see **Obituaries 82**
Baird, Tadeusz: see **Obituaries 82**
Bajon, Filip 539
Baker, T.C. 491
Bakr, Ahmad Hassan al-: see **Obituaries 83**
  Iraq 453
Balaguer, Joaquín 303
Balance of payments
  Latin-American deficits 476
  "You Can't Foreclose a Country" 62
Balance of terror
  "Great Disarmament Debate, The" 10
Balanchine, George 270
Balanus glandula (barnacle) 493
Baldwin, Roger Nash: see **Obituaries 82**
Ballantrae, Bernard Edward Fergusson: see **Obituaries 81**
Ballesteros, Severiano: see **Biographies 81**
Ballet Rambert, U.K. 272
Ballet West, U.S. 271
Ballinger, (Violet) Margaret Livingstone: see **Obituaries 81**
Ballooning 150
Ballykelly, N. Ire. 260
Balmain, Pierre Alexandre: see **Obituaries 83**
Balsemão, Francisco Pinto 575
Balukas, Jean il. 217
Banco Ambrosiano, Rome, Italy 460
  crime and law enforcement 261
  Vatican City State 721
  "You Can't Foreclose a Country" 60
Banda, Hastings Kamuzu 517
Bandaranaike, Sirimavo 632
Bangladesh 83, 82, 81
  agriculture and food supplies 156
  demography 289 (table)
  education 331 (table)
  health and disease 410
  India 424
  transportation 673 (table)
Bani-Sadr, Abolhassan: see **Biographies 81**
Banker Castelli (Turkey) 678
Bank for International Settlements
  "You Can't Foreclose a Country" 64
Banking: see Money and banking
Bankruptcy
  United States 692
Baptist Churches 593
Barbados 83, 82, 81
  demography 290 (table)
  unemployment benefits 614
Barber, Bill 422
Barber, Samuel: see **Obituaries 82**
Barbican Centre, London, U.K. 185, il. 186
Barbuda: see Antigua and Barbuda
"Barchester Chronicles" (TV drama) 655
Bareyev, Yevgeny 236
Bargum, Johan 509
Barnacle (Balanus glandula) 493
Barnetson, William Denholm: see **Obituaries 82**
Barnett, Lady Isobel: see **Obituaries 81**
Barnett, Stephen Frank: see **Obituaries 82**
Barr, Alfred Hamilton, Jr.: see **Obituaries 82**
Barr, Stringfellow: see **Obituaries 83**
Barrah, Muhammad Siyad
  African affairs 154, 616
Barrington, Kenneth Frank: see **Obituaries 82**
Barsky, Arthur Joseph: see **Obituaries 83**
Barth, John 502
Barthes, Roland Gérard: see **Obituaries 81**
Bar-Yosef, Ofar 177
Baryshnikov, Mikhail: see **Biographies 82**
  dance 270
Barzel, Rainer 398
Basalt 304
Baseball 83, 82, 81
  television and radio 654
Basketball 83, 82, 81
Bastyan, Sir Edric Montague: see **Obituaries 81**
Bates, L(ucius) C(hristopher): see **Obituaries 81**
Batovrin, Sergey 681
Baudouin I 214, il. 370
Baum, Gerhart 399
Baumann, Alex 643
Bauxite 532
Bayulken, Haluk il. 404
Bazin, Marc 408
BCA (Billiard Congress of America) 216
Beadle, Sir (Thomas) Hugh (William): see **Obituaries 81**

Beagle Channel, South America
  Argentina-Chile sovereignty dispute 190
  Latin American affairs 475
Beamon, Bob 668
Beaton, Sir Cecil Walter Hardy: see **Obituaries 81**
Beatrix, Queen: see **Biographies 81**
Beatty, Warren 536
"Beau Mariage, Le" (film) 537
"Bech Is Back" (Updike) 503
Bechtel, Stephen, Jr.: see **Biographies 83**
Beck, Joan 336
Beckmann, Max 545
Beckwith, Charles A.: see **Biographies 81**
Beddor, Frank 728
Beef 162
Beer 434
  United States (special report) 699
Beggs, James M. 622
Begin, Menachem: see **Biographies 82**
  Israel 457
  United States visit 696
Beheshti, Ayatollah Mohammad Hossein: see **Obituaries 82**. See **Biographies 81**
Behr, Mattias 246
Beirut, Lebanon
  defense 274
  international law 479
  Israeli invasion 457
  United Nations report 690
Bekaa Valley, region, Lebanon
  Syrian military affairs 645
Belaúnde Terry, Fernando: see **Biographies 81**
  Argentine mediation 188
  Peruvian political developments 563
Belgium 83, 82, 81
  demography 290 (table)
  foreign relations 516, 733
  industrial relations 429
  industrial review 447
  international law 479
  social security 613
  theatre 663
  transportation 673 (table)
Belize 83, 82
  archaeology 180
  demography 290 (table)
  dependent states 295
Beljavsky, Aleksandr 235
Bellini, Rosemary 256
Bell Laboratories (U.S.) 568
Bellow, Saul 501
Bell System (telephone co.) 693
Belmont Stakes (sports) 362
Belushi, John: see **Obituaries 83**
Belvoir, Vale of, U.K. 356
Benchley, Nathaniel Goddard: see **Obituaries 82**
Bendix (U.S. company) 693
Benelli, Giovanni Cardinal: see **Obituaries 83**
Benin 83, 82, 81
  demography 289 (table)
Benítez, Wilfred 244
Benn, Tony: see **Biographies 81**
  British domestic affairs 686
Bennett, Robert Russell: see **Obituaries 82**
Bennett, Sir Thomas Penberthy: see **Obituaries 81**
Benoxaprofen (drug) 410
Benyahia, Muhammad Seddik: see **Obituaries 83**
Berardi, Joe 219
Bérégovoy, Pierre 390
Bereiter, Carl 335
Berenger, Paul 523
Berezovoy, Anatoly N. 623
Bergman, Ingrid: see **Obituaries 83**
Bergström, Sune K.
  Nobel Prizes 97
Beria, Lavrenty
  "Russian Giant: 60 Years after Formation of the Soviet Union, The" 18
Berling, Zygmunt: see **Obituaries 81**
Berlinguer, Enrico 460
Berlin Swimming Championships 642
Bermuda 300
  demography 290 (table)
  education 331 (table)
Bernac, Pierre (Pierre Bertin): see **Obituaries 81**
Bernardin, Joseph L. 592
Bernbach, William: see **Obituaries 83**
"Berry Patches" (Yevtushenko) 512
Berryman, Sir Frank Horton: see **Obituaries 82**
"Best Little Whorehouse in Texas, The" (film) 536
Betancourt, Rómulo: see **Obituaries 82**
Betancur Cuartas, Belisario: see **Biographies 83**
  Colombia 243
Béthouart, Antoine: see **Obituaries 83**
Bettis, Valerie Elizabeth: see **Obituaries 83**
BEUC (Bureau Européen des Unions de Consommateurs) 253
Bhave, Acharya Vinoba: see **Obituaries 83**
BHP (Broken Hill Proprietary Co. Ltd.) 200
Bhutan 83, 82, 81
  demography 289 (table)
Bhutto, Murtaza Ali 560

Bible
religion (special report) 602
Bicherova, Olga 408
Bignone, Reynaldo 189
Bilenchi, Romano 509
Bilingual education 330
Bill 101 (Quebec language law) 226
Billiard Congress of America (BCA)
216
Billiard Games 83, 82, 81
Binaisa, Godfrey 678
Bingo 393
Bintley, David 272
Bio-chemical genetics (zoology) 489
Bipedalism 175
Birch, Paul 198
Bird, Vere Cornwall: *see* **Biographies**
82
Birds: *see* Ornithology
"Birds of the Soviet Union: A Sound
Guide, The" (recording) 492
Birley, Sir Robert: *see* **Obituaries 83**
Birnbaum, Astrid il. 729
Birth and death statistics: *see*
Demography
"Birthplace of Herbert Hoover, The"
(painting) 545
Bishop, Maurice 405
bissett, bill 504
Bitar, Salah ad-Din: *see* **Obituaries 81**
Biya, Paul 224
Bjørnson, Bjørnstjerne 508
Blach, Helena il. 729
Blackburne, Sir Kenneth William: *see*
Obituaries 81
Black-footed ferret (*Mustela nigripes*)
360
zoology 490
Blackjack (Ram-K, U.S.S.R. bomber)
277
Black June (terrorist group) 258
Black Muslims 600
Blacks
race relations 584
Black stilt 360
"Blade Runner" (film) 535
Blagosklonov, K. N.
ornithology 492
Blais, Marie-Claire 506
Blake, Eubie: *see* **Biographies 81**
jazz music 548
Blandos (wets) 237
Blanshard, Paul: *see* **Obituaries 81**
Bliss, Ray Charles: *see* **Biographies**
82
Blister 532
Blood
chemical substitute 232
"Blood and Honor" (W.Ger. TV dra-
ma) 655
"Bloodsmoor Romance, A" (Oates)
literature 502
Bloom, Benjamin 335
Blum, Yehuda 689
Blumenthal, Erwin 261
Bluth, Don 536
BMA (British Medical Association)
357
BMRI (British Meat Research Insti-
tute) 382
Bobsledding 729
Bodaveli, David 247
Bodley Scott, Sir Ronald: *see* **Obituar-
ies 83**
Boeing 757
industrial review 433
Boeing 767
industrial review 432
Böhm, Karl: *see* **Obituaries 82**
Bohusz-Szyszko, Zygmunt: *see* **Obitu-
aries 83**
Bolden, Jeanette 669
Bolivia 83, 82, 81
demography 291 (table)
education 331 (table)
transportation 673 (table)
Bolshoi Ballet 273
Bolton, Sir George Lewis French: *see*
Obituaries 83
Bombardier Inc. (Can.) 228
Bonanno group (crime syndicate) 261
Bonds 634
Bonham, John: *see* **Obituaries 81**
Bonin, William 260
Boodhoo, Harisun 523
Booker, Christopher 500
Booker Prize (literature) 500
Bookmaker (gambling) 393
Books
art sales 195
libraries (special report) 485
publishing 582
Boonchu Rojanastien 660
Boone, Richard Allen: *see* **Obituaries**
82
Boone, William 588
Bophuthatswana, region, S.Af. 619
demography 289 (table)
Borg, Björn 658
Borges, Jorge Luis 511
Borg Olivier, George: *see* **Obituaries**
81
Boris the Gypsy 681
Borobudur, monument, Indon.
historic preservation 417, il.
Borsos, Phillip 537
Bosporus, strait, Tur. 356
Bossy, Mike 420, il.

Boston Ballet 271
Boston Museum of Fine Art, Boston,
Mass. 544
architecture 184
Botanical Gardens: *see* Zoos and Bo-
tanical Gardens
Botany 493
Botha, Pieter Willem: *see* **Biographies**
82
Kaunda meeting 735
Botham, Ian Terence: *see* **Biographies**
82
Botswana 83, 82, 81
demography 289 (table)
education 331 (table)
Botswana Vaccine Institute 219
Boun Oum na Champassak, Prince: *see*
Obituaries 81
Bourguiba, Habib 676
Boussac, Marcel: *see* **Obituaries 81**
Boustead, Sir (John Edmund) Hugh:
see **Obituaries 81**
Bouterse, Daysi: *see* **Biographies 81**
Suriname 640
Bowling 83, 82, 81
Boxing 319
Boyd, Julian Parks: *see* **Obituaries 81**
Boyle of Handsworth, Edward Charles
Gurney Boyle, (Baron): *see* **Obitu-
aries 82**
"Boy Scout Handbook and Other Ob-
servations, The" (Fussell) 504
Braa, Oddvar 727
Bradford, The Rev. Robert John: *see*
Obituaries 82
Bradley, Omar Nelson: *see* **Obituaries**
82
Bradley University, Peoria, Ill. 213
Brady, Pam 588
Brahms, Caryl: *see* **Obituaries 83**
"Braided Lives" (Piercy) 502
Brain
tissue transplant 410
Bramly, Serge 506
Brandt, Willy 399
Braniff International Corp. 692
air transportation 671
Brassens, Georges: *see* **Obituaries 82**
Brazil 83, 82, 81
agriculture and food supplies 164
Antarctica 173
demography 291 (table)
education 331 (table)
energy production 342
engineering projects 350
environment 356
industrial review 447
literature 511
mining and quarrying 530
motion pictures 539
transportation 673 (table)
United States relations 697
"You Can't Foreclose a Country"
64
Bread 380
Breeding (zoos) 737
Breit, Gregory: *see* **Obituaries 82**
Breitenbach, Gary 490
Brett, George: *see* **Biographies 81**
Breuer, Marcel (Lajos): *see* **Obituaries**
82
Brezhnev, Leonid Ilyich: *see* **Obituar-
ies 83**
China policy 242
"Great Disarmament Debate, The"
13
"Russian Giant: 60 Years after For-
mation of the Soviet Union, The"
17
Union of Soviet Socialist Republics
679
United States 695
"Brideshead Revisited" (TV drama)
655
fashion influence 374
Bridges 348
Brisbane, XII Commonwealth Games
643
"Britannia Hospital" (film) 537
"British Architecture 1982" (exhibi-
tion) 183
British Broadcasting Corp.: *see* BBC
British Indian Ocean Territory 301
demography 289 (table)
British Meat Research Institute
(BMRI) 382
British Medical Association (BMA)
357
British Museum, London, U.K. 545
art exhibition 191
British Open (golf tournament) 401
British Telecom (BT) 440
British Virgin Islands 300
demography 290 (table)
Brizola, Leonel 221
Broadcasting: *see* Television and radio
Broadway, New York, N.Y. 665
Brodhead, William 699
Broken Hill Proprietary Co. Ltd.
(BHP) 200
Brombacher, Bruce il. 329
Bromfield, Rex 537
Bromine 531
Brooks, Louise 504
Brosio, Manlio: *see* **Obituaries 81**
Brown, Charles Lee: *see* **Biographies**
83
Brown, Christy: *see* **Obituaries 82**
Brown, Robert 197
Brown, Walter E. 179
Brown alga (*Macrocystis*) 493

Browne, E(lliot) Martin: *see* **Obituaries**
81
Brunei 295
demography 289 (table)
education 331 (table)
energy production 345
Brunhart, Hans 488
Brushy Mountain State Penitentiary,
Tenn. 577
Bruton, John 454
Bryant, David 220
Bryant, Paul ("Bear"): *see* **Biographies**
82
football retirement 388
BT (British Telecom) 440
Buddhism 598
art exhibition 192
Budget cuts 585
Budget deficit 312
Building and construction 437
engineering projects 348
Bulawayo, Zimbabwe 736
Bulgaria 83, 82, 81
aerial sports 151
demography 290 (table)
education 331 (table)
gymnastics and weight lifting 403
theatre 664
transportation 673 (table)
Bullard, Sir Edward Crisp: *see* **Obitu-
aries 81**
Bundesbank (Fed. Rep. of Ger.) 318
Bureau Européen des Unions de Con-
sommateurs (BEUC) 253
Burger King 432
Burgess, Anthony 499
Burma 83, 82, 81
demography 289 (table)
education 331 (table)
transportation 673 (table)
Burn, Joshua Harold: *see* **Obituaries**
82
Burnett, Carol: *see* **Biographies 82**
Burnett, Tommy 701
Burpee, David: *see* **Obituaries 81**
Burrowing shrimp (*Alpheus mackayi*)
493
Burton, Charles 187
Burundi 83, 82, 81
demography 289 (table)
Busch, Ernst: *see* **Obituaries 81**
Buses 675
Bush, George: *see* **Biographies 81**
Chinese visit 241
Taiwan trip 647
Bushmiller, Ernest Paul: *see* **Obituar-
ies 83**
Busing 330
Buthelezi, Gatsha 618
Butler, Reg (Reginald Cotterell But-
ler): *see* **Obituaries 82**
Butler of Saffron Walden, Richard
Austen Butler: *see* **Obituaries 83**
Butlin, Sir William ("Billy") Edmund:
see **Obituaries 81**
Butter 163
Buyer's premium 194
Byrd, Henry Roeland (Roy Byrde: *see*
Obituaries 81
Bythograea thermydon (crab) 492

C

CAB (Civil Aeronautics Board) 253
Cable television
ice hockey contracts 421
industrial review 432
television networks 650
Cabral, Luis de Almeida 407
Cabrera, Blas 198, 569
Cabrini, Antonio il. 383
CACM (Central American Common
Market) 476
Caetano, Marcelo José das Neves
Alves: *see* **Obituaries 81**
Cain, John 199
Calanus pacificus 493
Caldiara Marques, Antonio 231
Caldwell, Bettye 335
Calendar of Events of 1983 22
California 700
entomology 491
environment 356
wine industry 435
California Angels (baseball team) 209
California Federal Savings & Loan As-
sociation 693
Callado, Antônio 512
Callwood, June: *see* **Biographies 82**
Calvi, Roberto 261, 591
Calvin, Melvin 234
Calvo Sotelo y Bustelo, Leopoldo: *see*
Biographies 82
Spain 629
Cambodia: *see* Kampuchea
Cameroon 83, 82, 81
demography 289 (table)
education 331 (table)
foreign relations
Gabon 392
Nigeria 555
Camon, Ferdinando 509
Campaign (politics) 698
Campaign for European Nuclear Dis-
armament 13

Campaign for Lead-Free Air (CLEAR,
U.K.) 357
Campbell and Cosans v. United Kingdom
478
Camus, Marcel: *see* **Obituaries 83**
Canada 83, 82, 81
agriculture and food supplies 157
Arctic regions 187
arts
literature 504
motion pictures 537
theatre 666
Commonwealth of Nations 248
demography 290 (table)
education 334
energy production 343
engineering projects 351
fisheries 379
international law 480
machinery and machine tools 442
migration, international 528
mining and quarrying 530
sports
ice hockey 422
equestrian sports 362
swimming competitions 643
stock exchanges 635
transportation 673 (table)
world economy 324
Canada Act 225
Canadian Football League (CFL) 388
Canadian literature 504
Canaletto 192
Canal Zone 480
Cancer
demography 288
health and disease 409
Cancún, Mex.: *see* North-South
conference
Candu (nuclear reactor) 443
Canham, Erwin Dain: *see* **Obituaries**
83
Canning industry 378
Canoe competition 725
Canon (camera company) 567
Canton and Enderbury Islands
demography 291 (table)
CAP (Common agricultural policy)
167
Capacity utilization rate
world economy 313
Cape Cod, Mass. 308
Cape Verde 83, 82, 81
demography 289 (table)
Guinea-Bissau 407
Sao Tomé and Principe 609
Cape vulture (*Gyps coprotheres*) 360
Capitalism
"China's Uncertain Future" 130
Japan (special report) 465
Capital punishment 577
United States statistics 702
Captive Breeding Specialist Group
zoos 737
Caracas, Venezuela il. 722
Caracas Lions (baseball team) 211
Caraion, Ion 514
Carajás Range, Braz. 530
Caravaggio 190
Carcani, Adil 169
"Card Players" (painting) il. 192
Cardwell, Vicki 588
Cargill, Sir (Ian) Peter Macgillivray: *see*
Obituaries 82
Cargo ship 446
Caribbean Basin Initiative (CBI)
Costa Rican allocation 255
economic development 476
El Salvador 339
Guatemala 406
Jamaica 461
U.S.-Cuba relations 265
Caribbean Community (Caricom)
Grenada 405
summit 176
Trinidad and Tobago 676
Caribbean Sea 450
Caribbean Series (baseball) 211
Caricom: *see* Caribbean Community
Carlsen, Henning 538
Carlton, Steve 210
Carmichael, Hoagy (Hoagland How-
ard Carmichael): *see* **Obituaries 82**
Carner, JoAnne 403
"Carnival" (painting) 545
Caro, Robert 503
Caroe, Sir Olaf Kirkpatrick: *see* **Obitu-
aries 82**
Carpenter, Connie il. 266
Carpentier y Valmont, Alejo: *see* **Obit-
uaries 81**
Carr, Edward Hallett: *see* **Obituaries**
83
Carrington, Peter Alexander Rupert
Carington, 6th Baron 685, il. 370
Carritt, (Hugh) David Graham: *see*
Obituaries 83
Cars: *see* Motor vehicles
CART (Championship Auto Racing
Team) 541
Carter, Billy: *see* **Biographies 81**
Carter, Harry Graham: *see* **Obituaries**
83

Carter, Jimmy: *see* **Biographies 81**
  "China's Uncertain Future" 136
  "Great Disarmament Debate, The" 11
Carton, Cheryl 588
Cartwright, B. A. 491
Casamance, Senegal 611
Casino (gambling) 393
Caspar-Klug quasi-equivalence theory
  Nobel Prizes 98
Cassava (manioc) 160
Casserly, Joseph W. 183
Castillo, Jaime 238
Castro, Fidel 265
Cato, Milton 608
"Cats" (musical) 665, il. 662
Cattle 722
Caulfield, Michael 537
Cavalcanti, Alberto de Almeida: *see* **Obituaries 83**
Cavenaugh, Frank 540
Caves 630
Cavities 414
Cayman Islands 300
  demography 290 (table)
CBI: *see* Caribbean Basin Initiative
CBOE (Chicago Board of Trade Options Exchange) 634
CBS: *see* Columbia Broadcasting System
CBW (Chemical and biological weapons) 283
CCM (Chama Cha Mapinduzi; Revolutionary Party, Tan.) 648
CDC: *see* Central American Democratic Community
CDU (Christian Democratic Union)
  Germany, Federal Republic of 397
Ceausescu, Nicolae 604
Celenk, Bekir 459
Celibacy 592
Cellulosics (fibre) 448
Celtic art 177
Cement 532
Cenac, Winston Francis: *see* **Biographies 82**
Censorship
  libraries (special report) 485
  literature 511
Census Bureau, U.S. 292
"Center Ring: The Artist" exhibition 191
Central African Republic 83, 82, 81
  demography 289 (table)
Central America
  international refugee status 590
Central American Common Market (CACM) 476
Central American Democratic community (CDC) 476
  Costa Rica 255
  El Salvador 340
  Guatemala's admission 406
Centrally planned economies
  agriculture and food supplies 156
  "China's Uncertain Future" 133
  world economy 320, 325
Central TV (U.K.) 650
Centre Party (Norway) 558
Centrowitz, Matt 669
Ceramics 520
Cereals: *see* Grains
Cerqueda Pascuet, Francesc 171
Cerro Matoso (mine) 530
CETA (Comprehensive Employment and Training Act) 615
CFL (Canadian Football League) 388
CFTC (Commonwealth Fund for Technical Cooperation) 518
Chad 83, 82, 81
  demography 289 (table)
  international refugee status 589
Chagla, Mohomedali Currim: *see* **Obituaries 82**
Chagos Archipelago, Ind. O.
  Mauritius foreign relations 523
Chakela, Koenyame 482
Chakkri dynasty 660
"Challenger" (space shuttle) 623
Chama Cha Mapinduzi (CCM; Revolutionary Party, Tan.) 648
Chambers, George: *see* **Biographies 82**
  Trinidad and Tobago 675
Chambers, Sir (Stanley) Paul: *see* **Obituaries 82**
Champagne, region, Fr. 434
Champion, Gower: *see* **Obituaries 81**
Championship Auto Racing Team (CART) 541
Champion Stakes (horse racing) 364
Chan, Sir Julius: *see* **Biographies 81**
  Papua New Guinea 562
Chandler, Jeff 245
Chang Ai-p'ing (Zhang Aiping) 240
Chang Yong Ja 472 il.
Chanine, Youssef 539
"Chan Is Missing" (film) 536
Chan Kui-Yao 613
Channel 4 (U.K. television) 536, 650
Channel Islands
  demography 290 (table)
Channel Tunnel project 348
Channon, Paul 661
Chan Sy 468
Chao Tzu-yang: *see* Zhao Ziyang
Chapin, Harry: *see* **Obituaries 82**
Chapman, (Anthony) Colin: *see* **Obituaries 83**
"Chariots of Fire" (film) 536
Charles, Mary Eugenia: *see* **Biographies 81**
  Dominica's economy 302
Charter of Rights and Freedom, Can. 225
Chase Manhattan Bank (U.S.) 691
Chaudhri, Fazal Elahi: *see* **Obituaries 83**
Chavanon, Christian: *see* **Obituaries 82**
Chayefsky, Paddy (Sidney Stychevsky): *see* **Obituaries 82**
Chebrikov, Viktor 680
Checker Motors Corp. 437
Cheese 163
Cheever, Eddie 540
Cheever, John: *see* **Obituaries 83**
  literature 502
Chekova, Olga: *see* **Obituaries 81**
Chelonians (zoology) 360
Chemical and biological weapons (CBW) 283
Chemical element 109
  identification 233
Chemicals 437
Chemistry 83, 82, 81
  Nobel Prizes 98
Chen Boda (Ch'en Po-ta) 131
Chen Changjie 588
Chenchikova, Olga 273, il. 272
Cheney, Sheldon Warren: *see* **Obituaries 81**
Ch'en Hsi-lien (Chen Xilian) 240
Chenoweth, Dean: *see* **Obituaries 83**
  water sports 724
Chen Pixian: *see* **Biographies 83**
Ch'en Yün (Chen Yun) 240
Chernenko, Konstantin 680
Chervenkov, Vulko: *see* **Obituaries 81**
Chess 83, 82, 81
Chevènement, Jean-Pierre: *see* **Biographies 83**
"Chèvre, Le" (film) 537
Cheysson, Claude: *see* **Biographies 82**
  European Communities il. 369, 370
Chiang Ch'ing (Jiang Jing)
  "China's Uncertain Future" 131
Chicago, Ill. 545
Chicago Board of Trade Options Exchange (CBOE) 634
Chiesa, Carlo Alberto Dalla; *see* Dalla Chiesa, Carlo Alberto
Children
  United States statistics 701
Chile 83, 82, 81
  Antarctica 173
  Argentine dispute 190
  demography 291 (table)
  education 331 (table)
  international law 480
  literature 511
  mining and quarrying 532
  transportation 673 (table)
China 83, 82, 81
  agriculture and food supplies 156
  Antarctica expedition 173
  archaeology 178
  defense 284
  demography 293
  dependent states 301
  energy production 340
  education 333
  engineering projects 350
  foreign relations
    Africa 155, 734
    Burma 223
    Kampuchea's coalition 468
    Korea 473
    Southeast Asian affairs 621
    Soviet foreign affairs 683
    Soviet-Vietnamese relations 724
  Taiwan 647
  Japanese text-book issue 464
  literature 515
  mining and quarrying 532
  silk industry 448
  sports 256, 588, 643, 646, 649
  transportation 673 (table)
China National Offshore Oil Corporation 241
Chin A Sen, Hendrick R. 640
"China's Uncertain Future" (Solomon) 129
Chinese literature 515
Chin-ho, Kim 649
Ch'in Shih Huang (Qin Shi Huang)
  archaeology 178
Chirico, Giorgio de 193
Chirwa, Orton 517
Chiyonofuji 247
Chloros, Alexander George: *see* **Obituaries 83**
Choudhury, Abul Fazal Mohammad Ahsanuddin 206
Chou En-lai (Zhou Enlai) 131
Chrétien, Jean-Loup 624
Christian Church (Disciples of Christ) 594
Christian Democratic Party (It.) 459
Christian Democratic Union (CDU)
  Germany, Federal Republic of 397
Christianity: *see* Orthodox Church; Protestant Churches; Roman Catholic Church
Christian People's Party (Nor.) 558
Christian Social Union (CSU) 397
Christie's (art dealers) 194
Christmas Island 296
  demography 291 (table)
Christmas Past (race horse) 363
Christopher, Warren: *see* **Biographies 82**
Chromium 532
Chronology of Events of 1982 26
Chrysler Corp. 435
  industrial relations 428, il. 427
Chun Doo Hwan: *see* **Biographies 81**
  Korea 471
Chung Il-Choi 245
Church, Sam: *see* **Biographies 81**
Churches of Christ 594
Churchill, Sarah (Sarah Lady Audley): *see* **Obituaries 83**
Church of Christ, Scientist 594
Church of Jesus Christ of Latter-day Saints 594
Chuykov, Vasily Ivanovich: *see* **Obituaries 83**
CIAB (Coal Industry Advisory Board) 343
Cigarettes 449
  consumer warning label 254
  health and disease 409
Cinema: *see* Motion pictures
Circus art 191
Ciskei, region, S. Af. 620
  demography 289 (table)
Ciskei Development Corporation (S. Af.) 620
Cisneros, Henry: *see* **Biographies 82**
Cities Service Co. 693
City Museum and Art Gallery, Stoke-on-Trent, U.K. 544
Civil Aeronautics Board (CAB) 253
Civil rights and liberties
  education 330
  libraries (special report) 486
  see also various countries
Clair, René (René Chomette): *see* **Obituaries 82**
Clampett, Bobby 401
"Clare Boothe Luce" (Sheed) 504
Clark, Barney 411
Clark, William P.: *see* **Biographies 83**
Classical music 545
Classicism (arch.) 183
Claude, Sylvio 408
Clausen, A.W.: *see* **Biographies 82**
Clean Water Act, (U.S.) 355
CLEAR (Campaign for Lead-Free Air, U.K.) 357
Clinch River project, Tenn. 342
Cloud seeding 309
Clurman, Harold Edgar: *see* **Obituaries 81**
CMEA: see Council for Mutual Economic Assistance
Coal
  energy 343
  metallurgy 520
  transporation 672
Coal Industry Advisory Board (CIAB) 343
Coal-oil dispersion 343
Cobbett, William 501
Cochran, Jacqueline: *see* **Obituaries 81**
Cockburn, Claud: *see* **Obituaries 82**
Cocoa 164
Cocorp (Consortium for Continental Reflection Profiling) 304
Cocos (Keeling) Islands 296
  demography 291 (table)
Cody, John Patrick Cardinal: *see* **Obituaries 83**
Coe, Sebastian 667
Coghill, Nevill Henry Kendal Aylmer: *see* **Obituaries 81**
Cohen, Albert: *see* **Obituaries 82**
Coia, Jack (Iacomo Antonio Coia): *see* **Obituaries 82**
Coins: *see* Philately and Numismatics
Cole, "Cozy" (William Randolph Cole): *see* **Obituaries 82**
Cole, Dame Margaret Isabel: *see* **Obituaries 81**
Colean, Miles Lanier: *see* **Obituaries 81**
Coleman, Mel 603
Coleraine, Richard Kidston Law, 1st Baron: *see* **Obituaries 81**
Collage tectonics 304
Collective bargaining (Nor.) 558
Colleges 333, 387
Collett, T.S. 491
Collins, the Rev. Canon (Lewis) John: *see* **Obituaries 83**
Collins, Norman Richard: *see* **Obituaries 83**
Colombia 83, 82, 81
  demography 291 (table)
  education 331 (table)
  literature 511
  mining and quarrying 530
  motion pictures 539
  transportation 673 (table)
Colombo, Emilio il. 370
Colorado
  United States statistics 702
Colour additives 254
Colour printing 567
"Columbia" (space shuttle) 623
  aerial sports 150
  transportation 671
Columbia Broadcasting System (CBS)
  publishing 582
  television and radio 394, 652
Combat Sports 83, 82, 81
Comecon: *see* Council for Mutual Economic Assistance
Comédi Française 663
Commerce, U.S. Department of 437
Commission to Organize the Party of the Working People of Ethiopia (COPWE) 367
Committee of Enquiry into the Education of Children of Ethnic Minorities, The (U.K.) 584
Commodities trade 638
  agriculture and food supplies 166
  world economy 311
  "You Can't Foreclose a Country" 62
Common agricultural policy (CAP) 167
Common Market: *see* European Communities
Commonwealth Championships (India) 646
Commonwealth Fund for Technical Cooperation (CFTC) 518
Commonwealth Games
  Australian protests 199
  swimming competition 643
Commonwealth of Nations 83, 82, 81
  see also individual Commonwealth nations
Communications
  Portuguese news agency 575
  television and radio 650
Communist Party of Czechoslovakia (CPC) 269
Communist Party of China
  "China's Uncertain Future" 132
Communist Party Congress
  China 240
  Vietnam 723
Communist Party of Thailand 661
Comoros 83, 82, 81
  demography 289 (table)
"Compass Rose, The" (LeGuin) 503
Comprehensive Employment and Training Act (CETA) 615
Compressed-air power plant 342
Compton, John George Melvin: *see* **Biographies 83**
  Saint Lucia politics 607
Computers 83, 82, 81
  chemistry research 232
  crime (special report) 263
  libraries 484
  publishing 581
"Computers Don't Sin: People Do" (Special Report) 263
Computer Software Mangement and Information Center (COSMIC)
  space exploration (special report) 627
"Conan the Barbarian" (film) 536
Concessional terms (banking)
  "You Can't Foreclose a Country" 61
Concorde (aircraft) 433
Concrete 348
Conestoga I (U.S. launch vehicle) 624
"Confessions of Felix Krull" (TV drama) 655
Confindustria
  industrial relations 429
  Italian federation 460
  stock exchanges 636
Congdon, Justin D. 490
Congo 83, 82, 81
  demography 289 (table)
  education 331 (table)
  transportation 673 (table)
Congregational Churches 595
Congress (U.S.) 693
Congressional Budget Measure (U.S.)
  world economy 314
Connell, Amyas Douglas: *see* **Obituaries 81**
Connelly, Marc(us Cook): *see* **Obituaries 81**
Conner, Bart 408
Conner, William 491
Connes, Alain 521
Connolly, Gerard 184
Connolly, Patrick 454
Connors, Jimmy 658
Conquistador Cielo (race horse) 362, il. 365
Conried, Hans: *see* **Obituaries 83**
Conservative Party (U.K.) 684
Consumerism
  United States statistics 702
Conseils généraux (Fr.) 390
Conservation: *see* Environment; Historic Preservation
Conservative Party (CP, S.Af.) 617
Consortium for Continental Reflection Profiling (Cocorp) 304
Constitution
  Brazil 221
  China 241
  Portugal 575
Constitutional monarchy
  Norway 558
"Consul, The" (film) 539
Consumer bill of rights (U.S.) 252
Consumer Interpol 252
Consumerism 83, 82, 81
Consumer price index (econ.) 313
Consumer prices (econ.) 320
Consumers' Association of Penang (Malaysia) 253
Consumption (econ.)
  Soviet economic goals 682

Contact group
African politico-military activity 153
South African foreign relations 618
"Continental Drift: The Theory of Plate Tectonics" (film) 540
Continental Illinois National Bank 692
Contraceptives 411
Contract Bridge 83, 82, 81
Conventional weapons
"Stresses in the Western Alliance" 67
Convention of Wetlands of International Importance (Ramsar Convention) 360
Convention on the Conservation of Antarctic Marine Living Resources 173
Convention on the Conservation of European Wildlife and Natural Habitats 361
Cook, Betty: *see* **Biographies 81**
water sports 724
Cook Islands 301
demography 291 (table)
Coon, Carleton S(tevens): *see* **Obituaries 82**
Cooper, Christin 727
Coote, Robert: *see* **Obituaries 83**
Copeland, Al 724
Coper, Hans: *see* **Obituaries 82**
Copper 532
Coppola, Francis Ford 536
Coppola, Frank J. 577
Coptic Church 598
COPWE (Commission to Organize the Party of the Working People of Ethiopia) 367
Copyright 582
Corbett Ashby, Dame Margery (Irene): *see* **Obituaries 82**
Corbett, Harry H.: *see* **Obituaries 83**
Corcoran, Thomas Gardiner: *see* **Obituaries 82**
Cordero, Ángel 362
Cordillera (geology) 304
Cordovez, Diego 151
Corgi toys 394
Corn 160
Corner, George Washington: *see* **Obituaries 82**
Corn gluten 167
Corning Glass Works (U.S.) 440
Corona, Juan 260
Coronograph (research) 195
Corporation for Public Broadcasting (CPB) 650
Corrosion 235
Corruption
Syrian government crackdown 646
COSMIC (Computer Software Management and Information Center)
space exploration (special report) 627
Cosmology 198
Cosmos 1374 (U.S.S.R. shuttle) 624
Cosmos 1383 (U.S.S.R. satellite) 626
Costa-Gavras: *see* **Biographies 83**
motion pictures 536
Costakis, George 191
Costa Rica 83, 82, 81
demography 290 (table)
education 331 (table)
transportation 673 (table)
Cost-exchange ratio
defense (special report) 286
Costigan, Frank 200
Cotton 448
agriculture and food supplies 165
Couch grass (*Agropyron repens*) 395
Council for Mutual Economic Assistance (CMEA; Comecon)
"Russian Giant: 60 Years after Formation of the Soviet Union, The" 17
world economy 320
"You Can't Foreclose a Country" 63
Council of Lloyd's (U.K.) 440
Council of the Revolution
Portuguese constitution 575
Counter-purchase policies 324
Coup
Dominican domestic disorder 302
Mauritanian domestic unrest 522
Court Games 83, 82, 81
Courtneidge, Dame Cicely: *see* **Obituaries 81**
Cox, Paul 537
CP (Conservative Party, S.Af.) 617
CPB (Corporation for Public Broadcasting) 650
CPC (Communist Party of Czechoslovakia) 269
Craig, Jim: *see* **Biographies 81**
Crawley, Randall 588
Creationism 592
Creation science
life sciences (special report) 498
Creatonotos (Arctiid moth) 491
Credit and debt
"You Can't Foreclose a Country" 61
Cresson, Edith: *see* **Biographies 83**
Crete, island, Greece 178
Cricket 83, 82, 81
Crime and Law Enforcement 83, 82, 81
Mexican government 525
prisons and penology 576
Critical point (physics)
Nobel Prizes 98
Cronin, A(rchibald) J(oseph): *see* **Obituaries 82**
Crosby, Nathaniel 402
Cross country running 670
Cross-country skiing 727
Crow 492
Crowther, Bosley (Francis Bosley Crowther, Jr.): *see* **Obituaries 82**
"Great Disarmament Debate, The" 12
Crustaceans 492
Cryptographic secret coding 264
Crystallographic electron microscopy
Nobel Prizes 98
CSU (Christian Social Union)
Germany, Federal Republic of 397
Cuba 83, 82, 81
African affairs 154
Angola 172
Argentine alliance 189
South Africa 618
defense 284
demography 290 (table)
education 331 (table)
transportation 673 (table)
"You Can't Foreclose a Country" 63
Cuban-Americans
race relations (special report) 587
Cuban missile crisis
"Great Disarmament Debate, The" 10
Cullberg Ballet (Swed.) 273
Culshaw, John Royds: *see* **Obituaries 81**
Cult of Personality (Chin. hist.) 132
Cultural Revolution
"China's Uncertain Future" 130
Cuomo, Mario M.: *see* **Biographies 83**
Curfew 471
Curling 730
Curran, Sir Charles John: *see* **Obituaries 81**
Curran, Joseph Edward: *see* **Obituaries 82**
Currency reserves (banking)
"You Can't Foreclose a Country" 62
Curry, Lisa 643
"Curse of an Aching Heart, The" (play) 665
Curzon, Sir Clifford Michael: *see* **Obituaries 83**
Cuzco, department, Peru 180
Cycling 83, 82, 81
Cyclones 667
Cyprus 83, 82, 81
archaeology 178
demography 289 (table)
education 331 (table)
Greece 404
transportation 673 (table)
Czechoslovakia 83, 82, 81
defense 281
demography 290 (table)
disability pensions 614
education 331 (table)
ice hockey 422
literature 513
television and radio 655
transportation 673 (table)

D

Dagover, Lil (Marta-Maria Lillits): *see* **Obituaries 81**
Dahl, Tor Edvin 508
Dahrendorf, Ralf 333
Dai Houying (Tai Hou-ying) 515
Dail (Irish parliament) 454
Dailey, Dan 603
Dai Rakuda Kan (dance group) il. 271
Dairy products
agriculture and food supplies 163
consumer hazards 252
food processing 381
Dakhileh oasis, Egypt
archaeology 177
Dalai Lama il. 599
Dali, Salvador 544
Dal Khalsa (Sikh group)
religion 599
Dalla Chiesa, Carlo Alberto 262, 459
"Dallas" (TV show) 656
Dallas, Texas 434
Dalton, van Dijk, Johnson and Partners 184
Dams 349
Dams Referendum
Australia (special report) 202
Dance 83, 82, 81
Dance Theatre of Harlem 271
Dani, Fadel ad- il. 390
Danielson, G. Edward 196
Dannay, Frederic: *see* **Obituaries 83**
"Danse du loup, La" (Bramly) 506
"Dans la main de l'ange (Fernández) 505
Dantine, Helmut: *see* **Obituaries 83**
"Dark Crystal, The" (film) 536
Darlington, Cyril Dean: *see* **Obituaries 82**
Darnell, August 549
Darwin, Charles Robert 489, 497
Data diddling (computers) 264
Data processing 628
Datsun 436
D'Aubisson, Roberto: *see* **Biographies 83**
El Salvadoran political crisis 339
Davies, Robertson il. 505
Davies, Wayne 589
Davis, Jim: *see* **Obituaries 82**
Davis, Miles 548
Davis, Victor 642
Davis, William: *see* **Biographies 82**
Davis Cup 659
Day, Dorothy: *see* **Obituaries 81**
Dayan, Moshe: *see* **Obituaries 82**
Daytona 500 (race) 541
DBCP (dibromochloropropane)
environment 356
DBS (Direct broadcasting satellite) 651
"Dead Men Don't Wear Plaid" (film) 536
Dead Sea 468
Dean, Christopher 729
Dean, Paul ("Daffy"): *see* **Obituaries 82**
Dean, William Ralph ("Dixie"): *see* **Obituaries 81**
"Dean's December, The" (Bellow) 501
D'Eath, Tom 724
Death penalty 478
Death statistics: *see* Demography
De Banzie, Brenda: *see* **Obituaries 82**
De Carlo, Andrea 509
Decentralization (econ.)
South African economy 619
Sudanese domestic unrest 639
Decker Tabb, Mary: *see* **Biographies 83**
track and field 668
Deep Seabed Hard Mineral Resources Act of 1980 (U.S) 353
Deep-sea drilling 307
Defense 83, 82, 81
African affairs 155
see also various countries
Defense Bill (Visiting Warships Bill, Austr.) 199
Defferre, Gaston: *see* **Biographies 83**
De Freitas, Sir Geoffrey Stanley: *see* **Obituaries 83**
De Graff, Robert F(air): *see* **Obituaries 82**
De Klerk, Fredrik Willem: *see* **Biographies 83**
South African affairs 617
De la Espriella, Ricardo 561
Delblanc, Sven 509
Delbrück, Max: *see* **Obituaries 82**
Delivery system, (military) 286
Del Monaco, Mario: *see* **Obituaries 83**
De Lorean, John Zachary: *see* **Biographies 83**
crime and law enforcement 261
industrial review 435
United States 694
De Lorean Motor Co. 435
Del Portillo, Very Rev. Álvaro il. 597
De Lullo, Giorgio: *see* **Obituaries 82**
Del Vecchio, John M. 502
Democracy Wall.
"China's Uncertain Future" 133
Democratic Action Party (PAD, Spain) 629
Democratic Alliance (AD, Port.) 575
Democratic Party (U.S) 691
Democratic Union of the Malian People 519
Demography 83, 82, 81
international migration 528
race relations (special report) 586
see also various countries
Demonstrations and riots il. 214
De-nationalization
Peru economy 564
Dene Nation (Canadian Indians) 187
Deng Xiaoping (Teng Hsiao-p'ing): *see* **Biographies 82**
China 238, il. 239
"China's Uncertain Future" 131
Soviet foreign affairs 683
Denmark 83, 82, 81
demography 290 (table)
dependent states 296
education 330
European Communities role 371
fisheries 379
literature 507
motion pictures 538
transportation 673 (table)
Denny-Brown, Derek Ernest: *see* **Obituaries 82**
Dense pack system 276
Dentistry 414
Deoxyribonucleic acid (DNA) 496
Dependent States 83, 82, 81
Depo-Provera (drug)
health regulations 411
Deportation 584
DeRoburt, Hammer 550
De Rochemont, Richard Guertis: *see* **Obituaries 83**
Desaparecidos (missing persons)
Argentina 189
Desaulniers, Michael 588
Desegregation: *see* Civil rights and liberties; Race relations
Designated hitter (baseball) 208
Des Moines Art Center 545
"De Stijl—1917–1931: Visions of Utopia" (art exhibition) 192
Dètente
"Great Disarmament Debate, The" 10
"Russian Giant: 60 Years after Formation of the Soviet Union, The" 19
West Germany's position 399
Detroit Red Wings (team) 421
Deutscher Gewerkschaftsbund (DGB)
industrial relations 428
Devaluation and revaluation 450
"You Can't Foreclose a Country"
see also various countries
Developing nations
agriculture and food supplies 156
demography 288
world economy 319, 324
"You Can't Foreclose a Country" 61
Devine, Grant: *see* **Biographies 83**
Canada elections 226
DeVries, William C. 411
DGB (Deutscher Gewerkschaftsbund)
industrial relations 428
Dhaulāgiri, mt., Nepal 543
Diacodexis
life sciences 488, il. 490
Diamond 439
mining 531
Botswanan industry 219
Lesotho 482
Diana, Princess of Wales: *see* **Biographies 82**
Diarrhea (scours) 722
Dibba, Mustapha 392
Dibromochloropropane (DBCP)
environment 356
Diego Garcia, Island 300
Diet
hyperactivity treatment 414
"Different Seasons" (King) 503
Dilhorne, Reginald Edward Manningham-Butler: *see* **Obituaries 81**
Dillard, Annie 504
DiMichele, Leonard 489
"Diner" (film) 536
"Dinner at the Homesick Restaurant" (Tyler) 502
Diop, Alioune: *see* **Obituaries 81**
Diouf, Abdou: *see* **Biographies 82**
Senegalese foreign relations 611
Dirac, P.A.M. 569
Direct broadcasting satellite (DBS)
telecommunications industry 447
television and radio 651
Direct reduction metallurgy 520
Disarmament
defense 283
"Great Disarmament Debate, The" 10
Nobel Prizes 96
United Nations report 690
Independent Commission on Disarmament and Security Issues 14
Disasters 56
Italy 460
Japan 463
Mexico 525
Disc camera 566, il. 567
Disciples of Christ (Christian Church) 594
Discount rate (econ.) 312
Discrimination
race relations 584
Disease: *see* Health and Disease
District of Columbia 700
Diuretics (drugs) 410
Diversification (econ.)
Nigeria (special report) 556
Diving 643
Divorce
demography 292
Djibouti 83, 82, 81
demography 289 (table)
DNA (deoxyribonucleic acid)
biology 496
Dodecahedrane (cycloalkane molecule) 233
Doe, Samuel Kanyon: *see* **Biographies 81**
Liberian 482, il. 483
Doesburg, Theo van il. 192
Doig, Ivan 502
Dolgikh, Vladimir 680
Dollar (U.S. currency) 312
Mexican monetary crisis 524
Doman, Glenn 335
Dome Petroleum Ltd. (Canada) 227
Domingo, Placido: *see* **Biographies 83**
Dominica 83, 82, 81
demography 290 (table)
Dominica Labour Party 302
Dominican Republic 83, 82, 81
demography 290 (table)
Domoto, Hisao: *see* **Biographies 82**
Donaldson, Simon 521
Dönitz, Karl: *see* **Obituaries 81**
Donovan, Raymond J. 261
Donskoy, Mark (Semyonovich): *see* **Obituaries 82**
Dornberger, Walter Robert: *see* **Obituaries 81**
Dorsett, Tony 386

Dorst, Tankred 507
Dost, Shah Mohammad 151
Doubrovska, Felia (Felizata Dluzh-nevska): *see* **Obituaries 82**
Douglas, Donald Wills: *see* **Obituaries 82**
Douglas, Helen Gahagan: *see* **Obituaries 81**
Douglas, Melvyn (Melvyn Edouard Hesselberg): *see* **Obituaries 82**
Douglas, William O(rville): *see* **Obituaries 81**
Douglas-Home, Charles Cospatrick: *see* **Biographies 83**
Dourado, Autran 512
Dow Jones Industrial Average 633
Downer, Sir Alexander Russell: *see* **Obituaries 82**
Dozier, James Lee: *see* **Biographies 83**
  crime and law enforcement 258
  Italian terrorist activity 458
DPR (House of People's Representatives, Indon.) 426
Draper, James T. 594
"Draughtsman's Contract, The" (film) 537
Drought
  agricultural output effect 156
  Australian economic crisis 201
  Malaysian agricultural problems 518
  Moroccan economic effect 535
Drug abuse
  health and disease (Special report) 415
  United States statistics 701
Drugs, pharmaceutical: *see* Pharmaceuticals
Drysdale, Sir (George) Russell: *see* **Obituaries 82**
Drysdale Government Securities Inc. 691
Duarte, José Napoleón: *see* **Biographies 82**
  El Salvadoran political crisis 339
Dubai 684
Dubinsky, David (David Dobnievski): *see* **Obituaries 83**
Dubos, René Jules: *see* **Obituaries 83**
Dubuffet, Jean 183
Duckworth (U.K. publisher) 500
Dudgeon v. United Kingdom 478
Duerr, Heinz 438
Dugong (*Dugong dugong*)
  environment 360
Duisenberg, Willem 551
Dukore, Margaret Mitchell 502
Duncan, Ronald Frederick Henry: *see* **Obituaries 83**
Dunlop, Bill 607
Dunn, Dennis 336
Dunn, Douglas 501
Durant, Henry William: *see* **Obituaries 83**
Durant, Will (William James Durant): *see* **Obituaries 82**
Durante, Jimmy (James Francis Durante): *see* **Obituaries 81**
Durbin, Mike 219
Duros (hard-liners)
  Chilean economic policies 237
Düsseldorf, Federal Republic of Germany 445
Duvalier, Jean-Claude 408
Duvall, Sammy 725
Dzhanibekov, Vladimir 624

E

Eakins, Thomas 191
Eanes, António Ramalho 575
Earthquakes 305
  disasters 57
  engineering projects 352
  Yemen 731
Earth Sciences 83, 82, 81
Easter 597
Eastern European literature 513
Eastern Non-Chalcedonian Churches 598
East Germany: *see* German Democratic Republic
Eastman Kodak Co. 566
East Pacific Rise (oceanography) 309
East Timor, island, Indonesia 427
"Eating Raoul" (film) 536
EBC (European Brewery Convention) 434
Eberhard, Fritz: *see* **Obituaries 83**
Eberly, Bob: *see* **Obituaries 82**
Ebert, Carl (Anton Charles): *see* **Obituaries 81**
EC: *see* European Communities
"Eccezzzionale... Veramente" (film) 537
Ecevit, Bulent 677
Echeverriay, Pierre 256
Eclogite (geology) 305

Economic Community of West African States (ECOWAS) 479
  Nigeria (special report) 557
Economic Recovery Act (1981, U.S.) 314
Economics
  Japan (special report) 465
  Nigeria (special report) 556
  Nobel Prizes 96
  "Russian Giant: 60 Years after Formation of the Soviet Union, The" 19
Economic Stabilization Act (Nigeria) 555
Economy, World **83, 82, 81**
  health care 413
  industrial review 430
  see also various countries
ECOWAS: *see* Economic Community of West African States
ECSC: *see* European Coal and Steel Community
ECT (electroconvulsive therapy) 413, il. 414
Ecuador 83, 82, 81
  demography 291 (table)
  education 331 (table)
  social insurance 614
  transportation 673 (table)
Ecumenism (religion) 592
Edmonds, Ron 568
Edmonton Eskimos (football team) 388
Education 83, 82, 81
  libraries (special report) 485
  life sciences (special report) 498
  United States statistics 701
  see also various countries
Edwards, Blake 537
EEC: *see* European Communities
Egbert, Sundar 596
Egypt 83, 82, 81
  archaeology 177
  defense 274
  demography 289 (table)
  education 331 (table)
  Middle Eastern affairs 526
    Israel 455
  motion pictures 539
  transportation 673 (table)
"Egyptian Story, An" (film) 539
Eichstätt, W. Ger. 349
"Eighteenth-Century Woman, The" (art exhibition) 193
Eisenman/Robertson Architects 183
Eisner, Thomas 491
Eizenstat, Stuart 699
Ek, Mats 273
Elbe River, Europe 354
El Chichón, volcano, Mex. 306, il. 305
Eldjarn, Kristján: *see* **Obituaries 83**
Electricity 438
  energy production 343
Electrochromic display (ceramics) 520
Electroconvulsive therapy (ECT) 413, il. 414
Electron 568
Electronics
  energy production 344
  games 393
  music 549
Electron microscopy 232
Electronorte (Brazil) 358
Element 109 (chemistry) 233
"El Greco of Toledo" (art exhibition) 190
Eli Lilly and Co.
  health and disease 410
  pharmaceutical industry 443
Elizabeth II, Queen il. 226
El Juyo, cave, Spain 631
Elkin, Stanley 502
Eller, Enten il. 480
Ellesmere Island, Canada 188
Elliott, James F. ("Jumbo"): *see* **Obituaries 82**
Ellis, Perry: *see* **Biographies 82**
El Salvador 83, 82, 81
  defense 284
  demography 290 (table)
  earth sciences 305
  education 331 (table)
  Netherlands 552
  transportation 673 (table)
Emmet of Amberley, Evelyn Violet Elizabeth Emmet, Baroness: *see* **Obituaries 81**
Emmy awards (television) 654
Emney, Fred: *see* **Obituaries 81**
Employment, wages, and hours
  crime factors 577
  European unemployment 370
  hospital workers 413
  industrial relations 447
  social security and welfare services 613
  world economy 310
  see also various countries
Encyclopaedia Britannica 250
Enders, Thomas 553
Endicott, James G. 596
Endrom, Eric 361
Energy 83, 82, 81
  metallurgy 520
  United States statistics 702
  see also various countries
Energy, U.S. Department of 342
Engel, Lehman: *see* **Obituaries 83**
Engelmann, Siegfried 335

Engelmann, Therese 336
Engineering 83, 82, 81
England: *see* United Kingdom
England, Church of 593
English literature 499
Enmund v. Florida 478
Enoxy (It. company) 438
Entomology 491
Environment 83, 82, 81
  Australian (special report) 202
  Sweden 642
  United States statistics 702
Environmental Protection Agency (EPA) 355
"Environment 82" (conference) 354
Enzymes 381
EPA (Environmental Protection Agency) 355
Epcot Center, Lake Buena Vista, Fla. il. 450
Epple, Irene 727
Epple, Maria il. 728
Equal Rights Amendment
  religion (special report) 601
  United States 694
  United States statistics 702
Equatorial Guinea 83, 82, 81
  demography 289 (table)
Equestrian Sports 83, 82, 81
Erechtheum temple, Athens, Greece il. 418
Eriksen, Lars Erik 727
Eriksson, Thomas 727
Erim, Nihat: *see* **Obituaries 81**
Ernst, Max 191
Ershad, Hossain Mohammad: *see* **Biographies 83**
  Bangladesh coup 206
Ertl, Josef 399
Erving, Julius ("Dr. J.") il. 212
ESA (European Space Agency) 622
Esaki, Masumi 463
Escherichia coli (bacterium)
  life sciences 494
  veterinary science 722
Esquivel, Adolfo Pérez 563
Essay: *see* Literature
Essequibo, region, Guyana 722
Esso Resources Canada, Ltd. 187
ETA (Euzkadi ta Azkatasuna, Basque terrorists) 171
Etchebaster, Pierre: *see* **Obituaries 81**
Ethics
  United States statistics 701
Ethiopia 83, 82, 81
  African affairs 154, 616
  archaeology 177
  demography 289 (table)
  international refugee status 589
  religion 598
  transportation 673 (table)
Ethylene (chemistry) 444
"Étrange Affaire, Une" (film) 537
"E.T. The Extra-Terrestrial" (film) 535
Eufriesia purpurata (bee) 491
Euphrates River, Asia 177
Euratom: *see* European Communities
Eurocommunism 684
Eurodollars
  "You Can't Foreclose a Country" 62
European Brewery Convention (EBC) 434
European Champion's Cup (soccer) 383
European Championships (track) 667
European Coal and Steel Community (ECSC) 369
  British foreign affairs 687
  iron and steel industry 442
European Communities (EC) 369
  agriculture and food supplies 166
  education 333
  environment 353
  Falkland Islands conflict 188, 475
  fisheries 379
  industrial review 441
  "Stresses in the Western Alliance" 68
  world economy 322
  "You Can't Foreclose a Country" 61
  see also various countries
European Court of Human Rights 478
European Court of Justice 372, 477
European Cup-Winner's Cup (soccer) 384
European Economic Community: *see* European Communities
European Investment Bank, 349
European Monetary System 318
European otter 361
European Parliament 372
European Space Agency (ESA) 622
European Unity 83, 82, 81
  Stock exchanges 635
Euwe, Max: *see* **Biographies 82**
Euzkadi ta Azkatasuna (ETA, Basque terrorists) 171
Evander, Per Gunnar 509
Evangelical Women's Caucus 602
Evans, Harold Matthew: *see* **Biographies 82**
Evans of Hungershall, Benjamin: *see* **Obituaries 83**
Everest, Mount, Nepal 228, 542
Evert Lloyd, Chris 659
Evolution 497
  anthropology 175
  life sciences 488

Evren, Kenan 677
Exchange and payments, international
  world economy 311, 325
Exeter, David George Brownlow Cecil: *see* **Obituaries 82**
Exocet (missile) 285
Expansionist policy (econ.)
  France 318
Exports: *see* Trade, international
Exxon Corp. 342, 529
Eyadema, Gnassingbe 666

F

Fabbri, Diego: *see* **Obituaries 81**
Fabiola, Queen il. 370
Faeroe Islands 296
  demography 290 (table)
Fagan, Michael 259
Fahd ibn (Abd al-)Aziz Al Saud: *see* **Biographies 83**
  Middle Eastern affairs 526, 609
FAI (Fédération Aéronautique Internationale) 150
Falkland Islands 295
  demography 291 (table)
Falkland Islands conflict
  Argentine invasion 188
  British recovery 684
  Commonwealth position 248
    Australia 201
  defense 282
  European Communities 372
    France 391
    West Germany 400
  industrial review 434
  international law 479
  Latin-American affairs 474
    Cuba's position 265
    Grenada's position 405
    Panama's position 561
    Uruguay economy 720
  Nepal 551
  stock exchange 636
  "Stresses in the Western Alliance" 66
  United Nations report 690
  United States position 697
  world economy 317
Falkland Islands Naval Task Force (U.K.) 286, 685
Fallaci, Oriana: *see* **Biographies 81**
Fälldin, Thorbjörn 641
False data entry (computers)
  crime (special report) 264
Falwell, Jerry: *see* **Biographies 81**
Family
  demography 292
  juvenile crime prevention 577
"Family Rock" (film) 537
FAN (Armed Forces of the North)
  Chad civil war 231
Fanfani, Amintore 459
Food and Agriculture Organization, U.N.) 156
Farago, Ladislas: *see* **Obituaries 81**
Farming, *see* Agriculture and Food Supplies
Farrakhan, Louis 600
Farrell, Edelmiro J.: *see* **Obituaries 81**
Fashion and Dress 83, 82, 81
Fassbinder, Rainer Werner: *see* **Obituaries 83**
  motion pictures 538
Fast breeder reactor 344
"Fate of the Earth, The" (Schell) 503
  publishing 583
Fauna and Flora Preservation Society (FFPS) 359
Fawzi, Mahmoud: *see* **Obituaries 82**
FCC (Federal Communications Commission) 650
FDA: *see* Food and Drug Administration
FDP (Free Democratic Party, Federal Republic of Germany) 397
Federal Communications Commission (FCC) 650
Federal Funds Rate 314
Federal Reserve Board (U.S.) 312
Federal Trade Commission (FTC) 698
  consumer information 254
Federated States of Micronesia 301
Fédération Aéronautique Internationale (FAI) 150
Fédération Internationale des Quilleurs (FIQ) 219
Fedorchuk, Vitaly: *see* **Biographies 83**
Feingold, Ben 414
Feinstein, Dianne il. 479
Feld Ballet 271
Feldman, Marty: *see* **Obituaries 83**
Felici, Pericle Cardinal: *see* **Obituaries 83**
"Felix" (film) 538
Femtoseconds (physics) 568
Fencing 246
Fenton, Clyde Cornwall: *see* **Obituaries 82**
Fenton, James 501
Ferguson, Mark W. J. 490
Fernandez, Dominique 505
Fernandez, Maurice 151
Fernandez, Royes: *see* **Obituaries 81**
Fernández Krohn, Juan 258

Fernández-Miranda y Hevia, Torcuato: *see* **Obituaries 81**
Ferranti, Sir Vincent Zianide: *see* **Obituaries 81**
Ferras, Christian: *see* **Obituaries 83**
Fertility rate 288
Fez summit 337, 610
FFPS (Fauna and Flora Preservation Society) 359
FGD (Flue gas desulfurization) 343
Fianna Fail (Irish party) 454
Fibre optics 520
  energy production 345
Fiction: *see* Literature
Field Hockey and Lacrosse 83, 82, 81
Fields medals (math) 521
Fiennes, Sir Ranulph 187
Fierstein, Harvey 665, il. 666
"Fighting Back" (film) 537
Figueiredo, João Baptista de Oliveira
  Brazil 220
Figure skating 728
Fiji 83, 82, 81
  demography 291 (table)
  education 331 (table)
Filipov, Grisha 222
Film (photography) 567
Films: *see* Motion pictures
Financial futures 634
Fine Gael (Irish party) 454
Finland 83, 82, 81
  accident insurance 614
  demography 290 (table)
  education 331 (table)
  paint and varnish production 443
  transportation 673 (table)
Finletter, Thomas Knight: *see* **Obituaries 81**
Finnbogadóttir, Vigdís: *see* **Biographies 81**
  Iceland 423
FIQ (Fédération Internationale des Quilleurs) 219
FIRA (Foreign Investment Review Agency) 229
Fire (anthro.) 176
First, Ruth: *see* **Obituaries 83**
  Mozambique internal disorder 543
  South African foreign relations 619
First Amendment
  libraries (special report) 486
First City Tower, Houston, Texas 349
First International Plaza, San Antonio, Texas 186
Fish and fish products 378, 382
  Iceland 423
Fisheries 83, 82, 81
  food processing 382
  veterinary science 722
Fisk, James Brown: *see* **Obituaries 82**
"Fitzcarraldo" (film) 538
FitzGerald, Garret: *see* **Biographies 82**
Fitzmaurice, Sir Gerald Gray: *see* **Obituaries 83**
Fitzsimmons, Frank Edward: *see* **Obituaries 82**
Fitzwilliam Museum, Cambridge, U.K. 545
Five-year plan (U.S.S.R.) 681
Fix, Greg 217
Flagella (biology) 494
Flat-panel display (ceramics) 520
Flat-water competition 725
Fleetguard International Corp. (Fr.) 349
Fleming, Peter 658
Fletcher, Harvey: *see* **Obituaries 82**
"Fleurs Sauvages, Les" (film) 537
"Flight of the Eagle, The" (film) 538
Flindt, Flemming 273
FLN (National Liberation Front, Algeria) 171
Flooding 307
Flórez, Florencio 561
Floyd, Ray 402
Flue-cured tobacco 449
Flue gas desulfurization (FGD) 343
Fluorescent lamp 344
Fluorocarbons 449
Fluorspar 531
Foam insulation 628
Fogarty, Anne Whitney: *see* **Obituaries 81**
Fonda, Henry Jaynes: *see* **Obituaries 83**
  motion pictures 536
Fondazione Giorgio Cini, Venice, It. 192
Fontanet, Joseph: *see* **Obituaries 81**
Food: *see* Agriculture and food supplies
Food and Agriculture Organization, U.N. (FAO) 156
Food and Drug Administration (FDA)
  consumer information 254
  pharmaceutical industry 444
Food Processing 83, 82, 81
  agriculture and food supplies 163
  fish products 380
Food security 167
Food sharing 176
Food stamps 614
Foot, Michael: *see* **Biographies 81**
  British domestic affairs 686
Football 83, 82, 81
  industrial review 432
  television and radio 654
  United States 694
Football pool (gambling) 393

Forché, Carolyn il. 503
Ford Motor Co. 372, 428, il. 429, 435
  motor sports 541
Foreign debt (banking) 61
Foreign Interference Act (Malta) 519
Foreign Investment Review Agency (FIRA) 229
Forestry 450
Forlani, Arnold: *see* **Biographies 81**
Fortas, Abe: *see* **Obituaries 83**
Fossils
  life sciences 488, 498
  zoology 490, il. 489
Foster, Coy 150
Foster, Harold R.: *see* **Obituaries 83**
Foster Associates (architecture) 183
Fouché, Jacobus Johannes: *see* **Obituaries 81**
"Foundation's Edge" (Asimov) 508
Fourier-transform infrared spectroscopy (GC-FTIR) 234
Four Fundamental Principles
  "China's Uncertain Future" 133
Four modernizations (Chin. hist.)
  "China's Uncertain Future" 131
"Fous de Bassan, Les" (Hébert) 506
Fox, Carol: *see* **Obituaries 82**
Fox, Terrence ("Terry") Stanley: *see* **Obituaries 82**. See **Biographies 81**
Fox, Virgil Keen: *see* **Obituaries 81**
Franc (currency) 390, 516
  world economy 312
France 83, 82, 81
  African affairs 154
    Algeria 171
    Comoros 249
    Congo 252
    Gabon 392
    Guinea 406
    Ivory Coast 461
    Madagascar 517
    Mali 519
    Mauritania 522
    Togo 667
    Tunisia 676
  archaeology (special report) 181
  arts
    literature 505
    motion pictures 537
    music 547
    television and radio 651
    theatre 661
  consumerism 253
  defense 282
  demography 290 (table)
  dependent states 300
  education 328
  energy production 344
  environment 354
  equestrian sports 363
  foreign relations
    Egypt 338
    Hungary 420
    Romania 604
    Soviet Union 684
    Vanuatu 720
  industrial relations 428
  industrial review 438
  international law 480
  law 478
  libraries 484
  migration, international 529
  prisons and penology 577
  social security 613
  stock exchanges 636
  sports and games
    aerial sports 151
    contract bridge 254
    court games 256
  transportation 673 (table)
  world economy 318, 324
Francis, Dick: *see* **Biographies 82**
Franco, Rubén Oscar 189
Franjieh, Hamid: *see* **Obituaries 82**
Frank, Otto: *see* **Obituaries 81**
Frankfurt am Main, W.Ger. 352
Frankfurt Book Fair 582
Fraser, Malcolm
  Australia 198
  Korean visit 472
  Southeast Asian affairs 622
Fraser of North Cape, Bruce Austin Fraser, 1st Baron: *see* **Obituaries 82**
Frasyniuk, Wladyslaw, 571
Frazier, Brenda (Brenda Diana Duff Frazier Kelly Chatfield-Taylor): *see* **Obituaries 83**
Frederika: *see* **Obituaries 82**
Free Democratic Party (FDP, Federal Republic of Ger.) 397
Freedman, Lawrence
  "Great Disarmament Debate, The" 9
Freedman, Michael 521
Freeze Resolution
  "Great Disarmament Debate, The" 13
Frei Montalva, Eduardo: *see* **Obituaries 83**
Freight (trans.) 672
French Guiana 296
  demography 291 (table)
French literature 505
French Polynesia 301
  demography 291 (table)
French Southern and Antarctic Lands
  demography 289 (table)
Frenzel, Bill
  United States (special report) 699

Freud, Anna: *see* **Obituaries 83**
Friedman, Elizabeth Smith: *see* **Obituaries 81**
Friedman, Murray 598
Friends, Religious Society of (Quakers) 595
Friis, E.M. 488
Frisch, Karl von: *see* **Obituaries 83**
Frog 490
Froman, Jane: *see* **Obituaries 81**
Fromm, Erich: *see* **Obituaries 81**
"From Village to City in Ancient India" (art exhibition) 191
Front Line Urban Guerrilla Organization (Italy) 459
FTC: *see* Federal Trade Commission
Fujairah
  United Arab Emirate member 684
Fuller, Hoyt William: *see* **Obituaries 82**
Fullerton, C. Gordon 150, 623
Funk (music) 549
Furniture 438
Furs 439
Fürstenberg, Prince 196
Fussell, Paul 504

G

G-1 (Lenin, U.S.S.R. launch vehicle) 624
Gabés, Gulf of, Tunisia 676
Gabler, Mel and Norma: *see* **Biographies 83**
Gabon 83, 82, 81
  demography 289 (table)
  transportation 673 (table)
Gaines, Ervin
  libraries (special report) 486
Gaines, Rowdy
  swimming record 642
Galamian, Ivan Alexander: *see* **Obituaries 82**
Galápagos Islands, Ecuador 360
Galaxy 197, 569
Gale, Sir Richard Nelson: *see* **Obituaries 83**
Galíndez, Victor: *see* **Obituaries 81**
"Gallery of the Louvre, The" (painting) 195, il. 194
Gallium arsenide (chemical compound)
  microelectronics 443
Galtieri, Leopoldo Fortunato: *see* **Biographies 83**
  Argentina 188
  British foreign relations 685
Galway Crystal 440
Gambia, The 83, 82, 81
  African political systems 154
  demography 289 (table)
Gambling 83, 82, 81
  United States statistics 702
"Game of Disarmament: How the United States and Russia Run the Arms Race, The" (Myrdal)
  Nobel Prizes 96
Games and Toys 83, 82, 81
Gance, Abel: *see* **Obituaries 82**
"Gandhi" (film) 537
Gandhi, Indira: *see* **Biographies 81**
  defense 285
  education policies 334
Gandhi, Maneka
  India 425, 426
Gandhi, Rajiv: *see* **Biographies 82**
Gandhi, Sanjay: *see* **Biographies 81**
Gang of four (China) 131
Ganz, JoAnn and Julian 191
Gaos, Vicente 510
Gaprindashvili, Nona 236
García, Matías William: *see* **Biographies 81**
García Márquez, Gabriel il. 499, 510
  Nobel Prizes 96, il. 97
García Meza Tejada, Maj. Gen. Luis: *see* **Biographies 81**
García Robles, Alfonso
  Nobel Prizes 96
Gardening 83, 82, 81
Gardner, John Champlin, Jr.: *see* **Obituaries 83**
  literature 502
Garfield: *see* **Biographies 83**
Garnett, David: *see* **Obituaries 82**
Garroway, David Cunningham: *see* **Obituaries 83**
Garvey, Ed: *see* **Biographies 83**
  football 386
Gary, Romain: *see* **Obituaries 81**
Gas: *see* Natural gas
Gas-chromatography-mass spectrometry (GC-MS) 234
Gasoline (petrol) 357
Gas-plasma display 520
Gato del Sol (race horse) 362, il. 363
GATT (General Agreement on Tariffs and Trade) 167
Gaunt, Caughey 596
Gay, Don 603
Gayoom, Maumoon Abdul 518
Gaz de France (Fr. gas co.) 346
GCC: *see* Gulf Cooperation Council
GC-FTIR (Fourier-transform infrared spectroscopy) 234

GC-MS (Gas-chromatography-mass spectrometry) 234
GE: *see* General Electric Co.
GEC (General Electric Co. Ltd.) (U.K.) 438
Gelli, Licio 261
"Gelo, Il" (Bilenchi) 509
Gemayel, Amin: *see* **Biographies 83**
  Lebanon 481
Gemayel, Bashir: *see* **Obituaries 83**. See **Biographies 81**
  Middle Eastern affairs 457, 481, 527
Gemstones 439
Gene (biology) 496
General Agreement on Tariffs and Trade (GATT) 167
"General Belgrano" (ship) 285
General Electric (GE) 432, 438
General Electric Co. Ltd. (GEC) (U.K.) 438
General Motors 435
General People's Congress (Libyan pol.) 487
Geneva Disarmament Conference
  Nobel Prizes 96
Geneva Opera Ballet 273
Genevoix, Maurice Charles Louis: *see* **Obituaries 81**
Geng Biao (Keng Piao) 240
Genome (biology) 496
Genscher, Hans-Dietrich 397
  European Communities il. 369
Gentile, Claudio il. 383
Geochemistry 303
Geography (special report) 285
Geology 303
Geophysics 305
Georg Eckert Institute (W. Ger.)
  education and history 332
"George Mills" (Elkin) 502
Georgia 700
Georgia, University of 387
Gerhardt, Lillian 486
Gérin, Winifred (Mrs. John Lock): *see* **Obituaries 82**
German Democratic Republic 83, 82, 81
  defense 281
  demography 290 (table)
  education 329
  energy production 343
  literature 507
  religion 594
  sports
    ice hockey 422
    rowing 605
    swimming 642
    women's track and field 668
  theatre 664
  transportation 673 (table)
  world economy 321
German literature 506
Germany, Federal Republic of 83, 82, 81
  Antarctica 175
  consumerism 253
  defense 279
  demography 290 (table)
  education 329
  energy production 343
  engineering projects 348
  environment 352
  France 391
  German Democratic Republic 396
  industrial relations 428
  industrial review 438
  law 478
  libraries 483
  literature 506
  migration, international 529
  motion pictures 538
  race relations 585
  social services 613
  stock exchanges 636
  television and radio 651
  theatre 664
  transportation 673 (table)
  world economy 317, 323
Gerö, Ernö: *see* **Obituaries 81**
Getty, J. Paul 544
Ghana 83, 82, 81
  demography 289 (table)
  Nigeria 555
  Togo 666
  transportation 673 (table)
Ghotbzadeh, Sadegh: *see* **Obituaries 83**
  Iranian internal politics 451 il.
Giauque, William Francis: *see* **Obituaries 83**
Gibbs-Smith, Charles Harvard: *see* **Obituaries 82**
Gibraltar 295
  demography 290 (table)
Gielgud, Val Henry: *see* **Obituaries 82**
Gillespie, William H. 488
Gillott, Jacky: *see* **Obituaries 81**
Gil Robles y Quinones, José María: *see* **Obituaries 81**
Gimbel, Sophie Haas: *see* **Obituaries 82**
"Gimcrack, with John Pratt up on Newmarket Heath" (painting) 545

Giri, Varahagari Venkata: *see* **Obituaries 81**
"Girl Eating Oysters" (paint.) il. 193
"Giro City" (film) 537
Giurgola, Romaldo 183
"Give Your Child a Superior Mind" (Engelmann) 336
Glass 439
GLC (Greater London Council) (U.K.) 359
Glemp, Jozef: *see* **Biographies 82**
    Polish domestic unrest 571
Glenbow Museum, Calgary, Can. 191
Gliding 150
"Glomar Challenger" (ship) 307
Glueckauf, Eugen: *see* **Obituaries 82**
GNP (Gross National Product) 313
"God's Grace" (Malamud) 501
Godunov, Aleksandr 270
Golan Heights, Middle East 688
Gold
    commodity market 638
    mining and quarrying 532
Gold Cup (motorboating) 724
Golden, Harry (Lewis): *see* **Obituaries 82**
Goldmann, Nahum: *see* **Obituaries 83**
Golf 83, 82, 81
Gómez, Andrés 658
Gómez, Wilfredo 245
Gomulka, Wladyslaw: *see* **Obituaries 83**
Gonçalves, Olga 511
Gonella, Guido: *see* **Obituaries 83**
González Márquez, Felipe: *see* **Biographies 83**
    Spain 630, il. 629
Goolden, Richard Percy Herbert: *see* **Obituaries 82**
Gopallawa, William: *see* **Obituaries 82**
Gordon, Diana 254
Gordon, S.T. 244
Gordon-Walker, Patrick Chrestien Gordon Walker, Baron: *see* **Obituaries 81**
Gorman, Patrick Emmet (Smith): *see* **Obituaries 81**
Gosden, Freeman F(isher): *see* **Obituaries 83**
Gotland II (W. Ger. ship) 173
Gotovac, Jakov: *see* **Obituaries 83**
Gottlieb, Adolph 191
Gould, Glenn Herbert: *see* **Obituaries 83**
Gould, Stephen Jay 489
Gouled Aptidon, Hassan 302
Goumba, Abel 231
Government regulation (econ.) 63
Grace, Princess, of Monaco (Grace Kelly): *see* **Obituaries 83**
    Monaco 533
Grade, Chaim 515
Graham, Billy 590, il. 593
Graigmillar, Edinburgh, Scotland 357
Grains 156
    Laotian rice crop 474
    U.S.-Soviet agreement 695
    Zambia corn crop 734
Grandmaster Flash and the Furious Five (band) 550
"Grand Pardon, Le" (film) 537
Grand Prix (tennis) 658
Grand Prix (automobile racing) 540
Grand Unified Theories (GUTS) 198
Grantcharova, Zoya il. 408
Granville, Joseph: *see* **Biographies 82**
Grasso, Ella T. (Ella Rosa Giovanna Oliva Tambussi): *see* **Obituaries 82**
Grätzel, Michael 234
Graves, Michael: *see* **Biographies 82**
    architecture 183
Gray, Robin 203
"Gray Fox, The" (film) 537
Great Britain: *see* United Kingdom
"Great Disarmament Debate, The" (Freedman) 8
Greater London Council (GLC) (U.K.)
    environment 359
Great Leap Forward
    "China's Uncertain Future" 134
Greco-Roman wrestling 246
Greece 83, 82, 81
    archaeology 178
    Cyprus 267
    demography 290 (table)
    education 334
    industrial relations 429
    social security 614
    transportation 673 (table)
    Turkey relations 678
Greek Communist Party (KKE) 403
Greek tortoise (*Testudo graeca*) 361
Green, Paul Eliot: *see* **Obituaries 82**
Greenaway, Peter 537
Greene, Graham 501
Greene, Harold H. 693
Greenland 180
    demography 290 (table)
    Denmark 294
    dependent states 299
    European relations 371
Green Party ("Greens," Grün-

Alternative-Liste, W.Ger.) 399
    environment 355
Greenpeace 359, il. 357
Green Revolution
    Nigeria (special report) 556
Green sea turtles 490
Greenwood of Rossendale, Arthur William James Greenwood (Anthony Greenwood): *see* **Obituaries 83**
Greer, William Alexander ("Sonny") jazz music 549
Gregory, Horace: *see* **Obituaries 83**
Grenada 83, 82, 81
    defense 284
    demography 291 (table)
Gretzky, Wayne: *see* **Biographies 82**
    ice hockey records 420, il. 421
Grey, Sir Edward 9
Griffin, John Howard: *see* **Obituaries 81**
Griffith, Darrell: *see* **Biographies 81**
Griffith, Hugh (Emrys): *see* **Obituaries 81**
Grigson, Geoffrey 501
Grittar (race horse) 365
Gromyko, Andrey 732
Gros-Gaudenier, Marie-Cecile 727
Grosvenor, Melville Bell: *see* **Obituaries 83**
Groupe Spéléo Vulcain (team) 630
"Growing Child" (Dunn and Hargitt) education (special report) 336
Growth hormones 722
Grumman, Leroy Randle: *see* **Obituaries 83**
Grün-Alternative-Liste (W.Ger.): *see* Green Party
Guadeloupe 296
    demography 291 (table)
Guam 301
    demography 291 (table)
Guardian Industries 440
Guare, John: *see* **Biographies 83**
Guatemala 83, 82, 81
    demography 291 (table)
    education 331 (table)
    Mexico 525
    transportation 673 (table)
Guayaquil, Ecuador 642
Guayule rubber 445
Guernsey 298
"Guerra del fin del mundo, La" (Vargas Llosa) 510
Guerreiro de Sousa, Américo 511
Guerrillas
    Colombia 243
    Mozambique 543
    Philippines 566
    Uganda 678
    Zimbabwe 735
Guevara, Angel Aníbal 405
Guggenheim Museum, N.Y., N.Y. 191
    museum loans 545
Guiazova, Naila 247
Guilloux, Louis: *see* **Obituaries 81**
Guinan, Edward F. 196
Guinea 83, 82, 81
    demography 289 (table)
Guinea, Gulf of 608
Guinea-Bissau 83, 82, 81
    Cape Verde 231
    demography 289 (table)
Gulf Cooperation Council 479
    Middle Eastern affairs 528
    Saudi foreign relations 610
Gum disease (periodontal disease) 414
Gundelach, Finn Olav: *see* **Obituaries 82**
Guney, Yilmaz 539
GUNT (Transitional Government of National Union, Chad) 231
Guo Yuehua 646
Gustafsson, Lars 509, il. 508
Guston, Philip: *see* **Obituaries 81**
Guthrie, William Keith Chambers: *see* **Obituaries 82**
GUTS (Grand Unified Theories) 198
Guttman, Sir Ludwig: *see* **Obituaries 81**
Guyana 83, 82, 81
    demography 291 (table)
    Venezuela 722
Guzmán Fernández, Silvestre Antonio: *see* **Obituaries 83**
    Dominican Republic 303
Gwathmey–Siegel & Associates (architects) 184
Gwynne-Jones, Allan: *see* **Obituaries 83**
Gyenyes, Andras 420
Gymnastics and Weightlifting 83, 82, 81
Gyps caprotheres (Cape vulture) 360
Gypsy moth 395

H

Habib, Philip Charles: *see* **Biographies 83**
    defense 274

Israel 457
    Lebanon 481
    United States negotiations 696
Habré, Hissen: *see* **Biographies 83**
    Chadian civil war 231, il. 232
    OAU membership dispute 153
Habyarimana, Juvénal 606
Hackford, Taylor 536
Hadar, site, Ethiopia
    anthropology 175
Haddad, Saad: *see* **Biographies 83**
    Lebanon 481
Haggie Rand Ltd., S. Af.
    mining technology 531
Hagler, Marvin 244
Hagman, Larry: *see* **Biographies 81**
HAI (Health Action International) 252
Haidalla, Lieut. Col. Mohamed Khouna Ould: *see* **Biographies 81**
    Mitterrand visit il. 522
Haig, Alexander M., Jr.: *see* **Biographies 82**
    British foreign relaitons 685
    Latin-American affairs
        Argentine mediation 188
        Falkland Islands conflict 474
    Turkey visit 678
    United States 695
Hailwood, (Stanley) Michael Bailey: *see* **Obituaries 82**
Haimanot, Tekle 598
Haircut 100 (band) 549
Haiti 83, 82, 81
    demography 291 (table)
    migration, international 528
Haley, Bill (William John Clifton Haley, Jr.): *see* **Obituaries 82**
Haley, Leroy 245
Hall, Joyce Clyde: *see* **Obituaries 83**
Hall, Paul: *see* **Obituaries 81**
Halley's Comet 196
Hallon, Carlos 216
Hallstein, Walter: *see* **Obituaries 83**
Hama, Boubou: *see* **Obituaries 83**
    Niger 554
Hamad, Abdel Latif al-: *see* **Biographies 83**
    Kuwait 473
Hamah, Syria
    Syrian domestic disorders 645
Hambleton, Hugh 228
Hamilton, Scott 728
"Hammett" (film) 536
Hammond, Norman 180
Hampton, Hope: *see* **Obituaries 83**
Hanauer, Chip 724
Handball 255
Handguns
    crime and law enforcement 260
    target sports 649
Handler, Philip: *see* **Obituaries 82**
Hanika, Sylvia 659
Han Jian 588
"Hannah Arendt: For Love of the World" (Young-Bruel) 504
"Hannibal segraren" (Ahlin) 508
Hansen, Curt 235
Hanson, Howard: *see* **Obituaries 82**
Harare, Zimbabwe 736
Harburg, E.Y. (Edgar "Yip" Harburgh): *see* **Obituaries 82**
Hardliners (duros)
    Chilean economic policies 237
Hardy, Holzman, Pfeiffer Associates 184
Hare, Richard 500
Hargeisa, Somalia 616
Hargitt, Edwin 336
Harijans (untouchables)
    Hinduism 599
Harkarvy, Benjamin 271
Harkness, Rebekah West: *see* **Obituaries 83**
Harlow v. Fitzgerald 477
Harmon, Bonnie 650
Harness racing
    equestrian sports 365
Harris, Craig C. 196
Harrison, Wallace Kirkman: *see* **Obituaries 84**
Hartford Tower, CityPlace, Hartford, Conn. 186
Hartling, Paul 590
Hartman-Cox 185
Hartsfield, Henry W., Jr. 623
Hartzenberg, Ferdinand 617
Harun Idris 518
Hasenmayer, Jochen 631
Haskell, Arnold Lionel: *see* **Obituaries 81**
Hassan II
    Middle Eastern affairs 526
    Morocco 535
Hassel, Odd: *see* **Obituaries 82**
Hatano, Yasukichi il. 464
Hatfield, Richard 227
Hatta, Mohammad: *see* **Obituaries 81**
Hauamura Nihachiro 466
Haughey, Charles: *see* **Biographies 81**
    Ireland 454
Havel, Vaclav 513
Havemann, Robert: *see* **Obituaries 83**
Hawaii
    archaeology 179
    United States statistics 702
Hawke, Robert J. 198
Hawker, Willem 640
Hawley, Sandy: *see* **Biographies 81**
Hayden, William George: *see* **Biographies 81**
    Australian political crises 198

Hayes, Dennis: *see* **Biographies 81**
Haymes, Dick: *see* **Obituaries 81**
Hays, Lee: *see* **Obituaries 82**
Hays, Paul R.: *see* **Obituaries 81**
Hayward Gallery, London, U.K. 191
H-chain genes 496
Head, Alice Maud: *see* **Biographies 82**
Head, Edith: *see* **Obituaries 82**
Head Start (education) 336
Heald, Sir Lionel Frederick: *see* **Obituaries 82**
Healey, Denis Winston: *see* **Biographies 81**
Health Action International (HAI) 252
Health and Disease 83, 82, 81
    Nobel Prizes 97
    United States statistics 701
Hearns, Thomas 244
Heart disease
    demography 288
    health and disease 409
Heath, Edward 65
Heavy Ion Research Laboratory, W.Ger. 233
Hébert, Anne 506
Hebrew literature 514
"Heidelberg Manifesto," (W.Ger) race relations 585
Heiden, Eric: *see* **Biographies 81**
Heinze, Sir Bernard Thomas: *see* **Obituaries 83**
Helen, Queen of Romania: *see* **Obituaries 83**
Hell scanner (printing) 445
Helmers v. Sweden 478
Helms, Jesse: *see* **Biographies 82**
Henderson, Rickey: *see* **Biographies 83**
    baseball 210
Hendy, Sir Philip Anstiss: *see* **Obituaries 81**
Heng Samrin 468
Henley Royal Regatta, U.K. il. 605
Hennessy, Sir Patrick: *see* **Obituaries 82**
Henry, Albert Royle: *see* **Obituaries 82**
Henry VIII 181
Henson, Jim 536
Hepburn, Katharine 536
Heppenstall, (John) Rayner: *see* **Obituaries 82**
Herculaneum, ancient site, Italy 178, il. 179
"Hero" (film) 537
Herrera Campins, Luis 721
Herring, Sir Edmund Francis: *see* **Obituaries 83**
Herriot, James: *see* **Biographies 82**
Hersant, Robert 579
Herstigte Nasionale Party (HNP, S.Af.) 617
Hertzog, Albert: *see* **Obituaries 83**
Hervás, Graciano (Luis Romero) 510
Herzog, Werner 538
Heseltine, Michael: *see* **Biographies 82**
    environment 356
Hess, Erika 727
Hess, Roberta 488
Heym, Stefan 507
Hicks, Granville: *see* **Obituaries 83**
Hicks, Roy E. 595
Higgins, Colin 536
Higgins, Gary 588
High blood pressure 410
Higher education 333
High Plains Aquifer
    earth sciences 308
Hightower, Stephanie 669
Hijackings
    Air Tanzania il. 648
Hill, George Roy 536
"Hill Street Blues" (TV program) 654
Hinault, Bernard: *see* **Biographies 83**
    cycling 267
Hinckley, John, Jr.
    courts and penology 576
    crime and law enforcement 259, il. 260
    United States 694
Hinduism 599
Hingsen, Jurgen 667
Hirshhorn, Joseph Herman: *see* **Obituaries 82**
Hispanics: *see* Spanish-speaking people
Historic Preservation 83, 82, 81
Hitachi Ltd., (Jap.)
    alleged computer data theft 464
    computers 250
Hitchcock, Sir Alfred Joseph: *see* **Obituaries 81**
HNP (Herstigte Nasionale Party, S.Af.) 617
Hoare, Michael "Mad Mike" 611
Hockey 420
Hoffman, Linda 217
Hoffmann, Heinz 396
Hogan, Marty 589
Holden, William (William Franklin Beedle, Jr.): *see* **Obituaries 82**
Holgate, Harry 203
Hollai, Imre 691
Holloway, Stanley: *see* **Obituaries 83**
Hollowood, (Albert) Bernard: *see* **Obituaries 82**
Holmes, Larry 243, il. 244
Hominidae (humans) 175
Homosexuals
    health and disease 409
Honduras 83, 82, 81
    demography 291 (table)
    education 331 (table)

Panama refuge 561
transportation 673 (table)
Honecker, Erich 395, il. 396
Honegger, Fritz 644
Hong Kong
China-U.K. relations 242
demography 289 (table)
dependent states 298
education 331 (table)
stock exchange 637
transportation 674
Hong Kong Consumer Council 253
Hooker Chemicals and Plastics Corp.,
U.S. 356
Hopkins, Sam ("Lightnin' ") *see* **Obituaries 83**
Hops 434
Horan, Cheyne 726
Hörbiger, Paul: *see* **Obituaries 82**
Horikoshi, Jiro: *see* **Obituaries 83**
Horn, Rebecca 538
Horne, Lena: *see* **Biographies 82**
Horn of Africa 154
Horse racing 393
Horwood, Owen 619
Hospital, Janette Turner 505
Hotel New Japan, Tokyo, Japan 463
"Hothouse" (play) 665
Houphouët-Boigny, Felix 460
House of People's Representatives
(DPR, Indon.) 426
House of Representatives (U.S.) 691
Housing 437
United States mortgage rates 692
Houston Ship Canal Bridge, Houston,
Texas 348
Howard, Elston Gene: *see* **Obituaries 81**
Howard, John 200
Howard, Sir Edward 181
"How to Multiply Your Baby's Intelligence" (Doman) 336
"How to Raise a Brighter Child" (Beck) 336
"How to Teach Your Baby to Read" (Doman) 335
Hoxha, Enver 169
Hrabal, Bohumil 513
Hsia Nai (Xia Nai) 178
Hua Guofeng (Hua Kuo-feng)
China 240
"China's Uncertain Future" 131
Huang Hua
China 240
Soviet foreign affairs 683
Huari, site, Peru 180
Hudson, Hugh 536
Hughes, Augusto Jorge 189
Humana Headquarters, Louisville, Ky.
185
Human League (band) 549, il. 548
Human rights
Argentina 189
Humans (Hominidae) 175
Humes, Helen: *see* **Obituaries 82**
"Hundarnas himmel" (Evander) 509
Hung, Geoffrey 588
Hungary 83, 82, 81
defense 281
demography 290 (table)
education 332
literature 514
motion pictures 538
table tennis 646
transportation 673 (table)
water sports 726
world economy 321
Hunt, Joseph McVicker 335
Hunt, Lord 651
Hunt, (Nelson) Bunker: *see* **Biographies 81**
Hunthausen, Raymond il. 591
Hurricane Ina 309
Hurstfield, Joel: *see* **Obituaries 81**
Hurtado Larrea, Osvaldo 328
Husak, Gustav 269
Husani, Ali Nasir Muhammad 730
Hussein, Kamal 459
Hussein, King
Jordan 467
Middle Eastern affairs 527
Hussein at-Tikriti, Saddam: *see* **Biographies 83**
Iranian military forces 451
Iraq 453
Huston, John 536
Hutchings, Geoffrey 662, il. 661
Hutt River Province, region, Austr.
201
Hu Yaobang: *see* **Biographies 82, 81**
"China's Uncertain Future" 132
Chinese Communist Congress 240
Hybrid photonic device 520
Hydroelectricity
Argentina project 190
energy production 344
Hydrology 307
Hydroplane 724
Hydro-thermal energy 550
Hyperactivity 414

I

IAAF (International Amateur Athletic
Federation) 670

IATA (International Air Transport Association) 671
Iatrogenic disease 410
IBA (Independent Broadcasting Authority) 650
Ibarra Muñoz, David 523
IBFAN (International Baby Food Action Network) 252
IBM Corp. 250
United States 693
Ibuka, Masaru: *see* **Biographies 83**
ICARA (International Conference on
Assistance to Refugees in Africa)
589
ICBM (intercontinental ballistic missiles) 276
Ice Hockey 83, 82, 81
Iceland 83, 82, 81
demography 290 (table)
international law 480
Ice skating 728
Ich. (white spot, fish disease) 722
Ichikawa, Fusae: *see* **Biographies 82**
ICI (Imperial Chemical Industries)
444
ICTI (International Committee of Toy
Industries) 394
IDA (International Development Association) 168
Ida, Don 150
Idaho 701
IDB: *see* Inter-American Development
Bank
Idemitsu Museum of Arts (Japan) 192
IEA (International Energy Agency)
343
IFAD (International Fund for Agricultural Development) 168
Iguanas 360
Illegal aliens
race relations (special report) 586
Illinois 700
Illinois Regional Library for the Blind
and Physically Handicapped, Chicago, Ill. 183
Illiteracy 328
Ilmenite (chemistry) 533
Ilois (people) 300
IMF: *see* International Monetary Fund
Immigration 585
Immune system
health and disease 409
molecular biology 495
Immunization 496
Immunoglobulins (biology) 495
Imperial Chemical Industries (ICI)
444
Imports: *see* Trade, international
Imran, Khan: *see* **Biographies 83**
I/MRBM (intermediate/medium range
ballistic missile) 278
Inca empire 180
Inco. Ltd. (Canada) 533
Sudbury smelter 230
"Indecent Exposure" (McClintick) 504
Independence Party (Iceland) 423
Independent Broadcasting Authority
(IBA) 650
Independent Television (ITV) 650
India 83, 82, 81
agriculture and food supplies 160
Antarctica research 173
art exhibition 191
cricket 257
defense 283
demography 289 (table)
education 334
engineering projects 351
foreign relations
Bangladesh 207
Bhutan 216
Pakistan 561
motion pictures 539
printing industry 445
transportation 673 (table)
Indianapolis Ballet Theater 271
Indianapolis Motor Speedway 541
"Indian Heritage: Court Life and Arts
under Mughal Rule, The" (art exhibition) 191
Indians, Canadian 187
"India Observed" (art exhibition) 192
Indonesia 83, 82, 81
badminton 588
demography 289 (table)
education 331 (table)
energy production 345
Southeast Asian affairs 622
transportation 673 (table)
world economy 324
Induction heating (metallurgy) 521
Induction motor 344
Industrial Relations 83, 82, 81
see also various countries
Industrial Review 83, 82, 81
world economy 316
see also various countries
Industry Hills Aquatic Club 726
Infant mortality 292
Inflation
industrial review 430
world economy 311
see also various countries
Ingrams, Richard 500
Inkster, Juli 403
Inmos factory, U.K. 349
"Innamorato Pazzo" (film) 537
Institute for Religious Works (Vatican
bank)
crime and law enforcement 261
Italian foreign affairs 460

religion 591
Vatican City State 721
Institute of Life Insurance 440
Institute of Medicine 409
Insurance 440
social security and welfare services
613
Insurance Companies Act (U.K.) 440
Insurance Institute for Highway Safety
(U.S.) 253
Intellectual liberalization (pol.)
"China's Uncertain Future" 133
"Intelligence and Experience" (Hunt)
335
Inter-American Development Bank
(IDB)
engineering projects 351
Latin-American affairs 475
Intercity rail transportation 674
Intercontinental ballistic missiles
(ICBM) 276
Intercontinental Centre, Los Angeles,
Calif. 186
Interest rates
Canada (special report) 229
"Stresses in the Western Alliance"
66
United States 692
"You Can't Foreclose a Country"
61
Intergovernmental Maritime Consultative Organization 480
Intergráfica (Latin American trading
house) 445
Intermediate/medium range ballistic
missile (I/MRBM) 278
Intermediate range ballistic missile
(IRBM) 278
Internal Revenue Service (IRS) 330
International Air Transport Association (IATA) 671
International Amateur Athletic Federation (IAAF) 670
International Atomic Energy Agency
443
International Baby Food Action Network (IBFAN) 252
International Balloon Festival 150
International Committee of Toy Industries (ICTI) 394
International Conference of Donors
361
International Conference on Assistance to Refugees in Africa
(ICARA) 589
International Congress of Mathematicians 521
International Court of Justice 430
International Convention Concerning
the Protection of the World Cultural and Natural Heritage
(World Heritage Convention) 417
International Development Association (IDA) 168
International Energy Agency (IEA)
343
International Fund for Agricultural
Development (IFAD) 168
International law 478
United Nations report 690
International League for Human
Rights 238
International Machine Tool Show 442
International Maritime Organization
480
International Monetary Fund (IMF)
African affairs
Morocco loan 535
South African economy 619
Sudan economy 639
Zaire penalty 732
Zambia refusal 734
Zimbabwe 737
Hungary's admission 419
Latin-American affairs 476
Argentine economy 190
Brazilian economy 222
Costa Rican aid 255
Guyana's request 407
world economy 320
"You Can't Foreclose a Country"
64
International Organization of Consumers Unions (IOCU) 252
International Philatelic Federation 564
International Press Institute 578
International Professional Surfers
(IPS) 726
International Program for the Development of Communications 578
International relations
"Great Disarmament Debate, The"
9
"Russian Giant: 60 Years after Formation of the Soviet Union, The"
21
International Resource Development
Inc. 722
International Seabed Authority 352
International Squash Professional Association 588
International Table Tennis Federation
646
International Tin Agreement (ITA)
533
International Whaling Commission
(IWC)
environment 361
fisheries 380
international law 480
Intersind (Italian organization) 429

"In the Image of Man" (art exhibition) 191
Intsoy (U.S. org.) 380
Investment: *see* Savings and
Investment
"Invincible" (U.K. warship) 201
Inuit (Eskimo) Circumpolar Conference 188
Invisible account balances 323
IOCU (International Organization of
Consumers Unions) 252
Iowa, University of 246
IPS (International Professional Surfers) 726
IRA (Irish Republican Army) 259
Iran 83, 82, 81
defense 274
demography 289 (table)
education 331 (table)
international law 480
Middle Eastern affairs 525
Afghanistan 152
Bahrain 206
Iraq 452
Saudi Arabia 609
Syria 645
mining and quarrying 531
petroleum production 340
transportation 673 (table)
Iran-Iraq War
Iranian military forces 451
Jordan's role 468
Kuwait's involvement 473
Saudi foreign relations 610
United Nations report 690
Iraq 83, 82, 81
defense 274
demography 289 (table)
education 331 (table)
Middle Eastern affairs 525
Jordan 467
Kuwait 473
Syria 645
transportation 673 (table)
IRBM (intermediate range ballistic
missile) 278
Ireland 83, 82, 81
demography 290 (table)
education 331 (table)
football 385
industrial relations 429
international law 480
law 478
television and radio 655
theatre 663
transportation 673 (table)
Irish, Edward Simmons ("Ned"): *see*
Obituaries 83
Irish Ballet 273
Irish National Liberation Army 260
Irish Republican Army (IRA) 259
Iron and steel 440
engineering projects 348
metallurgy 520
mining and quarrying 532
Nigeria (special report) 556
U.S.-European trade 369
world economy 322
Irrigation 487
IRS (Internal Revenue Service) 330
Isaac (cyclone) 667
Iskara 2 (U.S.S.R. satellite) 626
Islam 599
archaeology 178
education 332
Egypt 338
Nigeria 555
Pakistan 560
Islamic art 192
Islamic Front for the Liberation of
Bahrain 206
Islamic Republican Party (Iran) 451
Isle of Man: *see* Man, Isle of
Israel 83, 82, 81
African affairs 155
Zaire 733
archaeology 177
defense 274
demography 289 (table)
education 334
European relations 371
industrial review 434
international law 479
Middle Eastern affairs 525
Egypt 337
Lebanon 481
Syria 645
motion pictures 539
religion 598
theatre 665
transportation 673 (table)
United Nations report 688
United States relations 696
Israel Museum, Jerusalem, Israel 192
Istanbul Technical University 356
"Is There Anyone Who Understands
Me?" (Irish TV documentary)
655
ITA (International Tin Agreement)
533
Itaipú hydroelectric project, Braz. 222,
il. 221
Italian literature 509

Italy 83, 82, 81
archaeology 178
arts
literature 509
motion pictures 537
theatre 664
demography 290 (table)
education 333
energy production 345
engineering projects 351
industrial relations 428
industrial review 438
Middle Eastern affairs 527
stock exchanges 636
target sports 649
transportation 673 (tale)
world economy 324
Ito, Ritsu: see **Biographies 81**
Iturbi, José: see **Obituaries 81**
ITV (Independent Television) 650
Ivanchenkov, Aleksandr 624
Ivory Coast 83, 82, 81
cocoa production 164
demography 289 (table)
education 331 (table)
transportation 673 (table)
"Ivory Swing, The" (Hospital) 505
Iwama, Kazuo: see **Obituaries 83**
Iwaszkiewicz, Jaroslaw: see **Obituaries 81**
IWC: see International Whaling Commission

J

Jabbar, Kareem Abdul il. 212
Jackson, Laura (Riding) 503
Jackson, Maynard: see **Biographies 82**
Jackson of Lodsworth, Barbara Mary Jackson (Barbara Mary Ward): see **Obituaries 82**
Jacoby, Jerry 724
Jacques, Hattie (Josephine Edwina): see **Obituaries 81**
Jaeger, Andrea 659
Jaffee, Irving: see **Obituaries 82**
Jahn, Helmut 186
Jai alai 256
Jakobson, Roman: see **Obituaries 83**
Jamaica 83, 82, 81
demography 291 (table)
Jan Mayen 297
demography 290 (table)
Janssen, David: see **Obituaries 81**
Japan 83, 82, 81
Antarctica 174
arts
art exhibitions 192
literature 515
motion pictures 539
television and radio 650
automobile industry 435
defense 284
demography 289 (table)
education 332
energy production 343
engineering projects 351
food processing 382
foreign relations
China 242
Europe 370
Southeast Asia 622
South Korea 472
prisons and penology 577
social insurance 613
sports
baseball 211
combat sports 247
ice hockey 422
table tennis 646
stock exchanges 637
transportation 674
world economy 315, 323
Japanese literature 515
"Japan's Economic Secret" (Special Report) 465
Japan Teachers' Union 332
Jari Project, Brazil 356
Jaruzelski, Wojciech Witold: see **Biographies 82**
Polish crisis 570
Jarvik, Robert: see **Biographies 83**
Jarvik-7 (artificial heart device) 411
Javan rhinoceros (*Rhinoceros sondaicus*) 361
"Java Surfing" (film) 540
Jawara, Sir Dawda Kairaba: see **Biographies 82**
Gambia 392
Jaworski, Leon: see **Obituaries 83**
Jayawardene, Junius 631
Jazz 548
"Jazz" (film) 540
Jehovah's Witnesses 594
Jelinek, A.J. 177
Jenkins, Roy Harris: see **Biographies 82**

British domestic affairs 686
Jerash, ancient site, Jordan 178
Jeriova, Kvetoslava 728
Jeritza, Maria (Mitzi Jedlicka): see **Obituaries 83**
Jersey 298
Jessel, George: see **Obituaries 82**
Jesuits (religious order) 597
Jet Propulsion Laboratory (JPL) 622
Jewish literature 514
Jews: see Judaism
Jiang Qing (Chiang Ch'ing)
"China's Uncertain Future" 131
Jiménez Alfarao, Tucapel 238
Joanen, Ted 490
Joffrey Ballet 270
John, Patrick 302
Johncock, Gordon
motor sports 541
John Paul II: see **Biographies 82**
crime and law enforcement 258
foreign travel
Argentina 189
Benin 215
Equatorial Guinea il. 362
Nigeria il. 555
San Marino 608
Spain 630
Italian terrorists 459
religion 597, il. 593
Vatican City State 720
Johns Hopkins University, Baltimore, Md. 375
Johnson, Dame Celia: see **Obituaries 83**
Johnson, Earvin ("Magic") 211, il. 212
Johnson, L.B. 414
Johnson, Pamela Hansford: see **Obituaries 82**
Johnson & Johnson Inc.
pharmaceutical industry 444
see also Tylenol
Johnston Island
demography 291 (table)
Jones, Amanda 266
Jones, George: see **Biographies 82**
Jordan 83, 82, 81
archaeology 177
defense 274
demography 289 (table)
education 331 (table)
Jorge, Lídia 511
Jorge Blanco, Salvador 303
Jørgensen, Anker 294
Jørgensen, Marianne il. 729
Jorn, Asger 545
José Limón Dance Company 271
Joseph, Sir Maxwell: see **Obituaries 83**
philately and numismatics 564
Journiac, René: see **Obituaries 81**
Joyce, James 499
J. Paul Getty Museum of Art, Malibu, Calif. 544
JPL (Jet Propulsion Laboratory) 622
Juan Carlos I: see **Biographies 82**
Spain 630
Judaism 598
Soviet domestic affairs 681
Judo 247
Jugnauth, Aneerood 523
Julien, Claude (Norbert): see **Biographies 81**
Jumbe, Aboud 648
Jurgens, Curt (Curd Jürgens): see **Obituaries 83**
Justice, U.S. Department of 693

K

Kadanoff, Leo 98
Kadar, Janos: see **Biographies 83**
Hungary 420
Kaempfert, Berthold: see **Obituaries 81**
Kagera River Basin project 224
Kalaglow (race horse) 364
Kamanin, Nikolai Petrovich: see **Obituaries 83**
space exploration 622
Kamougue, Wadal Abdelkader 232
Kampuchea 83, 82. see **Cambodia 81**
demography 289 (table)
Southeast Asian affairs 621
Vietnamese occupation 724
transportation 673 (table)
United Nations report 690
Kangaroo 361
KaNgwane, region, South Africa 640
Kania, Stanislaw: see **Biographies 81**
KANU (Kenya African National Union) 470
Kappafloat (glass) 440
Kapwepwe, Simon Mwansa: see **Obituaries 81**
Kara-Bogaz-Gol, gulf, U.S.S.R. 356
Karakorum Range, Asia 542
Karate 247
Karayev, Kara Abulpaz: see **Obituaries 83**
Kardiner, Abram: see **Obituaries 82**
Karmal, Babrak: see **Biographies 81**
Afghan insurgency problems 151
Karolinska Institute, Stockholm, Swed. 410
Karpov, Anatoly 235

Karpov, Viktor P. 696
Katanyan, Vasily Abgarovich: see **Obituaries 81**
Kaunda, Kenneth
Tanzanian visit 648
Zambia 735
Kautner, Helmut: see **Obituaries 81**
Kayaking 725
Kaysone, Phomvihan 474
Kedir, Mohamed 670
Kelly, Patsy (Bridget Veronica Kelly): see **Obituaries 82**
Kelly, Petra Karin: see **Biographies 83**
Kemp, Jack: see **Biographies 83**
Kemper, James Scott: see **Obituaries 82**
Kempowski, Walter 506
Kendo 248
Keneally, Thomas 500
Keng Piao (Geng Biao) 240
"Kenguru" (Aleshkovsky) 512
Kennecott Minerals Co. 530
Kennedy, Daisy: see **Obituaries 82**
Kennedy, Edward 691
Kennedy, John F., Center for the Performing Arts, Washington, D.C. 185
"Kennedy Imprisonment: A Meditation on Power, The" (Wills) 503
Kentucky Derby 362
Kenya 83, 82
African military coup 154
archaeology 177
demography 289 (table)
education and politics 334
transportation 673 (table)
Kenya African National Union (KANU) 470
Kerekou, Ahmed 215
Keynes, Sir Geoffrey Langdon: see **Obituaries 83**
Khalid ibn 'Abd al-'Aziz Al Saud: see **Obituaries 83**
Saudi Arabia 609
Khalifah, Khalifah ibn Sulman al- 206
Khama, Sir Seretse: see **Obituaries 81**
Khamenei, Hojatoleslam Sayyed Ali: see **Biographies 82**
Khan, Fazlur R(ahman): see **Obituaries 83**
engineering projects 348
Khan, Jahangir 588
Khan, Sahabzada Yaqub 151
Khartoum, Sudan 639
Khieu Samphan 469
Khmer Rouge 468
Southeast Asian affairs 621
Bhutan support 216
Vietnamese opposition 724
Khomeini, Ayatollah Ruhollah
Iranian internal politics 451
Islamic education 332
Khrushchev, Nikita
"Russian Giant: 60 Years after Formation of the Soviet Union, The" 17
Khun Sa
Thai domestic unrest 661
Khuzestan, province, Iran 451
Kid Creole and the Coconuts (band) 549
Kidnapping 258
Kielder water tunnel (U.K.) 352
Kim Duk Koo 245
Kimbell Art Museum, Fort Worth, Texas 192
Kim Chong Il 473
Kim Dae Jung 472
Kim Il Sung 470
China visit il. 240
King, Billie Jean 659
King, Henry: see **Obituaries 83**
King, Stephen: see **Biographies 81**
literature 503
King Sunny Ade (band) 549
Kinmonth, John Bernard: see **Obituaries 83**
Kipphardt, Heinar: see **Obituaries 83**
Kiribati 83, 82, 81
demography 291 (table)
Kirkland, Gelsey 270
Kirkpatrick, Jeane J.: see **Biographies 82**
Kirov Ballet (U.S.S.R.) 273
Kirvesniemi, Harri 727
Kissinger, Henry
"China's Uncertain Future" 135
"Great Disarmament Debate, The" 11
literature 503
KKE (Greek Communist Party) 403
Klindt-Jensen, Ole: see **Obituaries 81**
Klug, Aaron
chemistry research 232
Nobel Prizes 98, il. 97
Knight, John Shively: see **Obituaries 82**
Knickers (fashion) 372
Kobbekaduwa, Hector 632
Koch, Bill 727
Koch, Marita 668
Koenigswald, G.H. Ralph von: see **Obituaries 83**
Kogan, Leonid (Borisovich): see **Obituaries 83**
Kogler, Armin 728
Kohl, Helmut: see **Biographies 83**
defense 279
West Germany 399
Kohn, Pedersen, Fox Associates (architects) 186

Koirala, Bisheshwar Prasad: see **Obituaries 83**
Nepal 550
Koivisto, Mauno Henrik: see **Biographies 83**
Finland 376
Iceland visit 423
Kojima, Nobuo 515
Kokoschka, Oskar: see **Obituaries 81**
Kolbe, Maximilian 597
Kolingba, André: see **Biographies 82**
Central African Republic coup 231
Kollsman, Paul: see **Obituaries 83**
Komatiite (geology) 305
Kondrashin, Kyril: see **Obituaries 82**
Konwicki, Tadeusz 513
Korchnoi, Victor 235
Korea 83, 82, 81
defense 284
demography 289 (table)
North Korea
Zimbabwe training 736
South Korea
education 331 (table)
industrial review 447
Japanese textbook issue 464
transportation 673 (table)
Koriceva, Larisa 151
Koshland, Daniel E., Jr. 494
Kosovo, Yugoslavia 731
Kostelanetz, Andre: see **Obituaries 81**
Kosygin, Aleksey Nikoleyevich: see **Obituaries 81**
"Russian Giant: 60 Years after Formation of the Soviet Union, The" 18
Kotarbinski, Tadeusz Marian: see **Obituaries 82**
Kountché, Seyni 554
Krebs, Sir Hans Adolf: see **Obituaries 82**
Kreisky, Bruno 204
"Kriticky sbornik" (Czech. journal) 513
Krleza, Miroslav: see **Obituaries 82**
Krug, Judith 485
Kuala Lumpur, Malaysia 518
Kubo, Sotaro 192
Kuenen, L.P.S. 491
Kuenn, Harvey 209
Kuhn, Bowie 210
Kuk, Zvi Yehuda 598
Kukrit Pramoj 660
Kumin, Maxine 504
Kupreichik, Viktor 236
Kuron, Jacek: see **Biographies 82**
Kuwait 83, 82, 81
demography 289 (table)
education 331 (table)
Middle Eastern affairs 528
Kuznetsov, Vasily 679
Kvalfoff, Erik 728
ZwaZulu, region, South Africa 640
Kyprianou, Spyros 267
Greek relations 404

L

Labour Party (U.K.) 686
Lacan, Jacques: see **Obituaries 82**
Laciar, Santos 245
"Ladies and gentlemen embarking for the Isle of Cythera" (paint.) 195
Laetoli, site, Tanzania
anthropology 175
LAIA (Latin American Integration Association) 475
Lake Forest College, Ill. 256
Laker Airways 671
Lalonde, Marc 226, 229
Lamas, Fernando: see **Obituaries 83**
Lamb 162
Lambsdorff, Count Otto Graf 397
Lami Dozo, Basilio 189
"Lancaster Sound Region, 1980–2000, The" 187
Lancefield, Rebecca Craighill: see **Obituaries 82**
Landaluce (race horse) 362
Langley, Noel A.: see **Obituaries 81**
Lansing, Sherry Lee: see **Biographies 81**
Lao People's Revolutionary Party (LRPR) 474
Laos 83, 82, 81
demography 290 (table)
education 331 (table)
engineering projects 350
LaPorte, Juan 245
La Rochefoucauld, Fr. 177
La Scala, Italy 547
Lascaux cave, Fr. 177
Laser 568
metallurgy 521
Lasker, Edward: see **Obituaries 83**
Laskov, Haim: see **Obituaries 83**
Las Vegas, Nevada 393
Latin American Affairs 83, 82, 81
archaeology 180
defense 284
energy production 347
literature 499, 510
Nobel Prizes 96
United States relations 697
see also Latin American countries

Latin American Economic System (SELA) 476
Latin American Integration Association (LAIA) 475
"Latinization of the U.S., The" (Special Report) 586
Latinos: *see* Spanish-speaking people
Lauda, Niki 540
Laurens, André: *see* **Biographies 83**
Laurie, John: *see* **Obituaries 81**
Laut, David 669
Lauwerys, Joseph Albert: *see* **Obituaries 82**
Law 83, 82, 81
  hockey suit 421
  industrial review 432
  United States statistics 701
  see also various countries
Law enforcement: *see* Crime and Law enforcement
Lavilla Alsina, Landelino 629
Laye, Camara: *see* **Obituaries 81**
Lazar, Irving 336
L-chain genes
  molecular biology 496
LDPE (Low-density polyethylene) 444
Leach, James 699
Lead
  environment 357
  mining and quarrying 532
  paint and varnish industry 443
Leander, Zarah Stina: *see* **Obituaries 82**
Leatherheads (antiterrorists) 258
Leavis, Q(ueenie) D(orothy): *see* **Obituaries 82**
Lebanon 83, 82, 81
  defense 274
  demography 290 (table)
  education 331 (table)
  European Communities 371
  international law 479
  Middle Eastern Affairs 525
    Israel 456
    Syria 645
  motion pictures 539
  refugee status 589
  Tunisia relations 676
  United Nations report 689
  United States position 696
Lebedev, Valentin V. 623
Leder, Philip 496
Le Duan 723
Lee, Bernard: *see* **Obituaries 82**
Lee, James 227
Lee Chul Hi 472
Leeder, Sigurd: *see* **Obituaries 82**
Leek, Sybil: *see* **Obituaries 83**
Lee Kuan Yew 621
  Singapore 612
Lefebvre, Jean-Pierre 537
Léger, Fernand 193
Léger, Jules: *see* **Obituaries 81**
LeGuin, Ursula 503
Lejarreta, Marino 267
Le Mans (sports car race) 541
Lemelin, Roger 506
Lemhi Gold (race horse) 362
Lender-of-last-resort 63
Lendl, Ivan 658
Lenin
  "Russian Giant: 60 Years after Formation of the Soviet Union, The" 15
Lenin (G-1, U.S.S.R. launch vehicle) 624
Lennon, John (Winston): *see* **Obituaries 81**
Lenses 567
Lenya, Lotte (Karoline Blamauer): *see* **Obituaries 82**
Leonard, Shelagh 219
Leonard, Sugar Ray 245
Le Patourel, John Herbert: *see* **Obituaries 82**
Leroi-Gourhan, Arlette 177
Lesage, Jean: *see* **Obituaries 81**
Leshi, Haxhi 170
Lesney Products & Company Ltd. (U.K.) 394
Lesotho 83, 82, 81
  demography 289 (table)
  education 331 (table)
  South African foreign relations 619
Lesser, Sol: *see* **Obituaries 81**
Lessing, Doris 501
"Lessing J. Rosenwald: Tribute to a Collector" (art exhibition) 191
"Lessons from the Falklands" (Special Report) 285
Let a hundred flowers bloom 133
Levene, Sam (Samuel Levine): *see* **Obituaries 81**
Levenson, Sam: *see* **Obituaries 81**
Lévesque, René 225
Levi, Primo 509 il.
Levinson, Barry 536
Lewis, Carl 668, il. 669
Lewis, David: *see* **Obituaries 82**
Lewis, James and LeAnn 260
Liability insurance 440
Libby, Willard Frank: *see* **Obituaries 81**
Liberia 83, 82, 81
  demography 289 (table)
  education 331 (table)
  energy production 347
  transportation 673 (table)
Libraries 83, 82, 81
Library of Congress, Washington, D.C. 484

Libreville, University of, Gabon 392
Libya 83, 82, 81
  defense 274
  demography 289 (table)
  education 331 (table)
  foreign relations
    Algeria 171
    Chadian civil war 154
    Malta 519
    Saudi Arabia 610
    Tunisia 676
  international law 480
  transportation 673 (table)
Lidell, (Tord) Alvar Quan: *see* **Obituaries 82**
Lieberman, Nancy: *see* **Biographies 81**
Liebman, Max: *see* **Obituaries 82**
Liechtenstein 83, 82, 81
  demography 290 (table)
  law 477
Life expectancy 288
Life insurance 440
Life Sciences 83, 82, 81
Light Rail Transit (LRT) 675
"Light Unto My Path, A" (exhibit) 594
Li Hsien-nien (Li Xiannian) 240
Lilienthal, David E(li): *see* **Obituaries 82**
Lillak, Tiina 668, il. 670
Limann, Hilla 401
Limiler, John 588
Limited nuclear war
  "Stresses in the Western Alliance" 67
Limón, Rafael 245
Lin Biao (Lin Piao) 131
Lincoln cent (currency) 565
Linde, A.D. 198
Lindstrom, Fred Charles ("Lindy"): *see* **Obituaries 82**
Linear low-density polyethylene (LLDPE) 445
Linehan, Kim 642
Ling, Hung-hsün: *see* **Obituaries 82**
Lini, the Rev. Walter Hadye: *see* **Biographies 81**
  Vanuatu 720
Li Ning 403
Link, Edwin Albert: *see* **Obituaries 82**
Lin Piao (Lin Biao) 131
Liquefied natural gas (LNG) 345
Liqueurs 434
Liquidity 326
  "You Can't Foreclose a Country" 60
Lisberger, Steven 535
Literature 83, 82, 81
  Nobel Prizes 95
Lithography 442
Little Cornwallis Island, Can. 530
Little curlew (bird) 492
Litvinov, Sergey 668
Liver disease 288
Liverpool, U.K. 448
Livestock 162
"Living by Fiction" (Dillard) 504
Livingstone, Kenneth: *see* **Biographies 82**
Li Xiannian (Li Hsien-nien) 240
Lleras Restrepo, Carlos 243
Llewelyn-Davies, Richard Llewelyn-Davies, Baron: *see* **Obituaries 82**
Lloyd, Albert Lancaster: *see* **Obituaries 83**
Lloyd, Norman: *see* **Obituaries 81**
Lloyd, Sir Hugh Pughe: *see* **Obituaries 82**
Lloyd's Act, U.K. 440
LLDPE (Linear low-density polyethylene) 445
LNG (Liquefied natural gas) 345
LOADS (low-altitude defensive system) 276
Loans
  "You Can't Foreclose a Country" 60
LOAPA (Organic Law on the Harmonization of the Autonomy Process, Spain) 629
Lockheed Aircraft 433
  Japanese trial outcome 462
Lockridge, Richard: *see* **Obituaries 83**
Loeb, William: *see* **Obituaries 82**
Lombard rate (economics) 318
Lomé convention 154
  Mozambique economy 543
  Nigeria (special report) 557
London, U.K. 393
London Festival Ballet 272
"Lonely Hearts" (film) 537
Long March
  "China's Uncertain Future" 130
Longo, Luigi: *see* **Obituaries 81**
Long Valley Caldera, Calif. 306
Longworth, Alice Lee Roosevelt: *see* **Obituaries 81**
"Looking for Jesus" (film) 537
Loos, Anita: *see* **Obituaries 82**
López Portillo, José 524
Lopokova, Lydia Vasilievna (Lady Keynes): *see* **Obituaries 82**
Loring, Eugene: *see* **Obituaries 83**
Los Angeles County Museum of Art, Los Angeles, Calif. 184, 191
Los Angeles Lakers (team) 211
Los Angeles Raiders (team) 386
Lottery 393
Louganis, Greg 643
Lougheed, (Edgar) Peter: *see* **Biographies 82**

Canada elections 226, il. 227
Loughran, Tommy: *see* **Obituaries 83**
Louis, Joe (Joseph Louis Barrow): *see* **Obituaries 82**
Lousma, Jack R.
  aerial sport record 150
  space exploration 623
Love Canal, N.Y. 357
Low-altitude defensive system (LOADS) 276
Low-density polyethylene (LDPE) 444
Lowe, Arthur: *see* **Obituaries 83**
Lowe, Doug 203
Lowenstein, Allard K.: *see* **Obituaries 81**
LRPR (Lao People's Revolutionary Party) 474
LRT (Light Rail Transit) 675
Luan Jin 588
Lubalin, Herb(ert), Frederick: *see* **Obituaries 82**
Lubbers, Rudolphus Franciscus Marie: *see* **Biographies 83**
  Netherlands 552
Lubetkin, Berthold 184
Lucayan Caverns, Bahamas 631
Ludden, Allen Ellsworth: *see* **Obituaries 82**
Lüders, Rolf 237
Ludlum, Robert: *see* **Biographies 83**
  literature 503
Ludwig, Daniel K.: *see* **Biographies 83**
  environment 356
Lule, Yusufu 678
"Lulu in Hollywood" (Brooks) 504
Lumea (Rom. newspaper) 604
Lumet, Sidney 536
Luminescence 493
Lunar rocks 305
Lundquist, Steve 642
Luns, Joseph il. 370
Lustiger, Msgr. Jean Marie: *see* **Biographies 82**
Lutheran Churches 594
Lutyens, Sir Edwin 183
Luxembourg 83, 82, 81
  demography 290 (table)
  education 331 (table)
  industrial review 440
  international law 479
Lybbert, Chris 603
Lynd, Helen Merrell: *see* **Obituaries 83**
Lynde, Paul: *see* **Obituaries 83**
Lyon, J. G. A. 588
Lyons, Dame Enid Muriel: *see* **Obituaries 82**
Lysianassid amphipod crustaceans 492

M

M-19 (guerrillas)
  Colombia 243
Maazel, Lorin 546
Macau 297
  demography 290 (table)
McClintick, David 504
McConachy, Clark: *see* **Obituaries 81**
McCormack, John William: *see* **Obituaries 81**
MacCready, Paul: *see* **Biographies 82**
MacDonald, Dwight: *see* **Obituaries 83**
MacDonald, Malcom John: *see* **Obituaries 82**
McDonald's 432
McDonnell, James Smith, Jr.: *see* **Obituaries 81**
McDonnell Douglas 433
MacEachen, Allan 226
McEnroe, John 658
McEwen, Sir John: *see* **Obituaries 81**
McGraw, Tug: *see* **Biographies 81**
MacGregor, Ian: *see* **Biographies 81**
Machel, Samora 543
McHenry, Donald F.: *see* **Biographies 81**
Machinery and machine tools 442
  mining and quarrying 531
McKay Trading Estate, London, U.K.
  classical revival 183, il., 184
McKelway, St. Clair: *see* **Obituaries 81**
McKenzie, Dave 669
MacKenzie, Rachel: *see* **Obituaries 81**
McKenzie, Robert Trelford: *see* **Obituaries 81**
McKinney, Rick 648
MacLeish, Archibald: *see* **Obituaries 83**
McLuhan, (Herbert) Marshall: *see* **Obituaries 81**
McNamara, Julianne il. 408
McNeil Consumer Products Co. 444
  United States 694
Macphee, Ian 199
McQueen, Steve: *see* **Obituaries 81**
McQuirter, Alexander J. 302
Macrocystis (brown alga) 493
McWilliams, Carey: *see* **Obituaries 81**
Madagascar 83, 82, 81
  African political developments 154
  demography 289 (table)
  Madagascar National Independence Movement (Monima) 516
Madero, Pablo Emilio 524
"Madone à l'escalier" (painting) 195

Madrid Hurtado, Miguel de la: *see* **Biographies 83**
  Mexico 524
Maeght, Aimé: *see* **Obituaries 82**
Mafia 459
Magaña Borjo, Alvaro Alfredo 339
Magazines 580
Magee, Patrick: *see* **Obituaries 83**
Magma (geology) 304
Magnesium 532
Magnetic monopole (physics) 569
Magnetism 568
  astronomical observations 198
Mahathir bin Mohamad Iskandar: *see* **Biographies 82**
  Malaysia 517
Mahre, Phil 727
Mahre, Steve 727
Maianni, Giuseppe 608
Maillet, Antonine: *see* **Biographies 81**
"Mail On Sunday" (newspaper) 578
Maine 702
Mainz, W. Ger. 178
Majlis al-shura 609
Majluta Azar, Jacobo 303
Makarov, Sergey 422
Makarova, Natalia 270
Makieda Motofumi 332
Makk, Karoly 538
Malamud, Bernard 501 il.
"Malattia chiamata uomo, La" (Camon) 509
Malawi 83, 82, 81
  demography 289 (table)
  education 331 (table)
  transportation 673 (table)
Malaysia 83, 82, 81
  cocoa production 164
  demography 290 (table)
  education 331 (table)
  environment 356
  mining and quarrying 533
  transportation 673 (table)
Maldives 83, 82, 81
  Commonwealth membership 248
  demography 290 (table)
Mali 83, 82, 81
  demography 289 (table)
  education 331 (table)
  Upper Volta's relations 719
Malina, Frank Joseph: *see* **Obituaries 82**
Mallalieu, Sir (Joseph Percival) William: *see* **Obituaries 81**
Maloney, Frank P. 196
Malta 83, 82, 81
  demography 290 (table)
Maltese, Michael: *see* **Obituaries 82**
Malthus, Thomas 497
Malting barley 434
Malvinas, Islas: *see* Falkland Islands
Mamaloni, Solomon 616
Man, Isle of 299
  demography 290 (table)
Mancini, Ray 245
Mandlikova, Hana 659
"Man from Snowy River, The" (film) 537
Manganese 532
Manica, province, Mozambique 543
Manioc (cassava) 160
Manley, Michael 461
Man-made fibres 448
Manned Maneuvering Unit
  space exploration (special report) 627
Manning, Olivia: *see* **Obituaries 81**
Mansouri, Lofti: *see* **Biographies 82**
Mantovani (Annunzio Paolo): *see* **Obituaries 81**
Manufacturers Hanover Trust Co. 691
Manufacturing: *see* Industrial Review
Manville Corp.
  environment 358
  United States 692
Mao Dun (Mao Tun): *see* **Obituaries 82**
Mao Zedong (Mao Tse-tung) 130
Mara, Sir Kamisese 376
Maradona, Diego Armando: *see* **Biographies 82**
Marais, Jacob Albertus: *see* **Biographies 82**
Marathon Oil Co. 693
Marathon running 670
Marcinkus, Msgr. Paul Casimir: *see* **Biographies 83**
  Italian foreign affairs 460
  religion 591
  Vatican City State il. 721
"Marco Polo" (TV program) 654
Marcos, Ferdinand E. 565, 622
Marcos, Imee 566
Marcos, Imelda 566, il. 565
Margai, Sir Albert M.: *see* **Obituaries 81**
Margulies, Leo: *see* **Obituaries 83**
Mar Ignatius Yacoub III: *see* **Obituaries 81**
Marijuana 409
Marine biology 492
Marine Corps, U.S. 277
Marine environment 354

Marini, Marino: see **Obituaries 81**
Marjai, Jozsef 419
Mark (Ger. currency) 312
Market economies 96, 313
Markey, Lucille Parker: see **Obituaries 83**
Marley, Bob (Robert Nesta Marley): see **Obituaries 82**
Marquard, Richard: see **Obituaries 81**
Marriage 292
Marrinet, Neville: see **Biographies 81**
symphonic music 546
Marsh, Dame (Edith) Ngaio: see **Obituaries 83**
Marshall, Thomas Humphrey: see **Obituaries 82**
Marshall Islands 301
Martel, Chip 254
Martella, Ilario 459
Martenot, Maurice Louis Eugène: see **Obituaries 81**
Martens, Wilfried 214, 516
Martial law
Philippines 566
Polish crisis 570
Martin, Bob 256
Martin Marietta (U.S. co.) 693
Martin, Ross (Martin Rosenblatt): see **Obituaries 82**
Martin, Sir James: see **Obituaries 82**
Martínez, María: see **Obituaries 81**
Martínez, Verdugo, Arnaldo 524
Martinique 296
demography 291 (table)
Martin-Kuntz, Marty 728
Martins, Peter 270
Maruya, Saiichi 515
"Mary Rose" (Eng. warship) 418
archaeology (special report) 181
Masi, Victor 557
Masire, Quett Ketumile Jonny: see **Biographies 81**
Massachusetts 701
"Master Harold . . . and the Boys" (play) 665
Matabeleland Province, Zimb. 735
Matanzima, Kaiser 620
Matchbox toys 394
Material Sciences 83, 82, 81
Maternal mortality
demography 292
Mathematics 83, 82, 81
Mathis, F. John (author)
"You Can't Foreclose a Country" 60
Matilsky, T. 198
"Matinée chez la princesse de Guermantes" (Proust) 506
Matos Moctezuma, Eduardo 180
Mattheison, Leroy T. 591
Matter (phys.)
Nobel Prizes 98
Matthews, Jessie: see **Obituaries 82**
Mattingly, Thomas K.
aerial sport record 150
space exploration 623
Maudslay, Ronald Harling: see **Obituaries 82**
Maugham, Robin (Robert Cecil Romer Maugham, 2nd Viscount Maugham): see **Obituaries 82**
Mauritania 83, 82, 81
demography 289 (table)
Mauritius 83, 82, 81
African political developments 154
demography 289 (table)
education 331 (table)
Mauritshuis, The Hague, Neth.
art exhibition 193
museums 545
Mauroy, Pierre: see **Biographies 82**
France 391
Gabon's grant confirmation 392
Mavica (camera) 567
"Max Ernst—From the Collection of Mr. and Mrs. Jimmy Ernst" (art exhibition) 191
Maxwell, Cedric: see **Biographies 82**
Maya (archae.) 179
Mayer, Norman 259
Mayer, Stefan Antoni: see **Obituaries 82**
Mayotte 300
demography 289 (table)
Mayr, Ernst 499
Mazda (automobile) 436
Meagher, Mary T. 642
Meany, (William) George: see **Obituaries 81**
Mears, Rick 541
Meat and meat products
agriculture and food supplies 162
consumerism 254
food processing 381
industrial review 432
Medfly (Mediterranean fruit fly) 491
Medicaid 615
Medicine: see Health and Disease
Mediterranean Action Plan 354
Mediterranean fruit fly (Medfly) 491
Mediterranean land tortoise (*Testudo hermanni*) 361

Medvedev, Roy
"Russian Giant: 60 Years after Formation of the Soviet Union, The" 15
Medvedev, Zhores
"Russian Giant: 60 Years after Formation of the Soviet Union, The" 15
Meek, Marvin il. 162
Meese, Edwin, III: see **Biographies 82**
"Melanesian Alliance" 616
"Melanie" (film) 537
Mellon, Paul 544
"Memory of War, The" (Fenton) 501
Mendès-France, Pierre: see **Obituaries 83**
Menéndez, Mario Benjamín 189
defense 287
Mengistu Haile Mariam 368
African politico-military activity 154
Men's International Tennis Professional Council (MITPC) 658
Mental health 413
Menuhin, Hephzibah (Hephzibah Menuhin Hauzer): see **Obituaries 82**
Mercer, David: see **Obituaries 81**
Merchant, Vivien: see **Obituaries 83**
Mercouri, Melina: see **Biographies 83**
archaeology 177
Greece 404
Mercury (element) 353, 532
"Merlin" (Dorst) 507
Merrill, Henry Tindall (Dick Merrill): see **Obituaries 83**
"Message from the Falklands, A" (Tinker) 501
Messenger RNA (MRNA) 490
Messner, Reinhold: see **Biographies 81**
Metal
chemical bonding 233
metallurgy's laser use 521
mining and quarrying 531
Metalloproteins 233
Metallurgy 520
Meteorology 308
Methodist Churches 595
Methylation (biology) 495
Métis Association (Can. Indians)
Arctic regions 187
Metropolitan Handicap (horse racing) 362
Metropolitan Museum of Art, N.Y., N.Y.
art exhibition 193
museum acquisitions 545
Metropolitan Opera (N.Y., N.Y.) 271
Metropolitan Police of London 584
Mettoy Company Ltd. 394
"Meurtre d'Ovide Plouffe, Le" (Lemelin) 506
Mexican-Americans
race relations (special report) 586
Mexico 83, 82, 81
archaeology 180
baseball 211
demography 291 (table)
education 331 (table)
industry and mining
machinery and machine tools 442
mining and quarrying 530
petroleum production 340
tuna industry 378
literature 511
Nobel Prizes 96
transportation 673 (table)
world economy 312, 325
"You Can't Foreclose a Country" 60
Miami, Fla. 416, il. 415
Miami Dolphins (team) 386
Michael Graves & Associates 185
Michelene, Danial 256
Michels, Donald J. 196
Michener, James 503
Michigan 357
"Mickelson's Ghosts" (Gardner) 502
Microelectronics 442
Microelectronics and Computer Technology Corp. 250
Micronesia: see Federated States of Micronesia
Microprocessors 442
libraries 484
Micropropagation 395
Micunovic, Veljko: see **Obituaries 83**
Middle Eastern Affairs 83, 82, 81
defense 274
energy production 346
European Communities 371
Morocco 535
United States' role 696
United Nations report 688
world economy 320
Zaire 733
see also Middle Eastern countries
"Midnight Clear, A" (Wharton) 502
"Midsummer Night's Sex Comedy, A" (film) 536
Midway Islands
demography 291 (table)
Midwest Stock Exchange 633
Migrant labor
race relations (special report) 586
Migration, International 83, 82, 81
Australian policies 201
New Zealand 553
Sweden's Polish refugees 641
Miles, Bernard James Miles, Baron: see **Biographies 82**

Milestone, Lewis Milstein: see **Obituaries 81**
Militarism
"Stresses in the Western Alliance" 65
Military Council for National Salvation (Poland) 570
Milk 163
Miller, Henry (Valentine): see **Obituaries 81**
Mills, Harry: see **Obituaries 83**
Milward, Sir Anthony Horace: see **Obituaries 82**
Milwaukee Art Center, Wisc. 191
Milwaukee Brewers (team) 208
Minerals 529
Mining and Quarrying 83, 82, 81
Brazilian economic conditions 221
British economic crisis 687
Minne, Georg 193
Minneapolis Institute of Arts
museum acquisition 545
"Minneapolis Star" (newspaper) 580
Minnesota 700
Minnesota Orchestra 546
Mintoff, Dom 519
"Mio figlio non sa leggere" (Pirro) 509
MIRV (multiple independently targetable reentry vehicle) 276
Miskito Indians 554
"Missing" (film) 536
Mississippi University for Women v. Joe Hogan 477
Mitchell, Sir Godfrey Way: see **Obituaries 83**
MITPC (Men's International Tennis Professional Council) 658
Mitsubishi Corp. (Jap.) 464
computers 250
industrial review 437
Mitsui & Co.
Japan 464
Mittelman, George 254
Mitterrand, François Maurice: see **Biographies 82**
European meeting il. 370
foreign travel
Burundi il. 224
Mauritania il. 522
Niger 554
West Germany 399
France 389
Guinea president's visit il. 406
Hungarian relations 420
Mizerak, Steve il. 217
MNR (Mozambican National Resistance) 543
Möbius strip
chemical structure 233
Mobutu Sese Seko
crime and law enforcement 261
Zaire 733
Moffat, George 150
Mohammad Ali, Chaudhri: see **Obituaries 81**
Mohammad Reza Pahlavi: see **Obituaries 81**
Mohen jo-daro, site, Pakistan 417
Mohieddin, Ahmad Fuad 337
Moi, Daniel Torotich arap: see **Biographies 83**
Chad 232
Kenya 469
Mojsov, Lazar 732
Molecular biology 494
Molybdenum 532
Monaco 83, 82, 81
demography 290 (table)
Mondale, Walter Frederick: see **Biographies 84**
Mondiacult (World Conference on Cultural Policies) 417
Monetarism
Chilean economic crisis 237
"Stresses in the Western Alliance" 69
world economy 310
Money and banking
Latin-American affairs 475
stock exchange 634
world economy 312, 327
"You Can't Foreclose a Country" 60
see also various countries
Money market funds 634
Monge Álvarez, Luis Alberto 255
Mongolia 83, 82, 81
demography 290 (table)
Monima (Madagascar National Independence Movement) 516
Monk, Thelonious Sphere: see **Obituaries 83**
jazz music 548
Monopoly (game) il. 393
Monreal, Alfonso 256
"Monsignor Quixote" (Greene) 501
Montana 701
Montale, Eugenio: see **Obituaries 82**
Montevideo Treaty (South America)
trade and tariffs 475
Montgomery, Robert (Henry Montgomery, Jr.): see **Obituaries 82**
Montreal Stock Exchange 635
Montserrat 300
demography 291 (table)
"Monumentum" (journal) 417
Moon 305
Moon, Rev. Sun Myung 592
Moon, Warren 388
"Moonlighting" (film) 537

Moorcroft, Dave 668
Moore, Davey 245
Moore, Grover, Harper (firm) 183
Moore, Henry il. 195
Moore, Jeremy 289
Moore, Stanford: see **Obituaries 83**
Moraes, Vinicius de: see **Obituaries 81**
"Moral Thinking: Its Levels, Methods, and Point" (Hare) 500
Moravia, Alberto 509
More, Kenneth Gilbert: see **Obituaries 83**
Morena (Movement for National Renewal) 392
Morgan Field, oil field, Egypt 338
Morillo, Jaime 328
Morocco 83, 82, 81
demography 289 (table)
education 331 (table)
mining and quarrying 531
transportation 673 (table)
Western Sahara conflict 154
Moro National Liberation Front (Phil. separatist) 566
Morreale, Stephen J. 490
Morris, Margaret: see **Obituaries 81**
Morrow, Patrick 228
Morrow, Vic: see **Obituaries 83**
Morton, Thruston Ballard: see **Obituaries 83**
Moscone Convention Center, San Francisco, Calif. 349
Moseley, Mark: see **Biographies 83**
football 386
Mosely, Sir Oswald Ernald: see **Obituaries 81**
literature 501
Moses, Robert: see **Obituaries 82**
"Mosquito Coast, The" (Theroux) 501
Mostyn, Lord 195
Motal, Gloria 256
Motion Pictures 83, 82, 81
libraries (special report) 485
Motlana, Nthato 585
Motorboating 724
Motorcycles 542
Motors 531
Motor Sports 83, 82, 81
Motor vehicles
European imports 372
industrial review 435
theft 261
United States statistics 702
world economy 317, 322
Mountaineering 83, 82, 81
Mountains
earth sciences 303
Mouzaoir, Abdallah 249
Movement for National Renewal (Morena)
Gabon 392
Movement for the Restoration of Democracy (Pakistan) 560
Movies: see Motion Pictures
Mozambican National Resistance (MNR) 543
Mozambique 83, 82, 81
demography 289 (table)
education 331 (table)
Zimbabwe pipeline 736
MPR (People's Consultative Assembly, Indon.) 426
MRFIT (Multiple Risk Factor Intervention Trial) 410
MRNA (messenger RNA) 496
Mroudjae, Ali 249
Mubarak, Muhammad Hosni: see **Biographies 82**
Egyptian political economy 337
Israel 455
Mugabe, Robert: see **Biographies 81**
Zimbabwe 735
Muggeridge, Malcolm 499
Muldoon, Robert 552
Muldowney, Shirley: see **Biographies 82**
Müller, Erwin 150
Multilateral integration (econ.) 321
Multiphase loom 448
Multiple independently targetable reentry vehicle (MIRV) 276
Multiple Risk Factor Intervention Test (MRFIT) 410
Muluzi, Bakili
Malawi 517
Mummichog (fish) 489
Mummification 488
Muncey, Bill: see **Obituaries 82**
Mungai, Joseph 648
Muñoz Marín, Luis: see **Obituaries 81**
Murase Hisao 247
Murdani, Benny: see **Biographies 81**
Murdoch, (Keith) Rupert: see **Biographies 82**
publishing 578
Murjani, Mohan: see **Biographies 81**
Museo Civico, Pistoia, Italy 545
Museo Correr, Venice, Italy 192
Museum of Modern Art, N.Y., N.Y. 193
Museums 83, 82, 81
Music 83, 82, 81
television and radio 655
theatre 665
Muskie, Edmund Sixtus: see **Biographies 81**
Muslim Brotherhood
Syrian domestic disorder 645

Muslims: *see* Islam
Mustela nigripes: see Black-footed ferret
Musto, William V. 701
Mutual funds 634
Muus, Flemming B.: *see* **Obituaries 83**
"Muzhiki" (film) 538
Mwanga, Abel 648
MX missile program 693
"My Favorite Year" (film) 536
Myrdal, Alva Reimer
  Nobel Prizes 96

N

NADA (National Automobile Dealers
  Association) 698
Nakagome, Kiyoshi 183
Nakano, Koichi 266
Nakasone, Yasuhiro: *see* **Biographies
  83**
  Japan 462
Nam Duck Woo 471
Namgyal, Palden Thondup: *see* **Obituaries 83**
Namibia 300
  African affairs 154
    Angola 172
    South Africa 618
    Zambia 735
  defense 284
  demography 289 (table)
NAS (National Academy of Sciences)
  409
NASA: *see* National Aeronautics and
  Space Administration
NASCAR (National Association for
  Stock Car Auto Racing) 541
Nasdaq composite index
  stock exchange 632
National Aboriginal Conference 200
National Academy of Sciences (NAS)
  409
National Aeronautics and Space Ad-
  ministration (NASA)
  European Space Agency 622
  space exploration (special report)
  627
National Association for Stock Car
  Auto Racing (NASCAR) 541
National Association of Realtors 699
National Automobile Dealers Associa-
  tion (NADA) 698
National Bank of Hungary 419
National Broadcasting Company
  (NBC) 652
National Center for Health Statistics
  288
National Conservative Political Action
  Committee (NCPAC) 699
National Democratic Front (NDF, Ye-
  men Arab Republic) 730
National Economic Review Committee
  401
National Finals Rodeo 603
National Football League (NFL)
  football 386
  television 654
  United States 694
National Front (Malaysia) 517
National Gallery of Art, London, U.K.
  184
National Gallery of Art, Washington,
  D.C.
  art exhibition 191
  museums 544
National Health Service (U.K.) 687
National Highway Traffic Safety Ad-
  ministration (NHTSA) 446
National Hockey League (NHL) 420
National Liberation Front (FLN, Alg.)
  171
National League (baseball) 210
National Military Council (NMC, Suri-
  name) 640
National Museum of Civilization, Que-
  bec City, Quebec, Can. 184
National Party (NP, S.Af) 617
National Party of Nigeria (NPN) 554
National People's Congress (China)
  241
National Revolutionary Development
  Movement 606
National Security Council (NSC, Tur.)
  677
National Theatre (U.K.) 662
National Water Council (U.K.) 356
Nationalization
  Libyan economic developments
  487
  Mexican banking system 524
  Nigeria (special report) 557
Nation of Islam (U.S.) 600
NATO: *see* North Atlantic Treaty
  Organization
Nattrass, Susan: *see* **Biographies 83**
Natural gas
  Algerian pricing 170
  Arctic regions 187
  energy production 345
Natural selection
  life sciences (special report) 497
Nauru 83, 82, 81
  demography 291 (table)
Naval Research Laboratory 196
Navarrete, Rolando 245

Navratilova, Martina 659
Navy, U.S. 276
Nayef, Prince 610
NBC (National Broadcasting Compa-
  ny) 652
NCPAC (National Conservative Politi-
  cal Action Committee) 699
NDF (National Democratic Front, Ye-
  men Arab Republic) 730
Nebraska
  United States statistics 702
Nebraska, University of 388
Neel, Louis Boyd: *see* **Obituaries 82**
Negri Sembilan, state, Malaysia 517
Nehemiah, Renaldo 667
Nelson, Todd E. 623
Nenni, Pietro Sandro: *see* **Obituaries
  81**
Nepal 83, 82, 81
  demography 290 (table)
  education 331 (table)
  mountaineering 542
Neptune (planet) 196
Nereis virens (polychaete worm) 493
Nesbitt, Cathleen: *see* **Obituaries 83**
Net exchange rate 327
Netherlands, The 83, 82, 81
  demography 290 (table)
  dependent states 296
  education 329
  field hockey 374
  prisons and penology 577
  social security and welfare services
  613
  transportation 673 (table)
Netherlands Antilles 296
  demography 291 (table)
Neufert, Detlev F. 538
Neutron bomb
  "Great Disarmament Debate, The"
  12
  "Stresses in the Western Alliance"
  65
Neutrophils (cells) 414
Neveux, Georges: *see* **Obituaries 83**
"New American Art Museums" (exhi-
  bition) 544
Newberry Library, Chicago, Ill. 484
New Brunswick, province, Canada
  Canada elections 227
  earth sciences 305
New Caledonia 301
  demography 291 (table)
" 'New' Censors, The" (Special Re-
  port) 485
New federalism 615
Newfoundland, province, Canada 226
New Hebrides: *see* Vanuatu
New Jersey
  law 478
  United States statistics 702
New Jersey Devils (hockey team) 421
Newman, Sir Kenneth 584
New People's Army (Phil.) 566
"New Prohibition, The" (Special Re-
  port) 415
"New Roles for Women" (Special Re-
  port) 601
News broadcasting 653
"New Society" (magazine) 581
New Society Movement (Phil.) 566
Newspapers 578
  Moon's publication 592
  Singapore press 613
Newton, Ivor: *see* **Obituaries 82**
New York (state)
  law 478
  United States statistics 702
New York, N.Y.
  archaeology 179
  theatre 665
New York City Ballet (NYCB) 270
New York Cosmos (soccer team) 385
"New York Daily News" (newspaper)
  580
New York Islanders (hockey team) 420
New York Stock Exchange (NYSE)
  632
  United States 692
New Zealand 83, 82, 81
  Antarctica 174
  cricket 257
  demography 291 (table)
  dependent states 301
  education 331 (table)
  environment 360
  equestrian sports 366
  transportation 673 (table)
  Western Samoa 736
Ney, Marie: *see* **Obituaries 82**
Neyhorst, Henry 640
NFDM (nonfat dry milk) 163
NFL: *see* National Football League
Ngugi wa Thiong'o 470
Nguyen Co Thach 724
NHL (National Hockey League) 420
NHTSA (National Highway Traffic
  Safety Administration) 446
Niagara River, U.S.–Canada 356
Nicaragua 83, 82, 81
  demography 291 (table)
  education 331 (table)
  social security reform 614
  transportation 673 (table)
  United Nations report 690
Nichol s, Paul 589
Nicholson, Ben: *see* **Obituaries 83**
Nicholson, William 358
Nicklaus, Jack 401
Nickel 532
Nicolaides, Cristino 189

Nielsen, Arthur Charles: *see* **Obituar-
  ies 81**
Nielsen rating 652
Niger 83, 82, 81
  demography 289 (table)
Nigeria 83, 82, 81
  demography 289 (table)
  education 332
  table tennis 646
  transportation 673 (table)
Nigerian Advance Party 555
Nigerian Civil War 557
"Night of 100 Stars" (TV show) 654
"Night Shift" (film) 536
Nikon (camera company) 566
Nimeiry, Gaafar 639
"Nine" (musical) 665
"1934" (Moravia) 509
Nishimura Seiji 247
Nishio, Suehiro: *see* **Obituaries 82**
Nitrogen 493
Nitze, Paul H. 696
Niue 297
  demography 291 (table)
Niven, Douglas 184
Nixon, Agnes 656
Nixon, Richard 135
Nixon v. Fitzgerald 476
Nkomo, Joshua 735
NMC (National Military Council, Suri-
  name) 640
Noah, Yannick 659
Nobel Prizes 96
Noel-Baker, Philip John Noel-Baker:
  see **Obituaries 83**
Noguchi, Isamu: *see* **Biographies 81**
Nonaligned movement
  Cuba 265
  India 426
  Korea 472
Nonfat dry milk (NFDM) 163
Noonan, the Rev. James P.: *see* **Biogra-
  phies 82**
Nordbrandt, Henrik 508, il. 507
Norfolk and Western Railway 693
Norfolk Island 296
  demography 291 (table)
Norse: *see* Vikings
North America 229
North American Soccer League 385
North Atlantic Treaty Organization
  (NATO) 279
  "Stresses in the Western Alliance"
  65
  West Germany's commitment 399
North Carolina, University of 375
North Carolina State University 212,
  il. 213
North Dakota
  United States statistics 702
Northern Ireland 688
North Field, oil field, Qatar 583
North Korea: *see* Korea
North-South conference 557
Northrop, John Knudsen: *see* **Obituar-
  ies 82**
Northwest Territories, Canada 188
North Yemen: *see* Yemen Arab
  Republic
Norton, Richard
  education (special report) 336
Norway 83, 82, 81
  Antarctica 175
  demography 290 (table)
  dependent states 297
  education 331 (table)
  energy production 344
  engineering projects 351
  environment 356
  fisheries 379
  industrial relations 429
  international law 480
  literature 508
  rowing 605
  stock exchange 637
  transportation 673 (table)
Nott, John 685
"Notte di San Lorenzo, La" (film) 537
"Notte di Varennes, La" (film) 538
Nouhak, Phoumsavan 474
Novak, Kim 591
"Novel Called Heritage, A" (Dukore)
  502
Noyce, Philip 537
NP (National Party, S.Af.) 617
NPN (National Party of Nigeria) 554
NRK (Norsk Rikskringkasting) 651
NSC (National Security Council, Tur.)
  677
Nuclear ballistic missile submarines
  (SSBN) 275
Nuclear energy
  energy production 342
  industrial review 443
  protest il. 358
  reactor 443
  United States statistics 702
  see also various countries
Nuclear-freeze movement
  Australian political crises 199
  "Great Disarmament Debate, The"
  13
Nuclear Non-proliferation Treaty
  "Great Disarmament Debate, The"
  10
  Nobel Prizes 96
Nuclear Regulatory Commission 443
Nuclear Test-Ban Treaty
  "Great Disarmament Debate, The"
  10

Nuclear weapons
  defense 275
  European affairs
    German Democratic Republic 396
    Greece and U.S. military bases
    403
    "Great Disarmament Debate, The"
    9
    literature 501
    religion 597
    "Stresses in the Western Alliance"
    67
    United Nations 690
    United States 696
Nueva Razón de Patria (Bolivian
  army) 218
Numismatics: *see* Philately and
  Numismatics
Nummi, Seppo: *see* **Obituaries 82**
Nunavut, proposed territory, Can. 188
Nureyev, Rudolf 271
Nutrition 409
NYCB (New York City Ballet) 270
Nyerere, Julius 648
Nylon 449
NYSE (New York Stock Exchange)
  632

O

Oakley, Kenneth Page: *see* **Obituaries
  82**
Oates, Joyce Carol 502
OAU: *see* Organization of African
  Unity
Obasanjo, Olusegun 557
Oberg, Margo 726
Obiang Nguema Mbasogo, Teodoro
  361
Obote, Milton: *see* **Biographies 81**
  Uganda 678
O'Brien v. Sim
  law 477
"O Cais das Merendas" (Jorge) 511
Ocasio, Ossie 244
Occidental Petroleum Co. 693
Oceanography 309
Ochiai Hiromitsu 211
O'Connor, Sir Richard Nugent: *see* **Bi-
  ographies 82**
O'Connor, Sandra Day: *see* **Obituaries
  82**
Odinga, Oginga 470
O'Donoghue, Martin 454
OECD (Organization for Econom-
  ic Cooperation and Development
"Officer and a Gentleman, An" (film)
  536
"Official History of Postage Stamps of
  Japan" (publication) 564
Offshore lending
  "You Can't Foreclose a Country"
  61
Ogaden, region, Eth. 617
Ogarkov, Nikolay 680
O'Gorman, Juan: *see* **Obituaries 83**
Ohira, Masayoshi: *see* **Obituaries 81**
"Oh What a Paradise It Seems"
  (Cheever) 502
OIA (Organización Internacional del
  Antimonio) 532
Oil: *see* Petroleum
Oil and gas device il. 354
Oilseeds 161
Oil shale 529
Ojukwu, Odumuegwu 555
Oklahoma
  United States statistics 701
Okun, Arthur Melvin: *see* **Obituaries
  81**
Oldenbourg, Zoé 505
Oldfield, Sir Maurice: *see* **Obituaries
  82**
Oldowan industry 176
Old Stone Age 177
Olivier, Sir Laurence 501
Olsen, Jette il. 729
Olson, Billy 668, il. 670
Olympic Dam project, Austr.
  mining 531
Olympus (camera company) 567
O'Malley, Desmond 454
Oman 83, 82, 81
  demography 290 (table)
  South Yemen relations 730
"One from the Heart" (film) 536
"One Hundred Years of Solitude"
  (García Márquez)
  Nobel Prizes 96
"One Man's War" (film) 537
"On Golden Pond" (film) 536
"On the Origin of Species by Means
  of Natural Selection" (Darwin)
  life sciences (special report) 497
OPEC: *see* Organization of Petroleum
  Exporting Countries
Open-end spinning machine 448

Opera 547
Opie, Lisa 588
Opie, Peter Mason: see **Obituaries 83**
Opren (drug) 410
Optical fibres 440
Options trading 634
Opus Dei (religious org.) 597
"Ora esguardae" (Gonçalves) 511
Oraflex (drug)
  health and disease 410
  pharmaceutical industry 444
Oranges 432
Orbital Test Satellite 624
Orchestra Makassay 549
Oregon
  United States statistics 702
Orff, Carl: see **Obituaries 83**
Organic Law on the Harmonization of
  the Autonomy Process (LOAPA,
  Spain) 629
Organización Internacional del Anti-
  monio (OIA) 532
Organization for Economic Coopera-
  tion and Development (OECD)
  311
  agriculture and food supplies 168
Organization of African Unity (OAU)
  153
  Benin 216
  Ethiopia 368
  international refugee status 589
  Ivory Coast 461
  Libya 487
  Mali 519
  Morocco 534
  Nigeria 555
  Senegal 611
  Tunisia 676
  Zaire 733
Organization of American States 475
Organization of East Caribbean States
  176
Organization of Petroleum Exporting
  Countries (OPEC)
  energy demand 340
  Saudi economic developments 610
  Tunisian economic relations 676
  world economy 311, 320
Organized crime 261
Oriental Institute, Chicago, Il. 178
Ornithology 491
Orogens (geology) 304
Orono, Rafael 245
Orser, Brian 728
Ortega, Eduardo 328
Ortega Saavedra, Daniel 553
Orthodox Church 597
Oryx (*Oryx leucoryx*) 359
"Os Cornos de Cronos" (Guerreiro
  de Sousa) 511
Other End, The (billiard team) 216
O'Toole, Peter 536
Otrag Corp., W. Ger. 624
Oueddei, Goukouni
  Chad civil war 231
  OAU membership dispute 153
Ouedraogo, Jean-Baptist 719
"Our Ground Time Here Will Be
  Brief" (Kumin) 504
Outer Space Treaty 10
Outram, John 183
Ovando Candía, Alfredo: see **Obituar-
  ies 83**
Over-the-counter stocks 632
Overton, William R. 592
Ovett, Steve: see **Biographies 81**
  track and field 667
Owen, Johnny: see **Obituaries 81**
Owens, Jesse: see **Obituaries 81**
Ozal, Turgut 678
Ozdogan, Mehmet 178
Ozone
  botany 494
  environment 359

P

P2 (Masonic lodge) 261
Paasio, Rafael: see **Obituaries 81**
PAC (Political Action Committee) 698
Pacific Association of Tax Administra-
  tors 479
Pacific Islands, Trust Territory of the
  demography 291 (table)
Pacific Stock Exchange 633
Pacificism
  "Stresses in the Western Alliance"
  67
Packaging
  aseptic paper bottle il. 381
  glass industry 440
  tamper-resistant pharmaceuticals
  411, il. 253
"PAC's—the New Force in Politics"
  (Special Report) 698
PAD (Democratic Action Party, Spain)
  629

Padua, Italy 458
Page, George: see **Biographies 82**
Pagliai, Pierluigi 258
Pagnani, Andreina: see **Obituaries 82**
Pahlavi, Mohammad Reza: see Moham-
  mad Reza Pahlavi
Paige, Leroy Robert ("Satchel"): see
  Obituaries 83
Paigen, Beverly 357
"Painting in Naples from Caravaggio
  to Giordano" 190
Paints and varnishes 443
Pajainne tunnel, Fin. 352
Pakistan 83, 82, 81
  defense 284
  demography 290 (table)
  education 331 (table)
  India 426
  international refugee status 589
  sports
    cricket 257
    field hockey 374
    mountaineering 542
    squash rackets 588
  transportation 673 (table)
Pal, George: see **Obituaries 81**
Palar, Lambertus Nicodemus: see **Obit-
  uaries 82**
Palau, Republic of 301
Paleckis, Justas: see **Obituaries 81**
Palermo, Italy 459
Palestine Liberation Organization
  (PLO)
  defense 274
  Greece 404
  international law 479
  Middle Eastern affairs 525, il. 526
    Israel 456
    Jordan 467
    Lebanon 481
  Tunisia 676
  United Nations report 689
Palestinians
  Middle Eastern affairs 525
  United States position 697
Palme, (Sven) Olof Joachim: see **Biog-
  raphies 83**
  industrial relations 429
  stock exchanges 637
  Sweden elections 641
Pamirs Mountains, U.S.S.R. 177
PAN (Pesticide Action Network) 252
Panama 83, 82, 81
  demography 291 (table)
  education 331 (table)
  international law 479
  transportation 673 (table)
Panama Canal 561
Pan–American Highway 351
Panda (bear) 737
Panhellenic Socialist Movement (Pa-
  sok, Greece) 403
Panjsher Valley, region, Afg. 152
Pap, Jeno 247
Papandreou, Andreas: see **Biographies
  82**
  Cyprus relations 267
  Greece 403, il. 404
Papua New Guinea 83, 82, 81
  demography 291 (table)
  education 331 (table)
Paper 450
"Pappas flicka" (Bargum) 509
Paprika 380
Parachuting 150
Paraguay 83, 82, 81
  demography 291 (table)
  education 331 (table)
  transportation 673 (table)
Paraquat (herbicide) 358
Paraskevin, Connie 266
Parathyroid hormone 232
Paredes del Río, Rubén Darío 561
"Parenting Advisor, The" (guide)
  education (special report) 336
Parimutuel betting 393
Parker, Rev. James 592
Parrington, (Francis) Rex: see **Obitu-
  aries 82**
Parrot, André: see **Obituaries 81**
Parry, Clive: see **Obituaries 83**
"Parsifal" (film) 538, il. 539
"Parsifal Mosaic, The" (Ludlum) 503
Partido Democrático Social (PDS,
  Braz.) 220
Partido de Liberación Nacional (Costa
  Rica) 255
Partido Socialista Obrero Español
  (PSOE, Spain) 629
Pasok (Panhellenic Socialist Move-
  ment, Greece) 403
Patasse, Ange 231
  Togo foreign relations 667
Patent Extension Bill (U.S.) 444
Patrese, Riccardo 540
Patrick, Nigel: see **Obituaries 82**
Patriotic Front (PF, Zimbabwe) 735
Patrocinio Jiminez, José il. 266
Patterson, William Allan: see **Obituar-
  ies 81**
Paul, John, Jr. 541
Paul, John, Sr. 541
Paup, Don 588
Pavarotti, Luciano: see **Biographies 81**
Pawley, Howard: see **Biographies 83**
Payne, the Rev. Earnest Alexander: see
  Obituaries 81
Paz, Octavio 510 il.
PBS (Public Broadcasting Service) 650
PDS (Partido Democrático Social,
  Braz.) 220

Peace
  Nobel Prizes 96
Peacock, Andrew Sharp: see **Biogra-
  phies 82**
  Australian government 198
Peck, David 589, il. 588
Peckford, Brian 227
Pedini-Angelini, Maria Lea
  San Marino 608
Pedroza, Eusebio 245
Peete, Calvin 402
Pei, I.M. 184
Penne, Guy
  Central African Republic coup 231
Penn Square Bank
  United States banking 692
  "You Can't Foreclose a Country"
  60
Pennsylvania Ballet 271
Pennsylvania State University
  football 387
Penology: see Prisons and Penology
Pensions 613
  industrial review 400
Pen Sovan 468
Pentecostal Churches 595
People of the Year 70
People's Alliance (Ice.) 423
People's Consultative Assembly (MPR,
  Indon.) 426
People's Liberation Army
  "China's Uncertain Future" 133
People's Liberation Organization of
  Singapore 612
People's Peace Prize
  Nobel Prizes 96
People's Progressive Party (Gambia)
  392
Pepper, Art: see **Obituaries 83**
  jazz music 548
Pereira, Arístede (firm) 231
Pereira Associates 186
Pérez de Cuéllar, Javier: see **Biogra-
  phies 83**
  British foreign relations 685
  Peruvian foreign relations 564
  United Nations report 688
Perham, Dame Margery: see **Obituar-
  ies 83**
Peridotite (geology) 305
Periodontal (gum) disease 414
Permanent Fund Dividend
  Arctic regions 187
Peronist Confederación General de
  Tradbajo (Arg.) 188
Perrault (race horse) 363
Persian Gulf
  environment 354
Pershing missile
  "Great Disarmament Debate, The"
  12
Peru 83, 82, 81
  archaeology 180
  demography 291 (table)
  education 331 (table)
  fisheries 379
  literature 511
  mining and quarrying 532
  transportation 673 (table)
Peso (currency) 524
Pesticide Action Network (PAN) 252
Pesticides 252
PET (Polyethylene terephthalate) 445
Peterson, Bruce A.
  astronomy 197
Peterson, Roger Tory: see **Biographies
  83**
Petrehn, John 150
Petri, Elio: see **Obituaries 83**
Petroleum
  Arctic regions 187
  energy production 346
  environment 357
  world economy 311, 325
  "You Can't Foreclose a Country"
  62
  see also various countries
Pettersen, Brit 728
Petterson, Allan Gustaf: see **Obituaries
  81**
PF (Patriotic Front, Zimbabwe) 735
Pham Van Dong
  Vietnam 723
Pharmaceuticals
  consumer hazards 252
  health and disease 411, 415
  industrial review 443
  mental health treatment 414
Phatudi, Cedric 620
Phelps, Digger 213
Philadelphia Museum of Art, Pa. 191
Philately and Numismatics 83, 82, 81
PhilexFrance (exhibition) 564
Philip, Prince 202
Philippines 83, 82, 81
  demography 290 (table)
  education 331 (table)
  engineering projects 351
  Southeast Asian affairs 622
  transportation 673 (table)
Philip's (company) 440
Phosphate 533
  Togo economic crisis 666
Photography 83, 82, 81
Photosynthesis 234
Phoumi Nosavan 474
Physics 83, 82, 81
  Nobel Prizes 98
Physiology
  Nobel Prizes 97
Piaget, Jean: see **Obituaries 81**

Piccard, the Rev. Jeanette Ridlon: see
  Obituaries 82
Piercy, Marge 502
Pignedoli, Sergio Cardinal: see **Obitu-
  aries 81**
Pilinszky, Janos: see **Obituaries 82**
Pilyugin, Nikolay Alekseyevich: see
  Obituaries 83
  space exploration 622
Pimen, Patriarch 598
Pindling, Lynden O.
  Bahamas 205
Pines, Maya 335
Pinochet Ugarte, Augusto 236, il. 237
Pinter, Joseph 236
Pinto Balsemão, Francisco José Per-
  eira: see **Biographies 82**
Pinto da Costa, Manuel 608
Pintor, Lupe 245
Pioneer 10 (space probe) 626
Pipelines 672
  Africa
    Algeria 170
    Libya 487
    Zimbabwe 736
  Canada 227
  European economic sanctions 369
  Panama 561
Piquet, Nelson 540
Pironi, Didier 540
Pirro, Ugo 509
Pisarenko, Anatoly 408
Pistone, Joseph D. 261
Pitcairn Island 298
  demography 291 (table)
Pittsburgh Symphony 546
PKS 2000-330 (quasar) 197
Plamadeala, Antonie
  religion 598
Planck's constant (physics) 569
Planinc, Milka: see **Biographies 83**
  Yugoslavia 731, il. 732
Plastics
  chemical engineering 233
  industrial review 444
Plate tectonics 303
Platinum 533
Platts-Mills, Barney 537
Plays and Players (PP) awards 662
"Plaza del Diamante, La" (TV drama)
  655
Pleasant, Mount, Canada 530
PLO: see Palestine Liberation
  Organization
PLP (Progressive Liberal Party, Baha-
  mas) 205
Plugge, Leonard Frank: see **Obituaries
  82**
Plyer v. Doe 477
"P.M. Magazine" (TV program) 653
PNDC (Provisional National Defense
  Council, Ghana) 401
Pockar, Brian 728
Pocket billiards 216
Podborski, Steve: see **Biographies 83**
  winter sports 727
Podgorny, Nikolay
  "Russian Giant: 60 Years after For-
  mation of the Soviet Union, The"
  18
Podhoretz, Norman: see **Biographies
  83**
Poetry: see Literature
"Poets in Their Youth" (Simpson)
  504
Pohl, Dan 402
Poinar, George O., Jr.
  life sciences 488
Poincaré conjecture (mathematics)
  521
Point Conception, Calif.
  oil drilling 340, il. 347
Poland 83, 82, 81
  agriculture and food supplies 162
  Antarctica 174
  arts
    literature 513
    motion pictures 539
    theatre 664
  coal production 341
  defense 279
  demography 290 (table)
  education 331 (table)
  foreign relations
    Austrian immigration policies 204
    Canada 228
    European Communities 369
    Sweden refuge 641
    U.S.S.R. 683
  industrial relations 429
  iron and steel industry 440
  "Russian Giant: 60 Years after Formation of the Soviet Union, The"
  19
  "Stresses in the Western Alliance"
  65
  transportation 673 (table)
  world economy 312, 325
  "You Can't Foreclose a Country"
  63
Polaroid (company) 567
Polevoy, Boris (Boris Nikolayevich
  Kampov): see **Obituaries 82**
Poli, Robert Edmund: see **Biographies
  82**
Police 584
Polisario Front (Popular Front for the
  Liberation of Saguia el Hamra
  and Río de Oro)
  Morocco 534
  OAU membership dispute 153

Political Action Committee (PAC)
  United States (special report) 698
Political Parties 83, 82, 81
  television and radio broadcast 650
"Politics of Women's Spirituality,
  The" (Spretnak)
  religion (special report) 602
Pollution 358
  botany 494
Polo 367
Polychaete worm (*Nereis virens*) 493
Polyethylene terephthalate (PET) 445
Polymers 233
Polypropylene 449
Poncho (clothing) 372
Poniatowski, Prince Michel Casimir: *see*
  Biographies 81
Ponselle, Rosa (Rosa Melba Ponzillo):
  see **Obituaries 82**
Pontow, Don 588
Popov, Leonid I. 624
Popov, Zhivko 222
Popovic, Cvetko: *see* **Obituaries 81**
"Poppa John" (Woiwode) 502
Popular Front for the Liberation of
  Saguia el Hamra and Río de Oro:
  see Polisario Front
Popular music 549
Population statistics: *see* Demography
Pork 162
"Por qué y cómo mataron a Calvo So-
  telo" (Romero) 510
Porter, Darrell 208, il. 209
Porter, Katherine Anne: *see* **Obituaries
  81**
Porter, Sir George 234
Portraiture 191
Portsmouth, U.K.
  archaeology (special report) 181
Portugal 83, 82, 81
  demography 290 (table)
  dependent states 297
  literature 511
  Mozambique 543
  transportation 673 (table)
  world economy 324
Portuguese literature 511
Postan, Sir Michael Moissey: *see* **Obit-
  uaries 82**
Postmodernism 183
Potatoes 380
Potter, Mary: *see* **Obituaries 82**
Poultry 163
Powell, Eleanor Torrey: *see* **Obituaries
  83**
Powell, Enoch 584
Powell, Sandy: *see* **Obituaries 83**
Powers, Dennis A. 489
Poznan, Poland 571
PP (Plays and Players) awards 662
Prado, Ricardo 642
Pragmatic bureaucratism
  "China's Uncertain Future" 132
Pravda (Soviet newspaper) 321
Praz, Mario: *see* **Obituaries 83**
PRCA (Professional Rodeo Cowboy
  Association) 603
Preakness Stakes 362
Préfets (Fr. official) 390
Prem Tinsulanond: *see* **Biographies 81**
  Thai government elections 660
Prenn, John 588
Presbyterian Churches 595
Presidential Directive 59 (U.S.)
  "Great Disarmament Debate, The"
  12
President's Council (S.Af.) 617
Preter, Luc de 150
Price, George Cadle: *see* **Biographies
  82**
  Belize 215
Price, Nicky 401
Prices 449
  see also various countries
Primary education 329
Prime export markets 324
Prime rate (economics) 633
Primrose, William: *see* **Obituaries 83**
Prince Edward Island, prov. Can. 227
Printing 445
Prior, James 688
Prisons and Penology 83, 82, 81
  United States statistics 702
Pritchard, John Michael: *see* **Biogra-
  phies 83**
Pritzker Architecture Prize 184
"Private Eye" (journal) 499
Prix de l'Arc de Triomphe (horse rac-
  ing) 363
Prix Goncourt (literature) 505
"Procès du rêve, Le" (Oldenbourg)
  505
Procope, Russell Keith: *see* **Obituaries
  82**
Procter & Gamble Co.
  architecture 186
  industrial review 432
Production (economics) 321
  agriculture and food supplies 156
Professional Rodeo Cowboys Associa-
  tion (PRCA) 603
Programming
  crime (special report) 264
Progressive Liberal Party (PLP, Baha-
  mas) 205
Progressive Federal Party (S.Af.) 618
Progressive Parties' Alliance (Nigeria)
  555
Progressive Party (Ice.) 423
"Progress of Stories" (Jackson) 503
Progress 13 (satellite) 624

Prohibition
  health and disease (special report)
  415
"Promise of Early Learning, The"
  (Special Report) 335
Property insurance 440
Proposition 15 (Calif.) 260
Proprietary Association (U.S.)
  pharmaceutical industry 444
Prosser, Barry 576
Prost, Alain 540
Prostacyclins
  Nobel Prizes 97
Prostaglandins
  Nobel Prizes 97
Protectionism 322
  "Stresses in the Western Alliance"
  69
"Protégé, The" (film) 539
Protein
  Nobel Prizes 98
Protestant Churches 593
Proust, Marcel 506
Provisional National Defense Council
  (PNDC, Ghana) 401
Proxmire, William 698
Pryor, Aaron 245
Pryor, Richard: *see* **Biographies 83**
  motion pictures 536
Psakhis, Lev 235
PSOE (Partido Socialista Obrero Es-
  pañol, Spain) 629
Psychiatry 413
Puapua, Tomasi 678
Public Broadcasting Service (PBS) 650
Public Interest Research Group (U.S.)
  environment 356
Publishing 83, 82, 81
Publishers Databases Ltd. (U.K.) 582
Puerto Rico 500
  demography 291 (table)
  education 331 (table)
  United Nations report 691
Puica, Maricica 668
Pulitzer Prize 580
Punctuated equilibrium theory
  life sciences (special report) 498
Punjab, state, India 424
Purple glossy starlings 492
Puschino-on-Oka, U.S.S.R. 492
Putnam Publishing Group (U.S.) 582
Pym, Francis Leslie: *see* **Biographies
  83**
  British foreign relations 686

Q

Qaddafi, Muammar Muhammad al-: *see*
  Biographies 82
  African affairs 154, il. 153
  Austrian visit il. 204
  Libyan foreign relations 487
Qatar 83, 82, 81
  demography 290 (table)
Qawi, Dwight Muhammad 244
Qin Shi Huang (Ch'in Shih Huang)
  archaeology 178
Quakers (Religious Society of Friends)
  595
Quam, Howard 725
Quandt, Herbert: *see* **Obituaries 83**
Quantum theory 569
Quartz Hill, Alaska 530
Quasar 197
Quebec, province, Canada 226
"Querelle" (film) 538
Questiaux, Nicole Françoise: *see* **Biog-
  raphies 83**
Quigley, Derek 553
Quiser, Sohail 588
Quistgaard Erik 622

R

Race Relations 83, 82, 81
Racing (motor sports) 540
Racket games 83, 82, 81
Racquetball 589
Radiation 197
Radio: *see* Television and radio
Radio Martí (Spanish station) 265
Radio transmission 344
Radar 179
Raft, George: *see* **Obituaries 81**
Rahman, Ziaur: *see* **Obituaries 82**
"Raiders of the Lost Ark" (film) 536
Railways 674
Rainier III, Prince 533
"Raising of the 'Mary Rose', The"
  (Special Report) 181
Raja'i, Mohammad Ali: *see* **Obituaries
  82**. *see also* **Biographies 81**
Rakotomavo, Pascal 516
Rallies (motor sports) 541
Rallis, Georgios: *see* **Biographies 81**
Ramapithecus (anthropology) 175
Rambert, Dame Marie (Dame Marie
  Dukes): *see* **Obituaries 83**
  dance 272

Rambusch, Nancy 335
Ramgoolam, Sir Seewoosagur
  Mauritian developments 523
Ram-K (Blackjack, U.S.S.R. bomber)
  277
Ramsar Convention (Convention of
  Wetlands of International Impor-
  tance) 360
Rand, Ayn: *see* **Obituaries 83**
Randall, Sir Richard John: *see* **Obituar-
  ies 83**
Ranov, Vadim 177
Rap (music) 550
Ras al-Khaimah 684
Rather, Dan: *see* **Biographies 81**
Rationing
  Soviet economic goals 682
Rattle, Simon: *see* **Biographies 82**
Ratsiraka, Didier
  Madagascar elections 516
Raw cotton 448
Rawlings, Jerry John 401, il. 400
Ray, Satyajit 539
RCMP (Royal Canadian Mounted Po-
  lice) 262
RCP (Romanian Communist Party)
  604
Reader, (William Henry) Ralph: *see*
  Obituaries 83
Reagan, Nancy: *see* **Biographies 83**
  fashion trends 372
Reagan, Ronald Wilson: *see* **Biogra-
  phies 83, 82, 81**
  Canada (special report) 229
  "China's Uncertain Future" 137
  Doe visit il. 483
  Europe
    economic sanctions 369
    U.K. relations 688
    West Germany's support 399
  "Great Disarmament Debate, The"
    12
  Latin American affairs
    Brazilian foreign relations 222
    Falkland Islands conflict 475
  Middle Eastern affairs 525
  migration, international 528
  Nobel Prizes 96
  Southeast Asian affairs 622
  Taiwan policy 647
  transportation 672
  United States 693
    education policies 330
    energy policies 342
    religion 591
    social services 614
    world economy 313
Real de Angeles (mine) 530
Real growth (econ.) 319
Real productive output (econ.) 155
Real tennis 589
"Reasons for Separation" (Kojima)
  515
Receptors (biology) 494
Recession
  agriculture and food supplies 156
  iron and steel production 440
  world economy 311, 325
  see also various countries
"Reclining Figure" (sculpture) il 195
Record industry 547
Red Brigade (It. terrorists) 458
  crime and law enforcement 258
Redcliffe-Maud, John Primatt Red-
  cliffe Redcliffe-Maud: *see* **Obituar-
  ies 83**
Red Guards
  "China's Uncertain Future" 134
"Reds" (film) 536
Red Star Campaign (Ethiopia) 337
Reed, Stanley Forman: *see* **Obituaries
  81**
"Reevaluating Darwin" (Special Re-
  port) 497
Reeves, the Right Rev. (Richard) Am-
  brose: *see* **Obituaries 81**
Reeve, the Right Rev. Arthur Stretton:
  see **Obituaries 82**
  literature il. 503
Rees, Peter 475
Refining 347
Reformed, Presbyterian, and Congre-
  gational Churches 595
Refractory material
  space exploration (special report)
  628
Refugees 83, 82, 81
  Sweden asylum 641
  Uganda 679
Regan, Donald T.: *see* **Biographies 82**
Regionalism
  "Stresses in the Western Alliance"
  66
Reiniger, Lotte: *see* **Obituaries 82**
Reksten, Hilmar: *see* **Obituaries 81**
Religion 83, 82, 81
Remote Manipulator System
  space exploration (special report)
  628
Renaldo, Duncan: *see* **Obituaries 81**
Renault (automobile) 436, 540, il. 541
René, France-Albert 611
Rennie, Sir John Ogilvy: *see* **Obituar-
  ies 82**
Report of the Times" (Chinese jour-
  nal) 515
Representation (pol.)
  race relations (special report) 586
  South African domestic affairs 617
Republican Front (RF, Zimbabwe) 735
Republican Party (U.S.) 691

Rescheduled debt (banking)
  "You Can't Foreclose a Country"
  60
Resettlement program 585
Retirement 613
Returned Servicemen's League (RSL)
  199
Réunion 296
  demography 289 (table)
Reunification
  "China's Uncertain Future" 137
Reutemann, Carlos 540
Reuters United Kingdom commodity
  index 638
Revolutionary committees
  "China's Uncertain Future" 132
Revolutionary Party (Tanzania) 648
"Revolution in Learning" (Pines)
  (special report) 335
"Revolution in the Soaps" (Special
  Report) 656
Rexroth, Kenneth: *see* **Obituaries 83**
Reye's syndrome (disease) 411
RF (Republican Front, Zimbabwe) 735
Rhine, J(oseph) B(anks): *see* **Obituar-
  ies 81**
Rhinoceros sondaicus (Javan rhinoceros)
  361
Rhizobium (bacterium) 493
Rhode Island 702
Rhodesia: *see* Zimbabwe
Rhyl (Evelyn) Nigel Chetwode Birch:
  see **Obituaries 82**
Riad, Mohammed: *see* **Obituaries 82**
RIBA (Royal Institute of British Archi-
  tects) 184
Ribas Reig, Oscar 171
Rice 160
Richard Rodgers & Partners 185
Richard, Marthe (Marthe Betenfeld):
  see **Obituaries 83**
Richards, Mark 726
Richter, Karl: *see* **Obituaries 82**
Rieke, George 197
Rifbjerg, Klaus 508
Rifles 649
Riihivuori, Hilkka 728
Rimington, Dave 388
Ring system (astronomy) 196
Rio de Janeiro, Braz. 177
Ríos Montt, Efraín: *see* **Biographies 83**
  Guatemalan coup 405
Riots: *see* Demonstrations and riots
Ritchie-Calder, Peter Ritchie Ritchie-
  Calder: *see* **Obituaries 83**
Ritola, Ville: *see* **Obituaries 83**
Roads and highways 674
  engineering projects 351
Roa García, Raúl: *see* **Obituaries 83**
Robarts, John Parmenter: *see* **Obituar-
  ies 83**
Robbins, Marty: *see* **Obituaries 83**
Roberge, Carl 725
Roberge, Karin 725
Robert, Paul Charles Jules: *see* **Obitu-
  aries 81**
Roberts, Allison 256
Roberts, Donald 491
Roberts, John 230
Roberts, Rachel: *see* **Obituaries 81**
Roberts, Vern 256
Robinson, Frank il. 209
Rocha, Glauber: *see* **Obituaries 82**
Rock music 549
Rodeo 83, 82, 81
Rodgers, Bill: *see* **Biographies 81**
Rodriguez, Lucien 246
Roemer, Charles 701
Rogers, Kenny: *see* **Biographies 81**
Rogge, Bernard: *see* **Obituaries 83**
Roggy, Bob 669
Rohmer, Eric
  motion pictures 537
Roldós Aguilera, Jaime: *see* **Obituaries
  82**
Rolling Stones, The (band) 549
Roman art 177, il. 180
Roman Catholic Church 597
  Polish crisis 570
  race relations (special report) 586
Romania 83, 82, 81
  defense 281
  demography 290 (table)
  education 332
  literature 514
  religion 598
  transportation 673 (table)
  world economy 321
  "You Can't Foreclose a Country"
  63
Romanian Communist Party (RCP)
  604
Romankov, Aleksandr 247
Romero, Luis (Graciano Hervás) 510
Romero y Galdames, Oscar Arnulfo:
  see **Obituaries 81**
Ronaldson, Chris 589
Roofing (industry) 445
"Roofs or Ceilings?" (Stigler)
  Nobel Prizes 96
Root nodule 493
Rosales, Luis 510
Rosberg, Keke 540

Rosen, Samuel: *see* **Obituaries 82**
Rosenwald, Lessing J. 191
Roses 395
Roskill, Stephen Wentworth: *see* **Obituaries 83**
Rossi, Paolo: *see* **Biographies 83**
Rostow, Eugene: *see* **Biographies 83**
Rotha, Wanda: *see* **Obituaries 83**
Rothschild, Alain James Gustave Jules de: *see* **Obituaries 83**
Round Britain race (sailing) 606
Roving Boy (race horse) 363
Rowing 83, 82, 81
Rowlett, Ralph 180
Rowny, Edward L.
  United States negotiations 696
Royal Academy of Art, London, U.K. 190
Royal Botanic Gardens, Kew, England 738
Royal Canadian Mounted Police (RCMP) 262
Royal Commission on Environmental Pollution 355
Royal Institute of British Architects (RIBA) 184
Royal Naval Base, Portsmouth, U.K. 181
"Royal Opera House Retrospective 1732–1982, The" (art exhibition) 193
Royal Ontario Museum, Canada 177
Royal Shakespeare Company (RSC, U.K.) 662
Royo, Arístides 561
RSC (Royal Shakespeare Company, U.K.) 662
RSL (Returned Servicemen's League) 199
Rubber 445
Rubinstein, Arthur: *see* **Obituaries 83**
Ruby (gemstone) 439
Rudenko, Roman: *see* **Obituaries 82**
Rugby 385
Ruisdael, Jacob van 193
Rukeyser, Muriel: *see* **Obituaries 81**
Runaway Groom (race horse) 363
Running 670
Rurarz, Zdzizlaw S. 464
Rusev, Yanko 408
Russell of Liverpool, Edward Frederick Langley Russell: *see* **Obituaries 82**
"Russian Giant: 60 Years after Formation of the Soviet Union, The" (Medvedev and Medvedev) 15
Russian literature 512
Rutile (chemistry) 533
Rutter, Michael 358
Ruwais industrial zone, U.A.E. 684
Ruxton, Bruce 199
Rwanda 83, 82, 81
  demography 289 (table)
  education 331 (table)
  Uganda refuge 679
Ryan, Claude: *see* **Biographies 81**
Ryon, Luann 649
Rytov, Vladimir 681

S

Sá Carneiro, Francisco: *see* **Obituaries 81**
Saccharin 414
Sackler, Howard: *see* **Obituaries 83**
Sadat, (Muhammad) Anwar as-: *see* **Obituaries 82**
Sadler's Wells Royal Ballet 272, il. 273
Saarinen, Aarne 377
"Sabbatical: A Romance" (Barth) 502
SADR: *see* Saharan Arab Democratic Republic
Safeguards
  computers 264
Safety: *see* Accidents and safety
"Saga of Gisli, The" (film) 538
Saharan Arab Democratic Republic (SADR)
  Nigeria's support 555
  OAU membership dispute 153
Sa'id, Qabus ibn 559
Sailing 83, 82, 81
St. Christopher-Nevis: *see* St. Kitts-Nevis
St. Helena and Ascension Islands
  demography 289 (table)
  dependent states 298
St. Helens, Mount, Wash., U.S. 305
Saint Jean, Alfredo Oscar 189
St. John Ogilvie Church, Irvine, Scot. 184
St. Kitts-Nevis (St. Christopher-Nevis)
  demography 291 (table)
  dependent states 299
St. Louis Cardinals (baseball team) 208

Saint Lucia 83, 82, 81
  demography 291 (table)
"St. Martin and the Beggar" (painting) il. 190
St. Petersburg, Fla. 544
Saint-Pierre and Miquelon 296
  demography 291 (table)
Saint Vincent and the Grenadines 83, 82, 81
  demography 291 (table)
Saitoh Shinobu 220
Sajaa oil field, U.A.E. 684
Sakharov, Andrey 681
Salang Pass tunnel, Afg. 671
Salazar, Alberto 669
Salmon 378
Salnikov, Vladimir: *see* **Biographies 81**
  swimming record 642
Salomon Brothers Inc. 634
SALT: *see* Strategic Arms Limitation Talks
Salvation Army 596
Salyut (space stations) 623
Samaranch, Juan Antonio: *see* **Biographies 81**
Samrin, Heng 621
"Samuels döttrar" (Delblanc) 509
Samuelsson, Bengt I.
  Nobel Prizes 97
San'a': *see* Yemen Arab Republic
Sánchez, Salvador: *see* **Obituaries 83**
  boxing tragedy 245
Sanctions (econ.)
  European trade 369
  "Stresses in the Western Alliance" 65
Sandero Luminoso (Peru guerrillas) 563
Sanders, Carol 254
Sanders, "Colonel" Harland: *see* **Obituaries 81**
Sandham, Andrew: *see* **Obituaries 83**
San Diego Chargers (football team) 386
Sandinista National Liberation Front (Nicaragua) 553
Sands, Bobby (Robert Gerard Sands): *see* **Obituaries 82**
San Francisco, Calif. il. 185
San Francisco Ballet 271
San Francisco 49ers (football team) 386
"Sa N His Crystal Ball" (bissett) 504
Sankara, Thomas 719
San Marino 83, 82, 81
  demography 290 (table)
Sann, Son 621
Santamaría Cuadrado, Haydée: *see* **Obituaries 81**
Santos Costa, Fernando dos: *see* **Obituaries 83**
São Tomé and Príncipe 83, 82, 81
  demography 289 (table)
SAP (Social Action Party, Thailand) 660
SAR (synthetic aperture radar) 179
Sargeson, Frank: *see* **Obituaries 83**
Sarhupur, village, India 599
Saronni, Giuseppe 671
Saroyan, William (Sirak Goryan): *see* **Obituaries 82**
Sartre, Jean-Paul: *see* **Obituaries 81**
Saskatchewan, province, Canada 226
Sasol (coal facility) 343
Sassou-Nguesso, Denis 252
SAT (Scholastic Aptitude Test) 332
Satellite Communication 138
Satellites
  astronomy research 196
  space exploration 623
  television and radio 650
Sattar, Abdus: *see* **Biographies 82**
  Bangladesh coup 206
Saturn (planet) 626
Saudi Arabia 83, 82, 81
  demography 290 (table)
  education 329
  petroleum 340
  transportation 673 (table)
Sauter, Eddie (Edward Ernest Sauter): *see* **Obituaries 82**
Sauvé, Jeanne: *see* **Biographies 81**
Savage, Sir (Edward) Graham: *see* **Obituaries 82**
Savary, Alain 333
Savasta, Antonio il. 259
Saville, (Leonard) Malcolm: *see* **Obituaries 83**
Savimbi, Jonas 171
Saving of the President, The" (film) 539
Savings and investment
  Canada (special report) 229
  see also various countries
Savitskaya, Svetlana Y. 624
Scala mobile (Italian wage scale) 428
Scandinavian literature 507
Scandinavian theatre 665
Scargill, Arthur 687
Schäffner, Otto 150
Schary, Dore: *see* **Obituaries 81**
Schell, Jonathan: *see* **Biographies 83**
  literature 503
"Schindler's Ark" (Keneally) 500
Schizophrenia 413
Schlabrendorff, Fabian von: *see* **Obituaries 81**
Schlüter, Poul Holmskov: *see* **Biographies 83**
  Denmark 294

Schmid, Harald 667
Schmid, William 490
Schmidt, Helmut: *see* **Biographies 81**
  East German meeting il. 396
  environment 352
  European meeting il. 370
  West Germany 397
Schmidtke, Fredy 267
Schneider, Dietrich 491
Schneider, Petra 642
Schneider, Romy: *see* **Obituaries 83**
Schnurre, Wolfdietrich 507
Scholastic Aptitude Test (SAT) 332
Scholem, Gershom: *see* **Obituaries 83**
"Schöne Aussicht" (Kempowski) 506
School lunch program 615
Schools 329
Schramm, Norbert 728
Schuster, Sir George Ernest: *see* **Obituaries 83**
Sciascia, Leonardo 510
Scinteia (Romanian newspaper) 604
Scola, Ettore 534
Scorsese, Martin: *see* **Biographies 82**
Scotch whisky 434
Scotland: *see* United Kingdom
Scott, Gene 589
Scott, Hazel Dorothy: *see* **Obituaries 82**
Scott, Ridley 534
Scott, Sir Robert Heatlie: *see* **Obituaries 83**
Scott, Steve 667
Scottish National Portrait Gallery 545
Scours (diarrhea) 722
SDSF (Somali Democratic Salvation Front) 616
Seabed Treaty
  "Great Disarmament Debate, The" 10
Seafloor vents 309
Seafood 382
Seaga, Edward Philip George: *see* **Biographies 81**
  Jamaican political economy 461
Sea hare (aplysia) 493
Searle, Humphrey: *see* **Obituaries 83**
"Sea Runners, The" (Doig) 502
Seattle, Wash. 352
Seattle Art Museum, Wash. 192
Seattle First National Bank 692
Sea Wolf (missile) 285
Secondary education 329
Second-order phase transitions 98
Second Stride (dance group) 272
"Secret of N.I.M.H., The" (film) 536
Security (government)
  agriculture and food supplies 167
  South African domestic affairs 618
  "Stresses in the Western Alliance" 66
Security Council, U.N.
  Argentina-U.K. conflict 188
  United Nations report 688
Sedykh, Yury 668
Ségard, Norbert: *see* **Obituaries 82**
Seibu Lions (baseball team) 211
Seismology 305
SELA (Latin American Economic System) 476
Sellers, Peter Richard Henry: *see* **Obituaries 81**
Selye, Hans Hugo Bruno: *see* **Obituaries 83**
Sembene, Ousmane: *see* **Biographies 81**
Semenov, Sviatoslav 643
Seminal fluid 97
Sen, Aparna 539
Senate, U.S.: *see* United States Congress
Sendak, Maurice: *see* **Biographies 82**
Sender, Ramón José: *see* **Obituaries 83**
Senegal 83, 82, 81
  African political systems 154
  demography 289 (table)
  education 331 (table)
  transportation 673 (table)
Senegambia (confederation) 611
  African political systems 154
  Commonwealth of Nations 248
  international law 479
Senghor, Leopold Sedar 154
"Se non ora, quando?" (Levi) 509
Sensor (physics) 520
Seper, Franjo Cardinal: *see* **Obituaries 82**
Serebrov, Aleksandr A. 624
Sereni, Vittorio 510
Serocki, Kazimierz: *see* **Obituaries 82**
Serrano, Sammy 245
Seventh-day Adventist Church 596
Seveso directive (European Communities) 353
Sexually-transmitted diseases
  AIDS 410
Seychelles 83, 82, 81
  African military coup 154
  demography 289 (table)
  South African foreign relations 619
Shaffer, Peter: *see* **Biographies 81**
Shagari, Alhaji Shehu 554, 556
Shalamov, Varlam Tikhonovich: *see* **Obituaries 83**
Shale oil project
  energy 342
  mining and quarrying 529
Shamir, Yitzhak: *see* **Biographies 81**
Shanghai Communiqué
  "China's Uncertain Future" 136

Shank, C.V. 568
Shankly, Bill: *see* **Obituaries 82**
Shannon, James 699
Shao Shao (panda bear) 737
Sharjah
  United Arab Emirate member 684
Sharon, Ariel: *see* **Biographies 83, 82**
  Israel 457, il. 456
Sharpo (race horse) 364
Shaw Festival (Canada) 666
Shawl 372
Sheares, Benjamin Henry: *see* **Obituaries 82**
Sheed, Wilfred 504
Sheene, Barry 542
"Sheffield" (ship) 286
Shehu, Mehmet: *see* **Obituaries 82**
  Albania 169
Shell Coal (Botswana) 219
Shelley, Norman: *see* **Obituaries 81**
Sherindib, Pazarin 534
Sherrill, Henry Knox: *see* **Obituaries 81**
Shi'ah Muslims 560
Shimada, Yoko: *see* **Biographies 81**
Shimura, Takashi: *see* **Obituaries 83**
Shipbuilding 446
Shipham, U.K. 357
Ships and shipping 672
  archaeology (special report) 181
Shirley-Smith, Sir Hubert: *see* **Obituaries 82**
Shonfield, Sir Andre (Akiba): *see* **Obituaries 82**
Shooting 649
Short-term loan
  "You Can't Foreclose a Country" 64
Show jumping 367
Shriver, Pam 659
Shukairy, Ahmed Assad: *see* **Obituaries 81**
Shultz, George: *see* **Biographies 83**
  Middle Eastern affairs 525
  United States 695
Siberian gas pipeline
  energy 345, il. 346
  European economic sanctions 369
  Italian foreign affairs 460
  Soviet foreign affairs 682
  "Stresses in the Western Alliance" 65
  transportation 672
  United Kingdom 688
  United States position 695
Siemens (company, W. Ger.) 438
Sierra Leone 83, 82, 81
  demography 289 (table)
Sigel, Jay 402
Sihanouk, Prince Norodom
  Southeast Asian affairs 621
  Kampuchea coalition 468
  Singapore coalition 613
Sikhs (religion)
  Hinduism 599
  India 423
Siles Zuazo, Hernán: *see* **Biographies 83**
  Bolivia 218
Silicon (chemical element) 233
Silk 448
Silkeborg, Den. 545
Sillitoe, Alan 500
Silver
  dentistry substitute 414
  mining 533
Silverman, Leon 261
Simmons, Calvin: *see* **Obituaries 83**
Simon-Bellamy House, Stony Creek, Conn. 183
Simond, Jean-Christophe 728
Simonin, Albert Charles: *see* **Obituaries 81**
Simpson, Eileen 504
Simpson, William Hood: *see* **Obituaries 81**
Sinai Desert, Middle East
  environment 356
  Israel 455
Sindona, Michele 591
Singapore 83, 82, 81
  demography 290 (table)
  education 331 (table)
  stock exchange 637
"Singed Shadow" (Albur) 514
"Sing Kimigayo Falsetto" (Maruya) 515
Single-parent families
  demography 292
Sinn Fein (pol. party, Ire.) 688
Sipe, Brian: *see* **Biographies 81**
Sirch, Cornelia 642
Sivapithecus (anthropology) 175
"Six Feet in the Country" (W. Ger. TV drama) 655
Sjöberg, Alf: *see* **Obituaries 81**
Skalimov, Victor 422
Skarby, A. 488
Skating 727
Skidmore, Owings & Merrill (architecture firm) 186
Skiing 727
Skolimowski, Jerzy 537
Skreslet, Laurie 228
SLCM (submarine-launched cruise missile) 278
SLFP (Sri Lanka Freedom Party) 632
Sliwa, Curtis: *see* **Biographies 82**
Slone, Dennis: *see* **Obituaries 83**
Slurry shield (tunneling) 352
Small, Jerry 603

"Small Apocalypse, A" (Konwicki) 513
Smelter
  Canada (special report) 230
"Smiley's People" (TV program) 655
Smirnov, Vladimir 246
Smith, Bailey Ezell: see **Biographies** 82
Smith, Ian 736
Smith, Joe (Joe Sultzer): see **Obituaries** 82
Smith, Lucy Mack 594
Smith, Michael H. 490
Smith, Red (Walter Wellesley Smith): see **Obituaries** 83
Smith, Wayne 265
Smog 358
Smoking 409
Smolin, Victor 151
Smuggling 415
Smythe, Conn: see **Obituaries** 81
Snell, John 220
Snezhnaya Cave, U.S.S.R. 631
SNF (Strategic nuclear forces) 275
Snow, C(harles) P(ercy) Snow, Baron: see **Obituaries** 81
  literature 501
Snow, Philip 501
Sobhuza II: see **Obituaries** 83. See **Biographies** 82
  Swaziland royal succession 640
Soboul, Albert Marius: see **Obituaries** 83
Soccer 382
  television and radio 655
Social Action Party (SAP, Thailand) 660
Social Democratic Party (SPD Federal Republic of Germany) 397
Social Democratic Party (Sweden) 641
Social Democratic Party-Liberal Party Alliance (U.K.) 686
Socialist Party (Fr.)
  Gabon's relations 392
  Guinea's opposition 406
Socialist Party (Greece) 403
Social Security and Welfare Services 83, 82, 81
Society for the Scientific Study of Religion 590
Society of West End Theatre (SWET) awards 662
Soda ash mining 530
Softball 647
Sokolov, Andrey 236
Solar energy
  ceramics use 520
  energy production 342
  games and toys 394
  photochemical conversion 234
Solar Maximum Mission satellite 624
"Solar One" (power plant) 342
Solar system 196
Solidarity (Solidarnösc, Polish union)
  defense 279
  industrial relations 429
  Polish crisis 570
  religion 597
"Solitude of Latin America, The" (speech)
  Nobel Prizes 97
Solofoson, Georges 516
Solomon Islands 83, 82, 81
  demography 291 (table)
Solomon, Richard H.
  "China's Uncertain Future" 129
SOLWIND (orbiting coronograph) 196
Somalia 83, 82, 81
  African affairs 154
  demography 289 (table)
  transportation 673 (table)
Somali Democratic Salvation Front (SDSF) 616
Somali Revolutionary Socialist Party (SRSP) 616
Somare, Michael 560
Somoza Debayle, Anastasio: see **Obituaries** 81
Sondheimer, Franz: see **Obituaries** 82
Son Sann (Kampuchea coalition) 468
Sony (corporation) 567
Sorsa, Kalevi 376
Sotheby's (auction house)
  art sales losses 194
  philately and numismatics 564
"Soup for One" (film) 536
South Africa 83, 82, 81
  African affairs 153
    Angola 172
    Lesotho 482
    Mozambique 543
    Swaziland 640
    Zambia 735
    Zimbabwe 736
  Antarctica 174
  cricket 257
  defense 284
  demography 289 (table)
  dependent states 300
  education 331 (table)
  energy production 343
  environment 360
  industrial relations 429
  mining technology 531
  race relations 585
  religion 593
  stock exchange 637
  transportation 673 (table)
South Dakota
  United States statistics 700
Southeast Asian Affairs 83, 82, 81
  defense 283

international refugee status 590
  see also Southeast Asian countries
Southern Methodist University 387
South Georgia Island 685
South Korea: see Korea
South West Africa: see Namibia
South West Africa People's Organization (SWAPO)
  African affairs 153
  dependent states 300
  South African foreign relations 618
South Yemen: see Yemen, People's Democratic Republic of
Soutine, Chaim 193
Soybeans
  agriculture and food supplies 161
  botany 493
  food processing 380
"Space" (Michener) 503
Space Exploration 83, 82, 81
Spacek, Sissy: see **Biographies** 81
Space Services, Inc. 624
Space shuttle 623
  space exploration (special report) 627
  transportation 671
Spadolini, Giovanni: see **Biographies** 82
  stock exchange 636
Spain 83, 82, 81
  demography 290 (table)
  EC negotiations 371
  education 331 (table)
  environment 360
  Equatorial Guinea 361
  industrial relations 429
  literature 510
  "Stresses in the Western Alliance" 67
  television and radio 657
  tourism industry 449
  transportation 673 (table)
Spanish fly beetle 491
Spanish literature 510
Spanish-speaking people
  race relations (special report) 586
  U.S. population 238
Spater, George 501
SPD (Social Democratic Party, Federal Republic of Germany) 397
Spectroscopy 234
Speed skating 729
Speer, Albert: see **Obituaries** 82
Speleology 83, 82, 81
  archaeology 177
Spencer, Stanley 545
Spielberg, Steven: see **Biographies** 83
  motion pictures 535
Spinks, Mike 244
Spin-off (technology) 627
Spirit Lake, Wash. 507
Spirits (alcoholic beverages) 434
Spirulina (alga) 380
Spivak, Charlie: see **Obituaries** 83
Spohn, Dietmar 250
Sports broadcasting 654
Sposit, Joe 217
Springsteen, Bruce: see **Biographies** 82
  music 550
Spychalski, Marian: see **Obituaries** 81
Square-lipped rhinoceros (white rhinoceros) 361
Squash rackets 588
"Squizzy Taylor" (film) 537
Sri Lanka 83, 82, 81
  cricket 257
  demography 290 (table)
  education 331 (table)
Sri Lanka Freedom Party (SLFP) 632
SRSP (Somali Revolutionary Socialist Party) 616
SSBN (nuclear ballistic missile submarines) 275
"Stability and Change in Human Characteristics" (Bloom) 335
Stadler, Craig 401
Stalin, Joseph
  "Russian Giant: 60 Years after Formation of the Soviet Union, The" 16
Stambolic, Petar 732
Stamps: see Philately and Numismatics
Standard & Poor's 500 632
Stanford University 388
Stanley Cup (hockey) 420
Stanley Gibbons International (stamps) 564
Stanner, William Edward Hanley: see **Obituaries** 82
Starch blockers
  consumer hazards 254
  health regulation 412
START: see Strategic Arms Reduction Talks
State v. Hurd (N.J.) 478
Stearns, Cheryl 151
Steel: see Iron and steel
Steen, Jan il. 193
Steeplechasing 362
Stein, Jules Caesar: see **Obituaries** 82
Stein, William H(oward): see **Obituaries** 81
Steinberg, Donald 416
Steinberg, William (Sereni) 510
Stenmark, Ingemar 727
Stephanopoulos, Stephanos: see **Obituaries** 83
Stephen, Sir Ninian Martin: see **Biographies** 83

Stephenson, Jan il. 402
Stern, J.T. 490
Stevens, Jimmy Moli: see **Biographies** 81
Stevens, Siaka Probyn: see **Biographies** 81
  Sierra Leone 612
Stewart, Donald Ogden: see **Obituaries** 81
Stewart, Betty 151
Stewart, Ella Winter: see **Obituaries** 81
Stigler, George J.
  Nobel Prizes 96, il. 97
Still, Clyfford: see **Obituaries** 81
Stirling, James: see **Biographies** 81
Stitt, Edward ("Sonny"): see **Obituaries** 83
  jazz music 548
Stock Exchanges 83, 82, 81
Stockman, David: see **Biographies** 82
Stone tools 176
Stoph, Willi 395
"Story of the Wanderers" (Yasuoka) 515
"Strains along the Border" (Special Report) 229
"Stranger and Brother" (Snow) 501
Strasberg, Lee (Israel Strassberg): see **Obituaries** 83
Strategic Arms Limitation Talks (SALT)
  defense 283
  "Great Disarmament Debate, The" 10
Strategic arms reduction talks (START)
  defense 283
  "Great Disarmament Debate, The" 14
  "Stresses in the Western Alliance" 68
  United States 696
Strategic nuclear forces (SNF) 275
Strategy (military) 285
Stratford Festival (Canada) 666
Stratospheric aerosol cloud 306
Stratton, Monty Franklin Pierce: see **Obituaries** 83
Streep, Meryl: see **Biographies** 81
Street, G. Brian 233
Strelcyn, Stefan: see **Obituaries** 82
"Stresses in the Western Alliance" (Heath) 65
Strikes
  baseball 208
  football 386
  Pakistan universities 560
  Polish crisis 570
  Portuguese crisis 575
  teachers 332
  Tunisian domestic unrest 676
Stroessner, Alfredo 562
Strøm, Arne Svein 219
Strong, Sir Kenneth William Dobson: see **Obituaries** 83
Strougal, Lubomir 321
Stubbs, George 545
Student loans 333
Suárez González, Adolfo 629
Suazo Córdova, Roberto: see **Biographies** 83
  Honduras 418
Submarine-launched cruise missile (SLCM) 278
Submarines 641
Subsidies (economic) 559
"Substance or the Shadow: Images of Victorian Womanhood, The" (art exhibition) 193
Sucre (Ecuador currency) 328
Sudan 83, 82, 81
  demography 289 (table)
  education 331 (table)
  Ethiopian relations 367
  transportation 673 (table)
Sudbury, Canada il. 230
Sudets, Vladimir: see **Obituaries** 82
Suez Canal 338
Suez Oil Co. 338
Sugar 163
  Cuba 266
Sugimoto Katsuko 220
Suharto 426
Sulfur dioxide 494
Sultan, Prince 609
Summerskill, Edith Clara Summerskill, Baroness: see **Obituaries** 81
Summerson, Sir John 183
Sumo (wrestling) 247
Sun 196
"Sun" (newspaper) 578
Sunay, Cevdet: see **Obituaries** 83
Sungrazers (comets) 196
Sunni Muslims 560
Sunshine Skyway Bridge, Tampa Bay, Fla. 348
Sun Yat-sen, Madame (Soong Ch'ing-ling): see **Obituaries** 82
Super Bowl (football) 386
Super Etendard (aircraft) 285
Superzapping (computers) 264
Supply (military) 286
Supreme Court of the United States
  education of illegal aliens 330
  judicial decisions 476
Surfing 726
Suriname 83, 82, 81
  demography 291 (table)
  education 331 (table)
Surya Bahadur Thapa 550
Susan B. Anthony dollar 564

Suslov, Mikhail Andreyevich: see **Obituaries** 83
  Soviet domestic affairs 679
Susman, R.L. 490
Suspect terranes (allochthonous terranes, accreted terranes) 304
Sutherland, Graham Vivian: see **Obituaries** 81
  art exhibition 193
Sutherland, Dame Lucy Stuart: see **Obituaries** 81
Sutter, Bruce: see **Biographies** 83
  baseball 208, il. 209
Sutton Willie: see **Obituaries** 81
Suzuki, Zenko: see **Biographies** 81
  Japan 461, il. 463
Svalbard (archipelago)
  demography 290 (table)
  dependent states 299
SWAPO: see South West Africa People's Organization
Swart, Charles Robberts: see **Obituaries** 83
Swaziland 83, 82, 81
  Commonwealth land claims 248
  demography 289 (table)
  education 331 (table)
  South African foreign relations 619
Sweden 83, 82, 81
  art
    literature 508
    motion pictures 538
  demography 290 (table)
  education 329
  energy production 344
  engineering projects 350
  environment 354
  industrial relations 429
  international law 480
  Nobel Prizes 96
  Norwegian economic crisis 559
  social services 613
  sports
    bowling 219
    football 384
  stock exchanges 637
  transportation 673 (table)
Sweeteners 414
SWET (Society of West End Theatre) awards 662
Swimming 83, 82, 81
Swinnerton, Frank Arthur: see **Obituaries** 83
Switzerland 83, 82, 81
  demography 290 (table)
  international law 479
  migration, international 529
  social security 614
  theatre 664
  transportation 673 (table)
"Sword and the Sorcerer, The" (film) 536
Syberberg, Hans-Jürgen 538
Symbiotic zooxanthella algae 493
Symonette, Sir Roland Theodore: see **Obituaries** 81
Symphonic music 546
Synchronized swimming 643
Synthetic aperture radar (SAR) 179
Syria 83, 82, 81
  defense 274
  demography 290 (table)
  education 331 (table)
  Middle Eastern affairs 527
    Israel 456
    Lebanon 481
  religion 599
  transportation 673 (table)
Szmuness, Wolf: see **Obituaries** 83

T

Tabai, Ieremia 470
Table Tennis 83, 82, 81
Tabun cave, Mt. Carmel, Israel
  archaeology 177
  speleology 631
Tactics (military) 286
Tai Hou-ying (Dai Houying) 515
Taiwan 83, 82, 81
  "China's Uncertain Future" 136
  defense 284
  demography 290 (table)
  education 331 (table)
  food processing 382
  literature 515
  machinery and machine tool trade 442
  Sino-U.S. relations 241
  transportation 673 (table)
Takemitsu, Toru: see **Biographies** 82
Takamiyama 247
Takanosato 247
Tal, Mikhail 235
Talave irrigation tunnel, Spain 352
Talhi, Jadallah Azzuz at- 487
Talmon, Jacob Leib: see **Obituaries** 81

Taman Negara National Park, Malaysia 356
Tambay, Patrick 540
Tampa Financial Center, Fla. 186
Tanase, Virgil 604
Tanker
 energy 347
 industrial review 446
Tanzania 83, 82, 81
 demography 289 (table)
 Kenya refugees 470
 Mozambique foreign relations 543
 transportation 673 (table)
Tap dance 272
Tapir il. 737
Tardive dyskinesia (disease) 414
Target Sports 83, 82, 81
Tashkent, U.S.S.R. 352
Tasmania, state, Australia 202
"Tasmania Debates Progress" (Special Report) 202
Tasmanian Hydro Electric Commission 202
Tasmanian Wilderness Society 203
Tate Gallery, London, U.K.
 art exhibition 193
 museum acquisitions 545
Tati, Jacques (Jacques Tatischeff): see **Obituaries 83**
Tatrkiewicz, Wladyslaw: see **Obituaries 81**
Taurog, Norman: see **Obituaries 82**
Taxation
 pharmaceutical industry 444
 social security and welfare services 613
 see also various countries
Tax Equity and Fiscal Responsibility Act, U.S. 440
Taya, Maaouya Ould Sidi Ahmed 522
Taylor, Gordon Rattray: see **Obituaries 82**
Taylor, Kenneth: see **Biographies 81**
TBM (tunnel boring machine) 351
Teachers 329
Tebbit, Norman Beresford: see **Biographies 82**
Technology 322
Technology Transfer Network 627
Technology Utilization program (TU) 627
Tecopa pupfish 490
Ted Bates Worldwide Inc. 432
Telecommunications 447
 ceramics use 520
Teletex 447
 television experiments 650
Television and radio 83, 82, 81
 football contracts 387
 ice hockey contracts 421
 rodeo network 603
 U.S.–Cuba broadcasting 265
Television South (TVS, U.K.) 650
Television South West (TSW, U.K.) 650
Tell Yarmouth, archaeological site, Israel 177
Teng Hsiao-p'ing: see Deng Xiaoping
Tenneco Minerals Co. 530
Tennis 83, 82, 81
Ten wasted years
 "China's Uncertain Future" 131
Terra, Daniel J. il. 194
Terminalia ferdinandiana (fruit) 380
Terrorism
 crime and law enforcement 258
 France 390
 Italian domestic affairs 458
 Turkey 677
Terry, Walter: see **Obituaries 83**
Tesich, Steve 503
Teske, Charlotte 670
Testudo graeca (Greek tortoise) 361
Testudo hermanni (Mediterranean land tortoise) 361
Tewson, Sir (Harold) Vincent: see **Obituaries 82**
Texas 330
Texas, Univerity of 669
Texas Instruments, Inc. 520
Textiles 448
Thailand 83, 82, 81
 agriculture and food supplies 160
 demography 290 (table)
 education 331 (table)
 engineering projects 350
 mining and quarrying 533
 Southeast Asian affairs 622
 transportation 673 (table)
Thames, river, U.K. 356
Thatcher, Margaret Hilda: see **Biographies 83, 82, 81**
 China visit 242
 dependent states 302
 European meeting il. 370
 United Kingdom 684
 West Germany visit 399
Theatre 83, 82, 81
Theodosius, Metropolitan 598
Theorell, (Axel) Hugo Teodor: see **Obituaries 83**
Thermoplastics 444
Theroux, Paul 501

Thierbach, Tassilo 729
Thin-film electroluminescent panel 520
"13th Valley, The" (Del Vecchio) 502
"36 Chowringhee Lane" (film) 539
Thomas, C.E. 595
Thomas, Gwyn: see **Obituaries 82**
Thomas, Lowell: see **Obituaries 82**
Thomas, Percy, Partnership 184
Thomas, William Miles Webster Thomas, Baron: see **Obituaries 81**
Thomas Cup (badminton) 588
Thompson, Daley Francis: see **Biographies 81**
 track and field competitions 667
Thomson, Virgil: see **Biographies 82**
Thorn, Gaston: see **Biographies 81**
Thornton, Charles Bates ("Tex"): see **Obituaries 82**
Thoroughbred racing 362
Three Mile Island, Pa. 443
Thromboxane
 Nobel Prizes 97
Thunderbirds (U.S. Air Force) 151
Thurman, Howard: see **Obituaries 82**
Thurston, William 521
Tigerman, Stanley, and Associates 183
Tikhonov, Nicolay Aleksandrovich: see **Biographies 81**
 "Russian Giant: 60 Years after Formation of the Soviet Union, The" 18
Tilburg, Neth. 235
Time Charter (race horse) 364
Timely Writer (race horse) 362
Timerman, Jacobo: see **Biographies 82**
"Times, The" (newspaper) 578
Timman, Jan 236
Tin 533
Tindemans, Leo il. 369
Tinguely, Jean 193
Tinker, David 501
Tinker, Grant: see **Biographies 82**
Tires 445
Titanium 533
Tito, (Josip Broz): see **Obituaries 81**
Tlatelolco, Treaty of
 Nobel Prizes 96
Tobacco 449
 health and disease 409
Tobino, Mario 509
Tobogganing 729
Todd, Cindy 725
Togo 83, 82, 81
 demography 289 (table)
 education 331 (table)
Tojo, Teruo: see **Biographies 82**
Tokelau 297
 demography 291 (table)
Tolba, Mustafa il. 353
Tolbert, William Richard, Jr.: see **Obituaries 81**
Toledo Museum of Art, Ohio 190
Toleman, Ted 725
Tomori Tadashi 246
Tompkins, Middleton 649
Ton Duc Thang: see **Obituaries 81**
Tonegawa, Susumu 496
Tonga 83, 82, 81
 demography 291 (table)
Toronto Argonauts (football team) 388
Toronto Stock Exchange 635
Torrelio Villa, Celso: see **Biographies 82**
 Bolivia 217
Torres, Frank 216
Torrijos Herrera, Omar: see **Obituaries 82**
Tortoises 360
Torvill, Jayne 729
Touré, Ahmed Sékou
 African foreign relations 154
 Guinea 406
Tourism 449
 Saint Lucia economic crisis 607
Tourla, Vladas 649
Touloumdjian, Claude 631
Tower of London Armouries, London, U.K. 193
Toynbee, (Theodore) Philip: see **Obituaries 82**
Toyoda, Eiji: see **Biographies 81**
Toys: see Games and Toys
Toxic substances
 environment 356
 food processing 380
Toxic Substances Control Act (U.S.) 356
Track and Field Sports 83, 82, 81
Trade, international
 African economic conditions 155
 agriculture and food supplies 165
 Brazilian economic conditions 222
 energy strategy 343
 European affairs 369
  Norway 558
  United Kingdom 687
 Iranian economic crisis 452
 Syrian economic development 645
 U.S.S.R. 682
 United States sanctions 695
 world economy 310, 322
 "You Can't Foreclose a Country" 62
Trades Union Congress (U.K.) 687
Traffic Japan (organization) 361
Transportation 83, 82, 81
Traoré, Moussa 519
Tranquilizer 414
Trans-Arabian oil pipeline 467

Transfer RNA (TRNA) 232
Transitional Government of National Union (GUNT, Chad) 231
Transkei, region, S.Af. 620
 demography 289 (table)
Transkei Development Corporation 620
Trans-Mediterranean pipeline
 Algerian natural gas 170
 energy production 346
Transnational corporations 476
Trans-Panama Pipeline System 340
Transplants 410
Trap and skeet shooting 649
Travel 449
Travers, Ben: see **Obituaries 81**
"Treasures of Asian Art from the Idemitsu Collection" (exhibition) 192
Trepper, Leopold: see **Obituaries 83**
Trestrail, Michael 262
Treuernicht, Andries 617
Trichlorophenoxyacetic acid 353
Trifonov, Yury Valentinovich: see **Obituaries 82**
Trinidad and Tobago 83, 82, 81
 demography 291 (table)
Triple Crown (horse racing) 362
Triple-I system (printing) 445
Trippe, Juan Terry: see **Obituaries 82**
TriStar (airplane) 433
TRNA (Transfer RNA) 232
Troell, Jan 538
Trollope, Anthony 499
"Tron" (film) 535, il. 536
Trotskyite Militant Tendency (U.K.) 686
Trottier, Bryan: see **Biographies 83**
Trudeau, Pierre Elliott: see **Biographies 81**
 Canada 225, il. 226
 Canada (special report) 229
Truman, Bess (Elizabeth Virginia Wallace): see **Obituaries 83**
Trust Territory of the Pacific Islands (U.S.) 301
Tsedenbal, Yumzhagiyen 534
Tsvigun, Semyon Kuzmich: see **Obituaries 83**
TSW (Television South West, U.K.) 650
Tswanas (people) 585
TU (Technology Utilization program) (special report) 627
Tuaregs (people) 554
Tuna 378
Tune, Tommy: see **Biographies 83**
Tung, C. Y. (Tung Chao-yung): see **Obituaries 83**
Tungsten 533
Tunisia 83, 82, 81
 demography 289 (table)
 education 331 (table)
 international law 480
 transportation 673 (table)
Tunnel boring machine (TBM) 351
Tunnels 351
Tupou IV, King Taufa'ahau 667
Tupounuia, Mahe 667
Tupuola Efi 726
Turbay Ayala, Julio César 243
Turkey 83, 82, 81
 archaeology 177
 crime and law enforcement 258
 Cypriots 267
 demography 290 (table)
 education and Islamic principles 332
 Greek-Turkish talks 403
 motion pictures 539
 transportation 673 (table)
Turks and Caicos Islands
 demography 291 (table)
 dependent states 299
Turtle
 environment 360
 zoology 490
Tutu, the Rt. Rev. Desmond Mpilo: see **Biographies 83**
 religion 593
Tuve, Merle Antony: see **Obituaries 83**
"TV-Cable Week" (magazine) 581
TVS (Television South, U.K.) 650
12th Party Congress
 "China's Uncertain Future" 132
Twigg, Rebecca 266
Twining, Nathan Farragut: see **Obituaries 83**
Tworkov, Jack: see **Obituaries 83**
Tyerman, Donald: see **Obituaries 82**
Tylenol (drug)
 crime and law enforcement 260, il. 262
 health and disease 411
 pharmaceutical industry 444
 United States 694
Tyler, Anne 502
Tynan, Kenneth Peacock: see **Obituaries 81**

U

UAE: see United Arab Emirates

"Uccelli da gabbia e da voliera" (De Carlo) 509
UCD (Unión Centro Democrático, Spain) 629
UDPS (Union pour la Démocratie et le Progrès Social, Zaire) 733
UEFA Cup (soccer) 384
UF (ultrafiltration) 381
Uganda 83, 82, 81
 demography 289 (table)
 education 331 (table)
 environment 361
 transportation 673 (table)
UK: see United Kingdom
Ulloa Elías, Manuel 563
Ulmasova, Svyetlana 669
Ulrich, Bernhard 354
Ulrich, Frank 728
"Ultimi giorni di Magliano, Gli" (Tobino) 509
Ultrafiltration (UF) 381
Ultralights (airplane) il. 151
Ultrasonics 234
Ulusu, Bulent 678
"Umbra arsa" (Albu) 514
Umm al-Qaiwain
 United Arab Emirate member 684
UMNO (United Malays National Organization) 517
UN: see United Nations
Uncini, Franco 542
"UN City" (Aus. building project) 204
UNCLOS: see United Nations Conference on the Law of the Sea
UN Conference on the Human Environment 343
Underground Coordination Commission (Pol.) 571
Undocumented worker 586
Unemployment: see Employment, wages and hours
UNEP (United Nations Environment Program) 352
UNESCO: see United Nations Educational, Scientific, and Cultural Organization
"Unglücksfall, Ein" (Schnurre) 507
Ungo, Guillermo 525
UNHCR (United Nations High Commissioner for Refugees) 589
Uniform Tire Quality Grading (U.S.) 446
Unión Centro Democrático (UCD, Spain) 629
Union of Soviet Socialist Republics 83, 82, 81
 Afghanistan 152
 African affairs 155
  Congo 252
  Ethiopia 368
 agriculture and food supplies 156
 Antarctica 174
 Arctic regions 188
 arts
  literature 512
  motion pictures 538
  theatre 664
 Canada 228
 defense 274
 demography 291 (table)
 East Asian affairs
  China 242
  "China's Uncertain Future" 135
  North Korea 473
 education 329
 energy production 343
 engineering projects 350
 environment 353
 European affairs 369
  France 389
  Polish crisis 570
  West Germany 399
 "Great Disarmament Debate, The" 9
 Grenada 405
 industrial review 431
 international law 479
 mining and quarrying 532
 Panama 561
 religion 593
 "Russian Giant: 60 Years after Formation of the Soviet Union, The" 15
 social insurance 613
 Southeast Asian affairs 621
  Indonesia 426
  Singapore 612
  Vietnam 724
 sports
  aerial sports
   combat sports 246
   court games 256
   gymnastics and weight lifting 407
   ice hockey 422
   rowing 605
   target sports 649
   swimming 642
   water sports 725
  Syria 646
 television and radio 650
 transportation 673 (table)
 Turkey 678
 United Nations report 690
 United States 695
 world economy 321, 325
Union Oil Co. (U.S.) 529
Union pour la Démocratie et le Progrès Social (UDPS)
 Zaire 733
Unions 687
Unispace 82 (Vienna) 623

Unitarian (Universalist) Churches 596
United Arab Emirates 83, 82, 81
    demography 290 (table)
United Automobile Workers 428, il.
    429
United Church of Canada, The 596
United Church of Christ 596
United Environment Program (UNEP)
    352
United Kingdom 83, 82, 81
    Antarctica 174
    arts
        dance 272
        literature 499
        motion pictures 536
        music 546
        theatre 661
    Commonwealth of Nations 248
    consumerism 253
    defense 279, 285
    demography 290 (table)
    dependent states 295
    education 328
    energy production 343
    engineering projects 351
    environment 354
    European affairs 370
        France 391
        Germany, Federal Republic of
            400
        Ireland 455
    fisheries 379
    games and toys 394
    health and disease 410
    Hong Kong negotiations 242
    industrial relations 427
    industrial review 438
    international law 479
    Latin-American affairs
        Argentina dispute 188
        Falkland Islands conflict 478
    libraries 483
    Malaysian trade 518
    migration, international 529
    museums 544
    Nigeria (special report) 556
    philately and numismatics 565
    prisons and penology 576
    publishing 578
    race relations 584
    social security and welfare services
        613
    sports
        cricket 257
        equestrian sports 364
        field hockey 375
        football 383
        racket games 588
        swimming 643
        table tennis 646
        karate 247
    stock exchanges 635
    television and radio 650
    transportation 673 (table), 674
    United Nations report 690
    United States 697
    U.S.S.R. 684
    world economy 316, 324
United Malays National Organization
    (UMNO) 517
United Nationalist Democratic Organi-
    zation (Phil.) 566
United National Party (UNP, Sri Lan-
    ka) 632
United Nations 83, 82, 81
    "Great Disarmament Debate, The"
        9
    Latin-American affairs 475
    South African foreign relations 619
    see also various countries
United Nations Comission on Narcotic
    Drugs 416
United Nations Conference on the
    Human Environment 352
United Nations Conference on the
    Law of the Sea (UNCLOS) 691
    Commonwealth importance 248
    environment 352
    international law 480
United Nations Educational, Scientific,
    and Cultural Organization
    (UNESCO)
    education projections 328
    historic preservation 417
    libraries 484
United Nations Environment Program
    (UNEP) 352
United Nations Fund for Population
    Activities 293
United Nations High Commissioner
    for Refugees (UNHCR) 589
United Nations Resolution 435
    African affairs 154
United Press International 580
United States 83, 82, 81
    African affairs 155
        Morocco 534
        Somalia 617
        South Africa 618
        Tunisia 676
        Zaire 733
    agriculture and food supplies 165
    Antarctica 174
    archaeology 177
    arts
        dance 270
        literature 501
        motion pictures 535
        music 546
        theatre 665
    Canada (special report) 229

Caribbean affairs
    Bahamas 205
    Cuba 265
    Trinidad and Tobago 676
consumerism 253
defense 274
demography 288
dependent states 301
East Asian affairs
    China 241
    "China's Uncertain Future" 135
    Japan (special report) 466
    Korea 471
    Taiwan 647
education 331 (table)
energy production 340
engineering projects 351
environment 352
European affairs 369
    France 391
    Germany, Fed. Rep. of 399
    Greece 403
    Italy 460
    United Kingdom 685
games and toys 393
"Great Disarmament Debate, The"
    9
health and disease 410
industrial relations 428
industrial review 435
international law 479
Latin-American affairs 475
    Argentina 188
    El Salvador 339
    Guatemala 406
    Mexico 525
    Nicaragua 553
law 476
Middle Eastern affairs 525
    Egypt 338
    Israel 456
    Jordan 467
migration, international 528
mining and quarrying 529
philately and numismatics 564
prisons and penology 576
publishing 579
race relations 585, 586
social security and welfare services
    614
South Asian affairs
    Pakistan 561
    Turkey 678
Southeast Asian affairs 622
    Indonesia 427
    Vietnam 724
space exploration (special report)
    627
sports
    aerial sports 151
    auto racing 541
    equestrian sports 362
    lacrosse 375
    racket games 588
    swimming 642
    target sports 649
    water sports 724
stock exchange 632
"Stresses in the Western Alliance"
    65
television and radio 650
transportation 673 (table)
United Nations report 689
U.S.S.R. 682
world economy 313, 323
"You Can't Foreclose a Country"
    60
United States Congress
    television and radio budget 650
    United States 691
United States Football League 387
United States Supreme Court: *see* Su-
    preme Court of the United States
United Technologies (U.S.) 693
Universal International (Holdings)
    Ltd. of Hong Kong 394
Universalist (Unitarian) Churches 596
Universe 198
Universities 333
University of Utah Medical Center 411
UNP (United National Party, Sri Lan-
    ka) 632
Unser, Al 542
Untouchables (Harijans)
    Hinduism 599
Unusual but Noteworthy Events 52
Updike, John 503
Upper Volta 83, 82, 81
    African military coup 154
    demography 289 (table)
Uranium 342
Urban Institute (U.S.) 615
Urbanization
    race relations (special report) 586
Urban Mass Transit 675
Urey, Harold Clayton: *see* **Obituaries
    82**
Urrutia Lleó, Manuel: *see* **Obituaries
    82**
"Ur: The International Magazine of
    Arab Culture" (journal) 499
Uruguay 83, 82, 81
    demography 291 (table)
    education 331 (table)
    literature 511
    transportation 673 (table)
US: *see* United States
"USA Today" (newspaper) 580
USDA: *see* Agriculture, U.S. Depart-
    ment of
U.S. Open (tennis) 658

U.S. Open (golf) 401
U.S. Steel Corp. 693
U.S.S.R.: *see* Union of Soviet Socialist
    Republics
Ustinov, Dimitry 682
Utetheisa ornatrix (arctiid moth) 491

V

Va'ai Kolone 726
Vaccaroni, Dorina 247
Valenzuela, Fernando: *see* **Biographies
    82**
Valesul Aluminio (company) 530
Valladares, Armando 266
Valli, Romolo: *see* **Obituaries 81**
Van, Bobby: *see* **Obituaries 81**
Van Agt, Andreas 551
Van Bracht, Rini 216
Vanbremeersch, Claude: *see* **Obituar-
    ies 82**
Van der Stoel, Max il. 369
Van Dyke, T.E. 414
Vane, John R.
    Nobel Prizes 97
Vanuatu 83, 82, 81
    demography 291 (table)
Van Vleck, John H(asbrouck): *see*
    Obituaries 81
Vargas Llosa, Mario 510
"Världens tynstnad före Bach" (Gus-
    tafsson) 509
Vatican bank: *see* Institute for Reli-
    gious Works
Vatican City 83, 82, 81
    Argentine-Chile mediation 190
    demography 290 (table)
Vegetable oil 161
Venda, S. Af. 620
    demography 289 (table)
Venera (spacecrafts) 197
    space exploration 626
"Venezia: Piante e Vedute" (art exhi-
    bition) 192
Venezuela 83, 82, 81
    demography 291 (table)
    education 331 (table)
    Guyana 407
    transportation 673 (table)
    "You Can't Foreclose a Country"
        64
Venus (planet) 197
    space exploration 626
Veprintsev, Boris 492
Vera-Ellen (Vera-Ellen Rohe): *see*
    Obituaries 82
Verdet, Ilie 604
"Verdict, The" (film) 536
Verification (armaments)
    "Great Disarmament Debate, The"
        10
Vermont
    United States statistics 700
Vernov, Sergey Nikolayevich: *see* **Obit-
    uaries 83**
Versailles summit 369
Verstappen, Annemarie 642
Veterinary Science 83, 82, 81
Vertical/short take-off and landing
    (V/STOL) aircraft 434
Very Large Array radio telescope
    (New Mexico) 197
Victoria, state. Austr. 199
Victoria and Albert Museum, London,
    U.K. 191
    expansion 544
"Victor/Victoria" (film) 537
Video-cassette recorders 535
Video games 393
    computers 251
    microelectronics 442
Video Printing System 445
Videotext (telecommunications) 447
Vidor, King Wallis: *see* **Obituaries 83**
Vieira, João Bernardo 407
Vietnam 83, 82, 81
    defense 284
    demography 290 (table)
    race relations il. 584
    Southeast Asian affairs 621
        Kampuchea 468
        Singapore 613
    transportation 673 (table)
Viking Penguin (publisher) 583
Vikings 180
Viktoria Louise, Dowager Duchess of
    Brunswick and Lüneburg: *see*
    Obituaries 81
Vildoso Calderón, Guido 218
Villablanca, Benedicto 245
Villeneuve, Gilles: *see* **Obituaries 83**
    motor sports 540
Villette, La, Paris, Fr. 185
Villiers, Alan John: *see* **Obituaries 83**
Vincent Graves Greene Philatelic Re-
    search Foundation (Ottawa, Cana-
    da) 564
Vincent Wildlife Trust (U.K.) 361
Vinson, Carl: *see* **Obituaries 82**
Violence 507
Virata, Cesar: *see* **Biographies 82**
Virginia
    United States statistics 701

Virgin Islands 299
    demography 291 (table)
Virgin wool 448
Virology
    Nobel Prizes 98
Viruex-Molhin, Fr. 359
Vision Quest (rehabilitation organiza-
    tion) 577
"Visions d'Ana" (Blais) 506
Visiting Warships Bill (Australia) 199
Vista system (printing) 445
Vladimov, Georgy 513
Vlajkovic, Radovan 732
Vogel, Hans-Jochen 399
Volcanic dust 308
Volkswagen (company) 436
Volleyball (court game) 256
Von Euler, Ulf
    Nobel Prizes 97
Von Sydow, Max 538
Von Zell, Harry: *see* **Obituaries 82**
Voss, Torsten 668
Voting Rights Act (U.S., 1965) il. 585
Voyager (space probes) 626
Vriesekoop, Bettine 646
V/STOL (vertical/short take-off and
    landing) aircraft 434
Vulcan (bomber) 434
Vysotsky, Vladimir: *see* **Obituaries 81**

W

Wage-and-price freeze 319
Wage-earner funds 641
Wagner, Hermann
    entomology 491
Wagner, Winifred Williams: *see* **Obitu-
    aries 81**
Wain, John 500
Waitz, Grete 670
Wajda, Andrzej 539
Wakasa, Tokuji
    Japan 462
Wakashimazu 247
Wake Island
    demography 291 (table)
"Wake of Jamey Foster, The" (play)
    665
Waldock, Sir (Claud) Humphrey Mer-
    edith: *see* **Obituaries 82**
Waldrop, Duke il. 725
Walesa, Lech: *see* **Biographies 81**
    Polish crisis 570
Walhkoff, Irina 151
Walker, Fred ("Dixie") *see* **Obituaries
    83**
Walker, Herschel 387
Walker, Mickey (Edward Patrick Walk-
    er): *see* **Obituaries 82**
Walker Art Center, Minneapolis,
    Minn. 192
Wallaby (zool.) il. 738
Wallace, Alfred Russel
    life sciences (special report) 497
Wallace, (William Roy) DeWitt: *see*
    Obituaries 82
Wallenberg, Jacob: *see* **Obituaries 81**
Wallenberg, Marcus: *see* **Obituaries 83**
Wallis and Futuna 296
    demography 291 (table)
"Walsche, Die" (Zoderer) 507
Walsh, Raoul: *see* **Obituaries 81**
Walsh, Stella (Stanislawa Walasiewicz):
    see **Obituaries 81**
Walters, John 724
Waltrip, Darrell 541
Wang, Wayne 536
Wangchuk, Jigme Singye 216
Wang Debao
    chemistry research 232
Wan Li: *see* **Biographies 83**
    Chinese government 240
Warburg, Fredric John: *see* **Obituaries
    82**
Warburg, Sir Siegmund George: *see*
    Obituaries 83
WARC (World Alliance of Reformed
    Churches) 595
Ward of North Tynesie, Irene Mary
    Bewick Ward, Baroness: *see* **Obit-
    uaries 81**
Ward-Perkins, John Bryan: *see* **Obitu-
    aries 82**
Ware, Kallistos 598
Warner, Jack (John Waters): *see* **Obitu-
    aries 82**
Warren, Harry (Salvatore Guaragna):
    see **Obituaries 82**
Warren, Robert Penn: *see* **Biographies
    81**
Warsaw, Poland 571
Warsaw Pact
    defense 279
    Polish crisis 570
Washington, George 565
Washington Redskins (team) 386
Wassberg, Thomas 727

Watanabe, Jiro 245
"Watchfires" (Auchincloss) 502
Water 234
Waterbed Manufacturers Association 439
Water filter
  space exploration (special report) 628
Water Sports 83, 82, 81
Watson, John (auto racer) 540
Watson, John (bowler) 220
Watson, Tom 401
Watt, James Gaius: see **Biographies 82**
  environment 355
Waugh, Alex (Alexander Raban Waugh): see **Obituaries 82**
Wayne State University 247
Wazzan, Shafiq al- 481
WBA (World Boxing Association) 244
WBC (World Boxing Council) 243
WCC: see World Council of Churches
WCT (World Championship Tennis) 658
Weather 308
Weaver, Mike 244
Webb, Jack: see **Obituaries 83**
Weber, Frans 728
Weber, Pete 219, il. 220
Web-offset printing 445
Weedman, Daniel W.
  astronomical observations 197
Wehbe, Jorge
  Argentina 189
Weighted average rate (econ.) 320
Weightlifting: see Gymnastics and weightlifting
Weinberger, Caspar Willard: see **Biographies 82**
  Jordan tour il. 467
  Korea policy 471
  Southeast Asian affairs 622
  United States 697
Weiner, Joseph Sidney: see **Obituaries 83**
Weinstock, Lord 438
Weisner, Bernard 150
Weiss, Peter (Ulrich): see **Obituaries 83**
Weiss, Robert 271
Weld, Philip: see **Biographies 81**
Welfare
  social services 614
Welter, Erich: see **Obituaries 83**
Wendel, Heinrich: see **Obituaries 81**
Wenders, Wim 536
Wenzel, Hanni and Andreas: see **Biographies 81**
"We of the Never Never" (film) 537
Werner, Pierre
  Luxembourg 516
Wertheimer, Fred
  United States (special report) 699
Wertz, Richard
  United States statistics 701
West, Mae: see **Obituaries 81**
West African Monetary Union 519
Western Sahara
  demography 289 (table)
  Moroccan defense 534
Western Samoa 83, 82, 81
  demography 291 (table)
  education 331 (table)
  New Zealand citizenship 553
West Germany: see Germany, Federal Republic of
West Indies 257
Westinghouse Electric Corp. 438
West Virginia 701
Wets (blandos) 237
Weyman, Ray J.
  astronomy observations 197
WFC (World Food Council) 155
Whales and whaling 380
Wharton, William 502
Wheat 156
Whitaker, Rogers E.M.: see **Obituaries 82**
Whitbread Round the World race (sailing) 606
White, Antonia: see **Obituaries 81**
White, Ellen G.
  religion 596
White, John H.
  photography 568
White-headed flightless steamer duck il. 491
Whitelock, Dorothy: see **Obituaries 83**
White rhinoceros (square-lipped rhinoceros) 361
White spot (disease) 722
White-water competition 725
Whitney, John Hay ("Jock"): see **Obituaries 83**

Whitney Museum of American Art, N.Y., N.Y. 544
Whittaker, D. 588
WHO: see World Health Organization
Who, The (band) 549
"Who Benefits from the Shuttle?" (special report) 627
Widgery, John Passmore Widgery: see **Obituaries 82**
Wiener, Jean: see **Obituaries 83**
Wightman Cup (tennis) 660
Wilander, Mats 658
Wilder, Alec: see **Obituaries 81**
Wild-water competition 725
Wilhelmina (Wilhelmina Behmenburg Cooper): see **Obituaries 81**
Wilkie, David 642
Wilkins, Roy: see **Obituaries 82**
Willey, Mary
  Australia (special report) 203
William Esty Co. 432
Williams, Eric Eustace: see **Obituaries 82**
Williams, Frederick Ronald: see **Obituaries 83**
Williams, Gluyas: see **Obituaries 83**
Williams, Harrison A., Jr.
  crime and law enforcement 260
Williams, John: see **Biographies 81**
Williams, Mary Lou (Mary Elfrieda Scruggs): see **Obituaries 82**
Williams, Roy L.
  crime and law enforcement 260
Williams, Wayne Bertram
  crime and law enforcement 260
  United States 694
Williamson, Peter C.
  life sciences (special report) 498
Willoch, Kåre Issachsen: see **Biographies 82**
  Norwegian government crisis 558
Wills, Garry 503
Wilson, Bertha: see **Biographies 83**
Wilson, Don: see **Obituaries 83**
Wilson, Edwin: see **Biographies 83**
Wilson, Kenneth G.
  Nobel Prizes 98, il. 97
Wilson, Lanford: see **Biographies 82**
Wilson, Sandra Antoinette
  religion (special report) il. 601
Wilson cycle (geology) 303
Wimbledon championship (tennis) 658
Wind 345
Wine 434
Winkler, Paul: see **Obituaries 83**
Winter Sports 83, 82, 81
Wizards, The (team) 216
Woiwode, Larry 502
WOMAD (World of Music and Dance) 549
"Woman Called Golda, A" (T.V. drama) 653
Women
  art exhibition theme 193
  Liechtenstein voting right 488
  Pakistan Islamization 560
  religion (special report) 601
  San Marino nationality right 608
Women's Professional Council (tennis) 658
Women's Tennis Association 658
Wood, Natalie (Natasha Gurdin): see **Obituaries 82**
Woodburne, Michael 490
Wood products 450
Woods, George David: see **Obituaries 83**
Woodward, John: see **Biographies 83**
  defense (special report) 287
Wool 448
"Working" (Terkel) 485
"World According to Garp, The" (film) 536
World Bank 333
  agricultural development 168
World Boxing Association (WBA) 244
World Boxing Council (WBC) 243
World Championship Tennis (WCT) 658
World Conference of Religious Workers for Saving the Sacred Gift of Life from Nuclear Catastrophe 590, 598
World Conference on Cultural Policies (Mondiacult) 417
World Congress on Books
  libraries 484
  publishing 582
World Council of Churches (WCC) 590
World Cup competition
  gynastics 407
  rodeo 603
  skiing 727
  soccer 382
  soccer broadcast 655
World Fertility Survey 293
World Food Council (WFC) 155
World Food Day 252
World Health Assembly 410

World Health Organization (WHO) 409
World Heritage Convention (International Convention Concerning the Protection of the World Cultural and Natural Heritage) 417
World of Music and Dance (WOMAD) 549
World Pairs Olympiad (contract bridge) 254
World Series (baseball) 208
World Swimming Championships, IV 642
World Team Cup 659
World Tourism Organization (WTO) 449
World Union of Karate-do Organizations (WUKO) 247
World War II
  "Great Disarmament Debate, The" 9
Wormwood Scrubs (prison, U.K.) 577
Worthy, James: see **Biographies 83**
  basketball 212, il. 213
Wozniak, Stephen: see **Biographies 83**
Wrestling 246
Wright, Helena (Helena Rosa Lowenfeld): see **Obituaries 83**
WTO (World Tourism Organization) 449
Wu De (Wu Te) 240
Wu Hsüeh-ch'ien (Wu Xueqian) 240
WUKO (World Union of Karate-do Organizations) 247
Wuppertal Dance Theatre (W.G.) 273
Wurf, Jerry (Jerome Wurf): see **Obituaries 82**
Wu Te (Wu De) 240
Wu Xueqian (Wu Hsüeh-ch'ien) 240
Wyler, William: see **Obituaries 82**
Wyszynski, Stefan Cardinal: see **Obituaries 82**

X

Xia Nai (Hsia Nai) 178
X-ray microanalysis 235

Y

Yacyretá hydroelectric project
  Argentina 190
  Paraguay 563
Yahya Khan, Agha Mohammad: see **Obituaries 81**
Yale Center for British Art, New Haven, Conn. 193
Yalin-Mor, Nathan: see **Obituaries 81**
Yamamura Kazutoshi 247
Yamashita Yashuhiro 247
Yao Yilin (Yao I-lin)
  Chinese government 240
Yarmouk Brigade (Jordan) 467
Yasuoka, Shotaro 515
Yates, Dame Frances Amelia: see **Obituaries 82**
Yau Shing Tung
  mathematics award 521
"Year of the French, The" (Irish TV drama) 655
Year of the Knockout (horse racing) 393
"Years of Lyndon Johnson: The Path to Power, The" (Caro) 503
"Years of Upheaval" (Kissinger) 503
Ye Jianying (Yeh Chien-ying)
  Chinese Communist party 240
Yellen, Mike il. 588
Yellowlees, Sir Henry
  environment 357
Yemen, People's Democratic Republic of 83, 82, 81
  demography 290 (table)
  Oman foreign relation 559
Yemen Arab Republic 83, 82, 81
  demography 290 (table)
  earthquake 305
  South Yemen relations 730
Yen (currency) 312
"Yes Minister" (comedy) 655
Yevtushenko, Yevgeny 512, il. 513
Yiddish literature 514
"Yol" (film) 539
Yoo Chang Soon
  Korea 471
Yoshihara Yoshio 216
" 'You Can't Foreclose a Country' Debtor Nations Worry Bankers" (Mathis) 60

Young, Candy 669
Young-Bruehl, Elisabeth 504
Younghusband, Dame Eileen (Louise): see **Obituaries 82**
"Young Shoulders" (Wain) 500
Yount, Robin 208, il. 209
Yourcenar, Marguerite: see **Biographies 81**
"Your Money or Your Life" (film) 538
Y-shaped antibody molecule 495
Yue Po-Lock
  chemistry research 233
Yugoslavia 83, 82, 81
  demography 290 (table)
  education 331 (table)
  foreign relations
    Albania 170
    Iraq 453
  transportation 673 (table)
  "You Can't Foreclose a Country" 63
Yukawa, Hideki: see **Obituaries 82**
Yurchenko, Natalia 408

Z

Zagladin, Vadim 460
Zaid, Sheikh Sultan ibn
  U.A.E. politics 684
Zail Singh: see **Biographies 83**
  India 423, il. 424
Zaire 83, 82, 81
  African foreign relations 155
  crime and law enforcement 261
  demography 289 (table)
  education 331 (table)
  mining and quarrying 532
  transportation 673 (table)
Zambia 83, 82, 81
  demography 289 (table)
  education 331 (table)
  foreign relations
    South Africa 618
    Tanzania 648
    Zaire 733
  industrial review 439
  mining and quarrying 532
  transportation 673 (table)
ZANU (Zimbabwe African National Union) 735
Zanussi, Krzysztof 539
Zapata, Hilario 245
Zappa, Moon Unit 373
ZAPU (Zimbabwe African People's Union) 735
Zaviolov, Aleksandr 727
Zawawi, Qais al–
  Oman 559
Zenha, Francisco Salgado
  Portuguese constitutional crisis 575
Zeolites (minerals) 233
Zepler, Eric Ernest: see **Obituaries 81**
Zerbo, Saye: see **Biographies 82**
  Upper Volta 719
Zero-option (government)
  "Great Disarmament Debate, The" 14
Zhang Aiping (Chang Ai-p'ing) 240
Zhao Ziyang (Chao Tzu-yang): see **Biographies 81**
  China 239
  "China's Uncertain Future" 132
  Japanese meeting 464, il. 463
Zhivkov, Todor 222
  Romanian-Bulgarian hydroelectric project 604
Zhivkova, Lyudmila: see **Obituaries 82**
Zhou Enlai (Chou En-lai)
  "China's Uncertain Future" 131
Zia-ul-Haq, Mohammad 560
Ziefman, Jerome
  United States (special report) 699
Zimbabwe 83, 82, 81
  demography 289 (table)
  education 331 (table)
  foreign relations
    Mozambique 543
    South Africa 618
  transportation 673 (table)
Zimbabwe African National Union (ZANU) 735
Zimbabwe African People's Union (ZAPU) 735
Zimmermann, Friedrich 399
Zinc 533
Zoderer, Joseph 507
Zoff, Dino 382
Zoology 489
Zooplankton (biology) 492
Zoos and Botanical Gardens 83, 82, 81
Zuckerman, Yitzhak: see **Obituaries 82**
Zulfikar, Al 560
Zworykin, Vladimir Kosma: see **Obituaries 83**

N ow there's a way to identify all
your fine books with flair and style.
As part of our continuing service to you,
Britannica Home Library Service, Inc. is
proud to be able to offer you the fine quality
item shown on the next page.

B ooklovers will love the heavy-duty
personalized **Ex Libris** embosser.
Now you can personalize all your
fine books with the mark of distinction, just
the way all the fine libraries of the world do.

T o order this item,
please type or print your name,
address and zip code on a plain sheet
of paper. (Note special instructions for
ordering the embosser). Please send a check
or money order only (your money will be
refunded in full if you are not delighted) for
the full amount of purchase, including
postage and handling, to:

Britannica Home Library Service, Inc.
Attn: Yearbook Department
Post Office Box 6137
Chicago, Illinois 60680

17 68

(Please make remittance payable to: Britannica Home Library Service, Inc.)

IN THE
BRITANNICA
TRADITION
OF QUALITY...

EX LIBRIS
PERSONAL EMBOSSER

A mark of distinction for your fine books. A book embosser just like the ones used in libraries. The 1½" seal imprints "Library of _____" (with the name of your choice) and up to three centered initials. Please type or print clearly BOTH full name (up to 26 letters including spaces between names) and up to three initials.
Please allow six weeks for delivery.

Just **$20.00**

plus $2.00 shipping and handling

This offer available only in the United States.
Illinois residents please add sales tax

17 68

Britannica Home Library Service, Inc.